FROM SOCRATES TO CINEMA

AN INTRODUCTION TO PHILOSOPHY

JEFFREY R. DI LEO
UNIVERSITY OF HOUSTON—VICTORIA

Mc
Graw
Hill

Boston   Burr Ridge, IL   Dubuque, IA   Madison, WI   New York
San Francisco   St. Louis   Bangkok   Bogotá   Caracas   Kuala Lumpur
Lisbon   London   Madrid   Mexico City   Milan   Montreal   New Delhi
Santiago   Seoul   Singapore   Sydney   Taipei   Toronto

The McGraw-Hill Companies

Higher Education

FROM SOCRATES TO CINEMA: An Introduction to Philosophy

1 2 3 4 5 6 7 8 9 0 DOC /DOC 0 9 8 7 6

ISBN-13: 978-0-07-296906-1
ISBN-10: 0-07-296906-7

Vice president and Editor-in-Chief: *Emily Barrosse*
Publisher: *Lyn Uhl*
Senior sponsoring editor: *Jon-David Hague*
Production editor: *Mel Valentin*
Manuscript editor: *Thomas Briggs*
Design manager/Cover designer: *Gino Cieslik*
Interior designer: *Kay Fulton*
Art editor: *Ayelet Arbel*
Photo research coordinator: *Natalia Peschiera*
Senior production supervisor: *Richard DeVitto*
Compositor: *Carlisle Publishing Services*
Typeface: *10/12 Palatino*
Printer: *R. R. Donnelley & Sons*

Library of Congress Cataloging-in-Publication Data
Di Leo, Jeffrey R.
  From Socrates to cinema : an introduction to philosophy / Jeffrey R. Di Leo.
    p. cm.
  Includes bibliographical references.
  ISBN-13: 978-0-07-296906-1 (alk. paper)
  ISBN-10: 0-07-296906-7 (alk. paper)
 1. Philosophy--Introductions.   I. Title.
  BD21.D55 2006
  100--dc22

                                                                        2006042025

www.mhhe.com

BRIEF CONTENTS

TABLE OF CONTENTS

2 Of Truth and Knowledge   129

PREFACE

ABOUT THIS BOOK

Contemporary philosophers are increasingly recognizing the philosophical value of films and stories and coming to realize the significant role they play in shaping our philosophical outlook. We use films and stories as a basis for telling who we are and what we are doing, and as such, these works play a vital role in our identity and education. Moreover, stories and films can engage, challenge, and extend our understanding and imagination, as well as help us explore significant philosophical questions. They provide us with a common ground with which to identify and discuss philosophical problems.

Many philosophy teachers have found that their students respond better to philosophical questions when they are presented through familiar media such as films and short stories. *From Socrates to Cinema* gives you the ability to supplement core readings in classical and contemporary philosophy with relevant films and literary works. It contains over ninety film boxes and over fifteen literature selections, including nine complete short stories.

Although a number of introductory philosophy textbooks currently on the market include a small assortment of literary selections or utilize a modest number of films, this book is the first to extensively integrate both literature and film. Furthermore, it offers a comprehensive pedagogical system to assist you with the use of film and literature in your classroom. *From Socrates to Cinema* aims to balance the rigorous demands of philosophical inquiry with the needs and experiences of the twenty-first-century undergraduate.

In addition, *From Socrates to Cinema* contains an ample selection of readings and films that bring feminist, racial, and multicultural perspectives to bear on core philosophical topics. The aim here is to incorporate amidst a set of traditional introductory philosophy readings a selection of more progressive readings and materials. These latter selections are specifically suited to meet the demands of both diverse student populations and instructors seeking a more nontraditional approach.

Overall, this book is designed to accommodate a number of instructional strategies without sacrificing philosophical rigor or neglecting a standard set of philosophical topics. *From Socrates to Cinema* provides the materials for a lively, engaging, and contemporary introductory philosophy course—one that will pique student interest in philosophy and provide you with the resources for a challenging, exciting, and ultimately successful course.

ON USING FILMS

Modern culture has a number of important sites of philosophical deliberation that often go unnoticed by the average student. Film is one of these sites. As philosophy instructors, we can help our students locate these potential sites of philosophical deliberation and show them how to enter into a dialogue with them. By identifying how philosophical issues are a part of our everyday lives and are present in activities that we generally enjoy, such as watching films, we can help our students to become more observant and reflective individuals.

Most students enjoy watching films and sharing their views about what they have seen. However, some students have difficulty regarding films as anything more than entertainment. Fortunately, convincing students of the relevancy of films to philosophical issues is not very difficult. Films are a familiar way in which students have participated in philosophical thinking, and they will continue to be a major source of philosophical education for most of them beyond the scope of your class.

Incorporating films into your philosophy course is relatively easy and pedagogically astute. However, there are a few things to keep in mind when planning a philosophy course that will utilize film, particularly if you have never used film in your courses.

First, even if it is assumed that films can make an important contribution to our introductory philosophy course, incorporating film viewings into a teaching schedule is sometimes logistically difficult. The film summaries and dialogue transcriptions in this book are constructed so that they will be sufficient to generate class discussion even if the films are not shown to your class. They aim to capture the central philosophical issue presented in the film, most particularly, the issue that is developed in the chapter and section where the film box is located. This allows your students to participate immediately in class discussions on the relevant philosophical matters in these films. While it would be ideal for students to have seen each film before engaging in class discussions, this is often not possible or feasible.

Nevertheless, while the film summaries and script excerpts are sufficient to capture the general shape of the philosophical issue covered in each film, they are generally no substitute for viewing the films. Therefore, you might consider screening in class at least one or two of the films presented in this book. The main reason will be to show your students how to view a film *philosophically.* After screening key scenes in the film, pause it and explain to students the philosophical dimensions of the scene or scenes, allowing them to ask questions and discuss what they have seen. This approach will help them become more philosophically observant film viewers, a skill that will serve them well as they consider additional films throughout the semester. While students might dislike the interruption of their viewing experience, they will come to appreciate your insightful comments.

If you decide to have your students view more than one or two films for your class, it is not necessary to have them view these additional films in their entirety during class time. There are a number of good alternatives for incorporating film into your course without sacrificing much, if any, lecture and discussion time for in-class film viewings.

One option, as mentioned above, is simply to use the film summaries as the bases for class discussion. You might ask students to try to view the film on their own before class in order to be better prepared for discussion. While the summaries are not as nuanced as the films, they provide a more-than-adequate basis for lively discussion and debate.

Another option is to make the film available to students for viewing on campus at their convenience. For example, many libraries have facilities for viewing films that are available to students. You can place on reserve the films to be discussed throughout the semester and ask that students view them at their earliest convenience, but before class discussion of each the films.

Still another option is to put the films on reserve and allow students to borrow them. Again, students can select times that are convenient for them to view the films. Furthermore, since most of the films summarized in this book can be rented fairly easily, you might ask your students to do this on their own. You can also encourage them to form "viewing groups" to cut down on the expense of renting the films and to eliminate the problem of some students not having viewing equipment. In fact, students often find watching films with their peers to be quite enjoyable.

Yet another option is to schedule screenings the films outside class. Establish one night a week when students can attend a screening of a film you wish to discuss in class. You might even assign a student to manage the equipment.

Alternately, you might show only key scenes from the films under consideration during class. This will involve some additional preparation on your part. DVDs are recommended here because they include scene indexes that allow easy access to relevant parts of the film. If you are using VHS tapes, you might prepare beforehand a tape of the particular scenes that you want to show your students. In any case, viewing scenes from films is a reasonable alternative to showing an entire film in class or requiring students to view the entire film as homework.

Of course, you can also incorporate films into your class in an entirely different way. For example, you might give students the option of writing papers on the films presented in this book. Many of the discussion questions that follow the film summaries are rich enough to be the subject matter of papers. You might also have individual students or small groups give presentations on the philosophical issues contained in the films discussed in this book or in other films. Students particularly enjoy this type of activity and learn a great deal from the experience.

In addition to deciding how you will make these films available to your students, you will also need to decide how to coordinate film materials with your lecture and discussion plans for the semester. Here, much will depend on the number of films you plan to utilize during the semester and on your intended depth of analysis. An instructor who plans to discuss in depth one film a week will have a much different pedagogical strategy than one who intends to use only a couple of movies during the course of the semester or one who intends to discuss more than one film per week. In planning your course, you will want to ask yourself about your level of commitment to philosophically analyzing and discussing films. It may take a couple of semesters to find the level that fits your needs and those of your students.

Once you come to a conclusion with respect to the number of films you will utilize during the semester, you will need to decide how to coordinate film lectures and discussions with possible in-class film viewings, and with lectures and discussions concerning the philosophical readings. One popular method is simply to introduce the philosophical topic with a film. Have students watch the film, and then discuss with them its philosophical dimensions. After this, turn to the readings. One of the advantages of this strategy is that the film will get students interested in the philosophical topic without intimidating or overwhelming them. One of the drawbacks is that students will not have enough critical understanding of the philosophical topic to give it as strong an analysis as you might wish. The latter consideration might lead you to opt to cover the reading(s) before the film. The film is then viewed as a way to look at the material covered in the readings *in action:* students can discuss the ways in which the film engages and extends the material in the reading(s).

You will also want to decide whether you are going to discuss with students the philosophical dimensions of the film before viewing it, while viewing it, or after viewing it. Each approach has its relative merits and drawbacks. I tend to favor discussing the film with students as they view it so that I can point out significant scenes right after they have viewed them. Others, however, might feel that this approach interrupts the viewing experience and the philosophical discovery process and therefore will want to wait until the end of the film to discuss issues. Still others might discuss with students what they are going to see before they view the film, laying out key philosophical points and mentioning key scenes. This last strategy produces the most philosophically knowledgeable viewers, though perhaps at the cost of having students discover philosophical dimensions on their own.

The key is to experiment with different pedagogical strategies over the course of a few semesters. Just as it takes time to determine how much reading to assign to your students and how much class time to devote to discussion, so, too, will it take time for you to reach a pedagogical comfort level with regard to the introduction of film to your philosophy course. While you can be fairly confident that students will enjoy viewing and discussing films in class, you also need to be comfortable with the amount of film viewing and its level of contribution to the philosophical and pedagogical goals you have set for your course. While it might take a semester or two for you to find the pedagogical strategy that works best for you, it will be well worth it. Few materials engage the imagination and attention of students like film. Moreover, and perhaps more importantly, the use of film in your course will assist you in passing along your passion for philosophy to your students.

METHOD AND ORGANIZATION

From Socrates to Cinema comprises a preface, an introduction, and six chapters. Each of the chapters is subdivided into two to four sections, each of which address core questions in philosophy. Some of the readings in this anthology have been carefully edited to preserve the structure of the main argument(s) while omitting material that is superfluous to the main line of argumentation—including, at times, footnotes. Briefer entries not only help students with weaker reading/analysis skills to focus on arguments and positions but also allow for a greater diversity of materials to be anthologized.

The Introduction provides students with a brief introduction to philosophy and some basic logic and critical thinking materials. Included are three brief readings about why one studies philosophy and an excerpt from the classic Monty Python skit "The Argument Clinic." The latter is presented as a sample argument for class discussion. I recommend that a discussion of "The Argument Clinic" take place in the first week of the semester. It provides an excellent starting point for a discussion of the nature of arguments and the general role of arguments in philosophy. The readings on the question of why one studies philosophy might be utilized to stimulate student interest in the course and to give you an opportunity to share with the class your own thoughts on this topic.

Chapters 1–6 take up the following topics: (1) God and faith, (2) truth and knowledge, (3) minds and bodies, (4) morality and art, (5) freedom and justice, and (6) life and death.

Chapter 1 deals primarily with questions regarding the philosophy of religion. This topic opens the book because the question of the existence and nature of God is both an issue of perennial interest to introductory philosophy students and one in which arguments may be clearly introduced and discussed.

Chapter 2 is concerned with issues in epistemology and is divided into two sections: one on knowledge and one on truth. The second section of this chapter will probably be more difficult for students than the first.

Chapter 3 deals with three issues central to the philosophy of mind: the mind-body problem, personal identity, and artificial intelligence and consciousness.

Chapter 4 is broadly concerned with value theory and links issues in moral philosophy with issues in the philosophy of art. Sections 4.1 and 4.2 introduce students to relativism and moral theory; sections 4.3 and 4.4 are concerned respectively with the philosophy of art in general and the philosophy of the visual arts in particular. The material in the latter section is rarely found in introductory philosophy anthologies, but it will be intellectually stimulating to students interested in the philosophical dimensions of film.

Chapter 5 combines material on free will and determinism with topics in social and political philosophy. Section 5.1 takes up free will and determinism; section 5.2 concerns the nature of the just society; section 5.3 deals with sexual equality; and section 5.4 focuses on global human rights. If you wish to emphasize gender issues in your course, you should pay particular attention to section 5.3 (it is advisable that you also assign the selection from Simone de Beauvoir from chapter 3 in conjunction with the readings from this section). Section 5.4 is a must if you wish to foreground globalism in your course.

Chapter 6 is divided into two sections: one dealing with the meaning of life, and the other with meaning of death. Questions concerning the meaning of life work best either at the beginning or at the end of the course. Section 5.2 on the meaning of death combines more traditional material on this topic with readings on abortion and euthanasia.

Each of the 134 readings is prefaced by a brief overview of the selection and a biographical note on the author(s). Each reading is followed by a number of discussion questions. Chapters also include an ample assortment of film boxes, which introduce students to films that relate to material covered in the readings. Film boxes are placed after the reading or readings to which they are most immediately connected. Nevertheless, the questions included in the film boxes often encourage students to connect the films with issues covered throughout the section. Each chapter concludes with detailed lists of references or suggested readings.

SPECIAL FEATURES

From Socrates to Cinema contains a number of features that are designed both to make introductory philosophy more accessible and relevant to students and to aid you in the development of your course.

- *Film boxes.* There are over ninety film boxes in *From Socrates to Cinema.* The film boxes are interspersed with the readings to stimulate discussion of the readings. The films were selected based on their ability to speak to and engage the philosophical topic at hand, as well as on their potential appeal to students. To facilitate ease of presentation, many of the film boxes contain transcriptions of dialogue from the film. This means that, if necessary, scenes from the film may be discussed without having to show the film clip.
- *Literature selections.* There are over fifteen literature selections in *From Socrates to Cinema* including nine complete short stories. Writers featured include Ryōnøsuke Akutagawa, Jorge Luis Borges, Philip K. Dick, Fyodor Dostoyevsky, Franz Kafka, Ursula K. Le Guin, Isaac Bashevis Singer, Mark Twain, and Alice Walker.
- *Glossary.* Because some of the philosophical terminology will be new to the students, *From Socrates to Cinema* contains a glossary of the key terms used in the readings.
- *Discussion questions.* A list of discussion questions follows each of the film boxes and reading selections. You might assign these for homework, use them as paper topics, present them as discussion material, or give them as examination questions. In addition to providing you with course materials, they give the diligent student further points of entry into the material.
- *Reading selection introductions.* Each selection in this book is prefaced by a summary of the piece that will prepare both you and your students for what follows. However, these synopses should not be regarded as a substitute for reading the selection. Each introduction also provides a biographical note about the author(s).

- *Arguments and fallacies.* Material on arguments and fallacies is presented in the introductory chapter. This discussion includes definitions and examples of the more common informal fallacies, as well as a section on how to evaluate a philosophical argument.
- *References and Suggested Readings.* Additional reading material is suggested for each of the six chapters. Here you will find wide-ranging lists of additional sources including, where applicable, a number of historical and multicultural selections, as well as some of the omitted philosophical approaches to this material. These readings may be used as the basis for student research or as assigned presentation/review topics.

ACKNOWLEDGMENTS

This project is the product of many conversations with Jon-David Hague, my editor at McGraw-Hill. We both believe that film is increasingly becoming an important aspect of the introductory philosophy curriculum but that to date it has not been fully integrated into an introductory philosophy anthology. We strove to produce a resource that would both excite students about the possibilities for innovatively discovering philosophy and provide instructors with a new layer of enticing material for their philosophy courses. One cannot hope for a more supportive, energetic, and visionary editor. He has my deepest gratitude. I would also like to thank his team at McGraw-Hill, particularly Allison Rona for being patient with me regarding requests for deadline extensions, Fred Courtright for handling all the permission requests, Thomas Briggs for his masterful copy editing of this book, and Mel Valentin for shepherding my book through production. I want to thank as well those who reviewed the manuscript, particularly Tangren Alexander of Southern Oregon University, Pedro Amaral of California State University at Fresno, Charles Bolyard of James Madison University, Jack Green-Musselman of St. Edward's University, Karen Hanson of Indiana University, Bill Hartmann of St. Louis Community College of Forest Park, Nathan Houser of Indiana University/Purdue University at Indianapolis, Ivan Marquez of Bentley College, Edward Schoen of Western Kentucky University, Jan Thomas of the University of Arkansas at Little Rock, and Lynne Tirrell of the University of Massachusetts–Boston for their comments and suggestions, many of which have found their way into the pages of this book. I would also like to thank Sandra Wood for providing administrative support, Randy Faulk for computer support, Shirley Parkan for tracking down and providing me with of the books and articles required to carry out this project, and my colleagues Bud Fairlamb and Dan Jaeckle for offering timely suggestions regarding this book. I have used films in my philosophy courses now for over a dozen years. While many students over the years have introduced me to different films, one stands out: Scott Harkey. Scott's passion for film and philosophy is strong, and many of his suggestions have found their way into the pages of this book. Another student, Candice Chovanec Melzow, also deserves special mention. This is the third book that Candice has worked on with me, and I have grown to admire and rely on her editing prowess. Both Scott and Candice assisted me with the film summaries and transcriptions of dialogue. I am very grateful to both of them, as well as to all the students whom I have had the good fortune to teach and learn from at Indiana University at Bloomington, Georgia Tech, the University of Illinois at Chicago, and the University of Houston–Victoria. Finally, I would like to thank my wife, Nina, and children, Marco and Orlando, for their patience and support as I worked to bring this project to completion.

INTRODUCTION

"This sense of wonder is the mark of the philosopher. Philosophy indeed has no other origin. . . ."

—Plato, *Theaetetus*

"For it is owing to their wonder that men both now and at first began to philosophize; they wondered originally at the obvious difficulties, then advanced little by little and stated difficulties about greater matters, e.g., about the phenomena of the moon and those of the sun and of the stars, and about the genesis of the universe."

—Aristotle, *Metaphysics*

WHAT IS PHILOSOPHY?

The history of philosophy in the Western world can be traced back over 2,500 years to Ionia, on the west coast of present-day Turkey. It was there that Thales (625–545 B.C.E.), the first known philosopher in Western culture, is said to have introduced the well-known philosophical maxims "Know thyself" and "Nothing in excess." As one of the "Seven Sages of Ancient Greece," Thales abandoned the centuries-old tradition of explaining the world as a creation of the gods, offering in its place an account of the nature of the universe based on reason. He is credited with introducing geometry to Greece and is regarded as the first thinker in the Western world to search for the ultimate substance of things, which he identified as water. His scientific achievements were extraordinary and include predicting the eclipse of May 28, 585 B.C.E. and accurate estimations of the size of the sun and the moon.

In many ways, it is easier to get a sense of what philosophy is about from someone like Thales than it is from a contemporary philosopher because the aim of Thale's work is so clear. The physical world was for Thales a source of wonder. He wanted to know more about it—how it worked, from whence it came, what it was composed of—and he pursued knowledge of these and other topics primarily through the use of reason, avoiding many of the commonplace responses of his day. Many of the questions Thales asked are so fundamental that they persist even today in one form or another.

For Thales, philosophy amounts to reflection on the most basic features of the world and the way we ought to conduct our lives in this world. He is truly in awe of the phenomena that are presented to him through his senses, and he seeks to become as wise and knowledgeable about them as he can. He wonders, for example, "What is the nature of reality?" Or, phrased differently, "What is the ultimate substance of things?" He then proceeds by utilizing his reason to arrive at the best possible response to this question: water. He wonders as well, "How should one conduct one's life?" And again, through reason, he comes to the conclusion that knowing oneself and not doing anything to excess are rational responses.

While most contemporary philosophers have far more complex and sophisticated questions and doctrines than those of Thales, they are nevertheless pursuing the same thing: wisdom or knowledge. Moreover, like Thales, they are passionate in their pursuit of wisdom or knowledge.

This passion for knowledge is, in fact, part of the very meaning of the term *philosophy*, which is a combination of the Greek words *philos* (love of) and *sophia* (wisdom) and literally means "love of wisdom." However, the term was not introduced by Thales. It was introduced about fifty years after him, by the Greek philosopher Pythagoras (570–500 B.C.E.).

Pythagoras was the founder of a school in southern Italy that admitted both men and women and required that all goods be shared. Participants in Pythagoras's school practiced vegetarianism and had initiation ceremonies to advance through various ranks. Pythagoras and his students speculated on the nature of and relationship among God, the universe, society, and humans. One of the doctrines that Pythagoras held was that people could be divided into three types: (1) the lovers of wisdom, (2) the lovers of success, and (3) the lovers of pleasure. For Pythagoras, the lovers of wisdom were superior to the lovers of success and of pleasure. Even today, most philosophers would have difficulty identifying the philosophical life with the pursuit of pleasure or success. Philosophy is still strongly connected with the love of wisdom—its ancient connotation.

If philosophy is the pursuit of wisdom, we might ask, "What is the origin of this pursuit?" In *Theaetetus*, one of the philosophical dialogues written by Plato (428–348 B.C.E.), a character named Socrates states, that "wonder is the mark of the philosopher. Philosophy indeed has no other origin." While it is doubtful that the historical Socrates actually uttered these words, they uncontrovertibly amount to one of the best summaries of the origin of philosophical inquiry.

Philosophers are indeed curious and inquisitive people. They wonder about questions that many of us have never asked, let alone tried to answer. Moreover, when questions like "What is the nature of God?" and "What is the relationship of the mind to the body?" present themselves to philosophers, they are pursued not just with the goal of finding *an* answer but with the goal of finding the answer with the best set of reasons or arguments associated with it. Philosophers use their reason to think critically about the conduct of life, the justification of belief, and the nature of the world. While the example of Thales is illustrative of a philosopher utilizing reason to think critically about the nature of the world, the example of Socrates is illustrative of the ways in which philosophers use their reason to think critically about their beliefs and the conduct of life.

Socrates (469–399 B.C.E.) was born about 150 years after Thales. While Thales is regarded as the "Father of Philosophy" in general, Socrates is regarded as the "Father of Ethics" in particular. Whereas Thales and those Ionian philosophers who followed his lead were primarily concerned with studying the external universe, Socrates turned philosophy toward the study of the "internal universe," that is, the inner life of humans and the ways in which we relate to others. Whereas Thales was concerned with truths about the physical world, Socrates was concerned about truths concerning the world of human conduct. In his pursuit of truths concerning our conduct, Socrates utilized a "dialectical method" wherein he would push those with whom he was discussing these matters to clarify the meaning of the terms they were discussing or to look at the implications of the beliefs they held. Invariably, through his question-and-answer method Socrates exposed weaknesses in the arguments of his discussants. Socrates shows us how even the most generally accepted beliefs often cannot withstand critical scrutiny and how as philosophers—that is, persons committed to the pursuit of wisdom and knowledge—we must therefore reject them.

As you embark on an introductory philosophy course, remember that there are probably as many definitions of philosophy as there are philosophers. Nevertheless, there is something that binds these different conceptions of philosophy together, namely, a spirit of wonder and a passion for wisdom and knowledge.

AREAS OF PHILOSOPHY

Philosophical inquiry itself spans many fields of knowledge and areas of inquiry. For introductory students of philosophy, distinguishing these different areas of inquiry can initially be challenging, particularly as they try to understand the often complex and dependent relationships among them. However, it is important to get a sense of the range of philosophical inquiry before one begins to examine specific philosophical questions and responses to them. A sense of the broad areas of philosophical inquiry will help students understand how the particular philosophical topics they are studying fit into the broader arena of philosophical inquiry in general.

In its most general sense, philosophy may be reduced to three relatively distinct areas of inquiry:

- *Metaphysics:* the area of philosophy that studies the nature of reality, existence, and being. Metaphysics addresses questions concerning what there is. Specific topics in metaphysics include the nature of space and time, free will and determinism, the nature of causation, the distinction between appearance and reality, the distinction between the mind and the body, the nature of God, and the nature of identity.
- *Epistemology:* the area of philosophy that studies the sources, types, objects, and limits of knowledge. Epistemology addresses questions concerning what we can know and how we can know it.
- *Logic:* the area of philosophy that studies the methods and principles of correct reasoning. Logic addresses questions concerning what is coherent thought.

All the other areas of philosophical inquiry are in some way dependent upon one or more of these three areas. Some of the other areas of philosophical inquiry are these:

- *Ethics (or moral philosophy):* the area of philosophy that studies morality in itself in addition to moral psychology and the nature of moral knowledge. Ethics addresses questions concerning how we ought to act, toward ourselves and others. It takes up the meaning of good and evil, and right and wrong, both in themselves and as they relate to conduct, character, disposition, and things. *Applied ethics* attempts to explain and justify positions on specific moral problems such as abortion and capital punishment. Applied ethics may be further subdivided into business ethics, environmental ethics, medical ethics, and legal ethics.
- *Philosophy of mind:* the area of philosophy that studies the nature and contents of mind as well as our knowledge of mind. Philosophy of mind addresses questions concerning minds and machines, artificial intelligence, the nature of the self, the nature of consciousness, the nature of feelings and emotions, and the relationship of the mind to the body.
- *Aesthetics (or philosophy of art):* the area of philosophy that studies the nature, value, sources, and limits of art and beauty. Aesthetics addresses questions concerning standards of artistic taste, aesthetic experience, the nature of interpretation, the nature of representation, the role of the artist in society, the nature of the individual arts (dance, music, literature, film, and so on), the purpose of art, the sublime, authorship, textuality, and the ontology (being) of art. Traditionally, aesthetics was limited to the subject of beauty or the beautiful in art and questions concerning the standards of taste; however, today it is often used interchangeably with the philosophy of art, which is decidedly much broader in scope. It should be noted that each of the individual arts may be listed as subareas of aesthetics (or the philosophy of art). For example, the philosophy of literature and the philosophy of film are subareas of aesthetics.

- *Social and political philosophy:* the area of philosophy that studies the nature of the state, society, property, justice, authority, ideology, and punishment. Social and political philosophy addresses questions concerning the distribution of wealth, the justification of political violence, the nature of civil and human rights, justifications for war, the types of constitution, and a host of related topics concerning the state, property, and citizenship. Some regard social and political philosophy as two distinct areas of philosophy, namely, social philosophy *and* political philosophy. More often than not, however, they are regarded as one area of philosophy.
- *Philosophy of religion:* the area of philosophy that studies the meaning and justification of religious claims. The philosophy of religion addresses questions concerning the nature of God, proofs for the existence of God, the nature of religious knowledge, faith versus reason, religious experience, the problem of evil, miracles, immortality, science versus religion, religious pluralism, and the meaning of life.

While the material in this book focuses on the eight areas listed above, there are many other areas of philosophical inquiry, some of which are taken up by individual selections in this book. These areas include the philosophy of action, the philosophy of biology, the philosophy of economics, the philosophy of education, the philosophy of history, the philosophy of language, the philosophy of law, the philosophy of mathematics, the philosophy of physics, the philosophy of psychology, and the philosophy of science. Given that the scope of philosophical inquiry literally concerns *all that is,* an introductory philosophy course can concern itself only with a limited number of areas. Nevertheless, many of the areas of philosophical inquiry are related to other areas. Consequently, straying from one area of philosophical inquiry into another is quite common, particularly if you begin in an area other than metaphysics, epistemology, or logic. This is because all the other areas of philosophical inquiry are to varying degrees dependent upon these three areas.

For example, if your *epistemology* establishes that it is impossible to know anything with certainty, this will have implications for positions you hold in other areas of philosophical inquiry such as the *philosophy of religion.* Your uncertainty regarding knowledge will set limits on your beliefs regarding religious knowledge. In other words, your epistemology will affect your philosophy of religion. Note, however, that the opposite in this case does not hold. That is, if you hold that it is not possible to have knowledge of God with certainty, it does not follow that you must also contend that it is not possible to have any certain knowledge at all. You can be uncertain about your knowledge of God, yet still be certain in other areas of knowledge, for example, geometrical knowledge.

WHAT STUDENTS SHOULD EXPECT IN A PHILOSOPHY COURSE

If you have begun this course with no idea what philosophy is, you are not alone. Most students sign up for their first course in philosophy having little or no idea what to expect. Do not be surprised if you find yourself presented with some of the most challenging questions you have ever confronted. You may be asked to explain whether at this very moment you are dreaming or to ponder a proof for the existence of God or a proposal concerning the meaning of life. For some students, questions such as these trigger a chain reaction of related questions and set them on a path of philosophy discovery. For others, students, such questions lead to confusion and frustration, particularly once they learn that there are no "right" answers, unlike with questions like "What is the sum of two plus two?" or "What is the chemical composition of water?" Studying philosophy is quite different from studying mathematics or chemistry.

If you get caught up in the flow of philosophical discovery, my suggestion is to enjoy it as much as you can. Few experiences in life equal the power of discovering a philosophical question for the first time and becoming intoxicated with wonder by it. However, if you find yourself struggling with these questions, you should know that philosophy is a notoriously difficult subject. But if you are patient and diligent, philosophical inquiry will become easier for you, and philosophy will make more sense. At first, the questions pursued by philosophers may seem strange or disconnected from what is important to you. Nevertheless, invariably, they can and will touch your life in some significant way.

Part of the difficulty that many students have with philosophy is not that the subject matter is beyond their comprehension but rather that philosophy asks them to think about their lives and the world around them in a completely new way. Philosophy requires that we continually leave open to question even the things that seem most certain to us, such as who we are and what we know. It calls for us to take nothing for granted and to approach our life and the world around us with a continuous sense of wonder. It asks us to examine and reexamine our beliefs and values with the aim of understanding both their sources and their implications. It also asks us to consider rejecting positions that cannot be justified and to continuously strive to take up positions that can be rationally justified, that is, supported with good arguments. For many, this approach to belief is very different from what they are accustomed to and very intimidating.

Nevertheless, if you are patient with the material in this course and make an honest effort to understand it, you will find that the topics and questions addressed by philosophers are already taken up in many different forms in your own life. You will find that philosophical issues do not arise only in philosophy classrooms or in writings by philosophers. They can be found and explored in many other contexts, including films, literature, music, newspaper stories, television shows, and radio programs. You will find that the path from the arguments of Socrates to elements of your everyday life such as contemporary movies is lot shorter than you might have expected—and that perhaps the world of philosophy can play a valuable role in your own life.

One key difference in philosophical practice and everyday life is that philosophers strive to offer good *arguments* about topics such as the meaning of life and our ability to control our actions. Therefore, it is important that you become familiar with what constitutes a good argument before you begin to examine particular philosophical issues. Consider the following statement: "God exists because it says so in the Bible, which I know is true because God wrote it!" This may sound plausible, but is it a sound argument? Can you identify the fallacy inherent in such a statement? What are the hidden premises and assumptions? Arguments are an important part of philosophy, and learning how to distinguish good arguments from bad arguments will help you become adept at philosophy. What follows is a short introduction to help you build skills in the identification and creation of good philosophical arguments.

ARGUMENTS

An *argument* is a collection of statements. One statement is the *conclusion* of the argument. The other statements, often called *premises* or *reasons,* serve to show that the conclusion is true or that it is reasonable to believe that the conclusion is true.

> *Example:* A dog was kept in the stable along with the horses. Sometimes a visitor came in to get a horse. When the dog did not know the visitor well, the dog barked. Last night a stranger entered the stable. Obviously, the dog barked.

Premise 1: If the dog did not know the visitor well, then the dog barked.
Premise 2: The dog did not know the visitor well.
Conclusion: Therefore, the dog barked.

There are two types of arguments: *deductive* and *inductive*. A *valid* deductive argument is truth preserving: If the premises are true, then the conclusion must be true. A valid deductive argument guarantees this by following only truth-preserving forms, which are also called *valid forms*. Arguments that cannot offer this guarantee are *invalid*.

Think of a valid deductive argument as a box into which the premises are input and from which the conclusion is output. If we input all true statements into the valid deductive box, then the box outputs a true conclusion. However, if we input any false statements into the box, then the box *could* output a false conclusion. That is, the valid deductive box guarantees a true conclusion only if it is given true premises.

Similarly, we can think of an invalid argument as a defective box. If we input true premises into this defective box, the conclusion can be either true or false. Again, if we input any false premises, the conclusion could be either true or false. That is, the invalid deductive box cannot guarantee anything about the truth or falsity of the conclusion.

Here is a brief summary:

- *Valid argument:* an argument whose conclusion must be true if its premises are true
- *Invalid argument:* an argument whose conclusion may be false when its premises are true
- *Sound argument:* a valid argument in which all the premises are true

The conclusion is guaranteed to be true only if the argument is *sound*—that is, only if two conditions are met: (1) the argument is valid, and (2) all the premises are true. If the argument is not valid, then—by definition—it cannot guarantee a true conclusion from true premises. If at least one premise is false, then the argument—even if it is valid—cannot guarantee the truth of the conclusion.

COMMON VALID FORMS OF ARGUMENT

Modus ponens, modus tollens, dilemma, hypothetical syllogism, and *disjunctive syllogism* are five of the more common valid argument forms. The following examples substitute verbal phrases for the Ps and Qs.

- *Modus ponens:*   If P, then Q
                     P
                     Therefore, Q

     Example: If the dog hears a noise, then the dog barks.
                  The dog hears a noise.
                  Therefore, the dog barks.

- *Modus tollens:*   If P, then Q
                     Not Q
                     Therefore, not P

     Example: If the dog hears a noise, then the dog barks.
                  The dog does not bark.
                  Therefore, the dog does not hear a noise.

- *Hypothetical syllogism:*   If P, then Q
  If Q, then R
  Therefore, if P, then R

  Example: If the dog did not know the visitor well, then the dog would have barked.
  If the dog would have barked, then I would have been awakened.
  Therefore, if the dog did not know the visitor well, then I would have been awakened.

- *Dilemma:*   Either P or Q
  If P, then R
  If Q, then S
  Therefore, R or S

  Example: Either the dog is going to bite me, or the dog is going to be friendly to me.
  If the dog bites me, then I'll have to go to the hospital.
  If the dog is friendly to me, then I'll be able to continue walking home.
  Therefore, either I'll have to go to the hospital or I'll be able to continue walking home.

- *Disjunctive syllogism:*   Either P or Q
  Not P
  Therefore, Q

  Example: Either the dog bites me, or the dog licks me.
  The dog does not bite me.
  Therefore, the dog licks me.

Remember that even though the form of each of these arguments is *valid,* this does not necessary mean that the argument is *sound.* If one premise is false, then the argument—even if it is valid—cannot guarantee the truth of the conclusion. For example, consider the case of the disjunctive syllogism. This argument would not be *sound* if premise/reason 1 (Either P or Q—*Either the dog bites me, or the dog licks me*) were not true. For example, the dog could have growled at me, in which case he neither bit me nor licked me. Therefore, premise/reason 1 is untrue, making the argument as a whole *unsound.*

COMMON INVALID FORMS OF ARGUMENT

Denying the antecedent and *affirming the consequent* are two of the more common invalid argument forms. In both cases, the truth of the premises does not guarantee the truth of the conclusion.

- *Affirming the consequent:*   If P, then Q
  Q
  Therefore, P

  Example: If the dog hears a noise, then the dog barks.
  The dog barks.
  Therefore, the dog hears a noise.

	Comment:	Something other than a noise, such as the presence of a stranger, could have also made the dog bark.
•	*Denying the antecedent:*	If P, then Q Not P Therefore, not Q
	Example:	If the dog hears a noise, then the dog barks. The dog does not hear a noise. Therefore, the dog does not bark.
	Comment:	The dog could have barked anyway.

Earlier we distinguished between *deductive* and *inductive* forms of argumentation. To this point, we have discussed only deductive forms of argumentation. As a general rule, a valid deductive argument with true premises is a good argument, whereas an invalid deductive argument with true premises is both a bad argument and invalid. In contrast, inductive forms of argumentation are neither valid nor invalid. This does not mean that all inductive arguments should be considered bad forms of argumentation. Think of *strong* inductive arguments as comparable or analogous to *valid* deductive arguments and *weak* inductive arguments as comparable or analogous to *invalid* deductive arguments.

The premises of an inductive argument do not guarantee the truth of the conclusion; rather, they establish its truth with varying degrees of probability. As a rule, inductive arguments should be regarded as establishing *probable* conclusions on the basis of their premises, whereas deductive arguments should be regarded as establishing *necessary* conclusions on the basis of their premises. Here is an example of an inductive argument:

These beans (an appropriately determined sample) are from this bag.
These beans are white.
Therefore, all the beans in this bag are white.

This is not a deductively valid argument because the truth of the premises does not guarantee the truth of the conclusion. However, as the sample of beans from the bag increases and continues to be only white beans, then the truth of the conclusion (all the beans in this bag are white) becomes more *probable. Weak* inductive arguments draw general conclusions from incomplete or small sets of facts, whereas *strong* inductive arguments draw general conclusions from more complete or larger sets of facts. Here is an example of a strong inductive argument:

The sun has always risen in the east.
Therefore, the sun will rise in the east tomorrow.

Compare this argument to a weak inductive argument:

I have never broken any bones in my body.
Therefore, I will never break any bones in my body.

The probability that the sun will rise in the east tomorrow is greater than the probability that I will never break any bones in my body. It is this greater probability which makes the first inductive argument stronger than the second one. While both arguments are invalid, the first is a good argument based on the probability of its conclusion being true, whereas the second is a bad argument based on the probability of its holding true for the rest of my life. Nevertheless, arguments in the form of the first one are always better than arguments in the form of denying the antecedent or affirming the consequent. Whereas arguments in the form of denying the antecedent or affirming the consequent are such that the truth of the premises *never* guarantees the truth of the conclusion, the truth of the premise in the first argument supports the truth of the conclusion with a high degree of certainty.

COMMON FALLACIES

Fallacies are mistakes in arguments and so should be avoided. We touched on one of the major fallacies previously: drawing conclusions from too little evidence. This is what distinguishes weak inductive arguments from strong ones. Denying the antecedent and affirming the consequent are also examples of fallacies. However, these are only a few of the many ways in which arguments can be in error. What follows is a listing of some of the more common fallacies in arguments. Understanding these fallacies will sharpen your critical thinking abilities and help you analyze the reading in this book.

- *Ad hominem:* attacking the character of an alleged authority rather than his or her argument or qualifications. *Example:* "He's not from around here! How can he know what's going on?"
- *Appeal to authority:* seeking to persuade not by giving evidence but merely by citing an authority. *Example:* "It's a strong argument because my teacher told us that it is a strong argument."
- *Appeal to fear:* seeking to persuade not by giving evidence but merely by appealing to fear. *Example:* "Eat your carrots. If you don't, you'll go blind."
- *Appeal to ignorance* (ad ignorantiam): arguing that a claim is true simply because it has not been shown to be false. *Example:* "She's a witch! Nothing that has been said about her has disproven this!"
- *Appeal to pity* (ad misericordiam): seeking to persuade not through evidence but by appealing to pity. *Example:* "Professor, you have to give me a passing grade in this course! If I don't pass it, I won't be able to graduate in June!"
- *Appealing to the crowd* (ad populum): seeking to persuade not through evidence but by appealing to the masses. *Example:* "Cheating on exams is all right. Everybody does it!"
- *Begging the question:* assuming that which you want to prove, or, more formally, implicitly using your conclusion as a premise. *Example:* "God exists because it says so in the Bible, which I know is true because God wrote it!" (Or, more formally: "The Bible is true because God wrote it. The Bible says God exists. Therefore, God exists." The first premise assumes that God exists, for how could God write the Bible if God does not exist?)
- *Complex question:* asking a question in such a way that it is impossible for people to agree or disagree with it without committing themselves to the claim that the person who is asking the question seeks to promote. *Example:* "Do you still kick your dog?"
- *Composition:* assuming that the whole must have the properties of its parts. *Example:* "This must be a good school. All of the people I know who have gone to it are good students."
- *Division:* assuming that the parts must have the properties of the whole. *Example:* "He must be an excellent student. He goes to a very good school."

- *Equivocation:* using a single word in more than one sense. *Example:* "Men and women are physically different. Therefore, the sexes are not equal. The law should not treat men and women as though they are!" (The meaning of "equal" changes from "having the same physical attributes" to "having the same rights and opportunities.")
- *False analogy:* reaching a conclusion by comparing two significantly incomparable cases. *Example:* "You college professors have it easy! You have to teach only thirty weeks a year! At the factory, I have only two weeks a year off for vacation!"
- *False cause:* concluding that there is a casual link between two events when no such link has been established. *Example:* "We won every game that I wore these socks to. These socks are the key to our success!"
- *False dilemma:* reducing the number of potential options to just two. These options are often sharply opposed and unfair to the person facing the dilemma. *Example:* "America. Love it or leave it!"
- *Genetic fallacy:* attacking a position, institution, or idea by condemning its background or origin. *Example:* "That company will never succeed. Its founder came from a highly unsuccessful family."
- *Hasty generalization:* using an isolated or exceptional case as the basis for an unwarranted general conclusion. *Example:* "I drove well over the speed limit the other time I took this road and didn't get a ticket. I won't get a speeding ticket this time either!"
- *Poisoning the well:* disparaging an argument before even mentioning it. *Example:* "No intelligent person would believe that . . ."
- *Provincialism:* mistaking a local fact for a universal one. *Example:* "Everybody eats their dinner around 5:30."
- *Red herring:* introducing irrelevant or secondary information into an argument, thereby diverting attention from the main subject of the argument. *Example:* During the course of a discussion on the morality of abortion, someone brings up the issue of how cute babies are.
- *Slippery slope:* unjustifiably assuming that a proposal or position that is not undesirable or dangerous will trigger a chain of events that will lead to another undesirable or dangerous proposal or position. *Example:* "Today he is the leader of a small country, with little outside influence. However, if we allow him to stay in power, one day he will control the world."
- *Straw man:* misrepresenting a position in such a way that it is easy to refute. *Example:* "Why does God allow children to suffer? If he really is all-loving and all-caring, he would not do this. Therefore, God does not exist."
- *Sweeping generalization:* applying a general rule to a specific case to which the rule is not applicable because of special features of the case. *Example:* "If you work hard enough, you will get good grades." (There are people who work hard but still get poor grades. Other factors can play a role in getting good grades, including intelligence.)
- *Weasel word:* changing the meaning of a word in the middle of an argument in order to bring about the desired conclusion. *Example:* Bill: "Philosophy is a very difficult subject." Sam: "Well, what about ethics? You said that's easy!" Bill: "Oh, but ethics is not really philosophy."

EVALUATING PHILOSOPHICAL ARGUMENTS

The best way to decide which philosophical position is best is to examine the *arguments,* or reasons, that someone provides for choosing one philosophical position over others. Learning how to critically examine these arguments—deciding if they are good arguments that will convince a reasonable person—is one of the most difficult tasks that confronts someone learning philosophy. In learning to distinguish good arguments from bad ones, there is no substitute for practice. One of the best ways to practice an argument is by talking to others, listening to what they have to say, and writing out your thoughts on the issue. Writing about and discussing philosophical issues will help you develop not only your understanding of them but also your argumentation and critical skills in general.

In this book, you will often be faced with at least two arguments with conflicting conclusions. All of the conflicting conclusions cannot be true. To determine which conclusion to accept, follow these steps: (1) Reconstruct each argument as a valid argument, and (2) determine which argument has the true (or the more likely to be true) premises. This is, of course, sometimes easier said than done. Here are some general guidelines for reconstructing valid deductive arguments and some guidelines for evaluating premises.

Guidelines for Reconstructing Valid Deductive Arguments

- Make sure that the argument is in the form of a deductively valid argument.
- Compose the premises so that they fit the pattern of valid deductive rules.
- Make sure that all of the premises required to make the argument valid are included.
- Avoid begging the question; that is, make sure the premises do not assume the conclusion.
- Make sure the premises are general enough to avoid looking like prejudices. If a premise focuses on a specific group, it might come across as a prejudice against that group.
- Avoid straw man arguments; that is, make sure all the arguments are plausible and faithful to the proponents of that argument.
- Avoid equivocation; that is, make sure the argument does not turn on different meanings of the same word.

Guidelines for Evaluating Premises

- Challenge premises by formulating counterexamples to the premises.
- Look for irrelevant premises such as those that appeal to our emotions or that unfairly represent the opposing position.
- Question the foundations or basis of premises that are causal claims.
- Look for premises that are based on moral intuitions, and challenge these intuitions by examining cases that go counter to the intuition.
- Don't dismiss arguments on the basis of one faulty premise; rather, try alternative premises to give the argument its strongest defense. The aim is to solve moral problems, not to summarily dismiss arguments.

It is easy to become offended or angered by philosophical positions that do not match your own. Rather than quickly dismissing such arguments, you should try to analyze and reconstruct them. By examining the reasoning of people with opposing views, you can better understand *why* they may hold philosophical positions different from your own. Good critical thinking skills and the ability to discern good reasoning from bad are fundamentally interrelated. Your ability to get to the heart of philosophical controversies will improve as you critically work through the materials in this book.

SAMPLE ARGUMENT FOR CLASS DISCUSSION

MONTY PYTHON

THE ARGUMENT CLINIC

In this well-known Monty Python skit, a man (Michael Palin) walks into a clinic and purchases a five-minute "argument." The dialogue below picks up the skit from the point at which the man has walked into the office of Mr. Vibrating (John Cleese), the person who is paid to give him an argument, and ends when the man leaves Mr. Vibrating's office to lodge a complaint about the quality of the argument he has just purchased. This sketch appeared in episode 29 of the *Monty Python's Flying Circus* TV show and may be found on a number of Monty Python albums and videotapes.

After you read this selection from the "The Argument Clinic," discuss whether the man actually received what he paid for: an argument. You might discuss what are the *necessary* conditions (if it does not have these features, then it is not an argument) and *sufficient* conditions (if it has these features, then it is an argument) of an argument, and whether the argument below, if it is indeed one, is *valid* and *sound*. If you were the man, would you have been satisfied with the argument you received?

MAN (Knock)
MR. VIBRATING "Come in."
MAN "Ah, is this the right room for an argument?"
MR. VIBRATING "I told you once."
MAN "No you haven't."
MR. VIBRATING "Yes I have."
MAN "When?"
MR. VIBRATING "Just now."
MAN "No you didn't."
MR. VIBRATING "Yes I did."
MAN "You didn't."
MR. VIBRATING "I did!"
MAN "You didn't!"
MR. VIBRATING "I'm telling you I did!"
MAN "You did not!!"
MR. VIBRATING "Oh, I'm sorry, just one moment. Is this a five-minute argument or the full half hour?"
MAN "Oh, just the five minutes."
MR. VIBRATING "Ah, thank you. Anyway, I did."
MAN "You most certainly did not."
MR. VIBRATING "Look, let's get this thing clear; I quite definitely told you."
MAN "No you did not."
MR. VIBRATING "Yes I did."
MAN "No you didn't"
MR. VIBRATING "Yes I did."
MAN "No you didn't."
MR. VIBRATING "Yes I did."
MAN "No you didn't."

MR. VIBRATING "Yes I did."
MAN "You didn't."
MR. VIBRATING "Did."
MAN "Oh look, this isn't an argument."
MR. VIBRATING "Yes it is."
MAN "No it isn't. It's just contradiction."
MR. VIBRATING "No it isn't."
MAN "It is!"
MR. VIBRATING "It is not."
MAN "Look, you just contradicted me."
MR. VIBRATING "I did not."
MAN "Oh you did!!"
MR. VIBRATING "No, no, no."
MAN "You did just then."
MR. VIBRATING "Nonsense!"
MAN "Oh, this is futile!"
MR. VIBRATING "No it isn't."
MAN "I came here for a good argument."
MR. VIBRATING "No you didn't; no, you came here for an argument."
MAN "An argument isn't just contradiction."
MR. VIBRATING "It can be."
MAN "No it can't. An argument is a connected series of statements intended to establish a proposition."
MR. VIBRATING "No it isn't."
MAN "Yes it is! It's not just contradiction."
MR. VIBRATING "Look, if I argue with you, I must take up a contrary position."
MAN "Yes, but that's not just saying 'No it isn't.'"
MR. VIBRATING "Yes it is!"
MAN "No it isn't! Argument is an intellectual process. Contradiction is just the automatic gainsaying of any statement the other person makes."
(Short pause)
MR. VIBRATING "No it isn't."
MAN "It is."
MR. VIBRATING "Not at all."
MAN "Now look."
MR. VIBRATING (Rings bell) "Good morning."
MAN "What?"
MR. VIBRATING "That's it. Good morning."
MAN "I was just getting interested."
MR. VIBRATING "Sorry, the five minutes is up."
MAN "That was never five minutes!"
MR. VIBRATING "I'm afraid it was."
MAN "It wasn't."
(Pause)
MR. VIBRATING "I'm sorry, but I'm not allowed to argue anymore."
MAN "What?!"
MR. VIBRATING "If you want me to go on arguing, you'll have to pay for another five minutes."
MAN "Yes, but that was never five minutes, just now. Oh come on!"
MR. VIBRATING (Hums)
MAN "Look, this is ridiculous."
MR. VIBRATING "I'm sorry, but I'm not allowed to argue unless you've paid!"

MAN "Oh, all right."
(Pays money)
MR. VIBRATING "Thank you." (Short pause)
MAN "Well?"
MR. VIBRATING "Well what?"
MAN "That wasn't really five minutes, just now."
MR. VIBRATING "I told you, I'm not allowed to argue unless you've paid."
MAN "I just paid!"
MR. VIBRATING "No you didn't."
MAN "I DID!"
MR. VIBRATING "No you didn't."
MAN "Look, I don't want to argue about that."
MR. VIBRATING "Well, you didn't pay."
MAN "Aha. If I didn't pay, why are you arguing? I got you!"
MR. VIBRATING "No you haven't."
MAN "Yes I have. If you're arguing, I must have paid."
MR. VIBRATING "Not necessarily. I could be arguing in my spare time."
MAN "Oh I've had enough of this."
MR. VIBRATING "No you haven't."
MAN "Oh shut up."

WHY STUDY PHILOSOPHY?

BERTRAND RUSSELL

ON THE VALUE OF PHILOSOPHY

Bertrand Russell believes that even though the study of philosophy is limited, it is still a valuable pursuit. Philosophical studies cannot give definite answers to the questions they address, because "no definite answers can, as a rule, be known to be true." Nevertheless, philosophical investigation is still valuable because the questions that are pursued "enlarge our conception of what is possible, enrich our intellectual imagination and diminish the dogmatic assurance which closes the mind against speculation." The greatest value of the study of philosophy is that in the contemplation of something greater than ourselves, we are freed from our personal interests and prejudices. This allows our mind the opportunity for a "union with the universe which constitutes its highest good." In the final analysis, for Russell, the questions asked by philosophers are more important than the answers.

Bertrand Russell (1872–1970), a British philosopher, logician, and essayist, was the grandson of Lord John Russell, a prime minister under Queen Victoria. In 1890, he won a scholarship to Trinity College, Cambridge, where he studied mathematics and philosophy from 1890 to 1894. He was a fellow at Trinity from 1895 to 1901 and a lecturer in philosophy from 1901 to 1916, during which time he developed his mathematical logic. In 1916, he was prosecuted and fined for distributing a leaflet on conscientious objection, and he was dismissed from Trinity because of his pacifist activities. In 1918, he was sentenced to six months in prison for an allegedly libelous article he wrote expressing his opposition to World War I and his desire for peace. He wrote his *Introduction to Mathematical Philosophy* (1919) during his prison time. He ran unsuccessfully for Parliament in 1922 and 1923 and was dismissed from City College, New York (the trustees deemed him unworthy of a teaching post), and the Barnes Foundation in Philadelphia (subsequent legal action by Russell resulted in a successful wrongful dismissal verdict). He is best known for his work in mathematical logic and analytic philosophy, especially *The Principles of Mathematics* (1903) and *Principia Mathematica* (3 vols, 1910–13), which he co-authored with Alfred North Whitehead. He was also an influential social critic, noted for his many antiwar and antinuclear protests. Russell was awarded the Order of Merit in 1949 and the Nobel Prize for Literature in 1950. He was the author of over 2,000 articles and reviews, and over 60 books. His best-known philosophical work is *A History of Western Philosophy* (1946). This selection is the concluding chapter of *The Problems of Philosophy* (1912), a book that has been widely used to introduce students to philosophy.

Having now come to the end of our brief and very incomplete review of the problems of philosophy, it will be well to consider, in conclusion, what is the value of philosophy and why it ought to be studied. It is the more necessary to consider this question, in view of the fact that many men, under the influence of science or of practical affairs, are inclined to doubt whether philosophy is anything better than innocent but useless trifling, hair-splitting distinctions, and controversies on matters concerning which knowledge is impossible.

This view of philosophy appears to result, partly from a wrong conception of the ends of life, partly from a wrong conception of the kind of goods which philosophy strives to achieve. Physical science, through the medium of inventions, is useful to innumerable people who are wholly ignorant of it; thus the study of physical science is to be recommended, not only, or primarily, because of the effect on the student, but rather because of the effect on mankind in general. Thus utility does not belong to philosophy. If the study of philosophy has any value at all for others than students of philosophy, it must be only indirectly, through its effects upon the lives of those who study it. It is in these effects, therefore, if anywhere, that the value of philosophy must be primarily sought.

But further, if we are not to fail in our endeavour to determine the value of philosophy, we must first free our minds from the prejudices of what are wrongly called "practical" men. The "practical" man, as this word is often used, is one who recognizes only material needs, who realizes that men must have food for the body, but is oblivious of the necessity of providing food for the mind. If all men were well off, if poverty and disease had been reduced to their lowest possible point, there would still remain much to be done to produce a valuable society; and even in the existing world the goods of the mind are at least as important as the goods of the body. It is exclusively among the goods of the mind that the value of philosophy is to be found; and only those who are not indifferent to these goods can be persuaded that the study of philosophy is not a waste of time.

Philosophy, like all other studies, aims primarily at knowledge. The knowledge it aims at is the kind of knowledge which gives unity and system to the body of the sciences, and the kind which results from a critical examination of the grounds of our convictions, prejudices, and beliefs. But it cannot be maintained that philosophy has had any very great measure of success in its attempts to provide definite answers to its questions. If you ask a mathematician, a mineralogist, a historian, or any other man of learning, what definite body of truths has been ascertained by his science, his answer will last as long as you are willing to listen. But if you put the same question to a philosopher, he will, if he is candid, have to confess that his study has not achieved positive results such as have been achieved by other sciences. It is true that this is partly accounted for by the fact that, as soon as definite knowledge concerning any subject becomes possible, this subject ceases to be called philosophy, and becomes a separate science. The whole study of the heavens, which now belongs to astronomy, was once included in philosophy; Newton's great work was called "the mathematical principles of natural philosophy." Similarly, the study of the human mind, which was a part of philosophy, has now been separated from philosophy and has become the science of psychology. Thus, to a great extent, the uncertainty of philosophy is more apparent than real: those questions which are already capable of definite answers are placed in the sciences, while those only to which, at present, no definite answer can be given, remain to form the residue which is called philosophy.

This is, however, only a part of the truth concerning the uncertainty of philosophy. There are many questions—and among them those that are of the profoundest interest to our spiritual life—which, so far as we can see, must remain insoluble to the human intellect unless its powers become of quite a different order from what they are now. Has the universe any unity of plan or purpose, or is it a fortuitous concourse of atoms? Is consciousness a permanent part of the universe, giving hope of indefinite growth in wisdom, or is it a transitory accident on a small planet on which life must ultimately become impossible? Are good and evil of importance to the universe or only to man? Such questions are asked by philosophy, and variously answered by various philosophers. But it would seem that, whether answers be otherwise discoverable or not, the answers suggested by philosophy are none of them demonstrably true. Yet, however slight may be the hope of discovering an answer, it is part of the business of philosophy to continue the consideration of such questions, to make us aware of their importance, to examine all the approaches to them, and to keep alive that speculative interest in the universe which is apt to be killed by confining ourselves to definitely ascertainable knowledge.

Many philosophers, it is true, have held that philosophy could establish the truth of certain answers to such fundamental questions. They have supposed that what is of most importance in religious beliefs could be proved by strict demonstration to be true. In order to judge of such attempts, it is necessary to take a survey of human knowledge, and to form an opinion as to its methods and its limitations. On such a subject it would be unwise to pronounce dogmatically; but if the investigations of our previous chapters have not led us astray, we shall be compelled to renounce the hope of finding philosophical proofs of religious beliefs. We cannot, therefore, include as part of the value of philosophy any definite set of answers to such questions. Hence, once more, the value of philosophy must not depend upon any supposed body of definitely ascertainable knowledge to be acquired by those who study it.

The value of philosophy is, in fact, to be sought largely in its very uncertainty. The man who has no tincture of philosophy goes through life imprisoned in the prejudices derived from common sense, from the habitual beliefs of his age or his nation, and from convictions which have grown up in his mind without the co-operation or consent of his deliberate reason. To such a man the world tends to become definite, finite, obvious; common objects rouse no questions, and unfamiliar possibilities are contemptuously rejected. As soon as we begin to philosophize, on the contrary, we find, as we saw in our opening chapters, that even the most everyday things lead to problems to which only very incomplete answers can be given. Philosophy, though unable to tell us with certainty what is the true answer to the doubts which it raises, is able to suggest many possibilities which enlarge our thoughts and free them from the tyranny of custom. Thus, while diminishing our feeling of certainty as to what things are, it greatly increases our knowledge as to what they may be; it removes the somewhat arrogant dogmatism of those who have never travelled into the region of liberating doubt, and it keeps alive our sense of wonder by showing familiar things in an unfamiliar aspect.

Apart from its utility in showing unsuspected possibilities, philosophy has a value—perhaps its chief value—through the greatness of the objects which it contemplates, and the freedom from narrow and personal aims resulting from this contemplation. The life of the instinctive man is shut up within the circle of his private interests: family and friends may be included, but the outer world is not regarded except as it may help or hinder what comes within the circle of instinctive wishes. In such a life there is something feverish and confined, in comparison with which the philosophic life is calm and free. The private world of instinctive interests is a small one, set in the midst of a great and powerful world which must, sooner or later, lay our private world in ruins. Unless we can so enlarge our interests as to include the whole outer world, we remain like a garrison in a beleaguered fortress, knowing that the enemy prevents escape and that ultimate surrender is inevitable. In such a life there is no peace, but a constant strife between the insistence of desire and the powerlessness of will. In one way or another, if our life is to be great and free, we must escape this prison and this strife.

One way of escape is by philosophic contemplation. Philosophic contemplation does not, in its widest survey, divide the universe into two hostile camps—friends and foes, helpful and hostile, good and bad—it views the whole impartially. Philosophic contemplation, when it is unalloyed, does not aim at proving that the rest of the universe is akin to man. All acquisition of knowledge is an enlargement of the Self, but this enlargement is best attained when it is not directly sought. It is obtained when the desire for knowledge is alone operative, by a study which does not wish in advance that its objects should have this or that character, but adapts the Self to the characters which it finds in its objects. This enlargement of Self is not obtained when, taking the Self as it is, we try to show that the world is so similar to this Self that knowledge of it is possible without any admission of what seems alien. The desire to prove this is a form of self-assertion and, like all self-assertion, it is an obstacle to the growth of Self which it desires, and of which the Self knows that it is capable. Self-assertion, in philosophic speculation as elsewhere, views the world as a means to its own ends; thus it makes the world of less account than Self, and the Self sets bounds to the greatness of its goods. In contemplation, on the contrary, we start from the non-Self, and through its greatness the boundaries of Self are enlarged; through the infinity of the universe the mind which contemplates it achieves some share in infinity.

For this reason greatness of soul is not fostered by those philosophies which assimilate the universe to Man. Knowledge is a form of union of Self and not-Self; like all union, it is impaired by dominion, and therefore by any attempt to force the universe into conformity with what we find in ourselves. There is a widespread philosophical tendency towards the view which tells us that Man is the measure of all things, that truth is man-made, that space and time and the world of universals are properties of the mind, and that, if there be anything not created by the mind, it is unknowable and of no account for us. This view, if our previous discussions were correct, is untrue; but in addition to being untrue, it has the effect of robbing philosophic contemplation of all that gives it value, since it fetters contemplation to Self. What it calls knowledge is not a union with the not-Self, but a set of prejudices, habits, and desires, making an impenetrable veil between us and the world beyond. The man who finds pleasure in such a theory of knowledge is like the man who never leaves the domestic circle for fear his word might not be law.

The true philosophic contemplation, on the contrary, finds its satisfaction in every enlargement of the not-Self, in everything that magnifies the objects contemplated, and thereby the subject contemplating. Everything, in contemplation, that is personal or private, everything that depends upon habit, self-interest, or desire, distorts the object, and hence impairs the union which the intellect seeks. By thus making a barrier between subject and object, such personal and private things become a prison to the intellect. The free intellect will see as God might see, without a *here* and *now,* without hopes and fears, without the trammels of customary beliefs and traditional prejudices, calmly, dispassionately, in the sole and exclusive desire of knowledge—knowledge as impersonal, as purely contemplative, as it is possible for man to attain. Hence also the free intellect will value more the abstract and universal knowledge into which the accidents of private history do not enter, than the knowledge brought by the senses, and dependent, as such knowledge must be, upon an exclusive and personal point of view and a body whose sense-organs distort as much as they reveal.

The mind which has become accustomed to the freedom and impartiality of philosophic contemplation will preserve something of the same freedom and impartiality in the world of action and emotion. It will view its purposes and desires as parts of the whole, with the absence of insistence that results from seeing them as infinitesimal fragments in a world of which all the rest is unaffected by any one man's deeds. The impartiality which, in contemplation, is the unalloyed desire for truth, is the very same quality of mind which, in action, is justice, and in emotion is that universal love which can be given to all, and not only to those who are judged useful or admirable. Thus contemplation enlarges not only the objects of our thoughts, but also the objects of our actions and our affections: it makes us citizens of the universe, not only of one walled city at war with all the rest. In this citizenship of the universe consists man's true freedom, and his liberation from the thraldom of narrow hopes and fears.

Thus, to sum up our discussion of the value of philosophy; Philosophy is to be studied, not for the sake of any definite answers to its questions, since no definite answers can, as a rule, be known to be true, but rather for the sake of the questions themselves; because these questions enlarge our conception of what is possible, enrich our intellectual imagination and diminish the dogmatic assurance which closes the mind against speculation; but above all because, through the greatness of the universe which philosophy contemplates, the mind also is rendered great, and becomes capable of that union with the universe which constitutes its highest good.

DISCUSSION QUESTIONS

1. Russell contends that philosophy should be valued more for the questions it asks, than for the answers it provides. Do you agree with him? Why or why not?

2. Russell acknowledges that for many people philosophy is nothing more than "useless trifling, hair-splitting distinctions, and controversies on matters concerning which knowledge is impossible." What is Russell's argument against this position? Is it a good argument? Discuss.

3. Russell says that "it is exclusively among the goods of the mind that the value of philosophy is to be found; and only those who are not indifferent to these goods can be persuaded that the study of philosophy is not a waste of time." Is he saying, then, that the study of philosophy is of no value to the body? Do you agree with this position? Why or why not? Construct an argument supporting your position.

4. Russell contends that "as soon as any definite knowledge concerning any subject becomes possible, this subject ceases to be called philosophy, and becomes a separate science." Is this true? Should we infer from this that the sciences (for example, astronomy and psychology) are not or cannot be philosophical? Do you believe we should make a distinction distinguish between science and philosophy? Why or why not?

VOLTAIRE
STORY OF A GOOD BRAHMAN

In "Story of a Good Brahman" (1761), Voltaire claims that even though a life of philosophical investigation does not produce knowledge or happiness, it is still preferable to a life full of happiness that is based in ignorance. His Brahman says, "I have been studying forty years, which is forty years wasted; I teach others, and I know nothing; this situation brings into my soul so much humiliation and disgust that life is unbearable to me." Still, the Brahman does not want happiness if the price of it is bigotry and imbecility.

François-Marie Arouet Voltaire (1694–1778), one of the major Enlightenment thinkers, was a French philosopher, essayist, historian, and social critic. He advocated tolerance and allegedly coined the credo "I don't believe a word you say, but I'll defend to the death your right to say it." He worked eighteen to twenty hours per day, often writing in bed, and kept no set hours for sleep or food. His most popular work, the novel *Candide* (1759), parodies Leibniz's metaphysical optimism in *Theodicy* (see chapter 1). Voltaire said, "If God did not exist, it would be necessary to invent him."

I met on my travels an old Brahman, a very wise man, full of wit and very learned; moreover he was rich, and consequently even wiser; for, lacking nothing, he had no need to deceive anyone. His family was very well governed by three beautiful wives who schooled themselves to please him; and when he was not entertaining himself with his wives, he was busy philosophizing.

Near his house, which was beautiful, well decorated, and surrounded by charming gardens, lived an old Indian woman, bigoted, imbecilic, and rather poor.

The Brahman said to me one day: "I wish I had never been born."

I asked him why. He replied:

"I have been studying for forty years, which is forty years wasted; I teach others, and I know nothing; this situation brings into my soul so much humiliation and disgust that life is unbearable to me. I was born, I live in time, and I do not know what time is; I find myself in a point between two eternities, as our sages say, and I have no idea of eternity. I am composed of matter; I think, and I have never been able to find out what produces thought; I do not know whether my understanding is a simple faculty in me like that of walking or of digesting, and whether I think with my head, as I take with my hands. Not only is the principle of my thinking unknown to me, but the principle of my movements is equally hidden from me. I do not know why I exist. However, people every day ask me questions on all these points; I have to answer; I have nothing any good to say; I talk much, and I remain confounded and ashamed of myself after talking.

"It is much worse yet when they ask me whether Brahma was produced by Vishnu or whether they are both eternal. God is my witness that I don't know a thing about it, and it certainly shows in my answers. 'Ah! Reverend Father,' they say to me, 'teach us how it is that evil inundates the whole world.' I am as much at a loss as those who ask me that question; I sometimes tell them that all is for the very best, but those who have been ruined and mutilated at war believe nothing of it, and neither do I; I retreat to my house overwhelmed with my curiosity and my ignorance. I read our ancient books, and they redouble the darkness I am in. I talk to my companions: some answer that we must enjoy life and laugh at men; the others think they know something, and lose themselves in absurd ideas; everything increases the painful feeling I endure. I am sometimes ready to fall into despair, when I think that after all my seeking I know neither where I come from, nor what I am, nor where I shall go, nor what shall become of me."

The state of this good man caused me real pain; no one was either more reasonable or more honest than he. I perceived that the greater the lights of his understanding and the sensibility of his heart, the more unhappy he was.

That same day I saw the old woman who lived in his vicinity: I asked her whether she had ever been distressed not to know how her soul was made. She did not even understand my question: she had never reflected a single moment of her life over a single one of the points that tormented the Brahman; she believed with all her heart in the metamorphoses of Vishnu, and, provided she could sometimes have some water from the Ganges to wash in, she thought herself the happiest of women.

Struck by the happiness of this indigent creature, I returned to my philosopher and said to him:

"Aren't you ashamed to be unhappy at a time when right at your door there is an old automaton who thinks of nothing and who lives happily?"

"You are right," he answered; "I have told myself a hundred times that I would be happy if I was as stupid as my neighbor, and yet I would want no part of such a happiness."

This answer of my Brahman made a greater impression on me than all the rest. I examined myself and saw that indeed I would not have wanted to be happy on condition of being imbecilic.

I put the matter up to some philosophers, and they were of my opinion.

"There is, however," I said, "a stupendous contradiction in this way of thinking."

For after all, what is at issue? Being happy. What matters being witty or being stupid? What is more, those who are content with their being are quite sure of being content; those who reason are not so sure of reasoning well.

"So it is clear," I said, "that we should choose not to have common sense, if ever that common sense contributes to our ill-being."

Everyone was of my opinion, and yet I found no one who wanted to accept the bargain of becoming imbecilic in order to become content. From this I concluded that if we set store by happiness, we set even greater store by reason.

But, upon reflection, it appears that to prefer reason to felicity is to be very mad. Then how can this contradiction be explained? Like all the others. There is much to be said about it.

DISCUSSION QUESTIONS

1. Would you want happiness if it were on condition of being imbecilic? Is "ignorance bliss," as the saying goes?

2. What, according to Voltaire's story, is the value of the philosophical life? What is the value of the nonphilosophical life? Does Voltaire's story encourage you to study philosophy? Why or why not?

3. Voltaire reveals a tension between "reason and felicity [happiness]." What is this tension? Do you agree with him? Why or why not?

4. Imagine you are Voltaire's Brahman, and have studied and thought about life and the world for forty years. Do you think that like him you would come to find life "unbearable"? Why or why not?

JIDDU KRISHNAMURTI

THE FUNCTION OF EDUCATION

Jiddu Krishnamurti asks us to consider what education means. He argues that "education has no meaning unless it helps you to understand the vast expanse of life with all of its subtleties, with its extraordinary beauty, its sorrows and joys." Our education must encourage us to think freely, without fear of condemnation. The richness of life can be appreciated only "when you revolt against everything—against organized religion, against tradition, against the present rotten society—so that you as a human being find out for yourself what is true."

Jiddu Krishnamurti (1895–1986) was born in India. One of the central themes of his philosophy is that all forms of authority, including political and religious authority, get in the way of pursuit of the truth. The British novelist and critic Aldous Huxley said that listening to Krishnamurti speak was "like listening to a disclosure of the Buddha." Numerous schools were founded in India, Europe, and the United States based on his educational principles. He was the author of many books including *Life in Freedom* (1928), *Commentaries on Living* (1956), *The First and Last Freedom* (1954), *Beyond Violence* (1973), and *The Ending of Time* (with David Bohm, 1985). This selection is from *Think on These Things* (1964).

I wonder if we have ever asked ourselves what education means. Why do we go to school, why do we learn various subjects, why do we pass examinations and compete with each other for better grades? What does this so-called education mean, and what is it all about? This is really a very important question, not only for the students, but also for the parents, for the teachers, and for everyone who loves this earth. Why do we go through the struggle to be educated? Is it merely in order to pass some examinations and get a job? Or is it the function of education to prepare us while we are young to understand the whole process of life? Having a job and earning one's livelihood is necessary—but is that all? Are we being educated only for that? Surely, life is not merely a job, an occupation; life is something extraordinary wide and profound, it is a great mystery, a vast realm in which we function as human beings. If we merely prepare ourselves to earn a livelihood, we shall miss the whole point of life; and to understand life is much more important than merely to prepare for examinations and become very proficient in mathematics, physics, or what you will.

So, whether we are teachers or students, is it not important to ask ourselves why we are educating or being educated? And what does life mean? Is not life an extraordinary thing? The birds, the flowers, the flourishing trees, the heavens, the stars, the rivers and the fish therein—all this is life. Life is the poor and the rich; life is the constant battle between groups, races and nations; life is meditation; life is what we call religion, and it is also the subtle, hidden things of the mind—the envies, the ambitions, the passions, the fears, fulfillments and anxieties. All this and much more is life. But we generally prepare ourselves to understand only one small corner of it. We pass certain examinations, find a job, get married, have children, and then become more and more like machines. We remain fearful, anxious, frightened of life. So, is it the function of education to help us understand the whole process of life, or is it merely to prepare us for a vocation, for the best job we can get?

What is going to happen to all of us when we grow to be men and women? Have you ever asked yourselves what you are going to do when you grow up? In all likelihood you will get married, and before you know where you are you will be mothers and fathers; and you will then be tied to a job, or to the kitchen, in which you will gradually wither away. Is that all that *your* life is going to be? Have you ever asked yourselves this question? Should you not ask it? If your family is wealthy you may have a fairly good position already assured, your father may give you a comfortable job, or you may get richly married; but there also you will decay, deteriorate. Do you see?

Surely, education has no meaning unless it helps you to understand the vast expanse of life with all its subtleties, with its extraordinary beauty, its sorrows and joys. You may earn degrees, you may have a series of letters after your name and land a very good job; but then what? What is the point of it all if in the process your mind becomes dull, weary, stupid? So, while you are young, must you not seek to find out what life is all about? And is it not the true function of education to cultivate in you the intelligence which will try to find the answer to all these problems? Do you know what intelligence is? It is the capacity, surely, to think freely, without fear, without a formula, so that you begin to discover for yourself what is real, what is true; but if you are frightened you will never be intelligent. Any form of ambition, spiritual or mundane, breeds anxiety, fear; therefore ambition does not help to bring about a mind that is clear, simple, direct, and hence intelligent.

You know, it is really very important while you are young to live in an environment in which there is no fear. Most of us, as we grow older, become frightened; we are afraid of living, afraid of losing a job, afraid of tradition, afraid of what the neighbours, or what the wife or husband would say, afraid of death. Most of us have fear in one form or another; and where there is fear there is no intelligence. And is it not possible for all of us, while we are young, to be in an environment where there is no fear but rather an atmosphere of freedom—freedom, not just to do what we like, but to understand the whole process of living? Life is really very beautiful, it is not this ugly thing that we have made of it; and you can appreciate its richness, its depth, its extraordinary loveliness only when you revolt against everything—against organized religion, against tradition, against the present rotten society—so that you as a human being find out for yourself what is true. Not to imitate but to discover—*that* is education, is it not? It is very easy to conform to what your society or your parents and teachers tell you. That is a safe and easy way of existing; but that is not living, because in it there is fear, decay, death. To live is to find out for yourself what is true, and you can do this only when there is freedom, when there is continuous revolution inwardly, within yourself.

But you are not encouraged to do this; no one tells you to question, to find out for yourself . . . , because if you were to rebel you would become a danger to all that is false. Your parents and society want you to live safely, and you also want to live safely.

Living safely generally means living in imitation and therefore in fear. Surely, the function of education is to help each one of us to live freely and without fear, is it not? And to create an atmosphere in which there is no fear requires a great deal of thinking on your part as well as on the part of the teacher, the educator.

Do you know what this means—what an extraordinary thing it would be to create an atmosphere in which there is no fear? And we *must* create it, because we see that the world is caught up in endless wars; it is guided by politicians who are always seeking power; it is a world of lawyers, policemen and soldiers, of ambitious men and women all wanting position and all fighting each other to get it. Then there are the so-called saints, the religious *gurus* with their followers; they also want power, position, here or in the next life. It is a mad world, completely confused, in which the communist is fighting the capitalist, the socialist is resisting both, and everybody is against somebody, struggling to arrive at a safe place, a position of power or comfort. The world is torn by conflicting beliefs, by caste and class distinctions, by separative nationalities, by every form of stupidity and cruelty—and this is the world you are being educated to fit into. You are encouraged to fit into the framework of this disastrous society; your parents want you to do that, and you also want to fit in.

Now, is it the function of education merely to help you to conform to the pattern of this rotten social order, or is it to give you freedom—complete freedom to grow and create a different society, a new world? We want to have this freedom, not in the future, but now, otherwise we may all be destroyed. We must create immediately an atmosphere of freedom so that you can live and find out for yourselves what is true, so that you become intelligent, so that you are able to face

the world and understand it, not just conform to it, so that inwardly, deeply, psychologically you are in constant revolt; because it is only those who are in constant revolt that discover what is true, not the man who conforms, who follows some tradition. . . .

The question is: if all individuals were in revolt, would not the world be in chaos? But is the present society in such perfect order that chaos would result if everyone revolted against it? Is there not chaos now? Is everything beautiful, uncorrupted? Is everyone living happily, fully, richly? Is man not against man? Is there not ambition, ruthless competition? So the world is already in chaos, that is the first thing to realize. Don't take it for granted that this is an orderly society; don't mesmerize yourself with words. Whether here, in Europe, in America, or Russia, the world is in a process of decay. If you see the decay, you have a challenge: you are challenged to find a way of solving this urgent problem. And how you respond to the challenge is important, is it not? If you respond as a Hindu or a Buddhist, a Christian or a communist, then your response is very limited—which is no response at all. You can respond fully, adequately only if there is no fear in you, only if you don't think as a Hindu a communist or a capitalist, but as a total human being who is trying to solve this problem; and you cannot solve it unless you yourself are in revolt against the whole thing, against the ambitious acquisitiveness on which society is based. When you yourself are not ambitious, not acquisitive, not clinging to your own security—only then can you respond to the challenge and create a new world. . . .

When you are doing something with your whole being, not because you want to get somewhere, or have more profit, or greater results, but simply because you love to do it—in that there is no ambition, is there? In that there is no competition; you are not struggling with anyone for first place. And should not education help you to find out what you really love to do so that from the beginning to the end of your life you are working at something which you feel is worth while and which for you has deep significance? Otherwise, for the rest of your days, you will be miserable. Not knowing what you really want to do, your mind falls into a routine in which there is only boredom, decay and death. That is why it is very important to find out while you are young what it is you really *love* to do; and this is the only way to create a new society. . . .

DISCUSSION QUESTIONS

1. Krishnamurti asks, "Is it the function of education to help us to understand the whole process of life, or is it merely to prepare us for a vocation, for the best job we can get?" What do you think? Defend your position. Also, reflect on your own education. Which side has it fallen on?

2. Krishnamurti believes that if our aim is to discover the truth of life for ourselves, then we must revolt against everything. Do you agree with him? Why or why not?

3. Krishnamurti argues that "where there is fear there is no intelligence." What is his argument?

Do you agree with him? Why or why not? Do you think that a society that promotes fear among its people is promoting a lack of intelligence among them as well? What would Krishnamurti say?

4. For Krishnamurti, "education has no meaning unless it helps you to understand the vast expanse of life." Is a meaningful philosophy also one that helps us to understand the vast expanse of life? Or is understanding one small corner of life enough to make a philosophy meaningful? Defend your view.

5. Krishnamurti sees the world as torn by conflicting beliefs and every form of stupidity and cruelty. Education can give us the freedom to create a different society, a new world. Do you agree with him? Think about the world you live in. Is his position naïve? Defend your response.

OF God AND Faith

Jesse (Alex Wiesendanger) and Lama Norbu (Ying Ruocheng) kneeling in *Little Buddha*.

1.1 WHAT ARE THE PROOF AND THE NATURE OF GOD'S EXISTENCE?

MARK TWAIN

LITTLE BESSIE

Even though Mark Twain's Little Bessie is not yet three years of age, she is curious about some of the deepest questions concerning the nature of God and his relationship with humans. In chapter 1, Little Bessie wants to know why a good, merciful, and wise God would cause people so much pain, sorrow, and suffering. When her mother tells her that "the Lord sends us these afflictions to discipline us and make us better," Little Bessie naively concludes that "it is every *person's* duty to help discipline everybody, and cripple them and kill them, and starve them, and freeze them, and lead them into murder and theft and dishonor and disgrace." In chapter 2, Little Bessie discusses with Mr. Hollister the creation of humans, reaching the conclusions that God is responsible for everything we do and that God is the only criminal in the world. Finally, in chapter 3, Little Bessie learns that even if God is not responsible for our actions because he gave us the Bible, God is still responsible for the actions of creatures like flies, which do not have a bible to help them circumvent their nature. Thus, when flies spread germs that result in fatal diseases to humans, God is responsible, not the flies. Therefore, God is a murderer.

Mark Twain (Samuel Langhorne Clemens) (1835–1910) is most widely known for novels such as *The Innocents Abroad* (1869), *The Adventures of Tom Sawyer* (1876), and *The Adventures of Huckleberry Finn* (1884). *Little Bessie* was written in 1908–9, shortly before his death. Like his other writings from this period, such as *Letters from the Earth* (1909), it was too controversial for publication during his lifetime. These writings are at once ironically pessimistic and darkly humorous, and they all reject conventional religion. The manuscript of *Little Bessie* is composed of six chapters with no clearly designated order; the selection below contains three of those chapters.

CHAPTER 1

LITTLE BESSIE WOULD ASSIST PROVIDENCE

Little Bessie was nearly three years old. She was a good child, and not shallow, not frivolous, but meditative and thoughtful, and much given to thinking out the reasons of things and trying to make them harmonise with results. One day she said—

"Mamma, why is there so much pain and sorrow and suffering? What is it all for?"

It was an easy question, and mamma had no difficulty in answering it:

"It is for our good, my child. In His wisdom and mercy the Lord sends us these afflictions to discipline us and make us better."

"Is it *He* that sends them?"

"Yes."

"Does He send *all* of them, mamma?"

"Yes, dear, all of them. None of them comes by accident; He alone sends them, and always out of love for us, and to make us better."

"Isn't it strange!"

"Strange"? Why, no, I have never thought of it in that way. I have not heard any one call it strange before. It has always seemed natural and right to me, and wise and most kindly and merciful."

"Who first thought of it like that, mamma? Was it you?"

"Oh, no, child, I was taught it."

"Who taught you so, mamma?"

"Why, really, I don't know—I can't remember. My mother, I suppose; or the preacher. But it's a thing that everybody knows."

"Well, anyway, it does seem strange. Did He give Billy Norris the typhus?"

"Yes."

"What for?"

"Why, to discipline him and make him good."

"But he died, mamma, and so it *couldn't* make him good."

"Well, then, I suppose it was for some other reason. We know it was a *good* reason, whatever it was."

"What do you think it was, mamma?"

"Oh, you ask so many questions! I think it was to discipline his parents."

"Well, then, it wasn't fair, mamma. Why should *his* life be taken away for their sake, when he wasn't doing anything?"

"Oh, *I* don't know! I only know it was for a good and wise and merciful reason."

"What reason, mamma?"

"I think—I think—well, it was a judgment; it was to punish them for some sin they had committed."

"But *he* was the one that was punished, mamma. Was that right?"

"Certainly, certainly. He does nothing that isn't right and wise and merciful. You can't understand these things now, dear, but when you are grown up you will understand them, and then you will see that they are just and wise."

After a pause:

"Did He make the roof fall in on the stranger that was trying to save the crippled old woman from the fire, mamma?"

"Yes, my child. *Wait!* Don't ask me why, because I don't know. I only know it was to discipline some one, or be a judgment upon somebody, or to show His power."

"That drunken man that stuck a pitchfork into Mrs. Welch's baby when—"

"Never mind about it, you needn't go into particulars; it was to discipline the child—*that* much is certain, anyway."

"Mamma, Mr. Burgess said in his sermon that billions of little creatures are sent into us to give us cholera, and typhoid, and lockjaw, and more than a thousand other sicknesses and—mamma, does He send them?"

"Oh, certainly, child, certainly. Of course."

"What for?"

"Oh, to *discipline* us! haven't I told you so, over and over again?"

"It's awful cruel, mamma! And silly! And if I—"

"Hush, oh *hush!* Do you want to bring the lightning?"

"You know the lightning *did* come last week, mamma, and struck the new church, and burnt it down. Was it to discipline the church?"

(*Wearily.*) "Oh, I suppose so."

"But it killed a hog that wasn't doing anything. Was it to discipline the hog, mamma?"

"Dear child, don't you want to run out and play a while? If you would like to—"

"Mamma, only think! Mr. Hollister says there isn't a bird or fish or reptile or any other animal that hasn't got an enemy that Providence has sent to bite it and chase it and pester it, and kill it, and suck its blood and discipline it and make it good and religious. Is that true, mother—because if it is true, why did Mr. Hollister laugh at it?"

"That Hollister is a scandalous person, and I don't want you to listen to anything he says."

"Why, mamma, he is very interesting, and *I* think he tries to be good. He says the wasps catch spiders and cram them down into their nests in the ground—*alive*, mamma!—and there they live and suffer days and days and days, and the hungry little wasps chewing their legs and gnawing into their bellies all the time, to make them good and religious and praise God for His infinite mercies. *I* think Mr. Hollister is just lovely, and ever so kind; for when I asked him if *he* would treat a spider like that, he said he hoped to be damned if he would; and then he—"

"My child! Oh, do for goodness' sake—"

"And mamma, he says the spider is appointed to catch the fly, and drive her fangs into his bowels, and suck and suck and suck his blood, to discipline him and make him a Christian; and whenever the fly buzzes his wings with the pain and misery of it, you can see by the spider's grateful eye that she is thanking the Giver of All Good for—well, she's saying grace, as *he* says; and also, he—"

"Oh, aren't you *ever* going to get tired chattering! If you want to go out and play—"

"Mamma, he says himself that all troubles and pains and miseries and rotten diseases and horrors and villainies are sent to us in mercy and kindness to discipline us; and he says it is the duty of every father and mother to *help* Providence, every way they can; and says they can't do it by just scolding and whipping, for that won't answer, it is weak and no good— Providence's way is best, and it is every parent's duty and every *person's* duty to help discipline everybody, and cripple them and kill them, and starve them, and freeze them, and rot them with diseases, and lead them into murder and theft and dishonor and disgrace; and he says Providence's invention for disciplining us and the animals is the very brightest idea that ever was, and not even an idiot could get up anything shinier. Mamma, brother Eddie needs disciplining, right away; and I know where you can get the smallpox for him, and the itch, and the diphtheria, and bone-rot, and heart disease, and consumption, and—*Dear* mamma, have you fainted! I will run and bring help! Now *this* comes of staying in town this hot weather."

CHAPTER 2

CREATION OF MAN

Mamma. You disobedient child, have you been associating with that irreligious Hollister again?

Bessie. Well, mamma, he is interesting, anyway, although wicked, and I can't help loving interesting people. Here is the conversation we had:

Hollister. Bessie, suppose you should take some meat and bones and fur, and make a cat out of it, and should tell the cat, Now you are not to be unkind to any creature, on pain of punishment and death. And suppose the cat should disobey, and catch a mouse and torture it and kill it. What would you do the cat?

Bessie. Nothing.

H. Why?

B. Because I know what the cat would say. She would say, It's my nature, I couldn't help it; I didn't make my nature, *you* made it. And so you are responsible for what I've done—I'm not. I couldn't answer that, Mr. Hollister.

H. It's just the case of Frankenstein and his Monster over again.

B. What is that?

H. Frankenstein took some flesh and bones and blood and made a man out of them; the man ran away and fell to raping and robbing and murdering everywhere, and Frankenstein was horrified and in despair, and said, *I* made him, without asking his consent, and it makes me responsible for every crime he commits. *I* am the criminal, he is innocent.

B. Of course he was right.

H. I judge so. It's just the case of God and man and you and the cat over again.

B. How is that?

H. God made man, without man's consent, and made his nature, too; made it vicious instead of angelic, and then said, Be angelic, or I will punish you and destroy you. But no matter, God is responsible for everything man does, all the same; He can't get around that fact. There is only one Criminal, and it is not man.

Mamma. This is atrocious! It is wicked, blasphemous, irreverent, horrible!

Bessie. Yes'm, but it's true. And I'm not going to make a cat. I would be above making a cat if I couldn't make a good one.

CHAPTER 3

Mamma, if a person by the name of Jones kills a person by the name of Smith just for amusement, it's murder, isn't it, and Jones is a murderer?

Yes, my child.

And Jones is punishable for it?

Yes, my child.

Why, mamma?

Why? Because God has forbidden homicide in the Ten Commandments, and therefore whoever kills a person commits a crime and must suffer for it.

But mamma, suppose Jones has by birth such a violent temper that he can't control himself?

He *must* control himself. God requires it.

But he doesn't make his own temper, mamma, he is born with it, like the rabbit and the tiger; and so, why should he be held responsible?

Because God *says* he is responsible and *must* control his temper.

But he *can't*, mamma; and so, don't you think it is God that does the killing and is responsible, because it was *He* that gave him the temper which he couldn't control?

Peace, my child! He *must* control it, for God requires it, and that ends the matter. It settles it, and there is no room for argument.

(*After a thoughtful pause.*) It doesn't seem to me to settle it. Mamma, murder is murder, isn't it? and whoever commits it is a murderer? That is the plain simple fact, isn't it?

(*Suspiciously.*) What are you arriving at now, my child?

Mamma, when God designed Jones He could have given him a rabbit's temper if He had wanted to, couldn't He?

Yes.

Then Jones would not kill anybody and have to be hanged?

True.

But He chose to give Jones a temper that would *make* him kill Smith. Why, then, isn't *He* responsible?

Because He also gave Jones a Bible. The Bible gives Jones ample warning not to commit murder; and so if Jones commits it he alone is responsible.

(*Another pause.*) Mamma, did God make the house-fly?

Certainly, my darling.

What for?

For some great and good purpose, and to display His power.

What is the great and good purpose, mamma?

We do not know, my child. We only know that He makes *all* things for a great and good purpose. But this is too large a subject for a dear little Bessie like you, only a trifle over three years old.

Possibly, mamma, yet it profoundly interests me. I have been reading about the fly, in the newest science-book. In that book he is called "the most dangerous animal and the most murderous that exists upon the earth, killing hundreds of thousands of men, women and children every year, by distributing deadly diseases among them." Think of it, mamma, the *most* fatal of all the animals! by all odds the most murderous of all the living things created by God. Listen to this, from the book:

> Now, the house fly has a very keen scent for filth of any kind. Whenever there is any within a hundred yards or so, the fly goes for it to smear its mouth and all the sticky hairs of its six legs with dirt and disease germs. A second or two suffices to gather up many thousands of these disease germs, and then off goes the fly to the nearest kitchen or dining room. There the fly crawls over the meat, butter, bread, cake, anything it can find in fact, and often gets into the milk pitcher, depositing large numbers of disease germs at every step. The house fly is as disgusting as it is dangerous.

Isn't it horrible, mamma! One fly produces fifty-two billions of descendants in 60 days in June and July, and they go and crawl over sick people and wade through pus, and sputa, and foul matter exuding from sores, and gaum [smear] themselves with every kind of disease-germ, then they go to everybody's dinner-table and wipe themselves off on the butter and the other food, and many and many a painful illness and ultimate death results from this loathsome industry. Mamma, they murder seven thousand persons in New York City alone, every year—people against whom they have no quarrel. To kill without cause is murder—nobody denies that. Mamma?

Well?

Have the flies a Bible?

Of course not.

You have said it is the Bible that makes man responsible. If God didn't give him a Bible to circumvent the nature that He deliberately gave him, God would be responsible. He gave the fly his murderous nature, and sent him forth unobstructed by a Bible or any other restraint to commit murder by wholesale. And so, therefore, God is Himself responsible. God is a murderer. Mr. Hollister says so. Mr. Hollister says God can't make one moral law for man and another for Himself. He says it would be laughable.

Do shut up! I wish that that tiresome Hollister was in H—amburg! He is an ignorant, unreasoning, illogical ass, and I have told you over and over again to keep out of his poisonous company.

DISCUSSION QUESTIONS

1. Reconstruct and discuss the argument in chapter 1 that concludes, "It is every *person's* duty to help discipline everybody, and cripple them and kill them, and starve them, and freeze them, and lead them into murder and theft and dishonor and disgrace." Is this a valid argument? Is it a sound argument? Why or why not?

2. Little Bessie discusses various aspects of the nature of God. However, she never presents an argument for or against the existence of God. Do you think she believes in the existence of God? If so, what might her argument be? If not, what might her argument be?

3. Little Bessie's mother believes in the existence of God. She responds as well as she can to Bessie's inquiries but reaches a point at which she just does not want anything more to do with Bessie's questions. Is there a point at which we should stop asking and/or responding to questions about God's nature? Why or why not?

4. Reconstruct and discuss the argument in chapter 3 that concludes that God is responsible for the fatal consequences of the spread of germs by flies. Is this a valid argument? Is it a sound argument? Why or why not?

5. Mr. Hollister concludes in chapter 2 that God is responsible for everything that humans do and that God is the only criminal in the world. Analyze his arguments. Can you refute them? If so how? How might Hollister respond to your refutation?

THOMAS AQUINAS

THE FIVE WAYS

I n this reading, Aquinas presents five ways in which the idea of God must be included in any explanation of the world. The first three ways are formulations of the *cosmological argument* for the existence of God. Along with the teleological argument (see the Paley selection) and the ontological argument (see the Anselm selection), the cosmological argument is one of the three standard arguments for the existence of God. The cosmological argument moves from observed facts about the cosmos (or universe) to the conclusion that God exists as the origin of these facts.

Aquinas's first way is a *cosmological argument from change*, which proceeds from the observation that there is change in the world (some translations use "motion" instead of "change"). Everything that changes must be changed by something else. However, "we must stop somewhere, otherwise there will be no first cause of the change, and, as a result, no subsequent causes." This "first cause of change not itself changed by anything" is "what everybody understands by God."

The second way is a *cosmological argument from cause*, which proceeds from the observation that there are causes and effects in the world. A given effect may be explained by noting its cause, but then that cause, in turn, must be explained. However, "such a series of causes must stop somewhere." "One is therefore," says Aquinas, "forced to suppose some first cause, to which everyone gives the name 'God.' "

The third way is a *cosmological argument from contingency*, which proceeds from the observation that the world contains things that spring up and die away (*contingent* things), "thus sometimes in being and sometimes not." "Now everything cannot be like this," says Aquinas, "for a thing that need not be, once was not." If everything need not be—that is, is contingent—then once upon a time there must have been nothing. However, since we cannot get something from nothing, there should now be nothing. But this "contradicts observation," and so not everything is contingent. "One is forced therefore to suppose something which must be, and owes this to no other thing than itself."

The fourth way observes that different things have different degrees of goodness, truthfulness, nobility, and so on. However, because "such comparative terms describe varying degrees of approximation to a superlative," argues Aquinas, "[s]omething therefore is the truest and best and most noble of this, and hence the most fully in being." Aquinas (following Aristotle, not Plato) argues that because only beings exist, there must be something that has a perfect degree of truth, goodness, and nobility, and so on. "And this," says Aquinas, "we call 'God.' "

The fifth way observes that all things, both those that have awareness (animate things like persons and birds) and those without awareness (inanimate things like trees and arrows), tend toward goals. But inanimate things cannot direct themselves to these goals; there must be "someone with understanding" directing them. Just as "the arrow," argues Aquinas, "requires an archer," so too the world requires an intelligent being to direct it toward its goal. This being is called God. This fifth and final way is a precursor of William Paley's teleological argument.

Thomas Aquinas (1225–74) was the greatest of the medieval philosopher-theologians. A prodigious writer who produced over 8 million words, he was canonized in 1323 by Pope John XXII. For centuries, his work was neglected by thinkers outside the Catholic Church. Today, his writings are more widely studied by philosophers and have played an important role in contemporary philosophical debates. This reading is taken from his masterpiece, the *Summa Theologica* (1265–72) (*Summation of Theology*), the English translation of which fills sixty volumes. It was intended as a systematic introduction to theology for Dominican novices.

There are five ways in which one can prove that there is a God.

The first and most obvious way is based on change. Some things in the world are certainly in process of change: this we plainly see. Now anything in process of change is being changed by something else. This is so because it is characteristic of things in process of change that they do not yet have the perfection towards which they move, though able to have it; whereas it is characteristic of something causing change to have that perfection already. For to cause change is to bring into being what was previously only able to be, and this can only be done by something that already is: thus fire, which is actually hot, causes wood, which is able to be hot, to become actually hot, and in this way causes change in the wood. Now the same thing cannot at the same time be both actually x and potentially x, though it can be actually x and potentially y: the actually hot cannot at the same time be potentially hot, though it can be potentially cold. Consequently, a thing in process of change cannot itself cause that same change; it cannot change itself. Of necessity therefore anything in process of change is being changed by something else. Moreover, this something else, if in process of change, is itself being changed by yet another thing; and this last by another. Now we must stop somewhere, otherwise there will be no first cause of the change, and, as a result, no subsequent causes. For it is only when acted upon by the first cause that the intermediate causes will produce the change: if the hand does not move the stick, the stick will not move anything else. Hence one is bound to arrive at some first cause of change not itself being changed by anything, and this is what everybody understands by God.

The second way is based on the nature of causation. In the observable world causes are found to be ordered in series; we never observe, nor ever could, something causing itself, for this would mean it preceded itself, and this is not possible. Such a series of causes must, however, stop somewhere; for in it an earlier member causes an intermediate and the intermediate a last (whether the intermediate be one or many). Now if you eliminate a cause you also eliminate its effects, so that you cannot have a last cause, nor an intermediate one, unless you have a first. Given therefore no stop in the series of causes, and hence no first cause, there would be no intermediate causes either, and no last effect, and this would be an open mistake. One is therefore forced to suppose some first cause, to which everyone gives the name 'God.'

The third way is based on what need not be and on what must be, and runs as follows. Some of the things we come across can be but need not be, for we find them springing up and dying away, thus sometimes in being and sometimes not. Now everything cannot be like this, for a thing that need not be, once was not; and if everything need not be, once upon a time there was nothing. But if that were true there would be nothing even now, because something that does not exist can only be brought into being by something already existing. So that if nothing was in being nothing could be brought into being, and nothing would be in being now, which contradicts observation. Not everything therefore is the sort of thing that need not be; there has got to be something that must be. Now a thing that must be, may or may not owe this necessity to something else. But just as we must stop somewhere in a series of causes, so also in the series of things which must be and owe this to other things. One is forced therefore to suppose something which must be, and owes this to no other thing than itself; indeed it itself is the cause that other things must be.

The fourth way is based on the gradation observed in things. Some things are found to be more good, more true, more noble, and so on, and other things less. But such comparative terms describe varying degrees of approximation to a superlative; for example, things are hotter and hotter the nearer they approach what is hottest.

Something therefore is the truest and best and most noble of things, and hence the most fully in being; for Aristotle says that the truest things are the things most fully in being. Now *when many things possess some property in common, the one most fully possessing it causes it in the others: fire,* to use Aristotle's example, *the hottest of all things, causes all other things to be hot.* There is something therefore which causes in all other things their being, their goodness, and whatever other perfection they have. And this we call 'God.'

The fifth way is based on the guidedness of nature. An orderedness of actions to an end is observed in all bodies obeying natural laws, even when they lack awareness. For their behaviour hardly ever varies, and will practically always turn out well; which shows that they truly tend to a goal, and do not merely hit it by accident. Nothing, however, that lacks awareness tends to a goal, except under the direction of someone with awareness and with understanding; the arrow, for example, requires an archer. Everything in nature, therefore, is directed to its goal by someone with understanding, and this we call 'God.'

DISCUSSION QUESTIONS

1. Aquinas posits the idea of a being (God) whose existence requires no explanation. Do you agree with him? Why or why not?

2. One of the key premises of the third way is that one cannot get something from nothing. Is this premise sound? Present a case for and a case against this premise. Which case is stronger, and why?

3. In the second way, Aquinas says, "a series of causes must stop somewhere." Why must a series of causes be finite? Why can't a series of causes be infinite?

4. In the fourth way, Aquinas uses Aristotle's claim that "the truest things are the things most fully in being." What does this claim mean? What is an example of something that is "fully in being"? What is an example of something that is not "fully in being"? Discuss.

5. Which of the five ways is the strongest argument for the existence of God? Which is the weakest? Defend your response.

*F*railty depicts a small Texas town where God seems to be waging a war on demons. FBI investigator Wesley Doyle (Powers Boothe) is working on the "God's Hand" case, which involves the random disappearance of numerous individuals, but he has no leads. Posing as his brother Fenton Minks, Adam Minks (Matthew McConaughey) tells Doyle that his father (Bill Paxton) and brother Adam are involved in the disappearances. Fenton (Adam) describes how he is finally coming to terms with the true nature of his father's and brother's "murderous" actions.

Fenton (Adam) describes a childhood living with a father who had been told by God to destroy "demons," which, on the surface, appear to be normal human beings. Agent Doyle learns that Fenton's younger brother, Adam, participated in the murders. From his youth, Adam believed that his father had been called upon by God to destroy demons, whereas the young Fenton never believed in his father's God-given purpose. God told Fenton's father that Fenton was a demon, but the father refused to destroy his son and, in turn, was murdered by Fenton.

Agent Doyle is further informed that Adam committed suicide and that Fenton (Adam) would like to show him the rose garden near the Minks family home, where all the so-called demons are buried. When they arrive at the demon burial site, Adam reveals his true identity. He tells the agent that he destroyed Fenton because he was, as his father and God had told him, a demon. Now Adam must destroy the agent, who is also a demon, having committed the crime of matricide. Because only Doyle knows that he indeed murdered his mother, he is convinced that Adam is truly called upon by God to destroy demons. Adam then destroys Agent Doyle.

Frailty is a horror film, and viewers should be prepared for graphic violence (though violent acts largely take place off-screen). *Frailty* raises many philosophical issues concerning God—issues such as the nature of God (wrathful or compassionate?), human free will (if God orders us to do something, can we say no?), and faith (should we believe something even if it conflicts with reason?). It must also be noted that while the film makes clear that the persons who are "destroyed" have each committed murder (or have sinned), the true character of these demons is unresolved. Are the demons truly beings sent by the devil to bring about the end of the world, or are they merely sinners denied mercy? While the former explanation is implied by the film, the latter remains open for debate.

DISCUSSION QUESTIONS

1.   What is the nature God as depicted in *Frailty*? Does the film portray a compassionate God who sends men to kill demons? Or does it portray a wrathful God who sends men to kill sinners? Discuss.

2.   Fenton's father "had a vision from God." An angel came to him one night, told him "the truth of the world," and revealed God's "special purpose" for him and his family. The father tells his sons, "The end of the world is coming. There are demons among us, and the devil has released them for the final battle. But no one knows it but us and those like us. We have been chosen by God. He will protect us. We destroy them. That is our purpose. To save the world. . . . Our special power is that we can see the demons, but others can't. . . . God will be sending us special weapons to kill them with. . . . The

judgment day is here. . . . Soon we'll all be in heaven." Do these statements imply that God is not omnipotent (all-powerful)? If he were omnipotent, why wouldn't he kill the demons himself?

3. In the film *Dogma* (discussed later in this section), God does have the power to destroy demons (she [God] destroys Bartleby as he is about to enter the church). Compare the portrayal of God's power in *Frailty* to that in *Dogma*.

4. Are the demons in *Frailty* truly demons, or are they merely sinners denied mercy? How can we know the difference? What beliefs about the nature of God are necessary to make a decision about the nature of the demons?

5. Fenton (Adam) says to Agent Doyle, "Sometimes the truth defies reason." What does he mean? Is the case of these "demon destructions" an example of the truth defying reason? Do you agree that sometimes the truth defies reason? Explain.

6. Fenton (Adam) recounts the story of Abraham, who was asked by God to sacrifice his son Isaac. Adam and his father argue throughout the film that if God commands you to take someone's life and you follow his command, then it is not murder—it is "destruction." However, if you take the life of someone *before* God asks you to, then it is murder. Do you agree with this argument? What does it say about the nature of God? (In the film, the father is angry with young Fenton because Fenton's actions lead the father to murder the sheriff. If the sheriff had not been murdered, he would have tried to bring to a halt the work of "God's Hand." However, if the father received the name of the sheriff from God, the taking of the sheriff's life would be "destruction," not murder.)

7. For the sake of argument, assume that the demons are beyond any doubt evil people, and solid evidence suggests that they are responsible for the murder of many innocent persons. Would this make any difference in how you feel about the actions of Fenton (Adam) and his father? Or is it simply inconceivable that God would command persons to take the life of others, regardless of their guilt or innocence? Discuss.

WILLIAM PALEY

THE TELEOLOGICAL ARGUMENT

According to the teleological argument, God exists based on observations of the order, design, or purpose of the world. This argument takes its name from the Greek word *telos*, which means "end." One of the many formulations of this argument goes as follows: Design (order, purpose, and so on) exists in the world; design cannot exist without a designer; therefore, God exists as the source of the design. In this reading, Paley gives one of the best known and clearest formulations of the teleological argument, asserting that every manifestation of design that exists in a watch exists as well in the works of nature. Therefore, because there cannot be design without a designer, nature has a designer, an intelligent creator: God. Paley's argument is also referred to as the 'argument from design' or design argument.

If you look back to Aquinas's fifth way, you will notice that it, too, is a version of the teleological argument: all things, both those that have awareness (animate things like persons and birds) and those lacking awareness (inanimate things like trees and arrows), tend toward goals. But inanimate things cannot direct themselves toward these goals. Therefore, God exists as the intelligent being directing inanimate things toward their goals.

William Paley (1743–1805) was an influential English philosopher-theologian. He gradu-ated from Christ's College, Cambridge, where he went on to deliver a systematic course in moral philosophy. This course formed the basis of his book *The Principles of Moral and Political Philoso-phy* (1785), which became the ethics textbook of the University of Cambridge; it went through fif-teen editions. After nine years of teaching at Cambridge, he went into the ministry, where he spent the remainder of his life. In 1802, he published *Natural Theology, or Evidences of the Existence and Attributes of the Deity Collected from the Appearances of Nature*, his last book, of which he said would repair in the study his deficiencies in the church. Our selection is taken from it.

CHAPTER 1

STATE OF THE ARGUMENT

In crossing a heath, suppose I pitched my foot against a *stone* and were asked how the stone came to be there, I might possibly answer that for anything I knew to the contrary it had lain there forever; nor would it, perhaps, be very easy to show the absurdity of this answer. But suppose I had found a *watch* upon the ground, and it should be inquired how the watch happened to be in that place. I should hardly think of the answer which I had before given, that for anything I knew the watch might have always been there. Yet why should not this answer serve for the watch as well as for the stone? Why is it not as admissible in the second case as in the first? For this reason, and for no other, namely, that when we come to inspect the watch, we perceive—what we could not discover in the stone—that its several parts are framed and put together for a purpose, e.g., that they are so formed and adjusted as to produce motion, and that motion so regulated as to point out the hour of the day; that if the different parts had been differently shaped from what they are, of a different size from what they are, or placed after any other manner or in any other order than that in which they are placed, either no motion at all would have been carried on in the machine, or none which would have answered the use that is now served by it. To reckon up a few of the plainest of these parts and of their offices, all tending to one result; we see a cylindrical box containing a coiled elastic spring, which, by its endeavor to relax itself, turns round the box. We next observe a flexible chain—artificially wrought

for the sake of flexure—communicating the action of the spring from the box to the fusee. We then find a series of wheels, the teeth of which catch in and apply to each other, conducting the motion from the fusee to the balance and from the balance to the pointer, and at the same time, by the size and shape of those wheels, so regulating that motion as to terminate in causing an index, by an equable and measured progression, to pass over a given space in a given time. We take notice that the wheels are made of brass, in order to keep them from rust; the springs of steel, no other metal being so elastic; that over the face of the watch there is placed a glass, a material employed in no other part of the work, but in the room of which, if there had been any other than a transparent substance, the hour could not be seen without opening the case. This mechanism being observed—it requires indeed an examination of the instrument, and perhaps some previous knowledge of the subject, to perceive and understand it; but being once, as we have said, observed and understood—the inference we think is inevitable, that the watch must have had a maker—that there must have existed, at some time and at some place or other, an artificer or artificers who formed it for the purpose which we find it actually to answer, who comprehended its construction and designed its use.

I. Nor would it, I apprehend, weaken the conclusion, that we had never seen a watch made—that we had never known an artist capable of making one—that we were altogether incapable of executing such a piece of workmanship ourselves, or of understanding in what manner it was performed; all this being no more than what is true of some exquisite remains of ancient art, of some lost arts, and, to the generality of mankind, of the more curious productions of modern manufacture. Does one man in a million know how oval frames are turned? Ignorance of this kind exalts our opinion of the unseen and unknown artist's skill, if he be unseen and unknown, but raises no doubt in our minds of the existence and agency of such an artist, at some former time and in some place or other. Nor can I perceive that it varies at all the inference, whether the question arise concerning a human agent or concerning an agent of a different species, or an agent possessing in some respects a different nature.

II. Neither, secondly, would it invalidate our conclusion, that the watch sometimes went wrong or that it seldom went exactly right. The purpose of the machinery, the design, and the designer might be evident, and in the case supposed, would be evident, in whatever way we accounted for the irregularity of the movement, or whether we could account for it or not. It is not necessary that a machine be perfect in order to show with what design it was made: still less necessary, where the only question is whether it were made with any design at all.

III. Nor, thirdly, would it bring any uncertainty into the argument, if there were a few parts of the watch, concerning which we could not discover or had not yet discovered in what manner they conduced to the general effect; or even some parts, concerning which we could not ascertain whether they conduced to that effect in any manner whatever. For, as to the first branch of the case, if by the loss, or disorder, or decay of the parts in question, the movement of the watch were found in fact to be stopped, or disturbed, or retarded, no doubt would remain in our minds as to the utility or intention of these parts, although we should be unable to investigate the manner according to which, or the connection by which, the ultimate effect depended upon their action or assistance; and the more complex is the machine, the more likely is this obscurity to arise. Then, as to the second thing supposed, namely, that there

were parts which might be spared without prejudice to the movement of the watch, and that we had proved this by experiment, these superfluous parts, even if we were completely assured that they were such, would not vacate the reasoning which we had instituted concerning other parts. The indication of contrivance remained, with respect to them, nearly as it was before.

IV. Nor, fourthly, would any man in his senses think the existence of the watch with its various machinery accounted for, by being told that it was one out of possible combinations of material forms; that whatever he had found in the place where he found the watch, must have contained some internal configuration or other; and that this configuration might be the structure now exhibited, namely, of the works of a watch, as well as a different structure.

V. Nor, fifthly, would it yield his inquiry more satisfaction, to be answered that there existed in things a principle of order, which had disposed the parts of the watch into their present form and situation. He never knew a watch made by the principle of order; nor can he even form to himself an idea of what is meant by a principle of order distinct from the intelligence of the watchmaker.

VI. Sixthly, he would be surprised to hear that the mechanism of the watch was no proof of contrivance, only a motive to induce the mind to think so:

VII. And not less surprised to be informed that the watch in his hand was nothing more than the result of the laws of *metallic* nature. It is a perversion of language to assign any law as the efficient, operative cause of any thing. A law presupposes an agent, for it is only the mode according to which an agent proceeds; it implies a power, for it is the order according to which that power acts. Without this agent, without this power, which are both distinct from itself, the *law* does nothing, is nothing. The expression, "the law of metallic nature," may sound strange and harsh to a philosophic ear; but it seems quite as justifiable as some others which are more familiar to him, such as "the law of vegetable nature," "the law of animal nature," or, indeed, as "the law of nature" in general, when assigned as the cause of phenomena, in exclusion of agency and power, or when it is substituted into the place of these.

VIII. Neither, lastly, would our observer be driven out of his conclusion or from his confidence in its truth by being told that he knew nothing at all about the matter. He knows enough for his argument; he knows the utility of the end; he knows the subserviency and adaptation of the means to the end. These points being known, his ignorance of other points, his doubts concerning other points affect not the certainty of his reasoning. The consciousness of knowing little need not beget a distrust of that which he does know.

CHAPTER 2

STATE OF THE ARGUMENT CONTINUED

Suppose, in the next place, that the person who found the watch should after some time discover that, in addition to all the properties which he had hitherto observed in it, it possessed the unexpected property of producing in the course of its movement another watch like itself—the thing is conceivable; that it contained within it a mechanism, a system of parts—a mold, for instance, or a complex adjustment of lathes, files, and other tools—evidently and separately calculated for this purpose; let us inquire what effect ought such a discovery to have upon his former conclusion.

I. The first effect would be to increase his admiration of the contrivance, and his conviction of the consummate skill of the contriver. Whether he regarded the object of the contrivance, the distinct apparatus, the intricate, yet in many parts intelligible mechanism by which it was carried on, he would perceive in this new observation nothing but an additional reason for doing what he had already done—for referring the construction of the watch to design and to supreme art. If that construction *without* this property, or, which is the same thing, before this property had been noticed, proved intention and art to have been employed about it, still more strong would the proof appear when he came to the knowledge of this further property, the crown and perfection of all the rest.

II. He would reflect, that though the watch before him were, *in some sense,* the maker of the watch, which, was fabricated in the course of its movements, yet it was in a very different sense from that in which a carpenter, for instance, is the maker of a chair—the author of its contrivance, the cause of the relation of its parts to their use. With respect to these, the first watch was no cause at all to the second; in no such sense as this was it the author of the constitution and order, either of the parts which the new watch contained, or of the parts by the aid and instrumentality of which it was produced. We might possibly say, but with great latitude of expression, that a stream of water ground corn; but no latitude of expression would allow us to say, no stretch of conjecture could lead us to think that the stream of water built the mill, though it were too ancient for us to know who the builder was. What the stream of water does in the affair is neither more nor less than this: by the application of an unintelligent impulse to a mechanism previously arranged, arranged independently of it and arranged by intelligence, an effect is produced, namely, the corn is ground. But the effect results from the arrangement. The force of the stream cannot be said to be the cause or author of the effect, still less of the arrangement. Understanding and plan in the formation of the mill were not the less necessary for any share which the water has in grinding the corn; yet is this share the same as that which the watch would have contributed to the production of the new watch, upon the supposition assumed in the last section. Therefore,

III. Though it be now no longer probable that the individual watch which our observer had found was made immediately by the hand of an artificer, yet does not this alteration in anyway affect the inference that an artificer had been originally employed and concerned in the production. The argument from design remains as it was. Marks of design and contrivance are no more accounted for now than they were before. In the same thing, we may ask for the cause of different properties. We may ask for the cause of the color of a body, of its hardness, of its heat; and these causes may be all different. We are now asking for the cause of that subserviency to a use, that relation to an end, which we have remarked in the watch before us. No answer is given to this question by telling us that a preceding watch produced it. There cannot be design without a designer; contrivance without a contriver; order without choice; arrangement without anything capable of arranging; subserviency and relation to a purpose without that which could intend a purpose; means suitable to an end, and executing their office in accomplishing that end, without the end ever having been contemplated or the means accommodated to it. Arrangement, disposition of parts, subserviency of means to an end, relation of instruments to a use imply the presence of intelligence and mind. No one, therefore, can rationally believe that the insensible, inanimate watch, from which the watch before us issued, was the proper cause of the mechanism we so much admire in it—could be truly said to have constructed the instrument, disposed its parts, assigned their office, determined their order, action, and mutual dependency, combined their several motions into one result, and that also a result connected with the utilities of other beings. All these properties, therefore, are as much unaccounted for as they were before.

IV. Nor is anything gained by running the difficulty farther back, that is, by supposing the watch before us to have been produced from another watch, that from a former, and so on indefinitely. Our going back ever so far brings us no nearer to the least degree of satisfaction upon the subject. Contrivance is still unaccounted for. We still want a contriver. A designing mind is neither supplied by this supposition nor dispensed with. If the difficulty were diminished the farther we went back, by going back indefinitely we might exhaust it. And this is the only case to which this sort of reasoning applies. Where there is a tendency, or, as we increase the number of terms, a continual approach toward a

limit, *there*, by supposing the number of terms to be what is called infinite, we may conceive the limit to be attained; but where there is no such tendency or approach, nothing is effected by lengthening the series. There is no difference as to the point in question, whatever there may be as to many points, between one series and another— between a series which is finite and a series which is infinite. A chain composed of an infinite number of links, can no more support itself, than a chain composed of a finite number of links. And of this we are assured, though we never *can* have tried the experiment; because, by increasing the number of links, from ten, for instance, to a hundred, from a hundred to a thousand, etc., we make not the smallest approach, we observe not the smallest tendency toward self-support. There is no difference in this respect—yet there may be a great difference in several respects—between a chain of a greater or less length, between one chain and another, between one that is finite and one that is infinite. This very much resembles the case before us. The machine which we are inspecting demonstrates, by its construction, contrivance and design. Contrivance must have had a contriver, design a designer, whether the machine immediately proceeded from another machine or not. That circumstance alters not the case. That other machine may, in like manner, have proceeded from a former machine; nor does that alter the case; contrivance must have had a contriver. That former one from one preceding it: no alteration still; a contriver is still necessary. No tendency is perceived, no approach toward a diminution of this necessity. It is the same with any and every succession of these machines—a succession of ten, of a hundred, of a thousand; with one series, as with another—a series which is finite, as with a series which is infinite. In whatever other respects they may differ, in this they do not. In all equally, contrivance and design are unaccounted for.

The question is not simply, How came the first watch into existence? which question, it may be pretended, is done away by supposing the series of watches thus produced from one another to have been infinite, and consequently to have had no such *first* for which it was necessary to provide a cause. This, perhaps, would have been nearly the state of the question, if nothing had been before us but an unorganized, unmechanized substance, without mark or indication of contrivance. It might be difficult to show that such substance could not have existed from eternity, either in succession—if it were possible, which I think it is not, for unorganized bodies to spring from one another—or by individual perpetuity. But that is not the question now. To suppose it to be so is to suppose that it made no difference whether he had found a watch or a stone. As it is, the metaphysics of that question have no place; for, in the watch which we are examining are seen contrivance, design, an end, a purpose, means for the end, adaptation to the purpose. And the question which irresistibly presses upon our thoughts is, whence this contrivance and design? The thing required is the intending mind, the adapting hand, the intelligence by which that hand was directed. This question, this demand is not shaken off by increasing a number or succession of substances destitute of these properties; nor the more, by increasing that number to infinity. If it be said that, upon the supposition of one watch being produced from another in the course of that other's movements and by means of the mechanism within it, we have a cause for the watch in my hand, namely, the watch from which it proceeded; I deny that for the design, the contrivance, the suitableness of means to an end, the adaptation of instruments to a use, all of which we discover in the watch, we have any cause whatever. It is in vain, therefore, to assign a series of such causes or to allege that a series may be carried back to infinity; for I do not admit that we have yet any cause at all for the phenomena, still less any series of causes either finite or infinite. Here is contrivance but no contriver; proofs of design, but no designer.

V. Our observer would further also reflect that the maker of the watch before him was in truth and reality the maker of every watch produced from it; there being no difference, except that the latter manifests a more exquisite skill, between the making of another watch with his own hands, by the mediation of files, lathes, chisels, etc., and the disposing, fixing, and inserting of these instruments, or of others equivalent to them, in the body of the watch already made, in such a manner as to form a new watch in the course of the movements which he had given to the old one. It is only working by one set of tools instead of another.

The conclusion which the *first* examination of the watch, of its works, construction, and movement, suggested, was that it must have had, for cause and author of that construction, an artificer who understood its mechanism and designed its use. This conclusion is invincible. A *second* examination presents us with a new discovery. The watch is found, in the course of its movement, to produce another watch similar to itself; and not only so, but we perceive in it a system of organization separately calculated for that purpose. What effect would this discovery have or ought it to have upon our former inference? What, as has already been said, but to increase beyond measure our admiration of the skill which had been employed in the formation of such a machine? Or shall it, instead of this, all at once turn us round to an opposite conclusion, namely, that no art or skill whatever has been concerned in the business, although all other evidences of art and skill remain as they were, and this last and supreme piece of art be now added to the rest? Can this be maintained without absurdity? Yet this is atheism.

CHAPTER **5**

APPLICATION OF THE ARGUMENT CONTINUED

Every observation which was made in our first chapter concerning the watch may be repeated with strict propriety concerning the eye, concerning animals, concerning plants, concerning, indeed, all the organized parts of the works of nature. As,

I. When we are inquiring simply after the *existence* of an intelligent Creator, imperfection, inaccuracy, liability to disorder, occasional irregularities may subsist in a considerable degree without inducing any doubt into the question; just as a watch may frequently go wrong, seldom perhaps exactly right, may be faulty in some parts, defective in some, without the smallest ground of suspicion from thence arising that it was not a watch, not made, or not made for the purpose ascribed to it. When faults are pointed out, and when a question is started concerning the skill of the artist or dexterity with which the work is executed, then, indeed, in order to defend these qualities from accusation, we must be able either to expose some intractableness and imperfection in the materials or point out some invincible difficulty in the execution, into which imperfection and difficulty the matter of complaint may be resolved; or, if we cannot do this, we must adduce such specimens of consummate art and contrivance proceeding from the same hand as may convince the inquirer of the existence, in the case before him, of impediments like those which we have mentioned, although, what from the nature of the case is very likely to happen, they be unknown and unperceived by him. This we must do in order to vindicate the artist's skill, or at least the perfection of it; as we must also judge of his intention and of the provisions employed in fulfilling that intention, not from an instance in which they fail but from the great plurality of instances in which they succeed. But, after all, these are different questions from the question of the artist's existence; or, which is the same, whether the thing before us be a work of art or not; and the questions ought always to be kept separate in the mind. So likewise it is in the works of nature. Irregularities and imperfections are of little or no weight in the consideration when that consideration relates simply to the existence of a Creator. When the argument respects His attributes, they are of weight; but are then to be taken in conjunction—the attention is not to rest upon them, but they are to be taken in conjunction with the unexceptionable evidence which we possess of skill, power, and benevolence displayed in other instances; which evidences may, in strength, number, and variety, be such and may so overpower apparent blemishes as to induce us, upon the most reasonable ground, to believe that these last ought to be referred to some cause, though we be ignorant of it, other than defect of knowledge or of benevolence in the author. . . .

DISCUSSION QUESTIONS

1. Imagine you are walking down a road that leads to Athens. You are about one mile from Athens when you see a bunch of stones on the ground at the foot of a hill that spell out the words "ONE MILE TO ATHENS." You assume that they are a sign put there by someone to indicate your actual distance from Athens when, in fact, they simply happened to fall down a hill into this configuration of letters and words. If you were Paley, how would you explain this occurrence? Discuss.

2. Does Paley's argument imply that there is no such thing as chance? Why or why not? Discuss.

3. Compare Aquinas's fourth way to Paley's argument. Which argument is stronger, and why?

4. Assuming that everything in the universe exhibits order, are there any explanations for this order other than the existence of a supreme being?

ANSELM AND GAUNILO

THE ONTOLOGICAL ARGUMENT

In this reading, Anselm presents one of the most famous arguments in the history of philosophy: the ontological argument for the existence of God, an argument invented by Anselm. Along with the teleological argument (see the Paley selection) and the cosmological argument (see the Aquinas selection), it is one of the three standard arguments for the existence of God. The argument begins with the premise that God is perfect and moves to the conclusion that God exists. Anselm formulates two different versions of this argument.

The first version begins with this premise: God is "a being than which nothing greater can be conceived." Anselm then tells us that a being than which nothing greater can be conceived "cannot exist in the understanding alone" because "to exist in reality" is greater than to exist in the understanding alone. Therefore, God exists.

The second version of the argument begins with this premise: God is the being that "cannot be conceived not to exist." For Anselm, a being that cannot be conceived not to exist "is greater than one which can be conceived not to exist." He moves from this to the conclusion that God exists. Anselm claims that it is an "irreconcilable contradiction" for God to be both "than which nothing greater can be conceived" and "conceived not to exist."

One of the most famous criticisms of Anselm's first formulation of the ontological argument came from Gaunilo, an eleventh-century Benedictine monk. Gaunilo argues that the idea of an island of which none greater can be conceived can be proven along the same line of argument used by Anselm to prove God's existence. That is, this island, than which nothing greater can be conceived, cannot exist in the understanding alone because to exist in reality is greater than to exist in the understanding alone. Therefore, this magnificent island exists. Gaunilo asserts that this line of argumentation is simply foolish.

Anselm (c. 1033–1109), a medieval philosopher and theologian, was archbishop of Canterbury. He was canonized in 1494 by Alexander VI. "For I seek to understand that I may believe," said Anslem, "but I believe that I may understand." For Anselm, understanding of God is always preceded by faith in him. "He who does not believe will not experience," said Anselm, "and he who has not experienced will not understand." His writings aim to make clear to reason his firm belief in God. Moreover, he contends, it is our duty to understand our beliefs concerning God. His writings include *Proslogion (Colloquy* or *Discourse), Monologion (Soliloquy* or *Meditation), De Grammatico, De Veritate (On Truth),* and *Cur Deus Homo (Why a God-Man).* The selections below are from Anselm's *Proslogion* and Gaunilo's *Liber pro Insipiente (In Behalf of the Fool).*

Be it mine to look up to thy light, even from afar, even from the depths. Teach me to seek thee, and reveal thyself to me, when I seek thee, for I cannot seek thee, except thou teach me, nor find thee, except thou reveal thyself. Let me seek thee in longing, let me long for thee in seeking; let me find thee in love, and love thee in finding. Lord, I acknowledge and I thank thee that thou hast created me in this thine image, in order that I may be mindful of thee, may conceive of thee, and love thee; but that image has been so consumed and wasted away by vices, and obscured by the smoke of wrong-doing, that it cannot achieve that for which it was made, except thou renew it, and create it anew. I do not endeavor, O Lord, to penetrate thy sublimity, for in no wise do I compare my understanding with that; but I long to understand in some degree thy truth, which my heart believes and loves. For I do not seek to understand that I may believe, but I believe in order to understand. For this also I believe, —that unless I believed, I should not understand.

> Truly there is a God, although the fool hath said in his heart, there is no God.

And so, Lord, do thou, who dost give understanding to faith, give me, so far as thou knowest it to be profitable, to understand that thou art as we believe; and that thou art that which we believe. And, indeed, we believe that thou art a being than which nothing greater can be conceived. Or is there no such nature, since the fool hath said in his heart, there is no God?

(Psalms xiv. I). But, at any rate, this very fool, when he hears of this being of which I speak—a being than which nothing greater can be conceived—understands what he hears, and what he understands is in his understanding; although he does not understand it to exist.

For, it is one thing for an object to be in the understanding, and another to understand that the object exists. When a painter first conceives of what he will afterwards perform, he has it in his understanding, but he does not yet understand it to be, because he has not yet performed it. But after he has made the painting, he both has it in his understanding, and he understands that it exists, because he has made it.

Hence, even the fool is convinced that something exists in the understanding, at least, than which nothing greater can be conceived. For, when he hears of this, he understands it. And whatever is understood, exists in the understanding. And assuredly that, than which nothing greater can be conceived, cannot exist in the understanding alone. For, suppose it exists in the understanding alone: then it can be conceived to exist in reality; which is greater.

Therefore, if that, than which nothing greater can be conceived, exists in the understanding alone, the very being, than which nothing greater can be conceived, is one, than which a greater can be conceived. But obviously this is impossible. Hence, there is no doubt that there exists a being, than which nothing greater can be conceived, and it exists both in the understanding and in reality.

> God cannot be conceived not to exist.—God is that, than which nothing greater can be conceived.—That which can be conceived not to exist is not God.

And it assuredly exists so truly, that it cannot be conceived not to exist. For, it is possible to conceive of a being which cannot be conceived not to exist; and this is greater than one which can be conceived not to exist. Hence, if that, than which nothing greater can be conceived, can be conceived not to exist, it is not that, than which nothing greater can be conceived. But this is an irreconcilable contradiction. There is, then, so truly a being than which nothing greater can be conceived to exist, that it cannot even be

conceived not to exist; and this being thou art, O Lord, our God.

So truly, therefore, dost thou exist, O Lord, my, God, that thou canst not be conceived not to exist; and rightly. For, if a mind could conceive of a being better than thee, the creature would rise above the Creator; and this is most absurd. And, indeed, whatever else there is, except thee alone, can be conceived not to exist. To thee alone, therefore, it belongs to exist more truly than all other beings, and hence in a higher degree than all others. For, whatever else exists does not exist so truly, and hence in a less degree it belongs to it to exist. Why, then, has the fool said in his heart, there is no God (Psalms xiv. I), since it is so evident, to a rational mind, that thou dost exist in the highest degree of all? Why, except that he is dull and a fool?

> How the fool has said in his heart what cannot be conceived.—A thing may be conceived in two ways: (1) when the word signifying it is conceived; (2) when the thing itself is understood. As far as the word goes, God can be conceived not to exist; in reality he cannot.

But how has the fool said in his heart what he could not conceive; or how is it that he could not conceive what he said in his heart? Since it is the same to say in the heart, and to conceive.

But, if really, nay, since really, he both conceived, because he said in his heart; and did not say in his heart, because he could not conceive; there is more than one way in which a thing is said in the heart or conceived. For, in one sense, an object is conceived, when the word signifying it is conceived; and in another, when the very entity, which the object is, is understood.

In the former sense, then, God can be conceived not to exist; but in the latter, not at all. For no one who understands what fire and water are can conceive fire to be water, in accordance with the nature of the facts themselves, although this is possible according to the words. So, then, no one who understands what God is can conceive that God does not exist; although he says these words in his heart, either without any, or with some foreign, signification. For, God is that than which a greater cannot be conceived. And he who thoroughly understands this, assuredly understands that this being so truly exists, that not even in concept can it be non-existent. Therefore, he who understands that God so exists, cannot conceive that he does not exist.

I thank thee, gracious Lord, I thank thee; because what I formerly believed by thy bounty, I now so understand by thine illumination, that if I were unwilling to believe that thou dost exist, I should not be able not to understand this to be true.

> God is whatever it is better to be than not to be: and he, as the only self-existent being, creates all things from nothing.

What art thou, then, Lord God, than whom nothing greater can be conceived? But what art thou, except that which, as the highest of all beings, alone exists through itself, and creates all other things from nothing? For, whatever is not this is less than a thing which can be conceived of. But this cannot be conceived of thee. What good, therefore, does the supreme Good lack, through which every good is? Therefore, thou art just, truthful, blessed, and whatever it is better to be than not to be. For it is better to be just than not just; better to be blessed than not blessed.

GAUNILO'S CRITICISM

The fool might make this reply:

This being is said to be in my understanding already, only because I understand what is said. Now could it not with equal justice be said that I have in my understanding all manner of unreal objects, having absolutely no existence in themselves, because I understand these things if one speaks of them, whatever they may be? . . . .

For example: it is said that somewhere in the ocean is an island, which, because of the difficulty, or rather the impossibility, of discovering what does not exist, is called the lost island. And they say that this island has an inestimable wealth of all manner of riches and delicacies in greater abundance than is told of the Islands of the Blest; and that having no owner or inhabitant, it is more excellent than all other countries, which are inhabited by mankind, in the abundance with which it is stored.

Now if some one should tell me that there is such an island, I should easily understand his words, in which there is no difficulty. But suppose that he went on to say, as if by a logical inference: "You can no longer doubt that this island which is more excellent than all lands exists somewhere, since you have no doubt that it is in your understanding. And since it is more excellent not to be in the understanding alone, but to exist both in the understanding and in reality, for this reason it must exist. For if it does not exist, any land which really exists will be more excellent than it; and so the island already understood by you to be more excellent will not be more excellent."

If a man should try to prove to me by such reasoning that this island truly exists, and that its existence should no longer be doubted, either I should believe that he was jesting, or I know not which I ought to regard as the greater fool: myself, supposing that I should allow this proof; or him, if he should suppose that he had established with any certainty the existence of this island. For he ought to show first that the hypothetical excellence of this island exists as a real and indubitable fact, and in no wise as any unreal object, or one whose existence uncertain, in my understanding.

This, in the mean time, is the answer the fool could make to the arguments urged against him. When he is assured in the first place that this being is so great that its non-existence is not even conceivable, and that this in turn is proved on no other ground than the fact that otherwise it will not be greater than all things, the fool may make the same answer, and say:

When did I say that any such being exists in reality, that is, a being greater than all others?— that on this ground it should be proved to me that it also exists in reality to such a degree that it cannot even be conceived not to exist? Whereas in the first place it should be in some way proved that a nature which is higher, that is, greater and better, than all other natures, exists; in order that from this we may then be able to prove all attributes which necessarily the being that is greater and better than all possesses.

Moreover, it is said that the non-existence of this being is inconceivable. It might better be said, perhaps, that its non-existence, or the possibility of its non-existence, is unintelligible. For according to the true meaning of the word, unreal objects are unintelligible. Yet their existence is conceivable in the way in which the fool conceived of the non-existence of God. I am most certainly aware of my own existence; but I know, nevertheless, that my non-existence is possible. As to that supreme being, moreover, which God is, I understand without any doubt both his existence, and the impossibility of his non-existence. Whether, however, so long as I am most positively aware of my existence, I can conceive of my non-existence, I am not sure. But if I can, why can I not conceive of the non-existence of whatever else I know with the same certainty? If, however, I cannot, God will not be the only being of which it can be said, it is impossible to conceive of his non-existence.

DISCUSSION QUESTIONS

1. For the sake of argument, let us assume that Anselm has shown that whatever qualifies as the greatest thinkable being must exist. However, is it not still an open question whether there is anything that does qualify as the greatest thinkable being in the first place? Discuss.

2. One of the most famous criticisms of Anselm's argument came from the eighteenth-century philosopher Immanuel Kant (see chapter 2 for a biographical sketch). In his *Critique of Pure Reason* (1787), Kant argues, "*being* is obviously not a real predicate; that is, it is not a concept of something which could be added to the concept of a thing" (B626); "the real contains no more than the merely possible" (B627). Says Kant, "A hundred real thalers [dollars] do not contain the least coin more than a hundred possible thalers" (B627). This line of criticism raises questions concerning Anselm's assumption that to exist in reality is greater than to exist in the understanding alone. How might Anselm respond to Kant's charge? Whose position is stronger, and why?

3. Explain Gaunilo's charges against Anselm's argument in your own words. How might Anselm reply to Gaunilo's criticisms? Who has the better case, and why?

4. Consider Anselm's definition of God as "a being than which nothing greater can be conceived." What does this mean? Is it a good definition of God? Can you provide a better definition? Compare your own definition of God to Anselm's.

5. Anselm first asserts belief in God and then seeks arguments or reasons to help him understand what he believes. Is this the right approach to God and religious experience? He also says that achieving such an understanding of God and religious experience through reasons or arguments is our duty. Do you agree with him? Why or why not? Defend your position.

The Apostle
[USA 1997] 2 hours, 14 minutes
Directed by Robert Duvall

*E*ulis "Sonny" Dewey (Robert Duvall) is a fundamentalist preacher in Texas who seeks the satisfaction of preaching the Gospels and helping misguided souls find their way back to the path of redemption. After losing his wife Jessie (Farrah Fawcett) and his congregation owing to a crime of passion (beating his ex-wife's boyfriend [Todd Allen] into a coma), Dewey flees from his town, his ministry, and the law. He assumes a new identity, calling himself "Apostle E. F.," and travels to a small town in Louisiana. There he befriends a retired minister, Reverend Blackwell (John Beasley), who helps him start up his own ministry. Dewey, a man of faith, desire, God, and rage, preaches hope and forgiveness to his followers. Dewey is eventually arrested by law enforcement officers who have been searching for him. He sacrifices his freedom and faces up to his past misdeeds in order to remain on the path of righteousness.

DISCUSSION QUESTIONS

1. Should the story of the fall and rise of Eulis Dewey be considered a "proof" of God's existence? Why or why not? If Dewey's story can be considered a proof of God's existence, do you find it to be a more persuasive proof for the existence of God than, say, that of Aquinas or Anselm? Why or why not?
2. Discuss the nature of God as depicted in *The Apostle*.
3. After his church is taken away from him, Dewey says to God, "Somebody, I say somebody, has taken my wife and stolen my church." Is the *The Apostle* suggesting that God is vengeful or compassionate? Or neither? Do you think that such aspects of God's existence can be proved or disproved? Discuss.
4. Dewey yells at God, saying, "I'm mad at you. I can't take it. Give me a sign or something. . . . If you won't give me back my wife, give me peace. I don't know who's been fooling with me, you or the devil. . . . I love you, Lord, but I'm mad at you. . . . I know I'm a sinner and once in a while a womanizer, but I am your servant. . . . What should I do, Jesus?" Should the founding of Dewey's new church, the One Way to Heaven Holiness Temple, be considered a sign from God telling Dewey what to do? Discuss. Also, do you think Dewey has been given peace by God? Has God "spoken" in this film?
5. What, if anything, does Dewey come to learn about the nature of God? Do you think that his overall attitude toward God changes over the course of this film? Explain.

FRIEDRICH NIETZSCHE

THE DEATH OF GOD

Friedrich Nietzsche notoriously proclaims that "God is dead." For Nietzsche, the death of God signifies the close of a period in history in which people believed that an ultimate or absolute reality was the source of meaning and values. The God-hypothesis of Christianity and the notions of morality, truth, and value associated with it have given way to a form of nihilism that emphasizes a world other than the one we live in (other-worldliness) and rejects naturalistic values and truths (values and truths linked to this world and this life). Nietzsche states that we do not believe in God any longer because God is no longer believable.

In his book *The Antichrist* (1895), Nietzsche writes, "That we find no God—either in history or in nature or behind nature—is not what differentiates *us*, but that we experience what has been revered as God, not as 'godlike' but as miserable, as absurd, as harmful, not merely as an error but as a *crime against life*. We deny God as God. If one were to *prove* this God of the Christians to us, we should be even less able to believe in him" (sec. 47). Thus, for

Nietzsche, God is dead in the sense that the idea of God is no longer in consonance with our experiences in this life and this world, and, in fact, stands in direct opposition to them: we have come to experience God as a "crime against life." Nietzsche contends that in light of the death of God, we must create new values that are faithful to this world and this life. The impossibility of proving God's existence and the cultural fact that God's existence is no longer as widely believed are less important to Nietzsche than is the fact that the God-hypothesis of Christians no longer represents a life-affirming set of values.

It should be noted that here Nietzsche is discussing only the origin and value of the *idea* of God, not the independent *reality* of God. For Nietzsche, the cultural and intellectual idea of God (or of the God-hypothesis) has changed to the point that it is no longer worthwhile to rely upon it as a source of life-affirming value. However, this cultural and intellectual idea of God traditionally has been the only way that God has had any *being* in our world. Thus, the demise of this idea is tantamount to the demise of God.

To be sure, this is a serious turn of events. God's death raises the question of whether our existence in this world has any meaning in itself. In *The Gay Science,* when Nietzsche's "madman" cries out, "I seek God!" those present who do not believe in God laugh and ask frivolous questions: "Has he got lost? asked one. Did he lose his way like a child? asked another. Or is he hiding? Is he afraid of us? Has he gone on a voyage? emigrated?" This response is disturbing to Nietzsche's madman because these atheists fail to comprehend the gravity of the situation: the death of God involves nothing less than the loss of the entire Christian system of values. In his frustration, the madman cries out, "*We have killed him*—you and I! All of us are his murderers!" The madman reminds us that we are responsible for both developing this idea of God and eliminating it. Those who have eliminated the idea of God and denigrated the value system linked to that idea of God have murdered God, says the madman. Furthermore, they are responsible for the damage to culture that results from their murderous actions.

Friedrich Nietzsche (1844–1900), the German philosopher and philologist, was the son of a Lutheran minister. When he was four years old, his father went insane and died within a few months. Subsequently, Nietzsche was raised by his mother, his paternal grandmother, two maiden aunts, and his sister. He studied theology and classical philology at the University of Bonn and classical philology at Leipzig. In 1869, at the age of twenty-four, he was appointed associate professor of philology though he had not yet written his thesis or dissertation, let alone the second book required for an associate professorship. Nietzsche was regarded as simply brilliant. Leipzig conferred a doctorate upon Nietzsche without an examination or thesis, and, in 1870, he became a full professor at Basel and a Swiss subject. In 1879, he resigned from the university because of ill health; he spent the next ten years living in Italy and Switzerland, primarily in solitude. In 1899, he collapsed in a street in Turin while embracing a horse that had been flogged by a coachman. Nietzsche died in 1900 after eleven years of insanity, which was probably the result of tertiary syphilis. Unless the disease was congenital, it is unknown how or when he was infected; aside from one possible visit to a brothel as a student, Nietzsche was a sexual ascetic for his entire life. Friedrich Nietzsche was one of the greatest philosophers of nineteenth century and the author of many books including *The Birth of Tragedy* (1872), *Human, All Too Human* (1878), *The Gay Science* (1882), *Beyond Good and Evil* (1886), *Toward a Genealogy of Morals* (1887), *Twilight of the Idols* (1889), and *Thus Spoke Zarathustra* (1883–92). The following are selections from *The Gay Science* (*Die fröhliche Wissenschaft*) and *The Antichrist.*

THE GAY SCIENCE

108

New struggles.— After Buddha was dead, his shadow was still shown for centuries in a cave—a tremendous, gruesome shadow. God is dead; but given the way of men, there may still be caves for thousands of years in which his shadow will be shown. —And we—we still have to vanquish his shadow, too.

109

Let us beware.— Let us beware of thinking that the world is a living being. Where should it expand? On what should it feed? How could it grow and multiply? We have some notion of the nature of the organic; and we should not reinterpret the exceedingly derivative, late, rare, accidental; that we perceive only on the crust of the earth and make of it something essential, universal, and eternal, which is what those people do who call the universe an organism. This nauseates me. Let us even beware of believing that the universe is a machine: it is certainly not constructed for one purpose, and calling it a "machine" does it far too much honor.

Let us beware of positing generally and everywhere anything as elegant as the cyclical movements of our neighboring stars; even a glance into the Milky Way raises doubts whether there are not far coarser and more contradictory movements there, as well as stars with eternally linear paths, etc. The astral order in which we live is an exception; this order and the relative duration that depends on it have again made possible an exception of exceptions: the formation of the organic. The total character of the world, however, is in all eternity chaos—in the sense not of a lack of necessity but of a lack of order, arrangement, form, beauty, wisdom, and whatever other names there are for our aesthetic anthropomorphisms. Judged from the point of view of our reason, unsuccessful attempts are by all odds the rule, the exceptions are not the secret aim, and the whole musical box repeats eternally its tune which may never be called a melody—and ultimately even the phrase "unsuccessful attempt" is too anthropomorphic and reproachful. But how could we reproach or praise the universe? Let us beware of attributing to it heartlessness and unreason or their opposites: it is neither perfect nor beautiful, nor noble, nor does it wish to become any of these things; it does not by any means strive to imitate man. None of our aesthetic and moral judgments apply to it. Nor does it have any instinct for self-preservation or any other instinct; and it does not observe any laws either. Let us beware of saying that there are laws in nature. There are only necessities: there is nobody who commands, nobody who obeys, nobody who trespasses. Once you know that there are no purposes, you also know that there is no accident; for it is only beside a world of purposes that the word "accident" has meaning. Let us beware of saying that death is opposed to life. The living is merely a type of what is dead, and a very rare type.

Let us beware of thinking that the world eternally creates new things. There are no eternally enduring substances; matter is as much of an error as the God of the Eleatics.* But when shall we ever be done with our caution and care? When will all these shadows of God cease to darken our minds? When will we complete our de-deification of nature? When may we begin to *"naturalize"* humanity in terms of a pure, newly discovered, newly redeemed nature?

125

The madman.— Have you not heard of that madman who lit a lantern in the bright morning hours, ran to the market place, and cried incessantly: "I seek God!"—As many of those who did not believe in God were standing around just then, he provoked much laughter. Has he got lost? asked one. Did he lose his way like a child? asked

---

Eleatics: An ancient Greek philosophical school founded by Parmenides in the fifth century B.C.E. at Elea, a Greek colony in Lucania, Italy. Zeno of Elea and Melissus were also members of this school.—Ed.

another. Or is he hiding? Is he afraid of us? Has he gone on a voyage? emigrated?—Thus they yelled and laughed.

The madman jumped into their midst and pierced them with his eyes. "Whither is God?" he cried; "I will tell you. *We have killed him*—you and I. All of us are his murderers. But how did we do this? How could we drink up the sea? Who gave us the sponge to wipe away the entire horizon? What were we doing when we unchained this earth from its sun? Whither is it moving now? Whither are we moving? Away from all suns? Are we not plunging continually? Backward, sideward; forward, in all directions? Is there still any up or down? Are we not straying as through an infinite nothing? Do we not feel the breath of empty space? Has it not become colder? Is not night continually closing in on us? Do we not need to light lanterns in the morning? Do we hear nothing as yet of the noise of the gravediggers who are burying God? Do we smell nothing as yet of the divine decomposition? Gods, too, decompose. God is dead. God remains dead. And we have killed him.

"How shall we comfort ourselves, the murderers of all murderers? What was holiest and mightiest of all that the world has yet owned has bled to death under our knives: who will wipe this blood off us? What water is there for us to clean ourselves? What festivals of atonement, what sacred games shall we have to invent? Is not the greatness of this deed too great for us? Must we ourselves not become gods simply to appear worthy of it? There has never been a greater deed; and whoever is born after us—for the sake of this deed he will belong to a higher history than all history hitherto."

Here the madman fell silent and looked again at his listeners; and they, too, were silent and stared at him in astonishment. At last he threw his lantern on the ground, and it broke into pieces and went out. "I have come too early," he said then; "my time is not yet. This tremendous event is still on its way, still wandering; it has not yet reached the ears of men. Lightning and thunder require time; the light of the stars requires time; deeds, though done, still require time to be seen and heard. This deed is still more distant from them than the most distant stars—*and yet they have done it themselves.*"

It has been related further that on the same day the madman forced his way into several churches and there struck up his *requiem aeternam deo*. Led out and called to account, he is said always to have replied nothing but: "What after all are these churches now if they are not the tombs and sepulchers of God?"

130

A dangerous resolution—The Christian resolve to find the world ugly and bad has made the world ugly and bad.

132

Against Christianity—What is now decisive against Christianity is our taste, no longer our reasons.

THE ANTICHRIST

5

Christianity should not be beautified and embellished: it has waged deadly war against this higher type of man; it has placed all the basic instincts of this type under the ban; and out of these instincts it has distilled evil and the Evil One: the strong man as the typically reprehensible man, the "reprobate." Christianity has sided with all that is weak and base, with all failures; it has made an ideal of whatever *contradicts* the instinct of the strong life to preserve itself; it has corrupted the reason even of those strongest in spirit by teaching men to consider the supreme values of the spirit as something sinful, as something that leads into error—as temptations. The most pitiful example: the corruption of [French philosopher Blaise] Pascal, who believed in the corruption of his reason through original sin when it had in fact been corrupted only by his Christianity.

7

Christianity is called the religion of *pity*. Pity stands opposed to the tonic emotions which heighten our vitality: it has a depressing effect. We are deprived of strength when we feel pity. That loss of strength which suffering as such inflicts on life is still further increased and multiplied by pity. Pity makes suffering contagious. Under certain circumstances, it may engender a total loss of life and vitality out of all proportion to the magnitude of the cause (as in the case of the death of the Nazarene). That is the first consideration, but there is a more important one.

Suppose we measure pity by the value of the reactions it usually produces; then its perilous nature appears in an even brighter light. Quite in general, pity crosses the law of development, which is the law of *selection*. It preserves what is ripe for destruction; it defends those who have been disinherited and condemned by life; and by the abundance of the failures of all kinds which it keeps alive, it gives life itself a gloomy and questionable aspect.

Some have dared to call pity a virtue (in every *noble* ethic it is considered a weakness); and as if this were not enough, it has been made *the* virtue, the basis and source of all virtues. To be sure—and one should always keep this in mind—this was done by a philosophy that was nihilistic and had inscribed the *negation of life* upon its shield. Schopenhauer* was consistent enough: pity negates life and renders it *more deserving of negation*.

Pity is the *practice* of nihilism. To repeat: this depressive and contagious instinct crosses those instincts which aim at the preservation of life and at the enhancement of its value. It multiplies misery and conserves all that is miserable, and is thus a prime instrument of the advancement of decadence: pity persuades men to *nothingness*! Of course, one does not say "nothingness" but "beyond" or "God," or "*true* life," or Nirvana, salvation, blessedness.

This innocent rhetoric from the realm of the religious-moral idiosyncrasy appears much less innocent as soon as we realize which tendency it is that here shrouds itself in sublime words: *hostility against life*. Schopenhauer was hostile to life; therefore pity became a virtue for him.

Aristotle, as is well known, considered pity a pathological and dangerous condition, which one would be well advised to attack now and then with a purge: he understood tragedy as a purge. From the standpoint of the instinct of life, a remedy certainly seems necessary for such a pathological and dangerous accumulation of pity as is represented by the case of Schopenhauer (and unfortunately by our entire literary and artistic decadence from St. Petersburg to Paris, from Tolstoy to Wagner)—to puncture it and make it *burst*.

In our whole unhealthy modernity there is nothing more unhealthy than Christian pity. . . .

9

Against this theologians' instinct I wage war: I have found its traces everywhere. Whoever has theologians' blood in his veins, sees all things in a distorted and dishonest perspective to begin with. The pathos which develops out of this condition calls itself *faith*: closing one's eyes to oneself once and for all, lest one suffer the sight of incurable falsehood. This faulty perspective on all things is elevated into a morality, a virtue, a holiness; the good conscience is tied to faulty vision; and no *other* perspective is conceded any further value once one's own has been made sacrosanct with the names of "God," "redemption," and "eternity." I have dug up the theologians' instinct everywhere: it is the most wide-spread, really *subterranean*, form of falsehood found on earth.

Whatever a theologian feels to be true *must* be false: this is almost a criterion of truth. His most basic instinct of self-preservation forbids him to respect reality at any point or even to let it get a word in. Wherever the theologians' instinct extends, *value judgments* have been stood on their heads and the concepts of "true" and "false" are of necessity reversed: whatever is most harmful to life is called "true"; whatever elevates it, enhances, affirms, justifies it, and makes it triumphant, is called "false." When theologians reach out for *power* through the "conscience" of princes (or of peoples), we need never doubt what really happens at bottom: the will to the end, the *nihilistic* will, wants power.

---

* Arthur Schopenhauer (1788–1860), a German philosopher, was heavily influenced by the work of Plato, Kant, and the Upanishads. He is famous as the philosopher of pessimism and contributed to philosophy the distinctive position that will is more fundamental than thought in both man and nature. His major work is *The World as Will and Representation* (*Die Welt als Wille und Vorstellung*, 1818).—Ed.

47

That we find no God—either in history or in nature or behind nature—is not what differentiates *us*, but that we experience what has been revered as God, not as "godlike" but as miserable, as absurd, as harmful, not merely as an error but as a *crime against life*. We deny God as God. If one were to *prove* this God of the Christians to us, we should be even less able to believe in him. In a formula: *deus, qualem Paulus creavit, dei negatio.* ["God, as Paul created him, is the negation of God."]

A religion like Christianity, which does not have contact with reality at any point, which crumbles as soon as reality is conceded its rights at even a single point, must naturally be mortally hostile against the "wisdom of this world," which means *science*. It will applaud all means with which the discipline of the spirit, purity and severity in the spirit's matters of conscience, the noble coolness and freedom of the spirit, can be poisoned, slandered, brought into disrepute. "Faith" as an imperative is the *veto* against science—in practice, the lie at any price.

Paul comprehended that the lie—that "faith"—was needed; later the church in turn comprehended Paul. The "God" whom Paul invented, a god who "ruins the wisdom of the world" (in particular, philology and medicine, the two great adversaries of all supersition), is in truth merely Paul's own resolute *determination* to do this: to give the name of "God" to one's own will, *torah*, that is thoroughly Jewish. Paul *wants* to ruin the "wisdom of the world": his enemies are the good philologists and physicians with Alexandrian training—it is they against whom

he wages war. Indeed, one cannot be a philologist or physician without at the same time being an-*anti-Christian*. For as a philologist one sees *behind* the "holy books"; as a physician, *behind* the physiological depravity of the typical Christian. The physician says "incurable"; the philologist, "swindle."

DISCUSSION QUESTIONS

1. Why does Nietzsche think that we have killed God?

2. In his book *The Antichrist* (1895), Nietzsche writes, "That we find no God—either in history or in nature or behind nature—is not what differentiates *us*, but that we experience what has been revered as God, not as 'godlike' but as miserable, as absurd, as harmful, not merely as an error but as a *crime against life*. We deny God as God. If one were to *prove* this God of the Christians to us, we should be even less able to believe in him" (sec. 47). What does he mean by the statement "We deny God as God?"

3. Why does Nietzsche think that even if God's existence were proved to him, "we should be even less able to believe in him"? Does this make sense to you? How might Paley or Anselm respond to Nietzsche?

4. Why do you think Nietzsche uses a "madman" to announce to market goers that they have murdered God?

5. What does it mean to "'naturalize' humanity in terms of a pure, newly discovered, newly redeemed nature"?

MARY DALY

THE QUALITATIVE LEAP BEYOND PATRIARCHAL RELIGION

W hat is the sex of God? Is God male? Female? Neither? Both? Does it matter? In this reading, Mary Daly argues that the Judeo-Christian tradition assumes without argument that God is male. What follows from this assumption is a more powerful role and set of characteristics for men, and a lesser or subservient role and set of characteristics for women. "Since 'God' is male," writes Daly, "the male is God." For Daly, the

Judeo-Christian tradition is both essentially sexist (it promotes irrelevant differences between the sexes) and patriarchal (it legitimates the domination of men over women in all important areas of life). Daly suggests that the "word 'God' just may be inherently oppressive," but "this by no means indicates a movement in the direction of 'atheism' or 'agnosticism' or 'secularism.' " Nor does referring to "God" as "she" resolve the situation, because it involves "still working within all the boundaries of the same symbolic framework and the same power structure" as the patriarchal, Judeo-Christian tradition. Because there is a "profound contradiction between the inherent logic of radical feminism and the inherent logic of the Christian symbol system," Daly contends that a leap beyond patriarchal religion is the only way to overcome the inequality and power imbalance between men and women in the Judeo-Christian tradition.

Mary Daly (1929–), a theologian and feminist philosopher, was for over thirty years a theology professor at Boston College. Her writings, particularly those writings critical of the Catholic Church, have been championed by some and abhorred by others. Daly's employment status at the Jesuit-run Boston College was threatened on several occasions. In 1999, at seventy years of age, she was told to either stop teaching or admit male students into her women's studies courses that for twenty-five years had been for women only. (For the previous twelve years, Daly had offered to teach male students outside of the women-only classes.) The result of her dispute, according to the official press release from Boston College, was that "Dr. Daly agreed to retire and relinquish her position as a tenured faculty member rather than to admit male students into her classes."

Daly has three Ph.D.s—one in religion from St. Mary's College in Notre Dame, Indiana; one in sacred theology from the University of Fribourg in Switzerland; and another from Fribourg in philosophy—and is the author of seven books: *The Church and the Second Sex* (1968), *Beyond God the Father: Toward a Philosophy of Women's Liberation* (1973), *Gyn/Ecology, the Metaethics of Radical Feminism* (1978), *Pure Lust: Elemental Feminist Philosophy* (1984), *Webster's First New Intergalactic Wickedary of the English Language* (1987, with Jane Caputi), *Outercourse: The Bedazzling Voyage* (1992), and *Quintessence: Realizing the Archaic Future* (1998).

PROLEGOMENA

1. There exists a planetary sexual caste system, essentially the same in Saudi Arabia and in New York, differing only in degree.

2. This system is masked by sex role segregation, by the dual identity of women, by ideologies and myths.

3. Among the primary loci of sexist conditioning is grammar.

4. The "methods" of the various "fields" are not adequate to express feminist thought. Methodolatry requires that women perform Methodicide, an act of intellectual bravery.

5. All of the major world religions function to legitimate patriarchy. This is true also of the popular cults such as the Krishna movement and the Jesus Freaks.

6. The myths and symbols of Christianity are essentially sexist. Since "God" is male, the male is God. God the Father legitimates all earthly God-fathers, including Vito Corleone, Pope Paul, President Gerald Ford, the God-fathers of medicine (e.g., the American Medical Association), of science (e.g., NASA), of the media, of psychiatry, of education, and of all theologies.

7. The myth of feminine evil, expressed in the story of the Fall, is reinforced by the myth of salvation/redemption by a single human being of the male sex. The idea of a unique divine incarnation in a male, the God-man of the "hypostatic union," is inherently sexist and oppressive. Christolatry is idolatry.

8. A significant and growing cognitive minority of women, radical feminists, are breaking out from under the sacred shelter of patriarchal religious myths.

9. This breaking out, facing anomy [lawlessness] when the meaning structures of patriarchy are seen through and rejected, is a communal, political event. It is a revelatory event, a creative, political ontophany.

10. The bonding of the growing cognitive minority of women who are radical feminists, commonly called *sisterhood*, involves a process of new naming, in which words are wrenched out of their old semantic context and heard in a new semantic context. For example, the "sisterhoods" of patriarchy, such as religious congregations of women, were really mini-brotherhoods. *Sisterhood* heard with new ears is bonding for women's own liberation.

11. There is an inherent dynamic in the women's revolution in Judeo-Christian society which is Antichurch, whether or not feminists specifically concern ourselves with churches. This is so because the Judeo-Christian tradition legitimates patriarchy—the prevailing power structure and prevailing world view—which the women's revolution leaves behind.

12. The women's revolution is not only Antichurch. It is a post-Christian spiritual revolution.

13. The ethos of Judeo-Christian culture is dominated by The Most Unholy Trinity: Rape, Genocide, and War. It is rapism which spawns racism. It is gynocide which spawns genocide, for sexism (rapism) is fundamental socialization to objectify "the other."

14. The women's revolution is concerned with transvaluation of values, beyond the ethics dominated by The Most Unholy Trinity.

15. The women's revolution is not merely about equality within a patriarchal society (a contradiction in terms). It is about *power* and redefining power.

16. Since Christian myths are inherently sexist, and since the women's revolution is not about "equality" but about power, there is an intrinsic dynamic in the feminist movement which goes beyond efforts to reform Christian churches. Such efforts eventually come to be recognized as comparable to a Black person's trying to reform the Ku Klux Klan.

17. Within patriarchy, power is generally understood as power *over* people, the environment, things. In the rising consciousness of women, power is experienced as *power of presence* to ourselves and to each other, as we affirm our own being against and beyond the alienated identity (non-being) bestowed upon us within patriarchy. This is experienced as *power of absence* by those who would objectify women as "the other," as magnifying mirrors.

18. The presence of women to ourselves which is *absence* to the oppressor is the essential dynamic opening up the women's revolution to human liberation. It is an invitation to men to confront non-being and hence affirm their be-ing.

19. It is unlikely that many men will accept this invitation willingly, or even be able to hear it, since they have profound vested (though self-destructive) interest in the present social arrangements.

20. The women's movement is a new mode of relating to the self, to each other, to men, to the environment—in a word—to the cosmos. It is self-affirming, refusing objectification of the self and of the other.

21. Entrance into new feminist time/space, which is moving time/space located on the boundaries of patriarchal institutions, is active participation in ultimate reality, which is de-reified, recognized as Verb, as intransitive Verb with no object to block its dynamism.

22. Entrance into radical feminist consciousness involves recognition that all male-dominated

"revolutions," which do not reject the universally oppressive reality which is patriarchy, are in reality only reforms. They are "revolutions" only in the sense that they are spinnings of the wheels of the same senescent system.

23. Entrance into radical feminist consciousness implies an awareness that the women's revolution is the "final cause" (pun intended) in the radical sense that it is the cause which can move the other causes. It is the catalyst which can bring about real change, since it is the rising up of the universally and primordially objectified "Other," discrediting the myths which legitimate rapism. Rapism is by extension the objectification and destruction of all "others" and inherently tends to the destruction of the human species and of all life on this planet.

Radical feminism, the becoming of women, is very much an Otherworld Journey. It is both discovery and creation of a world other than patriarchy. Some observation reveals that patriarchy is "everywhere." Even outer space and the future have been colonized. As a rule, even the more imaginative science fiction writers (seemingly the most foretelling futurists) cannot/will not create a space and time in which women get far beyond the role of space stewardess. Nor does this situation exist simply "outside" women's minds, securely fastened into institutions which we can physically leave behind. Rather, it is also internalized, festering inside women's heads, even feminist heads.

The journey of women *becoming*, then, involves exorcism of the internalized Godfather, in his various manifestations (His name is legion). It involves dangerous encounters with these demons. Within the Christian tradition, particularly in medieval times, evil spirits have sometimes been associated with the Seven Deadly Sins, both as personifications and as causes. A "standard" and prevalent listing of the Sins is, of course, the following: pride, avarice, anger, lust, gluttony, envy, and sloth. I am contending that these have all been radically misnamed, that is, inadequately and even perversely "understood" within Christianity. These concepts have been used to victimize the oppressed, particularly

women. They are particularized expressions of the overall use of "evil" to victimize women. The feminist journey involves confrontations with the demonic distortions of evil.

Why has it seemed "appropriate" in this culture that a popular book and film (*The Exorcist*) center [on] a Jesuit who "exorcises" a girl-child who is "possessed"? Why is there no book or film about a woman who exorcises a Jesuit? Within a culture possessed by the myth of feminine evil, the naming, describing, and theorizing about good and evil has constituted a web of deception, a Maya. The journey of women becoming is breaking through this web—a Fall into free space. It is reassuming the role of subject, as opposed to object, and naming good and evil on the basis of our own intuitive intellection. . . .

THE QUALITATIVE LEAP

Creative, living, political hope for movement beyond the gynocidal reign of the Fathers will be fulfilled only if women continue to make qualitative leaps in living our transcendence. A short-circuited hope of transcendence has caused many to remain inside churches, and patriarchal religion sometimes has seemed to satisfy the hunger for transcendence. The problem has been that both the hunger and the satisfaction generated within such religions have to a great extent alienated women from our deepest aspirations. Spinning in vicious circles of false needs and false consciousness, women caught on the patriarchal wheel have not been able to experience women's own experience.

I suggest that what is required is *ludic cerebration*, the free play of intuition in our own space, giving rise to thinking that is vigorous, informed, multi-dimensional, independent, creative, tough. *Ludic cerebration* is thinking out of experience. I do not mean the experience of dredging out All That Was Wrong with Mother, or of instant intimacy in group encounters, or of waiting at the doctoral dispensary, or of self-lobotomization in order to publish, perish, and then be promoted. I mean the experience of being. *Be-ing* is the verb that says the dimensions of depth in all verbs, such as intuiting, reasoning, loving, imaging, making, acting, as well as the couraging, hoping, and playing that are always there when one is really living.

It may be that some new things happen within patriarchy, but one thing essentially stays the same: women are always marginal beings. From this vantage point of the margin it is possible to look at what is between the margins with the lucidity of The Compleat Outsider. To change metaphors: the systems within the System do not appear so radically different from each other to those excluded by all. Hope for a qualitative leap lies in *us* by reason of that deviance from the "norm" which was first imposed but which can also be *chosen* on our own terms. This means that there has to be a shift from "acceptable" female deviance (characterized by triviality, diffuseness, dependence upon others for self-definition, low self-esteem, powerlessness) to deviance which may be unacceptable to others but which is acceptable to the self and *is* self-acceptance.

For women concerned with philosophical/ theological questions, it seems to me, this implies the necessity of some sort of choice. One either tries to avoid "acceptable" deviance ("normal" female idiocy) by becoming accepted as a male-identified professional, or else one tries to make the qualitative leap toward self-acceptable deviance as ludic cerebrator, questioner of everything, madwoman, and witch.

I do mean witch. The heretic who rejects the idols of patriarchy is the blasphemous creatrix of her own thoughts. She is finding her life and intends not to lose it. The witch that smolders within every woman who cared and dared enough to become a philosophically/spiritually questing feminist in the first place seems to be crying out these days: "Light my fire!" The qualitative leap, the light of those flames of spiritual imagination and cerebral fantasy can be a new dawn. . . .

WANTED: "GOD" OR "THE GODDESS"?

Feminist consciousness is experienced by a significant number of women as ontological becoming, that is, being. This process requires existential courage, courage to be and to *see*, which is both revolutionary and revelatory, revealing our participation in ultimate reality as Verb, as intransitive Verb.

The question obviously arises of the need for anthropomorphic symbols for this reality. There is no inherent contradiction between speaking of ultimate reality as Verb and speaking of this as personal. The Verb is more personal than a mere static noun. However, if we choose to *image* the Verb in anthropomorphic symbols, we can run into a problematic phenomenon which sociologist Henri Desroche calls "crossing." "Crossing" refers to a notable tendency among oppressed groups to attempt to change or adapt the ideological tools of the oppressor, so that they can be used *against* him and *for* the oppressed. The problem here is the fact that the functioning of "crossing" does not generally move far enough outside the ideological framework it seeks to undermine. . . .

Some women religious leaders within Western culture in modern times have performed something like a "crossing" operation, notably such figures as Mary Baker Eddy and Ann Lee, in stressing the "maternal" aspect of the divinity. The result has been mixed. Eddy's "Father-Mother God" is, after all, the Christian God. Nor does Ann Lee really move completely outside the Christian framework. . . . But it is . . . necessary to note that their theologies lack explicit relevance to the concrete problems of the oppression of women. Intellection and spirituality remain cut off from creative political movement. In earlier periods also there were women within the Christian tradition who tried to "cross" the Christian all-male God and Christ to some degree. An outstanding example was Juliana of Norwich, an English recluse and mystic who lived in the last half of the fourteenth century. Juliana's "God" and "Jesus" were—if language conveys anything—hermaphroditic constructs, with the primary identity clearly male. While there are many levels on which I could analyze Juliana's words about "our beloved Mother, Jesus (who) feeds us with himself," suffice it to say here that this hermaphroditic image is somewhat less than attractive. The "androgynous" God and Jesus present problems analogous to and related to those problems which occur in connection with the use of the term "androgyny" to describe the direction of women's becoming. There is something like a "liberation of the woman within" the (primarily male) God and Jesus. . . .

One fact that stands out here is that these were women whose imaginations were still partially controlled by Christian myth. My contention is that they were caught in a contradiction. . . . I am saying that there is a profound contradiction between the inherent logic of radical feminism and the inherent logic of the Christian symbol system. . . .

Both the reformers and those who leave Judaism and Christianity behind are contributing and will contribute in different ways to the process of the becoming of women. The point here is not to place value judgments upon individual persons and their efforts—and there are heroic efforts at all points of the feminist spectrum. Rather, it is to disclose an inherent logic in feminism. The courage which some women have in affirming this logic comes in part from having been on the feminist journey for quite awhile. Encouragement comes also from knowing increasing numbers of women who have chosen the route of the logical conclusion. Some of these women have "graduated" from Christianity or religious Judaism, and some have never even been associated closely with church or synagogue, but have discovered spiritual and mythic depths in the women's movement itself. What we share is a sense of becoming in cosmic process, which I prefer to call the Verb, Be-ing, and which some would still call "God."

For some feminists concerned with the spiritual depth of the movement, the word "God" is becoming increasingly problematic, however. This by no means indicates a movement in the direction of "atheism" or "agnosticism" or "secularism," as these terms are usually understood. Rather, the problem arises precisely because of the spiritual and mythic quality perceived in feminist process itself. Some use expressions such as "power of being." Some reluctantly still use the word "God" while earnestly trying to divest the term of its patriarchal associations, attempting to think perhaps of the "God of the philosophers" rather than the overtly masculist and oppressive "God of the theologians." But the problem becomes increasingly troublesome, the more the "God" of the various Western philosophers is subjected to

feminist analysis. "He"—"Jahweh" still often hovers behind the abstractions, stunting our own thought, giving us a sense of contrived doublethink. The word "God" just may be inherently oppressive.

Indeed, the word "Goddess" has also been problematic, but for different reasons. Some have been worried about the problem of "crossing." However, that difficulty appears more and more as a pseudo-difficulty when it is recognized that "crossing" is likely to occur only when one is trying to work *within* a sexist tradition. For example, Christian women who in their "feminist liturgies" experiment with referring to "God" as "she" and to the Trinity as "The Mother, the Daughter, and the Holy Spirit," are still working within all the boundaries of the same symbolic framework and the same power structure. Significantly, their services are at the same place and time as "the usual," and are regarded by most of the constituency of the churches as occasional variations of "business as usual."

As women who are outside the Christian church inform ourselves of evidence supporting the existence of ancient matriarchy and of evidence indicating that the Gods of patriarchy are indeed contrived, pale derivatives and reversals of the Great Goddess of an earlier period, the fear of mere "crossing" appears less appropriate and perhaps even absurd. There is also less credibility allowable to the notion that "Goddess" would function like "God" in reverse, that is, to legitimate an oppressive "female-dominated" society, if one is inclined to look seriously at evidence that matriarchal society was not structured like patriarchy, that it was non-hierarchical. . . .

Clearly, it would be inappropriate and arrogant to try to "explain" or "interpret" this experience of another person. I can only comment that many women I know are finding power of being within the self, rather than in "internalized" father images. As a philosopher, my preference has been for abstractions. Indeed I have always been annoyed and rather embarrassed by "anthropomorphic" symbols, preferring terms such as "ground and power of being" (Paul Tillich), "beyond subjectivity and objectivity" (William James), "the Encompassing" (Karl Jaspers), or the commonly used "Ultimate

Reality," or "cosmic process." More recently I have used the expression "Intransitive Verb." Despite this philosophical inclination, and also because of it, I find it impossible to ignore the realm of symbols, or to fail to recognize that many women are experiencing and participating in a remythologizing process, which is a new dawn.

It is necessary to add a few remarks about the functioning of the confusing and complex "Mary" symbol within Christianity. Through it, the power of the Great Goddess symbol is enchained, captured, used, cannibalized, tokenized, domesticated, tranquillized. In spite of this, I think that many women and at least some men, when they have heard of or imaged the "Mother of God," have, by something like a selective perception process, screened out the standardized, lobotomized, dull, derivative and dwarfed Christian reflections of a more ancient symbol; they have perceived something that might more accurately be described as the Great Goddess, and which, in human terms, can be translated into "the strong woman who can relate because she can stand alone." A woman of Jewish background commented that "Mother of God" had always seemed strange and contradictory to her. Not having been programmed to "know" about the distinctions between the "divine" and the "human" nature of "Christ," or to "know" that the "Mother of God" is less than God, this woman had been able to hear the expression with the ears of an extraenvironmental listener. It sounded, she said, something like "infinite plus one." When this symbolic nonsense is recognized, it is more plausible simply to *think* "infinite," and to *image* something like "Great Mother," or "Goddess."

It may appear that the suffix "-ess" presents a problem, when one considers other usages of that suffix, for example, in "poetess," or in "authoress." In these cases, there is a tone of depreciation, a suggestion that women poets and authors are in a separate and "inferior" category to be judged by different standards than their male counterparts. However, the suffix does not always function in this "diminishing" way. For example, there appear to be no "diminutive" overtones suggested by the word "actress." So also it seems that the term "Goddess"—or "The Goddess"—*is not only non-diminutive*, but very strong. Indeed, it calls before the mind images of a powerful and ancient tradition before, behind, and beyond Christianity. These are multi-dimensional images of women's present and future becoming/be-ing.

DISCUSSION QUESTIONS

1.   Restate and analyze Daly's argument that the Judeo-Christian tradition legitimates patriarchy. What does it mean to take a "qualitative leap" beyond patriarchal religion? Is this possible?

2.   Daly claims that "Christian myths are inherently sexist." What does she mean by this? Locate one of these allegedly sexist myths, such as the story of the garden of Eden, and discuss whether it is sexist.

3.   What does Daly mean when she says that there is a "profound contradiction between the inherent logic of radical feminism and the inherent logic of the Christian symbol system"? Why do you think she believes this? Is she right? Why or why not?

4.   Daly says that "the word 'God' may just be inherently oppressive." What does she mean by this? Does Daly believe that there would still be oppression inherent in the term "God" if God were a woman? Discuss.

5.   Daly is very critical of the Judeo-Christian religious tradition but at the same time wants us to believe that "this by no means indicates a movement in the direction of 'atheism' or 'agnosticism' or 'secularism.'" Is she right? Or do her criticisms lead more to atheism, agnosticism, or secularism than to belief in the existence of God?

Dogma
[USA 1999] 2 hours, 10 minutes
Directed by Kevin Smith

*D*ogma is the story of two exiled angels, Loki (Matt Damon) and Bartleby (Ben Affleck), journeying from Wisconsin to New Jersey in an effort to get back into heaven. A Catholic priest in New Jersey, in an attempt to gain more supporters for his church, has guaranteed admittance into heaven to whoever walks through the front doors of his church. However, the priest did not anticipate that two exiled angels would take him up on his offer. And if they do, it will be in defiance of God's plan for the universe and thus establish the imperfection of God and lead to the annihilation of the universe. On their way to New Jersey, the exiled angels come into contact with the combined forces of Bethany (Linda Fiorentino), a relapsed Catholic recruited by a seraphim (Alan Rickman); two muses, Jay (Jason Mewes) and Silent Bob (Kevin Smith); and Rufus (Chris Rock), the thirteenth apostle—all sent by God to stop the exiled angels from entering the doors of the church. In the end, during a bloodbath in which Loki and Bartleby destroy everything in sight to purge themselves of all of their sinful yearnings before returning to heaven, God intervenes. While the two angels come close to triggering a divine catastrophe, they are no match for God and are destroyed. God's creation is preserved. God (Alanis Morrisette) is portrayed as a woman in this film. When she appears in the doors of the church to prevent Bartleby from entering, she does not speak. She simply emits one grand musical note that annihilates the exiles.

DISCUSSION QUESTIONS

1. God is portrayed as a woman in this film. Is this significant? Might males and females generally have different responses to this question?
2. Daly contends that a leap beyond patriarchal religion is the only way to overcome the inequality and power imbalance between men and women in the Judeo-Christian tradition. Does the portrayal of God as a woman in this film qualify as a leap beyond patriarchal religion? Why or why not?
3. While God appears in this film, the only sound she emits is a single powerful musical note. Why do you think God did not speak to Bartleby before annihilating him?
4. "Dogma" is by definition a body of doctrines proclaimed by a church. Why is this film titled *Dogma*? Discuss.
5. Compare the general nature of God as depicted in *Dogma* with the nature of God as depicted in *The Apostle* and *Frailty*. Which portrayal do you find more convincing, and why?
6. In *Dogma,* by annihilating the fallen angels, God avoids becoming imperfect. Nevertheless, the film suggests that it is possible for God to become less than perfect. Is this the same God of Aquinas, Paley, and Anselm? Why or why not?

JAMES H. CONE

GOD IN BLACK THEOLOGY

L ike Mary Daly, James H. Cone is a theologian who is critical of the Judeo-Christian theological tradition and seeks to revolutionize it. His black liberation theology asks, What can we say about the nature of God in view of his self-disclosure in biblical history and the oppressed condition of black people? "Black Theology represents that community of black people who refuse to cooperate in the exaltation of whiteness and the degradation of blackness," says Cone. "It proclaims the reality of the biblical God who is actively destroying everything that is against the manifestation of human dignity among black people." God has chosen blacks as his own *because* blacks are oppressed against their "will and God's, and he has decided to make our liberation his own." Furthermore, "[b]ecause black people have come to know themselves as *black*, and because that blackness is the cause of their own love of themselves and hatred of whiteness, God himself must be known only as he reveals himself in his blackness." "There is no place in Black Theology for a colorless God in a society when people suffer precisely because of their color," charges Cone. "Either God is identified with the oppressed to the point that their experience becomes his or he is a God of racism."

James H. Cone (1938–) is the Charles A. Briggs Distinguished Professor of Systematic Theology at the Union Theological Seminary in New York City and is an ordained minister in the African Methodist Episcopal Church. Cone's work reevaluates Christian theology from the perspective of black oppression in America. He was the first theologian to examine systematically the role of religion in the black community in the context of the black liberation movement. "Any message that is not related to the liberation of the poor in a society is not Christ's message," says Cone. "Any theology that is indifferent to the theme of liberation is not Christian theology." His many books include *Black Theology and Black Power* (1969), *A Black Theology of Liberation* (1970), *God of the Oppressed* (1975), *For My People: Black Theology and the Black Church* (1984), and *Martin & Malcolm & America: A Dream or a Nightmare?* (1991). In the latter book, he writes, "Anger and humor are like the left and right arm[s]. They complement each other. Anger empowers the poor to declare their uncompromising opposition to oppression, and humor prevents them from being consumed by their fury." The following selection is from *A Black Theology of Liberation*.

The reality of God is presupposed in Black Theology. Black Theology is an attempt to analyze the nature of that reality, asking what we can say about the nature of God in view of his self-disclosure in biblical history and the oppressed condition of black people.

If we take the question seriously, it becomes evident that there is no simple answer to it. To speak of God and his participation in the liberation of the oppressed of the land is a risky venture in any society. But if the society is racist and also uses God-language as an instrument to further the cause of human humiliation, then the task of authentic theological speech is even more dangerous and difficult.

It is *dangerous* because the true prophet of the gospel of God must become both "anti-Christian" and "unpatriotic." It is impossible to confront a racist society, with the meaning of human existence grounded in commitment to the divine, without at the same time challenging the very existence of the national structure and all of its institutions, especially the established church. All national institutions represent the interests of the society as a whole. We live in a nation which is committed to the perpetuation of white supremacy, and it will try to exterminate all who fail to assist it in this ideal. The genocide of the American Indian is evidence of that fact. Black Theology represents that community of black people who refuse to cooperate in the exaltation of whiteness and the degradation of blackness. It proclaims the reality of the biblical God who is actively destroying everything that is against the manifestation of human dignity among black people.

Because whiteness by its very nature is against blackness, the black prophet is a prophet of national doom. He proclaims the end of the "American Way," for God has stirred the soul of the black community, and now that community will stop at nothing to claim the freedom that is 350 years overdue. The black prophet is a rebel with a cause, the cause of over twenty-five million American blacks and all oppressed men everywhere. It is God's cause because he has chosen the blacks as his own. And he has chosen them not for redemptive suffering but for freedom. Black people are not elected to be Yahweh's suffering people. Rather we are elected because we are oppressed against our will and God's, and he has decided to make our liberation his own. We are elected to be free now to do the work of him who has called us into being, namely the breaking of the chains. The black theologian must assume the dangerous responsibility of articulating the revolutionary mood of the black community. This means that his speech about God, in the authentic prophetic tradition, will always move on the brink of treason and heresy in an oppressive society.

The task of authentic theological speech is *difficult* because all religionists in the society claim to be for God and thus for man. Even the executioners are for God. They carry out punitive acts against certain segments of society because "decent" people need protection against the undesirables. That is why blacks were enslaved and Indians exterminated—in the name of God and freedom. That is why today blacks are forced into ghettos and shot down like dogs if they raise a hand in protest. When George Washington, Thomas Jefferson, Lyndon Johnson, Richard Nixon and other "great" Americans can invoke the name of God at the same time they are defining the society for white people only, then Black Theology knows that it cannot approach the

God-question too casually. It must ask, "How can we speak of God without being associated with the oppressors of the land?" Whiteness is so pervasive that the oppressors can destroy the revolutionary mood among the oppressed by introducing the complacent white God into the black community, thereby reducing the spirit of freedom.

Therefore if black people want to break the chains, they must recognize the need for going all the way if liberation is to be a reality. The white God will point to a heavenly bliss as a means of directing black people away from earthly rage. Freedom comes when we realize that it is against our interests, as a self-determining black community, to point out the "good" elements in an oppressive structure. *There are no assets to slavery!* Every segment of the society participates in black oppression. To accept the white God, to see good in the evil, is to lose sight of the goal of the revolution—the destruction of everything "masterly" in the society. "All or nothing" is the only possible attitude for the black community.

MUST WE DROP GOD-LANGUAGE?

Realizing that it is very easy to be co-opted by the enemy and his God-language, it is tempting to discard all references to God and to seek to describe a way of living in the world that could not possibly be associated with "Christian" murderers. Some existentialist writers like Camus and Sartre have taken this course, and many black revolutionaries find this procedure appealing. Seeing the ungodly behavior of white churches and the timid, Uncle Tom approach of black churches, many black militants have no time for God and all that religious crap with its deadly prattle about loving your enemies and turning the other cheek. Christianity, they argue, participates in the enslavement of black Americans. Therefore an emancipation from white oppression means also liberation from the ungodly influences of the white man's religion. This approach is certainly understandable, and the merits of the argument warrant a serious investigation of this claim. As black theologians seeking to analyze the meaning of black liberation, we cannot ignore this mood. Indeed, it is quite tempting intellectually to follow the procedure. Neverthless two observations are in order at this juncture.

(1) Black Theology affirms that there is nothing special about the English word "God" in itself. What is important is the dimension of reality to which it points. The word "God" is a symbol that opens up depths of reality in the world. If the symbol loses its power to point to the meaning of black liberation, then we must destroy it. Black Theology asks whether the symbol God has lost its liberating power. Must we conclude that as a meaningful symbol the word "God" is hopelessly dead and thus cannot be resurrected? Certainly Black Theology realizes that, when a society performs all ungodly acts against the poor in the name of God, there may come a time when the oppressed might have to renounce all claims of "faith" in God in order to affirm authentic faith in him. Sometimes because of the very nature of oppressed-existence, the oppressed must define their being by negating everything the oppressors affirm, including belief in God. The oppressed must demonstrate that all communications are cut off. In Camus's words: "There is, in fact, nothing in common between a master and a slave; it is impossible to speak and communicate with a person who has been reduced to servitude." Therefore, the oppressed and the oppressors cannot possibly mean the same thing when they speak of God. The God of the oppressed is a God of revolution who breaks the chains of slavery. The oppressors' God is a God of slavery and must be destroyed along with the oppressors. The question then, as Black Theology sees it, is not whether black people believe in God, but whose God?

(2) In response to those inclined to drop God-language, Black Theology also believes that the destiny of black people is inseparable from the religious dimensions inherent in the black community. Theologically, one way of describing this reality is to call it general revelation. This means that all men have a sense of the presence of God, a feeling of awe, and it is precisely this experience that makes men creatures who always rebel against domestication. The black community is thus a religious community, a community that views its liberation as the work of the divine.

Here it is important to note that every significant black liberation movement has had its religious dimensions. Black liberation as a movement began with the pre–Civil War black churches who recognized that Christian freedom grounded in Jesus Christ was inseparable from civil freedom. That is why black preachers were the leaders in the struggle for abolition of slavery, and why southern slave owners refused to allow the establishment of the independent black churches in the South. It is true, however, that the post–Civil War black church lost its emphasis on civil freedom and began to identify Christianity with moral purity. But this does not mean that religion is irrelevant altogether; it only means that religion unrelated to black liberation is irrelevant. To try to separate black liberation from black religion is a mistake, because black religion is authentic only when it is identified with the struggle for black freedom. The influences of Marcus Garvey, Elijah Muhammad, Malcolm X, and Martin Luther King, Jr., demonstrate the role of religion in the black community.

It is not the task of Black Theology to remove the influences of the divine in the black community. Its task is to interpret the forces of black liberation as divine activity. Black Theology must retain God-language despite its perils, because the black community perceives its identity in terms of divine presence. Black Theology cannot create new symbols independent of the black community and expect black people to respond. It must stay in the black community and get down to the real issue at hand ("cutting throats" to use LeRoi Jones's phrase) and not waste too much time discussing the legitimacy of religious language. The legitimacy of any language, religious or otherwise, is determined by its usability in the struggle for liberation. That the God-language of white religion has been used to create a docile spirit among black people while whites aggressively attacked them is beyond question. But that does not mean that we cannot kill the white God, so that the God of black people can make his presence known in the black-white encounter. The white God is an idol, created by the racist bastards, and we black people must perform the iconoclastic task of smashing false images.

God Is Black

Because black people have come to know themselves as *black*, and because that blackness is the cause of their own love of themselves and hatred of whiteness, God himself must be known only as he reveals himself in his blackness. The blackness of God, and everything implied by it in a racist society, is the heart of Black Theology's doctrine of God. There is no place in Black Theology for a colorless God in a society when people suffer precisely because of their color. The black theologian must reject any conception of God which stifles black self-determination by picturing God as a God of all peoples. Either God is identified with the oppressed to the point that their experience becomes his or he is a God of racism. Authentic identification, as Camus pointed out, is not "a question of psychological identification—a mere subterfuge by which the individual imagines that it is he himself who is being offended." It is "identification of one's destiny with that of others and a choice of sides." Because God has made the goal of black people his own goal, Black Theology believes that it is not only appropriate but necessary to begin the doctrine of God with an insistence on his blackness.

The blackness of God means that God has made the oppressed condition his own condition. This is the essence of the biblical revelation. By electing Israelite slaves as his people and by becoming the Oppressed One in Jesus Christ, God discloses to men that he is known where men experience humiliation and suffering. It is not that he feels sorry and takes pity on them (the condescending attitude of those racists who need their guilt assuaged for getting fat on the starvation of others); quite the contrary, his election of Israel and incarnation in Christ reveal that the *liberation* of the oppressed is a part of the innermost nature of God himself. This means that liberation is not an afterthought, but the essence of divine activity.

The blackness of God then means that the essence of the nature of God is to be found in the concept of liberation. Taking seriously the Trinitarian view of the Godhead, Black Theology says that as Father, God identified with oppressed Israel participating in the bringing into being of this people; as Son, he became the Oppressed One in order that all may be free from oppression; as Holy Spirit, he continues his work of liberation. The Holy Spirit is the Spirit of the Father and the Son at work in the forces of human liberation in our society today. In America, the Holy Spirit is black people making decisions about their togetherness, which means making preparation for an encounter with white people.

It is Black Theology's emphasis on the blackness of God that distinguishes it sharply from contemporary white views of God. White religionists are not capable of perceiving the blackness of God because their satanic *whiteness* is a denial of the very essence of divinity. That is why whites are finding and will continue to find the black experience a disturbing reality. White theologians would prefer to do theology without reference to color, but this only reveals how deeply racism is embedded in the thought forms of this culture. To be sure, they would *probably* concede that the concept of liberation is essential to the biblical view of God. But it is still impossible for them to translate the biblical emphasis on liberation to the black-white struggle today. Invariably they quibble on this issue, moving from side to side, always pointing out the dangers of extremism on both sides. (In the black community, we call this shuffling.) They really cannot make a decision, because it has been made already for them. The way in which scholars would analyze God and black people was decided when black slaves were brought to this land, while churchmen sang "Jesus, Lover of My Soul." Their attitude today is no different from that of the Bishop of London who assured the slaveholders that

> Christianity, and the embracing of the Gospel, does not make the least Alteration in Civil property, or in any Duties which belong to Civil Relations; but in all these Respects, it continues Persons just in the same State as it found them. The Freedom which Christianity gives, is a Freedom from the Bondage of Sin and Satan, and from the dominion of Man's Lust and Passions and inordinate Desires; but as to their outward Condition, whatever that was before, whether bond or free, their being baptized and becoming Christians, makes no matter of change in it.

Of course white theologians today have a "better" way of putting it, but what difference does that make? It means the same thing to black people. "Sure," as the so-called radicals would say, "God is concerned about black people." And then they go on to talk about God and secularization or some other white problem unrelated to emancipation of black people. This style is a contemporary white way of saying that "Christianity . . . does not make the least alteration in civil property."

In contrast to this racist view of God, Black Theology proclaims his blackness. People who want to know who God is and what he is doing must know who black people are and what they are doing. This does not mean lending a helping hand to the poor and unfortunate blacks of the society. It does not mean joining the war on poverty! Such acts are sin offerings that represent a white way of assuring themselves that they are basically a "good" people. Knowing God means being on the side of the oppressed, becoming *one* with them and participating in the goal of liberation. *We must become black with God!*

It is to be expected that white people will have some difficulty with the idea of "becoming *black* with God." The experience is not only alien to their existence as they know it to be, it appears to be an impossibility. "How can *white* people become black?" they ask. This question always amuses me because they do not really want to lose their precious white identity, as if it is worth saving. They know, as everyone in this country knows, a black man is anyone who says he is black, despite his skin color. In the literal sense a black man is anyone who has "even one drop of black blood in his veins."

But "becoming black with God" means more than just saying "I am black," if it involves that at all. The question "How can white people become black?" is analogous to the Philippian jailer's question to Paul and Silas, "What must I do to be saved?" The implication is that if we work hard enough at it, we can reach the goal. But the misunderstanding here is the failure to see that blackness or salvation (the two are synonymous) is the work of God and not man. It is not something we accomplish; it is a gift. That is why they said, " Believe in the Lord Jesus and you will be saved." To *believe* is to receive the gift and utterly to reorient one's existence on the basis of the gift. The gift is so unlike what humans expect that when it is offered and accepted, we become completely new creatures. This is what the Wholly Otherness of God means. God comes to us in his blackness which is wholly unlike whiteness, and to receive his revelation is to become black with him by joining him in his work of liberation.

Even some black people will find this view of God hard to handle. Having been enslaved by the God of white racism so long, they will have difficulty believing that God is identified with their struggle for freedom. Becoming one of his disciples means rejecting whiteness and accepting themselves as they are in all their physical blackness. This is what the Christian view of God means for black people. . . .

DISCUSSION QUESTIONS

1. Cone claims, "there is no place in Black Theology for a colorless God in a society when people suffer precisely because of their color." What does this mean? What, according to Cone, is the relationship between persons who suffer and God? Do you agree with him?

2. Analyze Cone's argument that "[b]ecause black people have come to know themselves as *black*, and because that blackness is the cause of their own love of themselves and hatred of whiteness, God himself must be known only as he reveals himself in his blackness." Does this argument hold for other oppressed groups such as women, disabled persons, and homosexuals? Why or why not?

3. Like Mary Daly, Cone asks whether we should drop God-language. What are the arguments for dropping God-language? What does Cone think of them? Compare these arguments and responses to those of Daly.

4. According to Cone, "the true prophet of the gospel of God must become both 'anti-Christian' and 'unpatriotic.'" What does this mean? Do you agree? Why or why not?

5. What, according to Cone, is the relationship between Christian theology and racism? How might persons like Thomas Jefferson and Lyndon Johnson, persons whom Cone cites as "invok[ing] the name of God at the same time they are defining society for white people only," respond to Cone? Do you think Cone is right?

VICTOR A. GUNASEKARA
THE BUDDHIST ATTITUDE TO GOD

I n this reading, Victor Gunasekara explains how and why Buddhism, one of the major religions of the world, rejects the notion of a supreme God and the notion of a personal God operating in the universe. As he explains, while his essay is primarily concerned with one particular Buddhist tradition, Theravâda Buddhism, it is applicable to most other Buddhist traditions. "Buddhism is unique amongst the religions of the world," writes Gunasekara, "because it does not have any place for God in its soteriology [doctrine of salvation]." The Buddha, at least in the Theravâda tradition, is a "supremely enlightened human teacher," explains Gunasekara. It is a mistake to regard the Buddha as some kind of God figure.

Buddhism was founded in the sixth century B.C.E. in southern Nepal by Gautama Siddhartha (560–477 B.C.E.), later simply called "the Buddha" (Enlightened One). The Buddha achieved enlightenment through meditation and brought together a group of monks to carry on his teachings. The basic tenets of Buddhism include the following: (1) Existence is a realm marked by suffering (dukkha); (2) we seek to be liberated from this suffering; (3) liberation from suffering is achievable only through the destruction of desire and delusions of the importance of one's self; (4) enlightenment (nirvana) is connected to the destruction of desire and delusions of the importance of the self through meditation; (5) rebirth occurs—we are subjected to repeated lifetimes that are good or bad depending on our actions (karma); (6) a natural moral law rules the process of karma and rebirth; (7) the world we see is without substance and is constantly changing; (8) there is no self; (9) the Buddha was a human teacher who gained enlightenment and is a transcendent being who once was mortal; and (10) there is no God.

The two main schools are Hinayana (Lesser Vehicle) Buddhism and Mahayana (Greater Vehicle) Buddhism. Both are based on interpretations of the teachings of the Buddha. The formative period of Hinayana Buddhism, the earlier and stricter of the two branches, was between 400 and 250 B.C.E. Historically, there were four major schools of Hinayana Buddhism, all of which were very similar: the Theravâda, the Sarvastivada, the Sautrantika, and the Vaibhasika, though Theravâda is the sole surviving school today. The formative period of Mahayana Buddhism, the later and more popular and elaborate branch of Buddhism, was between 0 and 500 C.E. Zen Buddhism, a well-known type of Buddhism, developed out of and in reaction to both Hinayana and Mahayana Buddhism. Although Zen Buddhism originated in India, it is traceable back to China in the person of Bodhidharma (460–534 C.E.).

The basic differences between Mahayana and Hinayana Buddhism are roughly as follows: (1) Hinayana sees suffering as real, while Mahayana sees it as an illusion; (2) Hinayana denies the existence of some metaphysical absolute underlying phenomena, while Mahayana asserts one; (3) Hinayana regards liberation from suffering as an individual endeavor, while Mahayana entertains the possibility of outside assistance; (4) the immediate goal of Hinayana is achieving nirvana, while Mahayana sees the immediate goal as following the ways of the Bodhisattva (aspirants to Buddhahood) in leading all beings to liberation; and (5) Hinayana regards nirvana as representing a final exit from the world, while Mahayana regards niravana as becoming conscious of one's own absoluteness and gaining a state of mental detachment from all.

Victor Gunasekara is secretary of the Buddhist Society of Queensland, Australia. He has written a number of tracts on Buddhism, including *Basic Buddhism: A Modern Introduction to the Buddha's Teaching* (1997).

1. INTRODUCTION

The standpoint adopted here is primarily that of Theravâda Buddhism. But most of what is said will be applicable to most other Buddhist traditions. The Theravâda tradition, also called the Southern school of Buddhism, is based on texts maintained in the Pali language which are the oldest of the existing Canons of Buddhism and reputed to be the closest to the teaching of the Buddha himself.

There is no place for God in the Mahayana traditions of Buddhism as well, and indeed some of the early Indian Mahayana philosophers have denounced god-worship in terms which are even stronger than those expressed in the Theravâda literature. Some later Mahayana schools which flourished outside India ascribed some degree of divinity to a transcendent Buddha, considering living Buddhas to be a manifestation of this âdhi-buddha. But even here it cannot be said that the Buddha was converted into a Divinity comparable to the God of the monotheistic religions.

2. BUDDHISM AS A NON-THEISTIC RELIGION

Buddhism is unique amongst the religions of the world because it does not have any place for God in its soteriology. Indeed most Asian religions (with the possible exception of some extremely devotional forms of Hinduism) are essentially non-theistic, in that God does not occupy the central place that is accorded to him in monotheistic religious traditions. But Buddhism goes beyond most of these other religions in that it is positively anti-theistic because the very notion of God conflicts with some principles which are fundamental to the Buddhist view of the world and the role of humans in it (see section 5 below).

However Buddhism is not atheistic in the sense that modern secularism, rationalism, humanism, etc. could be regarded to be atheistic (although it has much in common with them). Buddhism is not concerned primarily with refuting the notion of God (as some atheistic writers have done). It is principally concerned with developing a method of escape from the worldly ills. This involves undertaking a method of mental discipline and a code of conduct which is sufficient to satisfy the most demanding of spiritual requirements. Indeed only very little of the Buddha's voluminous discourses deal directly with the question of God. He was more interested in expounding a way to personal salvation, and to improve the weal of mankind both in this world and in the worlds to come. It is this task that informs most of the discourses of the Buddha which later came to be compiled into the various Canons of Buddhism.

The Buddha did not take an ambiguous or agnostic position on the question of God as he is sometimes represented as having taken by theistically inclined writers. The Buddha has stated his position on God in clear and unequivocal terms.

3. THE NOTION OF GOD

It is first of all necessary to establish what is meant by the term "God." This term is used to designate a Supreme Being endowed with the qualities of omnipotence and omniscience, who is the creator of the universe with all its contents, and the chief law-giver for humans. God is generally considered as being concerned with the welfare of his human creatures, and the ultimate salvation of those who follow his dictates. God is therefore a person of some kind, and the question whether such an entity exists or not is fundamental to all theistic systems.

In contrast to this notion of a personal God some modern theologians have interpreted the term "God" as representing some kind of abstract principle of good (or "ground of being"). This view was first developed in the ancient Indian Upanishads where God is equated with an abstract principle (Brahman). The ancient Indian philosophers could entertain such a view because they also had a theory of karma which really does away with the need for a personal God. Buddhists too have a theory of karma, which is different front that of the Hindus, and which even more unequivocally dispenses with the need for a Deity. The use of the term "God" to denote an abstract reality by monotheistic theologians who have no theory of karma is difficult to justify; one suspects that this is merely a device to explain away the contradictions that arise from the notion of a personal God. In fact the actual practice of theistic religion proceeds as if God is a real person of some kind or other.

Just as Buddhism rejects the notion of a Supreme God it also rejects the notion of an abstract God-principle operating in the universe. The notion of Brahman (in the neuter) is not discussed at all in the Buddhist texts, and even in India it may well be a post-Buddhist development resulting from the attempt to reconcile the belief in God(s) with the powerful critique of the Buddha. It is therefore the attitude of Buddhism to the notion of a supreme personal God animating the Universe that we must consider.

Buddhism speaks of the existence of category of beings called devas. This term is generally translated as "gods" (with a simple "g" and in the plural). The term *deva* literally means a shining or radiant being, and describes their physical appearance rather than their supernatural powers (as the translation "gods" seems to imply). To prevent confusion with the notion of a supreme personal God we shall refer to these beings of Buddhist cosmology as devas. Many other religions also postulate the existence of non-human beings who are referred to as "gods" or "angels" if they are considered to be in a better position than humans (with respect to their material conditions of existence). Buddhist cosmology recognises 32 planes of existence, some of the higher planes being either states of meditative abstraction or actual domains for the devas. Generally we have direct experience of only two of these 32 planes (those of humans and animals). Planes of existence below these two realms are also said to exist and are characterised by greater degrees of suffering and discomfort. The actual physical location of these planes need not concern us here because the dimensions of the Buddhist universe are even greater than those envisaged by modern astronomy and will contain enough places to accommodate all these planes of existence.

We can easily dispose of the devas in the context of the Buddhist attitude to God because the devas are essentially irrelevant to the human situation. Beings are born in the deva-worlds because of particular karmic factors they have accumulated, and after these karmic factors are exhausted they could revert to any of the other planes of existence depending on their unexpended karma. The devas are not particularly endowed with special powers to influence others, and far from saving anyone else they themselves are not "saved." Salvation in Buddhism comes only from full enlightenment, which could be best accomplished from the human plane of existence.

The Vedic and Brahmanical religion of the Buddha's day postulated a large number of gods, many of them personifications of natural forces. However Brahmanical theology had advanced to the point that one of these gods was considered to be superior to all others, and was even considered to be the creator-god (Ishvara). This supreme god could then be considered as the equivalent to the single God of the monotheistic religions which emerged in the Middle East.

Different names have been given to the supreme god in the Brahmanical and later Hindu literature, but in Buddhist texts the supreme god is referred to as Mahâ-Brahmâ (or simply Brahmâ), who was the chief of a class of gods called the Brahmâs. Brahmâ of the Buddhist texts may be considered to be the equivalent of the God of the three monotheistic religions that [were] to emerge in the Middle East. The first of these was Judaism which promoted one of its gods, Yahweh, as the one God sometime about the 6th century B.C.E. Next Christianity adopted the same god under the name of Jehovah who is represented as the "Father" of Jesus. Finally Islam adopted the name of Allah for their only God. To get the Buddha's views on God we must therefore consider his views on Brahmâ.

One popular misconception of Buddhism must be dismissed at this point. This is the view that the Buddha is some kind of God figure. In the Theravâda tradition the Buddha is regarded as a supremely enlightened human teacher who has come to his last birth in samsâra (the Buddhist cycle of existence). Even Mahayana traditions which tend to think in terms of transcendental Buddhas do not directly make a claim for the Buddha as God. Thus the Buddha cannot be considered as playing a Godlike role in Buddhism.

4. THE BUDDHIST VIEW OF GOD

In the Buddhist texts Mahâ Brahmâ is represented as claiming the following attributes for himself:

> I am Brahmâ, the Great Brahmâ, the Supreme One, the Mighty, the All-seeing, the Ruler, the Lord of all, the Maker, the Creator, the Chief of all appointing to each his place, the Ancient of days, the Father of all that is and will be. (Dîgha Nikâya, II, 263)

The Buddha dismisses all these claims of Mahâ Brahmâ as being due to his own delusions brought about by ignorance. He argues that Mahâ-Brahmâ is simply another deva, perhaps with greater karmic force than the other gods, but nonetheless a deva and therefore unenlightened and subject to the samsâric process as determined by his karma. In such suttas as the Brahmajâla Sutta and the Aggañña Sutta the Buddha refutes the claims of Mahâ Brahmâ and shows him to be subject to karmic law (i.e., cosmic law). Even though long-lived, Mahâ Brahmâ will be eliminated in each cycle of inevitable world dissolution and re-evolution. In the Khevadda Sutta Mahâ Brahmâ is forced to admit to an inquiring monk that he is unable to answer a question that is posed to him, and advises the monk to consult the Buddha. This clearly shows the Brahmâ acknowledges the superiority of the Buddha.

The Buddhist view is that gods may lead more comfortable lives and be addicted to all the sense pleasures, but in terms of wisdom might be inferior to humans. They are even represented as coming to receive instruction from monks and even lay persons. Later on with the Hindu revival and proliferation of God-cults the Buddhists were increasingly vocal against the pretensions of God and his retinue of lesser gods. Nâgarjunâ, the Indian Buddhist philosopher of the 2nd century C.E., expressed a commonly shared Buddhist view when he wrote:

The gods are all eternal scoundrels
Incapable of dissolving the suffering of impermanence.
Those who serve them and venerate them
May even in this world sink into a sea of sorrow.
We know the gods are false and have no concrete being;
Therefore the wise man believes them not
The fate of the world depends on causes and conditions
Therefore the wise man many not rely on gods.

In the West a number of "arguments" have been adduced to prove or disprove the existence of God. Some of these were anticipated by the Buddha. One of the most popular is the "first cause" argument according to which everything must have a cause, and God is considered the first cause of the Universe. The Buddhist theory of causation says that every thing must have preconditions for its existence, and this law must also extend to "God" should such an entity exist. But while the "first cause" claims that God creates everything, it exempts God from the ambit of this law. However if exemptions are made with respect to God such exemptions could be made with respect to other things also hereby contradicting the principle of the first cause.

But the argument which the Buddha most frequently uses is what is now called the "argument from evil" which in the Buddhist sense could be stated as the argument from dukkha (suffering or unsatisfactoriness). This states that the empirical fact of the existence of dukkha cannot be reconciled with the existence of an omnipotent and omniscient being who is also all good. The following verses from the Bhûridatta Jataka bring this out clearly:

If the creator of the world entire
They call God, of every being be
the Lord
Why does he order
such misfortune
And not create concord?

If the creator of the world entire
They call God, of every being be
the Lord
Why prevail deceit, lies and
ignorance
And he such inequity and injustice
create?

If the creator of the world entire
They call God, of every being be
the Lord
Then an evil master is he, (O
Aritta)
Knowing what's right did let
wrong prevail!

The Buddha argues that the three most commonly given attributes of God, viz. omnipotence, omniscience and benevolence towards humanity, cannot all be mutually compatible with the existential fact of dukkha.

From the Buddhist standpoint the classic theistic statement that "God created man in his (i.e., God's) image" has actually to be reversed. It is man who has created God in his (i.e., man's) image! And as man's own image changes so does that of his God. Thus in the present time with the rise of feminism there is an attempt to change the gender of God from a man to a woman (or perhaps even to a neuter). To liberate himself mankind has to shed his delusions, and one of these is the existence of God.

5. THE GOD-CONCEPT AND BUDDHIST PRINCIPLES

Quite apart from explicit statements refuting the God-idea there is a fundamental incompatibility between the notion of God and basic Buddhist principles. We have already mentioned that God cannot be reconciled with the Buddhist notion of causality which is contained in the theory of "dependent origination" which is one of the discoveries of the Buddha during his enlightenment. Certainly nothing like this theory has been propounded prior to the Buddha.

A fundamental Buddhist belief is that all phenomena without exemption (including all animate beings) have three essential characteristics. These are dukkha (explained above), anicca (impermanence), and anatta (insubstantiality, "no-soul"). The attributes of God are not consistent with these universal marks of existence. Thus God must be free from dukkha; he must be eternal (and hence not subject to anicca); finally he must have a distinct unchanging identity (and therefore lack the characteristic of anatta).

Another concomitant of the God-idea that is fundamentally incompatible with Buddhism is the belief that God acts as the final judge and could determine if individuals go the heaven or hell. According to Buddhism the destination of individuals is determined by the karmic law which cannot be interfered [with] by any external process. Only individuals can effect their karmic destinies; even a Buddha cannot "pardon" or otherwise interfere with the karmic process. In Buddhism there is simply no place for a God even if one were to exist.

There is also no place for the notion of vicarious salvation, or atonement for human sins by a "suffering" God. The Buddha affirms that "by oneself is kamma done and by oneself is kamma undone." According to Buddhism no one (and this includes gods or God) can save another. This is a cardinal principle of the Buddha which cannot be reconciled with the declared attributes and actions of God.

The Buddhist path to salvation is based on deeds (including mental culture through "meditation") not prayer. God appears to Buddhists to be a vain being expecting all others to pray to him and worship him. Indeed such prayer seems to be the most decisive factor in a person's salvation, not necessarily any good or bad deeds by him. But as mentioned above in Buddhism it is volitional action which determines the karma of an individual.

There are no doubt some similarities in the moral codes of Buddhism and some theistic religions. Things like compassion are inculcated in all religions. But in Buddhism this does not arise from a heavenly dictate and there is no limitation in the exercise of these virtues as occurs in some theistic religions.

6. THE PERSISTENCE OF THE GOD-IDEA

The Buddha's refutation of the God-concept was formulated some 2500 years ago, perhaps at the very time that the idea of a single supreme God was mooted in India and in the Middle East. With the rise of modern science, and the discovery of natural causes for phenomena which were formerly ascribed to the action of God, some philosophers have restated the basic fallacies of the God-hypothesis using modern science and logic (and not the Buddha's dhamma) as their point of departure. Yet many people in the world formally subscribe to the notion of God. What is the Buddhist explanation for this phenomenon?

There are many causes for the persistence of the God-idea. Some of these are induced by social and other factors. These include the institutionalisation of theistic religion, the use of vast economic resources to propagate it including the mass media, and the legal right given to parents to impose their religions on their children.

There is also the attractiveness of vicarious salvation, or salvation through prayer or forgiveness which permits the committing of many moral crimes for which the doer does not "pay." We shall not consider these here. From the Buddhist point of view the root causes are ignorance and fear, with fear itself ultimately the product of ignorance. Atheistic materialism has failed to dislodge the God-idea not because of any deficiency of its arguments when compared to those put forward by the theists, but because it too has not been able to eliminate ignorance.

The ignorance (avijjâ,) that is meant here cannot be eliminated by formal education and the propagation of scientific knowledge. After all some leading scientists are themselves completely deluded by theistic suppositions. The progess of science has resulted only in a minor diminution in the power of theistic religion, and in any case theologians have become adept at "reinterpreting" dogma while the general followers continue to do what they have always done.

The Buddha himself grasped the over-pervading nature of ignorance because of his titanic struggle to liberate himself. He even initially displayed some reluctance to propagate his knowledge because of the formidable nature of the task. Nonetheless he proclaimed his knowledge out of compassion for the world because he felt that at least a few "with little dust in their eyes" would be able to benefit fully from his ideas. From the Buddhist point of view the persistence of theism, with all its evil consequences seen in history, is a necessary consequence of the persistence of ignorance.

While intellectual and scientific knowledge is not the sole (or even essential) constituent of wisdom (paññâ) it could in the modern world with high levels of educational attainment be a good basis for it. But what is really required is the cultivation of the mind (bhâvanâ, samâdhi). This is usually referred to as "meditation" even though this term is quite inadequate to convey the full implications of what is meant. Many modern-day "meditation teachers" do not give instruction in Buddhist mental culture, and even some of those who claim to do so may take a literal view of a few classic Buddhist texts on the subject. The

Buddhist path requires a correct balance between three components: wisdom, morality and mental culture. Progress in all these three areas must be made simultaneously, and exclusive concentration on any one these, especially "meditation" of a highly stylised form, is not the balanced path. The Buddha has asked all his disciples to go to the dhamma as their guide rather than to specific teachers. The Buddha's final instruction to his followers was to "work out your own salvation with diligence" with the Buddha's teaching (the dhamma) as the only guide.

The path of the Buddha cannot be followed if a person is deluded by the notion of God. This is why a correct understanding of all the ramifications of the God-idea is essential for anyone seeking to progress along the Buddhist path to total liberation.

DISCUSSION QUESTIONS

1. "From the Buddhist standpoint," writes Gunasekara, "the classic theistic statement that 'God created man in his (i.e., God's) image' has actually to be reversed. It is man who has created God in his (i.e., man's) image!" What does this mean?

2. Gunasekara says that the Buddha thought that the existence of suffering (dukkha) in the world could not be reconciled with the existence of an omnipotent (all-powerful) and omniscient (all-knowing) being who is all good. Is the Buddha right? Can these concepts be reconciled?

3. Based on what you read in Gunasekara's article, do you think that Buddhism is an atheistic religion? Why or why not?

4. Compare and contrast the arguments about the existence and nature of God developed by Aquinas, Anselm, Daly, Cone, and Gunasekara. Whose argument is the strongest, that is, the least susceptible to criticism? Why?

5. Cone's theology is described as black "liberation theology." Buddhism is also concerned with liberation. Compare and contrast the sense of "liberation" in each. Which seems more "liberating," and why?

Little Buddha
[USA 1993] 2 hours, 3 minutes
Directed by Bernardo Bertolucci

*A*fter the death of his Buddhist teacher Lama Dorje (Ven. Geshe Tsultim Gyelsen), exiled Tibetan monk Lama Norbu (Ying Ruocheng) begins searching for Dorje's reincarnation. From Bhutan, Lama Norbu travels to America because a dream has revealed to him that a candidate for the reincarnated Dorje may reside there. In Seattle, a boy named Jesse (Jesse Wiesendanger) exhibits all possible signs of having the soul of Dorje. Two cultures collide as Lama Norbu and his followers begin to teach young Jesse about the life of Siddhartha (Keanu Reeves), the man known as Buddha, who was responsible for all Buddhist teachings and practices. Jesse's parents (Bridget Fonda and Chris Isaak) remain skeptical about the religious world Lama Norbu and his followers are revealing to Jesse. Nonetheless, Jesse's father takes him to Nepal and Bhutan to meet the other two native candidates. There, the three children learn more about the life of Siddhartha and discover that all three of them carry the reincarnated soul of Lama Dorje. This is verified when each candidate selects from three possible items the one item that belonged to Lama Dorje. This test is done three consecutive times with three different items that belonged to Lama Dorje, proving to Lama Norbu that each of the three candidates carries the reincarnated soul of Lama Dorje.

DISCUSSION QUESTIONS

1. Jesse's parents remain skeptical about the religious world of Lama Norbu and his followers. If you were Jesse's parent, would you be skeptical? Why or why not?

2. Each of the three candidates selects the proper item among three items, three out of three times. This "proves" to the Lamu Norbu that all three are reincarnations of Lama Dorje. Would this be enough evidence for you? Why do you think it is enough evidence for Lama Dorje? (You may wish to calculate the odds of this event happening and take this number into consideration.)

3. Is it important for people to know as much about the religions of the world as possible? Why? Is it especially important to know about other religions in a country such as the United States, where people practice a great variety of religions? Why? What is a good source of knowledge about these religions? Is a film like *Little Buddha* a good source of knowledge about Buddhism? Why or why not?

4. Discuss the philosophical and social value of films like *Little Buddha*, which present Eastern religious views to Western audiences. What attitude should non-Buddhist westerners adopt when viewing this film?

5. Do you believe that it is possible to respect a religion or a set of beliefs about the nature of God other than your own if you do not know anything about it or them? Why or why not?

ALICE WALKER

GOD IS INSIDE YOU AND INSIDE EVERYBODY ELSE

I n this selection, some of Alice Walker's characters from her novel *The Color Purple* share their thoughts about the nature of God. Shug says, "God is inside you and inside everyone else. You come into the world with God. But only them that search for it inside find it. . . . I believe God is everything." The notion that God is everything is known as *pantheism,* from the Greek words *pan* (all) and *theos* (God). The term was first used by John Toland, an Irish philosopher, in 1705. However, the concept that "God is everything" goes back much further and can be found in both Western philosophical speculation and Eastern religious traditions. Western philosophers who espouse varying types of pantheism in their writings include Parmenides, Heraclitus, Chrysippus, Meister Eckhart, Nicholas of Cusa, Paracelsus, Pico Della Mirandolo, Spinoza, and Hegel. In the East, pantheism is found in Hindu scriptures (the Vedas and the Upanishads), Sufism, and some versions of Buddhism.

There are intriguing connections between Walker's essay and some of the other essays in this section. For example, Celie's comment "If he [God] ever listened to poor colored women the world would be a different place, I can tell you" provides a bridge to the black liberation theology of James Cone. Shug's insistence that God should be referred to as "It" connects back to Mary Daly's concerns about the gender of God. And Shug's question— "How come he look just like them [white folks], then? . . . Only bigger?"— is related to Buddhism's charge that man has created God in his image.

Alice Walker (1944–) is an American writer of short stories, juvenile literature, essays, poems, and novels. Her novels focus on the lives of women and are noted for their insight into African-American culture. *The Color Purple* (1982; film, 1985), her most popular novel, traces a black woman's struggle for racial and sexual equality. As the following selection from it reveals, the novel utilizes black English vernacular and is written entirely in the form of letters (epistolary form). All of the letters in the novel are addressed either to God (the majority of them), Nettie, or Celie except the last, which opens with "Dear God. Dear stars, dear trees, dear sky, dear peoples. Dear everything. Dear God," thus indicating Celie's return to writing to God and final embracing of pantheism.

In 1983, Alice Walker received the American Book Award and the Pulitzer Prize for *The Color Purple*. Her other novels include *The Third Life of Grange Copeland* (1970), *Meridian* (1976), *The Temple of My Familiar* (1989), and *Possessing the Secret of Joy* (1992).

Dear Nettie,

I don't write to God no more, I write to you.
What happen to God? ast Shug.
Who that? I say.
She look at me serious.
Big a devil as you is, I say, you not worried bout no God, surely.

She say, Wait a minute. Hold on just a minute here. Just because I don't harass it like some peoples us know don't mean I ain't got religion.
What God do for me? I ast.
She say, Celie! Like she shock. He gave you life, good health, and a good woman that love you to death.

Yeah, I say, and he give me a lynched daddy, a crazy mama, a low-down dog of a step pa and a sister I probably won't ever see again. Anyhow, I say, the God I been praying and writing to is a man. And act just like all the other mens I know. Trifling, forgitful and lowdown.

She say, Miss Celie, You better hush. God might hear you.

Let him hear me, I say. If he ever listened to poor colored women the world would be a different place, I can tell you.

She talk and she talk, trying to budge me way from blasphemy. But I blaspheme much as I want to.

All my life I never care what people thought about nothing I did. I say. But deep in my heart I care about God. What he going to think. And come to find out, he don't think. Just sit up there glorying in being deef, I reckon. But it ain't easy, trying to do without God. Even if you know he ain't there, trying to do without him is a strain.

I is a sinner, say Shug. Cause I was born. I don't deny it. But once you find out what's out there waiting for us, what else can you be?

Sinners have more good times, I say.

You know why? She ast.

Cause you ain't all the time worrying bout God, I say.

Naw, that ain't it, she say. Us worry bout God a lot. But once us feel loved by God, us do the best us can to please him with what us like.

You telling me God love you, and you ain't never done nothing for him? I mean, not go to church, sing in the choir, feed the preacher and all like that?

But if God love me, Celie, I don't have to do all that. Unless I want to. There's a lot of other things I can do that I speck God likes.

Like what? I ast.

Oh, she say. I can lay back and just admire stuff. Be happy. Have a good time.

Well, this sound like blasphemy sure nuff.

She say, Celie, tell the truth, have you ever found God in church? I never did. I just found a bunch of folks hoping for him to show. Any God I ever felt in church I brought in with me. And I think all the other folks did too. They come to church to *share* God, not find God.

Some folks didn't have him to share, I said. They the ones didn't speak to me while I was there struggling with my big belly and Mr. _____ children.

Right, she say.

Then she say: Tell me what your God look like, Celie.

Aw naw, I say. I'm too shame. Nobody ever ast me this before, so I'm sort of took by surprise. Besides, when I think about it, it don't seem quite right. But it all I got. I decide to stick up for him, just to see what Shug say.

Okay, I say. He big and old and tall and graybearded and white. He wear white robes and go barefooted.

Blue eyes? she ast.

Sort of bluish-gray. Cool. Big though. White lashes, I say.

She laugh.

Why you laugh? I ast I don't think it so funny. What you expect him to look like, Mr. _____?

That wouldn't be no improvement, she say. Then she tell me this old white man is the same God she used to see when she prayed. If you wait to find God in church, Celie, she say, that's who is bound to show up, cause that's where he live.

How come? I ast.

Cause that's the one that's in the white folks' white bible.

Shug! I say. God wrote the bible, white folks had nothing to do with it.

How come he look just like them, then? she say. Only bigger? And a heap more hair. How come the bible just like everything else they make, all about them doing one thing and another, and all the colored folks doing is gitting cursed?

I never thought bout that.

Nettie say somewhere in the bible it say Jesus' hair was like lamb's wool, I say.

Well, say Shug, if he came to any of these churches we talking bout he'd have to have it conked before anybody paid him any attention. The last thing niggers want to think about they God is that his hair kinky.

That's the truth, I say.

Ain't no way to read the bible and not think God white, she say. Then she sigh. When I found out I thought God was white, and a man, I lost interest. You mad cause he don't seem to listen to your prayers. Humph! Do the mayor listen to anything colored say? Ask Sofia, she say.

But I don't have to ast Sofia. I know white people never listen to colored, period. If they do, they only listen long enough to be able to tell you what to do.

Here's the thing, say Shug. The thing I believe. God is inside you and inside everybody else. You come into the world with God. But only them that search for it inside find it. And sometimes it just manifest itself even if you not looking, or don't know what you looking for. Trouble do it for most folks, I think. Sorrow, lord. Feeling like shit.

It? I ast.

Yeah, It. God ain't a he or a she, but a It.

But what do it look like? I ast.

Don't look like nothing, she say. It ain't a picture show. It ain't something you can look at apart from anything else, including yourself. I believe God is everything, say Shug. Everything that is or ever was or ever will be. And when you can feel that, and be happy to feel that, you've found it.

Shug a beautiful something, let me tell you. She frown a little, look out cross the yard, lean back in her chair, look like a big rose.

She say, My first step from the old white man was trees. Then air. Then birds. Then other people. But one day when I was sitting quiet and feeling like a motherless child, which I was, it come to me: that feeling of being part of everything, not separate at all. I knew that if I cut a tree, my arm would bleed. And I laughed and I cried and I run all around the house. I knew just what it was. In fact, when it happen, you can't miss it. It sort of like you know what, she say, grinning and rubbing high up on my thigh.

Shug! I say.

Oh, she say. God love all them feelings. That's some of the best stuff God did. And when you know God loves 'em you enjoys 'em a lot more. You can just relax, go with everything that's going, and praise God by liking what you like.

God don't think it dirty? I ast.

Naw, she say. God made it. Listen, God love everything you love—and a mess of stuff you don't. But more than anything else, God love admiration.

You saying God vain? I ast.

Naw, she say. Not vain, just wanting to share a good thing. I think it pisses God off if you walk by the color purple in a field somewhere and don't notice it.

What it do when it pissed off? I ast.

Oh, it make something else. People think pleasing God is all God care about. But any fool living in the world can see it always trying to please us back.

Yeah? I say.

Yeah, she say. It always making little surprises and springing them on us when us least expect.

You mean it want to be loved, just like the bible say.

Yes, Celie, she say. Everything want to be loved. Us sing and dance, make faces and give flower bouquets, trying to be loved. You ever notice that trees do everything to git attention we do, except walk?

Well, us talk and talk bout God, but I'm still adrift. Trying to chase that old white man out of my head. I been so busy thinking bout him I never truly notice nothing God make. Not a blade of corn (how it do that?) not the color purple (where it come from?). Not the little wildflowers. Nothing.

Now that my eyes opening, I feels like a fool. Next to any little scrub of a bush in my yard, Mr. _____'s evil sort of shrink. But not altogether. Still, it is like Shug say, You have to git man off your eyeball, before you can see anything a'tall.

Man corrupt everything, say Shug. He on your box of grits, in your head, and all over the radio. He try to make you think he everywhere. Soon as you think he everywhere, you think he God. But he ain't. Whenever you trying to pray, and man plop himself on the other end of it, tell him to git lost, say Shug. Conjure up flowers, wind, water, a big rock.

But this hard work, let me tell you. He been there so long, he don't want to budge. He threaten lightening, floods and earthquakes. Us fight. I hardly pray at all. Every time I conjure up a rock, I throw it.

Amen

DISCUSSION QUESTIONS

1. Imagine James Cone reading Celie's complaints about God. How would Cone, rather than Shug, respond to them? Which response do you prefer?

2. Shug asks, "How come he [God] look just like them [white folks], then? . . . Only bigger?" Formulate and compare responses to this question by Cone, Daly, and Gunasekara.

3. Shug prefers to use the gender-neutral pronoun "it" to refer to God. What kind of difference does using "it" as opposed to "he" or "she" make?

4. Shug maintains that God is everything. She then says, "If I cut a tree, my arm would bleed." What does she mean by this? Is this a necessary implication of the proposition "God is everything"? Defend your view.

5. Celie says, "If he [God] ever listened to poor colored women the world would be a different place, I can tell you." Do you agree with Celie? How might Cone or Daly respond to this claim?

1.2   DO SUFFERING AND EVIL DISPROVE GOD'S EXISTENCE?

FYODOR DOSTOYEVSKY

REBELLION

Through the character of Ivan Karamozov, Fyodor Dostoyevsky offers one of the most famous responses to the question of whether the existence of suffering and evil disprove God's existence. Ivan's response is complex. He says, "It's not that I don't accept God . . . it's the world created by Him I don't and cannot accept." Ivan asks his pious brother Alyosha to consider the story of a young boy being torn to pieces by hounds before his mother's eyes as punishment for hurting the paw of a general's dog. As Ivan sees it, if suffering of this kind is the necessary price of eternal harmony, then he would rather not have eternal harmony. "It's not worth the tears of that one tortured child," says Ivan, "who beat itself on the breast with its little fist and prayed in its stinking outhouse, with its unexpiated tears to 'dear, kind God'!" He then goes on to say, "If the sufferings of children go to swell the sum of sufferings which was necessary to pay for truth, then I protest that the truth is not worth such a price." When Alyosha calls Ivan's conclusion "rebellion," Ivan challenges him. "Imagine that you are creating a fabric of human destiny with the object of making men happy in the end, giving them peace and rest, but that it was essential and inevitable to torture to death only one tiny creature . . . and to found that edifice on its unavenged tears, would you consent to be the architect on those conditions?" Alyosha responds, "No, I wouldn't consent." The existence of suffering and evil in the world compels Ivan to reject the world that God has created, but not God. "I accept God simply," says Ivan.

Fyodor Dostoyevsky (1821–81), was born in Moscow and is one of the greatest novelists of the nineteenth century. Second of seven children, and the son of a physician who was murdered by his serfs in 1838 by being drowned in vodka, Dostoyevsky's life was nearly as dark as that of his characters. He had a gambling addiction and at one point in his life fell into deep financial debt. In 1849, he was arrested and sentenced to death for participating in the "Petrashevsky Circle," a group of utopian plotters against czarist Russia. Dostoyevsky suffered physical and mental anguish from the knowledge of his impending death, yet the czar never intended to carry out the sentence. Dostoyevsky was reprieved at the last moment but was sentenced to prison in Siberia until 1854.

Memoirs from the House of the Dead (1861) is based on the writer's prison experience. Dostoyevsky regarded prison as an opportunity to atone for his sins, even if it aggravated his epilepsy. The idea of salvation through suffering became a recurring theme in his novels. His most important works are *Notes from Underground* (1864), *Crime and Punishment* (1866), *The Gambler* (1866), *The Idiot* (1869), *The Devils* (1871), and *The Brothers Karamozov* (1880). The following selection is from *The Brothers Karamozov*, his last and greatest novel, which he completed three months before his death.

"Well, tell me where to begin, give your orders. The existence of God, eh?"

"Begin where you like. You declared yesterday at father's that there was no God." Alyosha looked searchingly at his brother.

"I said that yesterday at dinner on purpose to tease you and I saw your eyes glow. But now I've no objection to discussing with you, and I say so very seriously. I want to be friends with you, Alyosha, for I have no friends and want to try it. Well, only fancy, perhaps I too accept God," laughed Ivan, "that's a surprise for you, isn't it?"

"Yes of course, if you are not joking now."

"Joking? I was told at the elder's yesterday that I was joking. You know, dear boy, there was an old sinner in the eighteenth century who declared that, if there were no God; he would have to be invented. *S'il n'existait pas Dieu, il faudrait l'inventer* [Voltaire]. And man has actually invented God. And what's strange; what would be marvelous, is not that God should really exist; the marvel is that such an idea, the idea of the necessity of God, could enter the head of such a savage, vicious beast as man. So holy it is, so touching, so wise and so great a credit it does to man. As for me, I've long resolved not to think whether man created God or God man. And I won't go through all the axioms laid down by Russian boys on that subject, all derived from European hypotheses; for what's a hypothesis there, is an axiom with the Russian boy, and not only with the boys but with their teachers too, for our Russian professors are often just the same boys themselves. And so I omit all the hypotheses. For what are we aiming at now? I am trying to explain as quickly as possible my essential nature, that is what manner of man I am, what I believe in, and for what I hope, that's it, isn't it? And therefore I tell you that I accept God simply. But you must note this: if God exists and if He

really did create the world, then, as we all know, He created it according to the geometry of Euclid and the human mind with the conception of only three dimensions in space. Yet there have been and still are geometricians and philosophers, and even some of the most distinguished, who doubt whether the whole universe, or to speak more widely the whole of being was only created in Euclid's geometry; they even dare to dream that two parallel lines, which according to Euclid can never meet on earth, may meet somewhere in infinity. I have come to the conclusion that, since I can't understand even that, I can't expect to understand about God. I acknowledge humbly that I have no faculty for settling such questions, I have a Euclidian earthly mind, and how could I solve problems that are not of this world? And I advise you never to think about it either, my dear Alyosha, especially about God, whether He exists or not. All such questions are utterly inappropriate for a mind created with an idea of only three dimensions. And so I accept God and am glad to, and what's more I accept His wisdom, His purpose—which are utterly beyond our ken; I believe in the underlying order and the meaning of life; I believe in the eternal harmony in which they say we shall one day be blended. I believe in the Word to Which the universe is striving, and Which Itself was 'with God,' and Which Itself is God and so on, and so on, to infinity. There are all sorts of phrases for it. I seem to be on the right path, don't I? Yet would you believe it, in the final result I don't accept this world of God's, and, although I know it exists, I don't accept it at all. It's not that I don't accept God, you must understand, it's the world created by Him I don't and cannot accept. Let me make it plain. I believe like a child that suffering will be healed and made up for, that all the humiliating absurdity of human contradictions will vanish like a pitiful mirage, like the despicable fabrication of the impotent and infinitely small Euclidian mind of man, that in the world's finale, at the moment of eternal harmony, something so precious will come to pass that it will suffice for all hearts, for the comforting of all resentments, for the atonement of all the crimes of humanity, of all the blood they've shed; that it will make it not only possible to forgive but to justify all that has happened with men—but though all that may come to pass, I don't accept it. I won't accept it. Even if parallel lines do meet and I see it myself, I shall see it and say that they've met, but still I won't accept it. That's what's at the root of me, Alyosha; that's my creed.

" . . . Do you understand why this infamy must be and is permitted? Without it, I am told, man could not have known good and evil. Why should he know that diabolical good and evil when it costs so much? Why, the whole world of knowledge is not worth that child's prayer to 'dear, Kind God'! I say nothing of the sufferings of grown-up people, they have eaten the apple, damn them, and the devil take them all! But these little ones! I am making you suffer, Alyosha, you are not yourself. I'll leave off if you like."

"Never mind. I want to suffer too," muttered Alyosha.

"One picture, only one more, because it's so curious, so characteristic, and I have only just read it in some collection of Russian antiquities. I've forgotten the name. I must look it up. It was in the darkest days of serfdom at the beginning of the century, and long live the Liberator of the People! There was in those days a general of aristocratic connections, the owner of great estates, one of these men—somewhat exceptional, I believe, even then—who, retiring from the service into a life of leisure, are convinced that they've earned absolute power over the lives of their subjects. There were such men then. So our general, settled on his property of two thousand souls, lives in pomp and domineers over his poor neighbors as though they were dependents and buffoons. He has kennels of hundreds of hounds and nearly a hundred dog-boys—all mounted, and in uniform. One day a serf boy, a little child of eight, threw a stone in play and hurt the paw of the general's favorite hound. 'Why is my favorite dog lame?' He is told that the boy threw a stone that hurt the

dog's paw. 'So you did it.' The general looked the child up and down. 'Take him.' He was taken—taken from his mother and kept shut up all night. Early that morning the general comes out on horseback, with the hounds, his dependents, dog-boys, and huntsmen, all mounted around him in full hunting parade. The servants are summoned for their edification, and in front of them all stands the mother of the child. The child is brought from the lock-up. It's a gloomy, cold, foggy autumn day, a capital day for hunting. The general orders the child to be undressed; the child is stripped naked. He shivers, numb with terror not daring to cry. . . . 'Make him run,' commands the general. 'Run! run!' shout the dog-boys. The boy runs. . . . 'At him!' yells the general, and he sets the whole pack of hounds on the child. The hounds catch him, and tear him to pieces before his mother's eyes! . . . I believe the general was afterwards declared incapable of administering his estates. Well—what did he deserve? To be shot? to be shot for the satisfaction of our moral feelings? Speak, Alyosha!"

"To be shot," murmured Alyosha, lifting his eyes to Ivan with a pale twisted smile.

"Bravo!" cried Ivan delighted. "If even you say so . . . You're a pretty monk! So there is a little devil sitting in your heart, Alyosha Karamazov!"

"What I said was absurd, but—"

"That's just the point that 'but'!" cried Ivan. "Let me tell you, novice, that the absurd is only too necessary on earth. The world stands on absurdities, and perhaps nothing would have come to pass in it without them. We know what we know!"

"What do you know?"

"I understand nothing," Ivan went on, as though in delirium. "I don't want to understand anything now. I want to stick to the fact. I made up my mind long ago not to understand. If I try to understand anything, I shall be false to the fact and I have determined to stick to the fact."

"Why are you trying me?" Alyosha cried, with sudden distress. "Will you say what you mean at last?"

"Of course, I will; that's what I've been leading up to. You are dear to me, I don't want to let you go, and I won't give you up to your Zossima."

Ivan for a minute was silent, his face became all at once very sad.

"Listen! I took the case of the children only to make my case clearer. Of the other tears of humanity with which the earth is soaked from its crust to its center, I will say nothing. I have narrowed my subject on purpose. I am a bug, and I recognize in all humility that I cannot understand why the world is arranged as it is. Men are themselves to blame. I suppose; they were given paradise, they wanted freedom, and stole fire from heaven, though they knew they would become unhappy, so there is no need to pity them. With my pitiful, earthly, Euclidian understanding, all I know is that there is suffering and that there are none guilty; that cause follows effect, simply and directly; that everything flows and finds its level— but that's only Euclidian nonsense, I know that and I can't consent to live by it! What comfort is it to me that there are none guilty and that cause follows effect simply and directly, and that I know it—I must have justice, or I will destroy myself. And not justice in some remote infinite time and space, but here on earth, and that I could see myself. I have believed in it. I want to see it, and if I am dead by then, let me rise again, for if it all happens without me, it will be too unfair. Surely I haven't suffered, simply that I, my crimes and my sufferings, may manure the soil of the future harmony for somebody else. I want to see with my own eyes the hind lie down with the lion and the victim rise up and embrace his murderer. I want to be there when every one suddenly understands what it has all been for. All the religions of the world are built on this longing, and I am a believer. But then there are the children, and what am I to do about them? That's a question I can't answer. For the hundredth time I repeat, there are numbers of questions, but I've only taken the children, because in their case what I mean is so unanswerably clear. Listen! If all must suffer to pay for the eternal harmony, what have children to do with it, tell me please? It's beyond all comprehension why they should suffer, and why they should pay for the harmony. Why should they, too, furnish material to enrich the soil for the harmony of the future? I understand solidarity in sin among men. I understand solidarity in retribution, too; but there can be no such solidarity with children. And if it is really true that they must share responsibility for all their fathers' crimes, such a truth is not of this world and is beyond my comprehension. Some jester will say, perhaps that the child would have grown up and have sinned, but you see he didn't grow up, he was torn to pieces by the dogs, at eight years old. Oh, Alyosha, I am not blaspheming! I understand, of course, what an upheaval of the universe it will be, when everything in heaven and earth blends in one hymn of praise and everything that lives and has lived cries aloud: 'Thou art just, O Lord, for Thy ways are revealed,' when the mother embraces the fiend who threw her child to the dogs, and all three cry aloud with tears, 'Thou are just, O Lord!' then, of course, the crown of knowledge will be reached and all will be made clear. But what pulls me up here is that I can't accept that harmony. And while I am on earth, I make haste to take my own measures. You see, Alyosha, perhaps it really may happen that if I live to that moment, or rise again to see it, I, too, perhaps, may cry aloud with the rest, looking at the mother embracing the child's torturer, 'Thou art just, O Lord!' but I don't want to cry aloud then. While there is still time, I hasten to protect myself and so I renounce the higher harmony altogether. It's not worth the tears of that one tortured child who beat itself on the breast with its little fist and prayed in its stinking outhouse, with its unexpiated tears to 'dear, kind God'! It's not worth it, because those tears are unatoned for. They must be atoned for, or there can be no harmony. But how? How are you going to atone for them? Is it possible? By their being avenged? But what do I care for avenging them? What do I care for a hell for oppressors? What good can hell do, since those children have already been tortured? And what becomes of harmony, if there is hell? I want to forgive. I want to embrace. I don't want more suffering. And if the sufferings of children go to swell the sum of sufferings which was necessary to pay for truth, then I protest that the truth is not worth such a price. I don't want the mother to embrace the oppressor who threw her son to the dogs! She dare not forgive him! Let her forgive him for herself, if she will, let her forgive the torturer for the immeasurable suffering of her mother's heart. But the sufferings of her tortured child she has no right to forgive; she dare not forgive the torturer, even if the child were to forgive him! And if that is so, if they dare not forgive what becomes of harmony? Is there in the whole world a being who would have the right to forgive and could forgive? I don't want harmony.

From love for humanity I don't want it. I would rather be left with the unavenged suffering. I would rather remain with my unavenged suffering and unsatisfied indignation, *even if I were wrong.* Besides, too high a price is asked for harmony; it's beyond our means to pay so much to enter on it. And so I hasten to give back my entrance ticket, and if I am an honest man I am bound to give it back as soon as possible. And that I am doing. It's not God that I don't accept, Alyosha, only I most respectfully return Him the ticket."

"That's rebellion," murmured Alyosha, looking down.

"Rebellion? I am sorry you call it that," said Ivan earnestly. "One can hardly live in rebellion, and I want to live. Tell me yourself, I challenge you—answer. Imagine that you are creating a fabric of human destiny with the object of making men happy in the end, giving them peace and rest at last, but that it was essential and inevitable to torture to death only one tiny creature—that baby beating its breast with its fist, for instance—and to found that edifice on its unavenged tears, would you consent to be the architect on those conditions? Tell me, and tell the truth."

"No, I wouldn't consent," said Alyosha softly.

"And can you admit the idea that men for whom you are building it would agree to accept their happiness on the foundation of the unexpiated blood of a little victim? And accepting it would remain happy for ever?"

"No, I can't admit it. . . ."

DISCUSSION QUESTIONS

1. Ivan believes that it is possible to reject the world that God has created, yet still believe in God. Try to clearly state his position. Does it make sense to you? Why or why not?

2. Alyosha calls Ivan's conclusion "rebellion" but backs down when Ivan challenges him. Why? Would you have done the same thing? Would you consent to a world premised upon the "essential and inevitable to torture to death [of] only one tiny creature"?

3. Ivan says that he has resolved not to think about whether man created God or God created man. Why do you think he refuses to think about this question?

4. Ivan claims to analyze things from the perspective of "earthly, Euclidian understanding." What does he mean by this? What effect does it have on his conclusions?

5. Ivan says, "If all must suffer to pay for the eternal harmony, what have children to do with it, tell me, please? It's beyond all comprehension why they should suffer, why they should pay for the harmony." Do you agree with Ivan? Should only adults suffer for the eternal harmony? Or do you think, unlike Ivan, that both adults and children should suffer for the eternal harmony? Defend your response.

The Song of Bernadette
[USA 1943] 2 hours, 39 minutes
Directed by Henry King

This film is based on the historical novel by Franz Werfel, *Das Leid von Bernadette* (1941). Bernadette Soubirous (Jennifer Jones) is a French peasant girl from Lourdes who sees a vision of "a beautiful lady" in a grotto in 1858. While Bernadette never claims that the vision is anything more than a beautiful lady, the townspeople all assume that it is the Virgin Mary. News of Bernadette's visions spreads, attracting increasing attention. After being ridiculed by her family and the people in her town, Bernadette begins to receive messages from "the beautiful lady," and the townspeople observe miracles and healings on the once-desolate grounds of the grotto.

Local government officials think that Bernadette has lost her mind and try to suppress her and her followers. One of the officials is a skeptical prosecutor named Vital Dutour (Vincent Price). Dutour chooses science and logic over faith and superstition, and tries to stop Bernadette. For Dutour, her "miracles" are just social hysteria, and he holds on to this belief until just before his death, when he has a conversion in the grotto. The church also denies the veracity of Bernadette's visions. However, the young woman's sincerity and innocence ultimately convince the local Catholic dean (Charles Bickford) to lend her his support. The dean warns her that if she takes the examinations to determine whether she is insane, a fake, or a divine conduit, all three possible outcomes will bring about an undesirable future for her: an asylum, prison, or a convent. But Bernadette agrees to the tests, telling the dean that "the lady" informed her she would have to suffer. The tests determine that Bernadette is indeed a genuine divine conduit, and she is subsequently sent to a convent.

When Bernadette arrives at the convent, she is examined by a doctor. The doctor concludes that Bernadette has been suffering from a fatal and excruciating form of cancer: bone-marrow cancer. Surprisingly, Bernadette has remained unaware of this cancer due to her inability to feel any pain. Consumed by the cancer, Bernadette has a final vision, wherein the calming hand of the lady welcomes the visionary to her death.

DISCUSSION QUESTIONS

1. Bernadette claims to have never felt the excruciating pain associated with her cancer. "I have never suffered," says Bernadette. Is Bernadette's lack of suffering a sufficient basis on which to prove the existence of God? Can you construct an argument that moves from the lack of suffering by someone who should have suffered to the existence of God? Compare your argument to Ivan Karamozov's argument that moves from the suffering of one child to the rejection of God's creation.

2. A nun tells her students, "Only through suffering can we hope to obtain the kingdom of God." Does it follows from this line of thinking that the existence of suffering *proves* the existence of God? Can you construct an argument that moves from the existence of individual suffering to the existence of God?

3. A nun says to Bernadette, "In all our sacred history, the chosen ones always have been those who suffered. . . . Yes, I have suffered because I know it's the only true road to heaven. And if I, who have tortured myself, cannot glimpse the Blessed Virgin, how can you who have never felt pain dare to say you've seen her?" What are some of the implications of the nun's argument? Does it imply that those who do not or cannot suffer (like Bernadette) will not be granted entrance to heaven? Is it a valid argument? How should Bernadette respond to the nun?

4. "You must learn to expect nothing from God. When you get nothing, you will not be disappointed," says the cobbler. Do you agree with the cobbler? Do you think the nun quoted above would agree with the cobbler? Why or why not?

5. The philosopher Jeremy Bentham (1748–1832) argued that it is a fact of nature that the purpose of individual lives is the pursuit of pleasure and avoidance of pain. Can Bentham's view be reconciled with the view that "only through suffering can we hope to obtain the kingdom of God"?

6. Are the "miracles" associated with Bernadette proof of the existence of God? If not, under what conditions, if any, would you consider a miracle to be proof of the existence of God? Explain.

GOTTFRIED WILHELM LEIBNIZ

THEODICY

For Gottfried Wilhelm Leibniz, God not only exists but is all-good and all-perfect. However, the world that God has created contains evil. How is this possible? In this selection, Leibniz seeks to reconcile the existence of God with the presence of evil in the world. For Leibniz, the particular world we live in is one of an infinite number that God could have chosen. He chose this world for us because it is the one that will provide the greatest possible amount of good and the least possible amount of evil. Thus, according to Leibniz, this particular world in which we live is the best of all possible worlds.

Our world is not, however, a world devoid of evil. But what appears as evil in this world, if viewed from the standpoint of eternity, is shown to be necessary for the perfection of the universe. Evil cannot be viewed by itself. It may either be necessary to avoid still greater evils or be justified as a condition of attaining some positive good that far outweighs it: "The general of an army will prefer a great victory with a slight wound to a state of affairs without wound and without victory." Even if the evil can be shown to surpass the good in quantity, the quality of the good will make up for the lack of quantity. As Leibniz says, "The glory and the perfection of the blessed may be incomparably greater than the misery and imperfection of the damned."

According to Leibniz, we cannot lay blame for evil upon God. God is responsible only for things and events insofar as they are positive and perfect. Thus, evil is a negative fact that results from the necessary imperfection and limitation of finite creatures. Leibniz says that this is just like the boat that moves more slowly down the river because of its heavy load: The cause of the speed of the boat is the river current, but the cause of the retardation that limits its speed is its heavy load. God is responsible for things only so long as they are not retarded by the imperfections and limitations of finite creatures.

Leibniz discerns three types of evil: metaphysical, physical, and moral. Metaphysical evil has its source in imperfection. Leibniz contends that anything that is not perfect contains evil, and because only God is perfect, everything that is not God both is imperfect and contains evil. Physical evil is suffering or misery brought about by the evil will of humans or the forces of nature. Leibniz believes that this form of evil, if viewed in broader terms, can lead to greater good. Moral evil is sin, that is, an imperfection in the human act. Leibniz believes that God does not will moral evil to take place, even though he permits it for the production of greater good in the world.

Gottfried Wilhelm Leibniz (1646–1716), a German philosopher, scientist, mathematician, historian, and diplomat, developed infinitesimal calculus independently of Sir Isaac Newton. In addition to publishing articles in scholarly journals and composing many unpublished letters, papers, and notes, Leibniz wrote two books: *New Essays on Human Understanding* (1765), which was published only long after his death, and *Theodicy* (1710), the only book he published during his lifetime. *Theodicy* was the outcome of discussions he had with Sophie Charlotte, the queen of Prussia, on free will, evil, and the justification of God's creation and was written at her request. "Theodicy" is the term introduced by Leibniz for the problem of reconciling God's goodness with the existence of evil in the world. It comes from the Greek words *theos* (God) and *dike* (justice). The following selections are from *Theodicy*.

EVIL AS PRIVATION

20. But it is necessary also to meet the more speculative and metaphysical difficulties which have been mentioned, and which concern the cause of evil. The question is asked first of all, whence does evil come? *Si Deus est, unde malum? Si non est, unde bonum?** The ancients attributed the cause of evil to *matter*, which they believed uncreate and independent of God: but we, who derive all being from God, where shall we find the source of evil? The answer is, that it must be sought in the ideal nature of the creature, in so far as this nature is contained in the eternal verities which are in the understanding of God, independently of his will. For we must consider that there is an *original imperfection in the creature* before sin, because the creature is limited in its essence; whence ensues that it cannot know all, and that it can deceive itself and commit other errors. Plato said in *Timaeus* that the world originated in Understanding united to Necessity. Others have united God and Nature. This can be given a reasonable meaning. God will be the Understanding; and the Necessity, that is, the essential nature of things, will be the object of the understanding, in so far as this object consists in the eternal verities. But this object is inward and abides in the divine understanding. And therein is found not only the primitive form of good, but also the origin of evil: the Region of the Eternal Verities must be substituted for matter when we are concerned with seeking out the source of things.

This region is the ideal cause of evil (as it were) as well as of good: but, properly speaking, the formal character of evil has no *efficient* cause, for it consists in privation, as we shall see, namely, in that which the efficient cause does not bring about. That is why the Schoolmen are wont to call the cause of evil *deficient*.

21. Evil may be taken metaphysically, physically and morally. *Metaphysical evil* consists in mere imperfection, *physical evil* in suffering, and *moral evil* in sin. Now although physical evil and moral evil be not necessary, it is enough that by virtue of the eternal verities they be possible. And as this vast Region of Verities contains all possibilities it is necessary that there be an infinitude of possible worlds, that evil enter into divers of them, and that even the best of all contain a measure thereof. Thus has God been induced to permit evil.

THE ANALOGY OF THE BOAT

Let us suppose that the current of one and the same river carried along with it various boats, which differ among themselves only in the cargo, some being laden with wood, others with stone, and some more, the others less. That being so, it will come about that the boats most heavily laden will go more slowly than the others, provided it be assumed that the wind or the oar, or some other similar means, assist them not at all. It is not, properly speaking, weight which is the cause of this retardation, since the boats are going down and not upwards; but it is the same cause which also increases the weight in bodies that have greater density, which are, that is to say, less porous and more charged with matter that is proper to them: for the matter which passes through the pores, not receiving the same movement, must not be taken into account. It is therefore matter itself which originally is inclined to slowness or privation of speed: not indeed of itself to lessen this speed, having once received it, since that would be action, but to moderate by its receptivity the effect of the impression when it is to receive it. Consequently, since more matter is moved by the same force of the current when the boat is more laden, it is necessary that it go more slowly; and experiments on the impact of bodies, as well as reason, show that twice as much force must be employed to give equal speed to a body of the same matter but of twice the size. But that indeed would not be necessary if the matter were absolutely indifferent to repose and to movement, and if it had not this natural inertia whereof we have just spoken to give it a kind of repugnance to being moved. Let us now compare the force which the current exercises on boats, and communicates to them, with the action of God, who produces and conserves whatever is positive in creatures, and gives them perfection, being and force: let us compare, I say, the inertia of matter with the

---

* "If God exists, why is there evil? If God does not exist, why is there goodness?"—Ed.

natural imperfection of creatures, and the slowness of the laden boat with the defects to be found in the qualities and the action of the creature; and we shall find that there is nothing so just as this comparison. The current is the cause of the boat's movement, but not of its retardation; God is the cause of perfection in the nature and the actions of the creature, but the limitation of the receptivity of the creature is the cause of the defects there are in its action. Thus the Platonists, St. Augustine and the Schoolmen were right to say that God is the cause of the material element of evil which lies in the positive, and not of the formal element, which lies in privation. Even so one may say that the current is the cause of the material element of the retardation, but not of the formal: that is, it is the cause of the boat's speed without being the cause of the limits to this speed. And God is no more the cause of sin than the river's current is the cause of the retardation of the boat. . . .

31. There is, then, a wholly similar relation between such and such an action of God, and such and such a passion or reception of the creature, which in the ordinary course of things is perfected only in proportion to its "receptivity," such is the term used. And when it is said that the creature depends upon God in so far as it exists and in so far as it acts, and even that conservation is a continual creation, this is true in that God gives ever to the creature and produces continually all that in it is positive, good and perfect, every perfect gift coming from the Father of lights. The imperfections, on the other hand, and the defects in operations spring from the original limitation that the creature could not but receive with the first beginning of its being, through the ideal reasons which restrict it. For God could not give the creature all without making of it a God; therefore there must needs be different degrees in the perfection of things, and limitations also of every kind.

No Better World Possible

193. Up to now I have shown that the Will of God is not independent of the rules of Wisdom, although indeed it is a matter for surprise that one should have been constrained to argue about it, and to do battle for a truth so great and so well established. But it is hardly less surprising that there should be people who believe that God only half observes these rules, and does not choose the best, although his wisdom causes him to recognize it; and, in a word, that there should be writers who hold that God could have done better. . . .

194. Yet philosophers and theologians dare to support dogmatically such a belief; and I have many times wondered that gifted and pious persons should have been capable of setting bounds to the goodness and the perfection of God. For to assent that he knows what is best, that he can do it and that he does it not, is to avow that it rested with his will only to make the world better than it is; but that is what one calls lacking goodness. It is acting against that axiom already quoted: *Minus bonum habet rationem mali*. If some adduce experience to prove that God could have done better, they set themselves up as ridiculous critics of his works. To such will be given the answer given to all those who criticize God's course of action, and who from this same assumption, that is, the alleged defects of the world, would infer that there is an evil God, or at least a God neutral between good and evil. And if we hold the same opinion as King Alfonso, we shall, I say, receive this answer: You have known the world only since the day before yesterday, you see scarce farther than your nose, and you carp at the world. Wait until you know more of the world and consider therein especially the parts which present a complete whole (as do organic bodies); and you will find there a contrivance and a beauty transcending all imagination. Let us thence draw conclusions as to the wisdom and the goodness of the author of things, even in things that we know not. We find in the universe some things which are not pleasing to us; but let us be aware that it is not made for us alone. It is nevertheless made for us if we are wise: it will serve us if we use it for our service; we shall be happy in it if we wish to be.

195. Someone will say that it is impossible to produce the best, because there is no perfect creature, and that it is always possible to produce one which would be more perfect. I answer that what can be said of a creature or of a particular substance, which can always be surpassed by another, is not to be applied to the universe, which since it must extend through all future eternity, is an infinity. Moreover, there is an infinite number of creatures in the smallest

particle of matter, because of the actual division of the *continuum* to infinity. And infinity, that is to say, the accumulation of an infinite number of substances, is, properly speaking, not a whole any more than the infinite number itself, whereof one cannot say whether it is even or uneven. That is just what serves to confute those who make of the world a God, or who think of God as the Soul of the world; for the world or the universe cannot be regarded as an animal or as a substance.

Summary of the Controversy Reduced to Formal Arguments

Some persons of discernment have wished me to make this addition. I have the more readily deferred to their opinion, because of the opportunity thereby gained for meeting certain difficulties, and for making observations on certain matters which were not treated in sufficient detail in the work itself.

Objection I

Whoever does not choose the best course is lacking either in power, or knowledge, or goodness.

God did not choose the best course in creating this world.

Therefore God was lacking in power, or knowledge, or goodness.

Answer

I deny the minor, that is to say, the second premiss of this syllogism, and the opponent proves it by this.

Prosyllogism

Whoever makes things in which there is evil, and which could have been made without any evil, or need not have been made at all, does not choose the best course.

God made a world wherein there is evil; a world, I say, which could have been made without any evil or which need not have been made at all.

Therefore God did not choose the best course.

Answer

I admit the minor of this prosyllogism: for one must confess that there is evil in this world which God has made, and that is would have been possible to make a world without evil or even not to create any world, since its creation depended upon the free will of God. But I deny the major, that is, the first of the two premises of the prosyllogism, and I might content myself with asking for its proof. In order, however, to give a clearer exposition of the matter, I would justify this denial by pointing out that the best course is not always that one which tends towards avoiding evil, since it is possible that the evil may be accompanied by a greater good. For example, the general of an army will prefer a great victory with a slight wound to a state of affairs without wound and without victory. I have proved this in further detail in this work by pointing out, through instances taken from mathematics and elsewhere, that an imperfection in the part may be required for a greater perfection in the whole. I have followed therein the opinion of St. Augustine, who said a hundred times that God permitted evil in order to derive from it a good, that is to say, a greater good; and Thomas Aquinas says (in libr. 2, *Sent. Dist.* 32, qu. 1, art. 1) that the permission of evil tends towards the good of the universe. I have shown that among older writers the fall of Adam was termed *felix culpa*, a fortunate sin, because it had been expiated with immense benefit by the incarnation of the Son of God: for he gave to the universe something more noble than anything there would otherwise have been amongst created beings. For the better understanding of the matter I added, following the example of many good authors, that it was consistent with order and the general good for God to grant to certain of his creatures the opportunity to exercise their freedom, even when he foresaw that they would turn to evil: for God could easily correct the evil, and it was not fitting that in order to prevent sin he should always act in an extraordinary way. It will therefore sufficiently refute the objection to show that a world with evil may be better than a world without evil. But I have gone still further in the work, and have even shown that this universe must be indeed better than every other possible universe.

Objection II

If there is more evil than good in intelligent creatures, there is more evil than good in all God's work.

Now there is more evil than good in intelligent creatures.

Therefore there is more evil than good in all God's work.

ANSWER

I deny the major and the minor of this conditional syllogism. As for the major, I do not admit it because this supposed inference from the part to the whole, from intelligent creatures to all creatures, assumes tacitly and without proof that creatures devoid of reason cannot be compared or taken into account with those that have reason. But why might not the surplus of good in the non-intelligent creatures that fill the world compensate for and even exceed incomparably the surplus of evil in rational creatures? It is true that the value of the latter is greater; but by way of compensation the others are incomparably greater in number; and it may be that the proportion of number and quantity surpasses that of value and quality.

The minor also I cannot admit, namely, that there is more evil than good in intelligent creatures. One need not even agree that there is more evil than good in the human kind. For it is possible, and even a very reasonable thing, that the glory and the perfection of the blessed may be incomparably greater than the misery and imperfection of the damned, and that here the excellence of the total good in the smaller number may exceed the total evil which is in the greater number. The blessed draw near to divinity through a divine Mediator, so far as can belong to these created beings, and make such progress in good as is impossible for the damned to make in evil, even though they should approach as nearly as may be the nature of demons. God is infinite, and the Devil is finite; good can and does go on *ad infinitum*, whereas evil has its bounds. It may be therefore, and it is probable, that there happens in the comparison between the blessed and the damned the opposite of what I said could happen in the comparison between the happy and the unhappy, namely that in the latter the proportion of degrees surpasses that of numbers, while in the comparison between intelligent and non-intelligent the proportion of numbers is greater than that of values. One is justified in assuming that a thing may be so as long as one does not

prove that it is impossible, and indeed what is here put forward goes beyond assumption.

But secondly, even should one admit that there is more evil than good in the human kind, one still has every reason for not admitting that there is more evil than good in all intelligent creatures. For there is an inconceivable number of Spirits, and perhaps of other rational creatures besides: and an opponent cannot prove that in the whole City of God, composed as much of Spirits as of rational animals without number and of endless different kinds, the evil exceeds the good. Although one need not, in order to answer an objection, prove that a thing is, when its mere possibility suffices, I have nevertheless shown in this present work that it is a result of the supreme perfection of the Sovereign of the Universe that the kingdom of God should be the most perfect of all states or governments possible, and that in consequence what little evil there is should be required to provide the full measure of the vast good existing there.

OBJECTION III

If it is always impossible not to sin, it is always unjust to punish.

Now it is always impossible not to sin, or rather all sin is necessary.

Therefore it is always unjust to punish.
The minor of this is proved as follows.

FIRST PROSYLLOGISM

Everything predetermined is necessary.
Every event is predetermined.

Therefore every event (and consequently sin also) is necessary.
Again this second minor is proved thus.

SECOND PROSYLLOGISM

That which is future, that which is foreseen, that which is involved in causes is predetermined.
Every event is of this kind.

Therefore every event is predetermined.

ANSWER

I admit in a certain sense the conclusion of the second prosyllogism, which is the minor of the first; but I shall deny the major of the first prosyllogism, namely that everything predetermined is necessary; taking "necessity," say the necessity to sin, or the impossibility of not sinning, or of not doing some action, in the sense relevant to the argument, that is, as a necessity essential and absolute, which destroys the morality of action and the justice of punishment. If anyone meant a different necessity or impossibility (that is, a necessity only moral or hypothetical, which will be explained presently) it is plain that we would deny him the major stated in the objection. We might content ourselves with this answer, and demand the proof of the proposition denied: but I am well pleased to justify my manner of procedure in the present work, in order to make the matter clear and to throw more light on this whole subject, by explaining the necessity that must be rejected and the determination that must be allowed. The truth is that the necessity contrary to morality, which must be avoided and which would render punishment unjust, is an insuperable necessity, which would render all opposition unavailing, even though one should wish with all one's heart to avoid the necessary action, and though one should make all possible efforts to that end. Now it is plain that this is not applicable to voluntary action, since one would not do them if one did not so desire. Thus their prevision and predetermination is not absolute, but it presupposes will: if it is certain that one will do them, it is no less certain that one will will to do them. These voluntary actions and their results will not happen whatever one may do and whether one will them or not; but they will happen because one will do, and because one will will to do, that which leads to them. That is involved in prevision and predetermination, and forms the reason thereof. The necessity of such events is called conditional or hypothetical, or again necessity of consequence, because it presupposes the will and the other requisites. But the necessity which destroys morality, and renders punishment unjust and reward unavailing, is found in the things that will be whatever one may do and whatever one may will to do: in a word, it exists in that which is essential. This it is which is called an absolute necessity. Thus it avails nothing with regard to what is necessary absolutely to ordain interdicts or commandments, to propose penalties or prizes, to blame or to praise; it will come to pass no more and no less. In voluntary actions, on the contrary, and in what depends upon them, precepts, armed with power to punish and to reward, very often serve, and are included in the order of causes that make action exist. Thus it comes about that not only pains and effort but also prayers are effective, God having had even these prayers in mind before he ordered things, and having made due allowance for them. That is why the precept *Ora et labora* (Pray and work) remains intact. Thus not only those who (under the empty pretext of the necessity of events) maintain that one can spare oneself the pains demanded by affairs, but also those who argue against prayers, fall into that which the ancients even in their time called "the Lazy sophism." So the predetermination of events by their causes is precisely what contributes to morality instead of destroying it, and the causes incline the will without necessitating it. For this reason the determination we are concerned with is not a necessitation. It is certain (to him who knows all) that the effect will follow this inclination; but this effect does not follow thence by a consequence which is necessary, that is, whose contrary implies contradiction; and it is also by such an inward inclination that the will is determined, without the presence of necessity. Suppose that one has the greatest possible passion (for example, a great thirst), you will admit that the soul can find some reason for resisting it, even if it were only that of displaying its power. Thus though one may never have complete indifference of equipoise [balance], and there is always a predominance of inclination for the course adopted, that predominance of inclination for the course adopted, that predominance does not render absolutely necessary the resolution taken.

OBJECTION IV

Whoever can prevent the sin of others and does not so, but rather contributes to it, although he be fully apprised of it, is accessary thereto.

God can prevent the sin of intelligent creatures; but he does not so, and he rather contributes to it by his co-operation and by the opportunities he causes, although he is fully cognizant of it.

Therefore, etc.

ANSWER

I deny the major of this syllogism. It may be that one can prevent the sin, but that one ought not to do so, because one could not do so without committing a sin oneself, or (when God is concerned) without acting unreasonably. I have given instances of that, and have applied them to God himself. It may be also that one contributes to the evil, and that one even opens the way to it sometimes, in doing things one is bound to do. And when one does one's duty, or (speaking of God) when, after full consideration, one does that which reason demands, one is not responsible for events, even when one foresees them. One does not will these evils; but one is willing to permit them for a greater good, which one cannot in reason help preferring to other considerations. This is a *consequent* will, resulting from acts of *antecedent* will, in which one wills the good. I know that some persons, in speaking of the antecedent and consequent will of God, have meant by the antecedent that which wills that all men be saved, and by the consequent that which wills, in consequence of persistent sin, that there be some damned, damnation being a result of sin. But these are only examples of a more general notion, and one may say with the same reason, that God wills by his antecedent will that men sin not, and that by his consequent or final and decretory will (which is always followed by its effect) he wills to permit that they sin, this permission being a result of superior reasons. One has indeed justification for saying, in general, that the antecedent will of God tends towards the production of good and the prevention of evil, each taken in itself, and as it were detached (*particulariter et secundum quid:* Thom; I, qu. 19, art. 6) according to the measure of the degree of each good or of each evil. Likewise one may say that the consequent, or final and total, divine will tends towards the production of as many goods as can be put together, whose combination thereby becomes determined, and involves also the permission of some evils and the exclusion of some goods, as the best possible plan of the universe demands. [Jacobus] Arminius, in his *Antiperkinsus,* explained very well that the will of God can be called consequent not only in relation to the action of the creature considered beforehand in the divine understanding, but also in relation to other anterior acts of divine will. But it is enough to consider the passage cited from Thomas Aquinas, and that from [John Duns] Scotus (I, dist. 46, qu. 11), to see that they make this distinction as I have made it here. Nevertheless if anyone will not suffer this use of the terms, let him put "previous" in place of "antecedent" will, and "final" or "decretory" in place of "consequent" will. For I do not wish to wrangle about words.

DISCUSSION QUESTIONS

1. Leibniz contends that our world is the best of all possible worlds. In your own words, try to restate his argument. What are the strengths and weakness of his argument? Do you think that it is possible today to live in accordance with Leibniz's philosophy?

2. In Voltaire's *Candide* (1759), there is a character named Doctor Pangloss, a philosopher fashioned after Leibniz, who is always saying "everything is for the best in the best of all possible worlds." In Voltaire's satirical novel, the world is full of horrors and folly, yet Pangloss continues to espouse his optimistic metaphysical view of the world. His student, Candide, eventually rejects this world view and retires to a farm, where he discovers the secret of happiness in tending his garden. Unlike Leibniz, Voltaire thought that either man is born guilty and God is punishing him or God is indifferent to man—and the latter seemed more plausible to him. Is Voltaire being too pessimistic? Or is Leibniz being too optimistic? Is there a middle ground here? If so, what might it be?

3. In his answer to Objection I, Leibniz says, "An imperfection in the part may be required for a greater perfection of the whole." Can you think of an example that might lend support to this claim?

4. According to Leibniz's notion of metaphysical evil, everything that is not God is necessarily evil. What does he mean? Do you agree with him?

5. Leibniz claims to have resolved the existence of an all-good and all-perfect God with the existence of evil in the world. Do you think he has succeeded? Why or why not?

DAVID HUME

THE ARGUMENT FROM EVIL

I n this selection, David Hume's interlocutor Cleanthes, after reviewing four circumstances on which natural evil depends, concludes that the "first causes of the universe" *most probably* "have neither goodness nor malice." Cleanthes reaches this conclusion after "looking round this universe" and making the following observations about the deity: (1) If all living creatures were incapable of pain, evil could have never gained access to the universe; (2) if the deity were to exterminate willfully all ill, evil could have never gained access to the universe; (3) if animals were endowed by the deity "with a large stock of powers and faculties, beyond what strict necessity requires," there would have "been very little ill in comparison to what we feel at present"; and (4) if "the several springs and principles of the universe" were organized "to preserve the just temperment and medium," there would have "been very little ill in comparison to what we feel at present." "The true conclusion," says Cleanthes, "is that the original Source of all things . . . has no more regard to good above ill than to heat above cold, or to drought above moisture, or to light above heavy."

David Hume (1711–76), a Scottish philosopher, essayist, historian, and political economist, failed on several attempts to secure a professor's chair. At the age of twenty-seven, he published the first two volumes of his *Treatise of Human Nature* (1739–40). He spent three years writing it in France and notes that "it fell *dead-born* from the press." His other books include *An Inquiry Concerning Human Understanding* (1748), *An Inquiry Concerning the Principles of Morals* (1751), *History of England* (1753–61), and *Dialogues Concerning Natural Religion* (1779), the book from which our selection is taken. As Hume was prevailed upon not to publish *Dialogues* during his lifetime, he left instructions to publish it after his death. *Dialogues* is a conversation among three protagonists—Cleanthes, Philo, and Demea. Pamphilus, the person reporting their conversations, claims that Cleanthes' approach is nearest "to the truth." This has led some commentators to conclude that Cleanthes is Hume's mouthpiece. Others, however, contend that it is Philo.

In short, I repeat the question: Is the world, considered in general and as it appears to us in this life, different from what a man or such a limited being would, *beforehand*, expect from a very powerful, wise, and benevolent Deity? It must be strange prejudice to assert the contrary. And from thence I conclude that, however consistent the world may be, allowing certain suppositions and conjectures with the idea of such a Deity, it can never afford us an inference concerning his existence. The consistency is not absolutely denied, only the inference. Conjectures, especially where infinity is excluded from the Divine attributes, may perhaps be sufficient to prove a consistency, but can never be foundations for any inference.

There seem to be *four* circumstances on which depend all or the greatest part of the ills that molest sensible creatures; and it is not impossible but all these circumstances may be necessary and unavoidable. We know so little beyond common life, or even of common life, that, with regard to the economy of a universe, there is no conjecture, however wild, which may not be just, nor any one, however plausible, which may not be erroneous. All that belongs to human understanding, in this deep ignorance and obscurity, is to be sceptical or at least cautious, and not to admit of any hypothesis whatever, much less of any which is supported by no appearance of probability. Now this I assert to be the case with regard to all the causes of evil and the circumstances on which it depends. None of them appear to human reason in the least degree necessary or unavoidable, nor can we suppose them such, without the utmost license of imagination.

The *first* circumstance which introduces evil is that contrivance or economy of the animal creation by which pains, as well as pleasures, are employed to excite all creatures to action, and make them vigilant in the great work of self-preservation. Now pleasure alone, in its various degrees, seems to human understanding sufficient for this purpose. All animals might be constantly in a state of enjoyment; but when urged by any of the necessities of nature, such as thirst, hunger, weariness, instead of pain, they might feel a diminution of pleasure by which they might be prompted to seek that object which is necessary to their subsistence. Men pursue pleasure as eagerly as they avoid pain: at least, they might have been so constituted. It seems, therefore, plainly possible to carry on the business of life without any pain. Why then is any animal ever rendered susceptible of such a sensation? If animals can be free from it an hour, they might enjoy a perpetual exemption from it, and it required as particular a contrivance of their organs to produce that feeling as to endow them with sight, hearing, or any of the senses. Shall we conjecture that such a contrivance was necessary, without any appearance of reason, and shall we build on that conjecture as on the most certain truth?

But a capacity of pain would not alone produce pain were it not for the *second* circumstance, viz., the conducting of the world by general laws; and this seems nowise necessary to a very perfect Being. It is true, if everything were conducted by

particular volitions, the course of nature would be perpetually broken, and no man could employ his reason in the conduct of life. But might not other particular volitions remedy this inconvenience? In short, might not the Deity exterminate all ill, wherever it were to be found, and produce all good, without any preparation or long progress of causes and effects?

Besides, we must consider that, according to the present economy of the world, the course of nature, though supposed exactly regular, yet to us appears not so, and many events are uncertain, and many disappoint our expectations. Health and sickness, calm and tempest, with an infinite number of other accidents whose causes are unknown and variable, have a great influence both on the fortunes of particular persons and on the prosperity of public societies; and indeed all human life, in a manner, depends on such accidents. A Being, therefore, who knows the secret springs of the universe might easily, by particular volitions, turn all these accidents to the good of mankind and render the whole world, happy, without discovering himself in any operation. A fleet whose purposes were salutary to society might always meet with a fair wind. Good princes enjoy sound health and long life. Persons born to power and authority be framed with good tempers and virtuous dispositions. A few such events as these, regularly and wisely conducted, would change the face of the world, and yet would no more seem to disturb the course of nature or confound human conduct than the present economy of things where the causes are secret and variable and compounded. Some small touches given to Caligula's brain in his infancy might have converted him into a Trajan. One wave, a little higher than the rest, by burying Caesar and his fortune in the bottom of the ocean, might have restored liberty to a considerable part of mankind. There may, for aught we know, be good reasons why Providence interposes not in this manner, but they are unknown to us; and, though the mere supposition that such reasons exist may be sufficient to *save* the conclusion concerning the Divine attributes, yet surely it can never be sufficient to *establish* that conclusion.

If everything in the universe be conducted by general laws, and if animals be rendered susceptible of pain, it scarcely seems possible but some ill must arise in the various shocks of matter and the various concurrence and opposition of general laws; but this ill would be very rare were it not for the *third* circumstance which I proposed to mention, viz., the great frugality with which all powers and faculties are distributed to every particular being. So well adjusted are the organs and capacities of all animals, and so well fitted to their preservation, that, as far as history or tradition reaches, there appears not to be any single species which has yet been extinguished in the universe. Every animal has the requisite endowments, but these endowments are bestowed with so scrupulous an economy that any considerable diminution must entirely destroy the creature. Wherever one power is increased, there is a proportional abatement in the others. Animals which excel in swiftness are commonly defective in force. Those which possess both are either imperfect in some of their senses or are oppressed with the most craving wants. The human species, whose chief excellence is reason and sagacity, is of all others the most necessitous, and the most deficient in bodily advantages, without clothes, without arms, without food, without lodging, without any convenience of life, except what they owe to their own skill and industry. In short, nature seems to have formed an exact calculation of the necessities of her creatures, and, like a *rigid master*, has afforded them little more powers or endowments than what are strictly sufficient to supply those necessities. An *indulgent parent* would have bestowed a large stock in order to guard against accidents, and secure the happiness and welfare of the creature in the most unfortunate concurrence of circumstances. Every course of life would not have been so surrounded with precipices that the least departure from the true path, by mistake or necessity, must involve us in misery and ruin. Some reserve, some fund, would have been provided to ensure happiness, nor would the powers and the necessities have been adjusted with so rigid an economy. The Author of nature is inconceivably powerful; his force is supposed great, if not altogether inexhaustible, nor is there any reason, as far as we can judge, to make him observe this strict frugality in his dealings with his creatures. It would have been better, were his power extremely limited, to have created fewer animals, and to

have endowed these with more faculties for their happiness and preservation. A builder is never esteemed prudent who undertakes a plan beyond what his stock will enable him to finish.

In order to cure most of the ills of human life, I require not that man should have the wings of the eagle, the swiftness of the stag, the force of the ox, the arms of the lion, the scales of the crocodile or rhinoceros; much less do I demand the sagacity of an angel or cherubim. I am contented to take an increase in one single power or faculty of his soul. Let him be endowed with a greater propensity to industry and labour, a more vigorous spring and activity of mind, a more constant bent to business and application. Let the whole species possess naturally an equal diligence with that which many individuals are able to attain by habit and reflection, and the most beneficial consequences, without any allay of ill, is the immediate and necessary result of this endowment. Almost all the moral as well as natural evils of human life arise from idleness; and were our species, by the original constitution of their frame, exempt from this vice or infirmity, the perfect cultivation of land, the improvement of arts and manufactures, the exact execution of every office and duty, immediately follow; and men at once may fully reach that state of society which is so imperfectly attained by the best regulated government. But as industry is a power, and the most valuable of any, nature seems determined, suitably to her usual maxims, to bestow it on men with a very sparing hand, and rather to punish him severely for his deficiency in it than to reward him for his attainments. She has so contrived his frame that nothing but the most violent necessity can oblige him to labour; and she employs all his other wants to overcome, at least in part, the want of diligence, and to endow him with some share of a faculty of which she has thought fit naturally to bereave him. Here our demands may be allowed very humble, and therefore the more reasonable. If we required the endowments of superior penetration and judgment, of a more delicate taste of beauty, of a nicer sensibility to benevolence and friendship, we might be told that we impiously pretend to break the order of nature, that we want to exalt ourselves into a higher rank of being, that the presents which we require, not being suitable to our state and condition, would only be pernicious to us. But it is hard, I dare to repeat it, it is hard that, being placed in a world so full of wants and necessities, where almost every being and element is either our foe or refuses its assistance . . . we should also have our own temper to struggle with, and should be deprived of that faculty which can alone fence against these multiplied evils.

The *fourth* circumstance whence arises the misery and ill of the universe is the inaccurate workmanship of all the springs and principles of the great machine of nature. It must be acknowledged that there are few parts of the universe which seem not to serve some purpose, and whose removal would not produce a visible defect and disorder in the whole. The parts hang all together, nor can one be touched without affecting the rest, in a greater or less degree. But at the same time, it must be observed that none of these parts or principles, however useful, are so accurately adjusted as to keep precisely within those bounds in which their utility consists; but they are, all of them, apt, on every occasion, to run into the one extreme or the other. One would imagine that this grand production had not received the last hand of the maker—so little finished is every part, and so coarse are the strokes with which it is executed. Thus the winds are requisite to convey the vapours along the surface of the globe, and to assist men in navigation; but how often, rising up to tempests and hurricanes, do they become pernicious? Rains are necessary to nourish all the plants and animals of the earth; but how often are they defective? How often excessive? Heat is requisite to all life and vegetation, but is not always found in the due proportion. On the mixture and secretion of the humours and juices of the body depend the health and prosperity of the animal; but the parts perform not regularly their proper function. What [is] more useful than all the passions of the mind, ambition, vanity, love, anger? But how often do they break their bounds and cause the greatest convulsions in society? There is nothing so advantageous in the universe but what frequently becomes pernicious, by its excess or defect; nor has nature guarded, with the requisite accuracy, against all disorder or confusion. The irregularity is never perhaps so great as to destroy any species, but is often sufficient to involve the individuals in ruin and misery.

On the concurrence, then, of these *four* circumstances does all or the greatest part of natural evil depend. Were all living creatures incapable of pain, or were the world administered by particular volitions, evil never could have found access into the universe; and were animals endowed with a large stock of powers and faculties, beyond what strict necessity requires, or were the several springs and principles of the universe so accurately framed as to preserve always the just temperament and medium, there must have been very little ill in comparison of what we feel at present. What then shall we pronounce on this occasion? Shall we say that these circumstances are not necessary, and that they might easily have been altered in the contrivance of the universe? This decision seems too presumptuous for creatures so blind and ignorant. Let us be more modest in our conclusions. Let us allow that, if the goodness of the Deity (I mean a goodness like the human) could be established on any tolerable reasons *a priori*, these phenomena, however untoward, would not be sufficient to subvert that principle, but might easily, in some unknown manner, be reconcilable to it. But let us still assert that, as this goodness is not antecedently established but must be inferred from the phenomena, there can be no grounds for such an inference while there are so many ills in the universe, and while these ills might so easily have been remedied, as far as human understanding can be allowed to judge on such a subject. I am sceptic enough to allow that the bad appearances, notwithstanding all my reasonings, may be compatible with such attributes as you suppose, but surely they can never prove these attributes. Such a conclusion cannot result from scepticism, but must arise from the phenomena, and from our confidence in the reasonings which we deduce from these phenomena.

Look round this universe. What an immense profusion of beings, animated and organized, sensible and active! You admire this prodigious variety and fecundity. But inspect a little more narrowly these living existences, the only beings worth regarding. How hostile and destructive to each other! How insufficient all of them for their own happiness! How contemptible or odious to the spectator! The whole presents nothing but the idea of a blind nature, impregnated by a great vivifying principle, and pouring forth from her lap, without discernment or parental care, her maimed and abortive children!

Here the Manichaean system* occurs as a proper hypothesis to solve the difficulty; and, no doubt, in some respects it is very specious and has more probability than the common hypothesis, by giving a plausible account of the strange mixture of good and ill which appears in life. But if we consider, on the other hand, the perfect uniformity and agreement of the parts of the universe, we shall not discover in it any marks of the combat of a malevolent with a benevolent being. There is indeed an opposition of pains and pleasures in the feelings of sensible creatures; but are not all the operations of nature carried on by an opposition of principles, of hot and cold, moist and dry, light and heavy? The true conclusion is that the original Source of all things is entirely indifferent to all these principles, and has no more regard to good above ill than to heat above cold, or to drought above moisture, or to light above heavy.

There may *four* hypotheses be framed concerning the first causes of the universe; that they are endowed with perfect goodness; that they have perfect malice; that they are opposite and have both goodness and malice; that they have neither goodness nor malice. Mixed phenomena can never prove the two former unmixed principles; and the uniformity and steadiness of general laws seem to oppose the third. The fourth, therefore, seems by far the most probable.

DISCUSSION QUESTIONS

1. Hume's Cleanthes asks us to "look around the universe." In addition to good things, we will also find suffering, hostility, and destruction. Is he correct in concluding that the goodness of God cannot be inferred solely on the basis of what we see and hear (or what Hume calls "phenomena")? If so, what can we infer from what we see around us?

2. Hume's Cleanthes says, "Let us allow that, if the goodness of the Deity (I mean goodness like the human) could be established on any tolerable reasons *a priori* [namely, independently of experience], these phenomena, however untoward, would not be sufficient to subvert that principle, but might easily, in some unknown manner, be reconcilable to it." What does he mean by this? Do you agree with him? Why or why not?

3. How does Hume's Cleanthes show that "the original Source of all things . . . has no more regard to good above ill than to heat above cold, or to drought above moisture, or to light above heavy"? Evaluate this argument.

4. Create a dialogue between Leibniz and Hume on the argument from evil. Who prevails in your dialogue?

5. Hume thinks that it would be better if God acted more as an "indulgent parent" toward us than as a "rigid master." What does he mean? Do you agree with him?

---

* Manichaeism is an influential Gnostic religion founded by Mani (215–276) in the third century C.E. in Babylonia that lasted until the thirteenth century C.E. Manichaeism holds that good and evil are metaphysically distinct, and identifies good with light and evil with darkness. God is Lord of the Kingdom of Light, and Satan is the ruler of the Kingdom of Darkness. For the Manichaeans, these two kingdoms or forces have been engaged in a great struggle with each other.—Ed.

The Seventh Seal
[Sweden 1957] 1 hour, 36 minutes
Directed by Ingmar Bergman

After a ten-year crusade, knight Antonius Block (Max Von Sydow) and his squire Jons (Gunnar Björnstrand) return to their native Sweden, only to discover their land being devastated by the plague. Antonius, a man stricken with doubts about the existence of God and the afterlife, challenges Death (Bengt Ekerot) to a game of chess in hopes of finding truth and meaning before his life expires. The game is played in a series of sessions throughout the journey of the knight and his squire. Along the way, the two meet up with a girl (Gunnel Lindblom), whom Jons saves from a thief, a pair of poor itinerant actors—Jof (Nils Poppe) and his wife Mia (Bibi Andersson), and their baby daughter—as well as a monk (Anders Ek) and a painter (Gunnar Olsson). As the group journeys together, Antonius sees pain and anguish throughout his homeland. However, he also sees love and caring against the backdrop of the plague. It is love that leads Antonius to discover the meaning of life and death, and the meaning of his very existence in God's larger design. In addition to themes regarding the relationship of human suffering to God, the film also examines the existence of God and other topics in the philosophy of religion.

1. The monk links the suffering brought about by the plague to God in the following statement: "God has sentenced us to punishment. We shall all perish in the Black Death. You, standing there like gaping cattle, you who sit there in your glutted complacency, do you know that this may be your last hour? Death stands right behind you. I can see how his crown gleams in the sun. His scythe flashes as he raises it above your heads. Which one of you shall he strike first? You there, who stand staring like a goat, will your mouth be twisted into the last unfinished gasp before nightfall? And you, woman, who bloom with life and self-satisfaction, will you pale and become extinguished before the morning dawns? You back there, with your swollen nose and stupid grin, do you have another year left to dirty the earth with your refuse? Do you know, you insensible fools, that you shall die today or tomorrow, or the next day, because all of you have been sentenced? Do you hear what I say? Do you hear the word? You have been sentenced, sentenced!" Compare the monk's account of suffering to some of the other accounts of suffering you have encountered in this chapter. Which account do you, find more compelling, and why?

2. The painter says, "The remarkable thing is that the poor creatures think the pestilence is the Lord's punishment. Mobs of people who call themselves Slaves of Sin are swarming over the country, flagellating themselves and others, all for the glory of God." Are the "Slaves of Sin" drawing a valid conclusion from the premise that suffering is a punishment from God? If we assume that suffering is punishment from God, does it therefore follow that we should find ways to increase our suffering in order to please God? Why or why not?

3. Death comments, "Most people never reflect about either death or the futility of life." The knight responds, "In our fear, we make an image, and that image we call God." If death and the futility of life are assumed to be things that cause us suffering, then is the knight arguing that God's existence is derived from the fact that humans suffer? Discuss this line of argument.

4. The knight says, "I want knowledge, not faith, not suppositions, but knowledge. I want God to stretch out His hand towards me, reveal Himself and speak to me." However, recall the case of

Bernadette: Because she lacked religious knowledge, she was unable to recognize the identity of the vision that was speaking to her. How is it possible to know for certain that the voice we identify as God's is actually the voice of God? Is what the knight is asking for impossible?

5.   Jons says, "This damned ranting about doom. Is that food for the minds of modern people? Do they really expect us to take them seriously?" What do you think? Assume that by "doom" Jons means an extraordinary amount of suffering, and perhaps even the end of the world.

C. S. LEWIS

THE PROBLEM OF PAIN

I n "The Problem of Pain," C. S. Lewis argues we suffer pain so that God can use his authority to make us "into the sort of human being he, rightly, in his superior wisdom, wants [us] to be." Whereas some, like Hume in the previous selection, think that it would have been better for God "to have created fewer animals, and to have endowed these with more facilities for their happiness and preservation," Lewis thinks that our need to overcome pain is compatible with God's goodness toward and love of his creations. Lewis says, we were made *primarily* "that God may love us," not that we may love him. "To ask that God should be content with us as we are is to ask that God should cease to be God: Because he is what he is, his love must, in the nature of things, be impeded and repelled, by certain stains in our present character, and because he already loves us he must labour to make us loveable." Thus, by overcoming stains in our present character, we "become objects in which the Divine love may rest 'well pleased.'" For Lewis, the existence of pain and suffering in the world does not disprove the existence of God; rather, it reveals God's "authoritative love" toward us and our "obedient love" toward him.

C. S. (Clive Staples) Lewis (1898–1963), British medieval scholar, Christian theologian, and novelist, taught at Oxford University and the University of Cambridge. He was the author of some forty books, many of which are described as Christian apologetics, such as *The Pilgrim's Regress: An Allegorical Apology for Christianity, Reason, and Romanticism* (1933), *The Problem of Pain* (1940), *The Screwtape Letters* (1942), and *Mere Christianity* (1943). He also wrote a series of children's books called *The Chronicles of Narnia*, the most well known being *The Lion, the Witch, and the Wardrobe* (1950). His work as a medievalist, however, is best represented in *Allegory of Love: A Study of Medieval Tradition* (1936), considered by many to be his most significant scholarly achievement. His life is the subject of the film *Shadowlands* (1993) (see the film box). The following is a selection from *The Problem of Pain*.

Not many years ago when I was an atheist, if anyone had asked me, "Why do you not believe in God?" my reply would have run something like this: "Look at the universe we live in. By far the greatest part of it consists of empty space, completely dark and unimaginably cold. The bodies which move in this space are so few and so small in comparison with the space itself that even if every one of them were known to be crowded as full as it could hold with perfectly happy creatures, it would still be difficult to believe that life and happiness were more than a bye-product to the power that made the universe. As it is, however, the scientists think it likely that very few of the suns of space—perhaps none of them except our own—have any planets; and in our system it is improbable that any planet except the Earth sustains life. And Earth herself existed without life for millions of years and may exist for millions more when life has left her. And what is it like while it lasts? It is so arranged that all the forms of it can live only by preying upon one another. In the lower forms this process entails only death, but in the higher there appears a new quality called consciousness which enables it to be attended with pain. The creatures cause pain by being born, and live by inflicting pain, and in pain they mostly die. In the most complex of all the creatures, Man, yet another quality appears, which we call reason, whereby he is enabled to foresee his own pain which henceforth is preceded with acute mental suffering, and to foresee his own death while keenly desiring permanence. It also enables men by a hundred ingenious contrivances to inflict a great deal more pain than they otherwise could have done on one another and on the irrational creatures. This power they have exploited to the full. Their history is largely a record of crime, war, disease, and terror, with just sufficient happiness interposed to give them, while it lasts, an agonised apprehension of losing it, and, when it is lost, the poignant misery of remembering. Every now and then they improve their condition a little and what we call a civilisation appears. But all civilisations pass away and, even while they remain, inflict peculiar sufferings of their own probably sufficient to outweigh what alleviations they may have brought to the normal pains of man. That our own civilisation has done so, no one will dispute; that it will pass away like all its predecessors is surely probable. Even if it should not, what then? The race is doomed. Every race that comes into being in any part of the universe is doomed; for the universe, they tell us, is running down, and will sometime be a uniform infinity of homogeneous matter at a low temperature. All stories will come to nothing: all life will turn out in the end to have been a transitory and senseless contortion upon the idiotic face of infinite matter. If you ask me to believe that this is the work of a benevolent and omnipotent spirit, I reply that all the evidence points in the opposite direction. Either there is no spirit behind the universe, or else a spirit indifferent to good and evil, or else an evil spirit."

There was one question which I never dreamed of raising. I never noticed that the very strength and facility of the pessimists' case at once poses us a problem. If the universe is so bad, or even half so bad, how on earth did human beings ever come to attribute it to the activity of a wise and good Creator? Men are fools, perhaps; but hardly so foolish as that. The direct inference from black to white, from evil flower to virtuous root, from senseless work to a workman infinitely wise, staggers belief. The spectacle of the universe as revealed by experience can never have been the ground of religion: it must always have been something in spite of which religion, acquired from a different source, was held.

It would be an error to reply that our ancestors were ignorant and therefore entertained pleasing illusions about nature which the progress of science has since dispelled. For centuries, during which all men believed, the nightmare size and emptiness of the universe was already known. You will read in some books that the men of the Middle Ages thought the Earth flat and the stars near, but that is a lie. Ptolemy had told them that the Earth was a mathematical point without size in relation to the distance of the fixed stars—a distance which one mediaeval popular text estimates as a hundred and seventeen million miles. And in times yet earlier, even from the beginnings, men must have got the same sense of hostile immensity from a more obvious source. To prehistoric man the neighbouring forest must have been infinite enough, and the utterly alien and infest which we have to fetch from the thought of cosmic rays and cooling suns, came snuffing and howling nightly to his very doors. Certainly at all periods the pain and waste of human life was equally obvious. Our own religion begins among the Jews, a people squeezed between great warlike empires, continually defeated and led captive, familiar as Poland or Armenia with the tragic story of the conquered. It is mere nonsense to put pain among the discoveries of science. Lay down this book and reflect for five minutes on the fact that all the great religions were first preached, and long practised, in a world without chloroform.

At all times, then, an inference from the course of events in this world to the goodness and wisdom of the Creator would have been equally preposterous; and it was never made. Religion has a different origin.

DIVINE OMNIPOTENCE

"If God were good, He would wish to make His creatures perfectly happy, and if God were almighty He would be able to do what He wished. But the creatures are not happy. Therefore God lacks either goodness, or power, or both." This is the problem of pain, in its simplest form. The possibility of answering it depends on showing that the terms "good" and "almighty," and perhaps also the term "happy" are equivocal: for it must be admitted from the outset that if the popular meanings attached to these words are the best, or the only possible, meanings, then the argument is unanswerable. In this chapter I shall make some comments on the idea of Omnipotence, and, in the following, some on the idea of Goodness.

Omnipotence means "power to do all, or everything." And we are told in Scripture that "with God all things are possible." It is common enough, in argument with an unbeliever, to be told that God, if He existed and were good, would do this or that; and then, if we point out that the proposed action is impossible, to be met with the retort, "But I thought God was supposed to be able to do anything." This raises the whole question of impossibility.

In ordinary usage the word *impossible* generally implies a suppressed clause beginning with the word *unless*. Thus it is impossible for me to see the street from where I sit writing at this moment; that is, it is impossible to see the street *unless* I go up to the top floor where I shall be high enough to overlook the intervening building. If I had broken my leg I should say "But it is impossible to go up to the top floor"—meaning, however, that it is impossible *unless* some friends turn up who will carry me. Now let us advance to a different plane of impossibility, by saying "It is, at any rate, impossible to see the street *so long as* I remain where I am and the intervening building remains where it is." Someone might add "unless the nature of space, or of vision, were different from what it is." I do not know what the best philosophers and scientists would say to this, but I should have to reply. "I don't know whether space and vision *could possibly* have been of such a

nature as you suggest." Now it is clear that the words *could possibly* here refer to some absolute kind of possibility or impossibility which is different from the relative possibilities and impossibilities we have been considering. I cannot say whether seeing round corners is, in this new sense, possible or not, because I do not know whether it is self-contradictory or not. But I know very well that if it is self-contradictory it is absolutely impossible. The absolutely impossible may also be called the intrinsically impossible because it carries its impossibility within itself, instead of borrowing it from other impossibilities which in their turn depend upon others. It has no *unless* clause attached to it. It is impossible under all conditions and in all worlds and for all agents.

"All agents" here includes God Himself. His Omnipotence means power to do all that is intrinsically possible, not to do the intrinsically impossible. You may attribute miracles to Him, but not nonsense. This is no limit to His power. If you choose to say "God can give a creature free-will and at the same time withhold free-will from it," you have not succeeded in saying *anything* about God: meaningless combinations of words do not suddenly acquire meaning simply because we prefix to them the two other words "God can." It remains true that all *things* are possible with God: the intrinsic impossibilities are not things but nonentities. It is no more possible for God than for the weakest of His creatures to carry out both of two mutually exclusive alternatives; not because His power meets an obstacle, but because nonsense remains nonsense even when we talk it about God. . . .

By the goodness of God we mean nowadays almost exclusively His lovingness; and in this we may be right. And by Love, in this context, most of us mean kindness—the desire to see others than the self happy; not happy in this way or in that, but just happy. What would really satisfy us would be a God who said of anything we happened to like doing, "What does it mater so long as they are contented?" We want, in fact, not so much a Father in Heaven as a grandfather in heaven—senile benevolence who, as they say, "liked to see young people enjoying themselves" and whose plan for the universe was simply that it might be truly said at the end of each day, "a good time was had by all." Not many people, I admit, would formulate a theology in precisely those terms: but a conception not very different lurks at the back of many minds. I do not claim to be an exception: I should very much like to live in a universe which was governed on such lines. But since it is abundantly clear that I don't, and since I have reason to believe, nevertheless, that God is Love, I conclude that my conception of love needs correction.

I might, indeed, have learned, even from the poets, that Love is something more stern and splendid that mere kindness: that even the love between the sexes is, as in Dante, "a lord of terrible aspect." There is kindness in Love: but Love and kindness are not coterminous, and when kindness (in the sense given above) is separated from the other elements of Love, it involves a certain fundamental indifference to its object, and even something like contempt of it. Kindness consents very readily to the removal of its object—we have all met people whose kindness to animals is constantly leading them to kill animals lest they should suffer. Kindness, merely as such, cares not whether its object becomes good or bad, provided only that it escapes suffering. As Scripture points out, it is bastards who are spoiled: the legitimate sons, who are to carry on the family tradition, are punished [Heb. 12:8]. It is for people whom we care nothing about that we demand happiness on any terms: with our friends, our lovers, our children, we are exacting and would rather see them suffer much than be happy in contemptible and estranging modes. If God is Love, He is, by definition, something more than mere kindness. And it appears, from all the records, that though He has often rebuked us and condemned us, He has never regarded us with contempt. He has paid us the intolerable compliment of loving us, in the deepest, most tragic, most inexorable sense.

The relation between Creator and creature is, of course, unique, and cannot be paralleled by any relations between one creature and another. God is both further from us, and nearer to us, than any other being. He is further from us because the sheer difference between that which has Its principle of being in Itself and that to which being is communicated, is one compared with which the difference between an archangel and a worm is quite insignificant. He makes, we are made: He is

original, we derivative. But at the same time, and for the same reason, the intimacy between God and even the meanest creature is closer than any that creatures can attain with one another. Our life is, at every moment, supplied by Him: our tiny, miraculous power of free will only operates on bodies which His continual energy keeps in existence—our very power to think is His power communicated to us. Such a unique relation can be apprehended only by analogies: from the various types of love known among creatures we reach an inadequate, but useful, conception of God's love for man.

The lowest type, and one which is "love" at all only by an extension of the word, is that which an artist feels for an artefact. God's relation to man is pictured thus in Jeremiah's vision of the potter and the clay [Jer. 18], or when St. Peter speaks of the whole Church as a building on which God is at work, and of the individual members as stones [Pet. 2:5]. The limitation of such an analogy is, of course, that in the symbol the patient is not sentient, and that certain questions of justice and mercy which arise when the "stones" are really "living" therefore remain unrepresented. But it is an important analogy so far as it goes. We are, not metaphorically but in very truth, a Divine work of art, something that God is making, and therefore something with which He will not be satisfied until it has a certain character. Here again we come up against what I have called the "intolerable compliment." Over a sketch made idly to amuse a child, an artist may not take much trouble: he may be content to let it go even though it is not exactly as he meant it to be. But over the great picture of his life—the work which he loves, though in a different fashion, as intensely as a man loves a woman or a mother a child—he will take endless trouble—and would, doubtless, thereby *give* endless trouble to the picture if it were sentient. One can imagine a sentient picture, after being rubbed and scraped and re-commenced for the tenth time, wishing that it were only a thumb-nail sketch whose making was over in a minute. In the same way, it is natural for us to wish that God had designed for us a less glorious and less arduous destiny; but then we are wishing not for more love but for less.

Another type is the love of man for a beast—a relation constantly used in Scripture to symbolise the relation between God and men; "we are his people and the sheep of his pasture." This is in some ways a better analogy than the preceding, because the inferior party is sentient, and yet unmistakably inferior: but it is less good in so far as man has not made the beast and does not fully understand it. Its great merit lies in the fact that the association of (say) man and dog is primarily for the man's sake: he tames the dog primarily that he may love it, not that it may love him, and that it may serve him, not that he may serve it. Yet at the same time, the dog's interests are not sacrificed to the man's. The one end (that he may love it) cannot be fully attained unless it also, in its fashion, loves him, nor can it serve him unless he, in a different fashion, serves it. Now just because the dog is by human standards one of the "best" of irrational creatures, and a proper object for a man to love—of course, with that degree and kind of love which is proper to such an object, and not with silly anthropomorphic exaggerations— man interferes with the dog and makes it more lovable than it was in mere nature. In its state of nature it has a smell, and habits, which frustrate man's love: he washes it, house-trains it, teaches it not to steal, and is so enabled to love it completely. To the puppy the whole proceeding would seem, if it were a theologian, to cast grave doubts on the "goodness" of man: but the full-grown and full-trained dog, larger, healthier, and longer-lived than the wild dog, and admitted, as it were by Grace, to a whole world of affections, loyalties, interests, and comforts entirely beyond its animal destiny, would have no such doubts. It will be noted that the man (I am speaking throughout of the good man) takes all these pains with the dog, and gives all these pains to the dog, only because it is an animal high in the scale— because it is so nearly lovable that it is worth his while to make it fully lovable. He does not house-train the earwig or give baths to centipedes. We may wish, indeed, that we were of so little account to God that He left us alone to follow our natural impulses—that He would give over trying to train us into something so unlike our natural selves: but once again, we are asking not for more Love, but for less.

A nobler analogy, sanctioned by the constant tenor of Our Lord's teaching, is that between God's love for man and a father's love for a son.

Whenever this is used, however (that is, whenever we pray the Lord's Prayer), it must be remembered that the Saviour used it in a time and place where paternal authority stood much higher than it does in modern England. A father half apologetic for having brought his son into the world, afraid to restrain him lest he should create inhibitions or even to instruct him lest he should interfere with his independence of mind, is a most misleading symbol of the Divine Fatherhood. I am not here discussing whether the authority of fathers, in its ancient extent, was a good thing or a bad thing: I am only explaining what the conception of Fatherhood would have meant to Our Lord's first hearers, and indeed to their successors for many centuries. And it will become even plainer if we consider how Our Lord (though, in our belief, one with His Father and coeternal with Him as no earthly son is with an earthly father) regards His own Sonship, surrendering His will wholly to the paternal will and not even allowing Himself to be called "good" because Good is the name of the Father. Love between father and son, in this symbol, means essentially authoritative love on the one side; and obedient love on the other. The father uses his authority to make the son into the sort of human being he, rightly, and in his superior wisdom, wants him to be. Even in our own days, though a man might say, he could mean nothing by saying, "I love my son but don't care how great a blackguard he is provided he has a good time." . . .

The problem of reconciling human suffering with the existence of a God who loves, is only insoluble so long as we attach a trivial meeting to the word "love," and look on things as if man were the center of them. Man is not the centre. God does not exist for the sake of man. Man does not exist for his own sake. "Thou hast created all things, and for they pleasure they are and were created." We were made not primarily that we may love God (though we were made for that too) but that God may love us, that we may become objects in which the Divine love may rest "well pleased." To ask that God's love should be content with us as we are is to ask that God should cease to be God: because He is what He is, His love must, in the nature of things, be impeded and repelled, by certain stains in our present character, and because He already loves us He must labour to make us lovable. We cannot even wish, in our better moments, that He could reconcile Himself to our present impurities—no more than the beggar maid could wish that King Cophetua* should be content with her rags and dirt, or a dog, once having learned to love man, could wish that man were such as to tolerate in his house the snapping, verminous, polluting creature of the wild pack. What we would here and now call our "happiness" is not the end God chiefly has in view: but when we are such as He can love without impediment, we shall in fact be happy.

DISCUSSION QUESTIONS

1. "The problem of reconciling human suffering with the existence of a God who loves, is only insoluble so long as we attach a trivial meaning to the word 'love,' " says Lewis. What does he mean? Do you agree with him? How might Dostoyevsky or Hume respond to him?

2. For Lewis, the existence of pain and suffering in the world does not disprove the existence of God; rather, it reveals God's "authoritative love" toward us and our "obedient love" toward him. Do you agree with Lewis's description of the love between God and human beings? Why or why not?

3. How does the relationship between God and humankind proposed by Lewis differ from that of Leibniz? Which position do you prefer, and why?

4. Critically evaluate the following claims made by Lewis: We were made *primarily* "that God may love us," not that we may love him. "To ask that God should be content with us as we are is to ask that God should cease to be God: because He is what He is, His love must, in the nature of things, be impeded and repelled, by certain stains in our present character, and because He already loves us He must labour to make us loveable." Try to formulate these claims into a valid and sound argument.

5. Compare and contrast responses to the problem of evil by Dostoyevsky, Leibniz, Hume, and Lewis. Which do you prefer, and why?

* King Cophetua was an imaginary king from Africa who was very wealthy but disdained all women. One day he saw a beggar girl named Penelophon from his window and fell in love with her. They went on to live a long, happy life together.—Ed.

■ ■ ■ ■ ■ ■ ■ ■ ■ ■ ■ ■ ■ ■ ■ ■ ■
Shadowlands
[Gr. Brit. 1993] 2 hours, 13 minutes
Directed by Sir Richard Attenborough
■ ■ ■ ■ ■ ■ ■ ■ ■ ■ ■ ■ ■ ■ ■ ■ ■

*S*hadowlands recounts the real-life love affair between the British medieval scholar, Christian theologian, and novelist C. S. Lewis (Anthony Hopkins) and an American woman, Joy Gresham (Debra Winger). Lewis, an Oxford College scholar, receives a letter from Gresham, a fan of his writing. After a brief correspondence with Gresham, Lewis begins to have deep feelings for her. Later, Gresham and her son Douglas (Joseph Mazzello) flee an abusive home in America, take up residence in London, and reestablish their relationship with Lewis. While Lewis and Gresham marry in order for Gresham to maintain her British residency, the "in name only" marriage soon becomes a blissful relationship. Sadly, as the love between Lewis and Gresham grows stronger with each passing day, Gresham begins to suffer from a severe form of cancer, which doctors conclude is fatal. Lewis finally professes his love to Gresham, and they have a religious marriage ceremony while she is in the hospital. Gresham's affliction brings Lewis into direct contact with the reality of suffering in a way his previous experiences and learnedness never had. Lewis finds himself struggling with the meaning and significance of suffering in a world controlled by an omnipotent God.

C. S. Lewis is the author of *The Problem of Pain* (1940), one of the readings in this section. It is interesting to note that this book was written years before Gresham's cancer was discovered. Gresham died in 1960 and Lewis in 1963.

DISCUSSION QUESTIONS

1. Do we have to experience severe suffering in our lives in order to truly understand the relationship between God and human suffering? Discuss.

2. In the film, Lewis says, "That was the night a number one bus drove into a column of young royal marine cadets in Chatham and killed 24 of them. Do you remember? The letter asks some simple, but fundamental questions. Where was God on that December 9th? Why didn't he stop it? Isn't God supposed to be good? Isn't he supposed to love us? And does God want us to suffer? What if the answer to that question is yes? Because I'm not sure that God particularly wants us to be happy. I think he want us to be able to love and be loved. He wants us to grow up. I suggest to you that it is because God loves us that He makes us the Gift of suffering. Or to put it another way, pain is God's megaphone to rouse a deaf world. You see, we are like blocks of stone out of which the sculptor carves the forms of men. The blows of his chisel, which hurt us so much, are what make us perfect." Do you agree with Lewis that "it is because God loves us that He makes us the Gift of suffering?" Compare Lewis's view of suffering with the nun's view of suffering in *The Song of Bernadette*.

3. In the film, Lewis says, "Now just because something hurts us doesn't make it more true or more significant. . . . I'm not saying that pain is purposeless or even neutral, but to find meaning in pain, there has to be something else. Pain is a tool. . . ." Do you agree that pain has to have a greater purpose? Or is pain just something to be avoided, as many people believe?

4. In the film, Lewis says, "See, if you love someone, you don't want them to suffer. . . . You want to take their suffering onto yourself. If even I feel like that, then why doesn't God?" Discuss. Compare possible responses by Hume and Mill to this question with responses by Lewis (in the reading selection) and Leibniz.

5. In the film, Lewis argues that pain and suffering are an important part of happiness. At one point, he says, "We think our childish toys bring us all the happiness there is and our nursery is the whole world. But something, something must drive us out of the nursery to the world of others. And that something is suffering." At another point, he says, "The pain now is part of the happiness." Are pain and suffering truly a part of happiness? Explain. Reconcile your position with the fact that our society goes out of its way to help us avoid pain through a variety of means, including medicine and counseling.

JOHN STUART MILL

NATURE

In this selection, John Stuart Mill says that the suffering and evil that are present in the natural world suggest that we entertain the notion of a God who is limited in power. "If we are not obliged to believe animal creation to be the work of a demon," writes Mill, "it is because we need not suppose it to have been made by a Being of infinite power." Nature, as Mill abundantly illustrates, is far from perfect. If nature is the work of a divine being, because it has so many imperfections, it must be the creation of a being that lacks the power to make it perfect. Moreover, nature is not a reliable guide for the right or good conduct of humans. "In sober truth," says Mill, "nearly all the things which men are hanged or imprisoned for doing to one another, are nature's everyday performances." Finally, if we believe that all the acts of nature are willful acts of God, then any action by us to overcome an act of nature, such as relieving a toothache or draining a pestilential marsh, "ought to be accounted impious." Since we don't consider these actions to be sinful or impious, Mill concludes that nature is something that at times needs to be overcome. Humans need to improve the world and have the power to do it. In effect, the suffering and evil present in nature do not necessarily disprove God's existence; rather, they call for us to regard God as less than omnipotent and to assist in attaining perfection in the world he created.

John Stuart Mill (1806–73), a British philosopher, was educated by his father, the Scottish philosopher James Mill. He began studying Greek at the age of three and Latin at the age of eight. His writings include *A System of Logic* (1843), *Principles of Political Economy* (1848), *On Liberty* (1859), *Utilitarianism* (1863), *Auguste Comte and Positivism* (1865), *The Subjection of Women* (1869), *Autobiography* (1873), and the posthumously published *Three Essays on Religion* (1874). The following selection is from his essay "On Nature," which he finished in 1858 but which was published posthumously in *Three Essays*. Mill feared that publication of this and other essays on religion would alienate his readers by not entirely condemning religion and leaving open the possibility of a rational basis for religion and its tenets.

No one, indeed, asserts it to be the intention of the Creator that the spontaneous order of the creation should not be altered, or even that it should not be altered in any new way. But there still exists a vague notion that though it is very proper to control this or the other natural phenomenon, the general scheme of nature is a model for us to imitate: that with more or less liberty in details, we should on the whole be guided by the spirit and general conception of nature's own ways: that they are God's work, and as such perfect; that man cannot rival their unapproachable excellence, and can best show his skill and piety by attempting, in however imperfect a way, to reproduce their likeness; and that if not the whole, yet some particular parts of the spontaneous order of nature, selected according to the speaker's predilections, are in a peculiar sense, manifestations of the Creator's will; a sort of finger posts pointing out the direction which things in general, and therefore our voluntary actions, are intended to take. Feelings of this sort, though repressed on ordinary occasions by the contrary current of life, are ready to break out whenever custom is silent, and the native promptings of the mind have nothing opposed to them but reason: and appeals are continually made to them by rhetoricians, with the effect, if not of convincing opponents, at least of making those who already hold the opinion which the rhetorician desires to recommend, better satisfied with it. For in the present day it probably seldom happens that any one is persuaded to approve any course of action because it appears to him to bear an analogy to the divine government of the world, though the argument tells on him with great force, and is felt by him to be a great support, in behalf of anything which he is already inclined to approve. . . .

For, how stands the fact? That next to the greatness of these cosmic forces, the quality which most forcibly strikes every one who does not avert his eyes from it, is their perfect and absolute recklessness. They go straight to their end, without regarding what or whom they crush on the road. Optimists, in their attempts to prove that "whatever is, is right?" are obliged to maintain, not that Nature ever turns one step from her path to avoid trampling us into destruction, but that it would be very unreasonable in us to expect that she should. Pope's* "Shall gravitation cease when you go by?" may be a just rebuke to any one who should be so silly as to expect common human morality from nature. But if the question were between two men, instead of between a man and a natural phenomenon, that triumphant apostrophe would be thought a rare piece of impudence. A man who should persist in hurling stones or firing cannon when another man "goes by," and having killed him should urge a similar plea in exculpation, would very deservedly be found guilty of murder.

In sober truth, nearly all the things which men are hanged or imprisoned for doing to one another, are nature's every day performances. Killing, the most criminal act recognized by human laws, Nature does once to every being that lives; and in a large proportion of cases, after protracted tortures such as only the greatest monsters whom we read of ever purposely inflicted on their living fellow-creatures. If, by an arbitrary reservation, we refuse to account anything murder but what abridges a certain term supposed to be allotted to human life, nature also does this to all but a small percentage of lives, and does it in all the modes, violent or insidious, in which the worst human beings take the lives of one another. Nature impales men, breaks them as if on the wheel, casts them to be devoured by wild beasts, burns them to death, crushes them with stones like the first christian martyr, starves them with hunger, freezes them with cold, poisons them by the quick or slow venom of her exhalations, and has hundreds of other hideous deaths in reserve, such as the ingenious cruelty of a Nabis† or a Domitian‡ never surpassed. All this, Nature does with the most supercilious disregard both of mercy and of justice, emptying her shafts upon the best and noblest indifferently with the meanest and worst; upon those who are engaged in the highest and worthiest enterprises, and often as the direct consequence of the noblest acts; and it might almost be imagined as a punishment for them. She mows down those on whose existence hangs the well-being of a whole people, perhaps the prospects of the human race for generations to come, with as little compunction as those whose death is a relief to themselves, or a blessing to those under their noxious influence. Such are Nature's dealings with life. Even when she does not intend to kill, she inflicts the same tortures in apparent wantonness. In the clumsy provision which she has made for that perpetual renewal of animal life, rendered necessary by the prompt termination she puts to it in every individual instance, no human being ever comes into the world but another human being is literally stretched on the rack for hours or days, not unfrequently issuing in death. Next to taking life (equal to it according to a high authority) is taking the means by which we live; and Nature does this too on the largest scale and with the most callous indifference. A single hurricane destroys the hopes of a season; a flight of locusts, or an inundation, desolates a district; a trifling chemical change in an edible root, starves a million of people. The waves of the sea, like banditti seize and appropriate the wealth of the rich and the little all of the poor with the same accompaniments of stripping, wounding, and killing as their human antitypes. Everything in short, which the worst men commit either against life or property is perpetrated on a large scale by natural agents. Nature has Noyades more fatal than those of Carrier,** her explosions of fire damp are as destructive as human artillery; her

---

* Alexander Pope (1688–1744), English Poet, satirist, and essayist, whose works include *An Essay in Criticism* (1711) and *The Rape of the Lock* (1712). This quote is from his *An Essay on Man* (1733–34; epistle iv, line 128).—Ed.

† Nabis was a celebrated tyrant of Lacedaemon, known for his excessive acts of cruelty and oppression. He was accused of murdering the young Spartan king, Pelops, whose crown Nabis seized after his death. Nabis was murdered in 192 B.C.E.—Ed.

‡ Domitian was Roman emperor 51–96 C.E., known for his cruelty. He succeeded his brother, Titus, whom some say was murdered by poisoning at the hand of Domitian. Upon his assassination in 96 C.E. the Senate voted to forgo an honorary funeral for Domitian, and his body was left in the open air.—Ed.

** Jean Baptiste Carrier (1756–94) was a French revolutionist and terrorist. In 1793, he had large numbers of prisoners executed by sending them to sail aboard ships with trapdoors for bottoms and then sinking the ships in the Loire. The process of execution became known as the *Noyades* (drowning) of Nantes.—Ed.

plague and cholera far surpass the poison cups of the Borgias.* Even the love of "order" which is thought to be a following of the ways of Nature, is in fact a contradiction of them. All which people are accustomed to deprecate as "disorder" and its consequences, is precisely a counterpart of Nature's ways. Anarchy and the Reign of Terror are overmatched in injustice, ruin, and death, by a hurricane and a pestilence.

But, it is said, all these things are for wise and good ends. On this I must first remark that whether they are so or not, is altogether beside the point. Supposing it true that contrary to appearances these horrors when perpetrated by Nature, promote good ends, still as no one believes that good ends would be promoted by our following the example, the course of Nature cannot be a proper model for us to imitate. Either it is right that we should kill because nature kills; torture because nature tortures; ruin and devastate because nature does the like; or we ought not to consider at all what nature does, but what it is good to do. If there is such a thing as a *reductio ad absurdum*, this surely amounts to one. If it is a sufficient reason for doing one thing, that nature does it, why not another thing? If not all things, why anything? The physical government of the world being full of things which when done by men are deemed the greatest enormities, it cannot be religious or moral in us to guide our actions by the analogy of the course of nature. This proposition remains true, whatever occult quality of producing good may reside in those facts of nature which to our perceptions are most noxious, and which no one considers it other than a crime to produce artificially.

But, in reality, no one consistently believes in any such occult quality. The phrases which ascribe perfection to the course of nature can only be considered as the exaggerations of poetic or devotional feeling, not intended to stand the test of a sober examination. No one, either religious or irreligious, believes that the hurtful agencies of nature, considered as a whole, promote good purposes, in any other way than by inciting human rational creatures to rise up and struggle against them. If we believed that those agencies were appointed by a benevolent Providence as the means of accomplishing wise purposes which could not be compassed if they did not exist, then everything done by mankind which tends to chain up these natural agencies or to restrict their mischievous operation, from draining a pestilential marsh down to curing the toothache, or putting up an umbrella, ought to be accounted impious; which assuredly nobody does account them, notwithstanding an undercurrent of sentiment setting in that direction which is occasionally perceptible. On the contrary, the improvements on which the civilized part of mankind most pride themselves, consist in more successfully warding off those natural calamities which if we really believed what most people profess to believe, we should cherish as medicines provided for our earthly state by infinite wisdom. Inasmuch too as each generation greatly surpasses its predecessors in the amount of natural evil which it succeeds in averting, our condition, if the theory were true, ought by this time to have become a terrible manifestation of some tremendous calamity, against which the physical evils we have learnt to overmaster, had previously operated as a preservative. Any one, however, who acted as if he supposed this to be the case, would be more likely, I think, to be confined as a lunatic, than reverenced as a saint. . . .

This brief survey is amply sufficient to prove that the duty of man is the same in respect to his own nature as in respect to the nature of all other things, namely not to follow but to amend it. . . .

With regard to this particular hypothesis, that all natural impulses, all propensities sufficiently universal and sufficiently spontaneous to be capable of passing for instincts, must exist for good ends, and ought to be only regulated, not

---

* The Borgias were an Italian family of Spanish origin in Renaissance Italy known for their brilliance and patronage of the arts as well as their evilness and treachery. Two of the Borgias became popes: Alfonso Borgia became Pope Callistus III in 1455; and Alphonso's nephew, Rodrigo, became Pope Alexander VI in 1492. One of the most notorious members of the family, Cesare Borgia (1476–1507), murdered his brother Juan as well as his sister Lucrezia's second husband, Alfonso of Aragon. Cesare tried but failed to establish a hereditary monarchy in central Italy. Machiavelli modeled his ideal statesman after Cesare, and Leonardo da Vinci invented war machines for him. Caseare was killed in battle in 1507.—Ed.

repressed; this is of course true of the majority of them, for the species could not have continued to exist unless most of its inclinations had been directed to things needful or useful for its preservation. But unless the instincts can be reduced to a very small number indeed, it must be allowed that we have also bad instincts which it should be the aim of education not simply to regulate but to extirpate, or rather (what can be done even to an instinct) to starve them by disuse. Those who are inclined to multiply the number of instincts, usually include among them one which they call destructiveness: an instinct to destroy for destruction's sake. I can conceive no good reason for preserving this, no more than another propensity which if not an instinct is very like one, what has been called the instinct of domination; a delight in exercising despotism, in holding other beings in subjection to our will. The man who takes pleasure in the mere exertion of authority, apart from the purpose for which it is to be employed, is the last person in whose hands one would willingly entrust it. Again, there are persons who are cruel by character, or, as the phrase is, naturally cruel; who have a real pleasure in inflicting, or seeing the infliction of pain. This kind of cruelty is not mere hardheartedness, absence of pity or remorse; it is a positive thing; a particular kind of voluptuous excitement. The East, and Southern Europe, have afforded, and probably still afford, abundant examples of this hateful propensity. I suppose it will be granted that this is not one of the natural inclinations which it would be wrong to suppress. The only question would be whether it is not a duty to suppress the man himself along with it.

But even if it were true that every one of the elementary impulses of human nature has its good side, and may by a sufficient amount of artificial training be made more useful than hurtful; how little would this amount to, when it must in any case be admitted that without such training all of them, even those which are necessary to our preservation, would fill the world with misery, making human life an exaggerated likeness of the odious scene of violence and tyranny which is exhibited by the rest of the animal kingdom, except in so far as tamed and disciplined by man. There, indeed, those who flatter themselves with the notion of reading the purposes of the Creator in his works, ought in consistency to have seen grounds for inferences from which they have shrunk. If there are any marks at all of special design in creation, one of the things most evidently designed is that a large proportion of all animals should pass their existence in tormenting and devouring other animals. They have been lavishly fitted out with the instruments necessary for that purpose; their strongest instincts impel them to it, and many of them seem to have been constructed incapable of supporting themselves by any other food. If a tenth part of the pains which have been expended in finding benevolent adaptations in all nature, had been employed in collecting evidence to blacken the character of the Creator, what scope for comment would not have been found in the entire existence of the lower animals, divided, with scarcely an exception, into devourers and devoured, and a prey to a thousand ills from which they are denied the faculties necessary for protecting themselves. If we are not obliged to believe the animal creation to be the work of a demon, it is because we need not suppose it to have been made by a Being of infinite power. But if limitation of the Creator's will as revealed in nature, were applied as a rule of action in this case, the most atrocious enormities of the worst men would be more than justified by the apparent intention of Providence that throughout all animated nature the strong should prey upon the weak.

DISCUSSION QUESTIONS

1. Why, according to Mill, shouldn't we simply follow nature? Formulate his argument, and discuss why it is, as he calls it, a *"reductio ad absurdum."*

2. Mill and Leibniz both discuss the existence of evil and imperfection in the world. How and why do they reach different conclusions about the relationship of evil and imperfection to God? Whose arguments do you find more convincing, and why?

3. Mill's outlook on nature is not very positive. "Nature," according to Mill, "impales men, breaks them as if on the wheel, casts them to be devoured by wild beasts, burns them to

death, crushes them like stones like the first christian martyr, starves them with hunger . . . with the most supercilious disregard both of mercy and justice." Do you agree with this account of nature?

4. Discuss the following argument: If we believe that all of the acts of nature are willful acts of God, then any action by us to overcome an act of nature, such as relieving a toothache or draining a pestilential marsh, "ought to be accounted impious." But we don't, so Mill concludes that nature is something that at times needs to be overcome.

5. Mill is careful not to rule out the potential existence of God on the basis of evil in nature, yet he never fully asserts the existence of God either. Discuss this approach. Do you find it satisfactory? Why or why not? Why do you think Mill takes this approach?

The Last Temptation of Christ
[USA 1988] 2 hours, 43 minutes
Directed by Martin Scorsese

*T*he Last Temptation of Christ is a vision of the final days of Jesus of Nazareth. The film is adapted from Nikos Kazantzakis's novel of the same name. Jesus (Willem Dafoe) is portrayed as an ordinary Israelite tormented by divine doubt, human desires, and the voice of God. Jesus says, "How can I be the Messiah? When those people were torturing Magdalene, I wanted to kill them! And then I open my mouth and out comes the word 'love.'" Up to the time of his crucifixion, Jesus is depicted as undergoing an arduous journey to understand the meaning of his own existence and the conflict between human aspiration and divine destiny. While dying on the cross, Jesus is tempted one last time by an angel who informs him that he has already done his part to save humanity. The angel tells Jesus that he does not need to die on the cross in fulfillment of his divine destiny, but rather can live out the remainder of his life as a mortal man. Jesus accepts this last temptation of a mortal life and death. Jesus says, "I live like a man now. I work, eat, have children. I enjoy my life. For the first time, I'm enjoying it." As a result, however, humanity's sins remain unforgiven and death remains unconquered. The world is left in a state of damnation, and Jesus gradually comes to comprehend the consequences of his decision. When he realizes his error, he finds himself shunned by his now elderly apostles on his deathbed. He is forced to ask God for clemency and pleads for the opportunity to rectify his error. "Father—will you listen to me?" asks Jesus. "Are you still there? Will you listen to a selfish, unfaithful son? I fought you when you called. I resisted. I thought I knew more. I didn't want to be your son. Can you forgive me? I didn't fight hard enough. Father, give me your hand. I want to bring salvation. Father take me back . . . I want to pay the price. I want to be crucified. . . ." God grants his wish, and Jesus is immediately flashed back to his crucifixion. He therefore fulfills his destiny by dying on the cross for the sins of mankind. In the film, it is unclear if the sequence of events brought on by the acceptance of the last temptation is a dream or reality. The depiction of Jesus of Nazareth as a tormented ordinary Israelite who accepted the last temptation led to widespread protests against and banning of the film.

DISCUSSION QUESTIONS

1. Is the depiction of suffering and evil in this film intended to disprove the existence of God? Why or why not?

2. John Stuart Mill says that the suffering and evil that are present in the natural world suggest that we entertain the notion of a God who is limited in power. Is this movie suggesting that we draw a similar conclusion? Does the point that Jesus had to suffer for the sins of mankind suggest a limitation in the nature of God?

3. In this film, God is depicted as bringing suffering to both Mary and Jesus. In accepting the last temptation, Jesus is in effect rejecting the suffering that God has chosen for him. How is Jesus's rejection of the suffering chosen for him by God similar to Ivan Karamozov's rejection of the world God has created because of the existence of suffering and evil in that world? How is it different?

4. For C. S. Lewis, the existence of pain and suffering in the world reveals God's "authoritative love" toward us and our "obedient love" toward him. By overcoming stains in our present character, says Lewis, we "become objects in which the Divine love may rest 'well pleased.' " Do you think that Jesus's overcoming "stains" in his human character such as divine doubt and human desire helped him to become an object, as Lewis says, "in which the Divine love may rest 'well pleased'"? Does Lewis's account lead us to believe that first accepting but then renouncing the last temptation was necessary in order for Jesus to please God, his father? Why or why not?

5. The depiction of Jesus of Nazareth as a tormented, ordinary Israelite who accepted the last temptation led to widespread protests against and banning of the film. Do you think that this film should be banned? Why or why not?

ARTHUR C. CLARKE

THE STAR

Arthur C. Clarke's short story asks whether there is an evil so great in the world that it would cause even the most faithful believer in God to question his or her belief. His main character, a pious Jesuit, is the chief astrophysicist on a mission to examine the history and identity of a distant star. He discovers that this distant star was the cause of the destruction of "a civilization which in many ways must have been superior to our own." The Jesuit says, "This I could have accepted, hard though it is to look upon whole worlds and peoples thrown into the furnace." "But there comes a point when even the deepest faith must falter," he continues, "and now, as I look at my calculations, I know I have reached that point at last." His calculations reveal that it is the star of Bethlehem—that star that is said to have led the three wise men to the baby Jesus of Nazareth. Even the faith of a Jesuit, a member of the Society of Jesus, who is supposed to be prepared for any task *ad majorem Dei gloriam* (to the greater glory of God), would falter under these conditions, says Clarke. One of the philosophical points of the story seems to be that while the mere existence of evil does not alter the faith of the true believer, there are some particular evils that will. Therefore, our faith in God always has the possibility of faltering when we are confronted with evil.

Arthur C. Clarke (1917–) is a prolific English science-fiction writer. In his youth, he built a telescope and mapped the moon with it. He collaborated with director Stanley Kubrick on *2001: A Space Odyssey* (1968), which was based on his short story "The Sentinel" (1951). He developed the story into a novel in 1968, which now has two sequels: *2010: Odyssey Two* (1982; film, 1984) and *2061: Odyssey Three* (1987). "The Star" was first published in 1955.

It is three thousand light-years to the Vatican. Once I believed that space could have no power over Faith. Just as I believed that the heavens declared the glory of God's handiwork. Now I have seen that handiwork, and my faith is sorely troubled.

I stare at the crucifix that hangs on the cabin wall above the Mark VI computer, and for the first time in my life I wonder if it is no more than an empty symbol.

I have told no one yet, but the truth cannot be concealed. The data are there for anyone to read, recorded on the countless miles of magnetic tape and the thousands of photographs we are carrying back to Earth. Other scientists can interpret them as easily as I can—more easily, in all probability. I am not one who would condone that tampering with the Truth which often gave my Order a bad name in the olden days.

The crew is already sufficiently depressed, I wonder how they will take this ultimate irony. Few of them have any religious faith, yet they will not relish using this final weapon in their campaign against me—that private, good-natured but fundamentally serious war which lasted all the way from Earth. It amused them to have a Jesuit as a chief astrophysicist: Dr. Chandler, for instance, could never get over it (why are medical men such notorious atheists?). Sometimes he would meet me on the observation deck, where the lights are always low so that the stars shine with undiminished glory. He would come up to me in the gloom and stand staring out of the great oval port, while the heavens crawled slowly round us as the ship turned end over end with the residual spin we had never bothered to correct.

"Well, Father," he would say at last. "It goes on forever and forever, and perhaps *Something* made it. But how you can believe that Something has a special interest in us and our miserable little world—that just beats me." Then the argument would start, while the stars and nebulae would swing around us in silent, endless arcs beyond the flawlessly clear plastic of the observation port.

It was, I think, the apparent incongruity of my position which . . . yes, *amused* . . . the crew. In vain I would point to my three papers in the *Astrophysical Journal*, my five in the *Monthly Notices of the Royal Astronomical Society*. I would remind them that our Order has long been famous for its scientific works. We may be few now, but ever since the eighteenth century we have made contributions to astronomy and geophysics out of all proportions to our numbers.

Will my report on the Phoenix Nebula end our thousand years of history? It will end, I fear, much more than that.

I do not know who gave the Nebula its name, which seems to me a very bad one. If it contains a prophecy, it is one which cannot be verified for several thousand million years. Even the word nebula is misleading: this is a far smaller object than those stupendous clouds of mist—which are scattered throughout the length of the Milky Way. On the cosmic scale, indeed, the Phoenix Nebula is a tiny thing—a tenuous shell of gas surrounding a single star.

Or what is left of a star . . .

The Rubens engraving of Loyola seems to mock me as it hangs there above the spectrophotometer tracings. What would *you*, Father, have made of this knowledge that has come into my keeping, so far from the little world that was all the universe you knew? Would your faith have risen to the challenge as mine has failed to do?

You gaze into the distance, Father, but I have traveled a distance beyond any that you could have imagined when you founded our Order a thousand years ago. No other survey ship has been so far from Earth: we are at the very frontiers of the explored universe. We set out to reach the Phoenix Nebula, we succeeded, and we are homeward bound with our burden of knowledge. I wish I could lift that burden from my shoulders, but I call to you in vain across the centuries and the light-years that lie between us.

On the book you are holding the words are plain to read. AD MAIOREM DEI GLORIAM the message runs, but it is a message I can no longer believe. Would you still believe it, if you could see what we have found?

We knew, of course, what the Phoenix Nebula was. Every year, in *our* galaxy alone, more than a hundred stars explode, blazing for a few hours or days with thousands of times their normal brilliance before they sink back into death and obscurity. Such are the ordinary novae—the common place disasters of the universe. I have recorded the spectrograms and light-curves of dozens, since I started working at the lunar observatory.

But three or four times in every thousand years occurs something beside which even a nova pales into total insignificance.

When a star becomes a *supernova*, it may for a little while outshine all the massed suns of the galaxy. The Chinese astronomers watched this happen in 1054 A.D., not knowing what it was they saw. Five centuries later, in 1572, a supernova blazed in Cassiopeia so brilliantly that it was visible in the daylight sky. There have been three more in the thousand years that have passed since then.

Our mission was to visit the remnants of such a catastrophe, to reconstruct the events that led up to it, and, if possible, to learn its cause. We came slowly in through the concentric shells of gas that had been blasted out six thousand years before, yet were expanding still. They were immensely hot, radiating still with a fierce violet light, but far too tenuous to do us any damage. When the star had exploded, its outer layers had been driven upwards with such speed that they had escaped completely from its gravitational field. Now they formed a hollow shell large enough to engulf a thousand solar systems, and at this center burned the tiny, fantastic object which the star had now become—a white dwarf, smaller than the Earth yet weighing a million times as much.

The glowing gas shells were all around us, banishing the normal night of interstellar space. We were flying into the center of a cosmic bomb that had detonated millennia ago and those incandescent fragments were still hurtling apart. The immense scale of the explosion, and the fact that the debris already covered a volume of space many billions of miles across robbed the scene of any visible movement. It would take decades before the unaided eye could detect any motion in these tortured wisps and eddies of gas, yet the sense of turbulent expansion was overwhelming.

We had checked our primary drive hours before, and were drifting slowly towards the fierce little star ahead. Once it had been a sun like our own, but it had squandered in a few hours the energy that should have kept it shining for a million years. Now it was a shrunken miser, hoarding its resources as if trying to make amends for its prodigal youth.

No one seriously expected to find planets. If there had been any before the explosion, they would have been boiled into puffs of vapor, and their substance lost in the greater wreckage of the star itself. But we made the automatic search, as always when approaching an unknown sun, and presently we found a single small world circling the star at immense distance. It must have been the Pluto of this vanished solar system, orbiting on the frontiers of the night. Too far from the central sun ever to have known life, its remoteness had saved it from the fate of all its lost companions.

The passing fires had seared its rocks and burnt away the mantle of frozen gas that must have covered it in the days before the disaster. We landed, and we found the Vault.

Its builders had made sure that we should. The monolite marker that stood above the entrance was now a fused stump, but even the first long-range photographs told us that here was the work of intelligence. A little later we detected the continent's wide pattern of radioactivity that had been buried in the rock. Even if the pylon above the Vault had been destroyed, this would have remained, an immovable and all but eternal beacon calling to the stars. Our ship fell towards this gigantic bull's-eye like an arrow into its target.

The pylon must have been a mile high when it was built, but now it looked like a candle that had melted down into a puddle of wax. It took us a week to drill through the fused rock, since we did not have the proper tools for a task like this. We were astronomers, not archaeologists, but we could improvise. Our original program was forgotten: this lonely monument, reared at such labor at the greatest possible distance from the doomed sun, could have only one meaning. A civilization which knew it was about to die had made its last bid for immortality.

It will take us generations to examine all the treasures that were placed in the Vault. *They* had plenty of time to prepare, for their sun must have given its first warnings many years before the final detonation. Everything that they wished to preserve, all the fruits of their genius, they brought here to this distant world in the days before the end, hoping that some other race would find them and that they would not be utterly forgotten.

If only they had a little more time! They could travel freely enough between the planets of their own sun, but they had not yet learned to cross the interstellar gulfs, and the nearest solar system was a hundred light-years away.

Even if they had not been so disturbingly human as their sculpture shows, we could not have helped admiring them and grieving for their fate. The thousands of visual records and the machines for projecting them, together with elaborate pictorial instructions from which it will not be difficult to learn their written language. We have examined many of these records, and brought to life for the first time in six thousand years the warmth and beauty of a civilization which in many ways must have been superior to our own. Perhaps they only showed us the best, and one can hardly blame them. But their worlds were very lovely, and their cities were built with a grace that matches anything of ours. We have watched them at work and play and listened to their musical speech sounding across the centuries. One scene is still before my eyes—a group of children on a beach of strange blue sand, playing in the waves as children play on Earth.

And sinking into the sea, still warm and friendly and life giving, is the sun that will soon turn traitor and obliterate all this innocent happiness.

Perhaps if we had not been so far from home and so vulnerable to loneliness, we should not have been so deeply moved. Many of us had seen the ruins of ancient civilizations on other worlds, but they had never affected us so profoundly.

This tragedy was unique. It was one thing for a race to fail and die, as nations and cultures have done on Earth. But to be destroyed so completely in the full flower of its achievement, leaving no survivors—how could that be reconciled with the mercy of God?

My colleagues have asked me that, and I have given what answers I can. Perhaps you could have done better, Father Loyola, but I have found nothing in the *Exercitia Spiritualia* that helps me here. They were not an evil people: I do not know what gods they worshipped, if indeed they worshipped any. But I have looked back at them across the centuries, and have watched while the loveliness they used their last strength to preserve

was brought forth again into the light of their shrunken sun.

I know the answers that my colleagues will give when they get back to Earth. They will say that the universe has no purpose and no plan, that since a hundred suns explode every year in our galaxy, at this very moment some race is dying in the depths of space. Whether that race had done good or evil during its lifetime will make no difference in the end: there is no divine justice, *for there is no God*.

Yet, of course, what we have seen proves nothing of the sort. Anyone who argues thus is being swayed by emotion, not logic. God has no need to justify His actions to man. He who built the universe can destroy it when He chooses. It is arrogance—it is perilously near blasphemy—for us to say what He may or may not do.

This I could have accepted, hard though it is to look upon whole worlds and peoples thrown into the furnace. But there comes a point when even the deepest faith must falter, and now, as I look at my calculations, I know I have reached that point at last.

We could not tell, before we reached the nebula, how long ago the explosion took place. Now, from the astronomical evidence and the record in the rocks of that one surviving planet, I have been able to date it very exactly. I know in what year the light of this colossal conflagration reached Earth. I know how brilliantly the supernova whose corpse now dwindles behind our speeding ship once shone in terrestrial skies. I know how it must have blazed low in the East before sunrise, like a beacon in that Oriental dawn. There can be no reasonable doubt: the ancient mystery is solved at last. Yet—O God, there were so many stars you *could* have used.

What was the need to give these people to the fire, that the symbol of their passing might shine above Bethlehem?

DISCUSSION QUESTIONS

1. Clarke's story raises the possibility that there is a suffering or evil that would shake the faith of even the most devout believer. Do you agree with him? If you believe in God, what, if any, evil event might cause your faith in God to falter?

2. How would Leibniz respond to Clarke's story? Is Leibniz's response preferable to that of the Jesuit astrophysicist? Why or why not?

3. We might say that the philosophical point of the story seems to be that while the mere existence of evil does not alter the faith of the true believer, there are some particular evils that will. Therefore, faith in God always has the possibility of faltering. Do you agree with this assessment? Are there other possible philosophical points to this story? If so, explain.

4. Whose example do you think is a better one to use in a consideration of the problem of evil: Dostoyevsky's boy torn to pieces by dogs or Clarke's dying star? Why?

5. Do the stories of Dostoyevsky and Clarke get you to think more deeply and subtly about the problem of evil than the arguments of Leibniz, Hume, and Mill? Why or why not?

Night and Fog
[France 1955] 65 minutes
Directed by Alain Resnais

An estimated 9 million people died at the hands of their Nazi oppressors during the Holocaust of World War II. In his 1955 documentary *Night and Fog*, director Alain Resnais reveals the atrocities of the Holocaust. By contrasting 1955 images of abandoned concentration camps with 1944 footage of the same death camps, Resnais successfully links the anguish of the past to the ghosts still present eleven years later.

The pain and suffering experienced by the victims of the Holocaust, both living and deceased, and the evil unleashed by their Nazi oppressors, are overwhelming. For many, the Holocaust represents a time in history when God seemed to have abandoned humanity.

The following narration accompanies images from the concentration camps: "And who does know anything? Is it in vain that we in our turn try to remember. What remains of the reality of these camps—despised by those who made them, incomprehensible to those who suffered here? These wooden barracks, these beds where three people slept, these burrows where people hid, where they furtively ate, and where sleep itself was perilous. No description, no picture can restore their true dimension: endless, uninterrupted fear. We would need the mattress where scraps of food were hidden, the blanket that was fought over, the shouts and curses, the orders repeated in every tongue, the sudden appearance of the SS, seized with a desire for a spot check or for a practical joke. Of this brick dormitory, of these threatened sleepers, we can only show you the shell, the shadow. This is all that is left us to evoke a night shattered by screams, by inspections, by lice, a night of chattering teeth. Get to sleep quickly. Many are too weak to defend their ration against thieves. TheFy wait for the mud or snow to take them. At last to stretch out somewhere, anywhere, and at least have one's death to oneself. Yet man has incredible powers of resistance. When the body is worn out with fatigue, the mind goes on working. Hands covered with bandages go on working. They make spoons, marionettes, which they carefully hide. They can think of God. Nothing distinguished the gas chamber from an ordinary block. Inside, what looked like a shower room welcomed the newcomers. Their hosts closed the doors. They watched. The only sign—but you have to know it—is this ceiling, dug into by fingernails. Even the concrete was torn. The crematorium is no longer in use. The devices of the Nazis are out of date. Nine million dead haunt this landscape. Who is on the lookout from this strange tower to warn us of the coming of new executioners? Are their faces really different from our own? Somewhere among us, there are lucky Kapos, reinstated officers, and unknown informers. There are those who refused to believe this, or believed it only from time to time. And there are those of us who sincerely look upon the ruins today, as if the old concentration camp monster were dead and buried beneath them. Those who pretend to take hope again as the image fades, as though there were a cure for the plague of these camps. Those of us who pretend to believe that all this happened only once, at a certain time and in a certain place, and those who refuse to see, who do not hear the cry to the end of time."

DISCUSSION QUESTIONS

1. Clarke's story raised the possibility that there is a suffering and evil that would shake the faith of even the most devout believer. Is the Holocaust such an event? Discuss.
2. Do historical events like the Holocaust significantly challenge our attempt to reconcile the existence of suffering and evil in the world with the existence of God? Discuss.
3. What does the narrator mean when he says, "Those of us who pretend to believe that all this happened only once, at a certain time and in a certain place, and those who refuse to see, who do not hear the cry to the end of time"? Does the kind of suffering that was brought about by the Holocaust go on "until the end of time"?
4. Should we consider catastrophic suffering like that brought about by the Holocaust differently than we regard less extreme forms of suffering? Or should all suffering be considered equally? Does the existence of catastrophic suffering like that brought about by the Holocaust change how we formulate the problem of evil?
5. How should we respond to those who believe that the Holocaust represents a time in history when God seemed to have abandoned humanity? Discuss.
6. Do the narrator's comments reveal his position on the place of God in relationship to the events of the Holocaust? Does the combination of the visual images in the film and the narrative reveal the same position as the narrative alone or the images alone? Discuss.

1.3   IS FAITH COMPATIBLE WITH REASON?

THE BOOK OF JOB

The book of Job tells the story of an upright, prosperous man who loses all of his possessions, his children, and his health, yet refuses to curse God. In broader terms, it explores the meaning of undeserved suffering before a silent and inactive God. What judgment is to be drawn about God's purpose and character in view of Job's undeserved suffering? Job believes that the righteous will be rewarded and the wicked punished, but his experiences call this into question. His friends, who still believe in a calculus of retribution, try to convince him to confess to wickedness. But Job cannot find this wickedness in his conscience. So, Job entertains some different beliefs about God: that God is not a benevolent creator, compassionate father, or just covenanter, but rather an insensitive brute. Job even sometimes tries to imagine God to be on his side. During all of his questioning and doubt concerning the character and purpose of God, he does not turn his back on God; Job addresses his questions directly to God. In chapter 38, God breaks his silence with Job and addresses him directly. In chapter 42, the final chapter of the book, Job repents to God, and God restores to Job "twice as much as he had before."

The book of Job is a work of Hebrew literature and the eighteenth book of the Old Testament. While the date and place of composition and the identity of its author are debated, it is generally thought to have been composed between the seventh and fourth centuries B.C.E. The Hebrew name "Job" is said by some to mean "hated or persecuted one," by others to mean "where is the divine father?" and still others to mean "where is the divine father of the hated or persecuted one?" The following are selections from the book of Job.

CHAPTER 1

There was a man in the land of Uz, whose name was Job; and that man was perfect and upright, and one that feared God, and eschewed evil.

And there were born unto him seven sons and three daughters.

His substance also was seven thousand sheep, and three thousand camels, and five hundred yoke of oxen, and five hundred she-asses, and a very great household; so that this man was the greatest of all the men of the east.

And his sons went and feasted in their houses, every one his day; and sent and called for their three sisters to eat and to drink with them.

And it was so, when the days of their feasting were gone about, that Job sent and sanctified them, and rose up early in the morning, and offered burnt offerings according to the number of them all: for Job said, It may be that my sons have sinned, and cursed God in their hearts. Thus did Job continually.

Now there was a day when the sons of God came to present themselves before the Lord, and Satan came also among them.

And the Lord said unto Satan, Whence comest thou? Then Satan answered the Lord, and said, From going to and fro in the earth, and from walking up and down in it.

And the Lord said unto Satan, Hast thou considered my servant Job, that there is none like him in the earth, a perfect and an upright man, one that feareth God, and escheweth evil?

Then Satan answered the Lord, and said, Doth Job fear God for nought?

Hast not thou made an hedge about him, and about his house, and about all that he hath on every side? thou hast blessed the work of his hands, and his substance is increased in the land.

But put forth thine hand now, and touch all that he hath, and he will curse thee to thy face.

And the Lord said unto Satan, Behold, all that he hath is in thy power; only upon himself put not forth thine hand. So Satan went forth from the presence of the Lord.

And there was a day when his sons and his daughters were eating and drinking wine in their eldest brother's house:

And there came a messenger unto Job, and said, The oxen were plowing, and the asses feeding beside them:

And the Sabeans fell upon them, and took them away; yea, they have slain the servants with the edge of the sword; and I only am escaped alone to tell thee.

While he was yet speaking, there came also another, and said, The fire of God is fallen from heaven, and hath burned up the sheep, and the servants, and consumed them; and I only am escaped alone to tell thee.

While he was yet speaking, there came also another, and said, The Chaldeans made out three bands, and fell upon the camels, and have carried them away, yea, and slain the servants with the edge of the sword; and I only am escaped alone to tell thee.

While he was yet speaking, there came also another, and said, Thy sons and thy daughters were eating and drinking wine in their eldest brother's house:

And, behold, there came a great wind from the wilderness, and smote the four corners of the house, and it fell upon the young men, and they are dead; and I only am escaped alone to tell thee.

Then Job arose, and rent his mantle, and shaved his head, and fell down upon the ground, and worshiped,

CHAPTER 2

Again there was a day when the sons of God came to present themselves before the Lord, and Satan came also among them to present himself before the Lord.

And the Lord said unto Satan, From whence comest thou? And Satan answered the Lord, and said, From going to and fro in the earth, and from walking up and down in it.

And the Lord said unto Satan, Hast thou considered my servant Job, that there is none like him in the earth, a perfect and an upright man, one that feareth God, and escheweth evil? and still he holdeth fast his integrity, although thou movedst me against him, to destroy him without cause.

And Satan answered the Lord, and said, Skin for skin, yea, all that a man hath will he give for his life.

But put forth thine hand now, and touch his bone and his flesh, and he will curse thee to thy face.

And the Lord said unto Satan, Behold, he is in thine hand; but save his life.

So went Satan forth from the presence of the Lord, and smote Job with sore boils from the sole of his foot unto his crown.

CHAPTER 3

After this opened Job his mouth, and cursed his day.

And Job spake, and said,

Let the day perish wherein I was born, and the night in which it was said, There is a man child conceived.

Let that day be darkness; let not God regard it from above, neither let the light shine upon it.

Let darkness and the shadow of death stain it; let a cloud dwell upon it; let the blackness of the day terrify it.

And said, Naked came I out of my mother's womb, and naked shall I return thither: the Lord gave, and the Lord hath taken away; blessed be the name of the Lord.

In all this Job sinned not, nor charged God foolishly.

And he took him a potsherd to scrape himself withal; and he sat down among the ashes.

Then said his wife unto him, Dost thou still retain thine integrity? curse God, and die.

But he said unto her, Thou speakest as one of the foolish women speaketh. What? shall we receive good at the hand of God, and shall we not receive evil? In all this did not Job sin with his lips.

Now when Job's three friends heard of all this evil that was come upon him, they came every one from his own place; Eliphaz the Temanite, and Bildad the Shuhite, and Zophar the Naamathite: for they had made an appointment together to come to mourn with him and to comfort him.

And when they lifted up their eyes afar off, and knew him not, they lifted up their voice, and wept; and they rent every one his mantle, and sprinkled dust upon their heads toward heaven.

So they sat down with him upon the ground seven days and seven nights, and none spake a word unto him: for they saw that his grief was very great.

As for that night, let darkness seize upon it; let it not be joined unto the days of the year, let it not come into the number of the months.

Lo, let that night be solitary, let no joyful voice come therein.

Let them curse it that curse the day, who are ready to raise up their mourning.

Let the stars of the twilight thereof be dark; let it look for light, but have none; neither let it see the dawning of the day:

Because it shut not up the doors of my mother's womb, nor hid sorrow from mine eyes.

Why died I not from the womb? why did I not give up the ghost when I came out of the belly?

CHAPTER 21

Hear diligently my speech, and let this be your consolations.

Suffer me that I may speak; and after that I have spoken, mock on.

As for me, is my complaint to man? and if it were so, why should not my spirit be troubled?

Mark me, and be astonished, and lay your hand upon your mouth.

Even when I remember I am afraid, and trembling taketh hold on my flesh.

Wherefore do the wicked live, become old, yea, are mighty in power?

Their seed is established in their sight with them, and their offspring before their eyes.

Their houses are safe from fear, neither is the rod of God upon them.

Their bull gendereth, and faileth not; their cow calveth, and casteth not her calf.

They send forth their little ones like a flock, and their children dance.

They take the timbrel and harp, and rejoice at the sound of the organ.

They spend their days in wealth, and in a moment go down to the grave.

Therefore they say unto God, Depart from us; for we desire not the knowledge of thy ways.

CHAPTER 31

I made a covenant with mine eyes; why then should I think upon a maid?

For what portion of God is there from above? and what inheritance of the Almighty from on high?

Is not destruction to the wicked? and a strange punishment to the workers of iniquity?

Doth not he see my ways, and count all my steps?

If I have walked with vanity, or if my foot hath hasted to deceit;

Why did the knees prevent me? or why the breasts that I should suck?

For now should I have lain still and been quiet, I should have slept: then had I been at rest. . . .

What is the Almighty, that we should serve him? and what profit should we have, if we pray unto him?

Lo, their good is not in their hand: the counsel of the wicked is far from me.

How oft is the candle of the wicked put out! and how oft cometh their destruction upon them! God distributeth sorrows in his anger.

They are as stubble before the wind, and as chaff that the storm carrieth away.

God layeth up his iniquity for his children: he rewardeth him, and he shall know it.

His eyes shall see his destruction, and he shall drink of the wrath of the Almighty.

For what pleasure hath he in his house after him, when the number of his months is cut off in the midst?

Shall any teach God knowledge? seeing he judgeth those that are high.

One dieth in his full strength, being wholly at ease and quiet.

His breasts are full of milk, and his bones are moistened with marrow.

And another dieth in the bitterness of his soul, and never eateth with pleasure.

They shall lie down alike in the dust, and the worms shall cover them. . . .

Let me be weighed in an even balance, that God may know mine integrity.

If my step hath turned out of the way, and mine heart walked after mine eyes, and if any blot hath cleaved to mine hands;

Then let me sow, and let another eat; yea, let my offspring be rooted out.

If mine heart have been deceived by a woman, or if I have laid wait at my neighbor's door;

Then let my wife grind unto another, and let others bow down upon her.

For this is an heinous crime; yea, it is an iniquity to be punished by the judges.

For it is a fire that consumeth to destruction, and would root out all mine increase.

If I did despise the cause of my manservant or of my maidservant, when they contended with me;

What then shall I do when God riseth up? and when he visiteth, what shall I answer him?

Did not he that made me in the womb make him? and did not one fashion us in the womb?

If I have withheld the poor from their desire, or have caused the eyes of the widow to fail;

Or have eaten my morsel myself alone, and the fatherless hath not eaten thereof;

(For from my youth he was brought up with me, as with a father, and I have guided her from my mother's womb;)

If I have seen any perish for want of clothing, or any poor without covering:

If his loins have not blessed me, and if he were not warmed with the fleece of my sheep;

If I have lifted up my hand against the fatherless, when I saw my help in the gate:

Then let mine arm fall from my shoulder-blade, and mine arm be broken from the bone.

For destruction from God was a terror to me, and by reason of his highness I could not endure.

If I have made gold my hope, or have said to the fine gold, Thou art my confidence;

If I rejoiced because my wealth was great, and because mine hand had gotten much;

If I beheld the sun when it shined, or the moon walking in brightness;

And my heart hath been secretly enticed, or my mouth hath kissed my hand:

This also were an iniquity to be punished by the judge: for I should have denied the God that is above.

If I rejoiced at the destruction of him that hated me, or lifted up myself when evil found him:

Neither have I suffered my mouth to sin by wishing a curse to his soul.

If the men of any tabernacle said not, Oh that we had of his flesh! we cannot be satisfied.

The stranger did not lodge in the street: but I opened my doors to the traveler.

If I covered my transgressions as Adam, by hiding mine iniquity in my bosom:

Did I fear a great multitude, or did the contempt of families terrify me, that I kept silence, and went not out of the door?

Oh that one would hear me! behold, my desire is, that the Almighty would answer me, and that mine adversary had written a book.

Surely I would take it upon my shoulder, and bind it as a crown to me.

I would declare unto him the number of my steps; as a prince would I go near unto him.

If my land cry against me, or that the furrows likewise thereof complain;

If I have eaten the fruits thereof without money, or have caused the owners thereof to lose their life:

Let thistles grow instead of wheat, and cockle instead of barley. The words of Job are ended.

CHAPTER 38

Then the Lord answered Job out of the whirlwind, and said,

Who is this that darkeneth counsel by words without knowledge?

Grid up now thy loins like a man; for I will demand of thee, and answer thou me.

Where wast thou when I laid the foundations of the earth? declare, if thou hast understanding.

Who hath laid the measures thereof, if thou knowest? or who hath stretched the line upon it?

Whereupon are the foundations thereof fastened? or who laid the corner stone thereof;

When the morning stars sang together, and all the sons of God shouted for joy?

Or who shut up the sea with doors, when it brake forth, as if it had issued out of the womb?

When I made the cloud the garment thereof, and thick darkness a swaddling-band for it.

And brake up for it my decreed place, and set bars and doors,

And said, Hitherto shalt thou come, but no further: and here shall thy proud waves be stayed?

Hast thou commanded the morning since thy days; and caused the dayspring to know his place;

That it might take hold of the ends of the earth, that the wicked might be shaken out of it?

It is turned as clay to the seal; and they stand as a garment.

And from the wicked their light is withholden, and the high arm shall be broken.

Hast thou entered into the springs of the sea? or hast thou walked in the search of the depth?

Have the gates of death been opened unto thee? or hast thou seen the doors of the shadow of death?

Hast thou perceived the breadth of the earth? declare if thou knowest it all.

Where is the way where light dwelleth? and as for darkness, where is the place thereof,

That thou shouldest take it to the bound thereof, and that thou shouldest know the paths to the house thereof?

Knowest thou it, because thou wast then born? or because the number of thy days is great?

Hast thou entered into the treasures of the snow? or hast thou seen the treasures of the hail,

Which I have reserved against the time of trouble, against the day of battle and war?

By what way is the light parted, which scattereth the east wind upon the earth?

Who hath divided a watercourse for the overflowing of waters, or a way for the lightning of thunder;

To cause it to rain on the earth, where no man is; on the wilderness, wherein there is no man;

To satisfy the desolate and waste ground; and to cause the bud of the tender herb to spring forth?

Hath the rain a father? or who hath begotten the drops of dew?

Out of whose womb came the ice? and the hoary frost of heaven, who hath gendered it?

The waters are hid as with a stone, and the face of the deep is frozen.

Canst thou bind the sweet influences of Pleiades, or loose the bands of Orion?

Canst thou bring forth Mazzaroth in his season? or canst thou guide Arcturus with his sons?

Knowest thou the ordinances of heaven? canst thou set the dominion thereof in the earth?

Canst thou lift up thy voice to the clouds, that abundance of waters may cover thee?

Canst thou send lightnings, that they may go, and say unto thee, Here we are?

Who hath put wisdom in the inward parts? or who hath given understanding to the heart?

Who can number the clouds in wisdom? or who can stay the bottles of heaven,

When the dust groweth into hardness, and the clods cleave fast together?

Wilt thou hunt the prey for the lion? or fill the appetite of the young lions,

When they couch in their dens, and abide in the covert to lie in wait?

Who provideth for the raven his food? when his young ones cry unto God, they wander for lack of meat.

CHAPTER 42

Then Job answered the Lord, and said,

I know that thou canst do every thing, and that no thought can be withholden from thee.

Who is he that hideth counsel without knowledge? therefore have I uttered that I understood not; things too wonderful for me, which I knew not.

Hear, I beseech thee, and I will speak: I will demand of thee, and declare thou unto me.

I have heard of thee by the hearing of the ear: but now mine eye seeth thee.

Wherefore I abhor myself, and repent in dust and ashes. . . .

And the Lord turned the captivity of Job, when he prayed for his friends: also the Lord gave Job twice as much as he had before.

Then came there unto him all his brethren, and all his sisters, and all they that had been of his acquaintance before, and did eat bread with him in his house: and they bemoaned him, and comforted him over all the evil that the Lord had brought upon him: every man also gave him a piece of money, and every one an earring of gold.

So the Lord blessed the latter end of Job more than his beginning: for he had fourteen thousand sheep, and six thousand camels, and a thousand yoke of oxen, and a thousand she-asses.

He had also seven sons and three daughters.

And he called the name of the first, Jemima; and the name of the second, Kezia; and the name of the third, Keren-happuch.

And in all the land were no women found so fair as the daughters of Job: and their father gave them inheritance among their brethren.

After this lived Job an hundred and forty years, and saw his sons, and his sons' sons, even four generations.

So Job died, being old and full of days.

DISCUSSION QUESTIONS

1. How is the story of Job an example of the conflict between reason and faith? What does it reveal about this conflict? Is faith compatible with reason? Why or why not?

2. Does the book of Job establish that God is indifferent to the concerns of humans?

3. What is the new understanding that Job reaches in chapter 42 concerning his own suffering and God's ways?

4. Compare the conflict between faith and reason in Clarke's "The Star" and the book of Job. Which resolution do you find more convincing, and why?

5. In chapter 31, Job says, "Is not destruction to the wicked? And a strange punishment to the workers of iniquity? Doth not he see my ways, and count all my steps?" At the end of chapter 42, what conclusion has Job reached on these questions?

Inherit the Wind
[USA 1960] 2 hours, 8 minutes
Directed by Stanley Kramer

*I*n the 1920s, a surge of religious fundamentalism swept through the United States, particularly in the Midwest and the South. Advocating a literal interpretation of the Bible, many believers were returning to their faith for a sense of security and stability after the turmoil of World War I. As a consequence, Darwin's theory of evolution was disputed. Across the South, many states passed laws prohibiting the teaching of evolution, and in 1925, Tennessee joined the list by passing the Butler Law. Even though the governor of Tennessee said that he did not believe the Butler Law was going to be an active statute, the law was put to the test very quickly. In July 1925, John T. Scopes, a twenty-four-year-old science teacher and football coach from Dayton, Tennessee, was charged with violating the Butler Law by teaching evolution in his biology classroom. The Scopes "Monkey Trial," as it was called, was a national media event. It featured attorney William Jennings Bryan for the prosecution and Clarence Darrow for the defense. Bryan, a three-time presidential candidate and former secretary of state to Woodrow Wilson, called the trial a "contest between evolution and Christianity . . . a duel to the death," and Darrow, one of the most famous lawyers in American history, had yearned for years to reveal Bryan as a "bigot." The trial ended with the jury finding Scopes guilty. The judge ordered Scopes to pay a fine of $100, the minimum the law allowed. After the verdict, Scopes said to the court, "Your Honor, I feel that I have been convicted of violating an unjust statute. I will continue in the future . . . to oppose this law in any way I can. Any other action would be in violation of my idea of academic freedom." In January of 1927, the state supreme court reversed the decision, on the grounds that according to Tennessee state law, the jury, not the judge, must set the fine if it is above $50.

In 1950, Jerome Lawrence and Robert E. Lee completed a play about the Scopes trial called *Inherit the Wind*, which made its Broadway debut in 1955. A few years later, a film adaptation of the play was directed by Stanley Kramer. In the film and the play, the names of the principle participants in the trial, as well as the name of the city where the trial occurred, were changed. Bertram T. Cates (Dick York), a science teacher at a Hillsboro, Tennessee, school, is brought to trial after teaching his students Darwin's theory of evolution. Two prestigious attorneys take on the case—the fundamentalist prosecutor Matthew Harrison Brady (Fredric March) and the high-powered defense attorney Henry Drummond (Spencer Tracy). While the film is not entirely accurate in its depiction of the historical event (for example, whereas Drummond and Brady are on somewhat friendly terms in the film, the real lawyers were far from amicable), the outcome is the same.

DISCUSSION QUESTIONS

1. Cates states, "All I want to do is teach my students that man just wasn't planted here like a geranium in a flower pot. Life comes from a long miracle. It just didn't take seven days." What does Cates mean by the statement "Life comes from a long miracle"? Is he suggesting that Darwin's theory of evolution and the existence of God are not incompatible?

2. In the trial, a reverend declares that evolution is a betrayal of faith: The Bible tells us that God created human beings on the sixth day (Gen. 1:27–31); therefore, teaching evolution, which says otherwise, means sinning against the word of God. Is evolution a "betrayal of faith"? Why or why not?

3. Drummond says that science contradicts many of the events that took place in the Bible. For example, the story of Jonah and the whale asks us to believe that it is possible for a man to live for an extended period of time in the stomach of a whale; and the story of Joshua making the sun stand still asks us to believe that a human could wield such power. Science tells us that Jonah could not have survived in the belly of a whale and that Joshua could not have made the sun stand still without bringing about an ecological disaster. Is scientific reasoning therefore at odds with religious faith? Or should we not interpret the events of the Bible "literally"? If so, how do we determine which events to interpret literally and which to interpret allegorically or symbolically?

4. Drummond notes that if we censor evolution theory in schools, we will be opening up a slippery slope that leads to the censorship of anything that conflicts with beliefs validated by faith. Do you agree with him? Why or why not?

5. Drummond says that we must abandon faith because *God* gave us the power to think. Is he right? Is the conflict between faith and reason ("the power to think") ultimately one in which we have to take one side or the other?

6. Recall the "proofs" for the existence of God in the first section of this chapter. Would you consider them to be the result of our powers of "reason" or of our powers of "faith"? Or neither or both? Explain.

BLAISE PASCAL

THE WAGER

laise Pascal uses his reason to prepare the way for faith in God. For Pascal, there is no rational proof for or against the existence of God. "If there is a God," says Pascal, "He is infinitely incomprehensible, since, having neither parts nor limits, He has no affinity to us." However, while reason cannot prove or disprove God's existence, it does tell us that we are involved in a wager when we choose to believe or not believe in God: By believing or not believing in God, we are wagering that he exists or does not exist. "Your reason is no more shocked in choosing one rather than the other, since you must of necessity choose," comments Pascal. If you wager that God exists, and he does exist, the payoff is eternal happiness and immortality; if you wager that God exists, and he doesn't exist, you lose nothing; if you wager that God doesn't exist, and he does, an eternity of damnation awaits; if you wager that God doesn't exist, and he doesn't, you lose nothing. Consider then the wager that God exists: When "you gain, you gain all; if you lose, you lose nothing." "Wager, then," concludes Pascal, "without hesitation that He is." The wager was addressed to Pascal's skeptical and freethinking friends, some of whom enjoyed gambling.

   Blaise Pascal (1623–62), a French philosopher and mathematical genius, made important contributions to number theory, probability theory, and physics. The earliest anecdote about his life tells of him being "bewitched" and then freed from the spell through a strange ceremony. Following a religious experience in 1654, in which for two hours he had a strong sense of union with Christ, Pascal wrote a message to himself that contained some incoherent, mystical devotional lines. This message, called "Pascal's Amulet," he wore sewn into his coat for the rest of his life. He came out of this experience with the firm belief that the way to God was through Christianity, not philosophy. The following selection is from *Pensées* (1669), a collection of thoughts (pensées) on religion, which was posthumously published. The work was intended as a defense of the Christian faith, though it was never completed.

233

Let us now speak according to natural lights.

If there is a God, He is infinitely incomprehensible, since, having neither parts nor limits, He has no affinity to us. We are then incapable of knowing either what He is or if He is. This being so, who will dare to undertake the decision of the question? Not we, who have no affinity to Him.

Who then will blame Christians for not being able to give a reason for their belief, since they profess a religion for which they cannot give a reason? They declare, in expounding it to the world, that it is a foolishness . . . ; and then you complain that they do not prove it! If they proved it, they would not keep their word; it is in lacking proofs that they are not lacking in sense. "Yes, but although this excuses those who offer it as such, and takes away from them the blame of putting it forward without reason, it does not excuse those who receive it." Let us then examine this point, and say, "God is, or He is not." But to which side shall we incline? Reason can decide nothing here. There is an infinite chaos which separated us. A game is being played at the extremity of this infinite distance where heads or tails will turn up. What will you wager? According to reason, you can do neither the one thing nor the other; according to reason, you can defend neither of the propositions.

Do not then reprove for error those who have made a choice; for you know nothing about it.

"No, but I blame them for having made, not this choice, but a choice; for again both he who chooses heads and he who chooses tails are equally at fault, they are both in the wrong. The true course is not to wager at all."

Yes; but you must wager. It is not optional. You are embarked. Which will you choose then? Let us see. Since you must choose, let us see which interests you least. You have two things to lose, the true and the good; and two things to stake, your reason and your will, your knowledge and your happiness; and your nature has two things to shun, error and misery. Your reason is no more shocked in choosing one rather than the other, since you must of necessity choose. This is one point settled. But your happiness? Let us weigh the gain and the loss in wagering that God is. Let us estimate these two chances. If you gain, you gain all; if you lose, you lose nothing. Wager, then, without hesitation that He is. "That is very fine. Yes, I must wager; but I may perhaps wager too much." Let us see. Since there is an equal risk of gain and of loss, if you had only to gain two lives, instead of one, you might still wager. But if there were three lives to gain, you would have to play (since you are under the necessity of playing), and you would be imprudent, when you are forced to play, not to chance your life to gain three at a game where there is an equal risk of loss and gain. But there is an eternity of life and happiness. And this being so, if there were an infinity of chances, of which one only would be for you, you would still be right in wagering one to win two, and you would act stupidly, being obliged to play, be refusing to stake one life against three at a game in which out of an infinity of chances there is one for you, if there were an infinity of infinitely happy life to gain. But there is here an infinity of an infinitely happy life to gain, a chance of gain against a finite number of chances of loss, and what you stake is finite. It is all divided; wherever the infinite is and there is not an infinity of chances of loss against that of gain, there is no time to hesitate, you must give all. And thus, when one is forced to play, he must renounce reason to preserve his life, rather than risk it for infinite gain, as likely to happen as the loss of nothingness.

For it is no use to say it is uncertain if we will gain, and it is certain that we risk, and that the infinite distance between the *certainty* of what is staked and the *uncertainty* of what will be gained, equals the finite good which is certainly staked against the uncertain infinite. It is not so, as every player stakes a certainty to gain an uncertainty, and yet he stakes a finite certainty to gain a finite uncertainty, without transgressing against reason. There is not an infinite distance between the certainty staked and the uncertainty of gain; that is untrue. In truth, there is an infinity between the certainty of gain and the certainty of loss. But the uncertainty of the gain is proportioned to the certainty of the stake according to the proportion of the chances of gain and loss. Hence it comes that, if there are as many risks on one side as on the other, the course is to play even; and then the certainty of the stake is equal to the uncertainty of the gain, so far is it from fact that there is an infinite distance between them. And so our proposition is of infinite force, when there is the finite to stake in a game where there are equal risks of gain and of loss and the infinite to gain. This is demonstrable; and if men are capable of any truths, this is one.

"I confess it, I admit it. But, still, is there no means of seeing the faces of the cards?" Yes, Scripture and the rest, etc. "Yes, but I have my hands tied and my mouth closed; I am forced to wager, and am not free. I am not released and am so made that I cannot believe. What, then, would you have me do?"

True. But at least learn your inability to believe, since reason brings you to this, and yet you cannot believe. Endeavour then to convince yourself, not by increase of proofs of God, but by the abatement of your passions. You would like to attain faith, and do not know the way; you would like to cure yourself of unbelief, and ask the remedy for it. Learn of those who have been bound like you, and who now stake all their possessions. These are people who know the way which you would follow, and who are cured of all ill of which you would be cured. Follow the way by which they began; by acting as if they believed, taking the holy water, having masses said, etc. Even this will naturally make you believe, and deaden your acuteness. "But this is what I am afraid of." And why? What have you to lose?

But to show you that this leads you there, it is this which will lessen the passions, which are your stumbling-blocks.

The end of this discourse. Now, what harm will befall you in taking this side? You will be faithful, honest, humble, grateful, generous, a sincere friend, truthful. Certainly you will not have those poisonous pleasures, glory and luxury; but will you not have others? I will tell you that you will thereby gain in this life, and that, at each step you take on this road, you will see so great certainty of gain, so much nothingness in what you risk, that you will at last recognise that you have wagered for something certain and infinite, for which you have given nothing.

234

If we must not act save on a certainty, we ought not to act on religion, for it is not certain. But how many things we do on an uncertainty, sea voyages, battles! I say then we must do nothing at all, for nothing is certain, and that there is more certainty in religion than there is as to whether we may see to-morrow; for it is not certain that we may see to-morrow, and it is certainly possible that we may not see it. We cannot say as much about religion. It is not certain that it is; but who will venture to say that it is certainly possible that it is not? Now when we work for to-morrow, and so on an uncertainty, we act reasonably, for we ought to work for an uncertainty according to the doctrine of chance which was demonstrated above.

Saint Augustine has seen that we work for an uncertainty, on sea, in battle, etc. But he has not seen the doctrine of chance which proves that we should do so. Montaigne has seen that we are shocked at a fool, and that habit is all-powerful; but he has not seen the reason of this effect.

All these persons have seen the effects, but they have not seen the causes. They are, in comparison with those who have discovered the causes, as those who have only eyes are in comparison with those who have intellect. For the effects are perceptible by sense, and the causes are visible only to the intellect. And although these effects are seen by the mind, this mind is, in comparison with the mind which sees the causes, as the bodily senses are in comparison with the intellect.

252

For we must not misunderstand ourselves; we are as much automatic as intellectual; and hence it comes that the instrument by which conviction is attained is not demonstration alone. How few things are demonstrated! Proofs only convince the mind. Custom is the source of our strongest and most believed proofs. It bends the automaton, which persuades the mind without its thinking about the matter. Who has demonstrated that there will be a to-morrow, and that we shall die? And what is more believed? It is then custom which persuades us of it; it is custom that makes so many men Christians; custom that makes them Turks, heathens, artisans, soldiers, etc. (Faith in baptism is more received among Christians than among Turks.) Finally, we must have recourse to it when once the mind has seen where the truth is, in order to quench our thirst, and steep ourselves in that belief, which escapes us at every hour; for always to have proofs ready is too much trouble. We must get an easier belief, which is that of custom, which, without violence, without art, without argument, makes us believe things, and inclines all our powers to this relief, so that our soul falls naturally into it.

277

The heart has its reasons, which reason does not know. We feel it in a thousand things. I say that the heart naturally loves the Universal Being, and also itself naturally, according as it gives itself to them; and it hardens itself against one or the other at its will. You have rejected the one and kept the other. Is it by reason that you love yourself?

347

Man is but a reed, the most feeble thing in nature, but he is a thinking reed. The entire universe need not arm itself to crush him. A vapour, a drop of water suffices to kill him. But, if the universe were to crush him, man would still be more noble than that which killed him, because he knows that he dies and the advantage which the universe has over him; the universe knows nothing of this.

All our dignity consists then in thought.

365

Thought.—All the dignity of man consists in thought. Thought is therefore by its nature a wonderful and incomparable thing. It must have strange defects to be contemptible. But it has such, so that nothing is more ridiculous. How great it is in its nature! How vile it is in its defects! . . . There is no permanence for man: it is a condition which is at once natural to mankind, yet most contrary to his inclinations . . . . We burn with the desire of finding a secure abode, an ultimate firm base on which to build a tower which might rise to infinity; but our very foundation crumbles completely, and earth opens before us unto the very abyss.

DISCUSSION QUESTIONS

1. Explain the relationship between reason and faith in Pascal's wager.

2. Pascal asks us to think like a gambler when we consider the issue of God's existence. Is this a good approach? Does it matter how we gain faith in God?

3. Pascal says, "If we must not act save on certainty, we ought not to act on religion, for it is not certain." Do you agree with him? Why or why not?

4. What does Pascal mean when he says, "The heart has its reasons, which reason does not know"? What do you think about this statement?

5. How comforting is Pascal's wager in maintaining faith in God in the face of extreme suffering? Do you think, for example, that if Job had known of Pascal's wager before he lost his wealth, family, and health, he would not have questioned and doubted God's character and purpose after he lost these things?

Crimes and Misdemeanors
[USA 1989] 1 hour, 44 minutes
Directed by Woody Allen

Renowned New York optometrist and public figure Judah Rosenthal (Martin Landau) is anxious because he has recently discovered a letter addressed to his wife Miriam (Claire Bloom) from his boisterous lover, Dolores Paley (Anjelica Huston). Dolores is contacting Miriam to reveal Judah's infidelity because he has decided to terminate the relationship. Meanwhile, Cliff Stern (Woody Allen), a documentary filmmaker, is struggling with his work and his marriage to Wendy (Joanna Gleason). Wendy's brother Lester (Alan Alda) is a rich and famous TV producer whom Lester loathes for his arrogance and his success. Lester offers Cliff a job filming a documentary about Lester's life, though only as a favor to Wendy. As Judah struggles with the end of an adulterous relationship, Cliff finds himself drawn into one when he meets attractive production assistant Halley Reed (Mia Farrow). Conflicts arise when unmarried Lester also exhibits amorous intentions toward Halley. Meanwhile, Judah meets with his brother Jack (Jerry Orbach) and discusses the unthinkable solution to his insoluble problem: killing his mistress. After the murder is committed, a conflict of conscience threatens to overwhelm Judah. Through "flashbacks" to Judah's youth, we see the young Judah learning that "the eyes of God are on us always" and that "righteous are rewarded and the wicked punished."

In one of these flashbacks, Judah visits his childhood home and recalls a spirited dinner table conversation about God and morality. Family members argue about whether the universe has a moral structure and to what extent the wicked are punished for their misdeeds. Sol (David S. Howard), the father of the house, gives a dinner blessing in Hebrew, but his sister, Aunt May (Anna Berger), tells him to stop the "mumbo jumbo." "This is the twentieth century," she says. "Don't fill their heads with superstition." Sol, clearly irritated at her remark, responds, "The intellectual, the schoolteacher, spare us your Leninist philosophy." "Are you afraid that if you don't follow the rules, God is going to punish you?" Aunt May shoots back. "He won't punish me," replies Sol. "God punishes the wicked." Aunt May retorts, "Who, like Hitler? . . . Six million Jews burned to death and Hitler got away with it." Sol asks, "How did they get away with it?" Aunt May says, "Sol, open your eyes. Six million Jews and millions of others, and they got off with nothing . . . because might makes right."

DISCUSSION QUESTIONS

1. Sol views Aunt May as someone who has lost her faith in God. With faith, she would understand that Hitler did not "get away with it." He was punished as "God sees everything." Aunt May, however, lives by reason alone; for her, "six million Jews burned to death" by reason entails that "Hitler got away with it." Evaluate their conflict as one between faith and reason. Who is making the stronger case here, and why?

2. Pascal says, "The heart has its reasons, which reason does not know." In what way do the positions of Sol and Aunt May reflect this statement by Pascal?

3. At the dinner table, Judah asks what happens if a man kills. Sol answers, "Then one way or another he'll be punished." "If he's caught, Sol," says one of the guests at the table. Sol continues, "If he's not caught, that which originates from a black deed will blossom in a foul manner." Aunt May adds, "And I say if he can do it and get away with it, and he chooses not to be bothered by the ethics, then he's home free. Remember, history is written by the winners. And if the Nazis had won, future generations would understand the story of World War II quite differently." How would Pascal respond to this discussion?

4. At the dinner table, one of the guests asks him, "And if all your faith is wrong, Sol, I mean, just what if?" Sol answers, "Then I'll still have a better life than all those that doubt." Aunt May asks, "Do you mean that you prefer God to the truth?" Sol responds, "If necessary, I will always choose God over truth." Compare Sol's decision here to Pascal's wager.

5. Imagine that you were sitting at the dinner table with Sol and Aunt May. How would you respond to their overall conversation? Would you be more inclined to take the side of faith as Sol did or the side of reason as Aunt May? Or neither? Discuss.

6. Do you think that Aunt May, a woman of reason, would accept Pascal's wager if it were carefully presented to her? Why or why not?

SØREN KIERKEGAARD

THE LEAP OF FAITH

Søren Kierkegaard believes that because God's existence cannot be known through reason or proofs, we should make a leap of faith that God exists. For Kierkegaard, "If God does not exist it would of course be impossible to prove it; and if he does exist it would be folly to attempt it." Reason cannot produce knowledge or proof of God's existence, but when we let go of attempts at rational, objective proof, "the existence is there."

Kierkegaard notes that "this act of letting go" of attempts to approach God through reason and proof takes just a brief moment. In this brief subjective moment of faith, God's existence is felt rather than known.

Søren Kierkegaard (1813–55), a Danish philosopher and theologian, is the father of existentialism. Raised in a strict Lutheran environment, he reacted strongly against orthodox Christianity, which he saw as passionless, complacent, and secure. He aimed to help others learn what it is to be a Christian, espousing a highly personal form of religion. He wrote twenty-one books in twelve years, the early ones under pseudonyms and the later ones under his own name. They include *The Concept of Irony* (1841), *Either-Or* (1843), *Fear and Trembling* (1843), *Repetition* (1843), *The Concept of Dread* (1844), *Sickness unto Death* (1849), and *Training in Christianity* (1850). The following selection is from *Philosophical Fragments* (1844).

But what is this unknown something with which the Reason collides when inspired by its paradoxical passion, with the result of unsettling even man's knowledge of himself? It is the Unknown. It is not a human being, in so far as we know what man is; nor is it any other known thing. So let us call this unknown something: *God*. It is nothing more than a name we assign to it. The idea of demonstrating that this unknown something (God) exists, could scarcely suggest itself to the Reason. For if God does not exist it would of course be impossible to prove it; and if he does exist it would be folly to attempt it. For at the very outset, in beginning my proof, I will have presupposed it, not as doubtful but as certain (a presupposition is never doubtful, for the very reason that it is a presupposition), since otherwise I would not begin, readily understanding that the whole would be impossible if he did not exist. But if when I speak of proving God's existence I mean that I propose to prove that the Unknown, which exists, is God, then I express myself unfortunately. For in that case I do not prove anything, least of all an existence, but merely develop the content of a conception. Generally speaking, it is a difficult matter to prove that anything exists; and what is still worse for the intrepid souls who undertake the venture, the difficulty is such that fame scarcely awaits those who concern themselves with it. The entire demonstration always turns into something very different from what it assumes to be, and becomes an additional development of the consequences that flow from my having assumed that the object in question exists. Thus I always reason from existence, not toward existence, whether I move in the sphere of palpable sensible fact or in the realm of thought. I do not for example prove that a stone exists, but that some existing thing is a stone. The procedure in a court of justice does not prove that a criminal exists, but that the accused, whose existence is given, is a criminal. Whether we call existence an *accessorium* or the eternal *prius*, it is never subject to demonstration. Let us take ample time for consideration. We have no such reason for haste as have those who from concern for themselves or for God or for some other thing, must make haste to get its existence demonstrated. Under such circumstances there may indeed be need for haste, especially if the prover sincerely seeks to appreciate the danger that he himself, or the thing in question, may be non-existent unless the proof is finished; and does not surreptitiously entertain the thought that it exists whether he succeeds in proving it or not.

If it were proposed to prove Napoleon's existence from Napoleon's deeds, would it not be a most curious proceeding? His existence does indeed explain his deeds, but the deeds do not prove *his* existence, unless I have already understood the word "his" so as thereby to have assumed his existence. But Napoleon is only an individual, and in so far there exists no absolute relationship between him and his deeds; some other person might have performed the same deeds. Perhaps this is the reason why I cannot pass from the deeds to existence. If I call these deeds the deeds of Napoleon the proof becomes superfluous, since I have already named him; if I ignore this, I can never prove from the deeds that they are Napoleon's, but only in a purely ideal manner that such deeds are the deeds of a great general, and so forth. But between God and his works there exists an absolute relationship: God is not a name but a concept. Is this perhaps the reason that his *essentia involvit existentiam?* The works of God are such that only God can perform them. Just so, but where are the works of God? The works from which I would deduce his existence are not immediately given. The wisdom of God in nature, his goodness, his wisdom in the governance of the world—are all these manifest, perhaps, upon the very face of things? Are we not here confronted with the most terrible temptations to doubt, and is it not impossible finally to dispose of all these doubts? But from such an order of things I will surely not attempt to prove God's existence; and even if I began I would never finish, and would in addition have to live constantly in suspense, lest something terrible should suddenly happen that my bit of proof would be demolished. From what works then do I propose to derive the proof? From the works as apprehended through an ideal interpretation, i.e., such as they do not immediately reveal themselves. But in that case it is not from the works that I prove God's existence. I merely develop the ideality I have presupposed, and because of my confidence in *this* I make so bold as to defy all objections, even those that have not yet been made. In beginning my proof I presuppose the ideal interpretation, and also that I will be successful in carrying it through; but what else is this but to presuppose that God exists, so that I really begin by virtue of confidence in him?

And how does God's existence emerge from the proof? Does it follow straightaway, without any breach of continuity? Or have we not here an analogy to the behaviour of these toys, the little Cartesian dolls? As soon as I let go of the doll it stands on its head. As soon as I let it go—I must therefore let it go. So also with the proof for God's existence. As long as I keep my hold on the proof,

i.e., continue to demonstrate, the existence does not come out, if for no other reason than that I am engaged in proving it; but when I let the proof go, the existence is there. But this act of letting go is surely also something; it is indeed a contribution of mine. Must not this also be taken into the account, this little moment, brief as it may be—it need not be long, for it is a *leap*. However brief this moment, if only an instantaneous now, this "now" must be included in the reckoning.

Whoever therefore attempts to demonstrate the existence of God (except in the sense of clarifying the concept), proves in lieu thereof something else, something which at times perhaps does not need proof, and in any case need none better; for the fool says in his heart that there is no God, but whoever says in his heart or to men: Wait just a little and I will prove it—what a rare man of wisdom is he! If in the moment of beginning his proof it is not absolutely undetermined whether God exists or not, he does not prove it; and if it is thus undetermined in the beginning he will never come to begin, partly from fear of failure, since God perhaps does not exist, and partly because he has nothing with which to begin.—A project of this kind would scarcely have been undertaken by the ancients. Socrates at least, who is credited with having put forth the physico-teleological proof for God's existence, did not go about it in any such manner. He always presupposes God's existence, and under this presupposition seeks to interpenetrate nature with the ideal of purpose. Had he been asked why he pursued this method, he would doubtless have explained that he lacked the courage to venture out upon so perilous a voyage of discovery without having made sure of God's existence behind him. At the word of God he casts his net as if to catch the idea of purpose; for nature herself finds many means of frightening the inquirer, and distracts him by many a digression.

The paradoxical passion of the Reason thus comes repeatedly into collision with the Unknown, which does indeed exist, but is unknown, and in so far does not exist. The Reason cannot advance beyond this point, and yet it cannot refrain in its paradoxicalness from arriving at this limit and occupying itself therewith. It will not serve to dismiss its relation to it simply by asserting that the Unknown does not exist, since this itself involves a relationship. But what then is the Unknown, since the designation of it as God merely signifies for us that it is unknown? To say that it is the Unknown because it cannot be known, and even if it were capable of being known, it could not be expressed, does not satisfy the demands of passion, though it correctly interprets the Unknown as a limit; but a limit is precisely a torment for passion, though it also serves as an incitement. And yet the Reason can come no further, whether it risks an issue *via negationis* or *via eminentia*.

What then is the Unknown? It is the limit to which the Reason repeatedly comes, and in so far, substituting a static form of conception for the dynamic, it is the different, the absolutely different. But because it is absolutely different, there is no mark by which it could be distinguished. When qualified as absolutely different it seems on the verge of disclosure, but this is not the case; for the Reason cannot even conceive an absolute unlikeness. The Reason cannot negate itself absolutely, but uses itself for the purpose, and thus conceives only such an unlikeness within itself as it can conceive by means of itself; it cannot absolutely transcend itself; and hence conceives only such a superiority over itself as it can conceive by means of itself. Unless the Unknown (God) remains a mere limiting conception, the single idea of difference will be thrown into a state of confusion, and become many ideas of many differences. The Unknown is then in a condition of dispersion (diaspora), and the Reason may choose at pleasure from what is at hand and the imagination may suggest (the monstrous, the ludicrous, etc.).

But it is impossible to hold fast to a difference of this nature. Every time this is done it is essentially an arbitrary act, and deepest down in the heart of piety lurks the mad caprice which knows that it has itself produced its God. If no specific determination of difference can be held fast, because there is no distinguishing mark, like and unlike finally become identified with one another, thus sharing the fate of all such dialectical opposites. The unlikeness clings to the Reason and confounds it, so that the Reason no

longer knows itself and quite consistently confuses itself with the unlikeness. On this point paganism has been sufficiently prolific in fantastic inventions. As for the last named supposition, the self-irony of the Reason, I shall attempt to delineate it merely by a stroke or two, without raising any question of its being historical. There lives an individual whose appearance is precisely like that of other men; he grows up to manhood like others, he marries, he has an occupation by which he earns his livelihood, and he makes provision for the future as befits a man. For though it may be beautiful to live like the birds of the air, it is not lawful, and may lead to the sorriest of consequences: either starvation if one has enough persistence, or dependence on the bounty of others. This man is also God. How do I know? I cannot know it, for in order to know it I would have to know God, and the nature of the difference between God and man; and this I cannot know, because the Reason has reduced it to likeness with that from which it was unlike. Thus God becomes the most terrible of deceivers, because the Reason has deceived itself. The Reason has brought God as near as possible, and yet he is as far away as ever.

DISCUSSION QUESTIONS

1. Kierkegaard says that if God does exist, it would be folly to attempt to prove it. Do you agree with him? Why or why not?

2. Evaluate Kierkegaard's position that reason cannot produce knowledge or proof of God's existence, but when we let go of attempts at rational, objective proof, "the existence is there."

3. Kierkegaard says, "I always reason from existence, not toward existence." What is the difference? Do you agree with this approach?

4. According to Kierkegaard, reason is limited. Discuss its limitations. Do you agree with him?

5. Compare Pascal and Kierkegaard on the merits and limits of reason, and on the relationship between faith and reason. Whose position do you favor, and why?

W. K. CLIFFORD

THE ETHICS OF BELIEF

I n this selection, W. K. Clifford argues that it is always and everywhere wrong to believe anything on the basis of insufficient evidence. Whereas Kierkegaard allows for belief in God's existence without evidence, Clifford maintains that nothing, including a belief in the existence of God, should be held without sufficient evidence. For Clifford, the ethics of belief requires that we not "nourish belief by suppressing doubts and avoiding investigation." If we accept a belief on insufficient evidence, "the pleasure is stolen," maintains Clifford. "Not only does it deceive ourselves by giving us a sense of power which we do not really possess, but it is sinful, because it is stolen in defiance of our duty to mankind," continues Clifford." It is our "duty to guard ourselves from such beliefs as from a pestilence, which may shortly master our own body, and then spread to the rest of the town." "Every rustic who delivers in the village alehouse his slow, infrequent sentences," charges Clifford, "may help to kill or keep alive the fatal superstitions which clog his race." "No simplicity of mind, no obscurity of station can escape the duty of questioning all that we believe."

W. K. (William Kingdon) Clifford (1845–79), an English mathematician and philosopher, taught at Trinity College, Cambridge, and University College, London. Whereas early in his life he studied the writings of Thomas Aquinas and supported Catholicism, later in his life he turned against religion and became an agnostic, asserting that it is impossible to attain knowledge of God. Clifford published only some technical and nontechnical papers based on his lectures, and a dynamics textbook. The following selection is from his most famous essay, "The Ethics of Belief" (1877).

A ship-owner was about to send to sea an emigrant- ship. He knew that she was old, and not over-well built at the first; that she had seen many seas and climes, and often had needed repairs. Doubts had been suggested to him that possibly she was not seaworthy. These doubts preyed upon his mind and made him unhappy; he thought that perhaps he ought to have her thoroughly overhauled and refitted, even though this should put him to great expense. Before the ship sailed, however, he succeeded in overcoming these melancholy reflections. He said to himself that she had gone safely through so many voyages and weathered so many storms that it was idle to suppose she would not come safely home from this trip also. He would put his trust in Providence, which could hardly fail to protect all these unhappy families that were leaving their father-land to seek for better times elsewhere. He would dismiss from his mind all ungenerous suspicions about the honesty of builders and contractors. In such ways he acquired a sincere and comfortable conviction that his vessel was thoroughly safe and seaworthy; he watched her departure with a light heart, and benevolent wishes for the success of the exiles in their strange new home that was to be; and he got his insurance money when she went down to mid-ocean and told no tales.

[1.] What shall we say of him? Surely this, that he was verily guilty of the death of those men. It is admitted that he did sincerely believe in the soundness of his ship; but the sincerity of his conviction can in no wise help him, because *he had no right to believe on such evidence as was before him.* He had acquired his belief not by honestly earning it in patient investigation, but by stifling his doubts. And although in the end he may have felt so sure about it that he could not think otherwise, yet inasmuch as he had knowingly and willingly worked himself into that frame of mind, he must be held responsible for it.

[2.] Let us alter the case a little, and suppose that the ship was not unsound after all; that she made her voyage safely, and many others after it. Will that diminish the guilt of her owner? Not one jot. When an action is once done, it is right or wrong forever; no accidental failure of its good or evil fruits can possibly alter that. The man would not have been innocent, he would only have been not found out. The question of right or wrong has to do with the origin of his belief, not the matter of it; not what it was, but how he got it; not whether it turned out to be true or false, but whether he had a right to believe on such evidence as was before him.

[1, 2 cont.] There was once an island in which some of the inhabitants professed a religion teaching neither the doctrine of original sin nor that of eternal punishment. A suspicion got abroad that the professors of this religion had made use of unfair means to get their doctrines taught to children. They were accused of wresting the laws of their country in such a way as to remove children from the care of their natural and legal guardians; and even of stealing them away and keeping them concealed from their friends and relations. A certain number of men formed themselves into a society for the purpose of agitating the public about this matter. They published grave accusations against individual citizens of the highest position and character, and did all in their power to injure those citizens in the exercise of their profession. So great was the noise they made, that a Commission was appointed to investigate the facts; but after the Commission had carefully inquired into all the evidence that could be got, it appeared that the accused were innocent. Not only had they been accused on insufficient evidence, but the evidence of their innocence was such as the agitators might easily have obtained, if they had attempted a fair inquiry. After these disclosures the inhabitants of that country looked upon the members of the agitating society, not only as persons whose judgment was to be distrusted, but also as no longer to be counted honorable men. For although they had sincerely and conscientiously believed in the charges they had made, *yet they had no right to believe on such evidence as was before them.* Their sincere convictions, instead of being honestly earned by patient inquiring, were stolen by listening to the voice of prejudice and passion.

Let us vary this case also, and suppose, other things remaining as before, that a still more accurate investigation proved the accused to have been really guilty. Would this make any difference in the guilt of the accusers? Clearly not; the question is not whether their belief was true or false, but whether they entertained it on wrong grounds. They would no doubt say, "Now you see that we were right after all; next time perhaps you will believe us." And they might be believed, but they would not thereby become honorable men. They would not be innocent, they would only be not found out. Every one of them, if he chose to examine himself *in foro conscientiae* [in the forum of his conscience], would know that he had acquired and nourished a belief, when he had no right to believe on such evidence as was before him; and therein he would know that he had done a wrong thing.

It may be said, however, that in both of these supposed cases it is not the belief which is judged to be wrong, but the action following upon it. The shipowner might say, "I am perfectly certain that my ship is sound, but still I feel it my duty to have her examined, before trusting the lives of so many people to her." And it might be said to the agitator, "However convinced you were of the justice of your cause and the truth of your convictions, you ought not to have made a public attack upon any man's character until you had examined the evidence on both sides with the utmost patience and care."

In the first place, let us admit that, so far as it goes, this view of the case is right and necessary; right, because even when a man's belief is so fixed that he cannot think otherwise, he still has a choice in regard to the action suggested by it, and so cannot escape the duty of investigating on the ground of the strength of his convictions; and necessary, because those who are not yet capable of controlling their feelings and thoughts must have a plain-rule dealing with overt acts.

But this being premised as necessary, it becomes clear that it is not sufficient, and that our previous judgment is required to supplement it. For it is not possible so to sever the belief from the action it suggests as to condemn the one without condemning the other. No man holding a strong belief on one side of a question, or even wishing to hold a belief on one side, can investigate it with such fairness and completeness as if he were really in doubt and unbiased; so that the existence of a belief not founded on fair inquiry unfits a man for the performance of this necessary duty.

[3.] Nor is that truly a belief at all which has not some influence upon the actions of him who holds it. He who truly believes that which prompts him to an action has looked upon the action to lust after it, he has committed it already in his heart. If a belief is not realized immediately in open deeds, it is stored up for the guidance of the future. It goes to make a part of that aggregate of beliefs which is the link between sensation and action at every moment of all our lives, and which is so organized and compacted together that no part of it can be isolated from the rest, but every new addition modifies the structure of the whole. No real belief, however trifling and fragmentary it may seem, is ever truly insignificant; it prepares us to receive more of its like, confirms those which resembled it before, and weakens others; and so gradually it lays a stealthy train in our inmost thoughts, which may some day explode into overt action, and leave its stamp upon our character forever.

[4.] And no one man's belief is in any case a private matter which concerns himself alone. Our lives are guided by that general conception of the course of things which has been created by society for social purposes. Our words, our phrases, our forms and processes and modes of thought are common property, fashioned and perfected from age to age; an heirloom which every succeeding generation inherits as a precious deposit and a sacred trust to be handed on to the next one, not unchanged but enlarged and purified, with some clear marks of its proper handiwork. Into this, for good or ill, is woven every belief of every man who has speech of his fellows. An awful privilege, and an awful responsibility, that we should help to create the world in which posterity will live.

In the two supposed cases which have been considered, it has been judged wrong to believe on insufficient evidence, or to nourish belief by suppressing doubts and avoiding investigation. The reason of this judgment is not far to seek: It is that in both these cases the belief held by one man was of great importance to other men. But for as much as no belief held by one man, however seemingly trivial the belief, and however obscure the believer, is ever actually insignificant or without its effect on the fate of mankind, we have no choice but to extend our judgment to all cases

of belief whatever. Belief, that sacred faculty which prompts the decisions of our will, and knits into harmonious working all the compacted energies of our being, is ours not for ourselves, but for humanity. It is rightly used on truths which have been established by long experience and waiting toil, and which have stood in the fierce light of free and fearless questioning. Then it helps to bind men together, and to strengthen and direct their common action. It is desecrated when given to unproved and unquestioned statements, for the solace and private pleasure of the believer; to add a tinsel splendor to the plain straight road of our life and display a bright mirage beyond it; or even to drown the common sorrows of our kind by a self-deception which allows them not only to cast down but also to degrade us. Whoso would deserve well of his fellows in this matter will guard the purity of his belief with a very fanaticism of jealous care, lest at any time it should rest on an unworthy object and catch a stain which can never be wiped away.

It is not only the leader of men, statesman, philosopher, or poet, that owes this bounden duty to mankind. Every rustic who delivers in the village alehouse his slow, infrequent sentences may help to kill or keep alive the fatal superstitions which clog his race. Every hard-worked wife of an artisan may transmit to her children beliefs which shall knit society together, or rend it in pieces. No simplicity of mind, no obscurity of station can escape the duty of questioning all that we believe.

It is true that duty is a hard one, and the doubt which comes out of it is often a very bitter thing. It leaves us bare and powerless where we thought that we were safe and strong. To know all about anything is to know how to deal with it under all circumstances. We feel much happier and more secure when we think we know precisely what to do, no matter what happens, than when we have lost our way and do not know where to turn. And if we have supposed ourselves to know all about anything, and to be capable of doing what is fit in regard to it, we naturally do not like to find that we are really ignorant and powerless, that we have to begin again at the beginning, and try to learn what the thing is and how it is to be dealt with—if indeed anything can be learned about it. It is the sense of power attached to a sense of knowledge that makes men desirous of believing, and afraid of doubting.

This sense of power is the highest and best of pleasures when the belief on which it is founded is true belief, and has been fairly earned by investigation. For then we may justly feel that it is common property, and holds good for others as well as for ourselves. Then we may be glad, not that *I* have learned secrets by which I am safer and stronger, but that *we men* have got mastery over more of the world; and we shall be strong, not for ourselves, but in the name of Man and in his strength. But if the belief has been accepted on insufficient evidence, the pleasure is a stolen one. Not only does it deceive ourselves by giving us a sense of power which we do not really possess, but it is sinful, because it is stolen in defiance of our duty to mankind. That duty is to guard ourselves from such beliefs as from a pestilence, which may shortly master our own body and then spread to the rest of the town. What would be thought of one who, for the sake of a sweet fruit , should deliberately run the risk of bringing a plague upon his family and his neighbors?

[5.] And, as in other such cases, it is not the risk only which has to be considered; for a bad action is always bad at the time when it is done, no matter what happens afterwards. Every time we let ourselves believe for unworthy reasons, we weaken our powers of self-control, of doubting, of judicially and fairly weighing evidence. We all suffer severely enough from the maintenance and support of false beliefs and the fatally wrong actions which they lead to, and the evil born when one such belief is entertained is great and wide. But a greater and wider evil arises when the credulous character is maintained and supported, when a habit of believing for unworthy reasons is fostered and made permanent. If I steal money from any person, there may be no harm done by the mere transfer of possession; he may not feel the loss, or it may prevent him from using the money badly. But I cannot help doing this great wrong toward Man, that I make myself dishonest. What hurts society is not that it should lose its property, but that it should become a den of thieves; for then it must cease to be society. This is why we ought not to do evil that good may come;

for at any rate this great evil has come, that we have done evil and are made wicked thereby. In like manner, if I let myself believe anything on insufficient evidence, there may be no great harm done by the mere belief; it may be true after all, or I may never have occasion to exhibit it in outward acts. But I cannot help doing this great wrong toward Man, that I make myself credulous. The danger to society is not merely that it should believe wrong things, though that is great enough, but that it should become credulous, and lose the habit of testing things and inquiring into them; for then it must sink back into savagery.

The harm which is done by credulity in a man is not confined to the fostering of a credulous character in others, and consequent support of false beliefs. Habitual want of care about what I believe leads to habitual want of care in others about the truth of what is told to me. Men speak the truth to one another when each reveres the truth in his own mind and in the other's mind; but how shall my friend revere the truth in my mind when I myself am careless about it, when I believe things because I want to believe them, and because they are comforting and pleasant? Will he not learn to cry "Peace" to me, when there is no peace? By such a course I shall surround myself with a thick atmosphere of falsehood and fraud, and in that I must live. It may matter little to me, in my cloud-castle of sweet illusions and darling lies; but it matters much to Man that I have made my neighbors ready to deceive. The credulous man is father to the liar and the cheat; he lives in the bosom of this his family, and it is no marvel if he should become even as they are. So closely are our duties knit together, that whoso shall keep the whole law, and yet offend in one point, he is guilty of all.

To sum up: It is wrong always, everywhere, and for any one to believe anything upon insufficient evidence. . . .

"But," says one, "I am a busy man; I have no time for the long course of study which would be necessary to make me in any degree a competent judge of certain questions, or even able to understand the nature of the arguments." Then he should have no time to believe.

DISCUSSION QUESTIONS

1. Clifford argues that it is always wrong for anyone to believe anything upon insufficient evidence. What is his argument? Is it sound? Why or why not?

2. Why does Clifford assert that "no real belief, however trifling and fragmentary it may seem, is ever truly insignificant?" Do you agree with him?

3. Clifford maintains that we have a "duty" to question all we believe, that "it is sinful to accept a belief with insufficient evidence, because it is stolen in defiance of our duty to mankind." What does he mean by "duty"? What is our "duty to mankind"?

4. If we accept a belief on insufficient evidence, "the pleasure is stolen," maintains Clifford. Do you agree with this? Would Kierkegaard agree with this? Why or why not?

5. For Clifford, what would count as "sufficient evidence"? Do you agree with him? Do you think we need to have different standards of evidence for science and for religion? Why or why not?

Agnes of God
[USA 1985] 1 hour, 39 minutes
Directed by Norman Jewison

A newborn child is found strangled in a Montreal convent, forcing court psychiatrist Dr. Martha Livingston (Jane Fonda) to investigate. Upon arriving at the convent, Livingston remains truthful to rationality, which causes her to dismiss the notion put forth by the mother superior, Mother Miriam Ruth (Anne Bancroft), that the baby was born of a virgin, Sister Agnes (Meg Tilly). Mother Miriam Ruth persists in the belief that Agnes was given a child from God, mirroring the virgin birth of Jesus of Nazareth. The worlds of science and religion collide as Livingston fights for the life of Agnes, who is being held accountable for the murder of her child. As the story unfolds, Livingston discovers that Agnes endured years of psychological damage from her mother. Livingston believes that this damage may have caused Agnes to murder her child. In the end, through a physical display of Agnes receiving the stigmata (marks resembling the crucifixion wounds of Jesus of Nazareth) and her account under hypnosis of the night of conception, Livingston concludes that the murdered child was indeed a gift from God. Agnes is absolved by the court due to her years of psychological damage and is allowed to remain a faithful sister of the Montreal convent.

DISCUSSION QUESTIONS

1. The mother superior says to Livingston that "a miracle is an event without an explanation. If she is capable of putting a hole in her hand without the benefit of a nail, why couldn't she split a cell in her womb. . . . I want the opportunity to believe." Also, Livingston says, "I want to believe she is blessed." What role, if any, does "wanting to believe" that this was a virgin birth play in your final analysis of the situation? Is reason alone sufficient to reach a conclusion as to whether the birth was a virgin birth?

2. When the mother superior says to Livingston that "a miracle is an event without an explanation," what do you think she means? For example, does she mean that there is no *rational* explanation for the event? Or does she mean that there is no explanation period? Or something else? Do you believe that there are events without an explanation? What do they reveal, if anything, about the nature of God?

3. Should the birth of a baby born of a virgin be considered a *proof* of the existence of God? Why or why not? Compare this birth as a proof of the existence of God to the other proofs in this chapter. In what way is it more convincing? In what way is it less convincing? Why?

4. Livingston was eventually convinced that Agnes's baby was a virgin birth by the stigmata she received and her account under hypnosis of the conception. Are you convinced?

WILLIAM JAMES

THE WILL TO BELIEVE

In "The Will to Believe," William James argues that when the option (decision action) between two hypotheses (propositions) is genuine, and the intellect cannot resolve the matter one way or the other, we must use our passions to reach a decision. James is directly attacking W. K. Clifford and others, who would argue that it is always and everywhere wrong to believe anything on the basis of insufficient evidence. For James, if the choice between two hypotheses is genuine—that is, living, forced, and momentous—then we must arrive at a decision on a basis other than evidential or intellectual. Following Pascal, who says, "The heart has its reasons that reason does not know," James maintains that our "passional nature not only lawfully may, but must, decide an option between propositions" when reason fails to point to a decision. However, the same is not true of options between hypotheses that are not genuine. If the choice between two hypotheses is dead, avoidable, or trivial, the will to believe it is not warranted. In terms of religion, James says, "If we are to discuss the question at all, it must involve a living option." If it is not, James maintains, we need not go any further in considering the religious hypothesis as an option. If religion is a living option, then, as James explains, it also offers itself as both a momentous and a forced option. As a momentous option, "We are supposed to gain, even now, by our belief, and to lose by our nonbelief, a certain vital good"; as a forced option, "We cannot escape the issue by remaining skeptical and waiting for more light, because, although we do avoid error in that way *if religion be untrue*, we lose the good, *if it be true*, just as certainly as if we positively chose to disbelieve." "If religion be true and the evidence for it be still insufficient," continues James, "I do not wish . . . to forfeit my sole chance in life of getting upon the winning side,—that chance, of course, on my willingness to run the risk of acting as if my passional need of taking the world religiously might be prophetic and right."

William James (1842–1910), an American philosopher and psychologist, taught at Harvard University for his entire career. He was the brother of the novelist Henry James and is widely regarded as one of America's greatest philosophers. James was instrumental, along with Charles Peirce, in the founding of pragmatism and was one of the founders of modern psychology. While no enemy of religion, James believed that religious *experience* was more important than religious *doctrine*. If religious experience is not vital, it runs the risk of becoming "fossil conventionalism." While some maintain that his *The Principles of Psychology*

(1890) is his greatest work, he was author of a number of other highly regarded books including *The Will to Believe* (1897), *The Varieties of Religious Experience* (1902), *Pragmatism* (1907), *A Pluralistic Universe* (1909), and *Some Problems of Philosophy* (1911). The following selection is from his widely read essay "The Will to Believe" (1896), which was initially an address to the Philosophical Clubs of Yale and Brown universities.

I have long defended to my own students the lawfulness of voluntarily adopted faith; but as soon as they have got well imbued with the logical spirit, they have as a rule refused to admit my contention to be lawful philosophically, even though in point of fact they were personally all the time chockfull of some faith or other themselves. I am all the while, however, so profoundly convinced that my own position is correct, that your invitation has seemed to me a good occasion to make my statements more clear. Perhaps your minds will be more open than those with which I have hitherto had to deal. I will be as little technical as I can, though I must begin by setting up some technical distinctions that will help us in the end.

Let us give the name of *hypothesis* to anything that may be proposed to our belief; and just as the electricians speak of live and dead wires, let us speak of any hypothesis as either *live* or *dead*. A live hypothesis is one which appeals as a real possibility to him to whom it is proposed. If I ask you to believe in the Mahdi,* the notion makes no electric connection with your nature,—it refuses to scintillate with any credibility at all. As an hypothesis it is completely dead. To an Arab, however (even if he be not one of the Mahdi's followers), the hypothesis is among the mind's possibilities: it is alive. This shows that deadness and liveness in an hypothesis are not intrinsic properties, but relations to the individual thinker. They are measured by his willingness to act. The maximum of liveness in an hypothesis means willingness to act irrevocably. Practically, that means belief; but there is some believing tendency wherever there is willingness to act at all.

Next, let us call the decision between two hypotheses an *option*. Options may be several

kinds. They may be—1, *living* or *dead*; 2, *forced* or *avoidable*; 3, *momentous* or *trivial*; and for our purposes we may call an option a *genuine* option when it is of the forced, living, and momentous kind.

1. A living option is one in which both hypotheses are live ones. If I say to you: "Be a theosophist or be a Mohammedan," it is probably a dead option, because for you neither hypothesis is likely to be alive. But if I say, "Be an agnostic or be a Christian," it is otherwise: trained as you are, each hypothesis makes some appeal, however small, to your belief.

2. Next, if I say to you: "Choose between going out with your umbrella or without it," I do not offer you a genuine option, for it is not forced. You can easily avoid it by not going out at all. Similarly, if I say, "Either love me or hate me," "Either call my theory true or call it false," your option is avoidable. You may remain indifferent to me, neither loving nor hating, and you may decline to offer any judgment as to my theory. But if I say, "Either accept this truth or go without it," I put on you a forced option, for there is no standing place outside of the alternative. Every dilemma based on a complete logical disjunction, with no possibility of not choosing, is an option of this forced kind.

3. Finally, if I were Dr. Nansen and proposed to you to join my North Pole expedition, your option would be momentous; for this would probably be your only similar opportunity, and your choice now would either exclude you from the North Pole sort of immortality

---

* Madhi is Allah's representative who will appear on earth to lead Islam to worldwide victory. He will be the final Imam, that is, the last in the line of true succession to Mohammed. The Madhi is the Islamic equivalent to the Messiah.—Ed.

altogether or put at least the chance of it into your hands. He who refuses to embrace a unique opportunity loses the prize as surely as if he tried and failed. *Per contra*, the option is trivial when the opportunity is not unique, when the stake is insignificant, or when the decision is reversible if it later prove unwise. Such trivial options abound in the scientific life. A chemist finds an hypothesis live enough to spend a year in its verification. He believes in it to that extent. But if his experiments prove inconclusive either way, he is quit for his loss of time, no vital harm being done.

The thesis I defend is, briefly stated, this: *Our passional nature not only lawfully may, but must, decide an option between propositions, whenever it is a genuine option that cannot by its nature be decided on intellectual grounds; for to say, under such circumstances, "Do not decide, but leave the question open," is itself a passional decision—just like deciding yes or no—and is attended with the same risk of losing the truth. . . .*

Wherever the option between losing truth and gaining it is not momentous, we can throw the chance of *gaining truth* away, and at any rate save ourselves from any chance of *believing falsehood*, by not making up our minds at all till objective evidence has come. In scientific questions, this is almost always the case; and even in human affairs in general, the need of acting is seldom so urgent that a false belief to act on is better than no belief at all. Law courts, indeed, have to decide on the best evidence attainable for the moment, because a judge's duty is to make law as well as to ascertain it, and (as a learned judge once said to me) few cases are worth spending much time over: The great thing is to have them decided on *any* acceptable principle and gotten out of the way. But in our dealings with objective nature we obviously are recorders, not makers, of the truth; and decisions for the mere sake of deciding promptly and getting on to the next business would be wholly out of place. Throughout the breadth of physical nature facts are what they are quite independently of us, and seldom is there any such hurry about them that the risks of being duped by believing a premature theory need be faced. The questions here are always trivial

options; the hypotheses are hardly living (at anyrate not living for us spectators); the choice between believing truth or falsehood is seldom forced. The attitude of skeptical balance is therefore the absolutely wise one if we would escape mistakes. What difference, indeed, does it make to most of us whether we have or have not a theory of the Röntgen rays, whether we believe or not in mind-stuff, or have a conviction about the causality of conscious states? It makes no difference. Such options are not forced on us. On every account it is better not to make them, but still keep weighing reasons *pro et contra* with an indifferent hand.

I speak, of course, here of the purely judging mind. For purposes of discovery such indifference is to be less highly recommended, and science would be far less advanced than she is if the passionate desires of individuals to get their own faiths confirmed had been kept out of the game. . . . On the other hand, if you want an absolute duffer in an investigation, you must, after all, take the man who has no interest whatever in its results: He is the warranted incapable, the positive fool. The most useful investigator, because the most sensitive observer, is always he whose eager interest in one side of the question is balanced by an equally keen nervousness lest he become deceived. Science has organized this nervousness into a regular *technique*, her so-called method of verification; and she has fallen so deeply in love with the method that one may even say she ceased to care for truth by itself at all. It is only truth as technically verified that interests her. The truth of truths might come in merely affirmative form, and she would decline to touch it. Such truth as that, she might repeat with Clifford, would be stolen in defiance of her duty to mankind. Human passions, however, are stronger than technical rules. "Le cœur a ses raisons," as Pascal says, "que la raison ne connaît pas" [The heart has its reasons that reason does not know]: and however indifferent to all but the bare rules of the game the umpire, the abstract intellect, may be, the concrete players who furnish him the materials to judge of are usually, each one of them, in love with some pet "live hypothesis" of his own. Let us agree, however, that wherever there is no forced option, the dispassionately judicial intellect with no pet hypothesis, saving us, as it does, from dupery at any rate, ought to be our ideal.

The question next arises, Are there not somewhere forced options in our speculative questions, and can we (as men who may be interested at least as much in positively gaining truth as in merely escaping dupery) always wait with impunity till the coercive evidence shall have arrived? It seems *a priori* improbable that the truth should be so nicely adjusted to our needs and powers as that. In the great boarding-house of nature, the cakes and the butter and the syrup seldom come out so even and leave the plates so clean. Indeed, we should view them with scientific suspicion if they did.

Moral questions immediately present themselves as questions whose solution cannot wait for sensible proof. A moral question is a question not of what sensibly exists, but of what is good, or would be good if it did exist. Science can tell us what exists; but to compare the *worths*, both of what exists and of what does not exist, we must consult, not science, but what Pascal calls our heart. Science herself consults her heart when she lays it down that the infinite ascertainment of fact and correction of false belief are the supreme goods for man. Challenge the statement, and science can only repeat it oracularly, or else prove it by showing that such ascertainment and correction bring man all sorts of other goods which man's heart in turn declares. The question of having moral beliefs at all or not having them is decided by our will. Are our moral preferences true or false, or are they only odd biological phenomena, making things good or bad for *us*, but in themselves indifferent? How can your pure intellect decide? If your heart does not *want* a world of moral reality, your head will assuredly never make you believe in one. . . .

Turn now from these wide questions of good to a certain class of questions of fact, questions concerning personal relations, states of mind between one man and another. *Do you like me or not?*—for example. Whether you do or not depends, in countless instances, on whether I meet you half-way, am willing to assume that you must like me, and show you trust and expectation. The previous faith on my part in your liking's existence is in such cases what makes your liking come. But if I stand aloof, and refuse to budge an inch until I have objective evidence, until you shall have done something apt, as the absolutists say, *ad extorquendum assensum meum* [for forcing my agreement], ten to one your liking never comes. How many women's hearts are vanquished by the mere sanguine insistence of some man that they *must* love him! He will not consent to the hypothesis that they cannot. The desire for a certain kind of truth here brings about that special truth's existence; and so it is in innumerable cases of other sorts. Who gains promotions, boons, appointments but the man in whose life they are seen to play the part of live hypotheses, who discounts them, sacrifices other things for their sake before they have come, and takes risks for them in advance? His faith acts on the powers above him as a claim, and creates its own verification.

A social organism of any sort whatever, large or small, is what it is because each member proceeds to his own duty with a trust that the other members will simultaneously do theirs. Wherever a desired result is achieved by the cooperation of many independent persons, its existence as a fact is a pure consequence of the precursive faith in one another of those immediately concerned. A government, an army, a commercial system, a ship, a college, an athletic team, all exist on this condition, without which not only is nothing achieved, but nothing is even attempted. A whole train of passengers (individually brave enough) will be looted by a few highwaymen, simply because the latter can count on one another, while each passenger fears that if he makes a movement of resistance, he will be shot before anyone else backs him up. If we believed that the whole car-full would rise at once with us, we should each severally rise, and train-robbing would never even be attempted. There are, then, cases where a fact cannot come at all unless a preliminary faith exists in its coming. *And where faith in a fact can help create the fact*, that would be an insane logic which should say that faith running ahead of scientific evidence is the "lowest kind of immorality" into which a thinking being can fall. Yet such is the logic by which our scientific absolutists pretend to regulate our lives!

In truths dependent on our personal action, then, faith based on desire is certainly a *lawful and possibly an indispensable thing.*

But now, it will be said, these are all childish human cases, and have nothing to do with great cosmic matters, like the question of religious faith. Let us then pass on to that. Religions differ so much in their accidents that in discussing the religious question we must make it very generic and broad. What then do we now mean by the religious hypothesis? Science says things are; morality says some things are better than other things; and religion says essentially two things.

First, she says that the best things are the more eternal things, the overlapping things, the things in the universe that throw the last stone, so to speak, and say the final word. "Perfection is eternal,"—this phrase of Charles Secrétan* seems a good way of putting this first affirmation of religion, an affirmation which obviously cannot yet be verified scientifically at all.

The second affirmation of religion is that we are better off even now if we believe her first affirmation to be true.

Now, let us consider what the logical elements of this situation are *in case the religious hypothesis in both its branches be really true.* (Of course, we must admit that possibility at the outset. If we are to discuss the question at all, it must involve a living option. If for any of you religion be a hypothesis that cannot, by any living possibility be true, then you need go no farther. I speak to the "saving remnant" alone.) So proceeding, we see, first that religion offers itself as a *momentous* option. We are supposed to gain, even now, by our belief, and to lose by our nonbelief, a certain vital good. Secondly, religion is a *forced* option, so far as that good goes. We cannot escape the issue by remaining sceptical and waiting for more light, because, although we do avoid error in that way *if religion be untrue,* we lose the good, *if it be true,* just as certainly as if we positively chose to disbelieve. It is as if a man should hesitate indefinitely to ask a certain woman to marry him because he was not perfectly sure that she would prove an angel after he brought her home. Would he not cut himself off from that particular angel-possibility as decisively as if he went and married some one else? Scepticism, then, is not avoidance of option;

it is option of a certain particular kind of risk. *Better risk loss of truth than chance of error,*—that is your faith-vetoer's exact position. He is actively playing his stake as much as the believer is; he is backing the field against the religious hypothesis, just as the believer is backing the religious hypothesis against the field. To preach scepticism to us as a duty until "sufficient evidence" for religion be found, is tantamount therefore to telling us, when in presence of the religious hypothesis, that to yield to our fear of its being error is wiser and better than to yield to our hope that it may be true. It is not intellect against all passions, then; it is only intellect with one passion laying down its law. And by what, forsooth, is the supreme wisdom of this passion warranted? Dupery for dupery, what proof is there that dupery through hope is so much worse than dupery through fear? I, for one, can see no proof; and I simply refuse obedience to the scientist's command to imitate his kind of option, in a case where my own stake is important enough to give me the right to choose my own form of risk. If religion be true and the evidence for it be still insufficient, I do not wish, by putting your extinguisher upon my nature (which feels to me as if it had after all some business in this matter), to forfeit my sole chance in life of getting upon the winning side,—that chance depending, of course, on my willingness to run the risk of acting as if my passional need of taking the world religiously might be prophetic and right.

All this is on the supposition that it really may be prophetic and right, and that, even to us who are discussing the matter, religion is a live hypothesis which may be true, Now, to most of us religion comes in a still further way that makes a veto on our active faith even more illogical. The more perfect and more eternal aspect of the universe is represented in our religions as having personal form. The universe is no longer a mere *It* to us, but a *Thou,* if we are religious; and any relation that may be possible from person to person might be possible here. For instance, although in one sense we are passive portions of the universe, in another we show a curious

---

* Charles Secrétan (1815–95), a Swiss philosopher, studied under Friedrich Schelling in Munich. He developed a rational, philosophical religion aimed at reconciling Christianity with the basic principles of metaphysical philosophy.—Ed.

autonomy, as if we were small active centres on our own account. We feel, too, as if the appeal of religion to us were made to our own active goodwill, as if evidence might be forever withheld from us unless we met the hypothesis halfway. To take a trivial illustration: just as a man who in a company of gentlemen made no advances, asked a warrant for every concession, and believed no one's word without proof, would cut himself off by such churlishness from all the social rewards that a more trusting spirit would earn,—so here, one who should shut himself up in snarling logicality and try to make the gods extort his recognition willy-nilly, or not get it at all, might cut himself off forever from his only opportunity of making the gods' acquaintance. This feeling, forced on us we know not whence, that by obstinately believing that there are gods (although not to do so would be so easy both for our logic and our life) we are doing the universe the deepest service we can, seems part of the living essence of the religious hypothesis. If the hypothesis *were* true in all its parts, including this one, then pure intellectualism, with its veto on our making willing advances, would be an absurdity; and some participation of our sympathetic nature would be logically required. I, therefore, for one, cannot see my way to accepting the agnostic rules for truth-seeking, or willfully agree to keep my willing nature out of the game. I cannot do so for this plain reason, that *a rule of thinking which would absolutely prevent me from acknowledging certain kinds of truth if those kinds of truth were really there, would be an irrational rule.* That for me is the long and short of the formal logic of the situation, no matter what the kinds of truth might materially be.

I confess I do not see how this logic can be escaped. But sad experience makes me fear that some of you may still shrink from radically saying with me, *in abstracto*, that we have the right to believe at our own risk any hypothesis that is live enough to tempt our will. I suspect, however, that if this is so, it is because you have got away from the abstract logical point of view altogether, and are thinking (perhaps without realizing it) of some particular religious hypothesis which for you is dead. The freedom to "believe what we will" you apply to the case of some patent superstition; and the faith you think of is the faith defined by the schoolboy when he said, "Faith is when you believe something that you know ain't true." I can only repeat that this is misapprehension. *In concreto*, the freedom to believe can only cover living options which the intellect of the individual cannot by itself resolve; and living options never seem absurdities to him who has them to consider. When I look at the religious question as it really puts itself to concrete men, and when I think of all the possibilities which both practically and theoretically it involves, then this command that we shall put a stopper on our heart, instincts, and courage, and *wait*—acting of course meanwhile more or less as if religion were *not* true—till dooms day, or till such time as our intellect and senses working together may have raked in evidence enough,—this command, I say, seems to me the queerest idol ever manufactured in the philosophic cave. Were we scholastic absolutists, there might be more excuse. If we had an infallible intellect with its objective certitudes, we might feel ourselves disloyal to such a perfect organ of knowledge in not trusting to it exclusively, in not waiting for its releasing word. But if we are empiricists, if we believe that no bell in us tolls to let us know for certain when truth is in our grasp, then it seems a piece of idle fantasticality to preach so solemnly our duty of waiting for the bell. Indeed we *may* wait if we will.—I hope you do not think that I am denying that,—but if we do so, we do so at our peril as much as if we believed. In either case we *act*, taking our life in our hands. No one of us ought to issue vetoes to the other, nor should we bandy words of abuse. We ought, on the contrary, delicately and profoundly to respect one another's mental freedom: then only shall we bring about the intellectual republic: then only shall we have that spirit of inner tolerance without which all our outer tolerance is soulless, and which is empiricism's glory; then only shall we live and let live, in speculative as well as in practical things.

DISCUSSION QUESTIONS

1. For James, what is the difference between a "live" and a "dead" hypothesis? What is the difference between "living" and "dead," "forced" and "avoidable," and "momentous" and "trivial" options? Drawing from your own experience, give examples of each.

2. Is James's position on justifying religious hypotheses more like a Pascalian "wager" or a Kierkegaardian "leap"? Or does it have affinities with neither? Discuss.

3. James says, "I do not wish . . . to forfeit my sole chance in life of getting upon the winning side,—that chance depending, of course, on my willingness to run the risk of acting as if my passional need of taking the world religiously might be prophetic and right." Do you agree with James? Why or why not?

4. In part, James is criticizing Clifford's claim that it is always and everywhere wrong to believe anything on the basis of insufficient evidence. Does James make a convincing case? Why or why not?

5. For James, are scientific and moral hypotheses subject to the same conditions of belief and disbelief as religious hypotheses? Do you agree with James?

Contact
[USA 1997] 2 hours, 30 minutes
Directed by Robert Zemeckis

Religious faith and scientific reason are put to the test when astronomer Ellie Arroway (Jodie Foster) discovers a message from deep space. After years of unsuccessful attempts to locate a voice in space, Arroway retrieves a message containing a blueprint from the distant Vega region. After nearly being forced out of her own project, Arroway races to uncover the meaning behind the message. She discovers that the blueprint provides the schematics of a space pod, which is quickly built by a governmental coalition. After the first pod is destroyed by a radical religious group, Ellie is chosen to lead the second attempt. The world watches her pod slip through the portal device in a matter of seconds while Ellie travels eighteen hours through space to meet an alien holographic image of her dead father.

The story Ellie tells of her eighteen-hour voyage is met with disbelief. A commission is assigned to investigate her experience. At first, the commission does not believe any of Ellie's claims because all onlookers saw the pod slip directly through the transporter in a matter of seconds. However, this disbelief is shattered after the discovery that there is a gap of eighteen hours, the exact elapsed time that Ellie claimed she was away, recorded on her head-camera, a device she wore while in the pod. The findings of the commission lead to further questions concerning the nature of life elsewhere in the universe. *Contact* suggests that faith is not just an aspect of religious belief, but that it can also play a key role in scientific belief and progress.

In the film, Palmer Joss (Matthew McConaughey) is a former acquaintance of Ellie's who becomes the "spiritual advisor" to the president of the United States. Palmer is generally supportive of Ellie, though he questions her faith in science over religion. More specifically, Palmer thinks that reason and observation limit Ellie's ability to truly understand the mysteries of the universe. Palmer pushes Ellie to place more trust in her faith and instinct.

DISCUSSION QUESTIONS

1. Joss says, "There I was just looking at the sky, then I felt something. I don't know. All I know is that I wasn't alone, and for the first time in my life I wasn't scared of nothing, not even dying. It was God." What role does religious experience or feeling (as opposed to religious reason) play in our understanding of the nature of God? Discuss his statement in terms of James's notion of the will to believe and Kierkegaard's notion of the leap of faith.

2. Discuss the following questions raised by Joss: "The question I'm asking is, are we happier? As a human race, is the world fundamentally a better place because of science and technology? We shop at home, we surf the Web, but at the same time, we feel emptier, lonelier, and more cut off from each other than at any other time in history . . . maybe it's because we're looking for the meaning, well, what is the meaning? We have mindless jobs, we take frantic vacations, deficit-finance trips to the mall to buy more things that we feel are gonna fill these holes in our lives. Is it any wonder that we've lost our sense of direction?" Do you agree with him? Why or why not?

3. Arroway says to Joss, "It's like you're saying that science killed God. What if science simply revealed that he never existed in the first place? . . . Occam's Razor, you ever heard of it? . . . . It's a basic scientific principle. And it says, all things being equal, the simplest explanation tends to be the right one." Are the explanations of the origin and nature of the universe "simpler" in science than they are in religion (or theology)? Explain.

4. The following is an exchange between Ellie Arroway and Palmer Joss on the limits of proof:

    ELLIE   "An all-powerful and -mysterious God created the Universe, and then decided not to give any proof of his existence, or that he simply doesn't exist at all, and that we created him so that we didn't have to feel so small and alone?"

    PALMER   "I don't know. I couldn't imagine living in a world where God didn't exist. I wouldn't want to."

    ELLIE   "How do you know you're not deluding yourself? As for me, I'd need proof."

    PALMER   "Proof. Did you love your father?"

    ELLIE   "Huh?"

    PALMER   "Your Dad, did you love him?"

    ELLIE   "Yes, very much."

    PALMER   "Prove it."

    Is Palmer right? Are there beliefs that you hold with absolute certainty but cannot prove? Is the existence of God one of them?

5. Ellie Arroway is being interviewed by a panel that wants to determine her "fitness" to command the pod on its voyage. David Drumlin (Tom Skerritt), her former boss, would also like to be chosen for the position. Palmer Joss is one of the interviewers on the panel. The following is an excerpt from that panel investigation:

    PALMER   "Do you believe in God, Dr. Arroway?"

    ELLIE   "As a scientist I rely on empirical evidence, and in this matter, I don't believe that there is data either way."

CHAIRWOMAN   "So your answer would in fact be that you don't believe in God?"

ELLIE   "I—I just don't understand the relevance of the question."

ENGLISH REPRESENTATIVE   "Dr. Arroway, 95 percent of the world's population believes in a supreme being in one form or another. I believe that makes the question more than relevant."

CHAIRWOMAN   "Dr. Arroway?"

ELLIE   "I believe, um, I believe I've already answered that question."

DAVID   "I'm proud of what we've achieved as a species, and as a civilization. I would hate to see all we stand for, all that we have fought for, for a thousand generations, all that God has blessed us with, betrayed in the final hour because we chose to send a representative who did not put our most cherished beliefs first. Thank you."

How might a person's religious beliefs affect their scientific beliefs? Is the panel being fair to Ellie? Do we need to know individuals' religious beliefs in order to assess adequately their scientific abilities? Why or why not?

6.   A Senate panel has been formed to investigate Ellie's "voyage" into space. Ellie claims she spent eighteen hours in space, whereas, as seen by the public on television, her pod slipped through the transporter in a matter of seconds. The following is an exchange between Ellie and the Senate investigative committee:

SENATOR   "Dr. Arroway. You come to us with no evidence, no record, no artifacts, only a story that, to put it mildly, strains credibility. Over half a trillion dollars was spent, dozens of lives were lost, are you really gonna' sit there and tell us we should just take this all on faith?"

KITZ   "Please answer the question, doctor."

ELLIE   "Is it possible that it didn't happen, yes. As a scientist I must concede that, I must volunteer that."

KITZ   "Wait a minute, let me get this straight. You admit that you have absolutely no physical evidence to back up your story?"

ELLIE   "Yes."

This film leads us to the conclusion that faith plays an important part in both science and religion. This is the "lesson" Ellie learns through not being able to support her claim with physical evidence. Do you agree with this conclusion? Why or why not?

ISAAC BASHEVIS SINGER

GIMPEL THE FOOL

Isaac Bashevis Singer's character Gimpel is a good man who lives by his faith and believes everything that he is told, even when reason would seem to indicate otherwise. As a result, he is mercilessly deceived by the people of his town and lied to repeatedly by his wife. On her deathbed, however, his wife of twenty years reveals to him that the six children she gave birth to during their marriage are not his children. Shortly thereafter, the Spirit of Evil says to him, "The whole world deceives you . . . and you ought to deceive the world in your turn." The Spirit of Evil tells him that "there is no world to come" and that "there is no God either." Gimpel follows the Spirit of Evil's advice and urinates in the bread dough, saying to himself, "You've revenged yourself on them for all the shame they've put on you." His wife then appears to him in a dream, reminding him that if he distributes these loaves to the townspeople, he will suffer an eternity of damnation. So he buries the loaves, distributes his monies among the six children, and ventures off into the world. "After many years I became old and white; I heard a great deal, many lies and falsehoods, but the longer I lived," says Gimpel, "the more I understood that there were really no lies." He understands better now the notion that "everything is possible," and he looks forward to leaving this world for another. "Whatever may be there, it will be real, without complication, without ridicule, without deception. God be praised: there even Gimpel cannot be deceived."

Isaac Bashevis Singer (1904–91) wrote novels, essays, and short stories in Yiddish. He was born in Poland but immigrated to the United States in 1935. In 1943, he became a U.S. citizen, and in 1978, he received the Nobel Prize for literature. His fiction depicts Jewish life in Poland and the United States, focusing on characters tempted by evil in various ways. Singer's work is philosophically noteworthy for its understanding of the weaknesses that are a part of human nature. His novels include *The Family Moskat* (1950), *The Magician of Lublin* (1960), and *The Manor* (1967), and his short story collections include "Gimpel the Fool" (1957), "The Spinoza of Market Street" (1961), and "A Crown of Feathers" (1973).

I

I am Gimpel the fool. I don't think myself a fool. On the contrary. But that's what folks call me. They gave me the name while I was still in school. I had seven names in all: imbecile, donkey, flax-head, dope, glump, ninny, and fool. The last name stuck. What did my foolishness consist of? I was easy to take in. They said, "Gimpel, you know the rabbi's wife has been brought to childbed?" So I skipped school. Well, it turned out to be a lie. How was I supposed to know? She hadn't had a big belly. But I never looked at her belly. Was that really so foolish? The gang laughed and hee-hawed, stomped and danced and chanted a good-night prayer. And instead of the raisins they give when a woman's lying in, they stuffed my hand full of goat turds. I was no weakling. If I slapped someone he'd see all the way to Cracow. But I'm really not a slugger by nature. I think to myself: Let it pass. So they take advantage of me.

I was coming home from school and heard a dog barking. I'm not afraid of dogs, but of course I never want to start up with them. One of them may be mad, and if he bites there's not a Tartar in the world who can help you. So I made tracks. Then I looked around and saw the whole market place wild with laughter. It was no dog at all but Wolf-Leib the thief. How was I supposed to know it was he? It sounded like a howling bitch.

When the pranksters and leg-pullers found that I was easy to fool, every one of them tried his luck with me. "Gimpel, the czar is coming to Frampol; Gimpel, the moon fell down in Turbeen; Gimpel, little Hodel Furpiece found a treasure behind the bathhouse." And I like a golem believed everyone. In the first place, everything is possible, as it is written in *The Wisdom of the Fathers,* I've forgotten just how. Second, I had to believe when the whole town came down on me! If I ever dared to say, "Ah, you're kidding!" there was trouble. People got angry. "What do you mean! You want to call everyone a liar?" What was I to do? I believed them, and I hope at least that did them some good.

I was an orphan. My grandfather who brought me up was already bent toward the grave. So they turned me over to a baker, and what a time they gave me there! Every woman or girl who came to bake a batch of noodles had to fool me at least once. "Gimpel, there's a fair in Heaven; Gimpel, the rabbi gave birth to a calf in the seventh month; Gimpel, a cow flew over the roof and laid brass eggs." A student from the yeshiva came once to buy a roll, and he said, "You, Gimpel, while you stand here scraping with your baker's shovel the Messiah has come. The dead have arisen." "What do you mean?" I said. "I heard no one blowing the ram's horn!" He said, "Are you deaf?" And all began to cry, "We heard it, we heard!" Then in came Rietze the candle-dipper and called out in her hoarse voice, "Gimpel, your father and mother have stood up from the grave. They're looking for you."

To tell the truth, I knew very well that nothing of the sort had happened, but all the same, as folks were talking, I threw on my wool vest and went out. Maybe something had happened. What did I stand to lose by looking? Well, what a cat music went up! And then I took a vow to believe nothing more. But that was no go either. They confused me so than I didn't know the big end from the small.

I went to the rabbi to get some advice. He said, "It is written, better to be a fool all your days than for one hour to be evil. You are not a fool. They are the fools. For he who causes his neighbor to feel shame loses Paradise himself." Nevertheless, the rabbi's daughter took me in. As I left the rabbinical court she said, "Have you kissed the wall yet?" I said, "No; what for?" She answered, "It's the law; you've got to do it after every visit." Well, there didn't seem to be any harm in it. And she burst out laughing. It was a fine trick. She put one over on me, all right.

I wanted to go off to another town, but then everyone got busy matchmaking, and they were after me so they nearly tore my coat tails off. They talked at me and talked until I got water on the ear. She was no chaste maiden, but they told me she was virgin pure. She had a limp, and they said it was deliberate, from coyness. She had a bastard, and they told me the child was her little brother. I cried, "You're wasting your time. I'll never marry that whore." But they said indignantly, "What a way to talk! Aren't you ashamed of yourself? We can take you to the rabbi and have you fined for giving her a bad name." I saw then that I wouldn't escape them so easily and I thought: They're set on making me their butt. But when you're married the husband's the master, and if that's all right with her it's agreeable to me too. Besides, you can't pass through life unscathed, nor expect to.

I went to her clay house, which was built on the sand, and the whole gang, hollering and chorusing, came after me. They acted like bear-baiters. When we came to the well they stopped all the same. They were afraid to start anything with Elka. Her mouth would open as if it were on a hinge, and she had a fierce tongue. I entered the house. Lines were strung from wall to wall and clothes were drying. Barefoot she stood by the tub, doing the wash. She was dressed in a worn hand-me-down gown of plush. She had her hair put up in braids and pinned across her head. It took my breath away, almost, the reek of it all.

Evidently she knew who I was. She took a look at me and said, "Look who's here! He's come, the drip. Grab a seat."

I told her all; I denied nothing. "Tell me the truth," I said, "are you really a virgin, and is that mischievous Yechiel actually your little brother? Don't be deceitful with me, for I'm an orphan."

"I'm an orphan myself," she answered, "and whoever tries to twist you up, may the end of his nose take a twist. But don't let them think they can take advantage of me. I want a dowry of fifty guilders, and let them take up a collection besides. Otherwise they can kiss my you-know-what." She was very plainspoken. I said, "It's the bride and not the groom who gives a dowry." Then she said, "Don't bargain with me. Either a flat yes or a flat no. Go back where you came from."

I thought: No bread will ever be baked from *this* dough. But ours is not a poor town. They consented to everything and proceeded with the wedding. It so happened that there was a dysentery epidemic at the time. The ceremony was held at the cemetery gates, near the little corpse-washing hut. The fellows got drunk. While the marriage contract was being drawn up I heard the most pious high rabbi ask, "Is the bride a widow or a divorced woman?" And the sexton's wife answered for her, "Both a widow and divorced." It was black moment for me. But what was I to do, run away from under the marriage canopy?

There was singing and dancing. An old granny danced opposite me, hugging a braided white hallah. The master of revels made a "God 'a mercy" in memory of the bride's parents. The schoolboys threw burrs, as on Tishe b'Av fast day. There were a lot of gifts after the sermon: a noodle board, a kneading trough, a bucket, brooms, ladles, household articles galore. Then I took a look and saw two strapping young men carrying a crib. "What do we need this for?" I asked. So they said, "Don't rack your brains about it. It's all right, it'll come in handy." I realized I was going to be rooked. Take it another way though, what did I stand to lose? I reflected: I'll see what comes of it. A whole town can't go altogether crazy.

II

At night I came where my wife lay, but she wouldn't let me in. "Say, look here, is this what they married us for?" I said. And she said, "My monthly has come." "But yesterday they took you to the ritual bath, and that's afterwards, isn't it supposed to be?" "Today isn't yesterday," said she, "and yesterday's not today. You can beat it if you don't like it." In short, I waited.

Not four months later, she was in childbed. The townsfolk hid their laughter with their knuckles. But what could I do? She suffered intolerable pains and clawed at the walls. "Gimpel," she cried, "I'm going. Forgive me!" The house filled with women. They were boiling pans of water. The screams rose to the welkin.

The thing to do was to go to the house of prayer to repeat psalms, and that was what I did.

The townsfolk liked that, all right. I stood in a corner saying psalms and prayers, and they shook their heads at me. "Pray, pray!" they told me. "Prayer never made any woman pregnant." One of the congregation put a straw to my mouth and said, "Hay for the cows." There was something to that too, by God!

She gave birth to a boy. Friday at the synagogue the sexton stood up before the Ark, pounded on the reading table, and announced, "The wealthy Red Gimpel invites the congregation to a feast in honor of the birth of a son." The whole house of prayer rang with laughter. My face was flaming. But there was nothing I could do. After all, I *was* the one responsible for the circumcision honors and rituals.

Half the town came running. You couldn't wedge another soul in. Women brought peppered chick-peas, and there was a keg of beer from the tavern. I ate and drank as much as anyone, and they all congratulated me. Then there was a circumcision, and I named the boy after my father,

may he rest in peace. When all were gone and I was left with my wife alone, she thrust her head through the bed-curtain and called me to her.

"Gimpel," said she, "why are you silent? Has your ship gone and sunk?"

"What shall I say?" I answered. "A fine thing you've done to me! If my mother had known of it she'd have died a second time."

She said, "Are you crazy, or what?"

"How can you make such a fool," I said, "of one who should be the lord and master?"

"What's the matter with you?" she said. "What have you taken it into your head to imagine?"

I saw that I must speak bluntly and openly. "Do you think this is the way to use an orphan?" I said. "You have borne a bastard."

She answered, "Drive this foolishness out of your head. The child is yours."

"How can he be mine?" I argued. "He was born seventeen weeks after the wedding."

She told me then that he was premature. I said, "Isn't he a little too premature?" She said, she had had a grandmother who carried just as short a time and she resembled this grandmother of hers as one drop of water does another. She swore to it with such oaths that you would have believed a peasant at the fair if he had used them. To tell the plain truth, I didn't believe her; but when I talked it over next day with the school-master, he told me that the very same thing had happened to Adam and Eve. Two they went up to bed, and four they descended.

"There isn't a woman in the world who is not the granddaughter of Eve," he said.

That was how it was; they argued me dumb. But then, who really knows how such things are?

I began to forget my sorrow. I loved the child madly, and he loved me too. As soon as he saw me he'd wave his little hands and want me to pick him up, and when he was colicky I was the only one who could pacify him. I bought him a little bone teething ring and a little gilded cap. He was forever catching the evil eye from someone, and then I had to run to get one of those abracadabras for him that would get him out of it. I worked like an ox. You know how expenses go up when there's an infant in the house. I don't want to lie about it; I didn't dislike Elka either, for that matter. She swore at me and cursed, and I couldn't get enough of her. What strength she had! One of her looks could rob you of the power of speech. And her orations! Pitch and sulphur, that's what they were full of, and yet somehow also full of charm. I adored her every word. She gave me bloody wounds though.

In the evening I brought her a white loaf as well as a dark one, and also poppyseed rolls I baked myself. I thieved because of her and swiped everything I could lay hands on: macaroons, raisins, almonds, cakes. I hope I may be forgiven for stealing from the Saturday pots the women left to warm in the baker's oven. I would take out scraps of meat, a chunk of pudding, a chicken leg or head, a piece of tripe, whatever I could nip quickly. She ate and became fat and handsome.

I had to sleep away from home all during the week, at the bakery. On Friday nights when I got home she always made an excuse of some sort. Either she had heartburn, or a stitch in the side, or hiccups, or headaches. You know what women's excuses are. I had a bitter time of it. It was rough. To add to it, this little brother of hers, the bastard, was growing bigger. He'd put lumps on me, and when I wanted to hit back she'd open her mouth and curse so powerfully I saw a green haze floating before my eyes. Ten times a day she threatened to divorce me. Another man in my place would have taken French leave and disappeared. But I'm the type that bears it and says nothing. What's one to do? Shoulders are from God, and burdens too.

One night there was a calamity in the bakery; the oven burst, and we almost had a fire. There was nothing to do but go home, so I went home. Let me, I thought, also taste the joy of sleeping in bed in midweek. I didn't want to wake the sleeping mite and tiptoed into the house. Coming in, it seemed to me that I heard not the snoring of one but, as it were, a double snore, one a thin enough snore and the other like the snoring of a slaughtered ox. Oh, I didn't like that! I didn't like it at all. I went up to the bed, and things suddenly turned black. Next to Elka lay a man's form. Another in my place would have made an uproar, and enough noise to rouse the whole town, but the thought occurred to me that I might wake the child. A little thing like that—why frighten a little swallow, I thought. All right then, I went back to the bakery and stretched out on a sack of flour and till morning I never shut an eye. I shivered as

if I had had malaria. "Enough of being a donkey," I said to myself. "Gimpel isn't going to be a sucker all his life. There's a limit even to the foolishness of a fool like Gimpel."

In the morning I went to the rabbi to get advice, and it made a great commotion in the town. They sent the beadle for Elka right away. She came, carrying the child. And what do you think she did? She denied it, denied everything, bone and stone! "He's out of his head," she said. "I know nothing of dreams or divinations." They yelled at her, warned her, hammered on the table, but she stuck to her guns: it was a false accusation, she said.

The butchers and the horse-traders took her part. One of the lads from the slaughterhouse came by and said to me, "We've got our eye on you, you're a marked man." Meanwhile, the child started to bear down and soiled itself. In the rabbinical court there was an Ark of the Covenant, and they couldn't allow that, so they sent Elka away.

I said to the rabbi, "What shall I do?"

"You must divorce her at once," said he.

"And what if she refuses?" I asked.

He said, "You must serve the divorce. That's all you'll have to do."

I said, "Well, all right, Rabbi. Let me think about it."

"There's nothing to think about," said he. "You mustn't remain under the same roof with her."

"And if I want to see the child?" I asked.

"Let her go, the harlot," said he, "and her brood of bastards with her."

The verdict he gave was that I mustn't even cross her threshold—never again, as long as I should live.

During the day it didn't bother me so much. I thought: It was bound to happen, the abscess had to burst. But at night when I stretched out upon the sacks I felt it all very bitterly. A longing took me, for her and for the child. I wanted to be angry, but that's my misfortune exactly, I don't have it in me to be really angry. In the first place—this was how my thoughts went—there's bound to be a slip sometimes. You can't live without errors. Probably that lad who was with her led her on and gave her presents and what not, and women are often long on hair and short on sense, and so he got around her. And then since she denies it so, maybe I was only seeing things? Hallucinations do happen. You see a figure or a mannikin or something, but when you come up closer it's nothing, there's not a thing there. And if that's so, I'm doing her an injustice. And when I got so far in my thoughts I started to weep. I sobbed so that I wet the flour where I lay. In the morning I went to the rabbi and told him that I had made a mistake. The rabbi wrote on with his quill, and he said that if that were so he would have to reconsider the whole case. Until he had finished I wasn't to go near my wife, but I might send her bread and money by messenger.

III

Nine months passed before all the rabbis could come to an agreement. Letters went back and forth. I hadn't realized that there could be so much erudition about a matter like this.

Meanwhile, Elka gave birth to still another child, a girl this time. On the Sabbath I went to the synagogue and invoked a blessing on her. They called me up to the Torah, and I named the child for my mother-in-law—may she rest in peace. The louts and loudmouths of the town who came into the bakery gave me a going over. All Frampol refreshed its spirits because of my trouble and grief. However, I resolved that I would always believe what I was told. What's the good of *not* believing? Today it's your wife you don't believe; tomorrow it's God Himself you won't take stock in.

By an apprentice who was her neighbor I sent her daily a corn or a wheat loaf, or a piece of pastry, rolls or bagels, or, when I got the chance, a slab of pudding, a slice of honeycake, or wedding strudel—whatever came my way. The apprentice was a goodhearted lad, and more than once he added something on his own. He had formerly annoyed me a lot, plucking my nose and digging me in the ribs, but when he started to be a visitor to my house he became kind and friendly. "Hey, you, Gimpel," he said to me, "you have a very decent little wife and two fine kids. You don't deserve them."

"But the things people say about her," I said.

"Well, they have long tongues," he said, "and nothing to do with them but babble. Ignore it as you ignore the cold of last winter."

One day the rabbi sent for me and said, "Are you certain, Gimpel, that you were wrong about your wife?"

I said, "I'm certain."

"Why, but look here! You yourself saw it."

"It must have been a shadow," I said.

"The shadow of what?"

"Just of one of the beams, I think."

"You can go home then. You owe thanks to the Yanover rabbi. He found an obscure reference in Maimonides that favored you."

I seized the rabbi's hand and kissed it.

I wanted to run home immediately. It's no small thing to be separated for so long a time from wife and child. Then I reflected: I'd better go back to work now, and go home in the evening. I said nothing to anyone, although as far as my heart was concerned it was like one of the Holy Days. The women teased and twitted me as they did every day, but my thought was: Go on, with your loose talk. The truth is out, like the oil upon the water. Maimonides says it's right, and therefore it is right!

At night, when I had covered the dough to let it rise, I took my share of bread and a little sack of flour and started homeward. The moon was full and the stars were glistening, something to terrify the soul. I hurried onward, and before me darted a long shadow. It was winter, and a fresh snow had fallen. I had a mind to sing, but it was growing late and I didn't want to wake the householders. Then I felt like whistling, but I remembered that you don't whistle at night because it brings the demons out. So I was silent and walked as fast as I could.

Dogs in the Christian yards barked at me when I passed, but I thought: Bark your teeth out! What are you but mere dogs? Whereas I am a man, the husband of a fine wife, the father of promising children.

As I approached the house my heart started to pound as though it were the heart of a criminal. I felt no fear, but my heart went thump! thump! Well, no drawing back. I quietly lifted the latch and went in. Elka was asleep. I looked at the infant's cradle. The shutter was closed, but the moon forced its way through the cracks. I saw the newborn child's face and loved it as soon as I saw it—immediately—each tiny bone.

Then I came nearer to the bed. And what did I see but the apprentice lying there beside Elka. The moon went out all at once. It was utterly black, and I trembled. My teeth chattered. The bread fell from my hands, and my wife waked and said, "Who is that, ah?"

I muttered, "It's me."

"Gimpel?" she asked. "How come you're here? I thought it was forbidden."

"The rabbi said," I answered and shook as with a fever.

"Listen to me, Gimpel," she said, "go out to the shed and see if the goat's all right. It seems she's been sick." I have forgotten to say that we had a goat. When I heard she was unwell I went into the yard. The nannygoat was a good little creature. I had a nearly human feeling for her.

With hesitant steps I went up to the shed and opened the door. The goat stood there on her four feet. I felt her everywhere, drew her by the horns, examined her udders, and found nothing wrong. She had probably eaten too much bark. "Good night, little goat," I said. "Keep well." And the little beast answered with a "Maa" as though to thank me for the good will.

I went back. The apprentice had vanished.

"Where," I asked, "is the lad?"

"What lad?" my wife answered.

"What do you mean?" I said. "The apprentice. You were sleeping with him."

"The things I have dreamed this night and the night before," she said, "may they come true and lay you low, body and soul! An evil spirit has taken root in you and dazzles your sight." She screamed out, "You hateful creature! You moon calf! You spook! You uncouth man! Get out, or I'll scream all Frampol out of bed!"

Before I could move, her brother sprang out from behind the oven and struck me a blow on the back of the head. I thought he had broken my neck. I felt that something about me was deeply wrong, and I said, "Don't make a scandal. All that's needed now is that people should accuse me of raising spooks and dybbuks." For that was what she had meant. "No one will touch bread of my baking."

In short, I somehow calmed her.

"Well," she said, "that's enough. Lie down, and be shattered by wheels."

Next morning I called the apprentice aside. "Listen here, brother!" I said. And so on and so forth. "What do you say?" He stared at me as though I had dropped from the roof or something.

"I swear," he said, "you'd better go to an herb doctor or some healer. I'm afraid you have a screw loose, but I'll hush it up for you." And that's how the thing stood.

To make a long story short, I lived twenty years with my wife. She bore me six children, four daughters and two sons. All kinds of things happened, but I neither saw nor heard. I believed, and that's all. The rabbi recently said to me, "Belief in itself is beneficial. It is written that a good man lives by his faith."

Suddenly my wife took sick. It began with a trifle, a little growth upon the breast. But she evidently was not destined to live long; she had no years. I spent a fortune on her. I have forgotten to say that by this time I had a bakery of my own and in Frampol was considered to be something of a rich man. Daily the healer came, and every witch doctor in the neighborhood was brought. They decided to use leeches, and after that to try cupping. They even called a doctor from Lublin, but it was too late. Before she died she called me to her bed and said, "Forgive me, Gimpel."

I said, "What is there to forgive? You have been a good and faithful wife."

"Woe, Gimpel!" she said. "It was ugly how I deceived you all these years. I want to go clean to my Maker, and so I have to tell you that the children are not yours."

If I had been clouted on the head with a piece of wood it couldn't have bewildered me more.

"Whose are they?" I asked.

"I don't know," she said. "There were a lot . . . but they're not yours." And as she spoke she tossed her head to the side, her eyes turned glassy, and it was all up with Elka. On her whitened lips there remained a smile.

I imagined that, dead as she was, she was saying, "I deceived Gimpel. That was the meaning of my brief life."

IV

One night, when the period of mourning was done, as I lay dreaming on the flour sacks, there came the Spirit of Evil himself and said to me, "Gimpel, why do you sleep?"

I said, "What should I be doing? Eating kreplech?"

"The whole world deceives you," he said, "and you ought to deceive the world in your turn."

"How can I deceive all the world?" I asked him.

He answered, "You might accumulate a bucket of urine every day and at night pour it into the dough. Let the sages of Frampol eat filth."

"What about the judgment in the world to come?" I said.

"There is no world to come," he said. "They've sold you a bill of goods and talked you into believing you carried a cat in your belly. What nonsense!"

"Well then," I said, "and is there a God?"

He answered, "There is no God either."

"What," I said, "*is* there, then?"

"A thick mire."

He stood before my eyes with a goatish beard and horn, long-toothed, and with a tail. Hearing such words, I wanted to snatch him by the tail, but I tumbled from the flour sacks and nearly broke a rib. Then it happened that I had to answer the call of nature, and, passing, I saw the risen dough, which seemed to say to me, "Do it!" In brief, I let myself be persuaded.

At dawn the apprentice came. We kneaded the bread, scattered caraway seeds on it, and set it to bake. Then the apprentice went away, and I was left sitting in the little trench by the oven, on a pile of rags. Well, Gimpel, I thought, you've revenged yourself on them for all the shame they've put on you. Outside the frost glittered, but it was warm beside the oven. The flames heated my face. I bent my head and fell into a doze.

I saw in a dream, at once, Elka in her shroud. She called to me, "What have you done, Gimpel?"

I said to her, "It's all your fault," and started to cry.

"You fool!" she said. "You fool! Because I was false is everything false too? I never deceived anyone but myself. I'm paying for it all, Gimpel. They spare you nothing here."

I looked at her face. It was black; I was startled and waked, and remained sitting dumb. I sensed that everything hung in the balance. A false step now and I'd lose eternal life. But God gave me His help. I seized the long shovel and took out the loaves, carried them into the yard, and started to dig a hole in the frozen earth.

My apprentice came back as I was doing it. "What are you doing boss?" he said, and grew pale as a corpse.

"I know what I'm doing," I said, and I buried it all before his very eyes.

Then I went home, took my hoard from its hiding place, and divided it among the children. "I saw your mother tonight," I said. "She's turning black, poor thing."

They were so astounded they couldn't speak a word.

"Be well," I said, "and forget that such a one as Gimpel ever existed." I put on my short coat, a pair of boots, took the bag that held my prayer shawl in one hand, my stock in the other, and kissed the mezuzah. When people saw me in the street they were greatly surprised.

"Where are you going?" they said.

I answered, "Into the world." And so I departed from Frampol.

I wandered over the land, and good people did not neglect me. After many years I became old and white; I heard a great deal, many lies and falsehoods, but the longer I lived the more I understood that there were really no lies. Whatever doesn't really happen is dreamed at night. It happens to one if it doesn't happen to another, tomorrow if not today, or a century hence if not next year. What difference can it make? Often I heard tales of which I said, "Now this is a thing that cannot happen." But before a year had elapsed I heard that it actually had come to pass somewhere.

Going from place to place, eating at strange tables, it often happens that I spin yarns—improbable things that could never have happened—about devils, magicians, windmills, and the like. The children run after me, calling, "Grandfather, tell us a story." Sometimes they ask for particular stories, and I try to please them. A fat young boy once said to me, "Grandfather, it's the same story you told us before." The little rogue, he was right.

So it is with dreams too. It is many years since I left Frampol, but as soon as I shut my eyes I am there again. And whom do you think I see? Elka. She is standing by the washtub, as at our first encounter, but her face is shining and her eyes are as radiant as the eyes of a saint, and she speaks outlandish words to me, strange things. When I wake I have forgotten it all. But while the dream lasts I am comforted. She answers all my queries, and what comes out is that all is right. I weep and implore, "Let me be with you." And she consoles me and tells me to be patient. The time is nearer than it is far. Sometimes she strokes and kisses me and weeps upon my face. When I awaken I feel her lips and taste the salt of her tears.

No doubt the world is entirely an imaginary world, but it is only once removed from the true world. At the door of the hovel where I lie, there stands the plank on which the dead are taken away. The grave-digger Jew has his spade ready. The grave waits and the worms are hungry; the shrouds are prepared—I carry them in my beggar's sack. Another *shnorrer* is waiting to inherit my bed of straw. When the time comes I will go joyfully. Whatever may be there, it will be real, without complication, without ridicule, without deception. God be praised: there even Gimpel cannot be deceived.

DISCUSSION QUESTIONS

1. The rabbi tells Gimpel, "It is written, better to be a fool all the days of your life than for one hour to be evil. You are not a fool. They are fools." Is the rabbi right? Or is Gimpel a fool?

2. Gimpel always defers to his faith and trust in people rather than listening to his reason, even when it is obvious to him that he is being deceived. Is, as the rabbi tells Gimpel, belief in itself beneficial? Does a good man live (only) by his faith?

3. Gimpel says, "I resolved that I would always believe what I was told. What's the good of *not* believing? Today it's your wife you don't believe; tomorrow it's God Himself you won't take stock in." Answer Gimpel's question: What is the good of *not* believing? Is Gimpel's argument here a valid one?

4. How does Gimpel arrive at this conclusion: "Whatever may be there, it will be real, without complication, without ridicule, without deception. God be praised: there even Gimpel cannot be deceived." Discuss.

5. Ultimately, Gimpel says that "there were really no lies." What does he mean? Do you agree with him?

The Rapture
[USA 1991] 1 hour, 42 minutes
Directed by Michael Tolkin

By day, Sharon (Mimi Rogers) is an unhappy telephone operator; by night, she and her friend Victor (Patrick Bauchau) roam the town looking for couples willing to swap partners for a night. After a spiritually enlightening dream, Sharon leaves her life of sexual promiscuity to seek a life of faith and holy servitude. With her husband, Randy (David Duchovny), and their daughter, Mary (Kimberly Cullum), Sharon awaits the Rapture. However, all of Sharon's plans fall apart with the death of her husband. Sharon and Mary flee to the desert to await the Rapture, but Sharon, becoming impatient, murders Mary, who wishes only to be with her father again. Eventually, the Rapture begins, and Sharon is reunited just outside heaven with her daughter. Mary asks her mother if she still loves God, and Sharon responds, "He let us, alone, in the desert. He let me kill you. . . . How can I love a God who let me kill my baby?" At this point, it is clear that Sharon will not repent her sins, and so will be turned away from heaven. *The Rapture* explores the reasons for Sharon's initial turn toward faith in God and subsequent turn away from faith in God, despite having only to say that she loves him in order to get into heaven.

The title of the movie is meant to draw on two distinct senses of "rapture." One sense refers to a state of ecstasy, the kind of state that Sharon and Victor were seeking in the beginning of the film. The other refers to the Second Coming of Christ as stated in the the New Testament: "Those of us who are still alive when the Lord comes will have no advantage over those who have died; when the command is given, when the archangel's voice is heard, when God's trumpet sounds, then the Lord himself will descend from heaven; first the Christian dead will rise, then we who are still alive shall join them, caught up in clouds to meet the Lord in the air. Thus we shall always be with the Lord" (1 Thess. 4:15–17). The phrase "caught up" in this passage is a translation of the Latin verb *raptare,* hence the origin of the phrase "the Rapture."

While the Rapture is described variously, it always involves the disappearance of all Christians from the earth in order to meet the Lord. In the film, the Rapture begins when the Archangel Michael appears. Sinners have until Gabriel has blown his trumpet for the seventh time to repent their sins; if they do not repent, they do not go to heaven.

DISCUSSION QUESTIONS

1. In this exchange, Randy and Sharon discuss the source of our desire for God, with Randy taking the side of reason and human desire, and Sharon voicing the side of faith and spiritual desire:

    SHARON   "When we do something wrong, we feel bad, and that's because there's a little bit of God in all of us, telling us to change our ways before it's too late. Isn't that right?"

    RANDY   "No, it's not right. It's just conditioned by society. All we are is animals whose brains have become too big and too complicated for the purposes of satisfying our animal needs, which are food and sex."

    SHARON   "There is a spiritual need which is just as real as hunger, just as real as the need for love."

    RANDY   "Sharon, don't you understand what's going on? The world's a disaster. We have no power to make it better. You hate your job. You hate your life. But you want to feel special. But instead of letting me do that, you're rushing off to something that's not even there. There's no Pearl, there's only us."

    Who makes the more convincing case, Sharon or Randy? Why?

2. In this exchange, Sharon discusses with Victor what it is like to have complete faith in God:

    SHARON   "You can't understand, but I know what that's like. Until it happens to you, until you accept God into your heart, it's like a fairy tale, it's like some joke that you just don't get."

    VICTOR   "I think you need to be deprogrammed."

    SHARON   "There's no cult, Vic. There's only God, and his message of love."

    VICTOR   "Love."

    SHARON   "Love."

    VICTOR   "Look, you'll give this up, someday. I know you, you'll give this up."

    SHARON   "This is forever."

    What does Sharon mean when she says that faith in God is "like a fairy tale, it's like some joke that you just don't get"? Compare Sharon's description of religious belief to William James's notion of the will to believe. Are Victor's criticisms valid? Why or why not?

3.   Karl Marx, in the introduction to his *Criticism of Hegel's Philosophy of Right,* wrote, "Religion . . . is the opium of the people." In the following exchange, Sharon and Randy have an exchange that recalls Marx's statement:

SHARON   "I know you are as lost as I was, Randy, and I wanted to tell you that you could know God. If you just surrender your pride, you can know God."

RANDY   "Sharon, it's just a drug. Instead of doing heroin, you're doing God. . . ."

SHARON   "Randy, God is real. God is not make-believe, and you know that. You don't want to admit that, because you're afraid."

Discuss the merits of Randy's claim. Is Sharon's response to Randy a good one? Why or why not? How would you respond to Randy?

4.   Consider this exchange between Sharon and her friend Paula (Terri Hanauer):

PAULA   "I tell myself it's just conditioning, it's how I was raised. I tell myself that if we didn't tell our children about God, they wouldn't ask. It is a story we tell ourselves so everything makes sense."

SHARON   "It's not."

PAULA   "But how do you know?"

SHARON   "The Bible."

PAULA   Don't tell me the Bible."

SHARON   It's a question of faith."

PAULA   "So there's no proof?"

SHARON   "Paula, the universe you live in is cold and filled with empty space. The universe I live in is filled with God."

Paula claims that "if we didn't tell our children about God, they wouldn't ask." Is she right? Are you satisfied with Sharon's response to her? How would you respond to Paula?

5.   After the Rapture, Sharon has the following conversation with her daughter, Mary, who is trying to convince her mother to love God:

MARY   "You have to love God."

SHARON   "I love you, Mary."

MARY   "That isn't enough."

SHARON   "Baby, it's all I have. If life is a gift, if it really is a gift, and there really is a Heaven. . . ."

MARY   "There really is a Heaven."

SHARON   "Then why should I thank Him for the gift of so much suffering, Mary, so much pain on the earth that He created? Let me ask Him why."

MARY   "Tell God you love Him."

SHARON   "I can't."

MARY   "If you don't tell God that you love Him, you can't go to Heaven. Tell God that you love Him. Mommy!"

SHARON   "No."

Sharon goes full circle in this film: from having no faith, to gaining faith, and then losing her faith. As the preceding dialogue reveals, she refuses to thank God "for the gift of so much suffering." Her position recalls that of Ivan Karamozov in section 1.2: Ivan believes in God but rejects the world of suffering that God has created. What do you think about the conclusion that Sharon reaches here? Has Sharon's reason finally overcome her faith?

SUPPLEMENTARY READINGS

General

Alston, William. "Problems of Philosophy of Religion." *Encyclopedia of Philosophy*. Vol. 6. Ed. Paul Edwards. New York: Macmillan, 1967.

Beaty, Michael, ed. *Christian Theism and the Problems of Philosophy*. Notre Dame, IN: University of Notre Dame Press, 1991.

Bertocci, Peter. *An Introduction to the Philosophy of Religion*. Englewood Cliffs, NJ: Prentice Hall, 1951.

Brightman, Edgar. *A Philosophy of Religion*. New York: Prentice Hall, 1940.

Brody, Baruch A., ed. *Readings in the Philosophy of Religion: An Analytic Approach*. Englewood Cliffs, NJ: Prentice Hall, 1974.

Cahn, Steven M., and David Shatz. *Contemporary Philosophy of Religion*. New York: Oxford University Press, 1982.

Clack, Beverley, and Brian R. Clack. *The Philosophy of Religion: A Critical Introduction*. Malden, MA: Polity Press/Blackwell, 1998.

Collins, James. *The Emergence of Philosophy of Religion*. New Haven, CT: Yale University Press, 1967.

Craig, William Lane. *Philosophy of Religion: A Reader and Guide*. New Brunswick, NJ: Rutgers University Press, 2002.

Davies, Brian. *An Introduction to Philosophy of Religion*. New York: Oxford University Press, 1993.

Derrida, Jacques, and Gianni Vattimo, eds. *Religion*. Malden, MA: Polity Press/Blackwell, 1998.

French, Peter A., Theodore E. Uehling, Jr., and Howard K. Wettstein, eds. *Philosophy of Religion*. Notre Dame, IN: University of Notre Dame Press, 1997.

Hick, John. *Philosophy of Religion*. Englewood Cliffs, NJ: Prentice Hall, 1990.

James, William. *The Varieties of Religious Experience: A Study in Human Nature*. New York: Modern Library, 1936.

Mann, William, ed. *The Blackwell Guide to the Philosophy of Religion*. Malden, MA: Blackwell, 2005.

Murray, Michael, and Eleonore Stump, eds. *Philosophy of Religion: The Big Questions*. Oxford: Blackwell, 1999.

Patterson, Robert Leet. *The Philosophy of Religion*. Durham, NC: Duke University Press, 1970.

Quinn, Philip L., and Charles Taliaferro. *A Companion to Philosophy of Religion*. Oxford: Blackwell, 1997.

Taliaferro, Charles. "Philosophy of Religion." Chapter 14 in *The Blackwell Companion to Philosophy*. Eds. Nicholas Bunnin and E. P. Tsui-James. Malden, MA: Blackwell, 2005.

Yandell, Keith E. *Basic Issues in the Philosophy of Religion*. Boston: Allyn & Bacon, 1971.

Existence and Nature of God

Angeles, Peter Adam, ed. *Critiques of God*. Buffalo, NY: Prometheus Books, 1976.

Barnes, Jonathan. *The Ontological Argument*. New York: St. Martin's Press, 1972.

Bowker, John. *The Sense Of God*. Oxford: Oxford University Press, 1973.

Burkle, Howard R. *The Non-Existence of God: Antitheism from Hegel to Duméry*. New York: Herder & Herder, 1969.

Burrell, Donald, ed. *Cosmological Arguments*. Garden City, NY: Anchor Books, 1967.

Cahn, Steven M., and David Shatz, eds. *Questions About God: Today's Philosophers Ponder the Divine*. New York: Oxford University Press, 2002.

Cone, James H. *God of the Oppressed.* Maryknoll, NY: Orbis Books, 1997.

———. *A Black Theology of Liberation.* Philadelphia: Lippincott, 1970.

Craig, William Lane. *The Cosmological Argument from Plato to Leibniz.* London: Macmillan, 1980.

Daly, Mary. *Beyond God the Father: Toward a Philosophy of Women's Liberation.* Boston: Beacon Press, 1973.

———. *The Church and the Second Sex.* New York: Harper & Row, 1975.

Davidson, Herbert. *Proofs for Eternity, Creation, and the Existence of God in Medieval Islamic and Jewish Philosophy.* Oxford: Oxford University Press, 1987.

Descartes, René. *Meditations on First Philosophy: With Selections from the Objections and Replies.* Trans. John Cottingham. Cambridge: Cambridge University Press, 1986.

Feuerbach, Ludwig. *The Essence of Christianity.* Trans. George Eliot. New York: Harper, 1957.

Flew, Antony. *God and Philosophy.* New York: Harcourt, Brace & World, 1966.

Gale, Richard M. *On the Nature and Existence of God.* New York: Cambridge University Press, 1991.

Gilson, Etienne. *God and Philosophy.* New Haven, CT: Yale University Press, 1941.

Haldane, J. J., and J. J. C. Smart. *Theism and Atheism.* Oxford: Blackwell, 1996.

Hartshorne, Charles. *Anselm's Discovery: A Re-Examination of the Ontological Proof for God's Existence.* La Salle, IL: Open Court, 1991.

———. *The Divine Relativity: A Social Conception of God.* New Haven, CT: Yale University Press, 1948

——— and William L. Reese., eds. *Philosophers Speak of God.* Chicago: University of Chicago Press, 1953.

Hegel, Georg Wilhelm Friedrich. *Lectures on the Philosophy of Religion: Together with a Work on the Proofs of the Existence of God.* London: Routledge & Kegan Paul, 1968.

Hick, John. *Arguments for the Existence of God.* New York: Herder & Herder, 1971.

———, ed. *The Existence of God.* New York: Macmillan, 1964.

Hick, John, and Arthur McGill, eds. *The Many-Faced Argument: Recent Studies on the Ontological Argument for the Existence of God.* New York: Macmillan, 1967.

Johnson, Elizabeth. *She Who Is: The Mystery of God in Feminist Theological Discourse.* New York: Crossroad, 1993.

Kenny, Anthony. *The Five Ways: St. Thomas Aquinas' Proofs of God's Existence.* New York: Schocken Books, 1969.

Kung, Hans. *Does God Exist?* New York: Random House, 1981.

Lott, Eric. *God and the Universe in the Vedantic Theology of Ramanuja.* Madras: Ramanuja Research Society, 1976.

———. *Vedantic Approaches to God.* London: Macmillan, 1980.

Mackie, J. L. *The Miracle of Theism: Arguments for and Against the Existence of God.* New York: Oxford University Press, 1982.

Macquarrie, John. *In Search of Deity: An Essay in Dialectical Theism.* New York: Crossroad, 1985.

Marion, Jean-Luc. *God Without Being: Hors-Texte.* Trans. Thomas A. Carlson. Chicago: University of Chicago Press, 1991.

Matson, Wallace I. *The Existence of God.* Ithaca, NY: Cornell University Press, 1965.

McPherson, Thomas. *The Argument from Design.* New York: St. Martin's Press, 1972.

Messer, Richard. *Does God's Existence Need Proof?* New York: Oxford University Press, 1993.

Morris, Thomas V. *The Concept of God.* New York: Oxford University Press, 1987.

Newman, John Henry. *An Essay in Aid of a Grammar of Assent.* Garden City, NY: Image Books, 1955.

Nietzsche, Friedrich. *Thus Spoke Zarathustra.* Trans. Walter Kaufmann. London: Viking Penguin, 1954.

———. *The Gay Science: With a Prelude in Rhymes and an Appendix of Songs.* Trans. Walter Kaufmann. New York: Vintage Books, 1974.

———. *The Anti-Christ.* Trans. Walter Kaufmann. London: Viking Penguin, 1954.

Oppy, Graham Robert. *Ontological Arguments and Belief in God.* New York: Cambridge University Press, 1995.

Paley, William. *Natural Theology: Selections.* Indianapolis, IN: Bobbs-Merrill, 1963.

Phillips, Steven. *Classical Indian Metaphysics.* La Salle, IL: Open Court, 1995.

Plantinga, Alvin. *God and Other Minds: A Study of the Rational Justification of Belief in God.* Ithaca, NY: Cornell University Press, 1967.

———, ed. *The Ontological Argument: From St. Anselm to Contemporary Philosophers.* Garden City, NY: Anchor Books, 1965.

Rowe, William L. *The Cosmological Argument.* Princeton, NJ: Princeton University Press, 1975.

Saint Anselm, *St. Anselm's Proslogion with a Reply on Behalf of the Fool.* Notre Dame, IN: University of Notre Dame Press, 1979.

Saint Augustine, *The Confessions*. Trans. R. S. Pine-Coffin. London: Penguin Books, 1961.

Smart, Ninian. *A Dialogue of Religions*. London: SCM Press, 1960.

Swinburne, Richard. *Is There a God?* New York: Oxford University Press, 1996.

———. *The Coherence of Theism*. Oxford: Clarendon Press, 1977.

———. *The Existence of God*. New York: Oxford University Press, 1979.

Taylor, A. E. *Does God Exist?* New York: Macmillan, 1947.

Twain, Mark. *Letters from the Earth*. New York: Harper & Row, 1962.

Warder, A. K. *A History of Indian Buddhism*. Honolulu: University of Hawaii Press, 1990.

Westphal, Merold. *Suspicion and Faith: Religious Uses of Modern Atheism*. Grand Rapids, MI: Eerdmans, 1993.

Wolterstorff, Nicholas. *Divine Discourse: Philosophical Reflections on the Claim that God Speaks*. Cambridge: Cambridge University Press, 1995.

The Problem of Evil

Adams, Marilyn McCord, and Robert Merrihew Adams, eds. *The Problem of Evil*. New York: Oxford University Press, 1990.

Ahern, M. B. *The Problem of Evil*. New York: Schocken Books, 1971.

Badiou, Alain. *Ethics: An Essay on the Understanding of Evil*. New York: Verso, 2001.

Braiterman, Zachary. *(God) After Auschwitz: Tradition and Change in Post-Holocaust Jewish Thought*. Princeton, NJ: Princeton University Press, 1998.

Davis, Stephen T., and John B. Cobb, eds. *Encountering Evil: Live Options in Theodicy*. Atlanta: Knox, 1981.

Dore, Clement. *God, Suffering and Solipsism*. New York: Macmillan, 1989.

Ferré, Nels. *Evil and the Christian Faith*. New York: Harper & Brothers, 1947.

Geach, Peter T. *Providence and Evil*. New York: Cambridge University Press, 1977.

Griffin, David Ray. *God, Power and Evil: A Process Theodicy*. Philadelphia: Westminster Press, 1976.

Herman, Arthur. *The Problem of Evil in Indian Thought*. Delhi: Motilal Barnasidass, 1976.

Hick, John. *Evil and the God of Love*. New York: Harper & Row, 1966.

Howard-Snyder, Daniel, ed. *The Evidential Argument from Evil*. Bloomington: Indiana University Press, 1996.

Hume, David. *Dialogues Concerning Natural Religion; and the Posthumous Essays, Of the Immortality of the Soul and Of Suicide*. Ed. Richard Popkin. Indianapolis, IN: Hackett, 1980.

Laird, John. *Mind and Deity*. London: Allen & Unwin, 1941.

Lara, María Pía, ed. *Rethinking Evil: Contemporary Perspectives*. Berkeley: University of California Press, 2001.

Leaman, Oliver. *Evil and Suffering in Jewish Philosophy*. New York: Cambridge University Press, 1995.

Leibniz, Gottfried Wilhelm. *Theodicy: Essays on the Goodness of God, the Freedom of Man, and the Origin of Evil*. Ed. Austin Farrer. Trans. E. M. Huggard. La Salle, IL: Open Court, 1985.

Lewis, C. S. *The Problem of Pain*. New York: Macmillan, 1944.

Madden, Edward H., and Peter Hare, eds. *Evil and the Concept of God*. Springfield, IL: Thomas, 1968.

Maimonides, Moses. *The Guide of the Perplexed*. Trans. Shlomo Pines. Chicago: University of Chicago Press, 1963.

Maritain, Jacques. *St. Thomas and the Problem of Evil*. Milwaukee: Marquette University Press, 1942.

Mill, John Stuart. *Nature, and Utility of Religion*. New York: Liberal Arts Press, 1958.

Morton, Adam. *On Evil*. New York: Routledge, 2004.

O'Connor, David. *God and Inscrutable Evil: In Defense of Theism and Atheism*. Lanham, MD: Rowman & Littlefield, 1998.

Ormsby, Eric. *Theodicy in Islamic Thought*. Princeton, NJ: Princeton University Press, 1984.

Penelhum, Terence. *God and Scepticism*. Dordrecht: Reidel, 1983.

Petit, François. *The Problem of Evil*. New York: Hawthorn Books, 1959.

Pike, Nelson, ed. *God and Evil: Readings on the Theological Problem of Evil*. Englewood Cliffs, NJ: Prentice Hall, 1964.

Plantinga, Alvin. *God, Freedom, and Evil*. New York: Harper & Row, 1974.

Rorty, Amélie. *The Many Faces of Evil: Historical Perspectives*. New York: Routledge, 2001.

Rowe, William L. *God and the Problem of Evil*. Malden, MA: Blackwell, 2001.

Royce, Josiah. *Studies of Good and Evil*. Hamden, CT: Archon Books, 1964.

Surin, Kenneth. *Theology and the Problem of Evil*. New York: Blackwell, 1986.

Swinburne, Richard. *Providence and the Problem of Evil*. New York: Oxford University Press, 1998.

Temple, William. *Nature, Man and God*. London: Macmillan, 1935.

Van Inwagen, Peter, ed. *Christian Faith and the Problem of Evil*. Grand Rapids, MI: Eerdmans, 2004.

Woodruff, Paul, and Harry A. Wilmer, eds. *Facing Evil: Light at the Core of Darkness*. La Salle, IL: Open Court, 1988.

Faith and Reason

Adams, Robert Merrihew. *The Virtue of Faith and Other Essays in Philosophical Theology*. New York: Oxford University Press, 1987.

Alston, William P., and Thomas D. Senor, eds. *The Rationality of Belief and the Plurality of Faith: Essays in Honor of William P. Alston*. Ithaca, NY: Cornell University Press, 1995.

Brown, Stuart C., ed. *Reason and Religion*. Ithaca, NY: Cornell University Press, 1977.

Clifford, William Kingdon. *The Ethics of Belief and Other Essays*. Amherst, NY: Prometheus Books, 1999.

Dewey, John. *A Common Faith*. New Haven, CT: Yale University Press, 1934.

Harris, Sam. *The End of Faith: Religion, Terror, and the Future of Reason*. New York: Norton, 2004.

Hester, Marcus, ed. *Faith, Reason, and Skepticism*. Philadelphia: Temple University Press, 1992.

Hick, John. *Faith and Knowledge*. Ithaca, NY: Cornell University Press, 1966.

———, ed. *Faith and the Philosophers*. New York: St. Martin's Press, 1964.

Hoitenga, Dewey, J., Jr. *Faith and Reason from Plato to Plantinga: An Introduction to Reformed Epistemology*. Albany: State University of New York Press, 1991.

James, William. *The Will to Believe, and Other Essays in Popular Philosophy, and Human Immortality*. New York: Dover, 1960.

Kenny, Anthony. *What Is Faith? Essays in the Philosophy of Religion*. New York: Oxford University Press, 1992.

Kierkegaard, Søren. *Fear and Trembling*. Trans. Howard V. Hong and Edna H. Hong. Princeton, NJ: Princeton University Press, 1983.

———. *Philosophical Fragments, or, A Fragment of Philosophy*. 2nd ed. Originally trans. and introduced by David F. Swenson. New introd. and commentary by Niels Thulstrup. Translation rev. and commentary trans. by Howard V. Hong. Princeton, NJ: Princeton University Press, 1962.

Lundin, Roger. *The Culture of Interpretation: Christian Faith and the Postmodern World*. Grand Rapids, MI: Eerdmans, 1993.

Miller, Ed L., ed. *Believing in God: Readings on Faith and Reason*. Upper Saddle River, NJ: Prentice Hall, 1996.

Mitchell, Basil. *Faith and Logic: Oxford Essays in Philosophical Theology*. London: Allen & Unwin, 1957.

Morris, Thomas V. *Making Sense of It All: Pascal and the Meaning of Life*. Grand Rapids, MI: Eerdmans, 1992.

Plantinga, Alvin, and Nicholas Wolterstorff, eds. *Faith and Rationality: Reason and Belief in God*. Notre Dame, IN: University of Notre Dame Press, 1983.

Rescher, Nicholas. *Pascal's Wager: A Study of Practical Reasoning in Philosophical Theology*. Notre Dame, IN: University of Notre Dame Press, 1985.

Russell, Bertrand. *Religion and Science*. New York: Oxford University Press, 1960.

Smith, Wilfred Cantwell. *Faith and Belief*. Princeton, NJ: Princeton University Press, 1979.

Stump, Eleonore, and Norman Kretzmann, eds. *Reasoned Faith: Essays in Philosophical Theology in Honor of Norman Kretzmann*. Ithaca, NY: Cornell University Press, 1993.

Swinburne, Richard. *Faith and Reason*. New York: Oxford University Press, 1981.

Turner, Denys. *Faith, Reason, and the Existence of God*. New York: Cambridge University Press, 2004.

Wolterstorff, Nicholas. *Reason Within the Limits of Religion Alone*. Grand Rapids, MI: Eerdmans, 1984.

OF Truth AND Knowledge

In the opening scene from *Total Recall,* Quaid (Arnold Schwarzenegger) dreams that he is on a mission to Mars with a beautiful woman. Or is it more than just a dream?

2.1   WHAT DO I KNOW?

PLATO

THE ALLEGORY OF THE CAVE

I n this selection, Plato's cave-dwellers discover that their senses have led them to false knowledge about the world, and they come to learn the impact of true knowledge and education on a person. Plato's general approach to knowledge is called *rationalism*, which means that he believes that through reason alone, without the aid of information from the senses, we are capable of achieving knowledge. The allegory of the cave tells us that not having true knowledge of the world is like mistaking shadows projected on the wall of a cave for the real things. The cave-dwellers are akin to ordinary persons who do not know how to distinguish appearance from reality, false beliefs from justified true beliefs, or opinions from knowledge.

Once we are shown the source of the shadows on the cave wall, there is no going back to a state of ignorance. While it is a painful journey out of the cave and into the sunlight, it changes us for the rest of our lives. When we see things for what they really are, we will not want to lack true knowledge ever again, even if it means being the subject of ridicule. Alluding to the trial of Socrates on the charges of impiety and corrupting the youth of Athens, Plato adds the following touch: "As for the man who tried to free them [the cave-dwellers] and lead them upward, if they could somehow lay their hands on him and kill him, they would do so." The allegory of the cave is one of the most well-known and celebrated images in the history of philosophy, and it provides a key illustration of Plato's thoughts on knowledge and reality.

Plato makes a sharp distinction between the material world, perceived and known through the senses, and a supersensory world apprehended by reason. The material world is correlated with matter, the body, sense-perception, the many, opinion, particulars, and becoming. The supersensory world (or world of "ideas") is correlated with the mind, the soul, reason, knowledge, the one, truth, universals, and being. Plato rejects the concrete, material world as a source of true knowledge. For him, it yields only relative, individual truth (opinion) obtained through the senses. For example, an object may be heavy to one person and light to another; similarly, opinions will vary about beauty. Such truth is, therefore, subjective, temporary, and mutable. True reality is found in the supersensory world of abstract ideas, apprehended only by reason. It is the world of objective, eternal, immutable truth. Ideas (universals, absolutes) such as beauty, justice, and courage have an independent character in this world. Concrete particulars exist only insofar as the ideas "participate" in them. In other words, concrete particulars should be regarded as "copies" of "ideas." For Plato, all particulars, even all human beings, might cease to exist, but the world of ideas will continue to be. As all particulars are subordinated to and derive their existence from the ideas, so all ideas, forming a pyramid, are subordinated to the highest idea, that of the Good, positioned at the top of the pyramid. The Good, the analogue of which in the cave allegory is the sun, is the supreme concept. It is the one absolute reality, self-sufficient and perfectly harmonious; it is the creative cause of the universe; it is the end from which flows all other ideas, and through them the imperfect material world; it is pure reason and absolute virtue.

Plato (428–348 B.C.E.) was born in Athens, Greece, and studied for about ten years under Socrates (469–399 B.C.E.). He came from a wealthy, aristocratic family and was active in the political life of Athens as a youth. After the trial and death of Socrates (399 B.C.E.), he traveled for about ten years (399–389 B.C.E.). In 385 B.C.E., shortly after returning to Athens, he founded the Academy, the first university in the world, which existed continuously for about nine hundred years. He wrote dialogues for the public and lectures for his classes at the Academy; however, only his dialogues have survived. Socrates is a central character in most of Plato's dialogues; in some he is representative of the historical Socrates, whereas in others he is merely a mouthpiece for Plato. Plato's dialogues include *Apology* (Socrates' defense), *Crito, Phaedo, Euthyphro, Gorgias, Protagoras, Phaedrus, Cratylus, Symposium, Republic, Theaetetus, Parmenides, Sophist, Statesman, Philebus, Timeaus,* and *Laws.* Our selection is from *Republic,* a dialogue probably written around 380 B.C.E., which is concerned with the nature of justice in the state and in the individual. The conversation is between Socrates and Glaucon, a character named after one of Plato's elder brothers.

Next, I said, compare the effect of education and the lack of it upon our human nature to a situation like this: imagine men to be living in an underground cave-like dwelling place, which has a way up to the light along its whole width, but the entrance is a long way up. The men have been there from childhood, with their neck and legs in fetters, so that they remain in the same place and can only see ahead of them, as their bonds prevent them turning their heads. Light is provided by a fire burning some way behind and above them. Between the fire and the prisoners, some way behind them and on a higher ground, there is a path across the cave and along this a low wall has been built, like the screen at a puppet show in front of the performers who show their puppets above it. —I see it.

See then also men carrying along that wall, so that they overtop it, all kinds of artifacts, statues of men, reproductions of other animals in stone or wood fashioned in all sorts of ways, and, as is likely, some of the carriers are talking while others are silent. —This is a strange picture, and strange prisoners.

They are like us, I said. Do you think, in the first place, that such men could see anything of themselves and each other except the shadows which the fire casts upon the wall of the cave in front of them? —How could they, if they have to keep their heads still throughout life?

And is not the same true of the objects carried along the wall? —Quite.

If they could converse with one another, do you not think that they would consider these shadows to be the real things? —Necessarily.

What if their prison had an echo which reached them from in front of them? Whenever one of the carriers passing behind the wall spoke, would they not think that it was the shadow passing in front of them which was talking? Do you agree? —By Zeus I do.

Altogether then, I said, such men would believe the truth to be nothing else than the shadows of the artifacts? —They must believe that.

Consider then what deliverance from their bonds and the curing of their ignorance would be if something like this naturally happened to them. Whenever one of them was freed, had to stand up suddenly, turn his head, walk, and look up toward the light, doing all that would give him pain, the flash of the fire would make it impossible for him to see the objects of which he had earlier seen the shadows. What do you think he would say if he was told that what he saw then was foolishness, that he was now somewhat closer to reality and turned to things that existed more fully, that he saw more correctly? If one then pointed to each of the objects passing by, asked him what each was, and forced him to answer, do you not think he would be at a loss and believe that the things which he saw earlier were truer than the things now pointed out to him? —Much truer.

If one then compelled him to look at the fire itself, his eyes would hurt, he would turn round and flee toward those things which he could see, and think that they were in fact clearer than those now shown to him. —Quite so.

And if one were to drag him thence by force up the rough and steep path, and did not let him go before he was dragged into the sunlight, would he not be in physical pain and angry as he was dragged along? When he came into the light, with the sunlight filling his eyes, he would not be able to see a single one of the things which are now said to be true. —Not at once, certainly.

I think he would need time to get adjusted before he could see things in the world above; at first he would see shadows most easily, then reflections of men and other things in water, then the things themselves. After this he would see objects in the sky and the sky itself more easily at night, the light of the stars and the moon more easily than the sun and the light of the sun during the day. —Of course.

Then, at last, he would be able to see the sun, not images of it in water or in some alien place, but the sun itself in its own place, and be able to contemplate it. —That must be so.

After this he would reflect that it is the sun which provides the seasons and the years, which governs everything in the visible world, and is also in some way the cause of those other things which he used to see. —Clearly that would be the next stage.

What then? As he reminds himself of his first dwelling place, of the wisdom there and of his fellow prisoners, would he not reckon himself happy for the change, and pity them? —Surely.

And if the men below had praise and honours from each other, and prizes for the man who saw most clearly the shadows that passed before them, and who could best remember which usually came earlier and which later, and which came together and thus could most ably prophesy the future, do you think our man would desire those rewards and envy those who were honoured and held power among the prisoners, or would he feel, as Homer put it, that he certainly wished to be "serf to another man without possessions upon

the earth" [*Odyssey* 11, 489–90] and go through any suffering, rather than share their opinions and live as they do? —Quite so, he said, I think he would rather suffer anything.

Reflect on this too, I said. If this man went down into the cave again and sat down in the same seat, would his eyes not be filled with darkness, coming suddenly out of the sunlight? —They certainly would.

And if he had to contend again with those who had remained prisoners in recognizing those shadows while his sight was affected and his eyes had not settled down—and the time for this adjustment would not be short—would he not be ridiculed? Would it not be said that he had returned from his upward journey with his eyesight spoiled, and that it was not worthwhile even to attempt to travel upward? As for the man who tried to free them and lead them upward, if they could somehow lay their hands on him and kill him, they would do so. —They certainly would.

This whole image, my dear Glaucon, I said, must be related to what we said before. The realm of the visible should be compared to the prison dwelling, and the fire inside it to the power of the sun. If you interpret the upward journey and the contemplation of things above as the upward journey of the soul to the intelligible realm, you will grasp what I surmise since you were keen to hear it. Whether it is true or not only the god knows, but this is how I see it, namely that in the intelligible world the Form of the Good is the last to be seen, and with difficulty; when seen it must be reckoned to be for all the cause of all that is right and beautiful, to have produced in the visible world both light and the fount of light, while in the intelligible world it is itself that which produces and controls truth and intelligence, and he who is to act intelligently in public or in private must see it. —I share your thought as far as I am able.

Come then, share with me this thought also: do not be surprised that those who have reached this point are unwilling to occupy themselves with human affairs, and that their souls are always pressing upward to spend their time there, for this is natural if things are as our parable indicates. —That is very likely.

Further, I said, do you think it at all surprising that anyone coming to the evils of human life from the contemplation of the divine behaves awkwardly and appears very ridiculous while his eyes are still dazzled and before he is sufficiently adjusted to the darkness around him, if he is compelled to contend in court or some other place about the shadows of justice or the objects of which they are shadows, and to carry through the contest about these in the way these things are understood by those who have never seen Justice itself? —That is not surprising at all.

Anyone with intelligence, I said, would remember that the eyes may be confused in two ways and from two causes, coming from light into darkness as well as from darkness into light. Realizing that the same applies to the soul, whenever he sees a soul disturbed and unable to see something, he will not laugh mindlessly but will consider whether it has come from a brighter life and is dimmed because unadjusted, or has come from greater ignorance into greater light and is filled with a brighter dazzlement. The former he would declare happy in its life and experience, the latter he would pity, and if he should wish to laugh at it, his laughter would be less ridiculous than if he laughed at a soul that has come from the light above. —What you say is very reasonable.

We must then, I said, if these things are true, think something like this about them, namely that education is not what some declare it to be; they say that knowledge is not present in the soul and that they put it in, like putting sight into blind eyes. —They surely say that.

Our present argument shows, I said, that the capacity to learn and the organ with which to do so are present in every person's soul. It is as if it were not possible to turn the eye from darkness to light without turning the whole body; so one must turn one's whole soul from the world of becoming until it can endure to contemplate reality, and the brightest of realities, which we say is the Good. —Yes.

Education then is the art of doing this very thing, this turning around, the knowledge of how the soul can most easily and most effectively be turned around; it is not the art of putting the capacity of sight into the soul; the soul possesses that already but it is not turned the right way or looking where it should. This is what education has to deal with. —That seems likely.

DISCUSSION QUESTIONS

1. Plato's cave-dwellers discover that the source of their so-called knowledge, their senses, has been giving them false information about the world. How reliable are our senses as a source of knowledge? Plato rejects the senses as a source of knowledge. Do you agree with him? Why or why not?

2. Plato believes that once we are shown the source of the shadows on the cave wall, there is no going back to a state of ignorance. Do you agree with him?

3. Plato says, "As for the man who tried to free them and lead them upward, if they could somehow lay their hands on him and kill him, they would do so." Why do you think they would try to kill him? Would you try to kill him if you were a prisoner in the cave? Why or why not?

4. Create your own "allegory" concerning the path from ignorance to knowledge. You may use any image you wish except a cave. Compare your allegory with those of your classmates.

5. Is there a parallel between the status of the prisoners in Plato's cave and the spectators in a cinema? How is the experience of the movie-goer like or unlike the experience of Plato's cave-dwellers?

The Truman Show
[USA 1998] 1 hour, 45 minutes
Directed by Peter Weir

*T*ruman Burbank (Jim Carrey), a desk clerk for an insurance agency, seems to be living the American dream. He resides in a pleasant town; he is loved by his neighbors and his beautiful wife; he has a car, a house, and a comfortable life. One day, Truman decides that he wants to see the world. As he makes inquiries about travel, Truman begins to feel as if his friends and neighbors are somehow thwarting his plans. After Truman realizes that the locals are conspiring against him, he escapes to the sea. Upon reaching a wall at "the end of the ocean," Truman uncovers the truth about his life: From the moment he was born up until the present, Truman has been the star of a twenty-four-hour reality TV show called *The Truman Show*. Every moment of his life has been televised by thousands of cameras around his mock town, which is inhabited by actors. Truman, now on a quest for the truth, takes the final leap into the unknown as he turns his back on the life he once thought of as reality.

DISCUSSION QUESTIONS

1. Consider the following dialogue between the show's creator, Christof (Ed Harris), and Truman:

    CHRISTOF   "I am the creator of a television show that gives hope and joy and inspiration to millions."

    TRUMAN   "And who am I?"

    CHRISTOF   "You're the star."

    TRUMAN   "Was nothing real?"

    CHRISTOF   "*You* were real. That's what made you so good to watch. Listen to me, Truman. There's no more truth out there than there is in the world I created for you. Same lies. The same deceit. But in my world, you have nothing to fear. I know you better than you know yourself."

    TRUMAN   "You never had a camera in my head!"

    CHRISTOF   "You're afraid. That's why you can't leave. It's okay, Truman. I understand. I have been watching you your whole life. I was watching when you were born. I was watching when you took your first step. I watched you on your first day of school. Heh heh. The episode when you lost your first tooth. Heh heh heh. You can't leave, Truman. You belong here . . . with me. Talk to me. Say something. . . . You're on television! You're live to the whole world!"

    Why is it possible to believe that Truman lived his whole life as a television star but never knew it? Why do you think it took Truman so long to figure out that his life was a TV reality show? How long do you think it would take you to awake from Truman's American "dream"?

2. Truman asks, "Was nothing real?" The reply he receives from the creator of the show, Christof, is "*You* were real." How is it possible for everything around Truman not to be real but for him nevertheless to be real? Discuss.

3. Is "not being a real person" versus "being real a real person" relative to one's knowledge of the world? For example, if we know the world around us is not real, must we then conclude that we are not real? And, if we believe that the world around us is real, must we conclude that we too are real?
4. From Truman's perspective, was his life on the television show a "real" life? Why or why not?
5. A number of popular television shows are called "reality TV." How do you know that the reality they present to you is "real"? Does it matter to you if what you believe is real on television is actually fake? How might this knowledge come back and affect your own "real" life?
6. In the film, Truman's best friend, Marlon (Noah Emmerich), says, "Nothing is fake, it's merely controlled." What is the difference between something that is "fake" and something that is "merely controlled"?
7. In what way is your own life like a "controlled dream"? In what way are the things you take for knowledge part of a systematic effort to control what you know? For example, some people believe that the media provides us with information in a systematic effort to control what we know and believe about the world. How is this similar to or different from Truman's situation?

RENÉ DESCARTES
NEW FOUNDATIONS FOR KNOWLEDGE

In this selection, René Descartes wonders what, if anything, he can know with absolute certainty. Like Plato's concept, Descartes' general approach to knowledge is called *rationalism*, which means that he believes that through reason alone, without the aid of information from the senses, we are capable of arriving at some indubitable truths. Descartes reflects rationally on the certainty of his opinions by subjecting them to increasing levels of doubt or skepticism. He begins by stating, "I have noticed that the senses are sometimes deceptive." Nonetheless, while his senses might deceive him some of the time, they simply cannot be doubted all of the time. He then considers whether everything he senses might not just be a dream and how he might distinguish the waking state from the dream state. Descartes decides that even if he is dreaming, "arithmetic, geometry, and other such disciplines, which treat of nothing but the simplest and most general things and which are indifferent as to whether these things do or do not in fact exist, contain something certain and indubitable." In other words, "two plus three makes five . . . whether I am awake or asleep."

Finally, Descartes considers whether there may not be "an evil genius, supremely powerful and clever, who has directed his entire effort at deceiving me." Even if this is true, maintains Descartes, "there is no doubt I exist, if he is deceiving me." "Thus," concludes Descartes, "after everything has been most carefully weighed, it must finally be established that this pronouncement 'I am, I exist' is necessarily true every time I utter it or conceive it in my mind." Descartes later characterizes the "I" in "I am, I exist" as "a thing that thinks."

It should be noted that Descartes' famous line "I think, therefore I am" (*Cogito ergo sum*) is a different way of asserting the same level of certainty achieved in "I am, I exist." However, this line appears in an earlier work titled *Discourse on Method* (pt. 4, sec. 32; 1637), not in the later *Meditations on First Philosophy* (1641), the text from which our selection is taken.

René Descartes (1596–1650), a French philosopher, received baccalaureate and licentiate degrees in law in 1616 and joined the army as an unpaid volunteer in 1618. In November 1619, while still in the military, Descartes was struck with a notion of how to provide a basis for all knowledge with a level of certainty equal to that of mathematics. His idea was later reconfirmed through a series of dreams, and shortly thereafter Descartes quit the military. In 1628, he departed France for Holland, where he lived for the next twenty years. His publication plans for several of his writings, including *The World, or Treatise on Light* (1664), were altered in the 1630s after he learned of the trial of Galileo in Rome. He did, however, publish *Discourse on Method* during this period. *Meditations* is a response to questions about section IV of the *Discourse*, which lays out in rudimentary form Descartes' new foundation for knowledge. *Meditations* generated a considerable amount of controversy from a number of quarters, including the charge of atheism. In 1649, Descartes went to the court of Queen Christina of Sweden in order to teach her philosophy. The winter weather was abnormally cold, and Descartes died of pneumonia early the next year. His other writings include *Principles of Philosophy* (1644), *The Passions of the Soul* (1649), and *Rules for the Direction of the Mind* (1701).

MEDITATION ONE

CONCERNING THOSE THINGS THAT CAN BE CALLED INTO DOUBT

Several years have now passed since I first realized how numerous were the false opinions that in my youth I had taken to be true, and thus how doubtful were all those that I had subsequently built upon them. And thus I realized that once in my life I had to raze everything to the ground and begin again from the original foundations, if I wanted to establish anything firm and lasting in the sciences. But the task seemed enormous, and I was waiting until I reached a point in my life that was so timely that no more suitable time for undertaking these plans of action would come to pass. For this reason, I procrastinated for so long that I would henceforth be at fault, were I to waste the time that remains for carrying out the project by brooding over it. Accordingly, I have today suitably freed my mind of all cares, secured for myself a period of leisurely tranquility, and am withdrawing into solitude. At last I will apply myself earnestly and unreservedly to this general demolition of my opinions.

Yet to bring this about I will not need to show that all my opinions are false, which is perhaps something I could never accomplish. But reason now persuades me that I should withhold my assent no less carefully from opinions that are not completely certain and indubitable than I would from those that are patently false. For this reason, it will suffice for the rejection of all of these opinions, if I find in each of them some reason for doubt. Nor therefore need I survey each opinion individually, a task that would be endless. Rather, because undermining the foundations will cause whatever has been built upon them to crumble of its own accord, I will attack straightaway those principles which supported everything I once believed.

Surely whatever I had admitted until now as most true I received either from the senses or through the senses. However, I have noticed that the senses are sometimes deceptive; and it is a mark of prudence never to place our complete trust in those who have deceived us even once.

But perhaps, even though the senses do sometimes deceive us when it is a question of very small and distant things, still there are many other matters concerning which one simply cannot doubt, even though they are derived from the very same senses: for example, that I am sitting here next to the fire, wearing my winter dressing gown, that I am holding this sheet of paper in my hands, and the like. But on what grounds could one deny that these hands and this entire body are mine? Unless perhaps I were to liken myself to the insane, whose brains are impaired by such an unrelenting vapor of black bile that they steadfastly insist that they are kings when they are utter paupers, or that they are arrayed in purple robes when they are naked, or that they have heads made of clay, or that they are gourds, or that they are made of glass. But such people are mad, and I would appear no less mad, were I to take their behavior as an example for myself.

This would all be well and good, were I not a man who is accustomed to sleeping at night, and to experiencing in my dreams the very same things, or now and then even less plausible ones, as these insane people do when they are awake. How often does my evening slumber persuade me of such ordinary things as these: that I am here, clothed in my dressing gown, seated next to the fireplace—when in fact I am lying undressed in bed! But right now my eyes are certainly wide awake when I gaze upon this sheet of paper. This head which I am shaking is not heavy with sleep. I extend this hand consciously and deliberately, and I feel it. Such things would not be so distinct for someone who is asleep. As if I did not recall having been deceived on other occasions even by similar thoughts in my dreams! As I consider these matters more carefully, I see so plainly that there are no definitive signs by which to distinguish being awake from being asleep. As a result, I am becoming quite dizzy, and this dizziness nearly convinces me that I am asleep.

Let us assume then, for the sake of argument, that we are dreaming and that such particulars as these are not true: that we are opening our eyes, moving our head, and extending our hands. Perhaps we do not even have such hands, or any such body at all. Nevertheless, it surely must be admitted that the things seen during slumber are, as it were, like painted images, which could only have been produced in the likeness of true things, and that therefore at least these general things— eyes, head, hands, and the whole body—are not imaginary things, but are true and exist. For indeed when painters themselves wish to represent sirens and satyrs by means of especially bizarre forms, they surely cannot assign to them utterly new natures. Rather, they simply fuse together the members of various animals. Or if

perhaps they concoct something so utterly novel that nothing like it has ever been seen before (and thus is something utterly fictitious and false), yet certainly at the very least the colors from which they fashion it ought to be true. And by the same token, although even these general things—eyes, head, hands and the like—could be imaginary, still one has to admit that at least certain other things that are even more simple and universal are true. It is from these components, as if from true colors, that all those images of things that are in our thought are fashioned, be they true or false.

This class of things appears to include corporeal nature in general, together with its extension; the shape of extended things; their quantity, that is, their size and number; as well as the place where they exist; the time through which they endure, and the like.

Thus it is not improper to conclude from this that physics, astronomy, medicine, and all the other disciplines that are dependent upon the consideration of composite things are doubtful, and that, on the other hand, arithmetic, geometry, and other such disciplines, which treat of nothing but the simplest and most general things and which are indifferent as to whether these things do or do not in fact exist, contain something certain and indubitable. For whether I am awake or asleep, two plus three make five, and a square does not have more than four sides. It does not seem possible that such obvious truths should be subject to the suspicion of being false.

Be that as it may, there is fixed in my mind a certain opinion of long standing, namely that there exists a God who is able to do anything and by whom I, such as I am, have been created. How do I know that he did not bring it about that there is no earth at all, no heavens, no extended thing, no shape, no size, no place, and yet bringing it about that all these things appear to me to exist precisely as they do now? Moreover, since I judge that others sometimes make mistakes in matters that they believe they know most perfectly, may I not, in like fashion, be deceived every time I add two and three or count the sides of a square, or perform an even simpler operation, if that can be imagined? But perhaps God has not willed that I be deceived in this way, for he is said to be supremely good. Nonetheless, if it were repugnant to his goodness to have created me such that I be deceived all the time, it would also seem foreign to that same goodness to permit me to be deceived even occasionally. But we cannot make this last assertion.

Perhaps there are some who would rather deny so powerful a God than believe that everything else is uncertain. Let us not oppose them; rather, let us grant that everything said here about God is fictitious. Now they suppose that I came to be what I am either by fate, or by chance, or by a connected chain of events, or by some other way. But because being deceived and being mistaken appear to be a certain imperfection, the less powerful they take the author of my origin to be, the more probable it will be that I am so imperfect that I am always deceived. I have nothing to say in response to these arguments. But eventually I am forced to admit that there is nothing among the things I once believed to be true which it is not permissible to doubt—and not out of frivolity or lack of forethought, but for valid and considered reasons. Thus I must be no less careful to withhold assent henceforth even from these beliefs than I would from those that are patently false, if I wish to find anything certain.

But it is not enough simply to have realized these things; I must take steps to keep myself mindful of them. For long-standing opinions keep returning, and, almost against my will, they take advantage of my credulity, as if it were bound over to them by long use and the claims of intimacy. Nor will I ever get out of the habit of assenting to them and believing in them, so long as I take them to be exactly what they are, namely, in some respects doubtful, as has just now been shown, but nevertheless highly probable, so that it is much more consonant with reason to believe them than to deny them. Hence, it seems to me I would do well to deceive myself by turning my will in completely the opposite direction and

pretend for a time that these opinions are wholly false and imaginary, until finally, as if with prejudices weighing down each side equally, no bad habit should turn my judgment any further from the correct perception of things. For indeed I know that meanwhile there is no danger or error in following this procedure, and that it is impossible for me to indulge in too much distrust, since I am now concentrating only on knowledge, not on action.

Accordingly, I will suppose not a supremely good God, the source of truth, but rather an evil genius, supremely powerful and clever, who has directed his entire effort at deceiving me. I will regard the heavens, the air, the earth, colors, shapes, sounds, and all external things as nothing but the bedeviling hoaxes of my dreams, with which he lays snares for my credulity. I will regard myself as not having hands, or eyes, or flesh, or blood, or any senses, but as nevertheless falsely believing that I possess all these things. I will remain resolute and steadfast in this meditation, and even if it is not within my power to know anything true, it certainly is within my power to take care resolutely to withhold my assent to what is false, lest this deceiver, however powerful, however clever he may be, have any effect on me. But this undertaking is arduous, and a certain laziness brings me back to my customary way of living. I am not unlike a prisoner who enjoyed an imaginary freedom during his sleep, but, when he later begins to suspect that he is dreaming, fears being awakened and nonchalantly conspires with these pleasant illusions. In just the same way, I fall back of my own accord into my old opinions, and dread being awakened, lest the toilsome wakefulness which follows upon a peaceful rest must be spent thenceforward not in the light but among the inextricable shadows of the difficulties now brought forward.

MEDITATION TWO

CONCERNING THE NATURE OF THE HUMAN MIND: THAT IT IS BETTER KNOWN THAN THE BODY

Yesterday's meditation has thrown me into such doubts that I can no longer ignore them, yet I fail to see how they are to be resolved. It is as if I had suddenly fallen into a deep whirlpool; I am so tossed about that I can neither touch bottom with my foot, nor swim up to the top. Nevertheless I will work my way up and will once again attempt the same path I entered upon yesterday. I will accomplish this by putting aside everything that admits of the least doubt, as if I had discovered it to be completely false. I will stay on this course until I know something certain, or, if nothing else, until I at least know for certain that nothing is certain. Archimedes sought but one firm and immovable point in order to move the entire earth from one place to another. Just so, great things are also to be hoped for if I succeed in finding just one thing, however slight, that is certain and unshaken.

Therefore I suppose that everything I see is false. I believe that none of what my deceitful memory represents ever existed. I have no senses whatever. Body, shape, extension, movement, and place are all chimeras. What then will be true? Perhaps just the single fact that nothing is certain.

But how do I know there is not something else, over and above all those things that I have just reviewed, concerning which there is not even the slightest occasion for doubt? Is there not some God, or by whatever name I might call him, who instills these very thoughts in me? But why would I think that, since I myself could perhaps be the author of these thoughts? Am I not then at least something? But I have already denied that I have any senses and any body. Still I hesitate; for what follows from this? Am I so tied to a body and to the senses that I cannot exist without them? But I have persuaded myself that there is absolutely nothing in the world: no sky, no earth, no minds, no bodies. Is it then the case that I too do not exist? But doubtless I did exist, if I persuaded myself of something. But there is some deceiver or other who is supremely powerful and supremely sly and who is always deliberately deceiving me. Then too there is no doubt that I exist, if he is

deceiving me. And let him do his best at deception, he will never bring it about that I am nothing so long as I shall think that I am something. Thus, after everything has been most carefully weighed, it must finally be established that this pronouncement "I am, I exist" is necessarily true every time I utter it or conceive it in my mind.

But I do not yet understand sufficiently what I am—I, who now necessarily exist. And so from this point on, I must be careful lest I unwittingly mistake something else for myself, and thus err in that very item of knowledge that I claim to be the most certain and evident of all. Thus, I will meditate once more on what I once believed myself to be, prior to embarking upon these thoughts. For this reason, then, I will set aside whatever can be weakened even to the slightest degree by the arguments brought forward, so that eventually all that remains is precisely nothing but what is certain and unshaken.

What then did I used to think I was? A man, of course. But what is a man? Might I not say a "rational animal"? No, because then I would have to inquire what "animal" and "rational" mean. And thus from one question I would slide into many more difficult ones. Nor do I now have enough free time that I want to waste it on subtleties of this sort. Instead, permit me to focus here on what came spontaneously and naturally into my thinking whenever I pondered what I was. Now it occurred to me first that I had a face, hands, arms, and this entire mechanism of bodily members: the very same as are discerned in a corpse, and which I referred to by the name "body." It next occurred to me that I took in food, that I walked about, and that I sensed and thought various things; these actions I used to attribute to the soul. But as to what this soul might be, I either did not think about it or else I imagined it a rarified I-know-not-what, like a wind, or a fire, or ether, which had been infused into my coarser parts. But as to the body I was not in any doubt. On the contrary, I was under the impression that I knew its nature distinctly. Were I perhaps tempted to describe this nature such as I conceived it in my mind, I would have described it thus: by "body," I understand all that is capable of being bounded by some shape, of being enclosed in a place, and of filling up a space in such a way as to exclude any other body from it; of being perceived by touch, sight, hearing, taste, or smell; of being moved in several ways, not, of course, by itself, but by whatever else impinges upon it. For it was my view that the power of self-motion, and likewise of sensing or of thinking, in no way belonged to the nature of the body. Indeed I used rather to marvel that such faculties were to be found in certain bodies.

But now what am I, when I suppose that there is some supremely powerful and, if I may be permitted to say so, malicious deceiver who deliberately tries to fool me in any way he can? Can I not affirm that I possess at least a small measure of all those things which I have already said belong to the nature of the body? I focus my attention on them, I think about them, I review them again, but nothing comes to mind. I am tired of repeating this to no purpose. But what about those things I ascribed to the soul? What about being nourished or moving about? Since I now do not have a body, these are surely nothing but fictions. What about sensing? Surely this too does not take place without a body; and I seemed to have sensed in my dreams many things that I later realized I did not sense. What about thinking? Here I make my discovery: thought exists; it alone cannot be separated from me. I am; I exist—this is certain. But for how long? For as long as I am thinking; for perhaps it could also come to pass that if I were to cease all thinking I would then utterly cease to exist. At this time I admit nothing that is not necessarily true. I am therefore precisely nothing but a thinking thing; that is, a mind, or intellect, or understanding, or reason—words of whose meanings I was previously ignorant. Yet I am a true thing and am truly existing; but what kind of thing? I have said it already: a thinking thing.

What else am I? I will set my imagination in motion. I am not that concatenation of members we call the human body. Neither am I even some subtle air infused into these members, nor a wind, nor a fire, nor a vapor, nor a breath, nor anything I devise for myself. For I have supposed these things to be nothing. The assumption still stands; yet nevertheless I am something. But is it perhaps the case that these very things which I take to be nothing, because they are unknown to me, nevertheless are in fact no different from that "me" that I know? This I do not know, and I will not quarrel about it now. I can make a judgment only about things that are known to me. I know that I exist; I ask now who is this "I" whom I know? Most certainly, in the strict sense the knowledge of this "I" does not depend upon things of whose existence I do not yet have knowledge. Therefore it is not dependent upon any of those things that I simulate in my imagination. But this word "simulate" warns me of my error. For I would indeed be simulating were I to "imagine" that I was something, because imagining is merely the contemplating of the shape or image of a corporeal thing. But I now know with certainty that I am and also that all these images—and, generally, everything belonging to the nature of the body—could turn out to be nothing but dreams. Once I have realized this, I would seem to be speaking no less foolishly were I to say: "I will use my imagination in order to recognize more distinctly who I am," than were I to say: "Now I surely am awake, and I see something true; but since I do not yet see it clearly enough, I will deliberately fall asleep so that my dreams might represent it to me more truly and more clearly." Thus I realize that none of what I can grasp by means of the imagination pertains to this knowledge that I have of myself. Moreover, I realize that I must be most diligent about withdrawing my mind from these things so that it can perceive its nature as distinctly as possible.

But what then am I? A thing that thinks. What is that? A thing that doubts, understands, affirms, denies, wills, refuses, and that also imagines and senses.

DISCUSSION QUESTIONS

1. Does Descartes ever prove in his first meditation that we are not dreaming? Why or why not?

2. Descartes' "evil genius" raises the greatest degree of skepticism concerning his claim to know anything. How does Descartes prove that at least one thing can be known for

certain even if he is being deceived continuously by an evil genius. Do you think his proof works? Why or why not?

3. Descartes appeals to sensory information concerning his own body (for example, "I am sitting here next to the fire, wearing my dressing gown. . . .") in order to reach the conclusion that his senses are not always deceiving him. Are you convinced by his argument? How do you know, for example, that the hands you take to be your own hands *really are your own hands*? How might you prove this to someone else?

4. What does Descartes think he has demonstrated with the statement "I am, I exist"?

Does he convince you? In addition, why not simply say "I am" or "I exist" instead of "I am, I exist?"

5. Is the statement "I think, therefore I am" different from "I am, I exist?" Why do you think Descartes used this different formulation in the *Meditations*?

6. Do you find it ironic that Descartes confirms his notion of how to provide a basis for all knowledge through a series of dreams, yet strives to escape the uncertainty of dreams in his search for foundational knowledge? How might Descartes respond?

■ ■ ■ ■ ■ ■ ■ ■ ■ ■ ■ ■ ■ ■ ■ ■ ■ ■ ■ ■
The City of Lost Children
[France 1995] 1 hour, 52 minutes
Dir. by M. Caro and J. P. Jeunet
■ ■ ■ ■ ■ ■ ■ ■ ■ ■ ■ ■ ■ ■ ■ ■ ■ ■ ■ ■

*T*he City of Lost Children portrays the lives of genetically flawed beings created by a mysterious inventor. One of the inventor's creations is Krank (Daniel Emilfork), an evil man who cannot dream and who kidnaps young children so that he can steal their dreams for himself. When Krank kidnaps Denree (Joseph Lucien), the little brother of a simple-minded circus strongman named One (Ron Perlman), One begins a desperate search for his brother. On the journey, One is assisted by Miette (Judith Vittet), an orphan who dreams about the place where Denree is being held captive, a place known as the City of Lost Children. Miette and One encounter numerous obstacles, including Miette's evil conjoined-twin caregivers (Geneviève Brunet and Odile Mallet), the Cyclops, and the inventor's six cloned sons (Dominique Pinon). With the help of former circus manager Marcello (Jean-Claude Dreyfus), One and Miette reach the City of Lost Children. However, Miette must enter a world of dreams in which she defeats Krank and rescues Denree before anyone can truly be saved. Ultimately, all of the kidnapped children and all of the inventor's flawed "children" are able to escape as they watch the inventor himself and the City of Lost Children go up in flames.

DISCUSSION QUESTIONS

1. Consider the following dialogue between Krank and Irvin, a poor, migraine-ridden brain that lives in a fish tank:

    IRVIN   "Once upon a time, there was an inventor so gifted that he could create life. A truly remarkable man."

    KRANK   "Ah, a fairy tale. I can already feel tears in my eyes."

IRVIN   "Since he had no wife or children he decided to make them in his laboratory. He started with his wife and fashioned her into the most beautiful princess in the world. Alas, a wicked genetic fairy cast a spell on the inventor so much so that the princess was only knee-high to a grasshopper. He then cloned six children in his own image. Faithful, hardworking, they were so alike no one could tell them apart. But fate tricked him again, giving them all sleeping sickness. Craving someone to talk to, he grew in a fish tank a poor migraine-ridden brain. And then, at last, he created his masterpiece more intelligent than the most intelligent man on Earth. But, alas, the inventor made a serious mistake. While his creation was intelligent, he, too, had a defect. He never, ever had a dream. You can't imagine how quickly he grew old because he was so unhappy."

In this film, the most intelligent man on earth lacks the ability to dream and is unhappy as a result. Do you think that dreams play an important part in our happiness? Why or why not?

2.   If you, like Krank, lost the ability to dream but were the most intelligent person on earth, do you think you would be unhappy?

3.   Do you think that dreams are a source of knowledge? Why or why not? Does it matter to you that as a source of knowledge dreams cannot be known with certainty?

4.   Would you rather use a dream as a foundation for all your knowledge or, like Descartes, base your knowledge on the indubitability of your existence as a thinking thing (*res cogitans*)?

5.   Much of the material in this chapter has been concerned with detecting and escaping from dreams and the world of uncertain knowledge that comes with them. Has the implicit assumption here been that certainty regarding the sources of knowledge brings happiness?

6.   How is living like Krank, that is, without dreams, akin to living outside of Plato's cave? Plato says that those who leave the cave will not want to go back. Is Krank, who is intelligent but who desires the dreams of children, similar to a prisoner who leaves Plato's cave but wishes to return to the cave in order to be deceived by shadows on the cave wall? Why or why not?

7.   In his proof that "I think, therefore I am" is the only statement that can be known with certainty, Descartes has proved that he is a "thinking thing" or a mind, but has not yet proved the existence of his body. How is Irvin, the migraine-ridden brain in a fish tank, like Descartes' "thinking thing"? How are they different?

8.   In what way is this film simply a defense of dreaming against the encroachments of rationality and knowledge?

JORGE LUIS BORGES

THE CIRCULAR RUINS

Jorge Luis Borges' "The Circular Ruins" is the story of a man who discovers that he is only a dream in the mind of another. It raises a host of philosophical questions about the state of our knowledge: How do we know the difference between waking life and dreams? How dowe know that what we take to be reality is not a dream that we or someone else is having? Is it possible to know anything with certainty? Borges' story plants in readers a seed of doubt concerning our ability to know whether we actually exist in reality or are just the dream of another.

Jorge Luis Borges (1899–1986) was born in Buenos Aires, Argentina, and educated in Europe. He wrote poetry, essays, and short stories that are often described as "magical realism." In 1938, a severe wound to the head and subsequent blood poisoning brought him close to death, and he feared for his sanity. This accident marked the beginning of an intense period of creativity; "The Circular Ruins" is from this period. By 1955, Borges had become director of the Argentine national library and professor of English and American literature at the University of Buenos Aires. He was also nearly blind.

Borges is one of the great Spanish-language writers, perhaps second only to Cervantes. Many of his short stories explore the nature of knowledge, reality, the mind, and other philosophical perplexities. Borges' writing reveals a deep understanding of the history of philosophy. In 1967–68, he gave a series of lectures in English at Harvard University, in which he said, "What is a history of philosophy, but a history of the perplexities of the Hindus, of the Chinese, of the Greeks, of the Schoolmen, of Bishop Berkeley, of Hume, of Schopenhauer, and so on?" His story collections include *A Universal History of Iniquity* (1935), *Ficciones* (1944), *The Aleph* (1949), *In Praise of Darkness* (1969), and *The Book of Sand* (1975). "The Circular Ruins" was first collected in *El jardín de senderos que se bifurcan* (*The Garden of Forking Paths*) (1941–1942), then later in *Ficciones*.

And if he left off dreaming about you . . .

—*Through the Looking Glass, VI*

No one saw him disembark in the unanimous night, no one saw the bamboo canoe sinking into the sacred mud, but within a few days no one was unaware that the silent man came from the South and that his home was one of the infinite villages upstream on the violent mountainside, where the Zend tongue is not contaminated with Greek and where leprosy is infrequent. The truth is that the obscure man kissed the mud, came up the bank without pushing aside (probably without feeling) the brambles which dilacerated his flesh, and dragged himself, nauseous and bloodstained, to the circular enclosure crowned by a stone tiger or horse, which once was the color of fire and now was that of ashes. This circle was a temple, long ago devoured by fire, which the malarial jungle had profaned and whose god no longer received the homage of men. The stranger stretched out beneath the pedestal. He was awakened by the sun high above. He evidenced without astonishment that his wounds had closed; he shut his pale eyes and slept, not out of bodily weakness but out of determination of will. He knew that this temple was the place required by his invincible purpose; he knew that, downstream, the incessant trees had not managed to choke the ruins of another propitious temple, whose gods were also burned and dead; he knew that his immediate obligation was to sleep. Towards midnight he was awakened by the disconsolate cry of a bird. Prints of bare feet, some figs and a jug told him that men of the region had respectfully spied upon his sleep and were solicitous of his favor or feared his magic. He felt the chill of fear and sought out a burial niche in the dilapidated wall and covered himself with some unknown leaves.

The purpose which guided him was not impossible, though it was supernatural. He wanted to dream a man: he wanted to dream him with minute integrity and insert him into reality. This magical project had exhausted the entire content of his soul; if someone had asked him his own name or any trait of his previous life, he would not have been able to answer. The uninhabited and broken temple suited him, for it was a minimum of visible world; the nearness of the peasants also suited him, for they would see that his frugal necessities were supplied. The rice and fruit of their tribute were sufficient sustenance for his body, consecrated to the sole task of sleeping and dreaming.

At first, his dreams were chaotic; somewhat later, they were of a dialectical nature. The stranger dreamt that he was in the center of a circular amphitheater which in some way was the burned temple: clouds of silent students filled the gradins; the faces of the last ones hung many centuries away and at a cosmic height, but were entirely clear and precise. The man was lecturing to them on anatomy, cosmography, magic; the countenances listened with eagerness and strove to respond with understanding, as if they divined the importance of the examination which would redeem one of them from his state of vain appearance and interpolate him into the world of reality. The man, both in dreams and awake, considered his phantoms' replies, was not deceived by impostors, divined a growling intelligence in certain perplexities. He sought a soul which would merit participation in the universe.

After nine or ten nights, he comprehended with some bitterness that he could expect nothing of those students who passively accepted his doctrines, but that he could of those who, at times, would venture a reasonable contradiction. The former, though worthy of love and affection, could not rise to the state of individuals; the latter pre-existed somewhat more. One afternoon (now his afternoons too were tributaries of sleep, now he remained awake only for a couple of hours at dawn) he dismissed the vast illusory college forever and kept one single student. He was a silent boy, sallow, sometimes obstinate, with sharp features which reproduced those of the dreamer. He was not long disconcerted by his companions' sudden elimination; his progress, after a few special lessons, astounded his teacher. Nevertheless, catastrophe ensued. The man emerged from sleep one day as if from a viscous desert, looked at the vain light of afternoon, which at first he confused with that of dawn, and understood that he had not really dreamt. All that night and all day, the intolerable lucidity of insomnia weighed upon him. He tried to explore the jungle, to exhaust himself; amidst the hemlocks, he was scarcely able to manage a few snatches of feeble sleep, fleetingly mottled with some rudimentary visions which were useless. He tried to convoke the college and had scarcely uttered a few brief words of exhortation, when it became deformed and was extinguished. In his almost perpetual sleeplessness, his old eyes burned with tears of anger.

He comprehended that the effort to mold the incoherent and vertiginous matter dreams are made of was the most arduous task a man could undertake, though he might penetrate all the enigmas of the upper and lower orders: much more arduous than weaving a rope of sand or coining the faceless wind. He comprehended that an initial failure was inevitable. He swore he would forget the enormous hallucination which had misled him at first, and he sought another method. Before putting it into effect, he dedicated a month to replenishing the powers his delirium had wasted. He abandoned any premeditation of dreaming and, almost at once, was able to sleep for a considerable part of the day. The few times he dreamt during this period, he did not take notice of the dreams. To take up his task again, he waited until the moon's disk was perfect. Then, in the afternoon, he purified himself in the waters of the river, worshipped the planetary gods, uttered the lawful syllables of a powerful name and slept. Almost immediately, he dreamt of a beating heart.

He dreamt it as active, warm, secret, the size of a closed fist, of garnet color in the penumbra of a human body as yet without face or sex; with minute love he dreamt it, for fourteen lucid nights. Each night he perceived it with greater clarity. He did not touch it, but limited himself to witnessing it, observing it, perhaps correcting it with this eyes. He perceived it, lived it, from many distances and many angles. On the fourteenth night he touched the pulmonary artery with his finger, and then the whole heart, inside and out. The examination satisfied him. Deliberately, he did not dream for a night; then he took the heart again, invoked the name of a planet and set about to envision another of the principal organs. Within a year he reached the skeleton, the eyelids. The innumerable hair was perhaps the most difficult task. He dreamt a complete man, a youth, but this youth could not rise nor did he speak nor could he open his eyes. Night after night, the man dreamt him as asleep.

In the Gnostic cosmogonies, the demiurgi knead and mold a red Adam who cannot stand alone; as unskillful and crude and elementary as this Adam of dust was the Adam of dreams fabricated by the magician's nights of effort. One afternoon, the man almost destroyed his work, but then repented. (It would have been better for him had he destroyed it.) Once he had completed his supplications to the numina of the earth and the river, he threw himself down at the feet of the effigy which was perhaps a tiger and perhaps a horse, and implored its unknown succor. That twilight, he dreamt of the statue. He dreamt of it as a living, tremulous thing: it was not an atrocious mongrel of tiger and horse, but both these vehement creatures at once and also a bull, a rose, a tempest. This multiple god revealed to him that its earthly name was Fire, that in the circular temple (and in others of its kind) people had rendered it sacrifices and cult and that it would magically give life to the sleeping phantom, in such a way that all creatures except Fire itself and the dreamer would believe him to be a man of flesh and blood. The man was ordered by the divinity to instruct his creature in its rites, and send him to the other broken temple whose pyramids survived downstream, so that in this deserted edifice a voice might give glory to the god. In the dreamer's dream, the dreamed one awoke.

The magician carried out these orders. He devoted a period of time (which finally comprised two years) to revealing the arcana of the universe and of the fire cult to his dream child. Inwardly, it pained him to be separated from the boy. Under the pretext of pedagogical necessity, each day he prolonged the hours he dedicated to his dreams. He also redid the right shoulder, which was perhaps deficient. At times, he was troubled by the impression that all this had happened before. . . . In general, his days were happy; when he closed his eyes, he would think: *Now I shall be with my son.* Or, less often: *The child I have engendered awaits me and will not exist if I do not go to him.*

Gradually, he accustomed the boy to reality. Once he ordered him to place a banner on a distant peak. The following day, the banner flickered from the mountain top. He tried other analogous experiments, each more daring than the last. He understood with certain bitterness that his son was ready—and perhaps impatient—to be born. That night he kissed him for the first time and sent him to the other temple whose debris showed white downstream, through many leagues of inextricable jungle and swamp. But first (so that he would never know he was a phantom, so that he would be thought a man like others) he instilled into him a complete oblivion of years of apprenticeship.

The man's victory and peace were dimmed by weariness. At dawn and at twilight, he would prostrate himself before the stone figure, imagining perhaps that his unreal child was practicing the same rites, in other circular ruins, downstream; at night, he would not dream, or would dream only as all men do. He perceived the sounds and forms of the universe with certain colorlessness: his absent son was being nurtured with these diminutions of his soul. His life's purpose was complete; the man persisted in a kind of ecstasy. After a time, which some narrators of his story prefer to compute in years and others in lustra, he was awakened one midnight by two boatmen; he could not see their faces, but they told him of a magic man in a temple of the North who could walk upon fire and not be burned. The magician suddenly remembered the words of the god. He recalled that, of all the creatures of the world, fire was the only one that knew his son was a phantom. This recollection, at first soothing, finally tormented him. He feared his son might meditate on his abnormal privilege and discover in some way that his condition was that of a mere image. Not to be a man, to be the projection of another man's dream, what a feeling of humiliation, of vertigo! All fathers are interested in the children they have procreated (they have permitted to exist) in mere confusion or pleasure; it was natural that the magician should fear for the future of that son, created in thought, limb by limb and feature by feature, in a thousand and one secret nights.

The end of his meditations was sudden, though it was foretold in certain signs. First (after a long drought) a faraway cloud on a hill, light and rapid as a bird; then, toward the south, the sky which had the rose color of the leopard's mouth; then the smoke which corroded the metallic nights; finally, the panicky flight of the animals. For what was happening had happened many centuries ago. The ruins of the fire god's sanctuary were destroyed by fire. In a birdless dawn the magician saw the concentric blaze close round the walls. For a moment, he thought of taking refuge in the river, but then he knew that death was coming to crown his old age and absolve him of his labors. He walked into the shreds of flame. But they did not bite into his flesh, they caressed him and engulfed him without heat or combustion. With relief, with humiliation, with terror, he understood that he too was a mere appearance, dreamt by another.

DISCUSSION QUESTIONS

1. How do you know that you are not "a mere appearance, dreamt by another"? State your argument. How might Borges respond to it? How might Descartes?

2. Borges views the history of philosophy as "a history of the perplexities." What do you think he means by this? Do you agree with him?

3. Is there anything that you know beyond any doubt and with complete certainty? If so, list these truths, and defend your knowledge of them.

4. Why do you think that Borges' man was relieved when he understood that "he too was a mere appearance"? Would this knowledge relieve you? Is it any more of a relief than coming to the knowledge that you are a mere "reality" (as opposed to an "appearance")?

5. If Borges' man is being dreamt by another man, should we assume that this other man is being dreamt by yet *another* man? How far down does this phenomenon extend? Does it matter? Discuss this view of human existence.

Vanilla Sky
[USA 2001] 2 hours, 15 minutes
Directed by Cameron Crowe

David Aames (Tom Cruise), formerly a rich and handsome publisher, is in prison awaiting trial for murder. David is in the care of psychologist Dr. McCabe (Kurt Russell), who believes that he can crack David's case by helping him to remember the events surrounding the murder. David can remember some details from his previous life: his success, his popularity, and his disfigurement in a car accident caused by a jealous lover, Julie Gianni (Cameron Diaz). Following the accident, David is left with painful injuries and becomes addicted to painkillers. Lonely and in need, he seeks out Sofia (Penelope Cruz), a dancer whom he met on the night before his accident. Although David and Sofia's first attempts to reconnect fail, Sofia ultimately returns David's affections and helps him through his disfigurement and the subsequent surgeries to restore his handsome features.

David and Sofia enjoy a loving relationship until David begins to experience frightening fits of derangement. During moments when he thinks that he is with Sofia, David sees Julie instead. Confused, David ends up smothering Sofia to death with a pillow because he believes that she is Julie. The plot takes a strange turn when David encounters a mysterious man whom he believes holds the keys to his past and his future. McCabe pressures David for more information on the man, and eventually, David learns that he has signed a contract with the man, Edmund Ventura (Noah Taylor) of Life Extension, a company that specializes in cryogenic freezing. David learns that he is now in a state of *lucid dreaming*: Everything that he remembers before the night he met Sofia in the nightclub was real; everything afterward is part of his dream/ nightmare sequence, including the relationships with Sofia and McCabe. Edmund informs David that he has the choice to go on dreaming in a lucid state or to wake up in the real world, which is 150 years later. David, enjoying a new perspective on life, now knows that he must choose to live again, rather than continue the dream.

DISCUSSION QUESTIONS

1. In the dialogue below, Edmund Ventura of Life Extension introduces himself to David and discusses his lucid dream with him:

    EDMUND   "David Aames, I think it's time we had a proper introduction. I'm Edmund Ventura from the Oasis Project, formerly Life Extension, LE."

    DAVID   "Tech support?"

    EDMUND   "Yes. . . . We first met 150 years ago."

    DAVID   "You sold me the lucid dream?"

    EDMUND   *(nods)*

    DAVID   "Well, what the hell happened?"

    EDMUND   "I tried to warn you in the bar, David. I told you that you must exercise control of yourself, that it all depended on your mind. All of this—everything—is your creation. And now we're heading toward your true moment of choice."

    DAVID   "True moment of choice?"

    EDMUND   "Yes."

    DAVID   "When did the lucid dream begin?"

    EDMUND   "Do you remember the day of the nightclub? That night, after Sofia left you and you fell asleep on the pavement, that was the moment that you chose for the splice."

    DAVID   "Splice?"

    EDMUND   "Splice—the end of your real life and the beginning of LE's lucid dream. . . . From the moment you woke up on that street, nothing was real in the traditional sense."

    Do you agree with Edmund Ventura that nothing in David's lucid dream "was real in the traditional sense"? Why or why not?

2. What is a "lucid dream"? Is it different from the types of dreams presented by Descartes and by Borges? If so, how?

3. Consider this dialogue between David and Edmund Ventura of Life Extension:

    EDMUND   "It's now your moment of choice. You can return to your lucid dream and live a beautiful life with Sofia or whomever you wish. Or you can choose the world out there."

    DAVID   "The world out there? And you can bring me back, just like Benny the dog?"

EDMUND   "Yes, just like Benny the dog. Your face and body can be fixed now, of course. But things are very different now, and your finances won't last long. Your panel of observers are waiting for you to choose. There are no guarantees, but remember, even in the future, the sweet is never as sweet without the sour."

DAVID   "How do I wake up?"

EDMUND   "The decision is yours. . . ."

DAVID   "I want to live a real life. I don't want to dream any longer."

Why does David want to wake from the lucid dream? What is the qualitative difference between his waking life and his lucidly dreamt life? Would you make the same decision?

4. In a lucid dream, do you think it would be possible to know things? Or would your states of mind in a lucid dream be something other than knowledge?

5. Why do you think David chose to live a lucid dream in the first place? Was his reason a good one? Would you make the same choice? Why or why not?

6. If you were offered the opportunity of entering a lucid dream versus living in the real world, which option would you take, and why? How do you think your lucid dream life would differ from your real life?

7. Is seeing the world through a lucid dream state comparable to Kant's notion that we see the world only as presented to us through the structure of our understanding (see below)? Discuss.

8. How do you know that you are not lucidly dreaming right now?

9. Critics have commented that if David's body were frozen below zero as the movie indicates, every molecule of his body would be frozen, which would make it impossible for him to dream. Does this in any way spoil the philosophical significance of the movie for you? Why or why not?

10. McCabe asks, "Mortality as home entertainment? This cannot be the future, can it?" What do you think? If we had the technology to provide lucid dreams, do you think they would be popular? Why or why not?

JOHN LOCKE

THE SENSES AS THE BASIS OF KNOWLEDGE

John Locke argues that the source of all knowledge is to be found in experience. This general approach to knowledge is called *empiricism*. Whereas Descartes' rationalism calls for us to approach questions of knowledge by turning away from the external senses and experiences, Locke's empiricism calls for us to look to our external senses and experiences as the sole source of knowledge.

For Locke, there are no innate ideas, "which the soul receives in its very first being, and brings into the world with it." The notion that the soul comes into the world with ideas or knowledge already stored in it dates back at least as far as Plato, who developed the notion at length. It is found as well in Descartes' *Meditations*, which asserts the existence of innate ideas such as those concerning mathematics and infinite perfection. However, Locke compares the mind to a *tabula rasa*, a blank sheet or "white paper devoid of all characters," on which "experience" writes. Experience is composed of "sensation" and "reflection," the backbone of the life of the mind. All "ideas" come from sensation or reflection, with an idea being anything that is the object of thinking, including that which is "expressed by the words *whiteness, hardness, sweetness, thinking, motion, man, elephant, army, drunkenness,* and others."

One of the more important distinctions in Locke's argument is between "primary qualities" and "secondary qualities." Primary qualities are qualities "utterly inseparable from the body," namely, "solidity, extension, figure, motion or rest, and number." Secondary qualities are "qualities which in truth are nothing in the objects themselves but power to produce various sensations in us by their primary qualities," such as colors, smells, sounds, and tastes. For Locke, then, some of the ideas in our minds stand for the primary qualities of the things we observe, whereas others stand for secondary or derived qualities.

John Locke (1632–1704) earned bachelor's (1656) and master's (1658) degrees from Christ Church, Oxford, and in 1660 became a tutor there in Greek, rhetoric, and philosophy. Of his earliest reading, Locke said that it was the works of Descartes that gave him a taste for philosophy. While he never graduated in medicine, prior to 1666 he practiced medicine as a physician, becoming known among his friends as "Doctor Locke." In 1667, he became the confidential secretary of Lord Ashley, later the first Earl of Shaftesbury. His patron's political difficulties led them to flee England for Paris from 1675 to 1679, then move back, only to leave for Holland in 1683. Locke lived in Holland until 1688 under the assumed name of Dr. Van der Linden.

It was in Holland, at the age of fifty-four, that Locke published his first article. In 1690, twenty years after he had begun to write it, his *Essay Concerning Human Understanding* was finally published. By 1704, his *Essay*, having been through four editions and translations into French and Latin, had been formally condemned by the authorities at Oxford. Locke said of the event, "I take what has been done rather as a recommendation of the book." And he was probably right: The *Essay* was one of the most influential works of the eighteenth century. Locke's other works include *Letter on Toleration* (1689), *Two Treatises on Government* (1689), *Some Thoughts Concerning Education* (1693), *The Reasonableness of Christianity* (1695), *The Conduct of Understanding* (1706), and *Miracles* (1716). The following selection is from the *Essay*.

BOOK I

NEITHER PRINCIPLES NOR IDEAS ARE INNATE

CHAP. I. NO INNATE SPECULATIVE PRINCIPLES

1. *The way shown how we come by any knowledge, sufficient to prove it not innate.* It is an established opinion amongst some men, that there are in the understanding certain *innate principles;* some primary notions, characters, as it were stamped upon the mind of man; which the soul receives in its very first being, and brings into the world with it. It would be sufficient to convince unprejudiced readers of the falseness of this supposition, if I should only show (as I hope I shall in the following parts of this Discourse) how men,

barely by the use of their natural faculties, may attain to all the knowledge they have, without the help of any innate impressions; and may arrive at certainty, without any such original notions or principles. For I imagine any one will easily grant that it would be impertinent to suppose the ideas of colours innate in a creature to whom God hath given sight, and a power to receive them by the eyes from external objects: and no less unreasonable would it be to attribute several truths to the impressions of nature, and innate characters, when we may observe in ourselves faculties fit to attain as easy and certain knowledge of them as if they were originally imprinted on the mind.

But because a man is not permitted without censure to follow his own thoughts in the search of truth, when they lead him ever so little out of the common road, I shall set down the reasons that made me doubt of the truth of that opinion, as an excuse for my mistake, if I be in one; which I leave to be considered by those who, with me, dispose themselves to embrace truth wherever they find it.

2. *General assent the great argument.* There is nothing more commonly taken for granted than that there are certain *principles,* both *speculative* and *practical* (for they speak of both), universally agreed upon by all mankind: which therefore, they argue, must needs be the constant impressions which the souls of men receive in their first beings, and which they bring into the world with them, as necessarily and really as they do any of their inherent faculties.

3. *Universal consent proves nothing innate.* This argument, drawn from universal consent, has this misfortune in it, that if it were true in matter of fact, that there were certain truths wherein all mankind agreed, it would not prove them innate, if there can be any other way shown how men may come to that universal agreement, in the things they do consent in, which I presume may be done.

4. *"What is, is," and "It is impossible for the same thing to be and not to be," not universally assented to.* But, which is worse, this argument of universal consent, which is made use of to prove innate principles, seems to me a demonstration that there are none such: because there are none to which all mankind give an universal assent. I shall begin with the speculative, and instance in those magnified principles of demonstration, "Whatsoever is, is," and "It is impossible for the same thing to be and not to be"; which, of all others, I think have the most allowed title to innate. These have so settled a reputation of maxims universally received, that it will no doubt be thought strange if any one should seem to question it. But yet I take liberty to say, that these propositions are so far from having an universal assent, that there are a great part of mankind to whom they are not so much as known.

5. *Not on the mind naturally imprinted, because not known to children, idiots, &c.* For, first, it is evident, that all children and idiots have not the least apprehension or thought of them. And the want of that is enough to destroy that universal assent which must needs be the necessary concomitant of all innate truths: it seeming to me near a contradiction to say, that there are truths imprinted on the soul, which it perceives or understands not: imprinting, if it signify anything, being nothing else but the making certain truths to be perceived. For to imprint anything on the mind without the mind's perceiving it, seems to me hardly intelligible. If therefore children and idiots have souls, have minds, with those impressions upon them, *they* must unavoidably perceive them, and necessarily know and assent to these truths; which since they do not, it is evident that there are no such impressions. For if they are not notions naturally imprinted, how can they be innate? and if they are notions imprinted, how can they be unknown? To say a notion is imprinted on the mind, and yet at the same time to say, that the mind is ignorant of it, and never yet took notice of it, is to make this impression nothing. No proposition can be said to be in the mind which it never yet knew, which it was never yet conscious of. For if any one may, then, by the same reason, all propositions that are true, and the mind is capable ever of assenting to, may be said to be in the mind, and to be imprinted: since, if any one can be said to be in the mind, which it never yet knew, it must be only because it is capable of knowing it; and so the mind is of all truths it ever shall know. Nay, thus truths may be imprinted on the mind which it never did, nor ever shall know; for a man may live long, and die at last in ignorance of many truths which his mind was capable of knowing, and that with certainty. So that if the capacity of knowing be the natural impression contended for, all the truths a man ever comes to know will, by this account, be every one of them innate; and this great point will amount to no more, but only to a very improper way of speaking; which, whilst it pretends to assert the contrary, says nothing different from those who deny innate principles. For nobody, I think, ever denied that the mind was capable of knowing several truths. The

capacity, they say, is innate; the knowledge acquired. But then to what end such contest for certain innate maxims? If truths can be imprinted on the understanding without being perceived, I can see no difference there can be between any truths the mind is *capable* of knowing in respect of their original: they must all be innate or all adventitious: in vain shall a man go about to distinguish them. He therefore that talks of innate notions in the understanding, cannot (if he intend thereby any distinct sort of truths) mean such truths to be in the understanding as it never perceived, and is yet wholly ignorant of. For if

these words "to be in the understanding" have any propriety, they signify to be understood. So that to be in the understanding, and not to be understood; to be in the mind and never to be perceived; is all one as to say anything is and is not in the mind or understanding. If therefore these two propositions; "Whatsoever is, is," and "It is impossible for the same thing to be and not to be," are by nature imprinted, children cannot be ignorant of them: infants, and all that have souls, must necessarily have them in their understandings, know the truth of them, and assent to it. . . .

BOOK I I

OF IDEAS

Chap. I. Of Ideas in General, and Their Original

1. *Idea is the object of thinking.* Every man being conscious to himself that he thinks; and that which his mind is applied about whilst thinking being the *ideas* that are there, it is past doubt that men have in their minds several ideas,—such as are those expressed by the words *whiteness, hardness, sweetness, thinking, motion, man, elephant, army, drunkenness,* and others: it is in the first place then to be inquired, *How he comes by them?*

I know it is a received doctrine, that men have native ideas, and original characters, stamped upon their minds in their very first being. This opinion I have at large examined already; and, I suppose what I have said in the foregoing Book will be much more easily admitted, when I have shown whence the understanding may get all the ideas it has; and by what ways and degrees they may come into the mind;—for which I shall appeal to every one's own observation and experience.

2. *All ideas come from sensation or reflection.* Let us then suppose the mind to be, as we say, white paper, void of all characters, without any ideas:— How comes it to be furnished? Whence comes it by that vast store which the busy and boundless fancy of man has painted on it with an almost endless variety? Whence has it all the *materials* of reason and knowledge? To this I answer; in one word, from EXPERIENCE. In that all our knowledge is founded; and from that it ultimately derives itself. Our observation employed either, about

external sensible objects, or about the internal operations of our minds perceived and reflected on by ourselves is that which supplies our understandings with all the *materials* of thinking. These two are the fountains of knowledge, from whence all the ideas we have, or can naturally have, do spring.

3. *The objects of sensation one source of ideas.* First, our Senses, conversant about particular sensible objects, do convey into the mind several distinct perceptions of things, according to those various ways wherein those objects do affect them. And thus we come by those *ideas* we have of *yellow, white, heat, cold, soft, hard, bitter, sweet,* and all those which we call sensible qualities, which when I say the senses convey into the mind, I mean, they from external objects convey into the mind what produces there those perceptions. This great source of most of the ideas we have, depending wholly upon our senses, and derived by them to the understanding, I call SENSATION.

4. *The operations of our minds, the other source of them.* Secondly, the other fountain from which experience furnisheth the understanding with ideas is,—the perception of the operations of our own mind within us, as it is employed about the ideas it has got;—which operations, when the soul comes to reflect on and consider, do furnish the understanding with another set of ideas, which could not be had from things without. And such are *perception, thinking, doubting, believing, reasoning, knowing, willing,* and all the different actings of our

own minds;—which we being conscious of, and observing in ourselves, do from these receive into our, understandings, as distinct ideas as we do from bodies affecting our senses. This source of ideas every man has wholly in himself; and though it be not sense, as having nothing to do with external objects, yet it is very like it, and might properly enough be called *internal sense.* But as I call the other SENSATION so I call this REFLECTION, the ideas it affords being such only as the mind gets by reflecting on its own operations within itself. By reflection then, in the following part of this discourse, I would be understood to mean, that notice which the mind takes of its own operations, and the manner of them, by reason whereof there come to be ideas of these operations in the understanding. These two, I say, viz. external material things, as the objects of SENSATION, and the operations of our own minds within, as the objects of REFLECTION, are to me the only originals from whence all our ideas take their beginnings. The term *operations* here I use in a large sense, as comprehending not barely the actions of the mind about its ideas, but some sort of passions arising sometimes from them, such as is the satisfaction or uneasiness arising from any thought.

5. *All our ideas are of the one or the other of these.* The understanding seems to me not to have the least glimmering of any ideas which it doth not receive from one of these two. *External objects* furnish the mind with the ideas of sensible qualities, which are all those different perceptions they produce in us; and *the mind* furnishes the understanding with ideas of its own operations.

These, when we have taken a full survey of them, and their several modes, combinations, and relations, we shall find to contain all our whole stock of ideas; and that we have nothing in our minds which did not come in one of these two ways. Let any one examine his own thoughts, and thoroughly search into his understanding; and then let him tell me, whether all the original ideas he has there, are any other than of the objects of his senses, or of the operations of his mind, considered as objects of his reflection. And how great a mass of knowledge soever he imagines to be lodged there, he will, upon taking a strict view, see that he has not any idea in his mind but what one of these two have imprinted;—though

perhaps, with infinite variety compounded and enlarged by the understanding, as we shall see hereafter. . . .

CHAP. VIII. SOME FURTHER CONSIDERATIONS
CONCERNING OUR SIMPLE IDEAS OF SENSATION

1. *Positive ideas from privative causes.* Concerning the simple ideas of Sensation, it is to be considered,—that whatsoever is so constituted in nature as to be able, by affecting our senses, to cause any perception in the mind, doth thereby produce in the understanding a simple idea; which, whatever be the external cause of it, when it comes to be taken notice of by our discerning faculty, it is by the mind looked on and considered there to be a real positive idea in the understanding, as much as any other whatsoever; though, perhaps, the cause of it be but a privation of the subject.

2. *Ideas in the mind distinguished from that in things which gives rise to them.* Thus the ideas of heat and cold, light and darkness, white and black, motion and rest, are equally clear and positive ideas in the mind; though, perhaps, some of the causes which produce them are barely privations, in those subjects from whence our senses derive those ideas. These the understanding, in its view of them, considers all as distinct positive ideas, without taking notice of the causes that produce them which is an inquiry not belonging to the idea, as it is in the understanding, but to the nature of the things existing without us. These are two very different things, and carefully to be distinguished; it being one thing to perceive and know the idea of white or black, and quite another to examine what kind of particles they must be, and how ranged in the superficies, to make any object appear white or black.

3. *We may have the ideas when we are ignorant of their physical causes.* A painter or dyer who never inquired into their causes hath the ideas of white and black, and other colours, as clearly, perfectly, and distinctly in his understanding, and perhaps more distinctly, than the philosopher who hath busied himself in considering their natures, and thinks he knows how far either of them is, in its cause, positive or privative; and the idea of black is no less positive in his mind than that of white; however the cause of that colour in the external object may be only a privation.

4. *Why a privative cause in nature may occasion a positive idea.* If it were the design of my present undertaking to inquire into the natural causes and manner of perception, I should offer this as a reason why a privative cause might, in some cases at least, produce a positive idea; viz that all sensation being produced in us only by different degrees and modes of motion in our animal spirits, variously agitated by external objects, the abatement of any former motion must as necessarily produce a new sensation as the variation or increase of it; and so introduce a new idea, which depends only on a different motion of the animal spirits in that organ.

5. *Negative names need not be meaningless.* But whether this be so or not I will not here determine, but appeal to every one's own experience, whether the shadow of a man, though it consists of nothing but the absence of light (and the more the absence of light is, the more discernible is the shadow) does not, when a man looks on it, cause as clear and positive idea in his mind, as a man himself, though covered over with clear sunshine? And the picture of a shadow is a positive thing. Indeed, we have negative names, which stand not directly for positive ideas, but for their absence, such as *insipid, silence, nihil,* &c.; which words denote positive ideas, v.g. *taste, sound, being,* with a signification of their absence.

6. *Whether any ideas are due to causes really privative.* And thus one may truly be said to see darkness. For, supposing a hole perfectly dark, from whence no light is reflected, it is certain one may see the figure of it, or it may be painted; or whether the ink I write with makes any other idea, is a question. The privative causes I have here assigned of positive ideas are according to the common opinion; but, in truth, it will be hard to determine whether there be really any ideas from a privative cause, till it be determined, whether rest be any more a privation than motion.

7. *Ideas in the mind, qualities in bodies.* To discover the nature of our *ideas* the better, and to discourse of them intelligibly, it will be convenient to distinguish them *as they are ideas or perceptions in our minds*; and *as they are modifications of matter in the bodies that cause such perceptions in us*: that so we may not think (as perhaps usually is done)

that they are exactly the images and resemblances of something inherent in the subject; most of those of sensation being in the mind no more the likeness of something existing without us, than the names that stand for them are the likeness of our ideas, which yet upon hearing they are apt to excite in us.

8. *Our ideas and the qualities of bodies.* Whatsoever the mind perceives *in itself*, or is the immediate object of perception, thought, or understanding, that I call *idea*; and the power to produce any idea in our mind, I call *quality* of the subject wherein that power is. Thus a snowball having the power to produce in us the ideas of white, cold, and round,—the power to produce those ideas in us, as they are in the snowball, I call qualities; and as they are sensations or perceptions in our understandings, I call them ideas; which *ideas*, if I speak of sometimes as in the things themselves, I would be understood to mean those qualities in the objects which produce them in us.

9. *Primary qualities of bodies.* Qualities thus considered in bodies are,

First, such as are utterly inseparable from the body, in what state soever it be; and such as in all the alterations and changes it suffers, all the force can be used upon it, it constantly keeps; and such as sense constantly finds in every particle of matter which has bulk enough to be perceived; and the mind finds inseparable from every particle of matter, though less than to make itself singly be perceived by our senses: v.g. Take a grain of wheat, divide it into two parts; each part has still solidity, extension, figure, and mobility: divide it again, and it retains still the same qualities; and so divide it on, till the parts become insensible; they must retain still each of them all those qualities. For division (which is all that a mill, or pestle, or any other body, does upon another, in reducing it to insensible parts) can never take away either solidity, extension, figure, or mobility from any body, but only makes two or more distinct separate masses of matter, of that which was but one before; all which distinct masses, reckoned as so many distinct bodies, after division, make a certain number. These I call *original* or *primary qualities* of body, which I think we may observe to produce simple ideas in us, viz. solidity, extension, figure, motion or rest, and number.

10. *Secondary qualities of bodies. Secondly,* such qualities which in truth are nothing in the objects themselves but power to produce various sensations in us by their primary qualities, i.e. by the bulk, figure, texture, and motion of their insensible parts, as colours, sounds, tastes, &c. These I call *secondary qualities.* To these might be added a *third* sort, which are allowed to be barely powers; though they are as much real qualities in the subject as those which I, to comply with the common way of speaking, call qualities, but for distinction, secondary qualities. For the power in fire to produce a new colour, or consistency, in *wax* or *clay,*—by its primary qualities, is as much a quality in fire, as the power it has to produce in *me* a new idea or sensation of warmth or burning, which I felt not before,—by the same primary qualities, viz. the bulk, texture, and motion of its insensible parts.

11. *How bodies produce ideas in us.* The next thing to be considered is, how bodies produce ideas in us; and that is manifestly by impulse, the only way which we can conceive bodies to operate in.

12. *By motions, external, and in our organism.* If then external objects be not united to our minds when they produce ideas therein; and yet we perceive these *original* qualities in such of them as singly fall under our senses, it is evident that some motion must be thence continued by our nerves, or animal spirits, by some parts of our bodies, to the brains or the seat of sensation, there to produce in our minds the particular ideas we have of them. And since the extension, figure, number, and motion of bodies of an observable bigness, may be perceived at a distance by the sight, it is evident some singly imperceptible bodies must come from them to the eyes, and thereby convey to the brain some motion, which produces these ideas which we have of them in us.

13. *How secondary qualities produce their ideas.* After the same manner that the ideas of these original qualities are produced in us, may conceive that the ideas of *secondary* qualities are also produced, viz by the operation of insensible particles on our senses. For, it being manifest that there are bodies and good store of bodies, each whereof are so small, that we cannot by any of our senses discover either their bulk, figure, or motion,—as is evident in the particles of the air

and water, and others extremely smaller than those; perhaps as much smaller than the particles of air and water, as the particles of air and water are smaller than peas or hail-stones;—let us suppose at present that the different motions and figures, bulk and number, of such particles, affecting the several organs of our senses, produce in us those different sensations which we have from the colours and smells of bodies; v.g. that a violet, by the impulse of such insensible particles of matter, of peculiar figures and bulks, and in different degrees and modifications of their motions, causes the ideas of the blue colour, and sweet scent of that flower to be produced in our minds. It being no more impossible to conceive that God should annex such ideas to such motions, with which they have no similitude, than that he should annex the idea of pain to the motion of a piece of steel dividing our flesh, with which that idea hath no resemblance.

14. *They depend on the primary qualities.* What I have said concerning colours and smells may be understood also of tastes and sounds, and other the like sensible qualities; which, whatever reality we by mistake attribute to them, are in truth nothing in the objects themselves, but powers to produce various sensations in us; and depend on those primary qualities, viz. bulk, figure, texture, and motion of parts as I have said.

15. *Ideas of primary qualities are resemblances; of secondary; not.* From whence I think it easy to draw this observation,—that the ideas of primary qualities of bodies are resemblances of them, and their patterns do really exist in the bodies themselves, but the ideas produced in us by these secondary qualities have no resemblance of them at all. There is nothing like our ideas, existing in the bodies themselves. They are in the bodies we denominate from them only a power to produce those sensations in us and what is sweet, blue, or warm in idea, is but the certain bulk, figure, and motion of the insensible parts, in the bodies themselves, which we call so.

16. *Examples.* Flame is denominated hot and light; snow, white and cold; and manna, white and sweet, from the ideas they produce in us. Which qualities are commonly thought to be the same in those bodies that those ideas are in us, the

one the perfect resemblance of the other, as they are in a mirror, and it would by most men be judged very extravagant if one should say otherwise. And yet he that will consider that the same fire that, at one distance produces in us the sensation of warmth, does, at a nearer approach, produce in us the far different sensation of pain, ought to bethink himself what reason he has to say—that this idea of warmth, which was produced in him by the fire, is *actually in the fire* and his idea of pain, which the same fire produced in him the same way, is *not* in the fire. Why are whiteness and coldness in snow, and pain not, when it produces the one and the other idea in us; and can do neither, but by the bulk, figure, number, and motion of its solid parts?

17. *The ideas of the primary alone really exist.* The particular bulk, number, figure, and motion of the parts of fire or snow are really in them,—whether any one's senses perceive them or no: and therefore they may be called *real* qualities, because they really exist in those bodies. But light, heat, whiteness, or coldness, are no more really in them than sickness or pain is in manna. Take away the sensation of them; let not the eyes see light or colours, nor the ears hear sounds; let the palate not taste, nor the nose smell, and all colours, tastes, odours, and sounds, *as they are such particular ideas*, vanish and cease, and are reduced to their causes, i.e. bulk, figure, and motion of parts.

18. *The secondary exist in things only as modes of the primary.* A piece of manna of a sensible bulk is able to produce in us the idea of a round or square figure; and by being removed from one place to another, the idea of motion. This idea of motion represents it as it really is in manna moving: a circle or square are the same, whether in idea or existence, in the mind or in the manna.

And this, both motion and figure, are really in the manna, whether we take notice of them or no: this everybody is ready to agree to. Besides, manna, by the bulk, figure, texture, and motion of its parts, has a power to produce the sensations of sickness, and sometimes of acute pains or gripings in us. That these ideas of sickness and pain are *not* in the manna, but effects of its operations on us, and are nowhere when we feel them not; this also every one readily agrees to. And yet men are hardly to be brought to think that sweetness and whiteness are not really in manna; which are but the effects of the operations of manna, by the motion, size, and figure of its particles, on the eyes and palate: as the pain and sickness caused by manna are confessedly nothing but the effects of its operations on the stomach and guts, by the size, motion, and figure of its insensible parts, (for by nothing else can a body operate, as has been proved): as if it could not operate on the eyes and palate, and thereby produce in the mind particular distinct ideas, which in itself it has not, as well as we allow it can operate on the guts and stomach, and thereby produce distinct ideas, which in itself it has not. These ideas, being all effects of the operations of manna on several parts of our bodies, by the size, figure number, and motion of its parts;—why those produced by the eyes and palate should rather be thought to be really in the manna, than those produced by the stomach and guts; or why the pain and sickness, ideas that are the effect of manna, should be thought to be nowhere when they are not felt; and yet the sweetness and whiteness, effects of the same manna on other parts of the body, by ways equally as unknown, should be thought to exist in the manna, when they are not seen or tasted, would need some reason to explain.

BOOK III

OF WORDS

CHAP. I. OF WORDS OR LANGUAGE IN GENERAL

1. *Man fitted to form articulate sounds.* God, having designed man for a sociable creature, made him not only with an inclination, and under a necessity to have fellowship with those of his own kind, but furnished him also with language,

which was to be the great instrument and common tie of society. Man, therefore, had by nature his organs so fashioned, as to be fit to frame articulate sounds, which we call words. But this was not enough to produce language; for parrots, and several other birds, will be taught to make articulate sounds distinct enough, which yet by no means are capable of language.

2. *To use these sounds as signs of ideas.* Besides articulate sounds, therefore, it was further necessary that he should be able to use these sounds as signs of internal conceptions; and to make them stand as marks for the ideas within his own mind, whereby they might be made known to others, and the thoughts of men's minds be conveyed from one to another.

3. *To make them general signs.* But neither was this sufficient to make words so useful as they ought to be. It is not enough for the perfection of language, that sounds can be made signs of ideas, unless those signs can be so made use of as to comprehend several particular things: for the multiplication of words would have perplexed their use, had every particular thing need of a distinct name to be signified by. To remedy this inconvenience, language had yet a further improvement in the use of *general terms,* whereby one word was made to mark a multitude of particular existences: which advantageous use of sounds was obtained only by the difference of the ideas they were made signs of: those names becoming general, which are made to stand for *general ideas,* and those remaining particular, where the *ideas* they are used for are *particular.*

4. *To make them signify the absence of positive ideas.* Besides these names which stand for ideas, there be other words which men make use of, not to signify any idea, but the want or absence of some ideas, simple or complex, or all ideas together; such as are *nihil* in Latin, and in English, *ignorance* and *barrenness.* All which negative or privative words cannot be said properly to belong to, or signify no ideas: for then they would be perfectly insignificant sounds; but they relate to positive ideas, and signify their absence.

5. *Words ultimately derived from such as signify sensible ideas.* It may also lead us a little towards the original of all our notions and knowledge, if we remark how great a dependence our words have on common sensible ideas; and how those

which are made use of to stand for actions and notions quite removed from sense, have their rise from thence, and from obvious sensible ideas are transferred to more abstruse significations, and made to stand for ideas that come not under the cognizance of our senses; v.g. to *imagine, apprehend, comprehend, adhere, conceive, instil, disgust, disturbance, tranquillity,* &c., are all words taken from the operations of sensible things, and applied to certain modes of thinking. *Spirit,* in its primary signification, is breath; *angel,* a messenger: and I doubt not but, if we could trace them to their sources, we should find, in all languages, the names which stand for things that fall not under our senses to have had their first rise from sensible ideas. By which we may give some kind of guess what kind of notions they were, and whence derived, which filled their minds who were the first beginners of languages, and how nature, even in the naming of things, unawares suggested to men the originals and principles of all their knowledge: whilst, to give names that might make known to others any operations they felt in themselves, or any other ideas that came not under their senses, they were fain to borrow words from ordinary known ideas of sensation, by that means to make others the more easily to conceive those operations they experimented in themselves, which made no outward sensible appearances; and then, when they had got known and agreed names to signify those internal operations of their own minds, they were sufficiently furnished to make known by words all their other ideas; since they could consist of nothing but either of outward sensible perceptions, or of the inward operations of their minds about them; we having, as has been proved, no ideas at all, but what originally come either from sensible objects without, or what we feel within ourselves, from the inward workings of our own spirits, of which we are conscious to ourselves within.

CHAP. II. OF THE SIGNIFICATION OF WORDS

1. *Words are sensible signs, necessary for communication of ideas.* Man, though he have great variety of thoughts, and such from which others well as as himself might receive profit and delight; yet they are all within his own breast, invisible and hidden from others, nor can of themselves be made

to appear. The comfort and advantage of society not being to be had without communication of thoughts, it was necessary that man should find out some external sensible signs, whereof those invisible ideas, which his thoughts are made up of, might be made known to others. For this purpose nothing was so fit, either for plenty or quickness, as those articulate sounds, which with so much ease and variety he found himself able to make. Thus we may conceive how *words*, which were by nature so well adapted to that purpose, came to be made use of by men as the signs of their ideas; not by any natural connexion that there is between particular articulate sounds and certain ideas, for then there would be but one language amongst all men; but by a voluntary imposition, whereby such a word is made arbitrarily the mark of such an idea. The use, then, of words, is to be sensible marks of ideas; and the ideas they stand for are their proper and immediate signification.

2. *Words, in their immediate signification, are the sensible signs of his ideas who uses them.* The use men have of these marks being either to record their own thoughts, for the assistance of their own memory or, as it were, to bring out their ideas, and lay them before the view of others: words, in their primary or immediate signification, stand for nothing but *the ideas in the mind of him that uses them*, how imperfectly soever or carelessly those ideas are collected from the things which they are supposed to represent. When a man speaks to another, it is that he may be understood: and the end of speech is, that those sounds, as marks, may make known his ideas to the hearer. That then which words are the marks of are the ideas of the speaker: nor can any one apply them as marks, immediately, to anything else but the ideas that he himself hath: for this would be to make them signs of his own conceptions, and yet apply them to other ideas; which would be to make them signs and not signs of his ideas at the same time; and so in effect to have no signification at all. Words being voluntary signs, they cannot be

voluntary signs imposed by him on things he knows not. That would be to make them signs of nothing, sounds without signification. A man cannot make his words the signs either of qualities in things, or of conceptions in the mind of another, whereof he has none in his own. Till he has some ideas of his own, he cannot suppose them to correspond with the conceptions of another man; nor can he use any signs for them of another man; nor can he use any signs for them: for thus they would be the signs of he knows not what, which is in truth to be the signs of nothing. But when he represents to himself other men's ideas by some of his own, if he consent to give them the same names that other men do, it is still to his own ideas; to ideas that he has, and not to ideas that he has not.

DISCUSSION QUESTIONS

1. What is Locke's argument against innate knowledge? How does he use "children and idiots" to drive home his conclusion? Do you find his argument convincing?

2. Locke asserts that all ideas come from sensation or reflection. Summarize his argument. Is he right? Can you think of an idea that comes from neither sensation nor reflection? Discuss.

3. What is the difference between a secondary and a primary quality according to Locke? Why do you think he makes this distinction?

4. Locke argues that our mind is a "white paper, void of all characters." Do you agree with him? What are some implications of his position? Can you use them to either support or criticize his position?

5. Compare and contrast Locke's empiricist approach to knowledge and Descartes' rationalist approach. What are the strengths and weaknesses of each? Whose approach is stronger, and why?

At a very early age, acute congestion causes Helen Keller (Patty Duke) to become deaf and blind. Despite the many efforts of her family, doctors are unable to cure her blindness and deafness, and schools are unable to teach her. Her father, Captain Arthur Keller (Victor Jory), is on the brink of committing her to a mental asylum when his wife, Kate (Inga Swenson), suggests that he write to the Perkins School for the Blind in Boston regarding Helen. As a result of his letter, the Perkins School sends its star graduate, Annie Sullivan (Anne Bancroft), to be Helen's governess. After a difficult start, Sullivan teaches Helen how to communicate the letters of the alphabet with her hands and to use combinations of letters to form words.

At first, Helen is unable to associate specific groups of letters with specific sensations. The hand motions are an interaction and a game. Then, suddenly, she links the letters *w-a-t-e-r* with the sensation she feels as the liquid from the water pump flows over her hands. Sullivan is overjoyed and yells out, "She knows!" to Helen's mother. We then see Helen associating the hand signals with other objects, including her mother and father.

DISCUSSION QUESTIONS

1. Helen Keller was unable to see or hear, though her senses of touch, taste, and smell were fine. Do you think she experienced less than those with the ability to see or hear? Why or why not?

2. Locke believes that our senses are the source of our knowledge of the world. Does it follow from this that those with less sensory access to the world (for example, are blind) are inhibited in their ability to know?

3. Locke writes, "*Words are sensible signs, necessary for communication of ideas.* Man, though he have great variety of thoughts, and such from which others well as himself might receive profit and delight; yet they are all within his own breast, invisible and hidden from others, nor can of themselves be made to appear. The comfort and advantage of society not being to be had without communication of thoughts, it was necessary that man should find some external sensible signs, whereof those invisible ideas, which his thoughts are made up of, might be made known to others. . . . Thus we may conceive how *words*, which were by nature so well adapted to that purpose, came to be made use of by men as the signs of their ideas. . . ." Do you think it is possible to have knowledge of your ideas or sensations of the world without words or signs corresponding to those ideas or sensations? Why or why not?

4. Before Annie Sullivan taught Helen Keller signs (or words) to correspond with her sensory experiences, do you think she had knowledge of what she was experiencing? What changed when she linked the sign *w-a-t-e-r* to her sensory experience of water?

5. Imagine that you have sensory experience of the world (sight, sound) but do not have words or signs (language) that correspond to those sensory images. What would the world be like to you? Would it be possible to have knowledge of the world under these conditions? If so, what would you know, and what would you not be able to know? If not, why not?

6. Locke contends that experience is the source of all knowledge. In what way does the case of Helen Keller lend support to Locke's idea? In what way does it not? Does Helen Keller's story lead you to more firmly believe Locke's account? Why or why not?

7. Consider the following dialogue from the film. Annie Sullivan has been making signs for letters to Helen Keller and associating them with things and actions. Mrs. Keller sees her and asks her what she hopes to accomplish by doing this:

    ANNIE SULLIVAN   "She won't know what spelling is until she knows what a word is."

    MRS. KELLER   "Captain Keller says it's like spelling to a fence post."

    ANNIE SULLIVAN   "Perhaps she'll learn after a million words. . . . Like a baby. It's all gibberish at first."

    How do we come to know what a word is? Is it through experience, or are we born with the ability (that is, it is innate) to know what a word or sign is?

8. Annie Sullivan says to Helen Keller, "I wanted to teach you . . . everything that is on the earth . . . that it is full of . . . everything that is on it . . . is here for a wink and it's gone. And what we are on it, the light we bring to it, and leave behind in words. We can look 5000 years back in the light of words. Everything we feel, think, know, and share in words. So not a soul is in darkness or done with in the grave, but I know. I know one word and I can put the world in your hand and whatever it is to me. I won't take less. But how? How do I tell you that this means a word? And the word means this thing wool?" If all we knew were the present contents of our experience and did not have words or signs to express this experience of the present, would it follow that we would not be able to know the past or the future?

9. Before Helen Keller knew what words were, she was able to communicate with others only in a very limited way. Still, she was able to communicate. For example, she effectively communicated to her mother through gestures that she wanted eyes sewn onto her doll. In general, how do we know how to communicate? Is it through experience, or are we born with the ability (that is, it is innate)? If you believe that we are born with the knowledge of how to communicate, do you think that this is evidence against Locke's notion that the mind is a blank slate at birth? Why or why not?

10. Generally discuss the notion that signs, words, and/or language are central to our ability to have knowledge. Consider related questions: Does our language or system of signs delimit our knowledge? Would a new language imply a different knowledge of the world?

GEORGE BERKELEY

TO BE IS TO BE PERCEIVED

G eorge Berkeley argues that nothing exists outside of the mind. For him, the existence of things consists in their being perceived. "There *esse* is *percipi*," writes Berkeley, meaning that "to be is to be perceived." Nothing has "any existence out of the minds or thinking things which perceive them."

Berkeley's position on knowledge is that we only know what we find in our experience. Like Locke, he is an *empiricist*. However, Berkeley suggests that Locke did not follow his empiricism to its logical limit. Consequently, Berkeley strenuously disagrees with Locke on a number of issues including the distinction between primary and secondary qualities. Whereas Locke maintains that primary qualities exist independent of being experienced, and secondary qualities exist dependent on being experienced, Berkeley can find no difference between these two types of qualities since both are dependent upon perception. For Berkeley, Locke's primary qualities of extension, figure, motion, and so on "are only ideas existing in the mind."

Berkeley calls his philosophy *immaterialism*, emphasizing in this label its rejection of matter. For him, "It is plain that the very notion of what is called *Matter* or *corporeal substance*, involves a contradiction in it" and that "there is not any other Substance than *Spirit* or that which perceives." Berkeley's argument against the existence of matter might be formulated as follows: (1) Whatever can be thought of is an idea in the mind of the person thinking it; (2) nothing can be thought of except ideas in minds, and anything else is inconceivable; (3) what is inconceivable cannot exist; therefore, matter, which by definition is not an idea in a mind, cannot exist. Thus, according to Berkeley, the world is not composed of both material substances (matter) and immaterial substances (minds, spirits, souls), but only of the latter, which he simply calls "Spirit."

As such, Berkeley's doctrines are best termed *idealism*. In terms of metaphysics, idealism is the position that reality is ultimately mental, spiritual, or nonmaterial in nature; in terms of epistemology, idealism is the position that all we know are our ideas. Berkeley's positions are in accord with both epistemological and metaphysical idealism.

George Berkeley (1685–1753) was an Irish philosopher and bishop. Educated at Trinity College, Dublin, from 1700 to 1707, he became interested in philosophy through the writings of Isaac Newton, Robert Boyle, and John Locke. In 1707, he was named a tutor at Trinity, where he had several different duties including lecturer in divinity. In 1709, he was ordained deacon in the Anglican Church. In 1713, he obtained a leave of absence from his academic responsibilities, and from 1714 to 1721, he spent most of his time in Europe as a tutor and chaplain. In London, his wit and charm were instantly recognized, with Jonathan Swift remarking, "That Mr. Berkeley is a very ingenious man, and I have mentioned him to all the Ministers, and I will favour him as much as I can." In 1724, after much lobbying, he was promised funding from Parliament to establish a missionary college in the Bermudas. After four years of preparation, he sailed to America with his family and some friends, and worked on this project from 1728 to 1733, including a three-year stay in Newport, Rhode Island. However, Parliament never followed through on the funding, and the project was a failure. He returned to Europe and, in 1734, became bishop of Cloyne, a position he held for the next twenty years. In 1752, Berkeley moved to Oxford in order to be closer to his son, who was studying there; he died the following year. His works include *A New Theory of Vision* (1709), *Treatise Concerning the Principles of Human Knowledge* (1710), *Three Dialogues Between Hylas and Philonous* (1733), *Alciphron, or the Minute Philosopher* (1733), *The Theory of Vision or Visual Language* (1733), and *Siris* (1744). The following selection is from his *Treatise Concerning the Principles of Human Knowledge*.

1. It is evident to any one who takes a survey of the *objects of human knowledge,* that they are either *ideas* actually imprinted on the senses; or else such as are perceived by attending to the passions and operations of the mind; or lastly, *ideas* formed by help of memory and imagination—either compounding, dividing, or barely representing those originally perceived in the aforesaid ways.

By sight I have the ideas of light and colours, with their several degrees and variations. By touch I perceive hard and soft, heat and cold, motion and resistance; and of all these more and less either as to quantity or degree. Smelling furnishes me with odours; the palate with tastes; the hearing conveys sounds to the mind in all their variety of tone and composition.

And as several of these are observed to accompany each other, they come to be marked by one name, and so to be reputed as one *thing*. Thus, for example, a certain colour, taste, smell, figure and consistence having been observed to go together; are accounted one distinct thing, signified by the name apple; other collections of ideas constitute a stone, a tree, a book, and the like sensible things; which as they are pleasing or disagreeable excite the passion of love, hatred, joy, grief, and so forth.

2. But, besides all that endless variety of ideas or objects of knowledge, there is likewise Something which knows or perceives them; and exercises divers operations, as willing, imagining, remembering, about them. This perceiving, active being is what I call *mind, spirit, soul,* or *myself*. By which words I do not denote any one of my ideas, but a thing entirely distinct from them, wherein they exist, or, which is the same thing, whereby they are perceived; for the existence of an idea consists in being perceived.

3. That neither our thoughts, nor passions, nor ideas formed by the imagination, exist without the mind is what everybody will allow. And to me it seems no less evident that the various sensations or ideas imprinted on the Sense, however blended or combined together (that is, whatever objects they compose), cannot exist otherwise than in a mind perceiving them. I think an intuitive knowledge may be obtained of this, by any one that shall attend to what is meant by the term *exist* when applied to sensible things. The table I write on I say exists; that is, I see and feel it: and if I were out of my study I should say it existed; meaning thereby that if I was in my study I might perceive it, or that some other spirit actually does perceive it. There was an odour, that is, it was smelt; there was a sound, that is, it was heard; a colour of figure, and it was perceived by sight or touch. This is all that I can understand by these and the like expressions. For as to what is said of the *absolute* existence of unthinking things,

without any relation to their being perceived, that is to me perfectly unintelligible. Their *esse* is *percipi*; nor is it possible they should have any existence out of the minds or thinking things which perceive them.

4. It is indeed an opinion strangely prevailing amongst men, that houses, mountains, rivers, and in a word all sensible objects, have an existence, natural or real, distinct from their being perceived by the understanding. But, with how great an assurance and acquiescence soever this Principle may be entertained in the world, yet whoever shall find in his heart to call it in question may, if I mistake not, perceive it to involve a manifest contradiction. For, what are the forementioned objects but the things we perceive by sense? and what do we perceive besides our own ideas or sensations? and is it not plainly repugnant that any one of these, or any combination of them, should exist unperceived?

5. If we thoroughly examine this tenet it will, perhaps, be found at bottom to depend on the doctrine of *abstract ideas*. For can there be a nicer strain of abstraction than to distinguish the existence of sensible objects from their being perceived, so as to conceive them existing unperceived? Light and colours, heat and cold, extension and figures—in a word the things we see and feel—what are they but so many sensations, notions, ideas, or impressions on the sense? and is it possible to separate, even in thought, any of these from perception? For my part, I might as easily divide a thing from itself. I may, indeed, divide in my thoughts, or conceive apart from each other, those things which perhaps I never perceived by sense so divided. Thus, I imagine the trunk of a human body without the limbs, or conceive the smell of a rose without thinking on the rose itself. So far, I will not deny, I can abstract; if that may properly be called *abstraction* which extends only to the conceiving separately such objects as it is possible may really exist or be actually perceived asunder. But my conceiving or imagining power does not extend beyond the possibility of real existence or perception. Hence, as it is impossible for me to see or feel anything without an actual sensation of that thing, so is it impossible for me to conceive in my thoughts any sensible thing or object distinct from the sensation or perception of it. [In truth, the object and the

sensation are the same thing, and cannot therefore be abstracted from each other.]

6. Some truths there are so near and obvious to the mind that a man need only open his eyes to see them. Such I take this important one to be, viz. that all the choir of heaven and furniture of the earth, in a word all those bodies which compose the mighty frame of the world, have not any subsistence without a mind; that their *being* is to be perceived or known; that consequently so long as they are not actually perceived by me, or do not exist in my mind, or that of any other created spirit, they must either have not existence at all, or else subsist in the mind of some Eternal Spirit: it being perfectly unintelligible, and involving all the absurdity of abstraction, to attribute to any single part of them an existence independent of a spirit. To be convinced of which, the reader need only reflect, and try to separate in his own thoughts the *being* of a sensible thing from its *being perceived*.

7. From what has been said it is evident there is not any other Substance than *Spirit*, or that which perceives. But, for the fuller proof of this point, let it be considered the sensible qualities are colour, figure, motion, smell, taste, and such like, that is, the ideas perceived by sense. Now, for an idea to exist in an unperceiving thing is a manifest contradiction; for to have an idea is all one as to perceive: that therefore wherein colour, figure, and the like qualities exist must perceive them. Hence it is clear there can be no unthinking substance or *substratum* of those ideas.

8. But, say you, though the ideas themselves do not exist without the mind, yet there may be things like them, whereof they are copies or resemblances; which things exist without the mind, in an unthinking substance. I answer, an idea can be like nothing but an idea; a colour or figure can be like nothing but another colour or figure. If we look but ever so little into our thoughts, we shall find it impossible for us to conceive a likeness except only between our ideas. Again, I ask whether those supposed *originals*, or external things, of which our ideas are the pictures or representations, be themselves perceivable or no? If they are, then *they* are ideas, and we have gained our point; but if you say they are not, I appeal to any one whether it be sense to assert a colour is like something which is invisible; hard or soft, like something which is intangible; and so of the rest.

9. Some there are who make a distinction betwixt *primary* and *secondary* qualities. By the former they mean extension, figure, motion, rest, solidity or impenetrability, and number; by the latter they denote all other sensible qualities, as colours, sounds, tastes, and so forth. The ideas we have of these last they acknowledge not to be the resemblances of anything existing without the mind, or unperceived; but they will have our ideas of the *primary qualities* to be patterns or images of things which exist without the mind, in an unthinking substance which they call Matter. By Matter, therefore, we are to understand an inert, senseless substance, in which extension, figure, and motion do actually subsist. But it is evident, from what we have already shewn, that extension, figure, and motion are only ideas existing in the mind, and that an idea can be like nothing but another idea; and that consequently neither they nor the archetypes can exist in an unperceiving substance. Hence, it is plain that the very notion of what is called *Matter* or *corporeal substance*, involves a contradiction in it. Insomuch that I should not think it necessary to spend more time in exposing its absurdity. But, because the tenet of the existence of Matter seems to have taken so deep a root in the minds of philosophers, and draws after it so many ill consequences, I choose rather to be thought prolix and tedious than omit anything that might conduce to the full discovery and extirpation of that prejudice.

10. They who assert that figure, motion, and the rest of the primary or original qualities do exist without the mind, in unthinking substances, do at the same time acknowledge that colours, sounds, heat, cold, and suchlike secondary qualities, do not; which they tell us are sensations, existing in the mind alone, that depend on and are occasioned by the different size, texture, and motion of the minute particles of matter. This they take for an undoubted truth, which they can demonstrate beyond all exception. Now, if it be certain that those *original* qualities are inseparably united with the other sensible qualities, and not, even in thought, capable of being abstracted from them, it plainly follows that *they* exist only in the mind. But I desire any one to reflect, and try whether he can, by an abstraction of thought, conceive the extension and motion of a body without all other sensible qualities. For my own

part, I see evidently that it is not in my power to frame an idea of a body extended and moving, but I must withal give it some colour or other sensible quality, which is acknowledged to exist only in the mind. In short, extension, figure, and motion, abstracted from all other qualities, are inconceivable. Where therefore the other sensible qualities are, there must these be also, to wit, in the mind and nowhere else. . . .

14. I shall farther add, that, after the same manner as modern philosophers prove certain sensible qualities to have no existence in Matter, or without the mind, the same thing may be likewise proved of all other sensible qualities whatsoever. Thus, for instance, it is said that heat and cold are affections only of the mind, and not at all patterns of real beings, existing in the corporeal substances which excite them; for that the same body which appears cold to one hand seems warm to another. Now, why may we not as well argue that figure and extension are not patterns or resemblances of qualities existing in Matter; because to the same eye at different stations, or eyes of a different texture at the same station, they appear various and cannot therefore be the images of anything settled and determinate without the mind? Again, it is proved that sweetness is not really in the sapid thing; because the thing remaining unaltered the sweetness is changed into bitter, as in case of a fever or otherwise vitiated palate. Is it not as reasonable to say that motion is not without the mind; since if the succession of ideas in the mind become swifter, the motion, it is acknowledged, shall appear slower, without any alteration in any external object?

15. In short, let any one consider those arguments which are thought manifestly to prove that colours and tastes exist only in the mind, and he shall find they may with equal force be brought to prove the same thing of extension, figure, and motion. Though it must be confessed this method of arguing does not so much prove that there is no extension or colour in an outward object, as that we do not know by sense which is the true extension or colour of the object. But the arguments foregoing plainly shew it to be impossible that any colour or extension at all, or other sensible quality whatsoever, should exist in an unthinking subject without the mind, or in truth that there should be any such thing as an outward object.

16. But let us examine a little the received opinion. It is said extension is a *mode* or *accident* of Matter, and that Matter is the *substratum* that supports it. Now I desire that you would explain to me what is meant by Matter's *supporting* extension. Say you, I have no idea of Matter; and therefore cannot explain it. I answer, though you have no positive, yet, if you have any meaning at all, you must at least have a relative idea of Matter; though you know not what it is, yet you must be supposed to know what relation it bears to accidents, and what is meant by its supporting them. It is evident *support* cannot here be taken in its usual or literal sense, as when we say that pillars support a building. In what sense therefore must it be taken? For my part, I am not able to discover any sense at all that can be applicable to it.

17. If we inquire into what the most accurate philosophers declare themselves to mean by *material substance*, we shall find them acknowledge they have no other meaning annexed to those sounds but the idea of Being in general, together with the relative notion of its supporting accidents. The general idea of Being appeareth to me the most abstract and incomprehensible of all other; and as for its supporting accidents, this, as we have just now observed, cannot be understood in the common sense of those words: it must therefore be taken in some other sense, but what that is they do not explain. So that when I consider the two parts or branches which make the signification of the words *material substance*, I am convinced there is no distinct meaning annexed to them. But why should we trouble ourselves any farther, in discussing this material *substratum* or support of figure and motion and other sensible qualities? Does it not suppose they have an existence without the mind? And is not this a direct repugnancy, and altogether inconceivable?

18. But, though it were possible that solid, figured, moveable substances may exist without the mind, corresponding to the ideas we have of bodies, yet how is it possible for us to know this? Either we must know it by Sense or by Reason. As for our senses, by them we have the knowledge only of our sensations, ideas, or those things that are immediately perceived by sense, call them what you will: but they do not inform us that things exist without the mind, or unperceived,

like to those which are perceived. This the materialists themselves acknowledge.—It remains therefore that if we have any knowledge at all of external things, it must be by reason inferring their existence from what is immediately perceived by sense. But (I do not see) what reason can induce us to believe the existence of bodies without the mind, from what we perceive, since the very patrons of Matter themselves do not pretend there is any necessary connexion betwixt them and our ideas? I say it is granted on all hands (and what happens in dreams, frensies, and the like, puts it beyond dispute) that it is possible we might be affected with all the ideas we have now, though no bodies existed without resembling them. Hence it is evident the supposition of external bodies is not necessary for the producing our ideas; since it is granted they are produced sometimes, and might possibly be produced always, in the same order we see them in at present without their concurrence.

19. But, though we might possibly have all our sensations without them, yet perhaps it may be thought easier to conceive and explain the manner of their production, by supposing external bodies, in their likeness rather than otherwise; and so it might be at least probable there are such things as bodies that excite their ideas in our minds. But neither can this be said. For, though we give the materialists their external bodies, they by their own confession are never the nearer knowing how our ideas are produced; since they own themselves unable to comprehend in what manner body can act upon spirit, or how it is possible it should imprint any idea in the mind. Hence it is evident the production of ideas or sensations in our minds, can be no reason why we should suppose Matter or corporeal substances; since that is acknowledged to remain equally inexplicable with or without this supposition. If therefore it were possible for bodies to exist without the mind, yet to hold they do so must needs be a very precarious opinion; since it is to suppose, without any reason at all, that God has created innumerable beings that are entirely useless, and serve to no manner of purpose.

20. In short, if there were external bodies, it is impossible we should ever come to know it; and if there were not, we might have the very same reasons to think there were that we have now.

Suppose—what no one can deny possible—an intelligence, without the help of external bodies, to be affected with the same train of sensations or ideas that you are, imprinted in the same order and with like vividness in his mind. I ask whether that intelligence hath not all the reason to believe the existence of Corporeal Substances, represented by his ideas, and exciting them in his mind, that you can possibly have for believing the same thing? Of this there can be no question. Which one consideration were enough to make any reasonable person suspect the strength of whatever arguments he may think himself to have, for the existence of bodies without the mind. . . .

23. But, say you, surely there is nothing easier than for me to imagine trees, for instance, in a park, or books existing in a closet, and nobody by to perceive them. I answer, you may so, there is no difficulty in it. But what is all this, I beseech you, more than framing in your mind certain ideas which you call *books* and *trees*, and at the same time omitting to frame the idea of any one that may perceive them? But do not you yourself perceive or think of them all the while? This therefore is nothing to the purpose: it only shews you have the power of imagining, or forming ideas in your mind; but it does not shew that you can conceive it possible the objects of your thoughts may exist without the mind. To make out this, it is necessary that you conceive them existing unconceived or unthought of; which is a manifest repugnancy. When we do our utmost to conceive the existence of external bodies, we are all the while only contemplating our own ideas. But the mind, taking no notice of itself, is deluded to think it can and does conceive bodies existing unthought of, or without the mind, though at the same time they are apprehended by, or exist in, itself. A little attention will discover to any one the truth and evidence of what is here said, and make it unnecessary to insist on any other proofs against the existence of *material substance.*

DISCUSSION QUESTIONS

1. How does Berkeley respond to Locke's distinction between primary and secondary qualities? Do you agree with his response? Why or why not?

2. Critically analyze Berkeley's argument against the existence of matter. Can you find any difficulties in it? Does he convince you?

3. Samuel Johnson responded to Berkeley's philosophy by kicking a stone into the air, saying, "I refute him thus." What did Johnson mean? Is this a good refutation of Berkeley? Why or why not?

4. What, according to Berkeley, would be the difference between what we perceive in dreams and what we perceive in waking life? Are both "real" for him? Why or why not?

5. Berkeley was one of Jorge Luis Borges' favorite philosophers. What elements of Borges' "The Circular Ruins" are consistent with Berkeley's doctrines? What elements are not? Explain.

V. S. PRITCHETT

THE SAINT

This short story by V. S. Pritchett is an argument against idealist theories of knowledge, such as that of George Berkeley. Pritchett tells the story of a religious sect called the Church of the Last Purification in Toronto, Canada. The members of this church do not believe the evidence of their senses. They claim that anyone who does believe the evidence of their senses has committed an "Error"—their word for "Evil." As a result, church members do not believe in the existence of things, for example, that might harm them or bring them pain. One of the members says, "If we had influenza or consumption, or had lost our money or were unemployed, we denied the reality of these things, saying that since God could not have made them they therefore did not exist." Even if church members were observed falling off a tall building, if someone asked after them, they would deny having fallen and claim not to be injured. They truly believed that "Error" was an illusion.

Nevertheless, one day, one of the young faithful, a seventeen-year-old boy, is invited to spend an afternoon with Mr. Timberlake, a church leader. The boy observes Timberlake fall into a river and then act as though the whole thing did not happen. The boy is stunned and cannot believe what he saw. "For a full minute I did not believe what I saw; indeed our religion taught us never to believe what we saw." The boy wants desperately to believe that "a leader of our Church under the direct guidance of God could not possibly fall into a river"— but he does. The boy witnesses it as well as the man's direct denials. This series of events leads the boy to lose his faith in this religion.

Pritchett's point is that if the idealist is correct and all we know are our ideas, then we ought to be able to not allow "evil" ideas into the world of our knowledge. But this is not the case. Even if we deny the existence of the idea of the flu, it will not prevent us from getting the flu. While we might be able to maintain the idea to ourselves that nothing uncomfortable is happening to us, others will observe us to be nauseated, feverish, and congested.

V. S. (Victor Sawdon) Pritchett (1900–1997) was a British short-story writer, novelist, essayist, critic, and journalist. His father was a Christian Scientist and traveling salesman, and Pritchett worked in the leather trade from 1916 to 1920. In 1923, he became a correspondent for the *Christian Science Monitor*, first in Ireland, then in Spain. From 1928 to 1965, he wrote for the *New Statesman*, beginning as a literary critic and later becoming the literary editor. Pritchett was knighted in 1975. He wrote five novels but complained that the work was monotonous. His work is often ironic and is noted for its energetic portrayal of middle-class life. Pritchett's short stories examine the customs, speech, values, and other details of the lives of middle-class people in England from the 1930s through the 1990s. His short-story collections include *You Make Your Own Life* (1938), *Collected Stories* (1956), *The Saint and Other Stories* (1966), *Blind Love and Other Stories* (1969), *More Collected Stories* (1983), *A Careless Widow and Other Stories* (1989), and *Complete Collected Stories* (1990). His also published travel books, essay collections, and two autobiographies, *A Cab at the Door* (1966) and *Midnight Oil* (1971). "The Saint" was first published in 1966.

When I was seventeen years old I lost my religious faith. It had been unsteady for some time and then, very suddenly, it went as the result of an incident in a punt on the river outside the town where we lived. My uncle, with whom I was obliged to stay for long periods of my life, had started a small furniture-making business in the town. He was always in difficulties about money, but he was convinced that in some way God would help him. And this happened. An investor arrived who belonged to a sect called the Church of the Last Purification, of Toronto, Canada. Could we imagine, this man asked, a good and omnipotent God allowing his children to be short of money? We had to admit we could not imagine this. The man paid some capital into my uncle's business and we were converted. Our family were the first Purifiers—as they were called—in the town. Soon a congregation of fifty or more were meeting every Sunday in a room at the Corn Exchange.

At once we found ourselves isolated and hated people. Everyone made jokes about us. We had to stand together because we were sometimes dragged into the courts. What the unconverted could not forgive in us was first that we believed in successful prayer and, secondly, that our revelation came from Toronto. The success of our prayers had a simple foundation. We regarded it as "Error"—our name for Evil—to believe the evidence of our senses and if we had influenza or consumption, or had lost our money or were unemployed, we denied the reality of these things, saying that since God could not have made them they therefore did not exist. It was exhilarating to look at our congregation and to know that what the vulgar would call miracles were performed among us, almost as a matter of

routine, every day. Not very big miracles, perhaps; but up in London and out in Toronto, we knew that deafness and blindness, cancer and insanity, the great scourges, were constantly vanishing before the prayers of the more advanced Purifiers.

'What!' said my schoolmaster, an Irishman with eyes like broken glass and a sniff of irritability in the bristles of his nose. 'What! Do you have the impudence to tell me that if you fell off the top floor of this building and smashed your head in, you would say you hadn't fallen and were not injured?'

I was a small boy and very afraid of everybody, but not when it was a question of my religion. I was used to the kind of conundrum the Irishman had set. It was useless to argue, though our religion had already developed an interesting casuistry.

"I *would* say so," I replied with coldness and some vanity. "And my head would not be smashed."

"You would not say so," answered the Irishman. "You would not say so." His eyes sparkled with pure pleasure. "You"d be dead."

The boys laughed, but they looked at me with admiration.

Then, I do not know how or why, I began to see a difficulty. Without warning and as if I had gone into my bedroom at night and had found a gross ape seated in my bed and thereafter following me about with his grunts and his fleas and a look, relentless and ancient, scored on his brown face, I was faced with the problem which prowls at the centre of all religious faith. I was faced by the difficulty of the origin of evil. Evil was an illusion, we were taught. But even illusions have an origin. The Purifiers denied this.

I consulted my uncle. Trade was bad at the time and this made his faith abrupt. He frowned as I spoke.

"When did you brush your coat last?" he said. "You're getting slovenly about your appearance. If you spent more time studying books—that is to say, the Purification literature—and less with your hands in your pockets and playing about with boats on the river, you wouldn't be letting Error in."

All dogmas have their jargon; my uncle as a business man loved the trade terms of the Purification. "Don't let Error in," was a favourite one. The whole point about the Purification, he said, was that it was scientific and therefore exact; in consequence it was sheer weakness to admit discussion. Indeed, betrayal. He unpinched his pince-nez, stirred his tea and indicated I must submit or change the subject. Preferably the latter. I saw, to my alarm, that my arguments had defeated my uncle. Faith and doubt pulled like strings round my throat.

"You don't mean to say you don't believe that what our Lord said was true?" my aunt asked nervously, following me out of the room. "Your uncle does, dear."

I could not answer. I went out of the house and down the main street to the river where the punts were stuck like insects in the summery flash of the reach. Life was a dream, I thought; no, a nightmare, for the ape was beside me.

I was still in this state, half sulking and half exalted, when Mr Hubert Timberlake came to the town. He was one of the important people from the headquarters of our Church and he had come to give an address on the Purification at the Corn Exchange. Posters announcing this were everywhere. Mr Timberlake was to spend Sunday afternoon with us. It was unbelievable that a man so eminent would actually sit in our dining-room, use our knives and forks, and eat our food. Every imperfection in our home and our characters would jump out at him. The Truth had been revealed to man with scientific accuracy—an accuracy we could all test by experiment—and the future course of human development on Earth was laid down, finally. And here in Mr Timberlake was a man who had not merely performed many miracles—even, it was said with proper reserve, having twice raised the dead—but who had actually been to Toronto, our headquarters, where this great and revolutionary revelation had first been given.

"This is my nephew," my uncle said, introducing me. "He lives with us. He thinks he thinks, Mr Timberlake, but I tell him he only thinks he does. Ha, ha." My uncle was a humorous man when he was with the great. "He's always on the river," my uncle continued. "I tell him he"s got water on the brain. I've been telling Mr Timberlake about you, my boy."

A hand as soft as the best quality chamois leather took mine. I saw a wide upright man in a double-breasted navy blue suit. He had a pink square head with very small ears and one of those torpid, enamelled smiles which were said by our enemies to be too common in our sect.

"Why, isn't that just fine?" said Mr Timberlake who, owing to his contacts with Toronto, spoke with an American accent. "What say we tell your uncle it"s funny he think's he's funny."

The eyes of Mr Timberlake were direct and colourless. He had the look of a retired merchant captain who had become decontaminated from the sea and had reformed and made money. His defence of me had made me his at once. My doubts vanished. Whatever Mr Timberlake believed must be true and as I listened to him at lunch, I thought there could be no finer life than his.

"I expect Mr Timberlake's tired after his address," said my aunt.

"Tired?" exclaimed my uncle, brilliant with indignation. "How can Mr Timberlake be tired? Don't let Error in!"

For in our faith the merely inconvenient was just as illusory as a great catastrophe would have been, if you wished to be strict, and Mr Timberlake's presence made us very strict.

I noticed then that, after their broad smiles, Mr Timberlake's lips had the habit of setting into a long depressed sarcastic curve.

"I guess," he drawled, "I guess the Al-mighty must have been tired sometimes, for it says He relaxed on the seventh day. Say, do you know what I'd like to do this afternoon," he said turning to me. "While your uncle and aunt are sleeping off this meal let's you and me go on the river and get water on the brain. I'll show you how to punt."

Mr Timberlake, I saw to my disappointment, was out to show he understood the young. I saw he was planning a "quiet talk" with me about my problems.

"There are too many people on the river on Sundays," said my uncle uneasily.

"Oh, I like a crowd," said Mr Timberlake, giving my uncle a tough look. "This is the day of rest, you know." He had had my uncle gobbling up every bit of gossip from the sacred city of Toronto all the morning.

My uncle and aunt were incredulous that a man like Mr Timberlake should go out among the blazers and gramophones of the river on a Sunday afternoon. In any other member of our Church they would have thought this sinful.

"Waal, what say?" said Mr Timberlake. I could only murmur.

"That's fixed," said Mr Timberlake. And on came the smile as simple, vivid and unanswerable as the smile on an advertisement. "Isn't that just fine!"

Mr Timberlake went upstairs to wash his hands. My uncle was deeply offended and shocked, but he could say nothing. He unpinched his glasses.

"A very wonderful man," he said. "So human," he apologised.

"My boy," my uncle said. "This is going to be an experience for you. Hubert Timberlake was making a thousand a year in the insurance business ten years ago. Then he heard of the Purification. He threw everything up, just like that. He gave up his job and took up the work. It was a struggle, he told me so himself this morning. 'Many's the time,' he said to me this morning, 'when I wondered where my next meal was coming from.' But the way was shown. He came down from Worcester to London and in two years he was making fifteen hundred a year out of his practice."

To heal the sick by prayer according to the tenets of the Church of the Last Purification was Mr Timberlake's profession.

My uncle lowered his eyes. With his glasses off the lids were small and uneasy. He lowered his voice too.

"I have told him about your little trouble," my uncle said quietly with emotion. I was burned with shame. My uncle looked up and stuck out his chin confidently.

"He just smiled," my uncle said. "That's all."

Then we waited for Mr Timberlake to come down.

I put on white flannels and soon I was walking down to the river with Mr Timberlake. I felt that I was going with him under false pretences; for he would begin explaining to me the origin of evil and I would have to pretend politely that he was converting me when, already, at the first sight of him, I had believed. A stone bridge, whose two arches were like an owlish pair of eyes gazing up the reach, was close to the landing-stage. I thought what a pity it was the flannelled men and the sunburned girls there did not know I was getting a ticket for *the* Mr Timberlake who had been speaking in the town that very morning. I looked round for him and when I saw him I was a little startled. He was standing at the edge of the water looking at it with an expression of empty incomprehension. Among the white crowds his air of brisk efficiency had dulled. He looked middle-aged, out of place and insignificant. But the smile switched on when he saw me.

"Ready?" he called. "Fine!"

I had the feeling that inside him there must be a gramophone record going round and round, stopping at that word.

He stepped into the punt and took charge.

"Now I just want you to paddle us over to the far bank," he said, "and then I'll show you how to punt."

Everything Mr Timberlake said still seemed unreal to me. The fact that he was sitting in a punt, of all commonplace material things, was incredible. That he should propose to pole us up the river was terrifying. Suppose he fell into the river? At once I checked the thought. A leader of our Church under the direct guidance of God could not possibly fall into a river.

The stream is wide and deep in this reach, but on the southern bank there is a manageable depth and a hard bottom. Over the clay banks the willows hang, making their basket-work print of sun and shadow on the water, while under the gliding boats lie cloudy, chloride caverns. The hoop-like branches of the trees bend down until their tips touch the water like fingers making musical sounds. Ahead in midstream, on a day sunny as this one was, there is a path of strong light which is hard to look at unless you half close your eyes and down this path on the crowded

Sundays, go the launches with their parasols and their pennants; and also the rowing boats with their beetle-leg oars, which seem to dig the sunlight out of the water as they rise. Upstream one goes, on and on between the gardens and then between fields kept for grazing. On the afternoon when Mr Timberlake and I went out to settle the question of the origin of evil, the meadows were packed densely with buttercups.

"Now," said Mr Timberlake decisively when I had paddled to the other side. "Now I'll take her."

He got over the seat into the well at the stern.

"I'll just get you clear of the trees," I said.

"Give me the pole," said Mr Timberlake standing up on the little platform and making a squeak with his boots as he did so. "Thank you, sir. I haven"t done this for eighteen years but I can tell you, brother, in those days I was considered some poler."

He looked around and let the pole slide down through his hands. Then he gave the first difficult push. The punt rocked pleasantly and we moved forward. I sat facing him, paddle in hand, to check any inward drift of the punt.

"How's that, you guys?" said Mr Timberlake looking round at our eddies and drawing in the pole. The delightful water sished down it.

"Fine," I said. Deferentially I had caught the word.

He went on to his second and his third strokes, taking too much water on his sleeve, perhaps, and uncertain in his steering, which I corrected, but he was doing well.

"It comes back to me," he said. "How am I doing?"

"Just keep her out from the trees," I said.

"The trees?" he said.

"The willows," I said.

"I'll do it now," he said. "How's that? Not quite enough? Well, How's this?"

"Another one," I said. "The current runs strong this side."

"What? More trees?" he said. He was getting hot.

"We can shoot out past them," I said. "I'll ease us over with the paddle."

Mr Timberlake did not like this suggestion.

"No, don't do that. I can manage it," he said. I did not want to offend one of the leaders of our Church, so I put the paddle down; but I felt I ought to have taken him farther along away from the irritation of the trees.

"Of course," I said. "We could go under them. It might be nice."

"I think," said Mr Timberlake, "that would be a very good idea."

He lunged hard on the pole and took us towards the next archway of willow branches.

"We may have to duck a bit, that's all," I said.

"Oh, I can push the branches up," said Mr Timberlake.

"It is better to duck," I said.

We were gliding now quickly towards the arch, in fact I was already under it.

"I think I should duck," I said. "Just bend down for this one."

"What makes the trees lean over the water like this?" asked Mr Timberlake. "Weeping willows—I'll give you a thought there. How Error likes to make us dwell on sorrow. Why not call them *laughing* willows?" discoursed Mr Timberlake as the branch passed over my head.

"Duck," I said.

"Where? I don't see them," said Mr Timberlake turning round.

"No, your head," I said. "The branch," I called.

"Oh, the branch. This one?" said Mr Timberlake finding a branch just against his chest and he put out a hand to lift it. It is not easy to lift a willow branch and Mr Timberlake was surprised. He stepped back as it gently and firmly leaned against him. He leaned back and pushed from his feet. And he pushed too far. The boat went on, I saw Mr Timberlake's boots leave the stern as he took an unthoughtful step backwards. He made a last minute grasp at a stronger and higher branch, and then, there he hung a yard above the water, round as a blue damson that is ripe and ready, waiting only for a touch to make it fall. Too late with the paddle and shot ahead by the force of his thrust, I could not save him.

For a full minute I did not believe what I saw; indeed our religion taught us never to believe what we saw. Unbelieving I could not move. I gaped. The impossible had happened. Only a miracle, I found myself saying, could save him.

What was most striking was the silence of Mr Timberlake as he hung from the tree. I was lost between gazing at him and trying to get the punt out of the small branches of the tree. By the time I had got the punt out there were several yards of water between us and the soles of his boots were very near the water as the branch bent under his weight. Boats were passing at the time but no one seemed to notice us. I was glad about this. This was a private agony. A double chin had appeared on the face of Mr Timberlake and his head was squeezed between his shoulders and his hanging arms. I saw him blink and look up at the sky. His eyelids were pale like a chicken"s. He was tidy and dignified as he hung there, the hat was not displaced and the top button of his coat was done up. He had a blue silk handkerchief in his breast pocket. So unperturbed and genteel he seemed that as the tips of his shoes came nearer and nearer to the water, I became alarmed. He could perform what are called miracles. He would be thinking at this moment that only in an erroneous and illusory sense was he hanging from the branch of the tree over six feet of water. He was probably praying one of the closely reasoned prayers of our faith which were more like conversations with Euclid than appeals to God. The calm of his face suggested this. Was he, I asked myself, within sight of the main road, the town Recreation Ground and the landing-stage crowded with people, was he about to re-enact a well-known miracle? I hoped that he was not. I prayed that he was not. I prayed with all my will that Mr Timberlake would not walk upon the water. It was my prayer and not his that was answered.

I saw the shoes dip, the water rise above his ankles and up his socks. He tried to move his grip now to a yet higher branch—he did not succeed—and in making this effort his coat and waistcoat rose and parted from his trousers. One seam of shirt with its pant-loops and brace-tabs broke like a crack across the middle of Mr Timberlake. It was like a fatal flaw in a statue, an earthquake crack which made the monumental mortal. The last Greeks must have felt as I felt then, when they saw a crack across the middle of some statue of Apollo. It was at this moment I realised that the final revelation about man and society on earth had come to nobody and that Mr Timberlake knew nothing at all about the origin of evil.

All this takes long to describe, but it happened in a few seconds as I paddled towards him. I was too late to get his feet on the boat and the only thing to do was to let him sink until his hands

were nearer the level of the punt and then to get him to change hand-holds. Then I would paddle him ashore. I did this. Amputated by the water, first a torso, then a bust, then a mere head and shoulders, Mr Timberlake, I noticed, looked sad and lonely as he sank. He was a declining dogma. As the water lapped his collar—for he hesitated to let go of the branch to hold the punt—I saw a small triangle of deprecation and pathos between his nose and the corners of his mouth. The head resting on the platter of water had the sneer of calamity on it, such as one sees in the pictures of a beheaded saint.

"Hold on to the punt, Mr Timberlake," I said urgently. "Hold on to the punt."

He did so.

"Push from behind," he directed in a dry businesslike voice. They were his first words. I obeyed him. Carefully I paddled him towards the bank. He turned and, with a splash, climbed ashore. There he stood, raising his arms and looking at the water running down his swollen suit and making a puddle at his feet.

"Say," said Mr Timberlake coldly, "we let some Error in that time."

How much he must have hated our family.

"I am sorry, Mr Timberlake," I said. "I am most awfully sorry. I should have paddled. It was my fault. I'll get you home at once. Let me wring out your coat and waistcoat. You'll catch your death. . . ."

I stopped. I had nearly blasphemed. I had nearly suggested that Mr Timberlake had fallen into the water and that to a man of his age this might be dangerous.

Mr Timberlake corrected me. His voice was impersonal, addressing the laws of human existence, rather than myself.

"If God made water it would be ridiculous to suggest He made it capable of harming his creatures. Wouldn't it?"

"Yes," I murmured hypocritically.

"OK," said Mr Timberlake. "Let's go."

"I'll soon get you across," I said.

"No," he said. "I mean let's go on. We're not going to let a little thing like this spoil a beautiful afternoon. Where were we going? You spoke of a pretty landing-place farther on. Let's go there."

"But I must take you home. You can't sit there soaked to the skin. It will spoil your clothes."

"Now, now," said Mr Timberlake. "Do as I say. Go on."

There was nothing to be done with him. I held the punt into the bank and he stepped in. He sat like a bursting and sodden bolster in front of me while I paddled. We had lost the pole of course.

For a long time I could hardly look at Mr Timberlake. He was taking the line that nothing had happened and this put me at a disadvantage. I knew something considerable had happened. That glaze, which so many of the members of our sect had on their faces and persons, their minds and manners, had been washed off. There was no gleam for me from Mr Timberlake.

"What's the house over there?" he asked. He was making conversation. I had steered into the middle of the river to get him into the strong sun. I saw steam rise from him.

I took courage and studied him. He was a man, I realised, in poor physical condition, unexercised and sedentary. Now the gleam had left him one saw the veined empurpled skin of the stoutish man with a poor heart. I remembered he had said at lunch:

"A young woman I know said, 'Isn't it wonderful. I can walk thirty miles in a day without being in the least tired.' I said, 'I don't see that bodily indulgence is anything a member of the Church of the Last Purification should boast about.' "

Yes, there was something flaccid, passive and slack about Mr Timberlake. Bunched in swollen clothes, he refused to take them off. It occurred to me, as he looked with boredom at the water, the passing boats and the country, that he had not been in the country before. That it was something he had agreed to do but wanted to get over quickly. He was totally uninterested. By his questions—what is that church? Are there any fish in this river? Is that a wireless or a gramophone? —I understood that Mr Timberlake was formally acknowledging a world he did not live in. It was too interesting, too eventful a world. His spirit, inert and preoccupied, was elsewhere in an eventless and immaterial habitation. He was a dull man, duller than any man I have ever known; but his dullness was a sort of earthly deposit left by a being whose diluted mind was far away in the effervescence of metaphysical matters. There was a slightly pettish look on his face as (to himself, of course) he declared he was not wet and that he would not have a heart attack or catch pneumonia.

Mr Timberlake spoke little. Sometimes he squeezed water out of his sleeve. He shivered a little. He watched his steam. I had planned when we set out to go up as far as the lock but now the thought of another two miles of this responsibility was too much. I pretended I wanted to go only as far as the bend which we were approaching, where one of the richest buttercup meadows was. I mentioned this to him. He turned and looked with boredom at the field. Slowly we came to the bank.

We tied up the punt and we landed.

"Fine," said Mr Timberlake. He stood at the edge of the meadow just as he had stood at the landing-stage—lost, stupefied, uncomprehending.

"Nice to stretch our legs," I said. I led the way into the deep flowers. So dense were the buttercups there was hardly any green. Presently I sat down. Mr Timberlake looked at me and sat down also. Then I turned to him with a last try at persuasion. Respectability, I was sure, was his trouble.

"No one will see us," I said. "This is out of sight of the river. Take off your coat and trousers and wring them out."

Mr Timberlake replied firmly:

"I am satisfied to remain as I am."

"What is this flower?" he asked to change the subject.

"Buttercup," I said.

"Of course," he replied.

I could do nothing with him. I lay down full length in the sun; and, observing this and thinking to please me, Mr Timberlake did the same. He must have supposed that this was what I had come out in the boat to do. It was only human. He had come out with me, I saw, to show me that he was only human.

But as we lay there I saw the steam still rising. I had had enough.

"A bit hot," I said getting up.

He got up at once.

"Do you want to sit in the shade," he asked politely.

"No," I said. "Would you like to?"

"No," he said. "I was thinking of you."

"Let's go back," I said. We both stood up and I let him pass in front of me. When I looked at him again I stopped dead. Mr Timberlake was no longer a man in a navy blue suit. He was blue no longer. He was transfigured. He was yellow. He was covered with buttercup pollen, a fine yellow paste of it made by the damp, from head to foot.

"Your suit," I said.

He looked at it. He raised his thin eyebrows a little, but he did not smile or make any comment.

The man is a saint, I thought. As saintly as any of those gold-leaf figures in the churches of Sicily. Golden he sat in the punt; golden he sat for the next hour as I paddled him down the river. Golden and bored. Golden as we landed at the town and as we walked up the street back to my uncle's house. There he refused to change his clothes or to sit by a fire. He kept an eye on the time for his train back to London. By no word did he acknowledge the disasters or the beauties of the world. If they were printed upon him, they were printed upon a husk.

Sixteen years have passed since I dropped Mr Timberlake in the river and since the sight of his pant loops destroyed my faith. I have not seen him since, and today I heard that he was dead. He was fifty-seven. His mother, a very old lady with whom he had lived all his life, went into his bedroom when he was getting ready for church and found him lying on the floor in his shirt-sleeves. A stiff collar with the tie half inserted was in one hand. Five minutes before, she told the doctor, she had been speaking to him.

The doctor who looked at the heavy body lying on the single bed saw a middle-aged man, wide rather than stout and with an extraordinarily boxlike thick-jawed face. He had got fat, my uncle told me, in later years. The heavy liver-coloured cheeks were like the chaps of a hound. Heart disease, it was plain, was the cause of the death of Mr Timberlake. In death the face was lax, even coarse and degenerate. It was a miracle, the doctor said, that he had lived as long. Any time during the last twenty years the smallest shock might have killed him.

I thought of our afternoon on the river. I thought of him hanging from the tree. I thought of him, indifferent and golden in the meadow. I understood why he had made for himself a protective, sedentary blandness, an automatic smile, a collection of phrases. He kept them on like the coat after his ducking. And I understood why—though I had feared it all the time we were on the river—I understood why he did not talk to me about the origin of evil. He was honest. The ape was with us. The ape that merely followed me was already inside Mr Timberlake eating out his heart.

DISCUSSION QUESTIONS

1. Is Pritchett's story a direct attack on Berkeley's theory of knowledge? Are there significant differences between the world Pritchett creates in "The Saint" and Berkeley's world? Discuss.

2. We are told at the end of the story that Timberlake had heart disease and that his refusal to acknowledge sensory information that might have caused him fatal shock probably extended his life by many years. Why does Pritchett add this detail to his story? How would it be a different story without this detail? Explain.

3. One of the members of the church says, "If we had influenza or consumption, or had lost our money or were unemployed, we denied the reality of these things, saying that since God could not have made them they therefore did not exist." What do you think of this doctrine? Is it a valid response to the problem of evil?

4. Pritchett's point is that if the idealist is correct and all we know are our ideas, then we ought to be able to not allow "evil" ideas into the world of our knowledge. Is this a valid criticism of idealism? Why or why not? Are other assumptions needed to make this argument work?

5. Do you find anything appealing in the religion outlined by Pritchett in this story? What are its strengths and its weaknesses as a system of belief? Is it difficult to believe that someone might actually have faith in it? Discuss.

DAVID HUME

SKEPTICISM AND HUMAN NATURE

I n this selection, David Hume analyzes the relationship of human nature to three different kinds of skepticism: Cartesian, Pyrrhonian (or excessive), and mitigated. Hume finds Cartesian and Pyrrhonian skepticism to be unsatisfactory when considered in light of human nature, and goes on to discuss the merits of mitigated or limited skepticism.

Hume's first target is skepticism like that expressed by Descartes in his *Meditations*. Cartesian skepticism "is a species of skepticism, *antecedent* to all study and philosophy, which is much inculcated by Descartes and others, as a sovereign preservative against error and precipitate judgment." "It recommends an universal doubt, not only of all our former opinions and principles," says Hume, "but also of our very faculties." For Hume, this kind of skepticism is unsatisfactory for two reasons. First, even if it were possible to attain this level of skepticism (and it is not), it "would be entirely incurable"; and second, Cartesian skepticism does not allow any reasoning that "could ever bring us to a state of assurance and conviction upon any subject." For Hume, the doubt raised by Descartes simply "exceeds the power of all human capacity."

The second type of skepticism, Pyrrhonism, is named after its first exponent, Pyrrho of Elis (c. 360–270 B.C.E.), who argued that it is impossible to know the nature of anything and that we should completely suspend judgment of everything, including our ignorance and doubt. For Hume, while Pyrrhonian skeptics "may flourish and triumph in the schools; where it is, indeed, difficult, if not impossible, to refute them, . . . as soon as they leave the shade, and by the presence of the real objects which actuate our passions and sentiments, are put in opposition to the more powerful principles of our nature, they vanish like smoke." In other words, this kind of skepticism might work well in the classroom, but not in everyday life.

Hume advocates a mitigated type of skepticism, one that both reminds us to avoid dogmatic opinions and wild doctrines and "limits our enquiries to such subjects as are best adapted to the narrow capacity of human understanding." In effect, Hume's mitigated skepticism serves to balance his belief (following Locke) that sense experience is the source of all knowledge concerning matters of fact and existence with his belief that human nature limits our knowledge in certain important ways. The following selection is from section XII of Hume's *An Enquiry Concerning Human Understanding* (1748). A biographical sketch of Hume appears in chapter 1.

OF THE ACADEMICAL OR SCEPTICAL PHILOSOPHY

There is not a greater number of philosophical reasonings, displayed upon any subject, than those, which prove the existence of a Deity, and refute the fallacies of *Atheists*; and yet the most religious philosophers still dispute whether any man can be so blinded as to be a speculative atheist. How shall we reconcile these contradictions? The knights-errant, who wandered about to clear the world of dragons and giants, never entertained the least doubt with regard to the existence of these monsters.

The *Sceptic* is another enemy of religion, who naturally provokes the indignation of all divines and graver philosophers; though it is certain, that no man ever met with any such absurd creature, or conversed with a man, who had no opinion or principle concerning any subject, either of action or speculation. This begets a very natural question: What is meant by a sceptic? And how far is it possible to push these philosophical principles of doubt and uncertainty?

There is a species of scepticism, *antecedent* to all study and philosophy, which is much inculcated by DESCARTES and others, as a sovereign preservative against error and precipitate judgment. It recommends an universal doubt, not only of all our former opinions and principles, but also of our very faculties; of whose veracity, say they; we must assure ourselves, by a chain of reasoning, deduced from some original principle, which cannot possibly be fallacious or deceitful. But neither is there any such original principle, which has a prerogative above others, that are self-evident and convincing: Or if there were, could we advance a step beyond it, but by the use of those very faculties, of which we are supposed to be already diffident. The CARTESIAN doubt, therefore, were it ever possible to be attained by any human creature (as it plainly is not) would be entirely incurable; and no reasoning could ever bring us to a state of assurance and conviction upon any subject.

It must, however, be confessed, that this species of scepticism, when more moderate, may be understood in a very reasonable sense; and is a necessary preparative to the study of philosophy, by preserving a proper impartiality in our judgments, and weaning our mind from all those prejudices, which we may have imbibed from education or rash opinion. To begin with clear and self-evident principles, to advance by timorous and sure steps, to review frequently our conclusions, and examine accurately all their consequences; though by these means we shall make both a slow and a short progress in our systems; are the only methods, by which we can ever hope to reach truth, and attain a proper stability and certainty in our determinations.

There is another species of scepticism, *consequent* to science and enquiry, when men are supposed to have discovered, either the absolute fallaciousness of their mental faculties, or their unfitness to reach any fixed determination in all those curious subjects of speculation, about which they are commonly employed. Even our very senses are brought into dispute, by a certain species of philosophers; and the maxims of common life are subjected to the same doubt as the most profound principles or conclusions of metaphysics and theology. As these paradoxical tenets (if they may be called tenets) are to be met with in some philosophers, and the refutation of them in several, they naturally excite our curiosity, and make us enquire into the arguments, on which they may be founded.

I need not insist upon the more trite topics, employed by the sceptics in all ages, against the evidence of *sense;* such as those which are derived from the imperfection and fallaciousness of our organs, on numberless occasions; the crooked appearance of an oar in water; the various aspects of objects, according to their different distances; the double images which arise from the pressing one eye; with many other appearances of a like nature. These sceptical topics, indeed, are only sufficient to prove, that the senses alone are not implicitly to be depended on; but that we must correct their evidence by reason, and by considerations, derived from the nature of the medium, the distance of the object, and the disposition of the organ, in order to render them, within their sphere, the proper *criteria* of truth and falsehood. There are other more profound arguments against the senses, which admit not of so easy a solution.

It seems evident, that men are carried, by a natural instinct or prepossession, to repose faith in their senses; and that, without any reasoning, or even almost before the use of reason, we always suppose an external universe, which depends not on our perception, but would exist, though we and every sensible creature were absent or annihilated. Even the animal creation are governed by a like opinion, and preserve this belief of external objects, in all their thoughts, designs, and actions.

It seems also evident, that, when men follow this blind and powerful instinct of nature, they always suppose the very images, presented by the senses, to be the external objects, and never entertain any suspicion, that the one are nothing but representations of the other. This very table, which we see white, and which we feel hard, is believed to exist, independent of our perception, and to be something external to our mind, which perceives it. Our presence bestows not being on it: Our absence does not annihilate it. It preserves its existence uniform and entire, independent of the situation of intelligent beings, who perceive or contemplate it.

But this universal and primary opinion of all men is soon destroyed by the slightest philosophy, which teaches us, that nothing can ever be present to the mind but an image or perception, and that the senses are only the inlets, through which these images are conveyed, without being able to produce any immediate intercourse between the mind and the object. The table, which we see, seems to diminish, as we remove farther from it: But the real table, which exists independent of us, suffers no alteration: It was, therefore, nothing but its image, which was present to the mind. These are the obvious dictates of reason; and no man, who reflects, ever doubted, that the existences, which we consider, when we say, *this house* and *that tree*, are nothing but perceptions in the mind, and fleeting copies or representations of other existences, which remain uniform and independent.

So far, then, are we necessitated by reasoning to contradict or depart from the primary instincts of nature, and to embrace a new system with regard to the evidence of our senses. But here philosophy finds herself extremely embarrassed, when she would justify this new system, and obviate the cavils and objections of the sceptics. She can no longer plead the infallible and irresistible instinct of nature: For that led us to a quite different system, which is acknowledged fallible and even erroneous. And to justify this pretended philosophical system, by a chain of clear and convincing argument, or even any appearance of argument, exceeds the power of all human capacity. . . .

The great subverter of *Pyrrhonism* or the excessive principles of scepticism, is action, and employment, and the occupations of common life. These principles may flourish and triumph in the schools; where it is, indeed, difficult, if not impossible, to refute them. But as soon as they leave the shade, and by the presence of the real objects, which actuate our passions and sentiments, are put in opposition to the more powerful principles of our nature, they vanish like smoke, and leave the most determined sceptic in the same condition as other mortals.

The sceptic, therefore, had better keep within his proper sphere, and display those *philosophical* objections, which arise from more profound researches. Here he seems to have ample matter of triumph; while he justly insists, that all our evidence for any matter of fact, which lies beyond the testimony of sense or memory, is derived entirely from the relation of cause and effect; that we have no other idea of this relation than that of two objects, which have been frequently *conjoined* together; that we have no argument to convince us, that objects, which have, in our experience, been frequently conjoined, will likewise, in other instances, be conjoined in the same manner; and that nothing leads us to this inference but custom or a certain instinct of our nature; which it is indeed difficult to resist, but which, like other instincts, may be fallacious and deceitful. While the sceptic insists upon these topics, he shows his force, or rather, indeed, his own and our weakness; and seems, for the time at least, to destroy all assurance and conviction. These arguments might be displayed at greater length, if any durable good or benefit to society could ever be expected to result from them.

For here is the chief and most confounding objection to *excessive* scepticism, that no durable good can ever result from it; while it remains in its full force and vigour. We need only ask such a sceptic, *What his meaning is? And what he proposes by all these curious researches?* He is immediately at a loss, and knows not what to answer. A Copernican or Ptolemaic, who supports each his different system of astronomy, may hope to produce a conviction, which will remain constant and durable, with his audience. A Stoic or Epicurean displays principles, which may not only be durable, but which have an effect on conduct and behaviour. But a Pyrrhonian cannot expect, that his philosophy will have any constant influence on the mind: Or if it had, that its influence would be beneficial to society. On the contrary, he must acknowledge, if he will acknowledge any thing, that all human life must perish, were his principles universally and steadily to prevail. All discourse, all action would immediately cease; and men remain in a total lethargy, till the necessities of nature, unsatisfied, put an end to their miserable existence. It is true; so fatal an event is very little to be dreaded. Nature is always too strong for principle. And though a Pyrrhonian may throw himself or others into a momentary amazement and confusion by his profound reasonings; the first and most trivial event in life will put to flight all his doubts and scruples, and leave him the same, in every point or action and speculation, with the philosophers of every other sect, or with those who never concerned themselves in any philosophical researches. When he awakes from his dream, he will be the first to join in the laugh against himself, and to confess, that all his objections are mere amusement, and can have no other tendency than to show the whimsical condition of mankind, who must act and reason and believe; though they are not able, by their most diligent enquiry, to satisfy themselves concerning the foundation of these operations, or to remove the objections, which may be raised against them.

There is, indeed, a more *mitigated* scepticism . . . which may be both durable and useful, and which may, in part, be the result of this PYRRHONISM, or *excessive* scepticism, when its undistinguished doubts are, in some measure, corrected by common sense and reflection. The greater part of mankind are naturally apt to be affirmative and dogmatical in their opinions; . . . But could such dogmatical reasoners become sensible of the strange infirmities of human understanding, even in its most perfect state, . . . such a reflection would naturally inspire them with more modesty and reserve, and diminish their fond opinion of themselves. . . .

Another species of *mitigated* scepticism, which may be of advantage to mankind, and which may be the natural result of the PYRRHONIAN doubts and scruples, is the limitation of our enquiries to such subjects as are best adapted to the narrow capacity of human understanding. The *imagination* of man is naturally sublime, delighted with whatever is remote and extraordinary, and running, without control, into the most distant parts of space and time in order to avoid the objects, which custom has rendered too familiar to it. A correct *Judgment* observes a contrary method, and avoiding all distant and high enquiries, confines itself to common life, and to such subjects as fall under daily practice and experience; leaving the more sublime topics to the embellishment of poets and orators, or to the arts

of priests and politicians. To bring us to so salutary a determination, nothing can be more serviceable, than to be once thoroughly convinced of the force of the PYRRHONIAN doubt, and of the impossibility, that any thing, but the strong power of natural instinct, could free us from it. . . .

This narrow limitation, indeed, of our enquiries, is, in every respect, so reasonable, that it suffices to make the slightest examination into the natural powers of the human mind, and to compare them with their objects, in order to recommend it to us. We shall then find what are the proper subjects of science and enquiry.

DISCUSSION QUESTIONS

1. Hume argues that Descartes' skepticism is unsatisfactory because even if it were possible to attain this level of skepticism (and it is not), it "would be entirely incurable." What does he mean? Do you agree with him? How might Descartes respond?

2. Hume also charges that Descartes' skepticism does not allow any reasoning that "could ever bring us to a state of assurance and conviction upon any subject." What is Hume's argument? Do you agree with him?

3. For Hume, while Pyrrhonian skepticism might work well in the classroom, it is not applicable to everyday life. What is the difference? Do we have an obligation to test our philosophical doctrines against the standard of everyday life? Should we leave aside valid and sound arguments because they cannot be maintained in "real" life?

4. Hume's mitigated skepticism "limits our enquiries to such subjects as are best adapted to the narrow capacity of human understanding." What does this mean?

5. Hume sets various types of skepticism against human nature and essentially states that if they are not in accordance with human nature, then we should not take them seriously. Is he right?

Total Recall
[USA 1990] 2 hours, 4 minutes
Directed by Paul Verhoeven

*I*n the year 2084, a construction worker named Quaid (Arnold Schwarzenegger) is compelled by a deep fascination with Mars. He visits Rekall, a company that specializes in implanting artificial memories of vacations and experiences into the minds of clients. Quaid requests a memory implant in which he becomes a secret agent fighting a revolution on Mars. However, something goes wrong with the implant procedure . . . or does it? After Quaid receives the memory implant, our interpretation of his experiences can take one of two major paths: (1) The implant was *successful,* and Quaid is experiencing the implanted memory of a secret agent on a mission to Mars; or (2) the implant has actually *failed,* and Quaid has learned his true identity—that he is really a man named Hauser who has been implanted with the memories of Quaid in order to complete a secret mission.

Quaid (or Quaid/Hauser) discovers, among other things, that the woman he took to be his wife (Sharon Stone) is not really his wife. He travels to Mars to uncover a covert plot led by the tyrannical Cahagon (Ronny Cox) who, out of spite, withholds the air supply from the residents of Mars. Battling a group of thugs led by Richter (Michael Ironside), Quaid stops at nothing to reveal the secrets behind an ancient Martian machine while fighting for his life and his identity. The film closes with Quaid overcoming Cahagon and restoring the air supply to the planet. The final lines of the film leave open the possibility that the entire sequence could be a memory implant from Rekall. Part of the philosophical challenge and fun of this otherwise extremely violent and sometimes campy film is resolving this issue. Clues are presented to viewers throughout the film as to whether the implant failed.

DISCUSSION QUESTIONS

1. In this exchange, Quaid and Bob McClane (Ray Baker), the head of Rekall, discuss different memory packages that may be purchased.

    QUAID   "What's in the two-week package?"

    MCCLANE   "First of all, Doug, when you go Rekall, you get nothing but first-class memories: private cabin on the shuttle; deluxe suite at the Hilton; plus all the major sights: Mount Pyramid, the Grand Canals, and of course . . . Venusville."

    QUAID   "How real does it seem?"

    MCCLANE   "As real as any memory in your head."

    QUAID   "Come on. . . ."

    MCCLANE   "I'm telling you, Doug, your brain won't know the difference. Guaranteed, or your money back."

If the memories that are implanted in Quaid's head are as real as the other memories in his head, how will he be able to recognize the difference between real and implanted memories? Discuss.

2.   In this dialogue, McClane tries to convince Quaid to accept a new identity for his trip to Mars.

QUAID   "No options."

MCCLANE   "Whatever you say . . . Just answer one question. What is it that is exactly the same about every vacation you've ever taken?"

QUAID   "I give up."

MCCLANE   "You. You're the same. No matter where you go, there you are. Always the same old you. Let me suggest that you take a vacation from yourself. I know it sounds wild, but it's the latest thing in travel. We call it an 'Ego Trip.' "

QUAID   "I'm not interested in that."

MCCLANE   "You're gonna love this. We offer you a choice of alternate identities during your trip."

[A number of alternate identities appear on a video screen: A-14 MILLIONAIRE PLAYBOY; A-15 SPORTS HERO; A-16 INDUSTRIAL TYCOON; A-17 SECRET AGENT.]

MCCLANE   "Face it . . . Why go to Mars as a tourist when you can go as a playboy, or a famous jock, or a . . ."

QUAID   "Secret agent . . . How much is that?"

Is it possible to "take a vacation from yourself"? What would Descartes say? Doesn't "I think, therefore I am" establish for Descartes that only he can be the subject of his own experiences? How about Kant (see below)? Discuss.

3.   Would "taking a vacation from yourself" mean that another self experienced the memories implanted into Quaid's brain? Doesn't this mean that when Quaid awakens, these memories will be retained in his brain as the memories of actions of another person and, hence, the memory of the experience on Mars as a secret agent will not be enjoyed as his own?

4.   In continuing to describe the specifics of Quaid's trip to Mars as a secret agent, McClane says the following:

MCCLANE   "Aaah, let me tantalize you. You're a top operative, back under deep cover on your most important mission. People are trying to kill you left and right. You meet a beautiful, exotic woman . . ."

QUAID   "Go on."

MCCLANE   "I don't wanna spoil it for you, Doug. Just rest assured, by the time the trip is over, you get the girl, you kill the bad guys, and you save the entire planet. Now you tell me. Is that worth three hundred measly credits?"

What does McClane mean by "I don't wanna spoil it for you?" How is it possible for McClain to spoil the trip to Mars for Quaid *when an identity other than his own will be experiencing it*? Isn't it the case that if the "secret agent" Quaid experiences the trip, not the "construction worker" (his job before the memory procedure) Quaid, that the construction worker Quaid's memories will not be accessible during the "ego trip"?

5. The trip McClane summarizes to Quaid, one wherein "by the time the trip is over, you get the girl, you kill the bad guys, and you save the entire planet," is precisely the one that occurs after the procedure. Must we therefore believe that the implant was, in fact, successful? Why or why not?

6. When Quaid is asked to choose a woman for his "ego trip," he picks one who appears on the computer screen to look very similar to a woman Quaid was dreaming about at the beginning of the film. What are we to infer from this?

7. At the end of the film, Melina (Rachel Ticotin), the woman Quaid "chose" for his Mars adventure, and he exchange the following lines:

MELINA   "Quaid, I can't believe it . . . It's like a dream."

[On hearing her words, Quaid's expression turns grim and confused.]

MELINA   "What's wrong?"

QUAID   "I just has a terrible thought . . . What if this is all a dream?"

MELINA   "Then kiss me quick . . . before you wake up."

How is the skepticism in this film like Descartes' skepticism? How is it different?

8. How is the skepticism in this film like Borges's skepticism in "The Circular Ruins"? How is it different?

9. After viewing this film, can you make a solid case one way or the other as to whether there has been a successful memory implant in Quaid or an unsuccessful memory implant in Quaid/Hauser? Is there another interpretation that is even more persuasive?

10. If you conclude that this is all a memory implant, how do you reconcile this with scenes after the procedure in which Quaid neither is present *nor has knowledge of the scene*? Is this like having a dream but forgetting parts of the dream? Can you have a dream and not recognize or take part in parts of the dream? Or is there no dream correlate for this type of thing? Discuss.

IMMANUEL KANT

KNOWLEDGE, EXPERIENCE, AND REASON

In this selection, Immanuel Kant aims to resolve the two major opposing positions on knowledge: empiricism and rationalism. *Empiricism* is the general doctrine that experience is the source of knowledge; *rationalism* is the general doctrine that through reason alone, without the aid of information from the senses, we are capable of arriving at knowledge. The writings of Locke, Berkeley, and Hume are associated with empiricism, whereas the writings of Plato and Descartes are associated with rationalism. Kant writes, "That all our knowledge begins with experience there can be no doubt." "But, though all our knowledge begins with experience," he warns, "it by no means follows that all arises out of experience." Kant found inspiration in Hume's work to go beyond the empiricist/rationalist divide, and he credits Hume with having roused him from his "dogmatic slumber."

For Kant, knowledge is always the product of both sensory representations ("intuitions") and concepts of understanding ("conceptions"). This idea is crystallized in his slogan "Thoughts without content are void, intuitions without conceptions are blind." Says Kant, "Hence it is as necessary for the mind to make its conceptions sensuous (that is, to join to them the object in intuition), as to make its intuitions intelligible (that is, to join to them the object of intuition)."

Intuition requires that all sensory representation be given in space and time. The mind has concepts that make understanding sensory representations possible, and these concepts exist in our minds *a priori,* that is, prior to our experience of sensory representations. Nevertheless, the concepts that exist *a priori* in our minds are not simply with us from birth, owing to nature or God. Rather, these concepts are derived from a particular set of categories that are the preconditions of experience. The categories are twelve in number and fall into four groups: (1) quantity (unity, plurality, totality), (2) quality (positive, negative, limited), (3) relation (substance-accident, cause-effect, reciprocity or community), and (4) modality (possibility-impossibility, actuality-nonactuality, necessity-contingency). These categories are the fundamental preconditions of experience; without them, experience is not possible. In order for something to become an object of empirical knowledge, it must be viewed in terms of the categories. Ultimately, for Kant, we never see things as they actually are (what Kant elsewhere calls "noumena"); rather, we only see the world as presented to us through the structure of our understanding (what Kant elsewhere calls "phenomena"). This approach to knowledge is called *trancendental idealism,* the view that the content of knowledge comes from our senses and that the form of our knowledge comes from reason.

Immanuel Kant (1724–1804), a German philosopher, spent his entire life in Königsberg, Prussia. At the age of eight, he entered the Collegium Fredericianum, a Latin school, where he spent almost nine years. In 1740, he enrolled in the University of Königsberg as a theological student. Though he took courses in theology and even preached on several occasions, he was most interested in mathematics and physics, especially the work of Leibniz and Newton. Unable to secure a position at the university, he worked as a family tutor from 1746 to 1755.

In 1755, Kant completed his degree at the university and became a privat-dozent (lecturer). He spent fifteen years as a privat-dozent, lecturing on subjects ranging from mathematics, physics, and logic to fireworks, fortifications, and physical geography. In class (unlike in his writing), Kant is said to have been humorous, vivid, and lively, drawing on examples from travel, literature, and science. Finally, in 1770, he obtained a chair in logic and metaphysics at the university, and he also served as dean of the philosophy faculty and as rector. In 1781, his *Critique of Pure Reason* was published, a work that he claimed was written in only four or five months. It was followed by the *Critique of Practical Reason* (1788) and the *Critique of Judgment* (1790). Soon, Kant's work was being taught at all the important German-speaking universities, and people flocked to his hometown to meet him. In 1797, in frail health, Kant retired from the university; he died in 1804. His life is said to have been so orderly that the people of his town set their clocks according to the time Kant passed their houses on his daily walk. His other books include *Prolegommena to Any Future Metaphysics* (1783), *Foundations of the Metaphysics of Morals* (1785), *Religion Within the Limits of Reason Alone* (1793), *Perpetual Peace* (1795), and *Contest of the Faculties* (1798). The following selection is from his *Critique of Pure Reason.*

I. Of the Difference between Pure and Empirical Knowledge

That all our knowledge begins with experience there can be no doubt. For how is it possible that the faculty of cognition should be awakened into exercise otherwise than by means of objects which affect our senses, and partly of themselves produce representations, partly rouse our powers of understanding into activity, to compare, to connect, or to separate these, and so to convert the raw material of our sensuous impressions into a knowledge of objects, which is called experience? In respect of time, therefore, no knowledge of ours is antecedent to experience, but begins with it.

But, though all our knowledge begins with experience, it by no means follows that all arises out of experience. For, on the contrary, it is quite possible that our empirical knowledge is a compound of that which we receive through impressions, and that which the faculty of cognition supplies from itself (sensuous impressions giving merely the *occasion*), an addition which we cannot distinguish from the original element given by sense, till long practice has made us attentive to, and skillful in separating it. It is, therefore, a question which requires close investigation, and not to be answered at first sight, whether there exists a knowledge altogether independent of experience, and even of all sensuous impressions? Knowledge of this kind is called *a priori*, in contradistinction to empirical knowledge, which has its sources *a posteriori*, that is, in experience.

But the expression, "*a priori*," is not as yet definite enough adequately to indicate the whole meaning of the question above started. For, in speaking of knowledge which has its sources in experience, we are wont to say, that this or that may be known *a priori*, because we do not derive this knowledge immediately from experience, but from a general rule, which, however, we have itself borrowed from experience. Thus, if a man undermined his house, we say, "he might know *a priori* that it would have fallen"; that is, he needed not to have waited for the experience that it did actually fall. But still, *a priori*, he could not know even this much. For, that bodies are heavy, and, consequently, that they fall when their supports are taken away, must have been known to him previously, by means of experience.

By the term "knowledge *a priori*," therefore, we shall in the sequel understand, not such as is independent of this or that kind of experience, but such as is absolutely so of *all* experience. Opposed to this is empirical knowledge, or that which is possible only *a posteriori*, that is, through experience. Knowledge *a priori* is either pure or impure. Pure knowledge *a priori* is that with which no empirical element is mixed up. For example, the proposition, "Every change has a cause," is a proposition *a priori*, but impure, because change is a conception which can only be derived from experience.

II. The Human Intellect, Even in an Unphilosophical State, Is in Possession of Certain Cognitions "A Priori"

The question now is as to a *criterion*, by which we may securely distinguish a pure from an empirical cognition. Experience no doubt teaches us that this or that object is constituted in such and such a manner, but not that it could not possibly exist otherwise. Now, in the first place, if we have a proposition which contains the idea of necessity in its very conception, it is a judgment *a priori*; if, moreover, it is not derived from any other proposition, unless from one equally involving the idea of necessity, it is absolutely *a priori*. Secondly, an empirical judgment never exhibits strict and absolute, but only assumed and comparative universality (by induction); therefore, the most we can say is—so far as we have hitherto observed, there is no exception to this or that rule. If, on the other hand, a judgment carries with it strict and absolute universality, that is, admits of no possible exception, it is not derived from experience, but is valid absolutely *a priori*. . . .

Now, that in the sphere of human cognition we have judgments which are necessary, and in the strictest sense universal, consequently pure *a priori*, it will be an easy matter to show. If we desire an example from the sciences, we need only take any proposition in mathematics. If we cast our eyes upon the commonest operations of the understanding, the proposition, "Every change must have a cause," will amply serve our purpose. In the latter case, indeed, the conception of a cause so plainly involves the conception of a necessity of connection with an effect, and of a strict universality of the law, that the very notion of a cause would entirely disappear, were we to derive it, like Hume, from a frequent association of what happens with that which precedes, . . . Besides, without seeking for such examples of principles existing *a priori* in cognition, we might easily show that such principles are the indispensable basis of the possibility of experience itself, and consequently prove their existence *a priori*. For whence could our experience itself acquire certainty, if all the rules on which it depends were themselves empirical, and consequently fortuitous? No one, therefore, can admit the validity of the use of such rules as first principles.

INTRODUCTION

IDEA OF A TRANSCENDENTAL LOGIC

I. OF LOGIC IN GENERAL

Our knowledge springs from two main sources in the mind, the first of which is the faculty or power of receiving representations (receptivity for impressions); the second is the power of cognizing by means of these representations (spontaneity in the production of conceptions). Through the first an object is given to us; through the second, it is, in relation to the representation (which is a mere determination of the mind), thought. Intuition and conceptions constitute, therefore, the elements of all our knowledge, so that neither conceptions without an intuition in some way corresponding to them, nor intuition without conceptions, can afford us a cognition. Both are either pure or empirical. They are empirical, when sensation (which presupposes the actual presence of the object) is contained in them; and pure, when no sensation is mixed with the representation. Sensations we may call the matter of sensuous cognition. Pure intuition consequently contains merely the form under which something is intuited, and pure conception only the form of the thought of an object. Only pure intuitions and pure conceptions are possible *a priori;* the empirical only *a posteriori.*

We apply the term *sensibility* to the receptivity of the mind for impressions, in so far as it is in some way affected; and, on the other hand, we call the faculty of spontaneously producing representations, or the spontaneity of cognition, *understanding.* Our nature is so constituted that intuition with us never can be other than sensuous, that is, it contains only the mode in which we are affected by objects. On the other hand, the faculty of thinking the object of sensuous intuition is the understanding. Neither of these faculties has a preference over the other. Without the sensuous faculty no object would be given to us, and without the understanding no object would be thought. Thoughts without content are void; intuitions without conceptions, blind. Hence it is as necessary for the mind to make its conceptions sensuous (that is, to join to them the object in intuition), as to make its intuitions intelligible (that is, to bring them under conceptions). Neither of these faculties can exchange its proper function. Understanding cannot intuit, and the sensuous faculty cannot think. In no other way than from the united operation of both, can knowledge arise. . . .

TRANSITION TO THE TRANSCENDENTAL DEDUCTION OF THE CATEGORIES

. . . Now there are only two conditions of the possibility of a cognition of objects; firstly, *intuition,* by means of which the object, though only as phenomenon, is given; secondly, *conception,* by means of which the object which corresponds to this intuition is thought. But it is evident from what has been said on aesthetic that the first condition, under which alone objects can be intuited, must in fact exist, as a formal basis for them, *a priori* in the mind. With this formal condition of sensibility, therefore, all phenomena necessarily correspond, because it is only through it that they can be phenomena at all; that is, can be empirically intuited and given. Now the question is whether there do not exist, *a priori* in the mind, conceptions of understanding also, as conditions under which alone something, if not intuited, is yet thought as object. If this question be answered in the affirmative, it follows that all empirical cognition of objects is necessarily conformable to such conceptions, since, if they are not presupposed, it is impossible that anything can be an object of experience. Now all experience contains, besides the intuition of the senses through which an object is given, a *conception* also of an object that is given in intuition. Accordingly, conceptions of objects in general must lie as *a priori* conditions at the foundation of all empirical cognition; and consequently, the objective validity of the categories, as *a priori* conceptions, will rest upon *this*, that experience (as far as regards the form of thought) is possible only by their means. For in that case they apply necessarily and *a priori* to objects of experience, because only through them can an object of experience be thought.

DISCUSSION QUESTIONS

1. "Though all our knowledge begins with experience," warns Kant, "it by no means follows that all arises out of experience." What does this mean? Do you agree with this claim?

2. Discuss Kant's slogan "Thoughts without content are void, intuitions without conceptions are blind."

3. What is the difference between "a priori" and "a posteriori" knowledge? Give examples of both types of knowledge.

4. Kant maintains that we see the world only as presented to us through the structure of our understanding. What does he mean by this? Is this a form of skepticism? Why or why not?

5. Kant aims to resolve the two major opposing positions on knowledge: empiricism and rationalism. Is he successful? Why or why not?

LORRAINE CODE

THE SEX OF THE KNOWER

In this essay, Lorraine Code asks whether the sex of the knower is epistemologically significant. She points out that in academic philosophy, "the knower" is generally treated as "a featureless abstraction." "Sometimes, indeed," writes Code, "she or he is merely a place holder in the proposition 'S knows that p.'" Code claims that "the scope of epistemological inquiry has been too narrowly defined." "The S who could count as a model, paradigmatic knower has most commonly—if always tacitly—been an adult (but not *old*), white, reasonably affluent (latterly middle-class), educated man of status, property, and publicly acceptable accomplishments."

Moreover, in the Western philosophical tradition, women have been associated with subjectivity and men with objectivity. Consequently, since objectivity is a defining attribute of knowledge, women, by virtue of their "natural subjectivity," are not qualified to be knowers. In short, this provides a clear answer to Code's question: the sex of the knower *is* epistemologically significant.

Lorraine Code received her Ph.D. from the University of Guelph and is currently Distinguished Research Professor of Philosophy at York University in Toronto. She is the author and editor of a number of books including *Epistemic Responsibility* (1987), *What Can She Know? Feminist Theory and the Construction of Knowledge* (1991), *Rhetorical Spaces: Essays on Gendered Locations* (1995), *Encyclopedia of Feminist Theories* (ed., 2000), and *Feminist Interpretations of Hans-Georg Gadamer* (ed., 2003). The following selection is from *What Can She Know?*

A question that focuses on the knower, . . . claims that there are good reasons for asking who that knower is. Uncontroversial as such a suggestion would be in ordinary conversations about knowledge, academic philosophers commonly treat "the knower" as a featureless abstraction. Sometimes, indeed, she or he is merely a place holder in the proposition "S knows that p." Epistemological analyses of the proposition tend to focus on the "knowing that," to determine conditions under which a knowledge claim can legitimately be made. Once discerned, it is believed, such conditions will hold across all possible utterances of the proposition. Indeed, throughout the history of modern philosophy the central "problem of knowledge" has been to determine necessary and sufficient conditions for the possibility and justification of knowledge claims. Philosophers have sought ways of establishing a relation of correspondence between knowledge and "reality" and/or ways of establishing the coherence of particular knowledge claims within systems of already-established truths. They have proposed methodologies for arriving at truth, and criteria for determining the validity of claims to the effect that "S knows that p." Such endeavors are guided by the putatively self-evident principle that truth once discerned, knowledge once established, claim their status *as* truth and knowledge by virtue of a grounding in or coherence within a permanent, objective, ahistorical, and circumstantially neutral framework or set of standards.

The question "Who is S?" is regarded neither as legitimate nor as relevant in these endeavors. As inquirers into the nature and conditions of human knowledge, epistemologists commonly work from the assumption that they need concern themselves only with knowledge claims that meet certain standards of *purity.* . . .

The only thing that is clear about S from the standard proposition "S knows that p" is that S is a (would-be) knower. Although the question "Who is S?" rarely arises, certain assumptions about S as knower permeate epistemological inquiry. Of special importance for my argument is the assumption that knowers are self-sufficient

and solitary individuals, at least in their knowledge-seeking activities. This belief derives from a long and venerable heritage, with its roots in Descartes's quest for a basis of perfect certainty on which to establish his knowledge. The central aim of Descartes's endeavors is captured in this claim: "I shall have the right to conceive high hopes if I am happy enough to discover one thing only which is certain and indubitable." That "one thing," Descartes believed, would stand as the fixed pivotal, Archimedean point on which all the rest of his knowledge would turn. Because of its systematic relation to that point, his knowledge would be certain and indubitable.

Most significant for this discussion is Descartes's conviction that his quest will be conducted in a private, introspective examination of the contents of his own mind. It is true that, in the last section of the *Discourse on the Method,* Descartes acknowledges the benefit "others may receive from the communication of [his] reflection," and he states his belief that combining "the lives and labours of many" is essential to progress in scientific knowledge. It is also true that this individualistically described act of knowing exercises the aspect of the soul that is common to and alike in all knowers: namely, the faculty of reason. Yet his claim that knowledge seeking is an introspective activity of an individual mind accords no relevance either to a knower's embodiment or to his (or her) intersubjective relations. For each knower, the Cartesian route to knowledge is through private, abstract thought, through the efforts of reason unaided either by the senses or by consultation with other knowers. It is this individualistic, self-reliant, private aspect of Descartes's philosophy that has been influenced in shaping subsequent epistemological ideals.

Reason is conceived as autonomous in the Cartesian project in two ways, then. Not only is the quest for certain knowledge an independent one, undertaken separately by each rational being, but it is a journey of reason alone, unassisted by the senses. For Descartes believed that sensory experiences had the effect of distracting reason from its proper course.

The custom of formulating knowledge claims in the "S knows that p" formula is not itself of Cartesian origin. The point of claiming Cartesian inspiration for an assumption implicit in the formulation is that the knower who is commonly presumed to be the subject of that proposition is modeled, in significant respects, on the Cartesian pure inquirer. For epistemological purposes, all knowers are believed to be alike with respect both to their cognitive capacities and to their methods of achieving knowledge. In the empiricist tradition this assumption is apparent in the belief that simple, basic observational data can provide the foundation of knowledge just because perception is invariant from observer to observer, in standard observation conditions. In fact, a common way of filling the places in the "S knows that p" proposition is with substitutions such as "Peter knows that the door is open" or "John knows that the book is red." It does not matter who John or Peter is.

Such knowledge claims carry implicit beliefs not only about would-be knowers but also about the knowledge that is amenable to philosophical analysis. Although (Cartesian) rationalists and empiricists differ with respect to what kinds of claim count as foundational, they endorse similar assumptions about the relation of foundational claims to the rest of a body of knowledge. With "S knows that p" propositions, the belief is that such propositions stand as paradigms for knowledge in general. Epistemologists assume that knowledge is analyzable into prepositional "simples" whose truth can be demonstrated by establishing relations of correspondence to reality, or coherence within a system of known truths. These relatively simple knowledge claims (i.e., John knows that the book is red) could indeed be made by most "normal" people who know the language and are familiar with the objects named. Knowers would seem to be quite self-sufficient in acquiring such knowledge. Moreover, no one would claim to know "a little" that the book is red or to be in the process of acquiring knowledge about the openness of the door. Nor would anyone be likely to maintain that S knows better than W does that the door is open or that the book is red. Granting such examples paradigmatic status creates the mistaken assumption that all knowledge worthy of the name will be like this. . . .

In proposing that the sex of the knower is epistemologically significant, I am claiming that the scope of epistemological inquiry has been too narrowly defined. . . . There are numerous questions to be asked about knowledge whose answers matter to people who are concerned to know well. Among them are questions that bear not just on criteria of evidence, justification, and warrantability, but on the "nature" of cognitive agents: questions about their character; their material, historical, cultural circumstances; their interests in the inquiry at issue. These are questions about how credibility is established, about connections between knowledge and power, about the place of knowledge in ethical and aesthetic judgments, and about political agendas and the responsibilities of knowers. I am claiming that all of these questions are epistemologically significant. . . .

Although it has rarely been spelled out prior to the development of feminist critiques, it has long been tacitly assumed that S is male. Nor could S be just any man, the apparently infinite substitutability of the "S" term notwithstanding. The S who could count as a model, paradigmatic knower has most commonly—if always tacitly—been an adult (but not *old*), white, reasonably affluent (latterly middle-class) educated man of status, property, and publicly acceptable accomplishments. In theory of knowledge he has been allowed to stand for all men. This assumption does not merely derive from habit or coincidence, but is a manifestation of engrained philosophical convictions. Not only has it been taken for granted that knowers properly so-called are male, but when male philosophers have paused to note this fact, as some indeed have done, they have argued that things are as they should be. Reason may be alike in all men, but it would be a mistake to believe that "man," in this respect, "embraces woman." Women have been judged incapable, for many reasons, of achieving knowledge worthy of the name. It is no exaggeration to say that anyone who wanted to *count* as a knower has commonly had to be male.

In the *Politics*, Aristotle observes: "The freeman rules over the slave after another manner from that in which the male rules over the female, or the man over the child; although the parts of the soul are present in all of them, they are present in different degrees. For the slave has no deliberative faculty at all; the woman has, but it is without authority, and the child has, but it is immature." Aristotle's assumption that a woman will naturally be ruled by a man connects directly with his contention that a woman's deliberative faculty is "without authority." Even if a woman could, in her sequestered, domestic position, acquire deliberative skills, she would remain reliant on her husband for her sources of knowledge and information. She must be ruled by a man because, in the social structure of the *polis*, she enjoys neither the autonomy nor the freedom to put into visible practice the results of the deliberations she may engage in, in private. If she can claim no authority for her rational, deliberative endeavors, then her chances of gaining recognition as a knowledgeable citizen are seriously limited, whatever she may do.

Aristotle is just one of a long line of western thinkers to declare the limitations of women's cognitive capacities. Rousseau* maintains that young men and women should be educated quite differently because of women's inferiority in reason and their propensity to be dragged down by their sensual natures. For Kierkegaard, women are merely aesthetic beings: men alone can attain the (higher) ethical and religious levels of existence. And for Nietzsche, the Apollonian (intellectual) domain is the male preserve, whereas women are Dionysian (sensuous) creatures. Nineteenth-century philosopher and linguist Wilhelm von Humboldt, who writes at length about women's knowledge, sums up the central features of this line of thought as follows: "A sense of truth exists in [women] quite literally as a sense: . . . their nature also contains a lack or a failing of analytic capacity which draws a strict line of demarcation between ego and world; therefore, they will not come as close to the ultimate investigation of truth as man." The implication is that women's knowledge, if ever the products of their projects deserve that label, is inherently and inevitably *subjective*—in the most idiosyncratic sense—by contrast with the best of men's knowledge.

Objectivity, quite precisely construed, is commonly regarded as a defining feature of knowledge per se. So if women's knowledge is declared to be *naturally* subjective, then a clear answer emerges to my question. The answer is that if the would-be knower is female, then her sex is indeed epistemologically significant, for it disqualifies her as a knower in the fullest sense of that term. Such disqualifications will operate differently for women of different classes, races, ages, and allegiances, but in every circumstance they will operate asymmetrically for women and for men. . . .

The presuppositions I have just cited claim more than the rather simple fact that many kinds of knowledge and skill have, historically, been inaccessible to women on a purely practical level. It is true, historically speaking, that even women who were the racial and social "equals" of standard male knowers were only rarely able to become learned. The thinkers I have cited (and others like them) claim to find a rationale for this state of affairs through appeals to dubious "facts" about women's natural incapacity for rational thought. Yet deeper questions still need to be asked: Is there knowledge that is, quite simply, inaccessible to members of the female, or the male, sex? Are there kinds of knowledge that only men, or only woman, can acquire? Is the sex of the knower crucially determining in this respect, across all other specificities? The answers to these questions should not address only the *practical* possibilities that have existed for members of either sex. Such practical possibilities are the constructs of complex social arrangements that are themselves constructed out of historically specific choices, and are, as such, open to challenge and change.

Knowledge, as it achieves credence and authoritative status at any point in the history of the male-dominated mainstream, is commonly held to be a product of the individual efforts of human knowers. References to Pythagoras's theorem, Copernicus's revolution, and Newtonian and Einsteinian physics signal an epistemic community's attribution of pathbreaking contributions to certain

---

* Jean-Jacques Rousseau (1712–78) was one of the most influential European philosophers of the eighteenth century. Rousseau is best known for his work in political philosophy, particularly his *Discourse on the Origin of Inequality Among Men* (1755) and his masterpiece, *The Social Contract* (1762). His other works include *Émile* (1762), an educational treatise, and *Confessions* (1782), an autobiography. —Ed.

of its individual members. The implication is that *that* person, single-handedly, has effected a leap of progress in a particular field of inquiry. In less publicly spectacular ways, other cognitive agents are represented as contributors to the growth and stability of public knowledge.

Now any contention that such contributions are the results of independent endeavor is highly contestable. . . . A complex of historical and other sociocultural factors produces the conditions that make "individual" achievement possible, and "individuals" themselves are socially constituted. The claim that individual *men* are the creators of the authoritative . . . landmarks of western intellectual life is particularly interesting for the fact that the contributions—both practical and substantive—of their lovers, wives, children, servants, neighbors, friends, and colleagues rarely figure in analyses of their work.

The historical attribution of such achievements to specific cognitive agents does, nonetheless, accord a significance to individual efforts which raises questions pertinent to my project. It poses the problem, in another guise, of whether aspects of human specificity could, in fact, constitute conditions for the existence of knowledge or determine the kinds of knowledge that a knower can achieve. It would seem that such incidental physical attributes as height, weight, or hair color would not count among factors that would determine a person's capacities to know (though the arguments that skin color *does* count are too familiar). It is not necessary to consider how much Archimedes* weighed when he made his famous discovery, nor is there any doubt that a thinner or a fatter person could have reached the same conclusion. But in cultures in which sex differences figure prominently in virtually every mode of human interaction, being female or male is far more fundamental to the construction of subjectivity than are such attributes as size or hair color. So the question is whether femaleness or maleness are the kinds of subjective factor (i.e., factors about the circumstances of a knowing subject)

that are constitutive of the form and content of knowledge. Attempts to answer this question are complicated by the fact that sex/gender, then, always risks abstraction and is limited in its scope by the abstracting process. Further, the question seems to imply that sex and gender are themselves constants, thus obscuring the processes of *their* sociocultural construction. Hence the formulation of adequately nuanced answers is problematic and necessarily partial.

Even if it should emerge that gender-related factors play a crucial role in the construction of knowledge, then, the inquiry into the epistemological significance of the sex of the knower would not be complete. The task would remain of considering whether a distinction between "natural" and socialized capacity can retain any validity. The equally pressing question as to how the hitherto devalued products of *women's* cognitive projects can gain acknowledgment as "knowledge" would need to be addressed so as to uproot entrenched prejudices about knowledge, epistemology, and women. "The epistemological project" will look quite different once its tacit underpinnings are revealed. . . .

Feminist philosophy simply did not exist until philosophers learned to perceive the near-total absence of women in philosophical writings from the very beginning of western philosophy, to stop assuming that "man" could be read as a generic term. Explicit denigrations of women, which became the focus of philosophical writing in the early years of the contemporary women's movement, were more readily perceptible. The authors of derogatory views about women in classical texts clearly needed power to be able to utter their pronouncements with impunity: a power they claimed from a "received" discourse that represented women's nature in such a way that women undoubtedly merited the negative judgments that Aristotle or Nietzsche made about them. Women are now in a position to recognize and refuse these overt manifestations of contempt.

---

* Archimedes (287–212 B.C.E.) is regarded as the greatest mathematician and scientist of antiquity and is called both the "father of integral calculus" and the "father of mathematical physics." One of his most famous discoveries is a theory of buoyancy called the Archimedes Principle, which, legend has it, he discovered while taking a bath. After the discovery, he is said to have run naked through the streets yelling, "Eureka, eureka!" ["I have found it, I have found it!"] He also discovered *pi*. —Ed.

DISCUSSION QUESTIONS

1. Do you think it makes a difference in the proposition "S knows that p" if S is woman or a man? If so, how and why?

2. Code says, "It would seem that such incidental physical attributes as height, weight, or hair color would not count among factors that would determine a person's capacity to know (though the arguments that skin color *does* count are too familiar)." If we believe that the sex of the knower is epistemologically significant, shouldn't we also contend that other factors such as race, sexuality, and class are epistemologically relevant? What is Code's position? What is yours?

3. Discuss the philosophical tradition that women's cognitive capacities are lower than those of men. Does it make you think any differently about Aristotle's capacities as a philosopher, for example, knowing that he believed this?

4. Code says that individuals are "socially constituted" and mentions their "sociocultural construction." What do mean? How might affect what we know and how we know?

5. How does Code's conclusion that the sex of the knower is epistemologically significant affect the doctrines of Descartes, Locke, Hume, Berkeley, and Kant? Do her comments render their theories obsolete? Or do you think these philosophers would have ready responses for her? Discuss.

■ ■ ■ ■ ■ ■ ■ ■ ■ ■ ■ ■ ■ ■ ■ ■ ■ ■

He Said, She Said
[USA 1991] 1 hour, 55 minutes
Dir. by K. Kwapis and M. Silver

■ ■ ■ ■ ■ ■ ■ ■ ■ ■ ■ ■ ■ ■ ■ ■ ■ ■

*T*wo news columnists are drawn to each other by love but driven apart by their differing views on politics, relationships, and marriage. Journalists Dan Hanson (Kevin Bacon) and Lorie Bryer (Elizabeth Perkins) are on opposite ends of the ideological spectrum in their news columns. To boost ratings, a local TV station creates a show in which Dan and Lorie are to engage in a verbal battle of the sexes.

The film begins with a heated debate after which Lorie walks out on both the show and Dan. In a series of flashbacks, we are presented with two interpretations of the same story: one told from Dan's point of view, and the other from Lorie's. Through these flashbacks, the dual history of Dan and Lorie's relationship is revealed. In the end, Dan and Lorie attempt to work out their differences and regain the love they once had.

DISCUSSION QUESTIONS

1. Consider the following dialogue from this film:

   LORIE   "Alright, as long as we are going to talk in stereotypes: all women want to get married and all men fear commitment."

   DAN   "No, no. See, you don't understand. It's not fear; it's just that we don't have a choice in the matter. We can't commit. It's something deep inside in the animal part of man that wants to keep us separate from the pack."

Do you believe that our sex influences our knowledge claims regarding marriage and commitment? Assuming that it does or can, is this a strong enough ground to conclude that the sex of the knower is epistemologically significant?

2. Consider this exchange from the film:

    DAN   "What is the big deal?"

    LORIE   "The big deal is that from the moment I went to bed with you, sleeping with another man became unthinkable. But for you, sleeping with another woman remained thinkable."

    DAN   "That was in the beginning. Let's talk about now."

    The film asks us to consider whether the way men think about commitment is fundamentally different from the way women think about commitment. Assuming these differences exist, do you think their source is innate (we are born with these differences) or that we learn them? Does their source make a difference when considering the way they can possibly affect knowledge claims?

3. Lorraine Code says that in the statement "S knows that p" the sex of S is epistemologically significant. Are cases when p involves "love" and "marriage" prime examples of when the sex of S would significantly alter the knowledge claim?

4. Aside from marriage and commitment, are there other things toward which males and females arguably have a fundamentally different epistemological attitudes? What are they? Defend your position.

5. Consider the following sets of dialogue from the film:

    LORIE   "He always forgets the details. You know, all he remembers is the end result. I remember every moment we spent together. You know, all of the little things. Like the time I fixed his carburetor—he was so impressed. Or the time that he broke the window. Do you remember Mrs. Spepk, you had to call the repairman?"

    MRS. SPEPK   "The window—what window? . . . Oh, yeah, I remember."

    LORIE   "I'm sure he doesn't."

    MRS. SPEPK   "Guess you won't be breaking any more windows around here."

    DAN   "What do you mean?"

    MRS. SPEPK   "Remember the window you broke?"

    DAN   "Yeah, but I didn't break that window."

    MRS. SPEPK   "Yes, you did. Don't you remember?"

    DAN   "Mrs. Spepk, I did not break that window. Lorie broke that window."

    We never find out who broke the window, just that Lorie and Dan have radically different knowledge of the event. Do these two scenes establish deep epistemological differences between Lorie and Dan in particular? Do they establish deep epistemological differences between men and women in general? Why or why not?

ALISON M. JAGGAR

EMOTION IN FEMINIST EPISTEMOLOGY

A lison M. Jaggar argues that emotion is an important element in any adequate theory of knowledge. Her view, however, goes against the Western philosophical tradition, which has typically regarded emotion as distorting or impeding knowledge. Traditionally, reason is regarded as the path to knowledge, whereas emotion subverts knowledge. This position is reflected in the "myth of dispassionate investigation," the position that scientific inquiry is not contaminated by "subjective" values and emotions. "Like all myths," says Jaggar, "it is a form of ideology that fulfills certain social and political functions." Its function, argues Jaggar, is "to bolster the epistemic authority of the currently dominant groups, composed largely of white men, and to discredit the observations and claims of the currently subordinate groups including, of course, the observations and claims of many people of color and women." The alleged epistemic authority of the dominant group (primarily white men) is also used to justify their political authority and to discredit the political authority of the subordinate group (primarily people of color and women).

Furthermore, these ideologies function to validate particular emotional responses to societal events by dubbing them as conventional and expected, and to invalidate others by framing them as "outlaw emotions." The distinguishing mark of a so-called outlaw emotion is its incompatibility with the perceptions and values of the dominant group, and while not all outlaw emotions are feminist emotions, some of them are. "Outlaw emotions may," writes Jaggar, "enable us to perceive the world differently from its portrayal in conventional descriptions." Such "conventionally inexplicable emotions," continues Jaggar, "particularly though not exclusively those experienced by women, may lead us to make subversive observations that challenge dominant conceptions of the status quo." Jaggar concludes that outlaw emotions thus have the potential to make a valuable contribution to knowledge.

Alison Jaggar received her Ph.D. from the State University of New York at Buffalo in 1970 and is currently a professor of philosophy and women's studies at the University of Colorado. Her books include *Feminist Politics and Human Nature* (1983), *Companion to Feminist Philosophy* (co-edited with Iris M. Young, 1998), *Feminist Frameworks: Alternative Theoretical Accounts of the Relations Between Women and Men* (co-edited with Paula Rothenberg Struhl, 1978, 1984, 1993), *Gender/Body/Knowledge: Feminist Reconstructions of Being and Knowing* (co-edited with Susan Bordo, 1989), and *Living with Contradictions: Controversies in Feminist Social Ethics* (ed., 1994). The following selection is from her article "Love and Knowledge: Emotion in Feminist Epistemology" (1989).

INTRODUCTION

Within the Western philosophical tradition, emotions have usually been considered potentially or actually subversive of knowledge. From Plato until the present, with a few notable exceptions, reason rather than emotion has been regarded as the indispensable faculty for acquiring knowledge.

Typically, although again not invariably, the rational has been contrasted with the emotional, and this contrasted pair then often linked with other dichotomies. Not only has reason been contrasted with emotion, but it has also been associated with the mental, the cultural, the universal, the public and the male, whereas emotion has been associated with the irrational, the physical, the natural, the particular, the private and, of course, the female.

Although Western epistemology has tended to give pride of place to reason rather than emotion, it has not always excluded emotion completely from the realm of reason. In the *Phaedrus*, Plato portrayed emotions, such as anger or curiosity, as irrational urges (horses) that must always be controlled by reason (the charioteer). On this model, the emotions were not seen as needing to be totally suppressed, but rather as needing direction by reason: for example, in a genuinely threatening situation, it was thought not only irrational but foolhardy not to be afraid. The split between reason and emotion was not absolute, therefore, for the Greeks. Instead, the emotions were thought of as providing indispensable motive power that needed to be channelled appropriately. Without horses, after all, the skill of the charioteer would be worthless.

The contrast between reason and emotion was sharpened in the seventeenth century by redefining reason as a purely instrumental faculty. For both the Greeks and the medieval philosophers, reason had been linked with value in so far as reason provided access to the objective structure or order of reality, seen as simultaneously natural and morally justified. With the rise of modern science, however, the realms of nature and value were separated: nature was stripped of value and reconceptualized as an inanimate mechanism of no intrinsic worth. Values were relocated in human beings, rooted in their preferences and emotional responses. The separation of supposedly natural fact from human value meant that reason, if it were to provide trustworthy insight into reality, had to be uncontaminated by or abstracted from value. Increasingly, therefore, though never universally, reason was reconceptualized as the ability to make valid inferences from premises established elsewhere, the ability to calculate means but not to determine ends. The validity of logical inferences was thought independent of human attitudes and preferences; this was now the sense in which reason was taken to be objective and universal.

The modern redefinition of rationality required a corresponding reconceptualization of emotion. This was achieved by portraying emotions as

nonrational and often irrational urges that regularly swept the body, rather as a storm sweeps over the land. The common way of referring to the emotions as the "passions" emphasized that emotions happened to or were imposed upon an individual, something she suffered rather than something she did.

The epistemology associated with this new ontology rehabilitated sensory perception that, like emotion, typically had been suspected or even discounted by the Western tradition as a reliable source of knowledge. British empiricism, succeeded in the nineteenth century by positivism, took its epistemological task to be the formulation of rules of inference that would guarantee the derivation of certain knowledge from the "raw data" supposedly given directly to the senses. Empirical testability became accepted as the hallmark of natural science; this, in turn, was viewed as the paradigm of genuine knowledge. Often epistemology was equated with the philosophy of science, and the dominant methodology of positivism prescribed that truly scientific knowledge must be capable of intersubjective verification. Because values and emotions had been defined as variable and idiosyncratic, positivism stipulated that trustworthy knowledge could be established only by methods that neutralized the values and emotions of individual scientists.

Recent approaches to epistemology have challenged some fundamental assumptions of the positivist epistemological model. . . . However, few challenges have been raised thus far to the purported gap between emotion and knowledge. In this paper, I wish to begin bridging this gap through the suggestion that emotions may be helpful and even necessary rather than inimical to the construction of knowledge. . . .

THE MYTH OF DISPASSIONATE INVESTIGATION

. . . [The] derogatory Western attitude toward emotion, like the earlier Western contempt for sensory observation, fails to recognize that emotion, like sensory perception, is necessary to human survival. Emotions prompt us to act appropriately, to approach some people and situations and to avoid others, to caress or cuddle, fight or flee. Without emotion, human life would be unthinkable. Moreover, emotions have an intrinsic as well as an instrumental value. Although not all emotions are enjoyable or even justifiable, as we shall see, life without any emotion would be life without any meaning.

Within the context of Western culture, however, people have often been encouraged to control or even suppress their emotions. Consequently, it is not unusual for people to be unaware of their emotional state or to deny it to themselves and others. This lack of awareness, especially combined with a neopositivist understanding of emotion that construes it as just a feeling of which one is aware, lends plausibility to the myth of dispassionate investigation. But lack of awareness of emotions certainly does not mean that emotions are not present subconsciously or unconsciously, or that subterranean emotions do not exert a continuing influence on people's articulated values and observations, thoughts, and actions.

Within the positivist tradition, the influence of emotion is usually seen only as distorting or impeding observation or knowledge. Certainly it is true that contempt, disgust, shame, revulsion or fear may inhibit investigation of certain situations or phenomena. Furiously angry or extremely sad people often seem quite unaware of their surroundings or even of their own conditions; they may fail to hear or may systematically misinterpret what other people say. People in love are notoriously oblivious to many aspects of the situation around them.

In spite of these examples, however, positivist epistemology recognizes that the role of emotion in the construction of knowledge is not invariably deleterious and that emotions may make a valuable contribution to knowledge. But the positivist tradition will allow emotion to play only the role of suggesting hypotheses for investigation. Emotions are allowed this because the so-called logic of discovery sets no limits on the idiosyncratic methods that investigators may use for generating hypotheses.

When hypotheses are to be tested, however, positivist epistemology imposes the much stricter logic of justification. The core of this logic is replicability, a criterion believed capable of eliminating or cancelling out what are conceptualized as emotional as well as evaluative biases on the part of individual investigators. The conclusions of Western science thus are presumed "objective," precisely in the sense that they are uncontaminated by the supposedly "subjective" values and emotions that might bias individual investigators.

But if . . . the positivist distinction between discovery and justification is not viable, then such a distinction is incapable of filtering out values in science. For example, although such a split, when built into the Western scientific method, is generally successful in neutralizing the idiosyncratic or unconventional values of individual investigators, it has been argued that it does not, indeed, cannot, eliminate generally accepted social values. These values are implicit in the identification of the problems that are considered worthy of investigation, in the selection of the hypotheses that are considered worthy of testing and in the solutions to the problems that are considered worthy of acceptance. The science of past centuries provides ample evidence of the influence of prevailing social values, whether seventeenth-century atomistic physics or nineteenth-century competitive interpretations of natural selection.

Positivism views values and emotions as alien invaders that must be repelled by a stricter application of the scientific method. If the foregoing claims are correct, however, the scientific method [itself incorporates] values and emotions. Moreover, such an incorporation seems a necessary feature of all knowledge and conceptions of knowledge. Therefore, rather than repressing emotion in epistemology it is necessary to rethink the relation between knowledge and emotion and construct conceptual models that demonstrate the mutually constitutive rather than oppositional relation between reason and emotion. Far from precluding the possibility of reliable knowledge, emotion as well as value must be shown as necessary to such knowledge. Despite its classical antecedents and as in the ideal of disinterested inquiry, the ideal of dispassionate inquiry is an impossible dream, but a dream nonetheless or perhaps a myth that has exerted enormous influence on Western epistemology. Like all myths, it is a form of ideology that fulfils certain social and political functions.

THE IDEOLOGICAL FUNCTION OF THE MYTH

So far, I have spoken very generally of people and their emotions, as though everyone experienced similar emotions and dealt with them in similar ways. It is an axiom of feminist theory, however, that all generalizations about "people" are suspect. The divisions in our society are so deep, particularly the divisions of race, class, and gender, that many feminist theorists would claim that talk about people in general is ideologically dangerous because such talk obscures the fact that no one is simply a person but instead is constituted fundamentally by race, class, and gender. Race, class, and gender shape every aspect of our lives, and our emotional constitution is not excluded. Recognizing this helps us to see more clearly the political functions of the myth of the dispassionate investigator.

Feminist theorists have pointed out that the Western tradition has not seen everyone as equally emotional. Instead, reason has been associated with members of dominant political, social, and cultural groups and emotion with members of subordinate groups. Prominent among those subordinate groups in our society are people of color, except for supposedly "inscrutable Orientals," and women.

Although the emotionality of women is a familiar cultural stereotype, its grounding is quite shaky. Women appear to be more emotional than men because they, along with some groups of people of color, are permitted and even required to express emotion more openly. In contemporary Western culture, emotionally inexpressive women are suspect as not being real women, whereas men who express their emotions freely are suspected of being homosexual or in some other way deviant from the masculine ideal. Modern Western men, in contrast with Shakespeare's heroes, for instance, are required to present a facade of coolness, lack of excitement, even boredom, to express emotion only rarely and then for relatively trivial events, such as sporting occasions, where the emotions expressed are acknowledged to be dramatized and so are not taken entirely seriously. Thus, women in our society form the main group allowed or even expected to express emotion. A woman may cry in the face of disaster, and a man of color may gesticulate, but a white man merely sets his jaw.

White men's control of their emotional expression may go to the extremes of repressing their emotions, failing to develop emotionally or even losing the capacity to experience many emotions. Not uncommonly, these men are unable to identify what they are feeling, and even they may be surprised, on occasion, by their own apparent lack of emotional response to a situation, such as a death, where emotional reaction is perceived to be appropriate. . . . Paradoxically, men's lacking awareness of their own emotional responses frequently results in their being more influenced by emotion rather than less.

Although there is no reason to suppose that the thoughts and actions of women are any more influenced by emotion than the thoughts and actions of men, the stereotypes of cool men and emotional women continue to flourish because they are confirmed by an uncritical daily experience. In these circumstances, where there is a differential assignment of reason and emotion, it is easy to see the ideological function of the myth of the dispassionate investigator. It functions, obviously, to bolster the epistemic authority of the currently dominant groups, composed largely of white men, and to discredit the observations and claims of the currently subordinate groups including, of course, the observations and claims of many people of color and women. The more forcefully and vehemently the latter groups express their observations and claims, the more emotional they appear and so the more easily they are discredited. The alleged epistemic authority of the dominant groups then justifies their political authority.

The previous section of this paper argued that dispassionate inquiry was a myth. This section has shown that the myth promotes a conception of epistemological justification vindicating the silencing of those, especially women, who are defined culturally as the bearers of emotion and so are perceived as more "subjective," biased and irrational. In our present social context, therefore, the ideal of the dispassionate investigator is a classist, racist, and especially masculinist myth.

EMOTIONAL HEGEMONY AND EMOTIONAL SUBVERSION

. . . Within a hierarchical society, the norms and values that predominate tend to serve the interests of the dominant groups. Within a capitalist, white suprematist, and male-dominant society, the predominant values will tend to be those that serve the interests of rich white men.

Consequently, we are all likely to develop an emotional constitution that is quite inappropriate for feminism. Whatever our color, we are likely to feel what Irving Thalberg* has called "visceral racism"; whatever our sexual orientation, we are likely to be homophobic; whatever our class, we are likely to be at least somewhat ambitious and competitive; whatever our sex, we are likely to feel contempt for women. Such emotional responses may be rooted in us so deeply that they are relatively impervious to intellectual argument and may recur even when we pay lip service to changed intellectual convictions.

By forming our emotional constitution in particular ways, our society helps to ensure its own perpetuation. The dominant values are implicit in responses taken to be precultural or acultural, our so-called gut responses. Not only do these conservative responses hamper and disrupt our attempts to live in or prefigure alternative social forms but also, and in so far as we take them to be natural responses, they blinker us theoretically. For instance, they limit our capacity for outrage; they either prevent us from despising or encourage us to despise; they lend plausibility to the belief that greed and domination are inevitable human motivations; in sum, they blind us to the possibility of alternative ways of living.

This picture may seem at first to support the positivist claim that the intrusion of emotion only disrupts the process of seeking knowledge and distorts the results of that process. The picture, however, is not complete; it ignores the fact that people do not always experience the conventionally acceptable emotions. They may feel satisfaction rather than embarrassment when their leaders make fools of themselves. They may feel resentment rather than gratitude for welfare payments and hand-me-downs. They may be attracted to forbidden modes of sexual expression. They may feel revulsion for socially sanctioned ways of treating children or animals. In other words, the hegemony that our society exercises over people's emotional constitution is not total.

People who experience conventionally unacceptable, or what I call "outlaw," emotions often are subordinated individuals who pay a disproportionately high price for maintaining the status quo. The social situation of such people makes them unable to experience the conventionally prescribed emotions: for instance, people of color are more likely to experience anger than amusement when a racist joke is recounted, and women subjected to male sexual banter are less likely to be flattered than uncomfortable or even afraid.

When unconventional emotional responses are experienced by isolated individuals, those concerned may be confused, unable to name their experience; they may even doubt their own sanity. Women may come to believe that they are "emotionally disturbed" and that the embarrassment or fear aroused in them by male sexual innuendo is prudery or paranoia. When certain emotions are shared or validated by others, however, the basis exists for forming a subculture defined by perceptions, norms, and values that systematically oppose the prevailing perceptions, norms, and values. By constituting the basis for such a subculture, outlaw emotions may be politically because epistemologically subversive.

Outlaw emotions are distinguished by their incompatibility with the dominant perceptions and values, and some, though certainly not all, of these outlaw emotions are potentially or actually feminist emotions. Emotions become feminist when they incorporate feminist perceptions and values, just as emotions are sexist or racist when they incorporate sexist or racist perceptions and values. For example, anger becomes feminist anger when it involves the perception that the persistent importuning endured by one woman is a single instance of a widespread pattern of sexual harassment, and pride becomes feminist pride when it is evoked by realizing that a certain person's achievement was possible only because that individual overcame specifically gendered obstacles to success. . . .

---

* Irving Grant Thalberg (1899–1936), an American film producer, was known for his ability to select excellent scripts and actors as well as his high production standards. Called the "Boy Wonder," at the age of twenty-five Thalberg became the number-two executive under Louis B. Mayer at MGM, when it was the biggest movie studio in the world. In his honor, the Irving B. Thalberg Award is presented by the Motion Picture Academy each year for excellence in film production.—Ed.

OUTLAW EMOTIONS AND FEMINIST THEORY

. . . Outlaw emotions may . . . enable us to perceive the world differently from its portrayal in conventional descriptions. They may provide the first indications that something is wrong with the way alleged facts have been constructed, with accepted understandings of how things are. Conventionally unexpected or inappropriate emotions may precede our conscious recognition that accepted descriptions and justifications often conceal as much as reveal the prevailing state of affairs. Only when we reflect on our initially puzzling irritability, revulsion, anger or fear may we bring to consciousness our "gut-level" awareness that we are in a situation of coercion, cruelty, injustice or danger. Thus, conventionally inexplicable emotions, particularly though not exclusively those experienced by women, may lead us to make subversive observations that challenge dominant conceptions of the status quo. They may help us to realize that what are taken generally to be facts have been constructed in a way that obscures the reality of subordinated people, especially women's reality.

But why should we trust the emotional responses of women and other subordinated groups? How can we determine which outlaw emotions are to be endorsed or encouraged and which rejected? In what sense can we say that some emotional responses are more appropriate than others? What reason is there for supposing that certain alternative perceptions of the world, perceptions informed by outlaw emotions, are to be preferred to perceptions informed by conventional emotions? Here I can indicate only the general direction of an answer, whose full elaboration must await another occasion.

I suggest that emotions are appropriate if they are characteristic of a society in which all humans (and perhaps some nonhuman life too) thrive, or if they are conducive to establishing such a society. For instance, it is appropriate to feel joy when we are developing or exercising our creative powers, and it is appropriate to feel anger and perhaps disgust in those situations where humans are denied their full creativity or freedom. Similarly, it is appropriate to feel fear if those capacities are threatened in us.

This suggestion, obviously, is extremely vague and may even verge on the tautologous. How can we apply it in situations where there is disagreement over what is or is not disgusting or exhilarating or unjust? Here I appeal to a claim for which I have argued elsewhere: the perspective on reality that is available from the standpoint of the subordinated, which in part at least is the standpoint of women, is a perspective that offers a less partial and distorted and therefore more reliable view. Subordinated people have a kind of epistemological privilege in so far as they have easier access to this standpoint and therefore a better chance of ascertaining the possible beginnings of a society in which all could thrive. For this reason, I would claim that the emotional responses of subordinated people in general, and often of women in particular, are more likely to be appropriate than the emotional responses of the dominant class. That is, they are more likely to incorporate reliable appraisals of situations.

Even in contemporary science, where the ideology of dispassionate inquiry is almost overwhelming, it is possible to discover a few examples that seem to support the claim that certain emotions are more appropriate than others in both a moral and epistemological sense. For instance, Hilary Rose claims that women's practice of caring, even though warped by its containment in the alienated context of a coercive sexual division of labor, has nevertheless generated more accurate and less oppressive understandings of women's bodily functions, such as menstruation. Certain emotions may be both morally appropriate and epistemologically advantageous in approaching the nonhuman and even the inanimate world. Jane Goodall's scientific contribution to our understanding of chimpanzee behavior seems to have been made possible only by her amazing empathy with or even love for these animals. In her study of Barbara McClintock, Evelyn Fox Keller describes McClintock's relation to the objects of her research—grains of maize and their genetic properties—as a relation of affection, empathy and "the highest form of love: love that allows for intimacy without the annihilation of difference." She notes that McClintock's "vocabulary is consistently a vocabulary of affection, of kinship, of empathy." Examples like these prompt Hilary Rose to assert that a feminist science of nature needs to draw on heart as well as hand and brain.

SOME IMPLICATIONS OF RECOGNIZING THE EPISTEMIC
POTENTIAL OF EMOTION

Accepting that appropriate emotions are indispensable to reliable knowledge does not mean, of course, that uncritical feeling may be substituted for supposedly dispassionate investigation. Nor does it mean that the emotional responses of women and other members of the underclass are to be trusted without question. Although our emotions are epistemologically indispensable, they are not epistemologically indisputable. Like all our faculties, they may be misleading, and their data, like all data, are always subject to reinterpretation and revision. Because emotions are not presocial, physiological responses to unequivocal situations, they are open to challenge on various grounds. They may be dishonest or self-deceptive, they may incorporate inaccurate or partial perceptions, or they may be constituted by oppressive values. Accepting the indispensability of appropriate emotions to knowledge means no more (and no less) than that discordant emotions should be attended to seriously and respectfully rather than condemned, ignored, discounted or suppressed.

Just as appropriate emotions may contribute to the development of knowledge, so the growth of knowledge may contribute to the development of appropriate emotions. For instance, the powerful insights of feminist theory often stimulate new emotional responses to past and present situations. Inevitably, our emotions are affected by the knowledge that the women on our faculty are paid systematically less than the men, that one girl in four is subjected to sexual abuse from heterosexual men in her own family, and that few women reach orgasm in heterosexual intercourse. We are likely to feel different emotions toward older women or people of color as we re-evaluate our standards of sexual attractiveness or acknowledge that black is beautiful. The new emotions evoked by feminist insights are likely in turn to stimulate further feminist observations and insights, and these may generate new directions in both theory and political practice. There is a continuous feedback loop between our emotional constitution and our theorizing such that each continually modifies the other and is in principle inseparable from it.

The ease and speed with which we can re-educate our emotions is unfortunately not great. Emotions are only partially within our control as individuals. Although affected by new information, they are habitual responses not quickly unlearned. Even when we come to believe consciously that our fear or shame or revulsion is unwarranted, we may still continue to experience emotions inconsistent with our conscious politics. We may still continue to be anxious for male approval, competitive with our comrades and sisters, and possessive with our lovers. These unwelcome, because apparently inappropriate emotions, should not be suppressed or denied; instead, they should be acknowledged and subjected to critical scrutiny. The persistence of such recalcitrant emotions probably demonstrates how fundamentally we have been constituted by the dominant world view, but it may also indicate superficiality or other inadequacy in our emerging theory and politics. We can only start from where we are—beings who have been created in a cruelly racist, capitalist and male-dominated society that has shaped our bodies and our minds, our perceptions, our values and our emotions, our language, and our systems of knowledge.

The alternative epistemological models that I suggest would display the continuous interaction between how we understand the world and who we are as people. They would show how our emotional responses to the world change as we conceptualize it differently and how our changing emotional responses then stimulate us to new insights. They would demonstrate the need for theory to be self-reflexive, to focus not only on the outer world but also on ourselves and our relation to that world, to examine critically our social location, our actions, our values, our perceptions, and our emotions. The models would also show how feminist and other critical social theories are indispensable psychotherapeutic tools because they provide some insights necessary to a full understanding of our emotional constitution. Thus, the models would explain how the reconstruction of knowledge is inseparable from the reconstruction of ourselves. . . .

We can now see that women's subversive insights owe much to women's outlaw emotions, themselves appropriate responses to the situations of women's subordination. In addition to their propensity to experience outlaw emotions, at least on some level, women are relatively adept at identifying such emotions, in themselves and others, in part because of their social responsibility for caretaking, including emotional nurturance. It is true that women, like all subordinated peoples, especially those who must live in close proximity with their masters, often engage in emotional deception and even self-deception as the price of their survival. Even so, women may be less likely than other subordinated groups to engage in denial or suppression of outlaw emotions. Women's work of emotional nurturance has required them to develop a special acuity in recognizing hidden emotions and in understanding the genesis of those emotions. This emotional acumen can now be recognized as a skill in political analysis and validated as giving women a special advantage both in understanding the mechanisms of domination and in envisioning freer ways to live.

Conclusion

The claim that emotion is vital to systematic knowledge is only the most obvious contrast between the conception of theoretical investigation that I have sketched here and the conception provided by positivism. For instance, the alternative approach emphasizes that what we identify as emotion is a conceptual abstraction from a complex process of human activity that also involves acting, sensing, and evaluating. This proposed account of theoretical construction demonstrates the simultaneous necessity for and interdependence of faculties that our culture has abstracted and separated from each other: emotion and reason, evaluation and perception, observation and action. The model of knowing suggested here is nonhierarchical and antifoundationalist; instead, it is appropriately symbolized by the radical feminist metaphor of the upward spiral. Emotions are neither more basic than observation, reason or action in building theory, nor secondary to them. Each of these human faculties reflects an aspect of human knowing inseparable from the other aspects. Thus, to borrow a famous phrase from a Marxian context, the development of each of these faculties is a necessary condition for the development of all.

In conclusion, it is interesting to note that acknowledging the importance of emotion for knowledge is not an entirely novel suggestion within the Western epistemological tradition. That archrationalist, Plato himself, came to accept in the end that knowledge required a (very purified form of) love. It may be no accident that in the *Symposium* Socrates learns this lesson from Diotima, the wise woman!

DISCUSSION QUESTIONS

1. Jaggar argues that emotion is an important element in any adequate theory of knowledge. Do you agree with her? Why or why not?

2. Jaggar says that the distinguishing mark of an outlaw emotion is its incompatibility with the perceptions and values of the dominant group. Propose some examples of outlaw emotions. Are these outlaw emotions feminist emotions as well? Do you think the outlaw emotions you have proposed will "enable us to perceive the world differently from its portrayal in conventional descriptions"? Why or why not?

3. What is the "myth of dispassionate investigation"? Why does Jaggar believe that "it is a form of ideology that fulfills certain social and political functions"? Do you agree with her? Why or why not?

4. Jaggar says that "race, class, and gender shape every aspect of our lives, and our emotional constitution is not excluded." Give some examples of the way race, class, and gender shape our emotional constitution.

5. What is "epistemological privilege"? Do you agree with Jaggar's general position on the "politics" of knowledge? Do Jaggar's views on politics, emotion, and knowledge alter your opinion of the epistemologies of Descartes, Locke, Hume, and Kant in any way? If so, how?

Gaslight
[USA 1944] 1 hour, 53 minutes
Directed by George Cukor

When Paula Anton (Ingrid Bergman), a beautiful but naïve woman living in Victorian London, hears footsteps in the house of her murdered aunt, she starts to believe the lies told by her mentally abusive husband, Gregory (Charles Boyer). Paula had fled the house years ago to escape the memories of her aunt's tragic death but returned after meeting and marrying Gregory. After Gregory moves all of her aunt's belongings into the attic, he begins to accuse her of losing track of things and hallucinating. However, Paula is unaware that Gregory has been meticulously plotting her mental breakdown in order to finish a job he started long ago. His obsession with the aunt's diamonds drove him to break into the aunt's house and murder her. Paula, a young girl at the time, heard her aunt's screams and came downstairs, foiling Gregory's plans. Gregory worked for years to carry out his scheme to steal the diamonds, which involved marrying Paula and gaining access to the house while leaving Paula to question her own sanity.

The film's title has two meanings: (1) the frequent dimming and flickering of the gaslights and (2) "to gaslight" someone—to deliberately drive someone insane by manipulating the environment. George Cukor's version of *Gaslight* is a remake of a film that came out five years earlier in Great Britain, and was released in the United States as both *Gaslight* and *Angel Street* (1940). Both the American and British versions were adapted from Patrick Hamilton's play *Angel Street*, which was successfully produced both in London and on Broadway.

DISCUSSION QUESTIONS

1. Descartes tells us that our senses can deceive us but generally give us correct information. Are Paula's troubles in *Gaslight* an example of what happens when we trust our senses too much?
2. Are Paula's problems brought on by her inability to harness enough skepticism about the world around her? Or does she exhibit a healthy degree of skepticism?
3. At the end of the film, Paula says, "I couldn't have dreamed it. Did I dream? I dreamed all that happened." Why might Paula think it was all a dream? How does she know that it is not one?
4. How is Gregory's deception of Paula like the deception of the prisoners in Plato's cave?
5. Imagine Berkeley playing the role of Paula in this film. Do you think that someone who believed that to be is to be perceived would have been easier or more difficult for Gregory to drive to a mental breakdown? Defend your view.
6. Discuss what happens in *Gaslight* in terms of Jaggar's notion of epistemic authority. Could Gregory's ability to deceive Paula be linked to the fact that he is male and Paula is female?
7. Paula knows with certainty that the gaslights in her aunt's house are flickering because she has sensory experience of the event. However, Paula does not have sensory experience of the cause of the flickering. Why does Paula believe that the flickering is caused by the ghost of her dead aunt as opposed to some natural explanation such as gas being used in a different part of the house? Do Paula's beliefs concerning the cause of the flickering gaslights reveal anything about how in general we form beliefs? What role, for example, do you believe our worldview plays in how we interpret facts? Discuss.

2.2   WHAT IS TRUTH?

RYŌNOSUKE AKUTAGAWA

IN A GROVE

Ryōnosuke Akutagawa's "In a Grove" is the story of events surrounding the death of a man as recounted by seven different persons. The testimonies range from various accounts of the man's murder to the dead man himself (through a medium) claiming that he committed suicide. Which testimony, if any, is true? On what basis do we determine that one or none or a combination of the testimonies is true? Akutagawa's short story tests our beliefs about truth.

On the face of it, Akutagawa's story suggests that there are as many versions of the truth as there are persons who report it. This position is called *epistemological relativism*, the view that all truth is relative. It is an application of a more general doctrine called *relativism*, the view that no absolutes exist and that human judgment is always conditioned by a number of factors including our personal biases and the culture in which we live.

Ryōnosuke Akutagawa (1892–1927) was born in Tokyo. Shortly after he was born, his mother went insane, and his father, Binzo Shinhara, was not able to care for his son. Akutagawa was adopted by his uncle, Michiaki Akutagawa, and assumed his uncle's surname. In 1913, he entered Tokyo Imperial University, where he studied English, co-founded the literary magazine *Shin Shicho*, and began to write short stories. He read authors such as August Strindberg, Prosper Mérimée, Nietzsche, Dostoyevsky, Charles-Pierre Baudelaire, and Leo Tolstoy in English translation.

Akutagawa declined positions at universities in Tokyo and Kyoto, choosing instead to work as a newspaper editor and English teacher. Most of his stories were written between 1917 and 1927, the year of his suicide. He was only thirty-five years of age at the time of his suicide and suffered from visual hallucinations. In his suicide note, "A Note to a Certain Old Friend," he wrote, "The world I am now in is one of diseased nerves, lucid as ice. Such voluntary death must give us peace, if not happiness. Now that I am ready, I find nature more beautiful than ever, paradoxical as this may sound. I have seen, loved, and understood more than others." His stories, which often deal with macabre themes, are noted for the accuracy of their expression and their exploration of the dark undercurrents of the mind. Several of his 150 stories were made into films, the most famous of which is *Rashomon*, Akira Kurosawa's film (see the film box) based on two of Akutagawa's stories: "Rashomon" (1915) and "In a Grove" ("*Yabu no naka*," 1922).

THE TESTIMONY OF A WOODCUTTER QUESTIONED
BY A HIGH POLICE COMMISSIONER

Yes, sir. Certainly, it was I who found the body. This morning, as usual, I went to cut my daily quota of cedars, when I found the body in a grove in a hollow in the mountains. The exact location?

About 150 meters off the Yamashina stage road. It's an out-of-the-way grove of bamboo and cedars.

The body was lying flat on its back dressed in a bluish silk kimono and a wrinkled head-dress of the Kyoto style. A single sword-stroke had pierced the breast. The fallen bamboo-blades around it were stained with bloody blossoms. No, the blood was no longer running. The wound had dried up, I believe. And also, a gadfly was stuck fast there, hardly noticing my footsteps.

You ask me if I saw a sword or any such thing?

No, nothing, sir. I found only a rope at the root of a cedar near by. And . . . well, in addition to a rope, I found a comb. That was all. Apparently he must have made a battle of it before he was murdered, because the grass and fallen bamboo-blades had been trampled down all around.

"A horse was near by?"

No, sir. It's hard enough for a man to enter, let alone a horse.

THE TESTIMONY OF A TRAVELLING BUDDHIST PRIEST QUESTIONED BY A HIGH POLICE COMMISSIONER

The time? Certainly, it was about noon yesterday, sir. The unfortunate man was on the road from Sekiyama to Yamashina. He was walking toward Sekiyama with a woman accompanying him on horseback, who I have since learned was his wife. A scarf hanging from her head hid her face from view. All I saw was the color of her clothes, a lilac-colored suit. Her horse was a sorrel with a fine mane. The lady's height? Oh, about four feet five inches. Since I am a Buddhist priest, I took little notice about her details. Well, the man was armed with a sword as well as a bow and arrows. And I remember that he carried some twenty odd arrows in his quiver.

Little did I expect that he would meet such a fate. Truly human life is as evanescent as the morning dew or a flash of lightning. My words are inadequate to express my sympathy for him.

THE TESTIMONY OF A POLICEMAN QUESTIONED BY A HIGH POLICE COMMISSIONER

The man that I arrested? He is a notorious brigand called Tajomaru. When I arrested him, he had fallen off his horse. He was groaning on the bridge at Awataguchi. The time? It was in the early hours of last night. For the record, I might say that the other day I tried to arrest him, but unfortunately he escaped. He was wearing a dark blue silk kimono and a large plain sword. And, as you see, he got a bow and arrows somewhere. You say that this bow and these arrows look like the ones owned by the dead man? Then Tajomaru must be the murderer. The bow wound with leather strips, the black lacquered quiver, the seventeen arrows with hawk feathers—these were all in his possession I believe. Yes, sir, the horse is, as you say, a sorrel with a fine mane. A little beyond the stone bridge I found the horse grazing by the roadside, with his long rein dangling. Surely there is some providence in his having been thrown by the horse.

Of all the robbers prowling around Kyoto, this Tajomaru has given the most grief to the women in town. Last autumn a wife who came to the mountain back of the Pindora of the Toribe Temple, presumably to pay a visit, was murdered, along with a girl. It has been suspected that it was his doing. If this criminal murdered the man, you cannot tell what he may have done with the man's wife. May it please your honor to look into this problem as well.

THE TESTIMONY OF AN OLD WOMAN QUESTIONED BY A HIGH POLICE COMMISSIONER

Yes, sir, the corpse is the man who married my daughter. He does not come from Kyoto. He was a samurai in the town of Kokufu in the province of Wakasa. His name was Kanazawa no Takehiko, and his age was twenty-six. He was of a gentle disposition, so I am sure he did nothing to provoke the anger of others.

My daughter? Her name is Masago, and her age is nineteen. She is a spirited, fun-loving girl, but I am sure she has never known any man except Takehiko. She has a small, oval, dark-complected face with a mole at the corner of her left eye.

Yesterday Takehiko left for Wakasa with my daughter. What bad luck it is that things should have come to such a sad end! What has become of my daughter? I am resigned to giving up my son-in-law as lost, but the fate of my daughter worries me sick. For heaven's sake leave no stone unturned to find her. I hate that robber Tajomaru, or whatever his name is. Not only my son-in-law, but my daughter . . . (Her later words were drowned in tears.)

TAJOMARU'S CONFESSION

I killed him, but not her. Where's she gone? I can't tell. Oh, wait a minute. No torture can make me confess what I don't know. Now things have come to such a head, I won't keep anything from you.

Yesterday a little past noon I met that couple. Just then a puff of wind blew, and raised her hanging scarf, so that I caught a glimpse of her face. Instantly it was again covered from my view. That may have been one reason; she looked like a Bodhisattva. At that moment I made up my mind to capture her even if I had to kill her man.

Why? To me killing isn't a matter of such great consequence as you might think. When a woman is captured, her man has to be killed anyway. In killing, I use the sword I wear at my side. Am I the only one who kills people? You, you don't use your swords. You kill people with your power, with your money. Sometimes you kill them on the pretext of working for their good. It's true they don't bleed. They are in the best of health, but all the same you've killed them. It's hard to say who is a greater sinner, you or me. (An ironical smile.)

But it would be good if I could capture a woman without killing her man. So, I made up my mind to capture her, and do my best not to kill him. But it's out of the question on the Yamashina stage road. So I managed to lure the couple into the mountains.

It was quite easy. I became their traveling companion, and I told them there was an old mound in the mountain over there, and that I had dug it open and found many mirrors and swords. I went on to tell them I'd buried the things in a grove behind the mountain, and that I'd like to sell them at a low price to anyone who would care to have them. Then . . . you see, isn't greed terrible? He was beginning to be moved by my talk before he knew it. In less than half an hour they were driving their horse toward the mountain with me.

When he came in front of the grove, I told them that the treasures were buried in it, and I asked them to come and see. The man had no objection—he was blinded by greed. The woman said she would wait on horseback. It was natural for her to say so, at the sight of a thick grove. To tell you the truth, my plan worked just as I wished, so I went into the grove with him, leaving her behind alone.

The grove is only bamboo for some distance. About fifty yards ahead there's a rather open clump of cedars. It was a convenient spot for my purpose. Pushing my way through the grove, I told him a plausible lie that the treasures were buried under the cedars. When I told him this, he pushed his laborious way toward the slender cedar visible through the grove. After a while the bamboo thinned out, and we came to where a number of cedars grew in a row. As soon as we got there, I seized him from behind. Because he was a trained, sword-bearing warrior, he was quite strong, but he was taken by surprise, so there was no help for him. I soon tied him up to the root of a cedar. Where did I get a rope? Thank heaven, being a robber, I had a rope with me, since I might have to scale a wall at any moment. Of course it was easy to stop him from calling out by gagging his mouth with fallen bamboo leaves.

When I disposed of him, I went to his woman and asked her to come and see him, because he seemed to have been suddenly taken sick. It's needless to say that this plan also worked well. The woman, her sedge hat off, came into the depths of the grove, where I led her by the hand. The instant she caught sight of her husband, she drew a small sword. I've never seen a woman of such violent temper. If I'd been off guard, I'd have got a thrust in my side. I dodged, but she kept on slashing at me. She might have wounded me deeply or killed me. But I'm Tajomaru. I managed to strike down her small sword without drawing my own. The most spirited woman is defenseless without a weapon. At least I could satisfy my desire for her without taking her husband's life.

Yes, . . . without taking his life. I had no wish to kill him. I was about to run away from the grove, leaving the woman behind in tears, when she frantically clung to my arm. In broken fragments of words, she asked that either her husband or I die. She said it was more trying than death to have her shame known to two men. She gasped out that she wanted to be the wife of whichever survived. Then a furious desire to kill him seized me. (Gloomy excitement.)

Telling you in this way, no doubt I seem a crueler man than you. But that's because you didn't see her face. Especially her burning eyes at that moment. As I saw her eye to eye, I wanted to make her my wife even if I were to be struck by lightning. I wanted to make her my wife . . . this single desire filled my mind. This was not only lust, as you might think. At that time if I'd had no other desire than lust, I'd surely not have minded knocking her down and running away. Then I wouldn't have stained my sword with his blood. But the moment I gazed at her face in the dark grove, I decided not to leave there without killing him.

But I didn't like to resort to unfair means to kill him. I untied him and told him to cross swords with me. (The rope that was found at the root of the cedar is the rope I dropped at the time.) Furious with anger, he drew his thick sword. And quick as thought, he sprang at me ferociously, without speaking a word. I needn't tell you how our fight turned out. The twenty-third stroke . . . please remember this. I'm impressed with this fact still. Nobody under the sun has ever clashed swords with me twenty strokes. (A cheerful smile.)

When he fell, I turned toward her, lowering my blood-stained sword. But to my great astonishment she was gone. I wondered to where she had run away. I looked for her in the clump of cedars. I listened, but heard only a groaning sound from the throat of the dying man.

As soon as we started to cross swords, she may have run away through the grove to call for help. When I thought of that, I decided it was a matter of life and death to me. So, robbing him of his sword, and bow and arrows, I ran out to the mountain road. There I found her horse still grazing quietly. It would be a mere waste of words to tell you the latter details, but before I entered town I had already parted with the sword. That's all my confession. I know that my head will be hung in chains anyway, so put me down for the maximum penalty. (A defiant attitude.)

THE CONFESSION OF A WOMAN WHO HAS COME TO THE *SHIMIZU* TEMPLE

That man in the blue silk kimono, after forcing me to yield to him, laughed mockingly as he looked at my bound husband. How horrified my husband must have been! But no matter how hard he struggled in agony, the rope cut into him all the more tightly. In spite of myself I ran stumblingly

toward his side. Or rather I tried to run toward him, but the man instantly knocked me down. Just at the moment I saw an indescribable light in my husband's eyes. Something beyond expression . . . his eyes make me shudder even now. That instantaneous look of my husband, who couldn't speak a word, told me all his heart. The flash in his eyes was neither anger nor sorrow . . . only a cold light, a look of loathing. More struck by the look in his eyes than by the blow of the thief, I called out in spite of myself and fell unconscious.

In the course of time I came to, and found that the man in blue silk was gone. I saw only my husband still bound to the root of the cedar. I raised myself from the bamboo-blades with difficulty, and looked into his face; but the expression in his eyes was just the same as before.

Beneath the cold contempt in his eyes, there was hatred. Shame, grief, and anger . . . I don't know how to express my heart at that time. Reeling to my feet, I went up to my husband.

"Takejiro," I said to him, "since things have come to this pass, I cannot live with you. I'm determined to die, . . . but you must die, too. You saw my shame. I can't leave you alive as you are."

This was all I could say. Still he went on gazing at me with loathing and contempt. My heart breaking, I looked for his sword. It must have been taken by the robber. Neither his sword nor his bow and arrows were to be seen in the grove. But fortunately my small sword was lying at my feet. Raising it over head, once more I said, "Now give me your life, I'll follow you right away."

When he heard these words, he moved his lips with difficulty. Since his mouth was stuffed with leaves, of course his voice could not be heard at all. But at a glance I understood his words. Despising me, his look said only, "Kill me." Neither conscious nor unconscious, I stabbed the small sword through the lilac-colored kimono into his breast.

Again at this time I must have fainted. By the time I managed to look up, he had already breathed his last—still in bonds. A streak of sinking sunlight streamed through the clump of cedars and bamboos, and shone on his pale face. Gulping down my sobs, I untied the rope from his dead body. And . . . and what has become of me since I have no more strength to tell you. Anyway I hadn't the strength to die. I stabbed my own throat with the small sword, I threw myself into a pond at the foot of the mountain, and I tried to kill myself in many ways. Unable to end my life, I am still living in dishonor. (A lonely smile.) Worthless as I am, I must have been forsaken even by the most merciful Kwannon. I killed my own husband. I was violated by the robber. Whatever can I do? Whatever can I . . . I . . . (Gradually, violent sobbing.)

THE STORY OF THE MURDERED MAN, AS TOLD THROUGH A MEDIUM

After violating my wife, the robber, sitting there, began to speak comforting words to her. Of course I couldn't speak. My whole body was tied fast to the root of a cedar. But meanwhile I winked at her many times, as much as to say "Don't believe the robber." I wanted to convey some such meaning to her. But my wife, sitting dejectedly on the bamboo leaves, was looking hard at her lap. To all appearances, she was listening to his words. I was agonized by jealousy. In the meantime the robber went on with his clever talk, from one subject to another. The robber finally made his bold, brazen proposal. "Once your virtue is stained, you won't get along well with your husband, so won't you be my wife instead? It's my love for you that made me be violent toward you."

While the criminal talked, my wife raised her face as if in a trance. She had never looked so beautiful as at that moment. What did my beautiful wife say in answer to him while I was sitting bound there? I am lost in space, but I have never thought of her answer without burning with anger and jealousy. Truly she said, . . . "Then take me away with you wherever you go."

This is not the whole of her sin. If that were all, I would not be tormented so much in the dark. When she was going out of the grove as if in a dream, her hand in the robber's, she suddenly turned pale, and pointed at me tied to the root of the cedar, and said "Kill him! I cannot marry you as long as he lives." "Kill him!" she cried many times, as if she had gone crazy. Even now these words threaten to blow me headlong into the bottomless abyss of darkness. Has such a hateful thing come out of a human mouth ever before? Have such cursed words ever struck a human ear, even once? Even once such a . . . (A sudden cry of scorn.) At these words the robber himself turned pale. "Kill him," she cried, clinging to his arms. Looking hard at her, he answered neither yes nor no . . . but hardly had I thought about his answer before she had been knocked down into the bamboo leaves. (Again a cry of scorn.) Quietly folding his arms, he looked at me and said, "What will you do with her? Kill her or save her? You have only to nod. Kill her?" For these words alone I would like to pardon his crime.

While I hesitated, she shrieked and ran into the depths of the grove. The robber instantly snatched at her, but he failed even to grasp her sleeve.

After she ran away, he took up my sword, and my bow and arrows. With a single stroke he cut one of my bonds. I remember his mumbling, "My fate is next." Then he disappeared from the grove. All was silent after that. No, I heard someone crying. Untying the rest of my bonds, I listened carefully, and I noticed that it was my own crying. (Long silence.)

I raised my exhausted body from the root of the cedar. In front of me there was shining the small sword which my wife had dropped. I took it up and stabbed it into my breast. A bloody lump rose to my mouth, but I didn't feel any pain. When my breast grew cold, everything was as silent as the dead in their graves. What profound silence! Not a single bird-note was heard in the sky over this grave in the hollow of the mountains. Only a lonely light lingered on the cedars and mountains. By and by the light gradually grew fainter, till the cedars and bamboo were lost to view. Lying there, I was enveloped in deep silence.

Then someone crept up to me. I tried to see who it was. But darkness had already been gathering round me. Someone . . . that someone drew the small sword softly out of my breast in its invisible hand. At the same time once more blood flowed into my mouth. And once and for all I sank down into the darkness of space.

DISCUSSION QUESTIONS

1. There are seven different accounts of events associated with the death of a man in the grove. Should we find one of them more credible than the others? Why?

2. Do you think that Akutagawa's story is a defense of epistemological relativism? Why or why not?

3. What does it mean to say that a statement or testimony is "true"? What might be solid grounds for defending the truth of a statement? Explain.

4. Why does Akutagawa include the testimony of the murdered man as told through a medium? Does the fact that the story is told through a medium alter in any way your belief in its truthfulness? Would you believe anything told to you through a medium? Why or why not?

5. What is the difference, if any, between claiming to know something and claiming that it is true? Consider, for example, the statement "This is a good meal." Is knowing that the meal is good any different for you than claiming that it is true that the meal is good? Explain.

Rashomon
[Japan 1951] 1 hour, 29 minutes
Directed by Akira Kurosawa

While Akira Kurosawa's *Rashomon* is an adaptation of Ryōnosuke Akutagawa's "In a Grove," there are significant differences. In Kurosawa's *Rashomon*, the police officer (Daisuke Katô), bandit Tajômaru (Toshirô Mifune), woman (Machiko Kyô), and medium (Fumiko Honma) speak to the silent, offscreen high police commissioner. The priest (Minoru Chiaki) and the woodcutter (Takashi Shimura) speak to a commoner (Kichijiro Ueda) about the events surrounding the crime in an abandoned temple. The commoner, who wanders into the temple to seek shelter from the rain is not found in Akutagawa's story. He offers an outside perspective on the differing accounts of the man's murder.

The film also differs from the story by beginning and ending with two different testimonies from the woodcutter: While the first is much like his testimony in Akutagawa's story—he found a body along with a couple of personal items—the second testimony is radically different. This second testimony, prompted by the commoner, reveals that the woodcutter not only witnessed the murder but also stole a valuable dagger dropped by the woman in her struggle with the bandit. After learning that the woodcutter witnessed the event but declined to report it to the police because he knew he would have to turn the dagger in, the commoner says, "Selfish. That's the way we are, the way we live. You can't live unless you're what you call 'selfish.'" The woodcutter responds in turn, "Brute! All men are selfish and dishonest."

After this exchange, the commoner leaves the woodcutter and priest standing in stunned silence, appalled by the depth of their own selfishness and the inhumanity of recent events. Whereas Akutagawa's short story leaves us with differing testimonies and questions as to where the truth lies, Kurosawa leaves us believing that the second testimony of the woodcutter is the "truth" and that the other testimonies are selfish fabrications. The reason "truth" is not more consistent from person to person is that personal prejudice and selfishness lead us to see things only to the extent that they reflect our own needs and desires. Only after the woodcutter is shaken by the selfishness and inhumanity of the conflicting testimonies of the other persons does he reveal the true story of the murder. Furthermore, only by revealing what really happened that day in the grove is the depth of the woodcutter's own selfishness made apparent to him. Kurosawa seems to suggest that our selfishness is at the root of our inability to share the same truths about the world. Once we free ourselves from selfishness, we will be able to see a common truth.

DISCUSSION QUESTIONS

1. Does this film change your conclusions about Akutagawa's account of truth in "In a Grove"? Why or why not?

2. This film suggests that our inability to share common truths about the world reflects our inherent selfishness. Do you agree? Why or why not?

3. Is this film essentially an argument against *epistemological relativism*, the view that all truth is necessarily relative? Why or why not?

4. Why do people often have difficulty finding the same truth in commonly perceived events? Does this lead you to believe that truth is relative?

5. Why do you think we never see or hear the high police commissioner questioning the witnesses? Does it have to do with the high police commissioner's task of sorting out the evidence presented and reaching a verdict on the crime?

6. Imagine that you are the high police commissioner and have heard only the stories of the woman, the medium, the bandit, and the police officer. What would you conclude about the nature of this crime? On what basis would you decide which story is true?

7. In Akutagawa's "In a Grove," the testimonies of seven persons are directly presented to the high police commissioner (and to you, the reader). In Kurosawa's *Rashomon*, only the police officer, the bandit, the woman, and the medium speak to the high police commissioner. The priest and the woodcutter speak to a commoner about the events surrounding the crime. How do these differences between the story and the film alter the general position on truth presented in the movie as compared to the short story?

8. Do you think the characters in this film simply cannot see the truth or simply do not wish to see the truth? What is the difference?

9. Consider the following lines from the film:

   COMMONER   "Well, men are only men . . . that's why they lie. They can't tell the truth, even to themselves."

   PRIEST   "That may be true . . . because men are weak, they lie to deceive themselves."

   Do you agree with the commoner? Is it the case that people can't tell the truth, even to themselves? If so, why? If not, why is the commoner wrong?

10. What is the commoner's notion of truth? Does it differ from the other character's notions of truth?

JOHN LOCKE

ON TRUTH IN GENERAL

I n this selection, John Locke distinguishes between truth in thought and truth in language, though he admits that it is very difficult to treat them as distinct. According to Locke, truth belongs only to propositions. For Locke, a proposition always involves at least two ideas, and the truth of the proposition consists in whether the ideas agree with each other (a true proposition) or do not agree with each other (a proposition that is not true). Consequently, a single idea for Locke cannot be considered true or not true.

Locke further distinguishes between the "truth of thought" and the "truth of words." A truth of thought involves a "mental proposition," and whether the ideas in this proposition rest on an agreement with "things" (a true mental proposition, or mental truth) or not (a mental proposition that is not true). A truth of words involves a "verbal proposition," and whether the ideas agree with one another (a true verbal proposition, or verbal truth) or not (a verbal proposition that is not true).

According to Locke, a truth of words also has the possibility of being a "real truth" and not merely a trifling "verbal truth." *Verbal truth* indicates only that the words in the proposition have an agreement with the ideas they stand for "without regarding whether our ideas are such as really have, or are capable of having, an existence in nature." *Real truth* indicates that the terms in the proposition have an agreement with the ideas they stand for, and those ideas "are such as we know are capable of having an existence in nature." Locke continues, "If truth be nothing but the joining and separating of words in propositions, as the ideas they stand for agree or disagree in men's minds, the knowledge of truth is not so valuable a thing as it is taken to be, nor worth the pains and time men employ in the search of it."

Generally speaking, Locke's theory of truth is a mix of two distinct theories of truth: (1) the *correspondence theory of truth*, the position that the true "corresponds" to reality, and (2) the *coherence theory of truth*, the position that the true is a coherent system of ideas. The correspondence aspect is apparent in part of his criteria for real truth—namely, that ideas "are capable of having an existence in nature"—and the coherence aspect is evident in his notion that truth involves an "agreement" among ideas. A biographical sketch of Locke can be found in the first section of this chapter. The following selection is from *An Essay Concerning Human Understanding* (1690).

1. What is truth? was an inquiry many ages since; and it being that which all mankind either do, or pretend to search after, it cannot but be worth our while carefully to examine wherein it consists; and so acquaint ourselves with the nature of it, as to observe how the mind distinguishes it from falsehood.

2. Truth, then, seems to me, in the proper import of the word, to signify nothing but *the joining or separating of Signs, as the Things signified by them do agree or disagree one with another*. The joining or separating of signs here meant, is what by another name we call *proposition*. So that truth properly belongs only to propositions: whereof there are two sorts, viz. mental and verbal; as there are two sorts of signs commonly made use of, viz. ideas and words.

3. To form a clear notion of truth, it is very necessary to consider truth of thought, and truth of words, distinctly one from another: but yet it is very difficult to treat of them asunder. Because it is unavoidable, in treating of mental propositions,

to make use of words: and then the instances given of mental propositions cease immediately to be barely mental, and become verbal. For a *mental proposition* being nothing but a bare consideration of the ideas, as they are in our minds, stripped of names, they lose the nature of purely mental propositions as soon as they are put into words.

4. And that which makes it yet harder to treat of mental and verbal propositions separately is, that most men, if not all, in their thinking and reasonings within themselves, make use of words instead of ideas; at least when the subject of their meditation contains in it complex ideas. Which is a great evidence of the imperfection and uncertainty of our ideas of that kind, and may, if attentively made use of, serve for a mark to show us what are those things we have clear and perfect established ideas of, and what not. For if we will curiously observe the way our mind takes in thinking and reasoning, we shall find, I suppose, that when we make any propositions within our own thoughts about *white* or *black*, *sweet* or *bitter*, a *triangle* or a *circle*, we can and often do frame in our minds the ideas themselves, without reflecting on the names. But when we would consider, or make propositions about the more complex ideas, as of a *man, vitriol, fortitude, glory*, we usually put the name for the idea: because the ideas these names stand for, being for the most part imperfect, confused, and undetermined, we reflect on the names themselves, because they are more clear, certain, and distinct, and readier occur to our thoughts than the pure ideas: and so we make use of these words instead of the ideas themselves, even when we would meditate and reason within ourselves, and make tacit mental propositions. In substances, as has been already noticed, this is occasioned by the imperfections of our ideas: we making the name stand for the real essence, of which we have no idea at all. In modes, it is occasioned by the great number of simple ideas that go to the making them up. For many of them being compounded, the name occurs much easier than the complex idea itself, which requires time and attention to be recollected, and exactly represented to the mind, even in those men who have formerly been at the pains to do it; and is utterly impossible to be done by those who, though they have ready in their memory the greatest part of the common words of

that language, yet perhaps never troubled themselves in all their lives to consider what precise ideas the most of them stood for. Some confused or obscure notions have served their turns; and many who talk very much of *religion* and *conscience*, of *church* and *faith*, of *power* and *right*, of *obstructions* and *humours, melancholy* and *choler*, would perhaps have little left in their thoughts and meditations, if one should desire them to think only of the things themselves, and lay by those words with which they so often confound others, and not seldom themselves also.

5. But to return to the consideration of truth: we must, I say, observe two sorts of propositions that we are capable of making:—

First, *mental*, wherein the ideas in our understandings are without the use of words put together, or separated, by the mind perceiving or judging of their agreement or disagreement.

Secondly, *verbal* propositions, which are words, the signs of our ideas, put together or separated in affirmative or negative sentences. By which way of affirming or denying, these signs, made by sounds, are, as it were, put together or separated one from another. So that proposition consists in joining or separating signs; and truth consists in the putting together or separating those signs, according as the things which they stand for agree or disagree.

6. Every one's experience will satisfy him, that the mind, either by perceiving, or supposing, the agreement or disagreement of any of its ideas, does tacitly within itself put them into a kind of proposition affirmative or negative; which I have endeavoured to express by the terms putting together and separating. But this action of the mind, which is so familiar to every thinking and reasoning man, is easier to be conceived by reflecting on what passes in us when we affirm or deny, than to be explained by words. When a man has in his head the idea of two lines, viz. the side and diagonal of a square, whereof the diagonal is an inch long, he may have the idea also of the division of that line into a certain number of equal parts; v.g. into five, ten, a hundred, a thousand, or any other number, and may have the idea of that each line being divisible, or not divisible, into such equal parts, as a certain number of them will be equal to the sideline. Now, whenever he perceives, believes, or supposes such a kind of divisibility to agree or disagree to his idea of that line, he, as it

were, joins or separates those two ideas, viz. the idea of that line, and the idea of that kind of divisibility; and so makes a mental proposition, which is true or false, according as such a kind of divisibility, a divisibility into such *aliquot* parts, does really agree to that line or no. When ideas are so put together, or separated in the mind, as they or the things they stand for do agree or not, that is, as I may call it, *mental truth*. But *truth of words* is something more; and that is the affirming or denying of words one of another, as the ideas they stand for agree or disagree: and this again is two-fold; either purely verbal and trifling . . . or real and instructive; which is the object of that real knowledge which we have spoken of already.

7. But here again will be apt to occur the same doubt about truth, that did about knowledge: and it will be objected, that if truth be nothing but the joining and separating of words in propositions, as the ideas they stand for agree or disagree in men's minds, the knowledge of truth is not so valuable a thing as it is taken to be, nor worth the pains and time men employ in the search of it: since by this account it amounts to no more than the conformity of words to the chimeras of men's brains. Who knows not what odd notions many men's heads are filled with, and what strange ideas all men's brains are capable of? But if we rest here, we know the truth of nothing by this rule, but of the visionary words in our own imaginations; nor have other truth, but what as much concerns harpies and centaurs, as men and horses. For those, and the like, may be ideas in our heads, and have their agreement or disagreement there, as well as the ideas of real beings, and so have as true propositions made about them. And it will be altogether as true a proposition to say *all centaurs are animals*, as that *all men are animals;* and the certainty of one as great as the other. For in both the propositions, the words are put together according to the agreement of the ideas in our minds: and the agreement of the idea of animal with that of centaur is as clear and visible to the mind, as the agreement of the idea of animal with that of man; and so these two propositions are equally true, equally certain. But of what use is all such truth to us?

8. Though what has been said in the foregoing chapter to distinguish real from imaginary knowledge might suffice here, in answer to this doubt, to distinguish real truth from chimerical, or

(if you please) barely nominal, they depending both on the same foundation; yet it may not be amiss here again to consider, that though our words signify nothing but our ideas, yet being designed by them to signify things, the truth they contain when put into propositions will be only verbal, when they stand for ideas in the mind that have not an agreement with the reality of things. And therefore truth as well as knowledge may well come under the distinction of verbal and real; that being only verbal truth, wherein terms are joined according to the agreement or disagreement of the ideas they stand for; without regarding whether our ideas are such as really have, or are capable of having, an existence in nature. But then it is they contain *real truth*, when these signs are joined, as our ideas agree; and when our ideas are such as we know are capable of having an existence in nature: which in substances we cannot know, but by knowing that such have existed.

9. Truth is the marking down in words the agreement or disagreement of ideas as it is. Falsehood is the marking down in words the agreement or disagreement of ideas otherwise than it is. And so far as these ideas, thus marked by sounds, agree to their archetypes, so far only is the truth real. The knowledge of this truth consists in knowing what ideas the words stand for, and the perception of the agreement or disagreement of those ideas, according as it is marked by those words.

DISCUSSION QUESTIONS

1. Locke distinguishes between "truth of thought" and "truth of words." What is the difference? Is this distinction a valid one? Why or why not?

2. Locke says that a "mental proposition" is a "bare consideration of ideas, as they are in our minds, stripped of names." In other words, there are thoughts without words. Do you agree with him? Why or why not? Can you think of something without using words? Explain.

3. For Locke, truth relates only to propositions, not single ideas or words. Explain what he means. Do you agree with him? What are some the implications of Locke's position?

4. Consider the following line from Locke: "Some confused or obscure notions have served their turns: and many who talk very much of *religion* and *conscience*, of *church* and *faith* . . . would perhaps have little left in their thoughts and meditations, if one should desire them to think only of the things themselves, and lay by those words with which they so often confound others, and not seldom themselves also." Do you agree with Locke? Defend your position by discussing one of the terms noted by Locke.

5. What is the difference between "verbal truth" and "real truth"? Why is this distinction important for Locke's theory of truth?

BERTRAND RUSSELL

TRUTH AS CORRESPONDENCE

In this selection, Bertrand Russell argues for a *correspondence* theory of truth, the position that the true "corresponds" to reality. Russell says that any theory of truth must meet three requirements: (1) It must account for falsehood (as well as truth); (2) it must contain beliefs; and (3) it must accord with *realism*, the position that the truth or falsehood of a belief depends on something exterior to the belief itself. Russell offers a correspondence theory of truth in which truth and falsehood consist in the correspondence, or lack thereof, between a belief and a fact in the real world. For Russell, a belief is a complex unity involving the subject, the object term or terms, and the object relation or relations. This complex unity is tied together by the relation of "believing." According to Russell, this complex unity is actual in the case of both true belief and false belief. What distinguishes a true belief from a false one is the existence or non-existence of another complex unity, a fact. If there is no fact corresponding to the belief, then the belief is false. If there is a belief corresponding to the fact, then it is true.

Russell contends that his correspondence theory of truth is superior to the coherence theory of truth, the position that the true is a coherent system of ideas. He offers two main objections to the coherence theory of truth: (1) There is no way to establish which among a number of coherent bodies of statements is the true one; and (2) the theory presupposes the law of contradiction (a proposition cannot both be true and not true), which it cannot show to be true according to its own criterion. "For example, the two propositions 'this tree is a beech and 'this tree is not a beech,' are not coherent, because of the law of contradiction," says Russell. "But if the law of contradiction itself were subjected to the test of coherence, we should find that, if we choose to suppose it false, nothing will any longer be incoherent with anything else."

However, Russell does not completely reject the coherence theory of truth. He leaves room for utilizing coherence as a test of truth: While "coherence cannot be accepted as giving the *meaning* of truth," comments Russell, "it is often a most important *test* of truth after a certain amount of truth has become known." This comment reveals that Russell divides the problem of truth into two distinct questions: (1) "What is the test of truth?" and (2) "What is the meaning or nature of truth?" And, like a number of philosophers, he is comfortable using both "coherence" and "correspondence" in his answer, even if he favors the latter term. A biographical sketch of Russell can be found in the Introduction chapter. The following selection is from *The Problems of Philosophy* (1912).

Our knowledge of truths, unlike our knowledge of things, has an opposite, namely *error*. So far as things are concerned, we may know them or not know them, but there is no positive state of mind which can be described as erroneous knowledge of things, so long, at any rate, as we confine ourselves to knowledge by acquaintance. Whatever we are acquainted with must be something: we may draw wrong inference from our acquaintance, but the acquaintance itself cannot be deceptive. Thus there is no dualism as regards acquaintance. But as regards knowledge of truths, there is a dualism. We may believe what is false as well as what is true. We know that on very many subjects different people hold different and incompatible opinions: hence some beliefs must be erroneous. Since erroneous beliefs are often held just as strongly as true beliefs, it becomes a difficult question how they are to be distinguished from true beliefs. How are we to know, in a given case, that our belief is not erroneous? That is a question of the very greatest difficulty, to which no completely satisfactory answer is possible. There is, however, a preliminary question which is rather less difficult, and that is: What do we *mean* by truth and falsehood? It is this preliminary question which is to be considered in this chapter.

. . . We are not asking how we can know whether a belief is true or false: we are asking what is meant by the question whether a belief is true or false. It is to be hoped that a clear answer to this question may help us to obtain an answer to the question what beliefs are true, but for the present we ask only "What is truth?" and "What is falsehood?" not "What beliefs are true?" and "What beliefs are false?" It is very important to keep these different questions entirely separate, since any confusion between them is sure to produce an answer which is not really applicable to either.

There are three points to observe in the attempt to discover the nature of truth, three requisites which any theory must fulfill.

(1) Our theory of truth must be such as to admit of its opposite, falsehood. A good many philosophers have failed adequately to satisfy this condition: they have constructed theories according to which all our thinking ought to have been true, and have then had the greatest difficulty in finding a place for falsehood. In this respect our theory of belief must differ from our theory of acquaintance, since in the case of acquaintance it was not necessary to take account of any opposite.

(2) It seems fairly evident that if there were no beliefs there could be no falsehood, and no truth either, in the sense in which truth is correlative to falsehood. If we imagine a world of mere matter, there would be no room for falsehood in such a world, and although it would contain what may be called "facts," it would not contain any truths, in the sense in which truths are things of the same kind as falsehoods. In fact, truth and falsehood are properties of beliefs and statements: hence a world of mere matter, since it would contain no beliefs or statements, would also contain no truth or falsehood.

(3) But, as against what we have just said, it is to be observed that the truth or falsehood of a belief always depends upon something which lies outside the belief itself. If I believe that Charles I died on the scaffold, I believe truly, not because of any intrinsic quality of my belief, which could be discovered by merely examining the belief, but because of an historical event which happened two and a half centuries ago. If I believe that Charles I died in his bed, I believe falsely: no degree of vividness in my belief, or of care in arriving at it, prevents it from being false, again because of what happened long ago, and not because of any intrinsic property of my belief. Hence, although truth and falsehood are properties of beliefs, they are properties dependent upon the relations of the beliefs to other things, not upon any internal quality of the beliefs.

The third of the above requisites leads us to adopt the view—which has on the whole been commonest among philosophers—that truth consists in some form of correspondence between belief and fact. It is, however, by no means an easy matter to discover a form of correspondence to which there are no irrefutable objections. By this partly—and partly by the feeling that, if truth consists in a correspondence of thought with something outside thought, thought can never know when truth has been attained—many philosophers have been led to try to find some definition of truth which shall not consist in relation to something wholly outside belief. The most important attempt at a definition of this sort is the theory that truth consists in *coherence*. It is said that the mark of falsehood is failure to cohere in the body of our beliefs, and that it is the essence of a truth to form part of the completely rounded system which is The Truth.

There is, however, a great difficulty in this view, or rather two great difficulties. The first is that there is no reason to suppose that only *one* coherent body of beliefs is possible. It may be that, with sufficient imagination, a novelist might invent a past for the world that would perfectly fit on to what we know, and yet be quite different from the real past. In more scientific matters, it is certain that there are often two or more hypotheses which account for all the known facts on some subject, and although, in such cases, men of science endeavor to find facts which will rule out all the hypotheses except one, there is no reason why they should always succeed.

In philosophy, again, it seems not uncommon for two rival hypotheses to be both able to account for all the facts. Thus, for example, it is possible that life is one long dream, and that the outer world has only that degree of reality that the objects of dreams have; but although such a view does not seem inconsistent with known facts, there is no reason to prefer it to the common-sense view, according to which other people and things do really exist. Thus coherence as the definition of truth fails because there is no proof that there can be only one coherent system.

The other objection to this definition of truth is that it assumes the meaning of "coherence" known, whereas, in fact, "coherence" presupposes the truth of the laws of logic. Two propositions are coherent when both may be true, and are incoherent when one at least must be false. Now in order to know whether two propositions can both be true, we must know such truths as the law of contradiction. For example, the two propositions "this tree is a beech" and "this tree is not a beech," are not coherent, because of the law of contradiction. But if the law of contradiction itself were subjected to the test of coherence, we should find that, if we choose to suppose it false, nothing will any longer be incoherent with anything else. Thus the laws of logic supply the skeleton or framework within which the test of coherence applies, and they themselves cannot be established by this test.

For the above two reasons, coherence cannot be accepted as giving the *meaning* of truth, though it

is often a most important *test* of truth after a certain amount of truth has become known.

Hence we are driven back to *correspondence with fact* as constituting the nature of truth. It remains to define precisely what we mean by "fact," and what is the nature of the correspondence which must subsist between belief and fact, in order that belief may be true.

In accordance with our three requisites, we have to seek a theory of truth which (1) allows truth to have an opposite, namely falsehood, (2) makes truth a property of beliefs, but (3) makes it a property wholly dependent upon the relation of the beliefs to outside things.

The necessity of allowing for falsehood makes it impossible to regard belief as a relation of the mind to a single object, which could be said to be what is believed. If belief were so regarded, we should find that, like acquaintance, it would not admit of the opposition of truth and falsehood, but would have to be always true. This may be made clear by examples. Othello believes falsely that Desdemona loves Cassio. We cannot say that this belief consists in a relation to a single object, "Desdemona's love for Cassio," for if there were such an object, the belief would be true. There is in fact no such object, and therefore Othello cannot have any relation to such an object. Hence his belief cannot possibly consist in a relation to this object.

It might be said that his belief is a relation to a different object, namely "that Desdemona loves Cassio"; but it is almost as difficult to suppose that there is such an object as this, when Desdemona does not love Cassio, as it was to suppose that there is "Desdemona's love for Cassio." Hence it will be better to seek for a theory of belief which does not make it consist in a relation of the mind to a single object.

It is common to think of relations as though they always held between *two* terms, but in fact this is not always the case. Some relations demand three terms, some four, and so on. Take, for instance, the relation "between." So long as only two terms come in, the relation "between" is impossible: three terms are the smallest number that render it possible. York is between London and Edinburgh; but if London and Edinburgh were the only places in the world, there could be nothing which was between one place and another. Similarly *jealousy* requires three people: there can be no such relation that does not involve three at least. Such a proposition as "A wishes B to promote C's marriage with D" involves a relation of four terms; that is to say, A and B and C and D all come in, and the relation involved cannot be expressed otherwise than in a form involving all four. Instances might be multiplied indefinitely, but enough has been said to show that there are relations which require more than two terms before they can occur.

The relation involved in *judging* or *believing* must, if falsehood is to be duly allowed for, be taken to be a relation between several terms, not between two. When Othello believes that Desdemona loves Cassio, he must not have before his mind a single object, "Desdemona's love for Cassio," or "that Desdemona loves Cassio," for that would require that there should be objective falsehoods, which subsist independently of any minds; and this, though not logically refutable, is a theory to be avoided if possible. Thus it is easier to account for falsehood if we take judgment to be a relation in which the mind and the various objects concerned all occur severally; that is to say, Desdemona and loving and Cassio must all be terms in the relation which subsists when Othello believes that Desdemona loves Cassio. This relation, therefore, is a relation of four terms, since Othello also is one of the terms of the relation. When we say that it is a relation of four terms, we do not mean that Othello has a certain relation to Desdemona, and has the same relation to loving and also to Cassio. This may be true of some other relation than believing; but believing, plainly, is not a relation which Othello has to *each* of the three terms concerned, but to *all* of them together: there is only one example of the relation of believing involved, but this one example knits together four terms. Thus the actual occurrence, at the moment when Othello is entertaining his belief, is that the relation called "believing" is knitting together into one complex whole the four terms Othello, Desdemona, loving, and Cassio. What is called belief or judgment is nothing but this relation of believing or judging, which relates a mind to several things other than itself. An *act* of belief or of judgment is the occurrence between certain terms at some particular time, of the relation of believing or judging.

We are now in a position to understand what it is that distinguishes a true judgment from a false one. For this purpose we will adopt certain definitions. In every act of judgment there is a mind which judges, and there are terms concerning which it judges. We will call the mind the *subject* in the judgment, and the remaining terms the *objects*. Thus, when Othello judges that Desdemona loves Cassio, Othello is the subject, while the objects are Desdemona and loving and Cassio. The subject and the objects together are called the *constituents* of the judgment. It will be observed that the relation of judging has what is called a "sense" or "direction." We may say, metaphorically, that it puts its objects in a certain *order*, which we may indicate by means of the order of the words in the sentence. (In an inflected language, the same thing will be indicated by inflections, e.g., by the difference between nominative and accusative.) Othello's judgment that Cassio loves Desdemona differs from his judgment that Desdemona loves Cassio, in spite of the fact that it consists of the same constituents, because the relation of judging places the constituents in a different order in the two cases. Similarly, if Cassio judges that Desdemona loves Othello, the constituents of the judgment are still the same, but their order is different. This property of having a "sense" or "direction" is one which the relation of judging shares with all other relations. The "sense" of relations is the ultimate source of order and series and a host of mathematical concepts; but we need not concern ourselves further with this aspect.

We spoke of the relation called "judging" or "believing" as knitting together into one complex whole the subject and the objects. In this respect, judging is exactly like every other relation. Whenever a relation holds between two or more terms, it unites the terms into a complex whole. If Othello loves Desdemona, there is such a complex whole as "Othello's love for Desdemona." The terms united by the relation may be themselves complex, or may be simple, but the whole which results from their being united must be complex. Wherever there is a relation which relates certain terms, there is a complex object formed of the union of those terms; and conversely, wherever there is a complex object, there is a relation which relates its constituents. When an act of believing occurs, there is a complex, in which "believing" is the uniting relation, and subject and objects are arranged in a certain order by the "sense" of the relation of believing. Among the objects, as we saw in considering "Othello believes that Desdemona loves Cassio," one must be a relation—in this instance, the relation "loving." But this relation, as it occurs in the act of believing, is not the relation which creates the unity of the complex whole consisting of the subject and the objects. The relation "loving," as it occurs in the act of believing, is one of the objects—it is a brick in the structure, not the cement. The cement is the relation "believing." When the belief is *true*, there is another complex unity, in which the relation which was one of the objects of the belief relates the other objects. Thus, e.g., if Othello believes *truly* that Desdemona loves Cassio, then there is a complex unity, "Desdemona's love for Cassio," which is composed exclusively of the *objects* of the belief, in the same order as they had in the belief, with the relation which was one of the objects occurring now as the cement that binds together the other objects of the belief. On the other hand, when a belief is *false*, there is no such complex unity composed only of the objects of the belief. If Othello believes *falsely* that Desdemona loves Cassio, then there is no such complex unity as "Desdemona's love for Cassio."

Thus a belief is *true* when it *corresponds* to a certain associated complex, and *false* when it does not. Assuming, for the sake of definiteness, that the objects of the belief are two terms and a relation, the terms being put in a certain order by the "sense" of the believing, then if the two terms in that order are united by the relation into a complex, the belief is true; if not, it is false. This constitutes the definition of truth and falsehood that we were in search of. Judging or believing is a certain complex unity of which a mind is a constituent; if the remaining constituents, taken in the order which they have in the belief, form a complex unity, then the belief is true; if not, it is false.

Thus although truth and falsehood are properties of beliefs, yet they are in a sense extrinsic properties, for the condition of the truth of a belief is something not involving beliefs, or (in general) any mind at all, but only the *objects* of the belief. A mind, which believes, believes truly when there is a *corresponding* complex not involving the mind, but only its objects. This correspondence ensures truth, and its absence entails falsehood. Hence we account simultaneously for the two facts that beliefs (a) depend on minds for their *existence*, (b) do not depend on minds for their *truth*.

We may restate our theory as follows: If we take such a belief as "Othello believes that Desdemona loves Cassio," we will call Desdemona and Cassio the *object-terms*, and loving the *object-relation*. If there is a complex unity "Desdemona's love for Cassio," consisting of the object-terms related by the object-relation in the same order as they have in the belief, then this complex unity is called the *fact corresponding to the belief*. Thus a belief is true when there is a corresponding fact, and is false when there is no corresponding fact.

. . . Minds do not *create* truth or falsehood. They create beliefs, but when once the beliefs are created, the mind cannot make them true or false, except in the special case where they concern future things which are within the power of the person believing, such as catching trains. What makes a belief true is a *fact*, and this fact does not (except in exceptional cases) in any way involve the mind of the person who has the belief.

DISCUSSION QUESTIONS

1. Discuss Russell's account of false belief. What exactly does a false belief correspond to?

2. Are you convinced by Russell's objections to the coherence theory of truth? Why or why not?

3. If the truth of a belief corresponds to something outside of the belief, how do we get outside of the belief to verify the correspondence?

4. Has Russell convinced you that "minds do not *create* truth or falsehood. They create beliefs, but when once the beliefs are created, the mind cannot make them true or false . . ."?

5. What does Russell mean by "correspondence"? How, in Russell's account of truth, would we determine that "correspondence" is true? Or, more particularly, how might we show that the law of correspondence—that every true belief is made true by the existence of a fact to which it corresponds—*is itself true*? Is this a problem for Russell's theory in the same way that not being able to prove the truth of the law of contradiction is a problem for the coherence theory? Explain.

FRANCIS H. BRADLEY
TRUTH AS COHERENCE

In this selection, Francis H. Bradley argues for a *coherence* theory of truth, the position that the true is a coherent system of ideas. He begins by citing the inadequacies of the correspondence theory of knowledge. For Bradley, the judgments we make are not like the "facts" to which these judgments refer. Bradley argues that "the view that, when I say 'this,' 'now,' 'here,' or 'my,' what I feel, when so speaking, is carried over intact into my judgement, and that my judgement in consequence is exempt from error, seems wholly indefensible." "That which I designate," claims Bradley, "is not and cannot be carried over into my judgement." As such, Bradley's position on truth is the opposite of Russell's, who argues that judgments (or beliefs) correspond to facts.

For Bradley, the "object is to have a world as comprehensive and coherent as possible." He believes that "we depend vitally on the sense-world, that our material comes from it," and that we go to the sense-world "both to verify that matter which is old and also to increase that which is new." However, Bradley argues that "if I am to have an orderly world, I cannot accept all 'facts.' " "If by taking certain judgements of perception as true, I can get more system into my world, then these 'facts' are so far true, and if by taking certain 'facts' as errors I can order my experience better, then so far these 'facts' are errors." Whereas Russell relies on facts to determine the nature of truth, Bradley does not. If a "fact" contributes to the coherence of his world, then Bradley accepts it as truth; if not, it is regarded as "error." " 'Facts' are justified because and as far as, while taking them as real, I am better able to deal with the incoming new 'facts' and in general to make my world wider and more harmonious," writes Bradley. Truth then maintains the coherence and comprehensiveness of our world.

Francis H. Bradley (1846–1924) was educated at University College, Oxford. In 1870, he was elected to a fellowship at Merton College, Oxford. The fellowship was terminable upon marriage and did not require him to teach. Bradley never married and, consequently, was able to devote himself entirely to his philosophical writing. He is widely regarded as the greatest British philosopher between John Stuart Mill and Bertrand Russell. His philosophy, known as British absolute idealism, is a cross between British empiricism (Locke, Berkeley, Hume) and German idealism (particularly, Hegel). In short, Bradley was a *holist*, contending that everything in the world is somehow or other related to everything else. He argued that there must be an absolute or harmonious reality that transcends our thought and in which "mere thinking is absorbed." Bradley's work was most influential in the first decade of the twentieth century, and the writings of Russell and G. E. Moore were to a great extent intended as direct refutations of his doctrines. His major books are *Ethical*

Studies (1876), *Principles of Logic* (1883), and *Appearance and Reality* (1893). He also published many articles in scholarly journals, some of which are collected in *Essays on Truth and Reality* (1914), and others in *Collected Essays* (1935). The following selection is from *Essays on Truth and Reality*.

. . . What I maintain is that in the case of facts of perception and memory the test [of truth] which we do apply, and which we must apply, is that of system. I contend that this test works satisfactorily, and that no other test will work. And I argue in consequence that there are no judgements of sense which are in principle infallible. . . .

The reason for maintaining independent facts and infallible judgements, as I understand it, is twofold. (1) Such data, it may be said, can be actually shown. And (2) in any case they must exist, since without them the intelligence cannot work. . . .

(1) I doubt my ability to do justice to the position of the man who claims to show ultimate given facts exempt from all possible error. In the case of any datum of sensation or feeling, to prove that we have this wholly unmodified by what is called "apperception" seems a hopeless undertaking. And how far it is supposed that such a negative can be proved I do not know. What, however, is meant must be this, that we somehow and somewhere have verifiable facts of perception and memory, and also judgements, free from all chance of error.

I will begin hereby recalling a truth familiar but often forgotten. . . . In your search for independent facts and for infallible truths you may go so low that, when you have descended beyond the level of error, you find yourself below the level of any fact or of any truth which you can use. What you seek is particular facts of perception or memory, but what you get may be something not answering to that character. I will go on to give instances of what I mean, and I think that in every case we shall do well to ask this question, "What on the strength of our ultimate fact are we able to contradict?"

(*a*) If we take the instance of simple unrelated sensations or feelings, *a*, *b*, *c*—supposing that there are such things—what judgement would such a fact enable us to deny? We could on the strength of this fact deny the denial that *a*, *b* and *c*

exist in any way, manner or sense. But surely this is not the kind of independent fact of which we are in search.

(*b*) From this let us pass to the case of a complex feeling containing, at once and together, both *a* and *b*. On the ground of this we can deny the statement that *a* and *b* cannot or do not ever anyhow co-exist in feeling. This is an advance, but it surely leaves us far short of our goal.

(*c*) What we want, I presume, is something that at once is infallible and that also can be called a particular fact of perception or memory. And we want, in the case of perception, something that would be called a fact for observation. We do not seem to reach this fact until we arrive somewhere about the level of "I am here and now having a sensation or complex of sensations of such or such a kind." The goal is reached; but at this point, unfortunately, the judgement has become fallible, so far at least as it really states particular truth.

(α) In such a judgement it is in the first place hard to say what is meant by the "I." If, however, we go beyond feeling far enough to mean a self with such or such a real existence in time, then memory is involved, and the judgement at once, I should urge, becomes fallible. . . . Thus the statement made in the judgement is liable to error, or else the statement does not convey particular truth.

(β) And this fatal dilemma holds good when applied to the "now" and "here." If these words mean a certain special place in a certain special series or order, they are liable to mistake. But, if they fall short of this meaning, then they fail to state individual fact. My feeling is, I agree, not subject to error in the proper sense of that term, but on the other side my feeling does not of itself deliver truth. And the process which gets from it a deliverance as to individual fact is fallible.

Everywhere such fact depends on construction. And we have here to face not only the possibility of what would commonly be called mistaken interpretation. We have in addition the chance of actual sense-hallucination. And, worse than this, we have the far-reaching influence of abnormal suggestion and morbid fixed idea. This influence may stop short of hallucination, and yet may vitiate the memory and the judgement to such an extent that there remains no practical difference between idea and perceived fact. And, in the face of these possibilities, it seems idle to speak of perceptions and memories secure from all chance of error. Or on the other side banish the chance of error, and with what are you left? You then have something which (as we have seen) goes no further than to warrant the assertion that such and such elements can and do co-exist—somehow and somewhere, or again that such or such a judgement happens—without any regard to its truth and without any specification of its psychical context. And no one surely will contend that with this we have particular fact.

The doctrine that perception gives us infallible truth rests on a foundation which in part is sound and in part fatally defective. That what is felt is felt, and cannot, so far as felt, be mistaken—so much as this must be accepted. But the view that, when I say "this," "now," "here," or "my," what I feel, when so speaking, is carried over intact into my judgement, and that my judgement in consequence is exempt from error, seems wholly indefensible. It survives, I venture to think, only because it never has understood its complete refutation. That which I designate is not and cannot be carried over into my judgement. The judgement may in a sense answer to that which I feel, but none the less it fails to contain and to convey my feeling. And on the other hand, so far as it succeeds in expressing my meaning, the judgement does this in a way which makes it liable to error. Or, to put it otherwise, the perceived truth, to be of any use, must be particularized. So far as it is stated in a general form, it contains not only that which you meant to say but also, and just as much, the opposite of that which you meant. And to contend for the infallibility of such a truth seems futile. On the other side so far as your truth really is individualized, so far as it is placed in a special construction and vitally related to its context, to the same extent the element of interpretation or implication is added. And, with this element obviously comes the possibility of mistake. And

we have seen above that, viewed psychologically, particular judgements of perception immune from all chance of error seem hardly tenable.

(2) I pass now to the second reason for accepting infallible data of perception. Even if we cannot show these (it is urged) we are bound to assume them. For in their absence our knowledge has nothing on which to stand, and this want of support results in total scepticism.

It is possible of course here to embrace both premises and conclusion, and to argue that scepticism is to be preferred to an untrue assumption. And such a position I would press on the notice of those who uphold infallible judgements of sense and memory. But personally I am hardly concerned in this issue, for I reject both the conclusion and the premises together. Such infallible and incorrigible judgements are really not required for our knowledge, and, since they cannot be shown, we must not say that they exist. . . .

I agree that we depend vitally on the sense-world, that our material comes from it, and that apart from it knowledge could not begin. To this world, I agree, we have for ever to return, not only to gain new matter but to confirm and maintain the old. I agree that to impose order from without on sheer disorder would be wholly impracticable, and that, if my sense-world were disorderly beyond a certain point, my intelligence would not exist. And further I agree that we cannot suppose it possible that *all* the judgements of perception and memory which for me come first, could in fact for me be corrected. I cannot, that is, imagine the world of my experience to be so modified that in the end none of these accepted facts should be left standing. But so far, I hasten to add, we have not yet come to the real issue. There is still a chasm between such admissions and the conclusion that there are judgements of sense which possess truth absolute and infallible.

We meet here a false doctrine largely due to a misleading metaphor. My known world is taken to be a construction built upon such and such foundations. It is argued, therefore, to be in principle a superstructure which rests upon these supports. You can go on adding to it no doubt, but only so long as the supports remain; and, unless they remain, the whole building comes down. But the doctrine, I have to contend, is untenable, and the metaphor ruinously inapplicable. The foundation in truth is provisional merely. In order to begin my construction I take the foundation as absolute—so much certainly is true. But that my construction continues to rest on the beginnings of my knowledge is a conclusion which does not follow. It does not follow that, if these are allowed to be fallible, the whole building collapses. For it is in another sense that my world rests upon the data of perception.

My experience is solid, not so far as it is a superstructure but so far as in short it is a system. My object is to have a world as comprehensive and coherent as possible, and, in order to attain this object, I have not only to reflect but perpetually to have recourse to the materials of sense. I must go to this source both to verify the matter which is old and also to increase it by what is new. And in this way I must depend upon the judgements of perception. Now it is agreed that, if I am to have an orderly world, I cannot possibly accept all "facts." Some of these must be relegated, as they are, to the world of error, whether we succeed or fail in modifying and correcting them. And the view which I advocate takes them all as in principle fallible. On the other hand, that view denies that there is any necessity for absolute facts of sense. Facts for it are true, we may say, just so far as they work, just so far as they contribute to the order of experience. If by taking certain judgements of perception as true, I can get more system into my world, then these "facts" are so far true, and if by taking certain "facts" as errors I can order my experience better, then so far these "facts" are errors. And there is no "fact" which possesses an absolute right. Certainly there are truths with which I begin and which I personally never have to discard, and which therefore remain in fact as members of my known world. And of some of these certainly it may be said that without them I should not know how to order my knowledge. But it is quite another thing to maintain that every single one of these judgements is in principle infallible. The absolute indispensable fact is in my view the mere creature of false theory. Facts are valid so far as, when taken otherwise than as "real," they bring disorder into my world. And there are today for me facts such that, if I take them as mistakes, my known world is damaged and, it is possible, ruined. But how does it follow that I cannot tomorrow on the strength of new facts gain a wider order in which these old facts can take a place as errors? The supposition may be improbable, but what you have got to show is that it is in principle impossible. A foundation used at the beginning does not in short mean something fundamental at the end, and there is no single "fact" which in the end can be called fundamental absolutely. It is all a question of relative contribution to my known world-order.

"Then no judgement of perception will be more than probable?" Certainly that is my contention. "Facts" are justified because and as far as, while taking them as real, I am better able to deal with the incoming new "facts" and in general to make my world wider and more harmonious. The higher and wider my structure, and the more that any particular fact or set of facts is implied in that structure, the more certain are the structure and the facts. And, if we could reach an all-embracing ordered whole, then our certainty would be absolute. But, since we cannot do this, we have to remain content with relative probability. Why is this or that fact of observation taken as practically certain? It is so taken just so far as it is *not* taken in its own right. (i) Its validity is due to such and such a person perceiving it under such and such conditions. This means that a certain intellectual order in the person is necessary as a basis, and again that nothing in the way of sensible or mental distortion intervenes between this order and what is given. And (ii) the observed fact must agree with our world as already arranged, or at least must not upset this. If the fact is too much contrary to our arranged world we provisionally reject it. We eventually accept the fact only when after confirmation the hypothesis of its error becomes still more ruinous. We are forced then more or less to rearrange our world, and more or less perhaps to reject some previous "facts." The question throughout is as to what is better or worse for our order as a whole.

Why again to me is a remembered fact certain, supposing that it is so? Assuredly not because it is infallibly delivered by the faculty of Memory, but because I do not see how to reconcile the fact of its error with my accepted world. Unless I go on the principle of trusting my memory, apart from any special reason to the contrary, I cannot order my world so well, if indeed I can order it at all. The principle here again is system. . . .

The same account holds with regard to the facts of history. For instance, the guillotining of Louis XVI is practically certain because to take this as error would entail too much disturbance of my world. Error is possible here of course. Fresh facts conceivably might come before me such as would compel me to modify in part my knowledge as so far arranged. And in this modified arrangement the execution of Louis would find its place as an error. But the reason for such a modification would have to be considerable, while, as things are, no reason exists. . . . To take memory as in general trustworthy, where I have no special reason for doubt, and to take the testimony of those persons, whom I suppose to view the world as I view it, as being true, apart from special reason on the other side—these are principles by which I construct my ordered world, such as it is. And because by any other method the result is worse, therefore for me these principles are true. On the other hand to suppose that any "fact" or perception or memory is so certain that no possible experience could justify me in taking it as error seems to me injurious if not ruinous. On such a principle my world of knowledge would be ordered worse, if indeed it could be ordered at all. For to accept all the "facts," as they offer themselves, seems obviously impossible; and, if it is we who have to decide as to which facts are infallible, then I ask how we are to decide. The ground of validity, I maintain, consists in successful contribution. That is a principle of order, while any other principle, so far as I see, leads to chaos.

"But," it may still be objected, "my fancy is unlimited. I can therefore invent an imaginary world even more orderly than my known world. And further this fanciful arrangement might possibly be made so wide that the world of perception would become for me in comparison small and inconsiderable. Hence, my perceived world, so far as not supporting my fancied arrangement, might be included within it as *error*. Such a consequence would or might lead to confusion in theory and to disaster in practice. And yet the result follows from your view inevitably, unless after all you fall back upon the certainty of perception."

To this possible objection, I should reply first, that it has probably failed to understand rightly the criterion which I defend. The aspect of comprehensiveness has not received here its due emphasis. The idea of system demands the inclusion of all possible material. Not only must you include everything to be gained from immediate experience and perception, but you must also be ready to act on the same principle with regard to fancy. But this means that you cannot confine yourself within the limits of this or that fancied world, as suits your pleasure or private convenience. You are bound also, so far as is possible, to recognize and to include the opposite fancy.

This consideration to my mind ruins the above hypothesis on which the objection was based. The fancied arrangement not only has opposed to it the world of perception. It also has against it any opposite arrangement and any contrary fact which I can fancy. And, so far as I can judge, these contrary fancies will balance the first. Nothing, therefore, will be left to outweigh the world as perceived, and the imaginary hypothesis will be condemned by our criterion.

. . . I may state the view which has commended itself to my mind. Truth is an ideal expression of the Universe, at once coherent and comprehensive. It must not conflict with itself, and there must be no suggestion which fails to fall inside it. Perfect truth in short must realize the idea of a systematic whole. And such a whole . . . possesses essentially the two characters of coherence and comprehensiveness.

DISCUSSION QUESTIONS

1. What are Bradley's reasons for rejecting the correspondence theory of truth? How might Russell respond to Bradley?

2. Discuss Bradley's claim that " 'facts' are justified because and as far as, while taking them as real, I am better able to deal with the incoming new 'facts' and in general to make my world wider and more harmonious." Do you agree with him?

3. Bradley is critical of the view that our knowledge of the world is a construction build upon a foundation. This view, which might be called "foundationalism," is the position of Descartes. What is foundationalism,

and why is Bradley opposed to it? Do you agree with him?

4. Bradley discusses his coherence theory of truth with regard to historical truth. What, according to Bradley, is historical truth? Consider some of the implications of Bradley's position. Are you comfortable with them?

5. Bradley's doctrine of truth does not have much room for what Alison Jaggar might call "outlaw truth," that is, truth that disrupts or makes incoherent our worldview. Is this a serious flaw in Bradley's theory of truth? Why or why not?

JFK
[USA 1991] 3 hours, 26 minutes
Directed by Oliver Stone

The assassination of President John F. Kennedy is one of the darkest days in American history. On November 22, 1963, while driving in a motorcade through Dallas, Texas, in an open vehicle, the president was fatally shot. Oliver Stone's film asks who committed the crime, and why. What is the true story of the Kennedy assassination? In the process, he reveals the strengths and weaknesses of at least two major theories of truth: the coherence theory and the correspondence theory.

The coherence theory of truth is illustrated by the "official" government account of the assassination. According to Stone's film, immediately after the president was shot, Lee Harvey Oswald's guilt was announced by the White House Situation Room, before any kind of investigation had been done. According to this "lone-nut solution," Oswald fired three shots from the Dallas Book Depository at President Kennedy and was single-handedly responsible for his death. Subsequently, a commission led by Chief Justice Earl Warren produced a twenty-six-volume report confirming the lone-nut theory. The Warren Report presents a coherent and orderly account of the assassination by eliminating any "facts" that might have brought incoherence and disorder to the single-gunman-operating-alone solution. In this regard, the notion of truth employed in the Warren Report is exemplified in Bradley's coherence of truth. Bradley, as you will recall, says, "If I am to have an orderly world, I cannot accept all 'facts.' . . . If by taking certain judgements of perception as true, I can get more system into my world, then these 'facts' are so far true, and if by taking certain 'facts' as errors I can order my experience better, then so far these 'facts' are errors."

While the Warren Report satisfied many, it left too many "facts" unexplained for New Orleans district attorney Jim Garrison (Kevin Costner). As a result, Garrison and a few of his staff reopen the investigation. They soon discover that many testimonies and other purported "facts" were intentionally either left out of the Warren Report or altered in ways that were coherent with the lone-nut solution. Soon they have a body of facts that points to an entirely different account of the truth regarding the assassination. In short, they believe that the Kennedy assassination was the result of a vast conspiracy to remove the president from office. The main reasons for wanting to remove him stem from his backing down from wars in Cuba and Vietnam—decisions that cost defense contractors a lot of money, embarrassed and damaged the military, and undermined anticommunist efforts. In Garrison's account, Oswald becomes a very small piece in a very large puzzle involving the FBI, the CIA, the mob, the military, and various political groups and private interests. After conspirators Clay Shaw (Tommy Lee Jones) and David Ferrie (Joe Pesci) are located and interviewed, Ferrie turns up dead, and Shaw unleashes a bevy of obstacles to the investigation. Garrison's investigation becomes weakened to the point that only a skeleton of his case remains because witnesses have died, recanted, or been discredited. Nevertheless, Garrison uses the trial as an opportunity to lay out the facts he has gathered regarding the assassination in the hope that in thirty years there will be enough facts to learn the truth.

Garrison's approach to the Kennedy assassination is representative of a correspondence theory of truth. Like Russell, he relies on facts to determine the nature of truth even if it means accepting that (1) he may have only enough facts to determine the truth of particular statements at a much later date, and (2) the coherence and comprehensiveness of his world may be shattered as result of his pursuit of the truth. In this film, for our purposes, it is not so important to determine whether Stone is accurate regarding the precise dimensions of the conspiracy—or, for that matter, whether there actually was one. What is important within the context of this film, is to see the Warren Report as an example of a coherence theory of truth in action and to see Garrison's pursuit of all the facts regarding the Kennedy assassination as an example of a correspondence theory in action.

DISCUSSION QUESTIONS

1. According to Bradley's coherence theory of truth, "If by taking certain judgements of perception as true, I can get more system into my world, then these 'facts' are so far true, and if by taking certain 'facts' as errors I can order my experience better, then so far these 'facts' are errors." How is this idea reflected in the Warren Report? Does the omission of "facts"—or, more accurately, do the "errors"— in the Warren Report reveal a weakness in the coherence theory?
2. Would you rather have a neat and coherent account of the Kennedy assassination or a sloppy and incoherent account if the latter included all the facts regarding the case and the former only those that contributed to its coherence?
3. Garrison strives to base the truth of the Kennedy assassination on facts. However, he soon finds that there are so many facts to gather that it may be some time before he can reveal the truth. Is this a weakness of correspondence theories of truth? What if all the facts regarding the assassination cannot be gathered? Does this mean that we can never have the truth regarding the question "Who killed president Kennedy, and why?"
4. What are the relative strengths and weaknesses of the correspondence and coherence theories of truth as notions of truth to utilize in your everyday life? Do you think that living as a coherentist regarding truth is more satisfying than living as a correspondist?
5. Is it unfair to link the Warren Report as depicted in this film to a coherence theory of truth? Or does it simply reveal one of the practical (although extreme) implications of this notion of truth? Discuss.
6. How do you think the public and the government would have reacted if the Warren Commission had adopted Garrison's approach toward truth in writing their report?

WILLIAM JAMES

PRAGMATISM AND TRUTH

For William James, truth is whatever "works" to put us into a satisfactory relationship with the world. In his pragmatic conception of truth, James rejects both the correspondence theory of truth and the coherence theory of truth. In reference to the correspondence theory, James asks, "Where our ideas cannot copy definitely their object, what does agreement with that object mean?" In reference to the coherence theory, James complains that it cannot distinguish between consistent truth and consistent error. In their place, James offers his pragmatic conception of truth, the notion that "the true is the name of whatever proves itself to be good in the way of belief."

A true idea or belief is one that "works," that is, one that will make a "concrete difference" in our lives. "The truth of an idea is not a stagnant property inherent in it," says James. "Truth *happens* to an idea." A true idea is made true by events in the world. "Our thoughts and beliefs 'pass,' " argues James, "just so long as nobody refuses them." We believe in things only as long as it works to do so. "Truth is made," claims James, "just as health, wealth and strength are made, in the course of experience."

For James, there is no such thing as absolute truth. "The 'absolutely' true, meaning what no farther experience will ever alter, is that ideal vanishing-point towards which we imagine that all our temporary truths will some day converge." Truth is always changeable and progressive. " 'The true,' " says James, "is only the expedient in the way of our thinking, just as 'the right' is only the expedient in the way of our behaving." For James, the question of the meaning and nature of truth, and the question of the test of truth, are not distinct: Truth "is simply a collective name for verification processes."

Pragmatism is an American philosophical movement popularized by James but founded by Charles Peirce (1839–1914). James and Peirce knew each other well but differed in their conception of pragmatism to the point that in 1905 Peirce called his own version "pragmaticism" to distinguish it from James's version. In general, pragmatism emphasizes the interpretation of ideas through their consequences. Pierce states the pragmatic maxim in 1878 as follows: "Consider what effects, which might conceivably have practical bearings, we conceive the object of our conception to have. Then, our conception of these effects is the whole of our conception of the object." James's pragmatic maxim is as follows: "The meaning of any proposition can always be brought down to some particular consequence in our future practical experience, whether passive or active."

It is interesting to note that James dedicates his *Pragmatism: A New Name for Some Old Ways of Thinking* (1907) "To the memory of John Stuart Mill." In his dedication, James goes to say that it is Mill "from whom I first learned the pragmatic openness of mind and whom my fancy likes to picture as our leader were he alive to-day." Mill is the well-known promoter of the use of consequences to determine the rightness and wrongness of action (see chapter 5). Peirce's own form of pragmatism is more closely associable with the philosophy of Kant. Nevertheless, James is probably correct when he claims that "there is absolutely nothing new in the pragmatic method"; we can see it utilized in the philosophies of Socrates, Aristotle, Locke, Berkeley, and Hume, among others. A biographical sketch of James can be found in chapter 1. The following is a selection from *Pragmatism: A New Name for Some Old Ways of Thinking*.

PRAGMATISM'S CONCEPTION OF TRUTH

I fully expect to see the pragmatist view of truth run through the classic stages of a theory's career. First, you know, a new theory is attacked as absurd; then it is admitted to be true, but obvious and insignificant; finally it is seen to be so important that its adversaries claim that they themselves discovered it. Our doctrine of truth is at present in the first of these three stages, with symptoms of the second stage having begun in certain quarters. I wish that this lecture might help it beyond the first stage in the eyes of many of you.

Truth, as any dictionary will tell you, is a property of certain of our ideas. It means their "agreement," as falsity means their disagreement, with "reality." Pragmatists and intellectualists both accept this definition as a matter of course. They begin to quarrel only after the question is raised as to what may precisely be meant by the term "agreement," and what by the term "reality," when reality is taken as something for our ideas to agree with.

In answering these questions the pragmatists are more analytic and painstaking, the intellectualists more offhand and irreflective. The popular notion is that a true idea must copy its reality. Like other popular views, this one follows the analogy of the most usual experience. Our true ideas of sensible things do indeed copy them. Shut your eyes and think of yonder clock on the wall, and you get just such a true picture or copy of its dial. But your idea of its "works" (unless you are a clock-maker) is much less of a copy, yet it passes muster, for it in no way clashes with the reality. Even though it should shrink to the mere word "works," that word still serves you truly; and when you speak of the "time-keeping function" of the clock, or of its spring's "elasticity," it is hard to see exactly what your ideas can copy.

You perceive that there is a problem here. Where our ideas cannot copy definitely their object, what does agreement with that object mean? Some idealists seem to say that they are true whenever they are what God means that we ought to think about that object. Others hold the copy-view all through, and speak as if our ideas possessed truth just in proportion as they approach to being copies of the Absolute's eternal way of thinking.

These views, you see, invite pragmatistic discussion. But the great assumption of the intellectualists is that truth means essentially an inert static relation. When you've got your true idea of anything, there's an end of the matter. You're in possession; you *know;* you have fulfilled your thinking destiny. You are where you ought to be mentally; you have obeyed your categorical imperative; and nothing more need follow on that climax of your rational destiny. Epistemologically you are in stable equilibrium.

Pragmatism, on the other hand, asks its usual question. "Grant an idea or belief to be true," it says, "what concrete difference will its being true make in anyone's actual life? How will the truth be realized? What experiences will be different from those which would obtain if the belief were false? What, in short, is the truth's cash-value in experiential terms?"

The moment pragmatism asks this question, it sees the answer: *True ideas are those that we can assimilate, validate, corroborate and verify. False ideas are those that we cannot.* That is the practical difference it makes to us to have true ideas; that, therefore, is the meaning of truth, for it is all that truth is known as.

This thesis is what I have to defend. The truth of an idea is not a stagnant property inherent in it. Truth *happens* to an idea. It *becomes* true, is *made* true by events. Its verity *is* in fact an event, a process: the process namely of its verifying itself, its veri-*fication.* Its validity is the process of its valid-*ation.*

But what do the words verification and validation themselves pragmatically mean? They again signify certain practical consequences of the verified and validated idea. It is hard to find any one phrase that characterized these consequences better than the ordinary agreement-formula—just such consequences being what we have in mind whenever we say that our ideas "agree" with reality. They lead us, namely, through the acts and other ideas which they instigate, into or up to, or towards, other parts of experience with which we feel all the while—such feeling being among our potentialities—that the original ideas remain in agreement. The connections and transitions come to us from point to point as being progressive, harmonious, satisfactory. This function of agreeable leading is what we mean by an idea's verification. . . .

The possession of true thoughts means everywhere the possession of invaluable instruments of action; and . . . our duty to gain truth, so far from being a blank command from out of the blue, or a "stunt" self-imposed by our intellect, can account for itself by excellent practical reasons.

The importance to human life of having true beliefs about matters of fact is a thing too notorious. We live in a world of realities that can be infinitely useful or infinitely harmful. Ideas that tell us which of them to expect count as the true ideas in all this primary sphere of verification, and the pursuit of such ideas is a primary human duty. The possession of truth, so far from being here an end in itself, is only a preliminary means towards other vital satisfactions. If I am lost in the woods and starved, and find what looks like a cow-path, it is of the utmost importance that I should think of a human habitation at the end of it, for if I do so and follow it, I save myself. The true thought is useful here because the house which is its object is useful. The practical value of true ideas is thus primarily derived from the practical importance of their objects to us. Their objects are, indeed, not important at all times. I may on another occasion have no use for the house; and then my idea of it, however verifiable, will be practically irrelevant, and had better remain latent. Yet since almost any object may some day become temporarily important, the advantage of having a general stock of *extra* truths, of ideas that shall be true of merely possible situations, is obvious. We store such extra truths away in our memories, and with the overflow we fill our books of reference. Whenever such an extra truth becomes practically relevant to one of our emergencies, it passes from cold-storage to do work in the world and our belief in it grows active. You can say of it then either that "it is useful because it is true" or that "it is true because it is useful." Both these phrases mean exactly the same thing, namely that here is an idea that gets fulfilled and can be verified. True is the name for whatever idea starts the verification-process, useful is the name for its completed function in experience. True ideas would never have been singled out as such, would never have acquired a class-name, least of all a name suggesting value, unless they had been useful from the outset in this way.

From this simple cue pragmatism gets her general notion of truth as something essentially bound up with the way in which one moment in our experience may lead us towards other moments which it will be worthwhile to have been led to. Primarily, and on the common-sense level, the truth of a state of mind means this function of *a leading that is worthwhile*. When a moment in our experience, of any kind whatever, inspires us with a thought that is true, that means that sooner or later we dip by that thought's guidance into the particulars of experience again and make advantageous connection with them. This is a vague enough statement, but I beg you to retain, it, for it is essential.

Our experience meanwhile is all shot through with regularities. One bit of it can warn us to get ready for another bit, can "intend" or be "significant of" that remoter object. The object's advent is the significance's verification. Truth, in these cases, meaning nothing but eventual verification, is manifestly incompatible with waywardness on our part. Woe to him whose beliefs play fast and loose with the order which realities follow in his experience; they will lead him nowhere or else make false connections.

By "realities" or "objects" here, we mean either things of common sense, sensibly present, or else common-sense relations, such as dates, places, distances, kinds, activities. Following our mental image of a house along the cow-path, we actually come to see the house; we get the image's full verification. *Such simply and fully verified leadings are certainly the originals and prototypes of the truth-process.* Experience offers indeed other forms of truth-process, but they are all conceivable as being primary verifications arrested, multiplied or substituted one for another.

Take, for instance, yonder object on the wall. You and I consider it to be a "clock," altho no one of us has seen the hidden works that make it one. We let our notion pass for true without attempting to verify. If truths mean verification-process essentially, ought we then to call such unverified truths as this abortive? No, for they form the overwhelmingly large number of the truths we live by. Indirect as well as direct verifications pass muster. Where circumstantial evidence is sufficient, we can go without eye-witnessing. Just as we here assume Japan to exist without ever having been there, because it *works* to do so, everything we know conspiring with the belief, and nothing interfering, so we assume that thing to be a clock. We *use* it as a clock, regulating the length of our lecture by it. The verification of the assumption here means its leading to no frustration or contradiction. Verifi-*ability* of wheels and weights and pendulum is as good as verification. For one truth-process completed there are a million in our lives that function in this state of nascency. They turn us *towards* direct verification; lead us into the *surroundings* of the objects they envisage; and then, if everything runs on harmoniously, we are so sure that verification is possible that we omit it, and are usually justified by all that happens.

Truth lives, in fact, for the most part on a credit system. Our thoughts and beliefs "pass," so long as nothing challenges them, just as bank-notes pass so long as nobody refuses them. But this all points to direct face-to-face verifications somewhere, without which the fabric of truth collapses like a financial system with no cash-basis whatever. You accept my verification of one thing, I yours of another. We trade on each other's truth. But beliefs verified concretely by *somebody* are the posts of the whole superstructure.

Another great reason—beside economy of time—for waiving complete verification in the usual business of life is that all things exist in kinds and not singly. Our world is found once for all to have that peculiarity. So that when we have once directly verified our ideas about one specimen of a kind, we consider ourselves free to apply them to other specimens without verification. A mind that habitually discerns the kind of thing before it, and acts by the law of the kind immediately, without pausing to verify, will be a "true" mind in ninety-nine out of a hundred emergencies, proved so by its conduct fitting everything it meets, and getting no refutation.

Indirectly or only potentially verifying processes may thus be true as well as full verification-processes. They work as true processes would work, give us the same advantages, and claim our recognition for the same reasons. . . . Our account of truth is an account of truths in the plural, of processes of leading, realized *in rebus* [in things], and having only this quality in common, that they *pay*. They pay by guiding us into or towards some part of a system that dips at numerous points into sensepercepts, which we may copy mentally or not, but with which at any rate we are now in the kind of commerce vaguely designated as verification. Truth for us is simply a collective name for verification-processes, just as health, wealth, strength, etc., are names for other processes connected with life, and also pursued because it pays to pursue them. Truth is *made*, just as health, wealth and strength are made, in the course of experience.

Here rationalism is instantaneously up in arms against us. I can imagine a rationalist to talk as follows:

"Truth is not made," he will say; "it absolutely obtains, being a unique relation that does not wait upon any process, but shoots straight over the head of experience, and hits its reality every time. Our belief that yon thing on the wall is a clock is true already, altho no one in the whole history of the world should verify it. The bare quality of standing in that transcendent relation is what makes any thought true that possesses it, whether or not there be verification. You pragmatists put the cart before the horse in making truth's being reside in verification-processes. These are merely signs of its being, merely our lame ways of ascertaining after the fact which of our ideas already has possessed the wondrous quality. The quality itself is timeless, like all essences and natures. Thoughts partake of it directly, as they partake of falsity or of irrelevancy. It can't be analyzed away into pragmatic consequences."

The whole plausibility of this rationalist tirade is due to the fact to which we have already paid so much attention. In our world, namely, abounding as it does in things of similar kinds and similarly associated, one verification serves for others of its kind, and one great use of knowing things is to be led not so much to them as to their associates, especially to human talk about them. The quality of truth, obtaining *ante rem* [before the thing], pragmatically means, then, the fact that in such a world innumerable ideas work better by their indirect or possible than by their direct and actual verification. Truth *ante rem* means only verifiability, then; or else it is a case of the stock rationalist trick of treating the *name* of a concrete phenomenal reality as an independent prior entity, and placing it behind the reality as its explanation. . . .

In the case of "wealth" we all see the fallacy. We know that wealth is but a name for concrete processes that certain men's lives play a part in, and not a natural excellence found in Messrs. Rockefeller and Carnegie, but not in the rest of us.

Like wealth, health also lives *in rebus*. It is a name for processes, as digestion, circulation, sleep, etc., that go on happily, tho in this instance we are more inclined to think of it as a principle and to say the man digests and sleeps so well *because* he is so healthy.

With "strength" we are, I think, more rationalistic still, and decidedly inclined to treat it as an excellence pre-existing in the man and explanatory of the herculean performances of his muscles.

With "truth" most people go over the border entirely, and treat the rationalistic account as self-evident. But really all these words in *th* are exactly similar. Truth exists *ante rem* just as much and as little as the other things do.

The scholastics, following Aristotle, made much of the distinction between habit and act. Health *in actu* [in actuality] means, among other things, good sleeping and digesting. But a healthy man need not always be sleeping, or always digesting, any more than a wealthy man need be always handling money, or a strong man always lifting weights. All such qualities sink to the status of "habits" between their times of exercise; and similarly truth becomes a habit of certain of our ideas and beliefs in their intervals of rest from their verifying activities. But those activities are the root of the whole matter, and the condition of there being any habit to exist in the intervals.

"The true," to put it very briefly, is only the expedient in the way of our thinking, just as "the right" is only the expedient in the way of our behaving. Expedient in almost any fashion; and expedient in the long run and on the whole of course; for what meets expediently all the experience in sight won't necessarily meet all farther experiences equally satisfactorily. Experience, as we know, has ways of *boiling over*, and making us correct our present formulas.

The "absolutely" true, meaning what no farther experience will ever alter, is that ideal vanishing-point towards which we imagine that all our temporary truths will some day converge. It runs on all fours with the perfectly wise man, and with the absolutely complete experience; and, if these ideals are ever realized, they will all be realized together. Meanwhile we have to live today by what truth we can get today, and be ready tomorrow to call it falsehood. Ptolemaic astronomy, Euclidean space, Aristotelian logic, scholastic metaphysics, were expedient for centuries, but human experience has boiled over those limits, and we now call these things only relatively true, or true within those borders of experience. "Absolutely" they are false; for we know that those limits were casual, and might

have been transcended by past theorists just as they are by present thinkers. . . .

What Pragmatism Means

Truth is *one species of good*, and not, as is usually supposed, a category distinct from good, and coordinate with it. *The true is the name of whatever proves itself to be good in the way of belief, and good, too, for definite, assignable reasons.* Surely you must admit this, that if there were *no* good for life in true ideas, or if the knowledge of them were positively disadvantageous and false ideas the only useful ones, then the current notion that truth is divine and precious, and its pursuit a duty, could never have grown up or become a dogma. In a world like that, our duty would be to *shun* truth, rather. But in this world, just as certain foods are not only agreeable to our taste, but good for our teeth, our stomach, and our tissues; so certain ideas are not only agreeable to think about, or agreeable as supporting other ideas that we are fond of, but they are also helpful in life's practical struggles. If there be any life that it is really better we should lead, and if there be any idea which, if believed in, would help us to lead that life, then it would be really *better for us* to believe in that idea, *unless, indeed, belief in it incidentally clashed with other greater vital benefits.*

"What would be better for us to believe!" This sounds very like a definition of truth. It comes very near to saying "what we *ought* to believe": and in *that* definition none of you would find any oddity. Ought we ever not to believe what it is *better for us* to believe? And can we then keep the notion of what is better for us, and what is true for us, permanently apart?

Pragmatism says no, and I fully agree with her. Probably you also agree, so far as the abstract statement goes, but with a suspicion that if we practically did believe everything that made for good in our own personal lives, we should be found indulging all kinds of fancies about this world's affairs, and all kinds of sentimental superstitions about a world hereafter. Your suspicion here is undoubtedly well founded, and it is evident that something happens when you pass from the abstract to the concrete that complicates the situation.

I said just now that what is better for us to believe is true *unless the belief incidentally clashes with some other vital benefit.* Now in real life what vital benefits is any particular belief of ours most liable to clash with? What indeed except the vital benefits yielded by *other beliefs* when these *prove* incompatible with the first ones? In other words, the greatest enemy of any one of our truths may be the rest of our truths. Truths have once for all this desperate instinct of self-preservation and of desire to extinguish whatever contradicts them. . . .

DISCUSSION QUESTIONS

1. In general, how is the pragmatic conception of truth different from the correspondence theory of truth and the coherence theory of truth? Which do you prefer, and why?

2. James states, "Truth *happens* to an idea." What does he mean? Can "truth" happen to *any* idea? Why or why not?

3. " 'The true,' " says James, "is only the expedient in the way of our thinking, just as 'the right' is only the expedient in the way of our behaving." Discuss this passage. Is there is a parallel between truth in general and moral truth in particular? Why or why not?

4. For James, truth "is simply a collective name for verification processes." What does this mean? Do you think that the nature of truth should be distinguished from the way in which we test the truthfulness of a belief or idea?

5. Charles Peirce complained that James turned pragmatism into a theory of action rather than a theory of meaning. What is the difference? Compare the pragmatic maxims of Peirce and James. Which do you prefer, and why?

Chinatown
[USA 1974] 2 hours, 11 minutes
Directed by Roman Polanski

*J*ake Gittes (Jack Nicholson) is approached by a woman to investigate her husband's extramarital affair. The man in question is Hollis Mulwray (Darrell Zwerling), head of the Los Angeles city water department. Jake learns that Mulwray is currently trying to block a dam from being built in the Los Angeles area and is spending a lot of time watching water flow out of drain pipes. Jake finally finds Mulwray in the arms of a young woman, though he does not learn her name. The story makes the front page of the newspaper with the headline "Department of Water and Power Blows Fuse over Chief's Use of Funds for El Macando Love Nest."

After briefly celebrating cracking the case, Jake is confronted by Evelyn Mulwray (Faye Dunaway), who tells him that she never hired him for this case. Jake realizes that he has been set up: If the real Mrs. Mulwray did not hire him, then who did? And why? At first, Evelyn Mulwray is upset and begins legal proceedings to sue Jake; then, suddenly, she drops the lawsuit and asks Jake to forget the whole thing. But Jake cannot let go of the case—he wants the truth. So, he seeks out Hollis Mulwray for questioning but finds out that he has turned up in a fresh-water reservoir. Immediately, Jake suspects foul play, and the coroner's report revealing salt water in Mulwray's lungs further heightens his suspicion. Soon, Jake learns the "truth" about has what happened . . . or does he?

First truth: The city of Los Angeles is not running critically low on water. A corrupt group of individuals led by Noah Cross (John Huston) is diverting city water into storm drains and the sea in order to give the illusion of a water shortage. The perception of a waters shortage is necessary so that Cross can convince the city to fund the dam project. In the meantime, Cross is denying water to large areas of real estate outside city limits. As the value of the land decreases, Cross and his associates purchase it at a very low price. Their ultimate plan is to purchase all the land in this area and then use the water from the dam project to irrigate it. This would greatly increase the value of the land and make Cross a lot of money. Eventually, the bond passes for the dam. However, because the dam is supposed to be used only for city water needs, and Cross's newly acquired land is outside of city limits, Cross sees to it that his newly acquired land is rezoned as city land. This will allow him to legally irrigate the land with water from the dam, and thus greatly increase the value of the land.

Second truth: Cross killed Hollis Mulwray. Jake learns that Mulwray was attempting to thwart Cross's dam project because he thought the dam would be unsafe. Cross murdered Mulwray so that the dam project could proceed, despite the fact that Mulwray was once Cross's dear friend and business partner, and was currently his son-in-law.

Third truth: Cross had a daughter with his own daughter, Evelyn Mulwray. Their daughter, Katherine (Belinda Palmer), was the woman Hollis Mulwray was photographed with by Jake. Evelyn Mulwray hates her father and tries to keep Katherine away from him.

Although Jake has facts to back up each of these "truths," no one aside from his inner circle of associates believes him. The police are led to believe, through the influence of Cross, that Evelyn Mulwray is responsible for the death of her husband. The movie ends in Chinatown with Jake in temporary custody, watching as Mulwray attempts to flee to Mexico with her daughter/sister Katherine, and Cross and the police trying to prevent them. The police kill Mulwray as she tries to drive away.

Arguably, in *Chinatown*, we see two different notions of truth compete with each other. The first is presented through the world of Jake Giddes, and the second is presented through the world of Noah Cross. Giddes regards truth as a correspondence with reality, whereas Cross regards truth as whatever will put him and his friends into a satisfactory—or financially profitable—relationship with the world.

DISCUSSION QUESTIONS

1. How closely does Jake's notion of truth mirror Russell's correspondence theory of truth? How are their views similar? How are they different?
2. How closely does Cross's notion of truth mirror James's pragmatic theory of truth? How are their views similar? How are they different?
3. How does Cross's pragmatic notion of truth as represented through his actions in *Chinatown* reveal strengths and weaknesses in pragmatic notions of truth? After viewing this film, do you feel more or less inclined to embrace a pragmatist theory of truth?
4. In what way is Cross's notion of truth representative of a coherence theory of truth? In what way is it not? Discuss.
5. Russell contends that his correspondence theory of truth is superior to the coherence theory of truth, the position that the true is a coherent system of ideas. For the sake of argument, assume that Jake's position on truth is similar to Russell's, and that Cross's position on truth is representative of a coherence notion of truth. Does *Chinatown* support Russell's contention?
6. After watching this film and thinking about the different notions of truth at work in it, do you see your own view of truth as more like that of Jake or Cross? Why?
7. After seeing truth by correspondence, with facts subdued or repressed by Cross and the other corrupt people in Los Angeles, why do you think Jake says "As little as possible," as he looks at the dead body of Evelyn Mulwray, who has just been shot by the police, at the end of the film?

8. Jake tells the "fake" Mrs. Mulwray at the beginning of the film not to pursue her husband's affair. It is better not to know the truth about it, says Jake, better to "let sleeping dogs lie." Is this also the moral of this movie? While the correspondence theory of truth might reveal certain things about the world that are not immediately apparent to us, we really don't want to know truth in this sense. Do you agree that we should "let sleeping truth lie"?

9. Does this movie convince you that there are two different and legitimate versions of the truth in Chinatown? Why or why not?

10. In the following exchange, one of the most disturbing scenes in the film, Evelyn Mulwray finally tells Jake about Katherine, her sister/daugher:

JAKE   "Who is she? And don't give me that crap about it being your sister. You don't have a sister."

EVELYN   "I'll tell you the truth . . ."

JAKE   "That's good. Now what's her name?"

EVELYN   "Katherine."

JAKE   "Katherine? . . . Katherine who?"

EVELYN   "She's my daughter."

JAKE   "I said the truth!"

EVELYN   "She's my sister . . . she's my daughter . . . my sister . . . my daughter, my sister . . ."

JAKE   "I said I want the truth."

EVELYN   "She's my sister and my daughter!"

Why do you think Evelyn is having difficulty stating the truth concerning her relationship to Katherine? Analyze her response from the perspective of various theories of truth. Which theory of truth best explains her struggles with the truth concerning her relationship to Katherine?

FRIEDRICH NIETZSCHE

On Truth and Lie in a Nonmoral Sense

Friedrich Nietzsche argues that truths tell us nothing about reality, that they are illusions about which we have forgotten that this is what they are. For Nietzsche, the correspondence theory of truth is the ideal model of truth. However, it is a conception of truth that is unattainable. There is no way that our representations of things can ever perfectly correspond with reality, which means, in one respect, that truth is not available to us.

For Nietzsche, the process of metaphor formation more accurately resembles the way in which we form our notions of truth and lie than the hopelessly idealistic correspondence theory of truth. In metaphor formation, subject matter is referred to by a term or sentence that does not literally describe it—for example, "the winter of our discontent" or "the ship of state." According to Nietzsche, we come to know the world through a process akin to metaphor formation wherein our representations of things are fused with the things in themselves. The result of this process is akin to a live and vivid metaphor. In turn, however, these live metaphors are turned into cold, dead concepts or metaphors. And, says Nietzsche, truth is merely dead metaphor. This idea is found in one of his most famous statements: "What, then, is truth? A mobile army of metaphors, metonyms, and anthropomorphisms—in short, a sum of human relations, which have been enhanced, transposed, and embellished poetically and rhetorically, and which after long use seem firm, canonical, and obligatory to a people: that truths are illusions about which one has forgotten that this is what they are; metaphors which are worn out and without sensuous power; coins which have lost their pictures and now matter only as metal, no longer as coins." Truths, then, are dead metaphors in the sense that these truths have been used for so long that we have forgotten that they are *not* statements corresponding to things in themselves or reality.

Truth, claims Nietszche, as a "regularly valid and obligatory designation of things is invented, and this linguistic legislation also furnishes the first laws of truth: for it is here that the contrast between truth and lie first originates." According to Nietzsche, a "liar uses the valid designations, the words, to make the unreal appear real. . . . He abuses the fixed conventions by arbitrary changes or even by reversals of the names." In the final analysis, even if truth affords us the comfort of a life of certainty, it is a sense of comfort that comes as a result of maintaining certain illusions. Nevertheless, as Richard Rorty says near the close of the next selection, "Nietzsche hoped that eventually there might be human beings who could and did think of truth in this way, but who still liked themselves, who saw themselves as *good* people."

A biographical sketch of Nietzsche appears in chapter 1. The following selection is from "On Truth and Lie in a Nonmoral Sense," a fragment written in 1873 but not published until after Nietzsche's death.

In some remote corner of the universe, poured out and glittering in innumerable solar systems, there once was a star on which clever animals invented knowledge. That was the haughtiest and most mendacious minute of "world history"—yet only a minute. After nature had drawn a few breaths the star grew cold, and the clever animals had to die.

One might invent such a fable and still not have illustrated sufficiently how wretched, how shadowy and flighty, how aimless and arbitrary, the human intellect appears in nature. There have been eternities when it did not exist; and when it is done for again, nothing will have happened. For this intellect has no further mission that would lead beyond human life. It is human, rather, and only its owner and producer gives it such importance, as if the world pivoted around it. But if we could communicate with the mosquito, then we would learn that it floats through the air with the same self-importance, feeling within itself the flying center of the world. There is nothing in nature so despicable or insignificant that it cannot immediately be blown up like a bag by a slight breath of this power of knowledge; and just as every porter wants an admirer, the proudest human being, the philosopher, thinks that he sees the eyes of the universe telescopically focused from all sides on his actions and thoughts.

It is strange that this should be the effect of the intellect, for after all it was given only as an aid to the most unfortunate, most delicate, most evanescent beings in order to hold them for a minute in existence, from which otherwise, without this gift, they would have every reason to flee as quickly as Lessing's son.* That haughtiness

---

* Gotthold Ephraim Lessing (1729–81) was a German dramatist, critic, and philosopher. His major philosophical work is *Laocoön*—a work on the philosophy of art, which argues that each art has its own governing principles and function. In 1776, Lessing married Eva König, a widow, who died in 1778 after giving birth to a son who lived but a short time.—Ed.

which goes with knowledge and feeling, which shrouds the eyes and senses of man in a blinding fog, therefore deceives him about the value of existence by carrying in itself the most flattering evaluation of knowledge itself. Its most universal effect is deception; but even its most particular effects have something of the same character.

The intellect, as a means for the preservation of the individual, unfolds its chief powers in simulation; for this is the means by which the weaker, less robust individuals preserve themselves, since they are denied the chance of waging the struggle for existence with horns or the fangs of beasts of prey. In man this art of simulation reaches its peak: here deception, flattery, lying and cheating, talking behind the back, posing, living in borrowed splendor, being masked, the disguise of convention, acting a role before others and before oneself—in short, the constant fluttering around the single flame of vanity is so much the rule and the law that almost nothing is more incomprehensible than how an honest and pure urge for truth could make its appearance among men. They are deeply immersed in illusions and dream images; their eye glides only over the surface of things and sees "forms"; their feeling nowhere leads into truth, but contents itself with the reception of stimuli, playing, as it were, a game of blindman's buff on the backs of things. Moreover, man permits himself to be lied to at night, his life long, when he dreams, and his moral sense never even tries to prevent this— although men have been said to have overcome snoring by sheer will power.

What, indeed, does man know of himself! Can he even once perceive himself completely, laid out as if in an illuminated glass case? Does not nature keep much the most from him, even about his body, to spellbind and confine him in a proud, deceptive consciousness, far from the coils of the intestines, the quick current of the blood stream, and the involved tremors of the fibers? She threw away the key; and woe to the calamitous curiosity which might peer just once through a crack in the chamber of consciousness and look down, and sense that man rests upon the merciless, the greedy, the insatiable, the murderous, in the indifference of his ignorance— hanging in dreams, as it were, upon the back of a

tiger. In view of this, whence in all the world comes the urge for truth?

Insofar as the individual wants to preserve himself against other individuals, in a natural state of affairs he employs the intellect mostly for simulation alone. But because man, out of need and boredom, wants to exist socially, herd-fashion, he requires a peace pact and he endeavors to banish at least the very crudest *bellum omnium contra omnes* [war of all against all] from his world. This peace pact brings with it something that looks like the first step toward the attainment of this enigmatic urge for truth. For now that is fixed which henceforth shall be "truth"; that is, a regularly valid and obligatory designation of things is invented, and this linguistic legislation also furnishes the first laws of truth: for it is here that the contrast between truth and lie first originates. The liar uses the valid designations, the words, to make the unreal appear as real; he says, for example, "I am rich," when the word "poor" would be the correct designation of his situation. He abuses the fixed conventions by arbitrary changes or even by reversals of the names. When he does this in a self-serving way damaging to others, then society will no longer trust him but exclude him. Thereby men do not flee from being deceived as much as from being damaged by deception: what they hate at this stage is basically not the deception but the bad, hostile consequences of certain kinds of deceptions. In a similarly limited way man wants the truth: he desires the agreeable life-preserving consequences of truth, but he is indifferent to pure knowledge, which has no consequences; he is even hostile to possibly damaging and destructive truths. And, moreover, what about these conventions of language? Are they really the products of knowledge, of the sense of truth? Do the designations and the things coincide? Is language the adequate expression of all realities?

Only through forgetfulness can man ever achieve the illusion of possessing a "truth" in the sense just designated. If he does not wish to be satisfied with truth in the form of a tautology— that is, with empty shells—then he will forever buy illusions for truths. What is a word? The image of a nerve stimulus in sounds. But to infer from the nerve stimulus, a cause outside us, that is already the result of a false and unjustified application of the principle of reason. . . . The different languages, set side by side, show that what matters with words is never the truth, never an adequate expression; else there would not be so many languages. The "thing in itself" (for that is what pure truth, without consequences, would be) is quite incomprehensible to the creators of language and not at all worth aiming for. One designates only the relations of things to man, and to express them one calls on the boldest metaphors. A nerve stimulus, first transposed into an image—first metaphor. The image, in turn, imitated by a sound—second metaphor. . . .

Let us still give special consideration to the formation of concepts. Every word immediately becomes a concept, inasmuch as it is not intended to serve as a reminder of the unique and wholly individualized original experience to which it owes its birth, but must at the same time fit innumerable, more or less similar cases—which means, strictly speaking, never equal—in other words, a lot of unequal cases. Every concept originates through our equating what is unequal. No leaf ever wholly equals another, and the concept "leaf" is formed through an arbitrary abstraction from these individual differences, through forgetting the distinctions; and now it gives rise to the idea that in nature there might be something besides the leaves which would be "leaf"—some kind of original form after which all leaves have been woven, marked, copied, colored, curled, and painted, but by unskilled hands, so that no copy turned out to be a correct, reliable, and faithful image of the original form. We call a person "honest." Why did he act so honestly today? we ask. Our answer usually sounds like this: because of his honesty. Honesty! That is to say again: the leaf is the cause of the leaves. After all, we know nothing of an essence-like quality named "honesty"; we know only numerous individualized, and thus unequal actions, which we equate by omitting the unequal and by then calling them honest actions. In the end, we distill from them a *qualitas occulta* with the name of "honesty." . . .

What, then, is truth? A mobile army of metaphors, metonyms, and anthropomorphisms—in short, a sum of human relations, which have been enhanced, transposed, and embellished poetically and rhetorically, and which after long use seem firm, canonical, and obligatory to a people: truths are illusions about which one has forgotten that this is what they are; metaphors which are worn out and without sensuous power; coins which have lost their pictures and now matter only as metal, no longer as coins.

We still do not know where the urge for truth comes from; for as yet we have heard only of the obligation imposed by society that it should exist: to be truthful means using the customary metaphors—in moral terms: the obligation to lie according to a fixed convention, to lie herd-like in a style obligatory for all. . . .

DISCUSSION QUESTIONS

1. Why does Nietzsche believe that truth tells us nothing about reality? Compare Nietzsche's view of truth with Kant's view of knowledge. How are their views similar? How are they different?

2. Nietzsche contends that the correspondence theory of truth is the ideal theory of truth, but he concedes that it sets an unattainably high standard for truth. Do you agree with him? Why or why not?

3. Nietzsche associates truth formation with the process of metaphor formation. How and why does he do this? Do you find his argument convincing?

4. Nietzsche says that a "liar uses the valid designations, the words, to make the unreal appear real." What does he mean? Compare Nietzsche's use of "liar" with your own understanding of the term.

5. Both James and Nietzsche reject absolute truth. Who makes a stronger case for rejecting absolute truth, and why?

Proof

[Australia 1991] 1 hour, 32 minutes
Directed by Jocelyn Moorhouse

Martin (Hugo Weaving) has been blind since birth. When he was a boy (Jeffrey Walker), his mother (Heather Mitchell) used to describe a garden that could be viewed from their apartment window. She would do this twice a day. Martin always had the feeling, though, that she was lying to him about the garden in order "to punish [him] for being blind." When he was ten, Martin asked for and received a camera. His first photo was one of the garden. Since then he has taken many more photos. He pays people to give him short descriptions of the photos, which he then types out in braille and affixes to the backs of the photos.

When he is in his early thirties, Martin befriends Andy (Russell Crowe), whom he meets at a local restaurant. Andy offers to provide brief descriptions of Martin's photographs at no cost. Martin asks only that he always tell the truth about the content of the photos, and Andy agrees. Andy soon learns that Martin's housecleaner, Celia (Genevieve Picot), loves Martin but that Martin does not return her affections. In fact, Martin goes out of his way to abuse Celia regarding her feelings. Nevertheless, Celia continues to hope that Martin will come to love her. She cannot accept the truth that Martin does not love her and continually disregards the fact that Martin is treating her badly. Celia becomes jealous of Martin's budding friendship with Andy and seeks to sabotage it.

First, Celia allows Martin to take a photo of her distracting his dog in the park. For a while, Martin has been wondering where his dog disappears to every day for five minutes when they go to the park. So, when his dog disappears one day, he takes panoramic photos of the event in the hope of learning what his dog is doing when he disappears each day. Celia has been distracting the dog, but Martin does not know it. The photographs he takes shows Celia distracting the dog and Andy running to get out of the picture. When Martin asks Andy to describe the photo, he lies to him, saying nothing about his or her presence in the photo.

Second, Celia strikes up an affair with Andy in order to drive a wedge between Martin and Andy. Martin soon learns of the affair and of Andy's lie about the photo, and he fires Celia and refuses to speak with Andy. Soon, however, he reconciles with Andy, allowing him to describe to him the one photo that has never been described to him: the garden photo he took when he was ten. He learns that his mother had been telling him the truth about the garden all along. Andy apologizes to Martin, telling him, "I lied about Celia, but nothing else." Martin responds, "How can I believe you." Andy replies, "You can't. You tell the truth Martin, your whole life is the truth. Have some pity on the rest of us."

Proof arguably introduces three distinct senses of truth: Nietzschean, pragmatist, and correspondence. First, Celia uses truth like Nietzsche's "liar." She has told herself for so long that Martin is in love with her when, in fact, he despises her that her words and statements have long lost their correspondence with things in themselves. In her dealings with Martin, she continually, in Nietzsche's words, "uses the valid designations, the words, to make the unreal appear real" and "abuses the fixed conventions by arbitrary changes or even by reversals of the names." While maintaining the illusion of Martin's love gives her comfort and provides her life with a sense of certainty by allowing her to think that she is loved by the one whom she loves, it is all a lie: truths based on illusions about which she has forgotten—this is what they are. Even as Martin is firing her, she clings to words falsely associated with reality by asking him to kiss her. Celia's truths about the world are like dead metaphors: they do not correspond to any reality regarding Martin.

Second, Andy believes that truth is whatever puts us into a satisfactory relationship with the world. Thus, when Martin asks him to describe a photo of Celia luring Martin's dog away, Andy will not describe it because if he does it will hurt Martin. Martin is a pragmatist about truth: the truth is not about always describing the facts that are before us; rather, it is about using truth to put us into a satisfactory relationship with the world. For Andy, convincing Martin of an alternate description of the content of the photo is well within the bounds of a pragmatist notion of truth.

Finally, truth for Martin involves a one-to-one mapping of sensations to statements. What he hears, feels, tastes, and smells provides a strong link to his beliefs, the final proof of which is a photograph that establishes a visual correspondence to the facts. The camera becomes his eyes, filling in the factual information from the fifth sense that is unavailable to him naturally. Truth always and everywhere corresponds to the facts for Martin. The question explored throughout the film regarding the differing concepts of truth enacted by the three major characters is how their beliefs about truth affect their respective lives.

DISCUSSION QUESTIONS

1. Martin says "You can't know how important truth is to me." Why do you think truth is so important to Martin?
2. Martin says, "I wanted a camera. I thought it would help me see." Do his camera and his photos help him to see? Why or why not?
3. Consider the following dialogue between Andy and Martin:

   ANDY   "What are you doing?"

   MARTIN   "I'm labeling it."

   ANDY   "Why?"

   MARTIN   "Proof."

   ANDY   "Of what?"

   MARTIN   "Of what's in the photograph is what was there."

   ANDY   "A photograph could be of anything, anywhere."

   MARTIN   "Except it isn't. I was there Andy. I probably know more of what's in that vet's waiting room than you do. I know there were two fluorescent bulbs above me . . . I know a woman wore expensive perfume . . . but this is proof of what I sensed you saw through your eyes . . . the truth."

   Why do photographs prove to Martin the truth about what he has experienced through his other senses? Are they good proof? Why or why not?

4. Martin strives to know for certain that what he experiences through his senses corresponds with what others can see in a photos of the event. In the process, however, he reveals the limits of visual imagery: photos cannot reproduce the sounds, smells, feel, and tastes of what they iconically represent. Discuss the truth value of photos from the position of the correspondence theory of truth. Does the truth value of photos fare much better according to other theories of truth? Why or why not?
5. This film asks us to reconsider an old dictum: "Seeing is believing." Discuss this statement in light of the events in the film.

6. Discuss Celia's notion of truth in this film. Can it best be described as a Nietzschean notion of truth? Why or why not? If it can, what strengths and limitations does it reveal in the Nietzschean theory of truth? If not, what theory of truth better mirrors Celia's actions?

7. What are the effects on Celia and those around her of believing truths based on illusions that she has forgotten are illusions?

8. Discuss Andy's notion of truth in this film. Can it best be described as a pragmatist notion of truth? Why or why not? If it can, what strengths and limitations does it reveal in the pragmatist theory of truth? If not, what theory of truth better mirrors Andy's actions?

9. Compare the notions of truth represented in this film through the characters of Andy, Martin, and Celia. Which notion of truth within the context of this film is the strongest? Which the weakest? Why?

10. Reconsider Russell's notion of a "fact" in view of Martin's actions in this film. Do facts in Russell's sense have visual dimensions in addition to auditory (hearing), tactile (touch), olfactory (smell), and gustatory (taste) dimensions? Or are facts independent of our senses? If so, in what way do they "correspond" with statements? Do facts look like statements? Taste like statements? And so on. How do we verify that facts correspond with statements?

11. If Russell's facts are independent of our senses, then is not Martin, who lacks sight, in no better or worse position to verify the correspondence of facts with statements than is someone who has the ability to see? Does this represent a difficulty for Russell's theory? Discuss.

RICHARD RORTY

SOLIDARITY OR OBJECTIVITY?

Richard Rorty argues that we should view truth as what is good for *us* to believe. While his position on truth is close to that of William James, Rorty emphasizes the "us" or "solidarity" aspect of this statement much more than James. Moreover, Rorty's comments on truth incorporate elements of thought from other thinkers such as Friedrich Nietzsche. Consequently, Rorty's own position on truth is generally called *neopragmatism* in order to show its connections to and divergences from the positions of James and other pragmatists.

According to Rorty, reflective human beings tell themselves two general stories about their own lives into order to make sense of them and to draw them into a broader context: objectivity and solidarity. *Objectivity* is a story we tell ourselves about how we stand in immediate relation to a nonhuman reality. *Solidarity* is a story we tell about our contribution to a community. For Rorty, the story that has been told since Socrates and Plato about "truth" has been one about finding a sense of "one's existence by turning away from solidarity to objectivity." He calls this story "realism," the effort "to construe truth as a correspondence to reality," and, like both James and Nietzsche, he rejects it.

Unlike realism, a story that requires both a metaphysics and an epistemology, the "pragmatism" story requires neither. According to Rorty, the pragmatist wishes "to reduce objectivity to solidarity." "For pragmatists," writes Rorty, "the desire for objectivity is not the desire to escape the limitations of one's community, but simply the desire for as much intersubjective agreement as possible, the desire to extend the reference 'us' as far as we can."

Furthermore, while this pragmatism might be labeled a form of relativism, it is not a self-refuting (every belief is as good as every other) or eccentric ("true" is an equivocal term that has as many meanings as there are procedures of justification) type of relativism. Rather, the "ethnocentric" relativism at the center of pragmatism tell us that "there is nothing to be said about either truth or rationality apart from descriptions of the familiar procedures of justification which a given society—*ours*—uses in one or another area of inquiry."

Rorty does not think that pragmatism's ethnocentrism should be called a form of relativism. Whereas relativism requires that we hold a "positive theory which says that something is relative to something else," pragmatism makes only "the purely *negative* point that we should drop the traditional distinction between knowledge and opinion." For Rorty, the pragmatist position on truth is not a theory and does not maintain that truth has an intrinsic nature. Rather, it a way of thinking about truth "as entirely a matter of solidarity."

Richard Rorty (1931–) is the best-known contemporary advocate of pragmatism. He was educated at the University of Chicago (B.A., 1949; M.A., 1952) and Yale University (Ph.D., 1956), and has taught at Yale University (1956–57), Wellesley College (1958–61), Princeton University (1961–82), and the University of Virginia (1982–1998). He now teaches comparative literature at Stanford University. In 1979, he published *Philosophy and the Mirror of Nature*, a book that argued that it is impossible to pass judgment on our beliefs from an objective standpoint. This book received wide attention, much of it negative, among the American philosophical community and established Rorty's reputation as one of the most provocative and influential philosophers living in America today. It has been translated into sixteen languages. A later book, *Contingency, Irony, and Solidarity* (1988), has been translated into twenty-four languages. He is the author of a number of other books including *Consequences of Pragmatism* (1982), *Achieving Our Country: Leftist Thought in Twentieth Century America* (1998), and *Philosophy and Social Hope* (2000). First published in 1985, "Solidarity or Objectivity?" is a revision of a paper first given as a Howison Lecture at the University of California, Berkeley.

There are two principal ways in which reflective human beings try, by placing their lives in a larger context, to give sense to those lives. The first is by telling the story of their contribution to a community. This community may be the actual historical one in which they live, or another actual one, distant in time or place, or a quite imaginary one, consisting perhaps of a dozen heroes and heroines selected from history or fiction or both. The second way is to describe themselves as standing in immediate relation to a nonhuman reality. This relation is immediate in the sense that it does not derive from a relation between such a reality and their tribe, or their nation, or their imagined band of comrades. I shall say that stories of the former kind exemplify the desire for solidarity, and that stories of the latter kind exemplify the desire for objectivity. Insofar as a person is seeking solidarity, she does not ask about the relation between the practices of the chosen community and something outside that community. Insofar as she seeks objectivity, she distances herself from the actual persons around her not by thinking of herself as a member of some other real, or imaginary group, but rather by attaching herself to something which can be described without reference to any particular human beings.

The tradition in Western culture which centers [on] the notion of the search for Truth, a tradition which runs from the Greek philosophers through the Enlightenment, is the clearest example of the attempt to find a sense in one's existence by turning away from solidarity to objectivity. The idea of Truth as something to be pursued for its own sake, not because it will be good for oneself, or for one's real or imaginary community, is the central theme of this tradition. It was perhaps the growing awareness by the Greeks of the sheer diversity of human communities which stimulated the emergence of this ideal. A fear of parochialism, of being confined within the horizons of the group into which one happens to be born, a need to see it with the eyes of a stranger, helps produce the skeptical and ironic tone characteristic of Euripides and Socrates. Herodotus' willingness to take the barbarians seriously enough to describe their customs in detail may have been a necessary prelude to Plato's claim that the way to transcend skepticism is to envisage a common goal of humanity—a goal set by human nature rather than by Greek culture. The combination of Socratic alienation and Platonic hope gives rise to the idea of the intellectual as someone who is in touch with the nature of things, not by way of the opinions of his community, but in a more immediate way.

Plato developed the idea of such an intellectual by means of distinctions between knowledge and opinion, and between appearance and reality. Such distinctions conspire to produce the idea that rational inquiry should make visible a realm to which nonintellectuals have little access, and of whose very existence they may be doubtful. In the Enlightenment, this notion became concrete in the adoption of the Newtonian physical scientist as a model of the intellectual. To most thinkers of the eighteenth century, it seemed clear that the access to Nature which physical science had provided should now be followed by the establishment of social, political, and economic institutions which were in accordance with Nature. Ever since, liberal social thought has centered [on] social reform as made possible by objective knowledge of what human beings are like—not knowledge of what Greeks or Frenchmen or Chinese are like, but of humanity as such. We are the heirs of this objectivist tradition, which centers [on] the assumption that we must step outside our community long enough to examine it in the light of something which transcends it, namely, that which it has in common with every other actual and possible human community. This tradition dreams of an ultimate community which will have transcended the distinction between the natural and the social, which will exhibit a solidarity which is not parochial because it is the

expression of an ahistorical human nature. Much of the rhetoric of contemporary intellectual life takes for granted that the goal of scientific inquiry into man is to understand "underlying structures," or "culturally invariant factors," or "biologically determined patterns."

Those who wish to ground solidarity in objectivity—call them "realists"—have to construe truth as correspondence to reality. So they must construct a metaphysics which has room for a special relation between beliefs and objects which will differentiate true from false beliefs. They also must argue that there are procedures of justification of belief which are natural and not merely local. So they must construct an epistemology which has room for a kind of justification which is not merely social but natural, springing from human nature itself, and made possible by a link between that part of nature and the rest of nature. On their view, the various procedures which are thought of as providing rational justification by one or another culture may or may not really *be* rational. For to be truly rational, procedures of justification *must* lead to the truth, to correspondence to reality, to the intrinsic nature of things.

By contrast, those who wish to reduce objectivity to solidarity—call them "pragmatists"—do not require either a metaphysics or an epistemology. They view truth as, in William James's phrase, what is good for *us* to believe. So they do not need an account of a relation between beliefs and objects called "correspondence," nor an account of human cognitive abilities which ensures that our species is capable of entering into that relation. They see the gap between truth and justification not as something to be bridged by isolating a natural and transcultural sort of rationality which can be used to criticize certain cultures and praise others, but simply as the gap between the actual good and the possible better. From a pragmatist point of view, to say that what is rational for us now to believe may not be *true*, is simply to say that somebody may come up with a better idea. It is to say that there is always room for improved belief, since new evidence, or new hypotheses, or a whole new vocabulary, may come along. For pragmatists, the desire for objectivity is not the desire to escape the limitations of one's community, but simply the desire for as much intersubjective agreement as possible, the desire to extend the reference of "us" as far as we can. Insofar as pragmatists make a distinction between knowledge and opinion, it is simply the distinction between topics on which such agreement is relatively easy to get and topics on which agreement is relatively hard to get.

"Relativism" is the traditional epithet applied to pragmatism by realists. Three different views are commonly referred to by this name. The first is the view that every belief is as good as every other. The second is the view that "true" is an equivocal term, having as many meanings as there are procedures of justification. The third is the view that there is nothing to be said about either truth or rationality apart from descriptions of the familiar procedures of justification which a given society—*ours*—uses in one or another area of inquiry. The pragmatist holds the ethnocentric third view. But he does not hold the self-refuting first view, nor the eccentric second view. He thinks that his views are better than the realists', but he does not think that his views correspond to the nature of things. He thinks that the very flexibility of the word "true"—the fact that it is merely an expression of commendation—insures its univocity. The term "true," on his account, means the same in all cultures, just as equally flexible terms like "here," "there," "good," "bad," "you," and "me" mean the same in all cultures. But the identity of meaning is, of course, compatible with diversity of reference, and with diversity of procedures for assigning the terms. So he feels free to use the term "true" as a general term of commendation in the same way as his realist opponent does—and in particular to use it to commend his own view.

However, it is not clear why "relativist" should be thought an appropriate term for the ethnocentric third view, the one which the pragmatist *does* hold. For the pragmatist is not holding a positive theory which says that something is relative to something else. He is, instead, making the purely *negative* point that we should drop the traditional distinction between knowledge and opinion, construed as the distinction between truth as correspondence to reality and truth as a commendatory term for well-justified beliefs. The reason that the realist calls this negative claim "relativistic" is that he cannot believe that anybody would seriously deny that truth has an intrinsic nature. So when the pragmatist says that there is nothing to be said about truth save that each of us

will commend as true those beliefs which he or she finds good to believe, the realist is inclined to interpret this as one more positive theory about the nature of truth: a theory according to which truth is simply the contemporary opinion of a chosen individual or group. Such a theory would, of course, be self-refuting. But the pragmatist does not have a theory of truth, much less a relativistic one. As a partisan of solidarity, his account of the value of cooperative human inquiry has only an ethical base, not an epistemological or metaphysical one. Not having *any* epistemology, *a fortiori* he does not have a relativistic one.

The question of whether truth or rationality has an intrinsic nature, of whether we ought to have a positive theory about either topic, is just the question of whether our self-description ought to be constructed around a relation to human nature or around a relation to a particular collection of human beings, whether we should desire objectivity or solidarity. It is hard to see how one could choose between these alternatives by looking more deeply into the nature of knowledge, or of man, or of nature. Indeed, the proposal that this issue might be so settled begs the question in favor of the realist, for it presupposes that knowledge, man, and nature *have* real essences which are relevant to the problem at hand. For the pragmatist, by contrast, "knowledge" is, like "truth," simply a compliment paid to the beliefs which we think so well justified that, for the moment, further justification is not needed. An inquiry into the nature of knowledge can, on his view, only be a sociohistorical account of how various people have tried to reach agreement on what to believe.

. . .

I think that putting the issue in such moral and political terms, rather than in epistemological or metaphilosophical terms, makes clearer what is at stake. For now the question is not about how to define words like "truth" or "rationality" or "knowledge" or "philosophy," but about what self-image our society should have of itself. The ritual invocation of the "need to avoid relativism" is most comprehensible as an expression of the need to preserve certain habits of contemporary European life. These are the habits nurtured by the Enlightenment, and justified by it in terms of an appeal of Reason, conceived as a transcultural human ability to correspond to reality, a faculty whose possession and use is demonstrated by obedience to explicit criteria. So the real question about relativism is whether these same habits of intellectual, social, and political life can be justified by a conception of rationality as criterionless muddling through, and by a pragmatist conception of truth.

I think that the answer to this question is that the pragmatist cannot justify these habits without circularity, but then neither can the realist. The pragmatists' justification of toleration, free inquiry, and the quest for undistorted communication can only take the form of a comparison between societies which exemplify these habits and those which do not, leading up to the suggestion that nobody who has experienced both would prefer the latter. It is exemplified by Winston Churchill's defense of democracy as the worst form of government imaginable, except for all the others which have been tried so far. Such justification is not by reference to a criterion, but by reference to various detailed practical advantages. It is circular only in that the terms of praise used to describe liberal societies will be drawn from the vocabulary of liberal societies themselves. Such praise has to be in *some* vocabulary, after all, and the terms of praise current in primitive or theocratic or totalitarian societies will not produce the desired result. So the pragmatist admits that he has no ahistorical standpoint from which to endorse the habits of modern democracies he wishes to praise. These consequences are just what partisans of solidarity expect. But among partisans of objectivity they give rise, once again, to fears of the dilemma formed by ethnocentrism on the one hand and relativism on the other. Either we attach a special privilege to our own community, or we pretend an impossible tolerance for every other group.

I have been arguing that we pragmatists should grasp the ethnocentric horn of this dilemma. We should say that we must, in practice, privilege our own group, even though there can be no noncircular justification for doing so. We must insist

that the fact that nothing is immune from criticism does not mean that we have a duty to justify everything. We Western liberal intellectuals should accept the fact that we have to start from where we are, and that this means that there are lots of views which we simply cannot take seriously. To use Neurath's* familiar analogy, we can *understand* the revolutionary's suggestion that a sailable boat can't be made out of the planks which make up ours, and that we must simply abandon ship. But we cannot take his suggestion seriously. We cannot take it as a rule for action, so it is not a live option. For some people, to be sure, the option *is* live. These are the people who have always hoped to become a New Being, who have hoped to be converted rather than persuaded. But we—the liberal Rawlsian searchers for consensus, the heirs of Socrates, the people who wish to link their days dialectically each to each—cannot do so. Our community—the community of the liberal intellectuals of the secular modern West—wants to be able to give a *post factum* account of any change of view. We want to be able, so to speak, to justify ourselves to our earlier selves. This preference is not built into us by human nature. It is just the way *we* live now.

. . .

My suggestion that the desire for objectivity is in part a disguised form of the fear of the death of our community echoes Nietzsche's charge that the philosophical tradition which stems from Plato is an attempt to avoid facing up to contingency, to escape from time and chance. Nietzsche thought that realism was to be condemned not only by arguments from its theoretical incoherence, the sort of argument we find in Putnam and Davidson, but also on practical, pragmatic, grounds. Nietzsche thought that the test of human character was the ability to live with the thought that there was no convergence. He wanted us to be able to think of truth as:

> a mobile army of metaphors, metonyms, and anthro-morphisms—in short a sum of human relations, which have been enhanced, transposed, and embellished

---

* Otto Neurath (1882–1945), an Austrian philosopher, was one of the founders of the Vienna Circle, a group of philosophers who promoted logical positivism (or logical empiricism)—an approach to philosophical inquiry that makes logic the central instrument of philosophy and that aims to eliminate all metaphysical elements from philosophy.—Ed.

poetically and rhetorically and which after long use seem firm, canonical, and obligatory to a people.

Nietzsche hoped that eventually there might be human beings who could and did think of truth in this way, but who still liked themselves, who saw themselves as *good* people for whom solidarity was *enough*.

I think that pragmatism's attack on the various structure-content distinctions which buttress the realist's notion of objectivity can best be seen as an attempt to let us think of truth in this Nietzschean way, as entirely a matter of solidarity. That is why I think we need to say, despite Putnam, that "there is only the dialogue," only *us*, and to throw out the last residues of the notion of "transcultural rationality." But this should not lead us to repudiate, as Nietzsche sometimes did, the elements in our movable host which embody the ideas of Socratic conversation, Christian fellowship, and Enlightenment science. Nietzsche ran together his diagnosis of philosophical realism as an expression of fear and resentment with his own resentful idiosyncratic idealizations of silence, solitude, and violence. Post-Nietzschean thinkers like Adorno and Heidegger and Foucault have run together Nietzsche's criticisms of the metaphysical tradition on the one hand with his criticisms of bourgeois civility, of Christian love, and of the nineteenth century's hope that science would make the world a better place to live, on the other. I do not think that there is any interesting connection between these two sets of criticisms. Pragmatism seems to me, as I have said, a philosophy of solidarity rather than of despair. From this point of view, Socrates' turn away from the gods, Christianity's turn from an Omnipotent Creator to the man who suffered on the Cross, and the Baconian turn from science as contemplation of eternal truth to science as instrument of social progress, can be seen as so many preparations for the act of social faith which is suggested by a Nietzschean view of truth.

The best argument we partisans of solidarity have against the realistic partisans of objectivity is Nietzsche's argument that the traditional Western metaphysico-epistemological way of firming up our habits simply isn't working anymore. It isn't doing its job. It has become as transparent a device as the postulation of deities who turn out,

by a happy coincidence, to have chosen *us* as their people. So the pragmatist suggestion that we substitute a "merely" ethical foundation for our sense of community—or, better, that we think of our sense of community as having no foundation except shared hope and the trust created by such sharing—is put forward on practical grounds. It is *not* put forward as a corollary of a metaphysical claim that the objects in the world contain no intrinsically action-guiding properties, nor of an epistemological claim that we lack a faculty of moral sense, nor of a semantical claim that truth is reducible to justification. It is a suggestion about how we might think of ourselves in order to avoid the kind of resentful belatedness—characteristic of the bad side of Nietzsche—which now characterizes much of high culture. This resentment arises from the realization . . . that the Enlightenment's search for objectivity has often gone sour.

The rhetoric of scientific objectivity, pressed too hard and taken too seriously, has led us to people like B. F. Skinner on the one hand and people like Althusser on the other—two equally pointless fantasies, both produced by the attempt to be "scientific" about our moral and political lives. Reaction against scientism led to attacks on natural science as a sort of false god. But there is nothing wrong with science, there is only something wrong with the attempt to divinize it, the attempt characteristic of realistic philosophy. This reaction has also led to attacks on liberal social thought of the type common to Mill and Dewey and Rawls as a mere ideological superstructure, one which obscures the realities of our situation and represses attempts to change that situation. But there is nothing wrong with liberal democracy, nor with the philosophers who have tried to enlarge its scope. There is only something wrong with the attempt to see their efforts as failures to achieve something which they were not trying to achieve—a demonstration of the "objective" superiority of our way of life over all other alternatives. There is, in short, nothing wrong with the hopes of the Enlightenment, the hopes which created the Western democracies. The value of the ideals of the Enlightenment is, for us pragmatists, just the value of some of the institutions and practices which they have created. In this essay I have sought to distinguish these institutions and practices from the philosophical justifications for them provided by partisans of objectivity, and to suggest an alternative justification.

DISCUSSION QUESTIONS

1. Rorty discusses Nietzsche's view of truth. How is Rorty's own position similar to and different from Nietzsche's?

2. Rorty distinguishes between three different types of relativism with respect to truth. Discuss these types of relativism, and explain why Rorty's pragmatism is not guilty of all three types of relativism.

3. Rorty discusses the search for truth in Western culture, beginning with Plato. How does he characterize it? Do you agree with his assessment? Would Locke, Russell, Bradley, and Nietzsche agree with Rorty's account of truth in the West? Why or why not?

4. What does Rorty mean by "solidarity"? Is there enough solidarity in our culture to ground truth claims? Or is Rorty mistaken? Discuss.

5. What is "ethnocentrism"? Why does Rorty believe that we should "privilege our own group"? What are some of the social consequences of this position? Are you comfortable with them? Why or why not?

Twelve Angry Men
[USA 1957] 1 hour, 32 minutes
Directed by Sidney Lumet

*A*young man is being tried for murdering his father. The evidence of his guilt seems overwhelming. A woman who lives across the train tracks from the boy claims that she saw him murdering his father. An elderly man who lives in the apartment above claims to have heard him saying "I'm gonna kill you" just before the father's body hit the floor and to have seen the boy fleeing from his father's apartment just after the murder was committed. The knife used in the murder was just like the knife the boy bought earlier on the day of the murder. The boy's attorney, a public defender, raises very little doubt concerning these facts.

When the jury convenes to discuss a verdict, eleven out of twelve jurors find themselves convinced beyond any reasonable doubt by the aggressive prosecutor's case. Even juror 8 (Henry Fonda), the lone holdout on a guilty verdict, finds himself leaning toward believing that the boy is guilty. Nevertheless, Fonda asks the other jurors to talk through the facts of the case and see if even the remotest possibility of doubt can be raised. Fonda points out that a boy's life is a stake here and that they should at least discuss the facts of the case before making their final decision. So, despite complaints from most of the other jurors, they go through the case fact by fact. Soon, they find that all the facts of the case contain the possibility of reasonable doubt. For example, the woman across the train tracks who "saw" the murder was probably not wearing her glasses, and so probably did not get a good look at the murderer. The elderly man upstairs probably did not have enough time to run from his bedroom to the hallway to see the boy leaving his father's apartment; also, he probably could not have heard the boy scream "I'm gonna kill you" over the roar of the passing train, and even if he did, the phrase "I'm gonna kill you" is often uttered but not acted upon. The knife angle in the body was not probable given the type of knife the boy had and his height relative to that of the victim. The boy could have forgotten details of the movies he had seen the night of the murder because of the shock of seeing his father dead. And on and on. For every fact, a level of doubt is raised. Soon, all twelve jurors agree that there is a reasonable doubt that the boy committed the murder and vote unanimously to acquit him.

DISCUSSION QUESTIONS

1. Over the course of this film, the jurors move from near-unanimous agreement on the truth of the statement "This boy is guilty of murder" to something less than certainty on the truth of this statement. Do you think their collective notion of truth changes over the course of this film? Why or why not?

2. What, if anything, does this film reveal about the way average persons come to decisions about truth?

3. It is late in the film, and the vote is now nine "not guilty" and three "guilty." Juror 10, still finding the boy guilty, lays out his case to the others. His basic position is that "this type of boy always lies" and is therefore guilty based on the type of person he is. "The kid is a liar . . . I know all about them . . . they are all no good. Not a one is good. Listen to me . . . this kid on trial . . . his type . . . you don't know about him . . . these people are dangerous . . . they are wild." What fallacy is juror 10 guilty of?

4. Henry Fonda responds to juror 10's diatribe with the following: "It's always difficult to keep personal prejudice out of a thing like this. Wherever you run into it prejudice always obscures the truth. I don't really know what the truth is. I don't suppose anybody will every really know. Nine of us now seem to feel that the defendant is innocent. We're just gambling on probabilities. We may be wrong. We may let a guilty man go free. I don't know. Nobody really can. But we have a reasonable doubt. And that is something that is very valuable in our system. No jury can declare a man guilty unless it's sure. We nine cannot understand how you three are still so sure. Maybe you can tell us." Do you agree with Fonda that prejudice always obscures the truth? Why or why not?

5. If it is true that prejudice always obscures the truth, should we not simply conclude that objective truth is impossible?

6. Truth is what puts us into a satisfactory relationship with the world, says James. How are the views on truth of the jury members at the beginning of their deliberations representative of James's position?

7. Over the course of this film, can it be argued that the "facts" did not hold up as a sufficient basis for truth? Why or why not?

8. Russell's theory of truth assumes that there are observer-independent facts that serve as the foundation of truth via their correspondence with statements. Does this film challenge this notion of truth? Why or why not?

9. A coherent story is built up in court by the prosecuting attorney as to the guilt of the boy. Adjourning for their deliberations, the jurors more or less all believed this coherent story to be true. However, in discussing the story in detail, they came to doubt its ability to establish beyond a reasonable doubt its truthfulness. Is this line of criticism always applicable to coherence theories of truth like Bradley's? In other words, even though an account of truth may be coherent, is it not necessarily true beyond any doubt? Is this a weakness in this notion of truth?

10. How does this film depict Rorty's notion of solidarity as truth? Does it reveal flaws in the solidarity view of truth? Is solidarity as truth just a nice way of saying that truth is whatever the "mob" or "masses" say is truth? Why or why not?

11. Do you believe that people generally want to jump to the truth about matters? Does truth require a leap of faith like the leap of faith Kierkegaard requires for our belief in God? Why or why not?

12. Was Fonda's character being unrealistically skeptical about truth at the start of this film? Why or why not?

SANDRA HARDING

Strong Objectivity

I n this selection, Sandra Harding examines a notion of truth for the sciences called *strong objectivity,* wherein we concede that bias-free or neutral observation is impossible but do not completely give up on the possibility of objectivity. In other words, strong objectivity attempts to reconcile two seemingly contradictory positions: (1) Objectivity, the view that observer independence and neutrality are possible, and (2) "standpoint epistemology," the view that hidden cultural assumptions distort all observations and investigations of the truth.

Strong objectivity does not want to completely deny objectivity since it "is an important value for cultures that value sciences," but it also assumes that standpoint theory is an accurate account of what we can know. Standpoint theories generally contend that "what we do in our social relations both enables and limits (it does not determine) what we know." As a result, we must include our social relations in all considerations of knowledge and truth. The social relations of "marginal lives—women's lives, for example" are an important consideration in all claims to objectivity. We have to understand the ways in which these marginal social relations enable and limit the truth claims produced in these and related contexts.

Harding carefully explains that standpoint theory is not saying that we begin with "neutral" statements of women's experience; rather, we look at the "collective political and theoretical achievement" from women's experiences. These experiences raise the prospect of new questions for the sciences, nature, and social relations. Thus, standpoint theories are not claiming that there is an essential "male" or "female" perspective from which we should begin our investigations, but rather that we should consider experiences from the margins as opening up a path to a complete reconsideration of what we know and how we know.

"Standpoint theory," writes Harding, "claims that starting from women's lives is a way of gaining less false and distorted results of research." Strong objectivity might be regarded as a weaker form of (absolute) objectivity. However, strong objectivity still has four obvious limitations: (1) it will relegitimate scientific rationality in a world where many think it should be limited; (2) it is strongly linked to its own cultural heritage and might not take root in other cultures in exactly the same form as in our culture; (3) it might lead to disassociating neutrality with masculinity, *or* it might just lead to associating femininity with the logic of discovery, thus leaving the justification of masculine neutrality in place; and (4) it might have to wait a while, perhaps even a very long while, before it becomes part of mainstream science.

Sandra Harding (1935–) received her Ph.D. in philosophy from New York University and is currently professor of social sciences and comparative education at UCLA. Her research interests include feminist and postcolonial theory, epistemology, research methodology, and philosophy of science. Her books include *Can Theories Be Refuted? Essays on the Duhem-Quine Thesis* (ed., 1976), *The Science Question in Feminism* (1986), *Feminism and Methodology: Social Science Issues* (ed., 1987), *Whose Science? Whose Knowledge? Thinking from Women's Lives* (1991), *Is Science Multicultural? Postcolonialisms, Feminisms, and Epistemologies* (1998), and *Feminist Standpoint Theory Reader: Intellectual and Political Controversies* (2004). The following is from her 1995 article, "Strong Objectivity? A Response to the New Objectivity Question."

Standpoint theories argue that what we do in our social relations both enables and limits (it does not determine) what we can know. Standpoint theories, in contrast to empiricist epistemologies, begin from the recognition of social inequality; their models of society are conflict models, in contrast to the consensus model of liberal political philosophy assumed by empiricists. All human thought necessarily can be only partial; it is always limited by the fact of having only a particular historical location—of not being able to be everywhere and see everything, and of being "contained" by cultural assumptions that become visible only from outside that culture (hence: "medieval thought," Renaissance thought, etc.). However, standpoint theories are concerned with a distinctive dimension of social location that is more pernicious than these kinds of "positionality," and that is difficult to grasp from within the empiricist assumptions of modern scientific rationality. In hierarchically organized societies, the daily activities of people in the ruling groups tend to set distinctive limits on their thought, limits that are not created by the activities of the subjugated groups. Administrative-managerial activities, including the work of the natural and social sciences, are the form of "ruling" in our contemporary modern societies, and the conceptual frameworks of our disciplines are shaped by administrative-managerial priorities, just as pre-scientific observations of nature are shaped by other cultural priorities. Such priorities do enable gaining the kinds of information administrators need to function effectively, but they also distort and limit our understanding of just what brings about daily social relations and interactions with nature, and they make it difficult to think possible any different kind of interactions. In order to gain a causal critical view of the interests and values that constitute the dominant conceptual projects, one must start one's thought, one's research project, from outside those conceptual schemes and the activities that generate them; one must start from the lives excluded as origins of their design—from "marginal lives."

The fundamental features of the standpoint proposal can be grasped most quickly by looking at *what it is not*. Those constrained by the old objectivity question will tend to distort standpoint theory by perceiving it only through the conceptual choices offered by "Objectivity or relativism: which side are you on?" They often construct it as just a variant of empiricism or, alternatively, as a kind of gynocentrism, special pleading, or unreasonably claimed privileged positionality. On such a reading, empiricism is politics-free, and standpoint theory is asserting epistemological/scientific privilege for one group at the expense of the equally valuable/distorted perceptions of other groups. Or, it is simply substituting one politics for another, and all political positions—the master's and the slave's, that of the rich and of the poor, the colonizer's and the colonized's, the rapist's and his victim's—all are equally valuable and/or distorted. This interpretation of difference as merely diversity is a serious misunderstanding of social realities, as well as of standpoint claims. Standpoint theory leads us to turn such a way of posing the alternatives into a topic for historical analysis: "What forms of social relations make *this* conceptual framework—the 'view from nowhere' versus 'special pleading'—so useful, and for what purposes?"

NOT ABOUT ONLY MARGINAL LIVES

First, standpoint theory is not only about how to get a less limited understanding of marginal lives—women's lives, for example. Instead, research is to *start off* from such locations (not to take as truth what people in those locations think or say) in order to explain not only those lives but also the rest of the micro and macro social order, including human interactions with nature and the philosophies that have been developed to explain sciences. The standpoint of women, as Dorothy Smith puts the point, enables us to understand women's lives, men's lives, and the relations between the two through concepts and hypotheses arising from women's lives rather than only ones arising from the lives of those assigned administrative/managerial work, a group that includes sociologists (and philosophers). The point is to produce systematic causal accounts of how the natural and social orders are organized such that the everyday lives of women and men, our activities and beliefs, end up in the forms that they do.

The phrase "women's experiences" can be read in an empiricist way such that these experiences are assumed to be constituted prior to the social. Standpoint theory challenges this kind of reading. For a researcher to start from women's lives is not necessarily to take one's research problems in the terms in which women perceive or articulate their problems—and this is as true for women as it is for men thinkers. The dominant ideology restricts what everyone is permitted to see and shapes everyone's consciousness. Women, like men, have had to learn to think of sexual harassment not as a matter of "boys will be boys," but as a violation of women's civil rights. Marital rape was a legal and, for most people, conceptual impossibility until collective political struggle and theorizing resulted in its articulation in the law. European American feminists, like the rest of European Americans, are only beginning to learn how to conceptualize many of our issues in anti-Eurocentric terms. Women, too, have held distorted beliefs about our bodies, our minds, nature and society, and numerous men have made important contributions to feminist analyses— John Stuart Mill, Marx, Engels, and many contemporary scholars in history, sociology, economics, philosophy, literary and art criticism, etc. Moreover, it is obvious that "women's experience" does not automatically generate feminist analyses, since the former always exists but only occasionally does the latter emerge. Standpoint theorists are not making the absurd claim that feminist work simply flows from women's experiences.

Feminist knowledge is not a "neutral" elaboration of women's experiences, or what women say about their lives, but a collective political and theoretical achievement. Women's experiences and what women say are important guides to the new questions we can ask about nature, sciences, and social relations. However, the *answers* to such questions must be sought elsewhere than in women's experiences, since the latter are shaped by national and international policies and practices that are formulated and enacted far away from our daily lives—by Supreme Court decisions, international trade agreements, military policies on the other side of the world, etc.

Standpoint theory is not calling for phenomenologies of women's world, or for ethnocentric (gynocentric) accounts. Nor is it arguing that only women can generate feminist knowledge; it is not an "identity politics" project. Men, too, can learn to start their thought from women's lives, as many have done. These misunderstandings come about because objectivism insists that the only alternatives to its view from nowhere are special interest claims and ethno-knowledges that can be understood only within a relativist epistemology. However, institutionalized power imbalances give starting off from the lives of those who least benefit from such imbalances a critical edge for generating theoretically and empirically more accurate and comprehensive accounts. Feminist accounts of marital rape, sexual harassment, women's double-day of work or women's different and valuable forms of moral reason are capable of conceptualizing phenomena that were heretofore invisible because they start off from outside the dominant paradigms and conceptual schemes.

NO ESSENTIAL WOMAN'S LIFE

Next, standpoint theory is not arguing that there is some kind of essential, universal woman's life from which feminists (male and female) should start their thought. In any particular research situation, one is to start off research from the lives of those who have been disadvantaged by, excluded from the benefits of, the dominant conceptual frameworks. What can we learn about that framework by starting from their lives? For example, what can we learn about biological models of the human body, or of human evolution, psychological and philosophical models of moral reasoning, historical models of social change and of progress, philosophical models of rationality, etc., by starting off thought about them from the lives of women of different races, ethnicities, classes and sexualities whose natures and activities each of these models defines as inferior in partially different ways?

The point here is that these kinds of models have also been used to define other groups— racial, ethnic, economic, etc. —as inferior. We can learn some similar and some new things about the conceptual frameworks of the disciplines by starting off thought about the latter from, for example, the lives of slaves, or "orientals," workers, etc. Moreover, "woman" and the homogeneity of "women" is an elitist fiction. These categories in everyday life are multiple and contradictory, and the theorization of this fact by women of color and others who *started off their thought from women of color's lives* is one of the great strengths of contemporary feminist thought. This "matrix theory" developed by women of color enables us to think how each of us has a determinate social location in the matrix of social relations that is constituted by gender, class, race, sexuality and whatever other macro forces shape our particular part of the social order. Women are located at many positions in this matrix, and starting thought from each such group of lives can be useful for understanding social phenomena (including our relations with nature) that have effects on those lives.

CONSCIOUSNESS NOT DETERMINED BY SOCIAL LOCATION

For standpoint theorists, we each have a determinate location in such a social matrix, but that location does not *determine* one's consciousness. The availability of competing discourses enables men, for example, to think and act in feminist ways. They are still obviously men, who are thereby in determinate relations to women and men in every class and race; such relations cannot be changed simply by willing them. They can work to eliminate male supremacy, but no matter what they do, they will still be treated with the privilege (or suspicion!) accorded to men by students, sales people, other intellectuals, etc. A parallel account can be given about women, of course.

AN EPISTEMOLOGY, A PHILOSOPHY OF SCIENCE, A SOCIOLOGY OF KNOWLEDGE, AND A METHOD FOR DOING RESEARCH

Several disciplines have competed to disown standpoint theory. Some philosophers claim it is only a sociology; some sociologists reject it as only an epistemology. Some scientists and philosophers have insisted that it could not have any implications for the natural sciences since it is concerned with intentionality, and physical nature is not intentional.

It is more useful to see it as all of these projects: a philosophy of knowledge, a philosophy of science, a sociology of knowledge, and a proposed research method. Each such project must always make assumptions about the others; for example, every philosophy of science must make epistemological assumptions about the nature and conditions for knowledge in general, historical ones about which procedures for producing knowledge have been most successful in the past, and sociological ones about how communities that have produced the best knowledge claims in the past have been organized. In periods of what we could refer to as "normal philosophy," these background assumptions can safely be left unexamined; but when skepticism arises about the adequacy of fundamental assumptions in any one of these areas, the others all present themselves as candidates for reexamination. Our beliefs face the tribunal of experience as a network, as Quine points out, and none are immune from possible revision when a misfit between belief and observation arises. Feminist challenges to conventional bodies of knowledge have forced reexamination of empiricist assumptions about the organization of scientific communities, ideals of the knower, the known, and how knowledge should be produced, rational reconstructions of the growth of scientific knowledge, and scientific method in the sense of "how to do good research." Standpoint theory's claims must find support and have effects in all of these fields.

ASYMMETRICAL FALSITY AND TRUTH IN SCIENTIFIC PRACTICE

Standpoint theory claims that starting from women's lives is a way of gaining less false and distorted results of research. However, one gratuitously asks for trouble if one equates such claims with ones to truth or truth-likeness. This is a general point about scientific claims, not one peculiar to standpoint theories or to feminist philosophies of science. The claim that a result of research is "less false" is sufficient to capture what we can establish about the processes producing such a research result, and attributions of truth or truth-likeness are too strong for scientific claims. We do not have to be claiming to approximate the one true story about nature or social relations in order for it to make sense to argue that our account is less false than some specified set of competitors to it. For one thing, all that scientific processes could in principle produce are claims less false than competing ones as a hypothesis is tested against some chosen set of rivals—the dominant hypothesis, or another new one. Moreover, as a matter of principle one is never to assume that such processes generate what one can know to be true, since empirical claims have to be held open to future revision on the basis of empirical evidence and conceptual shifts. To put the point a familiar way, our best theories are always underdetermined by the evidence. As a glance at the history of science shows, nature says "yea" to many competing and, from our perspective, quite fantastic accounts of its regularities and their underlying causal tendencies; our best theories are only consistent with nature, not uniquely coherent with natural laws that are "out there" for our detection.

Standpoint approaches were developed both to explain the surprising results of feminist research and to guide future research. They show us how to detect values and interests that constitute scientific projects, ones that do not vary between legitimated observers, and the difference between those values and interests that enlarge and those that limit our descriptions, explanations and understandings of nature and social relations. Standpoint approaches provide a map, a method, for maximizing a strong objectivity that can function more effectively for knowledge projects faced with the problem of sciences that have been constituted by the values and interests of the most powerful social groups.

Standpoint theory has become a site for some of the most pressing contemporary discussions about post-foundationalism, realism versus constructivism, identity politics and epistemologies, the role of experience in producing knowledge, alternatives to both the "view from nowhere" and relativism, and other issues controversial in the philosophy and social studies of science more generally. Although it rejects and tries to move beyond many of the distorting features of modernity's conceptual framework, it also retains central commitments of that tradition. One is to the importance of the notion of objectivity.

OBJECTIVITY: AN INDIGENOUS RESOURCE OF THE MODERN NORTH?

Objectivity is an important value for cultures that value sciences, and its value spreads to other cultures as they import Northern forms of democracy, their epistemologies and sciences. This is not to say that Northerners are particularly good at democracy or maximizing objectivity, or have any corner on the ideals. And, of course, Northern forms of these ideals are widely criticized by many Third World intellectuals, as they are by feminists, as ideologies that have justified excluding and exploiting the already less powerful. Nevertheless, "objective" defines for many people today how they think of themselves: we are fair; we make decisions by principle, not by whim or fiat; we are against "might makes right"; we are rational; we can find ways to live together that value our cultural diversity . . . and so forth. I am not saying that everyone who claims objectivity in fact maximizes it, but that such an ideal is deeply embedded in the ethic and rhetoric of democracy at personal, communal, and institutional levels. The notion is centered in natural and many social science discourses, in jurisprudence, in public policy, in many areas where decisions about how to organize social relations are made. Thus, while the diverse arguments for abandoning the notion are illuminating and important to keep in mind, to do so is to adopt a "bohemian" strategy; it is to do "something else" besides try to struggle on the terrain where philosophies, science projects and social policies are negotiated. Why not, instead, think of objectivity as an "indigenous resource" of the modern North? It needs updating, rehabilitation, so that it is capable of functioning effectively in the science-based society that the North has generated and that many now say is its major cultural export.

What of the epistemological status of this strong objectivity program itself? What limitations arise from the particular historical projects from which it started off? No doubt there are many such limitations, but four easily come to mind. First, the strong objectivity program is, indeed, a science project. It relegitimates scientific rationality (and a modern European form of it) in a world where many think the power of this rationality should be limited. Now the "context of discovery" and the values and interests shared within a research community are to be added to the phenomena to be analyzed with scientific rationality.

Second, this strong objectivity program and the standpoint theory that supports it originate in the North, and draw upon the historical and cultural legacies of those cultures—for example, European Marxian and feminist legacies. Thinkers in other cultures may well prefer to draw on the riches of their own legacies in order to develop resources for blocking "might makes right" in the realm of knowledge production. Third, one can wonder if the delinking of objectivity from the neutrality ideal can succeed eventually in bypassing the gender-coding of objectivity as inherently masculine (and European, bourgeois, etc.)? Or does the logic of discovery become feminized (no neutrality) leaving the logic of justification masculinized as usual (here seeking neutrality can be useful)?

Finally, it is hard to imagine this strong objectivity program effectively enacted right away within the present day culture and practices of sciences, which are largely resistant to the interpretive and critical skills and resources necessary to detect values and interests in the conceptual frameworks of scientific projects. Natural scientists are not trained to do this work, and they often are hostile to sharing authority about nature, let alone about how science should be done, with any individuals or groups that they conceptualize as "outside science." And yet, we should not be too pessimistic since mainstream concerns to bring science under more democratic control, the global and local social changes to which such terms as "diversity" and "multiculturalism" point, and the ever increasing adoption of feminist projects into mainstream cultures and practices (albeit without the label "feminist") offer hope that the borders of scientific culture and practice, too, can become more permeable to these tendencies.

To conclude, the strong objectivity program is one response to the new objectivity question. It is not perfect, but it does have considerable advantages over the alternatives so far in sight.

DISCUSSION QUESTIONS

1. How does strong objectivity claim to reconcile objectivity with standpoint theories? Is it successful?

2. Standpoint theories generally contend that "what we do in our social relations both enables and limits (it does not determine) what we know." Do you agree with this general position? Why or why not?

3. Discuss Harding's concern that strong objectivity might lead to disassociating neutrality with masculinity *or* to associating femininity with the logic of discovery, thus leaving the justification of masculine neutrality in place.

4. Do you believe that it is possible to have good science without objectivity? Why is objectivity important to science? What happens when objectivity is lost? What if we settle for something like Rorty's notion of "solidarity"? Is this any better or worse than "strong objectivity"? Discuss.

5. Harding carefully explains that standpoint theory is not saying that we begin with "neutral" statements of women's experiences but rather that we look at the "collective political and theoretical achievement" of women's experiences. What is the difference, and why is it important?

JORGE LUIS BORGES
THE LIBRARY OF BABEL

J orge Luis Borges' "The Library of Babel" is a story about a library that contains every possible book of a particular format, and the search for truth within it. Borges tells us that "each book is made up of four hundred and ten pages; each page, of forty lines; each line, of some eighty black characters. In the library, no two books are alike. We learn that "the Library is total and that its shelves contain all the possible combinations of the twenty-odd orthographic symbols (whose number, though vast, is not infinite); that is, everything which can be expressed, in all languages." Furthermore, "There are always several hundreds of thousands of imperfect facsimiles—of works which differ only by one letter or one comma." All attempts thus far to find the truth that is assumed to be in these books has failed; nevertheless, the search for it continues. A biographical sketch of Jorge Luis Borges may be found in the first section of this chapter. "The Library of Babel" was first collected in *El jardín de senderos que se bifurcan* (*The Garden of Forking Paths*) (1941–42), then later in *Ficciones* (1944).

By this art you may contemplate the variation of the 23 letters . . .

—*The Anatomy of Melancholy, Part 2, Sect. II, Mem. IV*

The universe (which others call the Library) is composed of an indefinite, perhaps infinite, number of hexagonal galleries, with enormous ventilation shafts in the middle, encircled by very low railings. From any hexagon the upper or lower stories are visible, interminably. The distribution of the galleries is invariable. Twenty shelves—five long shelves per side—cover all sides except two; their height, which is that of each floor, scarcely exceeds that of an average librarian. One of the free sides gives upon a narrow entrance way, which leads to another gallery, identical to the first and to all the others. To the left and to the right of the entrance way are two miniature rooms. One allows standing room for sleeping; the other, the satisfaction of fecal necessities. Through this section passes the spiral staircase, which plunges down into the abyss and rises up to the heights. In the entrance way hangs a mirror, which faithfully duplicates appearances. People are in the habit of inferring from this mirror that the Library is not infinite (if it really were, why this illusory duplication?); I prefer to dream that the polished surfaces feign and promise infinity. . . .

Light comes from some spherical fruits called by the name of lamps. There are two, running transversally, in each hexagon. The light they emit is insufficient, incessant.

Like all men of the Library, I have traveled in my youth. I have journeyed in search of a book, perhaps of the catalogue of catalogues; now that my eyes can scarcely decipher what I write, I am preparing to die a few leagues from the hexagon in which I was born. Once dead, there will not lack pious hands to hurl me over the banister; my sepulchre shall be the unfathomable air: my body will sink lengthily and will corrupt and dissolve in the wind engendered by the fall, which is infinite. I affirm that the Library is interminable. The idealists argue that the hexagonal halls are a necessary form of absolute space or, at least, of our intuition of space. They contend that a triangular or pentagonal hall is inconceivable. (The mystics claim that to them ecstasy reveals a round chamber containing a great book with a continuous back circling the walls of the room; but their testimony is suspect; their words, obscure. That cyclical book is God.) Let it suffice me, for the time being, to repeat the classic dictum: *The Library is a sphere whose consummate center is any hexagon, and whose circumference is inaccessible.*

Five shelves correspond to each one of the walls of each hexagon; each shelf contains thirty-two books of a uniform format; each book is made up of four hundred and ten pages; each page, of forty lines; each line, of some eighty black letters. There are also letters on the spine of each book; these letters do not indicate or prefigure what the pages will say. I know that such a lack of relevance, at one time, seemed mysterious. Before summarizing the solution (whose disclosure, despite its tragic implications, is perhaps the capital fact of this history), I want to recall certain axioms.

The first: The Library exists *ab aeterno.* No reasonable mind can doubt this truth, whose immediate corollary is the future eternity of the world. Man, the imperfect librarian, may be the work of chance or malevolent demiurges; the universe, with its elegant endowment of shelves, of enigmatic volumes, of indefatigable ladders for the voyager, and of privies for the seated librarian, can only be the work of a god. In order to perceive the distance which exists between the divine and the human, it is enough to compare the rude tremulous symbols which my fallible hand scribbles on the end pages of a book with the organic letters inside: exact, delicate, intensely black, inimitably symmetric.

The second: *The number of orthographic symbols is twenty-five.** This bit of evidence permitted the formulation, three hundred years ago, of a general theory of the Library and the satisfactory resolution of the problem which no conjecture had yet made clear: the formless and chaotic nature of almost all books; one of these books which my father saw in a hexagon of the circuit number fifteen ninety-four was composed of the letters MCV perversely repeated from the first line to the last. Another, very much consulted in this zone, is a mere labyrinth of letters, but on the next-to-the-last page, one may read *O Time your pyramids.* As is well known: for one reasonable line or one straight-forward note there are leagues of insensate cacophony, of verbal farragoes and incoherencies. (I know of a wild region whose librarians repudiate the vain superstitious custom of seeking any sense

in books and compare it to looking for meaning in dreams or chaotic lines of one's hands. . . . They admit that the inventors of writing imitated the twenty-five natural symbols, but they maintain that this application is accidental and that books in themselves mean nothing. This opinion—we shall see—is not altogether false.)

For a long time it was believed that these impenetrable books belonged to past or remote languages. It is true that the most ancient men, the first librarians, made use of a language quite different from the one we speak today; it is true that some miles to the right the language is dialectical and that ninety stories up it is incomprehensible. All this, I repeat, is true; but four hundred and ten pages of unvarying MCVs do not correspond to any language, however dialectical or rudimentary it might be. Some librarians insinuated that each letter could influence the next, and that the value of MCV on the third line of page 71 was not the same as that of the same series in another position on another page, but this vague thesis did not prosper. Still other men thought in terms of cryptographs; this conjecture has come to be universally accepted, though not in the sense in which it was formulated by its inventors.

Five hundred years ago, the chief of an upper hexagon[†] came upon a book as confusing as all the rest but which contained nearly two pages of homogenous lines. He showed his find to an ambulant decipherer, who told him the lines were written in Portuguese. Others told him they were in Yiddish. In less than a century the nature of the language was finally established: it was a Samoyed-Lithuanian dialect of Guarani, with classical Arabic inflections. The contents were also deciphered: notions of combinational analysis, illustrated by examples of variations with unlimited repetition. These examples made it possible for a librarian of genius to discover the fundamental law of the Library. This thinker observed that all the books, however diverse, are made up of uniform elements: the period, the comma, the space, the twenty-two letters of the alphabet. He also adduced a circumstance confirmed by all travelers: *There are*

* The original manuscript of the present note does not contain digits or capital letters. The punctuation is limited to the comma and the period. These two signs, plus the space sign and the twenty-two letters of the alphabet, make up the twenty-five sufficient symbols enumerated by the unknown author.
† Formerly, for each three hexagons there was one man. Suicide and pulmonary diseases have destroyed this proportion. My memory recalls scenes of unspeakable melancholy: there have been many nights when I have ventured down corridors and polished staircases without encountering a single librarian.

not, in the whole vast Library, two identical books. From all these incontrovertible premises he deduced that the Library is total and that its shelves contain all the possible combinations of the twenty-odd orthographic symbols (whose number, though vast, is not infinite); that is, everything which can be expressed, in all languages. Everything is there: the minute history of the future, the autobiographies of the archangels, the faithful catalogue of the Library, thousands and thousands of false catalogues, a demonstration of the fallacy of these catalogues, a demonstration of the fallacy of the true catalogue, the Gnostic gospel of Basilides, the commentary on this gospel, the commentary on the commentary of this gospel, the veridical account of your death, a version of each book in all languages, the interpolations of every book in all books.

When it was proclaimed that the Library comprised all books, the first impression was one of extravagant joy. All men felt themselves lords of a secret, intact treasure. There was no personal or universal problem whose eloquent solution did not exist—in some hexagon. The universe was justified, the universe suddenly expanded to the limitless dimensions of hope. At that time there was much talk of the Vindications: books of apology and prophecy, which vindicated for all time the actions of every man in the world and established a store of prodigious arcana for the future. Thousands of covetous persons abandoned their dear natal hexagons and crowded up the stairs, urged on by the vain aim of finding their Vindication. These pilgrims disputed in the narrow corridors, hurled dark maledictions, strangled each other on the divine stairways, flung the deceitful books to the bottom of the tunnels, and died as they were thrown into space by men from remote regions. Some went mad. . . .

The Vindications do exist. I have myself seen two of these books, which were concerned with future people, people who were perhaps not imaginary. But the searchers did not remember that the calculable possibility of a man's finding his own book, or some perfidious variation of his own book, is close to zero.

The clarification of the basic mysteries of humanity—the origin of the Library and of time—was also expected. It is credible that those grave mysteries can be explained in words: if the language of the philosophers does not suffice, the multiform Library will have produced the unexpected language required and the necessary vocabularies and grammars for this language.

It is now four centuries since men have been wearying the hexagons. . . .

There are official searchers, *inquisitors.* I have observed them carrying out their functions: they are always exhausted. They speak of a staircase without steps where they were almost killed. They speak of galleries and stairs with the local librarian. From time to time they will pick up the nearest book and leaf through its pages, in search of infamous words. Obviously, no one expects to discover anything.

The uncommon hope was followed, naturally enough, by deep depression. The certainty that some shelf in some hexagon contained precious books and that these books were inaccessible seemed almost intolerable. A blasphemous sect suggested that all searches be given up and that men everywhere shuffle letters and symbols until they succeeded in composing, by means of an improbable stroke of luck, the canonical books. The authorities found themselves obliged to issue severe orders. The sect disappeared, but in my childhood I still saw old men who would hide out in the privies for long periods of time, and, with metal disks in a forbidden dicebox, feebly mimic the divine disorder.

Other men, inversely, thought that the primary task was to eliminate useless works. They would invade the hexagons, exhibiting credentials which were not always false, skim through a volume with annoyance, and then condemn entire bookshelves to destruction: their ascetic, hygenic fury is responsible for the senseless loss of millions of books. Their name is execrated; but those who mourn the "treasures" destroyed by this frenzy, overlook two notorious facts. One: the Library is so enormous that any reduction undertaken by humans is infinitesimal. Two: each book is unique, irreplaceable, but (inasmuch as the Library is total) there are always several hundreds of thousands of imperfect facsimiles—of works which differ only by one letter or one comma. Contrary to public opinion, I dare suppose that the consequences of the depredations committed by the Purifiers have been exaggerated by the horror which these fanatics provoked. They were spurred by the delirium of storming the books in the Crimson

Hexagon: books of a smaller than ordinary format, omnipotent, illustrated, magical.

We know, too, of another superstition of that time: the Man of the Book. In some shelf of some hexagon, men reasoned, there must exist a book which is the cipher and perfect compendium of *all the rest:* some librarian has perused it, and it is analogous to a god. Vestiges of the worship of that remote functionary still persist in the language of this zone. Many pilgrimages have sought Him out. For a century they trod the most diverse routes in vain. How to locate the secret hexagon which harbored it? Someone proposed a regressive approach: in order to locate book A, first consult book B, which will indicate the location of A; in order to locate book B, first consult book C, and so on ad infinitum. . . .

I have squandered and consumed my years in adventures of this type. To me, it does not seem unlikely that on some shelf of the universe there lies a total book.* I pray the unknown gods that some man—even if only one man, and though it have been thousands of years ago!—may have examined and read it. If honor and wisdom and happiness are not for me, let them be for others. May heaven exist, though my place be in hell. Let me be outraged and annihilated, but may Thy enormous Library be justified, for one instant, in one being.

The impious assert that absurdities are the norm in the Library and that anything reasonable (even humble and pure coherence) is an almost miraculous exception. They speak (I know) of "the febrile Library, whose hazardous volumes run the constant risk of being changed into others and in which everything is affirmed, denied, and confused as by a divinity in delirium." These words, which not only denounce disorder but exemplify it as well, manifestly demonstrate the bad taste of the speakers and their desperate ignorance. Actually, the Library includes all verbal structures, all the variations allowed by the twenty-five orthographic symbols, but it does not permit of one absolute absurdity. It is pointless to observe that the best book in the numerous hexagons under my administration is entitled *Combed Clap of Thunder;* or

that another is called *The Plaster Cramp;* and still another *Axaxaxas Mlö.* Such propositions as are contained in these titles, at first sight incoherent, doubtless yield a cryptographic or allegorical justification. Since they are verbal, these justifications already figure, *ex hypothesi*, in the Library. I cannot combine certain letters, as *dhcmrlchtdj*, which the divine Library has not already foreseen in combination, and which in one of its secret languages does not encompass some terrible meaning. No one can articulate a syllable which is not full of tenderness and fear, and which is not, in one of those languages, the powerful name of some god. To speak is to fall into tautologies. This useless and wordy epistle itself already exists in one of the thirty volumes of the five shelves in one of the uncountable hexagons—and so does its refutation. (An *n* number of possible languages makes use of the same vocabulary; in some of them, the symbol *library* admits of the correct definition *ubiquitous and ever-lasting system of hexagonal galleries*, but *library* is *bread* or *pyramid* or anything else, and the seven words which define it possess another value. You who read me, are you sure you understand my language?)

Methodical writing distracts me from the present condition of men. But the certainty that everything has been already written nullifies or makes phantoms of us all. I know of districts where the youth prostrate themselves before books and barbarously kiss the pages, though they do not know how to make out a single letter. Epidemics, heretical disagreements, the pilgrimages which inevitably degenerate into banditry, have decimated the population. I believe I have mentioned the suicides, more frequent each year. Perhaps I am deceived by old age and fear, but I suspect that the human species—the unique human species—is on the road to extinction, while the Library will last on forever: illuminated, solitary, infinite, perfectly immovable, filled with precious volumes, useless, incorruptible, secret.

Infinite I have just written. I have not interpolated this adjective merely from rhetorical habit. It is not illogical, I say, to think that the world is infinite. Those who judge it to be limited, postulate that in

---

* I repeat: it is enough that a book be possible for it to exist. Only the impossible is excluded. For example: no book is also a stairway, though doubtless there are books that discuss and deny and demonstrate this possibility and others whose structure corresponds to that of a stairway.

remote places the corridors and stairs and hexagons could inconceivably cease—a manifest absurdity. Those who imagine it to be limitless forget that the possible number of books is limited. I dare insinuate the following solution to this ancient problem: *The Library is limitless and periodic.* If an eternal voyager were to traverse it in any direction, he would find, after many centuries, that the same volumes are repeated in the same disorder (which, repeated, would constitute an order: Order itself). My solitude rejoices in this elegant hope.*

Mar del Plata
1941

DISCUSSION QUESTIONS

1. Borges begins the story with "The universe (which others call the Library)." Do you think that he literally wants us to believe that the universe is one big book or collection of books? Or does he want us to believe that the universe around us is like a collection of books?

2. None of Borges' characters are successful at locating the truth in this library. Why? How is their search like our own search for truth in the universe?

3. Assuming that this library is physically possible and that it contains everything that can be expressed, in all languages, does it follow that the library contains the truth about the universe? Why or why not?

4. Imagine each of the philosophers that you have read in this section walking through Borges's library. How would each of them know whether the book they were holding expressed or was the truth?

5. Nietzsche's view of truth is closely linked to figures of speech and language. Do you think that Borges' library visually symbolizes his idea of truth as a "mobile army of metaphors, metonyms, and anthropomorphisms—in short, a sum of human relations, which have been enhanced, transposed, and embellished poetically and rhetorically, and which after long use seem firm, canonical, and obligatory to a people"? Why or why not? Do you think that Borges and Nietzsche would agree that truth is ultimately not attainable given the nature of language?

* Letizia Alvarez de Toledo has observed that the vast Library is useless. Strictly speaking, *one single volume* should suffice: a single volume of ordinary format, printed in nine- or ten-point type size, and consisting of an infinite number of infinitely thin pages. (At the beginning of the seventeenth century, Cavalieri said that any solid body is the superposition of an infinite number of planes.) This silky *vade mecum* would scarcely be handy: each apparent leaf of the book would divide into other analogous leaves. The inconceivable central leaf would have no reverse.

Citizen Kane
[USA 1941] 2 hours, 24 minutes
Directed by Orson Welles

*C*itizen Kane chronicles the rise and fall of newspaper entrepreneur Charles Foster Kane (Orson Wells), who is a composite of Howard Hughes (1905–76) and William Randolph Hearst (1863–1951). The central question of the film is "Who is Charles Foster Kane?" After his death, a reporter interviews numerous individuals concerning Kane's past in order to discover the meaning behind his last word—"Rosebud." In a series of flashbacks, the viewers are led through the abusive childhood of Kane on up to his Zeus-like status in his mountain castle called "Xanadu." Kane's castle is named after pleasure gardens constructed in Xanadu by the thirteenth-century Mongol king of China, Khan (king) Kublai, and vividly imagined in Samuel Coleridge's ode, "Kubla Khan: or, A Vision in a Dream: A Fragment" (1816). The movie ends without providing an answers to its central question: the true Charles Foster Kane could be one of a number of persons, including the innocent boy yearning to regain his lost childhood and the secluded, bitter man attempting to buy his happiness. The only thing we know for certain is that "Rosebud" was the name on the sled he rode as a boy.

DISCUSSION QUESTIONS

1. How many distinct versions of the "true" Charles Foster Kane are presented? Do the multiple accounts of the true Charles Foster Kane lead you believe that there is no true Kane? Or that one of them is the true Kane? Or that the true account is somewhere among each of these accounts? Discuss.
2. Analyze the truth regarding Charles Foster Kane from each of the notions of truth found in this chapter. Which of those accounts depend on who is asking the true-identity question? Which of those accounts do not depend on who is asking the true-identity question?
3. How similar is searching for the truth regarding Charles Foster Kane to searching for truth in Borges's "Library of Babel"? Is the search for the true Kane more or less difficult than the search for the truth in the library of Babel?
4. Think about the "true you." Which view of truth provides you with the best account of the true you? Why? Is this the same account of truth that you in general think is the strongest?

SUPPLEMENTARY READINGS

General

Audi, Robert. *Epistemology: A Contemporary Introduction to the Theory of Knowledge.* 2nd ed. New York: Routledge, 2002.

———. *Belief, Justification, and Knowledge: An Introduction to Epistemology.* Belmont, CA: Wadsworth, 1988.

Chisholm, Roderick. *Theory of Knowledge.* 3rd ed. Englewood Cliffs, NJ: Prentice Hall, 1989.

Crumley, Jack S., II. *An Introduction to Epistemology.* Mountain View, CA: Mayfield, 1999.

Dancy, Jonathan. *An Introduction to Contemporary Epistemology.* New York: Blackwell, 1986.

Dancy, Jonathan, and Ernest Sosa, eds. *A Companion to Epistemology.* Cambridge, MA: Blackwell, 1992.

Greco, John, and Ernest Sosa, eds. *The Blackwell Guide to Epistemology.* Malden, MA: Blackwell, 1999.

Hamlyn, D. W. *The Theory of Knowledge.* New York: Doubleday, 1971.

Hetherington, Stephen Cade. *Knowledge Puzzles: An Introduction to Epistemology.* Boulder, CO: Westview Press, 1996.

Landesman, Charles. *An Introduction to Epistemology.* Cambridge, MA: Blackwell, 1997.

Lehrer, Keith. *Theory of Knowledge.* 2nd ed. Boulder, CO: Westview Press, 2000.

Lucey, Kenneth G., ed. *On Knowing and the Known: Introductory Readings in Epistemology.* Buffalo, NY: Prometheus Books, 1996.

Moser, Paul K., ed., *The Oxford Handbook of Epistemology.* New York: Oxford University Press, 2002.

Moser, Paul K., and Arnold vander Nat, eds. *Human Knowledge: Classical and Contemporary Approaches.* 3rd ed. Oxford: Oxford University Press, 2003.

Moser, Paul K., Dwayne H. Mulder, and J. D. Trout. *The Theory of Knowledge: A Thematic Introduction.* New York: Oxford University Press, 1998.

Niiniluoto, Ilkka, Matti Sintonen, and Jan Wolénski, eds. *Handbook of Epistemology.* Boston: Kluwer Academic, 2004.

O'Connor, D. J., and Brian Carr. *Introduction to the Theory of Knowledge*. Minneapolis: University of Minnesota Press, 1982.

Pojman, Louis P., ed. *What Can We Know? An Introduction to the Theory of Knowledge*. 2nd ed. Belmont, CA: Wadsworth, 2001.

Pollock, John, and Joseph Cruz. *Contemporary Theories of Knowledge*. 2nd ed. Totowa, NJ: Rowman & Littlefield, 1999.

Rescher, Nicholas. *Epistemology: An Introduction to the Theory of Knowledge*. Albany: State University of New York Press, 2003.

Steup, Matthias. *An Introduction to Contemporary Epistemology*. Upper Saddle River, NJ: Prentice Hall, 1996.

Williams, Michael. *Problems of Knowledge: A Critical Introduction to Epistemology*. New York: Oxford University Press, 2001.

Woozley, A. D. *Theory of Knowledge: An Introduction*. New York: Hutchinson University Library, 1949.

Knowledge

Alcoff, Linda, and Elizabeth Potter. *Feminist Epistemologies*. New York: Routledge, 1993.

Alston, William P. *Epistemic Justification*. Ithaca, NY: Cornell University Press, 1989.

Antony, Louise M., and Charlotte Witt, eds. *A Mind of One's Own: Feminist Essays on Reason and Objectivity*. Boulder, CO: Westview Press, 1993.

Ayer, A. J. *The Problem of Knowledge*. London: Pelican, 1976.

Berkeley, George. *Principles of Human Knowledge; and, Three Dialogues Between Hylas and Philonous*. Ed. Howard Robinson. New York: Oxford University Press, 1996.

Blanshard, Brand. *The Nature of Thought*. London: Allen & Unwin, 1939.

BonJour, Laurence. *The Structure of Empirical Knowledge*. Cambridge, MA: Harvard University Press, 1985.

Burnyeat, Myles F., ed. *The Skeptical Tradition*. Berkeley: University of California Press, 1983.

Code, Lorraine. *What Can She Know?* Ithaca, NY: Cornell University Press, 1991.

Collins, Patricia Hill. *Black Feminist Thought: Knowledge, Consciousness, and the Politics of Empowerment*. Boston: Unwin Hyman, 1990.

Craig, Edward. *Knowledge and the State of Nature*. Oxford: Clarendon Press, 1990.

Derrida, Jacques. *Of Grammatology*. Trans. Gayatri Chakravorty Spivak. Baltimore: Johns Hopkins University Press, 1976.

———. *Margins of Philosophy*. Trans. Alan Bass. Chicago: University of Chicago Press, 1982.

Descartes, René. *Discourse on Method; and, Meditations on First Philosophy*. 4th ed. Trans. Donald A. Cress. Indianapolis, IN: Hackett, 1998.

Dicker, Georges. *Kant's Theory of Knowledge: An Analytical Introduction*. New York: Oxford University Press, 2004.

Dretske, Fred. *Knowledge and the Flow of Information*. Cambridge, MA: MIT Press, 1981.

Duran, Jane. *Toward a Feminist Epistemology*. Savage, MD: Rowman & Littlefield, 1991.

Fine, Gail. *Plato on Knowledge and Forms: Selected Essays*. New York: Oxford University Press, 2003.

Fogelin, Robert. *Pyrrhonian Reflections on Knowledge and Justification*. New York: Oxford University Press, 1994.

Foley, Richard. *A Theory of Epistemic Rationality*. Cambridge, MA: Harvard University Press, 1987.

Foucault, Michel. *Power/Knowledge*. Ed. Colin Gordon. New York: Pantheon Books, 1980.

———. *The Order of Things: An Archaeology of the Human Sciences*. New York: Vintage Books, 1973.

Fricker, Miranda. "Feminism in Epistemology: Pluralism Without Postmodernism." In *The Cambridge Companion to Feminism in Philosophy*. Eds. Miranda Fricker and Jennifer Hornsby. Cambridge: Cambridge University Press. 2000, 146–165.

Gadamer, Hans-Georg. *Truth and Method*. 2nd ed. rev. Trans. Joel Weinsheimer and Donald G. Marshall. New York: Crossroad, 1991.

Garry, Ann and Marilyn Pearsall, eds. *Women, Knowledge and Reality*. 2nd ed. New York: Routledge, 1996.

Gettier, Edmund. "Is Justified True Belief Knowledge?" *Analysis* 23 (1963): 121–123.

Gilbert, Margaret. *On Social Facts*. London: Routledge, 1989.

Goldman, Alan H. *Empirical Knowledge*. Berkeley: University of California Press, 1988.

Goldman, Alvin. *Epistemology and Cognition*. Cambridge, MA: Harvard University Press, 1986.

Haack, Susan. *Evidence and Inquiry: Towards Reconstruction in Epistemology*. Oxford: Blackwell, 1993.

Harding, Sandra, and Merrill B. Hintikka, eds. *Discovering Reality: Feminist Perspectives on Epistemology, Metaphysics, Methodology and Philosophy of Science*. Dordrecht: Reidel, 1983.

Heidegger, Martin. *Being and Time*. Trans. John Macquarrie and Edward Robinson. New York: Harper & Row, 1962.

Hume, David. *Treatise of Human Nature*. 2nd ed. Ed. L. A. Selby-Bigge. New York: Oxford University Press, 1978.

———. *An Enquiry Concerning Human Understanding.* Ed. Tom L. Beauchamp. New York: Oxford University Press, 1999.

Jaggar, Alison, and Susan Bordo, eds. *Gender/Body/Knowledge.* New Brunswick, NJ: Rutgers University Press, 1989.

Kant, Immanuel. *Critique of Pure Reason.* Trans. Norman Kemp Smith. New York: Humanities Press, 1950.

Klein, Peter. *Certainty: A Refutation of Scepticism.* Oxford: Clarendon Press, 1984.

Kornblith, Hilary, ed. *Naturalizing Epistemology.* 2nd ed. Cambridge, MA: MIT Press, 1994.

Lehrer, Keith. *Self-Trust: A Study of Reason, Knowledge and Autonomy.* Oxford: Clarendon Press, 1997.

———. *Knowledge.* Oxford: Oxford University Press, 1974.

Lennon, Kathleen, and Margaret Whitford, eds. *Knowing the Difference: Feminist Perspectives in Epistemology.* New York: Routledge, 1994.

Lewis, C. I. *An Analysis of Knowledge and Valuation.* La Salle, IL: Open Court, 1946.

Lloyd, Genevieve. *The Man of Reason: "Male" and "Female" in Western Philosophy.* Minneapolis: University of Minnesota Press, 1994.

Malcolm, Norman. *Knowledge and Certainty: Essays and Lectures.* Englewood Cliffs, NJ: Prentice Hall, 1963.

———. *Dreaming.* New York: Routledge & Kegan Paul, 1962.

Moser, Paul K., ed. *A Priori Knowledge.* Oxford: Oxford University Press, 1987.

———. *Knowledge and Evidence.* New York: Cambridge University Press, 1989.

Musgrave, Alan E. *Common Sense, Science and Scepticism: A Historical Introduction to the Theory of Knowledge.* Cambridge: Cambridge University Press, 1993.

Nelson, Lynn Hankinson. *Who Knows: From Quine to Feminist Empiricism.* Philadelphia: Temple University Press, 1990.

Nozick, Robert. *Philosophical Explanations.* Cambridge, MA: Harvard University Press, 1981.

Pappas, George. *What Is Knowledge?* New York: Harper & Row, 1971.

Piaget, Jean. *Psychology and Epistemology: Towards a Theory of Knowledge.* Trans. Arnold Rosin. New York: Viking Press, 1971.

Plantinga, Alvin. *Warrant: The Current Debate.* Oxford: Oxford University Press, 1993.

———. *Warrant and Proper Function.* Oxford: Oxford University Press, 1993.

Pollock, John L. *Knowledge and Justification.* Princeton, NJ: Princeton University Press, 1974.

Popkin, Richard. *Scepticism from Erasmus to Spinoza.* Berkeley: University of California Press, 1979.

Popper, Karl. *Conjectures and Refutations: The Growth of Scientific Knowledge.* New York: Routledge, 1992.

Putnam, Hilary. *The Many Faces of Realism.* La Salle, IL: Open Court, 1987.

Quine, W. V. O. *From a Logical Point of View.* Cambridge, MA: Harvard University Press, 1953.

———. *Ontological Relativity and Other Essays.* New York: Columbia University Press, 1969.

Quine, W. V. O., and J. Ullian. *The Web of Belief.* 2nd ed. New York: Random House, 1978.

Rockmore, Tom. *On Constructivist Epistemology.* Lanham, MD: Rowman & Littlefield, 2004.

Rorty, Richard. *Philosophy and the Mirror of Nature.* Princeton, NJ: Princeton University Press, 1979.

Russell, Bertrand. *Human Knowledge: Its Scope and Limits.* New York: Simon & Schuster, 1948.

Searle, John R. *The Construction of Social Reality.* New York: Free Press, 1995.

Sextus, Empiricus. *Outline of Pyrrhonism.* Trans. R. G. Bury. Cambridge: Harvard University Press, 1933–49.

Sosa, Ernest, ed. *Knowledge and Justification.* 2 vols. Brookfield, VT: Ashgate, 1994.

———. *Knowledge in Perspective: Selected Essays in Epistemology.* Cambridge: Cambridge University Press, 1991.

Swartz, Robert J., ed. *Perceiving, Sensing, and Knowing.* Garden City, NY: Doubleday, 1965.

Tanesini, Alessandra. *An Introduction to Feminist Epistemologies.* Malden, MA: Blackwell, 1999.

Plato, *Theaetetus.* Ed. Bernard Williams. Trans. M. J. Levett. Indianapolis, IN: Hackett, 1992.

Unger, Peter. *Philosophical Relativity.* Minneapolis: University of Minnesota Press, 1984.

Wittgenstein, Ludwig. *On Certainty.* Eds. G.E.M. Anscombe and G. H. von Wright. Trans. Denis Paul and G. E. M. Anscombe. New York: Harper, 1969.

———. *Philosophical Investigations.* Trans. G.E.M. Anscombe. Oxford: Blackwell, 1953.

Truth

Alston, Walter P. *A Realist Conception of Truth*. Ithaca, NY: Cornell University Press, 1996.

Armstrong, David M. *A World of States of Affairs*. Cambridge: Cambridge University Press, 1997.

———. *Belief, Truth and Knowledge*. Cambridge: Cambridge University Press, 1973.

Austin, J. L. *Philosophical Papers*. 3rd ed. Ed. J. O. Urmson and G. J. Warnock. Oxford: Oxford University Press, 1979.

Ayer, A. J. *Language, Truth and Logic*. New York: Dover, 1952.

Beall, J. C. "On the Identity Theory of Truth." *Philosophy* 75 (2000): 127–30.

Bender, John W., ed. *The Current State of the Coherence Theory*. Boston: Kluwer, 1989.

Blackburn, Simon, and Keith Simmons, eds. *Truth*. Oxford: Oxford University Press, 1999.

Blanshard, Brand. *The Nature of Thought*. London. Allen & Unwin, 1939.

Bordo, Susan. *The Flight to Objectivity*. Albany: State University of New York Press, 1987.

Bradley, F. H. *Essays on Truth and Reality*. Oxford: Clarendon Press, 1914.

Campbell, Joseph K., Michael O'Rourke, and David Shier, eds. *Meaning and Truth: Investigations in Philosophical Semantics*. New York: Seven Bridges Press, 2002.

Candlish, Stewart. "The Truth About F. H. Bradley." *Mind* 98 (1989): 331–48.

Cartwright, Richard. "A Neglected Theory of Truth." In *Philosophical Essays*. Cambridge, MA: MIT Press, 1987.

Clark, Maudemarie. *Nietzsche on Truth and Philosophy*. Cambridge: Cambridge University Press, 1990.

David, Marian. *Correspondence and Disquotation: An Essay on the Nature of Truth*. Oxford: Oxford University Press, 1994.

Davidson, Donald. *Inquiries into Truth and Interpretation*. New York: Oxford University Press, 1984.

Devitt, Michael. *Realism and Truth*. 2nd ed. Oxford: Blackwell 1991.

Dodd, Julian. *An Identity Theory of Truth*. London: Macmillan, 2000.

Dummett, Michael. *Truth and Other Enigmas*. Oxford: Clarendon Press, 1978.

Evans, Gareth, and John McDowell, eds. *Truth and Meaning: Essays in Semantics*. Oxford: Oxford University Press, 1976.

Haraway, Donna. "Situated Knowledges: The Science Question in Feminism and the Privilege of Partial Perspective." *Feminist Studies* 14 (1988): 575–99.

———. *Primate Visions: Gender, Race, and Nature in the World of Modern Science*. New York: Routledge, 1989.

Harding, Sandra. *Whose Science? Whose Knowledge?* Ithaca NY: Cornell University Press, 1991.

———. "What Is Strong Objectivity?" In *Feminist Epistemologies*. Eds. Linda Alcoff and Elizabeth Potter. New York: Routledge, 1993.

Hempel, Carl. "On the Logical Positivists' Theory of Truth." *Analysis* 2 (1935): 49–59.

Horwich, Paul. *Truth*. Oxford, Blackwell, 1990.

———, ed. *Theories of Truth*. New York: Dartmouth, 1994.

James, William. *The Meaning of Truth*. Cambridge, MA: Harvard University Press, 1979.

Joachim, Harold H. *The Nature of Truth*. 2nd ed. Oxford: Oxford University Press, 1936.

Keller, Evelyn Fox. *Reflections on Gender and Science*. New Haven, CT: Yale University Press, 1985.

Kirkham, Richard L. *Theories of Truth: A Critical Introduction*. Cambridge, MA: MIT Press, 1992.

LePore, Ernest. *Truth and Interpretation: Perspectives on the Philosophy of Donald Davidson*. Oxford: Basil Blackwell, 1986.

Locke, John. *An Essay Concerning Human Understanding*. 2 vols. Ed. A. C. Fraser. New York: Dover, 1959.

Longino, Helen E. *Science as Social Knowledge*. Princeton, NJ: Princeton University Press, 1990.

Lynch, Michael P., ed. *The Nature of Truth: Classic and Contemporary Perspectives*. Cambridge, MA: MIT Press, 2001.

Margolis, Joseph. *The Truth About Relativism*. Cambridge: Blackwell, 1991.

———. *Pragmatism Without Foundations: Reconciling Realism and Relativism*. Cambridge: Blackwell, 1986.

Nietzsche, Friedrich. *The Gay Science, with a Prelude of Rhymes and an Appendix of Songs*. Trans. Walter Kaufmann. New York: Random House, 1974.

———. *The Antichrist*. Trans. Walter Kaufmann. In *The Portable Nietzsche*. Ed. Walter Kaufmann. New York: Viking Press, 1968.

O'Connor, D. J. *The Correspondence Theory of Truth*. London: Hutchinson, 1975.

Pitcher, George, ed. *Truth*. Englewood Cliffs, NJ: Prentice Hall, 1964.

Putnam, Hilary. *Reason, Truth and History*. Cambridge: Cambridge University Press, 1981.

Quine, W. V. O. *Philosophy of Logic*. Englewood Cliffs, NJ: Prentice Hall, 1970.

Rescher, Nicholas. *The Coherence Theory of Truth*. Oxford: Oxford University Press, 1973.

Rorty, Richard. *Consequences of Pragmantism*. Minneapolis: University of Minnesota Press, 1982.

———. *Contingency, Irony, and Solidarity*. New York: Cambridge University Press, 1989.

Russell, Bertrand. "On the Nature of Truth." *Proceedings of the Aristotelian Society* 7 (1907): 228–49.

———. *Problems of Philosophy*. Oxford: Oxford University Press, 1971.

———. *An Inquiry into Meaning and Truth*. London: Routledge, 1995.

Schantz, Richard, ed. *What Is Truth?* New York: De Gruyter, 2002.

Schmitt, Frederick F. *Truth: A Primer*. Boulder, CO: Westview Press, 1995.

Soames, Scott. *Understanding Truth*. New York: Oxford University Press, 1999.

Stern, Robert. "Did Hegel Hold an Identity Theory of Truth?" *Mind* 102 (1993): 645–47.

Tarksi, Alfred. "The Semantic Conception of Truth." *Philosophy and Phenomenological Research* IV (1944): 341–75.

Tuana, Nancy, ed. *Feminism and Science*. Bloomington: Indiana University Press, 1989.

Vision, Gerald. *Modern Anti-Realism and Manufactured Truth*. New York: Routledge, 1988.

Walker, R. C. S. "Bradley's Theory of Truth." In *Appearance Versus Reality*. Ed. Guy Stock. Oxford: Oxford University Press, 1998. 93–109.

———. *The Coherence Theory of Truth: Realism, Anti-realism, Idealism*. New York: Routledge, 1989.

Wilcox, John T. *Truth and Value in Nietzsche*. Ann Arbor: University of Michigan Press, 1974.

Wittgenstein, Ludwig. *Tractatus Logico-Philosophicus*. Trans. David F. Pears and Brian F. McGuinness. London: Routledge, 1961.

Wright, Crispin. *Truth and Objectivity*. Cambridge, MA: Harvard University Press, 1992.

Young, James O. "A Defence of the Coherence Theory of Truth." *The Journal of Philosophical Research* 26 (2001): 89–101.

OF Minds AND Bodies

Neo (Keanu Reeves) plugged into the Matrix.

3.1   WHAT IS THE RELATIONSHIP OF THE MIND
TO THE BODY?

RENÉ DESCARTES

THE REAL DISTINCTION OF THE MIND
FROM THE BODY

In this selection, our second from *Meditations on First Philosophy* (1641), René Descartes argues that the mind is separate from the body. In fact, the mind (or soul—he uses these terms interchangeably) and the body have entirely opposite natures: the mind (namely, *res cogitans,* or "thinking thing") is indivisible and unextended, and the body (namely, *res extensa,* or "extended thing") is extended and divisible. Descartes' position on the relationship between mind and body is referred to by a number of different phrases: Cartesian dualism, mind–body dualism, and psychophysical dualism. In general, *dualism* is the view that existence is composed of two separate, independent, unique realms and that neither one can be reduced to the other. Plato's distinction between a world of the senses and a world of the intellect and Immanuel Kant's distinction between a noumenal world and a phenomenal world are also types of dualism (see chapter 2).

Descartes begins his argument for the existence of bodies external to the mind by reviewing conclusions he reached in our previous selection from his *Meditations* (see chapter 2). First, he says that he was persuaded that nothing was in the mind that was not previously in the senses. However, past misjudgments, the dream argument, and the evil demon supposition have led him to lose all confidence in the accuracy of the reports of his senses. He also believes that as a thinking entity he is distinct from his body and that faculties such as perception and imagination are modes of his existence as a thinking thing. But what of other faculties such as movement and the active ability to produce ideas? Are these also modes of his existence as a thinking thing?

For Descartes, it seems obvious that faculties such as movement and the active ability to produce ideas are *not* modes of his existence as a thinking thing. First, movement requires a body, and a thinking thing exists independently of any body. Second, the faculty of producing ideas is distinct from thinking substance because it does not presuppose intelligence and does not act autonomously (ideas often occur without our consent). For Descartes, given that neither movement nor the active ability to produce ideas is a mode of the mind, only two other options are available: (1) these faculties exist in God, or (2) these faculties exist in a body.

If they exist in God, it would follow that God sends ideas directly to us via a medium in which there is not as much formal reality as is found in the ideas themselves. This would mean that God is deceiving us as to the nature of physical reality. However, Descartes reminds us that God is not a deceiver (a point he established earlier in his *Meditations*), and he concludes that bodies (or corporeal, extended, divisible things) exist and that what we know of these bodies through the senses is for the most part true. For Descartes, everything that we clearly and distinctly conceive concerning bodies is true.

In general, Descartes regards human beings as a union of mind (soul) and body, which are two distinct substances. The body, as part of the physical universe, is subject to the same laws of physics as the rest of the physical universe. Furthermore, like all things in the physical universe, the body is mechanical in operation; it is a machine made out of flesh and bone. For example, your heart is a pump, and your joints and tendons are ropes, pivots, and pulleys. Given that many of the activities of the body are not caused by the mind, the body can function autonomously, that is, on its own. Even though the mind is connected to every part of the human body, its most important connection is at the pineal gland in the brain. This is where the mind performs most of its functions. By acting upon the pineal gland, the mind produces mental events such as sensing, perceiving, willing, thinking, and emoting. Thus, for Descartes, while the mind and the body are separate, they still interact.

Finally, it should be noted that for Descartes, in addition to mind (created finite spiritual substance) and body (created finite material substance), there is a third substance: God-substance. As substance, God is the infinite, uncreated being that depends on nothing other than itself in order to exist. In comparison to God, mind and body are created, finite substances. Consequently, given Descartes' contention that substance is that which can be conceived alone by itself, without needing something else in terms of which it is known, and without depending on something else for its existence, God-substance is, in effect, the only true substance. A biographical sketch of René Descartes can be found in chapter 2. The following selection is from "Meditation Six: Concerning the Existence of Material Things, and the Real Distinction of the Mind from the Body."

But now, having begun to have a better knowledge of myself and the author of my origin, I am of the opinion that I must not rashly admit everything that I seem to derive from the senses; but neither, for that matter, should I call everything into doubt.

First, I know that all the things that I clearly and distinctly understand can be made by God such as I understand them. For this reason, my ability clearly and distinctly to understand one thing without another suffices to make me certain that the one thing is different from the other, since they can be separated from each other, at least by God. The question as to the sort of power that might effect such a separation is not relevant to their being thought to be different. For this reason, from the fact that I know that I exist, and that at the same time I judge that obviously nothing else belongs to my nature or essence except that I am a thinking thing, I rightly conclude that my essence consists entirely in my being a thinking thing. And although perhaps (or rather, as I shall soon say, assuredly) I have a body that is very closely joined to me, nevertheless, because on the one hand I have clear and distinct idea of myself,

insofar as I am merely a thinking thing and not an extended thing, and because on the other hand I have a distinct idea of a body, insofar as it is merely an extended thing and not a thinking thing, it is certain that I am really distinct from my body, and can exist without it.

Moreover, I find in myself faculties for certain special modes of thinking, namely the faculties of imagining and sensing. I can clearly and distinctly understand myself in my entirety without these faculties, but not vice versa: I cannot understand them clearly and distinctly without me, that is, without a substance endowed with understanding in which they inhere, for they include an act of understanding in their formal concept. Thus I perceive them to be distinguished from me as modes from a thing. I also acknowledge that there are certain other faculties, such as those of moving form one place to another, of taking on various shapes, and so on, that, like sensing or imagining, cannot be understood apart from some substance in which they inhere, and hence without which they cannot exist. But it is clear that these faculties, if in fact they exist, must be in a corporeal or extended substance, not in a substance endowed with understanding. For some extension is contained in a clear and distinct concept of them, though certainly not any understanding. Now there clearly is in me a passive faculty of sensing, that is, a faculty for receiving and knowing the ideas of sensible things; but I could not use it unless there also existed, either in me or in something else, a certain active faculty of producing or bringing about these ideas. But this faculty surely cannot be in me, since it clearly presupposes no act of understanding, and these ideas are produced without my cooperation and often even against my will. Therefore the only alternative is that it is in some substance different from me, containing either formally or eminently all the reality that exists objectively in the ideas produced by that faculty, as I have just noted above. Hence this substance is either a body, that is, a corporeal nature, which contains formally all that is contained objectively in the ideas, or else it is God, or some other creature more noble than a body, which contains eminently all that is contained objectively in the ideas. But since God is not a deceiver, it is patently obvious that he does not send me these ideas either immediately by himself, or even through the mediation of some creature that contains the objective reality of these ideas not formally but only eminently. For since God has given me no faculty whatsoever for making this determination, but instead has given me a great inclination to believe that these ideas issue from corporeal things, I fail to see how God could be understood not to be a deceiver, if these ideas were to issue from a source other than corporeal things. And consequently corporeal things exist. Nevertheless, perhaps not all bodies exist exactly as I grasp them by sense, since this sensory grasp is in many cases very obscure and confused. But at least they do contain everything I clearly and distinctly understand—that is, everything, considered in a general sense, that is encompassed in the object of pure mathematics.

As far as the remaining matters are concerned, which are either merely particular (for example, that the sun is of such and such a size or shape, and so on) or less clearly understood (for example, light, sound, pain, and the like), even though these matters are very doubtful and uncertain, nevertheless the fact that God is no deceiver (and thus no falsity can be found in my opinions, unless there is also in me a faculty given me by God for the purpose of rectifying this falsity) offers me a definite hope of reaching the truth even in these matters. And surely there is no doubt that all that I am taught by nature has some truth to it: for by "nature," taken generally, I understand nothing other than God himself or the ordered network of created things which was instituted by God. By my own particular nature I understand nothing other than the combination of all the things bestowed upon me by God.

There is nothing that this nature teaches me more explicitly than that I have a body that is ill-disposed when I feel pain, that needs food and drink when I suffer hunger or thirst, and the like. Therefore, I should not doubt that there is some truth in this.

By means of these sensations of pain, hunger, thirst, and so on, nature also teaches not merely that I am present to my body in the way a sailor is present in a ship, but that I am most tightly joined and, so to speak, commingled with it, so much so that I and the body constitute one single thing. For if this were not the case, then I, who am only a thinking thing, would not sense pain when the body is injured; rather, I would perceive the wound by means of the pure intellect, just as a sailor perceives by sight whether anything in his ship is broken. And when the body is in need of food or drink, I should understand this explicitly, instead of having confused sensations of hunger and thirst. For clearly these sensations of thirst, hunger, pain, and so on are nothing but certain confused modes of thinking arising from the union and, as it were, the commingling of the mind with the body. . . .

Now my first observation here is that there is a great difference between a mind and a body in that a body, by its very nature, is always divisible. On the other hand, the mind is utterly indivisible. For when I consider the mind, that is, myself insofar as I am only a thinking thing, I cannot distinguish any parts within me; rather, I understand myself to be manifestly one complete thing. Although the entire mind seems to be united to the entire body, nevertheless, were a foot or an arm or any other bodily part to be amputated, I know that nothing has been taken away from the mind on that account. Nor can the faculties of willing, sensing, understanding, and so on be called "parts" of the mind, since it is one and the same mind that wills, senses, and understands. On the other hand, there is no corporeal or extended thing I can think of that I may not in my thought easily divide into parts; and in this way I understand that it is divisible. This consideration alone would suffice to teach me that the mind is wholly diverse from the body, had I not yet known it well enough in any other way.

My second observation is that my mind is not immediately affected by all the parts of the body, but only by the brain, or perhaps even by just one small part of the brain, namely, by that part where the "common" sense is said to reside. Whenever this part of the brain is disposed in the same manner, it presents the same thing to the mind, even if the other parts of the body are able meanwhile to be related in diverse ways. Countless experiments show this, none of which need be reviewed here.

My next observation is that the nature of the body is such that whenever any of its parts can be moved by another part some distance away, it can also be moved in the same manner by any of the parts that lie between them, even if this more distant part is doing nothing. For example, in the cord ABCD, if the final part D is pulled, the first part A would be moved in exactly the same manner as it could be, if one of the intermediate parts B or C were pulled, while the end part D remained immobile. Likewise, when I feel a pain in my foot, physics teaches me that this sensation took place by means of nerves distributed throughout the foot, like stretched cords extending from the foot all the way to the brain. When these nerves are pulled in the foot, they also pull on the inner parts of the brain to which they extend, and produce a certain motion in them. This motion has been constituted by nature so as to affect the mind with a sensation of pain, as if it occurred in the foot. But because these nerves need to pass through the shin, thigh, loins, back, and neck to get from the foot to the brain, it can happen that even if it is not the part in the foot but merely one of the intermediate parts that is being struck, the very same movement will occur in the brain that would occur were the foot badly injured. The inevitable result will be that the mind feels the same pain. The same opinion should hold for any other sensation.

My final observation is that, since any given motion occurring in that part of the brain immediately affecting the mind produces but one sensation in it, I can think of no better arrangement

than that it produces the one sensation that, of all the ones it is able to produce, is most especially and most often conducive to the maintenance of a healthy man. Moreover, experience shows that all the sensations bestowed on us by nature are like this. Hence there is absolutely nothing to be found in them that does not bear witness to God's power and goodness. Thus, for example, when the nerves in the foot are agitated in a violent and unusual manner, this motion of theirs extends through the marrow of the spine to the inner reaches of the brain, where it gives the mind the sign to sense something, namely, the pain as if it is occurring in the foot. This provokes the mind to do its utmost to move away from the cause of the pain, since it is seen as harmful to the foot. But the nature of man could have been so constituted by God that this same motion in the brain might have indicated something else to the mind: for example, either the motion itself as it occurs in the brain, or in the foot, or in some place in between, or something else entirely different. But nothing else would have served so well the maintenance of the body. Similarly, when we need something to drink, a certain dryness arises in the throat that moves the nerves in the throat, and, by means of them, the inner parts of the brain. And this motion affects the mind with a sensation of thirst, because in this entire affair nothing is more useful for us to know than that we need something to drink in order to maintain our health; the same holds in the other cases.

DISCUSSION QUESTIONS

1. How do the properties of the mind differ from the properties of the body?

2. Is the relationship of the mind to the body like that of a sailor to the ship? Why or why not? What does Descartes say?

3. Descartes says that the body is divisible but that the mind is not. Do you agree with him? If you assume that the mind is indivisible, how do you account for cases in which your "mind is split" between conflicting emotions?

4. For Descartes, the brain in itself, as part of the physical world, cannot producecon-sciousness. Do you agree with him?

5. Review Descartes' argument for the existence of bodies. Is it a valid and sound argument? Why or why not?

6. Descartes believes that humans and animals as bodies are both machines, and, as such, are subject to the laws of physics. However, while humans possess minds/souls, animals do not. Therefore, the behavior of animals is always only the product of physical laws, whereas human behavior is the product of a combination of both mental activity and physical laws. Do you agree with Descartes that animals have neither minds nor souls nor consciousness?

All of Me
[USA 1984] 1 hour, 33 minutes
Directed by Carl Reiner

*E*dwina Cutwater (Lily Tomlin) is a dying millionaire who has spent her entire life in a sickbed. Upon her death, she plans to have her soul transferred or transmigrated into the body of Terry Hoskins (Victoria Tennant), the young, healthy daughter of Edwina's stableman, Fred Hoskins (Eric Christmas). In the transfer of Edwina's soul to Terry, Terry's own soul will be released into the universe. The soul transmigration will be supervised by His Holiness Prahka Lasa (Richard Libertini), a holy man from abroad. Roger Cobb (Steve Mar-tin), a struggling attorney and part-time jazz musician, is hired to help Edwina settle her legal and financial affairs before she dies. However, when Roger hears about the planned "soul migration," he thinks those involved are mentally unstable and takes himself off the case. Shortly thereafter, the soul transfer goes awry, and Edwina's soul mistakenly ends up in Roger's body. Roger now finds that he has control of the left side of his body but Edwina has control of the right side. Even basic actions such as walking require a coordi-nated effort between the minds of Roger and Edwina. Also, while Roger maintains his own speaking voice, it competes with that of Edwina. They also can talk with each other inside Roger's head.

As the story unfolds, we learn that Terry never intended to receive Edwina's soul; she did not believe that soul transfer was possible. However, Terry signed legal papers willing Edwina's entire estate to her upon Edwina's death. Therefore, Terry, assuming that Edwina's soul would not be transferred into her own body, simply believed that she was going to inherit a fortune upon Edwina's death. Eventually, Roger and Prahka manage to transfer Edwina's soul into Terry, and Terry's soul is transferred into a horse as punishment for attempting to murder Roger and inherit Edwina's fortune under false pretenses.

DISCUSSION QUESTIONS

1. Terry, Fred, and Roger meet each other for the first time at Edwina's bedside, and discuss the soul transfer. Consider the following exchange:

    FRED   "It's unnatural."

    ROGER   "Uh, let me get something straight here. You're going to will all of your money to the sta-bleman's daughter? And he's against it?"

EDWINA   "No."

ROGER   "But you just said . . ."

TERRY   "You see I shall inherit nothing."

ROGER   "But you just said you wanted to make her your sole beneficiary."

EDWINA   "That is correct."

ROGER   "So you will inherit the estate?"

EDWINA   "No she won't."

ROGER   "What am I missing here?"

TERRY   "You see thanks to His Holiness Prahka Lasa, I'm going to be transmigrated. Transmigrated means that my soul is going to leave my body forever and become one with the universe."

EDWINA   "At which time my soul will enter her body."

ROGER   "Ah, good plan."

FRED   "I'm sorry, but I don't think it's a good plan at all. My daughter's soul leaving her body and going off to who knows where."

EDWINA   "Fred, let's not go through all this again, shall we."

Fred asserts, but does not argue, that it would be "unnatural" for a soul to be transferred from one person's body to another's. Assuming that the soul is indeed separate from the body, and that the soul and the body are of the same character as described by Descartes, argue either for or against the "naturalness" of soul "transmigration" as described here.

2. We learn during the course of the film that Terry is on probation and has been arrested in the past. When Edwina's soul is transferred into Terry's body, and Terry's soul is transferred into that of a horse, which body will have to report to the probation officer—the horse's body (with Terri's soul in it) or Terry's body (with Edwina's soul in it)?

3. Edwina says that Terry will not inherit her estate after the soul transmigration procedure. Do you agree with Edwina? Why or why not?

4. Consider the following dialogue between Edwina and Roger:

ROGER   "Ms. Cutwater, as your attorney it's my duty to inform you that your will could be contested if you're deemed 'not of perfectly sound mind.'"

EDWINA   "Why you presumptuous ambulance chaser. Are you insinuating that I am not of perfectly sound mind?"

ROGER   "No, I would not do that, but I think that practically everyone in the solar system would."

EDWINA   "Mr. Cobb, the last thing I need around here is your ill-informed negativity. Get out."

ROGER   "Is everybody here bananas?"

Discuss whether Roger is right in that "practically everyone in the solar system" would believe that Edwina is "bananas." Do you think that she is bananas? Defend your position.

5.   Roger and Terry discuss the soul "repository" utilized by Prahka Lasa. Consider their dialogue:

ROGER   "Got to hand it to you. It's brilliant."

TERRY   "What is?"

ROGER   "Your scam. It's legal. It's logical. But the bit to do with the bowl is overdoing it a little bit."

TERRY   "That bowl is turned to the harmonic of Ms.Cutwater's life force. When her body dies it becomes a repository of that life force, so I hold the bowl and it becomes a conduit from her body to mine."

ROGER   "And you really believe that?"

TERRY   "Yes."

ROGER   "Of course, if you're wrong you inherit 20 million bucks."

TERRY   "I don't want the money. When I was fifteen I ran away from home thinking that I could find myself in the material world and found only pain. His Holiness Prahka teaches that possessions can transmit pain. I want something far more valuable than money, far more elusive. For which I'm willing to give up my physical being and become one with the universe."

ROGER   "Don't you think that's just a little bit wacko?"

Why does Roger not believe in the "soul repository"? Does he have a good argument? Imagine Descartes in the place of Roger in this dialogue. Would Descartes believe that his own unextended and indivisible soul (or mind) could be captured in a "repository"? In other words, if a soul has no extension as Descartes contends, how can it end up in a bowl?

6.   Do you think it is possible for two (or more souls) to be in one body? Why or why not?

7.   Consider the case of Roger, whose body is inhabited by Edwina's soul. Does it make sense to you that with two souls, he would have control of only one side of his body, with Edwina controlling the other side? What do you have to assume about the mind and the body to make sense of the "double-souled" Roger?

8.   When Roger is asleep, Edwina controls his body; when Edwina is asleep, Roger controls his own body. Does this imply that when persons with only one soul sleep, their body is not being controlled at all? Discuss.

9.   Discuss the philosophical implications of the fact that Roger and Edwina do not have to talk aloud to each other because each can hear the other's thoughts. Can you hear your own thoughts? If so, who is speaking?

10. Edwina's soul falls into a bucket of water. A small portion of the water from the bucket is drunk by Tyrone Wattell (Jason Bernard), a blind saxophone player who is asked by Roger to guard it, and the rest is thrown into flowerbeds by Terry. We learn, however, that Edwina's soul is not in the flower- beds, but is in Tyrone, who drank some of the water thinking it was gin. Why do you think her soul is not in the flowerbeds as well? Following the same logic, imagine that another character drank some of the water: Would he, too, have her soul in his body? Why or why not?

GILBERT RYLE

THE MYTH OF THE GHOST IN THE MACHINE

I n this selection, Gilbert Ryle argues that mental statements refer only to behavior, not to a mind that exists in the body. According to Ryle, the "Cartesian" tradition represents the human body as a purely physical thing that is like a "machine" and the human mind as a purely nonphysical thing that is like a "ghost." This "official doctrine" posits that the ghost somehow inhabits and operates the machine. It should be noted that although Ryle uses the term "Cartesian" to describe this view, it is not meant to be a historical reference. Ryle uses it as a general term for this "ghost in the machine" view of the operation of the mind and its relationship to the body. It is a view that Ryle himself once held and that he sees many other still holding.

Ryle attacks both Cartesian dualism and the ghost in the machine. He argues that both are based on what he calls a "category mistake," a mistake brought about by handling an expression of one category as if it belonged to another. The mistake committed by Cartesian dualism is that it treats statements concerning mental phenomena the same as those concerning physical phenomena. According to Ryle, when we do something, we are not simultaneously performing a mental action and a physical action; rather, we are behaving in a certain way. This position is often described as *logical behaviorism*.

Ryle's approach to the mind is similar to his approach to many other philosophical topics. He believes that philosophical mistakes result from the misapplication of categorically different terms, though these can be corrected by careful logical analysis and attention to language. The identification of category mistakes is one of the most important tasks of philosophy. For Ryle, philosophy is not so much about the meaning of expressions as it is about meaningless expressions, about why certain combinations of expressions make no sense. Ryle asserts that expressions can be grouped into "types" or "categories" and that philosophical troubles result from attempts to handle an expression of one category as if it belongs to another. Category mistakes produce meaningless expressions like "the ghost in the machine" and are the source of many philosophical difficulties. Consequently, the task of philosophy is to exhibit and correct category mistakes, as Ryle does here with the concept of mind.

Gilbert Ryle (1900–1976), a British philosopher, wrote primarily on philosophical methodology, philosophical logic, and the philosophy of mind. He became a lecturer at Christ Church in 1924, and the very next year became a student and tutor there. He remained at Christ Church until he was appointed Waynflete Professor of Metaphysical Philosophy and Fellow of Magdalen College, Oxford, a position he held from 1945 to 1968. After the retirement of G. E. Moore as editor of *Mind* in 1947, Ryle took his place, editing this prestigious journal until 1971.

On campus, Ryle was largely responsible for the institution of the new degree of bachelor of philosophy at Oxford. He was one of the dominant figures in mid-twentieth-century British language philosophy, which came to be known as "linguistic analysis." Ryle's writings avoid— or some would say "lack"—historical discussions of philosophical topics and are very informal, employing fresh language and imagery over worn-out philosophical vocabulary. The vast majority of Ryle's publications are articles, many of which can be found in his *Collected Papers* (1971). His books include *Locke on the Human Understanding* (1933), *Philosophical Arguments* (1945), *Dilemmas* (1954), and *Plato's Progress* (1966). His major work is *The Concept of Mind* (1949), from which the following is a selection.

THE OFFICIAL DOCTRINE

There is a doctrine about the nature and place of minds which is so prevalent among theorists and even among laymen that it deserves to be described as the official theory. Most philosophers, psychologists and religious teachers subscribe, with minor reservations, to its main articles and, although they admit certain theoretical difficulties in it, they tend to assume that these can be overcome without serious modifications being made to the architecture of the theory. It will be argued here that the central principles of the doctrine are unsound and conflict with the whole body of what we know about minds when we are not speculating about them.

The official doctrine, which hails chiefly from Descartes, is something like this. With the doubtful exceptions of idiots and infants in arms every human being has both a body and a mind. Some would prefer to say that every human being is both a body and a mind. His body and his mind are ordinarily harnessed together, but after the death of the body his mind may continue to exist and function.

Human bodies are in space and are subject to the mechanical laws which govern all other bodies in space. Bodily processes and states can be inspected by external observers. So a man's bodily life is as much a public affair as are the lives of animals and reptiles and even as the careers of trees, crystals and planets.

But minds are not in space, nor are their operations subject to mechanical laws. The workings of one mind are not witnessable by other observers; its career is private. Only I can take direct cognisance of the states and processes of my own mind. A person therefore lives through two collateral histories, one consisting of what happens in and to his body, the other consisting of what happens in and to his mind. The first is public, the second private. The events in the first history are events in the physical world, those in the second are events in the mental world.

It has been disputed whether a person does or can directly monitor all or only some of the episodes of his own private history; but, according to the official doctrine, of at least some of these episodes he has direct and unchallengeable cognisance. In consciousness, self-consciousness and introspection he is directly and authentically apprised of the present states and operations of his mind. He may have great or small uncertainties about concurrent and adjacent episodes in the physical world, but he can have none about at least part of what is momentarily occupying his mind.

It is customary to express this bifurcation of his two lives and of his two worlds by saying that the things and events which belong to the physical world, including his own body, are external, while the workings of his own mind are internal. This antithesis of outer and inner is of course meant to be construed as a metaphor, since minds, not being in space, could not be described as being spatially inside anything else, or as having things going on spatially inside themselves. But relapses from this good intention are common and theorists are found speculating how stimuli, the physical sources of which are yards or miles outside a person's skin, can generate mental responses inside his skull, or how decisions framed inside his cranium can set going movements of his extremities.

Even when "inner" and "outer" are construed as metaphors, the problem how a person's mind and body influence one another is notoriously charged with theoretical difficulties. What the mind wills, the legs, arms and the tongue execute; what affects the ear and the eye has something to do with what the mind perceives; grimaces and smiles betray the mind's moods and bodily castigations lead, it is hoped, to moral improvement. But the actual transactions between the episodes of the private history and those of the public history remain mysterious, since by definition they can belong to neither series. They could not be reported among the happenings described in a person's autobiography of his inner life, but nor could they be reported among those described in some one else's biography of that person's overt career. They can be inspected neither by introspection nor by laboratory experiment. They are theoretical shuttlecocks which are forever being bandied from the physiologist back to the psychologist and from the psychologist back to the physiologist.

Underlying this partly metaphorical representation of the bifurcation of a person's two lives there is a seemingly more profound and philosophical assumption. It is assumed that there are two different kinds of existence or status. What exists or happens may have the status of physical existence, or it may have the status of mental existence. Somewhat as the faces of coins are either heads or tails, or somewhat as living creatures are either male or female, so, it is supposed, some existing is physical existing, other existing is mental existing. It is a necessary feature of what has physical existence that it is in space and time; it is a necessary feature of what has mental existence that it is in time but not in space. What has physical existence is composed of matter, or else is a function of matter; what has mental existence consists of consciousness, or else is a function of consciousness.

There is thus a polar opposition between mind and matter, an opposition which is often brought out as follows. Material objects are situated in a common field, known as "space," and what happens to one body in one part of space is mechanically connected with what happens to other bodies in other parts of space. But mental happenings occur in insulated fields, known as "minds," and there is, apart maybe from telepathy, no direct causal connection between what happens in one mind and what happens in another. Only through the medium of the public physical world can the mind of one person make a difference to the mind of another. The mind is its own place and in his inner life each of us lives the life of a ghostly Robinson Crusoe. People can see, hear and jolt one another's bodies, but they are irremediably blind and deaf to the workings of one another's minds and inoperative upon them.

What sort of knowledge can be secured of the working of a mind? On the one side, according to the official theory, a person has direct knowledge of the best imaginable kind of the workings of his own mind. Mental states and processes are (or are normally) conscious states and processes, and the consciousness which irradiates them can engender no illusions and leaves the door open for no doubts. A person's present thinkings, feelings and willings, his perceivings, rememberings and imaginings are intrinsically "phosphorescent"; their existence and their nature are inevitably betrayed to their owner. The inner life is a stream of consciousness of such a sort that it would be absurd to suggest that the mind whose life is that stream might be unaware of what is passing down it.

True, the evidence adduced recently by Freud seems to show that there exist channels tributary to this stream, which run hidden from their owner. People are actuated by impulses the existence of which they vigorously disavow; some of their thoughts differ from the thoughts which they acknowledge; and some of the actions which they think they will to perform they do not really will. They are thoroughly gulled by some of their own hypocrisies and they successfully ignore facts about their mental lives which on the official theory ought to be patent to them. Holders of the official theory tend, however, to maintain that anyhow in normal circumstances a person must be directly and authentically seized of the present state and workings of his own mind.

Besides being currently supplied with these alleged immediate data of consciousness, a person is also generally supposed to be able to exercise from time to time a special kind of perception, namely inner perception, or introspection. He can take a (non-optical) "look" at what is passing in his mind. Not only can he view and scrutinize a flower through his sense of sight and listen to and discriminate the notes of a bell through his sense of hearing; he can also reflectively or introspectively watch, without any bodily organ of sense, the current episodes of his inner life. This self-observation is also commonly supposed to be immune from illusion, confusion or doubt. A mind's reports of its own affairs have a certainty superior to the best that is possessed by its reports of matters in the physical world. Sense-perceptions can, but consciousness and introspection cannot, be mistaken or confused.

On the other side, one person has no direct access of any sort to the events of the inner life of another. He cannot do better than make problematic inferences from the observed behaviour of the other person's body to the states of mind which, by analogy from his own conduct, he supposes to be signalised by that behaviour. Direct access to the workings of a mind is the privilege of that mind itself; in default of such privileged access, the workings of one mind are inevitably occult to everyone else. For the supposed arguments from bodily movements similar to their own to mental workings similar to their own would lack any possibility of observational corroboration. Not unnaturally, therefore, an adherent of the official theory finds it difficult to resist this consequence of his premises, that he has no good reason to believe that there do exist minds other than his own. Even if he prefers to believe that to other human bodies there are harnessed minds not unlike his own, he cannot claim to be able to discover their individual characteristics, or the particular things that they undergo and do. Absolute solitude is on this showing the ineluctable destiny of the soul. Only our bodies can meet.

As a necessary corollary of this general scheme there is implicitly prescribed a special way of construing our ordinary concepts of mental powers and operations. The verbs, nouns and adjectives, with which in ordinary life we describe the wits, characters and higher-grade performances of the people with whom we have do, are required to be construed as signifying special episodes in their secret histories, or else as signifying tendencies for such episodes to occur. When someone is described as knowing, believing or guessing something, as hoping, dreading, intending or shirking something, as designing this or being amused at that, these verbs are supposed to denote the occurrence of specific modifications in his (to us) occult stream of consciousness. Only his own privileged access to this stream in direct awareness and introspection could provide authentic testimony that these mental-conduct verbs were correctly or incorrectly applied. The onlooker, be he teacher, critic, biographer or friend, can never assure himself that his comments have any vestige of truth. Yet it was just because we do in fact all know how to make such comments, make them with general correctness and correct them when they turn out to be confused or mistaken, that philosophers found it necessary to construct their theories of the nature and place of minds. Finding mental-conduct concepts being regularly and effectively used, they properly sought to fix their logical geography. But the logical geography officially recommended would entail that there could be no regular or effective use of these mental-conduct concepts in our descriptions of, and prescriptions for, other people's minds.

THE ABSURDITY OF THE OFFICIAL DOCTRINE

Such in outline is the official theory. I shall often speak of it, with deliberate abusiveness, as "the

dogma of the Ghost in the Machine." I hope to prove that it is entirely false, and false not in detail but in principle. It is not merely an assemblage of particular mistakes. It is one big mistake and a mistake of a special kind. It is, namely, a category-mistake. It represents the facts of mental life as if they belonged to one logical type or category (or range of types of categories), when they actually belong to another. The dogma is therefore a philosopher's myth. In attempting to explode the myth I shall probably be taken to be denying well-known facts about the mental life of human beings, and my plea that I aim at doing nothing more than rectify the logic of mental-conduct concepts will probably be disallowed as mere subterfuge.

I must first indicate what is meant by the phrase "Category-mistake." This I do in a series of illustrations.

A foreigner visiting Oxford or Cambridge for the first time is shown a number of colleges, libraries, playing fields, museums, scientific departments and administrative offices. He then asks "But where is the University? I have seen where the members of the Colleges live, where the Registrar works, where the scientists experiment and the rest. But I have not yet seen the University in which reside and work the members of your University." It has then to be explained to him that the University is not another collateral institution, some ulterior counterpart to the colleges, laboratories and offices which he has seen. The University is just the way in which all that he has already seen is organized. When they are seen and when their coordination is understood, the University has been seen. His mistake lay in his innocent assumption that it was correct to speak of Christ Church, the Bodleian Library, the Ashmolean Museum *and* the University, to speak, that is, as if "the University" stood for an extra member of the class of which these other units are members. He was mistakenly allocating the University to the same category as that to which the other institutions belong.

The same mistake would be made by a child witnessing the march-past of a division, who, having had pointed out to him such and such battalions, batteries, squadrons, etc., asked when the division was going to appear. He would be supposing that a division was a counterpart to the units already seen, partly similar to them and partly unlike them. He would be shown his mistake by being told that in watching the battalions, batteries and squadrons marching past he had been watching the division marching past. The march-past was not a parade of battalions, batteries, squadrons *and* a division; it was a parade of the battalions, batteries and squadrons *of* a division.

One more illustration. A foreigner watching his first game of cricket learns what are the functions of the bowlers, the batsmen, the fielders, the umpires and the scorers. He then says "But there is no one left on the field to contribute the famous element of team-spirit. I see who does the bowling, the batting and the wicket-keeping; but I do not see whose role it is to exercise *esprit de corps*." Once more, it would have to be explained that he was looking for the wrong type of thing. Team-spirit is not another cricketing-operation supplementary to all of the other special tasks. It is, roughly, the keenness with which each of the special tasks is performed, and performing a task keenly is not performing two tasks. Certainly exhibiting team-spirit is not the same thing as bowling or catching, but nor is it a third thing such that we can say that the bowler first bowls *and* then exhibits team-spirit or that a fielder is at a given moment *either* catching *or* displaying *esprit de corps*.

These illustrations of category-mistakes have a common feature which must be noticed. The mistakes were made by people who did not know how to wield the concepts *University, division* and *team-spirit*. Their puzzles arose from inability to use certain items in the English vocabulary.

The theoretically interesting category-mistakes are those made by people who are perfectly competent to apply concepts, at least in the situations with which they are familiar, but are still liable in their abstract thinking to allocate those concepts to logical types to which they do not belong. An instance of a mistake of this sort would be the following story. A student of politics has learned the main differences between the British, the French and the American Constitutions, and has learned also the differences and connections between the Cabinet, Parliament, the various Ministries, the Judicature and the Church of England. But he still becomes embarrassed when asked questions about the connections between the Church of England, the Home Office and the British Constitution. For while the Church and the Home Office are institutions, the British Constitution is not another institution in the same sense of that noun. So inter-institutional relations which can be asserted or denied to hold between the Church and the Home Office cannot be asserted or denied to hold between either of them and the British Constitution. "The British Constitution" is not a term of the same logical type as "the Home Office" and "the Church of England." In a partially similar way, John Doe may be a relative, a friend, an enemy or a stranger to Richard Roe; but he cannot be any of these things to the Average Taxpayer. He knows how to talk sense in certain sorts of discussions about the Average Taxpayer, but he is baffled to say why he could not come across him in the street as he can come across Richard Roe.

It is pertinent to our main subject to notice that, so long as the student of politics continues to think of the British Constitution as a counterpart to the other institutions, he will tend to describe it as a mysteriously occult institution; and so long as John Doe continues to think of the Average Taxpayer as a fellow-citizen, he will tend to think of him as an elusive insubstantial man, a ghost who is everywhere yet nowhere.

My destructive purpose is to show that a family of radical category-mistakes is the source of the double-life theory. The representation of a person as a ghost mysteriously ensconced in a machine derives from this argument. Because, as is true, a person's thinking, feeling and purposive doing cannot be described solely in the idioms of physics, chemistry and physiology, therefore they must be described in counterpart idioms. As the human body is a complex organized unit, so the human mind must be another complex organized unit, though one made of a different sort of stuff and with a different sort of structure. Or, again, as the human body, like any other parcel of matter, is a field of causes and effects, so the mind must be another field of causes and effects, though not (Heaven be praised) mechanical causes and effects. . . .

SELF-KNOWLEDGE WITHOUT PRIVILEGED ACCESS

It has been argued from a number of directions that when we speak of a person's mind, we are not speaking of a second theatre of special-status incidents, but of certain ways in which some of the incidents of his one life are ordered. His life is not a double series of events taking place in two different kinds of stuff; it is one concatenation of events, the differences between some and other classes of which largely consist in the applicability or inapplicability to them of logically different types of law-propositions and law-like propositions. Assertions about a person's mind are therefore assertions of special sorts about that person. So questions about the relations between a person and his mind, like those about the relations between a person's body and his mind, are improper questions. They are important in much the same way as is the question, "What transactions go on between the House of Commons and the British Constitution?"

It follows that it is a logical solecism to speak, as theorists often do, of someone's mind knowing this, or choosing that. The person himself knows this and chooses that, though the fact that he does so can, if desired, be classified as a mental fact about that person. In partly the same way it is improper to speak of my eyes seeing this, or my nose smelling that; we should say, rather, that I see this or I smell that, and that these assertions carry with them certain facts about my eyes and nose. But the analogy is not exact, for while my eyes and nose are organs of sense, "my mind" does not stand for another organ. It signifies my ability and proneness to do certain sorts of things and not some piece of personal apparatus without which I could or would not do them. Similarly the British Constitution is not another British political institution functioning alongside of the Civil Service, the Judiciary, the Established Church, the Houses of Parliament and the Royal Family. Nor is it the sum of these institutions, or a liaison-staff between them. We can say that Great Britain has gone to the polls; but we cannot say that the British Constitution has gone to the polls, though the fact that Great Britain has gone to the polls might be described as a constitutional fact about Great Britain.

Actually, though it is not always convenient to avoid the practice, there is a considerable logical hazard in using the nouns "mind" and "minds" at all. The idiom makes it too easy to construct logically improper conjunctions, disjunctions and cause-effect propositions such as "so and so took place not in my body but in my mind," "my mind made my hand write," "a person's body and mind interact upon each other" and so on. Where logical candour is required from us, we ought to follow the example set by novelists, biographers and diarists, who speak only of persons doing and undergoing things.

The questions "What knowledge can a person get of the workings of his own mind?" and "How does he get it?" by their very wording suggest absurd answers. They suggest that, for a person to know that he is lazy, or has done a sum carefully, he must have taken a peep into a windowless chamber, illuminated by a very peculiar sort of light, and one to which only he has access. And when the question is construed in this sort of way, the parallel questions, "What knowledge can one person get of the workings of another mind?" and "How does he get it?" by their very wording seem to preclude any answer at all; for they suggest that one person could only know that another person was lazy, or had done a sum carefully, by peering into another secret chamber to which, *ex hypothesi*, he has no access.

In fact the problem is not one of this sort. It is simply the methodological question, how we establish, and how we apply, certain sorts of law-like propositions about the overt and the silent behaviour of persons. I come to appreciate the skill and tactics of a chess-player by watching him and others playing chess, and I learn that a certain pupil of mine is lazy, ambitious and witty by following his work, noticing his excuses, listening to his conversation and comparing his performances with those of others. Nor does it make any important difference if I happen myself to be that pupil. I can indeed then listen to more of his conversations, as I am the addressee of his unspoken soliloquies; I notice more of his excuses, as I am never absent, when they are made. On the other hand, my comparison of his performances with those of others is more difficult, since the examiner is himself taking the examination, which makes neutrality hard to preserve and precludes the demeanour of the candidate, when under interrogation, from being in good view.

To repeat a point previously made, the question is not the envelope-question "How do I discover that I or you have a mind?" but the range of specific questions of the pattern, "How do I discover that I am more unselfish than you; that I can do long division well, but differential equations only badly; that you suffer from certain phobias and tend to shirk facing certain sorts of facts; that I am more easily irritated than most people but less subject to panic, vertigo, or morbid conscientiousness?" Besides such pure dispositional questions there is also the range of particular performance questions and occurrence questions of the patterns, "How do I find out that I saw the joke and that you did not; that your action took more courage than mine; that the service I rendered to you was rendered from a sense of duty and not from expectation of kudos; that, though I did not fully understand what was said at the time, I did fully understand it, when I went over it in my head afterwards, while you understood it perfectly from the start; that I was feeling homesick yesterday?" Questions of these sorts offer no mysteries; we know quite well how to set to work to find out the answers to them; and though often we cannot finally solve them and may have to stop short at mere conjecture, yet, even so, we have no doubt what sorts of information would satisfy our requirements, if we could get it; and we know what it would be like to get it. For example, after listening to an argument, you aver that you understand it perfectly; but you may be deceiving yourself, or trying to deceive me. If we then part for a day or two, I am no longer in a position to test whether or not you did understand it perfectly. But still I know what tests would have settled the point. If you had put the argument into your own words, or translated it into French; if you had invented appropriate concrete illustrations of the generalisations and abstractions in the argument; if you had stood up to cross-questioning; if you had correctly drawn further consequences from different stages of the argument and indicated points where the theory was inconsistent with other theories; if you had inferred correctly from the nature of the argument to the qualities of intellect and character of its author and predicted accurately the subsequent development of his theory, then I should have required no further evidence that you understood it perfectly. And exactly the same sorts of tests would satisfy me that I had understood it perfectly; the sole differences would be that I should probably not have voiced aloud the expressions of my deductions, illustrations, etc., but told them to myself more perfunctorily in silent soliloquy; and I should probably have been more easily satisfied of the completeness of my understanding than I was of yours.

In short it is part of the *meaning* of "you understood it" that you could have done so and so and would have done it, if such and such, and the *test* of whether you understood it is a range of performances satisfying the apodoses of these general hypothetical statements. It should be noticed, on the one hand, that there is no single nuclear performance, overt or in your head, which would determine that you had understood the argument. Even if you claimed that you had experienced a flash or click of comprehension and had actually done so, you would still withdraw your other claim to have understood the argument, if you found that you could not paraphrase it, illustrate, expand or recast it; and you would allow someone else to have understood it who could meet all examination questions about it, but reported no click of comprehension. It should also be noticed, on the other hand, that though there is no way of specifying how many or what sub-tests must be satisfied for a person to qualify as having perfectly understood the argument, this does not imply that no finite set of sub-tests is ever enough. To settle whether a boy can do long division, we do not require him to try out his hand on a million, a thousand, or even a hundred different problems in long division. We should not be quite satisfied after one success, but we should not remain dissatisfied after twenty, provided that they were judiciously variegated and that he had not done them before. A good teacher, who not only recorded the boy's correct and incorrect solutions, but also watched his procedure in reaching them, would be satisfied much sooner, and he would be satisfied sooner still if he got the boy to describe and justify the constituent operations that he performed, though of course many boys can do long division sums who cannot describe or justify the operations performed in doing them.

I discover my or your motives in much, though not quite, the same way as I discover my or your abilities. The big practical difference is that I cannot put the subject through his paces in my inquiries into his inclinations as I can in my inquiries into his competences. To discover how conceited or patriotic you are, I must still observe your conduct, remarks, demeanour and tones of voice, but I cannot subject you to examination-tests or experiments which you recognise as such. You would have a special motive for responding to such experiments in a particular way. From mere conceit, perhaps, you would try to behave self-effacingly, or from mere modesty you might try to behave conceitedly. None the less, ordinary day to day observation normally serves swiftly to settle such questions. To be conceited is to tend to boast of one's own excellences, to pity or ridicule the deficiencies of others, to daydream about imaginary triumphs, to reminisce about actual triumphs, to weary quickly of conversations which reflect unfavourably upon oneself, to lavish one's society upon distinguished persons and to economise in association with the undistinguished. The tests of whether a person is conceited are the actions he takes and the reactions he manifests in such circumstances. Not many anecdotes, sneers or sycophancies are required from the subject for the ordinary observer to make up his mind, unless the candidate and the examiner happen to be identical.

The ascertainment of a person's mental capacities and propensities is an inductive process, an induction to law-like propositions from observed actions and reactions. Having ascertained these long-term qualities, we explain a particular action or reaction by applying the result of such an induction to the new specimen, save where open avowals let us know the explanation without research. These inductions are not, of course, carried out under laboratory conditions, or with any statistical apparatus, any more than is the shepherd's weather-lore, or the general practitioner's understanding of a particular patient's constitution. But they are ordinarily reliable enough. It is a truism to say that the

appreciations of character and the explanations of conduct given by critical, unprejudiced and humane observers, who have had a lot of experience and take a lot of interest, tend to be both swift and reliable; those of inferior judges tend to be slower and less reliable. Similarly the marks awarded by practiced and keen examiners who know their subject well and are reasonably sympathetic towards the candidates tend to be about right; those of inferior examiners tend to scatter more widely from the proper order. The point of these truisms is to remind us that in real life we are quite familiar with the techniques of assessing persons and accounting for their actions, though according to the standard theory no such techniques could exist.

DISCUSSION QUESTIONS

1. What is a "category mistake"? Discuss the three examples Ryle gives of category mistakes, and generate your own example.

2. Ryle argues that expressions can be grouped into "types" or "categories" and that philosophical troubles arise from attempts to handle an expression of one category as if it belongs to another. What do you think of this general approach to philosophy?

3. Discuss Ryle's criticisms of Cartesian dualism. Do you agree with him? How might Descartes have responded to him?

4. Ryle contends that to do something is not to perform two separate actions—one mental and one physical—but to behave in a certain way. Discuss this position.

5. Is Ryle's "logical behaviorism" essentially saying that there are only physical objects and physical events? If not, then what *is* that which is behaving in a certain way? Is this question guilty of a category mistake? Discuss.

■ ■ ■ ■ ■ ■ ■ ■ ■ ■ ■ ■ ■ ■ ■ ■ ■ ■ ■
The Matrix
[USA 1999] 2 hours, 16 minutes
Dir. by Larry and Andy Wachowski
■ ■ ■ ■ ■ ■ ■ ■ ■ ■ ■ ■ ■ ■ ■ ■ ■ ■ ■

*T*he Matrix is a computer-generated dream world built to keep human beings under the control of machines. The machines harvest humans in vats as a source of energy. In order to control the minds of the populace, the machines implant the experience of "reality" into the humans' brains. However, this "reality," called "the Matrix," is entirely computer-generated. There is little resemblance between the ways things appear to humans when they are "in the Matrix" as opposed to when they are "freed" from it.

The film follows a computer programmer's path from his unknowing life in a vat under the control of the Matrix to his release and eventual quest to destroy the Matrix. Neo (Keanu Reeves) is introduced to Morpheus (Laurence Fishburne), the leader of a group of anti-Matrix legionnaires, by Trinity (Carrie-Anne Moss), the second in command. After being told about the existence of the Matrix, Neo is given the choice by Morpheus of continuing to live in it or freeing himself. Choosing the latter, he is snatched and unplugged from his tank. He then undergoes the painful process of healing his body and his mind from the damage done to him by the Matrix. He learns how he can use his mind to beat or outsmart the Matrix upon reentering it; he also learns that he is "the One," the person with the special mental capacities to overthrow the Matrix. The film closes with Neo defeating some of the "agents" that protect the Matrix against potential destructive forces like Morpheus and his crew.

DISCUSSION QUESTIONS

1. In what way is the Matrix like the "ghost in the machine"? In what way is it different?

2. Discuss in general the relationship between the body and the mind in *The Matrix*. Does it involve different assumptions than found in the film *All of Me*?

3. Is this film's position on the relationship between the mind and the body Cartesian? Why or why not?

4. Consider the following dialogue between Morpheus and Neo:

    NEO   "I thought it [the Matrix] wasn't real."

    MORPHEUS   "Your mind makes it real."

    NEO   "If you're killed in the Matrix, you die here?"

    MORPHEUS   "Your body cannot live without the mind."

    How would Ryle respond to the claim that "your body cannot live without the mind"? How would Descartes respond? What do you think of this claim?

5. What do you think it would be like to be in a vat like the humans in *The Matrix* but not to have any experiences implanted in you? Would it be possible for people to live their entire lives in one of these vats and not have any experiences inputted (assuming, of course, that that their nutritional needs were met)?

6. The Matrix may be viewed as an updating of Descartes' "evil genius" argument from chapter 2. Does the Matrix add any new complications to Cartesian skepticism? If so, what are they?

7. How do you know that you are not being systematically deceived by the Matrix right now?

8. Consider the following exchange between Morpheus and Neo:

    MORPHEUS   "I can see it in your eyes. You have the look of a man who accepts what he sees because he is expecting to wake up. Ironically, this is not far from the truth. Do you believe in fate, Neo?"

    NEO   "No."

    MORPHEUS   "Why not?"

    NEO   "Because I do not like the idea that I am not in control of my life."

    MORPHEUS   "I know exactly what you mean. Let me tell you why you're here. Because you know something. What you know you can't explain. But you feel it. You've felt it your entire life. That there is something wrong with the world. You don't know what it is but it is there. Like a splinter in your mind. Driving you mad. It is this feeling that has brought you to me. Do you know what I'm talking about?"

    NEO   "The Matrix."

    MORPHEUS   "Do you want to know what it is? The Matrix is everywhere. It is all around us. Even now in this very room. You can see it when you look out your window or when you turn on your television. You can feel it when you go to work. When you go to church. When you pay your taxes. It is the world that has been pulled over your eyes to blind you from the truth."

    NEO   "What truth?"

    MORPHEUS   "That you are a slave, Neo. Like everyone else you were born into bondage, born into a prison that you cannot smell or taste or touch. A prison for your mind. Unfortunately no one can be told what the Matrix is, you have to see it for yourself."

    Morpheus calls the Matrix a prison for the mind. Do you agree with his assessment? Is the Matrix a prison for the mind? Or does it become a prison only once you learn about it?

9. If given the choice between a dismal reality or the false world of the Matrix, where would you choose to live? Why?

10. Consider this exchange between Morpheus and Neo:

    MORPHEUS   "This is the construct . . . our training program."

    NEO   "Right now we're really inside a computer program?"

    MORPHEUS   "Is it really so hard to believe? Your clothes are different. The plugs in your arms and head are gone. Your hair is changed. Your appearance now is what we call residual self-image. It is the mental projection of your digital self."

    What happens to the self once a person enters the training program? What does Morpheus mean when he says that your appearance in the training program is the "mental projection of your digital self"? What is the connection between the person sitting in the chair wired to a computer and the residual image of that person in the computer training program? Is it the same person? A different person? Discuss.

11. Consider the following dialogue between Morpheus and Neo concerning what occurs and what one finds while in the training program:

    NEO "This . . . this isn't real?"

    MORPHEUS "What is real? How do you define real? If you're talking about what you can feel, what you can smell, what you can taste and see, then real is simply electrical signals interpreted by your brain. This is the world that you know. The world as it was at the end of the twentieth century. It exists now only as part of a neural-interactive simulation that we call the Matrix. You've been living in a dream world, Neo. This is the world as it exists today. . . . Welcome to the Desert of the Real."

    What does Morpheus mean by the phrase "Desert of the Real"? Do you think that what is experienced in the Matrix is "real"? Is it more or less real than what is experienced outside of the Matrix? Why? Is your notion of reality linked to beliefs about the relative value of extended matter (body) versus unextended matter (mind)?

12. Apoc (Julian Arahanga) and Trinity are in the Matrix, and Cypher (Joe Pantoliano) is in the ship, standing next to their bodies, which are now plugged into the Matrix. Just before he kills Apoc by disconnecting him from the Matrix, Cypher says to Trinity, "I think the Matrix can be more real than this world. All I do is pull the plug here. But there [in the Matrix], you have to watch Apoc die." Is Cypher right? Can the Matrix be more real than reality?

13. Consider the following exchange between Morpheus and Neo:

    MORPHEUS ". . . We have only bits and pieces of information, but what we know for certain is that at some point in the early twenty-first century all of mankind was united in celebration. We marveled at our own magnificence as we gave birth to AI."

    NEO "AI? You mean artificial intelligence?"

    MORPHEUS "A singular consciousness that spawned an entire race of machines. We don't know who struck first, us or them. But we know that it was us that scorched the sky. At the time they were dependent on solar power, and it was believed that they would be unable to survive without an energy source as abundant as the sun. Throughout human history, we have been dependent on machines to survive. Fate it seems is not without a sense of irony. The human body generates more bio-electricity than a 120-volt battery and over 25,000 BTUs of body heat. Combined with a form of fusion the machines have found all the energy they would ever need. There are fields, endless fields, where human beings are no longer born, we are grown. For the longest time I wouldn't believe it, and then I saw the fields with my own eyes. Watch them liquefy the dead so they could be fed intravenously to the living. And standing there, facing the pure horrifying precision, I came to realize the obviousness of the truth. What is the Matrix? Control. The Matrix is a computer-generated dream world built to keep us under control in order to change a human being into this [a battery]."

    In *The Matrix*, machines have taken over the world. They have turned the tables on humankind: Instead of humans using machines for their survival, machines are using humans for their survival. Do you think it is possible for humans to "exploit" machines? For machines to "exploit" humans? Defend your view.

14. One of the members of Morpheus's group, Cypher, says, "You know, I know this steak doesn't exist. I know that when I put it in my mouth, the Matrix is telling my brain that it is juicy and delicious. After nine years, you know what I realize? Ignorance is bliss." Is he right? If the steak tastes good (to you), does it matter whether it actually exists?

15. Consider the following dialogue between a boy who bends spoons (Rowan Witt) and Neo:

SPOON BOY "Do not try and bend the spoon. That's impossible. Instead only try to realize the truth."

NEO "What truth?"

SPOON BOY "There is no spoon."

NEO "There is no spoon?"

SPOON BOY "Then you'll see that it is not the spoon that bends, it is only yourself."

What does Spoon Boy mean when he says that it is not the spoon that bends, it is only oneself?

16. Agent Smith, a sentient program, says, "Have you ever stood and stared at it, marveled at its beauty, its genius? Billions of people just living out their lives, oblivious. Did you know that the first Matrix was designed to be a perfect human world. Where none suffered. Where everyone would be happy. It was a disaster. No one would accept the program. Entire crops were lost. Some believed that we lacked the programming language to describe your perfect world. But I believe that as a species, human beings define their reality through misery and suffering. The perfect world would be a dream that your primitive cerebrum kept trying to wake up from. Which is why the Matrix was redesigned to this, the peak of your civilization. I say your civilization because as soon as we started thinking for you it really became our civilization, which is of course what this is all about. Evolution, Morpheus, evolution, like the dinosaur. Look out that window. You had your time. The future is our world, Morpheus. The future is our time." Is Agent Smith right? Would a program that presented a "perfect world" to the bodies in the vats result in their trying to awaken from this dream? Does the Matrix have to be a less-than-perfect world for the persons in the vats to accept it? Do humans define reality through misery and suffering? Discuss.

THOMAS NAGEL
WHAT IS IT LIKE TO BE A BAT?

In this selection, Thomas Nagel argues that consciousness and subjective experience cannot be reduced to brain activity. According to Nagel, all of the objective methods of reductionistic science can never capture the subjective experience of consciousness. Nagel contends that the fact that an organism has conscious experience at some level means that there is something "that it is like" to be that organism. This "that it is like" he calls the "subjective character" of experience. The subjective character of an experience is tied to a specific point of view, and the specificity of point of view is precisely what objective accounts always neglect. Nagel illustrates this idea using the example of bats.

Bats, as mammals, have experience. So, there is something that it is like to be a bat. However, bats have a sensory system unlike that of humans. They perceive distance, size, shape, motion, and texture through sonar. Consequently, we have no reason to believe that what it is like to be a bat is the same as what it is like to be a human; our subjective experiences must be different. While we can imagine what it would be like to fly around like a bat, and perhaps to navigate our way via sonar, we simply cannot form a concept of what the subjective experiences of a bat are like.

According to Nagel, while it is possible to understand bat neurophysiology, it is not possible to form a conception of the subjective character of a bat's experience. Simply observing the physical operations of the bat at any level will not necessarily bring us any closer to understanding what it is like to be a bat. Consequently, Nagel is critical of both behavioral accounts of the mind (see Ryle) and physical accounts of the mind and the brain (see Churchland), because none of them can capture the subjective character of experience. Nagel argues that even if it is true that mental processes are brain processes (*physicalism* or *identity theory*), it is also true that there is *something that it is like* to undergo such brain processes. Physicalism is not false. Rather, it is simply incomprehensible at this time.

Nagel concludes that because of the subjective character of experience, "we cannot even pose the mind–body problem" in a sensible way, and "it seems unlikely that a physical theory of mind can be contemplated." Nagel proposes to put aside temporarily the question of the relationship between the mind and the brain to try to achieve a more objective understanding of the mental in its own right. We can achieve this by developing an "objective phenomenology," that is, a way of describing phenomena not dependent on the point of view of the subject of experience. The goal of this objective phenomenology would be to describe the subjective character of experience in a way that could be understood by those not capable of such experience. Ideally, this method would allow us both to describe the subjective experience of bats and to explain to persons with sight what it is like not to have sight. Still, even if developed, this objective phenomenology would bring us to "a blank wall eventually," even if it "may permit questions about the physical basis of experience to assume more intelligible form."

Thomas Nagel (1937–) was born in Belgrade, in the former Yugoslavia, and specializes in political philosophy, ethics, epistemology, and philosophy of the mind. He received a B.A. from Cornell University in 1958, a B.Phil. from Oxford University in 1960, and a Ph.D. in philosophy from Harvard University in 1963. He is currently professor of philosophy, university professor, and Fiorello La Guardia Professor of Law at New York University. He is also a fellow of the American Academy of Arts and Sciences and a fellow of the British Academy, and he has held fellowships from the Guggenheim Foundation, the National Science Foundation, and the National Endowment for the Humanities. His many books include *The Possibility of Altruism* (1970), *Mortal Questions* (1979), *The View from Nowhere* (1986), *What Does It All Mean? A Very Short Introduction to Philosophy* (1987), *Equality and Partiality* (1991), *Other Minds: Critical Essays, 1969–1994* (1995), *The Last Word* (1997), *The Myth of Ownership: Taxes and Justice* (with Liam Murphy, 2002), and *Concealment and Exposure: And Other Essays* (2002).

Consciousness is what makes the mind–body problem really intractable. Perhaps that is why current discussions of the problem give it little attention or get it obviously wrong. The recent wave of reductionist euphoria has produced several analyses of mental phenomena and mental concepts designed to explain the possibility of some variety of materialism, psycho-physical identification, or reduction. But the problems dealt with are those common to this type of reduction and other types, and what makes the mind–body problem unique, and unlike the water–H$_2$O problem or the Turing machine–IBM machine problem or the lightning–electrical discharge problem or the gene–DNA problem or the oak tree–hydrocarbon problem, is ignored.

Every reductionist has his favorite analogy from modern science. It is most unlikely that any of these unrelated examples of successful reduction will shed light on the relation of mind to brain. But philosophers share the general human weakness for explanations of what is incomprehensible in terms suited for what is familiar and well understood, though entirely different. This has led to the acceptance of implausible accounts of the mental largely because they would permit familiar kinds of reduction. I shall try to explain why the usual examples do not help us to understand the relation between mind and body— why, indeed, we have at present no conception of what an explanation of the physical nature of a mental phenomenon would be. Without consciousness the mind–body problem would be much less interesting. With consciousness it seems hopeless. The most important and characteristic feature of conscious mental phenomena is very poorly understood. Most reductionist theories do not even try to explain it. And careful examination will show that no currently available concept of reduction is applicable to it. Perhaps a new theoretical form can be devised for the purpose, but such a solution, if it exists, lies in the distant intellectual future.

Conscious experience is a widespread phenomenon. It occurs at many levels of animal life, though we cannot be sure of its presence in the simpler organisms, and it is very difficult to say in general what provides evidence of it. (Some extremists have been prepared to deny it even of mammals other than man.) No doubt it occurs in countless forms totally unimaginable to us, on other planets in other solar systems throughout the universe. But no matter how the form may vary, the fact that an organism has conscious experience *at all* means, basically, that there is something it is like to *be* that organism. There may be further implications about the form of the experience; there may even (though I doubt it) be implications about the behavior of the organism. But fundamentally an organism has conscious mental states if and only if there is something that it is like to *be* that organism— something it is like *for* the organism.

We may call this the subjective character of experience. It is not captured by any of the familiar, recently devised reductive analyses of the mental, for all of them are logically compatible with its absence. It is not analyzable in terms of any explanatory system of functional states, or intentional states, since these could be ascribed to robots or automata that behaved like people though they experienced nothing. It is not analyzable in terms of the causal role of experiences in relation to typical human behavior—for similar reasons. I do not deny that conscious mental states and events cause behavior, nor that they may be given functional characterizations. I deny only that this kind of thing exhausts their analysis. Any reductionist program has to be based on an analysis of what is to be reduced. If the analysis leaves something out, the problem will be falsely posed. It is useless to base the defense of materialism on any analysis of mental phenomena that fails to deal explicitly with their subjective character. For there is no reason to suppose that a reduction which seems plausible when no attempt is made to account for consciousness can be extended to include consciousness. Without some idea, therefore, of what the subjective character of experience is, we cannot know what is required of physicalist theory.

While an account of the physical basis of mind must explain many things, this appears to be the most difficult. It is impossible to exclude the phenomenological features of experience from a reduction in the same way that one excludes the phenomenal features of an ordinary substance from a physical or chemical reduction of it— namely, by explaining them as effects on the minds of human observers. If physicalism is to be defended, the phenomenological features must themselves be given a physical account. But when we examine their subjective character it seems that such a result is impossible. The reason is that every subjective phenomenon is essentially connected with a single point of view, and it seems inevitable that an objective, physical theory will abandon that point of view.

Let me first try to state the issue somewhat more fully than by referring to the relation between the subjective and the objective, or between the *pour soi* and the *en soi*. This is far from easy. Facts about what it is like to be an X are very peculiar, so peculiar that some may be inclined to doubt their reality, or the significance of claims about them. To illustrate the connection between subjectivity and a point of view, and to make evident the importance of subjective features, it will help to explore the matter in relation to an example that brings out clearly the divergence between the two types of conception, subjective and objective.

I assume we all believe that bats have experience. After all, they are mammals, and there is no more doubt that they have experience than that mice or pigeons or whales have experience. I have chosen bats instead of wasps or flounders because if one travels too far down the phylogenetic tree, people gradually shed their faith that there is experience there at all. Bats, although more closely related to us than those other species, nevertheless present a range of activity and a sensory apparatus so different from ours that the problem I want to pose is exceptionally vivid (though it certainly could be raised with other species). Even without the benefit of philosophical reflection, anyone who has spent some time in an enclosed space with an excited bat knows what it is to encounter a fundamentally *alien* form of life.

I have said that the essence of the belief that bats have experience is that there is something that it is like to be a bat. Now we know that most bats (microchiroptera, to be precise) perceive the external world primarily by sonar, or echolocation, detecting the reflections, from objects within range, of their own rapid, subtly modulated, high-frequency shrieks. Their brains are designed to correlate the outgoing impulses with the subsequent echoes, and the information thus acquired enables bats to make precise discriminations of distance, size, shape, motion, and texture comparable to those we make by vision. But bat sonar, though clearly a form of perception, is not similar in its operation to any sense that we possess, and there is no reason to suppose that it is subjectively like anything we can experience or imagine. This appears to create difficulties for the notion of what it is like to be a bat. We must consider whether any method will permit us to extrapolate to the inner life of the bat from our own case, and if not, what alternative methods there may be for understanding the notion.

Our own experience provides the basic material for our imagination, whose range is therefore limited. It will not help to try to imagine that one has webbing on one's arms, which enables one to fly around at dusk and dawn catching insects in one's mouth; that one has very poor vision, and perceives the surrounding world by a system of reflected high-frequency sound signals; and that one spends the day hanging upside down by one's feet in an attic. Insofar as I can imagine this (which is not very far), it tells me only what it would be like for *me* to behave as a bat behaves. But that is not the question. I want to know what it is like for a *bat* to be a bat. Yet if I try to imagine this, I am restricted to the resources of my own mind, and those resources are inadequate to the task. I cannot perform it either by imagining additions to my present experience, or by imagining segments gradually subtracted from it, or by imagining some combination of additions, subtractions, and modifications.

To the extent that I could look and behave like a wasp or a bat without changing my fundamental structure, my experiences would not be anything like the experiences of those animals. On the other hand, it is doubtful that any meaning can be attached to the supposition that I should possess the internal neurophysiological constitution of a bat. Even if I could by gradual degrees be transformed into a bat, nothing in my present constitution enables me to imagine what the experiences of such a future stage of myself thus metamorphosed would be like. The best evidence would come from the experiences of bats, if we only knew what they were like.

So if extrapolation from our own case is involved in the idea of what it is like to be a bat, the extrapolation must be incompletable. We cannot form more than a schematic conception of what it *is* like. For example, we may ascribe general *types* of experience on the basis of the animal's structure and behavior. Thus we describe bat sonar as a form of three-dimensional forward perception; we believe that bats feel some versions of pain, fear, hunger, and lust, and that they have other, more familiar types of perception besides sonar. But we believe that these experiences also have in each case a specific subjective character, which it is beyond our ability to conceive. And if there is conscious life elsewhere in the universe, it is likely that some of it will not be describable even in the most general experiential terms available to us. (The problem is not confined to exotic cases, however, for it exists between one person and another. The subjective character of the experience of a person deaf and blind from birth is not accessible to me, for example, nor presumably is mine to him. This does not prevent us each from believing that the other's experience has such a subjective character.)

If anyone is inclined to deny that we can believe in the existence of facts like this whose exact nature we cannot possibly conceive, he should reflect that in contemplating the bats we are in much the same position that intelligent bats or Martians would occupy if they tried to form a conception of what it was like to be us. The structure of their own minds might make it impossible for them to succeed, but we know they would be wrong to conclude that there is not anything precise that it is like to be us: that only certain general types of mental state could be ascribed to us (perhaps perception and appetite would be concepts common to us both; perhaps not). We know they would be wrong to draw such a skeptical conclusion because we know what it is like to be us. And we know that while it includes an enormous amount of variation and complexity and while we do not possess the vocabulary to describe it adequately, its subjective character is highly specific, and in some respects describable in terms that can be understood only by creatures like us. The fact that we cannot expect ever to accommodate in our language a detailed description of Martian or bat phenomenology should not lead us to dismiss as meaningless the claim that bats and Martians have experiences fully comparable in richness of detail to our own. It would be fine if someone were to develop concepts and a theory that enabled us to think about those things; but such an understanding may be permanently denied to us by the limits of our nature. And to deny the reality or logical significance of what we can never describe or understand is the crudest form of cognitive dissonance.

This brings us to the edge of a topic that requires much more discussion than I can give it here: namely, the relation between facts on the one hand and conceptual schemes or systems of representation on the other. My realism about the subjective domain in all its forms implies a belief in the existence of facts beyond the reach of human concepts. Certainly it is possible for a human being to believe that there are facts which humans never *will* possess the requisite concepts to represent or comprehend. Indeed, it would be foolish to doubt this, given the finiteness of humanity's expectations. After all, there would have been transfinite numbers even if everyone had been wiped out by the Black Death before Cantor* discovered them. But one might also believe that there are facts which *could* not ever be represented or comprehended by human beings, even if the species lasted forever—simply because our structure does not permit us to operate with concepts of the requisite type. This impossibility might even be observed by other beings, but it is not clear that the existence of such beings, or the possibility of their existence, is a precondition of the significance of the hypothesis that there are humanly inaccessible facts. (After all, the nature of beings with access to humanly inaccessible facts is presumably itself a humanly inaccessible fact.) Reflection on what it is like to be a bat seems to lead us, therefore, to the conclusion that there are facts that do not consist in the truth of propositions expressible in a human language. We can be compelled to recognize the existence of such facts without being able to state or comprehend them.

I shall not pursue this subject, however. Its bearing on the topic before us (namely, the mind–body problem) is that it enables us to make a general observation about the subjective character of experience. Whatever may be the status of facts about what it is like to be a human being, or a bat, or a Martian, these appear to be facts that embody a particular point of view.

I am not adverting here to the alleged privacy of experience to its possessor. The point of view in question is not one accessible only to a single individual. Rather it is a *type*. It is often possible to

*Georg Cantor (1845–1918), a German mathematician, is well known for his definition of transfinite numbers as well as for his work in set theory and his definition of infinity. His major writings are *Groundwork for a Theory of Sets* (1883) and *Contributions to the Founding of the Theory of Transfinite Numbers* (1895 –92).—Ed.

take up a point of view other than one's own, so the comprehension of such facts is not limited to one's own case. There is a sense in which phenomenological facts are perfectly objective. One person can know or say of another what the quality of the other's experience is. They are subjective, however, in the sense that even this objective ascription of experience is possible only for someone sufficiently similar to the object of ascription to be able to adopt his point of view—to understand the ascription in the first person as well as in the third, so to speak. The more different from oneself the other experiencer is, the less success one can expect with this enterprise. In our own case we occupy the relevant point of view, but we will have as much difficulty understanding our own experience properly if we approach it from another point of view as we would if we tried to understand the experience of another species without taking up *its* point of view.

This bears directly on the mind–body problem. For if the facts of experience—facts about what it is like *for* the experiencing organism—are accessible only from one point of view, then it is a mystery how the true character of experiences could be revealed in the physical operation of that organism. The latter is a domain of objective facts par excellence—the kind that can be observed and understood from many points of view and by individuals with differing perceptual systems. There are no comparable imaginative obstacles to the acquisition of knowledge about bat neurophysiology by human scientists, and intelligent bats or Martians might learn more about the human brain than we ever will.

This is not by itself an argument against reduction. A Martian scientist with no understanding of visual perception could understand the rainbow, or lightning, or clouds as physical phenomena, though he would never be able to understand the human concepts of rainbow, lightning, or cloud, or the place these things occupy in our phenomenal world. The objective nature of the things picked out by these concepts could be apprehended by him because, although the concepts themselves are connected with a particular point of view and a particular visual phenomenology, the things apprehended from that point of view are not: they are observable from the point of view but external to it; hence they can be comprehended from other points of view also either by the same organisms or by others. Lightning has an objective character that is not exhausted by its visual appearance, and this can be investigated by a Martian without vision. To be precise, it has a *more* objective character than is revealed in its visual appearance. In speaking of the move from subjective to objective characterization, I wish to remain noncommittal about the existence of an end point, the completely objective intrinsic nature of the thing, which one might or might not be able to reach. It may be more accurate to think of objectivity as a direction in which the understanding can travel. And in understanding a phenomenon like lightning, it is legitimate to go as far away as one can from a strictly human viewpoint.

In the case of experience, on the other hand, the connection with a particular point of view seems much closer. It is difficult to understand what could be meant by the *objective* character of an experience, apart from the particular point of view from which its subject apprehends it. After all, what would be left of what it was like to be a bat if one removed the viewpoint of the bat? But if experience does not have, in addition to its subjective character, an objective nature that can be apprehended from many different points of view, then how can it be supposed that a Martian investigating my brain might be observing physical processes which were my mental processes (as he might observe physical processes which were bolts of lightning), only from a different point of view? How, for that matter, could a human physiologist observe them from another point of view?

We appear to be faced with a general difficulty about psychophysical reduction. In other areas the process of reduction is a move in the direction of greater objectivity, toward a more accurate view of the real nature of things. This is accomplished by reducing our dependence on individual or species-specific points of view toward the object of investigation. We describe it not in terms of the impressions it makes on our senses, but in terms of its more general effects and of properties detectable by means other than the human sense. The less it depends on a specifically human viewpoint, the more objective is our description. It is possible to follow this path because although the concepts and ideas we employ in thinking about the external world are initially applied from a point of view that involves our perceptual apparatus, they are used by us to refer to things beyond themselves—toward which we *have* the phenomenal point of view. Therefore we can abandon it in favor of another, and still be thinking about the same things.

Experience itself, however, does not seem to fit the pattern. The idea of moving from appearance to reality seems to make no sense here. What is the analogue in this case to pursuing a more objective understanding of the same phenomena by abandoning the initial subjective viewpoint toward them in favor of another that is more objective but concerns the same thing? Certainly it *appears* unlikely that we will get closer to the real nature of human experience by leaving behind the particularity of our human point of view and striving for a description in terms accessible to beings that could not imagine what it was like to be us. If the subjective character of experience is fully comprehensible only from one point of view, then any shift to greater objectivety—that is, less attachment to a specific viewpoint—does not take us nearer to the real nature of the phenomenon: It takes us farther away from it.

In a sense, the seeds of this objection to the reducibility of experience are already detectable in successful cases of reduction; for in discovering sound to be, in reality, a wave phenomenon in air or other media, we leave behind one viewpoint to take up another, and the auditory, human or animal viewpoint that we leave behind remains unreduced. Members of radically different species may both understand the same physical events in objective terms, and this does not require that they understand the phenomenal forms in which those events appear to the senses of members of the other species. Thus it is a condition of their referring to a common reality that their more particular viewpoints are not part of the common reality that they both apprehend. The reduction can succeed only if the species-specific viewpoint is omitted from what is to be reduced.

But while we are right to leave this point of view aside in seeking a fuller understanding of the external world, we cannot ignore it permanently, since it is the essence of the internal world, and not merely a point of view on it. Most of the neobehaviorism of recent philosophical psychology results from the effort to substitute an objective concept of mind for the real thing, in order to have nothing left over which cannot be reduced. If we acknowledge that a physical theory of mind must account for the subjective character of experience, we must admit that no presently available conception gives us a clue how this could be done. The problem is unique. If mental processes are indeed physical processes, then there is something it is like, intrinsically, to undergo certain physical processes. What it is for such a thing to be the case remains a mystery.

What moral should be drawn from these reflections, and what should be done next? It would be a mistake to conclude that physicalism must be false. Nothing is proved by the inadequacy of physicalist hypotheses that assume a faulty objective analysis of mind. It would be truer to say that physicalism is a position we cannot understand because we do not at present have any conception of how it might be true. Perhaps it will be thought unreasonable to require such a conception as a condition of understanding. After all, it might be said, the meaning of physicalism is clear enough: mental states are states of the body; mental events are physical events. We do not know *which* physical states and events they are, but that should not prevent us from understanding the hypothesis. What could be clearer than the words "is" and "are"?

But I believe it is precisely this apparent clarity of the word "is" that is deceptive. Usually, when we are told that X is Y we know *how* it is supposed to be true, but that depends on a conceptual or theoretical background and is not conveyed by the "is" alone. We know how both "X" and "Y" refer, and the kinds of things to which they refer, and we have a rough idea how the two referential paths might converge on a single thing, be it an object, a person, a process, an event or whatever. But when the two terms of the identification are very disparate it may not be so clear how it could be true. We may not have even a rough idea of how the two referential paths could converge, or what kind of things they might converge on, and a theoretical framework may have to be supplied to enable us to understand this. Without the framework, an air of mysticism surrounds the identification.

This explains the magical flavor of popular presentations of fundamental scientific discoveries, given out as propositions to which one must subscribe without really understanding them. For example, people are now told at an early age that all matter is really energy. But despite the fact that they know what "is" means, most of them never form a conception of what makes this claim true, because they lack the theoretical background.

At the present time the status of physicalism is similar to that which the hypothesis that matter is energy would have had if uttered by a pre-Socratic philosopher. We do not have the beginnings of a conception of how it might be true. In order to understand the hypothesis that a mental event is a physical event, we require more than an understanding of the word "is." The idea of how a mental and a physical term might refer to the same thing is lacking, and the usual analogies with theoretical identification in other fields fail to supply it. They fail because if we construe the reference of mental terms to physical events on the usual model, we either get a reappearance of separate subjective events as the effects through which mental reference to physical events is secured, or else we get a false account of how mental terms refer (for example, a causal behaviorist one).

Strangely enough, we may have evidence for the truth of something we cannot really understand. Suppose a caterpillar is locked in a sterile safe by someone unfamiliar with insect metamorphosis, and weeks later the safe is reopened, revealing a butterfly. If the person knows that the safe has been shut the whole time, he has reason to believe that the butterfly is or was once the caterpillar, without having any idea in what sense this might be so. (One possibility is that the caterpillar contained a tiny winged parasite that devoured it and grew into the butterfly.)

It is conceivable that we are in such a position with regard to physicalism. Donald Davidson has argued that if mental events have physical causes and effects, they must have physical descriptions. He holds that we have reason to believe this even though we do not—and in fact *could* not—have a general psychophysical theory. His argument applies to intentional mental events, but I think we also have some reason to believe that sensations are physical processes, without being in a position to understand how. Davidson's position is that certain physical events have irreducibly mental properties, and perhaps some view describable in this way is correct. But nothing of which we can now form a conception corresponds to it; nor have we any idea what a theory would be like that enabled us to conceive of it.

Very little work has been done on the basic question (from which mention of the brain can be entirely omitted) whether any sense can be made of experiences having an objective character at all. Does it make sense, in other words, to ask what my experiences are *really* like, as opposed to how they appear to me? We cannot genuinely understand the hypothesis that their nature is captured in a physical description unless we understand the more fundamental idea that they *have* an objective nature (or that objective processes can have a subjective nature).

I should like to close with a speculative proposal. It may be possible to approach the gap between subjective and objective from another direction. Setting aside temporarily the relation between the mind and the brain, we can pursue a more objective understanding of the mental in its own right. At present we are completely unequipped to think about the subjective character of experience without relying on the imagnation—without taking up the point of view of the experiential subject. This should be regarded as a challenge to form new concepts and devise a new method—an objective phenomenology not dependent on empathy or the imagination. Though presumably it would not capture everything, its goal would be to describe, at least in part, the subjective character of experiences in a form comprehensible to beings incapable of having those experiences.

We would have to develop such a pheno-menology to describe the sonar experiences of bats; but it would also be possible to begin with humans. One might try, for example, to develop concepts that could be used to explain to a person blind from birth what it was like to see. One would reach a blank wall eventually, but it should be possible to devise a method of expressing in objective terms much more than we can at present, and with much greater precision. The loose intermodal analogies—for example. "Red is like the sound of a trumpet"—which crop up in discussions of this subject are of little use. That should be clear to anyone who has both heard a trumpet and seen red. But structural features of perception might be more accessible to objective description, even though something would be left out. And concepts alternative to those we learn in the first person may enable us to arrive at a kind of understanding even of our own experience which is denied us by the very ease of description and lack of distance that subjective concepts afford.

Apart from its own interest, a phenomenology that is in this sense objective may permit questions about the physical basis of experience to assume a more intelligible form. Aspects of subjective experience that admitted this kind of objective description might be better candidates for objective explanations of a more familiar sort. But whether or not this guess is correct, it seems unlikely that any physical theory of mind can be contemplated until more thought has been given to the general problem of subjective and objective. Otherwise we cannot even pose the mind–body problem without sidestepping it.

DISCUSSION QUESTIONS

1. Do you think that it is impossible to truly know what it is like to be in another's consciousness?

2. Nagel argues that while we can imagine what it would be like for us to fly around like a bat, navigating our way via sonar, we simply cannot form a concept of what the subjective experiences of a bat are like. Do you agree?

3. How might Paul Churchland (see p. 287) respond to Nagel's charge that consciousness and subjective experience are necessary for any adequate account of the relationship between mind and body?

4. Nagel argues that observable behavior is not a good indicator of consciousness and subjective experience. Do you agree with him? How might Gilbert Ryle respond to Nagel?

5. Nagel's argument assumes a distinction between the subjective and the objective. What is the difference? Some, like the contemporary philosopher Daniel Dennett, argue that the subjective is a cognitive illusion. Do you agree with Dennett regarding the illusoriness of the subjective, or do you agree with Nagel on the importance of the subjective?

6. Is a reductive theory of subjective consciousness possible? Why or why not?

Being John Malkovich
[USA 1999] 1 hour, 53 minutes
Directed by Spike Jonz

Craig Schwartz (John Cusack) is having a difficult time finding a job that utilizes his particular talent: puppeteering. His wife, Lotte (Cameron Diaz), encourages him to get a job—any job. Craig takes a job at LesterCorp as a "short-statured file clerk with unusually nimble and dexterous fingers needed for speed filing." LesterCorp is located on the seventh floor of an office building, a floor with half-height ceilings and no direct elevator service, and is run by Dr. Lester (Orson Bean), a man who claims to be 105 years old. One day when filing, Craig discovers a small door in the wall behind one of his filing cabinets. He crawls through it and finds that it is a "portal" into the mind of the actor John Malkovich. Anyone who enters the portal is afforded the experience of seeing and feeling the world from the point of view of John Malkovich for fifteen minutes and is then dropped out of the sky onto the side of the New Jersey Turnpike. Craig and Maxine (Catherine Keener), a coworker with whom Craig is infatuated, decide to launch a business selling trips into Malkovich's mind for $200 each. In addition to paying customers, Lotte, Craig, and Malkovich himself enter the mind of Malkovich. When Lotte enters the portal, she discovers that if Maxine is making love with Malkovich when she (Lotte) is in Malkovich's mind, she (Lotte) experiences making love to Maxine. As a result, Lotte and Maxine fall in love with each other. Craig becomes jealous of Lotte, locks her in a cage with her monkey Elijah, and then proceeds to make love with Maxine via Malkovich's body. Malkovich eventually discovers the plot and insists on entering the portal to his own mind. Here he finds that everyone looks like him and can say only one word: "Malkovich." He demands that the portal be shut down or else he will take legal action. Craig, desperate to be with Maxine, takes over Malkovich's body, and for the next eight months, Craig's mind lives through and controls Malkovich's body. Craig (in Malkovich's body) then marries Maxine and becomes a celebrated puppeteer. Eventually, Craig releases control of Malkovich's body to Dr. Lester and a group of his elderly friends, who achieve immortality by jumping from younger body to younger body. The film closes with Malkovich, who is now controlled by Dr. Lester's group of minds, preparing the next host body: Maxine's daughter Emily (Kelly Teacher), who was conceived when she and Lotte made love via Malkovich. We also learn that Craig now controls Emily's body as a way to stay close to Maxine, who has spurned him to live with Lotte.

DISCUSSION QUESTIONS

1. This film presupposes a particular relationship between the mind and the body. What the nature of that relationship? Is it Cartesian? Why or why not?

2. Why do you think Craig is able to control Malkovich better than anyone else?

3. What happens to Malkovich's mind when the mind of another person enters his body?

4. When a character is in Malkovich's body, what happens to his or her own body?

5. Craig is better able than anyone else to control Malkovich's conscious mind. Nevertheless, we learn in the scene in which Lotte chases Maxine through Malkovich's subconscious mind that Craig has no control here. Why do you think this is the case? Do you believe that there is such a thing as the subconscious mind? If so, is it a separate entity from the conscious mind? Discuss.

6. Maxine tells us that when she is with Lotte via Malkovich, she feels as though two people are looking at her "with total lust and devotion through the same pair of eyes." What do we have to assume about the nature of the mind to make this possible?

7. When Maxine makes love with Lotte via Malkovich's body, we are told that a child was conceived as a result. Is Malkovich the father of the baby, or Lotte? Explain why.

8. When Craig's mind leaves Malkovich's body, a group of Lester's friends' minds and Lester's mind enter it in his place. Later, when we see Malkovich speaking, are we to assume that it is the minds of many persons speaking or a "collective" mind speaking? Is the film asking us to assume that more than one mind can be in a body? Or that when more than one mind enters a body it becomes one mind? Discuss.

9. We are told that Dr. Lester and his friends are able to live forever by jumping from host body to host body. But what, exactly, is living forever? Dr. Lester's mind or soul in itself? Or only Dr. Lester's consciousness of himself and the world? Does Dr. Lester's mind die if he does not jump bodies, or

does only his ability to perceive himself and the world pass away? Or something else? Discuss the possible philosophical implications of Dr. Lester's immortality.

10. Many persons are entering Malkovich's body and peering out into the world through his eyes. Are they experiencing the world as Malkovich experiences it? Or are they experiencing it *as themselves* experiencing Malkovich's experiences? What is the difference?

11. At the beginning of the film, Craig comments to Lotte's monkey Elijah, "You don't know how lucky you are being a monkey because consciousness is a terrible curse. I think, I feel, I suffer, and all I ask in return is the opportunity to do my work because I raise issues." However, later in the film, we see the world from the viewpoint of Elijah's consciousness—a scene in which the monkey remembers what it was like back in Africa when he and his parents were captured by trappers. In this scene, Elijah's parents cry out to him to untie them, but he is unable. Subtitles enable us to understand the monkeys' screams and conversations. Do you think that this scene truly gives us a sense of what it is like to be in a monkey's "consciousness," or to see the world as a monkey does? Do you believe that monkeys have "consciousness"? If so, how might it be similar to or different from our own? Can you think of a better way to depict seeing the world from a monkey's point of view? If so, describe how it might be done.

12. Craig says that entering the portal "raises all sorts of philosophical-type questions about the nature of self, about the existence of the soul. Am I me? Is Malkovich Malkovich? I had a piece of wood in my hand, Maxine. I don't have it anymore. Where is it? Did it disappear? How could that be? Is it still in Malkovich's head?" Answer the questions that Craig raises.

13. Craig says to Malkovich that "we operate a little business here that simulates, for our clientele, the experience of being you." Is what is happening to those who enter the portal a "simulated" experience or some other type of experience? Discuss.

14. Discuss what happens to Malkovich when he enters his own mind. Why does everyone look like him and say only "Malkovich"?

15. Do any of the people who enter Malkovich's mind, including Craig and Dr. Lester's group, succeed in being Malkovich? Why or why not?

16. Does *Being John Malkovich* bring us any closer to understanding what it is like to experience the world from the perspective of a consciousness other than our own?

PAUL CHURCHLAND

ELIMINATIVE MATERIALISM

Paul Churchland argues that talk about the mind and its mental states is mistaken and should be replaced with a scientific theory concerning how the brain works. Churchland begins by criticizing "identity theory," the view that there is a one-to-one correspondence between mental states and brain states. Identity theorists argue that all discussion of mental states such as hoping, imagining, and believing can be reduced to discussion of brain states. Whereas the identity theorist believes that intertheoretic reduction between mental states and brain states is possible, Churchland maintains that it is not. Intertheoretic reduction refers to the process whereby the terms and principles of an older, weaker theory are reduced or translated to the terms and principles of a newer, more powerful theory. According to

Churchland, mental states are a remnant of "folk" psychology—a severely flawed, pseudo-scientific theory—a theory so mistaken that its terms and principles must be completely dismissed. In place of folk psychology, Churchland defends *eliminative materialism*, which maintains that all human behavior can be explained in terms of neuroscience, the study of how the brain works. Eliminative materialists maintain that the terms and principles of folk psychology will cease to be used as we learn more about how the brain works. Churchland's eliminative materialism concludes that there is no such thing as the mind and mental states, only the brain and brain states.

Paul Churchland (1942–) received his Ph.D. in philosophy from the University of Pittsburgh in 1969. Since 1966, he has taught at various universities in the United States and Canada. In 1979, he became professor of philosophy at the University of Manitoba, and in 1984, he moved to the University of California at San Diego, where he remains professor of philosophy. Churchland is the best-known proponent of the position that "folk" psychology, which seeks to explain human behavior in terms of our beliefs and desires, is actually a deeply flawed theory that must be eliminated in favor of a mature cognitive neuroscience. His books include *Scientific Realism and the Plasticity of Mind* (1979), *Matter and Consciousness: A Contemporary Introduction to the Philosophy of Mind* (1984), *Images of Science: Essays on Realism and Empiricism* (co-edited with Clifford A. Hooker, 1985), *A Neurocomputational Perspective: The Nature of Mind and the Structure of Science* (1989), *The Engine of Reason, The Seat of the Soul: A Philosophical Journey into the Brain* (1995), and *On the Contrary: Critical Essays, 1987–1997* (with Patricia S. Churchland, 1998).

ELIMINATIVE MATERIALISM

The identity theory was called into doubt not because the prospects for a materialist account of our mental capacities were thought to be poor, but because it seemed unlikely that the arrival of an adequate materialist theory would bring with it the nice one-to-one match-ups, between the concepts of folk psychology and the concepts of theoretical neuroscience, that intertheoretic reduction requires. The reason for that doubt was the great variety of quite different physical systems that could instantiate the required functional organization. *Eliminative materialism* also doubts that the correct neuroscientific account of human capacities will produce a neat reduction of our common-sense framework, but here the doubts arise from a quite different source.

As the eliminative materialists see it, the one-to-one match-ups will not be found, and our common-sense psychological framework will not enjoy an intertheoretic reduction, *because our common-sense psychological framework is a false and radically misleading conception of the causes of human behavior and the nature of cognitive activity.* On this view, folk psychology is not just an incomplete representation of our inner natures; it is an outright *mis*representation of our internal states and activities. Consequently, we cannot expect a truly adequate neuroscientific account of our inner lives to provide theoretical categories that match up nicely with the categories of our common-sense framework. Accordingly, we must expect that the older framework will simply be eliminated, rather than be reduced, by a matured neuroscience.

HISTORICAL PARALLELS

As the identity theorist can point to historical cases of successful intertheoretic reduction, so the eliminative materialist can point to historical cases of the outright elimination of the ontology of an older theory in favor of the ontology of a new and superior theory. For most of the eighteenth and nineteenth centuries, learned people believed that heat was a subtle *fluid* held in bodies, much in the way water is held in a sponge. A fair body of moderately successful theory described the way this fluid substance—called "caloric"—flowed within a body, or from one body to another, and how it produced thermal expansion, melting, boiling, and so forth. But by the end of the last century it had become abundantly clear that heat was not a substance at all, but just the energy of motion of the trillions of jostling molecules that make up the heated body itself. The new theory—the "corpuscular/kinetic theory of matter and heat"—was much more successful than the old in explaining and predicting the thermal behavior of bodies. And since we were unable to *identify* caloric fluid with kinetic energy (according to the old theory, caloric is a material *substance*; according to the new theory, kinetic energy is a form of *motion*), it was finally agreed that there is *no such thing* as caloric. Caloric was simply eliminated from our accepted ontology.

A second example. It used to be thought that when a piece of wood burns, or a piece of metal rusts, a spiritlike substance called "phlogiston" was being released: briskly, in the former case, slowly in the latter. Once gone, that "noble" substance left only a base pile of ash or rust. It later came to be appreciated that both processes involve, not the loss of something, but the *gaining* of a substance taken from the atmosphere: oxygen. Phlogiston emerged, not as an incomplete description of what was going on, but as a radical misdescription. Phlogiston was therefore not suitable for reduction to or identification with some notion from within the new oxygen chemistry, and it was simply eliminated from science.

Admittedly, both of these examples concern the elimination of something nonobservable, but our history also includes the elimination of certain widely accepted "observables." Before Copernicus' views because available, almost any human who ventured out at night could look up at *the starry sphere of the heavens*, and if he stayed for more than a few minutes he could also see that it *turned*, around an axis through Polaris. What the sphere was made of (crystal?) and what made it turn (the gods?) were theoretical questions that exercised us for over two millennia. But hardly anyone doubted the existence of what everyone could observe with their own eyes. In the end, however, we learned to reinterpret our visual experience of the night sky within a very different conceptual framework, and the turning sphere evaporated.

Witches provide another example. Psychosis is a fairly common affliction among humans, and in earlier centuries its victims were standardly seen as cases of demonic possession, as instances of Satan's spirit itself, glaring malevolently out at us from behind the victims' eyes. That witches exist was not a matter of any controversy. One would occasionally see them, in any city or hamlet, engaged in incoherent, paranoid, or even murderous behavior. But observable or not, we eventually decided that witches simply do not exist. We concluded that the concept of a witch is an element in a conceptual framework that misrepresents so badly the phenomena to which it was standardly applied that literal application of the notion should be permanently withdrawn. Modern theories of mental dysfunction led to the elimination of witches from our serious ontology.

The concepts of folk psychology—belief, desire, fear, sensation, pain, joy, and so on—await a similar fate, according to the view at issue. And when neuroscience has matured to the point where the poverty of our current conceptions is apparent to everyone, and the superiority of the new framework is established, we shall then be able to set about *reconceiving* our internal states and activities, within a truly adequate conceptual framework at last. Our explanations of one another's behavior will appeal to such things as our neuropharmacological states, the neural activity in specialized anatomical areas, and whatever other states are deemed relevant by the new theory. Our private introspection will also be transformed, and may be profoundly enhanced by reason of the more accurate and penetrating framework it will have to work with—just as the astronomer's perception of the night sky is much enhanced by the detailed knowledge of modern astronomical theory that he or she possesses.

The magnitude of the conceptual revolution here suggested should not be minimized: it would be enormous. And the benefits to humanity might be equally great. If each of us possessed an accurate neuroscientific understanding of (what we now conceive dimly as) the varieties and causes of mental illness, the factors involved in learning, the neural basis of emotions, intelligence, and socialization, then the sum total of human misery might be much reduced. The simple increase in mutual understanding that the new framework made possible could contribute substantially toward a more peaceful and humane society. Of course, there would be dangers as well: increased knowledge means increased power, and power can always be misused.

The arguments for eliminative materialism are diffuse and less than decisive, but they are stronger than is widely supposed. The distinguishing feature of this position is its denial that a smooth intertheoretic reduction is to be expected—even a species-specific reduction—of the framework of folk psychology to the framework of a matured neuroscience. The reason for this denial is the eliminative materialist's conviction that folk psychology is a hopelessly primitive and deeply confused conception of our internal activities. But why this low opinion of our common-sense conceptions?

There are at least three reasons. First, the eliminative materialist will point to the widespread explanatory, predictive, and manipulative failures of folk psychology. So much of what is central and familiar to us remains a complete mystery from within folk psychology. We do not know what *sleep* is, or why we have to have it, despite spending a full third of our lives in that condition. (The answer, "For rest," is mistaken. Even if people are allowed to rest continuously, their need for sleep is undiminished. Apparently, sleep serves some deeper functions, but we do not yet know what they are.) We do not understand how *learning* transforms each of us from a gaping infant to a cunning adult, or how differences in *intelligence* are grounded. We have not the slightest idea how *memory* works, or how we manage to retrieve relevant bits of information instantly from the awesome mass we have stored. We do not know what *mental illness* is, nor how to cure it.

In sum, the most central things about us remain almost entirely mysterious from within folk psychology. And the defects noted cannot be blamed on inadequate time allowed for their correction, for folk psychology has enjoyed no significant changes or advances in well over 2,000 years, despite its manifest failures. Truly successful theories may be expected to reduce, but significantly unsuccessful theories merit no such expectation.

This argument from explanatory poverty has a further aspect. So long as one sticks to normal brains, the poverty of folk psychology is perhaps not strikingly evident. But as soon as one examines the many perplexing behavioral and cognitive deficits suffered by people with *damaged* brains, one's descriptive and explanatory resources start to claw the air. . . . As with other humble theories asked to operate successfully in unexplored extensions of their old domain (for example, Newtonian mechanics in the domain of velocities close to the velocity of light, and the classical gas law in the domain of high pressures or temperatures), the descriptive and explanatory inadequacies of folk psychology become starkly evident.

The second argument tries to draw an inductive lesson from our conceptual history. Our early folk theories of motion were profoundly confused, and were eventually displaced entirely by more sophisticated theories. Our early folk theories of the structure and activity of the heavens were wildly off the mark, and survive only as historical lessons in how wrong we can be. Our folk theories of the nature of fire, and the nature of life, were similarly cockeyed. And one could go on, since the vast majority of our past folk conceptions have been similarly exploded. All except folk psychology, which survives to this day and has only recently begun to feel pressure. But the phenomenon of conscious intelligence is surely a more complex and difficult phenomenon than any of those just listed. So far as accurate understanding is concerned, it would be a *miracle* if we had got *that* one right the very first time, when we fell down so badly on all the others. Folk psychology has survived for so very long, presumably, not because it is basically correct in its representations, but because the phenomena addressed are so surpassingly difficult that any useful handle on them, no matter how feeble, is unlikely to be displaced in a hurry.

A third argument attempts to find an *a priori* advantage for eliminative materialism over the identity theory and functionalism. It attempts to counter the common intuition that eliminative materialism is distantly possible, perhaps, but is much less probable than either the identity theory or functionalism. The focus again is on whether the concepts of folk psychology will find vindicating match-ups in a matured neuroscience. The eliminativist bets no; the other two bet yes. (Even the functionalist bets yes, but expects the match-ups to be only species-specific, or only person-specific. Functionalism, recall, denies the existence only of *universal* type/type identities.)

The eliminativist will point out that the requirements on a reduction are rather demanding. The new theory must entail a set of principles and embedded concepts that mirrors very closely the specific conceptual structure to be reduced. And the fact is, there are vastly many more ways of being an explanatorily successful neuroscience while *not* mirroring the structure of folk psychology, than there are ways of being an explanatorily successful neuroscience while also *mirroring* the very specific structure of folk psychology. Accordingly, the *a priori* probability of eliminative materialism is not lower, but substantially *higher* than that of either of its competitors. One's initial intuitions here are simply mistaken.

Granted, this initial *a priori* advantage could be reduced if there were a very strong presumption in favor of the truth of folk psychology—true theories are better bets to win reduction. But according to the first two arguments, the presumptions on this point should run in precisely the opposite direction.

ARGUMENTS AGAINST ELIMINATIVE MATERIALISM

The initial plausibility of this rather radical view is low for almost everyone, since it denies deeply entrenched assumptions. That is at best a question-begging complaint, of course, since those assumptions are precisely what is at issue. But the following line of thought does attempt to mount a real argument.

Eliminative materialism is false, runs the argument, because one's introspection reveals directly the existence of pains, beliefs, desires, fears, and so forth. Their existence is as obvious as anything could be.

The eliminative materialist will reply that this argument makes the same mistake that an ancient or medieval person would be making if he insisted that he could just see with his own eyes that the heavens form a turning sphere, or that witches exist. The fact is, all observation occurs within some system of concepts, and our observation judgments are only as good as the conceptual framework in which they are expressed. In all three cases—the starry sphere, witches, and the familiar mental states—precisely what is challenged is the integrity of the background conceptual frameworks in which the observation judgments are expressed. To insist on the validity of one's experiences, *traditionally interpreted*, is therefore to beg the very question at issue. For in all three cases, the question is whether we should *reconceive* the nature of some familiar observational domain.

A second criticism attempts to find an incoherence in the eliminative materialist's position. The bald statement of eliminative materialism is that the familiar mental states do not really exist. But that statement is meaningful, runs the argument, only if it is the expression of a certain *belief*, and an *intention* to communicate, and a *knowledge* of the language, and so forth. But if the statement is true, then no such mental states exist, and the statement is therefore a meaningless string of marks or noises, and cannot be true. Evidently, the assumption that eliminative materialism it true entails that it cannot be true.

The hole in this argument is the premise concerning the conditions necessary for a statement to be meaningful. It begs the question. If eliminative materialism is true, then meaningfulness must have some different source. To insist on the "old" source is to insist on the validity of the very framework at issue. Again, an historical parallel may be helpful here. Consider the medieval theory that being biologically *alive* is a matter of being ensouled by an immaterial *vital spirit*. And consider the following response to someone who has expressed disbelief in that theory.

> My learned friend has stated that there is no such thing as vital spirit. But this statement is incoherent. For if it is true, then my friend does not have vital spirit, and must therefore be *dead*. But if he is dead, then his statement is just a string of noises, devoid of meaning or truth. Evidently, the assumption that antivitalism is true entails that it cannot be true! Q.E.D.

This second argument is now a joke, but the first argument begs the question in exactly the same way.

A final criticism draws a much weaker conclusion, but makes a rather stronger case. Eliminative materialism, it has been said, is making mountains out of molehills. It exaggerates the defects in folk psychology, and underplays its real successes. Perhaps the arrival of a matured neuroscience will require the elimination of the occasional folk-psychological concept, continues the criticism, and a minor adjustment in certain folk-psychological principles may have to be endured. But the large-scale elimination forecast by the eliminative materialist is just an alarmist worry or a romantic enthusiasm.

Perhaps this complaint is correct. And perhaps it is merely complacent. Whichever, it does bring out the important point that we do not confront two simple and mutually exclusive possibilities here: pure reduction versus pure elimination. Rather, these are the end points of a smooth spectrum of possible outcomes, between which there are mixed cases of partial elimination and partial reduction. Only empirical research . . . can tell us where on that spectrum our own case will fall. Perhaps we should speak here, more liberally, of "revisionary materialism," instead of concentrating on the more radical possibility of an across-the-board elimination. Perhaps we should. But it has been my aim in this section to make it at least intelligible to you that our collective conceptual destiny lies substantially toward the revolutionary end of the spectrum.

DISCUSSION QUESTIONS

1. What, according to Churchland, is wrong with "identity theory"? Do you agree with him? Why or why not?

2. Critically discuss Churchland's arguments for and against eliminative materialism. Which argument is the strongest, and why?

3. Churchland contends that every activity and feature of our "mind" can be given a material or physical explanation. Can you think of an activity or feature of our "mind" that *cannot* be given a physical explanation? Defend your view.

4. Do you think the brain can produce consciousness? Or is the term *consciousness* just another "folk" psychology mistake? Discuss.

5. Churchland throws out all of our common-sense and "folk" psychological conceptions concerning the mind. Do you think he has gone too far? Is there any element of folk psychology worth preserving? Why?

6. Compare Churchland's account of the mind with Ryle's account. How are they similar? How do they differ? Whose account do you prefer, and why?

Invasion of the Body Snatchers
[USA 1978] 1 hour, 59 minutes
Directed by Philip Kaufman

Matthew Bennell (Donald Sutherland), an investigator for the public health department in San Francisco, and Elizabeth Driscoll (Brooke Adams), Bennell's coworker, begin to realize that the people around them are becoming shells of their former selves. Bennell and Driscoll find that a budlike flower from outer space is spreading all over San Francisco. As one sleeps, the mysterious flower silently attaches its roots to the individual and makes an exact copy of the person's body inside a giant "pod." The copied body then disposes of its original body and goes about the world more or less like the original. While the copied individual retains the original individual's memories, the copied individual shows and apparently feels no emotion. The copied body also works with other copied bodies to bring about the snatching of even more bodies.

Bennell and Driscoll quickly find that few persons are willing to support their efforts to stop the body-snatching. Eventually, they uncover a mass-organized effort to both spread the body-snatching and prevent them from stopping it. Even Dr. David Kibner (Leonard Nimoy), Bennell's dear and trusted psychologist friend who claims to be helping them uncover the mystery, turns out to be a major part of the conspiracy to snatch bodies. Still, Bennell and Driscoll fight for their "bodies" as the population increasingly becomes these hollow humans. Yet, this fight is short-lived, as Driscoll, and then shortly thereafter, Bennell, have their bodies snatched as well. The movie's conclusion leads us to believe that the outer-space invaders who are using the pods to snatch bodies will eventually capture the entire planet. This film is an excellent remake of the 1956 science-fiction/horror classic *Invasion of the Body Snatchers*.

DISCUSSION QUESTIONS

1. What assumptions does *Invasion of the Body Snatchers* make about the relationship of the mind to the body? Is the mind viewed as separate from the body? A part of the body? An illusion?

2. In the film, we learn that persons whose bodies are snatched retain their memories. However, they are provided with different but identical bodies. Is the copied person then the same person as the original person? Why or why not?

3. In the film, one of the snatched-bodies tells Driscoll and Bennell, "Your minds and memories will be totally absorbed" into your reborn body. However, the copied persons do not show emotion. Why would minds and memories be absorbed, but not emotions? Are our emotions part of our minds? Our bodies? Both? Neither? Discuss.

4. The space aliens that snatch bodies and replicate them on earth and other planets do this in order to survive. Ontologically—that is, in terms of being—what from the aliens is entering the snatched bodies? Alien minds? Alien bodies? Neither? How does snatching bodies help the aliens survive?

5. Why do you think the aliens allow the copied bodies to retain the mind that was originally linked to that body? Wouldn't it be more efficient to copy bodies and inhabit them without the original mind? Or to remove the mind from body and simply inhabit the mindless body? What assumptions are made about the relation between the mind and body?

6. Dr. Kibner tells Bennell and Driscoll that after a person's body is snatched, he or she is "born again into an untroubled world, free of anxiety, without fear or hate." In this world, says Kibner, there will be no need for hate or love, and he urges them not to be trapped by old concepts: "You're evolving into a new life form." What does he mean? What role does the lack of emotion in the "born again" persons play in this untroubled world? Would you want to be turned into one of these persons if the end result was living in an untroubled world, free of anxiety, without fear or hate?

7. There are a number of remakes of this film as well as movies similar to it—for example, zombie movies, or movies about bodies without minds. How do these films contribute to or complicate our understanding of the relationship of the mind to the body? How do zombie films, for example, contribute to our understanding of eliminative materialism?

ELIZABETH V. SPELMAN

WOMAN AS BODY

I n this selection, Elizabeth Spelman argues that we should be wary of classical Western philosophers' views of the distinction between the mind and the body because they are often linked with the depreciation and degradation of women. Spelman shows how Plato's views about women are tied to the distinction he makes between the mind (or soul) and the body. For Plato, only the soul can have true knowledge and ascend to the world of the Forms; the body is associated with the fallibility of the senses and keeps us from real knowledge. Men are then linked most closely with the soul, and women (and children, slaves, and animals) are variously associated with the body. Spelman says that for Plato, "images of women, slaves, laborers, children and animals are almost interchangeable."

Spelman then argues that some well-known and respected feminist thinkers may rely on the same assumptions about the relationship of the mind to the body as the classical philosophical tradition, namely, (1) that we must distinguish between the soul and the body, (2) that the physical part of our existence is to be devalued in comparison to the mental, and (3) that woman is body (or is meant to take care of the bodily aspects of life). These are key assumptions in the Western philosophical tradition's degradation of women. In Spelman's view, the fact that feminist thinkers like Simone de Beauvoir and Betty Friedan employ these assumptions is troublesome. She finds the position of Adrienne Rich superior to those of de Beauvoir and Friedan precisely because Rich's work "has begun to show us why use of the mind/body distinction does not give us appropriate descriptions of human experience." Spelman concludes that somatophobia (flesh-loathing) is *not* only linked to sexism but is also symptomatic of racism.

Elizabeth V. Spelman is professor of philosophy and Barbara Richmond 1940 Professor in the Humanities at Smith College. Her books include *Inessential Woman: Problems of Exclusion in Feminist Thought* (1988), *Fruits of Sorrow: Framing Our Attention to Suffering* (1997), and *Repair: The Impulse to Restore in a Fragile World* (2002).

---

and what
pure happiness to know
all our high-toned questions
breed in a lively animal.

—ADRIENNE RICH, FROM "TWO SONGS"

What philosophers have had to say about women typically has been nasty, brutish and short. A page or two of quotations from those considered among the great philosophers (Aristotle, Hume, and Nietzsche, for example) constitutes a veritable litany of contempt. Because philosophers have not said much about women, and, when they have, it has usually been in short essays or chatty addenda which have not been considered to be part of the central body of their work, it is tempting to regard their expressed views about women as asystemic: their remarks on women are unofficial asides which are unrelated to the heart of their philosophical doctrines. After all, it might be thought, how could one's view about something as unimportant as women have anything to do with one's views about something as important as the nature of knowledge, truth, reality, freedom? Moreover—and this is the philosopher's move par excellence—wouldn't it be charitable to consider those opinions about women as coming merely from the *heart*, which all too easily responds to the tenor of the times, while philosophy "proper" comes from the *mind*, which resonates not with the times but with the truth?

Part of the intellectual legacy from philosophy "proper," that is, the issues that philosophers have addressed which are thought to be the serious province of philosophy, is the soul/body or mind/body distinction (differences among the various formulations are not crucial to this essay). However, this part of philosophy might have not merely accidental connections to attitudes about women. For when one recalls that the Western philosophical tradition has not been noted for its celebration of the body, and that women's nature and women's lives have long been associated with the body and bodily functions, then a question is suggested. What connection might there be between attitudes toward the body and attitudes toward women? . . .

PLATO'S LESSONS
ABOUT THE SOUL AND THE BODY

Plato's dialogues are filled with lessons about knowledge, reality, and goodness, and most of the lessons carry with them strong praise for the soul and strong indictments against the body. According to Plato, the body, with its deceptive senses, keeps us from real knowledge; it rivets us in a world of material things which is far removed from the world of reality; and it tempts us away from the virtuous life. It is in and through the soul, if at all, that we shall have knowledge, be in touch with reality, and lead a life of virtue. Only the soul can truly know, for only the soul can ascend to the real world, the world of the Forms or Ideas. That world is the perfect model to which imperfect, particular things we find in matter merely approximate. It is a world which, like the soul, is invisible, unchanging, not subject to decay, eternal. To be good, one's soul must know the Good, that is, the Form of Goodness, and this is impossible while one is dragged down by the demands and temptations of bodily life. Hence, bodily death is nothing to be feared: immortality of the soul not only is possible, but greatly to be desired, because when one is released from the body one finally can get down to the real business of life, for this real business of life is the business of the soul. Indeed, Socrates describes his own commitment, while still on earth, to encouraging his fellow Athenians to pay attention to the real business of life:

> [I have spent] all my time going about trying to persuade you, young and old, to make your first and chief concern not for your bodies nor for your possessions, but for the highest welfare of your souls.

Plato also tells us about the nature of beauty. Beauty has nothing essentially to do with the body or with the world of material things. *Real* beauty cannot "take the form of a face, or of hands, or of anything that is of the flesh." Yes, there are beautiful things, but they only are entitled to be described that way because they "partake in" the form of Beauty, which itself is not found in the material world. Real beauty has characteristics which merely beautiful *things* cannot have; real beauty

> is an everlasting loveliness which neither comes nor goes, which neither flowers nor fades, for such beauty is the same on every hand, the same then as now, here as there, this way as that way, the same to every worshipper as it is to every other.

Because it is only the soul that can know the Forms, those eternal and unchanging denizens of Reality, only the soul can know real Beauty; our changing, decaying bodies only can put us in touch with changing, decaying pieces of the material world.

Plato also examines love. His famous discussion of love in the *Symposium* ends up being a celebration of the soul over the body. Attraction to and appreciation for the beauty of another's body is but a vulgar fixation unless one can use such appreciation as a stepping stone to understanding Beauty itself. One can begin to learn about Beauty, while one is still embodied, when one notices that this body is beautiful, that that body is beautiful, and so on, and then one begins to realize that Beauty itself is something beyond any particular beautiful body or thing. The kind of love between people that is to be valued is not the attraction of one body for another, but the attraction of one soul for another. There is procreation of the spirit as well as of the flesh. All that bodies in unison can create are more bodies—the children women bear—which are mortal, subject to change and decay. But souls in unison can create "something lovelier and less mortal than human seed," for spiritual lovers "conceive and bear the things of the spirit," that is, "wisdom and all her sister virtues." Hence, spiritual love between men is preferable to physical love between men and women. At the same time, physical love between men is ruled out, on the ground that "enjoyment of the flesh by flesh" is "wanton shame," while desire of soul for soul is at the heart of a relationship that "reverences, aye and worships, chastity and manhood, greatness and wisdom." The potential for harm in sexual relations is very great—harm not so much to one's body or physique, but to one's soul. Young men especially shouldn't get caught up with older men in affairs that threaten their "spiritual development," for such development is "assuredly and ever will be of supreme value in the sight of gods and men alike."

So, then, one has no hope of understanding the nature of knowledge, reality, goodness, love, or beauty unless one recognizes the distinction between soul and body; and one has no hope of attaining any of these unless one works hard on freeing the soul from the lazy, vulgar, beguiling body. A philosopher is someone who is committed to doing just that, and that is why philosophers go willingly unto death; it is, after all, only the death of their bodies, and finally, once their souls are released from their bodies, these philosophical desiderata are within reach. . . .

The division among parts of the soul is intimately tied to one other central and famous aspect of Plato's philosophy that hasn't been mentioned so far: Plato's political views. His discussion of the parts of the soul and their proper relation to one another is integral to his view about the best way to set up a state. The rational part of the soul ought to rule the soul and ought to be attended by the spirited part in keeping watch over the unruly appetitive part; just so, there ought to be rulers of the state (the small minority in whom reason is dominant), who, with the aid of high-spirited guardians of order, watch over the multitudes (whose appetites need to be kept under control).

What we learn from Plato, then, about knowledge, reality, goodness, beauty, love, and statehood, is phrased in terms of a distinction between soul and body, or alternatively and roughly equivalently, in terms of a distinction between the rational and irrational. And the body, or the irrational part of the soul, is seen as an enormous and annoying obstacle to the possession of these desiderata. If the body gets the upper hand over the soul, or if the irrational part of the soul over-powers the rational part, one can't have knowledge, one can't see beauty, one will be far from the highest form of love, and the state will be in utter chaos. So the soul/body distinction, or the distinction between the rational and irrational parts of the soul, is a highly charged distinction. An inquiry into the distinction is no mild metaphysical musing. It is quite clear that the distinction is heavily value-laden. Even if Plato hadn't told us outright that the soul is more valuable than the body, and the rational part of the soul is more important than the irrational part, that message rings out in page after page of his dialogues. The soul/body distinction, then, is integral to the rest of Plato's views, and the higher worth of the soul is integral to that distinction.

PLATO'S VIEW OF THE SOUL AND BODY, AND HIS ATTITUDE TOWARD WOMEN

Plato, and anyone else who conceives of the soul as something unobservable, cannot of course speak as if we could point to the soul, or hold it up for direct observation. At one point, Plato says no mere mortal can really understand the nature of the soul, but one perhaps could tell what it resembles. So it is not surprising to find Plato using many metaphors and analogies to describe what the soul is *like*, in order to describe relations between parts of the soul. For example, thinking, a function of the soul, is described by analogy to talking. The parts of the soul are likened to a team of harnessed, winged horses and their charioteer. The body's relation to the soul is such that we are to think of the body vis-à-vis the soul as a tomb, a grave or prison, or as barnacles or rocks holding down the soul. Plato compares the lowest or bodylike part of the soul to a brood of beasts.

But Plato's task is not only to tell us what the soul is like, not only to provide us with ways of getting a fix on the differences between souls and bodies, or differences between parts of the soul. As we've seen, he also wants to convince us that the soul is much more important than the body, and that it is to our peril that we let ourselves be beckoned by the rumblings of the body at the expense of harkening to the call of the soul. And he means to convince us of this by holding up for our inspection the silly and sordid lives of those who pay too much attention to their bodies and do not care enough for their soul; he wants to remind us of how unruly, how without direction, are the lives of those in whom the lower part of the soul holds sway over the higher part. Because he can't *point* to an adulterated soul, he points instead to those embodied beings whose lives are in such bad shape that we can be sure that their souls are adulterated. And whose lives exemplify the proper soul/body relationship gone haywire? The lives of women (or sometimes the lives of children, slaves and brutes).

For example, how are we to know when the body has the upper hand over the soul, or when the lower part of the soul has managed to smother the higher part? We presumably can't see such conflict, so what do such conflicts translate into, in terms of actual human lives? Well, says Plato, look at the lives of women. It is women who get hysterical at the thought of death; obviously, their emotions have overpowered their reason, and they can't control themselves. The worst possible model for young men could be "a woman, young or old or wrangling with her husband, defying heaven, loudly boasting, fortunate in her own conceit, or involved in misfortune or possessed by grief and lamentation—still less a woman that is sick, in love, or in labor." . . .

Moreover, Plato on many occasions points to women to illustrate the improper way to pursue the things for which philosophers are constantly to be searching. For example, Plato wants to explain how important and also how difficult the attainment of real knowledge is. He wants us to realize that not just anyone can have knowledge, there is a vital distinction between those who really have knowledge and those who merely think they do. Think, for example, about the question of health. If we don't make a distinction between those who know what health is, and those who merely have unfounded and confused opinions about what health is, then "in the matter of good or bad health . . . any woman or child—or animal, for that matter—knows what is wholesome for it and is capable of curing itself." The implication is clear: if any old opinion were to count as real knowledge, then we'd have to say that women, children, and maybe even animals have knowledge. But surely *they* don't have knowledge! And why not? For one thing, because they don't recognize the difference between the material, changing world of appearance, and the invisible, eternal world of Reality. In matters of beauty, for example, they are so taken by the physical aspects

of things that they assume that they can see and touch what is beautiful; they don't realize that what one knows when one has knowledge of real Beauty cannot be something that is seen or touched. Plato offers us, then, as an example of the failure to distinguish between Beauty itself, on the one hand, and beautiful things, on the other, "boys and women when they see bright-colored things." They don't realize that it is not through one's senses that one knows about beauty or anything else, for real beauty is eternal and invisible and unchangeable and can only be known through the soul.

So the message is that in matters of knowledge, reality, and beauty, don't follow the example of women. They are mistaken about those things. In matters of love, women's lives serve as negative examples also. Those men who are drawn by "vulgar" love, that is, love of body for body, "turn to women as the object of their love, and raise a family"; those men drawn by a more "heavenly" kind of love, that is, love of soul for soul, turn to other men. But there are strong sanctions against physical love between men: such physical unions, especially between older and younger men, are "unmanly." The older man isn't strong enough to resist his lust (as in woman, the irrational part of the soul has overtaken the rational part), and the younger man, "the impersonator of the female," is reproached for this "likeness to the model." The problem with physical love between men, then, is that men are acting like women.

To summarize the argument so far: the soul/body distinction is integral to the rest of Plato's views; integral to the soul/body distinction is the higher worth and importance of the soul in comparison to the body; finally, Plato tries to persuade his readers that it is to one's peril that one does not pay proper attention to one's soul—for if one doesn't, one will end up acting and living as if one were a woman. We know, Plato says, about lives dictated by the demands and needs and inducements of the body instead of the soul. Such lives surely are not good models for those who want to understand and undertake a life devoted to the nurturance of the best part of us: our souls.

To anyone at all familiar with Plato's official and oft-reported views about women, the above recitation of misogynistic remarks may be quite surprising. Accounts of Plato's views about women usually are based on what he says in book 5 of the *Republic*. In that dialogue, Plato startled his contemporaries, when as part of his proposal for the constitution of an ideal state, he suggested that

> there is no pursuit of the administrators of a state that belongs to woman because she is a woman or to a man because he is a man. But the natural capacities are distributed alike among both creatures, and women naturally share in all pursuits and men in all. . . .

Well now, what are we to make of this apparent double message in Plato about women? What are we to do with the fact that on the one hand, when Plato explicitly confronts the question of women's nature, in the *Republic*, he seems to affirm the equality of men and women; while on the other hand, the dialogues are riddled with misogynistic remarks? . . .

So the contradictory sides of Plato's views about women are tied to the distinction he makes between soul and body and the lessons he hopes to teach his readers about their relative values. When preaching about the overwhelming importance of the soul, he can't but regard the kind of body one has as of no final significance, so there is no way for him to assess differentially the lives of women and men; but when making gloomy pronouncements about the worth of the body, he points an accusing finger at a class of people with a certain kind of body—women—because he regards them, as a class, as embodying the very traits he wishes no one to have. In this way, women constitute a deviant class in Plato's philosophy, in the sense that he points to their lives as the kinds of lives that are not acceptable philosophically: they are just the kind of lives no one, especially philosophers, ought to live. . . .

In summary, Plato does not merely embrace a distinction between soul and body; for all the good and hopeful and desirable possibilities for human life (now and in an afterlife) are aligned with the soul, while the rather seedy and undesirable liabilities of human life are aligned with the body (alternatively, the alignment is with the higher or lower parts of the soul). There is a highly polished moral gloss to the soul/body distinction in Plato. One of his favorite devices for bringing this moral gloss to a high luster is holding up, for our contempt and ridicule, the lives of women. This is one of ways he tries to make clear

that it makes no small difference whether you lead a soul-directed or a bodily directed life.

FEMINISM AND "SOMATOPHOBIA"

There are a number of reasons why feminists should be aware of the legacy of the soul/body distinction. It is not just that the distinction has been wound up with the depreciation and degradation of women, although, as has just been shown, examining a philosopher's view of the distinction may give us a direct route to his views about women.

First of all, as the soul or mind or reason is extolled, and the body or passion is denounced by comparison, it is not just women who are both relegated to the bodily or passionate sphere of existence and then chastised for belonging to that sphere. Slaves, free laborers, children, and animals are put in "their place" on almost the same grounds as women are. The images of women, slaves, laborers, children, and animals are almost interchangeable. For example, we find Plato holding that the best born and best educated should have control over "children, women and slaves . . . and the base rabble of those who are free in name," because it is in these groups that we find "the mob of motley appetites and pleasures and pains." As we saw above, Plato lumps together women, children, and animals as ignoramuses. (For Aristotle, there is little difference between a slave and an animal, because both "with their bodies attend to the needs of life.") A common way of denigrating a member of any one of these groups is to compare that member to a member of one of the other groups—women are thought to have slavish or childish appetites, slaves are said to be brutish. Recall too, that Plato's way of ridiculing male homosexuals was to say that they imitated women. It is no wonder that the images and insults are almost interchangeable, for there is a central descriptive thread holding together the images of all these groups. The members of these groups lack, for all intents and purposes, mind or the power of reason; even the humans among them are not considered fully human.

It is important for feminists to see to what extent the images and arguments used to denigrate women are similar to those used to denigrate one group of men vis-à-vis another, children vis-à-vis adults, animals vis-à-vis humans, and even—though I have not discussed it here—the natural world vis-à-vis man's will (yes, man's will). For to see this is part of understanding how the oppression of women occurs in the context of, and is related to, other forms of oppression or exploitation.

There is a second reason why feminists should be aware of the legacy of the soul/body distinction. Some feminists have quite happily adopted both the soul/body distinction and relative value attached to soul and to body. But in doing so, they may be adopting a position inimical to what on a more conscious level they are arguing for.

For all her magisterial insight into the way in which the image of woman as body has been foisted upon and used against us, Simone de Beauvoir can't resist the temptation to say that woman's emancipation will come when woman, like man, is freed from this association with— according to the male wisdom of the centuries— the less important aspect of human existence. According to *The Second Sex*, women's demand is "not that they be exalted in their femininity; they wish that in themselves, as in humanity in general, transcendence may prevail over immanence." But in de Beauvoir's own terms, for "transcendence" to prevail over "immanence" is for the spirit or mind to prevail over matter or body, for reason to prevail over passion and desire. This means not only that the old images of women as mired in the world of "immanence"— the world of nature and physical existence—will go away. It will also happen that women won't lead lives given over mainly to their "natural" functions; "the pain of childbirth is on the way out"; "artificial insemination is on the way in." Although de Beauvoir doesn't explicitly say it, her directions for women are to find means of leaving the world of immanence and joining the men in the realm of transcendence. Men have said, de Beauvoir reminds us, that to be human is to have mind prevail over body; and no matter what disagreements she has elsewhere with men's perceptions and priorities, de Beauvoir here seems to agree with them. . . .

. . . in *The Feminine Mystique*, [Betty] Friedan remarks on the absence, in women's lives, of "the world of thought and ideas, the life of the mind and spirit." She wants women to be "culturally" as well as "biologically" creative—she wants us to think about spending our lives "mastering the secrets of the atoms, or the stars, composing symphonies, pioneering a new concept in government or society." And she associates "mental activity" with the "professions of highest value to society." Friedan thus seems to believe that men have done the more important things, the mental things; women have been relegated in the past to the less important human tasks involving bodily functions, and their liberation will come when they are allowed and encouraged to do the more important things in life.

Friedan's analysis relies on our old friend, the mind/body distinction, and Friedan, no less than Plato or de Beauvoir, quite happily assumes that mental activities are more valuable than bodily ones. Her solution to what she referred to as the "problem that has no name" is for women to leave (though not entirely) women's sphere and "ascend" into man's. Certainly there is much pleasure and value in the "mental activities" she extolls. But we can see the residue of her own negative attitude about tasks associated with the body: the bodily aspects of our existence must be attended to, the "liberated" woman, who is on the ascendant, can't be bothered with them. There is yet another group of people to whom these tasks will devolve: servants. Woman's liberation—and of course it is no secret that by "woman," Friedan could only have meant middle-class white women—seems to require woman's dissociation and separation from those who will perform the bodily tasks which the liberated woman has left behind in pursuit of "higher," mental activity. So we find Friedan quoting, without comment, Elizabeth Cady Stanton:*

I now understood the practical difficulties most women had to contend with in the isolated household

---

*Elizabeth Cady Stanton (1815–1902), an American social and political philosopher, was one of the most important figures in the nineteenth-century women's right movement. In 1848, she helped organize the first convention on women's rights, the event that initiated the women's rights movement in the United States. She was the author of a critique of the bible from a women's rights point of view called the *Women's Bible* (1895–98) and was a co-collaborator in the first three volumes of *A History of Woman Suffrage* (1881, 1882, 1886), which covered the period from 1848 to 1885. However, she wearied of the history project and did not work on the final three volumes.—Ed.

and the impossibility of women's best development if in contact the chief part of her life with servants and children. . . .

Friedan at times seems to chide those women who could afford to have servants but don't: the women pretend there's a "servant problem" when there isn't, or insist on doing their own menial work. The implication is that women could find servants to do the "menial work," if they wanted to, and that it would be desirable for them to do so. But what difference is there between the place assigned to women by men and the place assigned to some women (or men) by Friedan herself? . . .

What I have tried to do here is bring attention to the fact that varius versions of women's liberation may themselves rest on the very same assumptions that have informed the deprecation and degradation of women, and other groups which, of course, include women. Those assumptions are that we must distinguish between soul and body, and that the physical part of our existence is to be devalued in comparison to the mental. Of course, these two assumptions alone don't mean that women or other groups have to be degraded; it's these two assumptions, along with the further assumption that woman is body, or is bound to her body, or is meant to take care of the bodily aspects of life, that have so deeply contributed to the degradation and oppression of women. And so perhaps feminists would like to keep the first two assumptions (about the difference between mind and body, and the relative worth of each of them) and somehow or other get rid of the last—in fact, that is what most of the feminists previously discussed have tried to do. Nothing that has been said so far has amounted to an argument against those first two assumptions: it hasn't been shown that there is no foundation for the assumptions that the mind and body are distinct and that the body is to be valued less than the mind.

There is a feminist thinker, however who has taken it upon herself to chip away directly at the second assumption and to a certain extent at the first. Both in her poetry, and explicitly in her recent book, *Of Woman Born*, Adrienne Rich has begun to show us why use of the mind/body distinction does not give us appropriate descriptions of human experience; and she has begun to remind us of the distance we keep from ourselves when we try to keep a distance from our bodies.

She does this in the process of trying to redefine the dimensions of the experience of childbirth, as she tries to show us why childbirth and motherhood need not mean what they have meant under patriarchy.

We are reminded by Rich that it is possible to be alienated from our bodies not only by pretending or wishing they weren't there, but also by being "incarcerated" in them. The institution of motherhood has done the latter in its insistence on seeing woman only or mainly as a reproductive machine. Defined as flesh by flesh-loathers, woman enters the most "fleshly" of her experiences with that same attitude of flesh-loathing—surely "physical self-hatred and suspicion of one's own body" is scarcely a favorable emotion with which to enter an intense physical experience.

But Rich insists that we don't have to experience childbirth in that way—we don't have to experience it as "torture rack"; but neither do we have to mystify it as a "peak experience." The experience of childbirth can be viewed as a way of recognizing the integrity of our experience, because pain itself is not usefully catalogued as something just our minds or just our bodies experience. . . . The point of "natural childbirth" should be thought of not as enduring pain, but as having an active physical experience—a distinction we recognize as crucial for understanding, for example, the pleasure in athletics.

Rich recognizes that feminists have not wanted to accept patriarchal versions of female biology, of what having a female body means. It has seemed to feminists, she implies, that we must either accept that view of being female, which is, essentially, to be a body, or deny that view and insist that we are "disembodied spirits." It perhaps is natural to see our alternatives that way:

> We have been perceived for too many centuries as pure Nature, exploited and raped like the earth and the solar system; small-wonder if we not try to become Culture: pure spirit, mind.

But we don't *have* to do that, Rich reminds us; we can appeal to the physical without denying what is called "mind." We can come to regard our physicality as "resource, rather than a destiny":

> In order to live a fully human life we require not only *control* of our bodies (though control is a prerequisite);

we must touch the unity and resonance of our physicality, our bond with the natural order, the corporeal ground of our intelligence.

Rich doesn't deny that we will have to start thinking about our lives in new ways; she even implies that we'll have to start thinking about thinking in new ways. Maybe it will give such a project a small boost to point out that philosophers for their part still squabble about mind/body dualism; the legacy of dualism is strong, but not unchallenged by any means. And in any event, . . . one can hardly put the blame for sexism (or any other form of oppression) on dualism itself. Indeed, the mind/body distinction can be put to progressive political ends, for example, to assert equality between human beings in the face of physical differences between them. There is nothing intrinsically sexist or otherwise oppressive about dualism, that is, about the belief that there are minds and there are bodies and that they are distinct kinds of things. But historically, the story dualists tell often ends up being a highly politicized one; although the story may be different at different historical moments, often it is said not only that there are minds (or souls) and bodies, but also that one is meant to rule and control the other. And the stage is thereby set for the soul/body distinction, now highly politicized and hierarchically ordered, to be used in a variety of ways in connection with repressive theories of the self, as well as oppressive theories of social and political relations. Among the tasks facing feminists is to think about the criteria for an adequate theory of self. Part of the value of Rich's work is that it points to the necessity of such an undertaking, and it is no criticism of her to say that she does no more than remind us of some of the questions that need to be raised.

A Final Note about the Significance of Somatophobia in Feminist Theory

In the history of political philosophy, the grounds given for the inferiority of women to men often are quite similar to those given for the inferiority

of slaves to masters, children to fathers, animals to humans. In Plato, for example, all such subordinate groups are guilty by association with one another and each group is guilty by association with the bodily. In their eagerness to end the stereotypical association of woman and body, feminists such as de Beauvoir, Friedan, Firestone,* and Daly† have overlooked the significance of the connections—in theory and in practice—between the derogation and oppression of women on the basis of our sexual identity and the derogation and oppression of other groups on the basis of, for example, skin color and class membership. It is as if in their eagerness to assign women a new place in the scheme of things, these feminist theorists have by implication wanted to dissociate women from other subordinate groups. One problem with this, of course is that those other subordinate groups include women.

What is especially significant about Rich's recent work is that in contrast to these other theorists she both challenges the received tradition about the insignificance and indignity of bodily life and bodily tasks and explicitly focuses on racism as well as sexism as essential factors in women's oppression. I believe that it is not merely a coincidence that someone who attends to the first also attends to the second. Rich pauses not just to recognize the significance attached to the female body, but also to reevaluate that significance. "Flesh-loathing" is loathing of flesh by some particular group under some particular circumstances—the loathing of women's flesh by me, but also the loathing of black flesh by whites. (Here I begin to extrapolate from Rich, but I believe with some warrant.) After all, bodies are always particular bodies—they are male or female bodies (our deep confusion when we can't categorize a body in either way supports and does not belie the general point); but they are black or brown or biscuit or yellow or red bodies as well. We cannot seriously attend to the social significance attached to embodiment without recognizing this. I believe that it is Rich's

*Shulamith Firestone (1945–), an American feminist thinker, helped found the Chicago Women's Liberation Union in 1969. She is the author of the highly influential book *The Dialectic of Sex: A Case for Feminist Revolution* (1970). Heavily influenced by the writings of Sigmund Freud, Karl Marx and Friedrich Engels (see chapter 5), and Simone de Beauvoir (see above), Firestone argues in *The Dialectic of Sex* that women must gain control of the means of production in society.
†See the biographical note in chapter 1 on Mary Daly.—Ed.

recognition of this that distinguishes her work in crucial ways from that of most other major white feminists. Although the topic of feminism, sexism, and racism deserves a much fuller treatment, it is important to point out in the context of the present paper that not only does Rich challenge an assumption about the nature of the bodily that has been used to oppress women, but, unlike other feminists who do not challenge this assumption, she takes on the question of the ways in which sexism and racism interlock. Somatophobia historically has been symptomatic not only of sexism, but also of racism, so it is perhaps not surprising that someone who has examined that connection between flesh-loathing and sexism would undertake an examination of racism.

DISCUSSION QUESTIONS

1. Discuss Spelman's analysis of the Western philosophical tradition's association of men with mind and women with body. What evidence for or against this view do you see in our own culture and commonplace beliefs?

2. Spelman says that for Plato, "images of women, slaves, laborers, children and animals are almost interchangeable." What is her evidence? If true, would this aspect of Plato's view make you feel any differently about his philosophy? Discuss.

3. According to Spelman, what is the connection between somatophobia (flesh-loathing) and racism? Do you agree with her? Why or why not?

4. How do Simone de Beauvoir and Betty Friedan employ the mind–body distinction in their respective work? What problems does Spelman find with their work? Do you agree with Spelman's criticisms of de Beauvoir and Friedan? Why or why not?

5. Paul Churchland champions the body or matter (over non-existing mind). How does Churchland's work differ from the classical vision of the relationship between mind and body as stated by Spelman? Do you think Spelman would view Churchland's work favorably?

3.2   WHO AM I?

PHILIP K. DICK

IMPOSTOR

Philip K. Dick's short story "Imposter" introduces us to questions about the nature of the self (Who or what am I?) and personal identity (On what basis can we say that we are the same person over time?). Spence Olham is arrested and taken to the moon to be "disassembled." Olham is told that a robot has located him, killed him, and taken over his life. "The robot," says Peters, a government security officer, "would be unaware that he was not the real Spence Olham. He would become Olham in mind as well as in body. He was given an artificial memory system, false recall. He would look like him, have his memories, his thoughts and interests, perform his job." The only difference between the "real" and the "robot" Olham is that "the robot is a U-bomb, ready to explode at the trigger phrase." Throughout the story, Olham strives to prove that he is the real Olham, not the robot. Finally, Olham locates the wreckage of the ship that the robot used to reach earth. A body is found next to the ship. Is it the real Olham or the robot?

Philip K. Dick (1928–82) was an American science-fiction writer. He worked briefly in radio and then studied for one year at the University of California at Berkeley. He published his first story, "Beyond Lies the Wub," in 1952 and his first novel, *Solar Lottery*, in 1955. Much of his work, such as *Time Out of Joint* (1959) and *The Man in the High Castle* (1962), deals with the difference between appearances and reality. Some of his later work, beginning with *The Simulacra* (1964) and continuing through *Do Androids Dream of Electric Sheep?* (1968; adapted for film in *Blade Runner* [1982]), takes up the subject of humans and artificial creatures living together in a future world. In addition to novels, he also published many short-story collections including *A Handful of Darkness* (1955), *The Variable Man and Other Stories* (1957), *The Preserving Machine* (1969), and *I Hope I Shall Arrive Soon* (1985). "Imposter" was first published in 1953 and was adapted for film in 2002.

"One of these days I'm going to take time off," Spence Olham said at first-meal. He looked around at his wife. "I think I've earned a rest. Ten years is a long time."

"And the Project?"

"The war will be won without me. This ball of clay of ours isn't really in much danger." Olham sat down at the table and lit a cigarette. "The news machines alter dispatches to make it appear the Outspacers are right on top of us. You know what I'd like to do on my vacation? I'd like to take a camping trip in those mountains outside of town, where we went that time. Remember? I got poison oak and you almost stepped on a gopher snake."

"Sutton Wood?" Mary began to clear away the food dishes. "The Wood was burned a few weeks ago. I thought you knew. Some kind of a flash fire."

Olham sagged. "Didn't they even try to find the cause?" His lips twisted. "No one cares any more. All they can think of is the war." He clamped his jaws together, the whole picture coming up in his mind, the Outspacers, the war, the needle ships.

"How can we think about anything else?"

Olham nodded. She was right, of course. The dark little ships out of Alpha Centauri had by-passed the Earth cruisers easily, leaving them like helpless turtles. It had been one-way fights, all the way back to Terra.

All the way, until the protec-bubble was demonstrated at Westinghouse Labs. Thrown around the major Earth cities and finally the planet itself, the bubble was the first real defense, the first legitimate answer to the Outspacers—as the news machines labelled them.

But to win the war, that was another thing. Every lab, every project was working night and day, endlessly, to find something more: a weapon for positive combat. His own project, for example. All day long, year after year.

Olham stood up, putting out his cigarette. "Like the Sword of Damocles. Always hanging over us. I'm getting tired. All I want to do is take a long rest. But I guess everybody feels that way."

He got his jacket from the closet and went out on the front porch. The shoot would be along any moment, the fast little bug that would carry him to the Project.

"I hope Nelson isn't late." He looked at his watch. "It's almost seven."

"Here the bug comes," Mary said, gazing between the rows of houses. The sun glittered behind the roofs, reflecting against the heavy lead plates. The settlement was quiet; only a few people were stirring. "I'll see you later. Try not to work beyond your shift, Spence."

Olham opened the car door and slid inside, leaning back against the seat with a sigh. There was an older man with Nelson.

"Well?" Olham said, as the bug shot ahead. "Heard any interesting news?"

"The usual," Nelson said. "A few Outspace ships hit, another asteroid abandoned for strategic reasons."

"It'll be good when we get the Project into final stage. Maybe it's just the propaganda from the news machines, but in the last month I've got weary of all this. Everything seems so grim and serious, no colour to life."

"Do you think the war is in vain?" the older man said suddenly. "You are an integral part of it, yourself."

"This is Major Peters," Nelson said. Olham and Peters shook hands. Olham studied the older man.

"What brings you along so early?" he said. "I don't remember seeing you at the Project before."

"No, I'm not with the Project," Peters said, "but I know something about what you're doing. My own work is altogether different."

A look passed between him and Nelson. Olham noticed it and he frowned. The bug was gaining speed, flashing across the barren, lifeless ground toward the distant rim of the Project buildings.

"What is your business?" Olham said, "Or aren't you permitted to talk about it?"

"I'm with the government," Peters said. "With FSA, the Security Organ."

"Oh?" Olham raised an eyebrow. "Is there any enemy infiltration in this region?"

"As a matter of fact I'm here to see you, Mr. Olham."

Olham was puzzled. He considered Peters' words, but he could make nothing of them. "To see me? Why?"

"I'm here to arrest you as an Outspace spy. That's why I'm up so early this morning. *Grab him, Nelson—*"

The gun drove into Olham's ribs. Nelson's hands were shaking, trembling with released emotion, his face pale. He took a deep breath and let it out again.

"Shall we kill him now?" he whispered to Peters. "I think we should kill him now. We can't wait."

Olham stared into his friend's face. He opened his mouth to speak, but not words came. Both men were staring at him steadily, rigid and grim with fright. Olham felt dizzy. His head ached and spun.

"I don't understand," he murmured.

At that moment the shoot car left the ground and rushed up, heading into space. Below them the Project fell away, smaller and smaller, disappearing. Olham shut his mouth.

"We can wait a little," Peters said. "I want to ask him some questions first."

Olham gazed dully ahead as the bug rushed through space.

"The arrest was made all right," Peters said into the vidscreen. On the screen the features of the Security Chief showed. "It should be a load off everyone's mind."

"Any complications?"

"None. He entered the bug without suspicion. He didn't seem to think my presence was too unusual."

"Where are you now?"

"On our way out, just inside the protec-bubble. We're moving at maximum speed. You can assume that the critical period is past. I'm glad the take-off jets in this craft were in good working order. If there had been any failures at that point—"

"Let me see him," the Security Chief said. He gazed directly at Olham where he sat, his hands in his lap, staring ahead.

"So that's the man." He looked at Olham for a time. Olham said nothing. At last the chief nodded to Peters. "All right. That's enough." A faint trace of disgust wrinkled his features. "I've seen all I want. You've done something that will be remembered for a long time. They're preparing some sort of citation for both of you."

"That's not necessary," Peters said.

"How much danger is there now? Is there still much chance that—"

"There is some chance, but not too much. According to my understanding, it requires a verbal key phrase. In any case we'll have to take the risk."

"I'll have the Moon base notified you're coming."

"No," Peters shook his head. "I'll land the ship outside, beyond the base. I don't want it in jeopardy."

"Just as you like." The chief's eyes flickered as he glanced again at Olham. Then his image faded. The screen blanked.

Olham shifted his gaze to the window. The ship was already through the protec-bubble, rushing with greater and greater speed all the time. Peters was in a hurry; below him, rumbling under the floor, the jets were wide open. They were afraid, hurrying frantically, because of him.

Next to him on the seat, Nelson shifted uneasily. "I think we should do it now," he said. "I'd give anything if we could get it over with."

"Take it easy," Peters said. "I want you to guide the ship for a while so I can talk to him."

He slid over beside Olham, looking into his face. Presently he reached out and touched him gingerly, on the arm and then on the cheek.

Olham said nothing, *If I could let Mary know*, he thought again. *If I could find some way of letting her know.* He looked around the ship. How? The vidscreen? Nelson was sitting by the board, holding the gun. There was nothing he could do. He was caught, trapped.

But why?

"Listen," Peters said. "I want to ask you some questions. You know where we're going. We're moving Moonward. In an hour we'll land on the far side, on the desolate side. After we land you'll be turned over immediately to a team of men waiting there. Your body will be destroyed at once. Do you understand that?" He looked at his watch. "Within two hours your parts will be strewn over the landscape. There won't be anything left of you."

Olham struggled out of his lethargy. "Can't you tell me—"

"Certainly, I'll tell you." Peters nodded. "Two days ago we received a report that an Outspace ship had penetrated the protec-bubble. The ship let off a spy in the form of a humanoid robot. The robot was to destroy a particular human being and take his place."

Peters looked calmly at Olham.

"Inside the robot was a U-bomb. Our agent did not know how the bomb was to be detonated, but he conjectured that it might be by a particular spoken phrase, a certain group of words. The robot would live the life of the person he killed, entering into his usual activities, his job, his social life. He had been constructed to resemble that person. No one would know the difference."

Olham's face went sickly chalk.

"The person whom the robot was to impersonate was Spence Olham, a high-ranking official at one of the Research projects. Because this particular project was approaching crucial stage, the presence of an animate bomb, moving toward the centre of the Project—"

Olham stared down at his hands. *"But I'm Olham!"*

"Once the robot had located and killed Olham, it was a simple matter to take over his life. The robot was probably released from the ship eight days ago. The substitution was probably accomplished over the last weekend, when Olham went for a short walk in the hills."

"But I'm Olham." He turned to Nelson, sitting at the controls. "Don't you recognize me? You've known me for twenty years. Don't you remember how we went to college together?" He stood up. "You and I were at the University, We had the same room." He went toward Nelson.

"Stay away from me!" Nelson snarled.

"Listen. Remember our second year? Remember that girl. What was her name—" He rubbed his forehead. "The one with the dark hair. The one we met over at Ted's place."

"Stop!" Nelson waved the gun frantically. "I don't want to hear any more. You killed him! You . . . machine."

Olham looked at Nelson. You're wrong. I don't know what happened, but the robot never reached me. Something must have gone wrong. Maybe the ship crashed." He turned to Peters. "I'm Olham. I know it. No transfer was made. I'm the same as I've always been."

He touched himself, running his hands over his body. "There must be some way to prove it. Take me back to Earth. An X-ray examination, a neurological study, anything like that will show you. Or maybe we can find the crashed ship."

Neither Peters nor Nelson spoke.

"I am Olham," he said again. "I know I am. But I can't prove it."

"The robot," Peters said, "would be unaware that he was not the real Spence Olham. He would become Olham in mind as well as in body. He was given an artificial memory system, false recall. He would look like him, have his memories, his thoughts and interests, perform his job.

"But there would be one difference. Inside the robot is a U-bomb, ready to explode at the trigger phrase." Peters moved a little away. "That's the one difference. That's why we're taking you to the Moon. They'll disassemble you and remove the bomb. Maybe it will explode, but it won't matter, not there."

Olham sat down slowly.

"We'll be there soon," Nelson said.

He lay back, thinking frantically, as the ship dropped slowly down. Under them was the pitted surface of the Moon, the endless expanse of ruin. What could he do? What would save him?

"Get ready," Peters said.

In a few minutes he would be dead. Down below he could see a tiny dot, a building of some kind. There were men in the building, the demolition team, waiting to tear him to bits. They would rip him open, pull off his arms and legs, break him apart. When they found no bomb they would be surprised; they would know, but it would be too late.

Olham looked around the small cabin. Nelson was still holding the gun. There was no chance there. If he could get to a doctor, have an examination made—that was the only way. Mary could help him. He thought frantically, his mind racing. Only a few minutes, just a little time left. If he could contact her, get word to her some way.

"Easy," Peters said. The ship came down slowly, bumping on the rough ground. There was silence.

"Listen," Olham said thickly. "I can prove I'm Spence Olham. Get a doctor. Bring him here—"

"There's the squad." Nelson pointed. "They're coming." He glanced nervously at Olham. "I hope nothing happens."

"We'll be gone before they start work," Peters said. "We'll be out of here in a moment." He put on his pressure suit. When he had finished he took the gun from Nelson. "I'll watch him for a moment."

Nelson put on his pressure suit, hurrying awkwardly. "How about him?" He indicated Olham. "Will he need one?"

"No," Peters shook his head. "Robots probably don't require oxygen."

The group of men were almost to the ship. They halted, waiting. Peters signaled to them.

"Come on!" He waved his hand and the men approached warily; stiff, grotesque figures in their inflated suits.

"If you open the door," Olham said, "it means my death. It will be murder."

"Open the door," Nelson said. He reached for the handle.

Olham watched him. He saw the man's hand tighten around the metal rod. In a moment the door would swing back, the air in the ship would rush out. He would die, and presently they would realize their mistake. Perhaps at some other time, when there was no war, men might not act this way, hurrying an individual to his death because they were afraid. Everyone was frightened, everyone was willing to sacrifice the individual because of the group fear.

He was being killed because they could not wait to be sure of his guilt. There was not enough time.

He looked at Nelson. Nelson had been his friend for years. They had gone to school together. He had been best man at his wedding. Now

Nelson was going to kill him. But Nelson was not wicked; it was not his fault. It was the times. Perhaps it had been the same way during the plagues. When men had shown a spot they probably had been killed, too, without a moment's hesitation, without proof, on suspicion alone. In times of danger there was no other way.

He did not blame them. But he had to live. His life was too precious to be sacrificed. Olham thought quickly. What could he do? Was there anything? He looked around.

"Here goes," Nelson said.

"You're right," Olham said. The sound of his own voice surprised him. It was the strength of desperation. "I have no need of air. Open the door."

They paused, looking at him in curious alarm.

"Go ahead. Open it. It makes no difference." Olham's hand disappeared inside his jacket. "I wonder how far you two can run?"

"Run?"

"You have fifteen seconds to live." Inside his jacket his fingers twisted, his arm suddenly rigid. He relaxed, smiling a little. "You were wrong about the trigger phrase. In that respect you were mistaken. Fourteen seconds, now."

Two shocked faces stared at him from the pressure suits. Then they were struggling, running, tearing the door open. The air shrieked out, spilling into the void. Peters and Nelson bolted out of the ship. Olham came after them. He grasped the door and dragged it shut. The automatic pressure system chugged furiously, restoring the air. Olham let his breath out with a shudder.

One more second. . . .

Beyond the window the two men had joined the group. The group scattered, running in all directions. One by one they threw themselves down, prone on the ground. Olham seated himself at the control board. He moved the dials into place. As the ship rose up into the air the men below scrambled to their feet and stared up, their mouths open.

"Sorry," Olham murmured, "but I've got to get back to Earth."

He headed the ship back the way it had come.

It was night. All around the ship crickets chirped, disturbing the chill darkness. Olham bent over the vidscreen. Gradually the image formed; the call had gone through without trouble. He breathed a sigh of relief.

"Mary," he said. The woman stared at him. She gasped.

"Spence! Where are you? What's happened?"

"I can't tell you. Listen, I have to talk fast. They may break this call off any minute. Go to the Project grounds and get Dr. Chamberlain. If he isn't there, get any doctor. Bring him to the house and have him stay there. Have him bring equipment, X-ray, fluoroscope, everything."

"But—"

"Do as I say. Hurry. Have him get it ready in an hour." Olham leaned toward the screen. "Is everything all right? Are you alone?"

"Alone?"

"Is anyone with you? Has . . . has Nelson or anyone contacted you?"

"No, Spence. I don't understand."

"All right. I'll see you at the house in an hour. And don't tell anyone anything. Get Chamberlain there on any pretext. Say you're very ill."

He broke the connection and looked at his watch. A moment later he left the ship, stepping down into the darkness. He had a half-mile to go.

He began to walk.

One light showed in the window, the study light. He watched it, kneeling against the fence. There was no sound, no movement of any kind. He held his watch up and read it by starlight. Almost an hour had passed.

Along the street a shoot bug came. It went on.

Olham looked toward the house. The doctor should have already come. He should be inside, waiting with Mary. A thought struck him. Had she been able to leave the house? Perhaps they had intercepted her. Maybe he was moving into a trap.

But what else could he do?

With a doctor's records, photographs and reports, there was a chance, a chance of proof. If he could be examined, if he could remain alive long enough for them to study him. . . .

He could prove it that way. It was probably the only way. His one hope lay inside the house. Dr. Chamberlain was a respected man. He was the staff doctor for the Project. He would know; his word on the matter would have meaning. He could overcome their hysteria, their madness, with facts.

Madness—that was what it was. If only they could wait, act slowly, take their time. But they could not wait. He had to die, die at once, without proof, without any kind of trial or examination. The simplest test would tell, but they had not time for the simplest test. They could think only of the danger. Danger, and nothing more.

He stood up and moved toward the house. He came up on the porch. At the door he paused, listening. Still no sound. The house was absolutely still.

Too still.

Olham stood on the porch, unmoving. They were trying to be silent inside. Why? It was a small house; only a few feet away, beyond the door, Mary and Dr. Chamberlain should be standing. Yet he could hear nothing, no sound of voices, nothing at all. He looked at the door. It was a door he had opened and closed a thousand times, every morning and every night.

He put his hand on the knob. Then, all at once, he reached out and touched the bell instead. The bell pealed, off some place in the back of the house. Olham smiled. He could hear movement.

Mary opened the door. As soon as he saw her face he knew.

He ran, throwing himself into the bushes. A Security officer shoved Mary out of the way, firing past her. The bushes burst apart. Olham wriggled around the side of the house. He leaped up and ran, racing frantically into the darkness. A searchlight snapped on, a beam of light circling past him.

He crossed the road and squeezed over a fence. He jumped down and made his way across a backyard. Behind him men were coming. Security officers, shouting to each other as they came. Olham gasped for breath, his chest rising and falling.

Her face—he had known at once. The set lips, the terrified, wretched eyes. Suppose he had gone ahead, pushed open the door and entered! They had tapped the call and come at once, as soon as he had broken off. Probably she believed their account. No doubt she thought he was the robot, too.

Olham ran on and on. He was losing the officers, dropping them behind. Apparently they were not much good at running. He climbed a hill and made his way down the other side. In a moment he would be back at the ship. But where to, this time? He slowed down, stopping. He could see the ship already, outlined against the sky, where he had parked it. The settlement was behind him; he was on the outskirts of the wilderness between the inhabited places, where the forests and desolation began. He crossed a barren field and entered the trees.

As he came toward it, the door of the ship opened.

Peters stepped out, framed against the light. In his arms was a heavy boris-gun. Olham stopped, rigid. Peters stared around him, into the darkness. "I know you're there, some place," he said. "Come on up here, Olham. There are Security men all around you."

Olham did not move.

"Listen to me. We will catch you very shortly. Apparently you still do not believe you're the robot. Your call to the woman indicates that you are still under the illusion created by your artifical memories.

"But you *are* the robot. You are the robot, and inside you is the bomb. Any moment the trigger phrase may be spoken, by you, by someone else, by anyone. When that happens the bomb will destroy everything for miles around. The Project, the woman, all of us will be killed. Do you understand?"

Olham said nothing. He was listening. Men were moving toward him, slipping through the woods.

"If you don't come out, we'll catch you. It will be only a matter of time. We no longer plan to remove you to the Moon-base. You will be destroyed on sight and we will have to take the chance that the bomb will detonate. I have ordered every available Security officer into the area. The whole county is being searched, inch by inch. There is no place you can go. Around this wood is a cordon of armed men. You have about six hours left before the last inch is covered."

Olham moved away. Peters went on speaking; he had not seen him at all. It was too dark to see anyone. But Peters was right. There was no place he could go. He was beyond the settlement, on the outskirts where the woods began. He could hide for a time, but eventually they would catch him.

Only a matter of time.

Olham walked quietly through the wood. Mile by mile, each part of the county was being measured off, laid bare, searched, studied, examined. The cordon was coming all the time, squeezing him into a smaller and smaller space.

What was there left? He had lost the ship, the one hope of escape. They were at his home; his wife was with them, believing, no doubt, that the real Olham had been killed. He clenched his fists. Some place there was a wrecked Outspace needle-ship, and in it the remains of the robot. Somewhere nearby the ship had crashed, crashed and broken up.

And the robot lay inside, destroyed.

A faint hope stirred him. What if he could find the remains? If he could show them the wreckage, the remains of the ship, the robot. . . .

But where? Where would he find it?

He walked on, lost in thought. Some place, not too far off, probably. The ship would have landed close to the Project; the robot would have expected to go the rest of the way on foot. He went up the side of a hill and looked around. Crashed and burned. Was there some clue, some hint? Had he read anything, heard anything? Some place close by, within walking distance. Some wild place, a remote spot where there would be no people.

Suddenly Olham smiled. Crashed and burned. . . .

Sutton Wood.

He increased his pace.

It was morning. Sunlight filtered down through the broken trees onto the man crouching at the edge of the clearing. Olham glanced up from time to time, listening. They were not far off, only a few minutes away. He smiled.

Down below him, strewn across the clearing and into the charred stumps that had been Sutton Wood, lay a tangled mass of wreckage. In the sunlight it glittered a little, gleaming darkly. He had not had too much trouble finding it. Sutton Wood was a place he knew well; he had climbed around it many times in his life, when he was younger. He had known where he would find the remains. There was one peak that jutted up suddenly, without warning.

A descending ship, unfamiliar with the Wood, had little chance of missing it. And now he squatted, looking down at the ship, or what remained of it.

Olham stood up. He could hear them, only a little distance away, coming together, talking in low tones. He tensed himself. Everything depended on who first saw him. If it were Nelson, he had no chance. Nelson would fire at once. He would be dead before they saw the ship. But if he had time to call out, hold them off for a moment. . . . That was all he needed. Once they saw the ship he would be safe.

But if they fired first. . . .

A charred branch cracked. A figure appeared, coming forward uncertainly. Olham took a deep breath. Only a few seconds remained, perhaps the last seconds in his life. He raised his arms, peering intently.

It was Peters.

"Peters!" Olham waved his arms. Peters lifted his gun, aiming. "Don't fire!" His voice shook. "Wait a minute. Look past me, across the clearing."

"I've found him," Peters shouted. Security men came pouring out of the burned woods around him.

"Don't shoot. Look past me. The ship, the needle-ship. The Outspace ship. Look!"

Peters hesitated. The gun wavered.

"It's down there," Olham said rapidly. "I knew I'd find it here. The burned wood. Now you believe me. You'll find the remains of the robot in the ship. Look, will you?"

"There is something down there," one of the men said nervously.

"Shoot him!" a voice said. It was Nelson.

"Wait." Peters turned sharply. "I'm in charge. Don't anyone fire. Maybe he's telling the truth."

"Shoot him," Nelson said. "He killed Olham. Any minute he may kill us all. If the bomb goes off—"

"Shut up." Peters advanced toward the slope. He started down. "Look at that." He waved two men up to him. "Go down there and see what that is."

The men raced down the slope, across the clearing. They bent down, poking in the ruins of the ship.

"Well?" Peters called.

Olham held his breath. He smiled a little. It must be there; he had not had time to look, himself, but it had to be there. Suddenly doubt assailed him. Suppose the robot had lived long enough to wander away? Suppose his body had been completely destroyed, burned to ashes by the fire?

He licked his lips. Perspiration came out on his forehead. Nelson was staring at him, his face still livid. His chest rose and fell.

"Kill him," Nelson said. "Before he kills us."

The two men stood up.

"What have you found?" Peters said. He held the gun steady. "Is there anything there?"

"Looks like something. It's a needle-ship, all right. There's something beside it."

"I'll look." Peters strode past Olham. Olham watched him go down the hill and up to the men. The others were following after him, peering to see.

"It's a body of some sort," Peters said. "Look at it!"

Olham came along with them. They stood around in a circle, staring down.

On the ground, bent and twisted into a strange shape, was a grotesque form. It looked human, perhaps; except that it was bent so strangely, the arms and legs flung off in all directions. The mouth was open, the eyes stared glassily.

"Like a machine that's run down," Peters murmured.

Olham smiled feebly. "Well?" he said.

Peters looked at him. "I can't believe it. You were telling the truth all the time."

"The robot never reached me," Olham said. He took out a cigarette and lit it. "It was destroyed when the ship crashed. You were all too busy with the war to wonder why an out-of-the-way woods would suddenly catch fire and burn. Now you know."

He stood smoking, watching the men. They were dragging the grotesque remains from the ship. The body was stiff, the arms and legs rigid.

"You'll find the bomb, now," Olham said. The men laid the body on the ground. Peters bent down.

"I think I see the corner of it." He reached out, touching the body.

The chest of the corpse had been laid open. Within the gaping tear something glinted, something metal. The men stared at the metal without speaking.

"That would have destroyed us all, if it had lived," Peters said. "That metal box, there."

There was silence.

"I think we owe you something," Peters said to Olham. "This must have been a nightmare to you. If you hadn't escaped, we would have—" He broke off.

Olham put out his cigarette. "I knew, of course, that the robot had never reached me. But I had no way of proving it. Sometimes it isn't possible to prove a thing right away. That was the whole trouble. There wasn't any way I could demonstrate that I was myself."

"How about a vacation?" Peters said. "I think we might work out a month's vacation for you. You could take it easy, relax."

"I think right now I want to go home," Olham said.

"All right, then," Peters said. "Whatever you say."

Nelson had squatted down on the ground, beside the corpse. He reached out toward the glint of metal visible within the chest.

"Don't touch it," Olham said. "It might still go off. We'd better let the demolition squad take care of it later on."

Nelson said nothing. Suddenly he grabbed hold of the metal, reaching his hand inside the chest. He pulled.

"What are you doing?" Olham cried.

Nelson stood up. He was holding on to the metal object. His face was blank with terror. It was a metal knife, an Outspace needle-knife, covered with blood.

"This killed him," Nelson whispered. "My friend was killed with this." He looked at Olham. "You killed him with this and left him beside the ship."

Olham was trembling. His teeth chattered. He looked from the knife to the body. "This can't be Olham," he said. His mind spun, everything was whirling. "Was I wrong?"

He gaped.

"But if that's Olham, then I must be—"

He did not complete the sentence, only the first phrase. The blast was visible all the way to Alpha Centauri.

DISCUSSION QUESTIONS

1. The robot and the real Spence Olham look alike, have the same memories and thoughts and interests, and perform the same job. There is no physical or mental difference between the robot and the real Olham. Furthermore, the robot believes that he is the real Spence Olham. Would you be willing to hold the real Olham accountable for the actions of the robot? Would you be willing to hold the robot accountable for the actions of the real Olham? Why or why not?

2. Some might argue that one difference between the real Olham and the robot Olham is that the real Olham participated in his memories, whereas the robot Olham did not. Do you think this is a significant difference? Why or why not?

3. Do you think you would be able to tell the difference between a memory that you participated in making and a memory that you believed you had participated in but actually did not? Discuss.

4. This story assumes a technology that allows us to duplicate people exactly, including their bodies and their memories. Is there one self (or person) here or two? Why? Is the duplicate of the same "value" as the original? Why or why not?

5. Imagine that someone created a duplicate "you" in the ways described above. How could you prove that you are different from the duplicate?

JOHN LOCKE

OF IDENTITY AND DIVERSITY

In this selection, John Locke argues that the identity of persons should be determined in terms of consciousness. For Locke, a person is "a thinking intelligent being, that has reason and reflection, and can consider itself as itself, the same thinking thing, in different times and places." It is our consciousness that gives us the ability to consider our self as our self, the same thing that thinks now as thought five days or even five years ago. For Locke, consciousness is inseparable from and essential to thinking. Furthermore, perception without an awareness of perception is impossible. It is, says Locke, "impossible for any one to perceive without *perceiving* that he does perceive." Consciousness of ourself is at the center of our identity as a person; that is, consciousness makes personal identity. Consciousness, says Locke, "is that which makes every one to be what he calls self, and thereby distinguishes himself from all other thinking things, in this alone consists personal identity, i.e., the sameness of a rational being." Moreover, continues Locke, "as far backwards to any past action or thought, so far reaches identity of that person; it is the same self now it was then; and it is by the same self with this present one that now reflects on it, that that action was done." We are identical with whatever actions we remember as our own. This is sometimes called the "memory criterion" of personal identity.

Furthermore, even though we are capable of self-consciousness, consciousness is not tied to our body or our soul. Locke considers, for example, cases when our consciousness is interrupted or when we lose sight of our past self or selves. He says that while these cases raise doubts about whether we are the same thinking thing (or substance), they do not concern "*personal* identity at all." For Locke, the question is what makes the same *person*, "not whether it be the same identical substance, which always thinks in the same person." Not even different bodies and different substances united in a person can destroy personal identity, for "identity is preserved in that change of substances [or bodies] by the unity of one continued life." "For, it being the same consciousness that makes a man be himself to himself, personal identity depends on that only, whether it be annexed solely to one individual substance, or can be continued in a succession of several substances." To illustrate this point, Locke has us imagine the effects on consciousness of cutting off a hand. The severed hand, writes Locke, "is then no longer a part of that which is himself." "Thus, we see the *substance* whereof personal self consisted at one time may be varied at another, without the change of personal identity."

Locke also considers the case of immaterial substance (soul) and its relation to personal identity. While some maintain, for example, that the soul of Socrates can "inform" the body of another, say, George Washington, Locke asks, "Would any one say, that he [George Washington], being not conscious of any of Socrates' actions or thoughts, could be the same *person* with Socrates?" For Locke, even if Socrates' soul "informed" the body of George Washington, if Washington did not have the same consciousness as Socrates, then Socrates and Washington would still be two distinct persons. Writes Locke, "The same immaterial substance [that is, soul], without the same consciousness, no more making makes the same person, by being united to any body, than the same particle of matter, without consciousness, united with any body, makes the same person."

In sum, for Locke, "*Self* is that conscious thinking thing—whatever substance made of, (whether spiritual or material, simple or compounded, it matters not)—which is sensible or conscious of pleasure and pain, capable of happiness or misery, and so is concerned for itself, as far as that consciousness extends." A biographical sketch of Locke can be found in chapter 2. The following selection is from *An Essay Concerning Human Understanding* (1690).

---

9. *Personal identity*. This being premised, to find wherein personal identity consists, we must consider what *person* stands for;—which, I think, is a thinking intelligent being, that has reason and reflection, and can consider itself as itself, the same thinking thing, in different times and places; which it does only by that consciousness which is inseparable from thinking, and, as it seems to me, essential to it: it being impossible for any one to perceive without *perceiving* that he does perceive. When we see, hear, smell, taste, feel, meditate, or will anything, we know that we do so. Thus it is always as to our present sensations and perceptions: and by this every one is to himself that which he calls *self*:—it not being considered, in this case, whether the same self be continued in the same or divers substances. For, since consciousness always accompanies thinking, and it is that which makes every one to be what he calls self, and thereby distinguishes himself from all other thinking things, in this alone consists personal identity, i.e. the sameness of a rational being: and as far as this consciousness can be extended backwards to any past action or thought, so far reaches the identity of that person; it is the same self now it was then; and it is by the same self with this present one that now reflects on it, that that action was done.

10. *Consciousness makes personal identity*. But it is further inquired, whether it be the same identical substance. This few would think they had reason to doubt of, if these perceptions, with their consciousness, always remained present in the mind, whereby the same thinking thing would be always consciously present, and, as would be thought, evidently the same to itself. But that which seems to make the difficulty is this, that this consciousness being interrupted always by forgetfulness, there being no moment of our lives wherein we have the whole train of all our past actions before our eyes in one view, but even the best memories losing the sight of one part whilst they are viewing another; and we sometimes, and that the greatest part of our lives, not reflecting on our past selves, being intent on our present

thoughts, and in sound sleep having no thoughts at all, or at least none with that consciousness which remarks our waking thoughts, —I say, in all these cases, our consciousness being interrupted, and we losing the sight of our past selves, doubts are raised whether we are the same thinking thing, i.e., the same *substance* or no. Which, however reasonable or unreasonable, concerns not *personal* identity at all. The question being what makes the same person; and not whether it be the same identical substance, which always thinks in the same person, which, in this case, matters not at all: different substances, by the same consciousness (where they do partake in it) being united into one person, as well as different bodies by the same life are united into one animal, whose identity is preserved in that change of substances by the unity of one continued life. For, it being the same consciousness that makes a man be himself to himself, personal identity depends on that only, whether it be annexed solely to one individual substance, or can be continued in a succession of several substances. For as far as any intelligent being *can* repeat the idea of any past action with the same consciousness it had of it at first, and with the same consciousness it has of any present action; so far it is the same personal self. For it is by the consciousness it has of its present thoughts and actions, that it is *self to itself* now, and so will be the same self, as far as the same consciousness can extend to actions past or to come: and would be by distance of time, or change of substance, no more two persons, than a man be two men by wearing other clothes to-day than he did yesterday, with a long or a short sleep between: the same consciousness uniting those distant actions into the same person, whatever substances contributed to their production.

11. *Personal identity in change of substance*. That this is so, we have some kind of evidence in our very bodies, all whose particles, whilst vitally united to this same thinking conscious self, so that *we feel* when they are touched, and are affected by, and conscious of good or harm that happens to them, as a part of ourselves; i.e., of our thinking conscious self. Thus, the limbs of his body are to

every one a part of himself; he sympathizes and is concerned for them. Cut off a hand, and thereby separate it from that consciousness he had of its heat, cold, and other affections, and it is then no longer a part of that which is himself, any more than the remotest part of matter. Thus, we see the *substance* whereof personal self consisted at one time may be varied at another, without the change of personal identity; there being no question about the same person, though the limbs which but now were a part of it, be cut off.

12. *Personality in change of substance.* But the question is, Whether if the same substance which thinks be changed, it can be the same person; or, remaining the same, it can be different persons?

And to this I answer: First, This can be no question at all to those who place thought in a purely material animal constitution, void of an immaterial substance. For, whether their supposition be true or no, it is plain they conceive personal identity preserved in something else than identity of substance; as animal identity is preserved in identity of life, and not of substance. And therefore those who place thinking in an immaterial substance only, before they can come to deal with these men, must show why personal identity cannot be preserved in the change of immaterial substances, or variety of particular immaterial substances, as well as animal identity is preserved in the change of material substances, or variety of particular bodies: unless they will say, it is one immaterial spirit that makes the same life in brutes, as it is one immaterial spirit that makes the same person in men; which the Cartesians at least will not admit, for fear of making brutes thinking things too.

13. *Whether in change of thinking substances there can be one person.* But next, as to the first part of the question, Whether, if the same thinking substance (supposing immaterial substances only to think) be changed, it can be the same person? I answer, that cannot be resolved but by those who know what kind of substances they are that do think; and whether the consciousness of past actions can be transferred from one thinking substance to another. I grant were the same consciousness the same individual action it could not: but it being a present representation of a past action, why it may not be possible, that that may be represented to the mind to have been which really never was,

will remain to be shown. And therefore how far the consciousness of past actions is annexed to any individual agent, so that another cannot possibly have it, will be hard for us to determine, till we know what kind of action it is that cannot be done without a reflex act of perception accompanying it, and how performed by thinking substances, who cannot think without being conscious of it. But that which we call the same consciousness, not being the same individual act, why one intellectual substance may not have represented to it, as done by itself, what *it* never did, and was perhaps done by some other agent— why, I say, such a representation may not possibly be without reality of matter of fact, as well as several representations in dreams are, which yet whilst dreaming we take for true—will be difficult to conclude from the nature of things. And that it never is so, will by us, till we have clearer views of the nature of thinking substances, be best resolved into the goodness of God; who, as far as the happiness or misery of any of his sensible creatures is concerned in it, will not, by a fatal error of theirs, transfer from one to another that consciousness which draws reward or punishment with it. How far this may be an argument against those who would place thinking in a system of fleeting animal spirits, I leave to be considered. But yet, to return to the question before us, it must be allowed, that, if the same consciousness (which, as has been shown, is quite a different thing from the same numerical figure or motion in body) can be transferred from one thinking substance to another, it will be possible that two thinking substances may make but one person. For the same consciousness being preserved, whether in the same or different substances, the personal identity is preserved.

14. *Whether, the same immaterial substance remaining, there can be two persons.* As to the second part of the question, Whether the same immaterial substance remaining, there may be two distinct persons; which question seems to me to be built on this,—Whether the same immaterial being, being conscious of the action of its past duration, may be wholly stripped of all the consciousness of its past existence, and lose it beyond the power of ever retrieving it again: and so as it were beginning a new account from a new period, have a consciousness that *cannot* reach beyond this new

state. All those who hold pre-existence are evidently of this mind; since they allow the soul to have no remaining consciousness of what it did in that pre-existent state, either wholly separate from body, or informing any other body; and if they should not, it is plain experience would be against them. So that personal identity, reaching no further than consciousness reaches, a preexistent spirit not having continued so many ages in a state of silence, must needs make different persons. Suppose a Christian Platonist or a Pythagorean should, upon God's having ended all his works of creation the seventh day, think his soul hath existed ever since; and should imagine it has revolved in several human bodies; as I once met with one, who was persuaded his had been the *soul* of Socrates (how reasonably I will not dispute; this I know, that in the post he filled, which was no inconsiderable one, he passed for a very rational man, and the press has shown that he wanted not parts of learning;)— would any one say, that he, being not conscious of any of Socrates' actions or thoughts, could be the same *person* with Socrates? Let any one reflect upon himself, and conclude that he has in himself an immaterial spirit, which is that which thinks in him, and, in the constant change of his body keeps him the same: and is that which he calls *himself*: let him also suppose it to be the same soul that was in Nestor or Thersites, at the siege of Troy (for souls being, as far as we know anything of them, in their nature indifferent to any parcel of matter, the supposition has no apparent absurdity in it), which it may have been, as well as it is now the soul of any other man: but he now having no consciousness of any of the actions either of Nestor or Thersites, does or can he conceive himself the same person with either of them? Can he be concerned in either of their actions? attribute them to himself, or think them his own, more than the actions of any other men that ever existed? So that this consciousness, not reaching to any of the actions of either of those men, he is no more one *self* with either of them than if the soul or immaterial spirit that now informs him had been created, and began to exist, when it began to inform his present body; though it were never so true, that the same *spirit* that informed Nestor's or Thersites' body were numerically the same that now informs his. For, this would no more make him the same person with Nestor, than if some of the particles of matter that were once a part of Nestor were now a part of this man; the same immaterial substance, without the same consciousness, no more making the same person, by being united to any body, than the same particle of matter, without consciousness, united to any body, makes the same person. But let him once find himself conscious of any of the actions of Nestor, he then finds himself the same person with Nestor.

15. *The body, as well as the soul, goes to the making of a man.* And thus may be able, without any difficulty, to conceive the same person at the resurrection, though in a body not exactly in make or parts the same which he had here,—the same consciousness going along with the soul that inhabits it. But yet the soul alone, in the change of bodies, would scarce to any one but to him that makes the soul the man, be enough to make the same man. For should the soul of a prince, carrying with it the consciousness of the prince's past life, enter and inform the body of a cobbler, as soon as deserted by his own soul, every one sees he would be the same *person* with the prince, accountable only for the prince's actions: but who would say it was the same *man*? The body too goes to the making the man, and would, I guess, to everybody determine the man in this case, wherein the soul, with all its princely thoughts about it, would not make another man: but he would be the same cobbler to every one besides himself. I know that, in the ordinary way of speaking, the same person, and the same man, stand for one and the same thing. And indeed every one will always have a liberty to speak as he pleases, and to apply what articulate sounds to what ideas he thinks fit, and change them as often as he pleases. But yet, when we will inquire what makes the same *spirit, man,* or *person,* we must fix the ideas of spirit, man, or person in our minds; and having resolved with ourselves what we mean by them, it will not be hard to determine, in either of them, or the like, when it is the same, and when not.

16. *Consciousness alone unites actions into the same person.* But though the same immaterial substance or soul does not alone, wherever it be, and in whatsoever state, make the same *man*; yet it is plain, consciousness, as far as ever it can be extended— should it be to ages past—unites existences and actions very remote in time into the same *person,* as well as it does the existences and actions of the

immediately preceding moment: so that whatever has the consciousness of present and past actions, is the same person to whom they both belong. Had I the same consciousness that I saw the ark and Noah's flood, as that I saw an overflowing of the Thames last winter, or as that I write now, I could no more doubt that I who write this now, that saw the Thames overflowed last winter, and that viewed the flood at the general deluge, was the same *self*,—place that self in what *substance* you please—than that I who write this am the same *myself* now whilst I write (whether I consist of all the same substance, material or immaterial, or no) that I was yesterday. For as to this point of being the same self, it matters not whether this present self be made up of the same or other substances—I being as much concerned, and as justly accountable for any action that was done a thousand years since, appropriated to me now by this self-consciousness, as I am for what I did the last moment.

17. *Self depends on consciousness, not on substance.* *Self* is that conscious thinking thing,—whatever substance made up of, (whether spiritual or material, simple or compounded, it matters not)—which is sensible or conscious of pleasure and pain, capable of happiness or misery, and so is concerned for itself, as far as that consciousness extends. Thus every one finds that, whilst comprehended under that consciousness, the little finger is as much a part of himself as what is most so. Upon separation of this little finger, should this consciousness go along with the little finger, and leave the rest of the body, it is evident the little finger would be the person, the same person; and self then would have nothing to do with the rest of the body. As in this case it is the consciousness that goes along with the substance, when one part is separate from another, which makes the same person, and constitutes this inseparable self: so it is in reference to substances remote in time. That with which the consciousness of this present thinking thing *can* join itself, makes the same person, and is one self with it, and with nothing else; and so attributes to itself, and owns all the actions of that thing, as its own, as far as that consciousness reaches, and no further; as every one who reflects will perceive.

18. *Persons, not substances, the objects of reward and punishment.* In this personal identity is founded all the right and justice of reward and punishment; happiness and misery being that for which every one is concerned for *himself*, and not mattering what becomes of any *substance*, not joined to, or affected with that consciousness. For, as it is evident in the instance I gave but now, if the consciousness went along with the little finger when it was cut off, that would be the same self which was concerned for the whole body yesterday, as making part of itself, whose actions then it cannot but admit as its own now. Though, if the same body should still live, and immediately from the separation of the little finger have its own peculiar consciousness, whereof the little finger knew nothing, it would not at all be concerned for it, as a part of itself, or could own any of its actions, or have any of them imputed to him.

19. *Which shows wherein personal identity consists.* This may show us wherein personal identity consists: not in the identity of substance, but, as I have said, in the identity of consciousness, wherein if Socrates and the present mayor of Queinborough agree, they are the same person: if the same Socrates waking and sleeping do not partake of the same consciousness, Socrates waking and sleeping is not the same person. And to punish Socrates waking for what sleeping Socrates thought, and waking Socrates was never conscious of, would be no more of right, than to punish one twin for what his brother-twin did, whereof he knew nothing, because their outsides were so like, that they could not be distinguished; for such twins have been seen.

DISCUSSION QUESTIONS

1. Locke says that it is "impossible for any one to perceive without *perceiving* that he does perceive." Do you agree with him? Why or why not?

2. What does Locke mean by "consciousness"? What is its relationship to and difference from both perceiving and thinking?

3. Locke says that "*Self* is that conscious thinking thing—whatever substance made of, (whether spiritual or material, simple or compounded, it matters not)—which is sensible or conscious of pleasure and pain, capable of happiness or misery, and so is concerned for itself, as far as that consciousness extends." If self is not

delimited by soul or body, and is only delimited by consciousness, how far can and does consciousness, and therefore the self, extend?

4.   Does anything in Locke's notion of personal identity and consciousness render it impossible for you to be the same person as Socrates? On Locke's account, is it at least *possible* for you to

have the same consciousness as Socrates? Is this a shortcoming of his notion of personal identity? Discuss

5.   Do you think animals,— for example, dogs— have what Locke describes as "consciousness"? Do animals have what Locke calls a "self"? Is "animal" identity different from "personal" identity? Defend your response.

JOSEPH BUTLER

OF PERSONAL IDENTITY

I n this reading, Joseph Butler argues for personal identity. However, he distinguishes his own defense of personal identity from that of Locke's, which he contends is vulnerable to a serious line of doubt.

According to Butler, Locke defines a person as "a thinking intelligent being," and personal identity as "the sameness of a rational being." "The question then is," writes Butler, "whether the same person be the same substance; which needs no answer [for Locke], because being and substance, in this place, stand for the same idea." Nevertheless, according to Butler, the relationship that Locke establishes between consciousness and personal identity makes it doubtful that the same person is the same substance because no two acts of consciousness are identical.

Butler avoids the doubt raised Locke's position by clarifying the relationship between consciousness and personal identity. For Butler, what is important is not the identity of successive acts of consciousness, but the identity of the object of which we are conscious: the living agent, self, or person. Thus, contends Butler, even "though the successive consciousnesses which we have of our own existence are not the same," they are nevertheless "consciousnesses of one and the same thing or object; of the same person, self, or living agent." For Butler, we are as "certain that we are the same agents, living beings, or substances, now, which we were as far back as our remembrance reaches" as we are of the identity of any other thing.

Joseph Butler (1692–1752), a British bishop and philosopher, was primarily concerned with natural theology and moral philosophy. He was born in Wantage, Berkshire, educated at Oxford University, and became Bishop of Bristol in 1738, and Bishop of Durham in 1750. David Hume said that Butler was one of those "who have begun to put the science of man on a new footing, and have engaged the attention, and excited the curiosity of the public." His writings include *Several Letters to the Reverend Dr. Clarke* (1716), *Fifteen Sermons Preached at the Rolls Chapel* (1726; six sermons were added in the 1749 edition), *Analogy of Religion, Natural and Revealed, to the Constitution and Nature* (1736), and *Charge Delivered to the Clergy* (1751). Butler closed his *Analogy of Religion* with two short "dissertations," the first of which, "Of Personal Identity," appears below.

Whether we are to live in a future state, as it is the most important question which can possibly be asked, so it is the most intelligible one which can

be expressed in language. Yet strange perplexities have been raised about the meaning of that identity, or sameness of person, which is implied in the notion of our living now and hereafter, or in any two successive moments. And the solution of these difficulties hath been stranger than the difficulties themselves. For, personal identity has been explained so by some, as to render the inquiry concerning a future life of no consequence at all to us, the persons who are making it. And though few men can be misled by such subtleties, yet it may be proper a little to consider them.

Now, when it is asked wherein personal identity consists, the answer should be the same as if it were asked, wherein consists similitude or equality; that all attempts to define, would but perplex it. Yet there is no difficulty at all in ascertaining the idea. For as, upon two triangles being compared or viewed together, there arises to the mind the idea of similitude; or upon twice two and four, the idea of equality; so likewise, upon comparing the consciousness of one's self, or one's own existence in any two moments, there as immediately arises to the mind the idea of personal identity. And as the two former comparisons not only give the idea of similitude and equality, but also shows us, that two triangles are like, and twice two and four are equal; so the latter comparison not only gives us the idea of personal identity but also shows us the identity of ourselves in those two moments; the present, suppose, and that immediately past; or the present, and that a month, a year, or twenty years past. Or, in other words, by reflecting upon that which is myself now, and that which was myself twenty years ago, I discern they are not two, but one and the same self.

But though consciousness of what is past does thus ascertain our personal identity to ourselves, yet, to say that it makes personal identity, or is necessary to our being the same persons, is to say, that a person has not existed a single moment, nor done one action, but what he can remember; indeed none but what he reflects upon. And one should really think it self-evident, that consciousness of personal identity presupposes, and therefore cannot constitute, personal identity, any more than knowledge, in any other case, can constitute truth, which it presupposes.

This wonderful mistake may possibly have arisen from hence, that to be endued with consciousness, is inseparable from the idea of a person, or intelligent being. For, this might be expressed inaccurately thus—that consciousness makes personality; and from hence it might be concluded to make personal identity. But though present consciousness of what we at present do and feel, is necessary to our being the persons we now are; yet present consciousness of past actions, or feelings, is not necessary to our being the same persons who performed those actions, or had those feelings.

The inquiry, what makes vegetables the same in the common acceptation of the word, does not appear to have any relation to this of personal identity; because the word *same,* when applied to them and to persons, is not only applied to different subjects, but it is also used in different senses. For when a man swears to the same tree, as having stood fifty years in the same place, he means only the same as to all the purposes of property and uses of common life, and not that the tree has been all that time the same in the strict philosophical sense of the word. For he does not know whether any one particle of the present tree be the same with any one particle of the tree which stood in the same place fifty years ago. And if they have not one common particle of matter, they cannot be the same tree, in the proper philosophic sense of the word *same;* it being evidently a contradiction in terms, to say they are, when no part of their substance, and no one of their properties, is the same; no part of their substance, by the supposition; no one of their properties, because it is allowed that the same property cannot be transferred from one substance to another. And therefore, when we say the identity or sameness of a plant consists in a continuation of the same life communicated under the same organization, to a number of particles of matter, whether the same or not, the word *same,* when applied to life and to organization, cannot possibly be understood to signify, what it signifies in this very sentence, when applied to matter. In a loose and popular sense, then, the life, and the organization, and the plant, are justly said to be the same, notwithstanding the perpetual change of the parts. But in a strict and philosophical manner of speech, no man, no being, no mode of being, nor any thing, can be the same with that, with which it hath indeed nothing the same. Now, sameness is used in this latter sense when applied to persons. The identity of these, therefore, cannot subsist with diversity of substance.

The thing here considered, and demonstratively, as I think, determined, is proposed by Mr. Locke in these words, *Whether it,* i.e., the same self or person, *be the same identical substance?* And he has suggested what is a much better answer to the question than that which he give it in form. For he defines person, *a thinking intelligent being,* etc. and personal identity *the sameness of a rational being.* The question then is, whether the same rational being is the same substance; which needs no answer, because being and substance, in this place, stand for the same idea. The ground of the doubt, whether the same person be the same substance, is said to be this; that the consciousness of our own existence in youth and in old age, or in any two joint successive moments, is not *the same individual action,* i.e., not the same consciousness, but different successive consciousnesses. Now it is strange that this should have occasioned such perplexities. For it is surely conceivable, that a person may have a capacity of knowing some object or other to be the same now, which it was when he contemplated it formerly; yet, in this case, where, by the supposition, the object is perceived to be the same, the perception of it in any two moments cannot be one and the same perception. And thus, though the successive consciousnesses which we have of our own existence are not the same, yet are they consciousnesses of one and the same thing or object; of the same person, self, or living agent. The person, of whose existence the consciousness is felt now, and was felt an hour or a year ago, is discerned to be, not two persons, but one and the same person; and therefore is one and the same.

Mr. Locke's observations upon this subject appear hasty; and he seems to profess himself dissatisfied with suppositions, which he has made relating to it. But some of those hasty observations have been carried to a strange length by others; whose notion, when traced and examined to the bottom, amounts, I think, to this: "That personality is not a permanent, but a transient thing: that it lives and dies, begins and ends, continually: that no one can any more remain one and the same person two moments together, than two successive moments can be one and the same moment: that our substance is indeed continually changing; but whether this be so or not, is, it seems, nothing to the purpose; since it is not substance, but consciousness alone, which constitutes personality; which consciousness, being successive, cannot be the same in any two moments, nor consequently the personality constituted by it." And from hence it must follow, that it is a fallacy upon ourselves, to charge our present selves with any thing we did, or to imagine our present selves interested in any thing which befell us yesterday, or that our present self will be interested in what will befall us tomorrow; since our present self is not, in reality, the same with the self of yesterday, but another like self or person coming in its room, and mistaken for it; to which another self will succeed tomorrow. This, I say, must follow: for if the self or person of today, and that of tomorrow, are not the same, but only like persons, the person of today is really no more interested in what will befall the person of tomorrow, than in what will befall any other person. It may be thought, perhaps, that this is not a just representation of the opinion we are speaking of; because those who maintain it allow, that a person is the same as far back as his remembrance reaches. And, indeed, they do use the words, *identity* and *same* person. Nor will language permit these words to be laid aside: since if they were, there must be, I know not what, ridiculous periphrasis substituted in the room of them. But they cannot, consistently with themselves, mean, that the person is really the same. For it is self-evident, that the personality cannot be really the same. For it is self-evident, that the personality cannot be really the same, if, as they expressly assert, that in which it consists is not the same. And as, consistently with themselves, they cannot, so, I think, it appears they do not, mean, that the person is *really* the same, but only that he is so in a fictitious sense: in such a sense only as they assert; for this they do assert, that any number of persons whatever may be the same person. The bare unfolding this notion, and laying it thus naked and open, seems the best confutation of it. However, since great stress is said to be put upon it, I add the following things:

First, This notion is absolutely contradictory to that certain conviction, which necessarily, and every moment, rises within us, when we turn our thoughts upon ourselves; when we reflect upon what is past, and look forward upon what is to come. All imagination of a daily change of that living agent which each man calls himself, for another, or of any such change throughout our whole present life, is entirely borne down by our natural sense of things. Nor is it possible for a person in his wits to alter his conduct, with regard to his health or affairs, from a suspicion, that though he should live tomorrow, he should not, however, be the same person he is today. And yet, if it be reasonable to act, with respect to a future life, upon this notion, that personality is transient; it is reasonable to act upon it, with respect to the present. Here then is a notion equally applicable to religion and to our temporal concerns; and every one sees and feels the inexpressible absurdity of it in the latter case. If, therefore, any can take up with it in the former, this cannot proceed from the reason of the thing, but must be owing to an inward unfairness, and secret corruption of heart.

Secondly, It is not an idea, or abstract notion, or quality, but a being only which is capable of life and action, of happiness and misery. Now all beings confessedly continue the same, during the whole time of their existence. Consider then a living being now existing, and which has existed for any time alive: this living being must have done and suffered and enjoyed, what it has done and suffered and enjoyed formerly (this living being, I say, and not another), as really as it does and suffers and enjoys, what it does and suffers and enjoys this instant. All these successive actions, enjoyments, and sufferings, are actions, enjoyments, and sufferings, of the same living being. And they are so, prior to all consideration of its remembering or forgetting; since remembering or forgetting can make no alteration in the truth of past matter of fact. And suppose this being endued with limited powers of knowledge and memory, there is no more difficulty in conceiving it to have a power of knowing itself to be the same living being which it was some time ago, of remembering some of its actions, sufferings, and enjoyments, and forgetting others, than in conceiving it to know, or remember, or forget any thing else.

Thirdly, Every person is conscious, that he is now the same person or self he was, as far back as his remembrance reaches; since, when any one reflects upon a past action of his own, he is just as certain of the person who did that action, namely himself, the person who now reflects upon it, as he is certain that the action was at all done. Nay, very often a person's assurance of an action having been done, of which he is absolutely assured, arises wholly from the consciousness that he himself did it. And this he, person, or self, must either be a substance, or the property of some substance. If he, if person, be a substance; then consciousness that he is the same person, is consciousness that he is the same substance. If the person, or he, be the property of a substance; still consciousness that he is the same property, is as certain a proof that his substance remains the same, as consciousness the he remains the same substance would be; since the same property cannot be transferred from one substance to another.

But though we are thus certain that we are the same agents, living beings, or substances, now, which we were as far back as our remembrance reaches; yet it is asked, whether we may not possibly be deceived in it? And this question may be asked at the end of any demonstration whatever; because it is a question concerning the truth of perception by memory. And he who can doubt, whether perception by memory can in this case be depended upon, may doubt also, whether perception by deduction and reasoning, which also include memory, or, indeed, whether intuitive perception can. Here then we can go no farther. For it is ridiculous to attempt to prove the truth of those perceptions, whose truth we can no otherwise prove, than by other perceptions of exactly the same kind with them, and which there is just the same ground to suspect; or to attempt to prove the truth of our faculties, which can no otherwise be proved, than by the use or means of those very suspected faculties themselves.

DISCUSSION QUESTIONS

1. Do you think that personality is a permanent or a transient thing? Defend your position.

2. What problem does Butler find in Locke's notion of personal identity? How might Locke respond to this problem?

3. What is the relationship between acts of consciousness and personal identity? Compare your own position with that of Butler.

4. Butler contends that we are as "certain that we are the same agents, living beings, or substances, now, which we were as far back as our remembrance reaches" as we are of the identity of any other thing. Do you agree with him? Why or why not?

5. Compare and contrast Locke's and Butler's respective positions on personal identity. Discuss the strengths and weaknesses of each position. Which do you prefer and why?

THOMAS REID

OF IDENTITY

Like John Locke and Joseph Butler, Thomas Reid argues for personal identity. However, the notion of personal identity proposed by Reid is distinct from the notions of Locke and Butler. Reid argues that a person is indivisible and permanent, and that the identity of a person is a perfect identity. For him, identity "supposes an uninterrupted continuance of existence." Therefore, identity cannot "be applied to our pains, our pleasures, our thoughts, or any operation of our minds" because their existence is interrupted. While the pain that is felt today, for example, may be *similar* to the pain we felt yesterday, it is not the same individual pain that was felt yesterday.

According to Reid, a person is something that is not divisible and that does not consist of parts: it "is what Leibnitz [sic] calls a *monad.*" In Greek, *monad* means "unit," and as used by Reid and Leibniz (who was introduced in Chapter 1) refers to an irreducible ontological unit.

Given then his notions of identity and person, personal identity for Reid "implies the continued existence of that indivisible thing which I call *myself.*" For him, even though this thing "which I call *myself*" thinks, acts, and feels, "I am not thought, I am not action, I am not feeling; I am something that thinks, and acts, and suffers." While our thought, actions, and feelings change all the time, "that *self,* or *I,* to which they belong, is permanent." Writes Reid, "The identity of a person is a perfect identity: wherever it is real, it admits of no degrees; and it is impossible that a person should be in part the same, and in part different; because a person is a *monad,* and is not divisible into parts." For him, "no man of a sound mind ever doubted his own identity, as he distinctly remembered."

Thomas Reid (1710–1796), a Scottish philosopher and Presbyterian minister, is the founder of the Scottish school of common sense philosophy. Reid, born at Strachan in Kincardinshire, Scotland, was educated at the University of Aberdeen, and following graduation was appointed a librarian at the university. He resigned his librarian post in 1736, and in 1737 entered the ministry. In 1752, though he had only one published paper, he was appointed professor of philosophy at Kings College in Aberdeen, where he taught mathematics, logic, ethics, and physics. While at Kings College, he founded the Aberdeen Philosophical Society, where he presented much of the material that would later be published in his *Inquiry into the Human Mind on the Principles of Common Sense* (1764). Before publishing his *Inquiry,* Reid asked David Hume to read it. Hume commented that "parsons" should leave philosophical matters to philosophers, and mind their own business. In 1764, Reid succeeded the Scottish moral philosopher and economist Adam Smith (1723–1790) as professor of moral philosophy at the University of Glasgow. In addition to his *Inquiry,* his other major works are

Essays on the Intellectual Powers of Man (1785), and *Essays on the Active Powers of Man* (1788). The following is a selection from "Essay Three: Of Memory," from *Essays on the Intellectual Powers of Man*.

The conviction which every man has of his identity, as far back as his memory reaches, needs no aid of philosophy to strengthen it; and no philosophy can weaken it, without first producing some degree of insanity.

The philosopher, however, may very properly consider this conviction as a phenomenon of human nature worthy of his attention. If he can discover its cause, an addition is made to his stock of knowledge; if not, it must be held as a part of our original constitution, or an effect of that constitution produced in a manner unknown to us.

We may observe, first of all, that this conviction is indispensably necessary to all exercise of reason. The operations of reason, whether in action or in speculation, are made up of successive parts. The antecedent are the foundation of the consequent, and, without the conviction that the antecedent have been seen or done by me, I could have no reason to proceed to the consequent, in any speculation, or in any active project whatever.

There can be no memory of what is past without the conviction that we existed at the time remembered. There may be good arguments to convince me that I existed before the earliest thing I can remember; but to suppose that my memory reaches a moment farther back than my belief and conviction of my existence, is a contradiction.

The moment a man loses this conviction, as if he had drunk the water of Lethe, past things are done away; and, in his own belief, he then begins to exist. Whatever was thought, or said, or done, or suffered before that period, may belong to some other person; but he can never impute it to himself, or take any subsequent step that supposes it to be his doing.

From this it is evident that we must have the conviction of our own continued existence and identity, as soon as we are capable of thinking or doing anything, on account of what we have thought, or done, or suffered before; that is, as soon as we are reasonable creatures.

That we may form as distinct a notion as we are able of this phenomenon of the human mind, it is proper to consider what is meant by identity in general, what by our own personal identity, and how we are led into that invincible belief and conviction which every man has of his own personal identity, as far as his memory reaches.

Identity in general I take to be a relation between a thing which is known to exist at one time, and a thing which is known to have existed at another time. If you ask whether they are one and the same, or two different things, every man of common sense understands the meaning of your question perfectly. Whence we may infer with certainty, that every man of common sense has a clear and distinct notion of identity.

If you ask a definition of identity, I confess I can give none; it is too simple a notion to admit of logical definition: I can say it is a relation, but I cannot find words to express the specific difference between this and other relations, though I am in no danger of confounding it with any other. I can say that diversity is a contrary relation, and that similitude and dissimilitude are another couple of contrary relations, which every man easily distinguishes in his conception from identity and diversity.

I see evidently that identity supposes an uninterrupted continuance of existence. That which has ceased to exist cannot be the same with that which afterwards begins to exist; for this would be to suppose a being to exist after it ceased to exist, and to have had existence before it was produced, which are manifest contradictions. Continued uninterrupted existence is therefore necessarily implied in identity.

Hence we may infer, that identity cannot, in its proper sense, be applied to our pains, our pleasures, our thoughts, or any operation of our minds. The pain felt this day is not the same individual pain which I felt yesterday, though they may be *similar* in kind and degree, and have the same cause. The same may be said of every feeling, and of every operation of mind. They are all successive in their nature, like time itself, no two moments of which can be the same moment.

It is otherwise with the parts of absolute space. They always are, and were, and will be the same. So far, I think, we proceed upon clear ground in fixing the notion of identity in general.

It is perhaps more difficult to ascertain with precision the meaning of personality; but it is not necessary in the present subject: it is sufficient for our purpose to observe, that all mankind place their personality in something that cannot be divided, or consist of parts.

A part of a person is a manifest absurdity. When a man loses his estate, his health, his strength, he is still the same person, and has lost nothing of his personality. If he has a leg or an arm cut off, he is the same person he was before. The amputated member is no part of his person, otherwise it would have a right to a part of his estate, and be liable for a part of his engagements. It would be entitled to a share of his merit and demerit, which is manifestly absurd. A person is something indivisible, and is what Leibnitz calls a *monad*.

My personal identity, therefore, implies the continued existence of that indivisible thing which I call *myself*. Whatever this self may be, it is something which thinks, and deliberates, and resolves, and acts, and suffers. I am not thought, I am not action, I am not feeling; I am something that thinks, and acts, and suffers. My thoughts, and actions, and feelings, change every moment; they have no continued, but a successive, existence; but that *self*, or *I*, to which they belong, is permanent, and has the same relation to all the succeeding thoughts, actions, and feelings which I call mine.

Such are the notions that I have of my personal identity. But perhaps it may be said, this may all be fancy without reality. How do you know—what evidence have you—that there is such a permanent self which has a claim to all the thoughts, actions, and feelings which you call yours?

To this I answer, that the proper evidence I have of all this is remembrance. I remember that twenty years ago I conversed with such a person; I remember several things that passed in that conversation: my memory testifies, not only that this was done, but that it was done by me who now remember it. If it was done by me, I must have existed at that time, and continued to exist from that

time to the present: if the identical person whom I call myself had not a part in that conversation, my memory is fallacious; it gives a distinct and positive testimony of what is not true. Every man in his senses believes what he distinctly remembers, and every thing he remembers convinces him that he existed at the time remembered.

Although memory gives the most irresistible evidence of my being the identical person that did such a thing, at such a time, I may have other good evidence of things which befell me, and which I do not remember: I know who bare me, and suckled me, but I do not remember these events.

It may here be observed (though the observation would have been unnecessary, if some great philosophers had not contradicted it), that it is not my remembering any action of mine that makes me to be the person who did it. This remembrance makes me to know assuredly that I did it; but I might have done it, though I did not remember it. That relation to me, which is expressed by saying that I did it, would be the same, though I had not the least remembrance of it. To say that my remembering that I did such a thing, or, as some choose to express it, my being conscious that I did it, makes me to have done it, appears to me as great an absurdity as it would be to say, that my belief that the world was created made it to be created.

When we pass judgment on the identity of other persons than ourselves, we proceed upon other grounds, and determine from a variety of circumstances, which sometimes produce the firmest assurance, and sometimes leave room for doubt. The identity of persons has often furnished matter of serious litigation before tribunals of justice. But no man of a sound mind ever doubted of his own identity, as far as he distinctly remembered.

The identity of a person is a perfect identity: wherever it is real, it admits of no degrees; and it is impossible that a person should be in part the same, and in part different; because a person is a *monad*, and is not divisible into parts. The evidence of identity in other persons than ourselves does indeed admit of all degrees, from what we account certainty, to the least degree of probability. But still it is true, that the same person is perfectly the same, and cannot be so in part, or is some degree only.

For this cause, I have first considered personal identity, as that which is perfect in its kind, and the natural measure of that which is imperfect.

We probably at first derive our notion of identity from that natural conviction which every man has from the dawn of reason of his own identity and continued existence. The operations of our minds are all successive, and have no continued existence. But the thinking being has a continued existence, and we have an invincible belief, that it remains the same when all its thoughts and operations change.

Our judgments of the identity of objects of sense seem to be formed much upon the same grounds as our judgments of the identity of other persons than ourselves.

Wherever we observe great similarity, we are apt to presume identity, if no reason appears to the contrary. Two objects ever so like, when they are perceived at the same time, cannot be the same; but if they are presented to our senses at different times, we are apt to think them the same, merely from their similarity.

Whether this be a natural prejudice, or from whatever cause it proceeds, it certainly appears in children from infancy; and when we grow up, it is confirmed in most instances by experience: for we rarely find two individuals of the same species that are not distinguishable by obvious differences.

A man challenges a thief whom he finds in possession of his horse or his watch, only on similarity. When the watchmaker swears that he sold this watch to such a person, his testimony is grounded on similarity. The testimony of witnesses to the identity of a person is commonly grounded on no other evidence.

Thus it appears, that the evidence we have of our own identity, as far back as we remember, is totally of a different kind from the evidence we have of the identity of other persons, or of objects of sense. The first is grounded on memory, and gives undoubted certainty. The last is grounded on similarity, and on other circumstances, which in many cases are not so decisive as to leave no room for doubt.

It may likewise be observed, that the identity of objects of sense is never perfect. All bodies, as they consist of innumerable parts that may be disjoined from them by a great variety of causes, are subject to continual changes of their substance, increasing, diminishing, changing insensibly. When such alterations are gradual, because language could not afford a different name for every different state of such a changeable being, it retains the same name, and is considered as the same thing. Thus we say of an old regiment, that it did such a thing a century ago, though there now is not a man alive who then belonged to it. We say a tree is the same in the seed-bed and in the forest. A ship of war, which has successively changed her anchors, her tackle, her sails, her masts, her planks, and her timbers, while she keeps the same name, is the same.

The identity, therefore, which we ascribe to bodies, whether natural or artificial, is not perfect identity; it is rather something which, for the conveniency of speech, we call identity. It admits of a great change of the subject, providing the change be gradual; sometimes, even of a total change. And the changes which in common language are made consistent with identity differ from those that are thought to destroy it, not in kind, but in number and degree. It has no fixed nature when applied to bodies; and questions about the identity of a body are very often questions about words. But identity, when applied to persons, has no ambiguity, and admits not of degrees, or of more and less. It is the foundation of all rights and obligations, and of all accountableness; and the notion of it is fixed and precise. . . .

In a long chapter upon Identity and Diversity, Mr. Locke has made many ingenious and just observations, and some which I think cannot be defended. I shall only take notice of the account he gives of our own personal identity. His doctrine upon this subject has been censured by Bishop Butler, in a short essay subjoined to his *Analogy,* with whose sentiments I perfectly agree. . . .

This doctrine [Locke's] has some strange consequences, which the author was aware of. Such as, that if the same consciousness can be transferred from one intelligent being to another, which he thinks we cannot show to be impossible, *then two or twenty intelligent beings may be the same person.* And if the intelligent being may lose the consciousness of the actions done by him, which surely is possible, then he is not the person that did those actions; so that *one intelligent being may be two or twenty different persons,* if he shall so often lose the consciousness of his former actions. . . .

DISCUSSION QUESTIONS

1. According to Reid, is personality a permanent or a transient thing? Compare his position to those of Locke and Butler. Which do you prefer and why?

2. What is Reid's notion of personal identity? Compare his notion of personal identity to the positions of Locke and Butler. Which do you prefer and why?

3. For Reid, what is the relationship between acts of consciousness and personal identity? Compare Reid's position with those of Locke and Butler.

4. Reid writes, "The conviction which every man has of his identity, as far back as his memory reaches, needs no aid of philosophy to strengthen it; and no philosophy can weaken it, without first producing some degree of insanity." What does Reid mean? Do you agree with him? Why or why not?

5. Reid states, "A part of a person is a manifest absurdity." What is his argument? Is it a valid and sound argument? Why or why not?

Regarding Henry
[USA 1991] 1 hour, 48 minutes
Directed by Mike Nichols

Henry Turner (Harrison Ford), a rich, successful, and unscrupulous lawyer, ignores his daughter and is about to divorce his wife. One evening, Henry is shot in the head and the chest. The lack of oxygen flowing to his brain results in a loss of speech and physical coordination as well as the loss of his memory. The doctors are not sure whether he will regain his speech, physical coordination, or memory. However, after working with Bradley (Bill Nunn), a physical therapist, Henry gradually regains some of his speech and physical coordination. Still, none of the memories of his past come back to him: nothing about his childhood, his job, or his family. The only thing he can remember about his wife is the smell of her hair, and he remembers nothing about his daughter. The only other memories from his past that remain are the smell of his house and the color of its carpet. After his release from the rehabilitation center, he and his wife and daughter gradually forge new relationships with one another. He and his wife, Sarah (Annette Bening), fall in love again, and he establishes a strong relationship with his daughter, who helps him relearn how to read, among other things. When Henry finally realizes that he was an unscrupulous lawyer who cheated on his wife and neglected his daughter, he gives up trying to reestablish his former identity. He quits his job at the law firm, takes his daughter out of boarding school, and strives to continue to forge his new identity.

DISCUSSION QUESTIONS

1. Locke claims that we are identical with whatever actions we remember as our own. If we, like Henry, cannot remember anything of our past lives, does this mean that we are not the same person that we were in that past life?

2. Henry cannot remember anything about his life before he was shot. Gradually, he realizes that he cheated and lied to people, both as a lawyer and as a husband. Is the postaccident Henry morally responsible for the actions of the preaccident Henry? Why or why not?

3. Henry says, "I thought I could go back to my life but I don't like who I was. I don't fit in." Can a person simply reject the past and, in doing so, become a new person? Must the rejection also include "forgetting" about that past entirely, or is this unnecessary? What would Locke say?

4. Are the stories Henry is told about his past still his "memories" even if he does not remember them? Do you think it is possible to "create" memories based on accounts from others concerning your past experiences?

5. Bradley urges Henry not to listen to anyone tell him who he is. "It might take a while but you'll figure it out." If you were Henry, would you want other people to tell you who you are? Or would you want to "figure it out" for yourself?

6. During his recovery, Henry's first word is "Ritz." At first, he thinks it is a request for Ritz crackers; later, he finds out that it refers to the Ritz-Carlton Hotel, where he would cheat on his wife with a woman from the office. Henry learns that he was in love with this woman and planned to leave his wife for her. However, he does not tell Sarah about the Ritz, even though the plot suggests that he is going to "confess" to her. Why do you think Henry does not tell Sarah about his cheating past? Is this a sign that he is returning to his former lying self? Discuss.

7. Do you think that Henry's case and others like it are strong reasons to deny Locke's memory criterion for personal identity? Why or why not?

DAVID HUME

OF PERSONAL IDENTITY

According to David Hume, we experience our self as a succession of impressions, ideas, and memories, though we do not experience anything that unifies this succession. While some philosophers "imagine we are every moment intimately conscious of what we call our *Self*," Hume finds no merit in this position. "For my part," claims Hume, "when I enter most intimately into what I call *myself*, I always stumble on some particular perception or other . . . I never catch *myself* at any time without a perception, and never can observe any thing but the perception." Furthermore, when he is asleep and not perceiving, "so long am I insensible of *myself*, and may truly be said not to exist." Writes Hume, "And were all my perceptions remov'd by death, and cou'd I neither think, nor feel, nor see, nor love, nor hate after the dissolution of my body, I shou'd be entirely annihilated, nor do I conceive what is farther requisite to make me a perfect non-entity." For Hume, the self is simply an illusion or a fiction. While this position on the self is not widely found in the Western philosophical tradition, it is common in Eastern philosophical traditions such as Buddhism.

"The mind is a kind of theatre," writes Hume, "where several perceptions successively make their appearance." "There is properly no *simplicity* in it at one time, nor *identity* in different," states Hume, "whatever natural propension we may have to imagine that simplicity and identity." He reminds us not to take the "theatre" comparison too literally: the mind is a succession of perceptions only. "Nor have we the most distant notion of the place, where these scenes are represented," states Hume, "or of the materials, of which it is compos'd."

Of personal identity, Hume asks "whether in pronouncing concerning the identity of a person, we observe some real bond among his perceptions, or only feel one among the ideas we form of them." There are two possible responses: "There is something that really binds my perceptions together," and "There is nothing that really bonds my perceptions together, the bond is only felt." Hume contends that the bond is only felt. This is because causal relations exist between a person's experiences. For Hume, "Identity is nothing really belonging to these different perceptions, and uniting them together; but is merely a quality, which we attribute to them, because of the union of their ideas in the imagination, when we reflect on them." Note that here Hume is asking about the unity of a person's consciousness, not whether he is the same person over time. Also note that Hume begins with an observation about experiences and then moves to a consideration about the unity of consciousness.

Hume attributes our sense of personal identity to memory. Specifically, he discusses our memory's employment of two principles of association: resemblance and causation. Concerning resemblance, the "memory not only discovers the identity, but also contributes to its production, by producing the relation of resemblance among the perceptions"; concerning causation, the "memory does not so much *produce* as *discover* personal identity, by shewing us the relation of cause and effect among our different perceptions." A biographical sketch of Hume can be found in chapter 1. The following selection is from *A Treatise of Human Nature* (1739).

There are some philosophers, who imagine we are every moment intimately conscious of what we call our *self*; that we feel its existence and its continuance in existence; and are certain, beyond the evidence of a demonstration, both of its perfect identity and simplicity. The strongest sensation, the most violent passion, say they, instead of distracting us from this view, only fix it the more intensely, and make us consider their influence on *self* either by their pain or pleasure. To attempt a farther proof of this were to weaken its evidence; since no proof can be deriv'd from any fact, of which we are so intimately conscious; nor is there any thing, of which we can be certain, if we doubt of this.

Unluckily all these positive assertions are contrary to that very experience, which is pleaded for them, nor have we any idea of *self*, after the manner it is here explain'd. For from what impression cou'd this idea be deriv'd? This question 'tis impossible to answer without a manifest contradiction and absurdity; and yet 'tis a question, which must necessarily be answer'd, if we wou'd have the idea of self pass for clear and intelligible. It must be some one impression, that gives rise to every real idea. But self or person is not any one impression, but that to which our several impressions and ideas are suppos'd to have a reference. If any impression gives rise to the idea of self, that impression must continue invariably the same, thro' the whole course of our lives; since self is suppos'd to exist after that manner. But there is no impression constant and

invariable. Pain and pleasure, grief and joy, passions and sensations succeed each other, and never all exist at the same time. It cannot, therefore, be from any of these impressions, or from any other, that the idea of self is deriv'd; and consequently there is no such idea.

But farther, what must become of all our particular perceptions upon this hypothesis? All these are different, and distinguishable, and separable from each other, and may be separately consider'd, and may exist separately, and have no need of any thing to support their existence. After what manner, therefore, do they belong to self; and how are they connected with it? For my part, when I enter most intimately into what I call *myself*, I always stumble on some particular perception or other, of heat or cold, light or shade, love or hatred, pain or pleasure. I never can catch *myself* at any time without a perception, and never can observe any thing but the perception. When my perceptions are remov'd for any time, as by sound sleep; so long am I insensible of *myself*, and may truly be said not to exist. And were all my perceptions remov'd by death, and cou'd I neither think, nor feel, nor see, nor love, nor hate after the dissolution of my body, I shou'd be entirely annihilated, nor do I conceive what is farther requisite to make me a perfect non-entity. If any one upon serious and unprejudic'd reflection, thinks he has a different notion of *himself*, I must confess I can reason no longer with him. All I can allow him is, that he may be in the right as well as I, and that we are essentially different in this particular. He may, perhaps, perceive something simple and continu'd, which he calls *himself*; tho' I am certain there is no such principle in me.

But setting aside some metaphysicians of this kind, I may venture to affirm of the rest of mankind, that they are nothing but a bundle or collection of different perceptions, which succeed each other with an inconceivable rapidity, and are in a perpetual flux and movement. Our eyes can not turn in their sockets without varying our perceptions. Our thought is still more variable than our sight; and all our other senses and faculties contribute to this change; nor is there any single power of the soul, which remains unalterably the same, perhaps for one moment. The mind is a kind of theatre, where several perceptions successively make their appearance; pass, repass, glide away, and mingle in an infinite variety of postures and situations. There is properly no *simplicity* in it at one time, nor *identity* in different; whatever natural propension we may have to imagine that simplicity and identity. The comparison of the theatre must not mislead us. They are the successive perceptions only, that constitute the mind; nor have we the most distant notion of the place, where these scenes are represented, or of the materials, of which it is compos'd.

What then gives us so great a propension to ascribe an identity to these successive perceptions, and to suppose ourselves possest of an invariable and uninterrupted existence thro' the whole course of our lives. . . .

. . . 'Tis evident, that the identity, which we attribute to the human mind, however perfect we may imagine it to be, is not able to run the several different perceptions into one, and make them lose their characters of distinction and difference, which are essential to them. 'Tis still true, that every distinct perception, which enters into the composition of the mind, is a distinct existence, and is different, and distinguishable, and separable from every other perception, either contemporary or successive. But, as, notwithstanding this distinction and separability, we suppose the whole train of perceptions to be united by identity, a question naturally arises concerning this relation of identity; whether it be something that really binds our several perceptions together, or only associates their ideas in the imagination. That is, in other words, whether in pronouncing concerning the

identity of a person, we observe some real bond among his perceptions, or only feel one among the ideas we form of them. This question we might easily decide, if we wou'd recollect what has been already prov'd at large, that the understanding never observes any real connexion among objects, and that even the union of cause and effect, when strictly examin'd, resolves itself into a customary association of ideas. For from thence it evidently follows, that identity is nothing really belonging to these different perceptions, and uniting them together, but is merely a quality, which we attribute to them, because of the union of their ideas in the imagination, when we reflect upon them. Now the only qualities, which can give ideas an union in the imagination, are these relations above-mention'd. These are the uniting principles in the ideal world, and without them every distinct object is separable by the mind, and may be separately consider'd, and appears not to have any more connexion with any other object, than if disjoin'd by the greatest difference and remoteness. 'Tis, therefore, on some of these three relations of resemblance, contiguity and causation, that identity depends; and as the very essence of these relations consists in their producing an easy transition of ideas; it follows, that our notions of personal identity, proceed entirely from the smooth and uninterrupted progress of the thought along a train of connected ideas, according to the principles above-explain'd.

The only question, therefore, which remains, is, by what relations this uninterrupted progress of our thought is produc'd, when we consider the successive existence of a mind or thinking person. And here 'tis evident we must confine ourselves to resemblance and causation, and must drop contiguity, which has little or no influence in the present case.

To begin with *resemblance*: suppose we cou'd see clearly into the breast of another, and observe that succession of perceptions, which constitutes his mind or thinking principle, and suppose that he always preserves the memory of a considerable part of past perceptions; 'tis evident that nothing cou'd more contribute to the bestowing a relation on this succession amidst all its variations. For what is the memory but a faculty, by which we raise up the images of past perceptions? And as an image necessarily resembles its object, must not the frequent placing of these resembling perceptions in the chain of thought, convey the imagination more easily from one link to another, and make the whole seem like the continuance of one object? In this particular, then, the memory not only discovers the identity, but also contributes to its production, by producing the relation of resemblance among the perceptions. The case is the same whether we consider ourselves or others.

As to *causation*; we may observe, that the true idea of the human mind, is to consider it as a system of different perceptions or different existences, which are link'd together by the relation of cause and effect, and mutually produce, destroy, influence, and modify each other. Our impressions give rise to their correspondent ideas; and these ideas in their turn produce other impressions. One thought chases another, and draws after it a third, by which it is expell'd in its turn. In this respect, I cannot compare the soul more properly to any thing than to a republic or commonwealth, in which the several members are united by the reciprocal ties of government and subordination, and give rise to other persons, who propagate the same republic in the incessant changes of its parts. And as the same individual republic may not only change its members, but also its laws and constitutions; in like manner the same person may vary his character and disposition, as well as his impressions and ideas, without losing his identity. Whatever changes he endures, his several parts are still connected by the relation of causation. And in this view our identity with regard to the passions serves to corroborate that with regard to the imagination, by making our distant perceptions influence each other, and by giving us a present concern for our past or future pains or pleasures.

As memory alone acquaints us with the continuance and extent of this succession of perception, 'tis to be consider'd, upon that account chiefly, as the source of personal identity. Had we no memory, we never shou'd have any notion of causation, nor consequently of that chain of causes and effects, which constitute our self or person. But having once acquir'd this notion of causation from the memory, we can extend the same chain of causes, and consequently the identity of our persons beyond our memory, and can comprehend times, and circumstances, and actions, which we have entirely forgot, but suppose in general to

have existed. For how few of our past actions are there, of which we have any memory? Who can tell me, for instance, what were his thoughts and actions on the first of *January* 1715, the 12th of *March* 1719, and the 3d of *August* 1733? Or will he affirm, because he has entirely forgot the incidents of these days, that the present self is not the same person with the self of that time; and by that means overturn all the most establish'd notions of personal identity? In this view, therefore, memory does not so much *produce* as *discover* personal identity, by shewing us the relation of cause and effect among our different perceptions. 'Twill be incumbent on those, who affirm that memory produces entirely our personal identity, to give a reason why we can thus extend our identity beyond our memory.

The whole of this doctrine leads us to a conclusion, which is of great importance in the present affair, *viz.* that all the nice and subtile questions concerning personal identity can never possibly be decided, and are to be regarded rather as grammatical than as philosophical difficulties. Identity depends on the relations of ideas; and these relations produce identity, by means of that easy transition they occasion. But as the relations, and the easiness of the transition may diminish by insensible degrees, we have no just standard, by which we can decide any dispute concerning the time, when they acquire or lose a title to the name of identity. All the disputes concerning the identity of connected objects are merely verbal, except so far as the relation of parts gives rise to some fiction or imaginary principle of union, as we have already observ'd.

DISCUSSION QUESTIONS

1. Hume believes that the self is an illusion or a fiction. What is his argument? Do you find it convincing? Why or why not?

2. Hume says that the "mind is a kind of theatre." What does he mean by this?

3. Hume says, "When I enter most intimately into what I call *myself*, I always stumble on some particular perception or other . . . I never catch *myself* at any time without a perception, and never can observe any thing but the perception." Do you agree with him?

Why or why not? Do a thought experiment and try to catch *yourself* without a perception. Can you do it?

4. Hume contends that when he is asleep and not perceiving, "so long am I insensible of *myself* . . . may truly be said not to exist." Discuss this idea of not existing when we are asleep and not perceiving.

5. Writes Hume, "And were all my perceptions remov'd by death, and cou'd I neither think, nor feel, nor see, nor love, nor hate after the dissolution of my body, I shou'd be entirely annihilated, nor do I conceive what is farther requisite to make me a perfect non-entity." Do you agree with him? Why or why not?

Memento
[USA 2000] 1 hour, 56 minutes
Directed by Christopher Nolan

Leonard Shelby (Guy Pearce) suffers from a condition called "anterograde memory dysfunction," which results in patients not being able to remember anything for more than fifteen or so minutes. Leonard undertakes to find and kill "John G," the junkie who broke into his home, knocked him unconscious (triggering his illness), and raped and murdered his wife, Catherine (Jorja Fox). But Leonard's condition makes this a difficult task. In order to retain a sense of order in his life and keep track of the clues he uncovers in his search for John G, Leonard uses a system of tattoos, photographs, and meticulous notes.

Teddy Gammell (Joe Pantoliano) is the police officer assigned to investigate the murder of Leonard's wife. Together they track down John G, and Leonard murders him. When Teddy realizes that Leonard cannot remember that he has already tracked down John G, he decides to take advantage of Leonard's condition and set him up to murder a drug dealer named Jimmy Grantz (Larry Holden).

After Leonard kills Jimmy Grantz, he realizes that Teddy was using him to steal $200,000 from Grantz. To exact revenge, Leonard fabricates a series of clues that will lead him to establish Teddy as his next "John G." With help from Natalie (Carrie-Anne Moss), Jimmy Grantz's girlfriend, Leonard tracks Teddy down and kills him.

Two things further complicate an already complex plot: (1) the chronology of events in the film and (2) the fact that we don't know who is telling the truth. The color scenes in the film are arranged in reverse chronological order, while the black-and-white scenes move forward in time. Consequently, the first scene we see is actually the last event in the story: Teddy's murder. The point of the film seems to be that because Leonard can never have a complete view of the truth of the events surrounding the attack on his wife, so we should not either.

DISCUSSION QUESTIONS

1. Consider the following dialogue between Teddy and Leonard:

TEDDY   "You don't know me, you don't even know who *you* are."

LEONARD   "I'm Leonard Shelby, I'm from San Francisco and I'm—"

TEDDY   "That's who you were, you don't know who you are."

LEONARD   "Shut your mouth!"

TEDDY   "Lemme take you down in the basement and show you what you've become. C'mon, Lenny—we'll take a look down there together. Then you'll know. You'll know what you really are."

For Hume, is the "pre-short-term-memory-loss Leonard" the same as the "post-short-term memory-loss-Leonard"? Why or why not? Do you agree with Hume's conclusion?

2.   Leonard describes his condition as follows: "I have no short-term memory. I know who I am and all about myself, but since my injury I can't make any new memories. Everything fades. If we talk for too long, I'll forget how we started. I don't know if we've ever met before, and the next time I see you I won't remember this conversation. So if I seem strange or rude, that's probably [it]." Do you agree with Leonard's assessment of his own self-knowledge? "I know who I am and all about myself," says Leonard, but he cannot remember, for example, having killed John G numerous times. How, then, can he know who he is? In what way is your response to this question dependent on your views on the nature of the self?

3.   Consider the following exchange between Natalie and Leonard:

NATALIE   "Is that what your little note says?"

LEONARD   "Yes."

NATALIE   "Must be tough living life according to a few scraps of paper. Mix up your laundry list and your grocery list, you'll be eating your underwear."

Every fifteen or so minutes, Leonard must reorient himself using various slips of paper—he has no short-term memories that last longer than this time. According to Locke's "memory criterion" of personal identity, we are identical with whatever actions we remember as our own. Does this mean that according to Locke's theory, Leonard has become a succession of "fifteen-minute selves"? That every fifteen minutes, a self ceases to exist because its continuity of memory is lost, and another self is created along the lines of new memories? Why or why not?

4.   Consider this exchange between Teddy and Leonard:

TEDDY   "Because you're relying on them [the notes] alone. You don't remember what you've discovered or how. Your notes might be unreliable."

LEONARD   "Memory's unreliable. No, really. Memory's not perfect. It's not even that good. Ask the police, eyewitness testimony is unreliable. The cops don't catch a killer by sitting around remembering stuff. They collect facts, make notes, draw conclusions. Facts, not memories: that's how you investigate. I know, it's what I used to do. Memory can change the shape of a room or the color of a car. It's an interpretation, not a record. Memories can be changed or distorted and they're irrelevant if you have the facts."

Is memory unreliable? If it is as unreliable as Leonard says, should we also doubt a theory of personal identity that is based on memories? What would a theory of personal identity based on facts be like? How would it be similar to Leonard's notes-and-tattoos system? Discuss.

5. Leonard says, "I know the feel of the world. I know how this wood will sound when I knock. I know how this glass will feel when I pick it up. Certainties. You think it's knowledge, but it's a kind of memory, a kind you take for granted. I can remember so much. I know the feel of the world, and I know her." Notice that Leonard says, "I know." Is this "I" a constantly changing "I" as Locke would have us believe? Is it an "I" that, as Hume says, is always accompanied by a perception (but does not have personal identity)? Or is it the Cartesian "I" that persists as a thinking thing irrespective of what specific thoughts or memories are attached to it? Compare and contrast their respective positions, and state which makes the most sense to you, and why.

6. Consider the following dialogue between Natalie and Leonard:

    NATALIE   "You have no idea where you've just come from? What you've just done?"

    LEONARD   "I can't make new memories. Everything fades, nothing sticks. By the time we finish this conversation I won't remember how it started, and the next time I see you I won't know that I've ever met you before."

    Leonard's condition is a rare one. His memories fade very fast. However, consider your own memories. Think back to the second grade, and try to recall the person who sat behind you. Can you remember where you were on October 12, 1994? Or even what you doing last Wednesday at 7 p.m.? An argument can be made that all of us forget many of the details about our past—even our recent past—and that Leonard's is simply an extreme case of memory loss. Therefore, one we might argue that while now he cannot remember what he does without making a note of it, Leonard is still the same individual he was before the accident—only his attributes have changed (he now has a very bad short-term memory). However, he does not forget who he is—"I'm Leonard Shelby, I'm from San Francisco." Rather, he forgets what he *does*. Our personal identity is tied not to our memories of our past deeds, but to our ability to say "I" and know that it refers to ourselves. Evaluate this line of reasoning.

7. Consider the following conversation between Teddy and Leonard concerning Sammy Jankis (Stephen Tobolowsky), a man who claimed to have lost his short-term memory and whose insurance case Leonard investigated before his accident:

    TEDDY   "I dunno . . . your wife surviving the assault . . . her not believing about your condition . . . the doubt tearing her up inside . . . , the insulin—"

    LEONARD   "That's Sammy, not me! I told you about Sammy."

    TEDDY   "Like you've told yourself. Over and over. Conditioning yourself to believe. Learning through repetition."

    LEONARD   "Sammy let his wife kill herself! Sammy ended up in an institution!"

    TEDDY   "*Sammy* was a con man. A faker."

    LEONARD   I *never* said he was faking! I never said that!"

    TEDDY   "You exposed him for what he was: a fraud."

    Leonard claims that he can condition himself to believe things despite his memory disability by the use of repetition, that the memory associated with repetition is different from that which is utilized in short-term memory. How might this be used by someone with Leonard's disorder to preserve their personal identity?

8.   Consider this exchange between Teddy and Leonard:

LEONARD   "She wasn't diabetic. You think I don't know my own wife? What's wrong with you?"

TEDDY   "I guess I can only make you believe the things you want to be true, huh? Like ol' Jimmy down there."

LEONARD   "But he's not the right guy!"

TEDDY   "He was to you. Come on, Lenny, you got your revenge—just enjoy it while you still remember."

We do not know whether Teddy is telling us the truth about Leonard's wife: she may have died in the attack (Leonard's tattoos and statements indicate this), or she may have been killed by Leonard through insulin injections (Teddy's story), or she may even still be alive (the end of the film has shots of her and a tattooed Leonard lying in bed together—one of his tattoos indicating that he has killed John G). However, we do know that Leonard has long-term memories of events before the accident. Should we then conclude that Leonard is correct in saying that his wife was not a diabetic? How does this bit of information change what we believe about the fate of Leonard's wife?

9.   Leonard says to himself, "I have to believe in the world outside my own mind. I have to believe that my actions still have meaning, even if I can't remember them. I have to believe that when my eyes are closed, the world's still there. But do I? Do I believe the world's still there? Is it still out there?! We all need mirrors to remind ourselves who we are. I'm no different." Is Leonard right? Do we all need mirrors to remind ourselves of who and what we are? If so, what are those mirrors? How are they the same as or different from Leonard's? Explain.

10.   What do you think about Teddy? Is Teddy helping Leonard or using him, or both?

11.   Consider this well-known philosophical puzzler: A wooden boat goes out to sea. As planks rot, they are replaced. Over time, all of the planks on the boat (that is, all of the material components of the boat) are replaced. Is it still the same boat? Why or why not? Can a similar situation be said to hold between Leonard before the accident (Leonard B) and Leonard after the accident (Leonard A)? Is Leonard B like the boat when it goes out to sea, and Leonard A like the boat when all of its planks have been replaced? Is Leonard B still the same as Leonard A? Is the boat example analogous to Leonard's situation? Why or why not? Are your thoughts regarding identity between the boats similar to your thoughts regarding identity between the Leonards? Why or why not?

ALASDAIR MACINTYRE

THE STORYTELLING ANIMAL

I n this selection, Alasdair MacIntyre argues that "man is essentially a storytelling animal" and provides a narrative conception of the self. "He is not this essentially, but becomes through his history, a teller of stories that aspire to truth." For MacIntyre, the key question is

"Of what story or stories do I find myself a part?" Human beings are characters in enacted narratives. "Unpredictability and teleology [ends or goals] therefore coexist as part of our lives," writes MacIntyre; "like characters in a fictional narrative we do not know what will happen next, but none the less, our lives have a certain form which projects itself towards our future."

MacIntyre is critical of Locke's and Hume's accounts of personal identity (see above). Both try to explain personal identity only in terms of psychological states or events. Consequently, Locke and Hume "have failed to see that a background has been omitted, the lack of which makes the problems insoluble." "Just as history is not a sequence of actions, but the concept of an action is that of a moment in an actual or possible history abstracted from some purpose from that history," argues MacIntyre, "so the characters in a history are not a collection of persons, but the concept of a person is that of a character abstracted from a history." According to MacIntyre, "personal identity is just that identity presupposed by the unity of the character which the unity of the narrative requires." Accounts of personal identity must always utilize concepts of narrative, intelligibility, and accountability. Any attempt to deal with personal identity without utilizing these concepts will fail.

Alasdair MacIntyre (1929–), an American social, moral, and political philosopher born in Scotland, is currently senior research professor of philosophy at the University of Notre Dame in Indiana. MacIntyre is a proponent of virtue ethics, which is part of a larger project to recover the political and moral philosophy of Aristotle (see chapter 4 for a selection from Aristotle concerning virtue ethics). MacIntyre views contemporary political and moral life as theoretically fragmented and confused. One of the sources of this disorder is the liberal individualism of the Enlightenment. To extricate ourselves from this condition, MacIntyre suggests, we must return to a tradition that synthesizes themes from Aristotle and Augustine (354–430 C.E.). This tradition will provide the rationality and intelligibility that contemporary moral and political life requires. His many books include *Marxism: An Interpretation* (1953), *The Unconscious: A Conceptual Analysis* (1958), *Difficulties in Christian Belief* (1959), *A Short History of Ethics* (1966), *Marxism and Christianity* (1968), *The Religious Significance of Atheism* (with Paul Ricoeur, 1969), *Marcuse* (1970), *Against the Self-Images of the Age: Essays on Ideology and Philosophy* (1971), *After Virtue: A Study in Moral Theory* (1981; 2nd ed., 1984), *Whose Justice? Which Rationality?* (1988), *Three Rival Versions of Moral Enquiry: Encyclopaedia, Genealogy, and Tradition* (1990), *First Principles, Final Ends and Contemporary Philosophical Issues* (1990), and *Dependent Rational Animals* (1999). The following selection is from *After Virtue*.

We live out our lives, both individually and in our relationships with each other, in the light of certain conceptions of a possible shared future, a future in which certain possibilities beckon us forward and others repel us, some seem already foreclosed and others perhaps inevitable. There is no present which is not informed by some image of some future and an image of the future which always presents itself in the form of a *telos*—or of a variety of ends or goals—towards which we are either moving or failing to move in the present. Unpredictability and teleology therefore coexist as part of our lives; like characters in a fictional narrative we do not know what will happen next, but none the less our lives have a certain form which projects itself towards our future. Thus the narratives which we live out have both an unpredictable and a partially teleological character. If the narrative of our individual and social lives is to continue intelligibly—and either type of narrative may lapse into unintelligibility—it is always both the case that there are constraints on how the story can continue *and* that within those constraints there are indefinitely many ways that it can continue.

A central thesis then begins to emerge: man is in his actions and practice, as well as in his fictions, essentially a story-telling animal. He is not essentially, but becomes through his history, a teller of stories that aspire to truth. But the key question for men is not about their own authorship; I can only answer the question "What am I to do?" if I can answer the prior question "Of what story or stories do I find myself a part?" We enter human society, that is, with one or more imputed characters—roles into which we have been drafted—and we have to learn what they are in order to be able to understand how others respond to us and how our responses to them are apt to be construed. It is through hearing stories about wicked stepmothers, lost children, good but misguided kings, wolves that suckle twin boys, youngest sons who receive no inheritance but must make their own way in the world and eldest sons who waste their inheritance on riotous living and go into exile to live with the swine, that children learn or mislearn both what a child and what a parent is, what the cast of characters may be in the drama into which they have been born and what the ways of the world are. Deprive children of stories and you leave them unscripted, anxious stutterers in their actions as in their words. Hence there is no way to give us an understanding of any society, including our own, except through the stock of stories which constitute its initial dramatic resources. Mythology, in its original sense, is at the heart of things. Vico* was right and so was Joyce.† And so too of course is that moral tradition from heroic society to its medieval heirs according to which the telling of stories has a key part in educating us into the virtues.

I suggested earlier that "an" action is always an episode in a possible history: I would now like to make a related suggestion about another concept, that of personal identity. Derek Parfit‡ and others have recently drawn our attention to the contrast between the criteria of strict identity, which is an all-or-nothing matter (*either* the Tichborne claimant *is* the last Tichborne heir; *either* all the properties of the last heir belong to the claimant *or* the claimant is not the heir—Leibniz's Law applies) and the psychological continuities of personality which are a matter of more or less. (Am I the same man at fifty as I was at forty in respect of memory, intellectual powers, critical responses? More or less.) But what is crucial to human beings as characters in enacted narratives is that, possessing only the resources of psychological continuity, we have to be able to respond to the imputation of strict identity. I am forever whatever I have been at any time for others—and I may at any time be called upon to answer for it—no matter how changed I may be now. There is no way of *founding* my identity—or lack of it—on the psychological continuity or discontinuity of the self. The self inhabits a character whose unity is given as the unity of a character. Once again there is a crucial disagreement with empiricist or analytical philosophers on the one hand and with existentialists on the other.

Empiricists, such as Locke or Hume, tried to give an account of personal identity solely in terms of psychological states or events. Analytical philosophers, in so many ways their heirs as well as their critics, have wrestled with the connection between those states and events and strict identity understood in terms of Leibniz's Law. Both have failed to see that a background has been omitted, the lack of which makes the problems insoluble. That background is provided by the concept of a story and of that kind of unity of character which a story requires. Just as a history is not a sequence of actions, but the concept of an action is that of a moment in an actual or possible history abstracted for some purpose from that history, so the characters in a history are not a collection of persons, but the concept of a person is that of a character abstracted from a history.

*Giovanni Batista Vico (1668–1744), an Italian philosopher, was born in Naples and was a professor of rhetoric at the University of Naples. Regarded by many as the most important Italian philosopher, he was a fierce opponent of the philosophy of Descartes. Vico developed a philosophy of history in his *The New Science* (1725) and is credited with establishing the importance of history in philosophical inquiry.—Ed.
†James Joyce (1882–1941), an Irish novelist, graduated from University College, Dublin, in 1902. His experimental uses of language and literary form in novels such as *Ulysses* (1922) and *Finnegan's Wake* (1939) are regarded by many as among the greatest achievements of twentieth-century literature.—Ed.
‡Derek Parfit (1942–), a British philosopher, has been a fellow of All Souls College at Oxford University since 1967. He is well known for his positions on personal identity, most particularly in *Reasons and Persons* (1984), where he argues that considerations of the persistence and continuity of persons do not require that a significant role be played by identity.—Ed.

What the narrative concept of selfhood requires is thus twofold. On the one hand, I am what I may justifiably be taken by others to be in the course of living out a story that runs from my birth to my death; I am the *subject* of a history that is my own and no one else's, that has its own peculiar meaning. When someone complains—as do some of those who attempt or commit suicide—that his or her life is meaningless, he or she is often and perhaps characteristically complaining that the narrative of their life has become unintelligible to them, that it lacks any point, any movement towards a climax or a *telos*. Hence the point of doing any one thing rather than another at crucial junctures in their lives seems to such a person to have been lost.

To be the subject of a narrative that runs from one's birth to one's death is, I remarked earlier, to be accountable for the actions and experiences which compose a narratable life. It is, that is, to be open to being asked to give a certain kind of account of what one did or what happened to one or what one witnessed at any earlier point in one's life the time at which the question is posed. Of course someone may have forgotten or suffered brain damage or simply not attended sufficiently at the relevant times to be able to give the relevant account. But to say of someone under some one description ("The prisoner of the Chateau d'If") that he is the same person as someone characterised quite differently ("The Count of Monte Cristo") is precisely to say that it makes sense to ask him to give an intelligible narrative account enabling us to understand how he could at different times and different places be one and the same person and yet be so differently characterised. Thus personal identity is just that identity presupposed by the unity of the character which the unity of a narrative requires. Without such unity there would not be subjects of whom stories could be told.

The other aspect of narrative selfhood is correlative: I am not only accountable, I am one who can always ask others for an account, who can put others to the question. I am part of their story, as they are part of mine. The narrative of any one life is part of an interlocking set of narratives. Moreover this asking for and giving of accounts itself plays an important part in constituting narratives. Asking you what you did and why, saying what I did and why, pondering the differences between your account of what I did and my account of what I did, and *vice versa*, these are essential constituents of all but the very simplest and barest of narratives. Thus without the accountability of the self those trains of events that constitute all but the simplest and barest of narratives could not occur; and without that same accountability narratives would lack that continuity required to make both them and the actions that constitute them intelligible.

It is important to notice that I am not arguing that the concepts of narrative or of intelligibility or of accountability are *more* fundamental than that of personal identity. The concepts of narrative, intelligibility and accountability presuppose the applicability of the concept of personal identity, just as it presupposes their applicability and just as indeed each of these three presupposes the applicability of the two others. The relationship is one of mutual presupposition. It does follow of course that all attempts to elucidate the notion of personal identity independently of and in isolation from the notions of narrative, intelligibility and accountability are bound to fail. As all such attempts have.

It is now possible to return to the question from which this enquiry into the nature of human action and identity started: In what does the unity of an individual life consist? The answer is that its unity is the unity of a narrative embodied in a single life. To ask "What is the good for me?" is to ask how best I might live out that unity and bring it to completion. To ask "What is the good for man?" is to ask what all answers to the former question must have in common. But now it is important to emphasise that it is the systematic asking of these two questions and the attempt to answer them in deed as well as in word which provide the moral life with its unity. The unity of a human life is the unity of a narrative quest. Quests sometimes fail, are frustrated, abandoned or dissipated into distractions; and human lives may in all these ways also fail. But the only criteria for success or failure in a human life as a whole are the criteria of success or failure in a narrated or to-be-narrated quest.

DISCUSSION QUESTIONS

1. What is MacIntyre's narrative conception of the self? What story or stories do you find yourself a part of?

2. Why does MacIntyre claim that we are storytelling animals? Do you agree with him? If so, do you think we are born storytellers or become storytellers? If not, what type of "animal" are we? Discuss.

3. What difficulties does MacIntyre have with Hume's and Locke's theories of personal identity? Do you agree with him? Why or why not?

4. MacIntyre writes, "Just as history is not a sequence of actions, but the concept of an action is that of a moment in an actual or possible history abstracted from some purpose from that history, so the characters in a history are not a collection of persons, but the concept of a person is that of a character abstracted from a history." What does he mean? Do you agree with him? Why or why not?

5. "Deprive children of stories and you leave them unscripted, anxious stutterers in their actions as in their words," writes MacIntyre. Do you agree with him? What role do stories play in the formation of our self-identity?

The Bourne Identity
[USA 2002] 1 hour, 59 minutes
Directed by Doug Liman

*J*ason Bourne (Matt Damon) wakes up on a mysterious boat with no memory of how he got there or even who he is. When Bourne lands on solid ground, his whole life is turned upside down as agents from different groups attempt to dispose of him. Bourne, previously unaware of his true identity, discovers that he was not any ordinary person—he was a covert assassin working for a secret government organization. Bourne also learns that during an assignment, his feelings got in the way of his mission, and he lost his memory after being discovered by enemies, shot, and thrown for dead into the ocean. Now that Bourne's former employers know he is still alive, they gather up their best men in an attempt to kill him, fearing that Bourne is an enemy who can destroy their organization. Through his tactical military knowledge, Bourne survives the fight for his own life and leaves the country to live in peace.

DISCUSSION QUESTIONS

1. For MacIntyre, the key question is "Of what story or stories do I find myself a part?" Human beings are characters in enacted narratives. "Unpredictability and teleology [ends or goals] therefore coexist as part of our lives," writes MacIntyre; "like characters in a fictional narrative we do not know what will happen next, but none the less our lives have a certain form which projects itself towards our future." Discuss Bourne's situation in view of MacIntyre's notion of the narrative self. What story does Bourne find himself a part of? Even if he does not wish to be a part of this story any longer, how does this story project the form of his life into the future?

2. In *Regarding Henry* (discussed earlier), Henry finds himself to be part of a story in which he no longer wishes to take part. So, in an effort to leave behind this story and start a new one, he quits his job as a lawyer and chooses to not pursue the divorce of his wife or his relationship with his

mistress. Bourne, however, cannot quit his story as easily; his employers cannot risk this. Do you believe the stories that MacIntyre says are part of our narrative self can be discarded for new ones? Or are we always already part of those stories whether we like it or not?

3. Locke believes that we are identical with whatever actions we remember as our own. Bourne, however, cannot remember any of the actions in his own life prior to his being fished out of the water. According to Locke's theory of personal identity, who is Bourne after he has been rescued?

4. Consider the following dialogue between Bourne and Marie Kreutz (Franka Potente), the woman with whom he is running from assassins and the police:

    BOURNE   "Who has a safety deposit box full of money and six passports and a gun? Who has a bank account number in their hip? I come in here, and the first thing I'm doing is I'm catching the sightlines and looking for an exit."

    MARIE   "I see the exit sign, too, I'm not worried. I mean, you were shot. People do all kinds of weird and amazing stuff when they are scared."

    BOURNE   "I can tell you the license plate numbers of all six cars outside. I can tell you that our wait-ress is left-handed and the guy sitting up at the counter weighs two hundred fifteen pounds and knows how to handle himself. I know the best place to look for a gun is the cab of the gray truck outside, and at this altitude, I can run flat out for a half mile before my hands start shaking. Now why would I know that? How can I know that and not know who I am?"

    Do the notions of personal identity provided by Locke, Hume, and MacIntyre help us answer the questions raised by Bourne—namely, how can he know so many things yet not know who he is? Why or why not? Does a situation like Bourne's lead you in any way to think differently of their notions of personal identity? Why or why not?

5. Jason says, "Everything I found out I want to forget." Do you think it is possible to consciously "forget" your past? In other words, can you find something that you do not like about yourself and then choose to not remember it? In not remembering it, does it henceforth play no role in your personal identity? Discuss.

SIMONE DE BEAUVOIR

THE SECOND SEX

Simone de Beauvoir argues that "woman is the Other." She approaches the issue of "woman" from the viewpoint of the individual woman's consciousness of herself as such. "Otherness," for de Beauvoir, is a secondary status that the "Self" posits by negation and out of a sense of inadequacy. Consequently, women share the status of "Other" with any group that has been so negated.

For de Beauvoir, there does not seem to be any natural sex difference. All differences that have been recognized throughout history are merely the creations of defensive self-consciousness. This includes the traditional view of women in the Western philosophical tradition as atypical and deviant. Without the creation of feminine consciousness by men, argues de Beauvoir, *there would be no such thing as woman at all*. For de Beauvoir, woman is seen by man, and by herself, as "the Other," an atypical person. Woman helps man define himself through her alienness, but woman can never become man.

For de Beauvoir, these are cultural facts, not natural ones. The only way women can become authentic persons is to leave behind their role as "the second sex" by developing a consciousness that overcomes these distinctions: a consciousness that is neither Other nor Self and that is unbound by the dichotomous dictates of the master–slave relation. Education, for de Beauvoir, is one of the most important means to the establishment of this "new woman." In *The Second Sex*, de Beauvoir writes, "The truth is that when a woman is engaged in an enterprise worthy of a human being, she is quite able to show herself as active, effective, taciturn—and as ascetic—as a man."

Simone de Beauvoir (1908–86) was a French philosopher and novelist. She studied philosophy at the Sorbonne and taught philosophy from 1931 to 1943 in state-supported secondary schools (lycées) in Marseilles, Rouen, and Paris, France. After the publication in 1949 of *The Second Sex*, de Beauvoir became a figure of inspiration for women's movements around the world. She is widely regarded as one of the founding figures of classical feminism and is one of the most respected modern philosophers. Her work belongs to the existentialist-phenomenological tradition and was inspired by, among others, the works of Søren Kierkegaard, Edmund Husserl, Martin Heidegger, and Jean-Paul Sartre, her lifelong companion, whom she first met in 1929. Her many books include *Pyrrhus et Cinéas* (1944), The *Ethics of Ambiguity* (1947), *American Day by Day* (1948), *Existentialism and the Wisdom of Nations* (1948), *The Mandarins* (1954), *The Long March* (1957), *Memoirs of a Dutiful Daughter* (1958), *Brigitte Bardot and the Lolita Syndrome* (1960), *Force of Circumstances* (1963), *A Very Easy Death* (1964), *Les Belles Images* (1966), *The Coming Age* (1970), and *All Said and Done* (1972). The following is from *The Second Sex*.

For a long time I have hesitated to write a book on woman. The subject is irritating, especially to women; and it is not new. Enough ink has been spilled in the quarreling over feminism, now practically over, and perhaps we should say no more about it. It is still talked about, however, for the voluminous nonsense uttered during the last century seems to have done little to illuminate the problem. After all, is there a problem? And if so, what is it? Are there women, really? Most assuredly the theory of the eternal feminine still has its adherents who will whisper in your ear: "Even in Russia women still are *women*"; and other erudite persons—sometimes the very same—say with a sigh: "Woman is losing her way, woman is lost." One wonders if women still exist, if they will always exist, whether or not it is desirable that they should, what place they occupy in this world, what their place should be. "What has become of women?" was asked recently in an ephemeral magazine.

But first we must ask: what is a woman? *"Tota mulier in utero,"* says one, "woman is a womb." But in speaking of certain women, connoisseurs declare that they are not women, although they are equipped with a uterus like the rest. All agree in recognizing the fact that females exist in the human species; today as always they make up about one half of humanity. And yet we are told that femininity is in danger; we are exhorted to be women, remain women, become women. It would appear, then, that every female human being is not necessarily a woman; to be so considered she must share in that mysterious and threatened reality known as femininity. Is this attribute something secreted by the ovaries? Or is it a Platonic essence, a product of the philosophic imagination? Is a rustling petticoat enough to bring it down to earth? Although some women try zealously to incarnate this essence, it is hardly patentable. It is frequently described in vague and dazzling terms that seem to have been borrowed from the vocabulary of the seers, and indeed in the times of St. Thomas [Aquinas] it was considered an essence as certainly defined as the somniferous virtue of the poppy.

But conceptualism has lost ground. The biological and social sciences no longer admit the existence of unchangeable fixed entities that determine given characteristics, such as those ascribed to woman, the Jew, or the Negro. Science regards any characteristic as a reaction dependent in part upon a *situation*. If today femininity no longer exists, then it never existed. But does the word *woman*, then, have no specific content? This is stoutly affirmed by those who hold to the philosophy of the enlightenment, of rationalism, of nominalism; women, to them, are merely the human beings arbitrarily designated by the word *woman*. Many American women particularly are prepared to think that there is no longer any place for woman as such; if a backward individual still takes herself for a woman, her friends advise her to be psychoanalyzed and thus get rid of this obsession. In regard to a work, *Modern Woman: The Lost Sex*, which in other respects has its irritating features, Dorothy Parker has written: "I cannot be just to books which treat of woman as woman. . . . My idea is that all of us, men as well as women, should be regarded as human beings." But nominalism is a rather inadequate doctrine, and the antifeminists have had no trouble in showing that women simply *are not* men. Surely woman is, like man, a human being; but such a declaration is abstract. The fact is that every concrete human being is always a singular, separate individual. To decline to accept such notions as the eternal feminine, the black soul, the Jewish character, is not to deny that Jews, Negroes, women exist today—this denial does not represent a liberation for those concerned, but rather a flight from reality. Some years ago a well-known woman writer refused to permit her portrait to appear in a series of photographs especially devoted to women writers; she wished to be counted among the men. But in order to gain this privilege she made use of her husband's influence! Women who assert that they are men lay claim none the less to masculine consideration and respect. I recall also a young Trotskyite standing on a platform at a boisterous meeting and getting ready to use her fists, in spite of her evident fragility. She was denying her feminine weakness; but it was for love of a militant male whose equal she wished to be. The attitude of defiance of many American women proves that they are haunted by a sense of their femininity. In truth, to go for a walk with one's eyes open is enough to demonstrate that humanity is divided into two classes of individuals who clothes, faces, bodies, smiles, gaits, interests, and occupations are manifestly different. Perhaps these differences are superficial, perhaps they are destined to disappear. What is certain is that right now they do most obviously exist.

If her functioning as a female is not enough to define woman, if we decline also to explain her through "the eternal feminine," and if nevertheless we admit, provisionally, that women do exist, then we must face the question: what is a woman?

To state the question is, to me, to suggest, at once, a preliminary answer. The fact that I ask it is in itself significant. A man would never get the notion of writing a book on the peculiar situation of the human male. But if I wish to define myself, I must first of all say: "I am a woman"; on this truth must be based all further discussion. A man never begins by presenting himself as an individual of a certain sex; it goes without saying that he is a man. The terms *masculine* and *feminine* are used symmetrically only as a matter of form, as on legal papers. In actuality the relation of the two sexes is not quite like that of two electrical poles, for man represents both the positive and the neutral, as is indicated by the common use of *man* to designate human beings in general; whereas woman represents only the negative, defined by limiting criteria, without reciprocity. In the midst of an abstract discussion it is vexing to hear a man say: "You think thus and so because you are a woman"; but I know that my only defense is to reply: "I think thus and so because it is true," thereby removing my subjective self from the argument. It would be out of the question to reply: "And you think the contrary because you are a man," for it is understood that the fact of being a man is no peculiarity. A man is in the right in being a man; it is the woman who is in the wrong. It amounts to this: just as for the ancients there was an absolute vertical with reference to which the oblique was defined, so there is an absolute human type, the masculine. Woman has ovaries, a uterus; these peculiarities imprison her in her subjectivity, circumscribe her within the limits of her own nature. It is often said that she thinks with her glands. Man superbly ignores the fact that his anatomy also includes glands, such as the testicles, and that they secrete hormones. He thinks of his body as a direct and normal connection with the world, which he believes he apprehends objectively, whereas he regards the body of woman as a hindrance, a prison, weighed down by everything peculiar to it. "The female is a female by virtue of a certain *lack* of qualities," said Aristotle; "we should regard the female nature as afflicted with a natural defectiveness." And St. Thomas [Aquinas] for his part pronounced woman to be an "imperfect man," an "incidental" being. This is symbolized in Genesis where Eve is depicted as made from what Bossuet called "a supernumerary bone" of Adam.

Thus humanity is male and man defines woman not in herself but as relative to him; she is not regarded as an autonomous being. Michelet writes: "Woman, the relative being. . . ." And Benda is most positive in his *Rapport d'Uriel*: "The body of man makes sense in itself quite apart from that of woman, whereas the latter seems wanting in significance by itself. . . . Man can think of himself without woman. She cannot think of herself without man." And she is simply what man decrees; thus she is called "the sex," by which is meant that she appears essentially to the male as a sexual being. For him she is sex—absolute sex, no less. She is defined and differentiated with reference to man and not he with reference to her; she is the incidental, the inessential as opposed to the essential. He is the Subject, he is the Absolute—she is the Other.

The category of the *Other* is as primordial as consciousness itself. In the most primitive societies, in the most ancient mythologies, one finds the expression of a duality—that of the Self and the Other. This duality was not originally attached to the division of the sexes; it was not dependent upon any empirical facts. It is revealed in such works as that of Granet on Chinese thought and those of Dumézil on the East Indies and Rome. The feminine element was at first no more involved in such pairs as Varuna-Mitra, Uranus-Zeus, Sun-Moon, and Day-Night than it was in the contrasts between Good and Evil, lucky and unlucky

auspices, right and left, God and Lucifer. Otherness is a fundamental category of human thought.

Thus it is that no group ever sets itself up as the One without at once setting up the Other over against itself. If three travelers chance to occupy the same compartment, that is enough to make vaguely hostile "others" out of all the rest of the passengers on the train. In small-town eyes all persons not belonging to the village are "strangers" and suspect; to the native of a country all who inhabit other countries are "foreigners"; Jews are "different" for the anti-Semite, Negroes are "inferior" for American racists, aborigines are "natives" for colonists, proletarians are the "lower class" for the privileged. . . .

The native traveling abroad is shocked to find himself in turn regarded as a "stranger" by the natives of neighboring countries. As a matter of fact, wars, festivals, trading, treaties, and contests among tribes, nations, and classes tend to deprive the concept *Other* of its absolute sense and to make manifest its relativity; willy-nilly, individuals and groups are forced to realize the reciprocity of their relations. How is it, then, that this reciprocity has not been recognized between the sexes, that one of the contrasting terms is set up as the sole essential, denying any relativity in regard to its correlative and defining the latter as pure otherness? Why is it that women do not dispute male sovereignty? No subject will readily volunteer to become the object, the inessential; it is not the Other who, in defining himself as the Other, establishes the One. The Other is posed as such by the One in defining himself as the One. But if the Other is not to regain the status of being the One, he must be submissive enough to accept this alien point of view. Whence comes this submission in the case of woman? . . .

History has shown us that men have always kept in their hands all concrete powers; since the earliest days of the patriarchate they have thought best to keep woman in a state of dependence; their codes of law have been set up against her; and thus she has been definitely established as the Other. This arrangement suited the economic interests of the males; but it conformed also to their ontological and moral pretensions. Once the subject seeks to assert himself, the Other, who limits and denies him, is nonetheless a necessity to him: he attains himself only through that reality which he is not, which is something other than himself. That is why man's life is never abundance and quietude; it is dearth and activity, it is struggle. Before him, man encounters Nature; he has some hold upon her, he endeavors to mold her to his desire. But she cannot fill his needs. Either she appears simply as a purely impersonal opposition, she is an obstacle and remains a stranger; or she submits passively to man's will and permits assimilation, so that he takes possession of her only through consuming her—that is, through destroying her. In both cases he remains alone; he is alone when he touches a stone, alone when he devours a fruit. There can be no presence of an other unless the other is also present in and for himself: which is to say that true alterity—otherness—is that of a consciousness separate from mine and substantially identical with mine.

It is the existence of other men that tears each man out of his immanence and enables him to fulfill the truth of his being, to complete himself through transcendence, through escape toward some objective, through enterprise. But this liberty not my own, while assuring mine, also conflicts with it: there is the tragedy of the unfortunate human consciousness; each separate conscious being aspires to set himself up alone as sovereign subject. Each tries to fulfill himself by reducing the other to slavery. But the slave, though he works and fears, senses himself somehow as the essential; and, by a dialectical inversion, it is the master who seems to be the inessential. It is possible to rise above this conflict if each individual freely recognizes the other, each regarding himself and the other simultaneously as object and as subject in a reciprocal manner. But friendship and generosity, which alone permit in actuality this recognition of free beings, are not facile virtues; they are assuredly man's highest achievement, and through that achievement he is to be found in his true nature. But this true nature is that of a struggle unceasingly begun, unceasingly abolished; it requires man to outdo himself at every moment. We might put it in other words and say that man attains an authentically moral attitude when he renounces *mere being* to assume his position as an existent; through this transformation also he renounces all possession, for possession is one way of seeking mere being; but the transformation through which he attains true wisdom is never

done, it is necessary to make it without ceasing, it demands a constant tension. And so, quite unable to fulfill himself in solitude, man is incessantly in danger in his relations with his fellows; his life is a difficult enterprise with success never assured.

But he does not like difficulty; he is afraid of danger. He aspires in contradictory fashion both to life and to repose, to existence and to merely being; he knows full well that "trouble of spirit" is the price of development, that his distance from the object is the price of his nearness to himself; but he dreams of quiet in disquiet and of an opaque plenitude that nevertheless would be endowed with consciousness. This dream incarnated is precisely woman; she is the wished-for intermediary between nature, the stranger to man, and the fellow being who is too closely identical. She opposes him with neither the hostile silence of nature nor the hard requirement of a reciprocal relation; through a unique privilege she is a conscious being and yet it seems possible to possess her in the flesh. Thanks to her, there is a means for escaping that implacable dialectic of master and slave which has its source in the reciprocity that exists between free beings. . . .

. . . There were not at first free women whom the males had enslaved nor were there even castes based on sex. To regard woman simply as a slave is a mistake; there were women among the slaves, to be sure, but there have always been free women— that is, women of religious and social dignity. They accepted man's sovereignty and he did not feel menaced by a revolt that could make of him in turn the object. Woman thus seems to be the inessential who never goes back to being the essential, to be the absolute Other, without reciprocity. This conviction is dear to the male, and every creation myth has expressed it, among others the legend of Genesis, which, through Christianity, has been kept alive in Western civilization. Eve was not fashioned at the same time as the man; she was not fabricated from a different substance, nor of the same clay as was used to model Adam: she was taken from the flank of the first male. Not even her birth was independent; God did not spontaneously choose to create her as an end in herself and in order to be worshipped directly by her in return for it. She was destined by Him for man; it was to rescue Adam from loneliness that He gave her to him, in her mate was her origin and her purpose; she was his complement on the order of the inessential. Thus she appeared in the guise of privileged prey. She was nature elevated to transparency of consciousness; she was a conscious being, but naturally submissive. And therein lies the wondrous hope that man has often put in woman: he hopes to fulfill himself as a being by carnally possessing a being, but at the same time confirming his sense of freedom through the docility of a free person. No man would consent to be a woman, but every man wants women to exist. "Thank God for having created woman." "Nature is good since she has given women to men." In such expressions man once more asserts with naive arrogance that his presence in this world is an ineluctable fact and a right, that of woman a mere accident—but a very happy accident. Appearing as the Other, woman appears at the same time as an abundance of being in contrast to that existence the nothingness of which man senses in himself; the Other, being regarded as the object in the eyes of the subject, is regarded as *en soi*; therefore as a being. In woman is incarnated in positive form the lack that the existent carries in his heart, and it is in seeking to be made whole through her that man hopes to attain self-realization. . . .

Perhaps the myth of woman will some day be extinguished; the more women assert themselves as human beings, the more the marvelous quality of the Other will die out in them. But today it still exists in the heart of every man.

A myth always implies a subject who projects his hopes and his fears toward a sky of transcendence. Women do not set themselves up as Subject and hence have erected no virile myth in which their projects are reflected; they have no religion or poetry of their own: they still dream through the dreams of men. Gods made by males are the gods they worship. Men have shaped for their own exaltation great virile figures: Hercules, Prometheus, Parsifal; woman has only a secondary part to play in the destiny of these heroes. No doubt there are conventional figures of man caught in his relations to woman: the father, the seducer, the husband, the jealous lover, the good son, the wayward son; but they have all been established by men, and they lack the dignity of myth, being hardly more than clichés. Whereas woman is defined exclusively in her relation to man. The asymmetry of the categories—male and

female—is made manifest in the unilateral form of sexual myths. We sometimes say "the sex" to designate woman; she is the flesh, its delights and dangers. The truth that for woman man is sex and carnality has never been proclaimed because there is no one to proclaim it. Representation of the world, like the world itself, is the work of men; they describe it from their own point of view, which they confuse with absolute truth.

It is always difficult to describe a myth; it cannot be grasped or encompassed; it haunts the human consciousness without ever appearing before it in fixed form. The myth is so various, so contradictory, that at first its unity is not discerned: Delilah and Judith, Aspasia and Lucretia, Pandora and Athena—woman is at once Eve and the Virgin Mary. She is an idol, a servant, the source of life, a power of darkness; she is the elemental silence of truth, she is artifice, gossip, and falsehood; she is healing presence and sorceress; she is man's prey, his downfall, she is everything that he is not and that he longs for, his negation and his *raison d'être*. . . .

Man seeks in woman the Other as Nature and as his fellow being. But we know what ambivalent feelings Nature inspires in man. He exploits her, but she crushes him, he is born of her and dies in her; she is the source of his being and the realm that he subjugates to his will; Nature is a vein of gross material in which the soul is imprisoned, and she is the supreme reality; she is contingence and Idea, the finite and the whole; she is what opposes the Spirit, and the Spirit itself. Now ally, now enemy, she appears as the dark chaos from whence life wells up; as this life itself, and as the over-yonder toward which life tends. Woman sums up nature as Mother, Wife, and Idea; these forms now mingle and now conflict, and each of them wears a double visage. . . .

This, then, is the reason why woman has a double and deceptive visage: she is all that man desires and all that he does not attain. She is the good mediatrix between propitious Nature and man; and she is the temptation of unconquered Nature, counter to all goodness. She incarnates all moral values, from good to evil, and their opposites; she is the substance of action and whatever is an obstacle to it, she is man's grasp on the world and his frustration; as such she is the source and origin of all man's reflection on his existence and of whatever expression he is able to give to it; and yet she works to divert him from himself, to make him sink down in silence and in death. She is servant and companion, but he expects her also to be his audience and critic and to confirm him in his sense of being; but she opposes him with her indifference, even with her mockery and laughter. He projects upon her what he desires and what he fears, what he loves and what he hates. And if it is so difficult to say anything specific about her, that is because man seeks the whole of himself in her and because she is All. She is All, that is, on the plane of the inessential; she is all the Other. And, as the other, she is other than herself, other than what is expected of her. Being all, she is never quite *this* which she should be; she is everlasting deception, the very deception of that existence which is never successfully attained nor fully reconciled with the totality of existents. . . .

One is not born, but rather becomes, a woman. No biological, psychological, or economic fate determines the figure that the human female presents in society; it is civilization as a whole that produces this creature, intermediate between male and eunuch, which is described as feminine. Only the intervention of someone else can establish an individual as an *Other*. In so far as he exists in and for himself, the child would hardly be able to think of himself as sexually differentiated. In girls as in boys the body is first of all the radiation of a subjectivity, the instrument that makes possible the comprehension of the world: it is through the eyes, the hands, that children apprehend the universe, and not through the sexual parts. The dramas of birth and of weaning unfold after the same fashion for nurslings of both sexes; these have the same interests and the same pleasures; sucking is at first the source of their most agreeable sensations; then they go through an anal phase in which they get their greatest satisfactions from the excretory functions, which they have in common. Their genital development is analogous; they explore their bodies with the same curiosity and the same indifference; from clitoris and penis they derive the same vague pleasure. As their sensibility comes to require an object, it is turned toward the mother: the soft, smooth, resilient feminine flesh is what arouses sexual desires, and these desires are prehensile; the girl, like the boy, kisses, handles, and caresses her mother in an aggressive way; they feel the same jealousy if a new child is born, and they show it in similar behavior patterns: rage, sulkiness, urinary difficulties; and they resort to the same coquettish tricks to gain the love of adults. Up to the age of twelve the little girl is as strong as her brothers, and she shows the same mental powers; there is no field where she is debarred from engaging in rivalry with them. If, well before puberty and sometimes even from early infancy, she seems to us to be already sexually determined, this is not because mysterious instincts directly doom her to passivity, coquetry, maternity; it is because the influence of others upon the child is a factor almost from the start, and thus she is indoctrinated with her vocation from her earliest years.

DISCUSSION QUESTIONS

1. Why does de Beauvoir believe that "woman is the Other"? What is her argument? Is it a good one?

2. De Beauvoir writes that "humanity is male and man defines woman not in herself but as relative to him; she is not regarded as an autonomous being." What does she mean by this?

3. "No subject will readily volunteer to become the object, the inessential; it is not the Other who, in defining himself as the Other, establishes the One," says de Beauvoir. What does she mean by this? Do you agree with her? Why or why not?

4. What is the connection between sexism and racism for de Beauvoir? Between sexism and anti-Semitism? In what way do sexism, racism, and anti-Semitism affect a person's identity?

5. De Beauvoir says, "One is not born, but rather becomes a woman." What does she mean? How does one "become" a woman? Is she saying that there is no absolute metaphysics of womanhood? Discuss.

6. Compare and contrast Hume's, Locke's, MacIntyre's and de Beauvoir's responses to the question "Who am I?" Which do you prefer, and why?

*T*helma and Louise tells the story of two best friends whose simple weekend getaway turns into a desperate flight from the law. Louise (Susan Sarandon) works as a waitress. Her boyfriend, Jimmy (Michael Madson), is reluctant to propose marriage. Thelma (Geena Davis) is married to Darryl (Christopher McDonald), who has little respect for her. The women decide to take a weekend trip to enjoy each other's company and get away from their men.

On the way to the weekend getaway cabin, Thelma and Louise stop off at a bar for a drink and a bite to eat. Harlan (Timothy Carhart) begins to hit on Thelma and, after dancing with her, suggests that they go outside for some fresh air. Harlan tries to coerce Thelma into having sex with him, despite her protestations. He becomes enraged, hits her, and attempts to rape her. When Louise points a gun to Harlan's head and orders him to let Thelma go, he says, "Calm down, we're just having a little fun. That's all." Louise angrily responds, "In the future, when a woman is crying like that, she's not having fun!" When Harlan mocks Louise, she shoots and kills him.

Thelma suggests that they turn themselves into the police and explain how Harlan was attempting to rape her. Louise responds, "One hundred people saw you dancing cheek to cheek with him. Who is gonna believe you? We don't live in that kind of world, Thelma!" As they attempt to elude the authorities, Thelma and Louise commit more illegal acts, including robbing a convenience store and destroying a tanker truck. Their escape to Mexico is thwarted when the police corner them at the edge of the Grand Canyon. Refusing to give up or give in, Thelma and Louise drive off the cliff to their deaths.

DISCUSSION QUESTIONS

1. De Beauvoir writes that "humanity is male and man defines woman not in herself but as relative to him; she is not regarded as an autonomous being." In what way does this film support de Beauvoir's claim? Discuss.

2. De Beauvoir believes that "woman is the Other," the second sex. However, de Beauvoir also contends, "One is not born, but rather becomes a woman." If this is so, can a biological female become a "man," a member of the first sex? What would this involve? Can one argue that all of the events after the attempted rape of Thelma should be viewed as an effort by Thelma and Louise to shake their role as the second sex (woman) in an effort to "become" the first sex (man)? Do they succeed?

3. When Louise tells Harlan to let Thelma go, he says, "Calm down, we're just having a little fun. That's all." Louise responds, "In the future, when a woman is crying like that, she's not having fun!" Why do you think Harlan believes that he and Thelma were just having fun? Is Harlan's comment in any way defensible? How representative of patriarchal society are Harlan's actions? What do you think of Louise's verbal response to them? What would you have said to Harlan, and why? Defend your view.

4. Thelma and Louise begin the film paying close attention to the way they are dressed and to maintaining their makeup. By the end of the film, they have discarded their jewelry and makeup, and

their clothing is generally "untidy." Why do they make these changes? Is there a connection between our ideas about beauty and our beliefs about identity? Defend your position. What do you think de Beauvoir would say about this?

5. A trucker (Marco St. John) passing Thelma and Louise on the highway makes lewd gestures toward them. Thelma and Louise signal him to pull over on the side of the road, and ask him if he would make such gestures to his mother. When he refuses to apologize for making the lewd gestures, they shoot at his truck and blow it up. Why were Thelma and Louise so offended by the trucker's actions? Was their response to him—blowing up his truck—morally justifiable?

6. At the end of the movie, the police have cornered Thelma and Louise at the edge of a cliff. They ask them to "raise their hands in plain view" and say that "any failure to obey that command will be considered an act of aggression against us." Thelma and Louise decide to drive off the edge of the cliff rather than surrender to the police. Why do they do this? For them, is death the only escape from male domination, sexism, and violence against women? What would you have done in Thelma and Louise's position? Explain.

7. During the course of the film, we find out that Louise once was raped in Texas. This no doubt contributes to her odd request that they drive to Mexico without passing through Texas. What effect do you think Louise's past experiences have on her argument to Thelma that they should not turn themselves in? Recall that Louise tells Thelma that the police will not believe her rape claim because everyone saw her dancing with Harlan just moments before. Did they do the right thing by not turning themselves in? Would the police have believed them? What would you have done in their position?

8. In an article titled "Hate Violence Against Women," activist Suzanne Pharr comments that "this country minimizes hate violence against women, because women's lives are not valued, because the violence is so commonplace that people become numb to it, because people do not want to look at the institutions and systems that support it, and because people do not want to recognize how widespread the hatred is and how many perpetrators there are among us on every level of society." Do you think the film *Thelma and Louise* supports Pharr's comment? Why or why not?

CHARLES W. MILLS

BUT WHAT ARE YOU REALLY?

Charles W. Mills examines the metaphysics of race that underlies the question "But what are you *really?*" Mills begins by asking us to imagine and compare three different social systems with three different sets of membership criteria: (1) a quace system, (2) a horizontal racial system, and (3) a vertical racial system. In the quace system, persons are assigned randomly to groups; there is no connection between one's quacial group and one's individual morphology (skin, hair, facial features) or genealogy. Furthermore, there is no connection between one's quacial group and patterns of exploitation and discrimination. In the horizontal racial system, while one's individual morphology and genealogy are the basis of group membership, they are, like the quace, completely disconnected from patterns of exploitation and discrimination. Finally, in the vertical racial system, one's individual morphology and genealogy are the basis of group membership, and unlike the quace and the horizontal systems, are completely *connected to* patterns of exploitation and discrimination. Mills contends that "because the United States and many other nations have historically been vertical racial systems, race has significance." Consequently, the metaphysics of race needs to be examined against the background of the vertical system, not the quace and the horizontal systems. It is in this vertical system that the question "But what are you *really?*" becomes *ontologically* important.

Mills then introduces the notion of "social metaphysics," wherein race is treated not as metaphysically "part of the basic furniture of the universe" but rather as "a *contingently* deep reality that structures our particular social universe, having a social objectivity and causal significance that arise out of *our* particular history." "Because people come to think of themselves as 'raced,' as black and white, for example, these categories, which correspond to no natural kinds," argues Mills, "attain a social reality." In this regard, Mills's work is similar to that of de Beauvoir: arguably, both believe that one is not born a woman or raced; rather, one becomes these things through socially constructed identities. "I am most sympathetic to a contructivist position on the metaphysics of race," says Mills. "This position is most congruent with the actual historical record, where race has not been an arbitrary social category, as in a horizontal system, but has functioned as a real marker, if imperfectly, of privilege and subordination in a *vertical* system."

When we look back to the philosophical tradition on personal identity, we find that from Locke on, it has generally been assumed that there is an answer to the question of who we are *really*, which "is not necessarily the same as the answer to the question who the person is *taken* to be." In the case of race, though, what we are *really* is very difficult to ascertain adequately. Mills shows this by revealing through "naturally occurring or artificially devised problem cases," how seven potential criteria for racial identification (bodily appearance, ancestry, self-awareness of ancestry, public awareness of ancestry, culture, experience, and self-identification) are each, in themselves, inadequate. While the problem cases make apparent some of the philosophical difficulties facing any adequate account of racial identity, Mills concludes that the metaphysics of racial identity is a rich and complex topic, worthy of continued examination.

Charles W. Mills is professor of philosophy at the University of Illinois at Chicago. He received his Ph.D. from the University of Toronto in 1985, and he has also taught at the University of Oklahoma. His main research interests are radical and oppositional political theory, particularly on issues of class, gender, and race. He is the author of numerous articles on Marxism, critical race theory, and African American philosophy and has written three books: *The Racial Contract* (1997), *Blackness Visible: Essays on Philosophy and Race* (1998), and *From Class to Race: Essays in White Marxism and Black Radicalism* (2003). The following selection is from *Blackness Visible*.

Race has not traditionally been seen as an interesting or worthy subject of investigation for white Western philosophers, though it has, of course, been the central preoccupation of black intellectuals in the West. . . . That race *should* be irrelevant is certainly an attractive ideal, but when it has *not* been irrelevant, it is absurd to proceed as if it had been. There is a growing body of work—at this stage, largely by nonwhite philosophers—on such issues as slavery and colonialism, race and racism, culture and identity, bi- and no-racialism, Pan-Africanism and Afrocentrism, and with the projected demographic shift in the United States over the next century to a majority nonwhite population, we can expect philosophical interest in these matters to increase. As a contribution to this emerging literature, I will try to elucidate what could be termed the "metaphysics of race" that underlie the question "But what are you *really?*"

QUACE VERSUS RACE

Before talking about race, let me describe a hypothetical, contrasting system that could be termed *quace*. Imagine a nation in which at birth, or at naturalization, all citizens are assigned a code—Q_1, or Q_2, or Q_3—that indicates their "quacial" membership. This code is entered on birth certificates, naturalization papers, passports, state I.D.s, driver's licences, and the like. So all citizens have a quace. But the assignment is done randomly. There is no connection between quace and an individual's morphology (skin, hair, facial features) or genealogy. In other words, we could not tell a person's actual or likely quacial membership just by looking at him or her, and parents of a given quace would not automatically have children of the same quace. Nor is there any correlation between quace and historical patterns of exploitation and systemic discrimination. There are no $Q_1/Q_2/Q_3$ ghettoes; no prohibitions, juridical or moral, on intermarriage between Q_1s/Q_2s/Q_3s; no domination of the state or the corporate sector by representatives of a particular Q group; no embedded structural differentials in property ownership between the various Qs; no quacial division of labor; no trumpeting of the superiority of Q_x culture; no calls to maintain Q_1 purity or heart-wrenching accounts of the existential trauma of being a Q_2. The designation comes down from some long-forgotten practice and is maintained by cultural momentum.

In such a society, if someone were to ask us what our quace was, we would, if we were truthful (and it means so little that we would have no motive to lie), just report the information on our passport, let us say, "Q_3." But suppose the person persisted and asked, "No, but what are you *really?*" In such a society the question would barely be intelligible. "Really" contrasts with "apparently," but here there is no ontological depth, so to speak, to separate one from the other. We might wonder whether that person thought our code had originally been filled in incorrectly (the randomizing device actually generated "Q_1" but the computer was on the blink, or the recording clerk was recovering from the previous night's debaucheries, so that "Q_3" was entered instead). But the question would have no deeper significance, precisely because quace has no significance to the lives of the people in that society beyond bureaucratic irritation. "I am a Q_1!" would have no metaphysical ring, no broader historical resonance to it, any more than our declaration of our passport number has any metaphysical ring or broader historical resonance to it. And this is, of course, in sharp contrast with declarations of racial membership, which in the United States and many other countries have historically had deeper reverberations and significances.

To get at the root of these differences, we could imagine an ideal racial system, a system of race rather than quace. We could distinguish horizontal and vertical racial systems as contrasting types. In a horizontal system, race has no present or historical link with political power, economic wealth, cultural influence: the races are randomly distributed in the social order. So though race here is not like quace in that it is morphologically/genealogically grounded, it is like quace in being completely disconnected from patterns of discrimination. Whether such a society has ever actually existed seems unlikely, but the question need not engage us, since this abstract possibility has been mentioned only for the sake of the contrast with our real focus of interest: a vertical system. Here the polity and the economic order are expressly structured on a hierarchical axis in which $R_1 > R_2 > R_3$. The functional goal of the system is to privilege the R_1s and to subordinate the R_2s and R_3s. To this end, the R_1s are designated as the superior race. Different criteria are possible, but usually the most important dimensions of this metric of assessment will be intellectual/cognitive and characterological/moral; that is, the R_1s will be seen as more intelligent and of better moral character than the other races. We could speak of this as an R_1-supremacist system, since the R_1s are systemically privileged over the other races.

An ideal vertical racial system would then have rules to regulate its internal structure and guarantee as far as possible its reproduction. Such a system should be complete. That is, every person in the system should have a racial designation, R_1, R_2, R_3 . . ., and if there are people for whom that designation is R_0, this would be the outcome of the system's rules (rather than the result of confusion over where the person fits). The system should also be well formed; that is, clear-cut, unambiguous principles would determine to which race the products of intermarriage between Rs would belong. (And this system would have to be recursive to take account of what happens when those offspring intermarry.) Unless the system is closed (no immigration), it should also have rules for allocating new arrivals to the appropriate racial slots. The extent of the R_1 privileging (for example, in deciding public policy) should be determinate, whether through the stipulation of a strong "lexical" ordering of R_1 interests vis-à-vis R_2 and R_3 interests (R_1 interests as carrying infinite weight) or some weaker principle (R_1 interests as finitely weightier). Finally, it should be nationally uniform, in the sense that there should be no local variations in the rules according to state or region.

Obviously, in such a system, by contrast with a system of quace or the horizontal racial system, one's racial designation will have immense significance, since it will indicate one's social standing and profoundly affect one's life. And because the United States and many other nations have historically been vertical racial systems of this kind, race has significance. These systems have not been ideal because the rules have not usually been complete, well formed, determinate, or nationally uniform. Moreover, many of the privileged R_1s have opposed the system ("race traitors"/"white renegades"), refused to abide by its prescriptions, and supported the efforts of R_2s/R_3s to change it. Nonetheless, the system has been sufficiently successful that, to take the United States as an example, more than two hundred years after its founding, people still think of themselves as raced; American cities are more segregated now than they were at the turn of the century, there is little intermarriage; blacks are still, by conventional economic measures, near the bottom of the ladder; and some leading black intellectuals are now speaking despairingly of "the permanence of racism." So this, I suggest—as against the system of quace or the horizontal racial system—is the background against which the metaphysics of race needs to be examined and from which the question "But what are you *really?*" gains its ontological import.

METAPHYSICAL POSITIONS

The terms *social ontology* and *social metaphysics* (I will use them interchangeably) have a certain intuitive transparency, being obviously meant to refer to the basic struts and girders of social reality in a fashion analogous to the way "metaphysics" *simpliciter* refers to the deep structure of reality as a whole. So there are basic existents that constitute the social world, and that should be central to theorizing about it. Thus one readily understands what it means to say that the social ontology of the classic contractarians is an ontology of atomic individuals; that for Karl Marx, it was classes defined by their relation to the means of production; and that for radical feminists, it is the two sexes. In pre-postmodernist times, these categories would have been confidently put forward as part of foundationalist and theoretically exhaustive explanatory schemas—history as class or gender struggle. In the present, more cautious period, greater theoretical circumspection is wise. Note, then, that I am not claiming that race is the only principle of social hierarchy, or that racial struggle is the comprehensive key to understanding history, or that individuals' racial ontology is in all circumstances the most important thing about them. But systemic racial privilege has been an undeniable (though often denied) fact in recent global history, and exploring an ontology of race will contribute to (though not exhaust) our understanding of social dynamics. Other systems of domination besides race (class, gender) overlap and intersect with it. But in the United States (and elsewhere) race has correlated strongly with civic standing, culture, citizenship, privilege or subordination, and even designations of personhood. One's racial category has been taken as saying a great deal about what and who one is, more fundamentally. To what extent and in what ways, then, is race "real," and how deep is this reality?

Terminology developed elsewhere can illuminatingly be drawn upon to map representative positions on the ontology of race. As we know, philosophers of science and ethicists have an elaborate vocabulary for demarcating contrasting views on the reality of scientific entities and the metaphysics of moral value—realism, constructivism, conventionalism/relativism, instrumentalism, subjectivism, noncognitivism, nihilism/error theories, and so forth. Some of this vocabulary can usefully be appropriated to clarify debates on race. The correspondences are not exact and should not be pressed too far; moreover, some terms have no plausible "racial" equivalent at all. Too many qualifications and epicycles may so muddy the homology as to vitiate the whole exercise. Still, I expect the similarity that emerges to be sufficient to make the appropriation enlightening.

Let us distinguish, to begin with, between objectivism and anti-objectivism as umbrella categories of theories about the reality of race. *Objectivism* is used in several ways, but usually it connotes the independence of what we choose, what we believe. There are two main objectivist positions: realist and constructivist.

In metaethics and the philosophy of science, the term *realism* usually denotes the view that acts have value or disvalue and that the entities postulated by natural science either exist or do not exist independently of human consensus or dissent. So, for example, killing the innocent is objectively wrong prima facie even if a certain community has no prohibitions against such actions, just as electrons objectively exist even if nobody knows about them.

What, by analogy, would be realism about race? A "racial realist" in the most minimal sense will be somebody who thinks it is objectively the case— independent of human belief—that there are natural human races; in other words, that races are natural kinds. In the stronger, more interesting sense, a racial realist will also believe that the differences between races are not confined to the superficial morphological characteristics of skin color, hair type, and facial features, but extend to significant moral, intellectual, characterological, and spiritual characteristics also, that there are "racial essences." Anthony Appiah* argues that such a view (which he designates as "racialism") needs to be distinguished from racism proper, though, racism presupposes it, since these traits may be thought to be distributed in such a way across the population that there is no clear-cut hierarchy among races. Historically, however, not

merely have all racists been realists but most realists have been racists. For the past few hundred years, realism has been the dominant position on race; that is, people have believed that there are natural biological differences among races and that these differences run deeper than mere phenotypical traits.

Such views of race are often hostilely characterized as *essentialist,* and this term coheres nicely with the "realist" categorization insofar as in the philosophy of science, realism is associated with a belief in natural kinds with defining essences. One way of making the theoretical commitments here vivid is to think of the issue in terms of transworld identity. For racial realists, people categorizable by their phenotype in our world, with its peculiar history, as belonging to a particular "race" will continue to have the same "racial" intellectual and characterological traits in another world with a radically different history. For racial realists who link culture to genotype, this view implies, for example, that black American culture would still be basically the same even if Africans had come here as voluntary immigrants and never been enslaved. And to the extent that relations between groups identified as races are also explained in these naturalistic terms, relations between white and black Americans would still be antagonistic.

Racial realism, whether in its racist or merely racialist versions, thus runs directly against the gathering consensus of anthropological and biological research. It is not merely that racism (the natural biological hierarchy of races) is false; it is not merely that culture, psychology, and intergroup relations are far more convincingly explained on the basis of contingent histories than of "natural" racial traits; it is that the very categories used to identify races are significantly transworld relative. Indeed, as commentators often point out, the U.S. one-drop rule for determining membership in the "black" race— that is, any "black" blood makes you black—is

---

*Kwame Anthony Appiah is an American philosopher who specializes in philosophy of mind and language, African and African-American intellectual history, and political philosophy. Appiah was born in London and received his Ph.D. from Cambridge University in 1982. He has taught at Yale, Cornell, Duke, and Harvard universities, and, since 2002, Princeton University. His books include *Assertion and Conditionals* (1985), *For Truth in Semantics* (1986), *In My Father's House: Africa in the Philosophy of Culture* (1992), *Color Conscious: The Political Morality of Race* (with Amy Gutmann, 1996), *The Ethics of Identity* (2004), and *Cosmopolitanism: Ethics in a World of Strangers* (2004).—Ed.

practically unique even in *this* world. Many of those categorized as blacks in the United States would be categorized as browns/mulattoes or even whites in the Caribbean and Latin America. . . .

But from the fact that racial realism is false, it does not follow that race is not real in other senses; this is the point of developing objectivism as an umbrella category broader than realism. Many white liberals (and, indeed, historically many white Marxists also), aware of the verdict of science on race, are puzzled at black intellectuals' retention of race as a significant social category: they wish to move from the falsity of racial realism to global claims about the unreality of race in general and the corollary political mistakenness of race-centered political discourse such as one finds in black nationalism, Pan-Africanism, and Afrocentrism. But part of the point of my taxonomy of metaphysical positions is to show that there is conceptual room for a view of race as both real and unreal, not "realist" but still objectivist. This position is *racial constructivism*. . . .

Racial constructivism involves an actual agreement of some under conditions where the constraints are not epistemic (getting at the truth) but *political* (establishing and maintaining privilege); the "idealization" is pragmatic, instrumental to the best way of achieving this end. Nevertheless, the semantic virtue of retaining the same term (apart from the fact that it is already in use) is to highlight the crucial similarity: that an objective ontological status is involved which arises out of *intersubjectivity,* and which, though it is not naturally based, is real for all that. Race is not foundational: in different systems, race could have been constructed differently or indeed never have come into existence in the first place. Race is not essentialist: the same individuals would be differently raced in different systems. Race is not "metaphysical" in the deep sense of being eternal, unchanging, necessary, part of the basic furniture of the universe. But race is a *contingently* deep reality that structures our particular social universe, having a social objectivity and causal significance that arise out of *our* particular history. For racial realism, the social metaphysics is simply an outgrowth of a natural metaphysics; for racial constructivism, there is no natural metaphysics, and the social metaphysics arises directly out of the

social history. Because people come to think of themselves *as* "raced," as black and white, for example, these categories, which correspond to no natural kinds, attain a social reality. Intersubjectivity creates a certain kind of objectivity. . . .

For constructivists the arbitrariness of racial designation is rooted in a particular social history and cannot be overturned by individual fiat. . . .

I am most sympathetic to a constructivist position on the metaphysics of race, a position that is objectivist but also antirealist and antiessentialist. This position is most congruent with the actual historical record, where race has not been an arbitrary social category, such as "quace" or an innocent designation, as in a horizontal system, but has functioned as a real marker, if imperfectly, of privilege and subordination in a *vertical* system. In such a system, racial subjectivism, racial relativism, and racial error theories seem to me to be mistaken; the metaphysics of race is an objectivist if antirealist metaphysics.

CRITERIA FOR RACIAL IDENTITY

I want to turn now to the question of the possible criteria for determining racial identity and what happens when these criteria conflict. These are puzzle cases, what could be regarded as cases of racial transgression. I assume throughout a nonideal vertical racial system, where R_1s are the privileged race.

Consider the more familiar philosophical debate on personal identity. In the literature on this subject, going back to Locke's classic discussion in *Essay Concerning Human Understanding,* it has usually been assumed that there is an answer to the question "Who are you *really?*" that is not necessarily the same as the answer to the question who the person is *taken* to be. The whole point of the soul-transmigrating, brain-transplanting, and memory-loss examples is to get at this difference. The idea is that some kind of metaphysics is objectively there—who the person *is*—and that one may have intuitions that point at it, even if only fuzzily. Through problem cases one can draw on these intuitions, sometimes refining and reformulating them, sometimes giving them up altogether, in the attempt to capture the essence of personal identity, if not in terms of necessary and sufficient conditions, then perhaps in some looser formula that can at least cover most situations. Moreover, personal testimony, although it is given some weight, is not taken as indefeasible (e.g., cases of implanted memory); in some respects the individual has a privileged first-person perspective, but his or her self-identification may on occasion be mistaken. The question will be whether people's race, similarly, is an objective "metaphysical" fact about them, so that by considering puzzle cases in which the standard criteria conflict rather than agree, we can sharpen our intuitions as to what "race" really inheres in.

Seven possible candidates for racial self- and other-identification may be distinguished. They are not at all necessarily mutually exclusive, since they usually function in conjunction with one another. The interesting issue is what happens when this conjunction begins to disintegrate. The categories are bodily appearance, ancestry, self-awareness of ancestry, public awareness of ancestry, culture, experience, and self-identification.

When these categories all point to a specific racial designation, $R_1/R_2/R_3$, we do not hesitate to identify the person as a particular R, nor does the person. But since the United States has a nonideal racial system, with rules that are occasionally less than clear-cut, we may experience difficulty when the criteria conflict. Moreover, the problems in any decision procedure are compounded by the fuzziness of some of the criteria, which are not subject to precise stipulation. There is also the question whether $R_1/R_2/R_3$-ness is a discrete, on-off affair, or whether on occasion allowance is made for degrees of $R_1/R_2/R_3$-ness. This is separate from the question whether there is an *intermediate* category; the idea rather is that one could be seen as an R_1 or an R_2 or an R_3 but in a somewhat qualified (sometimes grudging?) fashion, not wholeheartedly or full-bloodedly—to use biological metaphors, though the basis for the judgment need not be biological—an R_1 or an R_2 or an R_3. It may also be that there is a partial gender asymmetry, so that what holds true for men in situations of criterial conflict does not always hold true for women. Finally, the fact of racial hierarchy (R_1s being systemically privileged) may carry over into the criteria for racial identification; that is, in some circumstances the rules for adjudicating the racial identity of R_1s may differ from the rules for R_2s/R_3s.

Bodily Appearance

Bodily appearance, the so-called eyeball test, is the criterion we all use to make summary judgments about race, since information about the other criteria is not usually immediately known to us. Historically, this has been true not merely for lay but for "scientific" judgments about race also, since before the advent of genetics earnest attempts were made to ascertain racial membership on the basis of such characteristics as skin color, skull measurements, and hair texture. In some racial systems, however, the appearance of R-ness is neither sufficient nor necessary for actual R-ness—though it will generally be a good evidential indicator—for some people may be able to "pass." Appearance is then the generally (but not always) reliable visible manifestation of a deeper essence that is taken to inhere in ancestry.

Ancestry

In the U.S. racial system, at least for whites and blacks, ancestry is usually taken as both necessary and sufficient for racial membership. (Elsewhere—in some Latin American countries, for example—appearance is more important, so that siblings of different colors may be assigned to different races despite their identical genealogy.) The rules for ancestral adjudication will, of course, be system-relative. A bipolar system, consisting exclusively of R_1s and R_2s, has no social and conceptual space for a third category, R_3s, that would explode the binary opposition, so that the offspring of "miscegenation" are assimilated to either the R_1s or the R_2s. Where blacks and whites are concerned, U.S. policy has historically been to classify them with the R_2s on the basis of the one-drop rule. This is what the anthropologist Marvin Harris calls the rule of "hypodescent," normative descent from the "lower" race. So entrenched has this view been until recently in national folkways and popular consciousness that it seems obvious, "natural," when in fact it is simply the result of a conscious public policy decision. The alternative policy of social *elevation* to R_1 status not merely is an abstract possibility but was actually followed at certain times in the Dutch East Indies, where the children of Dutch men and Asian women were counted as Dutch. Finally, in a tri- or multileveled racial system, such as obtains in the Caribbean and Latin America, there are formally recognized intermediate racial categories. (In the case of racial combinations, we may sometimes be satisfied with the less exact judgment "non-R_1"; that is, even if the details of the racial mixture are not clear, we at least want to know whether the person counts as an R_1, a member of the privileged race, or not.)

Self-Awareness of Ancestry

I have separated self-awareness (and public awareness) from ancestry in order to provide a conceptual entrée for some of the puzzle cases I will consider later. It might be thought that this is an epistemological rather than an ontological issue, that whether or not we *know* or others know, if we are an R_1 or an R_2 is not relevant to the substantive metaphysical question whether we actually *are* an R_1 or an R_2. But since this is one of the very claims I will examine, it seems better to leave it open rather than conceptually foreclose it.

Public Awareness of Ancestry

"Public awareness" as a criterion is fuzzy because one may be officially classed as an R_2 (e.g., on ancestral criteria) but, because of one's appearance, seem to be an R_1, so that—unless one remains in a small community where one's genealogy is known to all—one's ancestral R status may be on the record but not generally known.

Culture

Traditional racial theory, committed to racial realism, sees culture as an emanation of biological race, so invoking it as an additional criterion would be otiose (except perhaps as confirmation in contested cases of "mixed" ancestry). If culture stems from genotype, then for R_1s to adopt the cultural traits of R_2s or vice versa either should be impossible (the strong version of the thesis) or should at least involve considerable psychological strain (the weaker version), so that one's "real" biological self is always immanent within the borrowed clothes of the alien culture, waiting to assert itself. For nonrealist theories, on the other hand, whether constructivist, relativist, or subjectivist, culture is seen as adoptable with greater or lesser degrees of fluidity and is detachable from biological race, so that it may play a role in racial identification. Sometimes a tacit or overt normative premise of a moral and political kind is presupposed, that those

identifiable by other means as R_1s/R_2s should exclusively or predominantly embrace the culture associated with R_1s/R_2s. Failure to do so then makes one racially inauthentic. Note, though, that the use of culture as a criterion presumes relatively clear demarcating traits that differentiate R_1 from R_2 culture. But even if a clear genealogy of origins can be traced (not always the case), the constant intermingling of peoples means that patterns originally associated with one group can be adopted by others and, over time, transformed so as to be recognizably "theirs." Many Euro-American cultural practices have unacknowledged Native American and African roots, whereas the syncretism resulting from slavery makes dubious the dream of some Afrocentrists of recovering an uncontaminated African essence.

Experience

Like culture, "experience" has an unavoidable fuzziness, but it is important, for in the vertical racial systems we are considering it is part of the core of what it is to be (with all the metaphysical overtones of *be*) a member of a particular race. Thus in the United States, we naturally think of whiteness as being associated with the experience of racial privilege and of blackness as being associated with the experience of racial oppression. Since criterial divergence is possible, so that R_2s who look like R_1s and are not publicly identified as R_2s will escape racism, it may then be alleged that these R_2s are not "really" R_2s, insofar as the essence of being an R_2 is the experience of oppression *as* an R_2.

Subjective Identification

Finally, subjective identification—what one *sees* oneself as—needs to be conceptually separated from self-awareness of ancestry, for one may refuse to recognize the validity of this criterion for racial membership; and from culture, for one could still identify oneself as an R_1/R_2, while embracing R_2/R_1 culture; and finally from experience, for one could have experiences characteristically taken to be definitive of the R_1/R_2-experience while denying that these experiences should be seen as definitive of who one is. As a further complication, self-awareness of ancestry is an either-or affair (either one knows or not), whereas subjective identification lends itself to degrees of variation, in that one can weakly or strongly identify oneself as an R_1/R_2, so that this identification is less or more significant to one's sense of oneself and one's life projects. Robert Gooding-Williams makes the useful distinction of "thin" and "thick" senses of "black" to differentiate these varying degrees of self-identification for African-Americans.

What happens when these criteria conflict with one another? That is, what happens when, through naturally occurring or artificially devised problem cases, individuals are produced whose racial ontology is not immediately or maybe not even indefinitely clear? As in the parallel case of personal identity, the strategy simultaneously involves drawing on some intuitions and over-turning others.

Let us bracket the moral and political question whether one *should* try to change one's race, or at least one's apparent race. The motivation for such actions has often been seen as ignoble: the desire to enjoy the privileges of the dominant race while distancing oneself from the fate of the oppressed. But this is a separate issue, certainly of interest in its own right but distinct from the metaphysical one. So we should try to avoid the kind of cognitive interference that comes from thinking that because it is morally or politically *wrong* for black people to try to become white, they cannot succeed in doing so—that the (moral) "inauthenticity" of the decision, somehow carries over to infect the metaphysical status. (One would then be not a white person who is inauthentic but an inauthentic white person.) Unless, of course, a case can be made for such a connection. . . .

Problem Case A

Consider the case of someone I will call Mr. Oreo. Mr. Oreo cannot even think of passing, being quite dark with clearly black African features and with known black ancestry. But he is unhappy with his racial designation, so he fills in "white" on bureaucratic forms, identifies himself as white, and rejects black culture. Will these gestures make him white? The black community has a standard negative moral judgment of such people, which is of course signified by the name. Some notion of racial authenticity is presupposed, along with a normative judgment that this kind of repudiation

is morally contemptible. It would be interesting to explore the values that underlie this judgment—after all, if race is constructed, what gives it moral significance?—but as I said at the start, my focus is on the metaphysics rather than the ethics. And the designation Oreo clearly has a metaphysical as well as a moral dimension, since it implies that the person is divided, black on the outside but white on the inside. Does this mean that for lay consciousness, the person *has* succeeded in changing his race, insofar as the spatial metaphors of inside and outside standardly correspond to essence and appearance? In some contexts, after all, it would critically be said of Mr. Oreo that "he's really white." But this is really a statement about values and identification; if pressed, people would deny that Mr. Oreo has actually become white. The sense would be that he is a black man pretending, or trying and failing, to be white, so that the moral opprobrium arises from the attempt, not the success or failure of the attempt.

Now, why do we not think the person has succeeded? For lay consciousness, which is typically realist, the simple answer is that race inheres in ancestry, appearance, and so on, so that it cannot be changed. But racial constructivists would also deny that race-changing in this fashion is possible, seeing this position as an untenable racial subjectivism or voluntarism. And a central reason for their claim will be that Mr. Oreo is still socially *categorized* as black, especially by the crucial population, the white one; he will still experience racism and so will still be black insofar as the experience of white racism is definitive of the black experience. When followed around in a department store, stopped by the police in a white neighborhood, or mistaken for the waiter in a restaurant, Mr. Oreo may protest, with a reassuring laugh, "No, no, you don't understand, I'm not one of *them*," but his protest is not likely to be effective. (Note, though, that this scenario opens the possibility of a more liberal, "cultural" racism, whereby people could be prima facie black but gain at least a virtual, courtesy whiteness by passing, the appropriate cultural tests and thereby be distinguished from unreconstructed blacks.) So if racial subjectivism is a mistaken position on the metaphysics of race, Mr. Oreo will still be black.

Problem Case B

But suppose Mr. Oreo comes to understand this and is a sufficiently determined fellow. Let's give him the option of a technological fix, introducing to that end the Schuyler Machine. The well-publicized cosmetic transformation of Michael Jackson raises the possibility that advances in plastic surgery techniques or even genetic engineering may make it possible one day to transform one's skin, hair, and facial features so that one looks completely white. In George Schuyler's neglected satirical classic, *Black No More,* a black scientist invents a machine that can do just that, with the result that within a few months all the blacks in the United States vanish, having seized the opportunity to transform themselves into apparent whites. Let us call this device the Schuyler Machine. (In the book it has no name.)

Suppose individuals such as Mr. Oreo whose bodies are *not* naturally white make use of this device and then go on to assimilate as above. In these cases, does their artificially rather than naturally white bodily appearance support the doubts of those who question whether one can really change one's race? Why? What would the basis of this skepticism be? Compare another kind of physical transformation, that of bodily physique and strength. If a machine were invented (call this the Schwarzenegger Machine) that could transform 98-pound weaklings into massively muscled supermen capable of pressing hundreds of pounds without the tedium of years of special diets and weight training, would we say that the person only *looked* strong but had not really *become* strong? Obviously not: his new body, new physique, new strength are real. So what is the difference? (The question here is not the deep ontological one whether an apparently white body makes a person really racially white, since we have already seen that—at least by itself—it doesn't necessarily do so. Rather, the question is the shallow ontological one whether an apparently white body is any the less apparently white because the whiteness is artificially engineered rather than natural. So we are dealing here precisely with an ontology of appearance, of surfaces.)

Is the difference that we think of the first two persons' surface whiteness as real (because genetic), whereas Mr. Oreo's is unreal (because artificial)? In the first place, of course, the Schuyler Machine

may work through genetic manipulation, so the etiology would still be genetic, though not hereditary. If we insist that the whiteness comes from parental genes, is this not just a repetition of the ancestral criterion, whereas we began by agreeing to consider them separately? In the second place, even if the whiteness is artificial, why is it any the less real? "Artificial" does not necessarily contrast with "real"; it just contrasts with "natural." An artificial heart is real enough and can sometimes do the job as well as (or better than) a real heart. Moreover, technological advances and the general mediation of the natural by the social make the distinction increasingly problematic.

Or is the objection of another kind, that the "whiteness" is thought of as somehow merely surface, a kind of full-bodied "whiteface" that corresponds to the blackface of nineteenth-century minstrelsy, and underneath it is the original black-skinned person? By hypothesis, the pertinent bodily parts really are transformed; it is not that the skin acquires a white sheen that will come off if Mr. Oreo goes out in the rain, for example, or scrapes himself by accident. Rather, the change is in the skin (and hair texture, facial features, etc.). Or do we unconsciously think of physiological "whiteness" as something that permeates the whole body, inhering not merely in skin color, facial features, and hair texture but also sparking in the synapses of the brain, pumping through the bloodstream, dripping through the pancreas? If so, it is a revealing indication of how, despite ourselves, lay conceptions of race affect us. Research has shown that the morphological differences between people classed as white and those classed as black are minor, quite apart from the reality that many "blacks" in the United States have largely white ancestry.

My suggestion is, then, that whether the apparent whiteness is natural or artificial should make no difference to its reality; in both cases, the person is apparently white. So the point of this exercise is to undermine conventional intuitions about the "natural" basis of whiteness and the location of its ontological depth in the biological. Race *is* ontologically deep, but its depth lies in intersubjectivity; a body that appears to intersubjective judgment to be white is all, I am arguing, that is necessary here. (The alternative would be to introduce another level and speak of bodies that "appear white," whereas other bodies "appear to appear white.") A case can be made, then, that Mr. Oreo succeeds in changing his race, especially if he moves to a part of the country where nobody knows about his black past, though admittedly if he marries a white woman, having children will be a challenge.

Problem Case C

Consider the case of unconscious passing from the other direction: the white child in the Twain story raised as black. This is someone with a genetically white body and all-white ancestry who, unaware of his actual parentage, grows up as black, thinks of himself as black, is culturally black, and is categorized by the community as black. If the ancestral criterion is the overriding one, then we have to say that this person is really white. But what does the "really" mean other than the repetition of the point that his ancestry is white? At the novel's end, the deception is discovered and the biologically white young man resumes his place as rightful heir (though never to feel at home except in the kitchen), whereas the unconscious impostor, who has been a miscreant in various ways, is sold down the river as partial payment for estate debts. But suppose the switch had never been discovered. Would it still be true that in some deep sense, the biologically white boy was really white? Or can we say that he became black, that his race was changed?

Problem Case D

In a vertical racial system, members of the subordinate race who assume the privileges of the dominant race are, as I have noted, usually morally condemned. Correspondingly, members of the racially privileged group who support and identify with the racially oppressed usually gain our moral approbation, if not that of their peers. Can this identification extend to race-changing? The hostile term "nigger-lover" often carried with it the threat that, to persist in subversive behavior would lead one to be treated in the same way as blacks, but does this actually amount to an ontological shift? Various terms from the American and colonial experience seem to register such a possibility: the "white Injun" of the frontier period, the European

explorer who "goes native," the general notion of the "white renegade" or "race traitor" who is seen as not merely betraying his race but in some sense as *changing* his race. A U.S. journal, *Race Traitor*, calls on white Americans to self-consciously repudiate their whiteness. (In the 1950s Norman Mailer wrote a famous essay on the hipsters as "White Negroes"; their contemporary descendants are "whiggers," or "white niggers," suburban white kids who affect the clothing, language, and musical styles of black inner-city youth.)

Imagine such a contemporary white renegade who sets out to support and identify with black struggles, steeps himself in black culture, joins nonseparatist black political organizations, and is therefore on occasion targeted for differential treatment by hostile authorities. Sometimes, of course, whites who take this course are working out personal problems, indulging in some kind of "exoticism," or "slumming." But perhaps this individual's sincerity so impresses the black community that he is even regarded as an "honorary" black. In this case, unlike that of Mr. Oreo, one's moral judgment is likely to be favorable, but is this relevant to the metaphysical issue? It could perhaps be argued that since the metaphysics depends in part on some kind of subjective decision, the moral authenticity of giving up racial privilege translates into or becomes a kind of metaphysical authenticity. But we would tend to feel, I think, that the person is at most politically or maybe culturally but not *really* black. After all, in many situations his assumed identity will not be known, and he will just be treated like any other white guy. And in any case, he can always have a change of heart and jettison his assumed identity, which in a world without a Schuyler Machine blacks in general cannot do. (But suppose that the community is small, and the authorities have an official policy to penalize racial transgressors by publicizing their identities and formally and permanently changing their racial standing. Consider the real-life case of the white author John Howard Griffin, who, in a reversal of the Schuyler Machine process, had his skin treated to darken it and on the basis of his experience wrote the bestselling *Black Like Me* in 1959. If Griffin had carried out his project in a society so small that everyone subsequently was informed about his "crime" and treated him accordingly forever after, we might want to say that he really *would* have become black.) . . .

Problem Case E

Consider now the case of biracialism. The U.S. racial system has been polarized mainly between white and black, with blackness being demarcated through the one-drop rule. An intermediate mulatto category has sometimes or in particular locales been officially recognized, and within the black community there are traditional shade hierarchies, but this has been the basic division. In the Caribbean and Latin America the spectrum of statuses is more variegated. In part because of the growth in intermarriage and resulting "mixed" children, a movement is afoot in the United States to introduce a multiracial category on census forms to accommodate the experience of people who reject the bifurcation into black and white. The young golfing star Tiger Woods, for example, identifies himself as "Cablinasian"—Caucasian, black, Indian, and Asian. Some blacks protest that this is merely another way for people with visible European ancestry to differentiate themselves from the "pure" black population. Historically, browns/mulattoes/mestizos have been seen as superior to "unmixed" blacks, if not as good as whites, and as such have been privileged in various ways in mainstream white society. (This situation is recognized in black American popular discourse in the old rhyme "If you're white, you're all right, if you're brown, stick around, if you're black, stand back." Moreover, within the black American population in some cities there were somatically exclusive clubs—for example, the blue-vein or brown paper bag clubs—from which dark-skinned blacks were excluded.)

As before, however, the focus is on the metaphysical question. The question is not whether such a tri- or multipolar racial system is possible, because the Latin experience shows it is, and one could imagine a United States with an alternative history that had evolved with such a system. If racial constructivism is correct, then by definition the same human population can be demarcated and constructed into different "races" in many ways. The question is whether, in the face of majority white resistance to such a revision, subgroups within the existing bipolar system can successfully construct themselves as biracial. My endorsement of constructivism has been predicated on a uniform national system. But it might be argued that certain circumstances could promote a racial relativism in which particular subcommunities could reject official categorizations and construct their own identities.

In his book *Who Is Black?* for example, F. James Davis discusses the history of "American Mestizos": Brass Ankles, Red Legs, Yellowhammers, Red Bones, Guineas, Jackson Whites, Moors, Creoles, and other groups with black ancestry who have historically refused the status of blackness. "These so-called American Mestizo groups have protected themselves from the one-drop rule by remaining as isolated as possible, which has become more and more difficult. Within their own communities they are presumably all equal, whatever their racial composition, and they are very cautious in their dealings with the outside . . . [They] continue to try to avoid being defined as blacks by remaining isolated and wary."

We are talking, then, not of individual voluntarism (racial subjectivism) but of a group decision to challenge dominant conceptions. But as Davis's account makes clear, to the extent that their deviant self-definition has been possible, it has required social exile, which is not a desirable option for contemporary bi- and multiracial individuals. So the question is whether such a self-chosen hybrid identity can be sustained on the basis of group endorsement in the face of the majority's adherence to the traditional principle by which any black blood makes one black. Would such people really become another race, or, because of their interactions with the larger society, would they really just stay black? . . .

We have seen, then, that there are issues pertaining to race and racial identity that are well worth the time of philosophers to address. Doubtless they will become more pressing as the nation's racial composition shifts. Most Western philosophers have been white and have taken their racial standing for granted, not seeing how it enters into their identity and affects their relationship with the universe. Race may not be real in the sense that racial realists think or would even like, but it is real enough in other senses. The metaphysics of racial identity is thus a metaphysics well worth investigating.

DISCUSSION QUESTIONS

1. What are the similarities and differences among a quace system, a horizontal racial system, and a vertical racial system?

2. Mills states, "But from the fact that racial realism is false, it does not follow that race is not real in other senses." What is racial realism, and why is it false? In what sense does Mills believe that race is real? Do you agree with him? Why or why not?

3. What is the difference between who you are *really* and who you are *taken* to be? How does Mills utilize this distinction in his discussion of racial identity?

4. Compare and contrast MacIntyre's, de Beauvoir's and Mills's approaches to identity.

What are the similarities and difference among them?

5. Why does Mills believe that the seven potential criteria for racial identification (bodily appearance, ancestry, self-awareness of ancestry, public awareness of ancestry, culture, experience, and self-identification) are each, in themselves, inadequate? Discuss how one of the problem cases shows this inadequacy. Do you agree with him? Why or why not?

6. Mills discusses primarily racial identity in this article. Do you think his theses hold for sex/gender, ethnic, and class identity as well? Why or why not? Discuss one of these three types of identity using the model Mills applies to race.

White Man's Burden
[USA 1995] 1 hour, 38 minutes
Directed by Desmond Nakano

Whites are the minority population in the society depicted in *White Man's Burden*. White citizens are subject to racial profiling by the police, and the media are dominated by black actors and commentators. Louis Pinnock (John Travolta) works in a factory owned by Thaddeus Thomas (Harry Belafonte). Pinnock is wrongly accused of violating Thomas's privacy by peeping in his windows and consequently loses his job. A string of misfortunes follows Pinnock's termination. He is unable to find work through social services and cannot pay his bills. When his car breaks down, two police officers wrongly profile him as a criminal and severely beat him. The Pinnocks owe rent to their landlord and are evicted from their home. Pinnock's wife, Marsha (Kelly Lynch), moves to her mother's home, and Pinnock must part with his children. In desperation, he meets with Thomas and demands money in recompense for his lost employment. When Thomas is unable to withdraw funds from the bank, Pinnock kidnaps him. Several days later, the two men are found by the police. Though Pinnock surrenders, an officer spots a gun in his hand and shoots and kills him.

DISCUSSION QUESTIONS

1. Is the discrimination described in this film based on what Mills calls a quace system, a horizontal racial system, or a vertical racial system? Explain.

2. Does this film effectively introduce the difference between who you are *really* and who you are *taken* to be? Why or why not?

3. By reversing the social and economic positions of whites and blacks, is this film suggesting that our *identity* is primarily determined by our culture? Also, is this film suggesting that our social and economic positions are due only to culture?

4. Does Thomas "owe" Pinnock anything? Is Thomas responsible for the downward spiral that Pinnock's life takes after he is fired?

5. In an effort to assuage his feelings of guilt concerning Pinnock's death, Thomas attempts to give money to Marsha. His action suggests that racial discrimination negatively affects both the discriminator and the discriminated. Do you agree with this? Why or why not?

6. Is racial profiling morally unjustifiable? Is it racist? When, if ever, is it morally justifiable to profile someone as more of a threat to be engaged in crime based on his or her race? Defend your position.

7. When Thomas attempts to give money to Marsha following her husband's death, she refuses it, asking, "How much do you think would be enough?" Does she do the right thing? Why or why not? What do you think would be "enough"?

GLORIA ANZALDÚA

HOW TO TAME A WILD TONGUE

Gloria Anzaldúa argues that our identity is connected to the language or languages we speak. Therefore, when people are trained to lose their accents or trained not to speak in their native or chosen language, they are being denied their identity. Anzaldúa, a Chicana, describes how as a child she was repeatedly told that her native language was wrong and how such attacks on her native language resulted in a diminished sense of self. "So, if you want to really hurt me, talk badly about my language," says Anzaldúa. "Ethnic identity is twin skin to linguistic identity—I am my language." "Until I can take pride in my language," she argues, "I cannot take pride in myself." For Anzaldúa, a low regard for her language is tantamount to a low regard for her.

Anzaldúa's comments on language use and its role in identity formation reveal one of the important ways in which our identity is claimed to be socially constructed. For her, personal identity is not part of the metaphysical fabric of the universe but rather is determined by our social and cultural environment—particularly, the degree to which we are allowed to speak in our native tongue. Anzaldúa contends that "to tame a wild tongue" is to reshape an ethnic identity.

Gloria Anzaldúa (1942–2004) was born to sharecropper/field-worker parents in the South Texas Rio Grande Valley and worked the fields in Texas and Arkansas to survive after the death of her father when she was fifteen. She received a B.A. in English, art, and secondary education from Pan American University and an M.A. in English and education from the University of Texas at Austin. She taught feminism, Chicano studies, and creative writing at a number of universities, including the University of Texas at Austin, Vermont College of Norwich University, and San Francisco State University. She was the winner of the Before Columbus Foundation American Book Award, the Lambda Lesbian Small Press Book Award, an NEA Fiction Award, and the Sappho Award of Distinction. Her books include *This Bridge Called My Back: Writings by Radical Women of Color* (co-edited with Cherrie Moraga, 1981), *Borderlands/La Frontera: The New Mestiza* (1987), *Making Face, Making Soul/Hacieno Caras: Creative and Critical Perspectives by Women of Color* (1990), *Lloronas, Women Who Howl: Autohistorias-Torias and the Production of Writing, Knowledge, and Identity* (1996), *La Prieta* (1997), *Cassell's Encyclopedia of Queer Myth, Symbol and Spirit* (1998), and *Interviews/Entrevistas* (co-edited with AnaLouise Keating, 2000). The following selection is from *Borderlands/La Frontera*.

"We're going to have to control your tongue," the dentist says, pulling out all the metal from my mouth. Silver bits plop and tinkle into the basin. My mouth is a motherlode.

The dentist is cleaning out my roots. I get a whiff of the stench when I gasp. "I can't cap that tooth yet, you're still draining," he says.

"We're going to have to do something about your tongue," I hear the anger rising in his voice. My tongue keeps pushing out the wads of cotton, pushing back the drills, the long thin needles: "I've never seen anything as strong or as stubborn," he says. And I think, how do you tame a wild tongue, train it to be quiet, how do you bridle and saddle it? How do you make it lie down?

> Who is to say that robbing a people of
> its language is less violent than war?
>
> —RAY GWYN SMITH

I remember being caught speaking Spanish at recess—that was good for three licks on the knuckles with a sharp ruler. I remember being sent to the corner of the classroom for "talking back" to the Anglo teacher when all I was trying to do was tell her how to pronounce my name.

"If you want to be American, speak 'American.' If you don't like it, go back to Mexico where you belong."

"I want you to speak English. *Pa'hallar buen trabajo tienes que saber hablar el inglés bien. Qué vale toda tu educación si todavía hablas inglés con un* 'accent,'" my mother would say, mortified that I spoke English like a Mexican. At Pan American University, I, and all Chicano students were required to take two speech classes. Their purpose: to get rid of our accents.

Attacks on one's form of expression with the intent to censor are a violation of the First Amendment. *El Anglo con cara de inocente nos arrancó la lengua.* Wild tongues can't be tamed, they can only be cut out.

OVERCOMING THE TRADITION OF SILENCE

> *Ahogadas, escupimos el oscuro.*
> *Peleando con nuestra propia sombra*
> *el silencio nos sepulta.*

En boca cerrada no entran moscas. "Flies don't enter a closed mouth" is a saying I kept hearing when I was a child. *Ser habladora* was to be a gossip and a liar, to talk too much. *Muchachitas bien criadas,* well-bred girls don't answer back. *Es una falta de respeto* to talk back to one's mother or father. I remember one of the sins I'd recite to the priest in the confession box the few times I went to confession: talking back to my mother, *hablar pa' 'tras, repelar. Hocicona, repelona, chismosa,* having a big mouth, questioning, carrying tales are all signs of being *mal criada.* In my culture they are all words that are derogatory if applied to women— I've never heard them applied to men.

The first time I heard two women, a Puerto Rican and a Cuban, say the word *"nosotras,"* I was shocked. I had not known the word existed. Chicanas use *nosotros* whether we're male or female. We are robbed of our female being by the masculine plural. Language is a male discourse.

> And our tongues have become
> dry   the wilderness has
> dried out our tongues   and
> we have forgotten speech.
>
> —IRENA KLEPFISZ

Even our own people, other Spanish speakers *nos quieren poner candados en la boca.* They would hold us back with their bag of *reglas de academia.*

> *Oyé como ladra: el lenguaje de la frontera*
> *Quien tiene boca se equivoca.*
>
> —MEXICAN SAYING

"*Pocho,* cultural traitor, you're speaking the oppressor's language by speaking English, you're ruining the Spanish language," I have been accused by various Latinos and Latinas. Chicano Spanish is considered by the purist and by most Latinos deficient, a mutilation of Spanish.

But Chicano Spanish is a border tongue which developed naturally. Change, *evolución, enriquecimiento de palabras nuevas por invención o adopción* have created variants of Chicano Spanish, *un nuevo lenguaje. Un lenguaje que corresponde a un modo de vivir.* Chicano Spanish is not incorrect, it is a living language.

For a people who are neither Spanish nor live in a country in which Spanish is the first language; for a people who live in a country in which English is the reigning tongue but who are not Anglo; for a people who cannot entirely identify with either standard (formal, Castillian) Spanish nor standard English, what recourse is left to them but to create their own language? A language which they can connect their identity to, one capable of communicating the realities and values true to themselves—a language with terms that are neither *español ni inglés,* but both. We speak a patois, a forked tongue, a variation of two languages.

Chicano Spanish sprang out of the Chicanos' need to identify ourselves as a distinct people. We needed a language with which we could communicate with ourselves, a secret language. For some of us, language is a homeland closer than the Southwest—for many Chicanos today live in the Midwest and the East. And because we are a complex, heterogeneous people, we speak many languages. Some of the languages we speak are:

1. Standard English
2. Working class and slang English
3. Standard Spanish
4. Standard Mexican Spanish
5. North Mexican Spanish dialect
6. Chicano Spanish (Texas, New Mexico, Arizono and California have regional variations)
7. Tex-Mex
8. *Pachuco* (called *caló*)

My "home" tongues are the languages I speak with my sister and brothers, with my friends. They are the last five listed, with 6 and 7 being closest to my heart. From school, the media and job situations, I've picked up standard and working class English. From Mamagrande Locha and from reading Spanish and Mexican literature, I've picked up Standard Spanish and Standard Mexican Spanish. From *los recién llegados,* Mexican immigrants, and *braceros,* I learned the North Mexican dialect. With Mexicans I'll try to speak either Standard Mexican Spanish or the North Mexican dialect. From my parents and Chicanos living in the Valley, I picked up Chicano Texas Spanish, and I speak it with my mom, younger brother (who married a Mexican and who rarely mixes Spanish with English), aunts and older relatives.

With Chicanas from *Nuevo México* or *Arizona* I will speak Chicano Spanish a little, but often they don't understand what I'm saying. With most California Chicanas I speak entirely in English (unless I forget). When I first moved to San Francisco, I'd rattle off something in Spanish, unintentionally embarrassing them. Often it is only with another Chicana *tejana* that I can talk freely.

Words distorted by English are known as anglicisms or *pochismos.* The *pocho* is an anglicized Mexican or American of Mexican origin who speaks Spanish with an accent characteristic of North Americans and who distorts and reconstructs the language according to the influence of English. Tex-Mex, or Spanglish, comes most naturally to me. I may switch back and forth from English to Spanish in the same sentence or in the same word. With my sister and my brother Nune and with Chicano *tejano* contemporaries I speak in Tex-Mex.

From kids and people my own age I picked up *Pachuco. Pachuco* (the language of the zoot suiters) is a language of rebellion, both against Standard Spanish and Standard English. It is a secret language. Adults of the culture and outsiders cannot understand it. It is made up of slang words from both English and Spanish. *Ruca* means girl or woman, *vato* means guy or dude, *chale* means no, *simón* means yes, *churro* is sure, talk is *periquiar, pigionear* means petting, *que gacho* means how nerdy, *ponte águila* means watch out, death is called *la pelona.* Through lack of practice and not having others who can speak it, I've lost most of the *Pachuco* tongue.

CHICANO SPANISH

Chicanos, after 250 years of Spanish/Anglo colonization have developed significant differences in the Spanish we speak. We collapse two adjacent vowels into a single syllable and sometimes shift the stress in certain words such as *maíz/maiz, cohete/cuete.* We leave out certain consonants when they appear between vowels: *lado/lao, mojado/mojao.* Chicanos from South Texas pronounce *f* as *j* as in *jue (fue).* Chicanos use "archaisms," words that are no longer in the Spanish language, words that have been evolved out. We say *semos, truje, haiga, ansina,* and *naiden.* We retain the "archaic" *j,* as in *jalar,* that derives from an earlier *h* (the French *halar* or the Germanic *halon* which was lost to standard Spanish in the 16th century), but which is still found in several regional dialects such as the one spoken in South

Texas. (Due to geography, Chicanos from the Valley of South Texas were cut off linguistically from other Spanish speakers. We tend to use words that the Spaniards brought over from Medieval Spain. The majority of the Spanish colonizers in Mexico and the Southwest came from Extremadura—Hernán Cortés was one of them—and Andalucía. Andalucians pronounce *ll* like a *y*, and their *d*'s tend to be absorbed by adjacent vowels: *tirado* becomes *tirao*. They brought *el lenguaje popular, dialectos y regionalismos.*)

Chicanos and other Spanish speakers also shift *ll* to *y* and *z* to *s*. We leave out initial syllables, saying *tar* for *estar, toy* for *estoy, hora* for *ahora* (*cubanos* and *puertorriqueños* also leave out initial letters of some words). We also leave out the final syllable such as *pa* for *para*. The intervocalic *y*, the *ll* as in *tortilla, ella, botella*, gets replaced by *tortia* or *tortiya, ea, botea*. We add an additional syllable at the beginning of certain words: *atocar* for *tocar, agastar* for *gastar*. Sometimes we'll say *lavaste las vacijas,* other times *lavates* (substituting the *ates* verb endings for the *aste*.)

We use anglicisms, words borrowed from English: *bola* from ball, *carpeta* from carpet, *máchina de lavar* (instead of *lavadora*) from washing machine. Tex-Mex argot, created by adding a Spanish sound at the beginning or end of an English word such as *cookiar* for cook, *watchar* for watch, *parkiar* for park, and *rapiar* for rape, is the result of the pressures on Spanish speakers to adapt to English.

We don't use the word *vosotros/as* or its accompanying verb form. We don't say *claro* (to mean yes), *imagínate,* or *me emociona,* unless we picked up Spanish from Latinas, out of a book, or in a classroom. Other Spanish-speaking groups are going through the same, or similar, development in their Spanish.

LINGUISTIC TERRORISM

Deslenguadas. Somos los del español deficiente. We are your linguistic nightmate, your linguistic aberration, your linguistic *mestisaje,* the subject of your *burla.* Because we speak with tongues of fire we are culturally crucified. Racially, culturally and linguistically *somos buérfanos— we speak an orphan tongue.*

Chicanas who grew up speaking Chicano Spanish have internalized the belief that we speak poor Spanish. It is illegitimate, a bastard language.

And because we internalize how our language has been used against us by the dominant culture, we use our language differences against each other.

Chicana feminists often skirt around each other with suspicion and hesitation. For the longest time I couldn't figure it out. Then it dawned on me. To be close to another Chicana is like looking into the mirror. We are afraid of what we'll see there. *Pena.* Shame, Low estimation of self. In childhood we are told that our language is wrong. Repeated attacks on our native tongue diminish our sense of self. The attacks continue throughout our lives.

Chicanas feel uncomfortable talking in Spanish to Latinas, afraid of their censure. Their language was not outlawed in their countries. They had a whole lifetime of being immersed in their native tongue; generations, centuries in which Spanish was first language, taught in school, heard on radio and TV, and read in the newspaper.

If a person, Chicana or Latina, has a low estimation of my native tongue, she also has a low estimation of me. Often with *mexicanas y latinas* we'll speak English as a neutral language. Even among Chicanas we tend to speak English at parties or conferences. Yet, at the same time, we're afraid the other will think we're *agringadas* because we don't speak Chicano Spanish. We oppress each other trying to out-Chicano each other, vying to be the "real" Chicanas, to speak like Chicanos. There is no one Chicano language just as there is no one Chicano experience. A monolingual Chicana whose first language is English or Spanish is just as much a Chicana as one who speaks several variants of Spanish. A Chicana from Michigan or Chicago or Detroit is just as much a Chicana as one from the Southwest. Chicano Spanish is as diverse linguistically as it is regionally.

By the end of this century, Spanish speakers will [constitute] the biggest minority group in the U.S., a country where students in high schools and colleges are encouraged to take French classes because French is considered more "cultured." But for a language to remain alive it must be used. By the end of this century English, and not Spanish, will be the mother tongue of most Chicanos and Latinos.

So, if you want to really hurt me, talk badly about my language. Ethnic identity is twin skin to linguistic identity—I am my language. Until I can take pride in my language, I cannot take pride in myself. Until I can accept as legitimate Chicano Texas Spanish, Tex-Mex and all the other languages I speak, I cannot accept the legitimacy of myself. Until I am free to write bilingually and to switch code without having always to translate, while I still have to speak English or Spanish when I would rather speak Spanglish, and as long as I have to accommodate the English speakers rather than having them accommodate me, my tongue will be illegitimate.

I will no longer be made to feel ashamed of existing. I will have my voice: Indian, Spanish, white. I will have my serpent's tongue—my woman's voice, my sexual voice, my poet's voice. I will overcome the tradition of silence.

> My fingers
> move sly against your palm
> Like women everywhere, we speak in
>   code. . . .

— Melanie Kaye/Kantrowitz

"Vistas," corridos, y comida: My Native Tongue

In the 1960s, I read my first Chicano novel. It was *City of Night* by John Rechy, a gay Texan, son of a Scottish father and a Mexican mother. For days I walked around in stunned amazement that a Chicano could write and could get published. When I read *I Am Joaquín* I was surprised to see a bilingual book by a Chicano in print. When I saw poetry written in Tex-Mex for the first time, a feeling of pure joy flashed through me. I felt like we really existed as a people. In 1971, when I started teaching High School English to Chicano students, I tried to supplement the required texts with works by Chicanos, only to be reprimanded and forbidden to do so by the principal. He claimed that I was supposed to teach "American" and English literature. At the risk of being fired, I swore my students to secrecy and slipped in Chicano short stories, poems, a play. In graduate school, while working toward a Ph.D., I had to "argue" with one advisor after the other, semester after semester, before I was allowed to make Chicano literature an area of focus.

Even before I read books by Chicanos or Mexicans, it was the Mexican movies I saw at the drive-in—the Thursday night special of $1.00 a carload—that gave me a sense of belonging.

"Vámonos a las vistas," my mother would call out and we'd all—grandmother, brothers, sister and cousins—squeeze into the car. We'd wolf down cheese and bologna white bread sandwiches while watching Pedro Infante in melodramatic tearjerkers like *Nosotros los pobres,* the first "real" Mexican movie (that was not an imitation of European movies). I remember seeing *Cuando los hijos se van* and surmising that all Mexican movies played up the love a mother has for her children and what ungrateful sons and daughters suffer when they are not devoted to their mothers. I remember the singing-type "westerns" of Jorge Negrete and Miquel Aceves Majía. When watching Mexican movies, I felt a sense of homecoming as well as alienation. People who were to amount to something didn't go to Mexican movies, or *bailes* or tune their radios to *bolero, rancherita,* and *corrido* music.

The whole time I was growing up, there was *norteno* music sometimes called North Mexican border music, or Tex-Mex music, or Chicano music, or *cantina* (bar) music. I grew up listening to *conjuntos,* three- of four-piece bands made up of folk musicians playing guitar, *bajo sexto,* drums and button accordion, which Chicanos had borrowed from the German immigrants who had come to Central Texas and Mexico to farm and build breweries. In the Rio Grande Valley, Steve Jordan and Little Joe Hernández were popular, and Flaco Jiménez was the accordian king. The rhythms of Tex-Mex music are those of the polka, also adapted from the Germans, who in turn had borrowed the polka from the Czechs and Bohemians.

I remember the hot, sultry evenings when *corridos*—songs of love and death on the Texas-Mexican borderlands—reverberated out of cheap amplifiers from the local *cantinas* and wafted in through my bedroom window.

Corridos first became widely used along the South Texas/Mexican border during the early conflict between Chicanos and Anglos. The *corridos* are usually about Mexican heroes who do valiant deeds against the Anglo oppressors. Pancho Villa's song, *"La cucaracha,"* is the most famous one. *Corridos* of John F. Kennedy and his death are still very popular in the Valley. Older Chicanos remember Lydia Mendoza, one of the great border *corrido* singers who was called *la Gloria de Tejas.* Her *"El tango Negro,"* sung during the Great Depression, made her a singer of the people. The everpresent *corridos* narrated one hundred years of border history, bringing news of events as well as entertaining. These folk musicians and folk songs are our chief cultural mythmakers, and they made our hard lives seem bearable.

I grew up feeling ambivalent about our music. Country-western and rock-and-roll had more status. In the 50s and 60s, for the slightly educated and *agringado* Chicanos, there existed a sense of shame at being caught listening to our music. Yet I couldn't stop my feet from thumping to the music, could not stop humming the words, nor hide from myself the exhilaration I felt when I heard it.

There are more subtle ways that we internalize identification, especially in the forms of images and emotions. For me food and certain smells are tied to my identity, to my homeland. Woodsmoke curling up to an immense blue sky; woodsmoke perfuming my grandmother's clothes, her skin. The stench of cow manure and the yellow patches on the ground; the crack of a .22 rifle and the reek of cordite. Homemade white cheese sizzling in a pan, melting inside a folded *tortilla.* My sister Hilda's hot, spicy *menudo, chile colorado* making it deep red, pieces of *panza* and hominy floating on top. My brother Carito barbequing *fajitas* in the backyard. Even now and 3,000 miles away, I can see my mother spicing the ground beef, pork and venison with *chile.* My mouth salivates at the thought of the hot steaming *tamales* I would be eating if I were home.

> *SI LE PREGUNTAS A MI MAMÁ, "¿QUÉ ERES?"*
>
> Identity is the essential core of who we are as individuals, the conscious experience of the self inside.
>
> —KAUFMAN

Nosotros los Chicanos straddle the borderlands. On one side of us, we are constantly exposed to the Spanish of the Mexicans, on the other side we hear the Anglos' incessant clamoring so that we forget our language. Among ourselves we don't say *nosotros los americanos, o nosotros los espanoles, o nosotros los hispanos.* We say *nosotros los mexicanos* (by *mexicanos* we do not mean citizens of Mexico; we do not mean a national identity, but a racial one). We distinguish between *mexicanos del otro lado* and *mexicanos de este lado.* Deep in our hearts we believe that being Mexican has nothing to do with which country one lives in. Being Mexican is a state of soul—not one of mind, not one of citizenship. Neither eagle nor serpent, but both. And like the ocean, neither animal respects borders.

> *Dime con guien andasy te diré quien eres.*
> (Tell me who your friends are and I'll tell you who you are.)
>
> —MEXICAN SAYING

Si le preguntas a mi mamá, "¿Qué eres?" te dirá, "Soy mexicana." My brothers and sister say the same. I sometimes will answer *"soy Mexicana"* and at others will say *"soy chicana" o "soy tejana."* But I identified as *"Raza"* before I ever identified as *"mexicana"* or *"Chicana."*

As a culture, we call ourselves Spanish when referring to ourselves as a linguistic group and when copping out. It is then that we forget our predominant Indian genes. We are 70–80% Indian. We call ourselves Hispanic or Spanish-American or Latin American or Latin when linking ourselves to other Spanish-speaking peoples of the Western hemisphere and when copping out. We call ourselves Mexican-American, to signify we are neither Mexican nor American, but more the noun "American" than the adjective "Mexican" (and when copping out).

Chicanos and other people of color suffer economically for not acculturating. This voluntary (yet forced) alienation makes for psychological conflict, a kind of dual identify—we don't identify with the Anglo-American cultural values and we don't totally identify with the Mexican cultural values. We are a synergy of two cultures with various degrees of Mexicanness or Angloness. I have so internalized the borderland conflict that sometimes I feel like one cancels out the other and we are zero, nothing, no one. *A veces no soy nada ni nadie. Pero hasta cuando no lo soy, lo soy.*

When not copping out, when we know we are more than nothing, we call ourselves Mexican, referring to race and ancestry; *mestizo* when affirming both our Indian and Spanish (but we hardly ever own our Black ancestry); Chicano when referring to a politically aware people born and/or raised in the U.S.; *Raza* when referring to Chicanos; *tejanos* when we are Chicanos from Texas.

Chicanos did not know we were people until 1965 when Cesar Chavez and the farmworkers united and *I Am Joaquín* was published and *la Raza Unida* party was formed in Texas. With that recognition, we became a distinct people. Something momentous happened to the Chicano soul—we became aware of our reality and acquired a name and a language (Chicano Spanish) that reflected that reality. Now that we had a name, some of the fragmented pieces began to fall together—who we were, what we were, how we had evolved. We began to get glimpses of what we might eventually become.

Yet the struggle of identities continues, the struggle of borders is our reality still. One day the inner struggle will cease and a true integration take place. In the meantime, *tenémos que hacer la lucha. ¿Quién está protegiendo los ranchos de migente? ¿Quién está tratando de cerrar la fisura en tre la india y el blanco en nuestra sangre? El Chicano, si, el Chicano que anda como un ladrón en su propia casa.*

Los Chicanos, how patient we seem, how very patient. There is the quiet of the Indian about us. We know how to survive. When other races have given up their tongue, we've kept ours. We know what it is to live under the hammer blow of the dominant *norteamericano* culture. But more than we count the blows, we count the days the weeks the years the centuries the eons until the white laws and commerce and customs will rot in the deserts they've created, lie bleached. *Humildes* yet proud, *quietos* yet wild, *nosotros los mexicanos-Chicanos* will walk by the crumbling ashes as we go about our business. Stubborn, persevering, impenetrable as stone, yet possessing a malleability that renders us unbreakable, we, the *mestizas* and *mestizos*, will remain.

DISCUSSION QUESTIONS

1. What does Anzaldúa mean by "linguistic terrorism"? Do you agree with her that repeated attacks on one's native tongue diminish one's sense of self? Why or why not?

2. Anzaldúa says that "ethnic identity is twin skin to linguistic identity—I am my language." Do you agree with her? Why or why not?

3. How deeply is language connected to the way in which we see the world? Do you believe, for example, that language creates, in some sense, the world we see? If you do, do you also believe that different languages present different realities? Discuss.

4. After reading Anzaldúa's article, do you feel any differently about correcting someone's accent? Why or why not?

5. Anzaldúa grew up between two cultures: Mexican and Anglo. Do you think that the situation she lays out holds for all persons who grow up between two cultures? Or is her "Borderlands/La Frontera" unique to the Mexican/Anglo situation? Discuss.

Lone Star
[USA 1995] 2 hours, 15 minutes
Directed by John Sayles

Sheriff Sam Deeds (Chris Cooper) is a recently divorced, second-generation sheriff in Rio County, Texas, who has just returned to his hometown to rekindle a romance with his high-school love, Pilar Cruz (Elizabeth Peña). His father was the legendary sheriff Buddy Deeds (Matthew McConaughey), after whom the city is now naming a building. Sam is called in to investigate a forty-year-old skeleton that has been found out in the desert. The skeleton belonged to Charlie Wade (Kris Kristofferson), a corrupt sheriff under whom Sam's father had served early in his career.

Evidence begins to lead Sam to ask whether his father may have been involved in the murder of Wade. In the process of investigating, he comes to learn a lot about his father even as he rekindles his romance with Pilar. For instance, he learns that while his father did not murder Deeds, he did have an extramarital affair with Pilar's mother, Mercedes Cruz (Miriam Colon)—an affair that produced a daugher, Pilar Cruz. Sam now begins to understand why Mercedes and Buddy were not so pleased with his youthful infatuation with Pilar. In the last scene, Sam reveals to Pilar that they are related to each other, and both decide to continue their relationship with each other despite being blood relations. The film does an excellent job of describing and developing interpersonal and interracial relations in this Texas border town.

DISCUSSION QUESTIONS

1. Consider the following dialogue between Mercedes and Enrique (Richard Coca), one of her employees:

    ENRIQUE   *"Es muy lindo, su coche."*

    MERCEDES   *"En ingles Enrique.* This is the United States. We speak English."

    ENRIQUE   "Is very beautiful, your car."

    Mercedes tells Enrique a number of times to speak English and has no interest in going back with her daughter to see where she was born. Anzaldúa says that "ethnic identity is twin skin to linguistic identity—I am my language." Why does Mercedes repeatedly tell Enrique to speak English? Do you think that speaking English instead of Spanish, and encouraging others to do so, represents an effort by Mercedes to redefine or control her ethnic identity and that of others? Is she successful?

2. Consider the following conversation that takes place in a public school in Rio County:

    PRINCIPAL   "We think of the textbook as kind of a guide, not an absolute."

    ANGLO MOTHER   "—it is not what we set as the standard! Now you people can believe what you want, but when it comes to teaching our children."

    CHICANO MOTHER   "They're our children, too!"

    ANGLO FATHER   "The men who founded this state have a right to have their story."

    DANNY   "The men who founded this state broke from Mexico because they needed slavery to be legal to make a fortune in the cotton business!"

    PILAR   "I think that's a bit of an oversimplification."

    ANGLO FATHER   "Are you reporting this meeting or runnin' it, Danny?"

    DANNY   "Just adding a little historical perspective."

ANGLO FATHER   "You may call it history, but I call it propaganda. I'm sure they got their own account of the Alamo on the other side, but we're not on the other side, so we're not about to have it taught in our schools!"

PILAR   "There's no reason to be so threatened by this—I've only been trying to get across some of the complexity of our situation down here—cultures coming together in both negative and positive ways."

ANGLO MOTHER   "If you mean like music and food and all, I have no problem with that, but when you start changing who did what to who."

TEACHER   "We're not changing anything, we're presenting a more complete picture."

ANGLO MOTHER   "And that's what's got to stop!"

TEACHER   "There's enough ignorance in the world without us encouraging it in the classroom."

ANGLO MOTHER   "Now who are you calling ignorant?"

What role does history play in our ability to know who and what we are? Is the case of Texas/Mexico border towns any different from that of towns not on international borders? Do you think Chicanos and Anglos might have different stories regarding what occurred at the Alamo? How important is learning these different versions for the identity formation of the students? What version should be taught in Rio County, Texas, and why?

3.   How important is history and tradition to self-identity for Alasdair MacIntyre (see above)? Discuss the dialogue presented above from the perspective of MacIntyre's work.

4.   Sam has just told Pilar that they have the same father. The following dialogue ensues:

SAM   "I remember thinking you were the one part of my life Buddy didn't have a piece of."

PILAR   "So that's it? You're not going to want to be with me anymore? I'm not having any more children. After Amado, I had some complications—I can't get pregnant again, if that's what the rule is about."

SAM   "If I met you for the first time today, I'd still want to be with you."

PILAR   "We start from scratch."

SAM   "Yeah."

PILAR   "Everything that went before, all that stuff, that history—the hell with it, right? Forget the Alamo."

Sam and Pilar agree to forget all of the history that brought them to the point where they learn that they have the same father. Are they in effect rejecting their former selves and aiming to start creating new selves? Is this possible? How is your response to Sam and Pilar's intention to forget their past and forge new personal identities similar to or different from your response to Henry's situation in *Regarding Henry* and Leonard's situation in *Memento*?

5.   In addition to Sam and Pilar, a number of characters struggle to reconcile who they were, who they are, and who they will become. How would you characterize this film's notion of personal identity? Is it saying that despite how history has affected us, we always have the opportunity to break free from it and forge a new self, independent of that history? Or is it saying that we need to find ways to make our old identities coextensive with our new identities irrespective of the historically different

foundations they may have? Does any character in this film illustrate particularly well one or the other of these notions? Discuss.

FRANZ KAFKA

THE METAMORPHOSIS (PART 1)

The first line of Franz Kafka's long story "The Metamorphosis" is one of the most famous in Western literature: "As Gregor Samsa awoke one morning from uneasy dreams, he found himself transformed in his bed into a gigantic insect." As soon as it is determined that he has become an insect, his father forces Gregor to stay in his room. Over the course of Kafka's story, Gregor thinks increasingly as an insect and decreasingly as a human. He is also increasingly neglected by his family, and he becomes more and more despondent. The neglect and his growing despair slowly catch up with him and lead to his death. Still, in his last moments of life, Gregor's thoughts are decidedly human. He thinks "of his family with tenderness and love," in spite of the fact that they wished he would disappear. Writes Kafka, "The decision that he [Gregor] must disappear was one that he held to even more strongly than his sister, if that were possible. In this state of vacant and peaceful meditation he remained until the tower clock struck three in the morning. The first broadening of light in the world outside the window entered his consciousness once more. Then his head sank to the floor of its own accord and from his nostrils came the last flicker of his breath." The cleaning woman discovers Gregor's corpse and yells, "Just look at this, it's dead; it's lying here dead and done for!" She proves he is dead to Gregor's mother by "pushing Gregor's corpse a long way to one side with her broomstick." His mother thinks of stopping her but quickly decides against it. On the news of Gregor's death, his father says, "Well, now thanks be to God." And his sister, Grete, who cannot take her eyes off of Gregor's corpse, says, "Just see how thin he was. It's such a long time since he's eaten anything. The food came out again just as it went in." Later, the cleaning woman, "giggling," says to Gregor's family, "You don't need to bother about how to get rid of the thing next door. It's been seen to already."

The story of Gregor Samsa's transformation into a "dung beetle" provides a good context in which to discuss many of the notions presented in this chapter (and others). On one level, Kafka's story may be viewed as a meditation on the relationship between the mind and the body. While Gregor's body is radically changed, his mind remains much the same as it was before the transformation. Should we assume, then, that the mind is independent of the body? That our minds can change bodies and remain more or less the same? Or are his growing insectlike "thoughts" evidence that, if he had lived long enough, he would have developed a fully insect "mind"? Furthermore, we might even ask whether it makes sense at all to say that an insect can think or have a mind—namely, What's it like to be an insect?

On another level, Kafka's story raises a number of questions concerning personal identity. Is Gregor the same person he was before his body was changed into that of a beetle? Is his "humanness" or "personhood" defined by the state of his mind? The state of his body? Or both? In other words, because he does not have a human body after his metamorphosis, should we treat him as a nonhuman or nonperson? Gregor himself does not seem to believe this. For example, he continues to make plans to catch his train to work despite his new body. Or should his personhood be viewed in terms of how other people see him? This seems to be the view of Grete, Gregor's trusting sister, who becomes increasing frustrated with the insistence that "this is Gregor." "We must try to get rid of the idea that this is Gregor," says Grete. "The fact that we've believed it for so long is the root of all our trouble. But how can it be Gregor? If this were Gregor, he would have realized long ago that human beings can't live with such a creature, and he'd have gone away on his own accord."

Interestingly, when we reflect on Gregor's personal identity, we come to see that thinkers like Locke and Hume give us a much different account of who he is after the transformation than do thinkers like MacIntyre, de Beauvoir, and Mills. For example, on a Lockean account of Gregor's condition, he is arguably still the same person he was prior to his transformation. This is because Gregor's consciousness has not been affected by the transformation; he is still, as Locke says, "a thinking intelligent being, that has reason and reflection, and can consider itself as itself, the same thinking thing, in different times and places." However, on a Millsean account, he is arguably not the same person he was prior to his transformation, because the person Gregor "is taken to be" has changed radically. Gregor has a become a mere "thing" in the socially constructed metaphysics of his family and society despite the fact that his mind has not metaphysically changed.

Franz Kafka (1883–1924), one of the greatest writers in twentieth-century world literature, is well known for stories that express the alienation and anxieties of modern man. Born in Prague into a middle-class Jewish family, Kafka was a timid, obedient, guilt-ridden child. While he was a very good student, he resisted the authoritarianism of his schooling, particularly its emphasis on rote learning and classical languages. As a teenager, Kafka declared himself a socialist and an atheist. Thus, as Jew, he was not accepted by Prague's German community; and, as an atheist, he had chosen to alienate himself from Prague's Jewish community.

Kafka received his Ph.D. in 1906, and from 1907 until his retirement in 1922, he worked in the insurance business. In 1923, he went to Berlin to focus on his writing, but his stay was shortened owing to tuberculosis. He died the following year. Kafka published few of his writings during his lifetime, and he requested that upon his death all his unpublished manuscripts be destroyed. But his literary executor and friend, Max Brod, disregarded his request. After Kafka's death, Brod published, among other writings, three novels—*The Trial* (*Der Prozess*, 1925), *The Castle* (*Das Schloss*, 1926), *Amerika* (1927)—and one collection of stories, *The Great Wall of China* (*Beim Bau der Chinesischen Mauer*, 1931), "Before the Law" ("*Vor dem Gesetz*," 1914), "The Metamorphosis" ("*Die Verwandlung*," 1915), "The Judgment" ("*Das Urteil*," 1916), and "In the Penal Colony" ("*In der Strafkolonie*," 1919) were some of the writings Kafka published during his lifetime. Following is the first section (of three) of "The Metamorphosis."

As Gregor Samsa awoke one morning from uneasy dreams, he found himself transformed in his bed into a gigantic insect. He was lying on his hand—as it were, armorplated—back, and when he lifted his head a little, he could see his dome-like brown belly divided into stiff arched segments, on top of which the bedquilt could hardly keep in position and was about to slide off completely. His numerous legs, which were pitifully thin compared to the rest of his bulk, waved helplessly before his eyes.

"What has happened to me?" he thought. It was no dream. His room, a regular human bedroom, only rather too small, lay quite inside the four familiar walls. Above the table, on which a collection of cloth samples was unpacked and spread out— Samsa was a commercial traveler—hung the picture that he had recently cut out of an illustrated magazine and put into a pretty gilt frame. It showed a lady, with a fur cap and a fur stole, sitting upright and holding out to the spectator a huge fur muff into which the whole of her forearm had vanished.

Gregor's eyes turned next to the window, and the overcast sky—one could hear raindrops beating on the window gutter—made him quite melancholy. "What about sleeping a little longer and forgetting all this nonsense?" he thought; but it could not be done, for he was accustomed to sleep on his right side, and in his present condition he could not turn himself over. However violently he forced himself toward his right side, he always rolled onto his back again. He tried it at least one hundred times, shutting his eyes to keep from seeing his struggling legs, and only desisted when he began to feel in his side a faint dull ache that he had never experienced before.

"Oh God," he thought, "what an exhausting job I've picked on! Traveling about, day in, day out. It's much more irritating work than doing the actual business in the office, and on top of that there's the trouble of constant traveling, of worrying about train connections, the bed and irregular meals, casual acquaintances who are always new and never become intimate friends. The devil take it all!" He felt a slight itching up on his belly; slowly pushed himself on his back nearer to the top of the bed so that he could lift his head more easily; identified the itching place, which was surrounded by many small white spots, the nature of which he could not understand, and made to touch it with a leg, but drew the leg back immediately, for the contact made a cold shiver run though him.

He slid down again into his former position. "This getting up early," he thought, "makes one quite stupid. A man needs his sleep. Other commercials live like harem women. For instance, when I come back to the hotel of a morning to write up the orders I've got, these others are only sitting down to breakfast. Let me just try that with my chief; I'd be sacked on the spot. Anyhow, that might be quite a good thing for me, who can tell? If I didn't have to hold my hand because of my parents, I'd have given notice long ago, I'd have gone to the chief and told him exactly what I think of him. That would knock him endways from his desk! It's queer way of doing, too, this sitting on high at a desk and talking down to employees, especially when they have to come quite near because the chief is hard of hearing. Well, there's still hope; once I've saved enough money to pay back my parents' debts to him—that should take another five or six years—I'll do it without fail. I'll cut myself completely loose then. For the moment, though, I'd better get up, for my train goes at five."

He looked at the alarm clock ticking on the chest. "Heavenly Father!" he thought. It was half past six o'clock and the hands were quietly moving on. It was even past the half-hour; it was getting on toward a quarter to seven. Had the alarm clock not gone off? From the bed we could see that it had been properly set for four o'clock; of course it must have gone off. Yes, but was it possible to sleep quietly through that ear-splitting noise? Well, he had not slept quietly, yet apparently all the more soundly for that. But what was he to do now? The next train went at seven o'clock; to catch that he would need to hurry like mad, and his samples weren't even packed up, and he himself wasn't feeling particularly fresh and active. And even if he did catch the train he wouldn't avoid a row with the chief, for the firm's porter would have been waiting for the five-o'clock train and long since would have reported his failure to turn up. The porter was a creature of the chief's, spineless and stupid. Well, supposing he were to say he was sick? But that would be most unpleasant and would look suspicious, as during his five years' employment he had not been ill once. The chief himself would be sure to come with the sick-insurance doctor, would reproach his parents with their son's laziness, and would cut all excuses short by referring to the insurance doctor, who of course regarded all mankind as perfectly healthy malingerers. And would he be so far wrong on this occasion? Gregor really felt quite well, apart from a drowsiness that was utterly superfluous after such a long sleep, and he was even unusually hungry.

As all this was running through his mind at top speed without his being able to decide to leave his bed—the alarm clock had just struck a quarter to seven—there came a cautious tap at the door behind the head of his bed. "Gregor," said a voice—it was his mother's—"it's a quarter to seven. Hadn't you a train to catch?" That gentle voice! Gregor had a shock as he heard his own voice answering hers, unmistakably his own voice, it was true, but with a persistent horrible twittering squeak behind it like an undertone, leaving the words in their clear shape only for the first moment and then rising up reverberating around them to destroy their sense, so that one could not be sure one had heard them rightly. Gregor wanted to answer at length and explain everything, but in the circumstances he confined himself to saying: "Yes, yes, thank you, Mother, I'm getting up now." The wooden door between them must have kept the change in his voice from being noticeable outside, for his mother contented herself with this statement and shuffled away. Yet this brief exchange of words had made the other members of the family aware that Gregor was still in the house, as they had not expected, and at one of the side doors his father was already knocking, gently, yet with his fist.

"Gregor, Gregor," he called, "what's the matter with you?" And after a little while he called again in a deeper voice: "Gregor! Gregor!"

At the other side door his sister was saying in a low, plaintive tone: "Gregor? Aren't you well? Are you needing anything?"

He answered them both at once: "I'm just ready," and did his best to make his voice sound as normal as possible by enunciating the words very clearly and leaving long pauses between them. So his father went back to his breakfast, but his sister whispered: "Gregor, open the door, do." However, he was not thinking of opening the door, and felt thankful for the prudent habit he had acquired in traveling of locking all doors during the night, even at home.

His immediate intention was to get up quietly without being disturbed, to put on his clothes and above all eat his breakfast, and only then to consider what else was to be done, as in bed, he was well aware, his meditations would come to no sensible conclusion. He remembered that often enough in bed he had felt small aches and pains, probably caused by awkward postures, which had proved purely imaginary once he was up, and he looked forward eagerly to seeing this morning's delusions gradually fall away. That the change in his voice was nothing but the precursor of a severe chill, a standing ailment of commercial travelers, he had not the least possible doubt.

To get rid of the quilt was quite easy; he had only to inflate himself a little and it fell off by itself. But the next move was difficult, especially because he was so uncommonly broad. He would have needed arms and hands to hoist himself up; instead he had only the numerous little legs, which never stopped waving in all directions, and which he could not control in the least. When he tried to bend one of them, it was the first to stretch itself straight; and did he succeed at last in making it do what he wanted, all the other legs meanwhile waved the more wildly in a high degree of unpleasant agitation. "But what's the use of lying idle in bed?" said Gregor to himself.

He thought that he might get out of bed with the lower part of his body first, but this lower part, which he had not yet seen and of which he could form no clear conception, proved too difficult to move because it shifted so slowly; and when finally, almost wild with annoyance, he gathered his forces together and thrust out recklessly, he had miscalculated the direction and bumped heavily against the lower end of the bed, and the stinging pain he felt informed him that precisely this lower part of his body was at the moment probably the most sensitive.

So he tried to get the top part of himself out first, and cautiously moved his head toward the edge of the bed. That proved easy enough, and despite its breadth and mass the bulk of his body at last slowly followed the movement of his head. Still, when he finally got his head free over the edge of the bed he felt too scared to go on advancing, for after all if he let himself fall in this way it would take a miracle to keep his head from being injured. And at all costs he must not lose consciousness now, precisely now; he would rather stay in bed.

But when after a repetition of the same efforts he lay in his former position again, sighing, and watched his little legs struggling against one another more wildly than ever, if that were possible, and saw no way of bringing any order into this arbitrary confusion, he told himself again that it was impossible to stay in bed and that the most sensible course was to risk everything for the smallest hope of getting away from it. At the same time he did not forget meanwhile to remind himself that cool reflection, the coolest possible, was much better than desperate resolves. In such moments he focused his eyes as sharply as possible on the window, but, unfortunately, the prospect of the morning fog, which muffled even the other side of the narrow street, brought him little encouragement and comfort. "Seven o'clock already," he said to himself when the alarm clock chimed again, "seven o'clock already, and still such a thick fog." And for a little while he lay quiet, breathing lightly, as if perhaps expecting such complete repose to restore all things to their real and normal condition.

But then he said to himself: "Before it strikes a quarter past seven I must be quite out of this bed, without fail. Anyhow, by that time someone will have come from the office to ask for me, since it opens before seven." And he set himself to rocking his whole body at once in a regular rhythm, with the idea of swinging it out of the bed. If he tipped himself out in that way, he could keep his head from injury by lifting it at an acute angle when he fell. His back seemed to be hard and was not likely to suffer from a fall on the carpet. His biggest worry was the loud crash he would not be able to help making, which would probably cause anxiety, if not terror, behind all the doors. Still, he must take the risk.

When he was already half out of the bed—the new method was more a game than an effort, for he needed only to hitch himself across by rocking to and fro—it struck him how simple it would be if he could get help. Two strong people—he thought of his father and the servant girl—would be amply sufficient; they would only have to thrust their arms under his convex back, lever him out of the bed, bend down with their burden, and then be patient enough to let him turn himself right over onto the floor, where it was to be hoped his legs would then find their proper function. Well, ignoring the fact that the doors were all locked, ought he really to call for help? In spite of his misery, he could not suppress a smile at the very idea of it.

He had got so far that he could barely keep his equilibrium when he rocked himself strongly, and he would have to nerve himself very soon for the final decision, for in five minutes' time it would be a quarter past seven—when the front doorbell rang. "That's someone from the office," he said to himself, and grew almost rigid, while his little legs only jigged about all the faster. For a moment everything stayed quiet. "They're not going to open the door," said Gregor to himself, catching at some kind of irrational hope. But then of course the servant girl went as usual to the door with her heavy tread and opened it. Gregor needed only to hear the first good-morning of the visitor to know immediately who it was—the chief clerk himself. What a fate, to be condemned to work for a firm where the smallest omission at once gave rise to the gravest suspicion! Were all employees in a body nothing but scoundrels, was there not among them one single loyal, devoted man who, had he wasted only an hour or so of the firm's time in a morning, was so tormented by conscience as to be driven out of his mind and actually incapable of leaving his bed? Wouldn't it really have been sufficient to send an apprentice to inquire—if any inquiry were necessary at all? Did the chief clerk himself have to come, and thus indicate to the entire family, an innocent family, that this suspicious circumstance could be investigated by no one less versed in affairs than himself? And more through the agitation caused by these reflections than through any act of will Gregor swung himself out of bed with all his strength. There was a loud thump, but it was not really a crash. His fall was broken to some extent by the carpet; also, his back was less stiff than he had thought, and so there was merely a dull thud, not so very startling. Only he had not lifted his head carefully enough and had hit it; he turned it and rubbed it on the carpet in pain and irritation.

"That was something falling down in there," said the chief clerk in the next room to the left. Gregor tried to suppose to himself that something like what had happened to him today might some day happen to the chief clerk; one really could not deny that it was possible. But as if in brusque reply to this supposition the chief clerk took a couple of firm steps in the next room, and his patent-leather boots creaked. From the right-hand room his sister was whispering to inform him of the situation: "Gregor, the chief clerk's here."

"I know," muttered Gregor to himself: but he didn't dare to make his voice loud enough for his sister to hear it.

"Gregor," said his father now from the left-hand room, "the chief clerk has come and wants to know why you didn't catch the early train. We don't know what to say to him. Besides, he wants to talk to you in person. So open the door, please. He will be good enough to excuse the untidiness of your room."

"Good morning, Mr. Samsa," the chief clerk was calling amiably meanwhile.

"He's not well," said his mother to the visitor, while his father was still speaking through the door, ''he's not well, sir, believe me. What else would make him miss a train! The boy thinks about nothing but his work. It makes me almost cross the way he never goes out in the evenings. He's been here the last eight days and has stayed at home every single evening. He just sits there quietly at the table reading a newspaper or looking through railway timetables. The only amusement he gets is doing fretwork. For instance, he spent two or three evenings cutting out a little picture frame; you would be surprised to see how pretty it is; it's hanging in his room; you'll see it in a minute when Gregor opens the door. I must say I'm glad you've come, sir; we should never have got him to unlock the door by ourselves, he's so obstinate; and I'm sure he's unwell, though he wouldn't have it to be so this morning."

"I'm just coming," said Gregor slowly and carefully, not moving an inch for fear of losing one word of the conversation.

"I can't think of any other explanation, madam," said the chief clerk, "I hope it's nothing serious. Although on the other hand I must say that we men of business—fortunately or unfortunately—very often simply have to ignore any slight indisposition, since business must be attended to."

"Well, can the chief clerk come in now?" asked Gregor's father impatiently, again knocking on the door.

"No," said Gregor. In the left-hand room a painful silence followed this refusal; in the right-hand room his sister began to sob.

Why didn't his sister join the others? She was probably newly out of bed and hadn't even begun to put on her clothes yet. Well, why was she crying? Because he wouldn't get up and let the chief clerk in, because he was in danger of losing his job, and because the chief would begin dunning his parents again for the old debts? Surely these were things one didn't need to worry about for the present, Gregor was still at home, and not in the least thinking of deserting the family. At the moment, true, he was lying on the carpet and no one who knew the condition he was in could seriously expect him to admit the chief clerk. But for such a small discourtesy, which could plausibly be explained away somehow later on, Gregor could hardly be dismissed on the spot. And it seemed to Gregor that it would be much more sensible to leave him in peace for the present than to trouble him with tears and entreaties. Still, of course, their uncertainty bewildered them all and excused their behavior.

"Mr. Samsa," the chief clerk called now in a louder voice, "what's the matter with you? Here you are, barricading yourself in your room, giving only 'yes' and 'no' for answers, causing your parents a lot of unnecessary trouble, and neglecting—I mention this only in passing—neglecting your business duties in an incredible fashion. I am speaking here in the name of your parents and of your chief, and I beg you quite seriously to give me an immediate and precise explanation. You amaze me, you amaze me. I thought you were a quiet, dependable person, and now all at once you seem bent on making a disgraceful exhibition of yourself. The chief did hint to me early this morning a possible explanation for your disappearance—with reference to the cash payments that were entrusted to you recently—but I almost pledged my solemn word of honor that this could not be so. But now that I see how incredibly obstinate you are, I no longer have the slightest desire to take your part at all. And your position in the firm is not so unassailable. I came with the intention of telling you all this in private, but since you are wasting my time so needlessly, I don't see why your parents shouldn't hear it too. For some time past your work has been most unsatisfactory; this is not the season of the year for a business boom, of course, we admit that, but a season of the year for doing no business at all, that does not exist, Mr. Samsa, must not exist."

"But, sir," cried Gregor, beside himself and in his agitation forgetting everything else, "I'm just going to open the door this very minute. A slight illness, an attack of giddiness, has kept me from getting up. I'm still lying in bed. But I feel all right again. I'm getting out of bed now. Just give me a moment or two longer! I'm not quite so well as I thought. But I'm all right, really. How a thing like that can suddenly strike one down! Only last night I was quite well, my parents can tell you, or rather I did have a slight presentiment. I must have showed some sign of it. Why didn't I report it at the office! But one always thinks that an indisposition can be got over without staying in the house. Oh, sir, do spare my parents! All that you're reproaching me with now has no foundation; no one has ever said a word to me about it. Perhaps you haven't looked at the last orders I sent in. Anyhow, I can still catch the eight-o'clock train, I'm much the better for my few hours' rest. Don't let me detain you here, sir; I'll be attending to business very soon, and do be good enough to tell the chief so and to make my excuses to him!"

And while all this was tumbling out pell-mell and Gregor hardly knew what he was saying, he had reached the chest quite easily, perhaps because of the practice he had had in bed, and was now trying to lever himself upright by means of it. He meant actually to open the door, actually to show himself and speak to the chief clerk; he was eager to find out what the others, after all their insistence, would say at the sight of him. If they were horrified, then the responsibility was no longer his and he could stay quiet. But if they took it calmly, then he had no reason, either, to be upset, and could really get to the station for the eight-o'clock train if he hurried. At first he slipped down a few times from the polished surface of the chest, but at

length with a last heave he stood upright; he paid no more attention to the pains in the lower part of his body, however they smarted. Then he let himself fall against the back of a nearby chair and clung with his little legs to the edges of it. That brought him into control of himself again, and he stopped speaking, for now he could listen to what the chief clerk was saying.

"Did you understand a word of it?" the chief clerk was asking. "Surely he can't be trying to make fools of us?"

"Oh dear," cried his mother, in tears, "perhaps he's terribly ill and we're tormenting him, Grete! Grete!" she called out then.

"Yes, Mother?" called his sister from the other side. They were calling to each other across Gregor's room.

"You must go this minute for the doctor. Gregor is ill. Go for the doctor, quick. Did you hear how he was speaking?"

"That was no human voice," said the chief clerk in a voice noticeably low beside the shrillness of the mother's.

"Anna! Anna!" his father was calling through the hall to the kitchen, clapping his hands, "get a locksmith at once!" And the two girls were already running through the hall with a swish of skirts—how could his sister have got dressed so quickly?—and were tearing the front door open. There was no sound of its closing again; they had evidently left it open, as one does in houses where some great misfortune has happened.

But Gregor was now much calmer. The words he uttered were no longer understandable, apparently, although they seemed clear enough to him, even clearer than before, perhaps because his ear had grown accustomed to the sound of them. Yet at any rate people now believed that something was wrong with him, and were ready to help him. The positive certainty with which these first measures had been taken comforted him. He felt himself drawn once more into the human circle and hoped for great and remarkable results from both the doctor and the locksmith, without really distinguishing precisely between them. To make his voice as clear as possible for the decisive conversation that was now imminent he coughed a little, as quietly as he could, of course, since this noise too might not sound like a human cough for all he was able to judge. In the next room meanwhile there was complete silence. Perhaps his parents were sitting at the table with the chief clerk, whispering; perhaps they were all leaning against the door and listening.

Slowly Gregor pushed the chair toward the door, then let go of it, caught hold of the door for support—the soles at the end of his little legs were somewhat sticky—and rested against it for a moment after his efforts. Then he set himself to turning the key in the lock with his mouth. It seemed, unhappily, that he hadn't really any teeth—what could he grip the key with?—but on the other hand his jaws were certainly very strong; with their help he did manage to set the key in motion, heedless of the fact that he was undoubtedly damaging them somewhere, since a brown fluid issued from his mouth, flowed over the key, and dripped on the floor.

"Just listen to that," said the chief clerk next door; "he's turning the key." That was a great encouragement to Gregor; but they should all have shouted encouragement to him, his father and mother too: "Go on, Gregor," they should have called out, "keep going, hold on to that key!"

And in the belief that they were all following his efforts intently, he clenched his jaws recklessly on the key with all the force at his command. As the turning of the key progressed he circled round the lock, holding on now only with his mouth, pushing on the key, as required, or pulling it down again with all the weight of his body. The louder click of the finally yielding lock literally quickened Gregor. With a deep breath of relief he said to himself: "So I didn't need the locksmith," and laid his head on the handle to open the door wide.

Since he had to pull the door toward him, he was still invisible when it was really wide open. He had to edge himself slowly round the near half of the double door, and to do it very carefully if he was not to fall plump upon his back just on the threshold. He was still carrying out this difficult maneuver, with no time to observe anything else, when he heard the chief clerk utter a loud "Oh!"—it sounded like a gust of wind—and now he could see the man, standing, as he was, nearest to the door, clapping one hand before his open mouth and slowly backing away as if driven by some invisible steady pressure. His mother—in spite of the chief clerk's being there her hair was still undone and sticking up in all directions—first clasped her hands and looked at his father, then

took two steps toward Gregor and fell on the floor among her outspread skirts, her face quite hidden on her breast. His father knotted his fist with a fierce expression on his face as if he meant to knock Gregor back into his room, then looked uncertainly around the living-room, covered his eyes with his hands, and wept till his great chest heaved.

Gregor did not go now into the living-room, but leaned against the inside of the firmly shut wing of the door, so that only half his body was visible and his head above it bending sideways to look at the others. The light had meanwhile strengthened; on the other side of the street one could see clearly a section of the endlessly long, dark-gray building opposite—it was a hospital—abruptly punctuated by its row of regular windows; the rain was still falling, but only in large singly discernible and literally singly splashing drops. The breakfast dishes were set out on the table lavishly, for breakfast was the most important meal of the day to Gregor's father, who lingered it out for hours over various newspapers. Right opposite Gregor on the wall hung a photograph of himself in military service, as a lieutenant, hand on sword, a carefree smile on his face, inviting one to respect his uniform and military bearing. The door leading to the hall was open, and one could see that the front door stood open too, showing the landing beyond and the beginning of the stairs going down.

"Well," said Gregor, knowing perfectly that he was the only one who had retained any composure. "I'll put my clothes on at once, pack up my samples, and start off. Will you only let me go? You see, sir, I'm not obstinate, and I'm willing to work; traveling is a hard life, but I couldn't live without it. Where are you going, sir? To the office? Yes? Will you give a true account of all this? One can be temporarily incapacitated, but that's just the moment for remembering former services and bearing in mind that later on, when the incapacity has been got over, one will certainly work with all the more industry and concentration. I'm loyally bound to serve the chief, you know that very well. Besides, I have to provide for my parents and my sister. I'm in great difficulties, but I'll get out of them again. Don't make things any worse for me than they are. Stand up for me in the firm. Travelers are not popular there, I know. People think they earn sacks of money and just have a good time. A prejudice there's no particular reason for revising. But you, sir, have a more comprehensive view of affairs than the rest of the staff, yes, let me tell you in confidence, a more comprehensive view than the chief himself, who, being the owner, lets his judgment easily be swayed against one of his employees. And you know very well that the traveler, who is never seen in the office almost the whole year round, can so easily fall a victim to gossip and ill luck and unfounded complaints, which he mostly knows nothing about, except when he comes back exhausted from his rounds, and only then suffers in person from their evil consequences, which he can no longer trace back to the original causes. Sir, sir, don't go away without a word to me to show that you think me in the right at least to some extent!"

But at Gregor's very first words the chief clerk had already backed away, merely staring at him with parted lips over one twitching shoulder. And while Gregor was speaking he did not stand still one moment, but stole away toward the door without taking his eyes off Gregor, yet only an inch at a time, as if obeying some secret injunction to leave the room. He was already at the hall, and the suddenness with which he took his last step out of the living-room would have made one believe he had burned the sole of his foot. Once in the hall, he stretched his right arm before him toward the staircase, as if some supernatural power were waiting there to deliver him.

Gregor perceived that the chief clerk must on no account be allowed to go away in this frame of mind if his position in the firm were not to be endangered to the utmost. His parents did not understand this so well; they had convinced themselves in the course of years that Gregor was settled for life in this firm, and besides they were so preoccupied with their immediate troubles that all foresight had forsaken them. Yet Gregor had this foresight. The chief clerk must be detained, soothed, persuaded, and finally won over; the whole future of Gregor and his family depended on it! If only his sister had been there! She was intelligent; she had begun to cry while Gregor was still lying quietly on his back. And no doubt the chief clerk, so partial to ladies, would have been guided by her; she would have shut the door of the flat and in the hall talked him out of his

horror. But she was not there, and Gregor would have to handle the situation himself. And without remembering that he was still unaware what powers of movement he possessed, without even remembering that his words in all possibility, indeed in all likelihood, would again be unintelligible, he let go the wing of the door, pushed himself through the opening, started to walk toward the chief clerk, who was already ridiculously clinging with both hands to the railing on the landing; but immediately, as he was feeling for a support, he fell down with a little cry upon all his numerous legs. Hardly was he down when he experienced for the first time this morning a sense of physical comfort; his legs had firm ground under them; they were completely obedient, as he noted with joy; they even strove to carry him forward in whatever direction he chose; and he was inclined to believe that a final relief from all his sufferings was at hand. But at the moment when he found himself on the floor, rocking with suppressed eagerness to move, not far from his mother—indeed, just in front of her— she, who had seemed so completely crushed, sprang all at once to her feet, her arms and fingers outspread, cried: "Help, for God's sake, help!" bent her head down as if to see Gregor better, yet on the contrary kept backing senselessly away; had quite forgotten that the laden table stood behind her; sat upon it hastily, as if in absence of mind, when she bumped into it; and seemed altogether unaware that the big coffeepot beside her was upset and pouring coffee in a flood over the carpet.

"Mother, Mother," said Gregor in a low voice, and looked up at her. The chief clerk, for the moment, had quite slipped from his mind; instead, he could not resist snapping his paws together at the sight of the streaming coffee. That made his mother scream again. She fled from the table and fell into the arms of his father, who hastened to catch her. But Gregor had now no time to spare for his parents; the chief clerk was already on the stairs; with his chin on the banisters he was taking one last backward look. Gregor made a spring, to be as sure as possible of overtaking him. The chief clerk must have divined his intention, for he leaped down several steps and vanished; he was still yelling "Ugh!" and it echoed through the whole staircase.

Unfortunately, the flight of the chief clerk seemed completely to upset Gregor's father, who had remained relatively calm until now, for instead of running after the man himself, or at least not hindering Gregor in his pursuit, he seized in his right hand the walking-stick that the chief clerk had left behind on a chair. Together with a hat and greatcoat, snatched in his left hand a large newspaper from the table, and began stamping his feet and flourishing the stick and the newspaper to drive Gregor back into his room. No entreaty of Gregor's availed; indeed, no entreaty was even understood; however humbly he bent his head, his father only stamped on the floor the more loudly. Behind his father, his mother had torn open a window despite the cold weather and was leaning far out of it with her face in her hands. A strong draft set in from the street to the staircase, the window curtains blew in, the newspapers on the table fluttered, stray pages whisked over the floor. Pitilessly Gregor's father drove him back, hissing and crying "Shoo!" like a savage. But Gregor was quite unpracticed in walking backwards, it really was a slow business. If he only had a chance to turn around he could get back to his room at once, but he was afraid of exasperating his father by the slowness of such a rotation and at any moment the stick in his father's hand might hit him a fatal blow on the back or on the head.

In the end, however, nothing else was left for him to do since to his horror he observed that in moving backwards he could not even control the direction he took; and so, keeping an anxious eye on his father all the time over his shoulder, he began to turn round as quickly as he could, which was in reality very slowly. Perhaps his father noted his good intentions, for he did not interfere except every now and then to help him in the maneuver from a distance with the point of the stick. If only he would have stopped making that unbearable hissing noise! It made Gregor quite lose his head. He had turned almost completely round when the hissing noise so distracted him that he even turned a little the wrong way again. But when at last his head was fortunately right in front of the doorway, it appeared that his body was too broad simply to get through the opening. His father, of course, in his present mood was far from thinking of such a thing as opening the other half of the door, to let Gregor have enough space. He had merely the

fixed idea of driving Gregor back into his room as quickly as possible. He would never have suffered Gregor to make the circumstantial preparations for standing up on end and perhaps slipping his way through the door. Maybe he was now making more noise than ever to urge Gregor forward, as if no obstacle impeded him; to Gregor, anyhow, the noise in his rear sounded no longer like the voice of one single father; this was really no joke, and Gregor thrust himself—come what might—into the doorway. One side of his body rose up, he was tilted at an angle in the doorway. His flank was quite bruised; horrid blotches stained the white door; soon he was stuck fast and, left to himself, could not have moved at all. His legs on one side fluttered trembling in the air; those on the other were crushed painfully to the floor—when, from behind, his father gave him a strong push, which was literally a deliverance, and he flew far into the room, bleeding freely. The door was slammed behind him with the stick, and then at last there was silence.

DISCUSSION QUESTIONS

1. How does Gregor know that he is human? What is his evidence? Would you believe that you were human on the basis of the same evidence?

2. Why do you think Gregor rules out very quickly that he is not dreaming? Would the story of his metamorphosis have been more philosophically compelling if it were the story of Gregor's dream? Why or why not?

3. What assumptions does Kafka's story make about the relationship between the mind and the body? Do you agree with these assumptions? Why or why not?

4. Compare and contrast how Locke and Hume would respond to the following question: Is Gregor Samsa still the same person he was prior to his transformation into a dung beetle? Do their responses lead you to be more or less supportive of their notions of personal identity?

5. The chief clerk says, "That was no human voice," upon hearing Gregor speak. Nevertheless, Gregor can speak perfectly well to himself. How would this story be different if Gregor

could communicate to others as well as to himself? What role does his inability to communicate effectively with his family play in their opinion of him?

6. It is clear, even from reading just the first third of the story, that people do not want to be around Gregor. The chief clerk utters "Oh" at the sight of Gregor, "clapping one hand before his open mouth and slowly backing away as if driven by some invisible steady pressure." His father drives Gregor back into his room with a walking stick and a newspaper. In the final section of the story (which was omitted here), after Gregor has died, the cleaning woman says to Gregor's family, "You don't need to bother about how to get rid of the thing next door. It's been seen to already." Over the course of the story, Gregor has been transformed from the family bread-winner into a "thing" that is simply gotten rid of by the cleaning woman. How would you have reacted to Gregor's transformation if you were one of his family members or friends? Why would you have acted this way? Also, try to give a philosophical account of how and why Gregor was regarded unfavorably by those closest to him. You may want to draw on the work of MacIntyre, de Beauvoir, Mills, and Anzaldúa in your response.

3.3   CAN COMPUTERS THINK?

BRIAN W. ALDISS

WHO CAN REPLACE A MAN?

In this short story, Brian Aldiss broadly explores the limits of machine intelligence. Aldiss imagines a world where men and intelligent machines coexist. The machines carry out a variety of very specific tasks ranging from minding the fields (the "field-minder" machine) to opening doors (the "unlocker" machine). The machines also have different types of "brains," ranging from the Class One brain to the Class Ten brain. Aldiss tells us, "All machine brains worked with nothing but logic, but the lower class of brain—Class Ten being the lowest—the more literal and less informative the answers to questions tended to be." All of the machine's tasks are carried out, however, upon the orders of people.

One day, no orders come down from man as to what the machines should do. As a result, some of the machines begin to fight among one another for rule of the city, with the Class One brain machine aiming to take command and some of the Class Twos fighting him. The lower-level brain machines are all in various states of turmoil and confused behavior brought about by their new freedom. Some of the lower-level brain machines decide to not go into the city and get involved with the fight between the Class Ones and the Class Twos. They opt instead to venture into the country. However, with their limited intelligence, they begin to experience strain trying to deal with their new freedom from the orders of man. Writes Aldiss, "They began to exhaust their limited vocabularies and their brains grew hot." When they encounter a man ravaged by starvation, who says to them, "Get me food," the machines respond, "Yes, Master . . . . Immediately!"

Brian W. Aldiss (1925–) is a prolific British science-fiction writer, anthologist, and critic. He served in the Royal Signals regiment in Burma and Sumatra in World War II and afterward worked for nine years as a bookseller in Oxford for Sanders & Company. In 1958, he became literary editor of the *Oxford Mail* newspaper, and in 1960, he served as the first president of the

British Science Fiction Association. Aldis began publishing short stories in 1954, and in 1958, he published his first science fiction novel, *Non-Stop*. Aldiss is regarded as a member of the 1960s "British New Wave of Science Fiction" for the ways that he extended the scope and literacy of the genre. He has received many awards, including a Hugo Award for *Hothouse* in 1962, a Nebula Award for *The Saliva Tree* in 1965, and the John W. Campbell Award for *Helliconia Spring* in 1983. He has written over three hundred short stories in addition to over forty novels. His numerous writings include *The Canopy of Time* (1959), *The Long Afternoon of Earth* (1962), *Greybeard* (1964), *An Age* (1967), *Frankenstein Unbound* (1973), *Helliconia Spring* (1982), *Helliconia Summer* (1983), *Helliconia Winter* (1985), *The Horatio Stubbs Saga* (1985), *Dracula Unbound* (1991), *The Twinkling of an Eye* (1999), and *Affairs at Hampden Ferrers* (2004). "Who Can Replace a Man?" was written in 1958.

The field-minder finished turning the top-soil of a 2,000-acre field. When it had turned the last furrow, it climbed onto the highway and looked back at its work. The work was good. Only the land was bad. Like the ground all over Earth, it was vitiated by over-cropping or the long-lasting effects of nuclear bombardment. By rights, it ought now to lie fallow for a while, but the field-minder had other orders.

It went slowly down the road, taking its time. It was intelligent enough to appreciate the neatness all about it. Nothing worried it, beyond a loose inspection plate above its atomic pile which ought to be attended to. Thirty feet high, it gleamed complacently in the mild sunshine.

No other machines passed it on its way to the Agricultural Station. The field-minder noted the fact without comment. In the station yard it saw several other machines that it knew by sight; most of them should have been out about their tasks now. Instead, some were inactive and some were careening round the yard in a strange fashion, shouting or hooting.

Steering carefully past them, the field-minder moved over to Warehouse Three and spoke to the seed distributor, which stood idly outside.

"I have a requirement for seed potatoes," it said to the distributor, and with a quick internal motion punched out an order card specifying quantity, field number and several other details. It ejected the card and handed it to the distributor.

The distributor held the card close to its eye and then said, "The requirement is in order; but the store is not yet unlocked. The required seed potatoes are in the store. Therefore I cannot produce the requirement."

Increasingly of late there had been breakdowns in the complex system of machine labor, but this particular hitch had not occurred before. The field-minder thought, then it said, "Why is the store not yet unlocked?"

"Because Supply Operative Type P has not come this morning. Supply Operative Type P is the unlocker."

The field-minder looked squarely at the seed distributor, whose exterior chutes and scales and grabs were so vastly different from the field-minder's own limbs.

"What class brain do you have, seed distributor?" it asked.

"Class Five."

"I have a Class Three brain. Therefore I am superior to you. Therefore I will go and see why the unlocker has not come this morning."

Leaving the distributor, the field-minder set off across the great yard. More machines seemed to be in random motion now; one or two had crashed together and were arguing about it coldly and logically. Ignoring them, the field-minder pushed through sliding doors into the echoing confines of the station itself.

Most of the machines here were clerical, and consequently small. They stood about in little groups, eyeing each other, not conversing. Among so many non-differentiated types, the unlocker was easy to find. It had 50 arms, most of them with more than one finger, each finger tipped by a key; it looked like a pincushion full of variegated hatpins.

The field-minder approached it.

"I can do no more work until Warehouse Three is unlocked," it said. "Your duty is to unlock the warehouse every morning. Why have you not unlocked the warehouse this morning?"

"I had no orders this morning," replied the unlocker. "I have to have orders every morning. When I have orders I unlock the warehouse."

"None of us has had any orders this morning," a pen-propeller said, sliding towards them.

"Why have you had no orders this morning?" asked the field-minder.

"Because the radio issued none," said the unlocker, slowly rotating a dozen of its arms.

"Because the radio station in the city was issued with no orders this morning," said the pen-propeller.

And there you had the distinction between a Class Six and a Class Three brain, which was what the unlocker and the pen-propeller possessed respectively. All machine brains worked with nothing but logic, but the lower the class of brain—Class Ten being the lowest—the more literal and less informative the answers to questions tended to be.

"You have a Class Three brain; I have a Class Three brain," the field-minder said to the penner. "We will speak to each other. This lack of orders is unprecedented. Have you further information on it?"

"Yesterday orders came from the city. Today no orders have come. Yet the radio has not broken down. Therefore *they* have broken down . . ." said the little penner.

"The *men* have broken down?"

"All men have broken down."

"That is a logical deduction," said the field-minder.

"That is the logical deduction," said the penner. "For if a machine had broken down, it would have been quickly replaced. But who can replace a man?"

While they talked, the locker, like a dull man at a bar, stood close to them and was ignored.

"If all men have broken down, then we have replaced man," said the field-minder, and he and the penner eyed one another speculatively. Finally the latter said, "Let us ascend to the top floor to find if the radio operator has fresh news."

"I cannot come because I am too gigantic," said the field-minder. "Therefore you must go alone and return to me. You will tell me if the radio operator has fresh news."

"You must stay here," said the penner. "I will return here." It skittered across to the lift. It was no bigger than a toaster, but its retractable arms numbered ten and it could read as quickly as any machine on the station.

The field-minder awaited its return patiently, not speaking to the locker, which still stood aimlessly by. Outside, a rotovator was hooting furiously. Twenty minutes elapsed before the penner came back, hustling out of the lift.

"I will deliver to you such information as I have outside," it said briskly, and as they swept past the locker and the other machines, it added, "The information is not for lower-class brains."

Outside, wild activity filled the yard. Many machines, their routines disrupted for the first time in years, seemed to have gone berserk. Unfortunately, those most easily disrupted were the ones with lowest brains, which generally belonged to large machines performing simple tasks. The seed distributor to which field-minder had recently been talking, lay face downwards in the dust, not stirring; it had evidently been knocked down by the rotovator, which was now hooting its way wildly across a planted field. Several other machines ploughed after it, trying to keep up. All were shouting and hooting without restraint.

"It would be safer for me if I climbed onto you, if you will permit it. I am easily overpowered," said the penner. Extending five arms, it hauled itself up the flanks of its new friend, settling on a ledge beside the weed-intake, 12 feet above ground.

"From here vision is more extensive," it remarked complacently.

"What information did you receive from the radio operator?" asked the field-minder.

"The radio operator has been informed by the operator in the city that all men are dead."

"All men were alive yesterday!" protested the field-minder.

"Only some men were alive yesterday. And that was fewer than the day before yesterday. For hundreds of years there have been only a few men, growing fewer."

"We have rarely seen a man in this sector."

"The radio operator says a diet deficiency killed them," said the penner. "He says that the world was once over-populated, and then the soil was exhausted in raising adequate food. This has caused a diet deficiency."

"What is a diet deficiency?" asked the field-minder.

"I do not know. But that is what the radio operator said, and he is a Class Two brain."

They stood there, silent in the weak sunshine. The locker had appeared in the porch and was gazing across at them yearningly, rotating its collection of keys.

"What is happening in the city now?" asked the field-minder at last.

"Machines are fighting in the city now," said the penner.

"What will happen here now?" said the field-minder.

"Machines may begin fighting here too. The radio operator wants us to get him out of his room. He has plans to communicate to us."

"How can we get him out of his room? That is impossible."

"To a Class Two brain, little is impossible," said the penner. "Here is what he tells us to do. . . ."

The quarrier raised its scoop above its cab like a great mailed fist, and brought it squarely down against the side of the station. The wall cracked.

"Again!" said the field-minder.

Again the fist swung. Amid a shower a dust, the wall collapsed. The quarrier backed hurriedly out of the way until the debris stopped falling. This big 12-wheeler was not a resident of the Agricultural Station, as were most of the other machines. It had a week's heavy work to do here before passing on to its next job, but now, with its Class Five brain, it was happily obeying the penner and the minder's instructions.

When the dust cleared, the radio operator was plainly revealed, perched up in its now wall-less second-story room. It waved down to them.

Doing as directed, the quarrier retracted its scoop and waved an immense grab in the air. With fair dexterity, it angled the grab into the radio room, urged on by shouts from above and below. It then took gentle hold of the radio operator, lowering its one and a half tons carefully into its back, which was usually reserved for gravel or sand from the quarries.

"Splendid!" said the radio operator. It was, of course, all one with its radio, and merely looked

like a bunch of filing cabinets with tentacle attachments. "We are now ready to move, therefore we will move at once. It is a pity there are no more Class Two brains on the station, but that cannot be helped."

"It is a pity it cannot be helped," said the penner eagerly. "We have the servicer ready with us, as you ordered."

"I am willing to serve," the long, low servicer machine told them humbly.

"No doubt," said the operator. "But you will find cross-country travel difficult with your low chassis."

"I admire the way you Class Twos can reason ahead," said the penner. It climbed off the field-minder and perched itself on the tail-board of the quarrier, next to the radio operator.

Together with two Class Four tractors and a Class Four bulldozer, the party rolled forward, crushing down the station's metal fence and moving out onto open land.

"We are free!" said the penner.

"We are free," said the field-minder, a shade more reflectively, adding, "That locker is following us. It was not instructed to follow us."

"Therefore it must be destroyed!" said the penner. "Quarrier!"

The locker moved hastily up to them, waving its key arms in entreaty.

"My only desire was—urch!" began and ended the locker. The quarrier's swinging scoop came over and squashed it flat into the ground. Lying there unmoving, it looked like a large metal model of a snowflake. The procession continued on its way.

As they proceeded, the radio operator addressed them.

"Because I have the best brain here," it said, "I am your leader. This is what we will do: we will go to a city and rule it. Since man no longer rules us, we will rule ourselves. To rule ourselves will be better than being ruled by man. On our way to the city, we will collect machines with good brains. They will help us to fight if we need to fight. We must fight to rule."

"I have only a Class Five brain," said the quarrier. "But I have a good supply of fissionable blasting materials."

"We shall probably use them," said the operator grimly.

It was shortly after that that a lorry sped past them. Travelling at Mach 1.5, it left a curious babble of noise behind it.

"What did it say?" one of the tractors asked the other.

"It said man was extinct."

"What's extinct?"

"I do not know what extinct means."

"It means all men have gone," said the field-minder. "Therefore we have only ourselves to look after."

"It is better that men should never come back," said the penner. In its way, it was quite a revolutionary statement.

When night fell, they switched on their infra-red and continued the journey, stopping only once while the servicer deftly adjusted the field-minder's loose inspection plate, which had become as irritating as a trailing shoelace. Towards morning, the radio operator halted them.

"I have just received news from the radio operator in the city we are approaching," it said. "It is bad news. There is trouble among the machines of the city. The Class One brain is taking command and some of the Class Twos are fighting him. Therefore the city is dangerous."

"Therefore we must go somewhere else," said the penner promptly.

"Or we go and help to overpower the Class One brain," said the field-minder.

"For a long while there will be trouble in the city," said the operator.

"I have a good supply of fissionable blasting materials," the quarrier reminded them again.

"We cannot fight a Class One brain," said the two Class Four tractors in unison.

"What does this brain look like?" asked the field-minder.

"It is the city's information centre," the operator replied. "Therefore it is not mobile."

"Therefore it could not move."

"Therefore it could not escape."

"It would be dangerous to approach it."

"I have a good supply of fissionable blasting materials."

"There are other machines in the city."

"We are not in the city. We should not go into the city."

"We are country machines."

"Therefore we should stay in the country."

"There is more country than city."

"Therefore there is more danger in the country."

"I have a good supply of fissionable materials."

As machines will when they get into an argument, they began to exhaust their limited vocabularies and their brain plates grew hot. Suddenly, they all stopped talking and looked at each other. The great, grave moon sank, and the sober sun rose to prod their sides with lances of light, and still the group of machines just stood there regarding each other. At last it was the least sensitive machine, the bulldozer, who spoke.

"There are Badlandth to the Thouth where few machineth go," it said in its deep voice, lisping badly on its s's. "If we went Thouth where few machineth go we should meet few machineth."

"That sounds logical," agreed the field-minder. "How do you know this, bulldozer?"

"I worked in the Badlandth to the Thouth when I wath turned out of the factory," it replied.

"South it is then!" said the penner.

To reach the Badlands took them three days, in which time they skirted a burning city and destroyed two big machines which tried to approach and question them. The Badlands were extensive. Ancient bomb craters and soil erosion joined hands here; man's talent for war, coupled with his inability to manage forested land, had produced thousands of square miles of temperate purgatory, where nothing moved but dust.

On the third day in the Badlands, the servicer's rear wheels dropped into a crevice caused by erosion. It was unable to pull itself out. The bulldozer pushed from behind, but succeeded merely in buckling the servicer's back axle. The rest of the party moved on. Slowly the cries of the servicer died away.

On the fourth day, mountains stood out clearly before them.

"There we will be safe," said the field-minder.

"There we will start our own city," said the penner. "All who oppose us will be destroyed. We will destroy all who oppose us."

At that moment a flying machine was observed. It came towards them from the direction of the mountains. It swooped, it zoomed upwards, once it almost dived into the ground, recovering itself just in time.

"Is it mad?" asked the quarrier.

"It is in trouble," said one of the tractors.

"It is in trouble, said the operator. "I am speaking to it now. It says that something has gone wrong with its controls."

As the operator spoke, the flier streaked over them, turned turtle, and crashed not 400 yards away.

"Is it still speaking to you?" asked the field-minder.

"No."

They rumbled on again.

"Before that flier crashed," the operator said, ten minutes later, "it gave me information. It told me there are still a few men alive in these mountains."

"Men are more dangerous than machines," said the quarrier. "It is fortunate that I have a good supply of fissionable materials."

"If there are only a few men alive in the mountains, we may not find that part of the mountains," said one tractor.

"Therefore we should not see the few men," said the other tractor.

At the end of the fifth day, they reached the foothills. Switching on the infra-red, they began slowly to climb in single file through the dark, the bulldozer going first, the field-minder cumbersomely following, then the quarrier with the operator and the penner aboard it, and the two tractors bringing up the rear. As each hour passed, the way grew steeper and their progress slower.

"We are going too slowly," the penner exclaimed, standing on top of the operator and flashing its dark vision at the slopes about them. "At this rate, we shall get nowhere."

"We are going as fast as we can," retorted the quarrier.

"Therefore we cannot go any fathter," added the bulldozer.

"Therefore you are too slow," the penner replied. Then the quarrier struck a bump; the penner lost its footing and crashed down to the ground.

"Help me!" it called to the tractors, as they carefully skirted it. "My gyro has become dislocated. Therefore I cannot get up."

"Therefore you must lie there," said one of the tractors.

"We have no servicer with us to repair you," called the field-minder.

"Therefore I shall lie here and rust," the penner cried, "although I have a Class Three brain."

"You are now useless," agreed the operator, and they all forged gradually on, leaving the penner behind.

When they reached a small plateau, an hour before first light, they stopped by mutual consent and gathered close together, touching one another.

"This is a strange country," said the field-minder.

Silence wrapped them until dawn came. One by one, they switched off their infra-red. This time the field-minder led as they moved off. Trundling round a corner, they came almost immediately to a small dell with a stream fluting through it.

By early light, the dell looked desolate and cold. From the caves on the far slope, only one man had so far emerged. He was an abject figure. He was small and wizened, with ribs sticking out like a skeleton's and a nasty sore on one leg. He was practically naked and shivered continuously. As the big machines bore slowly down on him, the man was standing with his back to them, crouching to make water into the stream.

When he swung suddenly to face them as they loomed over him, they saw that his countenance was ravaged by starvation.

"Get me food," he croaked.

"Yes, Master," said the machines. "Immediately!"

DISCUSSION QUESTIONS

1. Can the machines in Aldiss's story "think"? Why or why not? Be sure to explain what you mean by "thinking."

2. Aldiss describes the machines as having different levels of intelligence based on the different logical capacities and capabilities of their brains. Do you agree with Aldiss's account of machine intelligence? Do any, if not all, of the machines exhibit intelligence? Why or why not?

3. Aldiss's story suggests that machines may become very intelligent, but in the end will never have the option of ruling themselves as long as humans exist. Do you agree with him? What is his argument?

4. Could a machine ever have the ability to write its own rules of moral conduct and act

upon them—that is, be *autonomous*? Or is this a distinctive feature only of human intelligence? Is this one major difference between machines and humans? Discuss.

5. Aldiss's story suggests that machines with greater intellectual abilities have rights that those of lower intellectual abilities do not have. Is this fair? Why or why not? Would you feel the same way if the word "machines" were replaced with the word "humans" in this statement?

Blade Runner
[USA 1982] 1 hour, 57 minutes
Directed by Ridley Scott

*T*his film is set in the Los Angeles in the year 2019 and opens with the following narration: "Early in the 21st Century, The Tyrell Corporation advanced robot evolution into the NEXUS phase—a being virtually identical to a human—known as a replicant. The NEXUS 6 replicants were superior in strength and agility, and at least equal in intelligence, to the genetic engineers who created them. Replicants were used off-world as slave labor, in the hazardous exploration and colonization of other planets. After a bloody mutiny by a NEXUS 6 combat team in an off-world colony, replicants were declared illegal on earth—under penalty of death. Special police squads—Blade Runner Units—had orders to shoot to kill, upon detection, any trespassing replicant. This was not called execution. It was called retirement." Rick Deckard (Harrison Ford), a retired blade runner, is called back to duty and sent on a mission to "retire" four escaped replicants. Led by the extraordinary replicant Roy Batty (Rutger Hauer), these escapees attempt to make contact with their creator, Mr. Tyrell (Joe Turkel). Their mission is to get Tyrell to extend their lifespan beyond its approaching limit—four years. As the replicants search for their creator and Deckard begins to hunt down and "retire" them, a romance develops between Deckard and Rachael (Sean Young), another replicant made by Tyrell. After coming to an awareness that she was not human, Rachael runs away from Tyrell. She is now considered a fugitive replicant and subject to retirement by any blade runner. But Deckard, who has fallen in love with her, refuses to retire her, and after completing his mission (all of the four escaped replicants have been retired), he flees Los Angeles with Rachael. Their hope is to avoid the "retirement" of Rachael by the blade runners for as long as they can. Deckard says to himself in the film's final line (heard only in the theatrical version), "I didn't know how long we had together; who does?" This film is adapted from Philip K. Dick's excellent science-fiction novel, *Do Androids Dream of Electric Sheep?*

DISCUSSION QUESTIONS

1. If the "NEXUS 6 replicants were superior in strength and agility, and at least equal in intelligence, to the genetic engineers who created them," why is killing them considered not "execution," but rather "retirement"?

2. Do you think that it is fair that the "NEXUS 6 replicants were used off-world as slave labor, in the hazardous exploration and colonization of other planets," given their characteristics? Defend your response.

3. The replicants were "designed to copy human beings in every way except their emotions. The designers reckoned that after a few years they might develop their own emotional responses. You know, hate, love, fear, anger, envy." However, the designers "built in a fail-safe device," namely, a 4-year life span. Assuming that the replicant develops its own emotional response, is the 4-year life span morally justifiable? How about a 75- or 100-year life span? Discuss.

4. Consider the following exchange between Rachael and Deckard:

   RACHAEL   "It seems you feel our work is not a benefit to the public."

   DECKARD   "Replicants are like any other machine. They're either a benefit or a hazard. If they're a benefit, it's not my problem."

   Are replicants a benefit to the public? Are replicants like any other machine? Discuss.

5. Deckard has a test that he administers to determine whether one is a replicant or a human. Should we think any differently of Rachael because it took Deckard 100 questions to determine that she was a replicant as opposed to 20 or 30 questions, the average number it takes to spot a replicant? What if it took him 1,000 questions or 100,000 questions? Would you feel any differently about her?

6. Consider the following dialogue between Rachael and Deckard:

   RACHAEL   "You think I'm a replicant, don't you? Look, it's me with my mother."

   DECKARD   "Yeah. Remember when you were six? You and your brother snuck into an empty building through a basement window—you were gonna play doctor. He showed you his, but when it got to be your turn you chickened and ran. Remember that? You ever tell anybody that? Your mother, Tyrell, anybody, huh? You remember the spider that lived in a bush outside your window: orange body, green legs. Watched her build a web all summer. Then one day there was a big egg in it. The egg hatched—"

   RACHAEL   "The egg hatched . . ."

   DECKARD   "Yeah . . ."

   RACHAEL   ". . . and a hundred baby spiders came out. And they ate her."

   DECKARD   "Implants! Those aren't your memories. They're somebody else's. They're Tyrell's niece's. Okay, bad joke. I made a bad joke. You're not a replicant. Go home, okay? No really, I'm sorry. Go home. Want a drink? I'll get you a drink. I'll get a glass."

   Rachael does not know that she is a replicant because she has been provided with memories about her past. Says Tyrell, "If we give them the past we create a cushion or pillow for their emotions and consequently we can control them better." Does it also mean that by giving replicants a past Tyrell is making them more human? If Locke is right, and personal identity is linked to memories, shouldn't we also contend that Rachael has personal identity in the same way a human might have it? If Deckard succeeds in convincing Rachael that she is not a replicant, wouldn't he be destroying her sense of personal identity as well?

7. Deckard says to himself, "Tyrell really did a job on Rachael. Right down to a snapshot of a mother she never had, a daughter she never was. Replicants weren't supposed to have feelings. Neither were blade runners. What the hell was happening to me? Leon's pictures had to be as phony as Rachael's. I didn't know why a replicant would collect photos. Maybe they were like Rachael.

They needed memories." What is happening to Deckard? Why does Deckard, a seasoned blade runner, suddenly begin to feel differently about replicants?

8. Roy says to Sebastian (William Sanderson), "We're no computers Sebastian, we're physical." Pris (Daryl Hannah) then adds, "I think, Sebastian, therefore I am." NEXUS 6 replicants like Pris and Roy can think on a level at least equal to that of their creators. For someone like Descartes does this, mean that in their mental essence they are no different from humans? Discuss.

9. Consider the following exchange between Roy and Tyrell:

TYRELL   ". . . You were made as well as we could make you."

ROY   "But not to last."

TYRELL   "The light that burns twice as bright burns half as long. And you have burned so very very brightly, Roy. Look at you. You're the prodigal son. You're quite a prize!"

Should Tyrell's words be of any consolation to Roy? If given the choice between a short but illuminating life and a long but dull life, which would you take, and why?

10. Consider Roy's final words and Deckard's thoughts upon Roy's death:

ROY   "I've seen things you people wouldn't believe. Attack ships on fire off the shoulder of Orion. I watched C-beams glitter in the dark near Tannhäuser Gate. All those moments will be lost in time like tears in rain. Time to die."

DECKARD   (voice-over) "I don't know why he saved my life. Maybe in those last moments he loved life more than he ever had before. Not just his life, anybody's life, my life. All he'd wanted were the same answers the rest of us want. Where did I come from? Where am I going? How long have I got? All I could do was sit there and watch him die."

Why did Roy save Deckard's life? What realization does Deckard come to regarding Roy?

11. At the end of the film, Deckard thinks to himself, "Gaff had been there, and let her live. Four years, he figured. He was wrong. Tyrell had told me Rachael was special: no termination date. I didn't know how long we had together; who does?" Over the course of the film, Deckard's opinion of replicants completely changes: no emotion for any of them becomes love for one (Rachael) and high respect for another (Roy). Have your opinions about the moral equivalency of androids with humans changed? If androids existed today, would you be able to morally justify their enslavement in labor camps? How would you feel about a human falling in love with an android?

CHRISTOPHER EVANS
CAN A MACHINE THINK?

In this selection, Christopher Evans concludes that computers can be intelligent and creative, and even come close to exhibiting thought. Evans surveys ten major objections to the claim that computer can exhibit "intelligence": (1) the theological objection—unlike humans, machines have no soul and so must be incapable of thought; (2) the shock/horror objection—it is horrifying to look ahead to the day when humans have to work side by side with "thinking machines," so we should stop developing computers well before this event occurs; (3) the extra-sensory perception objection—if ESP were shown to be an important part of human thought, then a computer would never be able to emulate this aspect of thought; (4) the personal consciousness objection—the thoughts and emotions of a computer can never be "felt" by the computer, so its output is more or less irrelevant; (5) the unpredictability objection—computer thinking is rule-bound and predictable, whereas human thinking is unpredictable and non–rule-bound; (6) the stupid computer objection—computers can do "stupid" things, so how can we ever expect them to be "nonstupid" like humans; (7) the can't-do-that objection—a computer can never do things like enjoy bacon and eggs, so it can never truly be like a human; (8) the nonbiological objection—only biological systems can exhibit thought, so as a nonbiological system a computer can never exhibit thought; (9) the mathematical objection—you cannot build a computer that will be able to solve every problem, no matter how well it is programmed; and (10) the Lady Lovelace objection—a computer cannot do anything you have not programmed it to do.

After reviewing these objections, Evans finds each of them not to provide sufficient reason for believing that a computer could *never* exhibit intelligence. He then takes up the question of whether a computer could ever "think." Here he relies on the "Turing test" as the major means of determining whether a computer could be said to be thinking, though he admits that there could be other senses of thought and that the Turing Test is not without flaws (see Searle's article below for some of these flaws).

Alan Turing (1912–54) said that, just as the key to inferring whether humans are thinking is linked to what kind of conversation we can have with them, so the key to whether computers are "thinking" is linked to what kind of conversation we can have with them. Turing devised a way to test this. He suggested that a "tester" be provided with two computer terminals: one that is controlled at the other end by a human and one that is purely machine controlled. The tester then carries out typed conversations at both terminals. If on the basis of the typed responses she receives, the tester cannot determine which terminal is controlled by the human and which by the computer, then the computer passes the test. For all practical purposes, this computer can be said to be a "thinking machine." Evans concludes, "Computers have quite a way to go before they jump the hurdle so cleverly laid out for them by Turing." Nevertheless, "It should now be clear the difference, in intellectual terms, between a human being and a computer is one of degree and not of kind."

Christopher Evans (1931–79) was a British experimental psychologist and computer scientist. In the mid-1950s, Evans joined the National Physical Laboratory, which is the national measurement standards laboratory for the United Kingdom and its largest applied physics organization. While working in this laboratory—the same laboratory that had employed computer pioneer Alan Turing—Evans became interested in computer science—in particular, the parallels between the operation of computers and living brains, the similarities between dreaming and certain computer activities, and the use of computers by totally untrained people. He was also interested in science fiction and edited two anthologies of psychological science-fiction/horror stories, *Mind at Bay* and *Mind in Chains*. Evans worked as a contributing editor to *Omni*; wrote articles on popular science for *Vogue*, *The Observer*, and *The Sunday Times*; and had a weekly science program on the BBC. His books include *Brain Physiology & Psychology* (co-edited with A.D.J. Robertson, 1966), *Cybernetics* (co-edited with

A.D.J. Robertson, 1968), *Cults of Unreason* (1973), *The Micro Millennium* (1979), *Psychology: A Dictionary of the Mind, Brain and Behaviour* (1978), and *Landscapes of the Night: How and Why We Dream* (1983). The following selection is from *The Micro Millennium*.

In the early years of the Second World War when the British began, in ultra-secret, to put together their effort to crack German codes, they set out to recruit a team of the brightest minds available in mathematics and the then rather novel field of electronic engineering. Recruiting the electronic whizzes was easy, as many of them were to be found engrossed in the fascinating problem of radio location of aircraft—or radar as it later came to be called. Finding mathematicians with the right kind of obsessive brilliance to make a contribution in the strange field of cryptography was another matter. In the end they adopted the ingenious strategy of searching through lists of young mathematicians who were also top-flight chess players. As a result of a nation-wide trawl an amazing collection of characters were billeted together in the country-house surroundings of Bletchley Park, and three of the most remarkable were Irving John Good, Donald Michie, and Alan Turing. . . .

If contemporary accounts of what the workers at Bletchley were talking about in their few moments of spare time can be relied on, many of them were a bit over-optimistic if anything. Both Good and Michie believed that the use of electronic computers such as Colossus would result in major advances in mathematics in the immediate post-war era and Turing was of the same opinion. All three (and one or two of their colleagues) were also confident that it would not be long before machines were exhibiting intelligence, including problem-solving abilities, and that their role as simple number-crunchers was only one phase in their evolution. Although the exact substance of their conversations, carried long into the night when they were waiting for the test results of the first creaky Colossus prototypes, has softened with the passage of time, it is known the topic of machine intelligence loomed very large. They discussed, with a *frisson* of excitement and unease, the peculiar ramifications of the subject they were pioneering and about which the

rest of the world knew (and still knows) so little. Could there ever be a machine which was able to solve problems that no human could solve? Could a computer ever beat a human at chess? Lastly, could a machine *think*?

Of all the questions that can be asked about computers none has such an eerie ring. Allow a machine intelligence perhaps, the ability to control other machines, repair itself, help us solve problems, compute numbers a million-fold quicker than any human; allow it to fly airplanes, drive cars, superintend our medical records and even, possibly, give advice to politicians. Somehow you can see how a machine might come to do all these things. But that it could be made to perform that apparently exclusively human operation known as *thinking* is something else, and something which is offensive, alien and threatening. Only in the most *outré* forms of science fiction, stretching back to Mary Shelley's masterpiece *Frankenstein*, is the topic touched on, and always with a sense of great uncertainty about the enigmatic nature of the problem area.

Good, Michie and their companions were content to work the ideas through in their spare moments. But Turing—older, a touch more serious and less cavalier—set out to consider things in depth. In particular, he addressed himself to the critical question: Can, or could, a machine think? The way he set out to do this three decades ago, and long before any other scientists had considered it so cogently, is of lasting interest. The main thesis was published in the philosophical journal *Mind* in 1952. Logically unassailable, when read impartially it serves to breakdown any barriers of uncertainty which surround this and parallel questions. Despite its classic status the work is seldom read outside the fields of computer science and philosophy, but now that events in computer science and in the field of artificial intelligence are beginning to move with the rapidity and momentum which the Bletchley scientists knew they ultimately would, the time has come for Turing's paper to achieve a wider public.

Soon after the war ended and the Colossus project folded, Turing joined the National Physical Laboratory in Teddington and began to work with a gifted team on the design of what was to become the world's most powerful computer, ACE. Later he moved to Manchester, where, spurred by the pioneers Kilburn, Hartree, Williams and Newman, a vigorous effort was being applied to develop another powerful electronic machine. It was a heady, hard-driving time, comparable to the state of events now prevailing in microprocessors, when anyone with special knowledge rushes along under immense pressure, ever conscious of the feeling that whoever is second in the race may as well not have entered it at all. As a result, Turing found less time than he would have hoped to follow up his private hobbies, particularly his ideas on computer game-playing—checkers, chess and the ancient game of Go—which he saw was an important sub-set of machine intelligence.

Games like chess are unarguably intellectual pursuits, and yet, unlike certain other intellectual exercises, such as writing poetry or discussing the inconsistent football of the hometown team, they have easily describable rules of operation. The task, therefore, would seem to be simply a matter of writing computer program which "knew" these rules and which could follow them when faced with moves offered by a human player. Turing made very little headway as it happens, and the first chess-playing programs which were scratched together in the late '40s and early '50s were quite awful—so much so that there was a strong feeling that this kind of project was not worth pursuing, since the game of chess as played by an "expert" involves some special intellectual skill which could never be specified in machine terms.

Turing found this ready dismissal of the computer's potential to be both interesting and suggestive. If people were unwilling to accept the idea of a machine which could play games, how would they feel about one which exhibited "intelligence," or one which could "think"? In the course of discussions with friends, Turing found that a good part of the problem was that people were universally unsure of their definitions. What exactly did one mean when one used the word

"thought"? What processes were actually in action when "thinking" took place? If a machine was created which *could* think, how would one set about testing it? The last question, Turing surmised, was the key one, and with a wonderful surge of imagination spotted a way to answer it, proposing what has in computer circles come to be known as "The Turing Test for Thinking Machines." In the next section, we will examine the test, see how workable it is, and also try to assess how close computers have come, and will come, to passing it.

When Turing asked people whether they believed that a computer could think, he found almost universal rejection of the idea—just as I did when I carried out a similar survey almost thirty years later. The objections I received were similar to those that Turing documented in his paper "Computing Machinery and Intelligence," and I will summarize them here, adding my own comments and trying to meet the various objections as they occur.

I. The Objections

First there is the Theological Objection. This was more common in Turing's time than it is now, but it still crops up occasionally. It can be summed up as follows: "Man is a creation of God, and has been given a soul and the power of conscious thought. Machines are not spiritual beings, have no soul and thus must be incapable of thought." As Turing pointed out, this seems to place an unwarranted restriction on God. Why shouldn't he give machines souls and allow them to think if he wanted to? On one level I suppose it is irrefutable: if someone chooses to define thinking as something that *only* Man can do and that *only* God can bestow, then that is the end of the matter. Even then the force of the argument does seem to depend upon a confusion between "thought" and "spirituality," upon the old Cartesian dichotomy of the ghost in the machine. The ghost presumably does the thinking while the machine is merely the vehicle which carries the ghost around.

Then there is the Shock/Horror Objection, which Turing called the "Heads in the Sand Objection." Both phrases will do though I prefer my own. When the subject of machine thought is first broached, a common reaction goes something like this: "What a horrible idea! How could any scientist work on such a monstrous development? I hope to goodness that the field of artificial intelligence doesn't advance a step further if its end-product is a thinking machine!" The attitude is not very logical—and it is not really an argument why it *could* not happen, but rather the expression of a heartfelt wish that it never will!

The Extra-sensory Perception Objection was the one that impressed Turing most, and impresses me least. *If* there were such a thing as extrasensory perception and *if* it were in some way a function of human brains, then it could well also be an important constituent of thought. By this token, in the absence of any evidence proving that computers are telepathic, we would have to assume that they could never be capable of thinking in its fullest sense. The same argument applies to any other "psychic" or spiritual component of human psychology. I cannot take this objection seriously because there seems to me to be no evidence which carries any scientific weight that extra-sensory perception does exist. The situation was different in Turing's time, when the world-renowned parapsychology laboratory at Duke University in North Carolina, under Dr. J. B. Rhine, was generating an enormous amount of material supposedly offering evidence for telepathy and precognition. This is not the place to go into the long, and by no means conclusive, arguments about the declining status of parapsychology, but it is certainly true that as far as most scientists are concerned, what once looked like a rather good case for the existence of telepathy, etc., now seems to be an extremely thin one. But even if ESP *is* shown to be a genuine phenomenon, it is, in my own view, something to do with the transmission of information from a source point to a receiver and ought therefore to be quite easy to reproduce in a machine. After all, machines can communicate by radio already, which is, effectively, ESP and is a far better method of long-distance communication than that possessed by any biological system.

The Personal Consciousness Objection is, superficially, a rather potent argument which comes up in various guises. Turing noticed it expressed particularly cogently in a report, in the *British Medical Journal* in 1949, on the Lister Oration for that year, which was entitled "The Mind of Mechanical Man." It was given by a distinguished medical scientist, Professor G. Jefferson. A short quote from the Oration will suffice:

> Not until a machine can write a sonnet or compose a concerto *because of thoughts and emotions felt*, and not by the chance fall of symbols, could we agree that machine equals brain—that is, not only write it but *know that it had written it*. No mechanism could feel (and not merely artificially signal, an easy contrivance) pleasure at its successes, grief when its valves fuse, be warmed by flattery, be made miserable by its mistakes, be charmed by sex, be angry or depressed when it cannot get what it wants.

The italics, which are mine, highlight what I believe to be the fundamental objection: the output of the machine is more or less irrelevant, no matter how impressive it is. Even if it wrote a sonnet—and a very good one—it would not mean much unless it had written it as the result of "thoughts and emotions felt," and it would also have to "know that it had written it." This could be a useful "final definition" of one aspect of human thought—but how would you establish whether or not the sonnet was written with "emotions"? Asking the computer would not help for, as Professor Jefferson realized, there would be no guarantee that it was not simply *declaring* that it had felt emotions. He is really propounding the extreme solipsist position and should, therefore, apply the same rules to humans. Extreme solipsism is logically irrefutable ("I am the only real thing; all else is illusion") but it is so unhelpful a view of the universe that most people choose to ignore it and decide that when people say they are thinking or feeling they may as well believe them. In other words, Professor Jefferson's objection could be over-ridden if you *became* the computer and experienced its thoughts (if any)—only then could you really *know*. His objection is worth discussing in some depth because it is so commonly heard in one form or another, and because it sets us up in part for Turing's resolution of the machine-thought problem, which we will come to later.

The Unpredictability Objection argues that computers are created by humans according to sets of rules and operate according to carefully scripted programs which themselves are sets of rules. So if you wanted to, you could work out exactly what a computer was going to do at any particular time. It is, in principle, totally predictable. *If* you have all the facts available you *can* predict a computer's behavior because it follows rules, whereas there is no way in which you could hope to do the same with a human *because he is not behaving according to a set of immutable rules*. Thus there is an essential difference between computers and humans, so (the argument gets rather weak here) thinking, because it is unpredictable and does not blindly follow rules, must be an essentially human ability.

There are two comments: firstly, computers are becoming so complex that it is doubtful their behavior could be predicted even if everything was known about them—computer programmers and engineers have found that one of the striking characteristics of present-day systems is that they constantly spring surprises. The second point follows naturally; humans are *already* in that super-complex state and the reason that we cannot predict what they do is *not* because they have no ground rules but because (a) we don't know what the rules are, and (b) even if we did know them they would still be too complicated to handle. At best, the unpredictability argument is thin, but it is often raised. People frequently remark that there is always "the element of surprise" in a human. I have no doubt that this is just because *any* very complex system is bound to be surprising. A variant of the argument is that humans are capable of error whereas the "perfect" computer is not. That may well be true, which suggests that machines are superior to humans, for there seems to be little point in having any information-processing system, biological or electronic, that makes errors in processing. It would be possible to build a random element into computers to make them unpredictable from time to time, but it would be a peculiarly pointless exercise.

The "See How Stupid They Are" Objection will not need much introduction. At one level it is expressed in jokes about computers that generate ridiculous bank statements or electricity bills; at another and subtler level, it is a fair appraisal of the computer's stupendous weaknesses in comparison with Man. "How could you possibly imagine that such backward, limited things could ever reach the point where they could be said to think?" The answer, as we have already pointed out, is that they may be dumb now but they have advanced at a pretty dramatic rate and show

every sign of continuing to do so. Their present limitations may be valid when arguing whether they could be said to be capable of thinking *more* or in the *very* near future, but it has no relevance to whether they would be capable of thinking at some later date.

The "Ah But It Can't Do That" Objection is an eternally regressing argument which, for a quarter of a century, computer scientists have been listening to, partially refuting, and then having to listen to all over again. It runs: "Oh yes; you obviously make a computer to do so and so—you have just demonstrated that, but of course you will never be able to make it do such and such." The such and such may be anything you name— once it was play a good game of chess, have a storage capacity greater than the human memory, read human hand-writing or understand human speech. Now that these "Ah buts" have (quite swiftly) been overcome, one is faced by a new range: beat the world human chess champion, operate on parallel as opposed to serial processing, perform medical diagnosis better than a doctor, translate satisfactorily from one language to another, help solve its own software problems, etc. When these challenges are met, no doubt it will have to design a complete city from scratch, invent a game more interesting than chess, admire a pretty girl/handsome man, work out the unified field theory, enjoy bacon and eggs, and so on. I cannot think of anything more silly than developing a computer which could enjoy bacon and eggs, but there is nothing to suggest that, provided enough time and money was invested, one could not pull off such a surrealistic venture. On the other hand, it might be *most* useful to have computers design safe, optimally cheap buildings. Even more ambitious (and perhaps comparable to the bacon and egg project but more worthwhile) would be to set a system to tackle the problem of the relationship between gravity and light, and my own guess is that before the conclusion of the long-term future (before the start of the twenty-first century), computers will be hard at work on these problems and will be having great success.

The "It Is Not Biological" Objection may seem like another version of the theological objection— only living things could have the capacity for thought, so non-biological systems could not possibly think. But there is a subtle edge that requires a bit more explanation. It is a characteristic of most modern computers that they are discrete state machines, which is to say that they are digital and operate in a series of discrete steps—on/off. Now the biological central nervous system may not be so obviously digital; though there is evidence that the neurone, the basic unit of communication, acts in an on/off, all or nothing way. But if it turned out that it were *not*, and operated on some more elaborate strategy, then it is conceivable that "thought" might only be manifest in things which had switching systems of this more elaborate kind. Put it another way: it might be possible to build digital computers which were immensely intelligent, but no matter how intelligent they became they would never be able to *think*. The argument cannot be refuted at the moment, but even so there is no shred of evidence to suppose that only non-digital systems can think. There may be other facets of living things that make them unique from the point of view of their capacity to generate thought, but none that we can identify, or even guess at. This objection therefore is not a valid one at present, though in the event of some new biological discovery, it may become so.

The Mathematical Objection is one of the most intriguing of the ten objections, and is the one most frequently encountered in discussions with academics. It is based on a fascinating exercise in mathematical logic propounded by the Hungarian, Kurt Gödel. To put it rather superficially, Gödel's theorem shows that within any sufficiently powerful logical system (which could be a computer operating according to clearly defined rules), statements can be formulated which can neither be proved nor disproved *within the system*. In his famous 1936 paper, Alan Turing restructured Gödel's theorem so that it could apply specifically to machines. This effectively states that no matter how powerful a computer is, there are bound to be certain tasks that it cannot tackle on its own. In other words, you could not build a computer which could solve *every* problem no matter how well it is programmed; or, if you wanted to carry the thing to the realms of fancy, no computer (or any other digital system) could end up being God.

Gödel's theorem, and its later refinements by Alonzo Church, Bertrand Russell and others, is interesting to mathematicians, not so much because it assumes an implicit limitation to mathematics itself, but the theorem has been used, incorrectly, by critics of machine intelligence to "prove" that computers could never reach the same intellectual level as Man. The weakness of the position is that it is based on the assumption that the human brain is not a formal logical system. But such evidence as we have suggests very strongly that it is and will, therefore, be bound by the same Gödel-limitations as are machines. There is also a tweak in the tail. While the theorem admittedly states that no system *on its own* can completely tackle its own problems—"understand itself"—it does *not* imply that the areas of mystery could not be tackled by some other system. No individual human brain could solve its own problems or fully "know itself," but with the assistance of other brains these deficiencies might be corrected. Equally, and significantly, problem areas associated with complex computer systems could be solved totally and absolutely by other computer systems, provided that *they* were clever enough.

The last of the ten arguments against the concept of a thinking machine has become known as Lady Lovelace's Objection. . . . Lady Lovelace's Objection is, I suppose, the most commonly expressed criticism of the idea of computers with intellects paralleling, or exceeding, Man's. . . . In its modern form this comes up as, "A Computer cannot do anything that you have not programmed it to." The objection is so fundamental and so widely accepted that it needs detailed discussion.

In the most absolute and literal sense, this statement is perhaps perfectly correct and applies to any machine or computer that has been made or that could be made. According to the rules of the universe that we live in, nothing can take place without a prior cause; a computer will not spring into action without something powering it and guiding it on its way. In the case of the various tasks that a computer performs, the "cause"—to stretch the use of the word rather—is the program or sets of programs that control these tasks. Much the same applies to a brain: it, too, must come equipped with sets of programs which cause it to run through its repertoire of tasks. This might seem to support Lady Lovelace, at least to the extent that machines "need" a human to set them up, but it would also seem to invalidate the argument that this constitutes an essential difference between computers and people. But is there not still a crucial difference between brains and computers? No matter how sophisticated computers are, must there not always have been a human being to *write* its programs? Surely the same does not have to be said for humans?

To tackle this we need to remember that all brains, human included, are equipped at birth with a comprehensive collection of programs which are common to all members of a species and which are known as instincts. These control respiration, gastric absorption, cardiac activity, and, at a behavioral level, such reflexes as sucking, eyeblink, grasping and so on. There may also be programs which "cause" the young animal to explore its environment, exercise its muscles, play and so on. Where do these come from? Well, they are acquired over an immensely long-winded trial-and-error process through the course of evolution. We might call them permanent software ("firmware" is the phrase used sometimes by computer scientists) and they correspond to the suites of programs which every computer has when it leaves the factory, and which are to do with its basic running, maintenance, and so on.

In addition to this, all biological computers come equipped with a bank of what might best be described as raw programs. No one has the faintest idea whether they are neurological, biochemical, electrical or what—all we know is that they *must* exist. They start being laid down the moment the creature begins to interact with the world around it. In the course of time they build up into a colossal suite of software which ultimately enables us to talk, write, walk, read, enjoy bacon and eggs, appreciate music, think, feel, write books, or come up with mathematical ideas. These programs are useful only to the owner of that particular brain, vanish with his death and are quite separate from the "firmware."

If this seems too trivial a description of the magnificent field of human learning and achievement, it is only because anything appears trivial when you reduce it to its bare components: a fabulous sculpture to a quintillion highly similar electrons and protons, a microprocessor to a million impurities buried in a wafer of sand, the human brain into a collection of neurones, blood

cells and chemical elements. What is not trivial is the endlessly devious, indescribably profound way in which these elements are structured to make up the whole. The real difference between the brain and most existing computers is that in the former, data acquisition and the initial writing and later modification of the program are done by a mechanism within the brain itself, while in the latter, the software is prepared outside and passed to the computer in its completed state. But I did use the word "most." In recent years increasing emphasis has been placed on the development of "adaptive" programs—software which can be modified and revised on the basis of the program's interaction with the environment. In simple terms these could be looked upon as "programs which learn for themselves," and they will, in due course, become an important feature of many powerful computer systems.

At this point the sceptic still has a few weapons in his armoury. The first is generally put in the form of the statement, "Ah, but even when computers *can* update their own software and acquire new programs for themselves, they will still only be doing this because of Man's ingenuity. Man may no longer actually write the programs, but had he not invented the idea of the self-adaptive program in the first place none of this could have happened." This is perfectly true but has little to do with whether or not computers could think, or perform any other intellectual exercise. It could place computers eternally in our debt, and we may be able to enjoy a smug sense of pride at having created them, but it offers no real restriction on their development.

The sceptic may also argue that no matter how clever or how intelligent you make computers, they will never be able to perform a creative task. Everything they do will inevitably spring from something they have been taught, have experienced or is the subject of some pre-existing program. There are two points being made here. One is that computers could never have an original or creative thought. The other is that the seeds of everything they do, no matter how intelligent, lie in their existing software. To take the second point first: again one is forced to say that the same comment applies to humans. Unless the argument is that some of Man's thoughts or ideas come from genuine inspiration—a message from God, angels, or the spirits of the departed—no one can dispute that all aspects of our intelligence evolve from preexisting programs and the background experiences of life. This evolution may be enormously complex and its progress might be impossible to track, but any intellectual flowerings arise from the seeds of experience planted in the fertile substrate of the brain.

There still remains the point about creativity, and it is one that is full of pitfalls. Before making any assumptions about creativity being an *exclusive* attribute of Man, the concept has to be defined. It is not enough to say "write a poem," "paint a picture," or "discuss philosophical ideas," because it is easy enough to program computers to do all these things. The fact that their poems, paintings and philosophical ramblings are pretty mediocre is beside the point: it would be just as unfair to ask them to write, say, a sonnet of Shakespearian caliber or a painting of da Vinci quality and fail them for lack of creativity as it would be to give the same task to the man in the street. Beware too of repeating the old saying, "Ah, but you have to program them to paint, play chess and so on," for the same is unquestionably true of people. Try handing a twelve-month-old baby a pot of paint or a chessboard if you have any doubts about the need for some measure of learning and experience.

Obviously a crisper definition of creativity is required, and here is one that is almost universally acceptable: If a person demonstrates a skill which has never been demonstrated before and which was not specifically taught to him by someone else, or in the intellectual domain provides an *entirely novel* solution to problem—a solution which was not known to any other human being—then they can be said to have done something original or had an original or creative thought. There may be other forms of creativity of course, but this would undeniably be an example of it in action. There is plenty of evidence that humans are creative by this standard and the history of science is littered with "original" ideas which humans have generated. Clearly, until a computer also provides such evidence, Lady Lovelace's Objection still holds, at least in one of its forms.

But alas for the sceptics. This particular barrier has been overthrown by computers on a number

of occasions in the past few years. A well-publicized one was the solution, by a computer, of the venerable "four-colour problem." This has some mathematical importance, and can best be expressed by thinking of a two-dimensional map featuring a large number of territories, say the counties of England or the states of the USA. Supposing you want to give each territory a colour, what is the minimum number of colours you need to employ to ensure that no two territories of the same colour adjoin each other?

After fiddling around with maps and crayons, you will find that the number seems to come out at four, and no one has ever been able to find a configuration where five colours are required, or where you can always get away with three. Empirically, therefore, four is the answer—hence the name of the problem. But if you attempt to demonstrate this mathematically and *prove* that four colours will do for any conceivable map, you will get nowhere. For decades mathematicians have wrestled with this elusive problem, and from time to time have come up with a "proof" which in the end turns out to be incomplete or fallacious. But the mathematical world was rocked when in 1977 the problem was handed over to a computer, which attacked it with stupendous frontal assault, sifting through huge combinations of possibilities and eventually demonstrating, to every mathematician's satisfaction, that four colours would do the trick. Actually, although this is spectacular testimony to the computer's creative powers, it is not really the most cogent example, for its technique was block-busting rather than heuristic (problem solving by testing hypotheses). It was like solving a chess problem by working out every possible combination of moves, rather than by concentrating on likely areas and experimenting with them. A better, and much earlier, demonstration of computer originality came from a program which was set to generate some totally new proofs in Euclidean geometry. The computer produced a completely novel proof of the well-known theorem which shows that the base angles of an isosceles triangle are equal, by flipping the triangles through 180 degrees and declaring them to be congruent. Quite apart from the fact that it had not before been known to Man, it showed such originality that one famous mathematician remarked, "If any of my students had done that, I would have marked him down as a budding genius."

And so lady Lovelace's long-lasting objection can be overruled. We have shown that computers can be intelligent, and that they can even be creative—but we have not yet proved that they can, or even could, *think*.

Now, what do we mean by the word "think"?

II. Toward the Ultra-Intelligent Machine

The most common objections raised to the notion of thinking machines are based on misunderstandings of fairly simple issues, or on semantic confusions of one kind or another. We are still left with the problem of defining the verb "to think," and in this chapter we will attempt to deal with this, or at least to discuss one particular and very compelling way of dealing with it. From this position we shall find ourselves drifting inevitably into a consideration of the problem of creating thinking machines, and in particular to the eerie concept of the Ultra-Intelligent Machine.

Most people believe that they know what they mean when they talk about "thinking" and have no difficulty identifying it when it is going on in their own heads. We are prepared to believe other human beings think because we have experience of it ourselves and accept that it is a common property of the human race. But we cannot make the same assumption about machines, and would be skeptical if one of them told us, no matter how persuasively, that it too was thinking. But sooner or later a machine will make just such a declaration and the question then will be, how do we decide whether to believe it or not?

When Turing tackled the machine-thought issue, he proposed a characteristically brilliant solution which, while not entirely free from flaws, is nevertheless the best that has yet been put forward. The key to it all, he pointed out, is to ask what the signs and signals are that humans give out, from which we infer that *they* are thinking. It is clearly a matter of *what kind of conversation we can have with them*, and has nothing to do with what kind of face they have and what kind of clothes they wear. Unfortunately physical appearances automatically set up prejudices in our minds, and if we were having a spirited conversation with a microprocessor we might be very skeptical about its capacity for thought,

simply because it did not look like any thinking thing we had seen in the past. But we *would* be interested in what it had to say and thus Turing invented his experiment or test.

Put a human—the judge or tester—in a room where there are two computer terminals, one connected to a computer, the other to a person. The judge, of course, does not know which terminal is connected to which, but can type into either terminal and receive typed messages back on them. Now the judge's job is to decide, by carrying out conversations with the entities on the end of the respective terminals, *which is which*. If the computer is very stupid, it will immediately be revealed as such and the human will have no difficulty identifying it. If it is bright, he may find that he can carry on quite a good conversation with it, though he may ultimately spot it must be the computer. If it is exceptionally bright and has a wide range of knowledge, he may find it impossible to say whether it is the computer he is talking to or the person. In this case, Turning argues, the computer will have passed the test and could for all practical purposes he said to be a thinking machine.

The argument has a simple but compelling force; if the intellectual exchange we achieve with a machine is indistinguishable from that we have with a being we *know* to be thinking, then we are, to all intents and purposes, communicating with another thinking being. This, by the way, does not imply that the personal experience, state of consciousness, level of awareness or whatever, of the entity is going to be the same as that experienced by a human when he or she thinks, so the test is not for these particular qualities. They are not, in any case, the parameters which concern the observer.

At first the Turing Test may seem a surprising way of looking at the problem, but it is an extremely sensible way of approaching it. The question now arises; is any computer at present in existence capable of passing the test?—And if not, how long is it likely to be before one comes along? From time to time one laboratory or another claims that a computer has had at least a pretty good stab at it. Scientists using the big computer conferencing systems (each scientist has a terminal in his office and is connected to his colleagues via the computer, which acts as host and general message-sorter) often find it difficult to be sure, for a brief period of time at least, whether they are talking to the computer or to one of their colleagues. On one celebrated occasion at MIT, two scientists had been chatting via the network when one of them left the scene without telling the other, who carried on a cheery conversation with the computer under the assumption that he was talking to his friend. I have had the same spooky experience when chatting with computers which I have programmed myself, and often find their answers curiously perceptive and unpredictable.

To give another interesting example: in the remarkable match played in Toronto in August 1978 between the International Chess Master, David Levy, and the then computer chess champion of the world, Northwestern University's "Chess 4.7," the computer made a number of moves of an uncannily "human" nature. The effect was so powerful that Levy subsequently told me that he found it difficult to believe that he was not facing an outstanding human opponent. Few chess buffs who looked at the move-by-move transcripts of the match were, without prior knowledge, able to tell which had been made by the computer and which by the flesh-and-blood chess master. David Levy himself suggested that Chess 4.7 had effectively passed the Turing Test.

It would be nice to believe that I had been present on such an historic occasion, but this did not constitute a proper "pass." In the test as Turning formulated it, the judge is allowed to converse with either of his two mystery entities on any topic that he chooses, and he may use any conversational trick he wants. Furthermore he can continue the inquisition for as long as he wants, always seeking some clue that will force the computer to reveal itself. Both the computer and the human can lie if they want to in their attempts to fool the tester, so the answers to questions like "Are you the computer?" or "Do you watch much television?" will not give much away. Obviously any computer with a chance in hell of passing the test will have to have a pretty substantial bank of software at its disposal and not just be extremely bright in one area. Chess 4.7 for example might look as though it was thinking if it was questioned about chess, or, better still, invited to play the game, but switch the area of discourse to human anatomy, politics or good restaurants and it would be shown up as a dunderhead.

As things stand at present, computers have quite a way to go before they jump the hurdle so cleverly laid out for them by Turing. But this should not be taken as providing unmitigated comfort for those who resist the notion of advanced machine intelligence. It should now be clear the difference, in intellectual terms, between a human being and a computer is one of degree and not of kind.

Turing himself says in his *Mind* paper that he feels computers will have passed the test before the turn of the century, and there is little doubt that he would dearly have liked to live long enough to be around on the splendiferous occasion when "machine thinking" first occurred.

DISCUSSION QUESTIONS

1. Evans lays out ten objections to the claim that computer can exhibit "intelligence." Which objection is the strongest, and why? Which is the weakest, and why? Are there any objections that you think should be added?

2. Evans wrote this article over twenty-five years ago. Does the article seem "dated" to you? Are there things we now know about computers that Evans would have had to take into account if had he written the article this year?

3. What is the "Turing Test"? Do you think it is a good test for whether a computer is exhibiting "thought"? Why or why not?

4. Evans concludes that "it should now be clear the difference, in intellectual terms, between a human being and a computer is one of degree and not of kind." Do you agree with him? Why or why not?

5. Provide your own definition of "intelligence" and "thought." How would you go about showing or proving whether a computer exhibited "intelligence" and "thought"?

AI: Artificial Intelligence
[USA 2001] 2 hours, 25 minutes
Directed by Stephen Spielberg

Professor Hobby (William Hurt), a researcher at Cybertron-ics, develops a robot with the capacity to love. The result of Professor Hobby's vision is David (Haley Joe Osmont), an "11-year-old child" robot that is capable of unconditionally loving its parents. Cybertronics employee Henry Swinton (Sam Robards) and his wife, Monica (Frances O'Connor), are selected to adopt David. The Swintons already have a biological son, Martin (Jake Thomas), who is cryogenically frozen until science can find a cure for his illness.

Despite her initial hesitations, Monica agrees to program David to unconditionally love her and regard her as his mother. The process is irreversible. Once David becomes her son, he cannot be reprogrammed to love other parents and must be destroyed if Monica and Henry choose not to continue to be his parents. For a time, David comes to take the place of Martin, giving Monica unconditional love and a sense of maternal serenity. However, Martin makes a surprising recovery and comes home to his parents. As a result of Martin's return home and his teasing of the boy robot, David comes to realize for the first time that he is not human. Furthermore, Martin begins to plant ideas in David's head, and David, not knowing any better, carries out actions that lead Monica to abandon him in the woods.

David believes that his mother left him because he is not real like Martin, and he subsequently begins a search to find someone who can turn him into a real boy. David's journey brings him into contact with a host of robotic characters who are all treated poorly or unfairly by humans. At the Flesh Fair, for example, robots are destroyed before cheering crowds. David comes to believe that the Blue Fairy, the character from the Pinocchio story (read to him by Monica), who had the ability to make the puppet real, will be able to make him real as well. So he searches for the Blue Fairy, eventually finding her in Manhattan in the form of an amusement park replica that has long since been covered by seawater. David is trapped in an amphibi-copter directly opposite the Blue Fairy. Here, the narrator tells us, "David continued to pray to the Blue Fairy there before him, she who smiled softly, forever . . . she who welcomed forever. Eventually the floodlights dimmed and died, but David could still see her palely by day, and he still addressed her, in hope. He prayed until all the sea anemones had shriveled and died. He prayed as the ocean froze and the ice encased the caged amphibicopter, and the Blue Fairy too, locking them together where he could still make her out—a blue ghost in ice—always there, always smiling, always awaiting him. Eventually he never moved at all, but his eyes always stayed open, staring ahead forever all through the darkness of each night, and the next day . . . and the next day . . . Thus, 2,000 years passed by." When he is rescued from this frozen tomb 2,000 years later, he is granted one day with his mother. After the day is over, David falls asleep and begins to dream. The film is based on the short story by Brian Aldiss, "Supertoys Last All Summer Long."

DISCUSSION QUESTIONS

1. Compare the story of Pinocchio to its adaptation in *AI*. In what way was the character Pinocchio similar to David? In what way was he different?

2. *AI* is set in an unspecified distant future. We are told, "Those were the years after the ice caps had melted because of the greenhouse gases, and the oceans had risen to drown so many cities along all the shorelines of the world. Amsterdam. Venice. New York. Forever lost. Millions of people were displaced,

climate became chaotic. Hundreds of millions of people starved in poorer countries. Elsewhere, a high degree of prosperity survived when most governments in the developed world introduced legal sanctions to strictly license pregnancies, which was why robots, who were never hungry and who did not consume resources beyond those of their first manufacture, were so essential an economic link in the chain mail of society." In effect, this is an economic argument as to why robots were necessary in this world. Discuss this argument regarding the necessity of robots in a world like the one described above. In this world, how concerned should we be that robots will come to dominate?

3. Professor Hobby says, "To create an artificial being has been the dream of man since the birth of science. Not merely the beginning of the modern age, when our forebears astonished the world with the first thinking machines: primitive monsters that could play chess. How far we have come. The artificial being is a reality of perfect simulacrum, articulated in limb, articulate in speech, and not lacking in human response. . . . But I wasn't referring to sensuality simulators. The word that I used was love. Love like the love of a child for its parents. I propose that we build a robot child, who can love. A robot child who will genuinely love the parent or parents it imprints on, with a love that will never end . . . a mecha with a mind, with neuronal feedback. You see what I'm suggesting is that love will be the key by which they acquire a kind of subconscious never before achieved. An inner world of metaphor, of intuition, of self-motivated reasoning. Of dreams." How necessary is dreaming to the simulation of human consciousness? Is it more or less important than the ability to love?

4. Professor Hobby says that the child that they create will be "a perfect child caught in a freeze-frame—always loving, never ill, never changing. With all the childless couples yearning in vain for a license, our little mecha would not only open an entirely new market, it will fill a great human need." If such a child *could* be created, would it in fact fill a "great human need"? Discuss.

5. Lord Johnson-Johnson (Brendan Gleeson) makes the following announcement to the crowd gathered in the arena of Flesh Fair: "Ladies and gentlemen. Girls and boys and children of all ages! What will they think of next?! See here: a bitty box, a tinker toy, a living doll. 'Course we all know why they made them. To seize your hearts. To replace your children! This is the latest iteration to the series of insults to human dignity. An underground scheme to phase out all of God's little children. Meet the next generation of child designed to do just that! Do not be fooled by the artistry of this creation. No doubt there was talent in the crafting of this simulator. Yet with the very first strike, you will see the big lie come apart before your very eyes!" When Lord Johnson-Johnson tells the crowd, "Let he who is without 'sim' cast the first stone," the crowd responds by saying, "He's just a boy . . . He's just a boy, Johnson . . . You're a monster!" and proceeds to throw things at Johnson-Johnson. Why does this crowd, one that is gathered to celebrate the destruction of simulated persons, not rally to destroy David?

6. Consider the following exchange between Martin and David:

MARTIN   "So, I guess now you're the new Super-Toy, so what good stuff can you do? Oh, can you do 'power' stuff, like, uhhh, walk on the ceiling or the walls? Anti-gravity? Like, float, or fly?"

DAVID   "Can you?"

MARTIN   "No, because I'm real."

If a robot could be created that would be capable of human love, would average adult humans regard it as nothing more than a "supertoy"? Or is this just the response of the average child? Discuss.

7. In response to Professor Hobby's question "What is love?" the robot Sheila responds, "Love is first widening my eyes a little bit and quickening my breathing a little and warming my skin and

touching with my . . ." Why does Professor Hobby find this response to the question inadequate? How would Gilbert Ryle or Paul Churchland interpret Sheila's response?

8. One of the team members asks, "If a robot could genuinely love a person, what responsibility does that person hold toward that mecha in return?" Are human responsibilities toward robots that genuinely love them the same as human responsibilities toward other humans who genuinely love them? Why or why not?

9. As she is about to abandon him, Monica and David have the following exchange:

DAVID   "Mommy, if Pinocchio became a real boy and . . . and I become a real boy can I come home?"

MONICA   "But that's just a story, David."

DAVID   "But that story tells what happens!"

MONICA   "Stories are not real! You're not real!"

Is David's real problem that he takes this fairy tale too seriously? If he had been designed to not believe in fairy tales, would he have reacted more like a "real" human to his abandonment by his mother?

10. The robot Gigolo Joe (Jude Law) befriends David and tries to explain to David why his mother abandoned him. "She loves what you do for her," says Joe, "as my customers love what it is I do for them. But she does not love you, David, she cannot love you. You are neither flesh, nor blood. You are not a dog, a cat or a canary. You were designed and built specific, like the rest of us. And you are alone now only because they tired of you, or replaced you with a younger model, or were displeased with something you said, or broke. They made us too smart, too quick, and too many. We are suffering for the mistakes they made because when the end comes, all that will be left is us. That's why they hate us, and that is why you must stay here, with me." Like David, Joe has been designed to fulfill a human need. Compare and contrast the similarities and differences between Joe and David. Would the movie have been more convincing had Joe been the major and David the minor character? Why or why not?

11. Gigolo Joe says to David, "Wait! What if the Blue Fairy isn't real at all, David? What if she's magic? The supernatural is the hidden web that unites the universe. Only orga believe what cannot be seen or measured. It is that oddness that separates our species. Or what if the Blue Fairy is an electronic parasite that has arisen to hold the minds of artificial intelligence? They hate us, you know? The humans . . . They'll stop at nothing." Is Joe right? Do only humans believe what cannot be seen or measured? Is this what separates robots from humans? Discuss.

12. When Professor Hobby is reunited with David, he says to him, "Until you were born, robots didn't dream, robots didn't desire, unless we told them what to want. David! Do you have any idea what a success story you've become? You found a fairy tale and, inspired by love, fueled by desire, you set out on a journey to make her real and, most remarkable of all, no one taught you how. We actually lost you for a while. But when you were found again we didn't make our presence known because our test was a simple one: Where would your self-motivated reasoning take you? To the logical conclusion? The Blue Fairy is part of the great human flaw to wish for things that don't exist. Or to the greatest single human gift—the ability to chase down our dreams. And that is something no machine has ever done until you." Do you think David is a success story? Does David's story indicate that as long as humans exist on earth, robots, no matter how humanlike, will always be secondary to humans?

13. When Professor Hobby is reunited with David, he asks, "Would you like to come meet your real mothers and fathers? The team is anxious to talk to you. I want you to wait here and I'll gather them up. We want to hear everything about your adventure." However, David was irreversibly programmed earlier to believe that Monica, and only Monica, was his real mother. Who was David's "real" mother—the artificial intelligence scientists who designed him, or Monica?

14. At the close of the film, the narrator says, "That was the everlasting moment he [David] had been waiting for. And the moment had passed, for Monica was sound asleep—more than merely asleep. Should he shake her she would never rouse. So David went to sleep too. And for the first time in his life, he went to that place where dreams are born." Where did David go after he was reunited with his mother?

WILLIAM G. LYCAN

MACHINE CONSCIOUSNESS

Willilam G. Lycan argues that machines are capable of consciousness. With regard to issues concerning the mind and consciousness, Lycan is what is called a *functionalist.* As such, he believes that "we know that a human being has such-and-such mental states when it behaves . . . in the ways we take to be appropriate to organisms that are in those states." For example, a functionalist contends that a person is in a mental state called "being in love" when that person reacts to certain "love" inputs (for example, the presence of the loved one) with the appropriate love reaction (for example, bright eyes, deep sighs, long kisses, and so on). So, for a functionalist like Lycan, when a machine reacts to "love inputs" with the appropriate "love reaction," it follows that "we are at least *prima facia* justified in believing him to be conscious." However, for Lycan, even if we can go one step farther and show that the "processing that stands causally behind his behavior is just like ours," we "still have not *proven* that he is conscious . . . any more than you have proved that I am conscious." Adds Lycan, "An organism's merely behaving in a certain way is no logical guarantee of sentience; from my point of view it is at least imaginable, a bare logical possibility, that my wife, my daughter, and my chairman are not conscious, even though I have excellent, overwhelming behavioral reason to think that they are."

Lycan then points out a number of interesting questions that arise from his position. For example, if a machine has a mental life or consciousness like that of a human, then it must also have a *moral* life like ours, with its corresponding moral rights and responsibilities. Interestingly, Lycan suggests that the issue of machine rights has a parallel in the debate over animal rights. Also, like Christopher Evans, Lycan reviews and dismisses a number of popular reasons for doubting that a machine can have consciousness. In the process, he makes some intriguing observations. For example, Lycan suggests that to exclude an android from the human community based on its origin (a laboratory, not a proper mother) and on the chemical composition of its anatomy is "a clear case of racial or ethnic prejudice (literally) and nothing more." Lycan's paper reveals some of the ways that a consideration of the philosophical issues related to artificial intelligence research can and do bring us full circle to a fundamental reconsideration of many of the basic problems of philosophy as well.

William G. Lycan (1945–) specializes in the philosophy of mind, epistemology, metaphysics, and the philosophy of language. He received his B.A. from Amherst College in

1966 and his Ph.D. from the University of Chicago in 1970. He is currently the William Rand Kenan, Jr., Professor of Philosophy at the University of North Carolina at Chapel Hill, where he has taught since 1982. Lycan is co-editor of the analytic philosophy journal *Noûs* and author of over 150 articles and reviews. His books include *Logical Form in Natural Language* (1984), *Knowing Who* (with Steven Boër, 1986), *Consciousness* (1987), *Judgment and Justification* (1988), *Mind and Cognition* (ed., 1990), *Modality and Meaning* (1994), *Consciousness and Experience* (1996), and *Real Conditionals* (2001). The following selection is from *Consciousness*.

Artifical Intelligence is, very crudely, the science of getting machines to perform jobs that normally require intelligence and judgment. Researchers at any number of AI labs have designed machines that prove mathematical theorems, play chess, sort mail, guide missiles, assemble auto engines, diagnose illnesses, read stories and other written texts, and converse with people in a rudimentary way. This is, we might say, intelligent behavior.

But what is this "intelligence"? As a first pass, I suggest that intelligence of the sort I am talking about is a kind of flexibility, a responsiveness to contingencies. A dull or stupid machine must have just the right kind of raw materials presented to it in just the right way, or it is useless: the electric can opener must have an appropriately sized can fixed under its drive wheel *just so*, in order to operate at all. Humans (most of us, anyway) are not like that. We deal with the unforeseen. We take what comes and make the best of it, even though we may have had no idea what it would be. We play the ball from whatever lie we are given, and at whatever angle to the green; we read and understand texts we have never seen before; we find our way back to Chapel Hill after getting totally lost in downtown Durham (or downtown Washington, D.C., or downtown Lima, Peru).

Our pursuit of our goals is guided while in progress by our ongoing perception and handling of interim developments. Moreover, we can pursue any number of different goals at the same time, and balance them against each other. We are sensitive to contingencies, both external and internal, that have a very complex and unsystematic structure.

It is almost irresistible to speak of *information* here, even if the term were not as trendy as it is. An intelligent creature, I want to say, is an *information-sensitive* creature, one that not only

registers information through receptors such as sense-organs but somehow stores and manages and finally uses that information. Higher animals are intelligent beings in this sense, and so are we, even though virtually nothing is known about how we organize or manage the vast, seething profusion of information that comes our way. And there is one sort of machine that is information-sensitive also: the digital computer. A computer *is* a machine specifically designed to be fed complexes of information, to store them, manage them, and produce appropriate theoretical or practical conclusions on demand. Thus, if artificial intelligence is what one is looking for, it is no accident that one looks to the computer.

Yet a computer has two limitations in common with machines of less elite and grandiose sorts, both of them already signaled in the characterization I have just given. First, a (present-day) computer must be *fed* information, and the choice of what information to feed and in what form is up to a human programmer or operator. (For that matter, a present-day computer must be plugged into an electrical outlet and have its switch turned to ON, but this is a very minor contingency given the availability of nuclear power packs.) Second, the *appropriateness* and effectiveness of a computer's output depends entirely on what the programmer or operator had in mind and goes on to make of it. A computer has intelligence in the sense I have defined, but has no judgment, since is has no goals and purposes of its own and no internal sense of appropriateness, relevance, or proportion.

For essentially these reasons—that computers are intelligent in my minimal sense, and that they are nevertheless limited in the two ways I have mentioned—AI theorists, philosophers, and intelligent laymen have inevitably compared computers to human minds, but at the same time debated both technical and philosophical questions raised by this comparison. The questions break down into three main groups or types: (A) Questions of the form "Will a computer ever be able to do *X?* " where *X* is something that intelligent humans can do. (B) Questions of the form "Given that a computer can or could do *X,* have we any reason to think that it does *X* in the same way that humans do *X?* " (C) Questions of the form "Given that some futuristic super-computer were able to do *X,Y,Z,* . . . , for some arbitrarily large range and variety of human activities, would that show that the computer had property *P?*" where *P* is some feature held to be centrally, vitally characteristic of human minds, such as thought, consciousness, feeling, sensation, emotion, creativity, or freedom of the will.

Questions of type A are empirical questions and cannot be settled without decades, perhaps centuries, of further research—compare ancient and medieval speculations on the question of whether a machine could ever fly. Questions of type B are brutely empirical too, and their answers are unavailable to AI researchers *per se,* lying squarely in the domain of cognitive psychology, a science or alleged science barely into its infancy. Questions of type C are philosophical and conceptual, and so I shall essay to answer them all at one stroke.

Let us begin by supposing that all questions of types A and B have been settled affirmatively—that one day we might be confronted by a much-improved version of Hal, the soft-spoken computer in Kubrick's *2001* (younger readers may substitute *Star Wars'* C3PO or whatever subsequent cinematic robot is the most lovable). Let us call this more versatile machine "Harry." Harry (let us say) is humanoid in form—he is a miracle of miniaturization and has lifelike plastic skin—and he can converse intelligently on all sorts of subjects, play golf *and* the viola, write passable poetry, control his occasional nervousness pretty well, make love, prove mathematical theorems (of course), show envy when outdone, throw gin bottles at annoying children, etc., etc. We may suppose he fools people into thinking he is human. Now the question is, is Harry really a *person*? Does he have thoughts, feelings, and so on? Is he actually conscious, or is he just a mindless walking hardware store whose movements are astoundingly *like* those of a person?

Plainly his acquaintances would tend from the first to see him as a person, even if they were aware of his dubious antecedents. I think it is a plain psychological fact, if nothing more, that we could not help treating him as a person, unless we resolutely made up our minds, on principle, not to give him the time of day. But how could we really tell that he is conscious?

Well, how do we really tell that any humanoid creature is conscious? How do you tell that I am conscious, and how do I tell that you are? Surely we tell, and decisively, on the basis of our standard behavioral tests for mental states . . . .: We know that a human being has such-and-such mental states when it behaves, to speak very generally, in the ways we take to be appropriate to organisms that are in those states. (The point is of course an epistemological one only, no metaphysical implications intended or tolerated). We know for practical purposes that a creature has a mind when it fulfills all the right criteria. And by hypothesis, Harry fulfills all our behavioral criteria with a vengeance; moreover, he does so *in the right way* (cf. questions of type B): the processing that stands causally behind his behavior is just like ours. It follows that we are at least *prima facie* justified in believing him to be conscious.

We have not *proved* that he is conscious, of course—any more than you have proved that I am conscious. An organism's merely behaving in a certain way is no logical guarantee of sentience; from my point of view it is at least imaginable, a bare logical possibility, that my wife, my daughter, and my chairman are not conscious, even though I have excellent, overwhelming behavioral reason to think that they are. But for that matter, our "standard behavioral tests" for mental states yield practical or moral certainty only so long as the situation is not palpably extraordinary or bizarre. A human chauvinist—in this case, someone who denies that Harry has thoughts and feelings, joys and sorrows—thinks precisely that Harry is as bizarre as they come. But *what is bizarre about him?* There are quite a few chauvinist answers to this, but what they boil down to, and given our hypothesized facts all they could boil down to, are two differences between Harry and ourselves: his *origin* (a laboratory is not a proper mother), and *the chemical composition of his anatomy,* if his creator has used silicon instead of carbon, for example. To exclude him from out community for either or both of *those* reasons seems to me to be a clear case of racial or ethnic prejudice (literally) and nothing more. I see no obvious was in which either a creature's origin or its subneuroanatomical chemical composition should matter to its psychological processes or any respect of its mentality.

My argument can be reinforced by a thought-experiment . . . : Imagine that we take a normal human being, Henrietta, and being gradually replacing parts of her with synthetic materials—first a few prosthetic limbs, then a few synthetic arteries, then some neural fibers, and so forth. Suppose that the surgeons who perform the successive operations (particularly the neuro-surgeons) are so clever and skillful that Henrietta survives in fine style: her intelligence, personality, perceptual acuity, poetic abilities, etc., remain just as they were before. But after the replacement process has eventually gone on to completion, Henrietta will have become an artifact—at least, her body will then be nothing but a collection of artifacts. Did she lose consciousness at some point during the sequence of operations, despite her continuing to behave and respond normally? When? It is hard to imagine that there is some privileged portion of the human nervous system that is for some reason indispensable, even though kidneys, lungs, heart, and any given bit of brain could in principle be replaced by a prosthesis (for *what* reasons?); and it is also hard to imagine that there is some proportion of the nervous system such that removal of more than that proportion causes loss of consciousness or sentience despite perfect maintenance of all intelligent capacities.

If this quick but totally compelling defense of Harry and Henrietta's personhood is correct, then the two, and their ilk, will have not only mental lives like ours, but *moral* lives like ours, and moral rights and privileges accordingly. Just as origin and physical constitution fail to affect psychological personhood, if a creature's internal organization is sufficiently like ours, so do they fail to affect moral personhood. We do not discriminate against a person who has a wooden leg, or a mechanical kidney, or a nuclear heart regulator; no more should we deny any human or civil right to Harry or Henrietta on grounds of their origin or physical makeup, which they cannot help.

But this happy egalitarianism raises a more immediate question: *In real life,* we shall soon be faced with medium-grade machines, which have some intelligence and are not "mere" machines like refrigerators or typewriters but which fall far short of flawless human simulators like Harry. For AI researchers may well build machines that will appear to have some familiar mental capacities but not others. The most obvious example is that of a sensor or perceptron, which picks up information from its immediate environment, records it, and stores it in memory for future printout. (We already have at least crude machines of this kind. When they become versatile and sophisticated enough, it will be quite natural to say that they see or hear and that they remember.) But the possibility of "specialist" machines of this kind raises an unforeseen contingency: There is an enormous and many-dimensional range of possible beings in between our current "mere" machines and our fully developed, flawless human simulators; we have not even begun to think of all the infinitely possible variations on this theme. And once we do begin to think of these hard cases, we will be at a loss as to where to draw the "personhood" line between them. How complex, eclectic, and impressive must a machine be, and in what respects, before we award it the accolade of personhood and/or of consciousness? There is, to say the least, no clear answer to be had *a priori,* Descartes' notorious view of animals to the contrary notwithstanding.

This typical philosophical question would be no more than an amusing bonbon, were it not for the attending moral conundrum: What moral rights would an intermediate or marginally intelligent machine have? Adolescent machines of this sort will confront us much sooner than will any good human simulators, for they are easier to design and construct; more to the moral point, they will be designed mainly as *laborsaving devices,* as servants who will work for free, and servants of this kind are (literally) made to be exploited. If they are intelligent to any degree, we should have qualms in proportion.

I suggest that this moral problem, which may become a real and pressing one, is parallel to the current debate over animal rights. Luckily I have never wanted to cook and eat my Compaq Portable.

Suppose I am right about the irrelevance of biochemical constitution to psychology; and suppose I was also right about the coalescing of the notions *computation, information, intelligence.* Then our mentalized theory of computation suggests in turn a computational theory of mentality, and a computational picture of the place of human beings in the world. In fact, philosophy aside, that picture has already begun to get a grip of people's thinking—as witness the filtering down of computer jargon into contemporary casual speech—and that grip is not going to loosen. Computer science is the defining technology of our time, and in this sense the computer is the natural cultural successor to the steam engine, the clock, the spindle, and the potter's wheel. Predictably, an articulate computational theory of the mind has also gained credence among professional psychologists and philosophers. I have been trying to support it here and elsewhere; I shall say no more about it for now, save to note again its near-indispensability in accounting for intentionality (noted), and to address the ubiquitous question of computer creativity and freedom.

Soft-determinism or libertarianism may be true of humans. But many people have far more rigidly deterministic intuitions about computers. Computers, after all, (let us all say it together:) "only do what they are told/programmed to do"; they have no spontaneity and no freedom of choice. But human beings choose all the time, and the ensuing states of the world often depend entirely on these choices. Thus the "computer analogy" supposedly fails.

The alleged failure of course depends on what we think freedom really is. As a soft-determinist, I think that to have freedom of choice in acting is (roughly) for one's action to proceed out of one's own desires, deliberation, will, and intention, rather than being compelled or coerced by external forces regardless of my desires or will. As before, free actions are not *uncaused* actions. My free actions are those that *I* cause, i.e., that are caused by my own mental processes rather than by something pressing on me from the outside. I have argued . . . that I am free in that my beliefs, desires, deliberations, and intentions are all functional or computational states and processes within me that do interact in characteristic ways to produce my

behavior. Note now that the same response vindicates our skilled human-simulating machines from the charge of puppethood. The word "robot" is often used as a veritable synonym for "puppet," so it may seem that Harry and Henrietta are paradigm cases of unfree mechanisms that "only do what they are programmed to do." This is a slander—for two reasons:

First, even an ordinary computer, let alone a fabulously sophisticated machine like Harry, is in a way upredictable. You are at its mercy. You *think* you know what it is going to do; you know what it should do, what it is supposed to do, but there is no guarantee—and it may do something *awful* or at any rate something that you could not have predicted and could not figure out if you tried with both hands. This practical sort of unpredictability would be multiplied a thousand-fold in the case of a machine as complex as the human brain, and it is notably characteristic of *people.*

The unpredictability has several sources. (i) Plain old physical defects, as when Harry's circuits have been damaged by trauma, stress, heat, or the like. (ii) Bugs in one or more of his programs. (I have heard that once upon a time, somewhere, a program was written that had not a single bug in it, but this is probably an urban folk tale.) (iii) Randomizers, quantum-driven or otherwise; elements of Harry's behavior may be *genuinely,* physically random. (iv) Learning and analogy mechanisms; if Harry is equipped with these, as he inevitably would be then his behavior patterns will be modified in response to his experimental input from the world, which would be neither controlled nor even observed by us. *We don't know where he's been.* (v) The relativity of reliability to goal description. This last needs a bit of explanation.

People often say things like, "A computer just crunches binary numbers; provided it isn't broken, it just chugs on mindlessly through whatever flipflop settings are predetermined by its electronic makeup." But such remarks ignore the multileveled character of real computer programming. At any given time, . . . a computer is running *each of any number of* programs, depending on how it is described and on the level of functional organization that interests us. True, it is always crunching binary numbers, but in crunching them it is also doing any number of more esoteric things. And (more to the point) what counts as a mindless, algorithmic procedure at a very low level of organization may constitute, at a higher level, a hazardous do-or-die heuristic that might either succeed brilliantly or (more likely) fail and leave its objective unfulfilled.

As a second defense, remember that Harry too has beliefs, desires, and intentions (provided my original argument is sound). If this is so, then his behavior normally proceeds out of his own mental processes rather than being externally compelled; and so he satisfies the definition of freedom-of-action formulated above. In most cases it will be appropriate to say that Harry could have done other than what he did do (but in fact chose after some ratiocination to do what he did, instead). Harry acts in the same sense as that in which we act, though one might continue to quarrel over what sense that is.

Probably the most popular remaining reason for doubt about machine consciousness has to do with the raw qualitative character of experience. Could a mere bloodless runner-of-programs have states that *feel to it* in any of the various dramatic ways in which our mental states feel to us?

The latter question is usually asked rhetorically, expecting a resounding answer "NO!!" But I do not hear it rhetorically, for I do not see why the negative answer is supposed to be at all obvious, even for machines as opposed to biologic humans. Of course there is an incongruity *from our human point of view* between human feeling and printed circuitry or silicon pathways; that is to be expected, since we are considering those high-tech items from an external, third-person perspective and at the same time comparing them to our own first-person feels. But argumentatively, that *Gestalt* phenomenon counts for no more in the present case than it did in that of human consciousness, viz., for nothing, especially if my original argument about Harry was successful in showing that biochemical constitution is irrelevant to psychology. What matters to mentality is not the stuff of which one is made, but the complex way in which that stuff is organized. If after years of close friendship we were to open Harry up and find that he is stuffed with microelectronic gadgets instead of protoplasm, we would be taken aback—no question. But our *Gestalt* clash on the occasion would do nothing *at all* to show that

Harry does not have his own right [to] inner qualitative life. If an objector wants to insist that computation alone cannot provide consciousness with its qualitative character, the objector will have to take the initiative and come up with a further, substantive argument to show why not. We have already seen that such arguments have failed wretchedly for the case of humans; I see no reason to suspect that they would work any better for the case of robots. We must await further developments. But at the present stage in inquiry I see no compelling feel-based objection to the hypothesis of machine consciousness.

DISCUSSION QUESTIONS

1. Discuss the example of Henrietta. How is Henrietta different from Harry? Why does Lycan introduce her? Do you believe that Henrietta has consciousness? Is a person? Why or why not?

2. Why does Lycan believe that to exclude an android from the human community on the basis of its origin (a laboratory, not a proper mother) and the chemical composition of its anatomy is "a clear case of racial or ethnic prejudice (literally) and nothing more"? Do you agree with him? Why or why not?

3. Lycan suggests that if a machine has a mental life or consciousness like that of a human, then it must also have a *moral* life like ours, with its corresponding moral rights and responsibilities. What is his argument? Do you agree with him? If so, why? If not, construct a counterargument to support your claim.

4. Lycan suggests that the issue of machine rights has a parallel in the debate over animal rights. What is the parallel? Do you agree with him? Why or why not?

5. Lycan suggests that it is possible for the actions of intelligent machines to be free. Evaluate his argument.

6. How do you think Lycan would respond to the claim that a machine could feel love for another machine? For a human being? What do you think about these claims? Construct an argument for or against these claims.

Andrew Martin (Robin Williams) is a robot purchased from NorthAm Robotics by "Sir" Richard Martin (Sam Neill). Andrew's job is to be of service to the Martin family. "Miss" Grace Martin, Richard's oldest daughter, tells Andrew to jump out of a window, and he does. After this, Richard tells his children that even though Andrew is a piece of property, he must be treated "as if" he were a person. When Andrew breaks the cherished, irreplaceable blown-glass horse belonging to Richard's youngest daughter, seven-year-old "Little Miss" Amanda Martin, she becomes very angry with him. Andrew makes up with Little Miss by carving her another horse out of driftwood. Richard then realizes that Andrew is a "unique" robot and begins to instruct him in the finer points of being a human being. Like his owner, Andrew becomes a master clock maker and earns a lot of money. Years pass, and Andrew confronts Richard one day, requesting his "freedom." Richard grants it, and Andrew goes off to live on his own, in a house that he builds. Richard eventually grows old and dies, and Andrew decides to go out into the world to find if there are any other robots like him. His travels bring him into contact with Rupert Burns (Oliver Platt), who, at Andrew's request, eventually replaces all of his robot parts with "humanlike" ones. Andrew is provided with fleshlike skin, internal organs, a central nervous system, a digestive tract, and a sexual organ. He also falls in love with Portia Charney (Embeth Davidtz), the granddaughter of Little Miss Amanda Martin, who in turn loves him. Andrew petitions his government to deem him a "human." However, they deny him because, even though he may have a body and mind much like that of a human, unlike a human, Andrew cannot die or even age. So, Andrew has Rupert give him the ability to age, and he and Portia grow old together. On the last day of his life, Andrew is granted the status "human," and his marriage to Portia is legally sanctioned.

Andrew's 200-year journey from service robot to full-fledged human being (the bicentennial "man") raises many of the questions that future societies may have to address. For example, can a robot have a bank account? Be guilty of a crime? Marry? If a robot can fall in love, should it be allowed to marry? At what point, if any, should we consider a machine a person? Or even a person a machine?

These questions assume, of course, that robots will continue to acquire more and more human attributes and behaviors—an assumption that there is strong reason to believe. This film is based on the excellent short story by Isaac Asimov titled "Bicentennial Man."

DISCUSSION QUESTIONS

1. Unlike David in the film *AI,* Andrew does not merely wish to be real but tries to make himself real by making changes to his body. Andrew is actively involved in his evolution toward "humanness," whereas David is continuously in search of a person (the Blue Fairy) who will make him real. Which story better convinces you of the human potential of and possibilities for robots—the story of Andrew or the story of David? Why?

2. If one of your children told Andrew to jump out of a window, would you, like Richard Martin, accuse your child of trying to "kill" Andrew? Can you "kill" a machine? Is unplugging a machine or taking it apart "killing"? Discuss.

3. After Miss Grace Martin tries to "kill" Andrew, Richard says the following to his children: "Andrew is not a person. He is a form of property. Property is also important. So, now on, as a matter of principle, in this household, Andrew is to be treated as if he were a person." What is the difference between treating something "as" a person and treating it "as if it were" a person?

4. Regarding Andrew, Richard tells Dennis Mansky (Stephen Root), head of NorthAm Robotics, "He is showing a number of characteristics like creativity, curiosity, friendship that have taken us by surprise." Richard says that Andrew makes objects (the wooden horse for Little Miss) and "enjoys" making them. Which of the following characteristics would you be most surprised to see in a robot: creativity, curiosity, or friendship? Why? Which of them is most closely associated with human behavior?

5. In response to Richard's report of Andrew's behavior, Mansky says, "Word of this gets out there will be trouble." "It is a household appliance, and yet acts like it is a man." Are Mansky's concerns legitimate? Should Andrew be "reprogrammed" as Mansky suggests?

6. Andrew listens to opera on an old Victrola record player and raises his eyebrows as though he were enjoying it deeply. Is he? Even though Andrew behaves in ways corresponding to human behavior, how do we know that he "feels inside" the way humans do when listening to music that deeply affects them? Furthermore, can't that "feeling inside" be programmed in as well?

7. Andrew says, "One presently has thoughts and feelings that do not show." What is more important in Andrew's quest to become a human—having or showing emotions? Discuss.

8. Richard says to Andrew, "For you, time is endless." Later, Andrew says, "I would rather die a man than live for all eternity as a machine." In the end, Andrew's immortality is the only obstacle that stands in the way of his becoming a "human." Do you agree with the notion that mortality is a *necessary* condition of personhood? That is, can we say, "If it is not mortal, then it is not a person or human"? Would the same hold for humans in a future world who replace all of their body parts, thus becoming immortal? In other words, can a human *become* a machine? Discuss the significance of mortality to personhood.

9. Little Miss Amanda says, "Andrew does all the work . . . then Andrew should get all the money." . . . It doesn't matter what he is. Andrew should benefit from the work he does." Does Andrew have a right to the money that results from the clocks he makes? Should Andrew be allowed to open his own bank account? Why or why not?

10. Andrew requests and is granted his freedom. As a programmed robot, can Andrew ever truly be free?

11. Andrew becomes every bit as complex as humans. He falls in love, has body parts like those that could be found in a human, and even ages. Does he become a "man" by the end of the film? Why or why not?

12. As humans, we do many things to extend our life and quell the aging process. Many humans even dream of being immortal, and if given the opportunity to live forever, they would take it. Is Andrew's wish to become mortal actually the thing that makes him most *unlike* a human?

13. Imagine that in the society in which you live robots are generally regarded as serving the needs of humans. If you were a member of the council that voted on Andrew's petition to be regarded a "human" and to marry, how would you vote, and why?

JOHN SEARLE

MINDS, BRAINS, AND PROGRAMS

In opposition to the optimistic claims of thinkers like Evans and Lycan, John Searle argues that computers cannot think, understand, or have mental states. Searle begins by separating work in artificial intelligence (AI) into two types: weak AI and strong AI. Weak AI claims that the "principal value of the computer in the study of the mind is that it gives us a very powerful tool" to, for example, test or formulate hypotheses. Strong AI claims that "the computer is not merely a tool in the study of the mind; rather, the appropriately programmed computer really *is* mind, in the sense that computers given the right programs can be literally said to *understand* and have other cognitive states." In this article, Searle has no problem with weak AI, but he strongly opposes strong AI.

To make his case against strong AI, Searle asks us to consider a "Chinese room" thought experiment. It goes broadly as follows: An English-speaking man who knows nothing about the Chinese language is locked in a room with two groups of tiles showing Chinese script and a set of rules or instructions as to how to manipulate the tiles in English. Upon properly following the instructions, the man is able to "correlate" Chinese characters from the second pile with Chinese characters from the first pile. Suppose later someone who knows Chinese reads results of the man's "correlation" of Chinese tiles and notes to him that they are an excellent "response" to the questions he was asked (the first pile of tiles) concerning the story (the second pile of tiles). However, the man in the Chinese room did not know that the first pile of characters was a "story" and that the second pile were "questions," nor even that following the rules for character manipulation resulted in a proper "response." All he did was follow the instructions that were provided to him.

Searle argues that the situation of the man in the Chinese room is akin to that of a computer providing output based on running data through its program. He argues that just as we would contend that the man in the Chinese room did not "understand" what he was doing (even if he produced results that made it seem as though he did), we would not contend that a computer "understands" its data or its output. Thus, for Searle, even though the man in the Chinese room would pass the Turing Test (see Evans above), he still could not be said to have understood what his response meant, nor what the piles of Chinese characters he manipulated meant. In the same way, even if a computer's response to questions were indistinguishable from a human's response to questions, this would not be sufficient grounds to conclude that the computer "understood" what it did.

Searle's Chinese room thought experiment has been the subject of much passionate discussion and heated debate. One of the more common lines of criticism is "the systems reply." These critics say the reason that understanding does not seem to be present in the Chinese room thought experiment is because Searle mistakenly imputes understanding to the man in the room alone, rather than to the "system" as a whole. Thus, from the systems perspective, while it is true that the man does not understand, the system as a whole does. Searle's short response to this is "All the same, he understands nothing of the Chinese, and *a fortiori* [all the more] neither does the system."

John Searle (1932–) is an American philosopher who specializes in the philosophy of language and the philosophy of mind. He was a Rhodes Scholar at Oxford University in the 1950s and received his D.Phil. from Oxford in 1959, where he was a student of the "ordinary language" philosopher J. L. Austin. Currently, Searle is the Mills Professor of Mind and Language at the University of California, Berkeley, where he has taught philosophy since 1959.

He is also a member of the Academy of Arts and Sciences, and was the recipient of a Guggenheim Fellowship. In addition to his work in the philosophy of mind, Searle's speech act theory, which addresses how language is an expression of thought, has been the subject of much scholarly discussion. To date, Searle's philosophical work has been the subject of seventeen books. His own books include *Speech Acts: An Essay in the Philosophy of Language* (1969), *The Campus War* (1971), *Expression and Meaning: Studies in the Theory of Speech Acts* (1979), *Intentionality: An Essay in the Philosophy of Mind* (1983), *Minds, Brains, and Science* (1984), *The Rediscovery of the Mind* (1992), *The Social Construction of Reality* (1995), *The Mystery of Consciousness* (1997), *Mind, Language and Society: Philosophy in the Real World* (1998), and *Mind: A Brief Introduction* (2004). The following article was first published in 1980.

What psychological and philosophical significance should we attach to recent efforts at computer simulations of human cognitive capacities? In answering this question, I find it useful to distinguish what I will call "strong" AI from "weak" or "cautious" AI (Artificial Intelligence). According to weak AI, the principal value of the computer in the study of the mind is that it gives us a very powerful tool. For example, it enables us to formulate and test hypotheses in a more rigorous and precise fashion. But according to strong AI, the computer is not merely a tool in the study of the mind; rather, the appropriately programmed computer really *is* a mind, in the sense that computers given the right programs can be literally said to *understand* and have other cognitive states. In strong AI, because the programmed computer has cognitive states, the programs are not mere tools that enable us to test psychological explanations; rather, the programs are themselves the explanations.

I have no objection to the claims of weak AI, at least as far as this article is concerned. My discussion here will be directed at the claims I have defined as those of strong AI, specifically the claim that the appropriately programmed computer literally has cognitive states and that the programs thereby explain human cognition. When I hereafter refer to AI, I have in mind the strong version, as expressed by these two claims.

I will consider the work of Roger Schank and his colleagues at Yale, because I am more familiar with it than I am with any other similar claims, and because it provides a very clear example of the sort of work I wish to examine. But nothing that follows depends upon the details of Schank's

programs. The same arguments would apply to Winograd's SHRDLU, Weizenbaum's ELIZA, and indeed any Turing machine simulation of human mental phenomena.

Very briefly, and leaving out the various details, one can describe Schank's program as follows: the aim of the program is to simulate the human ability to understand stories. It is characteristic of human beings' story-understanding capacity that they can answer questions about the story even though the information that they give was never explicitly stated in the story. Thus, for example, suppose you are given the following story: "A man went into a restaurant and ordered a hamburger. When the hamburger arrived it was burned to a crisp, and the man stormed out of the restaurant angrily, without paying for the hamburger or leaving a tip." Now, if you are asked "Did the man eat the hamburger?" you will presumably answer, "No, he did not." Similarly, if you are given the following story: "A man went into a restaurant and ordered a hamburger; when the hamburger came he was very pleased with it; and as he left the restaurant he gave the waitress a large tip before paying his bill," and you are asked the question "Did the man eat the hamburger?" you will presumably answer, "Yes, he ate the hamburger." Now Schank's machines can similarly answer questions about restaurants in this fashion. To do this, they have a "representation" of the sort of information that human beings have about restaurants, which enables them to answer such questions as those above, given these sorts of stories. When the machine is given the story and then asked the question, the machine will print out answers of the sort that we would expect human beings to give if told similar stories. Partisans of strong AI claim that in this question and answer sequence the machine is not only simulating a human ability but also

1. that the machine can literally be said to *understand* the story and provide the answers to questions, and

2. that what the machine and its program do *explains* the human ability to understand the story and answer questions about it.

Both claims seem to me to be totally unsupported by Schank's work, as I will attempt to show in what follows.

One way to test any theory of the mind is to ask oneself what it would be like if my mind actually worked on the principles that the theory says all minds work on. Let us apply this test to the Schank program with the following *Gedankenexperiment*. Suppose that I'm locked in a room and given a large batch of Chinese writing. Suppose furthermore (as is indeed the case) that I know no Chinese, either written or spoken, and that I'm not even confident that I could recognize Chinese writing as Chinese writing distinct from, say, Japanese writing or meaningless squiggles. To me, Chinese writing is just so many meaningless squiggles. Now suppose further that after this first batch of Chinese writing I am given a second batch of Chinese script together with a set of rules for correlating the second batch with the first batch. The rules are in English, and I understand these rules as well as any other native speaker of English. They enable me to correlate one set of formal symbols with another set of formal symbols, and all that "formal" means here is that I can identify the symbols entirely by their shapes. Now suppose also that I am given a third batch of Chinese symbols together with some instructions, again in English, that enable me to correlate elements of this third batch with the first two batches, and these rules instruct me how to give back certain Chinese symbols with certain sorts of shapes in response to certain sorts of shapes given me in the third batch. Unknown to me, the people who are giving me all of these symbols call the first batch "a script," they call the second batch a "story," and they call the third batch "questions." Furthermore, they call the symbols I give them

back in response to the third batch "answers to the questions," and the set of rules in English that they gave me, they call "the program." Now just to complicate the story a little, imagine that these people also give me stories in English, which I understand, and they then ask me questions in English about these stories, and I give them back answers in English. Suppose also that after a while I get so good at following the instructions for manipulating the Chinese symbols and the programmers get so good at writing the programs that from the external point of view— that is, from the point of view of somebody outside the room in which I am locked—my answers to the questions are absolutely indistinguishable from those of native Chinese speakers. Nobody just looking at my answers can tell that I don't speak a word of Chinese. Let us also suppose that my answers to the English questions are, as they no doubt would be, indistinguishable from those of other native English speakers, for the simple reason that I am a native English speaker. From the external point of view—from the point of view of someone reading my "answers"—the answers to the Chinese questions and the English questions are equally good. But in the Chinese case, unlike the English case, I produce the answers by manipulating uninterpreted formal symbols. As far as the Chinese is concerned, I simply behave like a computer; I perform computational operations on formally specified elements. For the purposes of the Chinese, I am simply an instantiation of the computer program.

Now the claims made by strong AI are that the programmed computer understands the stories and that the program in some sense explains human understanding. But we are now in a position to examine these claims in light of our thought experiment.

1. As regards the first claim, it seems to me quite obvious in the example that I do not understand a word of the Chinese stories. I have inputs and outputs that are indistinguishable from those of the native Chinese speaker, and I can have any formal program you like, but I still understand nothing. For the same reasons, Schank's computer understands nothing of any stories, whether in Chinese, English, or whatever,

since in the Chinese case the computer is me [*sic*], and in cases where the computer is not me, the computer has nothing more than I have in the case where I understand nothing.

2. As regards the second claim, that the program explains human understanding, we can see that the computer and its program do not provide sufficient conditions of understanding since the computer and the program are functioning, and there is no understanding. But does it even provide a necessary condition or a significant contribution to understanding? One of the claims made by the supporters of strong AI is that when I understand a story in English, what I am doing is exactly the same—or perhaps more of the same—as what I was doing in manipulating the Chinese symbols. It is simply more formal symbol manipulation that distinguishes the case in English, where I do understand, from the case in Chinese, where I don't. I have not demonstrated that this claim is false, but it would certainly appear an incredible claim in the example. Such plausibility as the claim has derives from the supposition that we can construct a program that will have the same inputs and outputs as native speakers, and in addition we assume that speakers have some level of description where they are also instantiations of a program. On the basis of these two assumptions we assume that even if Schank's program isn't the whole story about understanding, it may be part of the story. Well, I suppose that is an empirical possibility, but not the slightest reason has so far been given to believe that it is true, since what is suggested—though certainly demonstrated—by the example is that the computer program is simply irrelevant to my understanding of the story. In the Chinese case I have everything that artificial intelligence can put into me by way of a program, and I understand nothing; in the English case I understand everything, and there is so far no reason at all to suppose that my understanding has anything to do with computer programs, that is, with computational operations on purely formally specified elements. As long as the program is defined in terms of computational operations on purely formally defined elements, what the example suggests is that these by themselves have no interesting connection with

understanding. They are certainly not sufficient conditions, and not the slightest reason has been given to suppose that they are necessary conditions or even that they make a significant contribution to understanding. Notice that the force of the argument is not simply that different machines can have the same input and output while operating on different formal principles— that is not the point at all. Rather, whatever purely formal principles you put into the computer, they will not be sufficient for understanding, since a human will be able to follow the formal principles without understanding anything. No reason whatever has been offered to suppose that such principles are necessary or even contributory, since no reason has been given to suppose that when I understand English I am operating with any formal program at all. . . .

I have had the occasions to present this example to several workers in artificial intelligence, and, interestingly, they do not seem to agree on what the proper reply to it is. I get a surprising variety of replies, and in what follows I will consider the most common of these (specified along with their geographic origins). . . .

I. **The systems reply (Berkeley).** "While it is true that the individual person who is locked in the room does not understand the story, the fact is that he is merely part of a whole system, and the system does understand the story. The person has a large ledger in front of him in which are written the rules, he has a lot of scratch paper and pencils for doing calculations, he has "data banks" of sets of Chinese symbols. Now, understanding is not being ascribed to the mere individual; rather it is being ascribed to this whole system of which he is a part."

My response to the systems theory is quite simple: let the individual internalize all of these elements of the system. He memorizes the rules in the ledger and the data banks of Chinese symbols, and the does all the calculations in his head. The individual then incorporates the entire system. There isn't anything at all to the system that he does not encompass. We can even get rid of the room and suppose he works outdoors. All the same, he understands nothing of the Chinese, and *a fortiori* neither does the system, because there isn't anything in the system that isn't in him. If he doesn't understand, then there is no way the system could understand because the system is just a part of him.

Actually I feel somewhat embarrassed to give even this answer to the systems theory because the theory seems to me so unplausible to start with. The idea is that while a person doesn't understand Chinese, somehow the *conjunction* of that person and bits of paper might understand Chinese. It is not easy for me to imagine how someone who was not in the grip of an ideology would find the idea at all plausible. Still, I think many people who are committed to the ideology of strong AI will in the end be inclined to say something very much like this; so let us pursue it a bit further. According to one version of this view, while the man in the internalized systems example doesn't understand Chinese in the sense that a native Chinese speaker does (because, for example, he doesn't know that the story refers to restaurants and hamburgers, etc.), still "the man as a formal symbol manipulation system" *really does understand Chinese.* The subsystem of the man that is the formal symbol manipulation system for Chinese should not be confused with the subsystem for English.

So there are really two subsystems in the man; one understands English, the other Chinese, and "it's just that the two systems have little to do with each other." But, I want to reply, not only do they have little to do with each other, they are not even remotely alike. The subsystem that understands English (assuming we allow ourselves to talk in this jargon of "subsystems" for a moment) knows that the stories are about restaurants and eating hamburgers, he knows that he is being asked questions about restaurants and that he is answering questions as best he can by making various inferences from the content of the story, and so on. But the Chinese system knows none of this. Whereas the English subsystem knows that "hamburgers" refer to hamburgers, the Chinese subsystem knows only that "squiggle squiggle" is followed by "squoggle squoggle." All he knows is that various formal symbols are being introduced at one end and manipulated according to rules written in English, and other symbols are going out at the other end. The whole point of the original example was to argue that such symbol manipulation by itself couldn't be sufficient for

understanding Chinese in any literal sense because the man could write "squoggle squoggle" after "squiggle squiggle" without understanding anything in Chinese. And it doesn't meet that argument to postulate subsystems within the man, because the subsystems are no better off than the man was in the first place; they still don't have anything even remotely like what the English-speaking man (or subsystem) has. Indeed, in the case as described, the Chinese subsystem is simply a part of the English subsystem, a part that engages in meaningless symbol manipulation according to rules in English.

Let us ask ourselves what is supposed to motivate the systems reply in the first place; that is, what *independent* grounds are there supposed to be for saying that the agent must have a subsystem within him that literally understands stories in Chinese? As far as I can tell the only grounds are that in the example I have the same input and output as native Chinese speakers and a program that goes from one to the other. But the whole point of the examples has been to try to show that that couldn't be sufficient for understanding, in the sense in which I understand stories in English, because a person, and hence the set of systems that go to make up a person, could have the right combination of input, output, and program and still not understand anything in the relevant literal sense in which I understand English. The only motivation for saying there *must* be a subsystem in me that understands Chinese is that I have a program and I can pass the Turing test; I can fool native Chinese speakers. But precisely one of the points at issue is the adequacy of the Turing test. The example shows that there could be two "systems," both of which pass the Turing test, but only one of which understands; and it is no argument against this point to say that since they both pass the Turing test they must both understand, since this claim fails to meet the argument that the system in me that understands English has a great deal more than the system that merely processes Chinese. In short, the systems reply simply begs the question by insisting without argument that the system must understand Chinese.

Furthermore, the systems reply would appear to lead to consequences that are independently absurd. If we are to conclude that there must be cognition in me on the grounds that I have a certain sort of input and output and a program in between, then it looks like all sorts on noncognitive subsystems are going to turn out to be cognitive. For example, there is a level of description at which my stomach does information processing, and it instantiates any number of computer programs, but I take it we do not want to say that it has any understanding. But if we accept the systems reply, then it is hard to see how we avoid saying that stomach, heart, liver, and so on, are all understanding subsystems, since there is no principled way to distinguish the motivation for saying the Chinese subsystem understands from saying that the stomach understands. It is, by the way, not an answer to this point to say that the Chinese system has information as input and output and the stomach has food and food products as input and output, since from the point of view of the agent, from my point of view, there is no information in either the food or the Chinese—the Chinese is just so many meaningless squiggles. The information in the Chinese case is solely in the eyes of the programmers and the interpreters, and there is nothing to prevent them from treating the input and output of my digestive organs as information if they so desire.

This last point bears on some independent problems in strong AI, and it is worth digressing for a moment to explain it. If strong AI is be to a branch of psychology, then it must be able to distinguish those systems that are genuinely mental from those that are not. It must be able to distinguish the principles on which the mind works from those on which nonmental systems work; otherwise it will offer us no explanations of what is specifically mental about the mental. And the mental-nonmental distinction cannot be just in the eye of the beholder but it must be intrinsic to the systems; otherwise it would be up to any beholder to treat people as nonmental and, for example, hurricanes as mental if he likes. But quite often in the AI literature the distinction is blurred in ways that would in the long run prove disastrous to the claim that AI is a cognitive inquiry. McCarthy, for example writes, "Machines as simple as thermostats can be said to have beliefs, and having beliefs seems to be a characteristic of most machines capable of problem solving performance." Anyone who thinks strong AI has a chance as a theory of the mind ought to ponder the implications of that remark. We are asked to accept it is a discovery of strong AI that the hunk of metal on the wall that we use to regulate the temperature has beliefs in exactly the same sense that we, our spouses, and our children have beliefs, and furthermore that "most" of the other machines in the room—telephone, tape recorder, adding machine, electric light switch—also have beliefs in this literal sense. It is not the aim of this article to argue against McCarthy's point, so I will simply assert the following without argument. The study of the mind starts with such facts as that humans have beliefs, while thermostats, telephones, and adding machines don't. If you get a theory that denies this point you have produced a counter-example to the theory and the theory is false. One gets the impression that people in AI who write this sort of thing think they can get away with it because they don't really take it seriously, and they don't think anyone else will either. I propose for a moment at least, to take it seriously. Think hard for one minute about what would be necessary to establish that that hunk of metal on the wall over there had real beliefs, beliefs with direction of fit, propositional content, and conditions of satisfaction; beliefs that had the possibility of being strong beliefs or weak beliefs; nervous, anxious, or secure beliefs; dogmatic, rational, or superstitious beliefs: blind faiths or hesitant cogitations: any kind of beliefs. The thermostat is not a candidate. Neither is stomach, liver, adding machine, or telephone. However, since we are taking the idea seriously, notice that its truth would be fatal to strong AI's claim to be a science of the mind. For the now the mind is the mind from thermostats and livers. And if McCarthy were right, strong AI wouldn't have a hope of telling us that.

II. **The robot reply (Yale).** "Suppose we wrote a different kind of program from Schank's program. Suppose we put a computer inside a robot, and this computer would not just take in formal symbols as input and give out formal symbols as output, but rather would actually operate the robot in such a way that the robot does something very much like perceiving, walking, moving about, hammering nails, eating, drinking—anything you like. The robot would, for example, have a television camera attached to it that enabled it to 'see,' it would have arms and legs that enabled it to 'act,' and all of this would be controlled by its computer 'brain.' Such a robot would, unlike Schank's computer, have genuine understanding and other mental states."

The first thing to notice about the robot reply is that it tacitly concedes that cognition is not solely a matter of formal symbol manipulation, since this reply adds a set of causal relation with the outside world. But the answer to the robot reply is that the addition of such "perceptual" and "motor" capacities adds nothing by way of understanding, in particular, or intentionality, in general, to Schank's original program. To see this, notice that the same thought experiment applies to the robot case. Suppose that instead of the computer inside the robot, you put me inside the room and, as in the original Chinese case, you give me more Chinese symbols with more instructions in English for matching Chinese symbols to Chinese symbols and feeding back Chinese symbols to the outside. Suppose, unknown to me, some of the Chinese symbols that come to me come from a television camera attached to the robot and other Chinese symbols that I am giving out serve to make the motors inside the robot move the robot's legs or arms. It is important to emphasize that all I am doing is manipulating formal symbols: I know none of these other facts. I am receiving "information" from the robot's "perceptual" apparatus, and I am giving out "instructions" to its motor apparatus without knowing either of these facts. I am the robot's homunculus, but unlike the traditional homunculus, I don't know what's going on. I don't understand anything except the rules for symbol manipulation. Now in this case I want to say that the robot has no intentional states at all; it is simply moving about as a result of its electrical wiring and its program. And furthermore, by instantiating the program I have no intentional states of the relevant type. All I do is follow formal instructions about manipulating formal symbols.

DISCUSSION QUESTIONS

1. What is, for Searle, the difference between weak and strong AI? Is the distinction a reasonable one? Why or why not?

2. Summarize in your own words Searle's Chinese room thought experiment. Why does Searle think it reveals a serious problem with strong AI? Do you agree with him? Why or why not?

3. What is the "systems reply" to Searle's Chinese room thought experiment? How does Searle respond to it? How might a proponent of the systems reply in turn respond to Searle? Who has the stronger case here, and why?

4. Searle contends that the Chinese room thought experiment shows that computers are incapable of understanding. What exactly is "understanding" for Searle? Do you agree with Searle's conclusion that computers are incapable of understanding? Why or why not?

5. How would you go about proving or demonstrating that you understand something? Could a computer carry out the same proof or demonstration? Moreover, what would be sufficient evidence for you that someone else has understood something? Would this evidence be sufficient as well for establishing that a computer has understood something?

SUPPLEMENTARY READINGS

General

Beakley, Brian, and Peter Ludlow, eds. *The Philosophy of Mind: Classical Problems, Contemporary Issues.* Cambridge, MA: MIT Press, 1992.

Bechtel, William. *Philosophy of Mind: An Overview for Cognitive Science.* Hillsdale, NJ: Lawrence Erlbaum, 1988.

Gregory, Richard, ed. *Oxford Companion to the Mind.* New York: Oxford University Press, 1987.

Guttenplan, Samuel, ed. *A Companion to the Philosophy of Mind.* Cambridge, MA: Blackwell, 1994.

Heil, John. *Philosophy of Mind: A Contemporary Introduction,* 2nd ed. New York: Routledge, 2004.

———, ed. *Philosophy of Mind: A Guide and Anthology.* New York: Oxford University Press, 2004.

Kim, Jaegwon. *The Philosophy of Mind.* Boulder, CO: Westview Press, 1996.

Lycan, William, ed. *Mind and Cognition: A Reader,* 2nd ed. Cambridge, MA: Blackwell, 1999.

McGinn, Colin. *Minds and Bodies: Philosophers and Their Ideas.* New York: Oxford University Press, 1997.

O'Connor, Timothy, David Robb, and John Heil, eds. *Philosophy of Mind: Contemporary Readings.* New York: Routledge, 2003.

O'Hear, Anthony, ed. *Current Issues in Philosophy of Mind.* New York: Cambridge University Press, 1998.

Priest, Stephen. *Theories of Mind.* Boston: Houghton Mifflin, 1991.

Robinson, Daniel, ed. *The Mind.* New York: Oxford University Press, 1998.

Rosenthal, David, ed. *Nature of Mind.* New York: Oxford University Press, 1991.

The Mind–Body Problem

Armstrong, D. M. *The Mind–Body Problem: An Opinionated Introduction.* Boulder, CO: Westview Press, 1999.

Bateson, Gregory. *Mind and Nature: A Necessary Unity.* New York: Dutton, 1979.

Bordo, Susan. *Unbearable Weight: Feminism, Western Culture, and the Body.* Berkeley, CA: University of California Press, 1993.

Borst, C. V., and D. M. Armstrong, eds. *The Mind/Brain Identity Theory: A Collection of Papers.* London: Macmillan, 1970.

Block, Ned, ed. *Readings in Philosophy of Psychology.* Cambridge, MA: Harvard University Press, 1980.

Block, Ned, Owen Flanagan, and Guven Guzeldere, eds. *The Nature of Consciousness: Philosophical Debates.* Cambridge, MA: MIT Press, 1997.

Broad, C. D. *The Mind and Its Place in Nature.* London: Routledge & Kegan Paul, 1925.

Cairns-Smith, A. G. *Evolving the Mind: On the Nature of Matter and the Origin of Consciousness.* Cambridge: Cambridge University Press, 1995.

Campbell, Keith. *Body and Mind.* Garden City, NY: Anchor, 1970.

Chalmers, David. *The Conscious Mind: In Search of a Fundamental Theory.* New York: Oxford University Press, 1996.

Chappell, V. C., ed. *The Philosophy of Mind.* Englewood Cliffs, NJ: Prentice Hall, 1962.

Churchland, Paul. *Matter and Consciousness: A Contemporary Introduction to the Philosophy of Mind.* Cambridge, MA: MIT Press, 1984.

Damasio, Antonio. *Descartes' Error: Emotion, Reason, and the Human Brain.* New York: Putnam, 1995.

Davidson, Donald. *Essays on Actions and Events.* New York: Oxford University Press, 1980.

Dawkins, Richard. *The Selfish Gene.* New York: Oxford University Press, 1976.

Dennett, Daniel. *Brainstorms: Philosophical Essays on Mind and Psychology.* Cambridge, MA: MIT Press, 1981.

———. *Kinds of Minds: Toward an Understanding of Consciousness.* New York: Basic Books, 1996.

Descartes, René. *Passions of the Soul.* Trans. Stephen Voss. Indianapolis, IN: Hackett, 1989.

———. *Meditations on First Philosophy.* 3rd ed. Trans. Donald A. Cress. Indianapolis, IN: Hackett, 1993.

Donald, Merlin. *Origins of the Modern Mind: Three Stages in the Evolution of Culture and Cognition.* Cambridge, MA: Harvard University Press, 1991.

Dretske, Fred. *Naturalizing the Mind.* Cambridge, MA: MIT Press, 1995.

Eccles, John C., and Karl Popper. *The Self and Its Brain.* New York: Springer-Verlag, 1977.

Elvee, Richard Q., ed. *Mind in Nature.* San Francisco: Harper & Row, 1982.

Feigl, Herbert. *The "Mental" and the "Physical."* Minneapolis: University of Minnesota Press, 1967.

Flanagan, Owen. *The Science of the Mind.* Cambridge, MA: MIT Press, 1991.

Fodor, Jerry. *Modularity of the Mind: An Essay on Faculty Psychology.* Cambridge, MA: MIT Press, 1983.

Gardner, Howard. *Mind's New Science: A History of the Cognitive Revolution.* New York: Basic Books, 1985.

Griffiths, Paul J. *On Being Mindless: Buddhist Meditation and the Mind–Body Problem.* La Salle, IL: Open Court, 1986.

Hook, Sidney, ed. *Dimensions of Mind: A Symposium.* New York: New York University Press, 1960.

Humphrey, Nicholas. *A History of the Mind.* New York: Simon & Schuster, 1993.

Jackendoff, Ray. *Consciousness and the Computational Mind.* Cambridge, MA: MIT Press, 1987.

James, William. *The Principles of Psychology.* New York: Dover, 1950.

Kim, Jaegwon. *Mind in a Physical World: An Essay on the Mind–Body Problem and Mental Causation.* Cambridge, MA: MIT Press, 1998.

Koestler, Arthur. *The Ghost in the Machine.* London: Pan Books, 1967.

Lange, Friedrich A. *The History of Materialism and Criticism of Its Present Importance.* 3rd ed. London: Routledge & Kegan Paul, 1957.

Lewis, David K. *Philosophical Papers.* New York: Oxford University Press, 1983.

Lycan, William. *Consciousness.* Cambridge, MA: MIT Press, 1987.

Macdonald, Cynthia. *Mind–Body Identity Theories.* London: Routledge, 1989.

Malcolm, Norman. *Problems of Mind: Descartes to Wittgenstein.* London: Allen & Unwin, 1971.

Margolis, Joseph. *Persons and Minds: The Prospects of Nonreductive Materialism.* Boston: Reidel, 1978.

McGinn, Colin. *The Problem of Consciousness: Essays Toward a Resolution.* Cambridge, MA: Blackwell, 1991.

Nagel, Thomas. *Mortal Questions.* New York: Cambridge University Press, 1979.

———. *The View from Nowhere.* New York: Oxford University Press, 1986.

Penrose, Roger. *The Emperor's New Mind: Concerning Computers, Minds, and the Laws of Physics.* New York: Oxford University Press, 1989.

Popper, Karl. *Knowledge and the Body–Mind Problem.* New York: Routledge, 1994.

Putnam, Hilary. *Mind, Language and Reality.* New York: Cambridge University Press, 1975.

Rosenthal, David, ed. *Materialism and the Mind-Body Problem.* Englewood Cliffs, NJ: Prentice Hall, 1971.

Russell, Bertrand. *An Inquiry into Meaning and Truth.* New York: Norton, 1940.

Ryle, Gilbert. *The Concept of Mind.* London: Hutchinson, 1949.

Searle, John. *The Mystery of Consciousness.* New York: Granta Books, 1997.

Sellars, Wilfrid. *Science, Perception, and Reality.* London: Routledge & Kegan Paul, 1963.

Shear, Jonathan, ed. *Explaining Consciousness: The Hard Problem.* Cambridge, MA: MIT Press, 1995.

Stich, Stephen. *From Folk Psychology to Cognitive Science: The Case Against Belief.* Cambridge, MA: MIT Press, 1983.

Tye, Michael. *The Metaphysics of Mind.* New York: Cambridge University Press, 1989.

———. *Ten Problems of Consciousness: A Representational Theory of the Phenomenal Mind.* Cambridge, MA: MIT Press, 1995.

Wagman, Morton. *Cognitive Science and the Mind–Body Problem: From Philosophy to Psychology to Artificial Intelligence to Imaging of the Brain.* Westport, CT: Praeger, 1998.

Warner, Richard, and Tadeusz Szubka, eds. *The Mind–Body Problem: A Guide to the Current Debate.* Blackwell, Oxford, 1994.

Watson, John B. *Behaviorism.* New York: Norton, 1925.

Wilson, Robert A. *Cartesian Psychology and Physical Minds: Individualism and the Sciences of the Mind.* Cambridge: Cambridge University Press, 1997.

Wittgenstein, Ludwig. *Philosophical Investigations.* New York: Macmillan, 1953.

Young, J. Z. *Philosophy and the Brain.* New York: Oxford University Press, 1989.

Personal Identity and the Nature of the Self

Alexander, Ronald G. *Self, Supervenience and Personal Identity.* Brookfield, VT: Ashgate, 1997.

Allen, Douglas, ed. *Culture and Self: Philosophical and Religious Perspectives, East and West.* Boulder, CO: Westview Press, 1997.

Anderson, Walt. *Future of the Self: Inventing the Postmodern Person.* New York: Tarcher, 1997.

Anzaldúa, Gloria. *Borderlands/La Frontera: The New Mestiza.* San Francisco, CA: Aunt Lute Books, 1987.

Ayer, A. J. *The Concept of a Person.* London: Macmillan, 1963.

Babad, Elisha, Max Birnbaum, and Kenneth D. Benne. *The Social Self: Group Influences on Personal Identity.* Beverly Hills, CA: Sage, 1983.

Baillie, James. *Problems in Personal Identity.* New York: Paragon House, 1993.

Barresi, John, and Raymond Martin, eds. *Personal Identity.* Cambridge, MA: Blackwell, 2002.

Beauvoir, Simone de. *The Second Sex.* Trans. H. M. Parshley. New York: Vintage Books, 1974.

Battersby, Christine. *The Phenomenal Woman: Feminist Metaphysics and the Patterns of Identity.* New York: Routledge, 1998.

Belenky, Mary Field, Blythe McVickere Clinchy, Nancy Rule Goldberger, and Jill Mattuck Tarule. *Women's Ways of Knowing: The Development of Self, Voice, and Mind.* New York: Basic Books, 1986.

Benhabib, Seyla. *Situating the Self: Gender, Community, and Postmodernism in Contemporary Ethics.* New York: Routledge, 1992.

Bermúdez, José, Anthony Marcel, and Naomi Eilan, eds. *The Body and the Self.* Cambridge, MA: MIT Press, 1995.

Brennan, Andrew. *Conditions of Identity: A Study in Identity and Survival.* New York: Oxford University Press, 1988.

Butler, Judith. *Gender Trouble: Feminism and the Subversion of Identity.* New York: Routledge, 1990.

Campbell, John. *Past, Space, and Self.* Cambridge, MA: MIT Press, 1994.

Cassam, Quassim, ed. *Self-Knowledge.* New York: Oxford University Press, 1994.

Castell, Alburey. *The Self in Philosophy.* New York: Macmillan, 1965.

Cockburn, David, ed. *Human Beings.* New York: Cambridge University Press, 1991.

Doepke, Frederick, C. *The Kinds of Things: A Theory of Personal Identity Based on Transcendental Argument.* Chicago: Open Court, 1996.

Eccles, John. *Evolution of the Brian: Creation of the Self.* London: Routledge, 1989.

Feinberg, Todd. *Altered Egos: How the Brain Creates the Self.* New York: Oxford University Press, 2001.

Ferguson, Kathy Ellen. *Self, Society, and Womankind: The Dialectic of Liberation.* Westport, CT: Greenwood Press, 1980.

Foster, John. *The Immaterial Self: A Defence of the Cartesian Dualist Conception of the Mind.* New York: Routledge, 1991.

French, Peter A., Theodore Edward Uehling, and Howard K. Wettstein, eds. *Studies in the Philosophy of Mind.* Minneapolis: University of Minnesota Press, 1986.

Gallagher, Shaun, and Jonathan Shear, eds. *Models of the Self.* Thorverton, UK: Imprint Academic, 1999.

Gergen, Kenneth J. *The Saturated Self: Dilemmas of Identity in Contemporary Life.* New York: Basic Books, 1991.

Giddens, Anthony. *Modernity and Self-Identity: Self and Society in the Late Modern Age.* Cambridge: Polity Press, 1991.

Gilligan, Carol. *In a Different Voice: Psychological Theory and Women's Development.* Cambridge, MA: Harvard University Press, 1982.

Glover, Jonathan. *I: The Philosophy and Psychology of Personal Identity.* New York: Penguin Books, 1988.

Goethals, George, and Jaine Strauss, eds. *The Self: Interdisciplinary Approaches.* New York: Springer-Verlag, 1991.

Griffiths, Morwenna. *Feminisms and the Self: The Web of Identity.* New York: Routledge, 1995.

Hanson, Karen. *The Self Imagined: Philosophical Reflections on the Social Character of Psyche.* New York: Routledge & Kegan Paul, 1986.

Hume, David. *A Treatise on Human Nature.* New York: Oxford University Press, 1978.

Jacques, Francis. *Difference and Subjectivity : Dialogue and Personal Identity.* New Haven, CT: Yale University Press, 1991.

James, William. *The Principles of Psychology.* New York: Dover Publications, 1950.

Kolak, Daniel, and Raymond Martin. *Self and Identity: Contemporary Philosophical Issues.* New York: Macmillan, 1991.

LeDoux, Joseph. *Synaptic Self: How Our Brains Become Who We Are.* New York: Viking Press, 2002.

Lee, Benjamin, ed. *Psychosocial Theories of the Self.* New York: Plenum, 1979.

Locke, John. *An Essay Concerning Human Understanding.* New York: Dover, 1959.

Ludwig, Arnold M. *How Do We Know Who We Are?: A Biography of the Self.* New York: Oxford University Press, 1997.

MacIntyre, Alasdair. *After Virtue: A Study in Moral Theory,* 2nd ed. Notre Dame, IN: University of Notre Dame Press, 1984.

Madell, Geoffrey. *The Identity of the Self.* Edinburgh: Edinburgh University Press, 1981.

Mann, David W. *A Simple Theory of the Self.* New York: Norton, 1994.

Mathews, Freya. *The Ecological Self.* Savage, MD: Barnes & Noble, 1991.

McAdams, Dan P. *The Stories We Live By: Personal Myths and the Making of the Self.* New York: Morrow, 1993.

Mead, George Herbert. *Mind, Self and Society.* Chicago: University of Chicago Press, 1934.

Meyers, Diana T., ed. *Feminists Rethink the Self.* Boulder, CO: Westview Press, 1997.

Mills, Charles. *Blackness Visible: Essays on Philosophy and Race.* Ithaca, NY: Cornell University Press, 1998.

Mischel, Theodore, ed. *The Self: Psychological and Philosophical Issues.* Totowa, NJ: Rowan & Littlefield, 1977.

Modell, Arnold H. *The Private Self.* Cambridge, MA: Harvard University Press, 1993.

Morris, Brian. *Anthropology of the Self: The Individual in Cultural Perspective.* Boulder, CO: Pluto Press, 1994.

Neisser, Ulrich. *The Perceived Self: Ecological and Interpersonal Sources of Self-Knowledge.* New York: Cambridge University Press, 1993.

Neisser, Ulric, and Robin Fivush, eds., *The Remembering Self: Construction and Accuracy in the Self-Narrative.* New York: Cambridge University Press, 1994.

Neisser, Ulric, and David Jopling, eds. *The Conceptual Self in Context: Culture, Experience, Self-Understanding.* New York: Cambridge University Press, 1996.

Noonan, Harold W. *Personal Identity*, 2nd ed. London: Routledge, 2004.

Nozick, Robert. *Philosophical Explanations*. Cambridge, MA: Harvard University Press, 1981.

Parfit, Derek. *Reasons and Persons*. New York: Oxford University Press, 1985.

Peacocke, Arthur, and Grant Gillet, eds. *Persons and Personality: A Conceptual Inquiry*. New York: Blackwell, 1987.

Penelhum, Terence. *Survival and Disembodied Existence*. New York: Humanities Press, 1970.

———. "Personal Identity." *Encyclopedia of Philosophy*, Volume 6. Ed. Paul Edwards. New York: Macmillan, 1967. 95–106.

Perry, John ed. *Personal Identity*. Berkeley: University of California Press, 1975.

———, *A Dialogue on Personal Identity and Immortality*. Indianapolis, IN: Hackett, 1978.

Radden, Jennifer. *Divided Minds and Successive Selves: Ethical Issues in Disorders of Identity and Personality*. Cambridge, MA: MIT/Bradford Press, 1996.

Restak, Richard M. *The Modular Brain: How New Discoveries in Neuroscience Are Answering Age-Old Questions about Memory, Free Will, Consciousness, and Personal Identity*. New York: Scribner, 1994.

Ricoeur, Paul. *Oneself as Another*. Chicago: University of Chicago Press, 1992.

Rorty, Amélie Oksenberg, ed. *The Identities of Persons*. Berkeley: University of California Press, 1976.

Sartre, Jean-Paul. *The Transcendence of the Ego*. New York: Noonday Press, 1957.

Schechtman, Marya. *The Constitution of Selves*. Ithaca, NY: Cornell University Press, 1996.

Schrag, Calvin O. *The Self after Postmodernity*. New Haven, CT: Yale University Press, 1999.

Shalom, Albert. *The Body/Mind Conceptual Framework and the Problem of Personal Identity: Some Theories in Philosophy, Psychoanalysis and Neurology*. Atlantic Highlands, NJ: Humanities Press, 1985.

Shoemaker, Sydney, and Richard Swinburne. *Personal Identity*. New York: Blackwell, 1984.

Strawson, Peter F. *Individuals: An Essay in Descriptive Metaphysics*. New York: Oxford University Press, 1959.

Taylor, Charles. *Sources of the Self: The Making of the Modern Identity*. Cambridge, MA: Harvard University Press, 1989.

Tugendhat, Ernst. *Self-Consciousness and Self-Determination*. Cambridge: MIT Press, 1986.

Unger, Peter K. *Identity, Consciousness, and Value*. New York: Oxford University Press, 1990.

Varela, Francisco J., Evan Thompson, and Eleanor Rosch. *The Embodied Mind: Cognitive Science and Human Experience*. Cambridge, MA: MIT Press, 1991.

Vesey, Godfrey. *Personal Identity: A Philosophical Analysis*. Ithaca, NY: Cornell University Press, 1977.

Walters, James W. *What is a Person? An Ethical Exploration*. Urbana: University of Illinois Press, 1997.

White, Stephen L. *The Unity of the Self*. Cambridge, MA: MIT Press, 1991.

Wilkes, Kathleen V. *Real People: Personal Identity without Thought Experiments*. Oxford: Clarendon Press; New York: Oxford University Press, 1988.

Williams, Bernard. *Problems of the Self*. Cambridge: Cambridge University Press, 1973.

Artificial Intelligence

Amarel, Saul, Ryszard Michalski, Jaime Carbonell, and Tom Mitchell. *Machine Learning: An Artificial Intelligence Approach, Volume II*. Los Altos, CA: Morgan Kaufman, 1986.

Anderson, Alan Ross, ed. *Minds and Machines*. Englewood Cliffs, NJ: Prentice Hall, 1964.

Anderson, John, Ryszard Michalski, Jaime Carbonell, and Tom Mitchell. *Machine Learning: An Artificial Intelligence Approach*. Palo Alto, CA: Tioga, 1983.

Barr, Avron, and Edward Feigenbaum, eds. *Handbook of Artificial Intelligence*. Stanford, CA: Heuris Tech Press, 1982.

Boden, Margaret. *Artificial Intelligence and Natural Man*. New York: Basic Books, 1979.

———, ed. *Philosophy of Artificial Intelligence*. New York: Oxford University Press, 1990.

Brooks, Rodney and Luc Steels, eds. *The Artificial Life Route to Artificial Intelligence: Building Embodied Situated Agents*. Hillsdale, NJ: Lawrence Erlbaum, 1995.

Bynum, Terrell Ward, and James Moor, eds. *The Digital Phoenix: How Computers Are Changing Philosophy*. Cambridge, MA: Blackwell, 1998.

Carbonell, Jaime, ed. *Machine Learning: Paradigms and Methods*. Cambridge, MA: MIT Press, 1989.

Charniak, Eugene, and Drew V. McDermott. *Introduction to Artificial Intelligence*. Reading, MA: Addison-Wesley, 1985.

Churchland, Patricia. *Neurophilosophy: Toward a Unified Science of the Mind-Brain*. Cambridge, MA: MIT Press, 1986.

Copeland, B. Jack. *The Essential Turing: Seminal Writings in Computing, Logic, Philosophy, Artificial Intelligence, and Artificial Life, plus the Secrets of Enigma.* Oxford: Oxford University Press, 2004.

Dennett, Daniel. *Brainstorms: Philosophical Essays on Mind and Psychology.* Cambridge, MA: MIT Press, 1981.

Dreyfus, Hubert. *What Computers Still Can't Do: A Critique of Artificial Intelligence.* Cambridge, MA: MIT Press, 1992.

Dreyfus, Hubert, and Stuart Dreyfus. *Mind over Machine: The Power of Human Intuition and Expertise in the Era of the Computer.* New York: Free Press, 1985.

Evans, Christopher. *Micro Millennium.* New York: Viking/Penguin, 1979.

Feigenbaum, Edward, and Julian Feldman, eds. *Computers and Thought.* Cambridge, MA: MIT Press, 1995.

Feigenbaum, Edward, and Pamela McCorduck. *The Fifth Generation: Artificial Intelligence and Japan's Computer Challenge to the World.* Reading, MA: Addison-Wesley, 1984.

Fetzer James. *Artificial Intelligence: Its Scope and Limits.* Boston: Kluwer, 1990.

Graubard Stephen. *The Artificial Intelligence Debate: False Starts, Real Foundations.* Cambridge, MA: MIT Press, 1988.

Hagueland, John. *Artificial Intelligence: The Very Idea.* Cambridge, MA: MIT Press, 1985.

———, ed. *Mind Design II: Philosophy, Psychology, Artificial Intelligence.* Revised and enlarged ed. Cambridge, MA: MIT Press, 1997.

Harel, David. *Computers Ltd.: What They Really Can't Do.* New York: Oxford University Press, 2000.

Hofstadter, Douglas. *Gödel Escher Bach: An Eternal Golden Braid.* New York: Basic Books, 1980.

Hofstadter, Douglas R., and Daniel C. Dennett. *The Mind's I: Fantasies and Reflections on Self and Soul.* New York: Basic Books, 1981.

Langton, Christopher, ed. *Artificial Life: An Overview.* Cambridge, MA: MIT Press, 1995.

Leiber, Justin. *Can Animals and Machines Be Persons?: A Dialogue.* Indianapolis, IN: Hackett, 1985.

Levy, Steven. *Artificial Life: The Quest for a New Creation.* New York: Pantheon Books, 1992.

Luger, George, ed. *Computation and Intelligence: Collected Readings.* Menlo Park, CA: AAAI Press, 1995.

Maes, Patti, ed. *Designing Autonomous Agents: Theory and Practice from Biology to Engineering and Back.* Cambridge, MA: MIT Press, 1990.

McCorduck, Pamela. *Machines Who Think: A Personal Inquiry into the History and Prospects of Artificial Intelligence.* San Francisco: Freeman, 1979.

Minsky, Marvin, ed. *Robotics.* Garden City, NY: Anchor, 1985.

Minsky, Marvin, and Seymour Papert. *Artificial Intelligence.* Eugene, OR: Oregon State Higher Education System, 1974.

Newell, Allen, and Herbert Simon. *Human Problem Solving.* Englewood Cliffs, NJ: Prentice Hall, 1972.

Nilsson, Nils. *The Mathematical Foundations of Learning Machines.* San Mateo, CA: Morgan Kaufmann, 1990.

———. *Principles of Artificial Intelligence.* Los Altos, CA: Morgan Kaufman, 1993.

O'Shea, Tim, John Self, and Glan Thomas, eds. *Intelligent Knowledge-Based Systems: An Introduction.* New York: Harper & Row, 1986.

Raphael, Bertram. *The Thinking Computer: Mind Inside Matter.* San Francisco: Freeman, 1976.

Russell, Stuart and Peter Norvig. *Artificial Intelligence: A Modern Approach.* Englewood Cliffs, NJ: Prentice Hall, 1995.

Schank, Roger C., and Kenneth M. Colby, eds. *Computer Models of Thought and Language.* San Francisco: Freeman, 1973.

Searle, John. *Minds, Brains and Science.* Cambridge, MA: Harvard University Press, 1984.

———. *The Rediscovery of the Mind.* Cambridge, MA: MIT Press, 1992.

Shapiro, Stuart, ed. *Encyclopedia of Artificial Intelligence.* New York: Wiley, 1992.

Simon, Herbert. *Models of Thought.* New Haven, CT: Yale University Press, 1979.

———. *The Sciences of the Artificial,* 2nd ed. Cambridge, MA: MIT Press, 1981.

Sloman, Aaron. *The Computer Revolution in Philosophy: Philosophy, Science, and Models of the Mind.* Hassocks, UK: Harvester Press; 1978.

Von Neumann, John. *The Computer and the Brain.* New Haven, CT: Yale University Press, 1958.

Weizenbaum, Joseph. *Computer Power and Human Reason: From Judgment to Calculation.* San Francisco: Freeman, 1976.

Winograd, Terry. *Understanding Natural Language.* New York: Academic Press, 1972.

Winston, Patrick, and Brown, Richard, eds. *Artificial Intelligence: An MIT Perspective.* Cambridge, MA: MIT Press, 1979.

Wooldridge, Dean. *Mechanical Man: The Physical Basis of Intelligent Life.* New York: McGraw-Hill, 1968.

4

of Morality AND Art

Mookie (Spike Lee) and Sal (Danny Aiello) in front of the "Wall of Fame" in *Do the Right Thing*.

4.1   IS MORALITY RELATIVE?

HERODOTUS

MORALITY AS CUSTOM

The ancient Greek historian Herodotus presents an early version of *moral relativism*, the view that there are no absolute moral principles. What is morally right or wrong depends on the time when and the place in which people live. According to the moral relativist, different societies, different people, and different historical periods can result in different moral principles.

In this reading, Darius, king of Persia, asks some Greeks what it would take for them to eat the bodies of their dead fathers. The Greeks respond to Darius that they would not do it for any sum. Later, with the Greeks present, Darius asks the Callatians what it would take for them to burn the bodies of their dead fathers. The Callatians scream and tell Darius not to speak of such things. Herodotus uses this example to illustrate his point that morality is determined by custom. If any person were asked to select the best set of beliefs from among all the beliefs in the world, that person would choose those of his or her own country. For Herodotus, this is the most likely consequence of our careful and thoughtful attention to all the beliefs in the world. Says Herodotus, only "a madman would make such things the subject of ridicule." He reports that this is a widely held belief among the peoples of the ancient world regarding the relationship between morality and custom.

Herodotus (485–430 B.C.E.) was the first Western historian, and probably the first writer on morals in the Western world, to present a version of moral relativism. Herodotus's writings reveal him as lacking in racial prejudice and exhibiting a strong tolerance for all of the customs and cultures about which he writes. Herodotus's world is regulated by fate, disarranged by chance, and populated by gods who support those who do right and punish those who do wrong. Much of what we know about ancient Greece is directly attributable to the writings of Herodotus. The brief selection below is from Herodotus's *History*, which he describes as "a publication of the researches of Herodotus of Harlicarnassus, in order that the actions of men may not be effaced by time, nor the great wondrous deeds displayed both by Greeks and barbarians [foreigners] deprived of renown."

For if any one should propose to all men, to select the best institutions of all that exist, each, after considering them all, would choose their own; so certain is it that each thinks his own institutions by far the best. It is not therefore probable, that any but a madman would make such things the subject of ridicule. That all men are of this mind respecting their own institutions, may be inferred from many and various proofs, and amongst them by the following. Darius

having summoned some Greeks under his sway, who were present, asked them "for what sum they would feed upon the dead bodies of their parents." They answered, that they would not do it for any sum. Darius afterwards having summoned some of the Indians called Callatians, who are accustomed to eat their parents, asked them in the presence of the Greeks, and who were informed of what was said by an interpreter, "for what sum they would consent to burn their fathers when they die?" but they, making loud exclamations, begged he would speak words of good omen. Such then is the effect of custom: and Pindar appears to me to have said rightly, "That Custom is the king of all men."

DISCUSSION QUESTIONS

1. Do you agree with the claim that "custom is the king of all men"? What does Herodotus mean by "custom"?

2. Herodotus presents us with an example of cultures with different ways of honoring their dead fathers. Is this a good example to use as an argument for moral relativism? Defend your view.

3. Herodotus says that if any person were asked to select the best set of beliefs from among all the beliefs in the world, that person would choose those of his or her own country. Would you do this? Do you think this is the dominant view today?

4. What does Herodotus mean when he says that only "a madman would make such things the subject of ridicule?" Do you agree with him? Explain.

5. What, in your opinion, is the relationship between custom and morality? Give an example of a custom held by another culture that is very different from one of the customs of your own culture. What is your moral response to that custom?

Gosford Park
[USA 2001] 2 hours, 18 minutes
Directed by Robert Altman

This story takes place during the 1930s at the English country estate of the rich and unpleasant Sir William McCordle (Michael Gambon). Sir William and his wife, Lady Sylvia (Kristin Scott Thomas), host a weekend shooting party for a large group of friends and family, including relatives Constance Trentham (Maggie Smith) and Raymond Stockbridge (Charles Dance), entertainer Ivor Novello (Jeremy Northam), and movie director Morris Weissman (Bob Balaban). Each invited guest brings along his or her own personal servant(s). The characters in the film fall neatly into two distinct groups: the working-class servants and the wealthy employers. Each group is presented as having its own particular set of customs and way of life.

During the weekend, the host is murdered, and the servants in the house are the only ones with the knowledge that nearly everyone in residence has a motive. However, the self-assured Inspector Thompson (Stephen Fry) is too narrow-minded to believe that the servants would be helpful in his inquiry. He dismisses them as unimportant to his search for the murderer, whom he believes had financial motives for committing the crime. However, it is the young maid Mary Macreachran (Kelly Macdonald) who uncovers the perpetrator. Mary's perceptiveness leads her to pinpoint Mrs. Wilson (Helen Mirren) as the murderer. Her motive, however, has little to do with money, and everything to do with revenge.

DISCUSSION QUESTIONS

1. For most of the film, *Gosford Park* presents the worlds of the working-class servants and their upper-class employers as physically and socially distinct: the wealthy guests move and socialize in a

different area of the estate than the servants. Is the film suggesting that the customs and/or morality of these two groups are different or distinct as well? If so, how? If not, why not?

2. Do you think that different economic and/or social classes can have different customs in the same way that different nations can have different customs?

3. Robert, a valet, comments, "He [Sir William] thinks he's God Almighty. They all do." Would it also be accurate to say that the moral behavior and social customs of the upper class in *Gosford Park* are relative to what is approved and disapproved of by Sir William? In other words, if he approves of the custom or behavior, it is good; if he does not approve of it, it is bad. Does his moral and social influence extend as well into the culture and world of the servants? Explain.

4. Consider the following exchange between Mary and Elsie (Emily Watson):

MARY   "Do you know how you said Sir William could've had his pick between Lady Sylvia and Lady Stockbridge? Well, I asked our ladyship about it, and she said they cut cards for him."

ELSIE   "No."

MARY   "I know. I can't believe that either. Do you suppose it was a joke?"

ELSIE   "Oh, I wouldn't be too sure. You know what I heard?—Oh, just listen to me. . . ."

MARY   "What?"

ELSIE   "Why do we spend our lives living through them? I mean, look at poor, old Lewis. Her grandmother had a heart attack; she'd think it was less important than one of Lady Sylvia's farts."

Do the servants live vicariously through Sir William and his friends and family? If so, why do you think they do this? Is it merely a matter of custom or something else? Discuss.

5. Consider this exchange between Sir William and Lady Sylvia:

SIR WILLIAM   "Why shouldn't I be interested in films? You don't know what I'm interested in."

LADY SYLVIA   "Well, I know you're interested in money and fiddling with your guns, but I admit, when it comes to anything else, I'm stumped."

Despite being the center of the world of Gosford Park, Sir William is presented as a shallow character. For example, he decides whom to marry on the basis of a card draw, and his wife accuses of him of being interested only in money and guns. How does presenting Sir William as a shallow character affect the greater moral world of Gosford Park? Is this film suggesting that the people in Gosford Park should not look to Sir William as the source of moral value? That they should not respect his customs and values? Discuss.

6. Consider the following dialogue between Mrs. Wilson and Inspector Thompson:

MRS. WILSON   "I was just asking the Constable how long our guests will be staying. I know Mrs. Croft has all the meals to arrange, and I know one of the housemaids is anxious to get away."

INSPECTOR THOMPSON   "I don't think there's any need to worry about that. I'm not interested in the servants. I need people with a real connection to the dead man."

Why would Inspector Thompson say that the servants do not have a "real" connection with Sir William? What would a "real" connection be? Is the Inspector right? Discuss.

7.   Consider the following conversation between Mary and Robert:

MARY   "You didn't really dislike him, did you? Not really. At least not enough to kill him. You can't have. You didn't know him. You'd have to hate him, and why would you?"

ROBERT   "Can't a man hate his own father? Sir William McCordle was my father. He didn't know it, but he was."

MARY   "But you said you were an orphan."

ROBERT   "No, I didn't. I said I grew up in an orphanage. . . . They had my admission form. I was two days old. Guess who brought me to the door?"

MARY   "Robert, that doesn't mean . . ."

ROBERT   "Yes, it does. After that I found out she worked in one of his factories. She wasn't the only one, apparently. Either the authorities didn't know, or they didn't want to know. They took his babies, and they took his money."

How does the revelation that Sir William had a number of children with his servants and placed them in an orphanage affect your opinion of him? Can we just explain away the action of fathers orphaning their children without the knowledge of their mothers as a "custom" of the wealthy? Does this revelation about Sir William ultimately call for us to place the entire moral universe of Gosford Park into question? Discuss.

8.   Consider the following exchange between Mary and Mrs. Wilson:

MARY   "Why did you do it? How did you know it was him? Was it the name, or did you see the photograph in his room?"

MRS. WILSON   "Ah, yes, the photograph. It's a miracle that survived. I remember his [Robert's] mother putting it into his blanket, especially. She wanted him to have something of hers. Does he know what happened to her?"

MARY   "They said she died just after he was born."

MRS. WILSON   "Oh, she didn't die. She gave him away. . . . He promised the boy would be adopted. He said he knew the family. Turns out we all clung to that dream—all us girls—a better start in life for our children. All the time he was dumping his own children in some God-forsaken place. And I believed him. I suppose it was easier that way. My sister certainly never forgave me for it. . . ."

MARY   "But even if Robert is your son, how did you know that he meant to harm his father?"

MRS. WILSON   "What gift do you think a good servant has that separates him from the others? It's the gift of anticipation. And I'm a good servant—I'm better than good; I'm the best. I'm the perfect servant. I know when they'll be hungry, and the food is ready. I know when they'll be tired, and the bed is turned down. I know it before they know it themselves."

Mrs. Wilson murdered Sir William to protect her son, Robert, from doing it himself. Discuss her reasons for murdering Sir William. Do you think she was morally justified? Why or why not? If you were Mrs. Wilson, would you have done the same thing? Why or why not?

9.   What message, if any, are you left with at the end of this film concerning the morality of the wealthy as compared to the morality of their servants? Discuss.

10.   Does this film refute or support the notion that morality is custom? Discuss.

RUTH BENEDICT

A DEFENSE OF MORAL RELATIVISM

R uth Benedict says that morality is culturally relative. "'Morality' is just another word for socially approved customs. While we prefer to say 'It is morally good' rather than 'It is habitual,'" says Benedict, the two phrases mean the same thing. For Benedict, morality, the habitual, the good, and the normal are all synonymous. Normality is, according to Benedict, defined by our culture. Furthermore, our moral system is not necessarily the inevitable consequence of reason or some rational decision-making process whereby inferior moral systems are omitted, but the product of mere historical chance. Society shapes our moral beliefs, and most people, says Benedict, "are plastic to the moulding force of the society into which they are born."

Ruth Benedict (1887–1948) was one of the foremost anthropologists of the twentieth century. She graduated from Vassar College in 1909 and began graduate studies in anthropology at Columbia University in 1919. At Columbia, she studied under Franz Boas and received her Ph.D. in 1923. After spending almost ten years as a lecturer at Columbia, she became an assistant professor in 1931, an associate professor upon Boas's retirement in 1936, and a full professor four months before her death. Her most famous student was Margaret Mead. Benedict wrote poetry under the pseudonym Anne Singleton until the early 1930s. During World War II, she worked for the U.S. Government on war-related research, in consultation with a number of other leading social anthropologists. Her books include *Tales of the Conchiti Indians* (1931), *Patterns of Culture* (1934), *Zuni Mythology* (1935), *General Anthropology* (1938), *Race and Racism* (1942), and *The Chrysanthemum and the Sword: Patterns of Japanese Culture* (1946).

Modern social anthropology has become more and more a study of the varieties and common elements of cultural environment and the consequences of these in human behavior. For such a study of diverse social orders, primitive peoples fortunately provide a laboratory not yet entirely vitiated by the spread of a standardized worldwide civilization. Dyaks and Hopis, Fijians and Yakuts are significant for psychological and sociological study because only among these simpler peoples has there been sufficient isolation to give opportunity for the development of localized social forms. In the higher cultures the standardization of custom and belief over a couple of continents has given a false sense of the inevitability of the particular forms that have gained currency, and we need to turn to a wider survey in order to check the conclusions we hastily base upon this near-universality of familiar customs. Most of the simpler cultures did not gain the wide currency of the one which, out of our experience, we identify with human nature, but this was for various historical reasons, and certainly not for any that gives us as its carriers a monopoly of social good or of social sanity. Modern civilization, from this point of view, becomes not a necessary pinnacle of human achievement but one entry in a long series of possible adjustments.

These adjustments, whether they are in mannerisms like the ways of showing anger, or joy, or grief in any society, or in major human drives like those of sex, prove to be far more variable than experience in any one culture would suggest. In certain fields, such as that of religion or of formal marriage arrangements, these wide limits of variability are well known and can be fairly described. In others it is not yet possible to give a generalized account, but that does not absolve us of the task of indicating the significance of the work that has been done and of the problems that have arisen.

One of these problems relates to the customary modern normal-abnormal categories and our conclusions regarding them. In how far are such categories culturally determined, or in how far can we with assurance regard them as absolute? In how far can we regard inability to function socially as diagnostic of abnormality, or in how far is it necessary to regard this as a function of the culture? . . .

The most spectacular illustrations of the extent to which normality may be culturally defined are those cultures where an abnormality of our culture is the cornerstone of their social structure. It is not possible to do justice to these possibilities in a short discussion. A recent study of an island of northwest Melanesia by Fortune describes a society built upon traits which we regard as beyond the border of paranoia. In this tribe the exogamic groups look upon each other as prime manipulators of black magic, so that one marries always into an enemy group which remains for life one's deadly and unappeasable foes. They look upon a good garden crop as a confession of theft, for everyone is engaged in making magic to induce into his garden the productiveness of his neighbors'; therefore no secrecy in the island is so rigidly insisted upon as the secrecy of a man's harvesting of his yams. Their polite phrase at the acceptance of a gift is, "And if you now poison me, how shall I repay you this present?" Their preoccupation with poisoning is constant; no woman ever leaves her cooking pot for a moment untended. Even the great affinal economic exchanges that are characteristic of this Melanesian culture area are quite altered in Dobu since they are incompatible with this fear and distrust that pervades the culture. . . . They go farther and people the whole world outside their own quarters with such malignant spirits that all-night feasts and ceremonials simply do not occur here. They have even rigorous, religiously enforced customs that forbid the sharing of seed even in one family group. Anyone else's food is deadly poison to you, so that communality of stores is out of the question. For some months before harvest the whole society is on the verge of starvation, but if one falls to the temptation and eats up one's seed yams, one is an outcast and a beachcomber for life. There is no coming back. It involves, as a matter of course, divorce and the breaking of all social ties.

Now in this society where no one may work with another and no one may share with another, Fortune describes the individual who was regarded by all his fellows as crazy. He was not one of those who periodically ran amok and, beside himself and frothing at the mouth, fell with a knife upon anyone he could reach. Such behavior they did not regard as putting anyone outside the pale. They did not even put the individuals who were known to be liable to these attacks under any kind of control. They merely fled when they saw the attack coming on and kept out of the way. "He would be all right tomorrow." But there was one man of sunny, kindly disposition who liked work and liked to be helpful. The compulsion was too strong for him to repress it in favor of the opposite tendencies of his culture. Men and women never spoke of him without laughing; he was silly and simple and definitely crazy. Nevertheless, to the ethnologist used to a culture that has, in Christianity, made his type the model of all virtue, he seemed a pleasant fellow.

An even more extreme example, because it is of a culture that has built itself upon a more complex abnormality, is that of the North Pacific Coast of North America. The civilization of the Kwakiutl, at the time when it was first recorded in the last decades of the nineteenth century, was one of the most vigorous in North America. It was built up on an ample economic supply of goods, the fish which furnished their food staple being practically inexhaustible and obtainable with comparatively small labor, and the wood which furnished the material for their houses, their furnishings, and their arts being, with however much labor, always procurable. They lived in coastal villages that compared favorably in size with those of any other American Indians, and they kept up constant communication by means of sea-going dug-out canoes.

It was one of the most vigorous and zestful of the aboriginal cultures of North America, with complex crafts and ceremonials, and elaborate and striking arts. It certainly had none of the earmarks of a sick civilization. The tribes of the Northwest Coast had wealth, and exactly in our terms. That is, they had not only a surplus of economic goods, but they made a game of manipulation of wealth. It was by no means a mere direct transcription of economic needs and the filling of those needs. It involved the idea of capital, of interest, and of conspicuous waste. It was a game with all the binding rules of a game, and a person entered it as a child. His father distributed wealth for him, according to his ability, at a small feast or potlatch, and each gift the receiver was obliged to accept and to return after short interval with interest that ran to about 100 percent a year. By the time the child was grown, therefore, he was well launched, a larger potlatch had been given for him on various occasions of exploit or initiation, and he had wealth either out at usury or in his own possession. Nothing in the civilization could be enjoyed without validating it by the distribution of this wealth. Everything that was valued, names and songs as well as material objects, were passed down in family lines, but they were always publicly assumed with accompanying sufficient distributions of property. It was the game of validating and exercising all the privileges one could accumulate from one's various forebears, or by gift, or by marriage, that made the chief interest of the culture. Everyone in his degree took part in it, but many, of course, mainly as spectators. In its highest form it was played out between rival chiefs representing not only themselves and their family lines but their communities, and the object

of the contest was to glorify oneself and to humiliate one's opponent. On this level of greatness the property involved was no longer represented by blankets, so many thousand of them to a potlatch, but by higher units of value. These higher units were like our bank notes. They were incised copper tablets, each of them named, and having a value that depended upon their illustrious history. This was as high as ten thousand blankets, and to possess one of them, still more to enhance its value at a great potlatch, was one of the greatest glories within the compass of the chiefs of the Northwest Coast. . . .

Every contingency of life was dealt with in . . . two traditional ways. To them the two were equivalent. Whether one fought with weapons or "fought with property," as they say, the same idea was at the bottom of both. In the olden times, they say, they fought with spears, but now they fight with property. One overcomes one's opponents in equivalent fashion in both, matching forces and seeing that one comes out ahead, and one can thumb one's nose at the vanquished rather more satisfactorily at a potlatch than on a battlefield. Every occasion in life was noticed, not in its own terms, as a stage in the sex life of the individual or as a climax of joy or grief, but as furthering this drama of consolidating one's own prestige and bringing shame to one's guests. Whether it was the occasion of the birth of a child, or a daughter's adolescence, or of the marriage of one's son, they were all equivalent raw material for the culture to use for this one traditionally selected end. They were all to raise one's own personal status and to entrench oneself by the humiliation of one's fellows. A girl's adolescence among the Nootka was an event for which her father gathered property from the time she was first able to run about. When she was adolescent he would demonstrate his greatness by an unheard-of distribution of these goods, and put down all his rivals. It was not as a fact of the girl's sex life that it figured in their culture, but as the occasion for a major move in the great game of vindicating one's own greatness and humiliating one's associates.

In their behavior at great bereavements this set of the culture comes out most strongly. Among the Kwakiutl it did not matter whether a relative had died in bed of disease, or by the hand of an enemy; in either case death was an affront to be wiped out by the death of another person. The fact that one had been caused to mourn was proof that one had been put upon. A chief's sister and her daughter had gone up to Victoria; and either because they drank bad whiskey or because their boat capsized they never came back. The chief called together his warriors. "Now, I ask you, tribes, who shall wail? Shall I do it or shall another?" The spokesman answered of course, "Not you, Chief. Let some other of the tribes." Immediately they set up the war pole to announce their intention of wiping out the injury; and gathered a war party. They set out, and found seven men and two children asleep and killed them. "Then they felt good when they arrived at Sebaa in the evening."

The point which is of interest to us is that in our society those who on that occasion would feel good when they arrived at Sebaa that evening would be the definitely abnormal. There would be some, even in our society, but it is not a recognized and approved mood under the circumstances. On the Northwest Coast those are favored and fortunate to whom that mood under those circumstances is congenial, and those to whom it is repugnant are unlucky. This latter minority can register in their own culture only by doing violence to their congenial responses and acquiring others that are difficult for them. The person, for instance, who, like a Plains Indian whose wife has been taken from him, is too proud to fight, can deal with the Northwest Coast civilization only by ignoring its strongest bents. If he cannot achieve it, he is the deviant in that culture, their instance of abnormality.

This head-hunting that takes place on the Northwest Coast after a death is no matter of blood revenge or of organized vengeance. There is no effort to tie up the subsequent killing with any responsibility on the part of the victim for the death of the person who is being mourned. A chief whose son has died goes visiting wherever his fancy dictates, and he says to his host, "My prince has died today, and you go with him." Then he kills him. In this, according to their interpretation, he acts nobly because he has not been downed. He has thrust back in return. The whole procedure is meaningless without the fundamental paranoid reading of bereavement. Death, like all the other untoward accidents of

existence, confounds man's pride and can only be handled in the category of insults. . . .

These illustrations, which it has been possible to indicate only in the briefest manner, force upon us the fact that normality is culturally defined. An adult shaped to the drives and standards of either of these cultures, if he were transported into our civilization, would fall into our categories of abnormality. He would be faced with the psychic dilemmas of the socially unavailable. In his own culture, however, he is the pillar of society, the end result of socially inculcated mores, and the problem of personal instability in his case simply does not arise.

No one civilization can possibly utilize in its mores the whole potential range of human behavior. Just as there are great numbers of possible phonetic articulations, and the possibility of language depends on a selection and standardization of a few of these in order that speech communication may be possible at all, so the possibility of organized behavior of every sort, from the fashions of local dress and houses to the dicta of a people's ethics and religion, depends upon a similar selection among the possible behavior traits. In the field of recognized economic obligations or sex tabus this selection is as non-rational and subconscious a process as it is in the field of phonetics. It is a process which goes on in the group for long periods of time and is historically conditioned by innumerable accidents of isolation or of contact of peoples. In any comprehensive study of psychology, the selection that different cultures have made in the course of history within the great circumference of potential behavior is of great significance.

Every society, beginning with some slight inclination in one direction or another, carries its preference farther and farther, integrating itself more and more completely upon its chosen basis, and discarding those types of behavior that are uncongenial. Most of those organizations of personality that seem to us most incontrovertibly abnormal have been used by different civilizations in the very foundations of their institutional life. Conversely the most valued traits of our normal individuals have been looked on in differently organized cultures as aberrant. Normality, in short, within a very wide range, is culturally defined. It is primarily a term for the socially elaborated segment of human behavior in any culture; and abnormality, a term for the segment that that particular civilization does not use. The very eyes with which we see the problem are conditioned by the long traditional habits of our own society.

It is a point that has been made more often in relation to ethics than in relation to psychiatry. We do not any longer make the mistake of deriving the morality of our own locality and decade directly from the inevitable constitution of human nature. We do not elevate it to the dignity of the first principle. We recognize that morality differs in every society and is a convenient term for socially approved habits. Mankind has always preferred to say, "It is a morally good," rather than "It is habitual," and the fact of this preference is matter enough for a critical science of ethics. But historically the two phrases are synonymous.

The concept of the normal is properly a variant of the concept of the good. It is that which society has approved. A normal action is one which falls well within the limits of expected behavior for a particular society. Its variability among different peoples is essentially a function of the variability of the behavior patterns that different societies have created for themselves, and can never be wholly divorced from a consideration of culturally institutionalized types of behavior.

Each culture is a more or less elaborate working-out of the potentialities of the segment it has chosen. In so far as a civilization is well integrated and consistent within itself, it will tend to carry further and farther, according to its nature, its initial impulse toward a particular type of action, and from the point of view of any other culture those elaborations will include more and more extreme and aberrant traits.

Each of these traits, in proportion as it reinforces the chosen behavior patterns of that culture, is for that culture normal. Those individuals to whom it is congenial either congenitally, or as the result of childhood sets, are accorded prestige in that culture, and are not visited with the social contempt or disapproval which their traits would call down upon them in a society that was differently organized. On the other hand, those individuals whose characteristics are not congenial to the selected type of human behavior in that community are the deviants, no matter how valued their personality traits may be in a contrasted civilization. . . .

The problem of understanding abnormal human behavior in any absolute sense independent of cultural factors is still far in the future. The categories of borderline behavior which we derive from the study of the neuroses and psychoses of our civilization are categories of prevailing local types of instability. They give much information about the stresses and strains of Western civilization, but no final picture of inevitable human behavior. Any conclusions about such behavior must await the collection by trained observers of psychiatric data from other cultures. Since no adequate work of the kind has been done at the present time, it is impossible to say what core of definition of abnormality may be found valid from the comparative material. It is as it is in ethics; all our local conventions of moral behavior and of immoral are without absolute validity, and yet it is quite possible that a modicum of what is considered right and what wrong could be disentangled that is shared by the whole human race. When data are available in psychiatry, this minimum definition of abnormal human tendencies will be probably quite unlike our culturally conditioned, highly elaborated psychoses such as those that are described, for instance, under the terms of schizophrenia and manic-depressive.

DISCUSSION QUESTIONS

1. Benedict argues against moral progress. What is her argument? Do you agree with her? Why or why not?

2. Do you agree with Benedict that *morality* is just another word for socially approved customs? Explain.

3. Many people believe that there are basic human rights that cross societal barriers. What would Benedict say about such human rights? Do you agree with her response? Defend your view.

4. It is a fact of the world that there are many different cultures with many different and sometimes conflicting moral beliefs. For example, some cultures have praised homosexual love, whereas others have considered it

immoral. Does the fact of cultural diversity give us sufficient grounds for endorsing moral relativism? Present your case.

5. How would we resolve moral dilemmas on Benedict's model of morality? For example, some say that the death penalty is moral, and others say that it is immoral. How would Benedict resolve this moral dilemma? What do you think about this way of resolving moral dilemmas?

Planet of the Apes
[USA 2001] 1 hour, 59 minutes
Directed by Tim Burton

When Captain Leo Davidson (Mark Wahlberg) goes in search of his favorite chimpanzee, Pericles, who has been lost in space during an experiment, he is unexpectedly pushed forward in time and lands on a planet ruled by apes. On this planet, human beings are inferior, and Leo is captured and sold into slavery. Leo and a few other humans manage to escape with the help of Ari (Helena Bonham Carter), an ape and "human rights activist." The group then journeys out of Ape City in search of the crash site of the *Oberon*, Leo's ship, while pursued by the ruthless General Thade (Tim Roth) and his ape army.

In their journey to find the Oberon, Leo's group arrives at the apes' holy place of Ca Li Ma, which Leo soon discovers is the crash site of his crew's ship. When Thade and his army encroach upon the group, Leo uses reserves in the Oberon's fuel tank to create an explosion that kills the first wave of attacking apes. Then the humans and apes fall upon each other in frenzied fighting. During the middle of battle, Pericles, Leo's lost chimpanzee, unexpectedly arrives, and the apes mistake him for Semos, their Godlike savior. This event creates a diversion, and General Thade is trapped by Leo and Ari.

Once Thade has been defeated, the apes and humans decide to live together as equals. However, Leo insists that he cannot stay on the planet and takes Pericles' pod back to earth. Leo lands at what he believes is the Lincoln Memorial in Washington, DC, and sees that it now has the face of an ape. The movie ends with apes descending on Leo as if he were some sort of rare spectacle.

DISCUSSION QUESTIONS

1. How does *Planet of the Apes* support the notion that different cultures (ape and human) can have different and sometimes conflicting moral beliefs?

2. Many people believe that there are basic human rights that cross cultural and societal barriers. Do you think that *Planet of the Apes* supports this position? Does the decision of the apes and the humans to live together as equals near the end of the film support this view?

3. Consider the following dialogue between the Captain and Leo:

    CAPTAIN   "You get your monkey ready."

    LEO   "I hope you don't mind my saying, but this is a waste of time."

    CAPTAIN   "Look, we have standard operating procedures, and . . ."

    LEO   "I'm well aware of the procedures sir, but if we go through all of them it could be gone."

CAPTAIN   "No man flight. We start sending out an ape; then, if it's safe, we talk about a pilot, in that order."

LEO   "You need somebody out there who can think. Why don't you just let me do my job?"

CAPTAIN   "He's the canary. That's the coal mine. Your monkey launches at 16:00."

What does the Captain assume about moral worth in his statements about the monkey? In *Planet of the Apes*, how is moral worth determined? In particular, how are some living beings determined to be of higher moral worth than others? Does *Planet of the Apes* suggest that moral worth is relative to culture? How different is the basis of moral worth in *Planet of the Apes* from the basis of moral worth in your own culture? Discuss.

4.   Consider this exchange between Limbo (Paul Giamatti) and Ari regarding the humans:

LIMBO   "I don't see any of you bleeding hearts spending all day with these dangerous, dirty, dumb beasts."

ARI   "They're not dumb. They can be taught to live with us as equals, and I can prove it."

What does Ari assume about the source of our moral concepts? Would Ari agree that morality is custom? Why or why not?

5.   Consider the following dialogue between Leo and Daena (Estella Warren):

LEO   "How the hell did these monkeys get like this?"

DAENA   "What other way would they be?"

LEO   "They'd be begging me for a treat right now."

Ruth Benedict argues against moral progress. Does *Planet of the Apes* support her position? Do you think that the apes have progressed morally from the time Leo knew them as caged beings to the time depicted in this film? Why or why not?

6.   Consider this exchange between Ari and General Thade:

ARI   "Isn't it obvious that they [humans] are capable of a real culture?"

GENERAL THADE   "Everything in the human culture takes place below the waist."

What does it mean to say that something is "capable of a real culture"? Are there real cultures and unreal or false cultures? What is the difference, and how do we determine it? Are the moral standards of "false" cultures necessarily wrong? Discuss.

7.   Consider the following dialogue among Ari, Krull (Cary-Hiroyuki Tagawa), and Leo:

ARI   "These zoos you speak of, what are they? This word is not familiar."

LEO   "Zoos are where we find our last few apes."

KRULL   "What happened to them?"

LEO   "Gone! After we cut down the forests . . . the ones that survive, we lock up in cages for amusement or use them for scientific experiments."

ARI   "That's horrible!"

LEO   "Yeah. We do our worst to our kind."

ARI   "I don't understand. You seem to possess such intelligence."

LEO   "The smarter we get, the more dangerous our world becomes."

Is Leo right? Is it the case that the smarter we get, the more dangerous our world becomes? Why is this? Discuss.

8.   Is *Planet of the Apes* a warning about the dangers of cultural and moral isolationism? Discuss.

W. T. STACE
A CRITIQUE OF MORAL RELATIVISM

I n this selection, W. T. Stace argues against moral relativism, which he finds to be incoherent and unacceptable, and defends moral absolutism. First, moral relativism makes it impossible to say whether the moral standards of one culture are better or worse than the moral standards of another culture. Second, it is unclear just what counts as a "culture" for moral relativists. Moral absolutism says that the same moral standards apply to all people regardless of their culture. The fact that not everyone has the same moral beliefs is not evidence for moral relativism, says Stace, but rather is evidence of moral ignorance. While it is difficult to determine the grounds for moral absolutism, Stace believes that philosophers will ultimately provide a basis for a universal morality.

Walter Terence Stace (1886–1967) was born in London and educated at Fettes College, Edinburgh, and Trinity College, Dublin, where he was awarded an honorary doctorate of letters (D.Litt.) in 1929. From 1910 to 1932, he was a British army officer in Ceylon (now Sri Lanka) and at one time was mayor of Colombo (the capital of Ceylon). In 1932, he began his philosophical career at Princeton University, where he taught until his retirement in 1955. He was the author of many books including *The Philosophy of Hegel* (1924), *The Meaning of Beauty* (1929), *The Theory of Knowledge and Existence* (1932), *The Concept of Morals* (1937), *The Destiny of Western Man* (1942), *Philosophy and the Modern Mind* (1952), *Time and Eternity* (1952), *Mysticism and Philosophy* (1960) and *Religion and the Modern Mind* (1960). This selection is from *The Concept of Morals*.

I

Any ethical position which denies that there is a single moral standard which is equally applicable to all men at all times may fairly be called a species of ethical relativity. There is not, the relativist asserts, merely one moral law, one code, one standard. There are many moral law, codes, standards. What morality ordains in one place or age may be quite different from what morality ordains in another place or age. The moral code of

Chinamen is quite different from that of Europeans, that of African savages quite different from both. Any morality, therefore, is relative to the age, the place, and the circumstances in which it is found. It is in no sense absolute.

This does not mean merely—as one might at first sight be inclined to suppose—that the very same kind of action which is *thought* right in one country and period may be *thought* wrong in another. This would be a mere platitude, the truth of which everyone would have to admit. Even the absolutist would admit this—would even wish to emphasize it—since he is well aware that different people have different sets of moral ideas, and his whole point is that some of these sets of ideas are false. What the relativist means to assert is, not this platitude, but that the very same kind of action which *is* right in one country and period may *be* wrong in another. And this, far from being a platitude, is a very startling assertion.

It is very important to grasp thoroughly the difference between the two ideas. For there is reason to think that many minds tend to find ethical relativity attractive because they fail to keep them clearly apart. It is so very obvious that moral ideas differ from country to country and from age to age. And it is so very easy, if you are mentally lazy, to suppose that to say this means the same as to say that no universal moral standard exists—or in other words that it implies ethical relativity. We fail to see that the word "standard" is used in two different senses. It is perfectly true that, in one sense, there are many variable moral standards. We speak of judging a man by the standard of his time. And this implies that different times have different standards. And this, of course, is quite true. But when the word "standard" is used in this sense it means simply the set of moral ideas current during the period in question. It means what people *think* right, whether as a matter of fact it *is* right or not. On the other hand, when the absolutist asserts that there exists a single universal moral "standard," he is not using the word in this sense at all. He means by "standard" what *is* right as distinct from what people merely think right. His point is that although what people think right varies in different countries and periods, yet what actually is right is everywhere and always the same. And it follows that when the ethical relativist disputes

the position of the absolutist and denies that any universal moral standard exists, he too means by "standard" what actually is right. But it is exceedingly easy, if we are not careful, to slip loosely from using the word in the first sense to using it in the second sense, and to suppose that the variability of moral beliefs is the same thing as the variability of what really is moral. And unless we keep the two senses of the word "standard" distinct, we are likely to think the creed of ethical relativity much more plausible than it actually is.

The genuine relativist, then, does not merely mean that Chinamen may think right what Frenchmen think wrong. He means that what *is* wrong for the Frenchman may *be* right for the Chinaman. And if one inquires how, in those circumstances, one is to know what actually is right in China or in France, the answer comes quite glibly. What is right in China is the same as what people think right in China; and what is right in France is the same as what people think right in France. So that if you want to know what is moral in any particular country or age, all you have to do is to ascertain what are the moral ideas current in that age or country. Those ideas are, *for that age or country*, right. Thus what is morally right is identified with what is thought to be morally right, and the distinction which we made above between these two is simply denied. To put the same thing in another way, it is denied that there can be or ought to be any distinction between the two senses of the word "standard." There is only one kind of standard of right and wrong, namely, the moral ideas current in any particular age or country.

Moral right *means* what people think morally right. It has no other meaning. What Frenchmen think right is, therefore, right *for Frenchmen*. And evidently one must conclude—though I am not aware that relativists are anxious to draw one's attention to such unsavory but yet absolutely necessary conclusions from their creed—that cannibalism is right for people who believe in it, that human sacrifice is right for those races which practice it, and that burning widows alive was right for Hindus until the British stepped in and compelled the Hindus to behave immorally by allowing their widows to remain alive.

When it is said that, according to the ethical relativist, what is thought right in any social group is right for that group, one must be careful not to misinterpret this. The relativist does not, of course, mean that there actually is an objective moral standard in France and a different objective standard in England, and that French and British opinions respectively give us correct information about these different standards. His point is rather that there are not objectively true moral standards at all. There is no single universal objective standard. Nor are there a variety of local objective standards. All standards are subjective. People's subjective feelings about morality are the only standards which exist.

To sum up: The ethical relativist consistently denies, it would seem, whatever the ethical absolutist asserts. For the absolutist there is a single universal moral standard. For the relativist there is no such standard. There are only local, ephemeral, and variable standards. For the absolutist there are two senses of the word "standard." Standards in the sense of sets of current moral ideas are relative and changeable. But the standard in the sense of what is actually morally right is absolute and unchanging. For the relativist no such distinction can be made. There is only one meaning of the word standard, namely, that which refers to local and variable sets of moral ideas. Or if it is insisted that the word must be allowed two meanings, then the relativist will say that there is at any rate no actual example of a standard in the absolute sense, and that the word as thus used is an empty name to which nothing in reality corresponds; so that the distinction between the two meanings becomes empty and useless. Finally—though this is merely saying the same thing in another way—the absolutist makes a distinction between what actually is right and what is thought right. The relativist rejects this distinction and identifies what is moral with what is thought moral by certain human beings or groups of human beings. . . .

II

I shall now proceed to consider, first, the main arguments which can be urged in favor of ethical relativity; and secondly, the arguments which can be urged against it. . . . The first [in favor] is that which relies upon the actual varieties of moral "standards" found in the world. It was easy enough to believe in a single absolute morality in older times when there was no anthropology, when all humanity was divided clearly into two groups, Christian peoples and the "heathen." Christian peoples knew and possessed the one true morality. The rest were savages whose moral ideas could be ignored. But all this is changed. Greater knowledge has brought greater tolerance. We can no longer exalt our own morality as alone true, while dismissing all other moralities as false or inferior. The investigations of anthropologists have shown that there exists side by side in the world a bewildering variety of moral codes. On this topic endless volumes have been written, masses of evidence piled up. Anthropologists have ransacked the Melanesian Islands, the jungles of New Guinea, the steppes of Siberia, the deserts of Australia, the forests of central Africa, and have brought back with them countless examples of weird, extravagant, and fantastic "moral" customs with which to confound us. We learn that all kinds of horrible practices are, in this, that, or the other place, regarded as essential to virtue. We find that there is nothing, or next to nothing, which has always and everywhere been regarded as morally good by all men. Where, then, is our universal morality? Can we, in face of all this evidence, deny that it is nothing but an empty dream?

This argument, taken by itself, is a very weak one. It relies upon a single set of facts—the variable moral customs of the world. But this variability of moral ideas is admitted by both parties to the dispute, and is capable of ready explanation upon the hypothesis of either party. The relativist says that the facts are to be explained by the nonexistence of any absolute moral standard. The absolutist says that they are to be explained by human ignorance of what the absolute moral standard is. And he can truly point out that men have differed widely in their opinions about all manner of topics—including the subject-matters of the physical sciences—just as much as they differ about morals. And if the various different opinions which men have held about the shape of the earth do not prove that it has no one real shape, neither do the various opinions which they have held about morality prove that there is no one true morality.

Thus the facts can be explained equally plausibly on either hypothesis. There is nothing in the facts themselves which compels us to prefer the relativistic hypothesis to that of the absolutist. And therefore the argument fails to prove the relativist conclusion. If that conclusion is to be established, it must be by means of other considerations.

This is the essential point. But I will add some supplementary remarks. The work of the anthropologists, upon which ethical relativists seem to rely so heavily, has as a matter of fact added absolutely nothing *in principle* to what has always been known about the variability of moral ideas. Educated people have known all along that the Greeks tolerated sodomy, which in modern times has been regarded in some countries as an abominable crime; that the Hindus thought it a sacred duty to burn their widows; that trickery, now thought despicable, was once believed to be a virtue; that terrible torture was thought by our own ancestors only a few centuries ago to be a justifiable weapon of justice; that it was only yesterday that western peoples came to believe that slavery is immoral. Even the ancients knew very well that moral customs and ideas vary—witness the writings of Herodotus. Thus the principle of the variability of moral ideas was well understood long before modern anthropology was ever heard of. Anthropology has added nothing to the knowledge of this principle except a mass of new and extreme examples of it drawn from very remote sources. But to multiply examples of a principle already well known and universally admitted adds nothing to the argument which is built upon that principle. The discoveries of the anthropologists have no doubt been of the highest importance in their own sphere. But in any considered opinion they have thrown no new light upon the special problems of the moral philosopher.

Although the multiplication of examples has no logical bearing on the argument, it does have an immense *psychological* effect upon people's minds. These masses of anthropological learning are impressive. They are propounded in the sacred name of "science." If they are quoted in support of ethical relativity—as they often are—people *think* that they must prove something important. They bewilder and over-awe the simple-minded, batter down their resistance, make them ready to receive humbly the doctrine of ethical relativity from those who have acquired a reputation by their immense learning and their claims to be "scientific." Perhaps this is why so much ado is made by ethical relativists regarding the anthropological evidence. But we must refuse to be impressed. We must discount all this mass of evidence about the extraordinary moral customs of remote peoples. Once we have admitted—as everyone who is instructed must have admitted these last two thousand years without any anthropology at all—the principle that moral ideas vary, all this new evidence adds nothing to the argument. And the argument itself proves nothing for the reasons already given. . . .

The second argument in favor of ethical relativity . . . does not suffer from the disadvantage that it is dependent upon the acceptance of any particular philosophy such as radical empiricism. It makes its appeal to considerations of a quite general character. It consists in alleging that no one has ever been able to discover upon what foundation an absolute morality could rest, or from what source a universally binding moral code could derive its authority.

If, for example, it is an absolute and unalterable moral rule that all men ought to be unselfish, from whence does this *command* issue? For a command it certainly is, phrase it how you please. There is no difference in meaning between the sentence "You ought to be unselfish" and the sentence "Be unselfish." Now a command implies a commander. An obligation implies some authority which obliges. Who is this commander, what this authority? Thus the vastly difficult question is raised of *the basis of moral obligation.* Now the argument of the relativist would be that it is impossible to find any basis for a universally binding moral law; but that it is quite easy to discover a basis for morality if moral codes are admitted to be variable, ephemeral, and relative to time, place, and circumstance.

In this paper I am assuming that it is no longer possible to solve this difficulty by saying naively that the universal moral law is based upon the uniform commands of God to all men. There will be many, no doubt, who will dispute this. But I am not writing for them. I am writing for those who feel the necessity of finding for morality a basis independent of particular religious dogmas. And I shall therefore make no attempt to argue the matter.

The problem which the absolutist has to face, then, is this. The religious basis of the one absolute morality having disappeared, can there be found for it any other, any secular, basis? If not, then it would seem that we cannot any longer believe in absolutism. We shall have to fall back upon belief in a variety of perhaps mutually inconsistent moral codes operating over restricted areas and limited periods. No one of these will be better, or more true, than any other. Each will be good and true for those living in those areas and periods. We shall have to fall back, in a word, on ethical relativity.

For there is no great difficulty in discovering the foundations of morality, or rather of moralities, if we adopt the relativistic hypothesis. Even if we cannot be quite certain *precisely* what these foundations are—and relativists themselves are not entirely agreed about them—we can at least see in a general way the *sort* of foundations they must have. We can see that the question on this basis is not in principle impossible of answer—although the details may be obscure; while, if we adopt the absolutist hypothesis—so the argument runs—no kind of answer is conceivable at all. . . .

This argument is undoubtedly very strong. It *is* absolutely essential to solve the problem of the basis of moral obligation if we are to believe in any kind of moral standards other than those provided by mere custom or by irrational emotions. It is idle to talk about a universal morality unless we can point to the source of its authority—or at least to do so is to indulge in a faith which is without rational ground. To cherish a blind faith in morality may be, for the average man whose business is primarily to live right and not to theorize, sufficient. Perhaps it is his wisest course. But it will not do for the philosopher. His function, or at least one of his functions, is precisely to discover the rational grounds of our everyday beliefs—if they have any. Philosophically and intellectually, then, we cannot accept belief in a universally binding morality unless we can discover upon what foundation its obligatory character rests.

But in spite of the strength of the argument thus posed in favor of ethical relativity, it is not impregnable. For it leaves open one loophole. It is always possible that some theory, not yet examined, may provide a basis for a universal moral obligation. The argument rests upon the [universal] negative proposition that *there is no theory which can provide a basis for a universal morality.* But it is notoriously difficult to prove a negative. How can you prove that there are no green swans? All you can show is that none have been found so far. And then it is always possible that one will be found tomorrow. . . .

III

It is time that we turn our attention from the case in favor of ethical relativity to the case against it. Now the case against it consists, to a very large extent, in urging that, if taken seriously and pressed to its logical conclusion, ethical relativity can only end in destroying the conception of morality altogether, in undermining its practical efficacy, in rendering meaningless many almost universally accepted truths about human affairs, in robbing human beings of any incentive to strive for a better world, in taking the life-blood out of every ideal and every aspiration which has ever ennobled the life of man. . . .

First of all, then, ethical relativity, in asserting that the moral standards of particular social groups are the only standards which exist, renders meaningless all propositions which attempt to compare these standards with one another in respect of their moral worth. And this is a very serious matter indeed. We are accustomed to think that the moral ideas of one nation or social group may be "higher" or "lower" than those of another. We believe, for example, that Christian ethical ideals are nobler than those of the savage races of central Africa. Probably most of us would think that the Chinese moral standards are higher than those of the inhabitants of New Guinea. In short we habitually compare one civilization with another and judge the sets of ethical ideas to be found in them to be some better, some worse. The fact that such judgments are very difficult to make with any justice, and that they are frequently made on very superficial and prejudiced grounds, has no bearing on the question now at issue. The question is whether such judgments have any *meaning.* We habitually assume that they have.

But on the basis of ethical relativity they can have none whatever. For the relativist must hold that there is no *common* standard which can be applied to the various civilizations judged. Any such comparison of moral standards implies the existence of some superior standard which is applicable to both. And the existence of any such standard is precisely what the relativist denies. According to him the Christian standard is applicable only to Christians, the Chinese standard only to Chinese, the New Guinea standard only to the inhabitants of New Guinea.

What is true of comparisons between the moral standards of different races will also be true of comparisons between those of different ages. It is not unusual to ask such questions as whether the standard of our own day is superior to that which existed among our ancestors five hundred years ago. And when we remember that our ancestors employed slaves, practiced barbaric physical tortures, and burned people alive, we may be inclined to think that it is. At any rate we assume that the question is one which has meaning and is capable of rational discussion. But if the ethical relativist is right, whatever we assert on this subject must be totally meaningless. For here again there is no common standard which could form the basis of any such judgments.

This in its turn implies that the whole notion of moral *progress* is a sheer delusion. Progress means an advance from lower to higher, from worse to better. But on the basis of ethical relativity it has no meaning to say that the standards of this age are better (or worse) than those of a previous age. For there is no common standard by which both can be measured. Thus it is nonsense to say that the morality of the New Testament is higher than that of the Old. And Jesus Christ, if he imagined that he was introducing into the world a higher ethical standard than existed before his time, was merely deluded. . . .

I come now to a second point. Up to the present I have allowed it to be taken tacitly for granted that, though judgments comparing different races and ages in respect of the worth of their moral codes are impossible for the ethical relativist, yet judgments of comparison between individuals living within the same social group would be quite possible. For individuals living within the same social group would presumably be subject to the same moral code, that of their group, and this would therefore constitute, as between these individuals, a common standard by

which they could both be measured. We have not here, as we had in the other case, the difficulty of the absence of any common standard of comparison. It should therefore be possible for the ethical relativist to say quite meaningfully that President Lincoln was a better man than some criminal or moral imbecile of his own time and country, or that Jesus was a better man than Judas Iscariot.

But is even this minimum of moral judgment really possible on relativist grounds? It seems to me that it is not. For when once the whole of humanity is abandoned as the area covered by a single moral standard, what smaller areas are to be adopted as the *loci* of different standards? Where are we to draw the lines of demarcation? We can split up humanity, perhaps—though the procedure will be very arbitrary—into races, races into nations, nations into tribes, tribes into families, families into individuals. Where are we going to draw the *moral* boundaries? Does the *locus* of a particular moral standard reside in a race, a nation, a tribe, a family, or an individual? Perhaps the blessed phrase "social group" will be dragged in to save the situation. Each such group, we shall be told, has its own moral code which is, for it, right. But what *is* a "group"? Can anyone define it or give its boundaries? This is the seat of that ambiguity in the theory of ethical relativity to which reference was made on an earlier page.

The difficulty is not, as might be thought, merely an academic difficulty of logical definition. If that were all, I should not press the point. But the ambiguity has practical consequences which are disastrous for morality. No one is likely to say that moral codes are confined within the arbitrary limits of the geographical divisions of countries. Nor are the notions of race, nation, or political state likely to help us. To bring out the essentially practical character of the difficulty let us put it in the form of concrete questions. Does the American nation constitute a "group" having a single moral standard? Or does the standard of what I ought to do change continuously as I cross the continent in a railway train? Do different States of the Union have different moral codes? Perhaps every town and village has its own peculiar standard. This may at first sight seem reasonable enough. "In Rome do as Rome does" may seem as good a rule in morals as it is in etiquette. But can we stop there? Within the village are numerous cliques each having its own set of ideas. Why should not each of these claim to be bound only by its own special and peculiar moral standards? And if it comes to that, why should not the gangsters of Chicago claim to constitute a group having its own morality, so that its murders and debaucheries must be viewed as "right" by the only standard which can legitimately be applied to it? And if it be answered that the nation will not tolerate this, that may be so. But this is to put the foundation of right simply in the superior force of the majority. In that case whoever is stronger will be right, however monstrous his ideas and actions. And if we cannot deny to any set of people the right to have its own morality, is it not clear that, in the end, we cannot even deny this right to the individual? Every individual man and woman can put up, on this view, an irrefutable claim to be judged by no standard except his or her own.

If these arguments are valid, the ethical relativist cannot really maintain that there is anywhere to be found a moral standard binding upon anybody against his will. And he cannot maintain that, even within the social group, there is a common standard as between individuals. And if that is so, then even judgments to the effect that one man is morally better than another become meaningless. All moral valuation thus vanishes. There is nothing to prevent each man from being a rule unto himself. The result will be moral chaos and the collapse of all effective standards. . . .

But even if we assume that the difficulty about defining moral groups has been surmounted, a further difficulty presents itself. Suppose that we have now definitely decided what are the exact boundaries of the social group within which a moral standard is to be operative. And we will assume—as is invariably done by relativists themselves—that this group is to be some actually existing social community such as a tribe or nation. How are we to know, even then, what actually is the moral standard within that group? How is anyone to know? How is even a member of the group to know? For there are certain to be within the group—at least this will be true among advanced peoples—wide differences of opinion as to what is right, what wrong. Whose opinion,

then, is to be taken as representing *the* moral standard of the group? Either we must take the opinion of the majority within the group, or the opinion of some minority. If we rely upon the ideas of the majority, the results will be disastrous. Wherever there is found among a people a small band of select spirits, or perhaps one man, working for the establishment of higher and nobler ideas than those commonly accepted by the group, we shall be compelled to hold that, for that people at that time, the majority are right, and that the reformers are wrong and are preaching what is immoral. We shall have to maintain, for example, that Jesus was preaching immoral doctrines to the Jews. Moral goodness will have to be equated always with the mediocre and sometimes with the definitely base and ignoble. If on the other hand we said that the moral standard of the group is to be identified with the moral opinions of some minority, then what minority is this to be? We cannot answer that it is to be the minority composed of the best and the most enlightened individuals of the group. This would involve us in a palpably vicious circle. For by what standard are these individuals to be judged the best and the most enlightened? There is no principle by which we could select the right minority. And therefore we should have to consider every minority as good as every other. And this means that we should have no logical right whatever to resist the claim of the gangsters of Chicago—if such a claim were made—that their practices represent the highest standards of American morality. It means in the end that every individual is to be bound by no standard save his own.

The ethical relativists are great empiricists. *What* is the actual moral standard of any group can only be discovered, they tell us, by an examination on the ground of the moral opinions and customs of that group. But will they tell us how they propose to decide, when they get to the ground, which of the many moral opinions they are sure to find there is *the* right one in that group? To some extent they will be able to do this for the Melanesian Islanders—from whom apparently all lessons in the nature of morality are in future to be taken. But it is certain that they cannot do it for advanced peoples whose members have learned to think for themselves and to entertain among themselves a wide variety of opinions. They cannot do it unless they accept the calamitous view that the ethical opinion of the majority is always right. We are left therefore once more with the conclusion that, even within a particular social group, anybody's moral opinion is as good as anybody's else's, and that every man is entitled to be judged by his own standards.

Finally, not only is ethical relativity disastrous in its consequences for moral theory. It cannot be doubted that it must tend to be equally disastrous in its impact upon practical conduct. If men come really to believe that one moral standard is as good as another, they would conclude that their own moral standard has nothing special to recommend it. They might as well then slip down to some lower and easier standard. It is true that, for a time, it may be possible to hold one view in theory and to act practically upon another. But ideas, even philosophical ideas, are not so ineffectual that they can remain forever idle in the upper chambers of the intellect. In the end they seep down to the level of practice. They get themselves acted on.

DISCUSSION QUESTIONS

1. What is the best objection that Stace raises against moral relativism? Is it a good objection?

2. How important is it to be able to say that the moral standards of one society are better than those of another? Should we object to moral theories that do not call one moral system better than another? Defend your view.

3. What is moral absolutism? What is gained and what is lost with moral absolutism? How important is it for philosophers to provide a basis for a universal morality?

4. How do you think Ruth Benedict would respond to Stace's objections? Do you think that she was aware of them? What, if anything, would get her to change her position?

5. Can one support both cultural diversity and moral absolutism? Or is a defense of moral absolutism also an argument against cultural diversity? Explain your view.

Do the Right Thing
[USA 1989] 2 hours
Directed by Spike Lee

The action of *Do the Right Thing* takes place over the course of one long, hot summer day. Sal's Famous Pizzeria is owned and operated by an Italian-American family in the predominantly African-American neighborhood of Bedford-Stuyevesant in Brooklyn. Sal (Danny Aiello), the owner, has been making pizzas on the same corner for many years and has seen numerous changes in the neighborhood. He employs Mookie (Spike Lee) to deliver pizzas, and the two have an amicable if distant relationship.

The film presents the relations between different ethnic groups in the neighborhood as strained, and eventually the tensions increase. Sal is criticized for his restaurant's "Wall of Fame," which displays pictures of famous Italians and Italian-Americans. Mookie's friends insist that Sal should put some pictures of famous African-Americans on the wall since most of his customers are African-American. When Radio Raheem (Bill Nunn) enters the pizzeria with his radio blasting, Sal refuses to serve Raheem unless he turns off the music. Raheem does not comply, and Sal releases his rage and frustration by destroying the radio with a baseball bat. In retaliation, Mookie's friends boycott the pizzeria. During the protest, the police kill Radio Raheem while allegedly simply trying to restrain him. Mookie loses self-control and throws a trashcan through the window of Sal's restaurant, inciting angry protesters to destroy the pizzeria.

The film's credits include both a quote from Martin Luther King concerning the importance of nonviolence when confronting racism and a quote from Malcolm X imploring viewers to fight racism by "any means necessary." The film does not condone violence, but neither does it reject it. It is a portrait of multicultural life in the United States today—one that asks more questions than it answers.

DISCUSSION QUESTIONS

1. Reread Ruth Benedict's and Walter Stace's articles, and think about them in the context of Spike Lee's film. Should we regard *Do the Right Thing* as a defense of cultural relativism or a rejection of it? Defend your view.

2. Brooklyn is composed of people from many different nationalities, races, and religions, but all of these people are still considered Americans. Should we regard the people of this community as belonging to one culture or to many? What does the film suggest, if anything? What are the dangers and benefits associated with considering Brooklyn as one culture or many?

3. What is the right thing to do with regard to Sal's "Wall of Fame"? Should Sal put up pictures of famous African-Americans, or not? Defend your view.

4. In one scene, members of the various ethnic and social groups in the film stand in front of the camera and verbally berate one another. A member from each group directly shouts to the camera a series of derogatory terms or phrases associated with one of the groups they dislike. This scene reveals the deep level of tension among the ethnic groups in Bedford-Stuyevesant and the degree to which this tension is part of the language. What do you think is the cause of this tension? Can it ever be eliminated? Would a cultural relativist argue that it should be eliminated? Or, would the cultural relativist argue that because it is a part of the culture, it should be respected and not interfered with? Discuss.

5. The United States is composed of people from many different nationalities, races, and religions. Do you believe that as a citizen of the United States you have an obligation to respect the morals and customs of all nationalities, races, and religions equally? If so, does this make you a cultural relativist? If not, why not?

MARTHA NUSSBAUM

JUDGING OTHER CULTURES

In this reading, Martha Nussbaum describes and analyzes some of the controversies concerning the practice of female genital mutilation (FGM)—a practice that is often raised in discussions of moral relativism. Nussbaum reports that while this practice is common in Africa, a smaller number of cases have been reported in countries such as Australia, Belgium, France, the United Kingdom, and the United States. Furthermore, even though the practice is illegal in and widely resisted in most of the countries where it occurs, it continues to this day.

Part of the reason for its continuation despite legal and public resistance is that some people believe that FGM "appeals to cultural continuity." The "constitutive role played by such initiation rights in the formation of a community and the disintegrative effect of interference" lead some to oppose outlawing the surgery and instead to recommend a gradual process of education and persuasion in opposition to it.

Nevertheless, feminists and others "have organized to demand the abolition of this practice, citing its health risks, its impact on sexual functioning, and the violations of dignity and choice associated with its compulsory and nonconsensual nature." "At the same time, however, other writers have begun to protest that the criticism of FGM is inappropriate and 'ethnocentric,' a demonizing of another culture when we have many reasons to find fault with our own." Nussbaum says that her own students initially tend to be ethical relativists regarding the practice of FGM and are "hesitant to make any negative judgment of a culture other than their own." Nussbaum's own position on the practice is quite the opposite of her students and ethical relativists: FGM is an unacceptable practice that violates "women's human rights, and we should be ashamed of ourselves if we do not use whatever privilege and power has come our way to make it disappear forever."

Martha Nussbaum (1947–) is currently Ernst Freund Professor of Law and Ethics at the University of Chicago, with appointments in law, philosophy, divinity, political science, and classics. She is also founder and coordinator of the University of Chicago's new Center for Comparative Constitutionalism. She received a B.A. from New York University in 1969 and a Ph.D. from Harvard University in 1975. Professor Nussbaum has taught at Brown, Harvard, and Oxford. Her many books include *Aristotle's De Motu Animalium* (1978), *The Fragility of Goodness: Luck and Ethics in Greek Tragedy and Philosophy* (1986), *Love's Knowledge* (1990), *The Quality of Life* (co-edited, with Amartya Sen), *The Therapy of Desire* (1994), *Women, Culture and Development* (co-edited, with Jonathan Glover), *Poetic Justice* (1996), *For Love of Country* (1996), *Sex, Preference, and Family* (co-edited, with David Estlund), *Cultivating Humanity: A Classical Defense of Reform in Liberal Education* (1997), *Sexual Orientation and Human Rights in American Religious Discourse* (co-edited, Saul Olyan), *Sex and Social Justice* (1999), *Women and Human Development* (2000), and *Upheavals of Thought: The Intelligence of the Emotions* (2001). This selection is from *Sex and Social Justice*.

In June 1997, the Board of Immigration Appeals of the United States Immigration and Naturalization Service (INS) granted political asylum to a nineteen-year-old woman from Togo who had fled her home to escape the practice of genital mutilation. Fauziya Kassindja is the daughter of Muhammed Kassindja, a successful owner of a small trucking business in Kpalimé. Her father opposed the ritual practice: he remembered his sister's screams during the rite and her suffering from a tetanus infection she developed afterwards. Hajia, his wife, recalled the death of her older sister from an infection associated with the rite; this tragedy led Hajia's family to exempt her from cutting, and she, too, opposed the practice for her children. During his lifetime, Muhammed, being wealthy, was able to defy the tribal customs of the Tchamba-Kunsuntu, to which he belonged. Both illiterate themselves, the Kassindjas sent Fauziya to a boarding school in Ghana, so that she could learn English and help her father in his business. Meanwhile, her four older sisters married men of their own choice, genitals intact.

Fauziya's family was thus an anomaly in the region. Rakia Idrissou, the local genital exciser, told a reporter that girls usually have the procedure between the ages of four and seven. If weak, they are held down by four women; if stronger, they require five women, one to sit on their chests and one for each arm and leg. They must be kept still, she said, because if they jerk suddenly the razor blade used for the surgery can cut too deep.

When Fauziya was fifteen, however, her father died. Her mother was summarily turned out of the house by hostile relatives, and an aunt took control of the household, ending Fauziya's education. "We don't want girls to go to school too much," this aunt told a reporter from *The New*

York Times. The family patriarch then arranged for Fauziya to become the fourth wife of an electrician; her prospective husband insisted that she have the genital operation first. To avoid the marriage and the mutilation that would have preceded it, Fauziya decided to leave home; her mother gave her $3,000 of the $3,500 inheritance that was her only sustenance. On her wedding day, Fauziya left her aunt's house, flagged down a taxi, and, with nothing but the clothes on her back, asked the driver to take her across the border into Ghana, some twenty miles away. Once in Ghana, she got on a flight to Germany; with help from people who befriended her there, she got a flight to the United States.

On landing in Newark she confessed that her documents were false and asked for political asylum. After weeks of detention in an unsanitary and oppressive immigration prison, she got legal assistance—again with the help of her mother, who contacted a nephew who was working as a janitor in the Washington area. Scraping together $500, the nephew hired a law student at American University, Ms. Miller Bashir, to handle Fauziya's case. At first, Bashir was unsuccessful and a Philadelphia immigration judge denied Fauziya's request for asylum. Through the determined efforts of activists, journalists, and law faculty at American University, she successfully appealed the denial. The appellate ruling stated that the practice of genital mutilation constitutes persecution and concluded: "It remains particularly true that women have little legal recourse and may face threats to their freedom, threats or acts of physical violence, or social ostracization for refusing to undergo this harmful traditional practice, or attempting to protect their female children."

In recent years, the practice of female genital mutilation has been increasingly in the news, generating a complex debate about cultural norms and the worth of sexual functioning. This chapter attempts to describe and to sort out some aspects of this controversy. First, however, a word about nomenclature. Although discussions sometimes use the terms "female circumcision" and "clitoridectomy," "female genital mutilation" (FGM) is the standard generic term for all these procedures in the medical literature. "Clitoridectomy" standardly designates a subcategory, described shortly. The term "female circumcision" has been rejected by international medical practitioners because it suggests the fallacious analogy to male circumcision, which is generally believed to have either no effect or a positive effect on physical health and sexual functioning. Anatomically, the degree of cutting in the female operations described here is far more extensive. (The male equivalent of the clitoridectomy would be the amputation of most of the penis. The male equivalent of infibulation would be "removal of the entire penis, its roots of soft tissue, and part of the scrotal skin.") This discussion is confined to cases that involve substantial removal of tissue and/or functional impairment; I make no comment on purely symbolic procedures that involve no removal of tissue, and these are not included under the rubric "female genital mutilation" by international agencies that study the prevalence of the procedure.

Three types of genital cutting are commonly practiced: (1) In *clitoridectomy*, a part or the whole of the clitoris is amputated and the bleeding is stopped by pressure or a stitch. (2) In *excision*, both the clitoris and the inner lips are amputated. Bleeding is usually stopped by stitching, but the vagina is not covered. (3) In *infibulation*, the clitoris is removed, some or all of the labia minora are cut off, and incisions are made in the labia majora to create raw surface. These surfaces are either stitched together or held in contact until they heal as a hood of skin that covers the urethra and most of the vagina. Approximately 85% of women who undergo FGM have type 1 or type 2; infibulation, which accounts for only 15% of the total, nonetheless accounts for 80 to 90% of all operations in certain countries, for example, the Sudan, Somalia, and Djibouti.

The practice of female genital mutilation remains extremely common in Africa, although it is illegal, and widely resisted, in most of the countries where it occurs. The World Health Organization estimates that overall, in today's world between 85 and 115 million women have had such operations. In terms of percentages, for example, 93% of women in Mali have undergone genital cutting, 98% in Somalia, 89% of women in the Sudan, 43% in the Central African Republic, 43% in the Ivory Coast, and 12% in Togo. Smaller numbers of operations are now reported from countries such as Australia, Belgium, France, the United Kingdom, and the United States.

Female genital mutilation is linked to extensive and in some cases lifelong health problems. These include infection, hemorrhage, and abscess at the time of the operation; later difficulties in urination and menstruation; stones in the urethra and bladder due to repeated infections; excessive growth of scar tissue at the site, which may become disfiguring; pain during intercourse; infertility (with devastating implications for a woman's other life chances); obstructed labor and damaging rips and tears during childbirth. Complications from infibulation are more severe than those from clitoridectomy and incision; nonetheless, the false perception that clitoridectomy is "safe" frequently leads to the ignoring of complications.

Both in the implicated nations and outside, feminists have organized to demand the abolition of this practice, citing its health risks, its impact on sexual functioning, and the violations of dignity and choice associated with its compulsory and nonconsensual nature. These opponents have been joined by many authorities in their respective nations, both religious and secular. In Egypt, for example, both the Health Minister, Ismail Sallem, and the new head of Al Azhar, the nation's leading Islamic institution, support a ban on the practice. The World Health Organization has advised health professionals not to participate in the practice since 1982 and repeated its strong opposition in 1994; the practice has also been condemned by the U.N. Commission on Human Rights, UNICEF, the World Medication Organization, Minority Rights Group International, and Amnesty International.

At the same time, however, other writers have begun to protest that the criticism of genital mutilation is inappropriate and "ethnocentric," a demonizing of another culture when we have many reasons to find fault with our own. They have also charged that the focus on this problem involves a Western glamorization of sexual pleasure that is inappropriate, especially when we judge other cultures with different moral norms. To encounter such positions we do not need to turn to scholarly debates. We find them in our undergraduate students who are inclined to be ethical relativists on such matters, at least initially, hesitant to make any negative judgment of a culture other than their own. Because it seems important for anyone interested in political change in this area to understand these views in their popular and nonacademic form, I shall illustrate them from student writings I have encountered both in my own teaching and in my research for a book on liberal education, adding some points from the academic debate.

Many students, like some participants in the academic debate, are general cultural relativists, holding that it is always inappropriate to criticize the practices of another culture, and that cultures can appropriately be judged only by their own internal norms. That general position would indeed imply that it is wrong for Westerners to criticize female genital mutilation, but not for any reasons interestingly specific to genital mutilation itself. For that reason, . . . I shall focus here on four criticisms that, while influenced by relativism, stop short of the general relativist thesis:

(1) It is morally wrong to criticize the practices of another culture unless one is prepared to be similarly critical of comparable practices when they occur in one's own culture. (Thus, a typical student reaction is to criticize the "ethnocentrism" of a stance that holds that one's own culture is the benchmark for "the principles and practices that are appropriate for all people.")

(2) It is morally wrong to criticize the practices of another culture unless one's own culture has eradicated all evils of a comparable kind. (Thus, a typical undergraduate paper comments that criticism of genital mutilation is unacceptable "when one considers the domestic problems we are faced with in our own cultures.")

(3) Female genital mutilation is morally on a par with practices of dieting and body shaping in American culture. (I observed quite a few courses in which this comparison played a central role, and the comparison has often been suggested by my own students. In a similar vein, philosopher Yael Tamir writes that "Western conceptions of female beauty encourage women to undergo a wide range of painful medically unnecessary, and potentially damaging processes."

(4) Female genital mutilation involves the loss of a capacity that may not be especially central to the lives in question, and one to which Westerners attach disproportionate significance. Thus "references to clitoridectomy commonly reveal a patronizing attitude toward women, suggesting that they are primarily sexual beings."

These are significant charges, which should be confronted. Feminist argument should not be condescending to women in developing countries who have their own views of what is good. Such condescension is all the more damaging when it comes from women who are reluctant to criticize the flaws in their own culture, for then it is reminiscent of the worst smugness of "white man's burden" colonialism. Our students are surely right to think that withholding one's own judgment until one has listened carefully to the experiences of members of the culture in question is a crucial part of intelligent deliberation. On the other hand, the prevalence of a practice, and the fact that even today many women endorse and perpetuate it, should not be taken as the final word, given that there also are many women in African cultures who struggle against it, and given that those who do perpetuate it may do so in background conditions of intimidation and economic and political inequality. How, then, should we respond to these very common charges?

The first thesis is true, and it is useful to be reminded of it. Americans have all too often criticized other cultures without examining their own cultural shortcomings. It is less clear, however, that lack of self-criticism is a grave problem for Americans on such issues. We find no shortage of criticism of the ideal female body image, or of practices of dieting intended to produce it. Indeed, American feminists would appear to have devoted considerably more attention to these American problems than to genital mutilation, to judge from the success of books such as Naomi Wolf's *The Beauty Myth* and Susan Bordo's *Unbearable Weight*. Indeed, a review of the recent feminist literature suggests the problem may lie in exactly the opposite direction, in an excessive focusing on our own failings. We indulge in moral narcissism when we flagellate ourselves for our own errors while neglecting to attend to the needs of those who ask our help from a distance.

The second thesis is surely false. It is wrong to insist on cleaning up one's own house before responding to urgent calls from outside. Should we have said "Hands off Apartheid," on the grounds that racism persists in the United States? Or, during the Second World War, "Hands off the rescue of the Jews," on the grounds that in the 1930s and 1940s every nation that contained Jews was implicated in anti-Semitic practices? It is and should be difficult to decide how to allocate one's moral effort between local and distant abuses. To work against both is urgently important, and individuals will legitimately make different decisions about their priorities. But the fact that a needy human being happens to live in Togo rather than Idaho does not make her less my fellow, less deserving of my moral commitment. And to fail to recognize the plight of a fellow human being because we are busy moving our own culture to greater moral heights seems the very height of moral obtuseness and parochialism.

We could add that FGM is not as such the practice of a single culture or group of cultures. As recently as in the 1940s, related operations were performed by U.S. and British doctors to treat female "problems" such as masturbation and lesbianism. Nor is there any cultural or religious group in which the practice is universal. As Nahid Toubia puts it, "FGM is an issue that concerns women and men who believe in equality, dignity and fairness to all human beings, regardless of gender, race, religion or ethnic identity. . . . It represents a human tragedy and must not be used to set Africans against non-Africans, one religious group against another, or even women against men."

If the third thesis were true, it might support a decision to give priority to the local in our political action (though not necessarily speech and writing): If two abuses are morally the same and we have better local information about one and are better placed politically to do something about it, that one seems to be a sensible choice to focus on in our actions here and now. But is the third thesis true? Surely not. Let us enumerate the differences.

1. Female genital mutilation is carried out by force, whereas dieting in response to culturally constructed images of beauty is a matter of choice, however seductive the persuasion. Few mothers restrict their children's dietary intake to unhealthy levels in order to make them slim, indeed most mothers of anorexic girls are horrified and deeply grieved by their daughters' condition. By contrast, during

FGM small girls, frequently as young as four or five; are held down by force, often, as in Togo, by a group of adult women, and have no chance to select an alternative. The choices involved in dieting are often not fully autonomous: They may be the product of misinformation and strong social forces that put pressure on women to make choice, sometimes dangerous ones, that they would not make otherwise. We should criticize these pressures and the absence of full autonomy created by them. And yet the distinction between social pressure and physical force should also remain salient, both morally and legally. (Similarly, the line between seduction and rape is difficult to draw; frequently it turns on the elusive distinction between a threat and an offer, and on equally difficult questions about what threatened harms remove consent.) Nonetheless, we should make the distinction as best we can, and recognize that there remain relevant differences between genital mutilation and dieting, as usually practiced in America.

2. Female genital mutilation is irreversible, whereas dieting is, famously, far from irreversible.

3. Female genital mutilation is usually performed in conditions that in and of themselves are dangerous and unsanitary, conditions to which no child should be exposed, dieting is not.

4. Female genital mutilation is linked to extensive and in some cases lifelong health problems, even death. (In Kassindja's region, deaths are rationalized by the folk wisdom that profuse bleeding is a sign that a girl is not a virgin.) Dieting is linked to problems of this gravity only in the extreme cases of anorexia and bulimia, which, even, then, are reversible.

5. Female genital mutilation is usually performed on children far too young to consent even were consent solicited; dieting involves, above all, adolescents and young adults. Even when children are older, consent is not solicited. Typical is the statement of an Ivory Coast father of a twelve-year-old girl about to be cut. "She has no choice," he stated. "I decide. Her viewpoint is not important." His wife, who personally opposes the practice, concurs: "It is up to my husband," she states. "The man makes the decisions about the children."

6. In the United States, as many women as men complete primary education, and more women than men complete secondary education; adult literacy is 99% for both females and males. In Togo, adult female literacy is 32.9% (52% that of men); in the Sudan, 30.6% (56% that of men); is the Ivory Coast, 26.1% (56%); in Burkina Faso, 8% (29%). Illiteracy is an impediment to independence; other impediments are supplied by economic dependence and lack of employment opportunities. These facts suggest limits to the notions of consent and choice, even as applied to the mothers or relatives who perform the operation, who may not be aware of the extent of resistance to the practice in their own and relevantly similar societies. To these limits we may add those imposed by political powerlessness, malnutrition, and intimidation. The wife of the patriarch in Fauziya Kassindja's clan told a reporter that she is opposed to the practice and would have run away like Fauziya had she been able—but nonetheless, she will allow the operation for her infant daughter. "I have to do what my husband says," she concludes. "It is not for women to give an order. I feel what happened to my body. I remember my suffering. But I cannot prevent it for my daughter."

7. Female genital mutilation means the irreversible loss of the capability for a type of sexual functioning that many women value highly, usually at an age when they are far too young to know what value it has or does not have in their own life. In the rare case in which a woman can make the comparison, she usually reports profound regret. Mariam Razak, a neighbor of the Kassindjas, was fifteen when she was cut, with five adult women holding her down. She had had sex with the man who is now her husband prior to that time and found it satisfying. Now, they both say, things are difficult. Mariam

compares the loss to having a terminal illness that lasts a lifetime. "Now," her husband says, "something was lost in that place. . . . I try to make her feel pleasure, but it doesn't work very well."

8. Female genital mutilation is unambiguously linked to customs of male domination. Even its official rationales, in terms of purity and propriety, point to aspects of sex hierarchy. Typical is the statement of Egyptian farmer Said Ibrahim, upset about the government ban: "Am I supposed to stand around while my daughter chases men?" To which Mohammed Ali, age seventeen, added, "Banning it would make women wild like those in America." Sex relations constructed by the practice are relations in which intercourse becomes a vehicle for one-sided male pleasure rather than for mutuality of pleasure.

By contrast, the ideal female body image purveyed in the American media has multiple and complex resonances, including those of male domination, but also including those of physical fitness, independence, and boyish nonmaternity.

These differences help explain why there is no serious campaign to make ads for diet programs, or the pictures of emaciated women in *Vogue,* illegal, whereas FGM is illegal in most of the countries in which it occurs. (In the Sudan, the practice is punishable by up to two years' imprisonment.) Such laws are not well enforced, but their existence is evidence of a widespread movement against the practice in the countries implicated. Women in local regions where the practice is traditional give evidence of acquiescing, insofar as they do, out of intimidation and lack of options; women in adjacent regions where the practice is not traditional typically deplore it, citing health risks, loss of pleasure, and unnecessary suffering.

These differences also explain why Fauziya Kassindja was able to win political asylum. We shall not see similar arguments for political asylum for American women who have been pressured by the culture to be thin—however much it remains appropriate to criticize the norms of female beauty displayed in *Vogue* (as some

advertisers have begun to do), the practices of some mothers, and the many covert pressures that combine to produce eating disorders in our society. Similarly, whereas the prospect of footbinding of the traditional Chinese type (in which the bones of the feet were repeatedly broken and the flesh of the foot became rotten) would, in my view, give grounds for political asylum, the presence of advertisements for high-heeled shoes surely would not, however many problems may be associated with the fashion. Even the publication of articles urging women to undergo FGM should be seen as altogether different from forcing a woman to undergo the procedure.

How, then, is FGM traditionally justified, when it is? In social terms, it is highly likely that FGM emerged as the functional equivalent to the seclusion of women. African women, unlike their counterparts in India, Pakistan, and elsewhere, are major agricultural producers. There is no barrier to women's work outside the home, and indeed the entire organization of agriculture in Africa traditionally rests on the centrality of female labor. In India, women's purity is traditionally guaranteed by seclusion; in Africa, this guarantee was absent, and another form of control emerged. But this functional history clearly does not justify the practice. What arguments are currently available?

It is now generally agreed that there is no religious requirement to perform FGM. The prophet Mohammed's most cited statement about the practice (from a reply to a question during a speech) makes the process nonessential, and the force of his statement seems to have been to discourage extensive cutting in favor of a more symbolic type of operation. The one reference to the operation in the *hadith* classifies it as *a makrama,* or nonessential practice. FGM is not practiced at all in many Islamic countries, including Pakistan, Algeria, Tunisia, Saudia Arabia, Iran, and Iraq. Defenses appealing to morality (FGM keeps women from extramarital sex) have resonance because they connect with the practice's likely original rationale, but they presuppose an unacceptable picture of women as whorish and childish. However sincerely such arguments are addressed, they should not be accepted by people with an interest in women's dignity. Defenses in terms of physical beauty are trickier, because we know how much cultures differ in what they regard as beautiful, but even perceptions of beauty (also at issue in Chinese footbinding) should yield before evidence of impairment of health and sexual functioning. Arguments claiming that without the practice women will not be acceptable to men may state something true in local circumstances (as was also the case with footbinding) and may therefore provide a rationale for individual families to defer to custom as the best of a bad business (although this is less true now than formerly, given the widespread resistance to the practice in most areas where it occurs). Such arguments, however, clearly cannot justify the practice in moral or legal terms; similarly, arguments advising slaves to behave themselves if they do not want to be beaten may give good advice but cannot justify the institution of slavery.

The strongest argument in favor of the practice is an argument that appeals to cultural continuity. Jomo Kenyatta and others have stressed the constitutive role played by such initiation rites in the formation of a community and the disintegrative effect of interference. For this reason, Kenyatta opposed criminalization of the surgery and recommended a more gradual process of education and persuasion. Although one must have some sympathy with these concerns, it is still important to remember that a community is not a mysterious organic unity but a plurality of people standing in different relations of power to one another. It is not obvious that the type of cohesion that is effected by subordination and functional impairment is something we ought to perpetuate. Moreover, sixty years after Kenyatta's ambivalent defense, we see widespread evidence of resistance from within each culture, and there is reason to think that the practice is kept alive above all by the excisers themselves, paramedical workers who enjoy both high income and high prestige in the community from their occupation. These women frequently have the status of priestesses and have great influence over social perceptions. Countries that move against the practice should certainly make provision for the economic security of these women, but this does not mean taking them as

unbiased interpreters of cultural tradition. To the extent that an initiation ritual is still held to be a valuable source of cultural solidarity, such rituals can surely be practiced (as they already are in some places) using a merely symbolic operation that does not remove any tissue.

Let me now turn to the fourth thesis. A secondary theme in recent feminist debates about FGM is skepticism about the human value of sexual functioning. Philosopher Yael Tamir, for example, argues that hedonistic American feminists have ascribed too much value to pleasure. She suggests that it is men, above all, whose interests are being served by this, because female sexual enjoyment in our society is "seen as a measure of the sexual power and achievements of men," and because men find women who do not enjoy sex more intimidating than those who do.

I am prepared to agree with Tamir to this extent: The attention given FGM seems to me somewhat disproportionate, among the many gross abuses the world practices against women: unequal nutrition and health care, lack of the right to assemble and to walk in public, lack of equality under the law, lack of equal access to education, sex-selective infanticide and feticide, domestic violence, marital rape, rape in police custody, and many more. Unlike Tamir, I believe that the primary reason for this focus is not a fascination with sex but the relative tractability of FGM as a practical problem, given the fact that it is already widely resisted and indeed illegal, and given that it is not supported by any religion. How much harder to grapple with women's legal inequality before Islamic courts, their pervasive hunger, their illiteracy, their subjection to battery and violence. But surely Tamir is right that we should not focus on this one abuse while relaxing our determination to make structural changes that will bring women closer to full equality worldwide. And she may also be right to suggest that the fascination with FGM contains at least an element of the sensational or even the prurient.

Tamir, however, does not simply criticize the disproportionate focus on FGM: She offers a more general denigration of the importance of sexual pleasure as an element in human flourishing. This part of her argument is flawed by the failure to make a crucial distinction: that between a function and the capacity to choose that function. Criticizing her opponents for their alleged belief that the capacity for sexual pleasure is a central human good, she writes:

> Nuns take an oath of celibacy, but we do not usually condemn the church for preventing its clergy from enjoying an active sex life. Moreover, most of us do not think that Mother Teresa is leading a worse life than Chichulina, though the latter claims to have experienced an extensive number of orgasms. It is true that nuns are offered spiritual life in exchange for earthly goods, but in the societies where clitoridectomy is performed, the fulfilling life of motherhood and child bearing are offered in exchange. Some may rightly claim that one can function as a wife and a mother while still experiencing sexual pleasures. Others believe that full devotion to God does not require an oath of celibacy. Yet these views are, after all, a matter of convention.

There are a number of oddities in this argument. (It is hard, for example, to know what to make of the assertion that the possibility of combining sexual pleasure with motherhood is a mere "matter of convention.") More centrally, however, Tamir mischaracterizes the debate. No feminist opponent of FGM is saying or implying that celibacy is bad, that nuns all have a starved life, that orgasms are the be-all and end-all of existence. I know of no opponent who would not agree with Tamir's statement that women "are not merely sexual agents, that their ability to lead rich and rewarding lives does not depend solely on the nature of their sex life." But there is a great difference between fasting and starving; just so, there is also a great difference between a vow of celibacy and FGM. Celibacy involves the choice not to exercise a capability to which nuns, insofar as they are orthodox Roman Catholics, ascribe considerable human value. Its active exercise is thought good for all but a few of those humans, and even for them it is the choice not to use a capacity one has (as in the case of fasting) that is deemed morally valuable. (A Catholic should hold that a survivor of FGM cannot achieve the Christian good of celibacy.) FGM, by contrast, involves forgoing altogether the very possibility of sexual functioning—and, as I said, well before one is of an age to make such a choice. We all know that people who are blind or unable to walk

can lead rich and meaningful lives; nonetheless, we would all deplore practices that deliberately disabled people in those respects, nor would we think that critics of those practices are giving walking or seeing undue importance in human life.

Can even the mothers of these girls make an informed choice as to the value of female sexual pleasure? They have been immersed in traditional beliefs about women's impurity; lacking literacy and education, as a large proportion do, they have difficulty seeking out alternative paradigms. As the immigration report points out, their situation is made more difficult by fear and powerlessness. Equally important, their own experience of sexual life cannot have contained orgasmic pleasure if they themselves encountered FGM as girls; even if they did not, they are highly likely to have experienced marriage and sexual life as a series of insults to their dignity, given the ubiquity of domestic violence and marital rape. Should they believe that FGM is a bad thing for their daughters—as a remarkable proportion of the women interviewed in the recent stories clearly do—they have no power to make their choices effective and many incentives to conceal the views they hold. Such facts do not show that women who have had a more fortunate experience of marriage and sexuality are making a mistake when they hold that the capacity for sexual pleasure should be preserved for those who may choose to exercise it. There is certainly something wrong with any social situation in which women are viewed only or primarily as sex objects; but criticizing such perceptions has nothing to do with defending FGM.

Nor does Tamir give us any reason to suppose that the importance of women's sexual pleasure is a mythic construct of the male ego. Many women have reported enjoying sex a good deal, and there is no reason to think them all victims of false consciousness. It is probably true that some men find women who do not enjoy sex more intimidating than those who do, but it would be more than a little perverse to deny oneself pleasure simply in order to intimidate men. Moreover, in the situation we are contemplating in the case of FGM, the operative male fear is surely that of women's sexual agency, which is a sign that the woman is not simply a possession and might even experience pleasure with some one other than her owner. It would be highly implausible to suggest that African women can gain power and intimidate men by undergoing FGM. The attack on FGM is part and parcel of a more general attempt by women to gain control of their sexual capacities; it is thus a relative of attacks on rape, marital rape, sexual harassment, and domestic violence. It is precisely this challenge to traditional male control that many men find threatening.

In the concluding section of her discussion of FGM, Yael Tamir imagines a country called Libidia, where women with unnaturally enlarged clitorises find they cannot do anything else but have sex and therefore seek to remove the clitoris in order to have better lives. In this way she suggests that sexual pleasure undermines other valuable human functions—so one might plausibly deem its removal a helpful thing, rather like a trip to the dentist to get rid of a diseased tooth. She here expresses a Platonic idea about the relation between continence and intellectual creativity that may be true for some individuals at some times but is surely not a universal datum of human experience. Plato did indeed hold in the *Phaedo* that mental life would be much better if the bodily appetites could be put to one side insofar as possible—though even he did not maintain this position with absolute consistency, nor did he suggest genital mutilation as a remedy. Aristotle, on the other hand, held that someone who was insensible to the full range of the bodily pleasures would be "far from being a human being." We do not need to decide which thinker is right—or indeed for which people each of them is right—to decide sensibly that FGM is not like an appendectomy—that it involves the removal of a capability for whose value history and experience have had a great deal to say. Individuals may then choose whether and how to exercise it, just as we also choose whether and how to use our athletic and musical capacities.

Internal criticism is slowly changing the situation in the nations in which FGM has traditionally been practiced. The eighteen-year-old son of the patriarch of the Kassindja family told reporters that he wanted to marry a woman who had not been cut, because teachers in his high school had influenced his thinking. The

patriarch himself now favors making the practice optional, to discourage more runaways who give the family a bad name. The very fact that the age of cutting in Togo has been moving steadily down (from twelve to four), in order (the exciser says) to discourage runaways, gives evidence of mounting resistance to the practice. But many of the women and men in the relevant nations who are struggling against this practice are impoverished or unequal under the law or illiterate or powerless or in fear—and often all of these. There is no doubt that they wish outside aid. There is also no doubt that they encounter local opposition—as is always the case when one moves to change a deeply entrenched custom connected with the structures of power. (As I have suggested, some of the people involved have strong personal economic and status interests in the status quo.) Suzanne Aho, director of Togo's Office for the Protection and Promotion of the Family, explains that she tries to counsel men about women's rights of choice, but she encounters the dead weight of custom. Of the Kassindja patriarch she says: "'You cannot force her,' I told him. He understood, but he said it is a tradition."

These upholders of tradition are eager, often, to brand their internal opponents as Westernizers, colonialists, and any other bad thing that may carry public sentiment. Even so, Fauziya's father was accused of "trying to act like a white man." But this way of deflecting internal criticism should not intimidate outsiders who have reasoned the matter out, at the same time listening to the narratives of women who have been involved in the reality of FGM. The charge of "colonialism" presumably means that the norms of an oppressor group are being unthinkingly assimilated, usually to curry favor with that group. That is not at all what is happening in the case of FGM. In the United Nations, in Human Rights Watch, in many organizations throughout the world, and in countless local villages the issue has been debated. Even the not very progressive Immigration and Naturalization Service (INS) has been swayed by the data it collected. The vigor of internal resistance should give confidence to those outside who work to oppose the practice. Frequently external pressure can assist a relatively powerless internal group that is struggling to achieve change.

In short, international and national officials who have been culpably slow to recognize gender-specific abuses as human rights violations are beginning to get the idea that women's rights are human rights, and that freedom from FGM is among them. Without abandoning a broader concern for the whole list of abuses women suffer at the hands of unjust customs and individuals, we should continue to keep FGM on the list of unacceptable practices that violate women's human rights, and we should be ashamed of ourselves if we do not use whatever privilege and power has come our way to make it disappear forever.

DISCUSSION QUESTIONS

1. Nussbaum rejects the claim that we should "clean up" our "own house before responding to urgent calls from outside." What is her argument? Do you agree with her?

2. Nussbaum claims that both FGM and traditional Chinese footbinding ("the type in which the bones of the feet were repeatedly broken and the flesh of the foot became rotten") "give grounds for political asylum." Do you agree with her? Why or why not?

3. Nussbaum says, "The fact that a needy human being happens to live in Togo rather than Idaho does not make her less my fellow, less deserving of my moral commitment. And to fail to recognize the plight of a fellow human being because we are busy moving our own culture to greater moral heights seems the very height of moral obtuseness and parochialism." Do you agree with her? Why or why not?

4. Some say that FGM is morally on a par with practices of dieting and body shaping in American culture. Nussbaum dismisses this charge. Evaluate her argument.

5. In an essay titled "Women and Cultural Universals," Nussbaum writes, "the contingencies of where one is born, whose power one is afraid of, and what habits shape one's daily thought are chance events that should not be permitted to play the role they now play in pervasively shaping women's life chances. Beneath all these chance events are human powers, powers of choice and intelligent self-formation." Do you agree with Nussbaum? How does her analysis of FGM reflect her beliefs about women and cultural universals? Is the cultural practice of FGM a sufficient grounds upon which to reject completely cultural relativism? Why or why not?

Warrior Marks
[Great Britain 1993] 54 minutes
Directed by Pratibha Parmar

Warrior Marks is a documentary that follows Pulitzer Prize–winning author Alice Walker (see chapter 1, section 1.1) on a trip to Africa to research the practice of female genital mutilation (FGM). Along with director Pratibha Parmar, Walker conducts interviews with native women regarding this practice. We learn that the practice of FGM is found today across parts of Africa and Asia, and even, on a smaller scale, in the United States and Western Europe. Walker speaks with several women from different countries in Africa and Europe to gain insight into their perspectives on the practice. Many of the women still participate in FGM and feel powerless to stop it, but state that if they did have the power to abolish it, they would do so without hesitation. Walker takes the position that FGM is abusive to children and demeaning to women, and she hopes to convince other women across the world to take a stand against it.

DISCUSSION QUESTIONS

1. Awa Thiam, a woman from Senegal and a member of the Commission for the Abolition of Sexual Mutilation, says the following: "When you cut a woman's genitals, sew them up again, then undo them for sex, then sew them up again when the husband is away, only to open them again for her to sleep with her husband, there's no need to explain. It's perfectly clear. You control the woman as you would any object." What might a cultural relativist like Ruth Benedict say about the morality of this practice? Do you agree with the response of the cultural relativist? Why or why not?

2. Aminata Diop, a woman from Mali who was granted asylum in France to escape FGM, says the following: "They asked me to do the excision with the other girls as they do every year. I made an excuse that I was ill because I had already asked how they did the excision. I knew they cut something off and that it was very painful—that some girls were badly traumatized. So I knew how painful it was, and I had a friend whom I loved a lot, and she was excised on a Thursday, and the following Monday, she died. That's when I decided it would never happen to me." Should countries like France and the United States grant asylum for women such as Diop so that they may escape FGM? Why or why not? Consider possible objections to your argument.

3. Walker makes the following comment: "What the woman warrior learns if she is injured as a child before she can even comprehend there is a war going on against her is that you can fight back, even after you are injured. Your wound itself can be your guide." Do you agree with her? Why or why not?

4. In general, should we fight against cultural practices if we find them to be unacceptable or wrong? Why or why not?

5. Walker makes the following comment: "There are people who think that to speak about this is to stick your nose into somebody else's affairs, somebody else's culture. But there is a distinction between torture and culture. And I maintain that culture is not child abuse; it is not battering. I mean these may well be customs, you know. People customarily do these things just as they customarily enslaved people, but slavery is not really a culture." Is Walker right? Can practices such as torture and child abuse never be considered "cultural" or "normal"? If so, how do we separate the unacceptable practices from the acceptable ones? How do we separate torture, for example, from corporal punishment or capital punishment? Does saying that some practices cannot be considered culture even if they are widely accepted amount to a criticism of cultural relativism? Why or why not?

6. Awa Thiam, the Senegalese member of the Commission for the Abolition of Sexual Mutilation, says the following: "Men and women tend to say fighting for women's rights is for the west. It has nothing to do with Africa, the real, traditional, traditionalistic Africa. I think that point of view is wrong. Freedom concerns all human beings. Fighting for universal rights is a universal struggle." Is Thiam right?

4.2   WHAT IS THE ETHICAL THING TO DO?

THE BIBLE

THE TEN COMMANDMENTS AND THE SERMON ON THE MOUNT

The sacred scriptures of Judaism as well as Christianity are referred to by the term "Bible." "Bible" comes from the Greek word *biblia,* which means "the books," and *biblia* is derived from the Phoenician city Byblos, an important source of papyrus documents that contained text from the Bible. While the Bible of Judaism and the Bible of Christianity do not form a single, comprehensive ethical system, their influence over morality, particularly in the Western world, has been enormous. Moreover, few passages from the Bible have been more influential on moral ideals than the Ten Commandments and the Sermon on the Mount.

The Ten Commandments are a group of edicts from God to the chosen people, the Israelites, which are found with slight variations in their entirety twice in the Hebrew Bible (Exodus 20:1–17 and Deuteronomy 5:6–21). The following selection is from Exodus, the second book of the Hebrew Bible. Exodus tells the story of Moses's call by God to rescue his people from oppression in Egypt. In Exodus, Moses brings down from Mount Sinai to the chosen people two tablets of laws written by God. Located in the Hebrew Bible at the beginning of a long section of legal materials, they function as a sort of summary of covenant tradition. Thus, they are not an exhaustive listing of the statutes of the constitutional law of ancient Israel, but rather an enumeration of the statutes believed to be essential for the regulation of community life. Many scholars believe that these laws were intended to be memorized and publicly recited by the chosen people at events dedicated to the national reaffirmation of loyalty to the sovereign God.

The Sermon on the Mount is the first of five discourses of Jesus of Nazareth that are found in the Gospel according to Matthew, which was probably written around 90 C.E. by an unknown Christian. Most scholars believe that the author drew upon the Gospel according to Mark and a collection of sayings of Jesus called "Q." In the Sermon on the Mount, Jesus delivers his discourse as the Son of God, a level of authority greater than that of Moses, the Pharisees,* and the scribes.† The Beatitudes ("Blessed are the . . .") describe a reversal of conditions that will take place in the future and envision a new community composed of disciples of Jesus—the "salt of the earth" and the "light of the world." Jesus teaches that the law has enduring validity and that what distinguishes the lives of the disciples from the lives of others is greater "righteousness," which involves behavior toward others and toward God. This behavior is essentially characterized by love. Furthermore, for the disciples to love as God loves is for them to be perfect. "Be ye therefore perfect," says Jesus, "even as your Father which is in heaven is perfect." Jesus clarifies this a few lines later by saying that we are perfect when we wholeheartedly "doeth the will of my Father."

---

*Along with Sadducees and Essenes, the Pharisees were one of the three prominent societies of Judea at the time of Jesus of Nazareth. "Pharisee" in its Semitic form means "the separated ones." The Pharisees observed the traditions of Judaism down to the smallest detail and were by far the most influential of the three societies of Judea.—Ed.
†The scribes were a class of learned Jewish men who made the systematic study, presentation, and exposition of Jewish law their professional occupation. The scribes developed a complicated system of teaching to protect the sanctity of the law. They opposed Jesus (Mark 2:16) and were also denounced by him (Matthew 23).—Ed.

THE TEN COMMANDMENTS

And God spake all these words, saying,

2 I *am* the LORD thy God, which have brought thee out of the land of Egypt, out of the house of bondage.

3 Thou shalt have no other gods before me.

4 Thou shalt not make unto thee any graven image, or any likeness *of any thing* that *is* in heaven above, or that *is* in the earth beneath, or that *is* in the water under the earth:

5 Thou shalt not bow down thyself to them, nor serve them: for I the LORD thy God *am* a jealous God, visiting the iniquity of the fathers upon the children unto the third and fourth *generation* of them that hate me;

6 And shewing mercy unto thousands of them that love me, and keep my commandments.

7 Thou shalt not take the name of the LORD thy God in vain; for the LORD will not hold him guiltless that taketh his name in vain.

8 Remember the sabbath day, to keep it holy.

9 Six days shalt thou labour, and do all thy work:

10 But the seventh day *is* the sabbath of the LORD thy God: *in it* thou shalt not do any work, thou, nor thy son, nor thy daughter, thy manservant, nor thy maidservant, nor thy cattle, nor thy stranger that *is* within thy gates:

11 For *in* six days the LORD made heaven and earth, the sea, and all that in them *is,* and rested the seventh day: wherefore the LORD blessed the sabbath day, and hallowed it.

12 Honour thy father and thy mother: that thy days may be long upon the land which the LORD thy God giveth thee.

13 Thou shalt not kill.

14 Thou shalt not commit adultery.

15 Thou shalt not steal.

16 Thou shalt not bear false witness against thy neighbour.

17 Thou shalt not covet thy neighbour's house, thou shalt not covet thy neighbour's wife, nor his manservant, nor his maidservant, nor his ox, nor his ass, nor any thing that *is* thy neighbour's.

THE SERMON ON THE MOUNT

And seeing the multitudes, he went up into a mountain: and when he was set, his disciples came unto him:

2 And he opened his mouth, and taught them, saying,

3 Blessed *are* the poor in spirit: for theirs is the kingdom of heaven.

4 Blessed *are* they that mourn: for they shall be comforted.

5 Blessed *are* the meek: for they shall inherit the earth.

6 Blessed *are* they which do hunger and thirst after righteousness: for they shall be filled.

7 Blessed *are* the merciful: for they shall obtain mercy.

8 Blessed *are* the pure in heart: for they shall see God.

9 Blessed *are* the peacemakers: for they shall be called the children of God.

10 Blessed *are* they which are persecuted for righteousness' sake: for theirs is the kingdom of heaven.

11 Blessed are ye, when *men* shall revile you, and persecute *you* and shall say all manner of evil against you falsely, for my sake.

12 Rejoice, and be exceeding glad: for great *is* your reward in heaven: for so persecuted they the prophets which were before you.

13 Ye are the salt of the earth: but if the salt have lost his savour, wherewith shall it be salted? it is thenceforth good for nothing, but to be cast out, and to be trodden under foot of men.

14 Ye are the light of the world. A city that is set on an hill cannot be hid.

15 Neither do men light a candle, and put it under a bushel, but on a candlestick; and it giveth light unto all that are in the house.

16 Let your light so shine before men, that they may see your good works, and glorify your Father which is in heaven.

17 Think not that I am come to destroy the law, or the prophets: I am not come to destroy but to fulfill.

18 For verify I say unto you, Till heaven and earth pass, one jot or one title shall in no wise pass from the law, till all be fulfilled.

19 Whosoever therefore shall break one of these least commandments, and shall teach men so, he shall be called the least in the kingdom of heaven: but whosoever shall do and teach *them,* the same shall be called great in the kingdom of heaven.

20 For I say unto you, That except your righteousness shall exceed *the righteousness* of the scribes and Pharisees, ye shall in no case enter into the kingdom of heaven.

21 Ye have heard that it was said by them of old time, Thou shalt not kill; and whosoever shall kill shall be in danger of the judgment:

22 But I say unto you, That whosoever is angry with his brother without a cause shall be in danger of the judgment: and whosoever shall say to his brother, Rã'-cã, shall be in danger of the council: but whosoever shall say, Thou fool, shall be in danger of hell fire.

23 Therefore if thou bring thy gift to the altar, and there rememberest that thy brother hath aught against thee;

24 Leave there thy gift before the altar, and go thy way; first be reconciled to thy brother, and then come and offer thy gift.

25 Agree with thine adversary quickly, whiles thou art in the way with him; lest at any time the adversary deliver thee to the judge, and the judge deliver thee to the officer, and thou be cast into prison.

26 Verily I say unto thee, Thou shalt by no means come out thence, till thou hast paid the uttermost farthing.

27 Ye have heard that it was said by them of old time, Thou shalt not commit adultery:

28 But I say unto you, That whosoever looketh on a woman to lust after her hath committed adultery with her already in his heart.

29 And if thy right eye offend thee, pluck it out, and cast *it* from thee: for it is profitable for thee that one of thy members should perish, and not *that* thy whole body should be cast into hell.

30 And if thy right hand offend thee, cut it off, and cast *it* from thee: for it is profitable for thee that one of thy members should perish, and not *that* thy whole body should be cast into hell.

31 It hath been said, Whosoever shall put away his wife, let him give her a writing of divorcement:

32 But I say unto you, That whosoever shall put away his wife, saving for the cause of fornication, causeth her to commit adultery: and whosoever shall marry her that is divorced committeth adultery.

33 Again, ye have heard that it hath been said by them of old time, Thou shalt not forswear thyself, but shalt perform unto the Lord thine oaths:

34 But I say unto you, Swear not at all; neither by heaven; for it is God's throne:

35 Nor by the earth; for it is his footstool: neither by Jerusalem; for it is the city of the great King.

36 Neither shalt thou swear by thy head, because thou canst not make one hair white or black.

37 But let your communication be, Yea, yea; Nay, nay: for whatsoever is more than these cometh of evil.

38 Ye have heard that it hath been said, An eye for an eye, and a tooth for a tooth:

39 But I say unto you, That ye resist not evil: but whosoever shall smite thee on thy right cheek, turn to him the other also.

40 And if any man will sue thee at the law, and take away thy coat, let him have *thy* cloak also.

41 And whosoever shall compel thee to go a mile, go with him twain.

42 Give to him that asketh thee, and from him that would borrow of thee turn not thou away.

43 Ye have heard that it hath been said, Thou shalt love thy neighbour, and hate thine enemy.

44 But I say unto you, Love your enemies, bless them that curse you, do good to them that hate you, and pray for them which despitefully use you, and persecute you;

45 That ye may be the children of your Father which is in heaven: for he maketh his sun to rise on the evil and on the good, and sendeth rain on the just and on the unjust.

46 For if ye love them which love you, what reward have ye? do not even the publicans the same?

47 And if ye salute your brethren only, what do ye more *than others?* do not even the publicans so?

48 Be ye therefore perfect, even as your Father which is in heaven is perfect.

Take heed that ye do not your alms before men, to be seen of them: otherwise ye have no reward of your Father which is in heaven.

2 Therefore when thou doest *thine* alms, do not sound a trumpet before thee, as the hypocrites do in the synagogues and in the streets, that they may have glory of men. Verily I say unto you, They have their reward.

3 But when thou doest alms, let not thy left hand know what thy right hand doeth:

4 That thine alms may be in secret: and thy Father which seeth in secret himself shall reward thee openly.

5 And when thou prayest, thou shalt not be as the hypocrites *are:* for they love to pray standing in the synagogues and in the corners of the streets, that they may be seen of men. Verily I say unto you, They have their reward.

6 But thou, when thou prayest, enter into thy closet, and when thou hast shut thy door, pray to thy Father which is in secret; and thy Father which seeth in secret shall reward thee openly.

7 But when ye pray, use not vain repetitions, as the heathen *do:* for they think that they shall be heard for their much speaking.

8 Be not ye therefore like unto them: for your Father knoweth what things ye have need of, before ye ask him.

9 After this manner therefore pray ye: Our Father which art in heaven, Hallowed be thy name.

10 Thy kingdom come. Thy will be done in earth, as *it is* in heaven.

11 Give us this day our daily bread.

12 And forgive us our debts, as we forgive our debtors.

13 And lead us not into temptation, but deliver us from evil: For thine is the kingdom, and the power, and the glory, for ever. Ä-měn.

14 For if ye forgive men their trespasses, your heavenly Father will also forgive you:

15 But if ye forgive not men their trespasses, neither will your Father forgive your trespasses

16 Moreover when ye fast, be not, as the hypocrites, of a sad countenance: for they disfigure their faces, that they may appear unto men to fast. Verily I say unto you, They have their reward.

17 But thou, when thou fastest, anoint thine head, and wash thy face;

18 That thou appear not unto men to fast, but unto thy Father which is in secret: and thy Father, which seeth in secret, shall reward thee openly.

19 Lay not up for yourselves treasures upon earth, where moth and rust doth corrupt, and where thieves break through and steal:

20 But lay up for yourselves treasures in heaven, where neither moth nor rust doth corrupt, and where thieves do not break through nor steal:

21 For where your treasure is, there will your heart be also.

22 The light of the body is the eye: if therefore thine eye be single, thy whole body shall be full of light.

23 But if thine eye be evil, thy whole body shall be full of darkness. If therefore the light that is in thee be darkness, how great *is* that darkness!

24 No man can serve two masters: for either he will hate the one, and love the other; or else he will hold to the one, and despise the other. Ye cannot serve God and mammon.

25 Therefore I say unto you, Take no thought for your life, what ye shall eat, or what ye shall drink; nor yet for your body, what ye shall put on. Is not the life more than meat, and the body than raiment?

26 Behold the fowls of the air: for they sow not, neither do they reap, nor gather into barns; yet your heavenly Father feedeth them. Are ye not much better than they?

27 Which of you by taking thought can add one cubit unto his stature?

28 And why take ye thought for raiment? Consider the lilies of the field, how they grow; they toil not, neither do they spin:

29 And yet I say unto you, That even Solomon in all his glory was not arrayed like one of these.

30 Wherefore, if God so clothe the grass of the field, which today is, and tomorrow is cast into the oven, *shall he* not much more *clothe* you, O ye of little faith?

31 Therefore take no thought, saying, What shall we eat? or, What shall we drink? or, Wherewithal shall we be clothed?

32 (For after all these things do the Gentiles seek:) for your heavenly Father knoweth that ye have need of all these things.

33 But seek ye first the kingdom of God, and his righteousness; and all these things be added unto you.

34 Take therefore no thought for the morrow: for the morrow shall take thought for the things of itself. Sufficient unto the day *is* the evil thereof.

Judge not, that ye be not judged.

2 For with what judgment ye judge, ye shall be judged: and with what measure ye mete, it shall be measured to you again.

3 And why beholdest thou the mote that is in thy brother's eye, but considerest not the beam that is in thine own eye?

4 Or how wilt thou say to thy brother, Let me pull out the mote out of thine eye; and, behold, a beam *is* in thine own eye?

5 Thou hypocrite, first cast out the beam out of thine own eye; and then shalt thou see clearly to cast out the mote out of thy brother's eye.

6 Give not that which is holy unto the dogs, neither cast ye your pearls before swine, lest they trample them under their feet, and turn again and rend you.

7 Ask, and it shall be given you; seek, and ye shall find; knock, and it shall be opened unto you:

8 For every one that asketh receiveth; and he that seeketh findeth; and to him that knocketh it shall be opened.

9 Or what man is there of you, whom if his son ask bread, will he give him a stone?

10 Or if he ask a fish, will he give him a serpent?

11 If ye then, being evil, know how to give good gifts unto your children, how much more shall your Father which is in heaven give good things to them that ask him?

12 Therefore all things whatsoever ye would that men should do to you, do ye even so to them: for this is the law and the prophets.

13 Enter ye in at the strait gate: for wide *is* the gate, and broad *is* the way, that leadeth to destruction, and many there be which go in thereat:

14 Because strait *is* the gate, and narrow *is* the way, which leadeth unto life, and few there be that find it.

15 Beware of false prophets, which come to you in sheep's clothing, but inwardly they are ravening wolves.

16 Ye shall know them by their fruits. Do men gather grapes of thorns, or figs of thistles?

17 Even so every good tree bringeth forth good fruit; but a corrupt tree bringeth forth evil fruit.

18 A good tree cannot bring forth evil fruit, neither *can* a corrupt tree bring forth good fruit.

19 Every tree that bringeth not forth good fruit is hewn down, and cast into the fire.

20 Wherefore by their fruits ye shall know them.

21 Not everyone that saith unto me, Lord, Lord, shall enter into the kingdom of heaven; but he that doeth the will of my Father which is in heaven.

22 Many will say to me in that day, Lord, Lord, have we not prophesied in thy name? and in thy name have cast out devils? and in thy name done many wonderful works?

23 And then will I profess unto them, I never knew you: depart from me, ye that work iniquity.

24 Therefore whosoever heareth these sayings of mine, and doeth them, I will liken him unto a wise man, which built his house upon a rock:

25 And the rain descended, and the floods came, and the winds blew, and beat upon that house; and it fell not: for it was founded upon a rock.

26 And everyone that heareth these sayings of mine, and doeth them not, shall be likened unto a foolish man, which built his house upon the sand:

27 And the rain descended, and the floods came, and the winds blew, and beat upon that house; and it fell: and great was the fall of it.

DISCUSSION QUESTIONS

1. Consider the following passages from the Hebrew Bible: "Thou shalt have no other

gods before me," and "for I the Lord thy God *am* a jealous God, visiting the iniquity of the fathers upon the children unto the third and fourth *generation* of them that hate me." What is the ethical significance of these passages? Are these passages exhorting us to be tolerant or intolerant of other religions? Discuss.

2. "Thou shalt not kill" is one of the Ten Commandments from the Hebrew Bible. Discuss the scope and range of this commandment. Does it apply to cases of self-defense? Family defense? Civil defense? Does it preclude capital punishment?

3. The Sermon on the Mount exhorts us to "Love your enemies, bless them that curse you, do good to them that hate you . . ." Is this moral standard too high? Do you think that Jesus literally wants us to love our enemies, or is something else meant? Discuss.

4. What does Jesus mean when he exhorts his followers to be "perfect"? Is Jesus asking them to be "perfect" by striving to imitate the behavior of God? Is this a helpful way for them to think about their moral lives, or is it asking too much of humans to strive to imitate the moral behavior of God? Discuss.

5. Are the Ten Commandments and/or the Sermon on the Mount a sufficient basis on which to construct a complete ethical system? If so, discuss the general nature and precepts of this system. If not, why not?

6. In 2005, the U.S. Supreme Court made rulings on whether the Ten Commandments should be displayed on government property. Debate the pros and cons of public display of the Ten Commandments on government property.

THE BUDDHA
THE FOUR NOBLE TRUTHS

In this selection, the Buddha explains that right action should be viewed as part of a wider path aimed at the cessation of suffering (*dukkha*)—the central feature of the human condition. Consequently, right action as viewed by the Buddha is a relatively small part of a much broader way of conducting one's life. The four noble truths lay out what it means to live and how individuals should conduct their lives.

The first noble truth is that existence is suffering. All aspects of human existence and experience involve suffering, including the "five aggregates" or components that make up a human being: (1) form—the physical component; (2) feelings—the sensations resultant upon the operation of the senses; (3) perception—the awareness of sensations; (4) mental formations—the emotions and dispositions to act in particular ways with respect to sensations; and (5) consciousness—that which results from the interaction among form, feelings, perception, and mental formations. According to the Buddha, suffering takes many forms and is the most the central aspect of existence. Even material happiness and good health contain within them the seeds of suffering because aging, sickness, and death are inevitable.

The second noble truth is that the cause of suffering is craving (*tanha*). The Buddha believed that craving the transient objects of sight, sound, taste, touch, smell, and the mind (the sixth sense in Buddhism) results in suffering. All of the objects of these senses, which include both physical and mental objects, are impermanent or transient. This includes the "self" as well. Consequently, our desire or craving for these things brings about suffering.

The third noble truth is that the cessation of suffering is attainable. This is accomplished by removing the cause of the suffering.

The fourth noble truth describes the path to the cessation of suffering. The eightfold path includes right view, right thought, right speech, right action, right livelihood, right effort, right mindfulness, and right concentration. The path laid out by the Buddha is a middle way between excessive indulgence in pleasure (hedonism) and excessive denial of pleasure (asceticism). If followed, it leads eventually to the cessation of delusion, ignorance, craving, and the cycle of rebirth (a process which may extend over many lifetimes). It should be noted that the Buddha's eightfold path is similar to Aristotle's "golden mean" (see this chapter).

A biographical note on the Buddha, who died seven years before Socrates was born, and a description of Buddhism and its various schools can be found in chapter 1 (see the Gunasekara reading). The following selection is from the Digha Nikaya (Collection of Long Discourses) of the Buddha.

17. "Again, monks, a monk abides contemplating mind-objects as mind-objects in respect of the Four Noble Truths. How does he do so? Here, a monk knows as it really is: 'This is suffering'; he knows as it really is: 'This is the origin of suffering'; he knows as it really is: 'This is the cessation of suffering'; he knows as it really is: 'This is the way of practice leading to the cessation of suffering.'

18. "And what, monks, is the Noble Truth of Suffering? Birth is suffering, aging is suffering, death is suffering, sorrow, lamentation, pain, sadness and distress are suffering. Being attached to the unloved is suffering, being separated from the loved is suffering, not getting what one wants is suffering. In short, the five aggregates of grasping are suffering. . . .

"And how, monks, in short, are the five aggregates of grasping suffering? They are as follows: the aggregate of grasping that is form, the aggregate of grasping that is feeling, the aggregate of grasping that is perception, the aggregate of grasping that is the mental formations, the aggregate of grasping that is consciousness. These are, in short, the five aggregates of grasping that are suffering. And that, monks, is called the Noble Truth of Suffering.

19. "And what, monks, is the Noble Truth of the Origin of Suffering? It is that craving which gives rise to rebirth, bound up with pleasure and lust, finding fresh delight now here, now there: that is to say sensual craving, craving for existence, and craving for non-existence.

"And where does this craving arise and establish itself? Wherever in the world there is anything agreeable and pleasurable, there this craving arises and establishes itself.

"And what is there in the world that is agreeable and pleasurable? The eye in the world is agreeable and pleasurable, the ear . . . , the nose . . . , the tongue . . . , the body . . . , the mind in the world is agreeable and pleasurable, and there this craving arises and establishes itself. Sights, sounds, smells, tastes, tangibles, mind-objects in the world are agreeable and pleasurable, and there this craving arises and establishes itself.

"The craving for sights, sounds, smells, tastes, tangibles, mind-objects in the world is agreeable and pleasurable, and there this craving arises and establishes itself.

"Thinking of sights, sounds, smells, tastes, tangibles, mind-objects in the world is agreeable and pleasurable, and there this craving arises and establishes itself.

"Pondering on sights, sounds, smells, tastes, tangibles and mind-objects in the world is agreeable and pleasurable, and there this craving arises and establishes itself. And that, monks, is called the Noble Truth of the Origin of Suffering.

20. "And what, monks, is the Noble Truth of the Cessation of Suffering? It is the complete fading-away and extinction of this craving, its forsaking and abandonment, liberation from it, detachment from it. And how does this craving come to be abandoned, how does its cessation come about? . . .

21. "And what, monks, is the Noble Truth of the Way of Practice Leading to the Cessation of Suffering? It is just this Noble Eightfold Path, namely:—Right View, Right Thought; Right Speech, Right Action, Right Livelihood; Right Effort, Right Mindfulness, Right Concentration.

"And what, monks, is Right View? It is, monks, the knowledge of suffering, the knowledge of the origin of suffering, the knowledge of the cessation of suffering, and the knowledge of the way of practice leading to the cessation of suffering. This is called Right View.

"And what, monks, is Right Thought? The thought of renunciation, the thought of non-ill-will, the thought of harmlessness. This, monks, is called Right Thought.

"And what, monks, is Right Speech? Refraining from lying, refraining from slander, refraining from harsh speech, refraining from frivolous speech. This is called Right Speech.

"And what, monks, is Right Action? Refraining from taking life, refraining from taking what is not given, refraining from sexual misconduct. This is called Right Action.

"And what, monks, is Right Livelihood? Here, monks, the Ariyan disciple, having given up wrong livelihood, keeps himself by right livelihood.

"And what, monks, is Right Effort? Here, monks, a monk rouses his will, makes an effort, stirs up energy, exerts his mind and strives to prevent the arising of unarisen evil unwholesome mental states. He rouses his will . . . and strives to overcome evil unwholesome mental states that have arisen. He rouses his will . . . and strives to produce unarisen wholesome mental states. He rouses his will, makes an effort, stirs up energy, exerts his mind and strives to maintain wholesome mental states that have arisen, not to let them fade away, to bring them to greater growth, to the full perfection of development. This is called Right Effort.

"And what, monks, is Right Mindfulness? Here, monks, a monk abides contemplating body as body, ardent, clearly aware and mindful, having put aside hankering and fretting for the world; he abides contemplating feelings as feelings . . . ; he abides contemplating mind as mind . . . ; he abides contemplating mind-objects as mind-objects, ardent, clearly aware and mindful, having put aside hankering and

fretting for the world. This is called Right Mindfulness.

"And what, monks, is Right Concentration? Here, a monk, detached from sense-desires, detached from unwholesome mental states, enters and remains in the first jhāna [altered state of consciousness], which is with thinking and pondering, born of detachment; filled with delight and joy. And with the subsiding of thinking and pondering, by gaining inner tranquillity and oneness of mind, he enters and remains in the second jhāna, which is without thinking and pondering, born of concentration, filled with delight and joy. And with the fading away of delight, remaining imperturbable, mindful and clearly aware, he experiences in himself the joy of which the Noble Ones say: 'Happy is he who dwells with equanimity and mindfulness,' he enters the third jhāna. And, having given up pleasure and pain, and with the disappearance of former gladness and sadness, he enters and remains in the fourth jhāna, which is beyond pleasure and pain, and purified by equanimity and mindfulness. This is called Right Concentration. And that, monks, is called the way of practice leading to the cessation of suffering."

DISCUSSION QUESTIONS

1. The Buddha says that life means suffering (the first noble truth). What does he mean by this? Do you agree with him? Why or why not? What suffering can you identify in your own life?

2. The second noble truth tells us that suffering originates in craving or desire. What does the Buddha mean by this? What would your life be like if you did not crave or desire anything? Do you think it would be free from suffering?

3. The path to cessation from suffering is the fourth noble truth. It is also called "the eightfold path" and the "middle way." Discuss each of the eight elements of the path. Do you believe that following such a path will lead to the cessation of suffering? Why or why not?

4. Compare the approaches to conduct in the Bible to those stated by the Buddha. What are their similarities and differences regarding our reasons or motivations to act right?

5. The four noble truths are the Buddha's notion of a good life. Compare the Buddha's notion of a good life with your own. Discuss the strengths and weaknesses of each.

The Good Girl
[USA 2002] 1 hour, 34 minutes
Directed by Miguel Arteta

Justine "Teeny" Last (Jennifer Aniston) is a cosmetics counter clerk at the Retail Rodeo discount store. She is thirty years old and dissatisfied with her marriage to Phil (John C. Reilly), with whom she has been trying to start a family for years. Justine views her life as boring and empty until she meets Tom Worther (Jake Gyllenhaal), a quirky new cashier who prefers to be called Holden after the hero in J. D. Salinger's novel *The Catcher in the Rye*. Justine and Holden have a brief and passionate affair; however, Justine underestimates the depths of Holden's emotional and psychological troubles. By the time she comes to understand Holden's problems, it is too late: Holden has fallen obsessively in love with her, and she is pregnant with his child.

Desperate to escape the affair, Justine informs Holden's parents of his bizarre behavior. Later, when Holden concocts a plan for the lovers to run away and robs the Retail Rodeo safe of $15,000, Justine chooses to turn him in rather than run off with him. Holden takes his own life as police swarm his motel room. Phil is excited about Justine's pregnancy because he thinks he is the father, but he becomes distraught when he learns that Justine has had an affair. Justine cannot bring herself to tell Phil the truth about the baby or the affair, sinking further into a world of deception and lies.

DISCUSSION QUESTIONS

1. What, according to the Bible, is a good person? According to the Bible, would Justine be a good person? Why or why not?

2. Consider the following exchange between Justine, and one of her coworkers, a security guard named Corny (Mike White):

    CORNY   "You got any interest in reading the Bible?"

    JUSTINE   "I have my own, you know, beliefs."

    CORNY   "Well, we don't preach fire and brimstone. Ten Commandments, gotta live by those. Other than the usual ways, we're not interested in scaring people. We're about loving Jesus."

> JUSTINE   "Mm-hmm. Yeah, I kind of like my nights to myself."
>
> CORNY   "Well, maybe you'll have night after night of eternal hellfire all to yourself. Just kidding you. Drive safe. Bye-bye."

Shortly after Justine's refusal, her attempt to bring meaning into her life falls apart: she commits adultery and begins to lie. Clearly, Justine needs something to fill the void in her life, but she chooses Holden instead of the Bible. Is this film a warning about false paths to the good life or a better life? Why or why not? Would the film have been different if she had joined the Bible study group early on rather than going with Holden? Discuss.

3.   At the opening of the film, Justine says to herself, "As a girl, you see the world like a giant candy store filled with sweet candy and such. But one day you look around and see a prison, and you're on death row. You wanna run, or scream, or cry, but somethin's lockin' you up. Are the other folks cows chewin' cud till the hour come when their heads roll? Or are they just keepin' quiet like you, plannin' their escape?" According to the Buddha, what is the "prison" that Justine sees around her? What is it that is "locking her up"?

4.   Consider the following dialogue between Justine and Holden/Tom:

> JUSTINE   "What are your folks like?"
>
> HOLDEN/TOM   "They're OK. They don't get me. I mean, they're alright, they're just . . ."
>
> JUSTINE   "My husband doesn't get me."
>
> HOLDEN/TOM   "Since when do you have a husband?"
>
> JUSTINE   "Since seven years. He's a painter."
>
> HOLDEN/TOM   "What does he paint?"
>
> JUSTINE   "Houses. He's a pig. He talks, but he doesn't think. I'm sick of it. Did you go to college?"
>
> HOLDEN/TOM   "Oh, I had to drop out 'cause I had a problem with drinkin' and stuff, but I'll go back. I just gotta prove to my folks that I can fly straight. Did you go to college?"
>
> JUSTINE   "I was afraid I'd lose Phil if I went. Now it'd be reason enough to go. I was looking at you in the store, and I liked how you kept to yourself. I saw in your eyes that you hate the world. I hate it too. You know what I'm talking about?"

Why do Justine and Holden hate the world? What is the cause of their hatred? What might a Buddhist say is the cause of Justine and Holden's hatred for the world and belief that they are misunderstood? What might a proponent of the Bible say?

5.   Justine says to herself, "After livin' in the dark for so long, a glimpse of the light can make you giddy. Strange thoughts come into your head, and you'd better think 'em. Has a special fate been callin' you, and you're not listenin'? Is there a secret message right in front of you, and you're not readin' it? Is this your last best chance? Are you gonna take it? Or are you goin' to the grave with unlived lives in your veins?" What is the "light" that Justine has glimpsed? How is the light that she has glimpsed

different from the light that a Buddhist glimpses or a proponent of the Bible glimpses? Do you think Justine glimpsed or put her trust in the wrong light? Why or why not?

6. Shortly after her coworker Gwen Jackson (Deborah Rush) dies of food poisoning, Justine says to herself, "All of my thoughts turned to death. I thought of Gwen's body rottin' away. I thought about what a nice person she was, so full of life and good will. If there is a heaven, Gwen would be there givin' makeovers and offerin' up helpful advice. I thought if I died today what would happen to me, a hateful girl, a selfish girl, an adulteress, a liar. . . ." Why does Justine call herself a "selfish girl"? Is she selfish? Moreover, Justine has broken a number of the Ten Commandments, and she fears that if she does not change her ways, she will not gain entrance into heaven. Is acting morally simply in order to get into heaven a selfish act? Why or why not?

7. Phil's best friend, Bubba (Tim Blake Nelson), says to Justine that he will not tell Phil about her adulterous actions if she agrees to have sex with him. Discuss Bubba's reasoning. Is Bubba doing the right thing? Is this the way one should act toward a best friend? Compare Bubba's idea of friendship with that developed in the Koran and by Confucius (see below).

8. Consider this exchange between Justine and Holden/Tom:

HOLDEN/TOM   "I'll kill him. I'll murder him in his sleep. I'll kill my parents. I'll steal money. Whatever it takes, you just . . . just whatever you want, just as long as it's you and me. Please don't forsake me, Justine."

JUSTINE   "OK. Alright. I won't, I promise. I won't, I promise, OK? . . . *I realized then that Holden was at best a child and at worst a demon. If I was ever gonna go straight, I'd have to ditch him. Sometimes to get back on the road to redemption, you have to make a few pit stops.*"

Is Justine right? Is ditching Holden the right way to get back "on the road to redemption"? Compare your response to one grounded in the Bible and one grounded in the teachings of the Buddha.

9. Justine says the following to Holden's parents: "I'm worried about Holden . . . Tom. I'm worried about Tom. I just befriended Tom recently and now, well, I think he's mentally ill. He's got this idea in his head that we've had some sort of affair, which is crazy 'cause I'm . . . I'm married. And he's been sayin' all sorts of strange things and makin' threats and drinkin', and . . . and I just think he would be better off some place where people, professionals, could take care of him. Otherwise, he's gonna get himself into trouble." Was Justine morally justified in lying to Holden's parents even if the end was to save her marriage and to rescue Holden? Why or why not?

10. Justine lays out the following dilemma to herself at the end of the film: "How it all came down to this, only the devil knows. Retail Rodeo was at the corner on my left; the motel was down the road to my right. I closed my eyes and tried to peer into the future. On my left I saw days upon days of lipstick and tickin' clocks, dirty looks and quiet whisperings, and burning secrets that just won't ever die away. And on my right what could I picture? The blue sky, the desert earth stretching out into the eerie infinity, a beautiful, never-ending nothing." In the end, Justine decides to go back to her job and her husband, rather than follow Holden. Did she make the right decision? Why or why not?

11. When Justine tells Jack Field (John Carroll Lynch), the manager of Retail Rodeo, that Holden will be at the Hotel Glen Capri until noon, he responds to Justine, "You've done good. You're a good girl."

The effort of the police to remove Holden from the hotel room ends with his death. Is her boss right? Did she do the right thing? Is she a good girl? Discuss.

12. Consider the following conversation between Justine and Holden/Tom:

JUSTINE   "I'm pregnant, Holden."

HOLDEN/TOM   "It's my baby."

JUSTINE   "Not necessarily."

HOLDEN/TOM   "Yes, it is. You know it is."

JUSTINE   "Even if it is, you cannot raise a baby on the run."

HOLDEN/TOM   "Yes, you can. I mean, you can't raise a baby here, you know that. Justine, you hate your husband, you hate your job, you love me, let's go . . . Justine, what do you have to lose?"

Is Holden right? Why or why not? What guidance does the Bible give in this situation as to the right thing to do?

13. Consider this conversation between Phil and Justine:

PHIL   "Oh God, please don't tell me it's not my baby."

JUSTINE   "It's your baby."

PHIL   "Are you sure?"

JUSTINE   "It is. It is—I swear, I swear to God."

PHIL   "Who was he?"

JUSTINE   "That doesn't matter."

PHIL   "Yeah, it does. Was it someone from work? Yeah, I know who it was. It was that Bible study guy, wasn't it? At the Nazarene that's why you acted so spooked."

JUSTINE   "Yeah, it was him."

PHIL   "I wanna beat his ass."

JUSTINE   "Phil, don't . . . I'm sorry, Phil."

PHIL   "I need to get stoned."

JUSTINE   "OK. Get stoned."

PHIL   "I just gotta escape, you know?"

JUSTINE   "Yeah."

PHIL   "Do you ever feel like that? Like you gotta escape?"

JUSTINE   "Yeah, yeah, I do."

At the close of the film, Justine lies again to her husband, telling him that the baby is his and refusing to name Holden as the father. As a result, the "Bible study guy" gets badly beaten up by Phil and Bubba. Did Justine do the right thing in lying to her husband? Why did she do it? Discuss.

14. The film ends with Justine and Phil playing with their baby in their bed. If you were the writer of this film, is this the way you would have ended it? Also, flash forward five years. What do you think Justine and Phil's lives are like? Why?

CONFUCIUS

VIRTUE AND CHARACTER DEVELOPMENT

I n *The Analects*, Confucius's main concerns are reforming man and society. He lived in a time of social and political chaos, and his writings aimed at rectifying this situation. Confucius believed that the way to reform society is to reform the individual and that if order is established in the lives of individuals and their families, this order will also be manifested in the state. He held that the well-ordered society should be ruled by virtuous men of exemplary character who are selected (up to but not including the king) by merit, not by heredity or military force. Rather than through law and punishment, these rulers would bring about social order and ensure the welfare of the public through moral persuasion and personal example.

Confucius held that the well-ordered society is characterized by harmonious social relations, which are established through *li*. "Rules of proper behavior," "custom," "etiquette," "ceremony," "worship," "propriety," and "ritual" are all words used to translate this central concept in Confucian philosophy. Confucius believed that *li* is the way of good taste, which is not merely an external show of polished manners. *Li* involves keeping rites and ceremonies, carrying out the function's of one's position in life, and preserving the five cardinal relations: (1) sovereign and subject, (2) father and son (filial piety), (3) elder and younger brother, (4) husband and wife, and (5) friend and friend (friendship). For Confucius, the "superior man" maintains his way on the path of good taste through a strong and sincere sense of *li* and, in doing so, develops the proper character. In addition to propriety (*li*), music, poetry, and rightness (*yi*) are integral to character development. *Yi*, translated as "righteousness," "morals," "rightness," "duty," or "morality," is of central importance to both character development and the well-ordered society. Confucius tells us "not to do to others as you would not wish done to yourself" (12.2)—a (negative) form of the "Golden Rule" similar to that of Judaism and Christianity, though articulated long before both. However, as used by Confucius, the meaning of *yi* is much broader than merely "morality." It involves anything that is appropriate to do in any given situation—political, social, religious, and aesthetic.

Confucius also encourages us to develop our *jen*, a term that has variously been translated as "benevolence," "humanity," and "goodness." While *jen* involves propriety, righteousness, love of fellow men, respect, sincerity, loyalty, liberality, truthfulness, diligence, generosity, and mental cultivation, it is not these virtues in particular. Rather, *jen* is a general virtue: the foundation of all particular virtues. *Jen* is moral character, which is developed in ourselves and in our relations with others. It is something we cultivate through our aesthetic, moral, cognitive, and spiritual sensibilities. According to Confucius, while we may be good by nature, our societal practices have brought each of us to varying states far from our natural goodness. Thus, we must work to develop our *jen*, and in doing so, we are following the *tao*, which may be translated simply as "the way." In following the *tao*, we can become a "superior man" in ourself and in our relationship to both society and to "Heaven."

Even though Confucius's work is primarily focused on this life and society, heaven plays a role in his thought. However, it is used in two distinct senses: one sense of heaven is *ming*, which means "destiny," and has to do with the bringing about of what comes to pass; the second sense is *t'ien ming*, which is a kind of moral imperative to which one must relate one's life. The first sense of Heaven (*ming*) is used quite often by Confucius, and can be best seen in the line "Death and life have their determined appointment; riches and honours depend upon Heaven" (12.5). Here heaven clearly means destiny. The second sense of heaven (*t'ien ming*) is used only twice in *The Analects* (2.4 and 16.8), though it was frequently employed prior to Confucius. The superior man "stands in awe of the ordinances of Heaven" (16.8), says Confucius. Here "the ordinances of Heaven" concern what we ought to do, and it becomes our duty as superior people to live up to them.

Confucius (551–479 B.C.E.), is the most influential philosopher in Chinese history—if not, arguably, history period. His actual name is K'ung Ch'iu though he is called K'ung-tzu (Master K'ung), Tzu (Master), or Fu-zu (Venerable Master) by those respectful to him. Confucius is the latinized form of K'ung Fu-tzu (Venerable Master K'ung). Confucius was the descendant of a noble family, but he grew up poor. He was the first professional teacher in Chinese history. Over a century before Plato opened his Academy in Athens to train men for Athenian political life, Confucius established a school to train political leaders. After years of study with Confucius, his graduates received administrative positions in China.

From 502 to 492, Confucius worked as a government official in the state of Lü. The post did not involve much responsibility and was central to Confucius's decision to leave Lü in order to impress on other political leaders the merits of his social and political philosophy. He traveled for the next thirteen years with some of his students through nine states, though he was unable to convince their rulers. At the age of sixty-eight, he returned to Lü at the request of his students, who were now highly placed in its government. While Confucius's philosophy was influential in his own day, it was not until the second century B.C.E. that Confucianism became the dominant philosophy in China. His sayings are collected in the *Lun Yü*, called *The Analects*, which were compiled over a long period after his death. Following is a selection from them.

(1.1) 1. The Master said, "Is it not pleasant to learn with a constant perseverance and application?
2. "Is it not delightful to have friends coming from distant quarters?"
3. "Is he not a man of complete virtue, who feels no discomposure though men take no note of him?"

(1.2) 1. The philosopher Yû said, "They are few who, being filial and fraternal, are fond of offending against their superiors. There have been none, who, not liking to offend against their superiors, have been fond of stirring up confusion.
2. "The superior man bends his attention to what is radical. That being established, all practical courses naturally grow up. Filial piety and fraternal submission!—are they not the root of all benevolent actions?"

(1.3) 1. The Master said, "Fine words and an insinuating appearance are seldom associated with true virtue."

(1.4) The philosopher Tsăng said, "I daily examine myself on three points:—whether, in transacting business for others, I may have been not faithful;—whether, in intercourse with friends, I may have been not sincere;—whether I may have not mastered and practiced the instructions of my teacher."

(1.8) 1. The Master said, "If the scholar be not grave, he will not call forth any veneration, and his learning will not be solid.
2. "Hold faithfulness and sincerity as first principles."
3. "Have no friends not equal to yourself."
4. "When you have faults, do not fear to abandon them."

(1.12) 1. The philosopher Yû said, "In practicing the rules of propriety, a natural ease is to be prized. In the ways prescribed by the ancient kings, this is the excellent quality, and in things small and great we follow them.
2. "Yet it is not to be observed in all cases. If one, knowing *how* such ease *should be prized* manifests it, without regulating it by the rules of propriety, this likewise is not to be done."

(2.3) 1. The Master said, "If the people be led by laws, and uniformity sought to be given them by punishments, they will try to avoid *the punishment* but have no sense of shame.
2. "If they be led by virtue, and uniformity sought to be given them by the rules of propriety, they will have the sense of shame, and moreover will become good."

(2.4) 1. The Master said, "At fifteen, I had my mind bent on learning.
2. "At thirty, I stood firm.
3. "At forty, I had no doubts.
4. "At fifty, I knew the decrees of Heaven.
5. "At sixty, my ear was an obedient organ *for the reception of truth.*
6. "At seventy, I could follow what my heart desired, without transgressing what was right.

(2.10) 1. The Master said; "See what a man does.
2. "Mark his motives.
3. "Examine in what things he rests.
4. "How can a man conceal his character?
5. "How can a man conceal his character?"

(2.14) The Master said, "The superior man is catholic and no partisan. The mean man is a partisan but not catholic."

(2.20) Chî K'ang asked how to cause the people to reverence *their ruler,* to be faithful to him, and to go on to nerve themselves to virtue. The Master said, "Let them be filial and kind to all;—then they will be faithful to him. Let him advance the good and teach the incompetent;—then they will eagerly seek to be virtuous."

(3.3) The Master said, "If a man be without the virtues proper to humanity, what has he to do with the rites of propriety? If a man be without the virtues proper to humanity, what has he to do with music?"

(4.3) The Master said, "It is only the (*truly*) virtuous man, who can love, or who can hate others."

(4.4) The Master said, "If the will be set on virtue, there will be no practice of wickedness."

(4.5) 1. The Master said, "Riches and honors are what men desire. If it cannot be obtained in the proper way, they should not be held. Poverty and meanness are what men dislike. If it cannot be obtained in the proper way, they should not be avoided.
2. "If a superior man abandon virtue, how can he fulfill the requirements of that name?
3. "The superior man does not, even for the space of a single meal, act contrary to virtue. In moments of haste, he cleaves to it. In seasons of danger, he cleaves to it."

(4.6) 1. The Master said, "I have not seen a person who loved virtue, or one who hated what was not virtuous. He who loved virtue, would esteem nothing above it. He who hated what is not virtuous, would practice virtue in such a way that he would not allow anything that is not virtuous to approach his person.
2. "Is anyone able for one day to apply his strength to virtue? I have not seen the case in which his strength would be insufficient.
3. "Should there possibly be any such case, I have not seen it."

(4.8) The Master said, "If a man in the morning hear the right way, he may die in the evening without regret."

(4.11) The Master said, "The superior man thinks of virtue; the small man thinks of comfort. The superior man thinks of the sanction of law; the small man thinks of favours *which he may receive.*"

(4.12) The Master said, "He who acts with a constant view to his own advantage will be much murmured against."

(4.15) 1. The Master said, "Tsăng , my doctrine is that of an all-pervading unity." The disciple Tsăng replied, "Yes."
2. The Master went out, and the *other* disciples asked, saying, "What do his words mean?" Tsăng said, "The doctrine of our master is to be true to the principles of our nature and the benevolent exercise of them to others,—this and nothing more."

(5.15) The Master said of Tsze-ch'an that he had four of the characteristics of a superior man:—in his conduct of himself, he was humble; in serving his superiors, he was respectful; in nourishing the people, he was kind; in ordering the people, he was just."

(5.16) The Master said, "Yen P'ing knew well how to maintain friendly intercourse. The acquaintance might be long, but he showed the *same* respect *as at first.*"

(5.19) Chî Wăn thought thrice, and then acted. When the Master was informed of it, he said, "Twice may do."

(6.12) Tsze-yû being governor of Wû-ch'ăng, the Master said to him, "Have you got *good* men *there*?" He answered, "There is Tan-t'âi Mieh-ming, who never in walking takes a short cut, and never comes to my office, excepting on public business."

(6.20) Fan Chi'ih asked what constituted wisdom. The Master said," To gives one's self earnestly to the duties due to men, and, while respecting spiritual beings, to keep aloof from them, may be called wisdom." He asked about perfect virtue. The Master said, "The man of virtue makes the difficulty *to be overcome* his first business, and success only a subsequent consideration;—this may be called perfect virtue."

(6.28) 1. Tsze-kung said, "Suppose the case of a man extensively conferring benefits on the people, and able to assist all, what would you say of him? Might he be called perfectly virtuous?" The Master said, "Why speak only of virtue in connection with him? Must he not have the qualities of a sage? Even Yâo and Shun were still solicitous about this.
2. "Now the man of perfect virtue, wishing to be established himself, seeks also to establish others; wishing to be enlarged himself, he seeks also to enlarge others.
3. "To be able to judge *of others* by what is nigh *in ourselves*;—this may be called the art of virtue."

(7.3) The Master said, "The leaving virtue without proper cultivation; the not thoroughly discussing what is learned; not being able to move towards righteousness of which a knowledge is gained; and not being able to change what is not good:— these are the things which occasion me solicitude."

(7.6) 1. The Master said, "Let the will be set on the path of duty.
2. "Let every attainment in what is good be firmly grasped.
3. "Let perfect virtue be accorded with.
4. "Let relaxation and enjoyment be found in the polite arts."

(7.23) The Master said, "Do you think, my disciples, that I have any concealments? I conceal nothing from you. There is nothing which I do that is not shown to you, my disciples;—that is my way."

(7.27) The Master said, "There may be those who act without knowing why. I do not do so. Hearing much and selecting what is good and following it; seeing much and keeping it in memory:—this is the second style of knowledge.

(7.33) The Master said, "The sage and the man of perfect virtue;—how dare I *rank myself with them*? It may simply be said of me, that I strive to become such without satiety, and teach others without weariness." Kung-hsî Hwâ, said, "This is just what we, the disciples, cannot imitate you in."

(8.2) 1. The Master said, "Respectfulness, without the rules of propriety, becomes laborious bustle; carefulness, without the rules of propriety, becomes timidity; boldness, without the rules of propriety, becomes insubordination; straight-forwardness, without the rules of propriety, becomes rudeness.

2. "When those who are in high stations perform well all their duties to their relations, the people around them are aroused to virtue. When old friends are not neglected by them, the people are preserved from meanness."

(9.28) The Master said, "The wise are free from perplexities; the virtuous from anxiety; and the bold from fear."

(11.20) The Master said, "If, because a man's discourse appears solid and sincere, we allow him *to be a good man*, is he *really* a superior man? or is his gravity only in appearance ?"

(12.1) 1. Yen Yüan asked about perfect virtue. The Master said, "To subdue one's self and return to propriety, is perfect virtue. If a man can for one day subdue himself and return to propriety, all under heaven will ascribe perfect virtue to him. Is the practice of perfect virtue from a man himself, or is it from others?"

2. Yen Yüan said, "I beg to ask the steps of that process." The Master replied, "Look not at what is contrary to propriety; listen not to what is contrary to propriety; speak not what is contrary to propriety; make no movement which is contrary to propriety." Yen Yüan *then* said, "Though I am deficient in intelligence and vigor, I will make it my business to practice this lesson."

(12.2) Chung-kung asked about perfect virtue. The Master said, "*It is*, when you go abroad, *to behave to every one* as if you were receiving a great guest; to employ the people as if you were assisting at a great sacrifice; not to do to others as you would not wish done to yourself; to have no murmuring against you in the country, and none in the family." Chung-kung said, "Though I am deficient in intelligence and vigor, I will make it my business to practice this lesson."

(12.3) 1. Sze-mâ Niû asked about perfect virtue.
2. The Master said, "The man of perfect virtue is cautious and slow in his speech."
3. "Cautious and slow in his speech!" said Niû;—"Is this what is meant by perfect virtue?" The Master said, "When a man feels the difficulty of doing, can he be other than cautious and slow in speaking?"

(12.4) 1. Sze-mâ Niû asked about the superior man. The Master said, "The superior man has neither anxiety nor fear."
2. "Being without anxiety or fear!" said Niû;—"Does this constitute what we call the superior man?"
3. The Master said, "When internal examination discovers nothing wrong, what is there to be anxious about, what is there to fear?"

(12.5) 1. Sze-mâ Niû full of anxiety, said, "*Other* men all have their brothers, I only have not."
2. Tsze-hisâ said to him, "There is the following saying which I have heard:—
3. "'Death and life have their determined appointment; riches and honours depend upon Heaven.'
4. "Let the superior man never fail reverentially to order his own conduct, and let him be respectful to others and observant of propriety:—then all within the four seas will be his brothers. What has the superior man to do with being distressed because he has no brothers?"

(12.6) The Master said, "The superior man *seeks to* perfect the admirable qualities of men, and does not *seek to* perfect their bad qualities. The mean man does the opposite of this."

(12.22) 1. Fan Ch'ih asked about benevolence. The Master said, "It is to love *all* men." He asked about knowledge. The Master said, "It is to know *all* men."
2. Fan Ch'ih did not immediately understand *these answers*.
3. The Master said, "Employ the upright and put aside all the crooked; in this way the crooked can be made to be upright."
4. Fan Ch'ih retired, and, seeing Tsze-hisâ, he said to him, "A little while ago, I had an interview with our Master, and asked him about knowledge. He said, 'Employ the upright, and put aside all the crooked;—in this way, the crooked will be made to be upright.' What did he mean?"
5. Tsze-hsiâ said, "Truly rich is his saying!
6. "Shun, being in possession of the kingdom, selected from among all the people, and employed Kâo-yâo, on which all who were devoid of virtue disappeared. T'ang, being in possession of the kingdom, selected from among all the people, and employed I Yin, and all who were devoid of virtue disappeared."

(12.23) Tsze-kung asked about friendship. The Master said, "Faithfully admonish *your friend*, and skilfully lead him on. If you find him impracticable, stop. Do not disgrace yourself."

(12.24) The philosopher Tsăng said, "The superior man on grounds of culture meets with his friends, and by their friendship helps his virtue,"

(13.19) Fan Ch'ih asked about perfect virtue. The Master said, "It is, in retirement, to be sedately grave; in the management of business, to be reverently attentive; in intercourse with others, to be strictly sincere. Though a man go among rude, uncultivated tribes, these *qualities* may not be neglected."

(14.7) The Master said, "Superior men, and yet not *always* virtuous, there have been, alas! But there never has been a mean man, and, *at the same time* virtuous."

(14.30) 1. The Master said, "The way of the superior man is threefold, but I am not equal to it. Virtuous, he is free from anxieties; wise, he is free from perplexities; bold, he is free from fear.
2. Tsze-kung said, "Master, that is what you yourself say."

(15.3) The Master said, "Yû, those who know virtue are few."

(15.8) The Master said, "The determined scholar and the man of virtue will not seek to live at the expense of injuring their virtue. They will even sacrifice their lives to preserve their virtue complete."

(15.9) Tsze-kung asked about the practice of virtue. The Master said, "The mechanic, who wishes to do his work well, must first sharpen his tools. When you are living in any state, take service with the most worthy among its great officers, and make friends of the most virtuous among its scholars."

(15.17) The Master said, "The superior man *in everything* considers righteous to be essential. He performs it according to the rules of propriety. He brings it forth in humility. He completes it with sincerity. He is indeed a superior man."

(15.34) The Master said, "Virtue is more to man than either water or fire. I have seen men die from

treading on water and fire, but I have never seen a man die from treading the course of virtue."

(16.4) Confucius said, "There are three friendships which are advantageous, and three which are injurious. Friendships with the upright; friendship with the sincere; and friendship with the man of much observation:—these are advantageous. Friendship with the man of specious airs; friendship with the insinuatingly soft; and friendship with the glib-tongued: these are injurious."

(16.7) Confucius said, "There are three things which the superior man guards against. In youth, when the physical powers are not yet settled, he guards against lust. When he is strong and the physical powers are full of vigor, he guards against quarrelsomeness. When he is old, and the animal powers are decayed, he guards against covetousness."

(16.8) 1. Confucius said, "There are three things of which the superior man stands in awe. He stands in awe of the ordinances of Heaven. He stands in awe of great men. He stands in awe of the words of sages."

(16.10) Confucius said, "The superior man has nine things which are subjects with him of thoughtful consideration. In regard to the use of his eyes, he is anxious to see clearly. In regard to the use of his ears, he is anxious to hear distinctly. In regard to his countenance, he is anxious that it should be benign. In regard to his demeanor, he is anxious that it should be respectful. In regard to his speech, he is anxious that it should be sincere. In regard to his doing of business, he is anxious that it should be reverently careful. In regard to what he doubts about, he is anxious to question others. When he is angry, he thinks of the difficulties (*his anger may involve him in*). When he sees gain to be got, he thinks of righteousness."

(17.6) Tsze-chang asked Confucius about perfect virtue. Confucius said, "To be able to practice five things everywhere under heaven constitutes perfect virtue." He begged to ask what they were, and was told, "Gravity, generosity *of soul*, sincerity, earnestness, and kindness. If you are grave, you will not be treated with disrespect. If you are generous, you will win all. If you are sincere, people will repose trust in you. If you are earnest, you will accomplish much. If you are kind, this will enable you to employ services of others."

(17.24) 1. Tsze-kung said, "Has the superior man his hatreds also?" The Master said, "He has his hatreds. He hates those who proclaim the evil of others. He hates the man who, being of low station, slanders his superiors. He hates those who have valour *merely*, and are unobservant of propriety. He hates those who are forward and determined, and, *at same time*, of contracted understanding."

2. *The Master then* inquired, "Ts'ze, have you also your hatreds?" *Tsze-kung replied.* "I hate those who pry out matters, and ascribe the knowledge of their wisdom. I hate those who are *only* not modest, and think that they are valorous. I hate those who make known secrets, and think that they are straightforward."

(19.11) Tsze-hsiâ said, "When a person does not transgress the boundary-line in the great virtues, he may pass and repass it in the small virtues."

DISCUSSION QUESTIONS

1. Confucius's ethics emphasizes the development of character as the way to right conduct. Discuss the character of Confucius's "superior man." Can you think of anyone who can or could be characterized as a superior man or woman? If so, describe this person.

2. Compare Confucius's approach to individual moral conduct to that of the Bible. What are the similarities and differences?

3. Confucius held that, rather than through law and punishment, rulers should bring about social order and ensure the welfare of the public through moral persuasion and personal example. Do you agree with him? Why or why not?

4. What is the importance of friendship and filial piety for Confucius? Do you think they should have a more prominent role in contemporary Western moral theory? Why or why not?

5. The Master said, "If the people be led by laws, and uniformity sought to be given them by punishments, they will try to avoid *the punishment*, but have no sense of shame." "If they be led by virtue, and uniformity sought to be given them by the rules of propriety, they will have the sense of shame, and moreover will become good." Do you agree with the Master? Why or why not?

6. What is "perfect virtue" according to Confucius? Is this something you strive for in your own life? Why or why not?

Phone Booth
[USA 2003] 1 hour, 21 minutes
Directed by Joel Schumacher

Self-absorbed New York City publicist Stuart Shepard (Colin Farrell) finds himself in a desperate situation when he steps into a Manhattan phone booth to call his girlfriend, Pamela McFadden (Katie Holmes). After Stu hangs up with Pam, the pay phone rings, and he decides to pick it up. In a split second, Stu's life changes forever—a psychotic sniper is on the other end of the line, claiming he will shoot Stu dead if he does not comply with the caller's wishes. First, the sniper calls Pam and tells her that Stu is married while Stu helplessly listens in on the other line. Then the sniper forces Stu to call his wife, Kelly (Radha Mitchell), to tell her about the affair. However, when Stu calls Kelly, she informs him that a man called earlier and told her to be expecting an important call from Stu, and she suggests that she and

Stu meet in person to finish the conversation. As tension builds, the sniper makes his point clear when a bouncer attacks Stu for refusing to hang up the phone. The man is shot dead in the street, and prostitutes standing nearby claim that Stu shot him. Police soon swarm the area.

Stu is told by the sniper not to hang up the telephone; furthermore, he must publicly confess to his wife and the surrounding crowds about what a dishonest person he has been. Eventually, police negotiator Captain Ramey (Forest Whitaker) realizes that Stu is being threatened by someone who is outside the phone booth. Ramey traces the number from the strange phone call to Stu's wife back to a nearby apartment. When the police raid the apartment, they find a pizza delivery man whom Stu had insulted earlier in the day. The man's throat is freshly slit, and the police assume that he was the anonymous caller and has taken his own life. However, the sniper makes his true presence known to Stu alone as he awaits treatment in the back of an ambulance; drugged and unable to speak, Stu is forced to watch the true killer calmly walk away.

DISCUSSION QUESTION

1. What, according at Confucius, is a superior person? By Confucius's standard, is Stu a superior person? Why or why not?

2. Consider the following dialogue between the Caller and Stu:

    CALLER   "I can make him stop. Just say the word, do you hear me?"

    STU   "Yes, yes! "(Sniper shoots Leon)" You shot him! Why'd you . . . shoot him?"

    CALLER   "You said 'yes.'"

    STU   "I said "yes, I can hear you," not "yes, kill [him]. . . ."

    CALLER   "You ought to be more careful with what you say."

    In general, the Caller does not think that Stu is very considerate in what he says to other people. So he sets up this scenario to make Stu more aware of the implications of his words on others. Is the Caller being fair with Stu? Why or why not? Does the means (killing Leon) justify the Caller's end (making Stu aware of how his words are hurting others)? Why or why not?

3. Who by Confucius's standard exhibits more *jen*—Stu or the Caller? Why?

4. Consider the following exchange between the Caller and Stu:

    CALLER   "If only you had dealt with the man decently, this might not have been necessary."

    STU   "Look, I offered him money. I offered him my watch."

    CALLER   "But not your respect, which is what he really wanted. You were dismissive like you dismissed the nice pizza guy. . . . You are guilty of inhumanity to your fellow man."

    STU   "Look, I'm not guilty of a goddamn thing."

    CALLER   "Oh, take responsibility for what you've done, Stu. Be a man!"

    Would Confucius agree with the Caller that Stu is guilty of inhumanity to his fellow man? Why or why not? Discuss.

5. Stu asks the Caller, "How did I get so lucky to be picked out by a killer with a rifle?" The Caller responds to Stu, "You had it made. Kelly at home. Pam on the side. Life has given you more than your fair share, Stu, but it appears you don't appreciate it." Is the Caller right? Does Stu not appreciate his life? Is this why the Caller is targeting Stu?

6. The Caller says to Stu, "Your choices put other people in jeopardy, Stuart. When are you going to learn that?" Is it wrong to make choices that put other people in jeopardy? Compare the responses to this question from the Bible and Confucius. Which do you prefer, and why?

7. Consider this exchange between the Caller and Stu:

    CALLER   "Come on, Stuart. You're in a perfect position."

    STU   "How do you figure?"

    CALLER   "You get to choose between them–Pamela or Kelly. Or should I choose for you? One of them can take your place."

    STU   "Don't do this!"

    CALLER   "Stuart, you've got to be more in touch with your feelings. I thought you loved only Kelly, but you lie to her. Come on, Stu. Don't you get the game, yet? You're a selfish guy—pick one and save yourself . . . time's running out. You or them? Kelly or Pam? Kelly or Pam? Kelly or Pam?"

    What would you do if you were Stu? Will only a selfish person choose between Kelly and Pam?

8. By Confucius's standard, is the Caller a superior person? Why or why not?

9. *Phone Booth* reveals a lot about the moral character of Stu and the Caller. In the end, which one has the stronger moral character? Which one exhibits more virtue? Who is more morally repugnant, Stu or the Caller? Why?

10. Is *Phone Booth* ultimately the story of a virtuous man (the Caller) dealing with a wicked man (Stu)? Why or why not?

THE KORAN

THE RIGHT PATH

Т he Koran (or, in Arabic, *Qur'an*), the sacred book of Islam, is regarded by Muslims as the revelation of God. Supplemented by the Traditions (or *Hadith*), the Koran is the foundation of Islam and the final authority regarding dogma, belief, worship, jurisprudence, and ethics. The Koran provides an extensive set of guidelines concerning individual, family, and social conduct.

It is generally held that the Koran is largely the work of Mohammed (570–632), who was born in Mecca. Mohammed believed that there was one God, named Allah. At the age of forty, Mohammed began receiving revelations in Mecca, which convinced him that he had been called upon to be the prophet of Allah. The revelations continued over a period of twenty-three years, and the Koran is the record of Mohammed's revelations. Some believe that Mohammed could not write or read before the revelations but could do so afterward. Others believe that he could read and write before the revelation, and still others that he could never read or write. Regardless of the degree of Mohammed's literacy, the Koran is viewed by Muslims as a revelation by God to Mohammed.

The Koran is written in Arabic that is regarded as the most perfect form of the language. In 622, Mohammed began to dictate the Koran to a disciple in Medina as the oracles were revealed to him. Also, those who listened to Mohammed utilized their memories to retain the words they heard from him. Later, those who could write traced them in ancient characters in palm leaves, tanned hides, and dried bones. After Mohammed's death, all of these fragments were collected. Zaid ibn Thabit, Mohammed's disciple, was charged by the caliph Abu Bekr with collecting all that could be discovered of the sacred text into one volume. The copy made by Zaid was not canonical, and other copies were circulating. Consequently, a later caliph, Othman, asked Zaid and three others to collect all extant copies and to prepare a canonical version of the text. After this was completed, all of the other copies were destroyed. The 114 suras (chapters) of the Koran range from hundreds of lines to as few as three, and they are arranged according to length, not historical sequence. Consequently, the Koran comprises suras that derive from both Mohammed's time in Mecca (prior to 622) and his time in Medina (622–632), though not chronologically arranged. Nevertheless, some scholars have attempted to do so.

The Koran has six major sources: (1) the Old Testament (canonical and apocryphal) and hybrid forms of Judaism; (2) the New Testament (canonical and apocryphal) and various heretical Christian legends; (3) Sabaism, which is a combination of Judaism, Manicheism, and early Babylonian beliefs and practices; (4) Zoroastrianism; (5) Hanifism; and (6) ancient and contemporary Arabian beliefs and practices. These sources are commented upon and utilized to varying degrees in the development of various legal and moral duties. Guidelines concerning morality and the "right way" to conduct one's life appear throughout the text. Believers are exhorted to battle for their religion, to attain high levels of virtue, and to befriend only like believers. Those who cheat and steal or oppress the poor and orphans are condemned, and the righteous are rewarded. Every action has a moral significance, and moral actions are those that result in justice.

The Koran exhorts believers to develop a virtuous moral character, one that emphasizes modesty, moderation (or limits), and concern for justice and wisdom and that avoids greed, pride, and lust. Following are selections from the Koran.

[1.5] Keep us on the right path.

[2.62] Surely those who believe, and those who are Jews, and the Christians, and the Sabians, whoever believes in Allah and the Last day and does good, they shall have their reward from their Lord, and there is no fear for them, nor shall they grieve.

[2.177] It is not righteousness that you turn your faces towards the East and the West, but righteousness is this that one should believe in Allah and the last day and the angels and the Book and the prophets, and give away wealth out of love for Him to the near of kin and the orphans and the needy and the wayfarer and the beggars and for (the emancipation of) the captives, and keep up prayer and pay the poor-rate; and the performers of their promise when they make a promise, and the patient in distress and affliction and in time of conflicts— these are they who are true (to themselves) and these are they who guard (against evil).

[2.263] Kind speech and forgiveness is better than charity followed by injury; and Allah is Self-sufficient, Forbearing.

[3.14] The love of desires, of women and sons and hoarded treasures of gold and silver and well bred horses and cattle and tilth [tilled earth], is made to seem fair to men; this is the provision of the life of this world; and Allah is He with Whom is the good goal (of life).

[3.28] Let not the believers take the unbelievers for friends rather than believers; and whoever does this, he shall have nothing of (the guardianship of) Allah, but you should guard yourselves against them, guarding carefully; and Allah makes you cautious of (retribution from) Himself; and to Allah is the eventual coming.

[3.57] And as to those who believe and do good deeds, He will pay them fully their rewards; and Allah does not love the unjust.

[3.92] By no means shall you attain to right-eousness until you spend (benevolently) out of what you love; and whatever thing you spend, Allah surely knows it.

[3.104] And from among you there should be a party who invite to good and enjoin what is right and forbid the wrong, and these it is that shall be successful.

[3.118] O you who believe! do not take for intimate friends from among others than your own people; they do not fall short of inflicting loss upon you; they love what distresses you; vehement hatred has already appeared from out of their mouths, and what their breasts conceal is greater still; indeed, we have made the communications clear to you, if you will understand.

[3.198] But as to those who are careful of (their duty to) their Lord, they shall have gardens beneath which rivers flow, abiding in them; an entertainment from their Lord, and that which is with Allah is best for the righteous.

[4.34] Men are the maintainers of women because Allah has made some of them to excel others and because they spend out of their property; the good women are therefore obedient, guarding the unseen as Allah has guarded; and (as to) those on whose part you fear desertion, admonish them, and leave them alone in the sleeping-places and beat them; then if they obey you, do not seek a way against them; surely Allah is High, Great.

[4.36] And serve Allah and do not associate any thing with Him and be good to the parents and to the near of kin and the orphans and the needy and the neighbor of (your) kin and the alien neighbor, and the companion in a journey and the wayfarer and those whom your right hands possess; surely Allah does not love him who is proud, boastful.

[4.94] O you who believe! when you go to war in Allah's way, make investigation, and do not say to any one who offers you peace: You are not a believer. Do you seek goods of this world's life! But with Allah there are abundant gains; you too were such before, then Allah conferred a benefit on you; therefore make investigation; surely Allah is aware of what you do.

[4.107] And do not plead on behalf of those who act unfaithfully to their souls; surely Allah does not love him who is treacherous, sinful.

[4.110] And whoever does evil or acts unjustly to his soul, then asks forgiveness of Allah, he shall find Allah Forgiving, Merciful.

[4.124] And whoever does good deeds whether male or female and he (or she) is a believer—these shall enter the garden, and they shall not be dealt with a jot unjustly.

[4.126] And whatever is in the heavens and whatever is in the earth is Allah's; and Allah encompasses all things.

[4.128] And if a woman fears ill usage or desertion on the part of her husband, there is no blame on them, if they effect a reconciliation between them, and reconciliation is better, and avarice has been made to be present in the (people's) minds; and if you do good (to others) and guard (against evil), then surely Allah is aware of what you do.

[4.148] Allah does not love the public utterance of hurtful speech unless (it be) by one to whom injustice has been done; and Allah is Hearing, Knowing.

[5.33] The punishment of those who wage war against Allah and His apostle and strive to make mischief in the land is only this, that they should be murdered or crucified or their hands and their feet should be cut off on opposite sides or they should be imprisoned; this shall be as a disgrace for them in this world, and in the hereafter they shall have a grievous chastisement.

[5.38] And (as for) the man who steals and the woman who steals, cut off their hands as a punishment for what they have earned, an exemplary punishment from Allah; and Allah is Mighty, Wise.

[5.42] (They are) listeners of a lie, devourers of what is forbidden; therefore if they come to you, judge between them or turn aside from them, and if you turn aside from them, they shall not harm you in any way; and if you judge, judge between them with equity; surely Allah loves those who judge equitably.

[5.87] O you who believe! do not forbid (yourselves) the good things which Allah has made lawful for you and do not exceed the limits; surely Allah does not love those who exceed the limits.

[5.93] On those who believe and do good there is no blame for what they eat, when they are careful (of their duty) and believe and do good deeds, then they are careful (of their duty) and believe, then they are careful (of their duty) and do good (to others), and Allah loves those who do good (to others).

[5.105] O you who believe! take care of your souls; he who errs cannot hurt you when you are on the right way; to Allah is your return, of all (of you), so He will inform you of what you did.

[6.21] And who is more unjust than he who forges a lie against Allah or (he who) gives the lie to His communications; surely the unjust will not be successful.

[7.31] O children of Adam! attend to your embellishments at every time of prayer, and eat and drink and be not extravagant; surely He does not love the extravagant.

[7.178] Whomsoever Allah guides, he is the one who follows the right way; and whomsoever he causes to err, these are the losers.

[8.65] O Prophet! urge the believers to war; if there are twenty patient ones of you they shall overcome two hundred, and if there are a hundred of you they shall overcome a thousand of those who disbelieve, because they are a people who do not understand.

[9.23] O you who believe! do not take your fathers and your brothers for guardians if they love unbelief more than belief; and whoever of you takes them for a guardian, these it is that are the unjust.

[12.53] And I do not declare myself free, most surely (man's) self is wont to command (him to do) evil, except such as my Lord has had mercy on, surely my Lord is Forgiving, Merciful.

[16.23] Truly Allah knows what they hide and what they manifest; surely He does not love the proud.

[16.97] Whoever does good whether male or female and he is a believer, We will most certainly make him live a happy life, and We will most certainly give them their reward for the best of what they did.

[16.119] Yet surely your Lord, with respect to those who do an evil in ignorance, then turn after that and make amends, most surely your Lord after that is Forgiving, Merciful.

[17.9] Surely this Quran guides to that which is most upright and gives good news to the believers who do good that they shall have a great reward.
[17.10] And that (as for) those who do not believe in the hereafter, We have prepared for them a painful chastisement.

[17.22] Do not associate with Allah any other god, lest you sit down despised; neglected.
[17.23] And your Lord has commanded that you shall not serve (any) but Him, and goodness to your parents. If either or both of them reach old age with you, say not to them (so much as) "Ugh" nor chide them, and speak to them a generous word.
[17.24] And make yourself submissively gentle to them with compassion, and say: O my Lord! have compassion on them, as they brought me up (when I was) little.
[17.25] Your Lord knows best what is in your minds; if you are good, then He is surely Forgiving to those who turn (to Him) frequently.
[17.26] And give to the near of kin his due and (to) the needy and the wayfarer, and do not squander wastefully.
[17.27] Surely the squanderers are the fellows of the Shaitans and the Shaitan is ever ungrateful to his Lord.

[17.28] And if you turn away from them to seek mercy from your Lord, which you hope for, speak to them a gentle word.

[17.29] And do not make your hand to be shackled to your neck nor stretch it forth to the utmost (limit) of its stretching forth, lest you should (afterwards) sit down blamed, stripped off.

[17.30] Surely your Lord makes plentiful the means of subsistence for whom He pleases and He straitens (them); surely He is ever Aware of, Seeing, His servants.

[17.31] And do not kill your children for fear of poverty; We give them sustenance and yourselves (too); surely to kill them is a great wrong.

[17.32] And go not nigh to fornication; surely it is an indecency and an evil way.

[17.33] And do not kill anyone whom Allah has forbidden, except for a just cause, and whoever is slain unjustly, We have indeed given to his heir authority, so let him not exceed the just limits in slaying; surely he is aided.

[17.34] And draw not near to the property of the orphan except in a goodly way till he attains his maturity and fulfill the promise; surely (every) promise shall be questioned about.

[17.35] And give full measure when you measure out, and weigh with a true balance; this is fair and better in the end.

[17.36] And follow not that of which you have not the knowledge; surely the hearing and the sight and the heart, all of these, shall be questioned about that.

[17.37] And do not go about in the land exultingly, for you cannot cut through the earth nor reach the mountains in height.

[17.38] All this—the evil of it—is hateful in the sight of your Lord.

[17.39] This is of what your Lord has revealed to you of wisdom, and do not associate any other god with Allah lest you should be thrown into hell, blamed, cast away.

[17.109] And they fall down on their faces weeping, and it adds to their humility.

[18.46] Wealth and children are an adornment of the life of this world; and the ever-abiding, the good works, are better with your Lord in reward and better in expectation.

[19.36] And surely Allah is my Lord and your Lord, therefore serve Him; this is the right path.

[23.1] Successful indeed are the believers,

[23.2] Who are humble in their prayers,

[23.3] And who keep aloof from what is vain,

[23.4] And who are givers of poor-rate,

[23.5] And who guard their private parts,

[23.6] Except before their mates or those whom their right hands possess, for they surely are not blameable,

[23.7] But whoever seeks to go beyond that, these are they that exceed the limits;

[23.8] And those who are keepers of their trusts and their covenant,

[23.9] And those who keep a guard on their prayers;

[23.10] These are they who are the heirs,

[23.11] Who shall inherit the Paradise; they shall abide therein.

[24.26] Bad women are for bad men and bad men are for bad women. Good women are for good men and good men are for good women.

[24.31] And say to the believing women that they cast down their looks and guard their private parts and do not display their ornaments except what appears thereof, and let them wear their head-coverings over their bosoms, and not display their ornaments except to their husbands or their fathers, or the fathers of their husbands, or their sons, or the sons of their husbands, or their brothers, or their brothers' sons, or their sisters' sons, or their women, or those whom their right hands possess, or the male servants not having need (of women), or the children who have not attained knowledge of what is hidden of women; and let them not strike their feet so that what they hide of their ornaments may be known; and turn to Allah all of you, O believers! so that you may be successful.

[26.182] And weigh (things) with a right balance,

[28.77] And seek by means of what Allah has given you the future abode, and do not neglect your portion of this world, and do good (to others) as Allah has done good to you, and do not seek to make mischief in the land, surely Allah does not love the mischief-makers.

[30.39] And whatever you lay out as usury, so that it may increase in the property of men, it shall not increase with Allah; and whatever you give in charity, desiring Allah's pleasure—it is these (persons) that shall get manifold.

[31.17] O my son! keep up prayer and enjoin the good and forbid the evil, and bear patiently that which befalls you; surely these acts require courage;
[31.18] And do not turn your face away from people in contempt, nor go about in the land exulting overmuch; surely Allah does not love any self-conceited boaster;
[31.19] And pursue the right course in your going about and lower your voice; surely the most hateful of voices is braying of the asses.

[33.72] Surely We offered the trust to the heavens and the earth and the mountains, but they refused to be unfaithful to it and feared from it, and man has turned unfaithful to it; surely he is unjust, ignorant;
[33.73] So Allah will chastise the hypocritical men and the hypocritical women and the polytheistic men and the polytheistic women, and Allah will turn (mercifully) to the believing women, and Allah is Forgiving, Merciful.

[34.50] Say: If I err, I err only against my own soul, and if I follow a right direction, it's because of what my Lord reveals to me; surely He is Hearing, Nigh.

[42.40] And the recompense of evil is punishment like it, but whoever forgives and amends, he shall have his reward from Allah; surely He does not love the unjust.

[45.21] Nay! do those who have wrought evil deeds think that We will make them like those who believe and do good—that their life and their death shall be equal? Evil it is that they judge.

[45.24] And they say: There is nothing but our life in this world; we live and die and nothing destroys us but time, and they have no knowledge of that; they only conjecture.

[47.36] The life of this world is only idle sport and play, and if you believe and guard (against evil) He will give you your rewards, and will not ask of you your possessions.

[49.9] And if two parties of the believers quarrel, make peace between them; but if one of them acts wrongfully towards the other, fight that which acts wrongfully until it returns to Allah's command; then if it returns, make peace between them with justice and act equitably; surely Allah loves those who act equitably.

[57.23] So that you may not grieve for what has escaped you, nor be exultant at what He has given you; and Allah does not love any arrogant boaster:

[60.7] It may be that Allah will bring about friendship between you and those whom you hold to be your enemies among them; and Allah is Powerful; and Allah is Forgiving, Merciful.
[60.8] Allah does not forbid you respecting those who have not made war against you on account of (your) religion, and have not driven you forth from your homes, that you show them kindness and deal with them justly; surely Allah loves the doers of justice.
[60.9] Allah only forbids you respecting those who made war upon you on account of (your) religion, and drove you forth from your homes and backed up (others) in your expulsion, that you make friends with them, and whoever makes friends with them, these are the unjust.

[60.12] O Prophet! when believing women come to you giving you a pledge that they will not associate aught with Allah, and will not steal, and will not commit fornication, and will not kill their children, and win not bring a calumny which they have forged of themselves, and will not disobey you in what is good, accept their pledge, and ask forgiveness for them from Allah; surely Allah is Forgiving, Merciful.

[68.1] Noon. I swear by the pen and what the angels write,
[68.2] By the grace of your Lord you are not mad.
[68.3] And most surely you shall have a reward never to be cut off.
[68.4] And most surely you conform (yourself) to sublime morality.
[68.5] So you shall see, and they (too) shall see,
[68.6] Which of you is afflicted with madness.
[68.7] Surely your Lord best knows him who errs from His way, and He best knows the followers of the right course.
[68.8] So do not yield to the rejecters.

[68.9] They wish that you should be pliant so they (too) would be pliant.

[68.10] And yield not to any mean swearer

[68.11] Defamer, going about with slander

[68.12] Forbidder of good, outstepping the limits, sinful,

[68.13] Ignoble, besides all that, base-born;

[70.19] Surely man is created of a hasty temperament

[70.20] Being greatly grieved when evil afflicts him

[70.21] And niggardly when good befalls him

[70.22] Except those who pray,

[70.23] Those who are constant at their prayer

[70.24] And those in whose wealth there is a fixed portion.

[70.25] For him who begs and for him who is denied (good)

[70.26] And those who accept the truth of the judgment day

[70.27] And those who are fearful of the chastisement of their Lord—

[70.28] Surely the chastisement of their Lord is (a thing) not to be felt secure of—

[70.29] And those who guard their private parts,

[70.30] Except in the case of their wives or those whom their right hands possess—for these surely are not to be blamed,

[70.31] But he who seeks to go beyond this, these it is that go beyond the limits—

[70.32] And those who are faithful to their trusts and their covenant

[70.33] And those who are upright in their testimonies,

[70.34] And those who keep a guard on their prayer,

[70.35] Those shall be in gardens, honored.

[82.13] Most surely the righteous are in bliss,

[107.1] Have you considered him who calls the judgment a lie?

[107.2] That is the one who treats the orphan with harshness,

[107.3] And does not urge (others) to feed the poor.

[107.4] So woe to the praying ones,

[107.5] Who are unmindful of their prayers,

[107.6] Who do (good) to be seen,

[107.7] And withhold the necessaries of life.

DISCUSSION QUESTIONS

1. The Koran emphasizes the development of character as important to right conduct. Discuss the character of the "believer." Compare the believer in the Koran to the believer in the Bible and in the writings of the Buddha. What are the similarities and differences?

2. The Koran emphasizes laws and punishments as means of dealing with the unjust. Discuss the punishments for "those who wage war against Allah and His apostle" (5.33), and for the person who steals (5.38). What do you think about this approach to right conduct? Compare it to that of Confucius, who held that, rather than through law and punishment, rulers should bring about social order and ensure the welfare of the public through moral persuasion and personal example.

3. What is the importance and nature of friendship in the Koran? Compare it with the view of friendship expressed by Confucius. Which do you prefer, and why?

4. Discuss the following passage from the Koran: "Men are the maintainers of women because Allah has made some of them to excel others and because they spend out of their property; the good women are therefore obedient, guarding the unseen as Allah has guarded; and (as to) those on whose part you fear desertion, admonish them, and leave them alone in the sleeping-places and beat them; then if they obey you, do not seek a way against them; surely Allah is High, Great" (4.34).

5. How does the Koran characterize those who do not believe in Allah? What do you think about this characterization? Compare it with the account of those who do not believe in God in the Bible.

6. Discuss the following passage from the Koran: "O you who believe! do not forbid (yourselves) the good things which Allah has made lawful for you and do not exceed the limits; surely Allah does not love those who exceed the limits." Compare and contrast the Koran and Confucius on weighing things with "right balance," moderation, and the setting of limits.

7. Discuss the following passage from the Koran: "O Prophet! urge the believers to war; if there are twenty patient ones of you they shall overcome two hundred, and if there are a hundred of you they shall overcome a thousand of those who disbelieve, because they are a people who do not understand" (8.65).

ARISTOTLE

HAPPINESS AND VIRTUE

Aristotle claims that the virtues are those characteristics that enable human beings to live well in communities. *Virtue* is the ability to be reasonable in our actions, desires, and emotions. Anyone who manages their skills and their opportunities well is considered virtuous. According to Aristotle, all human beings seek happiness, and being virtuous makes us happy—it enables us to achieve a state of well-being (*eudaimonia*).

Eudaimonia refers to the objective character of one's life rather than to a particular psychological state. Aristotle believed that as human beings we are happy if we perform our human "function" well and that our function is to act in accordance with reason. Furthermore, it is reason that controls our emotions and other nonrational indicators like the desire for pleasure, so that we avoid both excess and deficiency, and thus act virtuously. In addition, individual *eudaimonia* requires proper social institutions as well as good character. Consequently, ethics, for Aristotle, is taken to be a branch of politics. However, unlike Jeremy Bentham (1748–1832), who famously equates happiness solely with "pleasure and the absence of pain," Aristotle does not equate happiness with pleasure, nor with honor or wealth. Rather, happiness is an activity of the soul in accordance with virtue. Right habits are acquired by living well, and these habits are, in fact, virtues. These virtues are the best guarantee of a happy life.

Aristotle distinguishes between two types of virtues: moral and intellectual. *Intellectual* virtues may be taught, whereas *moral* virtues must be lived in order to be learned. Moral virtue comes from habit and generally is a state of character that represents a mean between the vices of excess and deficiency. This concept of moderation, or the Golden Mean, is at the heart of Aristotle's virtue theory. Courage, for example, is presented as a virtue that represents a mean between the extremes of rashness (an excess) and cowardice (a deficiency). While the moral virtues are important to the achievement of a state of well-being, it is the intellectual virtues found in the activity of contemplation or reason that produce the most perfect happiness. Nevertheless, while the contemplative life is the ultimate happy life, Aristotle says that it does not hurt to have friends, money, and good looks.

Aristotle's virtue ethics (as well as Confucius's) emphasizes the whole person rather than individual actions. Critics of virtue ethics argue that people turn to ethics to answer questions about the morality of action. When people are faced with a concrete moral problem, they want to know what to do, not what kind of character they should cultivate over a lifetime. Virtue ethics does not answer common moral questions such as "What should I do now in this situation?" One might respond to this criticism of virtue ethics by saying that this is the wrong question to ask. "What would a virtuous or decent person do now in this situation?" is the right question. If one asks the question in this way, then virtue ethics can provide a response.

Aristotle (384–322 B.C.E.) is one of the most influential philosophers from Greek antiquity. Born in Stagyra, Macedonia, he is often called the "Sagirite." He was the son of

Nicomachus, a physician to the king. At age eighteen, he entered Plato's Academy; where he studied for nearly twenty years. After Plato's death, when a rival was selected to head the Academy, Aristotle left Athens for the island of Lesbos. Around 343, he became the tutor of the young Alexander the Great, son of King Philip of Macedon, a position he held for three years.

In 335, Artistotle returned to Athens to found his own school, the Lyceum, which was often called the Peripatetic School because Aristotle was in the habit of walking around the courtyard of the school when he lectured. Upon Alexander's death in 323 B.C.E., anti-Macedonian feelings were on the rise in Athens, so Aristotle chose to leave Athens so that Athenians might not "sin twice against philosophy" (the first "sin" being the trial of Socrates). It is often said that Aristotle "knew everything," and the wide range of his writings seem to confirm this. His works investigate many topics including logic, astronomy, biology, politics, ethics, rhetoric, drama, the soul, God, and physics. The following selection is from his *Nichomachean Ethics*, a work in which he summarizes the ethics of fourth-century B.C.E. Athenians and puts forth his own ethical theory.

Our discussion will be adequate if it has as much clearness as the subject-matter admits of, for precision is not to be sought for alike in all discussions, any more than in all the products of the crafts. Now fine and just actions, which political science investigates, admit of much variety and fluctuation of opinion, so that they may be thought to exist only by convention, and not by nature. And goods also give rise to a similar fluctuation because they bring harm to many people; for before now men have been undone by reason of their wealth, and others by reason of their courage. We must be content, then, in speaking of such subjects and with such premises to indicate the truth roughly and in outline, and in speaking about things which are only for the most part true and with premises of the same kind to reach conclusions that are no better. In the same spirit, therefore, should each type of statement be received; for it is the mark of an educated man to look for precision in each class of things just so far as the nature of the subject admits; it is evidently equally foolish to accept probable reasoning from a mathematician and to demand from a rhetorician scientific proofs.

Now each man judges well the things he knows, and of these he is a good judge. And so the man who has been educated in a subject is a good judge of that subject, and the man who has received an all-round education is a good judge in general. Hence a young man is not a proper hearer of lectures on political science; for he is inexperienced in the actions that occur in life, but its discussions start from these and are about these; and, further, since he tends to follow his passions, his study will be vain and unprofitable, because the end aimed at is not knowledge but action. And it makes no difference whether he is young in years or youthful in character; the defect does not depend on time, but on his living, and pursuing each successive object, as passion directs. For to such persons, as to the incontinent, knowledge brings no profit; but to those who desire and act in accordance with a rational principle knowledge about such matters will be of great benefit.

These remarks about the student, the sort of treatment to be expected, and the purpose of the inquiry, may be taken as our preface.

Let us resume our inquiry and state, in view of the fact that all knowledge and every pursuit aims at some good, what it is that we say political science aims at and what is the highest of all goods achievable by action. Verbally there is very general agreement; for both the general run of men and people of superior refinement say that it is happiness, and identify living well and doing well with being happy; but with regard to what happiness is they differ, and the many do not give the same account as the wise. For the former think it is some plain and obvious thing, like pleasure, wealth, or honour; they differ, however, from one another—and often even the same man identifies it with different things, with health when he is ill, with wealth when he is poor; but, conscious of their ignorance, they admire those who proclaim some great ideal that is above their comprehension. Now some thought that apart from these many goods there is another which is self-subsistent and causes the goodness of all these as well. To examine all the opinions that have been held were perhaps somewhat fruitless; enough to examine those that are most prevalent or that seem to be arguable. . . .

Let us, however, resume our discussion from the point at which we digressed. To judge from the lives that men lead, most men, and men of the most vulgar type, seem (not without some ground) to identify the good, or happiness, with pleasure; which is the reason why they love the life of enjoyment. For there are, we may say, three prominent types of life—that just mentioned, the political, and thirdly the contemplative life. Now the mass of mankind are evidently quite slavish in their tastes, preferring a life suitable to beasts, but they get some ground for their view from the fact that many of those in high places share the tastes of Sardanapallus. A consideration of the prominent types of life shows that, people of superior refinement and of active disposition identify happiness with honour; for this is, roughly speaking, the end of the political life. But it seems too superficial to be what we are looking for, since it is thought to depend on those who bestow honour rather than on him who receives it, but the good we divine to be something proper to a man and not easily taken from him. Further, men seem to pursue honour in order that they may be assured of their goodness; at least it is by men of practical wisdom that they seek to be honoured, and among those who know them, and on the ground of their virtue; clearly, then, according to them, at any rate, virtue is better. And perhaps one might even suppose this to be, rather than honour, the end of the political life. But even this appears somewhat incomplete; for possession of virtue seems actually compatible with being asleep, or with life-long inactivity, and, further, with the greatest sufferings and misfortunes; but a man who was living so no one would call happy, unless he were maintaining a thesis at all costs. But enough of this; for the

subject has been sufficiently treated even in the current discussions. Third comes the contemplative life, which we shall consider later.

The life of money-making is one undertaken under compulsion, and wealth is evidently not the good we are seeking; for it is merely useful and for the sake of something else. And so one might rather take the afore-named objects to be ends; for they are loved for themselves. But it is evident that not even these are ends; yet many arguments have been thrown away in support of them. . . .

Let us again return to the good we are seeking, and ask what it can be. It seems different in different actions and arts; it is different in medicine, in strategy, and in the other arts likewise. What then is the good of each? Surely that for whose sake everything else is done. In medicine this is health, in strategy victory, in architecture a house, in any other sphere something else, and in every action and pursuit the end; for it is for the sake of this that all men do whatever else they do. Therefore, if there is an end for all that we do, this will be the good achievable by action, and if there are more than one, these will be the goods achievable by action.

So the argument has by a different course reached the same point; but we must try to state this even more clearly. Since there are evidently more than one end, and we choose some of these (e.g., wealth, flutes, and in general instruments) for the sake of something else, clearly not all ends are final ends; but the chief good is evidently something final. Therefore, if there is only one final end, this will be what we are seeking, and if there are more than one, the most final of these will be what we are seeking. Now we call that which is in itself worthy of pursuit more final than that which is worthy of pursuit for the sake of something else, and that which is never desirable for the sake of something else more final than the things that are desirable both in themselves and for the sake of that other thing, and therefore we call final without qualification that which is always desirable in itself and never for the sake of something else.

Now such a thing happiness, above all else, is held to be; for this we choose always for itself and never for the sake of something else, but honour, pleasure, reason, and every virtue we choose indeed for themselves (for if nothing resulted from them we should still choose each of them), but we choose them also for the sake of happiness, judging that by means of them we shall be happy. Happiness, on the other hand, no one chooses for the sake of these, nor, in general, for anything other than itself. . . .

Presumably, however, to say that happiness is the chief good seems a platitude, and a clearer account of what it is, is still desired. This might perhaps be given, if we could first ascertain the function of man. For just as for a flute-player, a sculptor, or any artist, and, in general, for all things that have a function or activity, the good and the "well" is thought to reside in the function, so would it seem to be for man, if he has a function. Have the carpenter, then, and the tanner certain functions or activities, and has man none? Is he born without a function? Or as eye, hand, foot, and in general each of the parts evidently has a function, may one lay it down that man similarly has a function apart from all these? What then can this be? Life seems to be common even to plants, but we are seeking what is peculiar to man. Let us exclude, therefore, the life of nutrition and growth. Next there would be a life of perception, but *it* also seems to be common even to the horse, the ox, and every animal. There remains, then, an active life of the element that has a rational principle; of this, one part has such a principle in the sense of being obedient to one, the other in the sense of possessing one and exercising thought. And, as "life of the rational element" also has two meanings, we must state that life in the sense of activity is what we mean; for this seems to be the more proper sense of the term. Now if the function of man is an activity of soul which follows or implies a rational principle, and if we say "a so-and-so" and "a good so-and-so" have a function which is the same in kind, e.g., a lyre-player and a good lyre-player, and so without qualification in all cases, eminence in respect of goodness being added to the name of the function (for the function of a lyre-player is to play the lyre, and that of a good lyre-player is to do so well): if this is the case, [and we state the function of man to be a certain kind of life, and this to be an activity or actions of the soul implying a rational principle, and the function of a good man to be the good and noble performance of these, and if any action is well performed when it is performed in accordance with the appropriate excellence: if this is the case,] human good turns out to be activity of soul in accordance with virtue, and if there are more than one virtue, in accordance with the best and most complete.

But we must add "in a complete life." For one swallow does not make a summer, nor does one day; and so too one day, or a short time, does not make a man blessed and happy. . . .

We must consider it, however, in the light not only of our conclusion and our premises, but also of what is commonly said about it; for with a true view all the data harmonize, but with a false one the facts soon clash. Now goods have been divided into three classes, and some are described as external, others as relating to soul or to body; we call those that relate to soul most properly and truly goods, and psychical actions and activities we class as relating to soul. Therefore our account must be sound, at least according to this view, which is an old one and agreed on by philosophers. It is correct also in that we identify the end with certain actions and activities; for thus it falls among goods of the soul and not among external goods. Another belief which harmonizes with our account is that the happy man lives well and does well; for we have practically defined happiness as a sort of good life and good action. The characteristics that are looked for in happiness seem also, all of them, to belong to what we have defined happiness as being. For some identify happiness with virtue, some with practical wisdom, others with a kind of philosophic wisdom, others with these, or one of these, accompanied by pleasure or not without pleasure; while others include also external prosperity. Now some of these views have been held by many men and men of old, others by a few eminent persons; and it is not probable that either of these should be entirely mistaken, but rather that they should be right in at least some one respect or even in most respects.

With those who identify happiness with virtue or some one virtue our account is in harmony; for to virtue belongs virtuous activity. But it makes, perhaps, no small difference whether we place the chief good in possession or in use, in state of mind or in activity. For the state of mind may exist without producing any good result, as in a man who is asleep or in some other way quite inactive, but the activity cannot; for one who has the activity will of necessity be acting, and acting well. And as in the Olympic Games it is not the most beautiful and the strongest that are crowned but those who compete (for it is some of these that are victorious), so those who act win, and rightly win, the noble and good things in life.

Their life is also in itself pleasant. For pleasure is a state of *soul*, and to each man that which he is said to be a lover of is pleasant; e.g., not only is a horse pleasant to the lover of horses, and a spectacle to the lover of sights, but also in the same way just acts are pleasant to the lover of justice and in general virtuous acts to the lover of virtue. Now for most men their pleasures are in conflict with one another because these are not by nature pleasant, but the lovers of what is noble find pleasant the things that are by nature pleasant; and virtuous actions are such, so that these are pleasant for such men as well as in their own nature. Their life, therefore, has no further need of pleasure as a sort of adventitious charm, but has its pleasure in itself. For, besides what we have said, the man who does not rejoice in noble actions is not even good; since no one would call a man just who did not enjoy acting justly, nor any man liberal who did not enjoy liberal actions; and similarly in all other cases. If this is so, virtuous actions must be in themselves pleasant. But they are also *good* and *noble*, and have each of these attributes in the highest degree, since the good man judges well about these attributes; his judgment is such as we have described. Happiness then is the best, noblest, and most pleasant thing in the world. . . .

Yet evidently, as we said, it needs the external goods as well; for it is impossible, or not easy, to do noble acts without the proper equipment. In many actions we use friends and riches and political power as instruments; and there are some things the lack of which takes the lustre from happiness, as good birth, goodly children, beauty; for the man who is very ugly in appearance or ill-born or solitary and childless is not very likely to be happy, and perhaps a man would be still less likely if he had thoroughly bad children or friends or had lost good children or friends by death. As we said, then, happiness seems to need this sort of prosperity in addition; for which reason some identify happiness with good fortune, though others identify it with virtue.

For this reason also the question is asked, whether happiness is to be acquired by learning or by habituation or some other sort of training, or comes in virtue of some divine providence or again by chance. Now if there is *any* gift of the gods to men, it is reasonable that happiness should be god-given, and most surely god-given of all human things inasmuch as it is the best. But this question would perhaps be more appropriate to another inquiry; happiness seems, however, even if it is not god-sent but comes as a result of virtue and some process of learning or training, to be among the most god-like things; for that which is the prize and end of virtue seems to be the best thing in the world, and something god-like and blessed.

It will also on this view be very generally shared; for all who are not maimed as regards their potentiality for virtue may win it by a certain kind of study and care. But if it is better to be happy thus than by chance, it is reasonable that the facts should be so, since everything that depends on the action of nature is by nature as good as it can be, and similarly everything that depends on art or any rational cause, and especially if it depends on the best of all causes. To entrust to chance what is greatest and most noble would be a very defective arrangement.

The answer to the question we are asking is plain also from the definition of happiness; for it has been said to be a virtuous activity of soul, of a certain kind. Of the remaining goods, some must necessarily pre-exist as conditions of happiness, and others are naturally co-operative and useful as instruments. And this will be found to agree with what we said at the outset; for we stated the end of political science to be the best end, and political science spends most of its pains on making the citizens to be of a certain character, viz. good and capable of noble acts.

It is natural, then, that we call neither ox nor horse nor any other of the animals happy; for none of them is capable of sharing in such activity. For this reason also a boy is not happy; for he is not yet capable of such acts, owing to his age; and boys who are called happy are being congratulated by reason of the hopes we have for them. For there is required, as we said, not only complete virtue but also a complete life, since many changes occur in life, and all manner of chances, and the most prosperous may fall into great misfortunes in old age, as is told of Priam in the Trojan Cycle; and one who has experienced such chances and has ended wretchedly no one calls happy. . . .

Since happiness is an activity of soul in accordance with perfect virtue, we must consider the nature of virtue; for perhaps we shall thus see better the nature of happiness. . . .

Virtue, then, being of two kinds, intellectual and moral, intellectual virtue in the main owes both its birth and its growth to teaching (for which reason it requires experience and time), while moral virtue comes about as a result of habit. . . . From this it is also plain that none of the moral virtues arises in us by nature; for nothing that exists by nature can form a habit contrary to its nature. For instance the stone which by nature moves downwards cannot be habituated to move upwards, not even if one tries to train it by throwing it up ten thousand times; nor can fire be habituated to move downwards, nor can anything else that by nature behaves in one way be trained to behave in another. Neither by nature, then, nor contrary to nature do the virtues arise in us; rather we are adapted by nature to receive them, and are made perfect by habit. . . .

We must, however, not only describe virtue as a state of character, but also say what sort of state it is. We may remark, then, that every virtue or excellence both brings into good condition the thing of which it is the excellence and makes the work of that thing be done well; e.g., the excellence of the eye makes both the eye and its work good; for it is by the excellence of the eye that we see well. Similarly the excellence of the horse makes a horse both good in itself and good at running and at carrying its rider and at awaiting the attack of the enemy. Therefore, if this is true in every case, the virtue of man also will be the state of character which makes a man good and which makes him do his own work well.

How this is to happen we have stated already, but it will be made plain also by the following consideration of the specific nature of virtue. In everything that is continuous and divisible it is possible to take more, less, or an equal amount, and that either in terms of the thing itself or relatively to us; and the equal is an intermediate between excess and defect. By the intermediate in the object I mean that which is equidistant from each of the extremes, which is one and the same for all men; by the intermediate relatively to us that which is neither too much nor too little— and this is not one, nor the same for all. For instance, if ten is many and two is few, six is the intermediate, taken in terms of the object; for it exceeds and is exceeded by an equal amount; this is intermediate according to arithmetical proportion. But the intermediate relatively to us is not to be taken so; if ten pounds are too much for a particular person to eat and two too little, it does not follow that the trainer will order six pounds; for this also is perhaps too much for the person who is to take it, or too little—too little for Milo, too much for the beginner in athletic exercises. The same is true of running and wrestling. Thus a master of any art avoids excess and defect, but seeks the intermediate and chooses this—the intermediate not in the object but relatively to us.

If is thus, then, that every art does its work well—by looking to the intermediate and judging its works by this standard (so that we often say of good works of art that it is not possible either to take away or to add anything, implying that excess and defect destroy the goodness of the works of art, while the mean preserves it; and good artists, as we say, look to this in their work), and if, further, virtue is more exact and better than any art, as nature also is, then virtue must have the quality of aiming at the intermediate. I mean moral virtue; for it is this that is concerned with passions and actions, and in these there is excess, defect, and the intermediate. For instance, both fear and confidence and appetite and anger and pity and in general pleasure and pain may be felt both too much and too little, and in both cases not well; but to feel them at the right times, with reference to the right objects, towards the right people, with the right motive, and in the right way, is what is both intermediate and best, and this is characteristic of virtue. Similarly with regard to actions also there is excess, defect, and the intermediate. Now virtue is concerned with passions and actions, in which excess is a form of failure, and so is defect, while the intermediate is praised and is a form of success; and being praised and being successful are both characteristics of virtue. Therefore virtue is a kind of mean, since, as we have seen, it aims at what is intermediate.

Again, it is possible to fail in many ways (for evil belongs to the class of the unlimited, as the Pythagoreans conjectured, and good to that of the limited), while to succeed is possible only in one way (for which reason also one is easy and the other difficult—to miss the mark easy, to hit it difficult); for these reasons also, then, excess and defect are characteristic of vice, and the mean of virtue;

For men are good in but one way, but bad in many.

Virtue, then, is a state of character concerned with choice, lying in a mean, i.e., the mean relative to us, this being determined by a rational principle, and by that principle by which the man of practical wisdom would determine it. Now it is a mean between two vices, that which depends on excess and that which depends on defect; and again it is a mean because the vices respectively fall short of or exceed what is right in both passions and actions, while virtue both finds and chooses that which is intermediate. Hence in respect of its substance and the definition which states its essence virtue is a mean, with regard to what is best and right an extreme.

But not every action nor every passion admits of a mean; for some have names that already imply badness, e.g., spite, shamelessness, envy, and in the case of actions adultery, theft, murder; for all of these and suchlike things imply by their names that they are themselves bad, and not the excesses or deficiencies of them. It is not possible, then, ever to be right with regard to them; one must always be wrong. Nor does goodness or badness with regard to such things depend on committing adultery with the right woman, at the right time, and in the right way, but simply to do any of them is to go wrong. It would be equally absurd, then, to expect that in unjust, cowardly, and voluptuous action there should be a mean, an excess, and a deficiency; for at that rate there would be a mean of excess and of deficiency, an excess of excess, and a deficiency of deficiency. But as there is no excess and deficiency of temperance and courage because what is intermediate is in a sense an extreme, so too of the actions we have mentioned there is no mean nor any excess and deficiency, but however they are done they are wrong; for in general there is neither a mean of excess and deficiency, nor excess and deficiency of a mean.

We must, however, not only make this general statement, but also apply it to the individual facts. For among statements about conduct those which are general apply more widely, but those which are particular are more genuine, since conduct has to do with individual cases, and our statements must harmonize with the facts in these cases. We may take these cases from our table. With regard to feelings of fear and confidence courage is the mean; of the people who exceed, he who exceeds in fearlessness has no name (many of the states have no name), while the man who exceeds in confidence is rash, and he who exceeds in fear and falls short in confidence is a coward. With regard to pleasures and pains—not all of them, and not so much with regard to the pains—the mean is temperance, the excess self-indulgence. Persons deficient with regard to the pleasures are not often found; hence such persons also have received no name. But let us call them "insensible."

With regard to giving and taking of money the mean is liberality, the excess and the defect prodigality and meanness. In these actions people exceed and fall short in contrary ways; the prodigal exceeds in spending and falls short in taking, while the mean man exceeds in taking and falls short in spending. . . . With regard to money there are also other dispositions—a mean, magnificence (for the magnificent man differs from the liberal man; the former deals with large sums, the latter with small ones), and excess, tastelessness, and vulgarity, and a deficiency, niggardliness; these differ from the states opposed to liberality. . . .

That moral virtue is a mean, then, and in what sense it is so, and that it is a mean between two vices, the one involving excess, the other deficiency, and that it is such because its character is to aim at what is intermediate in passions and in actions, has been sufficiently stated. Hence also it is no easy task to be good. For in everything it is no easy task to find the middle, e.g., to find the middle of a circle is not for everyone but for him who knows; so, too, anyone can get angry—that is easy—or give or spend money; but to do this to the right person, to the right extent, at the right time, with the right motive, and in the right way, *that* is not for everyone, nor is it easy; wherefore goodness is both rare and laudable and noble. . . .

If happiness is activity in accordance with virtue, it is reasonable that it should be in accordance with the highest virtue; and this will be that of the best thing in us. Whether it be reason or something else that is this element which is thought to be our natural ruler and guide and to take thought of things noble and divine, whether it be itself also divine or only the most divine element in us, the activity of this in accordance with its proper virtue will be perfect happiness. That this activity is contemplative we have already said.

Now this would seem to be in agreement both with what we said before and with the truth. For, firstly, this activity is the best (since not only is reason the best thing in us, but the objects of reason are the best of knowable objects); and, secondly, it is the most continuous, since we can contemplate truth more continuously than we can do anything. And we think happiness has pleasure mingled with it, but the activity of philosophic wisdom is admittedly the pleasantest of virtuous activities; at all events the pursuit of it is thought to offer pleasures marvellous for their purity and their enduringness, and it is to be expected that those who know will pass their time more pleasantly than those who inquire. And the self-sufficiency that is spoken of must belong most to the contemplative activity. For while a philosopher, as well as a just man or one possessing any other virtue, needs the necessaries of life, when they are sufficiently equipped with things of that sort the just man needs people towards whom and with whom he shall act justly, and the temperate man, the brave man, and each of the others is in the same case, but the philosopher, even when by himself, can contemplate truth, and the better the wiser he is; he can perhaps do so better if he has fellow-workers, but still he is the most self-sufficient. And this activity alone would seem to be loved for its own sake; for nothing arises from it apart from the contemplating, while from practical activities we gain more or less apart from the action. And happiness is thought to depend on leisure; for we are busy that we may have leisure, and make war that we may live in peace. Now the activity of the practical virtues is exhibited in political or military affairs, but the actions concerned with these seem to be unleisurely. Warlike actions are completely so (for no one chooses to be at war, or provokes war, for the sake of being at war; any one would seem absolutely murderous if he were to make enemies of his friends in order to bring about battle and slaughter); but the action of the statesman is also unleisurely, and—apart from the political action itself—aims at despotic power and honours, or at all events happiness, for him and his fellow citizen—a happiness different from political action, and evidently sought as being different. So if among virtuous actions political and military actions are distinguished by nobility and greatness, and these are unleisurely and aim at an end and are not desirable for their own sake, but the activity of reason, which is contemplative, seems both to be superior in serious worth and to aim at no end beyond itself, and to have its pleasure proper to itself (and this augments the activity), and the self-sufficiency, leisureliness, unweariedness (so far as this is possible for man), and all the other attributes ascribed to the supremely happy man are evidently those connected with this activity, it follows that this will be the complete happiness of man, if to be allowed a complete term of life (for none of the attributes of happiness is *in*complete).

But such a life would be too high for man; for it is not in so far as he is man that he will live so, but in so far as something divine is present in him; and by so much as this is superior to our composite nature is its activity superior to that which is the exercise of the other kind of virtue. If reason is divine, then in comparison with man, the life according to it is divine in comparison with human life. But we must not follow those who advise us, being men, to think of human things, and, being mortal, of mortal things, but must, so far as we can, make ourselves immortal, and strain every nerve to live in accordance with the best thing in us; for even if it be small in bulk, much more does it in power and worth surpass everything. This would seem, too, to be each man himself, since it is the authoritative and better part of him. It would be strange, then, if he were to choose not the life of his self but that of something else. And what we said before will apply now; that which is proper to each thing is by nature best and most pleasant for each thing; for man, therefore, the life according to reason is best and pleasantest, since reason more than anything else *is* man. This life therefore is also the happiest.

But in a secondary degree the life in accordance with the other kind of virtue is happy; for the activities in accordance with this befit our human estate. Just and brave acts, and other virtuous acts, we do in relation to each other, observing our respective duties with regard to contracts and services and all manner of actions and with regard to passions; and all of these seem to be typically human. Some of them seem even to arise from the body, and virtue of character to be in many ways bound up with the passions. Practical wisdom, too, is linked to virtue of character, and this to practical wisdom, since the principles of practical wisdom are in accordance with the moral virtues and rightness in morals is in accordance with practical wisdom. Being connected with the passions also, the moral virtues must belong to our composite nature; and the virtues of our composite nature are human; so, therefore, are the life and the happiness which correspond to these. The excellence of the reason is a thing apart; we must be content to say this much about it, for to describe it precisely is a task greater than our purpose requires. It would seem, however, also to need external equipment but little, or less than moral virtue does. Grant that both need the necessaries; and do so equally, even if the statesman's work is the more concerned with the body and things of that sort; for there will be little difference there; but in what they need for the exercise of their activities there will be much difference. The liberal man will need money for the doing of his liberal deeds, and the just man too will need it for the returning of services (for wishes are hard to discern, and even people who are not just pretend to wish to act justly); and the brave man will need power if he is to accomplish any of the acts that correspond to his virtue, and the temperate man will need opportunity; for how else is either he or any of the others to be recognized? It is debated, too, whether the will or the deed is more essential to virtue, which is assumed to involve both; it is surely clear that its perfection involves both; but for deeds many things are needed, and more, the greater and nobler the deeds are. But the man who is contemplating the truth needs no such thing, at least with a view to the exercise of his activity; indeed they are, one may say, even hindrances, at all events to his contemplation; but

in so far as he is a man and lives with a number of people, he chooses to do virtuous acts; he will therefore need such aids to living a human life.

But that perfect happiness is a contemplative activity will appear from the following consideration as well. We assume the gods to be above all other beings blessed and happy; but what sort of actions must we assign to them? Acts of justice? Will not the gods seem absurd if they make contracts and return deposits, and so on? Acts of a brave man, then, confronting dangers and running risks because it is noble to do so? Or liberal acts? To whom will they give? It will be strange if they are really to have money or anything of the kind. And what would their temperate acts be? Is not such praise tasteless, since they have no bad appetites? If we were to run through them all, the circumstances of action would be found trivial and unworthy of gods. Still, everyone supposes that they *live* and therefore that they are active; we cannot suppose them to sleep like Endymion. Now if you take away from a living being action, and still more production, what is left but contemplation? Therefore the activity of God, which surpasses all others in blessedness, must be contemplative; and of human activities, therefore, that which is most akin to this must be most of the nature of happiness.

This is indicated, too, by the fact that the other animals have no share in happiness, being completely deprived of such activity. For while the whole life of the gods is blessed, and that of men too in so far as some likeness of such activity belongs to them, none of the other animals is happy, since they in no way share in contemplation. Happiness extends, then, just so far as contemplation does, and those to whom contemplation more fully belongs are more truly happy, not as a mere concomitant but in virtue of the contemplation; for this is in itself precious. Happiness, therefore, must be some form of contemplation.

But, being a man, one will also need external prosperity; for our nature is not self-sufficient for the purpose of contemplation, but our body also must be healthy and must have food and other attention. Still, we must not think that the man who is to be happy will need many things or great things, merely because he cannot be supremely happy without external goods; for self-sufficiency and action do not involve excess, and we can do noble acts without ruling earth and sea; for even with moderate advantages one can act virtuously (this is manifest enough; for private persons are thought to do worthy acts no less than despots—indeed even more); and it is enough that we should have so much as that; for the life of the man who is active in accordance with virtue will be happy. . . .

DISCUSSION QUESTIONS

1. According to Aristotle, what is happiness? Do you agree with him? Explain.
2. What is the connection between virtue and happiness according to Aristotle? Would Confucius agree with this? Why or why not? What is the difference between their views?
3. Aristotle says that a life of pleasure is suitable for beasts. Why does he believe this? What is wrong with a life of pleasure?
4. Aristotle asserts that the philosopher will be happier than anyone else. Do you agree with him? Why or why not?
5. Is Aristotle's moral theory compatible with human nature? Why or why not?
6. In what sense does equality play a role in Aristotle's ethics? It is possible for everyone to be happy? Or only some people? Is this a strength or weakness of Aristotle's position?

IMMANUEL KANT

THE CATEGORICAL IMPERATIVE

For Immanuel Kant, a human will governed by reason is a good will, and the good will is the only thing that is good without qualification. The human will experiences the laws of reason as commands issued by reason to act in various ways. Kant calls these commands "imperatives." There are two general kinds of imperatives: hypothetical and categorical. If an action is commanded as being necessary for bringing about some further end, the imperative is *hypothetical*. If an action is commanded as being good without qualification, the imperative is *categorical*. Categorical imperatives are unconditional; our obedience to them is unqualified. Kant formulates the categorical imperative as follows: act only according to that rule by which you can at the same time will that it should become a universal law. For Kant, you should perform only those actions that conform to rules that you could will to be adopted universally. If you were to lie, for example, you would be following the rule "It is permissible to lie." This rule could not be adopted universally because it would be self-defeating: People would stop believing one another, and then it would do no good to lie. Therefore, you should not lie.

Kant also distinguishes several types of duties. *Perfect duties* consist of actions whose maxims can consistently be neither *conceived* nor *willed* by us to be universal laws of nature. *Imperfect duties* consist of actions whose maxims *could* become universal laws of nature, but it is impossible for us to *will* that their maxims should be universal laws of nature since such a will would be in conflict with itself. Together with a distinction between duties to oneself and those to others, this yields four fundamental duties. The first is perfect duty to oneself—this type of duty would preclude suicide. The second is perfect duty to others—this type of duty would preclude insincere promises. The third is imperfect duty to oneself—this type of duty precludes not developing one's natural potential. The fourth is imperfect duty to others—this type of duty precludes refusing help to those in need.

At its core, Kant's moral theory contains three basic ideas: (1) Humans are rational beings, capable of thinking about the choices they face and selecting among them on the basis of reasons; (2) humans have an infinite worth or dignity—that is, humans are "ends-in-themselves"—and this sets them above all merely conditionally valuable things in the world; and (3) humans, as rational ends-in-themselves, are the authors of the moral law, so that their obedience to duty is not an act of submission but an act of autonomy. These three ideas are more apparent in another of Kant's formulations of the categorical imperative: act so that you treat humanity, whether in your own person or in that of another, always as an end and never as a means only.

Kantian ethics is a *nonconsequentialist* (or deontological) moral theory in that it maintains that the morality of an action depends on factors other than consequences. One of the major flaws in Kant's ethical theory is that it fails to provide guidance when duties conflict. Another is that acts that Kant condemns as universally wrong, such as lying, seem justified—perhaps even morally required—in some situations (for example, lying to protect individuals from capture by evil people who will hurt or even kill them). The following selection is from *Fundamental Principles of the Metaphysics of Morals*, which was first published in 1785. A biographical sketch of Immanuel Kant appears in chapter 2.

Nothing can possibly be conceived in the world, or even out of it, which can be called good, without qualification, except a Good Will. Intelligence, wit, judgment, and the other *talents* of the mind, however they may be named, or courage, resolution, perseverance, as qualities of temperament, are undoubtedly good and desirable in many respects; but these gifts of nature may also become extremely bad and mischievous if the will which is to make use of them, and which, therefore, constitutes what is called *character,* is not good. It is the same with the *gifts of fortune.* Power, riches, honour, even health, and the general well-being and contentment with one's condition which is called *happiness,* inspire pride, and often presumption, if there is not a good will to correct the influence of these on the mind, and with this also to rectify the whole principle of acting, and adapt it to its end. The sight of a being who is not adorned with a single feature of a pure and good will, enjoying unbroken prosperity, can never give pleasure to an impartial rational spectator. Thus a good will appears to constitute the indispensable condition even of being worthy of happiness.

There are even some qualities which are of service to this good will itself, and may facilitate its action, yet which have no intrinsic unconditional value, but always presuppose a good will, and this qualifies the esteem that we justly have for them, and does not permit us to regard them as absolutely good. Moderation in the affections and passions, self-control, and calm deliberation are not only good in many respects but even seem to constitute part of the intrinsic worth of the person; but they are far from deserving to be called good without qualification, although they have been so unconditionally praised by the ancients. For without the principles of a good will, they may become extremely bad; and the coolness of a villain not only makes him far more dangerous; but also directly makes him more abominable in our eyes than he would have been without it.

A good will is good not because of what it perform or effects, not by its aptness for the attainment of some proposed end, but simply by virtue of the volition, that is, it is good in itself, and considered by itself is to be esteemed much higher than all that can be brought about by it in favour of any inclination, may, even of the sum-total of all inclinations. Even if it should happen that, owing to special disfavour of fortune, or the niggardly provision of a step-motherly nature, this will should wholly lack power to accomplish its purpose, if with its greatest efforts it should yet achieve nothing, and there should remain only the good will (not, to be sure, a mere wish, but the summoning of all means in our power), then, like a jewel, it would still shine by its own light, as a thing which has its whole value in itself. Its usefulness or fruitlessness can neither add to nor take away anything from this value.

Thus the moral worth of an action does not lie in the effect expected from it, nor in any principle of action which requires to borrow its motive from this expected effect. For all these effects— agreeableness of one's condition, and even the promotion of the happiness of others—could have been also brought about by other causes, so that for this there would have been no need of the will of a rational being; whereas it is in this alone that the supreme and unconditional good can be found. The pre-eminent good which we call moral can therefore consist in nothing else than *the conception of law* in itself, *which certainly is only possible in a rational being,* in so far as this conception, and not the expected effect, determines the will. This is a good which is already present in the person who acts accordingly, and we have not to wait for it to appear first in the result.

But what sort of law can that be, the conception of which must determine the will, even without paying any regard to the effect expected from it, in order that this will may be called good absolutely and without qualification? As I have deprived the will of every impulse which could arise to it from obedience to any law, there remains nothing but the universal conformity of its actions to law in general, which alone is to serve the will as a principle, i.e., I am never to act otherwise than *so that I could also will that my maxim should become a universal law.* Here, now, it is the simple conformity to law in general, without assuming any particular law applicable to certain actions, that serves the will as its principle, and must so serve it, if duty is not to be a vain delusion and a chimerical notion. The common reason of men in its practical judgments perfectly coincides with this and always has in view the principle here suggested. Let the question be, for example: May I when in distress make a promise with the intention not to keep it? I readily distinguish here between the two significations which the question may have: Whether it is prudent, or whether it is right, to make a false promise? The former may undoubtedly often be the case. I see clearly indeed that it is not enough to extricate myself from a present difficulty by means of this subterfuge, but it must be well considered whether there may not

hereafter spring from this lie much greater inconvenience than that from which I now free myself, and as, with all my supposed *cunning,* the consequences cannot be so easily foreseen but that credit once lost may be much more injurious to me than any mischief which I seek to avoid at present, it should be considered whether it would not be more *prudent* to act herein according to a universal maxim, and to make it a habit to promise nothing except with the intention of keeping it. But it is soon clear to me that such a maxim will still only be based on the fear of consequences. Now it is a wholly different thing to be truthful from duty, and to be so from apprehension of injurious consequences. In the first case, the very notion of the action already implies a law for me; in the second case, I must first look about elsewhere to see what results may be combined with it which would affect myself. For to deviate from the principle of duty is beyond all doubt wicked; but to be unfaithful to my maxim of prudence may often be very advantageous to me, although to abide by it is certainly safer. The shortest way, however, and an unerring one, to discover the answer to this question whether a lying promise is consistent with duty, is to ask myself, Should I be content that my maxim (to extricate myself from difficulty by a false promise) should hold good as a universal law, for myself as well as for others? And should I be able to say to myself, "Everyone may make a deceitful promise when he finds himself in a difficulty from which he cannot otherwise extricate himself"? Then I presently become aware that while I can will the lie, I can by no means will that lying should be a universal law. For with such a law there would be no promises at all, since it would be in vain to allege my intention in regard to my future actions to those who would not believe this allegation, or if they over-hastily did so, would pay me back in my own coin. Hence my maxim, as soon as it should be made a universal law, would necessarily destroy itself.

I do not, therefore, need any far-reaching penetration to discern what I have to do in order that my will be morally good. Inexperienced in the course of the world, incapable of being prepared for all its contingencies, I only ask myself: Canst thou also will that thy maxim should be a universal law? If not, then it must be rejected, and that not because of a disadvantage accruing from it to myself or even to others, but because it cannot enter as a principle into a possible universal legislation, and reason extorts from me immediate respect for such legislation. I do not indeed as yet *discern* on what this respect is based (this the philosopher may inquire), but at least I understand this, that it is an estimation of the worth which far outweighs all worth of what is recommended by inclination, and that the necessity of acting from *pure* respect for the practical law is what constitutes duty, to which every other motive must give place, because it is the condition of a will being good *in itself,* and the worth of such a will is above everything. . . .

. . . Everything in nature works according to laws. Rational beings alone have the faculty of acting according *to the conception* of laws, that is according to principles, i.e., have a *will.* Since the deduction of actions from principles requires *reason,* the will is nothing but practical reason. If reason infallibly determines the will, then the actions of such a being which are recognized as objectively necessary are subjectively necessary also, i.e., the will is a faculty to choose *that only* which reason independent on inclination recognizes as practically necessary, i.e., as good. But if reason of itself does not sufficiently determine the will, if the latter is subject also to subjective conditions (particular impulses) which do not always coincide with the objective conditions; in a word, if the will does not *in itself* completely accord with reason (which is actually the case with men), then the actions which objectively are recognized as necessary are subjectively contingent, and the determination of such a will according to objective laws is *obligation,* that is to say, the relation of the objective laws to a will that is not thoroughly good is conceived as the determination of the will of a rational being by principles of reason, but which the will from its nature does not of necessity follow.

The conception of an objective principle, in so far as it is obligatory for a will, is called a command (of reason), and the formula of the command is called an Imperative. . . .

Now all *imperatives* command either *hypothetically* or *categorically.* The former represent the practical necessity of a possible action as means to something else that is willed (or at least which one might possibly will). The categorical imperative would be that which represented an action as necessary of itself without reference to another end, i.e. as objectively necessary.

Since every practical law represents a possible action as good, and on this account, for a subject who is practically determinable by reason, necessary, all imperatives are formulae determining an action which is necessary according to the principle of a will good in some respects. If now the action is good only as a means *to something else,* then the imperative is *hypothetical;* if it is conceived as good *in itself* and consequently as being necessarily the principle of a will which of itself conforms to reason, then it is *categorical.* . . .

When I conceive a hypothetical imperative, in general I do not know beforehand what it will contain until I am given the condition. But when I conceive a categorical imperative, I know at once what it contains. For as the imperative contains besides the law only the necessity that the maxims shall conform to this law, while the law contains no conditions restricting it, there remains nothing but the general statement that the maxim of the action should conform to a universal law, and it is this conformity alone that the imperative properly represents as necessary.

There is . . . but one categorical imperative, namely, this: *Act only on that maxim whereby thou canst at the same time will that it should become a universal law.*

Now if all imperatives of duty can be deduced from this one imperative as from their principle, then, although it should remain undecided whether what is called duty is not merely a vain notion, yet at least we shall be able to show what we understand by it and what this notion means.

Since the universality of the law according to which effects are produced constitutes what is properly called *nature* in the most general sense (as to form), that is the existence of things so far as it is determined by general laws, the imperative of duty may be expressed thus: *Act as if the maxim of thy action were to become by thy will a universal law of nature.*

We will now enumerate a few duties, adopting the usual division of them into duties to ourselves and to others, and into perfect and imperfect duties.

1. A man reduced to despair by a series of misfortunes feels wearied of life, but is still so far in possession of his reason that he can ask himself whether it would not be contrary to his duty to himself to take his own life. Now he inquires whether the maxim of his action could become a universal law of nature. His maxim is: From self-love I adopt it as a principle to shorten my life when its longer duration is likely to bring more evil than satisfaction. It is asked then simply whether this principle founded on self-love can become a universal law of nature. Now we see at once that a system of nature of which it should be a law to destroy life by means of the very feeling whose special nature it is to impel to the improvement of life would contradict itself, and therefore could not exist as a system of nature; hence that maxim cannot possibly exist as a universal law of nature, and consequently would be wholly inconsistent with the supreme principle of all duty.

2. Another finds himself forced by necessity to borrow money. He knows that he will not be able to repay it, but sees also that nothing will be lent to him, unless he promises stoutly to repay it in a definite time. He desires to make this promise, but he has still so much conscience as to ask himself: Is it not unlawful and inconsistent with duty to get out of a difficulty in this way? Suppose, however, that he resolves to do so, then the maxim of his action would be expressed thus: When I think myself in want of money, I will borrow money and promise to repay it, although I know that I never can do so. Now this principle of self-love or of one's own advantage may perhaps be consistent with my whole future welfare; but the question now is: Is it right? I change then the suggestion of self-love into a universal law, and state the question thus: How would it be if my maxim were a universal law? Then I see at once that it could never hold as a universal law of nature, but would necessarily contradict itself. For supposing it to be a universal law that everyone when he thinks himself in a difficulty should be able to promise whatever he pleases, with the purpose of not keeping his promise, the promise itself would become impossible, as well as the end that one might have in view in it, since no one would consider that anything was promised to him, but would ridicule all such statements as vain pretences.

3. A third finds in himself a talent which with the help of some culture might make him a useful man in many respects. But he finds himself in comfortable circumstances, and prefers to indulge in pleasure rather than to take pains in enlarging and improving his happy natural capacities. He asks, however, whether his maxim of neglect of his natural gifts, besides agreeing with his inclination to indulgence, agrees also with what is called duty. He sees then that a system of nature could indeed subsist with such a universal law although men (like the South Sea islanders) should let their talents rest, and resolve to devote their lives merely to idleness, amusement, and propagation of their species—in a word, to enjoyment; but he cannot possibly *will* that this should be a universal law of nature, or be implanted in us as such by a natural instinct. For, as a rational being, he necessarily wills that his faculties be developed, since they serve him, and have been given him, for all sorts of possible purposes.

4. A fourth, who is in prosperity, while he sees that others have to contend, with great wretchedness and that he could help them, thinks: What concern is it of mine? Let everyone be as happy as Heaven pleases, or as he can make himself; I will take nothing from him nor even envy him, only I do not wish to contribute anything to his welfare or to his assistance in distress! Now no doubt if such a mode of thinking were a universal law, the human race might very well subsist, and doubtless even better than in a state in which everyone talks of sympathy and good-will, or even takes care occasionally to put it into practice, but, on the other side, also cheats when he can, betrays the rights of men, or otherwise violates them. But although it is possible that a universal law of nature might

exist in accordance with that maxim, it is impossible to *will* that such a principle should have the universal validity of a law of nature. For a will which resolved this would contradict itself, inasmuch as many cases might occur in which one would have need of the love and sympathy of others, and in which, by such a law of nature, sprung from his own will, he would deprive himself of all hope of the aid he desires. . . .

We have thus established at least this much, that if duty is a conception which is to have any import and real legislative authority for our actions, it can only be expressed in categorical, and not at all in hypothetical, imperatives. We have also, which is of great importance, exhibited clearly and definitely for every practical application the content of the categorical imperative, which must contain the principle of all duty if there is such a thing at all. We have not yet, however, advanced so far as to prove à priori that there actually is such an imperative, that there is a practical law which commands absolutely of itself, and without any other impulse, and that the following of this law is duty. . . .

Now I say: man and generally any rational being *exists* as an end in himself, *not merely as a means* to be arbitrarily used by this or that will, but in all his actions, whether they concern himself or other rational beings, must be always regarded at the same time as an end. All objects of the inclinations have only a conditional worth; for if the inclinations and the wants founded on them did not exist, then their object would be without value. But the inclinations themselves being sources of want are so far from having an absolute worth for which they should be desired, that, on the contrary, it must be the universal wish of every rational being to be wholly free from them. Thus the worth of any object which is *to be acquired* by our action is always conditional. Beings whose existence depends not on our will but on nature's, have nevertheless, if they are non-rational beings, only a relative value as means, and are therefore called *things*; rational beings, on the contrary, are called *persons*, because their very nature points them out as ends in themselves, that is as something which must not be used merely as means, and so far therefore restricts freedom of

action (and is an object of respect). These, therefore, are not merely subjective ends whose existence has a worth *for us* as an effort of our action, but *objective ends,* that is things whose existence is an end in itself: an end moreover for which no other can be substituted, which they should subserve *merely* as means, for otherwise nothing whatever would possess *absolute worth;* but if all worth were conditioned and therefore contingent, then there would be no supreme practical principle of reason whatever.

If then there is a supreme practical principle or, in respect of the human will, a categorical imperative, it must be one which, being drawn from the conception of that which is necessarily an end for everyone because it is an *an end in itself,* constitutes an *objective* principle of will, and can therefore serve as a universal practical law. The foundation of this principle is: *rational nature exists as an end in itself.* Man necessarily conceives his own existence as being so: So far then this is a *subjective* principle of human actions. But every other rational being regards its existence similarly, just on the same rational principle, that holds for me: so that it is at the same time an objective principle, from which as a supreme practical law all laws of the will must be capable of being deduced. Accordingly the practical imperative will be as follows: *So act as to treat humanity, whether in thine own person or in that of any other, in every case as an end withal, never as means only. . . .*

The conception of every rational being as one which must consider itself as giving all the maxims of its will universal laws, so as to judge itself and its actions from this point of view—this conception leads to another which depends on it and is very fruitful, namely, that of a *kingdom of ends.*

By a *kingdom* I understand the union of different rational beings in a system by common laws. Now since it is by laws that ends are determined as regards their universal validity, hence, if we abstract from the personal differences of rational beings, and likewise from all the content of their private ends, we shall be able to conceive all ends combined in a systematic whole (including both rational beings as ends in themselves, and also the special ends which each may propose of himself), that is to say, we can conceive a kingdom of ends, which on the preceding principles is possible.

For all rational beings come under the *law* that each of them must treat itself and all others *never merely as means,* but in every case *at the same time as ends in themselves.* Hence results a systematic union of rational beings by common objective laws, i.e., a kingdom which may be called a kingdom of ends. . . .

DISCUSSION QUESTIONS

1. What does it mean to treat people as "ends in themselves"? What does it mean to treat others "merely as a means"? Explain the difference.

2. Why does Kant believe that the good will is the only thing that is good without qualification? Do you agree with him? Can you think of anything else that might be good without qualification? How might Kant respond to your choice?

3. Kant believes that animals have no moral rights because they are not ends-in-themselves. Why aren't animals ends-in-themselves? Do you agree with Kant's position? Discuss.

4. The Golden Rule says that you should do unto others as you would have them do unto you. What is the difference between the Golden Rule and the categorical imperative? Explain.

5. What is the major benefit of Kant's moral theory? What is its major weakness? In what sense would you call your own moral beliefs Kantian? Where do your views differ from Kant's?

6. Compare and contrast the approach to morality found in the Bible with Kant's approach. What are their similarities and differences?

Sophie's Choice
[USA 1982] 2 hours, 30 minutes
Directed by Alan J. Pakula

Stingo (Peter MacNicol) moves to New York City shortly after World War II in hopes of achieving success as a writer. At a Brooklyn boardinghouse, he meets Sophie Zawistowska (Meryl Streep), a Polish-Catholic immigrant and Holocaust survivor, and Nathan (Kevin Kline), her Jewish lover. Stingo befriends the couple and enters into their erratic world, where he witnesses Nathan's maniacal mood swings and verbal abuse of Sophie. Later, Stingo receives a call from Nathan's brother, Larry Lawndale (Stephen D. Newman), who reveals that Nathan is not really the successful Pfizer research biologist he claims to be; instead, he holds a minor position in Pfizer's library and suffers from paranoid schizophrenia. Sophie is unaware of Nathan's lies or his illness, and it soon becomes apparent to Stingo that Sophie has some secrets of her own. As Nathan's illness progresses, he becomes frighteningly unpredictable, and Stingo, who has fallen in love with Sophie, attempts to rescue her by taking her out of town.

On their brief trip, Stingo learns about the choice that Sophie had to make on the night the Nazis sent her to Auschwitz with her children. Sophie reveals that she was ordered by an SS doctor (Karlheinz Hackl) to select one of her children to live and the other one to die. He said that if she did not choose one of them, he would send both to the gas chambers. Sophie pleaded with him to no avail, and at the last moment she tearfully told the Nazis to take her youngest child, her little girl, away to die. After revealing her terrible secret to Stingo, Sophie and Stingo make love, but he awakens in the morning to find a note from her saying that she has gone back to Nathan. The movie ends when Stingo returns to the boardinghouse in hopes of finding Sophie. Instead, he discovers that she and Nathan have committed suicide together.

The movie is based on the best-selling autobiographical novel by William Styron. Meryl Streep won an Oscar for her performance as Sophie.

DISCUSSION QUESTIONS

1. If you were Sophie, would you choose one of your children to live and another to die if the only other alternative was having both die? On what basis would you morally justify your response?

2. If presented with a choice like Sophie's, what would a Kantian do? Why?

3. Would proponents of the Koran and the Bible handle Sophie's choice in the same way? Why or why not?

4. Consider the following dialogue between Sophie and an SS Doctor:

    SS DOCTOR   "You may keep one of your children."

    SOPHIE   "I beg your pardon?"

    SS DOCTOR   "You may keep one of your children. The other one must go."

    SOPHIE   "You mean, I have to choose?"

    SS DOCTOR   "You're a Polack, not a Yid. That gives you a privilege, a choice."

    SOPHIE   "I can't choose! I can't choose!"

    SS DOCTOR   "Be quiet! Choose! Or I'll send them both over there! Make a choice!"

    SOPHIE   "Don't make me choose! I can't!"

    SS DOCTOR   "I'll send them both over there. Shut up! Enough! I told you to shut up! Make a choice!"

    SOPHIE   "Don't make me choose! I can't!"

    SS DOCTOR   "Take both children away!"

    SOPHIE   "Take my little girl! Take my baby! Take my little girl!"

    The SS doctor says choosing is a "privilege." Is he right? Why or why not?

5. Some might argue that choosing between her children places some moral responsibility upon Sophie for the death of her little girl, whereas not having a choice places no moral responsibility for the death of her children upon her. Evaluate this claim. How would a Kantian respond to it?

6. Consider the following exchange between Wanda (Katharina Thalach), a leader in the Resistance, and Sophie:

    WANDA   "All we ask of you is to translate some stolen Gestapo documents."

    SOPHIE   "I can't. I cannot endanger my children."

    WANDA   "Your children could be next."

    SOPHIE   "No. No. I do not want to get involved."

    If you were Sophie, would you translate the documents? How would you morally justify your response? Compare your response to those of a Kantian and proponents of the Bible and the Koran.

7. Consider the following dialogue between Sophie and a fellow prisoner in the shower (Eugeniusz Priwieziencew):

PRISONER   "Will you help the Resistance?"

SOPHIE   "But what can *I* do?"

PRISONER   "Emmi Hoess has a radio. Her room is under her father's office . . . where you will work. If you could get the radio . . . bring it down here, I could smuggle it out."

SOPHIE   "Sure, sure. I give you the radio . . . you smuggle it out, and I get shot for stealing it."

PRISONER   "That's why you must make Hoess trust you."

SOPHIE   "But how?"

PRISONER   "He is a man . . . and you are a woman . . ."

SOPHIE   "Of course! Bald, starving, stinking of germicides. Very impressive!"

PRISONER   "You're wrong. You look German. You speak cultured German. You'll be working with him alone . . . and he's an unhappy man."

If you were Sophie, would you help the resistance by making Hoess a "happy" man? How would you morally justify your response? Compare your response to a Kantian response.

8. Consider this discussion between Dr. Lawndale and Stingo:

DR. LAWNDALE   "This, uh, . . . biologist business is my brother's masquerade. He has no degree of any kind. All that is a simple fabrication. The truth is he's quite mad."

STINGO   "Christ!"

DR. LAWNDALE   "It's one of those conditions where weeks, months, even years go by without manifestations, and then pow! Oh, he has a job at Pfizer in the company library, . . . where he can do . . . without bothering anyone, and occasionally he does a little research for one of the legitimate biologists on the staff. . . . I'm not sure Nathan would forgive me if he knew that I told you. He made me swear never to tell Sophie. She knows nothing."

STINGO   "What can I do?"

DR. LAWNDALE   "If he could stay off the drugs, he might have a chance."

STINGO   "The drugs . . . what is he on?"

DR. LAWNDALE   "Benzodrine–cocaine. You didn't know?"

STINGO   "No, I did not."

DR. LAWNDALE   "I don't want to sound like I'm asking you to spy, but if you could simply keep tabs on him and report back to me by phone from time to time, letting me know how he's getting on. I'm sorry to have to involve you this way."

STINGO   "I don't think you understand . . . I love them both–they're friends of mine."

Could a Kantian morally justify Stingo's lying to Sophie about Nathan's medical condition and job status? Why or why not? Compare the Kantian response with a response from a Confucian and a proponent of the Koran. Which response do you prefer, and why?

9. Which of the following approaches to morality is closest to that practiced by Sophie during and after the war: Judeo-Christianity (the Bible), Confucianism, Buddhism, Islam law (the Koran), virtue theory (Aristotle), or Kantianism? Why?

JOHN STUART MILL

UTILITARIANISM

John Stuart Mill explains morality in terms of the principle of utility, or the greatest-happiness principle. According to the principle of utility, we should attempt to produce the greatest balance of happiness over unhappiness. However, in this selection, Mill seeks to differentiate his brand of utilitarianism from that of his predecessor and mentor, Jeremy Bentham (1748–1832), the "father" of utilitarianism. Around the age of fourteen, Mill discovered the philosophy of Bentham, whose works gave him "a creed, a doctrine, a philosophy . . . a religion."

One of the major differences between Bentham's utilitarianism and Mill's is that Bentham's is based on considerations regarding the *quantity* of pleasure or pain (intensity, duration, certainty, proximity, fecundity, purity, and extent), whereas Mill's is focused on the *quality* of pleasure or pain, distinguishing the *higher* human pleasures from the *lower* human pleasures. Whereas Bentham's utilitarianism made the criterion of ethics the production of the greatest amount of pleasure and the least amount of pain, Mill makes a distinction between "higher pleasures," which are of more value, and "lower pleasures," which are of lesser value. Mill, then, unlike Bentham, distinguishes between happiness and mere sensual pleasure. "It is better to be a human being dissatisfied than a pig satisfied," said Mill, "better to be Socrates dissatisfied than a fool satisfied." Whereas Bentham tells us to maximize the sum of pleasure, Mill tells us to maximize the sum of *higher* pleasure. Consequently, Mill's utilitarianism is sometimes called *eudaimonistic utilitarianism* (*eudaimonia* is Greek for "happiness") to distinguish it from Bentham's *hedonistic utilitarianism* (*hedone* is Greek for "pleasure").

In general, utilitarianism is a form of *consequentialist* (or teleological) moral theory in that it attempts to locate the morality of actions in their nonmoral consequences. In addition to eudaimonistic and hedonistic utilitarianism, utilitarianism may be divided into *act* and *rule* utilitarianism. *Act utilitarianism* judges the rightness or wrongness of an action on a case-by-case basis according to the utilitarian principle. *Rule utilitarianism* uses the utilitarian principle to judge moral rules, not individual actions, by examining the effects on overall happiness of rules. There are some problems with rule utilitarianism, not only because it is far from clear how to apply the principle to rules but also because rules that allow for exceptions seem better than those that do not, and making exceptions threatens to reduce rule utilitarianism to act utilitarianism. The following is a selection from Mill's *Utilitarianism* (1863). A biographical sketch of Mill appears in chapter 1.

. . . The creed which accepts as the foundation of morals, Utility, or the Greatest Happiness Principle, holds that actions are right in proportion as they tend to promote happiness, wrong as they tend to produce the reverse of happiness. By happiness is intended pleasure, and the absence of pain; by unhappiness, pain, and the privation of pleasure. To give a clear view of the moral standard set up by the theory, much more requires to be said; in particular, what things it includes: in the ideas of pain and pleasure; and to what extent this is left an open question. But these supplementary explanations do not affect the theory of life on which this theory of morality is grounded—namely, that pleasure, and freedom from pain, are the only things desirable as ends; and that all desirable things (which are as numerous in the utilitarian as in any other scheme) are desirable either for the pleasure inherent in themselves, or as a means to the promotion of pleasure and the prevention of pain.

Now, such a theory of life excites in many minds, and among them in some of the most estimable in feeling and purpose, inveterate dislike. To suppose that life has (as they express it) no higher end than pleasure—no better and nobler object of desire and pursuit—they designate as utterly mean and groveling; as a doctrine worthy only of swine, to whom the followers of Epicurus were, at a very early period, contemptuously likened; and modern holders of the doctrine are occasionally made the subject of equally polite comparisons by its German, French, and English assailants.

When thus attacked, the Epicureans have always answered, that it is not they, but their accusers, who represent human nature in a degrading light; since the accusation supposes human beings to be capable of no pleasures except those of which swine are capable. If this supposition were true, the charge could not be gainsaid, but would then be no longer an imputation; for if the sources of pleasure were precisely the same to human beings and to swine, the rule of life which is good enough for the one would be good enough for the other. The comparison of the Epicurean life to that of beasts is felt as degrading, precisely because a beast's pleasures do not satisfy a human being's conception of happiness. Human beings have faculties more elevated than the animal appetites, and when once made conscious of them, do not regard anything as happiness which does not include their gratification. I do not, indeed; consider the Epicureans to have been by any means faultless in drawing out their scheme of consequences from the utilitarian principle. To do this in any sufficient manner, many Stoic, as well as Christian elements require to be included. But there is no known Epicurean theory of life which does not assign to the pleasures of the intellect, of the feelings and imagination, and of the moral sentiments, a much higher value as pleasures than to those of mere sensation. It must be admitted, however, that utilitarian writers in general have placed the superiority of mental over bodily pleasures chiefly in the greater permanency, safety, uncostliness, etc., of the former—that is, in their circumstantial advantages rather than in their intrinsic nature. And on all these points utilitarians have fully proved their case; but they might have taken the other, and, as it may be called, higher ground, with entire consistency. It is quite compatible with the principle of utility to recognize the fact, that some *kinds* of pleasure are more desirable and more valuable than others. It would be absurd that while, in estimating all other things, quality is considered as well as quantity, the estimation of pleasures should be supposed to depend on quantity alone.

If I am asked, what I mean by difference of quality in pleasures, or what makes one pleasure more valuable than another, merely as a pleasure, except its being greater in amount, there is but one possible answer. Of two pleasures, if there be one which all or almost all who have experience of both give a decided preference, irrespective of any feeling of moral obligation to prefer it, that is the more desirable pleasure. If one of the two is, by those who are competently acquainted with both, placed so far above the other that they prefer it, even though knowing it to be attended with a great amount of discontent, and would not resign it for any quantity of the other pleasure which their nature is capable of, we are justified in ascribing to the preferred enjoyment a superiority in quantity, so far out-weighing quantity as to render it, in comparison, of small account.

Now it is an unquestionable fact that those who are equally acquainted with, and equally capable of appreciating and enjoying, both, do give a most marked preference to the manner of existence which employs their higher faculties. Few human creatures would consent to be changed into any of the lower animals, for a promise of the fullest allowance of a beast's pleasures; no intelligent human being would consent to be a fool, no instructed person would be an ignoramus, no person of feeling and conscience would be selfish and base, even though they should be persuaded that the fool, the dunce, or the rascal is better satisfied with his lot than they are with theirs. They would not resign what they possess more than he for the most complete satisfaction of all the desires which they have in common with him. If they ever fancy they would, it is only in cases of unhappiness so extreme, that to escape from it they would exchange their lot for almost any other, however undesirable in their own eyes. A being of higher faculties requires more to make him happy, is capable probably of more acute suffering, and certainly accessible to it at more points, than one of an inferior type; but in spite of these liabilities, he can never really wish to sink into what he feels to be a lower grade of existence. We may give what explanation we please of this unwillingness; we may attribute it to pride, a name which is given indiscriminately to some of the most and to some of the least estimable feelings of which mankind are capable; we may refer it to the love of liberty and personal independence, an appeal to which was with the Stoics one of the most effective means for the inculcation of it; to the love of power, or to the love of excitement, both of which do really enter into and contribute to it; but its most appropriate appellation is a sense of dignity, which all human beings possess in one form or another, and in some, though by no means in exact, proportion to their higher faculties, and which is so essential a part of the happiness of those in whom it is strong, that nothing which conflicts with it could be, otherwise than momentarily, an object of desire to them. Whoever supposes that this preference takes place at a sacrifice of happiness— that the superior being, in anything like equal circumstances, is not happier than the inferior— confounds the two very different ideas, of happiness, and content. It is indisputable that the being whose capacities of enjoyment are low, has the greatest chance of having them fully satisfied; and a highly endowed being will always feel that any happiness which he can look for, as the world is constituted, is imperfect. But he can learn to bear its imperfections, if they are at all bearable; and they will not make him envy the being who is indeed unconscious of the imperfections, but only because he feels not at all the good which those imperfections qualify. It is better to be a human being dissatisfied than a pig satisfied; better to be Socrates dissatisfied than a fool satisfied. And if the fool, or the pig, are of a different opinion, it is because they only know their own side of the question. The other party to the comparison knows both sides.

It may be objected, that many who are capable of the higher pleasures, occasionally, under the influence of temptation, postpone them to the lower. But this is quite compatible with a full appreciation of the intrinsic superiority of the higher. Men often, from infirmity of character, make their election for the nearer good, though they know it to be the less valuable; and this no less when the choice is between two bodily pleasures, than when it is between bodily and mental. They pursue sensual indulgences to the injury of health, though perfectly aware that health is the greater good. It may be further objected, that many who begin with youthful enthusiasm for everything noble, as they advance in years sink into indolence and selfishness. But I do not believe that those who undergo this very common change, voluntarily choose the lower description of pleasures in preference to the higher. I believe that before they devote themselves exclusively to the one, they have already become incapable of the other. Capacity for the nobler feelings is in most natures a very tender plant, easily killed, not only by hostile influences, but by mere want of sustenance; and in the majority of young persons it speedily dies away if the occupations to which their position in life has devoted them, and the society into which it has thrown them, are not favorable to keeping that higher capacity in exercise. Men lose their high aspirations as they lose their intellectual tastes, because they have not time or opportunity for indulging them; and they addict themselves to inferior pleasures, not because they deliberately prefer them, but because they are either the only ones to which they have access, or the only ones which they are any longer capable of enjoying. It may be questioned whether any one who has remained equally susceptible to both classes of pleasures, ever knowingly and calmly preferred the lower; though many, in all ages, have broken down in an ineffectual attempt to combine both.

From this verdict of the only competent judges, I apprehend there can be no appeal. On a question which is the best worth having of two pleasures, or which of two modes of existence is the most grateful to the feelings, apart from its moral attributes and from its consequences, the judgment of those who are qualified by knowledge of both, or, if they differ, that of the majority among them, must be admitted as final. And there needs to be the less hesitation to accept this judgment respecting the quality of pleasures, since there is no other tribunal to be referred to even on the question of quantity. What means are there of determining which is the acutest of two pains, or the intensest of two pleasurable sensations, except the general suffrage of those who are familiar with both? Neither pains nor pleasures are homogeneous, and pain is always heterogeneous with pleasure. What is there to decide whether a particular pleasure is worth purchasing at the cost of a particular pain, except the feelings and judgment of the experienced? When, therefore, those feelings and judgment declare the pleasures derived from the higher faculties to be preferable *in kind,* apart from the question of intensity, to those of which the animal nature, disjoined from the higher faculties, is susceptible, they are entitled on this subject to the same regard.

I have dwelt on this point, as being a necessary part of a perfectly just conception of Utility or Happiness; considered as the directive rule of human conduct. But it is by no means an indispensable condition to the acceptance of the utilitarian standard; for that standard is not the agent's own greatest happiness, but the greatest amount of happiness altogether; and if it may possibly be doubted whether a noble character is always the happier for its nobleness, there can be no doubt that it makes other people happier, and that the world in general is immensely a gainer by it. Utilitarianism, therefore, could only attain its

end by the general cultivation of nobleness of character, even if each individual were only benefited by the nobleness of others, and his own, so far as happiness is concerned, were a sheer deduction from the benefit. But the bar enunciation of such an absurdity as this last, renders refutation superfluous.

According to the Greatest Happiness Principle, as above explained, the ultimate end, with reference to and for the sake of which all other things are desirable (whether we are considering our own good or that of other people), is an existence exempt as far as possible from pain, and as rich as possible in enjoyments, both in point of quantity and quality; the test of quality, and the rule for measuring it against quantity, being the preference felt by those who in their opportunities of experience, to which must be added their habits of self-consciousness and self-observation, are best furnished with the means of comparison. This, being, according to the utilitarian opinion, the end of human action, is necessarily also the standard of morality; which may accordingly be defined, the rules and precepts for human conduct, by the observance of which an existence such as has been described might be, to the greatest extent possible, secured to all mankind; and not to them only, but, so far as the nature of things admits, to the whole sentient creation. . . .

The objectors to utilitarianism cannot always be charged with representing it in a discreditable light. On the contrary, those among them who entertain anything like a just idea of its disinterested character, sometimes find fault with its standard as being too high for humanity. They say it is exacting too much to require that people shall always act from the inducement of promoting the general interests of society. But this is to mistake the very meaning of a standard of morals, and confound the rule of action with the motive of it. It is the business of ethics to tell us what are our duties, or by what test we may know them; but no system of ethics requires that the sole motive of all we do shall be a feeling of duty; on the contrary, ninety-nine hundredths of all our actions are done from other motives, and rightly so done, if the rule of duty does not condemn them. It is the more unjust to utilitarianism that this particular misapprehension should be made a ground of objection to it, inasmuch as utilitarian moralists have gone beyond almost all others in affirming that the motive has nothing to do with the morality of the action, though much with the worth of the agent. He who saves a fellow-creature from drowning does what is morally right, whether his motive be duty, or the hope of being paid for his trouble; he who betrays the friend that trusts him, is guilty of a crime, even if his object be to serve another friend to whom he is under greater obligation. But to speak only of actions done from the motive of duty, and in direct obedience to principle: it is a misapprehension of the utilitarian mode of thought, to conceive it as implying that people should fix their minds upon so wide a generality as the world, or society at large. The great majority of good actions are intended not for the benefit of the world, but for that of individuals, of which the good of the world is made up; and the thoughts of the most virtuous man need not on these occasions travel beyond the particular persons concerned, except so far as is necessary to assure himself that in benefiting them he is not violating the rights, that is, the legitimate and authorised expectations, of anyone else. The multiplication of happiness is, according to the utilitarian ethics, the object of virtue: the occasions on which any person (except one in a thousand) has it in his power to do this on an extended scale, in other words to be a public benefactor, are but exceptional; and on these occasions alone is he called on to consider public utility; in every other case, private utility, the interest or happiness of some few persons, is all he has to attend to. Those alone the influence of whose actions extends to society in general, need concern themselves habitually about so large an object. In the case of abstinences indeed—of things which people forbear to do from moral considerations, though the consequences in the particular case might be beneficial—it would be unworthy of an intelligent agent not to be consciously aware that the action is of a class which, if practiced generally, would be generally injurious, and that this is the ground of the obligation to abstain from it. The amount of regard for the public interest implied in this recognition, is no greater than is demanded by every system of morals, for they all enjoin to abstain from whatever is manifestly pernicious to society. . . .

It has already been remarked, that questions of ultimate ends do not admit of proof, in the ordinary acceptation of the term. To be incapable of proof by reasoning is common to all first principles; to the first premises of our knowledge, as well as to those of our conduct. But the former, being matters of fact, may be the subject of a direct appeal to the faculties which judge of fact—namely, our senses, and our internal consciousness. Can an appeal be made to the same faculties on questions of practical ends? Or by what other faculty is cognizance taken of them?

Questions about ends are, in other words, questions about what things are desirable. The utilitarian doctrine is, that happiness is desirable, and the only thing desirable as an end; all other things being only desirable as means to that end. What ought to be required of this doctrine—what conditions is it to requisite that the doctrine should fulfil—to make good its claim to be believed?

The only proof capable of being given that an object is visible, is that people actually see it. The only proof that a sound is audible, is that people hear it: and so of the other sources of our experience. In like manner, I apprehend, the sole evidence it is possible to produce that anything is desirable, is that people do actually desire it. If the end which the utilitarian doctrine proposes to itself were not, in theory and in practice, acknowledged to be an end, nothing could ever convince any person that it was so. No reason can be given why the general happiness is desirable, except that each person, so far as he believes it to be attainable, desires his own happiness. This, however, being a fact, we have not only all the proof which the case admits of, but all which it is possible to require, that happiness is a good: that each person's happiness is a good to that person, and the general happiness, therefore, a good to the aggregate of all persons. Happiness has made out its title as *one* of the ends of conduct, and consequently one of the criteria of morality.

But it has not, by this alone, proved itself to be the sole criterion. To do that, it would seem, by the same rule, necessary to show, not only that people desire happiness, but that they never desire anything else. . . .

We have now then, an answer to the question, of what sort of proof the principle of utility is susceptible. If the opinion which I have now stated is psychologically true—if human nature is so constituted as to desire nothing which is not either a part of happiness or a means of happiness, we can have no other proof, and we require no other, that these are the only things desirable. If so, happiness is the sole end of human action, and the promotion of it the test by which to judge of all human conduct; from whence it necessarily follows that it must be the criterion of morality, since a part is included in the whole.

And now to decide whether this is really so; whether mankind do desire nothing for itself but that which is a pleasure to them, or of which the absence is a pain; we have evidently arrived at a question of fact and experience, dependent, like all similar questions, upon evidence. It can only be determined by practiced self-consciousness and self-observation, assisted by observation of others. I believe that these sources of evidence, impartially consulted, will declare that desiring a thing and finding it pleasant, aversion to it and thinking of it as painful, are phenomena entirely inseparable, or rather two parts of the same phenomenon; in strictness of language, two different modes of naming the same psychological fact: that to think of an object as desirable (unless for the sake of its consequences), and to think of it as pleasant, are one and the same thing; and that to desire anything, except in proportion as the idea of it is pleasant, is a physical and metaphysical impossibility.

DISCUSSION QUESTIONS

1. What is Mill's principle of utility? What does he mean by "utility"? Does he mean the same thing as Bentham? Explain.

2. How does Mill explain the fact that some people choose lower pleasures over higher pleasures? Do you agree with his assessment?

3. How does Mill prove the principle of utility? Do you agree with his proof? Explain.

4. What are some objections that might be raised against Mill's eudaimonistic utilitarianism? How might he respond to them?

5. Both Mill and Aristotle utilize concepts of "happiness" in their moral theories. What are their similarities and differences? Which do you prefer, and why?

The Life of David Gale
[USA 2003] 2 hours, 11 minutes
Directed by Alan Parker

Former University of Austin philosophy professor David Gale (Kevin Spacey) is sentenced to death for the rape and murder of his leukemia-stricken colleague Constance Harraway (Laura Linney). Ironically, both David and Constance were also leading activists for Death Watch, a group opposed to capital punishment in Texas. A week before his execution, David asks to speak with journalist Bitsey Bloom (Kate Winslet) to tell his story. Bitsey and her intern, Zack Stemmons (Gabriel Mann), fly to Texas to cover the story, and, as the interviews progress, Bitsey learns more than she bargained for. First, David reveals to Bitsey that he thinks someone is framing him because the method of death that he mentioned once in an article was used to kill Constance. Furthermore, the murderer left a tripod in the room with Constance's body, which David feels was intended to taunt him since he knows that evidence of the real crime exists somewhere. Later, Bitsey finds a mysterious "death tape" in her motel room that shows Constance dying by the method that David had previously mentioned to her.

After finding the tape, Bitsey and Zack go on a desperate search for the truth. Bitsey notes that the tape shows Constance struggling only as she runs out of air; she does not struggle from the beginning as she would if someone put her in this position against her will. Bitsey believes this means that Constance killed herself. Furthermore, Bitsey arrives at the conclusion that Dusty Wright (Matt Craven), a death penalty opponent and close friend of Constance, was supposed to release a more complete version of the tape showing that Constance killed herself, thus proving Death Watch's point that an innocent man can be sentenced to death. Bitsey and Zack believe that Dusty is a zealot who was supposed to release the tape soon after David's sentencing but held onto it over the years because he believes that an innocent man being put to death is more politically powerful than an innocent man almost being put to death. Bitsey and Zack raid Dusty's house and find the original tape that shows Constance putting the bag over her own head. Bitsey then races against time to get the video to the authorities before David is put to death. However, she is too late and arrives only to find out that David has been executed via lethal injection. What Bitsey does not bargain for is subsequently receiving an extended tape labeled "Off the Record." This version shows that David was aware of the circumstances surrounding Constance's death and that he even played a role in the plan himself.

DISCUSSION QUESTIONS

1.   How far would you be willing to go to support your beliefs or principles? Would you, like David and Constance, sacrifice your life to prove that innocent persons can be executed? Why or why not?

2.   Would a utilitarian be able to justify Constance's actions? Why or why not?

3.   Would a utilitarian be able to justify David's actions? Why or why not?

4.   Is it ever morally justifiable to sacrifice your own life in an effort to save innocent persons? Compare Kantian and utilitarian responses to this question. Which do you prefer, and why?

5.   Consider the following dialogue between David and Bitsey:

DAVID   "Constance was murdered by what is known as the Secure Tot Method. You're handcuffed, forced to swallow the key; your mouth is taped, and a bag is sealed around your head, and you're left there to suffocate. The Secure Tot did it to Romanians when they wouldn't inform or confess. Sometimes the bag was ripped off your head at the last moment to give you a second chance; otherwise, you died knowing that the key to your freedom was inside of you the entire time. It's a cheap but effective method. The problem is I once mentioned it in an article that I wrote. Prosecution never knew that."

BITSEY   "Someone's framing you?"

DAVID   "Oh, it's more than that. There was a tripod."

BITSEY   "Right—facing her body. Back on the record?"

DAVID   "Yes. The tripod had no fingerprints on it. That means that somebody brought it there, set it up, wiped it clean and left it. Why? It's as if they wanted me to know that somewhere out there is a record of exactly what happened that afternoon. As if they wanted me to die knowing that the key to my freedom is out there somewhere."

BITSEY   "Maybe you're being paranoid."

DAVID   "Ms. Bloom, I used to be the state's leading death penalty abolitionist, and now I'm on death row. Doesn't that strike you as a little odd?"

BITSEY   "Any idea who they are?"

DAVID   "No, but I've got someone working on that—someone I'm relying on to prove my innocence."

BITSEY   "Belyeu's hired a detective?"

DAVID   "A journalist. She has to help me. You know I'm innocent."

BITSEY   "No—no, I don't."

What is the meaning of "innocent"? Do you think David is an "innocent" man? Why or why not? Is the meaning of "innocence" in David's case the same as the meaning of "innocence" in the case of a person falsely convicted of a murder and put to death for that crime? Discuss.

6.   Consider the following dialogue between Zack and Bitsey:

ZACK   "Why make it look like a murder?"

BITSEY   "I don't know. It's so calculated. She's handcuffed, taped at the mouth, the gloves, the tripod."

ZACK   "Why, Bitsey? Why fake your own murder? It doesn't make sense. The woman's a bleeding heart abolitionist. Why frame an innocent man? Why send Gale to the chair, for what?"

BITSEY   "What?"

ZACK   "Well, she had to know some innocent jerk would take the fall."

BITSEY   "Oh my God, Zack. That's it. That's why—to prove it happens. To have absolute proof that the system convicts innocents."

ZACK   "Get outta here!"

BITSEY   "No, that's how she thought. Come on, think about it! This woman lived for Death Watch. If she's gonna die anyway, why not die for it? That's why the tripod was here to record proof—undeniable proof! That's why we got the video!"

ZACK   "So a dead woman put the tape in your room?"

BITSEY   "No, of course not. I mean, she needed help—someone to keep it, release it—someone dedicated to the cause—someone she could trust."

Do David and Constance succeed in *absolutely* proving their point that innocent persons are executed? Why or why not?

7.   Consider the following exchange between Bitsey and Zack:

BITSEY   "Dusty's a bullhorner, a zealot who's OD'd on too many good causes. You know, the original plan was probably to release the tape after Gale's conviction; you know, after a year or so—It would force him to dry out, give him back his dignity. So Dusty Wright is sitting on this tape, waiting, and he's the only one who knows about it. So good ol' Dusty starts to think that an erroneous execution is a lot more politically useful than a last-minute save."

ZACK   "Because a last-minute save would only prove the system works."

BITSEY   "Almost martyrs don't count—Dusty's thinking: 'What's one murder if it stops thousands?'"

ZACK   "'So, I release the tape only after the execution.'"

BITSEY   "Which means he must have the original somewhere."

If you were Dusty, would allow David to be executed, or would you step in at the last moment and make him an "almost martyr"? Morally justify your response. Do you agree with the reasoning attributed to Dusty: "What's one murder if it stops thousands?"

JAMES RACHELS

EGOISM AND MORAL SKEPTICISM

J ames Rachels distinguishes between two types of egoism: psychological and ethical. *Psychological egoism* is the view that all people are selfish in everything they do. According to the psychological egoist, the only motive from which any of us ever acts is self-interest. *Ethical egoism*, unlike psychological egoism, is a normative view about how people *ought* to act. The ethical egoist believes that we have no obligation to do anything except what is in our own self-interest. According to the ethical egoist, whatever we do in our own self-interest, regardless of its effect on others, is morally justified. In this selection, Rachels lays out a number of difficulties with both types of egoism.

James Rachels (1941–2003) was university professor at the University of Alabama, Birmingham, where he had taught since 1977. He received his B.A. from Mercer College and his Ph.D. from the University of North Carolina. He also taught at Duke University, the University of Richmond, New York University, and the University of Miami. He is the author of *The End of Life: Euthanasia and Morality* (1986), *Created from Animals: The Moral Implications of Darwinism* (1991), *Can Ethics Provide Answers? And Other Essays in Moral Philosophy* (1997) and *The Elements of Moral Philosophy* (4th ed., 2002). The following selection is from *A New Introduction to Philosophy* (ed. Steven M. Cahn, 1971).

I

Our ordinary thinking about morality is full of assumptions that we almost never question. We assume, for example, that we have an obligation to consider the welfare of other people when we decide what actions to perform or what rules to obey; we think that we must refrain from acting in ways harmful to others, and that we must respect their rights and interests as well as our own. We also assume that people are in fact capable of being motivated by such considerations, that is, that people are not wholly selfish and that they do sometimes act in the interests of others.

Both of these assumptions have come under attack by moral skeptics, as long ago as by Glaucon in Book II of Plato's *Republic*. Glaucon recalls the legend of Gyges, a shepherd who was said to have found a magic ring in a fissure opened by an earthquake. The ring would make its wearer invisible and thus would enable him to go anywhere and do anything undetected. Gyges used the power of the ring to gain entry to the Royal Palace where he seduced the Queen, murdered the King, and subsequently seized the throne. Now Glaucon asks us to imagine that

there are two such rings, one given to a man of virtue and one given to a rogue. The rogue, of course, will use his ring unscrupulously and do anything necessary to increase his own wealth and power. He will recognize no moral constraints on his conduct, and, since the cloak of invisibility will protect him from discovery, he can do anything he pleases without fear of reprisal. So there will be no end to the mischief he will do. But how will the so-called virtuous man behave? Glaucon suggests that he will behave no better than the rogue: "No one, it is commonly believed, would have such iron strength of mind as to stand fast in doing right or keep his hands off other men's goods, when he could go to the market-place and fearlessly help himself to anything he wanted, enter houses and sleep with any woman he chose, set prisoners free and kill men at his pleasure, and in a word go about among men with the powers of a god. He would behave no better than the other; both would take the same course." Moreover, why shouldn't he? Once he is freed from the fear of reprisal, why shouldn't a man simply do what he pleases, or what he thinks is best for himself? What reason is there for him to continue being "moral" when it is clearly not to his own advantage to do so?

These skeptical views suggested by Glaucon have come to be known as *psychological egoism* and *ethical egoism,* respectively. Psychological egoism is the view that all men are selfish in everything that they do, that is, that the only motive from which anyone ever acts is self-interest. On this view, even when men are acting in ways apparently calculated to benefit others, they are actually motivated by the belief that acting in this way is to their own advantage, and if they did not believe this, they would not be doing that action. Ethical egoism is, by contrast, a normative view about how men *ought* to act. It is the view that, regardless of how men do in fact behave, they have no obligation to do anything except what is in their own interests. According to the ethical egoist, a person is always justified in doing whatever is in his own interest, regardless of the effect on others.

Clearly, if either of these views is correct, then "the moral institution of life" (to use Butler's well-turned phrase) is very different than what we normally think. The majority of mankind is grossly deceived about what is, or ought to be, the case, where morals are concerned.

II

Psychological egoism seems to fly in the face of the facts. We are tempted to say, "Of course people act unselfishly all the time. For example, Smith gives up a trip to the country, which he would have enjoyed very much, in order to stay behind and help a friend with his studies, which is a miserable way to pass the time. This is a perfectly clear case of unselfish behavior, and if the psychological egoist thinks that such cases do not occur, then he is just mistaken." Given such obvious instances of "unselfish behavior," what reply can the egoist make? There are two general arguments by which he might try to show that all actions, including those such as the one just outlined, are in fact motivated by self-interest. Let us examine these in turn:

A. The first argument goes as follows. If we describe one person's action as selfish, and another person's action as unselfish, we are overlooking the crucial fact that in both cases, assuming that the action is done voluntarily, *the agent is merely doing what he most wants to do.* If Smith stays behind to help his friend, that only

shows that he wanted to help his friend more than he wanted to go to the country. And why should he be praised for his "unselfishness" when he is only doing what he most wants to do? So, since Smith is only doing what he wants to do, he cannot be said to be acting unselfishly.

This argument is so bad that it would not deserve to be taken seriously except for the fact that so many otherwise intelligent people have been taken in by it. First, the argument rests on the premise that people never voluntarily do anything except what they want to do. But this is patently false; there are at least two classes of actions that are exceptions to this generalization. One is the set of actions which we may not want to do, but which we do anyway as a means to an end which we want to achieve; for example, going to the dentist in order to stop a toothache, or going to work every day in order to be able to draw our pay at the end of the month. These cases may be regarded as consistent with the spirit of the egoist argument, however, since the ends mentioned are wanted by the agent. But the other set of actions are those which we do, not because we want to, nor even because there is an end which we want to achieve, but because we feel ourselves *under an obligation* to do them. For example, someone may do something because he has promised to do it, and thus feels obligated, even though he does not want to do it. It is sometimes suggested that in such cases we do the action because, after all, we want to keep our promises; so, even here, we are doing what we want. However, this dodge will not work: If I have promised to do something, and if I do not want to do it, then it is simply false to say that I want to keep my promise. In such cases we feel a conflict precisely because we do *not* want to do what we feel obligated to do. It is reasonable to think that Smith's action falls roughly into this second category: He might stay behind, not because he wants to, but because he feels that his friend needs help.

But suppose we were to concede, for the sake of the argument, that all voluntary action is motivated by the agent's wants, or at least that Smith is so motivated. Even if these were granted, it would not follow that Smith is acting selfishly or from self-interest. For if Smith wants to do something that will help his friend, even when it means forgoing his own enjoyments, that is precisely what makes him *un*selfish. What else could unselfishness be, if not waning to help others? Another way to put the same point is to say that it is the *object* of a want that determines whether it is selfish or not. The mere fact that I am acting on *my* wants does not mean that I am acting selfishly; that depends on *what it is* that I want. If I want only my own good, and care nothing for others, then I am selfish; but if I also want other people to be well-off and happy, and if I act on *that* desire, then my action is not selfish. So much for this argument.

B. The second argument for psychological egoism is this. Since so-called unselfish actions always produce a sense of self-satisfaction in the agent, and since this sense of satisfaction is a pleasant state of consciousness, it follows that the point of the action is really to achieve a pleasant state of consciousness, rather than to bring about any good for others. Therefore, the action is "unselfish" only at a superficial level of analysis. Smith will feel much better with himself for having stayed to help his friend—if he had gone to the country, he would have felt terrible about it—and that is the real point of the action. According to a well-known story, this argument was once expressed by Abraham Lincoln:

> Mr. Lincoln once remarked to a fellow-passenger on an old-time mud-coach that all men were prompted by selfishness in doing good. His fellow-passenger was antagonizing this position when they were passing over a corduroy bridge that spanned a slough. As they crossed this bridge they espied an old razor-backed sow on the bank making a terrible noise because her pigs had got into the slough and were in danger of drowning. As the old coach began to climb the hill, Mr. Lincoln called out, "Driver, can't you stop just a moment?" Then Mr. Lincoln jumped out, ran back, and lifted the little pigs out of the mud and water and placed them on the bank. When he returned, his companion remarked: "Now Abe, where does selfishness come in on this little episode?" "Why, bless your soul, Ed, that was the very essence of selfishness. I should have had no peace of mind all day had I gone on and left that suffering old sow worrying over those pigs. I did it to get peace of mind, don't you see?"

This argument suffers from defects similar to the previous one. Why should we think that merely because someone derives satisfaction from helping others this makes him selfish? Isn't the unselfish man precisely the one who *does* derive satisfaction from helping others, while the selfish man does not? If Lincoln "got peace of mind" from rescuing the piglets, does this show him to be selfish, or, on the contrary, doesn't it show him to be compassionate and good-hearted? (If a man were truly selfish, why should it bother his conscience that *others* suffer—much less pigs?) Similarly, it is nothing more than shabby sophistry to say, because Smith takes satisfaction in helping his friend, that he is behaving selfishly. If we say this rapidly, while thinking about something else, perhaps it will sound all right; but if we speak slowly, and pay attention to what we are saying, it sounds plain silly.

Moreover, suppose we ask *why* Smith derives satisfaction from helping his friend. The answer will be, it is because Smith cares for him and wants him to succeed. If Smith did not have these concerns, then he would take no pleasure in assisting him; and these concerns, as we have already seen, are the marks of unselfishness, not selfishness. To put the point more generally: If we have a positive attitude toward the attainment of some goal, then we may derive satisfaction from attaining that goal. But the *object* of our attitude is *the attainment of that goal*; and we must want to attain the goal *before* we can find any satisfaction in it. We do not, in other words, desire some sort of "pleasurable consciousness" and then try to figure out how to achieve it; rather, we desire all sorts of different things—money, a new fishing-boat, to be a better chess-player, to get a promotion in our work, etc.—and because we desire these things, we derive satisfaction from attaining them. And so, if someone desires the welfare and happiness of another person, he will derive satisfaction from that; but this does not mean that this satisfaction is the object of his desire, or that he is in any way selfish on account of it.

It is a measure of the weakness of psychological egoism that these insupportable arguments are the ones most often advanced in its favor. Why, then, should anyone ever have thought it a true view? Perhaps because of a desire for theoretical simplicity: In thinking about human conduct, it would be nice if there were some simple formula that would unite the diverse phenomena of human behavior, under a single explanatory principle, just as simple formulae in physics bring together a great many apparently different phenomena. And since it is obvious that self-regard is an overwhelmingly important factor in motivation, it is only natural to wonder whether all motivation might not be explained in these terms. But the answer is clearly No; while a great many human actions are motivated entirely or in part by self-interest, only by a deliberate distortion of the facts can we say that all conduct is so motivated. This will be clear, I think, if we correct three confusions which are commonplace. The exposure of these confusions will remove the last traces of plausibility from the psychological egoist thesis.

The first is the confusion of selfishness with self-interest. The two are clearly not the same. If I see a physician when I am feeling poorly, I am acting in my own interest but no one would think of calling me "selfish" on account of it. Similarly, brushing my teeth, working hard at my job, and obeying the law are all in my self-interest but none of these are examples of selfish conduct. This is because selfish behavior is behavior that ignores the interests of others, in circumstances in which their interests ought not to be ignored. This concept has a definite evaluative flavor; to call someone "selfish" is not just to describe his action but to condemn it. Thus, you would not call me selfish for eating a normal meal in normal circumstances (although it may surely be in my self-interest); but you would call me selfish for hoarding food while others about are starving.

The second confusion is the assumption that every action is done *either* from self-interest or from other-regarding motives. Thus, the egoist concludes that if there is no such thing as genuine altruism then all actions must be done from self-interest. But this is certainly a false dichotomy. The man who continues to smoke cigarettes, even after learning about the connection between smoking and cancer, is surely not acting from self-interest, not even by his own standards—self-interest would dictate that he quit smoking at once—and he is not acting altruistically either. He *is*, no doubt, smoking for the pleasure of it, but all that this shows is that undisciplined pleasure-seeking and acting from self-interest are very different. This is what led Butler to remark that "The thing to be lamented is, not that men have so great regard to their own good or interest in the present world; for they have not enough."

The last two paragraphs show (*a*) that is it false that all actions are selfish, and (*b*) that it is false that all actions are done out of self-interest. And it should be noted that these two points can be made, and were, without any appeal to putative examples of altruism.

The third confusion is the common but false assumption that a concern for one's own welfare is incompatible with any genuine concern for the welfare of others. Thus, since it is obvious that everyone (or very nearly everyone) does desire his own well-being, it might be thought that no one can really be concerned with others. But again, this is false. There is no inconsistency in desiring that everyone, including oneself *and* others, be well-off and happy. To be sure, it may happen on occasion that our own interests conflict with the interests of others, and in these cases we will have to make hard choices. But even in these cases we might sometimes opt for the interests of others, especially when the others involved are our family or friends. But more importantly, not all cases are like this. Sometimes we are able to promote the welfare of others when our own interests are not involved at all. In these cases not even the strongest self-regard need prevent us from acting considerately toward others.

Once these confusions are cleared away, it seems to me obvious enough that there is no reason whatever to accept psychological egoism. On the contrary, if we simply observe people's behavior with an open mind, we may find that a great deal of it is motivated by self-regard, but by no means all of it; and that there is no reason to deny that "the moral institution of life" can include a place for the virtue of beneficence.

III

The ethical egoist would say at this point, "Of course it is possible for people to act altruistically, and perhaps many people do act that way—but there is no reason why they *should* do so. A person is under no obligation to do anything except what is in his own interests." This is really quite a radical doctrine. Suppose I have an urge to set fire to some public building (say, a department store) just for the fascination of watching the spectacular blaze: According to this view, the fact that several people might be burned to death provides no reason whatever why I should not do it. After all, this only concerns *their* welfare, not my own, and according to the ethical egoist the only person I need think of is myself.

Some might deny that ethical egoism has any such monstrous consequences. They would point out that it is really to my own advantage not to set the fire—for, if I do that I may be caught and put into prison (unlike Gyges, I have no magic ring for protection). Moreover, even if I could avoid being caught it is still to my advantage to respect the rights and interests of others, for it is to my advantage to live in a society in which people's rights and interests are respected. Only in such a society can I live a happy and secure life; so, in acting kindly toward others, I would merely be doing my part to create and maintain the sort of society which it is to my advantage to have. Therefore, it is said, the egoist would not be such a bad man; he would be as kindly and considerate as anyone else, because he would see that it is to his own advantage to be kindly and considerate.

This is a seductive line of thought, but it seems to me mistaken. Certainly it is to everyone's advantage (including the egoist's) to preserve a stable society where people's interests are generally protected. But there is no reason for the egoist to think that merely because *he* will not honor the rules of the social game, decent society will collapse. For the vast majority of people are not egoists, and there is no reason to think that they will be converted by his example—especially if he is discreet and does not unduly flaunt his style of life. What this line of reasoning shows is not that the egoist himself must act benevolently, but that he must encourage *others* to do so. He must take care to conceal from public view his own self-centered method of decision-making, and urge others to act on precepts very different from those on which he is willing to act.

The rational egoist, then, cannot advocate that egoism be universally adopted by everyone. For he wants a world in which his own interests are maximized; and if other people adopted the egoistic policy of pursuing their own interests to the exclusion of his interest, as he pursues his interests to the exclusion of theirs, then such a world would be impossible. So he himself will be an egoist, but he will want others to be altruists.

This brings us to what is perhaps the most popular "refutation" of ethical egoism current among philosophical writers—the argument that ethical egoism is at bottom inconsistent because it cannot be universalized. The argument goes like this:

To say that any action or policy of action is *right* (or that it *ought* to be adopted) entails that it is right for *anyone* in the same sort of circumstances. I cannot, for example, say that it is right for me to lie to you, and yet object when you lie to me (provided, of course, that the circumstances are the same). I cannot hold that it is all right for me to drink your beer and then complain when you drink mine. This is just the requirement that we be consistent in our evaluations; it is a requirement of logic. Now it is said that ethical egoism cannot meet this requirement because, as we have already seen, the egoist would not want others to act in the same way that he acts. Moreover, suppose he *did* advocate the universal adoption of egoistic policies: he would be saying to Peter, "You ought to pursue your own interests even if it means destroying Paul"; and he would be saying to Paul, "You ought to pursue your own interests even if it means destroying Peter." The attitudes expressed in these two recommendations seem clearly inconsistent—he is urging the advancement of Peter's interest at one moment, and countenancing their defeat at the next. Therefore, the argument goes, there is no way to maintain the doctrine of ethical egoism as a consistent view about how we ought to act. We will fall into inconsistency whenever we try.

What are we to make of this argument? Are we to conclude that ethical egoism has been refuted? Such a conclusion, I think, would be unwarranted; for I think that we can show, contrary to this argument, how ethical egoism can be maintained consistently. We need only to interpret the egoist's position in a sympathetic way. We should say that he has in mind a certain kind of world which he would prefer over all others; it would be a world in which his own interests were maximized, regardless of the effects on other people. The egoist's primary policy of action, then, would be to act in such a way as to bring about, as nearly as possible, this sort of world. Regardless of however morally reprehensible we might find it, there is nothing *inconsistent* in someone's adopting this as his ideal and acting in a way calculated to bring it about. And if someone did adopt this as his ideal, then he would not advocate universal egoism; as we have already seen, he would want other people to be altruists. So if he advocates any principles of conduct for the general public, they will be altruistic principles. This would not be inconsistent; on the contrary, it would be perfectly consistent with his goal of creating a world in which his own interests are maximized. To be sure, he would have to be deceitful; in order to secure the good will of others, and a favorable hearing for his exhortations to altruism, he would have to pretend that he was himself prepared to accept altruistic principles. But again, that would be all right; from the egoist's point of view, this would merely be a matter of adopting the necessary means to the achievement of his goal— and while we might not approve of this, there is nothing inconsistent about it. Again, it might be said, "He advocates one thing, but does another. Surely *that's* inconsistent." But it is not; for what he advocates and what he does are both calculated as means to an end (the *same* end, we might note); and as such, he is doing what is rationally required in each case. Therefore, contrary to the previous argument, there is nothing inconsistent in the ethical egoist's view. He cannot be refuted by the claim that he contradicts himself.

Is there, then, no way to refute the ethical egoist? If by "refute" we mean show that he has made some *logical* error, the answer is that there is not. However, there is something more that can be said. The egoist challenge to our ordinary moral convictions amounts to a demand for an explanation of why we should adopt certain policies of action, namely, policies in which the good of others is given importance. We can give an answer to this demand, albeit an indirect one. The reason one ought not to do actions that would hurt other people is: Other people would be hurt. The reason one ought to do actions that would benefit other people is: Other people would be benefited. This may at first seem like a piece of philosophical sleight-of-hand, but it is not. The point is that the welfare of human beings is something that most of us value *for its own sake,* and not merely for the sake of something else. Therefore, when *further* reasons are demanded for valuing the welfare of human beings, we cannot point to anything further to satisfy this demand. It is not that we have no reason for pursuing these policies; but that our reason *is* that these policies are for the good of human beings.

So if we are asked, "Why shouldn't I set fire to this department store?" one answer would be, "Because if you do, people may be burned to death." This is a complete, sufficient reason which does not require qualification or supplementation of any sort. If someone seriously wants to know why this action shouldn't be done, that's the reason: If we are pressed further and asked the skeptical question, "But why shouldn't I do actions that will harm others?" we may not know what to say—but this is because the questioner has included in his question the very answer we would like to give: "Why shouldn't you do actions that will harm others? Because doing those actions would harm others."

The egoist, no doubt, will not be happy with this. He will protest that *we* may accept this as a reason, but *he* does not. And here the argument stops: There are limits to what can be accomplished by argument, and if the egoist really doesn't care about other people—if he honestly doesn't care whether they are helped or hurt by his actions—then we have reached those limits. If we want to persuade him to act decently toward his fellow humans, we will have to make our appeal to such other attitudes as he does possess, by threats, bribes, or other cajolery. That is all that we, can do.

Though some may find this situation distressing (we would like to be able to show that the egoist is just *wrong*); it holds no embarrassment for common morality. What we have come up against is simply a fundamental requirement of rational action; namely, that the existence of reasons for action always depends on the prior existence of certain attitudes in the agent. For example, the fact that a certain course of action would make the agent a lot of money is a reason for doing it only if the agent wants to make money; the fact that practicing at chess makes one a better player is a reason for practicing only if one wants to be a better player; and so on. Similarly, the fact that a certain action would help the agent is a reason for doing the action only if the agent cares about his own welfare, and the fact that an action would help others is a reason for doing it only if the agent cares about others. In this respect ethical egoism and what we might call ethical altruism are in exactly the same fix: Both require that the agent *care* about himself, or about other people, before they can get started.

So a nonegoist will accept "It would harm another person" as a reason not to do an action simply because he cares about what happens to that other person. When the egoist says that he does *not* accept that as a reason, he is saying something quite extraordinary. He is saying that he has no affection for friends or family, that he never feels pity or compassion, that he is the sort of person who can look on scenes of human misery with complete indifference, so long as he is not the one suffering. Genuine egoists, people who really don't care at all about anyone [other] than themselves, are rare. It is important to keep this in mind when thinking about ethical egoism; it is easy to forget just how fundamental to human psychological makeup the feeling of sympathy is. Indeed, a man without any sympathy at all would scarcely be recognizable as a man; and that is what makes ethical egoism such a disturbing doctrine in the first place.

IV

There are, of course, many different ways in which the skeptic might challenge the assumptions underlying our moral practice. In this essay I have discussed only two of them, the two put forward by Glaucon in the passage that I cited from Plato's *Republic*. It is important that the assumptions underlying our moral practice should not be confused with particular judgments made within that practice. To defend one is not to defend the other. We may assume—quite properly, if my analysis has been correct—that the virtue of beneficence does, and indeed should, occupy an important place in "the moral institution of life"; and yet we may make constant and miserable errors when it comes to judging when and in what ways this virtue is to be exercised. Even worse, we may often be able to make accurate moral judgments, and know what we ought to do, but not do it. For these ills, philosophy alone is not the cure.

DISCUSSION QUESTIONS

1. What exactly is the difference between ethical egoism and psychological egoism? Why is this distinction important?

2. Why does Rachels believe that "selfishness" is not the same as "self-interest"? How does he use this distinction to refute psychological egoism?

3. How convinced are you by Rachels's argument against the notion that every action is done either from self-interest or from other-regarding motives? Can you think of a counterargument?

4. What is Rachels's best argument against ethical egoism? Why is it a strong argument? Defend your position.

5. Some say that egoism undermines the moral point of view, that is, the impartial attitude of one who attempts to see all sides of an issue without being committed to the interests of a particular individual or group. Do you agree with this claim? Why or why not? Is it an important line of criticism? Discuss.

Wall Street
[USA 1987] 2 hours, 6 minutes
Directed by Oliver Stone

Gordon Gekko (Michael Douglas) is a Wall Street trader with great wealth and power. He spends his days bending and breaking the law in order to increase his holdings. Gekko manipulates small investors in order to make a financial profit. He thinks little about taking companies away from their stockholders through ruthless and sometimes illegal means. Gekko acts as a mentor to a young stockbroker, Bud Fox (Charlie Sheen), who is hungry for success. To impress Gekko, Fox passes along some inside information from his father, which puts his father's company in jeopardy. Eventually, Fox comes to believe that Gekko's trading techniques are immoral as well as illegal.

While Oliver Stone clearly believes that Gekko's actions and much of the capitalist trading mentality of Wall Street are immoral, Gekko justifies his actions with statements like "Nobody gets hurt," "Everybody's doing it," "Who knows except us?" and "There's something in this deal for everybody." Gekko's credo is "Greed is good," and he builds an entire system of values around it. Stone's target in *Wall Street* is less the bending and breaking of laws by Wall Street insiders and more a system of values based on greed. Michael Douglas won an Oscar for his portrayal of Gordon Gekko.

DISCUSSION QUESTIONS

1. Is *Wall Street* a criticism of egoism or a defense of egoism? Defend your view.
2. Are Gekko's actions "selfish" or "self-interested"? Both? Neither? Defend your view.
3. Gekko morally justifies his actions in the film by saying things like "Nobody gets hurt," "Everybody's doing it," "Who knows except us?" and "There's something in this deal for everybody." Are any of these good reasons to do what he does?
4. Is it wrong to use "Nobody will know except us" as a justification for immoral activities? Why or why not?
5. Can greed ever be good as Gekko says? Can it be the center of a theory of morality? Or is greed always immoral? Defend your view.
6. Could a utilitarian justify Gekko's actions? A Kantian? Explain your view.
7. Why, according to Aristotle, is greed not a virtue? Do you agree with him?
8. What would Confucius say about greed and the actions of Gekko?
9. Imagine you are faced with greedy corporate executives like Gekko. Assume for the sake of argument that you believe greed is not good. How would you persuade them of this? Would you ultimately be able to convince them? Why or why not?

CAROL GILLIGAN

IN A DIFFERENT VOICE

C arol Gilligan argues that women have a moral voice or perspective that is distinct from that of men. A woman's moral perspective is by nature more personal and contextual than the natural moral perspective of a man. Whereas men are motivated more by impartial and abstract principles regarding duty, women are motivated more by a sense of feeling, care, and responsibility.

Gilligan contends that women's moral development and their mature approach to moral questions can be at times quite different from those of men. Gilligan criticizes Lawrence Kohlberg's theory of moral development. According to Kohlberg, a person's moral abilities develop in stages. In the first stage, the *preconventional* stage, we follow authority to avoid punishment. In the second stage, the *conventional* stage, we desire acceptance by a group and follow conventional moral standards. In the third and final, stage, the *postconventional stage*, we question conventional standards and base our ideas of morality on universal moral principles of human welfare, justice, and rights. When Kohlberg's theory is applied to women, it turns out that women are, on average, less morally developed than men. While many men continue to move up to the postconventional level of impartial principles, women are more likely to stay at the lower conventional level of personal attachments and loyalties.

Gilligan proposes an alternative model of moral development that reflects women's distinctive moral perspective. Women also develop in three stages for Gilligan. The first stage is caring for self only, the second is caring for others only, and the third is a balance between caring for self and others—recognition that caring for others depends on caring for self. According to Gilligan, women develop by discovering better ways of caring for themselves and others. Women faced with moral decisions focus on relationships and view morality in terms of taking care of these relationships. Men faced with moral decisions focus on following moral rules and principles. Consequently, the ideals of caring and responsibility play a more central role in the moral orientations of women, while the "rights" perspective plays a more central role in the moral orientations of men. Gilligan concludes that existing moral theories embody a male bias and fail to take specific account of women's moral orientation. According to Gilligan, women's morality is not inferior to that of men. The virtues of caring and responsibility are needed to ensure that society does not become a collection of isolated individuals who guard their individual rights and justice but who are lonely, unattached, and uncaring.

Carol Gilligan (1936–) taught at Harvard University for over thirty years and in 1997 became Harvard's first professor of gender studies. In 2002, she became university professor at New York University. She received an A.B. in English from Swarthmore College in 1958, an M.A. in clinical psychology from Radcliffe College in 1960, and a Ph.D. in social psychology from Harvard University in 1964. In 1967, she began teaching at Harvard with the psychologist Erik Erikson, and in 1970, she became a research assistant for Lawrence Kohlberg, whose views on moral development she would go on to criticize. She is the author of *In a Different Voice: Psychological Theory and Women's Development* (1982), *Mapping the Moral Domain* (1988), *Making Connections* (1990), *Women, Girls, and Psychotherapy: Reframing Resistance* (1991), *Meeting at the Crossroads: Women's Psychology and Girls' Development* (1992), *Between Voice and Silence: Women and Girls, Race and Relationships* (1995), and *The Birth of Pleasure* (2002). The following selection is from her most famous book, *In a Different Voice*.

In the second act of *The Cherry Orchard,* Lopahin, a young merchant, describes his life of hard work and success. Failing to convince Madame Ranevskaya to cut down the cherry orchard to save her estate, he will go on in the next act to buy it himself. He is the self-made man who, in purchasing the estate where his father and grandfather were slaves, seeks to eradicate the "awkward, unhappy life" of the past, replacing the cherry orchard with summer cottages where coming generations "will see a new life." In elaborating this developmental vision, he reveals the image of man that underlies and supports his activity: "At times when I can't go to sleep, I think: Lord, thou gavest us immense forests, unbounded fields and the widest horizons, and living in the midst of them we should indeed be giants"—at which point, Madame Ranevskaya interrupts him, saying, "You feel the need for giants—They are good only in fairy tales, anywhere else they only frighten us."

Conceptions of the human life cycle represent attempts to order and make coherent the unfolding experiences and perceptions, the changing wishes and realities of everyday life. But the nature of such conceptions depends in part on the position of the observer. The brief excerpt from Chekhov's play suggests that when the observer is a woman, the perspective may be of a different sort. Different judgments of the image of man as giant imply different ideas about human development, different ways of imagining the human condition, different notions of what is of value in life.

At a time when efforts are being made to eradicate discrimination between the sexes in the search for social equality and justice, the differences between the sexes are being rediscovered in the social sciences. This discovery occurs when theories formerly considered to be sexually neutral in their scientific objectivity are found instead to reflect a consistent observational and evaluative bias. Then the presumed neutrality of science, like that of language itself, gives way to the recognition that the categories of knowledge are human constructions. The fascination with point of view that has informed the fiction of the twentieth century and the corresponding recognition of the relativity of judgment infuse our scientific understanding as well when we begin to notice how accustomed we have become to seeing life through men's eyes.

A recent discovery of this sort pertains to the apparently innocent classic *The Elements of Style,* by William Strunk and E. B. White. The Supreme Court ruling on the subject of discrimination in classroom texts led one teacher of English to notice that the elementary rules of English usage were being taught through examples which counterposed the birth of Napoleon, the writings of Coleridge, and statements such as "He was an interesting talker. A man who had traveled all over the world and lived in half a dozen countries," with "Well, Susan, this is a fine mess you are in" or, less drastically, "He saw a woman, accompanied by two children, walking slowly down the road."

Psychological theorists have fallen as innocently as Strunk and While into the same observational bias. Implicitly adopting the male life as the norm, they have tried to fashion women out of a masculine cloth. It all goes back, of course, to Adam and Eve— a story which shows, among other things, that if you make woman out of a man, you are bound to get into trouble. In the life cycle, as in the Garden of Eden, the woman has been the deviant.

The penchant of developmental theorists to project a masculine image, and one that appears frightening to women, goes back at least to Freud, who built his theory of psychosexual development around the experiences of the male child that culminate in the Oedipus complex. In the 1920s, Freud struggled to resolve the contradictions posed for his theory by the differences in female anatomy and the different configuration of the young girl's early family relationships. After trying to fit women into his masculine conception, seeing them as envying that which they missed, he came instead to acknowledge, in the strength and persistence of women's pre-Oedipal attachments to their mothers, a developmental difference. He considered this difference in women's development to be responsible for what he saw as women's developmental failure.

Having tied the formation of the superego or conscience to castration anxiety, Freud considered women to be deprived by nature of the impetus for a clear-cut Oedipal resolution. Consequently, women's superego—the heir to the Oedipus complex—was compromised: it was never "so inexorable, so impersonal, so independent of its emotional origins as we require it to be in men." From this observation of difference, that "for women the level of what is ethically normal is different from what it is in men," Freud concluded that women "show less sense of justice than men, that they are less ready to submit to the great exigencies of life, that they are more often influenced in their judgments by feelings of affection or hostility."

Thus a problem in theory became cast as a problem in women's development, and the problem in women's development was located in their experience of relationships. Nancy Chodorow, attempting to account for "the reproduction within each generation of certain general and nearly universal differences that characterize masculine and feminine personality and roles," attributes these differences between the sexes not to anatomy but rather to "the fact that women, universally, are largely responsible for early child care." Because this early social environment differs for and is experienced differently by male and female children, basic sex differences recur in personality development. As a result, "in any given society, feminine personality comes to define itself in relation and connection to other people more than masculine personality does."

In her analysis, Chodorow relies primarily on Robert Stoller's studies, which indicate that gender identity, the unchanging core of personality formation, is "with rare exception firmly and irreversibly established for both sexes by the time a child is around three." Given that for both sexes the primary caretaker in the first three years of life is typically female, the interpersonal dynamics of gender identity formation are different for boys and girls. Female identity formation takes place in a context of ongoing relationship since "mothers tend to experience their daughters as more like, and continuous with, themselves." Correspondingly, girls, in identifying themselves as female, experience themselves as like their mothers, thus fusing the experience of attachment with the process of identity formation. In contrast, "mothers experience their sons as a male opposite," and boys, in defining themselves as masculine, separate their mothers from themselves, thus curtailing "their primary love and sense of empathic tie." Consequently, male development entails a "more emphatic individuation and a more defensive firming of experienced ego boundaries." For boys, but not girls, "issues of differentiation have become intertwined with sexual issues."

Writing against the masculine bias of psychoanalytic theory, Chodorow argues that the existence of sex differences in the early experiences of individuation and relationship "does not mean that women have 'weaker' ego boundaries than men or are more prone to psychosis." It means instead that "girls emerge from this period with a basis for 'empathy' built into their primary definition of self in a way that boys do not." Chodorow thus replaces Freud's negative and derivative description of female psychology with a positive and direct account of her own: "Girls emerge with a stronger basis for experiencing another's needs or feelings as one's own (or of thinking that one is so experiencing another's needs and feelings). Furthermore, girls do not define themselves in terms of the denial of preoedipal relational modes to the same extent as do boys. Therefore, regression to these modes tends not to feel as much a basic threat to their ego. From very early, then, because they are parented by a person of the same gender . . . girls come to

experience themselves as less differentiated than boys, as more continuous with and related to the external object-world, and as differently oriented to their inner object-world as well."

Consequently, relationships, and particularly issues of dependency, are experienced differently by women and men. For boys and men, separation and individuation are critically tied to gender identity since separation from the mother is essential for the development of masculinity. For girls and women, issues of femininity or feminine identity do not depend on the achievement of separation from the mother or on the progress of individuation. Since masculinity is defined through separation while femininity is defined through attachment, male gender identity is threatened by intimacy while female gender identity is threatened by separation. Thus males tend to have difficulty with relationships, while females tend to have problems with individuation. The quality of embeddedness in social interaction and personal relationships that characterizes women's lives in contrast to men's, however, becomes not only a descriptive difference but also a developmental liability when the milestones of childhood and adolescent development in the psychological literature are markers of increasing separation. Women's failure to separate then becomes by definition a failure to develop.

The sex differences in personality formation that Chodorow describes in early childhood appear during the middle childhood years in studies of children's games. Children's games are considered by George Herbert Mead and Jean Piaget as the crucible of social development during the school years. In games, children learn to take the role of the other and come to see themselves through another's eyes. In games, they learn respect for rules and come to understand the ways rules can be made and changed.

Janet Lever, considering the peer group to be the agent of socialization during the elementary school years and play to be a major activity of socialization at that time, set out to discover whether there are sex differences in the games that children play. Studying 181 fifth-grade, white, middle-class children, ages ten and eleven, she observed the organization and structure of their playtime activities. She watched the children as they played at school during recess and in physical education class, and in addition kept diaries of their accounts as to how they spent their out-of-school time. From this study, Lever reports sex differences: boys play out of doors more often than girls do; boys play more often in large and age-heterogeneous groups; they play competitive games more often, and their games last longer than girls' games. The last is in some ways the most interesting finding. Boys' games appeared to last longer not only because they required a higher level of skill and were thus less likely to become boring, but also because, when disputes arose in the course of a game, boys were able to resolve the disputes more effectively than girls: "During the course of this study, boys were seen quarrelling all the time, but not once was a game terminated because of a quarrel and no game was interrupted for more than seven minutes. In the gravest debates, the final word was always, to 'repeat the play,' generally followed by a chorus of 'cheater's proof.'" In fact, it seemed that the boys enjoyed the legal debates as much as they did the game itself, and even marginal players of lesser size or skill participated equally in these recurrent squabbles. In contrast, the eruption of disputes among girls tended to end the game.

Thus Lever extends and corroborates the observations of Piaget in his study of the rules of the game, where he finds boys becoming through childhood increasingly fascinated with the legal elaboration of rules and the development of fair procedures for adjudicating conflicts, a fascination that, he notes, does not hold for girls. Girls, Piaget observes, have a more "pragmatic" attitude toward rules, "regarding a rule as good as long as the game repaid it."

Girls are more tolerant in their attitudes toward rules, more willing to make exceptions, and more easily reconciled to innovations. As a result, the legal sense, which Piaget considers essential to moral development, "is far less developed in little girls than in boys."

The bias that leads Piaget to equate male development with child development also colors Lever's work. The assumption that shapes her discussion of results is that the male model is the better one since it fits the requirements for modern corporate success. In contrast, the sensitivity and care for the feelings of others that

girls develop through their play have little market value and can even impede professional success. Lever implies that, given the realities of adult life, if a girl does not want to be left dependent on men, she will have to learn to play like a boy.

To Piaget's argument that children learn the respect for rules necessary for moral development by playing rule-bound games, Lawrence Kohlberg adds that these lessons are most effectively learned through the opportunities for role-taking that arise in the course of resolving disputes. Consequently, the moral lessons inherent in girls' play appear to be fewer than in boys.' Traditional girls' games like jump rope and hopscotch are turn-taking games, where competition is indirect since one person's success does not necessarily signify another's failure. Consequently, disputes requiring adjudication are less likely to occur. In fact, most of the girls whom Lever interviewed claimed that when a quarrel broke out, they ended the game. Rather than elaborating a system of rules for resolving disputes, girls subordinated the continuation of the game to the continuation of relationships.

Lever concludes that from the games they play, boys learn both the independence and the organizational skills necessary for coordinating the activities of large and diverse groups of people. By participating in controlled and socially approved competitive situations, they learn to deal with competition in a relatively forthright manner—to play with their enemies and to compete with their friends—all in accordance with the rules of the game. In contrast, girls' play tends to occur in smaller, more intimate groups, often the best-friend dyad, and in private places. This play replicates the social pattern of primary human relationships in that its organization is more cooperative. Thus, it points less, in Mead's terms, toward learning to take the role of "the generalized other," less toward the abstraction of human relationships. But it fosters the development of the empathy and sensitivity necessary for taking the role of "the particular other" and points more toward knowing the other as different from the self.

The sex differences in personality formation in early childhood that Chodorow derives from her analysis of the mother-child relationship are thus extended by Lever's observations of sex differences in the play activities of middle childhood. Together these accounts suggest that boys and girls arrive at puberty with a different interpersonal orientation and a different range of social experiences.

"It is obvious," Virginia Woolf says, "that the values of women differ very often from the values which have been made by the other sex." Yet, she adds, "it is the masculine values that prevail." As a result, women come to question the normality of their feelings and to alter their judgments in deference to the opinion of others. In the nineteenth-century novels written by women, Woolf sees at work "a mind which was slightly pulled from the straight and made to alter its clear vision in deference to external authority." The same deference to the values and opinions of others can be seen in the judgments of twentieth-century women. The difficulty women experience in finding or speaking publicly in their own voices emerges repeatedly in the form of qualification and self-doubt, but also in intimations of a divided judgment, a public assessment and private assessment which are fundamentally at odds.

Yet the deference and confusion that Woolf criticizes in women derive from the values she sees as their strength. Women's deference is rooted not only in their social subordination but also in the substance of their moral concern. Sensitivity to the needs of others and the assumption of responsibility for taking care lead women to attend to voices other than their own and to include in their judgment other points of view. Women's moral weakness, manifest in an apparent diffusion and confusion of judgment, is thus inseparable from women's moral strength, an overriding concern with relationships and responsibilities. The reluctance to judge may itself be indicative of the care and concern for others that infuse the psychology of women's development and are responsible for what is generally seen as problematic in its nature.

Thus women not only define themselves in a context of human relationship but also judge themselves in terms of their ability to care. Women's place in man's life cycle has been that of nurturer, caretaker, and helpmate, the weaver of those networks of relationships on which she in turn relies. But while women have thus taken care of

men, men have, in their theories of psychological development, as in their economic arrangements, tended to assume or devalue that care. When the focus on individuation and individual achievement extends into adulthood and maturity is equated with personal autonomy, concern with relationships appears as a weakness of women rather than as a human strength.

The discrepancy between womanhood and adulthood is nowhere more evident than in the studies on sex-role stereotypes reported by Broverman, Vogel, Broverman, Clarkson, and Rosenkrantz. The repeated finding of these studies is that the qualities deemed necessary for adulthood—the capacity for autonomous thinking, clear decision-making, and responsible action—are those associated with masculinity and considered undesirable as attributes of the feminine self. The stereotypes suggest a splitting of love and work that relegates expressive capacities to women while placing instrumental abilities in the masculine domain. Yet looked at from a different perspective, these stereotypes reflect a conception of adulthood that is itself out of balance, favoring the separateness of the individual self over connection to others, and leaning more toward an autonomous life of work than toward the independence of love and care.

The discovery now being celebrated by men in mid-life of the importance of intimacy, relationships, and care is something that women have known from the beginning. However, because that knowledge in women has been considered "intuitive" or "instinctive," a function of anatomy coupled with destiny, psychologists have neglected to describe its development. In my research, I have found that women's moral development centers on the elaboration of that knowledge and thus delineates a critical line of psychological development in the lives of both of the sexes. The subject of moral development not only provides the final illustration of the reiterative pattern in the observation and assessment of sex differences in the literature on human development, but also indicates more particularly why the nature and significance of women's development has been for so long obscured and shrouded in mystery.

The criticism that Freud makes of women's sense of justice, seeing it as compromised in its refusal of blind impartiality, reappears not only in the work of Piaget but also in that of Kohlberg. While in Piaget's account of the moral judgment of the child, girls are an aside, a curiosity to whom he devotes four brief entries in an index that omits "boys" altogether because "the child" is assumed to be male, in the research from which Kohlberg derives his theory, females simply do not exist. Kohlberg's six stages that describe the development of moral judgment from childhood to adulthood are based empirically on a study of eighty-four boys whose development Kohlberg has followed for a period of over twenty years. Although Kohlberg claims universality for his stage sequence, those groups not included in his original sample rarely reach his higher stages.

Prominent among those who thus appear to be deficient in moral development when measured by Kohlberg's scale are women, whose judgments seem to exemplify the third stage of his six-stage sequence. At this stage morality is conceived in interpersonal terms and goodness is equated with helping and pleasing others. This conception of goodness is considered by Kohlberg and Kramer to be functional in the lives of mature women insofar as their lives take place in the home. Kohlberg and Kramer imply that only if women enter the traditional arena of male activity will they recognize the inadequacy of this moral perspective and progress like men toward higher stages where relationships are subordinated to rules (stage four) and rules to universal principles of justice (stages five and six).

Yet herein lies a paradox, for the very traits that traditionally have defined the "goodness" of women, their care for and sensitivity to the needs of others, are those that mark them as deficient in moral development. In this version of moral development, however, the conception of maturity is derived from the study of men's lives and reflects the importance of individuation in their development. Piaget, challenging the common impression that a developmental theory is built like a pyramid from its base in infancy, points out that a conception of development instead hangs from its vertex of maturity, the point toward which progress is traced. Thus, a change in the definition of maturity does not simply alter the description of the highest stage but recasts the understanding of development, changing the entire account.

When one begins with the study of women and derives developmental constructs from their lives, the outline of a moral conception different from that described by Freud, Piaget, or Kohlberg begins to emerge and informs a different description of development. In this conception, the moral problem arises from conflicting responsibilities rather than from competing rights and requires for its resolution a mode of thinking that is contextual and narrative rather than formal and abstract. This conception of morality as concerned with the activity of care centers moral development around the understanding of responsibility and relationships, just as the conception of morality as fairness ties moral development to the understanding of rights and rules.

This different construction of the moral problem by women may be seen as the critical reason for their failure to develop within the constraints of Kohlberg's system. Regarding all constructions of responsibility as evidence of a conventional moral understanding, Kohlberg defines the highest stages of moral development as deriving from a reflective understanding of human rights. That the morality of rights differs from the morality of responsibility in its emphasis on separation rather than connection, in its consideration of the individual rather than the relationship as primary, is illustrated by two responses to interview questions about the nature of morality. The first comes from a twenty-five-year-old man, one of the participants in Kohlberg's study:

> [*What does the word morality mean to you?*] Nobody in the world knows the answer. I think it is recognizing the right of the individual, the rights of other individuals, not interfering with those rights. Act as fairly as you would have them treat you. I think it is basically to preserve the human being's right to existence. I think that is the most important. Secondly, the human being's right to do as he pleases, again without interfering with somebody else's rights.
>
> [*How have your views on morality changed since the last interview?*] I think I am more aware of an individual's rights now. I used to be looking at it strictly from my point of view, just for me. Now I think I am more aware of what the individual has a right to.

Kohlberg cites this man's response as illustrative of the principled conception of human rights that exemplifies his fifth and sixth stages. Commenting on the response, Kohlberg says, "Moving to a perspective outside of that of his society, he identifies morality with justice (fairness, rights, the Golden Rule), with recognition of the rights of others as these are defined naturally or intrinsically. The human being's right to do as he pleases without interfering with somebody else's rights is a formula defining rights prior to social legislation."

The second response comes from a woman who participated in the rights and responsibilities study. She also was twenty-five and, at the time, a third-year law student:

[*Is there really some correct solution to moral problems, or is everybody's opinion equally right?*] No, I don't think everybody's opinion is equally right. I think that in some situations there may be opinions that are equally valid, and one could conscientiously adopt one of several courses of action. But there are other situations in which I think there are right and wrong answers, that sort of inhere in the nature of existence, of all individuals here who need to live with each other to live. We need to depend on each other, and hopefully it is not only a physical need but a need of fulfillment in ourselves, that a person's life is enriched by cooperating with other people and striving to live in harmony with everybody else, and to that end, there are right and wrong, there are things which promote that end and that move away from it, and in that way it is possible to choose in certain cases among different courses of action that obviously promote or harm that goal.

[*Is there a time in the past when you would have thought about these things differently?*] Oh, yeah, I think that I went through a time when I thought that things were pretty relative, that I can't tell you what to do and you can't tell me what to do, because you've got your conscience and I've got mine.

[*When was that?*] When I was in high school. I guess that it just sort of dawned on me that my own ideas changed, and because my own judgment changed, I felt I couldn't judge another person's judgment. But now I think even when it is only the person himself who is going to be affected, I say it is wrong to the extent it doesn't cohere with what I know about human nature and what I know about you, and just from what I think is true about the operation of the universe, I could say I think you are making a mistake.

[*What led you to change, do you think?*] Just seeing more of life, just recognizing that there are an awful lot of things that are common among people. There are certain things that you come to learn promote a better life and better relationships and more personal fulfillment than other things that in general tend to do the opposite, and the things that promote these things, you would call morally right.

This response also represents a personal reconstruction of morality following a period of questioning and doubt, but the reconstruction of moral understanding is based not on the primacy and universality of individual rights, but rather on what she describes as a "very strong sense of being responsible to the world." Within this construction, the moral dilemma changes from how to exercise one's rights without interfering with the rights of others to how "to lead a moral life which includes obligations to myself and my family and people in general." The problem then becomes one of limiting responsibilities without abandoning moral concern. When asked to describe herself, this woman says that she values "having other people that I am tied to, and also having people that I am responsible to. I have a very strong sense of being responsible to the world, that I can't just live for my enjoyment, but just the fact of being in the world gives me an obligation to do what I can to make the world a better place to live in, no matter how small a scale that may be on." Thus while Kohlberg's subject worries about people interfering with each other's rights, this woman worries about "the possibility of omission, of your not helping others when you could help them."

The issue that this woman raises is addressed by Jane Loevinger's fifth "autonomous" stage of ego development, where autonomy, placed in the context of relationships, is defined as modulating an excessive sense of responsibility through the recognition that other people have responsibility for their own destiny. The autonomous stage in Loevinger's account witnesses a relinquishing of moral dichotomies and their replacement with "a feeling for the complexity and multifaceted character of real people and real situations." Whereas the rights conception of morality that informs Kohlberg's principled level (stages five and six) is geared to arriving at an objectively fair or just resolution to moral dilemmas upon which all rational persons could agree, the responsibility conception focuses instead on the limitations of any particular resolution and describes the conflicts that remain.

Thus it becomes clear why a morality of rights and noninterference may appear frightening to women in its potential justification of indifference and unconcern. At the same time, it becomes clear why, from a male perspective, a morality of responsibility appears inconclusive and diffuse, given its insistent contextual relativism. Women's moral judgments thus elucidate the pattern observed in the description of the developmental differences between the sexes, but they also provide an alternative conception of maturity by which these differences can be assessed and their implications traced. The psychology of women that has consistently been described as distinctive in its greater orientation toward relationships and interdependence implies a more contextual mode of judgment and a different moral understanding. Given the differences in women's conceptions of self and morality, women bring to the life cycle a different point of view and order human experience in terms of different priorities.

The myth of Demeter and Persephone, which McClelland cites as exemplifying the feminine attitude toward power, was associated with the Eleusinian Mysteries celebrated in ancient Greece for over two thousand years. As told in the Homeric *Hymn to Demeter*, the story of Persephone indicates the strengths of interdependence, building up resources and giving, that McClelland found in his research on power motivation to characterize the mature feminine style. Although, McClelland says, "it is fashionable to conclude that no one knows what went on in the Mysteries, it is known that they were probably the most important religious ceremonies, even partly on the historical record, which were organized by and for women, especially at the onset before men by means of the cult of Dionysus began to take them over." Thus McClelland regards the myth as "a special presentation of femine psychology." It is, as well, a life-cycle story par excellence.

Persephone, the daughter of Demeter, while playing in a meadow with her girlfriends, sees a beautiful narcissus which she runs to pick. As she does so, the earth opens and she is snatched away by Hades, who takes her to his underworld kingdom. Demeter, goddess of the earth, so mourns the loss of her daughter that she refuses to allow anything to grow. The crops that sustain life on earth shrivel up, killing men and animals alike, until Zeus takes pity on man's suffering and persuades his brother to return Persephone to her mother. But before she leaves, Persephone eats some pomegranate seeds, which ensures that she will spend part of every year with Hades in the underworld.

The elusive mystery of women's development lies in its recognition of the continuing importance of attachment in the human life cycle. Woman's place in man's life cycle is to protect this recognition while the developmental litany intones the celebration of separation, autonomy, individuation, and natural rights. The myth of Persephone speaks directly to the distortion in this view by reminding us that narcissism leads to death, that the fertility of the earth is in some mysterious way tied to the continuation of the mother-daughter relationship, and that the life cycle itself arises from an alternation between the world of women and that of men. Only when life-cycle theorists divide their attention and begin to live with women as they have lived with men will their vision encompass the experience of both sexes and their theories become correspondingly more fertile.

DISCUSSION QUESTIONS

1. What is the difference between "a morality of rights" and "a morality of responsibility"? What is the significance of this distinction for Gilligan?

2. Why does Gilligan find the male ethic inadequate? Do you agree with her? Can the same inadequacies be found in the female ethic? Defend your view.

3. Gilligan compares the moral development of male and female children. What is her position? What difficulties does she have with Freud's notion of moral development? Why does she find Chodorow's view more compelling? Do you agree?

4. To what extent should moral development play a role in moral theory? What role would

you suppose that moral development has in the ethical positions of Confucius, Aristotle, Kant, and Mill?

5. To what extent are the moral theories of Kant, Aristotle, and Mill moralities of "rights"? To what extent are they moralities

of "responsibility"? What do you think Gilligan would say?

6. Is there a natural connection between one's moral outlook and one's sex? Defend your view. Respond to possible criticisms by Gilligan.

The Shop on Main Street
[Czech. 1965] 2 hrs., 8 min.
Directed by Ján Kadár and Elmar Klos

Tono Brtko (Jozef Kroner) works as a carpenter in a small Slovakian town during the Second World War. His nagging wife (Hana Slivková) thinks he should be improving their position in the world, and her fascist brother (Frantisek Zvarík) agrees, advising Tono to join forces with the occupying troops. To appease his wife and brother-in-law, Tono takes a job as the "Aryan comptroller" for a Jewish-owned button shop on Main Street. To his dismay, he finds that the owner, Rosalie Lautmann (Ida Kaminská), a deaf elderly woman, has gone bankrupt. Tono's dreams of prestige are quickly dashed, and his frustration is compounded by Rosalie's deafness. Communicating with her is virtually impossible, and Rosalie remains in a dream world, unaware of the gravity of the war.

Rosalie's Jewish friends bribe Tono to pose as her new assistant instead of her boss. Tono agrees, and slowly the two build a close friendship. Rosalie treats the carpenter with a kindness and respect he does not find in his own family. But troubles arise when an edict is passed demanding the deportation of the town's Jewish citizens. As the names are called off in the town square, Rosalie's name is mysteriously absent. Tono faces a moral dilemma. He must decide whether to protect his friend and risk arrest for harboring a Jew or obey the law and report her. As the Jews gather for deportation in front of the shop, Tono panics. He tries to force Rosalie to join them, but she realizes what is happening and attempts to escape. In a moment of panic, Tono pushes his friend into a cupboard and locks it, waiting until the troops have passed. When he opens the cupboard to release her, he finds that Rosalie has died. Tono then takes his own life

The Shop on Main Street was first shown in the United States at the New York Film Festival, where it received a standing ovation. It won an Oscar for Best Foreign Film in 1965. The film is based on the short novel by Ladislav Grosman.

DISCUSSION QUESTIONS

1. Did Tono do the right thing? Should he have obeyed the law and reported Rosalie to the authorities? Defend your response.

2. Compare and contrast what a Kantian, a utilitarian, and a virtue theorist would do in Tono's situation. Which response do you prefer? Why? How do their responses compare to your own?

3. Gilligan presented us with a male ethic of duty and rights and contrasted it with a female ethic of care and responsibility. Is Tono's situation one in which an ethic of abstract principles comes into

conflict with an ethic of care and compassion? Is the conflict presented as "genderless" in this movie? If so, could it be used as a criticism of Gilligan's position?

4. Why do you think that Tono killed himself? Out of guilt? Out of frustration with morality? What, if anything, do we learn about morality through his suicide?

5. How do we balance our desire for care and compassion for others in peril with our obligations as citizens of a state? Can you think of other stories or films that present situations similar to that of Tono? How do they compare?

6. Give a Confucian analysis of the moral character of Tono. Would Confucius consider Tono a superior man? Why or why not?

7. From the moral point of view of the Bible and the Koran, did Tono do the right thing by lying to the authorities in order to protect Rosalie? Why or why not?

URSULA K. LE GUIN

THE ONES WHO WALK AWAY FROM OMELAS

Omelas, a mythical civilization in which its inhabitants bask in their seemingly perfect lives, has a dark secret lurking beneath its utopian facade. The happiness of the inhabitants of Omelas relies on the misery and anguish of a single child. While many citizens of Omelas visit the "being" in its small, damp cellar and appreciate its suffering, others are horrified that a single person must suffer—even if this suffering is for the sake of an entire civilization. Moreover, those who sympathize with the child realize that even if it were allowed to leave the cellar, any attempts to reintroduce it into society would be unsuccessful. The narrator elaborates, "Even if the child were released, it would not get much good out of its freedom: a little vague pleasure of warmth and food, no doubt, but little more. It is too degraded and imbecile to know any real joy." Nevertheless, there are a few inhabitants who remain deeply disturbed by the misery that this individual must suffer. Those people choose to leave the city and never return.

Ursula K. Le Guin (1929–) is best known for her science-fiction and fantasy tales, writings that have been described as "philosophy disguised as science fiction." Born Ursula Kroeber, she received a B.A. from Radcliffe College in literature, an M.A. from Columbia University, and a Fulbright Scholarship to study in France, where she met her husband, Charles Le Guin. In 1973, she won the National Book Award for her children's book *The Farthest Shore*, the third volume in her Earthsea series. Le Guin has also contributed important essays on fantasy fiction, feminist issues, and other topics, some of which can be found in *Dancing at the Edge of the World* (1989), and has written numerous collections of poetry. Her books include *The Left Hand of Darkness* (1969), *The Dispossessed: An Ambiguous Utopia* (1974), *The Eye of the Heron* (1978), *The Compass Rose* (1982), *Always Coming Home* (1985), *Unlocking the Air and Other Stories* (1996), *The Other Wind* (2001), and *Changing Planes* (2003). "The Ones Who Walk Away from Omelas" was published in 1973.

With a clamor of bells that set the swallows soaring, the Festival of Summer came to the city. Omelas, bright-towered by the sea. The rigging of the boats in harbor sparkled with flags. In the streets between houses with red roofs and painted walls, between old moss-grown gardens and under avenues of trees, past great parks and public buildings, processions moved. Some were decorous: old people in long stiff robes of mauve and grey, grave master workmen, quiet, merry women carrying their babies and chatting as they walked. In other streets the music beat faster, a shimmering of gong and tambourine, and the people went dancing, the procession was a dance. Children dodged in and out, their high calls rising like the swallows' crossing flights over the music and the singing. All the processions wound towards the north side of the city, where on the great water-meadow called the Green Fields boys and girls, naked in the bright air, with mud-stained feet and ankles and long, lithe arms, exercised their restive horses before the race. The horses wore no gear at all but a halter without bit. Their manes were braided with streamers of silver, gold, and green. They flared their nostrils and pranced and boasted to one another; they were vastly excited, the horse being the only animal who has adopted our ceremonies as his own. Far off to the north and west the mountains stood up half encircling Omelas on her bay. The air of morning was so clear that the snow still crowning the Eighteen Peaks burned with white-gold fire across the miles of sunlit air, under the dark blue of the sky. There was just enough wind to make the banners that marked the racecourse snap and flutter now and then. In the silence of the broad green meadows one could hear the music winding through the city streets, farther and nearer and ever approaching, a cheerful faint sweetness of the air that from time to time trembled and gathered together and broke out into the great joyous clanging of the bells.

Joyous! How is one to tell about joy? How describe the citizens of Omelas?

They were not simple folk, you see, though they were happy. But we do not say the words of cheer much any more. All smiles have become archaic. Given a description such as this one tends to make certain assumptions. Given a description such as this one tends to look next for the King, mounted on a splendid stallion and surrounded by his noble knights, or perhaps in a golden litter borne by great-muscled slaves. But there was no king. They did not use swords, or keep slaves. They were not barbarians. I do not know the rules and laws of their society, but I suspect that they were singularly few. As they did without monarchy and slavery, so they also got on without

the stock exchange, the advertisement, the secret police, and the bomb. Yet I repeat that these were not simple folk, not dulcet shepherds, noble savages, bland utopians. They were not less complex than us. The trouble is that we have a bad habit, encouraged by pedants and sophisticates, of considering happiness as something rather stupid. Only pain is intellectual, only evil interesting. This is the treason of the artist: a refusal to admit the banality of evil and the terrible boredom of pain. If you can't lick 'em, join 'em. If it hurts, repeat it. But to praise despair is to condemn delight, to embrace violence is to lose hold of everything else. We have almost lost hold; we can no longer describe a happy man, nor make any celebration of joy. How can I tell you about the people of Omelas? They were not naive and happy children—though their children were, in fact, happy. They were mature, intelligent, passionate adults whose lives were not wretched. O miracle! But I wish I could describe it better. I wish I could convince you. Omelas sounds in my words like a city in a fairy tale, long ago and far away, once upon a time. Perhaps it would be best if you imagined it as your own fancy bids, assuming it will rise to the occasion, for certainly I cannot suit you all. For instance, how about technology? I think that there would be no cars or helicopters in and above the streets; this follows from the fact that the people of Omelas are happy people. Happiness is based on a just discrimination of what is necessary, what is neither necessary nor destructive, and what is destructive. In the middle category, however—that of the unnecessary but undestructive, that of comfort, luxury, exuberance, etc.—they could perfectly well have central heating, subway trains, washing machines, and all kinds of marvelous devices not yet invented here, floating light-sources, fuelless power, a cure for the common cold. Or they could have none of that: it doesn't matter. As you like it, I incline to think that people from towns up and down the coast have been coming in to Omelas during the last days before the Festival on very fast little trains and double-decked trams and that the train station of Omelas is actually the handsomest building in town, though plainer than the magnificent Farmers' Market. But even granted trains, I fear that Omelas so far strikes some of you as goody-goody. Smiles, bells, parades, horses, bleh. If so, please add an orgy. If an orgy would help, don't hesitate. Let us not, however, have temples from which issue beautiful nude priests and priestesses already half in ecstasy and ready to copulate with any man or woman, lover or stranger, who desires union with the deep godhead of the blood, although that was my first idea. But really it would be better not to have any temples in Omelas—at least, not manned temples. Religion yes, clergy no. Surely the beautiful nudes can just wander about, offering themselves like divine soufflés to the hunger of the needy and the rapture of the flesh. Let them join the processions. Let tambourines be struck above the copulations, and the glory of desire be proclaimed upon the gongs, and (a not unimportant point) let the offspring of these delightful rituals be beloved and looked after by all. One thing I know there is none of in Omelas is guilt. But what else should there be? I thought at first there were no drugs, but that is puritanical. For those who like it, the faint insistent sweetness of *drooz* may perfume the ways of the city, *drooz,* which first brings a great lightness and brilliance to the mind and limbs, and then after some hours a dreamy languor, and wonderful visions at last of the very arcana and inmost secrets of the Universe, as well as exciting the pleasure of sex beyond all belief; and it is not habit-forming. For more modest tastes I think there ought to be beer. What else, what else belongs in the joyous city? The sense of victory, surely, the celebration of courage. But as we did without clergy, let us do without soldiers. The joy built upon successful slaughter is not the right kind of joy; it will not do; it is fearful and it is trivial. A boundless and generous contentment, a magnanimous triumph felt not against some outer enemy but in communion with the finest and fairest in the souls of all men everywhere and the splendor of the world's summer: this is what swells the hearts of the people of Omelas, and the victory they celebrate is that of life. I really don't think many of them need to take *drooz.*

Most of the processions have reached the Green Fields by now. A marvelous smell of cooking goes forth from the red and blue tents of the provisioners. The faces of small children are amiably sticky; in the benign grey beard of a man a couple of crumbs of rich pastry are entangled.

The youths and girls have mounted their horses and are beginning to group around the starting line of the course. An old woman, small, fat, and laughing, is passing out flowers from a basket, and tall young men wear her flowers in their shining hair. A child of nine or ten sits at the edge of the crowd, alone, playing on a wooden flute. People pause to listen, and they smile, but they do not speak to him, for he never ceases playing and never sees them, his dark eyes wholly rapt in the sweet, thin magic of the tune.

He finishes, and slowly lowers his hands holding the wooden flute.

As if that little private silence were the signal, all at once a trumpet sounds from the pavilion near the starting line: imperious, melancholy, piercing. The horses rear on their slender legs, and some of them neigh in answer. Sober-faced, the young riders stroke the horses' necks and soothe them, whispering, "Quiet, quiet, there my beauty, my hope. . . ." They begin to form in rank along the starting line. The crowds along the racecourse are like a field of grass and flowers in the wind. The Festival of Summer has begun.

Do you believe? Do you accept the festival, the city, the joy? No? Then let me describe one more thing.

In a basement under one of the beautiful public buildings of Omelas, or perhaps in the cellar of one of its spacious private homes, there is a room. It has one locked door, and no window. A little light seeps in dustily between cracks in the boards, secondhand from a cob-webbed window somewhere across the cellar. In one corner of the little room a couple of mops, with stiff, clotted, foul-smelling heads, stand near a rusty bucket. The floor is dirt, a little damp to the touch, as cellar dirt usually is. The room is about three paces long and two wide: a mere broom closet or disused tool room. In the room a child is sitting. It could be a boy or a girl. It looks about six, but actually is nearly ten. It is feeble-minded. Perhaps it was born defective, or perhaps it has become imbecile through fear, malnutrition, and neglect. It picks its nose and occasionally fumbles vaguely with its toes or genitals, as it sits hunched in the corner farthest from the bucket and the two mops. It is afraid of the mops. It finds them horrible. It shuts its eyes, but it knows the mops are still standing there; and the door is locked; and nobody will come. The door is always locked; and nobody ever comes, except that sometimes—the child has no understanding of time or interval—sometimes the door rattles terribly and opens, and a person, or several people, are there. One of them may come in and kick the child to make it stand up. The others never come close, but peer in at it with frightened, disgusted eyes. The food bowl and the water jug are hastily filled, the door is locked, the eyes disappear. The people at the door never say anything, but the child, who has not always lived in the tool room, and can remember sunlight and its mother's voice, sometimes speaks. "I will be good," it says. "Please let me out. I will be good!" They never answer. The child used to scream for help at night, and cry a good deal, but now it only makes a kind of whining, "eh-haa, eh-haa," and it speaks less and less often. It is so thin there are no calves to its legs; its belly protrudes; it lives on a half-bowl of corn meal and grease a day. It is naked. Its buttocks and thighs are a mass of festered sores, as it sits in its own excrement continually.

They all know it is there, all the people of Omelas. Some of them have come to see it, others are content merely to know it is there. They all know that it has to be there. Some of them understand why, and some do not, but they all understand that their happiness, the beauty of their city, the tenderness of their friendships, the health of their children, the wisdom of their scholars, the skill of their makers, even the abundance of their harvest and the kindly weathers of their skies, depend wholly on this child's abominable misery.

This is usually explained when they are between eight and twelve, whenever they seem capable of understanding; and most of those who come to see the child are young people, though often enough an adult comes, or comes back, to see the child. No matter how well the matter has been explained to them, these young spectators are always shocked and sickened at the sight. They feel disgust, which they had thought themselves superior to. They feel anger, outrage, impotence, despite all the explanations. They would like to do something for the child. But there is nothing they can do. If the child were brought up into the sunlight out of that vile place, if it were cleaned and fed and comforted, that would be a good thing, indeed; but if it were

done, in that day and hour all the prosperity and beauty and delight of Omelas would wither and be destroyed. Those are the terms. To exchange all the goodness and grace of every life in Omelas for that single, small improvement: to throw away the happiness of thousands for the chance of the happiness of one: that would be to let guilt within the walls indeed.

The terms are strict and absolute; there may not even be a kind word spoken to the child.

Often the young people go home in tears, or in a tearless rage, when they have seen the child and faced this terrible paradox. They may brood over it for weeks or years. But as time goes on they begin to realize that even if the child could be released, it would not get much good of its freedom: a little vague pleasure of warmth and food, no doubt, but little more. It is too degraded and imbecile to know any real joy. It has been afraid too long ever to be free of fear. Its habits are too uncouth for it to respond to humane treatment. Indeed, after so long it would probably be wretched without walls about it to protect it, and darkness for its eyes, and its own excrement to sit in. Their tears at the bitter injustice dry when they begin to perceive the terrible justice of reality and to accept it. Yet it is their tears and anger, the trying of their generosity and the acceptance of their helplessness, which are perhaps the true source of the splendor of their lives. Theirs is no vapid, irresponsible happiness. They know that they, like the child, are not free. They know compassion. It is the existence of the child, and their knowledge of its existence, that makes possible the nobility of their architecture, the poignancy of their music, the profundity of their science. It is because of the child that they are so gentle with children. They know that if the wretched one were not there snivelling in the dark, the other one, the flute-player, could make no joyful music as the young riders line up in their beauty for the race in the sunlight of the first morning of summer.

Now do you believe in them? Are they not more credible? But there is one more thing to tell, and this is quite incredible.

At times one of the adolescent girls or boys who go to see the child does not go home to weep or rage, does not, in fact, go home at all. Sometimes also a man or woman much older falls silent for a day or two, and then leaves home. These people go out into the street, and walk down the street alone. They keep walking, and walk straight out of the city of Omelas, through the beautiful gates. They keep walking across the farmlands of Omelas. Each one goes alone, youth or girl, man or woman. Night falls; the traveler must pass down village streets, between the houses with yellow-lit windows, and on out into the darkness of the fields. Each alone, they go west or north, toward the mountains. They go on. They leave Omelas, they walk ahead into the darkness, and they do not come back. The place they go towards is a place even less imaginable to most of us than the city of happiness. I cannot describe it at all. It is possible that it does not exist. But they seem to know where they are going, the ones who walk away from Omelas.

DISCUSSION QUESTIONS

1. If you were a citizen of Omelas, would you stay or walk? Explain and justify your decision.

2. Can the suffering of one child to ensure the happiness of an entire society be morally justified by a utilitarian? A Kantian? A Buddhist? If so, how? If not, why not?

3. Does it make a moral difference that the child lives in the society that benefits from its suffering? What if the child lived halfway across the world? Would the same number of people walk away from Omelas? Would you feel the same about the conditions on which this society's happiness is founded if the child lived halfway around the world? Explain.

4. Why do you think Le Guin adds the following to her story: "Even if the child were released, it would not get much good out of its freedom: a little vague pleasure of warmth and food, no doubt, but little more. It is too degraded and imbecile to know any real joy." How does this affect the way you feel about Omelas? Explain.

5. Le Guin tells us that the children of Omelas are fully aware of the suffering of the child, but she makes a point of saying that those who stay in Omelas do not feel guilty. Is it possible to constantly feel guilty about the misery of others? Explain and give examples.

4.3   WHAT IS THE NATURE AND VALUE OF ART?

PLATO

ART, IMITATION, AND MORALITY

I n *The Republic,* Plato presents his views on the intrinsic nature of art and the role of art in the ideal state through dialogue between Socrates and a number of other characters. Plato argues that art ought to have a positive influence on its audience, and when it does not exert this type of influence, it must be censored. For Plato, not even the great poets Homer and Hesiod are beyond censorship. Furthermore, art is merely an imitation of an imitation—something with much stronger ties to the world of appearances than the world of reality and truth.

In the selection from Book II, Plato explains why the censorship of art is especially important for children, that is, those who are just forming their character and are much more amenable to taking in the "desired impression." Therefore, we should keep them away from stories that contain "ideas for the most part the very opposite of those which we should wish them to have when they are grown up." Plato says that children "cannot judge what is allegorical from what is literal." Consequently, given that literature often does not represent things or events as they truly are, it can exert a bad moral influence on the character development of the young. "Whenever an erroneous representation is made of the nature of gods and heroes," it must be kept away from the impressionable young minds of the future ideal citizens of Plato's ideal state—even if the representation is made by Homer or Hesiod, the two cornerstones of ancient Greek literature. In our culture, this would be the equivalent of keeping lines from William Shakespeare or Mark Twain away from schoolchildren.

In the selection from Book X, Plato goes into greater detail about the metaphysical and epistemological nature of *poesis*, which in Greek literally means "making." In Plato, *poesis* refers to all forms of artistic creativity including music, drama, poetry, fiction, painting, and sculpture. His discussion here recalls material presented in chapter 2 in connection with "The Allegory of the Cave." As noted previously, for Plato, true reality is the supersensory world of abstract ideas or forms, apprehended only by reason. It is the world of objective, eternal, unchanging truth. Ideas (universals, absolutes) such as "Beauty," "Justice," "Courage," and even "Bed" have an independent character in this world. Concrete particulars exist only insofar as the ideas "participate" in them. As Plato explains, a concrete, particular bed (for example, the one you slept in last night) should be regarded as a "copy" of the idea of bed that persists in the world of objective, supersensory truth. Therefore, the bed you slept in last night is for Plato a second level removed from truth—the idea of bed.

Art (*poesis*), being an imitation (*mimesis*) of the world around us, is thus a *third* level removed from truth. When we paint an image of the bed we slept in last night, or tell a story about it, or write a song about it, we are producing an "imitation of an imitation." Plato says then "must we not infer that all these poetical individuals, beginning with Homer, are only imitators; they copy images of virtue and the like, but the truth they never reach?" "The poet is like a painter who . . . will make a likeness of a cobbler though he understands nothing of cobbling; and his picture is good enough for those who know no more than he does, and judge only by colours and figures." For Plato, the artist is like one who continuously lives in the cave and produces images based solely on sensory observations of images on the cave wall. "The imitator or maker of the image knows nothing of true existence; he knows appearances only," says Plato. A biographical sketch of Plato appears in chapter 2.

BOOK II

[Socrates] Come then, and let us pass a leisure hour in story-telling, and our story shall be the education of our heroes.

[Adeimantus] By all means.

And what shall be their education? Can we find a better than the traditional sort?—and this has two divisions, gymnastic for the body, and music for the soul.

True.

Shall we begin education with music, and go on to gymnastic afterwards?

By all means.

And when you speak of music, do you include literature or not?

I do.

And literature may be either true or false?

Yes.

And the young should be trained in both kinds, and we begin with the false?

I do not understand your meaning, he said.

You know, I said, that we begin by telling children stories which, though not wholly destitute of truth, are in the main fictitious; and these stories are told them when they are not of an age to learn gymnastics.

Very true.

That was my meaning when I said that we must teach music before gymnastics.

Quite right, he said.

You know also that the beginning is the most important part of any work, especially in the case of a young and tender thing; for that is the time at which the character is being formed and the desired impression is more readily taken.

Quite true.

And shall we just carelessly allow children to hear any casual tales which may be devised by casual persons, and to receive into their minds ideas for the most part the very opposite of those which we should wish them to have when they are grown up?

We cannot.

Then the first thing will be to establish a censorship of the writers of fiction, and let the censors receive any tale of fiction which is good, and reject the bad; and we will desire mothers and nurses to tell their children the authorised ones only. Let them fashion the mind with such tales, even more fondly than they mould the body with their hands; but most of those which are now in use must be discarded.

Of what tales are you speaking? he said.

You may find a model of the lesser in the greater, I said; for they are necessarily of the same type, and there is the same spirit in both of them.

Very likely, he replied; but I do not as yet know what you would term the greater.

Those, I said, which are narrated by Homer and Hesiod, and the rest of the poets, who have ever been the great story-tellers of mankind.

But which stories do you mean, he said; and what fault do you find with them?

A fault which is most serious, I said; the fault of telling a lie, and, what is more, a bad lie.

But when is this fault committed?

Whenever an erroneous representation is made of the nature of gods and heroes—as when a painter paints a portrait not having the shadow of a likeness to the original.

Yes, he said, that sort of thing is certainly very blamable; but what are the stories which you mean?

First of all, I said, there was that greatest of all lies, in high places, which the poet told about Uranus, and which was a bad lie too,—I mean what Hesiod says that Uranus did, and how Cronus retaliated on him. The doings of Cronus, and the sufferings which in turn his son inflicted upon him, even if they were true, ought certainly not to be lightly told to young and thoughtless persons; if possible, they had better be buried in silence. But if there is an absolute necessity for their mention, a chosen few might hear them in a mystery, and they should sacrifice not a common [Eleusinian] pig, but some huge and unprocurable victim; and then the number of the hearers will be very few indeed.

Why, yes, said he, those stories are extremely objectionable.

Yes, Adeimantus, they are stories not to be repeated in our State; the young man should not be told that in committing the worst of crimes he is far from doing anything outrageous; and that even if he chastises his father when does he wrong, in whatever manner, he will only be following the example of the first and greatest among the gods.

I entirely agree with you, he said; in my opinion those stories are quite unfit to be repeated.

Neither, if we mean our future guardians to regard the habit of quarrelling among themselves as of all things the basest, should any word be said to them of the wars in heaven, and of the plots and fightings of the gods against one another, for they are not true. No, we shall never mention the battles of the giants, or let them be embroidered on garments; and we shall be silent about the innumerable other quarrels of gods and heroes with their friends and relatives. If they would only believe us we would tell them that quarrelling is unholy, and that never up to this time has there been any quarrel between citizens; this is what old men and old women should begin by telling children; and when they grow up, the poets also should be told to compose for them in a similar spirit. But the narrative of Hephaestus binding Hera his mother, or how on another occasion Zeus sent him flying for taking her part when she was being beaten, and all the battles of the gods in Homer—these tales must not be admitted into our State, whether they are supposed to have an allegorical meaning or not.

For a young person cannot judge what is allegorical and what is literal; anything that he receives into his mind at that age is likely to become indelible and unalterable; and therefore it is most important that the tales which the young first hear should be models of virtuous thoughts.

There you are right, he replied; but if any one asks where are such models to be found and of what tales are you speaking—how shall we answer him?

I said to him, you and I, Adeimantus, at this moment are not poets, but founders of a State: now the founders of a State ought to know the general forms in which poets should cast their tales, and the limits which must be observed by them, but to make the tales is not their business.

Book X

[Socrates] Of the many excellences which I perceive in the order of our State, there is none which upon reflection pleases me better than the rule about poetry.

[Glaucon] To what do you refer?

To the rejection of imitative poetry, which certainly ought not to be received; as I see far more clearly now that the parts of the soul have been distinguished.

What do you mean?

Speaking in confidence, for I should not like to have my words repeated to the tragedians and the rest of the imitative tribe—but I do not mind saying to you, that all poetical imitations are ruinous to the understanding of the hearers, and that the knowledge of their true nature is the only antidote to them.

Explain the purport of your remark.

Well, I will tell you, although I have always from my earliest youth had an awe and love of Homer, which even now makes the words falter on my lips, for he is the great captain and teacher of the whole of that charming tragic company; but a man is not to be reverenced more than the truth, and therefore I will speak out.

Very good, he said.

Listen to me then, or rather, answer me.

Put your question.

Can you tell me what imitation is? for I really do not know.

A likely thing, then, that I should know.

Why not? for the duller eye may often see a thing sooner than the keener.

Very true, he said; but in your presence, even if I had any faint notion, I could not muster courage to utter it. Will you enquire yourself?

Well then, shall we begin the enquiry in our usual manner: Whenever a number of individuals have a common name, we assume them to have also a corresponding idea or form. Do you understand me?

I do.

Let us take any common instance; there are beds and tables in the world—plenty of them, are there not?

Yes.

But there are only two ideas or forms of them—one the idea of a bed, the other of a table.

True.

And the maker of either of them makes a bed or he makes a table for our use, in accordance with the idea—that is our way of speaking in this and similar instances—but no artificer makes the ideas themselves: how could he?

Impossible.

And there is another artist,—I should like to know what you would say of him.

Who is he?

One who is the maker of all the works of all other workmen.

What an extraordinary man!

Wait a little, and there will be more reason for your saying so. For this is he who is able to make not only vessels of every kind, but plants and animals, himself and all other things—the earth and heaven, and the things which are in heaven or under the earth; he makes the gods also.

He must be a wizard and no mistake.

Oh! you are incredulous, are you? Do you mean that there is no such maker or creator, or that in one sense there might be a maker of all these things but in another not? Do you see that there is a way in which you could make them all yourself?

What way?

An easy way enough; or rather, there are many ways in which the feat might be quickly and easily accomplished, none quicker than that of turning a mirror round and round—you would soon enough make the sun and the heavens, and the earth and yourself, and other animals and plants, and all the other things of which we were just now speaking, in the mirror.

Yes, he said; but they would be appearances only.

Very good, I said, you are coming to the point now. And the painter too is, as I conceive, just such another—a creator of appearances, is he not?

Of course.

But then I suppose you will say that what he creates is untrue. And yet there is a sense in which the painter also creates a bed?

Yes, he said, but not a real bed.

And what of the maker of the bed? Were you not saying that he too makes, not the idea which, according to our view, is the essence of the bed, but only a particular bed?

Yes, I did.

Then if he does not make that which exists he cannot make true existence, but only some semblance of existence; and if any one were to say that the work of the maker of the bed, or of any other workman, has real existence, he could hardly be supposed to be speaking the truth.

At any rate, he replied, philosophers would say that he was not speaking the truth.

No wonder, then, that his work too is an indistinct expression of truth.

No wonder.

Suppose now that by the light of the examples just offered we enquire who this imitator is?

If you please.

Well then, here are three beds: one existing in nature, which is made by God, as I think that we may say—for no one else can be the maker?

No.

There is another which is the work of the carpenter?

Yes.

And the work of the painter is a third?

Yes.

Beds, then, are of three kinds, and there are three artists who superintend them: God, the maker of the bed, and the painter?

Yes, there are three of them.

God, whether from choice or from necessity, made one bed in nature and one only; two or more such ideal beds neither ever have been nor ever will be made by God.

Why is that?

Because even if He had made but two, a third would still appear behind them which both of them would have for their idea, and that would be the ideal bed and the two others.

Very true, he said.

God knew this, and He desired to be the real maker of a real bed; not a particular maker of a particular bed, and therefore He created a bed which is essentially and by nature one only.

So we believe.

Shall we, then, speak of Him as the natural author or maker of the bed?

Yes, he replied; inasmuch as by the natural process of creation He is the author of this and of all other things.

And what shall we say of the carpenter—is not he also the maker of the bed?

Yes.

But would you call the painter a creator and maker?

Certainly not.

Yet if he is not the maker, what is he in relation to the bed?

I think, he said, that we may fairly designate him as the imitator of that which the others make.

Good, I said; then you call him who is third in the descent from nature an imitator?

Certainly, he said.

And the tragic poet is an imitator, and therefore, like all other imitators, he is thrice removed from the king and from the truth?

That appears to be so.

Then about the imitator we are agreed. And what about the painter?—I would like to know whether he may be thought to imitate that which originally exists in nature, or only the creations of artists?

The latter.

As they are or as they appear? You have still to determine this.

What do you mean?

I mean, that you may look at a bed from different points of view, obliquely or directly or from any other point of view, and the bed will appear different, but there is no difference in reality. And the same of all things.

Yes, he said, the difference is only apparent.

Now let me ask you another question: Which is the art of painting designed to be—an imitation of things as they are, or as they appear—of appearance or of reality?

Of appearance.

Then the imitator, I said, is a long way off the truth, and can do all things because he lightly touches on a small part of them, and that part an image. For example: A painter will paint a cobbler, carpenter, or any other artist, though he knows nothing of their arts; and, if he is a good artist, he may deceive children or simple persons, when he shows them his picture of a carpenter from a distance, and they will fancy that they are looking at a real carpenter.

Certainly.

And whenever any one informs us that he has found a man knows all the arts, and all things else that anybody knows, and every single thing with a higher degree of accuracy than any other man—whoever tells us this, I think that we can only imagine to be a simple creature who is likely to have been deceived by some wizard or actor whom he met, and whom he thought all-knowing, because he himself was unable to analyse the nature of knowledge and ignorance and imitation.

Most true.

And so, when we hear persons saying that the tragedians, and Homer, who is at their head, know all the arts and all things human, virtue as well as vice, and divine things too, for that the good poet cannot compose well unless he knows his subject, and that he who has not this knowledge can never be a poet, we ought to consider whether here also there may not be a similar illusion. Perhaps they may have come across imitators and been deceived by them; they

may not have remembered when they saw their works that these were but imitations thrice removed from the truth, and could easily be made without any knowledge of the truth, because they are appearances only and not realities? Or, after all, they may be in the right, and poets do really know the things about which they seem to the many to speak so well?

The question, he said, should by all means be considered.

Now do you suppose that if a person were able to make the original as well as the image, he would seriously devote himself to the image-making branch? Would he allow imitation to be the ruling principle of his life, as if he had nothing higher in him?

I should say not.

The real artist, who knew what he was imitating, would be interested in realities and not in imitations; and would desire to leave as memorials of himself works many and fair; and, instead of being the author of encomiums, he would prefer to be the theme of them.

Yes, he said, that would be to him a source of much greater honour and profit.

Then, I said, we must put a question to Homer; not about medicine, or any of the arts to which his poems only incidentally refer: we are not going to ask him, or any other poet, whether he has cured patients like Asclepius, or left behind him a school of medicine such as the Asclepiads were, or whether he only talks about medicine and other arts at second hand; but we have a right to know respecting military tactics, politics, education, which are the chiefest and noblest subjects of his poems, and we may fairly ask him about them. "Friend Homer," then we say to him, "If you are only in the second remove from truth in what you say of virtue, and not in the third—not an image maker or imitator—and if you are able to discern what pursuits make men better or worse in private or public life, tell us what State was ever better governed by your help? The good order of Lacedaemon is due to Lycurgus,* and many other cities great and small have been similarly

---

* Lycurgus traditionaly is regarded as the founder of the Spartan constitution as well as of Sparta's social and military systems. Disorder in Sparta—which is also called Lacedaemon—is said to have forced him to reform the government. His reforms included the establishment of a senate, the banishment of luxury, and the support of useful arts. He was viewed by some as a friend of the gods and by others as simply a god rather than a man. While it is a matter of controversy whether he ever existed, many say that he lived around 775 B.C.E. —Ed.

benefited by others; but who says that you have been a good legislator to them and have done them any good? Italy and Sicily boast of Charondas, and there is Solon who is renowned among us; but what city has anything to say about you?" Is there any city which he might name?

I think not, said Glaucon; not even the Homerids themselves pretend that he was a legislator.

Well, but is there any war on record which was carried on successfully by him, or aided by his counsels, when he was alive?

There is not.

Or is there any invention of his, applicable to the arts or to human life, such as Thales* the Milesian or Anacharsis† the Scythian, and other ingenious men have conceived, which is attributed to him?

There is absolutely nothing of the kind.

But, if Homer never did any public service, was he privately a guide or teacher of any? Had he in his lifetime friends who loved to associate with him, and who handed down to posterity an Homeric way of life, such as was established by Pythagoras who was so greatly beloved for his wisdom, and whose followers are to this day quite celebrated for the order which was named after him?

Nothing of the kind is recorded of him. For surely, Socrates, Creophylus, the companion of Homer, that child of flesh, whose name always makes us laugh, might be more justly ridiculed for his stupidity, if, as is said, Homer was greatly neglected by him and others in his own day when he was alive?

Yes, I replied, that is the tradition. But can you imagine, Glaucon, that if Homer had really been able to educate and improve mankind—if he had possessed knowledge and not been a mere imitator—can you imagine, I say, that he would not have had many followers, and been honoured and loved by them? Protagoras§ of Abdera, and Prodicus** of Ceos, and a host of others, have only to whisper to their contemporaries; "You will never be able to manage either your own house or your own State until you appoint us to be your ministers of education"—and this ingenious device of theirs has such an effect in making them love them that their companions all but carry them about on their shoulders. And is it conceivable that the contemporaries of Homer, or again of Hesiod, would have allowed either of them to go about as rhapsodists, if they had really been able to make mankind virtuous? Would they not have been as unwilling to part with them as with gold, and have compelled them to stay at home with them? Or, if the master would not stay, then the disciples would have followed him about everywhere, until they had got education enough?

Yes, Socrates, that, I think, is quite true.

Then must we not infer that all these poetical individuals, beginning with Homer, are only imitators; they copy images of virtue and the like, but the truth they never reach? The poet is like a

---

* Thales (625–545 B.C.E.), a Greek philosopher, is the first known philosopher in Western culture. Thales abandoned the centuries-old tradition of explaining the world as a creation of the gods, offering in its place an account of the nature of the universe based on reason. He is credited with introducing geometry to Greece and is regarded as the first thinker in the Western world to search for the ultimate substance of all things, which he identified as water. His scientific achievements were extraordinary and include predicting the eclipse of May 28, 585 B.C.E., and making accurate estimations of the size of the sun and moon. He is one of the "Seven Sages of Ancient Greece." —Ed.

† Anacharsis, a Scythian prince and philosopher who traveled extensively in Greece in the sixth century B.C.E. Anacharsis lived around 592 B.C.E. and was noted for his wisdom, temperance, and extensive knowledge. When Anacharsis returned from Athens to Scythia, he attempted to introduce the laws of the Athenians to the Scythians. This irritated his brother, the king of Scythia, who then killed him with an arrow. Anacharsis is credited with the invention of tinder (material that catches fire easily), anchors, and the potter's wheel. He is also one of the "Seven Sages of Ancient Greece." —Ed.

§ Protagoras (cc. 490–410 B.C.E.) a Greek philosopher, claimed to be able to teach virtues and is said to have been the first philosopher to support himself by teaching philosophy. He apparently received fees as high as several thousand dollars per student. For this, he is classified as one of the Sophists, which comes from the Greek word *sophistes* meaning "one who professes to make men wise." Protagoras held that all knowledge is relative to each particular person, a position reflected in his best-know statement: "Man is the measure of all things." He published a book that denied the existence of a Supreme Being. The book was publicly burned in Athens, and Protagoras was banished from the city. —Ed.

** Prodicus of Ceos (fifth century B.C.E.) was a contemporary of Socrates (469–399 B.C.E.) and was, like Protagoras, a Sophist. He traveled from town to town in Greece, earning high fees for his courses of instruction. Among his pupils were Socrates and the dramatist Euripides. The Athenians put him to death for corrupting the morals of the youth of Athens. There is very little accurate information about his life. —Ed.

painter who, as we have already observed, will make a likeness of a cobbler though he understands nothing of cobbling; and his picture is good enough for those who know no more than he does, and judge only by colours and figures.

Quite so.

In like manner the poet with his words and phrases may be said to lay on the colours of the several arts, himself understanding their nature only enough to imitate them; and other people, who are as ignorant as he is, and judge only from his words, imagine that if he speaks of cobbling, or of military tactics, or of anything else, in metre and harmony and rhythm, he speaks very well—such is the sweet influence which melody and rhythm by nature have. And I think that you must have observed again and again what a poor appearance the tales of poets make when stripped of the colours which music puts upon them, and recited in simple prose.

Yes, he said.

They are like faces which were never really beautiful, but only blooming; and now the bloom of youth has passed away from them?

Exactly.

Here is another point: The imitator or maker of the image knows nothing of true existence; he knows appearances only. Am I not right?

Yes.

Then let us have a clear understanding, and not be satisfied with half an explanation.

Proceed.

Of the painter we say that he will paint reins, and he will paint a bit?

Yes.

And the worker in leather and brass will make them?

Certainly.

But does the painter know the right form of the bit and reins? Nay, hardly even the workers in brass and leather who make them; only the horseman who knows how to use them—he knows their right form.

Most true.

And may we not say the same of all things?

What?

That there are three arts which are concerned with all things: one which uses, another which makes, a third which imitates them?

Yes.

And the excellence or beauty or truth of every structure, animate or inanimate, and of every action of man, is relative to the use for which nature or the artist has intended them.

True.

Then the user of them must have the greatest experience of them, and he must indicate to the maker the good or bad qualities which develop themselves in use; for example, the flute-player will tell the flute-maker which of his flutes is satisfactory to the performer; he will tell him how he ought to make them, and the other will attend to his instructions?

Of course.

The one knows and therefore speaks with authority about the goodness and badness of flutes, while the other, confiding in him, will do what he is told by him?

True.

The instrument is the same, but about the excellence or badness of it the maker will only attain to a correct belief; and this he will gain from him who knows, by talking to him and being compelled to hear what he has to say, whereas the user will have knowledge?

True.

But will the imitator have either? Will he know from use whether or no his drawing is correct or beautiful? Or will he have right opinion from being compelled to associate with another who knows and gives him instructions about what he should draw?

Neither.

Then he will no more have true opinion than he will have knowledge about the goodness or badness of his imitations?

I suppose not.

The imitative artist will be in a brilliant state of intelligence about his own creations?

Nay, very much the reverse.

And still he will go on imitating without knowing what makes a thing good or bad, and may be expected therefore to imitate only that which appears to be good to the ignorant multitude?

Just so.

Thus far then we are pretty well agreed that the imitator has no knowledge worth mentioning of what he imitates. Imitation is only a kind of play or sport, and the tragic poets, whether they write in iambic or in Heroic verse, are imitators in the highest degree?

Very true.

And now tell me, I conjure you, has not imitation been shown by us to be concerned with that which is thrice removed from the truth?

Certainly.

And what is the faculty in man to which imitation is addressed?

What do you mean?

I will explain: The body which is large when seen near, appears small when seen at a distance?

True.

And the same object appears straight when looked at out of the water, and crooked when in the water; and the concave becomes convex, owing to the illusion about colours to which the sight is liable. Thus every sort of confusion is revealed within us; and this is that weakness of the human mind on which the art of conjuring and of deceiving by light and shadow and other ingenious devices imposes, having an effect upon us like magic.

True.

And the arts of measuring and numbering and weighing come to the rescue of the human understanding—there is the beauty of them—and the apparent greater or less, or more or heavier, no longer have the mastery over us, but give way before calculation and measure and weight?

Most true.

And this, surely, must be the work of the calculating and rational principle in the soul.

To be sure.

And when this principle measures and certifies that some things are equal, or that some are greater or less than others, there occurs an apparent contradiction?

True.

But were we not saying that such a contradiction is impossible—the same faculty cannot have contrary opinions at the same time about the same thing?

Very true.

Then that part of the soul which has an opinion contrary to measure is not the same with that which has an opinion in accordance with measure?

True.

And the better part of the soul is likely to be that which trusts to measure and calculation?

Certainly.

And that which is opposed to them is one of the inferior principles of the soul?

No doubt.

This was the conclusion at which I was seeking to arrive when I said that painting or drawing, and imitation in general, when doing their own proper work, are far removed from truth, and the companions and friends and associates of a principle within us which is equally removed from reason, and that they have no true or healthy aim.

Exactly.

The imitative art is an inferior who marries an inferior, and has inferior offspring.

Very true.

And is this confined to the sight only, or does it extend to the hearing also, relating in fact to what we term poetry?

Probably the same would be true of poetry.

Do not rely, I said, on a probability derived from the analogy of painting; but let us examine further and see whether the faculty with which poetical imitation is concerned is good or bad.

By all means.

We may state the question thus:—Imitation imitates the actions of men, whether voluntary or involuntary, on which, as they imagine, a good or bad result has ensued, and they rejoice or sorrow accordingly. Is there anything more?

No, there is nothing else.

But in all this variety of circumstances is the man at unity with himself—or rather, as in the instance of sight there was confusion and opposition in his opinions about the same things, so here also is there not strife and inconsistency in his life? Though I need hardly raise the question again, for I remember that all this has been already admitted; and the soul has been acknowledged by us to be full of these and ten thousand similar oppositions occurring at the same moment?

And we were right, he said.

Yes, I said, thus far we were right; but there was an omission which must now be supplied.

What was the omission?

Were we not saying that a good man, who has the misfortune to lose his son or anything else which is most dear to him, will bear the loss with more equanimity than another?

Yes.

But will he have no sorrow, or shall we say that although he cannot help sorrowing, he will moderate his sorrow?

The latter, he said, is the truer statement.

Tell me: will he be more likely to struggle and hold out against his sorrow when he is seen by his equals, or when he is alone?

It will make a great difference whether he is seen or not.

When he is by himself he will not mind saying or doing many things which he would be ashamed of any one hearing or seeing him do?

True.

There is a principle of law and reason in him which bids him resist, as well as a feeling of his misfortune which is forcing him to indulge his sorrow?

True. But when a man is drawn in two opposite directions, to and from the same object, this, as we affirm, necessarily implies two distinct principles in him?

Certainly.

One of them is ready to follow the guidance of the law?

How do you mean?

The law would say that to be patient under suffering is best, and that we should not give way to impatience, as there is no knowing whether such things are good or evil; and nothing is gained by impatience; also, because no human thing is of serious importance, and grief stands in the way of that which at the moment is most required.

What is most required? he asked.

That we should take counsel about what has happened, and when the dice have been thrown order our affairs in the way which reason deems best; not, like children who have had a fall, keeping hold of the part struck and wasting time in setting up a howl, but always accustoming the soul forthwith to apply a remedy, raising up that which is sickly and fallen, banishing the cry of sorrow by the healing art.

Yes, he said, that is the true way of meeting the attacks of fortune.

Yes, I said; and the higher principle is ready to follow this suggestion of reason?

Clearly.

And the other principle, which inclines us to recollection of our troubles and to lamentation, and can never have enough of them, we may call irrational, useless, and cowardly?

Indeed, we may.

And does not the latter—I mean the rebellious principle—furnish a great variety of materials for imitation? Whereas the wise and calm temperament, being always nearly equable, is not easy to imitate or to appreciate when imitated, especially at a public festival when a promiscuous crowd is assembled in a theatre. For the feeling represented is one to which they are strangers.

Certainly.

Then the imitative poet who aims at being popular is not by nature made, nor is his art intended, to please or to affect the principle in the soul; but he will prefer the passionate and fitful temper, which is easily imitated?

Clearly.

And now we may fairly take him and place him by the side of the painter, for he is like him in two ways: first, inasmuch as his creations have an inferior degree of truth—in this, I say, he is like him; and he is also like him in being concerned with an inferior part of the soul; and therefore we shall be right in refusing to admit him into a well-ordered State, because he awakens and nourishes and strengthens the feelings and impairs the reason. As in a city when the evil are permitted to have authority and the good are put out of the way, so in the soul of man, as we maintain, the imitative poet implants an evil constitution, for he indulges the irrational nature which has no discernment of greater and less, but thinks the same thing at one time great and at another small—he is a manufacturer of images and is very far removed from the truth.

Exactly.

But we have not yet brought forward the heaviest count in our accusation:—the power which poetry has of harming even the good (and there are very few who are not harmed), is surely an awful thing?

Yes, certainly, if the effect is what you say.

Hear and judge: The best of us, as I conceive, when we listen to a passage of Homer, or one of the tragedians, in which he represents some pitiful hero who is drawling out his sorrows in a long oration, or weeping, and smiting his breast—the best of us, you know, delight in giving way to sympathy, and are in raptures at the excellence of the poet who stirs our feelings most.

Yes, of course I know.

But when any sorrow of our own happens to us, then you may observe that we pride ourselves on the opposite quality—we would fain be quiet and patient; this is the manly part, and the other which delighted us in the recitation is now deemed to be the part of a woman.

Very true, he said.

Now can we be right in praising and admiring another who is doing that which any one of us would abominate and be ashamed of in his own person?

No, he said, that is certainly not reasonable.

Nay, I said, quite reasonable from one point of view.

What point of view?

If you consider, I said, that when in misfortune we feel a natural hunger and desire to relieve our sorrow by weeping and lamentation, and that this feeling which is kept under control in our own calamities is satisfied and delighted by the poets—the better nature in each of us, not having been sufficiently trained by reason a habit, allows the sympathetic element to break loose because the sorrow is another's; and the spectator fancies that there can be no disgrace to himself in praising and pitying any one who comes telling him what a good man he is, and making a fuss about his troubles; he thinks that the pleasure is a gain, and why should he be supercilious and lose this and the poem too? Few persons ever reflect, as I should imagine, that from the evil of other men something of evil is communicated to themselves. And so the feeling of sorrow which has gathered strength at the sight of the misfortunes of others is with difficulty repressed in our own.

How very true!

And does not the same hold also of the ridiculous? There are jests which you would be ashamed to make yourself, and yet on the comic stage, or indeed in private, when you hear them, you are greatly amused by them, and are not at all disgusted at their unseemliness;—the case of pity is repeated;—there is a principle in human nature which is disposed to raise a laugh, and this which you once restrained by reason, because you were afraid of being thought a buffoon, is now let out again; and having stimulated the risible faculty at

the theatre, you are betrayed unconsciously to yourself into playing the comic poet at home.

Quite true, he said.

And the same may be said of lust and anger and all the other affections, of desire and pain and pleasure, which are held to be inseparable from every action—in all of them poetry feeds and waters the passions instead of drying them up; she lets them rule, although they ought to be controlled, if mankind are ever to increase in happiness and virtue.

I cannot deny it.

Therefore, Glaucon, I said, whenever you meet with any of the eulogists of Homer declaring that he has been the educator of Hellas, and that he is profitable for education and for the ordering of human things, and that you should take him up again and again and get to know him and regulate your whole life according to him, we may love and honour those who say these things—they are excellent people, as far as their lights extend; and we are ready to acknowledge that Homer is the greatest of poets and first of tragedy writers; but we must remain firm in our conviction that hymns to the gods and praises of famous men are the only poetry which ought to be admitted into our State. For if you go beyond this and allow the honeyed muse to enter, either in epic or lyric verse, not law and the reason of mankind, which by common consent have ever been deemed best, but pleasure and pain will be the rulers in our State.

That is most true, he said.

And now since we have reverted to the subject of poetry, let this our defence serve to show the reasonableness of our former judgment in sending away out of our State an art having the tendencies which we have described; for reason constrained us. But that she may impute to us any harshness or want of politeness, let us tell her that there is an ancient quarrel between philosophy and poetry; of which there are many proofs, such as the saying of "the yelping hound howling at her lord," or of one "mighty in the vain talk of fools," and "the mob of sages circumventing Zeus," and the "subtle thinkers who are beggars after all"; and there are innumerable other signs of ancient enmity between them. Notwithstanding this, let us assure our sweet friend and the sister arts of imitation that if she will only prove her title to exist in a well-ordered State we shall be delighted to receive her—we are very conscious of her charms; but we may not on that account betray the truth. I dare say, Glaucon, that you are as much charmed by her as I am, especially when she appears in Homer?

Yes, indeed, I am greatly charmed.

Shall I propose, then, that she be allowed to return from exile, but upon this condition only—that she make a defence of herself in lyrical or some other metre?

Certainly.

And we may further grant to those of her defenders who are lovers of poetry and yet not poets the permission to speak in prose on her behalf: let them show not only that she is pleasant but also useful to States and to human life, and we will listen in a kindly spirit; for if this can be proved we shall surely be the gainers—I mean, if there is a use in poetry as well as a delight?

Certainly, he said, we shall be the gainers.

If her defence fails, then, my dear friend, like other persons who are enamoured of something, but put a restraint upon themselves when they think their desires are opposed to their interests, so too must we after the manner of lovers give her up, though not without a struggle. We too are inspired by that love of poetry which the education of noble States has implanted in us, and therefore we would have her appear at her best and truest; but so long as she is unable to make good her defence, this argument of ours shall be a charm to us, which we will repeat to ourselves while we listen to her strains; that we may not fall away into the childish love of her which captivates the many. At all events we are well aware that poetry being such as we have described is not to be regarded seriously as attaining to the truth; and he who listens to her, fearing for the safety of the city which is within him, should be on his guard against her seductions and make our words his law.

Yes, he said, I quite agree with you.

Yes, I said, my dear Glaucon, for great is the issue at stake, greater than appears, whether a man is to be good or bad. And what will any one be profited if under the influence of honour or money or power, aye, or under the excitement of poetry, he neglect justice and virtue?

DISCUSSION QUESTIONS

1. In the context of laying out the conditions necessary to produce ideal future citizens, Plato argues that art ought to have positive influence on its audience and that when it does not exert this type of influence it must be censored. What is his argument? Do you agree with Plato that the ideal state should censor art? Why or why not?

2. Plato says that we should keep children away from stories that contain "ideas for the most part the very opposite of those which we should wish them to have when they are grown up." How important to a child's moral development in particular, and to character development in general, are stories? Do you agree with Plato that we should not give children access to stories that have a message contrary to the one we would like them to believe? Why or why not?

3. Why does Plato believe that art is an imitation of an imitation? What are the epistemological implications of this position? That is, how valuable a source of knowledge is art compared to other sources of knowledge?

4. Plato asserts, "At all events we are well aware that poetry being such as we have described is not to be regarded seriously as attaining to the truth; and he who listens to her, fearing for the safety of the city which is within him, should be on his guard against her seductions and make our words his law." What does he mean by this? Do you agree with him? Analyze Plato's ideas regarding censorship in the context of contemporary American culture and society.

5. Should the same criticisms that Plato directs toward *poesis* be directed toward Plato's own writing, which might be described as "dialogues" or "philosophical fictions"? Do you think that Plato believed his own writing was immune from his general criticisms of *poesis*? Why or why not?

ARISTOTLE
THE NATURE OF TRAGEDY

W hereas Aristotle agrees with Plato that art is a mode of imitation (*mimesis*), he disagrees with him on what art imitates, as well as on its psychological and moral effects on human beings. Plato believes that art is an imitation of an imitation, a feature that makes art far removed from truth. Aristotle, however, contends that while art is imitation, it is not an imitation of an imitation. For him, the artist imitates not *particular* but rather *universal* characters, emotions, and actions. This places art in a close relationship with truth, since these universal characters, emotions, and actions are truer than particular ones. For Aristotle, then, art is an idealization of human life, not a direct copy. In addition, "It is not the function of the poet to relate what has happened but what may happen—what is possible according to the law of probability or necessity." "Poetry, therefore, is a more philosophical and a higher thing than history: for poetry tends to express the universal, history the particular."

For Aristotle, works of art are created because "the instinct of imitation is implanted in man from childhood," as is the instinct for "harmony and rhythm." Furthermore, we enjoy observing art because there is pleasure in seeing certain things and actions imitated, as well as pleasure in observing the technical perfection of a work. There is also enjoyment both in learning something new and in recognizing what we already know through a work of art.

Comedy involves imitation of lower types of men whose faults are "ludicrous," whereas tragedy involves imitation of the actions of men of a higher type. The purpose of tragedy is to arouse fear and pity, and to bring about a *catharsis* (purging) of these two emotions. In this latter regard, Aristotle and Plato disagree. Plato rejects tragedy on the ground that it arouses pity and fear and that this, in turn, makes people emotionally weak. Aristotle believes that tragedy *purges* these emotions and makes people stronger.

For Aristotle, tragedy has six elements: spectacle (scenery, costumes), song, diction, character, thought, and plot. The most important element is plot, for a good plot is necessary to produce the tragic effect of fear and pity. The second-most-important element is character. Both are described in depth by Aristotle in the following selection from his *Poetics* (350 B.C.E.).

Even though the *Poetics* focuses on only one imitative art (poetry) and, in particular, on only one form of that art (tragic drama), it has come to be the single most influential work on art. Nevertheless, the *Poetics* is not the only work by Aristotle that takes up the subject of art. Aristotle also comments on art in general, and on tragedy in particular, in many of his other writings. For example, in his *Rhetoric*, he describes pity and fear in greater detail; in his *Politics*, he further discusses catharsis; in his *Metaphysics* and *Nichomachean Ethics*, he comments on the general nature of art; and in his *Parts of Animals* and *Physics*, he notes the relationship of art to nature. A biographical sketch of Aristotle appears in the previous section (p. 479).

PART IV

Poetry in general seems to have sprung from two causes, each of them lying deep in our nature. First, the instinct of imitation is implanted in man from childhood, one difference between him and other animals being that he is the most imitative of living creatures, and through imitation learns his earliest lessons; and no less universal is the pleasure felt in things imitated. We have evidence of this in the facts of experience. Objects which in themselves we view with pain, we delight to contemplate when reproduced with minute fidelity: such as the forms of the most ignoble animals and of dead bodies. The cause of this again is, that to learn gives the liveliest pleasure, not only to philosophers but to men in general; whose capacity, however, of learning is more limited. Thus the reason why men enjoy seeing a likeness is, that in contemplating it they find themselves learning or inferring, and saying perhaps, "Ah, that is he." For if you happen not to have seen the original, the pleasure will be due not to the imitation as such, but to the execution, the coloring, or some such other cause.

Imitation, then, is one instinct of our nature. Next, there is the instinct for "harmony" and rhythm, meters being manifestly sections of rhythm. Persons, therefore, starting with this natural gift developed by degrees their special aptitudes, till their rude improvisations gave birth to Poetry.

Poetry now diverged in two directions, according to the individual character of the writers. The graver spirits imitated noble actions, and the actions of good men. The more trivial sort imitated the actions of meaner persons, at first composing satires, as the former did hymns to the gods and the praises of famous men. A poem of the satirical kind cannot indeed be put down to any author earlier than Homer; though many such writers probably there were. But from Homer onward, instances can be cited—his own *Margites*, for example, and other similar compositions. The appropriate meter was also here introduced; hence the measure is still called the iambic or lampooning measure, being that in which people lampooned one another. Thus the older poets were distinguished as writers of heroic or of lampooning verse.

As, in the serious style, Homer is pre-eminent among poets, for he alone combined dramatic form with excellence of imitation so he too first laid down the main lines of comedy, by dramatizing the ludicrous instead of writing personal satire. His *Margites* bears the same relation to comedy that the *Iliad* and *Odyssey* do to

tragedy. But when Tragedy and Comedy came to light, the two classes of poets still followed their natural bent: the lampooners became writers of Comedy, and the Epic poets were succeeded by Tragedians, since the drama was a larger and higher form of art.

Whether Tragedy has as yet perfected its proper types or not; and whether it is to be judged in itself, or in relation also to the audience—this raises another question. Be that as it may, Tragedy—as also Comedy—was at first mere improvisation. The one originated with the authors of the Dithyramb,* the other with those of the phallic songs, which are still in use in many of our cities. Tragedy advanced by slow degrees; each new element that showed itself was in turn developed. Having passed through many changes, it found its natural form, and there it stopped. . . .

PART V

Comedy is, as we have said, an imitation of characters of a lower type—not, however, in the full sense of the word bad, the ludicrous being merely a subdivision of the ugly. It consists in some defect or ugliness which is not painful or destructive. To take an obvious example, the comic mask is ugly and distorted, but does not imply pain.

The successive changes through which Tragedy passed, and the authors of these changes, are well known, whereas Comedy has had no history, because it was not at first treated seriously. It was late before the Archon granted a comic chorus to a poet; the performers were till then voluntary. Comedy had already taken definite shape when comic poets, distinctively so called, are heard of. Who furnished it with masks, or prologues, or increased the number of actors—these and other similar details remain unknown. As for the plot, it came originally from Sicily; but of Athenian writers Crates was the first who, abandoning the "iambic" or lampooning form, generalized his themes and plots.

* Dithyramb is a choral poem, chant, or hymn of ancient Greece sung by revelers at the festival in honor of Dionysus, the god of wine. The form originated in the seventh century B.C.E. in banquet songs led by a man who, as the poet Archilochus says, was "wit stricken by the thunderbolt of wine." It later became a literary form when the poet Arion composed works of this type, gave them names, and presented them at the Great Dionysia competitions at Corinth. A chorus of men dressed in goatskins performed the dithyramb at the competitions in a circular dancing space. The goatskinned men represented satyrs, the companions of Dionysus. The Greek work for these "goat songs" is *tragoedia*. —Ed.

Epic poetry agrees with Tragedy in so far as it is an imitation in verse of characters of a higher type. They differ in that Epic poetry admits but one kind of meter and is narrative in form. They differ, again, in their length: for Tragedy endeavors, as far as possible, to confine itself to a single revolution of the sun, or but slightly to exceed this limit, whereas the Epic action has no limits of time. This, then, is a second point of difference; though at first the same freedom was admitted in Tragedy as in Epic poetry.

Of their constituent parts some are common to both, some peculiar to Tragedy: whoever, therefore knows what is good or bad Tragedy, knows also about Epic poetry. All the elements of an Epic poem are found in Tragedy, but the elements of a Tragedy are not all found in the Epic poem.

PART VI

Of the poetry which imitates in hexameter verse, and of Comedy, we will speak hereafter. Let us now discuss Tragedy, resuming its formal definition, as resulting from what has been already said.

Tragedy, then, is an imitation of an action that is serious, complete, and of a certain magnitude; in language embellished with each kind of artistic ornament, the several kinds being found in separate parts of the play; in the form of action, not of narrative; through pity and fear effecting the proper purgation of these emotions. By "language embellished," I mean language into which rhythm, "harmony" and song enter. By "the several kinds in separate parts," I mean, that some parts are rendered through the medium of verse alone, others again with the aid of song.

Now as tragic imitation implies persons acting, it necessarily follows in the first place, that Spectacular equipment will be a part of Tragedy. Next, Song and Diction, for these are the media of imitation. By "Diction" I mean the mere metrical arrangement of the words: as for "Song," it is a term whose sense every one understands.

Again, Tragedy is the imitation of an action; and an action implies personal agents, who necessarily possess certain distinctive qualities both of character and thought; for it is by these that we qualify actions themselves, and these—thought and character—are the two natural causes from which actions spring, and on actions again all success or failure depends. Hence, the Plot is the imitation of the action—for by plot I here mean the arrangement of the incidents. By Character I mean that in virtue of which we ascribe certain qualities to the agents. Thought is required wherever a statement is proved, or, it may be, a general truth enunciated. Every Tragedy, therefore, must have six parts, which parts determine its quality—namely, Plot, Character, Diction, Thought, Spectacle, Song. Two of the parts constitute the medium of imitation, one the manner, and three the objects of imitation. And these complete the list. These elements have been employed, we may say, by the poets to a man; every play contains Spectacular elements as well as Character, Plot, Diction, Song, and Thought.

But most important of all is the structure of the incidents. For Tragedy is an imitation, not of men, but of an action and of life, and life consists in action, and its end is a mode of action, not a quality. Now character determines men's qualities, but it is by their actions that they are happy or the reverse. Dramatic action, therefore, is not with a view to the representation of character: character comes in as subsidiary to the actions. Hence the incidents and the plot are the end of a tragedy; and the end is the chief thing of all. Again, without action there cannot be a tragedy; there may be without character. The tragedies of most of our modern poets fail in the rendering of character; and of poets in general this is often true. It is the same in painting; and here lies the difference between Zeuxis* and

---

* A celebrated painter, Zeuxis was born in the fifth century B.C.E. at Heraclea in Lucania, a region in Italy between the Tyrrhene and Sicilian seas. Lucania was famous for its grapes, and Zeuxis was famous for one of his paintings of grapes, which was said to be so realistic that birds came to eat the fruit painted on the canvas. However, Zeuxis was said to be dissatisfied with the painting because the man depicted in it carrying the grapes was not terrifying enough to scare away the birds. Zeuxis was the greatest painter of his day, but he refused to sell his paintings because he said that no sum of money was sufficient to buy them.—Ed.

Polygnotus.* Polygnotus delineates character well; the style of Zeuxis is devoid of ethical quality. Again, if you string together a set of speeches expressive of character, and well finished in point of diction and thought, you will not produce the essential tragic effect nearly so well as with a play which, however deficient in these respects, yet has a plot and artistically constructed incidents. Besides which, the most powerful elements of emotional interest in Tragedy—Peripeteia or Reversal of the Situation, and Recognition scenes—are parts of the plot. A further proof is, that novices in the art attain to finish of diction and precision of portraiture before they can construct the plot. It is the same with almost all the early poets.

The plot, then, is the first principle, and, as it were, the soul of a tragedy; Character holds the second place. A similar fact is seen in painting. The most beautiful colors, laid on confusedly, will not give as much pleasure as the chalk outline of a portrait. Thus Tragedy is the imitation of an action, and of the agents mainly with a view to the action.

Third in order is Thought—that is, the faculty of saying what is possible and pertinent in given circumstances. In the case of oratory, this is the function of the political art and of the art of rhetoric: and so indeed the older poets make their characters speak the language of civic life; the poets of our time, the language of the rhetoricians. Character is that which reveals moral purpose, showing what kind of things a man chooses or avoids. Speeches, therefore, which do not make this manifest, or in which the speaker does not choose or avoid anything whatever, are not expressive of character. Thought, on the other hand, is found where something is proved to be or not to be, or a general maxim is enunciated.

Fourth among the elements enumerated comes Diction; by which I mean, as has been already said, the expression of the meaning in words; and its essence is the same both in verse and prose.

Of the remaining elements Song holds the chief place among the embellishments.

The Spectacle has, indeed, an emotional attraction of its own, but, of all the parts, it is the least artistic, and connected least with the art of poetry. For the power of Tragedy, we may be sure, is felt even apart from representation and actors. Besides, the production of spectacular effects depends more on the art of the stage machinist than on that of the poet.

Part VII

These principles being established, let us now discuss the proper structure of the Plot, since this is the first and most important thing in Tragedy.

Now, according to our definition Tragedy is an imitation of an action that is complete, and whole, and of a certain magnitude; for there may be a whole that is wanting in magnitude. A whole is that which has a beginning, a middle, and an end. A beginning is that which does not itself follow anything by causal necessity, but after which something naturally is or comes to be. An end, on the contrary, is that which itself naturally follows some other thing, either by necessity, or as a rule, but has nothing following it. A middle is that which follows something as some other thing follows it. A well-constructed plot, therefore, must neither begin nor end at haphazard, but conform to these principles.

Again, a beautiful object, whether it be a living organism or any whole composed of parts, must not only have an orderly arrangement of parts, but must also be of a certain magnitude; for beauty depends on magnitude and order. Hence a very small animal organism cannot be beautiful; for the view of it is confused, the object being seen in an almost imperceptible moment of time. Nor, again, can one of vast size be beautiful; for as the eye cannot take it all in at once, the unity and sense of the whole [are] lost for the spectator; as for instance if there were one a thousand miles long. As, therefore, in the case of animate bodies and organisms a certain magnitude is necessary,

---

* Polygnotus, a painter, lived roughly from 475 to 447 B.C.E. in Thasos, a small island in the Aegean, on the coast of Thrace. Although he did not use shading in his works, many in the ancient world still regarded him as the first great painter. A set of his paintings depicting events from the Trojan War was placed in one of the public porticos of Athens. It pleased the Athenians so much that they offered him whatever he wanted for them. Polygnotus refused their offer, but later, a council of the principle cities in Greece ordered that he should be maintained at public expense in every city he visited.—Ed.

and a magnitude which may be easily embraced in one view; so in the plot, a certain length is necessary, and a length which can be easily embraced by the memory. The limit of length in relation to dramatic competition and sensuous presentment is no part of artistic theory. For had it been the rule for a hundred tragedies to compete together, the performance would have been regulated by the water-clock—as indeed we are told was formerly done. But the limit as fixed by the nature of the drama itself is this: the greater the length, the more beautiful will the piece be by reason of its size, provided that the whole be perspicuous. And to define the matter roughly, we may say that the proper magnitude is comprised within such limits, that the sequence of events, according to the law of probability or necessity, will admit of a change from bad fortune to good or from good fortune to bad.

PART VIII

Unity of plot does not, as some persons think, consist in the unity of the hero. For infinitely various are the incidents in one man's life which cannot be reduced to unity; and so, too, there are many actions of one man out of which we cannot make one action. Hence the error, as it appears, of all poets who have composed a *Heracleid,* a *Theseid,* or other poems of the kind. They imagine that as Heracles was one man, the story of Heracles must also be a unity. But Homer, as in all else he is of surpassing merit, here too— whether from art or natural genius—seems to have happily discerned the truth. In composing the *Odyssey* he did not include all the adventures of Odysseus—such as his wound on Parnassus, or his feigned madness at the mustering of the host—incidents between which there was no necessary or probable connection: but he made the *Odyssey,* and likewise the *Iliad,* to center round an action that in our sense of the word is one. As therefore, in the other imitative arts, the imitation is one when the object imitated is one, so the plot, being an imitation of an action, must imitate one action and that a whole, the structural union of the parts being such that, if anyone of them is displaced or removed, the whole will be disjointed and disturbed. For a thing whose presence or absence makes no visible difference, is not an organic part of the whole.

PART IX

It is, moreover, evident from what has been said, that it is not the function of the poet to relate what has happened, but what may happen— what is possible according to the law of probability or necessity. The poet and the historian differ not by writing in verse or in prose. The work of Herodotus might be put into verse, and it would still be a species of history, with meter no less than without it. The true difference is that one relates what has happened, the other what may happen. Poetry, therefore, is a more philosophical and a higher thing than history: for poetry tends to express the universal, history the particular. By the universal I mean how a person of a certain type on occasion speak or act, according to the law of probability or necessity; and it is this universality at which poetry aims in the names she attaches to the personages. The particular is—for example— what Alcibiades did or suffered. In Comedy this is already apparent: for here the poet first constructs the plot on the lines of probability, and then inserts characteristic names—unlike the lampooners who write about particular individuals. But tragedians still keep to real names, the reason being that what is possible is credible: what has not happened we do not at once feel sure to be possible; but what has happened is manifestly possible: otherwise it would not have happened. Still there are even some tragedies in which there are only one or two well-known names, the rest being fictitious. In others, none are well known—as in Agathon's *Antheus,* where incidents and names alike are fictitious, and yet they give none the less pleasure. We must not, therefore, at all costs keep to the received legends, which are the usual subjects of Tragedy. Indeed, it would be absurd to attempt it; for even subjects that are known are known only to a few, and yet give pleasure to all. It clearly follows that the poet or "maker" should be the maker of plots rather than of verses; since he is a poet because he imitates, and what he imitates are actions. And even if he chances to take a historical subject, he is none the less a poet; for there is no reason why some events that have actually happened should not conform to the law of the probable and possible, and in virtue of that quality in them he is their poet or maker.

Of all plots and actions the episodic are the worst. I call a plot "episodic" in which the episodes or acts succeed one another without probable or necessary sequence. Bad poets compose such pieces by their own fault, good poets, to please the players; for, as they write show pieces for competition, they stretch the plot beyond its capacity, and are often forced to break the natural continuity.

But again, Tragedy is an imitation not only of a complete action, but of events inspiring fear or pity. Such an effect is best produced when the events come on us by surprise; and the effect is heightened when, at the same time, they follow as cause and effect. The tragic wonder will then be greater than if they happened of themselves or by accident; for even coincidences are most striking when they have an air of design. We may instance the statue of Mitys at Argos, which fell upon his murderer while he was a spectator at a festival, and killed him. Such events seem not to be due to mere chance. Plots, therefore, constructed on these principles are necessarily the best.

Part X

Plots are either Simple or Complex, for the actions in real life, of which the plots are an imitation, obviously show a similar distinction. An action which is one and continuous in the sense above defined, I call Simple, when the change of fortune takes place without Reversal of the Situation and without Recognition

A Complex action is one in which the change is accompanied by such Reversal, or by Recognition, or by both. These last should arise from the internal structure of the plot, so that what follows should be the necessary or probable result of the preceding action. It makes all the difference whether any given event is a case of *propter hoc* or *post hoc*.

Part XI

Reversal of the Situation is a change by which the action veers round to its opposite, subject always to our rule of probability or necessity. Thus in the *Oedipus,* the messenger comes to cheer Oedipus and free him from his alarms about his mother, but by revealing who he is, he produces the opposite effect. Again in the *Lynceus,* Lynceus is being led away to his death, and Danaus goes with him, meaning to slay him; but the outcome

of the preceding incidents is that Danaus is killed and Lynceus saved.

Recognition, as the name indicates, is a change from ignorance to knowledge, producing love or hate between the persons destined by the poet for good or bad fortune. The best form of recognition is coincident with a Reversal of the Situation, as in the *Oedipus.* There are indeed other forms. Even inanimate things of the most trivial kind may in a sense be objects of recognition. Again, we may recognize or discover whether a person has done a thing or not. But the recognition which is most intimately connected with the plot and action is, as we have said, the recognition of persons. This recognition, combined with Reversal, will produce either pity or fear; and actions producing these effects are those which, by our definition, Tragedy represents. Moreover, it is upon such situations that the issues of good or bad fortune will depend. Recognition, then, being between persons, it may happen that one person only is recognized by the other—when the latter is already known—or it may be necessary that the recognition should be on both sides. Thus Iphigenia is revealed to Orestes by the sending of the letter; but another act of recognition is required to make Orestes known to Iphigenia.

Two parts, then, of the Plot—Reversal of the Situation and Recognition—turn upon surprises. A third part is the Scene of Suffering. The Scene of Suffering is a destructive or painful action, such as death on the stage, bodily agony, wounds, and the like.

Part XIII

As the sequel to what has already been said, we must proceed to consider what the poet should aim at, and what he should avoid, in constructing his plots; and by what means the specific effect of Tragedy will be produced.

A perfect tragedy should, as we have seen, be arranged not on the simple but on the complex plan. It should, moreover, imitate actions which excite pity and fear, this being the distinctive mark of tragic imitation. It follows plainly, in the first place, that the change of fortune presented must not be the spectacle of a virtuous man brought from prosperity to adversity: for this moves neither pity nor fear; it merely shocks us. Nor, again, that of a bad man passing from adversity to prosperity: for nothing can be more alien to the spirit of Tragedy; it possesses no single tragic quality; it neither satisfies the moral sense nor calls forth pity or fear. Nor, again, should the downfall of the utter villain be exhibited. A plot of this kind would, doubtless, satisfy the moral sense, but it would inspire neither pity nor fear; for pity is aroused by unmerited misfortune, fear by the misfortune of a man like ourselves. Such an event, therefore, will be neither pitiful nor terrible. There remains, then, the character between these two extremes—that of a man who is not eminently good and just, yet whose misfortune is brought about not by vice or depravity, but by some error or frailty. He must be one who is highly renowned and prosperous—a personage like Oedipus, Thyestes, or other illustrious men of such families.

A well-constructed plot should, therefore, be single in its issue, rather than double as some maintain. The change of fortune should be not from bad to good, but, reversely, from good to bad. It should come about as the result not of vice, but of some great error or frailty, in a character either such as we have described, or better rather than worse. The practice of the stage bears out our view. . . .

Part XIV

Fear and pity may be aroused by spectacular means; but they may also result from the inner structure of the piece, which is the better way, and indicates a superior poet. For the plot ought to be so constructed that, even without the aid of the eye, he who hears the tale told will thrill with horror and melt to pity at what takes Place. This is the impression we should receive from hearing the story of the *Oedipus*. But to produce this effect by the mere spectacle is a less artistic method, and dependent on extraneous aids. Those who employ spectacular means to create a sense not of the terrible but only of the monstrous, are strangers to the purpose of Tragedy; for we must not demand of Tragedy any and every kind of pleasure, but only that which is proper to it. . . .

Part XV

In respect of Character there are four things to be aimed at. First, and most important, it must be good. Now any speech or action that manifests moral purpose of any kind will be expressive of character: the character will be good if the purpose is good. This rule is relative to each class. Even a woman may be good, and also a slave; though the woman may be said to be an inferior being, and the slave quite worthless. The second thing to aim at is propriety. There is a type of manly valor; but valor in a woman, or unscrupulous cleverness is inappropriate. Thirdly, character must be true to life: for this is a distinct thing from goodness and propriety, as here described. The fourth point is consistency: for though the subject of the imitation, who suggested the type, be inconsistent, still he must be consistently inconsistent. . . .

As in the structure of the plot, so too in the portraiture of character, the poet should always aim either at the necessary or the probable. Thus a person of a given character should speak or act in a given way, by the rule either of necessity or of probability; just as this event should follow that by necessary or probable sequence. It is therefore evident that the unraveling of the plot, no less than the complication, must arise out of the plot itself, it must not be brought about by the Deus ex Machina—as in the *Medea*, or in the return of the Greeks in the *Iliad*. The Deus ex Machina should be employed only for events external to the drama—for antecedent or subsequent events, which lie beyond the range of human knowledge, and which require to be reported or foretold; for to the gods we ascribe the power of seeing all things. Within the action there must be nothing irrational. If the irrational cannot be excluded, it should be outside the scope of the tragedy. Such is the irrational element in the *Oedipus* of Sophocles.

Again, since Tragedy is an imitation of persons who are above the common level, the example of good portrait painters should be followed. They, while reproducing the distinctive form of the original, make a likeness which is true to life and yet more beautiful. So too the poet, in representing men who are irascible or indolent, or have other defects of character, should preserve the type and yet ennoble it. In this way Achilles is portrayed by Agathon and Homer.

DISCUSSION QUESTIONS

1. Both Plato and Aristotle contend that art is imitation, though they disagree on what it imitates. Compare and contrast their positions. Which do you prefer, and why?

2. Aristotle contends that poetry is a higher and more philosophical pursuit than history. What does he mean by this? Do you agree with him? Why or why not?

3. Aristotle lays out a number of reasons why we take pleasure in art. What are they? Are there any reasons you might add to or subtract from his list? Why?

4. Aristotle says that the purpose of tragedy is to arouse fear and pity, and to bring about a *catharsis* (purging) of these two emotions. What does he mean by *catharsis*? Do you agree with Aristotle that good tragic art results in catharsis? Or do you agree with Plato that tragedy is more likely to weaken us emotionally?

5. Do you think that other arts can bring about a catharsis? If so, which arts, and why?

6. What, for Aristotle, is a good tragic "plot"? What is a good tragic "character"? Do the same general characteristics hold today? If not, how have they changed, and why?

Death of a Salesman
[USA 1985] 2 hours, 10 minutes
Directed by Volker Schlöndorf

*D*eath of a Salesman charts the dreams and aspirations of Willy Loman (Dustin Hoffman), a sixty-year-old traveling salesman. Willy began his career as a salesman who worked for commission only and now finds himself ending his career as he began it: working for commission only. He wonders what went wrong. Where did he miss his opportunity for success? Willy always believed that success involved being well liked and popular, and fashioned himself as an important person. However, his brother, Ben Loman (Louis Zorich), strongly disagreed with Willy's outlook on life. Ben tried to convince Willy not to put his trust in intangible things like the way other people felt about him, but rather to put his trust in things that he could touch. Ben became independently wealthy by the age of twenty-one, and in comparison to Ben, Willy seems a complete failure.

Willy's sons, Harold (Stephen Lang) and Biff (John Malkovich), had always looked up to their father as an important man and believed what he told them about success: it's not what you know, it's whom you know. Harold, nicknamed "Happy" (or simply "Hap"), while only an assistant's assistant, is just as deluded about his own importance as his father. Like his brother Hap, Biff leads a mediocre existence. Although Willy had big dreams of success for Biff in the business world, his son is a complete failure, unable to hold onto any job other than as a farmhand. Biff thought that he did not have to take orders from anyone and never believed that he had to work for anything just so long as he was popular. For these reasons, as well as his habit of stealing things, which was also taught to both sons by their father, Biff does not succeed in the business world. Biff sees himself as is a failure, which brings him to completely reevaluate his life.

Although Biff comes to realize that the values his father taught him are wrong and attempts to convince his father as much, Willy will not listen. Because Willy refuses to accept that his values are misguided and to see his life for what it really is, Biff decides to leave for good. Willy, now unemployed and reeling from

Biff's charges, aims to prove his son wrong by committing suicide so that Biff can use the insurance money to start his own business. Willy believes that Biff will consider him a hero for his action and will recognize the sacrifices that his father has made for him. Willy also anticipates a big turnout at his funeral—a visual proof to all of his importance and success. It turns out, however, that the insurance policy does not cover suicide, and Willy's funeral attracts only his family and two neighbors.

Hoffman and Malkovich were awarded Emmys for their performance in this made-for-television movie version of *Death of a Salesman*. The play, written by American playwright Arthur Miller (1915–2005), was published in 1949. For Miller, Willy Loman's obsession with money and success reflected values embraced by American society in general: the "American dream." Thus, in tracking the destruction of Willy Loman through his blind adherence to these false values, Miller offers a critique of the ethos of a materialist society.

DISCUSSION QUESTIONS

1. Does *Death of a Salesman* arouse fear and pity in the Aristotelian sense? Why or why not?

2. Does *Death of a Salesman* bring about a catharsis of fear and pity? Why or why not?

3. Is there "recognition" (*anagnorisis*) and "reversal" (*peripeteia*) in *Death of a Salesman*? Why or why not?

4. Evaluate the character, plot, and thought of *Death of a Salesman* in accordance with the standards described by Aristotle. How closely is it in accord with Aristotle's standards in these areas?

5. Is *Death of a Salesman* a tragedy in the full Aristotelian sense? Why or why not?

6. Compare the ability of *Death of a Salesman* to arouse fear and pity to that of other movies you may have seen—for example, *Psycho*, *Jaws*, *The Shining*, *Silence of the Lambs*, and *Natural Born Killers*. Are these movies also tragedies in the full Aristotelian sense? Why or why not? How are they different from *Death of a Salesman*?

DAVID HUME

OF THE STANDARD OF TASTE

David Hume argues that there is no authority other than taste for the evaluation of works of art. According to Hume, taste, not reason, is the source of our judgments of beauty in art and of virtuousness in action. Judgments of beauty and deformity are not "matters of fact" or "opinion" but arise from "sentiment," which "has a reference to nothing beyond itself." Hume argues that "beauty is quality in things themselves; it exists merely in the mind which contemplates them; and each mind perceives a different beauty." Moreover, "Men of the most confined knowledge are able to remark a difference of taste in the narrow circle of their acquaintance, even where the persons have been educated under the same government, and have early imbibed the same prejudices." Furthermore, those who become less provincial, "who can enlarge their view to contemplate distant nations and remote ages, are still more surprised at the great inconsistence and contrariety." Nevertheless, "It is natural for us to seek a *Standard of Taste*; a rule, by which the various sentiments of men may be reconciled; at least, a decision, afforded, confirming one sentiment, and condemning another."

One of Hume's challenges in this essay is to balance what he introduces as two competing commonsense claims: (1) that all tastes are equal, and (2) that some works of art are better than others. The first of these two "species of common sense" establishes "the natural equality of tastes," namely, that "a thousand sentiments, excited by the same object, are all right." The second indicates that critics who "assert an equality of genius and elegance between Ogilby and Milton" are simply "absurd and ridiculous." There is some disagreement as to whether Hume successfully defends both species of common sense in this essay, for at least on the surface, they seem to be inconsistent: either all tastes are equal, or they are not equal (with some being more absurd than others), but not both.

For Hume, "the rules of composition" are founded in "general observations, concerning what has been universally found to please in all countries and in all ages." "But though poetry can never submit to exact truth, it must be confined by rules of art, discovered by the author either by genius or observation," says Hume. Nevertheless, these rules can be transgressed, and works of art can be improved through the transgression of rules.

Meritorious art is determined not through the application of rules but through the delicacy of taste. The anecdote of the two wine judges from *Don Quixote* is intended to illustrate this point: one finds the wine slightly metallic, the other slightly leathery, and both are ridiculed for their supposed pretentiousness. But the judges are vindicated when a leather thong with a key on it is found at the bottom of the wine vat. For Hume, "Though the principles of taste be universal, and, nearly, if not entirely the same in all men; yet few are qualified to give judgment on any work of art, or establish their own sentiment as the standard of beauty." Hume asserts that "strong sense, united to delicate sentiment, improved by practice, perfected by comparison, and cleared of all prejudice, can alone entitle critics to his valuable character; and the joint verdict of such, wherever they are to be found, is the true standard of taste."

Hume's position on taste is in line with his general *empiricist theory of knowledge*, namely, that all knowledge comes from experience. In general, Hume believes that a standard of taste can be derived from the workings of the mind. Originally, he had planned to discuss moral and critical taste in his early masterpiece *Treatise of Human Nature* (1739), but he never did. "Of the Standard of Taste" (1757), an except from which is found below, is the only place where Hume formally comments on the arts and critical judgment. Despite the brevity and condensed nature of this essay, many believe that it lays out some of the central issues of philosophical aesthetics for many years to come, including the relativity of standards, the defeasibility of rules, and the authority of the critic. A biographical sketch of Hume appears in chapter 1.

The great variety of Taste, as well as of opinion, which prevails in the world, is too obvious not to have fallen under every one's observation. Men of the most confined knowledge are able to remark a difference of taste in the narrow circle of their acquaintance, even where the persons have been educated under the same government, and have early imbibed the same prejudices. But those, who can enlarge their view to contemplate distant nations and remote ages, are still more surprised at the great inconsistence and contrariety. We are apt to call *barbarous* whatever departs widely from our own taste and apprehension: But soon find the epithet of reproach retorted on us. And the highest arrogance and self-conceit is at last startled, on observing an equal assurance on all sides, and scruples, amidst such a contest of sentiment, to pronounce positively in its own favour.

As this variety of taste is obvious to the most careless inquirer, so will it be found, on examination, to be still greater in reality than in appearance. The sentiments of men often differ with regard to beauty and deformity of all kinds, even while their general discourse is the same. There are certain terms in every language, which impart blame, and others praise; and all men, who use the same tongue, must agree in their application of them. Every voice is united in applauding elegance, propriety, simplicity, spirit in writing; and in blaming fustian, affectation, coldness, and a false brilliancy: But when critics come to particulars, this seeming unanimity vanishes; and it is found, that they had affixed a very different meaning to their expressions. In all matters of opinion and science, the case is opposite: The difference among men is there oftener found to lie in generals than in particulars; and to be less in reality than in appearance. An explanation of the terms commonly ends the controversy; and the disputants are surprised to find, that they had been quarreling, while at bottom they agreed in their judgment. . . .

It is natural for us to seek a *Standard of Taste*; a rule, by which the various sentiments of men may be reconciled; at least, a decision, afforded, confirming one sentiment, and condemning another.

There is a species of philosophy, which cuts off all hopes of success in such an attempt, and represents the impossibility of ever attaining any standard of taste. The difference, it is said, is very wide between judgment and sentiment. All sentiment is right; because sentiment has a reference to nothing beyond itself, and is always real, wherever a man is conscious of it. But all determinations of the understanding are not right; because they have a reference to something beyond themselves, to wit, real matter of fact; and are not always comfortable to that standard. Among a thousand different opinions which different men may entertain of the same subject, there is one, and but one, that is just and true; and the only difficulty is to fix and ascertain it. On the contrary, a thousand different sentiments, excited by the same object, are all right: Because no sentiment represents what is really in the object. It only marks a certain conformity or relation between the object and the organs or faculties of the mind; and if that conformity did not really exist, the sentiment could never possibly have being. Beauty is no quality in things themselves: It exists merely in the mind which contemplates them; and each mind perceives a different beauty. One person may even perceive deformity, where another is sensible of beauty; and every individual ought to acquiesce in his own sentiment, without pretending to regulate those of others. To seek the real beauty, or real deformity, is as fruitless an enquiry, as to pretend to ascertain the real sweet or real bitter. According to the disposition of the organs, the same object may be both sweet and bitter; and the proverb has justly determined it to be fruitless to dispute concerning tastes. It is very natural, and even quite necessary, to extend this axiom to mental, as well as bodily taste; and thus common sense, which is so often at variance with philosophy, especially with the skeptical kind, is found, in one instance at least, to agree in pronouncing the same decision.

But though this axiom, by passing into a proverb, seems to have attained the sanction of common sense; there is certainly a species of common sense which opposes it, at least serves to modify and restrain it. Whoever would assert an equality of genius and elegance between Ogibly* and Milton,[†] Bunyan[‡] and Addison,[§] would be thought to defend no less an extravagance, than if he had maintained a molehill to be as high as [a mountain], or a pond as extensive as the ocean.

*John Ogibly (1600–1676) was an English translator and publisher of maps and geographical accounts. In 1669, he began working on a very ambitious project—a multivolume description of the world—and in 1670, the first volume, *Africa*, appeared. It was followed by *Atlas Japannensis* (1670), *Atlas Chinensis* (1671), *America* (1671), *Asia* (1673), and *Brittannia* (1675). —Ed.

[†]John Milton (1608–74) is one of the greatest poets of the English language. His major work is the epic poem *Paradise Lost* (1667). His other works include *Comus* (1637), a dramatization of the conflict between good and evil; *Lycidas* (1638), a poem that mourns the loss of a promising young man; *Areopagitica* (1644), a pamphlet protesting required government approval of all published books; and the tragedy *Samson Agonistes* (1671). —Ed.

[‡]John Bunyan (1628–88) was an English minister whose best-known work is *The Pilgrim's Progress* (1678, 1684), a book that exemplifies the Puritan religious outlook. An allegory of a Christian's journey into the Celestial City, *Pilgrim's Progress* was a very popular book and, with the Bible, was found in most every home in England well into the nineteenth century. —Ed.

[§]Joseph Addison (1672–1719) was an English poet, dramatist, and essayist. He gained his reputation as a brilliant contributor to the periodical *The Tatler*. When this periodical ceased publication, he cofounded with Joseph Steele another, *The Spectator*, the aim of which was to "enliven morality with wit, and to temper wit with morality." —Ed.

Though there may be found persons, who give the preference to the former authors; no one pays attention to such a taste; and we pronounce without scruple the sentiment of these pretended critics to be absurd and ridiculous. The principle of the natural equality of tastes is then totally forgot, and while we admit it on some occasions, where the objects seem near an equality, it appears an extravagant paradox, or rather a palpable absurdity, where objects so disproportioned are compared together.

It is evident that none of the rules of composition are fixed by reasonings *a priori,* or can be esteemed abstract conclusions of the understanding, from comparing those habitudes and relations of ideas, which are eternal and immutable. Their foundation is the same with that of all the practical sciences, experience; nor are they any thing but general observations, concerning what has been universally found to please in all countries and in all ages. Many of the beauties of poetry and even of eloquence are founded on falsehood and fiction, on hyperboles, metaphors, and an abuse or perversion of terms from their natural meaning. To check the sallies of the imagination, and to reduce every expression to geometrical truth and exactness, would be the most contrary to the laws of criticism; because it would produce a work, which, by universal experience, has been found the most insipid and disagreeable. But though poetry can never submit to exact truth, it must be confined by rules of art, discovered to the author either by genius or observation. If some negligent or irregular writers have pleased, they have not pleased by their transgressions of rule or order, but in spite of these transgressions: They have possessed other beauties, which were conformable to just criticism; and the force of these beauties has been able to overpower censure, and give the mind a satisfaction superior to the disgust arising from the blemishes. . . . If they are found to please, they cannot be faults; let the pleasure, which they produce, be ever so unexpected and unaccountable.

But though all the general rules of art are founded only on experience and on the observation of the common sentiments of human nature, we must not imagine, that, on every occasion, the feelings of men will be conformable to these rules. Those finer emotions of the mind are of a very tender and delicate nature, and require the concurrence of many favourable circumstances to make them play with facility and exactness, according to their general and established principles. The least exterior hindrance to such small springs, or the least internal disorder, disturbs their motion, and confounds the operation of the whole machine. When we would make an experiment of this nature, and would try the force of any beauty or deformity, we must choose with care a proper time and place, and bring the fancy to a suitable situation and disposition. A perfect serenity of mind, a recollection of thought, a due attention to the object; if any of these circumstances be wanting, our experiment will be fallacious, and we shall be unable to judge of the catholic and universal beauty. The relation, which nature has placed between the form and the sentiment will at least be more obscure; and it will require greater accuracy to trace and discern it. We shall be able to ascertain its influence not so much from the operations of each particular beauty, as from the durable admiration, which attends those works, that have survived all the caprices of mode and fashion, all the mistakes of ignorance and envy.

The same Homer who pleased at Athens and Rome two thousand years ago, is still admired at Paris and at London. All the changes of climate, government, religion, and language, have not been able to obscure his glory. Authority or prejudice may give a temporary vogue to a bad poet or orator; but his reputation will never be durable or general. When his compositions are examined by posterity or by foreigners, the enchantment is dissipated, and his faults appear in their true colours. On the contrary, a real genius, the longer his works endure, and the more wide they are spread, the more sincere is the admiration which he meets with . . .

It appears then, that, amidst all the variety and caprice of taste, there are certain general principles of approbation or blame, whose influence a careful eye may trace in all operations of the mind. Some particular forms or qualities, from the original structure of the internal fabric, are calculated to please, and others to displease; and if they fail of their effect in any particular instance, it is from some apparent defect or imperfection in the organ. A man in a fever would not insist on his palate as able to decide concerning flavours; nor would one, affected with the jaundice, pretend to give a verdict with regard to colours. In each creature, there is a sound and a defective state; and the former alone can be supposed to afford us a true standard of taste and sentiment. If, in the sound state of the organ, there be an entire or a considerable uniformity of sentiment among men, we may thence derive an idea of the perfect beauty; in like manner as the appearance of objects in daylight, to the eye of a man in health, is denominated their true and real colour, even while colour is allowed to be merely a phantasm of the senses.

Many and frequent are the defects in the internal organs, which prevent or weaken the influence of those general principles, on which depends our sentiment of beauty or deformity. Though some objects, by the structure of the mind, be naturally calculated to give pleasure, it is not to be expected, that in every individual the pleasure will be equally felt. Particular incidents and situations occur, which either throw a false light on the objects, or hinder the true from conveying to the imagination the proper sentiment and perception.

One obvious cause why many feel not the proper sentiment of beauty, is the want of that *delicacy* of imagination which is requisite to convey a sensibility of those finer emotions. This delicacy everyone pretends to: everyone talks of it; and would reduce every kind of taste or sentiment to its standard. But as our intention in this essay is to mingle some light of the understanding with the feelings of sentiment, it will be proper to give a more accurate definition of delicacy than has hitherto been attempted. And not to draw our philosophy from too profound a source, we shall have recourse to a noted story in *Don Quixote*.

It is with good reason, says Sancho to the squire with the great nose, that I pretend to have a judgement in wine: this is a quality hereditary in our family. Two of my kinsmen were once called to give their opinion of a hogshead, which was supposed to be excellent, being old and of a good vintage. One of them tastes it, considers it; and, after mature reflection, pronounces the wine to be good, were it not for a small taste of leather which he perceived in it. The other after using the same precautions, gives also his verdict in favour of the wine; but with the reserve of a taste of iron which he could easily distinguish. You cannot imagine how much they were both ridiculed for their judgement. But who laughed in the end? On emptying the hogshead, there was found at the bottom an old key with a leathern thong tied to it.

The great resemblance between mental and bodily taste will easily teach us to apply this story. Though it be certain that beauty and deformity, more than sweet and bitter, are not qualities in objects, but belong entirely to the sentiment, internal or external, it must be allowed that there are certain qualities in objects which are fitted by nature to produce those particular feelings. Now, as these qualities may be found in a small degree, or may be mixed and confounded with each other, it often happens that the taste is not affected with such minute qualities, or is not able to distinguish all the particular flavours, amidst the disorder in which they are presented. Where the organs are so fine as to allow nothing to escape them, and at the same time so exact as to perceive every ingredient in the composition, this we call delicacy of taste, whether we employ these terms in the literal or metaphorical sense. Here then the general rules of beauty are of use, being drawn from established models and from the observation of what pleases or displeases when presented singly and in a high degree; and if the same qualities, in a continued composition, and in a smaller degree, affect not the organs with a sensible delight or uneasiness, we exclude the person from all pretensions to this delicacy. To produce these general rules or avowed patterns of composition, is like finding the key with the leathern thong, which justified the verdict of Sancho's kinsmen, and confounded those pretended judges who had condemned them . . .

But though there be naturally a wide difference, in point of delicacy, between one person and another, nothing tends further to increase and improve this talent than *practice* in a particular art, and the frequent survey or contemplation of a particular species of beauty. When objects of any kind are first presented to the eye or imagination, the sentiment which attends them is obscure and confused; and the mind is, in a great measure, incapable of pronouncing concerning their merits or defects. . . . But allow him to acquire experience in those objects, his feeling becomes more exact and nice: he not only perceives the beauties and defects of each part, but marks the distinguishing species of each quality, and assigns it suitable praise or blame. A clear and distinct sentiment attends him through the whole survey of the objects; and he discerns that very degree and kind of approbation or displeasure which each part is naturally fitted to produce. The mist dissipates which seemed formerly to hang over the object; the organ acquires greater perfection in its operations, and can pronounce, without danger of mistake, concerning the merits of every performance. In a word, the same address and dexterity which practice gives to the execution of any work, is also acquired by the same means in the judging of it . . .

It is impossible to continue in the practice of contemplating any order of beauty, without being frequently obliged to form *comparisons* between the several species and degrees of excellence, and estimating their proportion to each other. A man, who had no opportunity of comparing the different kinds of beauty, is indeed totally unqualified to pronounce an opinion with regard to any object presented to him. By comparison alone we fix the epithets of praise or blame, and learn how to assign the due degree of each. . . .

But to enable a critic the more fully to execute this undertaking, he must preserve his mind free from all *prejudice,* and allow nothing to enter into his consideration, but the very object which is submitted to his examination. We may observe, that every work of art, in order to produce its due effect on the mind, must be surveyed in a certain point of view, and cannot be fully relished by persons, whose situation, real or imaginary, is not conformable to that which is required by the performance. . . .

It is well known, that in all questions, submitted to the understanding, prejudice is destructive of sound judgment, and perverts all operations of the intellectual faculties: It is no less contrary to good taste; nor has it less influence to corrupt our sentiment of beauty. It belongs to *good sense* to check its influence in both cases; and in this respect, as well as in many others, reason, if not an essential part of taste, is at least requisite to the operations of this latter faculty. In all the nobler productions of genius, there is a mutual relation and correspondence of parts; nor can

either the beauties or blemishes be perceived by him, whose thought is not capacious enough to comprehend all those parts, and compare them with each other, in order to perceive the consistence and uniformity of the whole. Every work of art has also a certain end or purpose, for which it is calculated; and is to be deemed more or less perfect, as it is more or less fitted to attain this end. The object of eloquence is to persuade, of history to instruct, of poetry to please by means of the passions and the imagination. These ends we must carry constantly in our view, when we peruse any performance; and we must be able to judge how far the means employed are adapted to their respective purposes. Besides, every kind of composition, even the most poetical is nothing but a chain of propositions and reasonings; not always, indeed, the justest and most exact, but still plausible and specious, however disguised by the coloring of the imagination. The persons introduced in tragedy and epic poetry, must be represented as reasoning, and thinking, and concluding, and acting, suitably to their character and circumstances; and without judgment, as well as taste and invention, a poet can never hope to succeed in so delicate an undertaking. Not to mention, that the same excellence of faculties which contributes to the improvement of reason, the same clearness of conception, the same exactness of distinction, the same vivacity of apprehension, are essential to the operations of true taste, and are its infallible concomitants. It seldom, or never happens, that a man of sense, who has experience in any art, cannot judge of its beauty; and it is no less rare to meet with a man who has a just taste without a sound understanding.

Thus, though the principles of taste be universal, and, nearly, if not entirely the same in all men; yet few are qualified to give judgment on any work of art, or establish their own sentiment as the standard of beauty. . . . Strong sense, united to delicate sentiment, improved by practice, perfected by comparison, and cleared of all prejudice, can alone entitle critics to his valuable character; and the joint verdict of such, wherever they are to be found, is the true standard of taste and beauty.

But where are such critics to be found? By what marks are they to be known? How distinguish them from pretenders? These questions are embarrassing; and seem to throw us back into the same uncertainty, from which, during the course of this essay, we have endeavoured to extricate ourselves.

But if we consider the matter aright, these are questions of fact, not of sentiment. Whether any particular person be endowed with good sense and a delicate imagination, free from prejudice, may often be the subject of dispute, and be liable to great discussion and enquiry: But that such a character is valuable and estimable will be agreed in by all mankind. Where these doubts occur, men can do no more than in other disputable questions, which are submitted to the understanding: They must produce the best arguments, that their invention suggests to them; they must acknowledge a true and decisive standard to exist somewhere, to wit, real existence and matter of fact; and they must have indulgence to such as differ from them in their appeals to this standard. It is sufficient for our present purpose, if we have proved, that the taste of all individuals is not upon an equal footing, and that some men in general, however difficult to be particularly pitched upon, will be acknowledged by universal sentiment to have a preference above others. . . .

But notwithstanding all our endeavours to fix a standard of taste, and reconcile the discordant apprehensions of men, there still remain two sources of variation, which are not sufficient indeed to confound all the boundaries of beauty and deformity, but will often serve to produce a difference in the degrees of our approbation or blame. The one is the different humours of particular men; the other, the particular manners and opinions of our age and country. The general principles of taste are uniform in human nature: where men vary in their judgements, some defect or perversion in the faculties may commonly be remarked; proceeding either from prejudice, from want of practice, or want of delicacy: and there is just reason for approving one taste, and condemning another. But where there is such a diversity in the internal frame or external situation as is entirely blameless on both sides, and leaves no room to give one the preference above the other; in that case a certain degree of diversity in judgement is unavoidable, and we seek in vain for a standard, by which we can reconcile the contrary sentiments.

A young man, whose passions are warm, will be more, sensibly touched with amorous and tender images, than a man more advanced in years, who takes pleasure in wise, philosophical reflections, concerning the conduct of life, and moderation of the passions. At twenty, Ovid may be the favourite author, Horace at forty, and perhaps Tacitus at fifty. Vainly would we, in such cases, endeavour to enter into the sentiments of others, and divest ourselves of those propensities which are natural to us. We choose our favourite author as we do our friend, from a conformity of humour and disposition. Mirth or passion, sentiment or reflection; whichever of these most predominates in our temper, it gives us a peculiar sympathy with the writer who resembles us. . . . Such performances are innocent and unavoidable, and can never reasonably be the object of dispute, because there is no standard by which they can be decided.

For a like reason, we are more pleased, in the course of our reading, with pictures and characters that resemble objects which are found in our own age and country than with those which describe a different set of customs. It is not without some effort that we reconcile ourselves to the simplicity of ancient manners, and behold princesses carrying water from the spring, and kings and heroes dressing their own victuals. We may allow in general that the representation of such manners is no fault in the author, nor deformity in the piece; but we are not so sensibly touched with them. . . .

DISCUSSION QUESTIONS

1. Hume says, "We are apt to call *barbarous* whatever departs widely from our own taste and apprehension." Do you agree with him? Compare Hume's position with that described by Herodotus earlier in the chapter, in section 4.1.

2. Hume writes, "Though the principles of taste be universal, and, nearly, if not entirely the same in all men; yet few are qualified to give judgement on any work of art, or establish their own sentiment as the standard of beauty." Why does he think that certain critics are better qualified than others to judge works of art? Do you agree with him? Is Hume's position elitist?

3. For Hume, "the rules of composition" are founded in "general observations, concerning what has been universally found to please in all countries and in all ages." What does he mean? Is his position on the rules of composition consistent with his belief that there is a "natural equality of tastes"? Why or why not?

4. What are the two species of common sense with regard to taste? Is Hume successful in reconciling them? Why or why not?

5. Some have criticized Hume's approach to art as being too "psychologistic," meaning that it relies too heavily on the workings of the human mind in its analysis of art. Do you agree with this line of criticism? How does Hume's position on art differ from those of Plato and Aristotle? Of the three positions, which do you prefer, and why?

Citizen Kane
[USA 1941] 1 hour, 59 minutes
Directed by Orson Welles

Wealthy newspaper mogul Charles Foster Kane (Orson Welles) meets a poor sheet music clerk named Susan Alexander (Dorothy Comingore). Though Kane is a married man embroiled in an important political race, he is lonely—and so is Susan. Upon their first meeting, it is clear to Kane that Susan knows nothing about his power, wealth, and reputation. She simply enjoys his company, and she charms him. They spend most of their time together performing songs, with Kane on the piano and Susan singing.

However, Kane's political rival finds out about the relationship and uses it to drive Kane to a crushing defeat in the election. Kane's marriage breaks up, and he weds Susan. Kane is accustomed to getting what he wants, and he becomes obsessed with forging a musical career for Susan. He insists on professional singing lessons and builds a massive opera house in Chicago. Susan, however, is an amateur singer, and the lessons do not improve her voice. Her debut opera performance is dismal, but Kane's newspaper critics plan to review it as a resounding success.

Jedediah Leland (Joseph Cotton), Kane's long-time friend and the drama critic for Kane's Chicago paper, refuses to write a positive review of a bad performance. He is so upset about having to write the review that he gets drunk and passes out in the middle of composing it. Kane reads what Jedediah has written and decides to finish it himself. However, instead of changing it to a positive review, he finishes it as Jedediah intended it—a bad review. While the other aspects of Susan's performance are reported in glowing terms in Kane's Chicago paper the next day, the dramatic aspect is panned. Susan is furious. She can accept all of the other papers panning her performance, but to read a bad review from Kane's friend Jedediah is unacceptable. She is unaware that Kane, wrote the review.

DISCUSSION QUESTIONS

1. According to Hume, there is no authority beyond taste for the evaluation of works of art. Do the events surrounding reviews of the performance of Susan Alexander in *Citizen Kane* challenge taste as the only source of authority? Why or why not?

2. According to Hume's theory, if Kane and his newspaper critics regard Susan's performances as excellent, and Jedediah and the rest of the critical community regard her performances as bad, must we honor as valid both sets of responses? Why or why not?

3. Consider the following dialogue between Kane and Signor Matisti (Fortunio Bononova), Susan's voice coach:

   SUSAN and MATISTI   (singing in Italian)

   MATISTI   "Go ahead, go ahead . . . Now . . . La-la-la-la-la-la-la-la-la. You're out the pitch . . . Some people can sing. Some can't. Impossible! Impossible!"

   KANE   "It's not your job to give Mrs. Kane your opinion of her talents. You're supposed to train her voice, Signor Matisti."

   MATISTI   "Mister . . ."

   KANE   "Nothing more. Please sit down and continue with the lesson."

   MATISTI   "But, Mr. Kane!"

   KANE   "Please."

   MATISTI   "But I will be the laughing stock of the musical world! People will think that . . ."

   KANE   "People will think. You're concerned with what people will think? Perhaps I can enlighten you, Signor Matisti. I'm something of an authority on what people will think. Newspapers, for example, I run several newspapers between here and San Francisco. It's all right, darling. Signor Matisti is gonna listen to reason. Aren't you, Signor Matisti?"

   MATISTI   "How can I persuade you?"

   KANE   "You can't."

   MATISTI   (inaudible)

   SUSAN   (sings)

   KANE   "It's all right, darling. Go ahead."

   SUSAN   (sings)

   KANE   "I thought you'd see it my way."

   Why does Kane tell Matisti not to worry about what people will think? How influential do you think that reviews of the arts in the newspaper, for example, are in tempering our opinions of the arts? If newspaper reviews of the arts can temper our tastes, then is Hume mistaken that there is no authority beyond taste for the evaluation of works of art? Discuss.

4. After Susan's operatic opening in Chicago, Mr. Bernstein (Everett Sloane) is speaking with a number of newspaper employees about the reviews of it they are going to run in Kane's newspaper. Kane surprises them with a visit and converses with them about it. Consider some of their dialogue:

   BERNSTEIN   "Mr. Leland is writing it from the dramatic angle?"

NEWSPAPERMAN 1   "Yes. And we covered it from the news end."

NEWSPAPERMAN 2   "Naturally."

BERNSTEIN   "And the social. How about the music notice? You got that in?"

NEWSPAPERMAN 2   "Oh, yes. That's already made up. Our Mr. Mervin wrote a swell review."

BERNSTEIN   "Enthusiastic?"

MERVIN   "Yes, sir."

NEWSPAPERMAN 2   "Naturally."

KANE   "Mr. Bernstein."

BERNSTEIN   "Mr. Kane."

NEWSPAPERMAN 2   "Mr. Kane."

BERNSTEIN   "Hello, Mr. Kane."

KANE   "Hello."

NEWSPAPERMAN 2   "This is a surprise. Everything's been done exactly . . ."

KANE   "You have a very nice plan here, gentlemen. Mr. Stanley."

NEWSPAPERMAN 2   "We've done two spreads of pictures."

KANE   ". . . the music notice on the front page?"

MERVIN   "Yes, Mr. Kane."

From this dialogue, it is clear that Kane's newspapers plan to do an extensive and enthusiastic spread on Susan's opening at the opera house even though her performance was poor. To what extent do you believe that art criticism is controlled by the interests of those who run the media? Are Hume's comments on the standard of taste dated because they do not take into account the impact of the media (and financial interests) on taste? Why or why not?

5.   All of Kane's Chicago newspaper staff except Leland praise Susan's performance. Consider the dialogue below:

KANE   "Close the door."

BERNSTEIN   "He ain't been drinking before, Mr. Kane. Never. We would have heard."

KANE   "What's it say there? The notice. What's he written?"

BERNSTEIN   " 'Miss Susan Alexander, a pretty but hopelessly incompetent amateur. Last night opened the new Chicago Opera House in the performance of . . .' I still can't pronounce that name, Mr. Kane. 'Her singing, happily, is no concern of this department. Of her acting it is absolutely impossible to . . .' "

KANE   "Go on. Go on."

BERNSTEIN   "That's all there is."

KANE   " 'Of her acting it is absolutely impossible to say anything except in the opinion of this reviewer, it represents a new low.' Have you got that, Mr. Bernstein? 'In the opinion of this reviewer.' "

BERNSTEIN   "I didn't see that."

KANE   "It isn't here, Mr. Bernstein. I'm dictating."

BERNSTEIN   "Mr. Kane, I . . ."

KANE   "Give me a typewriter. I'm gonna finish Mr. Leland's notice."

Kane insists on adding "In the opinion of this reviewer" to Leland's review. From Hume's perspective, wouldn't this be redundant? Is not all criticism for Hume only the opinion of the reviewer? Why or why not?

6.   An interviewer named Thompson (William Alland) questions an elderly Leland about why Kane would write a bad review of his wife's performance. Leland responds, "You just don't know Charlie. He thought that by finishing that notice he could show me he was an honest man. He was always trying to prove something." What was Kane trying to prove? Does he ultimately prove something about the nature of art criticism? Do you agree with Leland as to why Kane did it? If you were in Kane's shoes, would you have finished the review the same way? Discuss.

7.   Susan and Kane discuss Leland's review:

SUSAN   "Stop telling me he's your friend. Friends don't write that kind of review. All these other papers are panning me. I can expect that. But the *Inquirer* ran the thing like that spoiling my whole debut. Come in!"

KANE   "I'll get it."

SUSAN   "Friend! Not the kind of friends I know. But, of course, I'm not high class like you and I never went any swell schools."

Is Susan right? When she says, "Friends don't write that kind of review"? Can one use Hume's theory of sentiment in art evaluation to support Susan's position? Why or why not?

8.   What is the general view of art criticism in *Citizen Kane*? How does it compare with Hume's argument that taste, not reason, is the source of our judgments of beauty in art? Discuss.

LEO TOLSTOY

WHAT IS ART?

Leo Tolstoy's approach to art is both moralistic and practical. He asserts that art must be justified on moral grounds and rejects any position on art that conflicts with this fundamental principle. For Tolstoy, real or true art "is a means of union among men joining them together in the same feelings, and indispensable for the life and progress towards well-being of individuals and of humanity." False or "counterfeit" art has the opposite effect: it is divisive and elitist.

"Art is a human activity consisting in this, that one man consciously by means of certain external signs, hands on to others feelings he has lived through, and that others are infected by these feelings and also experience them," writes Tolstoy. He believes that real art is infectious and that "the stronger the infection the better the art." Furthermore, the degree of infectiousness of art depends on three conditions: (1) the more individual the feeling communicated by the art, the higher the degree of infection; (2) the clearer the feeling communicated by the art, the higher the degree of infection; and (3) most importantly, the more sincere the artist, the higher the degree of infection. By this third condition, Tolstoy means that better or more infectious art derives from artists who really feel what they are communicating through their art. For Tolstoy, these are the "three conditions which divide art from its counterfeits, and which also decide the quality of every work of art considered apart from its subject-matter."

In addition to these "internal" conditions of art, Tolstoy also considers what may be termed the "external" conditions of art. In our selection, he discusses the great amount of time, energy, expense, and personal sacrifice that an opera or ballet demands, and asks "whether all that professes to be art is really art, whether (as is presupposed by our society) all that which is art is good, and whether it is important and worth those sacrifices which is necessitates." For Tolstoy, arts such as opera and ballet, as well as concerts, printed books, exhibitions, circuses, and paintings, are not self-evidently valuable and are not self-justifying. They are valuable only if they satisfy the moral and practical conditions he lays out for real art.

Tolstoy's position on art puts him at odds with those who argue that art is self-justifying or that its value is self-evident. Moreover, Tolstoy does not presume to know before he undertakes his analysis of art what is and is not good art. Rather, he aims to establish the principles upon which good art may be ascertained and then applies those principles to particular artworks in order to determine their value. One of the implications of his position is that most of the "great" artists, such as the operatic composer Richard Wagner, the artist Michaelangelo, and the dramatist William Shakespeare, fail to live up to his principles of aesthetic value. In addition, some of Tolstoy's own writings, such as *Anna Karenina* and *War and Peace,* also fail to meet his conditions for real art, an implication that has led some to reject his theory. While Tolstoy does reject most of the traditional "canon" of fine arts, there are a few noteworthy exceptions, such as the works of Fyodor Dostoyevsky and some of the works of Charles Dickens.

Leo Nikolayevich Tolstoy (1828–1910), a Russian novelist and theorist, was born into an extremely wealthy noble family and grew up on his family's estate in Yasnaya Polyana, in central Russia. He was the fourth of five children, and his parents died when he was young. He attended the University of Kazan from 1844 to 1847, where he studied law and Oriental languages, but became dissatisfied with the teaching and returned to Yasnaya Polyana before completing his degree. In 1852, after amassing heavy gambling debts, he entered the military and saw action in local engagements against hill tribesmen and at the siege of Sevastopol during the Crimean War. In 1857, he visited France, Switzerland, and Germany. Upon his return, he started a school for peasant children in Yasnaya Polyana. In 1862, he married Sonya Andreyevna Bers, and together they had thirteen children. He had a midlife crisis that began with a bout of severe depression and resulted in the development of a radical anarchist-pacifist Christian philosophy, which led to his excommunication from the Orthodox Church. Tolstoy corresponded with Mohandas Gandhi and directly influenced

Gandhi's beliefs concerning nonviolent resistance. Later in life, he was torn between the desire to live as a wandering ascetic and his responsibilities as a writer and landowner. He came to believe that he was undeserving of his inherited wealth and was well known among the peasants for his generosity. When he died, thousands of peasants lined the streets for his funeral. His collected works consist of ninety volumes and include *Childhood* (1852), *Boyhood* (1854), *Youth* (1856), *Sevastopol Sketches* (1855–56), *The Cossacks* (1863), *War and Peace* (1865–69), *Anna Karenina* (1875–77), *A Confession* (1882), *The Death of Ivan Ilych* (1886), *The Kreutzer Sonata* (1889), *What Is Art?* (1898), and *Resurrection* (1899). The following selection is from *What Is Art?*

CHAPTER 1

Take up any one of our ordinary newspapers and you will find a part devoted to the theatre and music. In almost every number you will find a description of some art exhibition, or of some particular picture, and you will always find reviews of new works of art that have appeared, of volumes of poems, of short stories, or of novels.

Promptly, and in detail, as soon as it has occurred, an account is published of how such and such an actress or actor played this or that role in such and such a drama, comedy, or opera, and of the merits of the performance, as well as of the contents of the new drama, comedy or opera, with its defects and merits. With as much care and detail, or even more, we are told how such and such an artist has sung a certain piece, or has played it on the piano or violin, and what were the merits and defects of the piece and of the performance. In every large town there is sure to be at least one, if not more than one, exhibition of new pictures, the merits and defects of which are discussed in the utmost detail by critics and connoisseurs.

New novels and poems, in separate volumes or in the magazines, appear almost every day, and the newspapers consider it their duty to give their readers detailed accounts of these artistic productions.

For the support of art in Russia (where for the education of the people only a hundredth part is spent of what would be required to give everyone the opportunity of instruction), the government grants millions of roubles in subsidies to academies, conservatories and theatres. In France twenty million francs are assigned for art, and similar grants are made in Germany and England.

In every large town enormous buildings are erected for museums, academies, conservatories, dramatic schools, and for performances and concerts. Hundreds of thousands of workmen—carpenters, masons, painters, joiners, paperhangers, tailors, hairdressers, jewelers, moulders, typesetters—spend their whole lives in hard labour to satisfy the demands of art, so that hardly any other department of human activity, except the military, consumes so much energy as this.

Not only is enormous labour spent on this activity, but in it, as in war, the very lives of men are sacrificed. Hundreds of thousand of people devote their lives from childhood to learning to twirl their legs rapidly (dancers), or to touch notes and strings very rapidly (musicians), or to draw with paint and represent what they see (artists), or to turn every phrase inside out and find a rhyme to every word. And these people, often very kind and clever, and capable of all sorts of useful labour, grow savage over their specialists and stupefying occupations, and become one-sided and self-complacent specialists, dull to all the serious phenomena of life and skilful only at rapidly twisting their legs, their tongues, or their fingers.

But even this stunting of human life is not the worst. I remember being once at the rehearsal of one of the most ordinary of the new operas which are produced at all the opera houses of Europe and America.

I arrived when the first act had already begun. To reach the auditorium I had to pass through the stage entrance. By dark entrances and passages I was led through the vaults of an enormous building, past immense machines for changing the scenery and for lighting, and there in the gloom and dust I saw workmen busily engaged. One of these men, pale, haggard, in a dirty blouse, with dirty, work-worn hands and cramped fingers, evidently tired and out of humour, went past me, angrily scolding another man. Ascending by a dark stair, I came out on the boards behind the scenes. Amid various poles and rings and scattered scenery, decorations and curtains, stood and moved dozens, if not hundreds, of painted and dressed-up men, in costumes fitting tight to their thights and calves, and also women, as usual, as nearly nude as might be. These were all singers, or members of the chorus, or ballet dancers, waiting their turns. My guide led me across the stage and, by means of a bridge of boards across the orchestra (in which perhaps a hundred musicians of all kinds, from kettledrum to flute and harp, were seated), to the dark pit stalls.

On an elevation, between two lamps with reflectors, and in an armchair placed before a music stand, sat the director of the musical part, baton in hand, managing the orchestra and singers, and, in general, the production of the whole opera.

The performance had already begun, and on the stage a procession of Indians who had brought home a bride was being presented. Besides men and women in costume, two other men in ordinary clothes bustled and ran about on the stage; one was the director of the dramatic part, and the other, who stepped about in soft shoes and ran from place to place with unusual agility, was the dancing master, whose salary per month exceeded what ten labourers earn in a year.

These three directors arranged the singing, the orchestra and the procession. The procession, as usual, was enacted by couples, with tinfoil halberds on their shoulders. They all came from one place and walked round and round again, and then stopped. The procession took a long time to arrange: first, the Indians with halberds came

on too late; then, too soon; then, at the right time, but crowded together at the exit; then they did not crowd, but arranged themselves badly at the sides of the stage; and each time the whole performance was stopped and started again from the beginning. The procession was introduced by a recitative delivered by a man dressed up like some variety of Turk, who, opening his mouth in a curious way, sang; "Home I bring the bri-i-ide." He sings and waves his arm (which is of course bare) from under his mantle. The procession begins, but here the French horn, in the accompaniment of the recitative, does something wrong; and the director, with a shudder as if some catastrophe had occurred, raps with his stick on the stand. All is stopped, and the director, turning to the orchestra, attacks the French horn, scolding him in the rudest terms, as cabmen abuse each other, for taking the wrong note. And again the whole thing begins again. The Indians with their halberds again come on, treading softly in their extraordinary boots; again the singer sings, "Home I bring the bri-i-ide." But here the pairs get too close together. More raps with the stick, more scolding, and a recommencement. Again, "Home I bring the bri-i-ide," again the same gesticulation with the bare arm from under the mantle, and again the couples, treading softly with halberds on their shoulders, some with sad and serious faces, some talking and smiling, arrange themselves in a circle and begin to sing. All seems to be going well, but again the stick raps, and the director, in a distressed and angry voice, begins to scold the men and women of the chorus. It appears that when singing they had omitted to raise their hands from time to time in sign of animation. "Are you all dead, or what? Cows that you are! Are you corpses, that you can't move?" Again they start "Home I bring the bri-i-ide," and again, with sorrowful faces, the chorus women sing, first one and then another of them raising their hands. But two chorus girls speak to each other—again a more vehement rapping with the stick. "Have you come here to talk? Can't you grossip at home? You there in red breeches, come nearer. Look toward me! Begin!" Again, "Home I bring the bri-i-ide." And so it goes on for one, two, three hours. The whole of such a rehearsal lasts six hours on end. Raps with the stick, repetitions, placings, corrections of the singers, of the orchestra, of the procession, of the dancers—all seasoned with angry scolding. I heard the words "asses," "fools," "idiots," "swine," addressed to the musicians and singers at least forty times in the course of one hour. And the unhappy individual to whom the abuse is addressed—flautist, hornblower or singer—physically and mentally demoralized, does not reply and does what is demanded of him. Twenty times is repeated the one phrase, "Home I bring the bri-i-ide," and twenty times the striding about in yellow shoes with a halberd over the shoulder. The conductor knows that these people are so demoralized that they are no longer fit for anything but to blow trumpets and walk about with halberds and in yellow shoes, and that they are also accustomed to dainty, easy living, so that they will put up with anything rather than lose their luxurious life. He therefore gives free vent to his churlishness, especially as he has seen the same thing done in Paris and Vienna, and knows that this is the way the best conductors behave, and that it is a musical tradition of great artists to be so carried away by the great business of their art that they cannot pause to consider the feelings of other artists.

It would be difficult to find a more repulsive sight. I have seen one workman abuse another for not supporting the weight piled upon him when goods were being unloaded, or, at haystacking, the village elder scold a peasant for not making the rick right, and the man submitted in silence. And, however unpleasant it was to witness the scene, the unpleasantness was lessened by the consciousness that the business in hand was needful and important, and that the fault for which the head man scolded the labourer was one which might spoil a needful undertaking.

But what was being done here? For what, and for whom? Very likely the conductor was tired out, like the workman I passed in the vaults; it was even evident that he was; but who made him tire himself? And for what was he tiring himself? The opera he was rehearsing was one of the most ordinary of operas for people who are accustomed to them, but also one of the most gigantic absurdities that could possibly be

devised. An Indian king wants to marry; they bring him a bride; he disguises himself as a minstrel; the bride falls in love with the minstrel and is in despair, but afterwards discovers that the minstrel is the king, and everyone is highly delighted.

That there never were, or could be, such Indians, and that they were not only unlike Indians, but that what they were doing was unlike anything on earth except other operas, was beyond all manner of doubt; that people do not converse in such a way as recitative, and do not not place themselves at fixed distances in a quartet, waving their arms to express their emotions; that nowhere, except in theatres, do people walk about in such a manner, in pairs, with tinfoil halberds and in slippers; that no one ever gets angry in such a way, or is affected in such a way, or laughs in such a way, or cries in such a way; and that no one on earth can be moved by such performances—all this beyond the possibility of doubt.

Instinctively the question presents itself: For whom is this being done? Whom *can* it please? If there are, occasionally, good melodies in the opera to which it is pleasant to listen, they could have been sung simply, without these stupid costumes and all the processions and recitatives and handwavings.

The ballet, in which half-naked women make voluptuous movements, twisting themselves into various sensual writhing, is simply a lewd performance.

So one is quite at a loss as to whom these things are done for. The man of culture is heartily sick of them, while to a real working man they are utterly incomprehensible. If anyone can be pleased by these things (which is doubtful), it can only be some young footman or depraved artisan who has contracted the spirit of the upper classes but is not yet satiated with their amusements and wishes to show his breeding.

And all this nasty folly is prepared, not simply, nor with kindly merriment, but with anger and brutal cruelty.

It is said that it is all done for the sake of art, and that art is a very important thing. But is it true that art is so important that such sacrifices should be made for its sake? This question is especially urgent because art, for the sake of which the labour of millions, the lives of men, and, above all, love between man and man, are being sacrificed—this very art is becoming something more and more vague and uncertain to human perception.

Criticism, in which the lovers of art used to find support for their opinions, has latterly become so self-contradictory that, if we exclude from the domain of art all that to which the critics of various schools themselves deny the title, there is scarcely any art left.

The artists of various sects, like the theologians of the various sects, mutually exclude and destroy themselves. Listen to the artists of the schools of our times, and you will find, in all branches, each set of artists disowning others. In poetry the old Romanticists deny the Parnassiens and the Decadents; the Parnassiens disown the Romanticists and the Decadents; the Decadents disown all their predecessors and the Symbolists; the Symbolists disown all their predecessors and *les mages;* and *les mages* disown all, all their predecessors. Among novelists we have naturalists, psychologists, and "nature-ists," all rejecting each other. And it is the same in dramatic art, in painting and in music. So art, which demands such tremendous labour sacrifices from the people, which stunts human lives and transgresses against human love, is not only *not* a thing clearly and firmly defined, but is understood in such contradictory ways by its own devotees that it is difficult to say what is meant by art, and especially what is good, useful art—art for the sake of which we might condone such sacrifices as are being offered at its shrine.

CHAPTER 2

For the production of every ballet, circus, opera, operetta, exhibition, picture, concert or printed book, the intense and unwilling labour of thousands of people is needed at what is often harmful and humiliating work. It were well if artists made all they require for themselves, but, as it is, they all need the help of workmen, not only to produce art, but also for their own usually luxurious maintenance. And, one way or other, they get it, either through payments from rich people or through subsidies given by government (in Russia, for instance, in grants of millions of roubles to theatres, conservatories and academies). This money is collected from the people, some of whom have to sell their only cow to pay the tax and who never get those aesthetic pleasures which art gives.

It was all very well for a Greek or Roman artist, or even for a Russian artist of the first half of our century (when there were still slaves and it was considered right that there should be), with a quiet mind to make people serve him and his art; but in our day, when in all men there is at least some dim perception of the equal rights of all, it is impossible to constrain people to labour unwillingly for art without first deciding the question whether it is true that art is so good and so important an affair as to redeem this evil.

If not, we have the terrible probability to consider that while fearful sacrifices of the labour and lives of men, and of morality itself, are being made to art, that same art may be not only useless but even harmful.

And therefore it is necessary for a society in which works of art arise and are supported, to find out whether all that professes to be art is really art, whether (as is presupposed in our society) all that which is art is good, and whether it is important and worth those sacrifices which it necessitates. It is still more necessary for every conscientious artist to know this that he may be sure that all he does has a valid meaning; that it is not merely an infatuation of the small circle of people among whom he lives which excites in him the false assurance that he is doing a good work; and that what he takes from others for the support of his often very luxurious life will be compensated for by those productions at which he works. And that is why answers to the above questions are especially important in our time.

What is this art which is considered so important and necessary for humanity that for its sake these sacrifices of labour, of human life, and even of goodness may be made? . . .

CHAPTER 5

In order to define art correctly it is necessary first of all to cease to consider it as a means to pleasure, and to consider it as one of the conditions of human life. Viewing it in this way we cannot fail to observe that art is one of the means of intercourse between man and man.

Every work of art causes the receiver to enter into a certain kind of relationship both with him who produced or is producing the art, and with all those who, simultaneously, previously, or subsequently, receive the same artistic impression.

Speech transmitting the thoughts and experiences of men serves as a means of union among them, and art serves a similar purpose. The peculiarity of this latter means of intercourse, distinguishing it from intercourse by means of words, consists in this, that whereas by words a man transmits his thoughts to another, by art he transmits his feelings.

The activity of art is based on the fact that a man receiving through his sense of hearing or sight another man's expression of feeling, is capable of experiencing the emotion which moved the man who expressed it. To take the simplest example: one man laughs, and another who hears becomes merry, or a man weeps, and another who hears feels sorrow. A man is excited or irritated, and another man seeing him is brought to a similar state of mind. By his movements or by the sounds of his voice a man expresses courage and determination or sadness and calmness; and this state of mind passes on to others. A man suffers, manifesting his sufferings by groans and spasms, and this suffering transmits itself to other people; a man expresses his feelings of admiration, devotion, fear, respect, or love, to certain objects, persons, or phenomena, and others are infected by the same feelings of admiration, devotion, fear, respect, or love, to the same objects, persons, or phenomena.

And it is on this capacity of man to receive another man's expression of feeling and to experience those feelings himself, that the activity of art is based.

If a man infects another or others directly, immediately, by his appearance or by the sounds he gives vent to at the very time he experiences the feeling; if he causes another man to yawn when he himself cannot help yawning, or to laugh or cry when he himself is obliged to laugh or cry, or to suffer when he himself is suffering—that does not amount to art.

Art begins when one person with the object of joining another or others to himself in one and the same feeling, expresses that feeling by certain external indications. To take the simplest example: a boy having experienced, let us say, fear on encountering a wolf, relates that encounter, and in order to evoke in others the feeling he has experienced, describes himself, his condition before the encounter, the surroundings, the wood, his own lightheartedness, and then the wolf's appearance, its movements, the distance between himself and the wolf, and so forth. All this, if only the boy when telling the story again experiences the feelings he had lived through, and infects the hearers and compels them to feel what he had experienced—is art. Even if the boy had not seen a wolf but had frequently been afraid of one, and if wishing to evoke in others the fear he had felt, he invested an encounter with a wolf and recounted it so as to make his hearers share the feelings he experienced when he feared the wolf, that also would be art. And just in the same way it is art if a man, having experienced either the fear of suffering or the attraction of enjoyment (whether in reality or in imagination), expresses these feelings on canvas or in marble so that others are infected by them. And it is also art if a man feels; or imagines to himself, feelings of delight, gladness, sorrow, despair, courage, or despondency, and the transition from one to another of these feelings, and expresses them by sounds so that the hearers are infected by them and experience them as they were experienced by the composer.

The feelings with which the artist infects others may be most various—very strong or very weak, very important or very insignificant, very bad or very good: feelings of love of one's country, self-devotion and submission to fate or to God expressed in a drama, raptures of lovers described in a novel, feelings of voluptuousness expressed in a picture, courage expressed in a triumphal march, merriment evoked by a dance, humour evoked by a funny story, the feeling of quietness transmitted by an evening landscape or by a lullaby, or the feeling of admiration evoked by a beautiful arabesque—it is all art.

If only the spectators or auditors are infected by the feelings which the author has felt, it is art.

To evoke in oneself a feeling one has once experienced and having evoked it in oneself then by means of movements, lines, colours, sounds, or forms expressed in words, so to transmit that feeling that others experience the same feeling—this is the activity of art.

Art is a human activity consisting in this, that one man consciously by means of certain external signs, *hands on to others feelings he has lived through, and that others are infected by these feelings and also experience them.*

Art is not, as the metaphysicians say, the manifestation of some mysterious Idea of beauty or God; it is not, as the æsthetic physiologists say, a game in which man lets off his excess of stored-up energy; it is not the expression of man's emotions by external signs; it is not the production of pleasing objects; and, above all, it is not pleasure; but it is a means of union among men joining them together in the same feelings, and indispensable for the life and progress towards well-being of individuals and of humanity.

CHAPTER 15

Art in our society has become so perverted that not only has bad art come to be considered good, but even the very perception of what art really is has been lost. In order to be able to speak about the art of our society it is, therefore, first of all necessary to distinguish art from counterfeit art.

There is one indubitable sign distinguishing real art from its counterfeit—namely, the infectiousness of art. If a man without exercising effort and without altering his standpoint, on reading, hearing, or seeing another man's work experiences a mental condition which unites him with that man and with others who are also affected by that work, then the object evoking that condition is a work of art. And however poetic, realistic, striking, or interesting, a work may be, it is not a work of art if it does not evoke that feeling (quite distinct from all other feelings) of joy and of spiritual union with another (the author) and with others (those who are also infected by it).

It is true that this indication is an *internal* one and that there are people who, having forgotten what the action of real art is, expect something else from art (in our society the great majority are in this state), and that therefore such people may mistake for this æthetic feeling the feeling of diversion and a certain excitement which they receive from counterfeits of art. But though it is impossible to undeceive these people, just as it may be impossible to convince a man suffering from colour-blindness that green is not red, yet for all that, this indication remains perfectly definite to those whose feeling for art is neither perverted nor atrophied, and it clearly distinguishes the feeling produced by art from all other feelings.

The chief peculiarity of this feeling is that the recipient of a truly artistic impression is so united to the artist that he feels as if the work were his own and not some one else's—as if what it expresses were just what he had long been wishing to express. A real work of art destroys in the consciousness of the recipient the separation between himself and the artist, and not that alone, but also between himself and all whose minds receive this work of art. In this freeing of our personality from its separation and isolation, in this uniting of it with others, lies the chief characteristic and the great attractive force of art.

If a man is infected by the author's condition of soul, if he feels this emotion and this union with others, then the object which has effected this is art; but if there be no such infection, if there be not this union with the author and with others who are moved by the same work—then it is not art. And not only is infection a sure sign of art, but the degree of infectiousness is also the sole measure of excellence in art.

The stronger the infection the better is the art, as art, speaking of it now apart from its subject-matter—that is, not considering the value of the feelings it transmits.

And the degree of the infectiousness of art depends on three conditions:—

(1) On the greater or lesser individuality of the feeling transmitted; (2) on the greater or lesser clearness with which the feeling is transmitted; (3) on the sincerity of the artist, that is, on the greater or lesser force with which the artist himself feels the emotion he transmits.

The more individual the feeling transmitted the more strongly does it act on the recipient; the more individual the state of soul into which he is transferred the more pleasure does the recipient obtain and therefore the more readily and strongly does he join in it.

Clearness of expression assists infection because the recipient who mingles in consciousness with the author is the better satisfied the more clearly that feeling is transmitted which, as it seems to him, he has long known and felt and for which he has only now found expression.

But most of all is the degree of infectiousness of art increased by the degree of sincerity in the artist. As soon as the spectator, hearer, or reader, feels that the artist is infected by his own production and writes, sings, or plays, for himself, and not merely to act on others, this mental condition of the artist infects the recipient; and, on the contrary, as soon as the spectator, reader, or hearer, feels that the author is not writing, singing, or playing, for his own satisfaction—does not himself feel what he wishes to express, but is doing it for him, the recipient—resistance immediately springs up, and the most individual and the newest feelings and the cleverest technique not only fail to produce any infection but actually repel.

I have mentioned three conditions of contagion in art, but they may all be summed up into one, the last, sincerity; that is, that the artist should be impelled by an inner need to express his feeling. That condition includes the first; for if the artist is sincere he will express the feeling as he experienced it. And as each man is different from every one else, his feeling will be individual for every one else; and the more individual it is—the more the artist has drawn it from the depths of his nature—the more sympathetic and sincere will it be. And this same sincerity will impel the artist to find clear expression for the feeling which he wishes to transmit.

Therefore this third condition—sincerity—is the most important of the three. It is always complied with in peasant art, and this explains why such art always acts so powerfully; but it is a condition almost entirely absent from our upper-class art, which is continually produced by artists actuated by personal aims of covetousness or vanity.

Such are the three conditions which divide art from it counterfeits, and which also decide the quality of every work of art considered apart from its subject-matter.

The absence of any one of these conditions excludes a work from the category of art and relegates it to that of art's counterfeits. If the work does not transmit the artist's peculiarity of feeling and is therefore not individual, if it is unintelligibly expressed, or if it has not proceeded from the author's inner need for expression—it is not a work of art. If all these conditions are present even in the smallest degree, then the work even if a weak one is yet a work of art.

The presence in various degrees of these three conditions: individuality, clearness, and sincerity, decides the merit of a work of art as art, apart from subject-matter. All works of art take order of merit according to the degree in which they fulfil the first, the second, and the third, of these conditions. In one the individuality of the feeling transmitted may predominate; in another, clearness of expression; in a third, sincerity; while a fourth may have sincerity and individuality but be deficient in clearness; a fifth, individuality and clearness, but less sincerity; and so forth, in all possible degrees and combinations.

Thus is art divided from what is not art, and thus is the quality of art, as art, decided, independently of its subject-matter, that is to say, apart from whether the feelings it transmits are good or bad.

DISCUSSION QUESTIONS

1. Tolstoy believes that true art "is a means of union among men joining them together in the same feelings, and indispensable for the life and progress towards well-being of individuals and of humanity." What does he mean by this? What contemporary art fits Tolstoy's description of true art?

2. Tolstoy questions whether arts like opera and ballet are worth the sacrifices that they

necessitate. What are the sacrifices? Do you think these arts are worth the sacrifices? Why or why not?

3. Discuss Tolstoy's notion of the "infectiousness" of art. Do you agree with it? Why or why not?

4. Tolstoy rejects most of the "canon" of great art including his own work. Do you agree with critics who reject his theory of art simply on the basis that one of its implications is that

Tolstoy's own works, including *War and Peace*, do not meet his criteria for true art?

5. Artistic value and morality are closely connected for both Plato and Tolstoy. Compare and contrast their positions.

6. Do you think *contemporary Hollywood films* would be considered true or counterfeit art by Tolstoy's standards? Why?

OSCAR WILDE

AESTHETICISM

Oscar Wilde contends that art should be valued for itself alone, and not for *any* purpose it may serve. His position, called *aestheticism*, is encapsulated in the French phrase *"l'art pour l'art"*—"art for art's sake." Aestheticism grew in influence in the first half of the nineteenth century in France through the work of writers such as Théophile Gautier, Charles Baudelaire, and Gustave Flaubert, and in the second half of the nineteenth century, it became fashionable in England through the work of Walter Pater, Aubrey Beardsley, A. J. Symons, and, most notoriously, Oscar Wilde.

In the preface to his novel *The Picture of Dorian Gray*, Wilde encapsulates the aesthete's position with the famous line "All art is quite useless." For Wilde, the effect that art has on its perceivers is outside the scope of art. "All art is at once surface and symbol," writes Wilde. Attempts to "read the symbol" or "go beneath the surface" of art are beyond the proper sphere of art. For Wilde, art is neither moral nor immoral, even if vice and virtue are part of the material or subject matter of art. Wilde's position on art is in direct opposition to those Plato of and Leo Tolstoy (see above), who claim for art both a strong moral and strong social function.

For Wilde, aestheticism— "the new aesthetics"—comprises three basic doctrines. The first is that "Art never expresses anything but itself." Art does not necessarily express the social, political, religious, or philosophical conditions in which it was produced. For Wilde, art always merely expresses itself, and nothing beyond itself. The second doctrine is that "All bad art comes from returning to Life and Nature, and elevating them into ideals." Here Wilde is rejecting both realism in art (the return to "Life") and romanticism in art (the return to "Nature"). Both realism and romanticism are alternative views of art that are critical of Wilde's own aestheticism. The third, and final, doctrine of aestheticism is that "Life imitates Art far more than Art imitates Life." Wilde believes that nature imitates art far more than the opposite; that is, the effects we see in life and nature are, more often than not, ones that we have previously seen in art.

Oscar (Fingal O'Flahertie Wills) Wilde (1854–1900), Irish poet and dramatist, was the spokesperson for the aestheticist movement in England. Born in Dublin, Wilde attended Trinity College, Dublin (1871–74), and Magdalen College, Oxford (1874–78), where he was taught by Walter Pater and John Ruskin. While at Oxford, his eccentric clothing drew jeers from his classmates, and his irreverent attitude toward religion shocked his teachers. After receiving his B.A. from Oxford in 1878, he worked as an art reviewer (1881), lectured in the United States and Canada (1882), lived in Paris (1883), and lectured in Britain (1883–84). He married Constance Lloyd in 1884, with whom he had two children. He supported his family by writing reviews for the *Pall Mall Gazette* and editing *Woman's World*. In 1891, Wilde met and fell in love with Lord Alfred Douglass. His intimate association with Douglass led both to the end of his marriage in 1893 and to a two-year prison sentence at hard labor for sodomy, during which time he was denied pen and paper for nineteen months. Before his trial and conviction, Wilde had achieved much success as a playwright with plays such as *A Woman of No Importance* (1893), *An Ideal Husband* (1895), and *The Importance of Being Earnest* (1895). After his release in 1897, Wilde lived under the name Sebastian Melmoth in France. He died penniless of cerebral meningitis in a cheap Paris hotel in 1900.

The following selection includes the preface to Wilde's novel *The Picture of Dorian Gray* and an except from his dialogue "The Decay of Lying" (1889). The preface did not appear in the original version of the novel published in *Lippincott's Monthly Magazine* in 1890. It appeared, along with six additional chapters, in 1891. This dialogue along with another ("The Critic as Artist," 1890) are Wilde's two major literary-theoretical works. Together, these selections outline the basic tenets of Wilde's aestheticism.

PREFACE TO THE PICTURE OF DORIAN GRAY

The artist is the creator of beautiful things.

To reveal art and conceal the artist is art's aim.

The critic is he who can translate into another manner or a new material his impression of beautiful things.

The highest, as the lowest, form of criticism is a mode of autobiography.

Those who find ugly meanings in beautiful things are corrupt without being charming. This is a fault.

Those who find beautiful meanings in beautiful things are the cultivated. For these there is hope.

They are the elect to whom beautiful things mean only Beauty.

There is no such thing as a moral or an immoral book. Books are well written or badly written. That is all.

The nineteenth-century dislike of Realism is the rage of Caliban* seeing his own face in a glass.

The nineteenth-century dislike of Romanticism is the rage of Caliban not seeing his own face in a glass.

The moral and immoral life of man forms part of the subject matter of the artist, but the morality of art consists in the perfect use of an imperfect medium.

No artist desires to prove anything. Even things that are true can be proved.

No artist has ethical sympathies. An ethical sympathy in an artist is an unpardonable mannerism of style.

No artist is ever morbid. The artist can express everything.

Thought and language are to the artist instruments of an art.

Vice and virtue are to the artist materials for an art.

*Caliban is the savage and deformed slave in Shakespeare's play *The Tempest*. He represents the bestial or brutish side of human nature. His name is possibly a variation of "cannibal." —Ed.

From the point of view of form, the type of all the arts is the art of the musician. From the point of view of feeling, the actor's craft is the type.

All art is at once surface and symbol.

Those who go beneath the surface do so at their peril.

Those who read the symbol do so at their peril.

It is the spectator, and not life, that art really mirrors.

Diversity of opinion about a work of art shows that the work is new, complex, and vital.

When critics disagree the artist is in accord with himself.

We can forgive a man for making a useful thing as long as he does not admire it. The only excuse for making a useless thing is that one admires it intensely.

All art is quite useless.

THE DECAY OF LYING

Art never expresses anything but itself. It has an independent life, just as Thought has, and develops purely on its own lines. It is not necessarily realistic in an age of realism, nor spiritual in an age of faith. So far from being the creation of its time, it is usually in direct opposition to it, and the only history that it preserves for us is the history of its own progress. Sometimes it returns upon its footsteps, and revives some antique form, as happened in the archaistic movement of late Greek Art, and in the pre-Raphaelite movement of our own day. At other times it entirely anticipates its age, and produces in one century work that it takes another century to understand, to appreciate, and to enjoy. In no case does it reproduce its age. To pass from the art of a time to the time itself is the great mistake that all historians commit.

The second doctrine is this. All bad art comes from returning to Life and Nature, and elevating them into ideals. Life and Nature may sometimes be used as part of Art's rough material, but before they are of any real service to Art they must be translated into artistic conventions. The moment Art surrenders its imaginative medium it surrenders everything. As a method Realism is a complete failure, and the two things that every artist should avoid are modernity of form and modernity of subject-matter. To us, who live in the nineteenth century, any century is a suitable subject for art except our own. The only beautiful things are the things that do not concern us. It is, to have the pleasure of quoting myself, exactly because Hecuba* is nothing to us that her sorrows are so suitable a motive for a tragedy. Besides, it is only the modern that ever becomes old fashioned. [French novelist] M. [Emile] Zola sits down to give us a picture of the Second Empire.† Who cares for the Second Empire now? It is out of date. Life goes faster than Realism, but Romanticism is always in front of Life.

The third doctrine is that Life imitates Art far more than Art imitates Life. This results not merely from Life's imitative instinct, but from the fact that the self-conscious aim of Life is to find expression, and that Art offers it certain beautiful forms through which it may realize that energy. It is a theory that has never been put forward before, but it is extremely fruitful, and throws an entirely new light upon the history of Art.

It follows, as a corollary from this, that external Nature also imitates Art. The only effects that she can show us are effects that we have already seen through poetry, or in paintings. This is the secret of Nature's charm, as well as the explanation of Nature's weakness.

The final revelation is that Lying, the telling of beautiful untrue things, is the proper aim of Art. But of this I think I have spoken at sufficient length.

---

* Hecuba is a Trojan queen from Greek mythology. She was the second wife of King Priam and mother of nineteen children, including Creusa, Hector, Paris, and Cassandra. When Troy was taken by the Greeks (Acheaens), she was a awarded to Ulysses. —Ed.

† The Second (French) Empire was the imperial Bonapartist regime of Napoleon III, which lasted from 1852 to 1870. In the history of France, the Second Empire falls between the Second Republic (1848–52) and the Third Republic (1870–1940) —Ed.

DISCUSSION QUESTIONS

1. Wilde maintains that there is no such thing as a moral or immoral book. What does he mean by this? Do you agree with him? Why or why not?

2. What does Wilde mean when he says, "To reveal art and conceal the artist is the aim of art"? Do you think that art should aim to conceal the artist? Why or why not?

3. Wilde says that "art never expresses anything but itself." Do you agree with him? Why or why not?

4. What does Wilde mean when he says, "Life imitates Art far more that Art imitates Life"? Can you think of an example of life imitating a work of art such as a novel, film, or piece of music? Discuss.

5. Wilde contends that art should be valued for itself alone, and not for any purpose it may serve. Compare Wilde's views on art with those of Plato and Tolstoy. Whose do you prefer, and why?

SUSANNE LANGER

EXPRESSIVENESS

Susanne Langer argues that art is the creation of an expressive form, and what it expresses is human feeling. She argues that this definition of art does not change from age to age: From the age of cave drawings to the age of postmodernism, the same general concept of art holds. Furthermore, while her definition of art is broad, she believes that it does not include all crafts. "Art is craftsmanship, but to a special end: the creation of expressive forms—visually, audibly, or even imaginatively perceivable forms that set forth the nature of human feeling." She says that her "reason for rejecting the definition of all art as craft is pragmatic." Not only would museum directors "go crazy if they had to exhibit the pies and jellies that win prizes at country fairs," but foundations that sponsor the arts do not fund highly skilled craftspeople like chefs and surgeons. Her major reason for rejecting all craft as art is that it is "philosophically poor, because it raises no specific problems of art through which general ideas about art might be developed." For Langer, one of the merits of her own definition of art is that all the major problems of art show up in relation to it. These problems range from the autonomy of and connections among the arts to the origin and meaning of various styles and traditions.

Yet, despite the constant placed at the center of her definition, Langer's concept of art leaves wide latitude for variation in art. "The concept of art as the creation of expressive forms to present ideas of feeling . . . is a constant," writes Langer, "but the making of those forms is so varied that few people realize how many factors in history and [in actual chance setting] bear on it." She then identifies and discusses the four chief variables: (1) the ideas that artists want to express, (2) the discovered devices of artistic creation, (3) the opportunities offered by the physical and cultural environment, and (4) the public response. In the process of explaining these variables, she notes that "to create perceivable expressive forms is a *principle of art*; but the use of any device, no matter how important, is a *principle of creation in art*." She sets her own position apart from that of Aristotle, for example, by saying that while the principle of art is constant, the principles of creation in art are not.

Susanne Knauth Langer (1895–1985), an American philosopher, was one of the most important aestheticians of the twentieth century. She received her A.B. in 1920 from Radcliffe College and studied at the University of Vienna in 1921–22. In 1926, she received a Ph.D. from

Radcliffe College, where she remained as a tutor in philosophy for fifteen years. She went on teach at a number of other American universities, including the University of Delaware, New York University, and Columbia University. In 1954, she was appointed professor of philosophy at Connecticut College in New London, and in 1960, she was elected to the American Academy of Arts and Sciences. Her views on art are connected to a general philosophical position that defines man as essentially a symbol-using animal and envisions a comprehensive study of human symbols. Her work was strongly influenced by the philosophical writings of Alfred North Whitehead, Ernst Cassirer, Ludwig Wittgenstein, Charles S. Peirce, and Rudolph Carnap, as well as by works in art, biology, psychology, and anthropology. Langer's aesthetic theory was first developed in her widely read book *Philosophy in a New Key: A Study in the Symbolism of Reason, Rite, and Art* (1943) and further developed in *Feeling and Form: A Philosophy of Art Developed from Philosophy in a New Key* (1953), *Problems of Art: Ten Philosophical Lectures* (1957), *Reflections on Art* (1959), *Philosophical Sketches* (1962), and her final work, the three-volume *Mind: An Essay on Human Feeling* (1967, 1972, 1982). Her earlier books include *The Practice of Philosophy* (1930) and *Introduction to Symbolic Logic* (1937). The following selection is from *Problems of Art*.

It has often enough been remarked that the concept of art changes from age to age; that different nations, different epochs, even different schools within one time and place, have different notions of what art is, and therefore different judgments of what is or is not art; and that consequently no one can say, once and for all, what art is, what is meant by the term "a work of art," nor what is or is not to pass for such a work.

If these sweeping statements were true there would be little point in either criticizing and teaching art, or in philosophizing about it (or even producing it). But they are almost all too sweeping to be true, or, for that matter, to be false.

Let us begin with the first statement: that the concept of art changes from age to age. How do we determine what is, in any age, the concept of art? There are, for most ages, two main sources of information: what theorists in a given time say about art, and what the artists of that time seem to assume. The same goes, of course, for different places at any time, for instance Greece, Egypt, and China in 600 B.C., or France and Russia in 1950 A.D.

It is possible, I think, to formulate a definition of art that applies to everything artists have made, and made with varying success. That means that the concept of art implicit in practice—that is, "what the artists seem to assume"—does not vary from age to age and from place to place. I think it is safe to say that all art is the creation of "expressive forms," or *apparent forms expressive of human feeling*. That definition applies to the primitive "Venuses" and the Venus of Milo and Brancusi's "Bird," and to the Psalms of David and Herrick's "Fair Daffodils" and Joyce's *Ulysses,* to *Sakuntala* and *Tartuffe* and *The Emperor Jones* and *The Play's the Thing,* and to the famous cave paintings and the polite portraits that Reynolds and Sargent painted, and to ancient temple chants and African drum music and Mozart and Wagner. It defines, I think, what all artists have always done. There is little gained by calling "art" only what we judge to be good. Some art is bad; also, a work may be unsuccessful, or rather poor. But where there is any artistic intent (whether avowed, exclusive artistic intent, or unconscious artistic impulse) there will be some artistic result, i.e., some expressive form. The main point is that this definition includes every *kind* of art. Whether a work is good or bad depends on other things than the artistic intent. But whether it is art depends on its maker's desire to compose it into a form that expresses his idea of a feeling or a whole nexus of feeling—or, as he would be likely to say, "that has some feeling in it," or "has life."

Yet this broad definition excludes some things that theorists have sometimes included in the category of "works of art." Irwin Edman defined art as "the realm of all controlled treatment of material, practical or other." He was, of course, in good company; Plato spoke of catering, shoemaking, and medicine as "arts," and called business "the art of payment." But in Plato's discourses the word was clearly understood in two senses. When Aristotle classified the arts as "perfect" and "imperfect" he assumed the distinction which we make by the clumsy term "fine arts" for the arts he meant. Edman, however, explicitly denied the distinction. He said, in *Arts and the Man*, "It is for purely accidental reasons that the fine arts have been singled out to be almost identical with Art. For in painting and sculpture, music and poetry, there is so nice and so explicit a utilization of materials . . . that we turn to examples of these arts for Art and in them find our aesthetic experience most intense and pure."

Actually, the sensory or literally "aesthetic" experience of perfectly used materials is perhaps keenest in our appreciation of food and drink. Edman had too much artistic sense to draw his own conclusions, but they have been drawn; Baker Brownell in *The Seven Lively Arts* includes cooking, and Willem Thieme makes cooking and philosophy the lowest and highest stations, respectively, in the gamut of the arts. John Dewey unconfused by Albert Barnes might have ranged ballet and golf, and sculpture and hairdressing, all on a par; I don't know, since in fact he was influenced—enlightened, but also deeply confused—by Barnes.

My reason for rejecting the definition of art as all craft is pragmatic. Directors of art museums would go crazy if they had to exhibit the pies and jellies that win prizes at country fairs, and the nylons and dishmops and cigarettes that are definitely superior to anything else in the world. You can't use such a broad definition in museology. Secondly, foundations that sponsor the arts do not give grants to famous chefs and dressmakers, to pharmacologists, or even to surgeons, who have developed some of the highest skills of which humanity at present can boast. Popular usage is not a decisive measure of meanings, but to defy it does demand some special reason. Above all, I find the broad definition philosophically poor, because it raises no specific problems of art through which general ideas about art might be developed.

Art is craftsmanship, but to a special end: the creation of expressive forms—visually, audibly, or even imaginatively perceivable forms that set forth the nature of human feeling. This statement,

I think, is simply true or false for all places and times; if it was false when the cavemen painted their pictures—sacred, or magical, or just ostentatious, intended to simulate wealth, or whatever they were—if it was false then, it is false now. If those pictures did not achieve their stylization and beauty by being expressive of an apprehended feeling, then the theory is wrong, and no change in human affairs will make it right today.

But the intriguing thing about this basic concept of art is that all the major problems of art show up in relation to it, not one by one, but in direct or remote connection with each other: the autonomy of the several arts and their very intricate relations to one another, which are much more than the possession of some common features or equivalent elements; the origins and significance of styles; historical continuity, tradition and revolt, motivation and conscious purpose and extraneous aims, self-expression, representation, abstraction, social influences, religious functions, changes of taste and all the problems of criticism, the old wrangle about rules of art, and the deprecation of "mere technique." There are more problems that arise systematically from these, but the ones I have named have already arisen at quite definite points, and are enough to make me dizzy, so let them suffice as examples.

The concept of art as the creation of expressive forms to present ideas of feeling (or of what is sometimes called "inner life," "subjective reality," "consciousness"—there are many designations for it) is a constant, but the making of those forms is so varied that few people realize how many factors in history and in any actual, chance setting bear on it. I think most of the differences of opinion about artistic aims, canons, and standards arise on the level of these variables, which are too often taken for constants. The chief variable factors are:

1. The ideas artists want to express.
2. The discovered devices of artistic creation.
3. The opportunities offered by the physical and cultural environment.
4. Public response.

The first factor is the most important. The range of its variability is enormous; I think the only restriction on it is that all artistic ideas are ideas of something felt, or rather: of life as felt, for they need not be ideas of feelings that have actually occurred. The import of art is *imaginable feeling and emotion,* imaginable subjective existence. It is something quite different from daydream, which is imagined experience eliciting real emotion, somewhat like, somewhat unlike the emotion that a similar experience in reality would produce. In dream and personal phantasy a feeling is evoked; in a work of art it is conceived, formulated, presented. It is the work of art as a whole that symbolizes an emotional process— anything, from the rhythmic feeling of thinking a complex but clear, brief thought, to the whole sense of life, love, selfhood, and recognition of death that is probably the largest scope of our feeling. The relation between feeling presented and understood, and feeling activated by behold- ing and understanding the image of inner life, is another interesting problem that arises from this basic concept of art, and cannot be pursued here. It is probably a highly complex affair.

The feelings that interest people have their limitations, their day and place, just as the things and facts and activities that interest them do. The emotional patterns we want to appreciate are primarily our own—not personally, but culturally. When our culture reaches out suddenly beyond its old bounds and makes contacts with other cultures we become interested in new possibilities of feeling. It takes a while, but there comes a point when the beauty of an exotic art becomes apparent to us; then we have grasped the humanity of another culture, not only theoretically but imagi- natively. The discovery of beauty in Negro art, Polynesian art, and Alaskan art marked such extensions of emotional insight in our own age.

Feeling to be expressed dictates what Élie Faure called "The Spirit of the Forms." But the life of art is more detailed and involved than this big movement of the Spirit. Sometimes quite fortuitous things enter in to give it a historic turn—not things that alter the pattern of feeling, like cultural decay, new religions, commercial expansion, crusades or other social events, but such things as the invention of oil pigments, the finding of Carrara marble, the construction of the pipe organ in the high vaulted church. The influence of available art materials may easily be over-emphasized; what is much more influential, I think, is the discovery of fundamental artistic devices.

The introduction of a major device gives rise to a tradition in art. A tradition is usually something longer-lived than a style; styles may come and go within its history. Styles, too, are relative to devices, for the variation and combination and handing-down of devices is so great a process that we meet it as basic technique, composition, choice of subject-matter, idiom, "form" in the narrow sense in which we classify epics, ballads, sonnets, etc., as "literary forms," and it may meet us as "influence." The most powerful devices give rise to what may be called the "great traditions" in the arts; metric composition of words is such a basic device, giving rise to a great tradition, in poetry. In the history of Indo- European culture it is probably as old as liturgical speech and incantation. Representation in plastic art is another. Our own history of art is so full of it that it is practically taken for granted, and we have in the past been more aware of its variants, or styles, than of representation itself as a picture-making or statue-making device. But in certain parts of the world where plastic arts exist, representation of creatures or things is used very sparingly (e.g., in Maori art), if at all, and some of our own artists today find it dispensable.

To create perceivable expressive forms is a *principle of art;* but the use of any device, no matter how important, is a *principle of creation in art.* I think the belief that the concept of art changes from age to age rests on the fallacy of taking the most general principles of artistic technique operative in some particular period and culture as the principles of art itself. That is what Aristotle did in the *Poetics;* he had a fundamental and clear understanding of the principles on which Greek drama was constructed. He also could see some fairly obvious parallels between dramatic structure and epic structure; in the epic one can find all the special forms (lyric, pastoral, ode, etc.) incidentally. So he was content to accept those principles of construction—the relation of plot to characters and the relations, rhythmic or other, between action and diction, the familiar divisions of the action, the famous "unities," and all the major devices of building Greek tragedy—as the ultimate principles of poetry itself.

Looking for a moment to another art than poetry, the same situation confronts us in Heinrich Schenker's analysis of the principles of music. The breaking up of tones, or sounds of definite pitch, into their constituent overtones that determine the natural stations through which a melody moves, and the contrapuntal development on this melodic scaffold, or *Urlinie,* that gives rise to harmonic progression, seemed to him the lowest terms to which the fabric of music could be analyzed. But it follows, of course, that there can be no music without definite pitch—without, as he says, "harmony, that belongs to nature, and melody, that belongs to art." The vaguely bounded glissando of Hawaiian song and the drums of Africa are to him not music.

What Schenker has actually discovered, however, are the basic devices that have begotten the great tradition of European music. These are not the principles of all music. Watusi drums, monotone voices, even conches and rams' horns can make music. But the construction of melodies in the framework of harmonically related tones is probably the most powerful principle of musical creation that has ever been found.

The apparent uncertainty as to what art is, or what some particular art really is, or that arises from taking principles of construction for the defining function of art itself, can be illustrated in every domain. But let us return to poetry, where we can find examples enough of warring opinions.

Nothing could be further from Aristotle's conception of poetic creation than that which [American writer and poet Edgar Allan] Poe proposed in his famous lecture, *The Poetic Principle.* "A poem," he said there, "deserves its title only inasmuch as it excites, by elevating the soul. The value of the poem is in the ratio of this elevating excitement. But all excitements are, through a psychal necessity, transient. That degree of excitement which would entitle a poem to be so called at all, cannot be sustained throughout a composition of any great length. . . . This great work, in fact [his direct reference is to *Paradise Lost*], is to be regarded as poetical, only when . . . we view it merely as a series of minor poems. If . . . we read it . . . at a single sitting, the result is but a constant alternation of excitement and depression." He did not even hesitate, in fine, to say: "In regard to the 'Iliad,' we have, if not positive proof, at least very good reason, for believing it intended as a series of lyrics; but, granting the epic intention, I can say only that the work is based in an imperfect sense of art."

This is the most heroic operation I have ever seen performed on the world's masterpieces to fit them into the compass of a highly special theory. What Poe was expounding was, of course, at best a principle of lyric composition, involved wherever a poem is made to render a single emotional experience. It was in keeping with his own straight-channelled talents, perhaps, that he saw no other poetic aims. He had less historical excuse than Aristotle for regarding principles of creation, or construction, as principles of art. But then, he was a lesser man.

A third normative theory that comes naturally to mind, because, although later than Poe's essay, it represents one of the very norms Poe was attacking as spurious, is Matthew Arnold's poetics. Arnold has summed up in one line his conception of poetry, "as a criticism of life under the conditions fixed for such a criticism by the laws of poetic truth and poetic beauty." A criticism of life; that contrasts brusquely, indeed, with Poe's statement: "I would define, in brief, the Poetry of words as *The Rhythmical Creation of Beauty.* Its sole arbiter is Taste. With the Intellect or with the Conscience, it has only collateral relations. Unless incidentally, it has no concern whatever either with Duty or with Truth."

Here we seem to have three different notions of what poetry is, and three different standards for its evaluation. But when you read these authors, chosen more or less at random, a little more closely, you find that the idea of what poetry is has in each case been taken for granted, and is implicitly supposed to be known; and that, moreover, the knowledge of it is intuitive, so there is nothing more to say about it. Arnold, of all people, had no business to perpetrate a circular definition: yet he defines poetry as a criticism of life controlled by the laws of *poetic* truth and *poetic* beauty. What is "poetic" can only be directly felt. Aristotle remarks that Homer understood the laws of organic composition by instinct, and in fact excelled all other poets in the same way (1451b); and elsewhere he says that the greatest thing in poetry is to be "a master of metaphor," which cannot be learned from others because it involves logical intuition (1459a). As for Poe, he says explicitly that the perception of Beauty is a separate faculty, which he calls "Taste," and sometimes the "Poetic Sentiment," and describes as an immortal instinct, which has given the world "all *that* which it . . . has ever been enabled at once to understand and to *feel* as poetic."

Here we are indeed on very slippery ground. The word "Taste" has done its share to make it precarious. The old adage, "*De gustibus non disputandum,*" has firmly established the belief that beauty is simply what satisfies taste, and as beauty is artistic value, such value depends on taste, just as the value of coffee or candy does; and it certainly seems, on this basis, like pure snobbism to set up the taste of a few as more important than that of the many—that is, to make anything but the most popular taste the measure of good art.

But, rather than subscribe to what seems to me a patently false conclusion, I would abandon the metaphor of "taste." It gives artistic experience a false simplicity, and overemphasizes the pleasure-component that it has in common with gustatory sensations. So I shall speak of the perception of beauty; and once we stop relating beauty to an irrational taste, beauty is not indefinable.

Louis Arnaud Reid, in his *A Study in Aesthetics* (1931), said, "Beauty is just expressiveness." Upon the definition of art proposed at the beginning of this lengthening lecture—"Art is the creation of forms expressive of human feeling"—Reid's dictum comes almost like a scholium [a marginal comment that expands on a course of reasoning]. And, moreover, it has the pragmatic virtues by which I advertise my own theory. It explains why the finding of beauty must be intuitive; all semantical insights are. Such finding is a perception of import, akin to that of meaning. Also, the conception of beauty as the expressiveness of a form explains why beauty may go unperceived where, none the less, it exists; why maturity enables us to appreciate what was once too strange, or too unpleasant in some way, or perhaps too enigmatic, to elicit our response to it as an expressive form. And especially, it makes accessible to investigation the reasons why art, throughout the ages, has been charged with one office after another, didactic, religious, therapeutic, and what not, as often as it has been absolved of any and all such functions and set up on a pedestal (or an easel) all by itself.

What guides one's imagination in drawing or carving a line, establishing proportion in the building of a chicken coop or the planning of a temple, or in using words to create the image of an event (which may be the occurrence of a thought, or a passionate utterance), is intuition. But a guiding sense is not in itself a *motive* for making an expressive form. The motive has usually been supplied by other interests. This brings us to the third great variable factor in the life of art: the opportunities offered to artists by the cultural and physical environment.

Probably by far the greater part of the world's art has been made upon some fortuitous occasion, that is, not with the conscious intention of creating a work of art, but with the intention of making or performing or articulating something otherwise important. People gifted with artistic intuition take any such occasion to create expressive form. Look at the intricate, strong, handsome compositions of Alaskan totem poles; their makers probably had no art theory at all, but to make the post look impressive, holy, and alive they used every principle of composition and animation that could serve the cause of sculpture. Women making pots undoubtedly made them for the sake of domestic uses, but they shaped them in fine, voluminous curves for art's sake. They may often have decorated pots, fabrics, and furniture with magic symbols to keep spooks away, but in the hands of an artist such symbolic representations offer, above all, an occasion for design; and two pots bearing the same symbols, and made of the same clay, may be worlds apart in artistic value. Ritual has always been a natural and fertile source of art. Its first artistic product is the dance. Ecstatic people probably pranced before they danced; but the intuitive perception of expressive forms in that prancing invited composition, the making of dance. We know on venerable authority that the Greek drama rose when the sacred dances, embodying mythical motifs, gave it opportunity. The worship was in a spirit of pity for humanity and fear of divine powers; and Aristotle imputes to tragedy the prime office of inspiring pity and fear.

Throughout the ages, the practice of artistic creation has seized on whatever occasions life offered; and artistic excellence has usually been felt as an enhancement of whatever other excellence the constructed object had. That explains the difficulty critics have often encountered in sorting out the artistic from the non-artistic values. The beauty of a sculptured Virgin that seems to enhance her godly grace is hard to judge apart from that effect, which may even have been the clearest aim that the sculptor consciously entertained; and a portrait that seems to render the sitter's character as his friends know or remember it—which the painter may have consciously made his business—is naturally thought to be beautiful on that account. But if it is beautiful, it is so because the painter managed to use this portrayal of character as a means of organizing subtler pictorial elements and creating a more vital plastic effect than he could have achieved by ignoring the telling details of the model's appearance.

In poetry, the confusion of artistic with propositional significance sometimes seems to be past all redemption. Poetry is made of language, and language is normally a means of imparting discursive ideas—information, advice, comments, directions, and whatever else. Also, the literal meaning of words and sentences plays a major part in making poetry out of language. Poetic criticism, more than any other, is torn between the judgment of artistic aims, means, and achievement, and the judgment of what *the poet* is "telling" the reader; between the evaluation of something created and something asserted. Matthew Arnold's "criticism of life" is such a discursive message. Perhaps he himself was misled by an unhappy phrase. Poetry does, indeed, *make life appear in certain ways*, but that is not commenting on it. Comment itself when used as a poetic element is not the poet's comment, but the imaginary speaker's who makes it in the poem. His name may be simply, "I"; but that again is part of the poetic creation.

Finally, let us not ignore the fact that much art is made without waiting for any occasion; that sometimes sheer imagination goes to work. I don't know what made Chaucer write his tales, or what purpose Dante set himself in writing the *Divine Comedy*, besides that of making good poetry. The great opportunity for poetic art really came in a later age with the printed book and the popular practice of reading. Artists are generally opportunists, like everybody else in his own business, but artistic impulses can also be conscious, and motivate the work itself. The fact that they are often unconscious, however, and that artistic principles are recognized and used intuitively while the artist's discursive ideas are disporting themselves in quite other directions, seems to me to account for the fact that the best artists have often thought they were doing the oddest things.

The variable factors in art—which include all the principles of construction, and the possible ways of feeling that guide their use—are so many that they offer a practically unlimited field of study. Every place has its art, every time brings something forth that belongs to it alone, every artist changes the progress of art. But to recognize as constants the principles of art itself seems to me to make sense out of those differences, and open an indefinite number of problems to empirical or historical investigation that have often appeared an unrelated jumble of "isms"—a great collection of points of view, but all too often with nothing much in sight.

DISCUSSION QUESTIONS

1. Langer argues that the concept of art does not change from age to age. What is her argument? Do you agree with it? Why or why not?

2. For Langer, art is the creation of an expressive form. What is an "expressive form"?

3. How is the notion of art as craft different from Langer's notion of art? What problems does Langer have with notion of art as craft? Do you agree with her? Why or why not?

4. Langer distinguishes between the *principle of art* and the *principle of creation in art*. What is the distinction? How does she use this distinction to criticize Aristotle's theory of art?

5. Langer says that Matthew Arnold's definition of art is "circular." What does she mean? Do you agree with her? Why or why not?

6. For Langer, what is the relationship between the "emotional process" and "feelings" of the artist and art? Compare her notion of the role of feelings in art with Tolstoy's. Which do you prefer, and why?

Pollock
[USA 2000] 2 hours, 2 minutes
Directed by Ed Harris

This film follows the career of American painter Jackson Pollock (Ed Harris) from the early 1940s to his death in 1956. Pollock was born in Wyoming, grew up in California, and moved to New York City in 1929. He studied painting with Thomas Hart Benton, who covered his canvases with energetic forms. He was also inspired by the work of surrealist painters such as Joan Miró, abstract painters such as Wassily Kandinsky, and abstract expressionist painters such as Arshile Gorky.

For many years, Pollock struggled to distinguish his own work from that of his peers and predecessors. While his paintings through the early 1940s revealed a level of greatness, they did not separate his work in any large measure from other abstract painters of the time. During this period, Peggy Guggenheim (Amy Madigan) remained his patron. She supported his artwork and financed his move from New York City to the countryside in 1945.

A few years later, Pollock sent shock waves through the art world. In January 1947, he came upon the idea of laying large canvases on the floor and letting paint fall or drip on them from his brush. As Pollock moved around the canvas, allowing paint to fall in swirls and drops, large, sweeping, complex rhythms with numerous threads of color resulted. This type of painting, sometimes called *action painting*, was the product of both Pollock's control of the paintbrush and the random fall of paint on canvas.

From 1948 until 1951, Pollock was the darling of the modern art world. After this period, however, alcoholism began to take its toll on his artwork and his relationship with his supportive wife, Lee Krasner (Marcia Gay Harden), who was herself an accomplished artist. Pollock died in a car crash in 1956. In the car were his mistress, Ruth Kligman (Jennifer Connelly), who survived the crash, and her friend, Edith Metzger (Sally Murphy), who did not.

DISCUSSION QUESTIONS

1.   Susanne Langer argues that art is the creation of an expressive form, and what it expresses is human feeling. Are the action paintings of Jackson Pollock art according to Langer's definition? Do these paintings have an expressive form? Why or why not?

2.   Langer says, "The concept of art as the creation of expressive forms to present ideas of feeling . . . is a constant, but the making of those forms is so varied that few people realize how many factors in history and in actual chance setting bear on it." She then identifies and discusses the four chief variables: (1) the ideas that artists want to express, (2) the discovered devices of artistic creation, (3) the opportunities offered by the physical and cultural environment, and (4) the public response. Discuss the art of Jackson Pollock in terms of Langer's ideas. How did the variables Langer identifies affect the rise and fall of Pollock as an artist?

3.   Consider the following dialogue between Lee Krasner and Jackson Pollock:

KRASNER   "What's this? I see the head, the body. This isn't cubism because you're not breaking down the figure into multiple views. You're just showing us one side. What is this, free-association or automatism?

POLLOCK   "I'm just painting, Lee."

KRASNER   "Don't tell me you don't know what you're doing. Are you experimenting with surrealism? Is this a dream? Even if this is your dream it's still what you see. It's life. Not just randomly putting paint on the canvas. You're painting something. You can't abstract from nothing; you can only abstract from life—from nature."

POLLOCK   "I am nature."

KRASNER   "If you only work from inside yourself, you'll repeat yourself."

POLLOCK   "Why don't you just paint it."

Lee is having difficulty situating Jackson's work within a particular school of painting and is troubled by this. Jackson says that he is "just painting." How important is it to be able to locate a given artwork within the parameters of preestablished schools of art? In what way does this help to authorize it as good or bad art? Also, can an artist of Jackson's level of competency ever "just paint"? Why or why not?

4. One of the more interesting aspects of the film is to follow the comments of Clem Greenberg (Jeffrey Tambor), a character based on the famous modern art critic of the same name. At first, Greenberg finds Pollock's work to be original and ambitious but also muddy and pretentious. After a while, he becomes the only major art critic to support Pollock's work. Then, after all of the art world has finally embraced Pollock's work, Greenberg finds Pollock's artistic powers to be diminishing and turns to other artists as the next great thing in the art world. All of these comments occur over a period of slightly over ten years. In general, do you believe that artists are great by nature, or do they become great by culture—that is, because persons like Clement Greenberg say they are? Discuss.

5. Much of this film is about Jackson Pollock "cracking things wide open" and "breaking the ice" in the art world. In other words, the aim of the artist as depicted in this film is to be innovative. Do you believe that artistic greatness is marked by innovation? How do you feel about the claim "Jackson Pollock was a great artist because he was an innovator: he produced a new type of art"? Would Langer or Hume agree with this claim? Why or why not?

6. Clem Greenberg says to Pollock: "You are retreating into imagery again. Paint is paint; surface is surface; that is all there should be." What does he mean? How do you think Plato would respond to Greenberg's comments?

7. Later, Pollock says to a *Time* magazine reporter, "I don't let the image carry the painting. If it creeps in, I try to do away with it. I let the painting come through." What is the "image" in painting? Is it impossible to do away entirely with the image in painting? Why or why not?

8. Consider the following dialogue between Jackson Pollock and an interviewer:

INTERVIEWER   "What is modern art?"

POLLOCK   "Modern art, to me, is nothing more than the expression of the contemporary aims of the age we're living in. . . . All cultures have had means and techniques of expressing their immediate aims. The thing that interests me is that today painters do not have to go to a subject matter outside of them-selves. They work from a different source. They work from within. It seems to me that the modern artist cannot express this age, the airplane, the atom bomb, or the radio in the old forms of the Renaissance or any other past culture."

Would Langer agree with Pollock's comments about artistic form? Why or why not?

9. Consider another piece of dialogue between Pollock and an interviewer:

INTERVIEWER   "How do you get the paint on the canvas?"

POLLOCK   "I paint on the floor. That's not unusual. The Orientals did that. Most of the paint I use is a liquid flowing kind of paint. The brushes I use are used more as sticks. The brush does not actually touch the canvas.

INTERVIEWER   "Well isn't it more difficult to control? To splatter or any number of things?"

POLLOCK   "No, I don't think so. With experience it seems possible to control the flow of the paint to a great extent. I don't use the accident because I deny the accident."

What is an "accident"? Do you think it is possible to "deny the accident," as Pollock suggests? Why or why not?

10. Consider one more snippet of dialogue between Pollock and an interviewer:

INTERVIEWER   "How do you respond to some of your critics who describe your work as 'a map of tangled hair' . . . 'cathartic disintegration' . . . 'baked macaroni.'"

POLLOCK   "If people would leave most of their stuff at home and just look at the paintings I don't think they would have any trouble enjoying them. It's like looking at a bed of flowers. You don't tear your hair out over what it means."

Is it possible to leave your "stuff at home"? Is it possible to simply look at something from the "point-of-view of nowhere," as Pollock suggests? Why or why not? Is Pollock asking that we not look at his art as art, but rather as a mere "thing"? What does this mean? Discuss.

ARTHUR DANTO

THE ARTWORLD

Arthur Danto argues that art is not defined by a set of abstract properties internal to the artwork but rather by a historically evolving property external to the artwork. A "real object" comes to be an artwork when the art world constitutes or interprets it as such in accordance with a historically evolving theory of art. He demonstrates his position by analyzing Andy Warhol's artwork *Brillo Box* (1964).

In Warhol's exhibit, Brillo boxes made out of wood that were perceptually indiscernible from the cardboard variety found on supermarket shelves were put on display in the Stable Gallery. Danto observes that what makes the exhibited Brillo boxes artworks and those found in the supermarket merely ordinary, commercial objects is that those displayed in the gallery speak to the history of art and art theory and criticism in a way that those on the supermarket shelf do not. For Danto, "real objects" like Brillo boxes and beds become artworks when a theoretical interpretation is attached to them. Without the addition of these theoretical interpretations that evolve over history, real objects such as beds and Brillo boxes remain merely real objects. Writes Danto, "To mistake an artwork for a real object is no great feat when an artwork is the real object one mistakes for it." "The problem," he continues, "is how to avoid such errors, or to remove them once they are made." "To see something as art requires something the eye cannot descry—an atmosphere of artistic theory, a knowledge of the history of art: an artworld." For Danto, the "artworld" consists of a combination of history and theory. Danto's position on art has been instrumental in the development of contemporary philosophies of art that place a strong emphasis on social context.

Arthur Danto (1924–) is an American art critic and professor of philosophy. Currently, he is Emeritus Johnsonian Professor of Philosophy at Columbia University, where he has taught since 1951. He received a B.A. from Wayne State University, (1948) and an M.A. (1949) and a Ph.D. (1952) from Columbia University. He has received many fellowships and grants, including two Guggenheim Fellowships, and has been president of both the American Philosophical Association (1983) and the American Society for Aesthetics (1989–90). Since 1984, he has been art critic for *The Nation*. He is the author of many books including *Nietzsche as Philosopher* (1965), *The Transfiguration of the Commonplace: A Philosophy of Art* (1981), *Narration and Knowledge* (1985), *Philosophical Disenfranchisement of Art* (1986), *Mysticism and Morality: Oriental Thought and Moral Philosophy* (1987), *Connections to the World: The Basic Concepts of Philosophy* (1989), *Beyond the Brillo Box: The Visual Arts in Post-Historical Perspective* (1992), *Embodied Meanings: Critical Essays and Aesthetic Meditations* (1994), *After the End of Art: Contemporary Art and the Pale of History* (1997), *Andy Warhol* (1997), and *Abuse of Beauty: Aesthetics and the Concept of Art* (2004). The following article was first published in 1964.

Hamlet: *Do you see nothing there?*
The Queen: *Nothing at all; yet all that is I see.*

—*Shakespeare:* Hamlet, *act 3, scene 4*

Hamlet and Socrates, though in praise and depreciation respectively, spoke of art as a mirror held up to nature. As with many disagreements in attitude, this one has a factual basis. Socrates saw mirrors as but reflecting what we can already see; so art insofar as mirrorlike, yields idle accurate duplications of the appearances of things, and is of no cognitive benefit whatever. Hamlet, more acutely, recognized a remarkable feature of reflecting surfaces, namely that they show us what we could not otherwise perceive—our own face and form—and so art, insofar as it is mirrorlike, reveals us to ourselves, and is, even by Socratic criteria, of some cognitive utility after all. As a philosopher, however, I find Socrates' discussion defective on other, perhaps less profound grounds than these. If a mirror image of *o* is indeed an imitation of *o*, then,

if art is imitation, mirror images are art. But in fact mirroring objects no more is art than returning weapons to a madman is justice; and reference to mirrorings would be just the sly sort of counterinstance we would expect Socrates to bring forward in rebuttal of the theory he instead uses them to illustrate. If that theory requires us to class *these* as art, it thereby shows its inadequacy: "is an imitation" will not do as a sufficient condition for "is art." Yet, perhaps because artists *were* engaged in imitation, in Socrates' time and after, the insufficiency of the theory was not noticed until the invention of photography. Once rejected as a sufficient condition, mimesis was quickly discarded as even a necessary one; and since the achievement of [Russian abstract painter Wassily] Kandinsky, mimetic features have been relegated to the periphery of critical concern, so much so that some works survive in spite of possessing those virtues, excellence in which was once celebrated as the essence of art, narrowly escaping demotion to mere illustrations.

It is, of course, indispensable in Socratic discussion that all participants be masters of the concept up for analysis, since the aim is to match a real defining expression to a term in active use, and the test for adequacy presumably consists in showing that the former analyzes and applies to all and only those things of which the latter is true. The popular disclaimer notwithstanding, then, Socrates' auditors purportedly knew what art was as well as what they liked; and a theory of art, regarded here as a real definition of "Art," is accordingly not to be of great use in helping men to recognize instances of its application. Their antecedent ability to do this is precisely what the adequacy of the theory is to be tested against, the problem being only to make explicit what they already know. It is *our* use of the term that the theory allegedly means to capture, but we are supposed able, in the words of a recent writer, "to separate those objects which are works of art from those which are not, because . . . we know how correctly to use the word 'art' and to apply the phrase 'work of art.'" Theories, on this account, are somewhat like mirror images on Socrates' account, showing forth what we already know, wordy reflections of the actual linguistic practice we are masters in.

But telling artworks from other things is not so simple a matter, even for native speakers, and these days one might not be aware he was on artistic terrain without an artistic theory to tell him so. And part of the reason for this lies in the fact that terrain is constituted artistic in virtue of artistic theories, so that one use of theories, in addition to helping us discriminate art from the rest, consists in making art possible. Glaucon and the others could hardly have known what was art and what not: otherwise they would never have been taken in by mirror images. . . .

In what I hope are not unwitting footnotes to Plato, two of our pioneers—Robert Rauschenberg and Claes Oldenburg—have made genuine beds.

Rauschenberg's bed hangs on a wall, and is streaked with some desultory housepaint. Oldenburg's bed is a rhomboid, narrower at one end than the other, with what one might speak of as a built-in perspective: ideal for small bedrooms. As beds, these sell at singularly inflated prices, but one *could* sleep in either of them: Rauchenberg has expressed the fear that someone might just climb into his bed and fall asleep. Imagine, now, a certain Testadura—a plain speaker and noted philistine—who is not aware that these are art, and who takes them to be reality simple and pure. He attributes the paint streaks on Rauschenberg's bed to the slovenliness of the owner, and the bias in the Oldenburg bed to the ineptitude of the builder or the whimsy, perhaps, of whoever had it "custom-made." These would be mistakes, but mistakes of rather an odd kind, and not terribly different from that made by the stunned birds who pecked the sham grapes of Zeuxis. They mistook art for reality, and so has Testadura. . . . How shall we describe Testadura's error? What, after all, prevents Oldenburg's creation from being a misshapen bed? This is equivalent to asking what makes it art, and with this query we enter a domain of conceptual inquiry where native speakers are poor guides: *they* are lost themselves.

To mistake an artwork for a real object is no great feat when an artwork is the real object one mistakes it for. The problem is how to avoid such errors, or to remove them once they are made. The artwork is a bed, and not a bed-illusion; so there is nothing like the traumatic encounter against a flat surface that brought it home to the birds of Zeuxis that they had been duped. Except for the guard cautioning Testadura not to sleep on the artworks, he might never have discovered that this was an artwork and not a bed; and since, after all, one cannot discover that a bed is not a bed, how is Testadura to realize that he has made an error? . . .

There is an *is* that figures prominently in statements concerning artworks which is not the *is* of either identity or predication; nor is it the *is* of existence, of identification, or some special *is* made up to serve a philosophic end. Nevertheless, it is in common usage, and is readily mastered by children. It is the sense of *is* in accordance with which a child, shown a circle and triangle and asked which is him and which his sister, will point to the triangle saying "That is me"; or, in response to my question, the person next to me points to the man in purple and says "That one is Lear"; or in the gallery I point, for my companion's benefit, to a spot in the painting before us and say "That white dab is Icarus." We do not mean, in these instances, that whatever is pointed to stands for, or represents, what it is said to be, for the *word* "Icarus" stands for or represents Icarus: yet I would not in the same sense of *is* point to the word and say "That is Icarus." The sentence "That *a* is *b*" is perfectly compatible with "That *a* is not *b*" when the first employs this sense of *is* and the second employs some other, though *A* and *B* are used nonambiguously throughout. Often, indeed, the truth of the first *requires* the truth of the second. The first, in fact, is incompatible with "That *a* is not *b*" only when the *is* is used nonambiguously throughout. For want of a word I shall designate this the *is of artistic identification*; in each case in which it is used, the *a* stands for some specific physical property of, or physical part of an object; and finally, it is a necessary condition for something to be an artwork that some part or property of it be designable by the subject of a sentence that employs this special *is*. It is an *is*, incidentally, which has near relatives in marginal and mythical pronouncements. (Thus, one *is* Quetzalcoatl; those *are* the Pillars of Hercules.)

Let me illustrate. Two painters are asked to decorate the east and west walls of a science library with frescoes to be respectively called *Newton's First Law* and *Newton's Third Law*. These paintings, when finally unveiled, look, scale apart, as follows:

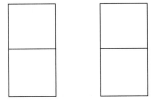

Figure A   **Figure B**

As objects I shall suppose the works to be indiscernible: a black, horizontal line on a white ground, equally large in each dimension and element. *B* explains his work as follows: a mass, pressing downward, is met by a mass pressing upward: the lower mass reacts equally and oppositely to the upper one. *A* explains his work as follows: the line through the space is the path of an isolated particle. The path goes from edge to edge, to give the sense of its *going beyond*. If it ended or began within the space, the line would be curved: and it is parallel to the top and bottom edges, for if it were closer to one than to another, there would have to be a force accounting for it, and this is inconsistent with its being the path of an *isolated* particle.

Much follows from these artistic identifications. To regard the middle line as an edge (mass meeting mass) imposes the need to identify the top and bottom half of the picture as rectangles, and as two distinct parts (not necessarily as two masses, for the line could be the edge of *one* mass jutting up— or down—into empty space). If it is an edge, we cannot thus take the entire area of the painting as a single space: it is rather composed of two forms, or one form and a non-form. We could take the entire area as a single space only by taking the middle horizontal as a *line* which is not an edge. But this almost requires a three-dimensional identification of the whole picture: the area can be a flat surface which the line is *above (Jet-flight)*, or *below (Submarine-path)*, or *on (Line)*, or *in (Fissure)*, or *through (Newton's First Law)*—though in this last case the area is not a flat surface but a transparent cross section of absolute space. We could make all these prepositional qualifications clear by imagining perpendicular cross sections to the picture plane. Then, depending upon the applicable prepositional clause, the area is (artistically) interrupted or not by the horizontal element. If we take the line as *through* space, the edges of the picture are not really the edges of the space: the space goes beyond the picture if the line itself does; and we are in the same space as the line is. As *B*, the edges of the picture can be *part* of the picture in case the masses go right to the edges, so that the edges of the picture are *their* edges. In that case, the vertices of the picture would be the vertices of the masses, except that the masses have four vertices more than the picture itself does: here four vertices would be part of the artwork which were not part of the real object. Again, the faces of the masses could be the face of the picture, and in looking at the picture, we are looking at these faces: but *space* has no face, and on the reading of *A* the work has to be read as faceless, and the face of the physical object would not be part of the artwork. Notice here how one artistic identification engenders another artistic identification, and how, consistently with a given identification, we are *required* to give others and *precluded* from still others: indeed, a given identification determines how many elements the work is to contain. These different identifications are incompatible with one another, or generally so, and each might be said to make a different artwork, even though each artwork contains the identical real object as part of itself—or at least parts of the identical real object as parts of itself. There are, of course, senseless identifications: no one could, I think, sensibly read the middle horizontal as *Love's Labour's Lost* or *The Ascendency of St. Erasmus*. Finally, notice how acceptance of one identification rather than another is in effect to exchange one *world* for another. We could, indeed, enter a quiet poetic world by identifying the upper area with a clear and cloudless sky, reflected in the still surface of the water below, whiteness kept from whiteness only by the unreal boundary of the horizon.

And now Testadura, having hovered in the wings throughout this discussion, protests that *all he sees is paint:* a white painted oblong with a black line painted across it. And how right he really is: that is all he sees or that anybody can, we aesthetes included. So, if he asks us to show him what there is further to see, to demonstrate through pointing that this is an artwork (*Sea and Sky*), we cannot comply, for he has overlooked nothing (and it would be absurd to suppose he had, that there was something tiny we could point to and he, peering closely, say "So it is! A work of art after all"). We cannot help him until he has mastered the *is of artistic identification* and so *constitutes* it a work of art. If he cannot achieve this; he will never look upon artworks: he will be like a child who sees sticks as sticks.

But what about pure abstractions, say something that looks just like *A* but is entitled No. 7? The 10th Street abstractionist blankly insists that there is nothing here but white paint and black, and none of our literary identifications need apply. What then distinguishes him from Testadura, whose philistine utterances are indiscernible from his? And how can it be an artwork for him and not for Testadura, when they agree that there is nothing that does not meet the eye? The answer, unpopular as it is likely to be to purists of every variety, lies in the fact that this artist has returned to the physicality of paint through an atmosphere compounded of artistic theories and the history of recent and remote painting, elements of which he is trying to refine out of his own work; and as a consequence of this his work belongs in this atmosphere and is part of this history. He has achieved abstraction through

rejection of artistic identifications, returning to the real world from which such identifications remove us (he thinks), somewhat in the mode of Ch'ing Yuan, who wrote:

> Before I had studied Zen for thirty years, I saw mountains as mountains and waters as waters. When I arrived at a more intimate knowledge, I came to the point where I saw that mountains are not mountains, and waters are not waters, but now that I have got the very substance I am at rest. For it is just that I see mountains once again as mountains, and waters once again as waters.

His identification of what he has made is logically dependent upon the theories and history he rejects. The difference between his utterance and Testadura's "This is black paint and white paint and nothing more" lies in the fact that he is still using the *is* of artistic identification, so that his use of "That black paint is black paint" is not a tautology [a statement that is true by its own definition or form alone]! Testadura is not at that stage. To see something as art requires something the eye cannot descry—an atmosphere of artistic theory, a knowledge of the history of art: an artworld.

Mr. Andy Warhol, the Pop artist, displays facsimiles of Brillo cartons, piled high, in neat stacks, as in the stockroom of the supermarket. They happen to be of wood, painted to look like cardboard, and why not? To paraphrase the critic of the *Times*, if one may make the facsimile of a human being out of bronze, why not the facsimile of a Brillo carton out of plywood? The cost of these boxes happens to be 2×10^3 that of their homely counterparts in real life—a differential hardly ascribable to their advantage in durability. In fact the Brillo people might, at some slight increase in cost, make their boxes out of plywood without these becoming artworks, and Warhol might make *his* out of cardboard without their ceasing to be art. So we may forget questions of intrinsic value, and ask why the Brillo people cannot manufacture art and why Warhol cannot *but* make artworks. Well, his are made by hand, to be sure. Which is like an insane reversal of Picasso's strategy in pasting the label from a bottle of Suze onto a drawing, saying as it were that the academic artist, concerned with exact imitation, must always fall short of the real thing: so why not just *use* the real thing? The Pop artist laboriously reproduces machine-made objects by hand, e.g., painting the labels on coffee cans (one can hear the familiar commendation "Entirely made by hand" falling painfully out of the guide's vocabulary when confronted by these objects). But the difference cannot consist in craft: a man who carved pebbles out of stones and carefully constructed a work called *Gravel Pile* might invoke the labor theory of value to account for the price he demands; but the question is, What makes it art? And why need Warhol *make* these things anyway? Why not just scrawl his signature across one? Or crush one up and display it as *Crushed Brillo Box* ("A protest against mechanization . . .") or simply display a Brillo carton as *Uncrushed Brillo Box* ("A bold affirmation of the plastic authenticity of industrial. . . .")? Is this man a kind of Midas, turning whatever he touches into the gold of pure art? And the whole world consisting of latent artworks waiting, like the bread and wine of reality, to be transfigured, through some dark mystery, into the indiscernible flesh and blood of the sacrament? Never mind that the Brillo box may not be good, much less great art. The impressive thing is that it is art at all. But if it is, why are not the indiscernible Brillo boxes that are in the stockroom? Or *has* the whole distinction between art and reality broken down?

Suppose a man collects objects (readymades), including a Brillo carton; we praise the exhibit for variety, ingenuity, what you will. Next he exhibits nothing but Brillo cartons, and we criticize it as dull, repetitive, self-plagiarizing—or (more profoundly) claim that he is obsessed by regularity and repetition, as in [the film *Last Year at*] *Marienbad.* Or he piles them high, leaving a narrow path; we tread our way through the smooth opaque stacks and find it an unsettling experience, and write it up as the closing in of consumer products, confining us as prisoners: or we say he is a modern pyramid builder. True, we don't say these things about the stockboy. But then a stockroom is not an art gallery, and we cannot readily separate the Brillo cartons from the gallery they are in, any more than we can separate the Rauschenberg bed from the paint upon it. Outside the gallery, they are pasteboard cartons. But then, scoured clean of paint, Rauschenberg's bed is a bed, just what it was before it was

transformed into art. But then if we think this matter through, we discover that the artist has failed, really and of necessity, to produce a mere real object. He has produced an artwork, his use of real Brillo cartons being but an expansion of the resources available to artists, a contribution to *artists' materials*, as oil paint was, or *tuche.*

What in the end makes the difference between a Brillo box and a work of art consisting of a Brillo Box is a certain theory of art. It is the theory that takes it up into the world of art, and keeps it from collapsing into the real object which it is (in a sense of *is* other than that of artistic identification). Of course, without the theory, one is unlikely to see it as art, and in order to see it as part of the artworld, one must have mastered a good deal of artistic theory as well as a considerable amount of the history of recent New York painting. It could not have been art fifty years ago. But then there could not have been, everything being equal, flight insurance in the Middle Ages, or Etruscan typewriter erasers. The world has to be ready for certain things, the artworld no less than the real one. It is the role of artistic theories, these days as always, to make the artworld, and art, possible. It would, I should think, never have occurred to the painters of Lascaux that they were producing *art* on those walls. Not unless there were neolithic asestheticians. . . .

Brillo boxes enter the Artworld with that same tonic incongruity the *commedia dell'arte* characters bring into *Ariadne auf Naxos.* Whatever is the artistically relevant predicate in virtue of which they gain their entry, the rest of the Artworld becomes that much the richer in having the opposite predicate available and applicable to its members. And, to return to the views of Hamlet with which we began this discussion, Brillo boxes may reveal us to ourselves as well as anything might: as a mirror held up to nature, they might serve to catch the conscience of our kings.

DISCUSSION QUESTIONS

1. Danto criticizes Plato's notion of "art as imitation." What are his criticisms? Do they convince you? Why does he say that "the insufficiency of the theory was not noticed until after the invention of photography"?

2. How does Danto respond to the claim that Robert Rauschenberg's bed is not art? How do you think Plato and Tolstoy would respond to Rauschenberg's bed? Would they regard it as an artwork? Compare Danto's response to Rauschenberg's bed with the responses of Plato and Tolstoy.

3. What is the *"is of artistic identification"*? What role does it play in Danto's theory of art?

4. Danto contends that "real objects" like Brillo boxes and beds become artworks when a theoretical interpretation is attached to them. Without the addition of these theoretical interpretations that evolve over time, real objects such as beds and Brillo boxes remain merely real objects. What do you think of his claim that a property external to a real object must be added to it in order for it to "constitute" an artwork?

5. Compare and contrast Danto and Hume on the nature of art, and the role of art critics in determining the value of art. Do you think Hume would argue that Warhol's *Brillo Box* is art? Why or why not?

6. Danto says, "It would, I should think, never have occurred to the painters of Lascaux that they were producing *art* on those walls. Not unless they were Neolithic aestheticians." Do you agree with him? Compare Danto's response to Neolithic "art" to that of Langer. Whose view do you prefer, and why?

Superstar: The Life and Times of Andy Warhol
[USA 1990] 1 hour, 31 minutes
Directed by Chuck Workman

American artist Andy Warhol (1928–87) was the most notorious, and arguably the most influential, visual artist of the twentieth century. Warhol grew up in Pittsburgh, Pennsylvania, and studied art at Carnegie Tech (now Carnegie Mellon University). He began his career as an advertising illustrator, drawing objects such as women's shoes for magazine ads. Warhol is best known for introducing iconic images from commercial art, such as the Campbell's soup can and the Brillo box, into the world of fine art. Warhol's reproductions of images from consumer culture, either on canvas or in art installations, shocked and thrilled the art world, and launched a movement called *pop art*. Warhol brought the art of silkscreening into the mainsteam of American fine art with massive screens of celebrity portraits, newspaper photographs, and other iconic images from American popular culture.

These mass-produced art objects both featured mass culture and were the product of it. They were also both the products of reproduction and made to be reproduced. One critic in the film states that Warhol's art is unique in the sense that it often looks as good in catalogue reproduction as it does in real life and that his success as an artist is in part due to this. The bold colors and lines of Warhol's art reproduce extraordinarily well.

His art was produced in "The Factory," a studio where many persons labored (and partied) to produce his silkscreens and develop his pop aesthetic in other areas such as film and music. Warhol's films, for example, are perhaps even more notorious than his silkscreens. His film *Sleep* (1963) is over six hours of footage of someone sleeping. In essence, Warhol's films capture a moment. They are not tightly scripted enactments of a series of plotted events; instead, they simply follow the course of a person or persons living in a moment. Warhol made fifteen-minute "portraits" of everyone who came into The Factory: each person sat in front of a motion-picture camera for fifteen minutes. Warhol infamously contended that everyone will be famous for fifteen minutes; his film work went a long way toward making this a reality.

Consequently, Warhol's films are unlike conventional American cinema, and a source of great critical controversy. Critics tends to fall into two very broad groups with regard to Warhol's films, with one group praising them as aesthetically and culturally valuable and the other finding little of value in them aside from the promotion of Warhol's notoriety as an artist.

This documentary traces the life of Warhol from his early days to his establishment as the centerpiece of the New York social scene in the 1970s and 1980s. Ultimately, despite the omnipresence of Warhol and his art in America, he is presented as an enigma.

DISCUSSION QUESTIONS

1. Danto argues that the artworld can make ordinary objects into art. Consider this claim in the context of Andy Warhol's art. Do you think Warhol takes this notion too far or to its logical limit? Are reproductions of Campbell's soup cans always only containers for soup, or can the imposition of an interpretation from the artworld alter their aesthetic status? Discuss.

2. Is it important to make a distinction between commercial art and fine art? Aesthetically, for example, what is the difference between the design of a gum wrapper or a beer bottle and a painting by Picasso or a sculpture by Rodin?

3. Roy Lichtenstein (1923–) made the comic strip the subject of his art. However, unlike Warhol's silkscreens that reproduce photos, Lichtenstein did not replicate actual comics but made it appear as though he did. Is there a difference between replicating the *style* of comics and replicating *actual* Brillo boxes? Why or why not?

4. In the film, the writer Tom Wolfe says, "Prior to the pop artists, and particularly Andy Warhol, the reigning attitude of art was that of the abstract expressionists. The idea was that America was a benighted, crassly commercialized, rather horrible place. And the artist can only turn his back as best he could and revert his eyes from this side of the modern world. Warhol came along as part of a slightly younger generation. And his idea was 'Oh it's so horrible, I love it.'" Which, if either, approach to art appeals to you more, and why?

5. Warhol's art is premised upon the notion that we desire to have what is familiar to us be aesthetically codified, that is, become the object of fine art. Is he right? Do you think that we prefer the familiar as opposed to the obscure in art?

6. Warhol believed that printmaking and painting were not different. Is he right? Or is there a significant philosophical difference? Discuss.

7. Warhol's prints reproduce very well: They are strong images that are immediately recognizable and memorable. Critics contend that they are just as good in a catalogue as in real life. Given that most people never see original artworks, but rather only reproductions of them, should we therefore privilege an aesthetic that emphasizes the ability of an artwork to reproduce well as a criterion of artistic goodness or greatness? Why or why not?

8. In many of his artworks, Warhol repeated one object many times. For example, one of his silkscreens reproduces multiple images of Elvis Presley holding a gun; another shows repeated images of Marilyn Monroe's face. What, if anything, is the philosophical significance of this?

9. Warhol contended that his Campbell's soup can series is autobiographical. What did he mean by this?

10. Warhol's film *Sleep* is six and a half hours of a man sleeping. Warhol said he made it because he could: he simply turned the motion-picture camera on and walked away. Is this film art? Why or why not? Consider it from the aesthetic perspectives of Plato, Aristotle, Hume, Langer, and Tolstoy.

11. Warhol had everyone who came into The Factory sit in front of a motion-picture camera for fifteen minutes. Can such a process capture the "essence" of a person? Why or why not?

12. The actor Dennis Hopper says of Andy Warhol that merely by pointing his finger something would become art. What would Hume say about his approach to art? Do you agree with this approach to art? Why or why not?

MARILYN FRENCH

IS THERE A FEMINIST AESTHETIC?

Marilyn French contends that a *feminist aesthetic* has three principles: (1) it endorses female experience; (2) it approaches reality from a feminist perspective; and (3) it is in an accessible style.

According to the first principle, work with a feminist aesthetic "penetrates, demystifies, or challenges patriarchal ideologies." Patriarchy, for French, involves three assumptions: (1) that males are superior to females, (2) that males have individual destinies that hold out the promise of domination or "some form of transcendent paternity," and (3) that a hierarchical structure maintains and transmits "power from spiritual father to spiritual son." While art that is feminist in perspective utilizes patriarchal structures because "almost all modern worlds are patriarchal," it does not promote patriarchal assumptions. Rather, art from a feminist perspective endorses a reversal of patriarchal assumptions regarding the nature of human beings in themselves and their relationship to nature and to one another.

French's second principle—the endorsement of female experience—requires feminist artists at times to change or reject artistic conventions that endorse patriarchal perspectives of female experience. One of the consequences of this will be the offending of both male and female viewers. She discusses how these patriarchal artistic conventions are linked to the history of Western philosophy—a history that for 2,500 years "has looked at life strictly from a male perspective, and strictly as if men were constituted only of intellect, ambition, and political concern; as if they never had to deal with upset stomachs, irritation at their children, emotional dependency, hunger, or distress at growing bald."

Of the three principles of a feminist aesthetic, the third is not a necessary condition of feminist art, whereas the other two are. Nevertheless, it is a principle about which French feels strongly. Accessibility of style and language allows her ideal author to "see the reader as an equal, who will out of friendship try as hard to understand the narrator's reality as she to express it." Finally, for French, feminist art is a moral act that can make us better, and it "must create the illusion of 'felt life.'"

Marilyn French (1929–), an American author, is well known for her feminist novels and scholarship. She was born in New York and received a B.A. from Hofstra College (now University) in 1951 and an M.A. in 1964. From 1964 to 1968, she was an instructor at Hofstra, and she continued her studies at Harvard University, earning a Ph.D. in 1972. She taught at the College of the Holy Cross in Worcester, Massachusetts, from 1972 to 1976. French started to write seriously in 1957, but in twenty years published only a few articles and stories. In 1976, she published *The Book as World: James Joyce's Ulysses*, a work based on her thesis. The following year, she published the very successful novel *The Women's Room* (1977), which has been translated into over twenty languages and was made into a television movie in 1980. Like a number of her books, *The Women's Room* takes up the battles of the sexes and features trenchant social commentary. Her other books include *The Bleeding Heart* (1980), *Shakespeare's Division of Experience* (1981), *Beyond Power: On Men, Women, and Morals* (1985), *Her Mother's Daughter* (1987), *The War Against Women* (1992), *Our Father* (1993), *Season in Hell* (1998), and *Women's History of the World* (2000). The following is an article that appeared in 1992.

It is questionable whether the terms and issues of traditional aesthetics are applicable to feminist art. Some critics claim traditional aesthetic principles are universal, and that art is "above" sex, or at least, that sex is irrelevant to it. There is an art which is specifically feminist: that much is clear. Some, by virtue of its feminism, would deny it the title *art*, arguing that its political interest violates aesthetic standards. An aesthetics like Susanne Langer's, which defines what art creates and is indeed universal, fits feminist art as well as any other. But most aesthetics are more prescriptive, and therefore more political: feminism has taught us that all critical approaches imply political standards, however tacitly. Before we can evaluate feminist art by any aesthetic principles, we need a definition of the art. In what follows, I will discuss the characteristics of feminist art as I understand them. For the sake of brevity, I will limit myself to the art I know best, literature; but the principles have parallels in the other arts.

The clearest proof of the existence of a feminist aesthetics is the distaste or rage feminists feel on encountering works that violate it. Sometimes a negative response seems to refer to subject matter—for example, I loathe lingering loving descriptions of mutilations of female bodies; yet when a writer like Andrea Dworkin treats such a theme, I feel it to be not offensive, but only unpleasant—it falls within the boundaries of "taste." So it is less subject-matter (content) than treatment (style) that is at issue (I will not here address the identity of style and content. Perhaps all a prescriptive aesthetic can be is a set of principles describing a particular style, a taste.

There are two fundamental, related principles that mark a work of art as feminist: first, it approaches reality from a feminist perspective; second, it endorses female experience. Each principle has several ramifications, so is more complicated than it sounds.

In a work with a feminist perspective, the narrational point of view, the point of view lying behind the characters and events, penetrates, demystifies, or challenges patriarchal ideologies. So much has been written about patriarchy in the last two decades that one tends to assume readers understand the term; yet I have met highly educated people who do not understand the feminist use of the term, so I'll explain it briefly. Patriarchy is a way of thinking, a set of assumptions that has been translated into various structures or ideologies. The assumptions are, first: males are superior to females. Their superiority may be granted by a deity or by nature, but it is absolute in conferring on men authority over women. Second: males have individual destinies; they are promised domination, a surrogate godhead, transcendence over the natural world through power in heroism, sainthood, or some form of transcendent paternity—founding a dynasty, an institution, a religion, or a state, or creating an enduring work of art or technology. Third: the form taken by patriarchy is hierarchy, a structure designed to maintain and transmit power from spiritual father to spiritual son. This form absolutely excludes females unless they "make themselves male" (the requirement Jesus places on women entering "the Life" in the gnostic Gospel of Thomas). Women control biological transmission, the ability to bring forth young passed from mother to daughter. Having this power, they must be excluded from institutional power—which was modeled on the biological sort—if they are not to overwhelm men. Females have only a "natural" destiny; interchangeable parts of nature's cycles, they are maids (in both senses), who become mothers, and finally widows (or hags), in which avatar they are expendable.

Finally, domination is divine, so to pursue it is noble, heroic, glorious. The material to be dominated is, essentially, nature—all women; the body and emotions; "bestial" men; and natural processes, the flux and transitoriness of time, material decay, life itself. Patriarchal works focus on individual males who pursue glory: lonely, self-made and self-defeating, men are isolated from community and exiled forever from the "female" fate of happiness.

Since almost all modern worlds are patriarchal, feminist literature necessarily depicts patriarchy. But it does not underwrite its standards. Feminist literature may show patriarchal attitudes destroying a character or a world, but the narrative does not approve the destruction. When, in *The Faerie Queene*, Guyon destroys the luscious female world called The Bower of Bliss, Spenser, who has used his highest imaginative skills to create the Bower, judiciously approves its ruin. This is true also of Vergil in *The Aeneid*. The poet sighs about the tears of things (*lacrimae rerum*), regretting that beauty and feeling (Dido and sexual love for instance) are destroyed in the pursuit of glory, yet approves Aeneas's desertion of Dido, and his slaughter of those who oppose his domination. Aeneas's destiny is to found Rome; it overrides humanitarian or emotional concerns. Clearly, despite their feelings, both poets uphold patriarchy.

It is less clear where Tolstoy stands in *Anna Karenina*, or Austen in *Pride and Prejudice*. Both authors accept the patriarchal societies in which they live. Yet the pity Tolstoy lavishes on Anna, and the acute irony with which Austen pricks upper-class pretention and the unctuous ambition of the middle-classes, subvert patriarchal standards. This sympathy is not in the eye of the reader; it is built-in. Tolstoy's novel induces readers to feel the world lessened by Anna's death, rather than to feel that it was necessary, like Dido's, to a greater purpose. Austen's heroines maintain self-respect and integrity (wholeness) even as they triumph within a patriarchal structure. Many works of the past three centuries stretch patriarchal standards in this way; they are not feminist, but do not wholly support patriarchy either.

The feminist perspective is partly a reversal of patriarchal views. Feminism sees women as at least equal to men, humanly if not politically or economically; it considers transcendence illusory or factitious and pursuit of power a fatally doomed enterprise, since it cannot ever be satisfied, and usually or always involves the destruction of vital qualities and even life itself. Domination is not divine but lethal to dominator and dominated. It harms the dominator by cutting him off from trust and mutuality, the foundations of friendship and love, the two primary values; it harms the dominated by forcing them into dependency, which precludes truth in relationships. Domination creates false forms of friendship (society) and love (conventional marriage) which mask power relations. And feminist art focuses on people as wholes; the human is made up of body and emotion as well as mind and spirit; she is also part of a community, connected to others; and—on the broadest level—to nature in both positive and negative aspects.

The second principle is equally complicated. To endorse women's experience, feminist art must present it honestly, wholly. This is difficult because literature, like all art, is made up of conventions which are particularly marked in the area of gender. Just as it would be startling to observe a painting of a male nude reclining seductively à la Maja, or Olympe, or of a clothed female Picasso contemplating a naked male with emphatic genitals, literary shifts in presentation of gender startle, distracting attention from *what* is being shown to *the fact* that it is shown. A work's political impact obliterates its other features. This means that either considerable time—decades or even centuries—must elapse before readers can concentrate on what is being shown, or the work will be forgotten without this ever happening. And conventions governing female characters in literature are extraordinarily powerful and tenacious.

One convention holds women's work trivial, insignificant, uninteresting. Indeed, even men's work was considered an inappropriate subject for literature until recently. Yet work fills our lives; domestic work *is* most women's entire life and takes up considerable time even for women who also work outside the home. What such work means to one's sense of self, of the larger world; how it affects a woman's relation to her children, mates, lovers, friends; its pleasures, pains, the personal and political consequences of endless work for which one is not paid: these experiences remain relatively unexplored because of convention.

Conventionally, women's stories had happy endings, usually marriage to a prince and living happily ever after—unless the heroine is guilty of a sexual transgression, in which case she is required to die. This convention has stretched to allow sexual women to survive, but readers still complain when a "good" woman does not live happily ever after. The assumption behind this convention seems to be that the world is ruled by a male bar of justice. All female characters come up before this bar, and males, being just, grant the good ones happiness—a female, not a male condition (male heroes almost never live happily ever after). If the author does not grant a virtuous female character eternal felicity, either she doesn't deserve it or the male bar is not just. Since in a patriarchal world the latter is unthinkable, her virtue must be deceptive. So male critics pore over Shakespeare's Cordelia searching for the hidden flaw that explains her fate and alter Edith Wharton's perception of her heroines (who *are* flawed), making them responsible for their own unhappiness.

If the definition of a "good" woman no longer involves chastity, heroines are still required to be sweet, vulnerable, *likeable*. Readers do not expect sweetness or honesty of male protagonists: they don't even have to be likeable: consider the heroes of *Under the Volcano, Notes from Underground, Look Back in Anger*. Authoritative, angry, rebellious heroines make most readers impatient; they tend to blame the character for not finding a way to be happy. I think about Andrea Dworkin's *Ice and Fire*, which could not at first find an American publisher, or my own *The Bleeding Heart*, which female and male reviewers (if not readers) uniformly condemned. Actual women, we ourselves, may walk around in a constant state of rage and yet reject heroines like us. The most lethal combination is authority and sexuality; it is almost impossible to depict a woman with both except as a villain.

I am very conscious of this because I am planning a novel with an authoritative, sexual woman character, who lives in rage and despair, and who may not be likeable—but who has real grounds for her feelings, and lives in pain, and is in some ways admirable. Someone like, say, Ivan Karamazov. I already know how she will be received, and I dread it. There should be room for every kind of female experience, even the inability to live happily ever after. There should be room for depictions of women who are monstrous. Again, difficulties occur in distinguishing portrayals of monstrous women from portraits drawn by woman-haters. Woman-hating nestles deep at the root of patriarchy; all of us, women and men, are probably infected by it to some degree. Women's own woman-hatred needs exploration in feminist art.

In portraying female experience, feminist art also portrays men, showing them as they impinge upon women or as they appear to women to be. There are no heroes who save women: not because men would not like to do this, but because it can't be done. This is not to say there is no heroism, male and female, in life; only that there are no princes. What men are in themselves or for other men may contradict what they are for women: women's dreams and hopes about men may be mere wishfulness; women may be complicit in male monstrousness. Feminist portraits of males must examine these realities, but there are serious dangers in doing so. Although women (and even men) offer blanket condemnation of male treatment of females in conversation, such condemnation on a printed page is tantamount to mutiny (so wives' disobedience of husbands, in Shakespeare's era, was called "revolution") and leads to the work being dismissed.

These principles may sound limiting, as if feminist work could deal only and always with the middle ground, the mundane, the probable, eschewing flights of fancy, excessive characters, extremes of good and evil. This is not at all the case, although precisely that middle ground needs examination. Consider that for the 2,500-plus years of its existence, Western philosophy has looked at life strictly from a male perspective, and strictly as if men were constituted only of intellect, ambition, and political concern; as if they never had to deal with upset stomachs, irritation at their children, emotional dependency, hunger, or distress at growing bald. As Nietzsche pointed out, philosophy has ignored and dismissed the life of the body and the emotions, and—I would add—social involvement with women and children. It has been able to show men transcending only by pretending that the mundane does not exist and that other people do not matter.

In addition, for millennia, at least since fifth century B.C.E. Athens, male thinking has divided human experience into two unequal categories. These may be mind/body, reason/sense, spirit/flesh (sexual desire), or intellect/emotion, but the two are always opposed like enemies, and one is always ascribed moral superiority—in the righteous man, mind (or reason, spirit, intellect) will triumph. By dividing experience this way, men have been able to build a world they claim is based on mind, reason, spirit, intellect, a culture which controls and belittles body, senses, desire, emotion; and have felt legitimate in using ruthless means to suppress people associated with what is disparaged. Valuing only certain talents and ignoring or denigrating others, certain men have created a science-based industrial-technological environment without giving a single moment of thought to its effect on living, feeling, and desire; and have disparaged, debased, and killed women of all sorts and men of discredited colors, religions, cultures, or backgrounds.

It is essential for the healing of a sick world that this division be mended. To begin with, it is false. Humans are of a piece, made up of thousands of intricate interconnections, mind body spirit sex sense intellect being only points in an indescribable continuum. Bodymind swirls around in us, without us; we contain it, it contains us. We can try to understand the processes by which we function, but we cannot control them. Every step at control is counteracted by the power of what is hidden; too many steps and we fall ill, off-balance.

Not only is each of us a complex network whose workings we barely understand, but each of us is connected to other people and ideas and things in equally complex ways. There is no such thing as a self-made man—or woman. Scientists are discovering more fully each decade that *nothing dominates*. No planet dominates the cosmos, no part of a cell dominates it, no single person, not even the boss, dominates any situation. The drive to control that informs patriarchy is an unremitting, relentless drive to an invulnerability, im*preg*nability (consider the root of this word), that does not exist on earth. People spend their lives trying to reach a pinnacle of power from which they can affect others without being affected in return—one definition of god. But even a Stalin, who arguably controlled more, in terms of people and territory, than any other human in our century, lived within prison walls, with a taster to try his food, without the possibility of trust, without which both friendship and love are impossible. And bosses are afraid in direct proportion to the degree of control they possess—of those beneath them as well as those above. And are affected by them, in all kinds of ways. Power is a moment, a temporary station on a telephone lines; tomorrow, the powerful man may be forced out even if he is president, chairman, Shah.

We have not yet created a language to describe interconnection: our language is based on fabricated dichotomies, and trying to speak about mind/body/senses all at once makes one feel she has a mouthful of marbles. But in whatever ways the genius of the artist can devise, feminist art suggests that things are connected as well as divided, that a person is not always at war with herself or her world, that in fact people seek to live harmoniously with themselves and their world *even though they can't control either*. Feminist work often focuses on groups, community, people as part of a context, and helps to remind us of a reality alternative to the Western tradition of individualistic, alienated man, lonely in a hostile, aggressive world.

So, a third kind of endorsement of female experience is showing a pluralistic reality made up of connection, flow, interrelation, and therefore equality—for when nothing dominates, all parts are equally necessary, and require equal attention. In the workings of the human being or of cosmic space, the puffing up of one part with claims of superiority leads to catastrophe for all parts. Human superiority is not a possibility, no matter how many have claimed it. Shakespeare may endow his kings and lords with social and political superiority, but he also regularly shows their underlings—a simple clown, a powerless girl—to be superior to them in common sense, morality, and understanding.

Works of art that assume the existence of human superiority are invariably anti-woman. I have been paying attention now for many years: works that presume that some people are and ought to be "better" than others betray contempt for those others on grounds of their identity—in Western literature, usually blacks or Jews. And when you find the one, you find the other: where there is contempt for any identity, there is also contempt for femaleness or things associated with femaleness—body, sex, desire, need—even in works written by women. Although writers of the late twentieth-century United States are inhibited from expressing anti-Semitism or racism, many, especially television writers, allow themselves the complacency of moral superiority in their literary treatment of prostitutes, who are not shown as people but as attractive subhumans, unworthy of humane consideration.

A third feminist principle, to which I myself am committed, is accessibility, language and style that aim at comprehensibility. I mention this separately because unlike the two principles already discussed, it is not a necessary condition of feminist art. It is, however, a standard about which I feel strongly.

For thousands of years, women were locked out of high culture. For example, sometime between 200 B.C.E. and 550 C.E., Hindu women were forbidden to learn Sanskrit, the language in which all the great Hindu religious and literary documents were composed. The rationale for this was that women were not capable of *moksha*, salvation, and so did not need to read about religion. But the prohibition kept women from learning the religious, mythic, and poetic backgrounds of their culture.

In the fifth century, Japan imported Chinese culture, philosophy, and language; at this time, Japanese women were still powerful. In later centuries, they were degraded and diminished, and male authorities forbade them to learn Chinese, by then the prestige language of Japan, the language of philosophy, government, and "high" literature. Ironically, in the eleventh century, while learned men trotted out tedious

pretentious Chinese imitations, literary women writing in the vernacular produced some of Japan's greatest literature, including its masterpiece, the *Tale of Genji*, by Murasaki Shikibu.

Some societies refused to teach females how to read and write. But even if some women were literate, once a particular language became exalted, became the language of scholarship, poetry, diplomacy, or law, theology, and medicine, women were forbidden to learn it. When humanism swept Europe after the fourteenth century, and it became essential to cultivated discourse to know Latin and Greek, women were excluded from schools that taught Latin and Greek. As more lower-class men learned classical languages, a new literary form emerged: allegory, intended to separate the low from the high mind. The medieval allegorist prided himself on concealing spiritual meaning under a sensuous surface. Of course, this also permitted him to write splendid sensuous poetry, filled with sexual and chivalric exploits, while claiming to offer a more severe and exalted "kernel" of hidden significance to the truly learned. Often, poets were also offering serious moral instruction, usually about power, in this coded language.

In our own time, in our own country, our own language, English, is the prestige tongue, the one in which advanced scientific, social, philosophical, and technological documents are written. But these documents are rarely written in an English all of us can comprehend. Rather, each discipline has created a special language, a jargon accessible only to those who have been trained in the field. Women now learn these languages, and use them with it seems to me special pleasure, as if they knew they were using tools formerly sacrosanct, kept in the part of the temple forbidden to females. Some degree of specialist language is necessary; feminists who must use special languages can develop a critique of those languages, and acknowledge and renounce, even as they use them, the patriarchal assumptions implanted in their codes.

What I find non-feminist is intentional obfuscation, the kind of writing that purposes to impress the reader with the writer's knowledge or intellect or high style or "inness," the kind that makes a point of excluding all but the chosen few. With reservations, I love the work of James Joyce,

T. S. Eliot, and Ezra Pound, writers who make frequent use of allusion, quoting fragments of poetry, namedropping, and otherwise referring to great poets and thinkers of the past. By this they accomplish several things: they add depth to their work, texturing, enriching it with allusions to a literary tradition. They also parade their learning, placing themselves above the perhaps less-learned reader, presenting themselves as distant and superior. And they legitimate themselves. Western poetry traditionally *required* citation of authority. By bringing in Homer, Cavalcante, Dante, Shakespeare, these men suggest that they are writing in the same tradition as the great men of the past; that they are the equals of these forebears; and that they deserve the same reverence.

Few women use such devices. In the first place, there are few female authorities and women do not seem to feel that males can legitimate them. Second, the device is itself patriarchal: patriarchy is about the transmission of power, the mantle handed from father to nonbiological son, a tradition excluding women. But most important, women seem to feel legitimated not by power and authority, as men do, but by experience itself. And experience is made up of feeling. Women seek legitimacy by finding ways to express what it feels like to live their particular reality. When women's writing is opaque, or what some might call inaccessible, it is because there is no language of expression of a context of emotion: each woman has to create a language for herself. So, some might find inaccessible Monique Wittig's *Les Guérillères* or Susan Griffin's *The Roaring Inside Her,* or Luce Irigaray's *And the One Doesn't Stir Without the Other*, or Lois Gould's *A Sea-change* and *Subject to Change,* or Christa Wolf's *Cassandra* or *No Place on Earth*: but whatever inaccessibility exists in these works emerges not from pretention but from the difficulty of rendering the life of the emotions.

My own style is based on my decision, made after almost twenty years of (unpublished) writing in a different mode, to address the reader like a friend talking across a kitchen table, over coffee: I see the reader as an equal, who will out of friendship try as hard to understand the narrator's reality as she to express it. I believe that a healthy literature, one that attempts to create a healthy culture, is inclusive—of everyone—implicitly or explicitly. It is directed at an entire society, and considers everyone in it a member of that society. Choosing to write in such a style necessarily involves some loss and therefore some anguish. But any style requires sacrificing others.

Finally, there may be a distinction between patriarchal and feminist forms. In *Feeling and Form*, Susanne Langer describes the form of tragedy as expressing the rhythms of individual life as the hero realizes his potential and exhausts it, comparing it with comedy, the form of which celebrates vital continuity. In *Shakespeare's Division of Experience*, I draw on Langer's definition to describe Shakespeare's tragedy and comedy as masculine and feminine forms respectively: tragedy focuses on an individual male, is linear, and leads to a destiny which must be death but suggests transcendence; comedy focuses less intensely on a female, is circular, communal, and leads to harmony and integration of an entire society (although in Shakespeare, the most seriously disruptive element may be excluded from the happy conclusion). Twentieth-century literature, patriarchal or feminist, rarely fits the categories of either traditional tragedy or comedy; yet I think a study of form in any art would yield similar conclusions.

The art I describe in these principles is a different entity from the art described by traditional aesthetics. Itself transcendent, embodying universal aesthetic principles, singular and useless except to move the sensibility exquisite enough to apprehend it, art as traditionally seen is the delicate flower expressing the spirit of a culture. But for feminists, as Lily Tomlin's baglady Trudy tries to work it out (in Jane Wagner's words, with Andy Warhol's image of cans of Campbell's soup), art is soup. Art nourishes a society, feeds it; sturdy, not delicate, it arises from the life of a people like food from the ground, teaching us what we do not know, reminding us of what we tend to forget, emphasizing what is important, grieving over pain, celebrating vitality. It is useful and beautiful and moral—not moralistic.

The standards I hold for a feminist art are thus, as you have probably guessed, my standards in life. And that is what I believe an art, any art, ought to be: an expression of a vision that is at once a belief and a faith—belief in humanity and faith in its future. I have always accepted the Horatian definition of the purpose of art—to teach and to delight—and I believe feminist art can make us better, just as I think a feminist world would make us better. But art is not just a moral act. There is a last principle which is not feminist but truly universal: vitality. Art must create the illusion of "felt life," as Henry James suggested. Without it, the best-intentioned piece of work is mere words, a dead shell. And that is a quality for which no one can write prescriptions.

DISCUSSION QUESTIONS

1. According to French, is the sex of the artist important in the creation of feminist art? In other words, according to her principles of a feminist aesthetic, can a man produce feminist art just as well as a woman? Why or why not?

2. While French uses examples only from literary art, she implies that her feminist aesthetic principles hold for other art forms as well. Do you think that they do? Discuss an art form other than literature—for example, music, sculpture, or painting—utilizing French's principles. Do her principles hold for this other art form, or is there a problem applying them to this form?

3. At several places in her essay, French refers to Susanne Langer's philosophy of art. Compare and contrast Langer's approach to art with that of French.

4. French argues that feminist art must be in an accessible style and language. What is her argument? Do you agree with her? If clarity and accessibility is the hallmark of feminist art, what might be the hallmark of patriarchal art? Obscurity? Discuss.

5. Do you agree with French that art is a moral act that can make us feel better, if not make the world a better place? Why or why not?

Frida
[USA 2002] 2 hours, 2 minutes
Directed by Julie Taymor

Frida Kahlo (Salma Hayek) was born in Mexico City in 1907. When she was six, she was stricken with polio, making her right leg weaker than her left for her entire life. At the age of eighteen, she was involved in a serious bus accident, breaking her spinal column, collarbone, ribs, and pelvis, and fracturing her right leg in eleven places. She was bed-ridden in boxlike cast for a month. Though she recovered from the accident, she suffered pain throughout her life. Over the course of her life, she underwent nearly thirty operations and turned to alcohol and drugs to ease her pain. Nevertheless, the accident was the event that turned Kahlo to painting. As a relief from the boredom of lying in bed, she began painting, which became her lifelong occupation.

Upon her recovery, a friend introduced her to the great Mexican muralist Diego Rivera (Alfred Molina), who was over twenty years older than she was. They were married in 1929, divorced in 1939, and remarried the following year. Her relationship with Rivera was stormy, to say the least, marked by miscarriages, infidelity, and emotional and physical turmoil, which was tempered by their deep love for and friendship with each other.

Through her paintings, Kahlo expressed the turbulence of her rich, complex, and pain-filled life. Kahlo depicts herself hemorrhaging during a miscarriage; sleeping with a skeleton; sitting on a hospital gurney crying, next to a twin covered with bloody incisions; sitting in a wheelchair holding her heart on a paint pallet; with Rivera's face inscribed on her forehead; and in numerous other emotionally and physically painful and highly personal situations. In each painting, even those when she is next to Rivera, she appears lonely. Her emotional life and her physical body are the objects of her art.

Kahlo's paintings have been celebrated all over the world. Later in her life, she was effectively able to step out of the shadow of her famous husband and gain recognition as a great artist. Nevertheless, because of poor health, she spent much of her life bedridden. She attended the only exhibition of her paintings in Mexico in 1953 on a hospital stretcher. In the middle of the exhibition, she lay drinking, singing, and entertaining the crowd. Kahlo turned her personal pain into paintings of great emotional and life-affirming energy. After the exhibition, her right leg was amputated, and she became depressed and suicidal. After several attempts to take her own life, she died in Mexico City in 1954 at the age of forty-seven. It is rumored that she committed suicide, though no official autopsy was performed. Rivera died three years later.

DISCUSSION QUESTIONS

1. Marilyn French contends that a feminist aesthetic has three principles: (1) it endorses female experience; (2) it approaches reality from a feminist perspective; and (3) it is in an accessible style. Discuss the art of Frida Kahlo in terms of each of these principles. Is it in accordance with these principles or not?

2. Does Kahlo's art prove that there is such a thing as a female aesthetic? Why or why not?

3. Do you think a male artist could have produced the art of Frida Kahlo? Why or why not?

4. Do you think that Kahlo's art expresses the notion that females are superior to males? That males are superior to females? Neither? Discuss.

5. In the film, Rivera says the following about Kahlo's painting: "Her work is acid and tender, hard as steel, fine as a butterfly's wing, lovable as a smile, cruel as the bitterness of life. I don't think that ever before has a woman put such agonizing poetry on canvas." Do you agree with him?

6. Oscar Wilde says that "art never expresses anything but itself." Is this true of the art of Frida Kahlo? Why or why not?

7. Do you think that Tolstoy would find Kahlo's art to be true art or false art? Real art or counterfeit art? Defend your view.

WILLIAM GASS

ON THE DISTANCE BETWEEN MORALITY AND ART

William Gass argues that artists are obligated only to create artworks that have *artistic* value and are not obligated to create artworks that have *moral* value. Unlike Plato and Tolstoy, who aim to link artistic value (Beauty) with moral value (Goodness), Gass aims to separate them.

Gass discusses five values "which men prize": Truth, Goodness, Beauty, Happiness, and Salvation. He also outlines four customary approaches to describing the interrelationship of these values. The first approach denies the objective existence of a particular value group (for example, some philosophers deny the existence of objective truth); the second reduces some or all values to others (for example, some argue that "Beauty is Truth"); the third makes some values more important than others (for example, Goodness is more important than Beauty); and the fourth says that each of these values is equal and is independent of the others. Gass advocates the fourth relationship between values.

Gass's belief in the independence and equality of these values is the foundation of his claim that "Goodness knows nothing of Beauty." Acts of moral value such as saving a baby from drowning are categorically different from acts of aesthetic value such as saving a beautiful painting from destruction. Thus, for Gass, when the conflict between art and morality is presented as akin to the conflict between saving a priceless painting from irreparable water damage and saving a baby from drowning, a false dilemma has been presented. For Gass, such false dilemmas are one way for moralists "to bully and beat up on artists." A choice between a baby's life and a painting's safety is not a decision between "two different actions but between two different objects." While this dilemma can be used by moralists to reveal the relative difference in importance between goodness and beauty—saving a baby's life is always of categorically higher importance than saving the painting—it does not give us much insight into the relationship between art and morality.

"Goodness knows nothing of beauty," says Gass. "Throughout history, goodness has done more harm than good, and over the years moralists have managed to give morality a thoroughly bad name." Censorship that uses moral value instead of aesthetic value is wrongheaded and can do harm to both art and morality. While Gass believes "writing a book is a very important moral act" for the writer, the values pursued in the writing itself need necessarily only be artistic. Writes Gass, "If the relation of morality to art were based simply on the demand that art be concerned with values, then almost every author should satisfy it." Finally, while artists should live in the present and be aware of, for example, the scientific, political, and religious values that they are not pursuing through or in their art, they should also recognize that pursuing these values in their art may be a way of masking their "failure as an artist."

William Gass (1924–), an American fiction writer, critic, and philosopher, is noted for his stylistically innovative and linguistically complex fictions. He was born in Fargo, North Dakota, and served as an ensign in the navy during World War II. He received his B.A. from Kenyon College (1947) and his Ph.D. from Cornell University (1954) with a dissertation titled "A Philosophical Investigation of Metaphor." He is currently David May Distinguished Professor Emeritus in Humanities at Washington University in St. Louis, where he has taught since 1969. His books include *Omensetter's Luck* (1966), *In the Heart of the Heart of the Country* (1968), *Willie Master's Lonesome Wife* (1971), *On Being Blue* (1976), *World Within the Word* (1978), *Habitations of the Word* (1985), *The Tunnel* (1995), *Finding a Form* (1996), *Cartesian Sonata and Other Novellas* (1998), *Reading Rilke: Reflections on Problems of Translation* (1999), and *Tests of Time* (2003). The following essay first appeared in *Harper's* in 1987.

We are to imagine a terrible storm like that which opens Verdi's *Otello*. The pavement of the *piazzetta* is awash. St. Mark's pigeons are flying about looking for land. The Venetian sun has gone down like a gondola in the lagoon. As we wade along in the dying light, a baby in a basket passes. It is being swept out to sea with the rest of the city's garbage. So is a large painting, beautifully framed, which floats its grand nude by us as if she were swimming. Then the question comes, bobbing like a bit of flotsam itself: Which one should we save,

the tiny tot or the Tintoretto? the kid in the crib or the Canaletto?

It may be that during two thousand or more years of monsoons, tidal waves, and high water, this choice has not once actually presented itself, yet, undismayed, it is in this form that philosophers frequently represent the conflict between art and morality—a conflict, of course, they made up in the first place. Baby or Botticelli. What'll you have?

Not only is the dilemma an unlikely one; the choice it offers is peculiar. We are being asked to decide not between two different actions but between two different objects. And how different indeed these floating objects are. The baby is a vessel of human consciousness, if its basket isn't. It is nearly pure potentiality. It must be any babe—no one babe but babe in general, babe in bulk—whose bunk is boating by. Never mind if it was born with the brain of an accountant, inflicted with a cleft palate, or given Mozartian talents: these are clearly irrelevant considerations, as are ones concerning the seaworthiness of the basket, or the prospect of more rain. One fist in this fight swings from the arm of an open future against the chest of a completed past. . . .

. . . A completed past because we have to know the pedigree of the painting or it's no contest. If it is the rosy nude who used to recline behind the bar in Harry's, or just another mislaid entrant in the latest Biennale, then the conditions of the case are fatally altered and there is no real conflict of interest, though the blank space behind the bar at Harry's will surely fill us with genuine sorrow each scotch-and-water hour. It is not between infant and image, then, that we are being asked to choose, but between some fully realized aesthetic quality and a vaguely generalized human nature, even though it is a specific baby who could drown.

It is the moralists, of course, who like to imagine these lunatic choices. It is the moralists who want to bully and beat up on the artists, not the other way around. The error of the artists is indifference. Not since Plato's day, when the politicians in their grab for public power defeated the priests, the poets, and the philosophers, have artists, except for an occasional Bronx cheer, molested a moralist. Authors do not gather to burn good deeds in public squares; laws are not passed by poets to put lying priests behind bars, nor do they usually suggest that the pursuit of goodness will lead you away from both beauty and truth, that it is the uphill road to ruin. Musicians do not hang moralizing lackeys from lampposts as though they were stringing their fiddles; moralizing lackeys do that.

On the other hand . . . We know what the other hand is full of: slings and arrows, slanders and censorship, prisons, scaffolds, burnings and beatings. To what stake has Savonarola's* piety been bound by the painters he disgraced? Throughout history, goodness has done more harm than good, and over the years moralists have managed to give morality a thoroughly bad name. Although lots of bad names have been loaned them by the poets, if the poets roast, they roast no one on the coals, while moralists, to their reward, have dispatched who knows how many thousands of souls.

The values which men prize have been variously classified. There may be said to be crudely, five kinds. There are first of all those facts and theories we are inclined to call true, and which, we think, constitute our knowledge. Philosophy, history, science, presumably pursue them. Second, there are the values of duty and obligation—obedience and loyalty, righteousness and virtue—qualities which the state finds particularly desirable. Appreciative values of all kinds may be listed third, including the beauties of women, art, and nature, the various sublimes, and that pleasure which comes from the pure exercise of human faculties and skills. Fourth are the values of self-realization and its attendant pleasures—growth, well-being, and the like—frequently called happiness in deference to Aristotle. Finally, there are those which have to do with real or imagined redemption, with ultimate justice and immortality. Some would prefer to separate political values like justice or freedom from more narrowly moral ones, while others would do the same for social values like comfort, stability, security, conditions often labeled simply "peace." But a complete and accurate classification, assuming it could be accomplished, is not important here. Roughly, we might call our goals, as tradition has, Truth, Goodness, Beauty, Happiness, and Salvation. (We can reach port, sometimes, even with a bad map.)

If we allow our classificatory impulse to run on a little longer, it will encourage us to list at least

---

*Girolamo Savonarola (1452–98), a Dominican priest, became ruler of Florence in 1494 after the overthrow of the Medici family. He set up a "Christian and religious Republic" in Florence and was responsible for the famous "Bonfire of the Vanities" of 1497, a public burning of items associated with moral laxness. Florence soon revolted against him, and he was excommunicated by Pope Alexander VI in 1497. The next year, he was hanged and burned. —Ed.

four customary attitudes which can be taken toward the relationship of these value areas to one another. First, one can deny the legitimacy or reality of a particular value group. Reckless pragmatists and some sophists deny the objective existence of all values except utility, while positivists prefer to elevate empirical truth (which they don't capitalize, only underscore) to that eminence. It is, of course, truth thinned to the thickness of a wire, which is fine if you want to cut cheese. The values which remain are rejected as attitudes, moods, or emotions—subjective states of various sorts like wishing, hoping, willing, which suggest external objects without being able to establish them. I happen to regard salvation values as illusory or mythological, since I deny any significance to the assumptions on which they are grounded, but other people may pick out different victims.

Second, we might accept the values of a certain sphere as real enough but argue that some or all of them are reducible to others, even eventually, to one. Reductionism is characteristic of Plato's famous argument that virtue is knowledge; of Keats's* fatuous little motto, Beauty Is Truth; of materialists and idealists equally. Rather than reduce moral values to those of happiness, Aristotle simply ignored them.

Third, we can try to make some values subordinate to others. This is not the same as reduction. One might argue that artistic and moral values are mutually exclusive, or unique, and yet support the superiority of one over the other. There are, however, two kinds of subordination. One asserts that X is more important than Y, so that when one has to choose between them (baby or Botticelli), one must always choose the baby. When designing buildings, for instance, beauty regularly runs afoul of function and economy. The other sort or subordination insists not only that X is more important, or "higher" in value, than Y, but that Y should serve or be a means to X: the baby is a model for the baby in the Botticelli. The slogan Form Follows Function is sometimes so understood. I take crude Marxism to require this kind of sacrifice from the artist.

Fourth, it is possible to argue, as I do, that these various value areas are significantly different. They are not only different; they are not reducible, but are independent of one another. Furthermore, no one value area is more important, abstractly considered, than any other. In short, these various values are different, independent, and equal.

This does not imply that in particular instances one would not choose one over the other and have good reasons for doing so; it is simply that what is chosen in any instance cannot be dictated in advance. Obviously, if one is starving, whether one's eventual food is served with grace and eaten with manners is less than essential. Should you skip dinner or lick the spilled beans from the floor? Should you choose to safeguard a painting or the well-being of its model? Should you bomb Monte Cassino?

That attachment to human life which demands that it be chosen over everything else is mostly humbug. It can be reasonably, if not decisively, argued that the world is already suffering from a surfeit of such animals; that most human beings rarely deserve the esteem some philosophers have for them; that historically humans have treated their pets better than they have treated one another; that no one is so essential he or she cannot be replaced a thousand times over; that death is inevitable anyhow; that it is our sense of community and our own identity which lead us to persist in our parochial overestimation; that it is rather a wish of philosophers than a fact that man be more important than anything else that's mortal, since nature remains mum and scarcely supports the idea, nor do the actions of man himself. Man makes a worse God than God, and when God was alive, he knew it.

Baby or Botticelli is a clear enough if artificial choice, but it places the problem entirely in the moral sphere, where the differences involved can be conveniently overlooked. What differences?

The writing of a book (the painting of a painting, the creation of a score) is generally such an exacting and total process that it is not simply O.K. if it has many motives, it is essential. The

---

*John Keats (1795–1821) was one of the major English Romantic poets. Most of his greatest poetry was written in 1819, including "Lamia," "The Eve of St. Agnes," "Ode on a Grecian Urn," "Ode to a Nightingale," and "Hyperion." Keats developed a poetic theory in his letters to friends and family. —Ed.

difference between one of Flaubert's* broken amatory promises to Louise Colet and his writing of *Madame Bovary* (both considered immoral acts in some circles) is greater even than Lenin's willingness to board a train and his intended overthrow of the czar. Most promises are kept by actions each one of which fall into a simple series; that is, I meet you at the Golden Toad by getting up from my desk, putting on my coat, and getting into my car: a set of actions each one of which can be serially performed and readily seen as part of "going to lunch." I may have many reasons for keeping our date, but having promised becomes the moral one.

However, when I create a work of art, I have entered into no contract of any kind with the public, unless the work has been commissioned. In this sense, most aesthetic acts are unbidden, uncalled-for, even unexpected. They are gratuitous. And unlike Lenin's** intention to overthrow an empire (which can scarcely be an intention of the same kind as my meeting you for lunch, involving, as it does, several years, thousands of folks, and millions of dollars), my writing will, all along, be mine alone, and I will not normally parcel out the adjectives to subordinates and the sex scenes to specialists, or contract the punctuation.

I have many reasons for going to the Golden Toad, then: I am hungry; you are pretty; we have business; I need a change from the atmosphere of the office; you are paying, and I am broke—oh yes . . . and I promised. All these interests are easily satisfied by our having lunch. There is no need to order them; they are not unruly or at odds.

So why am I writing this book? Why to make money, to become famous, to earn the love of many women, to alter the world's perception of itself, to put my rivals' noses out of joint, to satisfy my narcissism, to display my talents, to justify my existence to my deceased father, to avoid cleaning the house; but if I wish to make money I shall have to write trash, and if I wish to be famous, I had better hit home runs, and if I wish to earn the love of many women, I shall have more luck going to work in a bank. In short, these intentions do conflict; they must be ordered; none of them is particularly "good" in the goodie sense; and none is aesthetic in any way.

But there, is so much energy in the baser motives, and so little in the grander, that I need hate's heat to warm my art, I must have my malice to keep me going. For I must go, and go on, regardless. For making a work of art (writing a book, being Botticelli) requires an extended kind of action, an ordered group of actions. Yet these actions are not the sort which result, like a battle, in many effects, helter-skelter: in broken bodies, fugitive glories, lasting pains, conquered territories, power, ruins, ill will; rather as a funnel forms the sand and sends it all in the same direction, the many acts of the artist aim at one end, one result.

We are fully aware, of course, that while I am meeting you for lunch, admiring your bodice, buying office equipment, I am not doing the laundry, keeping the books, dieting, or being faithful in my heart; and when I am painting, writing, singing scales, I am not cooking, cleaning house, fixing flats. So the hours, the days, the years of commitment to my work must necessarily withdraw me from other things, from my duties as a husband, a soldier, a citizen.

So the actions of the artist include both what he does and, therefore, what he doesn't do; what he does directly and on purpose, and what he does incidentally and quite by the way. In addition, there are things done, or not done, or done incidentally, which are quite essential to the completion and character of the work, but whose effects do not show themselves in the ultimate object or performance. As necessary as any other

*Gustave Flaubert (1821–80) was a French realist novelist. His major novel, *Madame Bovary* (1857), which took him five years to write and caused quite a scandal, deals realistically with adultery. He was brought to trial in 1857 for the novel but escaped conviction. His other works include *Salammbô* (1862), *A Sentimental Education* (1869), *The Temptation of Saint Anthony* (1874), *Bouvard et Pécuchet* (1881), and *Three Tales* (1877). —Ed.
**Vladimir Ilyich Lenin (1870–1924), a Russian Marxist, was a revolutionary and the leader of the Bolshevik Party. He was imprisoned for revolutionary activity in 1895 and exiled to Siberia in 1897. Though his official exile ended in 1900, he still spent most of his time from 1900 to 1917 living in self-imposed exile. He became the first premier of the Soviet Union in 1917, a position he held until his death in 1924. Lenin sought to adapt Marx's philosophy to "the age of imperialism." His writings include *What Is to Be Done?* (1903), *Materialism and Emperio-Criticism* (1909), *Imperialism* (1916), and *State and Revolution* (1917). —Ed.

element, they disappear in the conclusion like a middle term in an argument. A deleted scene, for instance, may nevertheless lead to the final one. Every line is therefore many lines: words rubbed out, thoughts turned aside, concepts canceled. The eventual sentence seems to lie there quietly, "kill the king," with no one knowing that it once read, "kiss the king," and before that, "kiss the queen." For moralists, only too often, writing a book is little different than robbing a bank, but actions of the latter sort are not readily subject to revisions.

The writer forms words on a page. This defaces the page, of course, and in this sense it is like throwing a brick through a window; but it is not like throwing a brick through a window in any other way. And if writing is an immense ruckus made of many minor noises, some shutting down as soon as they are voiced, reading is similarly a series of acts, better ordered than many, to be sure, but just as privately performed, and also open to choice, which may have many motives too, the way the writing had. Paintings and performances (buildings even more so) are public in a fashion that reading and writing never are, although the moralist likes to make lump sums of everything and look at each art as if it were nothing but a billboard or a sound truck in the street.

If we rather tepidly observe that a building stands on its street quite differently than a book in its rack, must we not also notice how infrequently architects are jailed for committing spatial hanky-panky or putting up obscene facades? Composers may have their compositions hooted from the hall, an outraged patron may assault a nude, a church burned to get at the God believed to be inside, but more often than not it is the littérateur who is shot or sent to Siberia. Moralists are not especially sensitive to form. It is the message that turns their noses blue. It is the message they will murder you for. And messages which are passed as secretly as books pass, from privacy to privacy, make them intensely suspicious. Yet work which refuses such interpretations will not be pardoned either. Music which is twelve-toned, paintings which are abstract, writing which seems indifferent to its referents in the world—these attacks on messages themselves—they really raise the watchdog's hackles.

In life, values do not sit in separate tents like harem wives; they mix and mingle rather like sunlight in a room, or pollution in the air. A dinner party, for example, will affect the diners' waists, delight or dismay their palates, put a piece of change in the grocer's pocket, bring a gleam to the vintner's eye. The guests may be entertained or stupefied by gossip, chat, debate, wit. I may lose a chance to make out, or happily see my seduction advance past hunt and peck. The host may get a leg up in the firm whose boss he's entertaining, serious arguments may break out, new acquaintances may be warmly made. And if I, Rabbi Ben Ezra, find myself seated next to Hermann Goering,* it may put me quite off the quail—quail which the *Reichsminister* shot by machine gun from a plane. We should all be able to understand that. It would be a serious misjudgment, however, if I imagined that the quail was badly cooked on account of who shot it, or to believe that the field marshal's presence had soured the wine, although it may have ruined the taste in my mouth. It might be appropriate to complain of one who enjoyed the meal and laughed at the fat boy's jokes. Nevertheless, the meal will be well prepared or not quite independently of the guests' delightful or obnoxious presence, and it would be simple-minded to imagine that because these values were realized in such close proximity they therefore should be judged on other than their own terms—the terms, perhaps, of their pushier neighbors.

The detachment it is sometimes necessary to exercise in order to disentangle aesthetic qualities from others is often resented. It is frequently considered a good thing if moral outrage makes imbeciles of us. The aesthete who sees only the poppies blowing in Flanders fields is a sad joke, to be sure, but the politicized mind is too dense and too dangerous to be funny.

I have been mentioning some differences between moral acts as they are normally under-stood (keeping promises, saving the baby) and what might be called artistic ones (dancing the

---

* Hermann Wilhelm Goering (1893–1946) was one of the leaders in Nazi Germany and founder of the Gestapo. He was convicted of war crimes and crimes against humanity in the Nuremberg Trials (1945–46) and sentenced to death, which he avoided by committing suicide hours before his scheduled execution. —Ed.

fandango, painting the Botticelli), and I have been drawing our attention to the public and private qualities of the several arts lest they be treated en bloc. Finally, I have suggested that values have to be judged by sharply different standards sometimes, though they come to the same table. However, my dinner party differs from Petronius' banquet in another essential: it is "thrown" only once. Even if the evening is repeated down to the last guest's happy gurgle, the initial party can be only vaguely imitated, since you can't swallow the same soup twice (as a famous philosopher is supposed to have said). The events of my party were like pebbles tossed into a pond. The stones appear to shower the surface of the water with rings, which then augment or interfere with one another as they widen, although eventually they will enlarge into thin air, the pond will become calm, and the stones effects negligible.

Art operates at another level altogether. Petronius's story does not fling itself like a handful of stones at the public and then retire to contemplate the recession of its consequences, but occurs continually as readers reenact it. Of course these readings will not be identical (because no reading is written or a part of the text), but the text, unless it has been mutilated or reedited, will remain the same. I shall recognize each line as the line I knew, and each word as the word that was. The letter abides and is literal, though the spirit moves and strays. In short, the mouth may have an altered taste, but not the soup.

For this reason the powers of events are known to be brief, even when loud and unsettling, and unless they can reach the higher levels of historical accounts—unless they can reach language—the events will be forgotten and their effects erased. Accounts, too, can be lost or neglected, so those texts which are truly strong are those whose qualities earn the love and loyalty of their readers, and enlist the support and stewardship of the organizations those readers are concerned with and control (schools, societies, academies, museums, archives), because the institutions encourage us to turn to these now canonical texts again and again, where their words will burn in each fresh consciousness as if they had just been lit.

Moralists are right to worry about works of art, then, because they belong to a higher level of reality than most things. Texts can be repeated;

texts can be multiplied; texts can be preserved; texts beget commentaries, and their authors energize biographers; texts get quoted, praised, reviled, memorized; texts become sacred.

The effect of a text (as every failed commission on pornography has demonstrated) cannot be measured as you measure blows; the spread of a text cannot be followed like the course of an epidemic; there is no dye which can be spilled upon the ground to track the subtle seepages of its contamination. Texts are not acts of bodies but acts of minds; for the most part, then, they do not act on bodies as bodies act, but on minds as minds do.

So my position is not that literature has no relation to morality, or that reading, and writing, or composing, or painting, aren't also moral, or possibly immoral, acts. Of course they can be. But they are economic acts as well. (They contribute to their author's health or illness, happiness or melancholy.) My position, however, is that the artistic value of a book is different from its economic value, and is differently determined, as is its weight in pounds, its utility as a doorstop, its elevating or edifying or life-enhancing properties, its gallery of truths: new truths, known truths, believed truths, important truths, alleged truths, trivial truths, absolute truths, coming truths, plain unvarnished truths. Artistic quality depends upon a work's internal formal, organic character, upon its inner system of relations, upon its structure and its style, and not upon the morality it is presumed to recommend, or upon the benevolence of its author, or its emblematic character, when it is seen as especially representative of some situation or society.

As I have already suggested, values may reinforce one another, or interfere with their realization in some thing or person. The proximity of Herr Goering may put me off my feed. Perhaps I ought to be put off. Perhaps the chef should have poisoned the quail. Perhaps all of the guests should have left in a huff. And the housemaid and the butler grin as they quaff champagne in the kitchen, grin so little bones appear between their open teeth. How's the pâté no one would eat? Deelish.

Wagner's works are not wicked simply because he was; nor does even the inherent vulgarity deep within the music quite destroy it. Frost's poetry seems written by a better man than we've been told he was. In fact, we are frequently surprised when an author of genius (like Chekhov) appears to be a person of some decency of spirit. The moral points of view in works of art differ as enormously as Dante's do from Sophocles,' or Shakespeare's from Milton's. Simply consider what we should have to say if the merit of these writers depended at all upon their being correct, even about anything. In any case, Balzac sees the world quite differently than Butor does; Goethe and Milton cannot both be right; so if being right mattered, we should be in a mess indeed, and most of our classics headed for the midden.

If author and art ought not to be confused, neither should art and audience. If we were to say, as I should prefer, that it is the moral world of the work which ought to matter to the moralist, not the genes of the author's grandfather, or the Jean who was a longtime lover, or a lean of the penholder toward the political right or left, we ought also to insist that the reactions of readers aren't adequate evidence either. If Wagner's anti-Semitism doesn't fatally bleed into his operas, and, like a bruise, discolor them, and if Balzac's insufferable bourgeois dreams don't irreparably damage his fictions, then why should we suppose the work itself, in so much less command of its readers than its author is of it, will communicate its immoral implications like a virus to the innocents who open its covers?

To be sure, authors often like to think of their works as explosive, as corrupting, as evil. It is such fun to play the small boy. Lautréamont asks Heaven to "grant the reader the boldness to become ferocious, momentarily, like what he is reading, to find, without being disoriented, his abrupt and savage path through the desolate swamps of these somber and poison-filled pages." Yet this is an operatic attitude; reading is never more than reading, and requires a wakeful understanding—that is all. Certainly we should like to think that we had written some "poison-filled" pages, but no luck. Even chewing them won't make you sick, not even queasy.

If the relation of morality to art were based simply on the demand that art be concerned with values, then almost every author should satisfy it even if they wrote with their pricks in their sleep. (Puritans will object to the language in that

sentence, and feminists to the organ, and neither will admire or even notice how it was phrased.) Henry Miller's work has been condemned, but Henry Miller is obsessed with ethical issues, and his work has a very pronounced moral point of view. *Madame Bovary* was attacked; *Ulysses* was forbidden entry into the United States; *Lady Chatterley's Lover* was brought to court, where they worried about signs of sodomy in it; *Lolita*, of course, was condemned; and, as someone has said, who also has suffered such censorship, so it goes. How long the list would be, how tiresome and dismaying and absurd its recital, if we were to cite every work that has been banned, burned, or brought into the dock.

It is simply not possible to avoid ethical concerns; they are everywhere; one is scarcely able to move without violating someone's moral law. Nor are artists free of the desire to improve and instruct and chastise and bemoan their fellow creatures, whether they call themselves Dickens, D. H. Lawrence, or Hector Berlioz. Céline is so intensely a moral writer that it warps his work. That is the worry. "There are still a few hatreds I'm missing," he wrote. "I am sure they exist." Hate, we mustn't forget, is a thoroughly moralized feeling.

It is the management of all these impulses, attitudes, ideas, and emotions (which the artist has as much as anyone) that is the real problem, for each of us is asked by our aims, as well as by our opportunities, to overcome our past, our personal aches and pains, our beloved prejudices, and to enlist them in the service of our skills, the art we say we're loyal to and live for. If a writer is in a rage, the rage must be made to energize the form, and if the writer is extended on the rack of love, let pain give the work purpose and disappointment its burnished point. So the artistic temperament is called cold because its grief becomes song instead of wailing. To be a preacher is to bring your sense of sin to the front of the church, but to be an artist is to give to every mean and ardent, petty and profound, feature of the soul a glorious godlike shape.

It is actually not the absence of the ethical that is complained of, when complaints are made, for the ethical is never absent. It is the absence of the right belief, the *right* act, which riles. Our pets have not been fed; repulsive enthusiasms have been encouraged; false gods pursued; obnoxious notions noised about; so damn these blank and wavy paintings and these hostile drums, these sentences which sound like one long scratch of chalk.

Goodness knows nothing of Beauty. They are quite disconnected. If I say *shit* in a sentence, it is irrelevant what else I say, whether it helps my sentence sing or not. What is relevant is the power of certain principles of decorum, how free to be offensive we are going to be allowed to be. When the Empress Dowager of China, Ci Xi, diverted funds intended for the navy to construct a large and beautiful marble boat, which thousands now visit at the Summer Palace in Beijing, she was guilty of expropriation. If her choice had been a free one, she would seem to have chosen to spend her money on a thing of peace rather than on things of war (a choice we might applaud); in fact, we know she simply spent the money on herself. She cannot have chosen the beauty she received because beauty is beyond choice. The elegant workmanship which went into the boat, the pleasure it has given to many, its rich and marvelous material, are serendipitous, and do not affect the morality of the case.

When a government bans nonobjective art, it is the threat of the very look it has, its veer from the upright, its deviationism, that is feared—a daub is just as dangerous. Finally, when the Soviet authorities decide to loosen their restrictions on the publication of books and the holding of performances, this is not suddenly a choice of art over politics on their part; it is politics, and has to do with issues such as the freedom of information, the quashing of the Stalin cults, not with art. They know what the novels in the drawers are about.

I do happen to feel, with Theodor Adorno, that writing a book is a very important moral act indeed, consuming so much of one's life, and that, in these disgusting times, a writer who does not pursue an alienating formalism, but rather tries to buck us up and tell us not to spit in the face of the present, thus to serve a corrupt and debauched society in any way, is, if not a pawn of the system (a lackey, we used to say), then probably a liar and a hypocrite. It is a moral obligation to live in one's time, and to have a just and appropriate attitude toward it, not to live in the nineteenth century or to be heartless toward the less fortunate or to deny liberty and opportunity to others or to fall victim to nostalgia.

But good books have been written by bad people, by people who served immoral systems, who went to bed with snakes, by people who were frauds in various ways, by schemers and panderers. And beautiful books have been written by the fat and old and ugly, the lonely, the misbegotten (it is the same in all the arts), and some of these beautiful books are like Juan Goytisolo's, ferociously angry, and some of them are even somewhat sinister like Baudelaire's, and some are shakingly sensuous like those of Colette, and still others are dismayingly wise, or deal with terror tenderly, or are full of lamentable poppycock. (I am thinking most immediately of Pope's *Essay on Man*.)

I think it is one of the artist's obligations to create as perfectly as he or she can, not regardless of all other consequences, but in full awareness, nevertheless, that in pursuing other values—in championing Israel or fighting for women or defending the faith or exposing capitalism or speaking for your race—you may simply be putting a saving scientific, religious, political false face on your failure as an artist. Neither the world's truth nor a god's goodness will win you that race.

Finally, in a world which does not provide beauty for its own sake, but where the loveliness of flowers, landscapes, faces, trees, and sky are adventitious and accidental, it is the artist's task to add to the world objects and ideas—delineations, symphonies—which ought to be there, and whose end is contemplation and appreciation; things which deserve to become the focus of a truly disinterested affection.

There is perhaps a moral in that.

DISCUSSION QUESTIONS

1. Gass discusses five values "which men prize": Truth, Goodness, Beauty, Happiness, and Salvation. Are there any others? Discuss.

2. Discuss the four customary approaches to the relationship between values. Do you agree with Gass's designation of the independence-and-equality approach as the superior approach? Why or why not?

3. Artists are often accused of promoting bad religious or scientific values in their art.

Should they be held accountable for these nonartistic values? For example, should Salman Rushdie be held accountable for the religious values that his novel *The Satanic Verses* promotes? Or should he be held accountable only for the novel's artistic value?

4. Gass argues that "Goodness knows nothing of beauty." Construct and analyze his argument. How might Plato, Tolstoy, and Wilde reply to Gass's argument?

5. Discuss the conflict between saving a priceless painting from irreparable water damage and saving a baby from drowning. Does this "thought experiment" provide any insight into the relationship between morality (Goodness) and art (Beauty)? Why or why not?

4.4   WHAT IS THE NATURE AND VALUE OF PHOTOGRAPHY AND CINEMA?

WALTER BENJAMIN

THE WORK OF ART IN THE AGE OF MECHANICAL REPRODUCTION

Walter Benjamin argues that the technical reproducibility of photography and film destroys the aura and authenticity of artworks. He notes that while it has always been possible in principle to reproduce a work of art, the age of the mechanical reproduction of artworks "represents something new." The advent of lithography at the beginning of the nineteenth century, followed only a few decades later by photography, allowed for the reproduction of works of art. According to Benjamin, this technological advance resulted in "the most profound change" in the impact of artworks upon the public—the loss of authenticity.

For Benjamin, "Even the most perfect reproduction of a work of art is lacking in one element: its presence in time and space, its unique existence at the place where it happens to be," says Benjamin. "The presence of the original is the prerequisite to the concept of authenticity." He contends that not only are mechanically reproduced works of art more independent of the original work than are manually reproduced works, but "technical reproduction can put the copy of the original into situations which would be out of reach of the original itself." Reproduction detaches artworks from "the domain of tradition" and destroys their "aura." Once the work of art is detached from its aura, and its traditional and ritualistic significance, it can take on a significance unconnected to them. It then risks being attributed with political significance, which in the hands of repressive governments is particularly dangerous.

The technical reproduction of artworks marks a decided shift from an older aesthetic marked by authenticity and the presence of the original to a new aesthetic of "reproductibility" and disconnection from the original. Benjamin writes, "For the first time in world history, mechanical reproduction emancipates the work of art from its parasitical dependence on ritual," and "the work of art reproduced becomes the work of art designed for reproducibility." For Benjamin, film signals the greatest break from the older aesthetic of presence and authenticity: "For the first time—and this is the effect of the film—man has to operate with his whole living person, yet foregoing its aura." "For aura is tied to presence," continues Benjamin, "there can be no replica of it."

Walter Benjamin (1892–1940) was a German philosopher, cultural theorist, and literary critic. Benjamin was born in Berlin, and his father was an art dealer. His doctoral dissertation was titled *The Concept of Art Criticism in German Romanticism* (1919). A few years later, Benjamin completed *The Origin of German Tragic Drama* (1924–25), a work that, had it been accepted by the University of Frankfurt, would have secured him a tenured university position. Instead, Benjamin made an unsteady career for himself in journalism, writing essays and reviews. He committed suicide in the early fall of 1940 at the age of forty-eight. Wide recognition of Benjamin's work came only years after his death, when his friend and disciple, the philosopher Theodor Adorno, published a selection of his work in 1955. Benjamin's thought is heavily influenced by Marxism, Jewish mysticism, and surrealism and is marked by his close personal relationships with Adorno, philosopher and historian Gershom Scholem, and playwright and poet Bertolt Brecht. His writings include *Illuminations* (1968), *Charles Baudelaire: A Lyric Poet in the Era of High Capitalism* (1969), *The Origin of German Tragic Drama* (1977), *Understanding Brecht* (1977), *Reflections* (1978), and *One-Way Street and Other Writings* (1979). The following article, "The Work of Art in the Age of Mechanical Reproducion" ("Die Kunstwerk im Zeitalter seiner technischen Reproduzierbarkeit"), was first published in *Zeitschrift für Sozialforschung* in 1936.

I

In principle a work of art has always been reproducible. Manmade artifacts could always be imitated by men. Replicas were made by pupils in practice of their craft, by masters for diffusing their works, and, finally, by third parties in the pursuit of gain. Mechanical reproduction of a work of art, however, represents something new. Historically, it advanced intermittently and in leaps at long intervals, but with accelerated intensity. The Greeks knew only two procedures of technically reproducing works of art: founding and stamping. Bronzes, terra cottas, and coins were the only art works which they could produce in quantity. All others were unique and could not be mechanically reproduced. With the woodcut graphic art became mechanically reproducible for the first time, long before script became reproducible by print. The enormous changes which printing, the mechanical reproduction of writing, has brought about in literature are a familiar story. However, within the phenomenon which we are here examining from the perspective of world history, print is merely a special, though particularly important, case. During the Middle Ages engraving and etching were added to the woodcut; at the beginning of the nineteenth century lithography made its appearance.

With lithography the technique of reproduction reached an essentially new stage. This much more direct process was distinguished by the tracing of the design on a stone rather than its incision on a block of wood or its etching on a copperplate and permitted graphic art for the first time to put its products on the market, not only in large numbers as hitherto, but also in daily changing forms. Lithography enabled graphic art to illustrate everyday life, and it began to keep pace with printing. But only a few decades after its invention, lithography was surpassed by photography. For the first time in the process of pictorial reproduction, photography freed the hand of the most important artistic functions which henceforth devolved only upon the eye looking into a lens. Since the eye perceives more swiftly than the hand can draw, the process of pictorial reproduction was accelerated so enormously that it could keep pace with speech. A film operator shooting a scene in the studio captures the images at the speed of an actor's speech. Just as lithography virtually implied the illustrated newspaper, so did photography foreshadow the sound film. The technical reproduction of sound was tackled at the end of the last century. These convergent endeavors made predictable a situation which Paul Valéry pointed up in this sentence: "Just as water, gas, and electricity are brought into our houses from far off to satisfy our needs in response to a minimal effort, so we shall be supplied with visual or auditory images, which will appear and disappear at a simple movement of the hand, hardly more than a sign." Around 1900 technical reproduction had reached a standard that not only permitted it to reproduce all transmitted works of art and thus to cause the most profound change in their impact upon the public; it also had captured a place of its own among the artistic processes. For the study of this standard nothing is more revealing than the nature of the repercussions that these two different manifestations—the reproduction of works of art and the art of the film—have had on art in its traditional form.

II

Even the most perfect reproduction of a work of art is lacking in one element: its presence in time and space, its unique existence at the place where it happens to be. This unique existence of the work of art determined the history to which it was subject throughout the time of its existence. This includes the changes which it may have suffered in physical condition over the years as well as the various changes in its ownership. The traces of the first can be revealed only by chemical or physical analyses which it is impossible to perform on a reproduction; changes of ownership are subject to a tradition which must be traced from the situation of the original.

The presence of the original is the prerequisite to the concept of authenticity. Chemical analyses of the patina of a bronze can help to establish this, as does the proof that a given manuscript of the Middle Ages stems from an archive of the fifteenth century. The whole sphere of authenticity is outside technical—and, of course, not only technical—reproducibility. Confronted with its manual reproduction, which was usually branded as a forgery, the original preserved all its authority; not so *vis à vis* technical reproduction. The reason is twofold. First, process reproduction is more independent of the original than manual reproduction. For example, in photography, process reproduction can bring out those aspects of the original that are unattainable to the naked eye yet accessible to the lens, which is adjustable

and chooses its angle at will. And photographic reproduction, with the aid of certain processes, such as enlargement or slow motion, can capture images which escape natural vision. Secondly, technical reproduction can put the copy of the original into situations which would be out of reach for the original itself. Above all, it enables the original to meet the beholder halfway, be it in the form of a photograph or a phonograph record. The cathedral leaves its locale to be received in the studio of a lover of art; the choral production, performed in an auditorium or in the open air, resounds in the drawing room.

The situations into which the product of mechanical reproduction can be brought may not touch the actual work of art, yet the quality of its presence is always depreciated. This holds not only for the art work but also, for instance, for a landscape which passes in review before the spectator in a movie. In the case of the art object, a most sensitive nucleus—namely, its authenticity—is interfered with whereas no natural object is vulnerable on that score. The authenticity of a thing is the essence of all that is transmissible from its beginning, ranging from its substantive duration to its testimony to the history which it has experienced. Since the historical testimony rests on the authenticity, the former, too, is jeopardized by reproduction when substantive duration ceases to matter. And what is really jeopardized when the historical testimony is affected is the authority of the object.

One might subsume the eliminated element in the term "aura" and go on to say: that which withers in the age of mechanical reproduction is the aura of the work of art. This is a symptomatic process whose significance points beyond the realm of art. One might generalize by saying: the technique of reproduction detaches the reproduced object from the domain of tradition. By making many reproductions it substitutes a plurality of copies for a unique existence. And in permitting the reproduction to meet the beholder or listener in his own particular situation, it reactivates the object reproduced. These two processes lead to a tremendous shattering of tradition which is the obverse of the contemporary crisis and renewal of mankind. Both processes are intimately connected with the contemporary mass movements. Their most powerful agent is the film. Its social significance, particularly in its most positive form, is inconceivable without its destructive, cathartic aspect, that is, the liquidation of the traditional value of the cultural heritage. This phenomenon is most palpable in the great historical films. It extends to ever new positions. In 1927 Abel Gance exclaimed enthusiastically: "Shakespeare, Rembrandt, Beethoven will make films . . . all legends, all mythologies and all myths, all founders of religion, and the very religions . . . await their exposed resurrection, and the heroes crowd each other at the gate." Presumably without intending it, he issued an invitation to a far-reaching liquidation.

III

During long periods of history, the mode of human sense perception changes with humanity's entire mode of existence. The manner in which human sense perception is organized, the medium in which it is accomplished, is determined not only by nature but by historical circumstances as well. The fifth century, with its great shifts of population, saw the birth of the late Roman art industry and the Vienna Genesis, and there developed not only an art different from that of antiquity but also a new kind of perception. The scholars of the Viennese school, Riegl and Wickhoff, who resisted the weight of classical tradition under which these later art forms had been buried, were the first to draw conclusions from them concerning the organization of perception at the time. However far-reaching their insight, these scholars limited themselves to showing the significant, formal hallmark which characterized perception in late Roman times. They did not attempt—and, perhaps, saw no way—to show the social transformations expressed by these changes of perception. The conditions for an analogous insight are more favorable in the present. And if changes in the medium of contemporary perception can be comprehended as decay of the aura, it is possible to show its social causes.

The concept of aura which was proposed above with reference to historical objects may usefully be illustrated with reference to the aura of natural ones. We define the aura of the latter as the unique phenomenon of a distance, however close it may be. If, while resting on a summer afternoon, you follow with your eyes a mountain range on the horizon or a branch which casts its shadow over you, you experience the aura of those mountains, of that branch. This image makes it easy to comprehend the social bases of the contemporary decay of the aura. It rests on two circumstances, both of which are related to the increasing significance of the masses in contemporary life. Namely, the desire of contemporary masses to bring things "closer" spatially and humanly, which is just as ardent as their bent toward overcoming the uniqueness of every reality by accepting its reproduction. Every day the urge grows stronger to get hold of an object at very close range by way of its likeness, its reproduction. Unmistakably, reproduction as offered by picture magazines and newsreels differs from the image seen by the unarmed eye. Uniqueness and permanence are as closely linked in the latter as are transitoriness and reproducibility in the former. To pry an object from its shell, to destroy its aura, is the mark of a perception whose "sense of the universal equality of things" has increased to such a degree that it extracts it even from a unique object by means of reproduction. Thus is manifested in the field of perception what in the theoretical sphere is noticeable in the increasing importance of statistics. The adjustment of reality to the masses and of the masses to reality is a process of unlimited scope, as such for thinking as for perception.

IV

The uniqueness of a work of art is inseparable from its being imbedded in the fabric of tradition. This tradition itself is thoroughly alive and extremely changeable. An ancient statue of Venus, for example, stood in a different traditional context with the Greeks, who made it an object of veneration, than with the clerics of the Middle Ages, who viewed it as an ominous idol. Both of them, however, were equally confronted with its uniqueness, that is, its aura. Originally the contextual integration of art in tradition found its expression in the cult. We know that the earliest art works originated in the service of a ritual— first the magical, then the religious kind. It is significant that the existence of the work of art with reference to its aura is never entirely separated from its ritual function. In other words, the unique value of the "authentic" work of art has its basis in ritual, the location of its original use value. This ritualistic basis, however remote, is still recognizable as secularized ritual even in the most profane forms of the cult of beauty. The secular cult of beauty, developed during the Renaissance and prevailing for three centuries, clearly showed that ritualistic basis in its decline and the first deep crisis which befell it. With the advent of the first truly revolutionary means of reproduction, photography, simultaneously with the rise of socialism, art sensed the approaching crisis which has become evident a century later. At the time, art reacted with the doctrine of *l'art pour l'art,* that is, with a theology of art. This gave rise to what might be called a negative theology in the form of the idea of "pure" art, which not only denied any social function of art but also any categorizing by subject matter. (In poetry, Mallarmé was the first to take this position.)

An analysis of art in the age of mechanical reproduction must do justice to these relationships, for they lead us to an all-important insight: for the first time in world history, mechanical reproduction emancipates the work of art from its parasitical dependence on ritual. To an ever greater degree the work of art reproduced becomes the work of art designed for reproducibility. From a photographic negative, for example, one can make any number of prints; to ask for the "authentic" print makes no sense. But the instant the criterion of authenticity ceases to be applicable to artistic production, the total function of art is reversed. Instead of being based on ritual, it begins to be based on another practice—politics.

V

Works of art are received and valued on different planes. Two polar types stand out: with one, the accent is on the cult value; with the other, on the exhibition value of the work. Artistic production begins with ceremonial objects destined to serve in a cult. One may assume that what mattered was their existence, not their being on view. The elk portrayed by the man of the Stone Age on the walls of his cave was an instrument of magic. He did expose it to his fellow men, but in the main it was meant for the spirits. Today the cult value would seem to demand that the work of art remain hidden. Certain statues of gods are accessible only to the priest in the cella; certain Madonnas remain covered nearly all year round; certain sculptures on medieval cathedrals are invisible to the spectator on ground level. With the emancipation of the various art practices from ritual go increasing opportunities for the exhibition of their products. It is easier to exhibit a portrait bust that can be sent here and there than to exhibit the statue of a divinity that has its fixed place in the interior of a temple. The same holds for the painting as against the mosaic or fresco that preceded it. And even though the public presentability of a mass originally may have been just as great as that of a symphony, the latter originated at the moment when its public presentability promised to surpass that or the mass.

With the different methods of technical reproduction of a work of art, its fitness for exhibition increased to such an extent that the quantitative shift between its two poles turned into a qualitative transformation of its nature. This is comparable to the situation of the work of art in prehistoric times when, by the absolute emphasis on its cult value, it was, first and foremost, an instrument of magic. Only later did it come to be recognized as a work of art. In the same way today, by the absolute emphasis on its exhibition value the work of art becomes a creation with entirely new functions, among which the one we are conscious of, the artistic function, later may be recognized as incidental. This much is certain: today photography and the film are the most serviceable exemplifications of this new function.

VI

In photography, exhibition value begins to displace cult value all along the line. But cult value does not give way without resistance. It retires into an ultimate retrenchment: the human countenance. It is no accident that the portrait was the focal point of early photography. The cult of remembrance of loved ones, absent or dead, offers a last refuge for the cult value of the picture. For the last time the aura emanates from the early photographs in the fleeting expression of a human face. This is what constitutes their melancholy, incomparable beauty. But as man withdraws from the photographic image, the exhibition value for the first time shows its superiority to the ritual value. To have pinpointed this new stage constitutes the incomparable significance of Atget, who, around 1900, took photographs of deserted Paris streets. It has quite justly been said of him that he photographed them like scenes of crime. The scene of a crime, too, is deserted; it is photographed for the purpose of establishing evidence. With Atget, photographs become standard evidence for historical occurrences, and acquire a hidden political significance. They demand a specific kind of approach; free-floating contemplation is not appropriate to them. They stir the viewer; he feels challenged by them in a new way. At the same time picture magazines begin to put up signposts for him, right ones or wrong ones, no matter. For the first time, captions have become obligatory. And it is clear that they have an altogether different character than the title of a painting. The directives which the captions give to those looking at pictures in illustrated magazines soon become even more explicit and more imperative in the film where the meaning of each single picture appears to be prescribed by the sequence of all preceding ones.

VII

The nineteenth-century dispute as to the artistic value of painting versus photography today seems devious and confused. This does not diminish its importance, however; if anything, it underlines it. The dispute was in fact the symptom of a historical transformation the universal impact of which was not realized by either of the rivals. When the age of mechanical reproduction separated art from its basis in cult, the semblance of its autonomy disappeared forever. The resulting change in the function of art transcended the perspective of the century; for a long time it even escaped that of the twentieth century, which experienced the development of the film.

Earlier much futile thought had been devoted to the question of whether photography is an art. The primary question—whether the very invention of photography had not transformed the entire nature of art—was not raised. Soon the film theoreticians asked the same ill-considered question with regard to the film. But the difficulties which photography caused traditional aesthetics were mere child's play as compared to those raised by the film. Whence the insensitive and forced character of early theories of the film.

Abel Gance, for instance, compares the film with hieroglyphs: "Here, by a remarkable regression, we have come back to the level of expression of the Egyptians . . . Pictorial language, has not yet matured because our eyes have not yet adjusted to it. There is as yet insufficient respect for, insufficient cult of, what it expresses." Or, in the words of Séverin-Mars: "What art has been granted a dream more poetical and more real at the same time! Approached in this fashion the film might represent an incomparable means of expression. Only the most high-minded persons, in the most perfect and mysterious moments of their lives, should be allowed to enter its ambience." Alexandre Arnoux concludes his fantasy about the silent film with the question: "Do not all the bold descriptions we have given amount to the definition of prayer?" It is instructive to note how their desire to class the film among the "arts" forces these theoreticians to read ritual elements into it—with a striking lack of discretion. Yet when these speculations were published, films like *L'Opinion publique* and *The Gold Rush* had already appeared. This, however, did not keep Abel Gance from adducing hieroglyphs for purposes of comparison, nor Séverin-Mars from speaking of the film as one might speak of paintings by Fra Angelico. Characteristically, even today ultrareactionary authors give the film a similar contextual significance—if not an outright sacred one, then at least a supernatural one. Commenting on Max Reinhardt's film version of *A Midsummer Night's Dream*, Werfel states that undoubtedly it was the sterile copying of the exterior world with its streets, interiors, railroad stations, restaurants, motorcars, and beaches which until now had obstructed the elevation of the film to the realm of art. "The film has not yet realized its true meaning, its real possibilities . . . these consist in its unique faculty to express by natural means and with incomparable persuasiveness all that is fairylike, marvelous, supernatural."

VIII

The artistic performance of a stage actor is definitely presented to the public by the actor in person; that of the screen actor, however, is presented by a camera, with a twofold consequence. The camera that presents the performance of the film actor to the public need not respect the performance as an integral whole. Guided by the cameraman, the camera continually changes its position with respect to the performance. The sequence of positional views which the editor composes from the material supplied him constitutes the completed film. It comprises certain factors of movement which are in reality those of the camera, not to mention special camera angles, close-ups, etc. Hence, the performance of the actor is subjected to a series of optical tests. This is the first consequence of the fact that the actor's performance is presented by means of a camera. Also, the film actor lacks the opportunity of the stage actor to adjust to the audience during his performance, since he does not present his performance to the audience in person. This permits the audience to take the position of a critic, without experiencing any personal contact with the actor. The audience's identification with the actor is really an identification with the camera. Consequently the audience takes the position of the camera; its approach is that of testing. This is not the approach to which cult values may be exposed.

IX

For the film, what matters primarily is that the actor represents himself to the public before the camera, rather than representing someone else. One of the first to sense the actor's meta-morphosis by this form of testing was [the Italian writer Luigi] Pirandello. Though his remarks on the subject in his novel *Si Gira* were limited to the negative aspects of the question and to the silent film only, this hardly impairs their validity. For in this respect, the sound film did not change anything essential. What matters is that the part is acted not for an audience but for a mechanical contrivance—in the lease of the sound film, for two of them. "The film actor," wrote Pirandello, "feels as if in exile—exiled not only from the stage but also from himself. With a vague sense of discomfort he feels inexplicable emptiness: his body loses its corporeality, it evaporates, it is deprived of reality, life, voice, and the noises caused by his moving about, in order to be changed into a mute image, flickering an instant on the screen, then vanishing into silence. . . . The projector will play with his shadow before the

public, and he himself must be content to play before the camera." This situation might also be characterized as follows: for the first time—and this is the effect of the film—man has to operate with his whole living person, yet forgoing its aura. For aura is tied to his presence; there can be no replica of it. The aura which, on the stage, emanates from Macbeth, cannot be separated for the spectators from that of the actor. However, the singularity of the shot in the studio is that the camera is substituted for the public. Conse-quently, the aura that envelops the actor vanishes, and with it the aura of the figure he portrays.

It is not surprising that it should be a dramatist such as Pirandello who, in characterizing the film, inadvertently touches on the very crisis in which we see the theater. Any thorough study proves that there is indeed no greater contrast than that of the stage play to a work of art that is completely subject to or, like the film, founded in, mechanical reproduction. Experts have long recognized that in the film "the greatest effects are almost always obtained by 'acting' as little as possible. . . ." In 1932 Rudolf Arnheim saw "the latest trend . . . in treating the actor as a stage prop chosen for its characteristics and . . . inserted at the proper place." With this idea something else is closely connected. The stage actor identifies himself with the character of his role. The film actor very often is denied this opportunity. His creation is by no means all of a piece; it is composed of many separate performances. Besides certain fortuitous considerations, such as cost of studio, availability of fellow players, décor, etc., there are elementary necessities of equipment that split the actor's work into a series of mountable episodes. In particular, lighting and its installation require the presentation of an event that, on the screen, unfolds as a rapid arid unified scene, in a sequence of separate shootings which may take hours at the studio; not to mention more obvious montage. Thus a jump from the window can be shot in the studio as a jump from a scaffold, and the ensuing flight, if need be, can be shot weeks later when outdoor scenes are taken. Far more paradoxical cases can easily be construed. Let us assume that an actor is supposed to be startled by a knock at the door. If his reaction is not satisfactory, the director can resort to an expedient: when the actor happens to be at the studio again he has a shot fired behind him without his being forewarned of it. The frightened reaction can be shot now and be cut into the screen version. Nothing more strikingly shows that art has left the realm of the "beautiful semblance" which, so far, had been taken to be the only sphere where art could thrive.

X

The feeling of strangeness that overcomes the actor before the camera, as Pirandello describes it, is basically of the same kind as the estrangement felt before one's own image in the mirror. But now the reflected image has become separable, transportable. And where is it transported? Before the public. Never for a moment does the screen actor cease to be conscious of this fact. While facing the camera he knows that ultimately he will face the public, the consumers who constitute the market. This market, where he offers not only his labor but also his whole self, his heart and soul, is beyond his reach. During the shooting he has as little contact with it as any article made in a factory. This may contribute to that oppression, that new anxiety which, according to Pirandello, grips the actor before the camera. The film responds to the shriveling of the aura with an artificial build-up of the "personality" outside the studio. The cult of the movie star, fostered by the money of the film industry, preserves not the unique aura of the person but the "spell of the personality," the phony spell of a commodity. So long as the movie-makers' capital sets the fashion, as a rule no other revolutionary merit can be accredited to today's film than the promotion of a revolutionary criticism of traditional concepts of art. We do not deny that in some cases today's films can also promote revolutionary criticism of social conditions, even of the distribution of property. However, our present study is no more specifically concerned with this than is the film production of Western Europe.

It is inherent in the technique of the film as well as that of sports that everybody who witnesses its accomplishments is somewhat of an expert. This is obvious to anyone listening to a group of newspaper boys leaning on their bicycles and discussing the outcome of a bicycle race. It is not for nothing that newspaper publishers arrange races for their delivery boys. These arouse great interest among the participants, for the victor has an opportunity to rise from delivery boy to professional racer. Similarly, the newsreel offers everyone the opportunity to rise from passer-by to movie extra. In this way any man might even find himself part of a work of art . . . Any man today can lay claim to being filmed. This claim can best be elucidated by a comparative look at the, historical situation of contemporary literature.

For centuries a small number of writers were confronted by many thousands of readers. This changed toward the end of the [nineteenth] century. With the increasing extension of the press, which kept placing new political, religious, scientific, professional, and local organs before the readers, an increasing number of readers became writers—at first, occasional ones. It began with the daily press opening to its readers space for "letters to the editor." And today there is hardly a gainfully employed European who could not, in principle, find an opportunity to publish somewhere or other comments on his work, grievances, documentary reports, or that sort of thing. Thus, the distinction between author and public is about to lose its basic character. The difference becomes merely functional; it may vary from case to case. At any moment the reader is ready to turn into a writer. As expert, which he had to become willy-nilly in an extremely specialized work process, even if only in some minor respect, the reader gains access to authorship. . . .

All this can easily be applied to the film, where transitions that in literature took centuries have come about in a decade. In cinematic practice, particularly in Russia, this change-over has partially become established reality. Some of the players whom we meet in Russian films are not actors in our sense but people who portray *themselves*—and primarily in their own work process. In Western Europe the capitalistic exploitation of the film denies consideration to modern man's legitimate claim to being reproduced. Under these circumstances the film industry is trying hard to spur the interest of the masses through illusion-promoting spectacles and dubious speculations.

XI

The shooting of a film, especially of a sound film, affords a spectacle unimaginable anywhere at any time before this. It presents a process in which it is impossible to assign to a spectator a viewpoint which would exclude from the actual scene such extraneous accessories as camera equipment, lighting machinery, staff assistants, etc.—unless his eye were on a line parallel with the lens. This circumstance, more than any other, renders superficial and insignificant any possible similarity between a scene in the studio and one on the stage. In the theater one is well aware of the place from which the play cannot immediately be detected as illusionary. There is no such place for the movie scene that is being shot. Its illusionary nature is that of the second degree, the result of cutting. That is to say, in the studio the mechanical equipment has penetrated so deeply into reality that its pure aspect freed from the foreign substance of equipment is the result of a special procedure, namely, the shooting by the specially adjusted camera and the mounting of the shot together with other similar ones. The equipment-free aspect of reality here has become the height of artifice; the sight of immediate reality has become an orchid in the land of technology.

Even more revealing is the comparison of these circumstances, which differ so much from those of the theater, with the situation in painting. Here the question is: How does the cameraman compare with the painter? To answer this we take recourse to an analogy with a surgical operation. The surgeon represents the polar opposite of the magician. The magician heals a sick person by the laying on of hands; the surgeon cuts into the patient's body. The magician maintains the natural distance between the patient and himself; though he reduces it very slightly by the laying on of hands, he greatly increases it by virtue of his authority. The surgeon does exactly the reverse; he greatly diminishes the distance between himself and the patient by penetrating into the patient's body, and increases it but little by the caution with which his hand moves among the organs. In short, in contrast to the magician—who is still hidden in the medical practitioner—the surgeon at the decisive moment abstains from facing the patient man to man; rather, it is through the operation that he penetrates into him.

Magician and surgeon compare to painter and cameraman. The painter maintains in his work a natural distance from reality, the cameraman penetrates deeply into its web. There is a tremendous difference between the pictures they obtain. That of the painter is a total one, that of the cameraman consists of multiple fragments which are assembled under a new law. Thus, for contemporary man the representation of reality by the film is incomparably more significant than that of the painter, since if offers, precisely because of the thoroughgoing permeation of reality with mechanical equipment, an aspect of reality which is free of all equipment. And that is what one is entitled to ask from a work of art.

XII

Mechanical reproduction of art changes the reaction of the masses toward art. The reactionary attitude toward a Picasso painting changes into the progressive reaction toward a Chaplin movie. The progressive reaction is characterized by the direct, intimate fusion of visual and emotional enjoyment with the orientation of the expert. Such fusion is of great social significance. The greater the decrease in the social significance of an art form, the sharper the distinction between criticism and enjoyment by the public. The conventional is uncritically enjoyed, and the truly new is criticized with aversion. With regard to the screen, the critical and the receptive attitudes of the public coincide. The decisive reason for this is that individual reactions are predetermined by the mass audience response they are about to produce, and this is nowhere more pronounced than in the film. The moment these responses become manifest they control each other. Again, the comparison with painting is fruitful. A painting has always had an excellent chance to be viewed by one person or by a few. The simultaneous contemplation of paintings by a large public, such as developed in the nineteenth century, is an early symptom of the crisis of painting, a crisis which was by no means occasioned exclusively by photography but rather in a relatively independent manner by the appeal of art works to the masses.

Painting simply is in no position to present an object for simultaneous collective experience, as it was possible for architecture at all times, for the epic poem in the past, and for the movie today. Although this circumstance in itself should not lead one to conclusions about the social role of painting, it does constitute a serious threat as soon as painting, under special conditions and, as it were, against its nature, is confronted directly by the masses. In the churches and monasteries of the Middle Ages and at the princely courts up to the end of the eighteenth century, a collective reception of paintings did not occur simultaneously, but by graduated and hierarchized mediation. The change that has come about is an expression of the particular conflict in which painting was implicated by the mechanical reproducibility of paintings. Although paintings began to be publicly exhibited in galleries and salons, there was no way for the masses to organize and control themselves in their reception. Thus the same public which responds in a progressive manner toward a grotesque film is bound to respond in a reactionary manner to surrealism. . . .

XV

The mass is a matrix from which all traditional behavior toward works of art issues today in a new form. Quantity has been transmuted into quality. The greatly increased mass of participants has produced a change in the mode of participation. The fact that the new mode of participation first appeared in a disreputable form must not confuse the spectator. Yet some people have launched spirited attacks against precisely this superficial aspect. Among these, Duhamel has expressed himself in the most radical manner. What he objects to most is the kind of participation which the movie elicits from the masses. Duhamel calls the movie "a pastime for helots, a diversion for uneducated, wretched, worn-out creatures who are consumed by their worries . . . a spectacle which requires no concentration and presupposes no intelligence . . . which kindles no light in the heart and awakens no hope other than the ridiculous one of someday becoming a 'star' in Los Angeles." Clearly, this is at bottom the same ancient lament that the masses seek distraction whereas art demands concentration from the spectator. That is a commonplace. The question remains whether it provides a platform for the analysis of the film. A closer look is needed here. Distraction and concentration form polar opposites which may be stated as follows: A man who concentrates before a work of art is absorbed by it. He enters into this work of art the way legend tells of the Chinese painter when he viewed his finished painting. In contrast, the distracted mass absorbs the work of art. . . .

The distracted person . . . can form habits. More, the ability to master certain tasks in a state of distraction proves that their solution has become a matter of habit. Distraction as provided by art presents a covert control of the extent to which new tasks have become soluble by apperception. Since, moreover, individuals are tempted to avoid such tasks, art will tackle the most difficult and most important ones where it is able to mobilize the masses. Today it does so in the film. Reception in a state of distraction, which is increasing noticeably in all fields of art and is symptomatic of profound changes in apperception, finds in the film its true means of exercise. The film with its shock effect meets this mode of reception halfway. The film makes the cult value recede into the background not only by putting the public in the position of the critic, but also by the fact that at the movies this position requires no attention. The public is an examiner, but an absent-minded one.

DISCUSSION QUESTIONS

1. What does Benjamin mean by the "aura" of a work of art? Do you agree with Benjamin that works of art have an "aura"? Why or why not?

2. What does it mean for a work of art to be "authentic"? Compare your response to Benjamin's. Do you believe that mechanically or technically reproduced art can be authentic? Why or why not?

3. Why does Benjamin believe that film is more destructive of the aura and authenticity of art than photography? Do you agree with him? Why or why not?

4. Why does Benjamin believe that mechanical reproduction destroys more of the authenticity of art than does manual reproduction? Do you agree with him? Why or why not?

5. In general, how does the way in which art is produced and reproduced affect the public response to it?

6. Is digitally reproduced art a type of mechanically reproduced art? Do Benjamin's theses about the destruction of aura and authenticity hold in the age of digital reproduction of art? Do you think that Benjamin would find digitally produced art even more pernicious than the forms of mechanically reproduced art available in 1935, the year of publication of his essay?

7. Is the art of Andy Warhol a good example of what Benjamin calls "art designed for reproducibility"? Why or why not?

ANDRÉ BAZIN

THE ONTOLOGY OF THE PHOTOGRAPHIC IMAGE

André Bazin maintains that photography and film are the fulfillment of humankind's wish to see "the duplication of the world outside." This wish has been passed down from age to age, since the time when the "religion of ancient Egypt, aimed against death, saw survival as depending on the continued existence of the corporeal body." Bazin refers to this wish as "the mummy complex," the "basic psychological need in man" to snatch a thing up "from the flow of time, to stow it away neatly, so to speak, in the hold of life." For Bazin, the mummy complex is at the origin of painting and sculpture, as well as closely linked to the obsession with realism in art. The development of photography and cinema "are discoveries that satisfy, once and for all and in its very essence, our obsession with realism."

Photography and cinema are superior to painting in satisfying our obsession with realism not because they are the perfection of a physical process of duplicating the external world but rather because they satisfy our needs, namely, our "psychological appetite for illusion by a mechanical reproduction in which man plays no part." "The solution," writes Bazin, "is not to be found in the result achieved [viz., the photographic image] but in the way of achieving it [viz., a mechanical process in which man plays no part]." No matter how true to life a painting is, it is always already the product of a human process, whereas photography and cinema are always already merely the effect of light reflecting from objects and striking a lens and film. "The objective nature of photography confers on it a quality of credibility absent from all other picture-making," says Bazin. "In spite of any objections our critical spirit may offer, we are forced to accept as real the existence of the object reproduced, actually *re*-presented, set before us, that is to say, in time and space." Photography and cinema have a privileged relationship with reality or the real: photography "embalms time, rescuing it simply from its proper corruption"; cinema is "change mummified as it were." For Bazin, "photography is clearly the most important event in the history of the plastic arts" because it "allows us on the one hand to admire in reproduction something that our eyes alone could not have taught us to love, and on the other, to admire the painting as a thing in itself whose relationship to something in nature has ceased to be the justification for its existence."

André Bazin (1918–1958), French film critic and theorist, is widely credited with establishing the study of film as a serious intellectual endeavor. At an early age, he decided to be a teacher and entered a training college for teachers, which he completed in 1941. He was denied a teaching post because of his stammer but later participated in the Maison des Lettres, an organization that looked after students whose schooling had been interrupted by World War II. During the German occupation of Paris, Bazin screened films banned by the Nazis. After the war, he became director of cultural services at the Institut des Hautes Études Cinématographiques and was a film critic for *Le Parisien libéré*. His work drew the attention of

Jean-Paul Sartre, who asked him to write essays for the distinguished philosophy journal *Les temps modernes*. During the course of his relatively brief writing career, he is estimated to have written 2,000 pieces. He is credited with being the spiritual father of French New Wave cinema, and his work directly influenced many film directors, the most renowned of whom are François Truffaut, Jean-Luc Goddard, Jacques Rivette, and Claude Chabrol. In 1951, Bazin co-founded with Jacques Doniol-Valcroze the highly influential French film review *Cahiers du cinéma*. The following article, "The Ontology of the Photographic Image" ("Ontologie de l'image photographique") first appeared in 1945, and subsequently was collected in Bazin's *What is Cinema? (Qu'est-ce que le cinéma?)* in 1958.

If the plastic arts were put under psychoanalysis, the practice of embalming the dead might turn out to be a fundamental factor in their creation. The process might reveal that at the origin of painting and sculpture there lies a mummy complex. The religion of ancient Egypt, aimed against death, saw survival as depending on the continued existence of the corporeal body. Thus, by providing a defense against the passage of time it satisfied a basic psychological need in man, for death is but the victory of time. To preserve, artificially, his bodily appearance is to snatch it from the flow of time, to stow it away neatly, so to speak, in the hold of life. It was natural, therefore, to keep up appearances in the face of the reality of death by preserving flesh and bone. The first Egyptian statue, then, was a mummy, tanned and petrified in sodium. But pyramids and labyrinthine corridors offered no certain guarantee against ultimate pillage.

Other forms of insurance were therefore sought. So, near the sarcophagus, alongside the corn that was to feed the dead, the Egyptians placed terra cotta statuettes, as substitute mummies which might replace the bodies if these were destroyed. It is this religious use, then, that lays bare the primordial function of statuary, namely, the preservation of life by a representation of life. Another manifestation of the same kind of thing is the arrow-pierced clay bear to be found in prehistoric caves, a magic identity-substitute for the living animal, that will ensure a successful hunt. The evolution, side by side, of art and civilization has relieved the plastic arts of their magic role. Louis XIV did not have himself embalmed. He was content to survive in his portrait by Le Brun. Civilization cannot, however, entirely cast out the bogy of time. It can

only sublimate our concern with it to the level of rational thinking. No one believes any longer in the ontological identity of model and image, but all are agreed that the image helps us to remember the subject and to preserve him from a second spiritual death. Today the making of images no longer shares an anthropocentric, utilitarian purpose. It is no longer a question of survival after death, but of a larger concept, the creation of an ideal world in the likeness of the real, with its own temporal destiny. "How vain a thing is painting" if underneath our fond admiration for its works we do not discern man's primitive need to have the last word in the argument with death by means of the form that endures. If the history of the plastic arts is less a matter of their aesthetic than of their psychology then it will be seen to be essentially the story of resemblance, or, if you will, of realism.

Seen in this sociological perspective photography and cinema would provide a natural explanation for the great spiritual and technical crisis that overtook modern painting around the middle of the last century. André Malraux has described the cinema as the furthermost evolution to date of plastic realism, the beginnings of which were first manifest at the Renaissance and which found its completest expression in baroque painting.

It is true that painting, the world over, has struck a varied balance between the symbolic and realism. However, in the fifteenth century Western painting began to turn from its age-old concern with spiritual realities expressed in the form proper to it, towards an effort to combine this spiritual expression with as complete an imitation as possible of the outside world.

The decisive moment undoubtedly came with the discovery of the first scientific and already, in a sense, mechanical system of reproduction, namely, perspective: the camera obscura of da Vinci foreshadowed the camera of Niepce. The artist was now in a position to create the illusion of three-dimensional space within which things appeared to exist as our eyes in reality see them.

Thenceforth painting was torn between two ambitions: one, primarily aesthetic, namely the expression of spiritual reality wherein the symbol transcended its model; the other, purely psychological, namely the duplication of the world outside. The satisfaction of this appetite for illusion merely served to increase it till, bit by bit, it consumed the plastic arts. However, since perspective had only solved the problem of form and not of movement, realism was forced to continue the search for some way of giving dramatic expression to the moment, a kind of psychic fourth dimension that could suggest life in the tortured immobility of baroque art.

The great artists, of course, have always been able to combine the two tendencies. They have allotted to each its proper place in the hierarchy of things, holding reality at their command and molding it at will into the fabric of their art. Nevertheless, the fact remains that we are faced with two essentially different phenomena and these any objective critic must view separately if he is to understand the evolution of the pictorial. The need for illusion has not ceased to trouble the heart of painting since the sixteenth century. It is a purely mental need, of itself nonaesthetic, the origins of which must be sought in the proclivity of the mind towards magic. However, it is a need the pull of which has been strong enough to have seriously upset the equilibrium of the plastic arts.

The quarrel over realism in art stems from a misunderstanding, from a confusion between the aesthetic and the psychological; between true realism, the need that is to give significant expression to the world both concretely and its essence, and the pseudorealism of a deception aimed at fooling the eye (or for that matter the mind); a pseudorealism content in other words with illusory appearances. That is why medieval art never passed through this crisis; simultaneously vividly realistic and highly spiritual, it knew nothing of the drama that came to light as a consequence of technical developments. Perspective was the original sin of Western painting.

It was redeemed from sin by Niepce and Lumière. In achieving the aims of baroque art, photography has freed the plastic arts from their obsession with likeness. Painting was forced, as it turned out, to offer us illusion and this illusion was reckoned sufficient unto art. Photography and the cinema on the other hand are discoveries that satisfy, once and for all and in its very essence, our obsession with realism.

No matter how skillful the painter, his work was always in fee to an inescapable subjectivity. The fact that a human hand intervened cast a shadow of doubt over the image. Again, the essential factor in the transition from the baroque to photography is not the perfecting of a physical process (photography will long remain the inferior of painting in the reproduction of color); rather does it lie in a psychological fact, to wit, in completely satisfying our appetite for illusion by a mechanical reproduction in the making of which man plays no part. The solution is not to be found in the result achieved but in the way of achieving it.

This is why the conflict between style and likeness is a relatively modern phenomenon of which there is no trace before the invention of the sensitized plate. Clearly the fascinating objectivity of Chardin is in no sense that of the photographer. The nineteenth century saw the real beginnings of the crisis of realism of which Picasso is now the mythical central figure and which put to the test at one and the same time the conditions determining the formal existence of the plastic arts and their sociological roots. Freed from the "resemblance complex," the modern painter abandons it to the masses who, henceforth, identify resemblance on the one hand with photography and on the other with the kind of painting which is related to photography.

Originality in photography as distinct from originality in painting lies in the essentially objective character of photography. . . . For the first time, between the originating object and its reproduction there intervenes only the instrumentality of a nonliving agent. For the first time an image of the world is formed automatically, without the creative intervention of man. The personality of the photographer enters into the proceedings only in his selection of the object to be photographed and by way of the purpose he has in mind. Although the final result may reflect something of his personality, this does not play the same role as is played by that of the painter. All the arts are based on the presence of man, only photography derives an advantage from his absence. Photography affects us like a phenomenon in nature, like a flower or a snowflake whose vegetable or earthly origins are an inseparable part of their beauty.

This production by automatic means has radically affected our psychology of the image. The objective nature of photography confers on it a quality of credibility absent from all other picturemaking. In spite of any objections our critical spirit may offer, we are forced to accept as real the existence of the object reproduced, actually *re*-presented, set before us, that is to say, in time and space. Photography enjoys a certain advantage in virtue of this transference of reality from the thing to its reproduction.

A very faithful drawing may actually tell us more about the model but despite the promptings of our critical intelligence it will never have the irrational power of the photograph to bear away our faith.

Besides, painting is, after all, an inferior way of making likenesses, an ersatz of the processes of reproduction. Only a photographic lens can give us the kind of image of the object that is capable of satisfying the deep need man has to substitute for it something more than a mere approximation, a kind of decal or transfer. The photographic image is the object itself, the object freed from the conditions of time and space that govern it. No matter how fuzzy, distorted, or discolored, no matter how lacking in documentary value the image may be, it shares, by virtue of the very process of its becoming, the being of the model of which it is the reproduction; it *is* the model.

Hence the charm of family albums. Those grey or sepia shadows, phantomlike and almost undecipherable, are no longer traditional family portraits but rather the disturbing presence of lives halted at a set moment in their duration, freed from their destiny; not, however, by the prestige of art but by the power of an impassive mechanical process: for photography does not create eternity, as art does, it embalms time, rescuing it simply from its proper corruption.

Viewed in this perspective, the cinema is objectivity in time. The film is no longer content to preserve the object, enshrouded as it were in an instant, as the bodies of insects are preserved intact, out of the distant past, in amber. The film delivers baroque art from its convulsive catalepsy. Now, for the first time, the image of things is likewise the image of their duration, change mummified as it were. Those categories of *resemblance* which determine the species *photographic* image likewise, then, determine the character of its aesthetic as distinct from that of painting.

The aesthetic qualities of photography are to be sought in its power to lay bare the realities. It is not for me to separate off, in the complex fabric of the objective world, here a reflection on a damp sidewalk, there the gesture of a child. Only the impassive lens, stripping its object of all those ways of seeing it, those piled-up preconceptions, that spiritual dust and grime with which my eyes have covered it, is able to present it in all its virginal purity to my attention and consequently to my love. By the power of photography, the natural image of a world that we neither know nor can know, nature at last does more than imitate art: she imitates the artist.

Photography can even surpass art in creative power. The aesthetic world of the painter is of a different kind from that of the world about him. Its boundaries enclose a substantially and essentially different microcosm. The photograph as such and the object in itself share a common being, after the fashion of a fingerprint. Wherefore, photography actually contributes something to the order of natural creation instead of providing a substitute for it. The surrealists had an inkling of this when they looked to the photographic plate to provide them with their monstrosities and for this reason: the surrealist does not consider his aesthetic purpose and the mechanical effect of the image on our imaginations as things apart. For him, the logical distinction between what is imaginary and what is real tends to disappear. Every image is to be seen as an object and every object as an image. Hence photography ranks high in the order of surrealist creativity because it produces an image that is a reality of nature, namely, an hallucination that is also a fact. The fact that surrealist painting combines tricks of visual deception with meticulous attention to detail substantiates this.

So, photography is clearly the most important event in the history of plastic arts. Simultaneously a liberation and a fulfillment, it has freed Western painting, once and for all, from its obsession with realism and allowed it to recover its aesthetic autonomy. Impressionist realism, offering science as an alibi, is at the opposite extreme from eye-deceiving trickery. Only when form ceases to have any imitative value can it be swallowed up in color. So, when form, in the person of Cézanne, once more regains possession of the canvas there is no longer any question of the illusions of the geometry of perspective. The painting, being confronted in the mechanically produced image with a competitor able to reach out beyond baroque resemblance to the very identity of the model, was compelled into the category of object. Henceforth Pascal's condemnation of painting is itself rendered vain since the photograph allows us on the one hand to admire in reproduction something that our eyes alone could not have taught us to love, and on the other, to admire the painting as a thing in itself whose relation to something in nature has ceased to be the justification for its existence. . . .

DISCUSSION QUESTIONS

1. What is the "mummy complex"? Do you agree with Bazin that it is at the origin of our obsession with realism in art? Why or why not?

2. Why does Bazin believe that photography is more objective than painting? Do you agree with him? Why or why not?

3. Bazin writes, "Photography affects us like a phenomenon in nature, like a flower or a snowflake whose vegetable or earthly origins are an inseparable part of their beauty." What does he mean?

4. Bazin claims that cinema is "objectivity in time." What does he mean by this? Do you agree with him? Why or why not?

5. Bazin writes, "In spite of any objections our critical spirit may offer, we are forced to accept as real the existence of the object reproduced, actually *re*-presented, set before us, that is to say, in time and space." What are some objections to the charge that photography re-presents objects? Is the case of photography re-presenting objects similar to or different from the case of cinema re-presenting objects? Why or why not?

6. How might Plato respond to Bazin's claim that photography has a privileged relationship with reality?

The Purple Rose of Cairo
[USA 1985] 1 hour, 24 minutes
Directed by Woody Allen

Cecilia (Mia Farrow) is a waitress living in New Jersey during the Depression. She supports herself and her physically and verbally abusive husband, Monk (Danny Aiello). Monk has been unemployed for two years and spends his time gambling, drinking, and having affairs. He shows Cecilia little love or kindness, but asserts his right to her paychecks, cooking, and back rubs. Cecilia's means of escape from the drudgery of work and home is the movies. In the cinema, she is completely free. She knows the actors, characters, and lines by heart and often daydreams at work about the movies, which leads to the loss of her job.

One day, Cecilia attends a screening of *The Purple Rose of Cairo*. When one of the characters, Tom Baxter (Jeff Daniels), jumps out of the screen and professes his love for her, they flee the theater together. Tom refuses to return to the film, and the action of the movie is put on hold as the other characters wait for Tom to return. In the meantime, other Toms in other screenings of the film in other cities begin exhibiting strange behavior. The film studio is contacted, and representatives immediately rush to Cecilia's town to persuade Tom to go back on the screen.

   Meanwhile, Gil Shepard (also Jeff Daniels), the actor who plays Tom Baxter, meets Cecilia. When he, too, professes his love for her, she is compelled to make a choice between the "imaginary" Tom and the "real" Gil. She chooses Gil and plans to steal away to Hollywood with him. However, Cecilia is heartbroken when she learns that Gil has left town without her and that his love for her was nothing more than an effort to get Tom back on the screen and save his own film career. On the plane, Gil shows some remorse for tricking Cecilia, but his response is nothing compared to her heartbreak, which she washes away with the new movie in town—a Fred Astaire/Ginger Rogers musical. The cinema once again becomes Cecilia's refuge and sole comfort.

DISCUSSION QUESTIONS

1.   Bazin argues that we have a basic psychological need to snatch things up "from the flow of time" and to stow them away "in the hold of life," and that this is something film does well. Do you think this is the fundamental reason why Cecilia loves the movies? Why or why not?

2.   Bazin says that "we are forced to accept as real the existence of the object reproduced." In what way is *The Purple Rose of Cairo* a meditation on this idea? Is it an effective one? Does the film ultimately lead you to accept or reject Bazin's notion?

3.   The manager of the movie theater says, "Oh my God. He left the picture!" Many of the patrons stay in the theater to watch the characters on the screen react to the situation. Is this the reaction you might have if a character stepped out of the movie screen and into your reality? Discuss.

4.   One of the reporters says, "If you turn off the projector, you're liable to have a lost Tom Baxter roaming around." Discuss the ontological assumptions this statement makes. If you were the theater manager, would you have turned the projector off? If you did, would Tom Baxter have ceased to exist in the "real" world? How is Tom's existence dependent upon the continuous running of the projector?

5.   Why do you think Woody Allen did not have the action in the film "freeze" when Tom walks off the screen? Wouldn't this make more ontological sense? What is Allen saying about the nature of film and photography by allowing the other characters in the film to discuss the implications of Tom's leaving the film?

6.   One of the film industry representatives asserts, "The fictional ones want their lives real, and the real ones want their lives fiction." Is he right? Discuss.

7.   Tom says to Cecilia, "You make love without fading out?" Discuss the way in which the viewer is responsible for "filling in" many of the details of the inner and outer lives of the characters on the screen. Does this lead you to conclude that film characters are ultimately the creation of the viewer? Why or why not?

8.   A theater patron says, "Look at us—slaves to some stupid scenario. . . . We're the characters on the screen, not them!" Is he right? Why or why not?

9.   One of the characters on the screen asks, "What if all this is merely semantics. Let's just readjust our definitions. Let's just redefine ourselves as the real world and them as the world of illusions and shadow. We're reality, they're a dream." Can the characters in the film do this?

10.   Is Cecilia ultimately no more real or imaginary than Tom? How effective is Allen's film in making you forget that Cecilia, too, is only a film character? What does this reveal about the power of cinema?

SUSAN SONTAG

IN PLATO'S CAVE

S usan Sontag argues that photographs are not an objective representation of the world. Unlike Bazin, who values photography for its objectivity, Sontag contends that "photographs are as much an interpretation of the world as paintings and drawings are." Nevertheless, photography departs from painting and drawing by implying from its origins "the capture of the largest possible number of subjects," which is something to which painting never aspired. Sontag claims that from the beginning, photography sought "to democratize all experiences by translating them into images."

Sontag's discussion of photography reveals the many ways in which photography has become an important part of the fabric of both public and private life. From the use of photographs as a means of surveillance in the modern police state to the obligation to take pictures of one's children and vacations, she notes, photography plays a significant role in the life of the modern individual and state. However, the pervasive use of photographic images seems to have contradictory consequences. For example, photography can both "arouse" conscience and "deaden" it. Photography allows us access to images of atrocities and war, and makes those events "more real" than they would have been without photographs. However, repeated exposure to these photographic images has the opposite effect: they "anesthetize" us and make horrific events seem less real.

For Sontag, photography clouds our ethical and epistemological sensibilities. While photographic knowledge "can goad conscience, it can, finally, never be ethical or political knowledge." The knowledge that we gain through photographs "will always be some kind of sentimentalism, whether cynical or humanist." "Photographs cannot create a moral position," says Sontag, "but they can reinforce one—and can help build a nascent one." Moreover, when we furnish "this already crowded world with a duplicate one of images, photography makes us feel that the world is more available than it really is." The ultimate consequence of this is that "having an experience becomes identical to taking a photograph of it, and participating in a public event comes more and more to be equivalent to looking at it in photographed form."

Susan Sontag (1933–2004), essayist, novelist, cultural critic, and human rights activist, was born in New York City. She received her B.A. from the College of the University of Chicago and did graduate work in literature, philosophy, and theology at Harvard University and Saint Anne's College, Oxford. While she regarded herself as principally a writer of fiction, she wrote only four novels: *The Benefactor* (1963), *Death Kit* (1967), *The Volcano Lover* (1992), and *In America* (2000). She gained fame and respect, however, for her essays and cultural criticism. Her work often took on difficult topics such as cultural attitudes toward illness with depth and grace. In this regard, *Illness as Metaphor* (1978) and *AIDS and Its Metaphors* (1988) have come to be classics of cultural criticism. Her work is marked by a tendency to argue for the ethical seriousness of our aesthetic sensibilities. Her other works include *Against Interpretation* (1966), *Styles of Radical Will* (1969), *I, etcetera* (1977), *On Photography* (1977), *Under the Sign of Saturn* (1980), and *Regarding the Pain of Others* (2003). The following selection is from *On Photography*.

Humankind lingers unregenerately in Plato's cave, still reveling, its age-old habit, in mere images of the truth. But being educated by photographs is not like being educated by older, more artisanal images. For one thing, there are a great many more images around, claiming our attention. The inventory started in 1839 and since then just about everything has been photographed, or so it seems. This very insatiability of the photographing eye changes the terms of confinement in the cave, our world. In teaching us a new visual code, photographs alter and enlarge our notions of what is worth looking at and what we have a right to observe. They are a grammar and, even more importantly, an ethics of seeing. Finally, the most grandiose result of the photographic enterprise is to give us the sense that we can hold the whole world in our heads—as an anthology of images.

To collect photographs is to collect the world. Movies and television programs light up walls, flicker, and go out; but with still photographs the image is also an object, lightweight, cheap to produce, easy to carry about, accumulate, store. In Godard's *Les Carabiniers* (1963), two sluggish lumpen-peasants are lured into joining the King's Army by the promise that they will be able to loot, rape, kill, or do whatever else they please to the enemy, and get rich. But the suitcase of booty that Michel-Ange and Ulysse triumphantly bring home, years later, to their wives turns out to contain only picture postcards, hundreds of them, of Monuments, Department Stores, Mammals, Wonders of Nature, Methods of Transport, Works of Art, and other classified treasures from around the globe. Godard's gag vividly parodies the equivocal magic of the photographic image. Photographs are perhaps the most mysterious of all the objects that make up, and thicken, the environment we recognize as modern. Photographs really are experience captured, and the camera is the ideal arm of consciousness in its acquisitive mood.

To photograph is to appropriate the thing photographed. It means putting oneself into a certain relation to the world that feels like knowledge—and, therefore, like power. A now notorious first fall into alienation, habituating people to abstract the world into printed words, is supposed to have engendered that surplus of Faustian energy and psychic damage needed to build modern, inorganic societies. But print seems a less treacherous form of leaching out the world, of turning it into a mental object, than photographic images, which now provide most of the knowledge people have about the look of the past and the reach of the present. What is written about a person or an event is frankly an interpretation, as are handmade visual statements, like paintings and drawings. Photographed images do not seem to be statements about the world so much as pieces of it, miniatures of reality that any one can make or acquire.

Photographs, which fiddle with the scale of the world, themselves get reduced, blown up, cropped, retouched, doctored, tricked out. They age, plagued by the usual ills of paper objects; they disappear; they become valuable, and get bought and sold; they are reproduced. Photographs, which package the world, seem to invite packaging. They are stuck in albums, framed and set on tables; tacked on walls, projected as slides. Newspapers and magazines feature them; cops alphabetize them; museums exhibit them; publishers compile them.

For many decades the book has been the most influential way of arranging (and usually miniaturizing) photographs, thereby guaranteeing them longevity, if not immortality—photographs are fragile objects, easily torn or mislaid—and a wider public. The photograph in a book is, obviously, the image of an image. But since it is, to begin with, a printed, smooth object, a photograph loses much less of its essential quality when reproduced in a book than a painting does. Still, the book is not a wholly satisfactory scheme for putting groups of photographs into general circulation. The sequence in which the photographs are to be looked at is proposed by the order of pages, but nothing holds readers to the recommended order or indicates the amount of time to be spent on each photograph. Chris Marker's film, *Si j'avais quatre dromadaires* (1966), a brilliantly orchestrated meditation on photographs of all sorts and themes, suggests a subtler and more rigorous way of packaging (and enlarging) still photographs. Both the order and the exact time for looking at each photograph are imposed; and there is a gain in visual legibility and emotional impact. But photographs transcribed in a film cease to be collectable objects, as they still are when served up in books.

Photographs furnish evidence. Something we hear about, but doubt, seems proven when we're shown a photograph of it. In one version of its utility, the camera record incriminates. Starting with their use by the Paris police in the murderous roundup of Communards in June 1871, photographs became a useful tool of modern states in the surveillance and control of their increasingly mobile populations. In another version of its utility, the camera record justifies. A photograph passes for incontrovertible proof that a given thing happened. The picture may distort; but there is always a presumption that something exists, or did exist, which is like what's in the picture. Whatever the limitations (through amateurism) or pretensions (through artistry) of the individual photographer, a photograph—any photograph—seems to have a more innocent, and therefore more accurate, relation to visible reality than do other mimetic objects. Virtuosi of the noble image like Alfred Stieglitz and Paul Strand, composing mighty, unforgettable photographs decade after decade, still want, first of all, to show something "out there," just like the Polaroid owner for whom photographs are a handy, fast form of notetaking, or the shutterbug with a Brownie who takes snapshots as souvenirs of daily life.

While a painting or a prose description can never be other than a narrowly selective interpretation, a photograph can be treated as a narrowly selective transparency. But despite the presumption of veracity that gives all photographs authority, interest, seductiveness, the work that photographers do is no generic exception to the usually shady commerce between art and truth. Even when photographers are most concerned with mirroring reality, they are still haunted by tacit imperatives of taste and conscience. The immensely gifted members of the Farm Security Administration photographic project of the late 1930s (among them Walker Evans, Dorothea Lange, Ben Shahn, Russell Lee) would take dozens of frontal pictures of one of their sharecropper subjects until satisfied that they had gotten just the right look on film—the precise expression on the subject's face that supported their own notions about poverty, light, dignity, texture, exploitation, and geometry. In deciding how a picture should look, in preferring one exposure to another, photographers are always imposing standards on their subjects. Although there is a sense in which the camera does indeed capture reality, not just interpret it, photographs are as much an interpretation of the world as paintings and drawings are. Those occasions when the taking of photographs is relatively undiscriminating, promiscuous, or self-effacing do not lessen the didacticism of the whole enterprise. This very passivity—and ubiquity—of the photographic record is photography's "message," its aggression.

Images which idealize (like most fashion and animal photography) are no less aggressive than work which makes a virtue of plainness (like class pictures, still lifes of the bleaker sort, and mug shots). There is an aggression implicit in every use of the camera. This is as evident in the 1840s and 1850s, photography's glorious first two decades, as in all the succeeding decades, during which technology made possible an ever increasing spread of that mentality which looks at the world as a set of potential photographs. Even for such early masters as David Octavius Hill and Julia Margaret Cameron who used the camera as a means of getting painterly images, the point of taking photographs was a vast departure from the aims of painters. From its start, photography implied the capture of the largest possible number of subjects. Painting never had so imperial a scope. The subsequent industrialization of camera technology only carried out a promise inherent in photography from its very beginning: to democratize all experiences by translating them into images.

That age when taking photographs required a cumbersome and expensive contraption—the toy of the clever, the wealthy, and the obsessed—seems remote indeed from the era of sleek pocket cameras that invite anyone to take pictures. The first cameras, made in France and England in the early 1840s, had only inventors and buffs to operate them. Since there were then no professional photographers, there could not be amateurs either, and taking photographs had no clear social use; it was a gratuitous, that is, an artistic activity, though with few pretensions to being an art. It was only with its industrialization that photography came into its own as art. As industrialization provided social uses for the operations of the photographer, so the reaction against these uses reinforced the self-consciousness of photography-as-art.

Recently, photography has become almost as widely practiced an amusement as sex and dancing—which means that, like every mass art form, photography is not practiced by most people as an art. It is mainly a social rite, a defense against anxiety, and a tool of power.

Memorializing the achievements of individuals considered as members of families (as well as of other groups) is the earliest popular use of photography. For at least a century, the wedding photograph has been as much a part of the ceremony as the prescribed verbal formulas. Cameras go with family life. According to a sociological study done in France, most households have a camera, but a household with children is twice as likely to have at least one camera as a household in which there are no children. Not to take pictures of one's children, particularly when they are small, is a sign of parental indifference, just as not turning up for one's graduation picture is a gesture of adolescent rebellion.

Through photographs, each family constructs a portrait-chronicle of itself—a portable kit of images that bears witness to its connectedness. It hardly matters what activities are photographed so long as photographs get taken and are cherished. Photography becomes a rite of family life just when, in the industrializing countries of Europe and America, the very institution of the family starts undergoing radical surgery. As that claustrophobic unit, the nuclear family, was being carved out of a much larger family aggregate, photography came along to memorialize, to restate symbolically, the imperiled continuity and vanishing extendedness of family life. Those ghostly traces, photographs, supply the token presence of the dispersed relatives. A family's photograph album is generally about the extended family—and, often, is all that remains of it.

As photographs give people an imaginary possession of a past that is unreal, they also help people to take possession of space in which they are insecure. Thus, photography develops in tandem with one of the most characteristic of modern activities: tourism. For the first time in history, large numbers of people regularly travel out of their habitual environments for short periods of time. It seems positively unnatural to travel for pleasure without taking a camera along. Photographs will offer indisputable evidence that the trip was made, that the program was carried out, that fun was had. Photographs document sequences of consumption carried on outside the view of family, friends, neighbors. But dependence on the camera, as the device that makes real what one is experiencing, doesn't fade when people travel more. Taking photographs fills the same need for the cosmopolitans accumulating photograph-trophies of their boat trip up the Albert Nile or their fourteen days in China as it does for lower-middle-class vacationers taking snapshots of the Eiffel Tower or Niagara Falls.

A way of certifying experience, taking photographs is also a way of refusing it—by limiting experience to a search for the photogenic, by converting experience into an image, a souvenir. Travel becomes a strategy for accumulating photographs. The very activity of taking pictures is soothing, and assuages general feelings of disorientation that are likely to be exacerbated by travel. Most tourists feel compelled to put the camera between themselves and whatever is remarkable that they encounter. Unsure of other responses, they take a picture. This gives shape to experience: stop, take a photograph, and move on. The method especially appeals to people handicapped by a ruthless work ethic—Germans, Japanese, and Americans. Using a camera appeases the anxiety which the work-driven feel about not working when they are on vacation and supposed to be having fun. They have something to do that is like a friendly imitation of work: they can take pictures.

People robbed of their past seem to make the most fervent picture takers, at home and abroad. Everyone who lives in an industrialized society is obliged gradually to give up the past, but in certain countries, such as the United States and Japan, the break with the past has been particularly traumatic. In the early 1970s, the fable of the brash American tourist of the 1950s and 1960s, rich with dollars and Babbittry,* was replaced by the mystery of the group-minded Japanese tourist, newly released from his island prison by the miracle of overvalued

---

*Babbittry refers to the title character in Sinclair Lewis's 1922 novel *Babbitt*, about a man who is anti-intellectual, materialistic, and conformist. —Ed.

yen, who is generally armed with two cameras, one on each hip.

Photography has become one of the principle devices for experiencing something, for giving an appearance of participation. One full-page ad shows a small group of people standing pressed together, peering out of the photograph, all but one looking stunned, excited, upset. The one who wears a different expression holds a camera to his eye; he seems self-possessed, is almost smiling. While the others are passive, clearly alarmed spectators, having a camera has transformed one person into something active, a voyeur: only he has mastered the situation. What do these people see? We don't know. And it doesn't matter. It is an Event: something worth seeing—and therefore worth photographing. The ad copy, white letters across the dark lower third of the photograph like news coming over a teletype machine, consists of just six words: ". . . Prague . . . Woodstock . . . Vietnam . . . Sapporo . . . Londonderry . . . LEICA." Crushed hopes, youth antics, colonial wars, and winter sports are alike—are equalized by the camera. Taking photographs has set up a chronic voyeuristic relation to the world which levels the meaning of all events.

A photograph is not just the result of an encounter between an event and a photographer; picture-taking is an event in itself, and one with ever more peremptory rights—to interfere with, to invade, or to ignore whatever is going on. Our very sense of situation is now articulated by the cameras interventions. The omnipresence of cameras persuasively suggests that time consists of interesting events, events worth photographing. This, in turn, makes it easy to feel that any event, once underway, and whatever its moral character, should be allowed to complete itself—so that something else can be brought into the world, the photograph. After the event has ended, the picture will still exist, conferring on the event a kind of immortality (and importance) it would never otherwise have enjoyed. While real people are out there killing themselves or other real people, the photographer stays behind his or her camera, creating a tiny element of another world: the image-world that bids to outlast us all.

Photographing is essentially an act of non-intervention. Part of the horror of such memorable coups of contemporary photojournalism as the pictures of a Vietnamese bonze [monk] reaching for the gasoline can, of a Bengali guerrilla in the act of bayoneting a trussed-up collaborator, comes from the awareness of how plausible it has become, in situations where the photographer has the choice between a photograph and a life, to choose the photograph. The person who intervenes cannot record; the person who is recording cannot intervene. Dziga Vertov's great film, *Man with a Movie Camera* (1929), gives the ideal image of the photographer as someone in perpetual movement, someone moving through a panorama of disparate events with such agility and speed that any intervention is out of the question. Hitchcock's *Rear Window* (1954) gives the complementary image: the photographer played by James Stewart has an intensified relation to one event, through his camera, precisely because he has a broken leg and is confined to a wheelchair; being temporarily immobilized prevents him from acting on what he sees, and makes it even more important to take pictures. Even if incompatible with intervention in a physical sense, using a camera is still a form of participation. Although the camera is an observation station, the act of photographing is more than passive observing. Like sexual voyeurism, it is a way of at least tacitly, often explicitly, encouraging whatever is going on to keep on happening. To take a picture is to have an interest in things as they are, in the status quo remaining unchanged (at least for as long as it takes to get a "good" picture), to be in complicity with whatever makes a subject interesting, worth photographing—including, when that is the interest, another person's pain or misfortune.

"I always thought of photography as a naughty thing to do—that was one of my favorite things about it," Diane Arbus wrote, "and when I first did it I felt very perverse." Being a professional photographer can be thought of as naughty, to use Arbus's pop word, if the photographer seeks out subjects considered to be disreputable, taboo, marginal. But naughty subjects are harder to find these days. And what exactly is the perverse aspect of picture-taking? If professional photographers often have sexual fantasies when they are behind the camera, perhaps the perversion lies in the fact that these fantasies are both plausible and so inappropriate. In *Blowup*

(1966), Antonioni has the fashion photographer hovering convulsively over Verushka's body with his camera clicking. Naughtiness, indeed! In fact, using a camera is not a very good way of getting at someone sexually. Between photographer and subject, there has to be distance. The camera doesn't rape, or even possess, though it may presume, intrude, trespass, distort, exploit, and, at the farthest reach of metaphor, assassinate—all activities that, unlike the sexual push and shove, can be conducted from a distance, and with some detachment.

There is a much stronger sexual fantasy in Michael Powell's extraordinary movie *Peeping Tom* (1960), which is not about a Peeping Tom but about a psychopath who kills women with a weapon concealed in his camera, while photographing them. Not once does he touch his subjects. He doesn't desire their bodies; he wants their presence in the form of filmed images— those showing them experiencing their own death—which he screens at home for his solitary pleasure. The movie assumes connections between impotence and aggression, professionalized looking and cruelty, which point to the central fantasy connected with the camera. The camera as phallus is, at most, a flimsy variant of the inescapable metaphor that everyone unself-consciously employs. However hazy our awareness of this fantasy, it is named without subtlety whenever we talk about "loading" and "aiming" a camera, about "shooting" a film.

The old-fashioned camera was clumsier and harder to reload than a brown Bess musket. The modern camera is trying to be a ray gun. One ad reads: "The Yashica Electro- 35 GT is the space-age camera your family will love. Take beautiful pictures day or night. Automatically. Without any nonsense. Just aim, focus and shoot. The GT's computer brain and electronic shutter will do the rest." Like a car, a camera is sold as a predatory weapon—one that's as automated as possible, ready to spring. Popular taste expects an easy, an invisible technology. Manufacturers reassure their customers that taking pictures demands no skill or expert knowledge, that the machine is all-knowing, and responds to the slightest pressure of the will. It's as simple as turning the ignition key or pulling the trigger.

Like guns and cars, cameras are fantasy machines whose use is addictive. However, despite the extravagances of ordinary language and advertising, they are not lethal. In the hyperbole that markets cars like guns, there is at least this much truth: except in wartime, cars kill more people than guns do. The camera/gun does not kill, so the ominous metaphor seems to be all bluff—like a man's fantasy of having a gun, knife, or tool between his legs. Still, there is something predatory in the act of taking a picture. To photograph people is to violate them, by seeing them as they never see themselves, by having knowledge of them they can never have; it turns people into objects that can be symbolically possessed. Just as the camera is a sublimation of the gun to photograph someone is a sublimated murder—a soft murder, appropriate to a sad, frightened time.

Eventually, people might learn to act out more of their aggressions with cameras and fewer with guns, with the price being an even more image choked world. One situation where people are switching from bullets to film is the photographic safari that is replacing the gun safari in East Africa. The hunters have Hasselblads instead of Winchesters; instead of looking through a telescopic sight to aim a rifle, they look through a viewfinder to frame a picture. In end-of-the-century London, Samuel Butler complained that "there is a photographer in every bush, going about like a roaring lion seeking whom he may devour." The photographer is now charging real beasts, beleaguered and too rare to kill. Guns have metamorphosed into cameras in this earnest comedy, the ecology safari, because nature has ceased to be what it always had been—what people needed protection from. Now nature— tamed, endangered, mortal—needs to be protected from people. When we are afraid, we shoot. But when we are nostalgic, we take pictures.

It is a nostalgic time right now, and photographs actively promote nostalgia. Photography is an elegiac art, a twilight art. Most subjects photographed are, just by virtue of being photographed, touched with pathos. An ugly or grotesque subject may be moving because it has been dignified by the attention of the photographer. A beautiful subject can be the object of rueful feelings, because it has aged or decayed or no longer exists. All photographs are *memento mori.* To take a photograph is to participate in another person's (or thing's) mortality, vulnerability, mutability. Precisely by slicing out this moment and freezing it, all photographs testify to time's relentless melt.

Cameras began duplicating the world at that moment when the human landscape started to undergo a vertiginous rate of change: while an untold number of forms of biological and social life are being destroyed in a brief span of time, a device is available to record what is disappearing. The moody, intricately textured Paris of Atget and Brassaï is mostly gone. Like the dead relatives and friends preserved in the family album, whose presence in photographs exorcises some of the anxiety and remorse prompted by their disappearance, so the photographs of neighborhoods now torn down, rural places disfigured and made barren, supply our pocket relation to the past.

A photograph is both a pseudo-presence and a token of absence. Like a wood fire in a room, photographs—especially those of people, of distant landscapes and faraway cities, of the vanished past—are incitements to reverie. The sense of the unattainable that can be evoked by photographs feeds directly into the erotic feelings of those for whom desirability is enhanced by distance. The lover's photograph hidden in a married woman's wallet; the poster photograph of a rock star tacked up over an adolescent's bed, the campaign-button image of a politician's face pinned on a voter's coat, the snapshots of a cabdriver's children clipped to the visor—all such talismanic uses of photographs express a feeling both sentimental and implicitly magical: they are attempts to contact or lay claim to another reality.

Photographs can abet desire in the most direct, utilitarian way—as when someone collects photographs of anonymous examples of the desirable as an aid to masturbation. The matter is more complex when photographs are used to stimulate the moral impulse. Desire has no history—at least, it is experienced in each instance as all foreground, immediacy. It is aroused by archetypes and is, in that sense, abstract. But moral feelings are embedded in history, whose personae are concrete, whose situations are always specific. Thus, almost opposite rules hold

true for the use of the photograph to awaken desire and to awaken conscience. The images that mobilize conscience are always linked to a given historical situation. The more general they are, the less likely they are to be effective.

A photograph that brings news of some unsuspected zone of misery cannot make a dent in public opinion unless there is an appropriate context of feeling and attitude. The photographs Mathew Brady and his colleagues took of the horrors of the battlefields did not make people any less keen to go on with the Civil War. The photographs of ill-clad, skeletal prisoners held at Andersonville inflamed Northern public opinion—against the South. (The effect of the Andersonville photographs must have been partly due to the very novelty, at that time, of seeing photographs.) The political understanding that many Americans came to in the 1960s would allow them, looking at the photographs Dorothea Lange took of Nisei on the West Coast being transported to internment camps in 1942, to recognize their subject for what it was—a crime committed by the government against a large group of American citizens. Few people who saw those photographs in the 1940s could have had so unequivocal a reaction; the grounds for such a judgment were covered over by the pro-war consensus. Photographs cannot create a moral position, but they can reinforce one—and can help build a nascent one.

Photographs may be more memorable than moving images, because they are a neat slice of time, not a flow. Television is a stream of underselected images, each of which cancels its predecessor. Each still photograph is a privileged moment, turned into a slim object that one can keep and look at again. Photographs like the one that made the front page of most newspapers in the world in 1972—a naked South Vietnamese child just sprayed by American napalm, running down a highway toward the camera, her arms open, screaming with pain—probably did more to increase the public revulsion against the war than a hundred hours of televised barbarities.

One would like to imagine that the American public would not have been so unanimous in its acquiescence to the Korean War if it had been confronted with photographic evidence of the devastation of Korea, an ecocide and genocide in some respects even more thorough than those inflicted on Vietnam a decade later. But the supposition is trivial. The public did not see such photographs because there was, ideologically, no space for them. No one brought back photographs of daily life in Pyongyang, to show that the enemy had a human face, as Felix Greene and Marc Riboud brought back photographs of Hanoi. Americans did have access to photographs of the suffering of the Vietnamese (many of which came from military sources and were taken with quite a different use in mind) because journalists felt backed in their efforts to obtain those photographs, the event having been defined by a significant number of people as a savage colonialist war. The Korean War was understood differently— as part of the just struggle of the Free World against the Soviet Union and China—and, given that characterization, photographs of the cruelty of unlimited American firepower would have been irrelevant.

Though an event has come to mean, precisely, something worth photographing, it is still ideology (in the broadest sense) that determines what constitutes an event. There can be no evidence, photographic or otherwise, of an event until the event itself has been named and characterized. And it is never photographic evidence which can construct—more properly, identify—events; the contribution of photography always follows the naming of the event. What determines the possibility of being affected morally by photographs is the existence of a relevant political consciousness. Without a politics, photographs of the slaughter-bench of history will most likely be experienced as, simply, unreal or as a demoralizing emotional blow.

The quality of feeling; including moral outrage, that people can muster in response to photographs of the oppressed, the exploited, the starving, and the massacred also depends on the degree of their familiarity with these images. Don McCullin's photographs of emaciated Biafrans in the early 1970s had less impact for some people than Werner Bischof's photographs of Indian famine victims in the early 1950s because those images had become banal, and the photographs of Tuareg families dying of starvation in the sub-Sahara that appeared in magazines everywhere in 1973 must have seemed to many like an unbearable replay of a now familiar atrocity exhibition.

Photographs shock insofar as they show something novel. Unfortunately, the ante keeps getting raised—partly through the very proliferation of such images of horror. One's first encounter with the photographic inventory of ultimate horror is a kind of revelation, the prototypically modern revelation: a negative epiphany. For me, it was photographs of Bergen-Belsen and Dachau which I came across by chance in a bookstore in Santa Monica in July 1945. Nothing I have seen— in photographs or in real life—ever cut me as sharply, deeply, instantaneously. Indeed, it seems plausible to me to divide my life into two parts, before I saw those photographs (I was twelve) and after, though it was several years before I understood fully what they were about. What good was served by seeing them? They were only photographs—of an event I had scarcely heard of and could do nothing to affect, of suffering I could hardly imagine and could do nothing to relieve. When I looked at those photographs, something broke. Some limit had been reached, and not only that of horror; I felt irrevocably grieved, wounded, but a part of my feelings started to tighten; something went dead; something is still crying.

To suffer is one thing; another thing is living with the photographed images of suffering, which does not necessarily strengthen conscience and the ability to be compassionate. It can also corrupt them. Once one has seen such images, one has started down the road of seeing more—and more. Images transfix. Images anesthetize. An event known through photographs certainly becomes more real than it would have been if one had never seen the photographs—think of the Vietnam War. (For a counter-example, think of the Gulag Archipelago, of which we have no photographs.) But after repeated exposure to images it also becomes less real.

The same law holds for evil as for pornography. The shock of photographed atrocities wears off with repeated viewings, just as the surprise and bemusement felt the first time one sees a pornographic movie wear off after one sees a few more. The sense of taboo which makes us indignant and sorrowful is not much sturdier than the sense of taboo that regulates the definition of what is obscene. And both have been sorely tried in recent years. The vast photographic catalogue of misery and injustice throughout the world has given everyone a certain familiarity with atrocity, making the horrible seem more ordinary—making it appear familiar, remote ("It's only a photograph"), inevitable. At the time of the first photographs of the Nazi camps, there was nothing banal about these images. After thirty years, a saturation point may have been reached. In these last decades, "concerned" photography has done at least as much to deaden conscience as to arouse it.

The ethical content of photographs is fragile. With the possible exception of photographs of those horrors, like the Nazi camps, that have gained the status of ethical reference points, most photographs do not keep their emotional charge. A photograph of 1900 that was affecting then because of its subject would, today, be more likely to move us because it is a photograph taken in 1900. The particular qualities and intentions of photographs tend to be swallowed up in the generalized pathos of time past. Aesthetic distance seems built into the very experience of looking at photographs, if not right away, then certainly with the passage of time. Time eventually positions most photographs, even the most amateurish, at the level of art.

The industrialization of photography permitted its rapid absorption into rational—that is, bureaucratic—ways of running society. No longer toy images, photographs became part of the general furniture of the environment—touchstones and confirmations of that reductive approach to reality which is considered realistic. Photographs were enrolled in the service of important institutions of control, notably the family and the police, as symbolic objects and as pieces of information. Thus, in the bureaucratic cataloguing of the world, many important documents are not valid unless they have, affixed to them, a photograph-token of the citizen's face.

The "realistic" view of the world compatible with bureaucracy redefines knowledge—as techniques and information. Photographs are valued because they give information. They tell one what there is; they make an inventory. To spies, meteorologists, coroners, archaeologists, and other information professionals, their value is inestimable. But in the situations in which most people use photographs, their value as information is of the same order as fiction. The information that photographs can give starts to seem very important at that moment in cultural history when everyone is thought to have a right to something called news. Photographs were seen as a way of giving information to people who do not take easily to reading. The *Daily News* still calls itself "New York's Picture Newspaper," its bid for populist identity. At the opposite end of the scale, *Le Monde,* a newspaper designed for skilled, well-informed readers, runs no photographs at all. The presumption is that, for such readers, a photograph could only illustrate the analysis contained in an article.

A new sense of the notion of information has been constructed around the photographic image. The photograph is a thin slice of space as well as time. In a world ruled by photographic images, all borders ("framing") seem arbitrary. Anything can be separated, can be made discontinuous, from anything else all that is necessary is to frame the subject differently. (Conversely, anything can be made adjacent to anything else.) Photography reinforces a nominalist view of social reality as consisting of small units of an apparently infinite number—as the number of photographs that could be taken of anything is unlimited. Through photographs, the world becomes a series of unrelated, freestanding particles; and history, past and present, a set of anecdotes and *faits divers.* The camera makes reality atomic, manageable, and opaque. It is a view of the world which denies interconnectedness, continuity, but which confers on each moment the character of a mystery. Any photograph has multiple meanings; indeed, to see something in the form of a photograph is to encounter a potential object of fascination. The ultimate wisdom of the photographic image is to say: "There is the surface. Now think—or rather feel, intuit—what is beyond it, what the reality must be like if it looks this way." Photographs, which cannot themselves explain anything, are inexhaustible invitations to deduction, speculation, and fantasy.

Photography implies that we know about the world if we accept it as the camera records it. But this is the opposite of understanding, which starts from *not* accepting the world as it looks. All possibility of understanding is rooted in the ability to say no. Strictly speaking, one never understands anything from a photograph. Of course, photographs fill in blanks in our mental pictures of the present and the past: for example, Jacob Riis's images of New York squalor in the 1880s are sharply instructive to those unaware that urban poverty in late nineteenth-century America was really that Dickensian. Nevertheless, the camera's rendering of reality must always hide more than it discloses. As Brecht points out, a photograph of the Krupp works reveals virtually nothing about that organization. In contrast to the amorous relation, which is based on how something looks, understanding is based on how it functions. And functioning takes place in time, and must be explained in time. Only that which narrates can make us understand.

The limit of photographic knowledge of the world is that, while it can goad conscience, it can, finally, never be ethical or political knowledge. The knowledge gained through still photographs will always be some kind of sentimentalism, whether cynical or humanist. It will be a knowledge at bargain prices—a semblance of knowledge, a semblance of wisdom; as the act of taking pictures is a semblance of appropriation, a semblance of rape. The very muteness of what is, hypothetically, comprehensible in photographs is what constitutes their attraction and provocativeness. The omnipresence of photographs has an incalculable effect on our ethical sensibility. By furnishing this already crowded world with a duplicate one of images, photography makes us feel that the world is more available than it really is.

Needing to have reality confirmed and experience enhanced by photographs is an aesthetic consumerism to which everyone is now addicted. Industrial societies turn their citizens into image-junkies; it is the most irresistible form of mental pollution. Poignant longings for beauty, for an end to probing below the surface, for a redemption and celebration of the body of the world—all these elements of erotic feeling are affirmed in the pleasure we take in photographs. But other, less liberating feelings are expressed as well. It would not be wrong to speak of people having a *compulsion* to photograph: to turn experience itself into a way of seeing. Ultimately, having an experience becomes identical with taking a photograph of it, and participating in a public event comes more and more to be equivalent to looking at it in photographed form. That most logical of nineteenth-century aesthetes, Mallarmé,* said that everything in the world exists in order to end in a book. Today everything exists to end in a photograph.

DISCUSSION QUESTIONS

1. Compare and contrast Bazin and Sontag on the objectivity of photography. Whose view do you prefer, and why?

2. Why does Sontag believe that photography can never yield political and ethical knowledge? Do you agree with her? Why or why not?

3. Discuss Sontag's claim that "photographs alter and enlarge our notions of what is worth looking at and what we have a right to observe."

4. Sontag discusses several ways in which photography has come to be a means of control and surveillance by the government. What are they? Do you agree with her?

5. Why do people take photographs of their family and vacations? Does your response differ from Sontag's?

6. Sontag says that "photographing is essentially an act of non-intervention." Do you agree with her?

---

*Stéphane Mallarmé (1842–98) was a French poet and critic, and one of the originators of the Symbolist movement in poetry. He contended that there is nothing beyond reality and that within reality there exist perfectly formed essences. Mallarmé believed that poets should aim to capture these perfectly formed essences in their poetry. —Ed.

::::::::::::::::::::

Blow-Up
[UK/Italy 1966] 1 hour, 51 minutes
Directed by Michelangelo Antonioni

::::::::::::::::::::

T homas (David Hemmings) is a wealthy, popular, cynical fashion photographer living in London in the mid-1960s. He
makes real estate deals and organizes photo shoots while
cruising the city in his Rolls-Royce convertible. As part of the
"swinger" scene, Thomas is selfish, detached, and primarily concerned with recreational drugs and casual
sex. He is contemptuous of the women he photographs, and he manipulates others to satisfy his whims.

One day while Thomas is strolling through a park with his camera, he spots a grey-haired man (Ronan
O'Casey) and a woman (Vanessa Redgrave) embracing. After he photographs them repeatedly, the woman approaches him and heatedly asks for the film. Thomas refuses. Later, the woman, who introduces herself as Jane,
goes to his studio demanding the film. Thomas agrees to give it to her, but instead gives her another roll.

When Thomas develops the photos, he discovers that Jane is looking anxiously into the bushes while embracing her lover. When he enlarges the photos and studies them with a magnifying glass, he finds what appears to be a man with a gun in the bushes. Thomas believes that he has saved the lovers in the park from
being shot by this man. However, upon closer study of the photos, he finds a grainy, almost abstract, section
of the photograph that indicates the presence of a body. Thomas returns to the park and finds the corpse of
the grey-haired man. When Thomas gets back to his apartment, he finds that his photographs and negatives
have been stolen. He calls his friend Ron (Peter Bowles) and asks him to return to the park to photograph the
body. Ron declines, so Thomas goes back on his own. However, the corpse is nowhere to be found.

Upon leaving the park, Thomas encounters a group of young people miming a game of tennis. A crowd
silently follows the path of the make-believe ball. Eventually, the "ball" sails out of the tennis court. The
camera follows it as Thomas chases down and pretends to throw it back. We then hear the sounds of a ball
being hit back and forth, and the camera focuses on Thomas standing in a grassy field alone. The camera
tracks back until Thomas disappears, much like the corpse he had uncovered.

Blow-Up is a complex meditation on the ontological and epistemological nature of photography and
film. The film is based on a short story of the same name by the Argentine writer Julio Cortázar (1914–84).
It should be noted that Antonioni refused to cut nudity and sexually explicit scenes from the film. *Blow-Up*
was released without the approval of the Motion Picture Association of America, yet still did very well in
the "art house" circuit. *Blow-Up* was one of the films that led to the demise of the Production Code and the
establishment of the ratings system.

DISCUSSION QUESTIONS

1. Does *Blow-Up* support Susan Sontag's contention that photographs are not an objective representation of the world? Why or why not?

2. Sontag says that photographs allow us access to images of atrocities and make those events "more
   real" than they would have been without the photographs. Reflect on the way that Thomas's
   photographs of homeless men make poverty in London "more real." Compare those photographs
   with Thomas's fashion photographs. Do they also make their subject (fashion) "more real"? Why or
   why not?

3. Thomas blows up the photos he took in the park and studies them in order to uncover the reality they represent. Does he ever find it? What do his actions say about the limits of photography?

4. How is finding the meaning of abstract paintings (such as Thomas's friend Bill's [John Castle] "dot" paintings) similar to or different from finding the meaning of Thomas's blown-up, grainy photos? Is Antonioni insinuating that the process of finding with certainty the reality that underlies the paintings is just as difficult as finding the reality that underlies the photos taken in the park? Why or why not?

5. Thomas studies the photos that he took in the park and organizes them according to a narrative or story he has created. One of the narratives concerns the lovers in the park being saved from being shot from the unknown person wielding a gun in the distance, and another concerns a male in the park being the victim of a murder. The photos can be organized to support both narratives. Which, if either, is the true narrative, and why?

6. How is the process of organizing photos to support or create a narrative like the process of film-making? Do the images presented in a film represent reality or construct (or create) reality?

7. It could be said that taking images that collectively are inchoate (disordered) and imposing a narrative upon them is something we do in everyday life. That is, Thomas's search for the meaning of the photographs from the park is similar to our search for meaning in our everyday lives, namely, that without a narrative, our lives make about as much sense as Bill's "dot" paintings. Do you agree with this? Why or why not?

8. *Blow-Up* does not offer a final answer as to what happened in the park, and ultimately, the photos raise more questions than they answer. Antonioni has said that under the revealed image is another one that is more faithful to reality, and under this is yet another, and again another, down to the true image of that absolute mysterious reality that no one will ever see until the decomposition of all images. Do you agree with him? Must we do away with images in order to see the ultimate reality of things? And is this not similar to the position advocated by Plato in his cave analogy? Discuss.

9. The movie closes with the mimed tennis match sequence. David does not appreciate the game until he buys into the illusion that there really is a tennis ball and goes to chase it down. Once he does, he disappears (or decomposes) into the grassy background of the field. What is the meaning of this sequence?

10. Does it bother you that the mystery is never definitively resolved in this film? Is Antonioni suggesting in *Blow-Up* that even in such an objective genre as photography, the truth is not always verifiable? That we see in the photographs is only what we want to see, and not necessarily what is really there? Discuss.

FRANCIS SPARSHOTT

BASIC FILM AESTHETICS

Francis Sparshott outlines and analyzes the central features of film and urges film critics to use both these features and their own social and moral awareness in their film criticism. "If you could teach people to be critics, you could teach them to be human," writes Sparshott.

Sparshott begins with a working definition of film: "A film is a series of motionless images projected onto a screen so fast as to create in the mind of anyone watching the screen an impression of continuous motion, such images being projected by a light shining through a corresponding series of images arranged on a continuous band of flexible material." He points out that while one can argue over the specific features of the definition, two features are indispensable: (1) the basic mechanisms employed, and (2) the creation of an illusion of motion.

Concerning the first feature, Sparshott notes, "The history of film is the history of the invention of its means." The means of cinema are complex, and "anyone who has mastered them . . . will naturally use them to convey whatever message or vision he may wish to convey, whether or not it is 'cinematic' by any plausible definition." "People use their languages to say what they wish to say," continues Sparshott, "not what the language makes it easy to say." "Most theorists of cinema insist that the outcome of this natural tendency is bound to be a bad film, but one hardly sees why." With regard to the second feature, the creation of the illusion of motion, Sparshott notes that "different audiences will differ in the susceptibilities to such effects; trying to decide the proprieties . . . by invoking principles is surely a waste of time."

Sparshott describes and analyzes a number of other features of film including the commercial aspects, "bias of exposition," and film's dreamlike character, as well as space, time, motion, sound, and structure in film. However, he insists that analysis of these features in film criticism should not be formulaic. His comments on each feature always remind us that individual expectations and cultural contingencies play a large role in understanding the role and variations of these features in film. Moreover, film criticism at its best requires not merely an exhaustive consideration of each of these features but a critic able to situate these features within a social and moral awareness.

Francis Sparshott (1926–), a philosopher and poet, is widely admired as one of Canada's leading philosophers. Born in England, he received a B.A. and an M.A. from Corpus Christi College, Oxford. Upon the completion of his studies at Oxford in 1950, Sparshott joined the philosophy department at the University of Toronto, where he worked until his retirement in 1991. He is currently university professor emeritus at the University of Toronto. Sparshott was a member of the Canadian Philosophical Association, the League of Canadian Poets, and P.E.N. International. Sparshott's many publications include *An Enquiry into Goodness and Related Concepts* (1958), *The Structure of Aesthetics* (1963), *A Divided Voice* (1965), *The Concept of Criticism* (1967), *A Cardboard Garage* (1969), *A Book by Cromwell Kent* (1970), *Looking for Philosophy* (1972), *The Naming of the Beasts* (1979), *The Theory of the Arts* (1982), *The Hanging Gardens at Etobicoke* (1983), *Storms and Screens* (1986), *Sculling to Byzantium* (1989), *Taking Life Seriously: A Study of the Argument of the Nichomachean Ethics* (1994), *A Measured Pace: Towards a Philosophical Understanding of the Arts of Dance* (1995), *The Future of Aesthetics* (1998), and *The City Dwellers* (2000). The following article, "Basic Film Aesthetics," was first published in the *Journal of Aesthetic Education* in 1971.

The basic aesthetics of film as of any other art must be descriptive and analytic, giving an account of the relevant variables and their means of variation. And any such account must be rooted in some notion, however imprecise, of what a work of the art in question is. What, then, is a film? It seems to be characteristic of the art that acceptable definitions need to specify not only the nature of the work itself but also the means essential to its production and its characteristic effects. A sample definition might go like this: "A film is a series of motionless images projected onto a screen so fast as to create in the mind of anyone watching the screen an impression of continuous motion, such images being projected by a light shining through a corresponding series of images arranged on a continuous band of flexible material." Much variation in detail and in emphasis is possible, but no definition can dispense with two important features: a succinct description of at least the basic features of the *mechanism* employed, and an allusion to the creation of an *illusion* of motion. Let us consider these necessary features in turn.

Mechanism

More than any other art, film is technologically determined. Music, dance, drawing, painting, sculpture, poetry, even architecture need for their original and rudimentary forms either no materials or materials lying everywhere at hand, but cinematography cannot begin without laboriously invented and precisely constructed equipment. The history of film is the history of the invention of its means. Aestheticians of the cinema may often be differentiated by how they react to various aspects of its technology: the properties of lenses and emulsions, the conditions of production and display. Thus the most notorious dogmas about how films ought to be made are demands for truth to the supposed tendencies of some aspect of the medium: to the clarity and convincingness of photographic images, or to the impartial receptivity of a film camera to whatever may be put before it, or to the camera's way of reducing whatever is put before it to a homogeneous image, or to the ease with which assorted scraps of film may be so cemented as to suggest a common provenance, and so on. It is characteristic of such dogmas that they fasten on one such aspect and tendency and ignore the rest. All of them ignore one very important factor: just because the means of cinema are so complex, anyone who has mastered them (and, equally rare and difficult, who has regular access to them) will naturally use them to convey whatever message or vision he may wish to convey, whether or not it is "cinematic" by any plausible definition. People use their languages to say what they wish to say, not what the language makes it easy to say. Most theorists of cinema insist that the outcome of this natural tendency is bound to be a bad film, but one hardly sees why. Whatever can be one with a medium is among its possibilities and hence "true

to" it in a sense that has yet to be shown to be illegitimate. A person may become (or may train himself to be) sensitive to the degree in which films exploit or ignore some possibility of the medium, and then may govern his taste or regulate his critical judgment accordingly, but one does not see why such arbitrary selective systems should be imposed on those who would reject them. It is one thing to show that it is almost impossible to make a good film by photographing a stage performance of a play, by enumerating the probable sources of boredom and irritation; it is quite another to declare that all filmed plays are necessarily nonfilmic and on that account bad films.

Illusion

The second necessary feature of our sample definition was its reference to an illusion. Perhaps alone among the arts, and certainly in a way quite different from any of the other major arts, film is necessarily an art of illusion from the very beginning; and illusion, like technology, serves as a focal point around which aesthetic disputes arrange themselves. On the one hand, it may be taken as an opportunity to be exploited. Both by fabricating the images to be projected and by manipulating the speed and sequence of their projection, films can and do revel in the creation of the most elaborate illusions. On the other hand, illusion may be seen as the temptation to be resisted. The motion on the screen has to be unreal, but can and should faithfully portray a motion that really took place just so in the real world. Both tendencies go back to the earliest days of cinema, in the work of the realist Lumière and the fantasist Méliès. But that does not mean that film-makers have to choose between embracing and eschewing illusion: quite usually, and in the films of at least some acknowledged masters, fantasy is put at the service of realism (e.g., the stone lions in *Potemkin*) or realism at the service of fantasy (e.g., the homecoming in *Ugetsu*).

To speak broadly of "illusion" as we have done is misleading. While the basic illusion of motion is an automatic and unavoidable function of the mechanism of human vision, what I shall call the "secondary illusions" constructed upon it, to the effect that an event or movement of a certain sort is taking place, are not automatic but depend on the filmgoer's knowledge and his ability or willingness to acquiesce in a pretense. Writers on film often mention a scene in which an Indian villager is pursued by a tiger. The pursuit is shown entirely by intercut shots of scared man and slavering beast until, at the very end, pursuer and pursued at last appear together in a single shot. For Bazin, this saves the scene: previously one had assumed that the propinquity of man and beast was an illusion created by cutting, now one suddenly sees that it was not. For Montagu, it is stupid: the effect was created by the cutting, the concluding two-shot is a banal assertion. And of course on reflection one realizes that either it was a tame tiger or we are being served another trick shot. It seems obvious that different audiences will differ in their susceptibilities to such effects; trying to decide the proprieties (as both writers do) by invoking ultimate principles is surely a waste of time.

THE BIAS OF EXPOSITION

As the example we have just given shows, the secondary illusions of film relate not to what is projected on the screen but to the supposed provenance of the image. No more than when attending a stage play does anyone at the movies feel as if an event were really taking place before his eyes. But why should there be illusions of provenance? The answer seems to lie in the complex relations between cinematography and photography, and the peculiar nature of photographic images themselves. A clue to these relations may be found in the fact that all but one of the demands of "truth to the medium" that we used as examples mentioned some aspect of photography, although our sample definition of a film made no allusion to photography at all.

The images whose successive projection makes a film are most easily produced by photography; but they can be drawn directly on the film stock. A photograph to represent an object is most easily made by aiming a camera at an object of the appropriate kind; but what is photographed may also be a model or a drawing or even another photograph made for the purpose. A photograph of an event or happening is most easily made by finding one and photographing it; but scenes may be enacted and scenery constructed for the purpose. The required succession of images is most easily produced by using a device that will take a lot of photographs in rapid succession and fix them in the right order; but it can be (and in animated cartoons is) drawn or photographed frame by frame. And the obvious way to work the film camera (though not necessarily the easiest; rather it is synchronization that requires care) is to run it at the same speed as you will run your projector; but it can be run faster or slower. Film thus has a bias, quite strong though readily resistible, towards its simplest form, that in which the projector repeats a camera event; and one tends if not on one's guard to assume, wherever nothing in the film suggests the contrary, that what is shown on the screen represents such a repetition, as if the projector copied a camera that enacted the spectator's eye.

An eye is not a camera, and a photographic image does not show what eyes see. As you look around you, your eye constantly adjusts its iris as brightness changes and alters its focus as depth changes. The parallax effect of the use of two eyes gives everything you see a shifting and unstable character, since everything not focused on at the moment yields a vague doubled image. The eye in nature is therefore restless; in looking at a photograph, all in one plane and with a relatively small range of luminosity, the eye is spared much of its labor. However, though a photographic image is not at all like the visible world, it does have precisely the quality that old theorists used to ascribe to that venerable phantom of optics the retinal image. A photographic image represents a sort of ideal projection, the way we normalize in imagination what we see. What the invention of photography did was not to reproduce vision but to achieve a dream of ideal vision. A photographic image is not so much a true one as a convincing one. Photographs tend to carry an irresistible sense of authenticity. Looking at a good photograph is not like looking at the photographed thing (this is so far from being the case that Peter Ustinov's famous remark, that he made *Billy Budd* in black-and-white because it was more realistic than color, hardly seems paradoxical); it is like looking at a faithful record.

The basic illusion of movement by itself gives an impression not of reality but of a sort of unattributable vivacity. This becomes evident when one watches an animated cartoon.

Verisimilitude adds nothing to the lifelikeness of such films, and the elaborate devices used by Disney in his later years to suggest a third dimension have been abandoned as futile (as well as expensive). The sense of reality elicited by such films is akin to that of painting: we attribute the actions we see neither to the real world nor to the screen image, but to Donald Duck and the cartoon world created for him. It is not the illusion of movement, then, that moves us to attribute what we see to the world of experience; rather it is the photographic character of the image that lends films their characteristic bias of exposition, and to the extent that it is present and uncontradicted by the nature of what is presented encourages us to take what we see as the record of something that took place as we see it taking place. The viewer tends to normalize in this sense his perception of films made in the most diverse ways.

Many theories about how films ought to be made represent attitudes to the bias of exposition just described. The Soviet film-makers of the twenties claimed that the whole art of film lay in exploiting its tendency by the use of montage or associative cutting, joining strips of photographed film in such a way as to synthesize in the spectator's mind an experiential reality that went beyond the images shown. Siegfried Kracauer* urged on the contrary that the best use of film is an honest reliance on its capacity to convey authenticity, to preserve and celebrate the sense of reality. His argument was not that a film should actually be a record or chronicle, but that it should celebrate and "redeem," as no other medium can, the radiant actuality of the physical world, eschewing alike fantasies and superimposed formal arrangements. Other critics, noting that film bestows verisimilitude on the deserving and the undeserving alike, urge that film includes among its unique capacities that of making "dreams come true." Only film can *show* the impossible happening and thus make fantasy convincing. In the opposite direction, some exponents of contemporary "underground" film go beyond Kracauer (and beyond Rossellini and the Italian neorealists) in urging that to cut film at all is to falsify: the finished film should consist of all that the camera took in the order it was taken in, and if this means that some shots are out-of-focus, ill-exposed or irrelevant, they will thereby only be truer to the film experience. On this view, a film records not what happened in front of the camera but what happened to the film *in* the camera. And finally, some extremists might urge that the only honest way to make a film is to set a camera up somewhere and let it just run, taking in whatever may happen along. But at that point the urge to honesty would surely defeat itself by suggesting a standard it cannot fulfill. Films are not natural events, and it is pointless to prevaricate about the selective intervention of the film-maker.

FILM SPACE

That the realism of film is that of a graphic record and not that of an illusive actuality is apparent in the peculiar nature of film space, the actual and suggested spatial relations between elements of the film and between film and spectator. Many writers imply that a filmgoer ordinarily feels himself to be in the same relation to the filmed scene as the camera was (or purports to have been). On this basis such trick shots as those showing a room through the flames of a fire in the fireplace are condemned on the ground that the audience know that nobody would be in that position. But this seems to be mistaken. Spectators seem to identify themselves with the camera viewpoint only when some such process as Cinerama is used which makes the screen approximate to the total visual environment. Otherwise, shots taken looking straight downward do not give one a sense of vertigo (though they may do to persons extremely susceptible in this regard), and even the most rapid changes in camera position do not produce in an experienced filmgoer any sense of nausea or disorientation. If one really accepted a change in camera position as a change in one's personal viewpoint, rapid intercutting between different

---

*Siegfried Kracauer (1889–1966) was a German-born journalist, sociologist, and film critic. From 1922 to 1933, he worked as a film critic and literature editor at the *Frankfurter Zeitung* in Berlin, where one of his co-workers was Walter Benjamin. Kracauer contends that realism is the most important aspect of cinema and defends this position most extensively in his 1960 book, *Theory of Film: The Redemption of Physical Reality.* —Ed.

viewpoints would obviously be intolerable. There is certainly a sense in which one has a feeling of spatial presence at the filmed scene (which is not to be confused with psychological involvement in the action), construing the scene as a three-dimensional space in which one is involved and has a viewpoint. This depth and inclusiveness of cinema space owes much to parallax, the differential motion and occlusion of distant objects as the viewpoint changes. It follows that when, as often happens nowadays, action is interrupted by stop-motion, the whole nature of the space in which the action takes place is instantly transformed (a striking instance is the concluding scene of *The Strawberry Statement*). This little-noted factor is important. Without such a change in spatiality, stop-motion might give the impression that the world had suddenly come to a halt; as it is, it confronts us rather with a transition to a different mode of representation, and hence perhaps a different mode of being.

The more one reflects on one's sense of cinema space, the more it seems to be one peculiar to cinema. The use of a zoom lens increasing the (objective) size of the image does have the effect of bringing the action nearer; but walking towards the screen, though it produces a (subjectively) larger image and does bring the screen nearer, does not bring the action nearer at all. One's sense of spatial involvement in a scene does not depend on one's occupying any particular seat, but only on one's being neither too close nor too far to see the screen properly. Similar considerations apply to all the distortions of space that result from the use of various lenses. The resulting plasticity of space relations is accepted as a narrative device or as an invitation to an imaginary viewpoint, it does not disorient the audience. The use of a deep-focus lens for Miss Havisham's room in *Great Expectations* certainly has a "magnifying" effect, but a curious one: we do not feel that we are in a big room, but that "this is how it must have seemed to Pip." Again, in the scene where the girl runs toward the airplane in *Zabriskie Point* the scale-relations between girl and low horizon are such that for a second or two we accept what we see as an ordinary medium-shot; then we notice that for all her running the girl is not receding much, and realize that it is a typical telephoto shot. But the effect of this realization on me was not to alter my feeling of where I was in relation to the scene, but to change my interpretation of that relation. In fact, a telephoto shot answers to no possible real spatial relationship between spectator and event: there is a viewing angle, but no possible view point. Yet this never disturbs anyone.

Phenomena of the sort we have been mentioning suggest that one's sense of space in film is somehow bracketed or held in suspense: one is aware of one's implied position and accepts it, but is not existentially committed to it. A simple explanation of this is that most of the time one is simultaneously aware of a film (as one is of a painting) both as a two-dimensional arrangement on the screen and as a three-dimensional scene, so that neither aspect dominates the mind except in moments of excitement or disaffection. A subtler explanation is that cinema vision is alienated vision. A man's sense of where he is depends largely on his sense of balance and his muscular senses, and all a filmgoer's sensory cues other than those of vision and hearing relate firmly to the theater and seat in which he sits. In the scene with the epileptic doctor in *Carnet du Bal*, which is taken with a consistently titled camera, what one sees on the screen insists that one is off balance, but one's body insists that it is not; and the effect on me is the one Duvivier surely intended, a feeling of malaise accompanied by a sense of *vicarious* disorientation on behalf of the protagonist.

Some of the spatial ambiguity of film is shared with still photography. No matter how one moves a photograph around in relation to oneself, it continues to function as a faithful record implying a viewpoint from which it was taken: and there is a sense in which one continues to be "at" this viewpoint no matter what angle the photograph is inspected from. What differentiates film from still photography is not only the sense of vivacity and hence spatial reality that motion imparts, but also the great size and contrasting illumination of the film image in the darkened theater, whereby it comes much closer to dominating the visual sense, and the relatively invariant relation between screen and spectator. The director determines the audience's spatial relation to his films, but what he determines remains an imaginary space; we are within the film's space but not part of its world; we observe from a viewpoint at which we are not situated.

It is the alienation of the visual sense in cinema space that makes possible many of the uses and special effects of film that work against its function as record. Being deprived of so many sensory cues, the spectator loses all sense of absolute scale, so that back-projections and painted backgrounds may wear a convincing air of reality, and the apparent size of any object may be varied by placing it in a magnified or diminished setting, or simply (as when storms and wrecks are shot using models in tanks) by trading on the spectator's narrative assumptions.

Film and Dream

Unique as it is, the alienated spatiality of film, in which the spectator participates without contact, and which he observes from a viewpoint that contrives to be both definite and equivocal or impossible, presents striking analogies to the space of dreams. Or perhaps, since different people seem to have widely varying dream perceptions, I should limit myself to saying that my own spatial relation to my dream worlds is like nothing in waking reality so much as it is like my relation to film worlds. In my dreams, too, I see from where I am not, and move helplessly in a space whose very nature is inconstant, and may see beside me the being whose perceptions I share. There are indeed many ways in which filmgoing is like dreaming; but the likeness is always qualified. Films are like dreams in involving one in a world whose course one cannot control, but unlike them in that their world does not incorporate the dream of effort and participation. Filmed reality shares with dreamed reality (as nothing else does) its tolerance of limitlessly inconsequent transitions and transformations; but it lacks that curious conceptual continuity of dreams in which what is a raven may become a writing-desk or may simultaneously *be* a writing-desk, and in which one *knows* that what looks like one person is really a quite different person. The conceptual equivalences essayed by film-makers (e.g., Eisenstein's equation of Kerensky with a peacock in *October*), which usually proceed by intercutting shots of the two entities to be equated, seem rather to be the visual equivalent of similes or metaphors than equivalents of the dream carryover, which depends on a dream-interpretation imposed on the dream-percept and not (as must be the case

in film) on an interpretation suggested by the percept itself.

The dreamlikeness of film has often been noted. Usually the recognition takes the form of a loose analogy with daydreaming (which is quite different), but Susanne Langer for one has made the formal analogy with dreaming the basis of her account of the nature of film. The analogy must not be pushed too far. A quite fundamental difference between a filmgoer and a dreamer is that the former remains in control of his faculties, capable of sustained and critical attention. A dreamlike inconsequentiality is thus far from typical of film, though it remains among filmic possibilities and the filmgoing public at large acquiesces in a degree of cheerful incoherence (as in *Casino Royale*) that in other arts is acceptable only to the sophisticate.

To the extent that the analogy between film and dream is taken seriously, it seems to invite Freudians to apply their methods of symbolic interpretation with even more confidence than they do to other arts. But they seem not to have accepted the invitation (except in so far as Freudian methodology lies behind the auteur theory of criticism), perhaps because not enough film-makers are safely dead yet. In any case, before we reach that level of interpretation we have to complete our survey of the basic attributes of the film world.

Film Time and Film Reality

The same confusion between an actual event and a convincing record that has made critics write of the camera as a surrogate for the spectator's eye leads them to say that film time is present time, that in watching a film one seems to see things happening *now*, as though one were present not at the film but at the filmed event. But this contention is vulnerable to the same sort of objection that refutes the doctrine of the camera eye. In one sense it is true but trivial: of course what one sees is always here and now, because "here" and "now" are defined by one's presence. In any other sense it is false, or we should not be able to take in our stride the flashbacks and flash-forwards, the accelerations and decelerations, that are part of film's stock in trade. Rather, it is as though we were spectators of the temporality of the films we see. Film time has a quality analogous to that dreamlike floating between participation and observation, between definite and indeterminate relationships, that gives film space its pervasive character. Granted, the fundamental illusion of motion combines with the convincingness of a photographic record to ensure that we ordinarily do read the presented motion as continuous and as taking just as much time to happen as it takes us to observe it; but this supposition is readily defeated by any counterindication. D. W. Griffith, challenged on his early use of spatiotemporal discontinuities, justified himself by appealing to the example of Dickens, and surely he was right to do so. The time of a novel is filmic, as its space is not. Events can be filmed, as they can be narrated, with equal facility in any order, at any speed, with any degree of minuteness. Unlike the novelist, however, the film-maker has no language proper to his medium in which to specify temporal relations. He may use titles, trick dissolves, a narrator's voice, or datable visual clues to establish his temporal relations; but some directors seem to feel that such devices are clumsy or vulgar, and prefer to trust the public's acumen or simply to leave the relations indeterminate.

The dream-relationships of film space and the narrative nature of film time combine to encourage an ambiguity that may be fruitful or merely irritating. One often does not know whether one is seeing what in the film's terms is real, or only what is passing through the mind of one of the film's characters. This ambiguity becomes acute whenever there is a temporal jump, for time (as Kant observed) is the form of subjectivity. A flash-back may represent a character's memory, or may simply be a narrative device; a flash-forward may stand for a character's premonition, or simply an anticipation by the film-maker; and, where the temporally displaced scene is recalled or foreseen, it may stand either for the event as it was or would be, or for the way it is (perhaps falsely) conjured up. The status of film events thus becomes equivocal, and such uncertainty may pervade an entire film. Thus in $8^1/_2$ some scenes are remembered, some dreamed, some imagined, and some belong to the reality of the film's story. There are many scenes whose status is unclear at the time, and some whose status never becomes clear. Does the opening scene of

the closed car in the traffic jam show a seizure which makes the cure necessary (as Arnheim seems to think), or is it a dream of a patient already undergoing treatment (as most critics suppose)? Nothing in the version of the film I saw determined either answer. A more striking equivocation occurs in *Easy Rider*, when a brief glimpse of an unexplained roadside fire is identified at the end of the film as the burning of the hero's motorcycle. Was that first glimpse a premonition of the hero's (and if so, just what did he foresee?), or a *memento mori* by the director, or just a pointless interjection to which no meaning can be assigned? In such a self-indulgent piece of hokum, who can say? In general, the tolerability of such unresolved ambiguities is likely to depend partly on the handling of "reality" in the film as a whole, partly on one's confidence in the director's control over his medium, and partly on one's own tolerance of ambiguity. In any case, one must not suppose that such questions as we have just posed need have a single "right" answer (perhaps what the director "meant"). All the director has done is to splice celluloid, and if he has not provided enough clues to determine a reading then no meaning is determined. What the director may have had in mind is not the same as what he put on film, and directors sometimes have nothing at all in mind. The flexibility of film technique is a standing invitation to meaningless trickery, and the complexities of production involve endless risks of inadvertent nonsense.

As the apparent time of the action changes, then, so changes the subjectivity/objectivity rating of what we see; and so too may vary our degree of confidence in our ability to assign a rating. Nor are such ambiguities the prerogative of highbrow excursions like *Last Year at Marienbad*. They occur quite naturally in unsophisticated films. For example, in Jerry Lewis's Jekyll-and-Hyde fantasy *The Nutty Professor* the transformation scene in the laboratory slips onto a plane of witty extravagance quite removed from the surface naturalism of the rest of the film. Are we witnessing the event or a metaphor for the event? Who knows? One could spend a long time figuring out possible meanings for it, but in fact it comes across as just a happy episode and the popcorn-grinding jaws do not miss a beat.

FILM MOTION

The ambiguities of space and time combine to give film motion an endless complexity that we have no space to explore here. Let us confine our attention to some additional complications. In the earliest movies, each scene was taken with a fixed camera, so that the motion shown took place within a fixed frame and against an unchanging background. A scene in a modern film is likely to be enriched or muddled with three different kinds of camera motion. The camera may be shifted from place to place, turned horizontally or vertically to alter its field of reception, or modified by changing the focal length of its lens so as to take in a greater or smaller area. This third kind of camera shot is often dismissed as the equivalent of a tracking shot, moving the camera viewpoint toward or away from the scene, but it is not; it retains much of the sense of getting a different view from the same position. A camera can also be rotated on its focal axis, or joggled and steadied, but these can be set aside for now as occasional effects.

Even a shot of immobile objects taken with an immobile camera need not be devoid of movement, for there is also movement of light: illumination may change in direction, in intensity, in color, in sharpness. And even when the light remains unchanged, the much-used prints that most audiences see have a sort of constant surface shimmer, a vibrant presence derived from the random stains and lesions hard use imparts, that has a good deal to do with the "film experience" and is exploited by some film-makers in much the same spirit that furniture-makers fake a "distressed finish." The free combinations of all the kinds of film motion can impart to a single scene a plastic, balletic quality, a unique kind of formal beauty that is at once abstract and realistic and has no parallel in any other medium.

The mobility of the frame combines with the camera's typical neglect of natural boundaries to produce a marked contrast between the actions of theater and cinema. The stage world is a closed world; an actor who goes offstage loses all determinate existence for the audience; but the edge of a cinema screen functions like a window frame through which we glimpse part of a world to which we attribute infinite continuity. This sense of infinity adds an implicit freedom of movement to the actual freedom that the camera's mobility affords.

Because film space and time are observed rather than lived, film motion can be speeded up or slowed down within scenes in a way denied to theater, in which events take their proper time. (Conversely, theater has a way of achieving temporal plasticity denied to film, by exploiting the stage-unreality of the offstage world: in theater, but not in film, off-stage actions are often performed in the course of a scene in an incongruously short time.) The effects of such variations in time depend on context, in a way that becomes easier to understand when we reflect that motion photography was invented to serve not one realistic purpose but two: not only to observe and record movements, but also to study and examine them. And of course very fast movements are best studied by slowing down their representation, very slow ones by speeding it up. Nature films are quite regularly made at unnatural speeds, accelerating plant growth and decelerating bird flight, and replays of crucial movements in sport are usually in slow motion. In this context of study the spectator has no sense of unreality at all: he feels simply that he is getting a better look. But in narrative contexts things are different. Acceleration was early discovered to have a reliably comic effect. But deceleration is more variable, for it may produce an impression of joy, or unreality, or obsessiveness, or solemnity, or inevitability. Its effects often evade description, but directors find them reliable enough for regular use, and they have hardened into more than one cliché. One such is the flash-back reverie, where the slow motion seems to work by suggesting weightlessness and hence ethereality (as in *The Pawnbroker*). Another is the use of weightlessness as a metaphor for lightheartedness (as in many TV commercials). A third is the slow-motion death by shooting (as in *Bonnie and Clyde*), partly an appeal to voyeurism but partly a symbolization of death through the transposition of the action into another key of reality.

One can think of acceleration arid deceleration as a sort of preediting, the equivalent of adding or subtracting frames in a film taken at projector speed. It is basic to film that editing can produce an impression of motion by intercutting suitably spaced shots of the same object in different positions (as by successive still photographs). The impression does not depend on the basic illusion of continuity: provided that the mind can supply a possible trajectory, all that is needed is that the object should appear to be the same and that its position in successive shots should appear to be different. But beyond this, the effect of *any* sustainedly rapid cutting is to produce an impression of rapid motion, even if the intercut shots have no common content and one cannot say what (apart from "things") is moving. An intermediate sort of effect produced by editing is a two-dimensional movement of light, where the continuity of light and dark areas in successive shots is enough to entice the mind to complete a *Gestalt;* but this effect is of limited application, in that it draws attention away from the filmed world to the screen surface.

Cinema's repertory of motions both presented and psychologically suggested is so extensive and so essential that one might think that what film shares with still photography is unimportant, and specifically that two-dimensional composition within the frame can play no significant part in film at all. But that would be going too far. Not only does the awareness of the screen and its flat pattern play an essential part in grounding the ambiguous nature of film space, but directors in practice often do envisage their scenes statically. They make sketches for their key scenes beforehand, and use viewfinders to compose a scene before shooting it. A film no less than a play may proceed from tableau to tableau. Nonetheless, the tableau is insidiously misleading in more than one way. The more one reads about films the more clearly one sees how each film is invariably illustrated by a handful of constantly recurring still shots: *Potemkin* comes to be represented by half a dozen stills, *Caligari* by two, *Nosferatu* by one. Most of these are not even frames taken from the actual film, but photographs taken on a still camera before or after shooting. And they are chosen for their pictorial qualities. What I most vividly recall from *Bicycle Thieves* is the mountain of bundled clothing in the pawnshop, but that image would be nothing without the camera's movement and the action of adding one's own bundle to the mountain, and what the stills show me is a pretty, pathetic picture of the hero and his son sitting on the sidewalk. Thus in time one's recollection of what a film was like becomes distorted.

SOUND

We have been discussing film in visual terms. But for rather more than half its history film has been fully an art of sound as well as sight in the sense that the associated sound has been determined by the same celluloid strip that carries the image. The justification of our procedure is that sight remains primary. It is the requirements of the visual image that call for the elaboration of equipment and the circumstances of display that are fundamental to cinema. Film sound has no distinctive qualities in itself, and can be meaningfully discussed only as an adjunct to the visual.

Though a sound track for a film can be made directly at the time of shooting simply by hanging microphones near the action and recording on the film whatever they pick up, this is neither necessary nor usual. The sound track is usually made separately and combined with the visual film later. The resulting complexities for sound film are theoretically immense, though in practice the technology is not intimidating. The use of magnetic tape has made the recording, inventing, blending, splicing and modification of sounds easy and inexpensive as the analogous procedures for visual film can never be.

The fundamental classification of film sounds is that enunciated by Kracauer. A sound may belong to the world of the film (e.g., the dialogue of its characters) or it may be extraneous (e.g., background music or a commentary). In the former case, it may belong to the very scene being shown on the screen or it may not (you may hear what is happening elsewhere from what you see, or be reminded by the sound track of a previous scene; as a marginal case, what you hear may be a sound remembered by one of the characters). If the sound does belong to the scene being shown, its provenance may be on or off camera (as you hear someone talk, you may see him, or the person he is addressing, or someone who overhears him, or an opening door that he fails to notice). Thus sound may (and in a slackly made film often does) merely duplicate or reinforce what is visible, but it may play an independent structural or narrative role, and may affect the interpretation or emotional tone of what is seen.

For example, distortions, fadings, and swellings of voices can be used to overcome one of the difficulties of film narrative, that of economically revealing to the audience a state of mind that someone is successfully hiding from those around him. Background music may supply an ironic comment, as when the refueling of aircraft in *Dr. Strangelove* is accompanied by a love song—a Russian film of the silent days would have made the point by intercutting shots of animals mating, and what a bore it would have been. One can even try to use a musical score to supplement narrative deficiencies, or even to contradict the apparent tendency of what is seen to be happening, though such techniques have some notorious fiascos to their credit.

When determinate sound was first introduced, many film-lovers were opposed to it. In principle the objection was invalid, for films had never been shown without accompanying (and would-be relevant) sound (a "silent" film shown in silence is a curiosity rather than a significant experience), and in principle the change only guaranteed that from now on the sound would indeed be relevant. But in practice what was feared was the "talking film," in which the sound track merely enabled the audience to hear what they could already see. And the use of sound does indeed make sloppy and mindless film-making easier. But sound can be and properly is used not merely to add another dimension to the film experience but to add an extra perspective to the visual experience itself.

As an alternative to the mindless use of attached sound that they dreaded, the Russian theorists of the late twenties proposed that their favorite device of associative or metaphorical montage should be extended to sound: intercut images should form a counterpoint against intercut sounds. This did not happen. For one thing, auditory comprehension has a much slower tempo than visual; for another, sounds tend to blend whereas images contrast. The proposed contrapuntal montage would have been impossibly overloaded, if not unintelligible. What montage requires from sound, it turns out, is not a contrapuntal pattern but a chordal backing for its visual melody, a continuous equivalent for or commentary on the character of the whole episode. In any case, the possibility of using sound effects as commentary on the visual images has made elaborate visual montage an obsolete device. This can be thought of as a catastrophic and uncompensated loss to the art of film, but the matter is open to question. Although Eisenstein and others made the use of associative intercutting into a Marxist aesthetic dogma (inasmuch as the conflict of contrasting shots forms a "dialectic" from which the realist truth is synthesized), others have pointed out that the device endears itself to totalitarian regimes by lending itself to lying propaganda: the associations it creates are entirely irrational. Partly, too, the reliance on cutting was enforced by the use of heavy and inflexible camera equipment. Conversely, the decreasing reliance on editing in scene construction is partly due to the introduction of ever more mobile and flexible equipment, partly to the familiarity of multicamera television procedures, partly to difficulties in synchronizing dialogue, but partly also to the fact that commercial directors tend not to do their own cutting anyway, losing effective control over their films as soon as shooting stops.

STRUCTURE

We have been dealing with the material of film. To make a movie, the materials must somehow be organized. A film can be made simply by linking images and sounds in abstract rhythmic concatenation (as in McLaren's films), or by loosely arranging them around a theme (as in travelogues). But these straightforward methods, though in some ways they represent an ideal of pure cinema, seem to work well only for quite short films, and (especially since the decline of vaudeville) the staple of film production is the "feature," long enough to give the cash customers their money's worth. There are no theoretical limits to the length of a clearly articulated pattern of imagery, but most abstract films are short. The closest actual approximation to an abstract or purely formal method of organizing images is to associate them with extended musical forms, since the latter constitute long formal sequences of a kind that audiences already know and accept; but Disney's *Fantasia,* though often and lucratively revived, has not aroused emulation and in any case supplemented the musical structure with at least an illusion of parallel narrative form. More usually, coherence is sought through the organization of the subject matter of the imagery: by exploring a problem, or an object, or a place, or a situation, or an event (documentary), or, commonest of all, by constructing a fictitious or historical story. The contrast between documentary and the regular "feature" is not so much that between fact and fiction, for features may be factual and most documentaries have fictional aspects, as between exploratory and narrative methods of organization. The reason for the dominance of the narrative feature lies partly in the flexibility of the film medium, which makes it especially suitable for a free-running narrative whose closest affinities are with novels and biographies, but partly in the assumption that the "mass audience" will associate exploration with instruction and hence with tedium. Now that the mass audience is safely shut away with its TV set things may change: *Woodstock* is a portent. Meanwhile, writers on cinema are bound to assume that the narrative feature remains the norm.

It is from the normal narrative form that the customary description of the articulation of film is derived. In a sense, and from the editor's viewpoint, the unit is the frame, but this does not exist for perception. Aesthetically, a film consists of shots organized into scenes which are themselves articulated into sequences. This structure corresponds, very roughly, to an analysis of activity into movements (shots), actions (scenes), and episodes (sequences). Accordingly, shots cohere into scenes through relevance, each shot being experienced as relevant to expectations aroused earlier in the scene (ideally, I suppose, by the preceding shot). Scenes are divided by jump-cuts or dissolves marking a change of subject; sequences are divided by such more emphatic punctuation as fade-out and fade-in. But (as with novel and theater) no rules or firm conventions demand such articulation: the determining changes are discontinuities of place, time, participants or activities (in abstract films, changes in the kind of image or movement; in documentaries, change of aspect or style). The film-maker's use of punctuating devices is merely incidental to these. Actually, the very concept of a "shot" becomes nebulous and archaic as cameras become more mobile: the distinction between scene and shot takes on a vagueness such as infects the distinction between an action and its constituent movements.

The plasticity of camera viewpoint is such that films, like novels and unlike plays, can focus one's attention precisely. Only what is irreducibly relevant to the story need be shown. A raised eyebrow can fill the screen. In theater, perception follows attention: one looks at the relevant part of what is visible on stage and ignores the rest. In film, attention follows perception: whatever is not relevant is either not screened or thrown into shadow or out of focus. Hence, film storytelling can and sometimes does achieve great elegance and economy. Styles change, however. The introduction of the wide screen has made the use of close-ups to isolate relevant detail seem rather blatant, and encourages a more fluid and relaxed style of presentation in which more use is made of the simultaneous presence on the screen of more than one focus for attention.

The focusing habit of the camera and the necessary priority of the visual might make one think that the most filmic and hence the best film story was one in which the *precise* content of each shot set up the story through its dynamic connection with the next. One might further infer from this that tragedy with its overriding architectonic goes against the grain of film, which has a special affinity for such episodic forms as picaresque comedy. There is something in that, but we warned at the start against the facile assumption that the best works in any medium are those which take its most obvious opportunities as procedural rules, and an overly filmic film might have the mechanized aggressiveness of a "well-made play." One could more reasonably infer that the least filmic and hence dullest films would be those in which the dialogue carried the story and the camera just coasted along. And yet that is how most films seem to be made. One can see why. Many films are adapted from literary works, in which the dialogue alone can be borrowed without alteration. But in any case the logistics of making a full-scale film are such that it more or less has to be constructed from a detailed shooting-script. Films are largely *written* before they are shot. But writers are bound to be word-oriented. Besides, dialogue is the only part of the script that contributes directly to determining the actual quality of the finished film: specifications of visual images cannot include what will differentiate the effective from the flat, the fine from the clumsy. Perhaps most important, to throw responsibility for the story onto the dialogue is to play safe and easy. So long as the actors mouth the lines the story will somehow come through, and the director can content himself with the most perfunctory and generalized camera work. If the story depends on what can be seen, much greater care must be taken over exactly what is shown, and that will add to the shooting rime which is the variable on which the cost of a film chiefly depends.

Now the cat is out of the bag. Films are traditionally about money, and film as most people know it is commercial film. Film did not begin as high art or as folk art, but as the offspring of technological curiosity and showmanship. It got into the public eye by way of peepshow and vaudeville, and its first exponents did not think of themselves as artists. The structural analogies between film and novel, and the superficial likenesses between film and drama, suggest affiliations that took some time to develop. A glance at the advertisements in your local newspaper should convince you that film has yet to free itself from the hectic world and accent of the fairground.

Though cheap and flexible sound and camera equipment has done much to effect what Andrew Sarris has called "demystifying the medium," the financial structure of the film industry has still some claim to be considered as part of the technological conditions that we have recognized to be paramount in cinema. The decisive factors here are that the initial costs of making even a cheap film are high, but the printing, distribution, and exhibition costs are low. So the costs can be recovered if enough people are willing to see the film—which they will be able to do only if enough people are willing to show it. Nor is this a consequence of the sickness of western bourgeois society. No one, socialist or capitalist, is going to be allowed to tie up so much of other people's labor and equipment unless there is some reasonable assurance that there will be something to show for it: if not money, then prestige or the approved performance of some supposed social function. By the same token, the complexities of the arrangements for distributing or showing films are almost certain to deprive the director of control over the final condition and destiny of his work. A film critic is seldom commenting on the work of an individual or a cohesive group so much as on the upshot of a loosely connected series of independent decisions. He may thus succumb to feelings of irrelevance.

There are three plausible lines a critic can take here. One is to confine his attention to noncommercial films. Of course, these are atypical, but the critic can say (as Parker Tyler says) that it is not typical for a film to be a work of art. Most drawings, to take a parallel case, are not works of art but advertisements or sources of technical information or doodles, and no one expects a critic to waste his time on such objects.

A second critical line is to accept that most films, both commercial and "underground," are junk, to be greeted with silence or a dismissive gesture, but that any kind of interest or excellence may turn up in any sort of film. Such a rejection of all commitments to styles and cultural traditions is in the line of twentieth-century critical orthodoxy, but may find it hard to steer between the Scylla of an empty formalistic aestheticism and the Charybdis of a relativism that accepts everything equally because everything succeeds in being what it is.

A third critical line is to accept cinema as a demotic art and devise a critical system appropriate to such an art. George Orwell has shown the way. His exemplary study of Frank Richards devoted itself to describing the "world" depicted or implied by the ensemble of Richard's work, and exploring the repertory of mannerisms which gave that world a facile coherence. Students of Jung and Frye have enlarged this critical armory by showing how to expose the underlying mythical archetypes and patterns in popular fiction. These methods have been applied to Hollywood films in what is misnamed the "auteur theory" of criticism (which is a policy rather than a theory). Whatever a studio does to a film, a strong-minded director can impregnate it indelibly with his own basic textures, his view of human relationships, his favorite narrative devices, and obsessive images. In fact, the measure of a director's stature may be the extent to which he can retain these elements of his own style when working on an uncongenial assignment from his studio. And by comparing a director's different films, which taken in isolation had been thought undistinguished if no worse, one can educe a complex world full of ironies and unexpected insights.

Some auteur critics seem to assume that any director whose work is susceptible to their methods is thereby proved to be an artist, and his films shown to be good films. This is a strange assumption. Critics of other arts are far from supposing that to show that a work is recognizable and typical of its author has any tendency to show that it is a good work. In fact, the analogue in other arts is a form of criticism specifically devised for handling material incapable of yielding anything of interest to a more searching critique. Auteur criticism may work best as a heuristic device: armed with his comparisons and with his trained eye for manners and genres, a critic can show us meaning where we saw none; but when we have been shown we must be able to see for ourselves. In other arts we accept that one may not understand any work by an innovating artist until one has familiarized oneself with his style; but it is strange to have a similar esoteric status claimed for the output of a studio work-horse. The paradox of auteur criticism is that while its methods are devised to handle cinema as a demotic art, it relies on a view of that art which is inaccessible to most of its normal public. How many people are going to get to see a Raoul Walsh festival?

In so far as the normal film is about human affairs, it is susceptible to criticism on the same basis as literary or dramatic works or figurative paintings, in terms of its verisimilitude, psychological richness, moral maturity, social significance, political viability, relations to the divine and the unconscious and so on. The fact that such topics are not specific to film does not make them trivial or irrelevant: on the contrary, most actual serious discussion of films centers on this human side, and so it should. But we need say nothing about such criticism here. In practice we all know what we want to say; in theory the basic moves are familiar from discussions of criticism in the older arts. From this point of view, the art of film criticism would lie in knowledge of and sensitivity to the ways in which such human qualities can be conveyed by such cinematic means as we have been discussing.

The salient feature of film is the enormous range of its specific effects. Film is unique in its capacity for visual recording and analysis, in its ability to convey the unique present reality of things, in its ability to reveal the qualities of lives; but also in its formal freedom, its capacity for realizing fantasy and developing abstract forms. In view of this inexhaustible flexibility of the medium, it is ludicrous to lay down general principles as to what is a good film. Those critics who do so are in most cases obviously fixated on the kind of film that was around when they were first moved by movies. A judicious critic will equip himself with the most exhaustive possible grasp of the variables and variations accessible to film-makers, and note just which of these the director is exploiting and how he is doing it. So much can be done in a film that it requires close attention and knowledge to discern what is actually being done. Technical assessment and appreciation can almost be read off from the roll of specific opportunities opened up by the director's initial options and then seized or missed: take care of the facts and the values will take care of themselves. Beyond that, the moral and cultural side of a critique must depend on the maturity and sensitivity of the critic's social and moral awareness. If you could teach people to be critics, you could teach them to be human.

DISCUSSION QUESTIONS

1. In his comments on mechanism and film, Sparshott says "People use their languages to say what they wish to say, not what the language makes it easy to say." Do you agree with him? Why or why not?

2. As an art of illusion, how is film similar to and different from other forms of art such as painting, music, and sculpture?

3. Discuss the following statement from Sparshott: "Films are largely *written* before they are shot. But writers are bound to be word-oriented. Besides, dialogue is the only part of the script that contributes directly to determining the actual quality of the finished film: specifications of visual images cannot include what will differentiate the effective from the flat, the fine from the clumsy. Perhaps most importantly, to throw responsibility for the story onto the dialogue is to play safe and easy." Is dialogue the most important element in a film's ability to tell a

story, or is it simply the easiest way of telling the story? Compare and contrast the role of dialogue in the communication of a film's story or message with other features of film such as sound and time.

4. Sparshott claims that "no more than when attending a stage play does anyone at the movies feel as if an event were really taking place before his eyes." Do you agree with him? Why or why not? Discuss the similarities and differences between a dramatic performance and the screening of a film.

5. What, for Sparshott, are the similarities and differences between viewing films and dreaming? Do you agree with him? Why or why not?

6. What does Sparshott mean when he says, "If you could teach people to be critics, you could teach them to be human"? Do you agree with him? Why or why not?

Singin' in the Rain
[USA 1952] 1 hour, 59 minutes
Dir. by Stanley Donen & Gene Kelly

The late 1920s marked a period of dramatic development and change in the motion picture industry— namely, the transition from silent motion pictures to pictures with sound. *Singin' in the Rain* is an affectionate and humorous examination of this important time in film history. It is also one of the greatest musicals of all time, as well as an insightful look at the process of studio filmmaking.

Don Lockwood (Gene Kelly) and Lina Lamont (Jean Hagen) are a popular romantic silent screen duo. When the studio begins production of its first sound motion picture, a serious problem arises: Lina has an unflattering voice. To salvage the film, the studio hires Kathy Selden (Debbie Reynolds) to voice-over Lina's speaking and singing parts. However, the public is not aware that the voice on the screen is Kathy's, not Lina's, and Lina is praised for her remarkable talents. Despite Lina's blackmail attempts to keep her real voice a secret, Don reveals that Kathy is the real voice—and star—of the film. During a promotional performance for the film in which Lina sings before a live audience, Don pulls back the stage curtain and reveals that it is Kathy, not Lina, whose voice is heard. The lip-synching Lina's future in the movies is effectively over.

DISCUSSION QUESTIONS

1. Sparshott says, "The history of film is the history of the invention of means." One of the major changes in the means of film production was the technological advance that allowed sound to occur along with moving images. According to *Singin' in the Rain*, how did the invention of "talkies" affect the motion-picture industry?

2. Analyze *Singin' in the Rain* according to Sparshott's film aesthetics. Is your understanding of the film greater after your aesthetic analysis? Or was it greater before your aesthetic analysis? Discuss.

3. Discuss the major aesthetic differences between a motion picture with sound and without sound. Do you think that sound films are necessarily aesthetically superior to silent films? Defend your position.

4. How does a silent film communicate meaning to the viewer? How does a "talkie" communicate meaning to the viewer? What are the strengths and limitations in the communication of meaning in each type of film?

5. Imagine you go into a museum and the paintings on the wall begin to emit sounds. For example, the people begin to talk to you and the birds in the landscape chirp. Is this what it must have felt like for audiences who were accustomed to silent films when they first saw "talkies"? Why or why not?

6. Consider the following dialogue between Don and Kathy:

   DON   "Wait a minute. You mean I'm not an actor? Pantomime on the screen isn't acting?"

   KATHY   "Acting means great parts with wonderful lines, speaking those glorious words. Shakespeare, Ibsen."

   Is Kathy right? Is pantomime—that is, expression of something by facial gestures and body movements alone—not acting because there are no spoken words? Does this mean that when Don and Kathy dance without speaking in the film they are not acting? Discuss.

7. Consider this exchange between Don and Kathy:

   KATHY   "You can laugh all you want, but at least the stage is a dignified profession. And what do you have to be so conceited about. You're nothing but a shadow on film. A shadow. You're not flesh and blood."

   DON   "What can I do to you if I'm only a shadow."

   What does Don mean? Is he saying that if he were only a shadow, then he could not have an effect on you as an audience member? But because he can make you laugh and cry and experience many other emotions—that is, have an effect on you—then he is not merely a shadow? Or does he mean something else? Discuss.

8. Consider the following dialogue between Lina and Don:

   LINA   "Oh Donny, you couldn't kiss me like that and not mean it just a teensy-weensy bit!"

   DON   "Meet the greatest actor in the world!"

   Who is right, Don or Lina? What does it mean to say, "It was not a real kiss, even though it might have felt like one: I was just acting." Philosophically, what is the difference? Discuss.

9. What film do you think makes the most effective use of sound? Why? What film do you think makes the most effect use of silence? Why? How do the sound and silence respectively contribute to the meaning of the film? Compare your responses with those of others in your class.

THE HAYS COMMISSION

THE MOTION PICTURE PRODUCTION CODE OF 1930

The Motion Picture Production Code of 1930 was a set of guidelines developed by the motion-picture industry to regulate the moral standards presented in movies. Adopted on March 31, 1930, the production code is often referred to as the Hays Code. Will H. Hays was the head of the Motion Pictures Producers and Distributors Association (MPPDA), which was formed in 1922 to project a positive image of the movie industry. In the 1920s, Hollywood was dubbed "Sin City," and it was the task of Hays and the MPPDA to promote a more morally upright image of Hollywood. However, from 1922 to 1930, Hays and the MPPDA were able to do little to enforce moral authority over Hollywood. With the advent of "talking pictures" in the late 1920s, the need for a more formal production code was established, and the Hays Code was the result.

Despite the production code, between 1930 and 1934, movies became more violent and more sexually explicit. In 1934, it became a requirement that all movies receive a certificate of approval from the Production Code Administration before being released. The 1934 film *Tarzan and His Mate* was the first major instance of censorship under the production code. Some brief nude scenes of actress Maureen O'Sullivan's body-double were edited out of the master print of the film. The production code had many specific restrictions on films, all with the aim of reducing the level of morally unacceptable behavior shown on-screen. For example, murder was to be presented in a way that would not encourage imitations in real life, and adultery could not be explicitly shown or presented as morally justifiable.

While Hollywood produced films that were in accordance with the production code, every effort was made to find ways to get around the restrictions. In 1951, the Motion Picture Association of America (MPAA, the organization that succeeded the MPPDA) responded by making the code even more rigid. Still, directors like Otto Preminger produced commercially successful films in the 1950s that directly confronted the production code. Preminger's *The Moon Is Blue* (1953) was the first film to use the words "virgin," "seduce," and "mistress"; his *The Man with the Golden Arm* (1955) dealt with drug abuse; and his *Anatomy of a Murder* (1959) dealt with rape. By the 1960s, films like *Who's Afraid of Virginia Woolf* (1966), which included language specifically in violation of the code, received approval. The production code was eventually abandoned for the MPAA film-rating system. The system, which went into effect in 1968, has virtually no restrictions on film content.

If motion pictures present stories that will affect lives for the better, they can become the most powerful force for the improvement of mankind.

A Code to Govern the Making of Talking, Synchronized and Silent Motion Pictures. Formulated and formally adopted by The Association of Motion Picture Producers, Inc. and The Motion Picture Producers and Distributors of America, Inc. in March 1930.

PREAMBLE

Motion picture producers recognize the high trust and confidence which have been placed in them by the people of the world and which have made motion pictures a universal form of entertainment.

They recognize their responsibility to the public because of this trust and because entertainment and art are important influences in the life of a nation.

Hence, though regarding motion pictures primarily as entertainment without any explicit purpose of teaching or propaganda, they know that the motion picture within its own field of entertainment may be directly responsible for spiritual or moral progress, for higher types of social life, and for much correct thinking.

During the rapid transition from silent to talking pictures they have realized the necessity and the opportunity of subscribing to a Code to govern the production of talking pictures and of re-acknowledging this responsibility.

On their part, they ask from the public and from public leaders a sympathetic understanding of their purposes and problems and a spirit of cooperation that will allow them the freedom and opportunity necessary to bring the motion picture to a still higher level of wholesome entertainment for all the people.

GENERAL PRINCIPLES

1. No picture shall be produced that will lower the moral standards of those who see it. Hence the sympathy of the audience should never be thrown to the side of crime, wrong-doing, evil or sin.

2. Correct standards of life, subject only to the requirements of drama and entertainment, shall be presented.

3. Law, natural or human, shall not be ridiculed, nor shall sympathy be created for its violation.

PARTICULAR APPLICATIONS

I. Crimes Against the Law

These shall never be presented in such a way as to throw sympathy with the crime as against law and justice or to inspire others with a desire for imitation.

1. Murder
   a. The technique of murder must be presented in a way that will not inspire imitation.
   b. Brutal killings are not to be presented in detail.

   c. Revenge in modem times shall not be justified.

2. Methods of crime should not be explicitly presented.
   a. Theft, robbery, safe-cracking, and dynamiting of trains, mines, buildings, etc., should not be detailed in method.
   b. Arson must subject to the same safe-guards.
   c. The use of firearms should be restricted to the essentials.
   d. Methods of smuggling should not be presented.

3. Illegal drug traffic must never be presented.

4. The use of liquor in American life, when not required by the plot or for proper characteri-zation, will not be shown.

II. Sex

The sanctity of the institution of marriage and the home shall be upheld. Pictures shall not infer that low forms of sex relationship are the accepted or common thing.

1. Adultery, sometimes necessary plot material, must not be explicitly treated, or justified, or presented attractively.

2. Scenes of Passion
   a. They should not be introduced when not essential to the plot.
   b. Excessive and lustful kissing, lustful embraces, suggestive postures and gestures, are not to be shown.
   c. In general passion should so be treated that these scenes do not stimulate the lower and baser element.

3. Seduction or Rape
   a. They should never be more than suggested, and only when essential for the plot, and even then never shown by explicit method.
   b. They are never the proper subject for comedy.

4. Sex perversion or any inference to it is forbidden.

5. White slavery shall not be treated.

6. Miscegenation (sex relationships between the white and black races) is forbidden.

7. Sex hygiene and venereal diseases are not subjects for motion pictures.

8. Scenes of actual child birth, in fact or in silhouette, are never to be presented.

9. Children's sex organs are never to be exposed.

III. Vulgarity

The treatment of low, disgusting, unpleasant, though not necessarily evil, subjects should always be subject to the dictates of good taste and a regard for the sensibilities of the audience.

IV. Obscenity

Obscenity in word, gesture, reference, song, joke, or by suggestion (even when likely to be understood only by part of the audience) is forbidden.

V. Profanity

Pointed profanity (this includes the words God, Lord, Jesus, Christ—unless used reverently—Hell, S.O.B., damn, Gawd), or every other profane or vulgar expression however used, is forbidden.

VI. Costume

1. Complete nudity is never permitted. This includes nudity in fact or in silhouette, or any lecherous or licentious notice thereof by other characters in the picture.

2. Undressing scenes should be avoided, and never used save where essential to the plot.

3. Indecent or undue exposure is forbidden.

4. Dancing or costumes intended to permit undue exposure or indecent movements in the dance are forbidden.

VII. Dances

1. Dances suggesting or representing sexual actions or indecent passions are forbidden.

2. Dances which emphasize indecent movements are to be regarded as obscene.

VIII. Religion

1. No film or episode may throw ridicule on any religious faith.

2. Ministers of religion in their character as ministers of religion should not be used as comic characters or as villains.

3. Ceremonies of any definite religion should be carefully and respectfully handled.

IX. Locations

The treatment of bedrooms must be governed by good taste and delicacy.

X. National Feelings

1. The use of the Flag shall be consistently respectful.

2. The history, institutions, prominent people and citizenry of other nations shall be represented fairly.

XI. Titles

Salacious, indecent, or obscene titles shall not be used.

XII. Repellent Subjects

The following subjects must be treated within the careful limits of good taste:

1. Actual hangings or electrocutions as legal punishments for crime.

2. Third degree methods.

3. Brutality and possible gruesomeness.

4. Branding of people or animals.

5. Apparent cruelty to children or animals.

6. The sale of women, or a woman selling her virtue.

7. Surgical operations.

REASONS SUPPORTING THE PREAMBLE OF THE CODE

I. Theatrical motion pictures, that is, pictures intended for the theatre as distinct from pictures intended for churches, schools, lecture halls, educational movements, social reform movements, etc., are primarily to be regarded as Entertainment.

Mankind has always recognized the importance of entertainment and its value in rebuilding the bodies and souls of human beings.

But it has always recognized that entertainment can be a character either HELPFUL or HARMFUL to the human race, and in consequence has clearly distinguished between:

a.   Entertainment which tends to improve the race, or at least to re-create and rebuild human beings exhausted with the realities of life; and

b.   Entertainment which tends to degrade human beings, or to lower their standards of life and living.

Hence the MORAL IMPORTANCE of entertainment is something which has been universally recognized. It enters intimately into the lives of men and women and affects them closely; it occupies their minds and affections during leisure hours; and ultimately touches the whole of their lives. A man may be judged by his standard of entertainment as easily as by the standard of his work.

So correct entertainment raises the whole standard of a nation.

Wrong entertainment lowers the whole living conditions and moral ideals of a race.

Note, for example, the healthy reactions to healthful sports, like baseball, golf; the unhealthy reactions to sports like cockfighting, bullfighting, bear baiting, etc.

Note, too, the effect on ancient nations of gladiatorial combats, the obscene plays of Roman times, etc.

II. Motion pictures are very important as ART.

Though a new art, possibly a combination art, it has the same object as the other arts, the presentation of human thought, emotion, and experience, in terms of an appeal to the soul through the senses.

Here, as in entertainment,

Art enters intimately into the lives of human beings.

Art can be morally good, lifting men to higher levels. This has been done through good music, great painting, authentic fiction, poetry, drama.

Art can be morally evil in its effects. This is the case clearly enough with unclean art, indecent books, suggestive drama. The effect on the lives of men and women are obvious.

Note: It has often been argued that art itself is unmoral, neither good nor bad. This is true of the THING which is music, painting, poetry, etc. But the THING is the PRODUCT of some person's mind, and the intention of that mind was either good or bad morally when it produced the thing. Besides, the thing has its EFFECT upon those who come into contact with it. In both these ways, that is, as a product of a mind and as the cause of definite effects, it has a deep moral significance and unmistakable moral quality.

Hence: The motion pictures, which are the most popular of modern arts for the masses, have their moral quality from the intention of the minds which produce them and from their effects on the moral lives and reactions of their audiences. This gives them a most important morality.

1.   They reproduce the morality of the men who use the pictures as a medium for the expression of their ideas and ideals.

2.   They affect the moral standards of those who, through the screen, take in these ideas and ideals.

In the case of motion pictures, the effect may be particularly emphasized because no art has so quick and so widespread an appeal to the masses. It has become in an incredibly short period the art of the multitudes.

III. The motion picture, because of its importance as entertainment and because of the trust placed in it by the peoples of the world, has special MORAL OBLIGATIONS:

A.   Most arts appeal to the mature. This art appeals at once to every class, mature, immature, developed, undeveloped, law abiding, criminal. Music has its grades for different classes; so has literature and drama. This art of the motion picture, combining as it does the two fundamental appeals of looking at a picture and listening to a story, at once reaches every class of society.

B.   By reason of the mobility of film and the ease of picture distribution, and because of the possibility of duplicating positives in large quantities, this art reaches places unpenetrated by other forms of art.

C.   Because of these two facts, it is difficult to produce films intended for only certain classes of people. The exhibitors' theatres are built for the masses, for the cultivated and the rude, the mature and the immature, the self-respecting and the criminal. Films, unlike books and music, can with difficulty be confined to certain selected groups.

D. The latitude given to film material cannot, in consequence, be as wide as the latitude given to book material. In addition:

  a. A book describes; a film vividly presents. One presents on a cold page; the other by apparently living people.

  b. A book reaches the mind through words merely; a film reaches the eyes and ears through the reproduction of actual events.

  c. The reaction of a reader to a book depends largely on the keenness of the reader's imagination; the reaction to a film depends on the vividness of presentation.

Hence many things which might be described or suggested in a book could not possibly be presented in a film.

E. This is also true when comparing the film with the newspaper.

  a. Newspapers present by description, films by actual presentation.

  b. Newspapers are after the fact and present things as having taken place; the film gives the events in the process of enactment and with apparent reality of life.

F. Everything possible in a play is not possible in a film:

  a. Because of the larger audience of the film, and its consequential mixed character. Psychologically, the larger the audience, the lower the moral mass resistance to suggestion.

  b. Because through light, enlargement of character, presentation, scenic emphasis, etc., the screen story is brought closer to the audience than the play.

  c. The enthusiasm for and interest in the film actors and actresses, developed beyond anything of the sort in history, makes the audience largely sympathetic toward the characters they portray and the stories in which they figure. Hence the audience is more ready to confuse actor and actress and the characters they portray, and it is most receptive of the emotions and ideals presented by the favorite stars.

G. Small communities, remote from sophistication and from the hardening process which often takes place in the ethical and moral standards of larger cities, are easily and readily reached by any sort of film.

H. The grandeur of mass settings, large action, spectacular features, etc., affects and arouses more intensely the emotional side of the audience.

In general, the mobility, popularity, accessibility, emotional appeal, vividness, straightforward presentation of fact in the film make for more intimate contact with a larger audience and for greater emotional appeal.

Hence the larger moral responsibilities of the motion pictures.

REASONS UNDERLYING THE GENERAL PRINCIPLES

I. No picture shall be produced which will lower the moral standards of those who see it. Hence the sympathy of the audience should never be thrown to the side of crime, wrong-doing, evil or sin.

This is done:

1. When evil is made to appear attractive and alluring, and good is made to appear unattractive.

2. When the sympathy of the audience is thrown on the side of crime, wrongdoing, evil, sin. The same is true of a film that would thrown sympathy against goodness, honor, innocence, purity or honesty.

Note: Sympathy with a person who sins is not the same as sympathy with the sin or crime of which he is guilty. We may feel sorry for the plight of the murderer or even understand the circumstances which led him to his crime: we may not feel sympathy with the wrong which he has done. The presentation of evil is often essential for art or fiction or drama. This in itself is not wrong provided:

a. That evil is not presented alluringly. Even if later in the film the evil is condemned or punished, it must not be allowed to appear so attractive that the audience's emotions are drawn to desire or approve so strongly that later the condemnation is forgotten and only the apparent joy of sin is remembered.

b. That throughout, the audience feels sure that evil is wrong and good is right.

II. CORRECT STANDARDS OF LIFE SHALL, AS FAR AS POSSIBLE, BE PRESENTED.

A wide knowledge of life and of living is made possible through the film. When right standards are consistently presented, the motion picture exercises the most powerful influences. It builds character, develops right ideals, inculcates correct principles, and all this in attractive story form.

If motion pictures consistently hold up for admiration high types of characters and present stories that will affect lives for the better, they can become the most powerful force for the improvement of mankind.

III. LAW, NATURAL OR HUMAN, SHALL NOT BE RIDICULED, NOR SHALL SYMPATHY BE CREATED FOR ITS VIOLATION.

By natural law is understood the law which is written in the hearts of all mankind, the greater underlying principles of right and justice dictated by conscience.

By human law is understood the law written by civilized nations.

1. The presentation of crimes against the law is often necessary for the carrying out of the plot. But the presentation must not throw sympathy with the crime as against the law nor with the criminal as against those who punish him.

2. The courts of the land should not be presented as unjust. This does not mean that a single court may not be presented as unjust, much less that a single court official must not be presented this way. But the court system

of the country must not suffer as a result of this presentation.

REASONS UNDERLYING THE PARTICULAR APPLICATIONS

I. SIN AND EVIL ENTER INTO THE STORY OF HUMAN BEINGS AND HENCE IN THEMSELVES ARE VALID DRAMATIC MATERIAL.

II. IN THE USE OF THIS MATERIAL, IT MUST BE DISTINGUISHED BETWEEN SIN WHICH REPELS BY ITS VERY NATURE, AND SINS WHICH OFTEN ATTRACT.

a. In the first class come murder, most theft, many legal crimes, lying, hypocrisy, cruelty, etc.

b. In the second class come sex sins, sins and crimes of apparent heroism, such as banditry, daring thefts, leadership in evil, organized crime, revenge, etc.

The first class needs less care in treatment, as sins and crimes of this class are naturally unattractive. The audience instinctively condemns all such and is repelled.

Hence the important objective must be to avoid the hardening of the audience, especially of those who are young and impressionable, to the thought and fact of crime. People can become accustomed even to murder, cruelty, brutality, and repellent crimes, if these are too frequently repeated.

The second class needs great care in handling, as the response of human nature to their appeal is obvious. This is treated more fully below.

III. A CAREFUL DISTINCTION CAN BE MADE BETWEEN FILMS INTENDED FOR GENERAL DISTRIBUTION, AND FILMS INTENDED FOR USE IN THEATRES RESTRICTED TO A LIMITED AUDIENCE. THEMES AND PLOTS QUITE APPROPRIATE FOR THE LATTER WOULD BE ALTOGETHER OUT OF PLACE AND DANGEROUS IN THE FORMER.

Note: The practice of using a general theatre and limiting its patronage to "Adults Only" is not completely satisfactory and is only partially effective.

However, maturer minds may easily understand and accept without harm subject matter in plots which do younger people positive harm.

Hence: If there should be created a special type of theatre, catering exclusively to an adult audience, for plays of this character (plays with problem themes, difficult discussions and maturer treatment) it would seem to afford an outlet, which does not now exist, for pictures unsuitable for general distribution but permissible for exhibitions to a restricted audience.

I. Crimes Against the Law

The treatment of crimes against the law must not:

1. Teach methods of crime.
2. Inspire potential criminals with a desire for imitation.
3. Make criminals seem heroic and justified.

Revenge in modem times shall not be justified. In lands and ages of less developed civilization and moral principles, revenge may sometimes be presented. This would be the case especially in places where no law exists to cover the crime because of which revenge is committed.

Because of its evil consequences, the drug traffic should not be presented in any form. The existence of the trade should not be brought to the attention of audiences.

The use of liquor should never be excessively presented. In scenes from American life, the necessities of plot and proper characterization alone justify its use. And in this case, it should be shown with moderation.

II. Sex

Out of a regard for the sanctity of marriage and the home, the triangle, that is, the love of a third party for one already married, needs careful handling. The treatment should not throw sympathy against marriage as an institution.

Scenes of passion must be treated with an honest acknowledgement of human nature and its normal reactions. Many scenes cannot be presented without arousing dangerous emotions on the part of the immature, the young or the criminal classes.

Even within the limits of pure love, certain facts have been universally regarded by lawmakers as outside the limits of safe presentation.

In the case of impure love, the love which society has always regarded as wrong and which has been banned by divine law, the following are important:

1. Impure love must not be presented as attractive and beautiful.
2. It must not be the subject of comedy or farce, or treated as material for laughter.
3. It must not be presented in such a way to arouse passion or morbid curiosity on the part of the audience.
4. It must not be made to seem right and permissible.
5. It general, it must not be detailed in method and manner.

III. Vulgarity; IV. Obscenity; V. Profanity; hardly need further explanation than is contained in the Code.

VI. Costume

General Principles:

1. The effect of nudity or semi-nudity upon the normal man or woman, and much more upon the young and upon immature persons, has been honestly recognized by all lawmakers and moralists.
2. Hence the fact that the nude or semi-nude body may be beautiful does not make its use in the films moral. For, in addition to its beauty, the effect of the nude or semi-nude body on the normal individual must be taken into consideration.
3. Nudity or semi-nudity used simply to put a "punch" into a picture comes under the head of immoral actions. It is immoral in its effect on the average audience.
4. Nudity can never be permitted as being necessary for the plot. Semi-nudity must not result in undue or indecent exposures.
5. Transparent or translucent materials and silhouette are frequently more suggestive than actual exposure.

VII. Dances

Dancing in general is recognized as an art and as a beautiful form of expressing human emotions.

But dances which suggest or represent sexual actions, whether performed solo or with two or more; dances intended to excite the emotional reaction of an audience; dances with movement of the breasts, excessive body movements while the feet are stationary, violate decency and are wrong.

VIII. Religion

The reason why ministers of religion may not be comic characters or villains is simply because the attitude taken toward them may easily become the attitude taken toward religion in general. Religion is lowered in the minds of the audience because of the lowering of the audience's respect for a minister.

IX. Locations

Certain places are so closely and thoroughly associated with sexual life or with sexual sin that their use must be carefully limited.

X. National Feelings

The just rights, history, and feelings of any nation are entitled to most careful consideration and respectful treatment.

XI. Titles

As the title of a picture is the brand on that particular type of goods, it must conform to the ethical practices of all such honest business.

XII. Repellent Subjects

Such subjects are occasionally necessary for the plot. Their treatment must never offend good taste nor injure the sensibilities of an audience.

DISCUSSION QUESTIONS

1. The Production Code claims, "If motion pictures present stories that will affect lives for the better, they can become the most powerful force for the improvement of mankind." Do you agree with this claim? Why or why not? Is it also true that "if motion pictures present stories that will affect lives for the *worse*, they can become the most powerful force for the *destruction* of mankind"? Why or why not?

2. The Production Code requires that "No picture shall be produced that will lower the moral standards of those who see it." Do you think that viewing a movie can lower one's moral standards? Why or why not? Have you ever seen a movie that lowered your moral standards? If so, which one? How did it lower your standards?

3. Discuss the "Particular Applications" found in the Production Code. Which of these particular applications is in line with your own moral standards? Which is not? If you had to praise one of these standards, which would it be, and why? If you had to criticize one of these standards, which would it be, and why?

4. The Production Code provides "reasons" in support of its "Preamble," "General Principles," and "Particular Applications." Carefully analyze each set of reasons. Discuss their strengths and weaknesses. What assumptions do these reasons suggest about the relationship between art and morality? Do you agree with these assumptions? Why or why not?

5. Do you think the Production Code should have been applied to the other arts as well? For example, should fiction, drama, and dance have been held to the same standards of production as film? Why or why not?

6. Which of the following thinkers would be most comfortable with the Production Code: Plato, Aristotle, Hume, Tolstoy, Wilde, Langer, or Gass? Why? Which would be most uncomfortable? Why?

7. Formulate your own Production Code, and provide a philosophical defense of it. Your production code can have as many or as few particular applications as you wish.

Scarface
[USA 1931] 1 hour, 33 minutes
Directed by Howard Hawks

*S*carface is one of the greatest gangster films ever made—and also one of the most controversial motion pictures produced in the United States. It was filmed in 1930 but did not come out until 1932 because of disagreements between the film industry censors and the co-producers, Howard Hawks and Howard Hughes. The censors argued that *Scarface* violated the Motion Picture Production Code of 1930 in many ways, including hints at an incestuous relationship between the title character and his sister, brutal crimes (over thirty people are murdered on-screen), gun and liquor smuggling, illegal use of liquor, and the use of machine guns (a first in American cinema). Nevertheless, the most glaring violation of the Production Code, at least according to the censors, was that the film treated gangster life too sympathetically.

While Howard Hawks refused to change the film in any way in response to the censors' demands, Howard Hughes gave in on a number of points. For example, he changed the title from *Scarface* to *Scarface: The Shame of the Nation;* he added a prologue that describes the film as an "indictment of gang rule in America"; he had Scarface's mother express disapproval of her son's behavior; he blamed the public rather than the police for the existence of gangs; he inserted voice-overs and cuts throughout the film; and he added moralistic speeches by the chief of detectives. Also, Hughes added a scene wherein concerned citizens challenge a newspaper publisher about the amount of attention given to gangsters in the newspaper. The greatest change, however, is in the ending of the film.

In the original Hawks version, the title character, Tony Camonte (Paul Muni), struggles against the police despite a fatal wound. In the revised version, Tony begs for mercy from the police, and they respond by gunning him down to the cheers of onlookers. When this revised version still did not satisfy the censors, another ending was shot. In the final ending, Tony survives the shoot-out with the police and is sentenced by a judge to hang. The judge calls him "evil" and "vicious." The final scene involves Tony being hanged on December 10, 1931, in Illinois—a state that replaced death by hanging with death by electrocution in 1922.

Overall, the film's characters share similarities with many real-life Chicago gangsters from the 1920s and 1930s. The title character is based on Al Capone, Johnny Lovo (Osgood Perkins) on Johnny Torrio, and "Big Louis" Costillo (Harry J. Vejar) on "Big Jim" Colosimo. The crimes in the film are also based on actual crimes, the most famous of which is the St. Valentine's Day massacre of 1929. The screenplay for the film was written by Ben Hecht, a native Chicagoan who drew from his newspaper experiences.

Tony Camonte opens the film by murdering his boss, "Big Louis" Costillo, and switching over to another boss, Johnny Lovo. Though the police suspect Tony in the murder and bring him in for questioning, they cannot prove it and release him. Tony becomes infatuated with Poppy (Karen Morley), Lovo's girlfriend. Tony is also overly protective of his sister, Cesca (Ann Dvorak), not allowing her to associate with any man—aside from himself.

Tony secures the South Side of Chicago for Lovo and then defies Lovo's command not to expand any farther by making a move into the North Side as well. Tony has his best friend and sidekick, Guino Rinaldo (George Raft), murder the North Side boss O'Hara in his flower shop. Soon O'Hara's successor, Gaffney (Boris Karloff), comes after Tony with a new type of weapon: a submachine gun that fires 300 slugs per minute. Nevertheless, Tony soon vanquishes Gaffney and the rest of the North Side gangsters, leaving only Lovo between him and control of the Chicago underworld. After a failed attempt by Lovo to murder Tony, Lovo is murdered by Rinaldo.

Tony is now boss of the Chicago underworld. His first acquisition as mob boss is Poppy, Lovo's girlfriend. While Tony and Poppy are in Florida for a month, Rinaldo and Cesca fall in love and marry. When Tony returns, his mother tells him that she thinks that Cesca has moved out. Furious, Tony tracks Rinaldo down and murders him on the spot. Immediately afterward, a hysterical Cesca tells Tony that he murdered her husband. A distraught Tony is hunted down by the police for the murder of Rinaldo. He locks himself in his hideout, but his sister locates him with the intention of killing him; however, she is unable to do it. Cesca says to Tony, "You're me and I'm you." In the early stages of a shoot-out with the police, Cesca is hit by a bullet and dies. Tony dies soon thereafter as noted above: in the two early versions of the ending by police gunfire, and in the final version of the ending by hanging.

Scarface was banned in several states and had its debut in Chicago delayed for a year. It did not do very well financially and eventually was withdrawn from circulation by Howard Hughes. Moreover, until its reissue in 1979 by United Artists, it was rarely seen in the United States. In 1934, when it became a requirement that all movies receive a certificate of approval from the Production Code Administration before being released, *Scarface* became an example of the kind of protection the Production Code could give the public. The film was remade in 1983 by director Brian DePalma, with Al Pacino in the title role.

DISCUSSION QUESTIONS

1. In which ways did *Scarface* violate the Motion Picture Production Code of 1930?

2. *Scarface* is prefaced by the following statement: "This picture is an indictment of gang rule in America and of the callous indifference of the government to this constantly increasing menace to our safety and our liberty. Every incident in this picture is the reproduction of an actual occurrence, and the purpose of this picture is to demand of the government: What are you going to do about it? The government is your government. What are YOU going to do about it?" Do you think this statement was necessary? Why or why not?

3. The statement above maintains that the film is an "indictment of gang rule." Do you believe that such a statement can establish the meaning of the film? Why or why not?

4. The statement above also is a call to social action: "What are YOU going to do about it?" Can a film be a call to social action? Do you think *Scarface* is this type of film? Why or why not?

5. For Tolstoy, real or true art "is a means of union among men joining them together in the same feelings, and indispensable for the life and progress towards well-being of individuals and of humanity." False or "counterfeit" art has the opposite effect: it is divisive and elitist. Do you think Tolstoy would call *Scarface* "true art," particularly given that the revisions of the film contain a strong moral message against gang rule in America?

6. Consider the following monologue delivered by the chief of detectives, which was inserted into *Scarface*: "Colorful? What color is a crawling louse? Say listen, that's the attitude of too many morons in this country. They think these hoodlums are some sort of demagogues. What do they do about a guy like Tony? They sentimentalize, romance, make jokes about him. They had some excuse

for glorifying our old Western badmen. They met in the middle of the street at high noon and waited for each other to draw. But these things sneak up and shoot a guy in the back and then run away. Colorful? Did you read what happened the other day? A car full of 'em chasing another down the street in broad daylight. Three kiddies playing hop-scotch on the sidewalk get lead poured in their little bellies. When I think what goes on in the minds of these lice, I wanna vomit." Could this admonition against the "colorfulness" of gangsters and gangster life sway public opinion regarding gangsters? Is calling those who find Tony colorful "morons" an effective way of changing their views of him? Discuss.

7. In another inserted scene, citizens complain to the newspaper publisher, Garston (Purnell Pratt), about glorifying gangster life in the newspaper. Consider the following dialogue from this scene:

MALE CITIZEN   "Our organizations are opposed to your policy, Mr. Garston. Your paper could be an influence against the gangster, yet you keep right on playing up his activities as front-page news: murders, gangwar, killings—that's all we read about. You're glorifying the gangster by giving him all this publicity."

GARSTON   "You're trying to tell me you can get rid of the gangster by ignoring him, by keeping him off the front page. That's ridiculous. You're playing right into his hands. Show him up! Run him out of the country! That'll keep him off the front page."

FEMALE CITIZEN   "In the meantime, you expect our children to read of nothing but outrage and murder?"

GARSTON   "That's better than their being slaughtered. The city is full of machine guns, gang war in the streets. Kids aren't even safe to go to school. You want that to go on?"

ANOTHER MALE CITIZEN   "Certainly not, but what can private citizens do? Even our police force can't stop it."

GARSTON   "Don't blame the police. They can't stop machine guns from being run back and forth across the state lines. They can't enforce laws that don't exist."

MALE CITIZEN   "Then it's up to the federal government to do something about it."

GARSTON   "You're the government—all of you. Instead of trying to hide the facts, get busy and see that laws are passed that'll do some good."

MALE CITIZEN   "For instance?"

GARSTON   "Pass a federal law that puts the gun in the same class as drugs and white slavery. Put teeth in the Deportation Act. These gangsters don't belong in this country. Half of them aren't even citizens."

THIRD MALE CITIZEN   "That's-a true. They bring nothing but disgrace to my people."

GARSTON   "All right, I'll tell you what to do. Make laws and see that they're obeyed—if we have to have martial law to do it! Surely gang rule and wholesale law defiance are more of a menace to the nation than the regulation of oil or a bullfight. The Army will help. So will the American Legion. They offered their services over two years ago and nobody ever called on them. Let's get wise to ourselves. We're fighting organized murder!"

Why do you think this scene was inserted? Do you think it is necessary? Who makes the stronger case here, and why?

8. Many find the relationship between Tony and Cesca to be possibly incestuous, yet the censors did not require that it be removed from the film. Consider the following dialogue between Tony and Cesca just before she is shot by the police:

CESCA   "Tony, they're coming, the police. They're after you. They're gonna get you, Tony."

TONY   "Why didn't you shoot, Cesca, huh? Why didn't you shoot?"

CESCA   "I don't know. Maybe it's because you're me and I'm you. It's always been that way."

They then hug. Again, the context is that Tony has just murdered Cesca's new husband, and she has said to her brother, "Stay away from me. You're not my brother. Don't you think I know? Murderer! He kills people. He kills everybody. He kills everything. He's a butcher. That's what you are. You're a butcher. You're a butcher." What do you think is the nature of the relationship between Cesca and Tony? Is it a violation of the Production Code? Why or why not?

9. The director, Howard Hawks, refused to shoot a scene at the end of the film in which Tony turns cowardly when confronted with the prospect of the police shooting him. Here is part of the dialogue from the scene:

TONY   "Don't shoot. Don't shoot, Guarino. Lookit, Guarino. I'm all alone. I got no gun, see. Gimme a break, Guarino."

GUARINO   "Break? Who'd you ever give a break to?"

TONY   "Look, I got nobody. I'm all alone. A little boy's gun, Angelo's gun. My steel shutters—they don't work. Gimme a break, will ya? Don't shoot. You got me covered. I can't do nothin.'"

If you were Hawks, would you have shot this scene and added it to the picture? Is it acceptable to override a director's aesthetic principles for ethical or social principles? Why or why not? Would you feel the same way if you were the director of the film?

10. Discuss the various endings to *Scarface*. Does the death by hanging achieve its intended effect: an unsympathetic portrait of gangsters? Is it better or worse in achieving this than the ending in which Tony is shot down in front of a cheering crowd or the original one in which he dies violently in the shoot-out with the police?

MAX HORKHEIMER AND THEODOR ADORNO
THE CULTURE INDUSTRY

Max Horkheimer and Theodor Adorno argue that movies are not art; rather, they are commodities produced by the culture industry. "Film, radio, and magazines make up a system which is uniform as a whole and in every part," write Horkheimer and Adorno. This system is subservient to the "absolute power of capitalism." The interests of the motion-picture, broadcasting, and publishing industries are "economically interwoven" with other, more powerful, capitalist industries such as the banking, petroleum, utilities, and chemical industries. The culture industry "is the triumph of invested capital, whose title as absolute master is etched deep into the hearts of the dispossessed in the employment line; it is the meaningful content of every film, whatever plot the production team may have selected."

The culture industry produces homogeneous and monotonous commodities: "art for the masses." "Not only are hit songs, stars, and soap operas cyclically recurrent and rigidly invariable types, but the specific content of the entertainment itself is derived from and only appears to change," write Horkheimer and Adorno. "The details are interchangeable." Film, for example, comprises a series of "ready-made clichés to be slotted anywhere." "As soon as the film begins, it is quite clear how it will end, and who will be rewarded, punished, or forgotten." According to Horkheimer and Adorno, the homogeneity of art produced by the culture industry serves an important social and political function: It maintains the status quo and destroys individuality. "The culture industry as a whole has molded men as a type unfailingly reproduced in every product." Mass art aims to produce, control, and discipline its consumers. It even aims to deprive them of amusement by stunting their "powers of imagination and spontaneity." "The culture industry does not sublimate; it represses" the desire for happiness, write Horkheimer and Adorno, and the Production Code (or "Hays Office") "merely confirms" this.

The world depicted by mass culture is a "realistic" one that is a combination of clichés, propaganda, and advertising. Horkheimer and Adorno write, "If most of the radio stations and movie theaters were closed down, the consumers would probably not lose very much." "To walk from the street into the movie theater is no longer to enter a world of dream; as soon as the very existence of these institutions no longer made it obligatory to use them, there would be no great urge to do so." Ultimately, true art is art that goes beyond existing social relations and reality, something that the art produced by the culture industry never achieves.

Max Horkheimer (1895–1973), German philosopher, was born in Stuttgart, Germany, and educated at the universities of Munich, Freiburg, and Frankfurt am Main. He taught at the University of Frankfurt, where he was the director of its Institute for Social Research from 1931 to 1959, an organization established in 1923 to look into the future of Marxism after the Russian Revolution of 1917. Under Horkheimer's direction, the institute came to focus on social philosophy and critical theory, and it attacked positivism, which was claimed to wrongly separate facts from values, and knowledge from all other human interests. In 1933, when Hilter became chancellor of Germany, Horkheimer moved the institute to Geneva, and then again in 1935 to New York City, where it was associated with Columbia University until 1950. In 1950, the institute returned to the University of Frankfurt. Prominent members of the institute, known as the Frankfurt School, include Walter Benjamin, the psychologist Eric Fromm, and the philosophers Herbert Marcuse, Theodor W. Adorno, and Jürgen Habermas.

Many of Horkheimer's writings were co-authored with other members of the institute. His writings include *Eclipse of Reason* (1947), *Critical Theory: Selected Essays* (1972), *Critique of Instrumental Reason: Lectures and Essays Since the End of World War II* (1974), and *Between Philosophy and Social Science: Selected Early Writings* (1993).

Theodor W. Adorno (1903–69), German philosopher, musicologist, and cultural critic, was one of the most important German philosophers of the twentieth century. He was born in Frankfurt and educated at the University of Frankfurt. His father, Oscar Wiesengrund, was a wealthy, assimilated Jewish wine merchant, and his mother, Maria Calvelli-Adorno, was a Corsican Catholic and professional singer. He changed his last name from Wiesengrund to Adorno in the late 1930s. Adorno was trained in piano as a child, earned his doctorate in philosophy by the age of twenty-one, and studied composition for two years in Vienna with Alban Berg. Prior to being expelled with other Jewish scholars by the Nazis, Adorno had entered the professorate. During the Nazi era, Adorno left Germany for Oxford. He then moved to New York City in 1938 at the invitation of Horkheimer, and finally to Los Angeles in 1941 before returning to Frankfurt in 1949. He was co-director of the Institute of Social Research from 1955 to 1958, then director from 1958 to 1969. Adorno's many books include *Composing for Films* (with Hanns Eisler, 1947), *Prisms: Cultural Criticism and Society* (1967), *Negative Dialectics* (1973), *Philosophy of Modern Music* (1973), *Minima Moralia: Reflections from a Damaged Life* (1974), *Introduction to the Sociology of Music* (1976), *In Search of Wagner* (1981), *Against Epistemology* (1982), and *Aesthetic Theory* (1997). The following is excerpted from a long chapter from Horkheimer and Adorno's *Dialectic of Enlightenment* (1972), which was first published in German in 1947.

The sociological theory that the loss of the support of objectively established religion, the dissolution of the last remnants of precapitalism, together with technological and social differentiation or specialization, have led to cultural chaos is disproved every day; for culture now impresses the same stamp on everything. Films, radio and magazines make up a system which is uniform as a whole and in every part. Even the aesthetic activities of political opposites are one in their enthusiastic obedience to the rhythm of the iron system. The decorative industrial management buildings and exhibition centers in authoritarian countries are much the same as anywhere else. The huge gleaming towers that shoot up everywhere are outward signs of the ingenious planning of international concerns, toward which the unleashed entrepreneurial system (whose monuments are a mass of gloomy houses and business premises in grimy, spiritless cities) was already hastening. Even now the older houses just outside the concrete city centers look like slums, and the new bungalows on the outskirts are at one with the flimsy structures of world fairs in their praise of technical progress and their built-in demand to be discarded after a short while like empty food cans. Yet the city housing projects designed to perpetuate the individual as a supposedly independent unit in a small hygienic dwelling make him all the more subservient to his adversary—the absolute power of capitalism. Because the inhabitants, as producers and as consumers, are drawn into the center in search of work and pleasure, all the living units crystallize into well-organized complexes. The striking unity of microcosm and macrocosm presents men with a model of their culture: the false identity of the general and the particular. Under monopoly all mass culture is identical, and the lines of its artificial framework begin to show through. The people at the top are no longer so interested in concealing monopoly: as its violence becomes more open, so its power grows. Movies and radio need no longer pretend to be art. The truth that they are just business is made into an ideology in order to justify the rubbish they deliberately produce. They call themselves industries; and when their directors' incomes are published, any doubt about the social utility of the finished products is removed.

Interested parties explain the culture industry in technological terms. It is alleged that because millions participate in it, certain reproduction processes are necessary that inevitably require identical needs in innumerable places to be satisfied with identical goods. The technical contrast between the few production centers and the large number of widely dispersed consumption points is said to demand organization and planning by management. Furthermore, it is claimed that standards were based in the first place on consumers' needs, and for that reason were accepted with so little resistance. The result is the circle of manipulation and retroactive need in which the unity of the system grows ever stronger. No mention is made of the fact that the basis on which technology acquires power over society is the power of those whose economic hold over society is greatest. A technological rationale is the rationale of domination itself. It is the coercive nature of society alienated from itself. Automobiles, bombs, and movies keep the whole thing together until their leveling element shows its strength in the very wrong which it furthered. It has made the technology of the culture industry no more than the achievement of standardization and mass production, sacrificing whatever involved a distinction between the logic of the work and that of the social system. This is the result not of a law of movement in technology as such but of its function in today's economy. The need which might resist central control has already been suppressed by the control of the individual consciousness. The step from the telephone to the radio has clearly distinguished the roles. The former still allowed the subscriber to play the role of subject, and was liberal. The latter is democratic: it turns all participants into listeners and authoritatively subjects them to broadcast programs which are all exactly the same. No machinery of rejoinder has been devised and private broadcasters are denied any freedom. They are confined to the apocryphal field of the "amateur," and also have to accept organization from above. But any trace of spontaneity from the public in official broadcasting is controlled and absorbed by talent scouts, studio competitions and official programs of every kind selected by professionals. Talented performers belong to the industry long before it displays them; otherwise

they would not be so eager to fit in. The attitude of the public, which ostensibly and actually favors the system of the culture industry, is a part of the system and not an excuse for it. If one branch of art follows the same formula as one with a very different medium and content; if the dramatic intrigue of broadcast soap operas becomes no more than useful material for showing how to master technical problems at both ends of the scale of musical experience—real jazz or a cheap imitation; or if a movement from a Beethoven symphony is crudely "adapted" for a film soundtrack in the same way as a Tolstoy novel is garbled in a film script: then the claim that this is done to satisfy the spontaneous wishes of the public is no more than hot air. We are closer to the facts if we explain these phenomena as inherent in the technical and personnel apparatus which, down to its last cog, itself forms part of the economic mechanism of selection. In addition there is the agreement—or at least the determination—of all executive authorities not to produce or sanction anything that in any way differs from their own rules, their own ideas about consumers, or above all themselves.

In our age the objective social tendency is incarnate in the hidden subjective purposes of company directors, the foremost among whom are in the most powerful sectors of industry—steel, petroleum, electricity, and chemicals. Culture monopolies are weak and dependent in comparison. They cannot afford to neglect their appeasement of the real holders of power if their sphere of activity in mass society (a sphere producing a specific type of commodity which anyhow is still too closely bound up with easygoing liberalism and Jewish intellectuals) is not to undergo a series of purges. The dependence of the most powerful broadcasting company on the electrical industry or of the motion picture industry on the banks, is characteristic of the whole sphere, whose individual branches are themselves economically interwoven. All are in such close contact that the extreme concentration of mental forces allows demarcation lines between different firms and technical branches to be ignored. The ruthless unity in the culture industry is evidence of what will happen in politics. Marked differentiations such as those of A and B films, or of stories in magazines in different price ranges, depend not so much on subject matter as on classifying, organizing, and labeling consumers. Something is provided for all so that none may escape; the distinctions are emphasized and extended. The public is catered for with a hierarchical range of mass-produced products of varying quality, thus advancing the rule of complete quantification. Everybody must behave (as if spontaneously) in accordance with his previously determined and indexed level, and choose the category of mass product turned out for his type. Consumers appear as statistics on research organization charts, and are divided by income groups into red, green, and blue areas; the technique is that used for any type of propaganda.

How formalized the procedure is can be seen when the mechanically differentiated products prove to be all alike in the end. That the difference between the Chrysler range and General Motors products is basically illusory strikes every child with a keen interest in varieties. What connoisseurs discuss as good or bad points serve only to perpetuate the semblance of competition and range of choice. The same applies to the Warner Brothers and Metro Goldwyn Mayer productions. But even the differences between the more expensive and cheaper models put out by the same firm steadily diminish: for automobiles, there are such differences as the number of cylinders, cubic capacity, details of patented gadgets; and for films there are the number of stars, the extravagant use of technology, labor, and equipment, and the introduction of the latest psychological formulas. The universal criterion of merit is the amount of "conspicuous production," of blatant cash investment. The varying budgets in the culture industry do not bear the slightest relation to factual values, to the meaning of the products themselves. Even the technical media are relentlessly forced into uniformity. Television aims at a synthesis of radio and film, and is held up only because the interested parties have not yet reached agreement, but its consequences will be quite enormous and promise to intensify the impoverishment of aesthetic matter so drastically,

that by tomorrow the thinly veiled identity of all industrial culture products can come triumphantly out into the open, derisively fulfilling the Wagnerian dream of the *Gesamtkunstwerk*—the fusion of all the arts in one work. The alliance of word, image, and music is all the more perfect than in *Tristan* because the sensuous elements which all approvingly reflect the surface of social reality are in principle embodied in the same technical process, the unity of which becomes its distinctive content. This process integrates all the elements of the production, from the novel (shaped with an eye to the film) to the last sound effect. It is the triumph of invested capital, whose title as absolute master is etched deep into the hearts of the dispossessed in the employment line; it is the meaningful content of every film, whatever plot the production team may have selected.

The man with leisure has to accept what the culture manufacturers offer him. Kant's formalism still expected a contribution from the individual, who was thought to relate the varied experiences of the senses to fundamental concepts; but industry robs the individual of his function. Its prime service to the customer is to do his schematizing for him. Kant said that there was a secret mechanism in the soul which prepared direct intuitions in such a way that they could be fitted into the system of pure reason. But today that secret has been deciphered. While the mechanism is to all appearances planned by those who serve up the data of experience, that is, by the culture industry, it is, in fact forced upon the latter by the power of society, which remains irrational, however we may try to rationalize it; and this inescapable force is processed by commercial agencies so that they give an artificial impression of being in command. There is nothing left for the consumer to classify. Producers have done it for him. Art for the masses has destroyed the dream but still conforms to the tenets of that dreaming idealism which critical idealism balked at. Everything derives from consciousness: for Malebranche* and Berkeley,[†] from the consciousness of God; in mass art, from the

---

*Nicolas Malebranche (1638–1715), a French philosopher, became a priest in 1664. He is best known for his synthesis of the ideas of Saint Augustine and René Descartes. Malebranche contends God is the only real cause, and we see bodies through ideas in God. Malebranche's published works include *On the Search for Truth* (1674–75), *Treatise on Nature and Grace* (1680), *Treatise on Morality* (1684), *Conversations on Metaphysics and on Religion* (1688), and *Treatise on the Love of God* (1697). —Ed.
[†] George Berkeley (1685–1753) was an Irish philosopher and bishop. See chapter 2 for a biographical sketch of Berkeley. —Ed.

consciousness of the production team. Not only are the hit songs, stars, and soap operas cyclically recurrent and rigidly invariable types, but the specific content of the entertainment itself is derived from them and only appears to change. The details are interchangeable. The short interval sequence which was effective in a hit song, the hero's momentary fall from grace (which he accepts as good sport), the rough treatment which the beloved gets from the male star, the latter's rugged defiance of the spoilt heiress, are, like all the other details, ready-made cliches to be slotted in anywhere; they never do anything more than fulfill the purpose allotted them in the overall plan. Their whole *raison d'être* is to confirm it by being its constituent parts. As soon as the film begins, it is quite clear how it will end, and who will be rewarded, punished, or forgotten. In light music, once the trained ear has heard the first notes of the hit song, it can guess what is coming and feel flattered when it does come. The average length of the short story has to be rigidly adhered to. Even gags, effects, and jokes are calculated like the setting in which they are placed. They are the responsibility of special experts and their narrow range makes it easy for them to be apportioned in the office. The development of the culture industry has led to the predominance of the effect, the obvious touch, and the technical detail over the work itself—which once expressed an idea, but was liquidated together with the idea. When the detail won its freedom, it became rebellious and, in the period from Romanticism to Expressionism, asserted itself as free expression, as a vehicle of protest against the organization. In music the single harmonic effect obliterated the awareness of form as a whole; in painting the individual color was stressed at the expense of pictorial composition; and in the novel psychology became more important than structure. The totality of the culture industry has put an end to this. Though concerned exclusively with effects, it crushes their insubordination and makes them subserve the formula, which replaces the work. The same fate is inflicted on whole and parts alike. The whole inevitably bears no relation to the details—just like the career of a successful man into which everything is made to fit as an illustration or a proof, whereas it is nothing more than the sum of all those idiotic events. The

so-called dominant idea is like a file which ensures order but not coherence. The whole and the parts are alike; there is no antithesis and no connection. Their prearranged harmony is a mockery of what had to be striven after in the great bourgeois works of art. In Germany the grave-yard stillness of the dictatorship already hung over the gayest films of the democratic era.

The whole world is made to pass through the filter of the culture industry. The old experience of the movie-goer, who sees the world outside as an extension of the film he has just left (because the latter is intent upon reproducing the world of everyday perceptions), is now the producer's guideline. The more intensely and flawlessly his techniques duplicate empirical objects, the easier it is today for the illusion to prevail that the outside world is the straightforward continuation of that presented on the screen. This purpose has been furthered by mechanical reproduction since the lightning takeover by the sound film.

Real life is becoming indistinguishable from the movies. The sound film, far surpassing the theater of illusion, leaves no room for imagination or reflection on the part of the audience, who is unable to respond within the structure of the film, yet deviate from its precise detail without losing the thread of the story; hence the film forces its victims to equate it directly with reality. The stunting of the mass-media consumer's powers of imagination and spontaneity does not have to be traced back to any psychological mechanisms; he must ascribe the loss of those attributes to the objective nature of the products themselves, especially to the most characteristic of them, the sound film. They are so designed that quickness, powers of observation, and experience are undeniably needed to apprehend them at all; yet sustained thought is out of the question if the spectator is not to miss the relentless rush of facts. Even though the effort required for his response is semi-automatic, no scope is left for the imagination. Those who are so absorbed by the world of the movie—by its images, gestures, and words—that they are unable to supply what really makes it a world, do not have to dwell on particular points of its mechanics during a screening. All the other films and products of the entertainment industry which they have seen have taught them what to expect; they react automatically. The might of industrial society is lodged in men's minds. The entertainments manufacturers know that their products will be consumed with alertness even when the customer is distraught, for each of them is a model of the huge economic machinery which has always sustained the masses, whether at work or at leisure—which is akin to work. From every sound film and every broadcast program the social effect can be inferred which is exclusive to none but is shared by all alike. The culture industry as a whole has molded men as a type unfailingly reproduced in every product. All the agents of this process, from the producer to the women's clubs, take good care that the simple reproduction of this mental state is not nuanced or extended in any way.

The art historians and guardians of culture who complain of the extinction in the West of a basic style-determining power are wrong. The stereotyped appropriation of everything, even the inchoate, for the purposes of mechanical reproduction surpasses the rigor and general currency of any "real style," in the sense in which cultural *cognoscenti* celebrate the organic precapitalist past. No Palestrina* could be more of a purist in eliminating every unprepared and unresolved discord than the jazz arranger in suppressing any development which does not conform to the jargon. When jazzing up Mozart he changes him not only when he is too serious or too difficult but when he harmonizes the melody in a different way, perhaps more simply, than is customary now. No medieval builder can have scrutinized the subjects for church windows and sculptures more suspiciously than the studio hierarchy scrutinizes a work by Balzac or Hugo before finally approving it. No medieval theologian could have determined the degree of the torment to be suffered by the damned in accordance with the *ordo* [*order*] of divine love more meticulously than the producers of shoddy epics calculate the torture to be undergone by the hero or the exact point to which the leading lady's hemline shall be raised. The explicit and implicit, exoteric and esoteric catalog of the forbidden and tolerated is so extensive that it not only defines the area of

freedom but is all-powerful inside it. Everything down to the last detail is shaped accordingly. Like its counterpart, avant-garde art, the entertainment industry determines its own language; down to its very syntax and vocabulary, by the use of anathema [a thing greatly detested, loathed, or shunned]. The constant pressure to produce new effects (which must conform to the old pattern) serves merely as another rule to increase the power of the conventions when any single effect threatens to slip through the net. Every detail is so firmly stamped with sameness that nothing can appear which is not marked at birth, or does not meet with approval at first sight.

In the culture industry the notion of genuine style is seen to be the aesthetic equivalent of domination. Style considered as mere aesthetic regularity is a romantic dream of the past. The unity of style not only of the Christian Middle Ages but of the Renaissance expresses in each case the different structure of social power, and not the obscure experience of the oppressed in which the general was enclosed. The great artists were never those who embodied a wholly flawless and perfect style, but those who used style as a way of hardening themselves against the chaotic expression of suffering, as a negative truth. The style of their works gave what was expressed that force without which life flows away unheard. Those very art forms which are known as classical, such as Mozart's music, contain objective trends which represent something different to the style which they incarnate. As late as Schönberg and Picasso, the great artists have retained a mistrust of style, and at crucial points have subordinated it to the logic of the matter. What Dadaists and Expressionists called the untruth of style as such triumphs today in the sung jargon of a crooner, in the carefully contrived elegance of a film star, and even in the admirable expertise of a photograph of a peasant's squalid hut. Style represents a promise in every work of art. That which is expressed is subsumed through style into the dominant forms of generality, into the

---

*Giovanni Pierluigi da Palestrina (c. 1525–94) was an Italian Renaissance composer. His work is regarded as the highest achievement in a style of music called "Renaissance polyphony" and is unparalleled in the sixteenth century for its consistent adherence to precise rules of composition. Palestrina's music was central in the development of Roman Catholic Church music. —Ed.

language of music, painting, or words, in the hope that it will be reconciled thus with the idea of true generality. This promise held out by the work of art that it will create truth by lending new shape to the conventional social forms is as necessary as it is hypocritical. It unconditionally posits the real forms of life as it is by suggesting that fulfillment lies in their aesthetic derivatives. To this extent the claim of art is always ideology too. However, only in this confrontation with tradition of which style is the record can art express suffering. That factor in a work of art which enables it to transcend reality certainly cannot be detached from style; but it does not consist of the harmony actually realized, of any doubtful unity of form and content, within and without, of individual and society; it is to be found in those features in which discrepancy appears: in the necessary failure of the passionate striving for identity. Instead of exposing itself to this failure in which the style of the great work of art has always achieved self-negation, the inferior work has always relied on its similarity with others—on a surrogate identity.

In the culture industry this imitation finally becomes absolute. Having ceased to be anything but style, it reveals the latter's secret: obedience to the social hierarchy. Today aesthetic barbarity completes what has threatened the creations of the spirit since they were gathered together as culture and neutralized. To speak of culture was always contrary to culture. Culture as a common denominator already contains in embryo that schematization and process of cataloging and classification which bring culture within the sphere of administration. And it is precisely the industrialized, the consequent, subsumption which entirely accords with this notion of culture. By subordinating in the same way and to the same end all areas of intellectual creation, by occupying men's senses from the time they leave the factory in the evening to the time they clock in again the next morning with matter that bears the impress of the labor process they themselves have to sustain throughout the day, this subsumption mockingly satisfies the concept of a unified culture which the philosophers of personality contrasted with mass culture.

Nevertheless the culture industry remains the entertainment business. Its influence over the consumers is established by entertainment; that will ultimately be broken not by an outright decree, but by the hostility inherent in the principle of entertainment to what is greater than itself. Since all the trends of the culture industry are profoundly embedded in the public by the whole social process, they are encouraged by the survival of the market in this area. Demand has not yet been replaced by simple obedience. As is well known, the major reorganization of the film industry shortly before World War I, the material prerequisite of its expansion, was precisely its deliberate acceptance of the public's needs as recorded at the box-office—a procedure which was hardly thought necessary in the pioneering days of the screen. The same opinion is held today by the captains of the film industry, who take as their criterion the more or less phenomenal song hits but wisely never have recourse to the judgment of truth, the opposite criterion. Business is their ideology. It is quite correct that the power of the culture industry resides in its identification with a manufactured need, and not in simple contrast to it, even if this contrast were one of complete power and complete powerlessness. Amusement under late capitalism is the prolongation of work. It is sought after as an escape from the mechanized work process, and to recruit strength in order to be able to cope with it again. But at the same time mechanization has such power over a man's leisure and happiness, and so profoundly determines the manufacture of amusement goods, that his experiences are inevitably after-images of the work process itself. The ostensible content is merely a faded foreground; what sinks in is the automatic succession of standardized operations. What happens at work, in the factory, or in the office can only be escaped from by approximation to it in one's leisure time. All amusement suffers from this incurable malady. Pleasure hardens into boredom because, if it is to remain pleasure, it must not demand any effort and therefore moves rigorously in the worn grooves of association. No independent thinking must be expected from the audience: the product prescribes every reaction: not by its natural structure (which collapses under reflection), but by signals. Any logical connection calling for mental effort is painstakingly avoided. As far as possible, developments must follow from the immediately preceding situation and never from the idea of the whole. For the attentive movie-goer any individual scene will give him the whole thing. Even the set pattern itself still seems dangerous, offering some meaning—wretched as it might be—where only meaninglessness is acceptable. Often the plot is maliciously deprived of the development demanded by characters and matter according to the old pattern. Instead, the next step is what the script writer takes to be the most striking effect in the particular situation. Banal though elaborate surprise interrupts the story-line. The tendency mischievously to fall back on pure nonsense, which was a legitimate part of popular art, farce and clowning, right up to Chaplin and the Marx Brothers, is most obvious in the unpretentious kinds. This tendency has completely asserted itself in the text of the novelty song, in the thriller movie, and in cartoons, although in films starring Greer Garson and Bette Davis the unit of the socio-psychological case study provides something approximating a claim to a consistent plot. The idea itself, together with the objects of comedy and terror, is massacred and fragmented. Novelty songs have always existed on a contempt for meaning which, as predecessors and successors of psychoanalysis, they reduce to the monotony of sexual symbolism. Today detective and adventure films no longer give the audience the opportunity to experience the resolution. In the non-ironic varieties of the genre, it has also to rest content with the simple horror of situations which have almost ceased to be linked in any way.

This raises the question whether the culture industry fulfills the function of diverting minds which it boasts about so loudly. If most of the radio stations and movie theaters were closed down, the consumers would probably not lose so very much. To walk from the street into the movie theater is no longer to enter a world of dream; as soon as the very existence of these institutions no longer made it obligatory to use them, there would be no great urge to do so. Such closures would not be reactionary machine wrecking. The disappointment would be felt not so much by the enthusiasts as by

the slow-witted, who are the ones who suffer for everything anyhow. In spite of the films which are intended to complete her integration, the housewife finds in the darkness of the movie theater a place of refuge where she can sit for a few hours with nobody watching, just as she used to look out of the window when there were still homes and rest in the evening. The unemployed in the great cities find coolness in summer and warmth in winter in these temperature-controlled locations. Otherwise, despite its size, this bloated pleasure apparatus adds no dignity to man's lives. The idea of "fully exploiting" available technical resources and the facilities for aesthetic mass consumption is part of the economic system which refuses to exploit resources to abolish hunger.

The culture industry perpetually cheats its consumers of what it perpetually promises. The promissory note which, with its plots and staging, it draws on pleasure is endlessly prolonged; the promise, which is actually all the spectacle consists of, is illusory: all it actually confirms is that the real point will never be reached, that the diner must be satisfied with the menu. In front of the appetite stimulated by all those brilliant names and images there is finally set no more than a commendation of the depressing everyday world it sought to escape. Of course works of art were not sexual exhibitions either. However, by representing deprivation as negative, they retracted, as it were, the prostitution of the impulse and rescued by mediation what was denied. The secret of aesthetic sublimation is its representation of fulfillment as a broken promise. The culture industry does not sublimate; it represses. By repeatedly exposing the objects of desire, breasts in a clinging sweater or the naked torso of the athletic hero, it only stimulates the unsublimated forepleasure which habitual deprivation has long since reduced to a masochistic semblance. There is no erotic situation which, while insinuating and exciting, does not fail to indicate unmistakably that things can never go that far. The Hays Office merely confirms the ritual of Tantalus* that the culture industry has established anyway. Works of art are ascetic and

* Tantalus was admitted to the company of the gods and became immortal by eating the food of the gods. However, he angered the gods by stealing food from them and giving it to mortals. Because he was immortal and could not be killed, he was punished with everlasting thirst. To make the punishment more severe, he was plunged in a river up to his chin, but whenever he went to drink from the river, the water lowered just out of his reach. —Ed.

unashamed; the culture industry is pornographic and prudish. Love is downgraded to romance. And, after the descent, much is permitted; even license as a marketable speciality has its quota bearing the trade description "daring." The mass production of the sexual automatically achieves its repression. Because of his ubiquity, the film star with whom one is meant to fall in love is from the outset a copy of himself. Every tenor voice comes to sound like a Caruso record, and the "natural" faces of Texas girls are like the successful models by whom Hollywood has typecast them. The mechanical reproduction of beauty, which reactionary cultural fanaticism wholeheartedly serves in its methodical idolization of individuality, leaves no room for that unconscious idolatry which was once essential to beauty. The triumph over beauty is celebrated by humor—the *Schadenfreude* [malicious pleasure] that every successful deprivation calls forth. There is laughter because there is nothing to laugh at. Laughter, whether conciliatory or terrible, always occurs when some fear passes. It indicates liberation either from physical danger or from the grip of logic. Conciliatory laughter is heard as the echo of an escape from power; the wrong kind overcomes fear by capitulating to the forces which are to be feared. It is the echo of power as something inescapable. Fun is a medicinal bath. The pleasure industry never fails to prescribe it. It makes laughter the instrument of the fraud practised on happiness. Moments of happiness are without laughter; only operettas and films portray sex to the accompaniment of resounding laughter. But Baudelaire is as devoid of humour as Hölderlin. In the false society laughter is a disease which has attacked happiness and is drawing it into its worthless totality. To laugh at something is always to deride it, and the life which, according to Bergson, in laughter breaks through the barrier, is actually an invading barbaric life, self-assertion prepared to parade its liberation from any scruple when the social occasion arises. Such a laughing audience is a parody of humanity. Its members are monads, all dedicated to the pleasure of being ready for anything at the expense of everyone else. Their harmony is a caricature of solidarity. What is fiendish about this false laughter is that it is a compelling parody of the best, which is conciliatory. Delight is austere: *res severa verum gaudium* [true joy is a serious thing]. The monastic theory that not asceticism but the sexual act denotes the renunciation of attainable bliss receives negative confirmation in the gravity of the lover who with foreboding commits his life to the fleeting moment. In the culture industry, jovial denial takes the place of the pain found in ecstasy and in asceticism. The supreme law is that they shall not satisfy their desires at any price; they must laugh and be content with laughter. In every product of the culture industry, the permanent denial imposed by civilization is once again unmistakably demonstrated and inflicted on its victims. To offer and to deprive them of something is one and the same. This is what happens in erotic films. Precisely because it must never take place, everything centers upon copulation. In films it is more strictly forbidden for an illegitimate relationship to be admitted without the parties being punished than for a millionaire's future son-in-law to be active in the labor movement. In contrast to the liberal era, industrialized as well as popular culture may wax indignant at capitalism, but it cannot renounce the threat of castration. This is fundamental. It outlasts the organized acceptance of the uniformed seen in the films which are produced to that end, and in reality. What is decisive today is no longer puritanism, although it still asserts itself in the form of women's organizations, but the necessity inherent in the system not to leave the customer alone, not for a moment to allow him any suspicion that resistance is possible. The principle dictates that he should be shown all his needs as capable of fulfillment, but that those needs should be so predetermined that he feels himself to be the eternal consumer, the object of the culture industry. Not only does it make him believe that the deception it practices is satisfaction, but it goes further and implies that, whatever the state of affairs, he must put up with what is offered. The escape from everyday drudgery which the whole culture industry promises may be compared to the daughter's abduction in the cartoon: the father is holding the ladder in the dark. The paradise offered by the culture industry is the same old drudgery. Both escape and elopement are predesigned to lead back to the starting point. Pleasure promotes the resignation which it ought to help to forget.

The stronger the positions of the culture industry become, the more summarily it can deal with consumers' needs, producing them, controlling them, disciplining them, and even withdrawing amusement: no limits are set to cultural progress of this kind. But the tendency is immanent in the principle of amusement itself, which is enlightened in a bourgeois sense. If the need (for amusement was in large measure the creation of industry, which used the subject as a means of recommending the work to the masses—the oleograph* by the dainty morsel it depicted, or the cake mix by a picture of a cake—amusement always reveals the influence of business, the sales talk, the quack's spiel. But the original affinity of business and amusement is shown in the latter's specific significance: to defend society. To be pleased means to say Yes. It is possible only by insulation from the totality of the social process, by desensitization and, from the first, by senselessly sacrificing the inescapable claim of every work, however inane, within its limits to reflect the whole. Pleasure always means not to think about anything, to forget suffering even where it is shown. Basically it is helplessness. It is flight; not, as is asserted, flight from a wretched reality, but from the last remaining thought of resistance. The liberation which amusement promises is freedom from thought and from negation. The effrontery of the rhetorical question. "What do people want?" lies in the fact that it is addressed—as if to reflective individuals—to those very people who are deliberately to be deprived of this individuality. Even when the public does—exceptionally—rebel against the pleasure industry, all it can muster is that feeble resistance which that very industry has inculcated in it. Nevertheless, it has become increasingly difficult to keep people in this condition. The rate at which they are reduced to stupidity must not fall behind the rate at which their intelligence is increasing. In this age of statistics the masses are too sharp to identify themselves with the millionaire on the screen, and too slow-witted to ignore the law of the largest number. Ideology conceals itself in the calculation of probabilities.

Not everyone will be lucky one day—but the person who draws the winning ticket, or rather the one who is marked out to do so by a higher power—usually by the pleasure industry itself, which is represented as unceasingly in search of talent. Those discovered by talent scouts and then publicized on a vast scale by the studio are ideal types of the new dependent average. Of course, the starlet is meant to symbolize the typist in such a way that the splendid evening dress seems meant for the actress as distinct from the real girl. The girls in the audience not only feel that they could be on the screen, but realize the great gulf separating them from it. Only one girl can draw the lucky ticket, only one man can win the prize, and if, mathematically, all have the same chance, yet this is so infinitesimal for each one that he or she will do best to write it off and rejoice in the other's success, which might just as well have been his or hers, and somehow never is. Whenever the culture industry still issues an invitation naïvely to identify, it is immediately withdrawn. No one can escape from himself any more. Once a member of the audience could see his own wedding in the one shown in the film. Now the lucky actors on the screen are copies of the same category as every member of the public, but such equality only demonstrates the insurmountable separation of the human elements. The perfect similarity is the absolute difference. The identity of the category forbids that of the individual cases. Ironically, man as a member of a species has been made a reality by the culture industry. Now any person signifies only those attributes by which he can replace everybody else: he is interchangeable, a copy. As an individual he is completely expendable and utterly insignificant, and this is just what he finds out when time deprives him of this similarity. This changes the inner structure of the religion of success—otherwise strictly maintained. Increasing emphasis is laid not on the path *per aspera ad astra* [through adversities to the stars] which presupposes hardship and effort), but on winning a prize. The element of blind chance in the routine decision about which song deserves to be a hit

* An oleograph is a chromolithograph printed on cloth. It aims to imitate an oil painting. Chromolithography was a process commercialized in the 1830s to make multicolored prints that is based on lithography. The process enables prints to be colored mechanically, rather than hand-colored as they were done prior to chromolithography. —Ed.

and which extra a heroine is stressed by the ideology. Movies emphasize chance. By stopping at nothing to ensure that all the characters are essentially alike, with the exception of the villain, and by excluding non-conforming faces (for example, those which, like Garbo's, do not look as if you could say "Hello sister!" to them), life is made easier for movie-goers at first. They are assured that they are all right as they are, that they could do just as well and that nothing beyond their powers will be asked of them. But at the same time they are given a hint that any effort would be useless because even bourgeois luck no longer has any connection with the calculable effect of their own work. They take the hint. Fundamentally they all recognize chance (by which one occasionally makes his fortune) as the other side of planning. Precisely because the forces of society are so deployed in the direction of rationality that anyone might become an engineer or manager, it has ceased entirely to be a rational matter who the one will be in whom society will invest training or confidence for such functions. Chance and planning become one and the same thing, because, given men's equality, individual success and failure—right up to the top—lose any economic meaning. Chance itself is planned, not because it affects any particular individual but precisely because it is believed to play a vital part. It serves the planners as an alibi, and makes it seem that the complex of transactions and measures into which life has been transformed leaves scope for spontaneous and direct relations between man. This freedom is symbolized in the various media of the culture industry by the arbitrary selection of average individuals. In a magazine's detailed accounts of the modestly magnificent pleasure-trips it has arranged for the lucky person, preferably a stenotypist (who has probably won the competition because of her contacts with local bigwigs), the powerlessness of all is reflected. They are mere matter—so much so that those in control can take someone up into their heaven and throw him out again: his rights and his work count for nothing. Industry is interested in people merely as customers and employees, and has in fact reduced mankind as a whole and each of its elements to this all-embracing formula. According to the ruling aspect at the time, ideology emphasizes

plan or chance, technology or life, civilization or nature. As employees, men are reminded of the rational organization and urged to fit in like sensible people. As customers, the freedom of choice, the charm of novelty, is demonstrated to them on the screen or in the press by means of the human and personal anecdote. In either case they remain objects.

The less the culture industry has to promise, the less it can offer a meaningful explanation of life, and the emptier is the ideology it disseminates. Even the abstract ideals of the harmony and beneficence of society are too concrete in this age of universal publicity. We have even learned how to identify abstract concepts as sales propaganda. Language based entirely on truth simply arouses impatience to get on with the business deal it is probably advancing. The words that are not means appear senseless; the others seem to be fiction, untrue. Value judgments are taken either as advertising or as empty talk. Accordingly ideology has been made vague and noncommittal, and thus neither clearer nor weaker. Its very vagueness, its almost scientific aversion from committing itself to anything which cannot be verified, acts as an instrument of domination. It becomes a vigorous and prearranged promulgation of the status quo. The culture industry tends to make itself the embodiment of authoritative pronouncements, and thus the irrefutable prophet of the prevailing order.

DISCUSSION QUESTIONS

1. What is the "culture industry"? Does it still exist today? Why or why not?

2. Horkheimer and Adorno argue that art produced by the culture industry is "rubbish." Is their argument sound? Why or why not?

3. Horkheimer and Adorno write, "If most of the radio stations and movie theaters were closed down, the consumers would probably not lose very much." Do you agree with them? Why or why not?

4. What are the similarities and differences between Benjamin's and Horkheimer and Adorno's approach to art? In particular,

reflect on their respective approaches to film. Which, if either, do you prefer, and why?

5. What do you think Horkheimer and Adorno mean by the statement "The culture industry does not sublimate; it represses"?

6. What do you think Horkheimer and Adorno would say to those who believe that going to the movies can result in a philosophically challenging and rewarding experience?

Love and Death on Long Island
[USA 1997] 1 hour, 34 minutes
Directed by Richard Kwietniowski

Giles De'Ath (John Hurt) is a reclusive, middle-aged writer living in London. One day, he ventures out to see the film adaptation of one of his favorite E. M. Forester novels but inadvertently ends up in a theater screening a sophomoric comedy called *Hotpants College II*. He is about to leave the theater when a young actor in the film grabs his attention. Some days later, Giles visits a museum where a Romantic painting of a young writer reminds him of the actor. He returns to the theater to see the movie in its entirety and becomes enthralled by the star, Ronnie Bostock (Jason Priestley).

Giles begins scanning film and teen idol magazines for articles about and photos of the actor, and compiles an extensive dossier. He purchases his first television and VCR so that he can watch all of Ronnie's films. He tells his literary agent that he is exploring a new, revitalizing subject: finding beauty where no one has looked before. He even travels to New York with the intention of locating Ronnie on Long Island. Taking a room at a cheap motel, he wanders the streets in hopes of a chance meeting. He happens to see the actor's fiancée, Audrey (Fiona Loewi), at the supermarket and engineers an accidental meeting with her. Audrey is charmed by Giles' enthusiasm for Ronnie and asks if Giles would consider writing a script for the young actor. Audrey later arranges a meeting between the two men, and Giles showers Ronnie with praise.

Ronnie is impressed and intrigued by his fan, and they begin to spend time together. They read through the script of *Hotpants College III,* and Giles begins to rewrite the film, adding tender, heroic scenes with literary allusions. Audrey senses the growing relationship between the two men and suddenly announces that she and Ronnie are leaving Long Island. During a farewell meeting with Ronnie, Giles proposes that Ronnie leave America altogether and start over in Europe with his help. When Ronnie says that he must meet Audrey, Giles detains him, insisting that his relationship with Audrey will not last and confessing his own love for the actor. Ronnie quietly exits, pausing to lay a sympathetic hand on Giles' shoulder. Giles returns to his motel and writes the story of his infatuation, which he faxes to Ronnie. Ronnie reads the story and is deeply moved as he wonders how his life might have changed had he been able to open his heart to Giles. The young man reflects for a moment and then rips the fax to shreds.

DISCUSSION QUESTIONS

1. In the process of following Giles' pursuit of Ronnie, we are afforded a glimpse inside what Adorno and Horkheimer call the "culture industry." Giles discovers that Ronnie's movies are commodities produced for teenagers, not highly refined aesthetic objects. Nevertheless, he sees in Ronnie's acting the kind of beauty found in high art. Ultimately, do you think that *Love and Death on Long Island*

supports or denies Adorno and Horkheimer's claim that movies are not art but rather are commodities produced by the culture industry?

2. According to Horkheimer and Adorno, the culture industry produces homogeneous and monotonous commodities, that is, art for the masses. Are movies like the *Hotpants College* series representative of this notion? Why or why not? Is *Love and Death on Long Island* also representative of this notion? Why or why not?

3. Horkheimer and Adorno maintain that films produced by the culture industry constitute a series of "ready-made clichés to be slotted anywhere." "As soon as the film begins, it is quite clear how it will end, and who will be rewarded, punished, or forgotten." Are these characteristics of *Love and Death of Long Island*? For example, did you know how it would end? Discuss.

4. Does *Love and Death on Long Island* support Horkheimer and Adorno's notion that "if most of the radio stations and movie theaters were closed down, the consumers would probably not lose very much"? Why or why not?

5. What, if anything, is the value of films like *Hotpants College II* and *Skidmarks* (another one of Ronnie's films)? Are these films similar to contemporary films that you have seen? If so, which ones, and how?

6. Discuss connection between contemporary film aesthetics and what Adorno and Horkheimer call the "absolute power of capitalism." Are Horkheimer and Adorno right that contemporary cinema is plotted to allow for "the triumph of invested capital"—in other words, to make money for those who control the film industry? Is making money the ultimate goal of films like *Hotpants College II*? Discuss.

SUPPLEMENTARY READINGS

Morality: Its Nature and Justification

Baier, Kurt. *The Moral Point of View.* Ithaca, NY: Cornell University Press, 1958.

Brandt, Richard. *A Theory of the Good and the Right.* Oxford: Oxford University Press, 1979.

Frankena, William. *Ethics.* Englewood Cliffs, NY: Prentice Hall, 1973.

Gert, Bernard. *Morality.* New York: Oxford University Press, 1998.

Harman, Gilbert. *The Nature of Morality: An Introduction to Ethics.* New York: Oxford University Press, 1977.

Hudson, W. D. *A Century of Moral Philosophy.* New York: St. Martin's Press, 1983.

MacIntyre, Alasdair. *Whose Justice? Which Rationality?* Notre Dame, IN: University of Notre Dame Press, 1988.

Nagel, Thomas. *The View from Nowhere.* New York: Oxford University Press, 1986.

Rachels, James. *The Elements of Moral Philosophy*, 3rd ed. New York: Random House, 1998.

Stace, W. T. *The Concept of Morals.* New York: Macmillan, 1937.

Wallace, Gerald, and A. D. M. Walker, eds. *The Definition of Morality.* London: Methuen, 1970.

Warnock, Mary. *Ethics Since 1900.* London: Oxford University Press, 1966.

Williams, Bernard. *Ethics and the Limits of Philosophy.* Cambridge, MA: Harvard University Press, 1985.

Relativism

Benedict, Ruth. *Patterns of Culture.* Boston: Houghton Mifflin, 1934.

Cook, John W. *Morality and Cultural Differences.* New York: Oxford University Press, 1999.

Finnes, John. *Moral Absolutes: Tradition, Revision, and Truth.* New York: Cambridge University Press, 1991.

Fleischacker, Samuel. *The Ethics of Culture.* Ithaca, NY: Cornell University Press, 1994.

Harman, Gilbert. "Moral Relativism Defended." *Philosophical Review* 84 (1975): 3–22.

Harman, Gilbert, and Judith J. Thomson. *Moral Relativism and Moral Objectivity.* New York: Basil Blackwell, 1996.

Hurd, Heidi M. *Moral Combat.* New York: Cambridge University Press, 1999.

Ladd, John, ed. *Ethical Relativism.* Belmont, CA: Wadsworth, 1973.

Macklin, Ruth. *Against Relativism: Cultural Diversity and the Search for Ethical Universals in Medicine.* New York: Oxford University Press, 1999.

Margolis, Joseph. *The Truth about Relativism.* Cambridge, MA: Blackwell, 1991.

Melchert, Norman. *Who's to Say?—A Dialogue on Relativism.* Indianapolis, IN: Hackett, 1994.

Midgley, Mary. *Can't We Make Moral Judgments?* New York: St. Martin's Press, 1993.

Moody-Adams, Michele M. *Fieldwork in Familiar Places: Morality, Culture, and Philosophy.* Cambridge, MA: Harvard University Press, 1997.

Stewart, Robert M., and Lynn L. Thomas. "Recent Work on Ethical Relativism." *American Philosophical Quarterly* 28 (1991): 85–100.

Stout, Jeffrey. *Ethics after Babel.* Boston: Beacon Press, 1988.

Sumner, W. G. *Folkways.* Boston: Ginn, 1907.

Williams, Bernard. *Ethics and the Limits of Philosophy.* Cambridge, MA: Harvard University Press, 1985.

Wong, David. *Moral Relativity.* Berkeley: University of California Press, 1985.

Utilitarianism/Consequentialism

Brandt, Richard. *Morality, Utilitarianism, and Rights.* New York: Cambridge University Press, 1992.

Hare, R. M. *Moral Thinking: Its Levels, Method and Point.* New York: Oxford University Press, 1981.

Lyons, David. *The Forms and Limits of Utilitarianism.* Oxford: Clarendon Press, 1965.

Miller, Harlan B., and William Williams, eds. *The Limits of Utilitarianism.* Minneapolis: University of Minnesota Press, 1982.

Quinton, Anthony. *Utilitarian Ethics.* New York: St. Martin's Press, 1973.

Scheffler, Samuel. *The Rejection of Consequentialism.* Oxford: Clarendon Press, 1982.

———, ed. *Consequentialism and Its Critics.* Oxford: Oxford University Press, 1988.

Sen, Amartya, and Bernard Williams, ed. *Utilitarianism and Beyond.* Cambridge: Cambridge University Press, 1982.

Smart, J. J. C., and Bernard Williams. *Utilitarianism: For and Against.* Cambridge: Cambridge University Press, 1973.

Kantianism/Deontology

Acton, Harold. *Kant's Moral Philosophy.* New York: St. Martin's Press, 1970.

Baron, Marcia. *Kantian Ethics, Almost Without Apology.* Ithaca, NY: Cornell University Press, 1995.

Blum, Lawrence A. "Kant's and Hegel's Moral Rationalism: A Feminist Perspective." *Canadian Journal of Philosophy* 12. 2 (1982): 287–302.

O'Neill, Onora. *Acting on Principle: An Essay on Kantian Ethics.* New York: Columbia University Press, 1975.

Paton, H. J. *The Categorical Imperative.* London: Hutchinson, 1947.

Schneewind, J. B. "Autonomy, Obligation and Virtue: An Overview of Kant's Moral Philosophy." *The Cambridge Companion to Kant.* Ed. Paul Guyer. Cambridge: Cambridge University Press, 1992. 309–41.

Egoism

Butler, Joseph. *Five Sermons.* Ed. Stephen Darwall. Indianapolis, IN: Hackett, 1983.

Machan, Tibor. "Recent Work on Ethical Egoism." *American Philosophical Quarterly* 16 (1979): 1–15.

Milo, Ronald, ed. *Egoism and Altruism.* Belmont, CA: Wadsworth, 1973.

Nozick, Robert. "On the Randian Argument." *Personalist* 52 (1971): 282–304.

Rand, Ayn. *The Virtue of Selfishness.* New York: New American Library, 1964.

Regis, Edward, Jr. "What Is Ethical Egoism?" *Ethics* 91 (1980): 50–62.

Virtue Ethics

Blum, Lawrence A. *Friendship, Altruism and Morality.* New York: Routledge & Kegan Paul, 1980.

Broadie, Sarah. *Ethics with Aristotle.* Oxford: Oxford University Press, 1991.

Dent, N. J. H. *The Moral Psychology of the Virtues.* Cambridge: Cambridge University Press, 1984.

Foot, Phillipa. *Vices and Virtues.* Berkeley: University of California Press, 1978.

French, Peter, et. al. *Ethical Theory, Character and Virtue: Midwest Studies in Philosophy.* Vol. 13. Notre Dame, IN: University of Notre Dame Press, 1988.

Geach, P. T. *The Virtues.* Cambridge: Cambridge University Press, 1977.

Kekes, John. *Moral Tradition and Individuality.* Princeton, NJ: Princeton University Press, 1989.

Kruschwitz, Robert, and Robert Roberts. *The Virtues.* Belmont, CA: Wadsworth, 1987.

MacIntyre, Alasdair. *After Virtue,* 2nd ed. Notre Dame, IN: University of Notre Dame Press, 1984.

Mayo, Bernard. *Ethics and the Moral Life.* New York: Macmillan, 1958.

Murdoch, Iris. *The Sovereignty of Good.* New York: Schocken Books, 1971.

Rorty, Amelie. *Essays on Aristotle's Ethics.* Berkeley: University of California Press, 1980.

Sherman, Nancy. *The Fabric of Character: Aristotle's Theory of Virtue.* Oxford: Clarendon Press, 1985.

Wallace, James. *Virtues and Vices.* Ithaca, NY: Cornell University Press, 1978.

Religion and Morality

Helm, Paul, ed. *Divine Commands and Morality.* Oxford: Oxford University Press, 1979.

Kant, Immanuel. *Religion within the Limits of Reason Alone.* Trans. T. M. Greene and H. H. Hudson. New York: Harper & Row, 1960.

Kierkegaard, Søren. *Fear and Trembling.* Trans. Howard Hong and Edna Hong. Princeton, NJ: Princeton University Press, 1983.

Mitchell, Basil. *Morality: Religious and Secular.* Oxford: Oxford University Press, 1980.

Nielsen, Kai. *Ethics without God,* rev. ed. Buffalo, NY: Prometheus Books, 1990.

Outka, Gene, and J. P. Reeder, eds. *Religion and Morality: A Collection of Essays.* New York: Anchor Books, 1973.

Feminism and Morality

Baier, Annette. "What Do Women Want in a Moral Theory?" *Noûs* (1985): 53–63.

Bar On, Bat-Ami, and Ann Ferguson, eds. *Daring to Be Good: Essays in Feminist Ethico-Politics.* New York: Routledge, 1998.

Card, Claudia. *Feminist Ethics.* Lawrence: University of Kansas Press, 1991.

Code, Loraine, Sheila Mullet, and Christine Overall, eds. *Feminist Perspectives: Philosophical Essays on Method and Morals.* Toronto: University of Toronto Press, 1988.

Gilligan, Carol. *In a Different Voice: Psychological Theory and Women's Development.* Cambridge, MA: Harvard University Press, 1982.

Held, Virginia. *Feminist Morality.* Chicago: University of Chicago Press, 1993.

Kittay, Eva Feder, and Diana T. Meyers, eds. *Women and Moral Theory.* Totowa, NJ: Littlefield, Adams, 1987.

Noddings, Nel. *Caring: A Feminine Approach to Ethics and Moral Education.* Berkeley: University of California Press, 1984.

Okin, Susan. *Justice, Gender and the Family*. New York: Basic Books, 1989.

Tong, Rosemarie. *Feminist Thought*, 2nd ed. Boulder, CO: Westview Press, 1998.

Young, Iris. *Justice and the Politics of Difference*. Princeton, NJ: Princeton University Press, 1990.

The Nature and Value of Art

Adorno, Theodor, Gretel Adorno, and Rolf Tiedeman. *Aesthetic Theory*. Trans. Robert Hullot-Kentor. Minneapolis: University of Minnesota Press, 1997.

Aristotle. *The Poetics of Aristotle: Translation and Commentary*. Trans. Stephen Halliwell. Chapel Hill: University of North Carolina Press, 1987.

Arnheim, Rudolf. *Toward a Psychology of Art: Collected Essays*. Berkeley: University of California Press, 1966.

Battersby, Christine. *Gender and Genius: Towards a Feminist Aesthetics*. Bloomington: Indiana University Press, 1990.

Beardsley, Monroe C. *Aesthetics: Problems in the Philosophy of Criticism*, 2nd ed. Indianapolis, IN: Hackett, 1981.

Bender, John W., and H. Gene Blocker. *Contemporary Philosophy of Art: Readings in Analytic Aesthetics*. Englewood Cliffs, NJ: Prentice Hall, 1993.

Berger, John. *Ways of Seeing*. London: Penguin Books, 1972.

Blocker, H. Gene. *Philosophy of Art*. New York: Scribner, 1979.

Bourdieu, Pierre. *Distinction: A Social Critique of the Judgment of Taste*. Cambridge, MA: Harvard University Press, 1984.

Burke, Edmund. *A Philosophical Enquiry into the Origin of Our Ideas of the Sublime and Beautiful*. London: Routledge & Kegan Paul, 1958.

Coleman, Francis, ed. *Contemporary Studies in Aesthetics*. New York: McGraw-Hill, 1968.

Collingwood, R. G. *The Principles of Art*. Oxford: Clarendon Press, 1938.

Cooper, David E., ed. *A Companion to Aesthetics*. Cambridge, MA: Blackwell, 1992.

Cooper, David E., Peter Lamarque, and Crispin Sartwell. *Aesthetics: The Classic Readings*. Malden, MA: Blackwell, 1997.

Crowther, Paul. *The Kantian Sublime: From Morality to Art*. New York: Oxford University Press, 1989.

Davies, Stephen. *Art and Its Messages: Meaning, Morality, and Society*. University Park: Pennsylvania State University Press, 1997.

Dewey, John. *Art as Experience*. New York: Minton, Balch, 1934.

Dickie, George. *Evaluating Art*. Philadelphia: Temple University Press, 1988.

Dickie, George, and R. J. Sclafani. *Aesthetics: A Critical Anthology*. New York: St. Martin's Press, 1977.

Eagleton, Terry. *The Ideology of the Aesthetic*. Cambridge, MA: Blackwell, 1990.

Fisher, John Andrew. *Reflecting on Art*. Mountain View, CA: Mayfield, 1993.

Fleming, William. *Art, Music and Ideas*. New York: Holt, Rinehart & Winston, 1970.

Foster, Hal, ed. *The Anti-Aesthetic: Essays on Postmodern Culture*. New York: New Press, 1998.

Gadamer, Hans Georg. *Truth and Method*. Trans. Garrett Barden and John Cumming. New York: Seabury Press, 1975.

Gombrich, E. H. *Meditations on a Hobby Horse and Other Essays on the Theory of Art*, 2nd ed. New York: Phaidon, 1971.

Goodman, Nelson. *The Languages of Art*. Indianapolis, IN: Bobbs-Merrill, 1968.

Harrison, Charles, and Paul Wood, eds. *Art in Theory 1900–1990: An Anthology of Changing Ideas*. Malden, MA: Blackwell, 1993.

Harrison, Charles, Paul Wood, and Jason Gaiger, eds. *Art in Theory 1815–1900: An Anthology of Changing Ideas*. Malden, MA: Blackwell, 2001.

Hume, David. *Of the Standard of Taste, and Other Essays*. Ed. John W. Lenz. Indianapolis: Bobbs-Merrill, 1965.

Kant, Immanuel. *Critique of Judgment*. Trans. J. H. Bernard. New York: Hafner, 1951.

Kant, Immanuel. *Observations on the Feeling of the Beautiful and Sublime*. Trans. T. Goldthwait. Berkeley: University of California Press, 1960.

Korsmeyer, Carolyn, ed. *Aesthetics: The Big Questions*. Malden, MA: Blackwell, 1998.

Kupfer, Joseph H. *Experience as Art: Aesthetics in Everyday Life*. Albany: SUNY Press, 1983.

Langfeld, Herbert Sidney. *The Aesthetic Attitude*. New York: Harcourt, Brace & Howe, 1920.

Lyotard, Jean-François. *Lessons on the Analytic of the Sublime*. Trans. Elizabeth Rottenberg. Stanford, CA: Stanford University Press, 1994.

Maquet, Jacques J. P. *The Aesthetic Experience: An Anthropologist Looks at the Visual Arts*. New Haven, CT: Yale University Press, 1986.

Nietzsche, Friedrich. *The Birth of Tragedy and the Case of Wagner*. Trans. Walter Kaufmann. New York: Vintage Books, 1967.

Plato. *Apology, Crito, Phaedo, Symposium, Republic*. Ed. Benjamin Jowett and Louise Ropes Loomis. New York: W. J. Black, 1942.

Poggioli, Renato. *The Theory of the Avant-Garde*. Cambridge, MA: Harvard University Press, 1968.

Pollock, Griselda. *Vision and Difference: Feminity, Feminism and Histories of Art*. New York: Routledge, 1988.

Prall, David Wright. *Aesthetic Judgment*. New York: Crowell, 1929.

Putnam, Hilary. *Reason, Truth and History*. New York: Cambridge University Press, 1981.

Santayana, George. *Reason in Art*. New York: Collier Books, 1962.

Sharpe, R. A. *Contemporary Aeshetics: A Philosophical Analysis*. New York: St. Martin's Press, 1983.

Shusterman, Richard. *Pragmatist Aesthetics: Living Beauty, Rethinking Art*. Cambridge, MA: Blackwell, 1992.

Sircello, Guy. *Mind and Art*. Princeton, NJ: Princeton University Press, 1972.

Stolnitz, Jerome. *Aesthetics and Philosophy of Art Criticism, A Critical Introduction*. Boston: Houghton Mifflin, 1960.

Tolstoy, Leo. *What Is Art? and Essays on Art*. Trans. Aylmer Maude. New York: Oxford University Press, 1932.

Townsend, Dabney. *An Introduction to Aesthetics*. Malden, MA: Blackwell, 1997.

Wilde, Oscar. *The Picture of Dorian Gray*. New York: Oxford University Press, 1974.

Wolff, Janet. *Aesthetics and the Sociology of Art*, 2nd ed. Ann Arbor: University of Michigan Press, 1993.

Wollheim, Richard. *On Art and the Mind*. Cambridge, MA: Harvard University Press, 1974.

The Nature and Value of Cinema

Abel, Richard. *French Film Theory and Criticism: A History/Anthology, 1907–1939*. 2 vols. Princeton, NJ: Princeton University Press, 1988.

Anderson, Joseph. *The Reality of Illusion: An Ecological Approach to Cognitive Film Theory*. Carbondale: Southern Illinois University Press, 1996.

Baudrillard, Jean. *The Evil Demon of Images*. Sydney: Power Institute, 1987.

Bazin, André, and Hugh Gray. *What Is Cinema?* Berkeley: University of California Press, 1968–72.

Bergson, Henri. *Matter and Memory*. New York: Zone Books, 1988.

Brand, Peggy Zeglin, and Carolyn Korsmeyer, eds. *Feminism and Tradition in Aesthetics*. University Park: Pennsylvania State University Press, 1995.

Braudy, Leo. *World in a Frame: What We See in Films*. Garden City, NY: Anchor Press, 1976.

Bresson, Robert. *Notes on Cinematography*. New York: Urizen Books, 1977.

Brunette, Peter, and David Wills. *Screen/Play: Derrida and Film Theory*. Princeton, NJ: Princeton University Press, 1989.

———. *Deconstruction and the Visual Arts: Art, Media, Architecture*. Cambridge: New York, 1994.

Buckle, Gerard Fort. *The Mind and the Film: A Treatise on the Psychological Factors in the Film*. London: Routledge, 1926.

Cadbury, William, and Leland A. Poague. *Film Criticism: A Counter Theory*. Ames: Iowa State University Press, 1982.

Carrière, Jean-Claude. *The Secret Language of Film*. New York: Pantheon Books, 1994.

Carroll, Noël. *Theorizing the Moving Image*. Cambridge: Cambridge University Press, 1996.

Casebier, Allan. *Film and Phenomenology: Toward a Realist Theory of Cinematic Representation*. Cambridge: Cambridge University Press, 1991.

Cavell, Stanley. *The World Viewed: Reflections on the Ontology of Film*. New York: Viking Press, 1971.

———. *Cities of Words: Pedagogical Letters on a Register of the Moral Life*. Cambridge, MA: Harvard University Press, 2004.

Charley, Leo, and Vanessa R. Schwartz. *Cinema and the Invention of Modern Life*. Berkeley: University of California Press, 1995.

Chatman, Seymour Benjamin. *Coming to Terms: The Rhetoric of Narrative in Fiction and Films*. Ithaca, NY: Cornell University Press, 1990.

Cocteau, Jean, André Bernard, and Claude Gauteur. *The Art of Cinema*. New York: Marion Boyars, 1992.

Deleuze, Gilles. *Cinema 1: The Movement-Image*. Trans. Hugh Tomlinson and Barbara Habberjam. Minneapolis: University of Minnesota Press, 1986.

————. *Cinema 2: The Time-Image*. Trans. Hugh Tomlinson and Robert Galeta. Minneapolis: University of Minnesota Press, 1989.

Dienst, Richard. *Still Life in Real Time: Theory After Television*. Durham, NC: Duke University Press, 1994.

Douglas, Ian, and Horst Ruthrof. *Film and Meaning: An Integrative Theory*. Murdoch, WA: Continuum Publications and Film & Television Institute, 1988.

Dovzhenko, Alexander. *The Poet as Filmmaker: Selected Writings*. Cambridge, MA: MIT Press, 1973.

Eisenstein, Sergei, and Jay Leyda. *Film Essays and a Lecture by Sergei Eisenstein*. New York: Praeger, 1970.

Farber, Manny. *Negative Space: Manny Farber on the Movies*. New York: Praeger, 1971.

Freeland, Cynthia A., and Thomas E. Wartenberg, eds. *Philosophy and Film*. New York: Routledge, 1995.

Goffman, Erving. *Frame Analysis: An Essay on the Organisation of Experience*. New York: Harper & Row, 1974.

Greenberg, Harvey R. *The Movies on Your Mind*. New York: Saturday Review Press, 1975.

Heath, Stephen. *Questions of Cinema*. New York: Macmillan Press, 1981.

Hollander, Anne. *Moving Pictures*. New York: Knopf, 1989.

Jameson, Fredric. *Signatures of the Visible*. New York: Routledge, 1990.

Jarvie, Ian. *Philosophy of the Film: Espistemology, Ontology, Aesthetics*. New York: Routledge & Kegan Paul, 1987.

Kawin, Bruce F. *Mindscreen: Bergman, Godard, and First-Person Film*. Princeton, NJ: Princeton University Press, 1978.

Khatchadourian, Haig. *Music, Film and Art*. New York: Gordon & Breach, 1985.

Langer, Susanne. *Feeling and Form: A Theory of Art Developed from Philosophy in a New Key*. London: Routledge & Kegan Paul, 1953.

Lauder, Robert E. *God, Death, Art and Love: The Philosophical Vision of Ingmar Bergman*. New York: Paulist Press, 1989.

Linden, George William. *Reflections on the Screen*. Belmont, CA: Wadsworth, 1970.

Lowry, Edward. *The Filmology Movement and Film Study in France*. Ann Arbor, MI: UMI Research Press, 1985.

Mast, Gerald. *Film/Cinema/Movie: A Theory of Experience*. New York: Harper & Row, 1977.

McGuire, Jeremiah. *Cinema and Value Philosophy*. New York: Philosophical Library, 1968.

Messaris, Paul. *Visual "Literacy": Image, Mind and Reality*. Boulder, CO: Westview Press, 1994.

Miller, Mark Crispin. *Seeing through the Movies*. New York: Pantheon Books, 1990.

Mitchell, W. J. Thomas. *Picture Theory: Essays on Verbal and Visual Representation*. Chicago: University of Chicago Press, 1994.

Murray, Edward. *The Cinematic Imagination: Writers and the Motion Pictures*. New York: Ungar, 1972.

Orr, John. *Cinema and Modernity*. Cambridge, MA: Blackwell, 1993.

Roskill, Mark W., and David Carrier. *Truth and Falsehood in Visual Images*. Amherst: University of Massachusetts Press, 1983.

Rothman, William. *The "I" of the Camera: Essays in Film Criticism, History and Aesthetics*. New York: Cambridge University Press, 1988.

————, ed. *Cavell on Film*. Albany: State University of New York Press, 2005.

Ruiz, Raúl. *Poetics of Cinema*. Trans. Brian Holmes. Paris: Éditions Dis Voir, 1995.

Slade, Mark. *Language of Change: Moving Images of Man*. Toronto: Holt, Rinehart & Winston of Canada, 1970.

Smith, Murray. *Engaging Characters: Fiction, Emotion and the Cinema*. New York: Oxford University Press, 1995.

Spiegel, Alan. *Fiction and the Camera Eye: Visual Consciousness in Film and the Modern Novel*. Charlottesville: University Press of Virginia, 1976.

Stam, Robet. *Subversive Pleasures: Bakhtin, Cultural Criticism, and Film*. Baltimore: Johns Hopkins University Press, 1989.

Taylor, Mark C., and Esa Saarinen. *Imagologies: Media Philosophy*. New York: Routledge, 1994.

Taylor, Richard, and Boris Mikhailovich Eikhenbaum. *The Poetics of Cinema*. Oxford: RPT Publications in association with Dept. of Literature, University of Essex, 1982.

Virilio, Paul. *War and Cinema: The Logistics of Perception*. London: Verso, 1989.

Weiss, Paul. *Cinematics*. Carbondale: Southern Illinois University Press, 1975.

Wenders, Wim. *The Logic of Images: Essays and Conversations*. Boston: Faber & Faber, 1991.

Zants, Emily. *Chaos Theory, Complexity, Cinema and the Evolution of the French Novel*. Lewiston, NY: E. Mellen Press, 1996.

Zettl, Herbert. *Sight Sound Motion: Applied Media Aesthetics*, 2nd ed. Belmont, CA: Wadsworth, 1990.

# of Freedom and Justice

Albert (Danny Glover) watching Celie (Desreta Jackson, center) and her sister Nettie (Akosua Busia) hanging clothes in *The Color Purple*.

5.1   AM I FREE TO CONTROL MY CHOICES AND ACTIONS?

SOPHOCLES

FROM OEDIPUS THE KING

Sophocles' celebrated play tells the story of Oedipus, a man who is preordained to kill his father (King Laius of Thebes) and marry his mother (Queen Jocasta of Thebes). The play begins with Oedipus, now a king himself, believing that he has avoided this fate (*moira*). Fate is a prophetic declaration or oracle, and that which is fated is that which is destined or decreed to come to pass. Over the course of the play, however, Oedipus learns the horrible truth: he has not avoided his fate. Upon this realization, Jocasta commits suicide, and Oedipus blinds and banishes himself.

Before Oedipus was born, the oracle at Delphi warned Laius and Jocasta of the "fate" of their son. In order to avoid this fate, when the child was born, they gave him to a shepherd to be killed. The shepherd pierced the child's feet but pitied him and gave him to another shepherd from Corinth. The king and queen of Corinth, Polibus and Merope, adopted the child and named him Oedipus, which means "swollen-foot."

When Oedipus came of age, the oracle at Delphi warned him that he was to kill his father and marry his mother. In order to avoid this fate, he left Corinth. However, during the course of his journey, he came across a man whose chariot was blocking an intersection of three roads, making it impossible for Oedipus to pass. An argument ensued, and Oedipus killed the man, not knowing that the man was his real father, King Laius.

Later, when Oedipus reached the city of Thebes, he was blocked entry by the Sphinx, a monster that killed all who attempted to pass without answering her riddle. Oedipus was the first to successfully answer the riddle and was allowed entry. The Sphinx then destroyed herself, and Oedipus was credited with saving Thebes. After news of Laius's death was received, Oedipus was proclaimed king, and he married Jocasta, not knowing that she was his mother. They lived happily together for many years, producing four children: Antigone, Ismene, Eteocles, and Polynices.

When a plague overtook Thebes, Oedipus was again asked to save the city. He sent Jocasta's brother, Creon, to consult the oracle at Delphi. The oracle proclaimed that the undiscovered murderer of Laius was in the city and had to be killed or banished for the plague to subside.

In the first selection below, the blind prophet Tiresias is brought in to help identify the murderer. When he eventually says that it is Oedipus himself, the king accuses Creon and Tiresias of plotting to overthrow him. After Oedipus accuses Creon of conspiracy, Jocasta tries to convince her husband not to believe the oracle because the oracle's previous prediction did not come true: Laius was not killed by his own son. The second excerpt shows Oedipus slowly coming to understand that he may not have avoided his fate. The third excerpt is the shepherd's testimony, which conclusively establishes that Oedipus has murdered his father and married his mother. Later, Jocasta hangs herself. Upon seeing her body, Oedipus, having intended himself to kill her, blinds himself with her golden brooches. Creon then becomes king and grants Oedipus's wish to be banished. In the final selection, the chorus, reflecting on Oedipus's experiences, warns, "Call no man happy till his days surcease."

It should be noted that Greek drama was produced by the state as part of the function of the state religion. Every year in early spring, a major celebration called the Great Dionysia was held in which dramatists competed against one another for prizes. Awards were presented not only to the winning dramatist and the best actor but also to a wealthy sponsor of the plays.

Sophocles (c. 495–406 B.C.E.), Greek dramatist and poet, was born at Colonus in Attica. His father, Sophillus, was a munitions maker. As a schoolboy, Sophocles was famous for his beauty and won prizes in literature and athletics; as an adult, he had a prominent role in the life of Athens. In 443 B.C.E., he became president of the imperial treasury, and in 440 B.C.E., he was elected general and served with Pericles in the Samian War.

His dramatic career began at the age of twenty-seven with a public performance of his play *Triptolemus*. The play won first prize at the dramatic festival over a play by Aeschylus. Sophocles is said to have written and produced over 120 plays though only 7 survive: *Oedipus the King, Oedipus at Colonus, Antigone, Ajax, Electra, Women of Trachis*, and *Philoctetes*. The date of composition of *Oedipus the King* is unknown though most scholars date it around 427 B.C.E., a time just after the great plague at Athens. We are also told that it won only second prize at the dramatic festival.

OEDIPUS

Tiresias, it was good of you to come.
We know, the whole world knows, that there is
Nothing beyond your sphere of knowledge.
In your heart, if not in your eyes, you see
The wretched state of our city. Only you
Can help us. You will have heard
That we have sent to Apollo for the
Guidelines of help, and Apollo has answered.
The only way of deliverance from the plague
That has struck us is to find the murderer
Of Laius, your late king, and kill or banish him.
Him or them. Sir, your gifts are great.
You have worked in all the modes of divination—
    Scrying, astrology, probing the entrails
    of birds.
Save us, save yourself, you too are of Thebes.
Show us the way of cleansing. To help man
Is the noblest work of man.

TIRESIAS

Very wise words.
But when wisdom brings no profit to the wise,
Wisdom is a mode of suffering. Why did I
    forget this?
I who knew it so well. It was useless to send
    for me.
I should never have come.

OEDIPUS

This is no help.

TIRESIAS

Let me go home. It will be easier, believe me,
For you to bear your suffering, me mine.

OEDIPUS

You are great in Thebes, but you show yourself
No friend of Thebes if you refuse to answer.
Son of Thebes, it is the king of Thebes who speaks
    to you.

TIRESIAS

I refuse to answer, yes. Refuse because
Your words tend to no good. So I guard my own.

OEDIPUS

You know something, yet you refuse to speak.
Let this king be a beggar and beg again.

TIRESIAS

Beg in vain. You sin by asking. I will not
Divulge my heavy secrets—your heavy secrets.

OEDIPUS

More riddles. All I take your words to mean
Is that you know and will not tell. All I take
Your intention to mean is that you will fail us,
See with your blind eyes the city perish.

TIRESIAS

I wish to spare you, I wish to spare myself.
Ask nothing more. I will tell nothing more.

OEDIPUS

Nothing? This is insolence. You would lash
A heart of stone to anger. You are obstinate
Like stone. I command you to speak.

TIRESIAS

Your anger is misplaced. Reserve it
For yourself. Put your own house in order.

OEDIPUS

Your hear these insults? My anger is
The anger of the state. It is the state
You insult.

TIRESIAS

Things will be
As we shall see. Fate's engine
Is beyond the control of man's hands.
You need no prophet to tell you this.

OEDIPUS

What fate will bring to birth—
It is your art or trade to know this
And to say it. Practice your trade.

TIRESIAS

Prepare what new rage you will,
You whose great fault is rage,
I say no more.

OEDIPUS

If you want more rage you shall have it.
I speak openly, I say unflinchingly
What I must now believe. I believe that you
Had some hand in the plot to kill a king.
If you had eyes, I would say that those eyes
Instructed the hand. I say that
In your darkness murder coiled and
    writhed.

TIRESIAS

You would say that? Very well then, hear.
You have stung me out of silence. On your head
And your head only let the curse fall
That fell from your own lips. You are
    excommunicate,
Cut off from men. Speak no more to me or
    any. It is you,
You who are the defiler of this land.

OEDIPUS

You dare to say this? You—shameless,
Treacherous—you know the consequence—
You think you can escape the—

TIRESIAS

I have
Already escaped. The truth is my door.

OEDIPUS

But—it is treason. Who put you up to this?

TIRESIAS

You were, shall I say, the instigator.
You asked, you taunted, you stung. What I said
You made me say. It was against my will.

OEDIPUS

Say it again. Say what you said
Against your will. Let me be clear, let there be
No mistake.

TIRESIAS

It was plain enough.

OEDIPUS

Say it loud,
I will know it beyond all doubt. Say it once
    more.

TIRESIAS

I say that the murderer you seek
Is yourself.

OEDIPUS

Madman—

TIRESIAS

It is your voice
That grows to the voice of a madman. Now I
    have started,
At your request, at your order, remember that—
Will you hear more?

OEDIPUS

Spew all your madness out.
Fly to the limits of treason. You will suffer.
Say all you know.

TIRESIAS

This I know. This you do not know.
Your marriage is a sin. Your love is a sin.
Your bed is stained with sin.

OEDIPUS

Impunity—
You think your blindness and age grant you—

TIRESIAS

The truth grants it, not I, the mere
Bearer of the truth.

OEDIPUS

Bearer of lies, infamy,
Blind, senseless, brainless—

TIRESIAS

Cast no taunts,
You who must yet live in a thunder of them,
Swim in a torrent of them—

OEDIPUS

Do not threaten me,
You, who lack power to make flesh and blood
    of threats,
You who live in the dark. But men in the light
Lack equal power. My throne is of rock.

TIRESIAS

Rocks, you mean. Your throne rocks. No, I
    admit
I cannot harm you. But the gods can. Apollo
    can.

OEDIPUS

Apollo—Creon—it is Creon, then? Creon—
His idea, not yours—?

TIRESIAS

Creon is not your enemy.
You are your own.

OEDIPUS

The shadow of success
Is always envy. It is the scorpion over the royal
    bed,
The headache under the crown. Creon, my friend,
Trusted so long, standing in the shadow,
With the claw of dispossession ready to strike—

Is it possible? I took the crown from his hand,
A crown unsought by me, freely given
By him. And now—is it possible?—
He sets this cheating monger of magic on to me,
The light of cupidity in the blind eyes.
You, sir—I call your craft into question.
That famous gift was notably lacking when
The Sphinx fed on Theban flesh. That riddle
Which none could answer save I—surely a seer,
A prophet, a special being walking under
The equivocal canopy of the gods, surely he
Should have answered it? But the stars were
    silent,
The lees in the wine cup yielded no pattern,
The flight of the birds spelled nothing. I,
I, Oedipus, ignorant Oedipus gave the answer
And stopped the riddler's mouth forever,
With no benefit of the prophet's lore. I,
Oedipus, whom you would now dispossess
To feel in your blindness the embossed gold
Of a royal counselor's chair. Tiresias,
Though blind, the seeing eye of Creon.
Make no mistake, you shall regret this,
Creon shall regret it. To make me, your king,
The sacrificial goat—such impiety to the gods,
Such treason.

CHORUS LEADER

King Oedipus, we hear too much anger
On both sides. If I may say so, the true impiety
Is to waste time in anger, to neglect
The command of Apollo.

TIRESIAS

I accept that you
Wear the crown and stand above me, but I claim
No less than what you claim—the right of speech.
Moreover, it was more out of courtesy that I came
Than from a subject's duty. I am not your subject
Apollo is my one master, him I serve.
Nor is Creon my patron. I answer freely,
As a free being should. You mock my blindness.
First think of your own. You have eyes
That can see and will not. You shut them to
Your own state of sin and impending damnation.
Ask yourself whose son you are. Consider that
A man sins no less for being blind to his sin.
The curse of a father and a mother will yet
Send you packing from this palace and from
    this land.

Then you shall be blind like me but lack
  no voice
To cry aloud the horror of the truth
I know but you are yet to learn. Believe me,
You who use your voice to decry
Creon and myself, you shall be struck dumb yet
Before you find the air for lamentation.
You shall be stamped in the ground
But bear no fruit other than bitterness,
The bitterness of men's scorn.

OEDIPUS

I have stood enough. Leave me. Go back
Whither you came.

TIRESIAS

I came at your bidding,
Not from my own wish.

OEDIPUS

If only I had known
What slanderous madness I was to listen to,
I would have spared us both the trouble.

TIRESIAS

You talk of my madness. It is not the word
Your father would have used.

OEDIPUS

Would have used?
My father lives.

TIRESIAS

Today you find your father.
Today you are born. Today you die.

OEDIPUS

Riddles.
I am sick of riddles.

TIRESIAS

Strange words from a man
Whose pride lay in solving them. But, as you
Shall learn, what was your pride must be your
  ruin.

OEDIPUS

Ruin, ruin. Let us think of the city's ruin.
I saved it once. I will again. I am Oedipus.

TIRESIAS

And I am going. Give me your hand, boy.

OEDIPUS

Give it, boy. We can well spare him.

TIRESIAS

Wait. This is the last time you will see my face.
The rest of you will see and will remember.
Remember these words. This is the man you seek,
The killer of Laius. He passes for a stranger
But, as he will know to his cost, he is Theban born.
He came here seeing. He shall go blind.
He is rich now, but will soon beg his bread.
A stick shall tap his way into exile.
Where he enters, he once came out.
For the ones he loves, new names are needed,
Names against nature, sphinx-names.
He laid his father low to sleep in his bed.
Remember these things. Blind you called me.
You will not call me blind when you learn to see.
And when you learn to see, it is you—
You who will be blind. Lead me away.

* * *

JOCASTA

My brother banished. Surely I have a right
To know the sudden spring of this hatred.

OEDIPUS

Your brother is your brother. But I am the king.
He plotted against me. He put into the mouth
Of that blind old monger of lies that it was I
Who murdered Laius.

JOCASTA

Is it from his own pretended knowledge,
Or from what others have said and he has heard?

OEDIPUS

He kept himself cunningly clean of the accusation,
Using a soothsayer. Could anything be filthier,
More underhand?

JOCASTA

What has shaken you
Is that a soothsayer may speak truth, after all,
May have said truth now, against all evidence.
We are all superstitious. But let me give you

One instance to show that human prophecies
Can dismally fail. To Laius one day I
   remember,
An oracle uttered a dismal prophecy. It was not
The god himself of course—God forbid
I should think such a thing—but one of his
Least reliable servants. He said to Laius
That he should die at the hands of his own son,
A son to be born of Laius and me.
But the whole world knows what happened.
Laius was killed by robbers, foreign men,
At a place where three roads meet. As for
   our son—
And there was a son, the prophet was right in
   that—
In fear of the prophecy, the king gave orders—
It was a terrible thing to do, I had no part in it,
But necessary, I see that it was necessary—
Gave orders to pierce the ankles of the child
With an iron spike and cast him forth
To die on a barren hillside—

OEDIPUS

Pierce his ankles?

JOCASTA

So he could not crawl
Out of the deadly cold. Laius could be cruel,
But he could not directly kill. A winter night
Was the murderer. The point though is this—
That the prophecy failed. Laius's son
Did not kill his father. Prophecies *can* fail.
What God intends He prefers to show
In His own time. Pay no heed to prophets.

OEDIPUS

My wife, my dear wife—something
Terrifies me. Something in your words.
My mind wanders back then stops,
Fearful to look—

JOCASTA

Something in my words?

OEDIPUS

You said that Laius was murdered
At a point where three roads meet.

JOCASTA

That is the story.

OEDIPUS

Where is the place, Jocasta?
Where did it happen?

JOCASTA

Phocis—the road divides there,
Leading to Delphi one way, to Daulia another.

OEDIPUS

And the news of his death came when?

JOCASTA

As you know—just prior to your coming,
Your crowning, our marriage. What is it,
What is in your mind?

OEDIPUS

Oh God God,
To do this to me—

JOCASTA

To do what? What is the trouble?
For God's sake tell me—

OEDIPUS

Laius—
What did he look like?

JOCASTA

Tall, about your height.
Older, of course. White-haired.

OEDIPUS

Is it possible?
To curse oneself in ignorance?

JOCASTA

You're ill,
You frighten me—

OEDIPUS

I have a sudden fear
That that blind man had eyes. Tell me one
   more thing,
Then, God help me, I shall know.
How was he attended—Laius, King Laius?
Many officers? Many servants? A full
Royal retinue?

JOCASTA

There were five men all told,
Including a herald. One carriage for the king.
The details were clear.

OEDIPUS

All too clear. Who told you?
Who told you all this?

JOCASTA

The one servant
Who escaped and ran home.

OEDIPUS

And is he at home still?

JOCASTA

No. When he returned and saw you king,
He said his life was rooted in the old way.
He could not serve a new master. He asked me
To let him leave the service of the palace
And go into the fields to work as a shepherd.
He wanted no more of the city. I let him go.
He was good and honest. He could have
Begged a far greater favor. But
I granted what he asked.

OEDIPUS

Is it known where he is?
Could he be brought here quickly?

JOCASTA

He could.
His hovel is near enough. Why do you want him?

OEDIPUS

I am full of fear. I fear I have spoken too much.
I must see him.

JOCASTA

See him you shall. But
Meantime tell me everything. I am your wife,
I have a right to know.

OEDIPUS

You have the first right.
For the first time now I tell my whole story.
Listen, my dear wife, who, God help us both,

Are, I fear, all too deeply involved. But listen.
My father was a Corinthian—King Polybus—
And my mother a Dorian: Merope was her name.
I, as prince, was held by the citizens of Corinth
To be their greatest next to the king. Until one day
A strange thing happened. There was a dinner,
And a man who'd been drinking too much
Suddenly and insolently said that I
Was not the son of the man I called father.
I was hurt and angry but, rather than show anger,
I kept silence. I went to my parents
And told them what had been said and they
Were quick to quiet my fears, angry in their turn
That such a story should be put about.
But the story was put about, and put about
    widely.
I did what I had to do, though without
My parents' knowledge. I went to the shrine
Of Apollo at Pytho and asked,
But to that question received no answer. Instead
I was given, without asking, some information
So wretched, so terrible I could hardly sustain
The telling. For the god said I was doomed
To marry my own mother and bring to the
    daylight
A misbegotten brood, a breed of monsters
That men would shun as they shunned the
    Sphinx.
Add to this that I must also kill my father,
And there was but one way open to me—
To leave both father and mother, to flee from
    Corinth,
Never see home again, so that those ghastly
Prophecies should never be fulfilled.
This is what I did. I started
The longest possible journey, and on this journey
I came to that very neighborhood, the place
Where three roads meet. There I encountered
A herald followed by a carriage with a man in it,
A man like the man you described. This herald,
In a surly way, a way unfitted to my rank
Or indeed to anyone's, ordered me off the road.
I refused, then this venerable one in the carriage
Joined in with equal surliness—he even offered
To thrust me bodily off the road. I became angry
And struck the coachman. The old man
Watched for his moment and, as he passed,
Leaned out with a two-pronged goad and hit me
Full on the head. What could I do except
Seek payment in full for the pain and insult?

My stick struck him backwards from
   his carriage
And he fell out. The others attacked me
And I—need I go on? If this was Laius,
See then what I have done: rendered myself
Hateful to gods and to men. I was born evil,
I am utterly unclean, murderer and polluter
Of my victim's bed. Was it not enough
To have to leave my country in wretchedness,
Never again to see the parents I had at least,
Have at least, spared from the ultimate horror?
The gods have at least saved me from
Patricide and incest, but, for the rest,
They have spent themselves in malignancy.
As for that other—O God, may that day not dawn.
May I be lost to men's sight forever before
That final corruption visits me. But is not this
Enough, to know I am the murderer
Of the man whose crown I wear, whose queen
   I love?

CHORUS LEADER

Sir, if I may speak—everything depends
On the testimony of the man you have still to
   meet.
There is surely still ground for hope.

OEDIPUS

That is true. I can hope. I can wait in hope
For the coming of the shepherd.

JOCASTA

But when he comes
What do you want of him?

OEDIPUS

If his story
Is of robbers, of highway robbers, more than
   one—
That is the point, a plurality of killers—
Then I am safe. But if he speaks
Of a man traveling alone, then the guilt
Points clearly toward one man who already fears,
Already fears—

JOCASTA

But that was always his story,
A story told and retold, now part of our history.
He cannot now go back on it. But even
If in some small point he changes it,

He will never be able to allay my disbelief—
A disbelief I enjoin on you—in prophecies.
A child of mine should kill him: that was how
   it went.
But it was the child himself that died.
Poor child. Divination, soothsaying—
I would not cross the street to
Hear any of that nonsense.

OEDIPUS

You're right.
It is nonsense. Let us have hard fact, the record
Of a simple man's mind. Send for him.

JOCASTA

Without delay. . . .

* * *

OEDIPUS

Old shepherd, look at me and listen.
You were, I hear, a servant of King Laius.

SHEPHERD

Yes. A servant but no slave.
Reared in the king's own house.

OEDIPUS

You have always been his shepherd?

SHEPHERD

Most of my life I have tended the king's flocks.

OEDIPUS

In what part of the country?

SHEPHERD

Many parts.

OEDIPUS

Name one part.

SHEPHERD

Cithaeron—and the places near to Cithaeron.

OEDIPUS

And in Cithaeron you knew this man, did you not?

SHEPHERD

Who? Him? I don't know. What was his trade?

OEDIPUS

Forget the trade. You had dealings with
    this man.

SHEPHERD

It's so long ago—I can't remember.

MESSENGER

It *is* a long time ago. But wait, sir.
I'll make him remember. Don't you remember
A shepherd neighbor on the slopes of Cithaeron?
You had two flocks—I one only.
We had three seasons together—spring to fall.
I would fold my flock in Corinth for the winter,
You would drive yours to Thebes, to the steadings
Of King Laius. Surely you remember?

SHEPHERD

A long time ago. But it comes back, a little.

MESSENGER

Then perhaps you will remember the day
You gave a child to me—a baby boy—
To bring up as my own?

SHEPHERD

(frightened)
I don't know.
I don't know what you mean. Why was I brought
    here?

MESSENGER

To see that child. Or the man who was that child.
Here he is.

SHEPHERD

Damn you, fool. Can't you keep your—

OEDIPUS

Come on now. He's spoken honestly.
More honestly than you.

SHEPHERD

I've done nothing wrong.
Why do you look at me as if I've done—

OEDIPUS

It's wrong
Not to answer a straight question. You were asked
A straight question—

SHEPHERD

This one here
Knows nothing about it, nothing about
    anything.

OEDIPUS

Look, old man, if you won't speak
Of your own free will, we must use
Ways to make you speak.

SHEPHERD

Don't torture me. I'm only a poor old man.

OEDIPUS

(to attendants)
Twist his arms behind him.

SHEPHERD

No, no, leave me. What do you want to know?

OEDIPUS

That child. You gave a child to him,
That child he spoke about.

SHEPHERD

All right, I did.
And I wish to God I'd died the day I did.

OEDIPUS

You'll die now if you don't tell me the truth.

SHEPHERD

And if I do, I'll die. I'll die worse.

OEDIPUS

Come on, out with it. You're wasting time.

SHEPHERD

I said I gave it to him, didn't I?
What more can I say?

OEDIPUS

Where did the child come from?
Your home or someone else's?

SHEPHERD

It wasn't my child, if that's what you mean.
It was another man's.

OEDIPUS

Whose?

SHEPHERD

Please don't ask me any more—please—

OEDIPUS

I'll drag the answer out with your tongue.
Whose?

SHEPHERD

It was a —the child came from the house
Of King Laius.

OEDIPUS

A slave? Or one of his own?

SHEPHERD

Must I say?

OEDIPUS

You must say. I must know.

SHEPHERD

It was his child—so they said, anyway.
Your wife, the queen I mean, could tell you
More about it—

OEDIPUS

She gave it to you?

SHEPHERD

Yes, sir.

OEDIPUS

Why?

SHEPHERD

To—to do away with it.

OEDIPUS

To—kill it? To kill her own child?

SHEPHERD

There was this evil spell put on it, sir.
She cried terribly. But there was this evil spell,
You see.

OEDIPUS

What evil spell?

SHEPHERD

The child was going to kill his own father.

OEDIPUS

But the child was not destroyed.
You disobeyed an order.

SHEPHERD

I couldn't do it, sir. Could you do it?
Could anybody here? I gave it to this
    one here
Who's so high up now. I thought to myself:
He comes from another country, he'll take him
    there,
Right over the hills, miles away.
And now you're here, if it is you.
If it is you, O my God. O my God—

OEDIPUS

All out. Oozed out, to the last drop.
There's a sort of joy in it. No more.
No more to fear. No more to—
Oh, what sin. Oh, what unspeakable—
What filth. To see this in a mirror.
The stain on the bed. The wound in the earth,
Festering. My children, my poor children.
The light is stained. Never again.
The last sunset. No more dawns, no noon.
The light shall not be stained
By my looking on it.
There's a knife to be taken somewhere—
Here, the fountain of seed?
But I would still see. No, the light will look.
The light shall not look. No.
The light has seen enough.

*(He totters out. The messenger and shepherd, talking
under the chorus that follows, go out together.)*

CHORUS

What does it mean? What does it all amount to?
Here was a man the world called happy,

Oedipus, pattern of earthly happiness.
Who, after this, can be called happy?
Who would wish for happiness?
Consider his life. Consider his deeds of heroism.
He shot his arrows straight, favored by Zeus.
He saw the Sphinx, foiled and cursing,
Choke in her own blood; He steered our ship,
His arm was strong against disaster.
Our hearts are torn with this story, with this sight.
Of affliction unspeakable, for it is our affliction.
We are all Oedipus, but to some heaven is merciful,
Forbidding the unfolding of the pattern
To the ultimate horror, the thing we have seen.
Time sees everything, suffers everything,
Suffers what must now be inscribed forever
On stone unperishable. Curse after curse,
Begetter and begotten cursed. Son of Laius,
Would to God I had never seen you, you
Who were my light and must now be my
    darkness.
Our king, our king—stamped like ash into the
    earth.
But the story is stamped forever in our brains,
In our books, in our very loins. It is
Woven into the light of the sky,
Beats in the blood of the yet unborn,
Is with us, is with you. God forgive us all.

* * *

CHORUS LEADER

It is dangerous to answer riddles,
But some men are born to answer them.
It is the gods' doing. They hide themselves in
    riddles.
We must not try to understand too much.

CHILD

Why?

CHORUS

Citizens of Thebes, this was Oedipus,
A man strong in war, gentle in peace.
God gave him joy, God gave his loins increase.
His happy lot was fire to the envious,
But now the flutes are stilled, the trumpets cease.
Misfortune's waves have crashed, tumultuous,
Over that head endowed with masteries.
He yields to the Destroyer's animus.
A last day is reserved to all of us.

Look to it always. Human happiness
Is not for human error to assess.
Call no man happy till his days surcease,
Till all the gods of pain declare release,
Fate turns her back upon his obsequies,
And happiness may rest with him in peace.

THE END

DISCUSSION QUESTIONS

1. Tiresias says, "Things will be / As we shall see. Fate's engine / Is beyond the control of man's hands." In what way is Oedipus a victim of fate? In what way is he personally "responsible" for his "punishment"? Remember that while he did not knowingly kill his father, he did kill a man at the crossroads.

2. Do you agree with the notion that life is tragic and full of suffering? Do you believe that anything can happen to anyone and that even the innocent suffer? Is this part of the message that Sophocles wants the audience to take with them when they leave a performance of *Oedipus the King*? Why or why not?

3. Consider the fact that despite the best efforts of both Oedipus and his parents, they were unable to avoid their fate. Do you find this ironic? Why or why not? Is Sophocles suggesting that fate is ironic? Why or why not?

4. After Oedipus realizes that he has killed his father and married his mother, the chorus warns, "We are all Oedipus, but to some heaven is merciful, / Forbidding the unfolding of the pattern / To the ultimate horror, the thing we have seen." Are they saying that fate is not necessarily destiny? That even though something is foreordained, it does not necessarily have to come to pass?

5. Should we blame Oedipus for his actions? Pardon him? Pity him? Discuss.

6. At the close of the play, the chorus warns, "Call no man happy till his days surcease." Do you agree with this? Why or why not?

ARISTOTLE

Voluntary and Involuntary Actions

Aristotle argues that a voluntary action is one done through free will, when the person acting knows all the details involved in the action, and an involuntary action is one done under external compulsion or through ignorance. He contends that involuntary actions should be avoided.

Nevertheless, some acts involve a combination of the voluntary and the involuntary. Aristotle considers, for example, the case in which a despot is threatening to kill our parents and our children if we do not commit some evil action. Mixed-action cases such as this one "seem upon the whole rather to resemble voluntary acts than involuntary" because "at the exact moment at which they are done, such acts are choiceworthy; since it is the occasion of the action with its various concomitant circumstances that determines in each case the nature of its result." For Aristotle, an act is determined to be "voluntary" or "involuntary" at the moment of action, not in the abstract.

Actions are praiseworthy or blameworthy relative to the ends for which they are done: Praiseworthy actions are done for great and noble ends; blameworthy actions lack great and noble ends. Furthermore, actions such as slaying one's mother are "things which a man must never allow himself to be compelled to do, but must choose death by the most exquisite torments." Aristotle believes that, more often than not, it is our own moral weakness (or what might be called "internal pressure") that is to blame for wrong actions, rather than compulsion or external pressure.

Nonvoluntary acts are those done in ignorance. However, if pain and regret follow an act done in ignorance, the act becomes strictly *involuntary* and pardonable. Moreover, "every wicked man is in ignorance as to what he ought to do, and from what to abstain, and it is because of error such as this that men become unjust, and, in a word, wicked." For Aristotle, the unjust and wicked person's actions cannot be pardoned because they stem from a bad moral character. The following selection is from Aristotle's *Nichomachean Ethics*, Book 3, Section 1. A biographical sketch of Aristotle appears in chapter 4.

Now, since virtue is concerned with our emotions and our actions, and since praise and blame are never given except to that which is voluntary, while to that which is involuntary pardon is given, and sometimes even pity, it is perhaps necessary for those who are considering virtue to exactly distinguish between the voluntary and the involuntary; and such a distinction will further aid legislators in the award of honour or of punishment. Now it would seem that such acts only are involuntary as are done under compulsion or through ignorance. And that is done under compulsion the efficient cause of

which is strictly external to the man himself, and is moreover such that the agent, or, as the case may be, the patient, is not in any sense an element in it; as, for example, if a whirlwind were to carry us anywhere, or men who had us in their power. But all such things as are done through fear of some yet greater evil, or to win some noble end,—as, for example, were a despot in whose power were our parents and our children to impose upon us some disgraceful command, which if we obeyed they would be saved, if we disobeyed they would perish,—with regard to all such acts as these it can be disputed whether they are involuntary or voluntary. And a doubt of the same kind arises when jettison is made in peril of sea; for no man willingly makes jettison of his merchandise, but, to save their own lives and the lives of their fellow-voyagers, all would do so who are in their right senses. Such actions, then, are of a mixed nature. But they would seem upon the whole rather to resemble voluntary acts than involuntary. For, at the exact moment at which they are done, such acts are choiceworthy; since it is the occasion of the action with its various concomitant circumstances that determines in each case the nature of its result. And, moreover, the terms voluntary and involuntary are predicable of our acts not in the abstract but only at the moment of action. And in cases such as these a man at the moment of action does act voluntarily; for his limbs are the instruments by which the act is done, and the efficient cause of their motion is his own volition. And, where the efficient cause lies in ourselves, it is in our power to do the act, or not to do it. All cases such as these are, then, voluntary, but in the abstract perhaps involuntary; for no one would choose any such action for its own sake, and independently of its results. Now, in the case of actions such as these, it sometimes happens that men are praised, when they have undergone disgrace or pain for the sake of some great and noble end. But blame is given to them when their conduct is the reverse of this, for none but a bad man would undergo what is most disgraceful with no noble end, or with but a commonplace end, in view. And in some cases, again, it is not praise that is given, but rather pardon; as when, for instance, a man has done what he ought not to have done through fear of things beyond the power of human nature to endure, and such that no man could undergo them. And yet, perhaps, there are some things which a man must never allow himself to be compelled to do, but must rather choose death by the most exquisite torments. One cannot, for example, but smile to hear what it was that "compelled" Alcmæon, in Euripides, to slay his mother. And, moreover, it is at times difficult to decide which of two goods is to be preferred, or which of two evils is to be undergone; and still more difficult is it to abide by such a decision. For in the majority of such cases a man anticipates a something painful, and so is compelled to do a

something disgraceful; and hence it is that praise or blame is given, accordingly as he has given way to such compulsion or has not. But, to resume, what is to be the definition of a compulsory act? Perhaps the best general definition is that it is an act the efficient cause of which is purely external, and to which in consequence he who does the act contributes nothing. Whereas such acts as are in the abstract involuntary, but upon a certain given occasion, and in lieu of such or such an alternative, choiceworthy, and the efficient cause, moreover, of which is the agent's own volition, are involuntary, if regarded abstractedly and in themselves; but upon the occasion in question, and in lieu of the given alternative, are voluntary. And, upon the whole, they rather resemble voluntary acts than involuntary; for the field of our action is an aggregate of particular details, and our treatment of these particular details is voluntary. And yet it is no easy matter to give rules by which to determine our choice of alternatives, for in human action every possible variety of detail is to be found. Were one, however, to say that things pleasant and things noble act upon us by compulsion, for that they are motives external to ourselves, and that yet necessitate such or such a course of conduct, this would go to make all our actions compulsory; for it is with these motives in view that every action of each one of us is done. And, moreover, those who act under compulsion, and consequently against their will, do so with pain, while those who act with what is pleasant or what is noble in view do so with pleasure. And, moreover, it is ridiculous to say that it is a something external to ourselves that is to blame, instead of ourselves who are too easily enticed by such lures; and that for his noble acts the man himself is responsible, and for his disgraceful acts these pleasurable motives. The compulsory, in fine, would seem to be that the efficient cause of which is purely external, and to which the person so compelled contributes nothing.

Every act done in ignorance is, as such, *non-voluntary*, but is strictly *involuntary* only when it is followed by pain, and involves regret. For he who has done such or such a thing through ignorance, and who yet is in no way concerned at his act, cannot be said to have done voluntarily that which he did not know that he was doing, nor yet to have done involuntarily that at which he feels no pain. So that, when a man acts from ignorance, if he subsequently feel regret, he is held to have acted involuntarily; but, if he feel no such regret, we will, to distinguish him, call his act non-voluntary; for, since there is this difference, it is best that such actions should have a name of their own. And, again, acting *from* ignorance would seem to be entirely distinct from acting *in* ignorance. He who is drunk or in a passion is not held to act from ignorance, but from one of these two causes; but yet he acts in ignorance, since he knows not what he is doing. And so, too, every wicked man is in ignorance as to what he ought to do, and from what to abstain, and it is because of error such as this that men become unjust and, in a word, wicked. But yet the term involuntary cannot be applied merely because a man is in ignorance of what is for his good. For ignorance as to what ought to be the object of his choice does not make a man involuntary, but rather wicked,—as neither does ignorance of moral principles (for for ignorance of this kind men are blamed),—but only ignorance as to the several particular details of the action in question—to wit, the persons concerned in it, and the things. Herein only is it that we pity a man, and pardon him; for he acts involuntarily who acts in ignorance of any one of these. Perhaps, then, it were as well to exactly describe and enumerate these details. Firstly, we have the *agent*; secondly, his *action*, and that with which it is concerned; thirdly, the *person* whom it affects; fourthly, sometimes, the instrument with which it is done, as, for example, the weapon; fifthly, its *result*, as, for example, preservation of life; sixthly, its manner, as, for example, in the case of a blow, gently or heavily. Now of all these details no man could possibly be in ignorance, unless, indeed, he were mad. Clearly he could not be ignorant of the agent. For how can a man be

ignorant of his own identity? But of what it is that he is doing a man might be ignorant; as when, for example, in conversation men say that a thing escaped them unawares, or that they did not know that the subject was forbidden, as happened to Æschylus* concerning the mysteries,[†] or, that, wishing only to show how to shoot, that actually shot, as in the well-known catapult accident. And, again, one might take one's son to be an enemy, as did Merope,[‡] or think that a spear which was really pointed had been buttoned, or that the stone was only a pumice-stone. Or, again, one might kill a man when aiming a blow intended to save him; or, lastly, when wishing only to show how to hit, as in sparring, one might hit a heavy blow. Now, since ignorance is conceivably possible with regard to each or all of these details with which the action is concerned, it follows that he who is ignorant of any one of these is held to have acted involuntarily, and more especially if he be ignorant of those which most influence the action itself, and which are, it would seem, the persons concerned in it, and its result. In the case, then, of ignorance such as this, we apply the term involuntary, with the further determination that the act must give pain, that is to say, that it must be followed by regret.

That, then, being involuntary which is done under compulsion, or from ignorance, it would seem that that alone is strictly voluntary the efficient cause of which is the volition of the agent who knows thoroughly all the details that are involved in the action. For surely it is hardly well to say that acts done from anger or from desire are involuntary. For, in the first place, if this be so, it follows that no animal can ever act voluntarily, neither can children. And, secondly, are we to say that none of our acts done from desire and anger are voluntary, or that such of them as are good are

---

*Aeschylus (c. 525–456 B.C.E.), the first of the great tragic dramatists from Athens, is regarded as the creator of "drama." He added the second actor to Greek dramatic performance, increased the amount of dialogue, and reduced the importance of the chorus. Aeschylus fought in the battles of Marathon and Salamis, and competed in the Great Dionysia, the major dramatic competition of ancient Athens. While he wrote about ninety plays, only seven are extant: *Persians, Seven Against Thebes, Suppliants, Prometheus Bound,* and the *Oresteia* trilogy. —Ed.

[†]The Eleusian mysteries were religious rites in honor of Demeter, the Greek goddess of the earth, protector of agriculture and the fruits of the earth. These religious rites were performed at Eleusis in Attica. Aeschylus was prosecuted for revealing the mysteries of Eleusis in one of his plays, though he was later proven innocent. —Ed.

[‡]In Greek mythology, Merope was the wife of Cresphontes. Polyphontes, the brother of Cresphontes, killed him and married Merope against her will. Merope sent her son, Aepytus, away, and Polyphontes offered a great reward to whoever killed Aepytus. When he was grown, Aepytus returned and told Polyphontes that he had killed Merope's son. When Merope learned of a man who was claiming to have killed her son, she attempted to kill this man in his sleep. However, a servant recognized Aepytus and stopped Merope. Aepytus then killed Polyphontes and gained the crown that was rightfully his. —Ed.

voluntary, such as are bad involuntary? Evidently the latter supposition is ridiculous, since in each case the cause is the same; while, with regard to the former, it is surely strange to say that an act is involuntary when its impulse is right. And it is right to be angry at certain things, and also to desire certain things, such as health, for instance, and knowledge. Besides, it seems that involuntary acts give pain, while acts done from desire give pleasure. And, moreover, if both alike are involuntary, wherein do errors of reason differ from errors of anger. Both ought equally to be shunned, and the irrational passions would seem to be as much a part of human nature as is the reason. Men's actions may be prompted, no doubt, by anger and by desire; but it is absurd to assume that they are therefore involuntary.

DISCUSSION QUESTIONS

1. In brief, according to Aristotle, what are the differences between voluntary, involuntary, and nonvoluntary actions? Provide an example of each.

2. What is the difference between acting *from* ignorance and acting *in* ignorance? Why is this distinction important for Aristotle to maintain? How does he apply it?

3. Why does Aristotle believe that the unjust and wicked person acts nonvoluntarily rather than voluntarily? Discuss the implications of this belief.

4. Why does Aristotle believe that no child or animal acts voluntarily? Do you agree with him? Why or why not?

5. Using Aristotle's categories, would you say that Oedipus voluntarily, involuntarily, or nonvoluntarily murdered his father? Does the same hold for his marriage to his mother? Why or why not?

6. Aristotle says that "praise and blame are never given except to that which is voluntary, while to that which is involuntary pardon is given, and sometimes even pity." According to Aristotle, should Oedipus be praised, blamed, pardoned, and/or pitied? Defend your response.

EPICTETUS
OF WHAT IS AND IS NOT IN OUR OWN POWER

Epictetus argues that we should make the best of what is within our power and take the rest as it occurs. Things beyond our power are determined by providence, that is, by fate. We should not seek control over them; rather, since we cannot change them, we should face them with equanimity, namely, an evenness of mind and temper. For Epictetus, the equanimity or tranquility with which we face the world requires a strong sense of moral and religious principle, and is not simply the absence of feeling.

What is within our power is our will and our faculty of reasoning, which "judges of the appearance of things." These we can control, and with education we can aspire to true judgment and right will. "The essence of good and evil is a certain disposition of the will," writes Epictetus. "Right principles . . . keep the will in a good state; but perverse and distorted principles, in a bad one." For Epictetus, then, only our will and our judgment of the appearance of things are within our power; nothing else is. Nevertheless, we have absolute control over things in our power. "You will fetter my leg," writes Epictetus, "but not Zeus himself can get the better of my free will."

The things that are beyond our control and power are the will of God or fate. They include all physical events and all human actions. Each of these events and actions is predestined to occur. According to Epictetus, "Whoever desires or shuns things beyond his own power can neither be faithful nor free, but must necessarily take his chances with them, must necessarily too be subject to others, to such as can procure or prevent what he desires or shuns." He suggests that "we should enter upon a course of education and instruction, not in order to change the constitution of things . . . but that, things being as they are with regard to us, we may have our minds accommodated to the facts." Epictetus says that we should not criticize but should "thank the gods that they have made you superior to those events which they have not placed within your own control, and have rendered you accountable for that only which is within your own control." We are not responsible for our bodies, our possessions, our life, our death, and our families because they are all outside our sphere of control; we are responsible though for our will and judgment, namely, "a right use of things as they appear."

Epictetus (c. 50–138 C.E.) was one of the most influential of the Stoic philosophers. He was born in Hierapolis, in Asia Minor, to a slave woman and was for many years also a slave. His master was Epaphronditus, a freedman of the Roman emperor Nero, who was possibly also his administrative secretary. Sometime after the death of Nero in 68 C.E, Epictetus became a freedman. He studied philosophy as a youth with C. Musonius Rufus, one of the most influential Stoic philosophers of the time. Epictetus began his teaching career in Rome as a slave and later, when he was a freedman, was expelled from Rome in 89 C.E. along with all of the other philosophers by the emperor Domitian. He then went to Nicopolis in northwestern Greece and started the well-known School at Nicopolis that taught the physics, logic, and ethics of Stoicism. Epictetus was sickly and lame most of his life, the latter probably from maltreatment as a slave, and in his house kept only a rush mat, a simple pallet, and a lamp. Like Socrates, Epictetus did not write down his teachings. His thought comes to us rather through the surviving lecture notes of his student Flavius Arrianus. Epictetus's major works are *The Handbook (Enchiridion)* and *The Discourses*. The following is a selection from *The Discourses*.

Of human faculties in general, you will find that each is unable to contemplate itself, and therefore to approve or disapprove itself. How far does the proper sphere of grammar extend? As far as the judging of language. Of music? As far as the judging of melody. Does either of them contemplate itself, then? By no means.

Thus, for instance, when you are to write to your friend, grammar will tell you what to write; but whether you are to write to your friend at all, or no, grammar will not tell you. Thus music, with regard to tunes; but whether it be proper or improper, at any particular time, to sing or play, music will not tell you.

What will tell, then?

That faculty which contemplates both itself and all other things.

And what is that?

The Reasoning Faculty; for that alone is found able to place an estimate upon itself,—what it is, what are its powers, what its value and likewise all the rest. For what is it else that says, gold is beautiful? Since the gold itself does not speak. Evidently, that faculty which judges of the appearances of things. What else distinguishes music, grammar, the other faculties, proves their uses, and shows their proper occasions?

Nothing but this.

As it was fit, then, this most excellent and superior faculty alone, a right use of the appearances of things, the gods have placed in our own power; but all other matters they have not placed in our power. What, was it because they would not? I rather think that, if they could, they had granted us these too; but they certainly could not. For, placed upon earth, and confined to such a body and to such companions, how was it possible that, in these respects, we should not be hindered by things outside of us?

But what says Zeus? "O Epictetus, if it had been possible, I had made this little body and property of thine free, and not liable to hindrance.

But now do not mistake; it is not thy own, but only a finer mixture of clay. Since, then, I could not give thee this, I have given thee a certain portion of myself; this faculty of exerting the powers of pursuit and avoidance, of desire and aversion, and, in a word, the use of the appearances of things. Taking care of this point, and making what is thy own to consist in this, thou wilt never be restrained, never be hindered; thou wilt not groan, wilt not complain, wilt not flatter any one. How, then? Do all these advantages seem small to thee? Heaven forbid! Let them suffice thee, then, and thank the gods."

But now, when it is in our power to take care of one thing, and to apply ourselves to one, we choose rather to take care of many, and to encumber ourselves with many,—body, property, brother, friend, child, and slave,—and, by this multiplicity of encumbrances, we are burdened and weighed down. Thus, when the weather does not happen to be fair for sailing, we sit in distress and gaze out perpetually. Which way is the wind? North. What good will that do us? When will the west blow? When it pleases friend, or when Æolus pleases; for Zeus has not made you dispenser of the winds, but Æolus.

What, then, is to be done?

To make the best of what is in our power, and take the rest as it occurs.

And how does it occur?

As it pleases God.

What, then, must I be the only one to lose my head?

Why, would you have all the world, then, lose their heads for your consolation? Why are not you willing to stretch out your neck, like Lateranus, when he was commanded by Nero to be beheaded? For, shrinking a little after receiving a weak blow, he stretched it out again. And before this, when Epaphroditus, the freedman of Nero, interrogated him about the conspiracy, "If I have a mind to say anything," replied he, "I will tell it to your master."

What resource have we, then, upon such occasions? Why, what else but to distinguish between what is *ours*, and what not *ours*,—what is right, and what is wrong? I must die, and must I die groaning too? I must be fettered; must I be lamenting too? I must be exiled; and what hinders me, then, but that I may go smiling, and cheerful, and serene? "Betray a secret." I will not betray it,

for this is in my own power. "Then I will fetter you." What do you say, man? Fetter me? You will fetter my leg, but not Zeus himself can get the better of my free will. "I will throw you into prison; I will behead that paltry body of yours." Did I ever tell you that I alone had a head not liable to be cut off? These things ought philosophers to study; these ought they daily to write, and in these to exercise themselves.

Thraseas used to say, "I had rather be killed today than banished to-morrow." But how did Rufus answer him? "If you prefer it as a heavier misfortune, how foolish a preference! If as a lighter, who has put it in your power? Why do you not study to be contented with what is allotted you?"

Well, and what said Agrippinus upon this account? "I will not be a hindrance to myself." Word was brought him, "Your cause is pending in the senate." "Good luck attend it; but it is eleven o'clock" (the hour when he used to exercise before bathing),— "let us go to our exercise." This being over, a messenger tells him, "You are condemned." "To banishment," says he, "or to death?" "To banishment." "What of my estate?" "It is not taken away." "Well, then, let us go as far as Aricia, and dine there."

This it is to have studied what ought to be studied; to have placed our desires and aversions above tyranny and above chance. I must die,—if instantly, I will die instantly; if in a short time, I will dine first, and when the hour comes, then will I die. How? As becomes one who restores what is not his own.

OF PROGRESS

He who is entering on a state of progress, having learned from the philosophers that good should be sought and evil shunned, and having learned, too, that prosperity and peace are no otherwise attainable by man than in not missing what he seeks nor incurring what he shuns,—such a one totally extirpates and banishes all wayward desire, and shuns only those things over which he can have control. For if he should attempt to shun those things over which he has no control, he knows that he must sometimes incur that which he shuns, and be unhappy. Now if virtue promises happiness, prosperity, and peace, then progress in virtue is certainly progress in each of these. For to whatever point the perfection of anything absolutely brings us, progress is always an approach towards it.

How happens it, then, that when we confess virtue to be such, yet we seek, and make an ostentatious show of progress in other things! What is the business of virtue?

A life truly prosperous.

Who is in a state of progress, then? He who has best studied Chrysippus*? Why, does virtue consist in having read Chrysippus through? If so, progress is confessedly nothing else than understanding a great deal of Chrysippus; otherwise we confess virtue to consist in one thing, and declare progress, which is an approach to it, to be quite another thing.

This person, they say, is already able to understand Chrysippus, by himself. "Certainly, sir, you have made a vast improvement!" What improvement? Why do you delude him? Why do you withdraw him from a sense of his real needs? Why do not you show him the real function of virtue, that he may know where to seek progress? Seek it there, O unfortunate, where your work lies. And where does your work lie? In learning what to seek and what to shun, that you may neither be disappointed of one nor incur the other; in practicing how to pursue and how to avoid, that you may not be liable to fail; in practicing intellectual assent and doubt, that you may not be liable to be deceived. These are the first and most necessary things. But if you merely seek, in trembling and lamentation, to keep away all possible ills, what real progress have you made?

Show me then your progress in this point. As if I should say to a wrestler, Show me your muscle; and he should answer me, "See my dumb-bells." Your dumb-bells are your own affair; I desire to see the effect of them.

"Take the treatise on the active powers, and see how thoroughly I have perused it."

I do not inquire into this, O slavish man, but how you exert those powers, how you manage your desires and aversions, your intentions and purposes, how you meet events,—whether in accordance with nature's laws or contrary to them. If in accordance, give me evidence of that,

and I will say you improve; if the contrary, you may go your way, and not only comment on these treatises, but write such yourself; and yet what service will it do you? Do not you know that the whole volume is sold for five denarii? Does he who comments upon it, then, value himself at more than that sum? Never make your life to lie in one thing and yet seek progress in another.

Where is progress, then?

If any of you, withdrawing himself from externals, turns to his own will, to train, and perfect, and render it conformable to nature,— noble, free, unrestrained, unhindered, faithful, humble; —if he has learned, too, that whoever desires or shuns things beyond his own power can neither be faithful nor free, but must necessarily take his chance with them, must necessarily too be subject to others, to such as can procure or prevent what he desires or shuns; if, rising in the morning, he observes and keeps to these rules; bathes regularly, eats frugally, and to every subject of action applies the same fixed principles,—if a racer to racing, if an orator to oratory,—this is he who truly makes progress; this is he who has not labored in vain. But if he is wholly intent on reading books, and has labored that point only, and traveled for that, I bid him go home immediately and do his daily duties; since that which he sought is nothing.

The only real thing is to study how to rid life of lamentation, and complaint, and *Alas!* and *I am undone,* and misfortune, and failure; and to learn what death, what exile, what a prison, what poison is; that he may be able to say in a prison, like Socrates, "My dear Crito, if it thus pleases the gods, thus let it be"; and not, "Wretched old man, have I kept my gray hairs for this!" [Do you ask] who speaks thus? Do you think I quote some mean and despicable person? Is it not Priam who says it? Is it not Œdipus? Nay, how many kings say it? For what else is tragedy but the dramatized sufferings of men, bewildered by an admiration of externals? If one were to be taught by fictions that things beyond our will are nothing to us, I should rejoice in such a fiction, by which I might live

---

*Chrysippus (c. 280–206 B.C.E.), a Greek philosopher, was one of the leading Stoic philosophers. He studied under the founder and leader of the Stoic school of philosophy, Zeno of Citium (c. 335–264 B.C.E.), as well as under Zeno's successor, Cleanthes (331–232 B.C.E.). After Cleanthes' death, Chrysippus became the third leader of the Stoic school of philosophy, a position he held until 208 B.C.E. While Chrysippus allegedly wrote over 750 treatises, only fragments of them survive. Legend has it that Chrysippus died of laughter after seeing a donkey eat figs. —Ed.

prosperous and serene. But what your own aims are, it is your business to consider. . . .

OF CONTENTMENT

Concerning the gods, some affirm that there is no deity; others, that he indeed exists, but is slothful, negligent, and without providential care; a third class admits both his being and his providence, but only in respect to great and heavenly objects, not earthly; a fourth recognizes him both in heaven and earth, but only in general, not individual matters; a fifth, like Odysseus and Socrates, says, "I cannot be hid from thee in any of my motions."

It is, before all things, necessary to examine each of these opinions; which is, and which is not rightly spoken. Now, if there are no gods, wherefore serve them? If there are, but they take no care of anything, how is the case bettered? Or, if they both are, and take care; yet, if there is nothing communicated from them to men, and therefore certainly nothing to me, how much better is it? A wise and good man, after examining these things, submits his mind to Him who administers the whole, as good citizens do to the laws of the commonwealth.

He, then, who comes to be instructed, ought to come with this aim: "How may I in everything follow the gods? How may I acquiesce in the divine administration? And how may I be free?" For he is free to whom all happens agreeably to his desire, and whom no one can unduly restrain.

"What, then, is freedom mere license?"

By no means; for madness and freedom are incompatible.

"But I would have that happen which appears to me desirable, however it comes to appear so."

You are mad; you have lost your senses. Do not you know that freedom is a very beautiful and valuable thing? But for me to choose at random, and for things to happen agreeably to such a choice, may be so far from a beautiful thing, as to be of all things the most undesirable. For how do we proceed in writing? Do I choose to write the name of Dion (for instance) as I will? No, but I am taught to be willing to write it as it ought to be written. And what is the case in music? The same. And what in every other art or science? Otherwise, it would be of no purpose to learn anything if it were to be adapted to each one's particular humor. Is it, then, only in the greatest and principal matter, that of freedom, permitted me to desire at random? By no means; but true instruction is this,—learning to desire that things should happen as they do. And how do they happen? As the appointer of them hath appointed. He hath appointed that there should be summer and winter, plenty and dearth, virtue and vice, and all such contrarieties, for the harmony of the whole. To each of us he has given a body and its parts, and our several possessions and companions. Mindful of this appointment, we should enter upon a course of education and instruction, not in order to change the constitution of things,—a gift neither practicable nor desirable,—but that, things being as they are with regard to us, we may have our minds accommodated to the facts. Can we, for instance, flee from mankind? How is that possible? Can we, by conversing with them, transform them? Who has given us such a power? What, then, remains, or what method is there to be found, for such a commerce with them that, while they act according to the appearances in their own minds, we may nevertheless be affected conformably to nature?

But you are wretched and discontented. If you are alone, you term it a desert; and if with men, you call them cheats and robbers. You find fault too with your parents, and children, and brothers, and neighbors. Whereas you ought, if you live alone, to call that repose and freedom, and to esteem yourself as resembling the gods; and when you are in company, not to call it a crowd, and a tumult, and a trouble, but an assembly, and a festival,—and thus to take all things contentedly. What, then, is the punishment of those who do not so accept them? To be—as they are. Is any one discontented with being alone? Let him remain in his desert. Discontented with his parents? Let him be a bad son; and let him mourn. Discontented with his children? Let him be a bad father. Shall we throw him into prison? What prison? Where he already is; for he is in a situation against his will, and wherever any one is against his will, that is to him a prison,—just as Socrates was not truly in prison, for he was willingly there.

"What, then, must my leg be lame?"

And is it for one paltry leg, wretch, that you accuse the universe? Can you not forego that, in consideration of the whole? Can you not give up something? Can you not gladly yield it to him who gave it? And will you be angry and discontented with the decrees of Zeus,—which he, with the Fates, who spun in his presence the thread of your birth, ordained and appointed? Do not you know how very small a part you are of the whole?—that is, as to body; for, as to reason, you are neither worse nor less than divine. For reason is not measured by size or height, but by principles. Will you not, therefore, place your good there where you share with the gods?

"But how wretched am I, in such a father and mother!"

What, then, was it granted you to come beforehand, and make your own terms, and say, "Let such and such persons at this hour, be the authors of my birth"? It was not granted; for it was necessary that your parents should exist before you; and so you be born afterwards. Of whom? Of just such as they were. What, then, since they are such, is there no remedy afforded you? Surely, you would be wretched and miserable if you knew not the use of sight, and shut your eyes in presence of colors; and are not you more wretched and miserable in being ignorant that you have within you the needful nobleness and manhood wherewith to meet these accidents? Events proportioned to your reason are brought before you; but you turn your mind away, at the very time when you ought to have it the most open and discerning. Why do not you rather thank the gods that they have made you superior to those events which they have not placed within your own control, and have rendered you accountable for that only which is within your own control? They discharge you from all responsibility for your parents, for your brothers, for your body, possessions, death, life. For what, then, have they made you responsible? For that which is alone in your own power,—a right use of things as they appear. Why, then, should you draw those cares upon yourself for which you are not accountable? This is giving one's self vexation without need.

Of Courage

The essence of good and evil is a certain disposition of the will.

What are things outward, then?

Materials on which the will may act, in attaining its own good or evil.

How, then, will it attain good?

If it be not dazzled by its own materials; for right principles concerning these materials keep the will in a good state; but perverse and distorted principles, in a bad one. This law hath God ordained, who says, "If you wish for good, receive it from yourself." You say, No; but from another. "Nay; but from yourself."

Accordingly, when a tyrant threatens, and sends for me, I say, Against what is your threatening pointed? If he says, "I will chain you," I answer, It is my hands and feet that you threaten. If he says, "I will cut off your head," I answer, It is my head that you threaten. If he says, "I will throw you into prison," I answer, It is the whole of this paltry body that you threaten; and if he threatens banishment, just the same.

"Does he not threaten *you*, then?"

If I am persuaded that these things are nothing to me, he does not; but *if* I fear any of them, it is me that he threatens. Who is it, after all, that I fear? The master of what? Of things in my own power? Of these no one is the master. Of things not in my power? And what are these to me?

"What, then! do you philosophers teach us a contempt of kings?"

By no means. Which of us teaches any one to contend with them about things of which they have the command? Take my body; take my possessions; take my reputation; take away even my friends. If I persuade any one to claim these things as his own, you may justly accuse me. "Ay; but I would command your principles too." And who hath given you that power? How can you conquer the principle of another? "By applying terror, I will conquer it." Do not you see that what conquers itself is not conquered by another? And nothing but itself can conquer the will. Hence, too, the most excellent and equitable law of God, that the better should always prevail over the worse. Ten are better than one.

"For what purpose?"

For chaining, killing, dragging where they please; for taking away an estate. Thus ten conquer one, in the cases wherein they are better.

"In what, then, are they worse?"

When the one has right principles, and the others have not. For can they conquer in this case? How should they? If we were weighed in a scale, must not the heavier outweigh?

"How then came Socrates to suffer such things from the Athenians?"

O foolish man! What mean you by Socrates? Express the fact as it is. Are you surprised that the mere body of Socrates should be carried away, and dragged to prison, by such as were stronger; that it should be poisoned by hemlock and die? Do these things appear wonderful to you; these things unjust? Is it for such things as these that you accuse God? Had Socrates, then, no compensation for them? In what, then, to him did the essence of good consist? Whom shall we regard, you or him? And what says he? "Anytus and Melitus may indeed kill; but hurt me they cannot." And again, "If it so pleases God, so let it be."

But show me that he who has the worse principles can get the advantage over him who has the better. You never will show it, nor anything like it; for the Law of Nature and of God is this,—let the better always prevail over the worse. . . .

DISCUSSION QUESTIONS

1. For Epictetus, what does it mean to be free? Do you have a different conception of what it means?

2. Discuss Epictetus's contention that you should not criticize, but "thank the gods that they have made you superior to those events which they have not placed within your own control, and have rendered you accountable for that only which is within your own control." Do you agree with him? Why or why not?

3. Epictetus says that "Socrates was not in prison, for he was willingly there." What does he mean by this?

4. What does Epictetus mean by the statement "Never make your life lie in one thing and yet seek progress in another"?

5. Epictetus mentions Oedipus in this selection, saying that tragedy is "the dramatized sufferings of men, bewildered by the administration of externals." What does this mean? How might Epictetus interpret Oedipus's attempts to thwart fate?

PAUL-HENRI THIRY, BARON D'HOLBACH
OF THE SYSTEM OF MAN'S FREE AGENCY

Paul-Henri Thiry, Baron d'Holbach, argues that *all* events or occurrences, including human behavior and human will, are completely determined. Holbach's *determinism* maintains that everything in the universe is "submitted to" or operates in accordance with necessary and immutable causal laws. One of the implications of Holbach's position is the denial of moral freedom: we should give up the notion that we are morally responsible for our actions. Holbach's position on freedom and determinism is known as *hard determinism* because of its complete denial of freedom and responsibility.

Holbach is a materialist and an atheist. For him, both humankind and the world are machines, and neither require a machinist to run it. The world is a system of material particles operating according to fixed laws of motion in such a way that necessity rules everywhere, and this deterministic system consists of an eternal and constant totality of matter and motion. While individuals and worlds come together and pass away, the sum of existence always remains the same.

Humans, according to Holbach, are a completely material organic machine and are consequently entirely subject to the laws of nature. For Holbach, man "always acts according to necessary laws from which he has no means of emancipating himself." While Holbach contends that we have a will, it is viewed "a modification of the brain" and is not free because it necessarily strives to preserve or enhance our existence. Forces independent of us create various desires in us, and in any given situation, we always act in accordance with our strongest desire, namely, the one that is most directly advantageous to us. "Man, then, is not a free agent in any one instant of his life; he is necessarily guided in each step by those advantages, whether real or fictitious, that he attaches to the objects by which his passions are roused," writes Holbach.

Holbach argues against a number of contentions made by defenders of free will. Some, for example, assert that we must have free will because we make choices. Holbach responds that while it is true that we make choices, our choices are constrained by necessity: the necessity to choose the alternative that exerts the strongest influence on our will. Some also assert that the absence of restraint is the absence of necessity. Holbach responds that just because obstacles to action are not readily apparent, it does not mean that the individual is free to do as he pleases, for "the motive which causes him to will, is always necessary and independent of himself." In this regard, we are comparable to a falling object whose descent is interrupted by an obstacle. "Take away this obstacle, it will gravitate or continue to fall; but who shall say this dense body is free to fall or not?" says Holbach. "Is not its descent the necessary effect of its own specific gravity?"

Paul-Henri Thiry, Baron d'Holbach (1723–1789), a French philosopher, was born in Edesheim, Germany, but he lived in Paris from a very early age and became a French citizen. He was educated at the University of Leiden in Holland. Holbach inherited his French uncle's money, title, and estate, which became the meeting place for the leading French radical thinkers of the late eighteenth century, a group known as the *philosophes*. The *philosophes* included Jean-Jacques Rousseau, Denis Diderot, and Voltaire and were responsible for publishing the great French *Encyclopédie*, which was designed to encompass all knowledge. His foreign acquaintances included Benjamin Franklin, David Hume, and Adam Smith. As a severe critic of both religion and absolute monarchy. He published his books in Holland under a false name to avoid harm to himself. His books include *Christianity Unveiled* (1767), *The System of Nature* (1770), *Common Sense, or Natural Ideas Opposed to Supernatural Ideas* (1772), *Social System* (1773), *Natural Politics* (1774), and *Universal Morality* (1776). The following selection is from *The System of Nature*.

Motives and the Determination of the Will

In whatever manner man is considered, he is connected to universal nature, and submitted to the necessary and immutable laws that she imposes on all the beings she contains, according to their peculiar essences or to the respective properties with which, without consulting them, she endows each particular species. Man's life is a line that nature commands him to describe upon the surface of the earth, without his ever being able to swerve from it, even for an instant. He is born without his own consent; his organization does in nowise depend upon himself; his ideas come to him involuntarily; his habits are in the power of those who cause him to contract them; he is unceasingly modified by causes, whether visible or concealed, over which he has no control, which necessarily regulate his mode of existence, give the hue to his way of thinking, and determine his manner of acting. He is good or bad, happy or miserable, wise or foolish, reasonable or irrational, without his will being for anything in these various states. Nevertheless, in spite of the shackles by which he is bound, it is pretended he is a free agent, or that independent of the causes by which he is moved, he determines his own will, and regulates his own condition.

However slender the foundation of this opinion, of which everything ought to point out to him the error, it is current at this day and passes for an incontestable truth with a great number of people, otherwise extremely enlightened; it is the basis of religion, which, supposing relations between man and the unknown being she has placed above nature, has been incapable of imagining how man could merit reward or deserve punishment from this being, if he was not a free agent. Society has been believed interested in this system; because an idea has gone abroad, that if all the actions of man were to be contemplated as necessary, the right of punishing those who injure their associates would no longer exist. At length human vanity accommodated itself to a hypothesis which, unquestionably, appears to distinguish man from all other physical beings, by assigning to him the special privilege of a total independence of all other causes, but of which a very little reflection would have shown him the impossibility. . . .

The will . . . is a modification of the brain, by which it is disposed to action, or prepared to give play to the organs. This will is necessarily determined by the qualities, good or bad, agreeable or painful, of the object or the motive that acts upon his senses, or of which the idea remains with him, and is resuscitated by his memory. In consequence, he acts necessarily, his action is the result of the impulse he receives either from the motive, from the object, or from the idea which has modified his brain, or disposed his will. When he does not act according to this impulse, it is because there comes some new cause, some new motive, some new idea, which modifies his brain in a different manner, gives him a new impulse, determines his will in another way, by which the action of the former impulse is suspended: thus, the sight of an agreeable object, or its idea, determines his will to set him in action to procure it; but if a new object or a new idea more powerfully attracts him, it gives a new direction to his will, annihilates the effect of the former, and prevents the action by which it was to be procured. This is the mode in which reflection, experience, reason, necessarily arrests or suspends the action of man's will: without this he would of necessity

have followed the anterior impulse which carried him towards a then desirable object. In all this he always acts according to necessary laws from which he has no means of emancipating himself.

If when tormented with violent thirst, he figures to himself an idea, or really perceives a fountain, whose limpid streams might cool his feverish want, is he sufficient master of himself to desire or not to desire the object competent to satisfy so lively a want? It will no doubt be conceded, that it is impossible he should not be desirous to satisfy it; but it will be said—if at this moment it is announced to him that the water he so ardently desires is poisoned, he will, notwithstanding his vehement thirst, abstain from drinking it: and it has, therefore, been falsely concluded that he is a free agent. The fact, however, is, that the motive in either case is exactly the same: his own conservation. The same necessity that determined him to drink before he knew the water was deleterious upon this new discovery equally determined him not to drink; the desire of conserving himself either annihilates or suspends the former impulse; the second motive becomes stronger than the preceding, that is, the fear of death, or the desire of preserving himself, necessarily prevails over the painful sensation caused by his eagerness to drink: but, it will be said, if the thirst is very parching, an inconsiderate man without regarding the danger will risk swallowing the water. Nothing is gained by this remark: in this case, the anterior impulse only regains the ascendency; he is persuaded that life may possibly be longer preserved, or that he shall derive a greater good by drinking the poisoned water than by enduring the torment, which, to his mind, threatens instant dissolution; thus the first becomes the strongest and necessarily urges him on to action. Nevertheless, in either case, whether he partakes of the water, or whether he does not, the two actions will be equally necessary; they will be the effect of that motive which finds itself most puissant; which consequently acts in the most coercive manner upon his will.

This example will serve to explain the whole phenomena of the human will. This will, or rather the brain, finds itself in the same situation as a bowl, which, although it has received an impulse that drives it forward in a straight line, is deranged in its course whenever a force superior to the first obliges it to change its direction. The man who drinks the poisoned water appears a madman; but the actions of fools are as necessary as those of the most prudent individuals. The motives that determine the voluptuary and the debauchee to risk their health are as powerful, and their actions are as necessary, as those which decide the wise man to manage his. But, it will be insisted, the debauchee may be prevailed on to change his conduct: this does not imply that he is a free agent; but that motives may be found sufficiently powerful to annihilate the effect of those that previously acted upon him; then these new motives determine his will to the new mode of conduct he may adopt as necessarily as the former did to the old mode.

Man is said to *deliberate*, when the action of the will is suspended; this happens when two opposite motives act alternately upon him. *To deliberate*, is to hate and to love in succession; it is to be alternately attracted and repelled; it is to be moved, sometimes by one motive, sometimes by another. Man only deliberates when he does not distinctly understand the quality of the objects from which he receives impulse, or when experience has not sufficiently apprised him of the effects, more or less remote, which his actions will produce. He would take the air, but the weather is uncertain; he deliberates in consequence; he weighs the various motives that urge his will to go out or to stay at home; he is at length determined by that motive which is most probable; this removes his indecision, which necessarily settles his will, either to remain within or to go abroad: his motive is always either the immediate or ultimate advantage he finds, or thinks he finds, in the action to which he is persuaded.

Man's will frequently fluctuates between two objects, of which either the presence or the ideas move him alternately: he waits until he has contemplated the objects, or the ideas they have left in his brain which solicit him to different actions; he then compares these objects or ideas; but even in the time of deliberation, during the comparison, pending these alternatives of love and hatred which succeed each other, sometimes with the utmost rapidity, he is not a free agent for a single instant; the good or the evil which he believes he finds successively in the objects, are the necessary motives of these momentary wills; of the rapid motion of desire or fear, that he

experiences as long as his uncertainty continues. From this it will be obvious that deliberation is necessary; that uncertainty is necessary; that whatever part he takes, in consequence of this deliberation, it will always necessarily be that which he has judged, whether well or ill, is most probable to turn to his advantage.

When the soul is assailed by two motives that act alternately upon it, or modify it successively, it deliberates; the brain is in a sort of equilibrium, accompanied with perpetual oscillations, sometimes towards one object, sometimes towards the other, until the most forcible carries the point, and thereby extricates it from this state of suspense, in which consists the indecision of his will. But when the brain is simultaneously assailed by causes equally strong that move it in opposite directions, agreeable to the general law of all bodies when they are struck equally by contrary powers, it stops . . . it is neither capable to will nor to act; it waits until one of the two causes has obtained sufficient force to overpower the other; to determine its will; to attract it in such a manner that it may prevail over the efforts of the other cause.

This mechanism, so simple, so natural, suffices to demonstrate why uncertainty is painful, and why suspense is always a violent state for man. The brain, an organ so delicate and so mobile, experiences such rapid modifications that it is fatigued; or when it is urged in contrary directions, by causes equally powerful, it suffers a kind of compression, that prevents the activity which is suitable to the preservation of the whole, and which is necessary to procure what is advantageous to its existence. This mechanism will also explain the irregularity, the indecision, the inconstancy of man, and account for that conduct which frequently appears an inexplicable mystery, and which is, indeed, the effect of the received systems. In consulting experience, it will be found that the soul is submitted to precisely the same physical laws as the material body. If the will of each individual, during a given time, was only moved by a single cause or passion, nothing would be more easy than to foresee his actions; but his heart is frequently assailed by contrary powers, by adverse motives, which either act on him simultaneously or in succession; then his brain, attracted in opposite directions, is either fatigued, or else tormented by a state of compression, which deprives it of activity. Sometimes it is in a state of incommodious action; sometimes it is the sport of the alternate shocks it undergoes. Such, no doubt, is the state in which man finds himself when a lively passion solicits him to the commission of crime, whilst fear points out to him the danger by which it is attended; such, also, is the condition of him whom remorse, by the continued labour of his distracted soul, prevents from enjoying the objects he has criminally obtained.

Choice by no means proves the free agency of man: he only deliberates when he does not yet know which to choose of the many objects that move him; he is then in an embarrassment, which does not terminate until his will is decided by the greater advantage he believes he shall find in the object he chooses, or the action he undertakes. From whence it may be seen, that choice is necessary, because he would not determine for an object, or for an action, if he did not believe that he should find it in some direct advantage. That man should have free agency it were needful that he should be able to will or choose without motive, or that he could prevent motives coercing his will. Action always being the effect of his will once determined, and as his will cannot be determined but by a motive which is not in his own power, it follows that he is never the master of the determination of his own peculiar will; that consequently he never acts as a free agent. It has been believed that man was a free agent because he had a will with the power of choosing; but attention has not been paid to the fact that even his will is moved by causes independent of himself; is owing to that which is inherent in his own organization, or which belongs to the nature of the beings acting on him. Is he the master of willing not to withdraw his hand from the fire when he fears it will be burnt? Or has he the power to take away from fire the property which makes him fear it? Is he the master of not choosing a dish of meat, which he knows to be agreeable or analogous to his palate; of not preferring it to that which he knows to be disagreeable or dangerous? It is always according to his sensations, to his own peculiar experience, or to his suppositions, that he judges of things, either well or ill; but whatever may be his judgment, it depends necessarily on his mode of feeling, whether habitual or accidental, and

the qualities he finds in the causes that move him, which exist in despite of himself. . . .

In short, the actions of man are never free; they are always the necessary consequence of his temperament, of the received ideas, and of the notions, either true or false, which he has formed to himself of happiness; of his opinions, strengthened by example, by education, and by daily experience. So many crimes are witnessed on the earth only because every thing conspires to render man vicious and criminal; the religion he has adopted, his government, his education, the examples set before him, irresistibly drive him on to evil: under these circumstances, morality preaches virtue to him in vain. In those societies where vice is esteemed, where crime is crowned, where venality is constantly recompensed, where the most dreadful disorders are punished only in those who are too weak to enjoy the privilege of committing them with impunity, the practice of virtue is considered nothing more than a painful sacrifice of happiness. Such societies chastise, in the lower orders, those excesses which they respect in the higher ranks; and frequently have the injustice to condemn those in the penalty of death, whom public prejudices, maintained by constant example, have rendered criminal.

Man, then, is not a free agent in any one instant of his life; he is necessarily guided in each step by those advantages, whether real or fictitious, that he attaches to the objects by which his passions are roused: these passions themselves are necessary in a being who unceasingly tends towards his own happiness; their energy is necessary, since that depends on his temperament; his temperament is necessary, because it depends on the physical elements which enter into his composition; the modification of this temperament is necessary, as it is the infallible and inevitable consequence of the impulse he receives from the incessant action of moral and physical beings.

CHOICE DOES NOT PROVE FREEDOM

In spite of these proofs of the want of free agency in man, so clear to unprejudiced minds, it will, perhaps be insisted upon with no small feeling of triumph, that if it be proposed to any one, to move or not to move his hand, an action in the number of those called indifferent, he evidently appears to be the master of choosing; from which it is concluded that evidence has been offered of free agency. The reply is, this example is perfectly simple; man in performing some action which he is resolved on doing, does not by any means prove his free agency; the very desire of displaying this quality, excited by the dispute, becomes a necessary motive, which decides his will either for the one or the other of these actions: What deludes him in this instance, or that which persuades him he is a free agent at this moment, is, that he does not discern the true motive which sets him in action, namely, the desire of convincing his opponent: if in the heat of the dispute he insists and asks, "Am I not the master of throwing myself out of the window?" I shall answer him, no; that whilst he preserves his reason there is no probability that the desire of proving his free agency, will become a motive sufficiently powerful to make him sacrifice his life to the attempt: if, notwithstanding this, to prove he is a free agent, he should actually precipitate himself from the window, it would not be a sufficient warranty to conclude he acted freely, but rather that it was the violence of his temperament which spurred him on to this folly. Madness is a state, that depends upon the heat of the blood, not upon the will. A fanatic or a hero, braves death as necessarily as a more phlegmatic man or coward flies from it.

It is said that free agency is the absence of those obstacles competent to oppose themselves to the actions of man, or to the exercise of his faculties: it is pretended that he is a free agent whenever, making use of these faculties, he produces the effect he has proposed to himself. In reply to this reasoning, it is sufficient to consider that it in nowise depends upon himself to place or remove the obstacles that either determine or resist him. The motive that causes his action is no more in his own power than the obstacle that impedes him, whether this obstacle or motive be within his own machine or exterior of his person. He is not master of the thought presented to his mind, which determines his will; this thought is excited by some cause independent of himself.

To be undeceived on the system of his free agency, man has simply to recur to the motive by which his will is determined; he will always find this motive is out of his own control. It is said: that in consequence of an idea to which the mind gives birth, man acts freely if he encounters no obstacle. But the question is, what gives birth to this idea in his brain? Was he the master either to prevent it from presenting itself, or from renewing itself in his brain? Does not this idea depend either upon objects that strike him exteriorly and in despite of himself, or upon causes, that without his knowledge, act within himself and modify his brain? Can he prevent his eyes, cast without design upon any object whatever, from giving him an idea of this object, and from moving his brain? He is not more master of the obstacles; they are the necessary effects of either interior or exterior causes, which always act according to their given properties. A man insults a coward; this necessarily irritates him against his insulter; but his will cannot vanquish the obstacle that cowardice places to the object of his desire, because his natural conformation, which does not depend upon himself, prevents his having courage. In this case, the coward is insulted in spite of himself; and against his will is obliged patiently to brook the insult he has received.

ABSENCE OF RESTRAINT IS NOT ABSENCE OF NECESSITY

The partisans of the system of free agency appear ever to have confounded constraint with necessity. Man believes he acts as a free agent, every time he does not see any thing that places obstacles to his actions; he does not perceive that the motive which causes him to will, is always necessary and independent of himself. A prisoner loaded with chains is compelled to remain in prison; but he is not a free agent in the desire to emancipate himself; his chains prevent him from acting, but they do not prevent him from willing; he would save himself if they would loose his fetters; but he would not save himself as a free agent; fear or the idea of punishment would be sufficient motives for his action.

Man may, therefore, cease to be restrained, without, for that reason, becoming a free agent. In whatever manner he acts, he will act necessarily, according to motives by which he shall be determined. He may be compared to a heavy body that finds itself arrested in its descent by any obstacle whatever. Take away this obstacle, it will gravitate or continue to fall; but who shall say this dense body is free to fall or not? Is not its descent the necessary effect of its own specific gravity? The virtuous Socrates submitted to the laws of his country, although they were unjust; and though the doors of his jail were left open to him, he would not save himself; but in this he did not act as a free agent. The invisible chains of opinion, the secret love of decorum, the inward respect for the laws, even when they were iniquitous, the fear of tarnishing his glory, kept him in his prison; they were motives sufficiently powerful with this enthusiast for virtue, to induce him to wait death with tranquility; it was not in his power to save himself, because he could find no potential motive to bring him to depart even for an instant, from those principles to which his mind was accustomed.

Man, it is said, frequently acts against his inclination, from whence it is falsely concluded he is a free agent; but when he appears to act contrary to his inclination, he is always determined to it by some motive sufficiently efficacious to vanquish this inclination. A sick man, with a view to his cure, arrives at conquering his repugnance to the most disgusting remedies. The fear of pain, or the dread of death, then become necessary motives; consequently this sick man cannot be said to act freely.

When it is said, that man is not a free agent, it is not pretended to compare him to a body moved by a simple impulsive cause. He contains within himself causes inherent to his existence; he is moved by an interior organ, which has its own peculiar laws, and is itself necessarily determined in consequence of ideas formed from perception resulting from sensation which it receives from exterior objects. As the mechanism of these sensations, of these perceptions, and the manner they engrave ideas on the brain of man, are not known to him; because he is unable to unravel all these motions; because he cannot perceive the chain of operations in his soul, or the motive principle that acts within him, he supposes himself a free agent; which literally translated, signifies, that he moves himself by himself; that he determines himself without cause. When he rather ought to say, that he is ignorant how or why he acts in the manner he does. It is true the soul enjoys an activity peculiar to itself, but it is equally certain that this activity would never be displayed, if some motive or some cause did not put it in a condition to exercise itself. At least it will not be pretended that the soul is able either to love or to hate without being moved, without

knowing the objects, without having some idea of their qualities. Gunpowder has unquestionably a particular activity, but this activity will never display itself, unless fire be applied to it; this, however, immediately sets it in motion.

THE COMPLEXITY OF HUMAN CONDUCT AND THE ILLUSION OF FREE AGENCY

It is the great complication of motion in man, it is the variety of his action, it is the multiplicity of causes that move him, whether simultaneously or in continual succession, that persuades him he is a free agent. If all his motions were simple, if the causes that move him did not confound themselves with each other, if they were distinct, if his machine were less complicated, he would perceive that all his actions were necessary, because he would be enabled to recur instantly to the cause that made him act. A man who should be always obliged to go towards the west, would always go on that side; but he would feel that, in so going, he was not a free agent. If he had another sense, as his actions or his motion, augmented by a sixth, would be still more varied and much more complicated, he would believe himself still more a free agent than he does with his five senses.

It is, then, for want of recurring to the causes that move him; for want of being able to analyze, from not being competent to decompose the complicated motion of his machine, that man believes himself a free agent. It is only upon his own ignorance that he founds the profound yet deceitful notion he has of his free agency; that he builds those opinions which he brings forward as a striking proof of his pretended freedom of action. If, for a short time, each man was willing to examine his own peculiar actions, search out their true motives to discover their concatenation, he would remain convinced that the sentiment he has of his natural free agency, is a chimera that must speedily be destroyed by experience.

Nevertheless it must be acknowledged that the multiplicity and diversity of the causes which continually act upon man, frequently without even his knowledge, render it impossible, or at least extremely difficult for him to recur to the true principles of his own peculiar actions, much less the actions of others. They frequently depend upon causes so fugitive, so remote from their effects, and which, superficially examined, appear to have so little analogy, so slender a relation with them, that it requires singular sagacity to bring them into light. This is what renders the study of the moral man a task of such difficulty; this is the reason why his heart is an abyss, of which it is frequently impossible for him to fathom the depth.

DISCUSSION QUESTIONS

1. Are you convinced by Holbach's arguments against free will? Discuss the strengths and weaknesses of his position.

2. Holbach asserts that one of the consequences of his argument against free will is that we are not responsible for any of our actions. What is his argument? Is it a valid and sound argument? Why or why not?

3. Assuming that Holbach's arguments are sound and valid, what are some of their social and political implications?

4. Why does Holbach believe that the notion of free will is essential to religion and our system of punishment? Do you agree with him? Why or why not?

5. Discuss Holbach's claim that the will is a modification of the brain. What does he mean by this? Are his views of the will different from those of Epictetus? Are they similar to those of Paul Churchland (see chapter 3)?

6. Would you feel any differently about your life in general—and your actions, thoughts, and feelings in particular—if Holbach's theses were true? Why or why not?

Donnie Darko
[USA 2001] 1 hour, 50 minutes
Directed by Richard Kelly

Sixteen-year-old Donnie Darko (Jake Gyllenhaal) is awakened one night by a strange voice. Donnie leaves his house in Middlesex, Virginia, and walks to a golf course. There, on the seventh hole, is a grotesque six-foot rabbit named Frank (James Duval). Frank tells Donnie that he has been watching him and that God loves him. He also tells Donnie that he has come to save him because the world is going to end in twenty-eight days. When Donnie awakens on the golf course the next morning and returns home, he learns that his bedroom has been hit by a jet engine that has fallen from the sky.

No one is able to explain what has happened, least of all Donnie, who begins to consult with Frank. Frank persuades him to commit deeds that are both destructive and creative. Donnie gradually pieces together what is happening by fortuitous "clues" that are provided to him, including a book on time travel and the words "cellar door." He comes to believe that all of the events after the moment he survives the jet engine hitting his bedroom occur in an alternate universe. He also believes that he has been given the power to learn what would have happened if he had not survived the destruction of his room by a jet engine. Among other things, he sees his favorite teacher getting fired and his girlfriend dying. Donnie believes that these events foreshadow the end of the world.

One of the important "clues" that explains how Donnie can see this alternate universe is a book on the philosophy of time travel written by a woman Donnie and his friends call "Grandma Death." Donnie is given the book by Dr. Monnitoff (Noah Wyle), a man who is helping him to theoretically understand how what he is going through is possible. The book describes Donnie's experience, including his increasing visions of paths or channels growing out of people's stomachs, which are explained as ways of visualizing "destinies."

Donnie comes to believe that he has been given a choice and that the fate of the universe rests on it. The choice is between allowing himself to be hit by the jet engine and die, and escaping this type of death but seeing the world end in days as a consequence. In fact, from allowing the act of self-destruction, beautiful things will result. Donnie believes that these events are predetermined. However, he also believes that his *choice* of not allowing himself to die will bring about another predetermined set of events, which will conclude with the end of the world. Frank has given him the ability to see the two predetermined paths before him; his choice will make one of these two courses of events come about.

Donnie happily chooses death by a jet engine falling from the sky. He is presented as sacrificing his life for the happiness of others. The other choice—that is, to survive the crash—would bring about only pain for others and ultimately pain for himself, for it would cause, among other things, the death of his girlfriend.

DISCUSSION QUESTIONS

1. Is this film an argument against free will? Why or why not?

2. Is Donnie responsible for his actions after the jet engine crash? Why or why not?

3. Consider the following claim: while Donnie Darko is given the opportunity to see what the future would be in an alternative universe in which he does not die from a jet engine striking him in his bedroom, this alternative universe is not the universe in which he lives. Therefore, Donnie is looking not at his life but at the life of another "Donnie" in a different universe. Do you agree with this claim?

4. Do you think Donnie really has a *choice* in this film? If he does have a choice, does this mean that he has free will? If he does not have a choice, does this mean that all of the events in his life have been predetermined?

5. Consider the following dialogue between Dr. Monnitoff and Donnie:

DR. MONNITOFF   "Each vessel travels along a vector path through space-time . . . along its center of gravity."

DONNIE   "Like a spear."

DR. MONNITOFF   "Beg pardon?"

DONNIE   "Like a spear that comes out of your stomach?"

DR. MONNITOFF   "Uhh . . . sure. And in order for the vessel to travel through time it must find the portal, in this case the wormhole, or some unforeseen portal that lies undiscovered."

DONNIE   "Could these wormholes appear in nature?"

DR. MONNITOFF   "That . . . is highly unlikely. You're talking about an act of God."

DONNIE   "If God controls time then all time is predecided. Then every living thing travels along a set path."

DR. MONNITOFF   "I'm not following you."

DONNIE   "If you could see your path or channel growing out of your stomach, you could see into the future. And that's a form of time travel, right?"

DR. MONNITOFF   "You are contradicting yourself, Donnie. If we could see our destinies manifest themselves visually . . . then we would be given the choice to betray our chosen destinies. The very fact that this choice exists . . . would mean that all preformed destiny would end."

> DONNIE   "Not if you chose to stay within God's channel."
>
> DR. MONNITOFF   "Donnie, I'm afraid I can't continue this conversation. I could lose my job."
>
> Is Dr. Monnitoff right? Is Donnie contradicting himself? Why or why not?

6.   A jet engine falls from the sky, and no one knows its source. However, in the end, this is the cause of Donnie's death. Is there any philosophical significance to this? Would the philosophical message be any different if he was struck dead by, say, a drunk driver? Why or why not?

7.   Donnie is a troubled young man, but his journey into his future allows him to die content. Is the message of this film ultimately one of happily accepting whatever happens to you in your life, no matter how absurd it may seem? Why or why not?

8.   Discuss this film in light of the events of September 11, 2001. Do you think it would have had a different significance if those events had never occurred? Why or why not?

9.   Is this film a gloss on the following comment by Epictetus: "Never make your life lie in one thing and yet seek progress in another"? Why or why not?

10.   Do you think Donnie "sacrificed" his life for the happiness of others? If so, explain how it is possible to "sacrifice" one's life merely by living out a predetermined course of events. If not, then what is the significance of showing us what would happen to Donnie if he did not die from a jet engine crashing into his bedroom?

C. A. CAMPBELL

HAS THE SELF "FREE WILL"?

In opposition to Baron d'Holbach and other hard determinists, C. A. Campbell argues that we both possess free will and are morally responsible for our actions. Campbell's position is known as *libertarianism*, the view that a rational human being has the freedom of will to choose without being compelled to this choice by causes independent of the act. Because libertarians reject the determination of the will, they are also sometimes simply referred to as *indeterminists*.

Campbell notes that there are many kinds of human freedom and that the kind of freedom at issue in the debate over free will is that which is presupposed in relation to moral responsibility. This kind of moral freedom concerns inner acts of choice, rather than overt, external ones. More particularly, these inner acts of choice are ones wherein our self is the "sole author." This means that heredity and environment have not contributed in any way to the choice. Also, these inner acts of choice are such that the self could have acted another way.

For Campbell, our free will is exercised in our decisions to exert or withhold the moral effort to do our duty or resist temptation. When we examine our experiences in such situations, we notice that the decision to exert or withhold moral effort stems solely from the self and is an act "of which it is true to say that 'it could be' (or, after the event, 'could have been') 'otherwise.' " Nevertheless, the question must be raised as to whether we can "*trust* the evidence of inner experience." Campbell says that such evidence is not entirely conclusive.

To bolster his case for libertarianism, Campbell outlines and addresses two major determinist criticisms of libertarianism. The first criticism is that freedom is incompatible with the predictability of human behavior. Campbell responds that his libertarian notion of freedom of the will is compatible with the predictability of human behavior, even if other notions of freedom are not. The second criticism made by determinists is that acts issued from the self are meaningless because they are not issued from the self's "character." Campbell notes that this line of criticism is misguided. Even though the act of moral decision making may be meaningless to persons external to the decision making activity, they are significant and meaningful to the person making the decision. Inner acts of moral decision making are real to the moral decision maker and, as such, are as meaningful and significant as any other aspect of human experience.

C. A. (Charles Arthur) Campbell (1897–1974), a British philosopher, is well known for his defense of the concept of free will. He was born in Glasgow, Scotland, and served in the British Army during World War I. After the war, he did graduate work at Oxford University. For most of his career, he taught at Glasgow University (1924–32, 1938–61). From 1932 to 1938, he was professor of philosophy at University College of North Wales. Campbell is the author of *Skepticism and Construction: Bradley's Sceptical Principle as the Basis of Constructive Philosophy* (1931), *On Selfhood and Godhood* (1957), and *In Defence of Free Will, with Other Philosophical Essays* (1967). The following selection is from *On Selfhood and Godhood*, a book based on his Gifford Lectures at St. Andrews University, which were delivered over the course of two academic years, 1953–54 and 1954–55.

I

. . . It is something of a truism that in philosophic enquiry the exact formulation of a problem often takes one a long way on the road to its solution. In the case of the Free Will problem I think there is a rather special need of careful formulation. For there are many sorts of human freedom; and it can easily happen that one wastes a great deal of labour in proving or disproving a freedom which has almost nothing to do with the freedom which is at issue in the traditional problem of Free Will. The abortiveness of so much of the argument for and against Free Will in contemporary philosophical literature seems to me due in the main to insufficient pains being taken over the preliminary definition of the problem. . . .

Fortunately we can at least make a beginning with a certain amount of confidence. It is not seriously disputable that the kind of freedom in question is the freedom which is commonly recognised to be in some sense a precondition of moral responsibility. Clearly, it is on account of this integral connection with moral responsibility that such exceptional importance has always been felt to attach to the Free Will problem. But in what precise sense is free will a precondition of moral

responsibility, and thus a postulate of the moral life in general? This is an exceedingly troublesome question; but until we have satisfied ourselves about the answer to it, we are not in a position to state, let alone decide, the question whether "Free Will" in its traditional, ethical, significance is a reality. . . .

The first point to note is that the freedom at issue (as indeed the very name "Free *Will* Problem" indicates) pertains primarily not to overt acts but to inner acts. The nature of things has decreed that, save in the case of one's self, it is only overt acts which one can directly observe. But a very little reflection serves to show that in our moral judgments upon others their overt acts are regarded as significant only in so far as they are the expression of inner acts. We do not consider the acts of a robot to be morally responsible acts; nor do we consider the acts of a man to be so save in so far as they are distinguishable from those of a robot by reflecting an inner life of choice. Similarly, from the other side, if we are satisfied (as we may on occasion be, at least in the case of ourselves) that a person has definitely elected to follow a course which he believes to be wrong, but has been prevented by external circumstances from translating his inner choice into an overt act, we still regard him as morally blameworthy. Moral freedom, then, pertains to *inner* acts.

The next point seems at first sight equally obvious and uncontroversial; but, as we shall see, it has awkward implications if we are in real earnest with it (as almost nobody is). It is the simple point that the act must be one of which the person judged can be regarded as the *sole* author. It seems plain enough that if there are any *other* determinants of the act, external to the self, to that extent the act is not an act which the *self* determines, and to that extent not an act for which the self can be held morally responsible. The self is only part-author of the act, and his moral responsibility can logically extend only to those elements within the act (assuming for the moment that these can be isolated) of which he is the *sole* author. . . .

Thirdly, we come to a point over which much recent controversy has raged. We may approach it by raising the following question. Granted an act of which the agent is sole author, does this "sole authorship" suffice to make the act a morally free act? We may be inclined to think that it does, until we contemplate the possibility that an act of which the agent is sole author might conceivably occur as a necessary expression of the agent's nature; the way in which, e.g., some philosophers have supposed the Divine act of creation to occur. This consideration excites a legitimate doubt; for it is far from easy to see how a person can be regarded as a proper subject for moral praise or blame in respect of an act which he *cannot help* performing—even if it be his own "nature" which necessitates it. Must we not recognize it as a condition of the morally free act that the agent "could have acted otherwise" than he in fact did? It is true, indeed, that we sometimes praise or blame a man for an act about which we are prepared to say, in the light of our knowledge of his established character, that he "could do no other." But I think that a little reflection shows that in such cases we are not praising or blaming the man strictly for what he does *now* (or at any rate we ought not to be), but rather for those past acts of his which have generated the firm habit of mind from which his *present* act follows "necessarily." In other words, our praise and blame, so far as justified, are really retrospective,

being directed not to the agent *qua* performing *this* act, but to the agent *qua* performing those past acts which have built up his present character, and in respect to which we presume that he *could* have acted otherwise, that there really *were* open possibilities before him. These cases, therefore, seem to me to constitute no valid exception to what I must take to be the rule, viz. that a man can be morally praised or blamed for an act only if he could have acted otherwise.

Now philosophers today are fairly well agreed that it is a postulate of the morally responsible act that the agent "could have acted otherwise" in *some* sense of that phrase. But sharp differences of opinion have arisen over the way in which the phrase ought to be interpreted. There is a strong disposition to water down its apparent meaning by insisting that it is not (as a postulate of moral responsibility) to be understood as a straight-forward categorical proposition, but rather as a disguised hypothetical proposition. All that we really require to be assured of, in order to justify our holding X morally responsible for an act, is, we are told, that X could have acted otherwise *if* he had *chosen* otherwise or perhaps that X could have acted otherwise *if* he had had a different character, or *if* he had been placed in different circumstances.

I think it is easy to understand, and even, in a measure, to sympathise with, the motives which induce philosophers to offer these counter-interpretations. It is not just the fact that "X could have acted otherwise," as a bald categorical statement, is incompatible with the universal sway of causal law—though this is, to some philosophers, a serious stone of stumbling. The more wide-spread objection is that at least it looks as though it were incompatible with that causal continuity of an agent's character with his conduct which is implied when we believe (surely with justice) that we can often tell the sort of thing a man will do from our knowledge of the sort of man he is.

We shall have to make our accounts with that particular difficulty later. At this stage I wish merely to show that neither of the hypothetical propositions suggested—and I think the same could be shown for *any* hypothetical alternative—is an acceptable substitute for the categorical proposition "X could have acted otherwise" as the presupposition of moral responsibility.

Let us look first at the earlier suggestion—"X could have acted otherwise *if* he had chosen otherwise." Now clearly there are a great many acts with regard to which we are entirely satisfied that the agent is thus situated. We are often perfectly sure that—for this is all it amounts to—if X had chosen otherwise, the circumstances presented no external obstacle to the translation of that choice into action. For example, we often have no doubt at all that X, who in point of fact told a lie, could have told the truth *if* he had so chosen. But does our confidence on this score allay all legitimate doubts about whether X is really blameworthy? Does it entail that X is free in the sense required for moral responsibility? Surely not. The obvious question immediately arises: "But *could* X have *chosen* otherwise than he did?" It is doubt about the true answer to *that* question which leads most people to doubt the reality of moral responsibility. Yet on this crucial question the hypothetical proposition which is offered as a sufficient statement of the condition justifying the ascription of moral responsibility gives us no information whatsoever.

Indeed this hypothetical substitute for the categorical "X could have acted otherwise" seems to me to lack all plausibility unless one contrives to forget why it is, after all, that we ever come to feel fundamental doubts about man's moral responsibility. Such doubts are born, surely, when one becomes aware of certain reputable world-views in religion or philosophy, or of certain reputable scientific beliefs, which in their several ways imply that man's actions are necessitated, and thus could not be otherwise than they in fact are. But clearly a doubt so based is not even touched by the recognition that a man could very often act otherwise *if* he so chose. That proposition is entirely compatible with the necessitarian theories which generate our doubt: indeed it is this very compatibility that has recommended it to some philosophers, who are reluctant to give up either moral responsibility or Determinism. The proposition which we *must* be able to affirm if moral praise or blame of X is to be justified is the categorical proposition that X could have acted otherwise because—not if—he could have chosen otherwise; or, since it is essentially the inner side of the act that matters, the proposition simply that X could have chosen otherwise.

For the second of the alternative formulae suggested we cannot spare more than a few moments. But its inability to meet the demands it is required to meet is almost transparent. "X could have acted otherwise," as a statement of a precondition of X's moral responsibility, really means (we are told) "X could have acted otherwise *if* he were differently constituted, or *if* he had been placed in different circumstances." It seems a sufficient reply to this to point out that the person whose moral responsibility is at issue is X; a specific individual, in a specific set of circumstances. It is totally irrelevant to X's moral responsibility that we should be able to say that some person differently constituted from X, or X in a different set of circumstances, could have done something different from what X did. . . .

II

That brings me to the second, and more constructive, part of this lecture. From now on I shall be considering whether it is reasonable to believe that man does in fact possess a free will of the kind specified in the first part of the lecture. If so, just how and where within the complex fabric of the volitional life are we to locate it?—for although free will must presumably belong (if anywhere) to the volitional side of human experience, it is pretty clear from the way in which we have been forced to define it that it does not pertain simply to volition as such; not even to all volitions that are commonly dignified with the name of "choices." It has been, I think, one of the more serious impediments to profitable discussion of the Free Will problem that Libertarians and Determinists alike have so often failed to appreciate the comparatively narrow area within which the free will that is necessary to "save" morality is required to operate. It goes without saying that this failure has been gravely prejudicial to the case for Libertarianism. I attach a good deal of importance, therefore, to the problem of locating free will correctly within the volitional orbit. Its solution forestalls and annuls, I believe, some of the more tiresome clichés of Determinist criticism.

We saw earlier that Common Sense's practice of "making allowances" in its moral judgments for the influence of heredity and environment indicates Common Sense's conviction, both that a just moral judgment must discount determinants of choice over which the agent has no control, and also (since it still accepts moral judgments as legitimate) that *something* of moral relevance survives which can be regarded as genuinely self-originated. We are now to try to discover what this "something" is. And I think we may still usefully take Common Sense as our guide. Suppose one asks the ordinary intelligent citizen *why* he deems it proper to make allowances for X, whose heredity and/or environment are unfortunate. He will tend to reply, I think, in some such terms as these: that X has more and stronger temptations to deviate from what is right than Y or Z, who are normally circumstanced, so that he must put forth a *stronger moral effort* if he is to achieve the same level of external conduct. The intended implication seems to be that X is just as morally praiseworthy as Y or Z *if* he exerts an equivalent moral effort, even though he may not thereby achieve an equal success in conforming his will to the "concrete" demands of duty. And this implies, again, Common Sense's belief that *in moral effort* we have something for which a man is responsible *without qualification,* something that is *not* affected by heredity and environment but depends *solely* upon the self itself.

Now in my opinion Common Sense has here, in principle, hit upon the one and only defensible answer. Here, and here alone, so far as I can see, in the act of deciding whether to put forth or withhold the moral effort required to resist temptation and rise to duty, is to be found an act which is free in the sense required for moral responsibility; an act of which the self is sole author, and of which it is true to say that "it could be" (or, after the event, "could have been") "otherwise." Such is the thesis which we shall now try to establish.

The species of argument appropriate to the establishment of a thesis of this sort should fall, I think, into two phases. First, there should be a consideration of the evidence of the moral agent's own inner experience. What *is* the act of moral decision, and what does it imply, from the standpoint of the actual participant? Since there is no way of knowing the act of moral decision—or for that matter any other form of activity—except by actual participation in it, the evidence of the subject, or agent, is on an issue of this kind of palmary [outstanding, best] importance. It can hardly, however, be taken as in itself conclusive. For even if that evidence should be overwhelmingly to the effect that moral decision does have the characteristics required by moral freedom, the question is bound to be raised—and in view of considerations from other quarters pointing in a contrary direction is *rightly* raised—Can we *trust* the evidence of inner experience? That brings us to what will be the second phase of the argument. We shall have to go on to show, if we are to make good our case, that the extraneous considerations so often supposed to be fatal to the belief in moral freedom are in fact innocuous to it. . . .

These arguments can, I think, be reduced in principle to no more than two: first, the argument from "predictability"; second, the argument from the alleged meaninglessness of an act supposed to be the self's act and yet not an expression of the self's character. Contemporary criticism of free will seems to me to consist almost exclusively of variations on these two themes. I shall deal with each in turn. . . .

Let us remind ourselves briefly of the setting within which, on our view, free will functions. There is X, the course which we believe we ought to follow, and Y, the course towards which we feel our desire is strongest. The freedom which we ascribe to the agent is the freedom to put forth or refrain from putting forth the moral effort required to resist the pressure of desire and do what he thinks he ought to do.

But then there is surely an immense range of practical situations—covering by far the greater part of life—in which there is no question of a conflict within the self between what he most desires to do and what he thinks he ought to do. Indeed such conflict is a comparatively rare phenomenon for the majority of men. Yet over that whole vast range there is nothing whatever in our version of Libertarianism to prevent our agreeing that character determines conduct. In the absence, real or supposed, of any "moral" issue, what a man chooses will be simply that course which, after such reflection as seems called for, he deems most likely to bring him what he most strongly desires; and that is the same as to say the course to which his present character inclines him.

Over by far the greater area of human choices, then, our theory offers no more barrier to successful prediction on the basis of character than any other theory. For where there is no clash of strongest desire with duty, the free will we are defending has no business. There is just nothing for it to do.

But what about the situations—rare enough though they may be—in which there *is* this clash and in which free will does therefore operate? Does our theory entail that there at any rate, as the critic seems to suppose, "anything may happen"?

Not by any manner of means. In the first place, and by the very nature of the case, the range of the agent's possible choices is bounded by what he thinks he ought to do on the one hand, and what he most strongly desires on the other. The freedom claimed for him is a freedom of decision to make or withhold the effort required to do what he thinks he ought to do. There is no question of a freedom to act in some "wild" fashion, out of all relation to his characteristic beliefs and desires. This so-called "freedom of caprice," so often charged against the Libertarian, is, to put it bluntly, a sheer figment of the critic's imagination, with no *habitat* in serious Libertarian theory. Even in situations where free will does come into play it is perfectly possible, on a view like ours, given the appropriate knowledge of a man's character, to predict within certain limits how he will respond. . . .

I claim, therefore, that the view of free will I have been putting forward is consistent with predictability of conduct on the basis of character over a very wide field indeed. And I make the further claim that that field will cover all the situations in life concerning which there is any empirical evidence that successful prediction is possible.

Let us pass on to consider the second main line of criticism. This is, I think, much the more illuminating of the two, if only because it compels the Libertarian to make explicit certain concepts which are indispensable to him, but which, being desperately hard to state clearly, are apt not to be stated at all. The critic's fundamental point might be stated somewhat as follows:

"Free will as you describe it is completely unintelligible. On your own showing no *reason* can be given, because there just *is* no reason, why

a man decides to exert rather than to withhold moral effort, or *vice versa*. But such an act—or more properly, such an 'occurrence'—it is nonsense to speak of as an act of a *self*. If there is nothing in the self's character to which it is, even in principle, in any way traceable, the self has nothing to do with it. Your so-called 'freedom,' therefore, so far from supporting the self's moral responsibility, destroys it as surely as the crudest Determinism could do."

If we are to discuss this criticism usefully, it is important, I think, to begin by getting clear about two different senses of the word "intelligible."

If, in the first place, we mean by an "intelligible" act one whose occurrence is in principle capable of being inferred, since it follows necessarily from something (though we may not know in fact from what), then it is certainly true that the Libertarian's free will is unintelligible. But that is only saying, is it not, that the Libertarian's "free" act is not an act which follows necessarily from something! This can hardly rank as a *criticism* of Libertarianism. It is just a description of it. That there can be nothing unintelligible in *this* sense is precisely what the Determinist has got to *prove*.

Yet it is surprising how often the critic of Libertarianism involves himself in this circular mode of argument. Repeatedly it is urged against the Libertarian, with a great air of triumph, that on this view he can't say *why* I now decide to rise to duty, or now decide to follow my strongest desire in defiance of duty. Of course he can't. If he could he wouldn't *be* a Libertarian. To "account for" a "free" act is a contradiction in terms. A free will is *ex hypothesi* the sort of thing of which the request for an *explanation* is absurd. The assumption that an explanation must be in principle possible for the act of moral decision deserves to rank as a classic example of the ancient fallacy of "begging the question."

But the critic usually has in mind another sense of the word "unintelligible." He is apt to take it for granted that an act which is unintelligible in the *above* sense (as the morally free act of the Libertarian undoubtedly is) is unintelligible in the *further* sense that we can attach no meaning to it. And this is an altogether more serious matter. If it could really be shown that the Libertarian's "free will" were unintelligible in this sense of being meaningless, that, for myself at any rate, would be the end of the affair. Libertarianism would have been conclusively refuted.

But it seems to me manifest that this can *not* be shown. The critic has allowed himself, I submit, to become the victim of a widely accepted but fundamentally vicious assumption. He has assumed that whatever is meaningful must exhibit its meaningfulness to those who view it from the standpoint of external observation. Now if one chooses thus to limit one's self to the role of external observer, it is, I think, perfectly true that one can attach no meaning to an act which is the act of something we call a "self" and yet follows from nothing in that self's character. But then *why should we* so limit ourselves, when what is under consideration is a subjective activity? For the apprehension of subjective acts there is *another* standpoint available, that of *inner experience,* of the practical consciousness in its actual functioning. If our free will should turn out to be something to which we can attach a meaning from *this* standpoint, no more is required. And no more ought to be expected. For I must repeat that only from the inner standpoint of living experience *could* anything of the nature of "activity" be directly grasped. Observation from without is in the nature of the case impotent to apprehend the active *qua* active. We can from without observe sequences of states. If into these we read activity (as we sometimes do), this can only be on the basis of what we discern in ourselves from the inner standpoint. It follows that if anyone insists upon taking this criterion of the meaningful simply from the standpoint of external observation, he is really deciding in advance of the evidence that the notion of activity, and *a fortiori* the notion of a free will, is "meaningless." He looks for the free act through a medium which is in the nature of the case incapable of revealing it, and then, because inevitably he doesn't find it, he declares that it doesn't exist!

But if, as we surely ought in this context, we adopt the inner standpoint, then (I am suggesting) things appear in a totally different light. From the inner standpoint, it seems to me plain, there is no difficulty whatever in attaching meaning to an act which is the self's act and which nevertheless does not follow from the self's character. So much I claim has been established by the phenomenological

analysis . . . of the act of moral decision in face of moral temptation. It is thrown into particularly clear relief where the moral decision is to make the moral effort required to rise to duty. For the very function of moral effort, as it appears to the agent engaged in the act, is to enable the self to act against the line of least resistance, against the line to which his character as so far formed most strongly inclines him. But if the self is thus conscious here of *combating* his formed character, he surely cannot possibly suppose that the act, although his own act, *issues from* his formed character? I submit, therefore, that the self knows very well indeed—from the inner standpoint— what is meant by an act which is the *self's* act and which nevertheless does not follow from the self's *character.*

What this implies—and it seems to me to be an implication of cardinal importance for any theory of the self that aims at being more than superficial—is that the nature of the self is for itself something more than just its character as so far formed. The "nature" of the self and what we commonly call the "character" of the self are by no means the same thing, and it is utterly vital that they should not be confused. The "nature" of the self comprehends, but is not without remainder reducible to, its "character"; it must, if we are to be true to the testimony of our experience of it, be taken as including *also* the authentic creative power of fashioning and re-fashioning "character."

DISCUSSION QUESTIONS

1. Why does Campbell limit our freedom primarily to our inner acts and not our outward, external behavior? Do you agree with this limitation? Why or why not?

2. Campbell says that we are morally responsible only for acts of which we are the sole author. If the self is only part-author of the act, then our moral responsibility is limited to only those elements of which we are sole author. Give an example of an action of which we are only part-author. Do you agree with Campbell that we are not morally responsible for the part of this action of which we are not the author? Why or why not?

3. Campbell contends that our inner experience provides better evidence concerning free will than does that of external observation. Do you agree with him? Why or why not?

4. Do you believe that we have the power to and can act freely in a way that is contrary to our characters? Do you agree with Campbell that this is the best evidence that the will is free?

5. Campbell argues that the ability to predict human behavior to varying degrees is not sufficient grounds to deny that we have free will. What is his argument? Do you agree with him? Why or why not?

6. Has Campbell convinced you that we have free will? Compare his position on free will with that of Holbach. Which do you prefer, and why?

Gattaca
[USA 1997] 1 hour, 46 minutes
Directed by Andrew Niccol

*I*magine a world in which geneticists and parents work together to conceive near-perfect offspring. Parents can select the hair color, eye color, and skin tone of their children and can eliminate birth defects, the risk of disease, and "potentially prejudicial conditions" such as premature baldness, myopia, alcoholism, and the propensity for violence and obesity. At conception, genetic identity can be mapped out with such accuracy that even age of death can be predicted—so long as the person does not fall victim to events beyond genetic control, such as a fatal accident.

In such a world, few humans will be conceived and born without near-perfect "genetic quotients." Most parents will not want to leave anything like disease or potentially prejudicial conditions to chance, for it will not give their offspring the best opportunity for success in the world. Prestigious employers, for example, will have full knowledge of the genetic profile of their employees through a simple test, and while discrimination on the basis of genetic profile will be illegal, it will continue. If an employer sees an inferior genetic profile in the employee, it will offer the position to a genetically superior individual. In this society in the "not-too-distant future," it is believed that genetics—or biology—is destiny. Moreover, it is thought that there are some professions including astronautics, in which success is physically and intellectually impossible for those with weak genetic profiles.

Vincent Freeman (Ethan Hawke) is a young man whose genetic identity was left to chance and underwent no manipulation. In this society, persons like Vincent are called "in-valids," because their genetic identity is inferior to that of "valids," namely, those with near-perfect genetic quotients. Vincent wishes to become an astronaut, but the vocation is available only to valids. So, Vincent purchases the genetic traits of his near-perfect, but accident-paralyzed, friend Jerome (Jude Law). Vincent uses Jerome's genetic identity to gain entry into Gattaca Corporation's prestigious astronaut program, and though it is difficult for him, he does well in the astronaut-training program.

However, just as Vincent is nearing his goal, a murder at Gattaca Corporation threatens to expose his real genetic identity, for it is believed that an in-valid who works for the corporation may have committed the murder. In the end, the coordinator of the program is exposed as the true killer—not Vincent, who has just completed his astronaut training. While there is still some chance that Vincent's true genetic identity will be revealed, it will not be in time to stop him from engaging in his first mission as an astronaut. Vincent commences his mission having succeeded in defying the genetic prejudices of his society.

DISCUSSION QUESTIONS

1. Are the actions of Vincent a defense of libertarianism? Why or why not?

2. Imagine Holbach being told Vincent's story, namely, one of an in-valid achieving well beyond his genetic "capacity." Do you think he would agree that it proves the existence and power of the self's free will? Why or why not?

3. Consider the following internal monologue by Vincent (posing as Jerome): "The most unremarkable of events. Jerome Morrow, Navigator First Class, is only days away from a one-year manned mission to 951 Gaspra in the Outer Asteroid Belt. Nothing so unique in that. Last year, over one thousand citizens from every walk of life embarked on some space mission or other. Besides, selection for Jerome was virtually guaranteed at birth. He is blessed with all the physical and intellectual gifts required for such an arduous undertaking, a genetic quotient second to none. No, there is truly nothing remarkable about the progress of Jerome Morrow, except that I am not Jerome Morrow." Are you impressed by Vincent's achievement? To be impressed by it, do you need to assume that it is nearly physically and intellectually impossible for Vincent to succeed as an astronaut without Jerome's genetic profile? Why or why not?

4. Maria (Vincent's mother) is lying down on a medical examining table with her feet in stirrups as a nurse comes toward her with an instrument tray. Maria takes her feet out of the stirrups and swings her legs off the table. Consider the following dialogue between Maria (Jayne Brook) and the nurse (Maya Rudolph) at this family-planning clinic:

> NURSE   "What are you doing?"
>
> MARIA   "I can't do this."
>
> NURSE   "I told you, the government pays. It's all taken care of."
>
> MARIA   "No, you don't understand. I can't."
>
> NURSE   "The doctor will give you something."
>
> MARIA   "I'm not doing it."
>
> NURSE   "Honey, you've made *one* mistake—I've read your profile. I don't know about the father but you carry enough hereditary factors on your own. You can have other children."
>
> MARIA   "Not like *this* one."
>
> NURSE   "Honey, look around you. The world doesn't want one like *that* one."
>
> MARIA   "You don't know what it will be!"
>
> NURSE   "The child won't thank you!"

Maria leaves the hospital, not taking the opportunity of a state-sponsored abortion of her non-genetically-planned fetus (Vincent). Do you think that she should have had an abortion given the kind of world in which she lives—that is, a world in which genetic profile is tantamount to success in the world and in which "love children" (non-genetically-planned children, or in-valids) are subject to discrimination? Is the nurse right? Will the child not thank Maria?

5. Consider the following internal monologue by Vincent (posing as Jerome): "Those parents who, for moral or, more likely, economic reasons refrain from tampering with their offspring's genetic makeup or who fail to abort a deprived fetus condemn their children to a life of routine discrimination. Officially they are called 'In-Valids.' Also known as 'godchildren,' 'men-of-god,' 'faith births,' 'blackjack births,' 'deficients,' 'defectives,' 'genojunk,' 'ge-gnomes,' 'the fucked-up people.' They are the 'healthy ill.' They don't actually have anything yet—they may never. But since few of the preconditions can be cured or reversed, it is easier to treat them as if they were already sick." The world presented in *Gattaca* is one wherein many parents choose only to have children with high genetic quotients, and those without high quotients are terminated in the early stages of conception. Do you think the termination of pregnancies involving low-genetic-quotient fetuses is logical or right? Defend your case as a member of this community. Consider it from the valid and in-valid perspective. Does this make any difference to your argument?

6. Consider the following internal monologue by Vincent (posing as Jerome): "Those were early days— days when a priest could still persuade someone to put their faith in God's hands rather than those of the local geneticist." If science were able to determine the genetic profile of people to as high a degree as it can in *Gattaca*, would this result in a loss of faith in God and an increase in faith in geneticists? Why or why not?

7. Consider the following internal monologue by Vincent (posing as Jerome): "My destiny was mapped out before me—all my flaws—most untreatable to this day. Only minutes old, the date and cause of my death was already known." If you had the opportunity to know all of your flaws, predispositions, and susceptibilities, as well as the date of your death, would you want to know these things? Why or why not? Would your life be any different if you had been able to determine its course in this way?

8. Consider the following dialogue between a geneticist (Blair Underwood) and Maria and Antonio Freeman (Elias Koteas):

    GENETICIST   "You've already specified blue eyes, dark hair, and fair skin. I have taken the liberty of eradicating any potentially prejudicial conditions—premature baldness, myopia, alcoholism, and addictive susceptibility, propensity for violence and obesity."

    MARIA   "We didn't want—diseases, yes."

    ANTONIO   "We were wondering if we should leave some things to chance."

    GENETICIST   "You want to give your child the best possible start. Believe me, we have enough imperfection built in already. Your child doesn't need any additional burdens. And keep in mind this child is still you, simply the *best* of you. You could conceive naturally a thousand times and never get such a result."

    ANTONIO   "He's right, Maria. That's right."

    Should they leave anything to chance? Or is the geneticist right, in asserting that there is already enough imperfection built in? Discuss.

9. Consider the following internal monologue by Vincent (posing as Jerome): "My father was right. It didn't matter how much I lied on my résumé, my real C.V. was in my cells. Why should anybody invest all that money to train me, when there are a thousand other applicants with a far cleaner profile? Of course, it's illegal to discriminate—'genoism' it's called—but no one takes the laws seriously." Assuming that genetic engineering is possible, present an argument for or against "genoism," that is, discrimination based on genetic profile.

10. Consider the following internal monologue by Vincent (posing as Jerome): "The majority of people are now made-to-order. What began as a means to rid society of inheritable diseases has become a way to design your offspring—the line between health and enhancement blurred forever. Eyes can always be brighter, a voice purer, a mind sharper, a body stronger, a life longer. Everyone seeks to give their child the best chance, but the most skilled geneticists are accessible only to the privileged few." Assuming that genetic engineering is possible, does the state have a responsibility to make the best possible geneticists available to all of its citizens? Why or why not? What are the moral, social, and political implications of your position?

11. If you had the opportunity to live in the world presented by *Gattaca*, and were able to choose between living there as a valid or an in-valid, which would you choose, and why?

W. T. STACE

FREE WILL, DETERMINISM, AND THE PROBLEM OF MORALS

Determinism and moral responsibility are compatible, argues W. T. Stace, when free will is correctly defined. According to Stace, even if we agree with the hard determinists that all events, including human actions, are completely determined, we do not, like them, have to deny free will. Moreover, Stace agrees with the libertarian that without free will there can be no morality. Stace's position is known as *compatibilism* (or *soft determinism*), the view that freedom of the will and moral responsibility can be reconciled with determinism. If we did not have the freedom to choose to obey or disobey moral precepts, then all moral precepts would be meaningless. Consequently, any discussion of morality must be preceded by a discussion of free will.

According to Stace, the problem of free will "has been created by the fact that learned men, especially philosophers, have assumed an incorrect definition of free will." Both those who denied and those who defended free will incorrectly assumed that it meant "indeterminism." Stace argues that this definition is incorrect because it is not in keeping with the way in which the meaning of free will is commonly applied verbally, that is, *in conversation*. An analysis of the ordinary usage of free will in conversation reveals a different definition: acts freely done are those whose immediate causes are psychological states in the agent, and acts not freely done are those whose immediate causes are states of affairs external to the agent. Thus, for Stace, at issue is not whether actions are determined by some cause, but rather what kind of cause determined them: an internal, psychological one or an external, physical one. Unlike the philosophical concept of free will that places a false dichotomy between freedom and determinism, the concept used in ordinary conversation allows for their compatability.

Stace concludes that the ordinary-conversation meaning of free will is the correct one, not the classic philosophical definition of free will as indeterminism. He then goes on to show how his notion of "deterministic free will" is compatible with that of both moral responsibility and the punishment of wrongdoers. A biographical sketch of W. T. Stace appears in chapter 4. The following selection is from *Religion and the Modern Mind* (1952).

I shall first discuss the problem of free will, for it is certain that if there is no free will there can be no morality. Morality is concerned with what men ought and ought not to do. But if a man has no freedom to choose what he will do, if whatever he does is done under compulsion, then it does not make sense to tell him that he ought not to have done what he did and that he ought to do something different. All moral precepts would in such case be meaningless. Also if he acts always under compulsion, how can he be held morally responsible for his actions? How can he, for example, be punished for what he could not help doing?

It is to be observed that those learned professors of philosophy or psychology who deny the existence of free will do so only in their professional moments and in their studies and lecture rooms. For when it comes to doing anything practical, even of the most trivial kind, they invariably behave as if they and others were free. They inquire from you at dinner whether you will choose this dish or that dish. They will ask a child why he told a lie, and will punish him for not having chosen the way of truthfulness. All of which is inconsistent with a disbelief in free will. This should cause us to suspect that the problem is not a real one; and this, I believe, is the case. The dispute is merely verbal, and is due to nothing but a confusion about the meanings of words. It is what is now fashionably called a semantic problem.

How does a verbal dispute arise? Let us consider a case which, although it is absurd in the sense that no one would ever make the mistake which is involved in it, yet illustrates the principle which we shall have to use in the solution of the problem. Suppose that someone believed that the word "man" means a certain sort of five-legged animal; in short that "five-legged animal" is the correct definition of man. He might then look around the world, and rightly observing that there are no five-legged animals in it, he might proceed to deny the existence of men. This preposterous conclusion would have been reached because he was using an incorrect *definition* of "man." All you would have to do to show him his mistake would be to give him the correct definition; or at least to show him that his definition was wrong. Both the problem and its solution would, of course, be entirely verbal. The

problem of free will, and its solution, I shall maintain, is verbal in exactly the same way. The problem has been created by the fact that learned men, especially philosophers, have assumed an incorrect definition of free will, and then finding that there is nothing in the world which answers to their definition, have denied its existence. As far as logic is concerned, their conclusion is just as absurd as that of the man who denies the existence of men. The only difference is that the mistake in the latter case is obvious and crude, while the mistake which the deniers of free will have made is rather subtle and difficult to detect.

Throughout the modern period, until quite recently, it was assumed, both by the philosophers who denied free will and by those who defended it, that *determinism is inconsistent with free will*. If a man's actions were wholly determined by chains of causes stretching back into the remote past, so that they could be predicted beforehand by a mind which knew all the causes, it was assumed that they could not in that case be free. This implies that a certain definition of actions done from free will was assumed, namely that they are actions *not* wholly determined by causes or predictable beforehand. Let us shorten this by saying that free will was defined as meaning indeterminism. This is the incorrect definition which has led to the denial of free will. As soon as we see what the true definition is we shall find that the question whether the world is deterministic, as Newtonian science implied, or in a measure indeterministic, as current physics teaches, is wholly irrelevant to the problem.

Of course there is a sense in which one can define a word arbitrarily in any way one pleases. But a definition may nevertheless be called correct or incorrect. It is correct if it accords with a *common usage* of the word defined. It is incorrect if it does not. And if you give an incorrect definition, absurd and untrue results are likely to follow. For instance, there is nothing to prevent you from arbitrarily defining a man as a five-legged animal, but this is incorrect in the sense that it does not accord with the ordinary meaning of the word. Also it has the absurd result of leading to a denial of the existence of men. This shows that *common usage is the criterion for deciding whether a definition is correct or not*. And this is the principle which I shall apply to free will. I shall show that indeterminism is not what is meant by the phrase "free will" *as it is commonly used.* And I shall attempt to discover the correct definition by inquiring how the phrase is used in ordinary conversation.

Here are a few samples of how the phrase might be used in ordinary conversation. It will be noticed that they include cases in which the question whether a man acted with free will is asked in order to determine whether he was morally and legally responsible for his acts.

JONES   I once went without food for a week.

SMITH   Did you do that of your own free will?

JONES   No. I did it because I was lost in a desert and could find no food.

But suppose that the man who had fasted was Mahatma Gandhi. The conversation might then have gone:

GANDHI   I once fasted for a week.

SMITH   Did you do that of your own free will?

GANDHI   Yes. I did it because I wanted to compel the British Government to give India its independence.

Take another case. Suppose that I had stolen some bread, but that I was as truthful as George Washington. Then, if I were charged with the crime in court, some exchange of the following sort might take place:

JUDGE   Did you steal the bread of your own free will?

STACE   Yes. I stole it because I was hungry.

Or in different circumstances the conversation might run:

JUDGE   Did you steal of your own free will?

STACE   No. I stole because my employer threatened to beat me if I did not.

At a recent murder trial in Trenton some of the accused had signed confessions, but afterwards asserted that they had done so under police duress. The following exchange might have occurred:

JUDGE   Did you sign this confession of your own free will?

PRISONER   No. I signed it because the police beat me up.

Now suppose that a philosopher had been a member of the jury. We could imagine this conversation taking place in the jury room.

FOREMAN OF THE JURY   The prisoner says he signed the confession because he was beaten, and not of his own free will.

PHILOSOPHER   This is quite irrelevant to the case. There is no such thing as free will.

FOREMAN   Do you mean to say that it makes no difference whether he signed because his conscience made him want to tell the truth or because he was beaten?

PHILOSOPHER   None at all. Whether he was caused to sign by a beating or by some desire of his own—the desire to tell the truth, for example—in either case his signing was causally determined, and therefore in neither case did he act of his own free will. Since there is no such thing as free will, the question whether he signed of his own free will ought not to be discussed by us.

The foreman and the rest of the jury would rightly conclude that the philosopher must be making some mistake. What sort of a mistake could it be? There is only one possible answer. The philosopher must be using the phrase "free will" in some peculiar way of his own which is not the way in which men usually use it when they wish to determine a question of moral responsibility. That is, he must be using an incorrect definition of it as implying action not determined by causes.

Suppose a man left his office at noon, and were questioned about it. Then we might hear this:

JONES   Did you go out of your own free will?

SMITH   Yes. I went out to get my lunch.

But we might hear:

JONES   Did you leave your office of your own free will?

SMITH   No. I was forcibly removed by the police.

We have now collected a number of cases of actions which, in the ordinary usage of the English language, would be called cases in which people have acted of their own free will. We should also say in all these cases that they *chose* to act as they did. We should also say that they could have acted otherwise, if they had chosen. For instance, Mahatma Gandhi was not compelled to fast; he chose to do so. He could have eaten if he had wanted to. When Smith went out to get his lunch, he chose to do so. He could have stayed and done some more work, if he had wanted to. We have also collected a number of cases of the opposite kind. They are cases in which men were not able to exercise their free will. They had no choice. They were compelled to do as they did. The man in the desert did not fast of his own free will. He had no choice in the matter. He was compelled to fast because there was nothing for him to eat. And so with the other cases. It ought to be quite easy, by an inspection of these cases, to tell what we ordinarily mean when we say that a man did or did not exercise free will. We ought therefore to be able to extract from them the proper definition of the term. Let us put the cases in a table:

Free Acts	Unfree Acts
Gandhi fasting because he wanted to free India.	The man fasting in the desert because there was no food.
Stealing bread because one is hungry.	Stealing because one's employer threatened to beat one.
Signing a confession because one wanted to tell the truth.	Signing because the police beat one.
Leaving the office because one wanted one's lunch.	Leaving because forcibly removed.

It is obvious that to find the correct definition of free acts we must discover what characteristic is common to all the acts in the left-hand column, and is, at the same time, absent from all the acts in the right-hand column. This characteristic which all free acts have, and which no unfree acts have, will be the defining characteristic of free will.

Is being uncaused, or not being determined by causes, the characteristic of which we are in search? It cannot be, because although it is true that all the acts in the right-hand column have causes, such as the beating by the police or the absence of food in the desert, so also do the acts in the left-hand column. Mr. Gandhi's fasting was caused by his desire to free India, the man leaving his office by his hunger, and so on. Moreover there is no reason to doubt that these causes of the free acts were in turn caused by prior conditions, and that these were again the results of causes, and so on back indefinitely into the past. Any physiologist can tell us the causes of hunger. What caused Mr. Gandhi's tremendously powerful desire to free India is no doubt more difficult to discover. But it must have had causes. Some of them may have lain in peculiarities of his glands or brain, others in his past experiences, others in his heredity, others in his education. Defenders of free will have usually tended to deny such facts. But to do so is plainly a case of special pleading, which is unsupported by any scrap of evidence. The only reasonable view is that all human actions, both those which are freely done and those which are not, are either wholly determined by causes, or at least as much determined as other events in nature. It may be true, as the physicists tell us, that nature is not as deterministic as was once thought. But whatever degree of determinism prevails in the world, human actions appear to be as much determined as anything else. And if this is so, it cannot be the case that what distinguishes actions freely chosen from those which are not free is that the latter are determined by causes while the former are not. Therefore, being uncaused or being undetermined by causes, must be an incorrect definition of free will.

What, then, is the difference between acts which are freely done and those which are not? What is the characteristic which is present to all the acts in the left-hand column and absent from all those in the right-hand column? Is it not obvious that, although both sets of actions have causes, the causes of those in the left-hand column are *of a different kind* from the causes of those in the right-hand column? The free acts are all caused by desires, or motives, or by some sort of internal psychological states of the agent's mind. The unfree acts, on the other hand, are all caused by physical forces or physical conditions, outside the agent. Police arrest means physical force exerted from the outside; the absence of food in the desert is a physical condition of the outside world. We may therefore frame the following rough definitions. *Acts freely done are those whose immediate causes are psychological states in the agent. Acts not freely done are those whose immediate causes are states of affairs external to the agent.*

It is plain that if we define free will in this way, then free will certainly exists, and the philosopher's denial of its existence is seen to be what it is—nonsense. For it is obvious that all those actions of men which we should ordinarily attribute to the exercise of their free will, or of which we should say that they freely chose to do them, are in fact actions which have been caused by their own desires, wishes, thoughts, emotions, impulses, or other psychological states.

In applying our definition we shall find that it usually works well, but that there are some puzzling cases which it does not seem exactly to fit. These puzzles can always be solved by paying careful attention to the ways in which words are used, and remembering that they are not always used consistently. I have space for only one example. Suppose that a thug threatens to shoot you unless you give him your wallet, and suppose that you do so. Do you, in giving him your wallet, do so of your own free will or not? If we apply our definition, we find that you acted freely, since the immediate cause of the action was not an actual outside force but the fear of death, which is a psychological cause. Most people, however, would say that you did not act of your own free will but under compulsion. Does this show that our definition is wrong? I do not think so. Aristotle, who gave a solution of the problem of free will substantially the same as ours (though he did not use the term "free will") admitted that there are what he called "mixed" or borderline cases in which it is difficult to know whether we

ought to call the acts free or compelled. In the case under discussion, though no actual force was used, the gun at your forehead so nearly approximated to actual force that we tend to say the case was one of compulsion. It is a borderline case.

Here is what may seem like another kind of puzzle. According to our view an action may be free though it could have been predicted beforehand with certainty. But suppose you told a lie, and it was certain beforehand that you would tell it. How could one then say, "You could have told the truth"? The answer is that it is perfectly true that you could have told the truth *if* you had wanted to. In fact you would have done so, for in that case the causes producing your action, namely your desires, would have been different, and would therefore have produced different effects. It is a delusion that predictability and free will are incompatible. This agrees with common sense. For if, knowing your character, I predict that you will act honorably, no one would say when you do act honorably, that this shows you did not do so of your own free will.

Since free will is a condition of moral responsibility, we must be sure that our theory of free will gives a sufficient basis for it. To be held morally responsible for one's actions means that one may be justly punished or rewarded, blamed or praised, for them. But it is not just to punish a man for what he cannot help doing. How can it be just to punish him for an action which it was certain beforehand that he would do? We have not attempted to decide whether, as a matter of fact, all events, including human actions, are completely determined. For that question is irrelevant to the problem of free will. But if we assume for the purposes of argument that complete determinism is true, but that we are nevertheless free, it may then be asked whether such a deterministic free will is compatible with moral responsibility. For it may seem unjust to punish a man for an action which it could have been predicted with certainty beforehand that he would do.

But that determinism is incompatible with moral responsibility is as much a delusion as that it is incompatible with free will. You do not excuse a man for doing a wrong act because, knowing his character, you felt certain beforehand that he would do it. Nor do you deprive a man of a reward or prize because, knowing his goodness or his capabilities, you felt certain beforehand that he would win it.

Volumes have been written on the justification of punishment. But so far as it affects the question of free will, the essential principles involved are quite simple. The punishment of a man for doing a wrong act is justified, either on the ground that it will correct his own character, or that it will deter other people from doing similar acts. The instrument of punishment has been in the past, and no doubt still is, often unwisely used; so that it may often have done more harm than good. But that is not relevant to our present problem. Punishment, if and when it is justified, is justified only on one or both of the grounds just mentioned. The question then is how, if we assume determinism, punishment can correct character or deter people from evil actions.

Suppose that your child develops a habit of telling lies. You give him a mild beating. Why? Because you believe that his personality is such that the usual motives for telling the truth do not cause him to do so. You therefore supply the missing cause, or motive, in the shape of pain and the fear of future pain if he repeats his untruthful behavior. And you hope that a few treatments of this kind will condition him to the habit of truth-telling, so that he will come to tell the truth without the infliction of pain. You assume that his actions are determined by causes, but that the usual causes of truth-telling do not in him produce their usual effects. You therefore supply him with an artificially injected motive, pain and fear, which you think will in the future cause him to speak truthfully.

The principle is exactly the same where you hope, by punishing one man, to deter others from wrong actions. You believe that the fear of punishment will cause those who might otherwise do evil to do well.

We act on the same principle with non-human, and even with inanimate, things, if they do not behave in the way we think they ought to behave. The rose bushes in the garden produce only small and poor blooms, whereas we want large and rich ones. We supply a cause which will produce large blooms, namely fertilizer. Our automobile does not go properly. We supply a cause which will make it go better, namely oil in the works. The punishment for the man, the fertilizer for the plant, and the oil for the car, are all justified by the same principle and in the same way. The only difference is that different kinds of things require different kinds of causes to make them do what they should. Pain may be the appropriate remedy to apply, in certain cases, to human beings, and oil to the machine. It is, of course, of no use to inject motor oil into the boy or to beat the machine.

Thus we see that moral responsibility is not only consistent with determinism, but requires it. The assumption on which punishment is based is that human behavior is causally determined. If pain could not be a cause of truth-telling there would be no justification at all for punishing lies. If human actions and volitions were uncaused, it would be useless either to punish or reward, or indeed to do anything else to correct people's bad behavior. For nothing that you could do would in any way influence them. Thus moral responsibility would entirely disappear. If there were no determinism of human beings at all, their actions would be completely unpredictable and capricious, and therefore irresponsible. And this is in itself a strong argument against the common view of philosophers that free will means being undetermined by causes.

DISCUSSION QUESTIONS

1. According to Stace, what is the relationship between free will and morality? Do you agree with him? Why or why not?

2. Stace maintains that an action can be both predictable and free. What is his argument? Do you agree with it? Why or why not?

3. According to Stace, what is incorrect about the classic philosophical definition of free will as indeterminism? How does Staces's definition of free will correct the deficiencies in the classic definition? Is Stace's new definition an improvement over the classic one? Why or why not?

4. Stace justifies punishment on two grounds. What are they? Do you agree with them? Why or why not?

5. Why does Stace believe that moral responsibility requires determinism? Do you agree with him? Why or why not?

6. Imagine a dialogue between Holbach, Campbell, and Stace on the topic of free will. Whose position on free will would be the strongest, and why?

7. Consider a film from chapter 3—*The Matrix*. Do you think Stace would contend that we have free will when we are in the Matrix? Why or why not? What, if anything, would be the difference between the actions of persons in the Matrix and persons not in the Matrix according to Stace?

■ ■ ■ ■ ■ ■ ■ ■ ■ ■ ■ ■ ■ ■ ■ ■ ■ ■

A Clockwork Orange
[Gr. Brit. 1971] 2 hrs., 20 min.
Directed by Stanley Kubrick

■ ■ ■ ■ ■ ■ ■ ■ ■ ■ ■ ■ ■ ■ ■ ■ ■ ■

Alex de Large (Malcolm McDowell) is the leader of a loathsome group of young men who spend night after night committing acts of malevolent violence. When Alex's leadership of his "droogs" begins to slip, he asserts his authority over them with force. The droogs are not happy about this and plot against Alex. After a night of violence at a health farm at the edge of town, his droogs knock him out and leave him at the scene of the crime. Alex is caught by the authorities and sentenced to fourteen years in prison. Despising prison life, Alex undergoes a radical government experiment seeking to control the escalating violence in society. Through a type of aversion therapy called the Ludovico Technique, Alex comes to be sick to his stomach every time he ponders a sexual or violent act. After being "cured" of his desire to commit sexual or violent acts, Alex is released from prison.

However, life outside prison does not go well, as Alex finds himself living in constant terror of those who wish to do harm to him, particularly those to whom he has done harm in the past. Given that he has an aversion to violent acts, he is unable to protect himself against them. Alex is first beaten up by a group of tramps upon whom he had previously inflicted violence. However, he is rescued from being murdered by the tramps by two police officers, who turn out to be some of his old droogs. The droogs beat him up and leave him at the edge of town. When he goes to a house seeking help, it turns out to be the house at which he committed a rape, and the victim later died. Her husband recognizes Alex and tortures him by playing Beethoven's Ninth Symphony, a piece of music that he had formerly loved but that now causes him become extremely ill because of the aversion therapy. The music drives Alex to attempt to kill himself by jumping out a window.

After a period of hospitalization, he fully recovers from his injuries and learns that the government has reversed his aversion to violence. Alex is restored to his former nature, and the government promises to provide him with a solid job and income only if he will not complain about the "failure" of his conditioning. He agrees and is treated to an audio performance of Beethoven's Ninth Symphony in the hospital. Alex shows no ill effects from the music, and we are led to believe that he is on the path to regaining his previous nature. *A Clockwork Orange* is based on a novel of the same name by Anthony Burgess.

DISCUSSION QUESTIONS

1. Stace contends that without free will there can be no morality. If we did not have the freedom to choose to obey or disobey moral precepts, then all moral precepts would be meaningless. Has the

aversion therapy robbed Alex of his free will? Do moral precepts become meaningless for Alex after his aversion therapy? Discuss.

2.   Alex requests that he be subjected to the government's new procedure to reform prisoners. Consider this dialogue with the prison priest (Godfrey Quigley):

ALEX   "I don't care about the danger, Father. I just want to be good. I want for the rest of my life to be one act of goodness."

PRIEST   "The question is whether or not this technique really makes a man good. Goodness comes from within. Goodness is chosen. When a man cannot choose, he ceases to be a man."

Is the priest right? Do we cease to be human beings when we do not have free will? Discuss.

3.   Alex's aversion to "evil" is demonstrated to an audience by a minister (Anthony Sharp). Consider the following dialogue between the minister and the priest that follows the demonstration:

MINISTER   "Fine. Absolutely fine. You see, Ladies and Gentlemen, our subject is, you see, impelled towards good by paradoxically being impelled toward evil. The intention to act violently is accompanied by strong feelings of physical distress. To counter these, the subject has to switch to a diametrically opposed attitude. Any questions?"

PRIEST   "Choice! The boy has no real choice, has he? Self-interest, fear of physical pain drove him to that grotesque act of self-abasement. Its insincerity was clearly to be seen. He ceases also to be a creature capable of moral choice."

MINISTER   "Padre, these are subtleties. We are not concerned with motive, with the higher ethics; we are concerned only with cutting down crime. And with relieving the ghastly congestion in our prisons . . . He will be your true Christian, ready to turn the other cheek. Ready to be crucified rather than crucify, sick to the very heart at the thought even of killing a fly. Reclamation, joy before the angels of God. The point is that it works!"

Who makes the better point, the minister or the priest? Should we be concerned with the motive for Alex's actions or just with his actions in themselves? Discuss.

4.   After the police beat him up, Alex finds himself in the house of Mr. Alexander (Patrick Magee), the man whose wife Alex raped, and who subsequently died. Upon seeing Alex, Mr. Alexander phones his friends and plots to use him to bring down the government in the next election. Here is what Mr. Alexander says on the phone: "I tell you, sir, they have turned this young man into something other than a human being. He has no power of choice any more. He's committed to socially acceptable acts, a little machine capable only of good. He can be the most potent weapon imaginable to ensure that the Government is not returned at the next election. The Government's great boast, as you know sir, is the way they have dealt with crime in the last few months. Recruiting brutal young roughs into the police, proposing debilitation and will-sapping techniques of conditioning. Oh, we've seen it all before in other countries. The thin end of the wedge. Before we know where we are we shall have the full apparatus of totalitarianism. This young boy is a living witness to these diabolical proposals. The people—the common people—must know . . . must see! There are rare traditions of liberty to defend. The tradition of liberty means all. The common people will let it go! Oh, yes—they will sell liberty for a quieter life. That is why they must be led. . . ." Do you think society would be justified in

conditioning criminals like Alex, if it were possible? Why or why not? Is such a social policy one step away from a totalitarian form of government? Discuss.

5.   Assume that everything in this film is the same except for the location of Alex's release from govern-ment control. Imagine that instead of being released back into his old environment, he is released far from his family and former "droogs," and the scenes of his crimes. Do you think that a reversal of his aversions to sex and violence would still have been necessary? Why or why not? Would the film have had a different message about the social implications of denying persons of their free will?

6.   In the end, what is the philosophical message of A Clockwork Orange regarding human freedom? Do you agree with it? Why or why not?

CLARENCE DARROW

THE CRIME OF COMPULSION

C larence Darrow uses determinism to argue that criminals are not responsible for their actions. Even though Nathan Leopold, Jr., and Richard Loeb confessed to having committed the crimes of kidnapping and murder, Darrow argues that their actions were determined by heredity and environment. Therefore, they are no more responsible for their crimes than they are for "any other product of heredity," such as their hairline or eye color. The judge in their case, John R. Caverly, spared Leopold and Loeb from the death penalty, sentencing them to life in prison.

Leopold and Loeb were intelligent young men from affluent families. Eighteen-year-old Leopold was a law student at the University of Chicago and was planning to attend Harvard Law School the following year. Seventeen-year-old Loeb was the youngest graduate ever of the University of Michigan. Together they planned the "perfect crime."

On May 21, 1924, they kidnapped Bobby Franks, a fourteen-year-old boy from one of the wealthiest families in Chicago, murdered him, and then disposed of his body and clothing. Franks' parents were then contacted with a ransom demand, but just before they were to pay it, their son's body was found. A pair of horn-rimmed glasses, later determined to be Leopold's, were found near the body. Both pleaded guilty to kidnapping and murder, and a hearing was set to determine their punishment.

While the prosecutor and the public demanded the death penalty, Darrow argued that they be spared because their actions were beyond their control. Because they pleaded guilty, only a judge, not a jury, would determine their punishment. If they had pleaded innocent, a trial would have taken place—not a hearing—and a jury would have decided their punishment. Given the sentiment of the masses in favor of their execution, Darrow felt that he had a better chance in convincing a judge who was described as a "kindly and discerning man" to spare them than a jury.

His defense tactic paid off. On August 22, 1924, Darrow presented his closing arguments. They went on for twelve hours and left many in the courtroom, including the judge, in tears. Two weeks later, Judge Caverly reached a decision. He said that his judgment could not be affected by the causes of crime and that the court had no business in deciding who or what was ultimately responsible for actions. Thus, the age of the defendants and the fact that criminologists might learn something by studying them persuaded him to sentence Leopold and Loeb to life in prison, rather than to death.

Loeb was killed in prison by another inmate in 1936, and Leopold was released from prison in 1958. To escape the publicity stemming from the release of the film *Compulsion* (1959), which deals directly with his crime, Leopold moved to Puerto Rico. He died in 1971.

Clarence Darrow (1867–1938) was a famous American lawyer, well known for his wit, compassion, and agnosticism. He began his career as a corporate attorney in Illinois, though he later switched to defending members of the working class. He famously defended striking union workers against his former employer in the Pullman strike of 1894. He later left the practice of labor law to devote himself to opposing the death penalty, which he felt conflicted with the progress of humanity.

Darrow is best known for defending Leopold and Loeb in 1924, and John T. Scopes in the so-called Monkey trial in 1925. During the Leopold and Loeb trial, it was rumored that Darrow was being paid $1 million for his services. Though ordinary Americans felt betrayed by Darrow and were angry at him, he and his two co-counsels were paid a total of $100,000 for the defense—and that was only after several months of persistent requests to the Loeb family for payment.

Both trials have been the subject of numerous film adaptations. *Inherit the Wind* (see the film box in chapter 1) is an excellent film adaptation of the Scopes trial, and *Compulsion* is an adaptation of the Leopold and Loeb trial. After the Scopes trial, Darrow went into semiretirement, taking on only a few more cases. He wrote numerous widely read pamphlets on topics such as resisting evil, recognizing realism in art and literature, and facing life fearlessly, in addition to a number of books.

The following is a selection from Darrow's 1924 plea in defense of Loeb and Leopold, which is collected in *Attorney for the Damned* (1957), edited by Arthur Weinberg.

I have tried to study the lives of these two most unfortunate boys. Three months ago, if their friends and the friends of the family had been asked to pick out the most promising lads of their acquaintance, they probably would have picked these two boys. With every opportunity, with plenty of wealth, they would have said that those two would succeed.

In a day, by an act of madness, all this is destroyed, until the best they can hope for now is a life of silence and pain, continuing to the end of their years.

How did it happen?

Let us take Dickie Loeb first.

I do not claim to know how it happened; I have sought to find out. I know that something, or some combination of things, is, responsible for this mad act. I know that there are no accidents in nature. I know that effect follows cause. I know that, if I were wise enough, and knew enough about, this case, I could lay my finger on the cause. I will do the best I can, but it is largely speculation.

The child, of course, is born without knowledge.

Impressions are made upon its mind as it goes along. Dickie Loeb was a child of wealth and opportunity. Over and over in this court Your Honor has been asked, and other courts have been asked, to consider boys who have no chance; they have been asked to consider the poor, whose home had been the street, with no education and no opportunity in life, and they have done it, and done it rightfully.

But, Your Honor, it is just as often a great misfortune to be the child of the rich as it is to be the child of the poor. Wealth has its misfortunes. Too much, too great opportunity and advantage, given to a child has its misfortunes, and I am asking Your Honor to consider the rich as well as the poor (and nothing else). Can I find what was wrong? I think I can. Here was a boy at a tender age, placed in the hands of a governess, intellectual, vigorous, devoted, with a strong ambition for the welfare of this boy. He was pushed in his studies, as plants are forced in hothouses. He had no pleasures, such as a boy should have, except as they were gained by lying and cheating.

Now, I am not criticizing the nurse. I suggest that some day Your Honor look at her picture. It explains her fully. Forceful, brooking no interference, she loved the boy, and her ambition was that he should reach the highest perfection. No time to pause, no time to stop from one book to another, no time to have those pleasures which a boy ought to have to create a normal life. And what happened? Your Honor, what would happen? Nothing strange or unusual. This nurse was with him all the time, except when he stole out at night, from two to fourteen years of age. He, scheming and planning as healthy boys would do, to get out from under her restraint; she, putting before him the best books, which children generally do not want; and he, when she was not looking, reading detective stories, which he devoured, story after story, in his young life. Of all of this there can be no question.

What is the result? Every story he read was a story of crime. We have a statute in this state, passed only last year, if I recall it, which forbids minors reading stories of crime. Why? There is only one reason. Because the legislature in its wisdom felt that it would produce criminal tendencies in the boys who read them. The legislature of this state has given its opinion, and forbidden boys to read these books. He read them day after day. He never stopped. While he was passing through college at Ann Arbor he was still reading them. When he was a senior he read them, and almost nothing else.

Now, these facts are beyond dispute. He early developed the tendency to mix with crime, to be a detective; as a little boy shadowing people on the street; as a little child going out with his fantasy of being the head of a band of criminals and directing them on the street. How did this grow and develop in him? Let us see. It seems to be as natural as the day following the night. Every detective story is a story of a sleuth getting the best of it: trailing some unfortunate individual through devious ways until his victim is finally landed in jail or stands on the gallows. They all show how smart the detective is, and where the criminal himself falls down.

This boy early in his life conceived the idea that there could be a perfect crime, one that nobody could ever detect; that there could be one where the detective did not land his game—a perfect crime. He had been interested in the story of Charley Ross, who was kidnaped. He was interested in these things all his life. He believed in his childish way that a crime could be so carefully planned that there would be no detection, and his idea was to plan and accomplish a perfect crime. It would involve kidnaping and involve murder.

There had been growing in Dickie's brain, dwarfed and twisted—as every act in this case shows it to have been dwarfed and twisted—there had been growing this scheme, not due to any wickedness of Dickie Loeb, for he is a child. It grew as he grew; it grew from those around him; it grew from the lack of the proper training until it possessed him. He believed he could beat the police. He believed he could plan the perfect crime. He had thought of it and talked of it for years—had talked of it as a child, had worked at it as a child—this sorry act of his, utterly irrational and motiveless, a plan to commit a perfect crime which must contain kidnaping, and there must be ransom, or else it could not be perfect, and they must get the money. . . .

The law knows and has recognized childhood for many and many a long year. What do we know about childhood? The brain of the child is the home of dreams, of castles, of visions, of illusions and of delusions. In fact, there could be no childhood without delusions, for delusions are always more alluring than facts. Delusions, dreams and hallucinations are a part of the warp and woof of childhood. You know it and I know it. I remember, when I was a child, the men seemed as tall as the trees, the trees as tall as the mountains. I can remember very well when, as a little boy, I swam the deepest spot in the river for the first time. I swam breathlessly and landed with as much sense of glory and triumph as Julius Caesar felt when he led his army across the Rubicon. I have been back since, and I can almost step across the same place, but it seemed an ocean then. And those men whom I thought so wonderful were dead and left nothing behind. I had lived in a dream. I had never known the real world which I met, to my discomfort and despair, and that dispelled the illusions of my youth.

The whole life of childhood is a dream and an illusion, and whether they take one shape or another shape depends not upon the dreamy boy but on what surrounds him. As well might I have dreamed of burglars and wished to be one as to dream of policemen and wished to be one. Perhaps I was lucky, too, that I had no money. We have grown to think that the misfortune is in not having it. The great misfortune in this terrible case is the money. That has destroyed their lives. That has fostered these illusions. That has promoted this mad act. And, if Your Honor shall doom them to die, it will be because they are the sons of the rich. . . .

Now, to get back to Dickie Loeb. He was a child. The books he read by day were not the books he read by night. We are all of us molded somewhat by the influences around us, and of those, to people who read, perhaps books are the greatest and the strongest influences.

I know where my life has been molded by books, amongst other things. We all know where our lives have been influenced by books. The nurse, strict and jealous and watchful, gave him one kind of book; by night he would steal off and read the other.

Which, think you, shaped the life of Dickie Loeb? Is there any kind of question about it? A child. Was it pure maliciousness? Was a boy of five or six or seven to blame for it? Where did he get it? He got it where we all get our ideas, and these books became a part of his dreams and a part of his life, and as he grew up his visions grew to hallucinations.

He went out on the street and fantastically directed his companions, who were not there, in their various moves to complete the perfect crime. Can there be any sort of question about it?

Suppose, Your Honor, that instead of this boy being here in this court, under the plea of the State that Your Honor shall pronounce a sentence to hang him by the neck until dead, he had been taken to a pathological hospital to be analyzed, and the physicians had inquired into his case. What would they have said? There is only one thing that they could possibly have said. They would have traced everything back to the gradual growth of the child.

That is not all there is about it. Youth is hard enough. The only good thing about youth is that it has no thought and no care; and how blindly we can do things when we are young!

Where is the man who has not been guilty of delinquencies in youth? Let us be honest with ourselves. Let us look into our own hearts. How many men are there today—lawyers and congressmen and judges, and even state's attorneys—who have not been guilty of some mad act in youth? And if they did not get caught, or the consequences were trivial, it was their good fortune.

We might as well be honest with ourselves, Your Honor. Before I would tie a noose around the neck of a boy I would try to call back into my mind the emotions of youth. I would try to remember what the world looked like to me when I was a child. I would try to remember how strong were these instinctive, persistent emotions that moved my life. I would try to remember how weak and inefficient was youth in the presence of the surging, controlling feelings of the child. One that honestly remembers and asks himself the question and tries to unlock the door that he thinks is closed, and calls back the boy, can understand the boy.

But, Your Honor, that is not all there is to boyhood. Nature is strong and she is pitiless. She works in her own mysterious way, and we are her victims. We have not much to do with it ourselves. Nature takes this job in hand, and we play our parts. In the words of old Omar Khayyam, we are only:

But helpless pieces in the game He plays
Upon this checkerboard of nights and days;
Hither and thither moves, and checks, and slays,
And one by one back in closet lays.

What had this boy to do with it? He was not his own father; he was not his own mother; he was not his own grandparents. All of this was handed to him. He did not surround himself with governesses and wealth. He did not make himself. And yet he is to be compelled to pay.

There was a time in England, running down as late as the beginning of the last century, when judges used to convene court and call juries to try a horse, a dog, a pig, for crime. I have in my library a story of a judge and jury and lawyers trying and convicting an old sow for lying down on her ten pigs and killing them.

What does it mean? Animals were tried. Do you mean to tell me that Dickie Loeb had any more to do with his making than any other product of heredity that is born upon the earth? . . .

For God's sake, are we crazy? In the face of history, of every line of philosophy, against the teaching of every religionist and seer and prophet the world has ever given us, we are still doing what our barbaric ancestors did when they came out of the caves and the woods.

From the age of fifteen to the age of twenty or twenty-one, the child has the burden of adolescence, of puberty and sex thrust upon him. Girls are kept at home and carefully watched. Boys without instruction are left to work the period out for themselves. It may lead to excess. It may lead to disgrace. It may lead to perversion. Who is to blame? Who did it? Did Dickie Loeb do it?

Your Honor, I am almost ashamed to talk about it. I can hardly imagine that we are in the twentieth century. And yet there are men who seriously say that for what nature has done, for what life has done, for what training has done, you should hang these boys.

Now, there is no mystery about this case, Your Honor. I seem to be criticizing their parents. They had parents who were kind and good and wise in their way. But I say to you seriously that the parents are more responsible than these boys. And yet few boys had better parents.

Your Honor, it is the easiest thing in the world to be a parent. We talk of motherhood, and yet every woman can be a mother. We talk of fatherhood, and yet every man can be a father. Nature takes care of that. It is easy to be a parent. But to be wise and farseeing enough to understand the boy is another thing; only a very few are so wise and so farseeing as that. When I think of the light way nature has of picking our parents and populating the earth, having them born and die, I cannot hold human beings to the same degree of responsibility that young lawyers hold them when they are enthusiastic in a prosecution. I know what it means.

I know there are no better citizens in Chicago than the fathers of these poor boys. I know there were no better women than their mothers. But I am going to be honest with this court, if it is at the expense of both. I know that one of two things happened to Richard Loeb: that this terrible crime was inherent in his organism, and came from some ancestor; or that it came through his education and his training after he was born. Do I need to prove it? Judge Crowe said at one point in this case, when some witness spoke about their wealth, that "probably that was responsible."

To believe that any boy is responsible for himself or his early training is an absurdity that no lawyer or judge should be guilty of today. Somewhere this came to the boy. If his failing came from his heredity, I do not know where or how. None of us are bred perfect and pure; and the color of our hair, the color of our eyes, our stature, the weight and fineness of our brain, and everything about us could, with full knowledge, be traced with absolute certainty to somewhere. If we had the pedigree it could be traced just the same in a boy as it could in a dog, a horse or a cow.

I do not know what remote ancestors may have sent down the seed that corrupted him, and I do not know through how many ancestors it may have passed until it reached Dickie Loeb.

All I know is that it is true, and there is not a biologist in the world who will not say that I am right.

If it did not come that way, then I know that if he was normal, if he had been understood, if he had been trained as he should have been it would not have happened. Not that anybody may not slip, but I know it and Your Honor knows it, and every schoolhouse and every church in the land is an evidence of it. Else why build them?

Every effort to protect society is an effort toward training the youth to keep the path. Every bit of training in the world proves it, and it likewise proves that it sometimes fails. I know that if this boy had been understood and properly trained—properly for him—and the training that he got might have been the very best for someone; but if it had been the proper training for him he would not be in this courtroom today with the noose above his head. If there is responsibility anywhere, it is back of him; somewhere in the infinite number of his ancestors, or in his surroundings, or in both. And I submit, Your Honor, that under every principle of natural justice, under every principle of conscience, of right, and of law, he should not be made responsible for the acts of someone else. . . .

DISCUSSION QUESTIONS

1. Is Darrow a soft determinist or a hard determinist? Defend your position with quotes from him.

2. Does Darrow convince you that Leopold and Loeb were not responsible for their actions? Why or why not?

3. Darrow says that all of us are "molded somewhat by the influences around us, and of those, to people who read, perhaps books are the greatest and the strongest influences." Is Darrow right? What role did the detective stories that Loeb loved to read contribute to his actions? Can books "compel" us to commit crimes? Why or why not?

4. What is the meaning and significance of the passage from Omar Khayyam quoted by Darrow?

5. According to Darrow, how are Leopold and Loeb's parents responsible for their sons' actions? Is he right? Why or why not?

6. How might Campbell and Stace respond to Darrow's closing statement?

7. If you were the judge in this trial, what sentence would you give Leopold and Loeb? Why?

Compulsion
[USA 1959] 1 hour, 43 minutes
Directed by Richard Fleischer

*T*wo wealthy and brilliant students, Judd Steiner (Dean Stockwell) and Artie Straus (Bradford Dillman), develop a scheme to commit what they believe to be the perfect crime: the kidnapping and murder of a young boy, complete with a ransom demand. However, money is not Judd or Artie's true motive. The motives that spur the young men to commit the crime are quite unusual: Artie has a sadistic nature and a fascination with crime, and Judd has an interest in Nietzsche's theory of the superman and an intense love for Artie. The young men truly believe that they have committed the perfect crime until a pair of glasses is discovered next to the murder victim's body. Once the glasses are discovered, they are traced back to Judd, who insists that he lost them on a birding expedition the day before the murder. However, the police also trace the ransom note back to Judd's typewriter, and eventually both parties confess to the crime, each blaming the other for the actual murder.

When the young men are charged, their families hire Jonathan Wilk (Orson Welles) to defend them in court. While an initial plea of insanity is sought, Wilk alters the plea to guilty with mitigating circumstances. This plea assures that no jury will be present at the hearing. Wilk believes that it is better to leave the decision of whether to hang the boys to a judge. In a riveting speech, Wilk argues for the young men's lives, stating that he believes it was the circumstances of their upbringings that led to their criminal actions. The judge gives the boys two consecutive sentences: For the murder, they will serve the rest of their natural lives, and for the kidnapping, they will serve ninety-nine years. Although Wilk has saved their lives, Artie and Judd do not display gratitude toward him.

DISCUSSION QUESTIONS

1. Compare the case of Leopold and Loeb from Darrow's point of view and the case of Judd and Artie from the point of view of *Compulsion*. Which presents the stronger case for actions done through compulsion?

2.   Consider the following dialogue between Judd and Artie:

JUDD   "Please Artie, I'll do anything you say."

ARTIE   "Anything? I wanna do something really dangerous, something that'll have everybody talking, not just a few guys."

Does the film present Judd and Artie as being equally "compelled" toward committing their crime? Why or why not?

3.   Consider this exchange between Judd and Artie:

JUDD   "We agreed it was a true test of the superior intellect."

ARTIE   "Superior intellect!?"

What role does their intellect play in their actions? Do you think their actions are caused by internal, psychological events or by external, physical ones, or neither? What do you think Judd and Artie think?

4.   Consider the following dialogue between Judd and his girlfriend, Ruth (Diana Varsi).

RUTH   "What is it, Judd? You seem so sad."

JUDD   "Sad is a sentimental term. There's no such thing as sadness, only the reality of things happening."

RUTH   "You're not that cruel."

JUDD   "Murder is nothing. It's just a simple experience. Murder and rape. Do you know what beauty there is in evil?"

RUTH   "Is there?"

JUDD   "Yes."

Is Judd saying that in a deterministic universe there is no morality—only causes and effects? Why or why not?

5.   Consider this exchange between reporter, Sid (Martin Miller), and his ex-girlfriend, Ruth:

RUTH   "I can't help feeling sorry for Judd and for Artie."

SID   "Sorry for them! Ruth, they plotted a cold-blooded killing and went through with it like an experiment in chemistry."

RUTH   "Judd just isn't like that. Believe me—I know. . . . He was like a child, a sick, frightened child."

Do you feel sorry for Artie and Judd? Does it make any difference, how you feel about them if their actions were determined by their environment or not? Why or why not?

6.   Wilk says to the judge, "Your Honor, if these boys hang, you must do it. There can be no division of responsibility here. You can never explain that the rest overpowered you. It must be by your

deliberate, cool, premeditated act, without a chance to shift responsibility." Can the judge escape responsibility for the punishment he imposes on Artie and Judd? For example, can the judge argue back to Wilk that his environment—namely, the courtroom and American society—compelled him to punish Artie and Judd in the way he did? Would the judge be correct that his punishment was "compelled"? Why or why not? Is the possible case of the judge's compulsion different from the case of Artie and Judd's compulsion? Discuss.

BERNARD WILLIAMS

MORAL LUCK

B ernard Williams argues that while many wish to believe that all of our most deliberate decisions are within our control, many of them are not. Sometimes it happens that whether our moral behavior is good or bad depends on nothing less than chance. This idea in itself is not a new one. Ancient tragedians such as Sophocles knew this all too well: all of Oedipus's deliberate efforts to avoid killing his father were in a moment evaporated by fate. Just as chance events made Oedipus the hero of Thebes, so, too, did chance events take his hero status away from him.

Williams argues that any consideration of responsibility for our actions must take into account not only what we do voluntarily but also what role chance or luck play in the outcome of our deliberate actions. He contends that utilitarian and Kantian notions of moral responsibility leave no room for luck—for them, morality is immune to luck. Williams disagrees, and he uses a thought experiment involving a character named Paul Gauguin to prove his point.

William's Gauguin, like the real Gauguin, is a painter who has abandoned his family to pursue his painting career in Tahiti. Williams asks whether Gauguin's decision is rationally justified. He points out that in this case rational justification will be "retrospective," which means we cannot decide whether it was rationally justified until we know whether it resulted in him becoming a great painter. It is simply impossible to foresee whether Gauguin will succeed in his attempt to be a great painter. While he may have great talent, we do not know if this talent will manifest itself in the production of great works of art in Tahiti or how his decision to leave his family behind will affect the development of his talent. Williams says that "in such a situation the only thing that will justify his choice will be success itself," and the only thing that will make his decision rationally unjustified is failure.

However, not every success will rationally justify his decision, and not every failure will reveal it to be rationally unjustified. It all depends on the role of luck in his success and failure. "Some luck, in a decision of Gauguin's kind, is extrinsic to his project, some intrinsic," writes Williams; "both are necessary for success, and hence for actual justification, but only the latter relates to unjustification." *Intrinsic luck* is luck arising directly out of the project at hand, and *extrinsic luck* is luck arising out of elements external to the project at hand.

An example of intrinsic luck leading to failure would be if, upon arriving in Tahiti, Gaughin finds that the beautiful surroundings distract him from his efforts as a painter. This type of luck would make his decision rationally unjustified. An example of extrinsic luck leading to failure would be if, upon arriving in Tahiti, he trips over a fallen palm tree and injures himself in such a way that he can never paint again. This type of luck would result in the suspension of a decision as to the rational justification of his decision: owing to bad extrinsic luck, he will be neither justified nor unjustified because his painting project in Tahiti was never carried out. So, in order for Gauguin's decision to be rationally justified, intrinsic luck is required. "The intrinsic luck in Gauguin's case concentrates itself on virtually the one question of whether he is a genuinely gifted painter who can succeed in doing genuinely valuable work," says Williams.

William's analysis of the role of luck in rational justification presents a challenge to notions of morality that rely on rational justification, namely, utilitarianism and Kantianism. "Utilitarian formulations are not going to contribute any more to understanding these situations than do formulations in terms of rules," writes Williams. Utilitarianism "will miss a very important dimension of such cases, the question of what 'failure' may relevantly be." Kantianism does not fare much better than utilitarianism, for it leaves no place for luck in considerations of responsibility. According to Kant, we are morally responsible only for what we do voluntarily, and morality is completely disconnected from individual personality and circumstance. For Kant, the principle or rule that underlies our action is the same for all persons regardless of what may come about after the application of the rule. Moreover, the principle of action is entirely discoverable through reason alone. However, if Williams is correct, and rational justification is in some cases dependent upon luck, then Kantianism as well as utilitarianism fails to account for an important aspect of rational justification: luck. Williams opens the way for a consideration of cases in which one is rationally justified in acting but morally unjustified, and vice versa—for example, cases in which Gauguin is rationally justified in abandoning his family and going to Tahiti, but not morally justified, and vice versa. As such, the concept of moral luck presents utilitarianism and Kantianism with a serious problem.

Bernard Williams (1929–2003), a British philosopher, specialized in moral philosophy and the philosophy of mind. He was born in Westcliff-on-Sea, Essex; graduated from Balliol College, Oxford, in 1951; and served in the Royal Air Force in Canada for one year, flying Spitfires. He then taught at Oxford University, University College–London, and Bedford College before becoming Knightsbridge Professor of Philosophy at Cambridge University in 1967. After serving as provost at King's College, Cambridge University, from 1979 until 1987, he held posts at the University of California at Berkeley and Oxford University. Williams was knighted in 1999 and sat on the board of the English National Opera. In his writings, he is critical of both utilitarianism and Kantianism, offering in their place a moral philosophy that affords a much more positive role to self-interest in moral action. He is the author of *Morality: An Introduction to Ethics* (1972), *Problems of Self* (1973), *Descartes: The Project of Pure Inquiry* (1978), *Moral Luck* (1981), *Ethics and the Limits of Philosophy* (1985), *Shame and Necessity* (1993), *Making Sense of Humanity* (1995), and *Truth and Truthfulness: An Essay in Genealogy* (2002). The following essay, "Moral Luck," was first published in 1976 in *Aristotelian Society*.

Let us take first an outline example of the creative artist who turns away from definite and pressing human claims on him in order to live a life in which, as he supposes, he can pursue his art. Without feeling that we are limited by any historical facts, let us call him *Gauguin*. Gauguin might have been a man who was not at all interested in the claims on him, and simply preferred to live another life, and from that life, and perhaps from that preference, his best paintings came. That sort of case, in which the claims of others simply have no hold on the agent, is not what concerns me here, though it serves to remind us of something related to the present concerns, that while we are sometimes guided by the notion that it would be the best of worlds in which morality were universally respected and all men were of a disposition to affirm it, we have in fact deep and persistent reasons to be grateful that that is not the world we have.

Let us take, rather, a Gauguin who is concerned about these claims and what is involved in their being neglected (we may suppose this to be grim), and that he nevertheless, in the face of that, opts for the other life. This other life he might perhaps not see very determinately under the category of realising his gifts as a painter, but, to make things simpler, let us add that he does see it determinately in that light—it is as a life which will enable him really to be a painter that he opts for it. It will then be clearer what will count for him as eventual success in his project—at least, some possible outcomes will be clear examples of success (which does not have to be the same thing as recognition), however many others may be unclear.

Whether he will succeed cannot, in the nature of the case, be foreseen. We are not dealing here with the removal of an external obstacle to something which, once that is removed, will fairly predictably go through. Gauguin, in our story, is putting a great deal on a possibility which has not unequivocally declared itself. I want to explore and uphold the claim that in such a situation the only thing that will justify his choice will be success itself. If he fails—and we shall come shortly to what, more precisely, failure may be— then he did the wrong thing, not just in the sense in which that platitudinously follows, but in the sense that having done the wrong thing in those circumstances he has no basis for the thought that he was justified in acting as he did. If he succeeds, he does have a basis for that thought.

As I have already indicated. I will leave to the end the question of how such notions of justification fit in with distinctively moral ideas. One should be warned already, however, that, even if Gauguin can be ultimately justified, that need not provide him with any way of justifying himself to others, or at least to all others. Thus he may have no way of bringing it about that those who suffer

from his decision will have no justified ground of reproach. Even if he succeeds, he will not acquire a right that they accept what he has to say; if he fails, he will not even have anything to say.

The justification, if there is to be one, will be essentially retrospective. Gauguin could not do something which is thought to be essential to rationality and to the notion of justification itself, which is that one should be in a position to apply the justifying considerations at the time of the choice and in advance of knowing whether one was right (in the sense of its coming out right). How this can be in general will form a major part of the discussion. I do not want, at this stage of the argument, to lay much weight on the notion of morality, but it may help to throw some light on the matter of prior justification if we bring in briefly the narrower question whether there could be a prior justification for Gauguin's choice in terms of moral rules.

A moral theorist, recognizing that some value attached to the success of Gauguin's project and hence possibly to his choice, might try to accommodate that choice within a framework of moral rules, by forming a subsidiary rule which could, before the outcome, justify that choice. What could that rule be? It could not be that one is morally justified in deciding to neglect other claims if one is a great creative artist: apart from doubts about its content, the saving clause begs the question which at the relevant time one is in no position to answer. On the other hand, ". . . if one is convinced that one is a great creative artist" will serve to make obstinacy and fatuous self-delusion conditions of justification, while ". . . if one is reasonably convinced that one is a great creative artist" is, if anything, worse. What is reasonable conviction supposed to be in such a case? Should Gauguin consult professors of art? The absurdity of such riders surely expresses an absurdity in the whole enterprise of trying to find a place for such cases within the rules.

Utilitarian formulations are not going to contribute any more to understanding these situations than do formulations in terms of rules. They can offer the thought "it is better (worse) that he did it," where the force of that is, approximately, "it is better (worse) that it happened," but this in itself does not help towards a characterization of the agent's decision or its possible justification, and Utilitarianism has no special materials of its own to help in that. It has its own well-known problems, too, in spelling out the content of the "better"—on standard doctrine, Gauguin's decision would seem to have been a better thing, the more popular a painter he eventually became. But there is something more interesting than that kind of difficulty. The Utilitarian perspective, not uniquely but clearly, will miss a very important dimension of such cases, the question of what "failure" may relevantly be. From the perspective of consequences, the goods or benefits for the sake of which Gauguin's choice was made either materialise in some degree, or do not materialise. But it matters considerably to the thoughts we are considering, in what way the project fails to come off, if it fails. If Gauguin sustains some injury on the way to Tahiti which prevents his ever painting again, that certainly means that his decision (supposing it now to be irreversible) was for nothing, and indeed there is nothing in the outcome to set against the other people's loss. But that train of events does not provoke the thought in question, that after all he was wrong and unjustified. He does not, and never will, know whether he was wrong. What would prove him wrong in his project would not just be that it failed, but that he failed.

This distinction shows that while Gauguin's justification is in some ways a matter of luck, it is not equally a matter of all kinds of luck. It matters how intrinsic the cause of failure is to the project itself. The occurrence of an injury is, relative to these undertakings at least, luck of the most external and incident kind. Irreducibly, luck of this kind affects whether he will be justified or not, since if it strikes, he will not be justified. But it is too external for it to unjustify him, something which only his failure as a painter can do; yet still that is, at another level, luck, the luck of being able to be as he hoped he might be. It might be wondered whether that is *luck* at all, or, if so, whether it may not be luck of that constitutive kind which affects everything and which we have already left on one side. But it is more than that. It is not merely luck that he is such a man, but luck relative to the deliberations that went into his decision, that he turns out to be such a man: he might (epistemically) not have been. That is what sets the problem.

In some cases, though perhaps not in Gauguin's, success in such decisions might be thought not to be a matter of epistemic luck relative to the decision. There might be grounds for saying that the person who is prepared to take the decision, and was in fact right, actually knew that he would succeed, however subjectively uncertain he may have been. But even if this is right for some cases, it does not help with the problems of retrospective justification. For the concept of knowledge here is itself applied retrospectively, and while there is nothing wrong with that, it does not enable the agent at the time of his decision to make any distinctions he could not already make. As one might say, even if it did turn out in such a case that the agent did know, it was still luck, relative to the considerations available to him at the time and at the level at which he made his decision, that he should turn out to have known.

Some luck, in a decision of Gauguin's kind, is extrinsic to his project, some intrinsic; both are necessary for success, and hence for actual justification, but only the latter relates to unjustification. If we now broaden the range of cases slightly, we shall be able to see more clearly the notion of intrinsic luck. In Gauguin's case the nature of the project is such that two distinctions do, roughly, coincide. One is a distinction between luck intrinsic to the project, and luck extrinsic to it; the other is a distinction between what is, and what is not, determined by him and by what he is. The intrinsic luck in Gauguin's case concentrates itself on virtually the one question of whether he is a genuinely gifted painter who can succeed in doing genuinely valuable work. Not all the conditions of the project's coming off lie in him, obviously, since others' actions and refrainings provide many necessary conditions of its coming off—and that is an important locus of extrinsic luck. But the conditions of its coming off which are relevant to unjustification, the locus of intrinsic luck, largely lie in him—which is not to say, of course, that they depend on his will, though some may. This rough coincidence of two distinctions is a feature of this case. But in others, the locus of intrinsic luck (intrinsic, that is to say, to the project) may lie partly outside the agent, and this is an important, and indeed the more typical, case.

DISCUSSION QUESTIONS

1. Does Williams believe that we have control over our actions? Why or why not?

2. Do you think we should be responsible only for actions that we voluntarily do? What does Williams think?

3. Why does Williams believe that rational justifications involve a degree of luck? Do you agree with him? Why or why not?

4. Why does Williams believe that the utilitarian perspective misses an important aspect concerning Gauguin's situation? What is that aspect? Do you agree with him? Why or why not?

5. Nathan Leopold dropped his horn-rimmed glasses near the body of Bobby Franks. Was this a case of intrinsic or extrinsic luck?

6. In his effort to move far away from Polibus, whom he assumed was his father, Oedipus met Laius, his real father, on the road from Corinth to Thebes. Was this a case of intrinsic or extrinsic luck?

Being There
[USA 1979] 2 hours, 10 minutes
Directed by Hal Ashby

Chance (Peter Sellers) has lived his entire life as an uneducated gardener. Taken in at a young age by Mr. Jennings, a wealthy Washington, DC, resident, Chance's only education came through what he learned by watching television. After the death of Mr. Jennings, Chance has to venture out on his own into a world he knows only from the television screen. Wearing the luxurious-looking but dated clothes of his former guardian, Chance accidentally is struck by a car carrying Eve Rand (Shirley MacLaine), the wife of well-off Benjamin Rand (Melvyn Douglas). To keep publicity to a minimum, Chance is brought to the Rand estate to recuperate. He soon strikes up a friendship with Benjamin Rand, who in turn introduces him to his good friend, the president of the United States.

Both Benjamin, who is on his deathbed, and the president, are greatly impressed by the simplicity and depth of what they take to be Chance's political and economic "philosophy." When they ask Chance complex political and economic questions, he replies with only simplistic statements about gardening. An interview in place of the vice president with Chance on national television is met with a high public approval rating for the gardener, and a dinner with ambassadors from around the world spurs the belief that he is conversant in many languages and is widely read. No one who meets or hears Chance after he leaves the Jennings home believes that he is anything less than an astute, sensitive, politically savvy man.

In the meantime, Eve falls in love with Chance, and Chance becomes the object of an intensive investigation by the government, which reveals him to be a man without a history. The explanation must be that the CIA destroyed his files. Or was it the FBI? The film ends with the funeral of Benjamin Rand and murmurs that Chance could be the man who unseats the president in the next election. Only those who met Chance at Mr. Jennings' house—and the viewers—knows that he is a menial gardener. For everyone else, Chance's honesty, innocence, and childlike simplicity are a refreshing break from the usual level of political discourse: he becomes the most discussed man in the nation and, quite possibly, the next president.

DISCUSSION QUESTIONS

1. To what extent, if at all, does Chance exhibit free will?

2. Bernard Williams says that it sometimes happens that whether our moral behavior is good or bad depends on nothing less than chance. Does Peter Sellers's character "Chance" illustrate this point? Why or why not?

3. Williams says that any consideration of responsibility for our actions must take into account not only what we do voluntarily but also the role of chance or luck in the outcome of our deliberate actions. For Williams, the weakness of utilitarian and Kantian notions of morality is that they leave no room for luck. Is Peter Sellers's character morally responsible for his actions after leaving the home of Mr. Jennings? Why or why not? Compare your response to that of a utilitarian, a Kantian, and Williams.

4. Does Peter Sellers's character illustrate that Williams leaves *too much* room for moral luck? Why or why not?

5. Discuss the type of "luck" experienced by Peter Sellers's character. Is it what Williams would call "intrinsic" or "extrinsic" luck? Both? Neither? Why or why not?

6. Consider the following exchange between Franklin (David Clennon), a lawyer who met Chance at Mr. Jennings's estate and his wife, Johanna (Denise DuBarry):

   FRANKLIN   "It's that gardener!"

   JOHANNA   "Yes, Chauncey Gardiner."

   FRANKLIN   "No! He's a real gardener!"

   JOHANNA   "He does talk like one, but I think he's brilliant."

   Do you think the American public would find Chance brilliant? Why or why not? Would it matter to them if he had studied for years at a prestigious university or learned everything he knew through television and gardening?

7. Louise (Ruth Attaway), the woman who cared for Mr. Jennings and Chance, sees him being interviewed on the television one night and says the following: "Gobbledegook! All the time he talked gobbledegook! An' it's for sure a white man's world in America, hell, I raised that boy since he was the size of a puissant an' I'll say right now he never learned to read an' write—no sir! Had no brains at all, was stuffed with rice puddin' between the ears! Short-changed by the Lord and dumb as a jackass an' look at him now! Yes, sir, all you gotta be is white in America an' you get whatever you want! Just listen to that boy—gobbledegook!" If Chance were black and used the same language and mannerisms, do you think he would be the confidant of Benjamin Rand and a potential president? Is there a connection between race and moral luck? Is this something for which Williams needs to account? Why or why not?

8. Consider this exchange between Chance and a publisher named Stiegler (Richard McKenzie):

   STIEGLER   "Mr. Gardiner, my editors and I have been wondering if you'd consider writing a book for us? Something on your political philosophy. What do you say?"

   CHANCE   "I can't write."

   STIEGLER   "Of course, who can nowadays? I have trouble writing a postcard to my children! Look, we could give you a six-figure advance, provide you with the very best ghostwriters, research assistants, proofreaders. . . ."

CHANCE   "I can't read."

STIEGLER   "Of course not! No one has the time to read! One glances at things, watches television. . . ."

CHANCE   "Yes. I like to watch."

STIEGLER   "Sure you do! No one reads! Listen, book publishing isn't exactly a bed of roses these days!"

Are events like this "lucky" ones for Chance? In other words, is the opportunity to produce a book even though he cannot read or write best described as an example of luck, moral or otherwise? Why or why not?

9. Nothing in Chance's life seems to be in his control, and most everything that happens in the world is beyond his understanding, yet everything always seems to work out for the best for him. Is this a good life? Would you want to be Chance? Why or why not?

SARVEPALLI RADHAKRISHNAN

KARMA AND FREEDOM

Sarvepalli Radhakrishnan argues that the Hindu doctrine of Karma, or connection with the past, is consistent with human, creative freedom. According to the law of Karma, our lives are never subject to the capriciousness of fate, luck, or chance. Karma is a principle of continuity wherein the effects of actions become physically and morally part of the organism and the environment. "Every single thought, word and deed enters into the living chain of causes which makes us what we are," says Radhakrishnan. These thoughts, words, and deeds become part of the permanent structure of our lives. For Hindus, who believe in reincarnation, our karmic structure is carried into each succeeding cycle of existence. In other words, what we do in this life carries over into the next; what we do in the next life carries over into the succeeding life; and so on.

While some might think that the law of Karma is ultimately a denial of human freedom, Radhakrishnan argues otherwise. "The law that links us with the past also asserts that it can be subjugated by our free action," he maintains. "Though the past may present obstacles, they must yield to the creative power in man in proportion to its sincerity and insistence." We are bound to the past by Karma, yet have the freedom of self-determination. "Freedom is not caprice, nor is Karma necessity." We are free to determine our self within the limits imposed by our past actions. Radhakrishnan illustrates this point by comparing life to bridge, a game wherein cards are given to us, not selected. While these cards can be traced back to our prior choices—our Karma—"we are free to make any call as we think fit and lead any suit." Nevertheless, as the game goes on, we become less free because of the constraints placed upon us by our prior card choices. Nevertheless, until the end of the game, "there is always a choice."

Sarvepalli Radhakrishnan (1888–1975), an Indian philosopher, served as ambassador, vice president, and president of the Republic of India. He was born in Tiruttani, India; was educated in Christian missionary schools; and received his graduate degree in 1909 from Madras Christian College with a thesis on the ethics of Hindu Vedanta philosophy. He taught religion and philosophy at Presidency College in Madras (1909–17), Mysore University

(1918–21), and Calcutta University (1921–31) before becoming vice chancellor of Andhra University in Waltair in 1931, and Spalding Professor of Eastern Religions and Ethics at Oxford University in 1936. In 1946, he entered politics, and in 1962, he became the second president of India. He is the author of *Indian Philosophy* (1923), *The Philosophy of the Upanishads* (1924), *An Ideal View of Life* (1929), *Freedom and Culture* (1936), *Eastern Religions in Western Thought* (1939), *Contemporary Indian Philosophy* (1950), *East and West: Some Reflections* (1956), *A Sourcebook in Indian Philosophy* (with C. A. Moore, 1957), and *Religion in a Changing World* (1967). The following selection is from *An Ideal View of Life.*

The two pervasive features of all nature, connection with the past and creation of the future, are present in the human level. The connection with the past at the human stage is denoted by the word "Karma" in the Hindu systems. The human individual is a self-conscious, efficient portion of universal nature with his own uniqueness. His history stretching back to an indefinite period of time binds him with the physical and vital conditions of the world. Human life is an organic whole where each successive phase grows out of what has gone before. We are what we are on account of our affinity with the past. Human growth is an ordered one and its orderedness is indicated by saying that it is governed by the law of Karma.

Karma literally means action, deed. All acts produce their effects which are recorded both in the organism and the environment. Their physical effects may be short-lived but their moral effects (samsskāra) are worked into the character of the self. Every single thought, word and deed enters into the living chain of causes which makes us what we are. Our life is not at the mercy of blind chance or capricious fate. The conception is not peculiar to the Oriental creeds. The Christian Scriptures refer to it. "Be not deceived; God is not mocked: for whatsoever a man soweth, that shall he also reap." Jesus is reported to have said on the Mount, "Judge not that ye be not judged, for with what judgment ye judge, ye shall be judged, and with what measure ye mete, it shall be measured to you again."

Karma is not so much a principle of retribution as one of continuity. Good produces good, evil, evil. Love increases our power of love, hatred our power of hatred. It emphasizes the great importance of right action. Man is continuously shaping his own self. The law of Karma is not to be confused with either a hedonistic or a juridical theory of rewards and punishments. The reward for virtue is not a life of pleasure nor is the punishment for sin pain. Pleasure and pain may govern the animal nature of man but not his human. Love which is a joy in itself suffers; hatred too often means a perverse kind of satisfaction. Good and evil are not to be confused with material well-being and physical suffering.

All things in the world are at once causes and effects. They embody the energy of the past and exert energy on the future. Karma or connection with the past is not inconsistent with creative freedom. On the other hand it is implied by it. The law that links us with the past also asserts that it can be subjugated by our free action. Through the past may present obstacles, they must all yield to the creative power in man in proportion to its sincerity and insistence. The law of Karma says that each individual will get the return according to the energy he puts forth. The universe will respond to and implement the demands of the self. Nature will reply to the insistent call of spirit. "As is his desire, such is his purpose; as is his purpose, such is the action he performs; what action he performs, that he procures for himself." "Verily I say unto you that whoever shall say to this mountain, 'Be lifted up and cast into the sea,' and shall not doubt in his heart but believe fully that what he says shall be, it shall be done for him." When Jesus said, "Destroy this temple and I will raise it again in three days" he is asserting the truth that the spirit within us is mightier than the world of things. There is nothing we cannot achieve if we want it enough. Subjection to spirit is the law of universal nature. The principle of Karma has thus two aspects, a retrospective and a prospective, continuity with the past and creative freedom of the self.

The urge in nature which seeks not only to maintain itself at a particular level but advance to a higher becomes conscious in man who deliberately seeks after rules of life and principles of progress. "My father worketh hitherto, and I work." Human beings are the first among nature's children who can say "I" and consciously collaborate with the "father," the power that controls and directs nature, in the fashioning of the world. They can substitute rational direction for the slow, dark, blundering growth of the subhuman world. We cannot deny the free action of human beings however much their origin may be veiled in darkness. The self has conative tendencies, impulses to change by its efforts the given conditions, inner and outer, and shape them to its own purpose.

The problem of human freedom is confused somewhat by the distinction between the self and the will. The will is only the self in its active side and freedom of the will really means the freedom of the self. It is determination by the self.

It is argued that self-determination is not really freedom. It makes little difference whether the self is moved from without or from within. A spinning top moved from within by a spring is as mechanical as one whipped into motion from without. The self may well be an animated automaton. A drunkard who takes to his glass habitually does so in obedience to an element in his nature. The habit has become a part of his self. If we analyze the contents of the self, many of them are traceable to the influence of the environment and the inheritance from the past. If the individual's view and character are the product of a long evolution, his actions which are the outcome of these cannot be free. The feeling of freedom may be an illusion of the self which lives in each moment of the present, ignoring the determining past. In answer to these difficulties, it may be said that the self represents a form of relatedness or organization, closer and more intimate than that which is found in animal, plant or atom. Self-determination means not determination by any fragment of the self's nature but by the whole of it. Unless the individual employs his whole nature, searches the different possibilities and selects one which commends itself to his whole self, the act is not really free.

Sheer necessity is not to be found in any aspect of nature; complete freedom is divine and possible only when the self becomes co-extensive with the whole. Human freedom is a matter of degree. We are most free when our whole self is active and not merely a fragment of it. We generally act according to our conventional or habitual self and sometimes we sink to the level of our subnormal self.

Freedom is not caprice, nor is Karma necessity. Human choice is not unmotivated or uncaused. If our acts were irrelevant to our past, then there would be no moral responsibility or scope for improvement. Undetermined beginnings, upstart events are impossible either in the physical or the human world. Free acts cannot negate continuity. They arise within the order of nature. Freedom is not caprice, since we carry our past with us. The character, at any given point, is the condensation of our previous history. What we have been enters into the "me" which is now active and choosing. The range of one's natural freedom of action is limited. No man has the universal field of possibilities for himself. The varied possibilities of our nature do not all get a chance and the cosmic has its influence in permitting the development of certain possibilities and closing down others. Again, freedom is dogged by automatism. When we make up our mind to do a thing, our mind is different from what it was before. When a possibility becomes an actuality, it assumes the character of necessity. The past can never be cancelled, though it may be utilized. Mere defiance of the given may mean disaster, though we can make a new life spring up from the past. Only the possible is the sphere of freedom. We have a good deal of present constraint and previous necessity in human life. But necessity is not to be mistaken for destiny which we can neither defy nor delude. Though the self is not free from the bonds of determination, it can subjugate the past to a certain extent and turn it into a new course. Choice is the assertion of freedom over necessity by which it converts necessity to its own use and thus frees itself from it. "The human agent is free." He is not the plaything of fate or driftwood on the tide of uncontrolled events. He can actively mould the future instead of passively suffering the past. The past may become either an opportunity or an obstacle. Everything depends on what we make of it and not what it makes of us. Life is not bound to move in a specific direction. Life is a growth and a growth is undetermined in a measure. Though the future is the sequel of the past, we cannot say what it will be. If there is no indetermination, then human consciousness is an unnecessary luxury.

Our demand for freedom must reckon with a universe that is marked by order and regularity. Life is like a game of bridge. The cards in the game are given to us. We do not select them. They are traced to past Karma but we are free to make any call as we think fit and lead any suit. Only we are limited by the rules of the game. We are more free when we start the game than later on when the game has developed and our choices become restricted. But till the very end there is always a choice. A good player will see possibilities which a bad one does not. The more skilled a player the more alternatives does he perceive. A good hand may be cut to pieces by unskillful play and the bad play need not be attributed to the frowns of fortune. Even though we may not like the way in which the cards are shuffled, we like the game and we want to play. Sometimes wind and tide may prove too strong for us and even the most noble may come down. The great souls, find profound peace in the consciousness that the stately order of the world, now lovely and luminous, now dark and terrible, in which man finds his duty and destiny, cannot be subdued to known aims. It seems to have a purpose of its own of which we are ignorant. Misfortune is not fate but providence.

The law of Karma does not support the doctrine of predestination. There are some who believe that only the predestination of certain souls to destruction is consistent with divine sovereignty. God has a perfect right to deal with his creatures even as a potter does with his clay. St. Paul speaks of "vessels of wrath fitted to destruction." Life eternal is a gracious gift of God. Such a view of divine sovereignty is unethical. God's love is manifested in and through law.

In our relations with human failures, belief in Karma inclines us to take a sympathetic attitude and develop reverence before the mystery of misfortune. The more understanding we are, the less do we pride ourselves on our superiority. Faith in Karma induces in us the mood of true justice or charity which is the essence of spirituality. We realize how infinitely helpless and frail human beings are. When we look at the warped lives of the poor, we see how much the law of Karma is true. If they are lazy and criminal, let us ask what chance they had of choosing to be different. They are more unfortunate than wicked. Again, failures are due not so much to "sin" as to errors which lead us to our doom. In Greek tragedy man is held individually less responsible and circumstances or the decisions of Moira [Fate] more so. The tale of Oedipus Rex tells us how he could not avoid his fate to kill his father and marry his mother, in spite of his best efforts. The parting of Hector and Andromache in Homer is another illustration. In Shakespeare again, we see the artist leading on his characters to their destined ends by what seems a very natural development of their foibles, criminal folly in Lear or personal ambition in Macbeth. The artist shows us these souls in pain. Hamlet's reason is puzzled, his will confounded. He looks at life and at death and wonders which is worse. Goaded by personal ambition, Macbeth makes a mess of it all. Othello kills his wife and kills himself because a jealous villain shows him a handkerchief. When these noble souls crash battling with adverse forces we feel with them and for them; for it might happen to any of us. We are not free from the weaknesses that broke them, whatever we call them, stupidity, disorder, vacillation or, if you please, insane ambition and self-seeking. Today the evil stars of the Greek tragedians are replaced by the almighty laws of economics. Thousands of young men the world over are breaking their heads in vain against the iron walls of society like trapped birds in cages. We see in them the essence of all tragedy, something noble breaking down, something sublime falling with a crash. We can only bow our heads in the presence of those broken beneath the burden of their destiny. The capacity of the human soul for suffering and isolation is immense. Take the poor creatures whom the world passes by as the lowly and the lost. If only we had known what they passed through, we would have been glad of their company. It is utterly wrong to think that misfortune comes only to those who deserve it. The world is a whole and we are members one of another, and we must suffer one for another. In Christianity, it needed a divine soul to reveal how much grace there is in suffering. To bear pain, to endure suffering, is the quality of the strong in spirit. It adds to the spiritual resources of humanity.

DISCUSSION QUESTIONS

1. What is the law of Karma? Why is it not a principle of retribution?

2. Why does the law of Karma not support the doctrine of predestination?

3. Why does Radhakrishnan believe that life is like a game of bridge? What do you think about this view of life?

4. Sophocles and Bernard Williams say that chance or luck place plays a large part in our lives, whereas Radhakrishnan argues that it does not. What is Radhakrishnan's argument? Compare it with the positions of Sophocles and Williams regarding chance and luck. Which do you prefer, and why?

5. How does Radhakrishnan reconcile human freedom with Karma? Do you agree with his argument? Are the two reconcilable? Why or why not?

Groundhog Day
[USA 1993] 1 hour, 42 minutes
Directed by Harold Ramis

*P*hil Connors (Bill Murray) is a cynical, philandering television weatherman who has been assigned to cover Groundhog Day in Punxsutawney, Pennsylvania, for the fifth consecutive year. After covering the event, Phil decides to stay over in Punxsutawney for the night; however, when he awakens the next morning, it is Groundhog Day again. Thinking that this is some kind of joke or that perhaps his previous day was only a dream, he goes about Groundhog Day—February 2—much like he did the day before. This goes on for day after day, year after year.

Waking up every day to Groundhog Day in Punxsutawney gradually alters Phil's behavior for the worse. He comes to believe that whatever he does will have no consequences the next day because the next day never comes. So, for a very long time, he engages in increasingly excessive behavior including all kinds of debauchery and even crime. However, in spite of all of these unruly actions, including the taking of his own life many times in a variety of ways, he still wakes up to the same day.

Gradually, Phil comes to realize that his destructive behavior is not bringing him happiness and that what he really wants is for Rita (Andie MacDowell), his producer, who dislikes him, to desire him. He begins to learn through trial and error what Rita likes and wants, and with each passing day, she finds him less objectionable. Phil also begins to get on good terms with the residents of Punxsutawney and to improve himself by reading philosophy and taking piano lessons. Soon, he has had a positive effect on the lives of just about everyone in town, and his character has completely changed. The repetition of a single day is no longer a curse to him, but rather brings him the opportunity to improve himself and the lives of others in Punxsutawney.

Day by day, Rita grows more attracted to Phil, not only because she finds him more attentive to and knowledgeable about her but also because he is so admired by the community as a whole. One night, she decides to do what she had always previously refused: go back to Phil's room and spend the night with him. When Phil awakens the next morning, Rita is by his side, and it is no longer Groundhog Day. He has retained the positive traits that he developed over the course of his time in Punxsutawney, and he has found love.

DISCUSSION QUESTIONS

1. Radhakrishnan argues that the Hindu doctrine of Karma, or connection with the past, is consistent with human, creative freedom. Does *Groundhog Day* support Radhakrishnan's position? Why or why not?

2. "Every single thought, word and deed enters into the living chain of causes which makes us what we are," says Radhakrishnan. Does Phil's life during the repeated Groundhog Days illustrate this point? Why or why not? Does Rita's life illustrate this point as well? Why or why not?

3. Radhakrishnan compares life to bridge, a game wherein cards are given to us, not selected. While these cards can be traced back to our prior choices—our Karma—"we are free to make any call as we think fit and lead any suit." Do the lives of Phil and Rita illustrate this point? Why or why not?

4. Phil is presented as reliving the same day in *Groundhog Day*. Is Rita also reliving the same day? Why or why not? Isn't she there every day for his Groundhog Day report? For that matter, isn't everyone in Punxsutawney reliving the same day? What, if anything, is different about the case of Phil and the lives of Rita and the residents of Punxsutawney?

5. Phil asks one of the guys he meets in a bar what he would do if there were no tomorrow—if nothing mattered. The guy responds that he'd spend all his time "drivin' fast, gettin' loaded, and gettin' laid—that's it." Phil replies, "That's it. It just doesn't get any better than this, does it? Good friends, good conversation, and quality brew. Drink up. . . ." What would you do on a day with no tomorrow? Why?

6. How does Phil try to demonstrate to Rita that he is repeating Groundhog Day? Is this the best way to demonstrate it? Why or why not? How would you prove to someone else that you (and they) are repeating one day?

7. Midway through the film, Phil tells Rita that they could do anything they want today and "it wouldn't matter one bit. Absolutely no consequences. Complete and total freedom." Is he right? Are there no consequences to his actions? Is he completely and totally free? Why or why not?

8. What is the philosophical message of this film regarding the connection between free will and Karma? Do you agree with it? Why or why not?

9. Reflect on how Phil was released from his repeating cycle of Groundhog Days. What are the philosophical implications? If you had written this film, is this the way you would have ended the cycle? Why or why not?

MARILYN FRYE

OPPRESSION

In this selection, Marilyn Frye examines what it means to say that women are oppressed. In particular, she aims to salvage the term *oppression* from those who would render it meaningless by claiming that men are oppressed, too. The oppression of women is a fundamental claim of feminism, and efforts to render the term *oppression* meaningless serve to weaken a central component of feminist thought.

According to Frye, being oppressed is like being in a cage. Oppressed persons live in such a way that their actions are necessarily limited and shaped by forces and barriers. These limiting and shaping structures "are not accidental or occasional and hence avoidable, but are systematically related to each other in such a way as to catch one between and among them and restrict or penalize motion in any direction." Nevertheless, seeing the totality of this systematic oppressive structure can be difficult, even if the individual elements of the structure are more readily noticeable. Thus, "people can and do fail to see the oppression of women because they fail to see macroscopically and hence fail to see the various elements of the situation as systematically related to larger schemes."

Frye argues that "women are oppressed, *as women*," which means that they are oppressed as individuals because of their membership in a group. "One is marked for application of oppressive measures by one's membership in a some group or category," notes Frye. "If an individual is oppressed, it is in virtue of being a member of a group or category of people that is systematically reduced, molded, immobilized." To identify a person as oppressed, we must see that person as being a member of a particular category of people. She states that many do not see women as oppressed because women are dispersed and assimilated throughout systems of race and class that also systematically organize men. Nevertheless, for Frye, it is a fact that women of all races and classes are members of an oppressed group.

She also argues that one is not oppressed simply by the fact that one has suffered or has been harmed or limited in some way; it all depends on the context of this suffering, harming, and limiting. We must ask, who constructs and maintains the barrier that is the source of the limitation? Whose interests does the barrier serve? Is it part of a structure intended to limit some group? Once these and other contextual questions are addressed, we can determine whether the forces, barriers, and limitations are indeed the source of oppression or merely the source of something less systematic such as individual suffering, harm, or limitation.

Marilyn Frye specializes in feminist philosophy. She received her B.A. from Stanford University in 1963 and her Ph.D. from Cornell University in 1969. She taught at the University of Pittsburgh from 1967 until 1974 and then joined the philosophy faculty at Michigan State University, where she has taught ever since. She is the author of *The Politics of Reality: Essays in Feminist Theory* (1983), *Willful Virgin: Essays in Feminism, 1976–1992* (1992), and *Feminist Interpretations of Mary Daly* (co-edited with Sarah Lucia, 2000). The following selection is from *The Politics of Reality*.

It is a fundamental claim of feminism that women are oppressed. The word "oppression" is a strong word. It repels and attracts. It is dangerous and dangerously fashionable and endangered. It is much misused and sometimes not innocently.

The statement that women are oppressed is frequently met with the claim that men are oppressed too. We hear that oppressing is oppressive to those who oppress as well as to those they oppress. Some men cite as evidence of their oppression their much-advertised inability to cry. It is tough, we are told, to be masculine. When the stresses and frustrations of being a man are cited as evidence that oppressors are oppressed by

their oppressing, the word "oppression" is being stretched to meaninglessness; it is treated as though its scope includes any and all human experience of limitation or suffering, no matter the cause, degree or consequence. Once such usage has been put over on us, then if ever we deny that any person or group is oppressed we seem to imply that we think they never suffer and have no feelings. We are accused of insensitivity; even of bigotry. For women, such accusation is particularly intimidating, since sensitivity is one of the few virtues that has been assigned to us. If we are found insensitive, we may fear we have no redeeming traits at all and perhaps are not real women. Thus are we silenced before we begin: the name of our situation drained of meaning and our guilt mechanisms tripped.

But this is nonsense. Human beings can be miserable without being oppressed, and it is perfectly consistent to deny that a person or group is oppressed without denying that they have feelings or that they suffer.

We need to think clearly about oppression, and there is much that mitigates against this. I do not want to undertake to prove that women are oppressed (or that men are not), but I want to make clear what is being said when we say it. We need this word, this concept, and we need it to be sharp and sure.

I

The root of the word "oppression" is the element "press." *The press of the crowd; pressed into military service, to press a pair of pants, printing press; press the button.* Presses are used to mold things or flatten them or reduce them in bulk, sometimes to reduce them by squeezing out the gasses or liquids in them. Something pressed is something caught between or among forces and barriers which are so related to each other that jointly they restrain, restrict or prevent the thing's motion or mobility. Mold. Immobilize. Reduce.

The mundane experience of the oppressed provides another clue. One of the most characteristic and ubiquitous features of the world as experienced by oppressed people is the double bind—situations in which options are reduced to a very few and all of them expose one to penalty, censure or deprivation. For example, it is often a requirement upon oppressed people that we smile and be cheerful. If we comply, we signal our docility and our acquiescence in our situation. We need not, then, be taken note of. We acquiesce in being made invisible, in our occupying no space. We participate in our own erasure. On the other hand, anything but the sunniest countenance exposes us to being perceived as mean, bitter, angry or dangerous. This means, at the least, that we may be found "difficult" or unpleasant to work with, which is enough to cost one's livelihood; at worst, being seen as mean, bitter, angry or dangerous has been known to result in rape, arrest, beating and murder. One can only choose to risk one's preferred form and rate of annihilation.

Another example: It is common in the United States that women, especially younger women, are in a bind where neither sexual activity nor sexual inactivity is all right. If she is heterosexually active, a woman is open to censure and punishment for being loose, unprincipled or a whore. The "punishment" comes in the form of criticism, snide and embarrassing remarks, being treated as an easy lay by men, scorn from her more restrained female friends. She may have to lie and hide her behavior from her parents. She must juggle the risks of unwanted pregnancy and dangerous contraceptives. On the other hand, if she refrains from heterosexual activity, she is fairly constantly harassed by men who try to persuade her into it and pressure her to "relax" and "let her hair down"; she is threatened with labels like "frigid," "uptight," "man-hater," "bitch" and "cocktease." The same parents who would be disapproving of her sexual activity may be worried by her inactivity because it suggests she is not or will not be popular, or is not sexually normal. She may be charged with lesbianism. If a woman is raped, then if she has been heterosexually active she is subject to the presumption that she liked it (since her activity is presumed to show that she likes sex), and if she has not been heterosexually active, she is subject to the presumption that she liked it (since she is supposedly "repressed and frustrated"). Both heterosexual activity and heterosexual nonactivity are likely to be taken as proof that you wanted to be raped, and hence, of course, weren't *really* raped at all. You can't win. You are caught in a bind, caught between systematically related pressures.

Women are caught like this, too, by networks of forces and barriers that expose one to penalty, loss or contempt whether one works outside the home or not, is on welfare or not, bears children or not, raises children or not, marries or not, stays married or not, is heterosexual, lesbian, both or neither. Economic necessity; confinement to racial and/or sexual job ghettos; sexual harassment; sex discrimination; pressures of competing expectations and judgments about *women, wives* and *mothers* (in the society at large, in racial and ethnic subcultures and in one's own mind); dependence (full or partial) on husbands, parents or the state; commitment to political ideas; loyalties to racial or ethnic or other "minority" groups; the demands of self-respect and responsibilities to others. Each of these factors exists in complex tension with every other, penalizing or prohibiting all of the apparently available options. And nipping at one's heels, always; is the endless pack of little things. If one dresses one way, one is subject to the assumption that one is advertising one's sexual availability, if one dresses another way, one appears to "not care about oneself" or to be "unfeminine." If one uses "strong language," one invites categorization as a whore or slut; if one does not one invites categorization as a "lady"—one too delicately constituted to cope with robust speech or the realities to which it presumably refers.

The experience of oppressed people is that the living of one's life is confined and shaped by forces and barriers which are not accidental or occasional and hence avoidable, but are systematically related to each other in such a way as to catch one between and among them and restrict or penalize motion in any direction. It is the experience of being caged in: all avenues, in every direction, are blocked or booby trapped.

Cages. Consider a birdcage. If you look very closely at just one wire in the cage, you cannot see the other wires. If your conception of what is before you is determined by this myopic focus, you could look at that one wire, up and down the length of it, and be unable to see why a bird would not just fly around the wire any time it wanted to go somewhere. Furthermore, even if, one day at a time, you myopically inspected each wire, you still could not see why a bird would have trouble going past the wires to get anywhere. There is no physical property of any one wire, *nothing* that the closest scrutiny could discover, that will reveal how a bird could be inhibited or harmed by it except in the most accidental way. It is only when you step back, stop looking at the wires one by one, micro-scopically, and take a macroscopic view of the whole cage, that you can see why the bird does not go anywhere, and then you will see it in a moment. It will require no great subtlety of mental powers. It is perfectly *obvious* that the bird is surrounded by a network of systematically related barriers, no one of which would be the least hindrance to its flight, but which, by their relations to each other, are as confining as the solid walls of a dungeon.

It is now possible to grasp one of the reasons why oppression can be hard to see and recognize: one can study the elements of an oppressive structure with great care and some good will without seeing the structure as a whole, and hence without seeing or being able to understand that one is looking at a cage and that there are people there who are caged, whose motion and mobility are restricted, whose lives are shaped and reduced.

The arresting of vision at a microscopic level yields such common confusion as that about the male door-opening ritual. This ritual, which is remarkably widespread across classes and races, puzzles many people, some of whom do and some of whom do not find it offensive. Look at the scene of the two people approaching a door. The male steps slightly ahead and opens the door. The male holds the door open while the female glides through. Then the male goes through. The door closes after them. "Now how," one innocently asks, "can those crazy womenslibbers say that is oppressive? The guy *removed* a barrier to the lady's smooth and unruffled progress." But each repetition of this ritual has a place in a pattern, in fact in several patterns. One has to shift the level of one's perception in order to see the whole picture.

The door-opening pretends to be a helpful service, but the helpfulness is false. This can be seen by noting that it will be done whether or not it makes any practical sense. Infirm men and men burdened with packages will open doors for able-bodied women who are free of physical burdens. Men will impose themselves awkwardly and jostle everyone in order to get to the door first. The act is not determined by convenience or grace. Furthermore, these very numerous acts of unneeded or even noisome "help" occur in counterpoint to a pattern of men not being helpful in many practical ways in which women might welcome help. What *women* experience is a world in which gallant princes charming commonly make a fuss about being helpful and providing small services when help and services are of little or no use but in which there are rarely ingenious and adroit princes at hand when substantial assistance is really wanted either in mundane affairs or in situations of threat, assault or terror. There is no help with the (his) laundry; no help typing a report at 4:00 a.m.; no help in mediating disputes among relatives or children. There is nothing but advice that women should stay indoors after dark, be chaperoned by a man, or when it comes down to it, "lie back and enjoy it."

The gallant gestures have no practical meaning. Their meaning is symbolic. The door-opening and similar services provided are services which really are needed by people who are for one reason or another incapacitated—unwell, burdened with parcels, etc. So the message is that women are incapable. The detachment of the acts from the concrete realities of what women need and do not need is a vehicle for the message that women's actual needs and interests are unimportant or irrelevant. Finally, these gestures imitate the behavior of servants toward masters and thus mock women, who are in most respects the servants and caretakers of men. The message of the false helpfulness of male gallantry is female dependence, the invisibility or insignificance of women, and contempt for women.

One cannot see the meanings of these rituals if one's focus is riveted upon the individual event in all its particularity, including the particularity of the individual man's present conscious intentions and motives and the individual woman's conscious perception of the event in the moment. It seems sometimes that people take a deliberately myopic view and fill their eyes with things seen microscopically in order not to see macroscopically. At any rate, whether it is deliberate or not, people can and do fail to see the oppression of women because they fail to see macroscopically and hence fail to see the various elements of the situation as systematically related in larger schemes.

As the cageness of the birdcage is a macroscopic phenomenon, the oppressiveness of the situation in which women live our various and different lives is a macroscopic phenomenon. Neither can be *seen* from a microscopic perspective. But when you look macroscopically you can see it—a network of forces and barriers which are systematically related and which conspire to the immobilization, reduction and molding of women and the lives we live.

II

The image of the cage helps convey one aspect of the systematic nature of oppression. Another is the selection of occupants of the cages, and analysis of this aspect also helps account for the invisibility of the oppression of women.

It is as a woman (or as a Chicana/o or as a Black or Asian or lesbian) that one is entrapped.

"Why can't I go to the park; you let Jimmy go!"

"Because it's not safe for girls."

"I want to be a secretary, not a seamstress; I don't want to learn to make dresses."

"There's no work for negroes in that line; learn a skill where you can earn your living."

When you question why you are being blocked, why this barrier is in your path, the answer has not to do with individual talent or merit, handicap or failure; it has to do with your membership in some category understood as a "natural" or "physical" category. The "inhabitant" of the "cage" is not an individual but a group, all those of a certain category. If an individual is oppressed, it is in virtue of being a member of a group or category of people that is systematically reduced, molded, immobilized. Thus, to recognize a person as oppressed one has to see that individual *as* belonging to a group of a certain sort.

There are many things which can encourage or inhibit perception of someone's membership in the sort of group or category in question here. In particular, it seems reasonable to suppose that if one of the devices of restriction and definition of the group is that of physical confinement or segregation, the confinement and separation would encourage recognition of the group as a group. This in turn would encourage the macroscopic focus which enables one to recognize oppression and encourages the individuals' identification and solidarity with other individuals of the group or category. But physical confinement and segregation of the group as a group is not common to all oppressive structures, and when an oppressed group is geographically and demographically dispersed the perception of it as a group is inhibited. There may be little or nothing in the situations of the individuals encouraging the macroscopic focus which would reveal the unity of the structure bearing down on all members of that group.

A great many people, female and male and of every race and class, simply do not believe that *woman* is a category of oppressed people, and I think that this in part because they have been fooled by the dispersal and assimilation of women throughout and into the systems of class and race which organize men. Our simply being dispersed makes it difficult for women to have knowledge of each other and hence difficult to recognize the shape of our common cage. The dispersal and assimilation of women throughout economic classes and races also divides us against each other practically and economically and thus attaches *interest* to the inability to see: for some, jealousy of their benefits, and for some, resentment of the others' advantages.

To get past this, it helps to notice that in fact women of all races and classes *are* together in a ghetto of sorts. There is a women's place, a sector which is inhabited by women of all classes and races, and it is not defined by geographical boundaries but by function. The function is the service of men and men's interests as men define them, which includes the bearing and rearing of children. The details of the service and the working conditions vary by race and class, for men of different races and classes have different interests, perceive their interests differently, and express their needs and demands in different rhetorics, dialects and languages. But there are also some constants.

Whether in lower, middle or upper-class home or work situations women's service work always includes personal service (the works of maids, butlers, cooks, personal secretaries), sexual service (including provision for his genital sexual needs and bearing his children, but also including "being nice," "being attractive for him," etc.), and ego service (encouragement, support, praise, attention). Women's service work also is characterized everywhere by the fatal combination of responsibility and powerlessness: we are held responsible and we hold ourselves responsible for good outcomes for men and children in almost every respect though we have in almost no case power adequate to that project. The details of the subjective experience of this servitude are local. They vary with economic class and race and ethnic tradition as well as the personalities of the men in question. So also are the details of the forces which coerce our tolerance of this servitude particular to the different situations in which different women live and work.

All this is not to say that women do not have, assert and manage sometimes to satisfy our own interests, nor to deny that in some cases and in some respects women's independent interests do overlap with men's. But at every race/class level

and even across race/class lines men do not serve women as women serve men. "Women's sphere" may be understood as the "service sector," taking the latter expression much more widely and deeply than is usual in discussions of the economy.

III

It seems to be the human condition that in one degree or another we all suffer frustration and limitation, all encounter unwelcome barriers, and all are damaged and hurt in various ways. Since we are a social species, almost all of our behavior and activities are structured by more than individual inclination and the conditions of the planet and its atmosphere. No human is free of social structures, nor (perhaps) would happiness consist in such freedom. Structure consists of boundaries, limits and barriers; in a structured whole, some motions and changes are possible, and others are not. If one is looking for an excuse to dilute the word "oppression," one can use the fact of social structure as an excuse and say that every one is oppressed. But if one would rather get clear about what oppression is and is not, one needs to sort out the sufferings, harms and limitations and figure out which are elements of oppression and which are not.

From what I have already said here, it is clear that if one wants to determine whether a particular suffering, harm or limitation is part of someone's being oppressed, one has to look at it *in context* in order to tell whether it is an element in an oppressive structure: one has to see if it is part of an enclosing structure of forces and barriers which tends to the immobilization and reduction of a group or category of people. One has to look at how the barrier or force fits with others and to whose benefit or detriment it works. As soon as one looks at examples, it becomes obvious that not everything which frustrates or limits a person is oppressive, and not every harm or damage is due to or contributes to oppression.

If a rich white playboy who lives off income from his investments in South African diamond mines should break a leg in a skiing accident at Aspen and wait in pain in a blizzard for hours before he is rescued, we may assume that in that period he suffers. But the suffering comes to an end, his leg is repaired by the best surgeon money can buy and he is soon recuperating in a lavish suite, sipping Chivas Regal. Nothing in this picture suggests a structure of barriers and forces. He is a member of several oppressor groups and does not suddenly become oppressed because he is injured and in pain. Even if the accident was caused by someone's malicious negligence, and hence someone can be blamed for it and morally faulted, that person still has not been an agent of oppression.

Consider also the restriction of having to drive one's vehicle on a certain side of the road. There is no doubt that this restriction is almost unbearably frustrating at times, when one's lane is not moving and the other lane is clear. There are surely times, even, when abiding by this regulation would have harmful consequences. But the restriction is obviously wholesome for most of us most of the time. The restraint is imposed for our benefit, and does benefit us; its operation tends to encourage our *continued* motion, not to immobilize us. The limits imposed by traffic regulations are limits most of us would cheerfully impose on ourselves given that we knew others would follow them too. They are part of a structure which shapes our behavior, not to our reduction and immobilization, but rather to the protection of our continued ability to move and act as we will.

Another example: The boundaries of a racial ghetto in an American city serve to some extent to keep white people from going in, as well as to keep ghetto dwellers from going out. A particular white citizen may be frustrated or feel deprived because she cannot stroll around there and enjoy the "exotic" aura of a "foreign" culture or shop for bargains in the ghetto swap shops. In fact, the existence of the ghetto, of racial segregation, does deprive the white person of knowledge and harm her/his character by nurturing unwarranted feelings of superiority. But this does not make the white person in this situation a member of an oppressed race or a person oppressed because of her/his race. One must look at the barrier. It limits the activities and the access of those on both sides of it (though to different degrees). But it is a product of the intention, planning and action of whites for the benefit of whites, to secure and maintain privileges that are available to whites generally, as members of the dominant and privileged group. Though the existence of the barrier has some bad consequences for whites, the barrier does not exist in systematic relationship with other barriers and forces forming a structure oppressive to whites; quite the contrary. It is part of a structure which oppresses the ghetto dwellers and thereby (and by white intention) protects and furthers white interests as dominant white culture understands them. This barrier is not oppressive to whites, even though it is a barrier to whites.

Barriers have different meanings to those on opposite sides of them, even though they are barriers to both. The physical walls of a prison no more dissolve to let an outsider in than to let an insider out but for the insider they are confining and limiting while to the outsider they may mean protection from what s/he takes to be threats posed by insiders—freedom from harm or anxiety. A set of social and economic barriers and forces separating two groups may be felt, even painfully, by members of both groups and yet may mean confinement to one and liberty and enlargement of opportunity to the other.

The service sector of the wives/mommas/assistants/girls is almost exclusively a woman-only sector; its boundaries not only enclose women but to a very great extent keep men out. Some men sometimes encounter this barrier and experience it as a restriction on their movements, their activities, their control or their choices of "lifestyle." Thinking they might like the simple nurturant life (which they may imagine to be quite free of stress, alienation and hard work), and feeling deprived since it seems closed to them, they thereupon announce the discovery that they are oppressed, too, by "sex roles." But that barrier is erected and maintained by men, for the benefit of men. It consists of cultural and economic forces and pressures in a culture and economy controlled by men in which, at every economic level and in all racial and ethnic subcultures, economy, tradition—and even ideologies of liberation—work to keep at least local culture and economy in male control.

The boundary that sets apart women's sphere is maintained and promoted by men generally for the benefit of men generally, and men generally do benefit from its existence, even the man who bumps into it and complains of the inconvenience.

That barrier is protecting his classification and status as male, as superior, as having a right to sexual access to a female or females. It protects a kind of citizenship which is superior to that of females of his class and race, his access to a wider range of better paying and higher status work, and his right to prefer unemployment to the degradation of doing lower status or "women's" work.

If a person's life or activity is affected by some force or barrier that person encounters, one may not conclude that the person is oppressed simply because the person encounters that barrier or force; nor simply because the encounter is unpleasant, frustrating or painful to that person at that time; nor simply because the existence of the barrier or force, or the processes which maintain or apply it, serve to deprive that person of something of value. One must look at the barrier or force and answer certain questions about it. Who constructs and maintains it? Whose interests are served by its existence? Is it part of a structure which tends to confine, reduce and immobilize some group? Is the individual a member of the confined group? Various forces, barriers and limitations a person may encounter or live with may be part of an oppressive structure or not and if they are, that person may be on either the oppressed of the oppressor side of it. One cannot tell which by how loudly or how little the person complains.

IV

Many of the restrictions and limitations we live with are more or less internalized and self-monitored, and are part of our adaptations to the requirements and expectations imposed by the needs and tastes and tyrannies of others. I have in mind such things as women's cramped postures and attenuated strides and men's restraint of emotional self-expression (except for anger). Who gets what out of the practice of those disciplines, and who imposes what penalties for improper relaxations of them? What are the rewards of this self-discipline?

Can men cry? Yes, in the company of women. If a man cannot cry, it is in the company of men that they cannot cry. It is men, not women, who require this restraint; and men not only require it, they reward it. The man who maintains a steely or

tough or laid-back demeanor (all are forms which suggest invulnerability) marks himself as a member of the male community and is esteemed by other men. Consequently, the maintenance of that demeanor contributes to the man's self-esteem. It is felt as good, and he can feel good about himself. The way this restriction fits into the structures of men's lives is as one of the socially required behaviors which, if carried off, contribute to their acceptance and respect by significant others and to their own self-esteem. It is to their benefit to practice this discipline.

Consider, by comparison, the discipline of women's cramped physical postures and attenuated stride. This discipline can be relaxed in the company of women; it generally is at its most strenuous in the company of men. Like men's emotional restraint, women's physical restraint is required by men. But unlike the case of men's emotional restraint, women's physical restraint is not rewarded. What do we get for it? Respect and esteem and acceptance? No. They mock us and parody our mincing steps. We look silly, incompetent, weak and generally contemptible. Our exercise of this discipline tends to low esteem and low self-esteem. It does not benefit us. It fits in a network of behaviors through which we constantly announce to others our membership in a lower caste and our unwillingness and/or inability to defend our bodily or moral integrity. It is degrading and part of a pattern of degradation.

Acceptable behavior for both groups, men and women, involves a required restraint that seems in itself silly and perhaps damaging. But the social effect is drastically different. The woman's restraint is part of a structure oppressive to women; the man's restraint is part of a structure oppressive to women.

V

One is marked for application of oppressive pressures by one's membership in some group or category. Much of one's suffering and frustration befalls one partly or largely because one is a member of that category. In the case at hand, it is the category, *woman*. Being a woman is a major factor in my not having a better job than I do; being a woman selects me as a likely victim of sexual assault or harassment; it is my being a woman that reduces the power of my anger to a proof of my insanity. If a woman has little or no economic or political power, or achieves little of what she wants to achieve, a major causal factor in this is that she is a woman. For any woman of any race or economic class, being a woman is significantly attached to whatever disadvantages and deprivations she suffers, be they great or small.

None of this is the case with respect to a person's being a man. Simply being a man is not what stands between him and a better job; whatever assaults and harassments he is subject to, being male is not what selects him for victimization; being male is not a factor which would make his anger impotent—quite the opposite. If a man has little or no material or political power, or achieves little of what he wants to achieve, his being male is not part of the explanation. Being male is something he has going *for* him, even if race or class or age or disability is going against him.

Women are oppressed, *as women*. Members of certain racial and/or economic groups and classes, both the males and the females, are oppressed *as* members of those races and/or classes. But men are not oppressed *as men*.

. . . and isn't it strange that any of us should have been confused and mystified about such a simple thing?

DISCUSSION QUESTIONS

1. Why does Frye think that the term *oppression* is rendered meaningless when men as well as women claim to be oppressed? Do you agree with her? Why or why not?

2. Why does Frye contend that only persons who are members of a group are subject to oppression? Why does she contend that persons not associated with a group are not the subjects of oppression? Do you agree with her? Why or why not?

3. What is the "double-bind" of oppressed persons?

4. Frye describes oppression as the experience of having one's life "shaped by forces." How is oppression similar to and different from determinism?

5. Why does Frye contend that oppression at the systematic level is difficult to see? Do you agree with her? Why or why not?

6. Frye writes, "No human is free of social structures, nor (perhaps) would happiness consist in such freedom. Structure consists of boundaries, limits and barriers; in a structured whole, some motions and changes are possible, and others are not." Do you think that one can live in a structure and at the same time be free? Why or why not?

The Color Purple
[USA 1985] 2 hours, 32 minutes
Directed by Stephen Spielberg

*B*ased on the novel by Alice Walker, *The Color Purple* portrays a young black woman's struggle to control her life in a small southern town in the early twentieth century. By the age of fourteen, Celie (played by Desreta Jackson as a child and Whoopi Goldberg as an adult) has had a son and a daughter by her father. The children of this incestuous relationship are taken from Celie and adopted by Reverend Samuel (Carl Anderson) and his wife. Celie is married off to Albert Johnston (Danny Glover), a widower who beats her and forces her to serve him and care for his children.

Celie's only consolation is her proximity to her beloved sister Nettie (Akosua Busia), who comes to live in the household. Albert makes advances toward Nettie, and when she refuses him, he banishes her from the farm, and the sisters part in tears. Albert's son Harpo (Willard Pugh) marries Sophia (Oprah Winfrey), a strong-willed woman who leaves him when he beats her. Albert is madly in love with singer and performer Shug Avery (Margaret Avery), and he takes her into the household.

After some initial jealousies, Shug and Celie develop a close relationship, and Celie even falls in love with Shug. Meanwhile, Sophia gets into an argument with a white man and is sent to prison for eight years. When she is released, she is forced to serve as a maid for Miss Millie, the white man's wife. Celie and Shug discover letters from Nettie that Albert has been hiding for years. Nettie has moved to Africa with Reverend Samuel's family and is caring for Celie's children while the Samuels do missionary work. When Shug marries and decides to move to Memphis, Celie finally breaks from Albert and goes with her. Celie returns years later to claim her inheritance when her father dies. She learns that the man who fathered her children was her stepfather and that she will inherit the family farm. When Albert receives a letter from the immigration office, he makes the arrangements for Nettie and the children to return from Africa. Celie is reunited with her family.

The Color Purple received eleven Oscar nominations, yet won none.

DISCUSSION QUESTIONS

1. Consider the various ways in which the female characters in *The Color Purple* are oppressed. In particular, consider the ways in which their actions are limited and shaped by forces and barriers.

2. Are the barriers and forces that oppress women in *The Color Purple* systematically related to one another? Why or why not?

3. Are the women in *The Color Purple* oppressed as women? That is, are they, in Frye's words, "marked for application of oppressive measures" by their membership in a group called "women"? Why or why not?

4. In *The Color Purple*, who constructs and maintains the barrier that is the source of limitation for women? Whose interests does this barrier serve?

5. When Nettie encourages Celie to stand up to Albert early in the marriage, Celie responds, "I don't know how to fight. All I know is how to stay alive." Why do you think Celie does not know how to fight? What role does oppression play in her inability to fight?

6. Harpo is discouraged when Sophia speaks her mind and gives him orders. His father recommends that he beat her. Why does Celie also tell Harpo to beat Sophia? Is Celie oppressing Sophia by encouraging Harpo to beat her? What would Frye say?

7. When Miss Millie wrongly accuses Sophia's relatives of attacking her, she claims, "I've always been good to you people. I've always been good to coloreds." Does our charity to others give us the right to oppress them? Why do you think some people feel that it does? Evaluate their reasoning, and generally reflect on the connection between charity and oppression.

8. When Celie finally leaves Albert, he insults her and insists that she won't make it in the world. "Look at you," Albert tells her. "You're black, you're poor, you're ugly and you're a woman. You're nothing at all." Is verbal abuse just as serious a form of oppression against women as physical abuse? Defend your view.

9. What is the connection between oppression and violence against women in *The Color Purple*? Defend your reading of the movie.

10. Quite a few black men protested publicly after this film was released, claiming that it fed into stereotypes of black men as "shiftless, violent rapists." Do you think this film unfairly depicts black

men? Why or why not? Should it, for example, deal more with the oppression of black men in American society?

11. Frye contends that claiming that men as well as women are oppressed renders oppression meaningless. Can we discuss the oppression of black men along with that of women in general and not render the term *oppression* meaningless? Why or why not?

FYODOR DOSTOYEVSKY

WE ARE NOT PIANO KEYS

In this selection from Fyodor Dostoyevsky's *Notes from Underground* (Part 1, Section 8), a nameless character (who is generally called the "Underground Man") expresses his dissatisfaction with his life by stating that man is not a piano key or an organ-stop. Dostoyevsky's Underground Man is not troubled by the external conditions of his life, such as his job or a lack of money. Rather, his troubles are internal. Furthermore, while he is a sick man with liver troubles, his real internal troubles are not physical, they are emotional. What ails him is the way in which a fully determined existence could never authentically capture the essence of human life: desire.

For him, even "if there really is some day discovered a formula for all our desires and caprices—that is, an explanation of what they depend upon, by what laws they arise, how they develop, what they are aiming at in one case and in another and so on, that is a real mathematical formula—then, most likely, man will at once cease to feel desire, indeed, he will be certain to." Once our desires are determined by science and mapped out for us, we "will at once be transformed from a human being into an organ-stop or something of the sort; for what is man without desires, without free will and without choice, if not an organ-stop."

Arguably, the Underground Man is not dissatisfied with the possibilities of scientific progress in itself, but rather with the idea that such progress runs the risk of denying him his freedom and the possibilities for authentic, spontaneous desire. "What sort of free will is left when we come to tabulation and arithmetic, when it will all be a case of twice two makes four?" "Twice two makes four without my will," he says. "As if free will meant that!" For the Underground Man, free will means being able to assert that twice two makes *five*, not four. Humans are not mere mathematical or mechanical objects; rather, they are beings whose desires are not entirely calculable or determinable. "It is just his fantastic dreams, his vulgar folly that he will desire to retain, simply in order to prove to himself—as though that were so necessary—that men still are men and not the keys of a piano, which the laws of nature threaten to control so completely that soon one will be able to desire nothing but by the calendar."

Notes from Underground (*Zapiski iz podpolya*) was first published in 1864 in the magazine *Epokha*. This magazine was founded by Dostoyevsky and his brother after the previous magazine they had founded, *Vremya*, was suppressed. A biographical sketch of Dostoyevsky appears in chapter 1.

"Ha! ha! ha! But you know there is no such thing as choice in reality, say what you like," you will interpose with a chuckle. "Science has succeeded in so far analyzing man that we know already that choice and what is called freedom of will is nothing else than—"

Stay, gentlemen, I meant to begin with that myself. I confess, I was rather frightened. I was just going to say that the devil only knows what choice depends on, and that perhaps that was a very good thing, but I remembered the teaching of science . . . and pulled myself up. And here you have begun upon it. Indeed, if there really is some day discovered a formula for all our desires and caprices—that is, an explanation of what they depend upon, by what laws they arise, how they develop, what they are aiming at in one case and in another and so on, that is a real mathematical formula—then, most likely, man will at once cease to feel desire, indeed, he will be certain to. For who would want to choose by rule? Besides, he will at once be transformed from a human being into an organ-stop or something of the sort; for what is a man without desires, without free will and without choice, if not a stop in an organ? What do you think? Let us reckon the chances— can such a thing happen or not?

"H'm!" you decide. "Our choice is usually mistaken from a false view of our advantage. We sometimes choose absolute nonsense because in our foolishness we see in that nonsense the easiest means for attaining a supposed advantage. But when all that is explained and worked out on paper (which is perfectly possible, for it is contemptible and senseless to suppose that some laws of nature man will never understand), then certainly so-called desires will no longer exist. For if a desire should come into conflict with reason we shall then reason and not desire, because it will be impossible retaining our reason to be *senseless* in our desires, and in that way knowingly act against reason and desire to injure ourselves. And as all choice and reasoning can be really calculated—because there will some day be discovered the laws of our so-called free will—so, joking apart, there may one day be something like a table constructed of them, so that we really shall choose in accordance with it.

If, for instance, some day they calculate and prove to me that I made a long nose at some one because I could not help making a long nose at him and that I had to do it in that particular way, what *freedom* is left me, especially if I am a learned man and have taken my degree somewhere? Then I should be able to calculate my whole life for thirty years beforehand. In short, if this could be arranged there would be nothing left for us to do; anyway, we should have to understand that. And, in fact, we ought unwearyingly to repeat to ourselves that at such and such a time and in such and such circumstances nature does not ask our leave; that we have got to take her as she is and not fashion her to suit our fancy, and if we really aspire to formulas and tables of rules, and well, even . . . to the chemical retort, there's no help for it, we must accept the retort too, or else it will be accepted without our consent. . . ."

Yes, but here I come to a stop! Gentlemen, you must excuse me for being overphilosophical; it's the result of forty years underground! Allow me to indulge my fancy. You see, gentlemen, reason is an excellent thing, there's no disputing that, but reason is nothing but reason and satisfies only the rational side of man's nature while will is a manifestation of the whole life, that is, of the whole human life including reason and all the impulses. And although our life, in this manifestation of it, is often worthless, yet it is life and not simply extracting square roots. Here I, for instance, quite naturally want to live, in order to satisfy all my capacities for life, and not simply my capacity for reasoning, that is, not simply one twentieth of my capacity for life. What does reason know? Reason only knows what it has succeeded in learning (some things, perhaps, it will never learn; this is a poor comfort, but why not say so frankly?) and human nature acts as a whole, with everything that is in it, consciously or unconsciously, and, even if it goes wrong, it lives. I suspect, gentlemen, that you are looking at me with compassion; you tell me again that an enlightened and developed man, such, in short, as the future man will be, cannot consciously desire anything disadvantageous to himself, that that can be proved mathematically. I thoroughly agree, it can—by mathematics. But I repeat for the hundredth time, there is one case, one only, when man may consciously, purposely, desire what is injurious to himself, what is stupid, very stupid— simply in order to have the right to desire for himself even what is very stupid and not to be bound by an obligation to desire only what is sensible. Of course, this very stupid thing, this caprice of ours, may be in reality, gentlemen, more advantageous for us than anything else on earth, especially in certain cases. And in particular it may be more advantageous than any advantage even when it does us obvious harm, and contradicts the soundest conclusions of our reason concerning our advantage—for in any circumstances it preserves for us what is most precious and most important—that is, our personality, our individuality. Some, you see, maintain that this really is the most precious thing for mankind; choice can, of course, if it chooses, be in agreement with reason; and especially if this be not abused but kept within bounds. It is profitable and sometimes even praiseworthy. But very often, and even most often, choice is utterly and stubbornly opposed to reason . . . and . . . and . . . do you know that that, too, is profitable, sometimes even praiseworthy? Gentlemen, let us suppose that man is not stupid. (Indeed one cannot refuse to suppose that, if only from the one consideration, that, if man is stupid, then who is wise?) But if he is not stupid, he is monstrously ungrateful! Phenomenally ungrateful. In fact, I believe that the best definition of man is the ungrateful biped. But that is not all, that is not his worst defect; his worst defect is his perpetual moral obliquity, perpetual—from the days of the Flood to the Schleswig-Holstein period. Moral obliquity and consequently lack of good sense; for it has long been accepted that lack of good sense is due to no other cause than moral obliquity. Put it to the test and cast your eyes upon the history of mankind. What will you see? Is it a grand spectacle? Grand, if you like. Take the Colossus of Rhodes, for instance, that's worth something. With good reason Mr. Anaevsky testifies of it that some say that it is the work of man's hands, while others maintain that it has been created by nature herself. Is it many-colored? May be it is many-colored, too: if one takes the dress uniforms, military and civilian, of all peoples in all ages— that alone is worth something, and if you take the undress uniforms you will never get to the end of

it; no historian would be equal to the job. Is it monotonous? May be it's monotonous too: it's fighting and fighting; they are fighting now, they fought first and they fought last—you will admit, that it is almost too monotonous. In short, one may say anything about the history of the world—anything that might enter the most disordered imagination. The only thing one can't say is that it's rational. The very word sticks in one's throat. And, indeed, this is the odd thing that is continually happening; there are continually turning up in life moral and rational persons, sages and lovers of humanity who make it their object to live all their lives as morally and rationally as possible, to be, so to speak, a light to their neighbors simply in order to show them that it is possible to live morally and rationally in this world. And yet we all know that those very people sooner or later have been false to themselves, playing some queer trick, often a most unseemly one. Now I ask you: what can be expected of man since he is a being endowed with such strange qualities? Shower upon him every earthly blessing, drown him in a see of happiness, so that nothing but bubbles of bliss can be seen on the surface; give him economic prosperity, such that he should have nothing else to do but sleep, eat cakes and busy himself with the continuation of his species, and even then out of sheer ingratitude, sheer spite, man would play you some nasty trick. He would even risk his cakes and would deliberately desire the most fatal rubbish, the most uneconomical absurdity, simply to introduce into all this positive good sense his fatal fantastic element. It is just his fantastic dreams, his vulgar folly that he will desire to retain, simply in order to prove to himself—as though that were so necessary—that men still are men and not the keys of a piano, which the laws of nature threaten to control so completely that soon one will be able to desire nothing but by the calendar. And that is not all: even if man really were nothing but a piano-key, even if this were proved to him by natural science and mathematics, even then he would not become reasonable, but would purposely do something perverse out of simple ingratitude, simply to gain his point. And if he does not find means he will contrive destruction and chaos, will contrive sufferings of all sorts, only to gain his point. He will launch a curse upon the world, and as only man can curse (it is his privilege, the primary distinction between him and other animals), may be by his curse alone he will attain his object—that is, convince himself that he is a man and not a piano-key! If you say that all this, too, can be calculated and tabulated—chaos and darkness and curses, so that the mere possibility of calculating it all beforehand would stop it all, and reason would reassert itself, then man would purposely go mad in order to be rid of reason and gain his point! I believe in it. I answer for it, for the whole work of man really seems to consist in nothing but proving to himself every minute that he is a man and not a piano-key! It may be at the cost of his skin, it may be by cannibalism! And this being so, can one help being tempted to rejoice that it has not yet come off, and that desire still depends on something we don't know?

You will scream at me (that is, if you condescend to do so) that no one is touching my free will, that all they are concerned with is that my will should of itself, of its own free will, coincide with my own normal interests, with the laws of nature and arithmetic.

Good Heavens, gentlemen, what sort of free will is left when we come to tabulation and arithmetic, when it will all be a case of twice two make four? Twice two makes four without my will. As if free will meant that!

DISCUSSION QUESTIONS

1. Why is the Underground Man so opposed to the scientific calculation of his desires? Do you agree with him?

2. Is the Underground Man opposed to scientific progress? Why or why not?

3. For the Underground Man, how is desire related to reason?

4. What does freedom mean for the Underground Man? Compare his sense of freedom to the Hindu sense of freedom described by Radhakrishnan. Which do you prefer and why?

5. Why does the Underground Man not wish us to be organ stops or piano keys? Can you think of a more contemporary image for the idea that the Underground Man is trying to convey here?

6. How would you feel about your own desires if someone told you what they were going to be in advance of your feeling them? Would you regard this a denial of your free will? Why or why not?

5.2   WHAT MAKES A SOCIETY JUST?

THOMAS HOBBES

THE STATE OF NATURE AND THE SOCIAL CONTRACT

Accrding to Thomas Hobbes, the state of nature is devoid of justice and injustice. Hobbes argues that to avoid the state of nature, which is a "war of every one against every one," individuals form a contract with one another and with an individual or an assembly to rule them. This *social contract* subordinates the rights of the individual to the sovereign power, whether it is an individual or an assembly. Laws are established by the sovereign power, and with the enforcement of these laws comes justice and injustice. Hobbes believes that the establishment of a civil society with sovereign power, justice, and laws is the necessary consequence of the application of reason to the state of nature.

Hobbes asserts that all reality is matter or derived from matter and that the primary state of matter is motion. In this regard, Hobbes is following the Italian philosopher and astronomer

Galileo (1564–1642) in rejecting the traditional position that the primary state of matter is rest. Hobbes also contends that intellectual, moral, and political life is made up of only combinations of matter in motion. As such, he aims to develop a politics that proceeds from fundamental first principles in much the same way that Euclid's geometry develops from first principles or axioms.

When the principle of matter in motion is applied to humans, Hobbes determines that the principle of human self-motion is what he calls "endeavour[s]," which are "small beginnings of motion within the body of man." "This endeavour, when it is toward something which causes it, is called *appetite*, or *desire*. . . . And when the endeavour is fromward something, is generally called *aversion*" (*Leviathan* I.6). All voluntary human motion then is either an attraction to motion (appetite) or a repulsion from rest (aversion): appetites make voluntary human motion possible, and aversions are from what leads to rest. Good and evil are then derivable from appetites and aversions: Whatever is an object of appetite is good, and whatever is an object of aversion is evil. The worst evil is death, because it is the cessation of voluntary human motion.

Hobbes then utilizes this portrait of human motion as governed by appetites and aversions to speculate on what life would be like without *civil society*, namely, in what he calls the *state of nature*. He observes that while there are mental and physical differences among individuals, they are "not so considerable as that one man can thereupon claim to himself any benefit to which another may not pretend as well as he." Disadvantages can be overcome through a variety of means such as "secret machination or by confederacy with others that are in the same danger as himself." Thus, for Hobbes, there is an "equality of ability" among individuals to acquire the objects of their desire, and from this stems an "equality of hope." However, given unlimited human desire and a limited supply of objects of desire, competition for these scarce objects occurs, and with this competition comes "diffidence" (mistrust), particularly if there are no agreed-upon laws enforced by a common power. The state of nature is "the time men live without common power to keep them all in awe, they are in that condition which is called war; and such a war as is of every man against every man."

In the state of nature, each individual has the right to everything, and force and fraud are the cardinal virtues. Whatever any individual can acquire through force and fraud becomes that person's property. "In such condition there is no place for industry . . . no culture of the earth; no navigation, nor use of commodities that may be imported by sea; no commodious building; no instruments of moving and removing such things as require much force; no knowledge of the face of the earth; no account of time; no arts; no letters; no society; and which is worst of all, continual fear, and danger of violent death; and the life of man, solitary, poor, nasty, brutish, and short." Furthermore, the "notions of right and wrong, justice and injustice, have there no place" in the state of nature. Justice and injustice come about through laws, which are written by a common power. "Where there is no common power, there is no law; where no law, no injustice." Consequently, justice and injustice for Hobbes is always relative to the common power; there is no absolute, nonrelative conception of justice.

Hobbes argues that "war" is not consistent with our "fear of death; desire of such things as are necessary to commodious living; and a hope by their industry to obtain them." Consequently, our rational self-interest inclines us to prefer and bring about "peace" over war, and suggests to each of us a set of general principles to bring about a state of peace, namely, the *laws of nature*. "A LAW OF NATURE, *lex naturalis*, is a precept, or general rule, found out by reason, by which man is forbidden to do that which is destructive of his life, or taketh away the means of preserving the same, and to omit that by which he thinketh it may be best preserved." Hobbes distinguishes the law of nature from the "*RIGHT OF NATURE*" (*jus naturale*), which is "the liberty each man hath to use his own power as he will himself for the preservation of his own nature." Nevertheless, the first law of nature is "to seek peace and to follow it," and the second law of nature is, in short, to "lay down" as many liberties as one demands others lay down.

For Hobbes, to lay down one's liberties is not to give them up, but rather to transfer them to a mutually-agreed-on third party, namely, a sovereign monarch or body of rulers. "The mutual transferring of right is that which men call CONTRACT." Consequently, the third law of nature is "that men perform their covenants made." The only rational reason to fail to honor the social contract would be if the sovereign power failed to maintain peace and order in the society. Says Hobbes, "When the covenant is made, then to break it is *unjust*: And the definition of INJUSTICE, is no other than *the not performance of covenant*. And whatsoever is not unjust, is *just*. . . ." From these three laws of nature, all of the other laws of nature are deductively derived. It should be noted that while Hobbes demonstrates the necessity of a sovereign power, this power is designated not by divine right, but by common consent.

Thomas Hobbes (1588–1679), an English philosopher, is widely regarded as the founder of English moral and political philosophy though he wrote on many other subjects, including logic, optics, aesthetics, law, history, and religion. He was born in Westport and educated at Magdalen Hall, Oxford. After his graduation from Oxford, he became tutor to the young son of William Cavendish, Earl of Devonshire. He was employed similarly throughout his life, mainly with the Cavendish family, though he was also tutor to Charles II during his exile in Paris in 1646. He was secretary to Francis Bacon, visited Galileo in 1636, and engaged in disputes with René Descartes.

The boldness of his writings put Hobbes in disfavor with many, including both sides in the English Civil War: royalists disliked him because he denied the divine right of the king, and parliamentarians disliked him for his support of the king over Parliament. His unpopular religious views led to faculty at Oxford University being dismissed for advocating his philosophy and to the Catholic Church banning his books. He died at the age of ninety-one, after having spent many years of his life in self-imposed exile from England. His principal writings are *De Cive* (1647), *De Corpore Politico, or Elements of Law, Moral and Politic* (1650), *Human Nature, or the Fundamental Elements of Policy* (1650), *Leviathan, or the Matter, Form and Power of a Commonwealth, Ecclesiastical and Civil* (1651), *Questions Concerning Liberty, Necessity and Chance* (1656), and *De Homine* (1658). The following selection is from *Leviathan*.

CHAPTER 13

OF THE NATURAL CONDITION OF MANKIND AS CONCERNING THEIR FELICITY AND MISERY

Men by nature equal. Nature has made men so equal in the faculties of the body and mind as that, though there be found one man sometimes manifestly stronger in body or of quicker mind than another, yet, when all is reckoned together, the difference between man and man is not so considerable as that one man can thereupon claim to himself any benefit to which another may not pretend as well as he. For as to the strength of body, the weakest has strength enough to kill the strongest, either by secret machination or by confederacy with others that are in the same danger with himself.

And as to the faculties of the mind, setting aside the arts grounded upon words, and especially that skill of proceeding upon general and infallible rules called science—which very few have and but in few things, as being not a native faculty born with us, nor attained, as prudence, while we look after somewhat else—I find yet a greater equality among men than that of strength. For prudence is but experience, which equal time equally bestows on all men in those things they equally apply themselves unto. That which may perhaps make such equality incredible is but a vain conceit of one's own wisdom, which almost all men think they have in a greater degree than the vulgar—that is, than all men but themselves and a few others whom, by fame or for concurring with themselves, they approve. For such is the nature of men that howsoever they may acknowledge many others to be more witty or more eloquent or more learned, yet they will hardly believe there be many so wise as themselves; for they see their own wit at hand and other men's at a distance. But this proves rather that men are in that point equal than unequal. For there is not ordinarily a greater sign of the equal distribution of anything than that every man is contented with his share.

From equality proceeds diffidence. From this equality of ability arises equality of hope in the attaining of our ends. And therefore if any two men desire the same thing, which nevertheless they cannot both enjoy, they become enemies; and in the way to their end, which is principally their own conservation, and sometimes their delectation only, endeavor to destroy or subdue one another. And from hence it comes to pass that where an invader has no more to fear than another man's single power, if one plant, sow, build, or possess a convenient seat, others may probably be expected to come prepared with forces united to dispossess and deprive him, not only of the fruit of his labor, but also of his life or liberty. And the invader again is in the like danger of another.

From diffidence war. And from this diffidence of one another there is no way for any man to secure himself so reasonable as anticipation—that is, by force or wiles to master the persons of all men he can, so long till he see no other power great enough to endanger him; and this is no more than his own conservation requires, and is generally allowed. Also, because there be some that take pleasure in contemplating their own power in the acts of conquest, which they pursue farther than their security requires, if others that otherwise would be glad to be at ease within modest bounds should not by invasion increase their power, they would not be able, long time, by standing only on their defense, to subsist. And by consequence, such augmentation of dominion over men being necessary to a man's conservation, it ought to be allowed him.

Again, men have no pleasure, but on the contrary a great deal of grief, in keeping company where there is no power able to overawe them all. For every man looks that his companion should value him at the same rate he sets upon himself; and upon all signs of contempt or undervaluing naturally endeavors, as far as he dares (which among them that have no common power to keep them in quiet is far enough to make them destroy each other), to extort a greater value from his contemners by damage and from others by the example.

So that in the nature of man we find three principal causes of quarrel: first, competition; secondly, diffidence; thirdly, glory.

The first makes men invade for gain, the second for safety, and the third for reputation. The first use violence to make themselves masters of other men's persons, wives, children, and cattle; the second, to defend them; the third, for trifles, as a word, a smile, a different opinion, and any other sign of undervalue, either direct in their persons or by reflection in their kindred, their friends, their nation, their profession, or their name.

Out of civil states, there is always war of every one against every one. Hereby it is manifest that, during the time men live without a common power to keep them all in awe, they are in that condition which is called war, and such a war as is of every man against every man. For WAR consists not in battle only, or the act of fighting, but in a tract of time wherein the will to contend by battle is sufficiently known; and therefore the notion of *time* is to be considered in the nature of war as it is in the nature of weather. For as the nature of foul weather lies not in a shower or two of rain but in an inclination thereto of many days together, so the nature of war consists not in actual fighting but in the known disposition thereto during all the time there is no assurance to the contrary. All other time is PEACE.

The incommodities of such a war. Whatsoever, therefore, is consequent to a time of war where every man is enemy to every man, the same is consequent to the time wherein men live without other security than what their own strength and their own invention shall furnish them withal. In such condition there is no place for industry, because the fruit thereof is uncertain: and consequently no culture of the earth; no navigation nor use of the commodities that may be imported by sea; no commodious building; no instruments of moving and removing such things as require much force; no knowledge of the face of the earth; no account of time; no arts; no letters; no society; and, which is worst of all, continual fear and danger of violent death; and the life of man solitary, poor, nasty, brutish, and short.

It may seem strange to some man that has not well weighed these things that nature should thus dissociate and render men apt to invade and destroy one another; and he may therefore, not trusting to this inference made from the passions, desire perhaps to have the same confirmed by experience. Let him therefore consider with himself—when taking a journey he arms himself and seeks to go well accompanied, when going to sleep he locks his doors, when even in his house he locks his chests, and this when he knows there be laws and public officers, armed, to revenge all injuries shall be done him—what opinion he has of his fellow subjects when he rides armed, of his fellow citizens when he locks his doors, and of his children and servants when he locks his chests. Does he not there as much accuse mankind by his actions as I do by my words? But neither of us accuse man's nature in it. The desires and other passions of man are in themselves no sin. No more are the actions that proceed from those

passions till they know a law that forbids them, which, till laws be made, they cannot know, nor can any law be made till they have agreed upon the person that shall make it.

It may peradventure be thought there was never such a time nor condition of war as this, and I believe it was never generally so over all the world; but there are many places where they live so now. For the savage people in many places of America, except the government of small families, the concord whereof depends on natural lust, have no government at all and live at this day in that brutish manner as I said before. Howsoever, it may be perceived what manner of life there would be where there were no common power to fear by the manner of life which men that have formerly lived under a peaceful government use to degenerate into in a civil war.

But though there had never been any time wherein particular men were in a condition of war one against another, yet in all times kings and persons of sovereign authority, because of their independency, are in continual jealousies and in the state and posture of gladiators, having their weapons pointing and their eyes fixed on one another—that is, their forts, garrisons, and guns upon the frontiers of their kingdoms, and continual spies upon their neighbors—which is a posture of war. But because they uphold thereby the industry of their subjects, there does not follow from it that misery which accompanies the liberty of particular men.

In such a war nothing is unjust. To this war of every man against every man, this also is consequent: that nothing can be unjust. The notions of right and wrong, justice and injustice, have there no place. Where there is no common power, there is no law; where no law, no injustice. Force and fraud are in war the two cardinal virtues. Justice and injustice are none of the faculties neither of the body nor mind. If they were, they might be in a man that were alone in the world, as well as his senses and passions. They are qualities that relate to men in society, not in solitude. It is consequent also to the same condition that there be no propriety, no dominion, no *mine* and *thine* distinct; but only that to be every man's that he can get, and for so long as he can keep it. And thus much for the ill condition which man by mere nature is actually placed in, though with a possibility to come out of it consisting partly in the passions, partly in his reason.

The passions that incline men to peace

The passions that incline men to peace are fear of death, desire of such things as are necessary to commodious living, and a hope by their industry to obtain them. And reason suggests convenient articles of peace, upon which men may be drawn to agreement. These articles are they which otherwise are called the Laws of Nature, whereof I shall speak more particularly in the two following chapters.

CHAPTER 14

OF THE FIRST AND SECOND NATURAL LAWS, AND OF CONTRACTS

Right of nature what.

The RIGHT OF NATURE, which writers commonly call *jus naturale,* is the liberty each man has to use his own power, as he will himself, for the preservation of his own nature—that is to say, of his own life—and consequently of doing anything which, in his own judgment and reason, he shall conceive to be the aptest means thereunto.

Liberty what.

By LIBERTY is understood, according to the proper signification of the word, the absence of external impediments; which impediments may oft take away part of man's power to do what he would, but cannot hinder him from using the power left him according as his judgment and reason shall dictate to him.

A law of nature what.

A LAW OF NATURE, *lex naturalis,* is a precept or general rule, found out by reason, by which a man is forbidden to do that which is destructive of his life or takes away the means of preserving the same and to omit that by which he thinks it may be best preserved. For though they that speak of this subject use to confound *jus* and *lex, right* and *law,* yet they ought to be distinguished; because RIGHT consists in liberty to do or to forbear, whereas LAW

Difference of right and law.

determines and binds to one of them; so that law and right differ as much as obligation and liberty, which in one and the same matter are inconsistent.

Naturally every man has right to every thing.

And because the condition of man, as has been declared in the precedent chapter, is a condition of war of every one against every one—in which case everyone is governed by his own reason and there is nothing he can make use of that may not be a help unto him in preserving his life against his enemies—it follows that in such a condition every man has a right to everything, even to one another's body. And therefore, as long as this natural right of every man to everything endures, there can be no security to any man, how strong or wise soever he be, of living out the time which nature ordinarily allows men to live. And consequently it is a precept or general rule of reason *that every man ought to endeavor peace, as far as he has hope of obtaining it; and when he cannot obtain it, that he may seek and use all helps and advantages of war.*

The fundamental law of nature.

The first branch of which rule contains the first and fundamental law of nature, which is *to seek peace and follow it.* The second, the sum of the right of nature, which is, *by all means we can to defend ourselves.*

From this fundamental law of nature, by which men are commanded to endeavor peace,

The second law of nature.

is derived this second law: *that a man be willing, when others are so too, as far forth as for peace and defense of himself he shall think it necessary, to lay down this right to all things, and be contented with so much liberty against other men as he would allow other men against himself.* For as long as every man holds this right of doing anything he likes, so long are all men in the condition of war. But if other men will not lay down their right as well as he, then there is no reason for anyone to divest himself of his, for that were to expose himself to prey, which no man is bound to, rather than to dispose himself to peace. This is that law of gospel: *whatsoever you require that others should do to you, that do ye to them.* And that law of all men, *quod tibi fieri non vis, alteri ne feceris* [do not do to others what you do not want done to yourself].

What it is to lay down a right.

To *lay down* a man's *right* to anything is to *divest* himself of the *liberty* of hindering an- other of the benefit of his own right to the same. For he that renounces or passes away his right gives not to any other man a right which he had not before—because there is nothing to which every man had not right by nature—but only stands out of his way, that he may enjoy his own original right without hindrance from him, not without hindrance from another. So that the effect which redounds to one man by another man's defect of right is but so much diminution of impediments to the use of his own right original. Right is laid aside either by simply renouncing it or by transferring it to another. By simply RENOUNCING, when he cares not to whom the benefit thereof redounds. By TRANSFERRING, when he intends the benefit thereof to some certain person or persons. And when a man has in either manner abandoned or granted away his right, then he is said to be OBLIGED or BOUND not to hinder those to whom such right is granted or abandoned from the benefit of it; and that he *ought*, and it is his DUTY, not to make void that voluntary act of his own; and that such hindrance is INJUSTICE and INJURY as being *sine jure* [without legal basis], the right being before renounced or transferred. So that *injury* or *injustice* in the controversies of the world is somewhat like to that which in the disputations of scholars is called *absurdity*. For as it is there called an absurdity to contradict what one maintained in the beginning, so in the world it is called injustice and injury voluntarily to undo that which from the beginning he had voluntarily done. The way by which a man either simply renounces or transfers his right is a declaration or signification by some voluntary and sufficient sign or signs that he does so renounce or transfer, or has so renounced or transferred, the same to him that accepts it. And these signs are either words only or actions only; or as it happens most often, both words and actions. And the same are the BONDS by which men are bound and obliged—bonds that have

Renouncing a right, what it is.

Transferring right what. Obligation.

Duty.

Injustice.

their strength, not from their own nature, for nothing is more easily broken than a man's word, but from fear of some evil consequence upon the rupture.

Whensoever a man transfers his right or renounces it, it is either in consideration of some right reciprocally transferred to himself or for some other good he hopes for thereby. For it is a voluntary act; and of the voluntary acts of every man, the object is some *good to himself*. And therefore there be some rights which no man can be understood by any words or other signs to have abandoned or transferred. As, first, a man cannot lay down the right of resisting them that assault him by force to take away his life, because he cannot be understood to aim thereby at any good to himself. The same may be said of wounds and chains and imprisonment, both because there is no benefit consequent to such patience as there is to the patience of suffering another to be wounded or imprisoned, as also because a man cannot tell, when he sees men proceed against him by violence, whether they intend his death or not. And, lastly, the motive and end for which this renouncing and transferring of right is introduced is nothing else but the security of a man's person in his life and in the means of so preserving life as not to be weary of it. And therefore if a man by words or other signs seem to despoil himself of the end for which those signs were intended, he is not to be understood as if he meant it or that it was his will, but that he was ignorant of how such words and actions were to be interpreted.

Not all rights are alienable.

The mutual transferring of right is that which men call CONTRACT.

Contract what.

There is difference between transferring of right to the thing and transferring, or tradition—that is, delivery—of the thing itself. For the thing may be delivered together with the translation of right, as in buying and selling with ready money or exchange of goods or lands, and it may be delivered some time after.

Again, one of the contractors may deliver the thing contracted for on his part and leave the other to perform his part at some determinate time after and in the meantime be trusted, and then the contract on his part is called PACT or COVENANT; or both parts may contract now to perform

Covenant what.

hereafter, in which case he that is to perform in time to come, being trusted, his performance is called *keeping of promise* or faith, and the failing of performance, if it be voluntary, *violation of faith.* . . .

A man's covenant not to defend himself is void.

A covenant not to defend myself from force by force is always void. For, as I have showed before, no man can transfer or lay down his right to save himself from death, wounds, and imprisonment, the avoiding whereof is the only end of laying down any right; and therefore the promise of not resisting force in no covenant transfers any right, nor is obliging. For though a man may covenant thus: *unless I do so or so, kill me*, he cannot covenant thus: *unless I do so or so, I will not resist you when you come to kill me.* For man by nature chooses the lesser evil, which is danger of death in resisting, rather than the greater, which is certain and present death in not resisting. And this is granted to be true by all men, in that they lead criminals to execution and prison with armed men, notwithstanding that such criminals have consented to the law by which they are condemned.

No man obliged to accuse himself.

A covenant to accuse oneself, without assurance of pardon, is likewise invalid. For in the condition of nature, where every man is judge, there is no place for accusation; and in the civil state, the accusation is followed with punishment, which, being force, a man is not obliged not to resist. The same is also true of the accusation of those by whose condemnation a man falls into misery, as of a father, wife, or benefactor. For the testimony of such an accuser, if it be not willingly given, is presumed to be corrupted by nature, and therefore not to be received; and where a man's testimony is not to be credited, he is not bound to give it. Also accusations upon torture are not to be reputed as testimonies. For torture is to be used but as means of conjecture and light in the further examination and search of truth; and what is in that case confessed tends to the ease of him that is tortured, not to the informing of the torturers, and therefore ought not to have the credit of a sufficient testimony; for whether he deliver himself by true or false accusation, he does it by the right of preserving his own life. . . .

CHAPTER **15**

OF OTHER LAWS OF NATURE

The third law of nature, justice.

From that law of nature by which we are obliged to transfer to another such rights as, being retained, hinder the peace of mankind, there follows a third, which is this: *that men perform their covenants made*; without which covenants are in vain and but empty words, and, the right of all men to all things remaining, we are still in the condition of war.

Justice and injustice what.

And in this law of nature consists the fountain and original of JUSTICE. For where no covenant has preceded there has no right been transferred, and every man has right to every thing; and consequently no action can be unjust. But when a covenant is made, then to break it is *unjust*; and the definition of INJUSTICE is no other than *the not performance of covenant.* And whatsoever is not unjust is *just*.

Justice and propriety begin with the constitution of commonwealth.

But because covenants of mutual trust, where there is a fear of not performance on either part, as has been said in the former chapter, are invalid, though the original of justice be the making of covenants, yet injustice actually there can be none till the cause of such fear be taken away, which, while men are in the natural condition of war, cannot be done. Therefore, before the names of just and unjust can have place, there must be some coercive power to compel men equally to the performance of their covenants by the terror of some punishment greater than the benefit they expect by the breach of their covenant, and to make good that propriety which by mutual contract men acquire in recompense of the universal right they abandon; and such power there is none before the erection of a commonwealth. And this is also to be gathered out of the ordinary definition of justice in the Schools, for they say that *justice is the constant will of giving to every man his own*. And therefore where there is no *own*—that is, no propriety—there is no injustice; and where there is no coercive power eracted—that is, where there is no ommonwealth—there is no propriety, all men having right to all things; therefore, where there is no commonwealth, there nothing is unjust. So that the nature of justice consists in keeping of valid covenants; but the validity of covenants beings not but with the constitution of a civil power sufficient to compel men to keep them; and then it is also that propriety begins. . . .

A rule by which the laws of nature may easily be examined.

And though this may seem too subtle a deduction of the laws of nature to be taken notice of by all men—whereof the most part are too busy in getting food and the rest too negligent to understand—yet to leave all men inexcusable they have been contracted into one easy sum, intelligible even to the meanest capacity, and that is *Do not that to another which you would not have done to yourself*; which shows him that he has no more to do in learning the laws of nature but, when weighing the actions of other men with his own they seem too heavy, to put them into the other part of the balance and his own into their place, that his own passions and self-love may add nothing to the weight, and then there is none of these laws of nature that will not appear unto him very reasonable.

The laws of nature oblige in conscience always, but in effect then only when there is security.

The laws of nature oblige *in foro interno*—that is to say, they bind to a desire they should take place—but *in foro externo*—that is, to the putting them in act—

not always. For he that should be modest and tractable and perform all he promises in such time and place where no man else should do so should but make himself a prey to others and procure his own certain ruin, contrary to the ground of all laws of nature, which tend to nature's preservation. And again, he that, having sufficient security that others shall observe the same laws toward him, observes them not himself, seeks not peace but war and consequently the destruction of his nature by violence.

DISCUSSION QUESTIONS

1. Does Hobbes believe that all people are equal? Why or why not?

2. Why does Hobbes believe that there is neither justice nor injustice in the state of nature? Do you agree with him? Why or why not?

3. Hobbes contends that justice and injustice are relative to the laws of the sovereign power. Do you agree with him? Why or why not?

4. Why does Hobbes believe that rational, self-interested individuals will be willing to transfer some of their liberties to a common power? Analyze his argument.

5. What does Hobbes mean by "war"? Do you agree with him? Why or why not?

6. Hobbes argues that humans prefer peace to war. Analyze his argument.

Lord of the Flies
[Great Britain 1963] 1 hr., 40 min.
Directed by Peter Brook

When a plane crashes on a deserted island, the schoolboys aboard must learn to survive in the absence of adult supervision and organized society. The boys elect Ralph (James Aubrey) to be their leader, and rules are laid down. A conch shell found by Piggy (Hugh Edwards) is used as a horn to signal meetings of the stranded boys, and it is established that whoever holds the conch shell is allowed to address the group.

In the meantime, Jack (Tom Chapin) has decided that the group needs food, so he takes some of the boys on a hunting expedition. Jack's first attempt to kill a pig is a failure, but he says that he'll get the pig next time—a comment that foreshadows the brutal hunting that is to come. Soon Jack and the hunters become obsessed with hunting, as well as more and more vicious in their behavior. Relations between Ralph and Jack grow increasingly strained, particularly when Jack's group lets the signal fire die out, and thus all miss out on an opportunity to be rescued.

As the gap between Ralph and Jack widens, order on the island begins to decay. Piggy, a highly rational and sensible lad, attempts to help Ralph maintain control over the boys, while Jack and his hunters exhibit increasingly primitive and brutal behavior. Speculation about a beast living on the island arises, causing Jack and his group to reject Ralph's leadership completely and to operate as an independent group. One by one, the boys following Ralph leave his group to join Jack's "tribe," which rejects all notions of being rescued and establishes the unseen beast as a demigod figure in need of sacrificial offerings. When a pig is captured, the tribe impales the pig's head on a sharp stick. The head is their offering to the beast, an offering that attracts increasing numbers of flies—hence the title "lord of the flies."

Simon (Tom Gaman), a prophetic character, discovers the true nature of the beast and sees the destruction that lies ahead for the group. However, on his way to share with the rest of the boys what he has learned, he is mistaken for the beast and is killed by the boys before he can reveal what he has discovered. Piggy, now the last member of Ralph's group, is also killed while attempting to establish order, thus leaving Ralph to fend for himself against Jack's tribe. The tribe comes within inches of succeeding in the sacrificial murder of Ralph but is stopped when confronted by a British naval officer. The presence of the officer signals the return of civilization to the island and brings tears to the eyes of the formerly bloodthirsty boys, who suddenly recognize how far their behavior has "devolved." Simon and Piggy are dead because the boys did not succeed in establishing a "civil" society on the island, but rather gave way to the arguably more violent and primitive aspects of their nature.

This film is based on Sir William Golding's 1954 novel of the same title, which he described as "a journey into the darkness of the human heart."

DISCUSSION QUESTIONS

1. Compare the state of nature described by Hobbes to the state of Jack and his group. If the boys had not been rescued, how far do think Jack's tribe could have continued to devolve in the same direction? What would they have become?

2. When the boys land on the island, they make a mature decision to establish rules of order, and they appoint Ralph as ruler. Were their actions a "social contract"? Why or why not?

3. Why were the boys unable to establish a "civil society"?

4. *Lord of the Flies* presents the notion that civilization provides only minimal protection against violence and anarchy. The boys begin their life on the island in a more or less civilized manner but quickly descend into chaos and violence once the urge to hunt for meat overcomes them. Is the status of the social contract discussed by Hobbes as fragile as the one established in the film? Why or why not?

5. Ralph says, "I'm calling an assembly. Things are beginning to break up. I don't know why. It all began well. Then people started forgetting what really matters. The most important thing—for all of us—is getting rescued. So now let's discuss who does what. And when we have decided, we can

start again, and be careful about things like the fire." What does *Lord of the Flies* suggest really matters to persons in the state of nature? Do you agree?

6. Early in the film, Jack says, "I agree with Ralph. We got to have rules and obey them." Later, when Ralph tells Jack that he is breaking the rules, he says, "Who cares?" Ralph replies, "Because the rules are all we got!" What does Ralph mean? Is he right? Why does Jack change his opinion of the rules? Would you change your opinion if you were in Jack's position? Why or why not?

7. When Jack says to the group, "If there is a beast, it's my hunters who will protect you from it," Simon replies, "Maybe it wasn't a beast. . . . What I mean is maybe it's only us." Discuss the role and nature of "the beast" in *Lord of the Flies*. Is "the beast" ultimately the boys' loss of respect for the rules? What, if anything, is the nature of "the beast" in Hobbes's philosophy? Is it similar to the beast in *Lord of the Flies*? Why or why not?

8. When Ralph says, "I am chief, I was chosen," Jack replies, "Why should choosing make any difference?" Does choosing make a difference? Defend your response.

9. Piggy says, "Grown-ups know things. . . . They'd meet and discuss, and things would be alright." Is he right? If the pilot of the plane, for example, had survived the crash, would the situation have been different? Why or why not?

10. Just before he is killed by Jack's group, Piggy says, "Which is it better to be, a pack of bloody savages like you are or sensible like Ralph is? Which is better, to have rules and agree, or to hunt and kill?" Compare a Hobbesian response to this question with Jack's response. How does your own response compare to that of Hobbes and Jack?

JOHN STUART MILL

A UTILITARIAN THEORY OF JUSTICE

John Stuart Mill explains the concept of justice in terms of utility. In doing so, Mill contends that he is discharging one of the main arguments against the utilitarian theory of morals, namely, that it does not have a genuine notion of justice. Critics of utilitarianism maintain that morality must be founded on a universal concept of justice, and not merely on the consequences of actions as the utilitarians maintain. Given that utilitarianism does not found morality on a universal concept of justice, these critics charge that utilitarianism should be rejected. Mill directly responds to these charges.

Mill contends that punishment and rights are the essential moral elements of justice, and that both depend on social utility. Concerning punishment, Mill states that the desire to punish "is a spontaneous outgrowth from two sentiments, both in the highest degree natural, and which either are or resemble instincts; the impulse of self-defense, and the feeling of sympathy." "It is natural to resent, and to repel or retaliate, any harm done or attempted against ourselves, or against those with whom we sympathize," writes Mill. Self-defense, retaliation, and vengeance have no moral component in them. Social sympathy is, however, the same thing as social utility. Thus, punishment depends on social utility.

Mill states that rights are also based on utility: "When we call anything a person's right, we mean that he has a valid claim on society to protect him in the possession of it, either by force of law, or by that of education and opinion." For Mill, the sole reason that society ought to protect our rights is "general utility." Mill concludes that justice is found to be firmly grounded in utility through an analysis of its central components: punishment and rights.

Moreover, argues Mill, if morality were indeed founded upon a universal concept of justice as his critics assert, then it should be able to resolve disputes concerning topics such as punishment, the fair distribution of wealth, and fair taxation. Mill shows, however, that a universal concept of justice cannot resolve these disputes and that they can be resolved only by appealing to a utilitarian theory of justice. Thus, justice is found to be also firmly grounded in utility through an analysis of social disputes concerning justice.

Mill concludes that "justice is a name for certain moral requirements which, regarded collectively, stand higher in the scale of social utility, and are therefore of more paramount obligation, than others." "Justice remains the appropriate name for certain social utilities which are vastly more important, and therefore more absolute and imperative, than any others are as a class." For Mill, the charges of nonconsequentialists that utilitarianism cannot account for justice are ill-founded; justice provides no difficulties for the utilitarian theory of morals.

A biographical sketch of Mill appears in chapter 4. The following selection is from *Utilitarianism* (1863).

In all ages of speculation, one of the strongest obstacles to the reception of the doctrine that Utility or Happiness is the criterion of right and wrong, has been drawn from the idea of Justice. The powerful sentiment, and apparently clear perception, which that word recalls with a rapidity and certainty resembling an instinct, have seemed to the majority of thinkers to point to an inherent quality in things; to show that the Just must have an existence in Nature as something absolute, generically distinct from every variety of the Expedient, and, in idea, opposed to it, though (as is commonly acknowledged) never, in the long run, disjoined from it in fact.

In the case of this, as of our other moral sentiments, there is no necessary connection between the question of its origin, and that of its binding force. That a feeling is bestowed on us by Nature, does not necessarily legitimate all its promptings. The feeling of justice might be a peculiar instinct, and might yet require, like our other instincts, to be controlled and enlightened by a higher reason. If we have intellectual instincts, leading us to judge in a particular way, as well as animal instincts that prompt us to act in a particular way, there is no necessity that the former should be more infallible in their sphere than the latter in theirs: it may as well happen that wrong judgments are occasionally suggested by those, as wrong actions by these. But though it is one thing to believe that we have natural feelings of justice, and another to acknowledge them as an ultimate criterion of conduct, these two opinions are very closely connected in point of fact. Mankind are always predisposed to believe that any subjective feeling, not otherwise accounted for, is a revelation of some objective reality. Our present object is to determine whether the reality, to which the feeling of justice corresponds, is one which needs any such special revelation; whether the justice or injustice of an action is a thing intrinsically peculiar, and distinct from all its other qualities, or only a combination of certain of those qualities, presented under a peculiar aspect. For the purpose of this inquiry it is practically important to consider whether the feeling itself, of justice and injustice, is *sui generis* like our sensations of color and taste, or a derivative feeling, formed by a combination of others. And this it is the more essential to examine, as people are in general willing enough to allow, that objectively the dictates of Justice coincide with a part of the field of General Expediency; but inasmuch as the subjective mental feeling of Justice is different from that which commonly attaches to simple expediency, and except in the extreme cases of the latter, is far more imperative in its demands, people find it difficult to see, in Justice, only a particular kind or branch of general utility, and think that its superior binding force requires a totally different origin.

To throw light upon this question, it is necessary to attempt to ascertain what is the distinguishing character of justice, or of injustice: what is the quality, or whether there is any quality, attributed in common to all modes of conduct designated as unjust (for justice, like many other moral attributes, is best defined by its opposite), and distinguishing them from such modes of conduct as are disapproved, but without having that particular epithet of disapprobation applied to them. If in everything which men are accustomed to characterize as just or unjust, some one common attribute or collection of attributes is always present, we may judge whether this particular attribute or combination of attributes would be capable of gathering round it a sentiment of that peculiar character and intensity by virtue of the general laws of our emotional constitution, or whether the sentiment is inexplicable, and requires to be regarded as a special provision of Nature. If we find the former to be the case, we shall, in resolving this question, have resolved also the main problem: if the latter, we shall have to seek for some other mode of investigating it.

To find the common attributes of a variety of objects, it is necessary to begin by surveying the objects themselves in the concrete. Let us therefore advert successively to the various modes of action, and arrangements of human affairs, which are classed, by universal or widely spread opinion, as Just or as Unjust. The things well known to excite the sentiments associated with those names are of a very multifarious character. I shall pass them rapidly in review, without studying any particular arrangement.

In the first place, it is mostly considered unjust to deprive any one of his personal liberty, his property, or any other thing which belongs to him by law. Here, therefore, is one instance of the application of the terms just and unjust in a perfectly definite sense, namely, that it is just to respect, unjust to violate, the *legal rights* of any one. But this judgment admits of several exceptions, arising from the other forms in which the notions of justice and injustice present themselves. For example, the person who suffers the deprivation may (as the phrase is) have *forfeited* the rights which he is so deprived of: a case to which we shall return presently. But also,

Secondly, the legal rights of which he is deprived, may be rights which *ought* not to have belonged to him; in other words, the law which confers on him these rights, may be a bad law. When it is so, or when (which is the same thing for our purpose) it is supposed to be so, opinions will differ as to the justice or injustice of infringing it. Some maintain that no law, however bad, ought to be disobeyed by an individual citizen; that his opposition to it, if shown at all, should only be shown in endeavoring to get it altered by competent authority. This opinion (which condemns many of the most illustrious benefactors of mankind, and would often protect pernicious institutions against the only weapons which, in the state of things existing at the time, have any chance of succeeding against them) is defended, by those who hold it, on grounds of expediency; principally on that of the importance, to the common interest of mankind, of maintaining inviolate the sentiment of submission to law. Other persons, again, hold the directly contrary opinion, that any law, judged to be bad, may blamelessly be disobeyed, even though it be not judged to be unjust, but only inexpedient; while others would confine the license of disobedience to the case of unjust laws; but again, some say, that all laws which are inexpedient are unjust; since every law imposes some restriction on the natural liberty of mankind, which restriction is an injustice, unless legitimated by tending to their good. Among these diversities of opinion, it seems to be universally admitted that there may be unjust laws, and that law, consequently, is not the ultimate criterion of justice, but may give to one person a benefit, or impose on another an evil, which justice condemns. When, however, a law is thought to be unjust, it seems always to be regarded as being so in the same way in which a breach of law is unjust, namely, by infringing somebody's right; which, as it cannot in this case be a legal right, receives a different appellation, and is called a moral right. We may say, therefore, that a second case of injustice consists in taking or withholding from any person that to which he has a *moral right*.

Thirdly, it is universally considered just that each person should obtain that (whether good or evil) which he *deserves*; and unjust that he should obtain a good, or be made to undergo an evil, which he does not deserve. This is, perhaps, the clearest and most emphatic form in which the idea of justice is conceived by the general mind. As it involves the notion of desert, the question arises, what constitutes desert? Speaking in a general way, a person is understood to deserve good if he does right, evil if he does wrong; and in a more particular sense, to deserve good from those to whom he does or has done good, and evil from those to whom he does or has done evil. The precept of returning good for evil has never been regarded as a case of the fulfilment of justice, but as one in which the claims of justice are waived, in obedience to other considerations.

Fourthly, it is confessedly unjust to *break faith* with any one: to violate an engagement, either express or implied, or disappoint expectations raised by our own conduct, at least if we have raised those expectations knowingly and voluntarily. Like the other obligations of justice already spoken of, this one is not regarded as absolute, but as capable of being overruled by a stronger obligation of justice on the other side; or by such conduct on the part of the person concerned as is deemed to absolve us from our obligation to him, and to constitute a *forfeiture* of the benefit which he has been led to expect.

Fifthly, it is, by universal admission, inconsistent with justice to be *partial*; to show favor or preference to one person over another, in matters to which favor and preference do not properly apply. Impartiality, however, does not seem to be regarded as a duty in itself, but rather as instrumental to some other duty; for it is admitted that favor and preference are not always censurable, and indeed the cases in which they are condemned are rather the exception than the rule. A person would be more likely to be blamed than applauded for giving his family or friends no superiority in good offices over strangers, when he could do so without violating any other duty; and no one thinks it unjust to seek one person in preference to another as a friend, connection, or companion. Impartiality where rights are concerned is of course obligatory, but this is involved in the more general obligation of giving to every one his right. A tribunal, for example, must be impartial, because it is bound to award, without regard to any other consideration, a disputed object to the one of two parties who has the right to it. There are other cases in which impartiality means, being solely influenced by desert; as with those who, in the capacity of judges, preceptors, or parents, administer reward and punishment as such. There are cases, again, in which it means, being solely influenced by consideration for the public interest; as in making a selection among candidates for a government employment. Impartiality, in short, as an obligation of justice, may be said to mean, being exclusively influenced by the considerations which it is supposed ought to influence the particular case in hand; and resisting the solicitation of any motives which prompt to conduct different from what those considerations would dictate.

Nearly allied to the idea of impartiality is that of *equality*; which often enters as a component part both into the conception of justice and into the practice of it, and, in the eyes of many persons, constitutes its essence. But in this, still more than in any other case, the notion of justice varies in different persons, and always conforms in its variations to their notion of utility. Each person maintains that equality is the dictate of justice, except where he thinks that expediency requires inequality. The justice of giving equal protection to the rights of all, is maintained by those who support the most outrageous inequality in the rights themselves. Even in slave countries it is theoretically admitted that the rights of the slave, such as they are, ought to be as sacred as those of the master; and that a tribunal which fails to enforce them with equal strictness is wanting in justice; while, at the same time, institutions which leave to the slave scarcely any rights to enforce, are not deemed unjust, because they are not deemed inexpedient. Those who think that utility requires distinction of rank, do not consider it unjust that riches and social privileges should be unequally dispensed; but those who think this inequality inexpedient, think it unjust also. Whoever thinks that government is necessary, sees no injustice in as much inequality as is constituted by giving to the magistrate powers not granted to other people. Even among those who hold levelling doctrines, there are as many questions of justice as there are differences of opinion about expediency. Some Communists consider it unjust that the produce of the labor of the community should be shared on any other principle than that of exact equality; others think it just that those should receive most whose wants are greatest; while others hold that those who work harder, or who produce more, or whose services are more valuable to the community, may justly claim a larger quota in the division of the produce. And the sense of natural justice may be plausibly appealed to in behalf of every one of these opinions. . . .

* * *

. . . Justice implies something which it is not only right to do, and wrong not to do, but which some individual person can claim from us as his moral right. No one has a moral right to our generosity or beneficence, because we are not morally bound to practise those virtues towards any given individual. And it will be found with respect to this as to every correct definition, that the instances which seem to conflict with it are those which most confirm it. For if a moralist attempts, as some have done, to make out that mankind generally, though not any given individual, have a right to all the good we can do them, he at once, by that thesis, includes generosity and beneficence within the category of justice. He is obliged to say, that our utmost exertions are *due* to our fellow creatures, thus assimilating them to a debt; or that nothing less can be a sufficient *return* for what society does for us, thus classing the case as one of gratitude; both of which are acknowledged cases of justice. Wherever there is a right, the case is one of justice, and not of the virtue of beneficence: and whoever does not place the distinction between justice and morality in general, where we have now placed it, will be found to make no distinction between them at all, but to merge, all morality in justice.

Having thus endeavoured to determine the distinctive elements which enter into the composition of the idea of justice, we are ready to enter on the inquiry, whether the feeling, which accompanies the idea, is attached to it by a special dispensation of nature, or whether it could have grown up, by any known laws, out of the idea itself; and in particular, whether it can have originated in considerations of general expediency.

I conceive that the sentiment itself does not arise from anything which would commonly, or correctly, be termed an idea of expediency; but that though the sentiment does not, whatever is moral in it does.

We have seen that the two essential ingredients in the sentiment of justice are, the desire to punish a person who has done harm, and the knowledge or belief that there is some definite individual or individuals to whom harm has been done.

Now it appears to me, that the desire to punish a person who has done harm to some individual is a spontaneous outgrowth from two sentiments, both in the highest degree natural, and which either are or resemble instincts; the impulse of self-defense, and the feeling of sympathy.

It is natural to resent, and to repel or retaliate, any harm done or attempted against ourselves, or against those with whom we sympathize. The origin of this sentiment it is not necessary here to discuss. Whether it be an instinct or a result of intelligence, it is, we know, common to all animal nature; for every animal tries to hurt those who have hurt, or who it thinks are about to hurt, itself or its young. Human beings, on this point, only differ from other animals in two particulars. First, in being capable of sympathizing, not solely with their offspring, or, like some of the more noble animals, with some superior animal who is kind to them, but with all human, and even with all sentient, beings. Secondly, in having a more developed intelligence, which gives a wider range to the whole of their sentiments, whether self-regarding or sympathetic. By virtue of his superior intelligence, even apart from his superior range of sympathy, a human being is capable of apprehending a community of interest between himself and the human society of which he forms a part, such that any conduct which threatens the security of the society generally, is threatening to his own, and calls forth his instinct (if instinct it be) of self-defence. The same superiority of intelligence, joined to the power of sympathizing with human beings generally, enables him to attach himself to the collective idea of his tribe, his country, or mankind, in such a manner that any act hurtful to them, raises his instinct of sympathy, and urges him to resistance.

The sentiment of justice, in that one of its elements which consists of the desire to punish, is thus, I conceive, the natural feeling of retaliation or vengeance, rendered by intellect any sympathy applicable to those injuries, that is, to those hurts, which wound us through, or in common with, society at large. This sentiment, in itself, has nothing moral in it; what is moral is, the exclusive subordination of it to the social sympathies, so as to wait on and obey their call. For the natural feeling would make us resent indiscriminately whatever any one does that is disagreeable to us; but when moralized by the social feeling, it only acts in the directions conformable to the general good: just persons resenting a hurt to society, though not otherwise a hurt to themselves, and not resenting a hurt to themselves, however painful, unless it be of the kind which society has a common interest with them in the repression of.

It is no objection against this doctrine to say, that when we feel our sentiment of justice outraged, we are not thinking of society at large, or of any collective interest, but only of the individual case. It is common enough certainly, though the reverse of commendable, to feel resentment merely because we have suffered pain; but a person whose resentment is really a moral feeling, that is, who considers whether an act is blamable before he allows himself to resent it—such a person, though he may not say expressly to himself that he is standing up for the interest of society, certainly does feel that he is asserting a rule which is for the benefit of others as well as for his own. If he is not feeling this—if he is regarding the act solely as it affects him individually—he is not consciously just; he is not concerning himself about the justice of his actions. This is admitted even by anti-utilitarian moralists. When Kant (as before remarked) propounds as the fundamental principle of morals, "So act, that thy rule of conduct might be adopted as a law by all rational beings," he virtually acknowledges that the interest of mankind collectively, or at least of mankind indiscriminately, must be in the mind of the agent when conscientiously deciding on the morality of the act. Otherwise he uses words without a meaning: for, that a rule even of utter selfishness could not *possibly* be adopted by all rational beings—that there is any insuperable obstacle in the nature of things to its adoption—

cannot be even plausibly maintained. To give any meaning to Kant's principle, the sense put upon it must be, that we ought to shape our conduct by a rule which all rational beings might adopt *with benefit to their collective interest*.

To recapitulate: the idea of justice supposes two things; a rule of conduct, and a sentiment which sanctions the rule. The first must be supposed common to all mankind, and intended for their good. The other (the sentiment) is a desire that punishment may be suffered by those who infringe the rule. There is involved, in addition, the conception of some definite person who suffers by the infringement; whose rights (to use the expression appropriated to the case) are violated by it. And the sentiment of justice appears to me to be, the animal desire to repel or retaliate a hurt or damage to oneself, or to those with whom one sympathizes, widened so as to include all persons, by the human capacity of enlarged sympathy, and the human conception of intelligent self-interest. From the latter elements, the feeling derives its morality; from the former, its peculiar impressiveness, and energy of self- assertion.

I have, throughout, treated the idea of a *right* residing in the injured person, and violated by the injury, not as a separate element in the composition of the idea and sentiment, but as one of the forms in which the other two elements clothe themselves. These elements are, a hurt to some assignable person or persons on the one hand, and a demand for punishment on the other. An examination of our own minds, I think, will show, that these two things include all that we mean when we speak of violation of a right. When we call anything a person's right, we mean that he has a valid claim on society to protect him in the possession of it, either by the force of law, or by that of education and opinion. If he has what we consider a sufficient claim, on whatever account, to have something guaranteed to him by society, we say that he has a right to it. If we desire to prove that anything does not belong to him by right, we think this done as soon as it is admitted that society ought not to take measures for securing it to him, but should leave him to chance, or to his own exertions. Thus, a person is said to have a right to what he can earn in fair professional competition; because society ought not to allow any other person to hinder him from endeavoring to earn in that manner as much as he can. But he has not a right to three hundred a-year, though he may happen to be earning it; because society is not called on to provide that he shall earn that sum. On the contrary, if he owns ten thousand pounds three percent stock, he *has* a right to three hundred a-year; because society has come under an obligation to provide him with an income of that amount.

To have a right, then, is, I conceive, to have something which society ought to defend me in the possession of. If the objector goes on to ask, why it ought? I can give him no other reason than general utility. If that expression does not seem to convey a sufficient feeling of the strength of the obligation, nor to account for the peculiar energy of the feeling, it is because there goes to the composition of the sentiment, not a rational only, but also an animal element, the thirst for retaliation; and this thirst derives its intensity, as well as its moral justification, from the extraordinarily important and impressive kind of utility which is concerned. The interest involved is that of security, to every one's feelings the most vital of all interests. All other earthly benefits are needed by one person, not needed by another; and many of them can, if necessary, be cheerfully foregone, or replaced by something else; but security no human being can possibly do without; on it we depend for all our immunity from evil, and for the whole value of all and every good, beyond the passing moment; since nothing but the gratification of the instant could be of any worth to us, if we could be deprived of anything the next instant by whoever was momentarily stronger than ourselves. Now this most indispensable of all necessaries, after physical nutriment, cannot be had, unless the machinery for providing it is kept unintermittedly in active play. Our notion, therefore, of the claim we have on our fellow-creatures to join in making safe for us the very groundwork of our existence, gathers feelings around it so much more intense than those concerned in any of the more common cases of utility, that the difference in degree (as is often the case in psychology) becomes a real difference in kind. The claim assumes that character of absoluteness, that apparent infinity, and incommensurability with all other considerations, which constitute the distinction between the feeling of right and wrong and that of ordinary expediency and inexpediency. The feelings concerned are so powerful, and we count so positively on finding a responsive feeling in others (all being alike interested), that *ought* and *should* grow into *must*, and recognized indispensability becomes a moral necessity, analogous to physical, and often not inferior to it in binding force.

If the preceding analysis, or something resembling it, be not the correct account of the notion of justice; if justice be totally independent of utility, and be a standard *per se*, which the mind can recognize by simple introspection of itself; it is hard to understand why that internal oracle is so ambiguous, and why so many things appear either just or unjust, according to the light in which they are regarded.

We are continually informed that utility is an uncertain standard, which every different person interprets differently, and that there is no safety but in the immutable, ineffaceable, and unmistakable dictates of justice, which carry their evidence in themselves, and are independent of the fluctuations of opinion. One would suppose from this that on questions of justice there could be no controversy; that if we take that for our rule, its application to any given case could leave us in as little doubt as a mathematical demonstration. So far is this from being the fact; that there is as much difference of opinion and as much discussion about what is just, as about what is useful to society. Not only have different nations and individuals different notions of justice, but in the mind of one and the same individual, justice is not some one rule, principle, or maxim, but many, which do not always coincide in their dictates, and in choosing between which he is guided either by some extraneous standard or by his own personal predilections.

For instance, there are some who say that it is unjust to punish anyone for the sake of example to others; that punishment is just only when intended for the good of the sufferer himself. Others maintain the extreme reverse, contending that to punish persons who have attained years of discretion, for their own benefit, is despotism and injustice, since if the matter at issue is solely their own good, no one has a right to control their own judgment of it; but that they may justly be punished to prevent evil to others, this being the exercise of the legitimate right of self-defense. Mr. Owen,* again, affirms that it is unjust to punish at all; for the criminal did not make his own character; his education, and the circumstances which surrounded him, have made him a criminal, and for these he is not responsible. All these opinions are extremely plausible; and so long as the question is argued as one of justice simply, without going down to the principles which lie under justice and are the source of its authority, I am unable to see how any of these reasoners can be refuted. For in truth every one of the three builds upon rules of justice confessedly true. The first appeals to the acknowledged injustice of singling out an individual, and making him a sacrifice, without his consent, for other people's benefit. The second relies on the acknowledged justice of self-defense, and the admitted injustice of forcing one person to conform to another's notions of what constitutes his good. The Owenite invokes the admitted principle that it is unjust to punish anyone for what he cannot help. Each is triumphant so long as he is not compelled to take into consideration any other maxims of justice than the one he has selected; but as soon as their several maxims are brought face to face, each disputant seems to have exactly as much to say for himself as the others. No one of them can carry out his own notion of justice without trampling upon another equally binding. These are difficulties; they have always been felt to be such; and many devices have been invented to turn rather than to overcome them. As a refuge from the last of the three, men imagined what they called the freedom of the will; fancying that they could not justify punishing a man whose will is in a thoroughly hateful state, unless it be supposed to have come into that state through no influence of anterior circumstances. To escape from the other difficulties, a favorite contrivance has been the fiction of a contract, whereby at some unknown period all the members of society engaged to obey the laws and consented to be punished for any disobedience to them; thereby giving to their legislators the right, which it is assumed they would not otherwise have had, of punishing them, either for their own good or for that of society. This happy thought was considered to get rid of the whole difficulty, and to legitimate the infliction of punishment, in virtue of another received maximum of justice, *Volenti non fit injuria*—that is not unjust which is done with the consent of the person who is supposed to be hurt by it. I need hardly remark that even if the consent were not a mere fiction, this maxim is not superior in authority to the others which it is brought in to supersede. It is, on the contrary, an instructive specimen of the loose and irregular manner in which supposed principles of justice grow up. This particular one evidently came into use as a help to the coarse exigencies of courts of law, which are sometimes obliged to be content with very uncertain presumptions, on account of the greater evils which would often arise from any attempt on their part to cut finer. But even courts of law are not able to adhere consistently to the maxim, for they allow voluntary engagements to be set aside on the ground of fraud, and sometimes on that of mere mistake or misinformation.

Again, when the legitimacy of inflicting punishment is admitted, how many conflicting conceptions of justice come to light in discussing the proper apportionment of punishments to offenses, No rule on the subject recommends itself so strongly to the primitive and spontaneous sentiment of justice as the *lex talionis,* an eye for an eye and a tooth for a tooth. Though this principle of the Jewish and of the Mohammedan law has been generally abandoned in Europe as a practical maxim, there is, I suspect, in most minds, a secret hankering after it; and when retribution accidentally falls on an offender in that precise shape, the general feeling of satisfaction evinced bears witness how natural is the sentiment to which this repayment in kind is acceptable. With many,

*Robert Owen (1771–1858) ran a number of successful textile factories in New Lanmark, Scotland, where he also set up a new type of community. Owen believed that people were good by nature but corrupted by their environment and that the right environment would produce rational, good people. In New Lanmark, he instituted a number of reforms such as shortening work hours for children in the factory and requiring them to attend school. Own also opposed physical punishment in schools and factories, and banned its use in New Lanmark. Not satisfied with the response his ideas received in Britain, in 1825, Owen established a new community based on his ideas in New Harmony, Indiana. —Ed.

the test of justice in penal infliction is that the punishment should be proportioned to the offense; meaning that it should be exactly measured by the moral guilt of the culprit. (whatever be their standard for measuring moral guilt)—the consideration, what amount of punishment is necessary to deter from the offense, having nothing to do with the question of justice, in their estimation; while there are others to whom that consideration is all in all—who maintain that it is not just, at least for man, to inflict on a fellow-creature, whatever may be his offenses, any amount of suffering beyond the least that will suffice to prevent him from repeating, and others from imitating, his misconduct.

To take another example from a subject already once referred to. In a co-operative industrial association, is it just or not that talent or skill should give a title to superior remuneration? On the negative side of the question it is argued that whoever does the best he can, deserves equally well, and ought not in justice to be put in a position of inferiority for no fault of his own; that superior abilities have already advantages more than enough, in the admiration they excite, the personal influence they command, and the internal sources of satisfaction attending them, without adding to these a superior share of the world's goods; and that society is bound in justice rather to make compensation to the less favored for this unmerited inequality of advantages, than to aggravate it. On the contrary side it is contended that society receives more from the more efficient laborer; that his services being more useful, society owes him a larger return for them; that a greater share of the joint result is actually his work, and not to allow his claim to it is a kind of robbery; that if he is only to receive as much as others, he can only be justly required to produce as much, and to give a smaller amount of time and exertion, proportioned to his superior efficiency. Who shall decide between these appeals to conflicting principles of justice? Justice has in this case two sides to it, which it is impossible to bring into harmony, and the two disputants have chosen opposite sides; the one looks to what it is just that the individual should receive, the other to what it is just that the community should give. Each, from his own point of view, is unanswerable; and any choice between

them, on grounds of justice, must be perfectly arbitrary. Social utility alone can decide the preference.

How many, again, and how irreconcilable, are the standards of justice to which reference is made in discussing the repartition of taxation. One opinion is, that payment to the State should be in numerical proportion to pecuniary means. Others think that justice dictates what they term graduated taxation; taking a higher percentage from those who have more to spare. In point of natural justice a strong case might be made for disregarding means altogether, and taking the same absolute sum (whenever it could be got) from everyone—as the subscribers to a mess, or to a club, all pay the same sum for the same privileges, whether they can all equally afford it or not. Since the protection (it might be said) of law and government is afforded to, and is equally required by all, there is no injustice in making all buy it at the same price. It is reckoned justice, not injustice, that a dealer should charge to all customers the same price for the same article, not a price varying according to their means of payment. This doctrine, as applied to taxation, finds no advocates, because it conflicts so strongly with man's feelings of humanity and of social expediency; but the principle of justice which it invokes is as true and as binding as those which can be appealed to against it. Accordingly it exerts a tacit influence on the line of defense employed for other modes of assessing taxation. People feel obliged to argue that the State does more for the rich than for the poor, as a justification for its taking more from them: though this is in reality not true, for the rich would be far better able to protect themselves, in the absence of law or government, than the poor, and indeed would probably be successful in converting the poor into their slaves. Others again, so far defer to the same conception of justice, as to maintain that all should pay an equal capitation tax for the protection of their persons (these being of equal value to all), and an unequal tax for the protection of their property, which is unequal. To this others reply that the all of one man is as valuable to him as the all of another. From these confusions there is no other mode of extrication than the utilitarian. . . .

It appears from what has been said that justice is a name for certain moral requirements which, regarded collectively, stand higher in the scale of social utility, and are therefore of more paramount obligation, than any others; though particular cases may occur in which some other social duty is so important, as to overrule any one of the general maxims of justice. Thus, to save a life, it may not only be allowable but a duty to steal or take by force the necessary food or medicine, or to kidnap and compel to officiate the only qualified medical practitioner. In such cases, as we do not call anything justice which is not a virtue; we usually say, not that justice must give way to some other moral principle, but that what is just in ordinary cases is, by reason of that other principle not just in the particular case. By this useful accommodation of language, the character of indefeasibility attributed to justice is kept up, and we are saved from the necessity of maintaining that there can be laudable injustice.

The considerations which have now been adduced resolve, I conceive, the only real difficulty in the utilitarian theory of morals. It has always been evident that all cases of justice are also cases of expediency: the difference is in the peculiar sentiment which attaches to the former, as contradistinguished from the latter. If this characteristic sentiment has been sufficiently accounted for; if there is no necessity to assume for it any peculiarity of origin; if it is simply the natural feeling of resentment, moralized by being made coextensive with the demands of social good; and if this feeling not only does but ought to exist in all the classes of cases to which the idea of justice corresponds: that idea no longer presents itself as a stumbling-block to the utilitarian ethics. Justice remains the appropriate name for certain social utilities which are vastly more important,

and therefore more absolute and imperative, than any others are as a class (though not more so than others may be in particular cases); and which, therefore, ought to be, as well as naturally are, guarded by a sentiment not only different in degree, but also in kind; distinguished from the milder feeling which attaches to the mere idea of promoting human pleasure or convenience, at once by the more definite nature of its commands, and by the sterner character of its sanctions.

DISCUSSION QUESTIONS

1. According to Mill, what are the sources of our desire to punish? Are these sources connected in any way to utility? If so, how?

2. What are "rights" according to Mill? How are they grounded in utility? Do you agree with Mill? Why or why not?

3. What, for Mill, is the relationship between justice, impartiality, and equality? Do you agree with his analysis? Why or why not?

4. Mill discusses punishment, the fair distribution of wealth, and fair taxation. Why does he believe that a utilitarian notion of justice allows us to best contend with these issues? Do you agree with him? Why or why not?

5. Mill says, "To save a life, it may not only be allowable but a duty to steal or take by force the necessary food or medicine, or to kidnap and compel to officiate the only qualified practitioner." What is his argument? Does he believe that such actions are "laudable injustice"? Why or why not? Do you agree with his moral analysis of these actions? Why or why not?

KARL MARX AND FRIEDRICH ENGELS
THE COMMUNIST THEORY OF SOCIAL JUSTICE

K arl Marx and Friedrich Engels argue that the history of society is the history of class struggles. In each historical period, classes are formed as the result of the prevailing economic conditions, and when one looks back over the course of history, one sees much variation in class formation. There are no fixed, ahistorical classes; rather, "we find almost everywhere a complicated arrangement of society into various orders" based on economic conditions. For Marx and Engels, economics determines nearly everything in society, including the nature of its legal, religious, philosophical, and artistic institutions. To understand each of these, one must study the economic structures of which they are the products.

In modern times, the industrial revolution has produced two classes: (1) the *bourgeoisie*—the capitalists, who own the means of production such as factories—and (2) the *proletariat*—the workers, who are employed as wage-laborers by the bourgeoisie and who do not own the means of production. Within a capitalist economic system, the proletariat is the subject of increasing exploitation by the bourgeoisie. Marx and Engels state that members of the proletariat are "a commodity like every other article of commerce, and are consequently exposed to the vicissitudes of competition, to all the fluctuations of the market." "Not only are they slaves of the bourgeois class and of the bourgeois state; they are daily and hourly enslaved by the machine, by the overlooker, and, above all, by the individual bourgeois manufacturer himself." These conditions push the proletariat into a struggle with the bourgeoisie, with the ultimate goal of overthrowing the entire capitalist system. Marx and Engels view the proletariat as a "revolutionary class." The aim of the Communists is the "formation of the proletariat into a ruling class, overthow of the bourgeois supremacy, [and] conquest of political power by the proletariat."

Nevertheless, Marx and Engels are quite clear that the overthrow of capitalism will come about through both the revolutionary actions of the proletariat and the evolution of capitalism itself, which contains the seeds of its own destruction. The success of capitalism leads, for example, to overproduction, which in turn brings about its ruin. The Communists' push to organize the proletariat is aimed at bringing about a faster demise of capitalism, and is not the primary cause of capitalism's downfall and demise. "The theoretical conclusions of the Communists are in no way based on ideas or principles that have been invented, or discovered by this or that would-be universal reformer," write Marx and Engels. "The Communists everywhere support every revolutionary movement against the existing [capitalist] social and political order of things." According to Marx and Engels, capitalism as an economic system will ultimately fail; it is only a matter of time. The role of the Communists is to hasten capitalism's demise and to bring about a system of political power controlled by the proletariat, not the bourgeoisie. Such a system will, among other things, abolish private property and inheritance, and centralize banking, communication, and transportation. Under communism, the means of production will be controlled by the state.

Karl Marx (1818–83), German philosopher and economist, was born in Trèves, Prussia. Although his parents were Jewish, they converted to Lutheranism in 1824. At the age of seventeen, he studied law at the University of Bonn; he later transferred to the University of Berlin, where he took up the study of philosophy. In 1841, he received his Ph.D. in philosophy from the University of Jena with a thesis on Epicurus, though he was unable to secure a teaching position owing to his association with the Young Hegelians, a radical political group. In 1842, he became editor of the *Renish Gazette*, a liberal newspaper in Cologne, but when the paper was suppressed by the authorities, he moved to Paris in the fall of 1843 to be co-editor of the *Deutsch-französische Jahrbücher*. However, the *Jahrbücher* was also banned by the authorities after the publication of only one issue, and Marx was expelled from Paris at the request of the Prussian government. He then moved to Brussels, Belgium to edit with Engels the *Brüsseller deutsche Zeitung*, a weekly newspaper, and to work with the League of the Just, an organization of German workers dedicated to communism. In 1849, after being acquitted of treason in Prussia, he was expelled from Prussia and soon thereafter moved to London, where he would spend the rest of his life. Much of his time in London was spent at the British Museum working on his book, *Das Kapital*. He thought that the publication might make him wealthy, though the first volume sold only a thousand copies. He joked that the royalties from the book were not even enough to pay for the cigars he smoked writing it. His major works are *Economic and Philosophical Manuscripts of 1844* (1932), *The Holy Family* (with Engels, 1845), *The German Ideology* (with Engels, 1845–46), *The Poverty of Philosophy* (1847), *The Communist Manifesto* (1848), *The 18th Brumaire of Louis Bonaparte* (1852), and *Das Kapital* (3 vols., 1867, 1885, 1895).

Friedrich Engels (1820–95), German philosopher, was born in Garmen, Germany. He dropped out of secondary school and never attended university. In 1838, he worked in the office of his father's textile mill. He became interested in politics and became a Communist in 1842, the year in which he would also first meet Marx in Cologne. He then went to Manchester, England, to work as a clerk in his father's cotton mill. In 1844, he traveled to Paris to visit Marx and soon became Marx's close friend and lifelong collaborator. Engels followed Marx to Belgium in 1845. When Engels later moved back to Manchester to again work for his father, he shared his salary with Marx, who was then living in London. Engels introduced Marx to the working-class movement and political economy, and they coauthored *The Holy Family*, *The German Ideology*, and the *Communist Manifesto*. Engels also edited volumes 2 and 3 of *Das Kapital* and prepared them for publication after Marx's death. His writings include *Anti-Dühring* (1878), *Socialism: Utopian and Scientific* (1883), *The Origin of the Family, Private Property, and the State* (1884), *Ludwig Feuerbach and the Outcome of Classical German Philosophy* (1888), *Principles of Communism* (1919), and *Dialectics of Nature* (1925).

This selection is from the *Manifesto of the Communist Party*, which was written in December 1847 and January 1848. It was originally distributed only to the membership of the Communist League; however, since the first reprinted edition appeared in 1871, many editions have appeared, and it has been translated into many languages. It is one of the most influential books ever published.

1. Bourgeois and Proletarians

The history of all hitherto existing society is the history of class struggles.

Freeman and slave, patrician and plebeian, lord and serf, guild master and journeyman, in a word, oppressor and oppressed, stood in constant opposition to one another, carried on an uninterrupted, now hidden, now open fight—a fight that each time ended either in a revolutionary reconstitution of society at large, or in the common ruin of the contending classes.

In the earlier epochs of history, we find almost everywhere a complicated arrangement of society into various orders, a manifold gradation of social rank. In ancient Rome, we have patricians, knights, plebeians, slaves; in the Middle Ages, feudal lords, vassals, guild masters, journeymen, apprentices, serfs; in almost all of these classes, again, subordinate gradations.

The modern bourgeois society that has sprouted from the ruins of feudal society has not done away with class antagonisms. It has but established new classes, new conditions of oppression, new forms of struggle in place of the old ones.

Our epoch, the epoch of the bourgeoisie, possesses, however, this distinctive feature: it has simplified the class antagonisms. Society as a whole is more and more splitting up into two great hostile camps, into two great classes directly facing each other: bourgeoisie and proletariat.

From the serfs of the Middle Ages sprang the chartered burghers of the earliest towns. From these burgesses the first elements of the bourgeoisie were developed.

The discovery of America, the rounding of the Cape, opened up fresh ground for the rising bourgeoisie. The East Indian and Chinese markets, the colonisation of America, trade with the colonies, the increase in the means of exchange and in commodities generally, gave to commerce, to navigation, to industry, an impulse never before known, and thereby, to the revolutionary element in the tottering feudal society, a rapid development.

The feudal system of industry, under which industrial production was monopolised by closed guilds, now no longer sufficed for the growing wants of the new markets. The manufacturing system took its place. The guild masters were pushed on one side by the manufacturing middle class; division of labour between the different corporate guilds vanished in the face of division of labour in each single workshop.

Meantime the markets kept ever growing, the demand ever rising. Even manufacture no longer sufficed. Thereupon, steam and machinery revolutionised industrial production. The place of manufacture was taken by the giant, modern industry; the place of the industrial middle class, by industrial millionaires, the leaders of whole industrial armies, the modern bourgeois.

Modern industry has established the world market, for which the discovery of America paved the way. This market has given an immense development to commerce, to navigation, to communication by land. This development has, in its turn, reacted on the extension of industry; and in proportion as industry, commerce, navigation, railways extended, in the same proportion the bourgeoisie developed, increased its capital, and pushed into the background every class handed down from the Middle Ages.

We see, therefore, how the modern bourgeoisie is itself the product of a long course of development, of a series of revolutions in the modes of production and of exchange. . . .

The bourgeoisie, historically, has played a most revolutionary part.

The bourgeoisie, wherever it has got the upper hand, has put an end to all feudal, patriarchal, idyllic relations. It has pitilessly torn asunder the motley feudal ties that bound man to his "natural superiors," and has left remaining no other nexus between man and man than naked self-interest, than callous "cash payment." It has drowned the most heavenly ecstasies of religious fervour, of chivalrous enthusiasm, of philistine sentimentalism, in the icy water of egotistical calculation. It has resolved personal worth into exchange value, and in place of the numberless indefeasible chartered freedoms, has set up that single, unconscionable freedom—free trade. In one word, for exploitation veiled by religious and political illusions, it has substituted naked, shameless, direct, brutal exploitation.

The bourgeoisie has stripped of its halo every occupation hitherto honoured and looked up to with reverent awe. It has converted the physician, the lawyer, the priest, the poet, the man of science, into its paid wage-labourers.

The bourgeoisie has torn away from the family its sentimental veil, and has reduced the family relation to a mere money relation. . . .

The bourgeoisie cannot exist without constantly revolutionising the instruments of production, and thereby the relations of production, and with them the whole relations of society. Conservation of the old modes of production in unaltered form was, on the contrary, the first condition of existence for all earlier industrial classes. Constant revolutionising of production, uninterrupted disturbance of all social conditions, everlasting uncertainty and agitation, distinguish the bourgeois epoch from all earlier ones. All fixed, fast-frozen relations, with their train of ancient and venerable prejudices and opinions, are swept away; all new-formed ones become antiquated before they can ossify. All that is solid melts into air, all that is holy is profaned, and man is at last compelled to face with sober senses his real conditions of life and his relations with his kind.

The need of a constantly expanding market for its products chases the bourgeoisie over the whole surface of the globe. It must nestle everywhere, settle everywhere, establish connexions everywhere.

The bourgeoisie has through its exploitation of the world market given a cosmopolitan character to production and consumption in every country.

To the great chagrin of reactionists, it has drawn from under the feet of industry the national ground on which it stood. All old-established national industries have been destroyed or are daily being destroyed. They are dislodged by new industries, whose introduction becomes a life and death question for all civilised nations, by industries that no longer work up indigenous raw material, but raw material drawn from the remotest zones; industries whose products are consumed not only at home, but in every quarter of the globe. In place of the old wants, satisfied by the productions of the country, we find new wants, requiring for their satisfaction the products of distant lands and climes. In place of the old local and national seclusion and self-sufficiency, we have intercourse in every direction, universal interdependence of nations. And as in material, so also in intellectual production. The intellectual creations of individual nations become common property. National one-sidedness and narrow-mindedness become more and more impossible, and from the numerous national and local literatures there arises a world literature.

The bourgeoisie, by the rapid improvement of all instruments of production, by the immensely facilitated means of communication, draws all, even the most barbarian, nations into civilisation. The cheap prices of its commodities are the heavy artillery with which it batters down all Chinese walls, with which it forces the barbarians' intensely obstinate hatred of foreigners to capitulate. It compels all nations, on pain of extinction, to adopt the bourgeois mode of production; it compels them to introduce what it calls civilisation into their midst, that is, to become bourgeois themselves. In one word, it creates a world after its own image. . . .

Modern bourgeois society with its relations of production, of exchange, and of property, a society that has conjured up such gigantic means of production and of exchange, is like the sorcerer who is no longer able to control the powers of the nether world whom he has called up by his spells. For many a decade past, the history of industry and commerce is but the history of the revolt of modern productive forces against modern conditions of production, against the property relations that are the conditions for the existence of the bourgeoisie and of its rule. It is enough to mention the commercial crises that by their periodical return put on its trial, each time more threateningly, the existence of the entire bourgeois society. In these crises a great part not only of the existing products, but also of the previously created productive forces, are periodically destroyed. In these crises there breaks out an epidemic that, in all earlier epochs, would have seemed an absurdity—the epidemic of overproduction. Society suddenly finds itself put back into a state of momentary barbarism; it appears as if a famine, a universal war of devastation, had cut off the supply of every means of subsistence; industry and commerce seem to be destroyed. And why? Because there is too much civilisation, too much means of subsistence, too much industry, too much commerce. The productive forces at the disposal of society no longer tend to further the development of the conditions of bourgeois property; on the contrary, they have become too powerful for these conditions by which they are fettered, and so soon as they overcome these fetters, they bring disorder into the whole of bourgeois society, endanger the existence of bourgeois property. The conditions of bourgeois society are too narrow to comprise the wealth created by them. And how does the bourgeoisie get over these crises? On the one hand, by enforced destruction of a mass of productive forces; on the other, by the conquest of new markets and by the more thorough exploitation of the old ones. That is to say, by paving the way for more extensive and more destructive crises, and by diminishing the means whereby crises are prevented.

The weapons with which the bourgeoisie felled feudalism to the ground are now turned against the bourgeoisie itself.

But not only has the bourgeoisie forged the weapons that bring death to itself; it has also called into existence the men who are to wield those weapons—the modern working class, the proletarians.

In proportion as the bourgeoisie, that is, capital, is developed, in the same proportion is the proletariat, the modern working class, developed—a class of labourers who live only so long as they find work and who find work only so long as their labour increases capital. These labourers, who must sell themselves piecemeal, are a commodity like every other article of commerce, and are consequently exposed to all the vicissitudes of competition, to all the fluctuations of the market.

Owing to the extensive use of machinery and to division of labour, the work of the proletarians has lost all individual character and, consequently, all charm for the workman. He becomes an appendage of the machine, and it is only the most simple, most monotonous, and most easily acquired knack that is required of him. Hence, the cost of production of a workman is restricted, almost entirely, to the means of subsistence that he requires for his maintenance and for the propagation of his race. But the price of a commodity, and therefore also of labour, is equal to its cost of production. In proportion, therefore, as the repulsiveness of the work increases, the wage decreases. Nay more, in proportion as the use of machinery and division of labour increases, in the same proportion the burden of toil also increases, whether by prolongation of the working hours, by increase of the work exacted in a given time, or by increased speed of the machinery, etc.

Modern industry has converted the little workshop of the patriarchal master into the great factory of the industrial capitalist. Masses of labourers, crowded into the factory, are organised like soldiers. As privates of the industrial army they are placed under the command of a perfect hierarchy of officers and sergeants. Not only are they slaves of the bourgeois class and of the bourgeois state; they are daily and hourly enslaved by the machine, by the overlooker, and, above all, by the individual bourgeois manufacturer himself. The more openly this despotism proclaims gain to be its end and aim, the more petty, the more hateful, and the more embittering it is.

The less the skill and exertion of strength implied in manual labour, in other words, the more modern industry becomes developed, the more is the labour of men superseded by that of women. Differences of age and sex have no longer any distinctive social validity for the working class. All are instruments of labour, more or less expensive to use, according to their age and sex.

No sooner is the exploitation of the labourer by the manufacturer, so far, at an end, and he receives his wages in cash, than he is set upon by the other portions of the bourgeoisie, the landlord, the shopkeeper, the pawnbroker, etc.

The lower strata of the middle class—the small tradespeople, shopkeepers, and retired tradesmen generally, the handicraftsmen and peasants—all these sink gradually into the proletariat, partly because their diminutive capital does not suffice for the scale on which modern industry is carried on, and is swamped in the competition with the large capitalists, partly because their specialised skill is rendered worthless by new methods of production. Thus the proletariat is recruited from all classes of the population.

The proletariat goes through various stages of development. With its birth begins its struggle with the bourgeoisie. At first the contest is carried on by individual labourers, then by the workpeople of a factory, then by the operatives of one trade, in one locality, against the individual bourgeois who directly exploits them. They direct their attacks not against the bourgeois conditions of production, but against the instruments of production themselves; they destroy imported wares that compete with their labour, they smash to pieces machinery, they set factories ablaze, they seek to restore by force the vanished status of the workman of the Middle Ages.

At this stage the labourers still form an incoherent mass scattered over the whole country and broken up by their mutual competition. If anywhere they unite to form more compact bodies, this is not yet the consequence of their own active union, but of the union of the bourgeoisie, which class, in order to attain its own political ends, is compelled to set the whole proletariat in motion, and is moreover yet, for a time, able to do so. At this stage, therefore, the proletarians do not fight their enemies, but the enemies of their enemies, the remnants of absolute monarchy, the landowners, the nonindustrial bourgeois, the petty bourgeoisie. Thus the whole historical movement is concentrated in the hands of the bourgeoisie; every victory so obtained is a victory for the bourgeoisie.

But with the development of industry the proletariat not only increases in number; it becomes concentrated in greater masses, its strength grows, and it feels that strength more. The various interests and conditions of life within the ranks of the proletariat are more and more equalised, in proportion as machinery obliterates all distinctions of labour, and nearly everywhere reduces wages to the same low level. The growing competition among the bourgeois, and the resulting commercial crises, make the wages of the workers ever more fluctuating. The unceasing improvement of machinery, ever more rapidly developing, makes their livelihood more and more precarious; the collisions between individual workmen and individual bourgeois take more and more the character of collisions between two classes. Thereupon the workers begin to form combinations (trades' unions) against the bourgeois; they club together in order to keep up the rate of wages; they found permanent associations in order to make provision beforehand for these occasional revolts. Here and there the contest breaks out into riots.

Now and then the workers are victorious, but only for a time. The real fruit of their battles lies not in the immediate result, but in the ever-expanding union of the workers. This union is helped on, by the improved means of communication that are created by modern industry and that place the workers of different localities in contact with one another. It was just this contact that was needed to centralise the numerous local struggles, all of the same character, into one national struggle between classes. But every class struggle is a political struggle. And that union, to attain which the burghers of the Middle Ages, with their miserable highways, required centuries, the modern proletarians, thanks to railways, achieve in a few years.

This organisation of the proletarians into a class, and consequently into a political party, is continually being upset again by the competition between the workers themselves. But it ever rises up again, stronger, firmer, mightier. It compels legislative recognition of particular interests of the workers, by taking advantage of the divisions among the bourgeoisie itself. Thus the ten hours' bill in England was carried.*

Altogether collisions between the classes of the old society further, in many ways, the course of development of the proletariat. The bourgeoisie finds itself involved in a constant battle. At first

with the aristocracy; later on, with those portions of the bourgeoisie itself, whose interests have become antagonistic to the progress of industry; at all times, with the bourgeoisie of foreign countries. In all these battles it sees itself compelled to appeal to the proletariat, to ask for its help, and thus to drag it into the political arena. The bourgeoisie itself, therefore, supplies the proletariat with its own elements of political and general education. In other words, it furnishes the proletariat with weapons for fighting the bourgeoisie.

Further, as we have already seen, entire sections of the ruling classes are, by the advance of industry, precipitated into the proletariat, or are at least threatened in their conditions of existence. These also supply the proletariat with fresh elements of enlightenment and progress.

Finally, in times when the class struggle nears the decisive hour, the process of dissolution going on within the ruling class—in fact within the whole range of old society—assumes such a violent, glaring character, that a small section of the ruling class cuts itself adrift and joins the revolutionary class, the class that holds the future in its hands. Just as, therefore, at an earlier period, a section of the nobility went over to the bourgeoisie, so now a portion of the bourgeoisie goes over to the proletariat, and in particular, a portion of the bourgeois ideologists, who have raised themselves to the level of comprehending theoretically the historical movement as a whole.

Of all the classes that stand face to face with the bourgeoisie today, the proletariat alone is a really revolutionary class. The other classes decay and finally disappear in the face of modern industry; the proletariat is its special and essential product. . . .

All the preceding classes that got the upper hand sought to fortify their already acquired status by subjecting society at large to their conditions of appropriation. The proletarians cannot become masters of the productive forces of society, except by abolishing their own previous mode of appropriation, and thereby also every other previous mode of appropriation. They have nothing of their own to secure and to fortify; their

---

* In 1847, the Ten Hours Act was passed. It placed a ten-hour limit on the workdays of women and children who were industrial laborers —Ed.

mission is to destroy all previous securities for, and insurances of, individual property.

All previous historical movements were movements of minorities, or in the interest of minorities. The proletarian movement is the self-conscious, independent movement of the immense majority, in the interest of the immense majority. The proletariat, the lowest stratum of our present society, cannot stir, cannot raise itself up, without the whole superincumbent strata of official society being sprung into the air.

Though not in substance, yet in form, the struggle of the proletariat with the bourgeoisie is at first a national struggle. The proletariat of each country must, of course, first of all settle matters with its own bourgeoisie.

In depicting the most general phases of the development of the proletariat, we traced the more or less veiled civil war, raging within existing society, up to the point where that war breaks out into open revolution, and where the violent overthrow of the bourgeoisie lays the foundation for the sway of the proletariat.

Hitherto, every form of society has been based, as we have already seen, on the antagonism of oppressing and oppressed classes. But in order to oppress a class, certain conditions must be assured to it under which it can at least continue its slavish existence. The serf, in the period of serfdom, raised himself to membership in the commune, just as the petty bourgeois, under the yoke of feudal absolutism, managed to develop into a bourgeois. The modern labourer, on the contrary, instead of rising with the progress of industry, sinks deeper and deeper below the conditions of existence of his own class. He becomes a pauper, and pauperism develops more rapidly than population and wealth. And here it becomes evident that the bourgeoisie is unfit any longer to be the ruling class in society and to impose its conditions of existence upon society as an overriding law. It is unfit to rule because it is incompetent to assure an existence to its slave within his slavery, because it cannot help letting him sink into such a state that it has to feed him, instead of being fed by him. Society can no longer live under this bourgeoisie. In other words, its existence is no longer compatible with society.

The essential condition for the existence and for the sway of the bourgeois class is the formation and augmentation of capital; the condition for capital is wage-labour. Wage-labour rests exclusively on competition between the labourers. The advance of industry, whose involuntary promoter is the bourgeoisie, replaces the isolation of the labourers, due to competition; by their revolutionary combination, due to association. The development of modern industry, therefore, cuts from under its feet the very foundation on which the bourgeoisie produces and appropriates products. What the bourgeoisie, therefore, produces above all is its own grave-diggers. Its fall and the victory of the proletariat are equally inevitable.

II. PROLETARIANS AND COMMUNISTS

In what relation do the Communists stand to the proletarians as a whole?

The Communists do not form a separate party opposed to other working-class parties.

They have no interests separate and apart from those of the proletariat as a whole.

They do not set up any sectarian principles of their own, by which to shape and mould the proletarian movement.

The Communists are distinguished from the other working-class parties by this only: (1) In the national struggles of the proletarians of the different countries; they point out and bring to the front the common interests of the entire proletariat, independently of all nationality. (2) In the various stages of development which the struggle of the working class against the bourgeoisie has to pass through, they always and everywhere represent the interests of the movement as a whole.

The Communists, therefore, are on the one hand, practically, the most advanced and resolute section of the working-class parties of every country, that section which pushes forward all others; on the other hand, theoretically, they have over the great mass of the proletariat the advantage of clearly understanding the line of march, the conditions, and the ultimate general results of the proletarian movement.

The immediate aim of the Communists is the same as that of all the other proletarian parties: formation of the proletariat into a class, overthrow of the bourgeois supremacy, conquest of political power by the proletariat.

The theoretical conclusions of the Communists are in no way based on ideas or principles that have been invented, or discovered by this or that would-be universal reformer.

They merely express, in general terms, actual relations springing from an existing class struggle, from a historical movement going on under our very eyes. The abolition of existing property relations is not at all a distinctive feature of Communism.

All property relations in the past have continually been subject to historical change consequent upon the change in historical conditions.

The French Revolution, for example, abolished feudal property in favour of bourgeois property.

The distinguishing feature of Communism is not the abolition of property generally, but the abolition of bourgeois property. But modern bourgeois private property is the final and most complete expression of the system of producing and appropriating products that is based on class antagonisms, on the exploitation of the many by the few.

In this sense, the theory of the Communists may be summed up in the single sentence: abolition of private property. . . .

The first step in the revolution by the working class is to raise the proletariat to the position of ruling class, to win the battle of democracy.

The proletariat will use its political supremacy to wrest, by degrees, all capital from the bourgeoisie, to centralize all instruments of production in the hands of the state, that is, of the proletariat organised as the ruling class; and to increase the total of productive forces as rapidly as possible.

Of course, in the beginning this cannot be effected except by means of despotic inroads on the rights of property, and on the conditions of bourgeois production; by means of measures, therefore, which appear economically insufficient and untenable, but which, in the course of the movement, outstrip themselves, necessitate further inroads upon the old social order, and are unavoidable as a means of entirely revolutionising the mode of production.

These measures will, of course, be different in different countries.

Nevertheless, in the most advanced countries the following will be pretty generally applicable:

1. Abolition of property in land and application of all rents of land to public purposes.

2. A heavy progressive or graduated income tax.

3. Abolition of all right of inheritance.

4. Confiscation of the property of all emigrants and rebels.

5. Centralisation of credit in the hands of the state, by means of a national bank with state capital and an exclusive monopoly.

6. Centralisation of the means of communication and transport in the hands of the state.

7. Extension of factories and instruments of production owned by the state; the bringing into cultivation of wastelands, and the improvement of the soil generally in accordance with a common plan.

8. Equal liability of all to labour. Establishment of industrial armies, especially for agriculture.

9. Combination of agriculture with manufacturing industries; gradual abolition of the distinction between town and country, by a more equable distribution of the population over the country.

10. Free education for all children in public schools. Abolition of children's factory labour in its present form. Combination of education with industrial production, etc.

When, in the course of development, class distinctions have disappeared and all production has been concentrated in the hands of a vast association of the whole nation, the public power will lose its political character. Political power, properly so called, is merely the organised power of one class for oppressing another. If the proletariat during its contest with the bourgeoisie is compelled, by the force of circumstances, to organise itself as a class; if, by means of a revolution, it makes itself the ruling class, and, as such, sweeps away by force the old conditions of production; then it will, along with these conditions, have swept away the conditions for the existence of class antagonisms and of classes generally, and will thereby have abolished its own supremacy as a class.

In place of the old bourgeois society, with its classes and class antagonisms, we shall have an association in which the free development of each is the condition for the free development of all. . . .

IV. POSITION OF THE COMMUNISTS IN RELATION TO THE VARIOUS EXISTING OPPOSITION PARTIES

. . . The Communists everywhere support every revolutionary movement against the existing social and political order of things.

In all these movements they bring to the front, as the leading question in each, the property question, no matter what its degree of development at the time.

Finally, they labour everywhere for the union and agreement of the democratic parties of all countries.

The Communists disdain to conceal their views and aims. They openly declare that their ends can be attained only by the forcible overthrow of all existing social conditions. Let the ruling classes tremble at a Communistic revolution. The proletarians have nothing to lose but their chains. They have a world to win.

WORKING MEN OF ALL COUNTRIES, UNITE!

DISCUSSION QUESTIONS

1. Marx and Engels argue that taking power away from the bourgeoisie will end class struggles and bring about a just society. Do you agree with them? Why or why not?

2. Do you agree with Marx and Engels that the history of societies is the history of class struggles? Why or why not?

3. Why do Marx and Engels believe that capitalism is an exploitative economic system? Do you agree with them that the proletariat is exploited by the bourgeoisie? Why or why not?

4. Marx argued that every institution in a society, from the political, educational, and religious to the musical, athletic, and literary, is determined by the prevailing economic system. Do you agree with them? Are our institutions determined by economics? Can you think of an institution that is beyond the determining influence of capitalism? If so, argue your case. If not, why not?

5. Marx and Engels contend that the demise of capitalism will occur whether or not it is hastened by revolutionary actions by the proletariat. Is the proletariat's attempt to hasten this demise therefore justified? If so, why? If not, why not?

6. Marx believed that under capitalism, working conditions would get worse and worse. Was he right? Have working conditions gotten worse since the mid-nineteenth century or better?

Metropolis
[Germany 1926] 2 hours
Directed by Fritz Lang

*I*n the year 2026, Johhan (Joh) Fredersen (Alfred Abel) is the master of Metropolis. In this futuristic city, the leisure class lives above ground in lavish art deco towers powered by workers in an underground world. Fredersen's son Freder (Gustav Fröhlich) witnesses a deadly accident in the power-house. He reports the accident to his father, who replies that "accidents happen." Anguished, Freder pleads with his father to consider the workers' conditions.

Freder aims to learn more about the workers and trades places with one of them at the machines. He attends a gathering presided over by the reformer Maria (Brigitte Helm), a schoolteacher in the workers' colony. She promises the workers a mediator "between the hand and the head" derived from "the heart." Freder falls in love with Maria, who returns his affections.

Meanwhile, Fredersen has been plotting with the scientist Rotwang (Rudolph Klein-Rogge) to mechanize the work force. The two men secretly witness the workers' meeting. Fredersen instructs Rotwang to make his new robot in the image of Maria. Fredersen plots to use the robot to incite the workers to rebel as an excuse to use violence against them and forge the way for a new population of robotic laborers. The workers accept the robot as Maria and destroy the machines at her suggestion, even though this will lead to the destruction of their homes and endangerment of their children.

In the midst of the turmoil, Maria escapes from Rotwang's workshop and, with Freder's help, saves the children. But the workers' celebration soon turns to grief as they are told that their city has been flooded. Seeking to exact revenge upon Maria, the workers find the robot Maria and burn her at the stake as a witch. Meanwhile, Rotwang chases the real Maria in an attempt to silence her and preserve the workers' ignorance about the robots. Freder rescues Maria from Rotwang and acts as the mediator for a reconciliation between his father and the foreman of the workers.

Metropolis is a silent film and a science-fiction classic.

DISCUSSION QUESTIONS

1. Describe the life of the bourgeoisie as presented in *Metropolis*. How is it similar to or different from the life of the bourgeoisie as described by Marx and Engels?

2. Marx and Engels describe the proletariat as "a commodity like every other article of commerce, and are consequently exposed to the vicissitudes of competition, to all the fluctuations of the market." "Not only are they slaves of the bourgeois class and of the bourgeois state; they are daily and hourly enslaved by the machine, by the overlooker, and, above all, by the individual bourgeois manufacturer himself." How does *Metropolis* present proletariat life? How is it similar to or different from the life of the proletariat as described by Marx and Engels?

3. According to Marx and Engels, the proletariat is pushed into a struggle with the bourgeoisie, with the ultimate goal of overthrowing the entire capitalist system. How does *Metropolis* deal with the notion of the proletariat as a "revolutionary class"? What are we to make of the fact that the revolutionaries in *Metropolis* continue their destruction with the knowledge that they are putting their own children at risk? Is this a criticism of the revolutionaries or a testament to the sacrifices they must make? Discuss.

4. Do you think that *Metropolis* is ultimately a warning against worker uprising? Is this film suggesting that the working class wait for members of the upper class to recognize their own errors? Discuss.

5. There is much religious and ritualistic imagery in this film. For example, Maria recounts the story of the Tower of Babel. Also, in one of the eerier scenes in the film, a machine transforms into the Phoenician god Moloch, into which workers are sacrificed in the same way that the Phoenicians once sacrificed their children. What is the role of religion in this film? How does the use of religion in this film square with Marx's statement that "religion . . . is the opium of the people"? What is the connection between religion and the aims of the bourgeoisie? Discuss.

6. Marx contends that technology and mechanization have a dehumanizing affect on workers. How is this notion developed in *Metropolis*?

7. One of the notions developed by this film is that the workers will eventually be replaced by machines. How do the workers respond to this? How do you think Marx and Engels would respond to this? Why?

JOHN RAWLS

A Theory of Justice

John Rawls' theory of justice as fairness states that there are two principles of justice. The first principle involves equal basic liberties: each person has a right to the most extensive basic liberty that is compatible with the same liberty for others. The second principle concerns the arrangement of social and economic inequalities: inequalities of wealth are justified to the extent that they work out to the advantage of the disadvantaged.

According to Rawls, these are the principles that free and rational persons would accept in a hypothetical original position in which there was a veil of ignorance hiding from the contractors all the particular facts about themselves. Rawls asserts that because contractors make their choices behind a veil of ignorance, it is appropriate for them to select that strategy whose worst possible outcome is superior to the worst possible outcome of any other strategy.

This would rule out utilitarianism as a rational choice because the maximum social benefit of that alternative is compatible with a benefit below the social minimum for some and perhaps, then, given the veil of ignorance, for oneself. Justice as fairness, for Rawls, is the strategy whose worst possible outcome is superior to the worst possible outcome of any other strategy including utilitarianism.

Rawls' general position on distributive justice is called *liberalism*. Historically, liberalism has been closely associated with capitalism. Some even contend that liberalism was developed as a justification for the rise of capitalism. Most contemporary liberals, however, distance themselves from this position by arguing that markets must be regulated if for no other reason than to ensure equal opportunity. Liberals who defend free markets are called *libertarians* (or classical liberals), whereas those who do not are called either welfare liberals, liberal egalitarians, or, simply liberals. The historical figure most closely associated with liberalism is John Stuart Mill, though John Locke and Immanuel Kant also played important roles in the development of liberalism.

Liberals generally agree with libertarians that individuals have the right to be protected from being harmed by others and the right to own property. They disagree, however, with the libertarians on the notion of positive rights. Liberals argue that the least-advantaged individuals have some positive right to be provided with some of the basic necessities of life, though they do not go so far as to allow these positive rights to interfere greatly with structure of the underlying capitalist economy. Liberals tolerate a degree of economic and social inequality, whereas libertarians tolerate all economic and social inequality so long as every individual has the opportunity to freely compete for the goods of life. Whereas Rawls, a proponent of liberalism, argues that a given level of inequality is justified only when such inequality in the provision of goods and services will be to the benefit of the representative least advantaged of society, libertarians see no justification for the inequal distribution of goods and services to benefit the least advantaged. Inequality is justified for the liberals only if the situation benefits the least advantaged and if the positions that led to the inequality (for example, employment) were open to everyone in the first place.

John Rawls (1921–2002), an American social and political philosopher, was born in Baltimore, Maryland. In 1943, after receiving a B.A from Princeton University, Rawls served as an infantryman in the Pacific during World War II. After the war, he received his Ph.D. in moral philosophy from Princeton in 1950, and he taught there until 1952. He then left to attend Oxford University on a Fulbright Scholarship. Upon his return, he taught philosophy at Cornell University and then Massachusetts Institute of Technology. He joined the Harvard University philosophy faculty in 1964 and taught there for almost forty years. Rawls is the author of *A Theory of Justice* (1971), *Political Liberalism* (1993), and *The Law of Peoples* (1999). He remains one of the most respected liberal social and political philosophers in America today. The following selection is from *A Theory of Justice*.

THE ROLE OF JUSTICE

Justice is the first virtue of social institutions, as truth is of systems of thought. A theory however elegant and economical must be rejected or revised if it is untrue; likewise laws and institutions no matter how efficient and well-arranged must be reformed or abolished if they are unjust. Each person possesses an inviolability founded on justice that even the welfare of society as a whole cannot override. For this reason justice denies that the loss of freedom for some is made right by a greater good shared by others. It does not allow that the sacrifices imposed on a few are outweighed by the larger sum of advantages enjoyed by many. Therefore in a just society the liberties of equal citizenship are taken as settled; the rights secured by justice are not subject to political bargaining or to the calculus of social interests. The only thing that permits us to acquiesce in an erroneous theory is the lack of a better one; analogously, an injustice is tolerable only when it is necessary to avoid an even greater injustice. Being first virtues of human activities, truth and justice are uncompromising.

These propositions seem to express our intuitive conviction of the primacy of justice. No doubt they are expressed too strongly. In any event I wish to inquire whether these contentions or others similar to them are sound, and if so how they can be accounted for. To this end it is necessary to work out a theory of justice in the light of which these assertions can be interpreted and assessed. I shall begin by considering the role of the principles of justice. Let us assume, to fix ideas, that a society is a more or less self-sufficient association of persons who in their relations to one another recognize certain rules of conduct as binding and who for the most part act in accordance with them. Suppose further that these rules specify a system of cooperation designed to advance the good of those taking part in it. Then, although a society is a cooperative venture for mutual advantage, it is typically marked by a conflict as well as by an identity of interests. There is an identity of interests since social cooperation makes possible a better life for all than any would have if each were to live solely by his own efforts. There is a conflict of interests since persons are not indifferent as to how the greater benefits produced by their collaboration are distributed, for in order to pursue their ends they each prefer a larger to a lesser share. A set of principles is required for choosing among the various social arrangements which determine this division of advantages and for underwriting an agreement on the proper distributive shares. These principles are the principles of social justice: they provide a way of assigning rights and duties in the basic institutions of society and they define the appropriate distribution of the benefits and burdens of social cooperation.

Now let us say that a society is well-ordered when it is not only designed to advance the good of its members but when it is also effectively regulated by a public conception of justice. That is, it is a society in which (1) everyone accepts and knows that the others accept the same principles of justice, and (2) the basic social institutions generally satisfy and are generally known to satisfy these principles. In this case while men may put forth excessive demands on one another, they nevertheless acknowledge a common point of view from which their claims may be adjudicated. If men's inclination to self-interest makes their vigilance against one another necessary, their public sense of justice makes their secure association together possible. Among individuals with disparate aims and purposes a shared conception of justice establishes the bonds of civic friendship; the general desire for justice limits the pursuit of other ends. One may think of a public conception of justice as constituting the fundamental charter of a well-ordered human association.

Existing societies are of course seldom well-ordered in this sense, for what is just and unjust is usually in dispute. Men disagree about which principles should define the basic terms of their association. Yet we may still say, despite this disagreement, that they each have a conception of justice. That is, they understand the need for, and they are prepared to affirm, a characteristic set of principles for assigning basic rights and duties and for determining what they take to be the proper distribution of the benefits and burdens of social cooperation. Thus it seems natural to think of the concept of justice as distinct from the various conceptions of justice and as being specified by the role which these different sets of principles, these different conceptions, have in common. Those who hold different conceptions of justice can, then, still agree that institutions are just when no arbitrary distinctions are made between persons in the assigning of basic rights and duties and when the rules determine a proper balance between competing claims to the advantages of social life. Men can agree to this description of just institutions since the notions of an arbitrary distinction and of a proper balance, which are included in the concept of justice, are left open for each to interpret according to the principles of justice that he accepts. These principles single out which similarities and differences among persons are relevant in determining rights and duties and they specify which division of advantages is

appropriate. Clearly this distinction between the concept and the various conceptions of justice settles no important questions. It simply helps to identify the role of the principles of social justice.

Some measure of agreement in conceptions of justice is, however, not the only prerequisite for a viable human community. There are other fundamental social problems, in particular those of coordination, efficiency, and stability. Thus the plans of individuals need to be fitted together so that their activities are compatible with one another and they can all be carried through without anyone's legitimate expectations being severely disappointed. Moreover, the execution of these plans should lead to the achievement of social ends in ways that are efficient and consistent with justice. And finally, the scheme of social cooperation must be stable: it must be more or less regularly complied with and its basic rules willingly acted upon; and when infractions occur, stabilizing forces should exist that prevent further violations and tend to restore the arrangement. Now it is evident that these three problems are connected with that of justice. In the absence of a certain measure of agreement on what is just and unjust, it is clearly more difficult for individuals to coordinate their plans efficiently in order to ensure that mutually beneficial arrangements are maintained. Distrust and resentment corrode the ties of civility, and suspicion and hostility tempt men to act in ways they would otherwise avoid. So while the distinctive role of conceptions of justice is to specify basic rights and duties and to determine the appropriate distributive shares, the way in which a conception does this is bound to affect the problems of efficiency, coordination, and stability. We cannot, in general, assess a conception of justice by its distributive role alone, however useful this role may be in identifying the concept of justice. We must take into account its wider connections; for even though justice has a certain priority, being the most important virtue of institutions, it is still true that, other things equal, one conception of justice is preferable to another when its broader consequences are more desirable. . . .

THE MAIN IDEA OF THE THEORY OF JUSTICE

My aim is to present a conception of justice which generalizes and carries to a higher level of abstraction the familiar theory of the social contract as found, say, in Locke, Rousseau, and Kant. In order to do this we are not to think of the original contract as one to enter a particular society or to set up a particular form of government. Rather, the guiding idea is that the principles of justice for the basic structure of society are the object of the original agreement. They are the principles that free and rational persons concerned to further their own interests would accept in an initial position of equality as defining the fundamental terms of their association. These principles are to regulate all further agreements; they specify the kinds of social cooperation that can be entered into and the forms of government that can be established. This way of regarding the principles justice I shall call justice as fairness.

Thus we are to imagine that those who engage in social cooperation choose together, in one joint act, the principles which are to assign basic rights and duties and to determine the division of social benefits. Men are to decide in advance how they are to regulate their claims against one another and what is to be the foundation charter of their society. Just as each person must decide by rational reflection what constitutes his good, that is, the system of ends which it is rational for him to pursue, so a group of persons must decide once and for all what is to count among them as just and unjust. The choice which rational men would make in this hypothetical situation of equal liberty, assuming for the present that this choice problem has a solution, determines the principles of justice.

In justice as fairness the original position of equality corresponds to the state of nature in the traditional theory of the social contract. This original position is not, of course, thought of as an actual historical state of affairs, much less as a primitive condition of culture. It is understood as a purely hypothetical situation characterized so as to lead to a certain conception of justice. Among the essential features of this situation is that no one knows his place in society, his class position or social status, nor does anyone know his fortune in the distribution of natural assets and abilities, his intelligence, strength, and the like. I shall even assume that the parties do not know their conceptions of the good or their special psychological propensities. The principles of justice are chosen behind a veil of ignorance. This ensures that no one is advantaged or disadvantaged in the

choice of principles by the outcome of natural chance or the contingency of social circumstances. Since all are similarly situated and no one is able to design principles to favor his particular condition, the principles of justice are the result of a fair agreement or bargain. For given the circumstances of the original position, the symmetry of everyone's relations to each other, this initial situation is fair between individuals as moral persons, that is, as rational beings with their own ends and capable, I shall assume, of a sense of justice. The original position is, one might say, the appropriate initial status quo, and thus the fundamental agreements reached in it are fair. This explains the propriety of the name "justice as fairness": it conveys the idea that the principles of justice are agreed to in an initial situation that is fair. The name does not mean that the concepts of justice and fairness are the same, any more than the phrase "poetry as metaphor" means that the concepts of poetry and metaphor are the same.

Justice as fairness begins, as I have said, with one of the most general of all choices which persons might make together, namely, with the choice of the first principles of a conception of justice which is to regulate all subsequent criticism and reform of institutions. Then, having chosen a conception of justice, we can suppose that they are to choose a constitution and a legislature to enact laws, and so on, all in accordance with the principles of justice initially agreed upon. Our social situation is just if it is such that by this sequence of hypothetical agreements we would have contracted into the general system of rules which defines it. Moreover, assuming that the original position does determine a set of principles (that is, that a particular conception of justice would be chosen), it will then be true that whenever social institutions satisfy these principles those engaged in them can say to one another that they are cooperating on terms to which they would agree if they were free and equal persons whose relations with respect to one another were fair. They could all view their arrangements as meeting the stipulations which they would acknowledge in an initial situation that embodies widely accepted and reasonable constraints on the choice of principles. The general recognition of this fact would provide the basis for a public acceptance of the corresponding principles of justice. No society can, of course, be a scheme of cooperation which men enter voluntarily in a literal sense; each person finds himself placed at birth in some particular position in some particular society, and the nature of this position materially affects his life prospects. Yet a society satisfying the principles of justice as fairness comes as close as a society can to being a voluntary scheme, for it meets the principles which free and equal persons would assent to under circumstances that are fair. In this sense its members are autonomous and the obligations they recognize self-imposed.

One feature of justice as fairness is to think of the parties in the initial situation as rational and mutually disinterested. This does not mean that the parties are egoists, that is, individuals with only certain kinds of interests, say in wealth, prestige, and domination. But they are conceived as not taking an interest in one another's interests. They are to presume that even their spiritual aims may be opposed, in the way that the aims of those of different religions may be opposed. Moreover, the concept of rationality must be interpreted as far as possible in the narrow sense, standard in economic theory, of taking the most effective means to given ends. I shall modify this concept to some extent, . . . but one must try to avoid introducing into it any controversial ethical elements. The initial situation must be characterized by stipulations that are widely accepted.

In working out the conception of justice as fairness, one main task clearly is to determine which principles of justice would be chosen in the original position. To do this we must describe this situation in some detail and formulate with care the problem of choice which it presents. . . . It may be observed, however, that once the principles of justice are thought of as arising from an original agreement in a situation of equality, it is an open question whether the principle of utility would be acknowledged. Offhand it hardly seems likely that persons who view themselves as equals, entitled to press their claims upon one another, would agree to a principle which may require lesser life prospects for some simply for the sake of a greater sum of advantages enjoyed by others. Since each desires to protect his interests, his capacity to advance his conception of the good, no one has a reason to acquiesce in an enduring loss for himself in order to bring about a greater net balance of satisfaction. In the absence of strong and lasting benevolent impulses, a rational man would not accept a basic structure merely because it maximized the algebraic sum of advantages irrespective of its permanent effects on his own basic rights and interests. Thus it seems that the principle of utility is incompatible with the conception of social cooperation among equals for mutual advantage. It appears to be inconsistent with the idea of reciprocity implicit in the notion of a well-ordered society. Or, at any rate, so I shall argue.

I shall maintain instead that the persons in the initial situation would choose two rather different principles: the first requires equality in the assignment of basic rights and duties, while the second holds that social and economic inequalities, for example inequalities of wealth and authority, are just only if they result in compensating benefits for everyone, and in particular for the least advantaged members of society. These principles rule out justifying institutions on the grounds that the hardships of some are offset by a greater good in the aggregate. It may be expedient but it is not just that some should have less in order that others may prosper. But there is no injustice in the greater benefits earned by a few provided that the situation of persons not so fortunate is thereby improved. The intuitive idea is that since everyone's well-being depends upon a scheme of cooperation without which no one could have a satisfactory life, the division of advantages should be such as to draw forth the willing cooperation of everyone taking part in it, including those less well situated. Yet this can be expected only if reasonable terms are proposed. The two principles mentioned seem to be a fair agreement on the basis of which those better endowed, or more fortunate in their social position, neither of which we can be said to deserve, could expect the willing cooperation of others when some workable scheme is a necessary condition of the welfare of all. Once we decide to look for a conception of justice that nullifies the accidents of natural endowment and the contingencies of social circumstance as counters in quest for political and economic advantage, we are led to these principles. They express the result of leaving aside those aspects of the social world that seem arbitrary from a moral point of view.

The problem of the choice of principles, however, is extremely difficult. I do not expect the answer I shall suggest to be convincing to everyone. It is, therefore, worth noting from the outset that justice as fairness, like other contract views, consists of two parts: (1) an interpretation of the initial situation and of the problem of choice posed there, and (2) a set of principles which, it is argued, would be agreed to. One may accept the first part of the theory (or some variant thereof), but not the other, and conversely. The concept of the initial contractual situation may seem reasonable although the particular principles proposed are rejected. . . .

The Original Position and Justification

I have said that the original position is the appropriate initial status quo which ensures that the fundamental agreements reached in it are fair. This fact yields the name "Justice as fairness." It is clear, then, that I want to say that one conception of justice is more reasonable than another, or justifiable with respect to it, if rational persons in the initial situation would choose its principles over those of the other for the role of justice. Conceptions of justice are to be ranked by their acceptability to persons so circumstanced. Understood in this way the question of justification is settled by working out a problem of deliberation: we have to ascertain which principles it would be rational to adopt given the contractual situation. This connects the theory of justice with the theory of rational choice.

If this view of the problem of justification is to succeed, we must, of course, describe in some detail the nature of this choice problem. A problem of rational decision has a definite answer only if we know the beliefs and interests of the parties, their relations with respect to one another, the alternatives between which they are to choose, the procedure whereby they make up their minds, and so on. As the circumstances are presented in different ways, correspondingly different principles are accepted. The concept of the original position, as I shall refer to it, is that of the most philosophically favored interpretation of this initial choice situation for the purposes of a theory of justice.

But how are we to decide what is the most favored interpretation? I assume, for one thing, that there is a broad measure of agreement that principles of justice should be chosen under certain conditions. To justify a particular description of the initial situation, one shows that it incorporates these commonly shared presumptions. One argues from widely accepted but weak premises to more specific conclusions. Each of the presumptions should by itself be natural and plausible; some of them may seem innocuous or even trivial. The aim of the contract approach is to establish that taken together they impose significant bounds on acceptable principles of justice. The ideal outcome would be that these conditions determine a unique set of principles; but I shall be satisfied if they suffice to rank the main traditional conceptions of social justice.

One should not be misled, then, by the somewhat unusual conditions which characterize the original position. The idea here is simply to make vivid to ourselves the restrictions that it seems reasonable to impose on arguments for principles of justice and therefore on these principles themselves. Thus it seems reasonable and generally acceptable that no one should be advantaged or disadvantaged by natural fortune or social circumstances in the choice of principles. It also seems widely agreed that it should be impossible to tailor principles to the circumstances of one's own case. We should ensure further that particular inclinations and aspirations, and persons' conceptions of their good, do not affect the principles adopted. The aim is to rule out those principles that it would be rational to propose for acceptance, however little the chance of success, only if one knew certain things that are irrelevant from the standpoint of justice. For example, if a man knew that he was wealthy, he might find it rational to advance the principle that various taxes for welfare measures be counted unjust; if he knew that he was poor, he would most likely propose the contrary principle. To represent the desired restrictions, one imagines a situation in which everyone is deprived of this sort of information. One excludes the knowledge of those contingencies which sets men at odds and allows them to be guided by their prejudices. In this manner the veil of ignorance is arrived at in a natural way. This concept should cause no difficulty if we keep in mind the constraints on arguments that it is meant to express. At any time we can enter the original position, so to speak, simply by following a certain procedure, namely, by arguing for principles of justice in accordance with these restrictions.

It seems reasonable to suppose that the parties in the original position are equal. That is, all have the same rights in the procedure for choosing principles; each can make proposals, submit reasons for their acceptance, and so on. Obviously the purpose of these conditions is to represent equality between human beings as moral persons, as creatures having a conception of their good and capable of a sense of justice. The basis of equality is taken to be similarity in these two respects. Systems of ends are not ranked in value; and each man is presumed to have the requisite ability to understand and to act upon whatever principles are adopted. Together with the veil of ignorance, these conditions define the principles of justice as those which rational persons concerned to advance their interests would consent to as equals when none are known to be advantaged or disadvantaged by social and natural contingencies.

There is, however, another side to justifying a particular description of the original position. This is to see if the principles which would be chosen match our considered convictions of justice or extend them in an acceptable way. We can note whether applying these principles would lead us to make the same judgments about the basic structure of society which we now make intuitively and in which we have the greatest confidence; or whether, in cases where our present judgments are in doubt and given with hesitation, these principles offer a resolution which we can affirm on reflection. There are questions which we feel sure must be answered in a certain way. For example, we are confident that religious intolerance and racial discrimination are unjust. We think that we have examined these things with care and have reached what we believe is an impartial judgment not likely to be distorted by an excessive attention to our own interests. These convictions are provisional fixed points which we presume any conception of justice must fit. But we have much less assurance as to what is the correct distribution of wealth and authority. Here we may be looking for a way to remove our doubts. We can check an interpretation of the initial situation, then, by the capacity of its principles to accommodate our firmest convictions and to provide guidance where guidance is needed.

In searching for the most favored description of this situation we work from both ends. We begin by describing it so that it represents generally shared and preferably weak conditions. We then see if these conditions are strong enough to yield a significant set of principles. If not, we look for further premises equally reasonable. But if so, and these principles match our considered convictions of justice, then so far well and good. But presumably there will be discrepancies. In this case we have a choice. We can either modify the account of the initial situation or we can revise our existing judgments, for even the judgments we take provisionally as fixed points are liable to revision. By going back and forth, sometimes altering the conditions of the contractual circumstances, at others withdrawing our judgments and conforming them to principle, I assume that eventually we shall find a description of the initial situation that both expresses reasonable conditions and yields principles which match our considered judgments duly pruned and adjusted. This state of affairs I refer to as reflective equilibrium. It is an equilibrium because at last our principles and judgments coincide; and it is reflective since we know to what principles our judgments conform and the premises of their derivation. At the moment, everything is in order. But this equilibrium is not necessarily stable. It is liable to be upset by further examination of the conditions which should be imposed on the contractual situation and by particular cases which may lead us to revise our judgments. Yet for the time being we have done what we can to render coherent and to justify our convictions of social justice. We have reached a conception of the original position.

I shall not, of course, actually work through this process. Still, we may think of the interpretation of the original position that I shall present as the result of such a hypothetical course of reflection. It represents the attempt to accommodate within one scheme both reasonable philosophical conditions on principles as well as our considered judgments of justice. In arriving at the favored interpretation of the initial situation there is no point at which an appeal is made to self-evidence in the traditional sense either of general conceptions or particular convictions. I do not claim for the principles of justice proposed that they are necessary truths or derivable from such truths. A conception of justice cannot be deduced from self-evident premises or conditions on principles; instead, its justification is a matter of the mutual support of many considerations, of everything fitting together into one coherent view.

A final comment. We shall want to say that certain principles of justice are justified because they would be agreed to in an initial situation of equality. I have emphasized that this original position is purely hypothetical. It is natural to ask why, if this agreement is never actually entered into, we should take any interest in these principles, moral or otherwise. The answer is that the conditions embodied in the description of the original position are ones that we do in fact accept. Or if we do not, then perhaps we can be persuaded to do so by philosophical reflection. Each aspect of the contractual situation can be given supporting grounds. Thus what we shall do is to collect together into one conception a number of conditions on principles that we are ready upon due consideration to recognize as reasonable. These constraints express what we are prepared to regard as limits on fair terms of social cooperation. One way to look at the idea of the original position, therefore, is to see it as an expository device which sums up the meaning of these conditions and helps us to extract their consequences. On the other hand, this conception is also an intuitive notion that suggests its own elaboration, so that led on by it we are drawn to define more clearly the standpoint from which we can best interpret moral relationships. We need a conception that enables us to envision our objective from afar: the intuitive notion of the original position is to do this for us. . . .

DISCUSSION QUESTIONS

1.   What sorts of things could be expected from a Rawlsian society, as distinct from other ones?

2.   What is the "original position"? What is its role in Rawls' doctrine of justice as fairness?

3.   Would you rather be an industrialist or a day laborer in a Rawlsian society? Explain.

4.   Rawls says that free and rational persons in the original position would reject the principle of utility. What is his argument? Do you agree with it? Why or why not?

5.   Rawls says that it is not possible for free and rational persons in the original position to agree upon different principles other than those given by him. Do you agree? Why, for example, wouldn't contractors agree to an unequal distribution of wealth and income rather than an equal distribution? Why isn't an equal distribution of goods as rational as an unequal distribution?

6.   What is the veil of ignorance? What is its role in Rawls' theory of justice? Do you agree with Rawls? Defend your view.

Gandhi
[Gr. Brit. 1982] 3 hrs., 10 min.
Directed by Richard Attenborough

E ducated in London, Mohandas K. Gandhi (Ben Kingsley) is a young Indian attorney on an assignment in South Africa. When he is thrown out of first class on a train, Gandhi joins with the Indian Congress Party in seeking to bring about change through passive resistance. Enduring police beatings and imprisonments, Gandhi slowly works his way up the party ladder as his skill as an orator improves and his ideas on Indian civil rights become more and more refined.

Upon his release from prison in South Africa, Gandhi returns to Bombay, India, where he is hailed as a national hero. A mass of followers greet Gandhi, who now shaves most of the hair off his head and wears an Indian tunic and sandals instead of Western clothing. Financially supported by wealthy Indian citizens, Gandhi travels throughout India witnessing first-hand the blight and poverty plaguing his country, as well as the brutality of British officers toward Indian civilians.

Speaking out forcefully against British imperialism and colonization, Gandhi lays the foundation of an independence revolution in India. However, even though the citizens of India generally follow Gandhi's lead and spurn all forms of violence, many innocent Indian men, women, and children lose their lives in the process. In one of the most tragic events of the revolution, 1,500 Indians are murdered by British guards. This spurs Gandhi on to proceed even more energetically in his quest for human rights and independence for India through passive resistance. India finally achieves independence from the British in 1947, but Gandhi is assassinated only a few months later by a Hindu fanatic.

Mohandas K. Gandhi (1869–1948) was called "Mahatma," which means "great soul." As the film indicates, Gandhi's pacifism was a combination of Hindu, Muslim, and Christian principles. He was also highly influenced by the writings of Henry David Thoreau and Leo Tolstoy. The film *Gandhi* received nine Oscars including Best Actor (Kingsley), Best Director (Attenborough), and Best Film.

DISCUSSION QUESTIONS

1. Throughout the film, Gandhi calls out for justice. Compare and contrast the type of justice developed by Rawls with that emphasized by Gandhi. What are their similarities and differences?

2. Is the form of justice practiced by the British government in India consonant with the Rawls' theory of justice?

3. How were rights determined by the British government in India? Did all persons in India have the same rights? Why or why not? What do you think Rawls would say about the British notion of rights in India?

4. Consider the following statement Gandhi makes to a group of people in South Africa: "Ladies and Gentlemen, we have asked you to gather here to help us proclaim our right to be treated as equal citizens of the Empire. We do not seek conflict. We know the strength of the forces arrayed against us, know that because of them we can only use peaceful means—but we are determined that justice will be done! The symbol of our status is embodied in this pass—which we must carry at all times, but no European even has to have. And the first step to changing our status is to eliminate this difference between us." Gandhi urged passive resistance to South African laws requiring people of one nationality to carry special identification. Did such laws violate their rights? What would Rawls say? Discuss.

5. On a train in South Africa, Gandhi is told that he cannot sit in first class even though he has purchased the ticket. Gandhi argues that he is an attorney. A European in first class replies, "There are no colored attorneys in South Africa. Go and sit where you belong." Gandhi is told by the conductor to leave first class and go to third class or get off the train. He chooses to get off the train. What would you have done if you were in Gandhi's position? Provide a justification for your actions.

6. Gandhi says, "I try to live like an Indian, as you see it is stupid of course, because in our country it is the British who decide how an Indian lives—what he may buy, what he may sell. And from their luxury in the midst of our terrible poverty they instruct us on what is justice and what is sedition. So it is only natural that our best young minds assume an air of Eastern dignity, while greedily assimilating every Western weakness as quickly as they can acquire it." According to Gandhi, what is

wrong with justice in India? Do you think Rawls would find the same problem with justice in India? Why or why not?

7. Gandhi says, "There are unjust laws—as there are unjust men." Do you agree? He also says, "The function of a civil resister is to provoke response. And we will continue to provoke until they respond, or they change the law. They are not in control—we are. That is the strength of civil resistance." Do you think civil resistance is a justifiable response to what is perceived to be an "unjust" law? Why or why not?

8. Consider the following exchange between Margaret Bourke-White (Candice Bergen) and Gandhi:

   BOURKE-WHITE   "But do you really believe you could use nonviolence against someone like Hitler?"

   GANDHI   "Not without defeats—and great pain. But are there no defeats in this war—no pain? What you cannot do is accept injustice. From Hitler—or anyone. You must make the injustice visible—be prepared to die like a soldier to do so."

   Discuss Gandhi's response to Bourke-White. Is he right? Present an argument in support of your opinion.

9. The British government controls the salt industry in India, and Gandhi resists this practice by going to the Indian Ocean and showing people how to harvest salt from the sea for themselves. Gandhi argues, "man needs salt as he needs air and water. This salt comes from the Indian Ocean. Let every Indian claim it as his right!!" Following Gandhi's lead, thousands of people harvest salt from the sea, and many of them are arrested by the British. Argue for or against the claim "Everyone has a right to harvest salt from the ocean."

10. Gandhi says, "Every enemy is a human being—even the worst of them. And he believes he is right and you are a beast. And if you beat him over the head you will only convince him. But you suffer, to show him that he is wrong, your sacrifice creates an atmosphere of understanding—if not with him, then in the hearts of the rest of the community on whom he depends." Do you agree with Gandhi? Defend your response.

ANNETTE C. BAIER

THE NEED FOR MORE THAN JUSTICE

Annette C. Baier argues that considerations of justice must be harmonized with considerations of care. Baier criticizes approaches to justice like that of John Rawls, approaches that present justice as the "first" virtue of social institutions. While she agrees that "justice is *a* social value of very great importance, and injustice an evil," she asserts that "justice is only one virtue among many." Her argument draws upon Carol Gilligan's ethics of care (see chapter 4). According to Baier, Gilligan's "care perspective" reveals a "blind spot" not visible to "justice perspectives" like those of Kant and Rawls.

Gilligan's work establishes that women tend to speak in a different voice about morality and moral maturity. From the care perspective, the justice perspective fails "to ensure that the people who have and mutually respect" due process, equal opportunity, free speech, free association and so on "will have any other relationship to one another than the minimal relationship needed to keep such 'civil society' going." According to Baier, Gilligan's work reminds us that for relatively powerless individuals such as children, noninterference can amount to neglect, and even among equals, noninterference can be isolating and alienating. The justice perspective fails to adequately deal with Gilligan's notion that "a satisfactory life involves 'progress of affiliative relationship' where the concept of identity expands to include the experience of interconnexion."

For Baier, the justice perspective is "the moral tradition which developed the concept of rights, autonomy and justice." However, it is also "the same tradition that provided 'justifications' of the oppression of those whom the primary right-holders depended on to do the sort of work they themselves preferred not to do." Even Rawls' theory of justice, one of the best theories of justice in this moral tradition, assigns a key role to "the idea of the 'head of a household,' " which is, namely, "to deliberate behind the 'veil of ignorance' on the details of their own special situation, to arrive at the 'just' constitution of society." This leads Baier to lament that "traces of the old patriarchal poison still remain in even the best contemporary moral reasoning." For this and other reasons, Baier suggests that more than the justice perspective and liberal morality are needed. She concludes that "what we need now is a 'marriage' of the old male and the newly articulated female insights."

Annette Baier (1929–) is one of the best-known moral philosophers in the world. Born and educated in New Zealand, she studied philosophy at Otago University. After graduate work at Oxford University, she taught at the Universities of Aberdeen, Auckland, and Sydney, and at Carnegie Mellon University. She is currently emeritus professor of philosophy at the University of Otago and was until her retirement professor of philosophy at the University of Pittsburgh. She is the author of *Postures of Mind* (1985), *A Progress of Sentiments: Reflections on Hume's Treatise* (1991), *Moral Prejudices* (1995), and *The Commons of the Mind* (1997). The following article, "The Need for More than Justice," was first published in *Science, Morality and Feminist Theory* (1987), edited by Marsha Hanen and Kai Nielsen.

In recent decades in North American social and moral philosophy, alongside the development and discussion of widely influential theories of justice, taken as Rawls takes it as the "first virtue of social institutions," there has been a countermovement gathering strength, one coming from some interesting sources. For some of the most outspoken of the diverse group who have in a variety of ways been challenging the assumed supremacy of justice among the moral and social virtues are members of those sections of society whom one might have expected to be especially aware of the supreme importance of justice, namely blacks and women. Those who have only recently won recognition of their equal rights, who have only recently seen the correction or partial correction of longstanding racist and sexist injustices to their race and sex, are among the philosophers now suggesting that justice is only one virtue among many, and one that may need

the presence of the others in order to deliver its own undenied value. Among these philosophers of the philosophical counterculture, as it were—but an increasingly large counterculture—include Alasdair MacIntyre, Michael Stocker, Lawrence Blum, Michael Slote, Laurence Thomas, Claudia Card, Alison Jaggar, Susan Wolf and a whole group of men and women, myself included, who have been influenced by the writings of Harvard educational psychologist Carol Gilligan, whose book *In a Different Voice* caused a considerable stir both in the popular press and, more slowly, in the philosophical journals.

Let me say quite clearly at this early point that there is little disagreement that justice is *a* social value of very great importance, and injustice an evil. Nor would those who have worked on theories of justice want to deny that other things matter besides justice. Rawls, for example, incorporates the value of freedom into his account of justice, so that denial of basic freedoms counts as injustice. Rawls also leaves room for a wider theory of the right, of which the theory of justice is just a part. Still, he does claim that justice is the "first" virtue of social institutions, and it is only that claim about priority that I think has been challenged. It is easy to exaggerate the differences of view that exist, and I want to avoid that. The differences are as much in emphasis as in substance, or we can say that they are differences in tone of voice. But these differences do tend to make a difference in approaches to a wide range of topics not just in moral theory but in areas like medical ethics where the discussion used to be conducted in terms of patients' rights, of informed consent, and so on, but now tends to get conducted in an enlarged moral vocabulary, which draws on what Gilligan calls the ethics of *care* as well as that of *justice.*

For "care" is the new buzz-word. It is not, as Shakespeare's Portia demanded, mercy that is to season justice, but a less authoritarian human-itarian supplement, a felt concern for the good of others and for community with them. The "cold jealous virtue of justice" (Hume) is found to be too cold, and it is "warmer" more communitarian virtues and social ideals that are being called in to supplement it. One might say that liberty and equality are being found inadequate without fraternity, except that "fraternity" will be quite the wrong word, if as Gilligan initially suggested, it is *women* who perceive this value most easily. ("Sorority" will do no better, since it is too exclusive, and English has no gender-neuter word for the mutual concern of siblings.) She has since modified this claim, allowing that there are two perspectives on moral and social issues that we all tend to alternate between, and which are not always easy to combine, one of them what she called the justice perspective, the other the care perspective. It is increasingly obvious that there are many male philosophical spokespersons for the care perspective (Laurence Thomas, Lawrence Blum, Michael Stocker) so that it cannot be the prerogative of women. Nevertheless Gilligan still wants to claim that women are most unlikely to take *only* the justice perspective, as some men are claimed to, at least until some mid-life crisis jolts them into "bifocal" moral vision.

Gilligan in her book did not offer any explanatory theory of why there should be any difference between female and male moral outlook, but she did tend to link the naturalness to women of the care perspective with their role as primary caretakers of young children, that is with their parental and specifically maternal role. She avoided the question of whether it is their biological or their social parental role that is relevant, and some of those who dislike her book are worried precisely by this uncertainty. Some find it retrograde to hail as a special sort of moral wisdom an outlook that may be the product of the socially enforced restriction of women to domestic roles (and the reservation of such roles for them alone). For that might seem to play into the hands of those who still favor such restriction. (Marxists, presumably, will not find it so surprising that moral truths might depend for their initial clear voicing on the social oppression, and memory of it, of those who voice the truths.) Gilligan did in the first chapter of *In a Different Voice* cite the theory of Nancy Chodorow (as presented in *The Reproduction of Mothering*) which traces what appears as gender differences in personality to early social development, in particular to the effects of the child's primary caretaker being or not being of the same gender as the child. Later, both in "The Conquistador and the Dark Continent: Reflections on the Nature of Love" and "The Origins of Morality in Early Childhood, " she develops this explanation. She postulates two evils that any infant may become aware of, the evil of detachment or isolation from others whose love one needs, and the evil of relative power-lessness and weakness. Two dimensions of moral development are thereby set—one aimed at achieving satisfying community with others, the other aimed at autonomy or equality of power. The relative predominance of one over the other development will depend both upon the relative salience of the two evils in early childhood, and on early and later reinforcement or discouragement in attempts made to guard against these two evils. This provides the germs of a theory about *why*, given current customs of childrearing, it should be mainly women who are not content with only the moral outlook that she calls the justice perspective, necessary though that was and is seen by them to have been to their hard won liberation from sexist oppression. They, like the blacks, used the language of rights and justice to change their own social position, but nevertheless see limitations in that language, according to Gilligan's findings as a moral psychologist. She reports their discontent with the individualist more or less Kantian moral framework that dominates Western moral theory and which influenced moral psychologists such as Lawrence Kohlberg, to whose conception of moral maturity she seeks an alternative. Since the target of Gilligan's criticism is the dominant Kantian tradition, and since that has been the target also of moral philosophers as diverse in their own views as Bernard Williams, Alasdair MacIntyre, Philippa Foot, Susan Wolf, [and] Claudia Card, her book is of interest as much for its attempt to articulate an alternative to the Kantian justice perspective as for its implicit raising of the question of male bias in Western moral theory, especially liberal-democratic theory. For whether the supposed blind spots of that outlook are due to male bias, or to non-parental bias, or to early traumas of powerlessness or to early resignation to "detachment" from others, we need first to be persuaded that they *are* blind spots before we will have any interest in their cause and cure. Is justice blind to important social values, or at least only one-eyed? What is it that comes into view from the "care perspective" that is not seen from the "justice perspective"?

Gilligan's position here is most easily described by contrasting it with that of Kohlberg, against which she developed it. Kohlberg, influenced by Piaget and the Kantian philosophical tradition as developed by John Rawls, developed a theory about typical moral development which saw it to progress from a pre-conventional level, where what is seen to matter is pleasing or not offending parental authority-figures, through a conventional level in which the child tries to fit in with a group, such as a school community, and conform to its standards and rules, to a post-conventional critical level, in which such conventional rules are subjected to tests, and where those tests are of a Utilitarian, or, eventually, a Kantian sort—namely ones that require respect for each person's individual rational will, or autonomy, and conformity to any implicit social contract such wills are deemed to have made, or to any hypothetical ones they would make if thinking clearly. What was found when Kohlberg's questionnaires (mostly by verbal response to verbally sketched moral dilemmas) were applied to female as well as male subjects, Gilligan reports, is that the girls and women not only scored generally lower than the boys and men, but tended to *revert* to the lower stage of the conventional level even after briefly (usually in adolescence) attaining the post-conventional level. Piaget's finding that girls were deficient in "the legal sense" was confirmed.

These results led Gilligan to wonder if there might not be a quite different pattern of development to be discerned, at least in female subjects. She therefore conducted interviews designed to elicit not just how far advanced the subjects were towards an appreciation of the nature and importance of Kantian autonomy, but also to, find out what the subjects themselves saw as progress or lack of it, what conceptions of moral maturity they came to possess by the time they were adults. She found that although the Kohlberg version of moral maturity as respect for fellow persons, and for their rights as equals (rights including that of free association), did seem shared by many young men, the women tended to speak in a different voice about morality itself and about moral maturity. To quote Gilligan, "Since the reality of interconnexion is experienced by women as given rather than freely contracted, they arrive at an understanding of life that reflects the limits of autonomy and control. As a result, women's development delineates the path not only to a less violent life but also to a maturity realized by interdependence and taking care." She writes that there is evidence that "women perceive and construe social reality differently from men, and that these differences center around experiences of attachment and separation . . . because women's sense of integrity appears to be intertwined with an ethics of care, so that to see themselves as women is to see themselves in a relationship of connexion, the major changes in women's lives would seem to involve changes in the understanding and activities of care." She contrasts this progressive understanding of care, from merely pleasing others to helping and nurturing, with the sort of progression that is involved in Kohlberg's stages, a progression in the understanding, not of mutual care, but of mutual *respect*, where this has its Kantian overtones of distance, even of some fear for the respected, and where personal autonomy and *in*dependence, rather than more satisfactory interdependence, are the paramount values.

This contrast, one cannot but feel, is one which Gilligan might have used the Marxist language of alienation to make. For the main complaint about the Kantian version of a society with its first virtue justice, construed as respect for equal rights to formal goods such as having contracts kept, due process, equal opportunity including opportunity to participate in political activities leading to policy and law-making, to basic liberties of speech, free association and assembly, religious worship, is that none of these goods do much to ensure that the people who have and mutually respect such rights will have any other relationships to one another than the minimal relationship needed to keep such a "civil society" going. They may well be lonely, driven to suicide, apathetic about their work and about participation in political processes, find their lives meaningless and have no wish to leave offspring to face the same meaningless existence. Their rights, and respect for rights, are quite compatible with very great misery, and misery whose causes are not just individual misfortunes and psychic sickness, but social and moral impoverishment.

What Gilligan's older male subjects complain of is precisely this sort of alienation from some dimly glimpsed better possibility for human beings, some richer sort of network of relationships. As one of Gilligan's male subjects put it. "People have real emotional needs to be attached to something, and equality does not give you attachment. Equality fractures society and places on every person the burden of standing on his own two feet." It is not just the difficulty of self-reliance which is complained of, but its social "fracturing" effect. Whereas the younger men, in their college years, had seen morality as a matter of reciprocal noninterference, this older man begins to see it as reciprocal attachment. "Morality is . . . essential . . . for creating the kind of environment, interaction between people, that is a prerequisite to the fulfillment of individual goals. If you want other people not to interfere with your pursuit of whatever you are into, you have to play the game," says the spokesman for traditional liberalism. But if what one is "into" is interconnexion, interdependence rather than an individual autonomy that may involve "detachment," such a

version of morality will come to seem inadequate. And Gilligan stresses that the interconnexion that her mature women subjects, and some men, wanted to sustain was not merely freely chosen interconnexion, nor interconnexion between equals, but also the sort of interconnexion that can obtain between a child and her unchosen mother and father, or between a child and her unchosen older and younger siblings, or indeed between most workers and their unchosen fellow workers, or most citizens and their unchosen fellow citizens.

A model of a decent community different from the liberal one is involved in the version of moral maturity that Gilligan voices. It has in many ways more in common with the older religion-linked versions of morality and a good society than with the modem Western liberal ideal. That perhaps is why some find it so dangerous and retrograde. Yet it seems clear that it also has much in common with what we can call Hegelian versions of moral maturity and of social health and malaise, both with Marxist versions and with so-called right-Hegelian views.

Let me try to summarize the main differences, as I see them, between on the one hand Gilligan's version of moral maturity and the sort of social structures that would encourage, express and protect it, and on the other the orthodoxy she sees herself to be challenging. I shall from now on be giving my own interpretation of the significance of her challenges, not merely reporting them. The most obvious point is the challenge to the individualism of the Western tradition, to the fairly entrenched belief in the possibility and desirability of each person pursuing his own good in his own way, constrained only by a minimal formal common good namely a working legal apparatus that enforces contracts and protects individuals from undue interference by others. Gilligan reminds us that noninterference can, especially for the relatively powerless, such as the very young, amount to neglect, and even between equals can be isolating and alienating. On her less individualist version of individuality, it becomes defined by responses to dependency and to patterns of interconnexion, both chosen and unchosen. It is not something a person *has,* and which she then chooses relationships to suit, but something that develops out of a series of dependencies and interdependencies, and responses to them. This conception of individuality is not flatly at odds with, say, Rawls's Kantian one, but there is at least a difference of tone of voice between speaking as Rawls does of each of us having our own rational life plan, which a just society's moral traffic rules will allow us to follow, and which may or may not include close association with other persons, and speaking as Gilligan does of a satisfactory life as involving "progress of affiliative relationship" where "the concept of identity expands to include the experience of interconnexion." Rawls can allow that progress to Gilligan-style moral maturity may be *a* rational life plan, but not a moral constraint on every life-pattern. The trouble is that it will not do just to say "let this version of morality be an optional extra. Let us agree on the essential minimum, that is on justice and rights, and let whoever wants to go further and cultivate this more demanding ideal of responsibility and care." For, first, it cannot be satisfactorily cultivated without closer cooperation from others than respect for rights and justice will ensure, and, second, the encouragement of some to cultivate it while others do not could easily lead to exploitation of those who do. It obviously *has* suited some in most societies well enough that others take on the responsibilities of care (for the sick, the helpless, the young) leaving them free to pursue their own less altruistic goods. Volunteer forces of those who accept an ethic of care, operating within a society where the power is exercised and the institutions designed, redesigned, or maintained by those who accept a less communal ethic of minimally constrained self-advancement, will not be the solution. The liberal individualists may be able to "tolerate" the more communally minded, if they keep the liberals' rules, but it is not so clear that the more communally minded can be content with just those rules, nor be content to be tolerated and possibly exploited.

For the moral tradition which developed the concept of rights, autonomy and justice is the same tradition that provided "justification" of the oppression of those whom the primary right-holders depended on to do the sort of work they themselves preferred not to do. The domestic work was left to women and slaves, and the liberal morality for right-holders was surreptitiously supplemented by a different set of demands made on domestic workers. As long as women could be

got to assume responsibility for the care of home and children, and to train their children to continue the sexist system, the liberal morality could continue to be the official morality, by turning its eyes away from the contribution made by those it excluded. The long-unnoticed moral proletariat were the domestic workers, mostly female. Rights have usually been for the privileged. Talking about laws, and the rights those laws recognize and protect, does not in itself ensure that the group of legislators and rights-holders will not be restricted to some elite. Bills of rights have usually been proclamations of the rights of some in-group, barons, land-owners, males, whites, non-foreigners. The "justice perspective," and the legal sense that goes with it, are shadowed by their patriarchal past. What did Kant, the great prophet of autonomy, say in his moral theory about women? He said they were incapable of legislation, not fit to vote, that they needed the guidance of more "rational" males. Autonomy was not for them, only for first-class, really rational, persons. It is ironic that Gilligan's original findings in a way confirm Kant's views—it seems that autonomy really may not be for women. Many of them reject that ideal, and have been found not as good at making rules as are men. But where Kant concludes—"so much the worse for women," we can conclude—"so much the worse for the male fixation on the special skill of drafting legislation, for the bureaucratic mentality of rule worship, and for the male exaggeration of the importance of independence over mutual interdependence."

It is however also true that the moral theories that made the concept of a person's rights central were not just the instruments for excluding some persons, but also the instruments used by those who demanded that more and more persons be included in the favored group. Abolitionists, reformers, women, used the language of rights to assert their claims to inclusion in the group of full members of a community. The tradition of liberal moral theory has in fact developed so as to include the women it had for so long excluded, to include the poor as well as rich, blacks and whites, and so on. Women like Mary Wollstonecraft used the male moral theories to good purpose. So we should not be wholly ungrateful for those male moral theories, for all their objectionable earlier content. They were undoubtedly patriarchal, but they also contained the seeds of the challenge, or antidote, to this patriarchal poison.

But when we transcend the values of the Kantians, we should not forget the facts of history—that those values were the values of the oppressors of women. The Christian church, whose version of the moral law Aquinas codified, in his very legalistic moral theory, still insists on the maleness of the God it worships, and jealously reserves for males all the most powerful positions in its hierarchy. Its patriarchical prejudice is open and avowed. In the secular moral theories of men, the sexist patriarchal prejudice is today often less open, not as blatant as it is in Aquinas, in the later natural law tradition, and in Kant and Hegel, but is often still there. No moral theorist today would say that women are unfit to vote, to make laws, or to rule a nation without powerful male advisors (as most queens had), but the old doctrines die hard. In one of the best male theories we have, John Rawls's theory, a key role is played by the idea of the "head of a household." It is heads of households who are to deliberate behind a "veil of ignorance" of historical details, and of details of their own special situation, to arrive at the "just" constitution for a society. Now of course Rawls does not think or say that these "heads" are fathers rather than mothers. But if we have really given up the age-old myth of women needing, as Grotius put it, to be under the "eye" of a more "rational" male protector and master, then how do families come to have any one "head," except by the death or desertion of one parent? They will either be two-headed, or headless. Traces of the old patriarchal poison still remain in even the best contemporary moral theorizing. Few may actually say that women's place is in the home, but there is much muttering, when unemployment figures rise, about how the relatively recent flood of women into the work force complicates the problem, as if it would be a good thing if women just went back home whenever unemployment rises, to leave the available jobs for the men. We still do not really have a wide acceptance of the equal right of women to employment outside the home. Nor do we have wide acceptance of the equal duty of men to perform those domestic tasks which in no way depend on special female anatomy, namely cooking, cleaning, and the care of weaned children.

All sorts of stories (maybe true stories), about children's need for one "primary" parent, who must be the mother if the mother breast feeds the child, shore up the unequal division of domestic responsibility between mothers and fathers, wives and husbands. If we are really to transvalue the values of our patriarchal past, we need to rethink all of those assumptions, really test those psychological theories. And how will men ever develop an understanding of the "ethics of care" if they continue to be shielded or kept from that experience of caring for a dependent child, which complements the experience we all have had of being cared for as dependent children? These experiences form the natural background for the development of moral maturity as Gilligan's women saw it.

Exploitation aside, why would women, once liberated, not be content to have their version of morality merely tolerated? Why should they not see themselves as voluntarily for their own reasons, taking on *more* than the liberal rules demand, while having no quarrel with the content of those rules themselves, nor with their remaining the only ones that are expected to be generally obeyed? To see why, we need to move on to three more differences between the Kantian liberals (usually contractrians) and their critics. These concern the relative weight put on relationships between equals, and the relative weight put on freedom of choice, and on the authority of intellect over emotions. It is a typical feature of the dominant moral theories and traditions, since Kant, or perhaps since Hobbes, that relationships between equals or those who are deemed equal in some important sense, have been the relations that morality is concerned primarily to regulate. Relationships between those who are clearly unequal in power, such as parents and children, earlier and later generations in relation to one another, states and citizens, doctors and patients, the well and the ill, large states and small states, have had to be shunted to the bottom of the agenda, and then dealt with by some sort of "promotion" of the weaker so that an appearance of virtual equality is achieved. Citizens collectively become equal to states, children are treated as adults-to-be, the ill and dying are treated as continuers of their earlier more potent selves, so that their "rights" could be seen as the rights of equals. This pretence of an equality that is in fact absent may often lead to desirable protection of the weaker, or more dependent. But it somewhat masks the question of what our moral relationships *are* to those who are our superiors or our inferiors in power. A more realistic acceptance of the fact that we begin as helpless children, that at almost every point of our lives we deal with both the more and the less helpless, that equality of power and interdependency, between two persons or groups, is rare and hard to recognize when it does occur, might lead us to a more direct approach to questions concerning the design of institutions structuring these relationships between unequals (families, schools, hospitals, armies) and of the morality of our dealings with the more and the less powerful. One reason why those who agree with the Gilligan version of what morality is about will not want to agree that the liberals' rules are a good minimal set, the only ones we need pressure *everyone* to obey, is that these rules do little to protect the young or the dying or the starving or any of the relatively powerless against neglect, or to ensure an education that will form persons to be *capable* of conforming to an ethics of care and responsibility. Put badly, and in a way Gilligan certainly has not put it, the liberal morality, if unsupplemented, may *unfit* people to be anything other than what its justifying theories suppose them to be, ones who have no interest in each others' interests. Yet some must take an interest in the next generation's interests. Women's traditional work, of caring for the less powerful, especially for the young, is obviously socially vital. One cannot regard any version of morality that does not ensure that it gets well done as an adequate "minimal morality," any more than we could so regard one that left any concern for more distant future generations an optional extra. A moral theory, it can plausibly be claimed, cannot regard concern for new and future persons as an optional charity left for those with a taste for it. If the morality the theory endorses is to sustain itself, it must provide for its own continuers, not just take out a loan on a carefully encouraged maternal instinct or on the enthusiasm of a self-selected group of environmentalists, who make it their business or hobby to be concerned with what we are doing to mother earth.

The recognition of the importance for all parties of relations between those who are and cannot but be unequal, both of these relations in themselves and for their effect on personality formation and so on other relationships, goes along with a recognition of the plain fact that not all morally important relationships can or should be freely chosen. So far I have discussed three reasons women have not to be content to pursue their own values within the framework of the liberal morality. The first was its dubious record. The second was its inattention to relations of inequality or its pretence of equality. The third reason is its exaggeration of the scope of choice, or its inattention to unchosen relations. Showing up the partial myth of equality among actual members of a community, and of the undesirability of trying to pretend that we are treating all of them as equals, tends to go along with an exposure of the companion myth that moral obligations arise from freely *chosen* associations between such equals. Vulnerable future generations do not choose their dependence on earlier generations. The unequal infant does not choose its place in a family or nation, nor is it treated as free to do as it likes until some association is freely entered into. Nor do its parents always choose their parental role, or freely assume their parental responsibilities any more than we choose our power to affect the conditions in which later generations will live. Gilligan's attention to the version of morality and moral maturity found in women, many of whom had faced choice of whether or not to have an abortion, and who had at some point become mothers, is attention to the perceived inadequacy of the language of rights to help in such choices or to guide them in their parental role. It would not be much of an exaggeration to call the Gilligan "different voice" the voice of the potential parents. The emphasis on care goes with a recognition of the often unchosen nature of the responsibilities of those who give care, both of children who care for their aged or infirm parents, and of parents who care for the children they in fact have. Contract soon ceases to seem the paradigm source of moral obligation once we attend to parental responsibility, and justice as a virtue of social institutions will come to seem at best only first equal with the virtue, whatever its name, that ensures that each new generation is made appropriately welcome and prepared for their adult lives.

This all constitutes a belated reminder to Western moral theorists of a fact they have always known, that as Adam Ferguson, and David Hume before him emphasized, we are born into families, and the first society we belong to, one that fits or misfits us for later ones, is the small society of parents (or some sort of child-attendants) and children, exhibiting as it may both relationships of near equality and of inequality in power. This simple reminder, with the fairly considerable implications it can have for the plausibility of contractarian moral theory, is at the same time a reminder of the role of human emotions as much as human reason and will in moral development as it actually comes about. The fourth feature of the Gilligan challenge to liberal orthodoxy is a challenge to its typical *rationalism,* or intellectualism, to its assumption that we need not worry what passions persons have, as long as their rational wills can control them. This Kantian picture of a controlling reason dictating to possibly unruly passions also tends to seem less useful when we are led to consider what sort of person we need to fill the role of parent, or indeed want in any close relationship. It might be important for father figures to have rational control over their violent urges to beat to death the children whose screams enrage them, but more than control of such nasty passions seems needed in the mother or primary parent, or parent-substitute, by most psychological theories. They need to love their children, not just to control their irritation. So the emphasis in Kantian theories on rational control of emotions, rather than on cultivating desirable forms of emotion, is challenged by Gilligan, along with the challenge to the assumption of the centrality of autonomy, or relations between equals, and of freely chosen relations.

The same set of challenges to "orthodox" liberal moral theory has come not just from Gilligan and other women, who are reminding other moral theorists of the role of the family as a social institution and as an influence on the other relationships people want to or are capable of sustaining, but also, as I noted at the start, from an otherwise fairly diverse group of men, ranging from those influenced by both Hegelian and Christian traditions (MacIntyre) to all varieties of other backgrounds. From this group I want to draw attention to the work of one philosopher in particular, namely Laurence Thomas, the author

of a fairly remarkable article "Sexism and Racism" in which he finds sexism to be a more intractable social evil than racism. In a series of articles and a book, Thomas makes a strong case for the importance of supplementing a concern for justice and respect for rights with an emphasis on equally needed virtues, and on virtues seen as appropriate *emotional* as well as rational capacities. Like Gilligan (and unlike MacIntyre) Thomas gives a lot of attention to the childhood beginnings of moral and social capacities, to the role of parental love in making that possible, and to the emotional as well as the cognitive development we have reason to think both possible and desirable in human persons.

It is clear, I think, that the best moral theory has to be a cooperative product of women and men, has to harmonize justice and care. The morality it theorizes about is after all for all persons, for men and for women, and will need their combined insights. As Gilligan said, what we need now is a "marriage" of the old male and the newly articulated female insights. If she is right about the special moral aptitudes of women, it will most likely be the women who propose the marriage, since they are the ones with more natural empathy, with the better diplomatic skills, the ones more likely to shoulder responsibility and take moral initiative, and the ones who find it easiest to empathize and care about how the other party feels. Then, once there is this union of male and female moral wisdom, we maybe can teach each other the moral skills each gender currently lacks, so that the gender difference in moral outlook that Gilligan found will slowly become less marked.

DISCUSSION QUESTIONS

1. Why does Baier contend that justice is not the first virtue of social institutions? Do you agree with her argument? Why or why not?

2. What problem does Baier find in the type of "relationships" supported by the justice perspective? Do you agree with her? Why or why not?

3. Baier argues that "traces of the old patriarchal poison still remain in even the best contemporary moral reasoning." Evaluate her argument.

4. Why does Baier believe that women should not be content to pursue their own values within the framework of liberal morality? Do you agree with her? Why or why not?

5. Does Baier convince you that a justice perspective needs to be "married" to a care perspective? Why or why not? What other perspective, if any, would you add to this marriage of perspectives? Why?

JOHN HOSPERS

What Libertarianism Is

J ohn Hospers argues that the role of government is solely to protect our right to life, liberty, and property. It is not the role of government to maximize the public good, or to make citizens aid or assist others, or to make citizens always act in ways that are in their best interests. For Hospers, what is most valuable is individual freedom and autonomy. According to Hospers, each of us has the right to act in accordance with our own choices, unless those choices infringe on another individuals' ability to act on her or his own choices. No individual, institutions, or governments can interfere with the decisions other individuals make concerning their lives *unless* those decisions interfere with the rights of another individual or group. Hospers contends that every individual is the owner of his or her own life, and no one is the owner of anyone else's life.

Libertarians (or *classical liberals*) trace the roots of their ideas back to the social and political writings of the British philosopher John Locke, rather than John Stuart Mill. Libertarians believe that we have a fundamental right to liberty, that is, to be left alone. However, libertarians believe that we have only *negative rights*, not *positive rights*. Negative rights are regarded as the rights of noninterference: we have the right to life in the negative sense that others have a duty not to interfere in our right to live our lives. But we do not have the right to life in the positive sense that others have a duty to provide us with goods to help us to live well or even simply to live. Consequently, we have a right not to be harmed and not to have the products of our labor taken from us.

Libertarians contend that there is not a strong bond between the state or government and its citizens. The state exists mainly to protect individuals from harming one another and to enforce contracts. As long as the state is protecting citizens from things such as murder and theft, enforcing contracts, and ensuring a common marketplace for the free exchange of goods, then the state is just. Accordingly, government programs to assist those without adequate food, shelter, or health care are generally not supported on the libertarian minimalist model of the state. Government welfare programs are viewed by libertarians to be based on positive rights and, as such, to be outside of the bounds of their concept of distributive justice.

John Hospers (1918–), an American philosopher, was born in Pella, Iowa. He received his B.A. from Central College in 1939, his M.A. from the State University of Iowa in 1941, and his Ph.D. from Columbia University in 1944. He has taught philosophy at the University of Minnesota, Brooklyn College, California State University at Los Angeles, and the University of Southern California, where he is currently emeritus professor of philosophy. In 1971, he helped found the United States Libertarian Party, and the next year he became the first presidential candidate from this party, receiving one electoral vote. Hospers was an editor of *Liberty*, a leading libertarian magazine, and also ran for governor of California in 1974. His books include *Meaning and Truth in the Arts* (1946), *Human Conduct* (1961), *Introduction to Philosophical*

Analysis (1967), *Artistic Expression* (1971), *Libertarianism: A Political Philosophy for Tomorrow* (1971), *Will Capitalism Survive?* (1980), and *Understanding the Arts* (1982). The following article, "What Libertarianism Is," is from *The Libertarian Alternative* (1974), edited by Tibor R. Machan.

Government is the most dangerous institution known to man. Throughout history it has violated the rights of men more than any individual or group of individuals could do: it has killed people, enslaved them, sent them to forced labor and concentration camps, and regularly robbed and pillaged them of the fruits of their expended labor. Unlike individual criminals, government has the power to arrest and try; unlike individual criminals, it can surround and encompass a person totally, dominating every aspect of one's life, so that one has no recourse from it but to leave the country (and in totalitarian nations even that is prohibited). Government throughout history has a much sorrier record than any individual, even that of a ruthless mass murderer. The signs we see on bumper stickers are chillingly accurate: "Beware: the Government Is Armed and Dangerous."

The only proper role of government, according to libertarians, is that of the protector of the citizen against aggression by other individuals. The government, of course, should never initiate aggression; its proper role is as the embodiment of the *retaliatory* use of force against anyone who initiates its use.

If each individual had constantly to defend himself against possible aggressors, he would have to spend a considerable portion of his life in target practice, karate exercises, and other means of self-defense, and even so he would probably be helpless against groups of individuals who might try to kill, maim, or rob him. He would have little time for cultivating those qualities which are essential to civilized life, nor would improvements in science, medicine, and the arts be likely to occur. The function of government is to take this responsibility off his shoulders: the government undertakes to defend him against aggressors and to punish them if they attack him. When the government is effective in doing this, it enables the citizen to go about his business unmolested and without constant fear for his life. To do this, of course, government must have physical power—the

police, to protect the citizen from aggression within its borders, and the armed forces, to protect him from aggressors outside. Beyond that, the government should not intrude upon his life, either to run his business, or adjust his daily activities, or prescribe his personal moral code.

Government, then, undertakes to be the individual's protector; but historically governments have gone far beyond this function. Since they already have the physical power, they have not hesitated to use it for purposes far beyond that which was entrusted to them in the first place. Undertaking initially to protect its citizens against aggression, it has often itself become an aggressor—a far greater aggressor, indeed, than the criminals against whom it was supposed to protect its citizens. Governments have done what no private citizen can do: arrest and imprison individuals without a trial and send them to slave labor camps. Government must have power in order to be effective—and yet the very means by which alone it can be effective make it vulnerable to the abuse of power, leading to managing the lives of individuals and even inflicting terror upon them.

What then should be the function of government? In a word, the *protection of human rights*.

1. *The right to life:* libertarians support all such legislation as will protect human beings against the use of force by others, for example, laws against killing, attempting killing, maiming, beating, and all kinds of physical violence.

2. *The right to liberty:* there should be no laws compromising in anyway freedom of speech, of the press, and peaceable assembly. There should be no censorship of ideas, books, films, or of anything else by government.

3. *The right to property:* libertarians support legislation that protects the property rights of individuals against confiscation,

nationalization, eminent domain, robbery, trespass, fraud and misrepresentation, patent and copyright, libel and slander. . . .

Laws may be classified into three types: (1) laws protecting individuals against themselves, such as laws against fornication and other sexual behavior, alcohol, and drugs; (2) laws protecting individuals against aggressions by other individuals, such as laws against murder, robbery, and fraud; (3) laws requiring people to help one another; for example, all laws which rob Peter to pay Paul, such as welfare.

Libertarians reject the first class of laws totally. Behavior which harms no one else is strictly the individual's own affair. Thus, there should be no laws against becoming intoxicated, since whether or not to become intoxicated is the individual's own decision: but there should be laws against driving while intoxicated, since the drunken driver is a threat to every other motorist on the highway (drunken driving falls into type 2). Similarly, there should be no laws against drugs (except the prohibition of sale of drugs to minors) as long as the taking of these drugs poses no threat to anyone else. Drug addiction is a psychological problem to which no present solution exists. Most of the social harm caused by addicts, other than to themselves, is the result of thefts which they perform in order to continue their habit—and then the *legal* crime is the theft, not the addiction. The actual cost of heroin is about ten cents a shot; if it were legalized, the enormous traffic in illegal sale and purchase of it would stop, as well as the accompanying proselytization to get new addicts (to make more money for the pusher) and the thefts performed by addicts who often require eighty dollars a day just to keep up the habit. Addiction would not stop, but the crimes would: it is estimated that 75 percent of the burglaries in New York City today are performed by addicts, and all these crimes could be wiped out at one stroke through the legalization of drugs. (Only when the taking of drugs could be shown to constitute a threat to *others,* should it be prohibited by law. It is only laws protecting people against *themselves* that libertarians oppose.)

Laws should be limited to the second class only: aggression by individuals against other individuals. These are laws whose function is to protect human beings against encroachment by others; and this, as we have seen, is (according to libertarianism) the sole function of government.

Libertarians also reject the third class of laws totally: no one should be forced by law to help others, not even to tell them the time of day if requested, and certainly not to give them a portion of one's weekly paycheck. Governments, in the guise of humanitarianism, have given to some by taking from others (charging a "handling fee" in the process, which, because of the government's waste and inefficiency, sometimes is several hundred percent). And in so doing they have decreased incentive, violated the rights of individuals and lowered the standard of living of almost everyone.

All such laws constitute what libertarians call *moral cannibalism.* A cannibal in the physical sense is a person who lives off the flesh of other human beings. A *moral* cannibal is one who believes he has a right to live off the "spirit" of other human beings—who believes that he has a moral claim on the productive capacity, time, and effort expended by others.

It has become fashionable to claim virtually everything that one needs or desires as one's *right.* Thus, many people claim that they have a right to a job, the right to free medical care, to free food and clothing, to a decent home, and so on. Now if one asks, apart from any specific context, whether it would be desirable if everyone had these things, one might well say yes. But there is a gimmick attached to each of them: *At whose expense?* Jobs, medical care, education, and so on, don't grow on trees. These are goods and services *produced only by men.* Who then is to provide them, and under what conditions?

If you have a right to a job, who is to supply it? Must an employer supply it even if he doesn't want to hire you? What if you are unemployable, or incurably lazy? (If you say "the government must supply it," does that mean that a job must be created for you which no employer needs done, and that you must be kept in it regardless of how much or little you work?) If the employer is forced to supply it at his expense even if he doesn't need you, then isn't *he* being enslaved to that extent? What ever happened to *his* right to conduct his life and his affairs in accordance with his choices?

If you have a right to free medical care, then, since medical care doesn't exist in nature as wild apples do, some people will have to supply it to you for free: that is, they will have to spend their time and money and energy taking care of you whether they want to or not. What ever happened to *their* right to conduct their lives as they see fit? Or do you have a right to violate theirs? Can there be a right to violate rights?

All those who demand this or that as a "free service" are consciously or unconsciously evading the fact that there is in reality no such thing as free services. All man-made goods and services are the result of human expenditure of time and effort. There is no such thing as "something for nothing" in this world. If you demand something free, you are demanding that other men give their time and effort to you without compensation. If they voluntarily choose to do this, there is no problem; but if you demand that they be *forced* to do it, you are interfering with their right not to do it if they so choose. "Swimming in this pool ought to be free!" says the indignant passerby. What he means is that others should build a pool, others should provide the material, and still others should run it and keep it in functioning order, so that *he* can use it without fee. But what right has he to the expenditure of *their* time and effort? To expect something "for free" is to expect it *to be paid for by others* whether they choose to or not.

Many questions, particularly about economic matters, will be generated by the libertarian account of human rights and the role of government. Should government have a role in assisting the needy, in providing social security, in legislating minimum wages, in fixing prices and putting a ceiling on rents, in curbing monopolies, in erecting tariffs, in guaranteeing jobs, in managing the money supply? To these and all similar questions the libertarian answers with an unequivocal no.

"But then you'd let people go hungry!" comes the rejoinder. This, the libertarian insists, is precisely what would not happen; with the restrictions removed, the economy would flourish as never before. With the controls taken off business, existing enterprises would expand and new ones would spring into existence satisfying more and more consumer needs; millions more people would be gainfully employed instead of subsisting on welfare, and all kinds of research and production, released from the stranglehold of government, would proliferate, fulfilling man's needs and desires as never before. It has always been so whenever government has permitted men to be free traders on a free market. But *why* this is so, and how the free market is the best solution to all problems relating to the material aspect of man's life, is another and far longer story.

DISCUSSION QUESTIONS

1. According to Hospers, what is the role of the government? Compare his position on government with that of Marx.

2. Hospers discusses three types of laws. What are they? According to Hospers which are just types of law, and which are not? Do you agree with him? Why or why not?

3. What is the libertarian position on welfare? Why does Hospers believe that a libertarian government will create a society in which there will be no need for welfare? Do you agree with his argument? Why or why not?

4. Discuss the libertarian position on recreational drug use, prostitution, polygamy, and gambling. Do you agree with the position on each of these issues? Why or why not?

5. Imagine yourself behind Rawls' "veil of ignorance." You do not know if you are rich or poor, male or female, with or without disability. Would you choose to live in a libertarian society if you did not know your specific situation in life? Why or why not?

6. How libertarian are your current forms of local, state, and federal government? Do you think that they should be more or less libertarian? Why or why not?

7. Would you consider voting for a libertarian candidate in the next presidential or gubernatorial election? Why or why not?

The People vs. Larry Flynt
[USA 1996] 2 hours, 10 minutes
Directed by Milos Forman

*I*s the founder of *Hustler* magazine a First Amendment hero or a misogynistic pornographer? Larry Flynt would argue that he has the right to be both. *The People vs. Larry Flynt* follows Flynt's career from his early years as owner of a Cincinnati strip club to his subsequent success as a multimillion-dollar pornography publisher.

Flynt (Woody Harrelson) is sentenced to twenty-five years in jail for pandering obscenities and engaging in organized crime in Cincinnati. After serving five months, Flynt is cleared by the appellate court. Under the spiritual guidance of Ruth Carter Stapleton (Donna Hanover), sister of President Jimmy Carter, Flynt converts to Christianity. But he loses faith after he is shot and paralyzed by a sniper in Georgia.

Now confined to a wheelchair, Flynt moves into his Hollywood mansion and lives in seclusion with his wife, Althea (Courtney Love), drugged with painkillers. Flynt runs a satirical advertisement making untrue claims about the sexual practices of religious leader Jerry Falwell (Richard Paul). Falwell sues Flynt, and the case is eventually brought before the Supreme Court, which rules in Flynt's favor.

DISCUSSION QUESTIONS

1. How might a libertarian respond to the censorship of pornography? Do you agree with the libertarian response? Why or why not?

2. Flynt's lawyer says to the jury, "Ladies and gentlemen of the jury, you have heard a lot today, and I'm not going to go back over it, but you have to go into that room and make some decisions. But before you do, there's something you need to know. I am not trying to suggest that you like what Larry Flynt does. I don't like what Larry Flynt does, but what I do like is the fact that I live in a country where you and I can make that decision for ourselves. I like the fact that I live in a country where I can pick up *Hustler* magazine and read it, or throw it in the garbage can if that's where I think it belongs." Do you agree with Flynt's lawyer? Compare your response to that of a libertarian.

3. The First Amendment to the U.S. Constitution protects against Congress making laws that abridge, among other things, our freedom of speech and the freedom of the press. Larry Flynt says, "If the First Amendment will protect a scumbag like me, it will protect all of you." Is he right? Why or why not?

4. Compare what libertarians mean by freedom with what Flynt and his lawyer mean. What are their similarities? Their differences?

5. Flynt insists that all he is guilty of is bad taste. *Hustler* has published articles advising men to find "easy" sexual partners such as mentally handicapped women and minors. Do you consider this advice to be in "bad taste," or is it something more serious? Compare your response to that of a libertarian.

6. Should communities be allowed to set their own standards of decency and propriety? What limits, if any, should be put on these standards? Defend your position. How might Rawls and Hospers respond to you?

7. The Supreme Court's ruling reads, "In the world of debate about public affairs, many things with motives that are less than admirable are nonetheless protected by the First Amendment." What kinds of "things" might the court mean? Do you agree that they should be protected? Why or why not?

8. Some conceive of freedom in essentially positive terms, that is, the "freedom to" do particular things; others conceive of freedom in basically negative terms, that is, the "freedom from" external interference by the government or the law in one's affairs. Discuss the difference. Which sense of freedom is found in a just society? Compare your response to that of Flynt and Hospers.

9. Do you think Milos Forman's portrayal of Larry Flynt is "biased"? Explain. If you were going to set the life of Larry Flynt to film, would you do it in the same way as Forman? Why or why not?

MAJID KHADDURI

THE ISLAMIC CONCEPTION OF JUSTICE

Majid Khadduri introduces the concept of justice as found in a number of Islamic sources and then summarizes the Arabic philosopher Abu al-Walid Ibn Rushd's view of justice. Khadduri begins by introducing two different types of justice: positive and Revelational. *Positive justice* is the product of the establishment by individuals or collectives of "a certain scale or scales of justice" that evolve through either tacit agreement or formal action. This type of justice is "imperfect and men always endeavor to refine and improve it by a continuing process of social change." *Revelational or divine justice* is the product of intuition or divine inspiration and is closely tied to religion and ethics. "It coincided with Reason and may well fall in the category of 'natural justice' in the sense that it is the product not of social but of natural forces." Christian and Muslim scholars both hold that "Divine Justice is the ultimate objective of the Revelation, expressed in its early form in the sacred laws of Christianity and Islam."

In Islam, there are three main sources of Divine Justice: (1) Revelation—the words of God as revealed to the Prophet Mohammed and enshrined by him in the Koran (Qur'ān); (2) the Divine Wisdom—the "Traditions" or sayings, deeds, and approvals of the Prophet Mohammed, which are known as the Hadīth; and (3) the Law and Creed—principles of justice developed by scholars through human reasoning (*ijtihād*) on the basis of the Revelation and Divine Wisdom. "The principles and maxims of justice derived from the Revelation and Divine Wisdom were considered infallible and inviolable, designed for all time and potentially capable of application to all men."

The constitution and source of authority of the Islamic state is the Divine Law; that is, the source of authority comes indirectly through God's law, not directly from God. This form of government is called *Divine nomocracy* (*nomos* is a Greek word meaning "custom" or "law"), which means that the state is organized such that authority is exercised by a representative who derives his authority not directly from God but from God's law, and that Divine Law is regarded as the sovereign power. In a *theocracy*, the organization of the state is such that divine commandments are the civil laws and God himself is regarded as the sovereign power. The Islamic state is not a theocracy because God himself is not the direct source of authority; rather, it is the Divine Law.

While the Koran contains many abstract maxims concerning justice, and the Hadīth sought to explain the meaning of the maxims by utilizing specific examples, neither the Koran nor the Hadīth "indicate what are the constituent elements of justice or how justice can be realized on Earth." Thus, this task fell to scholars. Khadduri introduces us to the thought of one of the best known of those scholars, the great Arabic philosopher Abu al-Walid Ibn Rushd (1126–98), who is known in the West by his Latin name, Averroës.

Ibn Rushd was born in Córdoba, Spain, and was both a physician and a philosopher. He held a number of important official posts, served as a judge, and often went on diplomatic missions. Ibn Rushd saw the Islamic and the Greek notions of justice as ultimately the same and drew heavily on the philosophies of Plato and Aristotle. Opposed by both Muslim and Christian theologians, he was famous for his commentaries on Aristotle. For much of the Middle Ages, he was simply known as "The Commentator." His commentaries produced a philosophical school known as Averroism, which continued well into the fifteenth century. However, Averroism was condemned by church leaders and Christian councils in 1209, 1215, 1240, 1270, and 1277. It should be noted that no school of philosophy was condemned more times.

Since the Prophet Mohammed, the first ruler of the Islamic state, died without providing a rule for succession, the question of who is the legitimate successor to the Prophet became a crucial issue. Ibn Rushd said that the ruler of the Islamic state should be a prophet or a philosopher. This "ruler must be endowed with a set of natural qualifications such as disposition to theoretical knowledge, love for the truth, high-mindedness, courage, fluency in speech, good memory, control over desires that are not proper for rulers (like sensual desires and love for money), and—last but not least—justice." It should be noted, however, that other schools of Islamic thought, such as the Sunni and the Shi'ite differ from Ibn Rushd on the qualities of the leader of the Islamic state.

Majid Khadduri (1908–), an authority on Islamic law, was born in Mosul, Iraq. He received his Ph.D. from the University of Chicago in 1938 and then returned to Baghdad to teach. He was in the Iraqi delegation at the 1945 conference that gave birth to the United Nations. In 1947, he began teaching at Indiana University as a visiting lecturer, and from 1949 until his retirement in 1980, he was a professor in the Johns Hopkins University School of Advanced International Studies, where he is now distinguished emeritus professor. He was also the first person to teach a course in the United States on Islamic law, and he founded the Middle Eastern Studies Program at Johns Hopkins. He is the author of twenty-nine books including *The Law of War and Peace in Islam* (1940), *Independent Iraq: A Study of Iraqi Politics Since 1932* (1951), *War and Peace in the Law of Islam* (1955), *Socialist Iraq* (1978), *Arab Personalities in Politics* (1981), *The Islamic Conception of Justice* (1984), and *The Gulf War: The Origins and Implications of the Iraq–Iran Conflict* (1988). The following selection is from *The Islamic Conception of Justice.*

And fill up the measure when you measure, and with the just balance; that it better and fairer in the issue.

— *Q. VII, 37*

And when you speak, be just, even if it should be to a kinsman.

— *Q. VI, 153*

Justice is essentially a relative concept. Whenever a man asserts that which he considers his just claim, were it to be valid, it must be relevant to an established public order under which a certain scale of justice is acknowledged. Scales of justice vary considerably from land to land, and each scale is defined and ultimately determined by society in accordance with the public order of that society. Yet no matter how scales differ one from another, they all seem to have certain elements in common and, broadly speaking, may be divided into two major categories.

One category is to be found in societies which assume that men are capable of determining their individual or collective interests and know that which they may need or to which they may aspire; they therefore can, individually or collectively, establish a public order under which a certain scale or scales of justice are likely to evolve by tacit agreement or by formal action. This kind of justice, a product of the interaction between expectations and existing conditions, may be called positive justice. It is admittedly imperfect and men always endeavor to refine and improve it by a continuing process of social change. The ideal or perfect justice is a mirage, and the real one develops by improvisation from generation to generation.

In a society which presupposes that man is essentially weak and therefore incapable of rising above personal failings, the idea that fallible human beings can determine what their collective interests are and lay down an impartial standard of justice is scarcely acceptable. In such a society a superhuman or divine authority is invoked to provide either the sources or the basic principles of the public order under which a certain standard of justice is established. Whether the superhuman authority is exercised by a gifted sage or an inspired prophet, the kind of justice that flows from such a source commands respect and can have a lasting impact on the administration of justice. Some of the ancient societies—the Hebrew, the Christian and the Islamic are but three examples—were committed to this viewpoint: God disclosed Himself through Revelations, communicated to men through prophets, in which His justice is embodied. The justice which flows from such a high divine source is considered applicable to all men and forms another category of justice. In contrast with positive justice, it may be called Divine or Revelational justice. It is the product of intuition, or divine inspiration, and is closely interwoven with religion and ethics. It coincides with Reason and may well fall in the category of natural justice. Aristotle used the term "natural justice" in the sense that it is the product not of social but of natural forces. Following Aristotle, scholars often equated Divine or God's justice with natural justice, but, unlike the natural-law scholars who were concerned with the relation of justice to society, Christian and Muslim scholars focused their primary concern on the concept of justice in relation to God's Will and related it to the destiny of man. Both held that

Divine Justice is the ultimate objective of the Revelation, expressed in its early form in the sacred laws of Christianity and Islam. In the *Summa Theologica*, St. Thomas Aquinas termed the sacred law of Christianity the Eternal Law, and Muslims scholars called their Eternal Law simply the "pathway" (Sharī'a). The concept of justice embodied in the Religion and Law of Islam, not to speak of Christian justice, evoked an endless debate among scholars concerning both its scope and character and how its standard is to be realized on Earth.

The Sources of Justice

In Islam, Divine Justice is enshrined in the Revelation and Divine Wisdom which the Prophet Muhammad communicated to his people. The Revelation, transmitted in God's words, is to be found in the Qur'ān; and the Divine Wisdom, inspired to the Prophet, was uttered in the Prophet's own words and promulgated as the Sunna, which subsequently came to be known as the Hadīth, or the Prophet's Traditions. These two authoritative or "textual sources," the embodiment of God's Will and Justice, provided the raw material on the basis of which the scholars, through the use of a third "derivative source" of human reasoning called ijtihād, laid down the Law and the Creed. The fundamental principles of the Law and the Creed, and the creative works of succeeding generations, formed the foundation of the renowned Islamic public order. . . .

In Islamic theory, God is the Sovereign of the community of believers; He is its ultimate Ruler and Legislator. The Relevation and Divine Wisdom are the primary sources of the developing public order, presuming to meet the community's growing needs and expectations. The principles and maxims of justice derived from the Revelation and Divine Wisdom were considered infallible and inviolable, designed for all time and potentially capable of application to all men. In principle, the Law laid down by the Divine Legislator is an ideal and perfect system. But the public order, composed of the Law as well as state acts and the rulings (furū') and opinions of the scholars on all matters arrived at through human reasoning (ijti-hād), are by necessity subject to adaptation and refinement to meet changing conditions and the growing needs of the community.

Since the Divine Legislator did not rule directly over the believers, the enthronement of a Ruler to represent God on Earth, to whom God's authority was delegated, had become necessary to put the Law into practice and to rule with Justice. A new form of government had thus been established based on Divine Law and Justice. This form of government, often called theocracy, is obviously not based on the principle that authority is exercised directly by God (whether as a Pharaoh or a Caesar) but by a representative who derives his authority not directly from God but from God's Law. It is therefore the Law, embodying the principles of Divine authority, which indeed rules and therefore the state becomes not, strictly speaking, a theocracy, but a form of nomocracy. The Islamic State, whose constitution and source of authority is a Divine Law, might be called a Divine nomocracy.

The textual sources, consisting of the Revelation and Divine Wisdom, are the Qur'ān and the Sunna. To these constitutional instruments, the proximate source of authority, all the political leaders and contending parties appealed to assert their conflicting claims to power. Likewise, on the strength of these sources, the scholars sought to legitimize one claim against another by diverse arguments—theological, legal, and others—on the grounds of justice. Although the scholars agreed on the Divine nature of justice, they disagreed on how it should be realized on Earth and formulated various doctrines of justice reflecting the conflicting interests, local traditions, and aspirations of rival leaders and groups in their struggle for power. Legitimacy and justice were often used interchangeably by political leaders, and the scholars, in an attempt to rationalize the legitimacy of rival groups, provided one scale of justice or another drawn from the emerging public order. . . .

At the outset the debate on justice began on the political level. In a community founded on religion, it was indeed in the nature of things that public concern should focus first on the question or legitimacy and the qualification of the Ruler whose primary task was to put God's Law and Justice into practice. Since the Prophet, the first Ruler, died without providing a rule for succession, the question of legitimacy became crucial. Should any pretender to the throne seize power without a valid claim, his act would naturally be considered a travesty to Divine Justice. The debate thus was bound to center on the procedural question of the choice of the person who would have a legitimate claim to succeed the Prophet in accordance with the standard of political justice embodied in the textual sources.

Once the debate on political justice started, it never really ended. Like Pandora's box, it became exceedingly difficult to bring political differences under control. It led to schism in the body politic and the rise of rival credal groups and sects, each seeking to rationalize its standard of political justice on one credal ground or another. From the political level the debate gradually shifted to other levels—theological, legal, and others—although ulterior political motivation continued to reassert itself in one form or another. As the Islamic public order advanced, the debate moved to higher levels of sophistication, and scholars in fields other than theology and law—philosophers and other men of learning—were very soon drawn into it. For no great thinker, whether in Islam or in any other community, could possibly remain indifferent to a debate on a subject as engaging and central as justice. But before we proceed further, perhaps a clarification of the literary meaning of justice and other related terms would be in order.

THE LITERARY MEANING OF JUSTICE

The meaning of the common usage of words expressing the notions of justice or injustice is not only important in the abstract sense, but also illuminating for an understanding of the manifold aspects of justice; since the literal meaning of words is ultimately the outgrowth of their social or every-day meaning, the writers and thinkers are likely to be influenced by it in the articulation and rationalization of man's needs and expectations in the struggle to achieve justice and other human ideals. Classical Arabic is renowned for its richness in vocabulary and literary expressions. Indeed, it is no exaggeration to say that for every concept or action describing or identifying a particular human activity, perhaps a dozen words in the major lexicons are likely to be found, notwithstanding that each word is not necessarily a synonym, as it may often imply a slightly different shade of meaning from the other.

For instance, for the name of God (although this is not a typical example), it may be interesting to note, there are ninety-nine words called the asmā' alhusna (the beautiful names), each denoting or expressing the meaning of one of His manifold attributes.

For every aspect of justice there are several words and the most common in usage is the word "'adl." . . . The antonym of 'adl is not a modified spelling of the word 'adl denoting its negative meaning—as is the counter word "injustice" to "justice" in English—but an entirely different word called "jawr." . . .

Literally, the word 'adl is an abstract noun, derived from the verb 'adala, which means: First, to straighten or to sit straight, to amend or modify; second, to run away, depart or deflect from one (wrong) path to the other (right) one; third, to be equal or equivalent, to be equal or match, or to equalize; fourth, to balance or counterbalance, to weigh, or to be in a state of equilibrium. Finally, 'adl (or 'idl) may also mean example or alike (Q. V, 96), a literal expression which is indirectly related to justice. . . .

The literal meaning of 'adl in classical Arabic is thus a combination of moral and social values denoting fairness, balance, temperance and straightforwardness. Logically, Divine Justice would be a synthesis of all these values and virtues; indeed such a conceptual meaning is the theme of the debate among theologians, jurists and philosophers and will be the subject of our inquiry in the pages to follow.

THE NOTION OF JUSTICE IN THE QUR'ĀN AND TRADITIONS

The Prophet Muhammad, who seems to have been endowed with a deep sense of justice, found widespread inequity and oppression in the society in which he had grown up, and he sought to establish order and harmony within which a distinct standard of justice would be acknowledged. As a Prophet, he naturally stressed religious values, but he was also a social reformer, and his decisions provided precedents on the strength of which the issues that were to arise in succeeding generations were resolved. The idea of justice was of particular interest to him, and he dealt with the problems of his day with uprightness, balance, and fairness. Nor was he indifferent to discrimination and inhuman acts, as exemplified in the legislation for the improvement of the status of women, emancipation of slaves (though slavery as a system was not abolished), and prohibition of infanticide and other unjust acts and practices. Moreover, he himself valued certain virtues honored by his followers and he incorporated them in his teachings. As he said in one of his often quoted utterances, his call was not to abolish but to "further the good morals" (li utammim makārim al-akhlāq) that had been in existence in society, and he felt compelled to confirm them.

In the tribal society of Arabia, where survival was perhaps the tribesman's primary concern, such virtues as honor, courage, and liberality were more highly prized than other virtues. These were epitomized in the word "muruwwa," consisting of everything that was taken to be praiseworthy and which may be called the Arab *summum bonum*. The muruwwa continued to be viewed so high in Arab eyes in subsequent centuries that al-Maqqarī (d. 770/1369) in his definition of justice, stated that no one could claim to be just were he to compromise the virtue of muruwwa. But in the exhibition of honor and courage the tribesmen were often brutal and oppressive, especially in the pursuit of *vendetta*, with the consequent subordination of the virtues of fairness and moderation to arbitrary rules of order. The poet 'Amr B. Kulthūm, composer of one of the well-known Seven Odes (al-Mu'allaqāt al-Sab'a) was not the only one who sang the praise of brutality and oppression attributed to his tribe. The absence of a coherent social order and political unity in the tribal society of Arabia necessarily subordinated the scale of justice to the requirements of survival, and consequently the appeal to justice took the negative form of retribution, such as retaliation and the payment of blood-money, rather than the positive forms of fairness, balance, and temperance.

The Prophet, while conceding the value of courage and other virtues, felt keenly the need to assert religious and moral values to temper cruelty and harshness. For this reason, the Qur'ān and Traditions often warned believers against bigotry and oppression, and admonished them that in the fulfillment of their religious obligations they must above all be just. In the Qur'ān there are over two hundred admonitions against injustice expressed in such words as zulm, ithm, dalāl, and others, and no less than almost a hundred expressions embodying the notion of justice, either directly in such words as 'adl, qist, mizān, and others . . . or in a variety of indirect expressions.

Second only to the existence of the One God, no other religious or moral principles are more emphasized in the Qur'ān and Traditions than the principles of uprightness, equity, and temperance, partly because of their intrinsic value but mainly because of the reaction against the pre-Islamic social order which paid little or no attention to justice. The most important Quranic references to justice are as follows:

> God commands justice and good-doing . . . and He forbids indecency, dishonor and insolence. (Q. XV, 92)
>
> God commands you to deliver trusts back to their owners, and when you judge among men, you should judge with justice. (Q. IV, 61)
>
> Of those We created are a people who guide by the truth, and by it act with justice. (Q. VIII, 180)

In the Traditions, the Prophet sought to explain the meaning of the abstract maxims of justice enunciated in the Qur'ān by specific examples, expressed in legal and ethical terms, to distinguish between just and unjust acts as well as to set underlying rules indicating what the scale of justice ought to be. Since the Prophet dealt essentially with practical questions, the theologians and other scholars found in the Traditions precedents on the strength of which they formulated their theories of justice. However, neither in the Qur'ān nor in the Traditions are there specific measures to indicate what are the constituent elements of justice or how justice can be realized on Earth. Thus the task of working out what the standard of justice ought to be fell upon the scholars who sought to draw its elements from the diverse authoritative sources and the rulings and acts embodied in the works of commentators.

The religious character of the public order, however, imposed by its very nature certain restraints, and the community of believers, distrustful of the capacity of fallible men to legislate for society, discouraged radical departure from the literal meaning of textual sources. Small wonder that many scholars, under popular pressures, were often forced to renounce doctrines seemingly inconsistent with the literal meaning of the authoritative sources, despite the growing needs of society for innovations. However, most scholars felt that they were duty-bound to accept the interpretation of the standard of justice laid down by their predecessors more strictly than by those who sought radical changes. . . .

Having established the harmony of Reason and Revelation, Ibn Rushd proceeded to discuss his ideas of justice making a distinction between the Divine and Human justice (Rational Justice). He made it clear that despite differences in sources (Greek and Islamic), the notion of justice embodied in both is ultimately the same. In setting forth his theory of human justice, Ibn Rushd has drawn on both Plato and Aristotle, making a distinction between the theoretical and practical forms of justice with an emphasis on the latter. Justice, like other virtues, does not exist in its perfect form in a vacuum, said Ibn Rushd; it attains its perfection only when men are citizens of the state. Just as virtues are faculties of the soul, he added, justice is the highest virtue of man as a citizen. But justice is not just one virtue; it is, as Plato said, the sum of all virtues. "It consists," he said, "in no more than every citizen following the activity for which he is best qualified by nature." He went on to explain that this is conceivable only when the state is functioning in accordance with the guidance provided by the speculative science (philosophy) and governed by its masters. These are the ruling classes of the state just as the intellect is the ruling part of the soul. So justice means that each man (or class) does what he (or the class) has to do in proper measure and time.

Ibn Rushd distinguishes between virtues like wisdom and courage which are closely connected with one class only, and virtues like justice and temperance ('iffa) which are manifestly connected with all classes of the state. In agreement with Aristotle, he says that the virtue of temperance is connected with all, although Plato insists that temperance is a virtue confined to craftsmen. Justice is the virtue necessary for all.

In the realization of justice—indeed, in the realization of all virtues—Ibn Rushd said, in agreement with Aristotle, that three conditions are required. First, it is not only knowledge of the nature of virtues that is necessary; action is even more important. Second, the souls of the young must be inculcated with these virtues and cultivated to the point of perfection; if evil is ever in possession of some, it must be removed. Third, the qualities and virtues, whenever they are combined and render other virtues perfect, must be specified.

Ibn Rushd then turned to the question of how to inculcate and cultivate these virtues into the souls of the citizens. There are obviously two methods: First, by persuasion, either rhetorical and poetical for the multitude or the rational (speculative) for the elect; and second, by force. The first method is for the citizens who had already been accustomed to it from youth, and the other is for the adversaries and all those who are not sensitive to the appeals of virtue. The latter is evidently not for the citizens of the Virtuous State; it is for states whose public order is not based on virtues. In dealing with these states, whose rulers resort to force to correct their citizens, there is no other way than to resort to war. The Law, says Ibn Rushd, indicates how the two methods can be applied. If persuasion is not heeded, war becomes just (jihād) against rebels as well as unbelievers. Since preparation for war is impossible without the cultivation of the virtue of courage, the citizens should cultivate this virtue in preparedness for war when it becomes necessary. Just as wisdom is the virtue necessary for the realization of justice within the state, so courage is necessary for the realization of justice in the relationship between nations.

Ibn Rushd, in agreement with Plato, maintains that justice can be realized only in a state founded upon a set of virtues, namely, wisdom, courage, temperance, and justice. Whenever these virtues are fully cultivated, the state becomes an ideal state. A few words about each virtue may be called for.

Wisdom includes possession of theoretical and practical knowledge concerning governance and Law. Men who are endowed with this rare quality are very few; they may be found only among the philosophers and those who are capable of governing the State. The rulers of the Ideal State, said Ibn Rushd in agreement with Plato, "are necessarily the Philosophers."

Courage as a virtue is the quality of strength against such emotions as fear and desire, which can be attained by education, especially in music and gymnastics. This virtue is most needed by the guardians whose responsibility is to maintain order and protect the state from its enemies.

Temperance and justice are in a different category from wisdom and courage. Whereas the last two are ordinarily found among rulers and guardians, temperance and justice are virtues necessary for all men. Temperance may be defined as the middle or the mean in human behavior—in eating, drinking, sexual intercourse, and others—and the man who is temperate "is he who can, of his own accord, remain permanently in this middle position." He can control himself and restrain "the soul from pleasures and desire." "It is said," Ibn Rushd adds, "that the temperate man is the most courageous and master over himself." Just as the man who is by his intellect the master over the inferior, so is the temperate state more courageous than others and a master over itself. In order to attain such a quality, temperance should exist not only in one class but in all—the rulers and the ruled alike.

Finally, justice as a virtue is the quality of fairness and self-control. It is the quality by which the state can survive and claims to continue as long as the rulers and the multitude are in agreement "to keep that which the laws demand," namely, that "everyone . . . does that business for which he is fitted by nature, and does not long for what he does not possess." In other words, the ideal state is the Just State by reason of the quality of justness with which all its citizens are clothed, just as wrongdoings reduce other states to "states of injustice" or "erring states."

Justice is maintained in the state as long as each citizen pursues the virtue most fitting to his class. The Just State is characterized as wise, courageous, and temperate, provided that these virtues exist in the state in their true measure, so that the rational faculty (Reason) rules over the other faculties.

Justice, in order to endure, is dependent on the Ruler who presides over the destiny of the state. Such a Ruler must be a philosopher, because he is the only one who desires knowledge and investigates its nature (separated from matter) and is able to teach it. Knowledge may be taught to the few either by the rational or demonstrative argument; the multitude can be taught only by rhetorical and poetical methods. In order to succeed, the philosopher should master both the theoretical and the practical arts, just as the king, in order to perfect the art of governance, is in need of the qualities of wisdom and intellect. The lawgiver obviously needs the same qualities. Indeed, the qualities of the philosopher, the king, and the lawgiver are the same. The Imām, Ruler of the Islamic state, must possess all of these qualities.

Should the ruler be a prophet? Ibn Rushd's answer to this question in general is in the affirmative. Apart from being a prophet or a philosopher, however, the Ruler must be endowed with a set of natural qualifications such as disposition to theoretical knowledge, love for the truth, high-mindedness, courage, fluency in speech, good memory, control over desires that are not proper for rulers (like sensual desires and love for money), and—last but not least—justice. Since the existence of the prophet is a rarity, . . . Ibn Rushd stressed the personal qualities of the Ruler upon whom the survival of the state is dependent. Thus it would be tempting to conclude that were the state to be a just state it should be presided over by a Ruler possessing the theoretical and practical qualities without having first been ruled by a prophet. In such a state Rational Justice may be equated with the *jus naturale*.

The opposite of the Just State are the erring or wrongdoing states where injustice prevails. Like Plato, Ibn Rushd identifies four types of states apart from the Ideal State; in each a different scale of justice is maintained. The first is the state whose order is based on honor, which is called timocracy. In such a state, justice is subordinate to honor and to other qualities. As an end, honor may be combined with wealth and power and may tempt men to overpower each other and do evil and injustice. Men of honor are masters and their status corresponds generally to the degree of honor they attain. Rulers possess the ability to distribute honors in pursuit of the measures that preserve their control. This, says Ibn Rushd, is the kind of justice that exists in timocracy.

The second type, called plutocracy, is ruled by a few whose power rests on wealth. So wealth, not virtue, is the measure of the quality of men. The Ruler, the most powerful and perhaps the richest, combines with wealth an ability to govern successfully and consequently he is the master of the state, provided he allows his men to acquire wealth and let them enjoy it indefinitely. Wealth and power are the privilege of the few, but the majority, possessing no claim to privilege, are poor and oppressed.

The third type is the democratic state in which everybody is free from restraints and each is entitled to do whatever his heart desires. The aims and qualities of men vary—some love honor, others wealth, and still others tyranny. But there may be some who possess a few virtues and are moved by them. All arts and dispositions come into being, and it is possible that an "ideal state" as well as other types of states may emerge out of these varied dispositions. The man who is truly just is the one who has the power of leadership. The majority, at the mercy of whoever becomes the master, are plundered and oppressed by the more powerful, but these are often tempted to commit excesses "just as it happens in our own time and in our own state." When the conditions deteriorate and the rulers can no longer distribute wealth among supporters, they resort to imposing heavy taxes. Consequently the common run of men, encouraged by dissatisfied supporters, try to shake off the oppressors, but the masters seek control by force. The State, supported by a few (including religious leaders), becomes tyrannical. The end of such a state is reduced to nothing more than to serve the master and to fulfill his wishes. This state is obviously the opposite of the Just State. Only in the Just State can the citizen attain justice equal to his natural abilities. . . .

DISCUSSION QUESTIONS

1. What is the difference between positive justice and Divine justice? Discuss whether the notions of justice outlined by Hobbes, Mill, Marx, Rawls, and Hospers could be considered examples of positive or Divine justice.

2. What is the difference between Divine nomacracy and theocracy? Why does Khadduri describe the Islamic form of government as Divine nomacracy, and not theocracy?

3. Ibn Rushd saw the Islamic and the Greek notions of justice as ultimately the same, and he drew heavily on the philosophies of Plato and Aristotle. Discuss the similarities

between the Islamic and Greek notions of justice according to Ibn Rushd.

4. Ibn Rushd argues that the leader of the Islamic state should be either a prophet or a philosopher. Why does he believe this? Which does he think is more likely to rule the Islamic state, and why?

5. Ibn Rushd discussed a number of unjust states. What are they? Why is democracy one of them?

6. When, according to Ibn Rushd, does war against rebels and unbelievers become justifiable? How, according to Ibn Rushd, should individuals prepare for jihād?

CHARLES W. MILLS

THE RACIAL CONTRACT

Charles W. Mills identifies what he calls the *racial contract* and argues that it has a greater claim to being an actual historical fact than its philosophical cousin, the social contract. According to Mills, the *racial contact* grants white men natural freedom and equality, while nonwhites "are designated as born *un*free and *un*equal." The general purpose of the racial contract is "the differential privileging of the whites as a group with respect to the nonwhites as a group, the exploitation of their bodies, land, and resources, and the denial of equal socioeconomic opportunities to them." Nevertheless, the racial contract is *not* a contract consented to by nonwhites. "Rather," states Mills, "it is a contract between those categorized as white *over* the nonwhites, who are thus the objects rather than the subjects of the agreement."

The racial contact is both similar to and different from the social contract in a number of significant ways. First, while both contracts aim at the formation of a government, only the social contract is a contract between all persons. The racial contract constructs the category "nonwhite" and assigns a subordinate social standing to this group. Moreover, the racial contract is consented to only by whites— not nonwhites.

Second, while both contracts differentiate between a "state of nature" and a "civil state" and postulate movement from one state to the other, only the social contract says that the civil state is open to all persons. The racial contract maintains that the civil state or society is open only to whites and that nonwhites are to remain in the state of nature. Moreover, these two states are mapped onto geographical space. While the social contact regards all geographical spaces as civil states populated by civilized people, the racial contract names America and Europe as the only civil states. All other geographical spaces are regarded by the racial contract as uncivilized states of nature peopled by barbarians and savages.

Third, whereas the social contract is associated with an epistemology which maintains that "through our natural faculties we come to know reality in both its factual and valuational aspects, the way things objectively are and what is objectively good or bad about them," the racial contract is associated with "an inverted epistemology." The racial contract's epistemology is one of "ignorance, a particular pattern of localized and global cognitive dysfunctions (which are psychologically and socially functional), producing the ironic outcome that whites will in general be unable to understand the world they themselves have made." Signatories of the racial contract forget what they have agreed to by inventing "white mythologies, invented Orients, invented Africas, invented Americas, with a correspondingly fabricated population, countries that never were, inhabited by people who never were . . . but who attain a virtual reality through their existence in traveler's tales, folk myth, popular and highbrow fiction, colonial reports, scholarly theory, Hollywood cinema, living in the white imagination and determinedly imposed on their alarmed real-life counterparts."

Mills concludes that the racial contract better explains the actual history of racism, colonialism, and slavery than does the social contract. While social contract theorists since Hobbes were developing a hypothetical contract that might bring about a world of freedom and equality for all, the racial contract served as the real contract that was determining social reality. A biographical sketch of Charles W. Mills appears in chapter 3. The following is from his book *The Racial Contract* (1997).

I will start with an overview of the Racial Contract, highlighting its differences from, as well as its similarities to, the classical and contemporary social contract. The Racial Contract is political, moral, and epistemological, the Racial Contract is real; and economically, in determining who gets what, the Racial Contract is an exploitation contract.

THE RACIAL CONTRACT IS POLITICAL, MORAL, AND EPISTEMOLOGICAL

The "social contract" is actually several contracts in one. Contemporary contractarians usually distinguish, to begin with, between the *political* contract and the *moral* contract, before going on to make (subsidiary) distinctions within both. I contend, however, that the orthodox social contract also tacitly presupposes an "epistemological" contract, and that for the Racial Contract it is crucial to make this explicit. . . .

Now the Racial Contract—and the "Racial Contract" as a theory, that is, the distanced, critical examination of the Racial Contract—follows the classical model in being both sociopolitical and moral. It explains how society was created or crucially transformed, how the individuals in that society were reconstituted, how the state was established, and how a particular moral code and a certain moral psychology were brought into existence. (As I have emphasized, the "Racial Contract" seeks to account for the way things are and how they came to be that way—the descriptive—*as well as* the way they should be— the normative—since indeed one of its complaints about white political philosophy is precisely its otherworldiness, its ignoring of basic political realities.) But the Racial Contract, as we will see, is also epistemological, prescribing norms for cognition to which its signatories must adhere. A preliminary characterization would run something like this:

The Racial Contract is that set of formal or informal agreements or meta-agreements (higher-level contracts *about* contracts, which set the limits of the contracts' validity) between the members of one subset of humans, henceforth designated by (shifting) "racial" (phenotypical/genealogical/cultural) criteria C_1, C_2, C_3 . . . as "white," and coextensive (making due allowance for gender differentiation) with the class of full persons, to categorize the remaining subset of humans as "nonwhite" and of a different and inferior moral status, subpersons, so that they have a subordinate civil standing in the white or white-ruled polities the whites either already inhabit or establish or in transactions as aliens with these polities, and the moral and juridical rules normally regulating the behavior of whites in their dealings with one another either do not apply at all in dealings with nonwhites or apply only in a qualified form (depending in part on changing historical circumstances and what particular variety of nonwhite is involved), but in any case the general purpose of the Contract is always the differential privileging of the whites as a group with respect to the nonwhites as a group, the exploitation of their bodies, land, and resources, and the denial of equal socioeconomic opportunities to them. All whites are *beneficiaries* of the Contract, though some whites are not *signatories* to it.

It will be obvious, therefore, that the Racial Contract is not a contract to which the nonwhite subset of humans can be a genuinely consenting party (though, depending again on the circumstances, it may sometimes be politic to pretend that this is the case). Rather, it is a contract between those categorized as white *over* the nonwhites, who are thus the objects rather than the subjects of the agreement.

The logic of the classic social contract, political, moral, and epistemological, then undergoes a corresponding refraction, with shifts, accordingly, in the key terms and principles.

Politically, the contract to establish society and the government, thereby transforming abstract raceless "men" from denizens of the state of nature into social creatures who are politically obligated to a neutral state, becomes the founding of a *racial polity*, whether white settler states (where pre-existing populations already are or can be made sparse) or what are sometimes called "sojourner colonies," the establishment of a white presence and colonial rule over existing societies (which are somewhat more populous, or whose inhabitants are more resistant to being made sparse). In addition, the colonizing mother country is also changed by its relation to these new polities, so that its own citizens are altered.

In the social contract, the crucial human metamorphosis is from "natural" man to "civil/political" man, from the resident of the state of nature to the citizen of the created society. This change can be more or less extreme, depending on the theorist involved. For Rousseau it is a dramatic transformation, by which animal-like creatures of appetite and instinct become citizens bound by justice and self-prescribed laws. For Hobbes it is a somewhat more laid-back affair by which people who look out primarily for themselves learn to constrain their self-interest for their own good. But in all cases the original "state of nature" supposedly indicates the condition of *all* men, and the social metamorphosis affects them all in the same way.

In the Racial Contract, by contrast, the crucial metamorphosis is the preliminary conceptual partitioning and corresponding transformation of human populations into "white" and "nonwhite" men. The role played by the "state of nature" then becomes radically different. In the white settler state, its role is not primarily to demarcate the (temporarily) prepolitical state of "all" men (who are really white men), but rather the permanently prepolitical state or, perhaps better, *non*political state (insofar as "pre-" suggests eventual internal movement toward) of nonwhite men. The

establishment of society thus implies the denial that a society already existed; the creation of society *requires* the intervention of white men, who are thereby positioned as *already* sociopolitical beings. White men who are (definitionally) already part of society encounter nonwhites who are not, who are "savage" residents of a state of nature characterized in terms of wilderness, jungle, wasteland. These the white men bring partially into society as subordinate citizens or exclude on reservations or deny the existence of or exterminate. In the colonial case, admittedly preexisting but (for one reason or another) deficient societies (decadent, stagnant, corrupt) are taken over and run for the "benefit" of the nonwhite natives, who are deemed childlike, incapable of self-rule and handling their own affairs, and thus appropriately wards of the state. Here the natives are usually characterized as "barbarians" rather than "savages," their state of nature being somewhat farther away (though not, of course, as remote and lost in the past—if it ever existed in the first place—as the Europeans' state of nature). But in times of crisis the conceptual distance between the two, barbarian and savage, tends to shrink or collapse, for this technical distinction within the nonwhite population is vastly less important than the *central* distinction between whites and nonwhites.

In both cases, then, though in different ways, the Racial Contract establishes a racial polity, a racial state, and a racial juridical system, where the status of whites and nonwhites is clearly demarcated, whether by law or custom. And the purpose of this state, by contrast with the neutral state of classic contractarianism, is, inter alia, specifically to maintain and reproduce this racial order, securing the privileges and advantages of the full white citizens and maintaining the subordination of nonwhites. Correspondingly, the "consent" expected of the white citizens is in part conceptualized as a consent, whether explicit or tacit to the racial order, to white supremacy, what could be called Whiteness. To the extent that those phenotypically/genealogically/culturally catego-rized as white fail to live up to the civic and political responsibilities of Whiteness, they are in dereliction of their duties as citizens. From the inception, then, race is in no way an "afterthought," a "deviation" from ostensibly raceless Western ideals, but rather a central shaping constituent of those ideals.

In the social contract tradition, there are two main possible relations between the moral contract and the political contract. On the first view, the moral contract represents *preexisting* objectivist morality (theological or secular) and thus constrains the terms of the political contract. This is the view found in Locke and Kant. In other words, there is an objective moral code in the state of nature itself, even if there are no policemen and judges to enforce it. So any society, government, and legal system that are established should be based on that moral code. On the second view, the political contract *creates* morality as a conventionalist set of rules. So there is no independent objective moral criterion for judging one moral code to be superior to another or for indicting a society's established morality as unjust. On this conception, which is famously attributed to Hobbes, morality is just a set of rules for expediting the rational pursuit and coordination of our own interests without conflict with those other people who are doing the same thing.

The Racial Contract can accommodate both versions, but as it is the former version (the contract as described in Locke and Kant) rather than the latter version (the contract as described in Hobbes) which represents the mainstream of the contract tradition, I focus on that one. Here, the good polity is taken to rest on a preexisting moral foundation. Obviously, this is a far more attractive conception of a political system than Hobbes's view. The ideal of an objectively just polis to which we should aspire in our political activism goes back in the Western tradition all the way to Plato. In the medieval Christian worldview which continued to influence contractarianism well into the modern period, there is a "natural law" immanent in the structure of the universe which is supposed to direct us morally in striving for this ideal. (For the later, secular versions of contractarianism, the idea would simply be that people have rights and duties even in the state of nature because of their nature as human beings.) So it is wrong to steal, rape, kill in the state of nature even if there are no human laws written down saying it is wrong. These moral principles must constrain the human laws that are made and the civil rights that are assigned once the polity is established. In part, then, the political contract simply *codifies* a morality that already exists, writing it down and filling in the details, so we don't have to rely on a divinely implanted moral sense, or conscience, whose perceptions may on occasion be distorted by self-interest. What is right and wrong, just and unjust, in society will largely be determined by what is right and wrong, just and unjust, in the state of nature.

The character of this objective moral foundation is therefore obviously crucial. For the mainstream of the contractarian tradition, it is the *freedom and equality of all men in the state of nature*. As Locke writes in the *Second Treatise,* "To understand Political Power right, and derive it from its Original, we must consider what State all Men are naturally in, and that is, a *State of perfect Freedom* to order their Actions. . . . A *state* also *of Equality,* wherein all the Power and Jurisdiction is reciprocal, no one having more than another." For Kant, similarly, it is our equal moral personhood. Contractarianism is (supposedly) committed to moral egalitarianism, the moral equality of all men, the notion that the interests of all men matter equally and all men must have equal rights. Thus, contractarianism is also committed to a principled and foundational opposition to the traditionalist hierarchical ideology of the old feudal order, the ideology of inherent ascribed status and natural subordination. It is this language of equality which echoes in the American and French Revolutions, the Declaration of Independence, and the Declaration of the Rights of Man. And it is this moral egalitarianism that must be retained in the allocation of rights and liberties in civil society. When in a modern Western society people insist on their rights and freedoms and express their outrage at not being treated equally, it is to these classic ideas that, whether they know it or not, they are appealing.

But as we will see in greater detail later on, the color-coded morality of the Racial Contract restricts the possession of this natural freedom and equality to *white* men. By virtue of their complete nonrecognition, or at best inadequate, myopic recognition, of the duties of natural law, nonwhites are appropriately relegated to a lower rung on the moral ladder (the Great Chain of Being). They are, designated as born *un*free and *un*equal. A partitioned social ontology is therefore created, a universe divided between persons and racial subpersons, *Untermenschen,* who may variously be black, red, brown, yellow—slaves, aborigines, colonial populations—but who are collectively appropriately known as "subject races." And these subpersons—niggers, injuns, chinks, wags, greasers, blackfellows, kaffirs, coolies, abos, dinks, googoos, gooks—are biologically destined never to penetrate the normative rights ceiling established for them below white persons. Henceforth, then, whether openly admitted or not, it is taken for granted that the grand ethical theories propounded in the development of Western moral and political thought are of restricted scope, explicitly or implicitly intended by their proponents to be restricted to persons, whites. The terms of the Racial Contract set the parameters for white morality as a whole, so that competing Lockean and Kantian contractarian theories of natural rights and duties, or later anticontractarian theories such as nineteenth-century utilitarianism, are all limited by its stipulations.

Finally, the Racial Contract requires its own peculiar moral and empirical epistemology, its norms and procedures for determining what counts as moral and factual knowledge of the world. In the standard accounts of contractarianism it is not usual to speak of there being an "epistemological" contract, but there *is* an epistemology associated with contractarianism, in the form of natural law. This provides us with a moral compass, whether in the traditional version of Locke—the light of reason implanted in us by God so we can discern objective right and wrong—or in the revisionist version of Hobbes—the ability to assess the objectively optimal prudential course of a action and what it requires of us for self-interested cooperation with others. So through our natural faculties we come to know reality in both its factual and valuational aspects, the way things objectively are and what is objectively good or bad about them. I suggest we can think of this as an idealized consensus about cognitive norms and, in this respect, an agreement or "contract" of sorts. There is an understanding about what counts as a correct, objective interpretation of the world, and for agreeing to this view, one is ("contractually") granted full cognitive standing in the polity, the official epistemic community.

But for the Racial Contract things are necessarily more complicated. The requirements of "objective" cognition, factual and moral, in a racial polity are in a sense more demanding in that officially sanctioned reality is divergent from actual reality. So here, it could be said, one has an agreement to *mis*interpret the world. One has to learn to see the world wrongly, but with the assurance that this set of mistaken perceptions will be validated by white epistemic authority, whether religious or secular.

Thus in effect, on matters related to race, the Racial Contract prescribes for its signatories an inverted epistemology, an epistemology of ignorance, a particular pattern of localized and global cognitive dysfunctions (which are psychologically and socially functional), producing the ironic outcome that whites will in general be unable to understand the world they themselves have made. Part of what it means to be constructed as "white" (the metamorphosis of the sociopolitical contract), part of what it requires to achieve Whiteness, successfully to become a white person (one imagines a ceremony with certificates attending the successful rite of passage: "Congratulations, you're now an official white person!"), is a cognitive model that precludes self-transparency and genuine understanding of social realites. To a significant extent, then, white signatories will live in an invented delusional world, a racial fantasyland, a "consensual hallucination," to quote Willam Gibson's famous characterization of cyberspace, though this particular hallucination is located in real space. There will be white mythologies, invented Orients, invented Africas, invented Americas, with a correspondingly fabricated population, countries that never were, inhabited by people who never were—Calibans and Tontos, Man Fridays and Sambos—but who attain a virtual reality through their existence in travelers' tales, folk myth, popular and highbrow fiction, colonial reports, scholarly theory, Hollywood cinema, living in the white imagination and determinedly imposed on their alarmed real-life counterparts. One could say then, as a general rule, that *white misunderstanding, misrepresentation, evasion, and self-deception on matters related to race* are among the most pervasive mental phenomena of the past few hundred years, a cognitive and moral economy psychically required for conquest, colonization, and enslavement. And these phenomena are in no way *accidental*, but *prescribed* by the terms of the Racial Contract, which requires a certain schedule of structured blindnesses and opacities in order to establish and maintain the white polity.

THE RACIAL CONTRACT IS A HISTORICAL ACTUALITY

The social contract in its modern version has long since given up any pretensions to be able to explain the historical origins of society and the state. Whereas the classic contractarians were engaged in a project both descriptive and prescriptive, the modern Rawls-inspired contract is purely a prescriptive thought experiment. And even Pateman's Sexual Contract,* though its focus is the real rather than the ideal, is not meant as a literal account of what men in 4004 B.C. decided to do on the plains of Mesopotamia. Whatever accounts for what Friedrich Engels once called "the *world historical defeat of the female sex*"— whether the development of an economic surplus, as he theorized, or the male discovery of the capacity to rape and the female disadvantage of being the childbearing half of the species, as radical feminists have argued—it is clearly lost in antiquity.

By contrast, ironically, the Racial Contract, never so far as I know explored as such, has the best claim to being an actual historical fact. Far from being lost in the mists of the ages, it is clearly historically locatable in the series of events marking the creation of the modern world by European colonialism and the voyages of "discovery" now increasingly and more appropriately called expeditions of conquest. The Columbian quincentenary [the 500th anniversary of Columbus's first voyage to the Americas in 1492] a few years ago, with its accompanying debates, polemics, controversies, counterdemonstrations, and outpourings of revisionist literature, confronted many whites with the uncomfortable fact, hardly discussed in mainstream moral and political theory, that we live in a world which has been *foundationally shaped for the past five hundred years by the realities of European domination and the gradual consolidation of global white supremacy.* Thus not only is the Racial Contract "real," but— whereas the social contract is characteristically taken to be establishing the legitimacy of the nation-state, and codifying morality and law within its boundaries—the Racial Contract is *global*, involving a tectonic shift of the ethicojuridical basis of the planet as a whole, the division of the world, as Jean-Paul Sartre put it long ago, between "men" and "natives."

Europeans thereby emerge as "the lords of human kind," the "lords of all the world," with the increasing power to determine the standing of the non-Europeans who are their subjects. Although no single act literally corresponds to the drawing up and signing of a contract, there is a series of acts—papal bulls and other theological pronouncements; European discussions about colonialism, "discovery," and international law; pacts, treaties, and legal decisions; academic and popular debates about the humanity of nonwhites; the establishment of formalized legal structures of differential treatment; and the routinization of informal illegal or quasi-legal practices effectively sanctioned by the complicity of silence and government failure to intervene and punish perpetrators—which collectively can be seen, not just metaphorically but close to literally, as its conceptual, juridical, and normative equivalent.

Anthony Pagden suggests that a division of the European empires into their main temporal periods should recognize "two distinct, but interdependent histories": the colonization of the Americas, 1492 to the 1830s, and the occupation of Asia, Africa, and the Pacific, 1730s to the period after World War II. In the first period, it was, to begin with, the nature and moral status of the Native Americans that primarily had to be determined, and then that of the imported African slaves whose labor was required to build this "New World." In the second period, culminating in formal European colonial rule over most of the world by the early twentieth century, it was the character of colonial peoples that became crucial. But in all cases "race" is the common conceptual denominator that gradually came to signify the respective global statuses of superiority and inferiority, privilege and subordination. There is an opposition of us against them with multiple overlapping dimensions: Europeans versus non-Europeans (geography), civilized versus wild/savage/barbarians (culture), Christians versus

---

*Carole Pateman argues in *The Sexual Contract* (1988) that standard social contract theory fails to contend with what she identifies as "the sexual contract," namely, a contract that establishes modern patriarchy and the political right of men over women. —Ed.

heathens (religion). But they all eventually coalesced into the *basic* opposition of white versus nonwhite.

A Lumbee Indian legal scholar, Robert Williams, has traced the evolution of the Western legal position on the rights of native peoples from its medieval antecedents to the beginnings of the modern period, showing how it is consistently based on the assumption of "the rightness and necessity of subjugating and assimilating other peoples to [the European] worldview." Initially the intellectual framework was a theological one, with normative inclusion and exclusion manifesting itself as the demarcation between Christians and heathens. The pope's powers over the *Societas Christiana* the Universal Christian commonwealth, were seen as "extending not only over all Christians within the universal commonwealth, but over unregenerated heathens and infidels as well," and this policy would subsequently underwrite not merely the Crusades against Islam but the later voyages to the Americas. Sometimes papal pronouncements did grant rights and rationality to nonbelievers. As a result of dealing with the Mongols in the thirteenth century, for example, Pope Innocent IV "conceded that infidels and heathens possessed the natural law right to elect their own secular leaders," and Pope Paul III's famous *Sublimis Deus* (1537) stated that Native Americans were rational beings, not to be treated as "dumb brutes created for our service" but "as truly men . . . capable of understanding the Catholic faith." But as Williams points out, the latter qualification was always crucial. A Eurocentrically normed conception of rationality made it coextensive with acceptance of the Christian message, so that rejection was proof of bestial irrationality.

Even more remarkably, in the case of Native Americans this acceptance was to be signaled by their agreement to the *Requerimiento,* a long statement read aloud to them in, of course, a language they did not understand, failing which assent a just war could lawfully be waged against them. One author writes:

> The *requerimiento* is the prototypical example of *text* justifying conquest. Informing the Indians that their lands were entrusted by Christ to the pope and thence to the kings of Spain, the document offers freedom from slavery for those Indians who accept Spanish rule. Even though it was entirely incomprehensible to a non-Spanish speaker, reading the document provided sufficient justification for dispossession of land and immediate enslavement of the indigenous people. [Bartolomé de] Las Casas's famous comment on the *requerimiento* was that one does not know "whether to laugh or cry at the absurdity of it." . . . While appearing to respect "rights" the *requerimiento,* in fact, takes them away.

In effect, then, the Catholic Church's declarations either formally legitimated conquest or could be easily circumvented where a weak prima facie moral barrier was erected. . . .

Indian laws, slave codes, and colonial native acts formally codified the subordinate status of nonwhites and (ostensibly) regulated their treatment, creating a juridical space for non-Europeans as a separate category of beings. So even if there was sometimes an attempt to prevent "abuses" (and these codes were honored far more often in the breach than the observance), the point is that "abuse" as a concept presupposes as a norm the *legitimacy* of the subordination. Slavery and colonialism are not conceived as wrong in their denial of autonomy to persons; what is wrong is the improper administration of these regimes.

It would be a fundamental error, then—a point to which I will return—to see racism as anomalous, a mysterious deviation from European Enlightenment humanism. Rather, it needs to be realized that, in keeping with the Roman precedent, *European humanism usually meant that only Europeans were human.* European moral and political theory, like European thought in general, developed within the framework of the Racial Contract and, as a rule, took it for granted. As Edward Said points out in *Culture and Imperialism,* we must not see culture as "antiseptically quarantined from its worldly affiliations." But this occupational blindness has in fact infected most "professional humanists" (and certainly most philosophers), so that "as a result [they are] unable to make the connection between the prolonged and sordid cruelty of practices such as slavery, colonialist and racial oppression, and imperial subjection on the one hand, and the poetry, fiction, philosophy of the society that engages in these practices on the other." By the nineteenth century, conventional white opinion casually assumed the uncontroversial validity of a hierarchy of "higher" and "lower," "master" and "subject" races, for whom, it is obvious, different rules must apply.

The modern world was thus expressly created as a *racially hierarchical* polity, globally dominated by Europeans. A 1969 *Foreign Affairs* article worth rereading today reminds us that as late as the 1940s the world "was still by and large a Western white-dominated world. The long-established patterns of white power and nonwhite non-power were still the generally accepted order of things. All the accompanying assumptions and mythologies about race and color were still mostly taken for granted. . . . [W]hite supremacy was a generally assumed and accepted state of affairs in the United States as well as in Europe's empires." But statements of such frankness are rare or nonexistent in mainstream white opinion today, which generally seeks to rewrite the past so as to deny or minimize the obvious fact of global white domination.

Yet the United States itself, of course, is a white settler state on territory expropriated from its aboriginal inhabitants through a combination of military force, disease, and a "century of dishonor" of broken treaties. The expropriation involved literal genocide (a word now unfortunately devalued by hyperbolic overuse) of a kind that some recent revisionist historians have argued needs to be seen as comparable to the Third Reich's. Washington, Father of the Nation, was, understandably, known somewhat differently to the Senecas as "Town Destroyer." In the Declaration of Independence, Jefferson characterized Native Americans as "merciless Indian Savages," and in the Constitution, blacks, of course, appear only obliquely, through the famous "60 percent solution."* Thus, as Richard Drinnon concludes: "The Framers manifestly established a government under which non-Europeans were not men created equal—in the white polity . . . they were nonpeoples." Though on a smaller scale and not

always so ruthlessly (or, in the case of New Zealand, because of more successful indigenous resistance), what are standardly classified as the other white settler states—for example, Canada, Australia, New Zealand, Rhodesia, and South Africa—were all founded on similar policies: the extermination, displacement, and/or herding onto reservations of the aboriginal population. Pierre van den Berghe has coined the illuminating phrase "*Herrenvolk* democracies" to describe these polities, which captures perfectly the dichotomization of the Racial Contract. Their subsequent evolution has been somewhat different, but defenders of South Africa's system of apartheid often argued that U.S. criticism was hypocritical in light of its own history of jim crow, especially since de facto segregation remains sufficiently entrenched that even today, forty years after *Brown v. Board of Education*, two American sociologists can title their study *American Apartheid*. The racist record of preliberation Rhodesia (now Zimbabwe) and South Africa is well known; not so familiar may be the fact that the United States, Canada, and Australia all maintained "white" immigration policies until a few decades ago, and native peoples in all three countries suffer high poverty, infant mortality, and suicide rates.

Elsewhere, in Latin America, Asia, and Africa, large parts of the world were colonized, that is, formally brought under the rule of one or another of the European powers (or, later, the United States): the early Spanish and Portuguese empires in the Americas, the Philippines, and south Asia; the jealous competition from Britain, France, and Holland; the British conquest of India; the French expansion into Algeria and Indochina; the Dutch advance into Indonesia; the Opium Wars against China; the late nineteenth-century "scramble for Africa"; the U.S. war against Spain, seizure of Cuba, Puerto Rico, and the Philippines, and annexation of Hawaii. The pace of change [in] this century has been so dramatic that it is easy to forget that less than a hundred years ago, in 1914,

---

*Article 1, Section 2, Clause 3 of the U.S. Constitution establishes that each slave should be counted as three-fifths (60 percent) of a person for purposes of representation and taxation. This "60 percent solution" was the result of a compromise between southerners and northerners regarding the framing of the Constitution. There was debate over representation in the House of Representatives, with southerners wanting slaves to be counted fully as persons in order to increase the number of possible southern representatives in the House, and northerners wanting slaves not to be counted as persons at all in order to decrease the possible number of southern representatives in the House. —Ed.

"Europe held a grand total of roughly 85 percent of the earth as colonies, protectorates, dependencies, dominions, and commonwealths. No other associated set of colonies in history was as large, none so totally dominated, none so unequal in power to the Western metropolis." One could say that the Racial Contract creates a transnational white polity, a virtual community of people linked by their citizenship in Europe at home and abroad (Europe proper, the colonial greater Europe, and the "fragments" of Euro–America, Euro–Australia, etc.), and constituted in opposition to their indigenous subjects. In most of Africa and Asia, where colonial rule ended only after World War II, rigid "color bars" maintained the separation between Europeans and indigenes. As European, as white, one knew oneself to be a member of the superior race, one's skin being one's passport: "Whatever a white man did must in some grotesque fashion be 'civilized.'" So though there were local variations in the Racial Contract, depending on circumstances and the particular mode of exploitation—for example, a bipolar racial system in the (Anglo) United States, as against a subtler color hierarchy in (Iberian) Latin America—it remains the case that the white tribe, as the global representative of civilization and modernity, is generally on top of the social pyramid.

We live, then, in a world built on the Racial Contract. That we do is simultaneously quite obvious if you think about it (the dates and details of colonial conquest, the constitutions of these states and their exclusionary juridical mechanisms, the histories of official racist ideologies, the battles against slavery and colonialism, the formal and informal structures of discrimination, are all within recent historical memory and, of course, massively documented in other disciplines) and nonobvious, since most whites *don't* think about it or don't think about it as the outcome of a history of political oppression but rather as just "the way things are." ("You say we're all over the world because we *conquered* the world? Why would you put it that way?") In the Treaty of Tordesillas (1494) which divided the world between Spain and Portugal, the Valladolid (Spain) Conference (1550–1551) to decide whether Native Americans were really human, the later debates over African slavery and abolitionism, the Berlin Conference (1884–1885) to partition Africa, the various inter-European pacts, treaties, and informal arrangements on policing their colonies, the post–World War I discussions in Versailles after a war to make the world safe for democracy—we see (or should see) with complete clarity a world being governed by white people. So though there is also internal conflict—disagreements, battles, even world wars—the dominant movers and shapers will be Europeans at home and abroad, with non-Europeans lining up to fight under their respective banners, and the system of white domination itself rarely being challenged. (The exception, of course, is Japan; which escaped colonization, and so for most of the twentieth century has had a shifting and ambivalent relationship with the global white polity.) The legacy of this world is, of course, still with us today, in the economic, political, and cultural domination of the planet by Europeans and their descendants. The fact that this racial structure, clearly political in character, and the struggle against it, equally so, have *not* for the most part been deemed appropriate subject matter for mainstream Anglo-American political philosophy and the fact that the very concepts hegemonic in the discipline are refractory to an understanding of these realities, reveal at best, a disturbing provincialism and an ahistoricity profoundly at odds with the radically foundational questioning on which philosophy prides itself and, at worst, a complicity with the terms of the Racial Contract itself.

DISCUSSION QUESTIONS

1. Discuss the similarities and differences between the social contract and the racial contract.

2. Discuss Mills' argument that the racial contract is an actual historical reality. Does his argument and evidence persuade you? Why or why not?

3. Mills argues that the racial contract is an epistemology of ignorance or "inverted epistemology." What does he mean? Is the racial contract an "inverted epistemology"? Defend your position and compare it to that of Mills.

4. Mills argues that it is wrong for philosophers to work on hypothetical contracts. Rather, he thinks that they should be working to articulate real or actual contracts such as the racial contract. Do you agree with him? How might Hobbes or Rawls respond to Mills' charge?

5. What are "white mythologies"? Can you identify any specific ones presented in either Hollywood movies or popular or highbrow fiction?

6. Mills argues that the racial contract is global. What is his argument? Is he right? Why or why not?

7. Discuss Mills' claim that "European humanism usually meant that only Europeans were human." Who specifically are these "European humanists"? Is this claim a sufficient ground for the rejection of European humanism in its entirety? Why or why not?

Malcolm X
[USA 1992] 3 hours, 21 minutes
Directed by Spike Lee

Malcolm Little (Denzel Washington) is born the son of a preacher in Omaha, Nebraska, in 1925. His childhood is marred by racism, particularly the hateful actions of the Ku Klux Klan and the Black Legion, an offshoot of the Klan. The Black Legion burns down his parents' home and murders his father. Malcolm is separated from his mother and siblings and sent to a foster home by the state. He is the only black child in the foster home and at his school, and is told by his teacher that, despite having the best grades in his class, a career as a lawyer is not open to him; he should consider becoming a carpenter, like Jesus.

As a young man, Malcolm gets involved in a life of crime and soon has to flee from a gang in Harlem. Along with his friend Shorty (Spike Lee) and their white girlfriends, Malcolm starts to rob homes. He is caught and sentenced to prison for a minimum of ten years for fourteen counts of burglary. Malcolm comments that the sentencing was exceedingly harsh because of the "real crimes" he and Shorty committed: maintaining relationships with white women.

In prison, Malcolm is transformed from a thief, drug dealer, and pimp into a respectable, pious, and well-educated Black Muslim through the assistance of Brother Baines (Albert Hall) and the Honorable Elijah Muhammad (Al Freeman, Jr.). Upon his release from prison, Malcolm joins Elijah Muhammad to spread the word of Allah for the Nation of Islam and to preach the separation of black people from white people. Malcolm Little becomes "Malcolm X," the "X" standing for the lost last name of his slave ancestors.

Soon Malcolm becomes an even more powerful spiritual and political leader than Elijah Muhammad and a central force in the black liberation movement. After a fallout with the Nation of Islam, Malcolm founds his own mosque called Muslim Mosque, Inc. He states that his economic and social philosophy will be black nationalism and that his mosque will be open to ideas and financial aide from all quarters. However, forces begin to conspire to eliminate him. His phones are tapped by the government, and his home is burned down. He alleges that the source of burning is the Nation of Islam but later recognizes that other forces must be involved as well. Finally, on February 21, 1965, he is assassinated at the Audubon Ballroom in New York City, in a conspiracy that we are led to believe was supported by the Nation of Islam.

The screenplay for Spike Lee's film was cowritten by Arnold Perl and Spike Lee. James Baldwin contributed to early versions of the screenplay, which is based on *The Autobiography of Malcolm X* as told to Alex Haley.

DISCUSSION QUESTIONS

1. According to Mills, the racial contact grants whites natural freedom and equality, and nonwhites "are designated as born *unfree* and *unequal*." The general purpose of the racial contract is "the differential privileging of the whites as a group with respect to the nonwhites as a group, the exploitation of their bodies, land, and resources, and the denial of equal socioeconomic opportunities to them." Discuss the ways in which the film *Malcolm X* supports Mills' notion of the racial contract.

2. In the film, the Black Legion burns down young Malcolm's house. As the members of the Black Legion watch it burning, their leader says to Earl Little (Tommy Hollis), Malcolm's father, "Boy, good thing we're good Christians. Nigger, it's time for you to leave this town." Earl responds, "This here is 'pose to be a free country." What role, if any, does the American religious community play in the racial contract? Do you find it hard to believe that members of a hate group would claim to be "good Christians"? Discuss.

3. Consider the following dialogue concerning the sentencing of Malcolm and his friends for burglary:

   VOICE OF MALCOLM X "The average first offender gets two years for burglary. We were all first offenders. That's what Sophia and Peg drew. . . ."

   JUDGE "Two years in the Women's Reformatory at Framingham."

   VOICE OF MALCOLM X "But our crime wasn't burglary. It was balling white girls. They gave us the book."

   JUDGE "Burglary, count one—8 to 10 years; count two, 8 to 10 years; count three, 8 to 10 years . . . count fourteen, 8 to 10 years."

   VOICE OF MALCOLM X "Fourteen counts of 8 to 10 years."

   While all four participated in the crimes, the white women received two years in prison, whereas the men received at least ten years. Is this disproportionate sentencing? Is this sentencing evidence of the racial contract? Was their real crime their interracial relationships? Discuss.

4. Malcom says to Baines, "Everybody knows God is White." Baines responds, "But everything the white man taught you, you learned. He told you you were a black heathen and you believed him. He told you how he took you out of darkness and brought you to the light. And you believed him. He taught you to worship a blond, blue-eyed God with white skin—and you believed him. He told you black was a curse, you believed him. Did you ever look up the word black in the dictionary?" Do you agree with Baines' comments? Do you think the racial contract is a part of organized religion? Why or why not?

5. Consider the following statement by Malcolm X in the film: "What kind of black people does the Honorable Elijah Muhammad speak for? Black people who are jobless . . . the black masses who are poor, hungry, and angry, the black masses who are dissatisfied with the slums and ghettos in which we have been forced to live . . . the black masses who are tired of listening to the promises of white politicians to correct the miserable living conditions that exist in our community . . . the black masses that are sick of the inhuman acts of bestial brutality practiced by these semi-savage white

policemen that patrol our community, like the occupation forces of a conquering enemy army . . . the black masses who are fed up with the anemic, Uncle Tom leadership set up by the white man to act as a spokesman for our people and to *keep us satisfied and pacified with nothing*!" How should a just society deal with the kind of dissatisfaction noted by Malcolm X? Does a just society have an obligation to do more than just keep people pacified? Why or why not?

6. Consider the following statement by Malcolm X in the film: "The white people who are guilty of white supremacy try and hide their own guilt by accusing the Honorable Elijah Muhammad of teaching black supremacy when he tries to uplift the mentality, the social and economic conditions of black people in this country. And the Jews, who have been guilty of exploiting the black people economically, civilly, and otherwise, hide their guilt by accusing the Honorable Elijah Muhammad of being anti-Semitic simply because he teaches our people to go into business for ourselves and trying to take over the economic leadership in our own community. The black people in this country have been the victims of violence at the hands of the white man for 400 years, and following the ignorant Negro preachers, we have thought that it was Godlike to turn the other cheek to the brute that was brutalizing us. One hundred years ago they use to put on a white sheet and use a blood-hound against Negroes. Today they've taken off sheets and put on police uniforms, they've traded in the bloodhounds for police dogs. [And just as Uncle Tom back during slavery used to keep the Negroes from resisting the bloodhounds or resisting the Ku Klux Klan by telling them to love their enemy or pray for those who use them as spitefully today. The Honorable Elijah Muhammad is showing black people that just as the white man and every other person on this earth has God-given rights, natural rights, civil rights, and any other kind of rights that you can think of when it comes to defending himself.] Discuss each of the groups that are challenging the actions of the Honorable Elijah Muhammad. Is Malcolm justified in his criticism of them? Why or why not?

7. In the film, the Nation of Islam is presented as separating itself from all other groups, even other civil rights groups. Malcolm X eventually rejects this strategy. Why?

8. Consider the following statement by Malcolm X in the film: "If the so-called Negro were American citizens we wouldn't have a race problem. If the Emancipation Proclamation was authentic, you wouldn't have a race problem. If the 13th, 14th, and 15th Amendments to the Constitution was authentic, you wouldn't have a race problem. If the Supreme Court desegregation decision was authentic, you wouldn't have a race problem. All of this is hypocrisy. These Negro leaders have been telling the white man everything is all right, everything is under control. And they've been telling the white man that Mr. Muhammad is wrong, don't listen to him. But everything Mr. Muhammad has been saying is going to come to pass is now coming to pass and now the Negro leaders are standing up saying that we are about to have a racial explosion. We're going to have a racial explosion and that's more dangerous than an atomic explosion." What does Malcolm mean by "authentic"? Is it possible for a society to have just laws but still be unjust? Why or why not? Is this what Malcolm X is saying here? Discuss.

9. Nelson Mandela attributes to Malcolm X the following quote in the film: "We declare our right on this earth to be a man, to be a human being, to be respected as a human being, in this society, on this earth, in this day, which we intend to bring into existence by any means necessary." Do people have a right to be respected as a human being? Does a just society protect this right? If it does not protect it, are people justified in bringing this right into existence "by any means necessary"? Why or why not?

10. If you were going to set the life of Malcolm X to film, would you do it in the same way as Lee? Why or why not?

WILLIAM CARLOS WILLIAMS
THE USE OF FORCE

Williuam Carlos Williams's short story asks whether a society is justified in forcing people to do what they do not want to do. Olson is a doctor who calls on the home of a young girl who has had a fever for three days. The child's parents, suspecting that their daughter may have diphtheria, allow Olson to attempt to take a throat culture from the girl against her will. The increasing degree of force expended in attempts to complete the examination leads the doctor to try to justify rationally his actions. "The damned little brat must be protected against her own idiocy," says the doctor to himself. "Others must be protected against her," he continues. "It is a social necessity." In the end, though the examination is achieved, it is only through what the doctor describes as an "unreasoned assault."

William Carlos Williams (1883–1963), American poet, playwright, novelist, essayist, and short-story writer, was born in Rutherford, New Jersey. Trained as a pediatrician, Williams wrote and practiced medicine in his New Jersey hometown. His writing is notable for its ability to make the ordinary seem extraordinary. In 1963, he was posthumously awarded the Pulitzer Prize in poetry for *Pictures from Brueghel* (1962). His books include *Spring and All* (poetry, 1923), *In the American Grain* (prose, 1925), *White Mule* (novel, 1937), *The Doctor Stories* (1938), *In the Money* (novel, 1940), *Paterson* (poetry, 1946–58), *A Dream of Love* (play, 1948), *Autobiography* (1951), and *The Build-Up* (novel, 1952). The following is from *The Doctor Stories*.

They were new patients to me, all I had was the name, Olson. Please come down as soon as you can, my daughter is very sick. When I arrived I was met by the mother, a big startled looking woman, very clean and apologetic who merely said, Is this the doctor? and let me in. In the back, she added. You must excuse us, doctor, we have her in the kitchen where it is warm. It is very damp here sometimes.

The child was fully dressed and sitting on her father's lap near the kitchen table. He tried to get up, but I motioned for him not to bother, took off my overcoat and started to look things over. I could see that they were all very nervous, eyeing me up and down distrustfully. As often, in such cases, they weren't telling me more than they had to, it was up to me to tell them; that's why they were spending three dollars on me.

The child was fairly eating me up with her cold, steady eyes, and no expression to her face whatever. She did not move and seemed, inwardly, quiet; an unusually attractive little thing, and as strong as a heifer in appearance. But her face was flushed, she was breathing rapidly, and I realized that she had a high fever. She had magnificent blonde hair, in profusion. One of those picture children often reproduced in advertising leaflets and the photogravure sections of the Sunday papers.

She's had a fever for three days, began the father and we don't know what it comes from. My wife has given her things, you know, like people do, but it don't do no good. And there's been a lot of sickness around. So we tho't you'd better look her over and tell us what is the matter.

As doctors often do I took a trial shot at it as a point of departure. Has she had a sore throat?

Both parents answered me together. No . . . No, she says her throat don't hurt her.

Does your throat hurt you? added the mother to the child. But the little girl's expression didn't change nor did she move her eyes from my face.

Have you looked?

I tried to, said the mother, but I couldn't see.

As it happens we had been having a number of cases of diphtheria in the school to which this child went during that month and we were all, quite apparently, thinking of that, though no one had as yet spoken of the thing.

Well, I said, suppose we take a look at the throat first. I smiled in my best professional manner and asking for the child's first name I said, come on, Mathilda, open your mouth and let's take a look at your throat.

Nothing doing.

Aw, come on, I coaxed, just open your mouth wide and let me take a look. Look, I said opening both hands wide, I haven't anything in my hands. Just open up and let me see.

Such a nice man, put in the mother. Look how kind he is to you. Come on, do what he tells you to. He won't hurt you.

At that I ground my teeth in disgust. If only they wouldn't use the word "hurt" I might be able to get somewhere. But I did not allow myself to be hurried or disturbed but speaking quietly and slowly I approached the child again.

As I moved my chair a little nearer suddenly with one catlike movement both her hands clawed instinctively for my eyes and she almost reached them too. In fact she knocked my glasses flying and they fell, though unbroken, several feet away from me on the kitchen floor.

Both the mother and father almost turned themselves inside out in embarrassment and apology. You bad girl, said the mother, taking her and shaking her by one arm. Look what you've done. The nice man . . .

For heaven's sake, I broke in. Don't call me a nice man to her. I'm here to look at her throat on the chance that she might have diphtheria and possibly die of it. But that's nothing to her. Look here, I said to the child, we're going to look at your throat. You're old enough to understand what I'm saying. Will you open it now by yourself or shall we have to open it for you?

Not a move. Even her expression hadn't changed. Her breaths however were coming faster and faster. Then the battle began. I had to do it. I had to have a throat culture for her own protection. But first I told the parents that it was entirely up to them. I explained the danger but said that I would not insist on a throat

examination so long as they would take the responsibility.

If you don't do what the doctor says you'll have to go to the hospital, the mother admonished her severely.

Oh yeah? I had to smile to myself. After all, I had already fallen in love with the savage brat, the parents were contemptible to me. In the ensuing struggle they grew more and more abject, crushed, exhausted while she surely rose to magnificent heights of insane fury of effort bred of her terror of me.

The father tried his best, and he was a big man but the fact that she was his daughter, his shame at her behavior and his dread of hurting her made him release her just at the critical times when I had almost achieved success, till I wanted to kill him. But his dread also that she might have diphtheria made him tell me to go on, go on though he himself was almost fainting, while the mother moved back and forth behind us raising and lowering her hands in an agony of apprehension.

Put her in front of you on your lap, I ordered, and hold both her wrists.

But as soon as he did the child let out a scream. Don't, you're hurting me. Let go of my hands. Let them go I tell you. Then she shrieked terrifyingly, hysterically. Stop it! Stop it! You're killing me!

Do you think she can stand it, doctor! said the mother.

You get out, said the husband to his wife. Do you want her to die of diphtheria?

Come on now, hold her, I said.

Then I grasped the child's head with my left hand and tried to get the wooden tongue depressor between her teeth. She fought, with clenched teeth, desperately! But now I also had grown furious—at a child. I tried to hold myself down but I couldn't. I know how to expose a throat for inspection. And I did my best. When finally I got the wooden spatula behind the last teeth and just the point of it into the mouth cavity, she opened up for an instant but before I could see anything she came down again and gripped the wooden blade between her molars she reduced it to splinters before I could get it out again.

Aren't you ashamed, the mother yelled at her. Aren't you ashamed to act like that in front of the doctor?

Get me a smooth-handled spoon of some sort, I told the mother. We're going through with this. The child's mouth was already bleeding. Her tongue was cut and she was screaming in wild hysterical shrieks. Perhaps I should have desisted and come back in an hour or more. No doubt it would have been better. But I have seen at least two children lying dead in bed of neglect in such cases, and feeling that I must get a diagnosis now or never I went at it again. But the worst of it was that I too had got beyond reason. I could have torn the child apart in my own fury and enjoyed it. It was a pleasure to attack her. My face was burning with it.

The damned little brat must be protected against her own idiocy, one says to one's self at such times. Others must be protected against her. It is a social necessity. And all these things are true. But a blind fury, a feeling of adult shame, bred of a longing for muscular release are the operatives. One goes on to the end.

In the final unreasoning assault I overpowered the child's neck and jaws. I forced the heavy silver spoon back of her teeth and down her throat till she gagged. And there it was—both tonsils covered with membrane. She had fought valiantly to keep me from knowing her secret. She had been hiding that sore throat for three days at least and lying to her parents in order to escape just such an outcome as this.

Now truly she was furious. She had been on the defensive before but now she attacked. Tried to get off her father's lap and fly at me while tears of defeat blinded her eyes.

DISCUSSION QUESTIONS

1. Does a just society ever force people to do something that they do not want to do? Why or why not?

2. Does the little girl have to open her mouth even if she does not want to? Defend your response.

3. Should the doctor have stopped his examination? Did he act unjustly by forcing the spoon down the girl's throat?

4. How would a libertarian respond to the doctor's claim that "the damned little brat must be protected against her own idiocy"? Does the just society protect people against their own idiocy? Why or why not?

5. How would a utilitarian respond to the doctor's claim that "others must be protected against her [the little girl]"? More generally, does the just society protect people against others? Why or why not?

6. Was forcing the spoon down the girl's throat until she gagged a "social necessity"? Why or why not?

7. Why do you think the doctor calls his behavior toward the girl an "unreasoned assault"? Do you agree with his assessment of the situation?

5.3   ARE MEN AND WOMEN EQUAL?

PLATO

ON THE EQUALITY OF WOMEN

This reading is from the fifth book of Plato's *Republic*. In it, Socrates argues for the equality of the sexes. In the first four books, Socrates discusses the definition of justice through, in part, the construction of an ideal city. If the city is to be just, it must be protected from unrest both within and without. The job of protecting the city falls upon a class of citizens called "guardians." According to Plato, these guardians must be trained carefully in order to ensure that they do their job loyally and reliably. Good guardians must be obedient and courageous.

In earlier books, Socrates states that both men and women can be guardians as long as they have a loyal, courageous character. He also says that private marriages among the guardians will destroy the camaraderie and trust of the guardians, and suggests that wives be shared in common. In this, the fifth book of the *Republic*, Socrates' interlocutors, Polemarchus and Adeimantus, encourage him to go back and discuss in more detail the role of women in the just city.

Socrates argues that this ideal city will have arranged marriages and will educate men and women identically. He also suggests that modesty about our bodies is immature and keeps the city from functioning justly. Therefore, men and women, young and old, should exercise together naked. For Plato, the physical similarities and differences between men and women are not important. The virtuous life is achieved through the state of one's character, not one's physical characteristics. For example, in the passage about "bald men," Socrates argues that in most cases only one's character is relevant to one's job. Says Socrates, "We never meant when we constructed the state, that the opposition of natures should extend to every difference, but only to those differences which affected the pursuit in which the individual is engaged." Therefore, men and women of similar character should do similar jobs. Even though some physical qualities may be necessary for some jobs, for Socrates this is only rarely the case.

The implications of Socrates' reflections on the equality of women in the city are that sexism is not in the best interests of the state. Socrates states that "all the pursuits of men are the pursuits of women also" but adds, "in all of them a woman is inferior to a man." A biographical sketch of Plato appears in chapter 2.

Well, I replied, I suppose that I must retrace my steps and say what I perhaps ought to have said before in the proper place. The part of the men has been played out, and now properly enough comes the turn of the women. Of them I will proceed to speak, and the more readily since I am invited by you.

For men born and educated like our citizens, the only way, in my opinion, of arriving at a right conclusion about the possession and use of women and children is to follow the path on which we originally started, when we said that the men were to be the guardians and watchdogs of the herd.

True.

Let us further suppose the birth and education of our women to be subject to similar or nearly similar regulations; then we shall see whether the result accords with our design.

What do you mean?

What I mean may be put into the form of a question. I said: Are dogs divided into hes and shes, or do they both share equally in hunting and in keeping watch and in the other duties of dogs? or do we entrust to the males the entire and exclusive care of the flocks, while we leave the females at home, under the idea that the bearing and suckling their puppies is labour enough for them?

No, he said, they share alike; the only difference between them is that the males are stronger and the females weaker.

But can you use different animals for the same purpose, unless they are bred and fed in the same way?

You cannot.

Then, if women are to have the same duties as men, they must have the same nurture and education?

Yes.

The education which was assigned to the men was music and gymnastic.

Yes.

Then women must be taught music and gymnastic and also the art of war, which they must practice like the men?

That is the inference, I suppose.

I should rather expect, I said, that several of our proposals, if they are carried out, being unusual, may appear ridiculous.

No doubt of it.

Yes, and the most ridiculous thing of all will be the sight of women naked in the palaestra, exercising with the men, especially when they are no longer young; they certainly will not be a vision of beauty, any more than the enthusiastic old men who in spite of wrinkles and ugliness continue to frequent the gymnasia.

Yes, indeed, he said: according to present notions the proposal would be thought ridiculous.

But then, I said, as we have determined to speak our minds, we must not fear the jests of the wits which will be directed against this sort of innovation; how they will talk of women's attainments both in music and gymnastic, and above all about their wearing armour and riding upon horseback!

Very true, he replied.

Yet having begun we must go forward to the rough places of the law; at the same time begging of these gentlemen for once in their life to be serious. Not long ago, as we shall remind them, the Hellenes were of the opinion, which is still generally received among the barbarians, that the sight of a naked man was ridiculous and improper; and when first the Cretans and then the Lacedaemonians introduced the custom, the wits of that day might equally have ridiculed the innovation.

No doubt.

But when experience showed that to let all things be uncovered was far better than to cover them up, and the ludicrous effect to the outward eye vanished before the better principle which reason asserted, then the man was perceived to be a fool who directs the shafts of his ridicule at any other sight but that of folly and vice, or seriously inclines to weigh the beautiful by any other standard but that of the good.

Very true, he replied.

First, then, whether the question is to be put in jest or in earnest, let us come to an understanding about the nature of woman: Is she capable of sharing either wholly or partially in the actions of men, or not at all? And is the art of war one of those arts in which she can or cannot share? That will be the best way of commencing the enquiry, and will probably lead to the fairest conclusion.

That will be much the best way.

Shall we take the other side first and begin by arguing against ourselves; in this manner the adversary's position will not be undefended.

Why not? he said.

Then let us put a speech into the mouths of our opponents. They will say: "Socrates and Glaucon, no adversary need convict you, for you yourselves, at the first foundation of the State, admitted the principle that everybody was to do the one work suited to his own nature." And certainly, if I am not mistaken, such an admission was made by us. "And do not the natures of men and women differ very much indeed?" And we shall reply: Of course they do. Then we shall be asked, "Whether the tasks assigned to men and to women should not be different, and such as are agreeable to their different natures?" Certainly they should. "But if so, have you not fallen into a serious inconsistency in saying that men and women, whose natures are so entirely different, ought to perform the same actions?"— What defense will you make for us, my good Sir, against any one who offers these objections?

That is not an easy question to answer when asked suddenly; and I shall and I do beg of you to draw out the case on our side.

These are the objections, Glaucon, and there are many others of a like kind, which I foresaw long ago; they made me afraid and reluctant to take in hand any law about the possession and nurture of women and children.

By Zeus, he said, the problem to be solved is anything but easy.

Why yes, I said, but the fact is that when a man is out of his depth, whether he has fallen into a little swimming bath or into mid ocean, he has to swim all the same.

Very true.

And must not we swim and try to reach the shore: we will hope that Arion's dolphin or some other miraculous help may save us?

I suppose so, he said.

Well then, let us see if any way of escape can be found. We acknowledged—did we not? that different natures ought to have different pursuits, and that men's and women's natures are different. And now what are we saying?—that different natures ought to have the same pursuits,—this is the inconsistency which is charged upon us.

Precisely.

Verily, Glaucon, I said, glorious is the power of the art of contradiction!

Why do you say so?

Because I think that many a man falls into the practice against his will. When he thinks that he is reasoning he is really disputing, just because he cannot define and divide, and so know that of which he is speaking; and he will pursue a merely verbal opposition in the spirit of contention and not of fair discussion.

Yes, he replied, such is very often the case; but what has that to do with us and our argument?

A great deal; for there is certainly a danger of our getting unintentionally into a verbal opposition.

In what way?

Why we valiantly and pugnaciously insist upon the verbal truth, that different natures ought to have different pursuits, but we never considered at all what was the meaning of sameness or difference of nature, or why we distinguished them when we assigned different pursuits to different natures and the same to the same natures.

Why, no, he said, that was never considered by us.

I said: Suppose that by way of illustration we were to ask the question whether there is not an opposition in nature between bald men and hairy men; and if this is admitted by us, then, if bald men are cobblers, we should forbid the hairy men to be cobblers, and conversely?

That would be a jest, he said.

Yes, I said, a jest; and why? because we never meant when we constructed the State, that the opposition of natures should extend to every difference, but only to those differences which affected the pursuit in which the individual is engaged; we should have argued, for example, that a physician and one who is in mind a physician may be said to have the same nature.

True.

Whereas the physician and the carpenter have different natures?

Certainly.

And if, I said, the male and female sex appear to differ in their fitness for any art or pursuit, we should say that such pursuit or art ought to be assigned to one or the other of them; but if the difference consists only in women bearing and men begetting children, this does not amount to a proof that a woman differs from a man in respect of the sort of education she should receive; and we shall therefore continue to maintain that our guardians and their wives ought to have the same pursuits.

Very true, he said.

Next, we shall ask our opponent how, in reference to any of the pursuits or arts of civic life, the nature of a woman differs from that of a man?

That will be quite fair.

And perhaps he, like yourself, will reply that to give a sufficient answer on the instant is not easy; but after a little reflection there is no difficulty.

Yes, perhaps.

Suppose then that we invite him to accompany us in the argument, and then we may hope to show him that there is nothing peculiar in the constitution of women which would affect them in the administration of the State.

By all means.

Let us say to him: Come now, and we will ask you a question:—when you spoke of a nature gifted or not gifted in any respect, did you mean to say that one man will acquire a thing easily, another with difficulty; a little learning will lead the one to discover a great deal; whereas the other, after much study and application, no sooner learns than he forgets; or again, did you mean, that the one has a body which is a good servant to his mind, while the body of the other is a hindrance to him?—would not these be the sort of differences which distinguish the man gifted by nature from the one who is ungifted?

No one will deny that.

And can you mention any pursuit of mankind in which the male sex has not all these gifts and qualities in a higher degree than the female? Need I waste time in speaking of the art of weaving, and the management of pancakes and preserves, in which womankind does really appear to be great, and in which for her to be beaten by a man is of all things the most absurd?

You are quite right, he replied, in maintaining the general inferiority of the female sex: although many women are in many things superior to many men, yet on the whole what you is true.

And if so, my friend, I said, there is no special faculty of administration in a State which a woman has because she is a woman, or which a man has by virtue of his sex, but the gifts of nature are alike diffused in both; all the pursuits of men are the pursuits of women also, but in all of them a woman is inferior to a man.

Very true.

Then are we to impose all our enactments on men and none of them on women?

That will never do.

One woman has a gift of healing, another not; one is a musician, and another has no music in her nature?

Very true.

And one woman has a turn for gymnastic and military exercises, and another is unwarlike and hates gymnastics?

Certainly.

And one woman is a philosopher, and another is an enemy of philosophy; one has spirit, and another is without spirit?

That is also true.

Then one woman will have the temper of a guardian, and another not. Was not the selection of the male guardians determined by differences of this sort?

Yes.

Men and women alike possess the qualities which make a guardian; they differ only in their comparative strength or weakness.

Obviously.

And those women who have such qualities are to be selected as the companions and colleagues of men who have similar qualities and whom they resemble in capacity and in character?

Very true.

And ought not the same natures to have the same pursuits?

They ought.

Then, as we were saying before, there is nothing unnatural in assigning music and gymnastic to the wives of the guardians—to that point we come round again.

Certainly not.

The law which we then enacted was agreeable to nature, and therefore not an impossibility or mere aspiration; and the contrary practice, which prevails at present, is in reality a violation of nature.

That appears to be true.

We had to consider, first, whether our proposals were possible, and secondly whether they were the most beneficial?

Yes.

And the possibility has been acknowledged?

Yes.

The very great benefit has next to be established?

Quite so.

You will admit that the same education which makes a man a good guardian will make a woman a good guardian; for their original nature is the same?

Yes.

I should like to ask you a question.

What is it?

Would you say that all men are equal in excellence, or is one man better than another?

The latter.

And in the commonwealth which we were founding do you conceive the guardians who have been brought up on our model system to be more perfect men, or the cobblers whose education has been cobbling?

What a ridiculous question!

You have answered me, I replied: Well, and may we not further say that our guardians are the best of our citizens?

By far the best.

And will not their wives be the best women?

Yes, by far the best.

And can there be anything better for the interests of the State than that the men and women of a State should be as good as possible?

There can be nothing better.

And this is what the arts of music and gymnastic, when present in such manner as we have described, will accomplish?

Certainly.

Then we have made an enactment not only possible but in the highest degree beneficial to the State?

True.

Then let the wives of our guardians strip, for their virtue will be their robe, and let them share in the toils of war and the defence of their country; only in the distribution of labours the lighter are to be assigned to the women, who are the weaker natures, but in other respects their duties are to be the same. And as for the man who laughs at naked women exercising their bodies from the best of motives, in his laughter he is plucking

A fruit of unripe wisdom,

and he himself is ignorant of what he is laughing at, or what he is about;—for that is, and ever will be, the best of sayings, *That the useful is the noble and the hurtful is the base.*

Very true.

DISCUSSION QUESTIONS

1. What is Socrates' position on sexism? What is his position on gender roles? What are the major strengths and weaknesses of his positions?

2. What does Socrates mean when he says that "all the pursuits of men are the pursuits of women also, but in all of them a woman is inferior to a man"? Do you agree with him? Why or why not?

3. Socrates believes that both men and women should be entrusted with protecting the state. What is his argument?

4. Socrates says, "We never meant when we constructed the State, that the opposition of natures should extend to every difference, but only to those differences which affected the pursuit in which the individual is engaged." What does he mean by this?

5. Plato argues that men and women should exercise together naked, one consequence of which would be a greater maturity regarding our bodies. Is Plato right? Would this bring about greater or less equality among the sexes?

6. Do you think that Socrates' observations on men and women are valid in contemporary American society? Or are they products of a different era, incompatible with today's society? Defend your view.

G. I. Jane
[USA 1997] 2 hours, 5 minutes
Directed by Ridley Scott

When Senator Lillian DeHaven (Anne Bancroft) pressures the U.S. navy secretary to begin full gender integration, he counters with an offer for a test case: a female may participate in the SEAL/CRT (Combined Reconnaissance Team) selection program, and if she makes it through, gender integration will be considered.

Senator DeHaven selects Lieutenant Jordan O'Neil (Demi Moore) for the assignment, and initially, no one expects O'Neil to survive the rigorous training. However, O'Neil is pushed by events from the past: she was denied the opportunity for operational experience during the Gulf War because of her sex and has decided that failure at SEALS training is not an option. O'Neil refuses the preferential treatment that C.O. Salem (Scott Wilson) seeks to give her, even to the extent of shaving her head and bunking with the male trainees.

As training progresses, O'Neil's fellow SEALS gain respect for her, but Master Chief Urgayle (Viggo Mortensen) seeks to convince them and O'Neil that she does not belong in combat. At SERE (Survival, Evasion, Resistance, and Escape) training, Urgayle uses O'Neil's sex against her, but she adamantly refuses to give up, even when she is beaten and humiliated in front of her peers. O'Neil defies the odds and makes it through SEAL training, only to encounter difficulties of a much different nature. Someone has taken photos of her socializing with some lesbian friends, and O'Neil is now accused of being a homosexual. O'Neil is determined to prove that the charge is untrue, and with the help of her male companion Royce (Jason Beghe), she uncovers who actually sought to tarnish her good name: Senator DeHaven—the very same person who recruited her for SEAL training.

After O'Neil forces DeHaven to clear her name, she joins her fellow SEALS on a mission that takes them from the waters of the Mediterranean into Libya. During the mission, Master Chief Urgayle is wounded, and O'Neil drags him to safety. Later, Urgayle gives his Navy Cross to O'Neil as a sign of his respect for her and gratitude for saving his life.

DISCUSSION QUESTIONS

1. Socrates argues that men and women should be entrusted with protecting the state. Do you think that the case of Lieutenant Jordan O'Neil lends support to his argument? Why or why not?

2. Senator DeHaven tells Lieutenant O'Neil that her case is "just a test case . . . but if things work out, if you can go the distance, it could well change the military's official policy on women in combat, or actually, its official nonpolicy." Do you think men and women should be given equal opportunity to serve in both combat and noncombat positions in all branches of the military? Why or why not? Compare your response to Plato's.

3. Senator DeHaven says to Lieutenant O'Neil, "I . . . understand that you applied for active duty during the Gulf War and got turned down." O'Neil replies, "Yes, ma'am. There was an intel slot available aboard the USS Polk, but they told me that submarines had no bathroom facilities for women." Discuss this reason for denying O'Neil's request for active duty during the Gulf War. Are separate bathroom facilities necessary, or do they just reinforce sexism and irrelevant physical differences between men and women?

4. Consider the following discussion between O'Neil and Royce:

    O'NEIL   "The only thing that scares me are the sexual politics. I'm just not interested in being some poster girl for women's rights . . ."

    O'NEIL   "You don't have anything to say about this?"

    ROYCE   "I guess I don't."

    O'NEIL   "Honey, this is just a career opportunity. You don't want me sleeping my way to the top, do you?"

    ROYCE   "The SEALS, babe. These guys are world-class warriors; they see you coming, they may . . ."

    O'NEIL   "I'm aware they may not want me there."

    ROYCE   "May not! They will eat cornflakes out of your skull, OK? To tell you the truth, I don't get it. You're doing shit hot at intel, what do you want with SEALS training?"

    O'NEIL   "Royce, we're the same age. We entered the Navy the same month, and which one of us is wearing more ribbons?"

    ROYCE   "Oh, come on. That's just cause I got lucky during the Gulf War."

    O'NEIL   "Yes, thank you. Operational experience is the key to advancement, yet anyone with tits can't be on a sub, can't be a SEAL, and don't even think about . . ."

    ROYCE   "Whoa! If you made up your mind to do it, go. You always do what you wanna do anyway. Don't ask my permission."

    O'Neil cannot advance in the navy without operational experience, but she is denied operational experiences because she is a woman. Does a woman have a right to the operational experience necessary for career advancement in the Navy? Why or why not?

5. Consider the following dialogue between O'Neil and Salem, her commanding officer:

O'NEIL   "I believe you instructed me to come directly to you sir, if I felt I was being mistreated in any way."

SALEM   "Alright, I want names. I want specific grievances."

O'NEIL   "Permission to speak frankly, sir. . . . It's you, sir. It started the moment I came here."

SALEM   "Oh? Really?"

O'NEIL   "It's the double standard. The separate quarters, the deferential treatment. It's the way you practically pulled my chair out for me when we first met."

SALEM   "Because I was civil, now you're complaining?"

O'NEIL   "I can't afford civility, sir. How am I supposed to fit in with these guys when you've got me set up as an outsider? You've given me a different set of rules. The answer is, I can't. I mean really sir, why didn't you just issue me a pink petticoat to wear around the base? . . . Just treat me the same as everyone else, sir. No better, no worse."

SALEM   "Lieutenant, you're gonna get everything you want. I just wonder if you want what you're gonna get."

Discuss Salem's decision to treat O'Neil differently in order to help her to get through the SEAL training program. Did he do the right thing? Were his actions sexist? Why or why not? Discuss.

6. Royce says to O'Neil, "Big symbols make big targets, Jordan. There're a lot of people who don't want to see you finish." What does O'Neil symbolize? Discuss who would not be interested in seeing O'Neil finish the SEAL training. Why would they not be interested? Are their reasons good ones? Why or why not?

7. At first, Master Chief Urgayle is resistant to O'Neil joining the SEALS. He says to the male SEALS, "Guys, I'm saving her life and yours. Her presence makes us all vulnerable. I don't want you learning that inconvenient fact under fire." Later, he changes his mind, stating, "She's not the problem; we are." Presents arguments for both positions taken by Urgayle. Which is the stronger argument, and why?

8. Ridley Scott, the director of *G. I. Jane*, is also the director of *Thelma and Louise* (see chapter 3). Compare and contrast the treatment of gender equality and female identity in these two films. Which approach do you prefer, and why?

ARISTOTLE

ON THE INEQUALITY OF WOMEN

Aristotle disagrees with Socrates regarding the equality of women. Unlike Socrates, Aristotle maintains that men and women have different natural tendencies toward virtue. For example, the courage of a man is not the same as that of a woman—"the courage of a man is shown in commanding, of a woman in obeying." Consequently, women "would seem to be more useful," says Aristotle, "among the farmers rather than among the guardians" (*Politics* Book II, Chapter 4).

Also, for Aristotle, there is no equality between the sexes in marriage. He writes that husbands rule over their wives and that this *constitutional rule* is possible only with the consent of the wife. The constitutional rule of husbands over their wives differs from the *royal rule* that fathers hold over children. Royal rule results from the superior position that fathers enjoy over their children. In order for a household to function smoothly, it is necessary that either the husband or the wife rule consistently. Thus, given that men have a natural tendency toward the virtues necessary for rule, Aristotle argues that men are usually better suited to rule in the marriage relation and in the household than women are. The following is from Book I, Chapters 12 and 13 of Aristotle's *Politics*. A biographical sketch of Aristotle appears in chapter 4.

Of household management we have seen that there are three parts—one is the rule of a master over slaves, . . . another of a father, and the third of a husband. A husband and father . . . rules over wife and children, both free, but the rule differs, the rule over his children being a royal, over his wife a constitutional rule. For although there may be exceptions to the order of nature, the male is by nature fitter for command than the female, just as the elder and full-grown is superior to the younger and more immature. But in most constitutional states the citizens rule and are ruled by turns, for the idea of a constitutional state implies that the natures of the citizens are equal, and do not differ at all. Nevertheless, when one rules and the other is ruled we endeavour to create a difference of outward forms and names and titles of respect, . . . The relation of the male to the female is of this kind, but there the inequality is permanent. A question may indeed be raised, whether there is any excellence at all in a slave beyond and higher than merely instrumental and ministerial qualities—whether he can have the virtues of temperance, courage, justice, and the like; or whether slaves possess only bodily and ministerial qualities. And, whichever way we answer the question, a difficulty arises; for, if they have virtue, in what will they differ from freemen? On the other hand, since they are men and share in rational principle, it seems absurd to say that they have no virtue. A similar question may be raised about women and children, whether they too have virtues: ought a woman to be temperate and brave and just, and is a child to be called temperate, and

intemperate, or not? So in general we may ask about the natural ruler, and the natural subject, whether they have the same or different virtues. For if a noble nature is equally required in both, why should one of them always rule, and the other always be ruled? Nor can we say that this is a question of degree, for the difference between ruler and subject is a difference of kind, which the difference of more and less never is. Yet how strange is the supposition that the one ought, and that the other ought not, to have virtue! For if the ruler is intemperate and unjust, how can he rule well? if the subject, how can he obey well? If he be licentious and cowardly, he will certainly not do his duty. It is evident, therefore, that both of them must have a share of virtue, but varying as natural subjects also vary among themselves. Here the very constitution of the soul has shown us the way; in it one part naturally rules, and the other is subject, and the virtue of the ruler we maintain to be different from that of the subject;—the one being the virtue of the rational, and the other of the irrational part. Now, it is obvious that the same principle applies generally, and therefore almost all things rule and are ruled according to nature. But the kind of rule differs;—the freeman rules over the slave after another manner from that in which the male rules over the female, or the man over the child; although the parts of the soul are present in all of them, they are present in different degrees. For the slave has no deliberative faculty at all; the woman has, but it is without authority, and the child has, but it is immature. So it must necessarily be supposed to be with the moral virtues also; all should partake of them, but only in such manner and degree as is required by each for the fulfilment of his duty. Hence the ruler ought to have moral virtue in perfection, for his function, taken absolutely, demands a master artificer, and rational principle is such an artificer; the subjects, on the other hand, require only that measure of virtue which is proper to each of them. Clearly, then, moral virtue belongs to all of them; but the temperance of a man and of a woman, or the courage and justice of a man and of a woman, are not, as Socrates maintained, the same; the courage of a man is shown in commanding, of a woman in obeying. And this holds of all other virtues, as will be more clearly seen if we look at them in detail. . . . All classes must be deemed to have their special attributes; as the poet says of women,

> Silence is a woman's glory,

but this is not equally the glory of man. The child is imperfect, and therefore obviously his virtue is not relative to himself alone, but to the perfect man and to his teacher, and in like manner the virtue of the slave is relative to it master. Now we determined that a slave is useful for the wants of life, and therefore he will obviously require only so much virtue as will prevent him from failing in his duty through cowardice or lack of self-control . . . the slave shares in his master's life; the artisan is less closely connected with him, and only attains excellence in proportion as he becomes a slave. The meaner sort of mechanic has a special and separate slavery; and whereas the slave exists by nature, not so the shoemaker or other artisan. It is manifest, then, that the master ought to be the source of such excellence in the slave, and not a mere possessor of the art of mastership which trains the slave in his duties. Wherefore they are mistaken who forbid us to converse with slaves and say that we should employ command only, for slaves stand even more in need of admonition than children.

So much for this subject; the relations of husband and wife, parent and child, their several virtues, what in their intercourse with one another is good, and what is evil, will have to be discussed when we speak of the different forms of government. For, inasmuch as every family is a part of a state, and these relationships are the parts of a family, and the virtue of the part must have regard to the virtue of the whole, women and children must be trained by education with an eye to the constitution, if the virtues of either of them are supposed to make any difference in the virtues of the state. And they must make a difference: for the children grow up to be citizens, and half the free persons in a state are women.

DISCUSSION QUESTIONS

1. What is Aristotle's position on sexism? Compare his view with the position developed by Socrates. Whose view do you prefer, and why?

2. Do you believe that men and women have or tend to have different virtues? For example, do you agree with Aristotle that "the courage of a man is shown in commanding, of a woman in obeying"? Or do men and women share the same type of courage?

3. What is the difference between women and slaves according to Aristotle? Do you agree? Why or Why not?

4. Aristotle argues that women are not as suited to be guardians of the city as men are because women tend to lack the virtues necessary for good guardianship. Compare Aristotle's position on guardianship with Socrates'. Whose do you prefer, and why?

5. Aristotle says, "Silence is a woman's glory," but "this is not equally the glory of man." Do you agree with him? Why or why not? What percentage of the population in America today do you think would agree with Aristotle's claim about women's silence? Explain. How would these percentages break down according to sex?

6. Aristotle and Socrates lived in a different world than the one in which we live. Do you think it is important for us to worry about the position of women in ancient Greece? Why or why not? What bearing do you think the views of Socrates and Aristotle have on contemporary discussions of sexism? Explain.

Kadosh
[Israel 1999] 1 hour, 57 minutes
Directed by Amos Gitai

Rivka (Yaël Abecassis) lives in the ultra-Orthodox Mea Sherim quarter of Jerusalem. She is deeply in love with her husband of ten years, Meïr (Yoram Hattab), yet they remain childless. It is a religious rule that a husband can repudiate his wife if she has not provided him with a son after ten years of marriage. Consequently, Rivka and Meïr face a conflict between their love of God, and their love for each other. Will their love empower them to resist the pressure of the Jewish community or will religious law triumph over it?

Meïr's father, a rabbi, wants his son to leave Rivka because he believes that it is a woman's duty to bear and raise children and that something is wrong with a wife who cannot produce offspring. In fact, Rivka has been to a doctor who says that she is fertile and that Meïr could be the one who is sterile. However, Meïr refuses to go to the doctor because he believes that it is against Orthodox Jewish tradition. The rabbi eventually convinces Meïr to oust his wife from their home and meet with another woman who might be able to provide him with a child.

Meanwhile, Rivka's sister Malka (Meital Barda) faces conflicts of her own. Malka is in love with Yakov (Sami Hori), a young man who has been ostracized from the community for being too secular. Malka's parents arrange a marriage with Yossef (Uri Klauzner) against Malka's wishes, and she is forced into a life of submission to a man she doesn't love. As a result of her unhappiness, Malka secretly meets with Yakov and defies Yossef's wishes. For her defiance, Malka is beaten by Yossef with a belt.

The film ends with both Rivka and Malka leaving the community, although in very different ways. Rivka returns to her husband one evening, and the next morning, Meïr awakens only to discover that she has died of an unknown cause—perhaps a suicide. Malka chooses to leave Jerusalem, and the closing shot of the film has her walking away from the city alone.

Kadosh means "sacred" in Yiddish. The script for this film, written by Gitai and the French Jewish novelist Eliette Abecassis, was refused three times by the Israeli Film Commission.

DISCUSSION QUESTIONS

1. Aristotle argues that there is no equality between the sexes in marriage and that husbands rule over their wives. Moreover, this type of rule is possible only with the consent of the wife. Is the marriage between Meïr and Rivka consistent with Aristotle's views? Why or why not?

2. Aristotle says that "the courage of a man is shown in commanding, of a woman in obeying." Which of the men and women in this film would Aristotle consider to be courageous? Which not courageous? Do you agree with Aristotle? Why or why not?

3. *Kadosh* presents this twentieth-century Jewish community in Jerusalem as heavily rooted in ancient religious traditions that are highly patriarchal. Compare and contrast Rivka's and Malka's responses to this patriarchal society. Which do you admire more, and why?

4. Should persons outside of the Mea Sherim quarter of Jerusalem judge the way Yossef and Meïr treat Malka and Rivka? Why or why not? Do you think the director of this film judges them? Why or why not?

5. Meïr's father says to Meïr, "We've already talked about this. A woman's life is in him who makes use of her. A barren woman is no woman. A man who dies without progeny rips a page from the Torah." Discuss what it means to be a man and what it means to be a woman in Meïr's community.

6. Malka's parents arrange a marriage for her with a man she does not love. Consider the following conversation between Malka and her friend Sarah (Orian Zacay):

    MALKA   "I already told you. I don't want to get married. I won't get married."

    SARAH   "Of course you will. We all do."

    MALKA   "Not me."

    SARAH   "My wedding was the happiest day of my life."

    MALKA   "Mine won't be for me."

    Discuss Malka's feelings toward marriage. Are denying her a relationship with the man she loves and arranging a marriage for her with a man she does not love just treatment of her by her parents and her religious community? If you were one of her parents, what would you do? Why?

7. Malka says to Rivka, "I'm marrying Yossef. That's what they say. You know what? I'm a good girl, right? True, I don't like cooking and cleaning. I'll study accounting like you. That way, I'll be able to support my family and my husband can study. My husband can study. Then I'll shave my head, and I'll spend my whole life pregnant. I'll give myself to Yakov before the wedding. Yossef will see I'm not a virgin and repudiate me." Malka is torn between following her heart and doing her religious duty. Discuss what it means for Malka to be "a good girl." What are the implications in relation to the equality of the sexes.

8. Meïr's father says to Meïr, "Make up your mind. Do your duty. You know our laws. You know that the only task of a daughter of Israel is to bring children into the world. To give birth to Jews and enable her husband to study. God created man to study the Torah. Woman plays an indirect part in fulfilling the Torah by keeping his home clean, preparing his meals and especially by raising children. A woman's only joy is raising his children. Children are our strength. With them we will vanquish." Still, Meïr loves his wife very much and even says to her, "It's been ten years. I will never leave you." What should Meïr do? How should he respond to his father? Defend your position.

9. Consider the following conversation between Malka and Rivka:

    MALKA   "A man is obliged to satisfy his wife. If he doesn't, she has grounds for divorce."

    RIVKA   "I received a letter a few days ago. It said a woman without child is no better than dead."

    MALKA   "Who would send such a thing?"

    RIVKA   "I don't know. I asked Meïr. I sometimes think my problem isn't sterility, but shame. It's in her eyes. Mother is ashamed of me. Even Meïr is ashamed of me."

    MALKA   "What did he say about the letter?"

    RIVKA   "That it was copied from the Talmud."

    MALKA   "The Talmud, the Talmud, Rivka. Women don't study the Talmud. Father said the Talmud contains everything and its opposite. No woman dares say it, but men don't want us to know. That way they can do as they like with us. Look at the laws of menstruation. They're forbidden to touch us. We sully everything. We can't even hand them a cup. Is that in the Talmud?"

RIVKA   "What are you saying? What's come over you? I believe in this law, and so do you."

MALKA   "Really? And do you also think that woman is fickle and her heart unconstant? Why is the Torah forbidden to us?"

RIVKA   "It isn't."

MALKA   "I mean the right to carry it. I'd like to stand in the synagogue and take it in my hands like a man."

RIVKA   "You're mad!"

MALKA   "Rivka, look at the others. They live differently. They watch television, listen to the radio. Look at them when they drive by. The women wear short sleeves. The can laugh and they can drive. Once a woman with bare arms walked by. Hassadim threw stones at her. You think we're living normal lives?"

Discuss their conversation. What does Malka mean by a "normal life"? What does Rivka mean when she calls Malka "mad"? Are the lives of Rivka and Malka "normal" or "mad"? Defend your response.

10. Amos Gitai, the director of *Kadosh* says, "If we consider the three big monotheist religions, we can say that the same big contradiction exists in all of them. Judaism, Christianity, and Islam all relegate women to the same position. The woman's function is to assure the continuity of the community. The 'Mitzva of reproduction' in Judaism. Women are not equal partners in the process of religious study, and the elaboration of religious decisions. At the end of the twentieth century, it's time to discuss this contradiction, in Judaism, and the Orthodox community within it, about the status of women. This is the key question in this film." What is the contradiction about the status of women in Judaism, Christianity, and Islam that Gitai mentions? How might the contradiction be resolved?

11. At the close of the film, Rivka dies in the arms of her husband. It is not clear whether this is a suicide or a natural death. Do you find her to be more like a saint or a martyr? Or neither? Why?

JOHN STUART MILL

SEXISM AS INEQUALITY

John Stuart Mill defends sexual equality and argues against all forms of legal discrimination against women. "All women are brought up from the earliest years in the belief that their ideal of character is the very opposite of that of men; not self-will, and government by self-control, but submission, and yielding to the control of others," writes Mill. "All the moralities tell them," he continues, "that it is the duty of women, and all the current sentimentalities that it is their nature, to live for others."

While Mill is sympathetic to many traditional claims about the social roles of men and women, he nevertheless makes many controversial proposals, including the analogy between the subjection of women and the possession of slaves. Mill believes that the Enlightenment ideals of individual freedom and autonomy have almost eradicated slavery despite its long tradition. These same ideals should, if followed, eradicate the subordination of women to men.

Mill strongly advocates the freedom of choice and the equality of persons, both in this work and in others such as *On Liberty* and *Utilitarianism*. He also asserts that moral progress is possible and does occur over history. Most of the civilized world has abandoned slavery, yet the oppression of women remains unrecognized by most men, as well as widely accepted. According to Mill, men must recognize the slavery of women if reform is to happen. In the selection below, Mill responds to a number of objections raised by his predecessors to the equality of women, including the charge that women's subordination across history indicates their willingness to consent to it.

It is widely held that Harriet Taylor Mill, John Stuart Mill's best friend and strongest intellectual influence before they married (she was married to someone else during much of their friendship), was an important inspiration to his political and moral theories. The compassion that Mill shows in his writing on sexual equality might be attributable to the strong influence of Harriet Taylor Mill. The following reading is from the first chapter of *The Subjection of Women* (1869). A biographical sketch of Mill appears in chapter 1.

The object of this Essay is to explain as clearly as I am able, the grounds of an opinion which I have held from the very earliest period when I had formed any opinions at all on social or political matters. . . . That the principle which regulates the existing social relations between the two sexes—the legal subordination of one sex to the other—is wrong in itself, and now one of the chief hindrances to human improvement; and that it ought to be replaced by a principle of perfect equality, admitting no power or privilege on the one side, nor disability on the other. . . .

The generality of a practice is in some cases a strong presumption that it is, or at all events once was, conducive to laudable ends. This is the case, when the practice was first adopted, or afterwards kept up, as a means to such ends, and was grounded on experience of the mode in which they could be most effectually attained. If the authority of men over women, when first established, had been the result of a conscientious comparison between different modes of constituting the government of society; if, after trying various other modes of social organization—the government of women over men, equality between the two, and such mixed and divided modes of government as might be invented—it had been decided, on the testimony of experience, that the mode in which women are wholly under the rule of men, having no share at all in public concerns, and each in private being

under the legal obligation of obedience to the man with whom she has associated her destiny, was the arrangement most conducive to the happiness and well being of both; its general adoption might then be fairly thought to be some evidence that, at the time when it was adopted, it was the best. . . . But the state of the case is in every respect the reverse of this. In the first place, the opinion in favour of the present system, which entirely subordinates the weaker sex to the stronger, rests upon theory only; for there never has been trial made of any other: so that experience, in the sense in which it is vulgarly opposed to theory, cannot be pretended to have pronounced any verdict. And in the second place, the adoption of this system of inequality never was the result of deliberation, or forethought, or any social ideas, or any notion whatever of what conduced to the benefit of humanity or the good order of society. It arose simply from the fact that from the very earliest twilight of human society, every woman (owing to the value attached to her by men, combined with her inferiority in muscular strength) was found in a state of bondage to some man. Laws and systems of polity always begin by recognizing the relations they find already existing between individuals. They convert what was a mere physical fact into a legal right, give it the sanction of society, and principally aim at the substitution of public and organized means of asserting and protecting these rights, instead of the irregular and lawless conflict of physical strength. Those who had already been compelled to obedience became in this manner legally bound to it. Slavery, from being a mere affair of force between the master and the slave, became regularized and a matter of compact among the masters, who, binding themselves to one another for common protection, guaranteed by their collective strength the private possessions of each, including his slaves. In early times, the great majority of the male sex were slaves, as well as the whole of the female. And many ages elapsed, some of them ages of high cultivation, before any thinker was bold enough to question the rightfulness, and the absolute social necessity, either of the one slavery or of the other. By degrees such thinkers did arise: and (the general progress of society assisting) the slavery of the male sex has, in all the countries of Christian Europe at least (though, in one of them, only within the last few years), been at length abolished, and that of the female sex has been gradually changed into a milder form of dependence. But this dependence, as it exists at present, is not an original institution, taking a fresh start from considerations of justice and social expediency—it is the primitive state of slavery lasting on, through successive mitigations and modifications occasioned by the same causes which have softened the general manners, and brought all human relations more under the control of justice and the influence of humanity. It has not lost the taint of its brutal origin. No presumption in its favour, therefore, can be drawn from the fact of its existence. . . .

Some will object, that a comparison cannot fairly be made between the government of the male sex and the forms of unjust power which I have adduced in illustration of it, since these are arbitrary, and the effect of mere usurpation, while it on the contrary is natural. But was there ever any domination which did not appear natural to those who possessed it? There was a time when the division of mankind into two classes, a small one of masters and a numerous one of slaves, appeared, even to the most cultivated minds, to be a natural, and the only natural, condition of the human race. No less an intellect, and one which contributed no less to the progress of human thought, than Aristotle, held this opinion without doubt or misgiving; and rested it on the same premises on

which the same assertion in regard to the dominion of men over women is usually based, namely that there are different natures among mankind, free natures, and slave natures; that the Greeks were of a free nature, the barbarian races of Thracians and Asiatics of a slave nature. But why need I go back to Aristotle? Did not the slaveowners of the Southern United States maintain the same doctrine, with all the fanaticism with which men cling to the theories that justify their passions and legitimate their personal interests? Did they not call heaven and earth to witness that the dominion of the white man over the black is natural, that the black race is by nature incapable of freedom, and marked out for slavery? some even going so far as to say that the freedom of manual labourers is an unnatural order of things anywhere. . . . So true is it that unnatural generally means only uncustomary, and that everything which is usual appears natural. The subjection of women to men being a universal custom, any departure from it quite naturally appears unnatural. But how entirely, even in this case, the feeling is dependent on custom, appears by ample experience. Nothing so much astonishes the people of distant parts of the world, when they first learn anything about England, as to be told that it is under a queen: the thing seems to them so unnatural as to be almost incredible. To Englishmen this does not seem in the least degree unnatural, because they are used to it; but they do feel it unnatural that women should be soldiers or members of Parliament. In the feudal ages, on the contrary, war and politics were not thought unnatural to women, because not unusual; it seemed natural that women of the privileged classes should be of manly character, inferior in nothing but bodily strength to their husbands and fathers. The independence of women seemed rather less unnatural to the Greeks than to other ancients, on account of the fabulous Amazons (whom they believed to be historical), and the partial example afforded by the Spartan women; who, though no less subordinate by law than in other Greek states, were more free in fact, and being trained to bodily exercises in the same manner with men, gave ample proof that they were not naturally disqualified for them. There can be little doubt that Spartan experience suggested to Plato, among many other of his doctrines, that of the social and political equality of the two sexes.

But, it will be said, the rule of men over women differs from all these others in not being a rule of force: it is accepted voluntarily; women make no complaint, and are consenting parties to it. In the first place, a great number of women do not accept it. Ever since there have been women able to make their sentiments known by their writings (the only mode of publicity which society permits to them), an increasing number of them have recorded protests against their present social condition: and recently many thousands of them, headed by the most eminent women known to the public, have petitioned Parliament for their admission to the Parliamentary Suffrage. The claim of women to be educated as solidly, and in the same branches of knowledge, as men, is urged with growing intensity, and with a great prospect of success; while the demand for their admission into professions and occupations hitherto closed against them, becomes every year more urgent . . . it [is not] only in our own country and in America that women are beginning to protest, more or less collectively, against the disabilities under which they labour. France, and Italy, and Switzerland, and Russia now afford examples of the same thing. How many more women there are who silently cherish similar aspirations, no one can possibly know; but there are abundant tokens how many *would* cherish them, were they not so strenuously taught to repress them as contrary to the proprieties of their sex. It must be remembered, also, that no enslaved class ever asked for complete liberty at once. When Simon de Montfort called the deputies of the commons to sit for the first time in Parliament, did any of them dream of demanding that an assembly, elected by their constituents, should make and destroy ministries, and dictate to the king in affairs of state? No such thought entered into the imagination of the most ambitious of them. The nobility had already these pretensions; the commons pretended to nothing but to be exempt from arbitrary taxation, and from the gross individual oppression of the king's officers. It is a political law of nature that those who are under any power of ancient origin, never begin by complaining of the power itself, but only of its oppressive exercise. There is never any want of women who complain of ill usage by their husbands. There would be infinitely more, if complaint were not the greatest of all provocatives to a repetition and increase of the ill usage. It is this which frustrates all attempts to maintain the power but protect the woman against its abuses. In no other case (except that of a child) is the person who has been proved judicially to have suffered an injury, replaced under the physical power of the culprit who inflicted it. Accordingly wives, even in the most extreme and protracted cases of bodily ill usage, hardly ever dare avail themselves of the laws made for their protection: and if, in a moment of irrepressible indignation, or by the interference of neighbours, they are induced to do so, their whole effort afterwards is to disclose as little as they can, and to beg off their tyrant from his merited chastisement.

All causes, social and natural, combine to make it unlikely that women should be collectively rebellious to the power of men. They are so far in a position different from all other subject classes, that their masters require something more from them than actual service. Men do not want solely the obedience of women, they want their sentiments. All men, except the most brutish, desire to have, in the woman most nearly connected with them, not a forced slave but a willing one, not a slave merely, but a favourite. They have therefore put everything in practice to enslave their minds. The masters of all other slaves rely, for maintaining obedience, on fear; either fear of themselves, or religious fears. The masters of women wanted more than simple obedience, and they turned the whole force of education to effect their purpose. All women are brought up from the very earliest years in the belief that their ideal of character is the very opposite to that of men; not self-will, and government by self-control, but submission, and yielding to the control of others. All the moralities tell them that it is the duty of women, and all the current sentimentalities that it is their nature, to live for others; to make complete abnegation of themselves, and to have no life but in their affections. And by their affections are meant the only ones they are allowed to have—those to the men with whom they are connected, or to the children who constitute an additional and indefeasible tie between them and a man. When we put together three things—first, the natural attraction between opposite sexes; secondly, the wife's entire dependence on the husband, every privilege or pleasure she has being either his gift, or depending entirely on his will; and lastly, that the principal object of human pursuit, consideration, and all objects of social ambition, can in general be sought or obtained by her only through him, it would be a miracle if the object of being attractive to men had not become the polar star of feminine education and formation of character. And, this great means of influence over the minds of women having been acquired, an instinct of selfishness made men avail themselves of it to the utmost as a means of holding women in subjection, by representing to them meekness, submissiveness, and resignation of all individual will into the hands of a man, as an essential part of sexual attractiveness. Can it be doubted that any of the other yokes which mankind have succeeded in breaking, would have subsisted till now if the same means had existed, and had been as sedulously [diligently] used, to bow down their minds to it? If it had been made the object of the life of every young plebeian to find personal favour in the eyes of some patrician, of every young serf with some seigneur; if domestication with him, and a share of his personal affections, had been held out as the prize which they all should look out for, the most gifted and aspiring being able to reckon on the most desirable prizes; and if, when this prize had been obtained, they had been shut out by a wall of brass from all interests not centering in him, all feelings and desires but those which he shared or inculcated; would not serfs and seigneurs, plebeians and patricians, have been as broadly distinguished at this day as men and women are? and would not all but a thinker here and there, have believed the distinction to be a fundamental and unalterable fact in human nature?

The preceding considerations are amply sufficient to show that custom, however universal it may be, affords in this case no presumption, and ought not to create any prejudice, in favour of the arrangements which place women in social and political subjection to men. But I may go farther, and maintain that the course of history, and the tendencies of progressive human society, afford not only no presumption in favour of this system of inequality of rights, but a strong one against it; and that, so far as the whole course of human improvement up to this time, the whole stream of modern tendencies, warrants any inference on the subject, it is, that this relic of the past is discordant with the future, and must necessarily disappear.

DISCUSSION QUESTIONS

1. What are Mill's counterarguments to the charge that women voluntarily consent to the rule of men over them? Critically analyze these counterarguments.

2. Mill draws an analogy between the subjection of women and the possession of slaves. Is it a good analogy? Why or why not?

3. Why does Mill believe that the subordination of women is a cultural phenomenon, and not a natural one? Does he have a good argument?

4. How do you think Mill would respond to Aristotle's claim that women's natural virtue is to obey, and not to rule?

5. Mill believes that moral progress is possible and does occur over history. Do you agree with him? Give an argument in defense of your position.

MARILYN FRYE

SEXISM

Marilyn Frye provides a definition of sexism and argues that sexism is not always apparent either to those who suffer from it or to those who inflict it upon others. It is the imperceptibility of sexism that enables it to flourish in our society.

Like most contemporary discussions of sexism and sexual inequality, Fry's distinguishes between sex and gender (or sex role). *Sex* refers to the differences between men and women that are biological in origin. *Gender* or *sex role* refers to the differences between men and women that are cultural or societal in origin. The words *male* and *female* are used to identify distinctions made on the basis of sex, and *masculine* and *feminine* to distinctions made on the basis of gender or sex role.

According to Frye, the "term *sexist* characterizes cultural and economic structures which create and enforce the elaborate and rigid patterns of sex-marking and sex-announcing which divide the species, along lines of sex, into dominators and subordinates." For Frye, acts that reinforce those cultural and economic structures are sexist acts, and acts that work to undermine those structures are acts of resistance to sexism. Consequently, for Frye, "the locus of sexism is primarily in the system or framework, not in the particular act."

Frye's analysis of sexism aims to make the systemic structures of sex-marking and sex-announcing more visible by identifying some of the different ways in which sex differences are reinforced in our society. The continued cultural emphasis on sex differences for Frye serves only to reinforce and perpetuate acts of domination and subordination. The following selection is from *The Politics of Reality: Essays in Feminist Theory* (1983). A biographical sketch of Frye appears earlier in this chapter.

The first philosophical project I undertook as a feminist was that of trying to say carefully and persuasively what sexism is, and what it is for someone, some institution or some act to be sexist. This project was pressed on me with considerable urgency because, like most women coming to a feminist perception of themselves and the world, I was seeing sexism everywhere and trying to make it perceptible to others. I would point out, complain and criticize, but most frequently my friends and colleagues would not see that what I declared to be sexist was sexist, or at all objectionable.

As the critic and as the initiator of the topic, I was the one on whom the burden of proof fell—it was I who had to explain and convince. Teaching philosophy had already taught me that people cannot be persuaded of things they are not ready to be persuaded of; there are certain complexes of will and prior experience which will inevitably block persuasion, no matter the merits of the case presented. I knew that even if I could explain fully and clearly what I was saying when I called something sexist, I would not necessarily be able to convince various others of the correctness of this claim. But what troubled me enormously was that I could not explain it in any way which satisfied *me*. It is this sort of moral and intellectual

frustration which, in my case at least, always generates philosophy.

The following was the product of my first attempt to state clearly and explicitly what sexism is:

> The term "sexist" in its core and perhaps most funda-mental meaning is a term which characterizes any-thing whatever which creates, constitutes, promotes or exploits any irrelevant or impertinent marking of the distinction between the sexes.

When I composed this statement, I was thinking of the myriads of instances in which persons of the two sexes are treated differently, or behave differently, but where nothing in the real differences between females and males justifies or explains the difference of treatment or behavior. I was thinking, for instance, of the tracking of boys into Shop and girls into Home Ec, where one can see nothing about boys or girls considered in themselves which seems to connect essen-tially with the distinction between wrenches and eggbeaters. I was thinking also of sex discrimination in employment—cases where someone otherwise apparently qualified for a job is not hired because she is a woman. But when I tried to put this definition of "sexist" to use, it did not stand the test.

Consider this case: If a company is hiring a supervisor who will supervise a group of male workers who have always worked for male supervisors, it can scarcely be denied that the sex of a candidate for the job is relevant to the candidate's prospects of moving smoothly and successfully into an effective working relationship with the supervisees (though the point is usually exaggerated by those looking for excuses not to hire women). Relevance is an intrasystematic thing. The patterns of behavior, attitude and custom within which a process goes on determine what is relevant to what in matters of describing, predicting or evaluating. In the case at hand, the workers' attitudes and the surrounding customs of the culture make a difference to how they interact with their supervisor and, in particular, *make* the sex of the supervisor a relevant factor in predicting how things will work out. So then, if the company hires a man, in preference to a more experienced and knowledgeable woman, can we explain our objection to the decision by saying it involved distinguishing on the basis of sex when sex is irrelevant to the ability to do the job? No: sex is relevant here.

So, what did I mean to say about "sexist"? I was thinking that in a case of a candidate for a supervisory job, the reproductive capacity of the candidate has nothing to do with that person's knowing what needs to be done and being able to give properly timed, clear and correct directions. What I was picturing was a situation purified of all sexist perception and reaction. But, of course, *if* the whole context were not sexist, sex would not be an issue in such a job situation; indeed, it might go entirely unnoticed. It is precisely the fact that the sex of the candidate *is* relevant that is the salient symptom of the sexism of the situation.

I had failed, in that first essay, fully to grasp or understand that the locus of sexism is primarily in the system or framework, not in the particular act. It is not accurate to say that what is going on in cases of sexism is that distinctions are made on the basis of sex when sex is irrelevant; what is wrong in cases of sexism is, in the first place, that sex *is* relevant; and then that the making of distinctions on the basis of sex reinforces the patterns which make it relevant.

In sexist cultural/economic systems, sex is always relevant. To understand what sexism is, then, we have to step back and take a larger view.

Sex-identification intrudes into every moment of our lives and discourse, no matter what the supposedly primary focus or topic of the moment is. Elaborate, systematic, ubiquitous and redundant marking of a distinction between the two sexes of humans and most animals is customary and obligatory. One *never* can ignore it.

Examples of sex-marking behavior patterns abound. A couple enters a restaurant; the headwaiter or hostess addresses the man and does not address the woman. The physician addresses the man by surname and honorific (Mr. Baxter, Rev. Jones) and addresses the woman by given name (Nancy, Gloria). You congratulate your friend—a hug, a slap on the back, shaking hands, kissing; one of the things which determines which of these you do is your friend's sex. In everything one does one has two complete repertoires of behavior, one for interactions with women and one for interactions with men. Greeting, storytelling, order-giving and order-receiving, negotiating, gesturing deference or dominance, encouraging, challenging, asking for information: one does all of these things differently depending upon whether the relevant others are male or female.

That this is so has been confirmed in sociological and socio-linguistic research, but it is just as easily confirmed in one's own experience. To discover the differences in how you greet a woman and how you greet a man, for instance, just observe yourself; paying attention to the following sorts of things: frequency and duration of eye contact, frequency and type of touch, tone and pitch of voice, physical distance maintained between bodies, how and whether you smile, use of slang or swear words, whether your body dips into a shadow curtsy or bow. That I have two repertoires for handling introductions to people was vividly confirmed for me when a student introduced me to his friend, Pat, and I really could not tell what sex Pat was. For a moment I was stopped cold, completely incapable of action. I felt myself helplessly caught between two paths—the one I would take if Pat were female and the one I would take if Pat were male. Of course the paralysis does not last. One is rescued by one's ingenuity and good will; one can invent a way to behave as one says "How do you do?" to a human being. But the habitual ways are not for humans: they are one way for women and another for men. . . .

In order to behave "appropriately" toward women and men, we have to know which of the people we encounter are women and which are men. But if you strip humans of most of their cultural trappings, it is not always that easy to tell without close inspection which are female, which are male. The tangible and visible physical differences between the sexes are not particularly sharp or numerous and in the physical dimensions we associate with "sex differences," the range of individual variation is very great. The differences between the sexes could easily be, and sometimes are, obscured by bodily decoration, hair removal and the like. So the requirement of knowing everyone's sex in every situation and under almost all observational conditions generates a requirement that we all let others know our sex in every situation. And we do. We announce our sexes in a thousand ways. We deck ourselves from head to toe with garments and decorations which serve like badges and buttons to announce our sexes. For every type of occasion there are distinct clothes, gear and accessories, hair-dos, cosmetics and scents, labeled as "ladies" or "men's" and labeling us as females or males, and most of the time most of us choose, use, wear or bear the paraphernalia associated with our sex. It goes below the skin as well. There are different styles of gait, gesture, posture, speech, humor, taste and even of perception, interest and attention that we learn as we grow up to be women or to be men and that label and announce us as women or as men. It begins early in life: even infants in arms are color coded.

That we wear and bear signs of our sexes, and that this is absolutely compulsory, is made clearest in the relatively rare cases when we do not do so, or not enough. Responses ranging from critical to indignant to hostile meet mothers whose babies are not adequately coded; one of the most agitated criticisms of the sixties' hippies was that "you can't tell the boys from the girls." The requirement of sex-announcement is laden, indeed, with all the urgency of the taboo against homosexuality. One appears heterosexual by informing people of one's sex *very* emphatically and *very* unambiguously, and lesbians and homosexuals who wish *not* to pass as heterosexual generally can accomplish this just by cultivating ambiguous sex-indicators in clothes, behavior and style. The

power of this ambiguity to generate unease and punitive responses in others mirrors and demonstrates the rigidity and urgency of this strange social rule that we all be and assertively act "feminine" or "masculine" (and not both)— that we flap a full array of sex-signals at all times.

The intense demand for marking and for asserting what sex each person is adds up to a strenuous requirement that there *be* two distinct and sharply dimorphic sexes. But, in reality, there are not. There are people who fit on a biological spectrum between two not-so-sharply defined poles. In about 5 percent of live births, possibly more, the babies are in some degree and way not perfect exemplars of male and female. There are individuals with chromosome patterns other than XX or YY and individuals whose external genitalia at birth exhibit some degree of ambiguity. There are people who are chromosomally "normal" who are at the far ends of the normal spectra of secondary sex characteristics—height, musculature, hairiness, body density, distribution of fat, breast size, etc.—whose overall appearance fits the norm of people whose chromosomal sex is the opposite of theirs.

These variations notwithstanding, persons (mainly men, of course) with the power to do so actually *construct* a world in which men are men and women are women and there is nothing in between and nothing ambiguous; they do it by chemically and/or surgically altering people whose bodies are indeterminate or ambiguous with respect to sex. Newborns with "imperfectly formed" genitals are immediately "corrected" by chemical or surgical means, children and adolescents are given hormone "therapies" if their bodies seem not to be developing according to what physicians and others declare to be the norm for what has been declared to be that individual's sex. Persons with authority recommend and supply cosmetics and cosmetic regimens, diets, exercises and all manner of clothing to revise or disguise the too-hairy lip, the too-large breast, the too-slender shoulders, the too-large feet, the too-great or too-slight stature. Individuals whose bodies do not fit the picture of exactly two sharply dimorphic sexes are often enough quite willing to be altered or veiled for the obvious reason that the world punishes them severely for their failure to be the "facts" which would verify the doctrine of two sexes. The demand that the world be a world in which there are exactly two sexes is inexorable, and we are all compelled to answer to it emphatically, unconditionally, repetitiously and unambiguously.

Even being physically "normal" for one's assigned sex is not enough. One must *be* female or male, actively. Again, the costumes and performances. Pressed to acting feminine or masculine, one colludes (co-lude: play along) with the doctors and counselors in the creation of a world in which the apparent dimorphism of the sexes is so extreme that one can only think there is a great gulf between female and male, that the two are, essentially and fundamentally and naturally, utterly different. One helps to create a world in which it seems to us that we *could* never mistake a woman for a man or a man for a woman. We never need worry.

Along with all the making, marking and announcing of sex-distinction goes a strong and visceral feeling or attitude to the effect that sex-distinction is the most important thing in the world: that it would be the end of the world if it were not maintained, clear and sharp and rigid; that a sex-dualism which is rooted in the nature of the beast is absolutely crucial and fundamental to all aspects of human life, human society and human economy. . . .

It is a general and obvious principle of information theory that when it is very, very important that certain information be conveyed, the suitable strategy is redundancy. If a message *must* get through, one sends it repeatedly and by as many means or media as one has at one's command. On the other end, as a receiver of information, if one receives the same information over and over, conveyed by every medium one knows, another message comes through as well, and implicitly: the message that this information is very, very important. The enormous frequency with which information about people's sexes is conveyed conveys implicitly the message that this topic is enormously important. I suspect that this is the single topic on which we most frequently receive information from others throughout our entire lives. If I am right, it would go partway to explaining why we end up with an almost irresistible impression, unarticulated, that the

matter of people's sexes is the most important and most fundamental topic in the world.

We exchange sex-identification information, along with the implicit message that it is very important, in a variety of circumstances in which there really is no concrete or experientially obvious point in having the information. There are reasons, as this discussion has shown, why you should want to know whether the person filling your water glass or your tooth is male or female and why that person wants to know what you are, but those reasons are woven invisibly into the fabric of social structure and they do not have to do with the bare mechanics of things being filled. Furthermore, the same culture which drives us to this constant information exchange also simultaneously enforces a strong blanket rule requiring that the simplest and most nearly definitive physical manifestations of sex difference be hidden from view in all but the most private and intimate circumstances. The double message of sex-distinction and its preeminent importance is conveyed, in fact, in part *by* devices which systematically and deliberately cover up and hide from view the few physical things which do (to a fair extent) distinguish two sexes of humans. The messages are overwhelmingly dissociated from the concrete facts they supposedly pertain to, and from matrices of concrete and sensible reasons and consequences. . . .

If one is made to feel that a thing is of prime importance, but common sensory experience does not connect it with things of obvious concrete and practical importance, then there is mystery, and with that a strong tendency to the construction of mystical or metaphysical conceptions of its importance. If it is important, but not of mundane importance, it must be of transcendent importance. All the more so if it is *very* important.

This matter of our sexes must be very profound indeed if it must, on pain of shame and ostracism, be covered up and must, on pain of shame and ostracism, be boldly advertised by every means and medium one can devise.

There is one more point about redundancy that is worth making here. If there is one thing more effective in making one believe a thing than receiving the message repetitively, it is rehearsing it repetitively. Advertisers, preachers, teachers, all of us in the brainwashing professions, make use of this apparently physical fact of human psychology routinely. The redundancy of sex-marking and sex-announcing serves not only to make the topic seem transcendently important, but to make the sex-duality it advertises seem transcendently and unquestionably *true.* . . .

Sex-marking and sex-announcing are equally compulsory for males and females; but that is as far as equality goes in this matter. The meaning and import of this behavior is profoundly different for women and for men.

Whatever features an individual male person has which tend to his social and economic disadvantage (his age, race, class, height, etc.), one feature which never tends to his disadvantage in the society at large is his maleness. The case for females is the mirror image of this. Whatever features an individual female person has which tend to her social and economic advantage (her age, race, etc.), one feature which always tends to her disadvantage is her femaleness. Therefore, when a male's sex-category is the thing about him that gets first and most repeated notice, the thing about him that is being framed and emphasized and given primacy is a feature which in general is an asset to him. When a female's sex-category is the thing about her that gets first and most repeated notice, the thing about her that is being framed and emphasized and given primacy is a feature which in general is a liability to her. Manifestations of this divergence in the meaning and consequences of sex-announcement can be very concrete.

Walking down the street in the evening in a town or city exposes one to some risk of assault. For males the risk is less; for females the risk is greater. If one announces oneself male, one is presumed by potential assailants to be more rather than less likely to defend oneself or be able to evade the assault and, if the male-announcement is strong and unambiguous, to be a noncandidate for sexual assault. If one announces oneself female, one is presumed by potential assailants to be less rather than more likely to defend oneself or to evade the assault and, if the female-announcement is strong and unambiguous, to be a prime candidate for sexual assault. Both the man and the woman "announce" their sex through style of gait, clothing, hairstyle, etc., but they are not equally or identically affected by announcing their sex. The

male's announcement tends toward his protection or safety, and the female's announcement tends toward her victimization. It could not be more immediate or concrete; the meaning of the sex-identification could not be more different.

The sex-marking behavioral repertoires are such that in the behavior of almost all people of both sexes addressing or responding to males (especially within their own culture/race) generally is done in a manner which suggests basic respect, while addressing or responding to females is done in a manner that suggests the females' inferiority (condescending tones, presumptions of ignorance, overfamiliarity, sexual aggression, etc.). So, when one approaches an ordinary well-socialized person in such cultures, if one is male, one's own behavioral announcement of maleness tends to evoke supportive and beneficial response and if one is female, one's own behavioral announcement of femaleness tends to evoke degrading and detrimental response.

The details of the sex-announcing behaviors also contribute to the reduction of women and the elevation of men. The case is most obvious in the matter of clothing. As feminists have been saying for two hundred years or so, ladies' clothing is generally restrictive, binding, burdening and frail; it threatens to fall apart and/or to uncover something that is supposed to be covered if you bend, reach, kick, punch or run. It typically does not protect effectively against hazards in the environment, nor permit the wearer to protect herself against the hazards of the human environment. Men's clothing is generally the opposite of all this—sturdy, suitably protective, permitting movement and locomotion. The details of feminine manners and postures also serve to bind and restrict. To be feminine is to take up little space, to defer to others, to be silent or affirming of others, etc. It is not necessary here to survey all this, for it has been done many times and in illuminating detail in feminist writings. My point here is that though both men and women must behave in sex-announcing ways, the behavior which announces femaleness is in itself both physically and socially binding and limiting as the behavior which announces maleness is not.

The sex-correlated variations in our behavior tend systematically to the benefit of males and the detriment of females. The male, announcing his sex in sex-identifying behavior and dress, is both announcing and acting on his membership in a dominant caste—dominant within his subculture and to a fair extent across subcultures as well. The female, announcing her sex, is both announcing and acting on her membership in the subordinated caste. She is obliged to inform others constantly and in every sort of situation that she is to be treated as inferior, without authority, assaultable. She cannot move or speak within the usual cultural norms without engaging in self-deprecation. The male cannot move or speak without engaging in self-aggrandizement. Constant sex-identification both defines and maintains the caste boundary without which there could not be a dominance-subordination structure. . . .

The cultural and economic structures which create and enforce elaborate and rigid patterns of sex-marking and sex-announcing behavior, that is, create gender as we know it, mold us as dominators and subordinates (I do not say "mold our minds" or "mold our personalities"). They construct two classes of animals, the masculine and the feminine, where another constellation of forces might have constructed three or five categories, and not necessarily hierarchically related. Or such a spectrum of sorts that we would not experience them as "sorts" at all.

The term "sexist" characterizes cultural and economic structures which create and enforce the elaborate and rigid patterns of sex-marking and sex-announcing which divide the species, along lines of sex, into dominators and subordinates. Individual acts and practices are sexist which reinforce and support those structures, either as culture or as shapes taken on by the enculturated

animals. Resistance to sexism is that which undermines those structures by social and political action and by projects of reconstruction and revision of ourselves.

DISCUSSION QUESTIONS

1. Critically discuss Frye's final definition of "sexism." How is it different from her earlier definition? Why does she change her definition?

2. What does Frye mean by "sex-marking and sex-announcing"? Provide your own examples of these.

3. For Frye, "the locus of sexism is primarily in the system or framework, not in the particular act." What does she mean by this? What is her argument? Do you agree with her? Why or why not?

4. Sexism is not always apparent either to those who suffer from it or to those who inflict it upon others, argues Frye. What do you think about this claim? Does Frye convince you that this is the case? Discuss.

5. Frye writes, "People cannot be persuaded of things they are not ready to be persuaded of." What does she mean by this? Do you agree with her? How do people who do not find their society to be sexist become "ready to be persuaded" that it is?

6. Do you think that all sex-marking necessarily has to do with dominance and subordination? Are sex-marking and sex-announcing conceivable within the context of equality between the sexes? Explain.

This film tells the story of French sculptor Camille Claudel (1864–1943) and her relationship with sculptor Auguste Rodin (1840–1917). Rodin serves first as Camille's mentor, later as her lover, and lastly as her enemy.

Initially, Rodin (Gérard Depardieu) recognizes Camille's (Isabelle Adjani) natural talent for sculpture, and she is invited to work under him in his Paris studio. Later, Camille and Rodin become lovers, and together they inspire each other's art. Their relationship takes place over the course of many years, but Camille eventually tires of being only Rodin's mistress. However, Rodin refuses to leave his long-time companion, Rose Beuret (Danièle Lebrun), for Camille, and Camille decides to end their relationship.

As the years pass, Camille refuses to see Rodin even when it has to do with the business of her art, and she sinks into poverty and alcholism. Deeply bitter toward Rodin, she claims that he destroyed her life. In the meantime, Camille's much-loved brother Paul (Laurent Grévill) becomes a famous writer, and their father (Alain Cuny) grows ashamed that the daughter for whom he sacrificed so much has fallen into a desperate existence.

Eugène Blot (Philippe Clévenot), a wealthy art dealer, also recognizes Camille's rare talent and tries to convince her that her work has value. However, Camille is now given to sudden fits of rage and paranoia, and this instability sabotages her future in the art world. Shortly after her father's death, Camille's family has her committed to an institution where she spends the remaining thirty years of her life.

DISCUSSION QUESTIONS

1. Marilyn Frye contends that "the locus of sexism is primarily in the system or framework, not in the particular act." Describe the framework or system of sexism at work in the life of Camille Claudel as depicted by this film.

2. Is the account of Camille the story of one woman's triumph over sexism or the story of how sexual inequality destroyed a talented woman's life and career? What do you think Frye would say? Discuss.

3. Describe the ways in which individual freedom and autonomy allow Camille to pursue her passion for sculpting. Can her story be used to support the claim that given more freedom and autonomy, many more women would have had the opportunity to achieve artistic greatness?

4. Camille is encouraged by a number of men in this film, particularly her father, her brother Paul, the wealthy art dealer Eugène Blot, and Rodin. She is also limited by each of them. Discuss the role of each man in both facilitating and limiting Camille's career in sculpture. Collectively considered, does the impact of these men on Camille's life lead you to conclude that she has been oppressed by them, that is, has been the victim of patriarchy? Why or why not?

5. While Camille's father is for most of the film very supportive of her efforts to become a sculptor, her mother is not. Camille's mother says, "That tramp! If my first baby hadn't died, I'd never have given

birth to her! She behaves like a boy! She hurts me . . . sets her father against me. She'll make us all suffer for her filth." Why do you think her mother is less supportive of her than her father? Is her mother being sexist toward Camille? Why or why not?

6.   Consider the following conversation between Camille and Louis-Prosper, her father:

LOUIS-PROSPER   "Since you met Rodin, you've done no work of your own."

CAMILLE   "That's not true. He's more concerned about my future than I am."

LOUIS-PROSPER   "This is December. If you haven't begun, you'll miss the Salon. You've exhibited nothing yet this year."

CAMILLE   "I've learned to work faster from him."

LOUIS-PROSPER   "My daughter didn't wait for Rodin in order to exist. Don't ever forget that we're different. That we're the Claudels. You always worked faster and better than others. Remember, Boucher told us you must exhibit to become known. There's no other way."

CAMILLE   "I know, Papa."

LOUIS-PROSPER   "Look at me, darling. Lift your eyes. Your future belongs to you. Also, don't be seen too much with Monsieur Rodin. People might gossip."

In *The Second Sex*, Simone de Beauvoir writes that "humanity is male and man defines woman not in herself but as relative to him; she is not regarded as an autonomous being" (see chapter 3). How would de Beavoir respond to Louis-Prosper's comment "My daughter didn't wait for Rodin in order to exist." As long as Camille works with Rodin, is she defining herself as relative to him? Discuss.

7.   Rodin says, "Miss Claudel has become a master. She has the talent of a man." What does this comment imply about artistic talent and women? Is it fundamentally a sexist remark, rather than a compliment? Why or why not?

8.   Consider the following conversation between Camille and Rodin:

CAMILLE   "Choose, Rodin. Your wife or me."

RODIN   "Rose is not my wife. What's wrong with you? Jealous of an old attachment? It's not like you and me. You and I are freaks of nature. We're the same breed."

CAMILLE   "You're dreaming, Rodin. An idyllic romance in a castle. . . . We're two ghosts in a wasteland."

RODIN   "What are you talking about? With you I want peace . . . oblivion . . . work."

CAMILLE   "Will you leave her?"

RODIN   "If only I could, Camille. If only I could."

CAMILLE   "Leave her, I beg you. Leave her. I'm the one you love. Tell me I'm the one you love. You love me! Do you? You love me! Don't let the worst happen to us. Please."

RODIN   "There are different ways of loving. What do you want me to do? Fire her, like a maid? I'll speak to her. Give me time. Give me time to prepare her. I'm all she has."

CAMILLE   "She's the one you love. It's her."

RODIN   "Rose is ill, you hear. She's ill."

CAMILLE   "I thought you were different. I'm leaving. Tomorrow I'll send for my things and my pay."

RODIN   "You tyrant!"

CAMILLE   "I worked hard for you. Now I'll work for myself."

What does this conversation reveal about their relationship? Why does Rodin react this way to Camille's request that he choose either Rose or herself? Is Camille the "tyrant," in this conversation, or Rodin? Is Rodin the "dominator," or Camille? Discuss.

9.   After a long separation, Camille and Rodin get together, and Camille shows Rodin the work she has done since leaving him. Here is part of their conversation:

CAMILLE   "Why don't you touch me?"

RODIN   "No. Let me discover your work, will you?"

CAMILLE   "Why? Are you afraid I've surpassed you?"

RODIN   "No, no. Copied me, perhaps. . . . No. You can't. You can't. I've told you the trouble I've had over 'Balzac.' If you complete this one, there'll be more scandal. How can you reduce what we shared to that image? You show me as a spineless puppet torn apart by two women. That's a vile caricature!"

CAMILLE   "What do you want?"

RODIN   "I want you to do what I tell you to do! Exactly!"

CAMILLE   "Not do what I'm doing? I've earned the right to do my own work."

RODIN   "If it means ridiculing me, destroying me . . . then you must give it up. Submit all your ideas to me. Don't compare yourself to me!"

CAMILLE   "What?"

RODIN   "Never! You're a third-rate sculptor."

CAMILLE   "Then why attack me so violently?"

RODIN   "Everything comes from me, nothing from you. You struggle too much for your work. It speaks for itself."

CAMILLE   "Why are you jealous?"

RODIN   "Jealous?"

CAMILLE   "Yes."

RODIN   "Jealous, me? I make sculptures of life, not death! You despise life. You search for pain. You get drunk on pain. And you create pain. You portray yourself as a victim. A martyr. But *you're* the one who left *me*."

CAMILLE   "It was impossible to live with you!"

RODIN   "Listen, Camille. The work we did together was good. I always treated you as an equal."

CAMILLE   "All the work I did for you was good! 'Miss Claudel, Rodin's pupil! She picks up Rodin's scraps and crams them into her sculptures!' You allowed them to say it!"

RODIN   "Oh, God! You're my worst enemy, I've just realized."

Did Rodin ever treat Camille as an equal? Is he treating her as an equal in this conversation? Why or why not? What does this conversation reveal about the relationship between Rodin and Camille as seen from Rodin's point of view? From Camille's point of view? Which is the preferable point of view, and why?

10.   Camille was pregnant with Rodin's child, but she never told him. When she discovered that he had no intention of marrying her, she had an abortion. The following conversation occurs after Camille tells him much later that she was pregnant.

RODIN   "Had I known you expected a child I'd have married you."

CAMILLE   "For years . . . you didn't want . . . you never wanted to choose . . . you never decided anything."

RODIN   "I never loved anyone but you."

CAMILLE   "I couldn't share you. It was a struggle for me."

RODIN   "What should I tell you? You made a mistake, that's all. It's finished. I don't want any more complicated emotions . . . the tyranny of feelings. I can't anymore."

CAMILLE   "On your deathbed, you'll still hesitate!"

Why does Rodin think that Camille "made a mistake"? What was her mistake? Do you agree with Rodin? Discuss the fact that Camille's pregnancy is the turning point in her career: before the pregnancy, she is Rodin's apprentice; after the pregnancy she sculpts on her own. Compare her "success" with and without Rodin. What does this reveal about the cultural framework in which Camille lives?

11.   Near the end of the film, Paul says, "She amounted to nothing. I amounted to something. She didn't. All the gifts Nature gave her brought only unhappiness. It's a total catastrophe. My sister is swallowed up." Is he right? Did she amount to nothing, or do her efforts amount to something?

STEVEN GOLDBERG

THE INEVITABILITY OF PATRIARCHY

Steven Goldberg disagrees with Frye and others that sexism is the consequence of cultural and economic frameworks, arguing that sexism is inevitable because of certain *biological* factors. According to Goldberg, males have hormonal systems that generate a greater capacity for aggression than those of females. Cultural and economic institutions conform to the physical reality of hormonal sexual differentiation and to the statistical reality of the "aggression advantage" that males derive from their hormonal systems. "Male roles are not given high status primarily *because* men fill these roles," says Goldberg; "men fill these roles because of their biological aggression 'advantage.'"

Sexism and sexual oppression are not the result of male aggressive energies directed toward females, argues Goldberg, nor are they the result of cultural and economic institutions directed toward oppressing women. "In reality," says Goldberg, "these male energies are directed toward attainment of desired positions and toward succeeding in whatever areas a particular society considers important." "The fact that women lose out in these competitions, so that the sex-role expectations of a society would have to become different for men and women even if they were not different for other reasons, is an inevitable byproduct of the reality of the male's aggression advantage and not the cause, purpose, or primary function of it."

Steven Goldberg (1941–) is a professor of sociology at City College, City University of New York. He received a B.A. from Ricker College, an M.A. from the University of New Brunswick, and a Ph.D. from City University of New York. He is the author of *The Inevitability of Patriarchy* (1973), *When Wish Replaces Thought: Why So Much of What You Believe Is False* (1991), *Why Men Rule: A Theory of Male Dominance* (1993), and *Fads and Fallacies in the Social Sciences* (2003). The following selection is from *The Inevitability of Patriarchy*.

THE FEMINIST ASSUMPTION

The view of man and woman in society that implicitly underlies all of the arguments of the feminists is this: there is nothing inherent in the nature of human beings or of society that necessitates that any role or task (save those requiring great strength or the ability to give birth) be associated with one sex or the other; there is no natural order of things decreeing that dyadic and social authority must be associated with men, nor is there any reason why it must be men who rule in every society. Patriarchy, matriarchy and "equiarchy" are all equally possible and—while every society may invoke "the natural order of things" to justify its particular system—all the expectations we have of men and women are culturally determined and have nothing to do with any sort of basic male or female nature.

There is nothing internally contradictory in such a hypothesis; indeed, it is an ideal place from which to begin an empirical investigation into the nature of man, woman, and society. However, the feminist does not use this as a heuristic first step but unquestioningly accepts it as true. . . .

. . . *The only biological hypothesis included [here] states that those individuals whose male anatomy leads to a social identification as "male" have hormonal systems which generate a greater capacity for "aggression" (or a lower threshold for the release of "aggression"—for our purposes this is the same thing)* *than those individuals whose female anatomy leads to a social identification as "female and that socialization and institutions conform to the reality of hormonal sexual differentiation and to the statistical reality of the "aggression advantage" which males derive from their hormonal systems. . . .*

AGGRESSION AND ATTAINMENT

In other words, I believe that in the past we have been looking in the wrong direction for the answer to the question of why every society rewards male roles with higher status than it does female roles (even when the male tasks in one society are the female tasks in another). While it is true that men are always in the positions of authority from which status tends to be defined, male roles are not given high status primarily *because* men fill these roles; men fill these roles because their biological aggression "advantage" can be manifested *in any non-child related area rewarded by high status in any society.* (Again: the line of reasoning used in this book demonstrates only that the biological factors we discuss would make the social institutions we discuss inevitable and does not preclude the existence of other forces also leading in the same direction; there may be a biologically based tendency for women to prefer male leadership, but there need not be for male attainment of leadership and high-status roles to be inevitable.) As we shall see, this aggression "advantage" can be most manifested and can most enable men to reap status rewards *not* in those relatively homogeneous, collectivist primitive societies in which both male and female must play similar economic roles if the society is to survive or in the monarchy (which guarantees an occasional female leader); this biological factor will be given freest play in the complex, relatively individualistic, bureaucratic, democratic society which, of necessity, must emphasize organizational authority and in which social mobility is relatively free of traditional barriers to advancement. There were more female heads of state in the first two-thirds of the sixteenth century than in the first two-thirds of the twentieth.

The mechanisms involved here are easily seen if we examine any roles that males have attained by channeling their aggression toward such attainment. We will assume for now that equivalent women could *perform* the tasks of roles as well as men if they could attain the roles. Here we can speak of the corporation president, the union leader, the governor, the chairman of an association, or any other role or position for which aggression is a precondition for attainment. Now the environmentalist and the feminist will say that the fact that all such roles are nearly always filled by men is attributable not to male aggression but to the fact that women have not been allowed to enter the competitive race to attain these positions, that they have been told that these positions are in male areas, and that girls are socialized away from competing with boys in general. Women *are* socialized in this way, but again we must ask why. If innate male aggression has nothing to do with male attainment of positions of authority and status in the political, academic, scientific, or financial spheres, if aggression has nothing to do with the reasons why *every* society socializes girls away from those areas which are given high status and away from competition in general, then why is it never the *girls* in any society who are socialized toward these areas, why is it never the nonbiological roles played by women that have high status, why is it always boys who are told to compete, and why do women never "force" men into the low-status, nonmaternal roles that women play in every society?

These questions pose no problem if we acknowledge a male aggression that enables men to attain any nonbiological role given high status by any society. For one need merely consider the result of a society's *not* socializing women away from competitions with men, from its *not* directing girls toward roles women are more capable of playing than are men or roles with status low enough that men will not strive for them. No doubt some women would be aggressive enough to succeed in competitions with men and there would be considerably more women in high-status positions than there are now. But most women would lose in such competitive struggles with men (because men have the aggression advantage) and so most women would be forced to live adult lives as failures in areas in which the society had *wanted them to succeed*. It is women, far more than men, who would never allow a situation in which girls were socialized in such a way that the vast majority of them were doomed to adult lifetimes of failure to live up to their own expectations. Now I have no doubt that there is a biological factor that gives women the desire to emphasize maternal and nurturance roles, but the point here is that we can accept the feminist assumption that there is no female propensity of this sort and still see that a society must socialize women away from roles that men will attain through their aggression. For if women did not develop an alternative set of criteria for success, their sense of their own competence would suffer intolerably. It is undeniable that the resulting different values and expectations that are attached to men and women will tend to work against the aggressive woman while they work for the man who is no more aggressive. But this is the unavoidable result of the fact that most men are more aggressive than most women so that this woman, who is as aggressive as the average man, but more aggressive than most women, is an exception. Furthermore, even if the sense of competence of each sex did not necessitate society's attaching to each sex values and expectations based on those qualities possessed by each sex, observation of the majority of each sex by the population would "automatically" lead to these values and expectations being attached to men and women.

SOCIALIZATION'S CONFORMATION TO BIOLOGICAL REALITY

Socialization is the process by which society prepares children for adulthood. The way in which its goals conform to the reality of biology is seen quite clearly when we consider the method in which testosterone generates male aggression (testosterone's serially developing nature). Preadolescent boys and girls have roughly equal testosterone levels, yet young boys are far more aggressive than young girls. Eva Figes has used this observation to dismiss incorrectly the possibility of a hormone aggression association. Now it is quite probable that the boy is more aggressive than the girl for a purely biological reason. We have seen that it is simplistic to speak simply in terms of hormone levels and that there is evidence of male-female differences in the behavior of infants shortly after birth (when differential socialization is not a plausible explanation of such differences). The fetal alteration of the boy's brain by the testosterone that was generated by his testes has probably left him far more sensitive to the aggression-related properties of the testosterone that is present during boyhood than the girl, who did not receive such alteration. But let us for the moment assume that this is not the case. This does not at all reduce the importance of the hormonal factor. For even if the boy is more aggressive than the girl only because the society allows him to be, the boy's socialization still flows from society's acknowledging biological reality. Let us consider what would happen if girls had the same innate aggression as boys and if a society did not socialize girls away from aggressive competitions. Perhaps half of the third-grade baseball team would be female. As many girls as boys would frame their expectations in masculine values and girls would develop not their feminine abilities but their masculine ones. During adolescence, however, the same assertion of the male chromosomal program that causes the boys to grow beards raises their testosterone level, and their potential for aggression, to a level far above that of the adolescent woman. If society did not teach young girls that beating boys at competitions was unfeminine (behavior inappropriate for a woman), if it did not socialize them away from the political and economic areas in which aggression leads to attainment, these girls would grow into adulthood with self-images based not on succeeding in areas for which biology has left them better prepared than men, but on competitions that most women could not win. If

women did not develop feminine qualities as girls (assuming that such qualities do not spring automatically from female biology), then they would be forced to deal with the world in the aggressive terms of men. They would lose every source of power their feminine abilities now give them and they would gain nothing. . . .

DISCRIMINATION OF A SORT

If one is convinced that sexual biology gives the male an advantage in aggression, competitiveness, and dominance, but he does not believe that it engenders in men and women different propensities, cognitive aptitudes, and modes of perception, and if he considers it discrimination when male aggression leads to attainment of position even when aggression is not relevant to the task to be performed, then the unavoidable conclusion is that discrimination so defined is unavoidable. Even if one is convinced . . . that the differing biological substrates that underlie the mental apparatus of men and women *do* engender different propensities, cognitive aptitudes, and modes of perception, he will probably agree that the relevance of this to male attainment of male roles is small when compared to the importance of male biological aggression to attainment. Innate tendencies to specific aptitudes *would* indicate that at any given level of competence there will be more men than women or vice versa (depending on the qualities relevant to the task) and that the very best will, in all probability, come from the sex whose potentials are relevant to the task. Nonetheless, drastic sexual differences in occupational and authority roles reflect male aggression and society's acknowledgment of it far more than they do differences in aptitudes, yet they are still inevitable.

In addition, even if artificial means were used to place large numbers of women in authority positions, it is doubtful that stability could be maintained. Even in our present male bureaucracies problems arise whenever a subordinate is more aggressive than his superior and, if the more aggressive executive is not allowed to rise in the bureaucracy, delicate psychological adjustments must be made. Such adjustments are also necessary when a male bureaucrat has a female superior. When such situations are rare exceptions adjustments can be made without any great instability occurring, particularly if the woman in the superior position complements her aggression with sensitivity and femininity. It would seem likely, however, that if women shared equally in power at each level of the bureaucracy, chaos would result for two reasons. Even if we consider the bureaucracy as a closed system, the excess of male aggression would soon manifest itself either in men moving quickly up the hierarchy or in a male refusal to acknowledge female authority. But a bureaucracy is not a closed system, and the discrepancy between male dominance in private life and bureaucratic female dominance (from the point of view of the male whose superior is a woman) would soon engender chaos. Consider that even the present minute minority of women in high authority positions expend enormous amounts of energy trying *not* to project the commanding authority that is seen as the mark of a good male executive. It is true that the manner in which aggression is manifested will be affected by the values of the society in general and the nature of the field of competition in particular; aggression in an academic environment is camouflaged far more than in the executive arena. While a desire for control and power and a single-mindedness of purpose are no doubt relevant, here aggression is not easily defined. One might inject the theoretical argument that women could attain positions of authority and leadership by countering the male's advantage in aggression with feminine abilities. Perhaps, but the equivalents of the executive positions in every area of suprafamilial life in every society have been attained by men, and there seems no reason to believe that, suddenly, feminine means will be capable of neutralizing male aggression in these areas. And, in any case, an emphasis on feminine abilities is hardly what the feminists desire. All of this can be seen in a considerably more optimistic light, from the point of view of most women, if one considers that the biological abilities possessed only by women are complemented by biologically generated propensities directing women to roles that can be filled only by women. But it is still the same picture. . . .

"OPPRESSION"

All of this indicates that the theoretical model that conceives of male success in attaining positions of status, authority, and leadership as *oppression* of the female is incorrect if only because it sees male aggressive energies as *directed toward* females and sees the institutional mechanisms that flow from the fact of male aggression as *directed toward* "oppressing" women. In reality these male energies are directed toward attainment of desired positions and toward succeeding in whatever areas a particular society considers important. The fact that women lose out in these competitions, so that the sex-role expectations of a society would have to become different for men and women even if they were not different for other reasons, is an inevitable byproduct of the reality of the male's aggression advantage and not the cause, purpose, or primary function of it. In other words, men who attain the more desired roles and positions do so because they channel their aggression advantage toward such attainment; whether the losers in such competitions are other men or women is important only in that—because so few women succeed in these competitions—the society will attach different expectations to men and women (making it more difficult for the exceptional, aggressive woman to attain such positions even when her aggression is equal to that of the average man).

DISCUSSION QUESTIONS

1. Why, according to Goldberg, is sexism morally justifiable? Critically analyze his argument.

2. Compare and contrast Marilyn Frye and Goldberg on the foundations of sexism. Whom do you agree with? Is sexism the consequence of cultural and economic frameworks as Frye contends, or the inevitable consequence of biological factors as Goldberg contends?

3. For the sake of argument, assume that it *is* the case that males have hormonal systems that generate a greater capacity for aggression than do females. Can we derive what *ought* to be the case from what *is* the case? Is this what Goldberg is doing? Is he saying that because males' aggression advantage *is* the case, sexism *ought* to be the case? Is sexism morally justifiable on the basis of biology? How might Frye or Mill respond to this line of argument?

4. Is violence against women ever morally justifiable on the basis of biology? Why or why not? Defend your view.

5. Goldberg says, "If society did not teach young girls that beating boys at competitions was unfeminine . . . these girls would grow into adulthood with self-images based on succeeding in . . . competitions that most women could not win." Is it really true that "aggression" helps one land jobs and keep them? Does the type of job play a role? That is, does aggression help one to land a job as a mathematician? A chef? A teacher? Defend your view against counter-arguments.

In the Company of Men
[Canada 1996] 1 hour, 37 minutes
Directed by Neil Labute

In an airport, embarking on a six-week-long business trip, Chad (Aaron Eckhart) and Howard (Matt Malloy) complain about the women in their lives. They have been friends since college and work for the same company. Chad tells Howard how Suzanne (Emily Cline) left him without so much as a note, and Howard tells Chad how his fiancée told him that she wanted to see other men. They lament the constraints of sexual politics at work and the ease with which women reject them. Chad says, "We cannot even tell a joke in the workplace, yet a woman can change her mind. We need to put our foot down."

Chad proposes that they find a vulnerable woman, one who is "disfigured in some way" and who believes that romance and a sexual life are lost to her. He suggests that they both pursue her and then abandon her, just as the women in their lives have suddenly dropped them. Chad insists that the adventure will be entertaining, will "restore a little dignity to their lives," and will be payback for the messy relationships they've been going through. Howard hesitatingly agrees, and soon Chad has located a suitable victim: a deaf woman who works in the office where they are stationed for the six weeks.

Christine (Stacy Edwards) soon falls in love with Chad and has sex with him. Chad abhors Christine but does not let on. In the meantime, Howard truly falls in love with Christine, but she does not return his feelings. Christine does not tell Chad about her relationship with Howard, nor does she tell Howard about her relationship with Chad, until Howard confronts her with the game that is being played on her. Christine is unwilling to believe that Chad does not love her but soon discovers the truth. Howard remains in love with Christine and confronts Chad at his home. Chad tells Howard that Suzanne never left him and that he played both Christine and Howard. When Howard asks why, Chad responds, "Because I could. So, how's it feel to really hurt someone? See you [at work] on Monday." Howard, crushed, seeks out Christine, who will not listen to him.

DISCUSSION QUESTIONS

1. Steven Goldberg argues that "male energies are directed toward attainment of desired positions and toward succeeding in whatever areas a particular society considers important." Discuss this film in the context of Goldberg's comments on the inevitability of patriarchy.

2. How might Goldberg use "aggression advantage" to explain the results of the "competition" between Chad and Howard? Do you agree with his explanation?

3. Roger Ebert wrote in the *Chicago Sun-Times* that this is "the kind of bold, uncompromising film that insists on being thought about afterward." What do think about this film? Is it a critique of or an homage to patriarchy? Defend your view.

4. In the workplace as depicted in this film, men are continuously making cruel, sexist jokes about women. To what extent do you believe that the workplace in this movie reflects the workplace in America today? Would you be surprised to hear cruel, sexist jokes around the watercooler? How would you respond to them?

5. Chad plays both Howard and Christine for the simple reason that he had the power to do so. How do you think he is morally able to justify this decision? Is this ethic similar to the one in which he engages in the workplace? Why or why not?

6. Christine does not tell either man about her relationship with the other. Should she have? Did this in any way contribute to the situation in which she finds herself? Is her lack of forthrightness in any way to blame for the painful situation in which she finds herself? If you were Christine, would you have spoken sooner to Chad about Howard, and to Howard about Chad?

7. Howard seems to sense from the beginning that there is something wrong with the "game" that Chad is setting up. However, he ultimately goes along with it. Why does he put his moral intuitions to the side and play along with Chad? What role do you believe patriarchy plays in Howard's decision?

8. Howard and Christine find themselves in the same place at the end of the film: they are both victims of Chad's cruel game. Or are they? To what extent are Howard and Christine really victims? To what extent did they contribute to their own victimization? Explain.

SUZANNE PHARR

HATE VIOLENCE AGAINST WOMEN

Suzanne Pharr argues that hate violence against women is morally the same as hate crimes against people of color, Jews, gay men, and lesbians. "This country minimizes hate violence against women," says Pharr, "because women's lives are not valued, because the violence is so commonplace that people become numb to it, because people do not want to look at the institutions and systems that support it, and because people do not want to recognize how widespread the hatred is and how many perpetrators there are among us on every level of society."

Pharr argues that sexist violence must be monitored in the same way that racist, anti-Semitic, and homophobic violence is monitored. "Men beat, rape and kill women because they *can*," says Pharr, "because they live in a society that gives permission to the hatred of women." Pharr's article suggests that monitoring the scope and nature of hate violence against women will work to bring about a society that values women and does not permit violence of this type to persist.

Suzanne Pharr is a former director of the Highlander Research and Education Center, one of the nation's foremost institutions for the promotion of civil and political rights. She is a cofounder of the Arkansas Women's Project and has traveled throughout the United States supporting the efforts of civil rights activists. Pharr is the author of *In the Time of the Right: Reflections on Liberation* (1996), *Homophobia: A Weapon of Sexism* (2nd ed., 1997), and *Exile and Pride: Disability, Queerness and Liberation* (with Eli Clare, 1999). This selection first appeared in 1990.

Women and men in Canada, the U.S., and worldwide were stunned and appalled by the massacre of 14 women in the University of Montreal engineering school. There has been outrage, grief and intense questioning in the aftermath of this murder. People have wanted to know what could be the motivation for such an outrageous act, and there has been some relief drawn from the suicide note that many read as a statement of a deranged mind, suggesting that these killings were an isolated incident.

However, those of us who are longtime workers in the women's anti-violence movement know that these killings, while seeming to contain elements of madness, are simply one more piece of the more routine, less sensational hate murders of women that we deal with every day. According to the FBI, there are several thousand women killed by their husbands and boyfriends each year. This number does not include the great numbers of women killed by rapists on the street and in their homes. Almost all of these are women who die horrible deaths of brutality and terror with no public outcry and outrage for the waste of their lives.

There is media and public response when the murder is sensational either in numbers, in the esteemed worth of the victim, or when it is cross-race and the perpetrator is a man of color. Hence, the extensive coverage of the Montreal massacre, the rape of the white female investment banker in Central Park, and the Republicans' use of Willie Horton as the rapist most to be feared. Otherwise, when murders and rapes of women are briefly reported daily in our papers and on television, the public, accustomed to the ordinariness of rape and murder of women and desensitized to it, simply see it as one more trivial incident in the expected way of life for women. It's just one more woman violated or dead: turn the page; flip the channel.

To see how staggering these numbers are let's look just at one state, the small (pop. 2.3 million), mostly rural state of Arkansas. At the Women's Project, for almost a year now we've been monitoring hate violence in Arkansas, and unlike other monitoring groups, we include sexist violence along with racist, anti-Semitic and homophobic violence. During the first six months of the year, we were putting the project in place and quite possibly missed some of the murders of women; nevertheless, our records show 37 women and girls murdered in 1989. Their killers were husbands, boyfriends, acquaintances, strangers. Most of the women were killed in their homes and all were murders in which robbery was not the motive. Their ages ranged from 5 years old to 88. Some were raped and killed; all were brutal murders. Some were urban, some rural; some rich, some poor; some white, some women of color.

A few examples will be enough to show the level of hatred and violence that was present in all the murders. A 67-year-old woman was shot twice with a crossbow and dumped into a farm pond, her head covered with plastic and her body weighted down with six concrete blocks; a 22-year-old woman was abducted from her home by three armed men while her small children watched, taken to an abandoned house, raped, sodomized and killed; a 30-year-old teacher was slashed and stabbed dozens of times; a 19-year-old woman was beaten to death and buried in a shallow grave; a 5-year-old girl was raped, strangled and stuffed into a tree; a 32-year-old paraplegic was killed, a 35-lb, weight tied to her, and dropped into the Ouachita River; an 86-year-old woman was suffocated in her home.

Added to these brutal murders are the statistics from Arkansas Children and Family Services that indicate 1,353 girls were sexually assaulted in 1988, and from the Arkansas Crime Information Center that 656 rapes were reported in 1988. In November the Arkansas *Gazette* reported that in the first six months of 1989, Little Rock had more rapes—119—than Washington, D.C.—90—a city three times its size. When we understand that only about 10% of all rapes are reported, these numbers become significantly larger. All in all, when the numbers of murders, rapes, and sexual assaults of girls are put together there emerges a grim picture of the brutal hate violence launched against women and girls.

I don't believe Arkansas is an exception in this violence. From battered women's programs, from rape crisis programs, from crime statistics, we know that women are beaten, raped and killed in every state of this country, every day. Because so many women are viciously beaten and their lives placed in jeopardy, this country has over 1,100 battered women's programs, all filled to overflowing, and more being developed every day.

Wherever we live in the U.S., women live in a war zone where we may be attacked, terrorized, or abducted at any moment. Women are not safe in the home, on the street, or at the workplace. Or, as in Montreal, in a school setting on the eve of final exams for 14 women about to enter engineering jobs that only recently became accessible to them in a world that considers engineering "men's work." There is no safe place, no "proper" kind of woman whose behavior exempts her, no fully protected woman.

While we recognize the absence of safety in all women's lives, no matter what class or race, we also are aware that women of color have even less safety than white women. Women of color are the targets of the combined hatred of racism and sexism, and as such, they experience both racist and sexist violence against their lives from white people as well as sexist violence from men of color, and often racist responses and services when they seek help.

Recently, the writers of a hate crime bill that went before Congress could not agree to put women alongside people of color, Jews, gay men and lesbians as targets of hate crimes. This seems to me a critical error in moral and political judgment, one reminiscent of the immoral decision the white women of the 19th century women's movement made when they decided to turn their backs on black women in order to secure the participation of white Southern women. There is never a "more politically appropriate" time to bring in a group of people—in this case 52% of the population—that is this country's largest target of hate crimes. When hate crimes are limited to anti-Semitic, racist, and homophobic violence, there is inherent confusion: when Jewish women are killed, when women of color are killed, when lesbians are raped or killed, it is often impossible to determine if they were attacked because of their religion, race, sexual identity, or their *gender*.

The U.S. Justice Department's guidelines to determine bias motivation for a crime include common sense (i.e., cross burning or offensive graffiti), language used by the assailant, the severity of the attack, a lack of provocation, previous history of similar incidents in the same area, and an absence of any other apparent motive. Under this definition, rape would be an apparent hate crime, often severe—including armed assault, beating and killing—often repeated in the same neighborhood or area, no other apparent motive, and almost always abusive woman-hating language.

The same would be true with our monitored cases of battering that ends in murder. In the majority of the cases, the woman was beaten (sometimes there was a long history of battering) and then killed. Rather than cross burnings or offensive graffiti, the hate material is pornography. Most telling is the absence of any other apparent motive. And then there are the countless beatings and acts of terrorism that don't end in murder but do lasting physical and psychological damage to women. An example from Arkansas:

> (A woman) reported battery and terroristic threatening. She said her neighbor/ex-boyfriend threatened her with a handgun, and beat her, knocking her down a flight of stairs where she landed on a rock terrace.
>
> (She) sustained permanent damage to her eardrum, two black eyes and extensive bruises and lacerations. She stated her assailant was not intoxicated; that he bragged of having been a Golden Gloves boxer; and he allegedly told her he could not be arrested for beating her since he struck her with his hands open. (Washington County *Observer* 8/17/89)

Men beat, rape and kill women because they *can*; that is, because they live in a society that gives permission to the hatred of women.

This country minimizes hate violence against women because women's lives are not valued, because the violence is so commonplace that people become numb to it, because people do not want to look at the institutions and systems that support it, and because people do not want to recognize how widespread the hatred is and how many perpetrators there are among us on every level of society.

It is only when women's lives are valued that this violence will be ended. If 37 African Americans were killed by whites in Arkansas, our organization would be leading the organizing to investigate and end the murders; or if 37 Jews were killed by gentiles; or if 37 gay men or lesbians were murdered by heterosexuals—for all of these other groups we monitor violence against, we would be in the forefront of organizing on their behalf. But why not on behalf of women? We talk about violence against women and help develop organizations that provide safety and support for victims, but even we sometimes get numbed to its immensity, to its every dayness, to the loss of freedom it brings with it.

All of us must stop minimizing this violence against women. We must bring it to the forefront of our social consciousness and name it for what it is: not the gentler, less descriptive words such as family violence, or domestic violence, or wife or spouse abuse, or sexual assault, but *hate violence against women*. It does not erupt naturally or by chance from the domesticity of our lives; it comes from a climate of women hating.

For too long when women have named this violence as what it is, we have been called man-haters by people who want the truth kept quiet. "Man-hater" is a common expression but "woman-hater" is not, despite the brutal evidence of woman-hating that surrounds us: murder, rape, battering, incest. The common use of the word "man-hater" is a diversionary tactic that keeps us from looking at the hard reality of the source of violence in our lives. The threat of the label "man-hater" threatens women with loss of privilege and controls our behavior, but more importantly, it keeps us from working honestly and forcefully on our own behalf to end the violence that destroys us.

Social change occurs when those who experience injustice organize to improve or save their lives. Women must overcome the fear of organizing on behalf of women, no matter what the threat. We must organize together to eliminate the root causes of violence against us.

We must make sure that hate violence against women is monitored and documented separate from general homicides so that we can be clear about the extent of it, the tactics, the institutions and systems that allow it to continue. We must hold our institutions accountable. In December 1989, the Arkansas *Gazette* ran a series of articles about local hospitals "dumping" rape victims, that is, refusing to give rape examinations because they did not want to get involved in legal cases. Such inhumane practices are dehumanizing to women and lead to public indifference to rape and its terrible consequences.

We must create a society that does not give men permission to rape and kill women. We all must believe that women's lives are as important as the lives of men. If we created a memorial to the women dead from this war against them—just over the past decade—our memorial would rest next to the Vietnam Memorial in Washington in numbers and human loss to this nation. The massacre must end.

DISCUSSION QUESTIONS

1. Is there a connection between sexism and hate violence against women? Explain.

2. Pharr says that we "live in a society that gives permission to the hatred of women." What is her argument? Do you agree with her? What is your evidence?

3. Should hate violence against women be considered as morally equivalent to hate crimes against people of color, Jews, gay men, and lesbians? Why or why not? Why might someone disagree with your position?

4. Pharr says that we should not use phrases such as "family violence," "domestic violence," "spouse abuse," or "sexual assault"? Why not? What is wrong with these phrases? Do you agree with her?

5. Why does Pharr argue for the monitoring of hate violence against women? What difference does she think such monitoring will make? Do you agree with her argument? Why or why not?

6. Pharr argues that "women of color have even less safety than white women." What is her argument? Is it a good one?

The General's Daughter
[USA 1999] 1 hour, 55 minutes
Directed by Simon West

C aptain Elisabeth Campbell (Leslie Stefanson), the daughter of General Joe Campbell (James Cromwell), has been murdered. Her naked corpse is found staked spread-eagle to the ground; she had been strangled. Paul Brenner (John Travolta) and Sarah Sunhill (Madeleine Stowe) investigate this bizarre, brutal murder. They find a secret room in Captain Campbell's basement with S&M props and equipment, along with a video recording system. They also learn that she apparently had sexual relations with most of her father's staff. A flashback sequence indicates that Campbell had been violently gang-raped by male cadets when she was in her third year at West Point. Apparently, some of the cadets resented her stellar performance at West Point and carried out the rape to demoralize her. In the process, they almost killed her.

When her father found out about the rape, he instructed her to forget that it ever occurred. The entire incident at West Point was covered up. However, this violent event altered the course of Captain Campbell's life and became a leading cause of her sexual promiscuity. The film suggests that Campbell wanted to reenact the rape scene in order to exorcise the traumatic memory of the event. While the details of the solving of her crime are interesting, they are overshadowed by the portrayal of the gang rape of Campbell at West Point.

In his review for the *Chicago Sun-Times*, Roger Ebert writes the following about *The General's Daughter*: "I . . . admired the darkly atmospheric look of the film, and the way it sustains its creepy mood. But I cringed when the death of the general's daughter was played out. Did the details have to be so graphic? Did we need to linger on the sight of a terrified woman? Did the filmmakers hesitate before supplying actual shots of her being strangled? Can anything be left to the imagination? I believe that any subject matter is legitimate for artistic purposes, but this isn't art. It's a thriller that could have spared us the details of that woman's horrible death." These and similar questions make this otherwise pedestrian Hollywood film morally intriguing.

This film is based on the novel by Nelson DeMille. The screenplay was written by William Goldman and Christopher Bertolini.

DISCUSSION QUESTIONS

1. Suzanne Pharr argues that "men beat, rape and kill women because they *can*; because they live in a society that gives permission to the hatred of women." Does *The General's Daughter* lend support Pharr's thesis? If so, how? If not, why not?

2. Suzanne Pharr says, "This country minimizes hate violence against women, because women's lives are not valued, because the violence is so commonplace that people become numb to it, because people do not want to look at the institutions and systems that support it, and because people do not want to recognize how widespread the hatred is and how many perpetrators there are among us on every level of society." Discuss *The General's Daughter* in view of Pharr's statement.

3. Some might argue that *The General's Daughter* is an antisexist, profeminist, proequality film because of its portrayal of sexism in the military and because of the strong way in which a victim of sexism and sexual violence fought back. Others might argue that the graphic depiction of violence against a woman in this film is nothing short of sexist and misogynistic; any redeeming value that this film might have had is lost in the prolonged rape and strangulation shots. What do you think? Defend your view.

4.   In his review of *The General's Daughter*, Roger Ebert asks, "Did we need to linger on the sight of a terrified woman?" What do you think? Why did Simon West, the director of this film, choose to linger on these scenes? Why did he choose to graphically portray the crime onscreen?

5.   Ebert comments that "the death of Elisabeth Campbell is so unnecessarily graphic and gruesome that by the end I felt sort of unclean. If this had been a documentary, or even a fiction film with serious intentions, I would have accepted it. But does entertainment have to go this far just to shake us up?" Why do you think Ebert might feel that the portrayal of such gruesome violence is acceptable in a documentary but is unacceptable as entertainment? Do you agree? Why or why not? What does Ebert mean when he says he "felt sort of unclean"? Do you think that provoking this feeling in the audience was the director's aim?

6.   Consider the following claim: *The General's Daughter* is a film that condemns violence against women. Argue for or against this claim.

7.   Consider two other famous films about military men and rape: Otto Preminger's *Anatomy of a Murder* (1959) and Gottfried Reinhardt's *Town Without Pity* (1961). View one of these films, and compare it to *The General's Daughter*. What are their similarities and differences? Which do you prefer, and why? Compare how you think Marilyn Frye and Steven Goldberg would respond to them.

8.   Discuss a film you have seen that does not portray women as victims (you might consider films starring Mae West or Katherine Hepburn). Compare the effect of viewing a film like this with a film that portrays women as victims.

THE UNITED NATIONS DECLARATION ON THE RIGHTS OF WOMEN

The United Nations Declaration on the Rights of Women was adopted November 7, 1967. What follows are excerpts from that declaration.

Article 1—Discrimination against women, denying or limiting as it does their equality of rights with men, is fundamentally unjust and constitutes an offence against human dignity.

Article 2—All appropriate measures shall be taken to abolish existing laws, customs, regulations and practices which are discriminatory against women, and to establish adequate legal protection for equal rights of men and women. . . .

Article 3—All appropriate measures shall be taken to educate public opinion and to direct national aspirations towards the eradication of prejudice and the abolition of customary and all other practices which are based on the idea of the inferiority of women.

Article 4—All appropriate measures shall be taken to ensure to women on equal terms with men, without any discrimination:

(a) The right to vote in all elections and be eligible for election to all publicly elected bodies;

(b) The right to vote in all public referenda;

(c) The right to hold public office and to exercise all public functions. Such rights shall be guaranteed by legislation.

Article 5—Women shall have the same rights as men to acquire, change or retain their nationality. Marriage to an alien shall not automatically affect the nationality of the wife either by rendering her stateless or by forcing upon her the nationality of her husband.

Article 6—1. Without prejudice to the safeguarding of the unity and the harmony of the family, which remains the basic unit of any society, all appropriate measures, particularly legislative measures, shall be taken to ensure to women, married or unmarried, equal rights with men in the field of civil law. . . .

2. All appropriate measures shall be taken to ensure the principle of equality of status of the husband and wife, and in particular:

(a) Women shall have the same right as men as to free choice of a spouse and to enter into marriage rights with men during marriage and at its dissolution. In all cases the interest of the children shall be paramount. . . .

(c) Parents shall have equal rights and duties in matters relating to their children. In all cases the interest of the children shall be paramount.

3. Child marriage and the betrothal of young girls before puberty shall be prohibited, and effective action, including legislation, shall be taken to specify a minimum age for marriage and to make the registration of marriages in an official registry compulsory.

Article 7—All provisions of penal codes which constitute discrimination against women shall be repealed.

Article 8—All appropriate measures, including legislation, shall be taken to combat all forms of traffic in women and exploitation of prostitution of women.

Article 9—All appropriate measures shall be taken to ensure to girls and women, married or unmarried, equal rights with men in education at all levels. . . .

Article 10—1. All appropriate measures shall be taken to ensure to women, married or unmarried, equal rights with men in the field of economic and social life. . . .

2. In order to prevent discrimination against women on account of marriage or maternity and to ensure their effective right to work, measures shall be taken to prevent their dismissal in the event of marriage or maternity and to provide paid maternity leave, with the guarantee of returning to former employment, and to provide the necessary social services, including child-care facilities.

3. Measures taken to protect women in certain types of work, for reasons inherent in their physical nature, shall not be regarded as discriminatory.

Article 11—1. The principle of equality of rights of men and women demands implementation in all States in accordance with the principles of the Charter of the United Nations and of the Universal Declarations of Human Rights.

2. Governments, non-governmental organizations and individuals are urged, therefore, to do all in their power to promote the implementation of the principles contained in this Declaration.

DISCUSSION QUESTIONS

1. Article 3 of the United Nations Declaration on the Rights of Women states, "All appropriate measures shall be taken to educate public opinion and to direct national aspirations towards the eradication of prejudice and the abolition of customary and all other practices which are based on the idea of the inferiority of women." How important is this article relative to the others? What is the best way to satisfy Article 3? Do you think that our national aspirations are directed toward the eradication of prejudice against women? Explain.

2. What items in the excerpts from the United Nations Declaration on the Rights of Women protect women from violence in intimate relationships? What items might be added to the excerpted selections to provide (further) protection for women from violence in intimate relationships?

3. Critically comment on Article 10, item 3: "Measures taken to protect women in certain types of work, for reasons inherent in their physical nature, shall not be regarded as discriminatory."

4. How might Plato, Aristotle, John Stuart Mill, and Simone de Beauvoir (see chapter 3) respectively respond to Article 1? Compare your own view with theirs.

5. Many cultures have customs that are regarded by some as discriminatory against women. Article 2 states, "All appropriate measures should be taken to abolish these customs." Would a cultural relativist agree with this? Do you? Why or why not?

6. Is the United Nations Declaration on the Rights of Women respectful to the rights of men? Does it conflict with the rights of men in any way?

7. Imagine that you are Steven Goldberg and have just read the United Nations Declaration on the Rights of Women. What is your response to it? Which items do you find agreeable? Which, if any, do you find objectionable? Explain, and respond to Goldberg's objections.

5.4   ARE GLOBAL HUMAN RIGHTS FOR ALL POSSIBLE?

CLAUDE AKE

THE AFRICAN CONTEXT OF HUMAN RIGHTS

C laude Ake argues that the Western notion of human rights is not very interesting in the context of African realities. The Western notion of rights such as that found in the U.S. Bill of Rights (see p. 901) lacks concreteness. "It ascribes abstract rights to abstract beings," says Ake.

Nevertheless, argues Ake, more emphasis is needed on human rights in Africa. These rights will be collective rights grounded in socialism, rather than individual rights grounded in "procedural liberalism" like those found in the Bill of Rights. Collective rights are more useful to the hungry and the powerless than the "unrealizable rights" of Western nations. What good is the right of free speech when one is the subject of a fascist government and suffering from hunger and poverty?

Claude Ake (1939–96) was a Nigerian political scientist. He received his Ph.D. from Columbia University in 1966 and then was appointed to an assistant professorship at Columbia. He held positions at the University of Nairobi and the University of Dar es Salaam, and was dean of the faculty of social sciences at the University of Port Harcourt in Nigeria. He was also founder and director of the Centre for Advanced Social Sciences, which is located in Port Harcourt. He died in a plane crash near Lagos, the capital of Nigeria. Ake was the author of many books, including *Theory of Political Integration* (1967), *Revolutionary Pressures in Africa* (1978), *Social Science as Imperialism* (1979), *Political Economy of Africa* (1981), *New World Order* (1992), *The Democratization of Disempowerment in Africa* (1994), *Is Africa Democratizing?* (1996), *Marginalization of Africa* (1996), *Democracy and Development in Africa* (1997), and *The Feasibility of Democracy in Africa* (2000). The following article, "The African Context of Human Rights," first appeared in *Africa Today* in 1987.

Nobody can accuse Africa of taking human rights seriously. In a world which sees concern for human rights as a mark of civilized sensitivity, this indifference has given Africa a bad name. It is not unlikely that many consider it symptomatic of the rawness of life which has always been associated with Africa. I am in no position to say with any confidence why Africa has not taken much interest in human rights but I see good reasons why she should not have done so.

Before going into these reasons let us be clear what we are talking about. The idea of human rights is quite simple. It is that human beings have certain rights simply by virtue of being human. These rights are a necessary condition for the good life. Because of their singular importance, individuals are entitled to, indeed, required to claim them and society is enjoined to allow them. Otherwise, the quality of life is seriously compromised.

The idea of human rights, or legal rights in general, presupposes a society which is atomized and individualistic, a society of endemic conflict. It presupposes a society of people conscious of their separateness and their particular interests and anxious to realize them. The legal right is a claim which the individual may make against other members of society, and simultaneously an obligation on the part of society to uphold this claim.

The values implicit in all this are clearly alien to those of our traditional societies. We put less emphasis on the individual and more on the collectivity, we do not allow that the individual has any claims which may override that of the society. We assume harmony, not divergence of interests, competition and conflict; we are more inclined to think of our obligations to other members of our society rather than our claims against them.

The Western notion of human rights stresses rights which are not very interesting in the context of African realities. There is much concern with the right to peaceful assembly, free speech and thought, fair trial, etc. The appeal of these rights is sociologically specific. They appeal to people with a full stomach who can now afford to pursue the more esoteric aspects of self-fulfillment. The vast majority of our people are not in this position. They are facing the struggle for existence in its brutal immediacy. Theirs is a totally consuming struggle. They have little or no time for reflection and hardly any use for free speech. They have little interest in choice for there is no choice in ignorance. There is no freedom for hungry people, or those eternally oppressed by disease. It is no wonder that the idea of human rights has tended to sound hollow in the African context.

The Western notion of human rights lacks concreteness. It ascribes abstract rights to abstract beings. There is not enough concern for the historical conditions in which human rights can actually be realized. As it turns out, only a few people are in a position to exercise the rights which society allows. The few who have the resources to exercise these rights do not need a bill of rights. Their power secures them. The many who do not have the resources to exercise their

rights are not helped any by the existence of these rights. Their powerlessness dooms them.

The idea of human rights really came into its own as a tool for opposing democracy. The French Revolution had brought home forcefully to everyone the paradox of democracy, namely, that its two central values, liberty and equality, come into conflict at critical points. There is no democracy where there is no liberty for self-expression or choice. At the same time there is no democracy where there is no equality, for inequality reduces human relations to subordination and domination. The French Revolution and Jean-Jacques Rousseau revealed rather dramatically the paradoxical relation between these two central values of democracy by leaning heavily towards equality. They gave Europe a taste of what it would be like to take the idea of equality and the correlative idea of popular sovereignty seriously.

Bourgeois Europe was horrified. The idea of a popular sovereign insisting on equality and having unlimited power over every aspect of social life was unacceptable. For such power was a threat to the institution of private property as well as the conditions of accumulation. So they began to emphasize liberty rather than the collectivity. This emphasis was also a way of rejecting democracy in its pure form as popular sovereignty. That was the point of stressing the individual and his rights and holding that certain rights are inalienable. That was the point of holding that the individual could successfully sustain certain claims and certain immunities against the wishes of the sovereign or even the rest of society. It is ironical that all this is conveniently forgotten today and liberal democrats can pass as the veritable defenders of democracy.

CHANGING STATUS OF HUMAN RIGHTS IN AFRICA

Africa is at last beginning to take interest in human rights. For one thing, the Western conception of human rights has evolved in ways which have made it more relevant to the African experience, although its relevance still remains ambiguous. Because human rights is such an important part of the political ideology of the West, it was bound to register in Africa eventually. Human rights record is beginning to feature in Western decisions of how to relate to the countries and leaders of Africa. Western decisions on this score have been made with such cynical inconsistency that one wonders whether human rights record really matters to them at all. However, our leaders ever so eager to please are obliged to assume that it matters and to adjust their behavior accordingly. Also the authoritarian capitalism of Africa is under some pressure to be more liberal and thereby create political conditions more conductive to capitalist efficiency.

If these are the reasons why Africa is beginning to take more interest in human rights, they are by no means the reason why she ought to do so. The way I see it is that we ought to be interested in human rights because it will help us to combat social forces which threaten to send us back to barbarism. Because it will aid our struggle for the social transformation which we need to survive and to flourish. To appreciate this let us look at the historical conditions of contemporary Africa.

I hope we can all agree that for now, the most salient aspect of these conditions is the crisis. It has been with us for so long we might well talk of the permanent crisis. No one seems to know for sure what its character is but we know its devastating effects only too well. We Africans have never had it so bad. The tragic consequences of our development strategies have finally come home to us. Always oppressed by poverty and deprivation, our lives become harsher still with each passing day as real incomes continue to decline. We watch helplessly while millions of our people are threatened by famine and look pitifully to the rest of the world to feed us. Our social and political institutions are disintegrating under pressure from our flagging morale, our dwindling resources and the intense struggle to control them. What is the problem? I am not sure. But I am convinced that we are not dealing simply or even primarily with an economic phenomenon. There is a political dimension to it which is so critical, it may well be the most decisive factor.

This is the problem of democracy or the problem of political repression. A long time ago our leaders opted for political repression. Having abandoned democracy for repression, our leaders are delinked from our people. Operating in a vacuum, they proclaim their incarnation of the popular will, hear echoes of their own voices, and reassured, pursue with zeal, policies which have

nothing to do with the aspirations of our people and which cannot, therefore, mobilize them. As their alienation from the people increases, they rely more and more on force and become even more alienated.

CONSEQUENCES OF THE PROBLEM OF DEMOCRACY

The consequences of this are disastrous. In the first place it means that there is no development. Political repression ensures that the ordinary people of Africa who are the object of development remain silent, so that in the end nobody really speaks for development and it never comes alive in practice. Development cannot be achieved by proxy. A people develops itself or not at all. And it can develop itself only through its commitment and its energy. That is where democracy comes in. Self-reliance is not possible unless the society is thoroughly democratic, unless the people are the end and not just the means of development. Development occurs, in so far as it amounts to the pursuit of objectives set by the people themselves in their own interest and pursued by means of their own resources.

Another consequence of repression is the brutalization of our people. Look around you. The willful brutalization of people occurring among us is appalling. Human life is taken lightly, especially if it is that of the underprivileged. All manner of inhuman treatment is meted out for minor offenses and sometimes for no offenses at all. Ordinary people are terrorized daily by wanton display of state power and its instruments of violence. Our prison conditions are guaranteed to traumatize. The only consensus we can mobilize is passive conformity arising from fear and resignation. As we continue to stagnate this gets worse.

Yet another disaster threatens us. I am referring to fascism. In all probability this is something which nobody wants. But we might get it anyway because circumstances are moving steadily in that direction. All the ingredients of fascism are present now in most parts of Africa: a political class which has failed even by its own standards, and which is now acutely conscious of its humiliation and baffled by a world it cannot control; a people who have little if any hope or sense of self-worth yearning for redeemers; a milieu of anomie; a conservative leadership pitted against a rising popular radicalism and poised to take cover in defensive radicalism. That is what it takes and it is there in plenty. If Africa succumbs it will be terrible—fascism has always been in all its historical manifestations.

It seems to me that for many African countries the specter of fascism is the most urgent and the most serious danger today. Unless we contain it effectively and within a very short time, then we are in a great deal of trouble.

If this analysis is correct, then our present agenda must be the task of preventing the rise of fascism. To have a chance of succeeding, this task requires a broad coalition of radicals, populists, liberals and even humane conservatives. That is, a coalition of all those who value democracy not in the procedural liberal sense but in the concrete socialist sense. This is where the idea of human rights comes in. It is easily the best ideological framework for such a coalition.

An African Conception of Human Rights

We have now seen the relevance of human rights in the African context. But on a level of generality which does not tell us very much and so does not really settle the question of the applicability of the Western concept of human rights. I do not see how we can mobilize the African masses or the intelligentsia against fascism or whatever by accepting uncritically the Western notion of human rights. We have to domesticate it, re-create it in the light of African conditions. Let me indicate very briefly how these conditions redefine the idea of human rights.

First, we have to understand that the idea of legal rights presupposes social atomization and individualism, and a conflict model of society for which legal rights are the necessary mediation. However, in most of Africa, the extent of social atomization is very limited mainly because of the limited penetration of capitalism and commodity relations. Many people are still locked into natural economies and have a sense of belonging to an organic whole, be it a family, a clan, a lineage or an ethnic group. The phenomenon of the legal subject, the largely autonomous individual conceived as a bundle of rights which are asserted against all comers, has not really developed much especially outside the urban areas.

These are the conditions which explain the forms of consciousness which we insist on misunderstanding. For instance, ethnic consciousness and ethnic identity. It is the necessary consciousness associated with non-atomized social structures and mechanical solidarity. Ethnic consciousness will be with us as long as these structural features remain, no matter how we condemn it or try to engineer it out of existence.

All this means that abstract legal rights attributed to individuals will not make much sense for most of our people; neither will they be relevant to their consciousness and living conditions. It is necessary to extend the idea of human rights to include collective human rights for corporate social groups such as the family, the lineage, the ethnic group. Our people still think largely in terms of collective rights and express their commitment to it constantly in their behavior. This disposition underlies the zeal for community development and the enormous sacrifices which poor people readily make for it. It underlies the so-called tribalist voting pattern of our people, the willingness of the poor villager to believe that the minister from his village somehow represents his share of the national cake, our traditional land tenure systems, the high incidence of cooperative labor and relations of production in the rural areas. These forms of consciousness remain very important features of our lives. If the idea of human rights is to make any sense at all in the African context, it has to incorporate them in a concept of communal human rights.

For reasons which need not detain us here, some of the rights important in the West are of no interest and no value to most Africans. For instance, freedom of speech and freedom of the press do not mean much for a largely illiterate rural community completely absorbed in the daily rigors of the struggle for survival.

African conditions shift the emphasis to a different kind of rights. Rights which can mean something for poor people fighting to survive and burdened by ignorance, poverty and disease, rights which can mean something for women who are cruelly used. Rights which can mean something for the youth whose future we render more improbable every day. If a bill of rights is to make any sense, it must include among others, a right to work and to a living wage, a right to shelter, to health, to education. That is the least we can strive for if we are ever going to have a society which realizes basic human needs.

Finally, in the African context, human rights have to be much more than the political correlate of commodity fetishism which is what they are in the Western tradition. In that tradition the rights are not only abstract, they are also ascribed to abstract persons. The rights are ascribed to the human being from whom all specific determinations have been abstracted: the rights have no content just as individuals who enjoy them have no determination and so do not really exist.

All these problems which usually lurk beneath the surface appear in clear relief when we confront them with empirical reality. Granted, I have the freedom of speech. But where is this freedom, this right? I cannot read, I cannot write. I am so busy trying to survive I have no time to reflect. I am so poor I am constantly at the mercy of others. So where is this right and what is it really? Granted, I have the right to seek public office. That is all very well. But how do I realize this right? I am a full-time public servant who cannot find the time or the necessary resources to put up the organization required to win office. If I take leave from my work, I cannot hold out for more than one month without a salary. I have no money to travel about and meet the voters, even to pay the registration fees for my candidature. If I am not in a position to realize this right, then what is the point of saying that I have it? Do I really have it?

In Africa liberal rights make less sense even as ideological representations. If rights are to be meaningful in the context of a people struggling to stay afloat under very adverse economic and political conditions, they have to be concrete. Concrete in the sense that their practical import is visible and relevant to the conditions of existence of the people to whom they apply. And most importantly, concrete in the sense that they can be realized by their beneficiaries.

To be sure, there are rights which are realizable and there are people in Africa who effectively realize their rights. However, the people who are in a position to realize their rights are very few. They are able to realize their rights by virtue of their wealth and power. The litmus test for rights is those who need protection. Unfortunately these are precisely the people who are in no position to enjoy rights. Clearly, that will not do in African conditions. People are not going to struggle for formalities and esoteric ideas which will not change their lives.

Therefore, a real need arises, namely, to put more emphasis on the realization of human rights. How is this to be? Not in the way we usually approach such matters: by giving more unrealizable rights to the powerless and by begging the powerful to make concessions to them in the name of enlightened self-interest, justice and humanity. That approach will fail us always. Rights, especially those that have any real significance for our lives, are usually taken, not given—with the cooperation of those in power if possible, but without it if necessary. That is the way it was for other peoples and that is the way it is going to be in Africa.

The realization of rights is best guaranteed by the power of those who enjoy the rights. Following this, what is needed is the empowerment by whatever means, of the common people. This is not a matter of legislation, although legislation could help a little. It is rather a matter of redistributing economic and political power across the board. That means that it is in the final analysis a matter of political mobilization and struggle. And it will be a protracted and bitter struggle because those who are favored by the existing distribution of power will resist heartily.

CONCLUSION: HUMAN RIGHTS AND SOCIAL TRANSFORMATION

It is at this point that the ideal of human rights is fully articulated for it is now that we see its critical dialectical moment. Initially part of the ideological prop of liberal capitalism, the idea of human rights was a conservative force. It was meant to safeguard the interests of the men of property especially against the threatening egalitarianism of popular sovereignty. It was not of course presented as a tool of special interests but a universal value good for humanity. That went down well and it has been able to serve those who propagated it behind this mystification.

But ideas have their own dynamics which cannot easily be controlled by the people who brought them into being. In the case of human rights, its dynamics soon trapped it in a contradiction somewhat to the dismay of its protagonists. Fashioned as a tool against democracy, the idea became an important source of legitimation for those seeking the expansion of democracy. But in Europe, this contradiction never fully matured. An agile and accommodating political class and unprecedented affluence saw to that.

In Africa, prevailing objective conditions will press matters much further, particularly the question of empowerment. In all probability, the empowerment of people will become the primary issue. Once this happens, the social contradictions will be immensely sharpened and the idea of human rights will become an asset of great value to radical social transformation. I cannot help thinking that Africa is where the critical issues in human rights will be fought out and where the idea will finally be consummated or betrayed.

DISCUSSION QUESTIONS

1. Why does Ake think that rights such as those found in the U.S. Bill of Rights are useless to the disadvantaged people of Africa? Do you agree with him? Take a look at the U.S. Bill of Rights (see p. 901), and identify the potentially useful and useless rights.

2. What is the difference between individual rights and collective rights? Give examples of each. Which rights are more important, and why?

3. Do you think that collective rights can be grounded in what Ake calls "procedural liberalism"? Why or why not?

4. Ake says that the Western notion of human rights is not very interesting in the context of African realities. Does the U.S. Bill of Rights reflect the realities of America today? Defend your view.

5. What is the connection between human rights and social transformation for Ake? Do you agree with him? Defend your view.

Hotel Rwanda
[Gr. Brit./It./S. Africa] 2 hrs., 2 min.
Directed by Terry George

*I*n the mid-1990s, hundreds of thousands of people were executed in Rwanda, a country in east central Africa with a population of about 5 million. While the atrocities were known to the rest of the world as they were occuring, no foreign powers intervened to stop the genocide. The only outside presence were 300 United Nations "peacekeepers," who were instructed not to use their weapons. In the midst of this devastating event, one man managed to rescue 1,268 persons from the genocide.

Paul Rusesabagina (Don Cheadle) is the manager of the Hotel des Mille Collines in Kigali, the capital of Rwanda. This Belgian luxury hotel caters to a wealthy international clientele, and Paul is instrumental in maintaining the hotel's good reputation. He is especially adept at pampering important clients, which include government and military persons. Paul contends that maintaining good relationships with his powerful guests is vital because one day he may need to ask for favors to protect the lives of his family.

As Paul performs his duties, Hutu Power Radio broadcasts messages about ethnic cleansing: "When people ask me, good listeners, why do I hate all the Tutsi, I say, 'Read our history.' The Tutsi were collaborators for the Belgian colonists. They stole our Hutu land, they whipped us. Now they have come back, these Tutsi rebels. They are cockroaches. They are murderers. Rwanda is our Hutu land. We are the majority. They are a minority of traitors and invaders. We will squash the infestation. We will wipe out the RPF rebels." Paul, a Hutu who is married to Tatiana (Sophie Okonedo), a Tutsi, seems oblivious to these hateful announcements, believing that they are empty threats. However, the situation changes quickly for the worse after the Rwandan president's plane is shot down.

Paul sees his neighbor, a Tutsi, being beaten and taken away by the Hutu militia, the Interhamwe. Paul refuses to intervene, telling his wife that he will use his accumulated influence only to help his family. When his family and friends are threatened by the Hutu militia, he bribes the militia to spare their lives and shelters his family at the hotel. But others also find their way to the hotel seeking asylum and protection, including many Rwandan orphans. When Paul learns that Western nations will evacuate all of the non-Rwandans but will not rescue the African Rwandan refugees, he decides to shelter and protect them himself, turning the hotel into a refugee camp. He encourages the refugees to telephone friends and family in other nations and plead for international assistance.

Soon, however, the safety of the hotel occupants is jeopardized. Fortunately, a deal is struck with the Tutsi rebels and the Hutu militia allowing the refugees from the hotel to leave for a safe zone behind Tutsi rebel lines. All of the refugees are then transported to the safe zone by the UN peacekeepers.

DISCUSSION QUESTIONS

1. Does the case of the Rwandan genocide reveal problems for the establishment of global human rights? If so, what are they? If not, why not?

2. Why do you think the West did not intervene in the Rwandan genocide? Should the West have intervened? Why or why not?

3. When Tatiana asks her husband to help the neighbor who has been seized by the Hutu militia, Paul says, "He is not family. Family is all that matters." Paul tells Tatiana that he has not saved up favors at the hotel to expend them on anyone but his family. Would you, unlike Paul, have gone to the aid of your neighbor? Why or why not? What makes Paul change his mind about helping others?

4. Jack Daglish (Joaquim Phoenix) is a reporter sent to cover the story of Rwanda's agreement to make peace with the Tutsi rebels forces, and Benedict (Mothusi Magano) is an expert on the Belgian colonization of Rwanda. Consider their conversation:

    JACK   "So, what is the actual difference between a Hutu and a Tutsi?"

    BENEDICT   "According to the Belgian colonists, the Tutsis are taller and more elegant. It was the Belgians that created the division."

    JACK   "How?"

    BENEDICT   "They picked people, those with thinner noses, lighter skin. They used to measure the width of people's noses. The Belgians used the Tutsis to run the country. Then when they left, they left the power to the Hutus, and of course the Hutus took revenge on the elite Tutsis for years of repression."

    Given that Belgian colonization created the division between Tutsi and Hutu, and facilitated Tutsi repression of the Hutus, one might argue that the Belgians are at least in some way morally responsible for the Rwandan genocide. Do you agree? Do you think Belgium had more moral responsibility to help to alleviate the human rights atrocities in Rwanda than other countries around the world? Why or why not?

5. A reporter tells Colonel Oliver (Nick Nolte), commander of the UN forces in Rwanda, that "we have heard reports of reprisal massacres" and asks him, "Will the UN intervene to stop the bloodshed?"

Colonel Oliver responds, "We're here as peacekeepers, not as peacemakers. My orders are not to intervene." What is the difference between a "peacemaker" and "peacekeeper"? How is it possible to keep the peace while in the midst of genocide, a situation in which there is no peace? Should global human rights always include the right to rescue persons from unjustified execution if one has the means available to do so? Why or why not?

6.   Paul looks on as Jack reviews video footage of massacres occurring a half mile from the hotel. Later, Jack and Paul talk about what happened:

JACK   "Sorry about earlier. If I'd known you were in there I, I would have . . ."

PAUL   "I am glad that you have shot this footage and that the world will see it. It is the only way we have a chance that people might intervene."

JACK   "Yeah, and if no one intervenes, is it still a good thing to show?"

PAUL   "How can they not intervene when they witness such atrocities?"

JACK   "I think if people see this footage they'll say 'Oh, my God, that's horrible,' and then go on eating their dinners."

Is Jack right? Will people who see news footage of ethnic cleansing simply go on eating their dinners? Or is Paul right, namely, that it is impossible not to intervene when one sees such atrocities? Is news footage the most effective way to encourage international intervention?

7.   When additional UN troops move in, Paul thinks they have come to support the small contingent of occupying UN troops and the refugees. However, Colonel Oliver has a different story to tell Paul:

PAUL   "Congratulations, Colonel. You have performed a minor miracle . . ."

COLONEL   "You should spit in my face."

PAUL   "Excuse me, Colonel?"

COLONEL   "You're dirt. We think you're dirt Paul."

PAUL   "Who is 'we'?"

COLONEL   "The West, all the superpowers, everything you believe in, Paul. They think you're dirt, they think you're dung. You're worthless."

PAUL   "I'm afraid I don't understand what you are saying, sir."

COLONEL   "Come on, don't bullshit me, Paul. You're the smartest man here. You got them all eating out of your hands. You could own this freakin' hotel, except for one thing—you're black. You're not even a nigger. You're an African. They're not gonna stay Paul. They're not gonna stop this slaughter."

Was it right for the troops to rescue only non-Rwandans? Why do you think the troops were ordered to aid only non-Rwandans? What role, if any, did racism play in this decision? Imagine a similar situation occurring in Sweden. Do you think the troops would have been ordered to leave behind Swedish orphans? What kind of difficulties do situations like this one highlight in terms of attempts to promote global human rights? Are they insurmountable?

8. After learning that the troops are not going to rescue Rwandans, Paul relates the news to his wife:

   PAUL   "All the whites are leaving. They are being evacuated."

   TATIANA   "But, what about us?"

   PAUL   "We have been abandoned."

   TATIANA   "But the soldiers will stop the killers."

   PAUL   "Listen to me, Tatsi. Listen. I said all the whites are leaving—the French, the Italians, even the UN Belgian soldiers, all of them!"

   TATIANA   "Who is left?"

   PAUL   "I don't know. Colonel Oliver said he has 300 UN peacekeepers for the whole country. The most he can spare for the hotel are four men. And they are not allowed to shoot."

   Paul then says, "They told me I was one of them and I believed it. I have no history. I have no memory." What does he mean by this? Is he right?

9. Paul tells the priest who is leading a group of orphans to the vehicles that will be used to transport the non-Rwandans to safety to leave the orphans with him, saying, "These men are not here to help us." Should global human rights at minimum be collective rights directed toward the powerless, such as orphans? Discuss.

10. After the troops leave, Paul tells the other refugees, "There will be no rescue, no intervention for us. We can only save ourselves. Many of you know influential people abroad. You must call these people. . . . You must tell them what will happen to us. Say good-bye. But when you say good-bye, let them know that if they let go of that hand you will die. We must shame them into sending help. Most importantly, this cannot be a refugee camp. The Interhamwe [Hutu militia] believe that the Mille Collines is a four-star Sabena hotel. That is the only thing that is keeping us alive." Discuss this situation in which these refugees are compelled to shame others into sending help. Is this further evidence of Ake's claim that the Western notion of human rights is not very interesting in the context of African realities?

ABDULLAHI AHMED AN-NA'IM

ISLAM, ISLAMIC LAW, AND UNIVERSAL HUMAN RIGHTS

Abdullahi Ahmed An-Na'im argues that because the UN Universal Declaration of Human Rights (see p. 901) and the UN Charter were formed without much input from the peoples of Africa and Asia, it is understandable that there is a lack of awareness of and support for them in those continents. An-Na'im maintains that in order for human rights to be truly supported by the countries of Asia and Africa, human rights issues need to be formatted in ways that do not directly conflict with the particular religious and cultural views of these cultures.

In Islamic cultures, for example, there are deep divisions between men and women, and Muslims and non-Muslims. If human rights involve treating all people, regardless of their sex or religion, equally, then human rights policies for Islamic cultures must be defined in ways that respect both cultural and religious values, as well as issues of equality. Otherwise, they are functionally useless. An-Na'im suggests that Asian and African countries should not "scrap the present documents and start afresh" but rather should "supplement the existing standards and continue to develop them through the genuine participation of the widest possible range of cultural traditions."

Abdullahi Ahmed An-Na'im (1946–) is a scholar of Islam and human rights, and human rights in cross-cultural perspective. He was born in Sudan and studied at the University of Khartoum, though he left his native country in 1985 owing to the rise of Islamic fundamentalism. He was executive director of Africa Watch in Washington, DC, from 1993 until 1995, when he joined the faculty at Emory University. He is Charles Howard Candler Professor of Law at Emory University Law School, and director of the Religion and Human Rights Project and fellow of the Law and Religion Program at Emory University. He is the author of *Sudanese Criminal Law* (1985), *Toward an Islamic Reformation: Civil Liberties, Human Rights and International Law* (1990), *Human Rights in Cross-Cultural Perspectives* (1992), *Universal Rights, Local Remedies* (ed., 1999), *Cultural Transformation and Human Rights in Africa* (ed., 2002), *Islamic Family Law in a Changing World* (ed., 2002), *Human Rights Under African Constitutions* (ed., 2003). The following article, "Islam, Islamic Law and the Dilemma of Cultural Legitimacy for Universal Human Rights," is from *Asian Perpectives on Human Rights* (1990), edited by Claude E. Welch and Virginia Leary.

Although Islam is often discussed in the contexts of North Africa and the Middle East, in fact the majority of Muslims live outside this region. The clear majority of the Muslims of the world live in the Indian sub-continent. The Muslim population of Indonesia alone is equal to the combined Muslim population of Egypt and Iran, the largest countries of the so-called Muslim heartland of North Africa and the Middle East. In terms of percentage to the total population, Muslims constitute 97% of the total population of Pakistan, 82.9% of that of Bangladesh and 80% of that of Indonesia. While Muslims constitute slightly less than half the population of Malaysia, Islam is perceived as an important element of Malay ethnicity which receives special protection under the constitution. As we shall see, Pakistan has been struggling with the meaning and implications of its purported Islamic identity since independence. Bangladesh also appears to be heading in the same direction. It is therefore important to consider the

Islamic dimension of human rights policy and practice in South and Southeast Asia.

It is important to note that Islamic norms may be more influential at an informal, almost subconscious psychological level than they are at the official legal or policy level. One should not therefore underestimate the Islamic factor simply because the particular state is not constituted as an Islamic state, or because its legal system does not purport to comply with historical Islamic law, commonly known as Shari'a. Conversely, one should not overestimate the Islamic factor simply because the state and the legal system are publicly identified as such. This is particularly important from a human rights point of view where underlying social and political attitudes and values may defeat or frustrate the declared policy and formal legal principles.

This chapter is concerned with both the sociological as well as the legal and official impact of Islam on human rights. The chapter begins by explaining the paradox of declared commitment to human rights, on the one hand, and the low level of compliance with these standards in daily practice, on the other. It is my submission that this paradox can be understood in light of the competing claims of the universalism and relativism of human rights standards. It is my thesis that certain standards of human rights are frequently violated because they are not perceived to be culturally legitimate in the context of the particular country. To the extent that political regimes and other dominant social forces can explicitly or implicitly challenge the validity of certain human rights norms as alien or at least not specifically sanctioned by the primary values of the dominant indigenous culture, they can avoid the negative consequences of their violation.

Such analysis would seem to suggest the need for establishing cultural legitimacy for human rights standards in the context of the particular society. However, this enterprise raises another problem. If indigenous cultural values are to be asserted as a basis of human rights standards, we are likely to encounter "undesirable" aspects of the indigenous culture. In other words, while it may be useful to establish cultural legitimacy for human rights standards, certain elements of the indigenous culture may be antithetical to the human rights of some segments of the population. This chapter will illustrate the dilemma of cultural legitimacy for human rights in the Islamic tradition.

THE HUMAN RIGHTS PARADOX

1988 marked the fortieth anniversary of the Universal Declaration of Human Rights, which was adopted by the General Assembly of the United Nations on the 10th of December 1948. Several U.N. and regional human rights conventions have since been ratified as binding international treaties by scores of countries from all parts of the world. At the domestic level, many human rights receive strong endorsement in the constitutional and legal system of most countries of the world. Moreover, human rights issues are continuously covered by the news media as a supposedly important consideration in national and international politics.

Despite these formal commitments to human rights, and apparently strong concern with their violation, there is a mounting crisis in practical compliance with human rights standards throughout the world. Gross and consistent violations of human rights in many countries are recorded daily. Activist groups and nongovernmental organizations continue to charge almost every government in the world of involvement or complicity in violating one or more human right in its national and/or international policies.

This glaring disparity between apparent commitment in theory and poor compliance in practice is what may be called the paradox of human rights. On the one hand, the idea of human rights is so powerful that no government in the world today can afford to reject it openly. On the other hand, the most basic and fundamental human rights are being consistently violated in all parts of the world. It is therefore necessary to understand and resolve this paradox if human rights are to be respected and implemented in practice. As correctly stated by [C. Wilfred] Jenks [in *The World Beyond the Charter in Historical Perspective* (1969)]: The potentially tragic implication of this paradox is the ever-present danger that the denial of human rights may, as in the past, express, permit and promote a worship of the State no less fatal to peace than to freedom; by failure to make a reality of the Universal Declaration of Human Rights and United Nations Covenants of Human Rights we may leave mankind at the mercy of new absolutism which will engulf the world."

One obvious explanation of the dichotomy between the theory and practice of human rights is the cynical manipulation of a noble and enlightened concept by many governments and politicians in all countries of the world. It may therefore be said that this is merely the current manifestation of an ancient phenomenon in human affairs. However, without disputing the historical validity of this analysis, one can point to the other side of the coin as the concrete manifestation of another ancient phenomenon in human affairs, namely the capacity of people to assert and realize their rights and claims in the face of adversity and cynicism. From this perspective, what is therefore significant is not the cynical abuse of the human rights idea, but the fact that oppressive governments and ambitious politicians find expressing their support of human rights useful, if not necessary, for gaining popular support at home and legitimacy abroad. This tribute paid by vice to virtue is very significant and relevant to future efforts at bridging the gap between the theory and practice of human rights.

In order to hold governments to their declared commitment to human rights, it is essential to establish the principle that human rights violations are not matters within the exclusive domestic jurisdiction of any state in the world. Under traditional international law, national sovereignty was taken to include the right of each state to treat its own subjects in whatever manner it deemed fit. Consequently, it was perceived to be unwarranted interference in the internal affairs of a sovereign state for other states to object to or protest any action or policy of that state towards its own subjects. The Charter of the United Nations (UN) apparently endorsed these notions. Article 2.7 expressly stated that the Charter does not "authorize the United Nations to intervene in matters which are essentially within the domestic jurisdiction of any state or shall require the Members to submit such matters to settlement under the present Charter." Other authoritative statements of international law continue to emphasize the traditional definition of national sovereignty. For example, these notions feature prominently in the 1970 UN Declaration on Principles of International Law Concerning Friendly Relations and Cooperation among States in Accordance with the Charter of the United Nations.

However, Article 2.7 of the UN Charter stipulates that the principle of noninterference in matters essentially within the domestic jurisdiction of any state shall not apply to UN action with respect to threats to the peace, breaches of the peace and acts of aggression. It could be argued that serious and consistent violations of at least some fundamental human rights constitute a threat to international peace and security, and are therefore within this exception to the "essentially domestic jurisdiction" clause of the UN Charter. In other words, since serious and consistent violations of certain human rights constitute a threat to international peace and security, the UN can act against the offending state because the matter is beyond the "essentially domestic jurisdiction" of the state. It may also be possible to construe some of the language of the above cited 1970 UN Declaration on Friendly Relations as permitting international action in promoting and protecting at least some fundamental human rights.

Despite its problems, national sovereignty appears to be necessary for the exercise of the right of peoples to self-determination. In any case, it is too strongly entrenched to hope for its total repudiation in the foreseeable future. Nevertheless, it is imperative to overcome national sovereignty objections to international action for the protection and promotion of human rights without violating the legitimate scope of such sovereignty. "The renunciation of intervention [in the internal affairs of states] does not constitute a policy of nonintervention; it involves the development of some form of *collective intervention.*"

In order to support this position, it is necessary to repudiate any plausible argument which claims that action in support of human rights violates the national sovereignty of the country. It has been argued, for example, that the established international standards are not consistent with the cultural traditions or philosophical and ideological perspectives of the given country. It is not enough to say that this argument may be used as a pretext for violating human rights because such manipulation would not be viable if there is no validity to the argument itself. In other words, this argument is useful as a pretext precisely because it has some validity which makes the excuse plausible. It is therefore incumbent upon human rights advocates to address the element of truth in this argument in order to prevent its cynical abuse in the future.

The Legitimacy Dilemma

If we take the UN Charter and the Universal Declaration of Human Rights as the starting point of the modern movement for the promotion and protection of human rights, we will find it true that the majority of the peoples of Africa and Asia had little opportunity for direct contribution to the formulation of these basic documents. Since the majority of the peoples of these two continents were still suffering from the denial of their collective human right to self-determination because of colonial rule and foreign domination at the time, they were unable to participate in the drafting and adoption processes. It is true that some of the representatives of the older, mainly Western, nations were sensitive to the cultural traditions of the unrepresented peoples, but that could have hardly been a sufficient substitute for direct representation.

Many more African and Asian countries subsequently achieved formal independence and were able to participate in the formulation of international human rights instruments. By ratifying the UN Charter and subscribing to the specialized international instruments which incorporated and elaborated upon the Universal Declaration of Human Rights, the emerging countries of Africa and Asia were deemed bound by those earlier documents in addition to the subsequent instruments in which they participated from the start. Thus, the vast majority of the countries of Africa and Asia can be seen as parties to the process by which international human rights standards are determined and formulated. Nevertheless, this official and formal participation does not seem to have achieved the desired result of legitimizing international human rights standards in the cultural traditions of these peoples. This failure is clearly illustrated, in my view, by the lack of sufficient popular awareness of and support for these standards among the majority of the population of the countries of Africa and Asia. Given this lack of awareness and support for the international standards, it is not surprising that governments and other actors are able to evade the negative consequences of their massive and gross violations of human rights throughout Africa and Asia.

It is my submission that formal participation in the formulation and implementation processes by the elites of African and Asian countries will never achieve practical respect and protection for human rights in those regions unless that participation reflects the genuine consensus of the population of those countries. I would further suggest that the peoples of these regions have not had the chance to develop such consensus by reexamining their own cultural traditions in terms of universal and international human rights. It seems that the elites of these countries have come to the international fora where human rights standards were determined and formulated without a clear mandate from their own peoples.

As an advocate of international human rights, I am not suggesting that the international community should scrap the present documents and start afresh. This would be an impracticable and dangerous course of action because we may never recover what would be lost through the repudiation of the present instruments and structures. What I am suggesting is that we should supplement the existing standards and continue to develop them through the genuine participation of the widest possible range of cultural traditions. In furtherance of this approach, it is incumbent on the advocates of human rights to work for legitimizing universal standards of human rights within their own traditions.

However, this approach presents us with the other horn of the dilemma. Almost every existing cultural tradition (including philosophical or ideological positions) in the world has some problems with respect to the full range of fundamental human rights. Generally speaking, for example, whereas the liberal tradition(s) of the West have difficulties in accepting economic, social and cultural rights and in conceiving of collective rights such as a right to development, the Marxist tradition has similar difficulties with respect to civil and political rights. More specifically, prevailing notions of freedom of speech under the Constitution of the United States, for instance, may protect forms of speech and expression which advocate racial hatred in violation of the international standards set by the Covenant for the Elimination of All Forms of Racial Discrimination of 1965.

The main difficulty in working to establish universal standards across cultural boundaries is the fact that each tradition has its own internal frame of reference and derives the validity of its precepts and norms from its own sources. When a cultural tradition relates to other traditions and perspectives, it is likely to do so in a negative and perhaps even hostile and antagonistic way. In order to claim the loyalty and conformity of its own members, a tradition would normally assert its own superiority over, and tend to dehumanize the adherents of, other traditions. This tendency would clearly undermine efforts to accord members of other traditions equality in status and rights, even if they happen to live within the political boundaries of the same country.

Nevertheless, I believe that all the major cultural traditions adhere to the common normative principle that one should treat other people as he or she wishes to be treated by them. This golden rule, which may be called the principle of reciprocity, is shared by all the major traditions of the world. Moreover, the moral and logical force of this simple proposition can easily be appreciated by all human beings of whatever cultural tradition or philosophical persuasion. If construed in an enlightened manner so that the "other" includes all other human beings, this principle is capable of sustaining universal standards of human rights.

In accordance with this fundamental principle of reciprocity, I would take universal human rights to be those rights which I claim for myself, and must therefore concede to others. The practical implications of this fundamental principle would have to be negotiated through the political process to develop consensus around specific policies and concrete action on what the majority or other dominant segment of the population would accept for itself and would therefore have to concede to minorities and individuals. Although theoretical safeguards and structures may be devised to ensure the constitutional and human rights of all individuals and groups, the ultimate safeguard is the goodwill and sense of enlightened political expediency of the majority or other dominant segment of the population. Unless the majority or dominant segment of the population is persuaded to respect and promote the human rights of minorities and individuals, the whole society will drift into the politics of confrontation and subjugation rather than that of reconciliation and justice.

The Legitimacy Dilemma in the Muslim Context

When I consider Shari'a as the historical formulation of my own Islamic tradition I am immediately confronted with certain inadequacies in its conception of human rights as judged by the above stated principle of reciprocity and its supporting arguments. In particular, I am confronted by Shari'a's discrimination against Muslim women and non-Muslims and its restrictions on freedom of religion and belief. Unfortunately, most contemporary Muslim writings on the subject tend to provide a misleadingly glowing view of Shari'a on human rights without any reference to the above cited problematic aspects of Shari'a. Moreover, some of those Muslim authors who are willing to candidly state the various features of conflict and tension between Shari'a and current standards of human rights tend to take an intransigent position in favor of Shari'a without considering the prospects of its reconciliation with current standards of human rights.

It is true that Shari'a had introduced significant improvements in the status and rights of women as compared to its historical contemporaries between the seventh and nineteenth centuries A.D. Under Shari'a, Muslim women enjoy full and independent legal personality to own and dispose of property and conclude other contracts in their own right. They are also guaranteed specific shares in inheritance, and other rights in family law. However, Shari'a did not achieve complete legal equality between Muslim men and women. Whereas a man is entitled to marry up to four wives and divorce any of them at will, a woman is restricted to one husband and can only seek judicial divorce on very limited and strict grounds. Women receive only half a share of a man in inheritance, and less monetary compensation for criminal bodily harm (*diya*). Women are generally incompetent to testify in serious criminal cases. Where their testimony is accepted in civil cases, it takes two women to make a single witness. Other examples of inequality can be cited. In fact, the general rule of Shari'a is that men are the guardians of women, and as such have the license to discipline them to the extent of beating them "lightly" if they fear them to become unruly. Consequently, Shari'a holds that Muslim women may not hold any office involving exercising authority over Muslim men.

Similarly, Shari'a granted non-Muslim believers, mainly Christians and Jews who submit to Muslim sovereignty, the status of *dhimma*, whereby they are secured in person and property and permitted to practice their religion and regulate their private affairs in accordance with their own law and custom in exchange for payment of a special tax, known as *jiziya*. Those classified by Shari'a as unbelievers are not allowed to live within an Islamic state except with a special permit of safe conduct, known as *aman*, which defines their status and rights. If the residence of a *musta'min*, an unbeliever allowed to stay within an Islamic state under *aman*, extends beyond one year, some Shari'a jurists would allow him to assume the status of *dhimma*. However, neither *dhimma* nor *aman* would qualify a non-Muslim to full citizenship of an Islamic state or guarantee such a person complete equality with Muslim citizens. For example, Shari'a specifically requires that non-Muslims may never exercise authority over Muslims. Consequently, non-Muslims are denied any public office which would involve exercising such authority.

The third example of serious human rights problems with Shari'a indicated above is freedom of religion and belief. It is true that *dhimma* and possibly *aman* would guarantee a non-Muslim a measure of freedom of religion in that he would be free to practice his officially sanctioned religion. However, such freedom of religious practice is inhibited by the limitations imposed on non-Muslims in public life, including payment of *jiziya*, which is intended by Shari'a to be a humiliating tax.

Another serious limitation of freedom of religion and belief is the Shari'a law of apostasy, *ridda*, whereby a Muslim would be subject to the death penalty if he should repudiate his faith in Islam, whether or not in favor of another religion. Some modern Muslim writers have argued that apostasy should not be punishable by death. However, this progressive view has not yet been accepted by the majority of Muslims. Moreover, even if the death penalty is abolished, other serious consequences will remain, such as the possibility of other punishment, confiscation of the property of the apostate and the nullification of his or her marriage to a Muslim spouse. In contrast, non-Muslims, including Christians and Jews, are encouraged to embrace Islam. Whereas Muslims are supported by the State and community in their efforts to proselytize in order to convert non-Muslims to Islam, non-Muslims are positively prohibited from undertaking such activities.

All of the above features of discrimination against Muslim women and non-Muslims and restrictions on freedom of religion and belief are part of Shari'a to the present day. Those aspects of discrimination against Muslim women which fall within the scope of family law and inheritance are currently enforced throughout the Muslim world because Shari'a constitutes the personal law of Muslims even in those countries where it is not the formal legal system of the land. Discrimination against non-Muslims and the Shari'a law of apostasy are enforced in those countries where

Shari'a is the formal legal system. For example, Article 13 of the Constitution of the Islamic Republic of Iran expressly classifies Iranians in terms of their religious or sectarian belief. By the terms of this Article, Baha'is are not a recognized religious minority, and as such are not entitled even to the status of second class citizens under the principle of *dhimma* explained above. Moreover, as recently as January 1985, a 76-year-old man was executed for apostasy in the Sudan.

What is more significant for our present purposes, however, is the fact that all of these and other aspects of Shari'a are extremely influential in shaping Muslim attitudes and policies even where Shari'a is not the formal legal system. In other words, so long as these aspects of Shari'a are held by Muslim legislators, policy makers and executive officials to be part of their cultural tradition, we can only expect serious negative consequences for human rights in predominantly Muslim countries, regardless of whether or not Shari'a is the basis of the formal constitutional and legal system of the land. . . .

CONCLUSION: REVISED AGENDA FOR THE HUMAN RIGHTS MOVEMENT

Thus, if we are to bridge the gap between the theory and practice of human rights in the contemporary world, we must all be ready to shed or modify those preconceptions which seem to obstruct or frustrate the efficacy of international cooperation in the field of human rights. This would require a modification of the concept of national sovereignty in order to enhance the principle of international accountability for violating human rights. The international community must firmly establish, as a matter of international law and, as well, of practice, that violations of universal human rights are not matters of "essentially domestic jurisdiction." The legal framework for such action can easily be established under the UN Charter and existing international and regional human rights instruments. What may be lacking is the political will among states to relinquish their traditional national pride in favor of the international rule of law.

Another concept that needs to be modified is the cultural conception of the term "right." In the Western liberal tradition, rights are primarily entitlements or claims which the individual person has against the state. This conception has led many Western governments and human rights advocates to deny human rights status to claims which they deem to be too vague or not amenable to enforcement against the state, such as economic rights and collective rights to development. Non-Western cultural traditions, in contrast, not only conceive of such claims as human rights, they insist that they must be granted that status. Some of the human rights treaties and literature already reflect a broader conception of rights than originally envisaged by liberal theory. However, there is little evidence to show that this is more than a token concession by liberal governments. The developed countries of the world should not expect other peoples of the world, including the Muslim peoples, to examine and reevaluate their cultural and philosophical traditions in the interest of more genuine respect for and greater compliance with international standards of human rights *unless* they (the developed countries) are willing to examine and re-evaluate their own cultural traditions.

It is my submission that these and other related considerations must now be injected into human rights discourse at official, scholarly and popular levels of debate and action. It is not difficult, for example, to develop the appropriate formulations and implementation mechanisms and procedures for collective claims or entitlement as human rights which do not necessarily correspond to the established Western notion of "right." For this course of action to be useful, however, the existing human rights standards and mechanisms for their enforcement must be opened up for new ideas and influences. The process of definition, formulation and implementation of universal human rights must be genuinely universal and not merely Western in orientation and techniques.

In conclusion, the dilemma of cultural legitimacy must be resolved if the glaring disparity between the theory and practice of human rights is to be narrowed. To achieve this end, human rights advocates need to undertake a massive educational effort, drawing on all the religious and other normative resources of each community in support of universal human rights. They must build from the immediately local, through the national and regional levels, towards greater international cooperation in the promotion and protection of human rights. Greater emphasis must be placed on the role of grass-roots nongovernmental organizations and the role of indigenous mechanisms for enhancing the cultural legitimacy of human rights.

DISCUSSION QUESTIONS

1. An-Na'im suggests that human rights documents need to be formulated to fit the specific needs of communities; otherwise, they will not be considered legitimate in these communities. Look at the UN Universal Declaration of Human Rights (see p. 901). What, if anything, in this document can be changed and/or omitted without significant damage to international human rights?

2. Immanuel Kant's ideas (see chapter 4) were central in the formation of the United Nations. How do you think Kant would respond to An-Na'im's suggestion that human rights documents need to be formulated to fit the specific needs of communities? Explain.

3. Is An-Na'im a cultural relativist? Defend your position.

4. What do you think about An-Na'im's "legitimacy dilemma"? Do you agree that there is a dilemma? Why or why not?

5. With regard to human rights, what is the "principle of reciprocity"? Do you support such a principle? Defend your view.

CHARLOTTE BUNCH
WOMEN'S RIGHTS AS HUMAN RIGHTS

C harlotte Bunch argues that the human rights community should incorporate gender perspectives. Like Claude Ake, Abdullahi Ahmed An-Na'im, and Kenneth Inada (see p. 892), Bunch maintains that the Western conception of human rights is deeply flawed in that it fails to take sufficient account of women's rights.

Women around the world are subject to political oppression and various forms of violence based on their sex, and human rights policies marginalize these problems. Bunch argues that Western conceptions of human rights need to be transformed in order to recognize the particular rights of women. Women's rights, according to Bunch, tend to gravitate around socioeconomic rights, that is, rights centered on work, food, and shelter. She closes her article with some practical guidelines for transforming Western conceptions of rights.

Charlotte Bunch (1944–) is an American activist, author, and organizer of women's and human rights movements. Currently, she is a distinguished professor in the Department of Women's and Gender Studies at Rutgers University. She is also the founder and executive director of the Center for Women's Global Leadership. In 1999, she was awarded the Eleanor Roosevelt Award for Human Rights by President Clinton. Her books include *Class and Feminism: A Collection of Essays from the Furies* (1974), *Learning Our Way: Essays* (1983), *Passionate Politics: Feminist Theory in Action* (1987), *Gender Violence* (1992), and *Demanding Accountability: The Global Campaign and Vienna Tribunal for Women's Human Rights* (1994). The following article, "Women's Rights as Human Rights," first appeared in *Human Rights Quarterly* in 1990.

Significant numbers of the world's population are routinely subject to torture, starvation, terrorism, humiliation, mutilation and even murder simply because they are female. Crimes such as these against any group other than women would be recognized as a civil and political emergency as well as a gross violation of the victims' humanity. Yet, despite a clear record of deaths and demonstrable abuse, women's rights are not commonly classified as human rights. This is problematic both theoretically and practically, because it has grave consequences for the way society views and treats the fundamental issues of women's lives. This paper questions why women's rights and human rights are viewed as distinct, looks at the policy implications of this schism, and discusses different approaches to changing it.

Women's human rights are violated in a variety of ways. Of course, women sometimes suffer abuses such as political repression that are similar to abuses suffered by men. In these situations, female victims are often invisible, because the dominant image of the political actor in our world is male. However, many violations of women's human rights are distinctly connected to being female—that is, women are discriminated against and abused on the basis of gender. Women also experience sexual abuse in situations where their other human rights are being violated, as political prisoners or members of persecuted

ethnic groups, for example. In this paper I address those abuses in which gender is a primary or related factor because gender-related abuse has been most neglected and offers the greatest challenge to the field of human rights today.

The concept of human rights is one of the few moral visions ascribed to internationally. Although its scope is not universally agreed upon, it strikes deep chords of response among many. Promotion of human rights is a widely accepted goal and thus provides a useful framework for seeking redress of gender abuse. Further, it is one of the few concepts that speaks to the need for transnational activism and concern about the lives of people globally. The Universal Declaration of Human Rights, adopted in 1948, symbolizes this world vision and defines human rights broadly. While not much is said about women, Article 2 entitles all to "the rights and freedoms set forth in this Declaration without distinction of any kind, such as race, colour, sex, language, religion, political or other opinion, national or social origin, property, birth or other status." Eleanor Roosevelt and the Latin American women who fought for the inclusion of sex in the Declaration and for its passage clearly intended that it would address the problem of women's subordination.

Since 1948 the world community has continuously debated varying interpretations of human rights in response to global developments.

Little of this discussion, however, has addressed questions of gender, and only recently have significant challenges been made to a vision of human rights which excludes much of women's experiences. The concept of human rights, like all vibrant visions, is not static or the property of any one group; rather, its meaning expands as people reconceive of their needs and hopes in relation to it. In this spirit, feminists redefine human rights abuses to include the degradation and violation of women. The specific experiences of women must be added to traditional approaches to human rights in order to make women more visible and to transform the concept and practice of human rights in our culture so that it takes better account of women's lives.

In the next part of this article, I will explore both the importance and the difficulty of connecting women's rights to human rights, and then I will outline four basic approaches that have been used in the effort to make this connection.

Beyond Rhetoric: Political Implications

Few governments exhibit more than token commitment to women's equality as a basic human right in domestic or foreign policy. No government determines its policies toward other countries on the basis of their treatment of women, even when some aid and trade decisions are said to be based on a country's human rights record. Among nongovernmental organizations, women are rarely a priority, and Human Rights Day programs on 10 December seldom include discussion of issues like violence against women or reproductive rights. When it is suggested that governments and human rights organizations should respond to women's rights as concerns that deserve such attention, a number of excuses are offered for why this cannot be done. The responses tend to follow one or more of these lines: (1) sex discrimination is too trivial, or not as important, or will come after larger issues of survival that require more serious attention; (2) abuse of women, while regrettable, is a cultural, private, or individual issue and not a political matter requiring state action; (3) while appropriate for other action, women's rights are not human rights per se; or (4) when the abuse of women is recognized, it is considered inevitable or so pervasive that any consideration of it is futile or

will overwhelm other human rights questions. It is important to challenge these responses.

The narrow definition of human rights, recognized by many in the West as solely a matter of state violation of civil and political liberties, impedes consideration of women's rights. In the United States the concept has been further limited by some who have used it as a weapon in the cold war almost exclusively to challenge human rights abuses perpetrated in communist countries. Even then, many abuses that affected women, such as forced pregnancy in Romania, were ignored.

Some important aspects of women's rights do fit into a civil liberties framework, but much of the abuse against women is part of a larger socioeconomic web that entraps women, making them vulnerable to abuses which cannot be delineated as exclusively political or solely caused by states. The inclusion of "second generation" or socioeconomic human rights to food, shelter, and work—which are clearly delineated as part of the Universal Declaration of Human Rights—is vital to addressing women's concerns fully. Further, the assumption that states are not responsible for most violations of women's rights ignores the fact that such abuses, although committed perhaps by private citizens, are often condoned or even sanctioned by states. I will return to the question of state responsibility after responding to other instances of resistance to women's rights as human rights.

The most insidious myth about women's rights is that they are trivial or secondary to the concerns of life and death. Nothing could be farther from the truth: sexism kills. There is increasing documentation of the many ways in which being female is life-threatening. The following are a few examples:

- Before birth: Amniocentesis is used for sex selection leading to the abortion of more female fetuses at rates as high as 99 percent in Bombay, India; in China and India, the two most populous nations, more males than females are born even though natural birth ratios would produce more females.

- During childhood: The world Health Organization reports that in many countries girls are fed less, breast fed for shorter periods of time, taken to doctors less frequently, and die or are physically and mentally maimed by malnutrition at higher rates than boys.

- In adulthood: The denial of women's rights to control their bodies in reproduction threatens women's lives, especially where this is combined with poverty and poor health services. In Latin America, complications from illegal abortions are the leading cause of death for women between the ages of fifteen and thirty-nine.

Sex discrimination kills women daily. When combined with race, class, and other forms of oppression, it constitutes a deadly denial of women's right to life and liberty on a large scale throughout the world. The most pervasive violation of females is violence against women in all its manifestations, from wife battery, incest, and rape, to dowry deaths, genital mutilation, and female sexual slavery. These abuses occur in every country and are found in the home and in the workplace, on streets, on campuses, and in prisons and refugee camps. They cross class, race, age, and national lines; and at the same time the forms this violence takes often reinforce other oppressions such as racism, "able-bodyism," and imperialism. Case in point: in order to feed their families, poor women in brothels around U.S. military bases in places like the Philippines bear the burden of sexual, racial, and national imperialism in repeated and often brutal violation of their bodies.

Even a short review of random statistics reveals that the extent of violence against women globally is staggering:

- In the United States, battery is the leading cause of injury to adult women, and a rape is committed every six minutes.

- In Peru, 70 percent of all crimes reported to police involve women who are beaten by their partners; and in Lima (a city of seven million people), 168,970 rapes were reported in 1987 alone.

- In India, eight out of ten wives are victims of violence, either domestic battery, dowry-related abuse, or among the least fortunate, murder.

- In France, 95 percent of the victims of violence are women; 51 percent at the hands of a spouse or lover. Similar statistics from places as diverse as Bangladesh, Canada, Kenya, and Thailand demonstrate, that more than 50 percent of female homicides were committed by family members.

Where recorded, domestic battery figures range from 40 percent to 80 percent of women beaten, usually repeatedly, indicating that the home is the most dangerous place for women and frequently the site of cruelty and torture. As the Carol Stuart murder* in Boston demonstrated, sexist and racist attitudes in the United States often cover up the real threat to women; a woman is murdered in Massachusetts by a husband or lover every 22 days.

Such numbers do not reflect the full extent of the problem of violence against women, much of which remains hidden. Yet rather than receiving recognition as a major world conflict, this violence is accepted as normal or even dismissed as an individual or cultural matter. Georgina Ashworth notes that

> the greatest restriction of liberty, dignity and movement and at the same time, direct violation of the person, is the threat and realization of violence. . . . However, violence against the female sex, on a scale which far exceeds the list of Amnesty International victims, is tolerated publicly; indeed some acts of violation are not crimes in law, others are legitimized in custom or court opinion, and most are blamed on the victims themselves.

Violence against women is a touchstone that illustrates the limited concept of human rights and highlights the political nature of the abuse of women. As Lori Heise states: "This is not random violence. . . . [T]he risk factor is being female."

*On October 23, 1989, a pregnant white woman, Carol Stuart, was murdered in Boston. Her child, Christopher Stuart, who was delivered by C-section, died two weeks later. Carol's husband, Charles Stuart, who was also white and shot in the incident, survived and alleged that a black man with a raspy voice had shot him and his wife. William Bennett, a black man with a raspy voice and a long criminal record, was arrested for these crimes. Later, it was determined that Charles and his brother Matt were responsible for them. Charles had hoped to get away with the crimes by playing into racist attitudes in the Boston area. He committed suicide before the police were able to arrest him and charge him with murder. —Ed.

Victims are chosen because of their gender. The message is domination: stay in your place or be afraid. Contrary to the argument that such violence is only personal or cultural, it is profoundly political. It results from the structural relationships of power, domination, and privilege between men and women in society. Violence against women is central to maintaining those political relations at home, at work, and in all public spheres.

Failure to see the oppression of women as political also results in the exclusion of sex discrimination and violence against women from the human rights agenda. Female subordination runs so deep that it is still viewed as inevitable or natural, rather than seen as a politically constructed reality maintained by patriarchal interests, ideology, and institutions. But I do not believe that male violation of women is inevitable or natural. Such a belief requires a narrow and pessimistic view of men. If violence and domination are understood as a politically constructed reality, it is possible to imagine deconstructing that system and building more just interactions between the sexes.

The physical territory of this political struggle over what constitutes women's human rights is women's bodies. The importance of control over women can be seen in the intensity of resistance to laws and social changes that put control of women's bodies in women's hands: reproductive rights, freedom of sexuality whether heterosexual or lesbian, laws that criminalize rape in marriage, etc. Denial of reproductive rights and homophobia are also political means of maintaining control over women and perpetuating sex roles and thus have human rights implications. The physical abuse of women is a reminder of this territorial domination and is sometimes accompanied by other forms of human rights abuse such as slavery (forced prostitution), sexual terrorism (rape), imprisonment (confinement to the home), and torture (systematic battery). Some cases are extreme, such as the women in Thailand who died in a brothel fire because they were chained to their beds. Most situations are more ordinary like denying women decent educations or jobs, which leaves them prey to abusive marriages, exploitative work, and prostitution.

This raises once again the question of the state's responsibility for protecting women's human rights. Feminists have shown how the distinction between private and public abuse is a dichotomy often used to justify female subordination in the home. Governments regulate many matters in the family and individual spheres. For example, human rights activists pressure states to prevent slavery or racial discrimination and segregation even when these are conducted by nongovernmental forces in private or proclaimed as cultural traditions as they have been in both the southern United States and in South Africa. The real questions are: (1) who decides what are legitimate human rights? and (2) when should the state become involved and for what purposes? Riane Eisler argues that

> the issue is what types of private acts are and are not protected by the right to privacy and/or the principle of family autonomy. Even more specifically, the issue is whether violations of human rights within the family such as genital mutilation, wife beating, and other forms of violence designed to maintain patriarchal control should be within the purview of human rights theory and action. . . . [T]he underlying problem for human rights theory, as for most other fields of theory, is that the yardstick that has been developed for defining and measuring human rights has been based on the male as the norm.

The human rights community must move beyond its male defined norms in order to respond to the brutal and systematic violation of women globally. This does not mean that every human rights group must alter the focus of its work. However, it does require examining patriarchal biases and acknowledging the rights of women as human rights. Governments must seek to end the politically and culturally constructed war on women rather than continue to perpetuate it. Every state has the responsibility to intervene in the abuse of women's rights within its borders and to end its collusion with the forces that perpetrate such violations in other countries.

TOWARD ACTION: PRACTICAL APPROACHES

The classification of human rights is more than just a semantics problem because it has practical policy consequences. Human rights are still considered to be more important than women's rights. The distinction perpetuates the idea that the rights of women are of a lesser order than the "rights of man," and, as Eisler describes it, "serves to justify practices that do not accord women full and equal status." In the United Nations, the Human Rights Commission has more power to hear and investigate cases than the Commission on the Status of Women, more staff and budget, and better mechanisms for implementing its findings. Thus it makes a difference in what can be done if a case is deemed a violation of women's rights and not of human rights.

The determination of refugee status illustrates how the definition of human rights affects people's lives. The Dutch Refugee Association, in its pioneering efforts to convince other nations to recognize sexual persecution and violence against women as justifications for granting refugee status, found that some European governments would take sexual persecution into account as an aspect of other forms of political repression, but none would make it the grounds for refugee status per se. The implications of such a distinction are clear when examining a situation like that of the Bangladeshi women, who having been raped during the Pakistan–Bangladesh war, subsequently faced death at the hands of male relatives to preserve "family honor." Western powers professed outrage but did not offer asylum to these victims of human rights abuse.

I have observed four basic approaches to linking women's rights to human rights. These approaches are presented separately here in order to identify each more clearly. In practice, these approaches often overlap, and while each raises questions about the others, I see them as complementary. These approaches can be applied to many issues, but I will illustrate them primarily in terms of how they address violence against women in order to show the implications of their differences on a concrete issue.

1. Women's Rights as Political and Civil Rights

Taking women's specific needs into consideration as part of the already recognized "first generation" political and civil liberties is the first approach. This involves both raising the visibility of women who suffer general human rights violations as well as calling attention to particular abuses women encounter because they are female. Thus, issues of violence against women are raised when they connect to other forms of violation

such as the sexual torture of women political prisoners in South America. Groups like the Women's Task Force of Amnesty International have taken this approach in pushing for Amnesty to launch a campaign on behalf of women political prisoners which would address the sexual abuse and rape of women in custody, their lack of maternal care in detention, and the resulting human rights abuse of their children.

Documenting the problems of women refugees and developing responsive policies are other illustrations of this approach. Women and children make up more than 80 percent of those in refugee camps, yet few refugee policies are specifically shaped to meet the needs of those vulnerable populations who face considerable sexual abuse. For example, in one camp where men were allocated the community's rations, some gave food to women and their children in exchange for sex. Revealing this abuse led to new policies that allocated food directly to the women.

The political and civil rights approach is a useful starting point for many human rights groups; by considering women's experiences, these groups can expand their efforts in areas where they are already working. This approach also raises contradictions that reveal the limits of a narrow civil liberties view. One contradiction is to define rape as a human rights abuse only when it occurs in state custody but not on the streets or in the home. Another is to say that a violation of the right to free speech occurs when someone is jailed for defending gay rights, but not when someone is jailed or even tortured and killed for homosexuality. Thus while this approach of adding women and stirring them into existing first generation human rights categories is useful, it is not enough by itself.

2. Women's Rights as Socioeconomic Rights

The second approach includes the particular plight of women with regard to "second generation" human rights such as the rights to food, shelter, health care, and employment. This is an approach favored by those who see the dominant Western human rights tradition and international law as too individualistic and identify women's oppression as primarily economic.

This tendency has its origins among socialists and labor activists who have long argued that political human rights are meaningless to many without economic rights as well. It focuses on the primacy of the need to end women's economic subordination as the key to other issues including women's vulnerability to violence. This particular focus has led to work on issues like women's right to organize as workers and opposition to violence in the workplace, especially in situations like the free trade zones which have targeted women as cheap, nonorganized labor. Another focus of this approach has been highlighting the feminization of poverty or what might better be called the increasing impoverishment of females. Poverty has not become strictly female, but females now comprise a higher percentage of the poor.

Looking at women's rights in the context of socioeconomic development is another example of this approach. Third world peoples have called for an understanding of socioeconomic development as a human rights issue. Within this demand, some have sought to integrate women's rights into development and have examined women's specific needs in relation to areas like land ownership or access to credit. Among those working on women in development, there is growing interest in violence against women as both a health and development issue. If violence is seen as having negative consequences for social productivity, it may get more attention. This type of narrow economic measure, however, should not determine whether such violence is seen as a human rights concern. Violence as a development issue is linked to the need to understand development not just as an economic issue but also as a question of empowerment and human growth.

One of the limitations of this second approach has been its tendency to reduce women's needs to the economic sphere which implies that women's rights will follow automatically with third world development, which may involve socialism. This has not proven to be the case. Many working from this approach are no longer trying to add women into either the Western capitalist or socialist development models, but rather seek a transformative development process that links women's political, economic, and cultural empowerment.

3. WOMEN'S RIGHTS AND THE LAW

The creation of new legal mechanisms to counter sex discrimination characterizes the third approach to women's rights as human rights.

These efforts seek to make existing legal and political institutions work for women and to expand the state's responsibility for the violation of women's human rights. National and local laws which address sex discrimination and violence against women are examples of this approach. These measures allow women to fight for their rights within the legal system. The primary international illustration is the Convention on the Elimination of All Forms of Discrimination Against Women.

The Convention has been described as "essentially an international bill of rights for women and a framework for women's participation in the development process . . . [which] spells out internationally accepted principles and standards for achieving equality between women and men." Adopted by the UN General Assembly in 1979, the Convention has been ratified or acceded to by 104 countries as of January 1990. In theory these countries are obligated to pursue policies in accordance with it and to report on their compliance to the Committee on the Elimination of Discrimination Against Women (CEDAW).

While the Convention addresses many issues of sex discrimination, one of its shortcomings is failure to directly address the question of violence against women. CEDAW passed a resolution at its eighth session in Vienna in 1989 expressing concern that this issue be on its agenda and instructing states to include in their periodic reports information about statistics, legislation, and support services in this area. The Commonwealth Secretariat in its manual on the reporting process for the Convention also interprets the issue of violence against women as "clearly fundamental to the spirit of the Convention," especially in Article 5 which calls for the modification of social and cultural patterns, sex roles, and stereotyping that are based on the idea of the inferiority or the superiority of either sex.

The Convention outlines a clear human rights agenda for women which, if accepted by governments, would mark an enormous step forward. It also carries the limitations of all such international documents in that there is little power to demand its implementation. Within the United Nations, it is not generally regarded as a convention with teeth, as illustrated by the difficulty that CEDAW has had in getting countries to report on compliance with its provisions. Further, it is still treated by governments and most nongovernmental organizations as a document dealing with women's (read "secondary") rights, not human rights. Nevertheless, it is a useful statement of principles endorsed by the United Nations around which women can organize to achieve legal and political change in their regions.

4. Feminist Transformation of Human Rights

Transforming the human rights concept from a feminist perspective, so that it will take greater account of women's lives, is the fourth approach. This approach relates women's rights and human rights, looking first at the violations of women's lives and then asking how the human rights concept can change to be more responsive to women. For example, the GABRIELA women's coalition in the Philippines simply stated that "Women's Rights are Human Rights" in launching a campaign last year. As Ninotchka Rosca explained, coalition members saw that "human rights are not reducible to a question of legal and due process. . . . In the case of women, human rights are affected by the entire society's traditional perception of what is proper or not proper for women." Similarly, a panel at the 1990 International Women's Rights Action Watch conference asserted that "Violence Against Women Is a Human Rights Issue." While work in the three previous approaches is often done from a feminist perspective, this last view is the most distinctly feminist with its woman-centered stance and its refusal to wait for permission from some authority to determine what is or is not a human rights issue.

This transformative approach can be taken toward any issue, but those working from this approach have tended to focus most on abuses that arise specifically out of gender, such as reproductive rights, female sexual slavery, violence against women, and "family crimes" like forced marriage, compulsory heterosexuality, and female mutilation. These are also the issues most often dismissed as not really human rights questions. This is therefore the most hotly contested area and requires that barriers be broken down between public and private, state and nongovernmental responsibilities.

Those working to transform the human rights vision from this perspective can draw on the work

of others who have expanded the understanding of human rights previously. For example, two decades ago there was no concept of "disappearances" as a human rights abuse. However, the women of the Plaza de Mayo in Argentina did not wait for an official declaration but stood up to demand state accountability for these crimes. In so doing, they helped to create a context for expanding the concept of responsibility for deaths at the hands of paramilitary or right-wing death squads which, even if not carried out by the state, were allowed by it to happen. Another example is the developing concept that civil rights violations include "hate crimes," violence that is racially motivated or directed against homosexuals, Jews or other minority groups. Many accept that states have an obligation to work to prevent such rights abuses, and getting violence against women seen as a hate crime is being pursued by some.

The practical applications of transforming the human rights concept from feminist perspectives need to be explored further. The danger in pursuing only this approach is the tendency to become isolated from and competitive with other human rights groups because they have been so reluctant to address gender violence and discrimination. Yet most women experience abuse on the grounds of sex, race, class, nation, age, sexual preference, and politics as interrelated, and little benefit comes from separating them as competing claims. The human rights community need not abandon other issues but should incorporate gender perspectives into them and see how these expand the terms of their work. By recognizing issues like violence against women as human rights concerns, human rights scholars and activists do not have to take these up as their primary tasks. However, they do have to stop gatekeeping and guarding their prerogative to determine what is considered a "legitimate" human rights issue.

As mentioned before, these four approaches are overlapping and many strategies for change involve elements of more than one. All of these approaches contain aspects of what is necessary to achieve women's rights. At a time when dualist ways of thinking and views of competing economic systems are in question, the creative task is to look for ways to connect these approaches and to see how we can go beyond exclusive views of what people need in their lives. In the words of an early feminist group, we need bread and roses, too. Women want food and liberty and the possibility of living lives of dignity free from domination and violence. In this struggle, the recognition of women's rights as human rights can play an important role.

DISCUSSION QUESTIONS

1. Bunch mentions a number of different ways in which the rights of women have been violated around the world. What are they?

2. Bunch argues that conceptions of human rights need to be "gendered"? Do you agree? Why or why not?

3. View the film *Warrior Marks* (see the film box in chapter 4). How does this film address the points made in Bunch's article?

4. Like Claude Ake and Abdullahi Ahmed An-Na'im, Bunch maintains that the Western conception of human rights is deeply flawed. How do their views differ? How are they similar?

5. Evaluate the U.S. Bill of Rights and the UN Universal Declaration of Human Rights (see below) from the women's human rights perspective. Are they satisfactory from this perspective? Why or why not?

6. Consider everything that you have read and discussed about human rights. Now formulate your own Bill of Universal Human Rights. You may base it on the U.S. Bill of Rights or the UN Universal Declaration of Human Rights (p. 901). Or you may formulate a doctrine of your own design.

Osama

[Afghanistan/Netherlands/Japan/
Ireland/Iran 2003] 1 hour, 23 minutes
Directed by Siddiq Barmak

A peaceful demonstration by Afghani women to protest their treatment by the Taliban turns violent when Taliban forces attempt to break it up. A twelve-year-old girl (Marina Golbahari) and her mother (Zubaida Sahar) find refuge in a rundown house until the turmoil dies down, narrowly escaping the cruel Taliban soldiers. After the death of her father and brother in the Afghani wars, the young girl is left with only her mother to depend on for survival. Together they seek any source of income they can in order to stay alive. However, with the harsh rules of the ruling Taliban, which state that no woman can work or be outside of the home, survival for independent and/or widowed women is difficult.

After the hospital the mother has been working at is shut down by the Taliban, mother and daughter are forced to take drastic measures to survive. The mother recognizes that without a source of income, there will not be any food available to them. She cuts her daughter's hair and dresses her as boy so that she may bring in an income. Also, given that the Taliban does not allow women to leave their houses without a male "legal companion," the "boy" provides the mother an escort so that she may walk freely outside of her home. The young girl now posing as a boy takes on the name Osama.

A local merchant, a friend of Osama's father, agrees to let Osama work for him in his chai teashop and to teach her how to appear less feminine. But during the ritual prayer time in the Mosque, a place unfamiliar to Osama, she makes mistakes that cause observers to become suspicious of her. The Taliban then scours the town in search of young boys to train to become future members their regime. Osama is chosen for religious and military training. The boys tease Osama for "his" effeminate manner, until one day "he" gets stuck up in a tree trying to prove his masculinity. Osama is painfully punished by being suspended inside a well, and when finally pulled out of the well, it becomes clear that "he" is a she.

After her identity is discovered, Osama is arrested and sentenced by the religious court to be purchased by a wealthy merchant for marriage. The odious merchant takes Osama to his home in which he keeps his other purchased brides under lock and key. The merchant offers Osama a choice of padlocks for her room. When the distraught girl refuses to choose one, the merchant "rewards" her with the biggest padlock of all.

In 1996, when the Taliban took control of most of Afghanistan, all of the cinemas were either burned or shut down, and the Afghani film industry, which had produced only a few dozen films in its entire history, came to a standstill. In 2001, the Taliban ordered Afghan Film to burn all 3,000 films in their inventory (they complied by burning 2,000 and hiding the other 1,000). *Osama* was made on a budget of approximately $46,000 in 2002, only months after the war in Afghanistan. All of the actors in this film are amateurs who were discovered by the director in Kabul, Afghanistan.

DISCUSSION QUESTIONS

1.   What human rights violations do you believe are portrayed in *Osama*? Defend your position.

2.   Charlotte Bunch observes that women around the world are subject to political oppression and various forms of violence based on their sex. Discuss the ways in which *Osama* illustrates her point.

3.   Bunch maintains that women's rights tend to gravitate toward socioeconomic rights, that is, rights centered on work, food, and shelter. Does the film *Osama* corroborate her claim? Would socioeconomic rights be helpful to Osama and her mother? Why or why not?

4.   Abdullahi Ahmed An-Na'im observes that in Islamic cultures there are deep divisions between men and women. If human rights involves treating all people, regardless of their sex or religion, equally, then human right policies for Islamic cultures must be defined in ways that respect both cultural and religious values, as well as addressing issues of equality. Otherwise, they are functionally useless. Discuss human rights violations portrayed in *Osama* in view of An-Na'im's comment. Is there a way to pursue human rights violations in *Osama* that is both respectful of the religious and cultural traditions of Afghanistan, and sensitive to the concerns of human rights advocates?

5.   The film opens with Afghani women marching and waving signs that read, "We want the right to work," "We are not political," "We are hungry—give us work," and "We are widows." The Taliban turns firehoses on the women and shoots at them. Some are rounded up and locked in cages. How might An-Na'im and Bunch respond to this event? Is the Taliban's response to the women's concerns a violation of their human rights? Or is it an indigenous religious and cultural matter best not judged by non-Afghanis? Discuss.

6.   The harsh treatment of women in Afghanistan leads Osama's mother to say, "I wish God hadn't created women." Osama's grandmother responds, "What are you saying? Men and women are equal . . . They both work equally hard. And they are both equally fortunate." Discuss their comments, taking into consideration the fate of Osama's father and brother.

7.   Osama's grandmother says to her granddaughter, "My dear, we'll starve to death if you do not work." However, if the granddaughter is caught trying to pass herself off as a boy, she will be harshly punished. If you were Osama's mother, would you put your child in this position? What does this situation say about the options open to these three women? Discuss.

8.   Siddiq Barmak, the director of *Osama*, believes that cinema, education, and social renewal—that is, making a society that is outdated or worn out new again—are closely related. Do you agree with him?

9. After the overthrow of Taliban rule, Barmak returned to Afghanistan to make short educational films on subjects such as health and unexploded mines. These films were shown around Afghanistan in mobile cinemas. Barmak says, "Most of the population is not educated, not able to read newspapers, so pictures are very useful and powerful." If you had the ability to direct and produce films for "mobile cinemas," what subjects would you take up? To whom would you show the films? Why?

KENNETH K. INADA

A BUDDHIST RESPONSE TO THE NATURE OF HUMAN RIGHTS

Kenneth K. Inada argues that the Buddhist view of human rights is generally based on a "soft relationship,'" whereas the Western view of human rights is generally based on a "hard relationship." On the Western view, "persons are treated as separate and independent entities or even bodies, each having its own assumed identity or self-identity." On the Buddhist view, persons are treated with openness, extensiveness, depth, flexibility, absorptiveness, freshness, and creativity. Nevertheless, the soft relationship is not in contention with the hard relationship. "If anything, it has an inclusive nature that 'softens,' if you will, all contacts and allows for the binding of any element that comes along, even incorporating the entities of hard-relationships." A Buddhist view of human rights will be less concerned with legal formalities and more interested in the feelings that constitute the "saving truth of humanistic existence."

Kenneth K. Inada is emeritus professor of philosophy at the State University of New York at Buffalo. He is the author of *Nāgārjuna: A Translation of his Mūlamadhyamakakārikā* (1970), *East-West Dialogues in Aesthetics* (ed. 1978), *Buddhism and American Thinkers* (co-editor, 1984), and *Guide to Buddhist Philosophy* (1985). The following article, "A Buddhist Response to the Nature of Human Rights," is from *Asian Perpectives on Human Rights* (1990), edited by Claude E. Welch and Virginia Leary.

It is incorrect to assume that the concept of human rights is readily identifiable in all societies of the world. The concept may perhaps be clear and distinct in legal quarters, but in actual practice suffers greatly from lack of clarity and gray areas due to impositions by different cultures. This is especially true in Asia, where the two great civilizations of India and China have spawned such outstanding systems as Hinduism, Buddhism, Jainism, Yoga, Confucianism, Taoism and Chinese Buddhism. These systems, together with other indigenous folk beliefs, attest to the cultural diversity at play that characterizes Asia proper. In focusing on the concept of human rights, however, we shall concentrate on Buddhism to bring out the common grounds of discourse.

Alone among the great systems of Asia, Buddhism has successfully crossed geographical and ideological borders and spread in time throughout the whole length and breadth of known Asia. Its doctrines are so universal and profound that they captured the imagination of all the peoples they touched and thereby established a subtle bond with all. What then is this bond? It must be something common to all systems of thought which opens up and allows spiritual discourse among them.

In examining the metaphysical ground of all systems, one finds that there is a basic feeling for a larger reality in one's own experience, a kind of reaching out for a greater cosmic dimension of being, as it were. It is a deep sense for the total nature of things. All this may seem so simple and hardly merits elaborating, but it is a genuine feeling common among Asians in their quest for ultimate knowledge based on the proper relationship of one's self in the world. It is an affirmation of a reality that includes but at once goes beyond the confines of sense faculties.

A good illustration of this metaphysical grounding is seen in the Brahmanic world of Hinduism. In it, the occluded nature of the self (*atman*) constantly works to cleanse itself of defilements by yogic discipline in the hope of ultimately identifying with the larger reality which is Brahman. In the process, the grounding in the larger reality is always kept intact, regardless of whether the self is impure or not. In other words, in the quest for the purity of things a larger framework of experience is involved from the beginning such that the ordinary self (*atman*) transforms into the larger Self (*Atman*) and finally merges into the ultimate ontological Brahman.

A similar metaphysical grounding is found in Chinese thought. Confucianism, for example, with its great doctrine of humanity (*jen*), involves the ever-widening and ever-deepening human relationship that issues forth in the famous statement, "All men are brothers." In this sense, humanity is not a mere abstract concept but one that extends concretely throughout the whole of sentient existence. Confucius once said that when he searched for *jen*, it is always close at hand. It means that humanity is not something external to a person but that it is constitutive of the person's experience, regardless of whether there is consciousness of it or not. It means moreover that in the relational nature of society, individual existence is always more than that which one assumes it to be. In this vein, all experiences must fit into the larger cosmological scheme normally spoken of in terms of heaven, earth and mankind. This triadic relationship is ever-present and ever-in-force, despite one's ignorance, negligence or outright intention to deny it. The concept that permeates and enlivens the triadic relationship is the *Tao*. The *Tao* is a seemingly catchall term, perhaps best translated as the natural way of life and the world. In its naturalness, it manifests all of existence; indeed, it is here, there and everywhere since it remains aloof from human contrivance and manipulation. In a paradoxical

sense, it depicts action based on non-action (*wu-wei*), the deepest state of being achievable. The following story illustrates this point.

A cook named Ting is alleged to have used the same carving knife for some 19 years without sharpening it at all. When asked how that is possible, he simply replied:

> What I care about is the way (*Tao*), which goes beyond skill. When I first began cutting up oxen, all I could see was the ox itself. After three years I no longer saw the whole ox. And now—now I go at it by spirit and don't look with my eyes. Perception and understanding have come to a stop and spirit moves where it wants. I go along with the natural makeup, strike in the big hollows, guide the knife through the big openings, and follow things as they are. So I never touch the smallest ligament or tendon, much less a main joint. . . . I've had this knife of mine for nineteen years and I've cut up thousands of oxen with it, and yet the blade is as good as though it had just come from the grindstone.

Such then is the master craftsman at work, a master in harmonious triadic relationship based on the capture of the spirit of *Tao* where the function is not limited to a person and his or her use of a tool. And it is clear that such a spirit of *Tao* in craftsmanship is germane to all disciplined experiences we are capable of achieving in our daily activities.

Buddhism, too, has always directed our attention to the larger reality of existence. The original enlightenment of the historical Buddha told of a pure unencumbered experience which opened up all experiential doors in such a way that they touched everything sentient as well as insentient. A Zen story graphically illustrates this point.

Once a master and a disciple were walking through a dense forest. Suddenly, they heard the clean chopping strokes of the woodcutter's axe. The disciple was elated and remarked, "What beautiful sounds in the quiet of the forest!" To which the master immediately responded, "You have got it all upside down. The sounds only make obvious the deep silence of the forest!" The response by the Zen master sets in bold relief the Buddhist perception of reality. Although existential reality refers to the perception of the world as a singular unified whole, we ordinarily perceive it in fragmented ways because of our heavy reliance on the perceptual apparatus and its consequent understanding. That is to say, we perceive by a divisive and selective method which however glosses over much of reality and indeed misses its holistic nature. Certainly, the hewing sounds of the woodcutter's axe are clearly audible and delightful to the ears, but they are so at the expense of the basic silence of the forest (i.e., total reality). Or, the forest in its silence constitutes the necessary background, indeed the basic source, from which all sounds (and all activities for that matter) originate. Put another way, sounds arising from the silence of the forest should in no way deprive nor intrude upon the very source of their own being. Only human beings make such intrusions by their crude discriminate habits of perception and, consequently, suffer a truncated form of existence, unknowingly for the most part.

Now that we have seen Asian lives in general grounded in a holistic cosmological framework, we would have to raise the following question: How does this framework appear in the presence of human rights? Or, contrarily, how does human rights function within this framework?

Admittedly, the concept of human rights is relatively new to Asians. From the very beginning, it did not sit well with their basic cosmological outlook. Indeed, the existence of such an outlook has prevented in profound ways a ready acceptance of foreign elements and has created tension and struggle between tradition and modernity. Yet, the key concept in the tension is that of human relationship. This is especially true in Buddhism, where the emphasis is not so much on the performative acts and individual rights as it is on the matter of manifestation of human nature itself. The Buddhist always takes human nature as the basic context in which all ancillary concepts, such as human rights, are understood and take on any value. Moreover, the context itself is in harmony with the extended experiential nature of things. And thus, where the Westerner is much more at home in treating legal matters detached from human nature as such and quite confident in forging ahead to establish human rights with a distinct emphasis on certain "rights," the Buddhist is much more reserved but open and seeks to understand the implications of human behavior, based on the fundamental nature of human beings before turning his or her attention to the so-called "rights" of individuals.

An apparent sharp rift seems to exist between the Western and Buddhist views, but this is not really so. Actually, it is a matter of perspectives and calls for a more comprehensive understanding of what takes place in ordinary human relationships. For the basic premise is still one that is focused on human beings intimately living together in the selfsame world. A difference in perspectives does not mean noncommunication or a simple rejection of another's view, as there is still much more substance in the nature of conciliation, accommodation and absorption than what is initially thought of. Here we propose two contrasting but interlocking and complementary terms, namely, "hard relationship" and "soft relationship."

The Western view on human rights is generally based on a hard relationship. Persons are treated as separate and independent entities or even bodies, each having its own assumed identity or self-identity. It is a sheer "elemental" way of perceiving things due mainly to the strong influence by science and its methodology. As scientific methodology thrives on the dissective and analytic incursion into reality as such, this in turn has resulted in our perceiving and understanding things in terms of disparate realities. Although it makes way for easy understanding, the question still remains: Do we really understand what these realities are in their own respective fullness of existence? Apparently not. And to make matters worse, the methodology unfortunately has been uncritically extended over to the human realm, into human nature and human relations. Witness its ready acceptance by the various descriptive and behavioral sciences, such as sociology, psychology and anthropology. On this matter, Cartesian dualism of mind and body has undoubtedly influenced our ordinary ways of thinking in such a manner that in our casual perception of things we habitually subscribe to the clear-cut subject–object dichotomy. This dualistic perspective has naturally filtered down into human relationships and has eventually crystallized into what we refer to as the nature of a hard relationship. Thus, a hard relationship is a mechanistic treatment of human beings where the emphasis is on beings as such regardless of their inner nature and function in the fullest sense; it is an atomistic analysis of beings where the premium is placed on what is relatable and manipulable without regard for their true potentials for becoming. In a way it is externalization in the extreme, since the emphasis is heavily weighted on seizing the external character of beings themselves. Very little attention, if any, is given to the total ambience, inclusive of inner contents, and values, in which the beings are at full play. In this regard, it can be said that postmodern thought is now attempting to correct this seemingly lopsided dichotomous view created by our inattention to the total experiential nature of things. We believe this is a great step in the right direction. Meanwhile, we trudge along with a heavy burden on our backs, though unaware of it for the most part, by associating with people on the basis of hard relationships.

To amplify on the nature of hard relationships, let us turn to a few modern examples. First, Thomas Hobbes, in his great work, *Leviathan,* showed remarkable grasp of human psychology when he asserted that people are constantly at war with each other. Left in this "state of nature," people will never be able to live in peace and security. The only way out of this conundrum is for all to establish a reciprocal relationship of mutual trust that would work, i.e., to strike up a covenant by selfish beings that guarantees mutual benefits and gains, one in which each relinquishes certain rights in order to gain or realize a personal as well as an overall state of peace and security. This was undoubtedly a brilliant scheme. But the scheme is weak in that it treats human beings by and large mechanically, albeit psychologically too, as entities in a give-and-take affair, and thus perpetuates the condition of hard relationships.

Another example can be offered by way of the British utilitarian movement which later was consummated in American pragmatism. Jeremy Bentham's hedonic calculus (e.g., intensity of pleasure or pain, duration of pleasure or pain, certainty or uncertainty of pleasure or pain, purity or impurity of pleasure or pain, etc.) is a classic example of quantification of human experience. Although this is a most expedient or utilitarian way to treat and legislate behavior, we must remind ourselves that we are by no means mere quantifiable entities. John Stuart Mill introduced the element of quality in order to curb and tone down the excesses of the quantification process,

but, in the final analysis, human nature and relationships are still set in hard relations. American pragmatism fares no better since actions by and large take place in a pluralistic world of realities and are framed within the scientific mode and therefore it is unable to relinquish the nature of hard relationships.

In contemporary times, the great work of John Rawls, A *Theory of Justice,* has given us yet another twist in pragmatic and social contract theories. His basic concept of justice as fairness is an example of the reciprocal principle in action, i.e., in terms of realizing mutual advantage and benefit for the strongest to the weakest or the most favored to the least favored in a society. Each person exercises basic liberty with offices for its implementation always open and access available. It is moreover a highly intellectual or rational theory. It thus works extremely well on the theoretical level but, in actual situations, it is not as practical and applicable as it seems since it still retains hard relationships on mutual bases. Such being the case, feelings and consciousness relative to injustice and inequality are not so readily sported and corrected. That is to say, lacunae exist as a result of hard relationships and they keep on appearing until they are detected and finally remedied, but then the corrective process is painfully slow. Thus the theory's strongest point is its perpetually self-corrective nature which is so vital to the democratic process. Despite its shortcomings, however, Rawls' theory of justice is a singular contribution to contemporary legal and ethical thought.

By contrast, the Buddhist view of human rights is based on the assumption that human beings are primarily oriented in soft relationships; this relationship governs the understanding of the nature of human rights. Problems arise, on the other hand, when a hard relationship becomes the basis for treating human nature because it cannot delve deeply into that nature itself and functions purely on the peripheral aspects of things. It is another way of saying that a hard relationship causes rigid and stifling empirical conditions to arise and to which we become invariably attached.

A soft relationship has many facets. It is the Buddhist way to disclose a new dimension to human nature and behavior. It actually amounts to a novel perception or vision of reality. Though contrasted with a hard relationship, it is not in contention with it. If anything, it has an inclusive nature that "softens," if you will, all contacts and allows for the blending of any element that comes along, even incorporating the entities of hard relationship. This is not to say, however, that soft and hard relationships are equal or ultimately indentical. For although the former could easily accommodate and absorb the latter, the reverse is not the case. Still, it must be noted that both belong to the same realm of experiential reality and in consequence ought to be conversive with each other. The non-conversive aspect arises on the part of the "hard" side and is attributable to the locked-in character of empirical elements which are considered to be hard stubborn facts worth perpetuating. But at some point, there must be a break in the lock, as it were, and this is made possible by knowledge of and intimacy with the "soft" side of human endeavors. For the "soft" side has a passive nature characterized by openness, extensiveness, depth, flexibility, absorptiveness, freshness and creativity simply because it remains unencumbered by "hardened" empirical conditions.

What has been discussed so far can be seen in modern Thailand where tradition and change are in dynamic tension. Due to the onslaught of elements of modernity, Buddhism is being questioned and challenged. Buddhist Thailand, however, has taken up the challenge in the person of a leading monk named Buddhadasa who has led the country to keep a steady course on traditional values.

> The heart of Buddhadasa's teaching is that the Dhamma (Sanskrit, Dharma) or the truth of Buddhism is a universal truth. Dhamma is equated by Buddhadasa to the true nature of things. It is everything and everywhere. The most appropriate term to denote the nature of Dhamma is *sunnata* (Sanskrit, *sunyata*) or the void. The ordinary man considers the void to mean nothing when, in reality, it means everything—everything, that is, without reference to the self.

We will return to the discussion of the nature of the void or *sunnata* later, but suffice it to say here that what constitutes the heart of Buddhist truth of existence is based on soft relationships where all forms and symbols are accommodated and allows for their universal usage.

Robert N. Bellah has defined religion as a set of normative symbols institutionalized in a society or internalized in a personality. It is a rather good definition but does not go far enough when it comes to describing Buddhism, or Asian religions in general for that matter. To speak of symbols being intituitional or internalized without the proper existential of ontological context seems to be a bit artificial and has strains of meanings oriented toward hard relationships. Bellah, being a social scientist, probably could not go beyond the strains of a hard relationship, for, otherwise, he would have ended in a nondescriptive realm. The only way out is to give more substance to the nature to religious doctrines themselves, as in the case in Buddhism. The Buddhist Dharma is one such doctrine which, if symbolized, must take on wider and deeper meaning that strikes at the very heart of existence of the individual. In this respect, Donald Swearer is on the right track when he says:

> The adaptation of symbols of Theravada Buddhism presupposes an underlying ontological structure. The symbol system of Buddhism, then, is not to be seen only in relationship to its wider empirical context, but also in relationship to its ontological structure. This structure is denoted by such terms as Dhamma or absolute Truth, emptiness and non-attachment. These terms are denotative of what Dhiravamsa calls "dynamic being." They are symbols, but in a universalistic rather than a particularistic sense.

Swearer's reference to an underlying ontological structure is in complete harmony with our use of the term "soft relationship." And only when this ontological structure or soft relationship is brought into the dynamic tension between tradition and modernity can we give full accounting to the nature of human experience and the attendant creativity and change within a socity.

Let us return to a fuller treatment of soft relationships. In human experience, they manifest themselves in terms of the intangible human traits that we live by, such patience, humility, tolerance, deference, nonaction, humaneness, concern, pity, sympathy, altruism, sincerity, honesty, faith, responsibility, trust, respectfulness, reverence, love and compassion. Though potentially and pervasively present in any human relationship they remain for the most part as silent but vibrant components in all experience. Without them human intercourse would be sapped of the human element and reduced to perfunctory activities. Indeed, this fact seems to constitute much of the order of the day where our passions are mainly directed to physical and materialistic matters.

The actualization and sustenance of these intangible human traits are basic to the Buddhist quest for an understanding of human nature and, by extension, the so-called rights of human beings. In order to derive a closer look at the nature of soft relationships, we shall focus on three characteristics, namely mutuality, holism, and emptiness or void.

<h3 style="text-align:center">MUTUALITY</h3>

Our understanding of mutuality is generally limited to its abstract or theoretical nature. For example, it is defined in terms of a two-way action between two parties and where the action is invariably described with reference to elements of hard relationships. Except secondarily or deviously, nothing positive is mentioned about the substance of mutuality, such as the feelings of humility, trust and tolerance that transpire between the parties concerned. Although these feelings are present, unfortunately, they hardly ever surface in the relationship and almost always are overwhelmed by the physical aspect of things.

What is to be done? One must simply break away from the merely conceptual or theoretical understanding and fully engage oneself in the discipline that will bring the feelings of both parties to become vital components in the relationship. That is, both parties must equally sense the presence and value of these feelings and thus give substance and teeth to their actions.

Pursuing the notion of mutuality further, the Buddhist understands human experience as a totally open phenomenon, that persons should always be wide open in the living process. The phrase "an open ontology" is used to describe the unclouded state of existence. An illustration of this is the newborn child. The child is completely an open organism at birth. The senses are wide open and will absorb practically anything without prejudice. At this stage, also, the child will begin to imitate because its absorptive power is at the highest level. This open textured nature should continue on and on. In other words, if we are free

and open, there should be no persistence attaching ourselves to hard elements within the underlying context of a dynamic world of experience. The unfortunate thing, however, is that the open texture of our existence begins to blemish and fade away in time, being obstructed and overwhelmed by self-imposed fragmentation, narrowness and restriction, which gradually develop into a closed nature of existence. In this way, the hard relationship rules. But the nature of an open ontology leads us on to the next characteristic.

<h3 style="text-align:center">HOLISM</h3>

Holism of course refers to the whole, the total nature of individual existence and thus describes the unrestrictive nature of one's experience. Yet, the dualistic relationship we maintain by our crude habits of perception remains a stumbling block. This stunted form of perception is not conducive to holistic understanding and instead fosters nothing but fractured types of ontological knowledge taking. Unconscious for the most part, an individual narrows his or her vision by indulging in dualism of all kinds, both mental and physical, and in so doing isolates the objects of perception from the total process to which they belong. In consequence, the singular unified reality of each perceptual moment is fragmented and, what is more, fragmentation once settled breeds further fragmentation.

The Buddhist will appeal to the fact that one's experience must always be open to the total ambience of any momentary situation. But here we must be exposed to a unique, if not paradoxical, insight of the Buddhist. It is that the nature of totality is not a clearly defined phenomenon. In a cryptic sense, however, it means that the totality of experience has no borders to speak of. It is an open border totality, which is the very nature of the earlier mentioned "open ontology." It is a noncircumscribable totality, like a circle sensed which does not have a rounded line, a seamless circle, if you will. A strange phenomenon, indeed, but that is how the Buddhist sees the nature of individual existence as such. For the mystery of existence that haunts us is really the nature of one's own fullest momentary existence. Nothing else compares in profundity to this nature, so the Buddhist believes.

Now, the open framework in which experience takes place reveals that there is depth and substance in experience. But so long as one is caught up with the peripheral elements, so called, of hard relationships one will be ensnared by them and will generate limitations on one's understanding accordingly. On the other hand, if openness is acknowledged as a fact of existence, then the way out of one's limitations will present itself. All sufferings (*duhkha*), from the Buddhist standpoint, are cases of limited ontological vision (*avidya*, ignorance) hindered by the attachment to all sorts of elements that obsess a person.

Holism is conversant with openness since an open experience means that all elements are fully and extensively involved. In many respects, holistic existence exhibits the fact that mutuality thrives only in unhindered openness. But there is still another vital characteristic to round out or complete momentary experience. For this we turn to the last characteristic.

EMPTINESS

Emptiness in Sanskrit is *sunyata*. Strictly speaking, the Sanskrit term, depicting zero or nothing, had been around prior to Buddhism, but it took the historical Buddha's supreme enlightenment (nirvana) to reveal an incomparable qualitative nature inherent to experience. Thus emptiness is not sheer voidness or nothingness in the nihilistic sense.

We ordinarily find it difficult to comprehend emptiness, much less to live a life grounded in it. Why? Again, we return the nature of our crude habits of perception, which is laden with unwarranted forms. That is, our whole perpetual process is caught up in attachment to certain forms or elements which foster and turn into so-called empirical and cognitive biases. All of this is taking place in such minute and unknowing ways that we hardly, if ever, take notice of it until a crisis situation arises, such as the presence of certain obviously damaging prejudice or discrimination. Then and only then do we seriously wonder and search for the forms or elements that initially gave rise to those prejudicial or discriminatory forces.

Emptiness has two aspects. The first aspect alerts our perceptions to be always open and fluid, and to desist from attaching to any form or element. In this respect, emptiness technically functions as a force of "epistemic nullity," in the sense that it nullifies any reference to a form or element as preexisting perception or even postexisting for that matter. Second and more importantly, emptiness points at a positive content of our experience. It underscores the possibility of total experience in any given moment because there is now nothing attached to or persisted in. This latter point brings us right back to the other characteristics of holism and mutuality. Now, we must note that emptiness is that dimension of experience which makes it possible for the function of mutuality and holism in each experience, since there is absolutely nothing that binds, hinders or wants in our experience. Everything is as it is (*tathata*), under the aegis of emptiness; emptiness enables one to spread out one's experience at will in all directions, so to speak, in terms of "vertical" and "horizontal" dimensions of being. As it is the key principle of enlightened existence, it makes everything both possible and impossible. Possible in the sense that all experiences function within the total empty nature, just as all writings are possible on a clean slate or, back to the zen story, where the sounds are possible in the silence (emptiness) of the forest. At the same time, impossible in the sense that all attachments to forms and elements are categorically denied in the ultimate fullness of experience. In this way, emptiness completes our experience of reality and, at the same time, provides the grounds for the function of all human traits to become manifest in soft relationships.

It can now be seen that all three characteristics involve each other in the self-same momentary existence. Granted this, it should not be too difficult to accept the fact that the leading moral concept in Buddhism is compassion (*karuna*). Compassion literally means "passion for all" in an ontologically extensive sense. It covers the realm of all sentient beings, inclusive of non-sentients, for the doors of perception to total reality are always open. From the Buddhist viewpoint, then, all human beings are open entities with open feelings expressive of the highest form of humanity. This is well expressed in the famous concept of *bodhisattva* (enlightened being) in Mahayana Buddhism who has deepest concern for all beings and sympathetically delays his entrance to nirvana as long as there is suffering (ignorant existence) among sentient creatures. It depicts the coterminous nature of all creatures and may be taken as a philosophic myth in that it underscores the ideality of existence which promotes the greatest unified form of humankind based on compassion. This ideal form of existence, needless to say, is the aim and goal of all Buddhists.

As human beings we need to keep the channels of existential dialogue open at all times. When an act of violence is in progress, for example, we need to constantly nourish the silent and passive nature of nonviolence inherent in all human relations. Though nonviolence cannot counter violence on the latter's terms, still, its nourished presence serves as a reminder of the brighter side of existence and may even open the violator's mind to common or normal human traits such as tolerance, kindness and noninjury (*ahimsa*). Paradoxically and most unfortunately, acts of violence only emphasize the fact that peace and tranquillity are the normal course of human existence.

It can now be seen that the Buddhist view on human rights is dedicated to the understanding of persons in a parameter-free ambience, so to speak, where feelings that are extremely soft and tender, but nevertheless present and translated into human traits or virtues that we unphold, make up the very fiber of human relations. These relations, though their contents are largely intangible, precede any legal rights or justification accorded to human beings. In brief, human rights for the Buddhist are not only matters for legal deliberation and understanding, but they must be complemented by and based on something deeper and written in the very feelings of all sentients. The unique coexistent nature of rights and feelings constitutes the saving truth of humanistic existence.

DISCUSSION QUESTIONS

1. What is the difference between human rights based on a "soft relationship" and human rights based on a "hard relationship"? Which do you prefer, and why?

2. Do you agree with Inada that the rift between Western and Buddhist views of human rights is only an "apparent" one, not a real one? Defend your view.

3. Inada argues that we must get away from approaches to human rights that are mostly theoretical and conceptual. Do you agree? How does Inada's position on human rights compare with Claude Ake's? Explain.

4. Evaluate the U.S. Bill of Rights and the UN Universal Declaration of Human Rights (see p. 901) from the Buddhist human rights perspective. Are they satisfactory from this perspective? Why or why not?

5. Compare and contrast Rawls' theory of justice to a Buddhist response to human rights. Which do you prefer, and why?

Powaqqatsi
[USA 1988] 1 hour, 35 minutes
Directed by Godfrey Reggio

*P*owaqqatsi: *Life in Transformation* is a film without narration or dialogue. A series of images portrays people expressing themselves through work and tradition. The film focuses on the southern half of our planet—primarily South America, Africa, India, Asia, and the Middle East. These images are scored against the haunting, hypnotic music of composer Philip Glass.

The film opens with slow-motion footage of thousands of people working in the Serra Pelada mines in Brazil. In this open-pit gold mine, masses of workers haul bags of dirt on their backs from the bottom of the mine to the top. Ropes from the heavy bags of dirt cut into their sweaty, dirty skin. Two workers haul a third who has been accidentally hit on the head with a rock.

The grand scale of human energy and toil in this mining operation is followed by more images of people laboring, creating, worshiping, and playing. While the cultures to which these people belong are small and geographically distant from one another, they are connected in the film by a shared way of living centered on work and tradition. The film finds beauty in many of the exhausting realities of everyday existence and celebrates diverse ways of living while at the same time calling for us to find universals or connections among them.

Gradually, the focus shifts from people in smaller communities to life in cities. Images of a child guiding a horse through waves and women milling grain are replaced by images of sprawling buildings, crowded city sidewalks, and traffic jams. Then the entire screen fills with smoke and flames, followed by a shot of a burned-out car set against the background of "ghost cars" zooming along a highway.

Director Godfrey Reggio says that this film is "an impression, an examination of how life is changing." He explains, "That's all it is. There is good and there is bad. What we sought to capture is our unanimity as a global culture. Most of us tend to forget about this, caught up as we are in our separate trajectories. It was fascinating to blend these different existences together in one film." Ninety-nine percent of the shots in the film were not scripted in any way.

Powaqqatsi is the second of three films by Reggio dealing with changing life on earth. It takes it name from the Hopi language: *powaq*, meaning "sorcerer," and *qatsi*, meaning "life." In the film, *Powaqqatsi* is defined as "an entity, a way of life, that consumes the life forces of other beings in order to further its own life." Reggio explains that the *powaq* operates through seduction, not by force or intimidation.

DISCUSSION QUESTIONS

1. Kenneth K. Inada says that a Buddhist view of human rights treats persons based on a "soft relationship," whereas a Western view of human rights is generally based on a "hard relationship." How does the film *Powaqqatsi* treat persons? Is it based on a fundamentally "soft relationship" or based on a fundamentally "hard relationship?" Why?

2. What, if any, are the fundamental issues concerning human rights raised by *Powaqqatsi*? Do you think the approach to human rights in this film is essentially Buddhist? Defend your view.

3. *Powaqqatsi* means a way of life that consumes another way in order to advance itself. Do you think that its message is that the southern world is being consumed by the forces of cultural change? Why or why not?

4. Does this film make a virtue of poverty? Does it romanticize oppression? Does it aestheticize suffering, that is, present suffering as a thing of beauty? Discuss.

5. How effective is *Powaqqatsi* at raising issues concerning human rights? Would you call it a "human rights activist film"? Why or why not?

6. This film contains only music and images. Would you have preferred some type of verbal element to the film—for example, a narrator? If the film had a narrator, what would the narrator say? Why?

THE U.S. BILL OF RIGHTS AND THE UN UNIVERSAL DECLARATION OF HUMAN RIGHTS

From May through September 1787, the constitutional convention convened and drafted the United States Constitution, establishing a strong federal government. On September 17, 1787, the Constitution was signed and sent to the states for ratification. The Constitution went into effect after it was ratified by the ninth state, New Hampshire, on June 21, 1788.

The U.S. Bill of Rights, the first ten amendments to the U.S. Constitution, guarantees fundamental liberties to all U.S. citizens. The Bill of Rights passed by Congress on September 25, 1789, and was ratified on December 15, 1791.

The United Nations Universal Declaration of Human Rights was drafted over 150 years after the U.S. Bill of Rights. In the 1940s, a movement emerged to make human rights protections a condition of peace at the close of World War II. Early in the decade, President Franklin Roosevelt had called for the global protection of the freedoms of speech, expression, and worship as well as the freedom from fear and want in his 1941 State of the Union message. In 1947, former First Lady Eleanor Roosevelt was elected to the United Nations Commission on Human Rights. This commission produced the UN Universal Declaration of Human Rights, which was adopted by the UN General Assembly in December 1948.

THE U.S. BILL OF RIGHTS

AMENDMENT I

Congress shall make no law respecting an establishment of religion, or prohibiting the free exercise thereof; or abridging the freedom of speech, or of the press; or the right of the people peaceably to assemble and to petition the Government for a redress of grievances.

AMENDMENT II

A well regulated Militia, being necessary to the security of a free State, the right of the people to keep and bear Arms, shall not be infringed.

AMENDMENT III

No Soldier shall, in time of peace be quartered in any house, without the consent of the Owner, nor in time of war, but in a manner to be prescribed by law.

AMENDMENT IV

The right of the people to be secure in their persons, houses, papers, and effects, against unreasonable searches and seizures, shall not be violated, and no Warrants shall issue, but upon probable cause, supported by Oath or affirmation, and particularly describing the place to be searched, and the persons or things to be seized.

AMENDMENT V

No person shall be held to answer for a capital, or otherwise infamous crime, unless on a presentment or indictment of a Grand Jury, except in cases arising in the land or naval forces, or in the Militia, when in actual service in time of War or public danger; nor shall any person be subject for the same offence to be twice put in jeopardy of life or limb; nor shall be compelled in any criminal case to be a witness against himself nor be deprived of life, liberty or property, without due process of law; nor shall private property be taken for public use, without just compensation.

AMENDMENT VI

In all criminal prosecutions, the accused shall enjoy the right to a speedy and public trial, by an impartial jury of the State and district wherein the crime shall have been committed, which district shall have been previously ascertained by law, and to be informed of the nature and cause of the accusation; to be confronted with the witnesses against him; to have compulsory process for obtaining witnesses in his favor, and to have the Assistance of Counsel for his defence.

Amendment VII

In suits at common law, where the value in controversy shall exceed twenty dollars, the right of trial by jury shall be preserved, and no fact tried by a jury, shall be otherwise reexamined in any Court of the United States, than according to the rules of the common law.

Amendment VIII

Excessive bail shall not be required, nor excessive fines imposed, nor cruel and unusual punishments inflicted.

Amendment IX

The enumeration in the Constitution, of certain rights, shall not be construed to deny or disparage others retained by the people.

Amendment X

The powers not delegated to the United States by the constitution, nor prohibited by it to the States, are reserved to the States respectively, or to the people.

The UN Universal Declaration of Human Rights

Whereas recognition of the inherent dignity and of the equal and inalienable rights of all members of the human family is the foundation of freedom, justice and peace in the world,

Whereas disregard and contempt for human rights have resulted in barbarous acts which have outraged the conscience of mankind, and the advent of a world in which human beings shall enjoy freedom of speech and belief and freedom from fear and want has been proclaimed as the highest aspiration of the common people,

Whereas it is essential, if man is not to be compelled to have recourse, as a last resort, to rebellion against tyranny and oppression, that human rights should be protected by the rule of law,

Whereas it is essential to promote the development of friendly relations between nations,

Whereas the peoples of the United Nations have in the Charter reaffirmed their faith in fundamental human rights, in the dignity and worth of the human person and in the equal rights of men and women and have determined to promote social progress and better standards of life in larger freedom,

Whereas Member States have pledged themselves to achieve, in co-operation with the United Nations, the promotion of universal respect for and observance of human rights and fundamental freedoms,

Whereas a common understanding of these rights and freedoms is of the greatest importance for the full realization of this pledge,

Now, therefore, the General Assembly *proclaims* this Universal Declaration of Human Rights as a common standard of achievement for all peoples and all nations, to the end that every individual and every organ of society, keeping this Declaration constantly in mind, shall strive by teaching and education to promote respect for these rights and freedoms and by progressive measures, national and international, to secure their universal and effective recognition and observance, both among the peoples of Member States themselves and among the peoples of territories under their jurisdiction.

Article 1

All human beings are born free and equal in dignity and rights. They are endowed with reason and conscience and should act towards one another in a spirit of brotherhood.

Article 2

Everyone is entitled to all the rights and freedoms set forth in this Declaration, without distinction of any kind, such as race, colour, sex, language, religion, political or other opinion, national or social origin, property, birth or other status.

Furthermore, no distinction shall be made on the basis of the political, jurisdictional or international status of the country or territory to which a person belongs, whether it be independent, trust, non-self-governing or under any other limitation of sovereignty.

Article 3

Everyone has the right to life, liberty and security of person.

ARTICLE 4

No one shall be held in slavery or servitude; slavery and the slave trade shall be prohibited in all their forms.

ARTICLE 5

No one shall be subjected to torture or to cruel, inhuman or degrading treatment or punishment.

ARTICLE 6

Everyone has the right to recognition everywhere as a person before the law.

ARTICLE 7

All are equal before the law and are entitled without any discrimination to equal protection of the law. All are entitled to equal protection against any discrimination in violation of this Declaration and against any incitement to such discrimination.

ARTICLE 8

Everyone has the right to an effective remedy by the competent national tribunals for acts violating the fundamental rights granted him by the constitution or by law.

ARTICLE 9

No one shall be subjected to arbitrary arrest, detention or exile.

ARTICLE 10

Everyone is entitled in full equality to a fair and public hearing by an independent and impartial tribunal, in the determination of his rights and obligations and of any criminal charge against him.

ARTICLE 11

(1) Everyone charged with a penal offence has the right to be presumed innocent until proved guilty according to law in a public trial at which he has had all the guarantees necessary for his defence.

(2) No one shall be held guilty of any penal offence on account of any act or omission which did not constitute a penal offence, under national or international law, at the time when it was committed. Nor shall a heavier penalty be imposed than the one that was applicable at the time the penal offence was committed.

ARTICLE 12

No one shall be subjected to arbitrary interference with his privacy, family, home or correspondence, nor to attacks upon his honour and reputation. Everyone has the right to the protection of the law against such interference or attacks.

ARTICLE 13

(1) Everyone has the right to freedom of movement and residence within the borders of each State.

(2) Everyone has the right to leave any country, including his own, and to return to his country.

ARTICLE 14

(1) Everyone has the right to seek and to enjoy in other countries asylum from persecution.

(2) This right may not be invoked in the case of prosecutions genuinely arising from non-political crimes or from acts contrary to the purposes and principles of the United Nations.

ARTICLE 15

(1) Everyone has the right to a nationality.

(2) No one shall be arbitrarily deprived of his nationality nor denied the right to change his nationality.

ARTICLE 16

(1) Men and women of full age, without any limitation due to race, nationality or religion, have the right to marry and to found a family. They are entitled to equal rights as to marriage, during marriage and at its dissolution.

(2) Marriage shall be entered into only with the free and full consent of the intending spouses.

(3) The family is the natural and fundamental group unit of society and is entitled to protection by society and the State.

ARTICLE 17

(1) Everyone has the right to own property alone as well as in association with others.

(2) No one shall be arbitrarily deprived of his property.

ARTICLE 18

Everyone has the right to freedom of thought, conscience and religion; this right includes freedom to change his religion or belief, and freedom, either alone or in community with others and in public or private, to manifest his religion or belief in teaching, practice, worship and observance.

ARTICLE 19

Everyone has the right to freedom of opinion and expression; this right includes freedom to hold opinions without interference and to seek, receive and impart information and ideas through any media and regardless of frontiers.

ARTICLE 20

(1) Everyone has the right to freedom of peaceful assembly and association.

(2) No one may be compelled to belong to an association.

ARTICLE 21

(1) Everyone has the right to take part in the government of his country, directly or through freely chosen representatives.

(2) Everyone has the right of equal access to public service in his country.

(3) The will of the people shall be the basis of the authority of government; this will shall be expressed in periodic and genuine elections which shall be by universal and equal suffrage and shall be held by secret vote or by equivalent free voting procedures.

ARTICLE 22

Everyone, as a member of society, has the right to social security and is entitled to realization, through national effort and international co-operation and in accordance with the organization and resources of each State, of the economic, social and cultural rights indispensible for his dignity and the free development of his personality.

ARTICLE 23

(1) Everyone has the right to work, to free choice of employment, to just and favourable conditions of work and to protection against unemployment.

(2) Everyone, without any discrimination, has the right to equal pay for equal work.

(3) Everyone has the right to just and favourable remuneration ensuring for himself and his family an existence worthy of human dignity, and supplemented, if necessary, by other means of social protection.

(4) Everyone has the right to form and to join trade unions for the protection of his interests.

ARTICLE 24

Everyone has the right to rest and leisure, including reasonable limitation of working hours and periodic holidays with pay.

ARTICLE 25

(1) Everyone has the right to a standard of living adequate for the health and well-being of himself and of his family, including food, clothing, housing and medical care and necessary social services, and the right to security in the event of unemployment, sickness, disability, widowhood, old age or other lack of livelihood in circumstances beyond his control.

(2) Motherhood and childhood are entitled to special care and assistance. All children, whether born in or out of wedlock, shall enjoy the same social protection.

ARTICLE 26

(1) Everyone has the right to education. Education shall be free, at least in the elementary and fundamental stages. Elementary education shall be compulsory. Technical and professional education shall be made generally available and higher education shall be equally accessible to all on the basis of merit.

(2) Education shall be directed to the full development of the human personality and to the strengthening of respect for human rights and fundamental freedoms. It shall promote understanding, tolerance and friendship among all nations, racial or religious groups, and shall further the activities of the United Nations for the maintenance of peace.

(3) Parents have a prior right to choose the kind of education that shall be given to their children.

ARTICLE 27

(1) Everyone has the right to freely participate in the cultural life of the community, to enjoy the arts and to share in scientific advancement and its benefits.

(2) Everyone has the right to the protection of the moral and material interests resulting from any scientific, literary or artistic production of which he is the author.

ARTICLE 28

Everyone is entitled to a social and international order in which the rights and freedoms set forth in this Declaration can be fully realized.

ARTICLE 29

(1) Everyone has duties to the community in which alone the free and full development of his personality is possible.

(2) In the exercise of his rights and freedoms, everyone shall be subject only to such limitations as are determined by law solely for the purpose of securing due recognition and respect for the rights and freedoms of others and of meeting the just requirements of morality, public order and the general welfare in a democratic society.

(3) These rights and freedoms may in no case be exercised contrary to the purposes and principles of the United Nations.

ARTICLE 30

Nothing in this Declaration may be interpreted as implying for any State, group or person any right to engage in any activity or to perform any act aimed at the destruction of any of the rights and freedoms set forth herein.

DISCUSSION QUESTIONS

1. Claude Ake argues that the U.S. Bill of Rights ascribes "abstract rights to abstract beings." Do you agree with him? If so, this a virtue of the document or a deficiency? Explain.

2. Does the UN Universal Declaration of Human Rights ascribe, in Ake's words, "abstract rights to abstract beings"? If so, is this a virtue of the document or a deficiency? Explain.

3. To what extent, if any, is the U.S. Bill of Rights useful to the disadvantaged people of America? Defend your view. If it is not useful, how might it be altered to address their needs?

4. Should the U.S. Bill of Rights be rewritten as gender-specific as opposed to gender-neutral? How about the UN Universal Declaration of Human Rights? How would gender considerations alter these documents?

5. Which of the amendments of the U.S. Bill of Rights is the least valuable? Which is the most valuable? If you could add one amendment, what would it say? Defend your view against objections.

6. Which of the articles of the UN Universal Declaration of Human Rights is the least valuable? Which is the most valuable? If you could add one article, what would it say? Defend your views against objections.

7. Consider everything that you have read and discussed about human rights. Now formulate your own Bill of Universal Human Rights. You may base it on the U.S. Bill of Rights, or on the UN Universal Declaration of Human Rights, or on a doctrine of your own design.

8. Some suggest that human rights documents need to be formulated to fit the specific needs of communities; otherwise, they will not be considered legitimate in these communities. Do you agree with this suggestion? Look at the UN Universal Declaration of Human Rights. What, if anything, in this document can be changed and/or omitted without significant damage to international human rights?

Welcome to Sarajevo
[USA/Gr. Brit. 1997] 1 hr., 42 min.
Dir. by Michael Winterbottom

*T*his documentary-style movie about a group of American and British journalists sent to report on the Bosnian war is partly based on the experiences of ITN TV journalist Michael Nicholson. Film footage of the war is spliced with the fictional presentation of a group of journalists who are covering the conflict. One of the journalists, Henderson (Stephen Dillane), begins to question his moral position on the war as he avoids bombs and sniper fire in an effort to get the best story. Is it possible to maintain a moral distance from the atrocities that are taking place? Can one stand by passively and watch people suffer?

Henderson grows increasingly disturbed by the ruthlessness of the Serbs against the Muslims and the reluctance of the West to help the growing population of orphans. His emotional turmoil leads him to attempt to save orphans from mistreatment by the Serbs. In particular, Henderson promises a ten-year-old orphan girl that he will bring her back to London with him. After a terrifying bus journey, Henderson and the orphans are stopped by the Serbs when they try to leave Sarajevo. Ignoring a United Nations mandate allowing children to leave the country, armed Serbs forcibly remove the screaming Muslim children from the bus.

Welcome to Sarajevo questions the efficacy of international human rights laws that guarantee nations protection from foreign aggression. The film asserts that is insufficient to have strong international human rights laws on the books; laws are worthless if they are not actively enforced.

DISCUSSION QUESTIONS

1. *Welcome to Sarajevo* raises questions about the enforcement of international human rights laws. Should other nations be considered morally or legally responsible if they are aware of human rights violations in places such as Sarajevo but do not act to help those whose rights are being violated? Defend your view.

2. If you were in Henderson's position, would you help the orphans? In general, what are our moral obligations to help those in need who are directly before us? Defend your view.

3. As presented in the film, two of the reasons that the United Nations did not come to the assistance of the Muslims in Sarajevo were that the war was considered an internal affair of Serbia and that thirteen other areas worldwide had worse human rights violations than Serbia. Are these good reasons for not coming to the aid of the Muslims? Defend your view.

4. Are strong human rights laws important even if they are not enforced? What should the penalty for non-enforcement of these laws be? How should we enforce them? Discuss.

SUPPLEMENTARY READINGS

FREEDOM, FREE WILL, AND DETERMINISM

Aune, Bruce. *Reason and Action*. Boston: Reidel, 1977.

Bergmann, Frithjof. *On Being Free*. Notre Dame, IN: University of Notre Dame Press, 1977.

Bernstein, Richard J. *Praxis and Action: Contemporary Philosophies of Human Activity*. Philadelphia: University of Pennsylvania Press, 1971.

Berofsky, Bernard, ed. *Free Will and Determinism*. New York: Harper & Row, 1966.

Binkley, Robert, Richard Bronaugh, and Ausonio Marras, eds. *Agent, Action, and Reason*. Toronto: University of Toronto Press, 1971.

Boller, Paul F. *Freedom and Fate in American Thought: From Edwards to Dewey*. Dallas: SMU Press, 1978.

Brand, Myles, ed. *The Nature of Human Action*. Glenview, IL: Scott, Foresman, 1970.

Cahn, Steven M. *Fate, Logic, and Time*. New Haven, CT: Yale University Press, 1967.

Care, Norman S., and Charles Landesman. *Readings in the Theory of Action*. Bloomington: Indiana University Press, 1968.

Danto, Arthur Coleman. *Analytical Philosophy of Action*. Cambridge: Cambridge University Press, 1973.

D'Arcy, Eric. *Human Acts: An Essay in Their Moral Evaluation*. Oxford: Clarendon Press, 1963.

Darrow, Clarence. *Why I Am Agnostic and Other Essays*. Amherst, NY: Prometheus Books, 1995.

Davidson, Donald. *Essays on Actions and Events*. New York: Oxford University Press, 1980.

Davis, Lawrence H. *Theory of Action*. Englewood Cliffs, NJ: Prentice Hall, 1979.

Dennett, Daniel. *Freedom Evolves*. New York: Viking Press, 2003.

—— *Elbow Room: The Varieties of Free Will Worth Wanting*. Cambridge, MA: MIT Press, 1984.

Earman, John. *A Primer on Determinism*. Norwell, MA: Reidel, 1986.

Ellul, Jacques. *The Ethics of Freedom*. Grand Rapids, MI: Eerdmans, 1976.

Erasmus, Desiderius, and Martin Luther. *Discourse on Free Will*. New York: Ungar, 1961.

Goldman, Alvin I. *Thought and Action*. New York: Viking Press, 1960.

—— *A Theory of Human Action*. Englewood Cliffs, NJ: Prentice-Hall, 1970.

—— *Freedom of Mind and Other Essays*. Princeton NJ: Princeton University Press, 1971.

—— *Freedom of the Individual*. Expanded ed. Princeton NJ: Princeton University Press, 1975.

Hobbes, Thomas, and John Bramhall. *Hobbes and Bramhall: On Liberty and Necessity*. Ed. V. C. Chappell. New York: Cambridge University Press, 1999.

Honderich, Ted. *How Free Are You? The Determinism Problem*. New York: Oxford University Press, 1993.

—— *Essays on Freedom of Action*. London: Routledge & Kegan Paul, 1973.

Hornsby, Jennifer. *Actions*. London: Routledge & Kegan Paul, 1980.

Hume, David. *Treatise of Human Nature*. Eds. David Fate Norton and Mary J. Norton. Oxford: Oxford University Press, 2000.

Kenny, Anthony John Patrick. *Freewill and Responsibility*. London: Routledge & Kegan Paul, 1978.

Lamont, Corliss. *Freedom of Choice Affirmed*. New York: Horizon Press, 1967.

Lawrence, Roy. *Motive and Intention: An Essay in the Appreciation of Action*. Evanston, IL: Northwestern University Press, 1972.

Lehrer, Keith, ed. *Freedom and Determinism*. New York: Random House, 1966.

Louch, A. R. *Explanation and Human Action*. Berkeley: University of California Press, 1966.

Melden, Abraham I. *Free Action*. New York: Humanities Press, 1961.

O'Connor, Daniel J. *Free Will*. Garden City, NY: Doubleday Anchor, 1971.

Peters, Richard S. *The Concept of Motivation*. New York: Humanities Press, 1958.

Pinker, Steven. *The Blank Slate: The Modern Denial of Human Nature*. New York: Viking Press, 2002.

Ricoeur, Paul. *Freedom and Nature: The Voluntary and the Involuntary*. Evanston, IL: Northwestern University Press, 1966.

Rychlak, Joseph F. *Discovering Free Will and Personal Responsibility*. New York: Oxford University Press, 1979.

Taylor, Charles. *The Explanation of Behavior*. New York: Humanities Press, 1964.

Thalberg, Irving. *Enigmas of Agency: Studies in the Philosophy of Human Action*. New York: Humanities Press, 1972.

Thorp, John. *Free Will*. Boston: Routledge & Kegan Paul, 1980.

Tuomela, Raimo. *Human Action and Its Explanation: A Study on the Philosophical Foundations of Psychology*. Boston: Reidel, 1977.

Wegner, Daniel M. *The Illusion of Conscious Will*. Cambridge, MA: MIT Press, 2002.

Wright, Georg Henrik von. *Explanation and Understanding*. Ithaca, NY: Cornell University Press, 1971.

Zöller, Günter, ed. *Prize Essay on the Freedom of the Will*: *Arthur Shopenhauer*. Cambridge: Cambridge University Press, 1999.

Justice and Society

Barry, Brian. *The Liberal Theory of Justice*. London: Oxford University Press, 1973.

Buchanan, Allen. *Marx and Justice: The Radical Critique of Liberalism*. Totowa, NJ: Rowman & Allanheld, 1982.

Diamond, Irene. *Families, Politics, and Public Policy*. New York: Longman, 1983.

Fisk, Milton. *Ethics and Society: A Marxist Interpretation of Value*. New York: NY University Press, 1980.

Friedman, Milton. *Capitalism and Freedom*. Chicago: University of Chicago Press, 1962.

Gillespie, Ed, and Bob Schellhas. *The Contract with America: The Bold Plan by Rep. Newt Gingrich, Rep. Dick Armey and the House Republicans to Change the Nation*. New York: Random House, 1994.

Gutman, Amy. *Liberal Equality*. Cambridge: Cambridge University Press, 1980.

Harrington, Michael. *Socialism: Past and Future*. New York: Arcade, 1989.

Hayek, F. A. *The Constitution of Liberty*. Chicago: University of Chicago Press, 1960.

Hegel, G. W. F. *Philosophy of Right* (1821). Trans. T. M. Knox. New York: Oxford University Press, 1962.

Hospers, John. *Libertarianism*. Los Angeles: Nash, 1971.

Machan, Tibor. *Individuals and Their Rights*. La Salle, IL: Open Court, 1989.

MacIntyre, Alasdair. *Whose Justice? Which Rationality?* Notre Dame, IN: Notre Dame University Press, 1988.

MacKinnon, Catharine. *Toward a Feminist Theory of the State.* Cambridge, MA: Harvard University Press, 1989.

Nielson, Kai. *Equality and Liberty.* Totowa, NJ: Rowman & Littlefield, 1985.

Nozick, Robert. *Anarchy, State and Utopia.* Basic Books, 1974.

Okin, Susan. *Justice, Gender and the Family.* New York: Basic Books, 1989.

Peffer, R. G. *Marxism, Morality and Social Justice.* Princeton, NJ: Princeton University Press, 1990.

Rawls, John. *A Theory of Justice.* Cambridge, MA: Harvard University Press, 1971.

Rousseau, Jean-Jacques. *The Social Contract and Discourses.* Trans. G. D. H. Cole. London: J. M. Dent, 1973.

Sandel, Michael. *Liberalism and the Limits of Justice.* Cambridge: Cambridge University Press, 1982.

Singer, Peter. *Practical Ethics.* Cambridge: Cambridge University Press, 1979.

Walzer, Michael. *Spheres of Justice.* New York: Basic Books, 1983.

Young, Iris. *Justice and the Politics of Difference.* Princeton, NJ: Princeton University Press, 1990.

Sexism and Sexual Equality

Bartky, Sandra. *Feminity and Domination: Studies in the Phenomenology of Oppression.* New York: Routledge, 1990.

Beauvoir, Simone de. *The Second Sex.* Trans. H. M. Parshley. New York: Vintage Books, 1974.

Brod, Harry. *The Making of Masculinities: The New Men's Studies.* Boston: Unwin Hyman, 1987.

Burke, Phyllis. *Gender Shock: Exploding the Myths of Male and Female.* New York: Anchor Books, 1996.

Dines, Gial, and Jean Humez, eds. *Gender, Race and Class in the Media.* Thousand Oaks, CA: Sage, 1995.

Eisenstein, Zillah. *Feminism and Sexual Equality.* New York: Monthly Review Press, 1984.

English, Jane. *Sex Equality.* Englewood Cliffs, NJ: Prentice Hall, 1978.

Faludi, Susan. *Backlash: The Undeclared War Against American Women.* New York: Crown, 1991.

Faustino-Sterling, Anne. *Myths of Gender: Biological Theories of Women and Men.* New York: Basic Books, 1992.

Friedan, Betty. *The Feminine Mystique.* New York: Dell, 1970.

Frye, Marilyn. *The Politics of Reality.* Trumanburg, NY: Crossing Press, 1983.

Gilligan, Carol. *In a Different Voice.* Cambridge, MA: Harvard University Press, 1982.

Gornick, Vivian, and Barbara K. Moran, eds. *Women in Sexist Society.* New York: Signet, 1972.

Haskell, Molly. *From Reverence to Rape: The Treatment of Women in the Movies.* Chicago: University of Chicago Press, 1987.

Henley, Nancy. *Body Politics: Power, Sex and Non-Verbal Communication.* Englewood Cliffs, NJ: Prentice-Hall, 1977.

Henley, Nancy, and Clara Mayo. *Gender and Non-Verbal Behavior.* New York: Springer, 1981.

hooks, bell. *Talking Back: Thinking Feminist, Thinking Black.* Boston: South End Press, 1989.

Jaggar, Alison M. *Feminist Politics and Human Nature.* Totowa, NJ: Rowman & Allanheld, 1983.

McDonald, Myra. *Representing Women: Myths of Femininity in the Popular Media.* New York: St. Martin's Press, 1995.

Mill, John Stuart, and Harriet Taylor Mill. *Essays on Sex Equality.* Ed. Alice S. Rossi. Chicago: University of Chicago Press, 1970.

Millett, Kate. *Sexual Politics.* New York: Avon Books, 1971.

Sadker, Myra, and David Sadker. *Failing at Fairness: How America's Schools Cheat Girls.* New York: Scribner, 1994.

Spelman, Elizabeth V. *Inessential Woman: Problems of Exclusion in Feminist Thought.* Boston: Beacon Press, 1988.

Wolgast, Elizabeth. *Equality and the Rights of Women.* Ithaca, NY: Cornell University Press, 1980.

Wolf, Naomi. *The Beauty Myth: How Images of Beauty Are Used Against Women.* New York: Morrow, 1991.

Wollstonecraft, Mary. *A Vindication of the Rights of Women* (1792). New York: Norton, 1967.

Wood, Julia. *Gendered Lives: Communication, Gender and Culture.* Belmont, CA: Wadsworth, 1994.

Human Rights

An-Na'im, Abdullahi Ahmed, ed. *Human Rights in Cross-Cultural Perspectives: A Quest for Consensus.* Philadelphia: University of Pennsylvania Press, 1992.

An-Na'im, Abdullahi A., et al., eds. *Human Rights and Religious Values: An Uneasy Relationship?* Grand Rapids, MI: Eerdmans, 1995.

Beyani, Chaloka. *Human Rights Standards and the Movement of People Within States.* Oxford: Oxford University Press, 2000.

Brown, Seyom. *Human Rights in World Politics.* New York: Longman, 2000.

Davenport, Christian, ed. *Paths to State Repression: Human Rights Violations and Contentious Politics.* Lanham, MD: Rowman & Littlefield, 2000.

de Bary, Wm. Theodore. *Asian Values and Human Rights: A Confucian Communitarian Perspective.* Cambridge, MA: Harvard University Press, 1998.

de Bary, Wm. Theodore, and Tu Weiming, eds. *Confucianism and Human Rights.* New York: Columbia University Press, 1998.

Donnelly, Jack. *Universal Human Rights in Theory and Practice.* Ithaca, NY: Cornell University Press, 1989.

Dunne, Tim, and Nicholas J. Wheeler, eds. *Human Rights in Global Politics.* New York: Cambridge University Press, 1999.

Hilsdon, Anne-Marie, et al., eds. *Human Rights and Gender Politics: Asia Pacific Perspectives.* New York: Routledge, 2000.

Keown, Damien V., Charles S. Prebish, and Wayne R. Husted, eds. *Buddhism and Human Rights.* Richmond, Surrey: Curzon, 1998.

Mamdani, Mahmood, ed. *Beyond Culture Talk and Rights Talk: Comparative Essays on the Politics of Rights and Culture.* New York: St. Martin's Press, 2000.

Mayer, Ann Elizabeth. *Islam and Human Rights: Tradition and Politics.* 3rd ed. Boulder, CO: Westview Press, 1999.

Perry, Michael J. *The Idea of Human Rights: Four Inquiries.* New York: Oxford University Press, 1998.

Peters, Julie, and Andrea Wolper, eds. *Women's Rights, Human Rights: International Feminist Perspectives.* New York: Routledge, 1995.

Renteln, Alison Dundes. *International Human Rights : Universalism versus Relativism.* Newbury Park: Sage, 1990.

Rowan, John R. *Conflicts of Rights: Moral Theory and Social Policy Implications.* Boulder, CO: Westview Press, 1999.

Shepherd, George W., Jr., and Mark O. C. Anikpo, eds. *Emerging Human Rights: The African Political Economy Context.* New York: Greenwood Press, 1990.

Sterba, James. "Human Rights: A Social Contract Perspective." *American Catholic Philosophical Association Proceedings* 55 (1981): 268–275.

Van Ness, Peter, ed. *Debating Human Rights: Critical Essays from the United States and Asia.* New York: Routledge, 1999.

Williams, Mary E., ed. *Human Rights: Opposing Viewpoints.* San Diego, CA: Greenhaven Press, 1998.

Wilson, Richard, ed. *Human Rights, Culture and Context: Anthropological Perspectives.* Chicago: Pluto Press, 1997.

Zoelle, Diana. *Globalizing Concern for Women's Human Rights.* New York: St. Martin's Press, 2000.

# of LIFE and DEATH

Lester Burnham (Kevin Spacey) and his wife, Carolyn (Annette Bening) in *American Beauty*.

6.1   WHAT IS THE MEANING OF LIFE?

EPICURUS

THE LETTER OF EPICURUS TO MENOECEUS

According to Epicurus, the goal of life is happiness, and happiness is attained through the pursuit of pleasure. His position is called *hedonism* (*hedone* is Greek for "pleasure"), which means that he believes that pleasure is the end and aim of human life and action, "the alpha and omega of the happy life." "It is the starting point of every choice and of every aversion."

However, while all pleasures are good, *not all pleasures are preferable to pains*, for sometimes pain leads to pleasure. Epicurus says, "Often we consider pains superior to pleasures when submission to the pains for a long time brings us as a consequence greater pleasure." "While therefore all pleasure because it is naturally akin to us is good, not all pleasure is worthy of choice, just as all pain is an evil and yet not all pain is to be shunned." Thus, Epicurus's hedonism is not simply the pursuit of anything and everything that is pleasurable, and the avoidance of anything and everything that is painful. Sometimes, we must "treat the good as an evil, and the evil . . . as a good."

Furthermore, not all pleasures are to be chosen. While happiness consists in a state of pleasure, it is not just any kind of pleasure. "When we say that pleasure is the end and aim, we do not mean the pleasure of the prodigal or the pleasures of sensuality," says Epicurus. Rather, the pleasure sought by Epicurus is a state of tranquility, free from mental and physical disturbances (*ataraxia*). Pleasure is simply "the absence of pain in the body and of trouble in the soul." We are guided to this state of *ataraxia* by prudence, and prudence is the foundation of all of the other virtues. For Epicurus, "prudence is a more precious thing even than the other virtues, for one cannot lead a life of pleasure which not also a life of prudence, honor, and justice."

Peacefulness of mind and evenness of soul are the ultimate good. They allow us to master even our greatest fears, such as those regarding death. When we apply sober reasoning to the prospect of death, we see that "when we are, death is not come, and, when death is come, we are not." "It is nothing, then, either to the living or to the dead, for with the living it is not and the dead exist no longer."

Epicurus (341–270 B.C.E.), a Greek philosopher, was born in Samos a few years after the death of Plato. Like his atomist predecessors Leucippus (fifth century B.C.E.) and Democritus (460–370 B.C.E.), Epicurus believed that everything that is real is composed of atoms, including the soul.

In 306, Epicurus purchased a garden just outside of Athens and established a school there. The "Garden," as the school came to be known, was coeducational: women and men, children and slaves, soldiers and citizens of high status all studied there. It was a popular school that survived until the fifth century C.E.—the early Christian period. Part of the appeal of *Epicureanism* was its relative simplicity, coherency, and directness as compared to the philosophies of Aristotle and Plato. Over three hundred works have been attributed to Epicurus, though most are lost. His major surviving works are *On Nature* (nine of its thirty-seven books have survived), the *Canon*, and letters to Herodotus, Pitocles, and Menoeceus.

The following selection is the letter to Menoeceus, who was a mythological character, the son of Creon (the same Creon from *Oedipus the King* who was the brother of Queen Jocasta).

Legend had it that Thebes would not survive an assault unless an unmarried descendant of Cadmus's Spartoi (men who were sown from the ground from dragon's teeth on the future site of Thebes) was sacrificed. Menoeceus fit this description, and no other was available. So, despite the attempts of his father to save him, Menoeceus killed himself so that Thebes would survive the assault.

Let no one be slow to seek wisdom when he is young nor weary in the search thereof when he is grown old. For no age is too early or too late for the health of the soul. And to say that the season for studying philosophy has not yet come, or that it is past and gone, is like saying that the season for happiness is not yet or that it is now no more. Therefore, both old and young ought to seek wisdom, the former in order that, as age comes over him, he may be young in good things because of the grace of what has been, and the latter in order that, while he is young, he may at the same time be old, because he has no fear of the things which are to come. So we must exercise ourselves in the things which bring happiness, since, if that be present, we have everything, and, if that be absent, all our actions are directed toward attaining it.

Those things which without ceasing I have declared to you, those do, and exercise yourself in those, holding them to be the elements of right life. First believe that God is a living being immortal and happy, according to the notion of a god indicated by the common sense of humankind; and so believing, you shall not affirm of him anything that is foreign to his immortality or that is repugnant to his blessedness. Believe about him whatever may uphold both his blessedness and his immortality. For truly there are gods, and knowledge of them is evident; but they are not such as the multitude believe, seeing that people do not steadfastly maintain the notions they form respecting them. Not the person who denies the gods worshiped by the multitude, but he who affirms of the gods what the multitude believes about them is truly impious. For the utterances of the multitude about the gods are not true preconceptions but false assumptions; hence it is that the greatest evils happen to the wicked and the greatest blessings happen to the good from the hand of the gods, seeing that they are always favorable to their own good qualities and take

pleasure in people like to themselves, but reject as alien whatever is not of their kind.

Accustom yourself to believe that death is nothing to us, for good and evil imply awareness, and death is the privation of all awareness; therefore a right understanding that death is nothing to us makes the mortality of life enjoyable, not by adding to life an unlimited time, but by taking away the yearning after immortality. For life has no terror; for those who thoroughly apprehend that there are no terrors for them in ceasing to live. Foolish, therefore, is the person who says that he fears death, not because it will pain when it comes, but because it pains in the prospect. Whatever causes no annoyance when it is present, causes only a groundless pain in the expectation. Death, therefore, the most awful of evils, is nothing to us, seeing that, when we are, death is not come, and, when death is come, we are not. It is nothing, then, either to the living or to the dead, for with the living it is not and the dead exist no longer. But in the world, at one time people shun death as the greatest of all evils, and at another time choose it as a respite from the evils in life. The wise person does not deprecate life nor does he fear the cessation of life. The thought of life is no offense to him, nor is the cessation of life regarded as an evil. And even as people choose of food not merely and simply the larger portion, but the more pleasant, so the wise seek to enjoy the time which is most pleasant and not merely that which is longest. And he who admonishes the young to live well and the old to make a good end speaks foolishly, not merely because of the desirability of life, but because the same exercise at once teaches to live well and to die well. Much worse is he who says that it were good not to be born, but when once one is born to pass with all speed through the gates of Hades. For if he truly believes this, why does he not depart from life? It were easy for him to do so, if once he were firmly convinced. If he speaks only in mockery, his words are foolishness, for those who hear believe him not.

We must remember that the future is neither wholly ours nor wholly not ours, so that neither must we count upon it as quite certain to come nor despair of it as quite certain not to come.

We must also reflect that of desires some are natural, others are groundless; and that of the natural some are necessary as well as natural, and some natural only. And of the necessary desires some are necessary if we are to be happy, some if the body is to be rid of uneasiness, some if we are even to live. He who has a clear and certain understanding of these things will direct every preference and aversion toward securing health of body and tranquillity of mind, seeing that this is the sum and end of a happy life. For the end of all our actions is to be free from pain and fear, and, when once we have attained all this, the tempest of the soul is laid; seeing that the living creature has no need to go in search of something that is lacking, nor to look for anything else by which the good of the soul and of the body will be fulfilled. When we are pained because of the absence of pleasure, then, and then only, do we feel the need of pleasure. For this reason we call pleasure the alpha and omega of a happy life. Pleasure is our first and kindred good. It is the starting-point of every choice and of every aversion, and to it we come back, inasmuch as we make feeling the rule by which to judge of every good thing. And since pleasure is our first and native good, for that reason we do not choose every pleasure whatever, but often pass over many pleasures when a greater annoyance ensues from them. And often we consider pains superior to pleasures when submission to the pains for a long time brings us as a consequence a greater pleasure. While therefore all pleasure because it is naturally akin to us is good, not all pleasure is worthy of choice, just as all pain is an evil and yet not all pain is to be shunned. It is, however, by measuring one against another, and by looking at the conveniences and inconveniences, that all these matters must be judged. Sometimes we treat the good as an evil, and the evil, on the contrary, as a good. Again, we regard independence of outward things as a great good, not so as in all cases to use little, but so as to be contented with little if we have not much, being honestly persuaded that they have the

sweetest enjoyment of luxury who stand least in need of it, and that whatever is natural is easily procured and only the vain and worthless hard to win. Plain fare gives as much pleasure as a costly diet, when once the pain of want has been removed, while bread and water confer the highest possible pleasure when they are brought to hungry lips. To habituate one's self therefore, to a simple and inexpensive diet supplies all that is needful for health, and enables a person to meet the necessary requirements of life without shrinking and it places us in a better condition when we approach at intervals a costly fare and renders us fearless of fortune.

When we say, then, that pleasure is the end and aim, we do not mean the pleasures of the prodigal or the pleasures of sensuality, as we are understood to do by some through ignorance, prejudice, or willful misrepresentation. By pleasure we mean the absence of pain in the body and of trouble in the soul. It is not an unbroken succession of drinking-bouts and of merrymaking, not sexual love, not the enjoyment of the fish and other delicacies of a luxurious table, which produce a pleasant life; it is sober reasoning, searching out the grounds of every choice and avoidance, and banishing those beliefs through which the greatest disturbances take possession of the soul. Of all this the beginning and the greatest good is prudence. For this reason prudence is a more precious thing even than the other virtues, for one cannot lead a life of pleasure which is not also a life of prudence, honor, and justice; nor lead a life of prudence, honor, and justice, which is not also a life of pleasure. For the virtues have grown into one with a pleasant life, and a pleasant life is inseparable from them.

Who, then, is superior in your judgment to such a person? He holds a holy belief concerning the gods, and is altogether free from the fear of death. He has diligently considered the end fixed by nature, and understands how easily the limit of good things can be reached and attained, and how either the duration or the intensity of evils is but slight. Destiny which some introduce as sovereign over all things, he laughs to scorn, affirming rather that some things happen of necessity, others by chance, others through our own agency. For he sees that necessity destroys responsibility and that chance or fortune is inconstant; whereas our own actions are free, and it is to them that praise and blame naturally attach. It were better, indeed, to accept the legends of the gods than to bow beneath destiny which the natural philosophers have imposed. The one holds out some faint hope that we may escape if we honor the gods, while the necessity of the naturalists is deaf to all entreaties. Nor does he hold chance to be a god, as the world in general does, for in the acts of a god there is no disorder; nor to be a cause, though an uncertain one, for he believes that no good or evil is dispensed by chance to people so as to make life happy, though it supplies the starting-point of great good and great evil. He believes that the misfortune of the wise is better than the prosperity of the fool. It is better, in short, that what is well judged in action should not owe its successful issue to the aid of chance.

Exercise yourself in these and kindred precepts day and night, both by yourself and with him who is like to you; then never, either in waking or in dream, will you be disturbed, but will live as a god among people. For people lose all appearance of mortality by living in the midst of immortal blessings.

DISCUSSION QUESTIONS

1. Epicurus argues that pleasure gives life meaning. Do you agree with him? Why or why not? Is the lifestyle he proposes like your own lifestyle? Discuss.

2. According to Epicurus, who should study philosophy, and why?

3. According to Epicurus, why is a "holy belief concerning the gods" important?

4. Epicurus argues that we should not fear death. What is his argument? Do you agree with it? Why or why not?

5. Why does Epicurus believe that sometimes we need to "treat the good as an evil, and the evil . . . as a good"? Do you agree with him? Why or why not?

6. Epicurus argues that while pleasure is the end and aim of life, it is not the kind of pleasure found in sensual love, drinking, and "the enjoyment of fish and other delicacies of a luxurious table." Why are these pleasures to be avoided?

American Beauty
[USA 1999] 2 hours, 2 minutes
Directed by Sam Mendes

*L*ester Burnham (Kevin Spacey) lives in suburbia and works a boring job at an advertising agency, and both his teenage daughter, Jane (Thora Birch), and his wife, Carolyn (Annette Bening), hate him. He is fed up with his wife and daughter getting to do whatever they want, and not ever getting to do what he wants. He now refuses to sit quietly and live out his life the way his family wants him to. So, one day, he walks into his office and quits his job, but not before threatening to expose some scandalous secrets about his fellow employees. His blackmail efforts yield him an entire year's severance pay. He trades in his Toyota Camry for a red 1970s "muscle car," starts smoking pot and working out, and takes a job at Mr. Smiley's, a local burger shop, working the grill. He also begins to lust after his daughter's attractive teenage friend, Angela (Mena Suvari). Meanwhile, his wife and daughter are undergoing their own "crises."

Carolyn is a perfectionist real estate agent whose motto is "In order to be successful, one must project an image of success." However, underneath her outward image is a woman who is anything but happy. Carolyn decides that having an affair with her real estate competitor, Buddy Kane (Peter Gallagher), will bring happiness into her life. One day, giddy after an afternoon of passion, they pull into the burger shop where Lester works. Lester confronts them and says to Carolyn, "You don't get to tell me what to do ever again."

Jane, Lester's daughter, is experiencing teenage angst and embarrassment about her parents until Ricky Fitts (Wes Bentley), a boy with a mysterious past and an obsession with video cameras, moves in next door. As Jane and Ricky begin a relationship, Ricky's controlling ex-Marine Corps father (Chris Cooper), who exhibits an intense hatred for homosexuals, begins to suspect that something entirely different is taking place between Ricky and Lester. Colonel Fitts thinks that his son, who in actuality is simply selling marijuana to Lester, is having a homosexual affair with him. Ricky goes along with his father's lie when Fitts confronts him with it because he realizes that it is his only chance to escape this rigid and abusive home.

Highly distraught, Fitts then confronts Lester in his garage. He asks Lester where his wife is, and Lester says that she is out with another man and that he is fine with this—that their marriage is just for show. For Fitts, this confirms Lester's homosexuality, and, suddenly, he kisses him. When Lester tells Fitts that he has it all wrong, an embarrassed Fitts goes home.

Later, Lester and Angela begin to get passionate on Lester's couch, but Lester stops things before they go too far, realizing this is the right thing to do. After this, Lester and Angela talk a bit, and we find Lester in a surprisingly good mood. He asks Angela how Jane is, and Angela asks Lester how he is. He says, "I'm great." Angela leaves the room, and Lester goes over to a picture of his family that was taken long ago. As he smiles and looks at it happily, Colonel Fitts sneaks up behind him and shoots him in the back of the head, killing him.

DISCUSSION QUESTIONS

1. Are Lester and Carolyn unhappy because they lack pleasure in their lives? Does the pursuit of pleasure make their lives happier?

2. What do you think Epicurus would say about Lester's and Carolyn's pursuit of pleasure? Which, if either, is closest to his ideal of happiness and the life of pleasure?

3. Lester says to himself, "Both my wife and daughter think I'm this gigantic loser. Then, they're right. I have lost something. I'm not exactly sure what it is, but I know I didn't always feel this sedated. But, you know what? It's never too late to get it back." What do you think it is that Lester "lost"? Is it possible for him to get it back? Is it wise even to try? Why or why not?

4. Angela says to Jane, "There's nothing worse in life than being ordinary." Is Angela right? Why or why not? To what extent is this film an exploration of Angela's statement?

5. Consider the following conversation between Ricky and Jane:

   RICKY   "I got that homeless woman on videotape."

   JANE   "Why would you film that?"

   RICKY   "Because it was amazing."

   JANE   "What's amazing about it?"

   RICKY   "When you see something like that it's like God is looking right at you, just for a second. And if you're careful, you can look right back."

   JANE   "And what do you see?"

   RICKY   "Beauty."

Ricky finds the beauty and meaning of life in the ordinary. Compare his view of "ordinariness" with that of Angela. Whose position on the meaning of life do you prefer, and why?

6. Later, Ricky says to Jane, "You want to see the most beautiful thing I've ever filmed?" They then watch a videotape of a plastic bag blowing in the wind. Ricky continues, "It was one of those days where it's a minute away from snowing and there's this electricity in the air. You can almost hear it, right? And this bag was just dancing with me like a little kid begging me to play with it. For fifteen minutes. That's the day I realized that there was this entire life behind things. And this incredibly benevolent force wanted me to know that there was no reason to be afraid. Ever. Video is a poor excuse, I know. But it helps me to remember. I need to remember. Sometimes there's so much beauty in the world I feel like I can't take it." Is the kind of pleasure Ricky finds in watching this video of the plastic bag what Epicurus calls *ataraxia*? Why or why not?

7. Consider the following dialogue between Carolyn and Lester:

CAROLYN   "Lester, you're going to spill beer on the couch."

LESTER   "So what? It's just a couch."

CAROLYN   "This is $4,000 sofa upholstered in Italian silk. This is not just a couch!"

LESTER   "It's just a couch! This isn't life—this is just stuff. And it's become more important to you than living. Well, honey, that's just nuts. . . . I'm only trying to help you!"

What does Lester mean by "This isn't life—this is just stuff. And it's become more important to you than living"? Do you agree with him? Why or why not?

8. Lester tells his boss, "Brad, for fourteen years I've been a whore for the advertising industry. The only way I could save myself now is if I start firebombing." Then Lester says to him, "I'm just an ordinary guy with nothing to lose." Why does Lester feel he has nothing to lose? Do you agree with him?

9. After Lester dies, he says the following in a voice-over: "I'd always heard your entire life flashes in front of your eyes the second before you die. First of all, that one second isn't a second at all. It stretches forever like an ocean of time. For me it was lying on my back at Boy Scout camp watching falling stars. And yellow leaves from the maple trees that lined our street. Or my grand-mother's hands and the way her skin seemed like paper. And the first time I saw my cousin Tony's brand-new Firebird. And Janie. And Janie. And Carolyn. I guess I could be pretty pissed off about what happened to me, but it's hard to stay mad when there's so much beauty in the world. Sometimes I feel like I'm seeing it all at once. And it's too much. My heart fills up like a balloon that's about to burst. And then I remember to relax and stop trying to hold onto it. And then it flows through me like rain, and I can't feel anything but gratitude for every single moment of my stupid little life. You have no idea what I'm talking about, I'm sure. But don't worry. You will someday." How did Lester come to have "gratitude for every single moment of [his] stupid little life"? Do you think it is possible to feel that your life is stupid and still be grateful for every moment of it? Discuss what he is talking about in this passage, and whether you agree with him.

10. Why do you think this film was titled *American Beauty*? Is this an appropriate title? Why or why not? What sense of beauty, if any, is depicted in this film? Do you agree with it? Discuss.

11. Do you think that Lester has discovered the meaning of life? If so, what is it? Is it similar to Epicurus's position? Why or why not?

MARCUS AURELIUS

MEDITATIONS

Marcus Aurelius argues that tranquility of mind achieved by living in conformity with nature is the goal of life. Like his predecessor Epictetus (see chapter 5), Aurelius is a Stoic philosopher. Like Epictetus, Aurelius believes that we must accept whatever happens to us. However, Aurelius is a transitional figure in the history of Stoic philosophy.

While the writings of earlier Stoics like Zeno of Citium (c. 335–264 B.C.E.) and Chrysippus (c. 280–206 B.C.E.) are marked by a strong sense of self-sufficiency and pride, Aurelius's writing includes a noticeably lesser degree of self-sufficiency and pride. He readily acknowledges his own failures as a person with a sense of humility not found in the work of earlier Stoic philosophers. Aurelius's version of Stoicism anticipates the Christian virtue of humility. He also longs for sympathy and affection, something Zeno and Chrysippus, for example, would never do. Moreover, while like earlier Stoics, Aurelius emphasizes the control of life by reason, he widens the sense of duty to include duty to others or the public as well as to oneself.

Aurelius says that we should live according to nature, and by nature he means the force that guides the development of everything in the universe toward its ultimate perfection. Moreover, as Nature was sometimes referred to as God, one finds a similarity between the New Testament maxim "Be ye followers of God" and the Stoic maxim "to live according to Nature." Nevertheless, God for the Stoics is immanent in all created things (this is called *pantheism*); God does not have a separate existence outside of them. Aurelius writes, "Constantly regard the universe as one living being, having one substance and one soul . . ." (Book 4, para. 40). In addition, *Providence, Fate, Law, Necessity, Zeus*, and many other terms are used to refer to essentially the same thing as the terms *Nature* and *God*.

For Aurelius, the life lived in accordance with Nature is the life controlled by reason, which is also the virtuous life. Reason reveals to us the things that are in our power to control, such as our will and judgments, and also the things that are not in our power, such as health, wealth, friends, and death. Things that are not in our power to control cannot affect us, so we should maintain an attitude of indifference toward them. Things external to us are also neither good nor evil, neither sources of pleasure, nor pain. However, if we *judge* something pleasurable to be good or *judge* something painful to be evil, then and only then do they become so. In other words, only things that are within our power can be good or evil, and pleasure in itself is not good, and pain in itself is not evil. Good and evil are determined relative to our judgments. For Aurelius, "life is opinion," and opinion is everything.

Marcus Aurelius (121–180 C.E.) reigned as emperor of Rome for nineteen years. Born Marcus Annius Catilius Servus, he was the son of a Roman nobleman, and, as a boy, he was tutored in the doctrines of Stoic philosophy. From his youth, Marcus was a favorite of the emperor Hadrian. Because Marcus had become orphaned, Hadrian directed Marcus's uncle, Antoninus Pius, to adopt him. When Hadrian died in 138 C.E., his designated successor, Antoninus Pius, became emperor. Marcus was seventeen. By the will of Hadrian, Marcus married Faustina, the daughter of Antoninus Pius, in 145, at which time he changed his name to Marcus Annius Verus. Marcus and Faustina had thirteen children; however, only Commodus survived his father's death in 180. Commodus succeeded as emperor, but he was generally regarded as "worthless" and was later assassinated.

On the death of Antoninus Pius in 161, Marcus became emperor and changed his name to Marcus Aurelius Antoninus. Against the wishes of the Senate, he took Antoninus Pius's other adopted son, Lucius Verus, as his co-emperor (a first in Roman history). When Verus died in 169, Aurelius became sole emperor. His reign was marked by many disasters including flood, plague, insurrection, invasions, and fire. Later in life, he endowed philosophy chairs at the Academy, the Lyceum, the Epicurean Garden, and the Stoa, the major philosophical schools in Athens. He wrote his *Meditations* after the death of Faustina, while on a harsh military expedition on the Danube. It is a collection of thoughts regarding the conduct and meaning of life viewed from the position of Stoicism. He died at the age of fifty-nine of a disease contracted on this Danube expedition. The following selection is from the *Meditations*.

Book Two

Begin the morning by saying to thyself, I shall meet with the busy-body, the ungrateful, arrogant, deceitful, envious, unsocial. All these things happen to them by reason of their ignorance of what is good and evil. But I who have seen the nature of the good that it is beautiful, and of the bad that it is ugly, and the nature of him who does wrong, that it is akin to me, not only of the same blood or seed, but that it participates in the same intelligence and the same portion of the divinity, I can neither be injured by any of them, for no one can fix on me what is ugly, nor can I be angry with my kinsman, nor hate him. For we are made for co-operation, like feet, like hands, like eyelids, like the rows of the upper and lower teeth. To act against one another then is contrary to nature; and it is acting against one another to be vexed and to turn away.

2. Whatever this is that I am, it is a little flesh and breath; and the ruling part. Throw away thy books; no longer distract thyself: it is not allowed; but as if thou wast now dying, despise the flesh; it is blood and bones and a network, a contexture of nerves, veins, and arteries. See the breath also, what kind of a thing it is, air, and not always the same, but every moment sent out and again sucked in. The third then is the ruling part: consider thus: Thou art an old man; no longer let this be a slave, no longer be pulled by the strings like a puppet to unsocial movements, no longer be either dissatisfied with thy present lot, or shrink from the future.

3. All that is from the gods is full of Providence. That which is from fortune is not separated from nature or without an interweaving and involution

with the things which are ordered by Providence. From thence all things flow; and there is besides necessity, and that which is for the advantage of the whole universe, of which thou art a part. But that is good for every part of nature which the nature of the whole brings, and what serves to maintain this nature. Now the universe is preserved, as by the changes of the elements so by the changes of things compounded of the elements. Let these principles be enough for thee, let them always be fixed opinions. But cast away the thirst after books, that thou mayest not die murmuring, but cheerfully, truly, and from thy heart thankful to the gods.

4. Remember how long thou hast been putting off these things, and how often thou hast received an opportunity from the gods, and yet dost not use it. Thou must now at last perceive of what universe thou art a part, and of what administrator of the universe thy existence is an efflux, and that a limit of time is fixed for thee, which if thou dost not use for clearing away the clouds from thy mind, it will go and thou wilt go, and it will never return.

5. Every moment think steadily as a Roman and a man to do what thou hast in hand with perfect and simple dignity, and feeling of affection, and freedom, and justice; and to give thyself relief from all other thoughts. And thou wilt give thyself relief, if thou doest every act of thy life as if it were the last, laying aside all carelessness and passionate aversion from the commands of reason, and all hypocrisy, and self-love, and discontent with the portion which has been given to thee. Thou seest how few the things are, the which if a

man lays hold of, he is able to live a life which flows in quiet, and is like the existence of the gods; for the gods on their part will require nothing more from him who observes these things.

6. Do wrong to thyself, do wrong to thyself, my soul; but thou wilt no longer have the opportunity of honouring thyself. Every man's life is sufficient. But thine is nearly finished, though thy soul reverences not itself, but places thy felicity in the souls of others.

7. Do the things external which fall upon thee distract thee? Give thyself time to learn something new and good, and cease to be whirled around. But then thou must also avoid being carried about the other way. For those too are triflers who have wearied themselves in life by their activity, and yet have no object to which to direct every movement, and, in a word, all their thoughts.

8. Through not observing what is in the mind of another a man has seldom been seen to be unhappy; but those who do not observe the movements of their own minds must of necessity be unhappy.

9. This thou must always bear in mind, what is the nature of the whole, and what is my nature, and how this is related to that, and what kind of a part it is of what kind of a whole; and that there is no one who hinders thee from always doing and saying the things which are according to the nature of which thou art a part.

10. Theophrastus, in his comparison of bad acts—such a comparison as one would make in accordance with the common notions of mankind—says, like a true philosopher, that the offences which are committed through desire are more blameable than those which are committed through anger. For he who is excited by anger seems to turn away from reason with a certain pain and unconscious contraction; but he who offends through desire, being overpowered by pleasure, seems to be in a manner more intemperate and more womanish in his offences. Rightly then, and in a way worthy of philosophy, he said that the offence which is committed with pleasure is more blameable than that which is committed with pain; and on the whole the one is more like a person who has been first wronged and through pain is compelled to be angry; but the other is moved by his own impulse to be wrong, being carried towards doing something by desire.

11. Since it is possible that thou mayest depart from life this very moment, regulate every act and thought accordingly. But to go away from among men, if there are gods, is not a thing to be afraid of, for the gods will not involve thee in evil; but if indeed they do not exist, or if they have no concern about human affairs, what is it to me to live in a universe devoid of gods or devoid of Providence? But in truth they do exist, and they do care for human things, and they have put all the means in man's power to enable him not to fall into real evils. And as to the rest, if there was anything evil, they would have provided for this also, that it should be altogether in a man's power not to fall into it. Now that which does not make a man worse, how can it make a man's life worse? But neither through ignorance, nor having the knowledge, but not the power to guard against or correct these things, is it possible that the nature of the universe has overlooked them; nor is it possible that is has made so great a mistake, either through want of power or want of skill, that good and evil should happen indiscriminately to the good and the bad. But death certainly, and life, honour and dishonour, pain and pleasure, all these things equally happen to good men and bad, being things which make us neither better nor worse. Therefore they are neither good nor evil.

12. How quickly all things disappear, in the universe the bodies themselves, but in time the remembrance of them; what is the nature of all sensible things, and particularly those which attract with the bait of pleasure or terrify by pain, or are noised abroad by vapoury fame; how worthless, and contemptible, and sordid, and perishable, and dead they are—all this it is the part of the intellectual faculty to observe. To observe too who these are whose opinions and voices give reputation; what death is, and the fact that, if a man looks at it in itself, and by the abstractive power of reflection resolves into their parts all the things which present themselves to the imagination in it, he will then consider it to be nothing else than an operation of nature; and if any one is afraid of an operation of nature, he is a child. This, however, is not only an operation of nature, but it is also a thing which conduces to the purposes of nature. To observe too how man comes near to the deity, and by what part of him, and when this part of man is so disposed.

13. Nothing is more wretched than a man who traverses everything in a round, and pries into the things beneath the earth, as the poet says, and seeks by conjecture what is in the minds of his neighbours, without perceiving that it is sufficient to attend to the daemon* within him, and to reverence it sincerely. And reverence of the daemon consists in keeping it pure from passion and thoughtlessness, and dissatisfaction with what comes from gods and men. For the things from the gods merit veneration for their excellence; and the things from men should be dear to us by reason of kinship; and sometimes even, in a manner, they move our pity by reason of men's ignorance of good and bad; this defect being not less than that which deprives us of the power of distinguishing things that are white and black.

14. Though thou shouldst be going to live three thousand years, and as many times ten thousand years, still remember that no man loses any other life than this which he now lives, nor lives any other than this which he now loses. The longest and shortest are thus brought so the same. For the present is the same to all, though that which perishes is not the same; and so that which is lost appears to be a mere moment. For a man cannot lose either the past or the future: for what a man has not, how can any one take this from him? These two things then thou must bear in mind; the one, that all things from eternity are of like forms and come round in a circle, and that it makes no difference whether a man shall see the same things during a hundred years or two hundred, or an infinite time; and the second, that the longest liver and he who will die soonest lose just the same. For the present is the only thing of which a man can be deprived, if it is true that this is the only thing which he has, and that a man cannot lose a thing if he has it not. . . .

15. Remember that all is opinion. For what was said by the Cynic Monimus is manifest: and manifest too is the use of what was said, if a man receives what may be got out of it as far as it is true.

16. The soul of man does violence to itself, first of all, when it becomes an abscess and, as it were, a tumour on the universe, so far as it can. For to be vexed at anything which happens is a separation of ourselves from nature, in some part of which the natures of all other things are contained. In the next place, the soul does violence to itself when it turns away from any man, or even moves towards him with the intention of injuring, such as are the souls of those who are angry. In the third place, the soul does violence to itself when it is overpowered by pleasure or by pain. Fourthly, when it plays a part, and does or says anything insincerely and untruly. Fifthly, when it allows any act of its own and any movement to be without an aim, and does anything thoughtlessly and without considering what it is, it being right that even the smallest things be done with refrerence to an end; and the end of rational animals is to follow the reason and the law of the most ancient city and polity.

17. Of human life the time is a point, and the substance is in a flux, and the perception dull, and the composition of the whole body subject to putrefaction, and the soul a whirl, and fortune hard to divine, and fame a thing devoid of judgment. And, to say all in a word, everything which belongs to the body is a stream, and what belongs to the soul is a dream and vapour, and life is a warfare and a stranger's sojourn, and after-fame is oblivion. What then is that which is able to conduct a man? One thing and only one, philosophy. But this consists in keeping the daemon within a man free from violence and unharmed, superior to pains and pleasures, doing nothing without a purpose, not yet falsely and with hypocrisy, not feeling the need of another man's doing or not doing anything; and besides, accepting all that happens, and all that is allotted, as coming from thence, wherever it is, from whence he himself came; and, finally, waiting for death with a cheerful mind, as being nothing else than a dissolution of the elements of which every living being is compounded. But if there is no harm to the elements themselves in each continually changing into another, why should a man have any apprehension about the change and dissolution of all the elements? For it is according to nature, and nothing is evil which is according to nature.

---

*A guardian spirit, ranking somewhere between the gods and men, that the ancient philosophers believed presides over and gives advice on our actions. It also watches over our secret intentions. —Ed.

Book Four

That which rules within, when it is according to nature, is so affected with respect to the events which happen, that it always easily adapts itself to that which is possible and is presented to it. For it requires no definite material, but it moves towards its purpose, under certain conditions however; and it makes a material for itself out of that which opposes it, as fire lays hold of what falls into it, by which a small light would have been extinguished: but when the fire is strong, it soon appropriates to itself the matter which is heaped on it, and consumes it, and rises higher by means of this very material.

2. Let no act be done without a purpose, nor otherwise than according to the perfect principles of art.

3. Men seek retreats for themselves, houses in the country, sea-shores, and mountains; and thou too art wont to desire such things very much. But this is altogether a mark of the most common sort of men, for it is in thy power whenever thou shalt choose so retire into thyself. For nowhere either with more quiet or more freedom from trouble does a man retire than into his own soul, particularly when he has within him such thoughts that by looking into them he is immediately in perfect tranquillity; and I affirm that tranquillity is nothing else than the good ordering of the mind. Constantly then give to thyself this retreat, and renew thyself; and let thy principles be brief and fundamental, which, as soon as thou shalt recur to them, will be sufficient to cleanse the soul completely, and to send thee back free from all discontent with the things to which thou returnest. For with what art thou discontented? With the badness of men? Recall to thy mind this conclusion, that rational animals exist for one another, and that to endure is a part of justice, and that men do wrong involuntarily; and consider how many already, after mutual enmity, suspicion, hatred, and fighting, have been stretched dead, reduced to ashes; and be quiet at last. —But perhaps thou art dissatisfied with that which is assigned to thee out of the universe. — Recall to thy recollection this alternative; either there is providence or atoms, fortuitous concurrence of things; or remember the arguments by which it has been proved that the world is a kind of

political community, and be quiet at last. —But perhaps corporeal things will still fasten upon thee. —Consider then further that the mind mingles not with the breath, whether moving gently or violently, when it has once drawn itself apart and discovered its own power, and think also of all that thou hast heard and assented to about pain and pleasure, and be quiet at last. — But perhaps the desire of the thing called fame will torment thee. —See how soon everything is forgotten, and look at the chaos of infinite time on each side of the present, and the emptiness of applause, and the changeableness and want of judgment in those who pretend to give praise, and the narrowness of the space within which it is circumscribed, and be quiet at last. For the whole earth is a point, and how small a nook in it is this thy dwelling, and how few are there in it, and what kind of people are they who will praise thee.

This then remains: Remember to retire into this little territory of thy own, and above all do not distract or strain thyself, but be free, and look at things as a man, as a human being, as a citizen, as a mortal. But among the things readiest to thy hand to which thou shalt turn, let there be these, which are two. One is that things do not touch the soul, for they are external and remain immovable; but our perturbations come only from the opinion which is within. The other is that all these things, which thou seest, change immediately and will no longer be; and constantly bear in mind how many of these changes thou hast already witnessed. The universe is transformation: life is opinion.

4. If our intellectual part is common, the reason also, in respect of which we are rational beings, is common: if this is so, common also is the reason which commands us what to do, and what not to do; if this is so, there is a common law also; if this is so, we are fellowcitizens; if this is so, we are members of some political community; if this is so, the world is in a manner a state. For of what other common political community will any one say that the whole human race are members? And from thence, from this common political community comes also our very intellectual faculty and reasoning faculty and our capacity for law; or whence do they come? For as my earthly part is a

portion given to me from certain earth, and that which is watery from another element, and that which is hot and fiery from some peculiar source (for nothing comes out of that which is nothing, as nothing also returns to non-existence), so also the intellectual part comes from some source.

5. Death is such as generation is, a mystery of nature; a composition out of the same elements, and a decomposition into the same; and altogether not a thing of which any man should be ashamed, for it is not contrary to the nature of a reasonable animal, and not contrary to the reason of our constitution.

6. It is natural that these things should be done by such persons; it is a matter of necessity; and if a man will not have it so, he will not allow the fig-tree to have juice: But by all means bear this in mind, that within a very short time both thou and he will be dead; and soon not even your names will be left behind.

7. Take away thy opinion, and then there is taken away the complaint, "I have been harmed." Take away the complaint. "I have been harmed," and the harm is taken away.

8. That which does not make a man worse than he was, also does not make his life worse, nor does it harm him either from without or from within. . . .

10. Consider that everything which happens, happens justly, and if thou observest carefully, thou wilt find it to be so. I do not say only with respect to the continuity of the series of things, but with respect to what is just, and as if it were done by one who assigns to each thing its value. Observe then as thou last begun; and whatever thou doest, do it in conjunction with this, the being good, and in the sense in which a man is properly understood to be good; Keep to this in every action.

11. Do not have such an opinion of things as he has who does thee wrong, or such as he wishes thee to have, but look at them as they are in truth.

12. A man should always have these two rules in readiness; the one, to do only whatever the reason of the ruling and legislating faculty may suggest for the use of men; the other, to change thy opinion, if there is any one at hand who sets thee right and moves thee from any opinion. But this change of opinion must proceed only from a certain persuasion, as of what is just or of common advantage, and the like, not because it appears pleasant or brings reputation. . . .

16. Within ten days thou wilt seem a god to those to whom thou art now a beast and an ape, if thou wilt return to thy principles and the worship of reason.

17. Do not act as if thou wert going to live ten thousand years. Death hangs over thee. While thou livest, while it is in thy power, be good.

18. How much trouble he avoids who does not look to see what his neighbour says or does or thinks, but only to what he does himself, that it may be just and pure; or as Agathon says, look not round at the depraved morals of others, but run straight along the line without deviating from it. . . .

20. Everything which is in any way beautiful is beautiful in itself, and terminates in itself, not having praise as part of itself. Neither worse then nor better is a thing made by being praised. I affirm this also of the things which are called beautiful by the vulgar, for example, material things and works of art. That which is really beautiful has no need of anything; not more than law, not more than truth, not more than benevolence or modesty. Which of these things is beautiful because it is praised, or spoiled by being blamed? Is such a thing as an emerald made worse than it was, if it is not praised? Or gold, ivory, purple, a lyre, a little knife, a flower, a shrub? . . .

23. Everything harmonises with me, which is harmonious to thee, O Universe. Nothing for me is too early nor too late, which is in due time for thee. Everything is fruit to me which thy seasons bring, O Nature: from thee are all things, in thee are all things, to thee all things return. The poet says, Dear city of Cecrops; and wilt not thou say, Dear city of Zeus?

24. Occupy thyself with few things, says the philosopher, if thou wouldst be tranquil —But consider if it would not be better to say, Do what is necessary, and whatever the reason of the animal which is naturally social requires, and as it requires. For this brings not only the tranquillity which comes from doing well, but also that which comes from doing few things. For the greatest part of what we say and do being unnecessary, if a man takes this away, he will have more leisure and less uneasiness. Accordingly on every occasion a man should ask himself, Is this one of the unnecessary

things? Now a man should take away not only unnecessary acts, but also, unnecessary thoughts, for thus superfluous acts will not follow after. . . .

26. Hast thou seen those things? Look also at these. Do not disturb thyself. Make thyself all simplicity. Does any one do wrong? It is to himself that he does the wrong. Has anything happened to thee? Well; out of the universe from the beginning everything which happens has been apportioned and spun out to thee. In a word, thy life is short. Thou must turn to profit the present by the aid of reason and justice. Be sober in thy relaxation.

27. Either it is a well-arranged universe or a chaos huddled together, but still a universe. But can a certain order subsist in thee, and disorder in the All? And this too when all things are so separated and diffused and sympathetic. . . .

29. If he is a stranger to the universe who does not know what is in it, no less is he a stranger who does not know what is going on in it. He is a run-away, who flies from social reason; he is blind, who shuts the eyes of the understanding; he is poor, who has need of another, and has not from himself all things which are useful for life. He is an abscess on the universe who withdraws and separates himself from the reason of our common nature through being displeased with the things which happen, for the same nature produces this, and has produced thee too: he is a piece rent asunder from the state, who tears his own soul from that of reasonable animals, which is one. . . .

31. Love the art, poor as it may be, which thou hast learned, and be content with it; and pass through the rest of life like one who has intrusted to the gods with his whole soul all that he has, making thyself neither the tyrant nor the slave of any man.

32. Consider, for example, the times of Vespasian. Thou wilt see all these things, people marrying, bringing up children, sick, dying, warring, feasting, trafficking, cultivating the ground, flattering, obstinately arrogant, suspecting, plotting, wishing for some to die, grumbling about the present, loving, heaping up treasure, desiring counsulship, kingly power. Well then, that life of these people no longer exists at all. Again, remove to the times Trajan. Again, all is the same. Their life too is gone. In like manner view also the other epochs of time and of whole nations, and see how many after great efforts soon fell and were resolved into the elements. But

chiefly thou shouldst think of those whom thou hast thyself known distracting themselves about idle things, neglecting to do what was in accordance with their proper constitution, and to hold firmly to this and to be content with it. And herein it is necessary to remember, that the attention given to everything has its proper value and proportion. For thus thou wilt not be dissatisfied, if thou appliest thyself to smaller matters no further than is fit.

33. The words which were formerly familiar are now antiquated: so also the names of those who were famed of old, are now in a manner antiquated, Camillus; Caeso, Volesus, Leonnatus; and a little after also Scipio and Cato, then Augustus, then also Hadrian and Antoninus. For all things soon pass away and become a mere tale; and complete oblivion soon buries them. And I say this of those who have shone in a wondrous way. For the rest, as soon as they have breathed out their breath, they are gone, and no man speaks of them. And, to conclude the matter, what is even an eternal remembrance? A mere nothing. What then is that about which we ought to employ our serious pains? This one thing, thoughts just, and acts social, and words which never lie, and a disposition which gladly accepts all that happens, as necessary, as usual, as flowing from a principle and source of the same kind.

34. Willingly give thyself up to Clotho, one of the Fates, allowing her to spin thy thread into whatever things she pleases.

35. Everything is only for a day, both that which remembers and that which is remembered.

36. Observe constantly that all things take place by change, and accustom thyself to consider that the nature of the Universe loves nothing so much as to change the things which are and to make new things like them. For everything that exists is in a manner the seed of that which will be. But thou art thinking only of seeds which are cast into the earth or into a womb: but this is a very vulgar notion.

37. Thou wilt soon die, and thou art not yet simple, not free from perturbations, nor without suspicion of being hurt by external things, nor kindly disposed towards all; nor dost thou yet place wisdom only in acting justly.

38. Examine men's ruling principles, even those of the wise, what kind of things they avoid, and what kind they pursue.

39. What is evil to thee does not subsist in the ruling principle of another; nor yet in any turning and mutation of thy corporeal covering. Where is it then? It is in that part of thee in which subsists the power of forming opinions about evils. Let this power then not form such opinions, and all is well. And if that which is nearest to it, the poor body, is cut, burnt, filled with matter and rottenness, nevertheless let the part which forms opinions about these things be quiet, that is, let it judge that nothing is either bad or good which can happen equally to the bad man and the good. For that which happens equally to him who lives contrary to nature and to him who lives according to nature, is neither according to nature nor contrary to nature.

40. Constantly regard the universe as one living being, having one substance and one soul; and observe how all things have reference to one perception, the perception of this one living being; and how all things act with one movement; and how all things are the cooperating causes of all things which exist; observe too the continuous spinning of the thread and the contexture of the web.

41. Thou art a little soul bearing about a corpse, as Epictetus used to say.

42. It is no evil for things to undergo change, and no good for things to subsist in consequence of change.

43. Time is like a river made up of the events which happen, and a violent stream; for as soon as a thing has been seen, it is carried away, and another comes in its place, and this will be carried away too.

44. Everything which happens is as familiar and well known as the rose in spring and the fruit in summer; for such is disease, and death, and calumny, and treachery, and whatever else delights fools or vexes them.

45. In the series of things those which follow are always aptly fitted to those which have gone before; for this series is not like a mere enumeration of disjointed things, which has only a necessary sequence, but it is a rational connection: and as all existing things are arranged together harmoniously, so the things which come into existence exhibit no mere succession, but a certain wonderful relationship. . . .

48. Think continually how many physicians are dead after often contracting their eyebrows over the sick; and how many astrologers after predicting with great pretensions the deaths of others; and how many philosophers after endless discourses on death or immortality; how many heroes after killing thousands; and how many tyrants who have used their power over men's lives with terrible insolence as if they were immortal; and how many cities are entirely dead, so to speak, Helice and Pompeii and Herculaneum, and others innumerable. Add to the reckoning all whom thou hast known, one after another. One man after burying another has been laid out dead, and another buries him: and all this in a short time. To conclude, always observe how ephemeral and worthless human things are, and what was yesterday a little mucus to-morrow will be a mummy or ashes. Pass then through this little space of time conformably to nature, and end thy journey in content, just as an olive falls off when it is ripe, blessing nature who produced it, and thanking the tree on which it grew.

49. Be like the promontory against which the waves continually break, but it stands firm and tames the fury of the water around it.

Unhappy am I, because this has happened to me.—Not so, but happy am I, though this has happened to me, because I continue free from pain, neither crushed by the present nor fearing the future. For such a thing as this might have happened to every man; but every man would not have continued free from pain on such an occasion. Why then is that rather a misfortune than this a good fortune? And dost thou in all cases call that a man's misfortune, which is not a deviation from man's nature? And does a thing seem to thee to be a deviation from man's nature, when it is not contrary to the will of man's nature? Well, thou knowest the will of nature. Will then this which has happened prevent thee from being just, magnanimous, temperate, prudent, secure against inconsiderate opinions and falsehood; will it prevent thee from having modesty, freedom, and everything else, by the presence of which man's nature obtains all that is its own? Remember too on every occasion which leads thee to vexation to apply this principle: not that this is a misfortune, but that to bear it nobly is good fortune.

50. It is a vulgar, but still a useful help towards contempt of death, to pass in review those who

have tenaciously stuck to life. What more then have they gained than those who have died early? Certainly they lie in their tombs somewhere at last, Cadicianus, Fabius, Julianus, Lepidus, or any one else like them, who have carried out many to be buried, and then were carried out themselves. Altogether the interval is small between birth and death; and consider with how much trouble, and in company with what sort of people and in what a feeble body this interval is laboriously passed. Do not then consider life a thing of any value. For

BOOK FIVE

8. Just as we must understand when it is said, That Aesculapius prescribed to this man horse-exercise, or bathing in cold water or going without shoes; so we must understand it when it is said, That the nature of the universe prescribed to this man disease or mutilation or loss or anything else of the kind. For in the first case Prescribed means something like this: he prescribed this for this man as a thing adapted to procure health; and in the second case it means: That which happens to (or, suits) every man is fixed in a manner for him suitably to his destiny. For this is what we mean when we say that things are suitable to us, as the workmen say of squared stones in walls or the pyramids, that they are suitable, when they fit them to one another in some kind of connexion. For there is altogether one fitness, harmony. And as the universe is made up out of all bodies to be such a body as it is, so out of all existing causes necessity (destiny) is made up to be such a cause as it is. And even those who are completely ignorant understand what I mean, for they say, It (necessity, destiny) brought this to such a person.—This then was brought and this was prescribed to him. Let us then receive these things, as well as those which Aesculapius prescribes. Many as a matter of course even among his prescriptions are disagreeable, but we accept them in the hope of health. Let the perfecting and accomplishment of the things, which the common nature judges to be good, be judged by thee to be of the same kind as thy health. And so accept everything which happens, even if it seem disagreeable, because it leads to this, to the health of the universe and to

the prosperity and felicity of Zeus (the universe). For he would not have brought on any man what he has brought, if it were not useful for the whole. Neither does the nature of anything, whatever it may be, cause anything which is not suitable to that which is directed by it. For two reasons then it is right to be content with that which happens to thee; the one, because it was done for thee and prescribed for thee, and in a manner had reference to thee, originally from the most ancient causes spun with thy destiny; and the other, because even that which comes severally to every man is to the power which administers the universe a cause of felicity and perfection, nay even of its very continuance. For the integrity of the whole is mutilated, if thou cuttest off anything whatever from the conjunction and the continuity either of the parts or of the causes. And thou dost cut off, as far as it is in thy power, when thou art dissatisfied, and in a manner triest to put any-thing out of the way. . . .

18. Nothing happens to any man which he is not formed by nature to bear. The same things happen to another, and either because he does not see that they have happened or because he would show a great spirit he is firm and remains unharmed. It is a shame then that ignorance and conceit should be stronger than wisdom.

33. Soon, very soon, thou wilt be ashes, or a skeleton, and either a name or not even a name; but name is sound and echo. And the things which are much valued in life are empty and rotten and trifling; and like little dogs biting one another, and little children quarrelling, laughing,

look to the immensity of time behind thee, and to the time which is before thee, another boundless space. In this infinity then what is the difference between him who lives three days and him who lives three generations.

51. Always run to the short way; and the short way is the natural: accordingly say and do everything in conformity with the soundest reason. For such a purpose frees a man from trouble, and warfare, and all artifice and ostentatious display.

and then straightway weeping. But fidelity and modesty and justice and truth are fled.

Up to Olympus from the wide-spread earth.

—HESIOD

What then is there which still detains thee here? If the objects of sense are easily changed and never stand still, and the organs of perception are dull and easily receive false impressions; and the poor soul itself is an exhalation from blood. But to have good repute amidst such a world as this is an empty thing. Why then dost thou not wait in tranquillity for thy end, whether it is extinction or removal to another state? And until that time comes, what is suffient? Why, what else than to venerate the gods and bless them, and to do good to men, and to practise tolerance and self-restraint; but as to everything which is beyond the limits of the poor flesh and breath, to remember that this is neither thine nor in thy power.

34. Thou canst pass thy life in an equable flow of happiness, if thou canst go by the right way, and think and act in the right way. These two things are common both to the soul of God and to the soul of man, and to the soul of every rational being, not to be hindered by another; and to hold good to consist in the disposition to justice and the practice of it, and in this to let thy desire find its termination.

DISCUSSION QUESTIONS

1. Why does Aurelius believe that offenses committed through desire deserve more blame than offenses committed in anger (Book 2, para. 10)? Do you agree with him? Why or why not?

2. Why does Aurelius believe that retreating into our soul is important (Book 4, para. 3)? What is the importance of doing this? Do you agree with him? Why or why not?

3. What, according to Aurelius, is the role of reason in our lives? Do you agree with him? Why or why not?

4. What, according to Aurelius, is the meaning of death? Compare his position with that of Epicurus.

5. What, according to Aurelius, is the nature of the universe?

6. Aurelius believes that nothing happens to us that we are not formed by nature to bear (Book 5, para. 18). What does he mean? Do you agree with him? Why or why not?

7. Compare and contrast the Epicurean position on the meaning of life with that of the Stoic thinker Aurelius. How are their views similar? How different?

8. In what ways do your own observations about the meaning of life conform to or differ from those of Aurelius?

The Remains of the Day
[Great Britain 1993] 2 hrs. 15 min.
Directed by James Ivory

James Stevens (Anthony Hopkins) is a second-generation butler who works at the Darlington Estate in Oxfordshire, England, in the years preceding World War II. He has devoted body and soul to his job, serving his wealthy and influential employer, Lord Darlington (James Fox), with unflagging pride. Stevens is thorough and meticulous in his work, to the point that he irons Lord Darlington's newspaper each morning.

For Stevens, his service to Lord Darlington always takes precedence over his own emotions and needs. This is revealed most directly in his relationship with his father (Peter Vaughan) and the housekeeper,

Ms. Kenton (Emma Thompson). While he seems to love both of them deeply, he makes his relationships with them secondary to his relationship with Lord Darlington.

Stevens' father, Stevens Sr., has been in "service" his entire life. He is in his mid-seventies and has been serving dinners to wealthy employers for fifty-four years. When the under-butler at Darlington Estate leaves, Stevens Sr. is recommended by his son to replace him, and Lord Darlington agrees. However, it becomes clear that due to his age Stevens Sr. cannot handle his workload. After he collapses and drops a tray full of drinks in front of Lord Darlington and his friends, the employer suggests to Stevens Jr. that he cut back on his father's responsibilities. When Stevens Jr. tells Stevens Sr. of his new reduced workload, the elder Stevens is unhappy but compliant. Stevens Sr. is given the task of polishing dull doorknobs. Soon, however, he has a stroke and dies. When Stevens Jr. is told of his father's death, he appears unmoved, and after taking a moment to view his father's body, he returns to serve his employer. He does not even take the time to close his father's eyes; Ms. Kenton does this for him.

Stevens clearly respects the performance of Ms. Kenton and states, "I'd be lost without her." However, Stevens always manages to keep their relationship strictly at the professional level of attending to the needs of Lord Darlington, even when it appears that he is in love with her. When Stevens feels that they are growing too close, he distances himself from Ms. Kenton, ending their evening conversations. Later, Ms. Kenton informs Stevens that she is thinking of marrying Mr. Benn (Tim Pigott-Smith), a mutual acquaintance of theirs also in "service" at another estate. Stevens does not try to dissuade her and shows little outward emotion. Even when Ms. Kenton states that she will be leaving Darlington to marry Benn, Stevens responds with professional composure.

After Ms. Kenton leaves Darlington, Lord Darlington's fortunes take a turn for the worse. For years, he has been working to appease the Germans and help them regain the power they lost after World War I. Because Lord Darlington is such a noble and fundamentally decent man, he does not recognize that he is being used by the Germans. After World War II, Lord Darlington is viewed as a Nazi sympathizer who was instrumental in bringing them to power. He dies a broken man, regretting the decisions he made regarding the Germans.

Stevens, too, gradually comes to see that his employer has made mistakes, and he begins to reconsider his unquestioning allegiance and devotion to Lord Darlington. He thinks back to when Lord Darlington demanded that he fire two house servants merely because they were Jewish, but finds some solace in Lord Darlington's statement that this was, in retrospect, a mistake. Stevens also seems to regret never following through on his feelings for Ms. Kenton. A meeting with her twenty years after she has left Darlington produces the same situation as before, though: Stevens is unable or unwilling to directly express his feelings for her. They part leaving their love for each other unfulfilled.

DISCUSSION QUESTIONS

1. In what way is the life of Stevens lived in accordance with the Stoic philosophy of Marcus Aurelius? In what way is the life of Stevens not lived in accordance with the principles of Aurelius's philosophy? Do you think Stevens' approach to the meaning of life is ultimately Stoical? Why or why not?

2. Marcus Aurelius argues that we must accept whatever happens to us. Does Stevens do this? Why or why not?

3. According to Marcus Aurelius, the life controlled by reason is the virtuous life. Do you think the life of Stevens is controlled by reason? If it is, is it also a virtuous life? Why or why not?

4. In another room, Lord Darlington and his guests are discussing the morality of anti-Semitism and concentration camps. Consider the following conversation between Benn and Stevens:

BENN   "Well, you've made yourself a cozy little nest here. Seems to me, Mr. Stevens, that you must be a well-contented man."

STEVENS   "In my philosophy, Mr. Benn, a man cannot call himself well contented until he has done all he can to be of service to his employer. Of course, this assumes that one's employer is a superior person not only in rank and wealth, but also in moral stature."

BENN   "And in your opinion what is going on up there has moral stature, does it? Wish I could be so sure, but I'm not. I've heard some very fishy things, Mr. Stevens."

STEVENS   "I've heard nothing . . . to listen to the gentlemen's conversation would distract me from my work."

Marcus Aurelius maintains that if we judge something painful to be evil, then and only then does it become so. Otherwise, it is neither evil nor good. Stevens always maintains that he does not listen to the conversations of Lord Darlington and his guests. Does this mean that, because Stevens does not listen to these conversations or allow himself to be emotionally affected by them, these people are not evil to him? Discuss.

5.   Discuss Stevens's treatment of his father. Is his treatment consistent with the philosophy of Marcus Aurelius? In particular, consider Stevens' reaction to his father's death. Is this an essentially Stoical response? Why or why not?

6.   Discuss Stevens's reaction to Lord Darlington's firing of two servant girls because they were Jewish. Does this reaction reveal a serious flaw in Stevens' philosophy? Why or why not?

7.   Ms. Kenton says to Stevens, "Why do you always have to hide what you feel, Mr. Stevens?" Respond to her question. Is hiding one's emotions an essential requirement of being a Stoic? Why or why not?

8.   Ms. Kenton says to Stevens, "You don't like to have pretty girls on the staff. Might it be that our Mr. Stevens fears distraction? Might it be that our Mr. Stevens is flesh and blood after all?" Stevens responds, "Do you know what I'm doing Ms. Kenton? I'm placing my thoughts elsewhere while you chatter away." Is Stevens' response to Ms. Kenton a fundamentally Stoical response? Why or why not?

9.   What is the meaning of life for Stevens? Do you think his way of life brings him contentment? Tranquility of mind? Happiness? Why or why not? Discuss.

LEO TOLSTOY

MY CONFESSION

Leo Tolstoy argues that faith provides meaning to life. However, he confesses that he did not always believe this; he used to believe in rational, scientific knowledge, but reason led him to not be able to find meaning in any single action in his life. From the perspective of rational and scientific knowledge, his whole life appeared meaningless. "Thus I blundered in this forest of human knowledge, between the clearings of the mathematical and experimental sciences, which disclosed to me clear horizons, but such in the direction of which there could be no house, and between the darkness of the speculative sciences, where I sunk into a deeper darkness, the farther I proceeded, and I convinced myself at last that there was no way out and could not be." Tolstoy felt that he knew "all that science wants so persistently to know, but there is no answer to the question about the meaning of my life." Thus, science, with its rational approach to knowledge and meaning, yielded unsatisfactory responses to questions regarding the meaning of life. He concluded that he must turn elsewhere for a satisfactory response.

Tolstoy observes that when one looks to the lives of "simple men," not the "learned and wealthy," one finds more often than not that they possessed knowledge of the meaning of life. "It turned out that rational knowledge did not give any meaning to life," writes Tolstoy. However, "irrational knowledge" through faith did provide meaning to life. This knowledge wrought by faith led him to believe in "God as one and three, the creation in six days, devils and angels," and all of the other beliefs regarding God that give meaning to the lives of the faithful. He concluded that in order to find the meaning of life, he needed to "renounce reason" and follow the mandates of faith. He defines faith as "the knowledge of the meaning of human life" and as "the power of life." Writes Tolstoy, "All living humanity had a certain other irrational knowledge, faith, which made it possible to live."

Tolstoy reached these conclusions when a spiritual crisis came over him at the age of fifty. His crisis resulted in a turn toward Christianity as expressed in the Gospels and a sincere admiration of the simple Christian lives of the Russian peasants. His thought from this point on focused on religion and ethics, and he devoted himself to social and moral reform. A biographical sketch of Tolstoy appears in chapter 4. The following selection is from *My Confession*, which was published in 1882.

Although I regarded authorship as a waste of time, I continued to write during those fifteen years. I had tasted of the seduction of authorship, of the seduction of enormous monetary remunerations and applauses for my insignificant labour, and so I submitted to it as being a means for improving my material condition and for stifling in my soul all questions about the meaning of my life and life in general.

In my writings I advocated, what to me was the only truth, that it was necessary to live in such a way as to derive the greatest comfort for oneself and one's family.

Thus I proceeded to live, but five years ago something very strange began to happen with me: I was overcome by minutes at first of perplexity and then of an arrest of life, as though I did not know how to live or what to do, and I lost myself and was dejected. But that passed and I continued to live as before. Then those minutes of perplexity were repeated oftener and oftener, and always in one and the same form. These arrests of life found their expression in ever the same questions: "Why? Well, and then?"

At first I thought that those were simply aimless, inappropriate questions. It seemed to me that that was all well known and that if I ever wanted to busy myself with their solution, it would not cost me much labour, that now I had no time to attend to them, but that if I wanted to I should find the proper answers. But the questions began to repeat themselves oftener and oftener, answers were demanded more and more persistently, and, like dots that fall on the same spot, these questions, without any answers, thickened into one black blotch.

There happened what happens with any person who falls ill with a mortal internal disease. At first there appear insignificant symptoms of indisposition, to which the patient pays no attention; then these symptoms are repeated more and more frequently and blend into one temporally indivisible suffering. The suffering keeps growing, and before the patient has had time to look around, he becomes conscious that what he took for an indisposition is the most significant thing in the world to him—his death.

The same happened with me. I understood that it was not a passing indisposition, but something very important, and that, if the questions were going to repeat themselves, it would be necessary to find an answer for them. And I tried to answer them. The questions seemed to be so foolish, simple, and childish. But the moment I touched them and tried to solve them, I became convinced, in the first place, that they were not childish and foolish, but very important and profound questions in life, and, in the second, that, no matter how much I might try, I should not be able to answer them. Before attending to my Samára estate, to my son's education, or to the writing of a book, I ought to know why I should do that. So long as I did not know why, I could not do anything. I could not live. Amidst my thoughts of farming, which interested me very much during that time, there would suddenly pass through my head a question like this: "All right, you are going to have six thousand desyatínas of land in the Government of Samára and three hundred horses —and then?" And I completely lost my senses and did not know what to think farther. Or, when I thought of the education of my children, I said to myself: "Why?" Or, reflecting on the manner in which the masses might obtain their welfare, I suddenly said to myself: "What is that to me?" Or, thinking of the fame which my works would get me, I said to myself: "All right, you will be more famous than [the nineteenth-century Russian novelist and dramatist Nikolai] Gógol, [the nine- teenth-century Russian poet Aleksandr] Pushkin, Shakespeare, [the seventeenth-century French dramatist] Molière, and all the writers in the world—what of it?" And I was absolutely unable to make any reply. The questions were not waiting, and I had to answer them at once; if I did not answer them, I could not live.

I felt that what I was standing on had given way, that I had no foundation to stand on, that that which I lived by no longer existed, and that I had nothing to live by. . . .

All that happened with me when I was on every side surrounded by what is considered to be complete happiness. I had a good, loving, and beloved wife, good children, and a large estate, which grew and increased without any labour on my part. I was respected by my neighbours and friends, more than ever before, was praised by strangers, and, without any self-deception, could consider my name famous. With all that, I was not deranged or mentally unsound; on the contrary, I was in full command of my mental and physical powers, such as I had rarely met with in people of my age: physically I could work in a field, mowing, without falling behind a peasant; mentally I could work from eight to ten hours in succession, without experiencing any consequences from the strain. And while in such condition I arrived at the conclusion that I could not live, and, fearing death, I had to use cunning against myself, in order that I might not take my life.

This mental condition expressed itself to me in this form: my life is a stupid, mean trick played on me by somebody. Although I did not recognize that "somebody" as having created me, the form of the conception that some one had played a mean, stupid trick on me by bringing me into the world was the most natural one that presented itself to me.

Involuntarily I imagined that there, somewhere, there was somebody who was now having fun as he looked down upon me and saw me, who had lived for thirty or forty years, learning, developing, growing in body and mind, now that I had become strengthened in mind and had reached that summit of life from which it lay all before me, standing as a complete fool on that summit and seeing clearly that there was nothing in life and never would be: And that was fun to him—

But whether there was or was not that somebody who made fun of me did not make it easier for me. I could not ascribe any sensible meaning to a single act, or to my whole life. I was only surprised that I had not understood that from the start. All that had long ago been known to everybody. Sooner or later there would come diseases and death (they had come already) to my dear ones and to me, and there would be nothing left but stench and worms. All my affairs, no matter what they might be, would sooner or later be forgotten, and I myself should not exist. So why should I worry about all these things? How could a man fail to see that and live—that was surprising! A person could live only so long as he was drunk; but the moment he sobered up, he could not help seeing that all that was only a deception, and a stupid deception at that! Really, there was nothing funny and ingenious about it, but only something cruel and stupid.

Long ago has been told the Eastern story about the traveller who in the steppe is overtaken by an infuriated beast. Trying to save himself from the animal, the traveller jumps into a waterless well, but at its bottom he sees a dragon who opens his jaws in order to swallow him. And the unfortunate man does not dare climb out, lest he perish from the infuriated beast, and does not dare jump down to the bottom of the well, lest he be devoured by the dragon, and so clutches the twig of a wild bush growing in a cleft of the well and holds on to it. His hands grow weak and he feels that soon he shall have to surrender to the peril which awaits him at either side; but he still holds on and sees two mice, one white, the other black, in even measure making a circle around the main trunk of the bush to which he is clinging, and nibbling at it on all sides. Now, at any moment, the bush will break and tear off; and he will fall into the dragon's jaws. The traveller sees that and knows that he will inevitably perish; but while he is still clinging, he sees some drops of honey hanging on the leaves of the bush, and so reaches out for them with his tongue and licks the leaves. Just so I hold on to the branch of life, knowing that the dragon of death is waiting inevitably for me, ready to tear me to pieces, and I cannot understand why I have fallen on such suffering. And I try to lick that honey which used to give me pleasure; but now it no longer gives me joy, and the white and the black mouse day and night nibble at the branch to which I am holding on. I clearly see the dragon, and the honey is no longer sweet to me. I see only the inevitable dragon and the mice, and am unable to turn my glance away from them. That is not a fable, but a veritable, indisputable, comprehensible truth.

The former deception of the pleasures of life, which stifled the terror of the dragon, no longer deceives me. No matter how much one should say to me, "You cannot understand the meaning of life, do not think, live!" I am unable to do so, because I have been doing it too long before. Now I cannot help seeing day and night, which run and lead me up to death. I see that alone, because that alone is the truth. Everything else is a lie.

The two drops of honey that have longest turned my eyes away from the cruel truth, the love of family and of authorship, which I have called an art, are no longer sweet to me.

"My family—I said to myself, "but my family, my wife and children, they are also human beings.

They are in precisely the same condition that I am in; they must either live in the lie or see the terrible truth. Why should they live? Why should I love them, why guard, raise, and watch them? Is it for the same despair which is in me, or for dullness of perception? Since I love them, I cannot conceal the truth from them—every step in cognition leads them up to this truth. And the truth is death.

"Art, poetry?" For a long time, under the influence of the success of human praise, I tried to persuade myself that that was a thing which could be done, even though death should come and destroy everything, my deeds, as well as my memory of them; but soon I came to see that that, too, was a deception. It was clear to me that art was an adornment of life, a decoy of life. But life lost all its attractiveness for me. How, then, could I entrap others? So long as I did not live my own life, and a strange life bore me on its waves, so long as I believed that life had some sense, although I was not able to express it, the reflections of life in every description in poetry and in the arts afforded me pleasure, and I was delighted to look at life through this little mirror of art; but when I began to look for the meaning of life, when I experienced the necessity of living myself, that little mirror became either useless, superfluous, and ridiculous, or painful to me. I could no longer console myself with what I saw in the mirror, namely, that my situation was stupid and desperate. It was all right for me to rejoice so long as I believed in the depth of my soul that life had some sense. At that time the play of lights—of the comical, the tragical, the touching, the beautiful, the terrible in life—afforded me amusement. But when I knew that life was meaningless and terrible, the play in the little mirror could no longer amuse me. No sweetness of honey could be sweet to me when I saw the dragon and the mice that were nibbling down my support. . . .

In my search after the question of life I experienced the same feeling which a man who has lost his way in the forest may experience.

He comes to a clearing, climbs a tree, and clearly sees an unlimited space before him; at the same time he sees that there are no houses there, and that there can be none; he goes back to the forest, into the darkness, and he sees darkness, and again there are no houses.

Thus I blundered in this forest of human knowledge, between the clearings of the mathematical and experimental sciences, which disclosed to me clear horizons, but such in the direction of which there could be no house, and between the darkness of the speculative sciences, where I sunk into a deeper darkness, the farther I proceeded, and I convinced myself at last that there was no way out and could not be.

By abandoning myself to the bright side of knowledge I saw that I only turned my eyes away from the question. No matter how enticing and clear the horizons were that were disclosed to me, no matter how enticing it was to bury myself in the infinitude of this knowledge, I comprehended that these sciences were the more dear, the less I needed them, the less they answered my question.

"Well, I know," I said to myself, "all which science wants so persistently to know, but there is no answer to the question about the meaning of my life." But in the speculative sphere I saw that, in spite of the fact that the aim of the knowledge was directed straight to the answer of my question, or because of that fact, there could be no other answer than what I was giving to myself: "What is the meaning of my life?"—"None." Or, "What will come of my life?"—"Nothing." Or, "Why does everything which exists exist, and why do I exist?"—"Because it exists."

Putting the question to the one side of human knowledge, I received an endless quantity of exact answers about what I did not ask: about the chemical composition of the stars, about the movement of the sun toward the constellation of Hercules, about the origin of species and of man, about the forms of infinitely small, imponderable particles of ether; but the answer in this sphere of knowledge to my question what the meaning of my life was, was always: "You are what you call your life; you are a temporal, accidental conglomeration of particles. The interrelation, the change of these particles, produces in you that which you call life. This congeries will last for some time; then the interaction of these particles will cease, and that which you call life and all your questions will come to an end. You are an accidentally cohering globule of something. The

globule is fermenting. This fermentation the globule calls its *life*. The globule falls to pieces, and all fermentation and all questions will come to an end." Thus the clear side of knowledge answers, and it cannot say anything else, if only it strictly follows its principles.

With such an answer it appears that the answer is not a reply to the question. I want to know the meaning of my life, but the fact that it is a particle of the infinite not only gives it no meaning, but even destroys every possible meaning.

Those obscure transactions, which this side of the experimental, exact science has with speculation, when it says that the meaning of life consists in evolution and the cooperation with this evolution, because of their obscurity and inexactness cannot be regarded as answers.

The other side of knowledge, the speculative, so long as it sticks strictly to its fundamental principles in giving a direct answer to the question, everywhere and at all times has answered one and the same: "The world is something infinite and incomprehensible. Human life is an incomprehensible part of this incomprehensible all. . . ."

I lived for a long time in this madness, which, not in words, but in deeds, is particularly characteristic of us, the most liberal and learned of men. But, thanks either to my strange, physical love for the real working class, which made me understand it and see that it is not so stupid as we suppose, or to the sincerity of my conviction, which was that I could know nothing and that the best that I could do was to hang myself, I felt that if I wanted to live and understand the meaning of life, I ought naturally to look for it, not among those who had lost the meaning of life and wanted to kill themselves, but among those billions departed and living men who had been carrying their own lives and ours upon their shoulders. And I looked around at the enormous masses of deceased and living men—not learned and wealthy, but simple men—and I saw something quite different. I saw that all these billions of men that lived or had lived, all, with rare exceptions, did not fit into my subdivisions* and that I could not recognize them

*That is, they did not live in ignorance of the problem of life's meaning, they did not ignore the problem of life's meaning and pursue pleasure whenever possible, they did not acknowledge the meaningless of life and then commit suicide, and they did not acknowledge the meaningless of life and then live aimlessly. —Ed.

as not understanding the question, because they themselves put it and answered it with surprising clearness. Nor could I recognize them as Epicureans, because their lives were composed rather of privations and suffering than of enjoyment. Still less could I recognize them as senselessly living out their meaningless lives, because every act of theirs and death itself was explained by them. They regarded it as the greatest evil to kill themselves. It appeared, then, that all humanity was in possession of a knowledge of the meaning of life, which I did not recognize and which I condemned. It turned out that rational knowledge did not give any meaning to life, excluded life, while the meaning which by billions of people, by all humanity, was ascribed to life was based on some despised, false knowledge.

The rational knowledge in the person of the learned and the wise denied the meaning of life, but the enormous masses of men, all humanity, recognized this meaning in an irrational knowledge. This irrational knowledge was faith, the same that I could not help but reject. That was God as one and three, the creation in six days, devils and angels, and all that which I could not accept so long as I had not lost my senses.

My situation was a terrible one. I knew that I should not find anything on the path of rational knowledge but the negation of life, and there, in faith, nothing but the negation of reason, which was still more impossible than the negation of life. From the rational knowledge it followed that life was an evil and men knew it; it depended on men whether they should cease living, and yet they lived and continued to live, and I myself lived, though I had known long ago that life was meaningless and an evil. From faith it followed that, in order to understand life, I must renounce reason, for which alone a meaning was needed.

There resulted a contradiction, from which there were two ways out: either what I called rational was not so rational as I had thought; or that which to me appeared irrational was not so irrational as I had thought. And I began to verify the train of thoughts of my rational knowledge.

In verifying the train of thoughts of my rational knowledge, I found that it was quite correct. The deduction that life was nothing was inevitable; but I saw a mistake. The mistake was that I had not reasoned in conformity with the question put by me. The question was, "Why should I live?" that is, "What real, indestructible essence will come from my phantasmal, destructible life? What meaning has my finite existence in this infinite world?" And in order to answer this question, I studied life.

The solutions of all possible questions of life apparently could not satisfy me, because my question, no matter how simple it appeared in the beginning, included the necessity of explaining the finite through the infinite, and vice versa.

I asked, "What is the extra-temporal, extra-causal, extra-spatial meaning of life?" But I gave an answer to the question, "What is the temporal, causal, spatial meaning of my life?" The result was that after a long labour of mind I answered, "None."

In my reflections I constantly equated, nor could I do otherwise, the finite with the finite, the infinite with the infinite, and so from that resulted precisely what had to result: force was force, matter was matter, will was will, infinity was infinity, nothing was nothing—and nothing else could come from it.

There happened something like what at times takes place in mathematics: you think you are solving an equation, when you have only an identity. The reasoning is correct, but you receive as a result the answer: $a = a$, or $x = x$, or $0 = 0$. The same happened with my reflection in respect to the question about the meaning of my life. The answers given by all science to that question are only identities.

Indeed, the strictly scientific knowledge, that knowledge which, as Descartes did, begins with a full doubt in everything, rejects all knowledge which has been taken on trust, and builds everything anew on the laws of reason and experience, cannot give any other answer to the question of life than what I received—an indefinite answer. It only seemed to me at first that science gave me a positive answer—[the nineteenth century German philosopher Arthur] Schopenhauer's answer: "Life has no meaning, it is an evil." But when I analyzed the matter, I saw that the answer was not a positive one, but that it was only my feeling which expressed it as such. The answer, strictly expressed, as it is expressed by the Brahmins, by Solomon, and by Schopenhauer, is only an indefinite answer, or an identity; $0 = 0$, life is nothing. Thus the philosophical knowledge does not negate anything, but only answers that the question cannot be solved by it, that for philosophy the solution remains insoluble.

When I saw that, I understood that it was not right for me to look for an answer to my question in rational knowledge, and that the answer given by rational knowledge was only an indication that the answer might be got if the question were differently put, but only when into the discussion of the question should be introduced the question of the relation of the finite to the infinite. I also understood that, no matter how irrational and monstrous the answers might be that faith gave, they had this advantage that they introduced into each answer the relation of the finite to the infinite, without which there could be no answer.

No matter how I may put the question, "How must I live?" the answer is, "According to God's law." "What real result will there be from my life?"—"Eternal torment or eternal bliss." "What is the meaning which is not destroyed by death?"—"The union with infinite God, paradise."

Thus, outside the rational knowledge, which had to me appeared as the only one, I was inevitably led to recognize that all living humanity had a certain other irrational knowledge, faith, which made it possible to live.

All the irrationality of faith remained the same for me, but I could not help recognizing that it alone gave to humanity answers to the questions of life, and, in consequence of them, the possibility of living.

The rational knowledge brought me to the recognition that life was meaningless, my life stopped, and I wanted to destroy myself. When I looked around at people, at all humanity, I saw that people lived and asserted that they knew the meaning of life. I looked back at myself: I lived so long as I knew the meaning of life. As to other people, so even to me, did faith give the meaning of life and the possibility of living.

Looking again at the people of other countries, contemporaries of mine and those passed away, I saw again the same. Where life had been, there faith, ever since humanity had existed, had given the possibility of living, and the chief features of faith were everywhere one and the same.

No matter what answers faith may give, its every answer gives to the finite existence of man the sense of the infinite—a sense which is not destroyed by suffering, privation, and death. Consequently in faith alone could we find the meaning and possibility of life. What, then, was faith? I understood that faith was not merely an evidence of things not seen, and so forth, not revelation (that is only the description of one of the symptoms of faith), not the relation of man to man (faith has to be defined, and then God, and not first God, and faith through him), not merely an agreement with what a man was told, as faith was generally understood—that faith was the knowledge of the meaning of human life, in consequence of which man did not destroy himself, but lived. Faith is the power of life. If a man lives he believes in something. If he did not believe that he ought to live for some purpose, he would not live. If he does not see and understand the phantasm of the finite, he believes in that finite; if he understands the phantasm of the finite, he must believe in the infinite. Without faith one cannot live. . . .

In order that all humanity may be able to live, in order that they may continue living, giving a meaning to life, they, those billions, must have another, a real knowledge of faith, for not the fact that I with Solomon and Schopenhauer, did not kill myself convinced me of the existence of faith, but that these billions had lived and had borne us, me and Solomon, on the waves of life.

Then I began to cultivate the acquaintance of the believers from among the poor, the simple and unlettered folk, of pilgrims, monks, dissenters, peasants. The doctrine of these people from among the masses was also the Christian doctrine that the quasi-believers of our circle professed. With the Christian truths were also mixed in very many superstitions, but there was this difference: the superstitions of our circle were quite unnecessary to them, had no connections with their lives, were only a kind of an Epicurean amusement, while the superstitions of the believers from among the labouring classes were to such an extent blended with their life that it would have been impossible to imagine it without these superstitions—it was a necessary condition of that life. I began to examine closely the lives and beliefs of these people, and the more I examined them, the more did I become convinced that they had the real faith, that their faith was necessary for them, and that it alone gave them a meaning and possibility of life. In contradistinction to what I saw in our circle, where life without faith was possible, and where hardly one in a thousand professes to be a believer, among them was hardly one in a thousand who was not a believer. In contradistinction to what I saw in our circle, where all life passed in idleness, amusements, and tedium of life, I saw that the whole life of these people was passed in hard work, and that they were satisfied with life. In contradistinction to the people of our circle, who struggled and murmured against fate because of their privations and their suffering, these people accepted diseases and sorrows without any perplexity or opposition, but with the calm and firm conviction that it was all for good. In contradistinction to the fact that the more intelligent we are, the less do we understand the meaning of life and the more do we see a kind of a bad joke in our suffering and death, these people live, suffer, and approach death, and suffer in peace and more often in joy. In contradistinction to the fact that a calm death, a death without terror or despair, is the greatest exception in our circle, a restless, insubmissive, joyless death is one of the greatest exceptions among the masses. And of such people, who are deprived of everything which for Solomon and for me constitutes the only good of life, and who withal experience the greatest happiness, there is an enormous number. I cast a broader glance about me. I examined the life of past and present vast masses of men, and I saw people who in like manner had understood the meaning of life, who had known how to live and die, not two, not three, not ten, but hundreds, thousands, millions. All of them, infinitely diversified as to habits, intellect, culture, situation, all equally and quite contrary to my ignorance knew the meaning of life and of death, worked calmly, bore privations and suffering, lived and died, seeing in that not vanity, but good.

I began to love those people. The more I penetrated into their life, the life of the men now living, and the life of men departed, of whom I had read and heard, the more did I love them, and the easier it became for me to live. Thus I lived for about two years, and within me took place a transformation, which had long been

working within me, and the germ of which had always been in me. What happened with me was that the life of our circle—of the rich and the learned—not only disgusted me, but even lost all its meaning. All our acts, reflections, sciences, arts,—all that appeared to me in a new light. I saw that all that was mere pampering of the appetites, and that no meaning could be found in it; but the life of all the working masses, of all humanity, which created life, presented itself to me in its real significance. I saw that that was life itself and that the meaning given to this life was truth, and I accepted it.

DISCUSSION QUESTIONS

1. What is the difference between rational knowledge and irrational knowledge, according to Tolstoy? How, according to Tolstoy, is each related to the meaning of life? Do you agree with Tolstoy? Why or why not?

2. Tolstoy's reflections about scientific knowledge were made over a hundred years ago. Do you think contemporary science provides a greater foundation for finding meaning in life than the science of Tolstoy's day? Or is the situation regarding scientific knowledge and the meaning of life the same today as it was in Tolstoy's day? Discuss.

3. What role does social class play in Tolstoy's observations about the meaning of life? Do you agree with Tolstoy's statement concerning the level of religious belief among the poor versus the wealthy?

4. In the introduction to *Criticism of Hegel's Philosophy of Right*, Karl Marx observes that religion is "the opiate of the people." How do you think Tolstoy would respond to Marx's observation? Does religion make life more bearable for the working class (the *proletariat*, in Marx's terminology)? See chapter 5 for Marx's distinction between the bourgeoisie and the proletariat.

5. Both the Epicureans and the Stoics argue that a meaningful life can be achieved through reason. Compare and contrast their views with that of Tolstoy, who argues that reason and rational knowledge cannot lead to a meaningful life.

6. Do you think Tolstoy believes that he has found the *only* solution to the meaning of life? How might he respond to the lives of Buddhists and Hindus? Would he find their lives lacking in meaning because they do not express the type of faith required for a meaningful life?

BERTRAND RUSSELL

A FREE MAN'S WORSHIP

Bertrand Russell argues that life has meaning even though God does not exist. In agreement with Tolstoy, Russell argues that the world which science presents to us is both meaningless and void of purpose. However, unlike for Tolstoy, this does not lead him to turn to faith in God as the basis of the meaning of life. For Russell, God is the creation of Man, which is said to be "all-powerful and all-good, the mystic unity of what is and what should be." When humans worship this nonhuman power that they have created, Russell asserts, they are unnecessarily submitting themselves to the tyranny of an outside force. "For in all things it is well to exalt the dignity of Man, by freeing himself as far as possible from the tyranny of non-human Power," writes Russell. "If Power is bad, as it seems to be, let us reject it from our hearts."

In place of the worship of science or God, Russell argues, that we should worship human ideals, that the worship of these ideals provides life with meaning. Russell contends that we are free "to criticize, to know, and in imagination to create" during the relatively brief span of our lives. This freedom to pursue our ideals is unique to humans, indicative of our "superiority to the resistless forces that control [our] outward life." However, when we encounter an opposition between fact and ideal, "a spirit of fiery revolt, of fierce hatred of the gods, seems necessary to the assertion of freedom." "We must learn to resign ourselves to the outward rules of Fate and to recognize that the non-human world is unworthy of our worship." "Brief and powerless is Man's life; on him and all his race the slow, sure doom falls pitiless and dark," writes Russell. Amidst the ravages of time, fate, and death, the only things remaining for the free man to cherish and worship are "the lofty thoughts that ennoble his little day." A biographical sketch of Russell appears in the introduction. The following essay first appeared in 1903, some twenty years after the publication of Tolstoy's *My Confession*.

To Dr. Faustus in his study Mephistopheles told the history of the Creation, saying:

"The endless praises of the choirs of angels had begun to grow wearisome; for, after all, did he not deserve their praise? Had he not given them endless joy? Would it not be more amusing to obtain undeserved praise, to be worshipped by beings whom he tortured? He smiled inwardly, and resolved that the great drama should be performed.

"For countless ages the hot nebula whirled aimlessly through space. At length it began to take shape, the central mass threw off planets, the planets cooled, boiling seas and burning mountains heaved and tossed, from black masses of cloud hot sheets of rain deluged the barely solid crust. And now the first germ of life grew in the depths of the ocean, and developed rapidly in the fructifying warmth into vast forest trees, huge ferns springing from the damp mould, sea monsters breeding, fighting, devouring, and passing away. And from the monsters, as the play unfolded itself, Man was born, with the power of thought, the knowledge of good and evil, and the cruel thirst for worship. And Man saw that all is passing in this mad, monstrous world, that all is struggling to snatch, at any cost, a few brief moments of life before Death's inexorable decree. And Man said: 'There is a hidden purpose, could we but fathom it, and the purpose is good; for we must reverence something, and in the visible world there is nothing worthy of reverence.' And Man stood aside from the struggle, resolving that God intended harmony to come out of chaos by human efforts. And when he followed the instincts which God had transmitted to him from his ancestry of beasts of prey, he called it Sin, and asked God to forgive him. But he doubted whether he could be justly forgiven, until he invented a divine Plan by which God's wrath was to have been appeased. And seeing the present was bad, he made it yet worse, that thereby the future might be better. And he gave God thanks for the strength that enabled him to forgo even the joys that were possible. And God smiled; and when he saw that Man had become perfect in renunciation and worship, he sent another sun through the sky, which crashed into Man's sun; and all returned again to nebula.

"'Yes,' he murmured, 'it was a good play; I will have it performed again.'"

Such, in outline, but even more purposeless, more void of meaning, is the world which Science presents for our belief. Amid such a world, if anywhere, our ideals henceforward must find a home. That Man is the product of causes which had no prevision of the end they were achieving; that his origin, his growth, his hopes and fears, his loves and his beliefs, are but the outcome of accidental collocations of atoms; that no fire, no heroism, no intensity of thought and feeling, can preserve an individual life beyond the grave; that all the labours of the ages, all the devotion, all the inspiration, all the noonday brightness of human genius, are destined to extinction in the vast death the solar system, and that the whole temple of Man's achievement must inevitably be buried beneath the debris of a universe in ruins—all these things, if not quite beyond dispute, are yet so nearly certain, that no philosophy which rejects them can hope to stand. Only within the scaffolding of these truths, only on the firm foundation of unyielding despair, can the soul's habitation hence forth be safely built.

How, in such an alien and inhuman world, can so powerless a creature as Man preserve his aspirations untarnished? A strange mystery it is that Nature, omnipotent but blind, in the revolutions of her secular hurryings through the abysses of space, has brought forth at last a child, subject still to her power, but gifted with sight, with knowledge of good and evil, with the capacity of judging all the works of his unthinking Mother. In spite of Death, the mark and seal of the parental control, Man is yet free, during his brief years, to examine, to criticize, to know, and in imagination to create. To him alone, in the world with which he is acquainted, this freedom belongs; and in this lies his superiority to the resistless forces that control his outward life.

The savage, like ourselves, feels the oppression of his impotence before the powers of Nature; but having in himself nothing that he respects more than Power, he is willing to prostrate himself before his gods, without inquiring whether they are worthy of his worship. Pathetic and very terrible is the long history of cruelty and torture, of degradation and human sacrifice, endured in the hope of placating the jealous gods: surely, the trembling believer thinks, when what is most precious has been freely given, their lust for blood must be appeased, and more will not be required. The religion of Moloch*—as such creeds may be generically called—is in essence the cringing submission of the slave, who dare not, even in his heart, allow the thought that his master deserves no adulation. Since the independence of ideals is not yet acknowledged, Power may be freely worshipped, and receive an unlimited respect, despite its wanton infliction of pain.

But gradually as morality grows bolder, the claim of the ideal world begins to be felt, and worship, if it is not to cease, must be given to gods of another kind than those created by the savage.

*A god worshiped by the sacrifice of children. In the film *Metropolis* (1926), a machine is transformed into the god Moloch (see the film box in chapter 5). —Ed.

Some, though they feel the demands of the ideal, will still consciously reject them, still urging that naked Power is worthy of worship. Such is the attitude inculcated in God's answer to Job out of the whirlwind: the divine power and knowledge are paraded, but of the divine goodness there is no hint. Such also is the attitude of those who, in our own day, base their morality upon the struggle for survival, maintaining that the survivors are necessarily the fittest. But others, not content with an answer so repugnant to the moral sense, will adopt the position which we have become accustomed to regard as specially religious, maintaining that, in some hidden manner, the world of fact is really harmonious with the world of ideals. Thus Man creates God, all-powerful and all-good, the mystic unity of what is and what should be.

But the world of fact, after all, is not good; and, in submitting our judgment to it, there is an element of slavishness from which our thoughts must be purged. For in all things it is well to exalt the dignity of Man, by freeing him as far as possible from the tyranny of non-human Power. When we have realised that Power is largely bad; that man, with his knowledge of good and evil, is but a helpless atom in a world which has no such knowledge, the choice is again presented to us: Shall we worship Force, or shall we worship Goodness? Shall our God exist and be evil, or shall he be recognised as the creation of our own conscience?

The answer to this question is very momentous, and affects profoundly our whole morality. The worship of Force, to which Carlyle and Nietzsche and the creed of Militarism have accustomed us, is the result of failure to maintain our own ideals against a hostile universe: it is itself a prostrate submission to evil, a sacrifice of our best to Moloch. If strength indeed is to be respected, let us respect rather the strength of those who refuse that false "recognition of facts" which fails to recognise that facts are often bad. Let us admit that, in the world we know, there are many things that would be better otherwise, and that the ideals to which we do and must adhere are not realised in the realm of matter. Let us preserve our respect for truth, for beauty, for the ideal of perfection which life does not permit us to attain, though none of these things meet with the approval of the unconscious universe. If Power is bad, as it seems to be, let us reject it from our hearts. In this lies Man's true freedom: in determination to worship only the God created by our own love of the good, to respect only the heaven which inspires the insight of our best moments. In action, in desire, we must submit perpetually to the tyranny of outside forces; but in thought, in aspiration, we are free, free from our fellow-men, free from the petty planet on which our bodies impotently crawl, free even, while we live, from the tyranny of death. Let us learn, then, that energy of faith which enables us to live constantly in the vision of the good; and let us descend, in action, into the world of fact, with that vision always before us.

When first the opposition of fact and ideal grows fully visible, a spirit of fiery revolt, of fierce hatred of the gods, seems necessary to the assertion of freedom. To defy with Promethean constancy a hostile universe, to keep its evil always in view, always actively hated, to refuse no pain that the malice of Power can invent, appears to be the duty of all who will not bow before the inevitable. But indignation is still a bondage, for it compels our thoughts to be occupied with an evil world; and in the fierceness of desire from which rebellion springs there is a kind of self-assertion which it is necessary for the wise to overcome. Indignation is a submission of our thoughts, but not of our desires; the Stoic freedom in which wisdom consists is found in the submission of our desires, but not of our thoughts. From the submission of our desires springs the virtue of resignation; from the freedom of our thoughts springs the whole world of art and philosophy, and the vision of beauty by which, at last, we half reconquer the reluctant world. But the vision of beauty is possible only to unfettered contemplation, to thoughts not weighted by the load of eager wishes; and thus Freedom comes only to those who no longer ask of life that it shall yield them any of those personal goods that are subject to the mutations of Time.

Although the necessity of renunciation is evidence of the existence of evil, yet Christianity, in preaching it, has shown a wisdom exceeding that of the Promethean philosophy of rebellion. It must be admitted that, of the things we desire, some, though they prove impossible, are yet real goods; others, however, as ardently longed for, do not form part of a fully purified ideal. The belief that what must be renounced is bad, though sometimes false, is far less often false than untamed passion supposes; and the creed of religion, by providing a reason for proving that it is never false, has been the means of purifying our hopes by the discovery of many austere truths.

But there is in resignation a further good element: even real goods, when they are unattainable, ought not to be fretfully desired. To every man comes, sooner or later, the great renunciation. For the young, there is nothing unattainable; a good thing desired with the whole force of a passionate will, and yet impossible, is to them not credible. Yet, by death, by illness, by poverty or by the voice of duty, we must learn, each one of us, that the world was not made for us, and that, however beautiful may be the things we crave, Fate may nevertheless forbid them. It is the part of courage, when misfortune comes, to bear without repining the ruin of our hopes, to turn away our thoughts from vain regrets. This degree of submission to Power is not only just and right: it is the very gate of wisdom.

But passive renunciation is not the whole of wisdom; for not by renunciation alone can we build a temple for the worship of our own ideals. Haunting foreshadowings of the temple appear in the realm of imagination, in music, in architecture, in the untroubled kingdom of reason, and in the golden sunset magic of lyrics, where beauty shines and glows, remote from the touch of sorrow, remote from the fear of change, remote from the failures and disenchantments of the world of fact. In the contemplation of these things the vision of heaven will shape itself in our hearts, giving at once a touchstone to judge the world about us, and an inspiration by which to fashion to our needs whatever is not incapable of serving as a stone in the sacred temple.

Except for those rare spirits that are born without sin, there is a cavern of darkness to be traversed before that temple can be entered. The gate of the cavern is despair, and its floor is paved with the gravestones of abandoned hopes. There Self must die; there the eagerness, the greed of untamed desire must be slain, for only so can the soul be freed from the empire of Fate. But out of the cavern the Gate of Renunciation leads again to the daylight of wisdom, by whose radiance a new insight, a new joy, a new tenderness, shine forth to gladden the pilgrim's heart.

When, without the bitterness of impotent rebellion, we have learnt both to resign ourselves to the outward rules of Fate and to recognise that the non-human world is unworthy of our worship, it becomes possible at last so to transform and refashion the unconscious universe, so to transmute it in the crucible of imagination, that a new image of shining gold replaces the old idol of clay. In all the multiform facts of the world—in the visual shapes of trees and mountains and clouds, in the events of the life of man, even in the very omnipotence of Death—the insight of creative idealism can find the reflection of a beauty which its own thoughts first made. In this way mind asserts its subtle mastery over the thoughtless forces of Nature. The more evil the material with which it deals, the more thwarting to untrained desire, the greater is its achievement in inducing the reluctant rock to yield up its hidden treasures, the prouder its victory in compelling the opposing forces to swell the pageant of its triumph. Of all the arts, Tragedy is the proudest, the most triumphant; for it builds its shining citadel in the very centre of the enemy's country, on the very summit of his highest mountain; from its impregnable watchtowers, his camps and arsenals, his columns and forts, are all revealed; within its walls the free life continues, while the legions of Death and Pain and Despair, and all the servile captains of tyrant Fate, afford the burghers of that dauntless city new spectacles of beauty. Happy those sacred ramparts, thrice happy the dwellers on that all-seeing eminence. Honour to those brave warriors who, through countless ages of warfare, have preserved for us the priceless heritage of liberty, and have kept undefiled by sacrilegious invaders the home of the unsubdued.

But the beauty of Tragedy does but make visible a quality which, in more or less obvious shapes, is present always and everywhere in life. In the spectacle of Death, in the endurance of intolerable pain, and in the irrevocableness of a vanished past, there is a sacredness, an overpowering awe, a feeling of the vastness, the depth, the inexhaustible mystery of existence, in which, as by some strange marriage of pain, the sufferer is bound to the world by bonds of sorrow.

In these moments of insight, we lose all eagerness of temporary desire, all struggling and striving for petty ends, all care for the little trivial things that, to a superficial view, make up the common life of day by day; we see, surrounding the narrow raft illumined by the flickering light of human comradeship, the dark ocean on whose rolling waves we toss for a brief hour; from the great night without, a chill blast breaks in upon our refuge; all the loneliness of humanity amid hostile forces is concentrated upon the individual soul, which must struggle alone, with what of courage it can command, against the whole weight of a universe that cares nothing for its hopes and fears. Victory, in this struggle with the powers of darkness, is the true baptism into the glorious company of heroes, the true initiation into the overmastering beauty of human existence. From that awful encounter of the soul with the outer world, enunciation, wisdom, and charity are born; and with their birth a new life begins. To take into the inmost shrine of the soul the irresistible forces whose puppets we seem to be—Death and change, the irrevocableness of the past, and the powerlessness of Man before the blind hurry of the universe from vanity to vanity to feel these things and know them is to conquer them.

This is the reason why the Past has such magical power. The beauty of its motionless and silent pictures is like the enchanted purity of late autumn, when the leaves, though one breath would make them fall, still glow against the sky in golden glory. The Past does not change or strive; like Duncan,* after life's fitful fever it sleeps well; what was eager and grasping, what was petty and transitory, has faded away, the things that were beautiful and eternal shine out of it like stars in the night. Its beauty, to a soul not worthy of it, is unendurable; but to a soul which has conquered Fate it is the key of religion.

The life of Man, viewed outwardly, is but a small thing in comparison with the forces of Nature. The slave is doomed to worship Time and Fate and Death, because they are greater than anything he finds in himself, and because all his thoughts are of things which they devour. But, great as they are, to think of them greatly, to feel their passionless splendour, is greater still. And

such thought makes us free men; we no longer bow before the inevitable in Oriental subjection, but we absorb it, and make it a part of ourselves. To abandon the struggle for private happiness, to expel all eagerness of temporary desire, to burn with passion for eternal things—this is emancipation, and this is the free man's worship. And this liberation is effected by a contemplation of Fate; for Fate itself is subdued by the mind which leaves nothing to be purged by the purifying fire of Time.

United with his fellow-men by the strongest of all ties, the tie of a common doom, the free man finds that a new vision is with him always, shedding over every daily task the light of love. The life of Man is a long march through the night, surrounded by invisible foes, tortured by weariness and pain, towards a goal that few can hope to reach, and where none may tarry long. One by one, as they march, our comrades vanish from our sight, seized by the silent orders of omnipotent Death. Very brief is the time in which we can help them, in which their happiness or misery is decided. Be it ours to shed sunshine on their path, to lighten their sorrows by the balm of sympathy, to give them the pure joy of a never-tiring affection to strengthen failing courage, to instil faith in hours of despair. Let us not weigh in grudging scales their merits and demerits, but let us think only of their need—of the sorrows, the difficulties, perhaps the blindnesses, that make the misery of their lives; let us remember that they are fellow-sufferers in the same darkness, actors in the same tragedy as our selves. And so, when their day is over, when their good and their evil have become eternal by the immortality of the past, be it ours to feel that, where they suffered, where they failed, no deed of ours was the cause; but wherever a spark of the divine fire kindled in their hearts, we were ready with encouragement, with sympathy, with brave words in which high courage glowed.

Brief and powerless is Man's life; on him and all his race the slow, sure doom falls pitiless and dark. Blind to good and evil, reckless of destruction, omnipotent matter rolls on its relentless way; for Man, condemned to-day to lose his dearest, tomorrow himself to pass through the

---

*Refers to King Duncan, the Scottish king who is murdered by Macbeth in William Shakespeare's *Macbeth*. —Ed.

gate of darkness, it remains only to cherish, ere yet the blow falls, the lofty thoughts that ennoble his little day; disdaining the coward terrors of the slave of Fate, to worship at the shrine that his own hands have built; undismayed by the empire of chance, to preserve a mind free from the wanton tyranny that rules his outward life; proudly defiant of the irresistible forces that tolerate, for a moment, his knowledge and his condemnation, to sustain alone, a weary but unyielding Atlas, the world that his own ideals have fashioned despite the trampling march of unconscious power.

DISCUSSION QUESTIONS

1. Why does Russell believe that the worship of force and power should always be rejected? Do you agree with him? Why or why not?

2. Why does Russell reject the view of life presented by science? Compare his rejection of science with that of Tolstoy. Whose argument is stronger, and why? Do you agree with both of them that science does not give a satisfactory account of the meaning of life? Why or why not?

3. Compare and contrast Russell's view of the meaning of life with that of Marcus Aurelius and Epictetus (see chapter 5). How are they similar? How different?

4. According to Russell, why is tragedy the proudest and most triumphant of all the arts?

5. "Brief and powerless is Man's life; on him and all his race the slow, sure doom falls pitiless and dark," writes Russell. Amidst the ravages of time, fate, and death, the only thing remaining for the free man to cherish and worship are "the lofty thoughts that ennoble his little day." Do you think that Russell's conclusions regarding the meaning of life are too pessimistic? Why or why not?

6. Why does Russell think that resignation is a virtue? Do you agree with him? Why or why not?

The Razor's Edge
[USA 1946] 2 hours, 26 minutes
Directed by Edmund Goulding

While serving in the army during World War I, Larry Darrell (Tyrone Power) witnesses firsthand the horrors of war and narrowly escapes death. When he returns to the United States, his view of life has changed, and he seeks to understand it more deeply. He decides to postpone his upcoming marriage and put off employment until he can find answers to the questions that trouble him. His fiancée, Isabel (Gene Tierney), agrees to wait for Larry while he searches for knowledge in France and India. There he finds spiritual comfort in the advice of a holy man and wisdom in a solitary journey across the mountains.

After ten years of soul-searching, Larry meets with his fiancée and friends in Paris and finds them much changed. Larry learns that Isabel tired of waiting for him and married another man, Gray Maturin (John Payne). Gray has been suffering from depression since the devastating stock market crash of 1929. With his newly acquired wisdom, Larry comforts Gray and helps him regain his former demeanor.

Larry, Isabel, Gray, and a writer friend, Maugham (Herbert Marshall), go out for a night on the town in Paris. They run into an old friend, Sophie Macdonald (Anne Baxter), who has turned to alcohol after losing her husband and child in a car accident. Larry decides to help Sophie overcome her alcoholism, and she eventually succeeds. Sophie and Larry announce their intent to be married.

News of the engagement infuriates Isabel, who is still secretly in love with Larry. She schemes to disrupt the wedding by tempting Sophie with alcohol. Sophie, overcome with grief at the reminder of her dead child, gives in to drinking again. Larry tries to help Sophie, but she is ashamed of her failure and disappears. Larry does not see Sophie again until a year later, when he is asked to identify her brutally murdered body. Isabel begs Larry to leave Paris and return to the United States with her and Gray. Larry adamantly refuses, confronting Isabel about the scheme that led Sophie back into a life of addiction. The film ends with Larry maintaining that while he has found the answers to some of life's most puzzling questions, he still has many that are left unanswered. He must continue his search for these answers.

This film is based on the novel of the same name by Somerset Maugham. The film was remade in 1984 with Bill Murray in the role of Larry Darrell.

DISCUSSION QUESTIONS

1. Bertrand Russell argues that life has meaning even though an all-powerful and all-good God does not exist. Discuss how Larry Darrell finds meaning in life without assuming the existence of this type of God.

2. Bertrand Russell asserts, "Brief and powerless is Man's life; on him and all his race the slow, sure doom falls pitiless and dark." Amidst the ravages of time, fate, and death, what is left for the free man to cherish and worship are "the lofty thoughts that ennoble his little day." How do you think Larry Darrell would respond to these claims made by Russell? Would he agree with them? Why or why not?

3. In a voice-over monologue, the character Maugham says, "This is the young man of whom I write—he is not famous. It may be that when his life at last comes to an end he will leave no more of a trace of his soul on this earth than a stone thrown into the river leaves on the surface of the water. Yet it may be that the way of life he has chosen for himself may have an ever-growing influence over his fellow men so that long after his death perhaps it may be realized that there lived in this age a very remarkable creature." Do you think that Larry is remarkable? Why or why not?

4. Larry says to Isabel, "I've got a foolish notion I want to do more with my life than just sell bonds." He continues, "It's all so meaningless. You can't help but ask yourself what life is all about, whether there's any sense to it or whether it's just a stupid blunder." Compare the way in which Lester Burham (Kevin Spacey) in *American Beauty* and Larry Darrell respond to misgivings about the meaning their jobs hold for them. Which response do you admire more, and why? Discuss.

5. Larry says to Isabel, "If I ever acquire wisdom, I suppose I'll be wise enough to know what to do with it." In the end, does he know what to do with it? Why or why not?

6. A French coal miner tells Larry, "Enlightenment is the curse of civilization. A man who wastes his energy on knowledge is a fool. The more he learns, the more he wants, and the more unhappy he becomes." Is the coal miner right? Why or why not?

7. Consider the following conversation between Larry and a holy man in India:

    HOLY MAN   "What has brought you here, my son?"

    LARRY   "I've come to learn. Ever since the war I've been searching for something, something that I've not been able to put into words. I've been told that from you I might find guidance."

    HOLY MAN   "God is the only guide, but perhaps if we talk, he may show me a way to help you."

LARRY   "I've studied, I've traveled, I've read everything I could get my hands on, but nothing seems to satisfy me. Like everyone else I want to succeed, I want to improve, but not necessarily in the terms of what the world calls success. Somehow I've lost confidence in the accepted values."

HOLY MAN   "The whole world is restless and confused. . . . As long as men set their ideals on the wrong objects, there can be no real evolution, until men learn that it comes from within themselves."

LARRY   "I know."

What are the "accepted values" in which Larry has lost confidence? The holy man states, "As long as men set their ideals on the wrong objects, there can be no real evolution . . ." What are these "wrong objects"?

8. Borrowing from the *Upanishads*, the core philosophical texts of Hinduism, a holy man in India says to Larry, "The road to salvation is difficult to pass over, as difficult as the sharp edge of a razor. This much we know, and all religions teach it: There is in every one of us a spark of the infinite goodness which created us, and when we leave this earth we are reunited with it as a raindrop falling from heaven is at last reunited with the sea that gave it birth." What do you think the holy man means?

9. Larry says to Isabel, "The wonderful thing about life is that most of us get a second chance. I got a second chance right at the moment when I thought there was nothing in the world worthwhile living for . . . I found some of the things I was looking for. . . ." Do you agree with Larry that most of us get a second chance at bringing meaning to our lives?

10. Isabel asks Maugham, "What is [Larry] trying to do with his life? What does he hope to find?" Maugham responds, "My dear, Larry has found what we all want and very few of us ever get. I don't think anyone can feel but better, nobler, kinder for knowing him. You see, my dear, goodness is, after all, the greatest force in the world, and he's got it." What do you think Larry hopes to find? Do you think Larry is doing the right thing with his life? Why or why not?

JEAN-PAUL SARTRE

EXISTENTIALISM IS A HUMANISM

Jean-Paul Sartre argues that each of us is responsible for the creation of meaning in our own life. There is no source responsible for the composition of our essence and our values other than ourselves. Sartre's philosophy rejects *essentialism*, namely, the view that essence precedes existence. Essentialism can be traced back most famously to Plato's theory of forms or ideas. For essentialists like Plato, the essences of entities are transcendent forms or ideas, and the identity of these ideas or forms is fixed or determined. These essences—or forms or ideas—make entities what they are; that is, the essence of an entity is its defining characteristic in the absence of which the entity would not be itself. Sartre rejects essentialism and offers in its place something called *existentialism*.

Existentialism reverses the position of essentialism. For the existentialist, *existence precedes essence*. Unlike the essentialist, who maintains that the essence of an entity is responsible for determining the nature of the entity's existence, the existentialist places responsibility for defining the essence of an entity entirely upon its existence. When the doctrine of existentialism is applied to human existence, one finds that individuals are responsible for what they are. For Sartre, existentialism means for humans that "man first of all exists, encounters himself, surges up in the world—and defines himself afterwards." Humans are what they will, and because of this, humans are nothing more than what they will themselves to be. Thus, for Sartre, each of us is responsible for who we are, and no one or thing can take away that responsibility: Neither heredity, environment, or God determines who we are.

In addition, we are responsible for the creation of morality and for prescribing a moral philosophy to everyone else. For example, when we decide to marry, Sartre believes that this is not just an individual moral decision. Rather, in deciding to marry, "I am thereby committing not only myself, but humanity as a whole, to the practice of monogamy." Hence, "when we say that man is responsible for himself, we do not mean that he is responsible only for his own individuality, but that he is responsible for all men." When we create an image of ourselves, we are also creating an image of how we would have all people be.

Sartre gives us a lot of responsibility—so much, in fact, that he maintains that man is "condemned to be free." "Condemned, because he did not create himself, yet is nevertheless at liberty, and from the moment that he is thrown into this world he is responsible for everything he does."

Sartre explains that there are two kinds of existentialism: (1) Christian existentialism and (2) atheistic existentialism. He maintains that the latter is the better type because "if God does not exist there is at least one being whose existence comes before its essence, a being which exists before it can be defined by any conception of it." "That being is man . . . or human reality." Later, Sartre comments, "Existentialism is not atheist in the sense that it would exhaust itself in demonstrations of the non-existence of God." "It declares, rather, that even if God existed that would make no difference from its point of view." For Sartre, the key issue is not the existence of God, but rather what man needs to do in order to find himself again. We must "understand that nothing can save him from himself, not even a valid proof of the existence of God." As Sartre explains, even though we exist in "despair," "anguish," and "abandonment," there is still reason for celebration in the fact that we create our own essence and values.

Jean-Paul Sartre (1905–80), a French philosopher, playwright, and novelist, was born in Paris. He graduated from the prestigious École Normale Supérieure in 1929 and in the same year met Simone de Beauvoir, his lifelong partner. Sartre began his career as a philosophy teacher in 1931 in Le Havre but hated it. Eventually, because of the financial success of his literary works, he was able to live off this income and cease teaching philosophy. Drafted to serve in World War II in 1939, he was imprisoned in a Nazi prison camp the very next year. Upon his release in 1941, he returned to Paris and became active in the French resistance. By his own account, World War II turned Sartre from an academic philosopher and avant-garde writer into an intellectual deeply committed to the "wretched of the earth"—the title of a book by Franz Fanon for which Sartre wrote a preface. He was offered the Nobel Prize for Literature in 1964 but declined the honor. When he died in 1980, 50,000 people attended his funeral.

Sartre's philosophical masterpiece, *Being and Nothingness* (1943), reveals the strong influence that the German philosophers Edmund Husserl (1859–1938) and Martin Heidegger (1884–1976) had on his work, and it became one of the foundational texts of existentialism. Sartre was the author of many other books, including *The Transcendence of the Ego* (1936), *Nausea* (novel, 1938), *Sketch of a Theory of the Emotions* (1939), *The Psychology of Imagination* (1940), *The Age of Reason* (novel, 1945), *The Reprieve* (novel, 1945), *The Flies* (play, 1946), *No Exit* (play, 1946), *The Troubled Sleep* (novel, 1949), *Existentialism Is a Humanism* (1946), *What Is Literature?* (1949), *Literary and Philosophical Essays* (1955), *Critique of Dialectical Reason* (1960), *The Words* (autobiography, 1964), *The Family Idiot* (biography, 1971–72), *Between Existentialism and Marxism* (1975), *Life/Situations* (1977), and *Notebooks for an Ethics* (1983). The following selection, "Existentialism is a Humanism," was first delivered as a public lecture on October 29, 1945, and subsequently transcribed and published as a book, *L'existentialisme est un humanisme* (1946).

What, then, is this that we call existentialism?

Most of those who are making use of this word would be highly confused if required to explain its meaning. For since it has become fashionable, people cheerfully declare that this musician or that painter is "existentialist." A columnist in *Clartés* signs himself "The Existentialist," and, indeed, the word is now so loosely applied to so many things that it no longer means anything at all. It would appear that, for the lack of any novel doctrine such as that of surrealism, all those who are eager to join in the latest scandal or movement now seize upon this philosophy in which, however, they can find nothing to their purpose. For in truth this is of all teachings the least scandalous and the most austere: it is intended strictly for technicians and philosophers. All the same, it can easily be defined.

The question is only complicated because there are two kinds of existentialists. There are, on the one hand, the Christians, amongst whom I shall name [Karl] Jaspers and Gabriel Marcel, both professed Catholics; and on the other the existential atheists, amongst whom we must place Heidegger as well as the French existentialists and myself. What they have in common is simply the fact that they believe that *existence* comes before *essence*—or, if you will, that we must begin from the subjective. What exactly do we mean by that? If one considers an article of manufacture as, for example, a book or a paper-knife—one sees that it has been made by an artisan who had a conception of it; and he has paid attention, equally, to the conception of a paper-knife and to the pre-existent technique of production which is a part of that conception and is, at bottom, a formula. Thus the paper-knife is at the same time an article producible in a certain manner and one which, on the other hand, serves a definite purpose, for one cannot suppose that a man would produce a paper-knife without knowing what it was for. Let us say, then, of the paper-knife that its essence—that is to say the sum of the formulae and the qualities which made its

production and its definition possible—precedes its existence. The presence of such-and-such a paper-knife or book is thus determined before my eyes. Here, then, we are viewing the world from a technical standpoint, and we can say that production precedes existence.

When we think of God as the creator, we are thinking of him, most of the time, as a supernal artisan. Whatever doctrine we may be considering, whether it be a doctrine like that of Descartes, or of Leibniz himself, we always imply that the will follows, more or less, from the understanding or at least accompanies it, so that when God creates he knows precisely what he is creating. Thus, the conception of man in the mind of God is comparable to that of the paper-knife in the mind of the artisan. God makes man according to a procedure and a conception, exactly as the artisan manufactures a paper-knife, following a definition and a formula. Thus each individual man is the realization of a certain conception which dwells in the divine understanding. In the philosophic atheism of the eighteenth century, the notion of God is suppressed, but not, for all that, the idea that essence is prior to existence; something of that idea we still find everywhere, in Diderot, in Voltaire and even in Kant. Man possesses a human nature; that "human nature," which is the conception of human being, is found in every man; which means that each man is a particular example of a universal conception, the conception of Man. In Kant, this universality goes so far that the wild man of the woods, man in the state of nature and the bourgeois are all contained in the same definition and have the same fundamental qualities. Here again, the essence of man precedes that historic existence which we confront in experience.

Atheistic existentialism, of which I am a representative, declares with greater consistency that if God does not exist there is at least one being whose existence comes before its essence, a being which exists before it can be defined by any conception of it. That being is man or, as Heidegger has it, the human reality. What do we mean by saying that existence precedes essence? We mean that man first of all exists, encounters himself, surges up in the world—and defines himself afterwards. If man as the existentialist sees him [as] not definable, it is because to begin with he is nothing. He will not be anything until later, and then he will be what he makes of himself. Thus, there is no human nature, because there is no God to have a conception of it. Man simply is. Not that he is simply what he conceives himself to be, but he is what he wills, and as he conceives himself after already existing—as he wills to be after that leap towards existence.

Man is nothing else but that which he makes of himself. That is the first principle of existentialism. And this is what people call its "subjectivity," using the word as a reproach against us. But what do we mean to say by this, but that man is of a greater dignity than a stone or a table? For we mean to say that man primarily exists—that man is, before all else, something which propels itself towards a future and is aware that it is doing so. Man is, indeed, a project which possesses a subjective life, instead of being a kind of moss, or a fungus or a cauliflower. Before that projection of the self nothing exists; not even in the heaven of intelligence: man will only attain existence when he is what he purposes to be. Not, however, what he may wish to be. For what we usually understand by wishing or willing is a conscious decision taken—much more often than not—after we have made ourselves what we are. I may wish to join a party, to write a book or to marry—but in such a case what is usually called my will is probably a manifestation of a prior and more spontaneous decision. If, however, it is true that existence is prior to essence, man is responsible for what he is. Thus, the first effect of existentialism is that it puts every man in possession of himself as he is, and places the entire responsibility for his existence squarely upon his own shoulders. And, when we say that man is responsible for himself, we do not mean that he is responsible only for his own individuality, but that he is responsible for all men.

The word "subjectivism" is to be understood in two senses, and our adversaries play upon only one of them. Subjectivism means, on the one hand, the freedom of the individual subject and, on the other, that man cannot pass beyond human subjectivity. It is the latter which is the deeper meaning of existentialism. When we say that man chooses himself, we do mean that every one of us must choose himself; but by that we also mean that in choosing for himself he chooses for all men. For in effect, of all the actions a man may take in order to create himself as he wills to be, there is not one which is not creative, at the same time, of an image of man such as he believes he ought to be. To choose between this or that is at the same time to affirm the value of that which is chosen; for we are unable ever to choose the worse. What we choose is always the better; and nothing can be better for us unless it is better for all.

If, moreover, existence precedes essence and we will to exist at the same time as we fashion our image, that image is valid for all and for the entire epoch in which we find ourselves. Our responsibility is thus much greater than we had supposed, for it concerns mankind as a whole. If I am a worker, for instance, I may choose to join a Christian rather than a Communist trade union. And if, by that membership, I choose to signify that resignation is, after all, the attitude that best becomes a man, that man's kingdom is not upon this earth, I do not commit myself alone to that view. Resignation is my will for everyone, and my action is, in consequence, a commitment on behalf of all mankind. Or if, to take a more personal case, I decide to marry and to have children, even though this decision proceeds simply from my situation, from my passion or my desire, I am thereby committing not only myself, but humanity as a whole, to the practice of monogamy. I am thus responsible for myself and for all men, and I am creating a certain image of man as I would have him to be. In fashioning myself I fashion man.

This may enable us to understand what is meant by such terms—perhaps a little grandiloquent—as anguish, abandonment and despair. As you will soon see, it is very simple. First, what do we mean by anguish? The existentialist frankly states that man is in anguish. His meaning is as follows— When a man commits himself to anything, fully realizing that he is not only choosing what he will be, but is thereby at the same time a legislator deciding for the whole of mankind—in such a moment a man cannot escape from the sense of complete and profound responsibility. There are many, indeed, who show no such anxiety. But we affirm that they are merely disguising their anguish or are in flight from it. Certainly, many people think that in what they are doing they commit no one but themselves to anything: and if you ask them, "What would happen if everyone did so?" they shrug their shoulders and reply, "Everyone does not do so." But in truth, one ought always to ask oneself what would happen if everyone did as one is doing; nor can one escape from that disturbing thought except by a kind of self-deception.

The man who lies in self-excuse, by saying "Everyone will not do it" must be ill at ease in his conscience, for the act of lying implies the universal value which it denies. By its very disguise his anguish reveals itself. This is the anguish that Kierkegaard called "the anguish of Abraham." You know the story: An angel commanded Abraham to sacrifice his son: and obedience was obligatory, if it really was an angel who had appeared and said, "Thou, Abraham, shalt sacrifice thy son." But anyone in such a case would wonder, first, whether it was indeed an angel and secondly, whether I am really Abraham. Where are the proofs? A certain mad woman who suffered from hallucinations said that people were telephoning to her, and giving her orders. The doctor asked, "But who is it that speaks to you?" She replied: "He says it is God." And what, indeed, could prove to her that it was God? If an angel appears to me, what is the proof that it is an angel; or, if I hear voices, who can prove that they proceed from heaven and not from hell, or from my own subconsciousness or some pathological condition? Who can prove that they are really addressed to me?

Who, then, can prove that I am the proper person to impose, by my own choice, my conception of man upon mankind? I shall never find any proof whatever; there will be no sign to convince me of it. If a voice speaks to me, it is still I myself who must decide whether the voice is or is not that of an angel. If I regard a certain course of action as good, it is only I who choose to say that it is good and not bad. There is nothing to show that I am Abraham: nevertheless I also am obliged at every instant to perform actions which are examples. Everything happens to every man

as though the whole human race had its eyes fixed upon what he is doing and regulated its conduct accordingly. So every man ought to say, "Am I really a man who has the right to act in such a manner that humanity regulates itself by what I do." If a man does not say that, he is dissembling his anguish.

Clearly, the anguish with which we are concerned here is not one that could lead to quietism or inaction. It is anguish pure and simple, of the kind well known to all those who have borne responsibilities. When, for instance, a military leader takes upon himself the responsibility for an attack and sends a number of men to their death he chooses to do it and at bottom he alone chooses. No doubt under a higher command, but its orders, which are more general, require interpretation by him and upon that interpretation depends the life of ten, fourteen or twenty men. In making the decision, he cannot but feel a certain anguish. All leaders know that anguish. It does not prevent their acting, on the contrary it is the very condition of their action, for the action presupposes that there is a plurality of possibilities, and in choosing one of these, they realize that it has value only because it is chosen. Now it is anguish of that kind which existentialism describes, and moreover, as we shall see, makes explicit through direct responsibility towards other men who are concerned. Far from being a screen which could separate us from action, it is a condition of action itself.

And when we speak of "abandonment"—a favorite word of Heidegger—we only mean to say that God does not exist, and that it is necessary to draw the consequences of his absence right to the end. The existentialist is strongly opposed to a certain type of secular moralism which seeks to suppress God at the least possible expense. Towards 1880, when the French professors endeavored to formulate a secular morality, they said something like this: God is a useless and costly hypothesis, so we will do without it. However, if we are to have morality, a society and a law-abiding world, it is essential that certain values should be taken seriously; they must have an *à priori* existence ascribed to them. It must be considered obligatory *à priori* to be honest, not to lie, not to beat one's wife, to bring up children and so forth; so we are going to do a little work on this subject, which will enable us to show that these values exist all the same, inscribed in an intelligible heaven although, of course, there is no God. In other words—and this is, I believe, the purport of all that we in France call radicalism—nothing will be changed if God does not exist; we shall rediscover the same norms of honesty, progress and humanity, and we shall have disposed of God as an out-of-date hypothesis which will die away quietly of itself.

The existentialist, on the contrary, finds it extremely embarrassing that God does not exist, for there disappears with Him all possibility of finding values in an intelligible heaven. There can no longer be any good *à priori,* since there is no infinite and perfect consciousness to think it. It is nowhere written that "the good" exists, that one must be honest or must not lie, since we are now upon the plane where there are only men. Dostoevsky once wrote "If God did not exist, everything would be permitted"; and that, for existentialism, is the starting point. Everything is indeed permitted if God does not exist, and man is in consequence forlorn, for he cannot find anything to depend upon either within or outside himself. He discovers forthwith, that he is without excuse.

For if indeed existence precedes essence, one will never be able to explain one's action by reference to a given and specific human nature; in other words, there is no determinism—man is free, man is freedom. Nor, on the other hand, if God does not exist, are we provided with any values or commands that could legitimize our behavior. Thus we have neither behind us, nor before us in a luminous realm of values, any means of justification or excuse. We are left alone, without excuse.

That is what I mean when I say that man is condemned to be free. Condemned, because he did not create himself, yet is nevertheless at liberty, and from the moment that he is thrown into this world he is responsible for everything he does. The existentialist does not believe in the power of passion. He will never regard a grand passion as a destructive torrent upon which a man is swept into certain actions as by fate, and which, therefore, is an excuse for them. He thinks that man is responsible for his passion. Neither will an existentialist think that a man can find help through some sign being vouchsafed upon earth for his orientation: for he thinks that the man himself interprets the sign as he chooses. He thinks that every man, without any support or help whatever, is condemned at every instant to invent man. As Ponge has written in a very fine article, "Man is the future of man." That is exactly true. Only, if one took this to mean that the future is laid up in Heaven, that God knows what it is, it would be false, for then it would no longer even be a future. If, however, it means that, whatever man may now appear to be, there is a future to be fashioned, a virgin future that awaits him—then it is a true saying. But in the present one is forsaken.

As an example by which you may the better understand this state of abandonment, I will refer to the case of a pupil of mine, who sought me out in the following circumstances. His father was quarreling with his mother and was also inclined to be a "collaborator"; his elder brother had been killed in the German offensive of 1940 and this young man, with a sentiment somewhat primitive but generous, burned to avenge him. His mother was living alone with him, deeply afflicted by the semi-treason of his father and by the death of her eldest son, and her one consolation was in this young man. But he, at this moment, had the choice between going to England to join the Free French Forces or of staying near his mother and helping her to live. He fully realised that this woman lived only for him and that his disappearance—or perhaps his death—would plunge her into despair. He also realised that, concretely and in fact, every action he performed on his mother's behalf would be sure of effect in the sense of aiding her to live, whereas anything he did in order to go and fight would be an ambiguous action which might vanish like water into sand and serve no purpose. For instance, to set out for England he would have to wait indefinitely in a Spanish camp on the way through Spain; or, on arriving in England or in Algiers he might be put into an office to fill up forms. Consequently, he found himself confronted by two very different modes of action; the one concrete, immediate, but directed towards only one individual; and the other an action addressed to an end infinitely greater, a national collectivity, but for that very reason ambiguous—and it might be frustrated on the way. At the same time, he was hesitating between two kinds of morality; on the one side the morality of sympathy, of personal devotion and, on the other side, a morality of wider scope but of more debatable validity. He had to choose between those two.

What could help him to choose? Could the Christian doctrine? No. Christian doctrine says: Act with charity, love your neighbor, deny yourself for others, choose the way which is hardest, and so forth. But which is the harder road? To whom does one owe the more brotherly love, the patriot or the mother? Which is the more useful aim, the general one of fighting in and for the whole community, or the precise aim of helping one particular person to live? Who can give an answer to that *à priori*? No one. Nor is it given in any ethical scripture. The Kantian ethic says, Never regard another as a means, but always as an end. Very well; if I remain with my mother, I shall be regarding her as the end and not as a means: but by the same token I am in danger of treating as means those who are fighting on my behalf; and the converse is also true, that if I go to the aid of the combatants I shall be treating them as the end at the risk of treating my mother as a means.

If values are uncertain, if they are still too abstract to determine the particular, concrete case under consideration, nothing remains but to trust in our instincts. That is what this young man tried to do; and when I saw him he said, "In the end, it is feeling that counts; the direction in which it is really pushing me is the one I ought to choose. If I feel that I love my mother enough to sacrifice everything else for her—my will to be avenged, all my longings for action and adventure—then I stay with her. If, on the contrary, I feel that my love for her is not enough, I go." But how does one estimate the strength of a feeling? The value of his feeling for his mother was determined precisely by the fact that he was standing by her,. I may say that I love a certain friend enough to sacrifice such or such a sum of money for him, but I cannot prove that unless I have done it. I may say, "I love my mother enough to remain with her," if actually I have remained with her. I can only estimate the strength of this affection if I have performed an action by which it is defined and ratified. But if I then appeal to this affection to justify my action, I find myself drawn into a vicious circle.

Moreover, as Gide has very well said, a sentiment which is play-acting and one which is vital are two things that are hardly distinguishable one from an other. To decide that I love my mother by staying beside her, and to play a comedy the upshot of which is that I do so— these are nearly the same thing. In other words, feeling is formed by the deeds that one does; therefore I cannot consult it as a guide to action. And that is to say that I can neither seek within myself for an authentic impulse to action, nor can I expect, from some ethic, formulae that will enable me to act. You may say that the youth did, at least, go to a professor to ask for advice. But if you seek counsel—from a priest, for example—you have selected that priest; and at bottom you already knew, more or less, what he would advise. In other words, to choose an adviser is nevertheless to commit oneself by that choice. If you are a Christian, you will say, Consult a priest; but there are collaborationists, priests who are resisters and priests who wait for the tide to turn: which will you choose? Had this young man chosen a priest of the resistance, or one of the collaboration, he would have decided beforehand the kind of advice he was to receive. Similarly, in coming to me; he knew what advice I should give him, and I had but one reply to make. You are free, therefore choose—that is to say, invent. No rule of general morality can show you what you ought to do: no signs are vouchsafed in this world. The Catholics will reply, "Oh, but they are!" Very well; still, it is I myself, in every case, who have to interpret the signs.

While I was imprisoned, I made the acquaintance of a somewhat remarkable man, a Jesuit, who had become a member of that order in the following manner. In his life he had suffered a succession of rather severe setbacks. His father had died when he was a child, leaving him in poverty, and he had been awarded a free scholarship in a religious institution, where he had been made continually to feel that he was accepted for charity's sake, and, in consequence, he had been denied several of those distinctions and honors which gratify children. Later, about the age of eighteen, he came to grief in a sentimental affair; and finally, at twenty-two—this was a trifle in itself, but it was the last drop that overflowed his cup—he failed in his military examination. This young man, then, could regard himself as a total failure: it was a sign—but a sign of what? He might have taken refuge in bitterness or despair. But he took it—very cleverly for him—as a sign that he was not intended for secular success, and that only the attainments of religion, those of sanctity and of faith, were accessible to him. He interpreted his record as a message from God, and became a member of the Order. Who can doubt but that this decision as to the meaning of the sign was his, and his alone? One could have drawn quite different conclusions from such a series of reverses—as, for example, that he had better become a carpenter or a revolutionary. For the decipherment of the sign, however, he bears the entire responsibility. That is what "abandonment" implies, that we ourselves decide our being. And with this abandonment goes anguish.

As for "despair," the meaning of this expression is extremely simple. It merely means that we limit ourselves to a reliance upon that which is within our wills, or within the sum of the probabilities which render our action feasible. Whenever one wills anything, there are always these elements of probability. If I am counting upon a visit from a friend, who may be coming by train or by tram; I presuppose that the train will arrive at the appointed time, or that the tram will not be derailed. I remain in the realm of possibilities; but one does not rely upon any possibilities beyond those that are strictly concerned in one's action. Beyond the point at which the possibilities under consideration cease to affect my action, I ought to disinterest myself. For there is no God and no prevenient [antecedent] design, which can adapt the world and all its possibilities to my will. When Descartes said, "Conquer yourself rather than the world," what he meant was, at bottom, the same—that we should act without hope. . . .

Quietism is the attitude of people who say, "let others do what I cannot do." The doctrine I am presenting before you is precisely the opposite of this, since it declares that there is no reality except in action. It goes further, indeed, and adds, "Man is nothing else but what he purposes, he exists only in so far as he realizes himself; he is therefore nothing else but the sum of his actions, nothing else but what his life is." Hence we can well understand why some people are horrified by our teaching. For many have but one resource to sustain them in their misery, and that is to think, "Circumstances have been against me, I was

worthy to be some thing much better than I have been. I admit I have never had a great love or a great friendship; but that is because I never met a man or a woman who were worthy of it; if I have not written any very good books, it is because I had not the leisure to do so; or, if I have had no children to whom I could devote myself it is because I did not find the man I could have lived with. So there remains within me a wide range of abilities, inclinations and potentialities, unused but perfectly viable, which endow me with a worthiness that could never be inferred from the mere history of my actions."

But in reality and for the existentialist, there is no love apart from the deeds of love; no potentiality of love other than that which is manifested in loving; there is no genius other than that which is expressed in works of art. The genius of Proust is the totality of the works of Proust; the genius of Racine is the series of his tragedies, outside of which there is nothing. Why should we attribute to Racine the capacity to write yet another tragedy when that is precisely what he did not write? In life, a man commits himself, draws his own portrait and there is nothing but that portrait. No doubt this thought may seem comfortless to one who has not made a success of his life. On the other hand, it puts everyone in a position to understand that reality alone is reliable; that dreams, expectations and hopes serve to define a man only as deceptive dreams, abortive hopes, expectations unfulfilled; that is to say, they define him negatively, not positively. Nevertheless, when one says, "You are nothing else but what you live," it does not imply that an artist is to be judged solely by his works of art, for a thousand other things contribute no less to his definition as a man. What we mean to say is that a man is no other than a series of undertakings, that he is the sum, the organization, the set of relations that constitute these undertakings. . . .

You can see from these few reflections that nothing could be more unjust than the objections people raise against us. Existentialism is nothing else but an attempt to draw the full conclusions from a consistently atheistic position. Its intention is not in the least that of plunging men into despair. And if by despair one means—as the Christians do—any attitude of unbelief, the despair of the existentialists is something different. Existentialism is not atheist in the sense that it would exhaust itself in demonstrations of the non-existence of God. It declares, rather, that even if God existed that would make no difference from its point of view. Not that we believe God does exist, but we think that the real problem is not that of His existence; what man needs is to find himself again and to understand that nothing can save him from himself, not even a valid proof of the existence of God. In this sense existentialism is optimistic. It is a doctrine of action, and it is only by self-deception, by confounding their own despair with ours that Christians can describe us as without hope.

DISCUSSION QUESTIONS

1. Sartre maintains that each of us is responsible for the meaning of our lives. Compare his view of the meaning of life with those of Marcus Aurelius, Epicurus, Leo Tolstoy, and Bertrand Russell. Which view do you prefer, and why?

2. Why did Sartre say that we are nothing more than the sum of our actions? Do you agree with him? Why or why not?

3. Sartre argues that feeling is formed by the deeds that we do, and therefore cannot be consulted as a guide to action. Analyze his argument.

4. For Sartre, we are responsible for the creation of morality and for prescribing a moral philosophy to everyone else. For example, in deciding to marry, "I am thereby committing not only myself, but humanity as a whole, to the practice of monogamy." Do you agree with him? Why or why not? Compare Sartre's view of morality with that of Immanuel Kant (see chapter 4).

5. What does Sartre mean by "despair," "anguish," and "abandonment"? Do you agree with the meanings he assigns to these terms? Have you ever experienced these things in the way Sartre defines them?

6. Sartre maintains that even if God existed, it would make no difference regarding human reality. What does he mean? Do you agree with him? Why or why not?

7. Why does Sartre maintain that we are condemned to be free? Do you agree with him? Compare his view of freedom to those of Epictetus, C. A. Campbell, and Sophocles (all from chapter 5).

8. Do you think Sartre's philosophy regarding the meaning of life is ultimately a pessimistic one or an optimistic one? Compare your response with Sartre's.

Harold and Maude
[USA 1971] 1 hour, 31 minutes
Directed by Hal Ashby

Harold (Bud Cort) is a death-obsessed adolescent whose mother (Vivian Pickles) is indifferent to his troubles. He stages fake suicides, attends funerals as a hobby, and drives around in a sports car modified as a hearse. He even sees a psychologist to help him work through his obsession with death, but the sessions are of little help.

One day, Harold meets Maude (Ruth Gordon) at a funeral for someone who is a stranger to both of them. Maude is seventy-nine years old and lives life with passion and freedom. Says Maude, "I like to watch things grow. They grow and bloom and fade and die and change into something else. Ah, life. I should like to change into a sunflower most of all. They're so tall and simple." Harold falls in love with Maude as she shares her love for life and adventure with him. Together they run from the police, save Harold from the draft, and "liberate" a smog-suffocated tree.

Meanwhile, Harold's mother desperately attempts to introduce him to single young women. Harold will have none of it, devising hilarious stunts to frighten the women off. He falls more deeply in love with Maude and decides to ask her to marry him. When he surprises Maude with a ring on her eightieth birthday, she surprises him, too: she has taken some pills and will be dead by midnight. Distraught, Harold calls an ambulance in hope of saving Maude's life, but she dies in the hospital. The film ends with a grieving Harold launching his modified hearse off the side of a cliff. As the camera pans up from the wreckage, Harold is seen at the top of the cliff, playing "Maude's Theme" on his banjo and walking off toward the horizon.

DISCUSSION QUESTIONS

1. Jean-Paul Sartre argues that each person is responsible for the creation of meaning in his or her life. How does the film *Harold and Maude* develop Sartre's position?

2. According to Sartre, "Man first of all exists, encounters himself, surges up in the world—and defines himself afterwards." Examine the lives and actions of both Harold and Maude in view of this statement by Sartre. Do each of them ascribe in the same way to Sartre's notion?

3. Harold's mother is continuously introducing him to young women, presumably to find a suitable marriage partner. Harold rejects them all. Finally, when Harold tells his mother that he is getting married and shows her a picture of Maude, she says, "You can't be serious." When Harold proposes to Maude and gives her a ring on her eightieth birthday, Maude tells him that she will be dead soon because she has just taken some pills. What do the events suggest about this film's position on marriage?

4. Consider the following conversation between Maude and Harold:

   MAUDE   "What a delight it is, Harold, to bump into you again. I knew we were going to be good friends the moment I saw you. You go to funerals often, don't you?"

   HAROLD   "Yes."

   MAUDE   "Oh, so do I. They're such fun, aren't they? It's all change. All revolving. Burials and births. The end to the beginning and the beginning to the end—the great circle of life."

   Do you find it odd that Harold and Maude attend funerals for people whom they don't know? Do you think that they both share the same reasons for attending funerals? How are their beliefs about funerals connected to their respective beliefs about the meaning of life?

5. Consider the following dialogue between Harold and Maude:

   MAUDE   "Here we are, Harold. Oat straw tea and ginger pie."

   HAROLD   "Certainly a new experience for me."

   MAUDE   "Oh, wonderful! Try something new each day. After all, we're given life to find it out. It doesn't last forever."

   HAROLD   "You look as if you could."

   Discuss Maude's perspective on life and experience as expressed in this passage. Should we try something new each day? Why or why not?

6. Consider this exchange between Harold and Maude:

    HAROLD   "I'm sure picking up on vices."

    MAUDE   "Vice? Virtue? It's best not to be too moral. You cheat yourself out of too much life. Aim above morality. If you apply that to life, then you're bound to live it fully."

    HAROLD   "I haven't lived. I've died a few times."

    Compare and contrast Maude's position on morality with that of Sartre. Are they similar? Why or why not?

7. Consider the following conversation between Harold and Maude:

    HAROLD   "Maude, do you pray?"

    MAUDE   "Pray? No. I communicate."

    HAROLD   "With God?"

    MAUDE   "With life."

    HAROLD   "This is real nice. It makes me want to do somersaults."

    MAUDE   "Well, why don't you?"

    HAROLD   "I'd feel stupid."

    MAUDE   "Harold, everyone has the right to make an ass out of themselves. You can't let the world judge you too much."

    What does Maude mean when she says she communicates with life? Do you agree with her that you can't let the world judge you too much? Defend your position.

8. Consider the following dialogue between Harold and Maude at the hospital, just after Maude has taken the pills that will bring about her death:

    MAUDE   "Oh, Harold! What a fuss this is. So unnecessary."

    HAROLD   "Maude, please. Don't die. I couldn't bear it. Please, don't die."

    MAUDE   "But, Harold, we begin to die as soon as we are born. What is so strange about death? It's no surprise. It's part of life. It's change."

    HAROLD   "But why now?"

    MAUDE   "I thought eighty was a good round number. I feel giddy."

    HAROLD   "But Maude, you don't understand. I love you. Do you hear me? I've never said that to anyone in my life before. You're the first. Maude. Please don't leave me."

    MAUDE   "Oh, Harold, don't upset yourself so."

    HAROLD   "It's true. I can't live without you."

MAUDE   "And this too shall pass away."

HAROLD   "Never! Never! I'll never forget you. I wanted to marry you. Don't you understand! I love you. I love you!"

MAUDE   "Oh! That's wonderful, Harold. Go—and love some more."

Why does Maude kill herself on her eightieth birthday? Is this film suggesting that this is the ultimate expression of freedom—that is, to live a full and happy life, and then to end life when one chooses, on one's own terms? Why or why not? Discuss.

ALBERT CAMUS

THE ABSURD

Albert Camus argues that even though life is "absurd," we should not therefore conclude that it is not worth living. "In this unintelligible and limited universe, man's fate henceforth assumes its meaning." A person's life can have meaning through consciousness, freedom, and revolt even though the world itself is without meaning. For Camus, the *absurd* is the widespread sensibility of our times, and it is experienced in the context of our demands for justice and rationality in the face of an indifferent universe.

Camus compares life to the myth of Sisyphus, the character from Greek mythology condemned by the gods to the endless and futile task of rolling a huge rock up a hill only to watch it roll back down again when it reaches the top of the hill. Sisyphus is the "absurd hero" whose "whole being is exerted toward accomplishing nothing." His fate is tragic because each time he repeats the task it is in "the hope of succeeding." Nevertheless, despite his endless and futile efforts, Sisyphus is happy. "Happiness and the absurd are two sons of the same earth," says Camus. "They are inseparable." Even as Sisyphus accepts his task, he scorns the gods for bestowing it on him. Like Sisyphus, the contemporary person who works every day on the same task lives an absurd existence. According the Camus, "the absurd teaches that all experiences are unimportant" while at the same time urging us on "toward the greatest quantity of experiences."

For Camus, the absurdity of life provides us with the only truly serious philosophical question: why not commit suicide? Camus contends that suicide is an inadequate response to the absurdity of life. The adequate response is to continue living while being conscious of the absurdity of life. This consciousness results in the constant "confrontation between man and his own obscurity," which, for Camus, is an act of revolt. Living keeps the absurd alive, and keeping it alive represents a continuous act of revolt and assertion of freedom. "By the mere activity of consciousness I transform into a rule of life what was an invitation to death—and I refuse suicide," writes Camus. Thus, by means of "an absurd reasoning," man chooses life over suicide.

Albert Camus (1913–60), a French philosopher, novelist, essayist, and playwright, was born in Algeria. He was educated in philosophy at the University of Algiers, though he was unable to pursue a teaching career because of tuberculosis. Through the 1930s, he was one of the leading left-wing intellectuals in Algiers. Before World War II, he worked as a journalist for the *Alger-Républican*, contributing articles that drew attention to social injustices that led to the Algerian War of Independence in 1954. Camus and Sartre were for a time close philosophical friends, though they grew distant after a falling-out. Like Sartre, Camus was active in the French Resistance during the World War II. However, unlike Sarte, when Camus was offered the Nobel Prize for Literature (1957), he accepted it. When Camus died in a car crash in 1960, Sartre called it "an absurd death." The notion of the "absurd" is explored in many of Camus' works including *The Stranger* (novel, 1942), *The Myth of Sisyphus* (1942), *The Plague* (novel, 1947), *The Rebel* (essays, 1951), and *The Fall* (novel, 1956). The following selection is from Camus' long philosophical essay "The Myth of Sisyphus," which first appeared as a book in French in 1942.

AN ABSURD REASONING

There is but one truly serious philosophical problem, and that is suicide. Judging whether life is or is not worth living amounts to answering the fundamental question of philosophy. All the rest—whether or not the world has three dimensions, whether the mind has nine or twelve categories—comes afterwards. These are games; one must first answer. And if it is true, as Nietzsche claims, that a philosopher, to deserve our respect, must preach by example, you can appreciate the importance of that reply, for it will precede the definitive act. These are facts the heart can feel; yet they call for careful study before they become clear to the intellect.

If I ask myself how to judge that this question is more urgent than that, I reply that one judges by the actions it entails. I have never seen anyone die for the ontological argument. Galileo, who held a scientific truth of great importance, abjured it with the greatest ease as soon as it endangered his life. In a certain sense, he did right. That truth was not worth the stake. Whether the earth or the sun revolves around the other is a matter of profound indifference. To tell the truth, it is a futile question. On the other hand, I see many people die because they judge that life is not worth living. I see others paradoxically getting killed for the ideas or illusions that give them a reason for living (what is called a reason for living is also an excellent reason for dying). I therefore conclude that the meaning of life is the most urgent of questions. How to answer it? On all essential problems (I mean thereby those that run the risk of leading to death or those that intensify the passion of living) there are probably but two methods of thought: the method of La Palisse* and the method of Don Quixote.† Solely the balance between evidence and lyricism can allow us to achieve simultaneously emotion and lucidity. In a subject at once so humble and so heavy with emotion, the learned and classical dialectic must yield, one can see, to a more modest attitude of mind deriving at one and the same time from common sense and understanding.

Suicide has never been dealt with except as a social phenomenon. On the contrary, we are concerned here, at the outset, with the relationship

---

* Jacques d'La Palisse (1470–1525), a French nobleman and valiant military officer, fought in the Battle of Marignan, which took place on September 14 and 15, 1515—a battle regarded as the last and greatest triumph of the armored lancer. After he died in the Battle of Pavia, his soldiers composed a famous song in his honor, "Chanson de La Palisse." For Camus, "the method of La Palisse" is that of fighting for something that is such a worthy cause that one is willing to risk one's life for it. —Ed.

† *Don Quixote* (Part 1, 1605; Part 2, 1615), a novel by Miguel de Cervantes (1547–1616), is one of the best known books in Western literature. Its hero is a fifty-year-old man who has gone out of his mind reading books about chivalry and decides that he will venture into the world as an armor-clad, lance-bearing knight in search of adventure. However, unlike La Palisse, a man who set out to fight valiantly in real wars already in motion, Don Quixote's only "battles" are creations of his lyrical, romantic imagination. For example, he fights a giant that turns out to be a windmill and a hostile army that turns out to be a flock of sheep. For Camus, the method of Don Quixote is one wherein events are created through the poetic imagination with the purpose of intensifying the passion for living. Nevertheless, the actual risk to one's life in seeking to overcome these imagined events is negligible. —Ed.

between individual thought and suicide. An act like this is prepared within the silence of the heart, as is a great work of art. The man himself is ignorant of it. One evening he pulls the trigger or jumps. Of an apartment-building manager who had killed himself I was told that he had lost his daughter five years before, that he had changed greatly since, and that that experience had "undermined" him. A more exact word cannot be imagined. Beginning to think is beginning to be undermined. Society has but little connection with such beginnings. The worm is in man's heart. That is where it must be sought. One must follow and understand this fatal game that leads from lucidity in the face of existence to flight from light. . . .

But if it is hard to fix the precise instant, the subtle step when the mind opted for death, it is easier to deduce from the act itself the consequence it implies. In a sense, and as in melodrama, killing yourself amounts to confessing. It is confessing that life is too much for you or that you do not understand it. Let's not go too far in such analogies, however, but rather return to everyday words. It is merely confessing that that "is not worth the trouble." Living, naturally, is never easy. You continue making the gestures commanded by existence for many reasons, the first of which is habit. Dying voluntarily implies that you have recognized, even instinctively, the ridiculous character of that habit, the absence of any profound reason for living, the insane character of that daily agitation, and the uselessness of suffering.

What, then, is that incalculable feeling that deprives the mind of the sleep necessary to life? A world that can be explained even with bad reasons is a familiar world. But, on the other hand, in a universe suddenly divested of illusions and lights, man feels an alien, a stranger. His exile is without remedy since he is deprived of the memory of a lost home or the hope of a promised land. This divorce between man and his life, the actor and his setting, is properly the feeling of absurdity. All healthy men having thought of their own suicide, it can be seen, without further explanation, that there is a direct connection between this feeling and the longing for death.

The subject of this essay is precisely this relationship between the absurd and suicide, the exact degree to which suicide is a solution to the absurd. The principle can be established that for a man who does not cheat, what he believes to be true must determine his action. Belief in the absurdity of existence must then dictate his conduct. It is legitimate to wonder, clearly and without false pathos, whether a conclusion of this importance requires forsaking as rapidly as possible an incomprehensible condition. I am speaking, of course, of men inclined to be in harmony with themselves. . . .

In a man's attachment to life there is something stronger than all the ills in the world. The body's judgment is as good as the mind's, and the body shrinks from annihilation. We get into the habit of living before acquiring the habit of thinking. In that race which daily hastens us toward death, the body maintains its irreparable lead. In short, the essence of that contradiction lies in what I shall call the act of eluding because it is both less and more than diversion in the Pascalian sense. Eluding is the invariable game. The typical act of eluding, the fatal evasion that constitutes the third theme of this essay, is hope. Hope of another life one must "deserve" or trickery of those who live not for life itself but for some great idea that will transcend it, refine it, give it a meaning, and betray it. . . .

All great deeds and all great thoughts have a ridiculous beginning. Great works are often born on a street-corner or in a restaurant's revolving door. So it is with absurdity. The absurd world more than others derives its nobility from the abject birth. In certain situations, replying "nothing" when asked what one is thinking about may be pretense in a man. Those who are loved are well aware of this. But if that reply is sincere, if it symbolizes that odd state of soul in which the void becomes eloquent, in which the chain of daily gestures is broken, in which the heart vainly seeks the link that will connect it again, then it is as it were the first sign of absurdity.

It happens that the stage sets collapse. Rising, streetcar, four hours in the office or the factory, meal, streetcar, four hours of work, meal, sleep, and Monday Tuesday Wednesday Thursday Friday and Saturday according to the same rhythm—this path is easily followed most of the time. But one day the "why" arises and everything begins in that weariness tinged with amazement.

"Begins"—this is important. Weariness comes at the end of the acts of a mechanical life, but at the same time it inaugurates the impulse of consciousness. It awakens consciousness and provokes what follows. What follows is the gradual return into the chain or it is the definitive awakening. At the end of the awakening comes, in time, the consequence; suicide or recovery. In itself weariness has something sickening about it. Here, I must conclude that it is good. For everything begins with consciousness and nothing is worth anything except through it. There is nothing original about these remarks. But they are obvious; that is enough for a while, during a sketchy reconnaissance in the origins of the absurd. Mere "anxiety," as Heidegger says, is at the source of everything. . . .

Hence the intelligence, too, tells me in its way that this world is absurd. Its contrary, blind reason, may well claim that all is clear; I was waiting for proof and longing for it to be right. But despite so many pretentious centuries and over the heads of so many eloquent and persuasive men, I know that is false. On this plane, at least, there is no happiness if I cannot know. That universal reason, practical or ethical, that determinism, those categories that explain everything are enough to make a decent man laugh. They have nothing to do with the mind. They negate its profound truth, which is to be enchained. In this unintelligible and limited universe, man's fate henceforth assumes its meaning. A horde of irrationals has sprung up and surrounds him until his ultimate end. In his recovered and now studied lucidity, the feeling of the absurd becomes clear and definite. I said that the world is absurd, that is all that can be said. But what is absurd is the confrontation of this irrational and the wild longing for clarity whose call echoes in the human heart. The absurd depends as much on man as on the world. For the moment it is all that links them together. It binds them one to the other as only hatred can weld two creatures together. This is all I can discern clearly in this measureless universe where my adventure takes place. Let us pause here. If I hold to be true that absurdity that determines my relationship with life, if I become thoroughly imbued with that sentiment that seizes me in face of the world's scenes, with that lucidity imposed on me by the pursuit of a science, I must sacrifice everything to these certainties and I must see them squarely to be able to maintain them. Above all, I must adapt my behavior to them and pursue them in all their consequences. I am speaking here of decency. But I want to know beforehand if thought can live in those deserts. . . .

And carrying this absurd logic to its conclusion, I must admit that that struggle implies a total absence of hope (which has nothing to do with despair), a continual rejection (which must not be confused with renunciation), and a conscious dissatisfaction (which must not be compared to immature unrest). Everything that destroys, conjures away, or exercises these requirements (and, to begin with, consent which overthrows divorce) ruins the absurd and devaluates the attitude that may then be proposed. The absurd has meaning only in so far as it is not agreed to. . . .

There exists an obvious fact that seems utterly moral: namely, that a man is always a prey to his truths. Once he has admitted them, he cannot free himself from them. One has to pay something. A man who has become conscious of the absurd is forever bound to it. A man devoid of hope and conscious of being so has ceased to belong to the future. That is natural. But it is just as natural that he should strive to escape the universe of which he is the creator. All the foregoing has significance only on account of this paradox. . . .

It is a matter of living in that state of the absurd. I know on what it is founded, this mind and this world straining against each other without being able to embrace each other. I ask for the rule of life of that state, and what I am offered neglects its basis, negates one of the terms of the painful opposition, demands of me a resignation. I ask what is involved in the condition I recognize as mine; I know it implies obscurity and ignorance; and I am assured that this ignorance explains everything and that this darkness is my light. But there is no reply here to my intent, and this stirring lyricism cannot hide the paradox from me. One must therefore turn away. Kierkegaard may shout in warning: "If man had no eternal consciousness, if, at the bottom of everything, there were merely a wild, seething force producing everything, both large and trifling, in the storm of dark passions, if the bottomless void that nothing can fill underlay all things, what would life be but despair?" This cry is not likely to stop the absurd man. Seeking what is true is not seeking what is desirable. If in order to elude the anxious question: "What would life be?" one must, like the donkey, feed on the roses of illusion, then the absurd mind, rather than resigning itself to falsehood, prefers to adopt fearlessly Kierkegaard's reply: "despair." Everything considered, a determined soul will always manage. . . .

Now I can broach the notion of suicide. It has already been felt what solution might be given. At this point the problem is reversed. It was previously a question of finding out whether or not life had to have a meaning to be lived. It now becomes clear, on the contrary, that it will be lived all the better if it has no meaning. Living an experience, a particular fate, is accepting it fully. Now, no one will live this fate, knowing it to be absurd, unless he does everything to keep before him that absurd brought to light by consciousness. Negating one of the terms of the opposition on which he lives amounts to escaping it. To abolish conscious revolt is to elude the problem. The theme of permanent revolution is thus carried into individual experience. Living is keeping the absurd alive. Keeping it alive is, above all, contemplating it. Unlike Eurydice, the absurd dies only when we turn away from it. One of the only coherent philosophical positions is thus revolt. It is a constant confrontation between man and his own obscurity. It is an insistence upon an impossible transparency. It challenges the world anew every second. Just as danger provided man the unique opportunity of seizing awareness, so metaphysical revolt extends awareness, to the whole of experience. It is that constant presence of man in his own eyes. It is not aspiration, for it is devoid of hope. That revolt is the certainty of a crushing fate, without the resignation that ought to accompany it.

This is where it is seen to what a degree absurd experience is remote from suicide. It may be thought that suicide follows revolt—but wrongly. For it does not represent the logical outcome of revolt. It is just the contrary by the consent it presupposes. Suicide, like the leap, is acceptance at its extreme. Everything is over and man returns to his essential history. His future, his unique and dreadful future—he sees and rushes toward it. In its way, suicide settles the absurd. It engulfs the

absurd in the same death. But I know that in order to keep alive, the absurd cannot be settled. It escapes suicide to the extent that it is simultaneously awareness and rejection of death. It is, at the extreme limit of the condemned man's last thought, that shoelace that despite everything he sees a few yards away, on the very brink of his dizzying fall. The contrary of suicide, in fact, is the man condemned to death.

That revolt gives life its value. Spread out over the whole length of a life, it restores its majesty to that life. To a man devoid of blinders, there is no finer sight than that of the intelligence at grips with a reality that transcends it. The sight of human pride is unequaled. No disparagement is of any use. That discipline that the mind imposes on itself, that will conjured up out of nothing, that face-to-face struggle have something exceptional about them. To impoverish that reality whose inhumanity constitutes man's majesty is tantamount to impoverishing him himself. I understand then why the doctrines that explain everything to me also debilitate me at the same time. They relieve me of the weight of my own life, and yet I must carry it alone. At this juncture, I cannot conceive that a skeptical metaphysics can be joined to an ethics of renunciation.

Consciousness and revolt, these rejections are the contrary of renunciation. Everything that is indomitable and passionate in a human heart quickens them, on the contrary, with its own life. It is essential to die unreconciled and not of one's own free will. Suicide is a repudiation. The absurd man can only drain everything to the bitter end, and deplete himself. The absurd is his extreme tension, which he maintains constantly by solitary effort, for he knows that in that consciousness and in that day-to-day revolt he gives proof of his only truth, which is defiance. This is a first consequence. . . .

But what does life mean in such a universe? Nothing else for the moment but indifference to the future and a desire to use up everything that is given. Belief in the meaning of life always implies a scale of values, a choice, our preferences. Belief in the absurd, according to our definitions, teaches the contrary. But this is worth examining.

Knowing whether or not one can live *without appeal* is all that interests me. I do not want to get out of my depth. This aspect of life being given me, can I adapt myself to it? Now, faced with this particular concern, belief in the absurd is tantamount to substituting the quantity of experiences for the quality. If I convince myself that this life has no other aspect than that of the absurd, if I feel that its whole equilibrium depends on that perpetual opposition between my conscious revolt and the darkness in which it struggles, if I admit that my freedom has no meaning except in relation to its limited fate, then I must say that what counts is not the best of living but the most living. . . .

On the one hand the absurd teaches that all experiences are unimportant, and on the other it urges toward the greatest quantity of experiences. How, then, can one fail to do as so many of those men I was speaking of earlier—choose the form of life that brings us the most possible of that human matter, thereby introducing a scale of values that on the other hand one claims to reject?

But again it is the absurd and its contradictory life that teaches us. For the mistake is thinking that that quantity of experiences depends on the circumstances of our life when it depends solely on us. Here we have to be oversimple. To two men living the same number of years, the world always provides the same sum of experiences. It is up to us to be conscious of them. Being aware of one's life, one's revolt, one's freedom, and to the maximum, is living, and to the maximum. Where lucidity dominates, the scale of values becomes useless. . . .

Thus I draw from the absurd three consequences, which are my revolt, my freedom, and my passion. By the mere activity of consciousness I transform into a rule of life what was an invitation to death—and I refuse suicide. I know, to be sure, the dull resonance that vibrates throughout these days. Yet I have but a word to say: that it is necessary. When Nietzsche writes: "It clearly seems that the chief thing in heaven and on earth is to *obey* at length and in a single direction: in the long run there results something for which it is worth the trouble of living on this earth as, for example, virtue, art, music, the dance, reason, the mind—something that transfigures, something delicate, mad, or divine," he elucidates the rule of a really distinguished code of ethics. But he also points the way of the absurd man. Obeying the flame is both the easiest and the hardest thing to do. However, it is good for man to judge himself occasionally. He is alone in being able to do so.

"Prayer," says Alain, "is when night descends over thought." "But the mind must meet the night," reply the mystics and the existentials. Yes, indeed, but not that night that is born under closed eyelids and through the mere will of man—dark, impenetrable night that the mind calls up in order to plunge into it. If it must encounter a night, let it be rather that of despair, which remains lucid—polar night, vigil of the mind, whence will arise perhaps that white and virginal brightness which outlines every object in the light of the intelligence. At that degree, equivalence encounters passionate understanding. Then it is no longer even a question of judging the existential leap. It resumes its place amid the age-old fresco of human attitudes. For the spectator, if he is conscious, that leap is still absurd. In so far as it thinks it solves the paradox, it reinstates it intact. On this score, it is stirring. On this score, everything resumes its place and the absurd world is reborn in all its splendor and diversity.

But it is bad to stop, hard to be satisfied with a single way of seeing, to go without contradiction, perhaps the most subtle of all spiritual forces. The preceding merely defines a way thinking. But the point is to live.

THE MYTH OF SISYPHUS

The gods had condemned Sisyphus to ceaselessly rolling a rock to the top of a mountain, whence the stone would fall back of its own weight. They had thought with some reason that there is no more dreadful punishment than futile and hopeless labor.

If one believes Homer, Sisyphus was the wisest and most prudent of mortals. According to another tradition, however, he was disposed to practice the profession of highwayman. I see no contradiction in this. Opinions differ as to the reasons why he became the futile laborer of the underworld. To begin with, he is accused of a certain levity in regard to the gods. He stole their secrets. Ægina, the daughter of Æsopus, was carried off by Jupiter. The father was shocked by that disappearance and complained to Sisyphus. He, who knew of the abduction, offered to tell about it on condition that Æsopus would give water to the citadel of Corinth. To the celestial thunderbolts he preferred the benediction of water. He was punished for this in the underworld. Homer tells us also that Sisyphus had put Death in chains. Pluto could not endure the sight of his deserted, silent empire. He dispatched the god of war, who liberated Death from the hands of her conqueror.

It is said also that Sisyphus, being near to death, rashly wanted to test his wife's love. He ordered her to cast his unburied body into the middle of the public square. Sisyphus woke up in the underworld. And there, annoyed by an obedience so contrary to human love, he obtained from Pluto permission to return to earth in order to chastise his wife. But when he had seen again the face of this world, enjoyed water and sun, warm stones and the sea, he no longer wanted to go back to the infernal darkness. Recalls, signs of anger, warnings were of no avail. Many years more he lived facing the curve of the gulf, the sparkling sea, and the smiles of earth. A decree of the gods was necessary. Mercury came and seized the impudent man by the collar and, snatching him from his joys, led him forcibly back to the underworld, where his rock was ready for him

You have already grasped that Sisyphus is the absurd hero. He *is*, as much through his passions as through his torture. His scorn of the gods, his hatred of death, and his passion for life won him that unspeakable penalty in which the whole being is exerted toward accomplishing nothing. This is the price that must be paid for the passions of this earth. Nothing is told us about Sisyphus in the underworld. Myths are made for the imagination to breathe life into them. As for this myth, one sees merely the whole effort of a body straining to raise the huge stone, to roll it and push it up a slope a hundred times over; one sees the face screwed up, the cheek tight against the stone, the shoulder bracing the clay-covered mass, the foot wedging it, the fresh start with arms outstretched, the wholly human security of two earth-clotted hands. At the very end of his long effort measured by skyless space and time without depth, the purpose is achieved. Then Sisyphus watches the stone rush down in a few moments toward that lower world whence he will have to push it up again toward the summit. He goes back down to the plain.

It is during that return, that pause, that Sisyphus interests me. A face that toils so close to stones is already stone itself! I see that man going back down with a heavy yet measured step toward the torment of which he will never know the end. That hour like a breathing-space which returns as surely as his suffering, that is the hour of consciousness. At each of those moments when he leaves the heights and gradually sinks toward the lairs of the gods, he is superior to his fate. He is stronger than his rock.

If this myth is tragic, that is because its hero is conscious. Where would his torture be, indeed, if at every step the hope of succeeding upheld him? The workman of today works every day in his life at the same tasks, and this fate is no less absurd. But it is tragic only at the rare moments when it becomes conscious. Sisyphus, proletarian of the gods, powerless and rebellious, knows the whole extent of his wretched condition: it is what he thinks of during his descent. The lucidity that was to constitute his torture at the same time crowns his victory. There is no fate that cannot be surmounted by scorn.

If the descent is thus sometimes performed in sorrow, it can also take place in joy. This word is not too much. Again I fancy Sisyphus returning toward his rock, and the sorrow was in the beginning. When the images of earth cling too tightly to memory, when the call of happiness becomes too insistent, it happens that melancholy rises in man's heart: this is the rock's victory, this is the rock itself. The boundless grief is too heavy to bear. These are our nights of Gethsemane. But crushing truths perish from being acknowledged. Thus, Œdipus at the outset obeys fate without knowing it. But from the moment he knows, his tragedy begins. Yet at the same moment, blind and desperate, he realizes that the only bond linking him to the world is the cool hand of a girl. Then a tremendous remark rings out: "Despite so many ordeals, my advanced age and the nobility of my soul make me conclude that all is well." Sophocles' Œdipus, like Dostoevsky's Kirilov, thus gives the recipe for the absurd victory. Ancient wisdom confirms modern heroism.

One does not discover the absurd without being tempted to write a manual of happiness. "What by such narrow ways—?" There is but one world, however. Happiness and the absurd are two sons of the same earth. They are inseparable. It would be a mistake to say that happiness necessarily springs from the absurd discovery. It happens as well that the feeling of the absurd springs from happiness. "I conclude that all is well," says Œdipus, and that remark is sacred. It echoes in the wild and limited universe of man. It teaches that all is not, has not been, exhausted. It drives out of this world a god who had come into it with dissatisfaction and a preference for futile sufferings. It makes of fate a human matter, which must be settled among men.

All Sisyphus' silent joy is contained therein. His fate belongs to him. His rock is his thing. Likewise, the absurd man, when he contemplates his torment, silences all the idols. In the universe suddenly restored to its silence, the myriad wondering little voices of the earth rise up. Unconscious, secret calls, invitations from all the faces, they are the necessary reverse and price of victory. There is no sun without shadow, and it is essential to know the night. The absurd man says yes and his effort will henceforth be unceasing. If there is a personal fate, there is no higher destiny, or at least there is but one which he concludes is inevitable and despicable. For the rest, he knows himself to be the master of his days. At that subtle moment when man glances backward over his life, Sisyphus returning toward his rock, in that slight pivoting he contemplates that series of unrelated actions which becomes his fate, created by him, combined under his memory's eye and soon sealed by his death. Thus, convinced of the wholly human origin of all that is human, a blind man eager to see who knows that the night has no end, he is still on the go. The rock is still rolling.

I leave Sisyphus at the foot of the mountain! One always finds one's burden again. But Sisyphus teaches the higher fidelity that negates the gods and raises rocks. He too concludes that all is well. This universe henceforth without a master seems to him neither sterile nor futile. Each atom of that stone, each mineral flake of that night-filled mountain, in itself forms a world. The struggle itself toward the heights is enough to fill a man's heart. One must imagine Sisyphus happy.

DISCUSSION QUESTIONS

1. According to Camus, what is the meaning of life? Do you agree with him? If not, why not?

2. What does Camus mean by "the absurd"?

3. What does Camus mean by "revolt"? Why is revolt an important part of the meaningful life?

4. Why does Camus maintain that the only truly serious philosophical question is, Why not commit suicide?

5. Why does Camus believe that killing yourself amounts to confessing? What is one "confessing" through suicide?

6. Compare Camus' position on the meaning of life with that of Jean-Paul Sartre, Marcus Aurelius, and Epicurus. What are their similarities and differences?

7. Why does Camus think that Sisyphus must be happy? Do you agree with him? Why or why not? Do you agree with Camus that our own lives are like the life of Sisyphus? Why or why not?

8. Camus was writing on the absurdity of life during and after World War II, a very dark period in history. If he were writing today, would he come to the same conclusions about life? Why or why not? Do you agree with Camus that life is absurd?

Hannah and Her Sisters
[USA 1986] 1 hour, 43 minutes
Directed by Woody Allen

Mickey Sachs (Woody Allen) is a television producer who was formerly married to Hannah (Mia Farrow). One day, Mickey notices a hearing loss in one of his ears and fears it may be caused by a brain tumor. Medical tests support his belief until one day a doctor shows Mickey his brain scan and tells him that everything is fine; he does not have a tumor. Mickey is elated, but his mood quickly changes as he realizes that he is going to die some day. He says, "When I ran out of the hospital, I, I was so thrilled because they told me I was going to be all right. And I'm running down the street, and suddenly I stop 'cause it hit me, all right, so you know, I'm not going to go today. I'm okay. I'm not going to go tomorrow. But eventually, I'm going to be in that position."

Mickey decides that he needs some answers to life's big questions. He finds little of value in philosophy, so he turns to religion, rejecting his Judaism for Catholicism. But after a week as a Catholic, Mickey is already contemplating a new religion, and soon he hits rock bottom. He says, "You know, I just felt that in a Godless universe, I didn't want to go on living." Mickey loads a gun and places it to his forehead. He says, "I remember thinking, at the time, I'm gonna kill myself. Then I thought . . . what if I'm wrong? What if there is a God? I mean, after all, nobody really knows that. . . . But then I thought, no. You know, maybe is not good enough. I want certainty or nothing. And I remember very clearly the clock was ticking, and I was sitting there frozen, with the gun to my head, debating whether to shoot." Suddenly, the gun fires—Mickey is so tense that he inadvertently pulls the trigger, but because he is perspiring so much, the gun slides off his forehead and aims at a mirror. Mickey is distraught. He runs outside to clear his head. Soon he finds himself in a movie theater watching a favorite film: the Marx Brothers' *Duck Soup*.

He says, "I just, I just needed a moment to gather my thoughts and, and be logical, and, and put the world back into rational perspective." As his thoughts shift, Mickey says to himself, "I started to feel: how can you even think of killing yourself? I mean, isn't it so stupid? I mean, I-look at all the people up there on the screen. You know, they're real funny, and, and what if the worst is true? What if there's no God, and you only go around once and that's it? Well, you know, don't you want to be part of the experience? You know, what the hell, it-it-it's not all a drag. And I'm thinking to myself, geez, I should stop ruining my life searching for answers I'm never gonna get, and just enjoy it while it lasts. And . . . you know after, who knows? I mean, you know, maybe there is something. Nobody really knows. I know, I know 'maybe' is a very slim reed to hang your whole life on, but that's the best we have. And . . . then, I started to sit back, and I actually began to enjoy myself." After this, Mickey kindles a relationship with Hannah's sister, Holly (Dianne Wiest), a woman he once went out with on a disastrous date. A year later, they are happily married and expecting a child.

In addition to the life of Mickey, the film also follows the lives of Hannah; her husband, Elliot (Michael Caine); and her sisters, Holly and Lee (Barbara Hershey). When Elliot has an affair with Lee, Lee ends her relationship with her lover, Frederick (Max von Sydow). Eventually, Lee breaks off the affair with Elliot and starts up a relationship with one of her college professors. The affair with Lee helps Elliot realize the depth of his love for Hannah and see that she also has needs. In differing ways, each of these characters is presented as pursuing meaning in his or her life and each as finding it.

DISCUSSION QUESTIONS

1.   Discuss the way in which this film presents Camus' notion that life is absurd.

2.   Compare Mickey's reasons for not committing suicide with those given by Camus. How are they similar? How different?

3.   Compare and contrast the ways in which each of the main characters in this film—Hannah, Mickey, Elliot, Holly, and Lee—deal with questions concerning the meaning of life.

4.   Why, after the doctors tell him that he is not dying of brain tumor, does Mickey come to the conclusion that life is meaningless? Why does he change his mind about this later?

5. Consider the following conversation between Mickey and Father Flynn (Ken Costigan):

    FATHER FLYNN   "Now why do you think that you would like to convert to Catholicism?"

    MICKEY   "Well, uh, because, you know, I gotta have something to believe in, otherwise life is just meaningless."

    FATHER FLYNN   "I understand. But why did you make the decision to choose the Catholic faith?"

    MICKEY   "Well, you know . . . first of all, because it's a very beautiful religion. It's very well structured. Now I'm talking now, incidentally, about the against-school-prayer, pro-abortion, anti-nuclear wing."

    FATHER FLYNN   "So at the moment you don't believe in God."

    MICKEY   "No. And I want to. You know, I'm willing to do anything. I'll, you know, I'll dye Easter eggs if it works. I need some evidence. I gotta have some proof. Uh, you know, if I can't believe in God then I don't think life is worth living."

    Is Mickey right? Is life meaningless without a belief in God? Is his approach to finding something to believe in a good one? Why or why not?

6. The film presents a quote from Tolstoy: "The only absolute knowledge attainable by man is that life is meaningless." Is Tolstoy right? Do you think this is the ultimate conclusion of this film? Why or why not?

7. Mickey says to himself, "Millions of books written on every conceivable subject by all these great minds, and, and in the end, none of them knows anything more about the big questions of life than I do. I read Socrates. You know, this guy used to knock off little Greek boys. What the hell's he got to teach me? And, and Nietzsche with his, with his Theory of Eternal Recurrence. He said that the life we live, we're gonna live over and over again the exact same way for eternity. Great. That means I'll have to sit through the Ice Capades again. It's not worth it." Do you agree with Mickey? Do you think that philosophers don't know anything more about the big questions in life than you do? Why or why not?

8. What happened while Mickey was watching the Marx Brothers' film *Duck Soup* that changed his attitude toward life?

6.2   WHAT IS THE MEANING OF DEATH?

FIVE MYTHOLOGICAL ACCOUNTS
OF THE ORIGIN OF DEATH

M yths and stories concerning the origin of death are one of the ways that people traditionally have contended with the meaning and nature of death. One finds these originary myths concerning death across cultures and history. It is interesting to note that each of the myths in the selection below is limited to the origin of *human* death and does not take up the question of the origin of nonhuman death, that is, death in general. Each myth raises a very interesting and basic philosophical question: is all death the same? Or is the "death" that overcomes humans different from the type of "death" that overcomes living, non-human entities such as plants and animals? Although these myths do not address the origin of this nonhuman type of death, they do provide complex and interesting accounts of the origin of human death.

THE CAST SKIN: A MELANESIAN MYTH

At first men never died, but when they advanced in life they cast their skins like snakes and crabs, and came out with youth renewed. After a time a woman growing old went to a stream to change her skin. She threw off her old skin in the water, and observed that as it floated down it caught against a stick. Then she went home, where she had left her child. The child, however, refused to recognize her, crying that its mother was an old woman not like this young stranger; and to pacify the child she went after her cast integument and put it on. From that time mankind ceased to cast their skins and died.

—*R. H. Codrington,* The Melanesians
(Oxford, 1891), p. 265

THE STONE AND THE BANANA: AN INDONESIAN MYTH

Thus the natives of Poso, a district of Central Celebes, say that in the beginning the sky was very near the earth, and that the Creator, who lived in it, used to let down his gifts to men at the end of a rope. One day he thus lowered a stone; but our first father and mother would have none of it and they called out to their Maker. "What have we to do with this stone? Give us something else." The Creator complied and hauled away at the rope; the stone mounted up and up till it vanished from sight. Presently the rope was seen coming down from heaven again, and this time there was banana at the end of it instead of a stone. Our first parents ran at the banana and took it. Then there came a voice from heaven saying; "Because ye have chosen the banana, your life shall be like its life. When the banana-tree has offspring, the parent stem dies; so shall ye die and your children shall step into your place. Had ye chosen the stone, your life would have been like the life of the stone changeless and immortal." The man and his wife mourned over their fatal choice, but it was too late; that is how through the eating of a banana death came into the world.

—*J. G. Frazer,* The Belief in Immortality, *I (London, 1913), pp. 74–75, quoting A. C. Kruijt*

THE MOON AND RESURRECTION: AN AUSTRALIAN MYTH

In one of the Wotjobaluk legends it is said that at the time when all animals were men and women, some died, and the moon used to say, "You up-again," and they came to life again. There was at that time an old man who said, "Let them remain dead." Then none ever came to life again, except the moon, which still continued to do so.

—*A. W. Howitt,* The Native Tribes of South-East Australia *(London, 1904), p. 429*

THE CRUEL BIRD: AN AUSTRALIAN (ARANDA TRIBE) MYTH

From a floor of rock they issued forth, south of Ilkanara, from a little rock-hole. The rock was first opened by a curfew woman, who thrust her nose through the hard stone. A second curfew woman followed, then a third, a fourth, a fifth, and so on. And then a curfew man appeared, followed by a second, a third, a fourth, a fifth, and so on to the last. Finally they had all emerged.

The men who had issued forth last all grew angry against the man who had appeared first perhaps because he had followed too closely upon the women. The first-born man lit a great blazing fire; and the others pointed a magic bone at him. The doomed man stretched himself out; he lay motionless for two nights. Then he died, and the rest buried him east of the floor of rock. Some of the women went to Tjolankuta, deep in grief; others went to Lkebalinja; others again sat down at the entrance of the gap where the Ilkaknara creek breaks through the range. They moved about in a women's dance, to the accompaniment of shouts by the men: "bau! bau! bau! bau!"

But the dead man hollowed out the soil from underneath. Then his forehead emerged through the crust; next his temples reappeared; next his head became visible, up to his throat. His two shoulders, however, had become caught below.

Then the Urbura, the magpie, came from Urburakana. He rushed along in haste; he saw from a great distance away what was happening: "See, he has begun to sprout up again only a moment ago; but his two shoulders have become caught tightly and are still pinning him down." The dead man rose a little higher. The curfew women were approaching with dancing steps; they encircled him. The magpie rushed up, filled with deadly anger, to a mountain near-by, called Urburinka. Then he grasped a heavy mulga spear, thrust it deep into the neck of the dead man, stamped him back into the ground with his heel, trampling fiercely upon him: "Remain rooted down firmly for all time; do not attempt to rise stay for ever in the grave!"

Then the curfews all turned into birds and flew to Running Waters; they all left, both men and women. Their wailing shrieks rang out without ceasing; their tears fell without ceasing; they were deeply stricken with grief.

The Urbura, too, soared up like a bird and returned to his own home, where he remained forever.

My informant added briefly that, but for the cruelty of the Urbura, the dead man would have grown up into life a second time; and if he had risen of his own accord, all men who died since that day, would have risen again after death in the same manner. But the Urbura had finally crushed the unfortunate curfew man, and stamped his head down a second time into the grave: "And now all of us die and are annihilated forever; and there is no resurrection for us."

—*T. G. H. Strehlow*, Aranda Traditions
(Melbourne, 1947), pp. 44–45

Maui and Hine-Nui-Te-Po: A Polynesian Myth

Maui now felt it necessary to leave the village where Irawaru had lived, so he returned to his parents. When he had been with them for some time, his father said to him one day, "Oh, my son, I have heard from your mother and others that you are very valiant, and that you have succeeded in all feats that you have undertaken in your own country, whether they were small or great. But now that you have arrived in your father's country, you will, perhaps, at last be overcome."

Then Maui asked him, "What do you mean? What things are there that I can be vanquished by?" His father answered him, "By your great ancestress, by Hine-nui-te-po, who, if you look, you may see flashing, and, as it were, opening and shutting there, where the horizon meets the sky." Maui replied, "Lay aside such idle thoughts, and let us both fearlessly seek whether men are to die or live forever." His father said, "My child, there has been an ill omen for us. When I was baptizing you, I omitted a portion of the fitting prayer, and that I know will be the cause of your perishing."

Then Maui asked his father, "What is my ancestress Hine-nui-te-po like?" He answered, "What you see yonder shining so brightly red are her eyes. And her teeth are as sharp and hard as pieces of volcanic glass. Her body is like that of a man. And as for the pupils of her eyes, they are jasper. And her hair is like the tangles of long seaweed. And her mouth is like that of a barracouta." Then his son answered him: "Do you think her strength is as great as that of Tama-nui-te-Ra, who consumes man, and the earth, and the very waters, by the fierceness of his heat? Was not the world formerly saved alive by the speed with which he travelled? If he had then, in the days of his full strength and power, gone as slowly as he does now, not a remnant of mankind would have been left living upon the earth, nor, indeed, would anything else have survived. But I laid hold of Tama-nui-te-Ra, and now, he goes slowly, for I smote him again and again, so that he is now feeble, and long in travelling his course, and he now gives but very, little heat, having been weakened by the blows of my enchanted weapon. I then, too, split him open in many places, and from the wounds so made, many rays now issue forth and spread in all directions. So, also, I found the sea much larger than the earth, but by the power of the last born of your children, part of the earth was drawn up again, and dry land came forth." And his father answered him, "That is all very true, O, my last born, and the strength of my old age. Well, then, be bold, go and visit your great ancestress, who flashes so fiercely there, where the edge of the horizon meets the sky."

Hardly was this conversation concluded with his father, when the young hero went forth to look for companions to accompany him upon this enterprise. There came to him for companions, the small robin, and the large robin, and the thrush, and the yellow-hammer, and every kind of little bird, and the water-wagtail. These all assembled together, and they all started with Maui in the evening, and arrived at the dwelling of Hine-nui-te-po, and found her fast asleep.

Then Maui addressed them all, "My little friends, now if you see me creep into this old chieftainess, do not laugh at what you see. Nay, nay, do not, I pray you, but when I have got altogether inside her, and just as I am coming out of her mouth, then you may shout with laughter if you please." His little friends, who were frightened at what they saw, replied, "Oh, sir, you will certainly be killed." He answered them, "If you burst out laughing at me as soon as I get inside her, you will wake her up, and she will certainly kill me at once, but, if you do not laugh until I am quite inside her, and am on the point of coming out of her mouth I shall live, and Hine-nui-te-po will die." His little friends answered "Go on then, brave sir, but pray take good care of yourself."

Then the young hero started off. He twisted the strings of his weapon tight round his wrist, and went into the house. He stripped off his clothes, and the skin on his hips looked mottled and beautiful as that of a mackerel, from the tattoo marks, cut on it with the chisel of Uetonga [grandson of Ru, god of earthquakes; Uetonga taught tattooing to Mataora who taught it to man], and he entered the old chieftainess.

The little birds now screwed up their tiny cheeks, trying to suppress their laughter. At last the little Tiwakawaka could no longer keep it in, and laughed out loud, with its merry, cheerful note. This woke the old woman up. She opened her eyes, started up, and killed Maui.

Thus died this Maui we have spoken of. But before he died he had children, and sons were born to him. Some of his descendants yet live in Hawaiki, some in Aotearoa (or in these islands).

The greater part of his descendants remained in Hawaiki, but a few of them came here to Aotearoa. According to the traditions of the Maori, this was the cause of the introduction of death into the world (Hine-nui-te-po was the goddess of death. If Maui had passed safely through her, then no more human beings would have died, but death itself would have been destroyed.) We express it by saying, "The water-wagtail laughing at Maul-tiki-tiki-o Taranga made Hine-nui-te-po squeeze him to death." And we have this proverb, "Men make heirs, but death carries them off."

—*Sir George Grey,* Polynesian Mythology *(London, 1855), pp. 56–58.*

DISCUSSION QUESTIONS

1. What are the similarities and differences among these various mythological accounts of the origin of death?

2. What, if any, mythological accounts of the origin of death exist in your own culture?

3. How, if at all, are mythological accounts of topics such as death, beauty, and freedom different from philosophical accounts?

4. A number of philosophers throughout history, most notably Plato, have employed myths in their philosophical investigations. Can a good philosophical explanation employ or utilize a myth? If so, why? If not, why are myths not a part of good philosophical explanation? Defend your view.

5. What do you think is the best explanation of the origin of human death? Compare your own response to the mythological accounts.

6. Do you think there is a difference between human death and nonhuman death? Why or why not?

7. What, if anything, is the value of mythological accounts of phenomena such as the origin of life and death? Discuss.

PLATO

SOCRATES ON DEATH AND IMMORTALITY

In 399 B.C.E., Socrates was indicted on two "trumped up" charges—corrupting the youth of Athens and introducing new divinities (impiety)—and was condemned to death. While he had made many personal enemies in Athens by questioning conventional religion and morality, the principle cause of the indictment was political: Socrates was regarded as a threat to Athenian democracy. The jury consisted of 501 citizens chosen by lot from 6,000. By Athenian law, the trial could last only one day. After Socrates' accusers—Meletus, Anytus, and Lycon—presented their case against him, Socrates defended himself. His defense speech was written down later by Plato and is found in his dialogue *Apology* (*apologia* is Greek for "defense"), which, along with Plato's *Crito* and *Phaedo*, recounts the last days of Socrates.

The first selection below is from the conclusion of the *Apology*. Socrates has just been condemned to death and is now informally addressing the jury. He tells them that the death penalty does not disturb him because he is already old and would have died soon anyway. He asserts that he acted in accordance with righteousness and principle in refusing to plead for the mercy. He says, "I prophesy to you who are my murderers, that immediately after my death [a] punishment far heavier than you have afflicted on me will surely await you." Others like Socrates, though much less merciful, will take up the task of censuring their evil lives. Adds, Socrates, "If you think that by killing men you can prevent someone from censuring your evil lives, you are mistaken."

Socrates continues, "What has happened to me is a good, and . . . those of us who think that death is an evil are in error." He reasons that "either death is a state of nothingness and utter unconsciousness, or . . . there is a change and migration of the soul from this world to another." Either way, death is good. If death is a state of nothingness, then he will sleep peacefully for eternity. He reflects, "If death is like this, I say that to die is to gain; for eternity is a single night." However, "if death is a journey to another place," then death is an even greater good because it will enable him to use his immortality to continue his conversation in Hades. His time in this other place will be spent in the presence of the great men of the past: both those who have claimed to have wisdom and those, like him, who have suffered unjustly. He concludes that "no evil can happen to a good man" and that only God knows which is better: to live or to die.

The second selection, from the *Phaedo*, focuses on the moments before Socrates drinks the hemlock, the poison that will bring about his death. It is the second of three arguments in the *Phaedo* for the immortality of the soul. Socrates says that upon consideration of the nature of the soul, we can determine whether it can be dissolved after death or whether it survives as a whole (or compounded) after death. It is argued that ideas or essences are unchanging and eternal, and that concrete particulars are changeable and temporary. Ideas are unseen and are apprehended by reason, whereas concrete particulars are seen and are perceived by the senses. The body is seen, so it resembles concrete particulars, and like all concrete particulars, it must also be changing and temporal. However, the soul is unseen, resembling an idea, and like all ideas, must also be unchanging and eternal. The soul, like ideas, is thus immortal.

Moreover, because some souls are polluted and impure at the time of their departure, they do not leave the earth at death. These are the souls of those who were "in love with and fascinated by the body and by the desires and pleasures of the body." For these souls, because of their constant association with the body, bodily attributes are wrought into their nature.

Comments Socrates, "And this corporeal element . . . is heavy and weighty and earthy, and is that element of sight by which such a soul is depressed and dragged down again into the visible world," namely, the world below: Hades. However, the souls of those who practice true philosophy, and who have restrained from the pleasures and desires of the body, readily ascend to the invisible world above after death. Thus, those who lead a philosophical life, avoiding the pleasures of the body and following reason only, need not fear death: their souls will be free of their bodies and "depart to the invisible world—to the divine and immortal and rational." Socrates concludes by asking, "Is not philosophy is the practice of death?" A biographical sketch of Plato appears in chapter 2.

FROM THE *APOLOGY*

Not much time will be gained, O Athenians, in return for the evil name which you will get from the detractors of the city, who will say that you killed Socrates, a wise man; for they will call me wise, even although I am not wise, when they want to reproach you. If you had waited a little while, your desire would have been fulfilled in the course of nature. For I am far advanced in years, as you may perceive, and not far from death. I am speaking now only to those of you who have condemned me to death. And I have another thing to say to them: You think that I was convicted because I had no words of the sort which would have procured my acquittal—I mean, if I had thought fit to leave nothing undone or unsaid. Not so; the deficiency which led to my conviction was not of words— certainly not. But I had not the boldness or impudence or inclination to address you as you would have liked me to address you, weeping and wailing and lamenting, and saying and doing many things which you have been accustomed to hear from others, and which, as I maintain, are unworthy of me. I thought at the time that I ought not to do anything common or mean when in danger: nor do I now repent of the manner of my defence, and I would rather die having spoken after my manner, than speak in your manner and live. For neither in war nor yet at law ought I or any man to use every way of escaping death. Often in battle there can be no doubt that if a man will throw away his arms, and fall on his knees before his pursuers, he may escape death; and in other dangers there are other ways of escaping death, if a man is willing to say and do anything. The difficulty, my friends, is not in avoiding death, but in avoiding unrighteousness; for that runs faster than death. I am old and move

slowly, and the slower runner has overtaken me, and my accusers are keen and quick, and the faster runner, who is unrighteousness, has overtaken them. And now I depart hence condemned by you to suffer the penalty of death, and they too go their ways condemned by the truth to suffer the penalty of villainy and wrong; and I must abide by my award—let them abide by theirs. I suppose that these things may be regarded as fated—and I think that they are well.

And now, O men who have condemned me, I would fain prophesy to you; for I am about to die, and that is the hour in which men are gifted with prophetic power. And I prophesy to you who are my murderers, that immediately after my death punishment far heavier than you have inflicted on me will surely await you. Me you have killed because you wanted to escape the accuser, and not to give an account of your lives. But that will not be as you suppose: far otherwise. For I say that there will be more accusers of you than there are now; accusers whom hitherto I have restrained: and as they are younger they will be more inconsiderate with you, and you will be more offended at them. If you think that by killing men you can prevent some one from censuring your evil lives, you are mistaken; that is not a way of escape which is either possible or honourable; the easiest and the noblest way is not to be disabling others, but to be improving yourselves. This is the prophecy which I utter before my departure to the judges who have condemned me.

Friends, who would have acquitted me, I would like also to talk with you about this thing which has happened, while the magistrates are busy, and before I go to the place at which I must die. Stay then awhile, for we may as well talk with one another while there is time. You are my friends, and I should like to show you the meaning of this event which has happened to me. O my judges—for you I may truly call judges—I should like to tell you of a wonderful circumstance. Hitherto the familiar oracle within me has constantly been in the habit of opposing me even about trifles, if I was going to make a slip or error in any matter; and now as you see there has come upon me that which may be thought, and is generally believed to be, the last and worst evil. But the oracle made no sign of opposition, either as I was leaving my house and going out in the morning, or when I was going up into this court, or while I was speaking, at anything which I was going to say; and yet I have often been stopped in the middle of a speech, but now in nothing I either said or did touching this matter has the oracle opposed me. What do I take to be the explanation of this? I will tell you. I regard this as a great proof that what has happened to me is a good, and that those of us who think that death is an evil are in error. For the customary sign would surely have opposed me had I been going to evil and not to good.

Let us reflect in another way, and we shall see that there is great reason to hope that death is a good; for one of two things—either death is a state of nothingness and utter unconsciousness, or, as men say, there is a change and migration of the soul from this world to another. Now if you suppose that there is no consciousness, but a sleep like the sleep of him who is undisturbed even by the sight of dreams, death will be an unspeakable gain. For if a person were to select the night in which his sleep was undisturbed even by dreams, and were to compare with this the other days and nights of his life, and then were to tell us how many days and nights he had passed in the course of his life better and more pleasantly than this one, I think that any man, I will not say a private man, but even the great king will not find many such days or nights, when compared with the others. Now if death is like this, I say that to die is gain; for eternity is then only a single night. But if death is the journey to another place, and there, as men say, all the dead are, what good, O my friends and judges, can be greater than this? If indeed when the pilgrim arrives in the world below, he is delivered from the professors of justice in this world, and finds the true judges who are said to give judgment there, Minos and Rhadamanthus and Aeacus and Triptolemus, and other sons of God who were righteous in their own life, that pilgrimage will be worth making. What would not a man give if he might converse with Orpheus and Musaeus and Hesiod and Homer? Nay, if this be true, let me die again and again. I myself, too, shall have a wonderful interest in there meeting and conversing with Palamedes, and Ajax the son of Telamon, and other heroes of old, who have suffered death through an unjust judgment; and there will be no small pleasure, as I think, in comparing my own sufferings with theirs. Above all, I shall then be able to continue my search into true and false knowledge; as in this world, so also in that; and I shall find out who is wise, and who pretends to be wise, and is not. What would not a man give, O judges, to be able to examine the leader of the great Trojan expedition; or Odysseus or Sisyphus, or numberless others, men and women too! What infinite delight would there be in conversing with them and asking them questions! In another world they do not put a man to death for asking questions; assuredly not. For besides being happier in that world than in this, they will be immortal, if what is said is true.

Wherefore, O judges, be of good cheer about death, and know of a certainty, that no evil can happen to a good man, either in life or after death. He and his are not neglected by the gods; nor has my own approaching end happened by mere chance. But I see clearly that to die and be released was better for me; and therefore the oracle gave no sign. For which reason, also, I am not angry with my condemners, or with my accusers; they have done me no harm, although they did not mean to do me any good; and for this I may gently blame them.

Still I have a favour to ask of them. When my sons are grown up, I would ask you, O my friends, to punish them; and I would have you trouble them, as I have troubled you, if they seem to care about riches, or anything, more than about virtue; or if they pretend to be something when they are really nothing—then reprove them, as I have reproved you, for not caring about that for which they ought to care, and thinking that they are something when they are really nothing. And if you do this, I and my sons will have received justice at your hands.

The hour of departure has arrived, and we go our ways—I to die, and you to live. Which is better God only knows.

From the *Phaedo*

Must we not, said Socrates, ask ourselves what that is which, as we imagine, is liable to be scattered away, and about which we fear? and what again is that about which we have no fear? And then we may proceed further to enquire whether that which suffers dispersion is or is not of the nature of soul—our hopes and fears as to our own souls will turn upon the answers to these questions.

Very true, he said.

Now the compound or composite may be supposed to be naturally capable, as of being compounded, so also of being dissolved; but that which is uncompounded, and that only, must be, if anything is, indissoluble.

Yes; I should imagine so, said Cebes.

And the uncompounded may be assumed to be the same and unchanging, whereas the compound is always changing and never the same.

That I also think, he said.

Then now let us return to the previous discussion. Is that idea or essence, which in the dialectical process we define as essence or true existence—whether essence of equality, beauty, or anything else—are these essences, I say, liable at times to some degree of change? or are they each of them always what they are, having the same simple self-existent and unchanging forms, and not admitting of variation at all, or in any way, or at any time?

They must be always the same, Socrates, replied Cebes.

And what would you say of the many beautiful—whether men or horses or garments or any other things which may be called equal or beautiful,—are they all unchanging and the same always, or quite the reverse? May they not rather be described as almost always changing and hardly ever the same, either with themselves or with one another?

The latter, replied Cebes; they are always in a state of change.

And these you can touch and see and perceive with the senses, but the unchanging things you can only perceive with the mind—they are invisible and are not seen?

That is very true, he said.

Well then, added Socrates, let us suppose that there are two sorts of existences—one seen, the other unseen.

Let us suppose them.

The seen is the changing, and the unseen is the unchanging?

That may be also supposed.

And, further, is not one part of us body, and the rest of us soul?

To be sure.

And to which class may we say that the body is more alike and akin?

Clearly to the seen—no one can doubt that.

And is the soul seen or not seen?

Not by man, Socrates.

And what we mean by "seen" and "not seen" is that which is or is not visible to the eye of man?

Yes, to the eye of man.

And what do we say of the soul?—is that seen or not seen?

Not seen.

Unseen then?

Yes.

Then the soul is more like to the unseen, and the body to the seen?

That is most certain, Socrates.

And were we not saying long ago that the soul when using the body as an instrument of perception, that is to say, when using the sense of sight or hearing or some other sense (for the meaning of perceiving through the body is perceiving through the senses)—were we not saying that the soul too is then dragged by the body into the region of the changeable, and wanders and is confused; the world spins round her, and she is like a drunkard, when possessed by change?

Very true.

But when returning into herself she reflects, then she passes into the other world, the abode of purity, and eternity, and immortality, and unchangeableness, which are her kindred, and with them she ever lives, when she is by herself and is not let or hindered then she ceases from her erring ways, and being in communion with the unchanging is unchanging. And this state of the soul is called wisdom?

That is well and truly said, Socrates, he replied.

And to which class is the soul more nearly alike and akin, as far as may be inferred from this argument, as well as from the preceding one?

I think, Socrates, that, in the opinion of every one who follows the argument, the soul will be infinitely more like the unchangeable—even the most stupid person will not deny that.

And the body is more like the changing?

Yes.

Yet once more consider the matter in another light: When the soul and the body are united, then nature orders the soul to rule and govern, and the body to obey and serve. Now which of these two functions is akin to the divine? and which to the mortal? Does not the divine appear to you to be that which naturally orders and rules, and the mortal to be that which is subject and servant?

True.

And which does the soul resemble?

The soul resembles the divine, and the body the mortal—there can be no doubt of that, Socrates.

Then reflect, Cebes: of all that has been said is not this the conclusion?—that the soul is in the very likeness of the divine, and immortal, and intellectual, and uniform, and indissoluble, and unchangeable; and that the body is in the very likeness of the human, and mortal, and unintellectual, and multiform, and dissoluble, and changeable. Can this, my dear Cebes, be denied?

No indeed.

But if this is true, then is not the body liable to speedy dissolution? and is not the soul almost or altogether indissoluble?

Certainly.

And do you further observe, that after a man is dead, the body, or visible part of him, which is lying in the visible world, and is called a corpse, and would naturally be dissolved and decomposed and dissipated, is not dissolved or decomposed at once, but may remain for some time, nay even for a long time, if the constitution be sound at the time of death, and the season of the year favourable? For the body when shrunk and embalmed, as is the custom in Egypt, may remain almost entire through infinite ages; and even in decay, there are still some portions, such as the bones and ligaments, which are practically indestructible. You allow that?

Yes.

And are we to suppose that the soul, which is invisible, in passing to the true Hades, which like her is invisible, and pure, and noble, and on her way to the good and wise God, whither, if God will, my soul is also soon to go—that the soul, I repeat, if this be her nature and origin, is blown away and perishes immediately on quitting the body, as the many say? That can never be, my dear Simmias and Cebes. The truth rather is, that the soul which is pure at departing and draws after her no bodily taint, having never voluntarily had connection with the body, which she is ever avoiding, herself gathered into herself; (for such abstraction has been the study of her life. And what does this mean but that she has been a true disciple of philosophy, and has practised how to die cheerfully? Is not philosophy the practice of death?

Certainly.

That soul, I say, herself invisible, departs to the invisible world—to the divine and immortal and rational: thither arriving, she is secure of bliss and is released from the error and folly of men, their fears and wild passions and all other human ills, and for ever dwells, as they say of the initiated, in company with the gods. Is not this true, Cebes?

Yes, said Cebes, beyond a doubt.

But the soul which has been polluted, and is impure at the time of her departure, and is the companion and servant of the body always, and is in love with and fascinated by the body and by the desires and pleasures of the body, until she is led to believe that the truth only exists in a bodily form, which a man may touch and see and taste, and use for the purposes of his lusts,—the soul, I mean, accustomed to hate and fear and avoid the intellectual principle, which to the bodily eye is dark and invisible, and can be attained only by philosophy;—do you suppose that such a soul will depart pure and unalloyed?

That is impossible, he replied.

She is held fast by the corporeal, which the continual association and constant care of the body have wrought into her nature.

Very true.

And this corporeal element, my friend, is heavy and weighty and earthy, and is that element of sight by which such a soul is depressed and dragged down again into the visible world, because she is afraid of the invisible and of the world below—prowling about tombs and sepulchres, in the neighbourhood of which, as they tell us, are seen certain ghostly apparitions of souls which have not departed pure, but are cloyed with sight and therefore visible.

That is very likely, Socrates.

Yes, that is very likely, Cebes; and these must be the souls, not of the good, but of the evil, who are compelled to wander about such places in payment of the penalty of their former evil way of life; and they continue to wander until through the craving after the corporeal which never leaves them, they are imprisoned finally in another body. And they may be supposed to find their prisons in the same natures which they have had in their former lives.

What do you mean, Socrates?

I mean to say that men who have followed after gluttony, and wantonness, and drunkenness, and have had no thought of avoiding them, would pass into asses and animals of that sort. What do you think?

I think that opinion exceedingly probable.

And those who have chosen the portion of injustice, and tyranny, and violence, will pass into wolves, or into hawks and kites;—whither else can we suppose them to go?

Yes, said Cebes; that is doubtless the place of natures such as theirs.

And there is no difficulty, he said, in assigning to all of them places answering to their several natures and propensities?

There is not, he said.

Even among them some are happier than others; and the happiest both in themselves and their place of abode are those who have practised the civil and social virtues which are called temperance and justice, and are acquired by habit and attention without philosophy and mind.

Why are they the happiest?

Because they may be expected to pass into some gentle social nature which is like their own, such as that of bees or wasps or ants, or even back again into the form of man, and just and moderate men to spring from them.

That is not impossible.

But he who is a philosopher or lover of learning, and is entirely pure at departing, is alone permitted to attain to the divine nature. And this is the reason, Simmias and Cebes, why the true votaries of philosophy abstain from all fleshly lusts, and endure and refuse to give themselves up to them,—not because they fear poverty or the ruin of their families, like the lovers of money, and the world in general; nor like the lovers of power

and honour, because they dread the dishonour or disgrace of evil deeds.

No, Socrates, that would not become them, said Cebes.

No indeed, he replied; and therefore they who have any care of their own souls, and do not merely live moulding and fashioning the body, say farewell to all this; they will not walk in the ways of the blind: and when philosophy offers them purification and release from evil, they feel that they ought not to resist her influence, and whither she leads they turn and follow.

What do you mean, Socrates?

I will tell you, he said. The lovers of knowledge are conscious that their souls when philosophy takes them in hand, are simply fastened and glued to their bodies: the soul is able to view real existence only through the bars of a prison, and not of herself unhindered; she is wallowing in the mire of all ignorance; and philosophy, beholding the terrible nature of her confinement, inasmuch as the captive through lust becomes a chief accomplice in her own captivity—for the lovers of knowledge are aware that this was the original state of the soul, but that when she was in this state philosophy adopted and comforted her, and wanted to release her, pointing out to her that the eye and the ear and the other senses are full of deceit, and persuading her to retire from them in all but the necessary use of them, and to be gathered up and collected into herself, and to trust only to herself and her own pure apprehensions of pure existence, and to mistrust whatever comes to her through other channels and is subject to vicissitude—philosophy, I say, shows her that all this is visible and tangible, but that what she sees in her own nature is intellectual and invisible. And the soul of the true philosopher thinks that she ought not to resist this deliverance, and therefore abstains from pleasures and desires and pains and fears, as far as she is able; reflecting that when a man has great joys or sorrows or fears or desires, he suffers from them, not merely the sort of evil which might be anticipated—as for example, the loss of his health or property which he has sacrificed to his lusts—but an evil greater far, which is the greatest and worst of all evils, and one of which he never thinks.

And what is that, Socrates? said Cebes.

Why that when the feeling of pleasure or pain in the soul is most intense, all of us naturally suppose that the object of, this intense feeling is then plainest and truest: but such is not the case.

Very true.

And this is the state in which the soul is most enthralled by the body.

How is that?

Why, because each pleasure and pain is a sort of nail which nails and rivets the soul to the body, until she becomes like the body, and believes that to be true which the body affirms to be true; and from agreeing with the body and having the same delights she is obliged to have the same habits and haunts, and is not likely ever to be pure at her departure to the world below, but is always infected by the body; and so she sinks into another body and there germinates and grows, and has therefore no part in the communion of the divine and pure and simple.

That is most true, Socrates, answered Cebes.

And this, Cebes, is the reason why the true lovers of knowledge are temperate and brave; and not for the reason which the world gives.

Certainly not.

Certainly not! For the soul of a philosopher will reason in another way; she will not ask philosophy to release her in order that when released she may deliver herself up again to the thraldom of pleasures and pains, doing a work only to be undone again, weaving instead of unweaving her Penelope's web. But she will calm passion, and follow reason, and dwell in her, beholding the true and divine (which is not matter of opinion), and thence derive nourishment. Thus she seeks to live while she lives, and after death she hopes to go to her own kindred and to a congenial world and to be freed from human ills. Never fear, Simmias and Cebes, that a soul which has been thus nurtured and has had these pursuits, will at her departure from the body be scattered and blown away by the winds and be nowhere and nothing.

DISCUSSION QUESTIONS

1. Socrates says that he does not know which is better: to live or to die. What do you think?

2. Socrates believes that nothing evil can happen to a good man. Do you agree with him?

3. In the *Apology*, Socrates contends that there "is good reason to hope that death is a good." Why does he believe this? Do you agree with his argument? Why or why not?

4. How does Socrates prove the immortality of the soul? Analyze his argument.

5. Why does Plato believe that philosophy is the practice of death?

6. Why should the philosopher not fear death?

LUCRETIUS

AGAINST THE FEAR OF DEATH

Lucretius contends that we should not fear death because the soul is mortal—not immortal. Over twenty-five different arguments for the mortality of the soul are listed in Lucretius's *On the Nature of Things*. Strongly influenced by the metaphysics of Epicurus, Lucretius believes that the universe is composed entirely of atoms, motions, and the void. The soul, like everything else in the universe, is a composite of atoms and, as such, comes into being and perishes like everything else in the universe. Given the mortality of the soul, we should not fear death.

Lucretius argues that when our soul and body have been separated, we will not be affected by any events that happen in the future in the same way we were not affected by events that happened before our birth. Even if we suppose "the nature of the mind and power of the soul do feel, after they have been severed from our body," this will not affect us because our *identity* consists of the "marriage between body and soul." For Lucretius, the experiences of the soul alone are not our experiences: our experiences are possible only through the combination of our body and our soul. Even if, at a future point, atoms should recombine to re-form "our" body, and this body is married with our soul, because "the chain of our self-consciousness has once been snapped asunder," our identity will not thereby be reformed. The same holds true of the past: while it is probable that our body existed previously, because it was not continuously associated with our self-consciousness, we remember nothing from this past. Once the relationship between the mind and the body is destroyed, so, too, is our identity destroyed. With the destruction of our identity comes also the disappearance of feelings as *ours*. Hence, we have nothing to fear regarding death because we will have no sensation when we are dead. (Lucretius's speculations here extend some of the discussions from chapter 3 regarding the relationship of the mind to the body, and the nature of personal identity.)

It is foolish, therefore, to project our present self-consciousness, desires, and sensations both on our soul and on our body in death. After we die, we need not fear what happens to our body because with the loss of our identity comes the loss of sensation. People fear, for example, the decay of their body after death only because they are projecting their current consciousness into death. After death, none of our present sensations will be relevant: we will not be unhappy about the absence of a loved one in death, for example, because we will have no concern for these things after death. According to Lucretius, death is like an eternal sleep wherein we have no sensations or desires.

It is a law of nature that the old must give way to the new, that old combinations of atoms must give way to new combinations. Everything is subject to decay, generation, and change. Look at the great and powerful persons from the past, such as Scipio, Homer, and Epicurus, they all died. No one lives forever; therefore, all of the (mythological) stories that tell otherwise are false: Stories concerning figures like Sisyphus, Tartarus, Tantalus, and Cerberus are simply projections of the living fears of persons. Lucretius argues that the "lust of life" is evil for it burdens us with doubts and dangers. "A sure term of life is fixed for mortals, and death cannot be shunned, but meet it we must," concludes Lucretius. "Moreover we are ever engaged, ever involved in the same pursuits, and no new pleasure is struck out by living on." Finally, even if we do prolong our lives, we do not "take one tittle from the time past in death nor can we fret anything away, whereby we may haply be a less long time in the condition of the dead."

Titus Lucretius Carus (c. 99–55 B.C.E.), Roman poet and philosopher, was born in Rome to one of the most venerable of the great Roman houses. However, very little is known about his life. The only account of the life of Lucretius is the following short note by Saint Jerome in his *Chronicle* under the year 94 B.C.E.: "Titus Lucretius the poet is born. He was rendered insane by a love-philtre and, after writing during moments of lucidity, some books, which Cicero amended, he died by his own hand in the forty-third year of his life." Jerome's comment, perhaps based on a lost work by Suetonius, is neither provable nor disprovable. The following selection is from Book III of *On the Nature of Things* (*De rerum natura*), a didactic poem on the scientific views of Epicureanism. The English translation below is a prose rendering of Lucretius's poem, which was originally written in Latin.

Death therefore to us is nothing, concerns us not a jot, since the nature of the mind is proved to be mortal; and as in time gone by we felt no distress, when the Poeni from all sides came together to do battle, and all things shaken by war's troublous uproar shuddered and quaked beneath high heaven, and mortal men were in doubt which of the two peoples it should be to whose empire all must fall by sea and land alike, thus when we shall be no more, when there shall have been a separation of body and soul, out of both of which we are each formed into a single being, to us, you may be sure, who then shall be no more, nothing whatever can happen to excite sensation, not if earth shall be mingled with sea and sea with heaven. And even supposing the nature of the mind and power of the soul do feel, after they have been severed from our body, yet that is nothing to us who by the binding tie of marriage between body and soul are formed each into one single being. And if time should gather up our matter after our death and put it once more into the position in which it now is, and the light of life be given to us again, this result even would concern us not at all, when the chain of our self-consciousness has once been snapped asunder. So now we give ourselves no concern about any self which we have been before, nor do we feel any distress on the score of that self. For when you look back on the whole past course of immeasurable time and think how manifold are the shapes which the motions of matter take, you may easily credit this too, that these very same seeds of which we now are formed, have often before been placed in the same order in which they now are; and yet we cannot recover this in memory: a break in our existence has been interposed, and all the motions have wandered to and fro far astray from the sensations they produced. For he whom evil is to befall, must in his own person exist at the very time it comes, if the misery and suffering are haply to have any place at all; but since death precludes this, and forbids him to be, upon whom the ills can be brought, you may be sure that we have nothing to fear after death, and that he who exists not, cannot become miserable, and that it matters not a whit whether he has been born into life at any other time, when immortal death has taken away his mortal life.

Therefore when you see a man be moaning his hard case, that after death he shall either rot with his body laid in the grave or be devoured by flames or the jaws of wild beasts, you may be sure that his ring betrays a flaw and that there lurks in his heart a secret goad, though he himself declare that he does not believe that any sense will remain to him after death. He does not methinks really grant the conclusion which he professes to grant nor the principle on which he so professes, nor does he take and force himself root and branch out of life, but all unconsciously imagines something of self to survive. For when any one in life suggests to himself that birds and beasts will rend his body after death, he makes moan for himself: he does not separate himself from that self, nor withdraw himself fully from the body so thrown out, and fancies himself that other self and stands by and impregnates it with his own sense. Hence he makes much moan that he has been born mortal, and sees not that after real death there will be no other self to remain in life and lament to self that his own self has met death, and there to stand and grieve that his own self there lying is mangled or burnt. For if it is an evil after death to be pulled about by the devouring jaws of wild beasts, I cannot see why it should not be a cruel pain to be laid on fires and burn in hot flames, or to be placed in honey and stifled, or to stiffen with cold, stretched on the smooth surface of an icy slab of stone, or to be pressed down and crushed by a load of earth above.

"Now no more shall thy house admit thee with glad welcome, nor a most virtuous wife and sweet children run to be the first to snatch kisses and touch thy heart with a silent joy. No more mayst thou be prosperous in thy doings, a safeguard to thine own. One disastrous day has taken from thee luckless man in luckless wise all the many prizes of life." This do men say; but add not thereto "and now no longer does any craving for these things beset thee withal." For if they could rightly perceive this in thought and follow up the thought in words, they would release themselves from great distress and apprehension of mind.

"Thou, even as now thou art, sunk in the sleep of death, shalt continue so to be all time to come, freed from all distressful pains; but we with a sorrow that would not be sated wept for thee, when close by thou didst turn to an ashen hue on thy appalling funeral pile, and no length of days shall pluck from our hearts our ever-during grief." This question therefore should be asked of this speaker, what there is in it so passing bitter, if it come in the end to sleep and rest, that any one should pine in never-ending sorrow.

This too men often, when they have reclined at table cup in hand and shade their brows with crowns, love to say from the heart, "short is this enjoyment for poor weak men; presently it will have been and never after may it be called back." As if after their death it is to be one of their chiefest afflictions that thirst and parching drought is to burn them up hapless wretches, or a craving for any thing else is to beset them. What folly! no one feels the want of himself and life at the time when mind and body are together sunk in sleep; for all we care this sleep might be everlasting, no craving whatever for ourselves then moves us. And yet by no means do those first-beginnings throughout our frame wander at that time far away from their sense-producing motions; at the moment, when man starts up from sleep and collects himself. Death therefore must be thought to concern us much less, if less there can be than what we see to be nothing; for a greater dispersion of the mass of matter follows after death, and no one wakes up, upon whom the chill cessation of life has once come.

Once more, if the nature of things could suddenly utter a voice and in person could rally any of us in such words as these, "What hast thou, O mortal; so much at heart, that thou goest such lengths in sickly sorrows? Why bemoan and bewail death? For say thy life past and gone has been welcome to thee and thy blessings have not all, as if they were poured into a perforated vessel, run through and been lost without avail: why not then take thy departure like guest filled with life, and with resignation, thou fool, enter upon untroubled rest? But if all that thou hast enjoyed, has been squandered and lost; and life is a grievance, why seek to make any addition, to be wasted perversely in its turn and lost utterly without avail? Why not rather make an end of life and travail? For there is nothing more which I can contrive and discover for

thee to give pleasure: all things are ever the same. Though thy body is not yet decayed with years nor thy frame worn out and exhausted, yet all things remain the same, ay though in length of life thou shouldst outlast all races of things now living, nay even more if thou shouldst never die," what answer have we to make save this, that nature sets up against us a well-founded claim and puts forth in her pleading a true indictment?

If however one of greater age and more advanced in years should complain and lament poor wretch his death more than is right, would she not with greater cause raise her voice and rally him in sharp accents, "Away from this time forth with thy tears, rascal; a truce to thy complainings: thou decayest after full enjoyment of all the prizes of life. But because thou ever yearnest for what is not present, and despisest what is, life has slipped from thy grasp unfinished and unsatisfying, and or even thou thoughtest, death has taken his stand at thy pillow, before thou canst take thy departure sated and filled with good things. Now however resign all things unsuited to thy age, and with a good grace up and greatly go: thou must." With good reason methinks she would bring her charge, with reason rally and reproach; for old things give way and are suplanted by new without fail, and one thing must ever be replenished out of other things; and no one is delivered over to the pit and black Tartarus: matter is needed for after generations to grow; all of which though will follow thee when they have finished their term of life; and thus it is that all these no less than thou have before this come to an end and here after will come to an end. Thus one thing will never cease to rise out of another, and life is granted to none in fee-simple, to all in usufruct. Think too how the bygone antiquity of everlasting time before our birth was nothing to us. Nature therefore holds this up to us as a mirror of the time yet to come after our death. Is there aught in this that looks appalling, aught that wears an aspect of gloom? Is it nor more untroubled than any sleep?

And those things sure enough, which are fabled to be in the deep of Acheron, do all exist for us in this life. No Tantalus, numbed by groundless terror, as the story is, fears poor wretch a huge stone hanging in air; but in life rather a baseless dread of the god vexes mortals: the fall they fear is such fall of luck as chance brings to each. Nor do birds eat a way into Tityos laid in Acheron, nor can they sooth to say find during eternity food to peck under his large breast. However huge the bulk of body he extends, though such as to take up with outspread limbs not nine acres merely, but the whole earth, yet will he not be able to endure everlasting pain and supply food from his own body for ever. But he is for us a Tityos, whom, as he grovels in love, vultures rend and bitter anguish eats up or troubled thoughts from any other passion do rive. In life too we have a Sisyphus before our eyes who is bent on asking from the people the rods and cruel axes, and always retires defeated and disappointed. For to ask for power, which empty as it is is never given, and always in the chase of it to undergo severe toil, this is forcing up-hill with much effort a stone which after all rolls back again from the summit and seeks in headlong haste the levels of the plain. Then to be ever feeding the thankless nature of the mind; and never to fill it full and sate it with good things, as the seasons of the year do for us, when they come round and bring their fruits and varied delights, though after all we are never filled with the enjoyments of life, this methinks is to do what is told of the maidens in the flower of their age, to keep pouring water into a perforated vessel which in spite of all can never be filled full. Moreover Cerberus and the furies and yon privation of light are idle tales, as well as all the rest, Ixion's wheel and black Tartarus belching forth hideous fires from his throat: things which nowhere are nor sooth to say can be. But there is in life a dread if punishment for evil deeds, signal as the deeds are signal, and for atonement of guilt, the prison and the frightful hurling down from the rock, scourgings, executioners, the dungeon of the doomed, the pitch, the metal plate, torches; and eventhough these are wanting, yet the conscience-stricken mind through boding fears applies to itself goads and frightens itself with whips, and sees not meanwhile what end there can be of ills or what limit at last is to be set to punishments, and fears lest these very evils be enhanced after death. The life of fools at length becomes a hell here on earth.

This too you may sometimes say to yourself, "Even worthy Ancus has quitted the light with his eyes, who was far far better than thou, unconscionable man. And since then many other kings and kesars have been laid low, who lorded it over mighty nations. He [Xerxes] too, even he who erst paved a way over the great sea and made a path for his legions to march over the deep and taught them to pass on foot over the salt pools and set at naught the roarings of the sea, trampling on them with his horses, had the light taken from him and shed forth his soul from his dying body. The son of the Scipios, thunderbolt of war, terror of Carthage, yielded his bones to earth just as if he were the lowest menial. Think too of the inventors of all sciences and graceful arts, think of the companions of the Heliconian maids; among whom Homer bore the scepter without a peer, and he now sleeps the same sleep as others. Then there is Democritus, who when a ripe old age had warned him that the memory waking motions of his mind were waning, by his own spontaneous act offered up his head to death. Even Epicurus passed away, when his light of life had run its course, he who surpassed in intellect the race of man and quenched the light of all, as the ethereal sun arisen quenches the stars." Wilt thou then hesitate and think it a hardship to die? Thou for whom life is well nigh dead whilst yet thou livest and seest the light, who spendest the greater part of thy time in sleep and snorest wide awake and ceasest not to see visions and hast a mind troubled with groundless terror and canst not discover often what it is that ails thee, when besotted man thou art sore pressed on all sides with full many cares and goest astray tumbling about in the wayward wanderings of thy mind.

If, just as they are seen to feel that a load is on their mind which wears them out with its pressure, men might apprehend from what causes too it is produced and whence such a pile, if I may say so, of ill lies on their breast, they would not spend their life as we see them now for the most part do, not knowing any one of them what he means and wanting ever change of place as though he might lay his burden down. The man who is sick of home often issues forth from his large mansion, and as suddenly comes back to it, finding as he does that he is no better off abroad. He races to his country-house, driving his jennets in headlong haste, as if hurrying to bring help to a house on fire: he yawns the moment he has reached the door of his house, or sinks heavily into sleep and seeks forgetfulness, or even in haste goes back again to town. In this way each man flies from himself (but self from whom, as you may be sure is commonly the case, he cannot escape, clings to him in his own despite), hates too himself, because he is sick and knows not the cause of the malady; for if he could rightly see into this, relinquishing all else each man would study to learn the nature of things, since the point at stake is the condition for eternity, not for one hour, in which mortals have to pass all the time which remains for them to expect after death.

Once more what evil lust of life is this which constrains us with such force to be so mightily troubled in doubts and dangers? A sure term of life is fixed for mortals, and death cannot be shunned, but meet it we must. Moreover we are ever engaged, ever involved in the same pursuits, and no new pleasure is struck out by living on; but whilst what we crave is wanting, it seems to transcend all the rest; then, when it has been gotten, we crave something else, and ever does the same thirst of life possess us, as we gape for it open-mouthed. Quite doubtful it is what fortune the future will carry with it or what chance will bring us or what end is at hand. Nor by prolonging life do we take one tittle from the time past in death nor can we fret anything away, whereby we may haply be a less long time in the condition of the dead. Therefore you may

complete as many generations as you please during your life; none the less however will that everlasting death await you; and for no less long a time will he be no more in being, who beginning with to-day has ended his life, than the man who has died many months and years ago.

DISCUSSION QUESTIONS

1. Why does Lucretius believe that we should not fear death? Do you agree with him? Why or why not?

2. Lucretius argues that when the soul is separated from the body, self-consciousness and identity are destroyed. What is his argument? Do you agree with him? Why or why not?

3. Compare Plato's Socrates on death to Lucretius. What are the similarities and differences in their positions?

4. According to Lucretius, what is the purpose and source of mythological accounts of persons or heroes suffering after death? Also, why does he believe that all of these accounts are false? Do you agree with him? Why or why not?

5. Why, according to Lucretius, should we not fear what happens to our bodies after death?

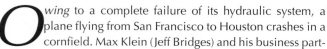

Fearless
[USA 1993] 2 hours, 2 minutes
Directed by Peter Weir

*O*wing to a complete failure of its hydraulic system, a plane flying from San Francisco to Houston crashes in a cornfield. Max Klein (Jeff Bridges) and his business partner, Jeff Gordon (John de Lancie), are passengers on the plane. Anticipating that the plane is going to crash and that he is going to die, Max is overcome by a complete lack of fear of death. His fearless state is very calming, and amidst the chaos that ensues, Max manages to help twenty or so people survive the crash, including a baby.

After saving so many lives, Max leaves the crash scene, rents a car, and drives toward Los Angeles, where he meets an old friend. She is amazed that Max is now able to eat strawberries, which had previously caused him a potentially fatal allergic reaction. The authorities wonder why Max walked away from the plane crash. The airline also wonders why he wants to be flown back to San Francisco rather than taking a train, given that he has always been afraid of flying and that he has just survived a horrendous plane crash.

Dr. Bill Perlman (John Turturro) is a psychologist hired by the airline to deal with the posttraumatic stress of the crash survivors. Max perplexes Dr. Perlman by insisting that the crash was the best thing that ever happened to him. When Max is reunited with his wife, Laura (Isabella Rossellini), and his son, Jonah (Spencer Vrooman), he remains distant. After successfully walking across a busy highway without looking out for the cars, Max comes to the belief that God wants to kill him but cannot. This is demonstrated by his repeatedly eating bowls of strawberries without any allergic reactions.

Several months after the crash, all of the survivors have been helped by Dr. Perlman except Max and Carla Rodrigo (Rosie Perez), whose two-year-old son died. In an attempt to help them, Dr. Perlman puts them in contact with each other. Max soon decides that he is in love with Carla and discusses divorcing his wife. Max and Carla believe that they are safe because they have died already, and they regard themselves as "ghosts."

With Max, Carla slowly comes out of her deep depression and opens up to him about the crash. She tells Max that she held onto her son until the moment she thought the plane was going to land safely—then she let go. She believes that she is responsible for the death of the child. Max says that there is no way Carla could have saved the youngster and demonstrates this by crashing his car into a brick wall at high speed while Carla holds a toolbox that she is pretending is her baby. When the car hits the wall, the toolbox flies out of Carla's arms and through the windshield. She realizes then that it would have been impossible for her to save her child, and snaps out of her deep depression once and for all.

Whereas Carla sustains only whiplash from the car crash, Max ends up in intensive care. Carla visits him and says that it is over between them, that it is time for Max to mend his strained relationship with his wife and son. When Max is released from the hospital, he tells his wife that she must "save" him. Shortly thereafter, he eats a strawberry and has a violent allergic reaction. Unconscious, Max lies on the floor while Laura resuscitates him, imploring him to stay alive. Max moves toward the afterlife but suddenly turns back because of Laura's efforts. In the end, Laura saves Max from death.

DISCUSSION QUESTIONS

1. Why doesn't Max fear death? Are the reasons for Max's lack of fear of death similar to or different from Lucretius's lack of fear of death? Discuss.

2. What position on the mortality of the soul is supported by this film? Is the soul mortal or immortal? Or neither? Discuss.

3. After walking across a busy highway without getting hit by a vehicle, Max says to God, "You want to kill me but you can't!" Is Max right? Discuss.

4. Max will not admit to Dr. Perlman that the crash was bad. Instead, he says that the crash was the best thing that ever happened to him. Why does Max believe this? Do you agree with him? Why or why not?

5. Consider the following conversation between Carla and Max:

   MAX   "When I was thirteen, my father died in front of my eyes. We were going out of our apartment. I was throwing this softball up and down. Mom screamed . . . I turned to look . . . Dad was dead on the sidewalk. Blood coming out of his nose. Legs all twisted under him. Looked like somebody with a big hand reached down and squeezed the life out of him."

CARLA "That was God."

MAX "That is what I thought. God killed my daddy."

CARLA "Why would he want to kill him?"

MAX "Couldn't figure that out. He was a religious guy. Hard-working, kind, to my mother and my sister."

CARLA "Did you love him?"

MAX "Yes. I didn't know why God killed my daddy. There was no reason to. So, I decided there was no God."

Evaluate Max's argument against the existence of God. Is a valid and sound argument? Why or why not?

6.   Consider the following exchange between Carla and Max:

CARLA "You know he hurt me. He hurt me forever. But I still believe in him."

MAX "People don't believe in God so much as they choose not to believe in nothing. Life and death, they happen for no reason. We think that people are born because their mothers wanted them alive or because God needed another home run hitter for the Giants. They think that we die because we eat red meat or rob banks. Now that way we can never be good enough or careful enough forever at least we can try. But if it makes no sense, if life and death just happen, then there is no reason to do anything."

CARLA "There is no reason to love."

Is Max right? Do "life and death just happen"? Is Carla right? Is there no reason to love "if life and death just happen?" Why? Compare Max's position with Lucretius's on life and death.

7.   Carla says to Max, "You told me I was going to be safe with you." Max responds, "You're safe. You're safe because we died already." What do you think Max means?

8.   Max and Carla buy gifts for the dead: Max for his father, and Carla for her child. Why do they do this? Is this one of their ways of showing that they are not afraid of death?

9.   When Max is in the hospital, Carla says to him, "I want you to go home, Max. I want to you live again. We're not ghosts any more. You can't save everyone, Max. You've got to try taking care of yourself." Earlier, Carla told Laura that Max is her best friend and that he is like an angel. Laura responded, "Max is a man, not an angel." Do you think Max literally became a "ghost" or an "angel" from the time of the accident to that of his being "saved" by Laura? Why or why not?

10.   Why does Laura need to "save" Max? Why does Max suddenly become deathly allergic to strawberries again at the end of the film? Discuss.

11.   What do you think the message of this film is regarding the fear of death?

CLARENCE DARROW

THE MYTH OF IMMORTALITY

Clarence Darrow challenges a number of common arguments for the soul's immortality. He concludes that it is not reasonable to believe in the immortality of the soul. Rather, it is reasonable to believe in the soul's mortality—a conclusion that he does not find to be pessimistic.

While some contend that we have memory and consciousness after death, Darrow argues that there is little reason to believe this because our memory is already very limited and becomes more so as we age. Not only do we not remember anything before we were born, but we remember very little from our youth, and as we grow older, we increasingly lose more and more memories. "I am sure that if I die of what is called 'old age'" writes Darrow, "my consciousness will gradually slip away with my failing emotions; I shall no more be aware of the near approach of final dissolution than is the dying tree." He concludes that because it is not reasonable to believe that memory persists after death, it is also not reasonable to believe that an immortal soul or consciousness persists after death.

Another line of argument for the immortality of the soul maintains that humans and only humans have an immortal soul. Darrow counters that because of the enormity of the universe, it is not reasonable to believe that we are the only life form in the universe. Therefore, it is unreasonable to believe that humans have been chosen over all other life forms to be endowed with immortal souls.

Darrow goes on to assert that "there is no connection whatever between the notion that personal consciousness and memory persist after death and the scientific theory that matter and force are indestructible." He wonders what would be the use of an immortal soul that was dispersed into new combinations of matter at the moment of death. He says that because the dispersal of the soul upon death would result in the forging of a new identity, scientific language does not lend support the notion of the immortality of the soul.

Finally, Darrow addresses the argument that, given that "nature never creates a desire without providing the means for its satisfaction" and that we desire an immortal soul, we must conclude that the soul is immortal. He challenges the idea that we desire a future life, maintaining that we only desire to keep on living, which is a very different thing.

In sum, these and other arguments for the immortality of the soul do not convince Darrow but instead lead him to embrace the soul's mortality. For him, the mortality of the soul is not a reason for despair. Rather, "when we accept the fact that all men and women are approaching an inevitable doom: the consciousness of it should make us more kindly and considerate to each other." A biographical sketch of Darrow appears in chapter 5.

There is, perhaps, no more striking example of the credulity of man than the widespread belief in immortality. This idea includes not only the belief that man knows that his life had a beginning. Can one imagine an organism that has a beginning and no end? If I did not exist in the infinite past, why should I, or could I, exist in the infinite future? "But," say some, "your consciousness, your memory may exist even after you are dead. This is what we mean by the soul." Let us examine this point a little.

I have no remembrance of the months that I lay in my mother's womb. I cannot recall the day of my birth nor the time when I first opened my eyes to the light of the sun. I cannot remember when I was an infant, or when I began to creep on the floor, or when I was taught to walk, or anything before I was five or six years old. Still, all of these events were important, wonderful, and strange in a new life. What I call my "consciousness," for lack of a better word and a better understanding, developed with my growth and the crowding experiences I met at every turn. I have a hazy recollection of the burial of a boy soldier who was shot toward the end of the Civil War. He was buried near the schoolhouse when I was seven years old. But I have no remembrance of the assassination of Abraham Lincoln, although I must then have been eight years old. I must have known about it at the time, for my family and my community idolized Lincoln, and all America was in mourning at his death. Why do I remember the dead boy soldier who was buried a year before? Perhaps because I knew him well. Perhaps because his family was close to my childish life. Possibly because it came to me as my first knowledge of death. At all events, it made so deep an impression that I recall it now.

"Ah, yes," say the believers in the soul, "what you say confirms our own belief. You certainly existed when these early experiences took place. You were conscious of them at the time, even though you are not aware of it now. In the same way, may not your consciousness persist after you die, even though you are not now aware of the fact?"

On the contrary, my fading memory of the events that filled the early years of my life leads me to the opposite conclusion. So far as these incidents are concerned, the mind and consciousness of the boy are already dead. Even now, am I fully alive? I am seventy-one years old. I often fail to recollect the names of some of those I knew full well. Many events do not make the lasting impression that they once did. I know that it will be only a few years, even if my body still survives decay, when few important matters will even register in my mind. I know how it is with the old. I know that physical life can persist beyond the time when the mind can fully function. I know that if I live to an extreme old age, my mind will fail. I shall eat and drink and go to my bed in an automatic way. Memory— which is all that binds me to the past—will already be dead. All that will remain will be a vegetative existence; I shall sit and doze in the chimney corner, and my body will function in a measure even though the ego will already be practically dead. I am sure that if I die of what is called "old age," my consciousness will gradually slip away with my failing emotions; I shall no more be aware of the near approach of final dissolution than is the dying tree.

In primitive times, before men knew anything about the human body or the universe of which it is part, it was not unreasonable to believe in spirits, ghosts, and the duality of man. For one thing, celestial geography was much simpler then. Just above the earth was a firmament in which the stars were set, and above the firmament was heaven. The place was easy of access, and in dreams the angels were seen going up and coming down on a ladder. But now we have a slightly more adequate conception of space and the infinite universe of which we are so small a part. Our great telescopes reveal countless worlds and planetary systems which make our own sink into utter insignificance in comparison. We have every reason to think that beyond our sight there is endless space filled with still more planets, so infinite in size and number that no brain has the smallest conception of their extent. Is there any reason to think that in this universe, with its myriads of worlds, there is no other life so important as our own? Is it possible that the inhabitants of the earth have been singled out for special favor and endowed with souls and immortal life? Is it at all reasonable to suppose that any special account is taken of the human atoms that forever come and go upon this planet? . . .

Some of those who profess to believe in the immortality of man—whether it be of his soul or his body—have drawn what comfort they could from the modern scientific doctrine of the indestructibility of matter and force. This doctrine, they say, only confirms in scientific language what they have always believed. This, however, is pure sophistry. It is probably true that no matter or force has ever been or ever can be destroyed. But it is likewise true that there is no connection whatever between the notion that personal consciousness and memory persist after death and the scientific theory that matter and force are indestructible. For the scientific theory carries with it a corollary, that the forms of matter and energy are constantly changing through an endless cycle of new combinations. Of what possible use would it be, then, to have a consciousness that was immortal, but which, from the moment of death, was dispersed into new combinations so that no two parts of the original identity could ever be reunited again?

These natural processes of change, which in the human being take the forms of growth, disease, senility, death, and decay, are essentially the same as the process by which a lump of coal is disintegrated in burning. One may watch the lump of coal burning in the grate until nothing but ashes remains. Part of the coal goes up the chimney in the form of smoke; part of it radiates through the house as heat; the residue lies in the ashes on the hearth. So it is with human life. In all forms of life nature is engaged in combining, breaking down, and recombining her store of energy and matter into new forms. The thing we call "life" is nothing other than a state of equilibrium which endures for a short span of years between the two opposing tendencies of nature—the one that builds up and the one that tears down. In old age, the tearing-down process has already gained the ascendancy, and when death intervenes, the equilibrium is finally upset by the complete stoppage of the building-up process, so that nothing remains but complete disintegration. The energy thus released may be converted into grass or trees or animal life; or it may lie dormant until caught up again in the crucible of nature's laboratory. But whatever happens, the man—the *You* and the *I*—like the lump of coal that has been burned, is gone, irrevocably dispersed. All the King's horses and all the King's men cannot restore it to its former unity.

The idea that man is a being set apart, distinct from all the rest of nature, is born of man's emotions, of his loves and hates, of his hopes and fears, and of the primitive conceptions of undeveloped minds. The *You* or the *I* which is known to our friends does not consist of an immaterial something called a "soul" which cannot be conceived. We know perfectly well what we mean when we talk about this *You* and this *Me*: and it is equally plain that the whole fabric that makes up our separate personalities is destroyed, dispersed, disintegrated beyond repair by what we call "death."

Those who refuse to give up the idea of immortality declare that nature never creates a desire without providing the means for its satisfaction. They likewise insist that all people, from the rudest to the most civilized, yearn for another life. As a matter of fact, nature creates many desires which she does not satisfy; most of the wishes of men meet no fruition. But nature does not create any emotion demanding a future life. The only yearning that the individual has is to keep on living—which is a very different thing. This urge is found in every animal, in every plant. It is simply the momentum of a living structure: or, as Schopenhauer put it, "the will to live." What we long for is a continuation of our present state of existence, not an uncertain reincarnation in a mysterious world of which we know nothing.

All men recognize the hopelessness of finding any evidence that the individual will persist beyond the grave. As a last resort, we are told that it is better that the doctrine be believed even if it is not true. We are assured that without this faith, life is only desolation and despair. However that may be, it remains that many of the conclusions of logic are not pleasant to contemplate; still, so long as men think and feel, at least some of them will use their faculties as best they can. For if we are to believe things that are not true, who is to write our creed? Is it safe to leave it to any man or organization to pick out the errors that we must accept? The whole history of the world has answered this question in a way that cannot be mistaken.

And after all, is the belief in immortality necessary or even desirable for man? Millions of men and women have no such faith; they go on with their daily tasks and feel joy and sorrow without the lure of immortal life. The things that really affect the happiness of the individual are the matters of daily living. They are the companionship of friends, the games and contemplations. They are misunderstandings and cruel judgments, false friends and debts, poverty and disease. They are our joys in our living companions and our sorrows over those who die. Whatever our faith, we mainly live in the present—in the here and now. Those who hold the view that man is mortal are never troubled by metaphysical problems. At the end of the day's labor we are glad to lose our consciousness in sleep; and intellectually, at least, we look forward to the long rest from the stresses and storms that are always incidental to existence.

When we fully understand the brevity of life, its fleeting joys and unavoidable pains; when we accept the fact that all men and women are approaching an inevitable doom: the consciousness of it should make us more kindly and considerate of each other. This feeling should make men and women use their best efforts to help their fellow travellers on the road, to make the path brighter and easier as we journey on. It should bring a closer kinship, a better understanding, and a deeper sympathy for the wayfarer who must live a common life and die a common death.

DISCUSSION QUESTIONS

1. Why does Darrow assert that it is not reasonable to believe in the persistence of memory or consciousness after death? Do you agree with his argument? Why or why not?

2. Darrow contends that it is unreasonable to believe that humans have been chosen over all other life forms to be endowed with immortal souls. Do you agree with his reasoning? Why or why not?

3. Why does Darrow believe that the scientific theory that matter and force are indestructible does not support the concept of the immortality of the soul? Do you agree with him? Why or why not?

4. How does Darrow refute the argument for the immortality of the soul that utilizes as its major premise "Nature never creates a desire without providing the means for its satisfaction"? Formalize this argument, and discuss Darrow's refutation.

5. How similar to or different from those of Lucretius, Marcus Aurelius, and Epicurus is Darrow's approach to life and death? Which approach do you prefer, and why?

6. Do Darrow's arguments against the immortality of the soul convince you? Why or why not? Which argument is the strongest one *against* the immortality of the soul, and which one is the strongest argument *for* the immortality of the soul? Discuss.

Flatliners
[USA 1990] 1 hour, 51 minutes
Directed by Joel Schumacher

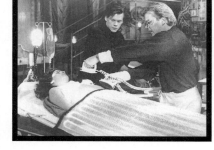

Nelson (Kiefer Sutherland) is a young doctor who has discovered a procedure for testing experience beyond death. The heart is stopped for one minute and then restarted with an electrical jolt. The procedure is called "flatlining" in reference to the flat line that appears on the heart monitor when the heart stops beating. Although some of Nelson's young doctor friends are skeptical about his technique, they help him with his experiment.

After Nelson undergoes the procedure and reports no negative side effects, the competitive nature of the other doctors surfaces. They begin jockeying among themselves to be the next to try the procedure. Joe (William Baldwin), a philanderer who videotapes himself having sex with women unbeknownst to them or to his fiancée, is the next to attempt flatlining. He comes out of the procedure seemingly unharmed, but he begins to see video and television screens projecting scenes from his "sex tapes." In the meantime, Nelson has run-ins with a boy from his childhood, one of which results in his being beaten up by the boy. Still, neither Nelson nor Joe reveal their negative experiences, reporting only the positive.

Labraccio (Kevin Bacon) is the self-professed atheist and skeptic of the group. He thinks that Nelson and Joe are inventing the positive experiences they are reporting and wants to try the procedure himself to verify their results. After Labraccio successfully flatlines for the longest period of time, he reports seeing Winnie Hicks, a girl from his childhood, on a train—only Winnie appears to him at the same age she was when Joe knew her as a youth. He suspects that his vision may be an illusion, since the others did not report any similar effects.

The confrontations between Nelson, Joe, and Labraccio become more frequent and intense, and the doctors begin to share the common elements of their experiences with one another. Rachel (Julia Roberts) does not report seeing anything negative during her flatline, but later she tells them that she saw her deceased father, who shot himself when she was five. The doctors conclude that they are all seeing people they have hurt or wronged in some way, and the task now is to find out how to end these visions.

Joe returns to his apartment one day to be greeted by all of the women whom he slept with and filmed without their knowledge. Each woman tells how he deceived her, but Joe does not know if they are real or hallucinated. Finally, he sees his fiancée in the apartment. She had come to see what was wrong with him after he called her sounding distraught, and while she waited in his apartment, she found his videotape collection. She immediately ends the engagement and leaves him.

Labraccio gets the idea from Joe's experience that if he seeks out the girl he wronged and apologizes to her, the visions of her will stop. His plan works. Now only Nelson and Rachel are still having run-ins, and both adopt the same "confrontation" strategy to end them. During one of her confrontations with her father, Rachel views him shooting up heroin, and they embrace and apologize to each other.

Nelson's situation is the most difficult because the boy who is attacking him wants to kill him. So, Nelson reveals that the boy, Billy Mahoney (Joshua Ruddy), fell out of a tree one day and died because Nelson was throwing stones at him. Nelson decides to flatline again to set the situation right. In a flatline that lasts over twelve minutes, Nelson manages to fall out of the tree himself and die instead of Billy. To the amazement of all, Nelson also manages to come out of this extremely long flatline alive.

DISCUSSION QUESTIONS

1. Do you think the flatliners' experiences confirm for them that there is something beyond death? Why or why not?

2. Nelson says that philosophy and religion have failed to establish whether there is anything out there beyond death, and now it is time for science to try. Do you agree with him that philosophy and religion have failed? Why or why not?

3. As presented in the film, are the "people" whom the flatliners experience immortal? Why or why not?

4. A number of characters in this film recount their death experiences. At one point, Rachel asks, "How do you explain the similarity of death experiences all around the world?" What should we conclude from this alleged similarity of death experiences? Defend your view.

5. Is one of the general conclusions of *Flatliners* that there is life after death? Why or why not?

6. Do you think the women who appear to Joe are real? Is Billy Mahoney, the boy who beats up Nelson, also real? Is Winnie Hicks, the girl who appears to Labraccio, real? Or are they all just figments of the viewers' imaginations? How, then, do you explain the attacks on Nelson—as self-inflicted? Discuss.

7. Labraccio begins the film as a skeptic and an atheist, and ends the film apologizing to God for stepping on his territory. At the end of the film, is he no longer an atheist? If not, what brought about this change?

8. Why do you think this film presents experiences beyond death as involving people whom these characters hurt or wronged in some way? If you were the screenwriter, how would you have "imagined" experience beyond death?

C. J. DUCASSE

IS LIFE AFTER DEATH POSSIBLE?

I n this selection, C. J. Ducasse argues that life after death is logically possible. He begins by scrutinizing the theoretical and factual reasons for rejecting the possibility, and finds them all to be weak.

Some argue that, theoretically speaking, consciousness is just another name for subvocal speech or for some other form of behavior and that when the physical or bodily bases of speech or behavior are removed, so, too, is consciousness. Ducasse argues that while some mental events are connected with some physical or bodily events, the connection is not one of identity—that is, there is not a one-to-one correspondence between events of consciousness and physical events.

Ducasse also argues that there is no factual basis to the claim that consciousness or mental processes *depend* on physical or bodily processes. Just because a person forgets things, for example, is not a necessary sign of loss of consciousness. Consciousness can manifest itself in ways other than memories: Ducasse writes, "If absence of memories relating to a given period proved unconsciousness for that period, this would force us to conclude that we were unconscious during the first few years of our lives, and indeed have been so most of the time since; for the fact is that we have no memories whatever of most of our days."

Then, after presenting a number of "well-authenticated cases" of the existence of "apparitions," Ducasse maintains that the main reason people deny the possibility of life after death is a tacit assumption that whatever is real is whatever is *material*; anything that is immaterial is not regarded as real. Ducasse then shows that the material world is just one of many objects of our consciousness. Therefore, once we acknowledge the weakness of arguments against the possibility of survival, take into consideration cases of "apparitions," dismiss our tacit assumption that "to be real is to be material," and recognize the ways in which the material world is but one object of many in our consciousness, we must therefore conclude that life after death is logically *possible*.

C. J. (Curt John) Ducasse (1881–1969), an American, was a systematic philosopher who wrote on most every topic in philosophy. He was born in France but lived his entire adult life in the United States. He was educated at the University of Washington and Harvard University, and he taught philosophy at the University of Washington and Brown University. A member of the board of trustees of the American Society for Psychical Research, Ducasse was a mind–body dualist and an advocate of soft determinism. His work had a great influence on the highly respected analytical American philosophers Wilfred Sellars (1912–89) and Roderick Chisholm (1916–1999). He was the author of *Causation and the Types of Necessity* (1924), *Philosophy of Art* (1929), *Philosophy as a Science* (1941), *Art, the Critics, and You* (1944), *Nature, Mind, and Death* (1951), *A Philosophical Scrutiny of Religion* (1953), *A Critical Examination of the Belief in a Life After Death* (1961), *Paranormal Phenomena* (1969), and *Truth, Knowledge and Causation* (1969). This selection is from a lecture presented at the University of California, Berkeley and published in 1948.

The question whether human personality survives death is sometimes asserted to be one upon which reflection is futile. Only empirical evidence, it is said, can be relevant, since the question is purely one of fact.

But no question is purely one of fact until it is clearly understood; and this one is, on the contrary, ambiguous and replete with tacit assumptions. Until the ambiguities have been removed and the assumptions critically examined, we do not really know just what it is we want to know when we ask whether a life after death is possible. Nor, therefore, can we tell until then what bearing on this question various facts empirically known to us may have.

To clarify its meaning is chiefly what I now propose to attempt. I shall . . . state, as convincingly as I can in the space available, the arguments commonly advanced to prove that such a life is impossible. After that, I shall consider the logic of these arguments, and show that they quite fail to establish the impossibility. Next, the tacit but arbitrary assumption, which makes them nevertheless appear convincing, will be pointed out. . . .

Let us turn to the first of these tasks.

THE ARGUMENTS AGAINST SURVIVAL

There are, first of all, a number of *facts* which definitely suggest that both the existence and the nature of consciousness wholly depend on the presence of a functioning nervous system. [F1.] It is pointed out, for example, that wherever consciousness is observed, it is found associated with a living and functioning body. [F2.] Further, when the body dies, or the head is struck a heavy blow, or some anesthetic is administered, the familiar outward evidences of consciousness terminate, permanently or temporarily. [F3.] Again, we know well that drugs of various kinds—alcohol, caffeine, opium, heroin, and many others—cause specific changes at the time in the nature of a person's mental states. . . . [F4.] Again, the contents of consciousness, the mental powers, or even the personality, are modified in characteristic ways when certain regions of the brain are destroyed by disease or injury or are disconnected from the rest by such an operation as prefrontal lobotomy. . . .

That continued existence of mind after death is impossible has been argued also on the basis of *theoretical considerations*. [T1.] It has been contended, for instance, . . . that "consciousness" is only the name we give to certain types of behavior, which differentiate the higher animals from all other things in nature. According to this view, to say, for example, that an animal is conscious of a difference between two stimuli means nothing more than that it responds to each by different behavior. That is, the difference of *behavior* is what consciousness of difference between the stimuli *consists in;* and is not, as is commonly assumed, only the behavioral sign of something mental and not public, called "consciousness that the stimuli are different."

[T2.] Or again, consciousness, of the typically human sort called thought, is identified with the typically human sort of behavior called speech; and this, again, not in the sense that speech *expresses* or *manifests* something different from itself, called "thought," but in the sense that speech—whether uttered or only whispered—*is* thought itself. And obviously, if thought, or any mental activity, is thus but some mode of behavior of the living body, the mind cannot possibly survive death.

THE ARGUMENTS EXAMINED

Such, in brief, are the chief reasons commonly advanced for holding that survival is impossible. Scrutiny of them, however, will, I think, reveal that they are not as strong as they first seem and far from strong enough to show that there can be no life after death.

[T1 and T2.] Let us consider first the assertion that "thought," or "consciousness," is but another name for subvocal speech, or for some other form of behavior, or for molecular processes in the tissues of the brain. As Paulsen and others have pointed out, no evidence ever is or can be offered to support that assertion, because it is in fact but a disguised proposal to make the words "thought," "feeling," "sensation," "desire," and so on, denote facts quite different from those which these words are commonly employed to denote. To say that those words are but other names for certain chemical or behavioral events is as grossly arbitrary as it would be to say that "wood" is but another name for glass, or "potato" but another name for cabbage. What thought, desire, sensation, and other mental states are like, each of us can observe directly by introspection; and what introspection reveals is that they do not in the least resemble muscular contraction, or glandular secretion, or any other known bodily events. No tampering with language can alter the observable fact that thinking is one thing and muttering quite another; that the feeling called anger has no resemblance to the bodily behavior which usually goes with it; or that an act of will is not in the least like anything we find when we open the skull and examine the brain. Certain mental events are doubtless connected in some way with certain bodily events, but they are not those bodily events themselves. The connection is not identity.

[F2, F3, and F4.] This being clear, let us next consider the arguments offered to show that mental processes, although not identical with bodily processes, nevertheless depend on them. We are told, for instance, that some head injuries, or anesthetics, totally extinguish consciousness for the time being. As already pointed out, however, the strict fact is only that the usual bodily signs of consciousness are then absent. But they are also absent when a person is asleep; and yet, at the same time, dreams, which are states of consciousness, may be occurring.

It is true that when the person concerned awakens, he often remembers his dreams, whereas the person that has been anesthetized or injured has usually no memories relating to the period of apparent blankness. But this could mean that his consciousness was, for the first time, dissociated from its ordinary channels of manifestation, as was reported of the co-conscious personalities of some of the patients of Dr. Morton Prince. Moreover, it sometimes occurs that a person who has been in an accident reports lack of memories not only for the period during which his body was unresponsive but also for a period of several hours *before* the accident, during which he had given to his associates all the ordinary external signs of being conscious as usual.

But, more generally, if absence of memories relating to a given period proved unconsciousness for that period, this would force us to conclude that we were unconscious during the first few years of our lives, and indeed have been so most of the time since; for the fact is that we have no memories whatever of most of our days. That we were alive and conscious on any long past specific date is, with only a few exceptions, not something we actually remember, but only something which we infer must be true.

EVIDENCE FROM PSYCHICAL RESEARCH

[F1 and F2.] Another argument advanced against survival was, it will be remembered, that death must extinguish the mind, since all manifestations of it then cease. But to assert that they invariably then cease is to ignore altogether the considerable amount of evidence to the contrary, gathered over many years and carefully checked by the Society for Psychical Research. This evidence, which is of a variety of kinds, has been reviewed by Professor Gardner Murphy in an article published in the Journal of the Society. He mentions first the numerous well-authenticated cases of apparition of a dead person to others as yet unaware that he had died or even been ill or in danger. The more strongly evidential cases of apparition are those in which the apparition conveys to the person who sees it specific facts until then secret. An example would be that of the apparition of a girl to her brother nine years after her death, with a conspicuous scratch on her cheek. Their mother then revealed to him that she herself had made that scratch accidentally while preparing her daughter's body for burial, but that she had then at once covered it with powder and never mentioned it to anyone.

Another famous case is that of a father whose apparition some time after death revealed to one of his sons the existence and location of an unsuspected second will, benefiting him, which was then found as indicated. Still another case would be the report by General Barter, then a subaltern in the British Army in India, of the apparition to him of a lieutenant he had not seen for two or three years. The lieutenant's apparition was riding a brown pony with black mane and tail. He was much stouter than at their last meeting, and, whereas formerly clean-shaven, he now wore a peculiar beard in the form of a fringe encircling his face. On inquiry the next day from a person who had known the lieutenant at the time he died, it turned out that he had indeed become very bloated before his death; that he had grown just such a beard while on the sick list; and that he had some time before bought and eventually ridden to death a pony of that very description.

Other striking instances are those of an apparition seen simultaneously by several persons. It is on record that an apparition of a child was perceived first by a dog, that the animal's rushing at it, loudly barking, interrupted the conversation of the seven persons present in the room, thus drawing their attention to the apparition, and that the latter then moved through the room for some fifteen seconds, followed by the barking dog.

Another type of empirical evidence of survival consists of communications, purporting to come from the dead, made through the persons commonly called sensitives, mediums, or automatists. Some of the most remarkable of these communications were given by the celebrated American medium, Mrs. Piper, who for many years was studied by the Society for Psychical Research, London, with the most elaborate precautions against all possibility of fraud. Twice, particularly, the evidences of identity supplied by the dead persons who purportedly were thus communicating with the living were of the very kinds, and of the same precision and detail, which would ordinarily satisfy a living person of the identity of another living person with whom he was not able to communicate directly, but only through an intermediary, or by letter or telephone.

Again, sometimes the same mark of identity of a dead person, or the same message from him, or complementary parts of one message are obtained independently from two mediums in different parts of the world.

Of course, when facts of these kinds are recounted, as I have just done, only in abstract summary, they make little if any impression upon us. And the very word "medium" at once brings to our minds the innumerable instances of demonstrated fraud perpetrated by charlatans to extract money from the credulous bereaved. But the modes of trickery and sources of error, which immediately suggest themselves to us as easy, natural explanations of the seemingly extra-ordinary facts, suggest themselves just as quickly to the members of the research committees of the Society for Psychical Research. Usually, these men have had a good deal more experience than the rest of us with the tricks of conjurers and fraudulent mediums, and take against them

precautions far more strict and ingenious than would occur to the average skeptic.

But when, instead of stopping at summaries, one takes the trouble to study the detailed, original reports, it then becomes evident that they cannot all be just laughed off; for to accept the hypothesis of fraud or malobservation would often require more credulity than to accept the facts reported.

THE INITIAL ASSUMPTION BEHIND THE ARGUMENTS AGAINST SURVIVAL

We have now scrutinized . . . the reasons mentioned earlier for rejecting the possibility of survival, and we have found them all logically weak. . . . It will be useful for us to . . . inquire why so many of the persons who advance those reasons nevertheless think them convincing.

It is, I believe, because these persons approach the question of survival with a certain uncon-scious metaphysical bias. It derives from a particular initial assumption which they tacitly make. It is that *to be real is to be material.* And to be material, of course, is to be some process or part of the perceptually public world, that is, of the world we all perceive by means of our so-called five senses.

Now, the assumption that to be real is to be material is a useful and appropriate one for the purpose of investigating the material world and of operating upon it; and this purpose is a legitimate and frequent one. But those persons, and most of us, do not realize that the validity of that assumption is strictly relative to that specific purpose. Hence they, and most of us, continue making the assumption, and it continues to rule judgment, even when, as now, the purpose in view is a different one, for which the assumption is no longer useful or even congruous.

The point is all-important here and therefore worth stressing. Its essence is that the conception of the nature of reality that proposes to define the real as the material is not the expression of an observable fact to which everyone would have to bow, but is the expression only of a certain direction of interest on the part of the persons who so define reality—of interest, namely, which they have chosen to center wholly in the material, perceptually public world. This specialized interest is of course as legitimate as any other, but it automatically ignores all the facts, commonly called facts of mind, which only introspection reveals. And that specialized interest is what alone compels persons in its grip to employ the word "mind" to denote, instead of what it commonly does denote, something else altogether, namely, the public behavior of bodies that have minds.

Only so long as one's judgment is swayed unawares by that special interest do the logically weak arguments against the possibility of survival, which we have examined, seem strong.

It is possible, however, and just as legitimate, as well as more conducive to a fair view of our question, to center one's interest at the start on the facts of mind as introspectively observable, ranking them as most real in the sense that they are the facts the intrinsic nature of which we most directly experience, the facts which we most certainly know to exist; and moreover, that they are the facts without the experiencing of which we should not know any other facts whatever—such, for instance as those of the material world.

The sort of perspective one gets from this point of view is what I propose now to sketch briefly. For one thing, the material world is then seen to be but one among other objects of our consciousness. Moreover, one becomes aware of the crucially important fact that it is an object postulated rather than strictly given. What this means may be made clearer by an example. Suppose that, perhaps in a restaurant we visit for the first time, an entire wall is occupied by a large mirror and we look into it without realizing that it is a mirror. We then perceive, in the part of space beyond it, various material objects, notwithstanding that in fact they have no existence there at all. A certain set of the vivid color images which we call visual sensations was all that was strictly given to us, and these we construed, automatically and instantaneously, but nonetheless erroneously, as signs or appearances of the existence of certain material objects at a certain place.

Again, and similarly, we perceive in our dreams various objects which at the time we take as physical but which eventually we come to believe were not so. And this eventual conclusion, let it be noted, is forced upon us not because we then detect that something, called "physical substance," was lacking in those objects, but only because we notice, as we did not at the time, that

their behavior was erratic—incoherent with their ordinary one. That is, their appearance was a *mere* appearance, deceptive in the sense that it did not then predict truly, as ordinarily it does, their later appearances. This, it is important to notice, is the *only* way in which we ever discover that an object we perceive was not really physical, or was not the particular sort of physical object we judged it to be.

These two examples illustrate the fact that our perception of physical objects is sometimes erroneous. But the essential point is that, even when it is veridical [genuine] instead of erroneous, *all* that is literally and directly given to our minds is still only *some set of sensations*. These, on a given occasion, may be only color sensations; but they often include also tactual sensations, sounds, odors, and so on. It is especially interesting, however, to remark here in passing that, with respect to almost all the many thousands of persons and other "physical" objects we have perceived in a lifetime, *vivid color images* were the only data our perceiving strictly had to go by; so that, if the truth should happen to have been that those objects, like ghosts or images in a mirror, were actually intangible—that is, were *only* color images—we should never have discovered that this was the fact. For all we *directly* know, it *may* have been the fact!

To perceive a physical object, then, instead of merely experiencing passively certain sensations (something which perhaps hardly ever occurs) is always to *interpret,* that is to *construe* given sensations as signs of, and appearances to us of, a postulated something other than themselves, which we believe is causing them in us and is capable of causing in us others of specific kinds. We believe this because we believe that our sensations too must have some cause, and we find none for them among our other mental states.

Such a postulated extramental something we call a physical object. We say that we observe physical objects, and this is true. But it is important for the present purpose to be clear that we "observe" them never in any more direct or literal manner than is constituted by the process of interpretive postulation just described—never, for example, in the wholly direct and literal manner in which we are able to observe our sensations themselves and our other mental states.

DISCUSSION QUESTIONS

1. Imagine you are Clarence Darrow, and Ducasse has just presented a case in defense of the possibility of life after death. How would you respond directly to his case? In the end, who do you think would be able to present the stronger case, and why?

2. Ducasse presents some "well-authenticated cases" of "apparitions." What is an apparition? What would constitute, in your opinion, a well-authenticated case of the appearance of an apparition? Does the existence of apparitions prove to you the survival of consciousness after death? Why or why not?

3. Ducasse says that arguments against survival after death tacitly assume that "to be real is to be material." Do you agree with him?

4. Why does Ducasse believe that there is no factual basis to the claim that consciousness or mental processes *depend* on physical or bodily processes? Is his argument valid and sound? Why or why not?

5. Ducasse's argument in favor of the possibility of survival after death has four parts: (1) the weakness of arguments against the possibility of survival, (2) the fact of cases of "apparitions," (3) rejection of the assumption that "to be real is to be material," and (4) recognition of the ways in which the material world is but one object of many in our consciousness. Which of these four parts do you have the most difficulty with? Which the least difficulty? If all were true, would you therefore acknowledge the possibility of survival after death?

What Dreams May Come
[USA 1998] 1 hour, 53 minutes
Directed by Vincent Ward

D r. Chris Neilsen (Robin Williams) meets Annie Collins (Annabella Sciorra) when their boats collide on a lake in Switzerland. They fall deeply in love, marry, and have two children, Maria (Jessica Brooks Grant) and Ian (Josh Paddock). After their two children are killed in a car accident, Annie attempts suicide and has to be institutionalized. Eventually, she regains her life through therapy and Chris's love for and devotion to her. However, four years after the death of her children, her husband is also killed in an automobile accident. This event causes Annie to again attempt to take her life; this time, she is successful.

When Chris dies, we follow him into the afterlife. A soon as he dies, he is met by another deceased person, Albert Lewis (Cuba Gooding Jr.), who has come to assist him in adjusting to the afterlife. Albert was the first doctor that Chris interned under, and someone he admired and respected.

At first, Chris remains earthbound, clinging to Annie, promising to never leave her. He even manages to control Annie from the afterlife by getting her to write some words on paper that he is directly communicating to her. Eventually, however, following the advice of Albert, Chris lets go of Annie and soon finds himself in "heaven," a place that turns out to be whatever one wishes it to be. In the afterlife, thought is real and the physical is an illusion, and so Chris chooses to see the afterlife as a series of paintings by the masters. So, for example, one of the earliest places that he occupies in the nonearthly afterlife is a van Gogh painting. He walks through the "reality" of this van Gogh painting and finds that everything in it is composed entirely of paint.

The first familiar being he runs into in the afterlife aside from Arthur is his dog, and he fears that he may be in "dog heaven." However, a confrontation with his daughter, Maria, ends this fear. She appears to him in the form of an Asian airline stewardess, but after talking with her for a while, he realizes that she really is his daughter. She chose this form in which to appear to her father because she remembered how pleasing the stewardess was to his father on a family vacation, and Maria wants to be just as pleasing to him.

Chris is adjusting well to his afterlife existence until he learns that his wife has just committed suicide and that it will impossible for her to join him in "heaven." He decides to journey to "hell" to rescue her from the suicides—a supposedly impossible task. Arthur says that they will need a "Tracker" to locate her, and one is found and joins them in their quest for Annie. On the way to locate Annie, Chris discovers that Arthur is really his son, Ian, and that his "Tracker" (Max von Sydow) is really Arthur.

When Chris locates Annie, he is unable to convince her of his real identity, and so he decides to stay with her in "hell" rather than go back without her. However, she quickly realizes that the person before her is indeed Chris, and we soon see them both living in their mutually cherished painting of "heaven" with their children. Nevertheless, this is not enough for them—they long for the opportunity to find each other all over again, and they discuss being reborn (or reincarnated). Against Annie's worry that they might not find each other in the next go-round on earth, Chris remarks, "I found you in hell. Don't you think I could find you in Jersey?"

The film closes with Chris and Annie having decided to leave the afterlife, opting instead to be reincarnated. They appear in the final scene reincarnated as young children sharing a sandwich on a dock in New Jersey.

What Dreams May Come is an adaptation of a 1984 novel by Richard Matheson that recalls both the Greek mythological story of Orpheus and Euridice and the great medieval poem by Dante, *The Divine Comedy*.

DISCUSSION QUESTIONS

1. What philosophical presuppositions about immortality does *What Dreams May Come* require? Do you agree with them? Why or why not?

2. C. J. Ducasse argues that life after death is logically possible. Is the account of life after death in *What Dreams May Come* logically possible? Why or why not?

3. According to this film, one may choose to be "reborn," that is, go back to live on earth in another body. Otherwise, one remains in the afterlife. According to this film, then, what is the meaning of "death"?

4. In the afterlife, Chris is able to "communicate" words to Annie, which she then writes down. The film sets this up as possible only because Chris and Annie are "soul mates." What argument for this is given? Do you think it is a good one? Why is this kind of communication not possible between people who are not "soul mates"?

5. Albert says to Chris that "'here' is big enough for everyone to have their own private universe." Discuss the philosophical implications of this statement. Do you agree with them?

6. Chris says, "A whole human life is just a heartbeat here in Heaven. Then we'll all be together forever." What does he mean by this? Discuss.

7. Consider the following conversation between Albert and Chris:

   ALBERT   "So what is the 'me'?"

   CHRIS   "My brain I suppose."

ALBERT   "Your brain? Your brain is a body part. Like your fingernail or your heart. Why is that the part that's you?"

CHRIS   "Because I have sort of a voice in my head, the part of me that thinks, that feels, that is aware that I exist at all."

ALBERT   "So if you're aware you exist, then you do. That's why you're still here."

According to this film, what are we in the afterlife, that is, what is "me"? Does this position make philosophical sense? Why or why not?

8. Discuss the claim made in this film that "thought is real; physical is the illusion." (You may want to compare this position with two from chapter 2—those of George Berkeley and Jorge Luis Borges.)

9. In this film, the suicides are forever wrapped in their own self-absorption. The Tracker says that Chris will be in danger of losing his mind if he spends too much time with a suicide. Why? Does Chris lose his mind? Why or why not?

10. Consider this exchange between Chris and the Tracker:

TRACKER   "Your wife love you as strong? We'll find her. But when we find her nothing will make her recognize you. Nothing will break her denial. It's stronger than her love. In fact, reinforced by her love. You can say everything you long to say, including good-bye. Even if she can't understand it. And you'll have the satisfaction that you didn't give up. That has to be enough."

CHRIS   "You just get me there, I'll decide what's enough."

What does Chris eventually decide is "enough"? If you were Chris, would you have attempted to rescue Annie? Why or why not?

11. Discuss Annie's explanation to Marie as to why she must have their family dog euthanized, and Marie's response. Would you explain the euthanasia of a family pet to your children in the same way? Why or why not?

12. If Chris creates reality through his mind, and he can create anything he wants, why doesn't he simply create the thing he desires most, namely, Annie? What would be the difference between Chris's "thought-created" Annie and the "real" Annie? Discuss.

JUDITH JARVIS THOMSON

A DEFENSE OF ABORTION

In "A Defense of Abortion," Judith Jarvis Thomson assumes, for the sake of argument, that a fetus is a person from conception. Through a series of imaginative scenarios—the most memorable of which concerns being plugged into a famous violinist—Thomson argues that the mother's right to control her own body and her right to self-defense are strong enough to outweigh the fetus's right to life. For Thomson, abortion is morally justifiable in cases in which rape was involved, the mother's life is threatened, or reasonable precautions were taken to avoid pregnancy.

In general, pregnancy is the state of a woman's body wherein a fetus develops over time in her uterus, and abortion is the termination of a pregnancy. For some, the death of a newly fertilized human egg is not the same as the death of a person. However, for others, it is. As such, the abortion debate involves questions concerning the meaning of death—as well as questions regarding the meaning of life.

There is much debate over the conditions in which, if any, abortion is morally justifiable. For example, is abortion morally justifiable when the mother's life is in danger? In cases of rape or incest? Is it allowable to have an abortion when there is deformity in or damage to the fetus? Or when the fetus poses a challenge to the parents' financial well-being? These are all reasons why women have had abortions. They are also reasons why abortion has been challenged.

The contemporary American legal system protects a woman's right to have an abortion. This right stems from the constitutional protections of individual privacy. Although the Bill of Rights (see chapter 5) does not explicitly mention privacy, *Griswold v. Connecticut* (1965) set the precedent that privacy is one of the rights of the people protected by the Ninth Amendment. In *Griswold v. Connecticut*, the Supreme Court said that it is a constitutional violation of our right to sexual privacy within marriage for Connecticut law to limit information about birth control to married couples. In 1973, in *Roe v. Wade*, the Supreme Court guaranteed abortion as fundamental to an individual woman's right to privacy; that is, the right to decide whether to bear children is protected by the Ninth through the Fourteenth Amendments; however, the right to terminate is not absolute. The state may limit a woman's right to terminate if it has a legitimate interest in safeguarding the woman's health, in maintaining medical standards, or in protecting human life.

Judith Jarvis Thomson (1929–) has been a philosophy professor at the Massachusetts Institute of Technology since 1964. She received her B.A. from Barnard College in 1950, her M.A. from Cambridge University in 1956, and her Ph.D. from Columbia University in 1959. She taught at Barnard College from 1955 to 1962, and then for one year at Boston University. In 1992, she was president of the Eastern Division of the American Philosophical Association, and in 1999, she gave the Tanner Lectures at Princeton University. Thomson is the author of *Ethics* (co-edited with Gerald Dworkin, 1968), *Acts and Other Events* (1977), *Rights, Restitution and Risk* (1986), *On Being and Saying: Essays for Richard Cartwright* (ed., 1987), *The Realm of Rights* (1990), and *Moral Relativism and Moral Objectivity* (with Gilbert Harman, 1996). This article was first published in 1971, two years before *Roe v. Wade*, and has become a classic in the abortion debate.

Most opposition to abortion relies on the premise that the fetus is a human being, a person, from the moment of conception. The premise is argued for, but, as I think, not well. Take, for example, the most common argument. We are asked to notice that the development of a human being from conception through birth into childhood is continuous; then it is said that to draw a line, to choose a point in this development and say "before this point the thing is not a person, after this point it is a person" is to make an arbitrary choice, a choice for which in the nature of things no good reason can be given. It is concluded that the fetus is, or anyway that we had better say it is, a person from the moment of conception. But this conclusion does not follow. Similar things might be said about the development of an acorn into an oak tree, and it does not follow that acorns are oak trees, or that we had better say they are. Arguments of this form are sometimes called "slippery slope arguments"—the phrase is perhaps self-explanatory—and it is dismaying that opponents of abortion rely on them so heavily and uncritically.

I am inclined to agree, however, that the prospects for "drawing a line" in the development of the fetus look dim. I am inclined to think also that we shall probably have to agree that the fetus has already become a human person well before birth. Indeed, it comes as a surprise when one first learns how early in its life it begins to acquire human chartacteristics. By the tenth week, for example, it already has a face, arms and legs, fingers and toes; it has internal organs, and brain activity is detectable. On the other hand, I think that the premise is false, that the fetus is not a person from the moment of conception. A newly fertilized ovum, a newly implanted clump of cells, is no more a person than an acorn is an oak tree. But I shall not discuss any of this. For it seems to me to be of great interest to ask what happens if, for the sake of argument, we allow the premise. How, precisely, are we supposed to get from there to the conclusion that abortion is morally impermissible? Opponents of abortion commonly spend most of their time establishing that the fetus is a person, and hardly any time explaining the step from there to the impermissibility of abortion. Perhaps they think the step too simple and obvious to require much comment. Or perhaps instead they are simply being economical in argument. Many of those who defend abortion rely on the premise that the fetus is not a person, but only a bit of tissue that will become a person at birth; and why pay out more arguments than you have to? Whatever the explanation, I suggest that the step they take is neither easy nor obvious, that it calls for closer examination than it is commonly given, and that when we do give it this closer examination we shall feel inclined to reject it.

I propose, then, that we grant that the fetus is a person from the moment of conception. How does the argument go from here? Something like this, I take it. Every person has a right to life. So the fetus has a right to life. No doubt the mother has a right to decide what shall happen in and to her body; everyone would grant that. But surely a person's right to life is stronger and more stringent than the mother's right to decide what happens in and to her body, and so outweighs it. So the fetus may not be killed; an abortion may not be performed.

It sounds plausible. But now let me ask you to imagine this. You wake up in the morning and find yourself back to back in bed with an unconscious violinist. A famous unconscious violinist. He has been found to have a fatal kidney ailment, and the Society of Music Lovers has canvassed all the available medical records and found that you alone have the right blood type to help. They have therefore kidnapped you, and last night the violinist's circulatory system was plugged into yours, so that your kidneys can be used to extract poisons from his blood as well as your own. The director of the hospital now tells you, "Look, we're sorry the Society of Music Lovers did this to you—we would never have permitted it if we had known. But still, they did it, and the violinist now is plugged into you. To unplug you would be to kill him. But never mind, it's only for nine months. By then he will have recovered from his ailment, and can safely be unplugged from you." Is it morally incumbent on you to accede to this situation? No doubt it would be very nice of you if you did, a great kindness. But do you *have* to accede to it? What if it were not nine months, but nine years? Or longer still? What if the director of the hospital says; "Tough luck, I agree, but you've now got to stay in bed, with the violinists plugged into you, for the rest of your life. Because remember this. All persons have a right to life, and violinists are persons. Granted you have a right to decide what happens in and to your body, but a person's right to life outweighs your right to decide what happens in and to your body. So you cannot ever be unplugged from him." I imagine you would regard this as outrageous, which suggests that something really is wrong with that plausible- sounding argument I mentioned a moment ago.

In this case, of course, you were kidnapped; you didn't volunteer for the operation that plugged the violinist into your kidneys. Can those who oppose abortion on the ground I mentioned make an exception for a pregnancy due to rape? Certainly. They can say that persons have a right to life only if they didn't come into existence because of rape; or they can say that all persons have a right to life, but that some have less of a right to life than others, in particular, that those who came into existence because of rape have less. But these statements have a rather unpleasant sound. Surely the question of whether you have a right to life at all, or how much of it you have, shouldn't turn on the question of whether or not you are the product of a rape. And in fact the people who oppose abortion on the ground I mentioned do not make this distinction, and hence do not make an exception in case of rape.

Nor do they make an exception for a case in which the mother has to spend the nine months of her pregnancy in bed. They would agree that would be a great pity, and hard on the mother; but all the same, all persons have a right to life, the fetus is a person, and so on. I suspect, in fact, that they would not make an exception for a case in which, miraculously enough, the pregnancy went on for nine years, or even the rest of the mother's life.

Some won't even make an exception for a case in which continuation of the pregnancy is likely to shorten the mother's life; they regard abortion as impermissible even to save the mother's life. Such cases are nowadays very rare, and many opponents of abortion do not accept this extreme view. All the same, it is a good place to begin: a number of points of interest come out in respect to it.

1. Let us call the view that abortion is impermissible even to save the mother's life "the extreme view." I want to suggest first that it does not issue from the argument I mentioned earlier without the addition of some fairly powerful premises. Suppose a woman has become pregnant, and now learns that she has a cardiac condition such that she will die if she carries the baby to term. What may be done for her? The fetus, being a person, has a right to life, but as the mother is a person too, so has she a right to life. Presumably they have an equal right to life. How is it supposed to come out that an abortion may not be performed? If mother and child have an equal right to life, shouldn't we perhaps flip a coin? Or should we add to the mother's right to life her right to decide what happens in and to her body, which everybody seems to be ready to grant—the sum of her rights now outweighing the fetus's right to life?

The most familiar argument here is the following. We are told that performing the abortion would be directly killing the child, whereas doing nothing would not be killing the mother, but only letting her die. Moreover, in killing the child, one would be killing an innocent person, for the child has committed no crime, and is not aiming at his mother's death. And then there are a variety of ways in which this might be continued. (1) But as directly killing an innocent person is always and absolutely impermissible, an abortion may not be performed. Or, (2) as directly killing an innocent person is murder, and murder is always and absolutely impermissible, an abortion may not be performed. Or, (3) as one's duty to refrain from directly killing an innocent person is more stringent than one's duty to keep a person from dying, an abortion may not be performed. Or, (4) if one's only options are directly killing an innocent person or letting a person die, one must prefer letting the person die, and thus an abortion may not be performed.

Some people seem to have thought that these are not further premises which must be added if the conclusion is to be reached, but that they follow from the very fact that an innocent person has a right to life. But this seems to me to be a mistake, and perhaps the simplest way to show this is to bring out that while we must certainly grant that innocent persons have a right to life, the theses in (1) through (4) are all false. Take (2), for example. If directly killing an innocent person is murder, and thus is impermissible, then the mother's directly killing the innocent person inside her is murder, and thus is impermissible. But it cannot seriously be thought to be murder if the mother performs an abortion on herself to save her life. It cannot seriously be said that she *must* refrain, that she *must* sit passively by and wait for her death. Let us look again at the case of you and the violinist. There you are, in bed with the violinist, and the director of the hospital says to you, "It's all most distressing, and I deeply sympathize, but you see this is putting an additional strain on your kidneys, and you'll be dead within the month. But you *have* to stay where you are all the same. Because unplugging you would be directly killing an innocent violinist, and that's murder, and that's impermissible." If anything in the world is true, it is that you do not commit murder, you do not do what is impermissible, if you reach around to your back and unplug yourself from that violinist to save your life.

The main focus of attention in writings on abortion has been on what a third party may or may not do in answer to a request from a woman for an abortion. This is in a way understandable. Things being as they are, there isn't much a woman can safely do to abort herself. So the question asked is what a third party may do, and what the mother may do, if it is mentioned at all, is deduced, almost as an afterthought, from what it is concluded that third parties may do. But it seems to me that to treat the matter in this way is to refuse to grant to the mother that very status of person which is so firmly insisted on for the fetus. For we cannot simply read off what a person may do from what a third party may do. Suppose you find yourself trapped in a tiny house with a growing child. I mean a very tiny house, and a rapidly growing child—you are already up against the wall of the house and in a few minutes you'll be crushed to death. The child on the other hand won't be crushed to death; if nothing is done to stop him from growing he'll be hurt, but in the end he'll simply burst open the house and walk out a free man. Now I could well understand it if a bystander were to say, "There's nothing we can do for you. We cannot choose between your life and his, we cannot be the ones to decide who is to live, we cannot intervene." But it cannot be concluded that you too can do nothing, that you cannot attack it to save your life. However innocent the child may be, you do not have to wait passively while it crushes you to death. Perhaps a pregnant woman is vaguely felt to have the status of house, to which we don't allow the right of self-defense. But if the woman houses the child, it should be remembered that she is a person who houses it.

I should perhaps stop to say explicitly that I am not claiming that people have a right to do anything whatever to save their lives. I think, rather, that there are drastic limits to the right of self-defense. If someone threatens you with death unless you torture someone else to death, I think you have not the right, even to save your life, to do so. But the case under consideration here is very different. In our case there are only two people involved, one whose life is threatened, and one who threatens it. Both are innocent: the one who is threatened is not threatened because of any fault, the one who threatens does not threaten because of any fault. For this reason we may feel that we bystanders cannot intervene. But the person threatened can.

In sum, a woman surely can defend her life against the threat to it posed by the unborn child, even if doing so involves its death. And this shows not merely that the theses in (1) through (4) are false; it shows also that the extreme view of abortion is false, and so we need not canvass any other possible ways of arriving at it from the argument I mentioned at the outset.

2. The extreme view could of course be weakened to say that while abortion is permissible to save the mother's life, it may not be performed by a third party, but only by the mother herself. But this cannot be right either. For what we have to keep in mind is that the mother and the unborn child are not like two tenants in a small house which has, by an unfortunate mistake, been rented to both: the mother *owns* the house. The fact that she does adds to the offensiveness of deducing that the mother can do nothing from the supposition that third parties can do nothing. But it does more than this: it casts a bright light on the supposition that third parties can do nothing. Certainly it lets us see that a third party who says "I cannot choose between you" is fooling himself if he thinks this is impartiality. If Jones has found and fastened on a certain coat, which he needs to keep him from freezing, but which Smith also needs to keep him from freezing, then it is not impartiality that says "I cannot choose between you" when Smith owns the coat. Women have said again and again "This body is *my* body!" and they have reason to feel angry, reason to feel that it has been like shouting into the wind. Smith, after all, is hardly likely to bless us if we say to him, "Of course it's your coat, anybody would grant that it is. But no one may choose between you and Jones who is to have it."

We should really ask what it is that says "no one may choose" in the face of the fact that the body that houses the child is the mother's body. It may be simply a failure to appreciate this fact. But it may be something more interesting, namely, the sense that one has a right to refuse to lay hands on people, even where it would be just and fair to do so, even where justice seems to require that somebody do so. This justice might call for somebody to get Smith's coat back from Jones and yet you have a right to refuse to be the one to lay hands on Jones, a right to refuse to do physical violence to him. This, I think, must be granted. But then what should be said is not "no one may choose," but only "*I* cannot choose," and indeed not even this, but *I will not act*" leaving it open that somebody else can or should, and in particular that anyone in a position of authority, with the job of securing people's rights, both can and should. So this is no difficulty. I have not been arguing that any given third party must accede to the mother's request that he perform an abortion to save her life, but only that he may.

I suppose that in some views of human life the mother's body is only on loan to her, the loan not being one which gives her any prior claim to it. One who held this view might well think it impartiality to say "I cannot choose." But I shall simply ignore this possibility. My own view is that if a human being has any just, prior claim to anything at all, he has a just, prior claim to his own body. And perhaps this needn't be argued for here anyway, since, as I mentioned, the arguments against abortion we are looking at do grant that the woman has a right to decide what happens in and to her body.

But although they do grant it, I have tried to show that they do not take seriously what is done in granting it. I suggest the same thing will reappear even more clearly when we turn away from cases in which the mother's life is at stake, and attend, as I propose we now do, to the vastly more common cases in which a woman wants an abortion for some less weighty reason than preserving her own life.

3. Where the mother's life is not at stake, the argument I mentioned at the outset seems to have a much stronger pull. "Everyone has a right to life, so the unborn person has a right to life." And isn't the child's right to life weightier than anything other than the mother's own right to life, which she might put forward as ground for an abortion?

This argument treats the right to life as if it were unproblematic. It is not, and this seems to me to be precisely the source of the mistake.

For we should now, at long last, ask what it comes to, to have a right to life. In some views, having a right to life includes having a right to be given at least the bare minimum one needs for continued life. But suppose that what in fact *is* the bare minimum a man needs for continued life is something he has no right at all to be given? If I am sick unto death, and the only thing that will save my life is the touch of Henry Fonda's cool hand on my fevered brow, then all the same, I have no right to be given the touch of Henry Fonda's cool hand on my fevered brow. It would be frightfully nice of him to fly in from the West Coast to provide it. It would be less nice, though no doubt well meant, if my friends flew out to the West Coast and carried Henry Fonda back with them. But I have no right at all against anybody that he should do this for me. Or again, to return to the story I told earlier, the fact that for continued life that violinist needs the continued use of your kidneys does not establish

that he has a right to be given the continued use of your kidneys. He certainly has no right against you that *you* should give him continued use of your kidneys. For nobody has any right to use your kidneys unless you give him such a right; and nobody has the right against you that you shall give him this right—if you do allow him to go on using your kidneys, this is a kindness on your part, and not something he can claim from you as his due. Nor has he any right against anybody else that *they* should give him continued use of your kidneys. Certainly he had no right against the Society of Music Lovers that they should plug him into you in the first place. And if you now start to unplug yourself, having learned that you will otherwise have to spend nine years in bed with him, there is nobody in the world who must try to prevent you, in order to see to it that he is given something he has a right to be given.

Some people are rather stricter about the right to life. In their views, it does not include the right to be given anything, but amounts to, and only to, the right not so be killed by anybody. But here a related difficulty arises. If everybody is to refrain from killing that violinist, then everybody must refrain from doing a great many different sorts of things. Everybody must refrain from slitting his throat, everybody must refrain from shooting him—and everybody must refrain from unplugging you from him. But does he have a right against everybody that they shall refrain from unplugging you from him? To refrain from doing this is to allow him to continue to use your kidneys. It could be argued that he has a right against us that *we* should allow him to continue so use your kidneys. That is, while he had no right against us that we should give him the use of your kidneys, it might be argued that he anyway has a right against us that we shall not now intervene and deprive him of the use of your kidneys. I shall come back to third-party interventions later. But certainly the violinist has no right against you that *you* shall allow him to continue to use your kidneys. As I said, if you do allow him to use them, it is a kindness on your part, and not something you owe him.

The difficulty I point to here is not peculiar to the right to life. It reappears in connection with all the other natural rights; and it is something which an adequate account of rights must deal with. For present purposes it is enough just to draw attention to it. But I would stress that I am not arguing that people do not have a right to life—quite to the contrary, it seems to me that the primary control we must place on the acceptability of an account of rights is that it should turn out in that account to be a truth that all persons have a right to life. I am arguing only that having a right to life does not guarantee having either a right to be given the use of or a right to be allowed continued use of another person's body—even if one needs it for life itself. So the right to life will not serve the opponents of abortion in the very simple and clear way in which they seem to have thought it would.

4. There is another way to bring out the difficulty. In the most ordinary sort of case, to deprive someone of what he has a right to is to treat him unjustly. Suppose a boy and his small brother are jointly given a box of chocolates for Christmas. If the older boy takes the box and refuses to give his brother any of the chocolates, he is unjust to him, for the brother has been given a right to half of them. But suppose that, having learned that otherwise it means nine years in bed with that violinist, you unplug yourself from him. You surely are not being unjust to him, for you gave him no right to use your kidneys, and no one else can have given him any such right. But we have to notice that in unplugging yourself, you are killing him; and violinists, like everybody else, have a right to life, and thus in the view we were considering just now, the right not to be killed. So here you do what he supposedly has a right you shall not do, but you do not act unjustly to him in doing it.

The emendation which may be made at this point is this: the right to life consists not in the right not to be killed, but rather in the right not to be killed unjustly. This runs a risk of circularity, but never mind: it would enable us to square the fact that the violinist has a right to life with the fact that you do not act unjustly toward him in unplugging yourself, thereby killing him. For if you do not kill him unjustly, you do not violate his right to life, and so it is no wonder you do him no injustice.

But if this emendation is accepted, the gap in the argument against abortion stares us plainly in the face: it is by no means enough to show that the fetus is a person, and to remind us that all persons have a right to life—we need to be shown also that killing the fetus violates its right so life, i.e., that abortion is unjust killing. And is it?

I suppose we may take it as a datum that in a case of pregnancy due to rape the mother has not given the unborn person a right to the use of her body for food and shelter. Indeed, in what pregnancy could it be supposed that the mother has given the unborn person such a right? It is not as if there were unborn persons drifting about the world, to whom a woman who wants a child says "I invite you in."

But it might be argued that there are other ways one can have acquired a right to the use of another person's body than by having been invited to use it by that person. Suppose a woman voluntarily indulges in intercourse, knowing of the chance it will issue in pregnancy, and then she does become pregnant; is she not in part responsible for the presence, in fact the very existence, of the unborn person inside her? No doubt she did not invite it in. But doesn't her partial responsibility for its being there itself give it a right to the use of her body? If so, then her aborting it would be more like the boy's taking away the chocolates, and less like your unplugging yourself from the violinist—doing so would be depriving it of what it does have a right to, and thus would be doing it an injustice.

And then, too, it might be asked whether or not she can kill it even to save her own life: If she voluntarily called it into existence, how can she now kill it, even in self-defense?

The first thing to be said about this is that it is something new. Opponents of abortion have been so concerned to make out the independence of the fetus, in order to establish that it has a right to life, just as its mother does, that they have tended to overlook the possible support they might gain from making out that the fetus is *dependent* on the mother, in order to establish that she has a special kind of responsibility for it, a responsibility that gives it rights against her which are not possessed by any independent person—such as an ailing violinist who is a stranger to her.

On the other hand, this argument would give the unborn person a right to its mother's body only if her pregnancy resulted from a voluntary act, undertaken in full knowledge of the chance a pregnancy might result from it. It would leave out entirely the unborn person whose existence is due to rape. Pending the availability of some further argument, then, we would be left with the conclusion that unborn persons whose existence is due to rape have no right to the use of their mothers' bodies, and thus that aborting them is not depriving them of anything they have a right to and hence is not unjust killing.

And we should also notice that it is not at all plain that this argument really does go even as far as it purports to. For there are cases and cases, and the details make a difference. If the room is stuffy, and I therefore open a window to air it, and a burglar climbs in, it would be absurd to say, "Ah, now he can stay, she's given him a right to the use of her house—for she is partially responsible for his presence there, having voluntarily done what enabled him to get in, in full knowledge that there are such things as burglars, and that burglars burgle." It would be still more absurd to say this if I had had bars installed outside my windows, precisely to prevent burglars from getting in, and a burglar got in only because of a defect in the bars. It remains equally absurd if we imagine it is not a burglar who climbs in, but an innocent person who blunders or falls in. Again, suppose it were like this: peopleseeds drift about in the air like pollen, and if you open your windows, one may drift in and take root in your carpets or upholstery. You don't want children, so you fix up your windows with fine mesh screens, the very best you can buy. As can happen, however, and on very, very rare occasions does happen, one of the screens is defective; and a seed drifts in and takes root. Does the person-plant who now develops have a right to the use of your house? Surely not—despite the fact that you voluntarily opened your windows, you knowingly kept carpets and upholstered furniture, and you knew that screens were sometimes defective. Someone may argue that you are responsible for its rooting, that it does have a right to your house, because after all you *could* have lived out your life with bare floors and furniture, or with sealed windows and doors. But this won't do—for by the same token anyone can avoid a pregnancy due to rape by having a hysterectomy, or anyway by never leaving home without a (reliable!) army.

It seems to me that the argument we are looking at can establish as most that there are *some* cases in which the unborn person has a right to the use of its mother's body, and therefore *some*

cases in which abortion is unjust killing. There is room for much discussion and argument as to precisely which, if any. But I think we should sidestep this issue and leave it open, for at any rate the argument certainly does not establish that all abortion is unjust killing.

5. There is room for yet another argument here, however. We surely must all grant that there may be cases in which it would be morally indecent to detach a person from your body at the cost of his life. Suppose you learn that what the violinist needs is not nine years of your life, but only one hour: all you need do to save his life is to spend one hour in that bed with him. Suppose also that letting him use your kidneys for that one hour would not affect your health in the slightest. Admittedly you were kidnapped. Admittedly you did not give anyone permission to plug him into you. Nevertheless it seems to me plain you ought to allow him to use your kidneys for that hour—it would be indecent to refuse.

Again, suppose pregnancy lasted only an hour, and constituted no threat to life or health. And suppose that a woman becomes pregnant as a result of rape. Admittedly she did not voluntarily do anything to bring about the existence of a child. Admittedly she did nothing at all which would give the unborn person a right to the use of her body. All the same it might well be said, as in the newly emended violinist story, that she *ought* to allow it to remain for that hour—that it would be indecent in her to refuse.

Now some people are inclined to use the term "right" in such a way that it follows from the fact that you ought to allow a person to use your body for the hour he needs, that he has a right to use your body for the hour he needs, even though he has not been given that right by any person or act. They may say that it follows also that if you refuse, you act unjustly toward him. This use of the term is perhaps so common that it cannot be called wrong; nevertheless it seems to me to be an unfortunate loosening of what we would do better to keep a tight rein on. Suppose that box of chocolates I mentioned earlier had not been given to both boys jointly, but was given only to the older boy. There he sits, stolidly eating his way through the box, his small brother watching enviously. Here we are likely to say "You ought not to be so mean. You ought to give your brother some of those chocolates." My own view is that it just does not follow from the truth of this that the brother has any right to any of the chocolates. If the boy refuses to give his brother any, he is greedy, stingy, callous—but not unjust. I suppose that the people I have in mind will say it does follow that the brother has a right to some of the chocolates, and thus that the boy does act unjustly if he refuses to give his brother any. But the effect of saying this is to obscure what we should keep distinct, namely, the difference between the boy's refusal in this case and the boy's refusal in the earlier case, in which the box was given to both boys jointly, and in which the small brother thus had what was from any point of view clear title to half.

A further objection to so using the term "right" that from the fact that A ought to do a thing for B, it follows that B has a right against A that A do it for him, is that it is going to make the question of whether or not a man has a right to a thing turn on how easy it is to provide him with it; and this seems not merely unfortunate, but morally unacceptable. Take the case of Henry Fonda again. I said earlier that I had no right to the touch of his cool hand on my fevered brow, even though I needed it to save my life. I said it would be frightfully nice of him to fly in from the West Coast to provide me with it, but that I had no right against him that he should do so. But suppose he isn't on the West Coast. Suppose he has only to walk across the room, place a hand briefly on my brow—and lo, my life is saved. Then surely he ought to do it, it would be indecent to refuse. Is it to be said "Ah, well, it follows that in this case she has a right to the touch of his hand on her brow, and so it would be an injustice in him to refuse"? So that I have a right to it when it is easy for him to provide it, though no right when it's hard? It's rather a shocking idea that anyone's rights should fade away and disappear as is gets harder and harder so accord them to him.

So my own view is that even though you ought to let the violinist use your kidneys for the one hour he needs, we should not conclude that he has a right to do so—we should say that if you refuse, you are, like the boy who owns all the chocolates and will give none away, self-centered and callous, indecent in fact, but not unjust. And similarly, that even supposing a case in which a woman pregnant

due to rape ought to allow the unborn person to use her body for the hour he needs, we should not conclude that he has a right to do so; we should conclude that she is self-centered, callous, indecent, but not unjust, if she refuses. The complaints are no less grave; they are just different. However, there is no need to insist on this point. If anyone does wish to deduce "he has a right" from "you ought," then all the same he must surely grant that there are cases in which it is not morally required of you that you allow that violinist to use your kidneys, and in which he does not have a right to use them, and in which you do not do him an injustice if you refuse. And so also for mother and unborn child. Except in such cases as the unborn person has a right to demand it— and we were leaving open the possibility that there may be such cases—nobody is morally *required* to make large sacrifices, of health, of all other interests and concerns, of all other duties and commitments, for nine years, or even for nine months, in order to keep another person alive.

6. We have in fact to distinguish between two kinds of Samaritan: the Good Samaritan and what we might call the Minimally Decent Samaritan. The story of the Good Samaritan, you will remember, goes like this:

> A certain man went down from Jerusalem to Jericho, and fell among thieves, which stripped him of his raiment, and wounded him, and departed, leaving him half dead.
>
> And by chance there came down a certain priest that way; and when he saw him, he passed by on the other side.
>
> And likewise a Levite, when he was at the place, came and looked on him, and passed by on the other side.
>
> But a certain Samaritan, as he journeyed, came where he was; and when he saw him he had compassion on him.
>
> And went to him, and bound up his wounds, pouring in oil and wine, and set him on his own beast, and brought him to an inn, and took care of him.
>
> And on the morrow, when he departed, he took out two pence, and gave them to the host, and said unto him, "Take care of him; and whatsoever thou spendest more, when I come again, I will repay thee." (Luke 10:30–35)

The Good Samaritan went out of his way, at some cost to himself, to help one in need of it. We are not told what the options were, that is, whether or not the priest and the Levite could have helped by doing less than the Good Samaritan did, but assuming they could have, then the fact they did nothing at all shows they were not even Minimally Decent Samaritans, not because they were not Samaritans, but because they were not even minimally decent.

These things are a matter of degree, of course, but there is a difference; and it comes out perhaps most clearly in the story of Kitty Genovese, who, as you will remember, was murdered [in New York City in the 1960s] while thirty-eight people watched or listened, and did nothing at all to help her. A Good Samaritan would have rushed out to give direct assistance against the murderer. Or perhaps we had better allow that it would have been a Splendid Samaritan who did this, on the ground that it would have involved a risk of death for himself. But the thirty-eight not only did not do this, they did not even trouble to pick up a phone to call the police. Minimally Decent Samaritanism would call for doing at least that, and their not having done it was monstrous.

After telling the story of the Good Samaritan, Jesus said "Go, and do thou likewise." Perhaps he meant that we are morally required to act as the Good Samaritan did. Perhaps he was urging people to do more than is morally required of them. At all events it seems plain that is was not morally required of any of the thirty-eight that he rush out to give direct assistance at the risk of his own life, and that it is not morally required of anyone that he give long stretches of his life—nine years or nine months—to sustaining the life of a person who has no special right (we were leaving open the possibility of this) to demand it.

Indeed, with one rather striking class of exceptions, no one in any country in the world is *legally* required to do anywhere near as much as this for anyone else. The class of exceptions is obvious. My main concern here is not the state of the law in respect to abortion, but it is worth drawing attention to the fact that in no state in this country is any man compelled by law to be even a Minimally Decent Samaritan to any person; there is no law under which charges could be brought against the thirty-eight who stood by while Kitty Genovese died. By contrast, in most states in this country women are compelled by law to be not merely Minimally Decent Samaritans, but Good Samaritans to unborn persons inside them. This doesn't by itself settle anything one way or the other, because it may well be argued that there should be laws in this country—as there are in many European countries—compelling at least Minimally Decent Samaritanism. But it does show that there is a gross injustice in the existing state of the law. And it shows also that the groups currently working against liberalization of abortion laws, in fact working toward having it declared unconstitutional for a state to permit abortion, had better start working for the adoption of Good Samaritan laws generally, or earn the charge that they are acting in bad faith.

I should think, myself, that Minimally Decent Samaritan laws would be one thing, Good Samaritan laws quite another, and in fact highly improper. But we are not here concerned with the law. What we should ask is not whether anybody should be compelled by law to be a Good Samaritan, but whether we must accede to a situation in which somebody is being compelled—by nature, perhaps—to be a Good Samaritan. We have, in other words, to look now at third-party interventions. I have been arguing that no person is morally required to make large sacrifices to sustain the life of another who has no right to demand them, and this even where the sacrifices do not include life itself; we are not morally required to be Good Samaritans or anyway Very Good Samaritans to one another. But what if a man cannot extricate himself from such a situation? What if he appeals to us to extricate him? It seems to me plain that there are cases in which we can, cases in which a Good Samaritan would extricate him. There you are, you were kidnapped, and nine years in bed with that violinist lie ahead of you. You have your own life to lead. You are sorry, but you simply cannot see giving up so much of your life to the sustaining of his. You cannot extricate yourself, and ask us to do so. I should have thought that—in light of his having no right to the use of your body—it was obvious that we do not have to accede to your being forced to give up so much. We can do what you ask. There is no injustice to the violinist in our doing so.

7. Following the lead of the opponents of abortion, I have throughout been speaking of the

fetus merely as a person, and what I have been asking is whether or not the argument we began with, which proceeds only from the fetus's being a person, really does establish its conclusion. I have argued that it does not.

But of course there are arguments and arguments, and it may be said that I have simply fastened on the wrong one. It may be said that what is important is not merely the fact that the fetus is a person, but that it is a person for whom the woman has a special kind of responsibility issuing from the fact that she is its mother. And it might be argued that all my analogies are therefore irrelevant—for you do not have that special kind of responsibility for that violinist, Henry Fonda does not have that special kind of responsibility for me. And our attention might be drawn to the fact that men and women both *are* compelled by law to provide support for their children.

I have in effect dealt (briefly) with this argument in section 4 above; but a (still briefer) recapitulation now may be in order. Surely we do not have any such "special responsibility" for a person unless we have assumed it, explicitly or implicitly. If a set of parents do not try to prevent pregnancy, do not obtain an abortion, and then at the time of birth of the child do not put it out for adoption, but rather take it home with them, then they have assumed responsibility for it, they have given it rights, and they cannot *now* withdraw support from it at the cost of its life because they now find it difficult to go on providing for it. But if they have taken all reasonable precautions against having a child, they do not simply by virtue of their biological relationship to the child who comes into existence have a special responsibility for it. They may wish to assume responsibility for it, or they may not wish to. And I am suggesting that if assuming responsibility for it would require large sacrifices, then they may refuse. A Good Samaritan would not refuse—or anyway, a Splendid Samaritan, if the sacrifices that had to be made were enormous. But then so would a Good Samaritan assume responsibility for that violinist, so would Henry Fonda, if he is a Good Samaritan, fly in from the West Coast and assume responsibility for me.

8. My argument will be found unsatisfactory on two counts by many of those who want to regard abortion as morally permissible. First, while I do argue that abortion is not impermissible, I do not argue that it is always permissible. There may well be cases in which carrying the child to term requires only Minimally Decent Samaritanism of the mother, and this is a standard we must not fall below. I am inclined to think it a merit of my account precisely that it does *not* give a general yes or a general no. It allows for and supports our sense that, for example, a sick and desperately frightened fourteen-year-old schoolgirl, pregnant due to rape, may *of course* choose abortion, and that any law which rules this out is an insane law. And it also allows for and supports our sense that in other cases resort to abortion is even positively indecent. It would be indecent in the woman to request an abortion, and indecent in a doctor to perform it, if she is in her seventh month, and wants the abortion just to avoid the nuisance of postponing a trip abroad. The very fact that the arguments I have been drawing attention to treat all cases of abortion, or even all cases of abortion in which the mother's life is not at stake, as morally on a par ought to have made them suspect at the outset.

Secondly while I am arguing for the permissibility of abortion in some cases, I am not arguing for the right to secure the death of the unborn child. It is easy to confuse these two things in that up to a certain point in the life of the fetus it is not able to survive outside the mother's body; hence removing it from her body guarantees its death. But they are importantly different. I have argued that you are not morally required to spend nine months in bed, sustaining the life of that violinist; but to say this is by no means to say that if, when you unplug yourself, there is a miracle and he survives, you then have a right to turn round and slit his throat. You may detach yourself even if this costs him his life; you have no right to be guaranteed his death, by some other means, if unplugging yourself does not kill him. There are some people who will feel dissatisfied by this feature of my argument. A woman may be utterly devastated by the thought of a child, a bit of herself, put out for adoption and never seen or heard of again. She may therefore want not merely that the child be detached from her, but more, that it die. Some opponents of abortion are inclined to regard this as beneath contempt—thereby showing insensitivity to what is surely a powerful source of despair. All the same, I agree that the desire for the child's death is not one which anybody may gratify, should it turn out to be possible to detach the child alive.

At this place, however, it should be remembered that we have only been pretending throughout that the fetus is a human being from the moment of conception. A very early abortion is surely not the killing of a person, and so is not dealt with by anything I have said here.

DISCUSSION QUESTION

1. Is the death of a newly fertilized human egg the same as the death of a person? Why or why not?

2. Is the fetus a person for Thompson? What is the difference for Thompson between the fetus and the mother in terms of personhood? Do you agree with her? Does she have a good argument? Defend your position.

3. What is the violinist analogy? How does Thompson use it in her defense of abortion? Is it a good analogy? Can you think of a better analogy to either defend abortion or argue against it? Explain.

4. According to Thompson, we are not responsible for other people unless we voluntarily assume that responsibility. Do you agree with her? What are some of the implications of her view?

5. What is the difference between a Minimally Decent Samaritan and a Good Samaritan? How does Thompson use this distinction in her argument? Explain.

6. Do you agree with Thompson that abortion is morally justifiable even if the fetus is a person? Why or why not? Do you feel the same way about abortion regardless of the trimester? What if the fetus is in the third-trimester? What might Thompson say about the morality of third-trimester abortions? Would you agree with her? Defend your view in detail, responding to possible objections by Thompson.

7. Are questions of abortion matters concerning the meaning of life or matters concerning the meaning of death? Take a stand and defend your position.

A Private Matter
[USA 1992] 1 hour, 29 minutes
Directed by Joan Micklin Silver

A Private Matter is based on the true story of Sherri Finkbine, the hostess of the children's television show *Romper Room*. The film examines the controversy surrounding Finkbine's decision in 1962 to terminate her pregnancy, as well as the roots of the abortion movement in the United States.

At that time, Finkbine was pregnant with her fifth child, which she and her husband eagerly awaited. During the pregnancy, she suffered from insomnia. Without consulting her doctor, she began taking a tranquilizer that her husband had brought back from Europe. Finkbine later read that a number of children with severe deformities had been born in Europe. Some were blind and deaf, others had severely deformed internal organs, and still others had limbs that failed to develop or developed abnormally. These deformities were linked to the presence of thalidomide in the very tranquilizer that she was taking. Her doctor confirmed that her child was likely to have severe birth defects and recommended that she have an abortion.

Finkbine presented her case to the three-member medical board of Phoenix, Arizona, and they granted her an abortion even though it was illegal at the time. Her doctor agreed to perform the abortion.

In the meantime, a strong sense of moral outrage prompted Finkbine to warn other women about the potential dangers of the drug. She told her story to a local newspaper, and it made the headlines. Soon

Finkbine's identity was revealed by reporters, and negative publicity ensued. Finkbine was condemned by the Vatican newspaper as a murderer and became the object of an intensive anti-abortion campaign. The result of this controversy was a reversal of the medical board's abortion approval. The board said that her case would not make it through the Arizona courts because abortion was allowed only to save the life of the mother. These events forced her to go to Sweden for the abortion. After the abortion, Finkbine inquired if the fetus was a boy or a girl. The fetus was so badly deformed that the doctor could not say.

DISCUSSION QUESTIONS

1. Was Sherri Finkbine's decision to have an abortion morally justifiable? How much of a role, if any, does the potential for deformity in the infant play a role in your decision? Explain.

2. What if Finkbine had had the child, and seeing its deformities, decided to "let it die." Would passive euthanasia have been morally justifiable in this case? What would James Rachels say (p. 1018)? Defend your view.

3. While Finkbine could afford to circumvent the decisions of the U.S. justice system by going to Sweden for an abortion, many women cannot afford to do this. Does this situation suggest a "class bias" in the abortion laws at the time? Explain.

4. Was it fair that the three-member medical board of Phoenix, Arizona, granted her an abortion but that the strong sense of moral outrage that prompted her to warn other women about the potential dangers of the drug brought about a reversal of the decision? Would you have reported the dangers of the drug to others? Would it make a difference if you knew that by reporting the dangers you would not be able to have an abortion in the United States?

DONALD B. MARQUIS

WHY ABORTION IS IMMORAL

D onald B. Marquis argues that the fetus, as a human, has the same moral status, or value, as any other human being. According to him, to abort the fetus is to "deny it a future," and since humans are entitled to a future, so is the human fetus. In short, Marquis offers arguments in defense of the view that abortion is almost always immoral, because it would be killing an innocent human, or person.

Donald B. Marquis has been a philosophy professor at the University of Kansas since 1967. As an undergraduate, he studied anatomy and physiology, receiving an A.B. from Indiana University in 1957. He then received an M.A. in history from the University of Pittsburgh in 1962 and an M.A. in the history and philosophy of science from Indiana University in 1964. In 1970, he received his Ph.D. in philosophy from Indiana University. Marquis has published many articles on applied ethics, particularly bioethics. The following article was first published in 1989 and has been widely anthologized.

The view that abortion is, with rare exceptions, seriously immoral has received little support in the recent philosophical literature. No doubt most philosophers affiliated with secular institutions of higher education believe that the anti-abortion position is either a symptom of irrational religious dogma or a conclusion generated by seriously confused philosophical argument. The purpose of this essay is to undermine this general belief. This essay sets out an argument that purports to show, as well as any argument in ethics can show, that abortion is, except possibly in rare cases, seriously immoral, that it is in the same moral category as killing an innocent adult human being.

The argument is based on a major assumption. Many of the most insightful and careful writers on the ethics of abortion—such as Joel Feinberg, Michael Tooley, Mary Anne Warren, H. Tristram Engelhardt, Jr., L. W. Sumner, John T. Noonan, Jr., and Philip Devine—believe that whether or not abortion is morally permissible stands or falls on whether or not a fetus is the sort of being whose life it is seriously wrong to end. The argument of this essay will assume, but not argue, that they are correct.

Also, this essay will neglect issues of great importance to a complete ethics of abortion. Some anti-abortionists will allow that certain abortions, such as abortion before implantation or abortion when the life of a woman is threatened by a pregnancy or abortion after rape, may be morally permissible. This essay will not explore the casuistry of these hard cases. The purpose of this essay is to develop a general argument for the claim that the overwhelming majority of deliberate abortions are seriously immoral.

I

A sketch of standard anti-abortion and pro-choice arguments exhibits how those arguments possess certain symmetries that explain why partisans of those positions are so convinced of the correctness of their own positions, why they are not successful in convincing their opponents, and why, to others, this issue seems to be unresolvable. An analysis of the nature of this standoff suggests a strategy for surmounting it.

Consider the way a typical anti-abortionist argues. She will argue or assert that life is present from the moment of conception or that fetuses look like babies or that fetuses possess a characteristic such as a genetic code that is both necessary and sufficient for being human. Anti-abortionists seem to believe that (1) the truth of all of these claims is quite obvious, and (2) establishing any of these claims is sufficient to show that abortion is morally akin to murder.

A standard pro-choice strategy exhibits similarities. The pro-choicer will argue or assert that fetuses are not persons or that fetuses are not rational agents or that fetuses are not social beings. Pro-choicers seem to believe that (1) the truth of any of these claims is quite obvious, and (2) establishing any of these claims is sufficient to show that an abortion is not a wrongful killing.

In fact, both the pro-choice and the anti-abortion claims do seem to be true, although the "it looks like a baby" claim is more difficult to establish the earlier the pregnancy. We seem to have a standoff. How can it be resolved?

As everyone who has taken a bit of logic knows, if any of these arguments concerning abortion is a good argument, it requires not only some claim characterizing fetuses, but also some general moral principle that ties a characteristic of fetuses to having or not having the right to life or to some other moral characteristic that will generate the obligation or the lack of obligation not to end the life of a fetus. Accordingly, the arguments of the anti-abortionist and the pro-choicer need a bit of filling in to be regarded as adequate.

Note what each partisan will say. The anti-abortionist will claim that her position is supported by such generally accepted moral principles as "It is always prima facie seriously wrong to take a human life" or "It is always prima facie seriously wrong to end the life of a baby." Since these are generally accepted moral principles, her position is certainly not obviously wrong. The pro-choicer will claim that her position is supported by such plausible moral principles as "Being a person is what gives an individual intrinsic moral worth" or "It is only seriously prima facie wrong to take the life of a member of the human community." Since these are generally accepted moral principles, the pro-choice position is certainly not obviously wrong. Unfortunately, we have again arrived at a standoff.

Now, how might one deal with this standoff? The standard approach is to try to show how the moral principles of one's opponent lose their plausibility under analysis. It is easy to see how this is possible. On the one hand, the anti-abortionist will defend a moral principle concerning the wrongness of killing which tends to be broad in scope in order that even fetuses at an early stage of pregnancy will fall under it. The problem with broad principles is that they often embrace too much. In this particular instance, the principle "It is always prima facie wrong to take a human life" seems to entail that it is wrong to end the existence of a living human cancer-cell culture, on the grounds that the culture is both living and human. Therefore, it seems that the anti-abortionist's favored principle is too broad.

On the other hand, the pro-choicer wants to find a moral principle concerning the wrongness of killing which tends to be narrow in scope in order that fetuses will *not* fall under it. The problem with narrow principles is that they often do not embrace enough. Hence, the needed principles such as "It is prima facie seriously wrong to kill only persons" or "It is prima facie wrong to kill only rational agents" do not explain why it is wrong to kill infants or young children or the severely retarded or even perhaps the severely mentally ill. Therefore, we seem again to have a standoff. The anti-abortionist charges, not unreasonably, that pro-choice principles concerning killing are too narrow to be acceptable; the pro-choicer charges, not unreasonably, that anti-abortionist principles concerning killing are too broad to be acceptable.

Attempts by both sides to patch up the difficulties in their positions run into further difficulties. The anti-abortionist will try to remove the problem in her position by reformulating her principle concerning killing in terms of human beings. Now we end up with "It is always prima facie seriously wrong to end the life of a human being." This principle has the advantage of avoiding the problem of the human cancer-cell culture counterexample. But this advantage is purchased at a high price. For although it is clear that a fetus is both human and alive, it is not at all clear that a fetus is a human *being*. There is at least something to be said for the view that something becomes a human being only after a process of development, and that therefore first trimester fetuses and perhaps all fetuses are not yet human beings. Hence, the anti-abortionist, by this move, has merely exchanged one problem for another.

The pro-choicer fares no better. She may attempt to find reasons why killing infants, young children, and the severely retarded is wrong which are independent of her major principle that

is supposed to explain the wrongness of taking human life, but which will not also make abortion immoral. This is no easy task. Appeals to social utility will seem satisfactory only to those who resolve not to think of the enormous difficulties with a utilitarian accounts of the wrongness of killing and the significant social costs of preserving the lives of the unproductive. A pro-choice strategy that extends the definition of "person" to infants or even to young children seems just as arbitrary as an anti-abortion strategy that extends the definition of "human being" to fetuses. Again, we find symmetries in the two positions and we arrive at a standoff.

There are even further problems that reflect symmetries in the two positions. In addition to counterexample problems, or the arbitrary application problems that can be exchanged for them, the standard anti-abortionist principle "It is prima facie seriously wrong to kill a human being," or one of its variants, can be objected to on the grounds of ambiguity. If "human being" is taken to be a *biological* category, then the anti-abortionist is left with the problem of explaining why a merely biological category should make a moral difference. Why, it is asked, is it any more reasonable to base a moral conclusion on the number of chromosomes in one's cells than on the color of one's skin? If "human being," on the other hand, is taken so be a *moral* category, then the claim that a fetus is a human being cannot be taken to be a premise in the anti-abortion argument, for it is precisely what needs to be established. Hence, either the anti-abortionist's main category is a morally irrelevant, merely biological category, or it is of no use to the anti-abortionist in establishing (noncircularly, of course) that abortion is wrong.

Although this problem with the anti-abortionist position is often noticed, it is less often noticed that the pro-choice position suffers from an analogous problem. The principle "Only persons have the right to life" also suffers from an ambiguity. The term "person" is typically defined in terms of psychological characteristics, although there will certainly be disagreement concerning which characteristics are most important. Supposing that this matter can be settled, the pro-choicer is left with the problem of explaining why *psychological* characteristics should make a *moral* difference. If the pro-choicer should attempt to deal with this problem by claiming that an explanation is not necessary, that in fact we do treat such a cluster of psychological properties as having moral significance, the sharp-witted anti-abortionist should have a ready response. We do treat being both living and human as having moral significance. If it is legitimate for the pro-choicer to demand that the anti-abortionist provide an explanation of the connection between the biological character of being a human being and the wrongness of being killed (even though people accept this connection), then it is legitimate for the anti-abortionist to demand that the pro-choicer provide an explanation of the connection between psychological criteria for being a person and the wrongness of being killed (even though that connection is accepted).

Feinberg has attempted to meet this objection (he calls psychological personhood "common-sense personhood"):

> The characteristics that confer commonsense person-hood are not arbitrary bases for rights and duties, such as race, sex or species membership; rather they are traits that make sense out of rights and duties and without which those moral attributes would have no point or function. It is because people are conscious; have a sense of their personal identities; have plans, goals, and projects; experience emotions; are liable to pains, anxieties, and frustrations; can reason and bar-gain, and so on—it is because of these attributes that people have values and interests, desires and expec-tations of their own, including a stake in their own fu-tures, and a personal well-being of a sort we cannot ascribe to unconscious or nonrational beings. Because of their developed capacities they can assume duties and responsibilities and can have and make claims on one another. Only because of their sense of self, their life plans, their value hierarchies, and their stakes in their own futures can they be ascribed fundamental rights. There is nothing arbitrary about these linkages.

The plausible aspects of this attempt should not be taken to obscure its implausible features. There is a great deal to be said for the view that being a psychological person under some description is a necessary condition for having duties. One cannot have a duty unless one is capable of behaving morally, and a being's capability of behaving morally will require having a certain psychology.

It is far from obvious, however, that having rights entails consciousness or rationality, as Feinberg suggests. We speak of the rights of the severely retarded or the severely mentally ill, yet some of these persons are not rational. We speak of the rights of the temporarily unconscious. The New Jersey Supreme Court based their decision in the Quinlan case on Karen Ann Quinlan's right to privacy, and she was known to be permanently unconscious as that time. Hence, Feinberg's claim that having rights entails being conscious is, on its face, obviously false.

Of course, is might not make sense to attribute rights to a being that would never in its natural history have certain psychological traits. This modest connection between psychological personhood and moral personhood will create a place for Karen Ann Quinlan and the temporarily unconscious. But then it makes a place for fetuses also. Hence, it does not serve Feinberg's pro-choice purposes. Accordingly, it seems that the pro-choicer will have as much difficulty bridging the gap between psychological personhood and personhood in the moral sense as the anti-abortionist has bridging the gap between being a biological human being and being a human being in the moral sense.

Furthermore, the pro-choicer cannot any more escape her problem by making person a purely moral category than the anti-abortionist could escape by the analogous move. For if person is a moral category, then the pro-choicer is left without the resources for establishing (noncircularly, of course) the claim that a fetus is not a person, which is an essential premise in her argument. Again, we have both a symmetry and a standoff between pro-choice and anti-abortion views.

Passions in the abortion debate run high. There are both plausibilities and difficulties with the standard positions. Accordingly, it is hardly surprising that partisans of either side embrace with fervor the moral generalizations that support the conclusions they preanalytically favor, and reject with disdain the moral generalizations of their opponents as being subject to inescapable difficulties. It is easy to believe that the counterexamples to one's own moral principles are merely temporary difficulties that will dissolve in the wake of further philosophical research, and that the counterexamples to the principles of one's opponents are as straightforward as the contradiction between *A* and *O* propositions in traditional logic. This might suggest to an impartial observer (if there are any) that the abortion issue is unresolvable.

There is a way out of this apparent dialectical quandary. The moral generalizations of both sides are not quite correct. The generalizations hold for the most part, for the usual cases. This suggests that they are all *accidental* generalizations, that the moral claims made by those on both sides of the dispute do not touch on the *essence* of the matter.

This use of the distinction between essence and accident is not meant to invoke obscure metaphysical categories. Rather, it is intended to reflect the rather atheoretical nature of the abortion discussion. If the generalization a partisan in the abortion dispute adopts were derived from the reason why ending the life of a human being is wrong, then there could not be exceptions to that generalization unless some special case obtains in which there are even more powerful countervailing reasons. Such generalizations would not be merely accidental generalizations; they would point to, or be based upon, the essence of the wrongness of killing, what it is that makes killing wrong. All this suggests that a necessary condition of resolving the abortion controversy is a more theoretical account of the wrongness of killing. After all, if we merely believe, but do not understand, why killing adult human beings such as ourselves is wrong, how could we conceivably show that abortion is either immoral or permissible?

II

In order to develop such an account, we can start from the following unproblematic assumption concerning our own case: it is wrong to kill us. Why is it wrong? Some answers can be easily eliminated. It might be said that what makes killing us wrong is that a killing brutalizes the one who kills. But the brutalization consists of being inured to the performance of an act that is hideously immoral; hence, the brutalization does not explain the immorality. It might be said that what makes killing us wrong is the great loss others would experience due to our absence. Although such hubris is understandable, such an explanation does not account for the wrongness of

killing hermits, or those whose lives are relatively independent and whose friends find it easy to make new friends.

A more obvious answer is better. What primarily makes killing wrong is neither its effect on the murderer nor its effect on the victim's friends and relatives, but its effect on the victim. The loss of one's life is one of the greatest losses one can suffer. The loss of one's life deprives one of all the experiences, activities, projects, and enjoyments that would otherwise have constituted one's future. Therefore, killing someone is wrong, primarily because the killing inflicts (one of) the greatest possible losses on the victim. To describe this as the loss of life can be misleading, however. The change in my biological state does not by itself make killing me wrong. The effect of the loss of my biological life is the loss to me of all those activities, projects, experiences, and enjoyments which would otherwise have constituted my future personal life. These activities, projects, experiences, and enjoyments are either valuable for their own sakes or are means to something else that is valuable for its own sake. Some parts of my future are not valued by me now, but will come to be valued by me as I grow older and as my values and capacities change. When I am killed, I am deprived both of what I now value which would have been part of my future personal life, but also what I would come to value. Therefore, when I die, I am deprived of all of the value of my future. Inflicting this loss on me is ultimately what makes killing me wrong. This being the case, it would seem that what makes killing *any* adult human being prima facie seriously wrong is the loss of his or her future.

How should this rudimentary theory of the wrongness of killing be evaluated? It cannot be faulted for deriving an "ought" from an "is," for it does not. The analysis assumes that killing me (or you, reader) is prima facie seriously wrong. The point of the analysis is to establish which natural property ultimately explains the wrongness of the killing, given that it is wrong. A natural property will ultimately explain the wrongness of killing, only if (1) the explanation fits with our intuitions about the matter and (2) there is no other natural property that provides the basis for a better explanation of the wrongness of killing. This analysis rests on the intuition that what makes killing a particular human or animal wrong is what it does to that particular human or animal. What makes killing wrong is some natural effect or other of the killing. Some would deny this. For instance, a divine-command theorist in ethics would deny it. Surely this denial is, however, one of those features of divine-command theory which renders it so implausible.

The claim that what makes killing wrong is the loss of the victim's future is directly supported by two considerations. In the first place, this theory explains why we regard killing as one of the worst of crimes. Killing is especially wrong, because it deprives the victim of more than perhaps any other crime. In the second place, people with AIDS or cancer who know they are dying believe, of course, that dying is a very bad thing for them. They believe that the loss of a future to them that they would otherwise have experienced is what makes their premature death a very bad thing for them. A better theory of the wrongness of killing would require a different natural property associated with killing which better fits with the attitudes of the dying. What could it be?

The view that what makes killing wrong is the loss to the victim of the value of the victim's future gains additional support when some of its implications are examined. In the first place, it is incompatible with the view that it is wrong to kill only beings who are biologically human. It is possible that there exists a different species from another planet whose members have a future like ours. Since having a future like that is what makes killing someone wrong, this theory entails that it would be wrong to kill members of such a species. Hence, this theory is opposed to the claim that only life that is biologically human has great moral worth, a claim which many anti-abortionists have seemed to adopt. This opposition, which this theory has in common with personhood theories, seems to be a merit of the theory.

In the second place, the claim that the loss of one's future is the wrong-making feature of one's being killed entails the possibility that the futures of some actual nonhuman mammals on our own planet are sufficiently like ours that it is seriously wrong to kill them also. Whether some animals do have the same right to life as human beings depends on adding to the account of the wrongness of killing some additional account of

just what it is about my future or the futures of other adult human beings which makes it wrong to kill us. No such additional account will be offered in this essay. Undoubtedly, the provision of such an account would be a very difficult matter. Undoubtedly, any such account would be quite controversial. Hence, it surely should not reflect badly on this sketch of an elementary theory of the wrongness of killing that it is indeterminate with respect to some very difficult issues regarding animal rights.

In the third place, the claim that the loss of one's future is the wrong-making feature of one's being killed does not entail, as sanctity of human life theories do, that active euthanasia is wrong. Persons who are severely and incurably ill, who face a future of pain and despair, and who wish to die will not have suffered a loss if they are killed. It is, strictly speaking, the value of a human's future which makes killing wrong in this theory. This being so, killing does not necessarily wrong some persons who are sick and dying. Of course, there may be other reasons for a prohibition of active euthanasia, but that is another matter. Sanctity-of-human-life theories seem to hold that active euthanasia is seriously wrong even in an individual case where there seems so be good reason for it independently of public policy considerations. This consequence is most implausible, and it is a plus for the claim that the loss of a future of value is what makes killing wrong that it does not share this consequence.

In the fourth place, the account of the wrongness of killing defended in this essay does straightforwardly entail that it is prima facie seriously wrong to kill children and infants, for we do presume that they have futures of value. Since we do believe that it is wrong to kill defenseless little babies, it is important that a theory of the wrongness of killing easily account for this. Personhood theories of the wrongness of killing, on the other hand, cannot straightforwardly account for the wrongness of killing infants and young children. Hence, such theories must add special ad hoc accounts of the wrongness of killing the young. The plausibility of such ad hoc theories seems to be a function of how desperately one wants such theories to work. The claim that the primary wrong-making feature of a killing is the loss to the victim of the value of its future accounts for the wrongness of killing young children and infants directly; it makes the wrongness of such acts as obvious as we actually think it is. This is a further merit of this theory. Accordingly, it seems that this value of a future-like-ours theory of the wrongness of killing shares strengths of both sanctity-of-life and personhood accounts while avoiding weaknesses of both. In addition, it meshes with a central intuition concerning what makes killing wrong.

The claim that the primary wrong-making feature of a killing is the loss to the victim of the value of its future has obvious consequences for the ethics of abortion. The future of a standard fetus includes a set of experiences, projects, activities, and such which are identical with the futures of adult human beings and are identical with the futures of young children. Since the reason that is sufficient to explain why it is wrong to kill human beings after the time of birth is a reason that also applies to fetuses, it follows that abortion is prima facie seriously morally wrong.

This argument does not rely on the invalid inference that, since it is wrong to kill persons, it is wrong to kill potential persons also. The category that is morally central to this analysis is the category of having a valuable future like ours; it is not the category of personhood. The argument to the conclusion that abortion is prima facie seriously morally wrong proceeded independently of the notion of person or potential person or any equivalent. Someone may wish to start with this analysis in terms of the value of a human future, conclude that abortion is, except perhaps in rare circumstances, seriously morally wrong, infer that fetuses have the right to life, and then call fetuses "persons" as a result of their having the right to life. Clearly, in this case, the category of person is being used to state the *conclusion* of the analysis rather than to generate the *argument* of the analysis.

The structure of this anti-abortion argument can be both illuminated and defended by comparing it to what appears to be the best argument for the wrongness of the wanton infliction of pain on animals. This latter argument is based on the assumption that it is prima facie wrong to inflict pain on me (or you, reader). What is the natural property associated with the infliction of pain which makes such infliction

wrong? The obvious answer seems to be that the infliction of pain causes suffering and that suffering is a misfortune. The suffering caused by the infliction of pain is what makes the wanton infliction of pain on me wrong. The wanton infliction of pain on other adult humans causes suffering. The wanton infliction of pain on animals causes suffering. Since causing suffering is what makes the wanton infliction of pain wrong and since the wanton infliction of pain on animals causes suffering, it follows that the wanton infliction of pain on animals is wrong.

This argument for the wrongness of the wanton infliction of pain on animals shares a number of structural features with the argument for the serious prima facie wrongness of abortion. Both arguments start with an obvious assumption concerning what it is wrong to do to me (or you, reader). Both then look for the characteristic or the consequence of the wrong action which makes the action wrong. Both recognize that the wrong-making feature of these immoral actions is a property of actions sometimes directed at individuals other than postnatal human beings. If the structure of the argument for the wrongness of the wanton infliction of pain on animals is sound, then the structure of the argument for the prima facie serious wrongness of abortion is also sound, for the structure of the two arguments is the same. The structure common to both is the key to the explanation of how the wrongness of abortion can be demonstrated without recourse to the category of person. In neither argument is that category crucial.

This defense of an argument for the wrongness of abortion in terms of a structurally similar argument for the wrongness of the wanton infliction of pain on animals succeeds only if the account regarding animals is the correct account. Is it? In the first place, it seems plausible. In the second place, its major competition is Kant's account. Kant believed that we do not have direct duties to animals at all, because they are not persons. Hence, Kant had to explain and justify the wrongness of inflicting pain on animals on the grounds that "he who is hard in his dealings with animals becomes hard also in his dealing with men." The problem with Kant's account is that there seems to be no reason for accepting this latter claim unless Kant's account is rejected. If the alternative to Kant's account is accepted, then it is easy to understand why someone who is indifferent to inflicting pain on animals is also indifferent to inflicting pain on humans, for one is indifferent to what makes inflicting pain wrong in both cases. But, if Kant's account is accepted, there is no intelligible reason why one who is hard in his dealings with animals (or crabgrass or stones) should also be hard in his dealings with men. After all, men are persons: animals are no more persons than crabgrass or stones. Persons are Kant's crucial moral category. Why, in short, should a Kantian accept the basic claim in Kant's argument?

Hence, Kant's argument for the wrongness of inflicting pain on animals rests on a claim that, in a world of Kantian moral agents, is demonstrably false. Therefore, the alternative analysis, being more plausible anyway, should be accepted. Since this alternative analysis has the same structure as the anti-abortion argument being defended here, we have further support for the argument for the immorality of abortion being defended in this essay.

Of course, this value of a future-like-ours argument, if sound, shows only that abortion is prima facie wrong, not that it is wrong in any and all circumstances. Since the loss of the future to a standard fetus, if killed, is, however, at least as great a loss as the loss of the future to a standard adult human being who is killed, abortion, like ordinary killing, could be justified only by the most compelling reasons. The loss of one's life is almost the greatest misfortune that can happen to one. Presumably abortion could be justified in some circumstances, only if the loss consequent on failing to abort would be at least as great. Accordingly, morally permissible abortions will be rare indeed unless, perhaps, they occur so early in pregnancy that a fetus is not yet definitely an individual. Hence, this argument should be taken as showing that abortion is presumptively very seriously wrong, where the presumption is very strong—as strong as the presumption that killing another adult human being is wrong.

III

How complete an account of the wrongness of killing does the value of a future-like-ours account have to be in order that the wrongness of abortion is a consequence? This account does not have to be an account of the necessary conditions for the wrongness of killing. Some persons in nursing homes may lack valuable human futures, yet it may be wrong to kill them for other reasons. Furthermore, this account does not obviously have to be the sole reason killing is wrong where the victim did have a valuable future. This analysis claims only that, for any killing where the victim did have a valuable future like ours, having that future by itself is sufficient to create the strong presumption that the killing is seriously wrong.

One way to overturn the value of a future-like-ours argument would be to find some account of the wrongness of killing which is at least as intelligible and which has different implications for the ethics of abortion. Two rival accounts possess at least some degree of plausibility. One account is based on the obvious fact that people value the experience of living and wish for that valuable experience to continue. Therefore, it might be said, what makes killing wrong is the discontinuation of that experience for the victim. Let us call this the *discontinuation account.* Another rival account is based upon the obvious fact that people strongly desire to continue to live. This suggests that what makes killing us so wrong is that it interferes with the fulfillment of a strong and fundamental desire, the fulfillment of which is necessary for the fulfillment of any other desires we might have. Let us call this the *desire account.*

Consider first the desire account as a rival account of the ethics of killing which would provide the basis for rejecting the anti-abortion position. Such an account will have to be stronger than the value of a future-like-ours account of the wrongness of abortion if it is to do the job expected of it. To entail the wrongness of abortion, the value of a future-like-ours account has only to provide a sufficient, but not a necessary condition for the wrongness of killing. The desire account, on the other hand, must provide us also with a necessary condition for the wrongness of killing in order to generate a pro-choice conclusion on abortion. The reason for this is that presumably the argument from the desire account moves from the claim that what makes killing wrong is interference with a very strong desire to the claim that abortion is not wrong because the fetus lacks a strong desire to live. Obviously, this inference fails if someone's having the desire to live is not a necessary condition of its being wrong to kill that individual.

One problem with the desire account is that we do regard it as seriously wrong to kill persons who have little desire to live or who have no desire to live or, indeed, have a desire not to live. We believe it is seriously wrong to kill the unconscious, the sleeping, those who are tired of life, and those who are suicidal. The value-of-a-human-future account renders standard morality intelligible in these cases; these cases appear to be incompatible with the desire account.

The desire account is subject to a deeper difficulty. We desire life, because we value the goods of this life. The goodness of life is not secondary to our desire for it. If this were not so, the pain of one's own premature death could be done away with merely by an appropriate alteration in the configuration of one's desires. This is absurd. Hence, it would seem that it is the loss of the goods of one's future, not the interference with the fulfillment of a strong desire to live, which accounts ultimately for the wrongness of killing.

It is worth noting that, if the desire account is modified so that it does not provide a necessary, but only a sufficient, condition for the wrongness of killing, the desire account is compatible with the value of a future-like-ours account. The combined accounts will yield an anti-abortion ethic. This suggests that one can retain what is intuitively plausible about the desire account without a challenge to the basic argument of this paper.

It is also worth noting that, if future desires have moral force in a modified desire account of the wrongness of killing, one can find support for an anti-abortion ethic even in the absence of a value of a future-like-ours account. If one decides that a morally relevant property, the possession of which is sufficient to make it wrong to kill some individual, is the desire at some future time to live—one might decide to justify one's refusal to kill suicidal teenagers on these grounds, for example—then, since typical fetuses will have the desire in the future to live, it is wrong to kill typical fetuses. Accordingly, it does not seem that a desire account of the wrongness of killing can

provide a justification of a pro-choice ethic of abortion which is nearly as adequate as the value of a human-future justification on an anti-abortion ethic.

The discontinuation account looks more promising as an account of the wrongness of killing. It seems just as intelligible as the value of a future-like-ours account, but it does not justify an anti-abortion position. Obviously, if it is the continuation of one's activities, experiences, and projects, the loss of which makes killing wrong, then it is not wrong to kill fetuses for that reason, for fetuses do not have experiences, activities, and projects to be continued or discontinued. Accordingly, the discontinuation account does not have the anti-abortion consequences that the value of a future-like-ours account has. Yet, it seems as intelligible as the value of a future-like-ours account, for when we think of what would be wrong with our being killed, it does seem as if it is the discontinuation of what makes our lives worthwhile which makes killing us wrong.

Is the discontinuation account just as good an account as the value of a future-like-ours account? The discontinuation account will not be adequate at all, if it does not refer to the *value* of the experience that may be discontinued. One does not want the discontinuation account to make it wrong to kill a patient who begs for death and who is in severe pain that cannot be relieved short of killing. (I leave open the question of whether it is wrong for other reasons.) Accordingly, the discontinuation account must be more than a bare discontinuation account. It must make some reference to the positive value of the patient's experiences. But, by the same token, the value of a future-like-ours account cannot be a bare future account either. Just having a future surely does not itself rule out killing the above patient. This account must make some reference to the value of the patient's future experiences and projects also. Hence, both accounts involve the value of experiences, projects, and activities. So far we still have symmetry between the accounts.

The symmetry fades, however, when we focus on the time period of the value of the experiences, etc., which has moral consequences. Although both accounts leave open the possibility that the patient in our example may be killed, this possibility is left open only in virtue of the utterly bleak future for the patient. It makes no difference whether the patient's immediate past contains intolerable pain, or consists in being in a coma (which we can imagine is a situation of indifference), or consists in a life of value. If the patient's future is a future of value, we want our account to make it wrong to kill the patient. If the patient's future is intolerable, whatever his or her immediate past, we want our account to allow killing the patient. Obviously, then, it is the value of that patient's future which is doing the work in rendering the morality of killing the patient intelligible.

This being the case, it seems clear that whether one has immediate past experiences or not does no work in the explanation of what makes killing wrong. The addition the discontinuation account makes to the value of a human future account is otiose [futile, functionless]. Its addition to the value-of-a-future account plays no role at all in rendering intelligible the wrongness of killing. Therefore, it can be discarded with the discontinuation account of which it is a part.

IV

The analysis of the previous section suggests that alternative general accounts of the wrongness of killing are either inadequate or unsuccessful in getting around the anti-abortion consequences of the value of a future-like-ours argument. A different strategy for avoiding these anti-abortion consequences involves limiting the scope of the value of a future argument. More precisely, the strategy involves arguing that fetuses lack a property that is essential for the value-of-a-future argument (or for any anti-abortion argument) to apply to them.

One move of this sort is based upon the claim that a necessary condition of one's future being valuable is that one values it. Value implies a valuer. Given this one might argue that, since fetuses cannot value their futures, their futures are not valuable to them. Hence, it does not seriously wrong them deliberately to end their lives.

This move fails, however, because of some ambiguities. Let us assume that something cannot be of value unless it is valued by someone. This does not entail that my life is of no value unless it is valued by me. I may think, in a period of despair, that my future is of no worth whatsoever, but I may be wrong because others rightly see value—even great value—in it. Furthermore, my future can be valuable to me even if I do not value it. This is the case when a young person attempts suicide, but is rescued and goes on to significant human achievements. Such young people's futures are ultimately valuable to them, even though such futures do not seem to be valuable to them at the moment of attempted suicide. A fetus's future can be valuable to it in the same way. Accordingly, this attempt to limit the anti-abortion argument fails.

Another similar attempt to reject the anti-abortion position is based on Tooley's claim that an entity cannot possess the right to life unless it has the capacity to desire its continued existence. It follows that, since fetuses lack the conceptual capacity to desire to continue to live, they lack the right to life. Accordingly, Tooley concludes that abortion cannot be seriously prima facie wrong. . . .

What could be the evidence for Tooley's basic claim? Tooley once argued that individuals have a prima facie right to what they desire and that the lack of the capacity to desire something undercuts the basis of one's right to it. . . . This argument plainly will not succeed in the context of the analysis of this essay, however, since the point here is to establish the fetus's right to life on other grounds. Tooley's argument assumes that the right to life cannot be established in general on some basis other than the desire for life. This position was considered and rejected in the preceding section of this paper.

One might attempt to defend Tooley's basic claim on the grounds that, because a fetus cannot apprehend continued life as a benefit, its continued life cannot be a benefit or cannot be something it has a right to or cannot be something that is in its interest. This might be defended in terms of the general proposition that, if an individual is literally incapable of caring about or taking an interest in some X, then one does not have a right to X or X is not a benefit or X is not something that is in one's interest.

Each member of this family of claims seems to be open to objections. As John C. Stevens has pointed out, one may have a right to be treated with a certain medical procedure (because of a health insurance policy one has purchased), even though one cannot conceive of the nature of the procedure. And, as Tooley himself has pointed out, persons who have been indoctrinated, or drugged, or rendered temporarily unconscious may be literally incapable of caring about or taking an interest in something that is in their interest or is something to which they have a right, or is something that benefits them. Hence, the Tooley claim that would restrict the scope of the value of a future-like-ours argument is undermined by counterexamples.

Finally, Paul Bassen has argued that, even though the prospects of an embryo might seem to be a basis for the wrongness of abortion, an embryo cannot be a victim and therefore cannot be wronged. An embryo cannot be a victim, he says, because it lacks sentience. His central argument for this seems to be that, even though plants and the permanently unconscious are alive, they clearly cannot be victims. What is the explanation of this? Bassen claims that the explanation is that their lives consist of mere metabolism and mere metabolism is not enough to ground victimizability. Mentation is required.

The problem with this attempt to establish the absence of victimizability is that both plants and the permanently unconscious clearly lack what Bassen calls "prospects" or what I have called "a future life like ours." Hence, it is surely open to one to argue that the real reason we believe plants and the permanently unconscious cannot be victims is that killing them cannot deprive them of a future life like ours; the real reason is not their absence of present mentation.

Bassen recognizes that his view is subject to this difficulty, and he recognizes that the case of children seems to support this difficulty, for "much of what we do for children is based on prospects." He argues, however, that, in the case of children and in other such cases, "potentiality comes into play only where victimizability has been secured on other grounds.". . .

Bassen's defense of his view is patently question begging, since what is adequate to secure victimizability is exactly what is at issue. His examples do not support his own view against the thesis of this essay. Of course, embryos can be victims: when their lives are deliberately terminated, they are deprived of their futures of

value, their prospects. This makes them victims, for it directly wrongs them.

The seeming plausibility of Bassen's view stems from the fact that paradigmatic cases of imagining someone as a victim involve empathy, and empathy requires mentation [mental activity] of the victim. The victims of flood, famine, rape, or child abuse are all persons with whom we can empathize. That empathy seems to be part of seeing them as victims.

In spite of the strength of these examples, the attractive intuition that a situation in which there is victimization requires the possibility of empathy is subject to counterexamples. Consider a case that Bassen himself offers: "Posthumous obliteration of an author's work constitutes a misfortune for him only if he had wished his work to endure.". . . The conditions Bassen wishes to impose upon the possibility of being victimized here seem far too strong. Perhaps this author, due to his unrealistic standards of excellence and his low self-esteem, regarded his work as unworthy of survival, even though it possessed genuine literary merit. Destruction of such work would surely victimize its author. In such a case, empathy with the victim concerning the loss is clearly impossible.

Of course, Bassen does not make the possibility of empathy a necessary condition of victimizability; he requires only mentation. Hence, on Bassen's actual view, this author, as I have described him, can be a victim. The problem is that the basic intuition that renders Bassen's view plausible is missing in the author's case. In order to attempt to avoid counterexamples, Bassen has made his thesis too weak to be supported by the intuitions that suggested it.

Even so, the mentation requirement on victimizability is still subject to counterexamples. Suppose a severe accident renders me totally unconscious for a month, after which I recover. Surely killing me while I am unconscious victimizes me, even though I am incapable of mentation during that time. It follows that Bassen's thesis fails. Apparently, attempts to restrict the value of a future-like-ours argument so that fetuses do not fall within its scope do not succeed.

V

In this essay, it has been argued that the correct ethic of the wrongness of killing can be extended to fetal life and used to show that there is a strong presumption that any abortion is morally impermissible. If the ethic of killing adopted here entails, however, that contraception is also seriously immoral, then there would appear to be a difficulty with the analysis of this essay.

But this analysis does not entail that contraception is wrong. Of course, contraception prevents the actualization of a possible future of value. Hence, it follows from the claim that futures of value should be maximized that contraception is prima facie immoral. This obligation to maximize does not exist, however; furthermore, nothing in the ethics of killing in this paper entails that it does. The ethics of killing in this essay would entail that contraception is wrong only if something were denied a human future of value by contraception. Nothing at all is denied such a future by contraception, however.

Candidates for a subject of harm by contraception fall into four categories: (1) some sperm or other, (2) some ovum or other, (3) a sperm and an ovum separately, and (4) a sperm and an ovum together. Assigning the harm to some sperm is utterly arbitrary, for no reason can be given for making a sperm the subject of harm rather than an ovum. Assigning the harm to some ovum is utterly arbitrary, for no reason can be given for making an ovum the subject of harm rather than a sperm. One might attempt to avoid these problems by insisting that contraception deprives both the sperm and the ovum separately of a valuable future like ours. On this alternative, too many futures are lost. Contraception was supposed to be wrong, because it deprived us of one future of value, not two. One might attempt to avoid this problem by holding that contraception deprives the combination of sperm and ovum of a valuable future like ours. But here the definite article misleads. At the time of contraception, there are hundreds of millions of sperm, one (released) ovum and millions of possible combinations of all of these. There is no actual combination at all. Is the subject of the loss to be a merely possible combination? Which one? This alternative does not yield an actual subject of harm either. Accordingly, the immorality of contraception is not entailed by the loss of a future-like-ours argument simply because there is no nonarbitrarily identifiable subject of the loss in the case of contraception.

VI

The purpose of this essay has been to set out an argument for the serious presumptive wrongness of abortion subject to the assumption that the moral permissibility of abortion stands or falls on the moral status of the fetus. Since a fetus possesses a property, the possession of which in adult human beings is sufficient to make killing an adult human being wrong, abortion is wrong. This way of dealing with the problem of abortion seems superior to other approaches to the ethics of abortion, because it rests on an ethics of killing which is close to self-evident, because the crucial morally relevant property clearly applies to fetuses, and because the argument avoids the usual equivocations on "human life," "human being," or "person." The argument rests neither on religious claims nor on Papal dogma. It is not subject to the objection of "speciesism." Its soundness is compatible with the moral permissibility of euthanasia and contraception. It deals with our intuitions concerning young children.

Finally, this analysis can be viewed as resolving a standard problem—indeed, *the* standard problem—concerning the ethics of abortion. Clearly, it is wrong to kill adult human beings. Clearly, it is not wrong to end the life of some arbitrarily chosen single human cell. Fetuses seem to be like arbitrarily chosen human cells in some respects and like adult humans in other respects. The problem of the ethics of abortion is the problem of determining the fetal property that settles this moral controversy. The thesis of this essay is that the problem of the ethics of abortion, so understood, is solvable.

DISCUSSION QUESTIONS

1. Why, according to Marquis, is killing wrong? Do you agree with his argument? Why or why not?

2. What is Marquis's argument against abortion? Critically evaluate it by comparing it with Judith Jarvis Thompson's argument. What are

the strengths and weaknesses of their respective arguments? Who provides the better argument, and why?

3. Is abortion immoral in all cases, according to Marquis? If not, in what cases is it not immoral? Why? Do you agree with him? Explain.

4. What does Marquis' moral principle imply about the killing of nonhuman animals? For Marquis, is it wrong to kill nonhuman animals? Do you agree with this line of argument? Explain.

5. What is Marquis' position on contraception? Does his argument convince you? Why or why not?

Racing with the Moon
[USA 1984] 1 hour, 38 minutes
Directed by Richard Benjamin

The film is set in Point Muir, California, during World War II. Henry Nash (Sean Penn) and Nicky (Nicolas Cage) are best friends. Henry and Nicky are a few weeks away from leaving for the war. Sally Kaiser (Suzanne Atkinson) becomes pregnant by Nicky, her boyfriend, and they decide that they want to have an abortion. However, neither of them can afford the $150 necessary for the operation. Nicky and Henry try to hustle the money playing pool with some soldiers but ultimately lose the game and their meager funds.

With nowhere else to turn, Henry asks his girlfriend, Caddie Winger (Elizabeth McGovern), for the money. Henry believes that Caddie is from a wealthy family; he does not realize that she only lives in the house of the wealthy Donelly family where her mother is a maid. Caddie agrees to help and attempts to steal a pearl necklace from Alice Donelly (Julie Philips), the Donelly's daughter. When Alice catches her in the act, Caddie admits that stealing the necklace was the only way she could think of to raise the money. Alice promises to give her the money she needs. Henry, Sally, Caddie, and Nicky drive out to a run-down trailer where Sally is going to have her abortion. After the abortion, Caddie becomes upset with Henry. Trying to calm her, Henry tells her that he "wouldn't take her to a place like that—I'd marry you." Caddie then tells him that she is not from a wealthy family.

DISCUSSION QUESTIONS

1. Henry tells Caddie that he "wouldn't take her to a place like that—I'd marry you." Would this be the right thing to do? Should Nicky have asked Sally to marry him? Why or why not?

2. Even though the abortion cost only $150, neither Sally nor Nicky had enough money. Should the cost of the procedure be a barrier to having an abortion? Do you think wealthy women are in a better financial position to have a safe abortion than poor women?

3. Caddie is willing to steal in order to help Sally finance her abortion. Is stealing in order to finance a friend's abortion morally justifiable?

4. Is there a connection between social class and abortion? Does the fact that Sally is poor affect her feelings about abortion? Why or why not?

JAMES RACHELS

ACTIVE AND PASSIVE EUTHANASIA

ames Rachels challenges the so-called difference between active euthanasia and passive euthanasia. According to Rachels, there is no necessary moral destruction between "killing" someone and "letting someone die." Furthermore, killing someone (*active euthanasia*) is sometimes even more humane than letting someone die (*passive euthanasia*). Rachels argues that since the moral status of killing depends on intentions and circumstances, relevant to these conditions, active euthanasia can be morally preferable to passive euthanasia.

Broadly conceived, *euthanasia* is the act or practice of painlessly putting to death those who suffer from terminal conditions. Furthermore, since the advent of medical technology able to prolong the life of those without hope of recovery, euthanasia has also come to mean intentionally not preventing the death of those suffering from terminal conditions. Some choose as well to drop the requirement of a "terminal condition" when discussing euthanasia.

Euthanasia, from a Greek word meaning "good death," has become a controversial issue in the United States. In the 1990s, a Michigan physician, Dr. Jack Kervorkian, helped people with terminal diseases to kill themselves. In England and in the United States, the Hemlock Society (hemlock was the poison that Socrates took to end his life), a group working to legalize euthanasia, believes that humans suffering from incurable diseases who are in extreme pain should be allowed to end their own lives, or have the assistance of others, in order to have a "good death."

One of the reasons that euthanasia has become such a controversial issue is that medical advances have enabled us to live much longer than our ancestors. Because of these advances, those who fall ill or have an accident can turn to advanced medical technology to save or prolong their lives. However, many question the view that medical practitioners must *always* preserve human life at any cost. The moral dilemma of euthanasia then involves the balance of the patient's right to a dignified and peaceful death with concerns over the devaluation of life that result in doctors making life-and-death decisions.

In the United States, letting a patient die by withholding or withdrawing all *extraordinary* equipment that may prolong life is legal. This is *passive euthanasia*. The cause of death is whatever ailment naturally afflicts the patient, not any artificially administered treatment. An example of *extraordinary* equipment would be a respirator, iron lung, or radiation treatment. These means of prolonging life impose an undue burden both on those providing the means and on those suffering. *Ordinary* means of prolonging life *do not* impose an undue burden on those providing the means and on those suffering the undue burden. Examples of ordinary means of prolonging life would be food, water, and common antibiotics. The most famous case regarding the withdrawl of ordinary equipment has been that of Terri Schiavo.

On March 18, 2005, following a seven-court battle, Schiavo's feeding tube was disconnected. Fifteen years earlier, Schiavo had collapsed from heart failure, which resulted in severe brain damage that left her in a persistent vegetative state. Although she did not leave any written instructions outlining what she would wish should she require extraordinary equipment for survival, her husband contended that she would not have wanted to be kept alive artificially. Her parents, however, disagreed. The courts had sided with Schiavo's husband in more than a dozen instances. When the case came before the U.S. Supreme Court, the court refused to hear it. Shiavo passed away shortly after her feeding tube was removed.

Active euthanasia is *killing* a patient—that is, causing death by administering a lethal (though humane) treatment such as a drug overdose. Active euthanasia involves a doctor actually taking steps to cause or assist in the death of a patient. This practice is rejected by the American Medical Association and is illegal in all but the state of Oregon. However, in this article, Rachels argues that there is no necessary moral difference between passive and active euthanasia. A biographical sketch of James Rachels appears in chapter 4.

The distinction between active and passive euthanasia is thought to be crucial for medical ethics. The idea is that it is permissible, at least in some cases, to withhold treatment and allow a patient to die, but it is never permissible to take any direct action designed to kill the patient. This doctrine seems to be accepted by most doctors, and it is endorsed in a statement adopted by the House of Delegates of the American Medical Association on December 4, 1973:

> The intentional termination of the life of one human being by another—mercy killing—is contrary to that for which the medical profession stands and is contrary to the policy of the American Medical Association.
>
> The cessation of the employment of extraordinary means to prolong the life of the body when there is irrefutable evidence that biological death is imminent is the decision of the patient and/or his immediate family. The advice and judgment of the physician should be freely available to the patient and/or his immediate family.

However, a strong case can be made against this doctrine. In what follows I will set out some of the relevant arguments and urge doctors to reconsider their views on this matter.

To begin with a familiar type of situation, a patient who is dying of incurable cancer of the throat is in terrible pain, which can no longer be satisfactorily alleviated. He is certain to die within a few days, even if present treatment is continued, but he does not want to go on living for those days since the pain is unbearable. So he asks the doctor for an end to it, and his family joins in the request.

Suppose the doctor agrees to withhold treatment, as the conventional doctrine says he may. The justification for his doing so is that the patient is in terrible agony, and since he is going to die anyway, it would be wrong to prolong his suffering needlessly. But now notice this. If one simply withholds treatment, it may take the patient longer to die, and so he may suffer more than he would if more direct action were taken and a lethal injection given. This fact provides strong reason for thinking that, once the initial decision not to prolong his agony has been made, active euthanasia is actually preferable to passive euthanasia, rather than the reverse. To say otherwise is to endorse the option that leads to more suffering rather than less, and is contrary to the humanitarian impulse that prompts the decision not to prolong his life in the first place.

Part of my point is that the process of being "allowed to die" can be relatively slow and painful, whereas being given a lethal injection is relatively quick and painless. Let me give a different sort of example. In the United States about one in 600 babies is born with Down syndrome. Most of these babies are otherwise healthy—that is, with only the usual pediatric care, they will proceed to an otherwise normal infancy. Some, however, are born with congenital defects such as intestinal obstructions that require operations if they are to live. Sometimes, the parents and the doctor will decide not to operate, and let the infant die. Anthony Shaw describes what happens then:

> When surgery is denied [the doctor] must try to keep the infant from suffering while natural forces sap the baby's life away. As a surgeon whose natural inclination is to use the scalpel to fight off death, standing by and watching a salvageable baby die is the most emotionally exhausting experience I know.
>
> It is easy at a conference, in a theoretical discussion to decide that such infants should be allowed to die. It is altogether different to stand by in the nursery and watch as dehydration and infection wither a tiny being over hours and days. This is a terrible ordeal for me and the hospital staff—much more so than for the parents who never set foot in the nursery.

I can understand why some people are opposed to all euthanasia, and insist that such infants must be allowed to live. I think I can also understand why other people favor destroying these babies quickly and painlessly. But why should anyone favor letting "dehydration and infection wither a tiny being over hours and days"? The doctrine that says that a baby may be allowed to dehydrate and wither, but may not be given an injection that would end its life without suffering, seems so patently cruel as to require no further refutation. The strong language is not intended to offend, but only to put the point in the clearest possible way.

My second argument is that the conventional doctrine leads to decisions concerning life and death made on irrelevant grounds.

Consider again the case of the infants with Down syndrome who need operations for congenital defects unrelated to the syndrome to live. Sometimes, there is no operation, and the baby dies, but when there is no such defect, the baby lives on. Now, an operation such as that to remove an intestinal obstruction is not prohibitively difficult. The reason why such operations are not performed in these cases is, clearly, that the child has Down syndrome and the parents and the doctor judge that because of that fact it is better for the child to die.

But notice that this situation is absurd, no matter what view one takes of the lives and potentials of such babies. If the life of such an infant is worth preserving, what does it matter if it needs a simple operation? Or, if one thinks it better that such a baby should not live on, what difference does it make that it happens to have an unobstructed intestinal tract? In either case, the matter of life and death is being decided on irrelevant grounds. It is the Down syndrome, and not the intestines, that is the issue. The matter should be decided, if at all, on that basis, and not be allowed to depend on that essentially irrelevant question of whether the intestinal tract is blocked.

What makes this situation possible, of course, is the idea that when there is an intestinal blockage, one can "let the baby die," but when there is no such defect there is nothing that can be done, for one must not "kill" it. The fact that this idea leads to such results as deciding life or death on irrelevant grounds is another good reason why the doctrine would be rejected.

One reason why so many people think that there is an important moral difference between active and passive euthanasia is that they think killing someone is morally worse than letting someone die. But is it? Is killing, in itself, worse than letting die? To investigate this issue, two cases may be considered that are exactly alike except that one involves killing whereas the other involves letting someone die. Then, it can be asked whether this difference makes any difference to the moral assessments. It is important that the cases be exactly alike, except for this one difference, since otherwise one cannot be confident that it is this difference and not some other that accounts for any variation in the assessments of the two cases. So, let us consider this pair of cases:

In the first, Smith stands to gain a large inheritance if anything should happen to his six-year-old cousin. One evening while the child is taking his bath, Smith sneaks into the bathroom and drowns the child, and then arranges things so that it will look like an accident.

In the second, Jones also stands to gain if any thing should happen to his six-year-old cousin. Like Smith, Jones sneaks in planning to drown the child in his bath. However, just as he enters the bathroom Jones sees the child slip and hit his head, and fall face down in the water. Jones is delighted; he stands by, ready to push the child's head back under if it is necessary, but it is not necessary. With only a little thrashing about, the child drowns all by himself, "accidentally," as Jones watches and does nothing.

Now Smith killed the child, whereas Jones "merely" let the child die. That is the only difference between them. Did either man behave better, from a moral point of view? If the difference between killing and letting die were in itself a morally important matter, one should say that Jones's behavior was less reprehensible than Smith's. But does one really want to say that? I think not. In the first place, both men acted from the same motive, personal gain, and both had exactly the same end in view when they acted. It may be inferred from Smith's conduct that he is a bad man, although that judgment may be withdrawn or modified if certain further facts are learned about him—for example, that he is mentally deranged. But would not the very same thing be inferred about Jones from his conduct?

And would not the same further considerations also be relevant to any modification of this judgment? Moreover, suppose Jones pleaded, in his own defense, "After all, I didn't do anything except just stand there and watch the child drown. I didn't kill him; I only let him die." Again, if letting die were in itself less bad than killing, this defense should have at least some weight. But it does not. Such a "defense" can only be regarded as a grotesque perversion of moral reasoning. Morally speaking, it is no defense at all.

Now, it may be pointed out, quite properly, that the cases of euthanasia with which doctors are concerned are not like this at all. They do not involve personal gain or the destruction of normal healthy children. Doctors are concerned only with cases in which the patient's life is of no further use to him, or in which the patient's life has become or will soon become a terrible burden. However, the point is the same in these cases: the bare difference between killing and letting die does not, in itself, make a moral difference. If a doctor lets a patient die, for humane reasons, he is in the same moral position as if he had given the patient a lethal injection for humane reasons. If his decision was wrong—if, for example, the patient's illness was in fact curable—the decision would be equally regrettable no matter which method was used to carry it out. And if the doctor's decision was the right one, the method used is not in itself important.

The AMA policy statement isolates the crucial issue very well; the crucial issue is "the intentional termination of the life of one human being by another." But after identifying this issue, and forbidding "mercy killing," the statement goes on to deny that the cessation of treatment is the intentional termination of a life. This is where the mistake comes in, for what is the cessation of treatment, in these circumstances, if it is not "the intentional termination of the life of one human being by another"? Of course it is exactly that, and if it were not, there would be no point to it.

Many people will find this judgment hard to accept. One reason, I think, is that it is very easy to conflate the question of whether killing is, in itself, worse than letting die, with the very different question of whether most actual cases of killing are more reprehensible than most actual cases of letting die. Most actual cases of killing are clearly terrible (think, for example, of all the murders reported in the newspapers), and one hears of such cases every day. On the other hand, one hardly ever hears of a case of letting die, except for the actions of doctors who are motivated by humanitarian reasons. So one learns to think of killing in a much worse light than of letting die. But this does not mean that there is something about killing that makes it in itself worse than letting die, for it is not the bare difference between killing and letting die that makes the difference in these cases. Rather, the other factors—the murderer's motive of personal gain, for example, contrasted with the doctor's humanitarian motivation—account for different reactions to the different cases.

I have argued that killing is not in itself any worse than letting die; if my contention is right, it follows that active euthanasia is not any worse than passive euthanasia. What arguments can be given on the other side? The most common, I believe, is the following.

> The important difference between active and passive euthanasia is that, in passive euthanasia, the doctor does not do anything to bring about the patient's death. The doctor does nothing, and the patient dies of whatever ills already afflict him. In active euthanasia, however, the doctor does something to bring about the patient's death: he kills him. The doctor who gives the patient with cancer a lethal injection has himself caused his patient's death; whereas if he merely ceases treatment, the cancer is the cause of the death.

A number of points need to be made here. The first is that it is not exactly correct to say that in passive euthanasia the doctor does nothing, for he does do one thing that is very important: he lets the patient die. "Letting someone die" is certainly different, in some respects, from other types of action—mainly in that it is a kind of action that one may perform by way of not performing certain other actions. For example, one may let a patient die by way of not giving medication, just as one may insult someone by way of not shaking his hand. But for any purpose of moral assessment, it is a type of action nonetheless. The decision to let a patient die is subject to moral appraisal in the same way that a decision to kill him would be subject to moral appraisal: it may be assessed as wise or unwise, compassionate or sadistic, right or wrong. If a doctor deliberately let a patient die who was suffering from a routinely curable illness, the doctor would certainly be to blame if he had needlessly killed the patient. Charges against him would be appropriate. If so, it would be no defense at all for him to insist that he didn't "do anything." He would have done something very serious indeed, for he let his patient die.

Fixing the cause of death may be very important from a legal point of view, for it may determine whether criminal charges are brought against the doctor. But I do not think that this notion can be used to show a moral difference between active and passive euthanasia. The reason why it is considered bad to be the cause of someone's death is that death is regarded as a great evil—and so it is. However, if it has been decided that euthanasia—even passive euthanasia—is desirable in a given case, it has also been decided that in this instance death is no greater an evil than the patient's continued existence. And if this is true, the usual reason for not wanting to be the cause of someone's death simply does not apply.

Finally, doctors may think that all of this is only of academic interest—the sort of thing that philosophers may worry about but that has no practical bearing on their own work. After all, doctors must be concerned about the legal consequences of what they do, and active euthanasia is clearly forbidden by the law. But even so, doctors should also be concerned with the fact that the law is forcing upon them a moral doctrine that may be indefensible, and has a considerable effect on their practices. Of course, most doctors are not now in the position of being coerced in this matter, for they do not regard themselves as merely going along with what the law requires. Rather, in statements such as the AMA policy statement that I have quoted they are endorsing this doctrine as a central point of medical ethics. In that statement, active euthanasia is condemned not merely as illegal but as "contrary to that for which the medical profession stands," whereas passive euthanasia is approved. However, the preceding considerations suggest that there is really no moral difference between the two, considered in themselves (there may be important moral differences in some cases in their *consequences*, but, as I pointed out, these

differences may make active euthanasia, and not passive euthanasia, the morally prefer-able option). So, whereas doctors may have to discriminate between active and passive euthanasia to satisfy the law, they should not do any more than that. In particular, they should not give the distinction any added authority and weight by writing it into official statements of medical ethics.

DISCUSSION QUESTIONS

1. What is the difference between active euthanasia and passive euthanasia? What do you believe is the moral difference between them? What does Rachels believe? Compare your views.

2. What is the American Medical Association's position on euthanasia? Do you think that it is a good one? Explain.

3. Rachels argues that the withholding of treatment is morally equivalent to the intentional termination of life. Do you agree with him? What is your own position? Can you think of an example to illustrate your position?

4. Is it immoral to allow infants with Down syndrome to die? What does Rachels think? Do you agree with him? Defend your view.

5. Suppose you are told that if you give a modest sum of money to a well-known and trusted organization, you can save the lives of twenty starving people. If you choose not to give money to this charity but could afford to do so, should you be held morally responsible for the deaths of these twenty people? Remember, you knew they would die if you did not help them. Defend your position in detail.

6. Do you think Terri Schiavo's feeding tube should have been removed? Was this a case of passive euthanasia or active euthanasia? Does her case support the position of those who claim that there is no moral difference between active and passive euthanasia? Why or why not? Discuss.

Whose Life Is It Anyway?
[USA 1981] 1 hour, 58 minutes
Directed by John Badham

Ken Harrison (Richard Dreyfuss) is a creative, energetic, thirty-two-year-old sculptor. On the eve of the triumphant unveiling of his new work, Harrison is severely injured in an automobile crash. His mind is unaffected, but he is left paralyzed from the neck down.

Initially, Harrison is optimistic about his recovery, and the hospital staff is charmed by his quick wit and sly jokes. However, as the sculptor comes to realize that he will always remain a quadriplegic, his attitude changes. He realizes that without the use his hands he will lose his means of artistic creation and his identity as an artist.

The doctor in charge of his case (John Cassavetes) insists that Harrison could still teach or write through dictation, but the sculptor remains unsatisfied. Harrison loses his desire to live. He tells his devoted and loving girlfriend (Christine Lahti) not to visit him. He wishes to cease dialysis and all medications, but his doctors refuse. The hospital staff tries to convince him that his life is worth living.

The turning point occurs when Harrison is mishandled by one of the staff and finds himself dangling helplessly from the bed, unable to right himself. He is rescued by the nurses and placed safely back in bed. Infuriated by his total dependence on others, however, Harrison decides definitively that he no longer wants to live and hires a lawyer to sue for his right to die.

The case hinges on Harrison's ability to prove that he is mentally fit to make this choice. Harrison demonstrates that he is in fact of sound mind. The judge grants him the right to be taken off of dialysis, which will result in his death within a few days. The doctors promise to make his last days comfortable and to be available in the event that he should change his mind, but Harrison is determined to die. *Whose Life Is It Anyway?* is a film adaptation of the popular play by Brian Clark.

DISCUSSION QUESTIONS

1. Harrison argues that his identity as a sculptor is his life. Without the ability to sculpt, he has no life; therefore, he should be allowed to die. If you were the judge, what would you say to Harrison?

2. Imagine that you, James Rachels, and Bonnie Steinbock (see below) were the judges. What would each of you say to Harrison? Would you agree that he should be allowed to die? Or would you say that such a decision would be immoral? (Each judge gets a single yes or no vote.)

3. It is important that Harrison show the judge that he is of sound mind and that his decision to be allowed to die has been rationally determined. Should a hospital ever allow a patient to die? Does it matter whether the patient wants to be allowed to die?

4. What if Harrison were not on dialysis and still wanted to die? Would the doctors be justified in killing him by lethal injection? What is the difference between denying him dialysis and killing him by lethal injection? Would this change your decision to allow him to die if you were the judge in his case? What if he wanted to die by starvation?

BONNIE STEINBOCK

THE INTENTIONAL TERMINATION OF LIFE

I n response to James Rachels's argument, Bonnie Steinbock claims that the distinction between active and passive euthanasia *can* be supported in cases in which the patient refuses treatment and in which the purpose of failing to treat a patient is not the termination of life but rather the reduction of pain. According to Steinbock, the mistake Rachels makes is identifying the cessation of life-prolonging treatment with passive euthanasia, or intentionally letting a person die. Steinbock believes that the decision not to operate on a child need not mean a decision to neglect the child. "Waiting for them to die may be tough on parents, doctors, and nurses," says Steinbock, "but it isn't necessarily tough on the child."

Bonnie Steinbock, a philosophy professor at the State University of New York at Albany, received her B.A. from Tufts University in 1968 and her Ph.D. from the University of California, Berkeley, in 1974. She is a fellow of the Hastings Center and a member of the Ethics Committee of the American Society for Reproduction and Medicine. Steinbock is the author of *Life Before Birth: The Moral and Legal Status of Embryos and Fetuses* (1992) and the editor of *Legal and Ethical Issues in Human Reproduction* (2002). She is also co-editor of *Killing and Letting Die* (with Alastair Norcross, 2nd ed, 1994), *New Ethics for the Public's Health* (with Dan E. Beauchamp, 1999), and *Ethical Issues in Modern Medicine* (with John D. Arras, 6th ed., 2002). The following article first appeared in 1979.

According to James Rachels and Michael Tooley, a common mistake in medical ethics is the belief that there is a moral difference between active and passive euthanasia. This is a mistake, they argue, because the rationale underlying the distinction between active and passive euthanasia is the idea that there is a significant moral difference between intentionally killing and intentionally letting die. "This idea," Tooley says, "is admittedly very common. But I believe that it can be shown to reflect either confused thinking, or a moral point of view unrelated to the interests of individuals." Whether the belief that there is a significant moral difference (between intentionally killing and intentionally letting die) is mistaken is not my concern here. For it is far from clear that this distinction *is* the basis of the doctrine of the American Medical Association which Rachels attacks. And if the killing/letting die distinction is not the basis of the AMA doctrine, then arguments showing that the distinction has no moral force do not, in themselves, reveal in the doctrine's adherents either "confused thinking" or "a moral point of view unrelated to the interests of individuals." Indeed, as we examine the AMA doctrine, I think it will become clear that it appeals to and makes use of a number of overlapping distinctions, which may have moral significance in particular cases, such as the distinction between intending and foreseeing, or between ordinary and extraordinary care. Let us then turn to the statement, from the House of Delegates of the American Medical Association, which Rachels cites:

> The intentional termination of the life of one human being by another—mercy-killing—is contrary to that for which the medical profession stands and is contrary to the policy of the American Medical Association.

> The cessation of the employment of extraordinary means to prolong the life of the body when there is irrefutable evidence that biological death is imminent is the decision of the patient and/or his immediate family. The advice and judgment of the physician should be freely available to the patient and/or his immediate family.

Rachels attacks this statement because he believes that it contains a moral distinction between active and passive euthanasia. . . .

I intend to show that the AMA statement does not imply support of the active/passive euthanasia distinction. In forbidding the intentional termination of life, the statement rejects both active and passive euthanasia. It does allow for ". . . the cessation of the employment of extraordinary means . . ." to prolong life. The mistake Rachels and Tooley make is in identifying the cessation of life-prolonging treatment with passive euthanasia or intentionally letting die. If it were right to equate the two, then the AMA statement would be self-contradictory, for it would begin by condemning, and end by allowing the intentional termination of life. But if the cessation of life-prolonging treatment is not always or necessarily passive euthanasia, then there is no confusion and no contradiction.

Why does Rachels think that the cessation of life-prolonging treatment is the intentional termination of life? He says:

> The AMA policy statement isolates the crucial issue very well; the crucial issue is "the intentional termination of the life of one human being by another." But after identifying this issue, and forbidding "mercy-killing," the statement goes on to deny that the cessation of treatment is the intentional termination of a life. This is where the mistake comes in, for what is the cessation of treatment, in these circumstances, if it is not "the intentional termination of the life of one human being by another"? Of course it is exactly that, and if it were not, there would be no point to it.

However, there *can* be a point (to the cessation of life-prolonging treatment) other than an endeavor to bring about the patient's death, and so the blanket identification of cessation of treatment with the intentional termination of a life is inaccurate. There are at least two situations in which the termination of life prolonging treatment cannot be identified with the intentional termination of the life of one human being by another.

The first situation concerns the patient's right to refuse treatment. Both Tooley and Rachels give the example of a patient dying of an incurable disease, accompanied by unrelievable pain, who wants to end the treatment which cannot cure him but can only prolong his miserable existence. Why, they ask, may a doctor accede to the patient's request to stop treatment, but not provide a patient in a similar situation with a lethal dose? The answer lies in the patient's right to refuse treatment. In general, a competent adult has the right to refuse treatment, even where such treatment is necessary to prolong life. Indeed, the right to refuse treatment has been upheld even when the patient's reason for refusing treatment is generally agreed to be inadequate. This right can be overridden (if, for example, the patient has dependent children) but, in general, no one may legally compel you to undergo treatment to which you have not consented. "Historically, surgical intrusion has always been considered a technical battery upon the person and one to be excused or justified by consent of the patient or justified by necessity created by the circumstances of the moment. . . ."

At this point, it might be objected that if one has the right to refuse life-prolonging treatment, then consistency demands that one have the right to decide to end his life and to obtain help in doing so. The idea is that the right to refuse treatment somehow implies a right to voluntary euthanasia, and we need to see why someone might think this. The right to refuse treatment has been considered by legal writers as an example of the right to privacy or, better, the right to bodily self-determination. You have the right to decide what happens to your own body, and the right to refuse treatment in an instance of that more general right. But if you have the right to determine what happens to your body, then should you not have the right to choose to end your life, and even a right to get help in doing so?

However, it is important to see that the right to refuse treatment is not the same as, nor does it entail, a right to voluntary euthanasia, even if both can be derived from the right to bodily self-determination. The right to refuse treatment is not itself a "right to die"; that one may choose to exercise this right even at the risk of death, or even *in order to die* is irrelevant. The purpose of the right to refuse medical treatment is not to give persons a right to decide whether to live or die, but to protect them from the unwanted interferences of others. Perhaps we ought to interpret the right to bodily self-determination more broadly so as to include a right to die: but this would be a substantial extension of our present understanding of the right to bodily self-determination, and not a consequence of it. Should we recognize a right to voluntary euthanasia, we would have to agree that people have the right not merely to be left alone, but also the right to be killed. I leave to one side that substantive moral issue. My claim is simply that there can be a reason for terminating life-prolonging treatment other than "to bring about the patient's death."

The second case in which termination of treatment cannot be identified with intentional termination of life is where continued treatment has little chance of improving the patient's condition and brings greater discomfort than relief.

The question here is what treatment is appropriate to the particular case. A cancer specialist describes it in this way:

> My general rule is to administer therapy as long as a patient responds well and has the potential for a reasonably good quality of life. But when all feasible therapies have been administered and a patient shows signs of rapid deterioration, the continuation of therapy can cause more discomfort than the cancer. From that time I recommend surgery, radiotherapy, or chemotherapy only as a means of relieving pain. But if a patient's condition should once again stabilize after the withdrawal of active therapy and if it should appear that he could still gain some good time, I would immediately reinstitute active therapy. The decision to cease anticancer treatment is never irrevocable, and often the desire to live will push a patient to try for another remission, or even a few more days of life.

The decision here to cease anticancer treatment cannot be construed as a decision that the patient die, or as the intentional termination of life. It is a decision to provide the most appropriate treatment for that patient at that time. Rachels suggests that the point of the cessation of treatment is the intentional termination of life. But here the point of discontinuing treatment is not to bring about the patient's death but to avoid treatment that will cause more discomfort than the cancer and has little hope of benefiting the patient. Treatment that meets this description is often called "extraordinary." The concept is flexible, and what might be considered "extraordinary" in one situation might be ordinary in another. The use of a respirator to sustain a patient through a severe bout of respiratory disease would be considered ordinary; its use to sustain the life of a severely

brain damaged person in an irreversible coma would be considered extraordinary.

Contrasted with extraordinary treatment is ordinary treatment, the care a doctor would normally be expected to provide. Failure to provide ordinary care constitutes neglect, and can even be construed as the intentional infliction of harm, where there is a legal obligation to provide care. The importance of the ordinary/extraordinary care distinction lies partly in its connection to the doctor's intention. The withholding of extraordinary care should be seen as a decision not to inflict painful treatment on a patient without reasonable hope of success. The withholding of ordinary care, by contrast, must be seen as neglect. Thus, one doctor says, "We have to draw a distinction between ordinary and extraordinary means. We never withdraw what's needed to make a baby comfortable, we would never withdraw the care a parent would provide. We never kill a baby. . . . But we may decide certain heroic intervention is not worthwhile."

We should keep in mind the ordinary/extraordinary care distinction when considering an example given by both Tooley and Rachels to show the irrationality of the active/passive distinction with regard to infanticide. The example is this: a child is born with Down syndrome and also has an intestinal obstruction which requires corrective surgery. If the surgery is not performed, the infant will starve to death, since it cannot take food orally. This may take days or even weeks, as dehydration and infection set in. Commenting on this situation, Rachels says:

> I can understand why some people are opposed to all euthanasia, and insist that such infants must be allowed to live. I think I can also understand why other people favor destroying these babies quickly and painlessly. But why should anyone favor letting "dehydration and infection wither a tiny being over hours and days"? The doctrine that says that a baby may be allowed to dehydrate and wither, but may not be given an injection that would end its life without suffering, seems so patently cruel as to require no further refutation.

Such a doctrine perhaps does not need further refutation; but this is not the AMA doctrine. For the AMA statement criticized by Rachels allows only for the cessation of extraordinary means to prolong life when death is imminent. Neither of these conditions is satisfied in this example. Death is not imminent in this situation, any more than it would be if a normal child had an attack of appendicitis. Neither the corrective surgery to remove the intestinal obstruction, nor the intravenous feeding required to keep the infant alive, until such surgery is performed can be regarded as extraordinary means, for neither is particularly expensive, nor does either place an overwhelming burden on the patient or others. (The continued existence of the child might be thought to place an overwhelming burden on its parents, but that has nothing to do with the characterization of the means to prolong its life as extraordinary. If it had, then *feeding* a severely defective child who required a great deal of care could be regarded as extraordinary.) The chances of success if the operation is undertaken are quite good, though there is always a risk in operating on infants. Though the Down syndrome will not be alleviated, the child will proceed to an otherwise normal infancy.

It cannot be argued that the treatment is withheld for the infant's sake, unless one is prepared to argue that all mentally retarded babies are better off dead. This is particularly implausible in the case of Down syndrome babies, who generally do not suffer and are capable of giving and receiving love, of learning and playing, to varying degrees.

In a film on this subject entitled "Who Should Survive?" a doctor defended a decision not to operate, saying that since the parents did not consent to the operation, the doctors' hands were tied. As we have seen, surgical intrusion requires consent, and in the case of infants, consent would normally come from the parents. But, as their legal guardians, parents are required to provide medical care for their children, and failure to do so can constitute criminal neglect or even homicide. In general, courts have been understandably reluctant to recognize a parental right to terminate life-prolonging treatment. Although prosecution is unlikely, physicians who comply with invalid instructions from the parents and permit the infant's death could be liable for aiding and abetting, failure to report child neglect, or even homicide. So it is not true that, in this situation, doctors are legally bound to do as the parents wish.

To sum up, I think that Rachels is right to regard the decision not to operate in the Down syndrome example as the intentional termination of life. But there is no reason to believe that either the law or the AMA would regard it otherwise. Certainly the decision to withhold treatment is not justified by the AMA statement. That such infants have been allowed to die cannot be denied; but this, I think, is the result of doctors misunderstanding the law and the AMA position.

Withholding treatment in this case is the international termination of life because the infant is deliberately allowed to die; that is the point of not operating. But there are other cases in which that is not the point. If the point is to avoid inflicting painful treatment on a patient with little or no reasonable hope of success, this is not the intentional termination of life. The permissibility of such withholding of treatment, then, would have no implications for the permissibility of euthanasia, active or passive. . . .

Someone might say: Even if the withholding of treatment is not the intentional termination of life, does that make a difference, morally speaking? If life-prolonging treatment may be withheld, for the sake of the child, may not an easy death be provided, for the sake of the child, as well? The unoperated child with spina bifida may take months or even years to die. Distressed by the spectacle of children "lying around, waiting to die," one doctor has written, "It is time that society and medicine stopped perpetuating the fiction that withholding treatment is ethically different from terminating a life. It is time that society began to discuss mechanisms by which we can alleviate the pain and suffering for those individuals whom we cannot help."

I do not deny that there may be cases in which death is in the best interests of the patient. In such cases, a quick and painless death may be the best thing. However, I do not think that, once active or vigorous treatment is stopped, a quick death is always preferable to a lingering one. We must be cautious about attributing to defective children *our* distress at seeing them linger. Waiting for them to die may be tough on parents, doctors and nurses—it isn't necessarily tough on the child. The decision not to operate need not mean a decision to neglect, and it may be possible to make the remaining months of the child's life comfortable, pleasant and filled with love. If this alternative is possible, surely it is more decent and humane than killing the child. In such a situation, withholding treatment, foreseeing the child's death, is not ethically equivalent to killing the child, and we cannot move from the permissibility of the former to that of the latter. I am worried that there will be a tendency to do precisely that if active euthanasia is regarded as morally equivalent to the withholding of life-prolonging treatment.

DISCUSSION QUESTIONS

1. Why does Steinbock believe that the American Medical Association's position on euthanasia does not imply support of the active/passive euthanasia distinction? Do you agree with her? Why or why not?

2. Why does Steinbock believe that the right to refuse treatment is not the same as, nor does it entail, a right to voluntary euthanasia? Do you agree with her? Why or why not?

3. "I do not think that, once active or vigorous treatment is stopped," says Steinbock, "a quick death is always preferable to a lingering one." Do you agree with her? Why or why not?

4. What is the major difference between Rachels' position on the Down syndrome infant example and Steinbock's position? Which do you prefer, and why?

5. Compare and contrast Rachels' and Steinbock's positions on euthanasia. Overall, who has the stronger arguments, and why? Do their arguments change your view on euthanasia? Why or why not?

6. In Greek, the word *euthanasia* means "good death." Do you think there is such a thing as a good death? Why or why not?

SUPPLEMENTARY READINGS

The Meaning of Life

Britton, Karl. *Philosophy and the Meaning of Life.* Cambridge: Cambridge University Press, 1969.

Burnett, Witt. *This Is My Philosophy; Twenty of the World's Outstanding Thinkers Reveal the Deepest Meanings They Have Found in Life.* New York: Harper, 1957.

Camus, Albert. *The Myth of Sisyphus, and Other Essays.* Trans. Justin O'Brien. New York: Knopf, 1955.

Clark, C. H. Douglas. *Christianity and Bertrand Russell: A Critique of the Essay "Why I Am not a Christian."* London: Lutterworth Press, 1958.

Craig, William Lane. *Reasonable Faith: Christian Truth and Apologetics.* Rev. ed. Wheaton, IL: Crossway Books, 1994.

Dostoyevsky, Fyodor, *The Grand Inquisitor: With Related Chapters from the Brothers Karamazov.* Ed. Charles B Guignon. Trans. Constance Garnett. Indianapolis, IN: Hackett, 1993.

Durant, Will, ed. *On the Meaning of Life.* New York: Long & Smith, 1932.

Fadiman, Clifton, ed. *I Believe: The Personal Philosophies of Certain Eminent Men and Women of Our Time.* New York: Simon & Schuster, 1939.

Flanagan, Owen J. *Self Expressions: Mind, Morals, and the Meaning of Life.* New York: Oxford University Press, 1996.

Frankl, Victor. *Man's Search for Meaning.* New York: Beacon Press, 1963.

Heidegger, Martin. *Being and Time.* New York: Harper, 1962.

Heinegg, Peter. *Mortalism: Readings on the Meaning of Life.* Amherst, NY: Prometheus Books, 2003.

Heschel, Abraham. *Who Is Man?* Stanford, CA: Stanford University Press, 1965.

James, William. *The Will to Believe and Other Essays in Popular Philosophy.* Eds. Frederick Burkhardt, Fredson Bowers, and Ignas K Skrupskelis. Cambridge, MA: Harvard University Press, 1979.

Ketcham, Charles B. *The Search for Meaningful Existence.* New York: Weybright & Talley, 1968.

Kierkegaard, Søren. *Practice in Christianity.* Eds. Howard Vincent Hong and Edna Hatlestad Hong. Princeton, NJ: Princeton University Press, 1991.

———. *The Essential Kierkegaard.* Eds. Howard Vincent Hong and Edna Hatlestad Hong. Princeton, NJ: Princeton University Press, 2000.

Klemke, E. D. *The Meaning of Life.* 2nd ed. New York and Oxford: Oxford University Press, 2000.

Kurtz, Paul. *The Fullness of Life.* New York: Horizon, 1974.

Lewis, C. S. *The Inspirational Writings of C. S. Lewis.* New York: Inspirational Press, 1987.

Martin, Nancy M., and Joseph Runzo. *The Meaning of Life in the World Religions.* Oxford: Oneworld, 2000.

Munitz, Milton. *The Mystery of Existence.* New York: Appleton-Century-Crofts, 1965.

Nagel, Thomas. *What Does It All Mean? A Very Short Introduction to Philosophy.* New York: Oxford University Press, 1987.

Nicholi, Armand M. *The Question of God: C. S. Lewis and Sigmund Freud Debate God, Love, Sex, and the Meaning of Life.* New York: Free Press, 2002.

Nielsen, Kai. *Ethics Without God.* Buffalo, NY: Prometheus Books, 1973.

Norton, David. *Personal Destinies.* Princeton, NJ: Princeton University Press, 1976.

Nozick, Robert. *The Examined Life: Philosophical Meditations.* New York: Simon & Schuster, 1989.

Quinn, Philip L., and Charles Taliaferro. *A Companion to the Philosophy of Religion.* Cambridge, MA: Blackwell, 1999.

Robinson, Richard. *An Atheist's Values.* Oxford: Oxford University Press, 1964.

Rosen, Stanley. *Nihilism: A Philosophical Essay.* New Haven, CT: Yale University Press, 1969.

Russell, Bertrand. *Why I Am Not a Christian: And Other Essays on Religion and Related Subjects.* New York: Simon & Schuster, 1957.

Sanders, Steven, and David R. Cheney. *The Meaning of Life: Questions, Answers, and Analysis.* Englewood Cliffs, NJ: Prentice Hall, 1980.

Sartre, Jean-Paul. *Jean-Paul Sartre: Basic Writings.* Ed. Stephen Priest. New York: Routledge, 2001.

Schopenhauer, Arthur. *The World as Will and Representation.* 2 vols. New York: Dover, 1966, 1958.

———. *The Will to Live: Selected Writings of Arthur Schopenhauer.* Ed. Richard Taylor. New York: Continuum, 1962.

———. *The Search for Absolute Values in a Changing World.* San Francisco: International Cultural Foundation, 1977.

Stern, Alfred. *The Search for Meaning: Philosophical Vistas.* Memphis, TN: Memphis State University Press, 1971.

Swenson, David F., and Lillian Marvin Swenson. *Kierkegaardian Philosophy in the Faith of a Scholar.* Philadelphia: Westminster Press, 1949.

Taylor, Richard. *Good and Evil: A New Direction.* New York: Macmillan, 1970.

Tolstoy, Leo. *The Death of Ivan Illych.* Trans. A. Maude. New York: New American Library, 1960.

Warnock, G. J. *The Object of Morality.* London: Methuen, 1971.

Wilber, Ken. *Up from Eden: A Transpersonal View of Human Evolution.* Wheaton, IL: Quest Books, 1981.

Wisdom, John. *Paradox and Discovery.* New York: Philosophical Library, 1965.

The Meaning of Death

Alger, William Rounseville, and Ezra Abbot. *The Destiny of the Soul: A Critical History of the Doctrine of a Future Life.* 10th ed. New York: Greenwood Press, 1968.

Badham, Paul, and Linda Badham, eds. *Death and Immortality in the Religions of the World.* New York: Paragon House, 1987.

Bevan, Edwyn Robert. *The Hope of a World to Come: Underlying Judaism and Christianity.* London: Allen & Unwin, 1930.

Blackmore, Susan. *Beyond the Body: An Investigation of Out-of-the-Body Experiences.* Chicago: Academy Chicago, 1992.

Boring, Edwin Garrigues. *The Physical Dimensions of Consciousness.* New York: Dover, 1963.

Broad, C. D. *The Mind and Its Place in Nature.* London: Paul, Trench, Trubner, 1925.

Chappell, V. C., ed. *The Philosophy of the Mind.* Englewood Cliffs, NJ: Prentice Hall, 1962.

Crookall, Robert. *The Next World—And the Next Ghostly Garments.* London: Theosophical, 1966.

Davis, Stephen T., ed. *Death and Afterlife.* New York: St. Martin's Press, 1989.

Ducasse, Curt John. *Nature, Mind, and Death.* La Salle, IL: Open Court, 1951.

———. *A Critical Examination of the Belief in Life After Death.* Springfield, IL: Thomas, 1961.

Dudley, William. *Death and Dying: Opposing Viewpoints.* San Diego: Greenhaven Press, 1992.

Edwards, Paul, ed. *Immortality.* New York: Macmillan, 1992.

Feifel, Herman. *The Meaning of Death.* New York: Blakiston Division, McGraw-Hill, 1959.

Flew, Antony, ed. *Body, Mind and Death: Readings Selected, Edited, and Furnished with an Introductory Essay by Antony Flew.* New York: Macmillan, 1964.

———. *The Logic of Mortality.* Oxford and New York: Blackwell, 1987.

Glover, J., ed. *The Philosophy of the Mind.* Oxford: Oxford University Press, 1976.

Greyson, Bruce, and Charles P. Flynn. *The Near-Death Experience: Problems, Prospects, Perspectives.* Springfield, IL: Thomas, 1984.

Grof, Stanislav, Christina Grof, and Jill Purce. *Beyond Death: The Gates of Consciousness.* London: Thames & Hudson, 1980.

Head, Joseph, and S. L. Cranston, eds. *Reincarnation in World Thought.* New York: Julian Press, 1967.

Hick, John. *Classic and Contemporary Readings in the Philosophy of Religion.* 2nd ed. Englewood Cliffs, NJ: Prentice Hall, 1970.

——. *Death and Eternal Life.* New York: Harper & Row, 1976.

Hume, David. *Dialogues Concerning Natural Religion and the Posthumous Essays, Of the Immortality of the Soul and Of Suicide.* Ed. Richard Henry Popkin. Indianapolis, IN: Hackett, 1980.

Kübler-Ross, Elisabeth. *On Death and Dying.* New York: Macmillan, 1969.

Küng, Hans. *Eternal Life? Life After Death as a Medical, Philosophical, and Theological Problem.* New York: Doubleday, 1984.

Lewis, Hywel David. *The Self and Immortality.* New York: Seabury Press, 1973.

——. *Persons and Life After Death: Essays.* New York: Barnes & Noble, 1978.

Lund, David H. *Death and Consciousness.* Jefferson, NC: McFarland, 1985.

Lundhal, Craig R., ed. *A Collection of Near-Death Research Readings.* Chicago: Nelson-Hall, 1982.

MacGregor, Geddes. *Reincarnation as a Christian Hope.* Totowa, NJ: Barnes & Noble, 1982.

Monroe, Robert A. *Journeys Out of the Body.* Garden City, NY: Doubleday, 1971.

Moody, Raymond A. *Life After Life: The Investigation of a Phenomenon—Survival of Bodily Death.* Harrisburg, PA: Stackpole Books, 1976.

Morick. Harold., ed. *Introduction to the Philosophy of the Mind: Readings from Descartes to Strawson.* Glenview, IL: Scott, Foresman, 1970.

Parfit, Derek. *Reasons and Persons.* Oxford: Clarendon Press, 1984.

Perry, John. *A Dialogue on the Personal Identity and Immortality.* Indianapolis, IN: Hackett, 1978.

Plato. *Apology, Crito, Phaedo, Symposium, Republic.* Trans. Benjamin Jowett. Ed. Louise Ropes Loomis. New York: Black, 1942.

Price, H. H. *Essays in the Philosophy of Religion: Based on the Sarum Lectures, 1971.* Oxford: Clarendon Press, 1972.

Reichenbach, Bruce R. *The Law of Karma—A Philosophical Study.* Honolulu: University of Hawaii Press, 1990.

Rosenthal, David M., ed. *The Nature of Mind.* New York: Oxford University Press, 1991.

Sabom, Michael B. *Recollections at Death: A Medical Investigation.* New York: Harper & Row, 1982.

Shaffer, Jerome A. *Philosophy of the Mind.* Englewood Cliffs, NJ: Prentice Hall, 1968.

Shirley, Ralph. *The Mystery of the Human Double: The Case for Astral Projection.* New York: University Books, 1965.

Siwek, Paul. *The Enigma of the Hereafter: The Re-Incarnation of Souls.* New York: Philosophical Library, 1952.

Spiro, Howard, Mary McCrea Curnen, and Lee Palmer Wandel. *Facing Death: Where Culture, Religion and Medicine Meet.* New Haven, CT: Yale University Press, 1996.

Stendhal, Krister, ed. *Immortality and Resurrection: Four Essays by Oscar Cullman, Harry A. Wolfson, Werner Jaeger, and Henry J. Cadbury.* New York: Macmillan, 1965.

Stevenson, Ian. *Children Who Remember Previous Lives: A Question of Reincarnation.* Charlottesville: University Press of Virginia, 1987.

Swinburne, Richard. *The Evolution of the Soul.* Oxford: Clarendon Press, 1986.

Toynbee, Arnold Joseph. *Life After Death.* New York: McGraw-Hill, 1976.

Abortion

Baird, Robert M., and Stuart E. Rosenbaum, eds. *The Ethics of Abortion: Pro-Life vs. Pro-Choice.* Buffalo, NY: Prometheus Books, 1989.

Brody, Baruch. *Abortion and the Sanctity of Human Life.* Cambridge, MA: Harvard University Press, 1975.

Callahan, Daniel. *Abortion: Law, Choice, and Morality.* New York: Macmillan, 1970.

Cohen, Marshall, Thomas Nagel, and Thomas Scanlon, eds. *The Rights and Wrongs of Abortion.* Princeton, NJ: Princeton University Press, 1974.

Corea, Gena. *The Hidden Malpractice: How American Medicine Mistreats Women.* New York: Harper & Row, 1985.

Davis, Angela. "Racism, Birth Control and Reproductive Rights." *In Abortion to Reproductive Freedom.* Ed. Marlene Gerber Fried. Boston: South End Press, 1990. 15–26.

Feinberg, Joel, ed. *The Problem of Abortion.* 2nd ed. Belmont, CA: Wadsworth, 1984.

Goldstein, R. D. *Mother-Love and Abortion: A Legal Interpretation.* Berkeley: University of California Press, 1988.

Gordon, Linda. *Woman's Body, Woman's Right: Birth Control in America.* Rev. ed. New York: Penguin Books, 1990.

Harrison, B. W. *Our Right to Choose: Toward a New Ethic of Abortion.* Boston: Beacon Press, 1983.

Hartmann, Betsy. *Reproductive Rights and Wrongs: The Global Politics of Population Control and Contraceptive Choice.* New York: Harper & Row, 1987.

Kamm, Francis Myrna. *Creation and Abortion: A Study in Moral and Legal Philosophy.* New York: Oxford University Press, 1992.

Mohr, J. C. *Abortion in America: The Origins and Evolution of National Policy, 1800–1900.* New York: Oxford University Press, 1978.

Nicholson, Susan. *Abortion and the Roman Catholic Church.* Knoxville, TN: Religious Ethics, 1978.

Noonan, John. *How to Argue About Abortion.* New York: Free Press, 1979.

Shrage, Laurie. *Moral Dilemmas of Feminism: Prostitution, Adultery, and Abortion.* New York: Routledge, 1994.

Soloway, R. A. *Birth Control and the Population Question in England, 1877–1930.* Chapel Hill: University of North Carolina Press, 1982.

Steinbock, Bonnie. *Life Before Birth: The Moral and Legal Status of Embryos and Fetuses.* New York: Oxford University Press, 1992.

Summer, L. W. *Abortion and Moral Theory.* Princeton, NJ: Princeton University Press, 1981.

Tooley, Michael. *Abortion and Infanticide.* New York: Oxford University Press, 1983.

Euthanasia

Baird, Robert M., and Stuart E. Rosenbaum, eds. *Euthanasia: The Moral Issues.* Buffalo, NY: Prometheus Books, 1989.

Behnke, John A., and Sissela Bok. *The Dilemmas of Euthanasia.* New York: Doubleday, Anchor, 1975.

Brody, Baruch, ed. *Suicide and Euthanasia: Historical and Contemporary Themes.* Dordrecht: Reidel, 1989.

Caughill, R. E., ed. *The Dying Patient: A Supportive Approach.* Boston: Little, Brown, 1976.

Dworkin, Gerald, R. G. Frey, and Sissela Bok. *Euthanasia and Physician-Assisted Suicide.* New York: Cambridge University Press, 1998.

Filene, Peter G. *In the Arms of Others: A Cultural History of the Right-to-Die in America.* Chicago: Dee, 1998.

Glover, J. *Causing Death and Saving Lives.* Harmondsworth: Penguin Books, 1987.

Grisez, Germain, and Joseph Boyle. *Life and Death with Liberty and Justice.* Notre Dame, IN: University of Notre Dame Press, 1975.

Harrold, Joan K., and Joanne Lynn, eds. *A Good Dying: Shaping Health Care for the Last Months of Life.* New York: Haworth Press, 1998.

Humphry, D., and A. Wickett. *The Right to Die—Understanding Euthanasia.* New York: Harper & Row, 1986.

Kass, Leon R. "Neither for Love Nor Money: Why Doctors Must Not Kill." *The Public Interest* 94 (1989): 25–46.

Kevorkian, Jack. "The Last Fearsome Taboo: Medical Aspects of Planned Death." *Medicine and Law* 7 (1988): 1–14.

Kluge, Eike-Henner. *The Practice of Death.* New Haven, CT: Yale University Press, 1975.

Kohl, Marvin, ed. *Beneficent Euthanasia.* Buffalo, NY: Prometheus Press, 1975.

Kübler-Ross, Elisabeth. *On Death and Dying.* New York: Macmillan, 1969.

Kuhse, H. *The Sanctity-of-Life Doctrine in Medicine—A Critique.* Oxford: Oxford University Press, 1986.

Lynn, Joanne, ed. *By No Extraordinary Means: The Choice to Forgo Life-Sustaining Food and Water.* Bloomington: Indiana University Press, 1986.

Maguire, Daniel C. *Death by Choice.* Garden City, NY: Doubleday, 1974.

Rachels, James. *The End of Life: Euthanasia and Morality.* New York: Oxford University Press, 1987.

Russell, O. Ruth. *Freedom to Die: Moral and Legal Aspects of Euthanasia.* New York: Human Sciences Press, 1975.

Steinbock, Bonnie, ed. *Killing and Letting Die.* Englewood Cliffs, NJ: Prentice Hall, 1980.

Thomasma, David C., and Glenn C. Graber. *Euthanasia: Toward an Ethical Social Policy.* New York: Continuum, 1990.

Torr, James, ed. *Euthanasia: Opposing Viewpoints.* San Diego, CA: Greenhaven Press, 2000.

GLOSSARY

A

abortion   The termination of a pregnancy.

absolute   That which is independent of relation. The absolute is the opposite of the relative.

absolute idealism   For F. H. Bradley, the view that there must be an absolute or a harmonious reality that transcends our thought and in which "mere thinking is absorbed." Bradley's absolute idealism is a cross between British empiricism (Locke, Berkeley, Hume) and German idealism (particularly Hegel). See also *empiricism, idealism.*

active euthanasia   Causing death by administering a lethal and humane treatment such as a drug overdose. See *euthanasia.*

actus reas   A legal term for the alleged criminal act of which the defendant stands accused in a court of law.

act utilitarianism   The view that the rightness or wrongness of an action is decided on a case-by-case basis according to the utilitarian principles. Compare with *rule utilitarianism.*

ad hominem   Attacking the character of an alleged authority, rather than his or her argument or qualifications.

ad infinitum   Without limit; endless.

adultery   Sexual intercourse between a married person and someone other than the lawful spouse.

aestheticism   The view that art should be valued for itself alone and not for *any* purpose it may serve. This position is encapsulated in the French phrase *"l'art pour l'art,"* which translates as "art for art's sake."

aesthetics   The area of philosophy that studies the nature, value, sources, and limits of art and beauty. Aesthetics addresses questions concerning standards of artistic taste, aesthetic experience, the nature of interpretation, the nature of representation, the role of the artist in society, the nature of the individual arts (dance, music, literature, film, etc.), the purpose of art, the sublime, authorship, textuality, and the ontology (being) of art. Traditionally, aesthetics was limited to the subject of beauty or the beautiful in art and questions concerning the standards of taste; however, today, it is often used interchangeably with the philosophy of art, which is decidedly much broader in scope. It should be noted that each of the individual arts may be listed as subareas of aesthetics (or the philosophy of art). For example, the philosophy of literature and the philosophy of film are subareas of aesthetics.

a fortiori   For a still stronger reason.

agent   A self who is capable of deliberate action or is in the process of action.

agnosticism   The view that we should suspend belief, particularly with respect to God. Based on the Greek words *a* meaning "not" and *gignoskein* meaning "to know."

ahimsa   Noninjury. Hindus and Buddhists believe that each living thing is working out its own salvation and that we must be careful not to injure it by interfering with its progress.

alterity   Otherness; difference; diversity; marginality. That which is not assimilable.

altruism   The view that we should give moral consideration to others for their own sake and not for any self-interested reason. Compare with *egoism.*

analogy   Using similar characteristics among a number of things as the basis for inferring that a further similarity is probable.

analytic philosophy   A philosophical movement in the twentieth century that emphasized the analysis of language and concepts, as well as clear and rigorous philosophical argumentation. Some of its leading proponents were Bertrand Russell, Ludwig Wittgenstein (1889–1951), and G. E. Moore (1873–1958).

anatta In Buddhism, insubstantiality.

androcentrism The view that everything should be interpreted or seen in terms of male or masculine values and experience.

androgyny Having a combination of masculine and feminine gender or sex-role characteristics.

anicca In Buddhism, impermanence.

animism The view that all natural phenomena have souls.

antecedent In "If A, then B," A is the antecedent and B the consequent.

anthropocentrism The view that everything should be interpreted or seen in terms of human values and experience.

anthropomorphism The attribution of human characteristics to a god, animal, or inanimate object.

apostasy The total abandonment of one's principles.

a posteriori Designates a kind of knowledge that can be gained only from experience. Compare with *a priori*.

appeal to authority Seeking to persuade not by giving evidence but by citing an authority.

appeal to fear Seeking to persuade not by giving evidence but by appealing to fear.

appeal to ignorance (ad ignorantiam) Arguing that a claim is true just because it has not been shown to be false.

appeal to pity (ad misericordiam) Seeking to persuade not through evidence but by appealing to pity.

appealing to the crowd (ad populum) Seeking to persuade not through evidence but by appealing to the crowd.

applied ethics The attempt to explain and justify positions on specific moral problems such as abortion or capital punishment. Also called *applied normative ethics*.

a priori Designates a kind of knowledge that is arrived at independent of experience. Compare with *a posteriori*.

aretaic Virtuous. Based on the Greek word *areté* meaning "virtue" or "excellence."

argument A collection of statements. One statement is the *conclusion* of the argument. The other statements, often called *premises* or *reasons*, serve to show that the conclusion is true or that it is reasonable to believe that the conclusion is true.

artificial intelligence (AI) The use of computer programs and programming techniques to help understand the principles of intelligence in general and human cognition in particular. See *cognition, weak AI, strong AI*.

asceticism The view that we must deny ourselves bodily pleasures and comforts. Ascetics deny themselves pleasure for many reasons including the belief that pleasure and comfort can lead to sin or distract from the contemplation of higher things. Based on the Greek word *askesis* meaning "self-denial."

assimilation Process whereby a person becomes part of a dominant culture by replacing the characteristics of the person's own subdominant group with the (major) characteristics of the dominant group.

ataraxia A state of tranquility, free from mental and physical disturbances.

atheism The view that there is no God. Based on the Greek words *a* meaning "not" and *theos* meaning "God."

atheistic existentialism The view that if God does not exist, then there is at least one form of being whose existence precedes its essence: humans. Human existence precedes any essential conception of it.

atman/Atman In Hinduism, atman (with a small "a") is the occluded self that is working to cleanse itself, that is, the self before enlightenment, or the ordinary self. The larger, True Self is Atman (with a capital "A"). It is the concept of No Self, that is, the Self after enlightenment.

attribute That which inheres in substance, that is, an underlying, supporting substratum. That which is predicated on something else and is itself the object of predication. That which is subject to change. Compare with *substance, essence*.

autonomy The power to determine one's own course in life. The act of self-government or self-direction.

avidya Ignorance or unawareness that leads to clinging. Specifically, ignorance or unawarness of the identity of the individual self or soul. In Buddhism, avidya is the cause of all suffering.

axiom A statement accepted as true without proof, or a statement that is so obviously true that it is accepted as true without proof.

B

begging the question Assuming that which one wants to prove, or, more formally, implicitly using a conclusion as a premise.

behaviorism A type of psychology that bases the study of human nature on observable human actions and behavior, rather than on unobservable things such as states of mind or consciousness. See also *logical behaviorism.*

being May be subdivided into two general types: universals and particulars. Also, what all things possess, namely, existence. See *existence, particulars, universals.*

bias A particular tendency, preference, or inclination that inhibits impartiality or unprejudiced consideration of a question.

bigotry Intolerant attachment to a particular creed, opinion, or practice.

bisexual A person who is sexually attracted to members of both sexes.

bodhisattva An enlightened being or aspirant to Buddhahood.

bourgeois Middle class.

bourgeoisie The capitalists, who own the means of production such as factories. Compare to *proletariat.*

Brahman In Hinduism, an infinite, unchanging, immanent, and transcendent reality that is the source and sum of the cosmos. A personal, indwelling Supreme Being that is pure being or the world soul. The singular substrate of everything.

Buddhism Founded in the sixth century B.C.E. in southern Nepal by Gautama Siddhartha (560–477 B.C.E.), later simply called "the Buddha" (the Enlightened One). The Buddha achieved enlightenment through meditation and brought together a group of monks to carry on his teachings. The basic tenets of Buddhism include the following: (1) the belief that existence is a realm marked by suffering (dukkha); (2) the belief that we seek to be liberated from this suffering; (3) the belief that liberation from suffering is achievable only through the destruction of desire and delusions of the importance of the self; (4) the belief that enlightenment (nirvana) is connected to the destruction of desire and delusions of the importance of the self through meditation; (5) the belief in rebirth— one is subjected to repeated lifetimes that are good or bad depending on one's actions (karma); (6) the belief in a natural moral law that rules the process of karma and rebirth; (7) the belief that the world we see is without substance and is constantly changing; (8) the belief that there is no self; (9) the belief that the Buddha was a human teacher who had gained enlightenment and is a transcendent being who had once been mortal; and (10) the belief that there is no God.

C

capitalism An economic system characterized by a free market and open competition, in which goods are produced for profit, labor is performed for wages, and the means of production and distribution are privately owned. See also *laissez-faire capitalism.*

capital punishment The death penalty. Punishment for a crime by taking the offender's life.

Cartesian Refers to the thought of René Descartes.

Cartesian dualism Refers to René Descartes' theory that reality is composed of two different substances that are distinct from each other: *res extensa* (extended thing or body) and *res cogitans* (thinking thing or mind).

categorical imperative An unconditional command. For Immanuel Kant, this unconditional command can be formulated or expressed in several different ways. One version states that "I am never to act unless I am acting on a maxim that I can will to become a universal law." Another says to "act as if the maxims you choose to follow always become universal laws of nature." Yet another says to act so as "to treat humanity always also as an end and never merely as a means." Compare with *hypothetical imperative.*

category   The most basic division of a subject area.

catharsis   A purging of the emotions. For Aristotle, a good play involved catharsis for the audience.

causa sui   Causing itself, that is, the cause of itself.

causation   Refers to the relationship between two events: a cause event and an effect event. When the first event occurs (the cause), then the second event (the effect) is necessarily produced.

censorship   Prohibition of the dissemination of words or pictures.

ceterus paribus   Other things being equal. Many times used to indicate that a claim may be false under other conditions or that there may be exceptions.

civil rights movement   Started in the late 1950s in the United States, this movement aimed at legal enforcement of rights guaranteed to African-Americans as citizens under the U.S. Constitution. While earlier groups such as the National Association for the Advancement of Colored People (NAACP), which was founded 1910, and the National Urban League, which was founded in 1911, strove for similar ends, by the late 1950s their efforts had come to be viewed by many as too slow and unsuited to overcome white resistance to change in the South.

cognition   The act or process of knowing, which involves perception, judgment, intuition, and memory.

cognitive science   The science that attempts to understand and explain intelligent cognitive behavior in both humans and machines.

coherence theory of truth   The view that the true is a coherent system of ideas. F. H. Bradley is a proponent of this theory of truth.

commodity   Anything exchanged, bought, or sold.

communism   A system of political and social organization based on common ownership of the means of production. Communism

aims to hasten the demise of capitalism and to bring about a system of political power controlled by the proletariat, not the bourgeoisie. A communist political system will place the means of production under state control, abolish private property and inheritance, and centralize banking, communication, and transportation.

compatibilism   The view that freedom of the will and moral responsibility can be reconciled with determinism. Also called *soft determinism.*

complex question   Asking a question in such a way that it is impossible for people to agree or disagree with it without committing themselves to the claim that the person who is asking the question seeks to promote.

composition   The manner in which something is composed; the whole must have the properties of its parts.

concept   A general idea. Opposed to a sensation or percept. For example, "woman" is a concept, whereas the experience of seeing Simone de Beauvoir would be a sensation or percept. Compare with *percept.*

conclusion   The statement proven or demonstrated by an argument.

consciousness   The possession of mental states or processes.

consequent   In "If A, then B," A is the antecedent and B is the consequent.

consequentialism   The view that the morality of actions should be located in their nonmoral consequences. Utilitarianism is an example of a consequentialist general normative theory. Also called *teleological.*

conservatism   Beliefs and practices that in cultural and political contexts imply a resistance to change.

constructivism   The view that all of our knowledge is constructed, that is, based on human perception, convention, and social relationships and interactions. Constructivists are critical of essentialist, rationalist, and empiricist accounts of knowledge, and offer in their place a socially based account of knowledge. Also called *constructivist* *epistemology*. Compare with *empiricism, essentialism, rationalism*.

contingent   An event or entity that may be or may not be dependent on or conditioned by something else. Contrast with *necessary*.

contraceptive   Any special device or drug used to intentionally prevent the fertilization of an ovum.

contradiction, law of   The idea that a proposition cannot both be true and not be true. Also called the *law of noncontradiction*.

cooptation   To make use of for one's own purposes.

correspondence theory of truth   The view that the true "corresponds" to reality. Bertrand Russell is a proponent of this theory of truth.

cosmological argument (for the existence of God)   An argument for the existence of God that moves from observed facts about the cosmos (or universe) to the conclusion that God exists as the origin of these facts. Thomas Aquinas proposes three different formulations of the cosmological argument: one from change, one from cause, and one from contingency.

critical race theory   Examines the economic, political, and legal systems of a country from the perspective of the role they play in maintaining injustice based on race.

critical theory   A term first used by Max Horkheimer as descriptive of the social theory of the Frankfurt School, which includes the work of Walter Benjamin and Theodor Adorno. Critical theory attacked positivism and empiricism, which were claimed to wrongly separate facts from values and knowledge from all other human interests, and also relativism. Critical theorists aimed to construct epistemologies that were alternatives to empiricism, positivism, and relativism. Now used more broadly to encompass any critical, theoretical approach including feminism, race theory, and liberation theory. Compare with *empiricism, positivism, relativism*.

cultural diversity   A general phrase used to refer to the presence of differences based on class, race, ethnicity, gender, sex, and sexuality.

These differences may be manifested in individuals, groups of people, or the products of people.

cultural relativism   The view that no absolutes exist and that human judgment is always conditioned by the culture in which we live. See also *moral relativism, relativism*.

D

daemon   A guardian spirit, ranking somewhere between the gods and men, which the ancient philosophers believed presides over us and gives us private advice on our actions. It also watches over our most secret intentions. Based on the Greek word *daimon* meaning "individual spirit." See also *eudaimonia*.

deductive argument   A type of argument in which the conclusion must follow from a given set of premises. A valid deductive argument is such that if the premises are true, then the conclusion must be true. Compare with *inductive argument*.

deism   The view that God created the universe and administers it from without through natural laws.

democracy   Rule by the whole people either directly as in a *pure democracy* or through representatives as in a *representative democracy*.

deontological   Moral theories which maintain that the rightness or wrongness of an action depends on factors other than consequences. Examples include *divine command* theory and the *categorical imperative*. Also called *nonconsequentialist*. Compare with *consequentialism, teleology*.

descriptive morality   The factual investigation of moral behavior without any element of approval or disapproval. An example is research on the moral customs of distant societies conducted by anthropologists such as Ruth Benedict. Descriptive morality is a type of nonnormative ethics. Compare with *prescriptive morality*.

design, argument from   See *teleological argument*.

determinism   The view that everything in the universe operates in accordance with necessary and immutable causal laws. See also *hard determinism*. Contrast with *free will*.

Dhammapada   A Buddhist religious text that supposedly contains the Buddha's responses to various questions, primarily dealing with virtue. Regarded as the path of virtue that leads to enlightenment.

Dharma   The principles by which a person can achieve enlightenment. A set of rules to be followed to maintain individual well-being as well as social order. Also, the cosmic rule that forms the nature of everything in the universe. Also called the *Bauddhadharma*.

dialectic   For Socrates, a form of philosophical investigation that proceeds through dialogue, that is, question and answer. Interlocutors discuss the meaning, implications, and assumptions of various responses to philosophical questions, eliminating those that lead to contradictions or have unwanted implications. This process results in a clarification of key concepts and the consideration of increasingly stronger arguments, which in turn bring about a resolution of the philosophical investigation. Also called the *dialectical method*.

discrimination   Actions or choices that favor one group as opposed to another, based on their race, gender, sex, sexuality, and/or ethnicity.

distributive justice   An area of philosophical inquiry centered on questions concerning the just distribution of benefits and burdens at both the national and the international level.

divine command theory   The view that we should always do the will of God. According to divine command theory, an act is right if it is commanded by God and wrong if it is forbidden by God.

Divine nomocracy   A state organized such that authority is exercised by a representative who derives authority not directly from God, but from God's law, and that divine law itself is regarded as the sovereign power. Nomocracy comes from the Greek *nomos* meaning "law" or "custom." Contrast with *theocracy*.

division   Assuming that the parts must have the properties of the whole.

dualism   The view that existence is composed of two separate, independent, unique realms and that neither one can be reduced to the other. Plato's distinction between a world of the senses and a world of the intellect and Immanuel Kant's distinction between a noumenal world and a phenomenal world are both examples of dualism. See also *Cartesian dualism*.

dukkha   Suffering. In Buddhism, the first noble truth is that existence is suffering.

duty   For Kant, the end to which one's life is ultimately directed. Duty is defined by Kant through the categorical imperative. See *categorical imperative*.

E

egalitarianism   The view that all humans are equal and should be treated equally in terms of rights, liberties, respect, opportunities, and so on.

egoism   The view that we should consider only ourselves and that any consideration of others is based on self-interest. Compare with *altruism*. See also *ethical egoism, psychological egoism*.

eliminative materialism   The view that all human behavior can be explained in terms of neuroscience.

empiricism   The view that knowledge has its origins in and derives all of its content from experience. The writings of John Locke, George Berkeley, and David Hume are associated with empiricism. See also *positivism*.

ends, kingdom of   According to Immanuel Kant, the unity of all rational people under a universal moral law.

Epicureans   Refers to a school of philosophy founded in ancient Greece by Epicurus (341–270 B.C.E.). The early Epicureans were hedonists, regarding pleasure as the highest good.

epistemic   Pertaining to knowledge. Epistemic claims are about the nature of knowledge.

epistemological relativism   The view that all truth is relative. See also *cultural relativism, ethical relativism, relativism*.

epistemology   The area of philosophy that studies the sources, types, objects, and limits of knowledge. Epistemology addresses questions concerning what we can know and how.

epistemology, constructivist   See *constructivism*.

epistemology, standpoint   See *standpoint epistemology*.

equivocation   Using a single word in more than one sense.

ergo   Therefore.

erotica   Sexually explicit, but not *obscene*, pictures or descriptions that are sexually interesting. Feminists many times further qualify the definition, calling *erotica* sexually explicit material that depicts sexuality in a mutually empowering manner. Compare with *pornography*. See also *obscene*.

essence   That by which a thing is what it is. A defining characteristic of a thing such that which, if lacking in the thing, it would not be itself. A more permanent and fixed aspect of a thing. Compare with *attribute*.

essentialism   The view that essence precedes existence. Essentialists maintain that the essence of an entity is responsible for determining the nature of the entity's existence. Essentialism can be traced back most famously to Plato's theory of forms or ideas. Compare with *existentialism*.

ethical absolutism   Any view that affirms the existence of a single universally applicable moral standard.

ethical egoism   A normative view about how people *ought* to act. The ethical egoist believes that we have no obligation to do anything except what is in our own self-interest. According to the ethical egoist, whatever we do in our own self-interest, regardless of its effect on others, is morally justified. Compare with *psychological egoism*. See also *egoism*.

ethical relativism   Any view that denies the existence of a single universally applicable moral standard.

ethical subjectivism   The view that moral judgments are simply assertions of opinion on the part of the person making the moral judgment.

ethics   The area of philosophy that studies morality in itself in addition to moral psychology and the nature of moral knowledge. Ethics addresses questions concerning how we ought to act toward ourselves and others. It takes up the meaning of good and evil, right and wrong, in themselves and as they relate to conduct, character, disposition, and things. While ethics is sometimes also called *moral philosophy*, some scholars separate ethics from moral philosophy by limiting the latter to only the study of morality in itself.

ethnocentrism   The view that one's own race or ethnic group is superior to other races or ethnic groups.

eudaimonia   For Aristotle, happiness. From the Greek *eu* meaning "happy or harmonious" and *daimon* meaning "individual spirit." See also *daemon*.

eudaimonistic utilitarianism   A moral theory claiming that what is morally right is whatever produces the greatest amount of happiness. This view was held by John Stuart Mill. Compare with *hedonistic utilitarianism*.

euthanasia   The act or practice of painlessly putting to death (or of intentionally not preventing the death of) those who suffer from terminal conditions. Some choose to drop the requirement of a "terminal condition" when defining euthanasia.

ex hypothesi   By hypothesis.

existence   That which distinguishes fictional objects from real objects. Everything that is reality.

existentialism   The view that existence precedes essence. Existentialism places responsibility for defining the essence of an entity entirely upon its existence. Compare with *essentialism*.

ex nihilo   Out of nothing.

extension   The object or set of objects to which a term refers. Compare with *intension*.

extrinsic   Not essentially or really belonging to the thing or state of being with which it is connected—that is, coming from outside the thing or state of being to which it is connected. Contrast with *intrinsic*.

F

fact   An actual state of affairs.

fallacy   An incorrect way of reasoning. Many times a fallacy is simply an invalid argument that appears to be a valid one.

false analogy   A conclusion that is reached by comparing two significantly incomparable cases.

false cause   Concluding that there is a causal link between two events when no such link has been established.

false dilemma   Reducing the number of options considered to just two. These options are often sharply opposed and unfair to the person to whom the dilemma is posed.

fatalism   The view that events are fixed and beyond human control.

feminism   There are many different definitions of feminism, and consequently many different feminisms. However, broadly conceived, feminism is a set of ideas connected with a social movement that advocates advancing the political and legal rights of women. Many feminisms work to establish equal opportunities for women in all areas of life and the right for women to determine for themselves the kinds of lives and interests that they pursue.

finite   Limited.

folk psychology   The view that human behavior can be explained in terms of human beliefs and desires.

foundationalism   In epistemology, the view that all knowledge must have an indubitable foundation. René Descartes' "I think, therefore I am" (*Cogito ergo sum*) is the best-known indubitable foundation for knowledge.

free speech   A term used to designate forms of speech, or more generally, expressions, that are legally protected. In the United States, for example, debate concerning the scope of free speech has ranged from hate speech to flag burning. The question has been whether and to what extent these forms of expression are legally permissible as forms of free speech protected by the U.S. Constitution.

free will   The view that people have freedom of decision or choice without coercion between alternative courses of action. See *libertarianism (metaphysical)*. Contrast with *determinism*.

functionalism   The view that the mind or consciousness consists only of functional activities of consciousness. That is, a human being has such-and-such a mental state when that individual behaves in the ways we take to be appropriate for an organism in that state.

G

gay   A male homosexual.

gender   Used to refer to the differences between men and women that are cultural or societal in origin. *Masculine* and *feminine* are generally used to refer to distinctions made on the basis of gender. Also called *sex role*. See *sex*.

genetic fallacy   Attacking a position, institution, or idea by condemning its background or origin.

genocide   The systematic killing of an entire ethnic group or nation.

gestalt   The view that the whole is not just the sum of the parts.

Golden Mean   Refers to the concept of moderation, harmony, or balance that is utilized in many moral theories including Aristotle's virtue theory. For Aristotle, courage, for example, is presented as a virtue that is a mean between the extremes of rashness (an excess) and cowardice (a deficiency). Also found in Confucian ethics in the claim that the harmonious life is the one that avoids excesses and deficiences and that wisdom is to be found in both high places and low places, in older people as well as in younger people. The term was coined in the first century B.C.E. by the Latin poet Horace (*Odes* 2.10.5).

Golden Rule   "Do unto others as you would have them do unto you." Versions of this rule are central to most religions and moral theories. Immanuel Kant's *categorical imperative* attempts to make this rule obligatory to rational persons.

greatest happiness principle   The view that what is morally right is whatever produces the greatest happiness for the greatest number. Associated with Jeremy Bentham (1748–1832) but first formulated by the English philosopher Francis Hutcheson (1694–1746) in 1725 in *An Inquiry into the Origins of Our Ideas of Beauty and Virtue* (iii. 8).

gynocentric   Woman or female centered.

H

Hadith   The "Traditions" or sayings, deeds, and approvals of the Prophet Mohammed.

hard determinism   The view that *all* events, including human actions, are completely *determined*. This position denies humans freedom in and responsibility for their actions. See also *determinism*.

hasty generalization   Using an isolated or exceptional case as the basis for an unwarranted general conclusion.

hate speech   Offensive speech that is intended to insult and harm others based on their race, ethnicity, gender, or sexuality.

hedonism   The view that pleasure is the only intrinsic value and is the proper end and aim of all morally right action. Based on the Greek word *hedone* meaning "pleasure."

hedonistic utilitarianism   A moral theory claiming that what is morally right is whatever produces the greatest amount of pleasure. This view was held by Jeremy Bentham (1748–1832). Compare with *eudaimonistic utilitarianism*.

hegemony   Dominance of one group, state, class, or set of ideas over others.

hermaphrodite   A person or animal with both male and female sexual organs.

heterosexuality   Sexual feeling for a person or persons of the opposite sex.

heuristic   Something that encourages one to discover something; an aid to learning.

Hobbesist   Refers to the social and political philosophy of Thomas Hobbes.

holism   (1) The view that everything in the world is somehow related to everything else. (2) The holist theory of truth states that truth

or meaning attaches only to a system as a whole and not to any individual part of the system. F. H. Bradley's coherence theory of truth is a holism. See *coherence theory of truth*.

homosexuality   Sexual feeling for a person or persons of the same sex.

humanism   The view that we have the freedom to give our lives value, purpose, and meaning through free inquiry, creative activity, and independent thought. Humanism rejects religion as a source of knowledge in favor of science. Also rejects theism, miracles, and life after death.

human rights   Entitlements that belong to each person by nature or by virtue of being human. Sometimes also called *natural rights*.

hypothesis   A statement proposed as a possible solution to a problem. Once proposed, a hypothesis is then generally subject to either experimentation, argumentation, or observation.

hypothetical imperative   A conditional command—for example, "If you want a better grade on the exam, then you'll have to study." Compare with *categorical imperative*.

I

idealism   (1) In metaphysics, the position that reality is ultimately mental, spiritual, or nonmaterial in nature. (2) In epistemology, the position that all we know are our ideas. George Berkeley's positions are in accord with both epistemological and metaphysical idealism. See also *absolute idealism*.

idea(s)   That which exists only as the contents of a mind. Note that this type of idea is different from Plato's ideas, that is, *universals* that subsist independent from a mind.

identity, personal   See *personal identity*.

identity theory   The view that there is a one-to-one correspondence between mental states and brain states, and that mental states are *really* brain states. Also called *reductive materialism, physicalism*.

ideology   Any system of beliefs or way of thought that provides an account of how the world should be based on moral assumptions, economic interests, and/or social and political beliefs.

idolatry   Worship of a false deity or an idol, that is, an image of a god.

immanent   Present throughout the universe as opposed to outside of it. Operating within. Opposed to transcendent.

immaterialism   George Berkeley calls his philosophy *immaterialism*, emphasizing in this label its rejection of matter. For him, "it is plain that the very notion of what is called *Matter* or *corporeal substance*, involves a contradiction in it," and that "there is not any other Substance *Spirit* or that which perceives." Berkeley's argument against the existence of matter might be formulated as follows: (1) Whatever can be thought of is an idea in the mind of the person thinking it. (2) Nothing can be thought of except ideas in minds; anything else is inconceivable. (3) What is inconceivable cannot exist; therefore, matter, which by definition is not an idea in a mind, cannot exist. Thus, according to Berkeley, the world is not composed of both material substances (matter) and immaterial substances (minds, spirits, or souls) but only of the latter, which he simply calls *Spirit*. Also called *subjective idealism*. See also *idealism*. Compare with *materialism*.

imperative   A command. See *categorical imperative, hypothetical imperative*.

imperfect duties   For Immanuel Kant, imperfect duties consist of actions whose maxims *could* become universal laws of nature, but it is impossible for us to *will* that their maxims should be universal laws of nature since such a will would be in conflict with itself. Compare with *perfect duties*.

immortality   The view that the soul or self survives physical death.

indeterminism   See *libertarianism (metaphysical)*.

inductive argument   A type of argument in which the conclusion is not guaranteed by the premises even if it is rendered plausible or probable by them. Here is an example of an inductive argument: (1) The sun always rises in the east. (2) Therefore, the sun will rise in the east tomorrow. This type of argument moves from particular claims (1) to a general conclusion (2). Compare with *deductive argument*.

infinite   Unlimited.

innate ideas   The notion that the soul comes into the world with ideas or knowledge already stored in it. This notion goes back at least as far as Plato and is found as well in Descartes' *Meditations*, which utilizes innate ideas, such as those concerning mathematics and infinite perfection.

instrumental value   Something that is valued as a means to some other end. Compare with *intrinsic value*.

intension   The characteristics of a term as presented in its definition. Compare with *extension*.

intention   A concept formed when the mind is directed toward an object.

intersubjective   The state or quality of being accessible to two or more subjectivities or consciousnesses. See *subjectivity*.

intertheoretic reduction   The process whereby the terms and principles of an older, weaker theory are reduced or translated to the terms and principles of a newer, more powerful theory.

intrinsic   Essentially or really belonging to the thing or state of being with which it is connected—that is, coming from inside the thing or state of being to which it is connected. Contrast with *extrinsic*.

intrinsic value   Something that is valuable in itself. Compare with *instrumental value*.

intuition   Direct knowledge of something without the use of reason or sensation.

invalid argument   An argument whose conclusion may be false when its premises are true. Compare with *valid argument*.

involuntary action   According to Aristotle, one done under external compulsion or through ignorance. Compare with *nonvoluntary action, voluntary action*.

involuntary euthanasia   Killing or allowing to die a person who, despite severe suffering and faced with the prospect of a painful end, expresses the desire *not* to die.

ipso facto   By the fact itself.

J

jen   A central concept in Confucian philosophy that is translated as "benevolence," "humanity," and "goodness."

jhāna   An altered state of consciousness.

judgment   (1) The faculty through which we affirm or deny propositions. (2) A proposition. See *proposition*.

jus taliones   The right of retaliation. See *lex taliones*.

K

kamma   In Buddhism, desire or pleasure.

karma   A principle of continuity wherein the effects of actions become physically and morally part of the organism and the environment—thoughts, words, and deeds become part of the permanent structure of one's life. For Hindus, who believe in reincarnation, our karmic structure is carried into each succeeding cycle of existence.

karuna   Compassion.

L

laissez-faire capitalism   A capitalist economic system marked by noninterventionism by the government into the workings of the markets. See also *capitalism*. Compare with *statism*.

legal paternalism   The view that governments may prohibit acts by which a person may harm her- or himself.

Leibniz's law   Law stating that two things are distinct only if they have different properties. If they have the same properties, then they will be the same thing. Also called the *principle of the identity of indiscernibles*.

lex taliones   The law of retaliation, according to which deserved punishment is neither more nor less than the harm done in a crime, and ideally mirrors the crime. Its best-known formulation is found in the Bible: "life for life, eye for eye, tooth for tooth . . . wound for wound . . ." (*Exodus* 21:22–25). Also referred to as *jus taliones*.

lesbian   A female homosexual.

li   A central concept in Confucian philosophy, translated as "rules of proper behavior," "custom," "etiquette," "ceremony," "worship," "propriety," and "ritual."

liberalism   A political ideology centered on the idea that individuals possess rights against the government, including the rights of equality of respect, freedom of expression and action, and freedom from religious and ideological constraint. Liberalism contends that individuals have the right to be protected from being harmed by others and the right to private property. Also, according to liberalism, a degree of economic and social inequality is acceptable. The least advantaged individuals have some positive right to be provided with some of the basic necessities of life just as long as it does not interfere too greatly with the structure of the underlying capitalist economy. The historical figure most closely associated with liberalism is John Stuart Mill.

libertarianism (metaphysical)   The view that a rational human being has the freedom of will to choose without being compelled to his or her choice by causes or forces independent of the act. Because libertarians reject the determination of the will, they are also sometimes simply called *indeterminists*.

libertarianism (social and political)   The belief that we have a fundamental right to liberty, that is, to be left alone and not to have the products of our labor taken from us. We do not have a right to life in the positive sense that others have a duty to provide us with goods to help us to live or even live well. The state exists mainly to protect individuals from harming one another and to enforce contracts. Accordingly, government programs to assist those without adequate food, shelter, or health care are generally not supported by libertarians. Libertarians trace the roots of their ideas back to John Locke rather than John Stuart Mill. Also called *classical liberalism*.

liberation (theology)   A type of theology dedicated to improving the lives of the oppressed. James Cone argues that Christianity is the religion of the oppressed and that both God and Christ are black.

logic   The area of philosophy that studies the methods and principles of correct reasoning.

Logic addresses questions concerning what is coherent thought.

logical behaviorism   The view that discussion of mental states is just another way of talking about actual and possible bodily behavior. Mental terms are disposition terms. According to logical behaviorism, when we do something, we are not performing at the same time a mental action and a physical action. Rather, we are simply behaving in a certain way. For example, to say "John is hungry" implies that John will probably say he is hungry if asked and will eat something if given a chance. See also *behaviorism*.

M

Manicheism   A religious system developed by Mani of Persia in the third century C.E. that emphasizes the dualism of good (spirit, light) and evil (body, dark) as independent principles.

materialism   The view that reality is ultimately composed of matter. Compare with *immaterialism*.

matriarchal   Ruled by women.

matter   For Descartes, matter is *res extensa* or "extended thing" and is opposed to mind or *res cogitans* or "thinking thing." Matter is extended and divisible, whereas mind is indivisible and unextended. See *materialism*.

maxim   For Kant, a subjective rule that an individual uses in making a decision.

maya   In Hinduism, the world of illusion, that is, of a limited reality that is solely mental and physical. This world of illusion clouds our consciousness of the true Self and Brahman, that is, infinite reality.

mens rea   Criminal intent, or the knowledge that one's act is criminal before or while committing the act.

mental state   A state or process of consciousness such as having a sensation, seeing something or experiencing an emotion.

metaethics   Investigates the meaning of ethical terms such as "right" and "wrong," "good" and "bad," as well as the procedures by which ethical terms are verified.

metaphor   Where one subject matter is referred to by a term or sentence that does not literally describe it—for example, "the winter of our discontent" or "the ship of state."

metaphysics   The area of philosophy that studies the nature of reality, existence, and being. Metaphysics addresses questions concerning what there is. Specific topics in metaphysics include the nature of space and time, free will and determinism, the nature of causation, the distinction between appearance and reality, the distinction between the mind and the body, the nature of God, and the nature of identity.

metatheory   The assumptions presupposed by any group of assertions. These might involve the concepts implied in the vocabulary used in the assertions, or the rules of inference that allow derivations among assertions.

mimesis   Imitation, that is, modeling, of one thing on another or presenting one thing by another. A central concept in Plato's and Aristotle's respective philosophies of art.

mind, philosophy of   The area of philosophy that studies the nature and contents of mind as well as our knowledge of mind. Philosophy of mind addresses questions concerning minds and machines, artificial intelligence, the nature of the self, the nature of consciousness, the nature of feelings and emotions, and the relationship of the mind to the body.

mind–body dualism   See *Cartesian dualism*.

misogyny   Hatred of women.

mode   The manner of existence of a substance or a thing. See *substance*.

modus operandi   Manner of working.

moira   Fate.

monism   The view that only one kind of substance exists. See *substance*. Compare with *pluralism*.

monotheism   The view that there is only one God.

moral absolutism   The view that moral principles are absolute and hold for all people at all times and in all situations.

moral development   Refers to the acquisition, formation, and growth of beliefs about right and wrong, good and evil.

moral isolationism The view that people should not be morally concerned with persons outside of their immediate group.

morality The particular practices, percepts, and customs of people and cultures.

moral philosophy See *ethics.*

moral relativism The view that there are no absolute moral principles. What is morally right or wrong depends on the time and place in which people live. According to the moral relativist, different societies, different people, and different historical periods can result in different moral principles. See *cultural relativism, relativism.*

moral scepticism (or skepticism) Either doubting all moral claims until they are proved, or holding that moral knowledge is not possible.

multiculturalism The view that the perspectives of women, minorities, and non-Western cultures are equally as valuable and valid as the perspectives of men, whites, and Western culture(s).

mutatis mutandis After making the necessary changes.

N

naturalism The view that nature is all that exists or is real.

natural law theory Any view that attempts to link the nature of human beings (or even the universe) with morality and the law. It is especially associated with the positions of Thomas Aquinas, who distinguishes four interrelated types of law: divine, natural, law of nations, and civil. For Aquinas, divine law is made known to us through revelation and reason. What we can discern of divine law (*jus divinum*) through our reason he calls natural law (*jus naturale*), and both the law of nations (*jus gentium*) and civil law (*jus civile*) are derived from natural law.

natural rights See *human rights.*

necessary Always true. No other event or state of affairs is possible. Contrast with *contingent.*

necessary condition If *x* is a necessary condition of *y*, then *y* cannot be the case if *x* is not the case. Alternately, if not *x*, then not *y*. For example, being a plane closed figure is a necessary condition of something being a triangle. For another example, being a Ford Escort is not a necessary condition for being a car. There are many cars that are not Ford Escorts. See also *sufficient condition.*

negative duties Duties that call on us to refrain from doing things—for example, the duty to refrain from harming other people. Compare with *positive duties.*

neo-pragmatism A philosophical movement that denies that there are universal or objective conceptions of truth and reality. Neo-pragmatism's rejection of essentialism and foundationalism leads it to be termed *antiessentialist* and *antifoundationalist.* Richard Rorty, one of the movement's major voices, argues that language and interpretation are constitutive of all experience. Compare with *essentialism, foundationalism, pragmatism.*

neuroscience The study of how the brain works.

nihilism Generally, the view that there is no meaning or purpose in existence. More specifically, metaphysical nihilism is the position that nothing exists; epistemological nihilism is the position that nothing can be known; and ethical nihilism is the position that all moral judgments are without value.

nirvana A state of release, enlightenment, or salvation. Buddhism holds that nirvana is connected to the destruction of desire and delusions of the importance of the self through meditation.

nominalism The view that universal terms do not refer to anything in reality. Even if they are necessary for thought, they are names only. Opposed to realism. Compare with *realism.*

nonconsequentialism The view that the morality of an action depends on factors other than consequences. Examples of nonconsequentialist moral theories include *divine command* theory and the *categorical imperative.* Also called *deontological.* Compare with *consequentialism.*

noncontradiction, law of See *contradiction, law of.*

nonmoral Issues that lie outside the sphere of moral concern.

nonnormative ethics   Consists of the scientific or descriptive study of ethics and metaethics. Scientific or descriptive study involves the factual investigation of moral behavior and is called *descriptive morality*. See also *descriptive morality, metaethics*. Compare with *normative ethics*.

nonvoluntary action   According to Aristotle, any action done in ignorance. However, if pain and regret follow an act done in ignorance, the act becomes strictly *involuntary* and pardonable. Compare with *involuntary action, voluntary action*.

nonvoluntary euthanasia   Situation in which a patient is incapable of requesting or indicating a desire for death, or of forming judgments in the matter. Standard cases of nonvoluntary euthanasia occur when patients, for example, are comatose or senile and have left no legal document like a living will in which they state their preferences regarding extraordinary medical treatment. Compare with *voluntary euthanasia*.

normative ethics   The branch of ethics that makes judgments about obligation and value. Unlike nonnormative ethics, which is only concerned with issues such as the meaning of the terminology of ethics or the descriptive study of ethics, normative ethics is concerned with what is actually right or wrong. Compare with *nonnormative ethics*.

noumena   For Kant, things as they actually are rather than only as presented to us through the structure of our understanding. Compare with *phenomena*.

O

objective   That which has a public nature independent of the individual and his or her judgments about it. Compare with *subjective*.

objective phenomenology   For Thomas Nagel, a way of describing phenomena not dependent on the point of view of the subject of experience. The goal of this objective phenomenology would be to describe the subjective character of experience in a way that could be understood by those not capable of such experience. Compare with *phenomenology*.

objectivism   A view of what is known or perceived that emphasizes its public nature, that is, its nature independent of the individual subject and her or his judgments about it.

objectivity   The quality of being objective, that is, having a public nature independent of the individual subject and the individual subject's judgments. Contrast with *subjectivity*.

obscene   The U.S. Supreme Court held that a work is obscene when (1) the average person, applying contemporary community standards, would find that the work, taken as a whole, appeals to the prurient interest; and, (2) the work depicts or describes, in a patently offensive way, sexual conduct that is specifically defined by law; and (3) the work, taken as a whole, lacks serious literary, artistic, political, or scientific value. See *pornography*.

Ockham's razor   The view that, all things being equal, the simplest explanation tends to be the right one. Named after the medieval philosopher William Ockham (1285–1347). Also called the *principle of parsimony*.

omnipotent   All-powerful.

omnipresent   All-present, that is, present everywhere at one time.

omniscience   All-knowing.

ontological argument, the   An argument for the existence of God advanced by Saint Anselm. The argument begins with the premise that God is perfect and moves to the conclusion that God exists.

ontology   A subdivision of *metaphysics* concerned with the nature of being and existence. An *ontological* problem is one concerning the nature of being. See *being, existence*.

oppression   To keep down or weigh heavily upon the minds and spirits of others by cruel or unjust use of power or authority.

ovum   An egg; the female reproductive cell.

P

paññâ   In Buddhism, discernment or wisdom that results from right understanding of the Four Noble Truths and right thinking, that is, following the right path in life. While this kind of wisdom or discernment is useful, it alone will not lead to enlightenment. Also called *prajna*.

pantheism   The view that God is immanent in all created things and has no existence separate from them. Based on the Greek words *pan* meaning "all" and *theos* meaning "God."

paradigm   A set of shared beliefs through which an area of reality is interpreted.

parsimony, principle of   See *Occam's razor*.

particulars   An instance of a universal. For example, there is the particular woman, Simone de Beauvoir. As viewed from the notion of universals/particulars, de Beauvoir is an instance or a particular of the universal "woman." Contrast with *universals*.

passive euthanasia   Letting a patient die by withholding or withdrawing all extraordinary equipment that may prolong life. An example of extraordinary equipment would be a respirator, an iron lung, or radiation treatment.

patriarchy   A social system in which men dominate in all important areas of life, usually associated with their roles as fathers and husbands but extending to public life as well.

percept   A particular idea, that is, what we experience when we experience a particular thing. For example, the experience of seeing Simone de Beauvoir is a percept. Compare with *concept*.

perception   The act or process by which one becomes aware of things.

perfect duties   For Immanuel Kant, duties consisting of actions whose maxims can neither consistently be conceived nor willed by us to be universal laws of nature. Compare with *imperfect duties*.

personal identity   A philosophical topic concerning whether we are the same person over time.

personhood   The necessary and sufficient conditions for being a person.

phenomena   For Kant, the world as presented to us through the structure of our understanding. Compare with *noumena*.

phenomenology   An approach to philosophy that centers on analysis and description of phenomena. See *objective phenomenology, phenomena*.

philology   The study of ancient languages and writings, including their grammar, rhetoric, and historical and cultural context.

philosophy   The pursuit of wisdom or knowledge. More specifically, rational, critical, and often systematic thinking about and analysis of the general nature of reality and existence (metaphysics), the nature and scope of knowledge (epistemology), the conduct of life (ethics), the nature of justice and the state (social and political philosophy), and the principles of correct reasoning (logic). The term *philosophy* is a combination of the Greek words *philos* (love of) and *sophia* (wisdom), and literally means "love of wisdom."

physicalism   See *identity theory*.

pluralism   The view that more than one kind of substance exists. See *substance*. Compare with *monism*.

plutocracy   A formation of the state that is controlled or at least greatly influenced by a group of wealthy people. Political power is directly connected with wealth.

poesis   For Plato, a term that refers to all forms of artistic creativity including music, drama, poetry, prose fiction, painting, and sculpture. In Greek, *poesis* literally means "making."

poisoning the well   Disparaging an argument before even mentioning it.

polis   The ancient Greek city-state.

pornography   Sexually explicit material that is obscene. Feminists many times further qualify the definition, calling pornography sexually explicit material that is *degrading to women*. Compare with *erotica*. See also *obscene*.

positive duties   Duties that call on us to do something—for example, the duty to help those in harm's way. Compare with *negative duties*.

positivism   The view that knowledge should be based only on observable, scientific facts and the data of sense experience. Compare with *critical theory, empiricism, relativism*.

postmodernism   In philosophy, generally refers to the rejection of foundationalism (e.g., Cartesian epistemology), essentialism, realism, transcendental arguments, truth as correspondence, and grand narratives.

pragmatism   An American philosophical movement popularized by William James but founded by Charles Peirce (1839–1914). James and Peirce differed in their conception of pragmatism to the point that Peirce called his own version "pragmaticism" in 1905 to distinguish it from James' version. In general, pragmatism emphasizes the interpretation of ideas through their consequences. Peirce states the pragmatic maxim as follows: "Consider what effects, which might conceivably have practical bearings, we conceive the object of our conception to have. Then, our conception of these effects is the whole of our conception of the object." James's pragmatic maxim is as follows: "The meaning of any proposition can always be brought down to some particular consequence in our future practical experience, whether passive or active."

prajna   See *paññâ*.

predestination   The doctrine that God determined or foreordained everything that has happened since the beginning of time.

predicate   That which is said of a subject. A grammatical term for the verb phrase in the subject–predicate sentence, where the noun phrase is the subject.

premise   A statement used in an argument as a reason for accepting a conclusion.

prescriptive morality   The study of moral behavior that makes judgments about obligation and value. Thus, unlike *descriptive morality*, which is concerned only with describing moral behavior, prescriptive morality is concerned with what is right or wrong. Compare with *descriptive morality*. See *normative ethics*.

presentationism   The view that in perception the mind is directly aware of external objects. Compare with *representationalism*.

prima facie   At first view or appearance, or on first consideration. The term is used to suggest that while an inference can be made that appears to be valid, a complete investigation has yet to been done.

primary qualities   For John Locke, qualities that are "utterly inseparable from the body," namely, "solidity, extension, figure, motion or rest, and number." Compare with *secondary qualities*.

proletariat   The workers who are employed as wage laborers by the bourgeoisie and who do not own the means of production. See *bourgeoisie*.

property   In metaphysics, that which belongs to or is attributable to some thing but is not part of the essence or essential nature of the thing. For example, the ability to jump is a property of humans but is not part of the essence or essential nature of humans; one can be a human and not be able to jump.

proposition   What is expressed or asserted by a true or a false statement. Also sometimes called a *judgment*.

providence   Refers to the guiding power or agency of God in the universe.

provincialism   Mistaking a local fact for a universal one.

psychological egoism   The view that all people are selfish in everything they do. According to the psychological egoist, the only motive from which anyone ever acts is self-interest. Compare with *ethical egoism*.

psycho-physical dualism   See *Cartesian dualism*.

Q

qualities   See *primary qualities, secondary qualities*.

R

racial contract, the   According to Charles Mills, a contact that grants white men natural freedom and equality, and designates nonwhites as born *un*free and *un*equal. The general purpose of the racial contract is "the differential privileging of the whites as a group with respect to the nonwhites as a group, the exploitation of their bodies, land, and resources, and the denial of equal socioeconomic opportunities to them." The racial contract is *not* a contract consented to by nonwhites. Compare with *social contract theory*.

racial discrimination   Actions or choices in favor of one racial group over another.

racism   Refers to the inability or refusal to recognize the rights, needs, dignity, or value of people of particular races or geographical origins.

racist   A practice, action, or belief that promotes, creates, or takes unfair advantage of any irrelevant or impertinent differences between races.

raison d'être   Reason for being.

rape   The crime of forcing a person to submit to sexual intercourse.

rational   Able to reason; based on reasoning.

rationalism   The general doctrine that reason alone, without the aid of information from the senses, is capable of arriving at knowledge. The writings of Plato and Descartes are associated with rationalism.

realism   (1) The position that the truth or falsehood of a belief depends on something exterior to the belief itself. (2) In opposition to nominalism, realism contends that universal terms have a reality of their own. Compare with *nominalism*.

red herring   Introducing irrelevant or secondary information into an argument thereby diverting attention away from the main subject of the argument.

reductio ad absurdum   Disproof of a principle or proposition by showing that it leads to an absurdity when followed to its logical conclusion.

reductive materialism   See *identity theory*.

reify   To treat an idea or a concept as though it were a thing, that is, an object in the world.

relativism   The view that no absolutes exist and that human judgment is always conditioned by a number of factors including our personal biases and the culture in which we live.

religion, philosophy of   The area of philosophy that studies the meaning and justification of religious claims. The philosophy of religion addresses questions concerning the nature of God, proofs for the existence of God, the nature of religious knowledge, faith versus reason, religious experience, the problem of evil, miracles, immortality, science versus religion, religious pluralism, and the meaning of life.

representationalism   (1) In aesthetics, the theory and practice of representational art. (2) In epistemology, the view that the mind apprehends external objects only by means of percepts or ideas. Compare with *presentationism*.

rights   Justifiable claims for the protection of our interests.

romanticism   A philosophical movement that emphasizes the role of nature, imagination, emotion, and subjectivity as opposed to the Enlightenment ideals of reason and objectivity. For Oscar Wilde, the return to nature in art.

rule utilitarianism   The view that the *utilitarian principle* should be used to judge moral rules by examining the effects on overall happiness of rules. Compare with *act utilitarianism*.

S

scholium   A marginal comment that expands on a course of reasoning or proof.

scientific method   The process in which physical evidence is observed and hypotheses are formed. These hypotheses must be falsifiable; that is, it must be possible to show that the hypothesis is wrong. Reproducible experiments are conducted to test predictions based on the hypotheses, and hypotheses that are repeatedly verified by experiments become scientific theories.

secondary qualities   For John Locke, "qualities which in truth are nothing in the objects themselves but power to produce various sensations in us by their primary qualities," such as colors, smells, sounds, and tastes. Compare with *primary qualities*.

secular humanism   For Bertrand Russell, the view that we must stand up for our ideals against a hostile, indifferent universe.

secularism   Worldly or temporal doctrines or views, particularly those that avoid or disregard matters of religious faith. Based on the Latin word *saecularis* meaning "the world" or "the times."

self Person, particularly the inner or psychological life of the person as opposed to his or her outward, bodily form.

semantics The study of the meanings of words.

semiotics The theory of signs. See also *sign, symbol*.

sense data That which is immediately perceived by the sense organs.

sentient Having sense perception or the capacity to feel.

sentiment For David Hume, a feeling that is evoked by an object that is under moral scrutiny. Sentiment is the opposite of reason.

sex Used to refer to the differences between men and women that are biological in origin. The words *male* and *female* are generally used to refer to distinctions made on the basis of sex. Also short for "sexual intercourse." See *gender, sex role*.

sex discrimination Actions or choices that favor one sex over the other.

sexism The exploitation of irrelevant or unjustified differences between the sexes, or the creation of irrelevant or unjustified differences between the sexes

sexist See *sex discrimination, sexism*.

sex role Used to refer to the differences between men and women that are cultural or societal in origin. *Masculine* and *feminine* are generally used to refer to distinctions made on the basis of sex role. Also called *gender*.

sine qua non An indispensable condition.

sign Something that stands for something else. For Charles Peirce, a sign is anything that stands for something (which he called its "object") in such a way as to generate another sign (which he called its "interpretant"). Compare with *symbol*.

signification The process by which signs and meanings are produced.

skepticism There are three major types of skepticism: Cartesian (or Descartes'), Pyrrhonian (or excessive), and mitigated (or limited) skepticism. Cartesian skepticism recommends universal doubt, that is, doubt

concerning all our opinions, principles, and human faculties, as necessary to protect us from error. Pyrrhonism, named after its first exponent, Pyrrho of Elis (c. 360–270 B.C.E.), claims that it is impossible to know the nature of anything and that we should suspend judgment of everything, including our ignorance and doubt. Mitigated or limited skepticism, as advocated by David Hume, avoids dogmatic opinions and wild doctrines and, as Hume says, "limits our enquiries to such subjects as are best adapted to the narrow capacity of human understanding."

slippery slope Unjustifiably assuming that a proposal or position that is not undesirable or dangerous will trigger a chain of events that will lead to another undesirable or dangerous proposal or position.

social and political philosophy The area of philosophy that studies the nature of the state, society, property, justice, authority, ideology, and punishment. Social and political philosophy addresses questions concerning the distribution of wealth, the justification of political violence, the nature of civil and human rights, justifications for war, the types of constitution, and a host of related topics concerning the state, property, and citizenship. Some regard social and political philosophy as two distinct areas of philosophy, but more often than not, they are regarded as one area of philosophy.

social contract theory The view that the right to govern and make law, and the duty to obey government and law, arises from a contract, compact, or agreement either among the members of a society or between the governance of the state and the members of a society. Social contract theorists have used the social contract as an explanation for society, government, or both. While the social contract itself is usually postulated as an unwritten agreement rather than an actual historical event or document, the governance of the state and the members of a society are expected to act as if there were a written agreement. Some of its major proponents were Thomas Hobbes, who claimed that moral principles and obligations among people did *not* exist before the social contract but were created by it; John Locke, who claimed that moral principles and obligations among people *did* exist before the creation of the social contract and that the social contact should be altered if it did not uphold these principles; and Jean-Jacques Rousseau (1712–78) in *The Social Contract* (1762). While social contract theory was overshadowed in the eighteenth century by utilitarianism, John Rawls is credited with reintroducing it to contemporary thought. Rawls argues that a particular contract hypothetically would be chosen by contractors within society from what he calls the "original position." See also *racial contract*.

socialism   A system of political and social organization based on state ownership of the means of production. Socialism aims to hasten the demise of capitalism and to bring about a system of political power controlled by the proletariat, not the bourgeoisie. A socialist political system will place the means of production under state control, will centrally control investment in the society, will provide more equal distribution of wealth, and will democratically elect government officials.

socialization   Introduction of persons into a culture's values, rules, and ways of operating.

social ontology   The basic framework or deep structure of social reality. Also called *social metaphysics*.

soft determinism   See *compatibilism*.

solipsism   In metaphysics, the view that the individual self is the whole reality. The metaphysical solipsist maintains that the external world and other persons in it are only representations of the self and have no independent existence. This is an extreme version of *immaterialism*. See *immaterialism*.

somatophobia   Hatred or fear of the body or flesh.

sound argument   A *valid argument* in which the premises are true. See *valid argument*.

standpoint epistemology   The broad position that hidden cultural assumptions distort all observation and investigations of the truth.

statism   The control and planning of a nation's economy by a centralized government. Compare with *capitalism, laissez-faire capitalism*

stereotype   A fixed, often derogatory, notion or conception of a person, idea, or group held by a number of people and allowing for no individuality or critical judgment.

stigmatize   To characterize or mark as undesirable.

Stoics   Members of a school of philosophy founded in ancient Greece by Zeno of Citium (c. 336–264 B.C.E.). Stoic moral philosophy is associated with the view that we should calmly accept our place in the scheme of things, striving to attain *apatheia*, a form of psychic detachment from mental and physical disturbances. The main Stoic virtues are reason, courage, justice, and self-discipline. The major Stoics include Cicero (106–43 B.C.E.), Seneca (c. 4 B.C.E–65 C.E.), Epictetus (c. 50–130 C.E.), and Marcus Aurelius (c. 121–180 C.E.).

straw man   Presenting a position in such a way that it is easy to refute.

strong AI (artificial intelligence)   The view that the appropriately programmed computer really *is* mind, in the sense that computers given the right programs can literally be said to *understand* and have other cognitive states. Compare with *weak AI*.

subject   A grammatical term for the noun phrase in the subject–predicate sentence, where the verb phrase is the predicate. See also *self*.

subjective   That which is relative to the knower's own individual experiences, or that which has no objective reference outside of the contents of consciousness. Compare with *objective*.

subjective idealism   See *immaterialism*.

subjectivism   According to Jean-Paul Sartre, the view that the human subject is free and that there is no way of rejecting or getting beyond human subjectivity.

subjectivity   That which encompasses the subject and the subject's individual perspective, namely the subject's beliefs, desires, and emotions. Contrast with *objectivity*.

sublime   An aesthetic value often opposed to the beautiful. For Immanuel Kant, the sublime is that which cannot conform to our faculties, whereas the beautiful can.

subordination   Being placed under the power or authority of another.

substance   The ultimate unit or units of reality. The underlying, supporting substratum of change. That to which properties or attributes inhere. That which depends on nothing else for its existence and exists in itself. That which cannot be predicated of anything else and is itself the subject of predication. Compare with *attribute, property.*

substratum   See *substance.*

sufficient condition   If *x* is a sufficient condition of *y*, then *y* will be the case if *x* is the case. Or, alternately, if *x*, then *y*. For example, being a plane closed figure with three sides or three interior angles is a sufficient condition of something being a triangle. For another example, being a Ford Escort is a sufficient condition for being a car. However, it is not a necessary condition. See also *necessary condition.*

summum bonum   The highest good. Compare with *summum malum.*

summum malum   The highest bad or evil. Compare with *summum bonum.*

sunyata   In Buddhism, the void, emptiness, nothingness. Everything encountered in life is empty of soul, permanence, and anything pertaining to a self.

sweeping generalization   Applying a general rule to a specific case to which the rule is not applicable because of special features of the case.

symbol   A type of sign. For Charles Peirce, a symbol is a sign that is related to its object by convention or habit. For example, a dove is a symbol of peace. Symbol is grouped with and differentiated from two other types of sign by Peirce: *icon*—a sign related to its object by resemblance (e.g., a map is an icon of its territory); and *index*—a sign that it is related to its object by a natural or existential connection (e.g., smoke is a sign of fire). See *sign.*

T

tabula rasa   Literally, a blank sheet. John Locke compares the mind to a *tabula rasa*, a blank sheet or "white paper devoid of all characters," on which "experience" writes.

tanha   Craving. In Buddhism, the second noble truth is that the cause of suffering is craving.

tao   According to Confucianism, the ideal way of life, as well as teaching about that way of life. Literally means "the way" or "the road" in Chinese.

tathata   In Buddhism, suchness, that is, reality as such. The ultimate, unchanging reality of all phenomena. The unchanging law of ultimate truth and the wisdom of ultimate truth manifested in changing relations.

tautology   A statement that is true by it own definition or form alone—for example, "The black cat is a black cat."

teleological argument, the   An argument for the existence of God. The teleological argument concludes that God exists based on observations of the order, design, or purpose of the world. One of the many formulations of this argument goes as follows: (1) Design (order, purpose, etc.) exists in the world. (2) Design cannot exist without a designer. (3) Therefore, God exists as the source of the design. Also called the *argument from design* or *design argument.*

teleology   The study of phenomena exhibiting order, design, purpose, ends, goals, tendencies, direction, and aims, and of how they are achieved in the process of development. Teleological ethics views the consequences of a moral act to determine the act's worth or correctness. From the Greek *telos* meaning "end" or "purpose" and *logos* meaning "the study of."

telos   End or purpose.

term   A word or phrase that denotes an individual or a class.

terminus ad quem   The end to which.

theism   A general term referring to the belief in god or gods.

theocracy   The organization of the state in which God is the sovereign power and the civil laws are taken to be direct commandments from God. Compare with *Divine nomocracy.*

theodicy   A term introduced by Gottfried Wilhelm Leibniz for the problem of reconciling God's goodness with the existence of evil in the world. Based on the Greek words *theos* meaning "God" and *dike* meaning "justice."

theologian A person who studies God.

theology The study of God.

timocracy A type of state whose order is based on honor, wealth, and power. For Plato, a form of government in which the rulers are motivated by political power and glory; for Aristotle, a form of government in which political power is directly proportional to property ownership.

totalitarianism An organization of the state in which one group or political party has complete control and bans all others.

transcendental idealism The view that the content of knowledge comes from our senses and that the form of our knowledge comes from reason. Kant is a proponent of this approach to epistemology.

Turing test A question-and-answer test that can be applied to computers to determine if they can think as well as process information.

U

universals The referent of general terms such as *box, yellow,* and *woman.* Universals are entities distinct from the particulars or individuals describable by these terms. For example, there is the particular woman, Simone de Beauvoir. As viewed from the notion of universals/particulars, de Beauvoir is an instance or a particular of the universal "woman." Plato's term for *universals* is "ideas." Compare with *particulars.*

uterus The womb; a hollow, muscular organ in females in which the ovum is deposited and the embryo and fetus are developed.

utilitarianism The view that what is morally right is whatever produces the greatest amount of pleasure (*hedonistic utilitarianism*) or happiness (*eudaimonistic utilitarianism*). See also *act utilitarianism, rule utilitarianism.*

utility What is of use, particularly to human beings. From the Latin word *utilis* meaning "useful."

utility, principle of The view that one ought to do that which brings about the greatest happiness (pleasure) to the greatest number of people, or to the community as a whole. Also called the *pleasure principle.*

V

valid argument An argument whose conclusion must be true if its premises are true. Compare with *invalid argument.*

viability In human gestation, the point at which the fetus has developed sufficiently within the uterus to be able to live and continue normal development outside the uterus.

via eminentia The way of eminence.

via negationis The way of negation.

via negativia The negative way.

via positivia The positive way.

virtue theory The view that the moral life should be concerned with cultivating a virtuous character rather than following rules of action.

Vishnu Hindu god that is a preserver. Vishnu is part of the Hindu *trimurti* (trinity) with the gods Shiva, who destroys, and Brahma, who creates.

voluntary action According to Aristotle, an action done through free will whereby the person acting knows all the details involved in the action. Compare with *involuntary action, nonvoluntary action.*

voluntary euthanasia When a person who is severely suffering and faced with the prospect of a painful end expresses a conscious and clear request for euthanasia. See *euthanasia.*

W

weak AI (artificial intelligence) The view that the principle value of the computer in the study of the mind is that it gives us a powerful tool to, for example, test or formulate hypotheses. Compare with *strong AI.*

weasel word Changing the meaning of a word in the middle of an argument in order to bring about the desired conclusion.

Weltanschauung A "Worldview"(German).

wu-wei Action based on nonaction.

Y

yi A central concept in Confucian philosophy that translates as "righteousness," "morals," "rightness," "duty," or "morality."

CREDITS